ITALIAN WIN

Gambero Rosso Editore

Slow Food Editore

ITALIAN WINES 2002

Slow Food Editore

Gambero Rosso Editore

italianwines

2002

ITALIAN WINES 2002
GAMBERO ROSSO EDITORE - SLOW FOOD EDITORE

EDITORIAL STAFF FOR THE ORIGINAL EDITION

CHIEF EDITORS
DANIELE CERNILLI AND CARLO PETRINI

SENIOR EDITORS
GIGI PIUMATTI AND MARCO SABELLICO

TECHNICAL SUPERVISION
GIANNI FABRIZIO, ERNESTO GENTILI, VITTORIO MANGANELLI, FABIO RIZZARI

MEMBERS OF THE FINAL TASTING PANEL
DARIO CAPPELLONI, GIULIO COLOMBA, NICOLA FRASSON, GIACOMO MOJOLI,
MARCO OREGGIA, PIERO SARDO

CONTRIBUTORS
NINO AIELLO, GILBERTO ARRU, STEFANO ASARO, ANTONIO ATTORRE, PAOLO BATTIMELLI,
ENRICO BATTISTELLA, ALBERTO BETTINI, WALTER BORDO, MICHELE BRESSAN,
DARIO CAPPELLONI, DIONISIO CASTELLO, ROBERTO CHECCHETTO, DANIELE CERNILLI,
VALERIO CHIARINI, ANTONIO CIMINELLI, GIULIO COLOMBA, EGIDIO FEDELE DELL'OSTE,
MASSIMO DI CINTIO, MASSIMO DOGLIOLO, GIANNI FABRIZIO, MAURIZIO FAVA,
NICOLA FRASSON, LUCA FURLOTTI, TIZIANO GAIA, ERNESTO GENTILI, FABIO GIAVEDONI,
VITO LACERENZA, GIANCARLO LO SICCO, GIACOMO MOJOLI, MARCO OREGGIA,
DAVIDE PANZIERI, STEFANO PASTOR, NEREO PEDERZOLLI, ANGELO PERETTI,
GUIDO PIRAZZOLI, GIGI PIUMATTI, MARIO PLAZIO, PIERPAOLO RASTELLI, FABIO RIZZARI,
LEONARDO ROMANELLI, GIOVANNI RUFFA, FABRIZIO RUSSO, MARCO SABELLICO,
DIEGO SORACCO, HERBERT TASCHLER, MASSIMO TOFFOLO, ANDREA VANNELLI,
RICCARDO VISCARDI, MASSIMO VOLPARI, PAOLO ZACCARIA, ALBERTO ZACCONE

PARTECIPANTS TASTING PANEL
PAOLA BERTINOTTI, SIMONE BROGI, ALESSANDRO BULZONI, TEODOSIO BUONGIORNO,
MARTA BUSQUETS, IRENE CALAMENTE, REMO CAMURANI, DARIO CAPPELLONI,
SERGIO CECCARELLI, VINCENZA COSTA, IAN DOMENICO D'AGATA, ANGELO DAL BON,
AURELIO DAMIANI, MARINO DEL CURTO, DAVID ESCOFET, ROSANNA FERRARO,
MICHELE FRANZAN, BEAT KOELLIKER, SIMONE GHIO, MARINA MARIANI, ENZO MERZ,
DANNY MURARO, DUILIO MURARO, UGO ONGARETTO, ROBERTO PALMIERI,
FRANCESCO PENSOVECCHIO, NICOLA PERULLO, LIANO PETROZZI, NICOLA PICCININI,
DOMENICO PICHINI, MARINO POERIO, CRISTIANA POLIMENO,
VALENTINO RAMELLI, GABRIELE RICCI ALUNNI, HELMUT RIEBSCHLÄGER, MAURIZIO ROSSI,
PAOLO VALDASTRI, GIULIANA VELISCECH, VALERIO ZORZI.

EDITING
MARCO OREGGIA, UMBERTO TAMBURINI, PAOLO ZACCARIA

EDITORIAL COORDINATOR
GIORGIO ACCASCINA

TRANSLATIONS COORDINATED AND EDITED BY
GILES WATSON

TRANSLATORS
MAUREEN ASHLEY, KAREN CHRISTENFELD, HELEN DONALD, STEPHEN JACKSON,
ANDREW L. MILLER, GILES WATSON, AILSA WOOD

PUBLISHER
GAMBERO ROSSO, INC.
636 BROADWAY - SUITE 1111 - NEW YORK, NY 10012
TEL. 212- 253-5653 FAX 212 253-8349 - E-MAIL: gamberousa@aol.com

DISTRIBUTION:
USA AND CANADA BY ANTIQUE COLLECTOR'S CLUB, MARKET STREET INDUSTRIAL PARK,
WAPPINGER FALLS, NY 12590, USA;
UK AND AUSTRALIA BY GRUB STREET, THE BASEMENT, 10 CHIVALRY ROAD,
LONDON SW11 1HT, UK.

COPYRIGHT© 2002 GAMBERO ROSSO EDITORE SPA - ROMA - ITALY
ALL RIGHTS RESERVED. NO PART OF THIS PUBLICATION MAY BE REPRODUCED, STORED IN A
RETRIEVAL SYSTEM OR TRANSMITTED BY ANY FORM OR BY ANY MEANS: ELECTRONIC,
ELECTROSTATIC, MAGNETIC TAPE, MECHANICAL, PHOTOCOPYING, RECORDING OR
OTHERWISE WITHOUT WRITTEN PERMISSION FROM THE PUBLISHER.
GAMBERO ROSSO IS A REGISTERED TRADE MARK

ITALIAN WINES 2002 WAS CLOSED SEPTEMBER 26, 2001

PRINTED IN ITALY BY TIPOGRAFICA LA PIRAMIDE SRL
VIA ANTON MARIA VALSALVA, 34 - ROMA

CONTENTS

INTRODUCTION	6
THREE GLASS AWARDS 2002	8
THE STARS	12
GUIDE TO VINTAGES	13
HOW TO USE THE GUIDE	14

THE REGIONS

VALLE D'AOSTA	15
PIEDMONT	21
LIGURIA	155
LOMBARDY	169
TRENTINO	215
ALTO ADIGE	239
VENETO	271
FRIULI VENEZIA GIULIA	331
EMILIA ROMAGNA	403
TUSCANY	429
MARCHE	577
UMBRIA	607
LAZIO	627
ABRUZZO AND MOLISE	639
CAMPANIA	653
BASILICATA	669
PUGLIA	675
CALABRIA	693
SICILY	699
SARDINIA	719

INDEXES

WINES	733
PRODUCERS	781

INTRODUCTION

In the past 15 years, many things have changed in the world of Italian wine. When we presented the first edition of the Guide in Florence, at the Palazzo Medici Riccardi, in November 1987, wine was hardly a fashionable subject. Only a year earlier, the tragic methanol scandal had undermined the very foundations of Italian winemaking. Consumption and exports headed rapidly south and even premium wines were regarded with suspicion. It was almost shameful to be writing about wineries and growers. Soon afterwards, many big names were hit by crises that were even more serious than the methanol emergency. For example, Barolo was thrown in by a number of wineries as a discount in kind for buyers of Dolcetto or Barbera. Chianti Classico achieved DOCG status in 1984 but was a long way from finding a viable commercial strategy. No one wanted to hear about Amarone and many producers decided to concentrate on making "ripasso" wines with the unpressed skins. Whites accounted for over 60 per cent of wines consumed in Italy. It looks like ancient history but all this was going on only 15 years ago. The Guide contained only 450 winery profiles, with 1,500 wines and 33 Three Glass distinctions. In the 2002 edition that you are reading, Tuscany alone can more or less match those numbers. Another phenomenon has been the proliferation of DOC zones. The traditional production areas have been joined by many new zones, some of which have swiftly achieved fame. Many wines once considered second or even third rate have acquired solid status. We could mention Barbera d'Asti, Sagrantino di Montefalco, Montepulciano d'Abruzzo and a host of reds from the south. Consider also the incredible advances made by entire regions, like Alto Adige or Marche. In successive editions of the Guide, we have attempted to follow, interpret and illustrate all these developments. We have done so by spotlighting rising stars and established names, acknowledging the quality of so many wines with our now celebrated Three Glasses. Well over 1,000 awards in 15 years. The Guide has met with growing success over the years. The 5,000 copies of the first edition's print run have risen to the current 80,000 of this year's Italian edition, and about 60,000 in English and German. It is likely that we have contributed to putting the world of wine at the centre of attention of a very large number of readers and wine enthusiasts. Add to that the educational initiatives, the courses and the tastings organized by Slow Food; the wine-related broadcasts on the Gambero Rosso Channel; all the books and periodicals from both publishers, from Vino Quotidiano to the Almanacco del Berebene and Jancis Robinson's book on vine types through to the Gambero Rosso practical guides; and you will realize just how firmly we believed in the wine sector, and how much effort has gone into explaining it to our readers. We are attempting to do so again this year, with the most comprehensive edition of the Guide to date. There are several changes and a host of new features. Let's deal with them one by one. In early May 2001, the 29 tasting panels scattered across the country, each with at least four members, set to work. They tasted about 25,000 wines, making a first selection of potential champions. All tastings were made from unidentifiable bottles, on samples that were comparable for wine type and vintage. This enormous initial round of tastings yielded about 800 wines that the panels forwarded to the final taste-offs. At that stage, the

Guide's experts met at three tasting sessions lasting for over ten days, at the St Regis in Rome, the Castello di Verduno and at the Là di Petros restaurant at Colloredo di Montalbano, near Udine. Those sessions selected the 241 Three Glass wines for 2002. Now let's move on to the new features which we were talking about, and which you will notice in this edition of the Guide. The first is that we have coloured the Three Glasses to make them instantly visible. We have also identified with the same colour the 800 or so wines that reached the final taste-offs but failed to win a third Glass. It didn't seem fair that such very good wines should come so close to a top award and then be relegated to the relative anonymity of the Two Glasses given to lesser bottles that had achieved significantly lower ratings. that's why you will now find a generous sprinkling of Two coloured Glasses. The third new feature is in the section reserved for the Other Wineries at the end of each region. This has been extended and now each cellar has its own, brief profile. All its wines are now reviewed, instead of being left in obscurity. These are, we hope, definite improvements that will help readers to form an all-round opinion of Italian winemaking, a sector that has made commendable progress in the last few years. All of this has enabled us to increase the number of cellars reviewed and provide a reasonably complete overview of wine in the peninsula. But let us make it quite clear that all the producers, wineries and wines are treated with absolute impartiality. This is a given imposed by our respect for the reader and sense of responsibility for the work of so many different people. It is for this reason that Gambero Rosso and Slow Food have agreed not to allow individual producers to buy advertising space in the Guide, even though this means forgoing a major source of income. In the same spirit, the system of cross-checking tasting results, involving the panels and final taste-offs, ensures that no individual panel member, and not even the Guide editors, can award points to specific wines on their own initiative. In addition, most of the panels meet in the offices of consortia or other bodies that have absolutely no connections with the publishers. Samples are procured, and tastings organized, in complete independence. We would therefore like to thank in particular the following consortia: Marchio Storico del Chianti Classico, Brunello di Montalcino, Rosso di Montalcino, Nobile di Montepulciano, Bolgheri, Franciacorta, Oltrepò Pavese, Valtellina, Soave, Valpolicella, the Istituto Agronomico Mediterraneo at Valenzano, the Centro Agroalimentare Umbro at Foligno, the Bolzano Chamber of Commerce, the Unione Provinciale Agricoltori di Caserta, the Enoteca Regionale di Dozza, the Enoteca Regionale di Gattinara, the Enoteca Regionale di Vignale Monferrato, Assivip at Majolati Spontini and Vinea at Offida, the Trento Chamber of Commerce and the Casa del Vino della Vallagarina. Our apologies, naturally, if we have left anyone out. Thanks are also due to the panel members who took part in tastings and to the dozens of profile authors. All this effort has enabled us to offer a record 1,770 producers and 12,610 wines reviewed. Finally, a word or two about this year's special awards. Cellar of the Year is Barone Ricasoli, the historic winery at Gaiole in Chianti. Oenologist of the Year is Giuseppe Caviola, known to one and all as Beppe, an extraordinarily talented young winemaker from Piedmont. The Sparkler of the Year prize goes to the Franciacorta Magnficentia from Uberti. White of the Year is the COF Tocai Vigne Cinquantanni '00 from Le Vigne di Zamò. Elio Grasso's Barolo Runcot '96 is Red of the Year. And the Sweet Wine of the Year, the Latinia '99, comes from the Cantina Sociale di Santadi, in Sardinia. That's it for this year.

Daniele Cernilli and Carlo Petrini

THREE GLASS AWARDS 2002

VALLE D'AOSTA

VALLE D'AOSTA CHARDONNAY CUVÉE FRISSONIÈRE LES CRÊTES CUVÉE BOIS '99	LES CRÊTES	17

PIEDMONT

BARBARESCO '98	GAJA	31
BARBARESCO ASILI RIS. '96	BRUNO GIACOSA	113
BARBARESCO BRICCO '97	PIO CESARE	25
BARBARESCO COTTÀ '98	SOTTIMANO	115
BARBARESCO VIGNETO LORETO '98	ALBINO ROCCA	34
BARBARESCO PAJORÉ '98	SOTTIMANO	115
BARBARESCO RABAJÀ '98	BRUNO ROCCA	35
BARBARESCO SORÌ BURDIN '98	FONTANABIANCA	112
BARBARESCO VIGNETI IN MONTESTEFANO RIS. '96	PRODUTTORI DEL BARBARESCO	34
BARBARESCO VIGNETO STARDERI '98	LA SPINETTA	54
BARBARESCO VIGNETO VALEIRANO '98	LA SPINETTA	54
BARBERA D'ALBA ASILI '99	CASCINA LUISIN	32
BARBERA D'ALBA CASCINA NUOVA '99	MAURO VEGLIO	90
BARBERA D'ALBA MARUN '99	MATTEO CORREGGIA	48
BARBERA D'ALBA MULASSA '99	CASCINA CA' ROSSA	47
BARBERA D'ALBA SCARRONE VIGNA VECCHIA '99	VIETTI	60
BARBERA D'ALBA VIGNETO GALLINA '99	LA SPINETTA	54
BARBERA D'ASTI COSTAMIÒLE '99	PRUNOTTO	26
BARBERA D'ASTI EMOZIONI '99	TENUTA LA TENAGLIA	132
BARBERA D'ASTI POMOROSSO '99	LUIGI COPPO E FIGLI	52
BARBERA D'ASTI SUP. ALFIERA '99	MARCHESI ALFIERI	124
BARBERA DEL M.TO SUP. BRICCO BATTISTA '99	GIULIO ACCORNERO E FIGLI	140
BAROLO BRUNATE '97	ENZO BOGLIETTI	83
BAROLO BRUNATE-LE COSTE '97	GIUSEPPE RINALDI	39
BAROLO BUSSIA VIGNA MUNIE '97	ARMANDO PARUSSO	103
BAROLO CANNUBI '96	GIACOMO BREZZA & FIGLI	36
BAROLO CANNUBI '97	E. PIRA & FIGLI - CHIARA BOSCHIS	38
BAROLO CASCINA FRANCIA '97	GIACOMO CONTERNO	99
BAROLO CEREQUIO '97	MICHELE CHIARLO	45
BAROLO CEREQUIO TENUTA SECOLO '97	GIUSEPPE CONTRATTO	51
BAROLO ENRICO VI '97	MONFALLETTO CORDERO DI MONTEZEMOLO	87
BAROLO ESTATE VINEYARD '97	MARCHESI DI BAROLO	37
BAROLO GRAN BUSSIA RIS. '95	ALDO CONTERNO	98
BAROLO LA SERRA '97	GIANNI VOERZIO	91
BAROLO MARGHERIA '97	VIGNA RIONDA - MASSOLINO	131
BAROLO MONDOCA DI BUSSIA SOPRANA '97	F.LLI ODDERO	88
BAROLO PERCRISTINA '96	DOMENICO CLERICO	98
BAROLO RAVERA '97	FLAVIO RODDOLO	104
BAROLO ROCCHE DELL'ANNUNZIATA '97	F.LLI REVELLO	89
BAROLO RUNCOT '96	ELIO GRASSO	101
BAROLO S. GIOVANNI '97	GIANFRANCO ALESSANDRIA	97
BAROLO S. LORENZO '97	F.LLI ALESSANDRIA	138
BAROLO VIGNA CONCA '97	MAURO MOLINO	87
BAROLO VIGNA DEL GRIS '97	CONTERNO FANTINO	100
BAROLO VIGNETO MARENCA '97	LUIGI PIRA	131
BAROLO VILLERO '96	GIUSEPPE MASCARELLO E FIGLIO	96
DOLCETTO D'ALBA BRICCO CARAMELLI '00	F.LLI MOSSIO	123
DOLCETTO DI DOGLIANI PAPÀ CELSO '00	MARZIANO E ENRICO ABBONA	69
DOLCETTO DI DOGLIANI S. LUIGI '00	F.LLI PECCHENINO	71
HARYS '99	GIOVANNI BATTISTA GILLARDI	74
LANGHE LA VILLA '99	ELIO ALTARE - CASCINA NUOVA	82
LANGHE LARIGI '99	ELIO ALTARE - CASCINA NUOVA	82
LANGHE ROSSO ALTA BUSSIA '99	ATTILIO GHISOLFI	101
LANGHE ROSSO BRIC DU LUV '99	CA' VIOLA	107
LANGHE ROSSO LUIGI EINAUDI '99	PODERI LUIGI EINAUDI	70
LANGHE ROSSO SORÌ TILDIN '97	GAJA	31
MONFERRATO ROSSO RIVALTA '99	VILLA SPARINA	80
NEBBIOLO D'ALBA '99	HILBERG - PASQUERO	120
NEBBIOLO D'ALBA MOMPISSANO '99	CASCINA CHICCO	47
ROERO RÒCHE D'AMPSÈJ '98	MATTEO CORREGGIA	48
ROERO SUP. '99	FILIPPO GALLINO	49

LOMBARDY

FRANCIACORTA BRUT CABOCHON '97	MONTE ROSSA	178

FRANCIACORTA DOSAGE ZERO '97	CA' DEL BOSCO	185
FRANCIACORTA BRUT MAGNIFICENTIA	UBERTI	188
FRANCIACORTA GRAN CUVÉE BRUT '97	BELLAVISTA	185
FRANCIACORTA SATEN '97	FERGHETTINA	186
LE ZALTE ROSSO '99	CASCINA LA PERTICA	196
OP PINOT NERO CL. NATURE	MONSUPELLO	202
TDF CHARDONNAY '99	CA' DEL BOSCO	185
VALTELLINA SFURSAT 5 STELLE '99	NINO NEGRI	179
VALTELLINA SFORZATO '99	TRIACCA	203
VALTELLINA SFORZATO CANUA '99	CONTI SERTOLI SALIS	202
VALTELLINA SFURSAT FRUTTAIO CA' RIZZIERI '98	ALDO RAINOLDI	179

TRENTINO

GIULIO FERRARI '93	FERRARI	234
GRANATO '99	FORADORI	228
STRAVINO DI STRAVINO '99	PRAVIS	222
TEROLDEGO ROTALIANO CLESURAE '99	CANTINA ROTALIANA	227
TRENTINO CHARDONNAY PRAISTEL '98	LONGARIVA	231

ALTO ADIGE

AUREUS '99	JOSEF NIEDERMAYR	244
A. A. CHARDONNAY CORNELL '99	C. PRODUTTORI COLTERENZIO	241
A. A. GEWÜRZTRAMINER BRENNTAL '00	CANTINA PRODUTTORI CORTACCIA	257
A. A. GEWÜRZTRAMINER KASTELAZ '00	CASTEL RINGBERG & KASTELAZ ELENA WALCH	265
A. A. GEWÜRZTRAMINER NUSSBAUMERHOF '00	CANTINA PRODUTTORI TERMENO	265
A. A. GEWÜRZTRAMINER PASSITO TERMINUM '99	CANTINA PRODUTTORI TERMENO	265
A. A. GEWÜRZTRAMINER ST. VALENTIN '00	C. PROD. SAN MICHELE APPIANO	242
A. A. LAGREIN SCURO '99	ANDREAS BERGER THURNHOF	245
A. A. LAGREIN SCURO RIS. '98	JOSEPHUS MAYR	249
A. A. LAGREIN SCURO ABTEI RIS. '98	CANTINA CONVENTO MURI-GRIES	246
A. A. LAGREIN SCURO RIS. '99	GEORG MUMELTER	249
A. A. LAGREIN SCURO TABERHOF RIS. '99	C. PROD. SANTA MADDALENA	247
A. A. MOSCATO GIALLO VINALIA '99	CANTINA GRIES	246
A. A. MOSCATO ROSA SCHWEIZER '00	FRANZ HAAS	261
A. A. SAUVIGNON PREMSTALERHOF '00	CANTINA VITICOLTORI DI CALDARO	253
A. A. SAUVIGNON ST. VALENTIN '00	C. PROD. SAN MICHELE APPIANO	242
A. A. TERLANO SAUVIGNON '00	IGNAZ NIEDRIST	243
A. A. VALLE VENOSTA RIESLING '00	TEN. FALKENSTEIN - FRANZ PRATZNER	262
A. A. VALLE VENOSTA RIESLING '00	TENUTA UNTERORTL-CASTEL JUVAL	264

VENETO

AMARONE DELLA VALPOLICELLA CL. '97	ALLEGRINI	277
AMARONE DELLA VALPOLICELLA CL. '97	BRIGALDARA	302
AMARONE DELLA VALPOLICELLA CL. '97	ZENATO	297
AMARONE DELLA VALPOLICELLA CL. TULIPANO NERO '97	VIVIANI	295
AMARONE DELLA VALPOLICELLA CL. VIGNETO MONTE CA' BIANCA '97	LORENZO BEGALI	301
AMARONE DELLA VALPOLICELLA VIGNETO DI MONTE LODOLETTA '96	ROMANO DAL FORNO	279
AMARONE DELLA VALPOLICELLA MITHAS '95	CORTE SANT'ALDA	285
CAPITEL CROCE '99	ROBERTO ANSELMI	288
COLLI EUGANEI ROSSO GEMOLA '99	VIGNALTA	312
FRATTA '99	MACULAN	274
LA POJA '97	ALLEGRINI	277
RECIOTO DELLA VALPOLICELLA CL. LE VIGNE CA' DEL PIPA '99	MICHELE CASTELLANI	282
RECIOTO DELLA VALPOLICELLA CL. TB '98	TOMMASO BUSSOLA	292
SOAVE CL. SUP. BUCCIATO '99	CA' RUGATE	289
SOAVE CL. SUP. CONTRADA SALVARENZA VECCHIE VIGNE '00	GINI	290
SOAVE CL. SUP. LA ROCCA '99	LEONILDO PIEROPAN	310
SOAVE CL. SUP. VIGNETO DU LOT '99	INAMA	298
SOAVE CL. SUP. VIGNETO MONTE GRANDE '00	PRÀ	291

FRIULI VENEZIA GIULIA

COF BIANCO POMÉDES '99	SCUBLA	381
COF MALVASIA '00	LE VIGNE DI ZAMÒ	370
COF MERLOT '98	MIANI	336
COF MERLOT CENTIS '99	ROCCA BERNARDA	380
COF MERLOT FOCUS '99	VOLPE PASINI	398
COF MERLOT RONC DI SUBULE '99	RONCHI DI MANZANO	371
COF ROSAZZO BIANCO TERRE ALTE '99	LIVIO FELLUGA	348
COF TOCAI FRIULANO '00	MIANI	336
COF TOCAI FRIULANO STORICO '00	ADRIANO GIGANTE	357
COF TOCAI FRIULANO VIGNE CINQUANT'ANNI '00	LE VIGNE DI ZAMÒ	370
COLLIO BIANCO DELLA CASTELLADA '99	LA CASTELLADA	366

COLLIO TOCAI FRIULANO '00	FERDINANDO E ALDO POLENCIC	350
COLLIO TOCAI FRIULANO '00	DARIO RACCARO	352
COLLIO TOCAI FRIULANO RONCO DELLE CIME '00	VENICA & VENICA	361
COLLIO CHARDONNAY GRÄFIN DE LA TOUR '99	VILLA RUSSIZ	340
COLLIO CHARDONNAY SEL. '99	BORGO DEL TIGLIO	344
COLLIO PINOT BIANCO '00	SCHIOPETTO	339
COLLIO PINOT BIANCO '00	FRANCO TOROS	355
COLLIO TOCAI FRIULANO '00	SCHIOPETTO	339
FRIULI ISONZO PINOT BIANCO '00	MAURO DRIUS	348
FRIULI ISONZO PINOT GRIGIO DESSIMIS '99	VIE DI ROMANS	373
FRIULI ISONZO SAUVIGNON '00	RONCO DEL GELSO	353
LIS '99	LIS NERIS - PECORARI	394
RUBRUM '99	IL CARPINO	390
TAL LUC '99	LIS NERIS - PECORARI	394
VESPA BIANCO '99	BASTIANICH	379
VINTAGE TUNINA '00	VINNAIOLI JERMANN	364

EMILIA ROMAGNA

COLLI BOLOGNESI CABERNET SAUVIGNON SEL. '99	VALLONA	407
COLLI PIACENTINI CABERNET SAUVIGNON CORBEAU '00	LURETTA	420
MARZIENO '99	FATTORIA ZERBINA	409
MONTEPIROLO '99	SAN PATRIGNANO - TERRE DEL CEDRO	409

TUSCANY

AVVOLTORE '99	MORIS FARMS	472
BOLGHERI SASSICAIA '98	TENUTA SAN GUIDO	434
BOLGHERI SUP. ORNELLAIA '98	TENUTA DELL' ORNELLAIA	433
BRANCAIA '99	LA BRANCAIA	521
BRUNELLO DI MONTALCINO '96	SIRO PACENTI	488
BRUNELLO DI MONTALCINO POGGIO ALL'ORO RIS. '95	BANFI	474
BRUNELLO DI MONTALCINO POGGIO AL VENTO RIS. '95	TENUTA COL D'ORCIA	479
BRUNELLO DI MONTALCINO RIS. '95	FANTI - SAN FILIPPO	481
BRUNELLO DI MONTALCINO RIS. '95	POGGIO DI SOTTO	489
BRUNELLO DI MONTALCINO VIGNA DI PIANROSSO RIS. '95	CIACCI PICCOLOMINI D'ARAGONA	478
BRUNELLO DI MONTALCINO VIGNA SPUNTALI '95	TENIMENTI ANGELINI - VAL DI SUGA	492
CAMARTINA '97	AGRICOLA QUERCIABELLA	465
CARMIGNANO RIS. '98	PIAGGIA	519
CARMIGNANO VILLA DI CAPEZZANA '99	CAPEZZANA	437
CASALFERRO '99	BARONE RICASOLI	456
CEPPARELLO '99	ISOLE E OLENA	431
CERVIOLO ROSSO '99	SAN FABIANO CALCINAIA	442
CHIANTI CL. CASASILIA '98	POGGIO AL SOLE	547
CHIANTI CL. CASTELLO DI BROLIO '98	BARONE RICASOLI	456
CHIANTI CL. DON TOMMASO '99	FATTORIA LE CORTI - CORSINI	531
CHIANTI CL. GIORGIO PRIMO '99	LA MASSA	512
CHIANTI CL. LA CASUCCIA '97	CASTELLO DI AMA	455
CHIANTI CL. RIS. '98	FATTORIA NITTARDI	441
CHIANTI RUFINA MONTESODI '99	MARCHESI DE' FRESCOBALDI	453
FONTALLORO '98	FATTORIA DI FELSINA	446
GALATRONA '99	FATTORIA PETROLO	509
SODI DI SAN NICCOLÒ '97	CASTELLARE DI CASTELLINA	439
IL CARBONAIONE '98	PODERE POGGIO SCALETTE	464
IL PARETO '98	TENUTE FOLONARI	452
LA GIOIA '98	RIECINE	460
LA VIGNA DI ALCEO '99	CASTELLO DEI RAMPOLLA	514
LIVERNANO '99	LIVERNANO	522
LUPICAIA '99	CASTELLO DEL TERRICCIO	442
LUENZO '99	VINCENZO CESANI	533
MASSETO '98	TENUTA DELL' ORNELLAIA	433
MESSORIO '98	LE MACCHIOLE	433
MILLANNI '99	GUICCIARDINI STROZZI	534
MONTECALVI '98	MONTECALVI	463
MORELLINO DI SCANSANO POGGIO VALENTE '99	LE PUPILLE	468
NOBILE DI MONTEPULCIANO VIGN. ANTICA CHIUSINA '98	FATTORIA DEL CERRO	499
NOBILE DI MONTEPULCIANO ASINONE '98	POLIZIANO	503
POGGIO GRANONI '95	FARNETELLA	541
REDIGAFFI '99	TUA RITA	545
ROMITORIO DI SANTEDAME '99	TENIMENTI RUFFINO	520
ROSSO DI SERA '99	FATTORIA POGGIOPIANO	532
SAN MARTINO '98	VILLA CAFAGGIO	516
SAXA CALIDA '99	PODERI DEL PARADISO	535
SIEPI '99	CASTELLO DI FONTERUTOLI	440
SYRAH '99	POGGIO AL SOLE	547
SYRAH CASE VIA '98	TENUTA FONTODI	512
SOLAIA '98	MARCHESI ANTINORI	452
VIN SANTO OCCHIO DI PERNICE '89	AVIGNONESI	497

MARCHE

AKRONTE '98	BOCCADIGABBIA	584
ANGHELOS '99	TENUTA DE ANGELIS	582
CAMERTE '99	LA MONACESCA	589
ROSSO CONERO SASSI NERI '99	FATTORIA LE TERRAZZE	593
ROSSO CONERO FIBBIO '99	LANARI	578
SANGIOVESE MOGGIO '98	SAN SAVINO	599
VERDICCHIO DEI CASTELLI DI JESI CL. SUP. PODIUM '99	GIOACCHINO GAROFOLI	588
VERDICCHIO DEI CASTELLI DI JESI CL. SUP. S. MICHELE '00	VALLEROSA BONCI	585
VERDICCHIO DEI CASTELLI DI JESI CL.VILLA BUCCI RIS. '98	F.LLI BUCCI	596

UMBRIA

CAMPOLEONE '99	LA FIORITA - LAMBORGHINI	620
CERVARO DELLA SALA '99	CASTELLO DELLA SALA	612
FOBIANO '99	LA CARRAIA	618
"IL" ROSSO '98	DECUGNANO DEI BARBI	617
MONTEFALCO SAGRANTINO '98	CÒLPETRONE	613
MONTEFALCO SAGRANTINO 25 ANNI '98	ARNALDO CAPRAI VAL DI MAGGIO	614

LAZIO

MONTIANO '99	FALESCO	634

ABRUZZO AND MOLISE

MOLISE DON LUIGI '99	DI MAJO NORANTE	641
MONTEPULCIANO D'ABRUZZO '95	EDOARDO VALENTINI	644
MONTEPULCIANO D'ABRUZZO VILLA GEMMA '97	GIANNI MASCIARELLI	647

CAMPANIA

BUE APIS '99	CANTINA DEL TABURNO	655
FALERNO DEL MASSICO VIGNA CAMARATO '98	VILLA MATILDE	655
MONTEVETRANO '99	MONTEVETRANO	662
PÀTRIMO '99	FEUDI DI SAN GREGORIO	663
SERPICO '99	FEUDI DI SAN GREGORIO	663
TERRA DI LAVORO '99	GALARDI	663

BASILICATA

AGLIANICO DEL VULTURE ROTONDO '98	PATERNOSTER	671

PUGLIA

NERO '99	CONTI ZECCA	683
PLATONE '98	TENUTE ALBANO CARRISI	678

CALABRIA

GRAVELLO '98	LIBRANDI	695

SICILY

CABERNET '00	FEUDO PRINCIPI DI BUTERA	701
CHARDONNAY '00	PLANETA	714
COMETA '00	PLANETA	714
DON ANTONIO '99	MORGANTE	704
FORTI TERRE DI SICILIA CABERNET SAUVIGNON '99	CANTINA SOCIALE DI TRAPANI	714
LITRA '99	ABBAZIA SANTA ANASTASIA	702
MERLOT '99	PLANETA	714
MOSCATO PASSITO DI PANTELLERIA MARTINGANA '98	SALVATORE MURANA	713
NOÀ '00	CUSUMANO	710

SARDINIA

ALGHERO MARCHESE DI VILLAMARINA '97	TENUTE SELLA & MOSCA	720
CAPICHERA V.T. '00	CAPICHERA	721
LATINIA '99	CANTINA SOCIALE DI SANTADI	726
TURRIGA '97	ANTONIO ARGIOLAS	728

WINERY OF THE YEAR
BARONE RICASOLI

OENOLOGIST OF THE YEAR
GIUSEPPE CAVIOLA

THE YEAR'S BEST WINES

THE BUBBLY		
FRANCIACORTA BRUT MAGNIFICENTIA	UBERTI	
THE WHITE		
COF TOCAI VIGNE CINQUANTANNI '00	LE VIGNE DI ZAMÒ	
THE RED		
BAROLO RUNCOT '96	ELIO GRASSO	
THE SWEET		
LATINIA '99	CANTINA SOCIALE DI SANTADI	

THE STARS

Stars indicate wineries that have, over the Guide's 15 years of publication, won at least ten Three Glass awards. In short, these are the best wineries over time, not just in one particular vintage. This year, Gaja, which leads the table with 29 Three Glass distinctions, has been joined in the Two Star category by Elio Altare and Ca' del Bosco, both of which have accumulated 20 top scores. Only one step away from a second Star is La Spinetta, owned by the Rivetti brothers and a fast-rising contender. Further back, we find Allegrini with 17. There are four new Stars this year, which went to Cantina Produttori di San Michele Appiano, the first Starred winery in Alto Adige, Miani in Friuli, Matteo Correggia in Piedmont, who so tragically and prematurely passed away during 2001, and Romano Dal Forno in Veneto. Five more producers could win a Star next year as they hold nine Three Glass awards. They are Cantina Produttori Colterenzio and Querciabella in Tuscany, Ceretto in Piedmont, and Maculan and Pieropan in Veneto.

★ ★

29
GAJA (Piedmont)

20
ELIO ALTARE
(Piedmont)
CA' DEL BOSCO
(Lombardy)

★

19
LA SPINETTA (Piedmont)

17
ALLEGRINI (Veneto)

15
FATTORIA DI FELSINA
(Tuscany)
CASTELLO DI FONTERUTOLI
(Tuscany)
VINNAIOLI JERMANN
(Friuli Venezia Giulia)

13
MARCHESI ANTINORI
(Tuscany)
DOMENICO CLERICO (Piedmont)
PAOLO SCAVINO
(Piedmont)
MARIO SCHIOPETTO
(Friuli Venezia Giulia)

12
BELLAVISTA (Lombardy)
CASTELLO DELLA SALA (Umbria)
PODERI ALDO CONTERNO
(Piedmont)
FERRARI (Trentino)
TENUTA FONTODI (Tuscany)
POLIZIANO (Tuscany)
TENIMENTI RUFFINO (Tuscany)
VIE DI ROMANS (Friuli Venezia Giulia)

11
CANTINA PRODUTTORI
SAN MICHELE APPIANO (Alto Adige)
CASTELLO DI AMA (Tuscany)
CASTELLO BANFI (Tuscany)
GIACOMO CONTERNO (Piedmont)
GIROLAMO DORIGO
(Friuli Venezia Giulia)
LIVIO FELLUGA
(Friuli Venezia Giulia)
ISOLE E OLENA (Tuscany)
LA BARBATELLA (Piedmont)
MIANI (Friuli Venezia Giulia)
TENUTA SAN GUIDO (Tuscany)
VALENTINI (Abruzzo)
VILLA RUSSIZ (Friuli Venezia Giulia)

10
MATTEO CORREGGIA (Piedmont)
ROMANO DAL FORNO (Veneto)
IOSKO GRAVNER
(Friuli Venezia Giulia)
TASCA D'ALMERITA (Sicily)
ROBERTO VOERZIO (Piedmont)

13

A GUIDE TO VINTAGES, 1971-1999

Year	BARBARESCO	BRUNELLO DI MONTALCINO	BAROLO	CHIANTI CLASSICO	NOBILE DI MONTEPULCIANO	AMARONE
1971	••••	•••	•••••	•••••	••••	••••
1973	••	•••	••	••	•••	••
1974	••••	••	••••	•••	•••	••••
1975	••	•••••	••	••••	•••	•••
1976	••	•	••	••	••	••••
1977	••	••••	••	••••	•••	•••
1978	•••••	••••	•••••	••••	••••	••••
1979	••••	••••	••••	••••	••••	••••
1980	••••	••••	••••	••••	•••	••••
1981	•••	•••	•••	•••	•••	•••
1982	•••••	•••••	•••••	••••	••••	•
1983	••••	••••	••••	••••	••••	•••••
1984	•	••	••	•	•	••
1985	•••••	•••••	•••••	•••••	•••••	••••
1986	•••	•••	•••	••••	••••	•••
1987	••	••	••	••	••	••
1988	•••••	•••••	•••••	•••••	•••••	•••••
1989	•••••	••	•••••	•	•	••
1990	•••••	•••••	•••••	••••	•••••	•••••
1991	•••	•••	•••	•••	•••	••
1992	••	••	••	•	•	•
1993	•••	••••	•••	••••	•••••	••••
1994	••	•••	••	••	••	••
1995	••••	•••••	••••	•••••	•••••	••••
1996	•••••	••••	•••••	•••	•••	•••
1997	•••••	•••••	•••••	•••••	•••••	•••••
1998	•••••	••••	••••	••••	•••	•••
1999	••••	••••	••••	••••	••••	•••

HOW TO USE THE GUIDE

KEY
- ○ WHITE WINES
- ● RED WINES
- ⊙ ROSÉ WINES

RATINGS

LISTING WITHOUT A GLASS SYMBOL:
A WELL-MADE WINE OF AVERAGE QUALITY IN ITS CATEGORY

🍷
ABOVE AVERAGE TO GOOD IN ITS CATEGORY, EQUIVALENT TO 70-79/100

🍷🍷
VERY GOOD TO EXCELLENT IN ITS CATEGORY, EQUIVALENT TO 80-89/100

🍷🍷🍷
VERY GOOD TO EXCELLENT WINE SELECTED FOR FINAL TASTINGS

🍷🍷🍷
EXCELLENT WINE IN ITS CATEGORY, EQUIVALENT TO 90-99/100

(🍷, 🍷🍷, 🍷🍷🍷) WINES RATED IN PREVIOUS EDITIONS OF THE GUIDE ARE INDICATED BY WHITE GLASSES, PROVIDED THEY ARE STILL DRINKING AT THE LEVEL FOR WHICH THE ORIGINAL AWARD WAS MADE

STAR ★
INDICATED WINERIES THAT WON TEN THREE GLASS AWARDS FOR EACH STAR

PRICE RANGES [1]
1 UP TO $ 8 AND UP TO £ 6
2 FROM $ 8 TO $ 12 AND FROM £ 6 TO £ 8
3 FROM $ 12 TO $ 18 AND FROM £ 8 TO £ 11
4 FROM $ 18 TO $ 27 AND FROM £ 11 TO £ 15
5 FROM $ 27 TO $ 40 AND FROM £ 15 TO £ 20
6 MORE THAN $ 40 AND MORE THAN £ 20

[1] Approx. retail prices in USA and UK

ASTERISK *
INDICATES ESPECIALLY GOOD VALUE FOR MONEY

NOTE
PRICES INDICATED REFER TO RETAIL AVERAGES. INDICATIONS OF PRICE NEXT TO WINES ASSIGNED WHITE GLASSES (AWARDS MADE IN PREVIOUS EDITIONS) TAKE INTO ACCOUNT APPRECIATION OVER TIME WHERE APPROPRIATE

ABBREVIATIONS

A. A.	Alto Adige
C.	Colli
Cl.	Classico
C.S.	Cantina Sociale (co-operative winery)
Cant.	Cantina (cellar or winery)
Cast.	Castello (castle)
COF	Colli Orientali del Friuli
Cons.	Consorzio (consortium)
Coop.Agr.	Cooperativa Agricola (farming co-operative)
DOC:	Denominazione di Origine Controllata (category of wines created in 1963)
DOCG:	Denominazione di Origine Controllata e Garantita (superior category of wines created in 1963)
Et.	Etichetta (label)
IGT	Indicazione Geografica Tipica (category of wines created in 1992)
M.	Metodo
M.to	Monferrato
OP	Oltrepò Pavese
P.R.	Peduncolo Rosso (red bunchstem)
P.	Prosecco
Rif. Agr.	Riforma Agraria (agrarian reform)
Ris.	Riserva
Sel.	Selezione
Sup.	Superiore
TdF	Terre di Franciacorta
V.	Vigna (vine)
Vign.	Vigneto (vineyard)
V. T.	Vendemmia Tardiva (late harvest)

VALLE D'AOSTA

There are 20 growers in Valle d'Aosta's small wine producers' association, "Viticulteur Encaveur" which continues to make its presence felt in the region. The group represents a significant proportion of local premium production and some members have their own profiles in the Guide. These are very small, boutique-style wineries, some of which make fewer than 5,000 bottles a year, but they are a fundamental part of the valley's winemaking fabric, which until a few years ago consisted almost entirely of co-operatives. The Lo Triolet winery run by Marco Martin is especially interesting. The number of bottles produced has grown, as has the general quality of the wines. Martin presents his tried and trusted Pinot Gris and an excellent red called Coteau Barrage from the new vintage. Maison Anselmet's excellent wines have scaled the heights of regional winemaking, achieving an admirable balance with the wood used for ageing. The Grosjean family, who own another of the top wineries of this mountainous region, will be enjoying a more comfortable and spacious new cellar next year. This will no doubt further improve on this year's already highly respectable products. We are delighted to note the products of the Blanc de Morgex et de La Salle DOC zone: a group of small producers have rescued from oblivion this wine, which is well-known for being made next to the glaciers of Mont Blanc. We have deliberately left the maestro of Valle d'Aosta winemaking until last. Costantino Charrère has proved that it is possible to make great wines in this strip of land huddling under the highest mountains in Europe. His philosophy is never to waste the excellent raw materials that nature makes available. That is why his vineyards are cared for like gardens, and that is why Costantino applies the knowledge and experience of the valley's older growers, the people who have turned the management of these steep vineyards into an art form. The wines presented this year are excellent and the Chardonnay Cuvée Bois yet again represents the best of Val d'Aosta winemaking. Let's conclude our look at the vintage with the region's leading winemaking institution, the Institut Agricole di Aosta. As well as making wines, including some particularly promising cask-conditioned selections, the Insititut focuses on viticulture, studying and analysing older local varieties now on the verge of extinction. In a few years, we will be hearing more about carnalin, mayolet, prëmetta and unillermin as they take their place alongside existing vines, lending new vigour to local wine production.

AOSTA

Institut Agricole Régional
Region La Rochere, 1/a
11100 Aosta
tel. 0165215811
e-mail: agriruda@interbusiness.it

The bottles of the Institut's latest vintage have a new design on their labels, taken from Francesco Nex's painting "Trente Six à la Table Ronde". Like the new Bordeaux bottle which is used for all the wines, the labels have been adopted for the whole range of Institut Agricole Régional products, whether basic wines or the more ostentatious barrique-aged selections. The Insititut's catalogue contains 13 wine types and offers the consumer an exhaustive panorama of the valley's wines, in fulfilment of its statutory aim to promote education and professional training in agriculture, to broaden the perspectives of growers and pursue ampelographic and winemaking research. We tasted products of two distinct kinds: fresh, fruity wines aged using traditional methods, and barrique-aged products with a more international style. The steel-aged wines are mainly whites, in particular Pinot Gris and Müller Thurgau. The Petite Arvine is also a good, unusual white obtained from a grape variety imported from nearby Vallese in Switzerland. A maximum of 1,000 bottles are made of each type of wine aged in barriques, including two extraordinary whites, the Chardonnay and the Élite, a monovarietal made from viognier grapes. Both were awarded Two Glasses. Best of the reds again this year was the Trésor du Caveau, which is a great syrah. The grenache-based Rouge du Prieur is good while the Vin du Prévôt is a rather over-oaked blend of 50 per cent cabernet sauvignon with 25 per cent cabernet franc and 25 per cent merlot.

AYMAVILLES (AO)

Costantino Charrère
Les Moulins, 28
11010 Aymavilles (AO)
tel. 0165902135

Costantino Charrère delights winelovers with the bottles from this family winery, which uses the same premises as Les Crêtes, of which Costantino is a founder. Costantino uses a different style for the wines in the range bearing his name, which differs from Les Crêtes not in quality but in the small number of labels released – only four – and the fact that it produces exclusively red wines. Charrère uses mainly native vines for his own winery, some of which have risked extinction: pride of place among these goes to the prëmetta, a red grown almost exclusively by Costantino which produces outstanding wines. The Prëmetta '00 is a pale but perky ruby red in colour, with delicate, aromas reminiscent of unripe berry fruit. The hint of acidity on the palate brightens the finish while the mid palate has notes of sweet spices. Although not over-endowed with structure, it is an eminently drinkable wine overall. This year only three of the four labels were tasted: Les Fourches, a monovarietal grenache, was missing because it was still ageing. The best was the Vin de la Sabla, a highly concentrated red made with petit rouge, fumin and barbera. At the tasting, we noted its attractive, almost impenetrable, ruby red colour, delicate blackcurrant aromas and mouthfilling, tangy flavour. This balanced wine has a noticeable, but by no means unpleasant, hint of acidity which perks up the finish. The Torrette is excellent and in fact the cellar's best wine of the year.

○ Valle d'Aosta Müller Thurgau '00	🍷🍷	4
○ Valle d'Aosta Pinot Gris '00	🍷🍷	4
○ Élite '99	🍷🍷	5
● Rouge du Prieur '99	🍷🍷	5
● Trésor du Caveau '99	🍷🍷	5
○ Valle d'Aosta Chardonnay Barrique '99	🍷🍷	5
○ Valle d'Aosta Petite Arvine '00	🍷	4
● Vin du Prévôt '99	🍷	5
● Valle d'Aosta Pinot Noir '00		4
● Trésor du Caveau '98	🍷🍷	5
● Vin du Prévôt '98	🍷🍷	5

● Valle d'Aosta Torrette '00	🍷🍷	4
● Vin de La Sabla '00	🍷🍷🍷	4
● Valle d'Aosta Prëmetta '00	🍷	4
● Valle d'Aosta Torrette '99	🍷🍷	4
● Vin de La Sabla '99	🍷🍷	4
● Vin Les Fourches '99	🍷🍷	4

AYMAVILLES (AO)

Les Crêtes
Loc. Villetos, 50
11010 Aymavilles (AO)
tel. 0165902274
e-mail: les.cretes@libero.it

This Val d'Aosta winery continues to make progress. It is the only privately owned cellar that turns out a really significant number of bottles, about 120,000 per year. Among the '99 wines, it was the Chardonnay Cuvée Bois that caught our eye. For a couple of years now, this selection, aged in barriques and vinified according to the precepts of the great Burgundy winemakers, has maintained superb standards of quality, more than good enough for a Three Glass award. It is a Chardonnay with a delightfully lustrous old gold hue and equally impressive aromas of aniseed, dried flowers and honey that blend well with charred oak from the wood. But it is the palate that astonishes. Mouthfilling, and almost oily, it has outstanding length in the elegantly well-balanced finish. This is probably the best ever version of the wine. Other whites well worth mentioning are the excellent Chardonnay, fermented in stainless steel, and the unusual Petite Arvine. Of the two, we again prefer the Chardonnay, although the Petite Arvine is elegant and subtle. The reds, too, are on the same high level of quality, with two really top-class labels: Fumin and Coteau La Tour. The former, a classic of the Val d'Aosta, is still young and rather vinous while the Coteau La Tour, the winery's top vineyard selection, is made from syrah grapes. We were not able to review the Coteau La Tour because the latest vintage, the 2000, will undergo an extra year of ageing. Our congratulations to Costantino Charrère for his skill and sagacity on the Coteau La Tour hill, one of the most beautiful and scenic in the valley. The other reds earned One Glass.

	Wine		
O	Valle d'Aosta Chardonnay Cuvée Frissonière Les Crêtes Cuvée Bois '99	🍷🍷🍷	5
O	Valle d'Aosta Chardonnay Cuvée Frissonière Les Crêtes '00	🍷🍷	4
O	Valle d'Aosta Petite Arvine Vigne Champorette '00	🍷🍷	4
●	Valle d'Aosta Fumin Vigne La Tour '99	🍷🍷	5
●	Valle d'Aosta Pinot Noir Vigne La Tour '00	🍷	4
●	Valle d'Aosta Torrette Vigne Les Toules '00	🍷	4
O	Valle d'Aosta Chardonnay Cuvée Frissonière Les Crêtes Cuvée Bois '97	🍷🍷🍷	5
O	Valle d'Aosta Chardonnay Cuvée Frissonière Les Crêtes Cuvée Bois '98	🍷🍷🍷	5

CHAMBAVE (AO)

La Crotta di Vegneron
P.zza Roncas, 2
11023 Chambave (AO)
tel. 016646670
e-mail: lacrotta@libero.it

The La Crotta di Vegneron producers' co-operative offers the best range of wines in the region. Its 130 members contribute grapes from small plots in two subzones of the Vallée d'Aoste DOC zone, Nus and, of course, Chambave. This is where the lower valley's most famous grape variety grows, the first to find success outside the region – moscato. This aromatic variety is vinified at Chambave as a Secco and as a Passito. In both versions, Chambave Moscatos are very good, the Passito coming very close to excellence. A well-deserved Two Glasses went to this version, with its lovely golden colour and aromas that are very reminiscent of the grape. The palate has hints of honey and toasted almonds in the finish and reveals a harmonious, concentrated progression. The Secco could do with a little more body but again the aromas are very true to type. The other Two Glass plaudit goes to the winery's second sweet wine, the Nus Malvoisie Flétri, from the pinot gris grapes known locally as malvoisie. Outstanding among the other varieties is the Fumin – only 1,500 bottles released – a well-structured red aged in oak, which smoothes off its rough edges. The fresh, tangy Chambave Rouge, made from petit rouge, dolcetto, gamay and pinot noir, and the unpretentious Müller Thurgau are also both good.

	Wine		
O	Valle d'Aosta Chambave Moscato Passito '99	🍷🍷	5
O	Valle d'Aosta Nus Malvoisie Flétri '99	🍷🍷	4
O	Valle d'Aosta Chambave Muscat '00	🍷	3*
●	Valle d'Aosta Fumin '99	🍷	4
●	Valle d'Aosta Chambave Rouge '00		3
O	Valle d'Aosta Müller Thurgau '00		3
O	Valle d'Aosta Chambave Moscato Passito '98	🍷🍷	5
●	Valle d'Aosta Fumin '98	🍷	4

INTROD (AO)

Lo Triolet - Marco Martin
Fraz. Junod, 4
11010 Introd (AO)
tel. 016595067 - 016595437

Last year, we mentioned that Marco Martin had plans for the future. Well, after just one year the future has arrived: with the '00 vintage, the Pinot Gris, previously the only wine made, in very limited numbers, reached a production of 8,000 bottles and the range has been extended to four labels. Most important of all, the quantum jump in quality involves the whole range and three of the four selections were awarded Two Glasses. The elegance of all this young producer's wines is astounding, especially as they all have plenty of body. An excellent example is the Coteau Barrage '00, in its first version. It is a red from 85 per cent syrah grapes, with the addition of fumin grown at the winery's Barrage estate in the municipality of Nus. Sixty per cent aged in barriques, it is a bright ruby red and the ripe berry fruit and autumn leaves aromas are balanced by toasty oak from the wood. The ripe, concentrated fruit adds harmony to the excellent flavour. Only 2,000 bottles are made but this is quite a lot for the valley's privately owned wineries. The barrique-aged Pinot Gris is also excellent but unfortunately, only 500 bottles are made. The standard Pinot Gris is fragrant and tangy, and more readily available (3,000 bottles). Last but not least, the Gamay, of which 3,000 bottles are released, is youthful and pleasantly drinkable. Marco Martin is a confident winemaker and continues to increase vine stock to produce a more substantial number of bottles. We will see the results in a few years but if the present evidence is anything to go by, they should be very good indeed.

- ● Coteau Barrage '00 ♇♇ 4
- ○ Valle d'Aosta Pinot Gris
  Élevé en Fût de Chêne '00 ♇♇ 5
- ○ Valle d'Aosta Pinot Gris
  Lo Triolet '00 ♇♇ 4
- ● Valle d'Aosta Gamay '00 ♇ 3

MORGEX (AO)

Cave du Vin Blanc de Morgex et de La Salle
Fraz. La Ruine - Chemin des Iles, 19
11017 Morgex (AO)
tel. 0165800331
e-mail: caveduvinblanc@hotmail.com

The Cave du Vin Blanc de Morgex operates in the mountain area overlooking Mont Blanc. The vineyards belonging to the members are the highest in Europe, at between 900 and 1,200 metres above sea level. The prié blanc, known as blanc de Morgex, variety has always been grown here and is one of the few to have survived phylloxera. It is not therefore necessary to graft it onto American rootstock. These are original vines and the growers in the area protect them carefully, using agricultural methods that in some cases are well nigh heroic. The Cave du Vin Blanc, founded in 1982, does its best not to squander this heritage and makes a series of good prié blanc-based wines. The range has been extended this year with a selection of Blanc de Morgex, called Rayon, alongside the traditional selection. The tasting results were more than satisfactory, and the Chaudelune, a late-vintage white, came out on top. It has good concentration of sugars and the honeyed aromas are subtle and delicate, with clear hints of stewed fruit. The two Blancs de Morgex won One Glass, the panel expressing a slight preference for the Rayon, which has greater weight, over the basic wine. Lastly, the Blanc de Morgex Spumante is a nice bottle.

- ○ Chaudelune Bianco ♇♇ 5
- ○ Valle d'Aosta Blanc
  de Morgex et de La Salle '00 ♇ 3*
- ○ Valle d'Aosta Blanc de Morgex
  et de La Salle Rayon '00 ♇ 4
- ○ Valle d'Aosta Blanc de Morgex
  et de La Salle M. Cl. '97 ♇ 5

QUART (AO)

F.lli Grosjean
Fraz. Ollignan, 1
11020 Quart (AO)
tel. 0165765283

The new cellar under construction near the old premises should be ready in time to accommodate the grapes from the 2001 harvest. Better use of space will make life easier for this winemaking family, who for years have been one of the most successful in the region. From this year, Vincent, the home-grown oenologist, will be working full-time, assisted by his brothers Piergiorgio, Marco, Fernando and Eraldo. Father Delfino will continue to supervise business and in fact, a very attractively priced white table wine is dedicated to him. As well as building a new cellar, the family has been looking to the future by expanding their agricultural activities. Having worked for many years in the viticulture sector for the regional authority, and personally followed the recovery of near extinct native varieties, Vincent Grosjean has decided to focus on prëmetta, cornalin and unillermin. We will taste the first results in a few years' time. Moving on to the wines themselves, we find the consistently good quality best expressed in the two major Grosjean reds, barrique-aged Pinot Nero and Fumin, which both easily merit Two Glasses. The former opens with small wild berry aromas mingling with fumé hints from the wood. The palate is lifted by good ripe fruit, which offsets the trademark acidity of a young Pinot Nero. The Fumin, a Valle d'Aosta variety that produces excellent, characterful red wines, has richly expressive aromas and flavours. The sweet note of balsam is a delight, and develops nicely in the long finish. The Petite Arvine is a fresh, fruity, out-of-the-ordinary white, with excellent fruit. The standard-label Torrette is refreshingly tangy.

● Valle d'Aosta Fumin '99	🍷🍷	4
● Valle d'Aosta Pinot Noir Élevé en Barrique '99	🍷🍷	4
○ Valle d'Aosta Petite Arvine '00	🍷	3
● Valle d'Aosta Torrette '00	🍷	3*
● Valle d'Aosta Gamay '00		3
● Valle d'Aosta Fumin '98	🍷🍷	4
● Valle d'Aosta Pinot Noir Élevé en Barrique '98	🍷🍷	4

VILLENEUVE (AO)

Renato Anselmet
Fraz. La Crete, 46
11018 Villeneuve (AO)
tel. 016595217 - 016595419
e-mail: renato.anselmet@tiscalinet.it

This very small family-run winery – Renato is helped by his son Giorgio, who works at the Cooperativa Onze Communes – has about one and a half hectares of vineyards, favourably aspected on the slopes in the municipalities of Saint-Pierre and Villeneuve. Annual production, consisting of the property's own grapes and others purchased from reliable sources, is around 13,000 bottles of the typical wines of the upper valley, the area from Aosta to Mont Blanc. The very good range presented for this edition of the Guide confirms the quality of winemaking in the Valle d'Aosta, which is boosted by private producers. Renato Anselmet has made a series of very good wines, some of which are aged in wood. In fact, the balance he has managed to achieve between toasty oak and fruit sensations is the real proof of his outstanding ability. Of the whites, the excellent oak-aged Chardonnay '00 is a deep straw yellow, with delicate, well-amalgamated herbal and vanilla aromas. The palate has finesse and good length, and its components are well balanced. The Pinot Gris '00 has an appealing green-flecked yellow hue and aromas reminiscent of a late-harvest wine: aromatic notes of ripe fruit with peach and apricot to the fore. The palate is full-bodied and compelling, with good nose-palate consistency and length. The interesting Müller Thurgau has an intriguing aromatic nose with ripe fruit nuances that give the wine a slightly super-ripe feel. The panel thought the best of the reds was the Pinot Nero, indeed it is the finest version of the wine type made in Valle d'Aosta. The Torrette, however, is a tad one-dimensional and short.

○ Valle d'Aosta Chardonnay Élevé en Fût de Chêne '00	🍷🍷	5
○ Valle d'Aosta Müller Thurgau '00	🍷🍷	3*
○ Valle d'Aosta Pinot Gris '00	🍷🍷	4
● Valle d'Aosta Pinot Noir Élevé en Fût de Chêne '00	🍷🍷	4
● Valle d'Aosta Torrette '00	🍷	4
○ Valle d'Aosta Chardonnay Élevé en Fût de Chêne '99	🍷🍷	4

OTHER WINERIES

CAVE DES ONZE COMMUNES
LOC. URBAINS, 14
11010 AYMAVILLES (AO)
TEL. 0165902912

The 220 members of the co-operative produce particularly interesting, good quality wines from their 57 hectares of vineyards. The excellent Müller Thurgau is fresh and aromatic; the Chardonnay is pleasant with well-balanced acidity; and the Torrette Superiore, aged in small oak casks, is more than decent.

○ Valle d'Aosta Chardonnay '00	♛	3
○ Valle d'Aosta Müller Thurgau '00	♛	3
● Valle d'Aosta Torrette Sup. '99	♛	4

GABRIELLA MINUZZO
FRAZ. SIZAN, 6
11020 CHALLAND SAINT VICTOR (AO)
TEL. 0125967365 - 0125967514

In Valle d'Aosta, as in other regions, smaller wineries are beginning to make their presence felt with wines that are sometimes surprisingly good. That is certainly the case with this Müller Thurgau, vibrant in hue with subtle aromatic herb nuances on the nose.

○ Vallée d'Aoste Müller Thurgau '00	♛♛	3*

CARLO CELEGATO
FRAZ. PREVILLAIR, 37
11017 MORGEX (AO)
TEL. 0165809461

Carlo Celegato is one of the smaller producers in the Blanc de Morgex et de La Salle DOC zone but he is determined and attracts attention for his consistently high quality. Celegato releases only 1,500 bottles of this wine but it is well worth trying if you can find it. Alpine herb aromas introduce a frank, tangily flavoursome palate.

○ Vallée d'Aoste Blanc de Morgex et de La Salle '00	♛	3*

MAISON ALBERT VEVEY
FRAZ. VILLAIR, 57
11017 MORGEX (AO)
TEL. 0165808930
E-MAIL: mariovevey@tiscalinet.it

Today, Maison Albert Vevey is run by Mario and Vevey has become a classic name in Italy's most altitude-enhanced DOC zone. The winery's Blanc de Morgex et de La Salle – no more than 5,000 bottles are made each year – is definitely one of the best: aniseed aromas accompany a vivacious palate, with the classic twist of acidity in the finish.

○ Valle d'Aosta Blanc de Morgex et de La Salle '00	♛	3*

PIEDMONT

The magic moment Piedmont winemaking has been enjoying goes on, and with it the success of the region's wines. The following pages offer space only to the very best of Piedmont producers (312 estates, of which 242 have full profiles and 70 are included in the Other Wineries section) but many others are queuing up with some very interesting bottles indeed. The number of up and coming wine areas is also on the increase and no DOC zone has failed to contribute at least one representative. We need only mention wines from the province of Alessandria, which until just three years ago were mere supporting actors on the cast list. Today, previously featured estates like Villa Sparina and Accornero have been joined by exciting newcomers, led by Tenuta La Tenaglia. However, the whole Piedmont wine sector is in splendid form. Estates like Vigneti Massa and Boveri in the Colli Tortonesi zone, Tenuta Gaiano near Casale and Ca' Bianca at Acqui all came very close to winning Three Glass awards. We are also witnessing the return to the limelight of a number of north Piedmont products, especially Gattinara. Travaglini, Antoniolo and Nervi are keeping this fine wine's flag flying high. After several years of success, Barbatella wines are no longer the leaders in the province of Asti, although they are still among the best. Coppo and Marchesi Alfieri wines have taken up the baton. Prunotto and the Michele Chiarlo cellar have confirmed their status: Prunotto won Three Glasses for a Barbera d'Asti, despite being an Alba-based estate, while Calamandrana's Michele Chiarlo gained top marks for one of the historic Barolo vineyard selections, the Cerequio. Another major award went to the Canelli-based Contratto estate, which have temporarily relinquished leadership in the spumante sector, won Three Glasses for a marvellous Barolo Cerequio. Still in Asti but over towards the border with the Langhe in the province of Cuneo, we find the cellar that obtained the greatest number of Three Glass awards in Piedmont this year, La Spinetta. Two stunning Barbarescos and a textbook Barbera Gallina put the rest of the La Spinetta line-up in the shade. Moving into the heart of the Langhe, we note the reassertion of Barbaresco and Barbera and especially the comeback of the old guard. Thanks to a series of superb vintages in '96, '97 and '98, the gap that separates traditionalists from innovators in Piedmont winemaking is closing perceptibly. Aldo and Giovanni Conterno were Three Glass winners again but there were also newcomers like Rinaldi, Brezza, Luigi Pira, Fontanabianca, Produttori di Barbaresco, Roddolo and Ghisolfi, all of whom left their mark. Dolcetto brought success for Pecchenino again and there were two rising stars in Mossio and Marziano Abbona. Roero is celebrating two Three Glass awards for the late Matteo Correggia. Finally, a word about two special awards: Beppe Caviola is Oenologist of the Year while Elio Grasso's Barolo Runcot '96 was adjudged Red of the Year.

AGLIANO TERME (AT)

DACAPO
STRADA ASTI MARE, 4
14041 AGLIANO TERME (AT)
TEL. 0141964921
E-MAIL: info@dacapo.it

The 2001 vintage saw Paolo Dania and Dino Riccomagno – the Dacapo "brothers" – inaugurated their new cellar in Agliano Terme, the Promised Land of the new Barbera d'Asti. Paolo and Rino, both of whom previously worked at other cellars, have put together their skills, resources and hopes to set up a new estate that has got off to a cracking start. Their mainstay in this new adventure is, of course, Barbera. For the time being, it is also the only wine in their range although there is a Monferrato Rosso in the pipeline that will blend Asti's favourite variety with a proportion of merlot, planted two years ago in front of the main estate building. Keeping a watchful eye on affairs is oenologist Olivieri, one of the area's best qualified professionals. But now for this year's wines. First comes the steel-vinified Barbera Sanbastiàn, a very approachable wine to drink through the meal. It has no great complexity but is undeniably refreshing and attractive. Bright, albeit not overly deep, ruby red in the glass, it proffers young, fruity aromas and a palate remarkable for its frankness and balance. All in all, an ideal choice at table to accompany traditional Piedmont cooking. The barrique-aged Vigna Dacapo vineyard selection is more of a heavyweight. A vibrant garnet leads into a nose whose fruit is enhanced by beautifully judged, fine quality wood. The palate is firm and the length good. We tasted these two wines a few days before they went into the bottle so they will certainly improve further.

- Barbera d'Asti Vigna Dacapo '99 ▼▼ 4
- Barbera d'Asti Sanbastiàn '99 ▼ 3
- Barbera d'Asti Vigna Dacapo '98 ▼▼ 4
- Barbera d'Asti Sanbastiàn '98 ▼ 3

AGLIANO TERME (AT)

TENUTA GARETTO
STRADA ASTI MARE, 30
14041 AGLIANO TERME (AT)
TEL. 0141954068
E-MAIL: tenutagaretto@garetto.it

Alessandro Garetto is the name of the young Monferrato winemaker who runs this estate, assisted by consultants Lorenzo Quinterno and Nicola Argamante. The team's aim is to make serious wines exploiting the potential of a territory with considerable, and in part unrealized, potential. There are 14 hectares under vine, which will increase to 20 in the next few years, and barbera occupies the lion's share. The Barbera d'Asti Tra Neuit e Dì '99, aged in stainless steel, has a ruby colour with purple highlights. Its fresh nose of red berry fruit precedes a palate where the bright acidity fails to integrate completely with the less than substantial structure. The dark ruby Barbera In Pectore '99 has a rich range of aromas that perhaps lack something in elegance but hint at the sumptuous fullness of the structure. The palate flaunts black cherry and cherry while the exuberance of barbera's trademark acidity is tempered by the fruit and alcohol. Barbera Favà '99 comes from very low-yield vines that show just what the variety can do. Fermented in vats and then barrique-aged, this is a wine that was made with tender loving care, and it shows. Its ruby red is impenetrably dark, the extract lusciously rich. It has softness, ripe fruit and a palate that blends power and elegance in a stunning balance, making this a very impressive wine indeed. Finally, the Chardonnay Diversamente is an attempt to break with the past and make a serious oak-conditioned white.

- Barbera d'Asti Sup. Favà '99 ▼▼ 4
- ○ Piemonte Chardonnay Diversamente '00 ▼▼ 4
- Barbera d'Asti Sup. In Pectore '99 ▼ 4
- Barbera d'Asti Tra Neuit e Dì '99 ▼ 3
- Barbera d'Asti Sup. Favà '97 ▼▼ 4
- Barbera d'Asti Sup. In Pectore '97 ▼▼ 3
- Barbera d'Asti Sup. Favà '98 ▼▼ 4
- Barbera d'Asti Sup. In Pectore '98 ▼ 4
- Barbera d'Asti Tra Neuit e Dì '98 ▼ 3

AGLIANO TERME (AT)

Agostino Pavia e Figli
Fraz. Bologna, 33
14041 Agliano Terme (AT)
tel. 0141954125

This fine estate, run by Agostino with the help of his sons Giuseppe and Mauro, is very much involved in the growing trend for Barbera d'Asti, which the Pavias release in three different versions. The Bricco Blina '99, made exclusively in stainless steel, is the most traditional, straightforward interpretation of the genre. Then there is Barbera d'Asti Moliss '99, 20,000 bottles of which are made with fruit from 25 year old vines. It ages first in barrels of Slavonian oak and then in 500 litre tonneaux. The resulting wine is attractive, its floral notes emerging strongly over a pleasantly soft, oak-tempered palate. This is altogether a much tidier wine than the '98. One of the most successful Barbera d'Astis of the vintage is the La Marescialla selection. The fruit used for this wine comes from a vineyard that is over 50 years old, which brings low natural yields and outstanding quality very much within reach. Although a very young wine, La Marescialla can already offer spicy notes from the toasty oak in which it aged for 12 months. In the pleasingly tannic palate, what really impresses is the long, long finish. To round off this report, a mention goes to the Grignolino d'Asti '00. It is a very interesting example of the type, with a slightly pale colour and faint floral aromas. Its main virtue is its moderate alcohol, which softens the typically bitterish varietal aftertaste and makes the wine distinctly moreish.

● Barbera d'Asti La Marescialla '99 🍷🍷	4
● Barbera d'Asti Moliss '99 🍷🍷	3
● Grignolino d'Asti '00 🍷	3
● Barbera d'Asti Bricco Blina '99 🍷	3
● Barbera d'Asti La Marescialla '96 🍷🍷	4
● Barbera d'Asti La Marescialla '98 🍷🍷	4
● Barbera d'Asti La Marescialla '97 🍷	4

AGLIE (TO)

Cieck
Fraz. San Grato
Strada Bardesono
10011 Aglie (TO)
tel. 0124330522 - 012432225
e-mail: info@cieck.it

The Canavese DOC zone has attracted less attention than other parts of Piedmont, such as the Langhe and Monferrato, but still manages to turn out admirable results thanks to estates like Cieck. Active for more than 15 years, it has shown uncommon consistency of quality. Again this year, the wines released demand respect: three out of eight bottles tasted gained Two Glass scores. Since '99, the two original proprietors – Remo Falconieri and Lodovico Bardesono – have been joined by a third partner, Domenico Caretto but the cellar philosophy remains unchanged. The trio aim to develop the potential of their territory by observing tradition and safeguarding local varieties. But let's leave the theory and look at the practice: all the wines released are from native varieties, with erbaluce for the whites and neretto, along with other locally grown grapes, for the reds. Best of the white offerings is the Erbaluce di Caluso Calliope. Although barrique-aged, it has a flavour only moderately nuanced by oak. The clean aromas and full, pervasive palate are instantly appealing. Another high scorer is the Spumante Metodo Classico Calliope '96 which, like the still version, is aged in wood. Pale straw yellow, it yields aromas that blend fruit, yeasts and toasty oak to perfection and a creamy, tangy palate with plenty of length. The Passito is also very tempting, both for its elegance and its ripe, caramel-covered fruit sensations. Among the reds, it is the Canavese Rosso Cieck, a blend of wood-aged local varieties, that stands out while the rather too quaffable Neretto '00 lacks complexity. Rounding off the range are a pleasant Erbaluce Misobolo '00 and an interesting '96 Spumante San Giorgio.

○ Caluso Passito Alladium Vigneto Runc '96 🍷🍷	5
○ Erbaluce di Caluso Spumante Brut Calliope '96 🍷🍷	5
○ Erbaluce di Caluso Calliope '99 🍷🍷	4
○ Erbaluce di Caluso Vigna Misobolo '00 🍷	4
○ Erbaluce di Caluso Spumante S. Giorgio Brut '96 🍷	5
● Canavese Rosso Cieck '99 🍷	4
● Canavese Rosso Neretto '00	3
○ Erbaluce di Caluso '00	3

ALBA (CN)

Silvano e Elena Boroli
Fraz. Madonna di Como, 34
12051 Alba (CN)
tel. 0173365477
e-mail: borolivini@borolivini.com

Silvano and Elena Boroli this year presented us with a range of wines from their two estates, Brunella at Castiglione Falletto and Bompé at Madonna di Como. The style tends towards balance and elegance yet without forgoing the complexity and power that have been the hallmark of recent Langhe harvests. For '97, two Barolo selections flank the base version that gained Two Glasses last year. The Villero impressed, its medium concentrated ruby red ushering in delicate aromas of red berry fruit laced with spices and tobacco. The structure on the palate is delicate, rather than muscular, with good balance and remarkable length. Equally good is the Bussia, its ruby colour shading into orange at the rim and opening on the nose with notes of fruit and roses. The palate unfolds over sweet, velvety tannins to a delicious liquorice-tinged finish. Scoring only a shade lower, we find the Barolo La Brunella, with its slightly forward fruit notes. This is a red that is better enjoyed now than laid down. The more impressive of the two Barberas is the Bricco dei Fagiani, which has greater structure and complexity. Its fruit-rich, spicy nose leads in to a palate noteworthy for its nicely judged acidity and fine balance. The powerful, soft Dolcetto Madonna di Coma is very much in the new style that aims produce an approachable, easy to drink wine. The sumptuously rich Moscato Aureum, from partially raisined fruit, is moderately effervescent and medium sweet. Finally, the Chardonnay Bel Amì is attractive and well-balanced.

	Wine	Glasses	Price
●	Dolcetto d'Alba Madonna di Como '00	♟♟	4
○	Moscato d'Asti Aureum '00	♟♟	4
●	Barolo Bussia '97	♟♟	6
●	Barolo La Brunella '97	♟♟	6
●	Barolo Villero '97	♟♟	6
●	Barbera d'Alba Bricco dei Fagiani '99	♟♟	5
○	Langhe Bianco Bel Amì '00	♟	4
●	Barbera d'Alba Bricco Quattro Fratelli '99	♟	4
●	Barolo La Brunella '96	♟♟	6
●	Dolcetto d'Alba Madonna di Como '99	♟♟	4
●	Langhe Nebbiolo Terranìn '98	♟	4

ALBA (CN)

Ceretto
Loc. San Cassiano, 34
12051 Alba (CN)
tel. 0173282582
e-mail: ceretto@ceretto.it

Here at the magnificent La Bernardina estate, the first outpost of the Barolo Langhe right on the border between the municipalities of Alba and Grinzane, you are looking out over the whole valley of this important DOC zone. It is here that all the Ceretto wines are made before release under the La Bernardina or Ceretto labels. In contrast, the two family jewels, Bricco Rocche and Bricco Asili, are in another category, in the municipality of Castiglione Falletto. La Bernardina is also a sort of laboratory for the Cerettos. This lovely property turns out international-style wines from cabernet sauvignon, syrah, chardonnay, riesling, merlot and viognier, in addition to the Langhe classics. Our report will start with the non-traditional varieties, specifically the remarkable Chardonnay La Bernardina. After the '99 vintage, an outstanding version, partly for its skilful use of oak, this wine will no longer be produced. A disastrous tornado destroyed the vineyard. Luckily, the Langhe Arbarei '99 has what it takes to carry on where the Chardonnay left off. It is a very elegant Riesling that reveals hints of green apple and a minerally note that is echoed in the long, tangy finish. Less impressive is the Langhe Arneis Blangé '00 but the Monsordo '98, a wine that for the past two years has brought together all the international varieties at La Bernardina, put up a very good show. The impenetrable colour tells you straight away that this is a wine with potential. The nose also comes up to scratch and while the palate may not be very muscular, it is softly enfolding and very well-sustained. The Barbaresco Asji '98 and Barbera d'Alba Piana '99 are well-made; the Nebbiolo d'Alba Lantasco '99 and Barolo Zonchera '97 are also decent.

	Wine	Glasses	Price
●	Langhe Rosso Monsordo La Bernardina '98	♟♟	6
●	Barbaresco Asji '98	♟♟	6
●	Barbera d'Alba Piana '99	♟♟	5
○	Langhe Chardonnay La Bernardina '99	♟♟	5
○	Langhe Arbarei '99	♟♟	5
○	Langhe Arneis Blangé '00	♟	4
●	Barolo Zonchera '97	♟	6
●	Nebbiolo d'Alba Lantasco '99	♟	5
○	La Bernardina Brut '95	♟♟	6
●	Langhe Rosso Monsordo La Bernardina '97	♟♟	6

ALBA (CN)

GIANLUIGI LANO
FRAZ. SAN ROCCO SENO D'ELVIO
STRADA BASSO, 38
12051 ALBA (CN)
TEL. 0173286958

This is a cellar that was set up relatively recently. In 1993, Gianluigi Lano decided to give up his job and devote his attentions to the family estate, bottling his first 600 bottles that year. After endless sacrifices and the invaluable contribution of oenologist Gianfranco Cordero, the modestly dimensioned cellar in San Rocco Seno d'Elvio is now producing 25,000 bottles a year from seven hectares under vine on the hillsides at San Rocco and Treiso. Our tastings this year confirmed that Gianluigi is enjoying particular success with barbera. The Fondo Prà '99, aged for 12 months in half new barriques, has a deep, vibrant ruby hue that introduces a lovely nose of vanilla spice, leather and mint. The palate is warm, with serious, close-knit tannins. The standard Barbera, again from '99, is aged in large vats. Slightly paler in colour than the Fondo Prà, it has a fruitier nose and a less explosive, but very well-balanced, palate. Two Glasses also went to the Barbaresco '98. Flaunting an eye-catchingly deep ruby red, it is a little closed on the nose, where hints of bramble jelly and Peruvian bark come through. On the palate, it is powerful, fresh-tasting and soft, with a satisfyingly long finish. The Favorita '00 also came close to Two Glasses, its 13 per cent alcohol giving it a soft attack and good structure. The Lano range concludes with two Dolcettos. The standard version is quaffable, with nice fruity touches, whereas the Ronchella, from the Bricco di Treiso vineyard, was still a little dumb when we tasted, showing morello cherry notes and roughish tannins.

●	Barbaresco '98	♛♛	5
●	Barbera d'Alba '99	♛♛	4
●	Barbera d'Alba Fondo Prà '99	♛♛	5
●	Dolcetto d'Alba '00	♛	3
●	Dolcetto d'Alba Ronchella '00	♛	3
○	Langhe Favorita '00	♛	3
●	Barbaresco '97	♛♛	5
●	Barbera d'Alba Fondo Prà '97	♛♛	4
●	Barbera d'Alba '98	♛♛	3
●	Barbera d'Alba Fondo Prà '98	♛♛	4

ALBA (CN)

PIO CESARE
VIA CESARE BALBO, 6
12051 ALBA (CN)
TEL. 0173440386
E-MAIL: piocesare@piocesare.it

The Pio Cesare range this year boasts a long list of Two Glass wines and a stunning Barbaresco Bricco '97 selection that, deservedly, again won Three Glasses. We say "deservedly" because of all the work that Pio Boffa and oenologist Paolo Fenocchio have done over the years to put this historic Alba estate back in the front rank of winemaking in the Langhe and beyond. The Bricco selection is made with near super-ripe fruit from one of the finest vineyards in Treiso. Its still-developing aromas disclose sweet notes of jam and tobacco with just the right hint of toasty oak. The palate is still tannic but already presents admirable balance. This is a bottle that will keep winelovers smiling for many years to come. A point or two lower on the scale came an excellent standard Barbaresco, a blend of grapes from several vineyards. Both Barolos are also exquisite, although we preferred the Ornato by a whisker. The Serralunga terroir has given the Ornato breadth, structure and a mouthfilling palate where the oak dominates the fruit without overwhelming it. The cherry, blackcurrant and bilberry-rich Barbera d'Alba Fides '98 is as good as it was in previous vintages. Its substantial body is complemented by a palate that is more refreshing than tannic. Both Chardonnays are very convincing, especially the PiodiLei, which in the '99 version has well-judged oak and serious structure as its strong points. The dry, minerally Langhe Arneis is nicely made and easy to drink, as is the Gavi '00, with its lovely fragrance of spring flowers.

●	Barbaresco Bricco '97	♛♛♛	6
●	Barolo Ornato '97	♛♛	6
●	Barolo '97	♛♛	6
●	Barbaresco '98	♛♛	6
●	Barbera d'Alba Fides '98	♛♛	6
○	Langhe Chardonnay PiodiLei '99	♛♛	6
○	Gavi '00	♛	4
○	Langhe Arneis '00	♛	4
●	Langhe Rosso Il Nebbio '00	♛	4
○	Piemonte Chardonnay L'Altro '00	♛	4
●	Barbera d'Alba '99	♛	4
●	Barolo Ornato '85	♛♛♛	6
●	Barolo Ornato '89	♛♛♛	6
●	Barbaresco Bricco '96	♛♛	6
●	Barolo Ornato '96	♛♛	6

ALBA (CN)

PODERI COLLA
FRAZ. SAN ROCCO SENO D'ELVIO, 82
12051 ALBA (CN)
TEL. 0173290148

The wine we like best of the many labels in the widely varied range of this historic San Rocco Seno d'Elvio cellar is the Barbaresco Tenuta Roncaglia '98, which has an attractive garnet hue and a nose of liqueur fruit laced with floral nuances. The elegantly even thrust on the palate is characterized by varietal notes, with evolved hints of liquorice and dried roses. While the structure may be a little lightweight, this does not detract from the brightness of either the palate or the finish, which is delicate rather than powerful, offers reasonable length and faithfully echoes the aromas of nose and palate. The Barolo Bussia is less successful, failing to make best use of the vintage's potential. Alternating broad, fairly complex aromas with a somewhat dull palate and a leanness that is inappropriate for a vintage like the '97. The Nebbiolo d'Alba '99 is bright ruby laced with garnet highlights. Its crushed flower aromas and its continuity from nose through to finish make it a very attractive glass. The Barbera d'Alba Tenuta Roncaglia '99 is an approachable, fruity little crowd-pleaser that offers balance and freshness. The Bonmé is a very unusual fortified wine with loads of personality. Made with moscato grapes from Cascine Drago, where the rows in the older vineyards and yield excellent quality fruit. The wine is fortified with 95 per cent alcohol and vegetable infusions containing herbs, roots and inflorescences, according to an ancient recipe handed down through the generations by the Colla family. On the nose, there are distinct notes of Italian bitters and absinthe while the thick but not cloyingly sweet palate unveils candied orange peel, chamomile and a tidy, well-balanced finish of new-mown grass.

● Barbaresco Tenuta Roncaglia '98	♈♈	6
○ Bonmé	♈♈	5
● Barolo Bussia Dardi Le Rose '97	♈	6
● Barbera d'Alba Tenuta Roncaglia '99	♈	4
● Nebbiolo d'Alba '99	♈	4
● Barolo Bussia Dardi Le Rose '95	♈♈	6
● Barbaresco Tenuta Roncaglia '96	♈♈	6
● Barolo Bussia Dardi Le Rose '96	♈♈	6
● Barbaresco Tenuta Roncaglia '97	♈♈	6
● Langhe Bricco del Drago '97	♈♈	5

ALBA (CN)

PRUNOTTO
LOC. SAN CASSIANO, 4/G
12051 ALBA (CN)
TEL. 0173280017
E-MAIL: prunotto@prunotto.it

The Antinori family continues to cultivate its ambitions plans for Piedmont with the invaluable assistance of Gianluca Torrengo, a very talented oenologist. The panel was particularly struck by two Prunotto wines. The first was the Barbera d'Asti Costamiòle '99, which made a triumphant return to Three Glass status, and the other was the Barolo Bussia '97. Vermilion in hue, and unveiling rich aromas of cocoa powder, black berry fruit and coffee, it explodes onto the palate, which mirrors the nose perfectly, expanding nicely into a balsamic finish. In contrast, the Bussia '97 has an austere and instinctively elegant character. Its thrillingly complex aromas are redolent of leather and elderflower, opening out on the palate into a broad, dynamic structure sustained by beautifully handled tannins. Ever reliable, the Nebbiolo d'Alba Occhetti '99 shows typically persistent notes of tobacco and spices with a soft counterpoint of tannins. Generous and elegant, the Barbaresco Bric Turot '98 boasts an attractive nose of fruit, fleshy roses and ripe black cherry from the wonderful hillslope grapes of Bric Turot, mellowed by the carefully gauged oak. The two Barberas, Pian Romualdo '99 and Fiulòt '00, are tidily made. In the former, stylish notes of black cherry and white pepper are to the fore whereas in the Fiulòt '00, the panel picked up an appealing overtone of mint which heralded an invitingly fruit-rich finish. The Barolo '97 and the Barbaresco '98 confirmed the estate's clean typicity. Our tasting was rounded off by the Dolcetto d'Alba '00, the Barbera d'Alba '99 and the Arneis '00, all very convincing.

● Barbera d'Asti Costamiòle '99	♈♈♈	6
● Barolo Bussia '97	♈♈	6
● Barbera d'Asti Fiulòt '00	♈♈	4
● Barbaresco '98	♈♈	6
● Barbaresco Bric Turot '98	♈♈	6
● Barbera d'Alba Pian Romualdo '99	♈♈	5
● Nebbiolo d'Alba Occhetti '99	♈♈	5
● Dolcetto d'Alba '00	♈	3
● Barolo '97	♈	6
● Barbera d'Alba '99	♈	4
○ Roero Arneis '00	♈	4
● Barbera d'Asti Costamiòle '96	♈♈♈	6
● Barolo Bussia '96	♈♈♈	6
● Barbera d'Asti Costamiòle '97	♈♈♈	6
● Barbaresco Bric Turot '97	♈♈	6

ALBA (CN)

MAURO SEBASTE
FRAZ. GALLO
VIA GARIBALDI, 222/BIS
12051 ALBA (CN)
TEL. 0173262148
E-MAIL: maurosebaste@areacom.it

The winery run by Mauro Sebaste and wife Maria Teresa is back in the Guide. They produce 100,000 bottles a year from 15 hectares of rented vineyards, tended under the supervision of Giovanni Bailo. Mauro graduated from the wine school in Alba and grew up among the family vines. His mother owned the historic Sylla Sebaste estate, which Mauro managed for several years. The offerings include a number of Barolos, which are aged in 1,500-litre vats and 500-litre tonneaux to give them a subtle hint of oak. Other wines are an Arneis, a Langhe Bianco, a Rosso and a Nebbiolo. The Barolo Prapò is garnet red, shading into brick red. The nose is intriguing, with hints of red and black berry fruit, autumn leaves and vanilla. On the palate, there is great structure underpinned by close-knit tannins taking you on to a long finish that mirrors the nose. The Barolo Monvigliero has a less complex nose of strawberry, rhubarb and leather. The palate has vigour and the fruit returns in the finish. The Sebastes also make a Barolo La Serra, which was still in the barrel when we came to taste. In the '99 vintage, it will be joined by the new Barolo Brunate. Centobricchi Rosso (80 per cent barbera and 20 per cent nebbiolo) has a dense hue and a nose of coffee and caramel over a faint vegetal notes. Full-bodied on the palate, it foregrounds fruit and toasty oak in the finish. Its stablemate, the Centobricchi Bianco, is from 90 percent sauvignon and 10 per cent arneis and presents notes of caramel-covered fruit with flowers. The palate is full and the finish slightly dominated by the wood. Finally, the Arneis is smooth and soft.

	Wine	Glasses	Score
●	Barolo Monvigliero '97	🍷🍷	6
●	Barolo Vigna Prapò '97	🍷🍷	6
○	Langhe Bianco Centobricchi '00	🍷	4
○	Roero Arneis '00	🍷	4
●	Langhe Rosso Centobricchi '99	🍷	5

ALBA (CN)

PODERI SINAGLIO
FRAZ. SAN ROCCO CHERASCA
12051 ALBA (CN)
TEL. 0173612209
E-MAIL: poderi.sinaglio@tiscalinet.it

The Accomo winery is making its Guide debut. Their 13 hectares of vineyard are scattered across the municipalities of Alba and Diano, where they grow dolcetto, nebbiolo, barbera, moscato, chardonnay and sauvignon. The estate, which has been bottling since 1995, is run by brothers Bruno and Silvano Accomo, and their parents Amabile and Olga. Several of their wines gained Two Glass ratings, beginning with the Dolcetto di Diano d'Alba Sörì Bricco Maiolica, one of the very finest of the modern-style Dianos. Intense in hue, it offers an entry on the nose of red fruit backed by vigorous alcohol. The fleshy, almost austere, mouthfeel precedes an almond-themed finish with the bitterish twist characteristic of the variety. The Rosso Sinaij (30 per cent freisa, 20 per cent nebbiolo and 50 per cent barbera) is dense in colour and on the nose offers notes of wild berries, autumn leaves and mint over faint toasty oak. The palate is generously rich, with a vibrant finish that reveals floral hints. Two Glasses also went to the vibrant straw yellow Chardonnay Boccabarile. The nose balances wood and fruit over minerally notes while the rich palate has good freshness. Next was the Barbera Vigna Erta, with its attractive entry on the nose, and plum, bramble and yeasted dough aromas. The vigorous palate is equally satisfying. To round off, the Nebbiolo Giachét is attractively rustic, the chardonnay and sauvignon Bianco Boccabarile is slightly in awe of the wood and the Moscato La Mimosa is nicely aromatic. The moscato-based Passito Le Monache has charm and the standard-label Barbera and Chardonnay are both well-made.

	Wine	Glasses	Score
●	Diano d'Alba Sörì Bricco Maiolica '00	🍷🍷	3*
○	Langhe Chardonnay Boccabarile '98	🍷🍷	3*
●	Langhe Rosso Sinaij '99	🍷🍷	4
●	Barbera d'Alba '00	🍷	3
○	Moscato d'Asti La Mimosa '00	🍷	3
○	Le Monache Passito '97	🍷	4
●	Barbera d'Alba Vigna Erta '99	🍷	4
○	Langhe Bianco Boccabarile '99	🍷	3
○	Langhe Chardonnay '99	🍷	3
●	Nebbiolo d'Alba Giachét '99	🍷	4

ALICE BEL COLLE (AL)

Ca' Bianca
Reg. Spagna, 58
15010 Alice Bel Colle (AL)
Tel. 0144745420
E-mail: giv@giv.it

Ca' Bianca is a Gruppo Italiano Vini estate. GIV owns a number of major cellars all round Italy and is a leading player in the international premium wine market. Ca' Bianca's annual output of around half a million bottles includes all of Piedmont's main wine types. The force behind Ca' Bianca is the very competent Marco Galeazzo. This was Barbera Chersì's year: on its first bottling, it came close to picking up Three Glasses. It is from a superb vineyard selection of more than 60 year old vines and impresses at once with its inky, ruby-flecked hue. The aromas of bilberry, bramble and coffee are enhanced by subtle overtones of tobacco and sweet spices. But you know you have a heavyweight on your hands when it crashes onto the palate with all the warmth of the stunning raw material. In the mouth, it is so full-bodied you can almost chew it and the variety's typical acidity provides support. The fruit is rich and well-sustained, holding the oak at a respectful distance. Two Glasses went to the Gavi '00, which unveils delicate fragrances of white peach, apple, pineapple and spring flowers. It's a wine that drinks as clean as a whistle. The combination of fresh notes and riper nuances is irresistible, with an overall harmony that lets the varietal character shine through. The Barolo puts the accent on warm, ripe notes of wild rose, violet, cinnamon and fennel seed while the palate is nicely balanced. The Barbera '99 offers aromas of ripe berry fruit, vanilla and cocoa powder and the fruit on the palate gives way somewhat tart acidity in the finish. Finally, the Dolcetto '00 is soft and fruity.

● Barbera d'Asti Chersì '99	ΨΨ	6
○ Gavi Ca' Bianca '00	ΨΨ	4
● Barolo '97	ΨΨ	6
● Dolcetto d'Acqui '00	Ψ	4
● Barbera d'Asti '99	Ψ	4
● Barolo '96	ΨΨ	6

ASTI

F.lli Rovero
Fraz. San Marzanotto
Loc. Val Donata
14100 Asti
Tel. 0141592460

Congratulations to the Rovero family. Claudio, Michele and Franco, who actually spends most of his time distilling, presented the panel with a very interesting range of wines. The Roveros firmly believe in organic farming and are gradually expanding their hospitality facilities. You certainly couldn't accuse them of underinvesting. We'll begin with the brace of Monferrato Bianco Sauvignons. The '00 vintage has fragrant, clean aromas that are reminiscent of apples and pears on the nose, tending towards a more vegetal note on the palate. In contrast, the '99 was fermented and aged in barriques. Obtained from a late, hillslope harvest, it opens on the nose with ripe hints of banana and melon. The palate progresses attractively, with a nice balance of wood-derived notes mingling with citrus fruit. Next came the impenetrably dark ruby Monferrato Rosso Cabernet '98. The notes of plum jam and fresh-cut hay on the nose are precisely mirrored on the palate, which delivers vigorous body and a refreshing, balsamic finish. Pepper, Peruvian bark and tobacco come across on the nose of the Monferrato Rosso Pinot Nero '99 while the blood-red Barbera d'Asti Vigneto Gustin '99 offers ripe notes of wild cherries and aromatic herbs, which are reflected on the fairly broad palate. The Barbera d'Asti Rouvé '98 comes from very ripe fruit, and releases austere aromas of stewed cherries, leather and spices on the nose. There is plenty of structure, and robust alcohol on the palate, which has benefited from judicious ageing in small oak barrels. We'll close with the rose, strawberry and pepper aromas of the Grignolino d'Asti La Casalina '00.

● Barbera d'Asti Sup. Rouvé '98	ΨΨ	4
● Monferrato Rosso Cabernet '98	ΨΨ	4
○ Monferrato Bianco Sauvignon Barrique '99	ΨΨ	4
● Monferrato Rosso Pinot Nero '99	ΨΨ	5
● Grignolino d'Asti Vigneto La Casalina '00	Ψ	3
○ Monferrato Bianco Sauvignon '00	Ψ	3
● Barbera d'Asti Sup. Vigneto Gustin '99	Ψ	3
● Monferrato Rosso Cabernet '97	ΨΨ	4
● Barbera d'Asti Rouvé '97	Ψ	4

BARBARESCO (CN)

Ca' Romé - Romano Marengo
Via Rabajà, 36
12050 Barbaresco (CN)
tel. 0173635126
e-mail: info@carome.com

Romano Marengo and his children Paola and Giuseppe make the nebbiolo-based Langhe classics at Ca' Romé but they also give due attention to Barbera. In fact, their La Gamberaja selection can justly be considered one of the cellar's flagship wines. Voluptuous violet and vegetal aromas already hint at complexity while the entry on the palate is full and very smooth. There is also plenty of length in the finish. These features are echoed by the Langhe Dapruvé '98, which we mentioned last time round but today is a more harmonious, complete product. Now let's move on to the Barbarescos and Barolos. And don't forget to let them breathe for while to get rid of the initial reductive notes that might otherwise detract from your pleasure. The Barbaresco Sorì Rio Sordo got off to a great start with the '98, its first vintage. In effect, it's right up there with the Ca' Romé's warhorse, the Barbaresco Maria di Brun. Both of these bottles have a lovely garnet hue and nice complexity on the nose, which ranges from bilberries to toasty balsamic notes. The standard-label Barbaresco is less genteel: the texture is looser while the tannins and alcohol have yet to settle down. The most convincing of the Ca' Romé Barolos was again the Rapet, which has good nose-palate consistency, decent structure and goodish length. On the nose, the Vigna Ceretta is a little closed and the alcohol tends to prevail over the tannins in the mouth.

• Barolo Rapet '97	🍷🍷	6
• Barbaresco Maria di Brun '98	🍷🍷	6
• Barbaresco Sorì Rio Sordo '98	🍷🍷	6
• Barbera d'Alba La Gamberaja '99	🍷🍷	5
• Barolo Vigna Cerretta '97	🍷	6
• Barbaresco '98	🍷	6
• Barbaresco Maria di Brun '95	🍷🍷	6
• Barbaresco Maria di Brun '96	🍷🍷	6
• Barolo Rapet '96	🍷🍷	6
• Barbaresco '97	🍷🍷	6
• Barbaresco Maria di Brun '97	🍷🍷	6
• Langhe Rosso Da Pruvé '98	🍷	5

BARBARESCO (CN)

Cantina del Pino
Via Ovello, 15
12050 Barbaresco (CN)
tel. 0173635147
e-mail: cantinadelpino@libero.it

A newcomer to the Guide last year, the Cantina del Pino has confirmed its status as a serious Barbaresco producer with a range of balanced and very well-made wines. Starting this year, Renato and his father Adriano have decided to vinify their Freisa – they only make 1,200 bottles – in a radically different manner. No longer will it be a quaffable, easy-going sparkler; now it is a serious red with a dense colour and clean aromas of rose petals and dried flowers, enhanced by a brief sojourn in pre-used wood. The 10,000 bottles of Dolcetto are made using a very short maceration. The very dark hue ushers in intense fruit aromas with a distinctive minty note. The palate is austere, almost to the point of stiffness, but the typically almondy finish lingers attractively. The Barbera Loreto, from a vineyard of barely one hectare, has a vibrant, purple-flecked ruby colour and a deliciously stylish fruit-rich nose. The palate is firm and fleshy while the sweet finish shows good length. About 15,000 bottles of the Barbaresco Ovello '98 were made, 70 per cent from the Loreto vineyard and the remainder from Albano. One third was aged in new barriques for 20 months and the rest in pre-used small and large barrels. This may only be the second bottling but it already reveals a sure hand in its garnet colour and vibrantly attractive style. The nose offers notes of ripe berry fruit and fragrant dried flowers before the palate contributes its rich texture, robust but not over-dry tannins and a dynamic, satisfying and very long finish, where berry fruit again comes through.

• Langhe Freisa '00	🍷🍷	4
• Barbaresco Ovello '98	🍷🍷	5
• Barbera d'Alba '99	🍷🍷	4
• Dolcetto d'Alba '00	🍷	3
• Barbaresco Ovello '97	🍷🍷	5
• Barbera d'Alba '98	🍷🍷	4

BARBARESCO (CN)

Tenute Cisa Asinari
dei Marchesi di Gresy
Via Rabajà, 43
12050 Barbaresco (CN)
tel. 0173635221 - 0173635222
e-mail: wine@marchesidigresy.com

The 38 hectares under vine of the Tenute Cisa Asinari are scattered across Treiso, Cassine and Barbaresco. Back in the cellar, Marco Dotta and his wine technician Alberto di Gresy vinify the grapes expertly and the results can be seen in the glass. There is a wide and successful range but this year it was the Barbaresco Gaiun '98 we liked best. The vibrant garnet heralds balsamic and liquorice aromas that have yet to develop fully but the full-bodied, fruit-rich palate, underpinned by robust tannins, holds up admirably to linger in the finish. The Martinenga '98 is nearer to being ready for drinking, its stylish violet and raspberry aromas coming through well. The palate is muscular and tannic without being dry and there is goodish fruit in the finish. In contrast, the release of the Camp Gros '98 has been delayed for a year for this is a wine that needs more time in the cellar. Ditto for one of the two Langhe Rossos, the Villa Martis '98. The Langhe Virtus, from 40 per cent cabernet and 60 per cent barbera, is very successful. Dark in hue, it melds its berry fruit and bramble aromas beautifully into the oak. On the palate, the tannins are sweet and the finish is very clean. The Dolcetto and Langhe Nebbiolo '00 are both very likeable while the Sauvignon, from this year Langhe Bianco, is the white that stands out. The vibrant straw-yellow introduces stylish aromas and a full, balanced palate with a nice tannic note in the finish. To round off, there was a very drinkable standard-label Chardonnay, a decent, if rather generously oaked, Chardonnay Gresy '99 and the ever-reliable Moscato d'Asti.

BARBARESCO (CN)

Giuseppe Cortese
Via Rabajà, 35
12050 Barbaresco (CN)
tel. 0173635131

Giuseppe Cortese and son Piercarlo have begin work on their cellars to create more space for ageing and a new cellar for the medium-sized barrels traditionally used for Nebbiolo and Barbaresco. The small wood is reserved for the Barbera, not yet ready for release, and Chardonnay. This impressive white, first released with the '99 vintage, comes from a small vineyard at Trifolera. It lives up to expectations, showing good potential for structure and finesse that can be built on in the future. The same subzone is the source of the steel-vinified Dolcetto d'Alba '00. A frank and typically quaffable wine, it reveals attractive notes of red berry jam and a faint almond twist in the finish. Grapes mainly from the lower part of the vineyard and older barrels are used for the Langhe Nebbiolo. Its garnet colour ushers in crisp aromas of cherry and more delicate balsamic notes while the tangy, elegant palate is tannin-rich, winding up with a nice, fruity finish. In line with its vintage, the Barbaresco Rabajà '98 is a stunner. Grape selection was relentless and after a ten-month sojourn in French oak, its mature garnet evokes magnificent hints of redcurrant, cocoa powder and fresh berry fruit. The palate is broad, deep and echoes the nose satisfyingly, foregrounding elegance rather than power. The prominent tannins lead in to a finish with attractive spicy nuances.

○ Langhe Bianco '00	▼▼	4
○ Moscato d'Asti La Serra '00	▼▼	3*
● Barbaresco Gaiun '98	▼▼	6
● Barbaresco Martinenga '98	▼▼	6
● Langhe Rosso Virtus '98	▼▼	5
● Dolcetto d'Alba Monte Aribaldo '00	▼	4
○ Langhe Chardonnay '00	▼	4
● Langhe Nebbiolo Martinenga '00	▼	4
○ Langhe Chardonnay Gresy '99	▼	5
● Barbaresco Gaiun '85	▼▼▼	6
● Barbaresco Gaiun '97	▼▼▼	6
● Barbaresco Camp Gros '97	▼▼	6
● Barbaresco Martinenga '97	▼▼	6

● Barbaresco Rabajà '98	▼▼	6
● Langhe Nebbiolo '99	▼▼	4
○ Dolcetto d'Alba Trifolera '00	▼	3
○ Langhe Chardonnay Scapulin '99	▼	4
● Barbaresco Rabajà '95	▼▼	5
● Barbaresco Rabajà '96	▼▼	5
● Barbaresco Rabajà '97	▼▼	6
● Langhe Nebbiolo '98	▼▼	4

BARBARESCO (CN)

★ ★ Gaja
Via Torino, 36
12050 Barbaresco (CN)
tel. 0173635158

You can go to the bank on Gaja wines. After 15 years in the Guide, the cellar has won so many Three Glass awards – fully 27, plus two more this year – that no other producer can match its performance. All six wines we tasted were impeccable but the panel like the Barbaresco '98 and the Sorì Tildin '97 best. The former may not be a vineyard selection, like the San Lorenzo, Costa Russi and Sorì Tildin, but it is one of the finest Barbarescos around. Its intense ruby hue opens the way for a perfect bouquet, where morello cherry and pencil lead meld brilliantly with oak-derived toastiness. On the palate, the mouthfeel is extraordinarily substantial and the fruit gently enfolds the taste buds. The beautifully long finish is characterized by a warm note of alcohol. The Sorì Tildin, one of the classic Gaja selections, also put up a fine performance. In the new Langhe DOC version, the '97 has a dense, attractive colour. A wine of superb class and elegance, it lives up admirably to the reputation it has acquired in its more than two decade-long career. Only a mark or two below came the other two Langhe DOC selection, the Costa Russi and the San Lorenzo. The slightly developed nose of the Costa Russi brought its score down but the palate is all you could wish for, rich in sweet, ripe fruit. Our notes on the San Lorenzo were similar, although here the acidity in the finish is a little more unruly. On the Langhe Barolo front, there were two excellent offerings in Sperss and Conteisa while the Chardonnay Gaja & Rey stood out among the whites.

BARBARESCO (CN)

Carlo Giacosa
Via Ovello, 8
12050 Barbaresco (CN)
tel. 0173635116

Carlo Giacosa knows very well that to make good wine you need to keep vineyard yields low and thin the bunches when nature is overgenerous. That's why this small cellar has been posting some very encouraging results for a few years now. The five hectares of vine in the municipalities of Barbaresco and Neive produce 35,000 bottles a year, half of them Barbaresco. There are two labels, the Montefico vinified in large oak barrels, and the Narin, the nickname of Carlo's father Donato, a barrique-aged wine made with fruit from the Canova, Asili and Cole vineyards. The '98 versions both obtained the same score at our tasting. The Montefico is very subtle, with hints of tobacco and raspberry and a balanced elegance on the palate. Less approachable on the nose, the Narin however reveals nice fruit and palate that stands out for its lovely tannins and long, dry finish. Another good performance came from the Barbera Lina, named after Carlo's mother. The '99 vintage, aged in barriques for 12 months, has a bright, attractive hue. The stylish nose is redolent of earth, vanilla and cherries while the well-structured palate is deliciously refreshing. The Mary Grace, a '00 table wine from almost 100 per cent nebbiolo named after Carlo's daughter, came close to a Two Glass rating. Its garnet colour introduces aromas of berry fruit and tobacco while the palate has plenty of power and character. Rounding off the tasting were the fresh-tasting and very drinkable Dolcetto Cuchet, with its almondy finish, and the vibrant colour and attractively fruity palate of the Barbera Mucin.

● Langhe Rosso Sorì Tildin '97	▼▼▼	6
● Barbaresco '98	▼▼▼	6
● Langhe Nebbiolo Conteisa '97	▼▼	6
● Langhe Nebbiolo Sperss '97	▼▼	6
● Langhe Rosso Costa Russi '97	▼▼	6
● Langhe Rosso Sorì S. Lorenzo '97	▼▼	6
○ Langhe Chardonnay Gaia & Rey '99	▼▼	6
● Barbaresco Sorì Tildin '93	▼▼▼	6
● Barbaresco Costa Russi '95	▼▼▼	6
● Barbaresco Sorì S. Lorenzo '95	▼▼▼	6
● Langhe Nebbiolo Sperss '96	▼▼▼	6
● Langhe Rosso Costa Russi '96	▼▼▼	6
● Langhe Rosso Darmagi '96	▼▼▼	6
● Barbaresco '97	▼▼▼	6

● Barbaresco Montefico '98	▼▼	5
● Barbaresco Narin '98	▼▼	5
● Barbera d'Alba Lina '99	▼▼	4
● Barbera d'Alba Mucin '00	▼	3*
● Dolcetto d'Alba Cuchet '00	▼	3*
● Mary Grace '00	▼	4
● Barbaresco Montefico '97	▼▼	5
● Barbaresco Narin '97	▼▼	5
● Mary Grace '99	▼▼	3
● Barbera d'Alba Lina '98	▼	3

BARBARESCO (CN)

I PAGLIERI
LOC. PAJÉ
VIA RABAJÀ, 8
12050 BARBARESCO (CN)
TEL. 0173635109

Now that Alfredo Roagna's son Luca, fresh from graduating as a wine technician, has joined the business, the energy level at this Barbaresco-based cellar, and its range of traditional-style products, have received a further boost. As ever, the '97 version of the Barbaresco Crichèt Pajé is a lovely wine, its ruby colour shading into garnet with an orange-tinged rim. On the nose, it is complex and dry, showing hints of dried flowers, cherry and hazelnut. The palate has good texture that comes through in the austere progression, supported by firm tannins and concluding in a long, well-sustained finish. The Barolo La Rocca e La Pira, moderately intense in hue, tempts the nose with notes of leather, fruit preserve and evolved floral notes. The palate has a close-knit, dry texture with lashings of robust tannins and a well-orchestrated finish redolent of cocoa powder and flowers. Opera Prima is a blend of nebbiolo from several vintages. The XIV version has an attractive colour that shades into garnet, a slightly creamy nose with hints of liqueur cherries and autumn leaves. There is remarkable power in the sustained, dry palate, nicely rounded off by a long finish that mirrors the nose. Finally, the Barbaresco '98 has an orange rim to its ruby colour in the glass. The nose is a little forward, with hints of coffee, raspberry and earth, while the satisfyingly full palate has a faintly bitterish twist in the finish.

● Barbaresco Crichèt Pajé '97	♟♟	6
● Barolo La Rocca e La Pira '97	♟♟	6
● Opera Prima XIV	♟♟	6
● Barbaresco '98	♟	6
● Barbaresco Crichèt Pajé '96	♟♟	6
● Barbaresco Ris. '96	♟♟	6
● Barolo La Rocca e La Pira '96	♟♟	6
● Opera Prima XIII	♟♟	6
● Barolo La Rocca e La Pira '95	♟	6
● Barbaresco '97	♟	6

BARBARESCO (CN)

CASCINA LUISIN
LOC. RABAJÀ, 23
12050 BARBARESCO (CN)
TEL. 0173635154

Luigi and Roberto Minuto, respectively father and son of one of the longest-established Barbaresco-producing families, make wine in a cellar that oozes history and tradition. On our last visit, we tasted a memorable Barbaresco '71. Perfectly conserved, it thrilled us with its freshness and superb aromas, worthy of the finest Burgundies from the same vintage. As was the case two years ago, the panel assigned Three Glasses to the Barbera Asili '99, a wine from a celebrated Barbaresco vineyard that ages in small oak barrels for 18 months. Its very deep, dark red heralds aromas of bramble jam mingling with oak-derived vanilla and mint. The attack on the palate is overwhelming, with close-knit, sweet tannins that carry it through to the warm, generous finish. The year 2000 was a fantastic one for the Barbera Maggiur. Made with grapes from a very old vineyard at San Rocco Seno d'Elvio, it is dark yet vibrant in the glass and unveils distinctly fruity notes, with hints of violets, on the nose. The palate is generously full-bodied and soft, the tannins delicious. Of the two Barbaresco '98s, we preferred the Rabajà to the Sorì Paolin. The pale garnet Rabajà has intense, evolved aromas of wild berries and astringent tannins, accompanied by good flesh and length. The Sorì Paolin is a comparable wine but rather less dense, not so full-bodied, and with less fruit on the nose. The Langhe Nebbiolo '99, from a San Rocco Seno d'Elvio vineyard, came within an ace of Two Glasses while the still greenish and rather hard Dolcetto '00 just managed One Glass.

● Barbera d'Alba Asili '99	♟♟♟	5
● Barbera d'Alba Maggiur '00	♟♟	3*
● Barbaresco Rabajà '98	♟♟	6
● Barbaresco Sorì Paolin '98	♟♟	6
● Dolcetto d'Alba Bric Trifüla '00	♟	3
● Langhe Nebbiolo '99	♟	4
● Barbera d'Alba Asili Barrique '97	♟♟♟	5
● Barbaresco Rabajà '95	♟♟	6
● Barbaresco Rabajà '96	♟♟	6
● Barbaresco Sorì Paolin '96	♟♟	6
● Barbaresco Rabajà '97	♟♟	6
● Barbera d'Alba Asili '98	♟♟	5
● Barbera d'Alba Maggiur '99	♟♟	3

BARBARESCO (CN)

MOCCAGATTA
VIA RABAJÀ, 24
12050 BARBARESCO (CN)
TEL. 01736355228 - 0173635152

Brothers Sergio and Franco Minuto run a 12-hectare property that produces about 70,000 bottles a year. The Minutos offer a wide range of fine wines, beginning with the Barbaresco Bric Balin. Its intense garnet introduces a complex nose where notes of cherry, cocoa powder and toasty oak mingles with tar. The firm, well-sustained palate pleases with firm tannins and a long finish. The hints of jam and cakes on the nose of the Basarin are sweeter. In the mouth, it delivers an attractive texture, laced with dry, oak-derived tannins, and a long finish swathed in floral notes. Good, too, was the Cole, although it didn't reach last year's heights. On the nose, there are nuances of wild berries, rhubarb, mint, liquorice and leather while the palate offers a solid and slightly austere progression with an attractive fruity after-aroma in the finish. Berry fruit and spices on the nose followed by a firm-textured mouthfeel: that's what earned the Barbera Basarin its comfortable Two Glasses. The Chardonnay Buschet offers fruit against a backdrop of super-ripe notes on the nose, followed by generous flesh on the palate. The standard-label Chardonnay is full-bodied and even, expressing all the typicity of its variety with laudable precision. Finally, the standard Freisa and Barbera were pleasingly rustic, the Freisa being lively while the uncomplicated Barbera put the accent on fruit.

	Wine	Glasses	Score
●	Barbaresco Bric Balin '98	♢♢	6
●	Barbaresco Basarin '98	♢♢	6
●	Barbaresco Cole '98	♢♢	6
●	Barbera d'Alba Basarin '99	♢♢	5
○	Langhe Chardonnay Buschet '99	♢♢	5
●	Barbera d'Alba '00	♢	4
○	Langhe Chardonnay '00	♢	3
●	Langhe Freisa '00	♢	3
●	Barbaresco Bric Balin '90	♢♢♢	6
●	Barbaresco Cole '97	♢♢♢	6
●	Barbaresco Cole '96	♢♢	6
●	Barbaresco Basarin '97	♢♢	6
●	Barbaresco Bric Balin '97	♢♢	6
●	Barbera d'Alba Basarin '98	♢♢	5
●	Barbaresco Basarin '96	♢	6

BARBARESCO (CN)

MONTARIBALDI
FRAZ. TRE STELLE
VIA RIO SORDO, 30/A
12050 BARBARESCO (CN)
TEL. 0173638220

Now that they have at last completed their new cellar, brothers Luciano and Roberto Taliano are gradually perfecting their vinification techniques, assisted by their parents. This may not be one of the DOC zone's better-known producers, but the Taliano's determination is paying off handsomely. The family, originally from Roero, for years managed vineyards for other people but now concentrate increasingly on their own labels. In this edition of the Guide, the Talianos confirmed their progress, particularly with a Barbera that easily achieved a Two Glasses score. It's a modern wine, very much in tune with the new-breed Barberas that pack sufficient complexity to make an impact on international markets. As you raise the glass, the colour impresses with its density and subtle purple highlights. There is intensity on the nose, too, where an explosive attack of morello cherry jam is lent depth by hints of roast coffee beans and plain chocolate. The keynotes on the palate are fullness and richness of flavour, leading in to an endlessly long, almost chewy, finish that still offers plenty of finesse. A mark or two lower came the Barbaresco '98, wine of class and complexity that are nonetheless not enough on their own to make up for a lack of softness in the fruity flesh. Not for the first time, the Dolcetto '00 earned Two Glasses for its combination of good structure on the palate and a richly vinous nose that also offers lots of fruit. The other Montaribaldi wines were a shade lower down the scale: pleasant and easy to drink, they managed One Glass apiece.

	Wine	Glasses	Score
●	Barbera d'Alba dü Gir '99	♢♢	5
●	Dolcetto d'Alba Nicolini '00	♢♢	4
●	Barbaresco Sörì Montaribaldi '98	♢♢	6
○	Roero Arneis '00	♢	4
○	Langhe Chardonnay Stissa d'le Favole '99	♢	4
●	Langhe Nebbiolo '99	♢	4
●	Barbaresco Sörì Montaribaldi '97	♢♢	6
●	Barbera d'Alba dü Gir '98	♢♢	4

BARBARESCO (CN)

Produttori del Barbaresco
Via Torino, 52
12050 Barbaresco (CN)
tel. 0173635139
e-mail: produttori@barbaresco.it

The Cantina dei Produttori del Barbaresco was set up in 1958 to bring together growers in the DOC zone. Since then, it has been devoting its energies to the promotion of the nebbiolo grape and, of course, Barbaresco. Today, there are 60 members who cultivate 100 hectares of outstanding vineyards in the zone's most important crus. Here are a few more numbers: it is impressive that, in such a small DOC zone as Barbaresco, one cellar should control fully 20 per cent of the nebbiolo terrain, for a total annual production of 400,000 bottles. Four out of five of those bottles contain Barbaresco, half released under the standard label and the rest split up among the Riserva labels. The remaining 20 per cent of the cellar's wine is Langhe Nebbiolo. In 2001, the '96 Riservas were released after a prolonged ageing. The results are good enough to satisfy the most demanding palates. The panel tasted nine selections – Asili, Moccagatta, Montefico, Montestefano, Ovello, Pajé, Pora, Rabajà and Rio Sordo – before awarding Two Glasses to seven of them. The remaining two contenders went into the final taste-off to compete for Three Glass ratings. Following a great harvest, the '96 looks like being a vintage for the record books. Traditional vinification and excellent fruit enabled the Produttori to make nine magnificent wines. Each one has its own subtle features but we will describe here the two most convincing. The Montestefano has a fruit and spice attack on the nose, contrasted by a rich, powerful palate. This is a wonderful, traditional Barbaresco, and it won for the Produttori their very first Three Glass award. The Pora was another lovely bottle and only a shade less delightful than its stablemate.

BARBARESCO (CN)

Albino Rocca
Via Rabajà, 15
12050 Barbaresco (CN)
tel. 0173635145

The cellar may bear the name of his father but it is Angelo Rocca who is now at the helm of this winery with its 12 hectares under vine, two of them rented. Angelo has been making every effort over the past decade to improve the quality of his wines and this Herculean labour is now bearing fruit. For the fifth time, the cellar has picked up Three Glasses, making it a prominent, and very dependable, landmark on the Barbaresco scene. The secret of Rocca's success has been improvement across the entire range so that it is not just the Barbarescos that excel. All the other wines are in the front rank of their respective categories. It was the Loreto, aged in large barrels, that turned out to be the more expressive of the two Barbarescos. It offers generous fruit on the nose, where hints of black berry fruit are enhanced by notes of violets, liquorice and sweet spices. On the palate, the muscular power is nicely offset by enviable balance and fine length. The Brich Ronchi grabs your attention with robust tannins but the still oak-dominated nose suggest that this is a wine to lay down for a few years until its innate elegance emerges. As ever, the Barbera d'Alba Gepin manages to combine a stylish and very varied nose with an incredibly full-bodied palate. Drink the Dolcetto Vignalunga while it is still young so that you can enjoy its fruit and alcohol without sacrificing its freshness and soft palate. Finally, the range is rounded off by the cortese-based white La Rocca and the Chardonnay da Bertü.

● Barbaresco Vigneti in Montestefano Ris. '96	▼▼▼	6
● Barbaresco Vigneti in Pora Ris. '96	▼▼	6
● Barbaresco Vigneti in Asili Ris. '96	▼▼	6
● Barbaresco Vigneti in Moccagatta Ris. '96	▼▼	6
● Barbaresco Vigneti in Montefico Ris. '96	▼▼	6
● Barbaresco Vigneti in Ovello Ris. '96	▼▼	6
● Barbaresco Vigneti in Pajé Ris. '96	▼▼	6
● Barbaresco Vigneti in Rabajà Ris. '96	▼▼	6
● Barbaresco Vigneti in Rio Sordo Ris. '96	▼▼	6

● Barbaresco Vigneto Loreto '98	▼▼▼	6
● Barbera d'Alba Gepin '99	▼▼	5
● Barbaresco Vigneto Brich Ronchi '98	▼▼	6
● Dolcetto d'Alba Vignalunga '00	▼▼	3*
○ Langhe Bianco La Rocca '00	▼▼	5
○ Langhe Chardonnay da Bertü '00	▼	3
● Barbaresco Vigneto Brich Ronchi '93	♛♛♛	6
● Barbaresco Vigneto Brich Ronchi '96	♛♛♛	6
● Barbaresco Vigneto Brich Ronchi '97	♛♛♛	6
● Barbaresco Vigneto Loreto '96	♛♛	6

BARBARESCO (CN)

Bruno Rocca
Via Rabajà, 29
12050 Barbaresco (CN)
Tel. 0173635112

Bruno Rocca may only have seven hectares under vine but, fortunately for him, much of the property lies in one of the finest of the Barbaresco crus, Rabajà. Another advantage Bruno enjoys is being able to offer his customers 20,000 bottles of Barbaresco every year, out of a total production that barely tops 40,000. And then there is Bruno himself, a man who has been championing Barbaresco for two decades. Everyone remembers when he heralded the comeback of this great wine in the early 1980s, creating softer, more elegant wines that could compete on equal terms with the more celebrated Barolos. It is good to hear, then, that Bruno's reds are reaping the international success they deserve. This time round, the Barbaresco Rabajà '98 won Three Glasses and the Barbera d'Alba '99 very nearly did so, too. The Rabajà '98 is a classic heavyweight Barbaresco for the cellar. Now in its youth, it has an intense ruby hue that flashes with garnet highlights while the bramble and raspberry fruit on the nose mingles with vanilla and cinnamon over hints of Peruvian bark and toasted hazelnut. Extraordinary power is the overriding impression on the palate: this wine will need at least five years to mellow out those wonderful tannins. The Barbera '99 is rich and well-rounded, its toasty notes superbly contrasted by hints of ripe cherry. On the other hand, the Barbaresco Coparossa lacks the finesse of the '97 version, where the new oak was handled with much more balance. Finally, the Dolcetto is well-made, although it lacks a little personality.

Wine	Rating	Price
● Barbaresco Rabajà '98	🍷🍷🍷	6
● Barbera d'Alba '99	🍷🍷	5
● Barbaresco Coparossa '98	🍷🍷	6
● Dolcetto d'Alba Vigna Trifolé '00	🍷	4
● Barbaresco Rabajà '88	🍷🍷🍷	6
● Barbaresco Rabajà '89	🍷🍷🍷	6
● Barbaresco Rabajà '93	🍷🍷🍷	6
● Barbaresco Rabajà '96	🍷🍷🍷	6
● Barbaresco Coparossa '97	🍷🍷🍷	6
● Barbaresco Rabajà '97	🍷🍷	6

BARBARESCO (CN)

Rino Varaldo
Via Secondine, 2
12050 Barbaresco (CN)
Tel. 0173635160

This year, the Varaldos are releasing a new wine, the Fantasia 4.20. It's a blend of nebbiolo, barbera, cabernet sauvignon and merlot, aged for 20 months in new barriques, hence the name. The garnet hue is very vivid and fully ripe notes of berry fruit on the nose fuse with elegant oak. The drinkable palate has substance and sweetness, well-sustained by tannins that lead into a long finish. A very successful experiment. There will be another new wine next year, when the cellar releases a Barolo made in Barolo itself. The other wines included a Dolcetto with a youthful colour and an intense, still alcohol-heavy nose of ripe fruit. In the mouth, there is breadth, power and body as the palate progresses to a juicy finish. The very dark Barbera d'Alba reveals intense notes of plum and damson, backed up by vanilla from the oak, before the chewy palate unveils nice acidity and good length. Not for the first time, the Varaldo Nebbiolo is a fine wine. Its lively colour heralds powerful notes of violets on the nose and a well-structured, assertive palate. But now for the two Barbarescos. The Bricco Libero, from the Gallina and Albesani crus, was 40 per cent aged in new barriques. It has a youthful colour and a nose where varietal notes meld attractively with sweet oak. In the mouth, it is sweet and muscular, with a full-bodied mid palate and a very long finish. The equally young-looking Sorì Loreto is aged in 15-hectolitre barrels. The nose has finesse, with notes of dried flowers and rose petals, then the solid palate contributes good fruit. In the long, clean finish, there are teasing hints of bramble and liquorice.

Wine	Rating	Price
● Barbaresco Bricco Libero '98	🍷🍷	6
● Barbaresco Sorì Loreto '98	🍷🍷	6
● Barbera d'Alba '99	🍷🍷	5
● Langhe Nebbiolo '99	🍷🍷	5
● Langhe Rosso Fantasia 4.20 '99	🍷🍷	5
● Dolcetto d'Alba '00	🍷🍷	3*
● Barbaresco Bricco Libero '97	🍷🍷🍷	6
● Barolo Vigna di Aldo '95	🍷🍷	6
● Barbaresco Bricco Libero '96	🍷🍷	6
● Barbaresco Sorì Loreto '96	🍷🍷	6
● Barbaresco Sorì Loreto '97	🍷🍷	6
● Barbera d'Alba '98	🍷🍷	5

BAROLO (CN)

GIACOMO BORGOGNO & FIGLI
VIA GIOBERTI, 1
12060 BAROLO (CN)
TEL. 017356108
E-MAIL: barologio@libero.it

The Barolo Liste '96 is the jewel in the crown of the range offered by the Boschis family. A wine of personality and vigour, it is very much in the traditional Barolo style. The garnet-tinged ruby hue shades into orange at the rim, introducing an intriguingly forward nose of red and black berry fruit jam, liquorice and tobacco over delightful notes of leather and dry earth. Entry on the palate is firm and assertive, progressing solidly over prominent tannins to conclude harmoniously on lingering notes of violets and liquorice. The Dolcetto '00 is another good wine, its intense ruby edged with purple in the glass. It unfolds fresh, youthful notes of redcurrant and cherry over subtle peach nuances. The palate is well-sustained, revealing a dry, spunky personality before the vigorous, fruit-rich finish. The Barbera has an intense hue and a nose that presents notes of cherry, mint and rosemary, laced with tobacco and coffee. The faintly acidic vein perceptible on the palate gives a slight edge to its character that is, however, kept well under control by the laudable weight of the body. The decently long finish echoes the nose nicely. And to finish our notes, the Nebbiolo '99 has evolved notes of leather and jam on the nose and a dry, less than challenging, palate that tails off with a slightly bitterish finish.

● Barolo Liste '96	♟♟	6
● Barbera d'Alba '00	♟	3
● Dolcetto d'Alba '00	♟	3
● Langhe Nebbiolo '99		4
● Barolo Cl. '93	♟♟	6
● Barolo Cl. '96	♟♟	6
● Barolo Liste '89	♟	6
● Barolo Cl. '95	♟	6
● Barbaresco '97	♟	5

BAROLO (CN)

GIACOMO BREZZA & FIGLI
VIA LOMONDO, 4
12060 BAROLO (CN)
TEL. 017356354 - 0173560921
E-MAIL: brezza@brezza.it

It's not hard to find this historic winery, which is located on the road leading into the town that gave its name to Italy's most famous wine. From the terrace of the Brezza family's hotel, there is a stunning view of the Barolo and the surrounding hill country that on its own makes your visit worthwhile. The profile of the castle that testifies to the town's origins stands proudly in the distance, providing a thrillingly beautiful backdrop. And the charm of Barolo's history, as well as the austere beauty of its countryside, can be found in the winemaking style of the Brezza cellar, to which all members of the family contribute. Tonino and Oreste are the elder statesmen, assisted by cousins Giacomo and Marco, Tonino's sons, and Oreste's son Enzo. Together, they make an admirable team. Tonino and Marco spend most of their time in the vineyards while Oreste, Giacomo and Enzo look after the cellar. This year, the Brezza wines were truly magnificent. The Barolo Cannubi '96 took full advantage of a great vintage to go to the top of the class with Three Glasses. Elegant, concentrated, and with a spectacular range of aromas, it discloses spicy and aromatic notes of mint and sage mingling with nuances of blackcurrant and bramble. On the palate, its slow, relentless progression is a triumph, backed up by firm but beautifully fine-grained tannins that take you through to the long, voluptuously soft finish. The Bricco Sarmassa '97 is also excellent and only a shade less convincing than the Cannubi while the Sarmassa, another '97, is just as good. Most interesting of the other Brezza wines is the Dolcetto d'Alba S. Lorenzo and the Barbera d'Alba Cannubi '98 achieved a comfortable One Glass rating, as did the Freisa Santa Rosalia '00.

● Barolo Cannubi '96	♟♟♟	6
● Barolo Bricco Sarmassa '97	♟♟	6
● Dolcetto d'Alba S. Lorenzo '00	♟♟	4
● Barolo Sarmassa '97	♟♟	6
● Langhe Freisa S. Rosalia '00	♟	3
● Barbera d'Alba Cannubi '98	♟	5
● Barolo Cannubi '93	♟♟	6
● Barolo Cannubi '90	♟♟	6
● Barolo Sarmassa '94	♟♟	6
● Barolo Sarmassa '96	♟♟	6
● Barolo Castellero Ris. '90	♟♟	6
● Barolo Cannubi '95	♟	6

BAROLO (CN)

Damilano
V.lo San Sebastiano, 2
12060 Barolo (CN)
Tel. 017356265 - 017356105
E-mail: damilanog@libero.it

It was in 1996 that the historic Damilano made a brusque change of direction. After a series of developments in the family, Giovanni Damilano, who until then been involved in other activities, took over the cellar with his children Mario and Paolo, niece Margherita and nephew Guido. Under their direction and with the input of consultants, agronomist Giampiero Romana and oenologist Beppe Caviola, the Damilano cellar today is firmly committed to obtaining the finest quality possible from the four hectares of estate-owned nebbiolo vineyards in the most prestigious subzones in the municipality of Barolo, Cannubi, Liste and Fossati. For the '97 harvest, grapes from Cannubi were vinified separately and aged in half new and half one-year-old barriques whereas the fruit from Liste and Fossati went into a traditional-style Barolo, aged mainly in 25-hectolitre Slavonian oak barrels and partly – 15 per cent by weight – in new barriques. The Cannubi has impeccable balance on nose and palate, yielding notes of raspberry and cinnamon laced with vanilla and dried flowers. Its velvet-smooth palate is remarkably long. In contrast, the Liste has a more evolved colour and less breadth on the nose, despite its complexity – liquorice, violets and sweet spices come through clearly – while the more austere palate also offers less breadth than the Cannubi. The range is completed by 1,000 bottles of an excellent Barbera '99, aged for 16 months in 70 per cent new barriques, and another 1,000 of a fruity, quaffable Dolcetto '00. We were impressed by the Barbera in particular, with its impenetrable purple hue, explosive attack on the nose, where intense notes of cherry and vanilla marry wonderfully, and powerful, long palate.

● Barolo '97	🍷🍷	6
● Barolo Cannubi '97	🍷🍷	6
● Barbera d'Alba '99	🍷🍷	5
● Docetto d'Alba '00	🍷	4

BAROLO (CN)

Marchesi di Barolo
Via Alba, 12
12060 Barolo (CN)
Tel. 0173564400
E-mail: marchesi.barolo@marchesibarolo.com

This prestigious estate is very strongly identified with Barolo, of which it releases as many as four top-level vineyard selections, showing that a huge range and quality are compatible. Well done the Barolo Estate Vineyard '97. Its civilized notes of black cherry and tobacco on the nose usher in a clean-tasting palate whose irresistible length is lifted by discreet, fine-grained tannins. A monster of a Barolo that puts Marchesi di Barolo back on the list of Three Glass winners. The Barolo Cannubi, another '97, presents charmingly crisp aromas of roses and ripe wild cherries before the nicely balanced structure enables the excellent texture and generous flavours to impress on the palate. The Sarmassa '97 is another nice wine. Its distinctive minty notes meld with the fruit and toasty oak on the nose then the stylish palate has very attractive depth. Less challenging but still well-made is the Coste di Rose '97, whose flower and spice notes on the nose are echoed on the palate. The Langhe Pi Cìt '99 is an exciting new blend of cabernet sauvignon and nebbiolo that tempts with notes of mint and berry fruit in an attractively complex bouquet. This is followed up by a palate with a firm tannic weave and a sweet toasty finish. The Barbera d'Alba Pajagal '99 has broad aromas of bramble and ripe raspberry, which are reflected attractively on the palate. It also has a good meaty mouthfeel. The Barbera d'Alba Ruvei '99 is a fresher, more alcoholic wine and the Dolcetto d'Alba Boschetti '00 has a bramble and violet finish that warm its faintly tannic palate. Finally, the Moscato d'Asti Zagara '00 is aromatic and tantalizing.

● Barolo Estate Vineyard '97	🍷🍷🍷	6
● Barolo Cannubi '97	🍷🍷	6
● Barolo Sarmassa '97	🍷🍷	6
● Barbera d'Alba Pajagal '99	🍷🍷	5
● Langhe Rosso Pi Cit '99	🍷🍷	6
● Dolcetto d'Alba Boschetti '00	🍷	4
○ Moscato d'Asti Zagara '00	🍷	4
● Barolo Coste di Rose '97	🍷	6
● Barbera d'Alba Ruvei '99	🍷	4
● Barolo Estate Vineyard '90	🍷🍷🍷	6
● Barolo Ris. '93	🍷🍷	6
● Barolo Estate Vineyard '95	🍷🍷	6
● Barolo Cannubi '96	🍷🍷	6
● Barolo Estate Vineyard '96	🍷🍷	6
● Barolo Sarmassa '96	🍷🍷	6

BAROLO (CN)

Bartolo Mascarello
Via Roma, 15
12060 Barolo (CN)
Tel. 017356125

Vintage after vintage, Bartolo Mascarello has been repeating the same winemaking rituals, defending them against the temptations of a modernity he sees as incompatible with typicity and tradition. Today, his wines continue to be the bond that links Bartolo to the land he loves intimately, the Langhe. His Barolo '97 is very similar to the spirited, charismatic 75 year old himself for it has immense character. Its vibrant ruby red has a garnet rim and the aromas, where the oak is undetectable, range from berry fruit to rain-soaked earth and ripe plum. On the palate, there is serious structure and marvellous balance, the alcohol and extract marrying perfectly with the prominent but not intrusive tannins. All this is in deference to a philosophy that disdains the easy applause won by emphasizing the softness and roundness prized by the international market. The finish may not be outstandingly long but it lets the austere yet elegant tannins take centre stage, presenting a crisp assertiveness that bode well for the future. The Barbera d'Alba '99 from the San Lorenzo vineyard had not yet gone into the bottle when the visited for the Guide tastings. We'll reserve judgement until next year. Last on the list was the bright ruby Dolcetto d'Alba '00, a crowd-pleaser with lots of fruit. Youthful notes of alcohol on the nose mingle with bramble and cherry while the tannins are perfectly at home in the generous fruit of the palate.

BAROLO (CN)

E. Pira & Figli - Chiara Boschis
Via Vittorio Veneto, 1
12060 Barolo (CN)
Tel. 017356247
E-mail: pirabc@libero.it

Ever since Chiara Boschis started making wine, she has been determined to make sure it is great wine. Sweeping aside all difficulties with a disarming nonchalance, she has now finished her impeccably tidy new cellar, where there is discreet evidence of a woman's touch. Starting next year, wine will be gravity-fed from vinification vats to the all-new barriques where they will undergo malolactic fermentation and then ageing. Chiara's efforts in the vineyard come through clearly in the Barolo '97, of which 13,000 bottles were made with fruit from the estate's two and a half hectares in the prestigious Cannubi subzone. Not for the first time, it waltzed away with Three effortless Glasses. You can see how concentrated it is in the vibrant, tight-knit colour in the glass. On the nose, there are intense aromas of berry fruit, nuanced with violets as well as the minty spice note typical of the cru. The elegance of the result is breath-taking, the wood lifting but not overwhelming the complexity of the bouquet. The attack on the mouth is soft but the mid palate never flinches, its superb body and balance staying taut and firm. Robust yet gentle tannins accompany the fruit through to the remarkably soft and very long finish, which unveils a delightful hint of liquorice. Our overall impression was of sturdiness and remarkable fruit. It's one of the finest Barolos to come out of a vintage that may turn out to be less memorable than was first thought. Chiara also makes 3,500 bottles of Barbera and 2,000 of Dolcetto, released too late to be included in the Guide.

● Dolcetto d'Alba Monrobiolo e Ruè '00	ΨΨ	4
● Barolo '97	ΨΨ	6
● Barolo '83	ΨΨΨ	6
● Barolo '84	ΨΨΨ	6
● Barolo '85	ΨΨΨ	6
● Barolo '89	ΨΨΨ	6
● Barolo '88	ΨΨ	6
● Barolo '90	ΨΨ	6
● Barolo '93	ΨΨ	6
● Barolo '96	ΨΨ	6
● Barbera d'Alba Vigna S. Lorenzo '98	ΨΨ	4

● Barolo Cannubi '97	ΨΨΨ	6
● Barolo Ris. '90	ΨΨΨ	6
● Barolo '94	ΨΨΨ	6
● Barolo Cannubi '96	ΨΨΨ	6
● Barolo '93	ΨΨ	6
● Barolo Cannubi '95	ΨΨ	6

BAROLO (CN)

GIUSEPPE RINALDI
VIA MONFORTE, 3
12060 BAROLO (CN)
TEL. 017356156

In this 15th edition of the Guide, it is with great pleasure that we award Three Glasses to a Barolo from the Giuseppe Rinaldi winery. The Brunate-Le Coste '97 selection is rather reminiscent of the great 1971 Barolo that Battista Rinaldi, father of the current owner, Beppe, delighted Barolo lovers with in the past. We hope the '97 will bear the years as lightly as its august predecessor, which we have been fortunate enough to taste twice over the past 30 years. True to tradition, the Giuseppe Rinaldi cellar produces almost exclusively Barolo, in addition to small quantities of Barbera, Dolcetto and, for a few years now, an unusual Ruché. The estate owns ten hectares in the subzones that have written the history of Barolo. Fruit for the Brunate comes from La Morra, the Ravera is towards Monforte, below the Le Coste cellar, and over in the direction of Alba lies the Cannubi San Lorenzo plot. All of these vineyards are planted to nebbiolo, from which Beppe obtains no more than 12,000 bottles a year. Most of these – around 10,000 bottles – are in the Brunate-Le Coste version. And it was stunning this year. The garnet-ruby colour has a depth that you rarely find in wines from this cellar and then the nose is even more astounding. Its vast range of aromas open out little by little, moving on from fruit-rich notes to more severe hints of tobacco, liquorice and spices. On the massive palate, the structure, breadth of fruit and vibrant tannins come together in delightful harmony. A marvellous wine that keeps the Rinaldi flag flying high. Neither should you underestimate the Barolo Cannubi San Lorenzo-Ravera, left a little in the shade by its – very – big brother.

● Barolo Brunate-Le Coste '97	▼▼▼	6
● Barolo Cannubi S. Lorenzo-Ravera '97	▼▼	6
● Barolo Brunate-Le Coste '93	▼▼	6
● Barolo Brunate-Le Coste '95	▼▼	6
● Barolo Cannubi S. Lorenzo-Ravera '95	▼▼	6
● Barolo Brunate-Le Coste '96	▼▼	6
● Barolo Cannubi S. Lorenzo-Ravera '96	▼▼	6

BAROLO (CN)

LUCIANO SANDRONE
VIA PUGNANE, 4
12060 BAROLO (CN)
TEL. 0173560023 - 0173560024
E-MAIL: info@sandroneluciano.com

Luciano Sandrone, backed up by the rest of the family, has nearly completed work on the new cellar in Via Pugnane, where he has already been making wine since 1999. The lovely, spacious structure is a restrained blend of tradition and modernity and has been designed with a strikingly rational approach that means every operation can carried out easily and efficiently. Luciano's Barolo Cannubi Boschis '97 is a classy wine with an intense garnet-ruby hue and a nose that layers attractive hints of violets over sweet spices and wild berries. The vigorous entry on the palate is not let down by the sustained progression. Deliciously fine-grained tannins come out in the long finish, which echoes the nose to perfection. The Le Vigne is a blend of fruit from four distinct vineyards in the municipalities of Barolo and Monforte. Its ruby hue has an orange-tinged rim and there are lovely salty notes in a bouquet that melds leather, dried flowers, autumn leaves and coffee. The palate is light, stylish and satisfyingly long. The '99 vintage added a new wine to the Sandrone list: the Pe Mol, a Langhe Rosso made with a 60-40 blend of barbera and nebbiolo from the municipality of Monforte. Its intense colour ushers in a fruit and mineral nose nuanced with cocoa powder. Lively and full on the palate, it rounds of with a finish that mirrors the nose. The intense ruby Dolcetto '00 has a fine range of aromas, from hay to morello cherry laced with intriguing hints of herbs in the sun. The attractive palate has good weight. The Barbera offers a fruit-rich nose with green notes and a smooth, surefooted palate. We finished with the Nebbiolo Valmaggiore, which has a creamy, faintly etheric nose and a vibrant, dry palate.

● Barolo Cannubi Boschis '97	▼▼	6
● Dolcetto d'Alba '00	▼▼	4
● Barbera d'Alba '99	▼▼	5
● Langhe Pe Mol '99	▼▼	5
● Barolo Le Vigne '97	▼	6
● Nebbiolo d'Alba Valmaggiore '99	▼	5
● Barolo '83	▼▼▼	6
● Barolo '84	▼▼▼	6
● Barolo Cannubi Boschis '86	▼▼▼	6
● Barolo Cannubi Boschis '87	▼▼▼	6
● Barolo Cannubi Boschis '89	▼▼▼	6
● Barolo Cannubi Boschis '90	▼▼▼	6
● Barolo Cannubi Boschis '96	▼▼	6
● Barolo Le Vigne '96	▼▼	6

BAROLO (CN)

GIORGIO SCARZELLO E FIGLI
VIA ALBA, 29
12060 BAROLO (CN)
TEL. 017356170
E-MAIL: cantina-scarzello@libero.it

Giorgio Scarzello's modest output of just over 20,000 bottles a year is marked by good overall quality, as is testified by the latest addition, the Barbera d'Alba Superiore that now lines up with the traditional Scarzello Barolo. The '98 Barbera Superiore delights with its rich, elegant fruit. The entry on the nose offers wild berries that are joined by rather forward toasty notes from the 600-litre tonneaux used for ageing. It is no coincidence that the Barolo is still aged in large barrels: the results for the '97 provide ample justification. The lively, tight-knit garnet introduces hints of jam and nuts on the nose that provide intensity and length. On the palate, the prominent but never intrusive tannins are already well incorporated, even though this is a very cellarable wine. The Dolcetto d'Alba '98 is another successful enterprise, enfolding nose and palate in aromas of berry fruit ranging from cherries through the whole gamut of wild berries. The panel was also impressed by how beautifully the palate mirrors the nose. The Langhe Nebbiolo '99 starts off with rather closed, indeed almost impenetrable, aromas before it opens out in the glass on greenish notes of Peruvian bark and liquorice. In contrast, the texture of the fruit is very close-knit and the finish lingers. The panel marked down the Barbera d'Alba '99 for its rather rustic nose. Still, the palate is refreshing and it drinks very nicely.

● Barolo '97	▼▼	6
● Barbera d'Alba Sup. '98	▼▼	4
● Barbera d'Alba '99	▼	3
● Dolcetto d'Alba '99	▼	3
● Langhe Nebbiolo '99	▼	4
● Barolo Vigna Merenda '90	▽▽	6
● Barolo '93	▽▽	6
● Barolo '95	▽▽	6
● Barolo '96	▽▽	6
● Barbera d'Alba Sup. '97	▽▽	4

BAROLO (CN)

TENUTA LA VOLTA - CABUTTO
VIA SAN PIETRO, 13
12060 BAROLO (CN)
TEL. 017356168

First class. That's what we thought of the range presented this year by the winery that dominates the village of Barolo, with the castle in the background, from its location on the La Volta hilltop. A pat on the back, then for the Cabuttos, especially Osvaldo, who has been working tirelessly for more than a decade to improve the quality of the cellar's wines. The results seem to be coming through for the four wines we tasted all gained high, if not quite stratospheric, scores, with the Barolo showing best. So we'll begin our round-up with the Vigna La Volta selection – 25,000 released – that impressed this year as never before. Its intense ruby red has a faint orangey rim. On the nose it offers delicacy and finesse, the sensations of ripe fruit marrying with notes of balsam and rain-soaked earth. It has sufficient structure for the length on the palate to offset the gentle, velvet-smooth tannins. This is a wine that was conceived in the vineyard. Yield per vine was minuscule and it easily reaches 14 per cent alcohol. The Barbera d'Alba Superiore Bricco delle Viole came close to matching it. It has a strikingly dark, almost impenetrable, colour and aromas that include super-ripe berry fruit and faint hints of oak. The long, mouthfilling palate verges is almost syrupy. The no-nonsense, deliciously quaffable Dolcetto is also attractive while the Vendemmiaio, from a blend of nebbiolo with generous helpings of barbera, is a little dominated by the wood, where it spends a year ageing. Presenting only four labels was the right thing to do. The Barolo Riserva del Fondatore, a tribute to the brothers' grandfather, is released only in truly exceptional years.

● Barolo Vigna La Volta '97	▼▼	6
● Barbera d'Alba Sup. Bricco delle Viole '99	▼▼	5
● Langhe Vendemmiaio '98	▼	5
● Dolcetto d'Alba Vigna La Volta '00	▼	3
● Barolo Ris. del Fondatore '90	▽▽	6
● Barolo Vigna La Volta '96	▽▽	6
● Barbera d'Alba Sup. Bricco delle Viole '98	▽▽	5

BAROLO (CN)

TERRE DA VINO
VIA BERGESIA, 6
12060 BAROLO (CN)
TEL. 0173564611
E-MAIL: info@terradivino.it

Terre da Vino was set up in 1980 by the agricultural development agency of the Piedmont regional authority and for 20 years was based at Moriondo Torinese. In September 2000, the facilities were transferred to new premises at Barolo, where the winery will be able to carry on the quality project it initiated with the magnificent '97 vintage. Ten or so growers, representing 15 hectares of vineyard, took part in the first stage and by 2000, the area under vine involved had risen to 50 hectares. The aim is to take that figure to 100, all planted to barbera to make the La Luna e I Falò selection, the wine that first established the cellar's reputation. In the new vintage, the '99, this Barbera d'Asti selection was again the best of the extensive range of wines produced. The palate in particular is long and well-sustained. Nor is the Barbera d'Alba Croere del '98, made with fruit from the Vezza d'Alba vineyards, any less interesting. The colour is intense and the aromas of ripe fruit merge nicely with the wood to introduce the full-bodied, tangy palate. The fruit lingers satisfyingly. Another Two Glass wine is the Langhe Rosso La Malora, from nebbiolo and barbera. Of the Barolos, the panel liked the Poderi Parussi '97 selection but the Paesi Tuoi version is less interesting and has less character. A honourable mention goes to the '00 Barbera d'Asti San Nicolao, a likeable, refreshing wine with a firm vein of acidity. There were two Gavis on show and it was the very pleasant Ca' da Bosio that we preferred. Finally, the sauvignon and chardonnay-based Monferrato Bianco Tra Donne Sole is a serious wine with good balance.

BAROLO (CN)

G. D. VAJRA
VIA DELLE VIOLE, 25
LOC. VERGNE
12060 BAROLO (CN)
TEL. 017356257
E-MAIL: gdvajra@tin.it

Aldo Vaira and his wife Milena are two of the most thoughtful, reflective producers in the Langhe. They refuse to be carried away by the euphoria that sweeps the hills when, as is the case at the moment, the cellars are virtually emptying themselves and some growers are grubbing up dolcetto to plant the more exalted nebbiolo. On their 20-hectare property, Aldo and Vaira produce a vast range of wines that still has space for quaffable wines that have less structure and are therefore easier on the pocket. A quick glance at the list of wines reviewed reveals that release of the Barolo Bricco delle Viole '97 and the Freisa Kyè '00 has been delayed for a year. That leaves three big-league wines for this Guide profile, the 9,000 bottles of Barbera Bricco delle Viole, the 17,000 of Dolcetto Coste & Fossati and the 6,000 of Langhe Bianco. Coste & Fossati '00 is an extraordinary Dolcetto with a great future, its strengths being balance and style rather than sheer strength. But it's another story with the barrel and tonneau-aged Barbera Bricco delle Viole, which unveils hints of cherry jam enhanced by elegant spicy nuances and a faint note of roast coffee beans before unleashing a long, muscular palate. As usual, the stainless steel-fermented and aged Riesling is a wine of quality but the minerally nose and the juicy acidity of the palate make it a bottle for connoisseurs of the genre. Our tasting also included a very moreish Dolcetto with intriguing hints of strawberry and white pepper, and a Nebbiolo with a balanced nose of violets and raspberry introducing a pleasantly tannic palate. And to round off, there was the very drinkable standard-label Barbera.

○	Monferrato Bianco Tra Donne Sole '00	ŸŸ	4
●	Barolo Poderi Parussi '97	ŸŸ	6
●	Barbera d'Alba Croere '98	ŸŸ	4
●	Barbera d'Asti La Luna e I Falò '99	ŸŸ	4
●	Langhe Rosso La Malora '99	ŸŸ	5
●	Barbera d'Asti San Nicolao '00	Ÿ	3*
○	Gavi Ca' da Bosio '00	Ÿ	4
●	Barolo Paesi Tuoi '97	Ÿ	6
○	Piemonte Moscato Passito La Bella Estate '99	Ÿ	5
○	Gavi Masseria dei Carmelitani '00		4
●	Barbera d'Alba Croere '97	♉	4
●	Barbera d'Asti La Luna e I Falò '97	♉	4
●	Barbera d'Asti La Luna e i Falò '98	♉	4

●	Dolcetto d'Alba Coste & Fossati '00	ŸŸ	5
●	Barbera d'Alba Bricco delle Viole '99	ŸŸ	5
○	Langhe Bianco '00	ŸŸ	5
●	Langhe Nebbiolo '00	ŸŸ	4
●	Barbera d'Alba '00	Ÿ	4
●	Dolcetto d'Alba '00	Ÿ	4
●	Barolo Bricco delle Viole '95	♉	6
●	Barolo Bricco delle Viole '96	♉	6
●	Barbera d'Alba Bricco delle Viole '98	♉	5
●	Langhe Freisa Kyè '99	♉	5

BASTIA MONDOVÌ (CN)

Bricco del Cucù
Fraz. Bricco, 21
12060 Bastia Mondovì (CN)
tel. 017460153

The life of Dario Sciolla, owner of Bricco del Cucù, has changed considerably in a relatively short space of time. Only a few years ago, the cellar sold most of its output in demijohns and one and a half-litre bottles to private customers in Genoa. Now, Dario manages to bottle himself almost all of the wine – about 50,000 bottles a year – produced by his eight hectares of vineyard. And, unbelievably if you know the man, he even sought advice this spring from Vin Conseil, an agency set up by a group of go-getting young oenologists, who immediately told him to throw out his old wooden barrels for fermenting vats and temperature-controlled stainless steel vats. There can be no doubt that the cellar will now be able to improve its already very good wines, obtained from the fruit that Dario nurtures in his very old and superbly aspected vineyards. This time round, it was the Dolcettos that stood out from the crowd, starting with the standard-label Langhe. For a very modest investment, winelovers will get a nose that ranges from bramble jam and cocoa powder and candied peel, followed by a warm and full-bodied, albeit slightly rustic, palate. The Dogliani has a deeper hue and convincingly characterful aromas of stewed fruit, bramble jam, Peruvian bark and rain-soaked earth as well as an astonishingly rich palate. If you give it time to breathe, the Bricco San Bernardo '99 will reward you with unusually complex aromas for a Dolcetto. There is a nice minerally hint, enticing spice and an elegant note of berry fruit. The rather severe palate punches its full weight, with a balanced structure and a very long finish that simply oozes class. Only the white, which is more oxidized than usual after the very warm harvest, failed to come up to expectations.

● Dolcetto di Dogliani '00	ŢŢ	3*
● Langhe Dolcetto '00	ŢŢ	2*
● Dolcetto di Dogliani Sup. Bricco S. Bernardo '99	ŢŢ	4
○ Langhe Bianco '00		3

BERZANO DI TORTONA (AL)

Terralba
Fraz. Inselmina
15050 Berzano di Tortona (AL)
tel. 0131866791

For four generations, the Terralba winery, owned by the Daffonchio family, has been transforming grapes into wine in the Berzano hills. Today Stefano, a young, determined winemaker, is in the saddle and his warhorse is a barbera-based Rosso that ages in small oak barrels. It carries the same name as the winery, Terralba. It has upfront aromas that range from toasty oak to cloves and red berries while on the palate there are equally distinct hints of liquorice, spring flowers and sun-dried hay. The other monovarietal Barbera has attractive structure founded on ripe fruit flavours that open to reveal nuances of sage and wild roses. Next in line was the Monleale. Aged in small barrels, it hails from a vineyard in the municipality from which it takes its name. A blend of barbera with about ten per cent croatina, it greets the nose with morello cherry and blackcurrant followed by a vigorously powerful palate with a distinctive note of ripe fruit. The croatina-based Montegrande and the Strà Loja, a Dolcetto, concluded the range of reds. The former came close to winning Two Glasses for its intense raspberry and black cherry aromas and warm violet-nuanced palate. While we wait for the Timorasso – early tastings have been very promising – we can uncork a bottle of the surprising La Vetta, a cortese-based white. It has good structure and the nose opens on mineral notes that shade into honey and citrus jam. Fruit, especially apricot, comes out on the palate, which closes with a faint after-aroma of sweet almonds.

○ Colli Tortonesi Bianco La Vetta '00	ŢŢ	3*
● Colli Tortonesi Rosso Terralba '98	ŢŢ	4
● Colli Tortonesi Rosso Monleale '99	ŢŢ	4
● Piemonte Barbera Identità '00	Ţ	3
● Colli Tortonesi Rosso Montegrande '99	Ţ	4
● Colli Tortonesi Rosso Strà Loja '99	Ţ	3

BORGONE SUSA (TO)

CARLOTTA
VIA CONDOVE, 61
10050 BORGONE SUSA (TO)
TEL. 0119646150
E-MAIL: rfrancesca@libero.it

The vineyards in the recently created Valsusa DOC zone stretch across countryside that is still almost unspoiled, where vine vies with woodland for the sunniest and steepest slopes between 500 and 1,000 metres above sea level. This small zone, where there are few hectares of vineyard registered is also where for more than ten years Carla Cometto and her husband have been fighting to conserve the plots they inherited from Carla's grandfather. Their efforts are even more admirable if we take into account the difficulties of vineyard management here. Mechanization is simply out of the question. Having said this, it also has to be mentioned that the estate's labelling policy is hard to follow. Wines like Rocca del Lupo, Costadoro and Vignacombe alternate Valsusa DOC status in '98 and '00 with that of a mere table wine for the '99. Neither do they seem able to settle on definitive names. For example, the Rocca del Lupo '98 and '00 was called Roche du Bau in '99, the Costadoro '98 and '00 became Il Conte in '99 and finally the Roceja, the cellar's front-running selection at the moment, started out in life as a sparkling red. As ever, the lightest, most quaffable wine is the Vignacombe, produced in Borgone from barbera, neretta cuneese, freisa, gamay and other native varieties. It has an uncomplicated fruit-rich nose and refreshingly clean acidity on the palate. The Costadoro, a blend of ciliegiolo, neretta cuneese and barbera from Borgone, is a shade better. Finally, the Rocca del Lupo, obtained from barbera and avanà di Chiomonte, and the Roceja, from a new barbera and nebbiolo vineyard, are both more powerful and tannin-rich, and thus more suitable for the cellar.

• Roceja '00	🍷🍷	4
• Valsusa Rocca del Lupo '00	🍷🍷	4
• Valsusa Costadoro '00	🍷	4
• Valsusa Vignacombe '00	🍷	4
• Il Conte '99	🍷🍷	4
• Valsusa Vignacombe '98	🍷	4

BOSIO (AL)

LA SMILLA
VICO GARIBALDI, 7
15060 BOSIO (AL)
TEL. 0143684245

For a long time, Bosio was one of the centres of the wine trade that travelled the road from Monferrato to Genoa. The village's steep vineyards were gradually grubbed up as it became more profitable to buy in grapes from other, flatter areas that could offer greater yields. But today, quantity is no longer the first priority. The new generations of Bosio's established wine families know this very well and look to own-labels, premium-quality wines, recovery of the remaining vineyards and the selection of growers of bought-in grapes as the way forward. That also sums up the recent history of Matteo Guido's Smilla cellar. The four hectares of estate-owned vines produce about 60,000 bottles a year, with the help of grapes from other growers. Matteo's son Danilo looks after the cellar, which is located around a courtyard in the centre of Bosio. Our tastings this year were very encouraging. The Gavi del Comune di Gavi has a youthful colour and a clean citrus nose. Refreshing on the palate, it reveals a bitterish twist in the finish. The I Bergi selection is equally creditable. Its straw yellow is flecked with green and the nose offers with flowers, citrus fruit and oak-derived vanilla that is echoed rather emphatically on the mellow, refreshing and very long finish. Two Glasses also went to the Dolcetto, whose ruby hue shades into purple at the rim. It has an attractive breadth of sweet fruit on the nose then the palate, after a soft entry, progresses warmly to a finish of average length. The Nsè Pesa '99 selection was a point or two down the scale. It has nice complexity but lacks structure.

• Dolcetto d'Ovada '00	🍷🍷	3*
○ Gavi del Comune di Gavi '00	🍷🍷	4
○ Gavi I Bergi '00	🍷🍷	4
• Dolcetto d'Ovada Nsè Pesa '99	🍷	4

BRA (CN)

Ascheri
Via Piumati, 23
12042 Bra (CN)
tel. 0172412394
e-mail: ascherivini@tin.it

Matteo Ascheri, with his very competent helpmate Giuliano Bedino, is determinedly and dynamically taking the family cellar to seriously good quality standards and a respectable production capacity. Matteo's successful experiments with imported vine types continue, as we confirmed when we retasted the Montelupa Bianca '99, from part barrique-aged viognier fruit. The Montalupa Rosso '98 is a monovarietal syrah that ages in large barrels. The nose of crisp cherry, bramble and spices is nuanced with rare smoky notes, then the palate delivers muscular structure that is nicely offset by well-judged tannins and understated acidity. Elegant as usual, the Barolo Sorano '97 delights with complex aromas of roses, white pepper and aromatic herbs. The body has wonderful texture, the wood melds in harmoniously and the length is refreshing. Less complete is the Barolo Vigna dei Pola '97, which combines liquorice with blackcurrant on a palate dried by astringent tannins. The Barbera d'Alba Vigna Fontanelle '00 presents warm notes of juicy fruit and spices then a complex, well-rounded palate. The characteristically uncompromising aromas of the Nebbiolo San Giacomo '99 lead in to a tangy, delicately tannic palate. The two '00 Dolcettos are different but both are as drinkable as they come. If the Vigna Nirane is softer and riper, the San Rocco foregrounds balsamic notes and a serious tannic weave.

● Barolo Sorano '97	㏘㏘	6
● Montalupa Rosso '98	㏘㏘	6
● Barbera d'Alba Vigna Fontanelle '00	㏘	4
● Dolcetto d'Alba S. Rocco '00	㏘	3
● Dolcetto d'Alba Vigna Nirane '00	㏘	3
● Barolo Vigna dei Pola '97	㏘	6
● Nebbiolo d'Alba Bricco S. Giacomo '99	㏘	4
● Barolo Sorano '96	㏘㏘	6
○ Montalupa Bianco '99	㏘㏘	6
● Barbera d'Alba Vigna Fontanelle '99	㏘	4

BRUSNENGO (BI)

Barni
Via Forte, 63
13082 Brusnengo (BI)
tel. 015985977

The Guide welcomes Giuseppe Filippo Barni, a young ambitious winemaker who has set off determinedly along the road to quality. Unusually for northern Piedmont, the five-hectare Barni cellar concentrates on specialty wines, with a particular regard for international varieties. However, the Mesolone, 70 per cent croatina blended with nebbiolo and uva rara, was inspired by the winemaking tradition of Brusnengo. The varieties in the blend have, in fact, always been cultivated in the historic vineyards of the Meisola area, from which the wine's name derives. Aged in large barrels of Slavonian oak, the Mesolone has an attractively intense ruby hue and a bouquet that discloses notes of bramble, raspberry and violets, nuanced with balsam. There is good breadth of well-sustained fruit on the palate, vigorous tannins and a pleasantly bitterish finish. The Torrearsa is also excellent. A blend of cabernet and vespolina, with a small proportion of uva rara, it flaunts an impenetrable ruby in the glass. The aromas are whistle-clean and tight-knit, the vanilla of the barrique enfolding the notes of bilberry, red pepper and cocoa powder. The very well-balanced palate offers rich, velvet-smooth fruit, backed up by a weave of sweet tannins. On the nose, the Albaciara, a 70-30 blend of chardonnay and erbaluce, is soft and intriguingly complex, proffering notes of pear, pineapple, tangerine and yellow roses. The palate is satisfyingly rich but never unbalanced. We nearly awarded Two Glasses to the Pian del Tufo, a very respectable Chardonnay. Varietal, stylish and well-rounded, it is on sale at a surprisingly low price. Finally, the fruity, clean-tasting Ca' del Forte is a slightly sparkling red that is ideal for the table on any day of the week.

○ Albaciara Bianco '00	㏘㏘	4
● Mesolone Rosso '98	㏘㏘	5
● Coste della Sesia Torrearsa '99	㏘㏘	5
● Ca' del Forte Rosso '00	㏘	3*
○ Pian del Tufo Bianco '00	㏘	3*

CALAMANDRANA (AT)

Michele Chiarlo
S.S. Nizza-Canelli, 99
14042 Calamandrana (AT)
tel. 0141769030
e-mail: chiarlo@tin.it

CALOSSO (AT)

Scagliola
Fraz. San Siro, 42
14052 Calosso (AT)
tel. 0141853183

Premium quality is the distinguishing characteristic of the Chiarlo cellar. The new, deep garnet Barbera Tardiva '97 discloses balsamic notes and hints of super-ripe black berry fruit while the admirable follow-through on the palate shows cocoa powder and fruit preserve. In contrast, the Cipressi della Court '99 has less structure, although it is still good. The varietal notes of fleshy fruit on the nose are picked up on the long, firm palate. But the La Court '98 is a stunner. This dark purple Barbera tempts the nose with spices and ripe fruit over a minerally backdrop, then the wonderful harmony and concentration of the endless palate bespeak an absolute mastery of oak conditioning. The barbera, nebbiolo and cabernet sauvignon Monferrato Countacc! '98 is reminiscent of tobacco and leather, and has a generously long palate. Then we sampled the Langhe Barilot '98. From barbera and nebbiolo, it shows autumn leaves and cherry on the nose, soft tannins and nice fruit in the finish. The ever-reliable Barbaresco Asili '98 has an elegantly broad range of aromas and its marked vein of acidity ushers in a sophisticated finish. What we liked about the Barolo Cerequio '97 was its complex nose, ranging from fresh berry fruit to bitter chocolate. It is followed by a fleshy, masculine palate that progresses unhurriedly to rediscover a hint of toastiness in the finish. This is a great '97 and well worth its Three Glasses. We were less convinced, though, by the traditional '97 Barolo Cannubi. The late-harvested Moscato d'Asti Smentiò 2000 is a classy bottle. Its aromas of pink grapefruit, meringue and talcum powder usher in a creamy entry on long palate. Although the Gavi '98 reveals its trademark apricot, it can offer no more than bright nose-palate consistency.

The two Scagliola Barberas, the Sansì and the Sansì Selezione, confirm the potential that this cellar, and the vineyard terrain in the municipality of Calosso, both possess. Barbera is king at Calosso and for some years now, the wines in this part of Asti have been among the best in the province, and indeed beyond. This year, the Barbera d'Asti Sansì Selezione '98 is excellent and scored very high indeed, only a whisker shy of Three Glasses. The intense garnet is accompanied by a complex nose that takes its time to open out. Initially, there are hints of toasty oak, then ripe fruit comes through with vanilla and tobacco. Already perfectly balanced on the palate, it delights the senses with its sensationally long sweet fruit. It is a great performance, and one that is endorsed by the overall standard of the cellar's wines. The Barbera Sansì '99 is only a little less good and easily won Two Glasses. But the Scagliola family also knows how to handle moscato, the other significant variety in this part of Monferrato. Their Volo di Farfalle selection is always one of the best, with its balanced fragrances that bring out the aromatic soul of the moscato grape. The pale straw-yellow colour and the palate are also very attractive. The lovely balance is matched by well-gauged sweetness and a measured finish, where refreshing notes of lemon peel emerge. The Chardonnay was decent, but nothing more.

Wine	Glasses	Score
● Barolo Cerequio '97	¶¶¶	6
● Barbera d'Asti Sup. La Court '98	¶¶	5
○ Moscato d'Asti Smentiò '00	¶¶	5
● Barbera d'Asti Sup. Tardiva '97	¶¶	6
● Barbaresco Asili '98	¶¶	6
● Langhe Barilot '98	¶¶	6
● Monferrato Countacc! '98	¶¶	6
● Barbera d'Asti Sup. Cipressi della Court '99	¶¶	4
● Barolo Cannubi '97	¶	6
○ Gavi Fornaci di Tassarolo '98	¶	5
● Barolo Cannubi '90	¶¶¶	6
● Barolo Cerequio '93	¶¶¶	6
● Barolo Cerequio '95	¶¶¶	6
● Barolo Cerequio '96	¶¶¶	6

Wine	Glasses	Score
● Barbera d'Asti SanSì Sel. '98	¶¶	5
○ Moscato d'Asti Volo di Farfalle '00	¶¶	3
● Barbera d'Asti SanSì '99	¶¶	5
○ Piemonte Chardonnay '00	¶	3
● Barbera d'Asti SanSì '96	¶¶	5
● Barbera d'Asti SanSì '97	¶¶	5
● Barbera d'Asti SanSì Sel. '97	¶¶	5
● Barbera d'Asti SanSì '98	¶¶	5

CALOSSO (AT)

Tenuta dei Fiori
Fraz. Rodotiglia
Via Valcalosso, 3
14052 Calosso (AT)
Tel. 0141826938
E-mail: info@tenutadeifiori.com

Walter Bosticardo's Barbera Rodotiglia '99 is a deliciously sumptuous wine with an impenetrably dark garnet colour. The generous bouquet hints at black berry fruit, eucalyptus and roasted coffee beans over vegetal notes of green leaf. In the mouth, it is just as impressive, its full-bodied structure backed up by dry tannins and a vigorous, lingering finish. We're looking at a very attractive, powerful wine that may be a little in thrall to the oak but is nonetheless enjoyable and well worth drinking. Walter's Barbera Is is also good, the intense colour framing notes of wild berries and toastiness in a very distinctive tasting profile. There is plenty of body on the palate, which only briefly lets a more spirited, dry note show through before finishing attractively on the liquorice notes of the nose. The nose of the rather pale Barbera Vigneto del Tulipano Nero is fairly forward, offering dry flowers and fruit over mineral notes and a dry, no-nonsense palate with a medium-length finish. Next came the Gamba di Pernice, its garnet shading off into orange at the rim. On the nose, roses, pepper, dried leaves and mushrooms are all apparent while the palate has good thrust. There is a faint bitterish twist in the decently long finish. The tight-knit colour of the Dolcetto Fiordaliso introduces a nose of fruit and autumn leaves over an earthy backdrop while the palate brooks no argument. Warm and rounded on the nose, the moscato-based Musica has aromas of peaches and new-mown grass then a full-bodied, nicely balanced palate. The Chardonnay Vento is well-made but the Rairì, also from moscato, is outstanding, confirming Walter Bosticardo's talent for wines of this kind.

○ Rairì Moscato '00	♊	3*
● Barbera d'Asti Rodotiglia Castello di Calosso '99	♊	6
○ Il Vento Chardonnay '00	♈	3
● Monferrato Dolcetto Fiordaliso '00	♈	3
○ Musica Moscato '00	♈	3
● Barbera d'Asti Is '98	♈	4
● Barbera d'Asti Vigneto del Tulipano Nero '98	♈	4
● Gamba di Pernice '99	♈	3
● Monferrato Rosso '95	♊	5
● Monferrato Rosso Cabernet '96	♊	4
● Barbera d'Asti Is '97	♊	4

CAMINO (AL)

Tenuta Gaiano
Via Trino, 8
15020 Camino (AL)
Tel. 0142469440
E-mail: tenutagaiano@tiscalinet.it

The winery owned by Gigi Lavander and Pier Iviglia is based in a mediaeval castle that for centuries served as a Cistercian monastery. The monks were keen viticulturists, as can be seen from the beautiful ancient cellars. Located in the extreme north of the Monferrato Casale area, the estate enjoys a site climate that benefits from the nearby rive Po and the ricefields round about. The wines are made in a proud, uncompromising Monferrato style, with the aid of oenologist Gianni Bailo. This year, the Barbera Vigna della Torretta came close to earning Three Glasses. Its impenetrable, inky colour ushers in deep, close-knit aromas of black berry fruit and vanilla. On the impressively structured palate, it unfolds all the power of the fruit in a well-balanced progression. The finish is generously varietal. The Grignolino Vigna del Convento is no slouch, either. The colour is surprisingly intense for a grignolino-based wine and the lingering aromas embrace notes of strawberry, raspberry, roses, almonds and distinct nuances of pepper. In the mouth, it shows very respectable structure and as much as 15 per cent alcohol which, however, is nicely offset by crisp, concentrated aromas on nose and palate. Birbarossa is a blend of freisa, ruché and various lesser varieties that aims for, and achieves, remarkable, immediately evident, approachability. The impenetrable purple-black colour is followed up by intensely fruit-rich notes with a light aromatic character lifted by ripe black berry fruit, violets and coffee. Soft and well-sustained by firm tannins on the palate, it tempts with a satisfying bilberry finish. Finally, the refreshingly drinkable Barbera Gallianum, vinified without recourse to wood, has open, varietal aromas and good structure.

● Barbera del M.to Vigna della Torretta '98	♊	5
● Barbera del M.to Gallianum '99	♊	4
● Grignolino del M.to Casalese Vigna del Convento '00	♊	4
● Birbarossa '00	♈	3
● Barbera del M.to Vigna della Torretta '96	♊♊	4
● Barbera del M.to Vigna della Torretta '97	♊♊	4
● Barbera del M.to Gallianum '98	♊♊	3

CANALE (CN)

Cascina Ca' Rossa
Loc. Cascina Ca' Rossa, 56
12043 Canale (CN)
tel. 017398348

The wines that Angelo Ferrio presented this year included the Mulassa '99, a characterful Barbera that soared away with Three Glasses. It is a selection with an intense, tight-knit garnet hue that precedes a thrillingly complex bouquet of cherries and ripe blackcurrants over nuances of chocolate, mint and black pepper. Entry on the palate is richly full-bodied, and the progression broad, its sinew kept well under control by the generous alcohol that comes through again in the warm, cocoa powder and liquorice finish. A welcome newcomer was the Roero Mompissano and the '99 vintage is the first to be released. It's a well-structured wine with an austere profile and comes from a vineyard of about two hectares in the Mompissano subzone in the municipal territory of Canale. The garnet ruby colour precedes an attractively evolved nose of fruit preserve, leather and dried flowers. There is plenty of muscle on the palate, as well as firm tannins that dry the lingering finish of mint and liquorice. In contrast, the Audinaggio '99 wasn't at its best, showing broad orange highlights in its garnet colour. The palate is dry and slightly austere and there is a bitterish twist in the finish. The excellent Barbera '00 has an intense colour and a rich nose with fresh nuances of bramble and raspberry over mint and tobacco. The palate is full-bodied and dynamic, the tannins firm and the finish long. The standard-label Roera is uncomplicated and pleasing while the Arneis Merica offers attractive, tangy notes.

● Barbera d'Alba Mulassa '99	🍷🍷🍷	5
● Barbera d'Alba '00	🍷🍷	3*
● Roero Mompissano '99	🍷🍷	5
● Roero Vigna Audinaggio '99	🍷🍷	5
● Roero '00	🍷	3
○ Roero Arneis Merica '00	🍷	3
● Roero Vigna Audinaggio '96	🍷🍷🍷	5
● Roero Vigna Audinaggio '97	🍷🍷	5
● Barbera d'Alba Mulassa '98	🍷🍷	4
● Roero Vigna Audinaggio '98	🍷🍷	5

CANALE (CN)

Cascina Chicco
Via Valentino, 144
12043 Canale (CN)
tel. 0173979069
e-mail: cascinachicco@cascinachicco.com

The Faccenda family offers all the typical Roero wines, interpreted in a rigorous yet modern style. Their Roero Mulino della Costa, from the Castellinaldo vineyard of the same name, is a newcomer that joins the Valmaggiore, the classic Cascina Chicco Roero which from the '99 vintage will be released after an extra year's ageing. The intense garnet-ruby Mulino della Costa delivers an intriguing nose of very ripe berry fruit and chocolate. The fleshy mouthfeel reveals robust tannins that are slightly astringent on the long, consistent finish. The Arcass is unusual: a dried-grape wine based on wood-fermented arneis with a lustrous gold hue and aromas of dried fruit and flowers. But it was the concentrated garnet Nebbiolo Mompissano, its nose marrying fruit notes superbly with oak-derived spice, that proved the thoroughbred of the stable, carrying off the Three Glasses that went last year to the Barbera Bric Loira. Hints of cloves, Peruvian bark and mint mingle with berry fruit, violets and almonds in a wonderfully complex but never difficult olfactory profile. The palate is right up to expectation, with its vigorous, tight-knit texture, nicely judged major-league tannins and a concentrated finish that beautifully echoes the nose. The Barbera Bric Loira brings together its famously outstanding structure and a delightfully complex palate that is only a shade less convincing than in previous vintages. Again this year, the Barbera Granera Alta picked up Two Glasses. And to round off, there was the ever-attractive Favorita and an Arneis Anterisio that was a little lean on the nose.

● Nebbiolo d'Alba Mompissano '99	🍷🍷🍷	5
● Barbera d'Alba Bric Loira '99	🍷🍷	5
● Barbera d'Alba Granera Alta '00	🍷🍷	4
● Roero Mulino della Costa '99	🍷🍷	5
○ Langhe Favorita '00	🍷	4
○ Arcass V. T.	🍷	5
○ Roero Arneis Anterisio '00		4
● Barbera d'Alba Bric Loira '97	🍷🍷🍷	5
● Barbera d'Alba Bric Loira '98	🍷🍷🍷	5
● Nebbiolo d'Alba Mompissano '97	🍷🍷	4
● Roero Valmaggiore '97	🍷🍷	4
● Nebbiolo d'Alba Mompissano '98	🍷🍷	4
● Roero Valmaggiore '98	🍷🍷	5

CANALE (CN)

★ Matteo Correggia
Case Sparse Garbinetto, 124
12043 Canale (CN)
tel. 0173978009
e-mail: matteo@matteocoreggia.com

If you look back over the years with Matteo Correggia, you retrace the story of one of Italy's finest producers. Matteo Corregia produced marvellous results from his first vintages during the late 1980s. These were followed up by his first Three Glass triumph, the Nebbiolo La Val dei Preti '93 and then an astounding series of successes with the Barbera Marun. There were also stunning wines like the Sauvignon Matteo Correggia and the Roero Ròche d'Ampsèj, as delicious as they were indicative of a mature winemaking style capable of masterfully interpreting very different wines. Just over a decade's endeavours were sufficient for Matteo to make his mark on the Piedmont wine scene. Then a tragic accident took him from us in June 2001. This modest and supremely competent man of wine will be sorely missed. Today, the cellar is run by Matteo's wife, Ornella, and mother Severina, helped this year by Matteo's sister Antonella and Luca Rostagno, a young wine technician from Roero. Their Marun is simply astounding. Its inky purple hue ushers in a concentrate nose of plums, spices and balsamic notes in an attractive and clearly defined olfactory profile. The palate is full-bodied, dense and well-sustained, the silky tannins melding perfectly in the long finish. The Ròche d'Ampsèj is also in a class of its own, with its irresistible hints of smoke and liquorice. The thrust on the palate of this wine takes your breath away. As ever, the Nebbiolo La Val dei Preti is a reliable bottle and the Sauvignon Matteo Correggia is a very welcome newcomer to this rock-solid range. Finally, there are all the remarkable wines, led by the Roero and Barbera, that the Correggias consider "standard".

● Barbera d'Alba Marun '99	🍷🍷🍷	5
● Roero Ròche d'Ampsèj '98	🍷🍷🍷	6
○ Langhe Bianco Matteo Correggia '99	🍷🍷	5
● Nebbiolo d'Alba La Val dei Preti '99	🍷🍷	5
● Barbera d'Alba '00	🍷🍷	4
● Roero '00	🍷🍷	4
○ Roero Arneis '00	🍷	4
● Barbera d'Alba Bricco Marun '95	🍷🍷🍷	5
● Barbera d'Alba Marun '96	🍷🍷🍷	5
● Nebbiolo d'Alba La Val dei Preti '96	🍷🍷🍷	5
● Roero Ròche d'Ampsèj '96	🍷🍷🍷	6
● Barbera d'Alba Marun '97	🍷🍷🍷	5
● Roero Ròche d'Ampsèj '97	🍷🍷🍷	6

CANALE (CN)

Deltetto
C.so Alba, 43
12043 Canale (CN)
tel. 0173979383
e-mail: deltetto@deltetto.com

Antonino Deltetto is an intelligent, enthusiastic producer who offers a wide range of premium-quality red, white and dessert wines. The list looks destined to lengthen for currently ageing is a pinot nero and chardonnay-based '99 Metodo Classico spumante, 2,000 bottles of which are due for release next year. In this year's range, there are two high-scoring Arneis, the Daivej and the San Michele. The former has a concentrated straw-yellow hue and an interesting nose with hints of apple, apricot and oregano but it is on the palate that it gives its best. The full texture is enlivened by a tangy note while the finish is dynamic and characterful. The San Michele is medium-intensity straw-yellow, introducing a distinctive nose of mulberry blossom, grapefruit, tomato and gunflint, with good overall complexity. The quality of the texture is immediately obvious on the palate, which offers smooth, well-sustained progression through to the consistent, lingering finish. All the nebbiolo-based wines are also excellent, the two Roero selections winning out over the more straightforward and less approachable Langhe Nebbiolo. The Madonna dei Boschi selection is less of a heavyweight but is temptingly well-balanced on the palate. In contrast, the concentrated colour of the Braja tells you that this is a wine with body. The subtle aromas are redolent of black berry fruit and the full body is lifted by sweet yet distinct tannins. The Barbera Bramé '99 wasn't quite up to its usual mark. Last on the list was the Bric du Liun, a golden dessert wine that releases hints of ripe apples and pears laced with honey on the nose. The palate has a distinct vein of sweetness, decent weight and good length.

○ Roero Arneis Daivej '00	🍷🍷	4
○ Roero Arneis S. Michele '00	🍷🍷	4
● Roero Braja '99	🍷🍷	5
● Roero Madonna dei Boschi '99	🍷🍷	5
○ Bric du Liun Passito '00	🍷	4
● Barbera d'Alba Bramè '99	🍷	4
○ Langhe Bianco Suasì '98	🍷🍷	4
● Roero Braja '98	🍷🍷	5
● Roero Madonna dei Boschi '98	🍷🍷	5

CANALE (CN)

FUNTANIN
VIA TORINO, 191
12043 CANALE (CN)
TEL. 0173979488

Emblematic of the sustained progress made by Bruno and Piercarlo Sperone's wines is their Barbera Ciabot Pierin '99, very much a bottle with attitude. The very dense ruby red has the narrowest of rims and the deep, intriguing nose releases elegant aromas of cherry and raspberry over attractively complex hints of mint and chocolate. The entry on the palate is impressively rich, progressing surefootedly with a barely perceptible sinewy note to a full-bodied, dynamic and deliciously long finish. The intense garnet-ruby Roero Bricco Barbisa is also outstanding. The nose offers mineral notes against a background of red berry jam, leather and coffee while the palate's generous progression is lifted by dry tannins that lend austerity to this very drinkable bottle. Lingering notes of cocoa powder, violets and caramel come through in the finish. Both the Arneis wines, the standard label and the Pierin di Soc, are good. The former has green highlights in a pale straw-yellow hue and a nose with faint nuances of spring flowers, aromatic herbs, fruit and yeast. Pleasantly fresh on the palate, it offers a well-balanced finish with a faint bitterish hint. The Pierin di Soc has a slightly more concentrated colour and a fairly broad nose that foregrounds notes of chamomile, apple and citrus fruits. Silky on the palate, it has a long finish that satisfyingly echoes the nose.

● Barbera d'Alba Ciabot Pierin '99	ŸŸ	5
● Roero Sup. Bricco Barbisa '99	ŸŸ	5
○ Roero Arneis '00	Ÿ	3
○ Roero Arneis Pierin di Soc '00	Ÿ	4
● Barbera d'Alba Sup. '97	ŸŸ	4
● Roero Sup. Bricco Barbisa '97	ŸŸ	5
● Barbera d'Alba Ciabot Pierin '98	ŸŸ	4
● Roero Sup. Bricco Barbisa '98	ŸŸ	5

CANALE (CN)

FILIPPO GALLINO
FRAZ. VALLE DEL POZZO, 63
12043 CANALE (CN)
TEL. 017398112
E-MAIL: gallino.filippo@libero.it

Filippo, Maria and Gianni Gallino's winery nestles among the vineyards at Valle del Pozzo, two and a half kilometres from Canale. The last two years have been very important ones for the Gallino family, who have increased output from 30,000 to 60,000 bottles over the period and also won a number of major awards, including our Three Glasses. Quality is ever the watchword, as is shown by the Three Glasses we awarded the Gallinos for their Roero Superiore again this year. And it's a very "superior" wine indeed, as is obvious from the garnet-ruby colour in the glass, with its compact rim, and the complex, concentrated nose with fresh notes of cherries, raspberries and violets nuanced with vanilla and toastiness. Full and compact on the palate, it unveils amazing extract and a generously long finish where hints of cocoa powder and liquorice peek through against a floral backdrop. The Barbera Superiore is another heavyweight. Dense in colour, it reveals an interesting nose of black and red berry fruit over a faint earthy background. The determined, full-bodied thrust concludes with a long finish and there is good nose-palate consistency. The standard-label reds, a Barbera and a Roero, are very good wines, the Barbera scoring a full Two Glasses. The less complex Roero can point to fruit and roasted almond aromas preceding a reasonably well-sustained palate and a finish with a hint of liquorice. Bringing up the rear is the Arneis. Its fruit and yeast aromas usher in a fresh and nicely balanced palate.

● Roero Sup. '99	ŸŸŸ	5
● Barbera d'Alba Sup. '99	ŸŸ	5
● Barbera d'Alba '00	ŸŸ	3*
● Roero '00	Ÿ	3
○ Roero Arneis '00		3
● Barbera d'Alba Sup. '97	ŸŸŸ	5
● Roero Sup. '98	ŸŸŸ	5
● Barbera d'Alba Sup. '96	ŸŸ	4
● Roero Sup. '96	ŸŸ	4
● Roero Sup. '97	ŸŸ	4
● Barbera d'Alba Sup. '98	ŸŸ	5

CANALE (CN)

Malvirà
Loc. Canova
Case Sparse, 144
12043 Canale (CN)
tel. 0173978145
e-mail: malvira@malvira.com

As usual, the Damonte brothers this year gave us an excellent series of wines, the whites proving consistently good as never before. The very stylish Tre Uve, a medium straw-yellow 40-40-20 blend of sauvignon, chardonnay and arneis, delights the nostrils with a bouquet of dried flowers, tomato leaf, apples and pears and aromatic herbs. Full-flavoured on the palate, it has good thrust and a long finish with complex variations on a vanilla theme. All the Arneis were good, starting with the Trinità. Lustrous straw-yellow, it has a distinctive nose of new-mown grass, grapefruit peel and apricot. In the mouth, it is full-bodied, vigorous and lingering. The Saglietto has an intense colour and aromas of ripe tropical fruit with tomato leaf. Well-structured on the palate, it unveils a long, vanilla-nuanced finish cakes. The Renesio, too, has a full colour that ushers in stylish hints of fruit, herbs and confectioner's cream. The full palate is perked up by a tangy note. There was a very full One Glass score for the standard Arneis, which has an individual nose of fruit over grassy notes. As for the reds, the San Gugliemo '98, from 55 per cent barbera, 40 per cent nebbiolo and five per cent bonarda, reveals a fairly firm garnet ruby hue. On the nose, aromas of minerals and autumn leaves mingle against a backdrop of violets, bramble, raspberry and mint. The very impressive palate is backed up by tannins and has complexity in the finish. The '98 version of the Roero Superiore '98 is only a tad less exciting than the fabulous '97. Its scrupulously selected nebbiolo grapes disclose hints of hay, cakes and liqueur fruit on the nose while the palate is muscular and long.

CANALE (CN)

Monchiero Carbone
Via Santo Stefano Roero, 2
12043 Canale (CN)
tel. 017395568
e-mail: info@monchierocarbone.com

Francesco Monchiero, with father Marco and mother Lucia Carbone, are the heart and soul of this impressive Roero estate. As winemakers, they have an open mind that looks to all the world's wines as possible opportunities for comparison. The ethos is reflected in their Barbera MonBirone, which this year brings out the variety's character in a serious, complex profile that is international in the best sense of the word. The deep garnet red has a narrow orangey rim then the nose opens on intriguing minerally and gamey notes over the typical barbera backdrop of black and red berry fruit. The palate makes no secret of its concentration, complexity and vigour, and is well-sustained through to the finish, which bows out on a note of mint and autumn leaves. The two Roeros, the Srü and the Printi, are excellent. The first of the pair has a fine garnet ruby colour and an interestingly broad nose, where aromas of violets, cocoa powder and liquorice meld over rain-soaked earth. The tight-knit palate is backed up by firm tannins and ends vigorously on notes of balsam and fruit. The Printi, which ages for a year longer than the Srü, has a fairly intense ruby hue and a forward nose of ripe fruit and flower. On the palate, it is full-bodied and sustained, with nice tannins and good length that plays out on notes of mint and cocoa powder. Finally, the Arneis Re Cit offers a fairly concentrated straw-yellow hue with green highlights. Yeasts and tropical fruit come across on the stylish nose while the attractive, fresh-tasting palate signs off with a faintly bitterish twist.

	Wine	Glasses	Score
●	Roero Sup. '98	¶¶	5
○	Roero Arneis Renesio '00	¶¶	3*
○	Roero Arneis Saglietto '00	¶¶	4
○	Roero Arneis Trinità '00	¶¶	3*
●	Langhe Rosso S. Guglielmo '98	¶¶	5
○	Langhe Bianco Tre Uve '99	¶¶	4
○	Roero Arneis '00	¶	3
●	Roero Sup. '90	¶¶¶	6
●	Roero Sup. '93	¶¶¶	6
●	Roero Sup. '97	¶¶¶	5
●	Langhe Rosso S. Guglielmo '97	¶¶	5
●	Roero '98	¶¶	4

	Wine	Glasses	Score
●	Roero Sup. Printi '98	¶¶	5
●	Barbera d'Alba MonBirone '99	¶¶	4
●	Roero Srü '99	¶¶	5
○	Roero Arneis Re Cit '00	¶	3
○	Langhe Bianco Tamardì '99	¶	4
●	Roero Srü '96	¶¶	4
●	Roero Srü '97	¶¶	4
●	Roero Sup. Printi '97	¶¶	5
●	Roero Srü '98	¶¶	5

CANELLI (AT)

Cascina Barisél
Reg. San Giovanni, 2
14053 Canelli (AT)
tel. 0141824849 - 03394165913
e-mail: barisel@inwind.it

This year, the Penna family presented the panel with two vintages of their excellent Barbera La Cappelletta. Both the '98 and the '99 easily scored Two Glass ratings, confirming the reliable quality of this wine. The '99 version has an intense garnet ruby hue and a vibrantly exciting nose of berry fruit, vanilla and toast oak aromas over subtle nuances of tobacco and autumn leaves. The good texture and fluent follow-through on the palate are highlighted by a dry note and conclude with a long finish where the spice and fruit of the nose re-emerge. The Barbera '98 is also intense in the glass, offering aromas of liquorice, plum, bramble and spices. The palate has good weight from entry, with a broad, dynamic progression through to a finish that may not be particularly long but is certainly very satisfying. Another very good wine is the deep straw-yellow Moscato '00, its golden flecks heralding a complex, well-defined nose of peaches, sage, vanilla sugar and lemon peel. Fat without being heavy on the palate, it has a discreet, refreshing prickle and a long, complex finish. To round off the tasting there was the Barbera '00. Its ruby hue ushers in aromas of fruit and mint while the fluent palate, backed up by dry tannins, has a decent a finish.

○	Moscato d'Asti '00	🍷🍷	3*
●	Barbera d'Asti Sup. La Cappelletta '98	🍷🍷	4
●	Barbera d'Asti Sup. La Cappelletta '99	🍷🍷	4
●	Barbera d'Asti '00	🍷	3
●	Barbera d'Asti Sup. La Cappelletta '97	🍷🍷	4
●	Barbera d'Asti '99	🍷	3

CANELLI (AT)

Contratto
Via G. B. Giuliani, 56
14053 Canelli (AT)
tel. 0141823349

Since the Bocchino family took over this historic Canelli winery, there have been major changes and the methods of the previous owners have been revolutionized. Brother and sister team Antonella and Carlo Bocchino, who also own the Bocchino grappa distillery, have restored the estate to its former glory. In addition to the excellent range of wines, the Bocchinos have promoted a series of gastronomic initiatives that have brought some of the world's greatest chefs to Canelli. But the farsightedness of the duo is best demonstrated by their stylish restructuring of the old cellars, where they have created a visitor's route which goes from the legendary Sempione tunnel where the spumantes are stocked to the ageing cellars and finally to the restaurant. Now let's look at the wines, vinified under the supervision of Giancarlo Scaglione. The range hinges on the classic regional bottles, from dry and sweet spumantes to the great reds of the Langhe and Monferrato. This year, it was a superb version of the Bocchinos' Barolo Cerequio that scored a Three Glass bull's eye. It's a monumental wine made with fruit from one of the most prestigious subzones of La Morra. Its concentrated garnet delights the eye and the nose enthrals at once, the balsamic notes melding superbly with fruit and oak-derived aromas to provide a complex, lingering olfactory profile. But it is on the palate that the wine really impresses: the stylish, creamy fruit is perfectly balanced and supported by firm but very docile tannins. Other high scorers were the Asti De Miranda Metodo Classico and the Barbera Solus Ad, a wine to match the most famous names in the DOC zone.

●	Barolo Cerequio Tenuta Secolo '97	🍷🍷🍷	6
○	Asti De Miranda M. Cl. '99	🍷🍷	5
○	Spumante M. Cl. Brut Ris. Giuseppe Contratto '97	🍷🍷	5
●	Barbera d'Asti Solus Ad '99	🍷🍷	6
○	Piemonte Chardonnay La Sabauda '99	🍷🍷	5
●	Barbera d'Asti Panta Rei '99	🍷	4
○	Spumante M. Cl. Brut Ris. Giuseppe Contratto '95	🍷🍷🍷	5
○	Asti De Miranda M. Cl. '96	🍷🍷🍷	5
○	Spumante M. Cl. Brut Ris. Giuseppe Contratto '96	🍷🍷🍷	5
○	Asti De Miranda M. Cl. '97	🍷🍷🍷	5

CANELLI (AT)

Luigi Coppo e Figli
Via Alba, 66
14053 Canelli (AT)
tel. 0141823146

This is a family business: Piero and Paolo Coppo look after the commercial side with the help of Piero's son Massimiliano, Roberto deals with production and Gianni takes care of administration and vineyard management. They are completing the restructuring of the cellar, a magnificent complex that links the main residence to the new entrance in Via Alba. In the cellar, the labyrinth of tunnels has been adapted without altering its character so that barrique ageing can be carried out in ideal conditions and the metodo classico spumantes can be produced at the appropriate controlled temperature and humidity. The long list of wines we tasted ranged from the good to the very good, with at least three candidates for top Guide honours but it was the magnificent Barbera d'Asti Pomorosso '99 that carried off the Three Glasses. The colour is almost impenetrable, hinting at the potential of a selection that also impresses with its delicate, complex nose, where bramble and ripe cherry allow stylishly sweet balsamic notes to come through. The palate is monumental. Full-bodied and creamy on entry, it unfolds in a seamlessly leisurely fashion to arrive at a sweet, intensely concentrated finish. The Alterego from the same vintage is equally impressive. It marries cabernet sauvignon and barbera from old vines quite remarkably. The '98 is good as well but falls down a little in the back palate, where there is a dry note. Next came the Monteriolo, a fine Chardonnay and one of the best in Piedmont, and beyond. The '96 Brut is almost as good as the absent Riserva del Fondatore, although it lacks some of the other wine's elegance, and the 100 per cent freisa Mondaccione is back on top form.

	Wine	Rating	Price
●	Barbera d'Asti Pomorosso '99	♀♀♀	6
●	Monferrato Alterego '99	♀♀	6
○	Coppo Brut Ris. '96	♀♀	5
●	Alterego '98	♀♀	6
●	Barbera d'Asti Camp du Rouss '99	♀♀	5
●	Langhe Rosso Mondaccione '99	♀♀	5
○	Piemonte Chardonnay Monteriolo '99	♀♀	6
○	Moscato d'Asti Moncalvina '00	♀	4
○	Piemonte Chardonnay Costebianche '00	♀	4
●	Barbera d'Asti Pomorosso '90	♀♀♀	5
●	Barbera d'Asti Pomorosso '96	♀♀	6
●	Barbera d'Asti Pomorosso '97	♀♀	6
●	Barbera d'Asti Pomorosso '98	♀♀	6

CANELLI (AT)

Villa Giada
Reg. Ceirole, 4
14053 Canelli (AT)
tel. 0141831100
e-mail: villagiada@atlink.it

Outstanding in this year's range from the Faccio family are two excellent Barberas, the Bricco Dani and La Quercia. Bricco Dani is made with fruit from the hillslope of the same name in the municipality of Agliano and presents a very close-knit garnet in the glass. The nose has an elegantly interesting profile with nuances of black berry fruit, aromatic herbs and liquorice over enticing hints of autumn leaves and Peruvian bark. On the palate, there is good body and width, with a nicely structured progression through to a lingering finish of fruit, violets and liquorice. The other outstanding Barbera, the La Quercia, has a fairly intense ruby colour and a satisfyingly deep nose where plum, bramble and dark leaves mingle with toastiness and cocoa powder. The front palate is reasonably full-bodied while the progression reveals slightly dryish tannins. The long finish echoes the nose, ending on a pleasantly bitterish note. One Glass went to the Barbera Superiore Ajan. The '90 has a moderately concentrated ruby hue that shades into garnet and a nose where the aromas of black berry preserve and violets succumb to the dominant oak-derived toastiness. The upfront and rather rustic palate reveals prominent tannins and a faintly bitterish finish.

	Wine	Rating	Price
●	Barbera d'Asti Sup. Bricco Dani '99	♀♀	5
●	Barbera d'Asti Sup. Vigneto La Quercia '99	♀♀	4
●	Barbera d'Asti Sup. Ajan '99	♀	4
●	Barbera d'Asti Sup. Bricco Dani '97	♀♀	4
●	Barbera d'Asti Sup. Vigneto La Quercia '97	♀♀	4
●	Barbera d'Asti Sup. Bricco Dani '98	♀♀	4
●	Barbera d'Asti Sup. Ajan '98	♀	4
●	Barbera d'Asti Sup. Vigneto La Quercia '98	♀	4

CAREMA (TO)

CANTINA DEI PRODUTTORI
NEBBIOLO DI CAREMA
VIA NAZIONALE, 28
10010 CAREMA (TO)
TEL. 0125811160
E-MAIL: cantinacarema@libero.it

At the helm of the Cantina dei Produttori Nebbiolo di Carema is Viviano Gassino, who has taken over from long-serving president Luciano Clerin. Assisting Gassino is the versatile Manlio Muggianu. The cellar has about 60 members, most of whom have very small estates, often of less than one hectare, located at between 300 and 600 metres above sea level. Total output is about 50,000 bottles a year. The cellar releases Carema under three labels. Two of these are well-established in the market but for a few years they have been flanked by a low-output – only 3,000 bottles – selection aged in small oak barrels. We'll start this year's round-up with the special selection, which is garnet with lustrous brick-red highlights. Its delicate aromas of spices and tobacco are deliciously offset by the wood and the palate, which is very traditional, puts the emphasis on style rather than muscle: a fine example of how best to marry tradition and innovation in a nebbiolo-based wine. The Carema Carema is good but not up to the standards of recent vintages. The aromas of tar and animal skins on the nose impress but the palate, while complex, is dominated by tannins. The standard '97, with its classic pale garnet colour, is more straightforward but its aromas are fresh and whistle-clean, and the palate has grace and style.
Concluding the range are two Canavese DOC wines, on sale at extremely interesting prices. Cellar door purchasers are welcome.

● Carema Selezione '96	🍷	5
● Carema Carema '96	🍷	4
● Carema Classico '97	🍷	3
● Carema Carema '93	🍷🍷	5
● Carema Carema '95	🍷🍷	4

CASSINASCO (AT)

KARIN E REMO HOHLER
REG. BRICCO BOSETTI, 85
14050 CASSINASCO (AT)
TEL. 0141851209
E-MAIL: remohohler@hotmail.com

Karin and Remo Hohler hail from Kaiseraugst, in German-speaking Switzerland, and always wanted to work together on a shared project. Ten years ago, they got their big break. They were offered a small winery at Cassinasco in the Asti part of the Langhe. There were risks a-plenty, of course, as well as the difficulties associated with a new country, a new langage and a new business. The Hohlers are made of stern stuff, though, and today their three-hectare property is a jewel of quality in the treasure trove that is Barbera d'Asti. The cellar itself is very simple but the aim is to concentrate on top-quality fruit by keeping yields low and selecting the grapes. The four small vineyards are managed so as to keep the environmental impact to a minimum and the Hohlers' consultant oenologist is Giuliano Noè. The team release two versions of their Barbera Pian del Bosco, identical in fruit and vinification but different in the method of ageing used. One sees no wood at all and the other spends seven or eight months in barriques. Both show what they are made of in the glass, where their impenetrable inky black has a purple-ruby rim. The crisply varietal aromas are tight-knit and enfolding, releasing stylish hints of ripe black berry fruit and violets. The broad, velvet-smooth mouthfeel caresses the palate, which presents a full-bodied structure and a balanced thrust that is perfectly sustained through to the long bramble-themed finish. In the barrique-aged version, the nose is enhanced by notes of tobacco and vanilla that exalt the fruit without covering it. The range is rounded off by an unusual dry moscato called Cenerentola, or Cinderella.

● Barbera d'Asti Pian del Bosco '99	🍷🍷	4
● Barbera d'Asti Pian del Bosco Barrique '98	🍷🍷	5

CASTAGNOLE DELLE LANZE (AT)

★ La Spinetta
Fraz. Annunziata, 17
14054 Castagnole delle Lanze (AT)
tel. 0141877396

Today, Bruno, Carlo and Giorgio Rivetti have an internationally famous winery that turns out world-class wines. This year sees the debut of a very convincing sauvignon-based Langhe Bianco that joins the excellent Chardonnay Lidia, named after their mother, who passed away in the summer. Produced at Mango and aged for 12 months in new barriques, it offers an elegant nose, a concentrated palate then a long finish. But there are other newcomers in the pipeline, including a Barolo '00 made at Grinzane Cavour and a Tuscan-style red from sangiovese grapes. Moving on to the Barbarescos, it is the Starderi that stands out. The colour is classic; the aromas reveal liquorice and balsamic notes with a background of dried flowers and mineral notes. The well-structured mouthfeel is backed up by sweet, succulent tannins and a never-ending finish. The Gallina is also very good but again it is the Valeirano that presents a stylish, youthful nose and notes of still evolving fruit. The palate is balanced through to the lingering finish, which discloses hints of violets and liquorice. Going back to the Gallina, we find a lively garnet hue and aromas of morello cherry with roses. The palate is robust and brimming with fruit while the long, juicy finish reveals remarkable balance. The Barbera d'Asti Superiore, grafted onto 50 to 60 year old "Vitis rupestris americana" rootstock, is equally lively and offers concentrated fruit on a nose lifted by exquisite mineral notes. The palate reveals unusual tannins for the variety. The Pin, with its minty fragrances, is also delicious. Firm and tannin-rich on the palate, it perhaps overplays the alcohol. As ever, the very attractive Barbera Ca' di Pian '00 and the two elegant Moscatos are very well made.

●	Barbaresco Vigneto Starderi '98	▼▼▼	6
●	Barbaresco Vigneto Valeirano '98	▼▼▼	6
●	Barbera d'Alba Vigneto Gallina '99	▼▼▼	6
●	Barbaresco Vigneto Gallina '98	▼▼	6
●	Monferrato Rosso Pin '99	▼▼	6
●	Barbera d'Asti Sup. '99	▼▼	6
●	Barbera d'Asti Ca' di Pian '00	▼▼	4
○	Moscato d'Asti Biancospino '00	▼▼	4
○	Moscato d'Asti Bricco Quaglia '00	▼▼	4
○	Langhe Bianco '99	▼▼	5
○	Piemonte Chardonnay Lidia '99	▼▼	5
●	Barbaresco Vigneto Gallina '97	▼▼▼	6
●	Barbaresco Vigneto Starderi '97	▼▼▼	6
●	Barbera d'Alba Vigneto Gallina '98	▼▼▼	6
●	Monferrato Rosso Pin '99	▼▼▼	6

CASTEL BOGLIONE (AT)

Araldica - Il Cascinone
V.le Laudano, 2
14040 Castel Boglione (AT)
tel. 014176319
e-mail: claudio@araldicavini.com

This year, Araldica, which selects and distributes wines from a number of co-operatives around Nizza Monferrato and Acqui Terme, inaugurated a new facility. It's a huge industrial building that may not be the last word in architectural aesthetics but it was accompanied by the consolidation of the Il Cascinone project. It is destined to become Alessandria's version of a "château" once it is restructured. Il Cascinone certainly has the makings. The 104 hectares of hillslopes include 37 planted to old barbera vines and other typical local varieties. The main residence includes a hospitality centre and accommodation for workers while the new winemaking cellar and ageing cellar for serious bottles are all promising factors. The property will be Araldica's flagship establishment and experimental centre where the company will produce its most cellarable labels. But let's get back to today and the wines that again impressed the panel, as they have in previous editions of the Guide. Top of the range is the Barbera Rive '99, a prestigious red, round and full-bodied, that bears comparison with the very best Barberas of the moment. Another distinctly superior bottle was the Roero Arneis Sorilaria, which benefited from a very ripe harvest and the skilful use of wood. The best of the international varieties on offer was the rich, buttery Chardonnay Roleto, vinified in new and used barriques. We preferred it to the Sauvignon Camillona. And going back to the reds, there was an honourable mention for the fine Luce Monaca, a 40-30-30 blend of barbera, cabernet and merlot, and the less exciting pinot nero-based Renero.

○	Piemonte Chardonnay Roleto '00	▼▼	4
●	Barbera d'Asti Sup. Rive '99	▼▼	5
●	Monferrato Rosso Luce Monaca '99	▼▼	5
○	Monferrato Bianco Camillona '00	▼	4
○	Roero Arneis Sorilaria '00	▼	4
○	Piemonte Brut M. Cl. '96	▼	4
●	Langhe Nebbiolo Castellero '99	▼	5
●	Monferrato Rosso Renero '99	▼	4

CASTEL BOGLIONE (AT)

Cascina Garitina
Via Gianola, 20
14040 Castel Boglione (AT)
Tel. 0141762162
E-mail: info@cascinagaritina.it

Father and son team Pasquale and Gianluca Morino own the Cascina Garitina, where they cultivate 13 hectares of vines for an annual production of about 70,000 bottles. This time round, they presented four wines, three of which earned Two Glass scores. We'll start with the Barbera Neuvsent, an intense garnet in the glass with the faintest hint of evolution at the rim. The nose offers a broad, enticing bouquet of ripe fruit, with hints of berry fruit, rhubarb, liquorice and mint over faint, and unexpected, touches of citrus. The palate is close-knit and full-bodied, ending with a vigorous finish that stylishly echoes the notes of cocoa powder and mint. The '99 version of the Barbera Bricco Garitta has a ruby colour of medium intensity and a nose of jam, spices and nutmeg. The attack in the mouth is reasonably concentrated, gaining momentum in mid palate to finish brightly on lingering notes of mint and liquorice. The Monferrato Rosso Amis is a blend of 50 per cent barbera, 40 per cent pinot nero and ten per cent cabernet with a fairly pronounced ruby colour that shades into garnet. On the nose, fruit notes mingle with autumn leaves and rhubarb while the palate is reasonably mouthfilling, the follow-through fluent and the finish satisfying. Finally, the monovarietal cabernet Estremis offers an intense hue and fragrances of dried flowers, jam and autumn leaves. The palate may lack a little power but the finish is decently long.

●	Monferrato Rosso Amis '99	🍷🍷	4
●	Barbera d'Asti Sup. Neuvsent '99	🍷🍷	5
●	Barbera d'Asti Bricco Garitta '99	🍷🍷	3*
●	Monferrato Rosso Estremis '99	🍷	5
●	Barbera d'Asti Sup. Neuvsent '96	🍷🍷	4
●	Barbera d'Asti Sup. Neuvsent '98	🍷🍷	4
●	Monferrato Rosso Amis '98	🍷🍷	4
●	Barbera d'Asti Bricco Garitta '98	🍷	3

CASTELLINALDO (CN)

Stefanino Morra
Via Castagnito, 22
12050 Castellinaldo (CN)
Tel. 0173213489

At present, this lovely estate at Castellinaldo produces 55,000 bottles a year from about eight hectares under vine but new vineyards will shortly be coming onstream. The stars of the show are Stefanino Morra, who looks after vineyards and cellar, his parents Margherita and Antonio, both of whom are tireless vinegrowers, Stefanino's wife Edda, who handles administration and packaging, and Edda's brother Gianni, in charge of sales. Starting this year, the Castellinaldo Barbera d'Alba will be released after a longer period of ageing so we will have to wait until next time to review the '99. We'll also have to skip the Arneis San Pietro, which was not produced in 1999, and the '00 will be released and distributed after this Guide has gone to press. The panel this year particularly liked the Barbera d'Alba '99, whose deep garnet colour has the narrowest of rims. On the nose, it mingles cherry, blackcurrant and black pepper in a well-defined profile while the palate impresses with its full-bodied progression and robust structure. Also good was the Roero Superiore, which presents a concentrated ruby colour and a distinctive nose of hazelnut, caramel-covered fruit, hay and dry earth. It is a little austere on the palate because of the dryish tannins. The standard Arneis is straw-yellow, flecked with flashes of green. Yielding aromas of fruit and yeasts, it is temptingly quaffable on the palate and ends with a trim, flowery finish.

●	Barbera d'Alba '99	🍷🍷	4
○	Roero Arneis '00	🍷	4
●	Roero Sup. '99	🍷	4
●	Castellinaldo Barbera d'Alba '97	🍷🍷	5
●	Roero Sup. '97	🍷🍷	4
●	Castellinaldo Barbera d'Alba '98	🍷🍷	5

CASTELLINALDO (CN)

FABRIZIO PINSOGLIO
FRAZ. MADONNA DEI CAVALLI, 8
12050 CASTELLINALDO (CN)
TEL. 0173213078

Fabrizio Pinsoglio and his mother Maria this year turned out a range of wines that confirm the excellent impression they made on our last visit, which led to their first full profile in the Guide. Our tastings revealed a very good Barbera Bric La Rondolina and an equally fine Roero. The Barbera has a concentrated garnet ruby colour and an intriguingly complex nose where aromas of cherries, wood resin and toastiness emerge over a faint background of tree sap. The full, concentrated palate is backed up by no-nonsense tannins, ending unhurriedly on notes of balsam and fruit. In the glass, the Roero '99 has a fairly close-knit ruby hue that ushers in an intriguing nose where notes of ripe black berry fruit and leather combine with coffee and aromatic wood. The vigorous thrust of the complex palate is complemented by serious tannins and crowned by a lingering finish, where berry fruit and violets emerge. The Nebbiolo d'Alba '99 offers a moderately intense ruby colour and a more straightforward nose that nevertheless has plenty of breadth, with hay, strawberries, hazelnuts and autumn leaves coming through. Its muscular tannins make their presence felt, dominating the less than massive texture to render the palate a touch astringent. Finally, the Arneis Vigneto Malinot has a medium straw-yellow hue and a likeable nose with hints of fruit and flowers. Soft on the palate, it takes its leave with a faintly bitterish finish that foregrounds grapefruit.

CASTELNUOVO DON BOSCO (AT)

CASCINA GILLI
VIA NEVISSANO, 36
14022 CASTELNUOVO DON BOSCO (AT)
TEL. 0119876984
E-MAIL: cascinagilli@libero.it

At Cascina Gilli, Gianni Vergnano produces attractive versions of the characteristic local wines, including an extremely tempting Barbera and, of course, a Malvasia that for years has been a benchmark for lovers of this wine. The Barbera Vigna delle More has a fairly intense ruby colour flecked with garnet. They nose may note be very complex but it is irresistible fresh and approachable. There are notes of berry fruit, autumn leaves and green leaf over earth and mineral nuances. On the palate, there is concentrated flesh and a solid, no-nonsense progression to the lively finish, where ripe notes of fruit come through. The relatively deep, purple-nuanced ruby of the Malvasia takes you into a nose of roses, lemon and berry fruit, where raspberry and strawberry are to the fore. The barbera and freisa-based Monferrato Rosso has a reasonably concentrated colour. Strawberry, roses and nutmeg emerge on the nose while the palate is tidy and deliciously dry. The Rafé, from chardonnay and cortese, is nice. The lustrous straw-yellow colour is a prelude to notes of banana, hazelnut, lemon peel and yeasts. Full and soft in the mouth, it ends with a finish that echoes the nose. There are three Cascina Gilli versions of Freisa: the uncomplicated Vivace; the Luna di Maggio, another lively wine but more intense than the Vivace; and the complex Vigna del Forno. Last on our list was a gutsy Bonarda with an appealing rustic attitude.

● Barbera d'Alba Bric La Rondolina '99	♇♇	4
● Roero '99	♇♇	4
● Nebbiolo d'Alba '99	♇	4
○ Roero Arneis Vigneto Malinot '00	♇	3
● Barbera d'Alba Bric La Rondolina '98	♇♇	4
● Roero '98	♇♇	4
● Barbera d'Alba '99	♇	3

● Barbera d'Asti Vigna delle More '00	♇♇	3*
● Malvasia di Castelnuovo Don Bosco '00	♇♇	3*
● Monferrato Rosso '00	♇	4
● Freisa d'Asti Luna di Maggio '00	♇	3
● Freisa d'Asti Vigna del Forno '00	♇	3
● Piemonte Bonarda '00	♇	3
○ Rafé Bianco '00	♇	3
● Freisa d'Asti Vivace '00		3
● Barbera d'Asti Vigna delle More '99	♇♇	3

CASTIGLIONE FALLETTO (CN)

AZELIA
VIA ALBA-BAROLO, 53
12060 CASTIGLIONE FALLETTO (CN)
TEL. 017362859

In the past ten years, Luigi and Lorella Scavino have come a long way, never losing sight of their goal – premium quality. Today, buyers queue up for the 60,000 bottles they turn out every year and their Barolo selections can be found on the wine lists of the world's finest restaurants. The Scavinos have achieved these results partly through new vinification techniques but principally by concentrating on vineyard management, a topic on which Luigi brooks no argument. Shoot thinning and very low yields – no more than 5,000 bottles per hectare – have enabled the family to come ever closer to inclusion in the winemaking aristocracy of the Langhe, and indeed Italy. The results are there in the glass. Barolo Bricco Fiasco '97, from the estate's historic vineyard, remains the panel's favourite. Around 9,000 bottles are produced of this bright, concentrated garnet wine. The entry on the nose is elegant and delicate, opening out with aromas of spices and tobacco enhanced by balsamic notes and ripe fruit. The rich, powerful palate is marvellous, the velvety, caressing mouthfeel takes you through to an unhurried finish where the ripe fruit of the nose returns. The fruit for the other leading estate selection, the San Rocco, comes from Serralunga d'Alba. In fact, it was the Scavinos that established San Rocco's reputation. A characterful wine with great personality, it needs more time in the cellar than the Bricco del Fiasco. The standard-label Barolo, although less complex than its big brothers, is still easily worth One Glass. Finally, the Barbera d'Alba Vigneto Punta and Dolcetto Bricco dell'Oriolo, from the Montelupo Albese vineyard, are both well up to scratch.

● Barolo Bricco Fiasco '97	♀♀	6
● Barolo S. Rocco '97	♀♀	6
● Dolcetto d'Alba Bricco dell'Oriolo '00	♀♀	4
● Barbera d'Alba Vigneto Punta '99	♀♀	5
● Barolo '97	♀	6
● Barolo '91	♀♀♀	6
● Barolo Bricco Fiasco '93	♀♀♀	6
● Barolo Bricco Fiasco '95	♀♀♀	6
● Barolo Bricco Fiasco '96	♀♀♀	6
● Barolo S. Rocco '96	♀♀	6
● Barbera d'Alba Vigneto Punta '98	♀♀	5

CASTIGLIONE FALLETTO (CN)

CASCINA BONGIOVANNI
VIA ALBA-BAROLO, 4
12060 CASTIGLIONE FALLETTO (CN)
TEL. 0173262184

Davide Mozzone always comes up with an exciting range. His two Barolos, the Langhe Rosso and the Dolcetto share a studiedly modern style and all earned Two Glasses. The Barolo Pernanno has a concentrated garnet colour with a narrow orangey rim. It offers notes of jam and leather over fascinating minerally notes of earth and truffles in a delightfully well-balanced nose. In the mouth, the entry is full-bodied and juicy, the mid palate revealing a powerful, richly extracted structure that sustains the progression before lingering on notes of liquorice in the finish. The ruby of the standard-label Barolo is flecked with orange, the etheric bouquet yielding notes of strawberry, cocoa powder and autumn leaves. Although not a heavyweight, the palate is very tidy and drinks deliciously. The barbera, nebbiolo and cabernet sauvignon-based Langhe Rosso Faletto has a narrow rim round its tight-knit garnet colour in the glass. On the nose, there are hints of strawberry, black cherry and liquorice nicely nuanced with dry leaves. The muscular, dry, well put together palate rounds things off unhurriedly, with attractive liquorice notes coming back. The impenetrable garnet of the Dolcetto heralds a concentrated, fairly complex nose with hints of black berry fruit, autumn leaves and pepper. The vibrant colour in the glass is reflected in the generous palate, which signs off with a lively finish that echoes the nose.

● Dolcetto d'Alba '00	♀♀	3*
● Barolo '97	♀♀	6
● Barolo Pernanno '97	♀♀	6
● Langhe Rosso Faletto '99	♀♀	5
● Barolo Pernanno '95	♀♀	6
● Barolo '96	♀♀	6
● Barolo Pernanno '96	♀♀	6
● Langhe Rosso Faletto '97	♀♀	5
● Langhe Rosso Faletto '98	♀♀	5

CASTIGLIONE FALLETTO (CN)

BRICCO ROCCHE - BRICCO ASILI
VIA MONFORTE, 63
12060 CASTIGLIONE FALLETTO (CN)
TEL. 0173282582
E-MAIL: ceretto@ceretto.it

Bruno and Marcello Ceretto are very proud of the family jewels: their Barolos from Bricco Rocche di Castiglione Falletto and Barbarescos from Bricco Asili di Barbaresco. This year, it was the Barolo Prapò '97 that performed best with its ravishingly elegant aromas of dried roses – almost a bouquet of dried flowers – and wild cherry jam. The entry on the palate is faintly sweetish and the progression delightful, even though the tannins poke through the extremely close-knit structure. The Barolo Bricco Rocche '97 has a less lively colour and vegetal aromas of new-mown grass and hays. On the palate, the tannins get the upper hand over the silky, caressing texture. The Barolo Brunate '97 also did well Its aromas of stewed prunes, mint and liquorice usher in a very long palate with warm alcohol to the fore. When a wine has won Three Glasses in the past, you expect it always to be outstanding so the merely good score earned by this year's Barbaresco Bricco Asili is news in itself. The '98 version is already evolved in hue. On the nose, it is clean but unexceptional, offering cassis, black pepper and an etheric finish. Although the tannins predominate, the palate already presents excellent balance and the wine's finest quality is its remarkable length. In fact, the '98 Barbaresco Faset was almost as good. More youthful in colour, it flaunts nice breadth on a nose of plums, liqueur morello cherries, tobacco and leather. On the more tannic palate, you note the wine's very decent structure. In contrast, the more problematic Barbaresco Bernardot '98 is let down by fairly inelegant etheric aromas that mask the fruit but the palate recovers some ground with its laudable structure.

- Barbaresco Bricco Asili Bricco Asili '98 ▽▽ 6
- Barolo Prapò Bricco Rocche '97 ▽▽ 6
- Barolo Bricco Rocche Bricco Rocche '97 ▽▽ 6
- Barolo Brunate Bricco Rocche '97 ▽▽ 6
- Barbaresco Faset Bricco Asili '98 ▽▽ 6
- Barbaresco Bernardot Bricco Asili '98 ▽ 6
- Barolo Prapò Bricco Rocche '83 ▽▽▽ 6
- Barbaresco Bricco Asili Bricco Asili '88 ▽▽▽ 6
- Barbaresco Bricco Asili Bricco Asili '89 ▽▽▽ 6
- Barbaresco Bricco Asili Bricco Asili '89 ▽▽▽ 6
- Barolo Bricco Rocche Bricco Rocche '89 ▽▽▽ 6
- Barolo Brunate Bricco Rocche '90 ▽▽▽ 6
- Barbaresco Bricco Asili Bricco Asili '96 ▽▽▽ 6
- Barbaresco Bricco Asili Bricco Asili '97 ▽▽▽ 6

CASTIGLIONE FALLETTO (CN)

F.LLI BROVIA
FRAZ. GARBELLETTO
VIA ALBA BAROLO, 54
12060 CASTIGLIONE FALLETTO (CN)
TEL. 017362852 - 017362934
E-MAIL: gibrovia@tin.it

Raffaele and Giacinto Brovia, with Giacinto's daughters Elena and Cristina, have put together a range of excellent Barolos in a style that interprets tradition with balance and a disciplined technique. Ca' Mio is very good but not quite up to last year's stunning level. The ruby colour is flecked with orange and the nose reveals mint and wild berries, laced with intriguing hints of tobacco. On the palate, the progression is marked by upfront tannins and concludes with a long finish that nicely echoes the nose. The Rocche dei Brovia unveils aromas of cakes and strawberries over leather and tar. Muscular and unyielding on the palate, it rounds off with a nice finish redolent of flowers and earth. The Barolo Villero is slightly subtler. Its ruby hue shades into brick red while the relatively uncomplicated nose offers notes of fruit, pepper and dried flowers that precede a sophisticated and fluent palate. The Dolcetto Solatìo is also very good, especially in this vintage where it has found the elegance and finesse of a thoroughbred. The colour is impenetrable and the nose opens out gradually to reveal confectioner's cream, cherries, green leaf and pepper. Lively and generous on the palate, it is sustained by vibrant tannins through to a finish of violets. Finally, the Barbera Brea greets you with aromas of fruit and hazelnuts. The determined palate has plenty of sinew and a lovely finish reminiscent of liquorice and autumn leaves.

- Dolcetto d'Alba Solatìo '99 ▽▽ 5
- Barbera d'Alba Brea '99 ▽▽ 4
- Barolo Ca' Mia '97 ▽▽ 6
- Barolo Rocche dei Brovia '97 ▽▽ 6
- Barolo Villero '97 ▽▽ 6
- Barolo Monprivato '90 ▽▽▽ 6
- Barolo Ca' Mia '96 ▽▽▽ 6
- Barolo Ca' Mia '95 ▽▽ 6
- Barolo Villero '95 ▽▽ 6
- Barolo Rocche dei Brovia '96 ▽▽ 6
- Barolo Villero '96 ▽▽ 6
- Dolcetto d'Alba Solatìo '98 ▽▽ 5

CASTIGLIONE FALLETTO (CN)

F.LLI CAVALLOTTO
LOC. BRICCO BOSCHIS
VIA ALBA-MONFORTE
12060 CASTIGLIONE FALLETTO (CN)
TEL. 017362814
E-MAIL: info@cavallotto.com

For some years, the Cavallotto family has been running one of Castiglione Falletto's most impressive wineries, vinifying only fruit grown on their 23-hectare property. Almost all of the estate is situated around the cellar at Bricco Boschis, although a small part lies lower down in the vineyard known as Vignolo. Over half of the winery's output is bottled as Barolo under three labels, the standard Bricco Boschis and the two Riservas, Vigna San Giuseppe and Vignolo. Currently, the historic Vigna Punta Marcello and Vigna Colle Sud-Ovest labels are not released. Fruit from those vineyards goes into the Bricco Boschis, making it a more serious contender. The '97 vintage was the best of recent years and the wine has a correspondingly deep colour. The fresh nose of raspberry fruit is crisp and clean and this very quaffable Barolo unfolds on the palate with power and warmth yet never loses its fullness and elegance. This year's three Riservas are definitely more challenging. The Barolo Vigna San Giuseppe '96, from the vineyard nearest to Castiglione Falletto, is still very young. It's a hefty, hard, tannin-heavy bottle that can safely be tucked away in the cellar. In contrast, the Vignolo from lower down the slope, grown on different soil, shows less typicity. The '96 has aromas of very ripe raspberry and dried fig fruit followed up by a soft palate with sweet tannins. The '95, with its aromatic herbs and cinnamon spices, has less body but is just as long as the '96. Rounding off the range were two well-made Dolcettos and an interesting Freisa that very nearly won Two Glasses. The Barbera Vigna del Cuculo '99 and the Nebbiolo '99 will go into the bottle in April 2002.

● Barolo Vignolo Ris. '95	🍷🍷	6
● Barolo Vigna S. Giuseppe Ris. '96	🍷🍷	6
● Barolo Vignolo Ris. '96	🍷🍷	6
● Barolo Bricco Boschis '97	🍷🍷	6
● Dolcetto d'Alba Vigna Scot '00	🍷	3
● Dolcetto d'Alba Vigna Melera '99	🍷	3
● Langhe Freisa '99	🍷	3
● Barolo Vigna S. Giuseppe Ris. '89	🍷🍷🍷	6
● Barolo Vigna S. Giuseppe Ris. '93	🍷🍷	6
● Barolo Vignolo Ris. '93	🍷🍷	6
● Barolo Bricco Boschis '95	🍷🍷	6
● Barolo Vigna S. Giuseppe '95	🍷🍷	6
● Barolo Bricco Boschis '96	🍷🍷	6
● Barbera d'Alba Vigna del Cuculo '98	🍷🍷	4

CASTIGLIONE FALLETTO (CN)

★ PAOLO SCAVINO
VIA ALBA BAROLO, 59
12060 CASTIGLIONE FALLETTO (CN)
TEL. 017362850

After 40 harvests, Enrico Savinio still has an appetite for new challenges. And they are of the particularly forbidding kind that only a determined Langhe grower could take up. The first presented itself this spring when two hectares under nebbiolo became available at Annunziata in La Morra. Immediately afterwards, there was another favourable opportunity on the hills at Roddi, a municipality in the Barolo DOC zone. Here, Enrico, with his family's support, decided to take another major step and secured two new hectares at Sant'Ambrogio. This lovely vineyard is magnificently aspected and it is here that Enrico will be producing a new Barolo selection. Having increased their estate from last year's 15 hectares under vine to this year's 19, the Scavinos are now looking to expand their cellar at Garbelletto, where work is due to start in the near future. Now let's move on to the fine series of wines that Enrico has released this time round. His five Barolos do not include the Rocche dell'Annunziata '95, which will only emerge from the cellar in 2002. The wine that most impressed the panel was the historic Scavino selection, the Bric dël Fiasc '97, which has lashings of personality. Not far behind came the smoother Cannubi, which still has a few rough edges to mellow out, and the Carobric, a blend of fruit from several vineyards. However, the big surprise was the standard-label Barolo. Thanks to an excellent vintage, it was just as convincing as its more exalted companions. And the grand finale was provided by a very attractive Barbera Affinata in Carati and the equally good nebbiolo, barbera and cabernet-based Corale.

● Barolo Bric dël Fiasc '97	🍷🍷	6
● Barolo Cannubi '97	🍷🍷	6
● Barolo '97	🍷🍷	6
● Barolo Carobric '97	🍷🍷	6
● Barbera d'Alba Affinata in Carati '98	🍷🍷	6
● Langhe Rosso Corale '98	🍷🍷	6
● Dolcetto d'Alba '00	🍷	4
● Barolo Bric dël Fiasc '90	🍷🍷🍷	6
● Barolo Rocche dell'Annunziata Ris. '90	🍷🍷🍷	6
● Barolo Bric dël Fiasc '93	🍷🍷🍷	6
● Barolo Bric dël Fiasc '95	🍷🍷🍷	6
● Barolo Bric dël Fiasc '96	🍷🍷🍷	6

CASTIGLIONE FALLETTO (CN)

Terre del Barolo
Via Alba-Barolo, 5
12060 Castiglione Falletto (CN)
Tel. 0173262749
E-mail: tdb@terredelbarolo.com

Terre del Barolo is a co-operative winery with a range that embraces all the classic Langhe wine types. Grapes come from over 800 hectares of vineyards managed by the 450 member growers to make 1,800,000 bottles every year. The wines we liked best on our visit were the Barbera d'Alba Superiore and the Dolcetto Raviole. The barrique-aged Barbera has a concentrated ruby colour and a pronounced, well-balanced nose of wild berries, mint and vanilla while the substantial, well-sustained palate is lent a hint of sinew by its slight acidity. The Dolcetto Raviole flaunts an intense, purple-flecked garnet and a warmly intriguing nose where berry fruit and confectioner's cream emerge over cocoa powder and hay. Concentrated on entry, the palate builds up beautifully to a vibrantly long finish. A medium colour and an interesting nose are the Barolo di Castiglione Falletto's visiting cards. The aromas of jam, tar, tobacco and toastiness usher in a generous palate backed up by abundant but unassertive tannins that dry out the finish. The Barolo Castello Riserva '95 has a rather evolved colour and a nose of leather and jam against a minerally backdrop. It also reveals lots of personality and vigour in the mouth. The extensive range is brought to a close by two attractive Dolcetto di Dianos, the uncomplicated but refreshing Dolcetto d'Alba Le Passere, that rustic Barbera Valdisera, the even, well-made Barbera Roncaglia and the pinot nero-based Langhe Rosso '98.

Wine	Glasses	Score
● Dolcetto d'Alba Raviole '00	♛♛	3*
● Barbera d'Alba Sup. '99	♛♛	4
● Dolcetto d'Alba Le Passere '00	♛	3
● Barolo Castello Ris. '95	♛	6
● Barolo di Castiglione Falletto '97	♛	6
● Langhe Rosso '98	♛	3
● Barbera d'Alba Söri della Roncaglia '99	♛	3
● Barbera d'Alba Valdisera '99	♛	3
● Diano d'Alba Cascinotto '99	♛	3
● Diano d'Alba Montagrillo '99	♛	3
● Barolo Codana '95	♛♛	6
● Barbera d'Alba Söri della Roncaglia '98	♛	3

CASTIGLIONE FALLETTO (CN)

Vietti
P.zza Vittorio Veneto, 5
12060 Castiglione Falletto (CN)
Tel. 017362825
E-mail: info@vietti.com

The Castiglione Falletto-based Vietti cellar, run with skill and passion by Mario Cordero and Luca Currado, is keeping up its very high standards of quality. There are 32 hectares under vine on the estate, about 24 of which are currently in production. The Barolo Lazzarito and the Barolo Brunate, both '97s, were every bit as good as we expected. The first melds toasty notes from the oak seamlessly into its flower and fruit aromas, without letting the wood dominate the progression of the rich bouquet, then the attack on the palate is dynamic and very impressive. In the attractive garnet-hued Brunate, flowers and spice anticipate a consistent, juicy, well-balanced palate with nice structure and balance. Down a notch, the Barolo Rocche '97 offers less structure than the preceding pair, following the liquorice, tobacco and dried rose aromas with a fairly one-dimensional palate of stewed fruit and cherry jam. On the way up again, the deep-hued Barbaresco Masseria '98 unveils a broad, well-orchestrated nose. But it was the Barbera Scarrone Vigna Vecchia '99 that swept all before it. An unbelievably good wine, it has now sorted out the occasional harsh notes it used to present on the nose in some previous vintages and is monumental from every point of view. Marrying cherry with black berry fruit in a seamless consistency, it combines concentration and muscle power with style and effortless length. A wonderful bottle that puts the Vietti cellar back on our list of Three Glass winners. Two full Glasses went to the Barbera d'Alba Scarrone, another '99, while the two Barbera d'Astis, Tre Vigne '99 and La Crena '98, both earned One Glass. The '00 Arneis and Dolcetto Sant'Anna were the last of a long series of wines presented to the panel.

Wine	Glasses	Score
● Barbera d'Alba Scarrone Vigna Vecchia '99	♛♛♛	6
● Barolo Lazzarito '97	♛♛	6
● Barolo Brunate '97	♛♛	6
● Barbaresco Masseria '98	♛♛	6
● Barbera d'Alba Scarrone '99	♛♛	5
● Barolo Rocche '97	♛	6
● Dolcetto d'Alba Sant'Anna '00	♛	4
○ Roero Arneis '00	♛	4
● Barbera d'Asti La Crena '98	♛	5
● Barbera d'Asti Tre Vigne '99	♛	5
● Barolo Villero '82	♛♛♛	6
● Barolo Rocche di Castiglione '85	♛♛♛	6
● Barolo Rocche di Castiglione '88	♛♛♛	6
● Barolo Brunate '96	♛♛	6

CASTIGLIONE TINELLA (CN)

CAUDRINA
STRADA BROSIA, 20
12053 CASTIGLIONE TINELLA (CN)
TEL. 0141855126

Romano and Bruna Dogliotti, with sons Alessandro, Sergio and Marco, have come up with an interesting new bottle this year. It's a barrique-aged Barbera d'Asti from a vineyard situated in the municipality of Nizza Monferrato and it joins the more straightforward, fresh-tasting La Solista. The garnet ruby of the new Barbera Monte Venere has a youthful rim and a soft nose with pleasing hints of cherry and chocolate over faint nuances of balsam and spices. There is nice weight on the palate, which has lively, gutsy sinew and a long finish that echoes the nose. As we said, La Solista is less challenging. Reasonably concentrated in colour, it reveals a fairly elegant nose and a fluent, unfussy palate. Both Moscatos, La Galeisa and La Caudrina, are very nice. La Galeisa has shimmering golden reflections in its straw yellow then the nose unveils ripe peach, candied citron and spring flowers over an attractive vegetal note of tomato. Well-extracted and full-bodied on the palate, it is effectively sustained by its prickle and acidity which lend the long finish freshness, as the citrus peel notes on the nose return in the after-aroma. In contrast, La Caudrina is a slightly less impressive proposition. The subtle nose has hints of elderflower mingling with peach, melon and lemon. In the mouth, the dynamic progression foregrounds the refreshing smoothness of the palate. In the glass, the straw yellow of the Asti La Selvatica reveals green highlights, taking you in to a moderately elegant nose of flowers and fruit while the bubbly palate is hard to resist. Finally, the Chardonnay Mej is direct and uncompromising.

O	Moscato d'Asti Caudrina '00	¶¶	3*
O	Moscato d'Asti La Galeisa '00	¶¶	3*
●	Barbera d'Asti Sup. Monte Venere '99	¶¶	4
O	Asti La Selvatica '00	¶	3
●	Barbera d'Asti La Solista '00	¶	3
O	Piemonte Chardonnay Mej '00	¶	3

CASTIGLIONE TINELLA (CN)

ICARDI
LOC. SAN LAZZARO - FRAZ. SANTUARIO
VIA BALBI, 30
12050 CASTIGLIONE TINELLA (CN)
TEL. 0141855159
E-MAIL: icardivino@libero.it

Claudio and Ornella Icardi are keeping up the good work, as the range of wines they presented shows. All that was missing was a Three Glass winner, although they came close with the Monferrato Rosso Cascina Bricco del Sole '99, a wonderfully balanced blend of barbera, nebbiolo and cabernet. The nose is rich in complex fruit aromas, ranging from strawberries to wild cherries in alcohol, while the softly enfolding mouthfeel has just the right degree of vigour. Neither was the Barbera d'Asti Nuj Suj '99 very far off the mark, with its splendidly tight-knit colour heralding a broad swathe of aromas from violets to nutmeg. The freshness and length of the palate also hit the spot. The monovarietal pinot nero Langhe Nej '99 is an essay in elegance, redolent of black cherry, blackcurrant and pomegranate. It's a highly successful and beautifully made wine that shows what can be done with this difficult variety. The Barbera d'Alba Surì di Mù '99 also came close to Two Glasses, although in comparison with its twin from Asti, it has less well-defined aromas. Next the nebbiolo-based wines: we are pleased to note that the Barolo Parej continues to improve, the palate in particular having now acquired serious weight, while the Langhe Pafoj and Langhe Nebbiolo Surìsjvan are well up to scratch. Moving on to the whites, the Piemonte Chardonnay Surìssara is stylish and flowery, and the Monferrato Pafoj, in line with the cellar's high standards, flaunts a generous array of chamomile flowers, tea leaves, aniseed and wild fennel. Hawthorn, citrus fruits and golden delicious apples are the keynotes of the Moscato d'Asti La Rosa Selvatica '00, which has a better balanced note of sweetness than in the past.

●	Monferrato Rosso Cascina Bricco del Sole '99	¶¶	6
●	Langhe Rosso Pafoj '00	¶¶	6
O	Monferrato Bianco Pafoj '00	¶¶	5
O	Piemonte Chardonnay Surìssara '00	¶¶	3
●	Barolo Parej '97	¶¶	6
●	Barbera d'Asti Nuj Suj '99	¶¶	5
●	Langhe Rosso Nej '99	¶¶	5
O	Moscato d'Asti La Rosa Selvatica '00	¶	3
●	Barbera d'Alba Surì di Mù '99	¶	4
●	Langhe Nebbiolo Surìsjvan '99	¶	4
●	Monferrato Rosso Cascina Bricco del Sole '98	¶¶	6

CASTIGLIONE TINELLA (CN)

La Morandina
Loc. Morandini, 11
12053 Castiglione Tinella (CN)
Tel. 0141855261
E-mail: lamorandina@tin.it

A 20-hectare estate turning out 70,000 bottles a year: that, in a nutshell, is La Morandina, run by Paolo and Giulio Morando with their parents, Emma and Corrado, and Paolo's wife, Giuliana. Their Barbera Varmat is always good and the '99 version offers a tight-knit garnet colour introducing a deliciously complex nose of berry fruit, toastiness and eucalyptus over biscuits. The dry palate is full-bodied and well-sustained through to the unhurried finish. The Moscato is a pale straw yellow, from which emerge intense notes of ripe peach, aromatic herbs and nutmeg. The fleshy palate has just the right degree of prickle to offset the sweet note before the long finish comes in to echo the nose. On the nose, the Chardonnay has plenty to say for itself, combining hazelnut with banana and spring flowers. The fluent, dynamic palate ends in a very satisfying finish. Bianco Verasis is a 60-40 blend of viognier and riesling with a tempting nose of apricots and flowers over intriguing mineral notes. The robust palate reveals good balance and lots of length. Finally, the Barbera Zucchetto has an intense hue and fairly ripe fruit aromas nuanced with coffee cream, all of which are mirrored on the palate.

○	Moscato d'Asti La Morandina '00	♀♀	4
○	Verasis Bianco '00	♀♀	4
●	Barbera d'Asti Varmat '99	♀♀	5
○	Langhe Chardonnay '00	♀	3
●	Barbera d'Asti Zucchetto '99	♀	4
●	Barbera d'Asti Varmat '96	♀♀	4
●	Barbera d'Asti Varmat '97	♀♀	5
●	Barbera d'Asti Varmat '98	♀♀	5

CASTIGLIONE TINELLA (CN)

Elio Perrone
Strada San Martino, 3/bis
12053 Castiglione Tinella (CN)
Tel. 0141855803
E-mail: elioperr@tin.it

In this superb Moscato area, Elio Perrone's Clarté and Sourgal are paragons of quality and fullness of body. The Clarté has a relatively concentrated straw-yellow hue and a broad, ripe nose that impresses at once, the aromas ranging from apricot cream to peaches and mint over subtle hints of pine resin. The progression on the rich, well-rounded palate is well-sustained and surefooted, the positive prickle and very tidy finish offering crisp notes of orange peel, apples, pears, peaches and melons. Scoring only a point or two lower, the Sourgal presents a vibrant straw-yellow colour and a slightly forward nose of fruit over balsamic nuances. Sustained and nicely balanced on the palate, it is perked up by the effervescence and finishes nicely on notes of peach and lemon liqueur. The intense ruby of the Barbera Grivò '99 shades into garnet and its aromas of cherries and flowers are layered over hints of autumn leaves and rain-soaked earth. The palate is lively and vigorous, the finish clean and lingering, taking its leave unhurriedly on notes of fruit and cocoa powder. Brachetto and moscato go into the blend for Bigarò, a cherry-coloured wine with nice purple highlights. The nose has notes of dried rose petals, lemon and tea leaves while the palate is fluent and eminently quaffable and easy to drink. Finally, the Char-de S is a bright and cheerful bottle that offers a very decent interpretation of chardonnay.

○	Moscato d'Asti Clarté '00	♀♀	3*
●	Barbera d'Asti Grivò '99	♀♀	4
●	Bigarò Rosso '00	♀	3
○	Moscato d'Asti Sourgal '00	♀	3
○	Char-de S.	♀	4
●	Barbera d'Asti Grivò '97	♀♀	4
●	Barbera d'Asti Grivò '98	♀	4

CASTIGLIONE TINELLA (CN)

PAOLO SARACCO
VIA CIRCONVALLAZIONE, 6
12053 CASTIGLIONE TINELLA (CN)
TEL. 0141855113

To write about the Paolo Saracco winery is to write about Moscato d'Asti made to superb standards, year after year. The best of the Saracco Moscatos, however, is the selection that goes into the standard-label product. About 250,000 bottles of this wine leave the cellar ever year and the quality has been outstanding for a long time, especially if we remember the quantities involved. Today, Paolo can be considered a master of the wine type and is certainly not awed by numbers. His '00 selection has delicious notes of citrus fruit, with pink grapefruit prominent, while the palate keeps a well-gauged balance between freshness and a sweetness that never cloys. As ever, the Moscato d'Autunno is excellent and the '00 vintage has gone out under the Piemonte DOC label. The most impressive of the Saracco dry whites was the Graffagno, only 3,000 bottles of which are released. The mineral and semi-aromatic notes of riesling, blended with sauvignon and especially the 30 per cent barrique-fermented chardonnay, all come together to infuse the wine with complexity and balance. The Chardonnay Bianch del Luv '99 has attractive hints of quince, yellow peaches and melon, melding with oak-derived aromas that are anything but aggressive after the wine's 11 months in barriques. Finally, the other Saracco Chardonnay, the Prasuè '00, is more direct and fresh-tasting.

○	Moscato d'Asti '00	🍷🍷	3*
○	Piemonte Moscato d'Asti Moscato d'Autunno '00	🍷🍷	3*
○	Langhe Bianco Graffagno '99	🍷🍷	4
○	Langhe Chardonnay Bianch del Luv '99	🍷🍷	5
○	Langhe Chardonnay Prasuè '00	🍷	3
○	Langhe Bianco Graffagno '97	🍷🍷	4
○	Langhe Chardonnay Bianch del Luv '97	🍷🍷	5
○	Langhe Bianco Graffagno '98	🍷🍷	4
○	Langhe Chardonnay Bianch del Luv '98	🍷🍷	5

COCCONATO (AT)

BAVA
STRADA MONFERRATO, 2
14023 COCCONATO (AT)
TEL. 0141907083
E-MAIL: bava@bava.com

The Bava winery is at Cocconato in the Asti part of Monferrato, on the border between the provinces of Turin and Alessandria. For the last 90 harvests, Bavas have made wine here: brothers Roberto, Giulio and Paolo, led by their father Piero, are in fact the fourth generation. The family philosophy remains unchanged. Today, as always, the Bavas respect tradition while using modern technology. Barbera is without doubt the number one variety, accounting for four estate labels and most of the vine stock. On the magnificent Piano Alto property at Agliano Terme, the Bavas have a 13-hectare plot planted to the most important grape type in the zone. It is here that they grow the fruit for their Barbera Piano Alto, the '98 version of which is admirably successful. The vibrant ruby colour ushers in fruit-rich aromas lifted by notes of spices and tobacco. On the palate, it presents a tangy, consistent progression that lacks a little power. The four-hectare estate-owned vineyard in Cocconato that in the 1950s provided the grapes for the memorable Cocconato Stravecchio today yields first-quality fruit for the Bava flagship wine, the Stradivario. We're talking about another Barbera but this wine is a cut above the previous selection. An unfiltered red, it impresses enormously on the palate, where the care that goes into its production is very obvious. The Barberas on offer did not include the Arbest or the Libera, the latest addition to the Bava range, but among the whites there was a new and very likeable Chardonnay as well as the good chardonnay-based Alteserre. And to round off, the Giulio Cocchi Brut '93 impressed the panel with its elegant palate.

○	Giulio Cocchi Brut '93	🍷🍷	4
●	Barbera d'Asti Sup. Piano Alto '98	🍷🍷	5
●	Barbera d'Asti Sup. Stradivario '98	🍷🍷	5
●	Malvasia di Castelnuovo Don Bosco Rosa Canina '00	🍷	3
○	Piemonte Chardonnay Thou Bianc '00	🍷	3
○	Monferrato Bianco Alteserre '99	🍷	4
●	Barbera d'Asti Sup. Piano Alto '96	🍷🍷	5
●	Barbera d'Asti Sup. Arbest '97	🍷🍷	4
●	Barbera d'Asti Sup. Piano Alto '97	🍷🍷	5
●	Barbera d'Asti Sup. Stradivario '97	🍷🍷	5

COSSOMBRATO (AT)

Carlo Quarello
Via Marconi, 3
14020 Cossombrato (AT)
tel. 0141905204

Carlo and Bianca Quarello, with the help of their son Valerio, make Cré Marcaleone, a Grignolino that year after year turns out to be one of the most full-flavoured, elegant wines in its category. The wine, which the Quarellos only turn out in the best years, is a sort of failsafe product that ensures this all too often underrated variety is not forgotten. Grignolino has, after all, played a major role in the winemaking history of the DOC zone. The '00 version has a cherry colour that shades into ruby, with an orangey rim. Varietal aspects come through strongly on the attractively broad nose whose hints of geraniums and black pepper marry well with complex notes of mushrooms and autumn leaves. On the palate, the Marcaleone is well-sustained and backed up by gutsy and very typical tannins that take you through to a deliciously long finish where notes of hazelnut provide a final flourish. The Monferrato Rosso Crebarné is a blend of barbera with about 20 per cent nebbiolo. Concentrated in colour, with a faintly orange-tinted rim, it offers a slightly forward nose of jam, dried rose petals and spices. All the wine's character comes out on the palate, with a hint of sinew and serious tannins that emerge on the rather long finish. The lovely after-aroma fades away on flowery notes of Parma violets.

COSTA VESCOVATO (AL)

Luigi Boveri
Via XX Settembre, 6
Fraz. Montale Celli
15050 Costa Vescovato (AL)
tel. 0131838165

Claudio and Ornella Icardi are keeping up the good work, as the range of wines they presented shows. Last year, we admired a Barbera Vignalunga that has come on apace and represents the cutting edge of the cellar's range. This time, the wine has improved even further to establish itself as a top-quality wine, confirming the exciting potential this zone has for the variety. Dark in colour, the Barber Vignalunga '99 opens on the nose with spices, tobacco and ripe berry fruit. Its velvet-soft, well-sustained mouthfeel and serious structure tells you all you need to know about its class. Also good is the stainless steel fermented and aged Poggio delle Amarene. Again dark in the glass, it tempts with a palate that strikes a beautiful balance between the ripeness of the fruit and the characteristic acidity of the grape. The uncomplicated but likeable Boccanera unfolds fragrances of cherry and plum that precede a refreshing palate. The Timorasso is another emblematic wine but has yet to find the right balance with the small oak barrels in which it is aged. Its golden colour is only moderately bright. It is followed by a palate with lots of substance that is however a tad muffled, like the varietal aromas, which struggle to come through. This is a wine that could happily stay a little longer in the ageing cellar, which will come as no surprise. This is after all a timorasso, a variety that has remarkable ageing potential. Finally, the cortese-based Vigna del Prete is an agreeable wine with subtle flowery aromas and a fresh palate that nicely echoes the nose.

● Grignolino del M.to Casalese Cré Marcaleone '00	3*
● Monferrato Rosso Crebarné '99	4
● Monferrato Rosso Crebarné '98	4
● Grignolino del M.to Casalese Cré Marcaleone '99	3

● Colli Tortonesi Barbera Vignalunga '99	4
● Colli Tortonesi Barbera Poggio delle Amarene '99	4
● Colli Tortonesi Barbera Boccanera '00	2*
○ Colli Tortonesi Cortese Vigna del Prete '00	2*
○ Colli Tortonesi Bianco Filari di Timorasso '99	4
● Colli Tortonesi Barbera Vignalunga '97	4
● Colli Tortonesi Barbera Vignalunga '98	4

COSTIGLIOLE D'ASTI (AT)

Carlo Benotto
Fraz. San Carlo, 52
14055 Costigliole d'Asti (AT)
tel. 0141966406

As usual, the Benotto brothers have come up with a fine range that includes some of the best Barberas in Asti. One of those is the Rupestris '99, which has a close-knit garnet hue with the narrowest of rims. On the nose, it shows complexity and charm, with notes of black and red berry fruit, autumn leaves and mulberry blossom over sweet toasty notes. Generous on the palate, its dry tannins are nicely mellowed by the warmth of the abundant alcohol while the long, vibrant finish echoes the nose with satisfying consistency. The Barbera Vigneto Casot offers a concentrated garnet hue and a fairly evolved nose of liqueur cherries, eucalyptus, cocoa powder and caramel. There is plenty of body on the fleshy, dry palate, which is muscular and tidy, releasing notes of cocoa powder and liquorice in the after-aroma. The Gamba di Pernice is called after the now-rare native grape of the same name, meaning "partridge leg", which refers to the red colour of the bunchstem. The wine's ruby colour shades into garnet at the slightly paler rim while the aromas on the nose are redolent of wild berries and roses. There is plenty of rustic energy on the palate and the finish bows out on a flowery note. Finally, the vibrantly lustrous straw yellow of the Cortese Lacrime di Gioia heralds an intriguing nose of apples, pears and flowers. Concentrated and full-bodied in the mouth, it signs off with a distinctive note of tangerines.

● Barbera d'Asti Sup. Rupestris '99 ΨΨ		4
● Barbera d'Asti Sup. Vigneto Casot '99	ΨΨ	3*
○ Piemonte Cortese Lacrime di Gioia '00	Ψ	3
● Gamba di Pernice '99	Ψ	3
● Barbera d'Asti Sup. Rupestris '97	ΨΨ	4
● Barbera d'Asti Sup. Balau '98	ΨΨ	3
● Barbera d'Asti Sup. Rupestris '98	ΨΨ	4

COSTIGLIOLE D'ASTI (AT)

Poderi Bertelli
Fraz. San Carlo, 38
14100 Costigliole d'Asti (AT)
tel. 0141966137

Alberto Bertelli takes admirable care of his cellar and an estate that embraces about seven hectares under vine. The cellar, with its fine stock of barriques, is actually something of a laboratory, turning out a few thousand bottles each of ten often unique labels. Alberto subscribes to the philosophy of the great French tradition according to which terroir, albeit tempered by the vagaries of the season, speaks louder than the winemaker. He is a firm believer in "laisser-faire" vinification and has no time for fashion. It is an approach that has put Bertelli's characterful wines right at the top of the heap, in Piedmont and in Italy. As we wait for his '99 Barberas, which will be released next year, we found two extraordinary wines already on the list, the San Marsan Rosso and the San Marsan Bianco. The red has a crystal-clear nose and unusual complexity that reveals aromas of white pepper, violets and leather. Two words sum up the palate - character and length. In the white version, an elegant nose of apricot, honey and incense combines with a powerful yet soft and intriguing palate. The Plissé, and Alsace-style Traminer, is also successful while the muscular Cabernet Fossaretti and the Chardonnay Giarone, a little closed on the nose, look promising but are still too young to be able to show off their full elegance. The crisp Monferrato Bianco Fossaretti, a Sauvignon, was however a little lean.

● Monferrato Cabernet Fossaretti '98	ΨΨ	5
● San Marsan Rosso '98	ΨΨ	5
○ Piemonte Chardonnay Giarone '99	ΨΨ	5
○ Plissé Traminer '99	ΨΨ	5
○ San Marsan Bianco '99	ΨΨ	5
○ Monferrato Bianco I Fossaretti '99	Ψ	5
● Barbera d'Asti Giarone '97	ΨΨ	5
● Barbera d'Asti Montetusa '98	ΨΨ	5
● Barbera d'Asti S. Antonio Vieilles Vignes '98	ΨΨ	5
● Monferrato Rosso Mon Mayor '98	ΨΨ	5

COSTIGLIOLE D'ASTI (AT)

Cascina Castlèt
Strada Castelletto, 6
14055 Costigliole d'Asti (AT)
tel. 0141966651
e-mail: castlet@tin.it

This year, Mariuccia Borio has released the '98 and '99 vintages of the Barbera Passum. It is excellent and both versions scored high, the '99 making it as far as the final tastings for the Three Glass awards. A moderately intense garnet ruby in the glass, the Barbera Passum '99 has great breadth on the nose, where wild berries, violets and leather hover over woodland notes of resin and rain-soaked earth. There is plenty of flesh and good structure in the mouth, although the tannins are a little forward in the mid palate, while the fruit-rich finish echoes the nose and lingers attractively. The '98 version has a reasonably intense ruby colour and a distinctive nose with a slightly rustic minerally nuance as well as berry fruit and geranium. Its resolute character comes through on the palate, where the mouthfeel is dried by the prominent tannins. The Monferrato Rosso Policalpo, a blend of barbera with a small proportion of cabernet, presents a fairly deep ruby colour and complex, stylish aromas that range from black berry fruit to pepper, closing on a green note. Compact and well-sustained in the mouth, it becomes a tad edgy on the mid palate. The Barbera Litina has a jolly, rustic nose leading in to a fluent, soft palate with decent energy and moderate length over its minty notes. Finally, the Moscato Passito Avié has a lovely golden colour and aromas of liqueur fruit and wax. It is sweet in the mouth and shows good nose-palate consistency.

● Barbera d'Asti Sup. Passum '99	ŶŶ	5
● Barbera d'Asti Sup. Passum '98	ŶŶ	5
● Monferrato Rosso Policalpo '99	ŶŶ	5
○ Piemonte Moscato Passito Avié '98	Ŷ	5
● Barbera d'Asti Sup. Litina '99	Ŷ	3
● Monferrato Rosso Policalpo '97	ŶŶ	4
○ Piemonte Moscato Passito Avié '97	ŶŶ	5
● Monferrato Rosso Policalpo '98	ŶŶ	5

COSTIGLIOLE D'ASTI (AT)

Claudio Rosso
Strada Roera, 32
14055 Costigliole d'Asti (AT)
tel. 0141968437

After welcoming the panel with a valid range of wines this year, Claudio Rosso has earned a full profile in the Guide. The property comprises only two and half hectares under vine so the annual output of 12-15,000 bottles is achieved by buying in fruit. Claudio has been working full-time at the winery since August 2000, when he decided to leave the insurance company where he was working to devote all of his energies to his life's passion. Unfortunately, the move was prompted by a bereavement, when his father Riccardo died in 1999. And it is to his father that Claudio has dedicated his excellent Barbera Cardin, a barrel-aged wine made entirely with grapes from the winery's vineyards. The ruby hue has a narrow rim and an interesting nose that proffers distinct notes of cherry, spices and leather. Then the sheer fullness of palate is irresistible and the balance quite impeccable. The concentrated entry is followed up by a broad, sturdy mid palate that takes you through to a long, vigorous finish, redolent of fruit, liquorice and pepper. The standard-label Barbera is pretty vigorous, too, as you can guess from the extremely dense colour. On the nose, it is a shade rustic but agreeable nonetheless, showing berry fruit and autumn leaves laced with faint vegetal notes. The generous, surefooted palate concludes with a long, fruit-rich finish. The Ciapin is a 60-30-10 blend of chardonnay, arneis and cortese. Its lustrous straw yellow ushers in upfront aromas of hazelnut, acacia blossom, apples and pears before the progression of the soft, delicious palate carries you through, without any hint of roughness, to the tidy finish.

● Barbera d'Asti Sup. Cardin '99	ŶŶ	4
● Barbera d'Asti '00	Ŷ	3
○ Ciapin Bianco '00	Ŷ	3

COSTIGLIOLE D'ASTI (AT)

SCIORIO
VIA ASTI NIZZA, 87
14055 COSTIGLIOLE D'ASTI (AT)
TEL. 0141966610

Mauro and Giuseppe Gozzelino, the owners of the Sciorio winery, make Barberas in the modern idiom that often bring out the fruit of the variety in their warm, mellow style. And that describes in a nutshell the Gozzelinos' very successful Barbera Vigna Beneficio '98. A concentrated garnet wine with a firm, youthful rim, it tempts the nose with intense notes of crushed berry fruit and dry earth over balsamic nuances. The palate is vigorous from the start, with a rich, powerful follow-through to the long finish, which echoes the nose and foregrounds the abundant alcohol. Equally concentrated in the glass is the La Barbera Superiore Sciorio, which offers crisp aromas of cherry, blackcurrant and pepper contrasted by delicious hints of mint and cocoa butter in a very impressive profile. There follows a full-bodied, rich and only faintly edgy palate that ends unhurriedly with the return of the aromas on the nose. The Barbera d'Asti Superiore Selezione is only a whisper less concentrated that the previous wine but the nose is rather more rustic, featuring insistent earthy notes alongside its aromatic herbs and wild berries. The palate is firm and undeniably satisfying, if not particularly muscular. Finally, the Monferrato Rosso Antico Vitigno also scored well. Ruby in colour, it reveals an interesting nose that delicately offers up hints of bilberry, rhubarb and tobacco. There is nice flesh on the palate, sturdy tannins and a good long finish with a faint bitterish twist.

● Barbera d'Asti Sup. Beneficio '98	▼▼	5
● Barbera d'Asti Sup. Sciorio '98	▼▼	4
● Monferrato Rosso Antico Vitigno '98	▼▼	4
● Barbera d'Asti Sup. Sel. '98	▼	4
● Barbera d'Asti Sup. Beneficio '97	♀♀	5
● Barbera d'Asti Sup. Sciorio '97	♀♀	4
● Monferrato Rosso Reginal '97	♀♀	4
● Monferrato Rosso Antico Vitigno '97	♀	4

COSTIGLIOLE D'ASTI (AT)

VALFIERI
STRADA LORETO, 5
14055 COSTIGLIOLE D'ASTI (AT)
TEL. 0141966881
E-MAIL: ncler@tin.it

For many years, the Valfieri cellar lived a quiet life, away from the passions that torment the great producers, and was happy to sell to its customers technically well-made wines with little or no personality. Today, Maria Chiara and Angelo Clerici, who co-own the cellar with their mother, have decided to change tack and go for quality. They are taking their first steps in this direction in the vineyards for they are looking for new plots to add to the estate's six hectares and are imposing ever stricter selection criteria on their suppliers. The policy has prompted the winery, traditionally active both in the province of Asti and in the Langhe, to cut back on purchases, concentrate on the local territory and neglect the Langhe to a certain extent, with the exception of their Barolo Roncaglie and Barbaresco Bric Mentina. Another crucial move was acquiring the consultancy services of Luca Caramellino, a promising young oenologist. On its first release, the '99 Barbera Filari Lunghi thoroughly convinced our panel. Made with fruit from a very young estate-owned vineyard at Agliano and aged in barrels of Slavonian oak, it has body and elegance, an uncompromising entry on the palate and a long, characterful finish where the cherry jam and white pepper of the nose return deliciously. Two other well-made wines were the barrique-aged monovarietal merlot Matot '99 and the Barbera '00. The Matot is rich and full of personality while the fruity, soft Barbera is distinctly attractive. Rounding up the Valfieri collection was a nice Barbera Superiore '99, a barbera and nebbiolo di Agliano blend called Cassabò and an international-style Chardonnay.

● Barbera d'Asti '00	▼▼	3*
● Barbera d'Asti Sup. I Filari Lunghi '99	▼▼	5
● Monferrato Rosso Matot '99	▼▼	5
○ Langhe Chardonnay Barricello '00	▼	4
● Barbera d'Asti Sup. '99	▼	4
● Cassabò Rosso '99	▼	5

CUCCARO MONFERRATO (AL)

Liedholm
Villa Boemia
15040 Cuccaro Monferrato (AL)
Tel. 0131771916
E-mail: c.liedholm@liedholm.com

Carlo Liedholm's winery has won its full Guide profile back thanks to the fine quality of this year's range. The winery is very much at the cutting edge in technical terms and it should be mentioned that in 1997, the cellar was awarded ISO certification. The Liedholm Barbera Tonneau, named after the barrel type used for ageing, is the product that scored highest. Its intense ruby heralds aromas of ripe black cherry, plum and white pepper, with the toastiness of the oak still pretty much to the fore. Powerful on the palate and full of ripe, velvet-smooth fruit, it reveals a well-gauged and characteristic hint of acidity. The excellent Liedholm Grignolino offers a very attractive nose of spices and flowers against a backdrop of berry fruit. The palate confirms the good impression left by the nose, the tannins emerging powerfully yet sweetly and the typicity of the variety coming through delightfully. Rosso della Boemia is an unusual blend of various native and international red grapes. It ages for two years in barriques and the results are very encouraging. Spices, cherry, bramble and redcurrant stand out on the nose over a faint backdrop of toastiness before the same aromas are echoed on the decently structured palate. Finally, the Bianco della Boemia, a part barrique-fermented blend of pinot bianco and cortese, is resplendent in a bright straw yellow that shades into gold. There are intriguing notes of ripe tropical fruit on the nose, where pineapple is prominent. The expert use of oak is evident on the concentrated and very distinctive palate.

● Grignolino del M.to Casalese '00	ΨΨ	3
● Barbera d'Asti Tonneau '98	ΨΨ	4
● Rosso della Boemia '99	ΨΨ	5
○ Bianco della Boemia '99	Ψ	4

DIANO D'ALBA (CN)

Claudio Alario
Via Santa Croce, 23
12055 Diano d'Alba (CN)
Tel. 0173231808

Year after year, the Alario family's lovely winery at Diano d'Alba lives up to our expectations. This time, the panel awarded five Two Glass ratings, confirming the excellent overall standard of production. Almost all of the eight-hectare property lies in the municipality of Diano and the cellar turns out an average of 35,000 bottles a year. The star of the show is the Barolo Riva, from a vineyard in the municipality of Verduno, and the '97 version is particularly outstanding, thanks in part to the vintage. The Nebbiolo Cascinotto '99, subtly redolent of new oak, also performed well. On the nose, it reveals mainly spicy notes of leather and liquorice while the palate is uncompromising, the sweet, close-knit tannins holding up admirably through to the long finish. Moving on to the Dolcettos, we found the Montagrillo '00 to be drinking better at the moment. Very dark in hue, it has aromas of raspberries and minty dried herbs. The entry on the palate is soft and the finish dryish. In contrast, the Costa Fiore '00 has a little way to go yet. It is closed and concentrated on the nose, where hints of cassis and bilberries come through, then it explodes onto the palate. The mouthfeel is concentrated, full-bodied and soft, despite the tight-knit tannic weave. A few marks behind the pack was the Barbera Valletta '99, which overplays its finesse, partly as a result of the very ripe vintage, and also seems to have succumbed a little to the wood. However, it has good balance on the palate, which is distinctly superior to the nose.

● Diano d'Alba Costa Fiore '00	ΨΨ	3*
● Diano d'Alba Montagrillo '00	ΨΨ	3*
● Barolo Riva '97	ΨΨ	6
● Barbera d'Alba Valletta '99	ΨΨ	4
● Nebbiolo d'Alba Cascinotto '99	ΨΨ	5
● Barolo Riva '96	ΨΨ	6
● Barbera d'Alba Valletta '98	ΨΨ	4
● Nebbiolo d'Alba Cascinotto '98	ΨΨ	5
● Diano d'Alba Costa Fiore '99	ΨΨ	3

DIANO D'ALBA (CN)

Bricco Maiolica
Fraz. Ricca
Via Bolangino, 7
12055 Diano d'Alba (CN)
tel. 0173612049

The 20 hectares under vine at Bricco Maiolica lie on steep hillsides that overlook the western part of Diano. Half lie in the municipality of Diano and the rest in the territory of Alba. Recently, the winery has recently acquired a lovely barrel cellar and almost all the wines are aged in oak, much of it new and the rest either one or two years old. Annual output comprises about 100,000 bottles of muscular, full-bodied wines that in warm years like 1999, with the help of low yields in the vineyard, are so concentrated they are sometimes short on finesse. When our panellists tasted this year's wines, they found a marvellous Sorì Bricco Maiolica. This very dark purplish ruby Dolcetto offers closed, concentrated aromas of bramble jelly, cinnamon, tobacco and fresh aromatic herbs. The temptingly close-knit, juicy palate is backed up by prominent but well-behaved tannins. Neither does the Langhe Lorié '98 disappoint, a monovarietal pinot nero dedicated to owner Beppe Accomo's wife, Loredana. Coming down the scale, the Vigna Vigia and the Cumot, both '99s, were a little less rich. The first is very dark and toasty, with a soft, warm mouthfeel, while the bright garnet red Cumot reveals mint and spices on the nose but the robust palate has yet to mellow out. As ever, the stylish, refreshing Dolcetto '00 and the chardonnay and sauvignon-based Langhe Bianco Rolando '00 are well-made, the latter foregrounding aromas of vanilla, yeast and tropical fruit.

DOGLIANI (CN)

Marziano e Enrico Abbona
Via Torino, 242
12063 Dogliani (CN)
tel. 0173721317
e-mail: abbona.marziano@tiscalinet.it

Marziano Abbona, his wife and their three daughters run one of the largest wineries in the DOC zone, with their 39 hectares of vineyard and 220,000 bottle annual production. Their Novello property, which from the '98 vintage on will be joined by the Pressenda vineyard at Monforte, yields more than 30,000 bottles of an excellent Barolo that ages first in one third new barriques and then for 18 months in 30 hectolitre barrels of Slavonian oak. The intensity of the colour is awesome and the still-closed nose barely lets you savour its fruit and spices. The palate is long but rather austere. In contrast, the Barbaresco Faset '98, which ages only in barriques, is a more complete bottle, delivering greater complexity and finesse on the nose and admirable balance, softness and length in the mouth. But it was the Dolcetto di Dogliani Papà Celso that really took the panel by storm. It's a quite wonderful Dolcetto that takes your breath away with its structure and then astounds you with its balance and length on the palate. There was no doubt about the Three Glass rating. Just a shade lower on the scale came the Barbera and the Langhe Rosso Due Ricu, from nebbiolo, barbera, cabernet and small proportions of other grapes, both aged in one third new barriques. We preferred the livelier personality of the Barbera, which has an impressive richness of flavour. Moving back to Dogliani, we find that the Bricco San Bernardo has been dropped from the range with the clear intention of improving the quality of the Vigneto Muntâ. Finally, the viognier-based Cinerino Bianco was less interesting than usual.

● Diano d'Alba Sörì Bricco Maiolica '00	♟♟	4
● Langhe Rosso Lorié '98	♟♟	5
● Barbera d'Alba Vigna Vigia '99	♟♟	4
● Nebbiolo d'Alba Cumot '99	♟♟	4
● Diano d'Alba '00	♟	3
○ Langhe Bianco Rolando '00	♟	4
● Barbera d'Alba Vigna Vigia '98	♟♟♟	4
● Langhe Rosso Lorié '97	♟♟	5
● Nebbiolo d'Alba Cumot '98	♟♟	4

● Dolcetto di Dogliani Papà Celso '00	♟♟♟	4
● Barbaresco Faset '98	♟♟	6
● Barolo Vigneto Terlo Ravera '97	♟♟	6
● Barbera d'Alba Rinaldi '99	♟♟	4
● Langhe Rosso I Due Ricu '99	♟♟	5
○ Cinerino Bianco '00	♟	4
● Dolcetto di Dogliani Vigneto Muntâ '00	♟	3
● Barolo Vigneto Terlo Ravera '96	♟♟	6
● Barbaresco Faset '97	♟♟	6
● Barbera d'Alba Rinaldi '98	♟♟	4
● Langhe Rosso I Due Ricu '98	♟♟	5
● Dolcetto di Dogliani Papà Celso '99	♟♟	4

DOGLIANI (CN)

Quinto Chionetti & Figlio
Fraz. San Luigi
B.ta Valdiberti, 44
12063 Dogliani (CN)
tel. 017371179

Here we are again with our profile of one of the great artists of Dolcetto di Dogliani. Quinto Chionetti is a scrupulous interpreter of the territory and continues to pursue his own philosophy of making just two wines. Obviously, the two wines come from different vineyards and every year succeed in expressing the unique characteristics of each. This time round, the panel preferred the cellar's traditional flagship wine, the Briccolero. Its inky-black hue is impenetrably deep, and the nose outstandingly concentrated, releasing complex notes of fruit and plum jam whose elegance is unhindered by the sheer power. The same aromas return on the palate, where structure just gains the upper hand over finesse but the overall balance is quite remarkable. The San Luigi echoes the Briccolero in its colour and nose where the fruit lacks a little of the latter's depth, but there is also an attractively fresh note of citrus. It was the palate that proved less convincing, although the wine is still very much a thoroughbred. There is plenty of weight but the tannins are still a little rough. Time, however, will bring out the class of the fruit and the winemaking technique that went into this bottle. The bitter almond finish already speaks volumes for Quinto's ability to make wines that perfectly reflect their terroir.

- Dolcetto di Dogliani Briccolero '00 ♀♀ 4
- Dolcetto di Dogliani S. Luigi '00 ♀♀ 4
- Dolcetto di Dogliani Briccolero '99 ♀♀ 4
- Dolcetto di Dogliani S. Luigi '99 ♀♀ 3

DOGLIANI (CN)

Poderi Luigi Einaudi
B.ta Gombe, 31/32
12063 Dogliani (CN)
tel. 017370191
e-mail: pleinaudi@libero.it

The Poderi Luigi Einaudi was founded in 1897 on the San Giacomo farm as a natural part of the rural scene at the time. Under the management of Italian President Luigi Einaudi, major strides were made towards modernizing the vineyards and the estate became a model for contemporary viticulturists. Then after a long period of stagnation, the combined efforts of Paola Einaudi and her husband Giorgio Ruffo restored the Luigi Einaudi estate to its former glory. Today, the property is involved in every aspect of Langhe winemaking, vinifying fruit not just from its historic vineyards at Dogliani but also from six hectares under nebbiolo at Barolo, including a lovely plot at Cannubi that has recently joined the Vigneto Terlo Vie Nuove. Top of the range for the third year running is the Langhe Luigi Einaudi, from cabernet, nebbiolo, barbera and merlot. As ever, it has a long, velvet-smooth palate and splendid aromas of balsam, mint and fruit. But all the other Einaudi wines performed well, starting with the three Barolos. The standard-label '97 is very pleasant while the Costa Grimaldi and the Cannubi are more redolent of oak. They are also more powerful and will need time to mellow out their tannins. Both Dolcettos were very nice indeed, each reflecting in its own way the typicity of the territory. Plum and cocoa powder aromas accompany a full, well-balanced body in the Vigna Tecc whereas the spicier I Filari is less fruity than its twin and has slightly harsher tannins. It is only a lack of years in the cellar that penalizes the balance of the richly extracted Piemonte Barbera.

- Langhe Rosso Luigi Einaudi '99 ♀♀♀ 6
- Barolo nei Cannubi '97 ♀♀ 6
- Barolo '97 ♀♀ 6
- Barolo Costa Grimaldi '97 ♀♀ 6
- Dolcetto di Dogliani I Filari '99 ♀♀ 4
- Dolcetto di Dogliani Vigna Tecc '99 ♀♀ 4
- Piemonte Barbera '99 ♀♀ 4
- Langhe Rosso Luigi Einaudi '97 ♀♀♀ 6
- Langhe Rosso Luigi Einaudi '98 ♀♀♀ 6
- Barolo nei Cannubi '95 ♀♀ 6
- Barolo Costa Grimaldi '96 ♀♀ 6
- Barolo nei Cannubi '96 ♀♀ 6

DOGLIANI (CN)

F.LLI PECCHENINO
B.TA VALDIBERTI, 59
12063 DOGLIANI (CN)
TEL. 017370686

When Orlando Pecchenino is talking about the future of Dolcetto di Dogliani, he bubbles with enthusiasm. He will start discussing the experiments that he and other local producers have made with Professor Di Stefano and which suggested the use of micro-aeration to fix dolcetto's phenolics without recourse to the frequent racking that the variety demands. In fact, you can see that something has changed in the 80,000 bottles that Orlando and his brother Attilio produce on their 25-hectare estate. It may also be the series of vintages warm enough to partially dry the grapes but the local wines have been reaching incredible, and indeed almost excessive, levels of concentration. With more attention to elegance and harmony, what was once a mere quaffing wine is becoming one of the greats. It is no surprise that the winery's highest scorers were the three Dolcetto di Doglianis. And the San Luigi is very high flier, its deep nose offering hints of jam, stewed fruit and Peruvian bark then a dense, almost chewy palate that never loses its freshness. This year, it was superior even to the Peccheninos' historic selection, the Sirì d'Jermu. Make no mistake, the Sirì d'Jermu is a very fine wine but perhaps overdoes richness on the palate to the detriment of finesse and elegance. It's a characterful wine but also one that is edgy and difficult. However, the Bricco Botti '99 is more balanced. Ageing – half the wine matured in new barriques – has lent it complexity on the nose and softness on the palate. The Langhe La Castella, from barbera, nebbiolo and cabernet, fails to match its great structure with the appropriate finesse on the nose while the Langhe Bianco is, as usual, the most straightforward of the Pecchenino wines.

- Dolcetto di Dogliani S. Luigi '00 ▼▼▼ 4
- Dolcetto di Dogliani
  Sirì d'Jermu '00 ▼▼ 4
- Langhe La Castella '98 ▼▼ 5
- Dolcetto di Dogliani
  Sup. Bricco Botti '99 ▼▼ 5
○ Langhe Bianco Vigna Maestro '99 ▼ 4
- Dolcetto di Dogliani
  Sirì d'Jermu '96 ▼▼▼ 4
- Dolcetto di Dogliani
  Sirì d'Jermu '97 ▼▼▼ 4
- Dolcetto di Dogliani
  Sirì d'Jermu '98 ▼▼▼ 4
- Dolcetto di Dogliani
  Sirì d'Jermu '99 ▼▼▼ 4

DOGLIANI (CN)

PIRA
B.TA VALDIBERTI, 69
12063 DOGLIANI (CN)
TEL. 017378538

According to the experts, some of the finest locations for growing dolcetto are to be found on the hillslopes between Monforte and Dogliani. This makes life very much easier for the likeable Gianmatteo Pira, whose aim in life is to vinify his estate-grown dolcetto and barbera, bringing out the typicity of the grapes and the strong personalities of the various subzones. As in previous years, there are no weak spots in Gianmatteo's range. In fact, his list is even more reliable than usual for all the wines are stupendously extracted. The Dolcetto d'Alba Vigna Fornaci '00 has a fruit-rich nose of mulberries and a full-bodied, juicy palate. The succulent but slightly aggressive tannins in the long finish will mellow out their rough edges in the cellar. The Dolcetto di Dogliani Vigna Landes '00 has a more complex nose as it allows hints of bramble and cocoa powder to emerge through its classic alcohol-rich aromas. On the palate, the tannins are cosseted by the remarkably dense fruit, which gives it a softer mouthfeel softer and a longer finish. With the Dolcetto Bricco dei Botti '99, which also has toasty and smoky nuances, we come to the barrique-aged wines. The enhanced tidiness of the aromas and the greater length on the palate combine to make a product with more class than the previous wines. In comparison with the Dolcettos, the Barbera Briccobotti '99, which replaces the old Barbera d'Alba Vendemmia Tardiva Secca on the Pira list, is less immediately drinkable. For the time being it is less delicate and harmonious but it is also undoubtedly more complex and more suitable for laying down.

- Dolcetto d'Alba Vigna Fornaci '00 ▼▼ 4
- Dolcetto di Dogliani
  Vigna Landes '00 ▼▼ 4
- Dolcetto di Dogliani
  Vigna Bricco dei Botti '99 ▼▼ 4
- Piemonte Barbera Briccobotti '99 ▼▼ 5
- Barbera d'Alba V. T. '98 ▼▼ 6
- Langhe Rosso Briccobotti '98 ▼▼ 5

DOGLIANI (CN)

SAN FEREOLO
BORGATA VALDIBÀ, 59
12063 DOGLIANI (CN)
TEL. 0173742075

In charge of this winery there are two people with completely different personalities, Nicoletta Bocca and Francesco Stralla. One – Nicoletta – is never, ever satisfied and the other has an iron will and unremitting determination. As a result, their seven hectares on the loveliest slopes in the entire DOC zone at Valdiberti and San Luigi produce wines that, true to the terroir, are powerful and austere but also have a strong personality. Stralla looks after the vineyards, finding ways to make all the oldest plots he is offered productive again. But in the cellar, it is Nicoletta Bocca's insight and imagination that set the tone. This odd couple work with healthy, concentrated fruit from a vine stock that is on average 40 years old, bringing to bear their considerable ageing skill with barrels of various sizes and origins. Their reward has come in the three consecutive Three Glass rating won by San Fereolo. For this edition of the Guide, Francesco and Nicoletta presented only two wines, the Dolcetto San Fereolo and the Brumaio. Brumaio is a barbera-based wine, aged in part-new barriques and tonneaux, that has an impenetrable colour and an intense, varied nose of berry fruit, cherry jam, roasted coffee, cocoa powder and vanilla. On the palate, the massive structure just fails to assimilate its marked acidity in the lingering finish. The other offering, the Dolcetto San Fereolo, has a purplish colour and a fruit-rich nose dominated by ripe black berry fruit and plum jam, with hints of cocoa powder emerging. There is good structure and even better balance on the palate.

● Dolcetto di Dogliani San Fereolo '00	ŶŶ	4
● Langhe Rosso Brumaio '99	ŶŶ	5
● Dolcetto di Dogliani San Fereolo '99	ŶŶŶ	4
● Dolcetto di Dogliani San Fereolo '97	ŶŶŶ	4
● Langhe Rosso Brumaio '97	ŶŶŶ	5
● Dolcetto di Dogliani Sup. 1593 '97	ŶŶ	4
● Langhe Rosso Brumaio '98	ŶŶ	5

DOGLIANI (CN)

SAN ROMANO
B.TA GIACHELLI, 8
12063 DOGLIANI (CN)
TEL. 017376289
E-MAIL: bchionetti@sanromano.com

Bruno Chionetti, with the very competent assistance of his wife and brother-in-law, has shown how good a winemaker he is. But in addition to running his own winery well, he is battling unsparingly on behalf of the dolcetto variety and, especially, of the local DOC zone. He firmly believes the way forward is in the promotion of the Dogliani name. For the time being, Bruno has the consultancy of Giampiero Romana in the vineyard and Beppe Caviola in the cellar to help him get the best out of the four hectares he currently has available, almost all of it planted to dolcetto. However, another four hectares will be coming onstream in 2003, which will take the annual production capacity of the estate to about 55,000 bottles. One of the most noteworthy new developments is the chardonnay planted in some less well-aspected locations. This will be blended with pinot nero to produce a metodo classico spumante. Despite the warm weather in 2001, Bruno's wines have maintained their balance. As ever, the best performer is the Vigna del Pilone. San Romano releases 12,000 bottles of this untamed nectar with its unusual notes of Peruvian bark and juniper merging with the classic varietal bramble and the close-knit, juicily robust tannic weave. The standard-label '00 can rightly claim to be a clone in a minor key of the Vigna del Pilone, and represents a more immediate and quaffable alternative. Dolianum '99 is another story. A Vigna del Pilone selection aged entirely in pre-used barriques and tonneaux, it adds intriguing aromas of vanilla to the other's nose. In contrast, the Langhe Martin Sec '99 is an interesting new monovarietal wine from pinot nero. It has greater complexity than the Dolcetto but is less harmonious on the palate.

● Dolcetto di Dogliani Vigna del Pilone '00	ŶŶ	4
● Dolcetto di Dogliani '00	ŶŶ	4
● Dolcetto di Dogliani Sup. Dolianum '99	ŶŶ	5
● Langhe Rosso Martin Sec '99	ŶŶ	5
● Dolcetto di Dogliani Vigna del Pilone '97	ŶŶŶ	4
● Dolcetto di Dogliani Vigna del Pilone '98	ŶŶŶ	4
● Dolcetto di Dogliani Vigna del Pilone '99	ŶŶŶ	4
● Dolcetto di Dogliani Sup. Dolianum '98	ŶŶ	5

FARA NOVARESE (NO)

DESSILANI
VIA CESARE BATTISTI, 21
28073 FARA NOVARESE (NO)
TEL. 0321829252
E-MAIL: dessilani@anw.net

As you walk into Enzio Lucca's large and lovely cellar, you note how clean and carefully looked after everything is, and how much attention is paid to detail. It is in that same spirit that Enzio continually seeks improvements in his wines. He has initiated consultancies with established experts and at the same time has made major investments in both vineyard and cellar. Best of the wines we tasted this time was the Fara Caramino, which was not far off a Three Glass score. The almost impenetrable ruby hue is remarkably concentrated. There follow clean, lingering aromas that highlight bramble and blackcurrant as well as elegant notes of spice. On the palate, balance, tidiness and a whistle-clean progression delight your taste receptors. The aromas of the Fara Lochera are a little in thrall to the balsamic notes of the oak but the palate has excellent weight, and is very well-sustained by the tannic weave. The Gattinara '96 is intense garnet in the glass, with a slightly orangey rim. On the nose, it has a modern style that features notes of ripe black cherries, cocoa powder and violets. There are powerful tannins on the palate but they will need time to assimilate. The Nebbiolo '98 has a lovely deep ruby hue. Intense on the nose, it reveals hints of violets that mingle with wild roses and strawberry against a minty, spice-rich backdrop. The palate is fluent but certainly not uninteresting for it is impeccably well-sustained, with clean, satisfying fruit.

●	Fara Caramino '98	▼▼	5
●	Gattinara '96	▼▼	6
●	Fara Lochera '98	▼▼	5
●	Colline Novaresi Nebbiolo '98	▼	4
●	Fara Caramino '95	♀♀	5
●	Fara Lochera '95	♀♀	5
●	Fara Caramino '97	♀♀	5
●	Fara Lochera '97	♀♀	5

FARIGLIANO (CN)

ANNA MARIA ABBONA
FRAZ. MONCUCCO, 21
12060 FARIGLIANO (CN)
TEL. 0173797228 - 01737342853
E-MAIL: annamaria.abbona@libero.it

Located in one of the highest and most beautiful parts of the Dolcetto di Dogliano zone, Anna Maria Abbona's estate now embraces about eight hectares under vine, most of it planted to dolcetto. The constant spur provided by the group of prestigious local producers has helped this winery to grow from what started almost as a hobby a few years ago to an enterprise that today bottles – about 50,000 of them – the entire production of its vines. Now that the vinification cellar has been modernized, the next job will be to create a climate-controlled bottle cellar. A quick glance at the range tells you that the estate policy is to combine maximum drinkability with moderate prices, starting with a refreshingly pleasant Langhe Dolcetto and a fruit and alcohol-rich Sorì dij But that still flaunts plenty of mouthfilling body. The Maioli vineyard, which has the winery's oldest vine stock, provides two Dolcettos, a standard-label version aged in stainless steel and a Superiore, aged for 12 months in new barriques, pre-used tonneaux and five-hectolitre barrels of Slavonian oak. Although they share the same raw material, these two high-quality wines have different personalities. The first is an explosion of ripe fruit backed by a decently balanced structure while the Superiore has its strengths in its complex nose and muscular tannins. The Cadò, from barbera with a small proportion of dolcetto, ages in French and Slovenian oak and is a worthy companion of the two Dolcettos. Deep vibrant red in the glass, it releases a nose of concentrated fruit followed up by a powerful yet well-balanced and lingering palate that very nearly earned it Three Glasses.

●	Dolcetto di Dogliani Maioli '00	▼▼	4
●	Dolcetto di Dogliani Sorì dij But '00	▼▼	3*
●	Dolcetto di Dogliani Sup. Maioli '99	▼▼	4
●	Langhe Rosso Cadò '99	▼▼	5
●	Langhe Dolcetto '00	▼	3
●	Langhe Rosso Cadò '97	♀♀	4
●	Langhe Rosso Cadò '98	♀♀	4
●	Dolcetto di Dogliani Maioli '99	♀♀	4

FARIGLIANO (CN)

GIOVANNI BATTISTA GILLARDI
CASCINA CORSALETTO, 69
12060 FARIGLIANO (CN)
TEL. 017376306
E-MAIL: gillardi@gillardi.it

Up there in the hills of Farigliano, some over 500 metres above sea level, Giovanni Battista Gillardi and his wife Giuseppina work the way they always have: making sure their vines do not yield to much fruit. What has changed over the past two years has been the average level of quality. No longer do these two likeable producers have any weak spots, not even in their newer wines such as Yeta, and they are firming in the front ranks of Piedmontese winemaking. Giacolino Gillardi, an oenologist and manager at the Ceretto estate, favours a laissez-faire approach in the cellar and here in the greater comfort of the new facilities manages to produce characterful wine that embody the typicity of their native soil. The Harys won Three Glasses for the second time with a version that has even greater finesse and elegance than the '98. On the splendidly complex nose it unveils sophisticated typical aromas of white pepper and raspberry, then the palate prefers well-balanced and unhurried length to a show of strength. This year, the Gillardis bottled for the first time a new blend of dolcetto with ten per cent cabernet sauvignon aged in pre-used 300-litre tonneaux, the Langhe Rosso Yeta. It's a more approachable wine with bramble jelly fruit and a mouthfilling palate, despite its rather alcohol-rich finish. But the Gillardi specialty is dolcetto, a variety that accounts for 90 per cent of their six hectares under vine. The Cursalet stands out thanks to its redoubtable character and full body, offering a nose of stewed fruit that is almost super-ripe. As usual, the Vigneto Maestra is more straightforward and down-to-earth.

● Harys '99	🍷🍷🍷	6
● Dolcetto di Dogliani Cursalet '00	🍷🍷	4
● Langhe Rosso Yeta '99	🍷🍷	5
● Dolcetto di Dogliani Vigneto Maestra '00	🍷	4
● Harys '98	🍷🍷🍷	6
● Harys '96	🍷🍷	6
● Harys '97	🍷🍷	6
● Dolcetto di Dogliani Cursalet '99	🍷🍷	4

FRASSINELLO MONFERRATO (AL)

CASTELLO DI LIGNANO
VIA LIGNANO
15035 FRASSINELLO MONFERRATO (AL)
TEL. 0142334529 - 0142925326
E-MAIL: vinidoc@castellodilignano.it

The castle at Lignano was built in the Middle Ages but today it is a modern multi-crop farm extending over 85 hectares, of which 14 are under vine. The owner is Giuseppe Gaiero, an enthusiastic champion of the territory's potential. He runs the estate with the aid of Ugo Bertana and the consultancy of Francesco Ferrero. The range of wines, all made with estate-grown fruit, includes all the classic Monferrato wine types. La Frassinella, a still Freisa aged briefly in barriques, is a welcome newcomer this year and will surprise winelovers who are unconvinced of the variety's potential. The intense ruby hue introduces clean notes of bramble and raspberry over pepper and vanilla. On the palate, it is elegant rather than muscular but shows good balance and is well-sustained by stylish tannins through to the typically bitterish finish. The Lhennius is a blend of 50 per cent barbera, 30 per cent cabernet and 20 per cent freisa. Its aromas of ripe black berry fruit and pepper are enhanced by grassy notes while the palate offers rich fruit and surefooted progression. The finish is concentrated and tidy, although not very long. After ageing for a year in barriques, the Barbera Vigna Stramba has aromas of cherry, tobacco and dried flowers that usher in a structured, varietal palate. Plum and cherry emerge on the nose of the Barbera Valisenda but the palate, while pleasant enough, is a tad short. The Grignolino greets the nose with notes of raspberry, pepper, roses and geranium. Stylish and subtle on the palate, it shows none of the rough edges that have in the past been a feature of this enticing Monferrato wine. The Grisello is soft and attractively tangy.

● Monferrato Freisa La Frassinella '99	🍷🍷	3*
● Monferrato Rosso Lhennius '99	🍷🍷	5
● Grignolino del M.to Casalese Vigna Tufara '00	🍷	3
○ Monferrato Bianco Grisello '00	🍷	3
● Barbera d'Asti Vigna Stramba '99	🍷	4
● Barbera del M.to Sup. Valisenda '99	🍷	3
● Barbera d'Asti Vigna Stramba '98	🍷🍷	5
● Monferrato Rosso Lhennius '98	🍷🍷	5

GATTINARA (VC)

ANTONIOLO
C.so VALSESIA, 277
13045 GATTINARA (VC)
TEL. 0163833612
E-MAIL: antoniolovini@gattinara.alpcom.it

The wines of the Antoniolo family have a prominent place in the panorama of northern Piedmontese premium quality wines. Rosanna runs things with the help of her son and daughter: Alberto manages the vineyards and cellar while Lorella looks after administration. Their consultant oenologist is Attilio Pagli, who took over from Giancarlo Scaglione in 1998. At this year's tasting, the panel very nearly gave the Gattinara Osso San Grato a Three Glass score. A deep garnet wine, it proffers a traditional-style nose with deep, intriguing notes of violets, liquorice, plum and fennel. The palate has the austere fascination of the great Nebbiolos from this area, with a close-knit, well-sustained structure backed up by very solid tannins. The Gattinara Vigneto Castelle is the only wine to have been aged in barriques. The aromas are complex and ripe on the nose then the uncompromising palate shows very decent structure. After some initial uncertainty, the nose of the Gattinara San Francesco opens out on notes of ripe black cherry, crushed roses and aniseed. The palate has a wide range of richly nuanced flavours and aromas but the tannins and acidity are slightly aggressive. The panel was pleasantly surprised by the lingering varietal aromas of the standard-label Gattinara, whose notes of violets, raspberry and tar mingle with spicy nuances against a faint vegetal backdrop. In the mouth, the fruit is clean and has satisfying depth. In contrast, the Nebbiolo Juvenia is more approachable, unveiling unusual hints of cocoa powder and bottled black cherries. Finally, don't forget the refreshingly tangy, clean-tasting Erbaluce di Caluso, which offers real value for money.

● Gattinara Vigneto Osso S. Grato '97	🍷🍷	6
● Gattinara '97	🍷🍷	4
● Gattinara Vigneto Castelle '97	🍷🍷	6
● Gattinara Vigneto S. Francesco '97	🍷🍷	6
● Coste della Sesia Nebbiolo Juvenia '00	🍷	3
○ Erbaluce di Caluso '00	🍷	3
● Gattinara Vigneto Osso S. Grato '95	🍷🍷	6
● Gattinara Vigneto Castelle '96	🍷🍷	6
● Gattinara Vigneto Osso S. Grato '96	🍷🍷	6
● Gattinara Vigneto S. Francesco '96	🍷🍷	6

GATTINARA (VC)

NERVI
C.so VERCELLI, 117
13045 GATTINARA (VC)
TEL. 0163833228
E-MAIL: avnervi@gattinara.alpcom.it

The time-worn cellars and 19th-century premises of the Nervi winery are on the outskirts of Gattinara. Visitors are welcomed in a sober but scrupulously well-kept area that includes a shop and tasting room. The winery's guiding spirit is Giorgio Aliata, a passionate, tenacious viticulturist who believes in his territory and spares no effort to promote it. The consultant oenologist, Giorgio Barbero, oversees 26 hectares under vine in the finest vinegrowing areas in Gattinara. From one such location comes the Gattinara Vigneto Molsino, a vibrant, nicely concentrated garnet wine. Its firm aromas are in the modern style without, however, making concessions to international tastes. The bouquet opens on notes of tobacco and dried flowers before adding hints of blackcurrant and violet. On the palate, the serious structure is immediately apparent, its uncompromising but aristocratic acidity and tannins melding into full-bodied, juicy fruit that crisply echoes the nose. The standard-label version is bright ruby with orange highlights at the rim. The lingering varietal fragrances delight with notes of flowers and autumn leaves lifted by understated spice. In the mouth, it shows decent structure and a well-sustained progression, and time will mellow the boisterous exuberance of the acid and tannic components. Coste della Sesia Rosso is a nebbiolo-based wine with croatina, vespolina and uva rara. Its translucent ruby hue introduces a nose of fascinating complexity, which is quite a surprise in a wine intended to be drunk through the meal. Its many nuances range from roses, violets, raspberries and cocoa powder to spice while the upfront palate has a stylish structure.

● Gattinara '96	🍷🍷	5
● Gattinara Vigneto Molsino '97	🍷🍷	5
● Coste della Sesia Rosso '00	🍷	4
● Gattinara Vigneto Molsino '93	🍷🍷	5
● Gattinara '95	🍷🍷	5
● Gattinara Vigneto Molsino '95	🍷🍷	5
● Gattinara Vigneto Molsino '96	🍷🍷	5

GATTINARA (VC)

Giancarlo Travaglini
Via delle Vigne, 36
13045 Gattinara (VC)
tel. 0163833588
e-mail: travaglini.gattinara@libero.it

With an annual production close to 300,000 bottles, nine out of ten destined for non-domestic markets, from his 42 hectares, Giancarlo Travaglini is Gattinara's ambassador abroad. Moreover, the winery's spacious cellars are equipped with the latest vinification technology. The Gattinara Riserva, from selected grapes, is a benchmark for the wine type and shows just how good it is as soon as you savour the nose. Clean as a whistle, it allows the bouquet to express all the noble complexity of a great Nebbiolo that is destined for the cellar. The aromas will intrigue with their endless range of nuances, including raspberry, plum, violets and a faint note of cinnamon and black pepper spice. It may not have the sheer muscle of some Langhe Nebbiolos bit it lacks nothing in style, consistency or crispness, and is backed by fine-grained tannins. The standard-label Gattinara is a short head behind. Its deep ruby colour is flecked with garnet and has concentrated aromas of bramble, plum, liquorice, cocoa powder and violets. The sensations on the palate are intense, clean and echo the nose delightfully while the attractive and anything but ordinary fruit is enlivened by an unexpected hint of zestiness. The nicely astringent finish reveals notes of blackcurrant and pomegranate. Finally, the Gattinara Tre Vigne is a blend of grapes from Gattinara's three historic crus, vinified together to make a more complete, harmonious wine. A dark wine, it has a modern-style nose of ripe black cherries, coffee and violets. The palate focuses on the softness and concentration of the fruit then the slightly edgy but intense finish mirrors the nose.

GAVI (AL)

Nicola Bergaglio
Fraz. Rovereto
Loc. Pedaggeri, 59
15066 Gavi (AL)
tel. 0143682195

It's the first time that Gianluigi Bergaglio's winery has earned a Guide profile. The wonderfully situated 12 hectares under vine at Rovereto are important, as is the estate's 30-year track record of reliable products, but a full profile is only awarded after the panel has tasted and approved the wines. On our visits this year, Nicola Bergaglio's '00 Gavis provided a very pleasant surprise, both gaining flattering Two Glass ratings. The historic Minaia label, one of the first selections in the DOC zone, has a bright straw-yellow colour. Its very subtle nose offers notes of apples, pears and flowers, with lily of the valley emerging. Attractive on the palate, it has a well-rounded, fresh-tasting style and nice acidity. The remarkable structure of this selection can be best appreciated in the deliciously long, tangy finish. The standard-label Gavi is simply excellent, its classic straw yellow flecked with youthful greenish highlights and the powerful nose vibrant and refreshingly redolent of citrus and flowers. The very fresh-tasting palate also delivers great flavour and structure, as well as admirable length.

●	Gattinara Ris. '97	ŸŸ	6
●	Gattinara '98	ŸŸ	5
●	Gattinara Tre Vigne '98	ŸŸ	6
●	Gattinara Ris. Numerata '88	ŸŸ	6
●	Gattinara Ris. Numerata '89	ŸŸ	6
●	Gattinara Ris. Numerata '90	ŸŸ	6
●	Gattinara Ris. '93	ŸŸ	6
●	Gattinara Ris. '95	ŸŸ	6
●	Gattinara Ris. '96	ŸŸ	6
●	Gattinara Tre Vigne '97	ŸŸ	6

○	Gavi del Comune di Gavi '00	ŸŸ	3*
○	Gavi del Comune di Gavi Minaia '00	ŸŸ	4

GAVI (AL)

GIAN PIERO BROGLIA
TENUTA LA MEIRANA
LOC. LOMELLINA, 14
15066 GAVI (AL)
TEL. 0143642998 - 0143743267
E-MAIL: broglia.azienda@tin.it

The 2000 vintage was another good one for Gavi. The very favourable weather gave winemakers almost perfect fruit, which the La Meirana cellar, run by the current president of Consorzio di Tutela del Gavi, vinified splendidly. Recently, Piero Broglia has given Federico Curtaz the job of looking after his vineyards and the excellent results can be found in the glass. Gavi La Meirana, in particular, stands out for its concentrated green-flecked straw yellow, introducing a broad, almost penetrating, nose that releases notes of green apple, raspberry and flowers. The deep, fruit-rich palate is tempting, and the tangy finish has a hint of mineral. The panel sampled the '99 version of the Bruno Broglia selection, a Gavi blend of stainless steel-fermented and small cask conditioned wine. The full, bright colour ushers in a deep nose that ranges from ripe apples and pears to super-ripe, almost tropical notes, honey, butter and oak-derived vanilla. Although rounded, rich and full-flavoured on the palate, it is still attractively fresh-tasting. The estate is soon to devote more attention to reds and the new facilities are close to completion. They've certainly got off to a good start with the delightful Bruno Broglia Rosso. This '98 won Two Glasses for its beautifully balanced aromas and the poise of the palate, achieved without detriment to the fresh varietal acidity of the barbera that accounts for a large proportion of the blend. Less of a heavyweight, but good nonetheless, is the Rosso Le Pernici. It combines aromas of ripe and stewed fruit, as well as roses, with a fresh, tannin-rich palate that could have been a little longer.

○ Gavi del Comune di Gavi La Meirana '00	♟♟ 3*
● Monferrato Rosso Bruno Broglia '98	♟♟ 5
○ Gavi del Comune di Gavi Bruno Broglia '99	♟♟ 5
● Monferrato Rosso Le Pernici '00	♟ 3
○ Gavi del Comune di Gavi Bruno Broglia '98	♟♟ 4
● Monferrato Rosso '98	♟♟ 4

GAVI (AL)

CASTELLARI BERGAGLIO
FRAZ. ROVERETO, 136
15066 GAVI (AL)
TEL. 0143644000
E-MAIL: gavi@castellaribergaglio.it

It is the good fortune of the Bergaglio family that they live in Rovereto, the part of Gavi where the finest vineyard terrain is located. For over ten years, Mario and Wanda Castellari have been working with their son Marco, who has now taken over the running of the cellar. From their perch atop the hill, they can look over the valley underneath, where they have ten hectares in the historic DOC subzones that provide superb quality cortese grapes. Vineyard management is the secret of their wines and the Castellari Bergaglio range is now a byword for quality. They release four labels, starting with the standard Rolona and Fornaci wines and moving on to the premium Rovereto Vignavecchia and Pilìn bottles. This year, the Pilìn is being presented as a "vino da tavola" for the last time: next year, it will be labelled DOCG. What happened was that in 1998, Marco had to forgo DOC status because Gavi regulations did not permit cask conditioning. But since spring 2001, producers who use wood can label their wines DOC, thanks to a modification of the Gavi regulations. In fact, the Pilìn is excellent and the extra year's ageing has enabled it to find a good balance with the oak. Also more than just good is the Rovereto Vignavecchia. Its straw yellow shades into gold then the sweet aromas of honey and ripe fruit make way for more complex sensations of almond and roasted walnuts. Rich and full-flavoured on the palate, it takes its leave with a long finish. The Rolona repeated its very good performance of last year and, bringing up the rear is the well-made Fornaci.

○ Pilìn Bianco '98	♟♟ 5
○ Gavi del Comune di Gavi Rolona '00	♟♟ 3*
○ Gavi Rovereto Vignavecchia '00	♟♟ 4
○ Gavi Fornaci '00	♟ 3
○ Gavi Rovereto Vignavecchia '99	♟♟ 4

GAVI (AL)

La Chiara
Loc. Vallegge, 24/2
15066 Gavi (AL)
tel. 0143642293

If you arrive in Gavi from the flatlands of Alessandria to the north, along the Lemme river valley on the provincial highway known as the Frascheta or Marengo road, you will find this lovely farmhouse at the foot of the sandstone ridge that frames the majestic spectacle of the fortress. The news from La Chiara regards the building programme under way on the estate offices but this hasn't distracted Roberto Bergaglio from his work in the cellar, where he is as attentive as ever. Both of his Gavi labels are well up to scratch, amply confirming the panel's opinions in previous editions of the Guide. Again, it was the barrique-fermented and aged Vigneto Groppella selection that caught our attention. Compared with previous vintages, it has a leaner feel, as if Roberto was trying to give it a lighter body, yet the colour is just as concentrated and the straw yellow is almost golden. The nose tells you that the wood used for fermentation and the fruit are happily married, the rich balanced aromas revealing concentrated hints of vanilla, flowers, honey and citrus. On the palate, it is pleasingly refreshing, showing very decent length. The Gavi '00 was vinified in stainless steel. It has a lighter straw-yellow hue with youthful greenish highlights. Attractive on the nose, it offers varietal notes of flowers, apples, pears and citrus fruit while the whistle-clean, fairly tangy and very approachable palate has goodish body and moderate length.

○ Gavi del Comune di Gavi Vigneto Groppella '99	▼▼	4
○ Gavi del Comune di Gavi La Chiara '00	▼	3*
○ Gavi del Comune di Gavi Vigneto Groppella '98	▼▼	4

GAVI (AL)

La Giustiniana
Fraz. Rovereto, 5
15066 Gavi (AL)
tel. 0143682132
e-mail: lagiustiniana@libarnanet.it

The Lombardinis are convinced that product and territory are inseparable. They are building up their Rovereto cellar and exploiting its considerable resources to the full: the vineyards, the 17th-century villa and the other farm buildings. Under Enrico Tomalino, La Giustiniana has found a winner in the Just label, which identifies the cellar's two top wines. The cortese-based Just Bianco will be released as a DOCG wine in future vintages. It has a vibrantly rich straw-yellow colour and a wide range of aromas from flowers to vanilla and honey, accompanied by notes of toasty oak. Fresh-tasting and tangy on the palate, it reveals good structure and fine length. Its stablemate, the barbera-based Just Rosso, is labelled DOC Monferrato. It, too, won a brace of Glasses for its deep ruby colour and notes of ripe fruit and jam. The palate is full, with slightly astringent tannins in the nice finish. The Lugarara earned a good score for an intense nose where mineral notes mingle with new-mown grass. Temptingly light on the fresh-tasting palate, it signs off with a longish finish. Only little below came the Montessora, its nose a swathe of flowers, hazelnut, vanilla and citrus fruit. Youthful and nice in the mouth, it is a very easy-drinking wine. The 2000 vintage was a good one for the La Giustiniana aromatic wines. The Brachetto d'Acqui and Moscato are released in both standard-cork and sparkling versions. The Moscato is an interesting representative from the future Strevi DOC subzone. Yellow, buttery and fragrant, it has a well-structured palate that never cloys. Finally, the Brachetto Spumante is very stylish.

○ Gavi del Comune di Gavi Lugarara '00	▼▼	4
● Monferrato Rosso Just '98	▼▼	4
○ Just Bianco '99	▼▼	4
● Brachetto d'Acqui Spumante Contero '00	▼	4
○ Gavi del Comune di Gavi Montessora '00	▼	4
○ Moscato d'Asti Contero '99	▼	3
○ Just Bianco '98	▼▼	5

GAVI (AL)

La Scolca
Fraz. Rovereto, 170/r
15066 Gavi (AL)
tel. 0143682176
e-mail: info@scolca.it

There's always something new going on at La Scolca, a winery that has left its mark on the history of Gavi. The Soldatis continue to beef up the estate staff and from the 2001 vintage have had Gian Luigi Zorio, a young wine technician from Alba who arrives in Gavi bringing with him several years' experience with the Gallo organization in Napa Valley. Assistant manager Luca Filippini is another recent acquisition. But those who know La Scolca will be astonished to learn that the cellar, for the very first time, now contains barriques, which are being used experimentally. It's almost a revolution and the extremely rigorous Giorgio Soldati only accepted their introduction when cask-conditioning was finally permitted by the DOC regulations. While we wait for the new Gavis, we are happy to confirm a number of positive judgements. The Gavi dei Gavi, the celebrated Etichetta Nera, is the best of recent years. Straw yellow with lustrous green highlights, it proffers a subtly elegant, almost etheric, nose and a fresh-tasting palate with a deliciously tangy, bitterish finish. The Gavi Brut, disgorged in 2001, performed even better. A cortese-based "blanc de blancs", it combines a textbook perlage and lovely colour with the delightful aromas of the fermentation less and classic crusty bread. On the palate, the sweetness of the liqueur d'expedition is perceptible in the creamy soft mouthfeel. The Villa Scolca has a deliciously varietal nose of pears, apples and citrus fruit and an equally attractive fresh-tasting progression on the palate. The white label version has a light rose of flowers and chamomile followed by a very approachable palate. Finally, One Glass went to the Oltrepò Pinot Nero.

○	Gavi Brut	🍷🍷	4
○	Gavi dei Gavi Etichetta Nera '00	🍷🍷	5
○	Gavi La Scolca '00	🍷	4
○	Gavi Villa Scolca '00	🍷	3
●	O. P. Pinot Nero '00	🍷	4
○	Soldati La Scolca Brut '90	🍷🍷	6
○	Soldati La Scolca Brut '87	🍷🍷	6

GAVI (AL)

Produttori del Gavi
Via Cavalieri di Vittorio Veneto, 45
15066 Gavi (AL)
tel. 0143642786
e-mail: cantina.prodgavi@libero.it

The Cantina Produttori del Gavi stands at the foot of the town's majestic fortress and its entry into the Guide this year is an important signal for the world of wine in the province of Alessandria. It is the first example of a co-operative winery that is aiming for quality, not quantity, an approach that for too long has held back winemaking in this part of Piedmont. Even more significant are the dimensions of the Cantina Produttori, which has 150 members, 190 hectares under vine an output of more that 9,000 hectolitres of DOCG Gavi wine. The model that the management team has identified is the winning formula adopted long ago by other co-operatives, for example in Alto Adige: greater care over selection of the fruit, encouraging growers to improve their vineyard techniques and cut back yields in return for higher prices. The cellar, under Roberto Sarotto, has adapted to the new regime and several good labels have been released in serious quantities. Cascine dell'Aureliana is a lustrous straw yellow with a nose that opens on super-ripe notes, giving way to fresh citrus aromas. In the mouth, the fresh progression is nicely offset by the warmth and softness of the length. The Gavi Maddalena is vibrant straw yellow in the glass, releasing a concentrated swathe of aromas including pear and apricots. The palate is rich and full-flavoured. Primuva has a concentrated straw-yellow colour and good breadth on the nose, where the intensity of the fruit is remarkable. In contrast, the palate is pleasantly refreshing. The DiVino '99 is a Cortese Piemonte as the DOCG regulations had to be interpreted very strictly. Until last year, barrique ageing was not permissible for Gavi.

○	Gavi Cascine dell'Aureliana '00	🍷🍷	4
○	Gavi Maddalena '00	🍷🍷	3*
○	Gavi Primuva '00	🍷🍷	3*
○	Piemonte Cortese DiVino '99	🍷	3

GAVI (AL)

Villa Sparina
Fraz. Monterotondo, 56
15066 Gavi (AL)
tel. 0143633835

The winery run by the Moccagatta family is never still. Investment in the soon to be opened Relais facility goes on and major operations are under way in the vineyard, where there has also been a change in management. The new vineyards, whose planting patterns reveal their high ambitions, are even now being joined by other that are coming onstream. The general impression is that at Monterotondo, no one is resting on the recently acquired laurels and ideas for the future are very clear. The wines presented this time round confirm the winery's style over the last few years, when concentration and structure have been the watchwords. Those are certainly the distinguishing features of the Monferrato Rosso Rivalta '99, which triumphed this year with Three glorious Glasses. An impenetrable ruby red in the glass, it reveals notes of ripe fruit opening over balsamic and minerally nuances. On the palate, it is stunning, the extract superbly supported by acidity and tannins. A marvellous red that the Moccagattas can be proud of. Excellent, too, if a little flabby, is the '00 Gavi Monte Rotondo while the müller thurgau-based Monferrato Bianco impresses with its aromatic notes and fullness of flavour. The Gavi '00 has a vivid, dark straw-yellow hue and a nose where crisply concentrated hints of apple and flowers emerge. The Bric Maioli '00 is the best of the standard-label Dolcettos from the province of Alessandria. Its bright ruby red is concentrated and impenetrable then the fruit-rich nose leads in to a full, warm palate. It big brother, d'Giusep, also has a challenging nose of etheric, gamey and spicy notes, with even cocoa powder coming through. Rounded and full-flavoured in the mouth, it signs off with a long, tannic finish.

GHEMME (NO)

Antichi Vigneti di Cantalupo
Via Michelangelo Buonarroti, 5
28074 Ghemme (NO)
tel. 0163840041
e-mail: info@cantalupovigneti.it

The vineyards at Ghemme stand on a stretch of the long alluvial-morainic hill that stretches from the entrance of Valsesia to the flatlands of Novara. It is on these slopes that the Arlunnos have been growing vines since the 16th century, the history of the family merging with that of the land. Alberto Alunno is in fact a local history enthusiast and today runs the estate with his wife Angela and the consultancy of Donato Lanati. Their vast range of wines is made entirely with estate-grown fruit. The Collis Carellae has a traditional nose with warm notes of plum, cinnamon and dried roses. On the palate, there is solid structure and, although it has the austere character of the local nebbiolo grapes, it is still delicious thanks to its fruit-rich thrust. Ghemme Signore di Bayard is the only barrique-aged wine. Its aromas meld hints of balsam vanilla with blackcurrant and violets then the full-flavoured, satisfying fruit in the mouth takes you through to an intense but rather mouth-drying finish. The '96 version of the Collis Breclemae turned out to be less attractive than usual. Its very ripe fragrances reveal a gamey note and the tannins on the broad, well-structured palate are very aggressive. The standard-label Ghemme '97, though, earned Two Glasses. An uncomplicated bottle that you can serve at table every day, it still has, thanks to its nebbiolo fruit, a complexity that similar wines can only dream of. The vespolina-based Villa Horta and the Primigenia, from uva rara and nebbiolo, are two light, crowd-pleasing reds. Finally, the Carolus white, from erbaluce, arneis and chardonnay, is soft and attractively tangy.

	Wine	Glasses	Score
●	Monferrato Rosso Rivalta '99	♟♟♟	6
●	Dolcetto d'Acqui Bric Maioli '00	♟♟	4
○	Gavi del Comune di Gavi Monte Rotondo '00	♟♟	6
○	Monferrato Müller Thurgau '00	♟♟	4
●	Dolcetto d'Acqui d'Giusep '99	♟♟	5
○	Gavi del Comune di Gavi '00	♟	3
○	Villa Sparina Brut M. Cl.	♟	5
○	Gavi del Comune di Gavi Monte Rotondo '99	♟♟♟	6
●	Barbera del M.to Rivalta '97	♟♟♟	6
○	Villa Sparina Brut M. Cl. '95	♟♟	5
○	Dolcetto d'Acqui d'Giusep '98	♟♟	4
●	Monferrato Rosso Rivalta '98	♟♟	6

	Wine	Glasses	Score
●	Ghemme '97	♟♟	4
●	Ghemme Collis Carellae '97	♟♟	6
●	Ghemme Signore di Bayard '97	♟♟	6
○	Carolus '00	♟	2*
●	Primigenia '00	♟	2*
●	Villa Horta '00	♟	2
●	Ghemme Collis Breclemae '96	♟	6
●	Colline Novaresi Agamium '99	♟	3
●	Ghemme Signore di Bayard '95	♟♟	5
●	Ghemme Collis Carellae '96	♟♟	5
●	Ghemme Signore di Bayard '96	♟♟	5
●	Ghemme Collis Breclemae '94	♟	5

GHEMME (NO)

Rovellotti
Via Privata Tamiotti, 3
28074 Ghemme (NO)
tel. 0163840478
e-mail: info@rovellotti.it

The walled mediaeval quarter of Ghemme is actually a fortress, erected long ago to protect the town's population, livestock and crops from the unwelcome attentions of passing marauders. Inside this "ricetto" is the winery owned by Paolo and Antonello Rovellotti, viticulturist and flower-growers who have been helped since the '97 vintage by the very competent oenologist Mario Ronco. Their Ghemme Riserva '97, earned a score that took it to the top of the Two Glass band for its lovely concentrated garnet hue and intense, tight-knit aromas of violets, tobacco and blackcurrant that show no signs of evolution. The attractive palate combines admirable structure with perfect balance. On the nose of the Ghemme '97, there is just the right equilibrium of freshness and ripeness in the notes of raspberry, violets and tar. A hint of spice enhances the approachable nose without jeopardizing complexity and in fact adding fresh nuances. The solid, well-sustained palate is let down by a slight lack of pulp. The patiently dried erbaluce grapes in the intriguing Valdenrico light up the glass with their sunflower hue. There are intense notes of hazelnut and chamomile on the nose then the muscular yet velvety palate unveils serious alcohol. The surprisingly good Colline Novaresi Bianco is from greco di Ghemme fruit, the local name for erbaluce. Its elegant flowers on the nose tell you that this is a clean, expertly made wine. On the temptingly fresh palate, there are hints of light-skinned plums and spring flowers, lifted by marked tanginess. And to round off, the Colline Novaresi Rosso, from nebbiolo with small proportions of vespolina and uva rara, is less challenging.

O	Colline Novaresi Bianco '00	♙♙	3*
●	Ghemme '97	♙♙	5
●	Ghemme Ris. '97	♙♙	6
O	Valdenrico Bianco '98	♙♙	6
●	Colline Novaresi Rosso '00	♙	2*

INCISA SCAPACCINO (AT)

Ermanno e Alessandra Brema
Via Pozzomagna, 9
14045 Incisa Scapaccino (AT)
tel. 014174019 - 014174617
e-mail: vinibrema@inwind.it

Ermanno and Alessandra Brema have had the input of celebrated Piedmontese oenologist Giancarlo Scaglione for the past couple of years and are now devoting all their attention to barbera, the local variety that has recently produced such good results in the Asti area. The Bremas have 13 hectares under vine, 80 per cent planted to barbera and the rest dolcetto and brachetto, in three farms – Cascina Croce, Cascina Giacomina and Cascina Bricconizza – on the hills around Nizza Monferrato. There are four Barberas, two of them exceptional selections. For the last two years the flagship wine has been the Barbera Bricco della Volpettona, which is a stunner again this year. The colour is almost impenetrable and the aromas of ripe fruit merge with the sweet, toasty wood and lovely balsamic notes. On the lovely, lingering palate, fruit is to the fore but the variety's elegance also comes through. The never-ending finish dallies over hints of bramble, bitter bilberries and tart wild cherries. Neither is the Bricconizza selection a disappointment. Even more closed than the Volpettona, it can still show a back palate that is quite delightful. The Barbera d'Asti Le Cascine is less concentrated than the previous wines but is drinkable enough thanks to a tangy palate and sweet fruit. Cascina Croce is a tad more rustic, though. Finally, a mention and a Glass for the Dolcetto d'Asti Impagnato, a wine type that few producers tackle nowadays, and the Piemonte Brachetto Carlotta.

●	Barbera d'Asti Sup. Bricco della Volpettona '99	♙♙	5
●	Barbera d'Asti Sup. Bricconizza '99	♙♙	5
●	Piemonte Brachetto Carlotta '00	♙	4
●	Barbera d'Asti Sup. Cascina Croce '99	♙	3
●	Barbera d'Asti Sup. Le Cascine '99	♙	4
●	Dolcetto d'Asti Vigna Impagnato '99	♙	3
●	Barbera d'Asti Sup. Bricco della Volpettona '98	♙♙	5
●	Barbera d'Asti Sup. Bricconizza '98	♙♙	5

IVREA (TO)

FERRANDO
FRAZ. SAN BERNARDO
VIA TORINO, 599/A
10015 IVREA (TO)
TEL. 0125641176
E-MAIL: info@ferrandovini.it

Luigi Ferrando is helped by his sons Roberto, who looks after the cellar, and Andrea, in charge of sales, and the family inaugurated their new complex in September 1999, when they moved production to the premises on the outskirts of Ivrea. Obviously, the Ferrando wine shop at Ivrea is still open, as is the cellar in Carema, where their Carema-label wine ages for more than four years before being released. Our tasting began with this classic bottle from the hills of Carema, right on the border with Valle d'Aosta. Carema Etichetta Nera is the Ferrandos' pride and joy, and the '97 vintage is again the finest in its category. The remarkably intense colour shades slightly into brick red at the rim and the tar, spice and tobacco aromas are deliciously elegant. Full and long on the palate, it has good balance and a caressing mouthfeel. Spices emerge again in the leisurely finish to vie with lively, prominent tannins. Not for the first time, the Erbaluce Cariola Etichetta Nera impressed. The '99 has a rich straw-yellow hue and complex aromas where the fruit melds seamlessly into the wood. There is plenty of breadth and richness on the palate. The standard-label Erbaluce is fresh and tangy in the mouth but nothing more. Best of the dried grape wines was the Caluso Vigneto Cariola '97, which is on top form, whereas the late-harvest Solativo is a touch rustic. Concluding the range are two Canavese DOC wines. We preferred the monovarietal erbaluce Bianco Castello di Loranzé, which was more convincing than the Rosso Montodo, from nebbiolo and barbera with additions of local varieties.

LA MORRA (CN)

★ ★ ELIO ALTARE - CASCINA NUOVA
FRAZ. ANNUNZIATA, 51
12064 LA MORRA (CN)
TEL. 017350835

The new millennium didn't get off to a good start for Elio Altare: a batch of about 30,000 corks used to seal the precious fruit of his hard work in the vineyard failed to do its job. Elio refused to take the blow lying down and complained to his multinational supplier, proving after many months of analyses and counter-analyses that the problem was not the wine but the corks. They were very expensive, first-quality corks but they prevented Altare from releasing his Barolo Arborina '97 and the '98 editions of the Langhe Larigi, the Arborina and the La Villa. All are outstanding products – the Arborina and the Larigi won Three Glass ratings – but Elio felt he could not send them out. There was too high a risk of their being corked. Still, the hullabaloo eventually died down. Elio acquired a batch of more reliable corks and he bottled the new vintages. Before we review the new products, we feel we should reassure winelovers: the bottles released in autumn 2001 range from good to exceptional. For instance, the Larigi is outstanding. A Barbera of great depth that marries elegance with big league extract, it embodies Elio's approach to winemaking, for he favours finesse over muscle power. La Villa, from barbera and nebbiolo, is equally extraordinary. Today, it is superior to the monovarietal nebbiolo Arborina, which requires further bottle age. The '98 version of the L'Insieme blend and the standard-label '97 Barolo, 4,500 bottles of which survived because their corks are from another batch, were also impressive. Finally, the Barbera d'Alba and Dolcetto were impeccable.

○ Caluso Passito Vigneto Cariola '97	ŶŶ	6
● Carema Etichetta Nera '97	ŶŶ	6
○ Erbaluce di Caluso Cariola Etichetta Nera '99	ŶŶ	4
○ Canavese Bianco Castello di Loranzé '00	Ŷ	4
● Canavese Rosso Montodo '00	Ŷ	4
○ Erbaluce di Caluso Cariola Etichetta Verde '00	Ŷ	4
○ Solativo '99	Ŷ	6
● Carema Etichetta Nera '95	ŶŶ	6
● Carema Etichetta Nera '96	ŶŶ	6

● Langhe La Villa '99	ŶŶŶ	6
● Langhe Larigi '99	ŶŶŶ	6
● Langhe Arborina '99	ŶŶ	6
● Barbera d'Alba '00	ŶŶ	4
● Dolcetto d'Alba '00	ŶŶ	4
● Barolo '97	ŶŶ	6
● L'Insieme	ŶŶ	6
● Barolo Vigneto Arborina '93	ŶŶŶ	6
● Langhe Larigi '95	ŶŶŶ	6
● Langhe Arborina '96	ŶŶŶ	6
● Langhe Arborina '97	ŶŶŶ	6
● Langhe Larigi '97	ŶŶŶ	6
● Barolo Vigneto Arborina '95	ŶŶ	6
● Barolo Vigneto Arborina '96	ŶŶ	6

LA MORRA (CN)

BATASIOLO
FRAZ. ANNUNZIATA, 87
12064 LA MORRA (CN)
TEL. 017350130 - 017350131
E-MAIL: info@batasiolo.com

Few wineries in the Langhe can boast Barolos like the Batasiolo range. All come from historic vineyard selections and in '97 all were outstandingly good. The new Barolo Cerequio '97, from the stupendous Cerequio vineyard at La Morra, was vinified as a selection for the first time and is every bit as good as the Batasiolo flagship wine, the Barolo Corda della Briccolina. The Cerequio has a close-knit, bright colour and complex fruit on the nose where jam and nuts emerge to make way for an intriguing hint of rhubarb. The Barolo Corda della Briccolina is barrique-aged and draws from the oak notes of mint, camphor and tobacco while still letting the fruit shine through. The palate already shows sufficient alcohol and body to offset the stylish tannins. In contrast, the Barolo Boscareto '97 is a much more approachable proposition. Two very full Glasses also went to the Barolo Bofani '97, whose nose is already evolving towards notes of spices and liquorice. Good, too, but less concentrated is the standard-label Barolo '97 while the Barbaresco '98 is attractively aristocratic. The first thing to strike the eye about the Barbera d'Alba Sovrana '99 is the dense hue, firm right to the rim. Then notes of roses and wild berries emerge, backed up by the wood, introducing the deliciously soft, refreshing palate. The cherry aromas of the Dolcetto d'Alba Bricco di Vergne '00 are tempting. Finally, the panel preferred the melon and white peach of the Langhe Chardonnay Serbato '00 to the mineral and vanilla of the Langhe Chardonnay Vigneto Morino '99.

● Barolo Bofani '97	🍷🍷	6
● Barolo Boscareto '97	🍷🍷	6
● Barolo Cerequio '97	🍷🍷	6
● Barolo Corda della Briccolina '97	🍷🍷	6
● Barbera d'Alba Sovrana '99	🍷🍷	4
● Dolcetto d'Alba Bricco di Vergne '00	🍷	4
○ Langhe Chardonnay Serbato '00	🍷	3
● Barolo '97	🍷	6
● Barbaresco '98	🍷	6
○ Langhe Chardonnay Morino '99	🍷	6
● Barolo Corda della Briccolina '88	🍷🍷🍷	6
● Barolo Corda della Briccolina '89	🍷🍷🍷	6
● Barolo Corda della Briccolina '90	🍷🍷🍷	6
● Barolo Corda della Briccolina '96	🍷🍷	6

LA MORRA (CN)

ENZO BOGLIETTI
VIA ROMA, 37
12064 LA MORRA (CN)
TEL. 017350330

Enzo and Gianni Boglietti make the classic wines of the Langhe in a modern style. Impeccably. The three Barolos presented include the absolutely exquisite Bruante '97, which won the coveted Three Glasses for the second time. It's a great wine with the classic Barolo garnet colour and a nose that marries sweet notes of oak with beautifully expressed hints of raspberry and violets. Full yet subtly elegant, it pampers the palate with fine-grained tannins and a juicy finish laced with refined minerally nuances. The youthful hue and vivacious personality of the Barolo Fossati '97 are also attractive, as is the balsam and fruit-rich nose of the Barolo Case Nere '07, a wine that owes more to its stay in oak. The firm attack on the palate ushers in tannins that have yet to mellow in the finish. The new Barbera Roscaleto '99 hails from a vineyard at La Morra that is more than 40 years old. A winner on its first outing, it reveals a dark colour and intense notes of raspberry and plum that will open further with bottle ageing. The full-bodied, pulp-rich palate has a long finish with just enough acidity to back up the fruit. The Barbera Vigna dei Romani '99 is a good, full-bodied proposition with lots of fruit but for now is dominated by the toastiness of the oak; the same could be said of the Buio '99, a 70-30 blend of nebbiolo and barbera with a powerfully tannic finish. A tip of the hat, too, for the Dolcetto Tigli Neri, obtained from vines some of which are 60 years old. Very fruity and sweet on the mouthfilling palate, it has an unusual note of strawberry in the balanced finish. Finally, the Barbera d'Alba '00 is admirably clean and varietal, unveiling barbera's trademark dried rose aromas.

● Barolo Brunate '97	🍷🍷🍷	6
● Barbera d'Alba '00	🍷🍷	4
● Dolcetto d'Alba Tigli Neri '00	🍷🍷	4
● Barolo Case Nere '97	🍷🍷	6
● Barolo Fossati '97	🍷🍷	6
● Barbera d'Alba Roscaleto '99	🍷🍷	4
● Barbera d'Alba Vigna dei Romani '99	🍷🍷	5
● Langhe Rosso Buio '99	🍷🍷	5
● Barbera d'Alba Vigna dei Romani '94	🍷🍷🍷	6
● Barolo Fossati '96	🍷🍷🍷	6
● Barolo Brunate '96	🍷🍷	6
● Barbera d'Alba Vigna dei Romani '98	🍷🍷	5

LA MORRA (CN)

GIANFRANCO BOVIO
FRAZ. ANNUNZIATA
BORGATA CIOTTO, 63
12064 LA MORRA (CN)
TEL. 017350190 - 017350604

This year, Giancarlo Bovio has added a new selection to his range of Barolos. It's called Rocchettevino, after a vineyard on the slope leading down from La Morra to Santa Maria. Let is be said that the cellar has chosen a great vintage, the '97, for this debut. This intensely fragrant wine offers aromatic notes of mint and thyme as well as blackcurrant and raspberry fruit. On the palate, the thrust is dynamic and elegant, the acidity and tannins complementing each other nicely. In contrast, the Barolo Arborina '97 is more sedate. Its aromas open gradually into fruit laced with tobacco and liquorice while the impressive, refreshing and deliciously tannic mouthfeel reveals attractively poised tannins. Austere and muscular, the Barolo Gattera '97 combines fruit aromas with truffle and a hint of autumn leaves. Liquorice and some minerally notes come through in the mouth and the palate foregrounds the tannins. Two Glasses went to the deep garnet Barbera Regiaveja '99, whose fruit-rich nose reveals gamey nuances and whose bright palate is slightly dry. The long finish is richly redolent of fruit and balsamic notes. The less exalted wines include a Langhe Freisa '00 from the Santa Lucia vineyard with frank, uncomplicated fruit and faint but clean aromas. Although the Dolcetto Dabbene lacks focus on the nose, the palate is firm and satisfying while the Barbera Il Ciotto is a no-nonsense wine with a nice touch of acidity in the finish. One Glass also went to the new Langhe Nebbiolo Annunziata for its soft, stylish palate. Moving on to the whites, we find one of the best Chardonnays in Piedmont, the Alessandra. Its golden yellow hue introduces buttery aromas over apples and pears, then a powerful, well-balanced palate.

•	Barolo Rocchettevino '97	YY	6
•	Barolo Vigna Arborina '97	YY	6
•	Barolo Vigna Gattera '97	YY	6
•	Barbera d'Alba Regiaveja '99	YY	5
○	Langhe Chardonnay Alessandra '00	YY	4
•	Barbera d'Alba Il Ciotto '00	Y	4
•	Langhe Freisa Santa Lucia '00	Y	4
•	Dolcetto d'Alba Dabbene '00	Y	3
•	Langhe Nebbiolo Annunziata '00	Y	4
•	Barolo Vigna Arborina '90	YYY	6
•	Barolo Vigna Arborina '95	YY	6
•	Barolo Vigna Arborina '96	YY	6
•	Barbera d'Alba Regiaveja '98	YY	5

LA MORRA (CN)

CASCINA BALLARIN
FRAZ. ANNUNZIATA, 115
12064 LA MORRA (CN)
TEL. 017350365
E-MAIL: cascina@cascinaballarin.it

Cascina Ballarin makes a triumphant entry into the Guide, thanks to the fine collection of wines that Luigi Viberti presented with the help of six hectares under vine and sons Giorgio and Gianni. The flagship selections have produced two impressive, heavyweight Barolos. The Bricco Rocca '97 is from a vineyard that lies only a stone's throw from the cellar. It is austere and dry in the mouth, with full ripe fruit and a long finish. In contrast, Bussia '97 has a concentrated and sweet, fruit-rich nose, attractively balanced structure and a lingering, delicious finish. It's a shame that only 1,500 bottles of the Bussia, and 3,000 of the Rocca, are released. Still, there is some consolation to be found in the 10,000 bottles of standard '97 Barolo. It is a blend of the preceding two selections whose most appealing characteristics are its austere aromas and substantial mouthfeel. Another wine the panel liked was the Barbera d'Alba Giuli '99, which comes from an old vineyard. Its complex nose, laced with sugared almonds and subtle oak-derived toastiness, precedes a fresh palate with a generous but stylish structure. Giorgio and Gianni also produce two Langhe DOC wines, the Ballarin Rosso and Ballarin Bianco. The '99 Rosso is a blend of nebbiolo, barbera and cabernet sauvignon with nicely concentrated fruit and aromas that lend elegance to the nose and substance in the mouth. The Bianco '00, from chardonnay, pinot nero and favorita, is a very pleasant surprise. The range is concluded by a Dolcetto d'Alba, which in the '00 version has impressive ripe fruit and a beefy structure.

•	Barolo Bricco Rocca '97	YY	6
•	Barolo Bussia '97	YY	6
•	Barbera d'Alba Giuli '99	YY	5
•	Dolcetto d'Alba Bussia '00	Y	4
○	Langhe Bianco Ballarin '00	Y	4
•	Barolo '97	Y	6
•	Langhe Rosso Ballarin '99	Y	5

LA MORRA (CN)

Giovanni Corino
Fraz. Annunziata, 24
12064 La Morra (CN)
Tel. 017350219 - 0173509452

LA MORRA (CN)

Silvio Grasso
Cascina Luciani, 112
Fraz. Annunziata
12064 La Morra (CN)
Tel. 017350322

For this edition of the Guide, brothers Renato and Giuliano Corino have added to the three family treasures another Barolo selection, the Vecchie Vigne '97. The total of 2,000 bottles and 158 magnums are obtained from a blend of small batches of nebbiolo from the three estate selections and its oldest vines. It's a Barolo that impressed the panel with its elegantly aromatic nose, where mint and thyme are prominent. The full-bodied, ripe fruit is well backed up by tangily fresh acidity and mellow tannins then the lingering finish is precisely what you would expect from a wine of breeding. Equally imposing is the Barolo Vigna Giachini '97, although it has a less complex nose and the tannins are a tad more aggressive. Still, this is a seriously good wine that will age in cellar for a very long time. The Barolo Vigneto Rocche '97 is elegant on the nose and decently balanced on the palate, where the sweetness of the fruit melds with the prominent tannic weave. The Barolo Vigneto Arborina '97 is still a little closed on the nose but the palate has good fresh fruit and attractive acidity. Next, the standard-label Barolo '97 has less body but is still nicely balanced and generous with its mineral notes on the nose. In total, the Corino cellar released 27,000 bottles of '97 Barolo. The Barbera d'Alba Pozzo is excellent, and brings to mind some of its finest versions. Its intense ruby hue releases hints of blackcurrant and morello cherry over notes of balsam. Potent and juicy on the palate, it can also point to a lingering finish. Finally, the standard-label Barbera and Dolcetto d'Alba were worth One Glass each.

If you taste Silvio Grasso's Barolo in their first year, as we do for the Guide, you will note that they have very marked, ripe fruit that hints at the fragrances and aromas that will develop during the leisurely ageing process in your cellar. There can be no doubt that the Barolo Bricco Luciani '97 will present an admirable complexity on the nose and palate in the future. The bouquet of red roses, blackcurrant and bramble allows hints of liquorice and liqueur cherries to come through. On the palate, the balance of acidity, tannins and alcohol is remarkable, making the mouthfeel full, warm and caressing and taking you through to the long finish. The Barolo Ciabot Manzoni '97 has a rather different nose of violets, aromatic herbs and vanillaed oak. Liquorice, albeit less intense, comes back in the finish. But in the mouth, the Ciabot Manzoni shows all its class, with dryish, fairly prominent tannins. A welter of different aromas, ranging from sugared almonds to cassis and spices, emerges on the nicely concentrated and reasonably long nose of the Barolo '97. The mouthfeel is firm and jammy, thanks to the notes of plum jam and slowly stewed cherries. As ever, the Barbera d'Alba Fontanile is excellent, showing admirable finesse and balance. Almost impenetrable in the glass, it offers equally concentrated, close-knit aromas with notes of blackcurrant and toasty oak. The broad, succulent palate marries power and finesse perfectly. And to round off, the L'Insieme (lotto 1.9.98) has good breadth and structure, although the alcohol emerges a little too strongly in the finish.

● Barolo Vecchie Vigne '97	♀	6
● Barolo Vigna Giachini '97	♀♀	6
● Barolo Vigneto Arborina '97	♀♀	6
● Barolo Vigneto Rocche '97	♀♀	6
● Barbera d'Alba Pozzo '99	♀♀	5
● Barbera d'Alba '00	♀	4
● Dolcetto d'Alba '00	♀	3
● Barolo '97	♀	6
● Barolo Vigna Giachini '89	♀♀♀	6
● Barolo Rocche '90	♀♀♀	6
● Barbera d'Alba Vigna Pozzo '96	♀♀♀	5
● Barbera d'Alba Vigna Pozzo '97	♀♀♀	5
● Barolo Vigna Giachini '96	♀♀	6
● Barolo Vigneto Rocche '96	♀♀	6
● Barbera d'Alba Pozzo '98	♀♀	5

● Barolo Bricco Luciani '97	♀♀	6
● Barolo '97	♀♀	6
● Barolo Ciabot Manzoni '97	♀♀	6
● Barbera d'Alba Fontanile '99	♀♀	5
● L'Insieme	♀♀	6
● Barolo Bricco Luciani '90	♀♀♀	5
● Barolo Bricco Luciani '95	♀♀♀	6
● Barolo Bricco Luciani '96	♀♀♀	6
● Barolo Ciabot Manzoni '95	♀♀	6
● Barolo Ciabot Manzoni '96	♀♀	6
● Barbera d'Alba Fontanile '98	♀♀	5

LA MORRA (CN)

Poderi Marcarini
P.zza Martiri, 2
12064 La Morra (CN)
tel. 017350222
e-mail: marcarini@marcarini.it

Luisa Bava and her husband Manuel Marchetti make two great Barolo selections which again this year have the nobility, as well as the hint of austerity, that has always been the hallmark of the estate's wines. The Barolo La Serra '97 has an elegant colour and an equally stylish bouquet, where flower and fruit notes dominate. The solid structure and juicy, ripe fruit combine in the mouth with attractively intense acidity that lends freshness to the palate. The Barolo Brunate is more austere and opens out more slowly but in the end wins out over its excellent stablemate. The fruit for this selection comes from one of Barolo's most prestigious crus and the wine behaves accordingly. The garnet hue has a faint orangey rim then the aromas, which open on notes of fruit, develop into more varietal hints of tobacco and liquorice. The palate is sheer Barolo, the sweet, fine-grained tannins backing up the serious structure. Next, the Barbera Ciabot Camerano has a deep colour and an impressive nose. Redcurrant and rain-soaked earth mingle with chocolate, apples and pears. The structure is full-bodied, with a marked note of acidity. Then we sampled the excellent Dolcetto Boschi di Berri. Although very young, its potential is obvious in the breadth and tannins of the palate, and in the finish enhanced by hints of bitter almonds. Finally, One Glass went to the Langhe Nebbiolo Lasarin '00. Its nose of cassis and caramel-covered fruit ushers in a soft front palate then dry tannins that emerge in mid palate.

Wine	Rating	Score
● Barolo Brunate '97	ŸŸ	6
● Barbera d'Alba Ciabot Camerano '00	ŸŸ	4
● Dolcetto d'Alba Boschi di Berri '00	ŸŸ	5
● Barolo La Serra '97	ŸŸ	6
● Langhe Nebbiolo Lasarin '00	Ÿ	4
● Barolo Brunate Ris. '85	ŸŸŸ	6
● Dolcetto d'Alba Boschi di Berri '96	ŸŸŸ	5
● Barolo La Serra '95	ŸŸ	6
● Barolo Brunate '96	ŸŸ	6
● Barolo La Serra '96	ŸŸ	6
● Barolo Brunate '95	Ÿ	6

LA MORRA (CN)

Mario Marengo
Via XX Settembre, 32
12064 La Morra (CN)
tel. 017350127 - 017350115

Sadly, Mario Marengo passed away during the winter. His son Marco has now taken over. As we were able to confirm at the tastings, the philosophy of the small cellar in the centre of La Morra remains unchanged, although expansion is planned for the future. As we wait for work to begin, we can savour a newcomer, the Barolo Bricco Viole '97, of which only 1,500 bottles were released. It comes from a tiny cru in Barolo itself and has the classic varietal orange-flecked ruby colour. The full, spicy nose has clear notes of liqueur cherries then the stylish, refreshing palate offers ripe, sweet fruit, as well as well-balanced tannins and acidity. The 7,000 bottles of Barolo Brunate '97 confirm its status as the Marengo estate's flagship wine. Still rather closed on the nose, where herbaceous notes come through, it has robust aromas and texture in the mouth, with ripe, velvet-soft fruit redolent of bramble, plum jam and cherry preserve. We will have to wait until the '00 Nebbiolo d'Alba Valmaggiore ages in small oak barrels before its first release but in the meantime there is a temptingly even Langhe Nebbiolo '99, albeit with a slight lack of definition on the nose

Wine	Rating	Score
● Barolo Bricco Viole '97	ŸŸ	6
● Barolo Brunate '97	ŸŸ	6
● Langhe Nebbiolo '99		4
● Barolo Brunate '95	ŸŸ	6
● Barolo Brunate '96	ŸŸ	6

LA MORRA (CN)

Mauro Molino
B.ta Gancia, 111
Fraz. Annunziata
12064 La Morra (CN)
tel. 017350814

Work has been completed on the new cellar that surrounds the ancient farmhouse at Gancia, in Annunziata at La Morra and Mauro Molino has confirmed his status as a great maker of Barolos. All three of his '97 Barolos met with the panel's approval, especially the estate's vineyard selections, Conca, just below the monastery of San Martino di Marcenasco, and Gancia, near the cellar. The Barolo Vigna Conca '97, a dark ruby wine with lustrous orangey highlights, has intense, delicately lingering aromas of roses and minty aromatic herbs, as well as redcurrant fruit. The entry on the palate is dry, then the lively mid palate offers an attractive balance of acidity and tannins, with round, ripe fruit and exceptional length that concludes with a sumptuous yet restrained finish. This is an outstanding performance by a winemaker who knows exactly what to do with the superb fruit yielded by this vineyard: Three very elegant Glasses. The stylish Barolo Vigna Gancia '97 is another serious wine that releases its complex aromas a little at a time, like the classic wine it is. Wild roses come through at first to make way for bramble fruit. The standard Barolo '97 has a fine range of crisp, lingering aromas with strawberry to the fore. It may have a tad less structure than its big brothers but the palate is fresh-tasting and generous with its fruit. As always, the Barbera Gattere is marvellous, showing good depth of fragrant and very refreshing fruit. Acanzio, a blend of nebbiolo, barbera and cabernet sauvignon, is complex on the palate and concentrated on the nose. L'Insieme (lotto 1.9.98.), obtained from nebbiolo, barbera, cabernet sauvignon and merlot, has a vibrant, powerful structure and finally the Chardonnay Livrot '00 tempts the nostrils with citrus and tropical fruit.

● Barolo Vigna Conca '97	▼▼▼	6
● Barolo Vigna Gancia '97	▼▼	6
● Barolo '97	▼▼	6
● Barbera d'Alba Vigna Gattere '99	▼▼	5
○ Langhe Chardonnay Livrot '00	▼▼	4
● Langhe Rosso Acanzio '99	▼▼	5
● L'Insieme	▼▼	6
● Barbera d'Alba Vigna Gattere '96	▼▼▼	5
● Barolo Vigna Conca '96	▼▼▼	6
● Barbera d'Alba Vigna Gattere '97	▼▼▼	5
● Barolo Vigna Gancia '95	▼▼	6
● Barolo Vigna Gancia '96	▼▼	6
● Langhe Rosso Acanzio '97	▼▼	5
● Langhe Rosso Acanzio '98	▼▼	5

LA MORRA (CN)

Monfalletto - Cordero di Montezemolo
Fraz. Annunziata, 67/Bis
12064 La Morra (CN)
tel. 017350344
e-mail:
monfalletto@corderodimontezemolo.com

There's always something going on at Gianni and Enrico Cordero's winery. It looked as if they had enough space but then they found they had to extend the barrel cellar. Their most exciting '97 Barolo, which for the second year running has earned itself Three Glasses, is a superb version of the Enrico VI. It throws a rich nose of liquorice, mint and ripe fruit, following this with a sweet, muscular palate well-sustained by attractive acidity and firm, juicy tannins. We can only congratulate the Corderos, who have in recent vintages achieved stupendous results all through the range. The better of the other two Barolos is the Bricco Gattera, from the vineyard that nestles under the winery's huge, stately cedar tree. Its delicately balsamic aromas join with classic Barolo violets and the follow-through on the palate is nicely balanced, offering a juicy mouthfeel and a finish that bespeaks the warm weather enjoyed in '97. The nose of the Barolo Monfalletto has the typical minty notes of its subzone, which mingle with hay and violet. Soft tannins and powerful alcohol come through on the attractively firm palate. The full body of the Barbera '99 is backed up by well-judged acidity. Its intense aromas of plum and strawberry usher in a deliciously quaffable palate. Meanwhile, the '99 Barbera Funtanì continues to age in the cellar. Our initial tastings indicate that this will be a wine to remember. The Curdè '99 is a blend for its pinot nero base has been joined by all the estate's other red grapes. Both the '00 Nebbiolo and the Dolcetto are very decent while the fragrant, acacia blossom Arneis is more than just well-made. The Chardonnay, barrique-aged for 12 months, is not bad.

● Barolo Enrico VI '97	▼▼▼	6
● Barolo Monfalletto '97	▼▼	6
● Barolo Vigna Bricco Gattera '97	▼▼	6
● Barbera d'Alba '99	▼▼	4
● Dolcetto d'Alba '00	▼	3
○ Langhe Arneis '00	▼	3
○ Langhe Chardonnay Elioro '99	▼	4
● Langhe Nebbiolo '00	▼	4
● Langhe Rosso Curdè '99	▼	5
● Barolo Enrico VI '96	▼▼▼	6
● Barolo Enrico VI '93	▼▼	6
● Barolo Monfalletto '93	▼▼	6
● Barolo Enrico VI '95	▼▼	6
● Barolo Monfalletto '95	▼▼	6
● Barolo Monfalletto '96	▼▼	6

LA MORRA (CN)

Andrea Oberto
Via G. Marconi, 25
12064 La Morra (CN)
tel. 0173509262

Andrea Oberto had an excellent Barolo Rocche waiting for us this year. What impressed the panel was its austere elegance and measured finesse, both the result of Andrea's decisions on how to handle the '97 vintage. Its dark garnet ruby hue introduces an impeccable nose then a dry, fresh-tasting palate. Tannins and acidity live together in harmony while the full, sweet flavour is laced with black cherries and bramble. The Barolo Albarella '97 is less shy on the nose, its fairly ripe fruit showing good complexity. In the mouth, it is soft and velvety, with nice sweet tannins. The Barolo '97 is a different proposition. Its intense aromas on the nose are less pronounced than those of its two stablemates but on the palate, it shows just how good it is: concentrated fruit, serious tannins and fresh acidity combine to convince. The '99 version of the ever attractive Barbera d'Alba Giada has a gracefully subtle nose, albeit a shade closed this early in its career. The chewy fruit is reminiscent of morello cherry and redcurrant preserve while there is a hint of spice in the finish. In the nebbiolo and barbera Fabio '99, it is the nebbiolo that comes out on top, lending the wine a dry, elegant style with its well-gauged tannins. Expertly made and well-balanced on the palate, it has raspberry and cherry as its main aromatic themes. Andrea started his line-up of '00 wines with three fine Dolcettos. The two vineyard selections are excellent, the San Francesco coming out ahead on points over the slightly less powerful Vantrino Albarella. Finally, the standard-label Dolcetto is pleasant and nicely extracted.

● Barolo Vigneto Rocche '97	ŸŸ	6
● Dolcetto d'Alba '00	ŸŸ	3*
● Dolcetto d'Alba Vigneto S. Francesco '00	ŸŸ	4
● Dolcetto d'Alba Vigneto Vantrino Albarella '00	ŸŸ	4
● Barolo '97	ŸŸ	6
● Barolo Albarella '97	ŸŸ	6
● Barbera d'Alba Giada '99	ŸŸ	5
● Langhe Fabio '99	ŸŸ	5
● Barbera d'Alba Giada '96	ŸŸŸ	6
● Barolo Vigneto Rocche '96	ŸŸŸ	6
● Barbera d'Alba Giada '97	ŸŸŸ	6
● Barolo Vigneto Rocche '95	ŸŸ	6
● Barbera d'Alba Giada '98	ŸŸ	5

LA MORRA (CN)

F.lli Oddero
Fraz. Santa Maria, 28
12064 La Morra (CN)
tel. 017350618
e-mail: info@odderofratelli.it

The Odderos have been making wine since 1878 and in over a century of activity at La Morra, they have built up a remarkable estate. The family owns vineyards in four municipalities, all in the Barolo DOCG zone, at Santa Maria di La Morra, where the cellar is located, at Monforte d'Alba, Castiglione Falletto and Serralunga d'Alba. The estate selections are the names that have written the history of Barolo: Vigna Rionda and Collareto at Serralunga; Mondoca di Bussia Soprana and Rocche di Bussia at Monforte; Rocche dei Rivera, Villero, Fiasco, Brunella and Bricco Boschetto at Castiglione Falletto; and Le Rive, Brunate and Bricco Chiesa at La Morra. There are 65 hectares all told, 35 planted to nebbiolo, and annual production of Barolo runs to 150,000 bottles. If we bear in mind that properties in the area are generally almost microscopic, these numbers are striking. Equally striking was the range of Barolos the panel tasted for the new edition of the Guide. Head and shoulders above the rest was the Mondoca di Bussia Soprana, from a southwest-facing vineyard at Bussia, Its vibrant, concentrated colour is followed by aromas of spice and ripe fruit that marry nicely with the oak. The fullness of the quite superbly concentrated, lavishly extracted palate never threatens the overall elegance of this stunning wine. Three Glasses for this great Barolo. Close behind came the Vigna Rionda which, like the Mondoca, contains a small proportion of barrique-aged wine. On the nose, the excellent Rocche di Castiglione opens with liquorice and dried flowers then the powerful, stiff palate reveals rather harsh tannins that emerge on the back palate. The Rocche dei Rivera, again from a Castiglione selection, is also a fine wine.

● Barolo Mondoca di Bussia Soprana '97	ŸŸŸ	6
● Barolo Rocche dei Rivera di Castiglione '97	ŸŸ	6
● Barolo Rocche di Castiglione '97	ŸŸ	6
● Barolo Vigna Rionda '97	ŸŸ	6
● Barolo '97	Ÿ	6
● Dolcetto d'Alba '00		3
● Barolo Vigna Rionda '89	ŸŸŸ	6
● Barolo Vigna Rionda '93	ŸŸ	6
● Barolo Vigna Rionda '95	ŸŸ	6
● Barolo Vigna Rionda '96	ŸŸ	6
● Langhe Furesté '97	ŸŸ	4
● Langhe Furesté '98	ŸŸ	4

LA MORRA (CN)

Renato Ratti
Fraz. Annunziata, 7
12064 La Morra (CN)
tel. 017350185

The Rattis are continuing the reorganization of the family winery. Bought-in fruit now accounts for only 20 per cent of total production. The 27 hectares the Rattis have yield seriously good Barolos, Barberas and Dolcettos while a further eight hectares at Villa Pattono in Costigliole d'Asti produce their Monferrato Rosso blend. Pietro Ratti manages the vineyards with the help of consultant Federico Curtaz, and Massimo Martinelli and Federico Oberto keep things going in the cellar. The most exciting Ratti wine this time is the Barolo Rocche Marcenasco '97. Its bright ruby hue shades into orange and the harmonious nose has notes of roses, ripe fruit and aromatic herbs. The palate has lovely texture and a nice balance of cherry and plum jam, with a hint of bramble in the finish. The Barolo Mercenasco '97, of which the cellar made 40,000 bottles, is more sedate yet warm in its fruit-rich, and faintly spicy, aromas. The lean, powerful body keeps the tannins on a tight rein. There was no '97 version of the Barolo Conca. On the nose, the Barbera d'Alba Torriglione '99 has elegant nuances of sugared almonds but the palate is less persuasive. Refreshing acidity combines with a soft body, and the raspberry and redcurrant fruit is very forward. The rather less convincing Dolcetto Colombè '00 fell down a little on the nose. The Monferrato Rosso Villa Pattono '99, from 60 per cent barbera with cabernet sauvignon and merlot, has a dark colour and varietal aromas, with vibrant blackcurrant fruit. Warm on the palate, it takes you through to a pleasing finish. The Nebbiolo d'Alba Ochetti has crisply elegant aromas on nose and palate.

- Barolo Rocche Marcenasco '97 ♀♀ 6
- Barolo Marcenasco '97 ♀♀ 6
- Barbera d'Alba Torriglione '99 ♀♀ 4
- Monferrato Villa Pattono '99 ♀♀ 5
- Nebbiolo d'Alba Ochetti '99 ♀♀ 5
- Dolcetto d'Alba Colombè '00 ♀ 4
- Barolo Rocche Marcenasco '83 ♀♀♀ 6
- Barolo Rocche Marcenasco '84 ♀♀♀ 6
- Barolo Rocche Marcenasco '96 ♀♀ 6
- Monferrato Villa Pattono '98 ♀♀ 5

LA MORRA (CN)

F.lli Revello
Fraz. Annunziata, 103
12064 La Morra (CN)
tel. 017350276

The Revellis now have nine hectares under vine, as well as a lovely "agriturismo", or farm holiday centre that Carlo looks after. Brother Enzo spends much of his time in the cellar, where he can rely on the advice of consultant Beppe Caviola. This year's impressive range includes a marvellous quartet of Barolos. The panel was spoilt for choice but in the end plumped for the '97 Rocche dell'Annunziata, which stormed home with a Three Glass score, barely a neck ahead of a great Barolo Vigna Conca from the same vintage. The winner has a rather concentrated garnet hue with the narrowest of rims. On the nose, it opens gradually with a delicious range of aromas, including wild berries, coffee and vanilla, over minerally hints of earth. Right from entry, the palate is firm and very broad. Underpinned by the well-judged tannins, it follows through faultlessly to the wonderful finish, where a flower and fruit theme emerges in the lingering after-aroma. The Barolo Vigna Conca manages to embody all the nobility of its august cru. The results are excellent and the wine has elegance and finesse. The other selection, the Giachini, and the standard-label Barolo were not far behind. L'Insieme (lotto 1.9.98.) is a wine of breeding. The nose releases notes of jam and mint over intriguing gamey and minerally nuances. The thrust on the palate is full-bodied and rich, showing lots of vigour and determination. We were fascinated by the earthy notes in the fruit of the Barbera Ciabot du Re. And to round things off, there were the creamy, morello cherry notes of the Dolcetto and the fruit and spice of the standard-label Barbera. Very well done.

- Barolo Rocche dell'Annunziata '97 ♀♀♀ 6
- Barolo Vigna Conca '97 ♀♀ 6
- Barbera d'Alba '00 ♀♀ 4
- Dolcetto d'Alba '00 ♀♀ 4
- Barolo '97 ♀♀ 6
- Barolo Vigna Giachini '97 ♀♀ 6
- Barbera d'Alba Ciabot du Re '99 ♀♀ 5
- L'Insieme ♀♀ 6
- Barolo '93 ♀♀♀ 6
- Barolo Rocche dell'Annunziata '96 ♀♀ 6
- Barolo Vigna Giachini '96 ♀♀ 6
- Barbera d'Alba Ciabot du Re '98 ♀♀ 5

LA MORRA (CN)

ROCCHE COSTAMAGNA
VIA VITTORIO EMANUELE, 8
12064 LA MORRA (CN)
TEL. 0173509225
E-MAIL: barolo@racchecostamagna.it

Rocche Costamagna's vineyards are in one of the most prestigious crus in the DOC zone, on the hillslope that leads down from La Morra to Annunziata. The estate takes its name from the former proprietors, who are related to the current owners. Alessandro Locatelli manages both the vineyards and the cellar, which is situated on the way into the village. This year, the Bricco Francesco vineyard in the Rocche dell'Annunziata has produced a wonderful, bright garnet Barolo with elegant, docile aromas redolent of dried roses and fresh-squeezed fruit. The structure on the palate may still be youthful but it will develop a measured austerity, thanks to the fairly prominent acidity and tannins. The other estate Barolo, the Rocche dell'Annunziata '97, has more evolved aromas and riper fruit. Black cherries, strawberries and bramble are evident in the soft, gentle body. We shall now move on to the Barbera d'Alba Rocche delle Rocche '99. A dark, intense ruby in the glass, it reveals great depth and nobility of structure. Aromas of vanilla and coffee-flavoured sugared almonds fail to mask the wood, which will mellow with the passage of time. Velvet-smooth and full-bodied, the palate is redolent of black cherry syrup and has a long, sweet finish. The panel also liked the Langhe Chardonnay Flavo '00 for its clean, concentrated aromas and vigorous citrus fruit. Last on the list was the interesting Dolcetto d'Alba Rubis '00, which has a fresh, upfront nose and good firmness on the palate.

● Barolo Bricco Francesco Rocche dell'Annunziata '97	♟♟	6
● Barolo Rocche dell'Annunziata '97	♟♟	6
● Barbera d'Alba Rocche delle Rocche '99	♟♟	4
● Dolcetto d'Alba Rubis '00	♟	3
○ Langhe Chardonnay Flavo '00	♟	4

LA MORRA (CN)

MAURO VEGLIO
FRAZ. ANNUNZIATA, 50
12064 LA MORRA (CN)
TEL. 0173509212
E-MAIL: mauro.veglio@libero.it

Mauro Veglio and his wife Daniela run a winery that aims consistently for quality. There are ten hectares of vineyards, almost all at La Morra. This year's wines included there ever reliable range of Barolos, starting with the Rocche. Its intense garnet hue has a narrow, firm rim. The generous and very distinctive nose reveals clear and remarkably varied notes of wild berries nuanced with mint, autumn leaves and chlorophyll. The palate is full-bodied, the powerful and almost aggressive tannins kept firmly in place by the alcohol. The Gattera is less concentrated, its aromas ranging from berry fruit to menthol, with hints of leather, earth and confectioner's cream. There is nice balance in the mouth, where the tannins are well-gauged and the finish full. In contrast, the Arborina has a slightly evolved nose but drinks very elegantly. The finish mirrors the nose and lingers attractively. The Castelletto comes from the vineyard of the same name at Monforte. Berry fruit, cocoa and spices emerge on the nose while the thrust on the palate is well-sustained. Faintly austere in personality, it yields notes of liquorice and menthol in the after-aroma. L'Insieme (lotto 1.9.98.) has good fruit and a very satisfying palate with plenty of breadth and depth. But the top of the range this time was the stunning Barbera Cascina Nuova. Yet again, it carried off Three Glasses, proving that Mauro Veglio's territory is a superb place to grow the variety. It's a selection that exploits the huge potential of its vintage to the limit. Dense and effortlessly stylish, it allows long, sweet notes of oak to emerge and lift its magnificent palate. And to round off, there was the excellent standard-label Barbera and a pleasing Dolcetto d'Alba '00.

● Barbera d'Alba Cascina Nuova '99	♟♟♟	5
● Barolo Vigneto Rocche '97	♟♟	6
● Barbera d'Alba '00	♟♟	4
● Barolo Arborina '97	♟♟	6
● Barolo Castelletto '97	♟♟	6
● Barolo Gattera '97	♟♟	6
● L'Insieme	♟♟	6
● Dolcetto d'Alba '00	♟	4
● Barbera d'Alba Cascina Nuova '96	♟♟♟	5
● Barolo Vigneto Rocche '96	♟♟♟	6
● Barolo Gattera '95	♟♟	6
● Barolo Arborina '96	♟♟	6
● Barolo Castelletto '96	♟♟	6
● Barolo Gattera '96	♟♟	6
● Barbera d'Alba Cascina Nuova '98	♟♟	5

LA MORRA (CN)

Eraldo Viberti
Fraz. Santa Maria
B.ta Tetti dei Turchi, 53
12064 La Morra (CN)
tel. 017350308

Our review of the Viberti winery this year kicks off with the Barolo '97, the cellar's most complex product and one that also stands out for its approachable warmth and elegance. Eraldo Viberti Barolo has an almost menacingly dark, orange-flecked garnet colour. Its aromas take time to open out into notes of vanilla and wild berries then the juicy palate offers delicious softness with hints of strawberry and black cherry. In the mouth, medium acidity finds a nice point of equilibrium with skilfully masked tannins, giving the wine a velvet-smooth mouthfeel and good roundness. The finish is very long. The panel awarded Two full Glasses. As usual, the Barbera d'Alba Vigna Clara is a good wine that behaves well and can offer rich, fresh-tasting fruit. Its wide range of aromas goes from roses to morello cherry and the robust texture on the palate has decent acidity. Notes of blackcurrant, raspberry and bramble prevail in the mouth. In the sweet finish, there is a faint hint of almonds. Newcomers to the Viberti list include the Gilat '99, a barbera and nebbiolo blend with a small proportion of cabernet sauvignon. This red "vino da tavola" with a spicy finish won the panel over with its bright ruby colour, upfront yet complex nose and soft, full-bodied palate that nicely complements its acidity with cassis fruit.

LA MORRA (CN)

Gianni Voerzio
Strada Loreto, 1
12064 La Morra (CN)
tel. 0173509194

Gianni Voerzio's Barolo La Serra is a wine with plenty of personality. Its charms derive from the rich, substantial fruit that goes into it and the impeccable technique with which it is made. The '97 vintage has a concentrated garnet colour with a youthful rim. Broad and generous on the nose, it unveils notes of wild berries, plum and Peruvian bark over complex minerally nuances. It has good weight on the palate right from entry, with a well-sustained follow-through that takes you to a long finish redolent of flowers and liquorice. It is a very fine interpretation of the vintage that allows Gianni to repeat his Three Glass success with the previous year's wine. Excellent, too, was the Barbera Ciabot della Luna. Its intense hue ushers in notes of black berry fruit, tar, autumn leaves and violets that come together delightfully in a nose laced with hints of new-mown grass. Fullness, power and remarkable length characterize the palate. Next came the full-flavoured Serrapiù, a nebbiolo and barbera blend whose '99 version throws a nose of fruit and liquorice. The Dolcetto Rocchettevino has an impenetrably close-knit colour and a varietal nose of great finesse and complexity. Its hints of black berry fruit and mint are followed up by delightfully unexpected nuances of mushrooms and hazelnut. The palate is equally satisfying, with breadth, vigour and complexity that are rounded off by a very long finish. There are metallic notes over the fruit in the nose of the Nebbiolo Ciabot della Luna, which goes on to offer a full-bodied, dry palate. Finally, the Arneis Bricco Cappellina '00 is well-made if a tad one-dimensional.

● Barolo '97	🍷🍷	6
● Barbera d'Alba Vigna Clara '98	🍷🍷	5
● Gilat Rosso '99	🍷🍷	5
● Barolo '93	🍷🍷🍷	6
● Barolo '94	🍷🍷	6
● Barolo '95	🍷🍷	6
● Barbera d'Alba Vigna Clara '96	🍷🍷	5
● Barolo '96	🍷🍷	6
● Barbera d'Alba Vigna Clara '97	🍷🍷	5

● Barolo La Serra '97	🍷🍷🍷	6
● Dolcetto d'Alba Rocchettevino '00	🍷🍷	4
● Barbera d'Alba Ciabot della Luna '99	🍷🍷	5
● Langhe Rosso Serrapiù '99	🍷🍷	5
○ Roero Arneis Bricco Cappellina '00	🍷	4
● Langhe Nebbiolo Ciabot della Luna '99	🍷	4
● Barolo La Serra '96	🍷🍷🍷	6
● Barolo La Serra '95	🍷🍷	6
● Langhe Rosso Serrapiù '97	🍷🍷	5
● Barbera d'Alba Ciabot della Luna '98	🍷🍷	5
● Langhe Rosso Serrapiù '98	🍷🍷	5

LA MORRA (CN)

★ Roberto Voerzio
Loc. Cerreto, 1
12064 La Morra (CN)
tel. 0173509196

Roberto Voerzio has a precise, modern style that highlights both variety and terroir. His '97 Barolos, for example, are a textbook exposition of the characteristics you would expect from each of their three crus. The Brunate is balanced and full-bodied, the Cerequio is austere and complex while the La Serra is a broader, more stately wine. All bear the mark of this master winemaker who can combine power with elegance astonishingly well. The Barolo Brunate has a tight-knit garnet colour with a narrow, compact rim. Its nose balances plum and bramble fruit in a frame of spices, eucalyptus and toastiness. The attack on the palate is full and robust extract backs up the progression on the palate through to the triumphantly long finish, where liquorice and violets call the tune. The Cerequio is equally concentrated in colour, offering intriguing notes of tar and autumn leaves over black berry jam, spices and tea biscuits. The succulence of the flesh in the mouth is matched by the vigour of the tannins, which dry out the lingering finish. There is good nose-palate consistency. Ripe and broad on the nose, the La Serra unfurls notes of black berry fruit, hay, almonds and autumn leaves, laced with unusual hints of Mediterranean herbs. It has massive texture on the broadish palate, the tannins are firm but not aggressive and the finish, with its notes of fruit and liquorice, has lots of vigour. Roberto's two superwines, released on in magnums, are convincing enough but not world-beaters. His Barolo Capalot e Brunate is stiff and powerful while the Barbera lacks elegance because of the sheer concentration of the extract. The nebbiolo and barbera Vignaserra is good and bringing up the rear is a pleasant Dolcetto.

Wine	Rating	Score
● Barolo Brunate '97	♈♈	6
● Barolo Cerequio '97	♈♈	6
● Barolo La Serra '97	♈♈	6
● Barolo Vecchie Viti dei Capalot e delle Brunate Ris. '96	♈♈	6
● Barbera d'Alba Vigneto Pozzo dell'Annunziata Ris. '98	♈♈	6
● Langhe Rosso Vignaserra '99	♈♈	6
● Dolcetto d'Alba La Pria '00	♈	4
● Barolo Cerequio '90	♈♈♈	6
● Barolo Brunate '93	♈♈♈	6
● Barbera d'Alba Vigneto Pozzo dell'Annunziata Ris. '96	♈♈♈	6
● Barolo Brunate '96	♈♈♈	6
● Barolo Cerequio '96	♈♈♈	6

LESSONA (BI)

Sella
Via IV Novembre, 110
13853 Lessona (BI)
tel. 01599455

It has been a few months since the death of Fabrizio Sella, the able and much respected head of this historic Piedmont family. The baton has now passed to his son Gioacchino while Pietro Marocchino stays in charge of winemaking, with the assistance of consultant Giancarlo Scaglione. All the wines share a distinctive Sella style, which emerges in the aromas and a warm, velvety mouthfeel. The San Sebastiano allo Zoppo is the estate's flagship bottle. The dark ruby hue precedes intriguing, close-knit aromas of black berry fruit over vanilla and spice. On the elegant, well-balanced palate, the concentrated fruit is presented over a backdrop of fine-grained tannins before oak-derived vanilla comes through again in the broad, velvet-smooth finish. Two Glasses also went to the deep ruby Lessona '97 whose deep, complex aromas foreground ripe black berry fruit and elegant spice. On the warm, mouthfilling palate, there is nice structure and a seamless progression. The Orbello, a 75-25 blend of barbera and cabernet, has an attractive nose where the cabernet's hallmark red pepper takes centre stage. Then it caresses the palate with soft but not cloying fruit. The Bramaterra combines a harmonious palate with aromas of autumn leaves, crushed roses and pepper. And to round off, the Piccone, a blend of 50 per cent nebbiolo with various local varieties, is a bright and jolly quaffing wine while the erbaluce-based La Doranda is subtle and tangy.

Wine	Rating	Score
● Lessona '97	♈♈	5
● Lessona S. Sebastiano allo Zoppo '97	♈♈	5
○ Coste della Sesia Bianco La Doranda '00	♈	4
● Bramaterra '97	♈	5
● Coste della Sesia Rosso Orbello '99	♈	3
● Coste della Sesia Rosso Piccone '99	♈	3
● Lessona Il Chioso '95	♈♈	5
● Lessona S. Sebastiano allo Zoppo '95	♈♈	5
● Lessona Il Chioso '96	♈♈	5

LOAZZOLO (AT)

BORGO MARAGLIANO
REG. SAN SEBASTIANO, 2
14050 LOAZZOLO (AT)
TEL. 014487132
E-MAIL: maragliano@inwind.it

Giuseppe and Carlo Galliano's winery vaunts a selection of products both traditional and modern, offering the consumer a full and comprehensive range of excellent wines. Their Loazzolo Vendemmia Tardiva '98, the vintage which best embodies the estate's strong territorial identity, is a lovely limpid gold with notes of confectioner's icing, peaches in syrup and almonds, set in a wonderfully intense framework. It opens out sweet and full-bodied on the palate, following through rich and solid into a lingering finish with undertones of dried fruit. The estate's two spumantes, the Giuseppe Galliano Brut '97 and the Giuseppe Galliano Chardonnay Brut, are both very good. The first, a "metodo classico", has a rich straw-yellow colour and an interesting nose suggesting tropical fruit and yeast, layered over a vegetal base. In the mouth, its sound structure and discreet, complex effervescence make it an immensely gratifying wine, nicely rounded off by fresh grapefruit. The Giuseppe Galliano Chardonnay Brut is a cuve close spumante that releases aromas of confectioner's cream, apples, pears and lemon. Harmonious and well structured, it has a pleasant fruity, citrussy finish. The subtle, coherent Moscato La Caliera is refreshing and not overly challenging on the palate, while the sweet El Calié is richer, with rather mature aromas and a weighty palate. The Chardonnay Marajan is redolent of tropical fruit and acacia blossom while the Chardonnay Crevoglio is less complex.

LOAZZOLO (AT)

FORTETO DELLA LUJA
REG. BRICCO CASA ROSSO, 4
14050 LOAZZOLO (AT)
TEL. 0141831596

Giancarlo Scaglione and his children, Gianni and Silvia, produce a Piasa Rischei with a relentless consistency that only the greatest of wines can boast. Every year, this Moscato becomes is a benchmark not only for Italian sweet wines but for dessert wines everywhere. The '98 vintage is deep gold with amber highlights. The complex, alluring nose offers up clear, intense but never obtrusive notes of confectioner's icing, raisins, vanilla cream and walnut over fascinating hints of super-ripeness. The palate opens out with a dense richness in a solid, powerful progression that leads to a lingering, beautifully coherent finish that leaves the mouth wonderfully clean. The estate's Brachetto Passito Pian dei Sogni '99 is a slightly transparent ruby red with a very agreeable nose of exquisite finesse. The bouquet harmoniously blends aromas of dried roses, small red berry fruit jam, spices and rhubarb then the complex, lively palate reveals a delightful sweet vein. Its great finish clearly echoes the aromas, notably the floral tones. The Rosso Le Grive '99, a barbera and pinot nero blend, has a fairly intense garnet-ruby colour and a nose that bursts with character, hinting at wild berry jam, mulberry blossom and leather, with barely discernible undertones of wood smoke. Its somewhat austere, well-contained palate boasts a long finish tinged with cocoa powder.

○	Giuseppe Galliano Brut M. Cl. '97	ΨΨ	5
○	Loazzolo Borgo Maragliano V. T. '98	ΨΨ	5
○	El Calié Moscato '00	Ψ	3
○	Moscato d'Asti La Caliera '00	Ψ	3
○	Piemonte Chardonnay Marajan '99	Ψ	4
○	Giuseppe Galliano Chardonnay Brut	Ψ	3
○	Piemonte Chardonnay Crevoglio '00		3
○	Loazzolo Borgo Maragliano V. T. '97	ΨΨ	5

○	Loazzolo Piasa Rischei '98	ΨΨ	6
●	Monferrato Rosso Le Grive '99	ΨΨ	5
●	Piemonte Brachetto Forteto Pian dei Sogni '99	ΨΨ	6
○	Loazzolo Piasa Rischei '93	ΨΨΨ	6
○	Loazzolo Piasa Rischei '94	ΨΨΨ	6
○	Loazzolo Piasa Rischei '95	ΨΨΨ	6
○	Loazzolo Piasa Rischei '96	ΨΨΨ	6
○	Loazzolo Piasa Rischei '97	ΨΨΨ	6
●	Piemonte Brachetto Forteto Pian dei Sogni '97	ΨΨ	5
●	Monferrato Rosso Le Grive '98	ΨΨ	5
●	Piemonte Brachetto Forteto Pian dei Sogni '98	ΨΨ	5

LU (AL)

Paolo Casalone
Via Marconi, 92
15040 Lu (AL)
tel. 0131741280
e-mail: info@casalone.com

The beautiful Paolo Casalone winery is situated right in the centre of Lu, an enchanting town steeped in the history of the little known Monferrato region. Although Monferrato has a very strong tradition, winemaking is not the area's only activity. A range of other crops is grown and the woods still swathe the hills in their shimmering colours, presenting the visitor with a varied panorama as yet unspoilt by the few tourists who pass through on their way to the more famous Langhe. One very good reason to dally here is the selection of wines offered by this estate. The Barbera d'Asti Rubermillo is very dense ruby red and boasts a nose loaded with ripe cherry, plums and spices. It is full-bodied and vigorous on the palate and the ripe fruit and spice aromas reverberate throughout the finish. The Barbera del Monferrato is obtained from a vineyard that stands atop the spectacular rolling tufa hill of the same name, Morlantino, a location that offers breathtaking views. The '99 reveals a gorgeous bouquet of ripe red berries, spices and almonds and a palate nicely poised between the velvety smoothness of the fruit and fresh varietal acidity. Then there is the Rus, a mix of barbera, merlot and pinot nero. Dark in hue, it has a spicy bouquet a gutsy palate. The Grignolino is also pleasant, with its fairly well balanced palate. Of the whites on offer, the Chardonnay possesses aromas of tropical and citrus fruits and a well-sustained palate with good length. The Munsret is also well worth a mention.

LU (AL)

Tenuta San Sebastiano
Cascina San Sebastiano, 41
15040 Lu (AL)
tel. 0131741353
e-mail: dealessi@libero.it

Roberto De' Alessi and his wife Noemi have just about finished the renovations to their winery, which are designed to improve the space for visitors. Chief among these is a very beautiful tasting room. But that's not all: the addition of new stainless steel vats and a barrique cellar will go a long way towards improving cellar management. Roberto belongs to a group of Monferrato wine producers who believe that if they are to make this a great region, they will have pull together and support each other. Combine this credo with the terrain at Lu and Roberto's skills in the vineyard, and how could his wines fail to be other than superb? Take, for example, the Barbera Mepari. Deep ruby, its aromas of spice, ripe plum and cherry rise up to caress the nose. The velvety palate is dense, fruity and lifted by an attractive, typically varietal, acid vein. The excellent LV is exceptional. A Moscato Vendemmia Tardiva aged in small casks, it has measured sweetness and a captivating bouquet whose typical Muscat grape aromas melt into the discreet vanilla notes from the oak. Full of flavour, dense and gutsy on the palate, it takes you through to a lovely long finish. The estate's solid, standard-label Barbera is very drinkable and refreshing, the Grignolino has a well-defined bouquet and quite a velvety palate for wine from this variety, and to round of the range there is a nice jolly Cortese.

● Barbera d'Asti Rubermillo '99	▼▼ 4
● Barbera del M.to Bricco Morlantino '99	▼▼ 3*
● Monferrato Rosso Rus '99	▼▼ 4
○ Monferrato Bianco Munsret '00	▼ 3
○ Piemonte Chardonnay '00	▼ 2
● Piemonte Grignolino '00	▼ 2
● Barbera d'Asti Rubermillo '98	▼▼ 4
● Barbera d'Asti Rubermillo Sel. '98	▼▼ 5

○ LV Passito '00	▼▼ 5
● Barbera del M.to Mepari '99	▼▼ 4
● Barbera del M.to '00	▼ 3
○ Monferrato Casalese Cortese '00	▼ 2
● Piemonte Grignolino '00	▼ 3
● Barbera del M.to Mepari '97	▼▼ 4
● Barbera del M.to Mepari '98	▼▼ 4

MANGO (CN)

Cascina Fonda
Loc. Cascina Fonda, 45
12056 Mango (CN)
tel. 0173677156
e-mail: cascinafonda@cascinafonda.com

The Barbero family's flagship product is Moscato and it comes in four versions, all excellent. The alluring Vendemmia Tardiva flaunts a rich straw yellow and a unique bouquet of cut flowers, apple and apricot with a very faint undercurrent of elderflower. It hits the palate with body and flavour, opening out generously and nicely bolstered by the fizz. The Driveri Metodo Classico is also very impressive, bottle fermentation lending it extra complexity. It is bright, gold-flecked straw yellow ushers in a bouquet that combines elements of peach, mint, rosemary and confectioner's cream with seductive mineral undertones and a suggestion of pine resin. There is great character on the palate and the lively sparkle keeps the strong sweet vein in check. The richly coloured Asti offers up notes of orange, delicate flowers, apples and pears, and sage in a well-balanced, beautifully orchestrated framework. On the palate, the insistent prickle takes you through to a fruity, lingering finish. The estate's standard-label Moscato hints at fruit and balsam, faintly tinged with sage. The Brachetto is cherry red with purple highlights introducing rather a ripe nose of dried roses and berry fruit then a supple, vibrant palate. The Barbera and the Dolcetto are simple, verging on the rustic.

MANGO (CN)

Degiorgis
Via Circonvallazione, 3
12056 Mango (CN)
tel. 014189107
e-mail: degiorgis.sergio@tin.it

Sergio and Patrizia Degiorgis have considerably improved the quality of a production that year after year yields an increasingly elegant range of wines. Witness their Langhe Riella, which in this vintage appears to have attained just the right balance of definition on the nose and structure in the mouth. Dense garnet with a short rim, it offers aromas of blackberry, plum, liquorice and mint, offset by traces of flowers and chilli pepper. It is invigorating on the solid, well-sustained palate, which reveals long flowery length. The exquisite '00 Dolcetto Bricco Peso is impenetrable almost to the rim. The nose is generous and complex for a Dolcetto, unveiling raspberry, almond and black pepper with hints of forest floor and mint peeking through. Full-bodied and generous on the palate, its marked, dry tannins usher in a warm, vigorous, never-ending finish where touches of violet and cocoa powder emerge. We awarded Two Glasses to the Degiorgis' Moscato Sorì del Re for its straw-yellow colour, its hints of resin over a peach base, and a full, rich palate bursting with aromatic overtones. This year's Accordo, obtained from chardonnay and pinot nero fermented without the skins, is a little dominated by the oak but still extremely agreeable. In contrast, Essenza, a dried-grape muscat-based bottle, can show a mature nose and sweet, full-bodied flavour. Last but not least, the Barbera has a somewhat over-evolved bouquet and a nice weighty palate.

○ Asti '00	▼▼	3*
○ Vendemmia Tardiva '00	▼▼	4
○ Asti Driveri M. Cl. '99	▼▼	4
○ Moscato d'Asti '00	▼	3
● Piemonte Brachetto '00	▼	3
● Dolcetto d'Alba Brusalino '00		3
● Barbera d'Alba Vigna Bruseisa '99		4

● Dolcetto d'Alba Bricco Peso '00	▼▼	4
○ Moscato d'Asti Sorì del Re '00	▼▼	3
● Langhe Rosso Riella '99	▼▼	5
○ Accordo Bianco '00	▼	4
● Barbera d'Alba '99	▼	4
○ Essenza Moscato '99	▼	4
○ Accordo Bianco '99	▼▼	4
● Dolcetto d'Alba Bricco Peso '99	▼▼	4

MOASCA (AT)

CASCINA LA GHERSA
VIA SAN GIUSEPPE, 19
14050 MOASCA (AT)
TEL. 0141856012
E-MAIL: info@laghersa.it

Massimo Barbero gave the panel a very impressive selection of wines to taste, four of which took Two Glasses. Two of the award winners are Barberas, the Vignassa and the Camparò. The Vignassa has great character. Ruby verging on garnet, it offers a nose of wild berry fruits, geraniums and green leaf through which filter intriguing mineral undertones. Fleshy on the palate, it builds up to a spirited climax that flows into an intense, lasting finish resonating with fruit, cocoa powder and spice. The Camparò is a not-quite-solid ruby with flashing garnet highlights that leads in to a pleasantly rustic nose with traces of red fruit jam, pine resin and forest floor. Robust on the palate, it offers a strong tannic vein and a lengthy fruit finish. The chardonnay and sauvignon-based Sivoj is very good indeed, with a gold-flecked straw-yellow colour and captivating aromas of lily, hazelnut and ripe apples and pears. It is well-structured and well-sustained on the palate and drives through to a long finish that recalls candied fruit. The Monferrato La Ghersa has a strongly mineral nose with undertones of berry fruit and almond. Vigorous on the palate, its very good length finishes on a balsamic note. The Piagé is a tad below par this year but the Gavi Il Poggio has notes of ripe apples and citrus fruit with a vegetal base and is eminently drinkable.

Wine	Rating	Score
● Barbera d'Asti Sup. La Vignassa '99	▼▼	5
● Monferrato Rosso La Ghersa '98	▼▼	4
● Barbera d'Asti Sup. Camparò '99	▼▼	4
○ Monferrato Bianco Sivoj '99	▼▼	4
○ Gavi Il Poggio '00	▼	4
● Monferrato Rosso Piagé '99	▼	4
● Barbera d'Asti Sup. La Vignassa '97	▼▼	5
● Barbera d'Asti Sup. La Vignassa '98	▼▼	5
● Monferrato Rosso Piagé '98	▼▼	4

MONCHIERO (CN)

GIUSEPPE MASCARELLO E FIGLIO
VIA BORGONUOVO, 108
12060 MONCHIERO (CN)
TEL. 0173792126
E-MAIL: mauromascarello@mascarello1881.com

The '96 was a tremendous vintage. It give us wines with lashings of Langhe character, austere tannins and pronounced acidity and Giuseppe Mascarello's winery has taken full advantage. The estate returns in triumph to the Three Glass ranks with its Barolo Villero. In the Monchiero cellars, which date back to the 1700s and were originally used for storing ice, Mauro Mascarello, wife Maria Teresa and son Giuseppe, make their wine in the traditional Piedmontese way. The Mascarellos still subject their wine to long macerations of up to 25 or 28 days and extended ageing (36 months) in used Slavonian oak barrels of 20 to 90 hectolitres. Occasionally, they use small French oak casks to modulate the nose of their wines. At our tasting, we concentrated mainly on the four '96 Barolos whose release has, as usual, been held over for a year. The Villero and the Monprivato, both celebrated Castiglione Falletto crus, are the cream of the crop. The Villero is an archetype of the great traditional Barolo, delivering a fabulously complex nose with delicious notes of liquorice and dried flowers, and a hugely powerful, beautifully orchestrated palate. The Monprivato, more tannic in character, shows all the signs of attaining the perfection of the Villero if it is left to age in the bottle for ten years or so. Every bit as potent, but not quite as noble, are the Santo Stefano di Perno and the Bricco, both very fine wines. The new Langhe Rosso Status, a blend of nebbiolo with a dash of barbera and freisa, and the Dolcetto Bricco are worthy of note. The two Barberas, the Langhe Nebbiolo and the Dolcetto Santo Stefano di Perno, are less inspired.

Wine	Rating	Score
● Barolo Villero '96	▼▼▼	6
● Barolo Bricco '96	▼▼	6
● Barolo Monprivato '96	▼▼	6
● Barolo S. Stefano di Perno '96	▼▼	6
● Langhe Rosso Status '96	▼▼	5
● Dolcetto d'Alba Bricco '99	▼▼	5
● Barbera d'Alba Codana '98	▼	6
● Dolcetto d'Alba S. Stefano di Perno '99	▼	4
● Langhe Nebbiolo '99	▼	5
● Barbera d'Alba '98		5
● Barolo Monprivato '85	▼▼▼	6
● Barolo Monprivato Ca' d' Morissio '93	▼▼	6
● Barolo Monprivato '95	▼▼	6

MONDOVÌ (CN)

Il Colombo - Barone Riccati
Via dei Sent, 2
12084 Mondovì (CN)
tel. 017441607

The enthusiasm of Carlo Riccati and his wife, Adriana Giusti, has made Il Colombo an undisputed leader around Mondovì, so much so that they now find themselves in friendly rivalry with their fellow researchers in Dogliani. The experiments of Professor Di Stefano in the laboratory and Beppe Caviola in the cellar, and put to the test on grapes from vines lovingly tended by Carlo and Adriana, have resulted in two resounding Three Glasses for the estate. This year, the Riccatis released their first Dolcetto Superiore, obtained from a small portion of the fruit obtained from their oldest and highest vineyard, grapes that usually go to make the standard-label Il Colombo. The wine, conditioned for 12 months in new and used 900-litre casks, seeks to rise above the simplicity of Dolcetto. It has an opaque hue, an etheric, complex nose and a powerful, mouthfilling palate bursting with personality. Il Colombo is, as ever, outstanding. Aged for six months in 900-litre casks, half of them new, it possesses aromas of black berries and sweet spices that blend perfectly into a round structure, borne up by a tannic twist in the tail that lends elegance and length to the finish. The Vigna della Chiesetta is exactly what it sets out to be, an everyday wine that for a few euros lets the drinker sample fresh raspberry, bitter almond and cocoa powder aromas and a pleasant palate that is neither simple nor banal.

● Dolcetto delle Langhe Monregalesi Sup. Monteregale '99 ♆♆	4
● Dolcetto delle Langhe Monregalesi Il Colombo '00 ♆♆	4
● Dolcetto delle Langhe Monregalesi Vigna della Chiesetta '00 ♆♆	3*
● Dolcetto delle Langhe Monregalesi Il Colombo '97 ♆♆♆	4
● Dolcetto delle Langhe Monregalesi Il Colombo '98 ♆♆♆	4
● Dolcetto delle Langhe Monregalesi Il Colombo '99 ♆♆	4

MONFORTE D'ALBA (CN)

Gianfranco Alessandria
Loc. Manzoni, 13
12065 Monforte d'Alba (CN)
tel. 017378576

Gianfranco Alessandria's Barbera Vittoria triumphs. Power, balance and complexity are the distinguishing characteristics of a wine that sustains its robust alcohol with a cornucopia of nose-palate aromas. The deep violet-tinged ruby introduces a nose that opens out in exciting notes of fruit and spice. On the palate, where the texture is opulent and balanced by the acidity, the influence of the oak makes itself felt but never intrudes. The length is fabulous. The standard-label Barbera '00 holds its own against this colossus. Similar in hue, it shows a bouquet that is already open, if not quite as complex as that of the Vittoria. Balance and firm structure meld seamlessly on the silkily refreshing palate. Insieme, a blend of almost equal proportions of nebbiolo, barbera and cabernet, comes from the '98 vintage, although it doesn't say so on the label. Dark ruby, its aromas of cherry, black cherry and redcurrant are tinged with notes of vanilla and spice that return on the soft, silky palate. Gianfranco also makes two wonderful Barolos. The standard-label version, ruby red with a slightly orange edge, has pleasantly minty, balsamic overtones and an attractive palate, with sweet, velvety tannins and traces of ripe fruit. But the estate's real tour de force is the San Giovanni, which scooped up Three Glasses for this year's exceptional selection. The gloweringly dark ruby ushers in clear notes of red fruit, mint and tobacco on the nose. Firm tannins, balsamic nuances and delicious fruity fragrances exalted by hints of liquorice set off the structure on the palate. And to round things off, the Dolcetto '00 is very drinkable.

● Barolo S. Giovanni '97	♆♆♆	6
● Barbera d'Alba Vittoria '99	♆♆	5
● Barbera d'Alba '00	♆♆	4
● Dolcetto d'Alba '00	♆♆	4
● Barolo '97	♆♆	6
● L'Insieme	♆♆	6
● Barolo '93	♆♆♆	6
● Barbera d'Alba Vittoria '96	♆♆♆	5
● Barbera d'Alba Vittoria '97	♆♆♆	5
● Barbera d'Alba Vittoria '98	♆♆♆	5
● Barolo S. Giovanni '95	♆♆	6
● Barolo S. Giovanni '96	♆♆	6

MONFORTE D'ALBA (CN)

★ Domenico Clerico
Loc. Manzoni, 67
12065 Monforte d'Alba (CN)
tel. 017378171

The amiable Domenico Clerico, who has been a leading figure in Piedmontese oenology for several years now, never lets up. Today, this is truer than ever for he has enlisted the help of the talented young Massimo Conterno, in whose capable hands vineyards and cellars run smoothly. Again, the estate's crowning glory is the Barolo Percristina: 4,200 bottles of nectar from the Mosconi vineyard. This Barolo comes from the '96 vintage, a historic year for the region. Aged in unusual 150-litre barrels of new oak, known as "cigarillos", it has a fresh nose that opens out to reveal remarkable complexity. Rich aromas of berry fruit, violets, liquorice, tobacco and leather usher in a dense, juicy tannic weave that flow through to a long, velvety, fruit-rich finish. Hot on the heels of this Barolo come the Pajana and the Ciabot Mentin Ginestra. They are from '97, a vintage notable for soft, alcoholic wines that drink earlier than the '96 vintages. The Ciabot Mentin Ginestra is fairly forward while the Pajana is spicier and more tannic. One step down in terms of structure is the Arte, a blend of 90 per cent nebbiolo with a dash of barbera and cabernet sauvignon. Conditioned in new barriques, it shows a less challenging palate. The Barbera Trevigne, aged half in new and half in two year old barriques, and the Langhe Dolcetto Visadì are both excellent, drinkable and faithful to their varieties. The Barbera unveils a fruity nose with strong notes of ripe cherry and a tangy, potent palate while the Dolcetto still has a rather alcohol-rich bouquet and no-nonsense tannins in the mouth.

• Barolo Percristina '96	♀♀♀	6
• Barolo Ciabot Mentin Ginestra '97	♀♀	6
• Langhe Dolcetto Visadì '00	♀♀	4
• Barolo Pajana '97	♀♀	6
• Barbera d'Alba Trevigne '99	♀♀	5
• Langhe Arte '99	♀♀	6
• Barolo Ciabot Mentin Ginestra '85	♀♀♀	6
• Barolo Ciabot Mentin Ginestra '89	♀♀♀	6
• Arte '90	♀♀♀	6
• Barolo Pajana '90	♀♀♀	6
• Barolo Pajana '91	♀♀♀	6
• Arte '93	♀♀♀	6
• Barolo Pajana '93	♀♀♀	6
• Barolo Pajana '95	♀♀♀	6
• Barolo Percristina '95	♀♀♀	6

MONFORTE D'ALBA (CN)

★ Aldo Conterno
Loc. Bussia, 48
12065 Monforte d'Alba (CN)
tel. 017378150

Aldo Conterno, who for the last ten years or so has been flanked by his sons, Franco, Giacomo and Stefano, always presents us with a superb selection of wines and again this year we gave his outstanding Barolo Gran Bussia Three Glasses. It undergoes a longer than usual period of ageing and has come to embody the tradition of the house of Conterno. It manages to be both rigorous in style and quite outstanding at the same time and, like all great Barolos, reveals its character very gradually. Already drinking exceptionally well, this is a wine that will only improve with cellaring. Of the other Barolos offered by the estate this year, we preferred the Cicala and the Colonnello to the standard-label version. Rich garnet with an orange rim, the Cicala has a seductive, mature nose suggesting wild berry jam and an appropriately austere character on the palate that resoundingly echoes all the fragrances of the bouquet. The Colonnello is redolent of almond and jam, with undertones ranging from vanilla to coffee. On the palate, it is weighty and opens out steadily to finish on a note of violets. The standard-label Barolo is quite dark and has aromas of liqueur cherries and cocoa powder set against a backdrop of spice. The gutsy tannins elegantly bolster up a rich texture that ushers in an invigorating, lengthy finish. The spunky Barbera has a crushed fruit and spice nose while the Dolcetto offers notes of hay, wild berries and green leaf, and a vigorous texture on the palate that is deliciously satisfying. The Printanié, a Chardonnay, is a good white.

• Barolo Gran Bussia Ris. '95	♀♀♀	6
• Barolo Cicala '97	♀♀	6
• Barolo Colonnello '97	♀♀	6
• Dolcetto d'Alba '00	♀	4
○ Langhe Bianco Printanié '00	♀	4
• Barolo '97	♀	6
• Barbera d'Alba '99	♀	5
• Barolo Gran Bussia Ris. '82	♀♀♀	6
• Barolo Gran Bussia Ris. '88	♀♀♀	6
• Barolo Vigna del Colonnello '88	♀♀♀	6
• Barolo Gran Bussia Ris. '89	♀♀♀	6
• Barolo Vigna del Colonnello '89	♀♀♀	6
• Barolo Gran Bussia Ris. '90	♀♀♀	6
• Barolo Vigna del Colonnello '90	♀♀♀	6
• Barolo Bussia Soprana '96	♀♀	6

MONFORTE D'ALBA (CN)

★ GIACOMO CONTERNO
LOC. ORNATI, 2
12065 MONFORTE D'ALBA (CN)
TEL. 017378221

In anticipation of the legendary Barolo Riserva Monfortino, only released in exceptional years – the 1995 vintage is due to make its appearance in 2002 - Giovanni Conterno this year offered us a stupendous Barolo Cascina Francia that earned his beautiful Monforte winery another Three Glass decoration. Garnet, with a slightly forward shade at the rim, it revels in a distinctive bouquet of fig jam, wild berries and leather, with alluring undertones of earth. The palate, which has remarkable weight and balance, starts out juicy and invigorating to rounds out beautifully in elegant, generous tannins. The long finish recalls the floral, minerally fragrances. The tangy '00 Barbera is also rich in mineral tones and sports a ruby red with violet highlights. The aromas range from fruit to dried flowers and the well-structured palate is topped off by plenty of warm length. The estate's Dolcetto Cascina Francia is a lovely dark garnet with distinct purple highlights at the rim. Hay, bilberry and raspberry aromas are layered over interesting undertones of forest floor and dried leaf, in an overall framework of impressive balance. This is a complex wine on the palate, with barely discernible tannins and a finish that mirrors the fragrant bouquet.

MONFORTE D'ALBA (CN)

PAOLO CONTERNO
LOC. GINESTRA, 34
12065 MONFORTE D'ALBA (CN)
TEL. 017378415
E-MAIL: ginestra@paoloconterno.com

Paolo Conterno and his son, Giorgio, own seven hectares planted to vine in Ginestra, one of the most important crus at Monforte. Five of those hectares are given over to the production of nebbiolo destined for Barolo. This year, we sampled the Barolo Ginestra '97, a fairly intense garnet wine with aromas of violets and alpine flowers, lifted by delicate notes of berry fruit. On the palate, it reveals a strong note of sweetness, fairly solid structure and good length, with attractive, unobtrusive tannins and a hint of berry fruit again. The Barolo Ginestra Riserva '96, a youthful garnet with a faint edge, offers intense violet overtones nuanced with menthol in its very refined bouquet. Entry in the mouth is full and sweet, then mid palate firms up with juicy flesh and muscular, but not dry, tannins that leave a distinct note of sweet liquorice in the after-aroma. The Brich Ginestra '99, from nebbiolo, has a fine, elegant nose of rose petals and morello cherry enhanced by sweet oaky tones. Sturdy on the palate with lots of fruit and flesh, it shows good length that the tannins never threaten to render astringent. The Dolcetto '00 is a fabulously deep, bright, vivacious ruby that heralds very intense bilberry and raspberry aromas through which a faint hint of balsam emerges. Richly fruity and fleshy on the palate, it shows excellent balance in the long, juicy finish. The Barbera on the other hand, is equally full and fleshy but lacks harmony on the palate.

● Barolo Cascina Francia '97	🍷🍷🍷	6
● Dolcetto d'Alba Cascina Francia '00	🍷🍷	4
● Barbera d'Alba Cascina Francia '00	🍷	5
● Barolo Monfortino Ris. '82	🍷🍷🍷	6
● Barolo Cascina Francia '85	🍷🍷🍷	6
● Barolo Monfortino Ris. '85	🍷🍷🍷	6
● Barolo Cascina Francia '87	🍷🍷🍷	6
● Barolo Monfortino Ris. '87	🍷🍷🍷	6
● Barolo Monfortino Ris. '88	🍷🍷🍷	6
● Barolo Cascina Francia '89	🍷🍷🍷	6
● Barolo Cascina Francia '90	🍷🍷🍷	6
● Barolo Monfortino Ris. '90	🍷🍷🍷	6
● Barolo Monfortino Ris. '93	🍷🍷	6
● Barolo Cascina Francia '95	🍷🍷	6
● Barolo Cascina Francia '96	🍷🍷	6

● Dolcetto d'Alba Ginestra '00	🍷🍷	4
● Barolo Ginestra Ris. '96	🍷🍷	6
● Barolo Ginestra '97	🍷🍷	6
● Langhe Rosso Brich Ginestra '99	🍷🍷	6
● Barbera d'Alba Ginestra '99	🍷	5
● Barolo Ginestra Ris. '93	🍷🍷	6
● Barolo Ginestra '95	🍷🍷	6
● Barolo Ginestra '96	🍷🍷	6
● Langhe Rosso Brich Ginestra '98	🍷🍷	6

MONFORTE D'ALBA (CN)

Conterno Fantino
Via Ginestra, 1
12065 Monforte d'Alba (CN)
tel. 017378204
e-mail: info@conternofantino.it

The Conterno Fantinos, who belong to the aristocracy of Italian winemaking, did not disappoint us this year with their 160,000 bottles. The pick of the range is the Barolo Vigna del Gris, whose extremely impressive performance scores a bull's-eye, taking a Three Glass award for the second year in a row. It's an impressive bottle for its deep, dark hue and typical oaky notes, flanked by sweet aromas of ripe fruit and tobacco. The fruit is very much in evidence on the palate, which possesses soft tannins and a finish that clearly echoes the oaky timbre, enfolding the flavour in sweet, satisfyingly warm tones. The Monprà, a nebbiolo, barbera and cabernet sauvignon blend, is also very good, its lively colour giving way to potent aromas of small berry fruits laced with new oak. Wonderfully round on the palate, it shows very firm tannins that never overpower. The range of Barolos is enhanced by the Parussi, from Castiglione Falletto. It has a distinctly modern style and a great deal more thrust than its stablemates, although it still lacks balance, particularly in the use of the new oak which is rather prominent and tends to cover the fruit. We liked the Sorì Ginestra, which blends very concentrated notes of violet with refined toasty oak. Coherent on the palate, it has a succulent, persistent finish that reveals deliciously sweet tannins. The very well put-together Barbera Vignota is dark and rather radiant, and boasts a heady, fruity bouquet and a well-structured palate with just the right amount of acidity, agreeable sweetness, and good long length. We preferred last year's Dolcetto Bricco Bastia to this year's offering, which is still very drinkable. The pleasing Chardonnay tastes rather oaky.

● Barolo Vigna del Gris '97	🍷🍷🍷	6
● Langhe Rosso Monprà '99	🍷🍷	6
● Barbera d'Alba Vignota '00	🍷🍷	4
● Barolo Sorì Ginestra '97	🍷🍷	6
○ Langhe Chardonnay Bastia '99	🍷🍷	5
● Barolo Parussi '97	🍷	6
● Dolcetto d'Alba Bricco Bastia '00	🍷	4
● Barolo Sorì Ginestra '90	🍷🍷🍷	6
● Barolo Sorì Ginestra '91	🍷🍷🍷	6
● Monprà '94	🍷🍷🍷	6
● Langhe Rosso Monprà '95	🍷🍷🍷	6
● Barolo Vigna del Gris '96	🍷🍷🍷	6
● Langhe Rosso Monprà '97	🍷🍷🍷	6
● Langhe Rosso Monprà '98	🍷🍷🍷	6
● Barolo Sorì Ginestra '86	🍷🍷🍷	6

MONFORTE D'ALBA (CN)

Alessandro e Gian Natale Fantino
Via G. Silvano, 18
12065 Monforte d'Alba (CN)
tel. 017378253

The renovations in the cellar area given over to barrel-ageing have been a resounding success and some very sophisticated lighting adds an elegant finishing touch. The two wells sunk into the floor are eye-catching, as well as serving to keep temperature and humidity at the right level. The Fantino winery is the only one in historic centre of Monforte d'Alba and it cost them considerable effort to wade through the bureaucracy involved in obtaining the necessary planning permission. They own seven hectares, all in the Vigna dei Dardi in Bussia. Alessandro, the first member of the family to devote himself fulltime to the business, spent ten years working at Bartolo Mascarello's famous cellars in Barolo. He and his brother both believe passionately in Langhe winemaking traditions and refuse to be beguiled by the fleeting trends that sway the market. They gave us a magnificent Barolo '97, a fine example of its vintage. The perfectly gauged oak and marked fruity character make this an eminently gratifying wine, which is drinking deliciously right now. The unusual Nebbiolo Passito has changed its name with the '98 vintage to become Nepas, an everyday table wine. On the palate, it reveals potent tannins and concentrated fruit, from the three months that the grapes spent drying naturally on rush mats. The fruit was pressed in January and aged in small barrels. The Barbera '99, elegant despite its big body, also takes home Two Glasses for its raspberry jam nose and its zesty, harmonious palate.

● Barolo Vigna dei Dardi '97	🍷🍷	6
● Nepas Rosso '98	🍷🍷	6
● Barbera d'Alba Vigna dei Dardi '99	🍷🍷	4
● Barolo Vigna dei Dardi '93	🍷🍷	6
● Barolo Vigna dei Dardi '95	🍷🍷	6
● Barolo Vigna dei Dardi '96	🍷🍷	6
● Nebbiolo Passito Vigna dei Dardi '96	🍷🍷	6
● Nebbiolo Passito Vigna dei Dardi '97	🍷🍷	6

MONFORTE D'ALBA (CN)

ATTILIO GHISOLFI
LOC. BUSSIA, 27
12065 MONFORTE D'ALBA (CN)
TEL. 017378345

Last year's announcement of a new recruit to the estate's ranks has led to a triumphant debut for the Langhe Rosso Alta Bussia, a wine whose sheer class impressed the panel. Obtained from 80 per cent barbera and 20 per cent nebbiolo, it displays all the character and verve of the vineyards at Bussia, a magnificent valley on the road from Castiglione Falletto to Monforte d'Alba. This subzone is home to some of the greatest Langhe wine and many Piedmontese critics claim, with good reason, that the terrain is among the best in the area. Gian Marco Ghisolfi makes the most of his six hectares under vine on the upper slopes of Bussia, producing a very interesting selection of wines. The fabulous Alta Bussia '99 combines to perfection the sophistication of nebbiolo with the fruitiness of barbera. Very dark, indeed almost opaque, it unveils aromas that range from cassis to redcurrant, underscored by sweet, balsamic notes that harmonize seamlessly. The palate is huge. Full of rich, potent extract, it fills the mouth in the most extraordinarily delicious manner. Three Glasses was the only score for this monumental offering. Slightly more aristocratic in its aromas, the Bricco Visette Barolo '97 is excellent while the Carlin, a nebbiolo and freisa mix rare for these latitudes, is interesting if somewhat dominated by the oak. The Barbera d'Alba Vigna Lisi '99 keeps pace with the rest of the range and the standard-label Barbera is very good.

MONFORTE D'ALBA (CN)

ELIO GRASSO
LOC. GINESTRA, 40
12065 MONFORTE D'ALBA (CN)
TEL. 017378491
E-MAIL: elio.grasso@isiline.it

Elio Grasso, with his wife Marina and son Gianluca, who has joined his parents in the winery, produced an outstanding Barolo Runcot from the exceptional harvest of '96. They only make this wine in the very best years, using the very best grapes from the Gavarini vineyard just below the estate's main building. The Grassos release it a year later than their other Barolos. This particular vintage is ruby red with orange flecks and offers a nose of berry fruit and spice, laced with balsam. Entry on the palate reveals the oakiness, then sweet, forceful tannins come through and a liquorice and tobacco finish. This is a truly great Barolo that can only benefit from cellaring. A magnificent Three Glasses go to one of the best wines of its kind in the last 10 years, with the Red of the Year award as an added bonus. The Gavarini Vigna Chiniera '97, from a powerful, sumptuous vintage, greets the nose with aromas of ripe berry fruit, violets, roses, hay and tobacco before dazzling the palate with succulence and a velvet-smooth texture. Casa Maté comes from Ginestra, a subzone long synonymous with great, cellar-worthy bottles. It's still closed but bottle age will undoubtedly give it the balance it currently lacks. The excellent barrique-conditioned Barbera Vigna Martina is very dark ruby with purple highlights. The raspberry, strawberry and cherry nose is enhanced by overtones of spice and the exceptional length is bolstered by perfect acidity. The elegant Dolcetto has a rich bouquet and the Chardonnay Educato is redolent of banana and vanilla.

	Wine	Glasses	Score
●	Langhe Rosso Alta Bussia '99	🍷🍷🍷	5
●	Barolo Bricco Visette '97	🍷🍷	6
●	Barbera d'Alba Vigna Lisi '99	🍷🍷	5
●	Langhe Rosso Carlin '99	🍷🍷	5
●	Barbera d'Alba '00	🍷	4
●	Barolo Bricco Visette '95	🍷🍷	6
●	Barolo Bricco Visette '96	🍷🍷	6
●	Barbera d'Alba Vigna Lisi '97	🍷🍷	4
●	Barbera d'Alba Vigna Lisi '98	🍷🍷	4
●	Langhe Rosso Alta Bussia '98	🍷🍷	5

	Wine	Glasses	Score
●	Barolo Runcot '96	🍷🍷🍷	6
●	Dolcetto d'Alba Gavarini Vigna dei Grassi '00	🍷🍷	4
●	Barolo Gavarini Vigna Chiniera '97	🍷🍷	6
●	Barolo Ginestra Vigna Casa Maté '97	🍷🍷	6
●	Barbera d'Alba Vigna Martina '98	🍷🍷	5
○	Langhe Chardonnay Educato '00	🍷	4
●	Barolo Gavarini Vigna Chiniera '89	🍷🍷🍷	6
●	Barolo Ginestra Vigna Casa Maté '90	🍷🍷🍷	6
●	Barolo Ginestra Vigna Casa Maté '93	🍷🍷🍷	6
●	Barolo Runcot '95	🍷🍷	6
●	Barolo Gavarini Vigna Chiniera '96	🍷🍷	6
●	Barolo Ginestra Vigna Casa Maté '96	🍷🍷	6

MONFORTE D'ALBA (CN)

GIOVANNI MANZONE
VIA CASTELLETTO, 9
12065 MONFORTE D'ALBA (CN)
TEL. 017378114

Giovanni Manzone has produced some truly magnificent wines this year, all from his scant seven hectares and annual production of about 30,000 bottles. This selection confirms his place among the ranks of the most important producers in the Langhe. He offered us three Barolos to taste and we liked the Gramolere for its coherence and clean, balsam and spice nose. The initial impression in the mouth is soft, then the flavour expands to caress and fill the palate. The Bricat is reminiscent of mint, aromatic herbs and freshly cut hay, these intense, stylishly sophisticated fragrances being enhanced by nicely judged oak. The aromas are faithfully mirrored on the palate, which is full-boded and finishes on a berry fruit note. The brilliant ruby Gramolere Riserva '96 has violet highlights and a complex, charming and eloquent nose with a trace of oak to give it definition. Exuberant and weighty on the palate, it tempts with sweet tannins and an elegant character. The finish is persistent, with sweet extracts. The ruby-and-purple Dolcetto d'Alba '00 lacks variety in the bouquet and is a little tart but the Barbera d'Alba La Serra '98 is soft and warm, laden with ripe cherry and redcurrant fruitiness. The Tris '98, a blend of dolcetto, barbera and nebbiolo, has a bigger structure than last year's version, as well as more character and complexity. The Rosserto, made from white rossese grapes, offers unusual notes of spring flowers and candied citron peel, which will no doubt attract critical attention.

MONFORTE D'ALBA (CN)

MONTI
FRAZ. CAMIA
LOC. SAN SEBASTIANO, 39
12065 MONFORTE D'ALBA (CN)
TEL. 017378391
E-MAIL: pie.monti@tiscalinet.it

Pier Paolo Monti set himself up in the wine business in 1996 when he acquired approximately eight hectares in Bussia, San Martino, Val di Sacco and Camia, all in the municipality of Monforte d'Alba. He is particularly fascinated by non-native varieties and has planted chardonnay, riesling, cabernet sauvignon and merlot alongside his nebbiolo and barbera. The estate's first Barolo selection, obtained from the generous '99 harvest, is slated for release in 2003. The wines that Pier Paolo offered us this year included the Aura, a white the panel liked from 70 per cent chardonnay and 30 per cent riesling. The chardonnay is fermented and conditioned in barriques while the riesling is vinified in stainless steel vats. Brilliant straw-yellow with green highlights, it offers nose of mineral and floral aromas with typical banana and vanilla undertones. It is well balanced on the palate, the solid body borne up by just the right dose of acidity before a long, pleasantly almondy finish. The Dossi Rossi, a '99 from 40 per cent cabernet sauvignon, 40 per cent merlot and the rest nebbiolo, makes its debut this year. Blood red, it unveils up a refined bouquet of berry fruit, freshly mown hay, vanilla and cocoa powder. Entry on the palate is soft and silky, then the progression reveals excellent balance, lifted by the varietal characteristics of the three grapes. The Barbera d'Alba is back on the form it showed in its debut vintage. Still rather closed when we tasted, it opens gradually on notes of fruit and spice, supported by the measured acidity of a solid structure, to end on a smoky, fruit-rich finish.

- Barolo Gramolere Ris. '96 ᵧᵧ 6
- Barolo Gramolere '97 ᵧᵧ 6
- Barolo Gramolere Bricat '97 ᵧᵧ 6
- Barbera d'Alba La Serra '98 ᵧᵧ 5
- Langhe Rosso Tris '98 ᵧᵧ 5
- ○ Rosserto Bianco '98 ᵧᵧ 4
- Dolcetto d'Alba '00 ᵧ 3
- Barolo Gramolere Ris. '90 ᵧᵧ 6
- Barolo Gramolere Bricat '94 ᵧᵧ 6
- Barolo Gramolere Bricat '95 ᵧᵧ 6
- Barolo Gramolere Ris. '95 ᵧᵧ 6
- Barolo Gramolere Bricat '96 ᵧᵧ 6
- Langhe Rosso Tris '96 ᵧᵧ 5
- Barbera d'Alba La Serra '97 ᵧᵧ 5
- Langhe Rosso Tris '97 ᵧᵧ 5

- ○ Langhe Bianco L'Aura '00 ᵧᵧ 4
- Barbera d'Alba '99 ᵧᵧ 5
- Langhe Rosso Dossi Rossi '99 ᵧᵧ 5
- Barbera d'Alba '97 ᵧᵧ 5

MONFORTE D'ALBA (CN)

Armando Parusso
Loc. Bussia, 55
12065 Monforte d'Alba (CN)
Tel. 017378257

Ten years ago, this winery was one of the smaller outfits in the area but it has grown to become a leading light in the Langhe wine world. Work to expand the cellars is almost complete and the space is now distributed over three floors, all well equipped, allowing the separation of the various phases in the winemaking process. The range of generally excellent wines amazed the panel. If the Dolcetto '00 is merely good, then the Barolo Vigna Munie '97 is head and shoulders above the rest and we again awarded it Three Glasses for its breadth and depth. Deep ruby shot with garnet highlights, it releases jammy fruit aromas that melt into notes of vanilla and chocolate. Entry on the palate is generous, and the intense softness in the progression is firm right through to the long, poised finish. In the subtler, sophisticated Vigna Rocche '97, the oak makes itself more apparent on both nose and palate. Very good, too, is the Mariondino '97, a balanced if a little predictable bottle, and the more traditional Piccole Vigne '97. It's the best version made so far but still not quite up to the standards of its more exalted companions. The two Barberas we tasted were stupendous. The Superiore '99, obtained from old vines, is full-flavoured and concentrated, and the uncomplicated Ornati '00 is fruity and harmonious, as well as being a snip at the price. We also liked the two Bricco Rovellas '99. The sauvignon-based Bianco is warm and well-balanced, suggesting grapefruit and bergamot, while the nebbiolo, barbera and cabernet-based Rosso is full of berry fruit aromas and already shows good balance on the palate, thanks to its sweet tannins.

●	Barolo Bussia Vigna Munie '97	🍷🍷🍷	6
●	Barolo Bussia Vigna Rocche '97	🍷🍷	6
●	Barbera d'Alba Ornati '00	🍷🍷	3*
●	Barolo Mariondino '97	🍷🍷	6
●	Barolo Piccole Vigne '97	🍷🍷	6
●	Barbera d'Alba Sup. '99	🍷🍷	5
○	Langhe Bianco Bricco Rovella '99	🍷🍷	5
●	Langhe Rosso Bricco Rovella '99	🍷🍷	6
●	Dolcetto d'Alba Piani Noci '00	🍷	3
●	Barolo Bussia Vigna Munie '96	🍷🍷🍷	6
●	Langhe Rosso Bricco Rovella '96	🍷🍷🍷	5
●	Barolo Bussia Vigna Munie '95	🍷🍷	6
●	Barolo Bussia Vigna Rocche '96	🍷🍷	6
●	Barolo Mariondino '96	🍷🍷	6
●	Langhe Rosso Bricco Rovella '98	🍷🍷	5

MONFORTE D'ALBA (CN)

Ferdinando Principiano
Via Alba, 19
12065 Monforte d'Alba (CN)
Tel. 0173787158

Important news from the Principiano estate. Ferdinando is seriously rethinking his vineyards, with new acquisitions and replantings. The makeover will change the face of the winery. The talented Monforte wine-maker has added another hectare to the three planted with nebbiolo he owns in the prestigious Boscareto cru. Recently, he replanted a further three to nebbiolo for Barolo, which will come onstream in 2005. Meanwhile at Pian Romualdo, the famous 70-year-old vines that have contributed so much to the estate's reputation continue to flourish. Other developments include a new approach in the cellar introduced by Principiano's new consultant, the legendary Beppe Caviola, who will undoubtedly do his bit to improve the quality of the estate's selections even further. Finally, we mourn the unexpected absence of hail victim Barolo Le Coste, which would have been making its second appearance this year. Turning to the wines we did taste, the Barolo Boscareto was up to its usual standards. Deep, seductive ruby, it flaunts a fresh, fruity nose redolent of raspberry and hay and a palate that attractively balances sophistication and power. The aromas of the bouquet echo throughout the long lingering palate. The Barbera La Romualda is, as usual, fabulous. The intense colour and wild berry nose herald a flavoursome, invigorating, well-balanced palate that ends in a mouthfilling finish. The Dolcetto Sant'Anna is also very agreeable.

●	Barbera d'Alba La Romualda '98	🍷🍷	5
●	Barolo Boscareto '97	🍷🍷	6
●	Dolcetto d'Alba S. Anna '00	🍷	3
●	Barolo Boscareto '93	🍷🍷🍷	6
●	Barolo Boscareto '95	🍷🍷	6
●	Barolo Boscareto '96	🍷🍷	6
●	Barolo Le Coste '96	🍷🍷	6
●	Barbera d'Alba La Romualda '97	🍷🍷	5

MONFORTE D'ALBA (CN)

PODERE ROCCHE DEI MANZONI
LOC. MANZONI SOPRANI, 3
12065 MONFORTE D'ALBA (CN)
TEL. 017378421

Almost 30 years after his arrival in Langhe, Valentino Migliorini's passion is undimmed. We'll start with the Barolo Vigna Cappella di Santo Stefano '97, just one of his vast selection of wines. Here, aromas of rose and cherry melt elegantly into exquisitely elegant notes of balsam then the palate displays solid, mouthfilling body with rich extract and a beautifully orchestrated finish of plum and roasted coffee beans. The other vineyard selections are equally impeccable. The Vigna Big 'd Big '97, balanced and bursting with flavour, mingles notes of raspberry and wild blackberry with lovely touches of dried fruit and aromatic herbs. The complex Vigna d'la Roul '97, melds wild cherry, elderflower and mint in a round, velvety palate. The Langhe Bricco Manzoni '98 and the Quatr Nas '98 bear the mark of the skilled hand that blended them. The first unfurls well-developed fruit that blends the verve of barbera with the strength of nebbiolo on the palate. The second, a blend of 50 per cent nebbiolo with barbera, pinot nero and cabernet, shows more complexity and luxuriates in berry fruit, fresh hay and tobacco aromas and a supple structure through to the finish. The Langhe Pinònero '98 is redolent of spice, with a touch of sweet oak. Finally, we have the Brut Riserva Elena '98, with its ultra-fine perlage. It combines notes of unripe banana and fresh crusty bread, leaving a creamy impression of peach, hazelnut and citrus fruits in the mouth. Valentino Migliorini shows a final touch of brilliance with his decision to postpone the release of his Barbera and Brut Zero selections so they can age further.

● Barolo Vigna Cappella di S. Stefano '97	♆♆	6
● Langhe Rosso Quatr Nas '98	♆♆	6
● Barolo Vigna Big 'd Big '97	♆♆	6
● Barolo Vigna d'la Roul '97	♆♆	6
● Langhe Rosso Pinònero '98	♆♆	6
● Langhe Rosso Bricco Manzoni '98	♆♆	6
○ Valentino Brut Ris. Elena '98	♆♆	5
● Barolo Vigna Big Ris. '89	♆♆♆	6
● Barolo Vigna Big Ris. '90	♆♆♆	6
● Barolo Vigna d'la Roul Ris. '90	♆♆♆	6
● Barolo Vigna Cappella di S. Stefano '96	♆♆♆	6
● Langhe Rosso Quatr Nas '96	♆♆♆	6
● Barbera d'Alba Sorito Mosconi '98	♆♆	5

MONFORTE D'ALBA (CN)

FLAVIO RODDOLO
LOC. SANT'ANNA, 5
BRICCO APPIANI
12065 MONFORTE D'ALBA (CN)
TEL. 017378535

When you have known a producer for years and hold him in great esteem, it gives immense satisfaction to award Three Glasses, especially when the "king" is flanked by a range of almost equally distinguished "courtiers". The monarch in question is the Barolo Ravera '97, of which 3,000 bottles were released. It is a stunningly brilliant garnet leading in to intense aromas of berry fruit and leather, which will develop in complexity. On the palate, it is a work of art. It starts out sweet, expands into a full-bodied roundness, and drives through to a finish full of robust yet soft, fruity tannins. The overall impression is of great weight and long length that lingers on a delicious note of spice. The Bricco Appiani '98, from 100 per cent cabernet sauvignon, is almost as good. Obtained from the very last grapes to be harvested, it is dark in the glass but sparkles and glints, releasing classic aromas of blackcurrant, blackberry and cassis enriched by a sophisticated undertone of fresh herbs. Entry on the palate is sweet, potent and velvety, despite a strong tannic presence, and it finishes on a lovely warm, vaguely balsamic note. The third heavyweight is a Dolcetto, which recaptures the sumptuousness of the legendary '90. Fermented in stainless steel and cement, it is remarkable for its radiant, purple-tinged hue introducing an explosion of cherry-dominated berry fruit on the nose and a flavoursome, full-bodied palate with vigorous tannins and endless length. All this, plus balance and drinkability rare in such a complex wine. The Barbera, an excellent wine, and the well put-together Nebbiolo, are also very enjoyable.

● Barolo Ravera '97	♆♆♆	6
● Bricco Appiani '98	♆♆♆	6
● Nebbiolo d'Alba '98	♆♆	4
● Barbera d'Alba Sup. '98	♆♆	4
● Dolcetto d'Alba Sup. '99	♆♆	3*
● Barolo '96	♆♆	6
● Bricco Appiani '96	♆♆	6
● Nebbiolo d'Alba '96	♆♆	4
● Bricco Appiani '97	♆♆	6
● Nebbiolo d'Alba '97	♆♆	4

MONFORTE D'ALBA (CN)

F.LLI SEGHESIO
FRAZ. CASTELLETTO, 20
12065 MONFORTE D'ALBA (CN)
TEL. 017378108

Aldo and Riccardo Seghesio's estate lies in the subzone of Castelletto di Monforte, encircled by the great Barolo vineyards. On the east, it is bordered by Serralunga, on the north by the vineyards of Castiglione Falletto, and to the west, in the distance are the crus of Barolo and La Morra. The Seghesios own just over ten hectares and produce about 50,000 bottles a year. Their Barbera d'Alba '00 was not ready for tasting for this edition of the Guide but we look forward to including it next year. We did taste the Barbera Vigneto della Chiesa '99, whose 18-month conditioning in new barriques renders it very dark and gives it a spicy nose with vanilla, roasted barley and coconut undertones from the oak. Entry on the palate is powerful, rich and mouthfilling but the finish is a little oak-dominated as yet. The Barolo '97 Vigneto La Villa merited Two Glasses for its garnet colour with brick-red highlights in the glass and a spicy bouquet of tobacco, lemon zest and vanilla. The palate is warm, velvety and already drinking well, with slightly dry tannins. Decidedly tangier, the Dolcetto '00 is deepest purple, almost black, as befits a nose that hints at rich aromas of bramble jam, wild herbs and India rubber. Uncomplicated and vigorous on the palate, it is flavoursome and zesty, if a tad hard. Last, we have the Langhe Rosso Bouquet, a blend of nebbiolo, cabernet sauvignon and merlot that shows off the skills of these capable vignerons. The colour is rich, the nose mingles toasty and ripe fruit aromas, and it is potent and austere on the palate. Mellow oaky tones return on the long, mouthfilling finish.

MONLEALE (AL)

VIGNETI MASSA
P.ZZA G. CAPSONI, 10
15059 MONLEALE (AL)
TEL. 013180302

The Three Glasses we awarded to Walter Massa last year were not just in acknowledgement of the wine, but also of the man himself and the vision he has pursued with pride and determination. Unfortunately, his moment of glory was marred by the death of his father, Augusto. Walter reacted to his loss by channelling even more energy into the realization of his ambitions. He set about restoring the cellars and acquiring new plots to put together the total of 20 hectares that he had set himself as a goal. The wines he offered us this year were all of a very high standard. We were unable to sample the estate's only Cerreta which, from now on, will be released one year on to give it the time to mature to perfection. We can, however, affirm that the Bigolla is a truly magnificent wine. This black Barbera has an opulent body, with a rich, ripe fruit velvetiness that in no way detracts from its strong character and complexity. The Monleale lacks the muscle power of the Bigolla but seduces with the extraordinary complexity of its cherry, plum, spice, leather and tobacco nose and its palate. The Sentieri, another Barbera, is very, very satisfying and exuberantly fruity. Walter sets great store by his Pertichetta, obtained from croatina grapes, and we were duly impressed. The Timorasso is rich and gutsy, proffering typical mineral notes that come through both on the nose and the palate. Last but not least, honourable there were Two Glass mentions for the excellent moscato-based Muscaté and the Freisa.

● Dolcetto d'Alba Vigneto della Chiesa '00	ΨΨ	3*
● Barolo Vigneto La Villa '97	ΨΨ	6
● Barbera d'Alba Vigneto della Chiesa '99	ΨΨ	5
● Langhe Rosso Bouquet '99	ΨΨ	5
● Barolo Vigneto La Villa '91	ΨΨΨ	6
● Barbera d'Alba Vigneto della Chiesa '97	ΨΨΨ	5
● Barolo Vigneto La Villa '90	ΨΨ	6
● Barolo Vigneto La Villa '93	ΨΨ	6
● Barolo Vigneto La Villa '95	ΨΨ	6
● Barolo Vigneto La Villa '96	ΨΨ	6
● Langhe Rosso Bouquet '98	ΨΨ	5

● Colli Tortonesi Bigolla '99	ΨΨ	6
○ Muscaté '00	ΨΨ	3*
● Piemonte Barbera Sentieri '00	ΨΨ	3*
● Colli Tortonesi Monleale '98	ΨΨ	5
○ Colli Tortonesi Costa del Vento Timorasso '99	ΨΨ	5
● Colli Tortonesi Pertichetta Croatina '99	ΨΨ	5
● Colli Tortonesi Pietra del Gallo Freisa '00	ΨΨ	3*
○ Colli Tortonesi Cortese Casareggio '00		3
● Colli Tortonesi Bigolla '98	ΨΨΨ	6
● Colli Tortonesi Monleale '97	ΨΨ	5
● Colli Tortonesi Cerreta '98	ΨΨ	6

MONTÀ (CN)

GIOVANNI ALMONDO
VIA SAN ROCCO, 26
12046 MONTÀ (CN)
TEL. 0173975256

MONTÀ (CN)

MICHELE TALIANO
C.SO A. MANZONI, 24
12046 MONTÀ (CN)
TEL. 0173976512 - 0173976100
E-MAIL: taliano@libero.it

In this small but beautifully appointed Roero winery, Domenico Almondo, the mayor of Montà, works diligently away with his parents, Giovanni and Teresina, and wife, Antonella. The annual production of 50,000 bottles, obtained from their ten hectares planted to vine, gives an idea of the family scale of the business. The wines we tasted this time around included two reds, the Barbera Valbianchera and the Roero Valdiana (the Roero Giovanni Almondo, a selection of the best barrique-conditioned wines bottled in magnums, was not produced in either '98 or '99) were, as ever, superb. The dense garnet Valbianchera shows a short, compact rim. Its very elegant bouquet offers up clear notes of fresh morello cherry, tobacco leaf and forest floor, and the full-bodied, generous palate is nicely bolstered by fine-grained tannins. There is good persistence that hints strongly at mint and liquorice. The Valdiana is intense ruby with garnet lights and possesses a complex nose of cherry aromas layered over vanilla cream and rain-soaked earth. It is juicy on the palate with lovely tannins that linger through to the final notes of violet and cocoa powder. The Arneis Bricco delle Ciliegie '00 is clear straw-yellow with sharp flecks of green, and has a fruit and chamomile bouquet. Entry on the palate is dense and tangy, and the back palate has reasonable persistency with a note of lemon. The Arneis Vigne Sparse shows a pale colour and hints of apricot on the nose. Its smooth, refreshing palate makes it an extremely gratifying and eminently moreish wine.

We are happy to welcome to the front ranks of the Guide this year the small winery run by the Taliano family, whose cellars are a stone's throw from the centre of Montà d'Alba. The young Taliano brothers, Alberto, who owns the business, and Ezio, who runs things on the technical side, have the assistance of father Michele in looking after their ten hectares of vines, split between Roero and the zone of San Rocco Seno d'Elvio just above Alba. They grow the typical wines of the zones: Roero and Roero Arneis from the Montà plots; and Barbaresco, Barbera d'Alba and Dolcetto from the property in San Rocco. We were extremely impressed by what we tasted and particularly liked the Barbera Laboriosa. Its dense purplish black colour was a pleasant surprise, as was the intense nose with lashings of flower, jam and fruit. The palate is powerful and has little to fear from the more famous versions of this wine. The two big reds are also very good. The bright ruby-coloured Roero Ròche dra Bòssora proffers heady fruity aromas with particularly strong hints of bramble and raspberry, then the palate successfully balances its truly remarkable structure with elegant finesse. It ends on an oaky note that does not jar in the least. The Barbaresco Ad Altiora is every bit as good, and stands out above all for the harmony of its fruity aromas. These make themselves felt both in the bouquet and on the palate, which also has great body and a rewarding finish. The Roero Arneis Sernì is tangy with lovely fruity overtones and to conclude, the standard-label Barbera is simple and agreeable.

● Roero Bric Valdiana '99	ŸŸ	5
○ Roero Arneis Bricco delle Ciliegie '00	ŸŸ	4
● Barbera d'Alba Valbianchera '99	ŸŸ	4
○ Roero Arneis Vigne Sparse '00	Ÿ	3*
● Barbera d'Alba Valbianchera '97	ŸŸ	4
● Roero Bric Valdiana '97	ŸŸ	4
● Roero Sup. Giovanni Almondo '97	ŸŸ	6
● Barbera d'Alba Valbianchera '98	ŸŸ	4
● Roero Bric Valdiana '98	ŸŸ	5

● Barbaresco Ad Altiora '98	ŸŸ	5
● Barbera d'Alba Laboriosa '99	ŸŸ	4
● Roero Ròche dra Bòssora '99	ŸŸ	4
○ Roero Arneis Sernì '00	Ÿ	3
● Barbera d'Alba '00		3

MONTEGROSSO D'ASTI (AT)

Tenuta La Meridiana
Fraz. Tana Bassa, 5
14048 Montegrosso d'Asti (AT)
Tel. 0141956250 - 0141956172
E-mail: meridiana@vininternet.com

Giampiero Bianco had something new and rather interesting for us this year: his Barbera d'Asti Superiore Tra Terra e Cielo, which debuted in '98 to a Two Glass rating. The wine is a blend of grapes from old vines that are subjected to radical pruning and consequently have a very low yield per plant. The end product is a fairly richly-coloured garnet Barbera, offering notes of cherries, redcurrants and aromatic herbs against a spicy background of rhubarb and juniper. Entry on the palate is solid and invigorating, topped off nicely by a warm, lingering finish that mirrors the notes of fruit and spice. This wine is produced with quite short macerations and, after it has been racked off the lees, is left to complete its fermentation in new barriques. The Monferrato Rosso Rivaia, a mix of 60 per cent nebbiolo, 30 per cent barbera and cabernet sauvignon all fermented together, undergoes the same process. Deep ruby in appearance, its bouquet hints at wild berries, mint, cut grass and forest floor. As soon as it hits the palate, the character becomes apparent, driving through steadily to a vigorous finish redolent of cocoa powder and fruit. The Barbera Bricco Sereno is produced with slightly longer submerged-cap macerations. Quite a rich ruby, it releases aromas of berry fruit and spice and reveals character on the slightly austere palate. The semi-sparkling dessert wine, Vigneto del Malaga, is delightfully sweet.

Wine	Rating	Price
● Barbera d'Asti Sup. Tra Terra e Cielo '98	🍷🍷	4
● Monferrato Rosso Rivaia '98	🍷🍷	5
● Barbera d'Asti Sup. Bricco Sereno '98	🍷	4
● Vigneto del Malaga '00		3
● Barbera d'Asti Sup. Bricco Sereno '97	🍷🍷	4
● Monferrato Rosso Rivaia '97	🍷🍷	5

MONTELUPO ALBESE (CN)

Ca' Viola
Via Langa, 17
12050 Montelupo Albese (CN)
Tel. 0173617570 - 0173617013
E-mail: caviola@caviola.com

Beppe Caviola's Bric du Luv has made regular appearances on the market over the last few years. This time, it is as outstanding as ever and again triumphs with Three Glasses. From the '99 harvest, it is sparely conceived, well-balanced, geometrically perfect and clean. Dark ruby, it has pure, sophisticated, elegant aromas, good structure and a silky, caressingly tangy palate that suggests black cherry and redcurrant. Its sweet, lingering finish recalls the aromas of dried, candied berries. The two Dolcettos also express the characteristics of the Alba terrain very well. The Barturot, as in previous vintages, has colour aplenty and a robust body. The bouquet is penetrating and pleasantly vinous, with traces of redcurrant. Entry on the palate is chewy, revealing a powerful fruitiness mingled with touches of violets, and the well-sustained progression hints at almond and hazelnut. The Vilot '00, tangier and less structured, is a very pleasant tipple. It may have less complex fruit but it is nevertheless quite agreeable. The Rangone '99, a Langhe Rosso with a pinot nero base, is rather a challenging wine. The nose proffers delightfully enfolding notes of raspberry and cherry jam with a discernible oaky overtone that blends in very nicely. Soft and sweet on the palate, it shows sensations of plum and black cherry. This small estate, owned by the renowned winemaker Beppe Caviola and Maurizio Anselma, is in the centre of Montelupo Albese. Here, Dolcetto di Langa has taken on new dimensions and prestige in a departure from the narrow confines imposed by its name and its terrain of origin.

Wine	Rating	Price
● Langhe Rosso Bric du Luv '99	🍷🍷🍷	6
● Dolcetto d'Alba Barturot '00	🍷🍷	4
● Dolcetto d'Alba Vilot '00	🍷🍷	4
● Langhe Rosso Rangone '99	🍷🍷	5
● Langhe Rosso Bric du Luv '95	🍷🍷🍷	5
● Langhe Rosso Bric du Luv '96	🍷🍷🍷	5
● Dolcetto d'Alba Barturot '96	🍷🍷🍷	4
● Dolcetto d'Alba Barturot '98	🍷🍷🍷	4
● Langhe Rosso Bric du Luv '98	🍷🍷🍷	5
● Langhe Rosso Bric du Luv '97	🍷🍷	5
● Langhe Rosso Rangone '98	🍷🍷	5

MONTELUPO ALBESE (CN)

DESTEFANIS
VIA MORTIZZO, 8
12050 MONTELUPO ALBESE (CN)
TEL. 0173617189
E-MAIL: marcodestefanis@marcodestefanis.com

Year after year, young Marco Destefanis' winery becomes increasingly well-established in Langhe wine-producing circles. Several factors have favoured the impressive progress of this estate, including Marco's close relationship with Beppe Caviola, his fellow townsman, consultant and personal friend, the acquisition of new vineyards in zones particularly suited for viticulture, and Marco's own natural inquisitiveness, which inspires him to discover every secret that the profession has to offer. This year, the wines presented for tasting were many and of a high level overall. Our own favourite is the Dolcetto Vigna Monia Bassa, obtained from the grapes of a long-established, low-yielding plot. The colour is impenetrable, its intense nose is redolent of fruit and Peruvian bark, and the potent, concentrated palate has a mouthfilling finish. We were also struck by the Nebbiolo d'Alba, one of the house of Destefanis' strongest products. The panel liked its alluring dark garnet hue with ruby highlights and the generous, complex bouquet, offering clear notes of liquorice, forest floor, and rain-soaked earth. On the palate, it shows structure, character, elegance and a glorious finish. The Barbera d'Alba Superiore, making its first appearance this year, is also well-structured. It offers refreshing fruit notes that come through on both nose and palate with attractive consistency. The standard-label Dolcetto and Barbera are very decent indeed. The Dolcetto is ready to drink but by no means simple while the Barbera has a satisfying note of varietal acidity in the finish. The very drinkable barrique-aged Chardonnay is a good example of how to use oak.

- ● Dolcetto d'Alba Vigna Monia Bassa '00 — 4
- ● Nebbiolo d'Alba '99 — 5
- ● Barbera d'Alba '00 — 3
- ● Barbera d'Alba Sup. '00 — 4
- ● Dolcetto d'Alba '00 — 3
- ○ Langhe Chardonnay Barrique '00 — 4
- ● Nebbiolo d'Alba '98 — 4
- ● Dolcetto d'Alba Vigna Monia Bassa '99 — 4

MONTEU ROERO (CN)

ANGELO NEGRO & FIGLI
FRAZ. SANT'ANNA, 1
12040 MONTEU ROERO (CN)
TEL. 017390252
E-MAIL: a.negro@areacom.it

The Negro family produces an excellent range of wines but there are several that stand out in this selection for structure and elegance. This year, it is the Barbera Nicolon and Bric Bertus that make their mark. Just for a change, though, we'll start our tasting notes not with a red but with a "passito" that for the last few years has consistently won a place among the ranks of the very best Roero dried-grape wines. We are, of course, talking about the arneis-based Perdaudin, which this year is gold flecked with brilliant amber highlights. The complex, captivating nose has notes of date, incense and acacia honey while the palate immediately reveals its full body and warmth, leading to an intense finish with refined notes of caramel-covered banana. The Barbera Nicolon is very deep ruby and shows mineral and toasty aromas with an undertone of bramble. Its flavoursome, concentrated palate recalls the nose's toastiness, with strong tannins that dry the warm, violet, cocoa powder and mint finish. The Barbera Bric Bertu is impenetrable in the glass, with a bouquet of charred oak, eucalyptus, cherry and plum. Entry on the palate is massive, and there is robust acidity and decent length capped by a touch of caramel. The Roero Sodisfà is ruby shading into garnet and has a sweet nose then on the palate reveals powerful nebbiolo tannins and a reasonably consistent texture. The two Arneis are both good.

- ○ Perdaudin Passito '98 — 6
- ● Barbera d'Alba Bric Bertu '99 — 4
- ● Barbera d'Alba Nicolon '99 — 4
- ● Roero Sup. Sodisfà '98 — 5
- ○ Roero Arneis Gianat '00 — 4
- ○ Roero Arneis Perdaudin '00 — 4
- ● Roero Sup. Sodisfà '96 — 4
- ● Barbera d'Alba Bric Bertu '97 — 4
- ○ Perdaudin Passito '97 — 6
- ● Roero Sup. Sodisfà '97 — 5
- ● Barbera d'Alba Bric Bertu '98 — 4

MONTEU ROERO (CN)

CASCINA PELLERINO
FRAZ. SANT'ANNA
12040 MONTEU ROERO (CN)
TEL. 0173978171 - 0173979083
E-MAIL: gythbo@tin.it

"Excellent" is the concise way to describe the range of wines presented young, accomplished Cristian Bono. His two crus, the Barbera Gran Madre and the Roero Vicot, dominate a selection that stands out for the quality of its base wines. We'll begin our tasting notes with the Barbera '99, which is fairly dark ruby with garnet highlights and proffers aromas of wild berry fruits and charred oak against a backdrop of woodland aromas suggested by hints of dried leaf, earth and mushrooms. It opens out on the palate, nicely punctuated by dense, slightly dry tannins, which hold up well into a long finish with a final sweet note of caramel and liquorice. The rich ruby red Vicot revels in a highly intriguing nose of red and black berry fruit over a toasty, minerally base. The palate has fullness and personality, with strong, oaky tannins and equally powerful alcohol that reverberates through to the finish, where there are notes of mint, violets and cocoa powder. The rich-hued basic Roero is a bit more rustic on the nose but the palate is robust and satisfying. The Barbera '00, also impenetrable in colour, is simple and coherent. The pale straw-yellow Arneis Boneur hints at subtle aromas of fruit and lemon liqueur and has a well-balanced, if unchallenging palate. The Poch ma Bon, obtained from sun-dried arneis grapes, shows dried fruit set against a mineral and balsam backdrop and has a sweet, slightly tannic palate.

MORSASCO (AL)

LA GUARDIA
REG. LA GUARDIA
15010 MORSASCO (AL)
TEL. 014473076
E-MAIL: guardia@libero.it

Situated in an amphitheatre of white earth that faces the midday sun, the Priarones' beautiful estate is a good example of how it is possible to make high-quality wines rooted in their territory of origin. The quality vintages from this cellar contrast with other volume-driven, low-priced wines. The estate makes it a policy to release wines only when they are ready, and this is what happened with the Dolcettos. The Bricco Riccardo '99 has a youthful ruby appearance with violet highlights. Its rich, complex bouquet offers nuances of roses, wild berry fruit and spice, and the palate, almost rustic and gamey, has nice character, progressing generously to a lingering finish. The Villa Delfini, conditioned in two-year-old oak barrels, is rich ruby with violet lights. Its intense nose heralds a flavoursome palate with reasonable length and good tannins. The Gamondino, a deep ruby red, has a sophisticated flower and berry fruit nose and a fresh-tasting, not very tannic palate. The Monferrato Rosso Innominabile '98 also contains dolcetto, blending local variety with the international grape and oak-derived aromas very successfully. It offers berry fruit fragrances, lovely astringency, freshness and flavour. The Sacroeprofano '99, a cabernet and barbera blend, has a brilliant appearance and a full, elegant nose hinting at rose and hay. It is refreshing and pleasant on the palate, with medium body and length. The Barbera Vigna di Dante '98 and the Gavi Camghé '00 just fall short of Two Glasses but we awarded a second Glass to the Cortese del Monferrato for its aromas of honey, sage and flowers, and its velvety, fresh palate.

● Barbera d'Alba Sup. Gran Madre '99	ÿÿ	4
● Roero Vicot '99	ÿÿ	4
● Barbera d'Alba '00	ÿ	3
○ Roero Arneis Boneur '00	ÿ	3
● Roero '99	ÿ	3
○ Arneis Passito Poch ma Bon	ÿ	4
● Barbera d'Alba Sup. Gran Madre '97	ÿÿ	4
● Roero Vicot '97	ÿÿ	4
● Barbera d'Alba Sup. Gran Madre '98	ÿÿ	4
● Roero Vicot '98	ÿÿ	4

○ Monferrato Cortese '00	ÿÿ	3*
● Monferrato Rosso Innominabile '98	ÿÿ	5
● Dolcetto di Ovada Sup. Vigneto Bricco Riccardo '99	ÿÿ	4
● Dolcetto di Ovada Sup. Villa Delfini '99	ÿÿ	4
● Monferrato Rosso Sacroeprofano '99	ÿÿ	5
○ Gavi Camghé '00	ÿ	4
● Barbera del M.to Vigna di Dante '98	ÿ	4
● Dolcetto di Ovada Sup. Il Gamondino '99	ÿ	4
● Barbera del M.to Ornovo '98	ÿÿ	4

MURISENGO (AL)

ISABELLA
FRAZ. CORTERANZO
VIA GIANOLI, 64
15020 MURISENGO (AL)
TEL. 0141693000
E-MAIL: calvo@isabellavini.com

This year, Gabriele Calvo's wines picked up a trio of Two Glasses. First, for the Bric Stupui, an impressive, oak-conditioned Barbera. Dark, almost opaque ruby, it shows notes of dark berry fruits and has a deep, powerful palate, well sustained by a typical varietal freshness. The Barbera Truccone, a lovely, rich, vibrant ruby wine, comes on a little less strong and proffers black cherry and hay aromas, then a refreshing, pleasantly rustic palate. The Freisa Bioc is notable for its elegance and balance. The nose is deep and complex, featuring bramble and cherry over a vanilla and spice base. The clean palate is perfectly harmonious, revealing concentrated, out-of-the-ordinary fruit and a nice bitterish finish. The Grignolino Montecastello is one of the best of its kind, with a characteristically brilliant cherry red hue. On the nose, it releases clear, generous aromas of rose and geranium flowers, raspberries, strawberries and white pepper and clove spice. The supple, well-balanced palate offers a final note of invigorating flavour. The Sobric, a lively Freisa, has a plum, raspberry, violet and macaroon nose and a fragrant, tangy palate with moderate prickle. Finally, the Barbera Vivace Bricco Montemà, is a simple, rugged wine. For wine tourists who come to this lovely area of Monferrato, the estate will soon be able to offer four well-appointed apartments in a country house right next to the vineyards.

MURISENGO (AL)

LA ZUCCA
FRAZ. SORINA
VIA SORINA, 53/55
15020 MURISENGO (AL)
TEL. 0118193343 - 0141993154
E-MAIL: info@lazucca.com

Big news from the Zucca estate. The ever-dynamic Ester Accornero has recently taken some new people on board with the aim of taking the quality of the estate's selection to even dizzier heights. Mario Ronco has been appointed consultant oenologist and Alberto Pansecchi now looks after things in the vineyard. To add to the original five, two new hectares of vines went into production in 1999 and another four were planted in 2001. Ester is a big fan of the local varieties, particularly barbera, the emblem of Monferrato. Her Barbera Martizza, obtained from a blend of the estate's best fruit, is up to its usual magnificent standards. In appearance, it is very dark, almost opaque, ruby, and has dense, enfolding aromas that suggest ripe dark berry fruits, coffee and sweet spices. The palate weds power with balance and floods the mouth with the pervasiveness and the silkiness of its fruit, well sustained through to a long bilberry finish. The Sulì, vinified entirely in stainless steel, is less of a heavyweight. The '99 vintage hints at ripe berry fruit and hay, and is supple on the palate, nicely soft and well-sustained. The Freisa, this year vinified as a still wine, is getting better and has managed to acquire tidiness and style without sacrificing any of its satisfaction. The limpid ruby has youthful violet highlights, offering very attractive aromas with unmistakable notes of bramble and Parma violet. The palate reveals medium structure, balance and fruit, echoing the aromas of the bouquet.

- Grignolino del M.to Casalese Montecastello '00 — ΨΨ 3
- Barbera d'Asti Bric Stupui '99 — ΨΨ 5
- Monferrato Freisa Bioc '99 — ΨΨ 3
- Monferrato Freisa Vivace Sobric '00 — Ψ 3
- Barbera d'Asti Truccone '99 — Ψ 3
- Barbera del M.to Vivace Bricco Montemà '00 — 2
- Barbera d'Asti Bric Stupui '97 — ΨΨ 4
- Barbera d'Asti Bric Stupui '98 — ΨΨ 4

- Barbera d'Asti Martizza '99 — ΨΨ 5
- Freisa d'Asti '00 — Ψ 4
- Barbera d'Asti 'l Sulì '99 — Ψ 4
- Barbera d'Asti Martizza '98 — ΨΨ 5

NEIVE (CN)

Piero Busso
Via Albesani, 8
12057 Neive (CN)
tel. 017367156
e-mail: goxxpierococc@libero.it

The Busso family won very flattering scores in this year's edition of the Guide with their two historic crus, in anticipation of the two new Barbarescos. One is the Gallina, to be released next year in magnums only, and the other is the Santo Stefanetto, from the newly acquired vineyards at Treiso. The excellent Bricco Mondino '98, aged in two-year-old barriques, has an intense ruby colour and caresses the nose with hints of berry fruits, mint, vanilla and spice. The palate opens out long and soft to reveal robust tannins, nicely finished off by a final note of leather, tobacco and cocoa powder. The Barbaresco Vigna Borgese, matured in big barrels, has a slightly orange edge and a complex, layered bouquet that suggests morello cherry, cherry, hay and leather. The palate boasts sweet, silky tannins with traces of cocoa powder, liquorice, and balsam. The Barbera Vigna Majano undergoes malolactic fermentation in large barrels before ageing for one year in barriques. The result is a deep, intense ruby wine that releases cherry, vanilla and spice tones, filling the palate with ripe pulp and refreshing acidity, enhanced by nice length. The yellow-gold Bianco di Busso, an interesting blend of barrique-conditioned chardonnay and sauvignon vinified in stainless steel vats, has an intense nose of peach, melon, butter and vanilla and a flavoursome, faintly spicy palate. Rounding off the selection, we have the well-managed and enjoyable Dolcetto Vigna Majano which, as always, comes into its own with the skilled coaxing of Piero Busso.

● Barbaresco Bricco Mondino '98	♛♛	6
● Dolcetto d'Alba Vigna Majano '00	♛♛	3*
● Barbaresco Vigna Borgese '98	♛♛	6
● Barbera d'Alba Vigna Majano '99	♛♛	4
○ Langhe Bianco di Busso '99	♛♛	4
● Barbaresco Vigna Borgese '97	♛♛♛	6
● Barbaresco Vigna Borgese '95	♛♛	5
● Barbaresco Vigna Borgese '96	♛♛	5
● Barbaresco Bricco Mondino '97	♛♛	5
● Barbaresco Bricco Mondino '96	♛	5

NEIVE (CN)

F.lli Cigliuti
Via Serraboella, 17
12057 Neive (CN)
tel. 0173677185
e-mail: cigliutirenato@libero.it

Renato Cigliuti, assisted by wife Dina and daughters Claudia and Silvia, runs his winery on the Bricco di Neive with a firm hand. All the wines he offered us for tasting this year stand out for being very well-made and for personality. The Serraboella cru, one of the best in Neive, is planted with vines that yield well-structured wines that can take prolonged ageing. The Barbaresco Serraboella is very good, deep ruby with a nose that shows a whole array of aromas from berry fruit to vanilla, cut grass, roses and violets. Entry on the palate reveals potent yet sweet tannins that are chewy and very persistent. Its wonderful structure does much to tone down the toasty element left over from its stay in oak barrels, only some of which are barriques. The Bricco Serra, a classic nebbiolo and barbera mix, again combines the two varieties to perfection, bringing out barbera's acidity and fruit as well as nebbiolo's complexity and power to finish on a note of balsam and cocoa powder. The Barbera di Cigliuti has for many years now been one of the best modern-style versions of the wine. A bright, intense ruby, it displays notes of bramble, cherry and mint in a very elegant framework. The palate has great structure and overtones of balsam and fruit. This year's Dolcetto d'Alba is excellent. Vinified in stainless steel vats and then aged in barrels – some large, some barriques – its purple-tinged ruby leads in to a fruit-rich, spicy nose.

● Barbaresco Serraboella '98	♛♛	6
● Dolcetto d'Alba Serraboella '00	♛♛	3*
● Barbera d'Alba Serraboella '99	♛♛	5
● Langhe Rosso Bricco Serra '99	♛♛	5
● Barbaresco Serraboella '90	♛♛♛	6
● Barbaresco Serraboella '96	♛♛♛	6
● Barbaresco Serraboella '97	♛♛♛	6
● Barbaresco Serraboella '93	♛♛	6
● Barbaresco Serraboella '95	♛♛	6
● Barbera d'Alba Serraboella '98	♛♛	4
● Langhe Rosso Bricco Serra '98	♛♛	5

NEIVE (CN)

FONTANABIANCA
VIA BORDINI, 15
12057 NEIVE (CN)
TEL. 0173 67195
E-MAIL: fontanabianca@libero.it

The harvest of '98 presented Aldo Pora and Bruno Ferro with two stupendous Barbarescos, the Sorì Burdin selection and their standard-label version. The first of these is so good that the panel, for the first time, deemed it worthy of Three Glasses. Hats off, then, to a young winery whose hard work has taken it in the space of a few years into the front rank of Langhe producers, and the forefront of Italian winemaking. The splendid Sorì Burdin possesses a slightly orange rim and a complex nose, full of fruit and dried flowers, that ushers in a harmonious finish of vanilla and cocoa powder. The same notes return on the palate, in a weave of blue-blooded, vigorous tannins that bolster the progression. Captivating tones of balsam and menthol come through strongly in the finish. The standard-label version, garnet in hue, has a complex bouquet in which bramble and raspberry fruit, spice, violets and vanilla all make their presence felt. The palate is just as good, revealing big tannins and great balance. The Nebbiolo, barrique–conditioned for a period of six months, is a credit to its variety while the Barbera d'Alba Brunet, from 50-year-old vines, is notable for its deep, impenetrable violet and a nose of fruit and vanilla. It is young as yet but will not take long to find a length. The Dolcetto d'Alba, a wine of body and character, is silky and persistent on the palate with ripe berry and coffee aromas. The delightful Arneis is yellow tinged with green and performs best on the nose with a bouquet of apple and spring flowers. On the palate, it is clean and refreshing.

Wine	Rating	Score
● Barbaresco Sorì Burdin '98	♟♟♟	6
● Dolcetto d'Alba Bordini '00	♟♟	3*
● Langhe Nebbiolo '00	♟♟	4
● Barbaresco '98	♟♟	6
● Barbera d'Alba Brunet '99	♟♟	4
○ Langhe Arneis '00	♟	3
● Barbaresco Sorì Burdin '95	♟♟	5
● Barbaresco '96	♟♟	5
● Barbaresco Sorì Burdin '96	♟♟	5
● Barbaresco Sorì Burdin '97	♟♟	6
● Barbera d'Alba '99	♟♟	4

NEIVE (CN)

GASTALDI
VIA ALBESANI, 20
12057 NEIVE (CN)
TEL. 0173 677400

Dino Gastaldi has a modern, balanced style and a strong personality. This gifted producer gets the best out of his 15-hectare estate and bottles only what he considers to be of high enough quality. "Compromise" is not a concept he will entertain. Dino offered us three wines for tasting in 2001 – the Rosso Castlé '97 will not be released until next year – and all three are very good. The '96 Barbaresco is a deep, vigorous ruby with garnet highlights introducing rich aromas of fruit and cakes against a mineral background. It is impressive on the palate for its rich mouthfeel and solidity of structure. It opens steadily and rather austerely to climax in a long finish that echoes the aromas on the nose. The Chardonnay is an intense straw-yellow verging on gold, and has an intriguing nose that hints at apricot, apple and aromatic herbs with pleasant fermented overtones in a powerful framework. Entry on the palate is smooth and silky, then the steady, refreshing mid palate culminates in an intense, persistent finish. The Langhe Bianco Gastaldi '99, 80 per cent sauvignon and 20 per cent chardonnay, is a pale, lustrous straw-yellow and has a complex nose of apple, hazelnut and vanilla with overtones of butter and citrus fruits. Good follow-through on the palate and overall harmony make this a winner.

Wine	Rating	Score
● Barbaresco '96	♟♟	6
○ Langhe Chardonnay '99	♟♟	5
○ Langhe Bianco Gastaldi '99	♟♟	5
● Gastaldi Rosso '88	♟♟♟	6
● Gastaldi Rosso '89	♟♟♟	6
● Dolcetto d'Alba Sup. Moriolo '90	♟♟♟	6
● Langhe Rosso Castlé '96	♟♟	6
○ Langhe Bianco Gastaldi '97	♟♟	5
○ Langhe Bianco Gastaldi '98	♟♟	5
● Dolcetto d'Alba Moriolo '99	♟♟	4

NEIVE (CN)

Bruno Giacosa
Via XX Settembre, 52
12057 Neive (CN)
tel. 017367027
e-mail: brunogiacosa@brunogiacosa.it

When we consider Bruno Giacosa and what he represents for Langhe wine, it has to be in terms of the utmost respect. His rather crusty exterior masks an introverted personality who shies away from the spotlight but who knows the Langhe like no one else. Today, the inimitable Bruno has several prestigious plots to his name: Falletto at Serralunga d'Alba, Asili and Rabajà at Barbaresco. The wines from the estate's own vineyards carry labels marked "Azienda Agricola Falletto" while those from bought-in grapes are labelled "Bruno Giacosa". This year, after a further selection in the vineyard, the Barolo Le Rocche del Falletto takes its place alongside the Barolo Falletto. This, too, is a very concentrated wine and like its stablemate, has a velvety mouthfeel lifted by robust alcohol and fairly low acidity. It reveals the fruit jam aromas typical of the '97 vintage. If the Falletto is not quite up to the standards it set last year, the Barbaresco Asili Riserva '96 steps into the breech as its natural heir. This intensely garnet wine, whose bouquet is still a tad closed but which can still show aromas of liquorice and tar, is a pure explosion of power. In a few years from now, it will be a historic Barbaresco, remembered as one of the greatest nebbiolo-based wines of all time. The Asili '97 may lacks the structure and rigorous character of its big brother but still delights with its elegance and softness. As for the other wines Bruno presented, his Extra Brut and Nebbiolo d'Alba Valmaggiore take home One Glass apiece and the Roero Arneis earned a mention in dispatches.

●	Barbaresco Asili Ris. '96	🍷🍷🍷	6
●	Barbaresco Asili '97	🍷🍷	6
●	Barolo Falletto '97	🍷🍷	6
●	Barolo Le Rocche del Falletto '97	🍷🍷	6
○	Bruno Giacosa Extra Brut '97	🍷	5
●	Nebbiolo d'Alba Valmaggiore '99	🍷	5
○	Roero Arneis '00		4
●	Barolo Ris. Collina Rionda '82	🍷🍷🍷	6
●	Barolo Rocche di Castiglione Falletto '85	🍷🍷🍷	6
●	Barolo Falletto '96	🍷🍷🍷	6
●	Barbaresco Santo Stefano '96	🍷🍷	6
●	Barbaresco Santo Stefano '97	🍷🍷	6
●	Barolo Falletto '95	🍷	6

NEIVE (CN)

F.lli Giacosa
Via XX Settembre, 64
12052 Neive (CN)
tel. 017367013
e-mail: giacosa@giacosa.it

The Giacosa family worked as tenant farmers in Langhe's Bricco di Neive vineyards as far back as 1895 but decided even then to set up on their own, starting a wine business and opening a cellar at Borgonuovo di Neive. Today, the fourth generation is at the helm: Valerio and Renzo, who inherited the business from their father, Leone, in the 1960s, have been joined by Maurizio, Valerio's eldest son, and Paolo, Renzo's second son. Over the course of the last century, the Giacosas, whose winery is big for the Langhe, have worked to improve the quality of their wines. Today, some of the selections released are very good indeed. One of these is the Barolo Vigna Mandorlo '97, of which only 9,000 bottles are produced. As soon as you pick up the glass, this wine from an important vineyard in Castiglione Falletto reveals its great character and personality in its garnet-tinged red hue. The nose displays aromas of berries and spice, enhanced by an attractive touch of charred oak. The palate shows good length and persistence, as well as robust yet fine-grained tannins. Also very good, if a little less intriguing, is the Barbaresco Rio Sordo, from one of the famous crus in the municipality of the same name. It opens on a floral note with undertones of forest floor and animal skins, then the rigorous palate reveals its concentration and vibrant, well-defined tannins. We were less impressed by the Barolo Bussia '97, a faithful rendition of the traditional Langhe style. The Barbera d'Alba Maria Gioana '98 is pleasant, if a little lacking in concentration. The refreshingly quaffable Chardonnay Roera, the slightly over-evolved Barbera d'Alba Bussia '99, and the Dolcetto d'Alba '00 all merit a mention.

●	Barolo Vigna Mandorlo '97	🍷🍷	6
●	Barbaresco Rio Sordo '98	🍷🍷	6
●	Barolo Bussia '97	🍷	6
●	Barbera d'Alba Maria Gioana '98	🍷	4
●	Dolcetto d'Alba Madonna di Como '00		4
○	Langhe Chardonnay Roera '00		3
●	Barbera d'Alba Bussia '99		3
●	Barbaresco Rio Sordo '95	🍷🍷	6
●	Barolo Vigna Mandorlo '95	🍷🍷	6
●	Barbaresco Rio Sordo '96	🍷🍷	6
●	Barolo Vigna Mandorlo '96	🍷🍷	6
●	Barbaresco Rio Sordo '97	🍷🍷	6
●	Barolo Bussia '95	🍷	6

NEIVE (CN)

Ugo Lequio
Via del Molino, 10
12057 Neive (CN)
Tel. 0173677224
E-mail: ugolequio@libero.it

Ugo Lequio produces a magnificent, massively structured Barbaresco Gallina that consistently replicates the quality of previous selections and that never fails to win lavish praise in blind tastings. The '98 vintage is a lovely garnet with an orange rim and a generous, complex nose of raspberry, bramble, dried violets and almond layered over an intriguing mineral base. In the mouth it thrills, swamping the palate with its flavour and mouthfilling presence, nicely punctuated by robust tannins. The finish is hearty, floral and fruity, with a lovely, clear note of chocolate. The Barbera '99, also obtained from the Gallina vineyard, is a little below par. Dense in appearance, its nose shows cherry jam, spice and cake aromas, and the well-rounded palate stands out for rich character and good length. The Arneis, a medium intense straw yellow, gives off notes of apple, apricot and spring flowers and has a complex, silky palate followed by a deliciously fruity finish. And finally there is the Dolcetto '99, rich ruby red with flashes of purple. Cream and berry fruit mingle on the nose with unusual peachy tones and the palate is well-structured and exuberant.

● Barbaresco Gallina '98	♟♟	5
○ Langhe Arneis '00	♟	3
● Barbera d'Alba Gallina '99	♟	4
● Dolcetto d'Alba '99	♟	4
● Barbaresco Gallina '96	♟♟	5
● Barbaresco Gallina '97	♟♟	5
● Barbera d'Alba Gallina '97	♟♟	4
● Barbera d'Alba Gallina '98	♟♟	4

NEIVE (CN)

Paitin
Via Serraboella, 20
12057 Neive (CN)
Tel. 017367343 - 0173363123
E-mail: paitin2@hotmail.com

The Pasquero Elia family has been making wine in Roero and Langhe for generations now but the decisive moves in its history were made first by Secondo, and then by his sons, Giovanni and Silvano. Beppe Caviola supports them as consultant winemaker. This year, the family presented us with three very characterful wines, the Barbaresco '98, the Langhe Rosso '99 and the Barbera Campolive '99. The first of these is very dense ruby with garnet highlights and shows a concentrated nose of berry fruit aromas mingled with flowers and dried grass, almost hay. But the real treat comes on the palate, where the sweet tannins, borne up by magnificent structure, expand into a lingering, harmonious, velvet-smooth mouthfeel. The Langhe Rosso is a blend of barbera, nebbiolo, cabernet sauvignon and syrah that impresses with its incredible power. It is so dark as to be opaque, and the nose tempts with notes of super-ripe fruit, jam and spice, then the palate explodes with concentration and rich extract. The Barbera Campolive has a very immature nose for its abundant fruit is somewhat overpowered by the toasty tones of the oak. The palate brims with ripe, still rather unruly, fruit aromas and seriously muscular flavours that are big enough to handle the strong acidity. It revealed fabulous progression through to a long, enfolding finish. The Dolcetto and the Barbera Serra Boella are up to their usual good standards, the first soft and eminently drinkable, the Barbera approachable and leaner.

● Barbaresco Sorì Paitin '98	♟♟	6
● Langhe Paitin '99	♟♟	6
● Dolcetto d'Alba Sorì Paitin '00	♟♟	4
● Barbera d'Alba Campolive '99	♟♟	5
● Barbera d'Alba Serra Boella '00	♟	4
● Barbaresco Sorì Paitin '95	♟♟♟	6
● Barbaresco Sorì Paitin '97	♟♟♟	6
● Langhe Paitin '97	♟♟♟	5
● Barbaresco Sorì Paitin '96	♟♟	6
● Langhe Paitin '98	♟♟	5

NEIVE (CN)

SOTTIMANO
FRAZ. COTTÀ, 21
12057 NEIVE (CN)
TEL. 0173635186

The harvest of '98 confirms our high opinion of this estate. This year, we awarded it no less than two Three Glasses, making it one of the biggest winners in Langhe. The austere Cottà has a bouquet that has yet to develop its full eloquence, with liquorice and fruit tones and a promising complexity. On the palate, the characteristic traits of nebbiolo re-emerge and the austere, fine-grained tannins never interfere with the long, seductive finish. The more traditional Pajoré, a Barbaresco, guards its aromas jealously at first, opening up slowly to delight the nose with notes of spice, truffle, berries, macerated rose petals and damp earth that reveal the wine's fullness and fascinating depth. On the palate, its fleshy chewiness reveals rich texture but with moderation, preferring to knock you off your feet with the elegance and the balance of its palate. If these two merited Three Glasses, the rest of this year's selection missed out by a whisker. At first sniff, the richly-coloured deep garnet Currà has a less pronounced bouquet but then it unleashes rich, exquisitely refined aromas. The palate, strong and satisfying, lacks the muscle of the other Barbarescos. The soft, classy Fausoni is a deep, brilliant garnet ushering in delicate, lingering notes of mint leaf and plum that give way to an opulent, consistent palate. The Barbera Pairolero '99 is deep ruby with an etheric, complex nose punctuated by refreshing touches of balsam and black berry fruit. Wonderfully dense on the palate, it is innocent of bitterness but may have a shade too much alcohol, though the acidity is respectfully muted. The Dolcetto Cottà '00, its youth rendering it a little unpolished as yet, shows more sophistication and balance than the Bric del Salto. The Brachetto Secco Maté '00 is interesting, fresh-tasting and varietal.

- Barbaresco Cottà '98 — 6
- Barbaresco Pajoré '98 — 6
- Barbaresco Currà '98 — 6
- Barbaresco Fausoni '98 — 6
- Barbera d'Alba Pairolero '99 — 5
- Dolcetto d'Alba Cottà '00 — 3*
- Dolcetto d'Alba Bric del Salto '00 — 3
- Maté Rosso '00 — 3
- Barbaresco Fausoni Vigna del Salto '96 — 6
- Barbaresco Cottà Vigna Brichet '97 — 6
- Barbaresco Cottà Vigna Brichet '96 — 5
- Barbaresco Currà Vigna Masué '97 — 6

NEIVE (CN)

CASCINA VANO
VIA RIVETTI, 9
12057 NEIVE (CN)
TEL. 017367263

Bruno and Beppe Rivetti obtain about 20-25,000 bottles a year from their eight hectares, five of which are estate-owned and three of which they rent. Almost without exception, the wines are matured in medium-sized oak barrels, macerated for a relatively short period, and flaunt an attractive, juicy drinkability. We loved this year's Barbaresco for its ruby red colour with garnet highlights and a nose that, although a little closed initially, opens out gradually to offer cherry, raspberry, dried rose and mint fragrances. Entry on the palate is full and succulent, with sweet, silky tannins that linger on into a long, long finish before the final note of cocoa powder and liquorice. The Duetto, equal parts barbera and nebbiolo, is rich ruby with an orange rim. The cornucopia of aromas ranges from berry fruits to cocoa powder and coffee, expanding on the palate with touches of vanilla and liquorice. The rich ruby Barbera d'Alba has garnet tones and caresses the nose with an intense bouquet of spice and fruit. The palate displays an acidity that backs up its robust structure and persistent length attractively. The vibrant purplish Dolcetto d'Alba, vinified in stainless steel, has fruity aromas, slightly marred by unpolished notes but is still very drinkable and fragrant.

- Barbaresco '98 — 6
- Barbera d'Alba '99 — 3
- Langhe Rosso Duetto '99 — 5
- Dolcetto d'Alba '00 — 3
- Barbaresco '96 — 5
- Barbaresco '97 — 6
- Barbera d'Alba '97 — 3
- Barbera d'Alba '98 — 4
- Langhe Rosso Duetto '98 — 5

NEVIGLIE (CN)

F.lli Bera
Cascina Palazzo, 12
12050 Neviglie (CN)
tel. 0173630194

Walter Bera offered the panel a tempting, dependable range of wines, three of which merit Two Glasses for their excellent character and fullness. The Barbera d'Alba Superiore is very dense garnet with a fascinating nose of red and black berry fruit, mint, forest floor and tar in a harmonious, elegant framework. On the palate, it reveals exceptional texture and progresses surefootedly to climax in a long, consistent finish that echoes the aromas of fruit, pepper and mint. The barbera and nebbiolo Langhe Sassisto is very dark in colour and has a sensation-rich nose of fragrances ranging from hay to tobacco, plum and fig. The well-sustained and well-rounded progression on the palate leads in to a persistent, vigorous finish with notes of candied fruit. The Moscato Su Reimond is a superb rendition of this zone's prince of wines. The bouquet evokes fresh grapes, peach, elderflower and lemon and the palate is complex, tidy, and very, very satisfying. The Asti has notes of fruit and flowers, then a tangy, sophisticated palate. The standard-label Moscato has rather a mature nose and is quite rounded on the palate. The Bera Brut, a "metodo classico" spumante, has lovely, complex aromas and reveals a slightly intrusive sparkle on the palate. The standard-label Barbera is simple and pleasant.

O	Moscato d'Asti Su Reimond '00	ŸŸ	4
●	Langhe Sassisto '98	ŸŸ	4
●	Barbera d'Alba Sup. '99	ŸŸ	4
O	Asti Cascina Palazzo '00	Ÿ	3
O	Moscato d'Asti '00	Ÿ	3
●	Barbera d'Alba '99	Ÿ	3
O	Bera Brut	Ÿ	4
●	Langhe Sassisto '97	ŸŸ	4
●	Barbera d'Alba Sup. '98	ŸŸ	4
●	Langhe Nebbiolo '96	Ÿ	4

NIZZA MONFERRATO (AT)

Bersano & Riccadonna
P.zza Dante, 21
14049 Nizza Monferrato (AT)
tel. 0141720211
e-mail: wine@bersano.it

Despite the changes that have taken place in the management of this famous Nizza Monferrato estate, the quality of the wines presented was as good as ever. We particularly liked the Monferrato Rosso Pomona and the Barbera d'Asti Generala, awarding both Two Glasses. The first is deep ruby-garnet and flaunts a seductive nose of raspberry, tobacco and dried leaf, layered over gorgeous notes of balsam. From the outset, the palate is juicy and generous, punctuated by rich tannins and culminating in a lingering finish full of sweet balsamic undertones. The Barbera d'Asti Superiore Generala, also concentrated in the glass, revels in a mature nose of wild berry fruit, pepper and vanilla, against a backdrop of cinnamon and mulberry blossom. The soft, concentrated palate takes you through to a delicious finish with a liquorice keynote. Only marginally lower down the scale, we have the garnet Barbera Cremosina with its aromas of ripe black berry fruits, tobacco and rosemary introducing a broad, well-sustained, hearty palate. The Gavi Marchese Raggio is straw yellow with delicate green flecks and releases notes of fruit, spring flowers and lemon. The Brachetto Castelgaro is a limpid cherry red with a purple edge, boasting notes of pear and rose in the bouquet and good balance between the sweet vein and the prickle on the palate.

●	Barbera d'Asti Sup. Generala '99	ŸŸ	6
●	Monferrato Pomona '99	ŸŸ	6
●	Brachetto d'Acqui Castelgaro '00	Ÿ	4
O	Gavi del Comune di Gavi Marchese Raggio '00	Ÿ	4
●	Barbera d'Asti Cremosina '99	Ÿ	4
●	Barbera d'Asti Sup. Generala '97	ŸŸŸ	6
●	Monferrato Pomona '97	ŸŸ	6
●	Barbera d'Asti Sup. Generala '98	ŸŸ	6
●	Monferrato Pomona '98	ŸŸ	6

NIZZA MONFERRATO (AT)

★ Cascina La Barbatella
Strada Annunziata, 55
14049 Nizza Monferrato (AT)
tel. 0141701434

Angelo Sonvico's and Giuliano Noè's range is always outstanding and this year it benefits from the addition of two very exciting wines, the Rosso Mystère, a barbera, cabernet sauvignon and pinot nero blend, and the Bianco Non è, a mix of cortese and sauvignon. The first is a fairly intense garnet with a range of aromas that run from jam to tobacco and leather. It is juicy and wide-ranging on the palate, with a steady progression and a long, vigorous liquorice finish. The lustrous straw yellow Bianco Non è has a nose redolent of citrus fruits and flowers layered over fine, complex notes of super-ripeness. The full texture lends breadth and roundness to the palate, which concludes in a lingering finish that mirrors the nose. An excellent performance came from the moderately dark ruby Sonvico, a barbera and cabernet blend with an enticing nose of bramble, plum, forest floor and leaf tobacco. The magnificent structure is borne aloft by robust tannins. The Barbera Vigna dell'Angelo is ruby verging on garnet and offers hints of jam, violet and leather with undertones of dry earth. The palate lacks the explosiveness of previous vintages but is still big, finishing on an elegant note of liquorice. These are two very good wines that do not, however, quite match the quality of the versions reviewed in previous editions of the Guide. The impeccably austere standard-label Barbera is a tour de force every time, and this year is no different. Fairly dense to the eye, it has a well-defined nose and a flavoursome, surefooted palate that offers harmony and deep satisfaction.

NIZZA MONFERRATO (AT)

Scarpa - Antica Casa Vinicola
Via Montegrappa, 6
14049 Nizza Monferrato (AT)
tel. 0141721331

Close scrutiny of the price list of the Nizza Monferrato-based Scarpa estate reveals the philosophy of Mario Pesce, the man at the helm of this historic winery. It features some incredible Barolo and Barbaresco vintages – there's a Barolo Riserva Speciale that goes all the way back to 1961 and the Barberas date from the 1980s. It does not, however, include any wines from the harvest of '00, as these are still maturing in oak casks and will not be released for several years yet. Only three wines are labelled '99, and they were all bottled in August 2001. The estate's most recent Barolos and Barbarescos are the 1990 and 1989 respectively. Mario Pesce has no time for poor or even average vintages, and we shall have to wait to sample his '95 Barolo and Barbaresco until he deems them to be fully mature. Indeed, the Moscato d'Asti, once a flagship product of this estate, has not been released since 1965, as Mario has not considered subsequent years good enough to produce a traditional Moscato using the jute-filtering process in vogue at the time. We tasted five wines on this visit, and were impressed by the performances, but there were no real champions. We liked the Freisa del Monferrato '99, a very dark red wine with a ripe fruit nose and a powerful palate whose acidity and tannins have still to settle down. The Selva Rosa, a sort of rosé from 45 per cent dolcetto and 55 per cent trebbianello, is good and above all has serious presence and structure. Enjoyable, too, are the Bogliona '98, which is still rather acidic, the Grignolino d'Asti and the Dolcetto d'Acqui.

● Barbera d'Asti Sup. Vigna dell'Angelo '99	ŸŸ	6
● Monferrato Rosso Sonvico '99	ŸŸ	6
● Barbera d'Asti La Barbatella '00	ŸŸ	4
○ Monferrato Bianco Non è '99	ŸŸ	5
● Monferrato Rosso Mystère '99	ŸŸ	6
● La Vigna di Sonvico '94	ŸŸŸ	6
● La Vigna di Sonvico '95	ŸŸŸ	6
● Barbera d'Asti Sup. Vigna dell'Angelo '96	ŸŸŸ	6
● La Vigna di Sonvico '96	ŸŸŸ	6
● Monferrato Rosso Sonvico '97	ŸŸŸ	6
● Barbera d'Asti Sup. Vigna dell'Angelo '98	ŸŸŸ	6
● Monferrato Rosso Sonvico '98	ŸŸŸ	6

● Monferrato Freisa La Selva di Moirano '99	ŸŸ	6
● Selva Rosa La Selva di Moirano	ŸŸ	5
● Dolcetto d'Acqui La Selva di Moirano '99	Ÿ	5
● Grignolino d'Asti Sandefendente '99	Ÿ	5
● Barbera d'Asti Sup. La Bogliona '98	Ÿ	6
● Rouchet Bricco Rosa '90	ŸŸŸ	6
● Barbera d'Asti Sup. La Bogliona '97	ŸŸ	6
● Barbera d'Asti Sup. I Bricchi di Castelrocchero '97	Ÿ	5

NIZZA MONFERRATO (AT)

Franco e Mario Scrimaglio
Strada Alessandria, 67
14049 Nizza Monferrato (AT)
Tel. 0141721385 - 0141727052
E-mail: info@scrimaglio.it

Year after year, the Scrimaglio estate turns out a selection of high-quality wines notable for their elegance and strong territorial identity. This time the cellar has taken a step closer to the upper reaches of Piedmont oenology, producing no less than four vintages worthy of Two Glasses. These include two Barbera d'Asti selections, the Acsé '99 and the Croutin '98. The first is rich ruby with garnet highlights followed by a lovely nose of blackcurrant, plum and almond aromas set against a backdrop of pepper and vanilla. Entry on the palate is soft and supple, picking up momentum in mid palate to climax in a long finish of liquorice, violet and cocoa powder. The Croutin has an intriguing, slightly ripe nose of cherry, strawberry and cocoa powder, layered over dry leaf and forest floor. The attack in the mouth is big, invigorating and characterful, then the warm finish lingers. The Crown Cap, a Piemonte DOC, is a young Barbera that boasts a fragrant, fruity, lively personality. Concentrated in appearance, this coherent, engrossing wine offers clean aromas of cherry, morello cherry and forest floor then a richly textured, well-structured palate. The Tantra, a barbera and cabernet blend, is also very decent. It has an opulent nose and a rich, complex taste profile with lingering after-aromas of liquorice and mint. Rounding off this year's range, there is the Futuro, a silky, aromatic white, and the Bricco Sant'Ippolito, a pleasantly rustic Barbera.

● Barbera d'Asti Sup. Acsé '99	ỸỸ	6
● Piemonte Barbera Crown Cap '00	ỸỸ	3*
● Barbera d'Asti Sup. Croutin '98	ỸỸ	5
● Monferrato Rosso Tantra '99	ỸỸ	5
○ Futuro Bianco '00	Ỹ	3
● Barbera d'Asti Sup. Bricco S. Ippolito '99	Ỹ	4
● Barbera d'Asti Sup. Acsé '97	ỸỸ	6
● Barbera d'Asti Sup. Acsé '98	ỸỸ	6
● Barbera d'Asti Sup. Il Sogno '98	ỸỸ	5
● Barbera d'Asti Sup. Croutin '97	Ỹ	5

NOVELLO (CN)

Elvio Cogno
Via Ravera, 2
12060 Novello (CN)
Tel. 0173744006
E-mail: elviocogno@elviocogno.com

Walter Fissore is a staunch believer in the potential of the Ravera cru, and he has good reason to do so. Soil composition, good exposure and a favourable site climate are on his side. And after we tasted his Barolo Vigna Elena '97, we came away completely convinced. A luxuriant garnet wine, it has complex, generous aromas of roses and fine-cut tobacco with hints of vanilla. Entry on the palate is strong and full, revealing fresh spices, berry fruit and liquorice, then the progression is packed with fragrance and flavour, well supported by the pleasant tannins. Equally classy, if more complex, is the rather austere, full-bodied Barolo Ravera '97. Its harmonious length combines tannic elegance with new leather and wild berry fruit, with plenty of room to evolve. The Langhe Rosso Montegrilli, a mix of nebbiolo and barbera, has come a long way and its lovely, lingering, clear, fruity aromas of raspberry and bramble attest to its depth and character. Walter's Barbera d'Alba Bricco dei Merli is very good indeed with its rich, seductive nose of fresh cherry and plum and a mouthfilling palate vibrant with enchanting notes of vanilla and balsam. The Nas-Cetta, a white, takes its name from the old vine that bears its grapes. Partially vinified in small barrels, it releases rich aromas of hedgerow, sage and citrus fruit, then shows off a delicate, beautifully orchestrated finish with a hint of bitter almonds. Last but not least, the Dolcetto d'Alba Vigna del Mandorlo evokes dried apricots and is very, very drinkable, thanks to well-gauged tannins and soft acidity.

● Barolo Vigna Elena '97	ỸỸ	6
● Dolcetto d'Alba Vigna del Mandorlo '00	ỸỸ	3*
● Barolo Ravera '97	ỸỸ	6
● Barbera d'Alba Bricco dei Merli '99	ỸỸ	5
● Langhe Rosso Montegrilli '99	ỸỸ	5
○ Nas-Cetta '00	Ỹ	4
● Barolo Ravera '93	ỸỸ	5
● Barolo Ravera '95	ỸỸ	6
● Barolo Ravera '96	ỸỸ	6
● Barbera d'Alba Bricco dei Merli '98	ỸỸ	4
● Langhe Rosso Montegrilli '98	Ỹ	5

NOVI LIGURE (AL)

IL VIGNALE
VIA GAVI, 130
15067 NOVI LIGURE (AL)
TEL. 014372715
E-MAIL: ilvignale@ilvignale.it

This beautiful estate, lying on the slopes of Mount Mesima and straddling the municipalities of Novi and Gavi, is a reliable source of the DOC zone's wines. The owners, Piero and Vilma Cappelletti, have boundless energy and an enviable attitude, which focuses on enjoying their work and getting the most out of what they do. This year, their customary stamina and the technical support of Giuseppe Bassi have presented us with the traditional three well-known labels while we wait for their new experimental vines to bear fruit. Again, it is the Gavi Vigne Alte that stands out, winning Two Glasses for its fairly deep straw-yellow colour and a fine nose of balsam and vanilla that opens out to embrace notes of peach and citrus fruit. The refreshing, tangy palate is nicely buttressed by structure that gives the classic almond finish decent length. The less sophisticated Gavi Vilma Cappelletti offers aromas of super-ripeness that give way to varietal spring flower and apple fragrances. The agreeably zesty palate is more immediate and less challenging than that of the Vigne Alte, balancing out the Il Vignale range to perfection. The Rosso di Malì is obtained from pinot nero and cabernet sauvignon grapes but the newly blended sample we tasted had yet to find a point of equilibrium. Despite this, the brilliant ruby and classic varietal aromas usher in a palate that satisfies for structure, body, length and zest.

○	Gavi Vigne Alte '00	ᵧᵧ	4
○	Gavi Vilma Cappelletti '00	ᵧ	3
●	Monferrato Rosso di Malì '99	ᵧ	3
○	Gavi Vigne Alte '99	ᵧᵧ	4
●	Monferrato Rosso di Malì '98	ᵧ	3

NOVI LIGURE (AL)

VIGNE DEL PARETO
VIA GAVI, 105
15067 NOVI LIGURE (AL)
TEL. 0108398776
E-MAIL: ilpareto@iol.it

Pietro Occhetti, an entrepreneur who originally hails from Genoa but who settled down in this area some time ago, is consolidating the dynamic image of his winery, which lies on the celebrated, scenic Lomellina road between Novi and Gavi on the old highway to Genoa. The new south-facing vineyards, planted to red varieties and next to the main house, are about to come onstream. All credit to Pietro, who has successfully reclaimed a plot that is well-suited to viticulture but stands on a steep incline. It had been left to run wild as it was considered too difficult to cultivate and not profitable enough. We look forward to heaping similar praise on the wines yielded by its red earth. In the meantime, however, we were more than satisfied by both of Pietro's Gavi del Paretos, which were supervised in the cellar by Mario Ronco from Monferrato. The Ricella Alta cru is a luminous straw-yellow flecked with green. It has a full, generous, floral bouquet full of vegetal and unexpected mineral tones, ranging from red pepper to basil, peach and balsam. The palate convinces with its fullness, elegance, complexity and gentle freshness. The Gavi Il Pareto, another freshly coloured, straw-yellow offering with green lights, possesses a lovely pure nose with a cornucopia of aromas including flowers, apples, pears and citrus fruit. Its magnificent structure is a perfect match for the tangy palate, rendered velvety and round by its substantial alcohol. The finish is long and pleasing.

| ○ | Gavi Ricella Alta '00 | ᵧᵧ | 4 |
| ○ | Gavi Vigne del Pareto '00 | ᵧᵧ | 4 |

PIOBESI D'ALBA (CN)

Tenuta Carretta
Loc. Carretta, 2
12040 Piobesi d'Alba (CN)
Tel. 0173619119
E-mail: t.carretta@tenutacarretta.it

Tenuta Carretta's new project was launched in 1996 when Paolo Dracone and the technical team, headed by Marco Monchiero and Gian Domenico Negro, joined the winery, Negro on a more or less full-time basis. That project is now a reality. A couple of final modifications to the company itself and in the vineyards, including perhaps a new plot or two in the Langhe, and this estate is poised to become a leading player not just in Roero but beyond. Meanwhile, we tasted some superb reds for this edition of the Guide. In contrast, the whites still have room for improvement, even though they have come a long way. The nebbiolo-based selections were by far the best, from three hectares planted to Barolo at Cannubi, four in Treiso in Cascina Bordino, and 11 in Piobesi, home of the Bric Paradiso. In fact, the Roero Superiore Bric Paradiso is a very fine wine, one of the best in its category. A rich, vibrant ruby, it offers aromas of fresh bramble and other ripe berry fruit, rounded off with a nicely judged dose of balsam and faint toasty notes that lift the entire bouquet. The palate is fruit-driven, caressing and long, with sweet tannins marking the typically Piedmontese finish. The Cannubi, a Barolo obtained from the grapes of one of the most famous Barolo crus, is an austere bottle that shuns modish trends. We also liked the Barbaresco Cascina Bordino, which returns to the Two Glass category with elegance, mouthfilling warmth, and a lingering, sweetly tannic finish. One notch below this is the Langhe Bric Quercia, a blend of 85 per cent barbera and 15 per cent nebbiolo while the Arneis Canorei has a richer taste profile than the standard-label version.

● Roero Sup. Bric Paradiso '99	ΨΨ	5
● Barolo Vigneti in Cannubi '97	ΨΨ	6
● Barbaresco Cascina Bordino '98	ΨΨ	6
○ Roero Arneis Vigna Canorei '00	Ψ	4
● Langhe Rosso Bric Quercia '99	Ψ	5
○ Roero Arneis '00		4
● Barolo Vigneti in Cannubi '95	ΨΨ	6
● Barbaresco Cascina Bordino '96	ΨΨ	6
● Barolo Vigneti in Cannubi '96	ΨΨ	6
● Langhe Bric Quercia '97	ΨΨ	4
● Langhe Bric Quercia '98	ΨΨ	4
● Roero Sup. Bric Paradiso '98	ΨΨ	4

PRIOCCA (CN)

Hilberg - Pasquero
Via Bricco Gatti, 16
12040 Priocca (CN)
Tel. 0173616197
E-mail: hilberg@libero.it

Assisted by wife Annette Hilberg and mother Clementina, Michele Pasquero runs this small Roero winery that produces a very good range of wines, good enough in fact to earn him Three Glasses for the last three years. His Nebbiolo d'Alba '99 is a thoroughbred that matches the Barbera d'Alba Superiore pace for pace in terms of elegance and delight but beats it into second place by a neck with a shade more complexity. This year's Three Glass champion is an opaque garnet with a brief rim and an opulent, fascinating nose that gives off aromas of ripe black berry fruits and tobacco leaf, layered over refined mineral notes. Full-bodied on the palate, it shows firm tannins and vigorous length that unhurriedly resonates with notes of cocoa powder and liquorice. The glorious Barbera d'Alba Superiore '99 is almost as impressive on the nose. Dense and complex, it precedes a challenging body and outstanding length. This year, the estate's superb range of wines welcomes a new recruit, a Langhe Rosso that immediately wins a resounding Two Glasses. It is a blend of nebbiolo and barbera, in proportions established each year according to the harvest to create a wine that is as harmonious as possible. The '99 vintage contains a lion's share of nebbiolo - 60 per cent - and is a wonderful, deep garnet. The lovely, complex bouquet foregrounds wild berry fruit, grass, almonds and mint. The attack on the palate is robust and rich, with strong tannins that make their presence felt in the dry, violet-tinged finish. The standard-label Barbera has a fresh, fruity nose with brief hints of mineral, then offers a palate of reasonably concentrated acidity and good length.

● Nebbiolo d'Alba '99	ΨΨΨ	5
● Barbera d'Alba Sup. '99	ΨΨ	5
● Langhe Rosso '99	ΨΨ	5
● Barbera d'Alba '00	Ψ	4
● Vareij Rosso '00	Ψ	3
● Barbera d'Alba Sup. '97	ΨΨΨ	5
● Barbera d'Alba Sup. '98	ΨΨΨ	5
● Nebbiolo d'Alba '97	ΨΨ	4
● Nebbiolo d'Alba '98	ΨΨ	5

PRIOCCA (CN)

Cascina Val del Prete
Strada Santuario, 2
12040 Priocca (CN)
Tel. 0173616534
E-mail: valdelprete@tiscalinet.it

The Roagnas' winery comprises about eight hectares planted to vine and turns out approximately 40,000 bottles a year. This winemaking family concentrates on producing typical Roero wines and bringing out their territorial identity. This year, they bowled us over with a magnificent Nebbiolo d'Alba Vigna di Lino that delighted the panel came very close to winning Three Glasses. This richly-hued beauty has a very well-knit nose of sweet spices and enticing notes of berry fruit, vanilla and Peruvian bark. On the palate, it reveals good character which, thanks to a judicious use of oak, balances the weighty extract to perfection. The long violet-themed finish pays tribute to the fullness of an elegant, velvet-smooth wine. The intense ruby Barbera Carolina has garnet highlights and an alluring bouquet that hints at wild berry fruit, vanilla, and cedarwood. Succulent and dynamic on the palate, it finishes on a lingering note of cocoa powder and caramel. Last of all, the Arneis Luet possesses floral and apricot tones and a pleasant, weighty palate punctuated by strong notes of fresh aromatic herbs. We did not have a chance to sample the Roero '99, however, as it has been left to age further in the bottle. We look forward to tasting it next year. The Roagnos are looking to the future and plan to increase production with another hectare planted to nebbiolo at Bricco Gatti, in the municipality of Priocca. A brand new Roero will bear the name of the cru on the label.

● Nebbiolo d'Alba Vigna di Lino '99	🍷🍷	5
● Barbera d'Alba '00	🍷🍷	3
● Barbera d'Alba Sup. Carolina '99	🍷🍷	5
○ Roero Arneis Luet '00	🍷	3
● Barbera d'Alba Sup. Carolina '97	🍷🍷	4
● Barbera d'Alba Sup. Carolina '98	🍷🍷	5
● Nebbiolo d'Alba Vigna di Lino '98	🍷🍷	5
● Roero '98	🍷🍷	4

ROCCA GRIMALDA (AL)

Cascina La Maddalena
Loc. Piani del Padrone, 258
15067 Rocca Grimalda (AL)
Tel. 0143876074 - 0143745989
E-mail: info@cascina-maddalena.com

For some years now, the top estates in upper Monferrato have been run by women. No longer content to stay in the home, the women of the wine world have become the guardians of the territory, demanding the best from vineyard and cellar with passion, skill and care. Again this year, Anna Poggio, Cristina Bozzano and Marilena De Gasperi have brought prestige to the Ovada area with a range of quality wines. Dolcetto and barbera are their mainstays for they firmly believe in native varieties. In this tasting, our favourite was the Rossa d'Ocra '99, a Barbera part aged in one year old barrels. Deep ruby with youthful violet highlights, it shows a refined nose of ripe berry fruit then a palate that happily weds warmth and softness without sacrificing any of its freshness or length. We have great hopes for the Bricco Maddalena. Already a Two Glass winner, cellaring will lend complexity and balance both to the nose and to the palate. The standard-label Dolcetto, a wonderful, vibrant ruby, releases delicious notes of fruit with gamey, almost tertiary, aromas. The palate is rustic with strong tannins. Warm tones and good persistence round it off nicely. We also liked the Bricco del Bagatto for its ruby red, perked up by purple highlights, and the rich array of aromas that include berry fruit, animal notes, charred oak and coffee. The palate is warm, mellow and moderately tannic.

● Barbera del M.to Rossa d'Ocra '99	🍷🍷	4
● Monferrato Rosso Bricco Maddalena '99	🍷🍷	5
● Dolcetto di Ovada '00	🍷	3*
● Dolcetto di Ovada Bricco del Bagatto '00	🍷	4
● Monferrato Rosso Bricco Maddalena '97	🍷🍷	5
● Monferrato Rosso Bricco Maddalena '98	🍷🍷	5
● Dolcetto di Ovada Bricco del Bagatto '99	🍷🍷	4

ROCCHETTA TANARO (AT)

BRAIDA
VIA ROMA, 94
14030 ROCCHETTA TANARO (AT)
TEL. 0141644113
E-MAIL: info@braida.it

This year, every single one of this Rocchetta Tanaro-based winery's offerings is quite excellent. The Grignolino d'Asti is pale, with evident tannins, and has a concentration of aromas reminiscent of moscato rosa and hints of bramble, geranium and white pepper. The palate is scrumptious, supple and similar to the vibrant, lively La Monella '00. The fragrant Brachetto d'Acqui and the varietal Dolcetto d'Alba '00 both put on a good show. The Fiore '00, a blend of chardonnay and riesling renano, is refreshing and simple with a clean, pleasant palate. At a different and altogether superior level, is the Asso di Fiori '99, a monovarietal barrique-aged chardonnay. Its nose is still dominated by the toasty notes of the oak but the wine promises to evolve well in the bottle. The lightweight Moscato d'Asti Vigna Senza Nome has delicate hints of fruit and orange blossom, leading in to a pleasant, well-balanced palate. Moving on to the big Barberas, the Ai Suma is absent this year but the Bricco dell'Uccellone and the Bigotta are resplendent in all their finery. The first of these is clear ruby with a nose that mingles oak with intense notes of plum and small berry fruit. Its authoritative entry on the palate reveals remarkable breadth. The Bigotta, one of the best versions we have seen of this wine, tends to the sophisticated rather than the powerful. Deep ruby with lovely, rich violet highlights, it has a luscious, complex nose full of spice and liquorice that play hide and seek with notes of wild berries and violets. Juicy but not too muscular on the palate, it shows clear acidity that never threatens to overwhelm the measured tannins.

ROCCHETTA TANARO (AT)

HASTAE
P.ZZA ITALIA, 1/BIS
14030 ROCCHETTA TANARO (AT)
TEL. 0141644113

Project Quorum forges ahead, collecting its first international plaudits. The brainchild of six big wineries, it is designed to promote Barbera d'Asti and create a wine that can hold its own against the best reds from Italy and elsewhere. Riccardo Cotarella, a very talented oenologist, is in the driving seat and he has the skills to take both indigenous and international varieties and get the very best from them with extraordinary results. The project stipulates very limited yields per hectare, careful vineyard management and winemaking techniques, all in the name of quality. The grapes, harvested from vineyards meticulously selected by each producer, are assembled in the cellar of the Coppo brothers, one of the participating wineries. Here, they are vinified separately and then blended. Quorum '99 lets you know straight away it is a serious proposition with its dark, almost opaque, ruby of incredible depth. Mineral and ripe fruit aromas rise up to greet the nose, ushering in a veritable treasure trove of extract. This is confirmed on the palate where the youthful qualities of the wine emerge even more evidently than in the bouquet. The oaky notes from barrel ageing have not yet found perfect harmony with the fruit and the first few seconds in the mouth are dominated by a strong toastiness. The lingering persistence on the palate underline the wine's power and softness, making it a stylish, fascinating bottle in the international idiom.

● Barbera d'Asti Bricco della Bigotta '99	▼▼ 6
● Barbera d'Asti Bricco dell'Uccellone '99	▼▼ 6
○ Langhe Bianco Asso di Fiori '99	▼▼ 4
● Barbera del M.to La Monella '00	▼ 3
● Brachetto d'Acqui '00	▼ 4
● Dolcetto d'Alba Serra dei Fiori '00	▼ 3
● Grignolino d'Asti '00	▼ 3
○ Langhe Bianco Il Fiore '00	▼ 3
○ Moscato d'Asti Vigna Senza Nome '00	▼ 3
● Bricco dell'Uccellone '91	▼▼▼ 6
● Barbera d'Asti Bricco dell'Uccellone '98	▼▼▼ 6

● Barbera d'Asti Quorum '99	▼▼ 6
● Barbera d'Asti Quorum '97	▼▼ 6
● Barbera d'Asti Quorum '98	▼▼ 6

RODELLO (CN)

F.lli Mossio
Fraz. Cascina Caramelli
Via Montà, 12
12050 Rodello (CN)
tel. 0173617149
e-mail: mossio@mossio.com

The large Mossio family has been making wine for a long time now. Cousins Valerio and Remo run the business full-time, but the rest of the tribe, who all have other jobs, also make an important contribution. Valerio's brothers, the explosive Mauro and Guido, their mother and aunt, and Remo's brother, Claudio, are all involved. The wines, produced with the collaboration of Beppe Caviola, are very good. We'll start our tasting notes with the Dolcetto Bricco Caramelli, from 50 year old vineyard. This Dolcetto more than holds its own against its peers and won Three Glasses in recognition of the tenacity and skills of a winemaking family that has yet to attract the attention it deserves. The '00 vintage is an impenetrable garnet and has an intense, generous nose of fruit syrup, eucalyptus, confectioner's cream and cocoa powder. The palate is full-bodied and flavoursome, opening out steadily to end in a captivating finish that focuses on liquorice. The Piano delli Perdoni reveals violet highlights in the glass and gorgeous fruity aromas of black cherry and cherry, contrasting with hints of coffee cream. It is complex and invigorating on the palate, with a hint of austerity, and ends on a note of balsam and fruit. The Langhe Rosso, a nebbiolo and barbera blend, is the estate's first ever. Only 1,200 bottles were released of a wine that offers aromas of almonds, black cherry and mint. On the palate, it is dense, with lashings of tannins and a dynamic finish. The Dolcetto Superiore '99 has a youthful colour, aromas that range from plum to peach to pepper, and a well-developed, robust palate that is a little taut but shows firm structure. The excellent standard-label Dolcetto is agreeably rustic and consistent.

● Dolcetto d'Alba Bricco Caramelli '00	🍷🍷🍷	4
● Dolcetto d'Alba '00	🍷🍷	3*
● Dolcetto d'Alba Piano delli Perdoni '00	🍷🍷	4
● Langhe Rosso '98	🍷🍷	5
● Dolcetto d'Alba Sup. '99	🍷🍷	4
● Dolcetto d'Alba Bricco Caramelli '99	🍷🍷	4

ROSIGNANO MONFERRATO (AL)

Vicara
Cascina Madonna delle Grazie, 5
15030 Rosignano Monferrato (AL)
tel. 0142488054
e-mail: vicara@vicara.it

Quality at the Vicara estate continues to improve. The three partners, Diego Visconti, Carlo Cassinis and Domenico Ravizza, are supported by oenologist Mario Ronco. Their Cantico della Crosia, a big barrique-aged Barbera, has a rich, pervasive bouquet that suggests tobacco and liquorice, with undertones of black berry fruit. The palate is well-rounded and well-structured. A blend of 70 per cent barbera, 20 per cent cabernet, with additions of nebbiolo and merlot, the Rubello offers aromas of bramble, red pepper and cocoa powder underscored by a lovely peachy tone. The palate reveals soft, well-sustained volume. The Sarnì, a barrique-conditioned Chardonnay, comes in half-litre bottles and suggests banana and summer flowers with an almost buttery sensation left by the wine's sojourn in new oak. The palate is full-bodied and well-structured. The Airales, 40 per cent cortese, 40 per cent chardonnay and the rest sauvignon, has refreshing aromas of pineapple, tangerine and summer flowers. The floral palate coyly reveals its roundness. The Uccelletta, a grignolino and pinot nero blend, reveals a distinctive bouquet of flowers, raspberry and pepper, with a hint of vanilla. The fruit spills over onto the clean, velvety palate, giving way to slightly mouth-drying tannins in the finish. The Barbera Superiore is traditional but not in the least rustic. The nose is a riot of flowers and mouth-watering minty tones. The palate has medium structure and attractive balance. The Grignolino shows raspberry and pomegranate aromas with notes of spice and balsamic mint. The palate has a softness unheard of in a Grignolino until a few years ago.

○ Monferrato Bianco Airales '00	🍷🍷	4
● Barbera del M.to Sup. Cantico della Crosia '99	🍷🍷	4
○ Monferrato Bianco Sarnì '99	🍷🍷	5
● Monferrato Rosso Rubello '99	🍷🍷	4
● Grignolino del M.to Casalese '00	🍷	3
● Barbera del M.to Sup. '99	🍷	3
● Monferrato Rosso l'Uccelletta '99	🍷	4
● Barbera del M.to Volpuva '00		3
● Monferrato Rosso Rubello '97	🍷🍷	4
● Barbera del M.to Sup. Cantico della Crosia '98	🍷🍷	4

SAN GIORGIO CANAVESE (TO)

Orsolani
Via Michele Chiesa, 12
10090 San Giorgio Canavese (TO)
Tel. 012432386
E-mail: orsolani@tiscalinet.it

Gigi Orsolani is a staunch advocate of the erbaluce variety and, in particular, of the wine that is obtained from the raisined grapes. Once you have tasted his Caluso Passito Sulé, it is impossible to demur. Without a shadow of a doubt, it is one of the best dried-grape wines in the zone. The initial customary note of super-ripeness is followed by an elegance rarely seen in these latitudes. Rich yellow, shading into gold, it unveils a bouquet of honeyed tones and ripe, raisined fruit. The palate reveals harmony, rich flavour, and near-perfect balance right through to the finish. From the same vineyard, the Orsolanis produce two Erbaluce di Caluso selections. This year, the La Rustìa was the more successful of the two. It's a white obtained from the very best of the estate's grapes, which are left on the vine until they turn amber in warmth of the sun. The elegant nose opens very gradually, showing hints of dried grapeskin that melt into ripe fruit sensations and toasted almond. The palate is fabulously long and persistent. The Sant'Antonio selection is not quite up to the same standards. Matured in barriques, the latest version is still dominated by oak, but it will no doubt age well and the edginess will mellow out. The Spumante Metodo Classico Brut, somewhat overshadowed by the Gran Riserva, wins one well-deserved Glass. We tasted the '95 again and are happy to report that we liked it just as much as we did last year. The Carema made a fine debut on its first official review in the Guide. The Orsolanis rely on technical assistance from the highly acclaimed Donato Lanati.

O	Erbaluce di Caluso La Rustìa '00	ΨΨ	4
O	Caluso Passito Sulé '96	ΨΨ	6
●	Carema Le Tappie '96	Ψ	5
O	Cuvée Storica Spumante M. Cl. '97	Ψ	5
O	Caluso Bianco Vignot S. Antonio '99	Ψ	4
O	Caluso Passito La Rustìa '94	ΨΨ	5
O	Cuvée Storica Spumante M. Cl. '96	ΨΨ	5
O	Cuvée Storica Spumante M. Cl. Gran Riserva '95	ΨΨ	5
O	Caluso Bianco Vignot S. Antonio '98	ΨΨ	4

SAN MARTINO ALFIERI (AT)

Marchesi Alfieri
Castello Alfieri
14010 San Martino Alfieri (AT)
Tel. 0141976288 - 0141976015
E-mail: latota@tin.it

Marchesi Alfieri has 18 hectares planted to vine with an annual production of about 80,000 bottles. These, in short, are the dimensions of this estate, which makes wines of excellent quality. The wines presented on our visit this year many and impressive. We'll start with the Barberas. All were excellent and one, the Alfiera '99, was a worthy Three Glass winner. We have regularly been impressed by this Barbera over the years and the '99 is a marvel. Dark in appearance, it flaunts sophisticated aromas of plum and bramble, offset by intriguing notes of balsam and juniper. The concentrated palate expands satisfyingly, showing depth and a wonderful finish that lingers on notes of liquorice and soft fruit. The Alfiera '98, another dense wine in the glass, hints at fruit over a base of thyme, eucalyptus and vanilla. The potent palate is rendered a little severe by prominent tannins. The La Tota '99 is a fairly intense ruby with a youthful rime. The intense, distinctive aromas of strawberry, peach, white pepper and geranium are well-defined and the palate is inviting and intense. The superb Grignolino Sansoero, a rich cherry red, has a clean nose suggesting black pepper and fruit. It is succulent, dry and persistent on the palate. The San Germano, a pinot nero-based red, is a moderately rich ruby with a bouquet that opens out gradually to reveal notes of violet, earth and rhubarb. The palate is well-structured and slightly austere. The Rosso dei Marchesi has a cakey nose and a palate of medium intensity. Finally, the riesling italico-based Bianco dei Marchesi is tidy and low-key, with a markedly floral nose.

●	Barbera d'Asti Sup. Alfiera '99	ΨΨΨ	5
●	Piemonte Grignolino Sansoero '00	ΨΨ	4
●	Barbera d'Asti Sup. Alfiera '98	ΨΨ	5
●	Barbera d'Asti La Tota '99	ΨΨ	4
O	Monferrato Bianco dei Marchesi '00	Ψ	3
●	Monferrato Rosso dei Marchesi '99	Ψ	3
●	Monferrato Rosso S. Germano '98	Ψ	5
●	Barbera d'Asti Sup. Alfiera '96	ΨΨ	5
●	Barbera d'Asti Sup. Alfiera '97	ΨΨ	5
●	Monferrato Rosso S. Germano '97	ΨΨ	5

SAN MARZANO OLIVETO (AT)

ALFIERO BOFFA
VIA LEISO, 50
14050 SAN MARZANO OLIVETO (AT)
TEL. 0141856115
E-MAIL: alfieroboffa@tin.it

Among the excellent wines offered by Rossano and Alfiero Boffa, there is one type that stands head and shoulders above the rest: the Barbera. Four out of the six we tasted were worthy of Two Glasses. Each has its own distinct personality and the skill of the Boffas lies in their ability to bring out the character of each cru. The Vigne delle More '99 is dark, intense ruby with garnet highlights and sports an alluring nose of ripe cherry and pepper with faint gamey undertones. On the palate, it is soft and nicely fleshy with a lingering finish. The more austere Collina della Vedova '98 is dark in appearance and has an elegant blackcurrant, cherry and cocoa powder nose layered over characteristic earthy tones. The attack on the palate is powerful and the progression shows notable structure. The mint and fruit finish is long and vigorous. The richly-hued Vigna Ronco '99 is refined and full-bodied, with aromas that range from fruit to mineral tones. The generous palate is nicely buttressed by fine tannins and has good length. The exciting, gutsy Muntrivé '99 is rich garnet in appearance and offers a nose of resin, dried mushrooms and rain-soaked earth over varietal ripe fruit. The Cua Longa '99 has rather an evolved nose but it is complex and deeply satisfying then the palate reveals a soft, generous texture. The Testimonium is evolved and rather severe, hinting at animal skins and tar. The Velo di Maya, 70 per cent barbera, is excellent, full-bodied and sophisticated with fruity, balsamic tones dominating. Finally, the Moscato Vigna Lupa is a pleasant bottle.

SAN MARZANO OLIVETO (AT)

TENUTA DELL'ARBIOLA
LOC. ARBIOLA
REG. SALINE, 56
14050 SAN MARZANO OLIVETO (AT)
TEL. 0141856194 - 0115187122
E-MAIL: arbiola@tin.it

Domenico and Carla Terzano, with son Riccardo, run this beautiful winery that lies between Agliano and Vinchio in a zone ideal for the cultivation of barbera. They are supported by Federico Curatz and Beppe Caviola, vineyard manager and oenologist respectively. Of the wines they gave us to taste for this year's Guide, we very much liked their Monferrato Rosso Dom, a barbera, pinot nero and cabernet blend. Dark garnet, its bouquet opens out gradually to reveal notes of berry fruit and vanilla cream. The palate shows lovely robust tannins that add to its already dense texture. The finish echoes the nose with refreshing touches of balsam. The Barbera La Romilda V, a deep garnet wine that shades into purple, releases notes of raspberry syrup, dried herbs, and cake. The palate is pleasantly vigorous and drives forward robustly to end on a note of cherry in a wonderfully warm framework. The Moscato Ferlingot '00 also merits Two Glasses for its hints of peach, aromatic herbs and lemon against a backdrop of nutmeg. The front palate is big and flavoursome, expanding firmly and nicely supported by the prickle and an agreeable acidulous vein. To finish off, we gave One Glass to the almost violet Barbera Carlotta, which boasts aromas of cherry and pepper in a framework notable for its youthful vinosity and no-nonsense, pleasantly rustic palate.

● Barbera d'Asti Sup. Collina della Vedova '98	ŸŸ	5
● Velo di Maya '98	ŸŸ	5
● Barbera d'Asti Sup. Vigna delle More '99	ŸŸ	4
● Barbera d'Asti Sup. Vigna Muntrivé '99	ŸŸ	4
● Barbera d'Asti Sup. Vigna Ronco '99	ŸŸ	4
○ Moscato d'Asti Vigna Lupa '00	Ÿ	3
● Barbera d'Asti Sup. Testimonium '97	Ÿ	5
● Barbera d'Asti Sup. Vigna Cua Longa '99	Ÿ	4

○ Moscato d'Asti Ferlingot '00	ŸŸ	3*
● Barbera d'Asti Sup. La Romilda V '99	ŸŸ	5
● Monferrato Rosso Dom '99	ŸŸ	5
● Barbera d'Asti La Carlotta '99	Ÿ	4
● Barbera d'Asti Sup. La Romilda IV '98	ŸŸ	4
● Monferrato Rosso Dom '98	ŸŸ	5
● Barbera d'Asti La Carlotta '98	Ÿ	4

SANTO STEFANO BELBO (CN)

Ca' d'Gal
Fraz. Valdivilla
Via Strada Vecchia, 108
12058 Santo Stefano Belbo (CN)
tel. 0141847103

This year, Alessandro Boido's consistent and valid range included one very good bottle in particular: the Moscato d'Asti Vigna Vecchia. Full of flavour, it is more rounded than refreshing and will be appreciated by all those who love this type of Moscato. A fairly rich straw-yellow, it has a nose packed with intense fruit aromas, especially peach, spring flowers and resin, with faint vegetal undertones. The palate immediately unveils the fullness of the wine and the progression is well-sustained through to the long finish, which mirrors the nose. The fairly deep straw yellow standard-label Moscato offers notes of wood resin, fruit, yeast and flowers, and has reasonable presence on the palate which is nicely rounded off by a complex finish of fresh lemon tones. The simple, well-sustained Chardonnay is a lustrous straw yellow, introducing a nose that hints at fermentation, hedgerow, banana and hazelnut. On the palate, it shows its easy drinkability and its tangy, invigorating acidity. The Langhe Pian del Gäje, obtained from freisa, barbera and dolcetto, is dense and dark, with a nose of charred oak, black berry fruit and dried leaf. Although well-structured, the palate is rather dry.

○ Moscato d'Asti Vigna Vecchia '00	♀♀	4
○ Langhe Chardonnay '00	♀	3
○ Moscato d'Asti Vigneti Ca' d'Gal '00	♀	3
● Langhe Rosso Pian del Gäje '98	♀	4
● Dolcetto d'Alba Vigneti Ca' d'Gal '99		3

SANTO STEFANO BELBO (CN)

Piero Gatti
Loc. Moncucco, 28
12058 Santo Stefano Belbo (CN)
tel. 0141840918

Piero Gatti's Moscato d'Asti is one of the best in its category. The '00 vintage is a fabulous blend of complexity and elegance in a framework of superlative balance. Its rich, vibrant straw yellow ushers in pure aromas of ripe peach, flowers and fresh aromatic herbs layered over delicious creamy undertones that all mingle richly and seductively. The palate immediately reveals this wine's fullness and flesh, with a clear sweet vein nicely held in check by the acidity and the carbon dioxide. The finish is intense and holds up well, lingeringly echoing the fruity notes of peach and apple. The Freisa Violetta del '99 is a rich ruby red with garnet highlights and a slightly pale edge. Its straightforward, candid nose suggests hay, candied cherries and liquorice, and the intriguing, full palate is refreshed by a restrained acidulous vein. The Verbeia, 80 per cent barbera and 20 per cent freisa, is very dark in hue and displays rather a rustic nose, a flavoursome palate, and exceptional vigour. Lastly, the Brachetto is a limpid cherry red with orange highlights ushering in a varietal nose with aromas of dried rose petals and berry fruit. The palate shows good balance between the sweet vein and the prickle, and the finish, which mirrors the nose, is dried by a faint tannic note.

○ Piemonte Moscato '00	♀♀	3*
● Piemonte Brachetto '00	♀	4
● Verbeia '99	♀	4
● Langhe Freisa La Violetta '99	♀	4

SANTO STEFANO BELBO (CN)

Sergio Grimaldi - Ca' du Sindic
Loc. San Grato, 15
12058 Santo Stefano Belbo (CN)
Tel. 0141840341

Sergio Grimaldi's Moscato Ca' du Sindic Capsula Oro, a new, more concentrated version that recalls the Moscatos of old, is without doubt one of the best in its category. It puts the emphasis more on fullness than on freshness, as is borne out by its distinctive, deep straw yellow hue, and has a nose of peaches in syrup, mint and wood resin in a rich mature framework. The palate mirrors the nose and is flavoursome, big, chewy and pleasantly fizzy, with lingering aromatic length. The Moscato Ca' du Sindic Capsula Argento is a rich straw yellow with faint green highlights. The nose, not quite as refined as that of its stablemate, contains notes of apples, pears, peaches, apricots and dried aromatic herbs. The cherry red Brachetto '00 is vibrant with violet lights. It offers aromas of dried roses and berry fruit, then the fluent, uncomplicated palate shows discreet sparkle and an ever so slightly dry tannic note. The deeply-hued Barbera Vivace '00 is a tad rustic. At the time of our tasting, the Barbera d'Asti '99 was still maturing, but we did sample the '98 selection again and are happy to report that it was every bit as good as we found it last year. The extra year has blunted the acidic edginess, rendering the palate softer.

○	Moscato d'Asti Ca' du Sindic Capsula Oro '00	4
○	Moscato d'Asti Ca' du Sindic Capsula Argento '00	3
●	Piemonte Brachetto Ca' du Sindic '00	3
●	Piemonte Barbera Vivace '00	2
●	Barbera d'Asti '98	3

SANTO STEFANO BELBO (CN)

I Vignaioli di S. Stefano
Fraz. Marini, 12
12058 Santo Stefano Belbo (CN)
Tel. 0141840419

Santo Stefano Belbo is an important spot for Moscato fans. These hills, perfect for the variety, traditionally produce some of the best Moscato d'Astis and I Vignaioli di Santo Stefano are among the best the leading exponents. The excellent Moscato d'Asti '00 is proof of this. A lovely lustrous straw yellow, it proffers a host of clean, alluring fragrances that form a sturdy aromatic framework where perfectly orchestrated notes of peach, apricot and candied orange mingle with refreshing touches of mint and lemon. The palate lets you know at once that this Moscato is big and round. It opens generously, very well buttressed by invigorating acidity and discreet spritz, leading into a lingering finish that echoes the nose and a wonderful after-aroma that recalls, amongst other things, elegant hints of peach and mint. This is a wine that balances to perfection the fullness of its palate with a bouquet of unparalleled elegance. Lower down on the harmony scale, but still pretty good, is the intense straw yellow Asti Spumante '00. It displays a pleasant, easy nose and a fairly even palate, with refreshing fizz and a relatively long, bitterish finish.

○	Moscato d'Asti '00	4
○	Asti '00	4

SAREZZANO (AL)

MUTTI
LOC. SAN RUFFINO, 49
15050 SAREZZANO (AL)
TEL. 0131884119

Andrea Muzzi is a shy chap but he transforms completely if you push the right buttons, namely those wired to his passion for wine. He has a wealth of technical knowledge and is very well versed in a whole range of subjects, including oenology. When he graduated with a degree in agriculture, Andrea made the decision to become, as he puts it, a "free man", and took up the reins of the family winery with determination. In our tasting notes, we feel compelled to pay tribute to the best Timorasso Castagnoli this estate has ever produced, a happy balance of the customary fullness with added complexity and sophistication. The nose offers grapefruit, spring flowers and honey aromas then the rich, gutsy palate keeps your interest with a pleasant acidic vein. Still on the whites, we found the Sauvignon Sull'Aia irresistible. This is a wine that never falls victim to the excesses that so often afflict the variety. Well balanced and very agreeable, its intense, varietal aromas lead into a consistent palate that reveals the juicy softness of the fruit, enlivened by just the right dose of tangy acidity. Of the reds we were offered, our favourite was the black Rivadestra, with its ripe berry and spice aromas that harmonize so nicely with the grassiness of the cabernet. Its dense, velvety palate follows through well with loads of ripe, vibrant fruit. The San Ruffino, 100 per cent barbera, shows great potential but could do with a bit longer in the bottle to come together fully. It offers aromas of ripe berry fruit, spice and leather, as well as a full-bodied palate with mildly domineering acidity and a finish of medium length.

	Wine	Glasses	Score
O	Colli Tortonesi Bianco Sull'Aia '00	ŸŸ	3*
O	Colli Tortonesi Bianco Timorasso Castagnoli '99	ŸŸ	3*
●	Colli Tortonesi Rosso Rivadestra '99	ŸŸ	4
●	Colli Tortonesi Rosso S. Ruffino '99	Ÿ	4
●	Colli Tortonesi Rosso Rivadestra '98	ŸŸ	4
O	Colli Tortonesi Bianco Sull'Aia '99	ŸŸ	3

SCURZOLENGO (AT)

CANTINE SANT'AGATA
REG. MEZZENA, 19
14030 SCURZOLENGO (AT)
TEL. 0141203186
E-MAIL: info@santagata.com

This beautiful Monferrato Asti estate north of Tanaro is owned by the Cavallero brothers, Franco and Claudio, who produce a range of good quality wines, many of which are the typical offerings of this zone. Their Monferrato Rosso Genesi, a barbera and ruché blend, is a Two Glass winner, thanks to a garnet hue with an orange edge that introduces aromas of wild berries, wild fennel and hazelnut. The palate has good weight and mirrors the nose. There is a markedly dry note and a nice long finish. The Barbera Piatin is relatively intense in colour and has a bouquet of strawberry, rhubarb and spice through which run faint traces of almond and mint. The palate is dry and smooth. The Barbera Cavalé boasts a vegetal, cakey nose with a varietal, fruity base, then a coherent, dry palate with a very enjoyable finish. The Monferrato Monterovere, a blend of barbera, cabernet and nebbiolo, has a lovely rich colour and aromas of fruit and black pepper. The palate is smooth and satisfying but lacks the fullness of the '98. The straw yellow Cortese Ciarea shows notes of tangerine and apple and a complex palate that echoes the nose. The Eliseo, a white, mingles vegetal and floral tones and its taste profile is simple and understated. The Grignolino Miravalle boasts fruity aromas, rare for this variety, with traces of wood resin, then a dry, light palate with reasonable length. We also liked the touches of rose and spice evident in the Ruché 'Na Vota, and its invigorating, no-nonsense palate.

	Wine	Glasses	Score
●	Monferrato Rosso Genesi '97	ŸŸ	5
●	Ruché di Castagnole M.to 'Na Vota '00	ŸŸ	4
O	Cortese dell'Alto M.to Ciarea '00	Ÿ	3
●	Barbera d'Asti Sup. Cavalé '98	Ÿ	4
●	Barbera d'Asti Sup. Piatin '98	Ÿ	3
●	Grignolino d'Asti Miravalle '00	Ÿ	3
O	Monferrato Bianco Eliseo '99	Ÿ	3
●	Monferrato Rosso Monterovere '99	Ÿ	4
●	Monferrato Rosso Monterovere '98	ŸŸ	4
●	Ruché di Castagnole M.to 'Na Vota '98	ŸŸ	4
●	Ruché di Castagnole M.to 'Na Vota '99	ŸŸ	4

SERRALUNGA D'ALBA (CN)

Luigi Baudana
Fraz. Baudana, 43
12050 Serralunga d'Alba (CN)
tel. 0173613354
e-mail: luigibaudana@bdv-serralunga.com

Luigi and Fiorina Baudana never disappoint us with the 25,000 bottles they so dedicatedly produce on their four and a half-hectare estate each year. Best of this year's offerings was the Langhe Rosso Lorenso, 55 per cent nebbiolo, 25 per cent barbera, and 20 per cent merlot, which stands out for its sophistication and balance. A fairly deep garnet, it can show aromas of violets, berry fruits, coffee and vanilla cakes. The palate echoes the nose, revealing great texture and well-balanced tannins that linger on into its lengthy finish. The Barolo Cerretta Piani is a good solid colour with a lovely bouquet of raspberry, bilberry and rosemary underscored by pleasant cakey tones. On the palate, it is full-bodied, with tight-knit, fine-grained tannins that are kept in check by the alcohol, which lends warmth to the harmonious fruity, balsamic finish. The standard-label Barolo is a bit simpler but still very good. The Bianco Lorenso, chardonnay and sauvignon in equal parts, flaunts a lovely, rich colour and floral, fruity and vegetal aromas topped off by a touch of butter. The palate reveals decent weight but the notes of new oak have yet to smooth out completely. The Barbera d'Alba Donatella has an enchanting nose that hints at black berry fruit, dry leaf, and yeasted dough, then a gratifying palate that displays serious presence, consistent backbone and long length.

● Langhe Rosso Lorenso '99	ŶŶ	4
● Barolo Cerretta Piani '97	ŶŶ	6
● Barbera d'Alba Donatella '99	ŶŶ	4
● Barolo '97	Ŷ	6
○ Langhe Bianco Lorenso '99	Ŷ	4
● Barbera d'Alba Donatella '96	ŶŶ	4
● Barolo Cerretta Piani '96	ŶŶ	6
● Langhe Rosso Lorenso '98	ŶŶ	4
● Barbera d'Alba Donatella '98	ŶŶ	4
● Dolcetto d'Alba Sörì Baudana '99	ŶŶ	3
● Barbera d'Alba Donatella '97	Ŷ	4

SERRALUNGA D'ALBA (CN)

Fontanafredda
Via Alba, 15
12050 Serralunga d'Alba (CN)
tel. 0173613161
e-mail: fontanafredda@fontanafredda.it

The large Fontanafredda estate at Serralunga d'Alba, under the guidance of manager Gian Minetti and oenologist Danilo Drocco, offered us a wide range of wines, all with great quality and personality. We tasted a selection emblematic of the full potential of this magnificent winery, which dominates the slope leading down to the town. This is the birthplace of the Barolos that have won the estate the recognition it enjoys, and which today are the prime focus of the new management. The Vigna Lazzarito is notable for its deep ruby-garnet colour and fruit and spice nose. In the mouth, it reveals great structure and a finish lengthened by sweet, balanced tannins. The Vigna La Delizia is every bit as good, as is the Vigna La Villa-Paiagallo, from the estate vineyards in the municipality of Barolo. The Barolo Vigna La Rosa cru rounds off the selection, offering aromas of spice, dried roses and liquorice on the nose and a full-bodied, concentrated palate with still rather rugged tannins. The Barolo Serralunga d'Alba is simpler but still very traditional. The Barbaresco Coste Rubìn '98 is superb. Aged for one year in big barrels and for a second year in barriques, it presents a brilliant garnet colour and a fine, elegant nose of vanilla, spice and light oak. The palate has fabulous persistence but the finish is somewhat dried by the wood. The Barbera d'Alba Papagena, which falls into the new category of Langhe reds based on the variety, performed very well and the Gatinera Brut is excellent. We also enjoyed both the Diano d'Alba La Lepre and the Eremo, the latest addition to the house of Fontanafredda, obtained from a blend of nebbiolo, barbera and other varieties.

● Barolo Vigna La Rosa '97	ŶŶ	6
● Diano d'Alba Vigna La Lepre '00	ŶŶ	4
○ Gatinera Brut Talento '92	ŶŶ	5
● Barolo Vigna La Delizia '97	ŶŶ	6
● Barolo Vigna La Villa-Paiagallo '97	ŶŶ	6
● Barolo Vigna Lazzarito '97	ŶŶ	6
● Barbaresco Coste Rubìn '98	ŶŶ	6
● Barbera d'Alba Papagena '99	ŶŶ	4
○ Asti '00	Ŷ	4
○ Langhe Chardonnay Ampelio '00	Ŷ	4
● Barolo Serralunga d'Alba '97	Ŷ	6
● Barbera d'Alba Raimonda '99	Ŷ	3
● Langhe Eremo '99	Ŷ	4
● Barolo Vigna La Villa '96	ŶŶ	6
● Barolo Vigna Lazzarito '96	ŶŶ	6

SERRALUNGA D'ALBA (CN)

GABUTTI - FRANCO BOASSO
B.ta GABUTTI, 3/A
12050 SERRALUNGA D'ALBA (CN)
TEL. 0173613165

The Gabutti subzone is one of the finest in the municipality of Serralunga. It is noted mainly for its nebbiolo and great Barolos characterized by their power, longevity and their ability to reveal new depths as they age. The Boassos live right in the middle of Gabutti and have five hectares planted to vine that turn out 30,000 bottles a year. The estate's flagships are, of course, the two Barolos. The standard-label '97 vintage, which is strongly influenced by the harvest, reveals sensations of slightly over-ripe fruit. Garnet with an orange edge, it has a nose of wild berries, rhubarb, dried flowers, hay and leather. The palate at once reveals its extraordinary texture and the austerity of its tannins, and the aromas of the nose return all through the lingering finish. The Barolo Gabutti, from 50 year old vines, has a more stylish, immediate nose redolent of bramble, raspberry, violet and cocoa powder. Its impressive structure promises great things for the future but it already possesses a wonderfully smooth mouthfeel, rounded off by a final note of liquorice and cocoa powder. We liked the Barbera and the Dolcetto, the first buttressed by a fresh acidity, the second rather rustic and edgy.

● Barolo '97	♈♈	6
● Barolo Gabutti '97	♈♈	6
● Barbera d'Alba '00	♈	3
● Dolcetto d'Alba Meriane '00	♈	3
● Barolo Gabutti '90	♆♆	6
● Barolo Gabutti '93	♆♆	6
● Barolo '96	♆♆	6
● Barolo Gabutti '96	♆♆	6
● Barolo Gabutti '95	♆	6

SERRALUNGA D'ALBA (CN)

ETTORE GERMANO
LOC. CERRETTA, 1
12050 SERRALUNGA D'ALBA (CN)
TEL. 0173613528
E-MAIL:
germanoettore@bdv-serralunga.com

The wines of Sergio and Ettore Germano are as good as ever. We'll start our tasting notes with the Barbera Vigna della Madre '99, a garnet offering with a nose of ripe black berry fruit, roasted coffee beans and forest floor. The palate is full and generous, and the progression dries out little by little before the long, liquorice-themed finish. The Barolo Prapò '97 releases aromas of jam, and almond and mint-flavoured cake. The palate is solidly structured and the finish warm. The Cerretta is more eloquent and more intense, with a rich colour and an alluring nose that blends fruit, vanilla and charred oak aromas quite beautifully in a complex framework of mineral and earthy tones. The palate opens nicely to climax in a burst of energy, borne up by an abundance of fine-grained tannins, then the finish revels in lingering cocoa powder and violet sensations. The Balàu, a blend of dolcetto and barbera, sports an intriguing nose of cherry, strawberry and cocoa powder and a gutsy, flavoursome palate nicely rounded off by a vigorous finish. The Dolcetto Lorenzino has a bouquet that suggests wild berries and hay, and a full, invigorating palate. From riesling and chardonnay, the Binel offers alluring notes of butter, incense and hazelnut, then a generous, tangy palate. The Chardonnay has a very complex varietal nose but the palate is not particularly challenging. Just before we closed our tasting for this edition of the Guide, we managed to sample the Dolcetto Pra di Pò, which is, as ever, superb, intense and powerful.

● Barbera d'Alba Vigna della Madre '99	♈♈	4
● Dolcetto d'Alba Vigneto Pra di Pò '00	♈♈	4
● Barolo Cerretta '97	♈♈	6
● Barolo Prapò '97	♈♈	6
● Langhe Rosso Balàu '99	♈♈	5
● Dolcetto d'Alba Vigneto Lorenzino '00	♈	3
○ Langhe Chardonnay '00	♈	3
○ Langhe Bianco Binel '99	♈	4
● Barolo Cerretta '93	♆♆	6
● Barolo Cerretta '94	♆♆	6
● Barolo Cerretta '95	♆♆	6
● Barolo Prapò '95	♆♆	6
● Barolo Cerretta '96	♆	6
● Barolo Prapò '96	♆♆	6
● Barbera d'Alba Vigna della Madre '98	♆♆	4

SERRALUNGA D'ALBA (CN)

Luigi Pira
Via XX Settembre, 9
12050 Serralunga d'Alba (CN)
tel. 0173613106

Luigi has been joined by his sons Giampaolo and Romolo who help him tend the family's eight hectares planted to vine. Nebbiolo, grown in the most prestigious crus at Serralunga d'Alba – Vigna Rionda, Marenca and Margheria – accounts for 70 per cent of the harvest. Giampaolo is the uncontested king of the cellars, among the barriques and the 900-litre casks, both new and used, which are interspersed with 30-litre barrels. The Piras only started to produce Barolo with the harvest of '93, and in a few short years, the combination of their determination and common sense has wrought miracles, earning them high praise from the international press and Three Glasses from us for their sublime Barolo '97. This time, too, there were two sure-fire winners, the Marenca again, aged in barriques and 900-litre casks, and the Vigna Rionda, conditioned entirely in barriques. We can only report how good the Vigna Ronda is for only 700 bottles were produced, putting it beyond the reach of most Barolo lovers. But the 10,000 bottles of Marenca took our breath away. It is, quite simply, a flawless Barolo that combines tradition and innovation to perfection. Potent and richly extracted, it displays the blue-blooded tannins of the grand Serralunga crus, sweetened by a skilful touch of oak. The Barolo '97, 6,000 bottles of which were released, is obtained from the grapes in the lowest rows of vines at Margheria and Marenca. A tad austere, it has good alcoholic weight. Matured partly in used barriques and partly in barrels, the 7,000 bottles of Barolo Margheria are notable for a harmonious palate that still has a few rough edges. And last of all, the delicious Pira Dolcetto d'Alba has a fresh, youthful nose and the tannic character typical of this terrain.

Wine	Rating	Price
● Barolo Vigneto Marenca '97	🍷🍷🍷	6
● Dolcetto d'Alba '00	🍷🍷	4
● Barolo Vigneto Margheria '97	🍷🍷	6
● Barolo '97	🍷	6
● Barolo Vigneto Marenca '95	🍷🍷	6
● Barolo Vigneto Marenca '96	🍷🍷	6
● Barolo Vigneto Margheria '96	🍷🍷	6
● Barolo Vigneto Margheria '95	🍷	6

SERRALUNGA D'ALBA (CN)

Vigna Rionda - Massolino
P.zza Cappellano, 8
12050 Serralunga d'Alba (CN)
tel. 0173613138
e-mail: vignarionda@libero.it

The Massolinis have produced a rich, varied range of offerings that will thrill winelovers with the perfection of their execution. We'll start our review with the Barolos, all excellent. The Parafada '97, the most innovative of the bunch, is dark ruby-garnet and shows aromas of liqueur cherries, cloves and vanilla with delightful undertones of chocolate. Full and flavoursome on the palate, it opens vigorously to finish with long length. But it is the Margheria from the same vintage that best embodies all the characteristics of the Serralunga terrain at its peak. This is a classic Barolo that pays little heed to fashion. The aromas of black berry fruits and forest floor are firmly in a distinctive, rigorous framework. The palate reveals excellent pulp and strong, fine-grained tannins that run on into the long, coherent finish. This is a magnificent Barolo, and as tribute to the Massolinos' skill in coaxing the very best out of their crus. We gave it Three well-deserved Glasses. We also liked the Vigna Rionda Riserva '95, and awarded One Glass to the standard-label '97 version. The lustrous Chardonnay is very good, boasting a vanilla, apple and pear nose and good presence on the palate, with a final note of candied fruit. The Barbera Gisep is very dark and the nose hints at wild berries and cocoa powder. The palate displays great character and the finish is warm and lingering. The Piria '98 offers a lovely bouquet of cherry, pepper and forest floor and a gutsy, dry palate. The rich, agreeable Moscato and the robust, forthright Langhe Nebbiolo round off the list.

Wine	Rating	Price
● Barolo Margheria '97	🍷🍷🍷	6
● Barolo Vigna Rionda Ris. '95	🍷🍷	6
● Barolo Parafada '97	🍷🍷	6
● Langhe Rosso Piria '98	🍷🍷	6
● Barbera d'Alba Gisep '99	🍷🍷	5
○ Langhe Chardonnay '99	🍷🍷	4
○ Moscato d'Asti di Serralunga '00	🍷	3
● Barolo '97	🍷	6
● Langhe Nebbiolo '98	🍷	4
● Barolo Parafada Ris. '90	🍷🍷🍷	6
● Barolo Vigna Rionda Ris. '90	🍷🍷🍷	6
● Barolo Parafada '96	🍷🍷🍷	6
● Barolo Margheria '95	🍷🍷	6
● Barolo Parafada '95	🍷🍷	6
● Barolo Margheria '96	🍷🍷	6

SERRALUNGA DI CREA (AL)

Tenuta La Tenaglia
Via Santuario di Crea, 6
15020 Serralunga di Crea (AL)
tel. 0142940252
e-mail: info@latenaglia.com

Delfina Quattrocolo has just celebrated 20 years winemaking on an estate that nestles among the rugged Monferrato hills but her passion for her work, which started out more as a hobby than as a real job, remains undimmed. In fact, the original project has expanded over the last couple of years and with the full-time collaboration of daughter Erika in administration and the cellars, and son-in-law, Pierpaolo Arturo, in the cellars, La Tenaglia is looking more and more like a north Italian "château". The lovely Monferrato winery, which owes its existence to the determination of this lady from Turin, now possesses all it needs to make it hugely successful. There are 18 hectares planted to vine, mainly barbera, a top-drawer fruitmaker, Federico Curtaz, and the support of skilled Tuscan oenologist, Attilio Pagli. This winning combination has already paid dividends in the form of a Three Glass award for the new vintage of the estate's veteran Barbera d'Asti Emozioni. Congratulations are in order for Delfina and her team. It is a dark garnet wine, proffering ripe fruit aromas exalted by perfectly dosed wood that seamlessly binds the fragrances together. The palate displays power, fullness and tremendous fruit-rich body before the magnificent finish, which is lingering and harmonious. These "emotions" somewhat dwarf the other wines in the range but the Barbera del Monferrato Tenaglia, aged in big barrels and one year old barriques, is also very good. The Giorgio Tenaglia, a monovarietal Barbera, recaptures its former glory but the Bricco Crea cru, based on a simpler, more immediate barbera, is only average. And finally, a solid Glass for the Grignolino, the Chardonnay and the 100 per cent syrah Paradiso.

● Barbera d'Asti Emozioni '99	🍷🍷🍷	6
● Barbera d'Asti Giorgio Tenaglia '99	🍷🍷	5
● Barbera del M.to Sup. Tenaglia è '99	🍷🍷	5
● Barbera d'Asti Bricco Crea '00	🍷	3
● Grignolino del M.to Casalese '00	🍷	3
○ Piemonte Chardonnay '00	🍷	4
● Paradiso Rosso '98	🍷	6
● Barbera d'Asti Emozioni '96	🍷🍷	6
● Barbera d'Asti Emozioni '97	🍷🍷	6
● Paradiso '97	🍷🍷	5
● Barbera d'Asti Emozioni '98	🍷🍷	6
● Barbera d'Asti Giorgio Tenaglia '98	🍷🍷	4

SPIGNO MONFERRATO (AL)

Cascina Bertolotto
Via Pietro Porro, 70
15018 Spigno Monferrato (AL)
tel. 014491223 - 014491551

Despite their different categories and vintages, all the wines from the Cascina Bertolotto estate have one thing in common – distinctive personality. When we tasted this time around, the Barbera I Cheini was head and shoulders above the rest. From of a vineyard more than 60 years old, the grapes are harvested at the end of October, laid in small cases to dry for a short period, and, after pressing, fermented in a 100-year-old wooden before they mature in large barrels. The resulting wine is dark ruby, with profound, enveloping aromas of bramble and bilberry and a warm, velvety palate that progresses surefootedly. Two Glasses go to the Dolcetto La Muïette, from the vine of the same name. It, too, is harvested late and fermented in wooden vats. The plum and cinnamon nose bears witness to the over-ripeness of the fruit without cloying and the palate, soft and well balanced, boasts lovely tannins. The Dolcetto La Cresta is a more traditional bottle. Brilliant ruby with violet highlights, it shows a bouquet of ripe cherry and almond with undertones of wild roses. The palate is powerful, soft and broad, with a nicely balanced, if rather short, finish. The La Tia, a dry red obtained from partially dried brachetto grapes, is rich in seductively fragrant, clean-tasting varietal aromas. The palate is not particularly dense but caresses the mouth with its delicious, velvety texture. We also liked the light, tangy Barigi, a 50-50 blend of cortese and favorita.

● Barbera del M.to I Cheini '99	🍷🍷	4
● Dolcetto d'Acqui La Muïette '99	🍷🍷	4
● Dolcetto d'Acqui La Cresta '00	🍷	3
● Rosso La Tia	🍷	4
○ Monferrato Bianco Il Barigi '00		3
● Dolcetto d'Acqui La Muïette '98	🍷🍷	4
● Barbera del M.to I Cheini '97	🍷	4

STREVI (AL)

MARENCO
P.zza Vittorio Emanuele, 10
15019 Strevi (AL)
Tel. 0144363133
E-mail: marencovini@libero.it

Michela, Patrizia and Doretta, the three Marenco sisters, inspire this cellar with their winemaking skills. Located near Strevi, Marenco has a splendid vine stock and their orderly rows do much to enhance the natural beauty of these hills. The estate, long famous for its sweet aromatic wines, has increased its production of dry reds over the last few years and the Barbera Ciresa '98 is the first outstanding product of those labours. Inky black in the glass with a purple rim, it has strong, persistent aromas that hint at bramble and cherry over a base of toasty oak. The palate is quite magnificent for structure and chewy fruit, progressing steadily without missing a beat. Less of a heavyweight, but nevertheless enjoyable, is the Barbera Bassina '99, whose ripe berry fruit nose with a faint touch of almond ushers in a fresh-tasting palate, which is well balanced and mirrors the nose. The Dolcetto Marchesa sports a fabulous black and purple hue and aromas of morello cherry and plum, slightly dominated by a note of hay. The palate is stylish and tangy, with good fruit and agreeable tannins. The straw yellow Moscato Scrapona is flecked with gold and shows an aromatic, mineral nose with unmistakable traces of peach. The palate is fluent, harmonious and sweet, but not too sweet. The Brachetto Pineto is a limpid purple ruby, with aromas of roses, strawberry and spice and a lovely, upfront. The Chardonnay Galet shows a delicately varietal bouquet and a palate that, although a bit short on complexity and structure, follows through well, displaying a nice tangy vein. A Glass and a mention for the Carialoso, too, from a native variety.

● Barbera d'Asti Ciresa '98	ΨΨ	5
● Barbera d'Asti Bassina '99	ΨΨ	4
● Brachetto d'Acqui Pineto '00	Ψ	4
● Dolcetto d'Acqui Marchesa '00	Ψ	4
○ Moscato d'Asti Scrapona '00	Ψ	3
○ Piemonte Chardonnay Galet '00	Ψ	4
○ Carialoso '00	Ψ	3

STREVI (AL)

VIGNE REGALI
Via Vittorio Veneto, 22
15019 Strevi (AL)
Tel. 0144363485

Vigne Regali is the Piedmontese "pied à terre" of Banfi, the prestigious winemaking house from Montalcino. The cellars where the wine is vinified are in Novi Ligure but ageing and bottling, including bottle fermentation for spumantes, are carried out in Strevi. Traditionally a spumante winery, Vigne Regali has for some years been showing renewed interest in still reds and has done much to improve their quality. The Barbera Banin, which caught our eye on first release, has a charming nose of black cherry, vanilla, tobacco and cinnamon, and a well-structured palate that follows through very nicely. The excellent Ardì is a Dolcetto that resembles a "vino novello" in its quest for pleasant youthful fruitiness while the Gavi Principessa Gavia is soft and easy to drink. Moving on to the spumantes, the Banfi Brut Metodo Classico is a winner. Made from grapes that come from the Oltrepò Pavese and from Trentino, its refined bouquet suggests crusty bread, citron and orange peel layered over a delicate vegetal undertone. The palate shows good, dense perlage, and long, harmonious length. The Brut Metodo Classico Alta Langa comes from a project undertaken by seven of the big producers to promote Piedmont's spumante-making tradition and the creation of a new Alta Langa DOC zone. This spumante releases hints of ripe apricot and gooseberry and has a moderate, creamy mousse. The Tener Brut is a bit more predictable, with a base of autoclave-fermented sauvignon and chardonnay, but shows very nice balance. The varietal Asti is sweet, but not cloyingly so.

○ Alta Langa Brut M. Cl. '97	ΨΨ	5
○ Talento Banfi Brut M. Cl. '97	ΨΨ	5
● Barbera d'Asti Banin '99	ΨΨ	5
● Dolcetto d'Acqui L'Ardì '00	Ψ	3
○ Gavi Principessa Gavia '00	Ψ	4
○ Asti	Ψ	3
○ Tener Brut N. M.	Ψ	3
● Dolcetto d'Acqui Argusto '98	Ψ	4

TASSAROLO (AL)

LA ZERBA
STRADA PER FRANCAVILLA, 1
15060 TASSAROLO (AL)
TEL. 0143342259
E-MAIL: lazerba@novaonline.com

The whole municipality of Tassarolo falls in the Gavi DOCG zone and boasts some of the very best crus made famous by some of the most prestigious Gavi labels. Most of the growers sell their grapes so it falls to the lot of two winemaking and bottling firms to carry the flag for the area. One of these is La Zerba, which lies on the extension of the Pessenti ridge, where it enjoys a commanding panorama. Its eight hectares under vine stand on deep, ancient alluvial deposits of sand and clay, which are dotted with red where patches of iron-bearing gravel emerge. The Lorenzi family made their way into the world of Piedmont wine via the somewhat unusual route of glassware. Today, the Lorenzis produce, vinify and bottle their Gavis with the guidance and co-ordination of Luigi and his brother-in-law Andrea Mascherini who, bitten by the wine bug, operate in the distribution and restaurant businesses. Their very pale straw yellow Gavi La Zerba has a generous, refreshing nose of flowers and citrus fruit and a fine, wonderfully tangy palate supported by good body that lends it flavour and length. The Gavi Terrarossa, one of the estate's own crus that is part macerated on the skins, is a vibrant straw yellow with flecks of green. The bouquet is complex and elegant, the palate fresh, soft and caressing.

○ Gavi La Zerba '00	🍷🍷	3*
○ Gavi Terrarossa '00	🍷🍷	3*

TASSAROLO (AL)

CASTELLO DI TASSAROLO
CASCINA ALBORINA, 1
15060 TASSAROLO (AL)
TEL. 0143342248

Last year, Paolo Spinola's estate did not appear in the Guide as we did not receive his wines in time. Unfortunately, there were various logistical problems. But this year, he's back with a vengeance and the absence may actually have worked to the advantage of some of his wines. This time around, they stand out for fullness and maturity. Yet further proof, we might add, that market requirements are often too impatient with a living product that rarely performs at its best if released too young. This is true of Gavi, which takes years to acquire its full density and nose, which is precisely why we liked the Vigneto Alborina '98 so much. The brilliant straw yellow heralds a deliciously fruit-rich nose of peachy notes, and a warm, mellow, chewy palate with good length. The Castello di Tassarolo '00 took home Two Glasses for its aromas of honey, citrus fruit, hazelnut, flowers, apples and pears, and a fresh-tasting palate that is satisfyingly thirst-quenching. A notch lower down the scale, the S label is very pale in colour and has a less harmonious nose, with honey aromas, and an agreeable, refreshing, soft palate. The Spinolas were the first in the Gavi zone to plant international black grape varieties and their cabernet and barbera Rosso '97 presents a vibrant purple ruby hue. Its intriguing bouquet, full of spice and aromatic herbs, ushers in an unusual, fresh-tasting palate that is perhaps a little heavy on the alcohol but still potent, rounded and redolent of aniseed.

○ Gavi Castello di Tassarolo '00	🍷🍷	4
○ Gavi Vigneto Alborina '98	🍷🍷	4
○ Gavi Tassarolo S '00	🍷	3
● Monferrato Rosso Castello di Tassarolo '97	🍷	4

TORINO

Franco M. Martinetti
Via San Francesco da Paola, 18
10123 Torino
tel. 0118395937
e-mail: gmartinetti@ciaoweb.it

Franco Martinetti co-ordinates all his oenological operations from his HQ in central Turin but he is constantly on the road, making sure that his products are receiving all the care they deserve in their three cellars in southern Piedmont. Before he had even released the Martin, an Alessandria white obtained from timorasso, than he was thinking about a sweet version. Moving from one new wine to the next, Franco Martinetti has arrived in the top ranks of Piedmont's winemaking elite. This year, he gives us his Barolo, a red he very much wanted to make. His Marasco, whose name in Italian conjures up sensations of morello cherry and ripe wild berries, is made from grapes grown in the municipality of Barolo. It embodies Franco's philosophy to the letter – he seeks sophistication and elegance in his wines, not muscle power – and is delicate, refined and harmonious. It has fabulous progression, even if it lacks the extra fullness that would make it truly great. The 100 per cent barbera Montruc, from plots on the slopes at Vinchio, triumphs once again. It has opulent colour, a range of aromas that run from ripe fruit to spice with fine, classy touches of oak, and a long, mouthfilling palate whose aromas are mellowed by the alcohol. The barbera and cabernet Sul Bric is also superb. It has a faint vegetal nuance, particularly notable on the nose, but this is immediately smothered by the rich fruitiness. The Martin is very good, slightly less concentrated than the first version, but very long and delightful on the palate. The understandably celebrated cortese-based Miaia and the Bric dei Banditi, a simple but never predictable Barbera, both put on a very good show.

●	Barbera d'Asti Sup. Montruc '99	ŸŸ	6
●	Monferrato Rosso Sul Bric '99	ŸŸ	6
○	Colli Tortonesi Martin '99	ŸŸ	6
●	Barolo Marasco '97	ŸŸ	6
○	Minaia '99	ŸŸ	5
●	Barbera d'Asti Bric dei Banditi '00	ŸŸ	4
●	Sul Bric '94	ŸŸŸ	6
●	Sul Bric '95	ŸŸŸ	6
●	Barbera d'Asti Sup. Montruc '96	ŸŸŸ	6
●	Barbera d'Asti Sup. Montruc '97	ŸŸŸ	6
○	Minaia '98	ŸŸŸ	5
●	Barbera d'Asti Sup. Montruc '98	ŸŸ	6
●	Monferrato Rosso Sul Bric '98	ŸŸ	6
○	Colli Tortonesi Martin '98	ŸŸ	6

TREISO (CN)

Ca' del Baio
Via Ferrere, 33
12050 Treiso (CN)
tel. 0173638219

From the '98 vintage, Giulio Grassi has obtained a brand new Barbaresco, the Valgrande, from the vineyard of the same name at Treiso, and aged entirely in large barrels. Giulio planted this vineyard only recently and it will no doubt yield better fruit as it matures. In the meantime, its first result did well in our tasting and merits One Glass. Deep garnet, it boasts moderately intense aromas of cake, rhubarb, fruit and mint and a nice pulpy palate with elegant tannins and quite a warm finish. The Asili, from the famed barbaresco cru, is aged half in barriques and half in barrels. It is intense garnet with a brief rim and has a generous nose that hints at wild berries, vanilla and almonds against a backdrop of pepper and hazelnut. The palate opens out gradually, building up to a dry, complex finish. The Chardonnay Sermine, half matured in small barrels, presents aromas of fruit and hazelnut with barely discernible mineral and vegetal undertones. The palate displays good weight and a balanced progression. The richly coloured Moscato '00 proffers a charming nose of fruit, aromatic herbs and nutmeg. On the palate, the vigorous effervescence keeps the sweet vein in check, lending balance. The coherent, well-made Nebbiolo Bric del Baio hints at strawberry and cocoa powder then reveals a robust, leisurely palate that finishes on a note of violets. Finally, the Dolcetto is jolly and well-managed.

○	Langhe Chardonnay Sermine '00	ŸŸ	4
●	Barbaresco Asili Barrique '98	ŸŸ	5
○	Moscato d'Asti '00	Ÿ	3
●	Barbaresco Valgrande '98	Ÿ	5
●	Langhe Nebbiolo Bric del Baio '99	Ÿ	4
●	Dolcetto d'Alba Lodoli '00		3
●	Barbaresco Asili '95	ŸŸ	5
●	Barbaresco Asili Barrique '95	ŸŸ	5
●	Barbaresco Asili '96	ŸŸ	5
●	Barbaresco Asili Barrique '96	ŸŸ	5
●	Barbaresco Asili '97	ŸŸ	5
●	Barbaresco Asili Barrique '97	ŸŸ	5

TREISO (CN)

ADA NADA
VIA AUSARIO, 12
12050 TREISO (CN)
TEL. 0173638127
E-MAIL: info@adanada.it

We welcome the estate of Giancarlo and Ada Nada to the Guide. With daughters Annalisa and Sara, the Nadas look after nine hectares planted to vine in Rombone, and rent two more planted with barbera at Altavilla in the municipality of Alba. The winery produces 30,000 bottles a year and also features a lovely farm holiday centre. Giancarlo, the oenologist, is careful to tread a balanced line between tradition and innovation. His style is evident in the tasting profile of the Barbaresco Valeirano, which is conditioned partly in large barrels and partly in barriques and 900-litre casks. A rich garnet ruby wine with an orange rim, it shows aromas of raspberry, mint, cocoa powder and forest floor. The palate unfolds a gradual, complex progression, firmly bolstered by potent, sophisticated tannins that linger on, pleasantly dry, into the long, warm finish that strongly recalls the fruity tones of the bouquet. The Barbaresco Cichin, 100 per cent barrel-conditioned, is named after Giancarlo's uncle, who passed away recently. Dark in appearance, it has a complex, evolved nose reminiscent of sun-dried flowers, earth and berry fruit. The palate ushers in rather dry, robust tannins that render the progression vigorous and persistent. The Rosso La Bisbetica, a blend of 40 per cent nebbiolo and 60 per cent barbera vinified together and aged in barriques, caresses the nose with alluring tones of black berry fruit, cloves, dry leaf and dried flowers. On the palate, the rich character is slightly marred by slightly forward acidity, and the long length has hints of liquorice. The sturdy Barbera Salgà and the fruity Vigna Pierin are both decent.

TREISO (CN)

FIORENZO NADA
LOC. ROMBONE
VIA AUSARIO, 12/C
12050 TREISO (CN)
TEL. 0173638254
E-MAIL: nadafiorenzo@nada.it

The second edition of Bruno Nada's Barbaresco Rombone '98 has personality in spades. It comes from extraordinarily high quality fruit and superlative winemaking. Dense garnet with a brief rim, it has a nose that at once reveals fascinating aromas of blackcurrant, mint, pepper and liquorice that come together harmoniously over seductive undertones of forest floor and powdery soil. The palate has a rich mouthfeel, bolstered by robust tannins that herald a lingering, finish that echoes the nose and is lifted by toasty oak. It didn't quite make Three Glasses but it wasn't far off. The standard-label Barbera is garnet with a faintly orange rim and tempts the nose with aromas of bilberry, cake and mint over faint traces of hay. The palate displays reasonable muscle and has solid extract that dries the long, very persistent finish. The after-aroma is exquisite, sweetened by lovely notes of cocoa powder. Excellent, too, is the Seifile '98, a blend of nebbiolo and barbera with a dense hue and a compact rim. The nose thrills with its complexity, hinting at cherry and leather layered over notes of earth and fresh fruit. From the outset, the palate is full, wide, well-sustained and very muscular. This splendid bottle boasts a long, vigorous, dry finish that clearly echoes the initial aromas on the nose. The cellar's Dolcetto never fails to please, perfectly embodying the characteristics of the variety.

● Barbaresco Cichin '98	♛♛	6
● Barbaresco Valeirano '98	♛♛	6
● Langhe Rosso La Bisbetica '98	♛♛	6
● Barbera d'Alba Salgà '98	♛	5
● Barbera d'Alba Vigna Pierin '99	♛	4

● Barbaresco Rombone '98	♛♛	6
● Langhe Rosso Seifile '98	♛♛	6
● Dolcetto d'Alba '00	♛♛	4
● Barbaresco '98	♛♛	6
● Seifile '93	♛♛♛	6
● Langhe Rosso Seifile '95	♛♛♛	6
● Langhe Rosso Seifile '96	♛♛♛	6
● Barbaresco Rombone '97	♛♛♛	6
● Barbaresco '94	♛♛	6
● Barbaresco '95	♛♛	6
● Barbaresco '96	♛♛	6
● Barbaresco '97	♛♛	6
● Langhe Rosso Seifile '97	♛♛	6

TREISO (CN)

Pelissero
Via Ferrere, 19
12050 Treiso (CN)
tel. 0173638136 - 0173638430

Giorgio Pelissero's beautiful estate of approximately 20 hectares gives him an annual production of some 100,000 bottles. As usual, the best of the wines he presented for tasting was the Barbaresco Vanotu, which was a head above the rest. The '98 vintage is deep garnet with an orange rim and has a slightly unruly nose of jam, croissant dough, leather and forest floor over intriguing mineral tones. The palate has prominent tannins and a long finish reminiscent of violet and mint. The standard-label Barbera is rich in colour and excellent on the nose, its flower and fruit aromas laced with notes of pepper and earth. The palate is dry and vigorous, then there is a nice floral finish. The opaque Barbera d'Alba Piani offers a nose of hay, plum, eucalyptus, coffee and caramel, and a full-bodied, wide-ranging palate capped by a consistent finish that follows through well. Two Glasses for the Favorita, which possesses an unusual personality and an authentically rustic character. The initial impression of edginess in the nose gives way to aromas of almond and fruit with a lovely mineral undertone. The palate shows maturity and weight and follows through well to the eminently gratifying finish. This is not an easy wine, but it is nevertheless very alluring. The Dolcetto Augenta is concentrated and enjoyable, with a flavoursome, dense palate, and the Nebbiolo possesses creamy notes of black berry fruits and a richly extracted palate. Up last, the Dolcetto Munfrina is well managed and the Grignolino is worthy of note.

● Barbaresco Vanotu '98	♟♟	6
● Barbera d'Alba I Piani '00	♟♟	4
● Dolcetto d'Alba Augenta '00	♟♟	4
○ Langhe Favorita '00	♟♟	3*
● Barbaresco '98	♟♟	6
● Dolcetto d'Alba Munfrina '00	♟	3
● Langhe Nebbiolo '00	♟	4
● Piemonte Grignolino '00		3
● Barbaresco Vanotu '95	♟♟♟	6
● Barbaresco Vanotu '97	♟♟♟	6
● Barbaresco Vanotu '93	♟♟	6
● Barbaresco '96	♟♟	5
● Barbaresco Vanotu '96	♟♟	6
● Barbaresco '97	♟♟	5
● Barbera d'Alba I Piani '99	♟♟	4

TREISO (CN)

Vignaioli Elvio Pertinace
Loc. Pertinace, 2
12050 Treiso (CN)
tel. 0173442238
e-mail: c.vignaioli@areacom.it

This co-operative winery, headed by Cesare Barbero, offers an impressive array of typical Langhe wines, among which, of course, the four versions of Barbaresco reign supreme. This year, we liked the Castellizzano for its complex, assertive nose that strongly recalls bramble, plum, cocoa powder and rosemary layered over faint traces of charred oak and animal skins. The palate, generous and moderately powerful, displays good texture and strong tannins whose astringency is muted by the potency of the alcohol. Very dark in colour with a youthful rim, the Vigneto Marcarini has rather an evolved nose of black berry fruit, tobacco and cocoa powder offset by toasty, minerally tones. The palate reveals an abundance of tannins and long length with vibrant notes of forest floor. But it is the Vigneto Nervo that gets our vote for its incredibly rich garnet colour with a brief rim, its refined notes of flowers and fruit, and its dense, invigorating palate rounded off by an attractive after-aroma redolent of liquorice and alcohol. This lends warmth and persistence to a finish that combines fruit and balsam. The standard-label Barbaresco, also very dark, has aromas of cherry, raspberry, leather and mint, a palate braced by muscular tannins, and good long length revealing notes of violet and persimmon. The Nervo vineyard has also given us the best of the estate's three Dolcettos. An austere wine, it shows attractively rounded varietal characteristics that earned it Two Glasses. The Castellizzano and the standard-label version are simpler, while the Barbera Gratia Piena has a somewhat earthy nose and a dry, well-structured palate.

● Dolcetto d'Alba Vigneto Nervo '00	♟♟	3*
● Barbaresco Vigneto Nervo '98	♟♟	6
● Dolcetto d'Alba '00	♟	3
● Dolcetto d'Alba Vigneto Castellizzano '00	♟	3
● Barbaresco '98	♟	5
● Barbaresco Vigneto Castellizzano '98	♟	6
● Barbaresco Vigneto Marcarini '98	♟	6
● Barbera d'Asti Gratia Plena '99	♟	4
● Barbaresco Vigneto Castellizzano '97	♟♟	5
● Barbaresco Vigneto Nervo '97	♟♟	5
● Barbaresco Vigneto Marcarini '97	♟	5

VERDUNO (CN)

F.LLI ALESSANDRIA
VIA BEATO VALFRÉ, 59
12060 VERDUNO (CN)
TEL. 0172470113

Gian Alessandria's excellent range of wines is made even better this year by the arrival of two new products, the Barolo San Lorenzo and the Langhe Rosso Luna. The first, from the cru of the same name in Verduno that faces Monvigliero, is garnet ruby with an orange rim and has a clean, stylish nose of strawberry, violet and coffee lifted by notes of vanilla and almond. The palate echoes these wonderfully in a solid, harmonious progression with prominent tannins. Its lingering, complex length guaranteed the San Lorenzo maximum points from the Guide, the second time this family-run estate has won Three Glasses. The Rosso Luna is a blend with equal proportions of barrique-aged barbera, freisa and nebbiolo. It has a vibrant, youthful colour and an alluring nose of black berry fruit, tobacco leaf, forest floor and pepper. Dense and vigorous, the palate unveils powerful, fine-grained tannins. Equally excellent is the Barolo Monvigliero, with its garnet hue and its clean, varietal aromas that hint at berry fruit, leather and menthol. The palate is soft, potent and austere. The standard-label Barolo is also superb. Enticingly dark in hue, it offers ripe fragrances of plum, bilberry, cocoa powder and damp earth. The fleshy, invigorating palate is nicely borne up by the measured tannins. The Barbera has a fruity nose, shot through with interesting vegetal tones, and a palate with marked acidity supported by a robust framework. The Chardonnay Buscat offers notes of butter, apricot and peach blossom and a full-bodied, fresh-tasting texture.

● Barolo S. Lorenzo '97	▼▼▼	6
● Barolo '97	▼▼	6
● Barolo Monvigliero '97	▼▼	6
● Barbera d'Alba '99	▼▼	4
● Langhe Rosso Luna '99	▼▼	5
● Dolcetto d'Alba '00	▼	3
○ Langhe Chardonnay Buscat '00	▼	4
○ Langhe Favorita '00	▼	3
● Verduno Pelaverga '00	▼	4
● Barolo Monvigliero '95	▼▼▼	6
● Barolo Monvigliero '96	▼▼	6

VERDUNO (CN)

BEL COLLE
FRAZ. CASTAGNI, 56
12060 VERDUNO (CN)
TEL. 0172470196

As usual, Paolo Torchio presented the panel with a fine range of wines, even if the Barbaresco Roncaglie and the Barolo Monvigliero were a little below par in comparison with recent vintages. The Roncaglie is ruby red with orange highlights and has quite an evolved nose that discloses notes of berry fruit and spice with minerally undertones. The palate opens out somewhat austerely, and the mid palate is rather rigid, but the lingering finish hints enticingly at violets and liquorice. The Barolo Monvigliero, which won Two Glasses, is garnet with an orange rim and redolent of dried flowers, jam and cake. The palate has nice weight and a finish that echoes the nose in a complex framework that will improve with cellaring. The simpler, more direct Barolo Boscato shows notes of jam with undertones of leather and earth. The palate has decent flesh with a hint of tannin and a very satisfying cocoa powder and violet finish. The Pelaverga is very well-made. It has a vibrant colour and whistle-clean aromas of almonds and pepper, laced with balsam. The palate is well-balanced, tidy and wonderfully exuberant. The Nebbiolo Bricco San Cristoforo has a minerally, fruity nose and a dry, even palate. The Chardonnay Le Masche is redolent of hazelnut, tropical fruit and vanilla, introducing a substantial palate. The Favorita and the Arneis are marred by notes of fermentation and could have been more exciting.

● Verduno Pelaverga '00	▼▼	4
● Barolo Monvigliero '97	▼▼	6
● Barolo Boscato '97	▼	6
● Barbaresco Roncaglie '98	▼	6
● Nebbiolo d'Alba Bricco S. Cristoforo '99	▼	4
○ Langhe Chardonnay Le Masche '00	▼	4
○ Langhe Favorita '00	▼	3
○ Roero Arneis '00	▼	4
● Barolo Monvigliero '96	▼▼	5
● Barbera d'Alba Le Masche '97	▼▼	4
● Barbaresco Roncaglie '97	▼▼	6

VERDUNO (CN)

G. B. BURLOTTO
VIA VITTORIO EMANUELE, 28
12060 VERDUNO (CN)
TEL. 0172470122
E-MAIL: burlotto@burlotto.com

Giuseppe and Marina Burlotto, with their son, Fabio, turn out a most impressive range of high quality wines. The first of these is the Barolo Cannubi '97, a moderately intense garnet glass with a youthful rim. Its aromas of raspberry, bilberry and violet are enhanced by balsamic nuances in an elegant framework. On the palate, where the rich flesh is buttressed by rich extract, the flavour is balanced by muscular alcohol and the velvet-smooth body. The magnificent, deep garnet Barbera Aves has notes of black berry fruit, pepper and mulberry blossom layered over seductive hints of rain-soaked earth. The powerful, rounded palate is braced by lively sinew and has long, vibrant length with good tannins. The standard-label Barolo has a fairly coherent nose with traces of strawberry, leather and mint, while the palate is smooth and complex. The Barbera Boscato proffers a youthful, fruit-rich nose and a full-bodied palate. The Sauvignon Dives never fails to please with its aromas of candied fruit, sage and tomato and intense, long progression. The forthright Pelaverga suggests almond, pepper and geranium and the Dolcetto Neirane has lots of juicy fruit and rather a rustic character.

VERDUNO (CN)

CASTELLO DI VERDUNO
VIA UMBERTO I, 9
12060 VERDUNO (CN)
TEL. 0172470125 - 0172470284

Gabriella Burlotto and Franco Bianco presented the panel with a fabulous Barbaresco Rabajà that flaunts an intense, intriguing and exuberant nose. The deep garnet has an orange rim and reveals notes of raspberry and bilberry, layered over alluring minerally, floral and balsamic tones. The palate is full and invigorating, progressing attractively with close-knit tannins, to end in a lingering finish that recalls cocoa powder, violet and mint. The Barolo Massara is a Two Glass bottle, ruby red with a fairly complex nose of berry fruit, sweet spices and forest floor over a minerally backdrop. The palate is austere and well-balanced, with good flesh and a nicely persistent violet-themed finish. The Barolo Monvigliero is forward, offering aromas of dried flowers, leather and jam. The palate is a little rigid, because of the tannins that the body fails to offset. All in all, a sound series of Langhe wines, born of careful, traditional-style vinification. Castello di Verduno also produces an enjoyable Pelaverga, whose '00 vintage is emblematic. Pale ruby in the glass, it releases pepper-rich spicy aromas leading in to a sober but very gratifying palate. The austere, lively Dolcetto Campot is good and the sweetly tannic Langhe Nebbiolo is pleasant.

● Barolo Vigneto Cannubi '97	ŸŸ	6
● Barbera d'Alba Aves '99	ŸŸ	5
○ Langhe Bianco Dives '99	ŸŸ	4
● Dolcetto d'Alba Vigneto Neirane '00	Ÿ	3
● Verduno Pelaverga '00	Ÿ	4
● Barolo '97	Ÿ	6
● Barbera d'Alba Vigneto Boscato '99	Ÿ	4
● Barolo '96	ŸŸ	6
● Barolo Vigneto Cannubi '96	ŸŸ	6
● Barbera d'Alba Vigneto Boscato '98	ŸŸ	4

● Verduno Pelaverga '00	ŸŸ	4
● Barolo Massara '97	ŸŸ	6
● Barbaresco Rabajà '98	ŸŸ	6
● Dolcetto d'Alba Campot '00	Ÿ	3
● Langhe Nebbiolo '00	Ÿ	4
● Barolo Monvigliero '97	Ÿ	6
● Barbaresco Rabajà '93	ŸŸ	6
● Barolo Monvigliero '93	ŸŸ	6
● Barbaresco Rabajà '95	ŸŸ	6
● Barbaresco Rabajà '96	ŸŸ	6
● Barolo Monvigliero '96	ŸŸ	6
● Barbaresco Rabajà '97	ŸŸ	6

VIGNALE MONFERRATO (AL)

GIULIO ACCORNERO E FIGLI
CA' CIMA, 1
15049 VIGNALE MONFERRATO (AL)
TEL. 0142933317
E-MAIL: azaccornero@tin.it

Ermanno and Massimo Accornero's estate again shows that it is a major player in the Monferrato wine scene. Over the last few years, Bricco Battista has been the cutting edge of a move towards centre stage and is again outstanding this year winning Three Glasses for the third year in a row. This is a Barbera bursting with character, with a remarkably intense dark ruby red colour and rich aromas of ripe berry fruits and spice. The magnificent entry on the palate is smoothly refreshing, and the structure underpins its length and freshness. The excellent Barbera Giulìn, aged entirely in stainless steel, is brilliant ruby and boasts a very generous, fruit-rich nose of gamey, spicy nuances and faint traces of hay. The palate is fresh-tasting but also alcohol-rich and mellow, showing good length. The new, oak-conditioned Barbera Cima comes from the vineyard next to the winery. Dense and impenetrable to the eye, it surprises on the nose with unusual aromas of animal skins and fruit. Rounded on the palate, it reveals a bitterish undertone and discreet tannins that come out in the dry finish. The estate has delayed releasing the Monferrato Rosso Centenario '98 for a year in response to the demands of fans who want wines that are properly aged. We liked both the mature and richly varietal Grignolino Bricco del Bosco and the sweet – but not too sweet - aromatic, red Brigantino, which has a fine floral nose and a softly refreshing palate.

Wine	Glasses	Score
● Barbera del M.to Sup. Bricco Battista '99	🍷🍷🍷	5
● Barbera del M.to Sup. Cima '98	🍷🍷	6
● Barbera del M.to Giulìn '99	🍷🍷	4
● Casorzo Malvasia Passito Pico '98	🍷🍷	6
● Casorzo Malvasia Brigantino '00	🍷	4
● Grignolino del M.to Casalese Bricco del Bosco '00	🍷	3
● Barbera d'Asti Bricco Battista '97	🍷🍷🍷	5
● Barbera del M.to Sup. Bricco Battista '98	🍷🍷🍷	5
● Monferrato Rosso Centenario '96	🍷🍷	6
● Monferrato Rosso Centenario '97	🍷🍷	6

VIGNALE MONFERRATO (AL)

BRICCO MONDALINO
REG. MONDALINO, 5
15049 VIGNALE MONFERRATO (AL)
TEL. 0142933204

Mauro Gaudio releases wines of dependable quality. Without fail, they win high scores at our tastings every year. The ruby Grignolino Bricco Mondalino '00, an estate classic, has a nose rich in fruity, spicy tones and a very full, wonderfully satisfying palate rounded off by a lingering finish of attractive rose petal fragrances and fine-grained tannins. The Barbera Gaudium Magnum and the Bergantino selection are Gaudio's great Barberas. The first is very dark and has an alluring nose of strawberry, vanilla and hay leading in to a richly textured palate that flaunts great personality and a long, intense finish. The Barbera Il Bergantino, also very dark, releases aromas of wild berries, peach, tobacco and mint. The palate is ever so slightly edgy but very satisfying with a lingering, finish of violets. The medium-coloured Barbera Zerolegno is pleasantly rustic with a mineral and fruit nose. The refreshing palate is uncomplicated. The other wines we tasted included a standard-label Grignolino we liked. It has always been a good starting point for the DOC zone but it lacks the personality of the Bricco Mondalino.

Wine	Glasses	Score
● Barbera d'Asti Sel. Gaudium Magnum '99	🍷🍷	6
● Grignolino del M.to Casalese Bricco Mondalino '00	🍷🍷	4
● Barbera d'Asti Il Bergantino '99	🍷🍷	4
● Barbera del M.to Zerolegno '00	🍷	3
● Grignolino del M.to Casalese '00	🍷	3
● Barbera d'Asti Sel. Gaudium Magnum '97	🍷🍷	6
● Barbera d'Asti Il Bergantino '98	🍷🍷	4
● Barbera d'Asti Sel. Gaudium Magnum '98	🍷🍷	6

VIGNALE MONFERRATO (AL)

Marco Canato
Cascina Baldea, 18
15049 Vignale Monferrato (AL)
tel. 0142933653
e-mail: canatovini@yahoo.it

Marco and Roberto Canato's Vignale Monferrato estate makes its first appearance in the Guide this year. The Canatos came to these parts as tenant farmers in the 1950s and, convinced that the terrain was perfect for cultivating grapes, they bought this lovely winery. Today, they are the proud owners of 12 hectares, mainly planted to barbera, and have enlisted the support of oenologist Enzo Bailo. Best of the wines we tasted was the Barbera Baldea, matured for six months in oak barrels. An extremely dark ruby, it shows deep, varietal aromas of cherry and plum lifted by hints of tobacco and spice. The well-structured palate has a pleasantly varietal acidic vein. Almost as good is the Barbera Rapet, conditioned for a year in barriques. It mirrors the qualities of the Baldea but is still a little in thrall to the oak. The clear ruby Grignolino has attractive aromas of spice and geranium. The palate is fairly soft but very varietal. We preferred the steel-aged Piasì of the two Chardonnays. It is a rich, vibrant straw yellow and has a nose of roses and ripe tropical fruits. On the palate, it is rich, dense and well-balanced, echoing the nose nicely despite its opulence. The Bric di Bric has a gold hue and the stupendous fruit of the previous edition. For the time being, though, it lacks its predecessor's balance.

○ Piemonte Chardonnay Piasì '00	ΨΨ	4
● Barbera del M.to Rapet '98	ΨΨ	4
● Barbera del M.to Sup. La Baldea '98	ΨΨ	4
● Grignolino del M.to Casalese Celio '00	Ψ	3
○ Piemonte Chardonnay Bric di Bric '00	Ψ	4

VIGNALE MONFERRATO (AL)

Colonna
Fraz. San Lorenzo
Ca' Accatino, 1
15049 Vignale Monferrato (AL)
tel. 0142933239
e-mail: vini.colonna@onw.net

Alessandra Colonna is passionate and enthusiastic about Monferrato. The farm holiday centre she runs on her estate is very successful and her Osteria dei Sapori has become a Mecca for friends and winelovers. We are particularly pleased to note that the winery has increased the quality of its production, too. The wines offered for tasting this year were very good indeed and some selections appeared in two editions. We'll start with the Barberas, faithful old warhorses not only of this estate but of the whole zone. Alessandra's simple La Rossa, in both the '99 and the '00 version, is most impressive and shows how even the estate's basic wines are driven by quality. Of the two, we preferred the '00 for its freshness and the power of its fruit but the earlier version also behaved impeccably. The Alessandra '99 is a fine bottle. So dark as to be almost opaque, it reveals elegant, concentrated aromas of ripe fruit that blend with sweet, caressing toasty tones. The palate is richly extracted and displays a harmonious balance of all its components. The finish is long and juicy. The Mondone '98, a blend of barbera, cabernet sauvignon and pinot nero, is our pick of the innovative wines on offer. It is notable for its dense ruby colour, its broad, fruit-rich nose and the powerful, elegant palate. Finally, a round of applause for the house of Colonna's new wine, a Cabernet available in magnums only. Its seductive appearance ushers in gorgeous aromas of blackcurrant, black cherry and dried fruit and a palate that astounds with its power and balance.

● Barbera del M.to La Rossa '00	ΨΨ	3*
● Barbera del M.to Alessandra '98	ΨΨ	5
● Monferrato Rosso Mondone '98	ΨΨ	5
● Barbera del M.to Alessandra '99	ΨΨ	5
● Barbera del M.to La Rossa '99	ΨΨ	3*
● Monferrato Rosso Cabernet '99	ΨΨ	6
● Monferrato Rosso Bigio '99	Ψ	3
● Grignolino del M.to Casalese Sansìn '00	Ψ	3
● Barbera del M.to Alessandra '97	ΨΨ	5
● Monferrato Rosso Mondone '97	Ψ	5

VIGUZZOLO (AL)

Cascina Montagnola
Strada Montagnola, 1
15058 Viguzzolo (AL)
tel. 0131898558
e-mail: cascina.montagnola@libero.it

In 1988, Donatella Giannotti and Bruno Carvi decided to buy the Cascina Montagnola estate in the Colli Tortonesi and embarked upon a series of major and time-consuming renovations. Today, strolling up the gentle hill that leads to the splendid 19th-century villa surrounded by vineyards and orchards, you cannot help but admire this charming corner of the countryside. Donatella and Bruno have equipped their cellars with all the necessary technology and, thanks to oenologist Giovanni Bailo and the quality of their grapes, they are able to offer some seriously textured wines, not least of which is the Barbera Superiore Rodeo. Obtained from pure barbera matured in oak casks for 12-14 months, its intense colour heralds a nose of spice and fruit in syrup. On the palate, its velvety tannins give way to berry fruit and vanilla sensations and a long, long aromatic finish. The Risveglio is also rather remarkable. A monovarietal barrique-aged Chardonnay, it has a rich colour and vanillaed aromas of almonds and tropical fruits. The palate is redolent of mouthfilling fragrances of nutmeg, coffee and cocoa powder. The white Vergato is obtained from cortese with a dash of chardonnay. The estate produces two other reds, the Pigmento, from croatina, has up notes of leather and berry fruit, and the Amaranto is a pleasant, monovarietal Barbera vinified in stainless steel.

O Risveglio Chardonnay '00	ŶŶ	4
● Colli Tortonesi Barbera Sup. Rodeo '99	ŶŶ	5
O Vergato Cortese '00	Ŷ	2*
● Colli Tortonesi Barbera Sup. Amaranto '99	Ŷ	3
● Pigmento Rosso '99	Ŷ	3
● Colli Tortonesi Barbera Sup. Amaranto '98	ŶŶ	3
● Colli Tortonesi Barbera Sup. Rodeo '98	ŶŶ	5

VINCHIO (AT)

Cantina Sociale
di Vinchio e Vaglio Serra
Strada Provinciale, 40
14040 Vinchio (AT)
tel. 0141950903
e-mail: info@vinchio.com

The Barbera d'Asti Superiore Vigne Vecchie, flagship product of this co-operative winery established in 1959, is one of the most interesting Barberas to come out of the province of Asti and this year we awarded it Two Glasses. The barrique-aged '99 vintage is ruby verging on garnet and releases well-defined, intriguing aromas of black berry fruit, cloves and pepper, layered over fascinating hints of liquorice. The palate immediately reveals solid weight, progressing steadily buttressed by slightly dry tannins that lead into a warm, finish that echoes the nose with lingering notes of menthol and ripe fruit. The Barbera d'Asti Superiore is rather pale and has a moderately refined nose of berry fruit - heavy on the raspberry and cherry – enhanced by notes of balsam and rosemary. Dry and coherent on the palate, it has a finish that follows through well with on a faintly bitterish note. The Barbera d'Asti '00, somewhat transparent in appearance, shows uncomplicatedly inviting aromas of wild berries and roses. The palate is approachable, with pleasant, dry tannins that spill over into the reasonably long finish. The cherry-coloured Grignolino is good, with violet, hay and pepper aromas. The palate displays a solid flavour profile and an attractively vigorous finish.

● Barbera d'Asti Sup. Vigne Vecchie '99	ŶŶ	5
● Barbera d'Asti '00	Ŷ	3
● Grignolino d'Asti '00	Ŷ	3
● Barbera d'Asti Sup. '99	Ŷ	3
● Barbera d'Asti Sup. Vigne Vecchie '96	ŶŶ	5
● Barbera d'Asti Sup. Vigne Vecchie '97	ŶŶ	5
● Barbera d'Asti Sup. Vigne Vecchie '98	ŶŶ	5

OTHER WINERIES

ROBERTO FERRARIS
FRAZ. DOGLIANI, 33
14041 AGLIANO TERME (AT)
TEL. 0141954234

Roberto Ferraris, who can count on advice from consultant Giuliano Noè, presented the panel with two Barberas. We preferred the stainless steel-fermented Nobbio, with its purplish ruby hue and intense fruit aromas. The generous, flavour-rich palate also has plenty of length. Roberto's La Cricca is barrique-aged.

- Barbera d'Asti Sup. Nobbio '99   3*
- Barbera d'Asti La Cricca '98   4

TRINCHERO
REG. VIANOCE, 56
14041 AGLIANO TERME (AT)
TEL. 0141954016
E-MAIL: trinchero@libero.it

A winery with a fine range of Barberas that get better every year. The wonderful Barbera Vigna del Noce '97, now drinking at its best, is not to be missed. It's a traditional-style bottle that requires patient cellaring to reach its peak.

- Barbera d'Asti Sup.
  Vigna del Noce '97   5

EUGENIO BOCCHINO
LOC. SERRE, 2
12051 ALBA (CN)
TEL. 0173364226
E-MAIL: laperucca@libero.it

Eugenio Bocchino has only been making wine for a few years but his bottles already stand out from the crowd for quality. In addition, his new cellar at Serra dei Turchi is now fully operational. For the meantime, we can enjoy his remarkable barbera and nebbiolo '99 Suo di Giacomo.

- Langhe Rosso
  Suo di Giacomo '99   5

TENUTA CASTELLO DI RAZZANO
FRAZ. CASARELLO
LOC. GESSI, 2
15021 ALFIANO NATTA (AL)
TEL. 0141922124 - 0141922426

Today, Castello di Razzano is a ravishingly beautiful agricultural concern and a traditional destination for wine tourists. The mature, varietal Barbera Campasso is excellent value for money. The nicely structured Barbera Vigna del Beneficio is aged in barriques and the Onero is obtained from pinot nero grapes.

- Barbera d'Asti Sup. Campasso '99   3*
- Barbera d'Asti Sup.
  Vigna del Beneficio '99   4
- Onero Rosso '99   5

Cascina Morassino
Loc. Ovello, 32
12050 Barbaresco (CN)
Tel. 0173635149

Roberto and Mauro Bianco's property only has four and a half hectares planted to vine but still manages to turn out two impressive Barbarescos, the Ovello and the Morassino. Also worth investigating are a robust yet elegant Nebbiolo and a full-flavoured, pleasantly rustic Dolcetto.

- Dolcetto d'Alba '00 — 3
- Barbaresco Morassino '98 — 6
- Barbaresco Ovello '98 — 6
- Langhe Nebbiolo '99 — 4

F.lli Barale
Via Roma, 6
12060 Barolo (CN)
Tel. 017356127
E-mail: barale.fratelli@areacom.it

The Barale family's Barolo Castellero has a nose of hay, leather and wild berries. On the palate, the texture is firm and attractively broad, with just the right note of austerity, and the finish has a nice flowery flourish. The gutsy Barbera Preda and the Dolcetto Bussia are also well made.

- Barolo Castellero '97 — 6
- Dolcetto d'Alba Bussia '00 — 3
- Barbera d'Alba Preda '99 — 4

Giacomo Grimaldi
Via Luigi Einaudi, 8
12060 Barolo (CN)
Tel. 017335256

The Grimaldis presented us with a Barolo Le Coste redolent of slowly dried flowers and jam, with a close-knit, well-sustained palate. Their Barbera also has good texture and a finish that foregrounds notes of caramel. The characterful Dolcetto has good grip. A winery that knows what it's doing.

- Barolo Le Coste '97 — 6
- Barbera d'Alba Pistin '00 — 4
- Dolcetto d'Alba '00 — 3

Domenico Ghio
Via Circonvallazione, 15
15060 Bosio (AL)
Tel. 0143684117
E-mail: ghiovini@novi.it

Only 1,000 bottles were released but the expertly made Two Glass winner, Drac Rosso di Ghio, demands our attention. Obtained from generously but not excessively concentrated fruit, it is a wine in the grand tradition of the territory. The Barbera Bricco del Tempo selection is also worth investigating.

- Dolcetto di Ovada Sup.
  Drac Rosso '99 — 5
- Piemonte Barbera
  Bricco del Tempo '98 — 4

Paolo Poggio
Via Roma, 67
15050 Brignano Frascata (AL)
Tel. 0131784929 - 0131784650

We were anxious to see what the Derio would offer this year. Often a great wine, this time round it is well up to expectations. Inky black in the glass, it has a silk-soft mouthfeel of ripe fruit laced with tangy acidity. The Timorasso is good but the standard-label Barbera is uninteresting.

- Colli Tortonesi Barbera Derio '99 — 4
- Colli Tortonesi Barbera '00 — 2*
- ○ Colli Tortonesi Bianco
  Timorasso '00 — 2

La Giribaldina
Fraz. San Vito, 39
14042 Calamandrana (AT)
Tel. 0141718043
E-mail: giribaldina@inwind.it

La Giribaldina is a lovely estate at Calamandrana run by the enthusiastic Colombo family, who moved to the area from the province of Varese. Currently, they have six hectares planted to vine and their range includes the DOC zone's classics, with Barbera leading the pack. Their Cala delle Mandrie selection is excellent.

- Barbera d'Asti Sup.
  Cala delle Mandrie '98 — 5
- Barbera d'Asti Sup.
  Rossoboldo '98 — 4

FABIO FIDANZA
FRAZ. RODOTIGLIA
14052 CALOSSO (AT)
TEL. 0141826921
E-MAIL: castellodicalosso@tin.it

Fabio Fidanza is a young Calosso-based producer who has the good fortune to live at Rodotiglia, where his barbera vines stand on the hillslopes of this exceptional subzone. Even if it is a bit of a wallet-punisher, don't miss Fabio's Castello di Calosso Barbera. His standard-label Barbera is also a very agreeable proposition.

● Barbera d'Asti Castello di Calosso Rodotiglia '99 ▼▼	6
● Barbera d'Asti '99 ▼	3*

CORNAREA
VIA VALENTINO, 150
12043 CANALE (CN)
TEL. 017365636 - 0173979091

Two of the wines in this Canale-based cellar's range are particularly interesting. One is the arneis-based dried-grape Tarasco, a pale amber wine with a nose of Peruvian bark and tamarind ushering in a sweet, broad palate, while the second is the Roero Superiore. This has rather forward aromas and a dry, vigorous progression in the mouth.

○ Tarasco Bianco '97 ▼	5
● Roero Sup. '99 ▼	4

PORELLO
C.SO ALBA, 71
12043 CANALE (CN)
TEL. 0173979324

Marco Porello has turned out a very good '99 Roero Bric Torretta. It reveals aromas of flowers, fruit, coffee and leather followed by a well-structured and slightly austere palate. His fresh, uncomplicated Arneis Camestrì and juicy, minerally Barbera Bric Torretta are also admirable.

● Roero Bric Torretta '99 ▼▼	4
○ Roero Arneis Camestrì '00 ▼	3
● Barbera d'Alba Bric Torretta '99 ▼	4

L'ARMANGIA
REG. SAN GIOVANNI, 14/C
14053 CANELLI (AT)
TEL. 0141824947
E-MAIL: armangia@inwind.it

Ignazio Giovine is the boss at L'Armangia, where for some years he has been turning out a rather exciting range that draws on local traditions with one or two concessions to international tastes. Don't miss his Barbera Castello di Calosso Vignali '99, a harmonious, mouthfilling wine with plenty of body.

● Barbera d'Asti Castello di Calosso Vignali '99 ▼▼	6
● Barbera d'Asti Sup. Titon '98 ▼	4

MAURIZIO NERVI
REG. SERRA MASIO, 30
14053 CANELLI (AT)
TEL. 0141831152

Good news from the hills at Canelli: Maurizio Nervi, cellarmaster at one of the best-known wineries in the Asti area, has been making his own wine for quite a few years now. His Barbera d'Asti Martleina '99 is outstanding for its structure and the sheer length of the fruit.

● Barbera d'Asti Martleina '99 ▼▼	4
○ Valon Chardonnay '00 ▼	4

TEO COSTA
VIA SAN SALVARIO, 1
12050 CASTELLINALDO (CN)
TEL. 0173213066
E-MAIL: teocosta@teocosta.it

Marco and Roberto Costa release a wide range of Roero wines, including an outstanding Castellinaldo Barbera d'Alba. The '99 vintage is concentrated and flaunts a caressing mouthfeel. This year, their already extensive list has been extended with a very satisfying Barbaresco.

● Castellinaldo Barbera d'Alba Castelli di Castellinaldo '99 ▼▼	5
● Barbaresco Lancaia '98 ▼	6

Raffaele Gili
Reg. Pautasso, 7
12050 Castellinaldo (CN)
Tel. 0173639011

Raffaele Gili's selection of typical Roero bottles is unfailingly reliable and modern in style. Best of the bunch are his full-bodied, vibrant Castellinaldo Barbera, the warm, dry Nebbiolo Sansivé and the refreshingly tangy Arneis.

- Castellinaldo Barbera d'Alba '99 🍷🍷 4
- Roero Arneis '00 🍷 3
- Nebbiolo d'Alba Sansivé '99 🍷 4

Marsaglia
Via Mussone, 2
12050 Castellinaldo (CN)
Tel. 0173213048

The Barbera San Cristoforo made by Marina and Emilio Marsaglia throws an intriguing nose of fruit and chocolate, followed by a robust, balanced palate. Also good are the Roero Bric d'America, with its sweet aromas and well-balanced palate, and the full-bodied, vigorous Castellinaldo Barbera d'Alba.

- Barbera d'Alba S. Cristoforo '99 🍷🍷 4
- Castellinaldo Barbera d'Alba '99 🍷 5
- Roero Sup. Bric d'America '99 🍷 5

Vielmin
Via San Damiano, 16
12050 Castellinaldo (CN)
Tel. 0173213298
E-mail: ivan.gili@tin.it

Best of Ivan Gili's wines are his gutsy, generous, cherry and cocoa powder-nuanced Castellinaldo Barbera d'Alba, the fairly forward and slightly stiff-backed Nebbiolo d'Alba and the earthily vigorous Barbera d'Alba.

- Castellinaldo Barbera d'Alba '99 🍷🍷 4
- Barbera d'Alba '99 🍷 3
- Nebbiolo d'Alba '99 🍷 4

Villa Fiorita
Via Case Sparse, 2
14034 Castello di Annone (AT)
Tel. 0141401231 - 0141401852
E-mail: villafiorita-wines@villafiorita-wines.com

Villa Fiorita is a breath-takingly beautiful estate set round an equally impressive farmhouse, owned by the Rondolino. The vineyards are on the ridge that leads from Asti to Castello d'Annone; the main variety is barbera. The Rondolino's Il Giorgione selection is skilfully made while their Grignolino is also attractive.

- Barbera d'Asti Sup. Il Giorgione '98 🍷🍷 5
- Grignolino d'Asti Pian delle Querce '00 🍷 3

Renzo Beccaris
Fraz. Madonnina, 26
14055 Costigliole d'Asti (AT)
Tel. 0141966592

There are some very nice Barbera d'Astis coming out of this attractive Costigliole estate, which for some years now has been clambering up the steep slope of quality. The Barbera San Lorenzo '98 has is a winning wine with plenty of personality and the Bric d'Alì selection is sincere and easy to like.

- Barbera d'Asti Sup. Bric d'Alì '98 🍷 4
- Barbera d'Asti Sup. S. Lorenzo '98 🍷 4

Alfonso Boeri
Via Bionzo, 2
14055 Costigliole d'Asti (AT)
Tel. 0141968171
E-mail: boeri@boerivini.it

On the slopes of Bricco Quaglia at Bionzo, the Boeris grow their outstandingly good barbera grapes and turn them into delicious, well-made wines. Try the two Barbera selections: we preferred the barrique-aged Pörlapà '98 version.

- Barbera d'Asti Sup. Pörlapà '98 🍷🍷 4
- Barbera d'Asti Martinette '99 🍷 3*

LUIGI NEBIOLO
VIA AIE, 3
14055 COSTIGLIOLE D'ASTI (AT)
TEL. 0141966030

Piero Nebiolo is a serious, skilful winemaker who concentrates his energies on Barbera. Both of his selections are good but the Superiore '98 has more substantial body and a caressing palate. Also good is the Piemonte Chardonnay, a pleasing white bottled with almost no sulphur dioxide.

● Barbera d'Asti Sup. '98	🍷🍷	4
○ Piemonte Chardonnay '00	🍷	3
● Barbera d'Asti San Martino '99	🍷	3

CASCINA FLINO
VIA ABELLONI, 7
12055 DIANO D'ALBA (CN)
TEL. 017369231

Paolo Monte is the owner of this lovely estate at Diano, which produces two excellent typical wines. The muscular, richly extracted Dolcetto Cascina Flino has an impenetrable colour while the Barbera d'Alba Flin stands out for its finesse and rich flavours.

● Diano d'Alba Cascina Flino Vigna Vecchia '00	🍷🍷	3*
● Barbera d'Alba Flin '99	🍷	4

MASSIMO ODDERO
VIA SAN SEBASTIANO, 1
12055 DIANO D'ALBA (CN)
TEL. 017369169
E-MAIL: massimo.oddero@isiline.it

Massimo Oddero has released a very well thought-out range of wines. His classic Dolcetto di Diano from the Sorba subzone is flanked by a convincingly generous, barbera and nebbiolo-based Rosso del Notaio, dedicated to his father, and an austere, tannin-rich Nebbiolo d'Alba.

● Rosso del Notaio	🍷🍷	5
● Diano d'Alba Sorba '00	🍷	4
● Nebbiolo d'Alba Rapalin '99	🍷	5

RICCHINO - TIZIANA MENEGALDO
CASCINA RICCHINO
12055 DIANO D'ALBA (CN)
TEL. 0142488884

There is interesting news from the hills of Diano d'Alba, where this family-run estate turns out just 7,000 bottles of very fine Dolcetto. The Rizieri selection is a winner with an impenetrable colour, fruit-rich aromas and an opulently rich palate.

● Diano d'Alba Rizieri '00	🍷🍷	4

OSVALDO BARBERIS
B.TA VALDIBÀ, 42
12063 DOGLIANI (CN)
TEL. 017370054
E-MAIL: brekos@jumpy.it

Barbera Brichat has a concentrated colour and a moderately elegant nose with all the variety's characteristic aromas. In the mouth, it shows good breadth of texture and an attractive tannic note in the finish, which echoes the nose nicely. The Dolcetto Puncin has a forceful personality and good grip.

● Dolcetto di Dogliani Puncin '00	🍷🍷	3*
● Piemonte Barbera Brichat '00	🍷	3

BOSCHIS
FRAZ. SAN MARTINO DI PIANEZZO, 57
12063 DOGLIANI (CN)
TEL. 017370574
E-MAIL: m.boschis@tiscalinet.it

This is a Dogliani estate with a good range of wines, particularly the Barbera Le Masserie, an intriguingly soft-textured wine. The series of Dolcetto di Dogliani wines is nice. We thought the Sorì San Martino was slightly better than the Vigna dei Prey.

● Barbera d'Alba Le Masserie '99	🍷🍷	4
● Dolcetto di Dogliani Vigna dei Prey '00	🍷	3
● Dolcetto di Dogliani Vigna Sorì S. Martino '00	🍷	3

RIBOTE
Fraz. San Luigi
B.ta Valdiberti, 24
12063 Dogliani (CN)
tel. 017370371

Bruno Porro's is the very competent hand at the helm of this lovely Dogliani estate, which has been quality-oriented for some years now. Bruno presented two Dolcettos and we liked the selection that takes its name from the cellar. The Monetti version is frank, approachable and very drinkable.

● Dolcetto di Dogliani Ribote '00	🍷🍷 4
● Dolcetto di Dogliani Monetti '00	🍷 3

ERALDO REVELLI
Loc. Pianbosco, 29
12060 Farigliano (CN)
tel. 0173797154
e-mail: eraldorevelli@tin.it

At Farigliano, the Revelli family runs a small cellar that specializes in making good wines, Dolcettos in particular. The San Matteo is remarkable for the intensity of its aromas and a robust structure that is anything but inelegant. The Autin Lungh is also nice.

● Dolcetto di Dogliani S. Matteo '00	🍷🍷 3*
● Dolcetto di Dogliani Autin Lungh '00	🍷 3

IL ROCCHIN
Loc. Vallemme, 39
15066 Gavi (AL)
tel. 0143642228

The bright straw-yellow Gavi releases fresh aromas of flowers leading in to a delicate but lively and tangy palate. In the Vigna del Bosco, varietal aromas are joined by unusual smoky notes and in the mouth the wine is full-flavoured and caressing. Although a little dryish, the Dolcetto is well worth its Glass.

○ Gavi del Comune di Gavi '00	🍷🍷 3
● Dolcetto di Ovada '00	🍷 3
○ Gavi del Comune di Gavi Vigna del Bosco '00	🍷 4

MORGASSI SUPERIORE
Case Sparse Sermoria, 7
15060 Gavi (AL)
tel. 0143642007
e-mail: info@morgassisuperiore.it

The syrah-based Tamino has a dark ruby hue and a varietal nose, followed by a fresh, full-bodied palate with generously warm alcohol. The bright straw-yellow Gavi offers refreshing citrus aromas. The Sarastro is a blend of barbera and cabernet.

○ Gavi del Comune di Gavi '00	🍷🍷 4
● Sarastro '98	🍷 5
● Tamino '99	🍷 5

SAN BARTOLOMEO
Loc. Vallegge
Cascina San Bartolomeo, 26
15066 Gavi (AL)
tel. 0143643180

Compared to the preceding, often exceptional, vintages, this year's performance by San Bartolomeo was low-key but the Bergaglio family and their estate-owned vines merit our faith and encouragement. The Gavi Pelöia gained a One Glass score for its generous fruit.

○ Gavi del Comune di Gavi Pelöia '00	🍷 4

SANTA SERAFFA
Loc. Colombare
15066 Gavi (AL)
tel. 0143643600
e-mail: santaseraffa@libarnanet.it

Ca' di Maggio has a concentrated, bright straw-yellow hue and a varietal nose sweetened by hints of vanilla. The wood used for ageing returns on the palate, which signs off with a long, bitterish finish. The Gavi Le Colombare is redolent of flowers and citrus fruit while the Dioniso red packs lots of fruit and extract.

○ Gavi Ca' di Maggio '99	🍷🍷 4
○ Gavi Le Colombare '00	🍷 3
● Dioniso Rosso	🍷 4

Torraccia del Piantavigna
Via Romagnano, 69/a
28074 Ghemme (NO)
Tel. 0163844711

Torraccia del Piantavigna is the winemaking arm of the well-known Francoli distillery. The Gattinara is an excellent example of its category while the well-made Ghemme is a point or two lower down the scale Ghemme. The Tre Confini is an uncomplicated but likeable and expertly vinified red.

● Gattinara '97	🍷🍷 5
● Colline Novaresi Nebbiolo Tre Confini '00	🍷 3*
● Ghemme '97	🍷 4

Tenuta Olim Bauda
Strada Prata, 22
14045 Incisa Scapaccino (AT)
Tel. 014174266
E-mail: giannibertolino@yahoo.it

Tenuta Olim Bauda is owned by Gianni Bertolino, who is backed up by consultant Beppe Caviola. The cellar has only one aim – to make premium-quality wines. The Superiore '98 selection makes its presence felt with its full body, honest approach and elegance.

● Barbera d'Asti Sup. '98	🍷🍷 4
● Barbera d'Asti '99	🍷 3*

F.lli Ferrero
Fraz. Annunziata, 12
12064 La Morra (CN)
Tel. 017350691
E-mail: renato.ferrero@tiscalinet.it

Renato Ferrero's winery is a very welcome newcomer to the Guide this year. The cellar has a small production of Barolo, in two interpretations, and Barbera, which impressed the panel with their intense but clean aromas and remarkable overall balance.

● Barolo Manzoni '97	🍷🍷 6
● Barbera d'Alba Goretta '99	🍷 5

Gianni Gagliardo
Fraz. Santa Maria
12064 La Morra (CN)
Tel. 017350829
E-mail: gagliardo@gagliardo.it

Gianni Gagliardo's extensive output totals 250,000 bottles a year. We would like to mention three interesting bottles, the Barolo Preve '97 from La Morra and Castiglione Falletto, the standard-label Barolo '97 and the Langhe Nebbiolo Batié, also from '97.

● Barolo '97	🍷 6
● Barolo Preve '97	🍷 6
● Langhe Nebbiolo Batié '97	🍷 5

Aurelio Settimo
Fraz. Annunziata, 30
12064 La Morra (CN)
Tel. 017350803
E-mail: a.settimo@winecompany.net

Aurelio Settimo is a historic estate at Annunziata in La Morra that makes an outstanding Barolo Rocche. The aromas of peach, wild berries and aromatic wood are laced with minerally touches then the palate offers lots of body and fine structure. The standard-label Barolo is less demanding and very easy to drink.

● Barolo Rocche '97	🍷🍷 6
● Barolo '97	🍷 6

Osvaldo Viberti
Fraz. Santa Maria
B.ta Serra dei Turchi, 95
12064 La Morra (CN)
Tel. 017350374

Osvaldo Viberti and his wife Carla make fine quality wines and presented the panel with a lovely range this year. The Barolo Serra dei Turchi '97 has a wealth of fine-grained tannins, Dolcetto d'Alba Galletto offers a ruby red hue and well-sustained palate while the Barbera d'Alba Mancine '99 is powerful yet harmonious.

● Barolo Serra dei Turchi '97	🍷🍷 6
● Barbera d'Alba Mancine '99	🍷 4
● Dolcetto d'Alba Galletto '00	🍷 3

MALGRÀ
Via Nizza, 8
14046 Mombaruzzo (AT)
tel. 0141726377
e-mail: vinibec@tin.it

After leaving the historic Bersano winery, Nico Conta and Massimiliano Diotto have embarked on this new and ambitious project. Malgrà is a winery to keep an eye on for the first year's range is very well-made, especially the Barbera Galana.

● Barbera d'Asti Superiore Galana '98	▼▼ 4
● Barbera d'Asti Superiore Mora di Sassi '99	▼ 4

CASCINA ORSOLINA
Via Caminata, 28
14036 Moncalvo (AT)
tel. 0141917277
e-mail: cascinaorsolina@tin.it

Cascina Orsolina is owned by the De Negri family and the estate's strong suit is Barbera d'Asti. There are two very reliable selections but this year, the Bricco dei Cappuccini was not released. In the absence of the cellar's flagship wine, we tasted a decent Caminata and a very nice Grignolino.

● Barbera d'Asti Caminata '99	▼ 3
● Grignolino d'Asti S. Giacu '00	▼ 3

BUSSIA SOPRANA
Loc. Bussia, 81
12065 Monforte d'Alba (CN)
tel. 039305182

Bussia Soprana presented three '97 Barolos. The Vigna Colonnello has a nose of herbs and redcurrant. Its soft palate may not have much body but it is stylish. There are hard vegetal notes followed by good body in the Mosconi and the Bussia offers a nose of coffee and bitter cocoa powder, echoed on the palate.

● Barolo Bussia '97	▼▼ 6
● Barolo Mosconi '97	▼ 6
● Barolo Vigna Colonnello '97	▼ 6

PAJANA - RENZO SEGHESIO
Via Circonvallazione, 2
12065 Monforte d'Alba (CN)
tel. 017378269

Renzo Seghesio vinifies grapes from the prestigious Pajana subzone. The Barolo he obtains is in the traditional mould. Orangey in colour, it has aromas of nuts and tobacco that shade into tar. The '97 is austere on the palate and will require more bottle age to firm up. The Barbera is a tad fuzzy on the nose.

● Barbera d'Alba Ars Vivendi '99	▼ 4
● Barolo Pajana '97	▼ 6

PODERE RUGGERI CORSINI
Via Garibaldi, 14
12065 Monforte d'Alba (CN)
tel. 017378625

This lovely Langhe estate is located at Monforte in the Barolo DOCG zone. The wines presented were generously extracted and rich in alcohol but could improve in terms of finesse. The Barbera Armujan is excellent, the Barolo is very concentrated and the Dolcetto is an attractively high-spirited wine.

● Barbera d'Alba Armujan '99	▼▼ 5
● Dolcetto d'Alba '00	▼ 4
● Barolo '97	▼ 6

VALERIO ALOI
Via Milano, 45
12052 Montà (CN)
tel. 0173975604

Valerio Aloi's Roero Bricco Morinaldo is ruby red, shading into garnet, with a nose of jam, leather and dried flowers. The palate is austere and dynamic, ending with a nice flowery finish. His Barbera Bricco Volpiana is a pleasingly rustic wine with a no-nonsense palate.

● Roero Bricco Morinaldo '99	▼▼ 4
● Barbera d'Alba Bricco Volpiana '99	▼ 4

CANTINA DEL GLICINE
VIA GIULIO CESARE, 1
12057 NEIVE (CN)
TEL. 017367215
E-MAIL: cantineglicine@tiscalinet.it

The cellars of this historic Neive winery are well worth a visit. From the long list of wines, we have chosen two excellent Barbarescos, the intriguing, uncompromising Marcorino, which is barrique aged, and the more austere, tannin-heavy Curà.

● Barbaresco Marcorino '98	🍷🍷	6
● Barbaresco Curà '98	🍷	6

PUNSET
FRAZ. MORETTA, 5
12057 NEIVE (CN)
TEL. 017367072
E-MAIL: punset@punset.com

Punset is a delightful Neive estate that uses organic farming methods. It turns out two good Barbarescos, as well. The Campo Quadro selection has a spicy nose, with notes of dried herbs and raspberry that sign off with minerally nuances. The palate is firm and tannic. In contrast, the standard-label Barbaresco is less challenging.

● Barbaresco Campo Quadro '98	🍷🍷	6
● Barbaresco '98	🍷	6

ANTONIO BALDIZZONE
CASCINA LANA
C.SO ACQUI, 187
14049 NIZZA MONFERRATO (AT)
TEL. 0141726734

We are in the heart of Barbera territory and there were two labels that caught the panel's eye. Only 2,000 bottles of the '98 Vin ed Michen selection are made, a wine that offers elegance and ripe fruit. The standard-label version is a very pleasant, quaffable '99.

● Barbera d'Asti Vin ed Michen '98	🍷🍷	4
● Barbera d'Asti '99	🍷	3

CASCINA GIOVENALE
STRADA SAN NICOLAO, 102
14049 NIZZA MONFERRATO (AT)
TEL. 0141793005

Cascina Giovenale is a small winery near Nizza Monferrato that has well-informed winelovers talking about two fine Barbera selections. The standard-label version is nice and approachable while the Superiore Ansemma '99 has exciting breadth and roundness on the palate. Don't miss it.

● Barbera d'Asti Sup. Ansemma '99	🍷🍷	4
● Barbera d'Asti '99	🍷	3

CASCINA ULIVI
STRADA MAZZOLA, 14
15067 NOVI LIGURE (AL)
TEL. 0143744598 - 01436756430
E-MAIL: cascinaulivi@libero.it

Stefano Bellotti is inaugurating his cellar at Montemarino. In the meantime, he has presented another range of wines from organically grown grapes. The Nibiô '00 has firm aromas and a lingering palate. The Barbera Mounbè and the Venta Quemada performed well, as did the Gavi Filagnotti.

● Monferrato Dolcetto Nibiô '00	🍷🍷	4
○ Gavi I Filagnotti '00	🍷	3
● Piemonte Venta Quemada '00	🍷	3
● Piemonte Barbera Mounbè '99	🍷	4

TENUTA LA MARCHESA
VIA GAVI, 87
15067 NOVI LIGURE (AL)
TEL. 0143743362
E-MAIL: info@tenutalamarchesa.it

The Tenuta la Marchesa is owned by the Giulini family. It is a fine Gavi estate that turns out a well-made range of the DOC zone's typical wines. This year, consultant Donato Lanati has supervised the production of a good Gavi Etichetta Nera and a tangy Gavi Etichetta Bianca.

○ Gavi Etichetta Bianca '00	🍷	3
○ Gavi Etichetta Nera '00	🍷	3

Valditerra
Strada Monterotondo, 75
15067 Novi Ligure (AL)
tel. 0143321451

Laura Valditerra, the owner of this delightful Gavi property, is diversifying her range. Today, her classic fruit-rich, tangy Gavi has been flanked by a good red from barbera with small proportions of merlot, freisa and cabernet. The newcomer's name is FiorDesAri.

○ Gavi Sel. Valditerra '00	4
● FiorDesAri Rosso	5

Favaro
Via Chiusure, 1/Bis
10010 Piverone (TO)
tel. 012572606
e-mail: favaro.chiusure@hotmail.com

A mini-profile this year for Benito Favaro and his one-hectare property in the excellent Vigna delle Chiusure vineyard. The pale straw-yellow Erbaluce di Caluso has varietal aromas of crusty bread, flowers and citron peel. On the palate, there is a refreshing but not overbearing acidity that lends delicious zest.

○ Erbaluce di Caluso Vigna delle Chiusure '00	3*

Castello del Poggio
Loc. Il Poggio, 9
14038 Portacomaro (AT)
tel. 0141202543
e-mail: info@poggio.it

Castello del Poggio is the Asti outpost of the Zonin empire. The 140 estate-owned hectares are located in the municipality of Portacomaro, a fine area in which to make Barbera and Grignolino d'Asti. Those are also the wines that are most representative of the Castello del Poggio cellar.

● Grignolino d'Asti '00	3
● Barbera d'Asti '99	3

Verrina
Via San Rocco, 14
15010 Prasco (AL)
tel. 0144375745

Verrina has eight hectares under vine. Yields are low and quality high, as in the case of the dolcetto antico dal raspo rosso plants. This year, the Vigna Oriali selection earned Two Glasses for its purplish ruby hue, ripe nose and warm, soft palate. There is an attractive note of liquorice in the finish.

● Dolcetto di Ovada Vigna Oriali '00	3*

Viticoltori Associati di Rodello
Fraz. Vay - Via Montà, 13
12050 Rodello (CN)
tel. 0173617318
e-mail: assovini@assovini.it

The Produttori di Rodello release a range of classic Dolcettos that are excellent value for money. Best of the four selections presented to the panel was the pleasingly long Vigna Deserto. But don't underrate the Vigna Buschin or Vigna Campasso.

● Dolcetto d'Alba Vigna Deserto '00	3*
● Dolcetto d'Alba Vigna Buschin '00	3
● Dolcetto d'Alba Vigna Campasso '00	3

Saccoletto
S. S. Casale-Asti, 82
15020 San Giorgio Monferrato (AL)
tel. 0142806509
e-mail: saccolettovini@libero.it

Daniele Saccoletto makes his wines according to the tenets of organic farming. His range is extensive, covering all the main Monferrato wine types. The Barbera Vigna Filari Lunghi is full-bodied while the Barbera Vigna Minerva is a more approachable, easy-to-drink prospect.

● Barbera del M.to Vigna I Filari Lunghi '00	3
● Barbera d'Asti Vigna Minerva '99	3

Guido Berta
Loc. Saline, 53
14050 San Marzano Oliveto (AT)
Tel. 0141856193
E-mail: bgpm@inwind.it

Guido Berta is a producer who has gained a reputation in recent years for his characterful wines, obtained from well-aspected plots. The Canto di Luna selection, of which only a limited number of bottles were released, is a very good wine and the Superiore '99 is also well-made.

● Barbera d'Asti Sup. Canto di Luna '99	🍷🍷 4
● Barbera d'Asti Sup. '99	🍷 3

Franco Mondo
Reg. Mariano, 33
14050 San Marzano Oliveto (AT)
Tel. 0141834096
E-mail: francomondo@inwind.it

Since Franco Mondo is in San Marzano Oliveto, one of the finest areas for Barbera d'Asti, there is little doubt about where the winery's strengths lie. The Superiore Vigna delle Rose '98 selection is a fine, well-structured wine while the '99 Vigna del Salice is also very attractive.

● Barbera d'Asti Sup. Vigna delle Rose '98	🍷🍷 4
● Barbera d'Asti Vigna del Salice '99	🍷 3

Tenuta Il Falchetto
Fraz. Ciombi - Via Valle Tinella, 16
12058 Santo Stefano Belbo (CN)
Tel. 0141840344
E-mail: tenuta@ilfalchetto.com

The Fornos make a very reliable range that includes whites, reds and dessert wines. Moscato is, of course, the main variety at this Santo Stefano Belbo winery, with two versions featuring on the list, the Tenuta dei Ciombi and the Tenuta del Fant.

○ Moscato d'Asti Tenuta dei Ciombi '00	🍷🍷 3*
○ Moscato d'Asti Tenuta del Fant '00	🍷 3

Cascina Cucco
Via Mazzini, 10
12050 Serralunga d'Alba (CN)
Tel. 0173613147

This year, the municipality of Serralunga d'Alba has a new source of premium wines. The Cascina Cucco, owned by the Stroppiana family, has decided to aim for quality and the early results are extremely encouraging. Their Barolo Vigna Cucco is excellent and the Vigna Cerrati is also very good.

● Barolo Vigna Cucco '97	🍷🍷 6
● Barolo Vigna Cerrati '97	🍷 6

Giovanni Rosso
Via Foglio, 18
12050 Serralunga d'Alba (CN)
Tel. 0173613142
E-mail: wine@giovannirosso.com

More good news from the hills around Serralunga: oenologist Davide Rosso has decided to settle down on the family property to make the classic wines of the Langhe. His Barolo Cerretta is austere and tannic while his Dolcetto d'Alba La Serra has a well-structured, mouthfilling palate.

● Barolo Cerretta '97	🍷🍷 6
● Dolcetto d'Alba La Serra '00	🍷 4

Bianchi
Via Roma, 37
28070 Sizzano (NO)
Tel. 0321810004
E-mail: e.bianchi@bianchibiowine.it

This estate, founded in 1785, makes wines using organic methods. The merlot, barbera and nebbiolo Primosole is clean, well-structured and broad in the mouth. The Eloise Bianco, a blend of erbaluce and barrique-fermented chardonnay, is concentrated. The DOCG-label products are also good.

● Primosole Rosso '99	🍷🍷 4
● Gattinara Vigneto Valferana '96	🍷 5
● Ghemme Colle Baraggiole '96	🍷 4
○ Eloise Bianco '99	🍷 3

La Colombera
Fraz. Vho
15057 Tortona (AL)
Tel. 0131867795
E-mail: la.semina@libero.it

La Colombera, owned by Pier Carlo Semino and his daughter Elisa, makes wines in the classic Tortona tradition. The stainless steel-vinified Vegia Rampana and the winery's flagship product, the Elisa, are both obtained from barbera. The cortese-based Brillo and the sweet Burgò are also attractive.

- Elisa Rosso '98 — 4
- Burgò Rosso '00 — 3
- ○ Colli Tortonesi Brillo '00 — 3
- Colli Tortonesi Vegia Rampana '00 — 3

Claudio Mariotto
Fraz. Vho
Strada per Sarrezzano, 29
15057 Tortona (AL)
Tel. 0131868500

Claudio Mariotto makes wine at Vho and that is the name he has given to his most successful bottle, an oak-aged Barbera that tempts the nose with notes of wild berries and a palate redolent of liquorice. The Profilo, a blend obtained mainly from cortese, is very good and the Barbera Territorio is also appealing.

- Piemonte Barbera Vho '99 — 4
- ○ Colli Tortonesi Bianco Profilo '00 — 3
- Piemonte Barbera Territorio '00 — 3

Orlando Abrigo
Via Cappelletto, 5
12050 Treiso (CN)
Tel. 0173630232 - 017356120
E-mail: orlandoabrigo@libero.it

The Abrigos make two Barbarescos. The Montersino, aged in new wood, has more depth and body whereas the Vigna Rongallo is a more traditional bottle, austere and tannic. Their Langhe Rosso Livraie, one of Piedmont's few merlot-based reds, is worth investigating.

- Barbaresco Vigna Montersino '98 — 6
- Barbaresco Rongallo '98 — 6
- Langhe Rosso Livraie '99 — 4

Il Mongetto
Via Piave, 2
15049 Vignale Monferrato (AL)
Tel. 0142933469
E-mail: info@mongetto.it

Carlo Sanpietro looks after both the winery and the adjoining farm holiday centre; brother Roberto makes sauces and preserves. All the wines are very good but the barrique-aged Barbera Vigneto Guera stands out. The Barbera Vigneto Mongetto is elegant and harmonious.

- Barbera d'Asti Sup. Vign. Guera '99 — 5
- Barbera del M.to Sup. Vigneto Mongetto '99 — 3*

La scamuzza
Cascina Pollina, 17
15049 Vignale Monferrato (AL)
Tel. 0142926214
E-mail: lascamuzza@tiscalinet.it

Laura Zavattaro's property is on the way from Vignale to Fubine, in the midst of the lovely Monferrato hills. Her remarkable barrique-aged Barbera Vigneto della Amorosa marries structure with balance whereas the Bricco San Tomaso is an intriguing blend of barbera and cabernet.

- Barbera del M.to Sup. Vigneto della Amorosa '99 — 5
- Monferrato Rosso Bricco San Tomaso '99 — 5

La Cella di San Michele
Via Cascine di Ponente, 21
13886 Viverone (BI)
Tel. 016198245

La Cella di San Michele, on the banks of the Viverone lake, turns out a fine range of wines but the Erbaluce di Caluso is the best. For years, the Enriettis have been making one of the most attractive wines of this type and again this time their Cella Grande selection is admirably full-bodied and flavoursome.

- ○ Erbaluce di Caluso Cella Grande '00 — 4

LIGURIA

Ligurian winemaking has built up a new, dependable image. It's not yet a bed of roses, and it is still early days to speak of a real boom. But the desire to really make the most of the region's resources is gradually spreading as a result of the realization – at long last – that quality pays, and also because it is not a good idea to get left behind. Even the deep-rooted, uncommunicative individualism typical of the region, and the lack of a sense of unity in Liguria itself, seem to have been overcome by a desire to compare experiences and get involved in a common project. Envy and diffidence are things of the past. Not everyone has the same level of awareness but the new mood seems to be meeting with general approval. Today, several wineries working with pigato grapes, and equipped with modern systems for controlling fermentation temperatures, are making the most of the potential of this extract-rich variety and the results are excellent. The quest is for aroma-endowed whites with the capacity to age for longer has already met with success. Some producers have left the cliché of accessible, obsequiously smooth, easy-to-drink wines far behind. Along this particular road, we encounter Riccardo Bruna who, true to form, has turned out great Pigato U Bacan and Le Russeghine selections; then Vladimiro Galluzzo of Terre Rosse offers his admirers an excellent selection of samples with a standard-label Pigato, the Apogeo selection and Le Banche, which has a percentage of vermentino grapes. Emanuele Trevia from Maria Donata Bianchi makes the grade with the standard-label Pigato and his Artemide. Keeping him company are Fausto De Andreis with a Pigato Crociata, La Rocca di San Nicolao with Pigato Proxi, Terre Bianche and Laura Aschero with their base Pigatos. This year, the harvest was hampered by rain and the vintage is not outstanding. This certainly widened the gap between quality producers and the rest. Those who make wine from bought-in grapes were especially held back by fruit that simply wasn't up to scratch. The Vermentinos were generally rather lacking in definition, with a few peaks here and there in the Ponente and Levante rivieras. The standard-label product and the Eretico from the Maria Donata Bianchi winery are both very good; La Vecchia Cantina's star continues to shine with a commendable wine; and Colle dei Bardellini's Vigna U Munte cru also performed well. Ottaviano Lambruschi's Saticola keeps up the winery's high standards and Pietra del Focolare released a delightful Salarancio. In the red sector, success stories are exciting but few and far between. Cascino delle Terre Rosse's Solitario is seductive with an international feel, like the Syrah from Tenuta Giuncheo, which also turned out a fine Rossese di Dolceacqua Pian del Vescovo. Finally, the Superiore Vigneto Morghe from Mandino Cane is a classy wine made in the same DOC zone.

ALBENGA (SV)

Fausto De Andreis
Fraz. Salea
Reg. Ruato, 4
17030 Albenga (SV)
tel. 018221175

Fausto De Andreis, owner of the winery, has a talent for interpreting the terroir of the Albenga plain. He delivered the goods this year, too. The wines have character, vigour and a personal touch that sets them apart from the rest of the – also good – production in the area. Fausto maintains that "with determination and a touch of daring, dreams can come true. And I am still working on my own: to revive the traditional Pigato, full-bodied and sunny, but with the capacity to age and develop well". His wines do not comply with DOC regulations, which Fausto considers to be restrictive, with very little to offer, and he has renamed them Spigàu. There are two, a basic version and the Crociata selection. The Crociata is straw yellow with golden highlights and an interesting, markedly aromatic, nose ranging from pine resin and scrubland to slight hints of musk. On the palate, there is a good balance of acidity, structure and body. Good alcohol gives the palate richness and a subtle softness while the finish is long and well-sustained. The standard-label version also has a bright straw yellow colour, which is almost a De Andreis trademark, from its long fermentation on the skins. This is followed by clearly defined but light aromas of eucalyptus, with fruity notes. The well-expressed palate is lifted by nice aromas, lending it great balance, clean flavour and exceptional quaffability.

○ Spigàu Crociata '00		4
○ Spigàu '00		3*

ALBENGA (SV)

Cascina Feipu dei Massaretti
Fraz. Bastia
Reg. Massaretti, 8
17031 Albenga (SV)
tel. 018220131

Pigato is a native variety found only in Liguria, and deserves promotion to enhance the distinction from the white vermentino grape, with which it was long confused. Luckily, pigato caught the attention of winegrowers and has often been made into wines of certain quality. The most prestigious pigato person, and the first to get full value from the grape, is Pippo Parodi. His winery is situated in Masseretti, a short distance from the Albenga exit from the autostrada, on a property of about four and a half hectares, all on sandy soil. Despite having recently turned 80, Pippo continues to work with his customary verve, which has made him one of the best-known figures in Ligurian winemaking. Although he is happy to have handed over running of the winery to his son-in-law Mirko, Pippo and his inseparable wife Bice continue to dispense opinions and suggestions. The 2000 vintage is a typical lustrous straw yellow, with stylish, uncomplicated aromas of broom, banana, peach and aromatic herbs. It offers nice balance on the palate and the aromas linger satisfyingly. The bright ruby red Rosso dei Massaretti is enjoyable. It has a fine attack on the nose with persistent notes of strawberry and raspberry fruit, accompanied by hints of spice. The palate is absolutely smooth and there is an intriguingly bitterish back palate, sustained by robust alcohol.

○ Riviera Ligure di Ponente Pigato '00		4
● Rosso dei Massaretti '00		4

ALBENGA (SV)

La Vecchia Cantina
Fraz. Salea
Via Corta, 3
17031 Albenga (SV)
tel. 0182559881

Umberto Calleri is the competent and very hospitable owner of La Vecchia Cantina and a convinced promoter of the local native grape varieties which flourish on his four hectares at Salea, in the heart of the Albenga plain. Serious hard work in the vineyard, followed by scrupulously careful vinification yield the positive results which have characterized the production of this winery for several years. The best wine is the Vermentino, which has a good straw yellow colour flecked with gold. The clean, complex nose has aromas of tree sap, scrubland, spring flowers and honey. It is fresh and aromatic on the palate, with good structure, mouthfilling warmth and a long finish. The Pigato is slightly less wonderful but not without charm. A white with intense persistent aromas featuring fruit and citrus, it has a palate that is fresh-tasting and still rather green, with good body and pleasant aromatic balance. The Passito makes its debut this year, the result of patient labour and the scrupulous selection of pigato grapes with a small addition of rossese. After a late harvest, the grapes were dried for two months and then underwent vinification by traditional local methods. The wine was aged for about eight months in 500-litre wooden barrels. The bright golden colour is attractive and the delicate nose has hints of honey, spring flowers and pineapple. The palate has decent structure and balance, while the unobtrusive sweetness is offset by a faint bitterish twist that leads into a long, clean finish.

○	Riviera Ligure di Ponente Vermentino '00	ŸŸ	4
○	Riviera Ligure di Ponente Pigato '00	Ÿ	4
○	Colline Savonesi Passito '98	Ÿ	5

CAMPOROSSO (IM)

Tenuta Giuncheo
Loc. Giuncheo
18033 Camporosso (IM)
tel. 0184288639

The range of the dynamic Camporosso winery is expanding, and for several years, it has enjoyed well-deserved success in the market as it single-mindedly pursues quality. Alongside the Vermentinos, which account for a large proportion of the wines sold, there is a new red. The Sirius '99 is a 100 per cent syrah aged in one-year-old barriques for 16 months. This is a splendid wine with good strong colour and deep, intense aromas. The black pepper and nutmeg on the nose are accompanied by notes of morello cherry and redcurrant berry fruit. The flavour is full and warm, echoing the nose well, with excellent sinew and a hint of sweetish tannin, closing with a long liquorice finish. Sirius is as stylish as the cellar's other flagship wine, the Rossese Pian del Vescovo '99. Generous and well-defined on the nose, it unveils well-integrated aromas of vanilla, spices, plum and strawberry. Entry on the palate is smooth, warm and mouthfilling, there is good texture and a bitterish finish. The basic Rossese is well-managed with varietal, but rather rustic, aromas. Balance and structure on the palate are decent and there is a noticeable vein of bitterness. Now for the whites. The Vermentino Le Palme is fairly undemanding but pleasant on the nose, with spring flower and herb aromas. It is smooth and fresh-tasting on the palate with good consistency, balance and stylish – though not particularly firm – structure. The standard-label Vermentino is less bright and offers less versatility. The flavour is over-smooth flavour and the wine lacks balance. However, the Eclis '99 is spot-on. A monovarietal barrique-fermented vermentino, it may not be excessively powerful but does have style, showing good freshness and length.

●	Rossese di Dolceacqua Vigneto Pian del Vescovo '99	ŸŸ	4
●	Sirius '99	ŸŸ	6
○	Riviera Ligure di Ponente Vermentino Le Palme '00	Ÿ	4
●	Rossese di Dolceacqua '00	Ÿ	3
○	Vermentino Eclis '99	Ÿ	5
○	Riviera Ligure di Ponente Vermentino '00		3

CASTELNUOVO MAGRA (SP)

GIACOMELLI
VIA PALVOTRISIA, 134
19030 CASTELNUOVO MAGRA
TEL. 0187674155
E-MAIL: giacomelli71@libero.it

Roberto Petacchi is a skilful young grower with a degree in political science who is not afraid of rolling his sleeves up to work in the vineyard and cellar. The vineyards are mostly family-owned and cover an area of six hectares, all situated in the Colli di Luni DOC zone, in the municipalities of Castelnuovo and Ortonovo. A small portion – about one hectare – is used for olive groves. Vermentino, albarola, trebbiano, sangiovese and canaiolo are grown in south and southeast-facing plots on this mainly clayey soil, at an average altitude of 200 metres above sea level. The yield per hectare is kept quite low, especially considering the average for this DOC zone. Roberto gets 50 quintals, in fact, from a planting density of 4,000 vines per hectare. The winery benefits from the valuable advice of respected local oenologist Giorgio Bacigalupi. The Vermentino '00 is well-made but is penalized by the poor vintage. Despite its intense straw yellow colour, the aromas are frank but lacking in breadth, with hints of scrubland, spring flowers and herbs. The wine shows perfect nose-palate consistency and is quite smooth and pleasantly tangy on the palate. Roberto also makes a light red with fresh fruity aromas, and a white from albarola, trebbiano and vermentino. The estate also makes a small quantity of good extravirgin olive oil using traditional methods and frantoio, pendolino and lavagnina cultivars.

○ Colli di Luni Vermentino '00	♀	3
○ Giacomelli Bianco '00		2
● I Campi Rosso '00		2

CASTELNUOVO MAGRA (SP)

IL TORCHIO
VIA PROVINCIALE, 202
19030 CASTELNUOVO MAGRA (SP)
TEL. 0187674075

This year, the wines of Giorgio Tendola, La Torchia's owner, aren't quite as good as those produced in recent vintages. Unfortunately, the poor weather did not allow this very competent grower to perform at his best and the wines are generally less complex and vigorous than his usual offerings. The Vermentino made the most favourable impression, thanks to its attractively intense straw yellow, lifted by warm golden highlights from prolonged fermentation on the skins. It has an interesting nose, the aromatic and green notes mingle with hazelnut and summer flowers. The palate, is smooth, tasty and decently structured, with a slightly excessive alcohol content. There's good length and a pleasant overall impression. The Di Giorgio is a white from albarola, trebbiano and vermentino. The former name, Linero, has been dropped in favour of that of the owner. Intense straw yellow, it has sweet floral aromas with hints of wild herbs. The noticeably acidic palate reflects the bouquet well, although the flavour lacks breadth, and the wine is fresh, easy going and drinkable. Lastly, the Rosso is from mainly sangiovese and merlot grapes. Aged in 25-hectolitre barrels, it has a rather faint nose that foregrounds gamey and plum jam notes. It is not especially long on the palate although it has plenty of tannins and nicely gauged alcohol.

○ Colli di Luni Vermentino '00	♀	3
○ Di Giorgio Bianco	♀	3
● Colli di Luni Rosso '99		4

CASTELNUOVO MAGRA (SP)

OTTAVIANO LAMBRUSCHI
VIA OLMARELLO, 28
19030 CASTELNUOVO MAGRA (SP)
TEL. 0187674261
E-MAIL: ottavianolambruschi@libero.it

Ottaviano Lambruschi is the grand old man of local winemaking and his son Fabio is no longer just a helper but the driving force behind the winery. The arena where they try their skills every day comprises five hectares of estate-owned vineyards and two which are rented. The Lambruschis grow their vines in two different places, Costa Marina and Sarticola, both considered to be particularly well-suited for the purpose. They are, as it were, two crus where the vines perform superbly, usually yielding aroma and extract-rich fruit. The Sarticola '00 is a really good vermentino-based wine that easily earned itself Two Glasses. This selection is deep straw yellow with a very aromatic nose that hints at scrubland, pine resin, flowers and pears, cosseted by sweet honey. Balanced and long on the palate, it is a no-nonsense, juicy Vermentino. A tad less exalted are the Costa Marina – fresh but with less character – and the well-made standard-label Vermentino. Ignoring the grumbles from his father, a dyed-in-the-wool white winemaker, Fabio continues to grow cabernet, sangiovese and merlot. Although the vines are still very young, he has bottled the Maniero after a brief stay in barriques. It's a fresh-tasting wine with bramble and raspberry aromas.

	Wine	Rating	Score
O	Colli di Luni Vermentino Sarticola '00	🍷🍷	4
O	Colli di Luni Vermentino Costa Marina '00	🍷	4
●	Colli di Luni Rosso Maniero '00		4
O	Colli di Luni Vermentino '00		4

CHIAVARI (GE)

ENOTECA BISSON
C.SO GIANELLI, 28
16043 CHIAVARI (GE)
TEL. 0185314462
E-MAIL: bisson@bissonvini.it

If his wine shop in Corso Gianelli were not so busy, Piero Lugano would already have closed it to devote all his time to his lifelong dream of making wine. But as the business is a success, reinforcements are hard to find and his daughter has yet to take over. Each working day is a minor battle for the popular Piero, who forced to face a multitude of tasks. The situation is made even more complicated by the long list of wines offered by this very simpatico grower who has done so much to make good wine better-known in the area. The products we tasted are well-made but lack a personal touch. The Acini Rari is the most serious Passito in the range and the best of the wines we sampled. It has a bright amber colour and immediate dried fig, dates and chestnut honey aromas which are pleasingly intense and persistent. The palate reveals that the wine will need a little longer to find the right balance and closes on a fragrant note of bitter almonds. The Caratello from bianchetta genovese grapes is goodish but rather simple. The faint apricot and beeswax aromas are accompanied by a rather lightweight structure. The monovarietal vermentino Vigna Erta is a pleasant wine with good nose-palate consistency. Straw yellow, it has green apple, pear and citrus fruit and vegetal aromas, like the Cinque Terre Marea. The two versions of Musaico are worth mentioning, as does the typical U Pastine, from 100 per cent bianchetta.

	Wine	Rating	Score
O	Cinque Terre Marea '00	🍷	4
O	Golfo del Tigullio Vermentino Vigna Erta '00	🍷	4
O	Acini Rari Passito '98	🍷	5
O	Caratello Passito '98	🍷	4
O	Golfo del Tigullio Bianchetta Genovese U Pastine '00		3
●	Golfo del Tigullio Rosso Il Musaico '00		4
●	Golfo del Tigullio Rosso Il Musaico Barrique '99		4

CHIUSANICO (IM)

La Rocca di San Nicolao
Fraz. Gazzelli
Via Dante, 10
18023 Chiusanico (IM)
tel. 018352850 - 018352304
e-mail: info@roccasannicolao.it

We have been following this young, determined winery's progress with interest for a few years, as it continually works its way up to premium production. The progress of Ligurian winemaking can sometimes be measured by the number of wineries with appropriate capital and first-rate technicians to make a forceful entry into the difficult top end of the wine market. La Rocca di San Nicolao has six hectares on hillslopes at between 350 and 600 metres above sea level, also buying in grapes from trusted growers. They make over 70,000 bottles, using pigato, vermentino and rossese grapes. Marco della Valle, the winery's manager, knows his job in both the vineyard and the cellar. He is helped by expert agronomist Franco Bessone and winemakers Marco Giamello and Luciano Empolesi. This is a good team, if the wines are anything to go by. The Pigato Vigna Proxi is outstanding, intense in colour, broad and complex on the nose, with hints of peach and apricot, wood resin and scrubland. On the palate, it is fresh-tasting, weighty and almost fat. The structure is well-balanced, the flavours linger and there is an intriguing aromatic herb finish. The standard-label Pigato is very decent. The soft vegetal aromas have hints of almonds and the palate is fresh and fairly full-bodied, with a marked varietal bitterish vein. Of the Vermentinos, the standard-label version is the most enjoyable. Expressive on the nose and rather complex, it reveals hints of peach, pear and summer flowers. Still a little green on the palate, it has a fresh, stylish and well-balanced progression. The barrique version is not entirely convincing, lacking originality in the aromas and balance on the palate.

○ Riviera Ligure di Ponente Pigato Vigna Proxi '00	4
○ Riviera Ligure di Ponente Pigato '00	3
○ Riviera Ligure di Ponente Vermentino '00	3
○ Riviera Ligure di Ponente Vermentino Vigna Proxi '00	4
○ Riviera Ligure di Ponente Vermentino Barricato '98	5

DIANO CASTELLO (IM)

Maria Donata Bianchi
Via delle Torri, 16
18010 Diano Castello (IM)
tel. 0183498233

Technology alone is not enough to scale the heights of quality. Love and a passion for winemaking are also required, and these are two qualities which Emanuele Trevia has in spades. His commitment has not stopped at developing the Vermentino and Pigato for he is now rising to a new challenge, red wines. New grenache and syrah vineyards have been planted and will enter production with next year's harvest. The whites are almost all above average in quality. This is certainly true of the Pigatos, starting with the standard-label version. Lustrous in colour, with well-defined aromas, it opens on green notes followed by aromatic herbs and yellow-skinned plums. The firm, enjoyable thrust on the palate reveals the winemaker's quest for balance and concentration of extract. The Artemide selection is even better, an excellent interpretation of the variety with very bright nose and palate. The gold-flecked straw yellow colour introduces a concentrated, generous nose. There is a hint of pine resin on the palate, which gives way to a pleasant bitterish finish. The Eretico Pigato, fermented and aged in barriques, is still fresh and balanced but less convincing on the palate, because of the rather intrusive wood. Both the basic Vermentino and the Eretico Vermentino, though, have lots of energy. The standard-label wine has laudable aromas of citrus fruit and good dynamism on the palate to take you through to a lingering finish. The Eretico Vermentino has a very intense, stylish nose, mirrored well on a palate that offers a no-nonsense, persistent flavour.

○ Riviera Ligure di Ponente Pigato '00	4
○ Riviera Ligure di Ponente Pigato Artemide '00	4
○ Riviera Ligure di Ponente Vermentino '00	4
○ Eretico Vermentino '98	5
○ Eretico Pigato '98	5

DOLCEACQUA (IM)

GIOBATTA MANDINO CANE
VIA ROMA, 21
18035 DOLCEACQUA (IM)
TEL. 0184206120

Mandino Cane owns two vineyards on hills almost directly opposite each other at Arcagna and Morghe, and a couple of hectares in an enviable position. These are planted mainly with rossese but also a small amount of syrah, which is giving excellent results, and viognier. Lower down, on the border with the municipality of Camporosso, a number of rows of vermentino provide a small amount of wine which is entirely sold to local restaurant. The cellar has been moved from its previous location in an old church to nearer the house, in properly equipped facilities. The winery's consultant oenologist is the very able Walter Bonetti, who makes sure the care and effort expended in the vineyard do not go to waste. Mandino makes his own contribution and his wines benefit from that touch of class he puts into all his endeavours. Top of the range this year is the Morghe selection. Lifted by flowery notes of roses and violets, the aroma expands into balsamic fragrances laced with spice. Full-bodied and tangy on the palate, with good alcohol, it offers pleasing warmth. A well-structured wine with good complexity on the palate, it signs of with an attractive almond twist. In the Rossese Vigneto Arcagna, the aromas are delicate rather than powerful, focusing on caressing notes of autumn leaves, scrubland and dried flowers. The well-sustained palate is fresh and balanced, with well-orchestrated tannins and fruit, good extract and a fairly long finish.

●	Rossese di Dolceacqua Sup. Vigneto Morghe '00	🍷🍷 4
●	Rossese di Dolceacqua Sup. Vigneto Arcagna '00	🍷 4
●	Rossese di Dolceacqua Sup. Vigneto Arcagna '99	🍷🍷 4
●	Rossese di Dolceacqua Sup. Vigneto Morghe '99	🍷🍷 4

DOLCEACQUA (IM)

TERRE BIANCHE
LOC. ARCAGNA
18035 DOLCEACQUA (IM)
TEL. 018431426 - 018431230
E-MAIL: terrebianche@terrebianche.com

To reach the stone buildings of the Terre Bianche holiday centre, the backdrop for the winery, you follow the Nervia valley up as far as the bridge after the town of Dolceacqua. Cross the bridge and bear left towards Arcagna. Up here in breathtaking scenery, Paolo Rondelli, his young nephew Filippo and brother-in-law Franco Laconi make their wines with an eye to constant improvement in quality. The results are more than flattering, thanks in part to the input of oenologist Mario Ronco. The Vermentino, for example, has a very distinctive nose, with intense scrubland and pine resin aromas. On the palate, it is well-textured, balanced and fresh-tasting with a moderately long flavour. The Arcana is also nice. Made from a blend of pigato and vermentino, the sweet, buttery boisé melds with hints of citrus fruit, flowers and coffee. The palate is smooth, warm and decently extracted. The Pigato is rather more stimulating, with its bright straw yellow and big nose of no-nonsense peach, summer flowers and almonds. The mouthfeel is temptingly velvety, and there is good extract and length. All in all, an elegant and very pleasant wine. The reds include a strikingly good standard-label Rossese, with a vibrant ruby red hue. The concentrated, persistent nose is rich in flower and fruit aromas laced with faint hints of balsam. Full-bodied and with a pleasing bitterish hint, it has warmth and softness to take you through to a clean finish. Lastly, the Bricco Arcagna has fair texture and distinctive fruity aromas.

○	Riviera Ligure di Ponente Pigato '00	🍷🍷 4
○	Riviera Ligure di Ponente Vermentino '00	🍷 4
●	Rossese di Dolceacqua '00	🍷 4
○	Arcana Bianco '99	🍷 5
●	Rossese di Dolceacqua Bricco Arcagna '99	🍷 5
●	Rossese di Dolceacqua Bricco Arcagna '98	🍷🍷 5
●	Arcana Rosso '98	🍷 5

FINALE LIGURE (SV)

Cascina delle Terre Rosse
Via Manie, 3
17024 Finale Ligure (SV)
tel. 019698782

The factors contributing to this winery's improvement in quality are the vineyards situated at 350 metres above sea level, scrupulous selection of grapes, late harvests, the invaluable help of oenologist Giuliano Noè and the determination of Vladimiro Galluzzo. His Pigato has been universally praised, and confirms its place in the front rank of Ligurian whites for structure and balance. The bouquet is broad and intense, with a characteristic aromatic note and hints of peaches, almonds and musk. Full-bodied in the mouth, it is stylish with plenty of temperament. The Apogeo selection is unusual. It spends rather longer in the cellar than most before release. The intense straw yellow ushers in subtle aromas that are full and complex, with hints of aromatic herbs and honey. The palate is more stylish than powerful, with excellent balance and a pleasant tangy finish with a twist of almond. The Le Banche '00, from barrique-aged pigato and vermentino, has well-judged oak that leaves room for notes of apricot and tropical fruit. The palate hinges on rich extract and delightful softness. The Vermentino is also good, with an intense, complex nose and a palate that marries finesse and sinew. The red Solitario, from grenache, barbera and rossese, has a concentrated nose with hints of black berry fruit blending well with the notes of chocolate, pepper and leather. Authoritative in the mouth, it reveals elegant structure and fresh-tasting acidity. An unquestionably good Ligurian red, with enjoyable thrust on the palate and a vibrant, lingering finish.

○	Riviera Ligure di Ponente Pigato Apogeo '00	♀♀	4
○	Le Banche '00	♀♀	5
○	Riviera Ligure di Ponente Pigato '00	♀♀	4
●	Solitario '99	♀♀	6
○	Riviera Ligure di Ponente Vermentino '00	♀	4
○	Riviera Ligure di Ponente Pigato '99	♀♀♀	4
●	Solitario '97	♀♀	6

IMPERIA

Colle dei Bardellini
Loc. Bardellini
Via Fontanarosa, 12
18100 Imperia
tel. 0183291370 - 010594513

The grapes growing on the Colle dei Bardellini estate enjoy wonderful exposure to the sun, and as they ripen, they are watched over by Giuliano Noè, the well-known oenologist. Noè is now a pillar of this excellent winery, which is run efficiently and without fuss by Pino Sola. Each year, Colle dei Bardellini further consolidates its place in the Guide as one of the region's best wineries. About 20,000 bottles were released of the Vermentino Vigna U Munte '00, a very fine wine. The intense, bright straw yellow is followed by a rich, lingering nose with hints of scrubland, apricots, citron, broom and musk. The palate follows through well with good balance and texture, backed up by attractive acidity that invigorates the warm, concentrated finish. The Pigato La Torretta is a notch or two lower, its fairly bright straw yellow ushering in faint apple, mimosa, chamomile and acacia blossom aromas. Smooth but vibrant in the mouth, with a vein of acidity. A nice Pigato, which will age in the cellar for a good while. The crystal clear standard-label Vermentino is also worth a mention for its easy-going quaffability. The nose is all freshness with aniseed, banana and summer flower aromas, and the palate follows suit, although the structure is not massive. Colle dei Bardellini also makes other wines, which brings total production up to about 80,000 bottles. A seriously large number for a Ligurian winery.

○	Riviera Ligure di Ponente Vermentino Vigna U Munte '00	♀♀	4
○	Riviera Ligure di Ponente Pigato Vigna La Torretta '00	♀	4
○	Riviera Ligure di Ponente Vermentino '00		3
○	Riviera Ligure di Ponente Vermentino Vigna U Munte '99	♀♀	4

ORTONOVO (SP)

LA PIETRA DEL FOCOLARE
VIA DOGANA, 209
19034 ORTONOVO (SP)
TEL. 0187662129
E-MAIL: lapietradelfocolare@libero.it

Stefano Salvetti and his wife Laura run this tiny winery in the municipality of Ortonovo, in the Colli di Luni DOC zone, with determination and an engaging modesty. The entire estate consists of six and a half hectares of vineyards in a wonderful position. The Salvettis know what they want and how to get it, starting with careful selection in the vineyard where the yield never goes above 40 quintals per hectare. The fruit is undergoes careful fermentation and then skilfully gauged extraction and skin contact to bring out the best in the grapes without the use of wood. The Solarancio is obtained from a selection of grapes grown in the prestigious Saricola and Bacchiano areas, and easily earns Two Glasses. Its rich, persistent, characterful nose has flower, fruit and aromatic notes, all enhanced by honey sensations. Rounded, balanced and satisfying on the palate, the wine is has good structure and concentration, as well as a finish with a faint twist of almonds. The standard-label Vermentino is also good. Straw yellow flecked with pale green, it has a clean, vegetal nose with fairly intense fruit aromas. Those notes are mirrored on the palate, which reveals a satisfyingly moreish texture. The fresh Villa Linda and the Santo Paterno are less convincing, though.

O Colli di Luni Vermentino Solarancio '00	ŸŸ	4
O Colli di Luni Vermentino '00	Ÿ	3
O Colli di Luni Vermentino Villa Linda '00		4
O Colli di Luni Vermentino Santo Paterno '00		4

PIEVE DI TECO (IM)

TOMMASO E ANGELO LUPI
VIA MAZZINI, 9
18026 PIEVE DI TECO (IM)
TEL. 018336161 - 0183291610

The Lupi brothers have 12 hectares of rented vineyards, supervised by Fabio and fruitmaker Franco Bessone. Wisely, they also buy in grapes from trusted growers. There are no outstanding performances this year but the winery's results confirm the good impressions made in the past, starting with the Vignamare. It's a blend of pigato and vermentino that stands out for its well-defined, delicately fruity aromas accompanied by a very faint note of toastiness. Initially, it is slightly vegetal on the palate, then a temptingly complex mid palate follows to lend quaffability and softness. The standard-label Vermentino is always enjoyable. The promisingly intense straw yellow ushers in moderately concentrated aromas of herbs and summer flower. The progression on the palate is textbook stuff, backed up by acidity and decent weight. We were expecting something more from the Le Serre Vermentino selection, which is closed the nose and has little dynamism on the palate. The standard-label Pigato, on the other hand, has bags of character. It opens gradually on the nose into complex aromas that are followed through on the palate, which has pretty good weight, freshness and attractive length. The Pigato Le Petraie, however, is not particularly exciting, its intensely varietal nose jarring with a palate that combines acidity with marked smoothness. One Glass for the Ormeasco Le Braje, a well-made red, though not especially rich or extracted. On the palate, it is a little thin in comparison with previous vintages of the same selection.

O Riviera Ligure di Ponente Pigato '00	Ÿ	4
O Riviera Ligure di Ponente Pigato Le Petraie '00	Ÿ	4
O Riviera Ligure di Ponente Vermentino '00	Ÿ	4
● Riviera Ligure di Ponente Ormeasco Sup. Le Braje '99	Ÿ	4
O Vignamare '99	Ÿ	5
O Riviera Ligure di Ponente Vermentino Le Serre '00		4
O Vignamare '98	ŸŸ	5
● Riviera Ligure di Ponente Ormeasco Sup. Le Braje '98	Ÿ	4

RANZO (IM)

A Maccia
Fraz. Borgo
Via Umberto I, 54
18028 Ranzo (IM)
tel. 0183318003

RANZO (IM)

Bruna
Fraz. Borgo
Via Umberto I, 81
18028 Ranzo (IM)
tel. 0183318082

Loredana Fiorito's skill and commitment have always borne good fruit. This year is no exception, with the Pigato and the Rossese both showing character and personality. The three hectares of vineyards are scattered over the sun-kissed hills of Ranzo and supervised in person by the enterprising, tenacious owner. Loredana adroitly juggles her roles as mother and winemaker, with the invaluable help of Piedmontese oenologist, Rossano Abbona. About 16,000 bottles are made, most of them Pigato, and the labels have recently undergone well thought-out restyling. The 2000 vintage must be tasted for the delicate flower – especially broom – and fruit aromas, with their fresh hint of sage. On the palate, the wine is warm and well-sustained, with good nose-palate consistency and acidity. The decent structure has its best point in its long almondy finish. The Rossese also impresses. It has an intriguing nose of cherry and raspberry, followed by a faint note of alcohol. Nicely balanced on the palate, it shows a fruity softness and quite good extract. The sensation of warmth in the clean finish is very attractive. Loredana Fiorito doesn't like to cut corners. She is aiming for a more densely textured red and hopes to get there little by little, planting a new vineyard from a shortlist of eligible plots still being evaluated. In the meantime, she has begun restructuring and enlarging the cellars to keep abreast of the work in hand.

Great wines could emerge from Riccardo Bruna's vineyards overlooking the Arroscia valley, in the strip of land at the far end of the province of Imperia. There are several factors pointing that way: the sea air, the sunny climate and the gravelly subsoil of the dry, permeable red earth. These are backed up by enthusiasm and solid hard work, as well as a strong belief in the potential and personality of the pigato variety, characteristics Riccardo shares with his daughters Francesca and Anna Maria. Only this kind of enthusiasm can make a white as good as the Pigato U Bacan. Bruna has won her bet, if this bright straw yellow wine is anything to go by. The full, seductive aromas of peach, honey, aromatic herbs and fragrant scrubland are sustained by good alcohol. The other selection, Le Russeghine, has plenty of concentration and good thrust but isn't quite as good. It has an interestingly concentrated range of aromas, and the palate proffers good acidity which perks up and complements the alcohol. The Villa Torrachetta is interesting, albeit simpler in structure, with faint fruity aromas. The winery has more than four hectares in Ranzo and Ortovero, where pigato and rossese grapes are grown. The bulk of production is accounted for by pigato, 34,000 bottles of which are released, while rossese is a familiar variety in western Liguria. This year about 3,000 bottles were made of this red variety, which has subtle floral aromas. Soft and tangy on the palate, it shows decent structure, nice fruit in the mid palate, balance and a good clean finish.

○ Riviera Ligure di Ponente Pigato '00	♀	3
● Riviera Ligure di Ponente Rossese '00	♀	3

○ Riviera Ligure di Ponente Pigato U Bacan '00	♀♀	5
○ Riviera Ligure di Ponente Pigato Le Russeghine '00	♀♀	4
○ Riviera Ligure di Ponente Pigato Villa Torrachetta '00	♀	4
● Riviera Ligure di Ponente Rossese '00	♀	3
○ Riviera Ligure di Ponente Pigato Le Russeghine '99	♀♀	4
○ Riviera Ligure di Ponente Pigato U Bacan '99	♀♀	5

RIOMAGGIORE (SP)

Walter De Battè
Via Trarcantu, 25
19017 Riomaggiore (SP)
Tel. 0187920127

We were very excited last year by Walter de Battè's Sciacchetrà '97, which had bags of personality and complex aromas. Unfortunately the new vintages, the Riserva '98 and the brand new standard label version, aged for only two years, did not inspire the same reaction. Neither of them possesses the same barrage of aromas that have always characterized the nectar made in this small Cinque Terre winery. The '98 Riserva was awarded Two Glasses, though. Amber in colour, with an immediately impressive nose, it offers notes of apricot, honey and bitter orange. The palate is a whisker too sweet, which tends to highlight the forward tannins, finding a point of equilibrium in the moderately powerful body. The Sciacchetrà '99 isn't quite as good. Younger, it also has a more limited range of aromas. We know how hard this committed producer works in the vineyard, and his natural winemaking ability, so we are sure that his Sciacchetrà selections will shine again in the future as they have in the past. The dry Cinque Terre is decent and, like the sweet version, is obtained from albarola, bosco and vermentino. Deep straw yellow with gold flecks in the glass, it offers a delicate nose with persistent fruit notes of apricot and yellow-skinned plum, and toasty vanilla and coffee aromas mingling with flowers. The palate reflects the nose well and is typically tangy, with nice freshness and balance.

SARZANA (SP)

Il Monticello
Via Groppolo, 7
19038 Sarzana (SP)
Tel. 0187621432
E-mail: sub@libero.it

For the last eight years, Alessandro and Davide Neri have been running this small family winery in the hills overlooking Sarzana. They join forces for the exhausting vineyard work, then split the other tasks more or less as follows: Alessandro is mainly responsible for vinification and Davide deals with the commercial side of the business. The estate covers an area of ten hectares but only five of these, in Monticello and Paterno, are used for vineyards. Guyot-trained vermentino, sangiovese, canaiolo, ciliegiolo, pollera and merlot are planted. The winery makes four wines, including standard labels and barrique-aged bottles. Podere Paterno, which is briefly aged in wood, has a deep straw yellow colour with pale gold highlights. It has a wide range of persistent, well-defined aromas, including coffee, vanilla, apricot, pear and honey. The palate echoes the nose, and is satisfying, clean and warm, if lacking a little bite. The standard-label Vermentino has a fresh, fruity nose of apricots, citron and apples, with a supple palate and an attractively invigorating citrus note. The red Poggio dei Magni is made from a selection of red grapes and while basically well-made, is a little lacking in personality. The Rupestro is rustic and engagingly uncomplicated. This year, the estate has opened two lovely, fully furnished flatlets, which would be the ideal base from which to explore the surrounding area.

○ Cinque Terre Sciacchetrà Ris. '98	ŶŶ	6	
○ Cinque Terre '00	Ŷ	5	
○ Cinque Terre Sciacchetrà '99	Ŷ	6	
○ Cinque Terre Sciacchetrà '96	ŶŶ	6	
○ Cinque Terre Sciacchetrà '97	ŶŶ	6	

○ Colli di Luni Vermentino '00	Ŷ	4
○ Colli di Luni Vermentino Podere Paterno '00	Ŷ	4
● Colli di Luni Rosso Poggio dei Magni '99	Ŷ	4
● Colli di Luni Rosso Rupestro '00		3

SARZANA (SP)

SANTA CATERINA
VIA SANTA CATERINA, 6
19038 SARZANA (SP)
TEL. 0187610129
E-MAIL: akih@libero.it

After graduating in philosophy, Andrea Kihlgren, whose father is Swedish, decided to help run his Italian mother's winery. He is personally involved in all aspects of the work and decision-making, aiming to make wines with personality. The total of 28,000 bottles produced come from about six and a half hectares of mainly sandy soil, planted with six or seven year old Guyot-trained vines. These are short pruned to ensure a fairly low yield of 50 quintals per hectare for the Vermentino and 40 for the Rosso. Of the six wines made – and six are perhaps too many – and tasted for this edition of the Guide, the best is the Bianco Giuncaro. A blend of several varieties, it includes fruit from old tocai vines which make a rich contribution to the bouquet. The wine has flowery, almondy and aniseed aromas on the nose, and a soft palate, which is pleasant if not powerful. The standard-label Vermentino also performs well, its attractive straw yellow flecked with green. The fresh vegetal nose has aromatic rosemary herb and peach fruit notes. On the palate, it shows typical varietal qualities with good balance and a confident progression. The Bianco's deep straw yellow and gold highlights tell you it has been aged in oak, an impression confirmed on the nose of coffee, wood resin and vanilla and on the palate. A notch or two below come the Poggio Alti selection, Rosso '00 and the barrique-aged Giaretolo, from merlot grapes grown where once the Magra river flowed.

○	Colli di Luni Bianco Giuncaro '00 ▼	3
○	Colli di Luni Vermentino '00 ▼	3
○	Colli di Luni Bianco '99 ▼	3
●	Colli di Luni Rosso '00	3
●	Colli di Luni Rosso Ghiaretolo '99	4
○	Colli di Luni Vermentino Poggi Alti '99	4

VENDONE (SV)

CLAUDIO VIO
FRAZ. CROSA, 16
17032 VENDONE (SV)
TEL. 018276338

Vendone is a small inland town between Val d'Arroscia and Val Pennavaira. Back in 1920, the Vio family began to cultivate vines in the lush countryside, to make wine for the family's own consumption. Their winery was built in 1970, and continues to produce the classic local whites. Claudio has followed in his father's footsteps, personally supervising all the winery's operations for some years now, from the vineyard, where he selects the bunches so that they can ripen fully, to the cellar, where he strives to bring out the characteristics of the grapes. Only two of the property's five hectares are used to grow vines and they are located in a beautifully sunny position. The vineyards are mainly around 300 metres above sea level, an important factor in the formation of aromas, which have always been a strong feature in Vio's wines. The Pigato '00 is very good, with a straw yellow colour and moderately full, delicately aromatic nose. The peach, apricot and floral aromas, with hints of broom, are followed by a dry but soft, pleasantly persistent and very varietal palate. The long warm finish has an attractive bitter twist in the after-aroma. The Vermentino also did well, revealing a subtle nose dominated by scrubland aromas, fragrant summer flowers, and varietal wood resin. Tangy and medium-long on the palate, it has a nice drinkable finish and a slightly off-centre note of alcohol.

○	Riviera Ligure di Ponente Pigato '00 ▼	3
○	Riviera Ligure di Ponente Vermentino '00 ▼	3

OTHER WINERIES

Anfossi
Fraz. Bastia - Via Paccini, 39
17030 Albenga (SV)
Tel. 018220024
E-mail: anfossi@aziendaagrariaanfossi.it

Anfossi is a large estate on the Albenga plain. As well as wine, they make a series of other quality products, from extra virgin olive oil to tempting sauces and preserves. The Pigato has light fruity aromas with a smooth, uncomplicated palate.

○ Riviera Ligure di Ponente Pigato '00	🍷 3

Cantine Calleri
Reg. Fratti, 2
17031 Albenga (SV)
Tel. 018220085
E-mail: iqpc@tin.it

Calleri is a good-sized winery that places 80,000 bottles of wine on the market each year. Of the five labels presented, we particularly liked the Vermentino I Muzazzi, with its fresh aromas of pear, citrus fruit and scrubland, and the fruity Ormeasco.

● Riviera Ligure di Ponente Ormeasco '00	🍷 4
○ Riviera Ligure di Ponente Vermentino I Muzazzi '00	🍷 4

'R Mesueto
Via Masignano, 12
19021 Arcola (SP)
Tel. 0187986190

The vineyards belonging to this small winery are located in a valley between Monte Masignano and Monte Misureto. The Vermentino has aromatic herb, resin and acacia flowers on the nose and a distinctly lemony note in the flavour. The good aromatic length is handicapped by a slight lack of body.

○ Colli di Luni Vermentino '00	🍷 4

Ruffino
Via Strada Vecchia, 19
Fraz. Varigotti
17024 Finale Ligure (SV)
Tel. 019698522

Mataossu is a markedly acidic wine made from lumassina grapes. The straw yellow colour has pale greenish highlights introducing a nose with distinctive overtones of country herbs. Vigorous and fairly long on the palate, it reveals a distinct, persistent vegetal sensation reminiscent of unripe berries.

○ Mataossu Vigneto Reinè '00	🍷 4

Enoteca Bruzzone
Via Bolzaneto, 94/r
16100 Genova
tel. 0107455157
e-mail: andreabruzz@libero.it

The bianchetta genovese is the typical variety of the Genoa area. This wine has fresh aromas of apple, aniseed and resin. Very drinkable, with a dry no-nonsense palate, it signs off with a pleasantly bitterish finish. Congratulations the Enoteca Bruzzone for their gritty commitment to a wine type that is too often neglected.

○ Val Polcevera Bianchetta
   Genovese '00   3

Laura Aschero
P.zza Vittorio Emanuele, 7
18027 Pontedassio (IM)
tel. 0183293515

Cesare and Marco Rizzo manage the family winery's four hectares of vineyards under the careful direction of skilled oenologist Giampaolo Ramò. The wines are very good this year, the Pigato in particular.

○ Riviera Ligure di Ponente
   Pigato '00   4

Massimo Alessandri
Fraz. Costa Parrocchia, 22
18028 Ranzo (IM)
tel. 018253458

Massimo Alessandri is a young producer with three hectares under vine. For the past four years, he has been turning out a good Pigato selection. This year's offering is straw yellow flecked with light green, ushering in fairly intense aromas. The warm palate is slightly short on weight.

○ Riviera Ligure di Ponente Pigato
   Costa de Vigne '00   4

Fiorenzo Guidi
Fraz. Borgo
Via Parrocchia, 4
18028 Ranzo (IM)
tel. 0183318076

There is news from the Ranzo hills – the Guidi Piansoprano selection. Bright straw yellow, it unveils varietal apricot, white peach, resin and musk aromas. The flavour is tangy and smooth, the texture attractive.

○ Riviera Ligure di Ponente Pigato
   Piansoprano '00   4

Forlini e Cappellini
Loc. Manarola
Via Riccobaldi, 45
19010 Riomaggiore (SP)
tel. 0187920496

Forlini e Cappellini is a family winery and one of very few in Liguria that is distributed beyond the regional boundaries. Their Cinque Terre is bright straw yellow with delicate floral aromas. On the palate, it has a touch of acidity and a typical almondy finish.

○ Cinque Terre '00   4

La Pollenza
Via San Bernardino, 24
Vernazza (SP)
tel. 0187821214

More good news. La Pollenza is a not long established winery with an interesting Cinque Terre selection. Bright straw yellow, with toasty overtones of honey and flowers in the nose. Pleasantly inviting on the palate.

○ Cinque Terre '99   5

LOMBARDY

With 12 wines winning top awards, three more than in the last Guide, Lombardy is sending out strong signals. The region is re-affirming its major role on the Italian scene and demonstrating that its estates, in every zone, are working quickly to achieve important quality goals. Up until now, Franciacorta, with its much loved sparklers, has been the leader of the pack of Lombardy's most distinguished winemaking zones. Today, however, this illustrious area is also accompanied by another prestigious wine district with a high concentration of seriously good bottles, Valtellina. Out of nine wineries mentioned in the Guide, four won Three Glasses this year. It's a record that looks even more incredible when you consider that there were also four taste-off finalists in Valtellina. We doubt that any other wine zone in Italy can boast as much. Goals like this are reached with hard work, quality-oriented strategic decisions and investments in vineyards and cellars. It's not only the commitment of individual producers that does the trick for input is needed from particularly enlightened and sensitive DOC consortia. This is the case with the Consorzio di Tutela della Valtellina that has, in just a few years, duplicated the extraordinary results reached by another famous Lombardy consortium, Franciacorta. For its part, Franciacorta has not been resting on its laurels. All it takes is a visit to the territory and a look at a few estates to see this. Wineries here now boast the best oenologists, the best equipment and most carefully chosen oak. Leaving aside the peaks – and there are many – the average quality level is much more than ordinary. This year, five Franciacortas won Three Glasses. Among them was the Magnificentia from Uberti, which was also adjudged to be the Sparkler of the Year. Add to this is an excellent '99 version of Chardonnay by Maurizio Zanella. With Antinori's Cervaro della Sala, Zanella is a benchmark in Italy for this wine type. One thing we should mention regarding the Franciacortas in this very positive scenario is the rise in prices that has become noticeable over the last two years. We hope the market is sufficiently mature to absorb this with no problems. Moving on to the Oltrepò, this is a zone rich in promise that is finding it difficult to take off. We hope many will follow the example of the Boatti family at Monsupello, who won the Three Glasses again with their excellent metodo classico O. P. Nature, and who also produce a range with a very high overall level of quality. An estate from Garda, Cascina La Pertica, has now been accepted into the exclusive circle of Three Glass estates with a great red, the Zalte '99. A Bordeaux blend with extraordinary concentration and style, it could spark off a wine Renaissance in the Garda area. We very much hope so.

ADRO (BS)

Contadi Castaldi
Loc. Fornace Biasca
Via Colzano, 32
25030 Adro (BS)
Tel. 0307450126
E-mail: contadicastaldi@contadicastaldi.it

The Contadi Castaldi saga continues. This booming Franciacorta winery is, along with Bellavista and the other Tuscan estates, part of the holding company owned by Vittorio Moretti. General manager Martino De Rose and estate manager and oenologist Mario Falcetti are determined to scale the oenological heights of Franciacorta and for the second consecutive year, are just a step away from reaching their objective. The centrepiece of our tastings this year was, in fact, the Franciacorta Brut Magno '94. A great vintage, it was disgorged only 12 months after the excellent '95. The Magno has a bright, intense straw-yellow colour and an extraordinarily fine, compact perlage. On the nose, it is fresh and fruity with sweet, fragrant notes that add complexity. The palate is succulent, full-flavoured and inviting. The structure has remarkable overall symmetry and the aromas linger. With their refined elegance, the Cuvée Brut and Satèn bear witness to how effectively the estate is organized. Only a mark or two below these this year we find the Franciacorta Rosé and Brut Zero, both enjoyably clean in style and full in flavour. Of the still wines, we would point out a Chardonnay, the Manca Pane '99, which has fresh, fruity tones and expresses elegant vanilla nuances both on the nose and the soft, big, lingering palate. Also good is the Marconero '98, a very successful Cabernet Sauvignon, with an intense ruby red colour and a tidy nose that hints at bramble and morello cherries. Full-bodied in the mouth, it has a soft, delicate texture and varietal notes. The other three labels from the estate are all excellent.

○	Franciacorta Magno Brut '94	♥♥	6
○	Franciacorta Brut	♥♥	5
○	Franciacorta Satèn '97	♥♥	5
●	Marconero '98	♥♥	5
○	TdF Bianco Manca Pane '99	♥♥	5
○	TdF Bianco '00	♥	4
●	TdF Rosso '99	♥	4
◉	Franciacorta Rosé	♥	5
○	Franciacorta Zéro	♥	5
○	Franciacorta Magno Brut '95	♥♥	6
○	Franciacorta Satèn '95	♥♥	5
○	TdF Bianco Manca Pane '98	♥♥	5
○	Pinodisé	♥♥	6

ADRO (BS)

Cornaleto
Via Cornaleto, 2
25030 Adro (BS)
Tel. 0307450507 - 0307450565

The prestige of Luigi Lancini's winery has for sometime been based on excellent vintages disgorged many years after the harvest. One of the most interesting Franciacortas tasted in this edition of the Guide is in fact a '92 that was disgorged in early 2001. For those who do not know this winery, we would say that Cornaleto produces around 150,000 bottles a year of both Franciacorta and still wines, all made from grapes grown on the 18 hectares of estate vineyards. The terrain is stony – "cornaleto" in the Brescian dialect means "stony ground" – along the slopes of Monte Alto in Adro. Cesare Ferrari, the house oenologist, presented us with a Franciacorta '92 that presents a beautiful straw-yellow colour flecked with brilliant green highlights, very fine perlage and a long persistent finish. The nose is just as good, opening up broad and complex on notes of ripe fruit and yeasts, lifted by fresh vegetal touches redolent of newly cut mountain pastures and wildflower honey. On the palate, it is big, fresh, elegant and dense. Very harmonious, it closes on complex, exciting nuances of minerals and spice. In other words, it's Italy's answer to a Bollinger RD, showing how a Franciacorta can elegantly age in stacks for a long period. Another excellent label from this estate is the Franciacorta Bianco Saline '99, fragrant with flower and fresh fruit aromas, expressed on the palate in a rich, well defined structure. It has freshness and fruity pulp, signing off delicately oaky notes. The Terre di Franciacorta Rosso Barricato '97 intrigued the panel, although it was marked by a slight excess of vegetal notes. The Franciacorta Brut was balanced and fresh.

○	Franciacorta Brut '92	♥♥	6
○	TdF Bianco V. Saline '99	♥♥	4*
●	TdF Rosso Barricato '97	♥	4
○	Franciacorta Brut	♥	5
○	Franciacorta Brut '89	♥♥	5
●	TdF Rosso Cornaleto '90	♥♥	3
●	TdF Rosso Poligono '90	♥♥	3
●	TdF Rosso Sarese '96	♥♥	4
○	Franciacorta Brut '88	♥	4
○	Franciacorta Brut '90	♥	5

BRESCIA

CASCINA NUOVA
LOC. PONCARALE
VIA CASCINA NUOVA, 10
25020 BRESCIA
TEL. 0302540058

The recently built Cascina Nuova winery, owned by Franco Poli, has introduced a largely unknown, small DOC zone into the inner circle of wines from Brescia. The zone is Capriano del Colle, on the high plain of Montenetto, south of Brescia, that rises up in the midst of the Po valley flatlands near the towns of Capriano and Poncarale. On this clay and limestone terrain grow the sangiovese, marzemino and barbera vines from which Capriano Rosso is made, along with the trebbiano di Lugana (or trebbiano toscano, though this is not quite the same thing) that goes into Capriano Bianco. Cascina Nuova had already made a favourable impression on us last year with its Rosso '97. In this edition, the Rosso '98 Vigna Tenuta Anna is even better. Macerated slowly in stainless steel and well-matured in oak, it has a deep ruby red colour and an expansive bouquet of bramble and raspberry jam with Parma violets and a measured hint of vanilla. In the mouth, it is warm, full-bodied and vigorous, supported by fine-grained tannins. An elegant wine with remarkable structure. The very cleanly made Capriano Rosso '98 is robust and uncompromising, showing an intense, fruit aroma and a palate that is still a bit rough. It will definitely improve in the bottle. This is also true for the Montenetto di Brescia Merlot '98, which will need an even longer period to settle down. At the moment, it is edgy and difficult to drink. The Capriano Bianco '00 was delicate, fresh and flowery but rather lacked body and persistence, probably because of the unfavourable vintage.

● Capriano del Colle Rosso Vigna Tenuta Anna '97	ŸŸ	4
● Capriano del Colle Rosso '98	ŸŸ	3
● Montenetto di Brescia Merlot '98	Ÿ	3
○ Capriano del Colle Bianco '00		3

CALVIGNANO (PV)

TRAVAGLINO
LOC. TRAVAGLINO, 6
27025 CALVIGNANO (PV)
TEL. 0383872222

Travaglino is a historic name in the Oltrepò and may come from the Piedmontese word "travaj" (work) or from "uga travajena", an ancient grape variety from Pavia. Founded around 1700, the estate presently extends over 400 hectares with around 70 of them planted to vine. It has been the property of the Comi family since the end of the 19th century. The cellar, currently undergoing reconstruction, is entrusted to the care of oenologist Fabrizio Maria Marzi, who turns out a range of very respectable wines. Outstanding among these is the Pajarolo, a late harvest Riesling in a central European style that, in the right vintages, might be a way to relaunch a noble grape variety that is going through a difficult period on the market. The grapes from the italico and renano subvarieties are selected on the vine when super-ripe and part attacked by botrytis. The very concentrated must is fermented in stainless steel. This is an elegant sweet wine that has touches of tropical fruit, acacia honey, vanilla and gunflint. It is more suitable for serving with strong cheeses and foie gras than freshly baked pastries. The Rosso Riserva Marc'Antonio '98 is also excellent. From mainly barbera, croatina and pinot nero, it aged for more than a year in small oak casks. Good, too, is the Pinot Nero Poggio della Buttinera '98. The Brut Classico '97 Classese was outstanding among the spumantes. From an 80-20 blend of pinot nero and chardonnay, it is disgorged 36 months after going into the bottle to ferment. It is very mature, complex and rich with hints of toasted hazel nuts and crusty bread. The softer, more approachable Pinot Nero Brut Classico Grand Cuvée was not bad.

○ O.P. Brut Class. Classese '97	ŸŸ	4
● O.P. Pinot Nero Poggio della Buttinera '98	ŸŸ	4
○ O.P. Riesling Vendemmia Tardiva Pajarolo '98	ŸŸ	4
● O.P. Rosso Ris. Marc'Antonio '98	ŸŸ	4
○ O.P. Riesling La Fojada '99	Ÿ	3
○ O.P. Pinot Nero Brut Class. Grand Cuvée	Ÿ	3

CANNETO PAVESE (PV)

F.LLI GIORGI
LOC. CAMPONOCE, 39/A
27044 CANNETO PAVESE (PV)
TEL. 0385262151
E-MAIL: fgiorgi@tin.it

The three wineries owned by brothers Gianfranco and Antonio Giorgi at Casa Chizzoli, Camponoce and Vigalone, in the immediate area around Canneto, work with the grapes from the 28 hectares of estate-owned vineyards and 300 hectares from various zones in the Oltrepò that regularly contribute fruit. F.lli Giorgi is an important producer that releases different ranges of quality and price. At the top end, we find the Pinot Nero '99 Monte Roso with a lovely varietal nose of blackcurrant jam, wild rose and pepper, a dry, elegant palate and clear tangy background of toasted almonds. Then come the two Buttafuocos, with the same blend as the Rosso Oltrepò, in both a "vivace" (semi-sparkling) and still version. The first, La Manna '00, has bubbles from its light refermentation and is fruity, tangy and forthright. The second, the '98 Casa del Corno, has a pleasant bouquet of bramble jam and violets but also a roughish palate from over-assertive tannins. This seems to be a common characteristic of Buttafuocos, especially those in the traditional style. It will improve, but for now, it is difficult to drink. The Rosso Vigna Casa del Corno '99 also has the same problem but a waiting period should make it more agreeable. The Cabernet Sauvignon '99 is more developed, but less rich in appearance than the preceding wine. It has a ruby red colour with garnet hints and an aroma of red berry jam with grassy notes. The palate is dry and well balanced. From the 2000 vintage, the Bonarda Vivace La Brughera and sweet, sparkling Malvasia, which reveals a marked note of sage, are both enjoyably fresh. Finally, the mature but very sound Pinot Nero Brut Classico Elith '96 confirmed our very favourable assessment last year.

● O.P. Buttafuoco Vivace La Manna '00	🍷🍷 3
● O.P. Pinot Nero Monte Roso '99	🍷🍷 4
● O.P. Bonarda Vivace La Brughera '00	🍷 3
○ O.P. Malvasia Dolce '00	🍷 3
● O.P. Buttafuoco Casa del Corno '98	🍷 4
● O.P. Cabernet Sauvignon '99	🍷 4
● O.P. Rosso Vigna Casa del Corno '99	🍷 4
○ O.P. Pinot Nero Brut Cl. Elith '96	🍷🍷 5

CANNETO PAVESE (PV)

BRUNO VERDI
VIA VERGOMBERRA, 5
27044 CANNETO PAVESE (PV)
TEL. 038588023
E-MAIL: azagrverdi@libero.it

Paolo Verdi's progressive improvement in quality is impressive. For the third consecutive year, Barbera Campo del Marrone went well beyond the Two Glass mark. In part, that is thanks to a series of very favourable harvests and in part to the commitment of a young grower to his vineyards. The Campo del Marrone '99, from 100 per cent barbera, shows the quality this ancient Piedmontese grape can achieve in the hills of the Oltrepò. Modern vinification methods have been used, including shorter maceration at high temperatures, continual rackings, delestage (racking the must off the pomace and returning it) and malolactic fermentation immediately after alcoholic fermentation. With serious oak-ageing for 12 months in five-hectolitre barrels, a third of them new, they have created a powerful, elegant wine with a complex bouquet of violets, pennyroyal, tobacco, jam and leather, and a deep ruby red colour. Already very good, it is capable of developing even further in the bottle. The Rosso Riserva Cavariola '98 is equally attractive, though slower to mature. It has aged for a year and a half in Allier oak barriques and comes from a blend of only native varieties: 65 per cent croatina, 20 per cent uva rara, 10 per cent ughetta and barbera. There is no pinot nero, or even cabernet. The Bonarda '00 Possessione di Vergomberra is fruity and fragrant and the Sangue di Giuda Paradiso is a very pleasant, sweet, slightly sparkling dessert wine. Best of the whites are the Pinot Grigio and Riesling Renano Vigna Costa, and above all the Moscato di Volpara '00, one of the best in the entire Oltrepò.

● OP Rosso Cavariola Ris. '98	🍷🍷 5
● OP Sangue di Giuda Dolce Paradiso '0	🍷🍷 3
● OP Bonarda Vivace Possessione di Vargomberra '00	🍷🍷 3
○ OP Moscato Volpara '00	🍷🍷 3
○ OP Pinot Grigio '00	🍷🍷 3
○ OP Riesling Renano Vigneto Costa '00	🍷🍷 3
● OP Barbera Campo del Marrone '99	🍷🍷 4
● OP Barbera del Marrone '96	🍷🍷 3
● OP Rosso Cavariola Ris. '96	🍷🍷 4
● OP Barbera Campo del Marrone '97	🍷🍷 3
○ OP Brut Cl. Vergomberra '97	🍷🍷 4
● OP Rosso Cavariola Ris. '97	🍷🍷 4
● OP Bonarda '98	🍷🍷 3

CAPRIOLO (BS)

Lantieri de Paratico
Via Simeone Paratico, 50
25031 Capriolo (BS)
Tel. 030736151
E-mail: lantierideparatico@numerica.it

The Lantieris are one of the oldest families in Franciacorta, with a long tradition in wine production. Nevertheless, the present winery was only started in the mid 1970s, specializing in the production of both Franciacorta and still wines from the territory. Today, Fabio Lantieri is at the helm of the winery and relies on the oenological advice of Cesare Ferrari. Grapes from the 15 hectares of vineyards on the property are used to produce excellent quality blends in the modern cellars, set in the walls of the old family palace in Capriolo. This year, the Franciacorta Brut has very few competitors for the title of the best non-vintage Brut of the year. It is a lustrous straw yellow, with a very fine perlage and a bouquet with elegantly developed, toasty mineral notes under an inviting layer of fresh fruit. The deep palate is full yet at the same time harmonious, a perfect full-bodied, supple Brut with great length. The Extra Brut is just as good with its lovely greenish, straw yellow and sweet touches of ripe apples and vanilla on the nose that promptly return on the palate, supported by a complex, dry structure with great freshness. The Satèn was also very pleasant. Perfectly in keeping with its type, it has rich, sweet notes of yeasts and vanilla, and well-controlled residual sugar. The Terre di Franciacorta Rosso Colzano '98 is dark ruby red, with an intense bouquet of red berries and vanilla. On the palate, its shows off a full structure, roundness and delicate tannins. Finally, the Bianco Colzano '99 is good, as is the basic 2000 white.

●	TdF Rosso Colzano '98	ΨΨ	4*
○	Franciacorta Brut	ΨΨ	5
○	Franciacorta Extra Brut	ΨΨ	5
○	Franciacorta Satèn	ΨΨ	5
○	TdF Bianco '00	Ψ	3
○	TdF Bianco Colzano '99	Ψ	4
○	Franciacorta Brut '90	ΨΨ	4
○	Franciacorta Brut '91	ΨΨ	4
○	Franciacorta Brut Arcadia '95	ΨΨ	5
○	TdF Bianco Colzano '95	ΨΨ	3
○	Franciacorta Brut '96	ΨΨ	5
○	Franciacorta Brut Arcadia '96	ΨΨ	6

CAPRIOLO (BS)

Ricci Curbastro
Via Adro, 37
25031 Capriolo (BS)
Tel. 030736094
E-mail: agrit.riccicur@imp.it

Riccardo Ricci Curbastro and his two oenologists, Alberto Musatti for the Franciacortas and New Zealander, Owen J. Bird for the still wines, have now become a remarkable team. They create a very wide range of labels every year, all of remarkable quality and, we might add, just slightly better every year than the previous edition. But no one at the winery is resting on the laurels of an already established reputation. Work has already begun to expand and modernize the cellar at Capriolo, now filled with small casks of new oak, and the vineyards have been expanded to around 30 hectares, some only recently planted. The Franciacorta Satèn from this winery has reached stylistic maturity and is among the best in the DOC zone. It has a straw yellow colour with golden highlights, a very fine perlage and the exuberant aromas of yeasts, vanilla and ripe apples. In the mouth, it has structure, concentration and elegance. If we really wanted to find a defect, it might be in the dosage, which is a bit over-generous, but on the whole, it is charming in its richness and complexity. Similar aromas are found in the Demi Sec, its sweetness supported by a good acid vein that renders it supple and caressing. A full Two Glasses also go to the Terre di Franciacorta Santella del Gröm '98 for its remarkable structure, elegantly expressed and supported by a smooth tannic weave and buttery softness that hints at notes of ripe dark berries. The white, sweet Brolo dei Passoni '98, from super-ripe chardonnay grapes, is as good as ever while the elegant and varietal Pinot Nero '98 has sweet tannins and good oak but lacks the concentration of some previous vintages.

○	Franciacorta Satèn	ΨΨ	5
○	Brolo dei Passoni '98	ΨΨ	5
●	TdF Rosso Santella del Gröm '98	ΨΨ	4*
○	Franciacorta Démi Sec	ΨΨ	4
○	TdF Bianco '00	Ψ	3*
○	Franciacorta Extra Brut '97	Ψ	5
●	Pinot Nero Sebino '98	Ψ	5
●	TdF Rosso '99	Ψ	3*
○	Franciacorta Brut	Ψ	5
●	Pinot Nero Sebino '97	ΨΨ	5
○	Franciacorta Extra Brut '95	Ψ	5
○	Franciacorta Extra Brut '96	Ψ	5

CASTEGGIO (PV)

RICCARDO ALBANI
LOC. LA CASONA
STRADA SAN BIAGIO, 46
27045 CASTEGGIO (PV)
TEL. 038383622
E-MAIL: Info@vinialbani.it

"There has never been so much richness in the Rosso della Casona. The old winemakers say a harvest like that only comes once every 20 years", claims Riccardo Albani, speaking about the Riserva '98. His flagship wine has extraordinary concentration and yet still manages to be elegant despite the abundance of alcohol in the structure. The credit here goes not only to nature but also to Riccardo, who knew how to make the best of his carefully tended grapes. The vines, between 35 and 40 years old, are grown on seven and a half hectares of clay terrain in a hollow with a southern exposure in the area of La Casona di San Biagio di Casteggio, considered one of the best crus in the Oltrepò. Harvested by hand between 15 and 18 October 1998, the bunches of barbera, croatina, uva rara and pinot nero were very healthy and ripe, and have produced a wine with an alcohol content of almost 15 per cent, decent acidity and a good measure of fine-grained tannins. Oak-aged for a year in small and medium casks, and French barriques, it has a deep ruby red colour and a broad, fragrant aroma of brambles, prunes, vanilla and cloves that blossoms into a complex bouquet. It is fruity and spicy in the mouth and has great vitality and elegance. Though it should be given time to mature in the bottle, it is difficult to resist the temptation to drink it right away. The Bonarda '00 is very good. "Mossa" or sparkling, from its slight refermentation in a pressure tank, it has captivating fragrances of blackcurrant and violets, a palate with well-integrated alcohol, acidity, tannins and barely noticeable residual sugar. The tangy Riesling Renano '99 shows off touches of fresh tropical fruit with good harmony and the Riesling '00 is even better, with a greater overall depth.

	Wine		Score
●	OP Rosso Vigna della Casona Ris. '98	♀♀	4
●	O.P. Bonarda Frizzante '00	♀♀	3
○	O.P. Riesling Renano '00	♀♀	3*
○	O.P. Riesling Renano '99	♀♀	3*
●	OP Rosso Vigna della Casona Ris. '96	♀♀	4
●	OP Rosso Vigna della Casona Ris. '97	♀♀	4
●	OP Bonarda '98	♀♀	3
○	O.P. Riesling Renano '98	♀♀	3

CASTEGGIO (PV)

CANTINA DI CASTEGGIO
VIA TORINO, 96
27045 CASTEGGIO (PV)
TEL. 0383806311
E-MAIL: cscaste@maxidata;it

An emphatic endorsement for this historic co-operative in Casteggio with 95 years of activity behind it. They presented several noteworthy products. Among these, the Brut Classico '98 offers a particularly favourable price-quality ratio. Oenologist Emilio Renato De Filippi selected pinot nero grapes, spumante clones obviously, from organically grown vineyards in the middle altitude range of the hills at Montalto and Calvignano. The base wine is refermented in the bottle and left to age for 18 months on the yeasts in tunnels 11 metres underground. At disgorgement, a reasonable dose - not too much, not too little - of liqueur is added. With its fine, bright straw-yellow colour, the Pinot Nero Brut Classico '98 has a persistent mousse, a fine, continuous perlage, and a well-pronounced bouquet of golden delicious apples, bay leaf and small red berries. The taste is elegant, soft and fresh, without being excessively dry. It could be drunk before dinner as an aperitif but is better with serious fish or shellfish. The dry, still Malvasia '00, with its clear aroma of sage, is even better than the '99. The Sauvignon from 2000 is surprising, with a very intense aroma of tomato leaves and figs, nettles and green bell peppers – consider serving it with asparagus. The Cabernet Sauvignon '99 only just missed Two Glasses. Aged partially in small oak casks, it has dominant grassy aromas more reminiscent of Cabernet Franc and probably needs further maturing in the bottle. The Bonarda Vivace Frambos, Moscato, Pinot Grigio and Riesling Vivace I Soli are all from the 2000 vintage and all good.

	Wine		Score
○	OP Malvasia '00	♀♀	2*
○	OP Sauvignon '00	♀♀	2*
○	OP Pinot Nero Brut Cl. '98	♀♀	3
●	OP Bonarda Vivace Frambos '00	♀	2
○	OP Moscato '00	♀	2
○	OP Pinot Grigio '00	♀	2
○	OP Riesling Vivace I Soli '00	♀	2
●	OP Cabernet Sauvignon '99	♀	2
○	OP Malvasia '99	♀♀	2
○	OP Moscato '99	♀♀	2
●	OP Bonarda '98	♀	2

CASTEGGIO (PV)

FRECCIAROSSA
VIA VIGORELLI, 141
27045 CASTEGGIO (PV)
TEL. 0383804465
E-MAIL: info@frecciarossa.com

Frecciarossa, a historic name in Oltrepò winemaking, returns to the Guide after a pause for reflection. Though Villa di Casteggio, in the middle of the vineyards, was built in 1860, a wine cellar was already operating there in the 18th century. Acquired by Giorgio Odero in 1923, it now belongs to his descendants who rebuilt the outbuildings and wine cellar in the early 1990s. Collaboration with oenologist Franco Bernabei began during the same period. In the near future, the Odero family plans to expand the estate's property from the present 22 to 35 hectares. Meanwhile, the work of renovating and replanting the vineyards will continue, managed by agronomist Claudio Giorgi. The estate's banner wine is the Riserva Villa Odero '97, not released in either '96 or '95. From traditional croatina, barbera and uva rara grapes aged partially in barriques and partially in Slavonian oak casks, it has a dark ruby colour, a broad bouquet of vanilla and wild berries and a lively flavour that is elegant in its fullness. Though already very sound, it should age further in the bottle. The Pinot Nero '97 is perfectly balanced after ageing in barriques and oak barrels. It reveals hints of cassis, liquorice and vanilla and signs off against a distinct background of autumn leaves. The new entry here is the Uva Rara '00, made entirely from the indigenous variety of the same name. Aged only in stainless steel so as to not alter the original aromas, it is a bright ruby red with a bouquet of morello cherries, faintly nuanced with citrus, and a straightforward, tangy, fruity taste. The Riesling Renano '00 is also good but rather immature at the moment and will definitely improve in the bottle.

● OP Pinot Nero '97	ΨΨ	4
● OP Rosso Villa Odero Ris. '97	ΨΨ	4
○ OP Riesling Renano '00	Ψ	3
● Provincia di Pavia Uva Rara '00	Ψ	3
● OP Rosso Villa Odero Ris. '90	ΨΨ	5
● OP Rosso Villa Odero Ris. '94	ΨΨ	4
○ OP Riesling Renano '98	ΨΨ	4
● OP Rosso Villa Odero Ris. '91	Ψ	4

CASTEGGIO (PV)

LE FRACCE
FRAZ. MAIRANO
VIA CASTEL DEL LUPO, 5
27045 CASTEGGIO (PV)
TEL. 038382526 - 0383805769
E-MAIL: info@le-fracce.it

Though Le Fracce, the estate owned by the Fondazione Bussolera-Branca, submitted only a few samples, all of them were good. The two flagship riservas, Cirgà and Bohemi, were missing since they are still ageing and will probably be reviewed in the next edition of the Guide. Also missing is the Brut Cuvée Bussolera, a "metodo Martinotti", or cuve close, Pinot Nero that normally makes a great impression. So while we wait for the wines made by oenologist Roberto Gerbino, who only arrived a short while ago to look after the estate, in the small but very well equipped cellar in Mairano di Casteggio, we tasted only three products from the 2000 vintage. But they more than merit Two Glasses. The first is the Riesling Renano from the vineyards in San Biagio di Mairano. It has a golden green colour, an intense bouquet of roses, white peach and gunflint, and a full, aristocratic flavour with zest and length. A long-lived white that will acquire more complexity over time. The second is the Pinot Grigio, a definite improvement in quality with respect to the '99 vintage. It has finesse and power, and an aroma of hay and honey. The third and last in this miniseries is the Bonarda La Rubiosa, sparkling because of its slight pressure tank refermentation. It has a red mousse, purplish colour, a fruity, bramble-dominated nose and a dry palate with a nice background of jam and autumn leaves.

● OP Bonarda La Rubiosa '00	ΨΨ	3*
○ OP Pinot Grigio '00	ΨΨ	4
○ OP Riesling Renano '00	ΨΨ	4
○ OP Pinot Grigio '95	ΨΨ	4
○ OP Riesling Renano '96	ΨΨ	4
○ OP Pinot Grigio '97	ΨΨ	4
● OP Rosso Cirgà '97	ΨΨ	4
● OP Bonarda La Rubiosa '98	ΨΨ	3
○ OP Pinot Grigio '98	ΨΨ	3
○ OP Riesling Renano '98	ΨΨ	3
● OP Bonarda La Rubiosa '99	ΨΨ	3
○ OP Riesling Renano '99	ΨΨ	3
○ OP Pinot Grigio '99	Ψ	3

CASTEGGIO (PV)

Ruiz de Cardenas
Fraz. Mairano
Via Mollie, 35
27045 Casteggio (PV)
tel. 038382301
e-mail: g.ruiz@tiscalinet.it

Gianluca Ruiz De Cardenas has dedicated himself to vineyards and wines with a passion that verges on asceticism. Since 1979, he has grown and vinified only two grape varieties: pinot nero and chardonnay, an illegitimate child of pinot nero from a spontaneous crossing with a very old French variety, gouais. He does everything both in the field and the cellar. He has no employees, only helpers and consultants, albeit very competent ones in oenologist Scaglione and agronomist Zatti, who he calls in when needed. The vineyards cover an area of five hectares: the Brumano and Miraggi vineyards in Casteggio with pinot nero clones for reds; the Le Moine vineyard in Oliva Gessi, again with pinot nero for reds; and the Galasta vineyard in Torricella Verzate, with chardonnay and pinot nero for still whites and spumantes. The clones, "noblesse oblige", come from Burgundy and Champagne. De Cardenas does his best in the small but well-equipped cellar beneath his house, with varying results. The spumantes were good last time and the reds are good this year. The Pinot Nero Vigna Brumano '98, from very ripe grapes, ages over a year in Allier and Vosges oak barriques. Harmonious and elegant, it shows clean varietal notes of blackcurrants and autumn leaves. The Baloss '99, Pinot Nero, aged exclusively in stainless steel, is simpler but just as valid. The Pinot Nero '98 Vigna Miraggi was good, but not good enough to reach Two Glasses. The Extra Brut Classico '97 was reasonable but seemed very mature while the Blanc de Blanc '98, which we had already tasted last year, just did not hold up.

● OP Pinot Nero Baloss '99	🍷🍷	3*
● OP Pinot Nero Brumano '98	🍷🍷	4
● OP Pinot Nero Vigna Miraggi '98	🍷	5
○ OP Extra Brut Cl. '97		4
● OP Pinot Nero Brumano '92	🍷🍷	4
○ OP Brut Cl. Réserve '93	🍷🍷	4
○ OP Extra Brut Cl. '95	🍷🍷	4
● OP Pinot Nero Brumano '96	🍷🍷	4
● OP Pinot Nero Baloss '97	🍷🍷	3
● OP Pinot Nero '94	🍷	3
● OP Pinot Nero Vigna Miraggi '97	🍷	4
○ OP Brut Cl. Blanc de Blanc '98	🍷	4

CASTEGGIO (PV)

Tenuta Pegazzera
Loc. Pegazzera
Via Vigorelli, 151
27045 Casteggio (PV)
tel. 0383804646 - 0383804647
e-mail: tenutapegazzera@libero.it

The Pegazzera estate has finally begun to express its full potential, not just with the spumantes, up till now its strong point, but also with its reds. Not as much with the Rosso del Cardinale (dedicated to Federico Borromeo since the lovely villa, Italian-style garden and vineyards were all the property of the Collegio Borromeo) which maintains a certain level of correctness but without any particular enthusiasm. No, the performers are the Petrae '99 and Ligna '98. The first is a Pinot Nero with a garnet red colour, a distinct bouquet of ripe blackcurrants and toasted cocoa beans, and spicy notes. The palate is dry, with a very persistent background note of jam and forest floor, so it won a well-deserved Two Glasses. The Ligna is a very rich Cabernet Sauvignon, aged for a year in barriques, with a complex bouquet of small dark berries, vanilla and liquorice and a full, warm, harmonious flavour. Another Two Glasses. While anxiously awaiting the other wines now ageing in the cellar, wines that promise an even rosier future, we tasted a dignified Barbera '98, the Safrana, from the vineyard of the same name. Now on to the spumantes. First, the Pinot Nero Brut Classico '97 Talento, which has 10 per cent chardonnay. After spending 24 months on the yeasts, it has a lovely bead and a penetrating aroma of crusty bread, small berries and dried bay leaf. It is dry on the mouth, yet not excessively so, and very elegant and harmonious. The Pinot Nero Brut, fermented in pressure tanks with the "metodo Martinotti", is soft, simpler and more immediate.

○ OP Pinot Nero Brut Cl. '97	🍷🍷	4
● OP Cabernet Sauvignon Ligna '98	🍷🍷	4
● OP Pinot Nero Petrae '99	🍷🍷	4
● OP Barbera Safrana '98	🍷	3
● OP Rosso Cardinale '99	🍷	4
○ OP Pinot Nero Brut	🍷	3
○ OP Chardonnay Bianco del Cardinale '00		3

CASTELLI CALEPIO (BG)

Il Calepino
Via Surripe, 1
24060 Castelli Calepio (BG)
tel. 035847178

Castelli Calepio is the town that gave its name to Valcalepio, a territory you won't find on any maps since it exists only in oenological terms. Here, the Plebani family turns out a substantial quantity of classic spumantes - around 60,000 bottles - with a very French style: firm colour, developed aromas and full, mature flavours. The most successful Brut in the last tasting was the '95 vintage of the Riserva di Fra Ambrogio, named after Ambrogio da Calepio, called Il Calepino, author of a massive 16th-century Latin dictionary. Disgorged in May 2001, this classic cuvée of chardonnay and 30 per cent pinot nero aged slowly on its own fermentation yeasts and shows a creamy mousse, a lovely fine, dense perlage, a golden colour and a bouquet of bay leaf and fragrant cakes, with touches of butter and vanilla. The flavour is dry without being excessive, mature but well supported, with a long finish of toasted hazelnuts. The Brut Classico '97 Il Calepino is almost at the same level and therefore well past the Two Glass mark. Disgorged in April of this year, it is soft and enjoyably harmonious. The Extra Brut '96, disgorged in March 2001, is slightly less successful. Now nearing the peak of its development, it lacks the complexity of its stablemates. Instead, we liked the Valcalepio Rosso Surie – the name, in the incomprehensible dialect of Bergamo, means "along the banks", those of the nearby Oglio river. It's a nice blend of cabernet and merlot, 70 per cent aged in barrels and the rest in barriques, and has well-gauged oak that does not cover the pleasant traces of raspberry jam.

○	Brut Cl. Ris. Fra Ambrogio '95	♛♛	5
○	Brut Cl. Il Calepino '97	♛♛	4
●	Valcalepio Rosso Surie '97	♛♛	4
○	Extra Brut M. Cl. '96	♛	4
○	Valcalepio Bianco '00		3
○	Brut Cl. Ris. Fra Ambrogio '93	♛♛	5
○	Extra Brut M. Cl. '95	♛♛	4
○	Extra Brut M. Cl. '90	♛	5
●	Valcalepio Rosso Surie '90	♛	4
○	Brut M. Cl. Linea 2000 '95	♛	4
○	Valcalepio Bianco '99	♛	3

CAZZAGO SAN MARTINO (BS)

Conti Bettoni Cazzago
Via Marconi, 6
25046 Cazzago San Martino (BS)
tel. 0307750875

Though the noble Bettoni Cazzago family has been producing wine for centuries in Franciacorta, the estate only took on a commercial orientation and began to produce Franciacorta at the end of the 1980s. Agronomist Vincenzo Bettoni Cazzago personally tends the estate's 15 hectares of vineyards and benefits from the consultancy of oenologist Cesare Ferrari. Annual production runs at around 30,000 bottles with the leading product being the vintage Franciacorta Tetellus. The '94 particularly impressed us. It has a full, bright straw-yellow colour, a creamy mousse and a perlage of particular finesse and persistence. On the nose, it opens out broad and complex, with soft, elegant notes of ripe fruit, vanilla and toastiness. Then comes a soft palate that shows both solid structure and remarkable overall harmony. It has freshness and a big, chewy quality, ending on the elegant, fruit-rich aromas, with spicy notes and touches of tobacco, which were evident on the nose. The Satèn is just as well-made. We recommend it to those who like very mature fruit and a soft, vanillaed character over freshness and structure in this type of wine. They will be pleasantly surprised by the intense nuances of butter, fresh cakes and white chocolate expressed by this cuvée. The basic Brut has a golden, straw-yellow colour, a bouquet with classic notes of yeast, toasted bread and caramelized sugar, then the palate shows off decent body and good overall balance. The Terre di Franciacorta Bianco Tetellus '00 seemed a little bit thin to us, though still correct and pleasant, perhaps because the fruit is weakish.

○	Franciacorta Brut Tetellus '94	♛♛	5
○	Franciacorta Satèn '95	♛♛	5
○	TdF Bianco Tetellus '00	♛	3*
○	Franciacorta Brut Tetellus	♛	5
○	Franciacorta Brut Tetellus '91	♛	4

CAZZAGO SAN MARTINO (BS)

MONTE ROSSA
FRAZ. BORNATO
VIA LUCA MARENZIO, 14
25040 CAZZAGO SAN MARTINO (BS)
TEL. 030725066 - 0307254614
E-MAIL: info@monterossa.com

Proof of remarkable continuity in quality again this year, the Rabotti family's Monte Rossa estate picked up the Three Glass prize. This time, to the joy of Emanuele and his parents, Paolo and Paola, it is the family jewel that earns our highest honour. The Franciacorta Cabochon '97 is by far the best cuvée ever to come out of this now celebrated estate at Cazzago San Martino. An elegant vintage from the very first glance at its brilliant, straw yellow with green highlights, it unfolds incredible breadth and complexity on the nose where clean, youthful aromas mingle sumptuously with mature notes of forest floor and yeasts, against a delicate toasty, mineral component. It unveils compact texture in the mouth, supported by a fresh acidity that offsets the soft fullness of the fruit in a firm structure. It is caressing and velvety in its effervescence, and fades away long and elegant on notes of spices, ripe fruit and vanilla. Simply exquisite. Alongside this grand Cabochon, we find other great wines, such as the Cabochon Rosé '95. An aristocratic pale rose, this wine shares its solid structure with the white and releases the graceful notes of wild berries and vanilla that remind us of the pinot nero that makes up almost 50 per cent of the cuvée. But all the sparkling wines from Monte Rossa deserve a round of applause. The Brut I Cuvée also impressed the panel with its overall harmony, and do did the Satèn, by now a classic, that plays across delicate registers of vanilla, pear and ripe white peaches. This parade of wines closes with a good Extra Brut '97, impeccably clean but not as enchanting as in previous vintages.

○	Franciacorta Brut Cabochon '97	🍷🍷🍷	6
⊙	Franciacorta Brut Cabochon Rosé '95	🍷🍷	6
○	Franciacorta Brut I Cuvée	🍷🍷	5
○	Franciacorta Satèn	🍷🍷	6
○	Franciacorta Extra Brut '97	🍷	5
○	Franciacorta Extra Brut Cabochon '93	🍷🍷🍷	5
○	Franciacorta Satèn	🍷🍷🍷	5
○	Franciacorta Brut Cabochon '90	🍷🍷	5
○	Franciacorta Brut Cabochon '92	🍷🍷	5
○	Franciacorta Brut Cabochon '94	🍷🍷	5
○	Franciacorta Sec	🍷🍷	5

CAZZAGO SAN MARTINO (BS)

RONCO CALINO
VIA SCALA, 88
25040 CAZZAGO SAN MARTINO (BS)
TEL. 035317788

The oenological adventures of Paolo Radici, a businessman from Bergamo with a great passion for wine, continue with undimmed enthusiasm. The Ronco Calino estate, boasting ten hectares of vineyards, woodlands and a lovely villa that once belonged to pianist Benedetti Michelangeli, earned flattering comments in the Guide last year. The results from this year's tastings confirmed that this was more than just a flash in the pan. A talented, well-matched team including cellar manager Paolo Zerboni, oenologist Francesco Polastri and Leonardo Valenti in the role of agronomist, has created wines and Franciacortas of an even higher quality than the very good bottles we enjoyed last year. If it is true that the measure of an estate is seen in the quality of its base wines, then Ronco Calino deserves high marks. Its Franciacorta Brut is solid, full, soft and structured, with fruit-rich pulp and freshness. The Brut '96 is excellent. A charming mix of complex notes of yeast, ripe fruit, vanilla and toasty hints emerges on both nose and palate, where the structure is solid and the persistence long. The Satèn is equally good with its inviting aromas of peach and ripe apricot and a soft chewiness that is supple in the mouth, and perked up by pleasant acidity and very gentle effervescence. But there is more. The Terre di Franciacorta Rosso '99 is a candidate for the best of the vintage and was awarded Two Glasses for its good concentration, clean fruit and the balanced touch of wood that enhances, and never masks, the palate. We also felt the Terre di Franciacorta Bianco Sottobosco '99 was agreeable and well-conceived.

○	Franciacorta Brut '96	🍷🍷	6
●	TdF Rosso '99	🍷🍷	4*
○	Franciacorta Brut	🍷🍷	5
○	Franciacorta Satèn	🍷🍷	5
○	TdF Bianco Sottobosco '99	🍷	4
○	Chardonnay Sottobosco '98	🍷🍷	4
●	Pinot Nero L'Arturo '98	🍷🍷	5
●	TdF Rosso '98	🍷🍷	3

CHIURO (SO)

Nino Negri
Via Ghibellini, 3
23030 Chiuro (SO)
Tel. 0342482521 - 0342483103
E-mail: giv@giv.it

If we were to create an award for the wine that has been awarded the highest number of Three Glasses in the various editions of the Guide, the 5 Stelle Sfursat by Casimiro Maule would be one of the leading contenders. Now, partly because of a particularly good vintage in Valtellina, the '99 also confirms itself as a magnificent Sforzato and for the seventh time receives our top honour. Everything conspires to create a wine that, thanks to the perfect raisining of its nebbiolo grapes, becomes powerful and elegant, with intense aromas of raspberry and wild rose. The palate is majestic and inviting, velvet-smooth with a rare balance, closing on persistent, final notes of spicy jam. The classic Sfursat '98 is a revelation and made the cut for our final tastings because of its concentration, harmony and fullness. Select nebbiolo grapes are the secret of a seductive Sassella, the Le Tense '98, made with brief maceration and 80 per cent aged in barriques. The Inferno Mazer '98 is among the best of its type. Spicy on the nose; warm and round on the palate. The Grumello Vigna Sassorosso '98 is fruity on the nose and tangy on the palate, with firm structure and a long finish. The Fracia Oro '97 is correctly made and pleasant to drink but much the leanest of the bottles submitted. Finally, the white Ca' Brione '00 is from sauvignon and chardonnay, subsequently blended with Incrocio Manzoni and with the addition of nebbiolo fermented without the skins. It is floral and exotic in its aromas, then dense and elegant in the mouth.

● Valtellina Sfursat 5 Stelle '99	♛♛♛	6
● Valtellina Sfursat '98	♛♛	5
○ Vigneto Ca' Brione Bianco '00	♛♛	4
● Valtellina Sup. Grumello Vigna Sassorosso '98	♛♛	4
● Valtellina Sup. Inferno Mazer '98	♛♛	4
● Valtellina Sup. Sassella Le Tense '98	♛♛	4
● Valtellina Sup. Valgella Fracia Oro '97	♛	4
● Valtellina Sfursat 5 Stelle '94	♛♛♛	5
● Valtellina Sfursat 5 Stelle '95	♛♛♛	5
● Valtellina Sfursat 5 Stelle '96	♛♛♛	5
● Valtellina Sfursat 5 Stelle '97	♛♛♛	6
● Valtellina Sfursat 5 Stelle '98	♛♛♛	6

CHIURO (SO)

Aldo Rainoldi
Loc. Casacce
Via Stelvio, 128
23030 Chiuro (SO)
Tel. 0342482225
E-mail: rainpoldi@rainoldi.com

Year after year, Peppino Rainoldi's estate never misses the mark and has become one of the most dynamic and consistent wineries in Valtellina. Over the past few years, capital has been invested in the cellar, the acquisition of new barriques is the order of the day and the selection of grapes represents a fundamental part of this winery's philosophy. This is how good wineries grow better and are able to create wines with great class, like the Sforzato Fruttaio Ca' Rizzieri '98 that takes Three Glasses for the third time. Fermented and aged in new oak, and more powerful than the '97, it has incredible concentration and balance. Complex in its aromas, with notes of prunes, the palate is soft and compact with a continually expanding finish. The standard-label Sfursat '98 has now become a classic because of its quality and correct execution. More developed in its aromas, it has a round entry on the palate, with sweet notes and the partial drying of the grape in evidence. Surprisingly elegant, the Sassella Riserva '97 has intense, balsamic aromas. Its flavour is dense, with well-sustained tannins and a dry, pleasant finish. The Inferno Barrique '97 is very sound. Elegant on the nose with hints of dried violet, it makes a soft entry on the palate to pleasant spicy notes. The Crespino '98, made with 100 per cent nebbiolo, is lively and solid in structure, fruit-led in its bouquet, and rich and harmonious on the palate. The finish may not be massive but it is still very pleasant. Both the Sassella and the Inferno '97 are typical, terroir-driven wines. Fresh and clean, they stand out for smooth drinkability. The Bianco Ghibellino '99 is altogether agreeable, with aromas that recall grapefruit, but a bit thin on the palate.

● Valtellina Sfursat Fruttaio Ca' Rizzieri '98	♛♛♛	6
● Valtellina Sup. Crespino '98	♛♛	5
● Valtellina Sup. Inferno Ris. Barrique '97	♛♛	5
● Valtellina Sup. Sassella Ris. '97	♛♛	5
● Valtellina Sfursat '98	♛♛	5
● Valtellina Sup. Inferno '97	♛	4
● Valtellina Sup. Sassella '97	♛	3
○ Bianco Ghibellino '99	♛	4
● Valtellina Sfursat Fruttaio Ca' Rizzieri '95	♛♛♛	5
● Valtellina Sfursat Fruttaio Ca' Rizzieri '97	♛♛♛	6

COCCAGLIO (BS)

TENUTA CASTELLINO
VIA SAN PIETRO, 46
25030 COCCAGLIO (BS)
TEL. 0307721015
E-MAIL: tcastel@inwinol.it

COCCAGLIO (BS)

LORENZO FACCOLI & FIGLI
VIA CAVA, 7
25030 COCCAGLIO (BS)
TEL. 0307722761

In this area of sparkling wine, it is the still wines that set the tone this year in the entry for Fausto Bonomi's estate. But do not get us wrong; the Franciacortas presented, though non-vintage, still made an impression and the credit goes to oenologist Cesare Ferrari, who oversees their production. The Brut is characterized by ripe touches of yeasts and minerals, and a good overall delicacy, even if it didn't set the panel's pulses racing. The Satèn '97 is juicy and rich with tones of apple preserves, vanilla and toasted oak, the latter a bit intrusive, and is fresh and caressing on the palate. The Capineto '98, overseen by Luca D'Attoma, like the other still wines, is a classic Bordeaux blend, aged in new oak. It introduces itself with a lovely dark, rich ruby then the nose opens out on a broad swathe of wild berries, currants and especially brambles, to shift toward the deeper tones of vanilla, tobacco and a toasty quality with a slight vegetal impression and a hint of printer's ink. It is just as pleasant and complex in the mouth, showing solid body and smooth tannins, then reprising the fruity, spicy tones of the nose with good persistence. The Terre di Franciacorta Bianco Solicano '98 - we reviewed a barrel sample last year – from 100 per cent chardonnay grapes, has freshness and balance, and is endowed with a vibrant suppleness where the touches of ripe fruit and the toasty vanillaed notes of the wood elegantly merge together, fading away in a soft, persistent finish. The Terre di Franciacorta Rosso '99 is pleasantly round, endowed with good concentration and sweet tannins, and is probably the best of its vintage. The presentation closed with a good Terre di Franciacorta Bianco '00 that boasts nice acidity, fruit and a good persistence.

This estate owned by the Faccoli family, Lorenzo and his sons Claudio, currently president of the Consorzio di Tutela dei Vini di Franciacorta, and Gian Mario, has fairly small harvests but still boasts a high level of quality in all its production. The Faccolis vinify the grapes from their four and a half hectares of vineyards and turn out around 40,000 bottles a year. The Franciacorta Brut we tasted this time has a lovely, bright straw-yellow colour, delicate perlage and remarkable persistence. Its very sweet bouquet leans toward notes of apples and tropical fruit, and the palate is fresh and smooth yet still elegant and solid in its structure, with caressing effervescence and good persistence. The Extra Brut runs along the same lines, showing good overall softness with a more spirited, controlled finish because of the very low dosage. The Rosé, a cuvée with 20 per cent pinot nero, has a lovely salmon pink colour but the roundness of the fruit in the mouth is undermined by a prominent acidic vein. The Terre di Franciacorta Bianco, in this case the '00, is as good as ever. Certainly not a complex wine, it can however be appreciated for its clean quality, clear fruity vein and fresh drinkability.

● Capineto '98	🍷🍷	5
○ TdF Bianco Solicano '98	🍷🍷	4*
● TdF Rosso '99	🍷🍷	4*
○ Franciacorta Satèn '97	🍷	5
○ Franciacorta Brut	🍷	5
○ TdF Bianco '00	🍷	4
○ Franciacorta Satèn '93	🍷🍷	5
○ Franciacorta Brut '95	🍷🍷	5
○ TdF Bianco Solicano '96	🍷🍷	4
● Capineto '97	🍷🍷	4
○ TdF Bianco Solicano '97	🍷🍷	4

○ Franciacorta Brut	🍷🍷	5
○ Franciacorta Extra Brut	🍷🍷	5
○ TdF Bianco '00	🍷	3*
○ Franciacorta Brut Rosé	🍷	5
○ Franciacorta Extra Brut '89	🍷🍷	6
○ Franciacorta Extra Brut '90	🍷🍷	6

CODEVILLA (PV)

MONTELIO
VIA D. MAZZA, 1
27050 CODEVILLA (PV)
TEL. 0383373090

More than a century and a half since it was founded, Montelio – the name comes from the Greek for "mountain of the sun" – keeps up the reputation of the Oltrepò with a prestigious range of reds and whites. The banner wine of this estate continues to be the monovarietal merlot Comprino, a variety introduced into the hills of the Oltrepò by Montelio. There are two versions of this wine. The younger one is pleasant in its simplicity and the second, aged in small oak casks, is more complex and vigorous. The latter is the Riserva Mirose, dedicated to estate owner Maria Rose Sesia, who recently passed away. In the '98 vintage, not reported on the label since it is a table wine, it has a broad developed aroma of vanilla and cinnamon spice with small red berry jam and a robust, warm, very harmonious flavour. Another good red is the Riserva Solarolo '97, from equal parts of barbera and croatina with 20 per cent pinot nero, which has touches of liquorice, vanilla and wild berries. The Müller Thurgau La Giostra is one of the top whites, from slightly super-ripe grapes fermented with cold maceration. In the '99 vintage, it has an intense bouquet of banana and pineapple tropical fruit and a full-bodied flavour with a long, aromatic finish. The Müller Thurgau '00 is fresher and more immediate but just as pleasant, with a bouquet that recalls vine blossoms and elderflower. The Oltrepò Pavese Rosso and Barbera Ferma '99 are both good, as is the Bonarda Frizzante '00. The Roseto, the Riesling Italico and Cortese '00 are all very fresh and captivating. The last of these, thanks to oenologist Mario Maffi, has an upfront flower and fruit nose that makes the most of an under-rated variety.

○ Provincia di Pavia Muller Thurgau '00	▼▼	3*
● OP Rosso Riserva Solarolo '97	▼▼	4
● Comprino Mirosa Ris. '98	▼▼	4
○ Provincia di Pavia Muller Thurgau La Giostra '99	▼▼	4
● OP Bonarda Frizzante '00	▼	3
○ OP Cortese '00	▼	3
○ OP Riesling Italico '00	▼	3
⊙ OP Rosato '00	▼	3
● OP Barbera '98	▼	3
● OP Rosso '99	▼	3
● OP Rosso Ris. Vigna Solarolo '96	♀♀	4
● Comprino Rosso '98	♀♀	3
● Comprino Rosso Legno '98	♀♀	4

COLOGNE (BS)

LA BOSCAIOLA
VIA RICCAFANA, 19
25033 COLOGNE (BS)
TEL. 030715596 - 030715596
E-MAIL: laboscaiola@tin.it

La Boscaiola, the estate of Giuliana Cenci and her father Nelson, is not one of the front-rank estates in Franciacorta in terms of production and sales. But if we were to evaluate the overall quality of its range, then this modest Cologne-based cellar would be right at the top of the list. Not least because of the excellent value for money offered by its wines. The base grapes for the Franciacortas, made under the guidance of Cesare Ferrari, and the red wines, supervised by oenologist Piotti, all come from its six hectares of vineyards. Again this year, the Franciacorta Brut received a more than flattering review. It has a lovely, bright, pale straw-yellow colour and floral aromas with sensations of vanilla. On the palate, the perfect bottle fermentation translates into a full, rich structure with a caressing effervescence, overall harmony and long persistence of fruit, with a vein of clear vanillaed tones running through the back palate. Another excellent piece of work is the Terre di Franciacorta Bianco Anna '99, from chardonnay and pinot bianco partially aged in new wood. It is an intense straw yellow and has a nose rich in ripe fruit, with tones of butter and white chocolate made more complex by the fresh touches of aromatic herbs. In the mouth, it is assertive and full, with a harmonious balance of fresh acidic notes and the richness of its body flowing through to a long, rounded finish. The Bordeaux blend Giuliana C. '99, where everything hinges on intense sensations of ripe red berry fruit, cherries in particular, lacks the extra structure and weight that would have earned it Two Glasses. Finally, the other red, the Terre di Franciacorta Ritorno '98, was harmonious and balanced on our second tasting.

○ TdF Bianco Anna '99	▼▼	4*
○ Franciacorta Brut	▼▼	5
● Sebino Giuliana C. '99	▼	4
○ Franciacorta Brut '96	♀♀	5
● Sebino Giuliana C. '98	♀♀	3
○ TdF Bianco Giuliana C. '98	♀♀	3
● TdF Rosso Ritorno '98	♀	4

CORTE FRANCA (BS)

Barone Pizzini
Fraz. Timoline
Via Brescia, 3/a
25050 Corte Franca (BS)
tel. 030984136
e-mail: info@baronepizzini.it

Barone Pizzini is one of the most dynamic wineries in the Franciacorta area. Over the last few years, the estate has invested significant resources in its vineyards, which now total 18 hectares, its cellars and consultants. The Franciacortas are made with the collaboration of Alberto Musatti, and still wines with the consultancy of Roberto Cipresso, while vineyard management is in the hands of Pierluigi Donna. The Franciacorta Rosé is at the top of our list this year, which is unusual for this zone, where great attention has never traditionally been paid to this type of wine. But this Rosé from Barone Pizzini has charm and fullness, and introduces itself with a brilliant rose colour, delicately nuanced with salmon pink. On the nose, it is intense, soft and fresh, everything turning on the elegant hints of ripe apricot, red berry fruit and vanilla. The palate has elegant structure and softness, rich fruit and a caressingly persistent length. The Chardonnay Polzina '99 is aged partially in small oak casks and partially in stainless steel. It has a brilliant, bright straw-yellow colour then boisé and flowery notes meld perfectly with fresh notes of apples on the nose. It is succulent, fresh and smooth on the palate, and signs off with whispers of pear, peach and ripe apricot, and persistent hints of butter and vanilla. Of the Franciacortas, the soft Extra Dry is also excellent. We did not enjoy the Satèn very much, since it is undefined on the nose and a bit heavy on the palate. We anxiously await the presentation of the new vintage of the Bagnadore and the red crus that were not ready in time for this edition.

○	Chardonnay Polzina '99	♛♛	5
○	Franciacorta Extra Dry	♛♛	5
⊙	Franciacorta Rosé	♛♛	5*
○	TdF Bianco '00	♛	3
●	TdF Rosso '99	♛	4
○	Franciacorta Brut	♛	5
○	Franciacorta Satèn	♛	6
○	Franciacorta Extra Brut Bagnadore V '92	♛♛	5
○	Franciacorta Brut Bagnadore V '93	♛♛	5
●	Pinot Nero '98	♛♛	5
●	San Carlo '98	♛♛	5
○	Franciacorta Brut Bagnadore I '95	♛	5

CORTE FRANCA (BS)

F.lli Berlucchi
Loc. Borgonato
Via Broletto, 2
25040 Corte Franca (BS)
tel. 030984451
e-mail: info@berlucchifranciacorta.com

The exact date of the Berlucchi family's arrival in Franciacorta has been lost in the mists of time. Their name has been tied to the history of this area for centuries. On their land in Borgonato, presently extending over 90 hectares, 50 of them under vine, they have always produced excellent wines and, since the 1960s, quality Franciacortas. With their oenological consultant Cesare Ferrari, Berlucchi this year presents an excellent quality Franciacorta Brut '97. It has a bright, straw-yellow colour and an intense, fresh nose where the fruit takes on buttery and vanillaed notes. It has good fullness in the mouth, and soft, gentle effervescence, with good length and persistence in the finish. We found the Satèn a bit less charming. It has a greenish straw-yellow colour, creamy mousse and fine perlage, followed by a tenuous nose that centres around flowery aromas. It is pleasant and balanced on the palate but perhaps has a bit too much dosage. The Franciacorta Rosé '97 is as good as ever, with its lovely salmon colour and aromas of red berries and toasted bread. But the Cuvée Casa delle Colonne '95 was slightly below our expectations, with slightly forward notes on the nose. The palate, though balanced and with good finesse, suggests a liqueur that has given it rather mature tones. The Terre di Franciacortas are all good, from the Dossi delle Querce '98, which is fresh and fruity, with touches of oak well integrated into the structure of the wine, to the richly tannic, admirably structured Dossi delle Querce Rosso '97 and the basic Bianco and Rosso.

○	Franciacorta Brut '97	♛♛	5
○	TdF Bianco Dossi delle Querce '98	♛♛	4*
○	TdF Bianco '00	♛	3
○	Franciacorta Casa delle Colonne Brut '95	♛	6
⊙	Franciacorta Rosé '97	♛	5
○	Franciacorta Satèn '97	♛	5
●	TdF Rosso Dossi delle Querce '97	♛	4
○	Franciacorta Brut '93	♛♛	4
○	Franciacorta 30 anni di Doc '93	♛♛	6
○	Franciacorta Brut '94	♛♛	4
○	Franciacorta Brut '95	♛♛	5
●	TdF Rosso Dossi delle Querce '95	♛♛	4
○	Franciacorta Brut Satèn '96	♛♛	5

CORTE FRANCA (BS)

Guido Berlucchi & C.
Fraz. Borgonato
P.zza Duranti, 4
25040 Corte Franca (BS)
tel. 030984381
e-mail: info@berlucchi.it

Guido Berlucchi & C. just celebrated its 40th birthday but has the dynamism and vitality of a newborn winery, thanks to the enthusiasm of Franco Ziliani and his children Arturo, Paolo and Cristina. At present, Berlucchi is a giant that produces more than 5,000,000 bottles of spumante a year, all at an absolutely sound quality level, and with some very interesting high points. Again this year, our favourite cuvée is the Cellarius, a Riserva Speciale from 60 per cent chardonnay, 30 per cent pinot bianco and pinot nero grapes that age for more than three years on the yeasts. It has a bright, greenish, straw-yellow colour, a very fine perlage and a bouquet that pivots around flower and fruit tones well-integrated with notes of yeast and toasty bread. It has decent density in the mouth and a fresh acid vein, good balance and persistence. But even the celebrated Cuvée Imperiale, with a production of 4,000,000 bottles a year, is an excellently made, clean, consistent brut. The variations on this theme are just as attractive, beginning with the soft, fruity Max Rosé and continuing with the Pas Dosé, dry and well-sustained, and ending with the Brut Extreme and the complex Brut Millesimato, whose '95 version we have already reviewed. In the Franciacorta area, we are still waiting for the new cuvées under the Berlucchi label so we tasted the excellent cuvées from the Antica Cantina Fratta in Monticelli Brusati, owned by Berlucchi. The Millesimato '95 is excellent, and the Franciacorta Brut is also good, rich in notes of yeast and toasty bread, with very firm structure. The fresh, fruity Terre di Franciacorta '00 intrigued us with its luscious personality. However, the other new label, the barrique-aged Terre di Franciacorta Le Arzelle '98, was less convincing.

CORTE FRANCA (BS)

Monzio Compagnoni
Fraz. Nigoline
C.da Monti della Corte
25040 Corte Franca (BS)
tel. 0309884157 - 035940311
e-mail: a.a.mc@gmcitalia.com

Marcello Monzio Compagnoni has a great passion for wine, especially spumante. Could this have been what lead him to add a new property in Franciacorta to an estate that already produces in the province of Bergamo, specializing in Valcalepio? Today, Marcello is happy to split his time between these two operations. Though it seems to us that Franciacorta gives him much more work, in terms of hectares (11 as opposed to eight and a half at the estate in Cenate Sotto), production and number of labels. The entire production of metodo classico spumante is now concentrated here in Cortefranca and all the sparklers made by Marcello are now Franciacorta DOCG. Leading our preferences this year is a superb quality Franciacorta Brut. It is concentrated and elegant, structured and smooth, supple, soft and winning with its tones of yeasts, aromatic herbs and the delicate citrus shadings we find on the nose as well as the palate. It has good length, too. The soft, round Satèn is just as good, sweet on the nose and "comme il faut" on the palate, where it reveals full, harmonious structure. This excellent threesome ends with an Extra Brut that plays on fresh tones of apples. Spirited but not edgy, long on the back palate, it is the perfect incarnation of its type. Both the Terre di Franciacorta Bianco and Rosso del Ronco della Seta seemed well-made to us, even though we expected something more from the Bianco '00. The Rosso di Nero '99, from pinot nero grapes, is balanced, fruity and varietal. The Valcalepio Bianco and Rosso are as good as ever.

○	Cellarius Brut Ris.	🍷🍷	5
○	TdF Bianco '00	🍷	4
○	TdF Bianco Le Arzelle '98	🍷	5
○	Cuvée Imperiale Brut	🍷	5
○	Cuvée Imperiale Brut Extrême	🍷	5
⊙	Cuvée Imperiale Max Rosé	🍷	5
○	Cuvée Imperiale Pas Dosé	🍷	5
○	Franciacorta Brut Antica Cantina Fratta	🍷	5
○	Bianco Imperiale		3
○	Franciacorta Brut Antica Cantina Fratta '92	🍷🍷	4
○	Franciacorta Brut Antica Cantina Fratta '95	🍷🍷	5
○	Cuvée Imperiale Brut '95	🍷🍷	5

○	Franciacorta Brut	🍷🍷	5
○	Franciacorta Extra Brut	🍷🍷	5
○	Franciacorta Satèn	🍷🍷	5
○	TdF Bianco Ronco della Seta '00	🍷	4
○	Valcalepio Bianco Colle della Luna '00	🍷	4
●	Rosso di Nero '99	🍷	5
●	TdF Rosso Ronco della Seta '99	🍷	4
●	Valcalepio Rosso Colle della Luna '99	🍷	4
○	Moscato di Scanzo Don Quijote '96	🍷🍷	5
○	TdF Bianco della Seta '98	🍷🍷	5
○	TdF Bianco Ronco della Seta '99	🍷🍷	3
●	TdF Rosso Ronco della Seta '98	🍷	3

CORVINO SAN QUIRICO (PV)

Tenuta Mazzolino
Via Mazzolino, 26
27050 Corvino San Quirico (PV)
tel. 0383876122 - 0383896657
e-mail: info@tenutamazzolino.com

Very few grape varieties – by Oltrepò standards – are grown on the 20 hectares of vineyards at the Mazzolino estate, owned by the Braggiotti family, in Corvino San Quirico: pinot nero, chardonnay and cabernet sauvignon, from Burgundy and Bordeaux, and bonarda (aka croatina), a bona fide indigenous variety. Two technicians from the French school, Jean François Coquard and Kyriakos Kynigopoulos, were hired to bring out the potential of these varieties. This year, they presented us with the results of their first vintage from Mazzolino. Already very good in past years, the Noir '99, a Pinot Nero, has made further progress and is now outstanding. Very cleanly fermented, without that "chicken coop" smell that you occasionally find in Burgundy, and aged in Allier and Tronçais oak barriques, it has elegance and richness on the nose of cassis, roses, autumn leaves and leather, as well as on the palate. It may improve in the bottle, smoothing over some minor edginess and acquiring completeness. The Blanc '99, from chardonnay fermented in barriques, is among the best ever. A golden straw yellow, it suggests spring flowers and vanilla, with slight citrus notes. It is full and warm in the mouth, with a distinct backdrop of acacia honey and roasted hazelnuts. Again from '99, the Corvino, a Cabernet Sauvignon, is excellent. Aged in small oak casks, it is dark garnet with a bouquet of wild berries, vanilla and sweet peppers, and a well-rounded, harmonious flavour with a finish of jam and toasted cocoa beans. The still Bonarda '99 is decent but these talented oenologists from beyond the Alps will have to gain more experience with the variety.

	Wine	Rating	Score
●	OP Cabernet Sauvignon Corvino '99	ƔƔ	4
○	OP Chardonnay Blanc '99	ƔƔ	4
●	OP Pinot Nero Noir '99	ƔƔ	5
●	OP Bonarda '00		3
●	OP Pinot Nero Noir '90	♀♀	6
●	OP Pinot Nero Noir '95	♀♀	5
○	OP Chardonnay Blanc '96	♀♀	4
●	OP Pinot Nero '96	♀♀	4
●	OP Pinot Nero '97	♀♀	4
●	OP Cabernet Sauvignon Corvino '98	♀♀	4
●	OP Pinot Nero Noir '98	♀♀	5
○	OP Chardonnay Blanc '98	♀	4

DESENZANO DEL GARDA (BS)

Provenza
Via dei Colli Storici
25015 Desenzano del Garda (BS)
tel. 0309910006
e-mail: provenza@provenza.it

This year, there are two designer wines by Fabio Contato. The first is the Lugana Selezione, from trebbiano with 10 per cent chardonnay. By now a classic, aged 24 months in barriques, it has more or less the same almond, white peach, vanilla, lime blossom and gunflint complexity and weight in the '98 vintage as the '97. Two hearty Glasses, in spite of the fact that the presence of wood continues to be a bit excessive. The other is a new entry: the Garda Classico Rosso '97 from groppello, marzemino, barbera and sangiovese, aged two years in barriques. Here, the structure of the red stands up better to the oak, in an overall ensemble of remarkable elegance, fullness and complexity. The Lugana Superiore Ca' Molin '99 is also remarkable, with 40 per cent aged for six months in barriques. The more measured oak shows off the flower, fruit and musky tones of the trebbiano di Lugana and chardonnay. Continuing with the Lugana theme, the Ca' Maiol is one of the best from 2000. Not a great compliment since the vintage was not a very satisfying one. However, this is a fresh, fragrant, zesty wine with clean varietal notes. The two spumantes also turned out to be very good: the Brut Classico Ca' Maiol '97, and Sebastian Metodo Charmat, the former from a Lugana base. The Garda Classico Chiaretto '00 is very nice and pleasantly fruity. The Negresco Rosso '99 was good, but no more, and needs further bottle-ageing. Finally, the Sol Doré '96 is a pleasant tipple from raisined trebbiano and chardonnay grapes, partially aged in oak.

	Wine	Rating	Score
●	Garda Cl. Rosso Sel. Fabio Contato '97	ƔƔ	6
○	Lugana Sup. Sel. Fabio Contato '98	ƔƔ	6
○	Lugana Sup. Cà Molin '99	ƔƔ	5
○	Lugana Brut Sebastian	Ɣ	3
◉	Garda Cl. Chiaretto '00	Ɣ	4
○	Lugana Cà Maiol '00	Ɣ	4
○	Sol Doré '96	Ɣ	5
○	Lugana Brut Cl. Cà Maiol '97	Ɣ	4
●	Garda Cl. Rosso Negresco '99	Ɣ	4
○	Lugana Sup. Sel. Fabio Contato '97	♀♀	5
●	Garda Cl. Rosso Negresco '98	♀♀	4
○	Lugana Sup. Cà Molin '98	♀♀	4
○	Lugana Cà Maiol '99	♀♀	3

ERBUSCO (BS)

★ BELLAVISTA
VIA BELLAVISTA, 5
25030 ERBUSCO (BS)
TEL. 0307762000
E-MAIL: info@bellavistasrl.it

At the end of the 1970s, Vittorio Moretti created one of the most prestigious estates in Italy, Bellavista. On this success, Moretti built a holding company that is still growing and includes, just to mention a couple, Contadi Castaldi in Franciacorta and Petra in Tuscany. With the help of oenologist Mattia Vezzola, Bellavista has established over the years an original style in the field of sparkling as well as still wines, all playing off delicate and elegant fruity tones and great purity of style. Again this year, Bellavista presented us with several cuvées out of the top drawer. The Franciacorta Gran Cuvée Pas Operé '96 has an elegant bouquet where notes of yeast shade into aromas of apricot, ripe pear and nuances of aromatic herbs. It caresses the mouth with its effervescence and closes out elegantly with fresh notes of fruit and vanilla. The Gran Cuvée Brut '97 focuses on sweet tones of ripe fruit. It has an intense nose and imposes structure and balance on the palate with rich pulp and an extraordinary overall harmony of composition. All this, along with an incredible aromatic persistence, we felt was worthy of Three Glasses. The Satèn throws a vast repertory of flower and apple aromas, mixed in with notes of vanilla. In the mouth, it is chewy and fresh, offering ripe fruit with notes of candied citrus, and finishing slightly sweet. The Franciacorta Brut has a bright, green-flecked straw-yellow colour, a sweet nose with a flowery touch and a smooth progression on the palate, which is soft and fresh with sensations of peach, apricot and vanilla. The rest of the range is excellent, from the Rosé to the Terre di Franciacorta and the outstandingly elegant, varietal Pinot Nero Casotte, along with the luxurious, harmonious Bianco del Convento dell'Annunciata '98.

ERBUSCO (BS)

★ ★ CA' DEL BOSCO
VIA CASE SPARSE, 20
25030 ERBUSCO (BS)
TEL. 0307766111 - 0307766136
E-MAIL: cadelbosco@cadelbosco.com

When its impressive expansion project is finished, Ca' del Bosco will probably have a cellar equipped with the most advanced technology in Europe, if not the world. Two wines were awarded Three Glasses this year. The Chardonnay '99, by Maurizio Zanella, has a bright straw-yellow colour with lovely greenish highlights and an intense, captivating bouquet where touches of apples, flower and butter meld, elegant and fresh, into the woody tones of the high quality oak used for ageing. It is sensuously dense in the mouth, succulent and complex, endowed with extraordinary persistence and outstanding cellarability. The Franciacorta Dosage Zero '97 is the elegant epitome of the Ca' del Bosco style. It has an intense, brilliant straw-yellow colour and introduces itself on the nose with a rich palette of sensations that run from fresh fruity notes to soft but exceptionally clear tones of yeast and pastries, lime and bergamot. All this comes back on the palate with a rare fullness, qualities that meld with an extraordinary finesse in the refermentation and a soft vanillaed note that fades out slowly on more complex mineral notes. In other words, this is a marvellous wine. In fact, it puts the Cuvée Annamaria Clementi slightly in the shade. Here in its '94 vintage, this wine plays elegantly across notes of ripe fruit with great overall harmony but does not quite show the depth of previous vintages. Exemplary as always are the Satèn '97, with intense notes of peach and apricot, the Brut '97, rich in accents of yeast and vanilla, the Pinéro '99 and the brand new Carmenero '98, from carmenère grapes, in addition to all the other labels of this extremely distinguished winery.

O	Franciacorta Gran Cuvée Brut '97	▼▼▼	6
O	Franciacorta Gran Cuvée Pas Operé '96	▼▼	6
⊙	Franciacorta Gran Cuvée Rosé '97	▼▼	4
●	Casotte '98	▼▼	5
O	TdF Bianco Convento dell'Annunciata '98	▼▼	5
O	TdF Bianco Uccellanda '98	▼▼	5
O	Franciacorta Cuvée Brut	▼▼	4
O	Franciacorta Gran Cuvée Satèn	▼▼	6
●	TdF Bianco '00	▼	4
●	TdF Rosso '99	▼	4
O	Franciacorta Extra Brut Vittorio Moretti Ris. '91	♀♀♀	6
O	Franciacorta Gran Cuvée Brut '93	♀♀♀	5
O	Franciacorta Gran Cuvée Brut '95	♀♀♀	6
O	Franciacorta Gran Cuvée Brut '96	♀♀♀	6

O	Franciacorta Dosage Zéro '97	▼▼▼	6
O	TdF Chardonnay '99	▼▼▼	6
O	Franciacorta Brut '97	▼▼	6
O	Franciacorta Cuvée Annamaria Clementi '94	▼▼	6
O	Franciacorta Satèn '97	▼▼	6
O	Elfo 10 '00	▼▼	5
O	TdF Bianco '00	▼▼	4
●	Carmenèro '98	▼▼	6
●	Pinéro '99	▼▼	6
O	Franciacorta Brut	▼▼	5
O	Franciacorta Cuvée Annamaria Clementi '91	♀♀♀	6
O	Franciacorta Cuvée Annamaria Clementi '93	♀♀♀	6
O	TdF Chardonnay '98	♀♀♀	6

ERBUSCO (BS)

CAVALLERI
VIA PROVINCIALE, 96
25030 ERBUSCO (BS)
TEL. 0307760217

Cavalleri's elegant cuvées have made history in Franciacorta. This is again proved by a recently disgorged, long-lived vintage, the Collezione Esclusiva '93, released only in magnums. An extraordinarily complex Brut, it has a soft mousse and incredibly fine, continuous perlage that has a bright, pale gold colour. The perlage has great finesse and continuity, while the nose touches on soft tones of ripe fruit, yeast and vanilla, run through with citrus and floral bursts that underline its freshness and complexity. On the palate, it has substantial but particularly elegant structure, and closes out long on touches of mineral and spice. Only the fact that just a few hundred bottles were released keeps us from awarding it Three Glasses. Though the Collezione Esclusiva '94 runs along lines similar to the '93, it cannot boast as much depth. The solid, rich Pas Dosé '97 is charming in its notes of ripe fruit, yeast and toasty bread while the fat and fruity Franciacorta Brut Blanc de Blancs, with its fresh tones of aromatic herbs, is probably the best of its type. This incredibly fine range is rounded off by the balanced, alluring Satèn, with its sweet vanilla and apple tones. Of the still wines this year, we felt the white Seradina '99 was particularly well made. Its lustrous, greenish straw yellow, and upfront aromas of peach and vanilla, lead into a succulent, fresh, concentrated palate. The Rampaneto '00 has rich mineral tones and its weight and length won it Two Glasses, along with the Terre di Franciacorta Bianco from the same vintage. The reds are all good, with the Tajardino '99 outstanding.

ERBUSCO (BS)

FERGHETTINA
VIA CASE SPARSE, 4
25030 ERBUSCO (BS)
TEL. 0307760120 - 0307268308

For a few years now, we have been mentioning Roberto Gatti as one of the most talented grower-producers in Franciacorta. The history of his estate began about a decade ago when he decided to take over a country house in Erbusco, rented several vineyards and started to put his long experience in the cellar to good use. From the very beginning, the wines and Franciacortas from Ferghettina made themselves known for their excellent quality and good value for money. Every year, we continued to point out that this winery had ambitious objectives and was constantly improving quality. Finally, Roberto and his daughter Laura, who actively collaborates in the winery, have made a significant step. In our tasting, the Satèn '97 proved itself one of the best made cuvées of those tasted this year and easily merits the first Three Glasses for the house of Ferghettina. A perfect expression of this type, enchanting in its fruity notes with their ripe apricot, white peach and vanilla on the nose that come right back on the palate, it offers a weighty, round mouthfeel with a balanced vein of acidity, controlled effervescence, and elegant, long aromatic persistence. It should be obvious this is no isolated feat. All the labels from Gatti are very interesting, from the Franciacorta Brut, one of the best buys in the DOC zone, to the concentrated, varietal Baladello Merlot, right down to the Terre di Franciacorta Bianco and Rosso and the Chardonnay Favento. Now on to even better wines!

O Franciacorta Collezione Esclusiva Brut '93	🍷🍷	6
O Franciacorta Satèn '97	🍷🍷	5
O TdF Bianco '00	🍷🍷	4*
O TdF Bianco Rampaneto '00	🍷🍷	4*
O Franciacorta Collezione Esclusiva Brut '94	🍷🍷	6
O Franciacorta Pas Dosé '97	🍷🍷	5
O TdF Bianco Seradina '99	🍷🍷	5
O Franciacorta Brut Blanc de Blancs	🍷🍷	5*
● TdF Rosso '99	🍷	4
● TdF Rosso Tajardino '99	🍷	5
O Franciacorta Collezione Brut '86	🍷🍷🍷	6
O Franciacorta Collezione Brut '93	🍷🍷🍷	6
O Franciacorta Collezione Brut '94	🍷🍷🍷	6

O Franciacorta Satèn '97	🍷🍷🍷	5*
O TdF Bianco '00	🍷🍷	4*
O TdF Bianco Favento '00	🍷🍷	4*
● Merlot Baladello '98	🍷🍷	6
O Franciacorta Brut	🍷🍷	5*
● TdF Rosso '99	🍷	4
● Merlot Sebino '95	🍷🍷	4
● Merlot Sebino '96	🍷🍷	4
● Merlot Baladello '97	🍷🍷	6
O TdF Bianco Favento '97	🍷🍷	4
O TdF Bianco Favento '98	🍷🍷	4

ERBUSCO (BS)

Enrico Gatti
Via Metelli, 9
25030 Erbusco (BS)
Tel. 0307267999 - 0307267157

Lorenzo and Paola Gatti, with the invaluable collaboration of their respective spouses, Sonia Cherif and Enzo Balzarini, and oenologist Alberto Musatti, within the space of ten years or so have transformed the family estate into one of the up and coming names in the crowded Franciacorta landscape. If things go well, this will not only be true for the sparkling wines but also in the very difficult field of still wines, while they continue to maintain an extraordinarily advantageous price-quality ratio. This year, the Franciacorta Satèn '97, on its debut, left several highly celebrated competitors behind and became a serious candidate for our highest score. It has a deep, bright, straw-yellow colour with golden highlights, a fine perlage and luxurious, sweet aromas of ripe fruit, white chocolate and vanilla. On the palate, it is thick, soft and round, supported by a fresh acidic vein, rich in pulp, fruity and persistent. The Franciacorta Brut is equally enjoyable for its compact structure, embracing effervescence and overall softness. It also offers backbone and vitality that make it one of the most successful labels in this type. The Gatti Rosso '99 is a Bordeaux blend of remarkable presence and density with a dark, deep ruby colour, rich on the nose with the soft tones of small red berries and a vegetal vein of tobacco and toasted oak well integrated into the fruit. The palate is concentrated, revealing a solid tannic structure and remarkable balance. The Terre di Franciacorta Bianco '00 is quite simply one of the best in the vintage, rich in structure and fruit, and supported by acidity that brings it to life and ensures longevity. The Terre di Franciacorta Rosso, in this case the '99, is as good as ever.

○	Franciacorta Satèn '97	🍷🍷	5*
○	TdF Bianco '00	🍷🍷	3*
●	Gatti Rosso '99	🍷🍷	4*
○	Franciacorta Brut	🍷🍷	4*
●	TdF Rosso '99	🍷	3
●	Gatti Rosso '95	🍷🍷	4
○	Gatti Bianco '96	🍷🍷	4
●	Gatti Rosso '96	🍷🍷	4
○	Gatti Bianco '97	🍷🍷	4
○	TdF Gatti Bianco '98	🍷🍷	4
●	Gatti Rosso '98	🍷🍷	4
●	TdF Rosso '98	🍷🍷	3
●	Gatti Rosso '97	🍷	4

ERBUSCO (BS)

San Cristoforo
Fraz. Villa
Via Villanuova, 2
25030 Erbusco (BS)
Tel. 0307760482

In just ten years or so, Bruno Dotti and his wife Claudia have made great strides with this winery, one that already enjoyed a good reputation in the past. Now their vineyards spread across 12 hectares and are supervised by agronomist Giacomo Gropetti, who is preparing them for better things. In the cellar, Bruno, with the consultancy of Alberto Musatti, turns out over 70,000 bottles a year. What counts the most is that the wines from San Cristoforo grow in quality vintage after vintage, and remain very good value for money. San Cristoforo submitted four labels. Of these, the Uno, already reviewed in the '98 version, is not yet available in the new vintage. Not to worry, since the Terre di Franciacorta Rosso '99 took Two Glasses hands down for its deep, dark ruby colour, and intense, sweet nose that hints at bramble, raspberries and ripe bilberries. Then it reveals a solid palate with ripe, round tannins, but also fat and rich in fruit. The Franciacorta Brut is just as good. It has a golden, straw-yellow colour, fine perlage, and an attractive bouquet marked by golden delicious apples, quince, pear and vanilla. The fullness, elegance, balance and remarkable persistence on the palate make this a wine not to miss. The parade closes with an excellent Terre di Franciacorta Bianco '00 that reveals a bright straw-yellow colour, aromas that foreground flowery tones and a soft and smooth palate marked by freshness.

●	TdF Rosso '99	🍷🍷	4*
○	Franciacorta Brut	🍷🍷	4*
○	TdF Bianco '00	🍷	4
●	San Cristoforo Uno '98	🍷🍷	4
○	TdF Bianco '98	🍷🍷	3
●	TdF Rosso '98	🍷🍷	3

ERBUSCO (BS)

UBERTI
LOC. SALEM
VIA E. FERMI, 2
25030 ERBUSCO (BS)
TEL. 0307267476

Agostino and Eleonora Uberti are two very retiring people whom you will rarely see away from their estate in Erbusco. Their entire world is in the winery, among the casks and clean, shiny vats or in their lovely, well-tended vineyards. The result of this deeply felt commitment, which leads to a perfectionism and special care for each minute detail, is a range of excellent wines with few equals in Franciacorta. The Magnificentia, for example, was awesome. We feel this is the best cuvée we tasted for this edition of the Guide and elected it Sparkler of the Year, but it's much more than a mere spumante. This is a Satèn from chardonnay grapes aged for around three years on the yeasts, It has a bright, deep straw-yellow colour, fine mousse and a dense, continuous perlage with an almost invisible grain. On the nose, there is a parade of sweet peach and ripe pear fruit sensations that veer towards hawthorn and acacia blossoms to then fade into medicinal herbs and vanilla. It has weight in the mouth and the soft opulence of fruit expressed with a fresh balance that ends in a very long aromatic finish. The other Uberti big gun is the Brut Comarì del Salem '96. It may not have put on a repeat performance of last year's vintage but it still has firm structure that reveals elegant tertiary notes of maturity, supported by a fresh acid vein and captivating overall lusciousness that make it, as usual, a minor classic. And speaking of classics, we would remind you that the Brut Francesco I and the Terre di Franciacorta Bianco dei Frati Priori and Maria dei Medici, the latter from '99, are as good as they ever have been. The rest of the broad Uberti range is all of very fine quality.

	Wine	Rating	Score
O	Franciacorta Brut Magnificentia	♛♛♛	6
O	Franciacorta Extra Brut Comarì del Salem '96	♛♛	6
O	TdF Bianco dei Frati Priori '99	♛♛	5
O	TdF Bianco Maria Medici '99	♛♛	5
O	Franciacorta Brut Francesco I	♛♛	5
●	TdF Rosso Augustus '99	♛	4
O	Franciacorta Extra Brut Francesco I	♛	5
⊙	Franciacorta Rosé Brut Francesco I	♛	5
O	TdF Bianco Augustus '00	♛	4
O	Franciacorta Extra Brut Comarì del Salem '88	♛♛♛	6
O	Franciacorta Extra Brut Comarì del Salem '95	♛♛♛	6
O	Franciacorta Brut Magnificentia	♛♛♛	5

GODIASCO (PV)

CABANON
LOC. CABANON, 1
27052 GODIASCO (PV)
TEL. 0383940912

In Piedmont and the Oltrepò, an area that was once under Piedmontese administration, the "infernot" is the corner of the cellar where the most valuable bottles are kept in special niches. And the Rosso Infernot '98 has to be one of the most prized wines of the Mercandelli family, owners of Cabanon. Made from late-harvest grapes left to dry for a short while, the very concentrated must is fermented in new barriques, after which the wine matures slowly in Slavonian oak casks. It has great body and, though it still is undergoing development, we can already see just how far it is able to go. All that is needed is the patience not to drink it right away. The Syra's '98 Vigna dei Gerbidi is from syrah grapes grown on poor, rocky terrain. One third fermented in barriques and the rest in oak barrels, it is a very deep ruby red with the typical aromas of toasted cocoa beans and jam, and a rich, warm flavour. The Botte n. 18 Cuoredivino '98, from super-ripe grapes fermented in small Slavonian oak casks, is mature and harmonious, with a distinct bouquet of spices and dried fruit. The Cabanon Noir '99, Pinot Nero from Burgundian clones, was made only in stainless steel to bring out the varietal notes of the grape. Though it has touches of blackcurrant and the gamey background characteristic of the variety, the tannins are still rather edgy and will have to mellow out. The Bonarda '97, aged in oak casks of different sizes and different toastings, is almost too concentrated. Again, it needs more time in the bottle.

	Wine	Rating	Score
●	Syra's '98	♛♛	4
●	OP Rosso Botte n. 18 '98	♛♛	4
●	OP Rosso Infernot Ris. '99	♛♛	5
●	OP Bonarda '97	♛	4
●	Cabanon Noir '99	♛	4
●	OP Bonarda Ris. '91	♛♛	4
●	OP Rosso Vino Cuore '91	♛♛	4
●	OP Barbera Piccolo Principe '97	♛♛	5
●	OP Passito Oro '97	♛♛	5
O	Opera Prima Cabanon Blanc '97	♛♛	3
O	Opera Prima Cabanon Blanc '98	♛♛	3
●	OP Bonarda Vivace '99	♛♛	3
O	OP Pinot Grigio '99	♛♛	3
O	OP Riesling Renano '99	♛♛	3
●	OP Barbera Prunello '97	♛	4

GRUMELLO DEL MONTE (BG)

CARLOZADRA
VIA CANDOSSE, 13
24064 GRUMELLO DEL MONTE (BG)
TEL. 035832066 - 035830244

A native of Trentino transplanted into the province of Bergamo, Carlo Zadra continues to create his classic spumantes and still wines from bases carefully selected in the province of Trento. He is quite right to do so. Here is his list. Of the four traditional spumantes that make up the range, two were not yet ready, the Nondosato Millesimato '98, still resting on its "pupitres" awaiting disgorgement, and the Millesimato Tradizionale, which is going through a long ageing process on its own fermentation yeasts and will not come out of the cellar before 2002. However, the other two are ready. The Liberty Extra Dry '98 vintage, disgorged on 12 September 2000, is a particularly fresh, agreeable Blanc de Blancs, with the almond and honeysuckle flower notes and fruity sensations of golden delicious apple sensations from Chardonnay. Less dry than a Brut, it can easily be drunk as either an aperitif or with delicate, fish-based dishes. It is another story for the Brut Millesimato '96, disgorged in September 2000, from a cuvée of Pinot Nero, Pinot Bianco and Chardonnay from the vineyards around San Michele all'Adige, and the glacial hills between Trento and Bolzano. It is mature but solid, full and harmonious. Dry yet not excessively so, with a developed and complex aroma, it earned Two well-deserved Glasses. The Don Ludovico '97 is also noteworthy. The vintage is not displayed on the label because it is a table wine. Aged for a year in small oak casks, it releases aromas of blackcurrants and pepper, ending on a pleasant bitter note. The Donna Nunzia '00, Moscato Giallo Secco is in a positive phase of development and destined to improve in the bottle.

○	Carlozadra Cl. Brut '96	▼▼	5
●	Don Ludovico Pinot Nero '97	▼▼	4
○	Carlozadra Extra Dry Liberty '98	▼▼	4
○	Donna Nunzia Moscato Giallo '00	▼	4
○	Carlozadra Cl. Brut '92	▼▼	4
○	Carlozadra Cl. Brut Nondosato '92	▼▼	5
○	Carlozadra Cl. Brut '93	▼▼	5
○	Carlozadra Cl. Brut Nondosato '93	▼▼	4
●	Don Ludovico Pinot Nero '93	▼▼	4
○	Carlozadra Cl. Brut Nondosato '94	▼▼	5
○	Carlozadra Cl. Brut '95	▼▼	4
○	Donna Nunzia Moscato Giallo '99	▼▼	3

MESE (SO)

MAMETE PREVOSTINI
VIA LUCCHINETTI, 65
23020 MESE (SO)
TEL. 034341003
E-MAIL: info@mameteprevostini.com

No one, especially those in the business, will be surprised at the triumphant entrance into the Guide of this small estate. In fact, we have been keeping its wines under observation for some time now and every time we have tasted them, in various contexts, our judgement has always been more than positive. The manager is young Mamete Prevostini who, in 1987, having just graduated in oenology, had the farsighted idea of working and professionally training at the school of Casimiro Maule, the oenologist who contributed so significantly to raising the prestige of wines from Valtellina. It was a long apprenticeship of harvests, clonal selection, small batch vinifications, the use of large and small oak casks, satisfaction and disappointments, until the decisive step that led the Prevostini family to acquire almost three hectares of vineyards. Located in a magnificent spot in the heart of the Sassella zone, they produce a total of around 30,000 bottles of wine, all made from nebbiolo, with harvests that run from 3,000 to 4,500 kilograms per hectare. This range had to have a Sassella, and it's the Sommarovina '98, a wine with personality to burn, clean aromas that recall raspberries, and a full flavour with a lovely, continually expanding fruit base. The Corte di Cama '97 was very good, made with the addition of partially dried grapes. Elegant on the nose with notes of black berry fruit and a light spiciness, it reveals a dense Barolo-style palate with good pulp and nice progression. The Sforzato Albareda '99 is spicy in its aromas, with shades of incense, chocolate and jam. It is full on the palate, with good concentration and length, soft tannins and an elegant finish.

●	Valtellina Sup. Corte di Cama '97	▼▼	5
●	Valtellina Sup. Sassella Sommarovina '98	▼▼	4
●	Valtellina Sforzato Albareda '99	▼▼	6

MONIGA DEL GARDA (BS)

COSTARIPA
VIA CIALDINI, 12
25080 MONIGA DEL GARDA (BS)
TEL. 0365502010

At the last edition of Vinitaly, Motoi Arima San, commercial director for one of the most important wine importers in Japan, tasted the Molmenti '99, the only Chiaretto from the classic Garda zone aged in oak, as it used to be at the end of the 19th century. From groppello, marzemino, sangiovese and barbera grapes, it is vinified "a lacrima" ("tear" vinification because the fruit is piled up and left to "weep" juice under its own weight to create the must), and fermented in 400-litre barrels with production limited to 4,000 bottles. "Can I have 1,200 bottles?" asked Arima San. "I have never tasted a wine that worked so well with Japanese cooking," explained the importer, astonishing Mattia Vezzola, Costaripa's owner. This very particular Chiaretto is worth remembering. With its hints of flowers, vanilla and almond, it goes well beyond the Two Glass mark. Of the other most successful wines from Costaripa, along with the Groppello Maim '99, fermented in barriques, we find the new Garda Classico Rosso, a blend of sangiovese, barbera, marzemino and groppello, aged in oak, made for the Christian Barnard Foundation. Proceeds from its sale go to the foundation created by the famous heart surgeon. With a dark ruby colour, it has the fragrant aroma of ripe wild berries and a warm, round taste. Several other wines are also good, though not as wonderful as the ones mentioned above. The reds include the Campo delle Starne and Pradamonte, from Cabernet Sauvignon, both from '99, and the Marzemino Le Manzane and Groppello Castellina '00. Of the whites, the Brut Classico '98, from chardonnay and pinot bianco, with 20 per cent pinot nero, and the Lugana '00 are both good and delicately fruity.

⊙ Garda Cl. Chiaretto Molmenti '99	▼▼	5
● Garda Cl. Groppello Maim '99	▼▼	5
● Garda Cl. Rosso Chr. Barnard '99	▼▼	5
● Benaco Bresciano Marzemino Le Mazane '00	▼	4
● Garda Cl. Groppello Vigneto Le Castelline '00	▼	4
○ Lugana '00	▼	4
○ Brut Cl. Costaripa '98	▼	4
● Garda Cabernet Sauv. Pradamonte '99	▼	4
● Garda Cl. Rosso Campo delle Starne '99	▼	4
● Garda Cl. Groppello Maim '97	▽▽	5
⊙ Garda Cl. Chiaretto Molmenti '98	▽▽	5

MONTALTO PAVESE (PV)

CA' DEL GÈ
VIA CA' DEL GÉ, 3
27040 MONTALTO PAVESE (PV)
TEL. 0383870179

From the 24 hectares of vineyards on their own property, and another 15 rented, the Padroggi family makes more than 150,000 bottles of whites, rosés and reds, still wines, semi-sparkling wines and spumantes, sweet and dry. If we were to trace a quality graph for these wines, we would come out with something similar to the outline of the Dolomites, with very high peaks alternating with deep valleys. What we have reported in years past is confirmed again in this edition of the Guide, with one difference. We found mainly reds at the peaks while the whites are almost invariably a bit lower. The Dolcetto Tormento '97 is at the summit and has never been so good. Made from super-ripe grapes, it is concentrated and powerful yet harmonious. The Barbera Vigna Varmasì '99 has a prominent nose of morello cherries and a robust palate that is a bit rough but still developing. The Bonarda Vivace '00 has an intense bouquet of bramble and Parma violets, and a pleasant finish of yellow peach. The Pinot Nero from '97 is garnet coloured with flecks of brick red. It throws an intense black pepper and tar nose, then a very mature palate. It's fairly solid but it would be better to drink it right away. The Barbera '00 is decent, dry and firm. The sweet, clean Moscato Vivace '00 is technically the best of the whites. The Pinot Nero Brut Classico '95 is right behind it, with crisp touches of bread crusts and toasted almond. The still Riesling Italico '00 is fresh and spirited while the oak has created some problems with the Renano Vigna Marinoni '99. The Müller Thurgau from the 2000 vintage is subtly aromatic but a bit tired.

● OP Bonarda Vivace '00	▼▼	4
○ OP Moscato '00	▼▼	3
● Dolcetto Tormento '97	▼▼	4
● OP Barbera Viga Varmasì '99	▼▼	4
● OP Barbera '00	▼	3
○ OP Riesling Italico '00	▼	3
○ OP Pinot Nero Brut Cl. '95	▼	4
● OP Pinot Nero '97	▼	3
○ OP Muller Thurgau '00		3
● OP Barbera Vigna Varmasì '90	▽▽	4
● OP Barbera Vigna Varmasì '97	▽▽	4
○ OP Riesling Italico '98	▽▽	2
○ OP Riesling Italico '99	▽	3

MONTALTO PAVESE (PV)

Doria
Loc. Casa Tacconi, 3
27040 Montalto Pavese (PV)
Tel. 0383870143

"A.D." in this case does not stand for "Anno Domini" but for Adriano Doria, the owner of this estate in Montalto, who firmly believes in the potential of the Oltrepò and the revival of old indigenous grape varieties. This grand red is dedicated to his memory. Made with nebbiolo grapes – it is no coincidence that the Oltrepò is known as "Ancient Piedmont" –cultivated in an eight-year-old vineyard, from a selection of clones brought to the hills of the Oltrepò by the University of Milan, the fruit was carefully vinified and blended into a special version of Rosso Oltrepò. A.D. '97 underwent malolactic fermentation in barriques that were half new and half one year old, where it was then aged for 14 months. A deep garnet with orange highlights, it has a bouquet of bramble, raspberry and strawberry preserves, with sweet vanilla spice, and a long austere, warmly vigorous palate. The fine-grained tannins are developing well and this will help its harmony in the mouth. The other wines created by Giuseppina Doria and her young agronomist Daniele Manini, under the supervision of Beppe Bassi, are of the usual high quality, thanks in part to their hard work in the vineyards. Doria is, in fact, one of the estates in the Oltrepò most committed to vineyard management. The Roncorosso '98, from barbera, croatina and uva rara, is very good. It ages for the most part in barriques, as does the Pinot Nero Querciolo '99. The Roncobianco '00, a Riesling Renano part cold macerated and aged for a time in oak, is greenish gold with intense aromas of tropical fruit and aromatic herbs and a good, zesty flavour. The Pinot Nero in bianco Querciolo '99 is fermented without the skins and spends six months in oak. It has the soft fragrances of artemisia and vanilla.

Wine	Rating	Score
● Rosso A.D. '97	♛♛	5
○ OP Riesling Renano Roncobianco '00	♛♛	3
○ OP Pinot Nero in bianco Querciolo '99	♛♛	3
● OP Pinot Nero Querciolo '99	♛♛	4
● OP Rosso Roncorosso '98	♛♛	4
● OP Pinot Nero Querciolo '93	♛♛	5
● OP Rosso Roncorosso V. Siura '93	♛♛	4
● OP Pinot Nero Querciolo '95	♛♛	5
○ OP Pinot Nero in bianco Querciolo '97	♛♛	4
● OP Pinot Nero Querciolo '98	♛♛	4
○ OP Riesling Renano Roncobianco V. Tesi '98	♛♛	4

MONTEBELLO DELLA BATTAGLIA (PV)

Tenuta La Costaiola
Via Costaiola, 11
27054 Montebello della Battaglia (PV)
Tel. 038383169 - 038382069

At Costaiola di Montebello, the Rossetti brothers, young men with very clear ideas, have thrown themselves into a programme of rebuilding the cellars and lavishing even greater care on their vineyards, and the results are starting to be seen. The Rosso Riserva La Vigna Bricca '98 goes far beyond the '97, which was itself not bad at all. A blend of 60 per cent croatina and barbera, with 10 per cent pinot nero added, its name comes from a vineyard on the top of the hill of Mairano, at Casteggio, with an output of barely 5,000 kilograms per hectare. Aged for ten months in oak casks, it is presently ageing in the bottle where it will improve even further, though it is a great wine even now. Its dark ruby introduces aromas of red berry fruit and sweet spices. The palate is full and generous, with a rich, elegant background of jam and liquorice. The Barbera Due Draghi from the 2000 vintage is simpler but just as pleasant. Aged only in stainless steel, it is purple-red, with a nose of ripe fruit and a dry, zesty, forthright, palate that is soft but still very firm. The Pinot Nero Bellarmino '98, after a year in Allier oak barriques, promises well with notes of blackcurrant, autumn leaves, crushed ferns and vanilla. However, it needs further bottle ageing because the tannins must develop. Refermented in a pressure tank, the Bonarda Giada '00 was agreeably fruity and showed good body. The only flaw of the Riesling Renano Attimo '00 is that it calls itself a Riesling, a variety that is no longer considered trendy. However, those who pay more attention to the wine than the name will definitely find it enjoyable for its hints of tropical fruit and gunflint. The Riesling Bellarmino '98, aged 25 per cent in oak, has great structure and a remarkably intense aroma.

Wine	Rating	Score
● OP Barbera I due Draghi '00	♛♛	3
● OP Bonarda Vivace Giada '00	♛♛	3
● OP Pinot Nero Bellarmino '98	♛♛	4
● Rosso La Vigna Bricca Ris. '98	♛♛	4
○ OP Moscato Fiori di Campo '00	♛	3
○ OP Riesling Renano Attimo '00	♛	3
○ OP Riesling Renano Bellarmino '98	♛	4

MONTICELLI BRUSATI (BS)

CASTELVEDER
VIA BELVEDERE, 4
25040 MONTICELLI BRUSATI (BS)
TEL. 030652308
E-MAIL: castelveder@libero.it

Renato Alberti, owner of this estate, and his oenologist Teresio Schiavi have presented us this year with a most interesting vintage Franciacorta, the Brut '96. This cuvée has done well in blind tastings and is widely considered one of the best interpretations of a vintage that, it should be recalled, was not one that gave particularly exciting results. This Franciacorta from Castelveder has a nice straw-yellow colour shimmering with greenish highlights, a soft, creamy mousse, very fine perlage and good continuity. It opens up sweet on the nose, with rich, complex tones of ripe fruit, yeasts and vanilla against a delicate mineral background. It is dense and compact in the mouth, showing a good acid backbone but at the same time a winning elegance. It finishes harmonious and persistent. The Brut is also enjoyable and well-made. It has the soft, full aromas of yeasts and vanilla, a refined palate with gentle effervescence and a fresh vein of acidity that supports the good structure. The juicy fruit fades into pleasant notes of peach. The Extra Brut rounds off this excellent threesome and also deserves Two Glasses for its very fine perlage, the excellent cleanliness of its fruity tones and its remarkable fullness on the palate. It is even more admirable if we remember the almost token dosage of this cuvée, which has a dry yet soft taste thanks to its lovely concentration. We also found the Terre di Franciacorta Rosso Vigna Monte della Rose '98 to be a good wine, albeit perhaps just a bit rough on the palate, and the two basic Terre di Franciacorta were nice.

○	Franciacorta Brut '96	🍷🍷	5
○	Franciacorta Brut	🍷🍷	5
○	TdF Bianco '00	🍷	3
●	TdFRosso Vigna Monte della Rosa '98	🍷	4
●	TdF Rosso '99	🍷	3
○	Franciacorta Extra Brut	🍷	5
○	Franciacorta Brut '91	🍷🍷	4
○	Franciacorta Brut '92	🍷🍷	4
○	Franciacorta Brut '94	🍷🍷	5

MONTICELLI BRUSATI (BS)

LA MONTINA
VIA BAIANA, 17
25040 MONTICELLI BRUSATI (BS)
TEL. 030653278
E-MAIL: info@lamontina.it

The ambitious estate of the Vittorio brothers, Giancarlo and Alberto Bozza, returns after a year of absence from these pages, caused by problems of space rather than any lack of merit. A good three labels from La Montina have in fact been awarded Two Glasses this time. To our mind, the most interesting is the Franciacorta Brut '96 made with the consultancy of Cesare Ferrari. In this vintage, the Brut presents a bright straw-yellow colour, a creamy mousse and wonderfully fine perlage. It has sweet, intense aromas that hinge on white peach, yeast and vanilla, and shows perfect consistency on the palate, where the solid structure melds into fresh, soft fruity tones and a long finish. The Satèn has a special charm that comes from the exuberant nose of sweet floral tones, with rose and violet to the fore. It is round, soft and harmonious on the full, lingering palate. Another label we recommend is the well-designed Rosé. The Demi Sec dosage suggests it is best drunk at the end of the meal, to accompany the dessert. It has a pale rose colour, a very fine, well-sustained perlage, and opens up on the nose with a rich swathe of ripe red berries, particularly wild strawberries. It is sweet and fresh in the mouth, rich in fruit, harmonious and persistent. The Extra Brut is only a point or two below this. It shows traces of excessive rigidity in a structure that hints at slightly forward tones of dried fruit and finishes a shade too bitter. Finally, the Terre di Franciacortas are all good, from the Rosso dei Dossi 98 to the Bianco Palanca '00 and Bianco '00.

○	Franciacorta Brut '96	🍷🍷	5
⊙	Franciacorta Rosé Demi Sec	🍷🍷	5
○	Franciacorta Satèn	🍷🍷	5
○	TdF Bianco '00	🍷	3*
○	TdF Bianco Vign. Palanca '00	🍷	3*
●	TdF Rosso dei Dossi '98	🍷	4
○	Franciacorta Extra Brut	🍷	4
○	Franciacorta Brut '91	🍷🍷	4
○	Franciacorta Brut '94	🍷🍷	5
○	Franciacorta Brut '95	🍷🍷	5

MONTICELLI BRUSATI (BS)

Lo Sparviere
Via Costa, 2
25040 Monticelli Brusati (BS)
Tel. 030652382
E-mail: losparviere@libero.it

In the space of just a few years, Ugo Gussalli Beretta and his wife Monique Poncelet have taken their estate to a position in the front ranks of Franciacorta winemaking. Lo Sparviere boasts 150 hectares of its own land, 23 planted to vine, surrounding the lovely villa of Monticelli Brusati in the town of Provaglio d'Iseo. With the collaboration of oenologist Francesco Polastri, Lo Sparviere at present boasts an annual production of over 100,000 bottles and an enviable standard of quality. Proof of this is the Franciacorta Brut that shows off a bright straw-yellow colour, a perlage of great finesse, and a sweet, fresh nose, fragrant with notes of white peach, yeasts and vanilla. Thick and round on the palate, with good structure, it has delicate, gentle effervescence, fading out long and elegant on notes of old wood and beeswax. The Terre di Franciacorta Bianco Lo Sparviere '98 is a Chardonnay with a silky texture, full body and great balance. It easily won Two Glasses thanks to its remarkable nose-palate consistency, playing off ripe fruit against softer notes of sweet pastries and butter. Slightly less rich than the Brut, but just as elegant, the Extra Brut boasts the fresh tones of apples on the nose and palate but does not have the same succulent fullness. The Terre di Franciacorta Rosso Il Sergnana '98 has good fruit and balance but shows no depth and is slightly masked by boisé notes that have got the better of its less than imposing structure. The Terre di Franciacorta Rosso Vino del Cacciatore '98 is inviting to drink, with a lean, smooth body. Finally the Terre di Franciacorta Bianco '00 and Rosso '99 are both well-designed, fruity and well-executed.

O	TdF Bianco Lo Sparviere Ris. '98	🍷🍷	5
O	Franciacorta Brut	🍷🍷	5
O	TdF Bianco '00	🍷	4
●	TdF Rosso Il Sergnana '98	🍷	5
●	TdF Rosso Vino del Cacciatore '98	🍷	5
●	TdF Rosso '99	🍷	4
O	Franciacorta Extra Brut	🍷	5
O	TdF Bianco Ris. '95	🍷🍷	3
●	TdF Rosso Il Sergnana '96	🍷🍷	5
●	TdF Rosso '96	🍷	4
●	TdF Rosso Vino del Cacciatore '97	🍷	4

MONTICELLI BRUSATI (BS)

Villa
Via Villa, 12
25040 Monticelli Brusati (BS)
Tel. 030652329 - 030652100
E-mail: infor@villa-franciacorta.it

Just looking through the list of this celebrated estate in Monticelli Brusati can cause dismay. There are more than a dozen labels of Franciacortas and still wines. But Villa is one of the few cases where the range of production has no detrimental effect on our notes, if anything rendering them more favourable. The fact is that every Franciacorta and still wine from Alessandro Bianchi's estate answers to its own precise logic, whether in bringing out the best in a cru or stylistic research into a particular wine type. Bianchi has worked very hard to obtain these excellent results. He has invested impressive resources and put together a very talented team, beginning with oenologist Corrado Cugnasco. But an important role is also played by agronomist Ermes Vianelli, who tends to the 30 hectares of vineyards at the Villa estate, and Giacomo Mela, who co-ordinates the tasting panels. Over the past few years, all this has given us the opportunity to taste some excellent Franciacorta cuvées and our expectations this year have once again not been disappointed. Two wines from Villa even came very close to winning Three Glasses: the excellent Satèn '97, with complex aromas that recall honey and aromatic herbs, and delicately elegant palate with close-knit texture; and the Brut Selezione '95 with its sweet, very fresh, complex bouquet that combines delicate aromatic nuances of gooseberry and tropical fruit, and reveals great structure in the elegant, harmonious palate, which is rich in fruit and fresh citrus notes. Space does not allow us to treat every wine individually but we would like to underline that the average level of production is high enough to put Villa up near the top of the Franciacorta hit parade.

O	Franciacorta Brut Sel. '95	🍷🍷	6
O	Franciacorta Satèn '97	🍷🍷	6
O	Franciacorta Extra Brut '97	🍷🍷	5
O	Franciacorta Brut '97	🍷🍷	5
●	TdF Rosso Gradoni '98	🍷🍷	4*
O	TdF Bianco Marengo '99	🍷🍷	4*
O	TdF Bianco '00	🍷	3*
O	TdF Bianco Pian della Villa '00	🍷	4
●	TdF Rosso '00	🍷	3*
O	Franciacorta Cuvette Sec '97	🍷	5
⊙	Franciacorta Rosé Démi Sec '97	🍷	5
O	Franciacorta Brut Sel. '94	🍷🍷	6
O	Franciacorta Brut '96	🍷🍷	4

MONTÙ BECCARIA (PV)

IL MONTÙ
VIA MARCONI, 10
27040 MONTÙ BECCARIA (PV)
TEL. 0385262252

This new winery, equipped with all the necessary technology, was founded on the same site where the first co-operative winery was built in the Oltrepò Pavese in 1902. The grapes come from 80 hectares of vineyards in Valle Versa. Oenologist Riccardo Ottina has decades of experience with vines and wines from the Oltrepò. With this kind of foundation, they should never miss a beat. But although Cantina Storica Il Montù presented several very valid products, others did not leave us with a very favourable impression: the Bonarda Vivace '00 could be cleaner; the Moscato '00 more fragrant; the Pinot Nero '98 Vigna Rosera more full-bodied. With another winery, we might be contented but it is only right to expect more from Il Montù. On the other hand, you only have to sip the "good" wines to realize the cellar's potential. The Pinot Nero Brut Classico '98 is worthy of a spumante-maker of Ottina's calibre. It has an excellent appearance and an elegant, attractively well-defined aroma. The palate is dry, harmonious and fresh, with no bitterness. The oak-aged Bonarda Ferma '98 Vigna del Vespero is very sound and offers aromas of bramble and spices. The Chardonnay '98 Vigna del Mattino has a bright golden colour, alluring aromas of vanilla, golden delicious apples and musk, and a full, forthright palate. The Buttafuoco '98 Vigna Letizia is good but has tannins that are still a bit edgy. The red Sangue di Giuda is clean, fruity, sweet and sparkling. In the last Guide, the Malvasia '99 Carpe Diem merited Two Glasses but at this year's retasting, it had developed a strange, unpleasant odour. We felt it was our duty to mention the fact.

●	OP Bonarda Vigna del Vespero '98	♟♟	4
○	OP Chardonnay Vigna del Mattino '98	♟	4
○	OP Pinot Nero Brut Cl. '98	♟♟	4
●	OP Sangue di Giuda '00	♟	3
●	OP Buttafuoco Vigna Letizia '98	♟	4
○	OP Pinot Nero Brut		3
○	OP Chardonnay '97	♟♟	4
○	OP Malvasia Passito '99	♟♟	4
●	OP Bonarda Vigna del Vespero '97	♟	4
○	OP Pinot Nero Brut Cl.	♟	4

MONTÙ BECCARIA (PV)

VERCESI DEL CASTELLAZZO
VIA AURELIANO, 36
27040 MONTÙ BECCARIA (PV)
TEL. 038560067 - 0385262098
E-MAIL: vercesicastellazzo@libero.it

The Vercesi of Castellazzo di Montù, the Beccaria castle converted into a monastery by Barnabite monks in the 16th century, did not have their family jewels ready to go on display yet. In other words, the Pinot Nero Luogo dei Monti, Oltrepò Pavese Rosso Orto di S. Giacomo and Bonarda Fatila from the 2000 vintage are all ageing either in oak or the bottle. So, relatively speaking, there were few gems on the table. We'll begin with a new entry, the Bonarda '00 Luogo della Milla, the only sparkling wine in a normally all-still series. Even though the "vivace", or sparkling, version of Bonarda is still the most popular in the Oltrepò, the Vercesi have always believed in the still version, aged in oak. Take the case of Fatila. Not changing their beliefs in the least, they now present a Bonarda that is lively, fragrant, pleasantly fruity, to be drunk young and fresh from the cellar, with salami, a savoury first course or meat, either boiled or in gravy. A unanimous Two Glasses. Another red that is ready to drink is the Vespolino '00, from the variety with almost the same name, vespolina or ughetta. Because of the vintage, this has more body and alcohol than the '99 but still maintains its characteristic fragrance of green pepper and wild fruits. Again from 2000, the Oltrepò Pavese Rosso Pezzalunga is very pleasant, with good structure, and endowed with a marked fragrance of morello cherries. As for the older wines, the Gugiarolo '99, from pinot nero fermented without the skins, has a generous aroma of ripe fruit and a properly balanced palate. The dry, still Barbera Clà '98, aged for a period in oak, is potentially interesting but needs further bottle ageing.

●	OP Bonarda Luogo della Milla '00	♟♟	3*
●	OP Rosso Pezzalunga '00	♟♟	3*
●	Provincia di Pavia Rosso Vespolino '00	♟♟	3*
●	OP Barbera Clà '98	♟	4
○	OP Pinot Nero in bianco Gugiarolo '99	♟	3
●	OP Bonarda Fatila '90	♟♟	4
●	OP Bonarda Fatila '91	♟♟	4
●	OP Pinot Nero Luogo dei Monti '95	♟♟	4
●	OP Pinot Nero Luogo dei Monti '96	♟♟	4
●	OP Pinot Nero Luogo dei Monti '97	♟♟	4
●	OP Rosso Orto di S. Giacomo '97	♟♟	4
●	OP Bonarda Fatila '97	♟♟	4
●	Vespolino '99	♟♟	3

MORNICO LOSANA (PV)

Ca' di Frara
Loc. Casa Ferrari, 1
27040 Mornico Losana (PV)
tel. 0383892299
e-mail: cadifrara@libero.it

Absolutely the best wine by Luca Bellani, the young owner of Ca' di Frara, continues to be the Pinot Grigio from late-harvest grapes. The 2000 vintage has a full bouquet of honey, rose and tropical fruit, and a mature palate that is almost too powerful because of the bountiful vintage. Continuing with the whites, the Malvasia Il Raro '00 has a marked aroma of sage and musk and a full palate with a lingering aromatic background. The series of whites closes with the Riesling Renano Apogeo '00 that has developed more rapidly with respect to the edgy '99. It has distinct mineral notes of gunflint that underline sensations of apple and lime blossom, and a nice tanginess. The red section opens with the Pinot Nero Il Raro '99, characterized by a deep garnet colour, a composite aroma of cassis jam and spices, and a rich, soft palate well-supported by nicely gauged acidity. The Oltrepò Pavese Rosso Riserva Il Frater '98 has a good dose of oak - just like the rest of the '97 vintage - but from underneath the hint of spices there emerges a still-developing, complex bouquet of small black berry fruit preserves and dried flowers. The flavour is elegant in its vigorous fullness. The Rosso Io '98 has great prospects but is still a little astringent and does not express itself very well, especially on the nose. It is one of those wines that require patience to wait for the development process to finish. Finally, the still Bonarda '99 La Casetta, despite its consistent texture, didn't quite make it to Two Glasses because of the slight hint of reduction that jeopardizes the bouquet.

○ OP Malvasia Il Raro '00	♟♟	4
○ OP Pinot Grigio V. T. '00	♟♟	4
○ OP Riesling Renano Apogeo '00	♟♟	3*
● OP Rosso Il Frater '98	♟♟	5
● OP Pinot Nero Il Raro '99	♟♟	4
● OP Rosso Io '98	♟	4
● OP Bonarda La Casetta '99	♟	4
○ OP Chardonnay '97	♟♟	3
● OP Bonarda La Casetta '98	♟♟	4
○ OP Malvasia Il Raro '98	♟♟	4
○ OP Pinot Grigio V. T. '98	♟♟	4
● OP Pinot Nero Il Raro '98	♟♟	4
○ OP Riesling Renano Apogeo '98	♟♟	3
○ OP Pinot Grigio V. T. '99	♟♟	4

OME (BS)

Majolini
Loc. Valle
Via Manzoni
25050 Ome (BS)
tel. 0306527378
e-mail: majolini@majolini.it

This year, Majolini again shows it is operating at a very respectable level of proficiency. Two cuvées from this model estate in Ome were serious candidates for our highest award, a result that few wineries can boast in Franciacorta, or even Italy. The other labels submitted for tasting by Majolini earned flattering scores. All this is the outcome of several years of serious investment in rebuilding, expanding the vineyards and constructing a large cellar for fermentation and ageing. Two skilled professionals, Jean Pierre Valade and Cesare Ferrari, manage vinification at this exemplary Franciacorta winery. This explains the performance in the tastings of a vintage like the Franciacorta Electo '95, which introduces itself with a creamy, fine mousse and an incredibly fine, dense, persistent perlage. The Electo opens up broad and complex on the nose with elegant aromas of ripe apricot, tropical fruit, vanilla and sweet notes of yeast. The palate echoes the nose admirably and expands assertively with good body, reproposing the soft fruit notes on a solid structure, then fading away unhurriedly on classic vanilla tones. And what can we say about the Satèn Ante Omnia '97? Those who love the soft chewiness and succulence of fruit in this type of wine will be won over by its aromas of orange blossom honey and its perfectly balanced palate, nuanced with fresh fruity notes, that closes out long on returning touches of honey and vanilla. One of the best Bruts of the vintage stands proudly alongside these Franciacortas and the excellently made still wines.

○ Franciacorta Electo Brut '95	♟♟	6
○ Franciacorta Ante Omnia Satèn '97	♟♟	6
○ Franciacorta Brut	♟♟	5
○ TdF Bianco Ronchello '00	♟	4
● TdF Rosso Dordaro '90	♟♟	4
● TdF Rosso Ruc di Gnoc '91	♟♟	4
○ Franciacorta Brut '92	♟♟	5
○ Franciacorta Brut '94	♟♟	5
○ Franciacorta Satèn '96	♟♟	5
● TdF Rosso Dordaro '98	♟♟	5

PASSIRANO (BS)

IL MOSNEL
LOC. CAMIGNONE
VIA BARBOGLIO, 14
25040 PASSIRANO (BS)
TEL. 030653117

What can we say to Giulio and Lucia Barzanò, who for some years now have managed this winery with their mother Emanuela Barboglio? Nothing except, "Well done and carry on as you are!" Every year our tastings show better results. Though the range of labels from the estate is extensive, it very well-made and average scores are high at Guide tastings. This puts Il Mosnel among the best wineries in Franciacorta. A policy of long ageing in stacks did not permit us to taste this year's successor to the excellent Franciacorta '93 we enjoyed last time. But while waiting for it, we were able to appreciate three quality cuvées. These are: the Satèn '97, elegant, full, harmonious in its fruity and vanillaed tones, with solid structure and remarkable freshness; the Franciacorta Brut, with its intriguingly complex bouquet of yeast, peach and aromatic herbs, caressing on the palate, fresh, with a solid, well-sculpted body and good persistence; and finally, the Extra Brut, which shows floral and vanillaed aromas, is dry but not edgy on the palate, showing finesse, freshness and concentration and then concluding on delicate toasty notes and hints of walnutskin. Three wines from the generous selection of still wines hit the Two Glass target, all Terre di Franciacorta crus. These are the Sulìf '99 and Campolarga '00. The latter seemed particularly excellent with its dynamic freshness and the distinct pulpiness of the fruit. In addition, we tasted the Terre di Franciacorta Rosso Fontecolo '98, which has good structure and soft tannins. We feel the Pinot Nero '98, with its lean, varietal lines, lacks a bit of concentration.

○ Franciacorta Satèn '97	ΨΨ	5
○ TdF Bianco Campolarga '00	ΨΨ	4*
● TdF Rosso Fontecolo '98	ΨΨ	4*
○ TdF Bianco Sulìf '99	ΨΨ	4*
○ Franciacorta Brut	ΨΨ	4*
○ Franciacorta Extra Brut	ΨΨ	5
○ TdF Bianco '00	Ψ	3
● Pinot Nero Sebino '98	Ψ	6
○ Franciacorta Brut '90	ΨΨ	5
○ Franciacorta Brut '91	ΨΨ	5
○ Franciacorta Brut '93	ΨΨ	5
○ Franciacorta Satèn '96	ΨΨ	5

POLPENAZZE DEL GARDA (BS)

CASCINA LA PERTICA
FRAZ. PICEDO
VIA PICEDO, 24
25080 POLPENAZZE DEL GARDA (BS)
TEL. 0365651471

Ruggero Brunori is a happy man. The Three Glasses for the Le Zalte Rosso '99, from cabernet sauvignon and merlot, are more important for him than a five per cent increase in turnover at his light engineering factory, Valsabbia. Obviously, we are joking but the truth is that Brunori has a real passion for wine and for him to win an award like this is a great satisfaction. However, he must share the credit with cellar manager Andrea Salvetti and Franco Bernabei, an internationally famous oenologist who collaborated in creating the Le Zalte '99, a truly impressive wine both for elegance and concentration. A red of this stature has never been made in the Valtenesi zone, which runs along the hillslopes that dominate the Lombard section of Lake Garda. With his typical Brescian stubbornness, Ruggero Brunori has finally shown everyone the potential of this zone. As well as Le Zalte, Le Sincette Brut, a "blanc de blancs" from chardonnay also performed well. The Garda Chiaretto Le Sincette '00 was not bad and the Garda Classico Le Sincette Rosso '99 was intriguing, obtained from an odd, complex blend of groppello, marzemino, sangiovese and barbera. It all adds up to a range that is limited but made of well-constructed wines, though not all are as stupendous as Le Zalte '99.

● Le Zalte Rosso '99	ΨΨΨ	5
○ Le Sincette Brut	ΨΨ	5
○ Garda Cl. Chiaretto Le Sincette '00	Ψ	4
● Garda Cl. Rosso Le Sincette '99	Ψ	4
● Le Zalte Rosso '90	ΨΨ	5
● Le Zalte Rosso '94	ΨΨ	5
● Le Zalte Rosso '97	ΨΨ	5
● Le Zalte Rosso '98	ΨΨ	5
● Le Zalte Rosso '95	Ψ	5
● Garda Cl. Rosso Le Sincette '98	Ψ	3

PROVAGLIO D'ISEO (BS)

BERSI SERLINI
VIA CERRETO, 7
25050 PROVAGLIO D'ISEO (BS)
TEL. 0309823338

Bersi Serlini has submitted several new entries this year that confirm the determination of this family-run winery to go for important goals. Oenologist Corrado Cugnasco works in tandem with Pierluigi Villa, the agronomist who manages the replanting and modernization of the 28 hectares under vine and, at the same time, the work of rebuilding the cellar and the old building where the estate has its headquarters. A new product was called for during this renovation phase. And here it is, in the Franciacorta Cuvée n. 4, made with selected grapes from four different estate crus. It has a lustrous, greenish straw-yellow colour and the intense, fresh aromas of apples are enlivened by pleasant citrus. In the mouth, it is fresh, complete and balanced, with moderate effervescence, and it finishes on soft, fruity tones. Then we tasted the Satèn, which offers elegant vanilla tones on both nose and palate, where they integrate nicely with the juicy fruit and brisk acidity that never threatens roundness of the flavour. Continuing with the sparkling theme, the Nuvola Demi Sec convincingly marries the freshness of the fruit with the sweetness of its sugars, and has a harmonious, full personality with a delicate aromatic vein of candied citrus. We felt the Franciacorta Extra Brut was slightly less intense and a bit veiled to the nose while the Franciacorta Brut showed good quality, rich in the sensations of yeast and toasty bread, with a fine perlage and decent fullness. Finally, the two Terre di Franciacortas were correct and pleasant.

O	Franciacorta Brut Cuvée n. 4	♉♉	5
O	Franciacorta Satèn	♉♉	5
O	Nuvola Démi Sec	♉♉	5
O	TdF Bianco '00	♉	3
●	TdF Rosso '99	♉	4
O	Franciacorta Brut	♉	5
O	Franciacorta Extra Brut	♉	5
O	Franciacorta Brut Cuvée Millennio '92	♉♉	6
O	Franciacorta Brut Cuvée Millennio '93	♉♉	6

ROCCA DE' GIORGI (PV)

ANTEO
LOC. CHIESA
27043 ROCCA DE' GIORGI (PV)
TEL. 038548583 - 038599073
E-MAIL: anteovini@libero.it

Thanks to the commitment of the Cribellati family, and the experience of oenologist Beppe Bassi, Anteo remains at the top of the Oltrepò spumante heap. The Nature '98, pinot nero with 20 per cent chardonnay and more than 30 months on its own yeasts with no final dosage, is dry without being bitter. It has a subtle, sustained perlage and an elegant aroma of hawthorn, artemisia and toasted bread. The non-vintage Brut Classico, from 70 per cent pinot nero and 30 per cent chardonnay, is on a par. It has a creamy mousse, very fine perlage and a lovely aroma of roasted hazelnuts, light vanilla, golden delicious apple and orange peel. The palate is fresh-tasting and agreeable, and lingers in the mouth. The Pinot Nero Brut Martinotti has a lovely appearance, a fragrant aroma of black berry fruit and a softly fruity flavour. Again from monovarietal pinot nero but fermented on the skins and aged in barriques, the Ca' dell'Oca '98 has a rich texture and appealing varietal notes of blackcurrant and pepper brought out by the oak, which are nicely gauged. The Coste del Roccolo '00 is original and pleasant, a marriage of bonarda from Rovescala and pinot nero from Rocca de' Giorgi. On the nose, it has notes of ripe bramble and blackcurrant and the palate is soft and easy drinking. The Moscato La Volpe and Uva '00 come from Volpara, the zone in Valle Versa most suited to this aromatic grape variety. It is sweet, fresh and redolent of apricot and peach fruit, with hints of orange blossom. The Bonarda Vivace '00 Staffolo is good while the Quattro Marzo '00, from chardonnay, pinot bianco and riesling renano, is a bit astringent but will improve with time.

●	Coste del Roccolo '00	♉♉	3*
O	OP Pinot Nero Cl. Anteo Nature '98	♉♉	4
O	OP Pinot Nero in bianco Ca' dell'Oca '98	♉♉	4
O	OP Brut Metodo Martinotti	♉♉	2*
O	OP Pinot Nero Brut Cl.	♉♉	4
●	OP Bonarda Staffolo '00	♉	3
O	OP Moscato La Volpe e L'Uva '00	♉	3
O	Quattro Marzo Bianco '00	♉	3
O	OP Pinot Nero in bianco Ca' dell'Oca '95	♉♉	4
●	Rosso Giublot '97	♉♉	4
O	Quattro Marzo Bianco '98	♉♉	3
●	OP Bonarda Staffolo '98	♉	3

ROVESCALA (PV)

AGNES
Via Campo del Monte, 1
27040 Rovescala (PV)
tel. 038575206 - 03385806773
E-MAIL: info@fratelliagnes.it

In the 2001 Guide, we said that some of the most representative wines by Bonarda specialists Cristiano and Sergio Agnes were not ready and that we would taste them again for this edition. With time, the yeasts have done their job and the Bonarda Vignazzo and Cresta del Ghiffi are finally ready for uncorking. As tradition dictates, they are slightly sparkling. The first, from a very steep vineyard with a southeasterly exposure where the grapes mature very early, has spent six months in oak barrels. The Cresta del Ghiffi, from late-harvest grapes grown in vineyard planted in the mid 1950s, never sees oak. Both are dark, dynamic and clearly varietal. The Cresta del Ghiffi has hints of raisins and bramble jam while the Vignazzo finishes on a bittersweet note of peach kernels. The Bonarda Possessione del Console '00, from a clone called "pignolo", is intensely fruity, generous and very solid. The Campo del Monte '00 needs further bottle ageing but promises great things. In contrast, the Bonarda Millennium '98 has maintained all the promises of a great vintage. From a selection of super-ripe bunches, it is a concentrate of croatina with an impenetrable purple, almost black, hue. It has a big, complex bouquet of wild berries, prunes and spices. The palate is lively, warm and zesty, with a clear backdrop of oak and fruit preserves. From extremely old vines, the Loghetto '99, a sweetish Bonarda, is delicious and ideal for drinking with fruit tarts and chestnuts.

ROVESCALA (PV)

MARTILDE
Fraz. Croce, 4/A1
27040 Rovescala (PV)
tel. 0385756280
E-MAIL: martilde@martilde.it

Rovescala, in the first row of hills in the Oltrepò, is the cradle of the croatina variety, which is called "bonarda" locally. The variety gives good results both as a "mossa", or sparkling wine, and as a still product. The Bonarda '97 Zaffo di Martilde is a monovarietal croatina from a particularly fortunate vintage. Aged in oak, it has a ruby colour with garnet flashes, a well pronounced aroma with dominant notes of bramble jam underlined by hints of clove and cinnamon spice and a robust, dry, slightly tannic palate, with a pleasantly persistent finish of peach kernels. It has good cellar potential and will improve as it ages. The other Bonarda '97, Ghiro Rosso d'Inverno, spent some time in barriques and confirms the assessment we made in the last edition of the Guide. Now it has taken on ethereal notes on the nose, and is more mature in the mouth and relatively soft. The Barbera '99 is forthright and heady with a reddish purple colour and good flavour. The Malvasia Piume '00 is excellent. A lustrous straw yellow, it has intense tones of sage, musk and fruit and a clean, dry flavour with a long finish. The dry, still Riesling Italico Gelo '00 is fresh with a subtle hint of flowers and citrus peel. The name derives from the Maremma sheepdog shown on the label, with all those cats – but there are also horses, chickens, geese and sheep – that appear on the bottles from this estate. The property is called Martilde from a conflation of the names of two cats, Martina and Matilde.

● Loghetto '00	🍷🍷	4
● OP Bonarda Campo del Monte '00	🍷🍷	3*
● OP Bonarda Possessione del Console '00	🍷🍷	3*
● OP Bonarda Millenium '98	🍷🍷	5
● OP Bonarda Cresta del Ghiffi '99	🍷🍷	4
● OP Bonarda Vignazzo '99	🍷🍷	4
● OP Bonarda Millenium '97	🍷	5
● OP Bonarda Possessione del Console '97	🍷	3
● Loghetto '98	🍷	3
● OP Bonarda Campo del Monte '98	🍷	3
● OP Bonarda Cresta del Ghiffi '98	🍷	3
● Rosso Poculum '98	🍷	4
● OP Bonarda Possessione del Console '99	🍷	3

○ OP Malvasia Piume '00	🍷🍷	4
● OP Bonarda Zaffo '97	🍷🍷	4
○ OP Riesling Italico Gelo '00	🍷	3
● OP Barbera '99	🍷	3
● OP Pinot Nero Martuffo '96	🍷	4
● OP Barbera La Strega, la Gazza, il Pioppo '97	🍷	5
● OP Bonarda Ghiro Rosso d'Inverno '97	🍷	5
● OP Bonarda '98	🍷	3
○ OP Riesling Italico Gelo '98	🍷	3
● OP Bonarda '99	🍷	3
○ OP Malvasia Piume '99	🍷	4
○ OP Riesling Italico Gelo '99	🍷	3

SAN PAOLO D'ARGON (BG)

CANTINA SOCIALE BERGAMASCA
VIA BERGAMO, 10
24060 SAN PAOLO D'ARGON (BG)
TEL. 035951098
E-MAIL: csbsanpaolo@libero.it

The San Paolo d'Argon co-operative, recently expanded and rebuilt – it now has modern vinification and bottling plant, and 2,000 hectolitres of barrel and small oak cask capacity –continues to amaze us with the value for money of its wines. Outstanding among them this year is the Valcalepio Rosso Riserva Akros '98 Vigna La Tordela, a Bordeaux blend with a predominance of cabernet. The perfectly ripened grapes, fermented with a leisurely maceration and aged for 36 months in 25-hectolitre French oak barrels, have created a product of particular richness with a deep ruby colour, a well-rounded aroma of morello cherry jam and sweet vanilla and cinnamon spice, and a warm, lively palate that is elegant in its harmonious fullness. The Riserva Vigneto Palma is not as concentrated but equally enjoyable, and destined to develop more rapidly. The Valcalepio Rosso from the '98 Orologio line is good, albeit simpler – it aged for nine months in large barrels – with fruity sensations supported by light, spicy notes,. The Rosso Doc '99 is leaner but well-balanced. A blend of pinot bianco, pinot grigio and chardonnay, the Valcalepio Bianco '00 is fresh and fragrant with captivating almond blossom and hawthorn floral aromas mingling with balsamic notes of green tobacco. The Pinot Spumante Metodo Charmat is nice and clean, offering nuances of ripe apple and toasted bread. A reassuring performance also came from the Aureo, a Moscato Giallo della Bergamasca from partially dried grapes. Sweet but not cloying, it's just the ticket with a tangy gorgonzola cheese.

○	Moscato Giallo Passito Aureo '00	🍷🍷	4
●	Valcalepio Rosso Riserva Akros Vigna La Tordela '98	🍷🍷	4
●	Valcalepio Rosso Riserva Akros Vigneto Palma '98	🍷🍷	4
○	Valcalepio Bianco '00	🍷	2
●	Valcalepio Rosso Orologio '98	🍷	3
○	Moscato Giallo Passito Perseo '99	🍷	5
●	Valcalepio Rosso '99	🍷	2
○	Pinot Brut	🍷	3
○	Moscato Giallo Passito Aureo '99	🍷🍷	2

SANTA GIULETTA (PV)

ISIMBARDA
LOC. CASTELLO
27046 SANTA GIULETTA (PV)
TEL. 0383899256
E-MAIL: isim@libero.it

Again, the Rosso Riserva Montezavo is at the top of the range of wines from Isimbarda, Luigi Meroni's winery and an estate that once belonged to the noble Isimbardi family. It confirmed the Two Glass status it acquired in the last edition of the Guide. The aroma has developed into an etheric bouquet, with refined spicy notes, and the palate has acquired greater completeness. Also tasted last time round was the Pinot Nero '98, which is almost as good. It comes from vineyards planted at 6,000 vines per hectare with French clones subjected to mass selection. Aged partially in new oak casks, it has a ruby colour and an aroma of wild berries with hints of leather and pepper. In the mouth it is warm, aristocratic and persistent. Another well-structured red is the Monplò '98, a blend of barbera, croatina, uva rara and pinot nero from the vineyard in Tramonto. By the way, we wonder why the estate has invented a name like Monplò when the vineyard is called, delightfully, Tramonto, or sunset. The wine has a deep ruby colour with flecks of garnet, then a nose of prunes, violets and vanilla. The palate is full-bodied and warm with robust alcohol (14.5 per cent). The Bonarda Frizzante '00, refermented in a pressure tank, has a purple colour, with aromas of morello cherry and bramble, leading in to a palate that is straightforward, lively and pleasantly sharp. The Riesling Renano Vigna Martina '00 is the best of the whites. With a greenish gold colour, it offers aromas of peach and lime blossom, then a soft, fresh, fruity palate with a tanginess emphasized by a clear mineral note. The Barbera Frizzante '00 della Vigna Picco dei Giganti is good but no more.

●	OP Bonarda Vivace '00	🍷🍷	3*
○	OP Riesling Renano Vigna Martina '00	🍷🍷	4
●	OP Rosso Monplò '98	🍷🍷	4
●	OP Barbera Frizzante '00	🍷	3
●	OP Rosso '96	🍷🍷	3
●	OP Barbera '98	🍷🍷	3
●	OP Bonarda Vivace '98	🍷🍷	3
●	OP Rosso Montezavo Ris. '98	🍷🍷	5
●	OP Rosso Vigna del Tramonto '98	🍷🍷	4
○	OP Riesling V. Belvedere '97	🍷	3
●	OP Pinot Nero '98	🍷	3
●	OP Barbera Frizzante '99	🍷	3
●	OP Bonarda Vivace '99	🍷	3

SANTA MARIA DELLA VERSA (PV)

Cantina Sociale La Versa
Via F. Crispi, 15
27047 Santa Maria della Versa (PV)
tel. 0385798411

The management of the La Versa co-operative winery co-ordinate 753 members who contribute 10,000,000 kilograms of grapes from 1,300 hectares of vineyards for a production of 8,000,000 bottles a year, mostly metodo classico and cuve close spumantes. In charge of winemaking is oenologist Francesco Cervetti, who is putting to good use his long experience gained in the Oltrepò. The more than satisfying results obtained by the wines presented for tasting confirm the desire of the Cantina di S. Maria della Versa to boost quality. The spumante classico cuvée Testarossa Extra Dry, less dry than a Brut, has a creamy mousse, a fine, compact perlage, the fragrant aromas of ripe fruit and hazelnuts, and a fresh, harmonious and very agreeable taste. The new Bonarda Frizzante Ca' Bella '00, from grapes harvested from the first hills in the Valle Versa, offers intense notes of bramble and Parma violets, then a lively, full and fruity flavour. The clean, well-balanced standard-label Bonardas from the 2000 vintage are also good, in both still and slightly sparkling versions. The Donelasco '99, a blend of 60 per cent croatina and barbera from vineyards in the village of Donelasco di S. Maria, is aged in oak, though the wood never overwhelms the fruit. More elegant than vigorous, it will last and improve over time. Part of the Pentagonon Antica Cantina 1905 line, the Bonarda '00 is good, zesty and full-bodied. The most well-managed of the whites is the Chardonnay '00, whose distinct varietal notes of apple and musk are underlined by hints of vanilla. Finally, a tip of the hat to the Pinot Nero Brut Metodo Martinotti, a fresh, clean wine with peach and almond aromas. Not bad, if you consider that more than 900,000 bottles are produced.

	Wine	Glasses	Score
●	OP Bonarda Frizzante Ca' Bella '00	♟♟	3
○	OP Chardonnay '00	♟♟	3*
○	Spumante Classico Cuvée Testarossa Extra Dry '98	♟♟	4
●	OP Rosso Donelasco '99	♟♟	3*
●	OP Bonarda '00	♟	3
●	OP Bonarda Pentagonon '00	♟	3
●	OP Bonarda Vivace '00	♟	3
○	OP Moscato Spumante	♟	3
○	OP Pinot Nero Brut	♟	3
○	OP Moscato Passito Lacrimae Vitis La Soleggia '96	♟♟	5
○	OP Pinot Nero Brut Mise en Cave '96	♟♟	4
●	OP Rosso Ris. Donelasco '97	♟♟	4

SCANZOROSCIATE (BG)

La Brugherata
Fraz. Rosciate
Via G. Medolago, 47
24020 Scanzorosciate (BG)
tel. 035655202
e-mail: info@labrugherata.it

With only ten or so hectares in all, five in vines set "a ritocchino", or following the line of maximum inclination along a steep slope, underneath an overhanging olive grove, La Brugherata is tended as if it were a botanical garden – it features roses, Mediterranean herbs and spices, and orchards – and is capable of creating great wines. First place goes to the Valcalepio Rosso Riserva Doglio '97, made from a very favourable vintage, although not the "vintage of the century" as it was too hastily defined: 1998 was in many ways better. Still, '97 produced few, well-ripened grapes. It has a clear, ruby colour and a complex aroma of morello cherry and blackcurrants leading in to a warm, round palate that is supported by a remarkable concentration of fine-grained tannins and a long finish of wild berry jam and vanilla. The Vescovado '00 is also very, very good, in fact the best of the Valcalepio whites we tasted this year. From a blend of pinot bianco and chardonnay, it brings together vitality and elegance in admirable harmony, with pronounced aromas of tropical banana and pineapple fruit, nuanced with honey. Of the two Alberico wines, the barrique-aged Rosso and Bianco, only the white hit the Two Glass mark with notes of sweet spices that do not overwhelm the fruit. The Rosso is good but lacks structure and persistence. The Vescovado '99 is not bad. An agreeable Bordeaux blend, it is already rather developed in colour and bouquet. The Doge '98, a Valcalepio Moscato di Scanzo Passito, has a bittersweet taste and an extremely complex bouquet of roses, sage, mace, black pepper and cinnamon. Though outstanding of its kind, it is hardly a bargain.

	Wine	Glasses	Score
○	Valcalepio Bianco Vescovado '00	♟♟	3
●	Valcalepio Rosso Ris. Doglio '97	♟♟	4
●	Moscato di Scanzo Passito Doge '98	♟♟	6
●	Rosso di Alberico '99	♟♟	4
●	Valcalepio Rosso Vescovado '99	♟	4
○	Bianco di Alberico '00	♟	4
●	Valcalepio Rosso Ris. Doglio '96	♟♟	4
●	Valcalepio Rosso Vescovado '96	♟♟	3
●	Rosso di Alberico '97	♟♟	4
○	Bianco di Alberico '98	♟♟	4
○	Valcalepio Bianco Vescovado '98	♟♟	3
●	Valcalepio Rosso Vescovado '98	♟♟	3
○	Bianco di Alberico '99	♟♟	4
●	Moscato di Scanzo Passito Doge '97	♟	6

SIRMIONE (BS)

Ca' dei Frati
Fraz. Lugana
Via Frati, 22
25010 Sirmione (BS)
tel. 030919468
e-mail: info@cadeifrati.it

On the Lugana plain, the 2000 harvest went so badly – terrible weather with violent hailstorms – that for the great majority of producers, it would have been better to relinquish DOC status so as not to damage the image of a white that can reach much higher quality in good years. Among the few that saved something from the disaster was the Lugana I Frati, which is a little lean and edgy but clean and pleasant, with fine floral notes. The Lugana from preceding vintages was very different and altogether superior. The Brolettino '99, even though it does not have the richness of the '98, is full and elegant and has a lovely complexity of aromas, underpinned by a touch of vanilla from its barrique-ageing. The same considerations go for the Pratto '99, an original blend of lugana and chardonnay in barriques and sauvignon blanc in stainless steel, that went beyond Two Glasses but is still far short of the legendary '96 that won Three Glasses in the 2000 Guide. There are two good, concentrated, complex wines here: the oak-aged Brolettino Grande Annata '97, with a bit too much wood showing, and the Tre Filer '98, from partially dried trebbiano, sauvignon and chardonnay, fermented in barriques. The Lugana series closes with the Brut Classico Cuvée dei Frati which has a creamy mousse, aromas of lime blossom and crusty bread, and a fresh, agreeable palate. The Ronchedone '99 is also good, a Benaco Bresciano Rosso obtained from a rather complicated blend of groppello, marzemino, barbera, cabernet, merlot and sangiovese. Its stay in small oak casks has created a harmony between the bouquet and palate that will become more complete with bottle ageing.

TEGLIO (SO)

Fay
Loc. San Giacomo
Via Pila Caselli, 1
23036 Teglio (SO)
tel. 0342786071
e-mail: elefay@tin.it

The high quality of Fay family wines is confirmed this year, as is the precise, very recognizable style of sweet, slightly super-ripe notes, rich in sunshine, warmth and softness. The wines of Sandro Fay are now made with the collaboration of his children Marco and Elena. You either love them or run the risk of misunderstanding them, and thus failing to appreciate them. We belong to the first category, so much so that four wines in this edition have been awarded Two Glass scores. The first is the excellent Sforzato Ronco del Picchio '98, which made it to our final taste-offs. It regales the nose with intense notes of morello cherry, cloves and liqueur fruit. The palate is a little too obviously sweet but very well balanced, with hints of chocolate and coffee to the fore, and there is a soft, characteristic finish. The Sassella Il Glicine is very good in the '98 version. Fresh and fruity in its bouquet, with a faint, spicy note, it follows with a palate that shows a harmonious, close-knit, pleasant texture and an attractively broad finish. A real cult favourite from the Fay winery is the Valgella Ca' Morei which, in the '98 vintage, confirms its traditional characteristics: intense aromas of ripe fruit and a soft, concentrated palate supported by sweet, nicely assertive tannins. This is a sort of anniversary for the Carteria '98 Trentennale label. An excellent wine from nebbiolo grapes with the addition of five per cent raisined grapes. Part aged in 900-litre tonneaux, it is a wine with an unmistakeable bouquet, appreciated for the multi-layered richness of its aromas, its sweetness and the length of its palate.

○	Lugana Brolettino Grande Annata '97	♀♀	5
○	Tre Filer '98	♀♀	5
○	Lugana Il Brolettino '99	♀♀	4
○	Pratto '99	♀♀	5
●	Benaco Bresciano Ronchedone '99	♀	4
○	Lugana Brut Cl. Cuvée dei Frati	♀	5
○	Pratto '96	♀♀♀	4
○	Tre Filer '90	♀♀	5
○	Tre Filer '95	♀♀	5
○	Tre Filer '96	♀♀	5
○	Lugana Il Brolettino '97	♀♀	4
○	Pratto '97	♀♀	5
○	Tre Filer '97	♀♀	5
○	Lugana Il Brolettino '98	♀♀	4
○	Pratto '98	♀♀	5

●	Valtellina Sforzato Ronco del Picchio '98	♀♀	6
●	Valtellina Sup. Sassella Il Glicine '98	♀♀	5
●	Valtellina Sup. Valgella Ca' Morei '98	♀♀	5
●	Valtellina Sup. Valgella Carteria Trentennale '98	♀♀	5
●	Valtellina Sforzato '97	♀♀	5
●	Valtellina Sforzato Ronco del Picchio '97	♀♀	6
●	Valtellina Sup. Valgella Ca' Morei '97	♀♀	5
●	Valtellina Sup. Valgella Carteria '97	♀♀	5

TIRANO (SO)

Conti Sertoli Salis
P.zza Salis, 3
23037 Tirano (SO)
tel. 0342710404
e-mail: info@sertolisalis.com

The Sforzato Canua '99 again brilliantly won Three Glasses, a distinguished result for Sertoli Salis as well as a recognition of the work carried out by oenologist Claudio Introini, one of the most respected professionals in Valtellina. So a round of applause for this producer who successfully exploited the potential of a very favourable vintage to create a major wine of exceptional elegance. It has an intense ruby red colour with garnet highlights, then the fruit is ripe and sustained on the nose, with obvious notes of elderberry jam and shades of spice. The entry on the palate is monumental, with tannins perfectly integrated into the velvety, fruity texture of a flavour that closes on delicious notes of cocoa powder. Made partially from nebbiolo grapes left to raisin and then added to the wine, the Corte della Meridiana '98 has an intense aroma of wild berries and is warm and comforting on the palate, which holds up well through to the lingering finish. Perhaps less effective on the nose, the Capo di Terra '98 is strikingly delicious to drink. Round and fruity, it has a warm, convincing finish. The Saloncello '00 just missed Two Glasses. Fruity and delicate on the nose, it has a soft palate with a precise, linear development. Instead, a very full One Glass went to the Sassella '98, a good example of how to interpret the terroir. The bouquet is classic, conjuring up dried roses and tobacco leaves, then the sound palate offers soft tannins and good nose-palate consistency in the finish. The Torre della Sirena '00, with its slightly pale, straw-yellowish colour, has clean aromas that hint at citrus with vegetal overtones. It is zesty, almost citrussy, on the palate and fresh and agreeable to drink.

TORRICELLA VERZATE (PV)

Monsupello
Via San Lazzaro, 5
27050 Torricella Verzate (PV)
tel. 0383896043

The Three Glasses awarded in the last edition to the spumante classico Pinot Nero Nature di Monsupello sparked a series of "me-too" reactions among the other producers in the Oltrepò. Not all, of course, but a growing number who were already skilful but were now looking to improve further. At the head of this laudable group, is Monsupello and the estate continues to shine under Carlo Boatti and his son Pierangelo, major players this year in an impressive growth in quality. Suffice it to say there is not enough space here for the complete list of deserving wines. We must limit ourselves to those that went beyond the Two Glass mark, emphasizing that none of the other wines dropped below a score of One Glass. We'll start with the spumante classicos: the Pinot Nero Nature, round, elegant and harmonious, continues to be a quality bottle; then come the Classese '96 and the non-vintage Brut, both from pinot nero. The top still white was the powerful, complex Chardonnay Senso '99. Then come the whites from the 2000 vintage: Chardonnay, Pinot Grigio, Riesling and Sauvignon, all rich and very varietal. In addition to the already well-known reds, the Pinot Nero 3309 from '98, the Rosso La Borla '98, the Great Ruby '00 and the Barbera Vivace Magenga '00, with their balanced structure, there are some interesting new entries from the '97 vintage: the Rosso Riserva Mosaico, the Barbera Pivena and the Cabernet Sauvignon Aplomb. All are impressive in the concentration of their aromas and flavour. Not many producers in Italy can produce a similar line-up.

● Valtellina Sforzato Canua '99	♟♟♟	6
● Valtellina Sup. Corte della Meridiana '98	♟♟	5
● Valtellina Sup. Capo di Terra '98	♟♟	5
● Il Saloncello '00	♟	4
○ Torre della Sirena '00	♟	4
● Valtellina Sup. Sassella '98	♟	4
● Valtellina Sforzato Canua '97	♟♟♟	6
● Valtellina Sforzato Canua '95	♟♟	5
● Valtellina Sforzato Canua '96	♟♟	6
● Valtellina Sup. Corte della Meridiana '97	♟♟	5
● Valtellina Sup. Sassella '97	♟♟	4
● Valtellina Sforzato Canua '98	♟♟	6

○ OP Pinot Nero Cl. Nature	♟♟♟	4
○ OP Chardonnay Senso '99	♟♟	4
● OP Barbera Magenga '00	♟♟	4
○ OP Chardonnay '00	♟♟	4
○ OP Pinot Grigio '00	♟♟	4
○ OP Riesling '00	♟♟	4
● OP Rosso Great Ruby '00	♟♟	4
○ OP Sauvignon '00	♟♟	4
○ OP Pinot Nero Brut Cl. '96	♟♟	4
● OP Barbera Pivena '97	♟♟	5
● OP Cabernet Sauvignon Aplomb '97	♟♟	5
● OP Rosso Riserva Mosaico '97	♟♟	5
● OP Pinot Nero 3309 '98	♟♟	5
○ OP Pinot Nero Brut	♟♟	4
● OP Pinot Nero Cl. Nature	♟♟♟	4

VILLA DI TIRANO (SO)

TRIACCA
VIA NAZIONALE, 121
23030 VILLA DI TIRANO (SO)
TEL. 0342701352
E-MAIL: info@triacca.com

Domenico Triacca has put on a great show. His Sforzato '99 charmed the members of the Guide's final awards commission so much that none of them hesitated to give it Three Glasses. This is in recognition of the producer's dedication and the fact that a wine like the Sforzato represents a national trend in winemaking. It is a unique style that is synonymous with a territory, Valtellina, that is still not widely known or appreciated. Made from nebbiolo grapes with a very low yield per hectare, the '99 vintage of this Sforzato is characterized by complexity and austerity. Round in its aromas, with notes of leather mixed with dried fruit and hints of graphite and eucalyptus, it is solid on the palate, with an excellent tannic weave, and a soft, spicy texture. The Sforzato '98, though less impressive, has great character. Intense on the nose and round on the palate, it is let down by a shortish finish. The Prestigio '99 makes a point of concentration, perhaps too much. Fruity in its aromas, with notes of cinnamon, it is succulent in the mouth and rather unchallenging in some ways but very pleasant to drink. The Riserva Triacca '97 is a captivating classic with light notes of hay on the nose and good structure. The Casa La Gatta '98, again from nebbiolo, came close to Two Glasses. It's a fine example of the wine from this area, which offers excellent value for money, a heady bouquet, and a round, traditional palate. The Sassella '98 is not completely clean on the nose but the palate is pleasant with typical mineral touches. Neither does the Sauvignon Del Frate '00 disappoint. Minerally on the nose, with notes of gunflint, it is long and elegant in the mouth.

● Valtellina Sforzato '99	♟♟♟	6
● Valtellina Prestigio '99	♟♟	6
○ Sauvignon Del Frate '00	♟♟	4
● Valtellina Sup. Ris. Triacca '97	♟♟	5
● Valtellina Sforzato '98	♟♟	6
● Valtellina Casa La Gatta '98	♟	4
● Valtellina Sup. Sassella '98	♟	4
● Valtellina Prestigio Millennium '97	♟♟♟	5
● Valtellina Prestigio '94	♟♟	4
● Valtellina Prestigio '95	♟♟	4
● Valtellina Prestigio '96	♟♟	5
● Valtellina Sforzato '96	♟♟	5
● Valtellina Sup. Ris. Triacca '96	♟♟	4
● Valtellina Sforzato '97	♟♟	5
● Valtellina Prestigio '98	♟♟	5

ZENEVREDO (PV)

TENUTA IL BOSCO
LOC. IL BOSCO
27049 ZENEVREDO (PV)
TEL. 0385245326
E-MAIL: info@ilbosco.com

On the whole, it was a good performance from Tenuta Il Bosco, part of the Zonin Group. There has been significant improvement with respect to past editions of the Guide and we hope that this progress continues. Certainly, the means are not lacking. There are the vineyards, 130 hectares in a single lot, there is a perfectly equipped cellar, comprising 6,000 square metres equipped with the latest technology, and the men are there, too, in young Domenico Zonin and oenologist Pier Nicola Olmo. While waiting for great wines that will hit the headlines and further raise the image of winemaking in the Oltrepò, let's look at the present situation. The Rosso Teodote '99 has returned to the level of the '97 vintage. A blend of 55 per cent croatina and barbera, with the addition of 10 per cent uva rara, it is fermented with five days' maceration and then aged six months in barriques. It has a dark ruby colour, a broad fragrance of berries and vanilla, and a dry, forthright, harmonious palate. In short, a modern red, from indigenous varieties. The Malvasia Frizzante '00 is also modern and pleasant, from malvasia di Candia grapes grown in vineyards at San Zeno and Laghetto. It has an intense aroma of sage and acacia blossom, and it is spirited in the mouth, very soft but fresh and lively, with a slightly bitter finish. The Bonarda Poggio Pelato '99, from the vineyard of the same name, is well-made, and aged only in stainless steel. It has notes of plum, bitter almonds and violets. In the spumante range, the Pinot Nero Classico Phileo, which spends a year on the lees, is fruity, soft and winning while the Pinot Nero Regal Cuvée, with two years' lees contact, is elegant and stands up well to the passage of time.

○ OP Malvasia Frizzante '00	♟♟	3
○ OP Brut Il Bosco '94	♟♟	4
● OP Bonarda Vivace Poggio Pelato '99	♟♟	3*
○ OP Pinot Nero Brut Cl. Phileo	♟♟	4
○ OP Pinot Nero Brut Cl. Regal Cuvée	♟	4
○ OP Pinot Nero Brut Cl. '94	♟♟	4
○ OP Malvasia '98	♟♟	3
○ OP Pinot Nero Brut Cl. '92	♟♟	2*
○ OP Brut Regal Cuvée	♟♟	4
● Rosso Teodote '98	♟	4

OTHER WINERIES

BATTISTA COLA
VIA SANT'ANNA, 22
25030 ADRO (BS)
TEL. 0307356195
E-MAIL: cola@virgilio.it

Stefano Cola cultivates around 10 hectares of vineyards on the slopes of Monte Alto at Adro. He makes excellent wines and Franciacortas as exemplified by the Tamino, a soft red with fine-grained tannins, and the good Franciacorta Brut. Both are offered at very reasonable prices.

○ Franciacorta Brut	🍷	4*
○ Franciacorta Extra Brut '95	🍷🍷	4
○ Franciacorta Extra Brut '96	🍷🍷	5
● TdF Rosso Tamino '98	🍷🍷	4

LEBOVITZ
LOC. GOVERNOLO
V.LE RIMEMBRANZE, 4
46037 BAGNOLO SAN VITO (MN)
TEL. 0376668115

The Lebovitz family began producing wines in the Mantua area at the beginning of the 20th century. Their pride and joy is the Rosso dei Concari, a Lambrusco aged on its yeasts to give it more strength. The standard-label Lambrusco is lighter but pleasant.

● Lambrusco Mantovano Rosso dei Concari '00	🍷	2
● Lambrusco Mantovano		2

CANTRINA
FRAZ. CANTRINA - VIA COLOMBERA, 7
25081 BEDIZZOLE (BS)
TEL. 0306871052
E-MAIL: cantrina@libero.it

Cristina Inganni submitted the same wines as she did in the last edition of the Guide. The Sole di Dario '97, a "passito" from partially dried sauvignon and sémillon, has hints of honey, vanilla and tropical fruit. The Corteccio Pinot Nero 1998 has a bouquet of blackcurrants and spices, then a full, solid taste.

○ Sole di Dario '97	🍷🍷	4
● Garda Pinot Nero Corteccio '98	🍷	4

MEDOLAGO ALBANI
LOC. TRESCORE BALNEARIO
VIA REDONA, 12 - 24069 BERGAMO
TEL. 035942022
E-MAIL: wine@medolagoalbani.it

Situated in a well-located valley, this historic winery has been producing wine since the beginning of the 16th century. Today, it occupies 80 hectares with 22 of them planted to vine. The cellar turns out an excellent, mature Rosso Riserva '97 and a good Valcalepio Bianco '00, with a bouquet of almond blossom.

● Valcalepio Rosso Ris. '97	🍷🍷	4
○ Valcalepio Bianco '00	🍷	2

PERCIVALLE
VIA TORCHI, 9
27040 BORGO PRIOLO (PV)
TEL. 0383871175

The estate of Paolo Percivalle has several wines worthy of mention. The top bottle is the Barbera Costa del Sole '99, with a great alcohol and extractive structure. The partially oak-aged Riesling Renano '00 Parsua is interesting, with clear notes of minerals and spices.

○ OP Riesling Renano Parsua '00	3
● OP Barbera Costa del Sole '99	4

EMILIO FRANZONI
VIA CAVOUR, 10
25080 BOTTICINO (BS)
TEL. 0302691134 - 0302691071
E-MAIL: franzoni@botticino.it

The Franzoni estate has devoted great effort to promoting Botticino, the small Brescia DOC zone. Its flagship wine is the Riserva Faja d'Or '97, a robust, austere and uncompromising blend of barbera, marzemino, sangiovese and schiava.

● Botticino Faja d'Or Ris. '97	3

CATTURICH-DUCCO
LOC. CAMIGNONE - FRAZ. PASSIRANO
VIA DEGLI EROI, 70
25040 BRESCIA
TEL. 0306850566 - 0306850576

From his 76 hectares of vineyards, Piero Catturich produces around 450,000 bottles a year that cover all the types of Franciacortas and wines from the territory. In the past few years, the estate has shown signs of strong growth in quality.

○ Franciacorta Pas Dosé Torre Ducco '97	5
○ Franciacorta Brut	4

FRANCESCO QUACQUARINI
VIA MONTEVENEROSO
27044 CANNETO PAVESE (PV)
TEL. 038560152

The Quacquarini family has 40 hectares of vineyards at Canneto, an area perfect for the production of red wines. The Buttafuoco Frizzante '00 is very good, fruity and forthright. The Pinot Nero Brut Classico and the Bonarda, with its hints of berries and spices, are also both well made.

● OP Buttafuoco Frizzante '00	2*
● OP Bonarda Vivace '00	2*
○ OP Pinot Nero Brut Cl.	3

LA VIGNA
VIA TORRAZZA
25020 CAPRIANO DEL COLLE (BS)
TEL. 0309748061

Anna Botti, whose surname means "barrels", has a seven-hectare estate in the Montenetto hills. Her Rosso Montebruciato '98 is impressive. Made from sangiovese, marzemino, barbera and merlot grapes aged in wood, it has aromas of jam and toast, and a persistent, powerful flavour.

● Capriano del Colle Rosso Monte Bruciato Ris. '98	3

TENUTA LA COSTA - CALVI
VIA COSTA, 68
27040 CASTANA (PV)
TEL. 0385241527

The Calvis have been growing vineyards on the hills of Castana since the end of the 17th century. The jewel in their crown is the historic Buttafuoco Vigna Montarzolo from croatina, barbera, uva rara and ughetta fruit. The '97, aged for 12 months in barriques, is still a tad rigid but will mellow out in the bottle.

● OP Buttafuoco Vigna Montarzolo '97	4

Marco Giulio Bellani
Via Manzoni, 75
27045 Casteggio (PV)
Tel. 038382122

Marco Bellani introduces a dark Barbera Vivace with a bouquet of red berries. The taste is full, supported by good acidity. The Bonarda Vivace is also noteworthy. It's straightforward and spirited, with a clear aroma of over-ripe wild brambles.

● OP Barbera Vivace '00	♀ 2*
● OP Bonarda Vivace '00	♀ 2

Bellaria
Fraz. Mairano
Via Castel del Lupo, 28
27045 Casteggio (PV)
Tel. 038383203 - 033523539

The Massone family cultivates 14 hectares of vineyards dedicated to the typical varieties from the Oltrepò DOC zone, in addition to cabernet and merlot. The Bricco Sturnel and La Macchia are both made from the two international varieties. Aged in oak, they are concentrated and lively.

● Bricco Sturnel '97	♀♀ 4
● La Macchia '98	♀ 4

Clastidio
Via San Biagio, 32
27045 Casteggio (PV)
Tel. 038382566

Ballabio is one of the historic estates in the Oltrepò. The grapes from the well-tended vines on the estate produce wines that should restore it to its former glory. The Bonarda Vivace '00 Le Cento Pertiche is forthright and fragrant; the Narbusto '98 must still mature.

● OP Bonarda Vivace Le Cento Pertiche '00	♀♀ 3*
● OP Rosso Narbusto '98	♀ 4

CastelFaglia
Fraz. Calino - Loc. Boschi, 3
25046 Cazzago San Martino (BS)
Tel. 030775104 - 059812424
E-mail: castelfaglia@cavicchioli.it

Owned by the Modena-based Cavicchioli winery, a specialist in Lambrusco, CastelFaglia creates excellent wines and Franciacortas with a well-made and elegant style. An excellent example is the Franciacorta Brut Cuvée Giunone, which is fresh fruity, soft and well-structured.

○ Franciacorta Brut Monogram Cuvée Giunone	♀♀ 6
○ Franciacorta Extra Brut	♀ 4
○ Franciacorta Brut Monogram mill. '91	♀♀ 6

Ca' del Vent
Via Stella, 2
25060 Cellatica (BS)
Tel. 0302770411
E-mail: p.clerici@cadelvent.com

Ca' del Vent makes its appearance in the Guide with an excellent Franciacorta Brut that reveals a greenish, straw-yellow colour, fine perlage and intense fruit and flower aromas. It has a full-bodied palate, velvet-smooth effervescence and a long finish with notes of white peach.

○ Franciacorta Brut	♀♀ 5

Agricola Gatta
via Stella, 27
25060 Cellatica (BS)
Tel. 0302772950
E-mail: invigna@inwind.it

Mario Gatta works his 10 hectares of vineyards at Cellatica, Gussago and Rodengo Saiano, with real dedication. In addition to a good Cellatica Rosso Superiore Negus, he produces Febo, an excellent white from chardonnay grapes, fermented and aged in barriques.

○ Febo '98	♀♀ 4

CAMINELLA
VIA DANTE ALIGHIERI, 13
24069 CENATE SOTTO (BG)
TEL. 035951828

This compact, four-hectare estate is beautifully looked after. Owned by Giovanna Terzi, releases a range that his its high points in the full-bodied, fruit-driven Valcalepio Bianco Ripa di Luna '00, the barrique-aged Verde Luna Bianco, and the Valcalepio Rosso Ripa di Luna '98, which is well-balanced and elegant.

○	Valcalepio Bianco Ripa di Luna '00	♀	3
●	Valcalepio Rosso Ripa di Luna '98	♀	3
○	Verde Luna Bianco	♀	4

CASA VINICOLA NERA
VIA IV NOVEMBRE, 43
23030 CHIURO (SO)
TEL. 0342482629

Nera continues its search for an identity in step with the advances made by winemaking in Valtellina. The Sforzato '96 is traditional in its bouquet, then generous and well-structured in the mouth. The Inferno Riserva '95 has a heady bouquet and round palate, with a faint acidic twist in its finish.

●	Valtellina Sforzato '96	♀♀	5
●	Valtellina Sup. Inferno Ris. '95	♀	4

BETTINZANA - CASCINA RONCO BASSO
LOC. MONTE ORFANO - VIA BUSSAGHE, 14
25030 COCCAGLIO (BS)
TEL. 0307721689 - 0307240579
E-MAIL: chrom@dfn.it

Though small, the Battista Bettinzana estate always offers wines with a clean style and excellent balance. We would point out a Franciacorta Brut with decent structure and remarkable delicacy, offered at an excellent price.

○	Franciacorta Brut	♀	4
○	Franciacorta Brut '95	♀♀	5

VISCONTI
VIA C. BATTISTI, 139
25015 DESENZANO DEL GARDA (BS)
TEL. 0309120681

Visconti has been making wines since just after the Second World War. This experience has produced their aromatic, full-bodied Lugana '98. Of their various Luganas from the '00 vintage, we felt the best was the Santa Onorata, for its clean taste and good finish of damsons.

○	Lugana Sup. '98	♀♀	4
○	Lugana Collo Lungo '00	♀	3
○	Lugana S. Onorata '00	♀	4
●	Benaco Bresciano Rosso Vigne Sparse '97	♀	4

LONGHI DE CARLI
VIA VERDI, 4
25030 ERBUSCO (BS)
TEL. 0307760280

Among the outstanding wines produced by the Alessandro Longhi estate is an excellent Satèn, rich in softness and fruit, with a long finish on sweet notes of vanilla. The Franciacorta Brut shows good structure and bouquet.

○	Franciacorta Satèn	♀♀	5
○	Franciacorta Brut	♀	4

PRINCIPE BANFI
VIA PER ISEO, 25
25030 ERBUSCO (BS)
TEL. 0307750387 - 022131322

This estate, owned by Roberto Principe, boasts nine hectares of vineyards and an annual production of 60,000 bottles. The overall quality level is excellent, thanks in part to the oenological advice of Cesare Ferrari. The Satèn in particular is stylistically very clean and remarkably full-bodied.

○	Franciacorta Satèn	♀♀	5
●	TdF Rosso '99	♀	3
○	Franciacorta Brut	♀	5

Attilio Vezzoli
Via Costa di Sopra, 22
25030 Erbusco (BS)
tel. 0307267601

The range presented by Attilio Vezzoli this year is carefully made, which hints that the estate is growing in quality. Its best bottle is the Franciacorta Satèn, which has enjoyably robust structure and successful balance.

○ Franciacorta Satèn		5
● TdF Rosso '99		3

Tallarini
Via Fontanile, 7/9
24060 Gandosso (BG)
tel. 035834003
e-mail: info@tallarini.com

This estate, owned by Vincenzo Tallarini, has 23 hectares of vineyards between Valcalepio and Franciacorta. His most interesting product is the Valcalepio Rosso Riserva San Giovannino '97. It's spicy – there is too much oak – but is developing well. The Rosso '99 is good and unveils an intense aroma of morello cherries.

● Valcalepio Rosso Riserva San Giovannino '97		4
● Valcalepio Rosso '99		3

Trevisani
Loc. Soprazocco
Via Galuzzo, 2
25085 Gavardo (BS)
tel. 036532825

This estate is called Ca' dei Venti, or "House of Winds" and in fact several of its wines take their names from the local breezes. Balì is a strong north wind that blows from Lake Garda as well as a good blend of chardonnay and sauvignon blanc. Sùer, another wind off the lake, is from merlot and rebo.

○ Benaco Bresciano Bianco Balì '00		3
● Benaco Bresciano Rosso Sùer '98		3

Castello di Grumello
Via Fosse, 11
24064 Grumello del Monte (BG)
tel. 0354420817 - 035830244
e-mail: info@castellodigrumelo.it

Though the Colle del Calvario '98 from cabernet sauvignon and merlot is a bit closed, the substance is there. The Valcalepio Bianco '00 is not bad. As for the Celebra, it shows a delicious bouquet of damask roses, sage and cloves but is a bit too dry on the palate.

○ Valcalepio Bianco '00		3
● Valcalepio Rosso Colle del Calvario '98		4
○ Chardonnay Aurito '99		4
● Valcalepio Rosso '99		3

Le Corne
Loc. Corne - Via San Pantaleone
24064 Grumello del Monte (BG)
tel. 035830215
e-mail: italia@lecorne.it

Gambarini and Perletti's Le Corne is housed in a 15th-century country villa surrounded by 50 hectares of vineyards. The Messernero '97, an oak-aged cabernet, is evolved and complex with notes of fruit jam, spices and animal fur leading in to a warm, full palate with well-gauged tannins.

● Cabernet della Bergamasca Messernero '97		4

Spia d'Italia
Via M. Cerutti, 61
25017 Lonato (BS)
tel. 0309130233 - 0309913414
e-mail: guettaandrea@libero.it

Andrea Guetta has reinvented and remade a dessert wine that was famous in the early 19th century but had been completely forgotten. His San Martino della Battaglia, from super-ripe tocai grapes, has notes of dried flowers and chestnut honey with a distinct tangy almond background.

○ San Martino della Battaglia Liquoroso '97		5

STEFANO SPEZIA
VIA MATTEOTTI, 90
46010 MARIANA MANTOVANA (MN)
TEL. 0376735012

Winemaker and merchant Stefano Spezia creates his Lambrusco Etichetta Blu directly in the bottle. It is exuberant and tangy, from a forthright country peasant tradition. The Etichetta Rossa is a clear and properly fruity Lambrusco that is pleasant in its simplicity.

● Lambrusco Provincia di Mantova Etichetta Blu '00	1*
● Provincia di Mantova Lambrusco Etichetta Rossa '00	1*

VILLA MAZZUCCHELLI
LOC. CILIVERGHE
VIA MATTEOTTI, 99
25080 MAZZANO (BS)
TEL. 0302301457 - 0302120394

Inside Villa Mazzucchelli at Ciliverghe, Piero Giacomini, oenologist and owner of the estate, has restored the old cellars for the production of both spumante classico and still wines. Best of the estate's spumantes is the Brut Carato Oro.

○ Brut Carato Oro	6
○ Brut Conte Giammaria Ris.	6
○ Brut Sauvage	5

CA' DEL SANTO
LOC. CAMPOLUNGO
27040 MONTALTO PAVESE (PV)
TEL. 0383870545

Estate owner Laura Bozzi grows her vineyards in the village of Campolungo at Montalto Pavese. From the well-ripened grapes of the '98 harvest, she has made an excellent Pinot Nero aged in barriques. The Bonarda Vivace '00 is also good, straightforward and fruity.

● Pinot Nero '98	3*
● OP Bonarda Vivace Riva degli Zingari '00	3

CANTINE VALTENESI - LUGANA
VIA PERGOLA, 21
25080 MONIGA DEL GARDA
TEL. 0365502002
E-MAIL: civielle@gardavino.it

This cellar produces 18 types of wines from the Garda area. The best product tasted this year was the well-structured Lugana Superiore Cios '98. The fruity, attractive Marzemino Vigna Balosse is not bad, either, or indeed the oak-aged Garda Rosso Superiore Brol.

○ Lugana Sup. Cios '98	4
● Garda Cl. Sup. Rosso Brol '98	4
● Garda Marzemino Vigna Balosse '99	2*

TENIMENTI CASTELROTTO - TORTI
FRAZ. CASTELROTTO, 6
27047 MONTECALVO VERSIGGIA (PV)
TEL. 0385951000
E-MAIL: patrizia@tortino.it

Dino Torti's Tenimenti Castelrotto submitted several wines for tasting that deserve attention. The Pinot Nero '98 has strength and elegance with a very typical bouquet of cassis and spices. The Barbera '98 shows off aromas of fruit preserves and vanilla.

● OP Pinot Nero '98	5
● OP Barbera '98	3

PIETRO TORTI
FRAZ. CASTELROTTO
27047 MONTECALVO VERSIGGIA (PV)
TEL. 038599763 - 038599344

For generations, the Torti family has cultivated its just under nine and a half hectares of vineyards at Castelrotto in Montecalvo. The Barbera "mossa" (sparkling) has a frank, zesty taste and fragrant bouquet. The full-bodied and fruity Bonarda Vivace has a pleasant bittersweet background of peach kernels.

● OP Barbera Vivace '00	2*
● OP Bonarda Vivace '00	2

Marco Vercesi
Loc. Montù Beccaria
Via F.R. Crosia, 1
27040 Montù Beccaria (PV)
Tel. 038561330

Marco Vercesi manages his small estate with great dedication. His Re di Bric '98, a monovarietal croatina, has a broad nose of bramble and raspberry and a vigorous palate. The oak-aged Chardonnay '98 displays notes of musk and ripe apples.

○ OP Chardonnay '98	♀	4
● Re di Bric '98	♀	3

Ricchi
Via Festoni, 13/D
46040 Monzambano (MN)
Tel. 0376800238
E-mail: vitivinicola.ricchi@libero.it

Brothers Claudio and Giancarlo Stefanoni tend 32 hectares of vineyards in the morainic hollow of the Garda area in the province of Mantua, growing both local and international varieties. The Cabernet '99 Ribò is full-bodied with an aroma of fruit preserves, leather and tobacco. The Merlot '00 is grassy and fruity.

● Garda Merlot '00	♀	2
● Garda Cabernet Ribò '99	♀	3

Cascina Gnocco
Fraz. Losana, 20
27040 Mornico Losana (PV)
Tel. 0383892280
E-mail: ca.gnocco@exite.it

This estate of Domenico Cuneo presently covers an area of 20 hectares, with 15 under vine. The Barbera '99, with 10 per cent croatina, is aged in medium-sized oak barrels and has a well-structured, uncompromising palate. The Moscato Adagetto '00 is full and sweet, with fruit and flower aromas.

● OP Bonarda Frizzante Vigna dei Frati '00	♀	3
○ OP Provincia di Pavia Moscato Adagetto '00	♀	3
● OP Barbera '99	♀	4

Al Rocol
Via Prov.le, 79
25050 Ome (BS)
Tel. 0306852542
E-mail: info@alrocol.com

On his estate in Ome, Gianluigi Vimercati creates a Franciacorta Brut that is much appreciated for its soft fullness and remarkable balance. His other wine, a red with a soft, fruity style, is also good.

○ Franciacorta Brut	♀♀	5
● TdF Rosso Borbone '98	♀	3

Ugo Vezzoli
Loc. San Pancrazio - Via G. B. Vezzoli, 20
25030 Palazzolo sull'Oglio (BS)
Tel. 030738018 - 0307386177
E-mail: agricola.vezzoli@libero.it

This is a small winery, with just five hectares of vineyards, that manages to produce 50,000 bottles annually of Franciacortas and still wines. Its list is fairly extensive and reasonably priced. We enjoyed both the Franciacorta and the two DOC wines.

○ TdF Bianco '00	♀	3*
● TdF Rosso '99	♀	3*
○ Franciacorta Brut	♀	4

Bredasole
Via San Pietro, 44
25030 Paratico (BS)
Tel. 035910407
E-mail: ferrari@bredasole.it

The Ferrari brothers presented a good red, the Terre di Franciacorta Rosso, and a white, the Pio Elemosiniere, created from a vineyard located on a morainic spur with sparse, pebbly soil. It has great structure, softness on the palate and richness on the nose.

○ TdF Bianco Pio Elemosiniere '99	♀♀	4*
● TdF Rosso Spigolato '98	♀	5

MARCHESI FASSATI DI BALZOLA
VIA CASTELLO, 2
25050 PASSIRANO (BS)
TEL. 0306850753 - 0276318315
E-MAIL: info@fassatidibalzola.com

Leonardo Fassati, with the advice of his consultant Corrado Cugnasco, produces around 30,000 bottles annually of Brut and Extra Brut Franciacorta with the grapes from his six hectares of vineyards. The products have a fresh, captivating style.

○ Franciacorta Brut	♟ 5
○ Franciacorta Extra Brut	♟ 5

LE MARCHESINE
VIA VALLOSA, 31
25050 PASSIRANO (BS)
TEL. 030657005

Giovanni Biatta's Marchesine winery specializes in making Franciacortas, turning out more than 100,000 bottles of good wine annually. Most of the grapes that make up the base cuvées come from the 15 hectares of estate-owned vineyards.

○ Franciacorta Brut	♟♟ 5
○ Franciacorta Brut Secolo Novo '95	♟♟ 5

MONTERUCCO
LOC. CICOGNOLA
VALLE CIMA, 38
27040 PAVIA
TEL. 038585151 - 038585411

Monterucco, owned by the Valenti brothers, vinifies the grapes harvested from its own 15 hectares of vineyards. The Bonarda Frizzante Vigna Il Modello is dark ruby red with a bouquet of roses and brambles. It is full-bodied in the mouth with a good almondy background.

● OP Bonarda Vivace Vigna Il Modello '00	♟♟ 2*

CANTINA SOCIALE VAL SAN MARTINO
VIA BERGAMO, 1195
24030 PONTIDA (BG)
TEL. 035795035

This co-operative makes wine from the grapes cultivated by its 50 or so members on 50 hectares of vineyards in the area between the Brembo and the Adda. The Riera '00 is an original white from a base of Incrocio Manzoni 6.0.13 with the addition of other fine grapes. The Valcalepio Bianco is also good.

○ Bianco della Bergamasca Riera '00	♟ 2*
○ Valcalepio Bianco '00	♟ 2

MARANGONA
ANTICA CORTE IALIDY
25010 POZZOLENGO (BS)
TEL. 030919379
E-MAIL: info@marangona.com

The property occupies part of the Antica Corte Ialidy estate and produces both wine and extravirgin olive oil. The Lugana Superiore Il Rintocco '98 is truly excellent and evidently vinified using grapes from very old vines. The Chiaretto '00 is pleasant and very tangy, despite the unfavourable year.

○ Lugana Il Rintocco '98	♟♟ 3
● Garda Cl. Rosso Sup. Corte Ialidy '00	♟ 2

TENUTA ROVEGLIA
LOC. ROVEGLIA, 1
25010 POZZOLENGO (BS)
TEL. 030918663
E-MAIL: tenuta.roveglia@gsnet.it

The Lugana Superiore Filo di Arianna '99 is the best of the products presented by the Roveglia estate. Fermented in barriques, it has a bouquet of vanilla spice and dried flowers leading in to a palate of ripe fruit and toasted almonds. The other wines are also good.

○ Lugana Sup. Filo di Arianna '99	♟♟ 4
○ Passito di Roveglia '97	♟ 5
○ Lugana Sup. Vigne di Catullo '99	♟ 4
○ Lugana '00	3

Pasini Produttori
Fraz. Raffa - Via Videlle, 2
25080 Puegnago sul Garda (BS)
Tel. 030266206 - 0365651419
E-mail: info@pasiniproduttori.com

Pasini Produttori is finishing its new cellar but has already opened a restaurant in an 18th century courtyard. The cabernet and groppello-based San Gioan I Carati '97 ages in barriques and stood out from the other wines we tasted. The Cap del Priu '99 and Lugana Brut Charmat Lungo '00 were also good.

○ Lugana Brut '00	♀	3
● Benaco Bresciano Rosso San Gioan I Carati '97	♀	4
● Garda Cl. Rosso Sup. Cap del Priu '99	♀	3

Cantina Sociale Coop. di Quistello
Via Roma, 46
46026 Quistello (MN)
Tel. 0376618118
E-mail: info@cantinasocialequistello.it

The Quistello co-operative cultivates various subvarieties of lambrusco on the principles of integrated vineyard management. Its lively, easy-drinking Lambrusco Banda Blu and Banda Rossa are both zesty and aromatic, showing notes of violets and morello cherries. It would be difficult to do better at this price.

● Lambrusco Mantovano Banda Blu '00	♀	1*
● Lambrusco Mantovano Banda Rossa '00	♀	1*

Mirabella
Via Cantarane, 2
25050 Rodengo Saiano (BS)
Tel. 030611197
E-mail: info@mirabellavini.it

Founded in 1979, the Mirabella estate has over the past few years boosted its quality levels with creditable enthusiasm. It is owned by a large group of partners that includes the estate oenologist, Teresio Schiavi.

○ Franciacorta Non Dosato '94	♀♀	5
● T. d F. Rosso Maniero '99	♀	3
⊙ Franciacorta Rosé	♀	4

Pusterla
Via F. Petrarca, 7
25038 Rovato (BS)
Tel. 0307702927

This estate takes its name from a 100 year old vineyard situated below the castle of Brescia. Covering four hectares, it is one of the largest urban vineyards in the world. Its best wine is the Merlorso '98, from merlot. The Pusterla Bianco and Pusterla are also excellent.

● Rosso Merlorso '98	♀♀	5
○ Pusterla Bianco '99	♀	3
● Pusterla Rosso '99	♀	2

Franco Bazzini
Via Castello, 16
27040 Rovescala (PV)
Tel. 038575205
E-mail: francobazzini@libero.it

Dark, concentrated, with a full aroma of bramble jam and a broad, vigorous flavour, the Bonarda '99 Vigna Butas of Franco Bazzini is well up to the standard of the '97. The Rosso Bonabà '97, is also noteworthy for its rustic nobility.

● OP Bonabà '97	♀	4
● OP Bonarda Vigna Butas '99	♀	2*

Antonio Panigada - Banino
Via della Vittoria, 13
20078 San Colombano al Lambro (MI)
Tel. 037189103

The Riserva La Merla '98, from very old vineyards, has a broad bouquet of fruit preserves underlined with hints of vanilla that do not dominate the fruit. It is rich and powerful in the mouth, with excellent extract, and will improve as the tannins develop. The other wines are also enjoyable.

● San Colombano Banino Ris. La Merla '98	♀♀	4
○ Colline del Milanese Banino '00	♀	3
● San Colombano Rosso Banino '00	♀	3

Enrico Riccardi
Via Capra, 17
20078 San Colombano al Lambro (MI)
Tel. 0371897381 - 0371200523
E-mail: info@viniriccardi.com

From barbera, croatina and uva rara, Enrico Riccardi has created a nice tangy San Colombano '99 with good personality. The Riserva '97 I Chiostri is more complex. Ruby, with penetrating aromas, it has a robust palate. The Verdea La Tonsa is pleasant, sparkling, fresh and fruity.

● San Colombano Rosso I Chiostri '97 ♀		3
● San Colombano Rosso Roverone '99 ♀		2
○ Collina del Milanese Verdea La Tonsa		2

Vanzini
Fraz. Barbaleone, 7
27040 San Damiano al Colle (PV)
Tel. 038575019
E-mail: vanzini@inwind.it

The Vanzini family began its winemaking career in 1890. Today, they create 800,000 bottles each year. The Pinot Nero Extra Dry is good, soft and fresh, as are the clean, fruity Moscato Spumante and the Bonarda Frizzante, fragrant with aromas of bramble and almond.

● OP Bonarda Frizzante '00	♀	2
○ OP Moscato Spumante	♀	3
○ OP Pinot Nero Extra Dry	♀	3

Le Chiusure
Fraz. Portese
Via Boschette, 2
25010 San Felice del Benaco (BS)
Tel. 0365626243

Agronomist Alessandro Luzzago tends four hectares of vineyards around his typical Garda country house. His Mal Borghetto '98 Benaco Bresciano Rosso is definitely very good. From a blend of merlot, rebo and barbera aged in barriques, it should be left to age in the cellar for a while.

● Benaco Bresciano Rosso Mal Borghetto '98	♀	4

Montini
Via Emilia, 21
27046 Santa Giuletta (PV)
Tel. 0383899231

The Montini estate started up in the early 19th century on land owned at the time by the noble Isimbardi family. The Rosso Riserva Eventi '94 is austere and very firm. The Bonarda Frizzante Vigna dei Frati is also very pleasant, chiefly because of its generous bouquet of wild berries.

● OP Bonarda Frizzante Vigna dei Frati '00	♀	3
● OP Rosso Riserva Eventi '94	♀	4

Bagnasco
Via Roma, 57
27047 Santa Maria della Versa (PV)
Tel. 0385278019 - 0385798033
E-mail: cantinabagnasco@virgilio.it

With the grapes from the ten hectares of vineyards on his property, Paolo Bagnasco has produced an excellent Bonarda Frizzante with an abundant bouquet of morello cherry and a tangy palate. The sweet, sparkling Sangue di Giuda, from barbera, croatina, uva rara and ughetta, is also pleasant.

● OP Bonarda Frizzante '00	♀	2*
● OP Sangue di Giuda '00	♀	3

Ca' Lojera
Loc. San Benedetto di Lugana
25019 Sirmione (BS)
Tel. 0457551901
E-mail: info@calojera.com

The Ca' Lojera estate of Franco Tiraboschi uses only the grapes grown on its 14 hectares of vineyards. The cellar releases an excellent Lugana Superiore '99, with notes of spices and exotic fruit, and a more than merely good Lugana '99 Vigna Silva that has been partially aged for a short time in oak.

○ Lugana Sup. '99	♀♀	4
○ Lugana Vigna Silva '99	♀	3

F.lli Bettini
Loc. San Giacomo
Via Nazionale, 4/a
23036 Teglio
Tel. 0342786068 - 0342786096

This estate produces numerous Valtellina wines. The Sfursat from '98 confirms its traditional elegance. It has a spicy bouquet and a very well-balanced palate with pleasant hints of cocoa. The Inferno '97 Prodigio is very well-made.

- Valtellina Sup. Sfursat '98 ŦŦ 6
- Valtellina Sup. Inferno Prodigio '97 Ŧ 4

Plozza
Via S. Giacomo, 22
23037 Tirano (SO)
Tel. 0342701297
E-mail: infa@plozza.ch

The Plozza style has been more modern for the last few years but one decision is clear: leisurely ageing is the rule. The Riserva La Scala '96 has spicy aromas and a full, concentrated taste. The Sfursat Vin da Ca' '96 is slightly toasty on the nose and lively on the palate.

- Valtellina Sfurzat Vin da Ca' '96 ŦŦ 6
- Valtellina Sup. Riserva
  La Scala '96 ŦŦ 5

La Tordela
Via Torricelli, 1
24060 Torre de' Roveri (BG)
Tel. 035580172
E-mail: info@latordela.it

This estate has 20 hectares of vineyards, on the hill between the hollow of Torre dei Roveri and the Serradesca valley. The vines stand round the main residence, built at the end of the 16th century. The Valcalepio Rosso '98 is good but will improve with bottle ageing and acquire greater balance on the palate. For the time being, it is still a bit edgy.

- Valcalepio Rosso '98 Ŧ 3

Reale Boselli
Via Volta, 34
46049 Volta Mantovana (MN)
Tel. 037683409
E-mail: cantina.boselli@tin.it

The ancient Boselli cellars were making wine as far back as 1532. Their most outstanding product is the Rubino Vigna del Moro '98, from cabernet, sangiovese and merlot. An austere wine, it shows a bouquet of fruit preserves. The Cabernet Riserva '98 has good promise but needs to age a little longer.

- Garda Colli Mantontovani
  Cabernet Ris. '98 Ŧ 3
- Garda Colli Mantovani Rubino
  Vigna del Moro '98 Ŧ 4

TRENTINO

Trentino winemaking longs to go up a gear. It wants to get back to the top of the quality tree in Italy, a commitment that all the publicly funded bodies in this autonomous province continue to support. It was the Trento Chamber of Commerce that gave us invaluable help in organizing the tastings of the 400 or so wines submitted, and the Vallagarina Casa del Vino in Isera that provided the premises. Promising signs of progress emerged. Mostly, Trentino wines are well made and technically faultless but often enough they are also one-dimensional, too "correct", and struggle to express any character. This year's selection often combined a rather slight structure with somewhat vegetal hints on tasting. This is the fault of poorish recent vintages and the intense competition between the two winemaking giants of the region, both determined to conquer the market abroad with huge volumes and high turnovers – remember that the entire crop in Trentino is only about 1,000,000 quintals of grapes. Or it may derive from rivalry between co-operative wineries on the one hand and small producers on the other. It remains to say that we haven't made any great discoveries. The usual producers come out on top again and show themselves to be the real power behind Trentino's vinous renaissance. But it's hard to make this group expand. In our opinion, even the co-operatives are going through a flat period. Those that embraced the path of quality some time ago, sacrificing quantity, are paying the price in fierce competition inside the Trentino region. On the legislative side of things, the Trentino Superiore DOC zone has been set up. This could be a benefit, but we hope it doesn't also mean price increases for the consumer. Coming to more welcome news, we are happy to announce two new recruits to the Three Glass category. Ferrari, Foradori and Longariva are old hands. All credit to the new arrivals, then. The Cantina Sociale Rotaliana is a solid company in the Teroldego zone that has achieved its goals without recourse to advertising, concentrating only on the improvement of its wines. Then there is Azienda Agricola Pravis, from Lasino, with a wine that justifies their efforts to safeguard the typicity of products from the Valle dei Laghi. Five wines altogether have been awarded the Guide's top accolade while another 20 will have to be content with "near misses" for a third Glass. A sign that something is changing. All things considered, for the better.

ALA (TN)

ALESSANDRO SECCHI
FRAZ. SERRAVALLE ALL' ADIGE
VIA CONI ZUGNA, 5
38060 ALA (TN)
TEL. 0464696647
E-MAIL: info@sechivini.it

The wines of Alessandro Secchi, the young grower oenologist from the Vallagarina area, were some of the few exciting surprises we discovered in the hundreds of Trentino wines submitted to us for tasting. He's been in charge for just five years of the ten hectare or so family agricultural estate, located in the vineyard-rich southern end of the valley. The rows of vines almost reach into the modern little winery itself, so close are the vineyards. This is grape growing on an artisanal scale, painstaking stuff, aimed at providing the raw material for small batch fermentation on the premises. The wine that impressed us most is the Berillo d'Oro, a blend of chardonnay, sauvignon and pinot grigio, assembled in steel tanks to give a typical straw yellow colour with bright reflections. Aromatic and attractive, it bears the mark of a sure hand during vinification. The Corindone Rosso is typically Trentino in style. An elegant, well-balanced Bordeaux blend and worthy son of the soil, it brings out like few others the typical characteristics of the great red wine-producing Bassa Vallagarina zone. Full-bodied on the palate with a good dose of tannins; fruity but evolving on the nose; well defined and spicy, too, with a caressing mouthfeel. The Pinot Nero also has a rich bouquet and a clean palate; fascinating colour, too, like a coral gemstone. Praise for the Marzemino, as well. Perhaps more concentrated than others, it displayed an enviable freshness, and was light and most enjoyable on the palate. The Cabernet Sauvignon, on the other hand, still needs some ageing. It's not yet fully balanced. Alessandro Secchi, however, is on the right road.

○	Berillo d'Oro '00	4
●	Corindone Rosso '99	4
●	Trentino Marzemino '00	3
●	Cabernet Sauvignon '99	4
●	Pinot Nero '99	4

AVIO (TN)

CANTINA SOCIALE DI AVIO
VIA DANTE, 14
38063 AVIO (TN)
TEL. 0464684008
E-MAIL: cantinasocialediavio.can@tin.it

Alfonso Iannelli runs this co-operative winery shrewdly. With his technical staff, he has launched a programme of radical rethinking, both in the vineyards and in the range of wines produced. Member-growers are changing their methods of cultivation, experimenting with new rootstocks to contain the natural vigour of the vines so as to reduce yields and increase quality. At the winery, rigorous selection in the vineyards is reflected in all phases of vinification and maturation to produce an excellent series of cru wines. It's a project based on teamwork, and there's no lack of enthusiasm. The early results are already in the glass. The Bordeaux-style red has more character with this vintage. Dark and opaque with a deep ruby red colour, it shows a well-developed berry fruit bouquet and is full-bodied and powerful on the palate. For centuries, this area has been the home of a very typical Lagarino grape called lambrusco a foglia frastagliata (literally "jagged leaf lambrusco"), which is used to make a wine called Enantio. The version produced here has a deep red colour with bright reflections, and a bouquet of cherries and quina, while examination on the palate shows it to be well-balanced and well-made. The Marzemino is equally good, with nice concentration, satisfying weight and an attractive bitter twist on the finish. The whites were not as successful, in our opinion. Both the Pinot Grigio and the Pinot Bianco were, however, correct enough – fresh and fruity. The Trentino Bianco blend lacked complexity while the late-harvest 11 Novembre was more interesting than ever, with hints of dried flowers and quinces on the palate.

●	Trentino Marzemino '00	3
●	Trentino Rosso Ris. '98	4
○	Trentino Vendemmia Tardiva '99	4
○	Trentino Pinot Bianco '00	3
○	Trentino Pinot Grigio '00	3
●	Enantio '99	3
○	Trentino Bianco '99	4
●	Trentino Rosso Ris. '96	4
●	Trentino Pinot Nero '97	3
●	Trentino Rosso Ris. '97	4
○	11 Novembre '97	4
●	Trentino Enantio '98	2
○	Trentino Vendemmia Tardiva '98	4
●	Trentino Pinot Nero '98	3
●	Trentino Marzemino '99	2

AVIO (TN)

TENUTA SAN LEONARDO
FRAZ. BORGHETTO ALL'ADIGE
LOC. SAN LEONARDO, 3
38060 AVIO (TN)
TEL. 0464689004
E-MAIL: info@sanleonardo.it

The absence of the San Leonardo in this year's list of award-winning wines is not as amazing as it seems. It simply doesn't exist. Mindful of his commitment to top quality, Carlo Guerrieri Gonzaga thought the 1998 vintage unworthy of consideration for the jewel in his vinous crown. A stark decision that allowed him to devote even more time to the development of his beautiful winemaking estate. And come out with something new. The first result was the construction of a new vinification cellar, technologically state-of-the-art and finished in record time. Vines of little commercial use have also been replaced with new graftings of cabernet and merlot, and there are innovative training methods, based on drastic reductions in yields per hectare. While the San Leonardo 1999 matures patiently in its casks, we took the opportunity to taste the other wine produced by this prize-winning winery, the Merlot. Beautiful garnet red colour, bright and intense; cherries and strawberries on the nose are balanced by elegant hints of vanilla; splendid palate, good depth of extract with firm mouthfeel and soft, sweet tannins; velvety texture. Such characteristics will do much for the prestige of this wine. Indeed, Carlo Guerrieri Gonzaga and his son Anselmo, who has joined the cellar team in recent months, are hoping for great things from it. There are 50,000 bottles of this top class Merlot, one of the best we have tasted in Trentino, and they have been put on the market at the very reasonable price of less than € 8.00 a bottle – at the cellar door, not in the wine shops. A great bargain.

AVIO (TN)

VALLAROM
FRAZ. VO' SINISTRO
VIA MASI, 21
38063 AVIO (TN)
TEL. 0464684297
E-MAIL: vallarom@libero.it

Barbara and Filippo Scienza have only been running this solid family business for a few vintages but they have already displayed both expertise and much enthusiasm. The wines that we tasted showed very well. Nine different wines, all well-made and showing good individual characteristics, with a special mention for the reds. To start with, the Syrah. It has good depth of flavour, with appropriate spicy tones and good length on the finish, and will keep well, growing in complexity over time. The Pinot Nero is just as good. A subtle and sophisticated wine, it shows greater bouquet than usual, probably because of the generally favourable 1999 vintage in the lower part of Vallagarina. The 1999 vintage also shows well in the Bordeaux-blend Campi Sarni, a powerful red that suffers from being tasted so young. It needs time to flesh out its intrinsic, and already emerging, qualities. The standard-label Cabernet Sauvignon is always good with its hints of wood and slight vegetal nuances. The last red, the Marzemino, is a full-bodied red made in the traditional local style that concentrates more on structure and flavour than fruitiness, but has good vinosity and characteristic hints of Parma violets on the nose. Of the whites, the Chardonnay Riserva Vigna Brioni is full and rich on the nose with a bouquet of tropical fruit mixed with hints of vanilla. The traditional-style Chardonnay is less well developed, like the other two whites, the Pinot Bianco and the Campi Sarni 2000. Both are too young as yet to show their undoubted quality.

● Trentino Merlot '99	🍷🍷	4
● San Leonardo '88	🍷🍷🍷	5
● San Leonardo '90	🍷🍷🍷	5
● San Leonardo '93	🍷🍷🍷	5
● San Leonardo '94	🍷🍷🍷	5
● San Leonardo '95	🍷🍷🍷	5
● San Leonardo '96	🍷🍷🍷	5
● San Leonardo '97	🍷🍷🍷	5
● Trentino Cabernet '93	🍷🍷	3
● Trentino Cabernet '94	🍷🍷	3
● Trentino Merlot '92	🍷🍷	3
● Trentino Merlot '95	🍷🍷	3
● Trentino Merlot '96	🍷🍷	3
● Trentino Merlot '97	🍷🍷	3
● Trentino Merlot '98	🍷🍷	4

● Campi Sarni '99	🍷🍷	4
● Syrah '99	🍷🍷	4
○ Trentino Chardonnay Vigna Brioni '99	🍷🍷	4
● Trentino Pinot Nero '99	🍷🍷	4
○ Campi Sarni Bianco '00	🍷	4
○ Trentino Chardonnay '00	🍷	4
● Trentino Marzemino '00	🍷	3
○ Trentino Pinot Bianco '00	🍷	4
● Trentino Cabernet Sauvignon '99	🍷	4
● Campi Sarni '98	🍷🍷	4
● Trentino Cabernet Sauvignon Vign. Belvedere '98	🍷🍷	4
○ Trentino Chardonnay Vign. Lavine '98	🍷🍷	4
● Trentino Pinot Nero Vign. Ventrat '98	🍷	4
● Trentino Marzemino Vign. Capitello '99	🍷	4

CALLIANO (TN)

Vallis Agri
Via Valentini, 37
38060 Calliano (TN)
tel. 0464834113

Rarely have we tasted such a good Marzemino. The Vigna Fornàs selection is truly delightful, a tangible sign of how this winery wants to develop in its drive for quality, concentrating its best efforts on Marzemino itself. It was no accident when SAV, the Società Agricoltori della Vallagarina, set up Vallis Agri specially to identify the best wines. Mission accomplished, you could say, because after a few years of ups and downs, Vallis Agri is forging ahead with confidence. Which is fully borne out by the selection of wines we were given for tasting. The Marzemino dei Ziresi Vigna Fornàs also won us over because of its touch of complexity, so rare with this grape type. The Merlot was complex, too. Simply named Borgosacco, after a vineyard-clad bowl in the Adige valley, it is soft, velvety and well-structured. Talking of selections, the winery has attributed a rural landmark, a campanile or a capital for example, to each of its special cuvées, to denote the origin of the wine. A worthy series of wines from a worthy selection of vineyards, scattered along Vallagarina. Don't miss the white Vigna Prà dei Fanti, a traditional blend of chardonnay and pinot bianco, which is good on both nose and palate. The Pinot Grigio Vigna Reselé is fruity with hints of pears and a good depth of flavour. The Aura is most unusual, an elegant blend of sauvignon and chardonnay, with a broad bouquet on the nose and a firm palate. Of the reds, praise goes to the two standard-label Marzeminos and the easy-drinking, well-structured Cabernet S. Ilario.

CIVEZZANO (TN)

Maso Cantanghel
Loc. Forte
Via Madonnina, 33
38045 Civezzano (TN)
tel. 0461859050

It's been an odd year for this fine grower-producer. Last year's vintage certainly didn't help the white grapes. Which you see in the chardonnay-based Vigna Piccola and the Solitaire, from sauvignon, two wines that are both well-made but unbalanced by excess acidity. The former has attractive hints of jasmine and hazelnuts, while the Solitaire is pleasingly confident with yellow plums and walnutskin both on nose and palate. The 1999 vintage wines are decidedly better, the reds in particular. To start with, Rosso di Pila. The mid ruby red leads in to an upfront nose of bitter cherries and spices. It is soft, full-bodied and elegant on the palate, thanks to the fine quality of the cabernet grapes that go into its make-up. The Pinot Nero is an established classic. The 1999 is excellent, with a more exciting bouquet than previous vintages. It's less full bodied, though, with a slight imbalance between the alcohol and the extract. Very soft and slightly astringent, perhaps it will improve with age. The Tajapreda shows a good colour, good nose and long finish, even if it will always be a simple wine deliberately made for easy drinking. Piero Zabini feels confident enough in his fascinating winery lodged in an old Austro-Hungarian fort that once defended the Sugana valley. He's right. All he needs are some better vintages.

○	Trentino Bianco Vigna Prà dei Fanti '00	♆♆	3*
●	Trentino Marzemino dei Ziresi V. Fornàs '00	♆♆	4
●	Trentino Merlot Borgosacco '98	♆♆	4
○	Aura '00	♆	3
●	Trentino Marzemino '00	♆	3
●	Trentino Marzemino dei Ziresi '00	♆	3*
○	Trentino Pinot Grigio Vigna Reselé '00	♆	3
●	Trentino Cabernet Sauvignon Sant'Ilario '98	♆	4
●	Trentino Cabernet Sauvignon Sant'Ilario '95	♆♆	4
●	Trentino Marzemino dei Ziresi '96	♆♆	3
○	Trentino Moscato Giallo '97	♆♆	3
●	Trentino Marzemino dei Ziresi '98	♆♆	3
○	Trentino Nosiola '99	♆♆	3
○	Trentino Pinot Bianco '99	♆♆	3
●	Trentino Marzemino dei Ziresi '99	♆	3

●	Trentino Cabernet Sauvignon Rosso di Pila '99	♆♆	5
○	Trentino Chardonnay Vigna Piccola '00	♆	4
●	Trentino Merlot Tajapreda '00	♆	4
○	Trentino Sauvignon Solitaire '00	♆	4
●	Trentino Pinot Nero Zabini '99	♆	5
●	Trentino Cabernet Sauvignon Rosso di Pila '95	♆♆	5
●	Trentino Cabernet Sauvignon Rosso di Pila '96	♆♆	5
●	Trentino Cabernet Sauvignon Rosso di Pila '97	♆♆	5
●	Trentino Merlot Tajapreda '97	♆♆	3
●	Trentino Pinot Nero Zabini '98	♆♆	5

FAEDO (TN)

Graziano Fontana
Via Case Sparse, 9
38010 Faedo (TN)
tel. 0461650400

If Faedo has gone from being a tiny village no one had heard of to one of the most important bastions of viticulture and winemaking in Trentino, then some of the credit should go to the Fontana family. In a few short vintages, this microscopic cellar has squeezed its way into the big league. And not just in Trentino. Graziano Fontana, though, is a fine wineman and hasn't let it go to his head. He carries on making wine. His peers look on him as an excellent maker of red wines, above all because of one or two Lagreins that he released to general amazement at their concentration and sheer complexity. Graziano's Lagrein is in fact one of the best in Trentino. This year's version is headily fragrant and full-bodied, with a delicious palate of ripe cherries. However, our hero has never neglected his whites and this year, the Sauvignon has garnered universal praise. At every competitive tasting, at local level or on larger, more selective stages, it has invariably stood out. We found the range of aromas on the nose was very broad, a tad green with subtle notes of elderflower and red peppers. The front palate reveals well-controlled acidity on the tongue, following on with well-sustained, rounded apple and peach fruit. The Müller Thurgau and Traminer are very good. Both are lean-bodied, fresh-tasting and very approachable while the Traminer is a little saltier than usual. The clean but rather subdued Chardonnay fails to convince entirely but we may have tasted it too young. Finally, the '99 vintage was unkind to the Pinot Nero, which is slightly vegetal and lacks length.

FAEDO (TN)

Pojer & Sandri
Loc. Molini, 4/6
38010 Faedo (TN)
tel. 0461650342
e-mail: info@pajeresandri.it

Pojer & Sandri, Faedo, Trentino. Three names that add up to success. And this year, the wines are worthy of the pivotal role the cellar has in Trentino winemaking. Mario Pojer and Fiorentino Sandri have been working together for almost three decades, and the results have been almost invariably exceptional. We need only say that four of the 12 wines presented at our tastings went on to the Three Glass finals. All the other labels sailed past the Two Glass cut-off point. The Spumante, a special cuvée of several vintages, is quite splendid. Masterfully put together, it has body, flavour and harmony. Equally laudable is the elegance on the palate of the Faye Bianco. The nose-palate consistency is impeccable and the marriage of fruit and wood is an idyllic one. In contrast, the '98 vintage was a difficult one for the nice Bordeaux blend Faye. The panel were astonished at the finesse and body of the Traminer. Then both the standard-label and Riserva versions of the Pinot Nero were beautifully behaved with crisply defined aromas, vibrantly vigorous body and lots of staying power. Your drinking pleasure is also guaranteed by the Essenzia, a delicate late-harvest blend of various white varieties. Picked at the end of November, the grapes sheltered under fine nets to keep hungry birds at bay. The other wines, from the Chardonnay to the Nosiola, the Sauvignon and Rosato Vin dei Molini, not to mention the Müller Thurgau Palai, are decidedly good.

	Wine	Glasses	Score
○	Trentino Müller Thurgau di Faedo '00	♀	3*
○	Trentino Sauvignon di Faedo '00	♀♀	3
○	Trentino Chardonnay di Faedo '00	♀	3
○	Trentino Traminer di Faedo '00	♀	3
●	Trentino Lagrein di Faedo '99	♀	4
●	Trentino Pinot Nero di Faedo '99		4
●	Trentino Lagrein di Faedo '95	♀♀	3
○	Trentino Chardonnay di Faedo '97	♀♀	3
●	Trentino Lagrein di Faedo '97	♀♀	4
○	Trentino Müller Thurgau '97	♀♀	3
○	Trentino Sauvignon di Faedo '97	♀♀	3
●	Trentino Lagrein di Faedo '98	♀♀	4

	Wine	Glasses	Score
○	Bianco Faye '98	♀♀	4
○	Cuveé Extra Brut	♀♀	5
○	Essenzia Vendemmia Tardiva '99	♀♀	5
○	Trentino Traminer '00	♀♀	4
○	Palai '00	♀♀	3*
●	Pinot Nero '00	♀♀	4
○	Sauvignon Atesino '00	♀♀	4
○	Trentino Chardonnay '00	♀♀	4
○	Trentino Nosiola '00	♀♀	3*
◉	Vin dei Molini Rosato '00	♀♀	3
●	Pinot Nero Ris. '98	♀♀	5
●	Rosso Faye '98	♀♀	5
○	Bianco Faye '97	♀♀	4
●	Rosso Faye '97	♀♀	5
○	Essenzia Vendemmia Tardiva '98	♀♀	4

ISERA (TN)

DE TARCZAL
FRAZ. MARANO
VIA G. B. MIORI, 4
38060 ISERA (TN)
TEL. 0464409134
E-MAIL: tarczal@tin.it

Few wines but good ones. Ruggero de Tarczal is a winemaker whose principles are as noble as his blood. He will only bottle wines that he believes worthy of the honour. Quantity and instant market appeal are the last of his worries. Ruggero manages his flourishing estate with an entrepreneur's flair but he has never relinquished the healthy habits of the past. He keeps in step with the slow rhythms of the seasons, the rhythms that also improves the quality of life. Lucky him. From his country residence, he directs operations not just in the adjoining vineyards. He also selects grapes from vineyards many kilometres away to ensure that only the finest fruit goes into his cellar. That's the story behind his latest wine, born in the hills of Matterello near Trento, the Pianilonghi, a monovarietal cabernet sauvignon. Already, this wine is showing the hallmarks of greatness. It has concentration, depth, subtle aromas and tannins that are still young. The Merlot comes from nearer home, in the vineyards at Campiano. It foregrounds vegetal notes on the nose, which lead in to a straightforward but clean palate. Then there's the Marzemino, another estate star, which combines approachable drinkability with more than decent structure. Finally, we sampled the delicious, traditional-style Pinot Bianco, the only white that Ruggero de Tarczal presented for tasting.

ISERA (TN)

CANTINA D'ISERA
VIA AL PONTE, 1
38060 ISERA (TN)
TEL. 0464433795
E-MAIL: info@cantinaisera.it

Few co-operative wineries in Trentino are prepared to go for real quality, the kind that demands severe selection in the vineyard and equally scrupulous cellar management. One such, however, is the Cantina d'Isera, which has 200 members, with 200 hectares under vine, bringing in 22,000 quintals of fruit. The facilities have been renewed, an alliance has been forged with Cavit, a prize for the best vineyard has been instituted and the average quality of the range has been further enhanced. We'll start with the Marzemino, the cellar's flagship wine. There were two versions at our tastings, one traditional and the Novecentosette selection, which has a distinctive green label. Both are ruby red, with subtle, alcohol-rich aromas where Parma violets come through. The palate is full and well-balanced. But there were other fine reds. Sentieri is a Bordeaux blend with complex aromas and a full, attractively tannic palate. The firmly structured Merlot is vinous and very fruity. The same can be said of the Cabernet, which is still a little edgy but well-made and attractively long. The rebo grape is a cross between marzemino and merlot, although DNA laboratory tests have identified the teroldego gene. The garnet red wine it produces offers a fine entry on the nose and a remarkably full, elegantly soft palate. We tasted many other wines from the cellar. The quaffable Moscato Giallo deserves a special mention for attractively light aromatic note. The well-made Müller Thurgau and Sauvignon, two authentic sons of the Trentino soil, round off the d'Isera range.

● Trentino Marzemino d'Isera Husar '00	♀♀	3*
● Trentino Cabernet Pianilonghi '99	♀♀	4
● Trentino Merlot Campiano '99	♀♀	4
○ Trentino Pinot Bianco '00	♀	3
● Trentino Marzemino d'Isera Husar '97	♀♀	4
● Trentino Merlot Campiano '97	♀♀	4
● Trentino Marzemino d'Isera Husar '98	♀♀	4
○ Trentino Chardonnay '99	♀♀	3
● Trentino Marzemino d'Isera Husar '99	♀♀	4
○ Trentino Pinot Bianco '99	♀♀	3

● Trentino Marzemino Etichetta Verde '00	♀♀	3*
● Trentino Rosso Sentieri '98	♀♀	4
● Trentino Cabernet '00	♀	3
● Trentino Merlot '00	♀	3
○ Trentino Moscato Giallo '00	♀	3
○ Trentino Müller Thurgau '00	♀	3
○ Trentino Sauvignon '00	♀	3
● Trentino Rebo Novecentosette '98	♀	3
● Trentino Rosso Novecentosette '97	♀♀	3
● Trentino Marzemino Etichetta Verde '99	♀♀	3

ISERA (TN)

ENRICO SPAGNOLLI
VIA G. B. ROSINA, 4/A
38060 ISERA (TN)
TEL. 0464409054
E-MAIL: cnrspagn@tin.it

Luigi Spagnolli is a cellarman who loves growing vines. In fact, you're more likely to find him out among the rows than indoors for he follows the growth cycle of his stock from close at hand, always ready to trim here, thin there or check up on the sugar content of the berries. At Villalagarina, a stone's throw from the winery, he is experimenting with ancient local varieties and other vines that he has acquired in distant lands. Spagnollis have been making wine here at Isera for more than half a century. Gigi, as his friends call him, has always loved marzemino, a native variety emblematic of Isera. But when he took over the family winery, he decided to focus on other grapes, pay more attention to what was happening elsewhere and generally look to the future. He has planted merlot and cabernet, for example, but also pinot nero, traminer aromatico and even nosiola. It is no coincidence that recent tastings have brought rewards for Gigi's intuition. His major Bordeaux blend is called Tebro. A seriously muscular red with a dense colour, it has a nose of bramble and cherry jam, ushering in a mouthfilling flavour and delicious fine-grained tannins. It will be even better after ageing in the bottle for while. There were good marks for the Pinot Nero, a very typical wine with upfront aromas. It just needs a tad more concentration to be perfect. The cellarman's skills are evident in the two whites, especially the Traminer Aromatico, an unusual wine to find in Vallagarina. Spagnolli manages to infuse it with rich colour, spicy aromas and notes of wild roses and jasmine. The full palate shows lovely weight. Next came the Nosiola, which is less lean than many similar wines, and to close the show is the nicely made Marzemino, which sells at very competitive prices.

○	Trentino Traminer Aromatico '00	▼▼	4
●	Trentino Pinot Nero '99	▼▼	4
●	Trentino Rosso Tebro '99	▼▼	4
●	Trentino Marzemino '00	▼	3*
○	Trentino Nosiola '00	▼	3
●	Trentino Rosso Tebro '96	▼▼	4
○	Trentino Gewürztraminer '97	▼▼	3
●	Trentino Pinot Nero '97	▼▼	4
●	Trentino Rosso Tebro '97	▼▼	4
●	Trentino Rosso Tebro '98	▼▼	4
○	Trentino Müller Thurgau '98	▼	3
●	Trentino Pinot Nero '98	▼	3
●	Trentino Marzemino '99	▼	3

LASINO (TN)

PISONI
LOC. SARGHE - FRAZ. PERGOLESE
VIA SAN SIRO, 7/B
38076 LASINO (TN)
TEL. 0461563216
E-MAIL: pisoagri@iol.it

The Pisonis have always made wine. In the mid 16th century, prelates ordered their tenants to make wine with grapes from Vallagarina, the "Valley of the Lakes", for banquets and daily Mass. The Pisonis still make communion wine but they have never stopped renewing their range and their vine stock. That's especially true since the estate was taken over by young Marco and Stefano, both graduates of the wine school at San Michele all'Adige and both determined to rethink the property's vineyard management. The vines are on the sun-drenched hillslopes that separate the lakes of Santa Massenza, Toblino and Cavedine from the plain that leads down to Lake Garda. The Pisonis were among the first to produce a classic method spumante. They've been making it for more than 30 years, leaving the bottles to age in a cave carved deep into the living rock. The sparklers are upfront and jolly, as you might expect from a jovial cellar like this. The still wines are just as affable. Sarica is a red named after the pair's eldest daughters, Sara and Federica, and comes from an unusual blend of syrah and pinot nero. As in the past, it is the best Pisoni wine. Warm, mouthfilling and lavish with its elegant varietal notes, it proffers a supple body and good length on the palate. There is a nice note of wild brambles in the after-aroma. Next, we tried the wines obtained from nosiola, a grape that is native to the valley. The traditional version is fresh-tasting, direct and clean. Vino Santo '93 is from dried grapes pressed during Easter week. It's not yet on top form, which may be because we tasted it too soon after bottling. It is one of the few decent examples of this wine type to be found in Trentino.

●	Sarica '99	▼▼	4
○	Trentino Nosiola '00	▼	3
○	Trentino Vino Santo '93	▼	5
○	Trento Brut	▼	4
○	Trentino Vino Santo '90	▼▼	5
○	Trentino Vino Santo '92	▼▼	5
●	Sarica '98	▼▼	4
○	Trento Brut Ris. '92	▼	4
○	Trentino Nosiola '98	▼	3
●	Trentino Rosso San Siro '98	▼	3
○	Trentino Nosiola '99	▼	3

LASINO (TN)

Pravis
Via Lagolo, 26
38076 Lasino (TN)
tel. 0461564305

Simplicity and authenticity can transform an apparently ordinary wine into one of rare fascination. Pravis is celebrating the completion of the new cellar, on the hill at Castel Madruzzo, in the best possible manner – with Three Glasses. The wine in question is Stravino di Stravino. It's a white from fruit harvested in the rows that point to the village of Stravino, in the heart of the "Valley of the Lakes", as Vallagarina is known, between Trento and Lake Garda. Gianni Chisté, Domenico Pedrini and Mario Zambarda spent years experimenting in cellar and vineyard to make this masterpiece. The planted special lots of riesling renano, incrocio Manzoni, chardonnay and sauvignon in carefully selected vineyards, harvesting as late as possible; in fact the riesling was left to become super-ripe on the vine. The chardonnay is oak-fermented and small-batch fermentation in stainless steel was used to preserve aromas. Put all that together and you get Stravino di Stravino. An exciting lustrous gold ushers in a range of spring flower aromas that mingle with quince and honey. The palate follows through, adding pineapple and peach over a satisfyingly rich, buttery structure with a very fresh finish. The cellar's progress can also be seen in the Syrae, a monovarietal syrah with a spicy personality, nice roundness and a muscular palate. Also impressive was the first edition of the Niergal, an anagram of "lagrein", the grape with which it is made. Alcohol-rich and concentrated, it reveals a delicious background note of balsam. The franconia-based Destrani and the El Filò, from groppello noneso, are very unusual wines. The rest of the range is well-made.

LAVIS (TN)

Nilo Bolognani
Via Stazione, 19
38015 Lavis (TN)
tel. 0461246354
e-mail: dibolog@tin.it

The lovely estate run by owner Diego Bolognani, with the help of his large family, served up four expertly made whites when the panel called. The Bolognanis are a winemaking dynasty that has always striven for perfection. That goes especially for Diego, a tireless experimenter and imaginative inventor of mechanical equipment, such as presses and special filters, to keep the must on top form after pressing. This technical bent comes through in the personality of the wines, although some of Diego's more eccentric adventures have never been repeated. All this points to maturity and a well-balanced production philosophy, founded on scrupulous selection of the fruit bought in from a few, tried and trusted growers at Laviso and in the nearby Val di Cembra. There were just the four whites because the eagerly awaited Teroldego, the first wine from grapes grown in estate-owned vineyards, is still ageing in its barrels. The Müller Thurgau, then, was the first wine we tasted. The light aromatic palate is offset by marked acidity that perhaps derives from the location of the vines, on the upper slopes of Val di Cembra. Also outstanding was the limpid, crystalline Sauvignon, whose shimmering hues are flecked with green. Faintly vegetal on the nose, it has a slightly sinewy palate, rich in fruit, as befits a wine of this type. As ever, the Nosiola and Moscato Giallo are very well-made. They may not be as rich as some but they are a delight to drink.

○	Stravino di Stravino '99	🍷🍷🍷	5
●	Syrae '99	🍷🍷	5
●	Niergal '99	🍷🍷	5
●	Destrani '00	🍷	4
●	El Filò '00	🍷	4
○	Nosiola Le Frate '00	🍷	4
○	Trentino Müller Thurgau St. Thomà '00	🍷	4
●	Syrae '96	🍷🍷	4
●	Syrae '97	🍷🍷	4
●	Trentino Rebo Rigotti '97	🍷🍷	3
●	Syrae '98	🍷🍷	4
●	Trentino Cabernet Fratagranda '98	🍷🍷	4
○	Trentino Müller Thurgau St. Thomà '99	🍷🍷	3

○	Trentino Müller Thurgau '00	🍷🍷	3
○	Trentino Sauvignon '00	🍷🍷	3
○	Trentino Moscato Giallo '00	🍷	3
○	Trentino Nosiola '00	🍷	3
○	Müller Thurgau della Val di Cembra '96	🍷🍷	3
○	Trentino Moscato Giallo '96	🍷🍷	3
○	Trentino Moscato Giallo '97	🍷🍷	3
○	Trentino Sauvignon '97	🍷🍷	3
○	Trentino Müller Thurgau '98	🍷🍷	3
○	Trentino Sauvignon '98	🍷🍷	3
○	Trentino Chardonnay '99	🍷🍷	3
○	Trentino Müller Thurgau '99	🍷🍷	3
○	Trentino Nosiola '99	🍷	3
○	Trentino Pinot Grigio '99	🍷	3

LAVIS (TN)

Casata Monfort
Via Garibaldi, 11
38015 Lavis (TN)
tel. 0461241484

Thinking at Casata Monfort seems at last to have embraced the best elements of local tradition. In short, it's back to the land, and back to the vineyard. This is a major, and very welcome, shift in the focus of an estate that has been making wine for more than half a century. The Simoni brothers will now only crush small lots of fruit to make their carefully crafted wines if the weather and developments in the field are favourable. Bottles like Credazi, a late-harvest Müller Thurgau, or Monfort Giallo, the sweet version of the Trentino Moscato Giallo, or the Monfort Rosa, from the hard-to-find moscato rosa variety. In fact, the quantities released are so tiny that you we have not included them in the Glass table under this profile. The '00 harvest was a good one for the Traminer, which is one of the best we have tasted. Deep straw yellow, it offers a generous range of aromas that hints at roses, figs and geraniums, showing good thrust on the palate, where the structure is broad and well-sustained. The fragrant, juicy Pinot Grigio is clean and even on the palate. Then comes the Chardonnay, which is anything but one-dimensional with crusty bread and ripe golden delicious apple aromas that shift from sweet to more acidulous notes. The other white, the Müller Thurgau, is very consistent, foregrounding freshness and tangy acidity. Rounding off the range are two reds, the Lagrein and the Pinot Nero, both aged in small oak barrels. Both – the former in particular – are thoroughbreds: full-bodied, rich and far removed from the rustic wines that are so often the norm among Trentino Lagreins.

○	Trentino Traminer Aromatico '00	♈♈	4
○	Trentino Chardonnay '00	♈	4
○	Trentino Müller Thurgau '00	♈	4
○	Trentino Pinot Grigio '00	♈	4
●	Trentino Lagrein Sel. '98	♈	4
○	Trentino Chardonnay '95	♈♈	3
○	Trentino Chardonnay '99	♈♈	3
○	Trentino Müller Thurgau '99	♈♈	3
○	Trentino Pinot Grigio '99	♈♈	3
○	Trentino Brut M. Cl.	♈♈	5
●	Trentino Lagrein '95	♈	3
●	Trentino Lagrein '98	♈	4
○	Trentino Traminer Aromatico '99	♈	4

LAVIS (TN)

Cesconi
Fraz. Pressano
Via Marconi, 39
38015 Lavis (TN)
tel. 0461240355
e-mail: cesconi@cr-surfing.net

Few other Trentino estates have olive groves planted so close to vines. This is true both in the lower Sarca valley, near Lake Garda, where the Cesconis grow exclusively red varieties, and up here on the hills at Lavis, where the olives grow right at the northern limit of their distribution in the Mediterranean. And it is the olive, or "olivar" in the local dialect, that has given its name to the white Cesconi blend that best represents the cellar style. You won't find Olivar in the list of Three Glass wines, but not for want of trying. An almost perfect white, it has body, well-gauged aromas and a well-defined, silky-soft mouthfeel. The other whites also impressed. Chardonnay, Pinot Grigio, Nosiola and Traminer are excellent. We particularly liked the Traminer, a spicy wine with hints of orange and tangerine mingling with mint and jasmine, and the Nosiola, as usual in a full-flavoured version with the sort of structure this grape rarely achieves. There were favourable comments for the Chardonnay, with its sweet notes of apple and pear fruit. Next was the Pinot Grigio, offering generous, inviting notes of pear. This year, the reds are ageing in the newly completed cellar. We'll be tasting them later on. In all likelihood, these highly competent winemakers will have to wait a few years for their vine stock to reach maturity.

○	Olivar '00	♈♈	4
○	Trentino Chardonnay '00	♈♈	4
○	Trentino Pinot Grigio '00	♈♈	4
○	Trentino Traminer Aromatico '00	♈♈	4
○	Trentino Nosiola '00	♈	4
○	Trentino Pinot Grigio '98	♈♈♈	4
●	Trentino Cabernet '98	♈♈	4
●	Trentino Merlot '98	♈♈	4
○	Trentino Sauvignon '98	♈♈	4
○	Olivar '99	♈♈	4
○	Trentino Chardonnay '99	♈♈	4
○	Trentino Nosiola '99	♈♈	4
○	Trentino Pinot Grigio '99	♈♈	4
○	Trentino Sauvignon '99	♈♈	4
○	Trentino Traminer Aromatico '99	♈♈	4

LAVIS (TN)

VIGNAIOLO GIUSEPPE FANTI
FRAZ. PRESSANO
P.ZZA CROCE, 3
38015 LAVIS (TN)
TEL. 0461240809
E-MAIL: alessandro.fanti@katamail.com

The Fantis have been making wine at Pressano for two centuries. They cultivate small plots scattered over the hills at Lavis, lavishing the same care on them as they would on a garden. This is craft winemaking in the traditional country style. And the cellar is very much in the same tradition. Located near the village church, its barrels and winemaking gear are tidily tucked away in an old house with a characteristic porticoed entrance. For the past few harvests, vineyard management has been the responsibility of Alessandro, a young graduate of the San Michele all'Adige wine school. He works with a will and the early results are seriously good. Alessandro's wines have great texture and character – a fine tribute to the Fanti winemaking heritage. One bottle made it through to the final tastings and it was only by the merest of margins that the Chardonnay Robur failed to win a third Glass. A gold wine, opulent in hue and flavour, it is full-bodied, rich and evolved, offering hints of tropical fruit splendidly veined with acidity. Equally good is the Portico Rosso, a 50-50 blend of cabernet franc and merlot. Dark ruby red in hue, it has a similarly intense, spicily etheric aroma and a harmonious palate, silky soft with a lingering tight-knit texture. Two outstanding wines, flanked by a very personal range. Such as the Incrocio Manzoni, a crossing of riesling and pinot bianco that melds mineral fragrances with tangy notes of ripe apples. The clear, green-flecked yellow Nosiola is also attractively zesty, if modestly aromatic. Finally, the Chardonnay is fresh-tasting, upfront, lean and appealingly coherent.

LAVIS (TN)

LA VIS
VIA CARMINE, 12
38015 LAVIS (TN)
TEL. 0461246325
E-MAIL: cantina@la-vis.com

"Vis" means "strength" in Latin and this co-operative winery, which brings together the best growers in Lavis, Sorni and Salorno, as well as a few in the hills leading to the nearby Val di Cembra, continues to show the way. It was the first co-operative winery in Trentino to set up a zoning-based quality project involving radical changes in vine management, strict environmental standards and a determination to make modern products that are still identifiable as authentically Trentino wines. In a few short years, they have restructured their offices, cellars and members' vineyards, establishing a new, mould-breaking way to make wine in Trentino. Recent tastings revealed no real stars, even though the latest edition of Ritratto Bianco behaved very well indeed, and has all the makings of a champion. Another very nice white is the Chardonnay from the Ritratti range. Full-bodied and still a little closed on the nose, it has lovely structure on the palate. The Pinot Grigio Ritratti is notably fruit-rich and the Pinot Nero from the same range is one of the best in Trentino. The vineyards of Salorno, a municipality in Alto Adige, supply fruit for the Ceolan range, which La Vis vinifies with all due respect. The Chardonnay is flavoursome, the Lagrein vigorous and attractive. Like all La Vis wines.

○	Trentino Chardonnay Robur '99	▼▼	4
●	Portico Rosso '98	▼▼	4
○	Incrocio Manzoni '00	▼▼	4
○	Trentino Chardonnay '00	▼	3
○	Trentino Nosiola '00	▼	3
●	Portico Rosso '97	▼▼	4
○	Trentino Chardonnay Robur '98	▼▼	3
○	Incrocio Manzoni '99	▼▼	3
○	Trentino Nosiola '99	▼	3

○	Ritratto Bianco '99	▼▼	4
○	A. A. Chardonnay Ceolan '00	▼▼	3
●	A. A. Lagrein Ceolan '00	▼▼	4
○	Trentino Chardonnay Ritratti '00	▼▼	4
○	Trentino Pinot Grigio Ritratti '00	▼▼	4
●	Trentino Pinot Nero Ritratti '99	▼▼	4
○	Ritratto '98	▼▼	4
●	Trentino Cabernet Sauvignon Ritratti '98	▼▼	4
○	A. A. Chardonnay Ceolan '99	▼▼	3
○	Mandolaia '99	▼▼	5
○	Trentino Chardonnay Ritratti '99	▼▼	4
●	Trentino Lagrein Maso Baldazzini '99	▼▼	3

LAVIS (TN)

Maso Furli
Via Furli, 32
38015 Lavis (TN)
tel. 0461240667

The Zanoni brothers are true winemen. The turn the fruit from the vines around their tiny property into excellent wines. Here, at their smallholding surrounded by densely planted rows in the only sun-favoured depression on the hills at Lavis, they make wines that connoisseurs clamour for. This year, the three Zanoni white masterpieces are joined by a red. All are outstanding. The Chardonnay is delicious, its superbly complex aromas, with their nuances of summer apples, putting it in a class of its own. Then the palate opens out irresistibly, its elegant notes showing faint nuances of super-ripeness. The Traminer is also marvellous. Crystal-clear both in hue and aromatic range, it proffers a rich, full body whose only, negligible, fault is a slight stiffening in the back palate. But these are mere details, which detract nothing from the vines. The less than favourable vintage is the real culprit. The year 2000 did little to help the growers of Lavis. The Sauvignon is very much in the same vein. A fragrant, intensely varietal wine, it will need to age in the bottle to be able reveal its true force. Finally, a word of praise for the first release of the red, the Maso Furli Rosso. A classic Bordeaux blend, it focuses on juicy, full-flavoured fruit, with hints of blackcurrant and bilberries backed up by solid, very fine-grained tannins. It's a great wine and beautifully rounds off the range from Marco and Giorgio Zanoni, two genuine wineman. As genuine as their exquisite wines.

MEZZOCORONA (TN)

Marco Donati
Via Cesare Battisti, 41
38016 Mezzocorona (TN)
tel. 0461604141

It didn't win Three Glasses this year but Marco Donati's Teroldego is still a super wine. The '99 Sangue del Drago is excellent: it just couldn't quite match the fullness of the previous vintage. A minor quibble, which detracts little or nothing from the quality of this austere Teroldego, an extraordinarily vigorous yet refined wine. Vino del Maso, a blend of teroldego, lagrein and merlo, has been released onto the market young so that winelovers can appreciate its warm, rich alcohol. The colour is dark and deep, the structure seriously robust. It will be interesting to see how it evolves in the next few years. The standard-label Teroldego deserves a comment to itself. Donati wants it to be purplish in colour and quaffable by nature. Notes of raspberry and bilberry are present on nose and palate. In short, it's a fleshy wine that is still fresh-tasting and very approachable. While the Novai, a blend of teroldego, cabernet and merlot, ages in the bottle prior to its imminent release, we enjoyed the tasty Terra del Noce, a well-structured white with a great range of aromas, and an exquisite Nosiola, before finishing with a delicious Lagrein Rosato, the more accessible blush version of the definitely demanding red.

○ Trentino Chardonnay '00	🍷🍷	4
○ Trentino Traminer Aromatico '00	🍷🍷	4
○ Trentino Sauvignon '00	🍷🍷	4
● Maso Furli Rosso '98	🍷🍷	4
○ Trentino Chardonnay '99	🍷🍷🍷	3
○ Trentino Sauvignon '98	🍷🍷	3
○ Trentino Traminer Aromatico '98	🍷🍷	3
○ Trentino Sauvignon '99	🍷🍷	3
○ Trentino Traminer Aromatico '99	🍷🍷	3
○ Trentino Chardonnay '98	🍷	3

● Teroldego Rotaliano Sangue del Drago '99	🍷🍷	4
● Teroldego Rotaliano '00	🍷🍷	3
○ Terre del Noce Bianco '00	🍷🍷	3
● Vino del Maso Rosso '99	🍷🍷	4
⊙ Trentino Lagrein Rosato '00	🍷	3
○ Trentino Nosiola '00	🍷	3
● Teroldego Rotaliano Sangue del Drago '98	🍷🍷🍷	4
○ Terre del Noce Bianco '95	🍷🍷	3
● Teroldego Rotaliano Sangue diel Drago '96	🍷🍷	4
○ Terre del Noce Bianco '96	🍷🍷	3
○ Terre del Noce Bianco '98	🍷🍷	4
● Vino del Maso Rosso '98	🍷🍷	4
● Teroldego Rotaliano '99	🍷🍷	3
○ Trentino Nosiola '99	🍷🍷	3

MEZZOCORONA (TN)

F.lli Dorigati
Via Dante, 5
38016 Mezzocorona (TN)
tel. 0461605313
e-mail: vini@dorigati.it

A nearly but not quite Three Glass thoroughbred and a fine sequence of excellent tasting results may not give the full picture. The wines from Fratelli Dorigati are very good indeed. Taste them and see. For five generations, Dorigatis have been growers and producers at Mezzocorona. Recently, young Michele, a qualified wine technician with a degree in biology, also joined the team. He adds his knowledge to that of father Franco and uncle Carlo. The Dorigatis have always made characterful wines and for the past few vintages, they have been making spumante with a few lots of chardonnay and pinot nero. Their sparkler, the Methius, is already in the front rank in Trentino and beyond. The bead is dense and lingering, the mousse firm, the aromas subtly expressive and the palate soft yet well-defined. We also found the rest of the range to be even better than usual. The standard-label Teroldego is purplish, headily aromatic and firmly structured. The Cabernet has finesse and a tempting, faintly grassy, nose of berry fruit and plenty of body. Then came the Pinot Grigio. Partly fermented in barriques, it is juicy and intriguingly acidulous. The very pale cherry, coppery pink Lagrein Rosato offers an intense, fruit-rich palate. Finally, the Dorigatis are among the very few producers of Rebo, from a crossing made by researcher Rebo Rigotti to combine the grace of merlot with the vigour of the native Trentino marzemino and teroldego varieties.

○ Trento Methius Ris. '94	♀♀	5
● Teroldego Rotaliano '00	♀♀	3*
○ Trentino Pinot Grigio '00	♀♀	3
◉ Trentino Lagrein Rosato '00	♀	3
● Trentino Rebo '00	♀	3
○ Trentino Cabernet '99	♀	3
○ Trento Methius Ris. '92	♀♀♀	5
○ Trento Methius Ris. '91	♀♀	5
○ Trento Methius Ris. '93	♀♀	5
● Teroldego Rotaliano '97	♀♀	3
● Teroldego Rotaliano Diedri Ris. '97	♀♀	5
● Teroldego Rotaliano Diedri Ris. '98	♀♀	5
○ Trentino Pinot Grigio '99	♀♀	3

MEZZOCORONA (TN)

MezzaCorona
Via IV Novembre, 127
38016 Mezzocorona (TN)
tel. 0461605163 - 0461616399

The large Mezzacorona co-operative winery is implementing its commercial strategy with determination and dynamism. The numbers are on their side. Turnover is up, the vine stock has grown – Mezzacorona has even purchased plots in Sicily – and the wines are consistently very good. Here, we have to say that reliability may be at the cost of a certain uniformity of style. But this is a transition period, we were assured by Mezzacorona executives. Further developments are imminent. In the meantime, it was again the Rotari spumante that stood out for personality. Both the Arte Italiana, as the traditional-style brut is called, and the Riserva are wines of character. Well-balance and well-made, they have a fine, persistent perlage, good structure and decent complexity. The latest Rotari Riserva, normally a very harmonious, concentrated wine, may lack a certain "je ne sais quoi" but it remains impressive. The other wines are as you would expect: fruit-rich, easy-drinking and occasionally intriguing. Such as the Pinot Grigio, a variety where Mezzacorona is a leading producer, turning out millions of bottles a year, and the Chardonnay. Moving on to the reds, only the Pinot Nero, and not the Merlot, won a second Glass this time. The Teroldego is well-balanced and has reasonable personality. Despite the large quantities produced, it shows attractive structure but cannot be counted as one of the best examples of the type.

● Trentino Pinot Nero '99	♀♀	3
○ Trento Rotari Ris. '97	♀♀	4
○ Trento Rotari Brut Arte Italiana	♀♀	4*
○ Trentino Chardonnay '00	♀	3
○ Trentino Pinot Grigio '00	♀	3
● Teroldego Rotaliano Ris. '98	♀	3*
● Trentino Merlot '99	♀	3
● Teroldego Rotaliano Ris. '94	♀♀	3
● Trentino Cabernet Sauvignon Oltresarca '94	♀♀	3
○ Trento Rotari Brut Ris. '94	♀♀	4
○ Trento Rotari Ris. '95	♀♀	4
● Teroldego Rotaliano Ris. '96	♀♀	3
● Teroldego Rotaliano Ris. '97	♀♀	3

MEZZOLOMBARDO (TN)

BARONE DE CLES
VIA G. MAZZINI, 18
38017 MEZZOLOMBARDO (TN)
TEL. 0461601081 - 0461602673
E-MAIL: baronedecles@tin.it

The historic Barone de Cles winery, always a reliable producer, regains its full Guide profile this year. The current range includes ten or so wines, obtained exclusively from estate-grown fruit. Much attention is focused on Teroldego, predictably enough. And the 2000 version is very exciting. Purplish ruby red, with clear, lustrous highlights, it offers crisp aromas of brambles and violets, and a vinous but well-defined flavour with lots of concentration and length. In a word, a Teroldego worthy of the Cles label. Another teroldego-based red, this time with a little added merlot, did very well at out tastings. It's the Rosso Cardinale, a wine that unveils great character after beguiling the palate with a velvet-soft attack. From mid palate through to the long finish, it is a robustly structured, surefooted red with a fine-grained tannic weave. This seriously good wine is dedicated to Bernardo Clesio, the cardinal who called the Council of Trent to launch the Counter-Reformation. Good as ever and a pleasure to drink, the traditional-style Lagrein is full-bodied, dark and richly fruity. In fact, it is very similar to the Teroldego, no surprise, really, as the original vines are thought to be genetic twins. The whites are good, if nothing really special. The Traminer has crisp, spicy aromas while the Chardonnay is a tad one-dimensional and considerably less complex than the reds from this blue-blooded cellar.

MEZZOLOMBARDO (TN)

CANTINA ROTALIANA
C.SO DEL POPOLO, 6
38017 MEZZOLOMBARDO (TN)
TEL. 0461601010 - 04616043323
E-MAIL: info@cantinarotaliana.it

We have to admit it. For several years, we have been passionate fans of the Teroldego made by this solid co-operative winery. We have believed in the quality and character of the wine, and in the ability of oenologist and cellar manager Luciano Lunelli's staff, not to mention the 280 member growers. Well, the '99 vintage was one for the record books. Not just here but for Teroldego all over Trentino. But especially at the Cantina Rotoliana, rightly considered the spiritual home of this powerful red wine. The Clesurae comes from experimental plantings, a project, monitored by technicians from the agricultural college at San Michele, which aims to exploit the full potential of the teroldego variety. Concentrated and muscular, yet approachable, flavoursome and instantly appealing: it has been some time since we last found such sheer quality in a wine from Trentino. Three Glasses and no mistake. The traditional versions of Teroldego are also excellent, and quite superb value for money, while the Canevarie selection whites are very persuasive. That goes for both the Pinot Bianco, with its distinctive fragrances and rock-solid structure, and the clean, fruity Pinot Grigio. Textbook wines, from a textbook co-operative winery, the Cantina Rotoliana.

Wine	Rating	Score
● Teroldego Rotaliano Maso Scari '00	🍷🍷	4
● Rosso del Cardinale '99	🍷🍷	5
○ Trentino Traminer '00	🍷	3
● Trentino Lagrein '98	🍷	4
○ Trentino Chardonnay '00		3
● Teroldego Rotaliano Maso Scari '96	🍷🍷	3
● Teroldego Rotaliano Maso Scari '97	🍷🍷	4
● Trentino Lagrein '96	🍷	3
● Trentino Lagrein '97	🍷	3

Wine	Rating	Score
● Teroldego Rotaliano Clesurae '99	🍷🍷🍷	4
● Teroldego Rotaliano '00	🍷🍷	2*
○ Trentino Pinot Bianco Canevarie '00	🍷🍷	4*
○ Trentino Pinot Grigio Canevarie '00	🍷🍷	4*
● Teroldego Rotaliano Ris. '98	🍷🍷	4*
● Teroldego Rotaliano '97	🍷🍷	2
● Teroldego Rotaliano Pieve Francescana '97	🍷🍷	4
● Teroldego Rotaliano '98	🍷🍷	2
● Teroldego Rotaliano '99	🍷	2

MEZZOLOMBARDO (TN)

FORADORI
VIA DAMIANO CHIESA, 1
38017 MEZZOLOMBARDO (TN)
TEL. 0461601046
E-MAIL: foradori@interline.it

Teroldego is a difficult customer. Not all growers are successful. In addition, the pre-harvest weather is crucial, as are the vineyard and cellar techniques adopted. And there's more. You also need a little bit of luck if everything is going to go well. Elisabetta Foradori has always done everything possible for her teroldego vines and this time, she had a helping hand from mother nature. Like a true grower, Elisabetta grasped her opportunity in both hands. The '99 Granato is again, at last, Teroldego at its exquisite best. A superb wine, it explodes onto the nose in a headily harmonious swathe of fragrances. Then the full-bodied, firm palate unfolds in all its meaty intensity, backed up by a velvet-smooth tannic weave. It doesn't take a rocket scientist to realize how much care Elisabetta has lavished on this masterpiece, a splendid demonstration of the vine's potential and, of course, the skill in vineyard and cellar of its maker. That same skill is equally obvious in the other reds. From the sweet tannins of the alcohol-rich, upfront Teroldego, we moved on to the challenging syrah-based Ailanpa. A peppery wine, laced with notes of bay leaf and incense, it unveils serious concentration. Also splendidly made is the easy-drinking Karanar, an eye-catching blend of cabernet, syrah, petit verdot and merlot. Finally, the estate's only white, the chardonnay and sauvignon-based Myrto, is always a good wine.

NOGAREDO (TN)

CASTEL NOARNA
FRAZ. NOARNA
VIA CASTELNUOVO, 1
38060 NOGAREDO (TN)
TEL. 0464413295 - 0464435222
E-MAIL: info@castelnoarna.com

Marco Zani is a wineman of many parts. He succeeds in combining his work in the vineyard with the main business of the Zani family, long-established hoteliers in the "city of the oak", as Rovereto is known. Marco's determination keeps him firmly oncourse to achieve the objectives of the wine project he so enthusiastically embarked upon in the late 1980s. The first thing he did was to redesign the planting patterns near his castle. He has recently added new lagrein and carmener stock to join his close-packed rows of cabernet, merlot, chardonnay, sauvignon and venerable nosiola vines. Few vineyards in Italy are as meticulously tended. This year, Marco presented no reds at all, preferring to skip the '98 reserves and focus on just a few whites. The Castelnuovo '00 was again one of the estate's best wines. Rich with classic fruit aromas of golden delicious apples, banana and pineapple, it is certain to further improve as it evolves, as did previous editions, and time will bring out its notes of moss, gunflint and hazelnut. The Nosiola Casot is more straightforward, its classic nose elusive but whistle-clean. The crisply, intense Sauvignon has more structure, as well as varietal notes of ripe figs and lively acidity that will stand it in good stead in the future. As we have said many times, Marco Zani's wines need patience and time in the cellar.

● Granato '99	￸￸￸	5
● Teroldego Rotaliano '00	￸￸	4
● Ailanpa '99	￸￸	5
● Karanar '99	￸￸	5
○ Myrto '00	￸￸	5
● Granato '91	￸￸￸	5
● Granato '93	￸￸￸	5
● Teroldego Rotaliano Sgarzon '93	￸￸￸	4
● Teroldego Rotaliano Sgarzon '94	￸￸￸	4
● Granato '96	￸￸￸	5
● Karanar '97	￸￸	4
● Granato '98	￸￸	5
● Teroldego Rotaliano '98	￸￸	3
○ Myrto '99	￸￸	4
● Teroldego Rotaliano '99	￸￸	4

○ Bianco di Castelnuovo '00	￸￸	4
○ Sauvignon Atesino '00	￸￸	4
○ Trentino Nosiola Casot '00	￸	4
● Trentino Cabernet Romeo '93	￸￸	4
● Trentino Cabernet Romeo '94	￸￸	4
○ Bianco di Castelnuovo '96	￸￸	3
● Trentino Cabernet Romeo '96	￸￸	4
○ Trentino Chardonnay Campo Grande '96	￸￸	4
○ Trentino Sauvignon '96	￸￸	3
○ Bianco di Castelnuovo '97	￸￸	4
● Trentino Cabernet Romeo '97	￸￸	5
● Trentino Cabernet Sauvignon Mercuria '97	￸￸	3
○ Trentino Chardonnay '97	￸￸	3
○ Trentino Chardonnay Campo Grande '97	￸￸	4
○ Trentino Nosiola '98	￸￸	3

NOMI (TN)

Cantina Sociale di Nomi
Via Roma, 1
38060 Nomi (TN)
Tel. 0464834195
E-mail: cantinanomi@tin.it

The cellar at Nomi is one of the benchmarks for Trentino's co-operative winemaking. It works away unassumingly, shunning the limelight and never flaunting its manufacturing muscle, even though its wines are interesting and very well-made. Nevertheless, Nomi doesn't shut itself away in a corner. The cellar is developing innovative ways of collaborating with neighbouring co-operative wineries and with member-growers who may be based as far away as Sicily. There were 11 wines at our tastings, all of which scored at least One Glass. Here they are, in no particular order: the attractively deep pink Schiava has a subtle note of almonds on the nose; the Müller Thurgau is fresh-tasting and aromatic; the Pinot Grigio is juicy and flavoursome; the Chardonnay, well-made as ever; and the youthful Teroldego foregrounds notes of plum. A word or two more about the wines that Nomi considers most representative of the range. The most outstanding of these is undoubtedly the Résorso, a typical blend of chardonnay and barrique-fermented pinot. Vibrantly bright golden yellow, it reveals vanillaed notes on the nose and a soft, well-sustained finish. Also very good are the sweet Moscato Giallo from the Le Comete selection, obtained from grapes harvested at Castel Beseno. Golden yellow, with notes of tropical fruit, apricots and peach jam, it unveils a deliciously sweet palate. The Merlot is spicy and offers great definition on nose and palate. This may be a non-Riserva version but it is still quite delicious. Finally, the Marzemino is as attractively even and nicely gauged as ever.

○	Trentino Bianco Résorso Le Comete '00	ŸŸ	4
○	Trentino Moscato Giallo Le Comete '00	ŸŸ	4
●	Trentino Marzemino '00	Ÿ	3
⊙	Valdadige Schiava '00	Ÿ	2*
●	Trentino Merlot '99	Ÿ	3*
●	Trentino Merlot Le Campagne '97	ŸŸ	4
●	Trentino Rosso Résorso '97	ŸŸ	4
●	Trentino Rosso Résorso Le Comete '98	ŸŸ	4
○	Trentino Bianco Résorso Le Comete '99	ŸŸ	4
●	Trentino Marzemino Le Fornas '98	Ÿ	3
○	Meditandum ad 2000	Ÿ	4

ROVERÈ DELLA LUNA (TN)

Gaierhof
Via IV Novembre, 51
38030 Roverè della Luna (TN)
Tel. 0461658527 - 0461658514

It could be because the estate lies athwart the border between Trentino and Alto Adige. Or it may be Gaierhof's desire to keep its cultivation zones distinct. Whatever the case, the cellar has again presented a premium range with two very different labels, Gaierhof and Maso Poli. And it was the Maso Poli wines in particular that had the panel nodding in approval at our tastings. To start with, the Costa Erta is magnificent, a mainly barrique-fermented Chardonnay with a golden yellow hue and an intensely fruit-rich nose of apples and peaches. On the palate, the honeyed mouthfeel is stylish, full-flavoured and complex. It's not often you taste a Chardonnay like this in Trentino. Maso Poli is also the label to look for when it comes to Pinot Nero, for all-round elegance and frank morello cherry on the palate. Comparable marks went to the other two Maso Poli wines, the chardonnay, pinot bianco and müller thurgau-based Sorni Bianco and the eminently drinkable Pinot Grigio, a clean, fresh-tasting wine with hints of fruit salad. The remaining bottles from this lovely "frontier" winery are true children of the Dolomites. The Müller Thurgau dei Settecento, so-called because the vines stand 700 metres above sea level, has grip and character, attractive acidity and a well-defined finish. Next is the beautifully crafted Merlot Riserva, with its cassis and plum aromas that also reveal nuances of cocoa powder and a soft, caressing mouthfeel. The rest of the range is attractively well-made, the Nosiola, the Pinot Grigio, the lovely Teroldego and the delicious Moscato Rosa, a wine the Togns dedicate to connoisseurs of this rare type.

○	Trentino Chardonnay Costa Erta '00	ŸŸ	4
○	Trentino Sorni Bianco Maso Poli '00	ŸŸ	4
●	Trentino Moscato Rosa '00	Ÿ	5
○	Trentino Müller Thurgau dei Settecento '00	Ÿ	4
○	Trentino Nosiola '00	Ÿ	3
○	Trentino Pinot Grigio '00	Ÿ	4
○	Trentino Pinot Grigio Maso Poli '00	Ÿ	4
●	Trentino Merlot Ris. '97	Ÿ	4
○	Trentino Pinot Nero '99	Ÿ	4
●	Teroldego Rotaliano '99	Ÿ	4
○	Trentino Trentino Müller Thurgau dei Settecento '99	ŸŸ	4

ROVERETO (TN)

Nicola Balter
Via Vallunga II, 24
38068 Rovereto (TN)
tel. 0464430101

Barbanico from the Balter cellar is a wine of uncommon force. Territory-driven and distinctively stylish, this exemplary bottle is created by Nicola Balter, a winemaker of breeding. The '98 came within a whisker of repeating the previous vintage's exploit but missed out on a third Glass for a hint of edginess in the tannins. It is likely that this blend of cabernet sauvignon, merlot and lagrein has paid the price of the inclement weather just before the pickers went out. Still, it remains a powerfully extracted, alcohol-rich bottle that offers a range of subtly intense aromas, shifting from bramble, "uva spinella", as blackcurrant is called in Trentino, and Parma violets. "Satisfying on eye, nose and palate" also sums up the Cabernet Sauvignon. The fruit-led thrust on the nose is remarkable, with grassy secondary notes also coming through, while the palate is broad, harmonious and lingering. Now on to the "ultima sboccatura", or recently disgorged, Brut that Nicola's spumante-making skills have produced. The rich straw yellow is flecked with green, the perlage finely beaded and persistent, and the fruity aromas soft and sweet. On the palate, it offers body and balance, with just a hint of candied tangerine peel. If we go back to Balter's still wines, we find a fresh, stylish Sauvignon with varietal character and elderflower aromas. We were, however, hoping for a little more from the Clarae, a white with an intense hue and good structure but with aromas that are a tad unfocused. Finally, the very quaffable Rossinot is a jolly rosé that is perfect for drinking in convivial company.

● Barbanico '98	🍷🍷	5
● Cabernet Sauvignon '98	🍷🍷	4
○ Sauvignon '00	🍷🍷	4
○ Trento Brut	🍷🍷	4
⊙ Rossinot '00	🍷	3
○ Clarae '99	🍷	4
● Barbanico '97	🍷🍷🍷	5
● Trentino Cabernet Sauvignon '91	🍷🍷	4
○ Clarae '95	🍷🍷	4
● Trentino Cabernet Sauvignon '95	🍷🍷	4
○ Clarae '96	🍷🍷	4
● Trentino Cabernet Sauvignon '96	🍷🍷	4
● Trentino Cabernet Sauvignon '97	🍷🍷	4
○ Trentino Sauvignon '98	🍷🍷	3
○ Trentino Chardonnay '98	🍷	3

ROVERETO (TN)

Letrari
Via Monte Baldo, 13/15
38068 Rovereto (TN)
tel. 0464480200
e-mail: info@letrari.it

The founder of this winery, Leonello Letrari, spent half a century in the cellar before he decided it was time to ease off and work as a consultant. He left the business to his children, Lucia in particular, to whom he transferred not just the estate but also his accumulated experience. The '00 wines are some of the first to emerge from the new, modern cellar the Letraris have built between Rovereto and Isera, among vineyards that have survived creeping urban development. All eleven wines presented at our tastings performed splendidly. Only lack of space forces us to make a selection and discuss those that the panel liked best. To start with, the two spumantes were great, the Riserva ever more complex and harmonious, the Brut quite correctly more immediately approachable. Next, we come to the Ballistarius, a Bordeaux-style red that Leonello had set his heart on, as he wants to leave future generations a seriously good red. The Ballistarius '97 aged in the bottle for longer than originally planned but now it is very convincing. In fact, it has the bearing of a great international-style red. Wild berry fruit on the nose mingles with leather and cocoa powder while the palate is well-structured and beautifully knit. There are still hints of grassiness but the tannins are remarkably fine-grained. Another newcomer is the Fossa Bandita white, a wine which owes its charms more to its primary – but very inviting – aromas than its structure. There's also an excellent Marzemino with concentrated fruit fragrances. Then, we enjoyed the solid Maso Lodron, a Bordeaux blend with notes of ripe cherries on the nose and a nicely balanced hint of sweetness on the palate. And to round off, we'll mention the delicious distinctive Moscato Rosa, a wine of style.

○ Fossa Bandita '00	🍷🍷	4
● Ballistarius '97	🍷🍷	5
○ Trento Brut Ris. '96	🍷🍷	5
● Trentino Marzemino Sel. '00	🍷🍷	4
○ Trento Brut	🍷	4
● Trentino Moscato Rosa '98	🍷	6
● Trentino Rosso Maso Lodron '99	🍷	3
○ Trento Brut Ris. '96	🍷🍷	5
● Trentino Cabernet Sauvignon Ris. '94	🍷🍷	3
● Trentino Moscato Rosa '94	🍷🍷	6
● Trentino Rosso Maso Lodron '95	🍷🍷	3
● Trentino Cabernet Sauvignon '96	🍷🍷	4
● Trentino Marzemino Sel. '97	🍷🍷	3
● Trentino Moscato Rosa '97	🍷🍷	5
● Ballistarius '98	🍷🍷	5
● Trentino Marzemino Sel. '99	🍷🍷	4

ROVERETO (TN)

LONGARIVA
FRAZ. BORGO SACCO
VIA ZANDONAI, 6
38068 ROVERETO (TN)
TEL. 0464437200 - 0464487322
E-MAIL: longariva@acg.it

It's curious to see how a convinced "red" man like Marco Manica – and his red wines are truly excellent – sets our panel's heads nodding in agreement mainly with his white bottles. Three Glasses went to Marco again this time for a white. He didn't manage to repeat the success of his fantastic Pergole, a Pinot Bianco from '99, but with an equally massive Praistel, a carefully wood-fermented Chardonnay that impeccably interprets a vintage, the '98, that had many Trentino winemakers struggling. That year was favourable only to winemakers who knew what they were about, and could transfer their expertise into the bottle. Marco came up with this richly aromatic Chardonnay with its full, firm attack on the nose and a softly stylish structure on both nose and palate. The Pergole had to be content with making it to the final tastings but this was perhaps because it had only gone into the bottle a few weeks before. In the past, bottle age has always worked in its favour. Best of the reds was the Tre Cesure, a selection created to celebrate Longariva's quarter century. It is fragrant, full and well-structured. Also excellent are the Marognon, a close-knit, meatily intense Cabernet, and the Tovi, a Merlot that flaunts its elegance and appealing agility. The Pinot Nero Zinzele wasn't up to form, however, and the coppery Graminé, the estate's Pinot Grigio, was only well-made. Still, never mind.

ROVERETO (TN)

ARMANDO SIMONCELLI
LOC. NAVESEL, 7
38068 ROVERETO (TN)
TEL. 0464432373

Armando Simoncelli has come a long way since 1977, when he decided to vinify the grapes from his vineyards and bottle the wine himself under the family name. His estate is a paragon of modern viticulture. It stands at Navesel, an ancient port on the river Adige, in warm, sun-drenched and very fertile countryside, and the site climate has the right range of temperatures for the vines to prosper. There are 12 or so hectares and the range of vine types is wide. The most important is Marzemino, the traditional Trentino variety. Simoncelli's version is amaranth-tinged ruby red with subtle, attractive aromas reminiscent of Parma violets. Full-bodied and robustly flavoured, it ends with a trademark bitterish twist. The cellar predilection for reds is also obvious in the Bordeaux-blend Navesel, a lustrous garnet red wine with an alcohol-rich and slightly grassy nose. Well-balanced, it flaunts a fine-grained tannic weave. Similar, albeit less compact, sensations are offered by the Cabernet Franc. Paler in colour, it has lashings of alcohol and a greenish note on the nose. The purplish Lagrein also has a strong suit in approachability, showing upfront, uncomplicated blackcurrant flavours. Simoncelli's whites included one of Trentino's most intriguing Pinot Biancos. Its vibrant greenish reflections introduce subtle aromas of artemisia, as well as citrus fruit and ripe apples. The palate is nicely structured and well-balanced. Finally, make a note of the spumante, one of the most reliable products in its category.

	Wine	Rating	Score
O	Trentino Chardonnay Praistel '98	♛♛♛	5
O	Trentino Pinot Bianco Pergole '00	♛♛	4
●	Trentino Cabernet Sauvignon Marognon Ris. '98	♛♛	5
●	Trentino Merlot Tovi '97	♛♛	5
●	Trentino Rosso Tre Cesure Sel. 25°. '97	♛♛	5
O	Pinot Grigio Graminè '00	♛	4
●	Trentino Pinot Nero Zinzèle '97	♛	5
O	Trentino Pinot Bianco Pergole '99	♛♛♛	3
●	Trentino Pinot Nero Zinzèle '96	♛♛	4
●	Trentino Cabernet Quartella '97	♛♛	4
●	Trentino Cabernet Sauvignon Marognon Ris. '97	♛♛	4
●	Trentino Rosso Tre Cesure Ris. '97	♛♛	4
O	Trentino Pinot Grigio Graminè '99	♛♛	3

	Wine	Rating	Score
●	Trentino Marzemino '00	♛♛	3*
O	Trentino Pinot Bianco '00	♛♛	3*
●	Trentino Rosso Navesèl '98	♛♛	4
●	Trentino Cabernet '00	♛	3
●	Trentino Lagrein '00	♛	3
O	Trento Brut	♛	4
●	Trentino Rosso Navesèl '91	♛♛	3
●	Trentino Marzemino '96	♛♛	3
●	Trentino Lagrein '97	♛♛	3
●	Trentino Marzemino '97	♛♛	3
●	Trentino Rosso Navesèl '97	♛♛	4
●	Trentino Lagrein '98	♛♛	3
●	Trentino Marzemino '98	♛♛	3
●	Trentino Marzemino '99	♛♛	3

SAN MICHELE ALL'ADIGE (TN)

Endrizzi
Loc. Masetto, 2
38010 San Michele all'Adige (TN)
Tel. 0461650129
E-mail: info@endrizzi.it

Paolo Endrici from the Endrizzi cellar. A tongue-twister if ever there was one. But this is one of the most interesting estates in Trentino, driven by the dynamism of an entrepreneur from good winemaking stock. The Endricis have expanded their facilities, purchased the neighbouring vineyards in the direction of Castel Monreale, and above all have focused even more attention on the vinification process itself. Fruit from estate-owned vineyards goes into riserva wines, which include two version of Masetto, a red and a white. The white is a chardonnay and pinot bianco blend. Its golden colour is flecked with green and introduces a fruit-rich, apple-themed nose, then a palate with plenty of structure and grip. The red, Masetto Nero, meshes well on the rich, solid palate. Drinking nicely now, it promises to be even better in a few years' time. There were good performances from the selections of Pinot Nero, a mouthfilling plum and morello cherry tipple, and the sinewy, alcohol-rich Teroldego. We have no hesitation, either, in recommending the Moscato Rosa, with its inviting nose and a palate for special occasions. The rest of the range is well-made.

O	Masetto Bianco '99	♈♈	4
●	Masetto Nero '99	♈♈	4
●	Trentino Moscato Rosa '00	♈	5
●	Teroldego Ris. '99	♈	4
●	Trentino Pinot Nero Ris. '99	♈	4
●	Teroldego Rotaliano Sup. Sel. '96	♈♈	4
●	Teroldego Rotaliano Maso Camorz '97	♈♈	4
●	Teroldego Rotaliano Maso Camorz '98	♈♈	4
O	Masetto Bianco '98	♈	4
●	Masetto Nero '98	♈	4
O	Trentino Chardonnay Collezione '98	♈	4

SAN MICHELE ALL'ADIGE (TN)

Istituto Agrario Provinciale
San Michele all'Adige
Via Edmondo Mach, 1
38010 San Michele all'Adige (TN)
Tel. 0461615252
E-mail: cantina@ismaa.it

The wine school at San Michele all'Adige is renowned. For more than a century, it has been helping agriculture in the province to progress and improve. No family in rural Trentino is without its graduate, or training certificate holder, from one branch or another of the Istituto Agrario Provinciale. The school's cellar was looking for a valid director when along came Enrico Paternoster, a former pupil of the school and imaginative innovator, bringing with him a solid track record. In a trice, the wines have gone back to the top of the class. The Pinot Bianco missed Three Glasses by the skin of its teeth. It is a distinctly varietal version, especially in its aromas of mountain apples. There is nice acidity on the palate, with a range of minerally notes and hints of pear. The Istituto can be just as proud of the other wines the panel enjoyed. Castel San Michele showed that it is still a red with finesse. It lives up to its name as the first Bordeaux blend ever to be officially recognized in Trentino, back in 1964. At the time, the Istituto's purchase of small oak barrels to age its Cabernet and Merlot raised more than a few eyebrows. Incrocio Manzoni, chardonnay and pinot bianco go into the latest version of the Castel San Michele Bianco. A well put-together, full-bodied and fruit-rich white, it unveils balanced weight on the palate and excellent prospects for the future. The other bottles in the range are much more approachable. The Sauvignon comes straight out of the textbook, foregrounding notes of elderflower and red peppers, while the Chardonnay and Pinot Grigio flaunt above all freshness, clean flavour and an all-round elegance.

O	Trentino Pinot Bianco '00	♈♈	4
O	Trentino Bianco Castel S. Michele '00	♈♈	4
●	Trentino Rosso Castel S. Michele '99	♈♈	4
O	Trentino Sauvignon '00	♈♈	3*
O	Trentino Chardonnay '00	♈	3
O	Trentino Pinot Grigio '00	♈	3
●	Trentino Merlot '96	♈♈	4
●	Trentino Rebo '97	♈♈	3
O	Trentino Bianco Castel S. Michele '99	♈♈	3
O	Trentino Pinot Bianco '99	♈♈	3
●	Trentino Rebo '99	♈♈	3
O	Trentino Chardonnay '99	♈	3

SAN MICHELE ALL'ADIGE (TN)

ZENI
FRAZ. GRUMO
VIA STRETTA, 2
38010 SAN MICHELE ALL'ADIGE (TN)
TEL. 0461650456

Each year, the Zeni brothers, Andrea and Roberto, strive to interpret the harvest just as the season has given it to them, without making drastic interventions in the cellar. That's why their wines are instantly recognizable and true to their vintage. The '00 vintage produced wines that have less acidity than usual, and are therefore rounder and more mouthfilling. The aromatic ones have crisp, well-defined noses that tend even more than ever towards flowery notes. Reds tend to be fuller and more opulent because of their low level of natural acidity. Sortì, based on pinot bianco, has apples on the nose and a round palate with a subtle note of barrique-derive vanilla. The Pini, a Teroldego Riserva, is excellent, the hallmark hints of bramble emerging in a rich framework that will age well in the cellar. The standard-label Teroldego is a classically quaffable crowd-pleaser in the Rotaliano mould. The monovarietal pinot nero Spiazol also shows a stylish nose and a lively palate. The Zenis are scrupulous growers and distillers who, for the past few years, have been making sparkling wine. Their Brut is perhaps the most enjoyable outcome of this development. A Trentino DOC aged on the lees for five years, it offers the nose a marked note of vanilla and chocolate, followed by a soft, well-rounded mouthfeel. Finally, there is another Zeni treat, the Moscato Rosa. Intense in the glass, it proffers aromas of rose petals, cinnamon and cloves.

O	Trentino Pinot Bianco Sortì '00	㏘	3
O	Trento Brut M. Cl. '95	㏘	4
●	Teroldego Rotaliano Pini '97	㏘	5
●	Trentino Pinot Nero Spiazol '98	㏘	4
●	Teroldego Rotaliano '00	㏑	4
●	Trentino Moscato Rosa '00	㏑	5
●	Teroldego Rotaliano Pini '93	㏘㏘	4
O	Trento Brut M. Cl. '93	㏘㏘	4
●	Teroldego Rotaliano Pini '95	㏘㏘	4
●	Teroldego Rotaliano '97	㏘㏘	4
●	Trentino Pinot Nero Spiazol '97	㏘㏘	4

TRENTO

CAVIT - CONSORZIO DI CANTINE SOCIALI
FRAZ. RAVINA
VIA DEL PONTE, 31
38040 TRENTO
TEL. 0461381711
E-MAIL: cavit@cavit.it

Cavit, one of Italy's most firmly established brands, belongs to a dynamic group of gargantuan size that is capable of taking Trentino wines into the global market and competing with the big boys in terms of quantity as well as quality. Backed by 15 or so co-operative wineries, Cavit can select from a wide range of wines, all of which are at least technically well-made. Firmato continues to be a thoroughbred spumante, with all the elegance, finesse and brio of a seriously great bubbly. The Millesimato is especially good, a fine example of a clean, well-sustained sparkler, with fine beading, a creamy mousse, lots of fruit and a soft mouthfeel. Cavit also focuses on short runs, a sector which it handles rather well. We'll start with a special wine, Vino Santo Aréle, named after the rush mats the nosiola grapes dry on until Easter week before pressing. This amazed the panel with its concentration, elegance, creamy texture and sheer length. The nose is well-defined and the palate never cloys. In fact, Aréle has enough class to stand alongside the world's great dessert wines. Maso Torresella is a white blend with heady aromas and lively acidity on the palate. The red version is a Bordeaux blend that manages to keep its grassy nuances well under control. Two other wines from the Bottega Vinai range are well worth investigating, the Chardonnay and the Pinot Nero. They may not have massive structure but they can offer lashings of fruit.

O	Trentino Vino Santo Aréle '94	㏘	6
O	Maso Torresella Cuvée '00	㏘	5
O	Trentino Chardonnay Bottega Vinai '00	㏘	4
O	Trento Brut Firmato mill. '97	㏘	4*
●	Maso Torresella '98	㏘	5
●	Trentino Pinot Nero Bottega Vinai '00	㏑	4
O	Trento Graal Brut Ris. '93	㏘㏘㏘	4
O	Trento Brut Firmato '96	㏘㏘	4
●	Teroldego Rotaliano Maso Cervara '97	㏘㏘	4
●	Teroldego Rotaliano Bottega Vinai '99	㏘㏘	3

TRENTO

★ FERRARI
FRAZ. RAVINA
VIA DEL PONTE, 15
38040 TRENTO
TEL. 0461972311
E-MAIL: info@cantineferrari.it

One Ferrari carried off the Formula One Grand Prix title this year but another triumphed in the world of wine. Riserva del Fondatore is a class act, a legend among Italian spumantes, again showing just how great it is. The Giulio Ferrari '93, with its redesigned label, is superb. Full-bodied and harmonious, it offers a never-ending perlage and intense yet utterly fresh aromas on the nose, despite almost a decade's ageing in the bottle. Progression in the mouth, from front to mid to back palate, is – quite simply – impeccable. The Trento Brut Perlé wasn't far off a third Glass, which in fact it very nearly won. Aromas and flavours of discreet elegance are accompanied by a thrust on the palate that is initially restrained, then gains momentum and cut. Mauro Lunelli, oenologist to the winemaking branch of the Ferrari clan, considers it his flagship spumante. It's hard to argue with him, especially since more than half a million bottles are released every year. Very creditable comments also went to the spumantes made for the mass market. The Brut is delightfully quaffable, the Brut Incontri invites closer inspection while the Brut Maximum is attractively made and soft on the palate. Then the rosé version of the Perlé is similar in style and tasting profile to the better-known standard Perlé.

TRENTO

LUNELLI
FRAZ. RAVINA
VIA MARGON, 19
38040 TRENTO
TEL. 0461972311
E-MAIL: info@cantineferrari.it

To make their still wines, the Lunellis carefully identified the best locations in their finest vineyards, striving to respect specific local winemaking traditions and changing only the planting patterns. Each wine is thus linked to a specific plot, a small group of farm buildings as carefully tended as a window box. The four wines presented won eight splendid Glasses. The 2000 vintage was a better one than usual for the two whites. Villa Margon, from chardonnay, has an attractively complex nose with clear hints of banana and a pleasant vanilla overtone. Equally convincing was the Villa San Nicolò, a Sauvignon with persuasive aromas of lemon, sage, peach and a curious hint of nettle followed by a palate well-sustained by fresh acidity. The Pinot Nero is the red that is closest to the owners' hearts and the one they are aiming to raise to the very highest levels. But the '99 vintage was not one of the best. A lovely purplish red hue introduces a fruity, elegantly soft palate that still lacks a little muscle. In contrast, the dark red Maso Le Viane is distinctly full-bodied. This Bordeaux-style blend comes from the lower Vallagarina, the heart of the Campi Sarni between Ala and Avio, long the home of great reds. There are notes of oak on the nose, as well as crisp fragrances of wild berries, then the stylish palate offers ripe, tight-knit tannins before the faintly grassy finish.

○ Giulio Ferrari '93	♛♛♛	6
○ Trento Brut Maximum	♛♛	5
○ Trento Brut Perlé '97	♛♛	5
◉ Trento Brut Perlé Rosé '96	♛♛	5
○ Trento Brut Incontri	♛♛	5
○ Trento Brut	♛	4
○ Giulio Ferrari '86	♛♛♛	6
○ Giulio Ferrari '88	♛♛♛	6
○ Giulio Ferrari '89	♛♛♛	6
○ Giulio Ferrari '90	♛♛♛	6
○ Giulio Ferrari '91	♛♛♛	6
○ Giulio Ferrari '92	♛♛♛	6
○ Trento Brut Perlé '94	♛♛	5
○ Trento Brut Perlé '95	♛♛	5
○ Trento Brut Perlé '96	♛♛	5

○ Trentino Chardonnay Villa Margon '00	♛♛	4
○ Trentino Sauvignon Villa San Nicolò '00	♛♛	5
● Trentino Rosso Maso Le Viane '98	♛♛	5
● Trentino Pinot Nero Maso Montalto '99	♛♛	5
● Trentino Pinot Nero Maso Montalto '96	♛♛	4
○ Trentino Chardonnay Villa Margon '97	♛♛	4
● Trentino Pinot Nero Maso Montalto '97	♛♛	4
● Trentino Rosso Maso Le Viane '97	♛♛	5
○ Trentino Chardonnay Villa Gentilotti '98	♛♛	4
○ Trentino Chardonnay Villa Margon '98	♛♛	4
○ Trentino Sauvignon Villa San Nicolò '99	♛♛	4

TRENTO

MASO MARTIS
LOC. MARTIGNANO
VIA DELL'ALBERA, 52
38040 TRENTO
TEL. 0461821057
E-MAIL: masomartis@tin.it

Maso Martis has 12 or so hectares on a hillside at Trento, on the sunny slopes that face Monte Calisio. The vines have been planted using innovative techniques that bring out the intrinsic qualities of each variety: short pruning, organic fertilization, drastic bunch thinning and similarly scrupulous treatment in the cellar, which is also equipped to host cultural events and wine tourism initiatives. Originally, Antonio Stelzer intended to concentrate on spumantes, a goal he achieved and left behind long ago. Nowadays, Maso Martis also releases a wide range of still wines. Antonio's spumantes have always been characterful. The latest version has fine beading and aromas redolent of the chardonnay base wine. Fresh-tasting and subtle, it shows nice length in the finish. The same characteristics are even more apparent in the Brut Riserva, one of the finest spumantes it was our privilege to taste during our Guide selections. An immensely refined wine, it has concentrated, richly nuanced aromas and full, lingering flavours on the palate. These are indeed serious sparklers and enable Maso Martis to regain its full Guide profile with this edition. Another contributing factor was the appeal of the remaining wines made by Stelzer and his gritty technical team, led by young oenologist Matteo Ferrari. The Chardonnay L'Incanto is exciting. Obtained from fruit harvested late in the autumn, it has lots of body, ripe melon and apricot fruit on nose and palate, spicy nuances and a soft, full body. Sole d'Autunno, a chardonnay-based sweet wine, has good balance, although it is a tad predictable.

○	Trento Brut Ris. '97	♈♈	5
○	Sole d'Autunno '00	♈	5
○	Trentino Chardonnay L'Incanto '00	♈	4
○	Trento Brut	♈	4
○	Trento Brut Ris. '92	♈♈	5
○	Trentino Chardonnay '94	♈♈	3
○	Trento Brut Ris. '94	♈♈	5
○	Trentino Chardonnay '95	♈♈	3
○	Trentino Chardonnay '97	♈♈	3
●	Trentino Moscato Rosa '95	♈	5
●	Trentino Moscato Rosa '97	♈	5

VOLANO (TN)

CONCILIO
ZONA INDUSTRIALE, 2
38060 VOLANO (TN)
TEL. 0464411000
E-MAIL: concilio@concilio.it

Undoubtedly one of Trentino's most exciting winemaking concerns, Concilio has been in operation now for ten years. But to view it as merely a selector and distributor of major quantities of wine would be to belittle the skills and competence of its executive staff. Above all, it would do scant justice to Concilio wines. They are scrupulously made in a traditional style for a market where quality is a given and quantity needs to be delivered at a competitive price. State-of-the-art technology and strictly selected Trentino grapes are the means used to obtain them. Finally, these are wines that have solid roots in their territory of origin. As in the case of the Teroldego Braide, a red with clean, concentrated aromas, hinting faintly at blackcurrant and bramble, that lead into a soft yet vigorously full-bodied mouthfeel. Elegance and finesse are the main virtues of the Merlot Novaline, a wine that is made with the same admirable skill year after year. The remaining reds were also well-made. The Marzemino, dedicated to Mozart, is unobtrusively alcohol-rich while the Cabernet Riserva puts varietal characteristics in centre stage, although it does tend to overdo the grassy note, a feature we have noted quite often in Trentino wines. To round off the show, there was the attractively quaffable Enantio, from lambrusco a foglia frastagliata, or "jagged leaf lambrusco", grapes, and the whites, including an interesting Pinot Grigio Maso Guà.

●	Trentino Merlot Novaline Ris. '98	♈♈	5
●	Teroldego Rotaliano Braide '99	♈♈	5
○	Trentino Pinot grigio Maso Guà '00	♈	3
●	Trentino Cabernet '98	♈	4
●	Enantio '99	♈	3
●	Trentino Marzemino Mozart '99	♈	4
●	Trentino Merlot Novaline Ris. '96	♈♈	4
●	Trentino Pinot Nero Novaline Ris. '97	♈♈	4
●	Trentino Rosso Mori Vecio '97	♈♈	4
○	Trentino Chardonnay '98	♈♈	3
○	Trentino Pinot Grigio '98	♈♈	3
○	Trentino Chardonnay '99	♈♈	3
○	Trentino Müller Thurgau '99	♈♈	3

OTHER WINERIES

La Cadalora
Loc. Santa Margherita
Via Trento, 44
38060 Ala (TN)
tel. 0464696443 - 0646696300

The Tomasi family has been working in the vineyards for six generations. They marry tradition with a more experimental approach. Their Chardonnay shows good acidic grip, nice fruit and the right concentration. The Sauvignon is varietal, the Vignalet, a Pinot Nero, is still a little dumb and the Bordeaux-blend Majere is decently made.

○ Chardonnay '00	3
○ Trentino Sauvignon '00	4
● Majere '98	5
● Trentino Pinot Nero Vignalet '99	5

Madonna delle Vittorie
Via Linfano, 81
38062 Arco (TN)
tel. 0464505432

This is a modern winery in the heart of the lower Sarca, over towards Lake Garda, and it makes a fine range of premium wines. There were good performances from the white Sommolago, a chardonnay-based blend, and the excellent Trento Talento.

○ Trentino Bianco Sommolago '00	4
○ Trento Talento Brut	4

Cantina Sociale di Toblino
Fraz. Sarche - Via Ponte Oliveti, 1
38070 Calavino (TN)
tel. 0461564168
E-mail: toblino@tin.it

The Cantina Sociale di Toblino lies in a lovely valley, next to one of Trentino's most impressive castles. The wines are making great progress and now show better structure. The winery image has been revamped and precise quality objectives set.

○ Trentino Nosiola '00	3
○ Trentino Vino Santo '93	6
○ Trento Brut Antàres	3

Arcangelo Sandri
Via Vanegge, 4
38010 Faedo (TN)
tel. 0461650935

Faedo seems to be full of growers. Arcangelo Sandri's estate has a number of small hillslope plots that produce wines with a very individual style. His Müller Thurgau is fruit-led and irresistible. The Lagrein, too, is deliciously complex and delicate.

○ Trentino Müller Thurgau '00	3
● Trentino Lagrein '99	4

Cipriano Fedrizzi
Via 4 Novembre, 1
38017 Mezzolombardo (TN)
Tel. 0461602328

This winery belongs to a likeable winemaking family that continue to improve their trademark wine, Teroldego. In the last two editions, their selection swept the board. The Fedrizzis are held back by the tiny quantities they release, which are still too niche-oriented. But their Due Vigneti is a superlative Teroldego.

● Teroldego Rotaliano Due Vigneti '98	🍷🍷	4

Zanini
Loc. Via Degasperi, 42
38017 Mezzolombardo (TN)
Tel. 0461601496

Oscar and Andrea are carrying on the good work started by their father, Luigi, 30 vintages ago when he founded the small estate with its strategically located plots for growing teroldego rotaliano. Their wines are frank. They may not be overly delicate but they are as honest as the day is long.

● Teroldego Rotaliano Le Cervare '99	🍷🍷	4
○ Trentino Chardonnay I Giardini '00	🍷	4

Riccardo Battistotti
Via 3 Novembre, 21
38060 Nomi (TN)
Tel. 0464834145
E-mail: mail@battistotti.com

Luciano Battistotti is a hard to dislike. A genuine, thoroughly competent cellarman, he always manages to turn out wines of excellent quality. Like any other craft worker, though, he is sometimes let down by lady luck or simply by bad weather. His Marzemino is still great and the infrequently seen Moscato Rosa is very good.

● Trentino Marzemino '00	🍷🍷	3*
● Trentino Moscato Rosa '00	🍷🍷	5
● Trentino Moscato Rosa '97	🍷🍷	5
● Trentino Marzemino '98	🍷🍷	3

Grigoletti
Via Garibaldi, 12
38060 Nomi (TN)
Tel. 0464834215
E-mail: grigolettivini@tin.it

Grigolettis have been making wine for generations and the range has been improving with each release. The Gonzalier is a fragrant Bordeaux blend with spice, leather and cocoa powder on the nose, good fruit and a velvety mouthfeel. The Merlot is excellent and the rest of the range well-made.

● Gonzialer '97	🍷🍷	5
● Trentino Merlot di Nomi '99	🍷🍷	4
○ Trentino Chardonnay L'Opera '00	🍷	4
● Trentino Marzemino '00	🍷	3

Conti Bossi Fedrigotti
Via Unione, 43
38068 Rovereto (TN)
Tel. 0464439250
E-mail: info@fedrigotti.it

A name you can bank on. Few other cellars in Trentino can boast such experience or such a history. The wines are well-made, with sufficient body to ensure they can be confidently cellared.

● Trentino Marzemino '00	🍷	3
● Fojaneghe Rosso '98	🍷	4

Dalzocchio
Loc. Bosco della Città
Via Vallelunga Seconda, 50
38068 Rovereto (TN)
Tel. 0464423580 - 0464413664

Dalzocchio is a new estate run by a dynamic winewoman who is determined to make her presence felt on the local wine scene. Low numbers and high quality are the watchwords. The stylish Chardonnay is well-pitched and full-bodied. The same goes for the fruit-rich, harmonious Pinot Nero.

○ Trentino Chardonnay '99	🍷🍷	5
● Trentino Pinot Nero '98	🍷	5

BAILONI
VIA MASERE, 7/A
38100 TRENTO
TEL. 0461911842

This small, recently renovated estate has been a feature of the winemaking scene in Trentino for many years. The young owners insist on selecting the grapes for some parcels of their wine. The results are encouraging for the range is very attractive and offers exceptional value for money.

○	Trentino Chardonnay '00	🍷	3*
●	Blu Perla '98	🍷	4

MASO BERGAMINI
LOC. COGNOLA - BERGAMINI, 3
38050 TRENTO
TEL. 0461983079
E-MAIL: masobergamini@tin.it

Maso Bergamini is in an area noted for whites. Remo Tomasi is a fine winemaker who has rethought his vineyard and cellar management. The few thousand bottles of wine released are good, and for connoisseurs only. The intriguing cuvée of chardonnay, riesling and incrocio Manzoni is an irresistible white.

●	Trentino Moscato Rosa '00	🍷🍷	5
○	Bianco Maso Bergamini '99	🍷🍷	4

VIGNETI DELLE MERIDIANE
LOC. AL CASTELLER, 6
38100 TRENTO
TEL. 0461920811 - 0464419343
E-MAIL: vigneti@vignetimeridiane.it

The cellar is on a hill to the south of Trento. Wines from this dynamic estate, which is re-organizing on all fronts, are always persuasive.

○	Trentino Chardonnay '00	🍷	4
●	Teroldego Atesino Cernidor '96	🍷🍷	4
●	Teroldego Atesino Cernidor '97	🍷🍷	4

GIULIO POLI
LOC. SANTA MASSENZA
VIA VEZZANO, 3
38070 VEZZANO (TN)
TEL. 0461864149

The name Poli means wine and grappa in this lakeside village. But the family wants to be known for products other than their exceptional grappas. So they have released a late-harvest white that is as good as it is rare, Saros. Which shows the competitive spirit.

○	Saros V. T. '98	🍷🍷	6
●	Schiava Valle dei Laghi '00	🍷	3

MASO BASTIE
LOC. BASTIE
38070 VOLANO (TN)
TEL. 0464412747

The Torelli family makes very seductive wines in their new winery. The bottles have lots of personality, good aromatic concentration and what it takes to age well in the cellar. The sweet wines, a specialty of the house, are particularly convincing.

○	Edys '00	🍷🍷	4
●	Moscato Rosa '00	🍷🍷	5

EUGENIO ROSI
VIA TAVERNELLE, 3/B
38060 VOLANO (TN)
TEL. 0464461375

Eugenio Rosi vinifies grapes that he has been personally growing and selecting in his pocket handkerchief vineyards for only two years. Already, the wines are concentrated, very well-made and thoroughly convincing.

●	Poiema Marzemino dei Ziresi '00	🍷🍷	5
●	Esegesi '98	🍷🍷	5

ALTO ADIGE

There are now 56 wineries from Alto Adige with their own profiles in the Guide and 16 in the Other Wineries section. This year, 19 wines were awarded Three Glasses and the Cantina Produttori di San Michele Appiano, the region's leading producer, has been awarded the star that indicates at least ten Three Glasses awards. That deals with Guide business. If we take a look at what is happening with consumers, then we clearly see this is a magical period for wines from the Alto Adige. The overwhelming success of the region's wines in the market created problems for many producers from other regions who have difficulty in competing with such excellent quality and still affordable prices. Wines as well made and competitively priced as those from Alto Adige are difficult, if not impossible, to find in other Italian regions. Part of the secret of this success lies in the "virtuous circle" the producers in this area have managed to create. Though some go a little too far with price hikes, such wineries are exceptions to the rule. But let us get back to the performance of the winemakers of Alto Adige. This year 17 wineries won awards for 19 wines, San Michele Appiano and Termeno earning two apiece. The most positive aspect here is that many award-winning wines are made from traditional grape varieties such as lagrein and gewürztraminer, a phenomenon due only in part to the fact that difficult vintages such as '98 and '99 somewhat penalized the Merlot and Cabernet and did little for oak-aged Chardonnay. The progress of relatively new production areas in the high quality wine sector should also be mentioned. With its Rieslings, the small zone of Valle Venosta seems to be making good progress. Valle Isarco, with Sylvaner, Kerner and Müller Thurgau, has become an important reference point for whites. Both are on a par with the Bolzano and Oltradige zones, perhaps not in the quantity produced but definitely in the average quality of the wines presented. In all of the very small subzones, many small privately owned wineries turn out surprisingly good products while the co-operative wineries confirm they are by far the best in Italy. We have mentioned San Michele Appiano and Termeno. We could also point to Santa Maddalena and Gries, which are merging to create the Cantina Produttori in Bolzano. Then there are the co-operative wineries of Caldaro, Colterenzio, Cortaccia and others besides. Many privately owned wineries confirmed their status, including Walch, Muri Gries, Josephus Mayr, Niedermayr and Haas, and there are newcomers, Ignaz Niedrist in particular. Things are coming together to make Alto Adige one of the most interesting wine-producing regions in Europe and a benchmark for wine aficionados everywhere.

ANDRIANO/ANDRIAN (BZ)

Cantina Produttori Andriano
Via della Chiesa, 2
39010 Andriano/Andrian (BZ)
tel. 0471510137
e-mail: info@andrianer-kellerei.it

The Cantina Produttori Andriano is the oldest co-operative winery in Alto Adige. Founded in 1893, it brings together 145 partners who work 140 hectares of vineyards, half planted to white varieties. The largest producer of organic wines in Alto Adige, the cellar has for years offered a broad range of always very dependable wines. This year, it presented the panel with an assortment of excellent wines. Eight out of 11 received Two Glasses, and one went through to the final taste-offs for the Three Glass award. We'll start with the Merlot Siebeneich '99 Tor di Lupo. Intense ruby, it has delicate, clear, fruity aromas with elegant hints of oak and a strong, complex structure on the stylish palate. Definitely the best red from the winery and one of the best Merlots from the region. The other reds were also excellent: the Lagrein Tor di Lupo '99 and Lagrein Riserva Selection Sonnengut '98 are two rich, powerful wines in the traditional mould; the Cabernet Tor di Lupo '98, a soft red, with sweet tannins and well-integrated hints of oak; the fragrant Santa Maddalena and Schiava St. Justina are both very drinkable. The whites from Andriano are just as good as the reds. The Terlano Sauvignon Preciosa Tor di Lupo '00 shows an intense, concentrated fruity bouquet, with hints of aniseed, sage and lime blossom. Then the characterful, tangy palate reveals good body and length. The Traminer Aromatico Selection Sonnengut '00 is a very well-typed, richly aromatic glass with inviting hints of roses. The Chardonnay Tor di Lupo '99 is also rich in flavour and aromas. It is soft and elegant, even if the oak is a bit dominant. Finally, don't forget the Müller Thurgau Classico, a white with an excellent price-quality ratio.

●	A. A. Merlot Siebeneich Tor di Lupo '99	▼▼	4
●	A. A. Lagrein Scuro Tor di Lupo '99	▼▼	4
○	A. A. Gewürztraminer Sel. Sonnengut '00	▼▼	4
○	A. A. Terlano Müller Thurgau Cl. '00	▼▼	2*
○	A. A. Terlano Sauvignon Preciosa Tor di Lupo '00	▼▼	3
●	A.A. Lagrein Riserva Sel. Sonnengut '98	▼▼	3*
○	A. A. Chardonnay Tor di Lupo '99	▼▼	4
●	A. A. Santa Maddalena '00	▼	2*
●	A. A. Schiava S. Giustina '00	▼	2
○	A. A. Terlano Pinot Bianco Cl. Sonnengut '00	▼	3
●	A. A. Merlot Siebeneich '97	▼▼	4
●	A. A. Cabernet Tor di Lupo '98	▼▼	5
●	A. A. Lagrein Scuro Tor di Lupo '98	▼▼	4
○	A. A. Chardonnay Tor di Lupo '98	▼	4

APPIANO/EPPAN (BZ)

Josef Brigl
Loc. Cornaiano/Girlan
Via San Floriano, 8
39057 Appiano/Eppan (BZ)
tel. 0471662419
e-mail: brigl@brigl.com

With around 2,000,000 bottles produced each year and 50 hectares of vineyards, this is the largest winery in Alto Adige in absolute terms. For several years, more precisely since the mid 1990s, Brigl has only been mentioned either for its vast production or the value for money offered by its wines. But we saw evidence of an overall improvement in quality in the tasting samples submitted to us this year. The most convincing was the Lagrein Scuro Briglhof '98, a well-typed red with good concentration. Equally impressive was the Santa Maddalena Classico Reierhof '00, which is right at the top of its category. And what about the excellent Sauvignon '00, an impeccably made white with nice varietal aromas? In other words, Brigl was a very pleasant surprise and we are the first to be satisfied. But there is more. The Terlano Pinot Bianco '00 and Pinot Nero Briglhof '98 are both at least correctly made while the Gewürztraminer Windegg '00 and Lago di Caldaro Haslhof '00, a fragrant, delicate red, are straightforward but well-executed. All in all, it was a creditable performance with every wine presented taking at least one Glass.

○	A. A. Santa Maddalena Reierhof '00	▼▼	3*
○	A. A. Sauvignon '00	▼▼	4*
●	A. A. Lagrein Scuro Briglhof '98	▼▼	5
○	A. A. Gewürztraminer Windegg '00	▼	4
●	A. A. Lago di Caldaro Scelto Haslhof '00	▼	3
●	A. A. Pinot Nero Briglhof '98	▼	5
○	A. A. Terlano Pinot Bianco '00	▼	3
○	A. A. Sauvignon '98	▼▼	3
○	A. A. Sauvignon '99	▼▼	3
●	A. A. Lagrein Scuro '97	▼	3
●	A. A. Merlot Windegg '97	▼	3
●	A. A. Pinot Nero Haslhof '97	▼	4
○	A. A. Chardonnay '99	▼	3

APPIANO/EPPAN (BZ)

Cantina Produttori Colterenzio
Loc. Cornaiano/Girlan
Strada del Vino, 8
39050 Appiano/Eppan (BZ)
Tel. 0471664246
E-mail: info@colterenzio.com

There were 20 Glasses for the ten wines presented by Colterenzio/Schreckbichl, with an average of Two Glasses per wine. A performance like that is only possible from cellars that belong to the aristocracy of Italian production. This is one such winery. The quality of its wines is always impressive and this time the Three Glass award went to the Chardonnay Cornell '99, which shows great character in spite of a difficult vintage. It may not have the strength of the '98 or '97 but the nose has refined aromas redolent of tropical fruit. Everything is in place in the well-balanced palate and the concentration is more than just good. The Gewürztraminer Cornell '00 also came close to our finals for it is one of the best versions of the last few years. But then we had to choose. The Pinot Bianco Weisshaus '00 was very good, fragrant and even in flavour. The Chardonnay Pinay '00, a younger brother to the Cornell, was also very decent, as was the Sauvignon Prail, again from 2000, a soft, varietal wine. The panel also heaped praise on the Pinot Grigio Puiten '00, the Lagrein Cornell '99 and the Cabernet Sauvignon-Merlot Cornelius Rosso '98. On the other hand, we were slightly perplexed by the Cabernet Sauvignon Lafoa '98, perhaps because of our memories of the truly impressive '97, and particularly by the Sauvignon Lafoa '00 where the varietal characteristics seem to veer a bit too much toward vegetal notes and the oaky component is less integrated than we would have liked. But critics have a job to do, pointing out what they consider minor faults, especially when dealing with fine wines at prices that are not exactly bargain basement.

○ A. A. Chardonnay Cornell '99	▼▼▼	6
○ A. A. Gewürztraminer Cornell '00	▼▼	6
○ A. A. Chardonnay Pinay '00	▼▼	5
○ A. A. Pinot Bianco Weisshaus '00	▼▼	4
○ A. A. Pinot Grigio Puiten '00	▼▼	5
○ A. A. Sauvignon Prail '00	▼▼	4
● A. A. Cabernet Sauvignon Lafoa '98	▼▼	6
● A. A. Cabernet-Merlot Cornelius Rosso '98	▼▼	6
● A. A. Lagrein Cornell '99	▼▼	6
○ A. A. Sauvignon Lafoa '00	▼	6
● A. A. Cabernet Sauvignon Lafoa '97	▼▼▼	6

APPIANO/EPPAN (BZ)

Cantina Produttori Cornaiano
Loc. Cornaiano/Girlan
Via San Martino, 24
39050 Appiano/Eppan (BZ)
Tel. 0471662403
E-mail: info@girlan.it

Hartmuth Spitaler, director of Cornaiano/Girlan, one of the oldest and most prestigious co-operative wineries in Alto Adige, is a very charismatic personality. One of his convictions is that Schiava could be a more serious wine than it is if it were produced to higher standards. This is not just a statement of principle. Spitaler has in fact for years presented what could be considered the Ferrari of Schiavas, the Von alten Reben aus Gschleier, or "Gschleier" for short. The '99 version is fairly pleasant, even though we are anxiously awaiting the '00 vintage, which should be superior. The nose has aromas of blackcurrants and other wild berries, then a full-bodied, concentrated palate that has little to do with the lightweight flavours you so often find in what passes for Schiava. But Cornaiano/Girlan also produces other excellent wines. The Sauvignon Select Art Flora '00 even reached our finals. The Cabernet Sauvignon Riserva '98, the Lagrein Riserva '98, the varietal Pinot Bianco Plattenriegl '00 and the Pinot Nero Patricia '99, the last of these one of the best in its category from the vintage, all easily took Two Glasses. The Chardonnay Select Art Flora '99, Pinot Nero Mazon Trattmannhof '99 and Lagrein-Merlot Cuvée Girlan scored a Glass apiece. All this gives you a clear picture of this excellent winery, with its commendably consistent quality and very professional management.

○ A. A. Sauvignon Select Art Flora '00	▼▼	5
○ A. A. Pinot Bianco Plattenriegl '00	▼▼	3*
● A. A. Cabernet Sauvignon Ris. '98	▼▼	5
● A. A. Lagrein Ris. '98	▼▼	5
● A. A. Pinot Nero Patricia '99	▼▼	4*
● A. A. Schiava Gschleier '99	▼▼	4
○ A. A. Chardonnay Select Art Flora '00	▼	5
● A. A. Lagrein-Merlot Cuvée Girlan '98	▼	4
● A. A. Pinot Nero Mazon Trattmannhof '99	▼	5
● A. A. Cabernet Sauvignon Ris. '97	▼▼	5
● A. A. Lagrein Ris. '97	▼▼	5

APPIANO/EPPAN (BZ)

★ Cantina Produttori
San Michele Appiano
Via Circonvallazione, 17/19
39057 Appiano/Eppan (BZ)
tel. 0471664466
e-mail: kellerei@stmichael.it

It is tempting to skip the tasting notes on wines from San Michele Appiano since there is a serious risk of repeating yourself. But this is a risk we'll just have to run. So let's begin by saying that this winery is the first in Alto Adige to be awarded a Guide Star for ten Three Glasses awards. With its two triumphs this year, the total actually comes to 11, which prompts us, again, to hazard the opinion that this is the best co-operative winery in Italy. The two wines we alluded to just now are the Sauvignon St. Valentin '00 and the Gewürztraminer St. Valentin, also from 2000, two superbly varietal whites, made with consummate skill. The Pinot Grigio and Chardonnay '99, barrique-aged whites, came close in the finals for the Three Glasses, missing out by a hair's breadth. But it is the entire range of wines presented here that is impressive and surprising in its constant quality. Take the Sauvignon Lahn '00, for example. It's almost as good this year as its thoroughbred stablemate, the St. Valentin. Or again there are the Pinot Nero Riserva and Cabernet Riserva '98, which utterly belie the long-standing reputation of cellarmaster Hans Terzer as a man who can only make whites. And how can we resist the delicious, aromatic allure of the Comtess '00, a sweet white from partially dried gewürztraminer grapes? Or the aristocratic profile of the Riesling Montiggl '00 in one of its best versions ever? Two wines are merely decent, the Pinot Grigio Anger '00 and, oddly enough, the Pinot Bianco Schulthauser '00, from which we expected something more.

APPIANO/EPPAN (BZ)

Cantina Produttori San Paolo
Loc. San Paolo/St. Pauls
Via Castel Guardia, 21
39050 Appiano/Eppan (BZ)
tel. 0471662183
e-mail: info@kzllereistpauls.com

We would have liked more convincing results from the Cantina Produttori San Paolo. The wines are correct, even well-made, and definitely pleasant. However, none are really exceptional; none are wines that would give the winery's production the distinction that comes from an exclusive, top of the range, selection. The quality objective is more than within reach of this important and relatively old (founded almost a century ago) Alto Adige winery. Coming back to the wines from this year, we can point out a decent version of Sauvignon Exclusiv Gfilhof, the '00, and Terlano Pinot Bianco Exclusiv Plötzner, again from 2000. These are well-typed whites with delicately fruity aromas, consistent flavour and decent balance. But they are still wines that, all things considered, are rather simple. They neither disappoint nor surprise. The Schiava Exclusiv Sarner '00 is pleasant, fruity, fragrant and pleasantly drinkable. The Lagrein Riserva '99 and Pinot Nero '99 from the DiVinus line are less brilliant than usual, perhaps because of problems connected with the unimpressive vintage. As you can see, all these wines are fairly good in general but the potential of a San Paolo has yet to be pushed to the limit.

○ A. A. Gewürztraminer St. Valentin '00	🍷🍷🍷	5
○ A. A. Sauvignon St. Valentin '00	🍷🍷🍷	5
○ A. A. Chardonnay St. Valentin '99	🍷🍷	5
○ A. A. Pinot Grigio St. Valentin '99	🍷🍷	5
○ A. A. Riesling Montiggl '00	🍷🍷	4
○ A. A. Sauvignon Lahn '00	🍷🍷	4
○ Comtess '00	🍷🍷	6
● A. A. Cabernet Ris. '98	🍷🍷	5
● A. A. Pinot Nero Ris. '98	🍷🍷	5
○ A. A. Pinot Bianco Schulthauser '00	🍷	4
○ A. A. Pinot Grigio Anger '00	🍷	4
○ A. A. Chardonnay St. Valentin '97	🍷🍷🍷	4
○ A. A. Sauvignon St. Valentin '98	🍷🍷🍷	4
○ Comtess '98	🍷🍷	5

○ A. A. Sauvignon Exclusiv Gfilhof '00	🍷	4
● A. A. Schiava Exclusiv Sarner '00	🍷	3
○ A. A. Terlano Pinot Bianco Exclusiv Plötzner '00	🍷	4
● A. A. Lagrein Scuro DiVinus Ris. '99	🍷	5
● A. A. Pinot Nero DiVinus '99	🍷	5
● A. A. Merlot DiVinus '97	🍷🍷	5
● A. A. Lagrein Scuro DiVinus Ris. '97	🍷	5
● A. A. Merlot DiVinus '98	🍷	5
○ A. A. Sauvignon Exclusiv Gfilhof '99	🍷	4

APPIANO/EPPAN (BZ)

Kössler - Praeclarus
Loc. San Paolo/St. Pauls
39050 Appiano/Eppan (BZ)
Tel. 0471660256 - 0471662182

The wines presented by this winery at San Paolo Appiano are as reliable and well-made as ever, thanks to impeccable technical management and careful selection of the grapes at harvest-time. We again note that part of the range is made up of still wines, almost all under the Kössler & Ebner label, while the other wines are metodo classico spumantes sold with the Praeclarus label. The most interesting of the still bottles this year was the Lagrein '98, a red with excellent body and the classic aromas of wild berries laced with slightly spicy hints. The Cabernet-Merlot Cuvée St. Pauls '98 was also decent; it is elegant but perhaps not as complex as we would have liked. This was probably because of the unexceptional vintage in the zone. The same holds true for the Cabernet '98. However, the truly low prices of both should be emphasized. Moving onto the sparklers, it is no news that the Praeclarus Noblesse Riserva '92 is very sound. It's a "blanc de blancs" from chardonnay grapes, with small additions of pinot bianco. This is one of the best Alto Adige spumantes and has a particularly complex bouquet, with smoky, mineral notes alongside more fruity aromas. The flavour is full and concentrated. The non-vintage Praeclarus Brut, which has a bit of pinot nero added to the blend, is also good, as is the fragrant Praeclarus Rosé.

APPIANO/EPPAN (BZ)

Ignaz Niedrist
Loc. Cornaiano/Girlan
Via Ronco, 5
39050 Appiano/Eppan (BZ)
Tel. 0471664494

We have already mentioned several times that Ignaz Niedrist was just a heartbeat away from his first Three Glass distinction. Knowing his talent and dedication, we were really hoping this would happen. Niedrist is a professional, an intelligent winemaker who looks for balance and elegance in his wines. It is no coincidence that he has always worked with difficult grape varieties such as riesling, pinot nero and sauvignon. Well, Ignaz hit the mark for the first time and earned Three Glasses with a formidable Terlano Sauvignon '00. A superb white, vinified "à la Niedrist", with aromas that are varietal but not excessively wild, showing notes of white peach and elderflower then a round, balanced flavour with hints of acidity well integrated into the structure of the wine. But it does not stop here. Niedrist is slowly bringing the small vineyard of Berger Gei, in the centre of Gries, back onstream. He now vinifies almost all the grapes from this vineyard himself, no longer handing them over to the local co-operative winery. The Lagrein Scuro Berger Gei Riserva '97 made it to our finals and shows excellent concentration with clean, caressing aromas. Another Niedrist speciality, the Riesling '00, also reached the final taste-offs in one of the best versions from the last few years. The Niedrist triumph was completed by the standard Lagrein Berger Gei '99, a red with heady aromas and a full, consistent, fairly well-balanced flavour. All this from just five hectares of vineyards. Hats off, then, to Ignaz Niedrist, a small producer who brings honour to winemaking in Alto Adige.

	Wine	Glasses	Score
○	A. A. Spumante Praeclarus Noblesse Ris. '92	🍷🍷	5
●	A. A. Lagrein Scuro '98	🍷🍷	5
○	A. A. Praeclarus Brut	🍷🍷	5
●	A. A. Cabernet Kössler & Ebner '98	🍷	4
●	A. A. Cabernet-Merlot S. Pauls '98	🍷	4
⊙	A. A. Praeclarus Rosé	🍷	5
○	A. A. Spumante Praeclarus Noblesse Ris. '91	🍷🍷	6
●	A. A. Cabernet Kössler & Ebner '97	🍷🍷	4
●	A. A. Merlot-Lagrein Ebner '97	🍷🍷	5
○	A. A. Bianco '99	🍷🍷	5

	Wine	Glasses	Score
○	A. A. Terlano Sauvignon '00	🍷🍷🍷	4*
○	A. A. Riesling Renano '00	🍷🍷	4
●	A. A. Lagrein Scuro Berger Gei Ris. '97	🍷🍷	5
●	A. A. Lagrein Scuro Berger Gei '99	🍷	4
●	A. A. Pinot Nero '95	🍷🍷	4
○	A. A. Riesling Renano '95	🍷🍷	4
●	A. A. Pinot Nero '96	🍷🍷	4
○	A. A. Riesling Renano '96	🍷🍷	4
●	A. A. Merlot '98	🍷🍷	5
○	A. A. Terlano Sauvignon '98	🍷🍷	4
○	A. A. Riesling Renano '99	🍷🍷	4
●	A. A. Pinot Nero '97	🍷	5
●	A. A. Pinot Nero '98	🍷	5

APPIANO/EPPAN (BZ)

Josef Niedermayr
Loc. Cornaiano/Girlan
Via Casa di Gesù, 15
39050 Appiano/Eppan (BZ)
tel. 0471662451
e-mail: info@niedermayr.it

The best products presented by Josef Niedermayr this year include more than just sweet wines. Sure, the Aureus '99 is always top of the range and you couldn't say it is not sweet. This white passito, mainly from partially dried chardonnay and sauvignon fruit, wins Three Glasses for the third time. The Aureus is by now a classic and it is difficult not to let oneself be charmed by its delicately botrytized bouquet and a flavour that is sweet, but not cloying, and well supported by generous acidity. But there are also several nice surprises among the other wines. This time the Euforius '99, a barrique-aged red from lagrein, cabernet and merlot, almost upstaged it, going through to the finals and coming close to a Third Glass. The palate is remarkably well-balanced palate and the nose elegant, intense and rich in particularly well-defined fruit and balsam notes. The Lagrein Aus Gries Riserva '99 was also very good. Though it does not match the concentration of the '97, it is still one of the best of its type. We felt the best of the whites was the Gewürztraminer Lage Doss '00, a well made bottle from an almost historic vintage for the variety. The other wines were all, at the very least, well-made, the Pinot Nero Riserva '99 being decent and the Sauvignon Allure '00 good, with nicely varietal aromas. A notch below these are the less exciting, aroma-rich Terlano Hof zu Pramol '00 and Santa Maddalena Egger-Larcherhof.

APPIANO/EPPAN (BZ)

Stroblhof
Via Pigano, 25
39057 Appiano/Eppan (BZ)
tel. 0471662250
e-mail: hotel@stroblhof.it

The Stroblhof winery in the village of San Michele Appiano adjoins the hotel and restaurant of the same name, which is well-known in the area. For more than 30 years, Stroblhof has released decent, well-made wines. For some time, it has also profited from the consultancy of Hans Terzer, the legendary cellarmaster from the Cantina Produttori di San Michele Appiano. The flagship product of the winery is definitely the Pinot Bianco Strahler, a real classic for the zone. This year, the 2000 version was not particularly great but neither was it a wine to pass over. It has varietal, rather one-dimensional aromas and a decently concentrated structure on the palate. The Pinot Nero Pigeno '98 was decidedly better, and in fact it was the best wine in the range. Here again we are dealing with a classic, given that Stroblhof has had a reputation for some time for its knack with Pinot Nero. The Pigeno '98, not the well-known Riserva, which has not yet been released this year, but a standard-label version, is elegant with well-defined varietal aromas. The Gewürztraminer Pigeno '00 is interesting though not exceptional. The Chardonnay Schwarzhaus '00, aged in large casks for nine months, was more convincing. It has a nice impact on the palate and a fairly delicate, varietal bouquet although the length is not that marvellous.

	Wine	Glasses	Score
○	Aureus '99	♛♛♛	6
●	Euforius '99	♛♛	5
○	A. A. Gewürztraminer Lage Doss '00	♛♛	5
●	A. A. Lagrein Aus Gries Ris. '99	♛♛	5
●	A. A. Santa Maddalena Cl. Egger-Larcherhof '00	♛	3
○	A. A. Sauvignon Allure '00	♛	5
○	A. A. Terlano Hof zu Pramol '00	♛	4
●	A. A. Pinot Nero Ris. '99	♛	5
○	Aureus '95	♛♛♛	6
○	Aureus '98	♛♛♛	6
○	Aureus '96	♛♛	6
○	Aureus '97	♛♛	6
●	Euforius '98	♛♛	5

	Wine	Glasses	Score
●	A. A. Pinot Nero Pigeno '98	♛♛	5
○	A. A. Chardonnay Schwarzhaus '00	♛	4
○	A. A. Gewürztraminer Pigeno '00	♛	4
○	A. A. Pinot Bianco Strahler '00	♛	4
●	A. A. Pinot Nero Strahler Ris. '90	♛♛	6
●	A. A. Pinot Nero Ris. '96	♛♛	5
○	A. A. Gewürztraminer '97	♛♛	4
○	A. A. Pinot Bianco Strahler '97	♛♛	4
●	A. A. Pinot Nero Ris. '97	♛♛	5
○	A. A. Gewürztraminer '98	♛♛	4
○	A. A. Pinot Bianco Strahler '98	♛♛	4
○	A. A. Pinot Bianco Strahler '99	♛♛	4
●	A. A. Pinot Nero Ris. '93	♛	5
●	A. A. Pinot Nero Ris. '95	♛	5

APPIANO/EPPAN (BZ)

Viticoltori Alto Adige
Via Circonvallazione, 17
39057 Appiano/Eppan (BZ)
Tel. 0471660060
E-mail: viticoltoria@tiscalinet.it

This was one of our biggest surprises in Alto Adige when we were tasting for this edition of the Guide. The Viticoltori Alto Adige, also known as the Torchio d'Oro, is a winery that markets products supplied by other co-operative wineries, including Colterenzio and San Michele Appiano. In technical terms, it could be defined as a second level co-operative. The fact is that sometimes the wines from this label are just as attractive as those from more celebrated wineries and cost decidedly less. This year, we were truly amazed by the four wines they presented. All went beyond the Two Glass cut-off point and two even went through to the finals. The Lagrein Torculum '98 was very good. An excellent red, it is powerful, full-bodied, very well-typed and incredible value for money. Jaws dropped in disbelief when the panel saw the price list. The Terlano Sauvignon Classico '00 is awesome, clean and varietal in its aromas, and they are almost giving this wine away as well. To put things in perspective, the quality is beyond that of some wines selling at twice the price. The lightly barrique-aged Chardonnay Torculum '99 was very good, coherent and elegant in its bouquet, and well-balanced on the palate. The series closes with the Santa Maddalena Classico Tenuta De Ferrari '00, which is one of the best in its category. Here again, no need to comment on the prices. If we were to award a prize to the winery with the best price-quality ratio in Italy, this would probably be the number one candidate. It goes to show that you superior quality can still be made at affordable prices.

○ A. A. Terlano Sauvignon Cl. '00	🍷🍷	3*
● A. A. Lagrein Scuro Torculum Ris. '98	🍷🍷	3*
● A. A. Santa Maddalena Tenuta De Ferrari '00	🍷🍷	2*
○ A. A. Chardonnay Torculum '99	🍷🍷	3*

BOLZANO/BOZEN

Andreas Berger Thurnhof
Via Castel Flavon, 7
39100 Bolzano/Bozen
Tel. 0471288460 - 0471285446
E-mail: info@thurnhof.com

Thurnhof is a small, family-run winery that has been around for a while. Since 1175, in fact. It is located on three hectares of vineyards in the Bolzano-Aslago area, a warm, sunny zone with high temperatures that guarantee complete ripening even for late-maturing red grapes. Andreas Berger, a young, enthusiastic winemaker and oenologist, makes wines with character. For years, we have closely followed the development of this estate and are very happy to be able to award it Three Glasses for the first time. They go to the Lagrein Scuro from the '99 vintage, one of the house specialities and one of the greatest reds in the history of Thurnhof. An impenetrable ruby, it throws intense aromas of bramble-dominated berries along with chocolate and spice, all beautifully defined and sustained. Delicate on the palate, it has concentration and roundness with a distinctly mature tannic structure. It's an exciting, truly impressive wine that literally explodes onto the palate. The Passaurum is also very interesting. A passito from partially dried moscato giallo, sauvignon and riesling grapes, it is clear amber with brilliant highlights. On the nose, it displays attractive aromas of ripe apricots, saffron and botrytis then offers plenty of body sweetness in the mouth. Too bad only a few hundred bottles are produced. The Cabernet Sauvignon Riserva '98 seemed a bit simple to us, with green notes on the nose and average structure on the palate. Finally, the Moscato Giallo was pleasant.

● A. A. Lagrein Scuro '99	🍷🍷🍷	4*
○ Passaurum '99	🍷🍷	5
○ A. A. Moscato Giallo '00	🍷	3
● A. A. Cabernet Sauvignon Ris. '98	🍷	5
● A. A. Cabernet '93	🍷🍷	4
● A. A. Cabernet Wienegg Ris. '94	🍷🍷	4
● A. A. Lagrein Scuro '95	🍷🍷	5
● A. A. Lagrein Scuro Ris. '97	🍷🍷	5
● A. A. Lagrein Scuro '98	🍷🍷	4
○ Passaurum	🍷🍷	5
○ A. A. Sauvignon '99	🍷	3

BOLZANO/BOZEN

Cantina Convento Muri-Gries
P.zza Gries, 21
39100 Bolzano/Bozen
tel. 0471282287
e-mail: muri-gries-kg@dnet.it

A brace of splendid wines and a tradition that continues to stand the test of time. Muri-Gries is a winery that sets the standard for Lagrein Scuro and never ceases to amaze us with the constant quality of its top wines. So it was with conviction, as well as the satisfaction of seeing how the cellar's ceaseless search for the best possible quality has never wavered, that this year we again give Three Glasses to the Lagrein Scuro Abtei Riserva '98. This exceptional wine manages to marry the complexity of the nose, coming from the base grape, with awesome power. As extract-rich a wine as a Hermitage by Chave or a Côte Rotie from Guigal, in its own way, but with all the personality and character of a fantastic representative Lagrein from the historic cru of Gries. To sip it is to fall in love with it. Along with this blockbuster is a real surprise, a white Alto Adige Bianco Abtei from '99, aged in barriques for about a year and blended mainly from pinot bianco plus chardonnay and pinot grigio. It is all that a good barrique-aged white should be: fruity on the nose, with only faint toasty notes, and a soft, caressing, concentrated mouthfeel. The other wines presented were decidedly less challenging. The decent Lagrein Scuro Abtei '00 was pleasant but with very fermented aromas, while the Lagrein Rosato '00 and Pinot Grigio '00 gave the impression of being there mainly to give some depth to the range.

	Wine	Glasses	Score
●	A. A. Lagrein Scuro Abtei Ris. '98	ŸŸŸ	5
○	A. A. Bianco Abtei '99	ŸŸ	5
○	A. A. Pinot Grigio '00	Ÿ	3
⊙	A. A. Lagrein Rosato '00	Ÿ	3
●	A. A. Lagreis Scuro Abtei. '00	Ÿ	4
●	A. A. Lagrein Scuro Abtei Ris. '96	ŸŸŸ	5
●	A. A. Lagrein Scuro Abtei Ris. '97	ŸŸŸ	5
●	A. A. Cabernet Ris. '91	ŸŸ	5
●	A. A. Lagrein Scuro Gries '95	ŸŸ	4
●	A. A. Lagrein Scuro Gries '97	ŸŸ	2
●	A. A. Lagrein Scuro Gries '98	Ÿ	4

BOLZANO/BOZEN

Cantina Gries
Fraz. Gries
P.zza Gries, 2
39100 Bolzano/Bozen
tel. 0471270909 - 0471280248
e-mail: info@cantina-gries.it

2000 was the last harvest vinified by the Cantina Gries on its own before its merger with the Cantina di Santa Maddalena. But nothing will change for the consumer. The names of the two wineries will remain, as will the renowned quality of their products. This year, Cantina Gries amazed us with an extraordinary sweet white, the Moscato Giallo Passito Vinalia '99, which was well worth its Three Glasses. Clear amber in the glass, it tempts the nose with an intense, concentrated bouquet of botrytis, honey and nuts, then charms the palate with its luxurious structure and elegant balance of residual sugar and fresh acidity. But more than anything, Cantina Gries is a watchword for the production of Lagrein. There are two outstanding Lagrein Scuros from this winery: the Collection Grieser Baron Carl Eyrl Riserva '99 and the Prestige Line Grieser Riserva '98. The former, from the vineyards of Barone Carl Eyrl, is vinified the traditional way, on the skins. Ruby in hue, it reveals delicately attractive aromas of berries and new wood, then a full-bodied, complex, velvety mouthfeel. The Grieser Riserva was pressed in the traditional manner and then aged for a year in barriques. It is convincing in its complex fruitiness, with hints of violet and chocolate, and rich tannic structure. The Mauritius '98 is a successful blend of merlot and lagrein that preserves the natural aromas of the fruit. The Cantina di Gries is also famous for its Santa Maddalenas and one of the best is the Collection Classico Tröglerhof '00. The Pinot Bianco Collection Fritz Dellago '00 stands out among the whites and the rest of the range is at least correct.

	Wine	Glasses	Score
○	A. A. Moscato Giallo Vinalia '99	ŸŸŸ	5
○	A. A. Pinot Bianco Fritz Dellago '00	ŸŸ	3
●	A. A. Santa Maddalena Cl. Tröglerhof '00	ŸŸ	3
●	A. A. Lagrein Scuro Grieser Prestige Line Ris. '98	ŸŸ	5
●	Mauritius '98	ŸŸ	5
●	A. A. Lagrein Scuro Grieser Baron Carl Eyrl Ris. '99	ŸŸ	5
○	A. A. Sauvignon '00	Ÿ	4
⊙	A. A. Lagrein Rosato '98	Ÿ	5
●	A. A. Lagrein Scuro Grieser '99	Ÿ	4
●	A. A. Lagrein Scuro Grieser Baron Carl Eyrl Ris. '97	ŸŸ	5
●	A. A. Lagrein Scuro Grieser Prestige Line Ris. '97	ŸŸ	5

BOLZANO/BOZEN

CANTINA PRODUTTORI
SANTA MADDALENA
VIA BRENNERO, 15
39100 BOLZANO/BOZEN
TEL. 0471972944
E-MAIL: info@kellereimagdalena.com

This year was a triumph for the wines of the Cantina Produttori di Santa Maddalena. The extensive, varied range at times achieves real excellence. This result is very important in terms of the winery's upcoming merger with the Cantina di Gries to create the Cantina Produttori di Bolzano. The new cellar will have an estimated capacity of more than 2,000,000 bottles. But getting back to this year's wine, as usual the best was the Lagrein Taberhof Riserva '99, an excellent version of one of the finest Lagreins from Alto Adige, despite the unsatisfactory vintage. It is concentrated, typical, powerful and very well-balanced: confirmation that the Taberhof Riserva is as good as they get. The Sauvignon Mockhof '00 is also very good and almost picked up a third Glass. It made it to our finals because of its varietal aromas of tropical fruit and a full body with a very refreshing, slightly acidic, varietal note. The Gewürztraminer and Chardonnay Kleinstein, both from 2000, are interesting, the first showing particularly clean aromatic notes on the nose. The Cabernet Mumelterhof '99 and Lagrein Perlhof '99 are a bit below par but nonetheless well-made from the technical point of view. In contrast, the Santa Maddalena Classico Huck am Bach '00 was excellent, perhaps the best of its type. The others were all decent, with a special mention for the Pinot Nero Greel '00, which is fresher and more varietal than the Riserva Sandlahner '99. The Santa Maddalena Classico '00, the Riesling Leitach '00, the Müller Thurgau '00 and the Pinot Bianco '00 were all easy-drinking but very pleasant, and with very reasonable price tags.

BOLZANO/BOZEN

FRANZ GOJER GLÖGGLHOF
FRAZ. S. MADDALENA
VIA RIVELLONE, 1
39100 BOLZANO/BOZEN
TEL. 0471978775

Franz Gojer has moved to the front this year with a series of incredible wines that are better than ever before. An excellent result for an enthusiastic winemaker like Franz, very much a real one man band at this winery, capable of producing 40,000 bottles a year. The Lagrein Riserva '99 made it to our finals. It's a typical, concentrated red as only a great country-style Lagrein can be. It may be a bit too rugged but it also has character and charm. The standard-label Lagrein '00 is also very good. It has intensely fruity aromas and obviously less strength than the Riserva but also has a perilous drinkability. All this at a cellar door price of around € 5.00. If that's not a steal then we do not know what is. The Merlot Spitz '99 is interesting. Its label comes from a local placename; it's not dedicated to the great American swimming champion from the 1970s. Franz's two most typical wines are always good. The Santa Maddalena Classico '00 and Santa Maddalena Rondell '00 are fragrant and so quaffable they just sweep you off your feet. What more can we say? Perhaps just that we would like to find winemakers as good as Gojer all over the world.

● A. A. Lagrein Scuro Taberhof Ris. '99	6
○ A. A. Sauvignon Mockhof '00	4
○ A. A. Chardonnay Kleinstein '00	4
○ A. A. Gewürztramier Kleinstein '00	4
● A. A. Pinot Nero Greel '00	4*
● A. A. Santa Maddalena Cl. Huck am Bach '00	4
● A. A. Cabernet Mumelterhof '99	6
○ A. A. Pinot Bianco '00	3*
○ A. A. Riesling Leitach '00	4
● A. A. Santa Maddalena Cl. '00	3
○ A. A. Valle Isarco Müller Thurgau '00	3*
● A. A. Lagrein Scuro Perlhof '99	4
● A. A. Pinot Nero Sandlahner Ris. '99	5

● A. A. Lagrein Scuro Ris. '99	4
● A. A. Lagrein Scuro '00	4*
● A. A. Santa Maddalena Cl. '00	3*
● A. A. Santa Maddalena Rondell '00	3*
● A. A. Merlot Spitz '99	4
● A. A. Lagrein Scuro Ris. '98	4
● A. A. Lagrein Scuro '99	3
● A. A. Santa Maddalena Cl. '99	2
● A. A. Santa Maddalena Rondell '99	2

BOLZANO/BOZEN

Loacker Schwarzhof
Via Santa Justina, 3
39100 Bolzano/Bozen
tel. 0471365125
e-mail: lo@cker.it

Famous in Italy for producing excellent bakery products, the Loacker family is also one of the main players in winemaking in the Santa Maddalena area. Their estate uses organic methods and the seven hectares of vineyard produce around 80,000 bottles. This year, Rainer and Hayo Loacker presented us with a range of wines that seemed to have made overall progress when compared with earlier years. One in particular, the part barrique-aged Chardonnay Ateyon '99, easily reached our finals. It's a full wine with good body, a bouquet of tropical fruit and hints of oak-derived vanilla. The Cuvée Jus Osculi '99 is fairly good, with a clear prevalence of schiava grapes and the addition of lagrein, cabernet and pinot nero. In other words, it's a sort of Santa Maddalena Classico with a bit of reinforcement. The typical Lagrein Pitz Thurü Riserva '99 is not bad and has a fragrant bouquet even though its structure is less than huge. The Cabernet Kastlet Riserva '98 is decent. The vintage year was only average but it's well-made technically. The other wines are less interesting but still very satisfactory in comparison with past performances.

BOLZANO/BOZEN

R. Malojer Gummerhof
Via Weggestein, 36
39100 Bolzano/Bozen
tel. 0471972885
e-mail: info@malojer.it

The wines of Urban and Alfred Malojer this year put on a show worthy of inclusion in the Guide. The cellar vinifies fruit from 30 hectares of vineyards, some estate-owned, some rented, and produces about 100,000 bottles of ten of so different types, almost all of them reds from the Bolzano area. The most prestigious product is the Cabernet-Lagrein Bautzanum Riserva '99, a powerful, aroma-rich red that integrates the distinguishing features of its two base grapes well. The '99 version is more decisive and concentrated than the '98, though that was also good. At any rate, both are more convincing than the simple Cabernet Riserva '98, which is well-made but without much character and slightly dilute in the mouth. The two Lagrein Riserva, '99 and '98 are both good but we preferred the former for its intensity on both nose and palate. The Lagrein Rahmhött '99 is less successful, though still well-typed. It's elegant enough but lacks personality. In contrast, the Merlot Riserva '99 is elegant, varietal, soft and concentrated, in short a truly lovely wine. The last two wines we tried were more predictable: the Santa Maddalena '00 is good but very simple and the Sauvignon Gur zur Sand '00 is correct and coherent, but offers no evident varietal notes.

○ A. A. Chardonnay Ateyon '99	♛♛	4*
● Cuvée Jus Osculi '99	♛♛	4
● A. A. Cabernet Kastlet Ris. '98	♛	5
● A. A. Lagrein Scuro Pitz Thurü Ris. '99	♛	4
● A. A. Cabernet Kastlet '96	♛♛	5

● A. A. Cabernet-Lagrein Bautzanum Ris. '99	♛♛	5
● A. A. Lagrein Scuro Ris. '99	♛♛	5
● A. A. Merlot Ris. '99	♛♛	5
● A. A. Santa Maddalena Cl. '00	♛	3
○ A. A. Sauvignon Gur zur Sand Classic '00	♛	4
● A. A. Cabernet Ris. '98	♛	5
● A. A. Cabernet-Lagrein Bautzanum '98	♛	5
● A. A. Lagrein Scuro Ris. '98	♛	5
● A. A. Lagrein Scuro Weingutt Rahmhütt '99	♛	3
● A. A. Lagrein Scuro Ris. '97	♛♛	5

BOLZANO/BOZEN

Josephus Mayr
Erbhof Unterganzner
Loc. Cardano/Kardaun
Via Campiglio, 15
39100 Bolzano/Bozen
Tel. 0471365582

We feel we ought to found a Josephus Mayr fan club. Why? Because he is one of the greats. First of all, a great grower, and then a great interpreter of his wines, which always have something personal, maybe a little crazy. Precisely because of this quirkiness, we feel they have a charm and charisma possessed by few other wines in Italy. It is very true that great wines are made by producers who identify themselves with their work and Josephus Mayr is that kind of man. This year, he presented us with some extraordinary wines. The Lamarein '99, from partially dried lagrein grapes – a little bit Amarone and a little bit Lagrein, if we interpreted it correctly – is fantastic. We didn't award it any Glasses because Josephus makes only 1,800 bottles and we do not want to be crucified by readers who can't get their hands on it. It is almost black, with a nose of bilberries and blackcurrants and a slightly sweet flavour that is very concentrated but not in the least cloying. If you do find it, try serving it with blue cheese. But the real jewel in the Mayr crown is the Lagrein Riserva '98, a delicious wine, with rare fullness and extraordinary class. The Cabernet Sauvignon '98 and Santa Maddalena Classico '99 are also good and in fact Mayr has released the Santa Maddalena after almost a year. Even the Lagrein Rosato '00 is pleasant and fragrant. It's a very simple wine that only Josephus Mayr could manage to make this well. So are we going to start this fan club or not?

BOLZANO/BOZEN

Georg Mumelter
Via Rencio, 66
39100 Bolzano/Bozen
Tel. 0471973090 - 03386137880
E-mail: mumelter@garolmail.net

With last year's results, Georg Mumelter has now entered the exclusive circle of the most promising winemakers in Alto Adige. He is a producer of few words and has worked his vineyards with great enthusiasm and commitment for years. Maybe Georg will be a bit more talkative after the publication of our Guide, especially with all those winelovers who will be asking for the Lagrein Scuro Riserva '99. The wine in question has in fact taken Three Glasses. Congratulations! The small, historic Griesbauerhof estate is located in the Santa Maddalena heartland and has three hectares of vineyards with excellent exposure. The Lagrein Scuro Riserva '99 is truly great. Aged in barriques, it has an intense ruby red colour, a well-typed bouquet with great intensity and a solid, powerful, rich structure with sweet, velvety tannins and long persistence in the mouth. A Lagrein that brings honour to its variety and, if there was ever any doubt, shows the great potential of this grape. The new wine from this estate is also interesting. The Isarcus '00 is made from the classic varieties of the Bolzano valley: schiava and a small percentage of lagrein. Special care in the vineyard, with partial drying on the vine, and long ageing in barriques give the wine great richness and variety in its fruit-driven yet delicate aromas, leading in to a velvety, full body. The Pinot Grigio, a white two thirds aged in stainless steel and one third in barriques, is sumptuous and has great structure, with concentrated aromas of quince and tropical fruit. The house Santa Maddalena is also a good drinking wine.

● A. A. Lagrein Scuro Ris. '98	🍷🍷🍷	5
● Lamarein '99	🍷🍷	6
● A. A. Cabernet Sauvignon '98	🍷🍷	5
● A. A. Santa Maddalena Cl. '99	🍷🍷	4
● A. A. Lagrein Scuro Ris. '97	🍷🍷🍷	5
● A. A. Lagrein Scuro Ris. '93	🍷🍷	5
● A. A. Lagrein Scuro Ris. '94	🍷🍷	5
● A. A. Cabernet Sauvignon '95	🍷🍷	5
● A. A. Lagrein Scuro Ris. '95	🍷🍷	5
● A. A. Cabernet Sauvignon '96	🍷🍷	5
● A. A. Lagrein Scuro Ris. '96	🍷🍷	5
● Lamarein '97	🍷🍷	5
● A. A. Lagrein Scuro '98	🍷🍷	3
● A. A. Santa Maddalena Cl. '98	🍷🍷	3
● Lamarein '98	🍷🍷	6

● A. A. Lagrein Scuro Ris. '99	🍷🍷🍷	5
○ A. A. Pinot Grigio Griesbauerhof '00	🍷🍷	4
● Isarcus '00	🍷🍷	5
● A. A. Santa Maddalena '00	🍷	3

BOLZANO/BOZEN

HEINRICH PLATTNER - WALDGRIES
SANTA GIUSTINA, 2
39100 BOLZANO/BOZEN
TEL. 0471973245

BOLZANO/BOZEN

GEORG RAMOSER - UNTERMOSERHOF
VIA SANTA MADDALENA DI SOTTO, 36
39100 BOLZANO/BOZEN
TEL. 0471975481

On not much more than four hectares on the hillslopes of Santa Giustina, in the classic Santa Maddalena zone in Bolzano, we find this completely family-run business where the father and son team of Heinrich and Christian Plattner work together with enthusiasm and skill. They produce just a few tens of thousands of bottles, mostly of wines typical to the zone. Their speciality however is sweet wines. This year, they presented us with two especially good ones: the Peperum '98, a passito from partially dried moscato giallo and gewürztraminer, and the Moscato Rosa '99, the Plattners' particular favourite. The Peperum is very well defined. It has obvious aromatic notes and the oak from the barriques is not at all intrusive. The second is a typically aromatic Moscato Rosa with very clear hints of wild rose. The other wines in the small Plattner range are all very decent with the Lagrein Riserva '99 just a shade better than the others. A very typical, if somewhat lightweight, Santa Maddalena Classico '00 and a more than decent Terlano Pinot Bianco Riol '00, partially aged in large casks, round off the list. Overall, this is one of the best small producers in Santa Maddalena and one of the wineries that helps to make wine in Alto Adige the thriving sector it is today.

An excellent Lagrein Riserva '99, perhaps less forceful than the monumental '97 version, but still very concentrated. That's the most interesting wine in the limited range presented to us by Georg Ramoser, owner of the tiny Untermoserhof winery in Santa Maddalena. This is a very typical red, with the classic aromas of blackcurrants mingling with hints of vanilla. The full, well-defined flavour shows faint tannins and a delicately bitter finish with excellent persistence. It reached our finals and came very close to a Third Glass. A good result, backed up by the panel's comments on the other two wines presented, both of which are very well-made. In particular, the Merlot '99 shows markedly varietal aromas, with notes of pencil lead and balsamic hints in addition to fruit. Just a few thousand bottles are produced from a vineyard barely larger than a single hectare. Because of this, the harvests are really small, never reaching 50 quintals. The last wine tasted was the Santa Maddalena Classico '00, the most typical product from this winery. It has a fruity bouquet, with hints of grassy herbs and yeast, a light flavour and great drinkability.

○ A. A. Bianco Passito Peperum '98	♛♛	5
● A. A. Moscato Rosa '99	♛♛	5
● A. A. Santa Maddalena Cl. '00	♛	3
○ A. A. Terlano Pinot Bianco Riol '00	♛	4
● A. A. Lagrein Scuro Ris. '99	♛	5
● A. A. Cabernet Sauvignon '94	♛♛	5
● A. A. Cabernet Sauvignon '95	♛♛	5
● A. A. Cabernet Sauvignon '96	♛♛	5
● A. A. Lagrein Scuro Ris. '97	♛♛	5
● A. A. Cabernet Sauvignon '98	♛♛	4
● A. A. Lagrein Scuro Ris. '98	♛♛	4
● A. A. Moscato Rosa '98	♛♛	5
● A. A. Cabernet Sauvignon '97	♛	5
● A. A. Santa Maddalena Cl. '99	♛	2

● A. A. Lagrein Scuro Ris. '99	♛♛	5
● A. A. Merlot '99	♛♛	5
● A. A. Santa Maddalena Cl. '00	♛	3
● A. A. Lagrein Scuro Ris. '97	♛♛♛	5
● A. A. Merlot '97	♛♛	5
● A. A. Lagrein Scuro Ris. '98	♛♛	5
● A. A. Merlot '98	♛♛	4
● A. A. Santa Maddalena Cl. '99	♛♛	3

BOLZANO/BOZEN

HANS ROTTENSTEINER
VIA SARENTINO, 1
39100 BOLZANO/BOZEN
TEL. 0471282015
E-MAIL: rottensteiner.weine@dnet.it

This winery, located at the entrance to Val Sarentino, northwest of the city of Bolzano, was founded in 1956 by Hans Rottensteiner. Presently, it is managed by Toni Rottensteiner, one of the leading winemaking personalities in Alto Adige, and his son Hannes, who has just finished his studies in oenology. Special attention and care are given to the grapes on the property's 15 hectares of vineyard, in the heart of the DOC zones for Lagrein and Santa Maddalena Classico. This year the Rottensteiners were well received at our tastings, especially with their Gewürztraminer. The Cresta '99, from grapes partially dried for five months in wicker baskets, and then pressed and fermented, is an extraordinary sweet wine, and among the best of its type in Alto Adige. The golden amber introduces an intensely aromatic bouquet of honey and roses, then there is a fullness on the concentrated palate where the powerful, creamy mouthfeel is offset by very pleasant acidity. The Traminer Aromatico Cancenai '00 is also very good and well-typed. Aromatic and delicate, it shows good structure and acidity. The Santa Maddalena Classico Premstallerhof is also excellent this year. Its clear ruby ushers in elegant, fruity aromas and a sweet, pleasant structure that fills the palate. The two Lagreins, the Grieser Riserva Select and Riserva, both from the '98 vintage, are concentrated and harmonious, with notes of berries on the nose and a velvet-smooth mouthfeel. The Pinot Nero Mazzon Riserva Select '98 shows good body and lovely drinkability. However, the Cabernet Riserva Select '98, a difficult vintage for this variety in Alto Adige, and the Pinot Bianco Carnol '00 were merely decent.

○	A. A. Traminer aromatico Cresta '99	🍷🍷	6
○	A. A. Gewürztraminer Cancenai '00	🍷🍷	4
●	A. A. Santa Maddalena Cl. Premstallerhof '00	🍷🍷	3*
●	A. A. Lagrein Scuro Grieser Select Ris. '98	🍷🍷	5
○	A. A. Pinot Bianco Carnol '00	🍷	3
●	A. A. Cabernet Select Ris '98	🍷	5
●	A. A. Lagrein Scuro Ris. '98	🍷	4
●	A. A. Pinot Nero Mazzon Select Ris. '98	🍷	5
●	A. A. Lagrein Scuro Grieser Select Ris. '97	🍷🍷	4
●	A. A. Pinot Nero Mazzon Select Ris. '97	🍷🍷	5

BOLZANO/BOZEN

HEINRICH & THOMAS ROTTENSTEINER
FRAZ. RENCIO
VIA SANTA MADDALENA DI SOTTO, 35
39100 BOLZANO/BOZEN
TEL. 0471973549 - 03356887019
E-MAIL: info@obermoser.it

The wines from this small estate are always good. Heinrich Rottensteiner and his son Thomas continue to produce no more than 30,000 bottles and have barely three hectares under vine. These are in Obermoser, in the heart of the Santa Maddalena hillslopes, and the wines they make come exclusively from their own grape harvest. In other words, it's a genuine family-run craft winery. Though their specialities are, obviously enough, all the classic wines from the zone, the most interesting one this year was the Cabernet-Merlot Putz Riserva '99, an excellent red that concedes something to the international style. It has all the varietal characteristics of any good Bordeaux blend from Alto Adige. The two Lagrein Grafenleitens from '98 and '99 are good but not exciting. The Santa Maddalena Classico is as pleasant as always. This time, the 2000 vintage was on show and behaved very creditably for this fragrant, delicate red wine type. The Sauvignon '00 is interesting, although it is produced in a very limited number of bottles. The Moscato Giallo Passito '99 is curious, aromatic and pleasant but again this sweet white is produced in very limited quantities. Overall, the Rottensteiner range is always one to look out for.

●	A. A. Cabernet-Merlot Putz Ris. '99	🍷🍷	5
●	A. A. Santa Maddalena Cl. '00	🍷	3
○	A. A. Sauvignon '00	🍷	4
●	A. A. Lagrein Scuro Grafenleiten Ris. '98	🍷	5
●	A. A. Lagrein Scuro Grafenleiten Ris. '99	🍷	5
○	A. A. Moscato Giallo Passito '99	🍷	5
●	A. A. Lagrein Scuro Grafenleiten Ris. '97	🍷🍷	5
●	A. A. Santa Maddalena Cl. '99	🍷	3
○	A. A. Sauvignon '99	🍷	3

BRESSANONE/BRIXEN (BZ)

Kuenhof - Peter Pliger
Loc. Mara, 110
39042 Bressanone/Brixen (BZ)
tel. 0472850546

The wines of Peter Pliger, one of the best winemakers in the Valle Isarco, need a bit more time than others to show their best characteristics. These whites are full of structure and personality but above all, they are true wines. In other words, they mature slowly and can stand the test of time even for several years. This is why we sometimes risk underrating them if we taste them too soon. We hope we did not make that mistake this time round because we found all the wines a bit closed to the nose. Though we retasted them more than once, and even put two of them into our final taste-offs, we were unable to award them our highest score. It was a bit of a disappointment for Pliger is a very serious, dedicated producer, one of the growers who should receive an honorary Three Glasses every year. In any case, his Sylvaner '00 is excellent. The aromas will take another few months to express themselves to the full but the wine has power and concentration in the mouth, so much so that even the high acidity turns out to be well merged into the overall palate. The Kaiton '00, from riesling renano grapes, is also an imposing, richly extracted wine. We are certain that in a couple of years it will give great satisfaction to anyone with the patience to wait for it. The Veltliner '00, a real Pliger speciality, is almost at the same level while the correct but simple Gewürztraminer '00 did not really impress us very much. At any rate, we can give an overall endorsement to the Kuenhof range. They are still very much part of the Alto Adige wine aristocracy.

BRESSANONE/BRIXEN (BZ)

Manfred Nössing - Hoandlhof
Fraz. Kranebih
Weinbergstrasse, 66
39042 Bressanone/Brixen (BZ)
tel. 0472832672

Manfred Nössing has for some years now been one of the rising stars on the winemaking scene in Alto Adige. This young, dynamic winemaker and grower could almost be defined as an artist, so full is he of ideas and innovative projects. He's a producer who has found his own path and is patiently putting together the characteristics and individual styles of his wines. The Tenuta Hoandlhof is located east of Bressanone in the Valle Isarco. Though Manfred Nössing bottled his first wines just two years ago, in 1999, he is more than convinced of what he is doing. "My objective is to produce white wines with complex aromas and good structure that represent the character of the variety, along with the terrain and climate of this zone". And how well he has done just that! We can confirm Manfred's success after tasting his wines from the 2000 vintage. We'll start with the Kerner, one of the best from the category. Its straw yellow ushers in a delicate, characteristically intense grassy aroma and an elegant, rich, full-bodied structure. The Gewürztraminer is still young and a bit closed to the nose but seems to have great potential for development. It is full, and has precise aromatic definition on the palate. The Müller Thurgau, which vinifies beautifully here in the Valle Isarco, has an intense, clean, fruity bouquet with decent body that is fresh and tangy. Finally, we found the Sylvaner this year to be below its stablemates. Grassy, with hints of camomile, it is rather one-dimensional and neutral in the mouth.

○ A. A. Kaiton '00	🍷🍷	4
○ A. A. Valle Isarco Sylvaner '00	🍷🍷	4*
○ A. A. Valle Isarco Veltliner '00	🍷🍷	4*
○ A. A. Valle Isarco Gewürztraminer '00	🍷	4
○ Kaiton '99	🍷🍷🍷	4
○ A. A. Valle Isarco Sylvaner '97	🍷🍷	4
○ A. A. Valle Isarco Veltliner '97	🍷🍷	4
○ Kaiton '97	🍷🍷	4
○ A. A. Valle Isarco Gewürztraminer '98	🍷🍷	4
○ A. A. Valle Isarco Sylvaner '98	🍷🍷	4
○ A. A. Valle Isarco Veltliner '98	🍷🍷	4
○ A. A. Valle Isarco Sylvaner '99	🍷🍷	4
○ A. A. Valle Isarco Veltliner '99	🍷🍷	4

○ A. A. Valle Isarco Kerner '00	🍷🍷	4
○ A. A. Valle Isarco Gewürztraminer '00	🍷🍷	4
○ A. A. Valle Isarco Müller Thurgau '00	🍷🍷	3*
○ A. A. Valle Isarco Sylvaner '00	🍷	4
○ A. A. Valle Isarco Kerner '99	🍷🍷	4
○ A. A. Valle Isarco Müller Thurgau '99	🍷🍷	3
○ A. A. Valle Isarco Sylvaner '99	🍷🍷	4
○ A. A. Valle Isarco Gewürztraminer '99	🍷	4

CALDARO/KALTERN (BZ)

CANTINA VITICOLTORI DI CALDARO
VIA DELLE CANTINE, 12
39052 CALDARO/KALTERN (BZ)
TEL. 0471963149 - 0471963124
E-MAIL: info@kellereikalterner.com

The same top score and the same Glass-filled cabinet. President, Johann Klauser, and "kellermeister", Helmuth Zozin, can be proud of their efforts and look with confidence to the future of this extraordinary co-operative winery. One wine with Three Glasses, two others in our finals and another three well into Two Glass country. We can say, without fear of being contradicted, that this is definitely the peak of oenological quality in Alto Adige. Top honours go to the Sauvignon Premstalerhof '00, absolutely one of the best in its category. The varietal aromas foreground delicate notes of tropical fruit and minerals then the powerful, richly concentrated palate lingers through to a long finish. The Gewürztraminer Campaner '00 is also excellent but then this classic never disappoints. Intensely aromatic on the nose, it reveals a full, round, flavour that is caressingly soft with barely a hint of a tangy, varietal finish. Then came the real surprise, the Pinot Bianco Vial '00. Fruity, typical, with aromas of fresh almonds and peach, it is a minor masterpiece. Alongside the three top wines from the winery, there is a delicious Chardonnay Wadleith '00, the Cabernet Sauvignon Pfarrhof Riserva '98 and the Pinot Nero Riserva '98, all three well worth Two Glasses. The series closes with an unexciting version of the Cabernet Sauvignon Campaner Riserva from '99, the Lago di Caldaro Classico Superiore Pfarrhof '00, Pinot Nero Saltnerhof '99 and Pinot Grigio Söll '00, each one at least well-made. Not bad at all, don't you think?

CALDARO/KALTERN (BZ)

CASTEL SALLEGG - GRAF KUENBURG
V.LO DI SOTTO, 15
39052 CALDARO/KALTERN (BZ)
TEL. 0471963132
E-MAIL: castellsallegg@kuemburg.it

This year, the noble Kuenburgs celebrate their family's 150th anniversary at Castel Sallegg, one of the most beautifully tended vineyards in the entire Caldaro subzone. Though the potential and preconditions for being competitive are there, the results are not always completely satisfying. While last year we liked the red wines from this winery very much, and decided to suspend our judgement on the whites, this year the situation has changed and become a bit more complicated. The best results were obtained by two whites and a red. The Gewürztraminer '00 has a golden, straw-yellow colour, an intense, aromatic fruitiness and elegance on the nose and a stylish structure that is strong in the mouth. In other words, it's a lovely wine of its type. The Sauvignon from the same vintage is fairly typical on the nose, with a delicate fruitiness that recalls grapefruit and elder blossoms, and a full, fresh-tasting varietal flavour with a touch of zest. The well-defined note of wood is nicely understated. We liked the Lagrein Riserva '98 very much – we retasted a wine we reviewed in the previous edition of the Guide – with its intense ruby red, complex, concentrated bouquet of ripe bramble and plum fruit and powerful, velvety flavour. The Pinot Nero Riserva '98 is slightly acidic, with fairly insistent oaky notes. Finally, the Moscato Rosa, once the estate's legendary showcase wine, is just fair. Its garnet ruby is a bit forward, it has aromas of medicinal herbs and the flavour is slightly astringent and sweetish.

	Wine	Glasses	Score
○	A. A. Sauvignon Premstalerhof '00	♉♉♉	4*
○	A. A. Gewürztraminer Campaner '00	♉♉	4*
○	A. A. Pinot Bianco Vial '00	♉♉	4*
○	A. A. Chardonnay Wadleith '00	♉♉	4
●	A. A. Cabernet Sauvignon Pfarrhof Ris. '98	♉♉	6
●	A. A. Lago di Caldaro Scelto Cl. Sup. Pfarrhof '00	♉	3
○	A. A. Pinot Grigio Söll '00	♉	4
○	A. A. Cabernet Sauvignon Campaner Ris. '99	♉	4
●	A. A. Pinot Nero Saltnerhof '99	♉	4
○	A. A. Gewürztraminer Campaner '99	♉♉	4
●	A. A. Pinot Nero Ris. '98	♉♉	6

	Wine	Glasses	Score
○	A. A. Gewürztraminer '00	♉♉	4
○	A. A. Sauvignon '00	♉♉	4
●	A. A. Moscato Rosa '97	♉	6
●	A. A. Pinot Nero Ris. '98	♉	5
●	A. A. Moscato Rosa '93	♉♉	6
●	A. A. Cabernet '95	♉♉	5
●	A. A. Merlot '95	♉♉	5
●	A. A. Moscato Rosa '95	♉♉	6
●	A. A. Merlot Ris. '96	♉♉	5
●	A. A. Cabernet Ris. '97	♉♉	5
●	A. A. Merlot '97	♉♉	5
●	A. A. Lagrein Ris. '98	♉♉	4
●	Rosso Conte Kuenburg	♉♉	6

CALDARO/KALTERN (BZ)

KETTMEIR
VIA DELLE CANTINE, 4
39052 CALDARO/KALTERN (BZ)
TEL. 0471963135

As usual, the good Pinot Grigio Maso Reiner, this time the 2000 version, is the most representative, best-made product from this large, famous winery, owned by the Marzotto-Santa Margherita group, at Caldaro/Kaltern. Evidently when Santa Margherita is involved, Pinot Grigio can be nothing less than particularly well-made. As everyone knows, the huge international success of this wine is attributable in great part specifically to the Portogruaro-based Santa Margherita winery that produced it and distributed it worldwide until the end of the 1960s. This same wine from Kettmeir is very good and has always received good reviews, from us and from other critics. It spends a six-month period in barriques and has fruity aromas with hints of pear and peach on the nose, excellent body and coherent, balanced flavour. It's the house speciality. The Chardonnay '00 Maso Reiner is also not bad. Also briefly barrique-aged, it shows notes of pineapple on the nose and has an elegant flavour with good length. All the other wines are decent, with the Cabernet Sauvignon Maso Castello '98 leading the rest of the pack. In conclusion, this year Kettmeir returns with its own profile after a year in the wilderness. We hope they can remain in the Guide in the future. If wines like the Pinot Grigio Maso Reiner can be duplicated, and the average quality level raised, there should be no problems. But this is linked to the winery's production philosophy. Certainly, this cellar deserves to be at the cutting-edge of Marzotto wines, so we'll be keeping our fingers crossed.

○ A. A. Chardonnay Maso Rainer '00	ŸŸ	4*
○ A. A. Pinot Grigio Maso Reiner '00	ŸŸ	4*
● A. A. Cabernet Sauvignon Maso Castello '98	Ÿ	4
○ A. A. Spumante Brut	Ÿ	4
○ A. A. Chardonnay Maso Rainer '99	Ÿ	4

CALDARO/KALTERN (BZ)

PRIMA & NUOVA/ERSTE & NEUE
VIA DELLE CANTINE, 5
39052 CALDARO/KALTERN (BZ)
TEL. 0471963122
E-MAIL: info@erste-neve.it

The wines from Erste & Neue made a decent showing this year though with no particularly evident high points. Aside from the Cabernet Puntay, the cellar's true star which was not presented in the '98 version, almost all the other most prestigious wines performed well. We felt the best was the Anthos '98, a white passito from partially dried moscato giallo, gewürztraminer and sauvignon varieties, rich in aromatic shadings, it has a sweet flavour, nicely offset by a pleasant acidic note. Right behind it is the excellent Cabernet-Merlot Feld '98, caressing and varietal in its bouquet with a very consistent structure, sweet tannins and nice length in the mouth. We continued with a classic from the winery, the Pinot Bianco Puntay '00, which is fragrant and elegant on both nose and palate, and then two Chardonnays, the Puntay '99, aged briefly in small casks, and the Salt '00, which ages in stainless steel vats. The first Chardonnay is obviously more complex and the second simpler, but extremely well-made from the technical point of view. The other wines in the range are less convincing but certainly deserve respect. The Gewürztraminer Puntay '00 seems slightly overripe and the aromatic tones are less delicate than in previous versions. The Pinot Bianco Brunar '00 is rather simple and less concentrated than the Puntay. The Sauvignon Stern '00 is well-made and sufficiently varietal but not much more than that. The Lago di Caldaro Puntay '00 is, as it should be, a light, fragrant red but definitely not a wine with any great pretensions.

○ A. A. Chardonnay Salt '00	ŸŸ	4*
○ A. A. Pinot Bianco Puntay '00	ŸŸ	4*
● A. A. Cabernet-Merlot Feld '98	ŸŸ	5
○ Anthos '98	ŸŸ	6
○ A. A. Chardonnay Puntay '99	ŸŸ	5
○ A. A. Gewürztraminer Puntay '00	Ÿ	5
● A. A. Lago di Caldaro Scelto Puntay '00	Ÿ	4
○ A. A. Pinot Bianco Brunar '00	Ÿ	4
○ A. A. Sauvignon Stern '00	Ÿ	4
● A. A. Cabernet Puntay '97	ŸŸŸ	5
○ A. A. Chardonnay Salt '99	ŸŸ	3
○ A. A. Gewürztraminer Puntay '99	ŸŸ	4

CALDARO/KALTERN (BZ)

Josef Sölva - Niklaserhof
Loc. San Nicolò
Via Brunner, 31a
39052 Caldaro/Kaltern (BZ)
Tel. 0471963432
E-mail: info@niklaserhof.it

With just three hectares of vineyards and a production of only 15,000 bottles, divided into seven different types, Josef and Johanna Sölva's Niklaserhof winery is a very small producer here in the Caldaro/Kaltern area. However, this year it again earned a review in our Guide thanks to a very admirable performance. "Small" does not necessarily mean "better" in the wine world but here at Niklaserhof the two concepts go together perfectly. We feel the best product is the Alto Adige Bianco Mondevinum, made from pinot bianco grapes with the addition of sauvignon and left to partially age in small casks for around a year. It is a white with intense aromas and a concentrated flavour. The wood is well-integrated into the bouquet and a pleasant, slightly acidic note runs through the palate. The Sauvignon '00 is also very good and very reasonably priced to boot. It has varietal aromas that are on the wild side but not excessively so, and shows excellent structure. All the other bottles are good and the remarkable Justinus Kerner '00, with its citrus-like aromas, has carved out a niche for itself because of its characteristic sensory profile. The Pinot Bianco '00 and Cabernet-Lagrein Klaser Riserva '98 are both not bad, the latter being the most representative red in the range. We are not reviewing the Pinot Bianco Klaser '00 since it was still in the cask and not in suitable condition for a serious tasting.

CALDARO/KALTERN (BZ)

Peter Sölva & Söhne - Paterbichl
Via d'Oro, 33
39052 Caldaro/Kaltern (BZ)
Tel. 0471964650

Only three wines submitted this time but all three were excellent. That's how we could sum up our review of Peter and Stephan Sölva's winery this year, one of the great cellars in Caldaro/Kaltern. There are barely five hectares of vineyards, some estate-owned and others rented, and a production of around 60,000 bottles distributed across up to five labels. As we have already mentioned, the Sölvas only submitted three to us. The best of the whole range turned out to be the Amistar Rosso '99, from lagrein and cabernet with a predominance of merlot. Barrique-aged for around a year and a half, its shows off excellent body and very clear complexity on the nose. There are hints of blackcurrants and bilberry, along with light toasty and smoky notes, in the rich, multi-layered bouquet of one of the best reds in the region. Moving down the list, we find the Amistar Bianco '99 from equal parts of gewürztraminer, sauvignon and chardonnay grapes. Aged for just over a year in small casks, it has rather intense aromatic notes on the nose and a soft, caressing palate where it shows body and roundness. This is well supported by a hint of acidity that perfectly melds into the structure. The Lagrein-Merlot '00 is good but less convincing, perhaps because it is a bit young. However, it is undeniably simpler and more immediate than the Amistar Rosso.

○	A. A. Bianco Mondevinum '00	ΨΨ	5
○	A. A. Sauvignon '00	ΨΨ	4*
●	A. A. Lago di Caldaro Scelto Cl. '00	Ψ	2*
○	A. A. Pinot Bianco '00	Ψ	3
○	Justinus Kerner '00	Ψ	3
●	A. A. Lagrein-Cabernet Klaser '98	Ψ	5
●	A. A. Lago di Caldaro Scelto Cl. '99	ΨΨ	2
○	A. A. Sauvignon '99	ΨΨ	2
●	A. A. Lagrein-Cabernet Klaser '97	Ψ	5
○	A. A. Pinot Bianco '99	Ψ	3
○	Justinus Kerner '99	Ψ	2

●	Amistar Rosso '99	ΨΨ	5
○	Amistar Bianco '99	ΨΨ	4
●	A. A. Lagrein-Merlot '00	Ψ	4

CERMES/TSCHERMS (BZ)

Graf Pfeil Weingut Kränzel
Via Palade, 1
39010 Cermes/Tscherms (BZ)
tel. 0473564549
e-mail: weingut@kraenzel-pfeil.com

The best Pinot Bianco from the 2000 vintage in Alto Adige is the Helios from the Kränzel estate. A good result, considering the fame and distribution Weissburgunder can count on around these parts. It is even more surprising if you consider that the tiny Graf Pfeil estate has, in this wine type, outclassed many much larger and more celebrated estates, both privately owned and co-operative. But let's get back to the Helios '00, a splendid Pinot Bianco aged for eight months in small casks. We put it into our final taste-off and, though it did not win the highest score of Three Glasses, it performed well, revealing fruity aromas with hints of fresh almond, and a full palate with good concentration, perhaps lacking a little length. The Cabernet Sauvignon-Merlot Sagittarius '98 was also very good but with barely 1,500 bottles produced, it is almost impossible to find. A firm yet elegant wine, it comes from a harvest that was by and large satisfactory though not great. The Dorado '98 is also sound. A passito from partially dried pinot bianco grapes, it is very personal, moderately concentrated and very well-balanced for a sweet wine. All the other wines were decent, with a curious Gewürztraminer Passito '00 scoring slightly above the rest and the usual, incredibly complex Schiava Schloss Baslan '99 confirming its position as one of the best in a very broad category.

	Wine	Glasses	Score
○	A. A. Pinot Bianco Helios '00	▼▼	5
○	A. A. Gewürztraminer Passito '00	▼▼	5
○	A. A. Bianco Passito Dorado '98	▼▼	6
●	A. A. Cabernet Sauvignon-Merlot Sagittarius '98	▼▼	6
●	A. A. Schiava Schloss Baslan '99	▼▼	5
●	A. A. Meranese '00	▼	3
○	A. A. Pinot Bianco '00	▼	4
●	A. A. Pinot Nero '99	▼	5
●	A. A. Pinot Nero '95	▽▽	5
●	Sagittarius '95	▽▽	6
●	Sagittarius '96	▽▽	6
○	Dorado '97	▽▽	6
●	Sagittarius '97	▽▽	6

CHIUSA/KLAUSEN (BZ)

Cantina Produttori Valle Isarco
Loc. Coste, 50
39043 Chiusa/Klausen (BZ)
tel. 0472847553
e-mail: info@cantinavalleisarco.it

This winery is a specialist in whites made mainly from the most typical varieties in this subzone, the most northerly in Alto Adige. Remember that the northernmost of its vineyards, beyond Varna, reach the 47th parallel. We are more or less on the same line of latitude here as Volnay in Burgundy. So from the Cantina Produttori Valle Isarco we should expect Müller Thurgau, Kerner, Veltliner, Sylvaner, some Gewürztraminer and some fragrant Pinot Grigio, in addition to a special type of Schiava, the Klausner Laitacher. And in fact we can begin our comments with a white, a Sylvaner '00 from the basic line that costs just € 3.75 or so plus VAT at the cellar door. We liked it so much that, in spite of its relative simplicity, we decided to send it on to the finals for Three Glasses. Even though it didn't win, we cannot forget its elegance, its very typical aromas of citrus and mountain herbs, and above all its very pleasant drinkability. The Pinot Grigio, Kerner and Veltliner were all almost at the same level. All of them are from the 2000 vintage and all are standard-label bottles. The wines from the Aristos line, which in theory should represent the winery's finest selections, were interesting and well-made but paradoxically a bit less immediate. On the other hand, the Gewürztraminer Passito Nectaris '99 was very good. This is a wine type that is gaining great popularity in Alto Adige. The oak-aged Sylvaner Dominus continues to be unconvincing, present this year on the market in the '98 version.

	Wine	Glasses	Score
○	A. A. Valle Isarco Sylvaner '00	▼▼	3*
○	A. A. Valle Isarco Kerner '00	▼▼	3*
○	A. A. Valle Isarco Pinot Grigio '00	▼▼	3*
○	A. A. Valle Isarco Sylvaner Aristos '00	▼▼	4
○	A. A. Valle Isarco Veltliner '00	▼▼	3
○	A. A. Gewürztraminer Passito Nectaris '99	▼▼	6
○	A. A. Chardonnay '00	▼	3
○	A. A. Valle Isarco Gewürztraminer '00	▼	3
●	A. A. Valle Isarco Klausener Laitacher '00	▼	3
○	A. A. Valle Isarco Müller Thurgau '00	▼	3

CORTACCIA/KURTATSCH (BZ)

Cantina Produttori Cortaccia
Strada del Vino, 23
39040 Cortaccia/Kurtatsch (BZ)
tel. 0471880115
e-mail: info@akellerei-kurtatsch.it

A breathtaking Gewürztraminer, the Brenntal '00 from the same zone as the famous Merlot produced by this co-operative winery, was the wine that had the panel talking this year. Along with the adjacent zone in the Termeno/Tramin area, the Cortaccia/Kurtatsch zone is very well-adapted to this grape variety, one that needs warmth and a good range of temperatures between day and night to reach its peak level of ripeness and aromatic concentration. So we were expecting a positive performance. But the reality went beyond even our wildest dreams. The Gewürztraminer Brenntal '00 is truly fantastic and the very positive vintage for the grape has given it extremely elegant and concentrated varietal characteristics. The Merlot Brenntal '98 is also very good and, though it does not reach the stratospheric levels of the '95 and '97 versions, it is still well up to our expectations. Among the other wines, special mention should go to the fragrant Chardonnay Felsenhof '00 and the Schiava Grigia Sonntaler, again from 2000, confirmed as being at the top of their respective categories. The '99 version was less enjoyable as this was certainly not an exciting vintage, especially for red wines. Neither were the panel overly impressed by the Cabernet Kirchhügel or the Lagrein Forhof or the Cabernet-Merlot Soma or even the Pinot Nero Vorhof, all very much below expectations. We were also a little disappointed, even if not as profoundly, by the Chardonnay Eberlehof '99. It's good but not comparable to the '98. The Sauvignon Milla '00 and Müller Thurgau Hofstatt '00 are as decent as ever, with very clean, varietal tones on the nose.

○	A. A. Gewürztraminer Brenntal '00	♆♆♆	5
●	A. A. Merlot Brenntal '98	♆♆	6
○	A. A. Chardonnay Felsenhof '00	♆♆	4*
●	A. A. Schiava Grigia Sonntaler '00	♆♆	4*
○	A. A. Müller Thurgau Hofstatt '00	♆	4
○	A. A. Sauvignon Milla '00	♆	4
●	A. A. Cabernet Kirchhügel '99	♆	5
●	A. A. Cabernet-Merlot Soma '99	♆	6
○	A. A. Chardonnay Eberlehof '99	♆	5
●	A. A. Lagrein Scuro Forhof '99	♆	5
●	A. A. Pinot Nero Vorhof '99	♆	5
●	A. A. Cabernet Freienfeld '95	♆♆♆	6
●	A. A. Merlot Brenntal '95	♆♆♆	5
●	A. A. Cabernet Freienfeld '97	♆♆♆	6
●	A. A. Merlot Brenntal '97	♆♆♆	5

CORTACCIA/KURTATSCH (BZ)

Tiefenbrunner
Fraz. Niclara
Via Castello, 4
39040 Cortaccia/Kurtatsch (BZ)
tel. 0471880122
e-mail: info@tiefenbrunner.com

Herbert and Cristof Tiefenbrunner's winery is one of the most famous and respected on the Alto Adige wine scene. In particular, it was one of the first to make the wines from this region known outside their production zones and German-speaking countries. This can be attributed to the consistent quality and reliability of the wines produced, in addition to their always excellent value for money. This year's performance is no exception. As always, the Linticlarus Cuvée '99 is excellent. From lagrein, merlot and cabernet sauvignon, it is still one of the showcase wines of the estate despite a vintage that was not exactly exceptional. The Alto Adige Bianco Cuvée Anna '00 is very interesting. A blend of pinot grigio, chardonnay and pinot bianco aged for five months in stainless steel vats, it is a coherent, elegant white in the best style of this winery. The partially barrique-aged Chardonnay Castel Turmhof '00, the Gewürztraminer '00, Lagrein Castel Turmhof '99 and Sauvignon Kirchleiten '00 are all decent. The famous Feldmarschall '00 wasn't at its best. From Müller Thurgau grapes cultivated in a vineyard almost 1,000 metres above sea level, it has the usual aromatic bouquet, but not the body, of the best versions. The Schiava Grigia Castel Turmhof '00 is simple and fragrant, in addition to being very pleasant to drink.

○	A. A. Bianco Cuvée Anna '00	♆♆	4
●	Linticlarus Cuvée '99	♆♆	5
○	A. A. Chardonnay Castel Turmhof '00	♆	4
○	A. A. Gewürztraminer '00	♆	4
○	A. A. Sauvignon Kirchleiten '00	♆	5
●	A. A. Schiava Grigia Castel Turmhof '00	♆	4
○	Feldmarschall von Fenner zu Fennberg '00	♆	5
●	A. A. Lagrein Scuro Castel Turmhof '99	♆	5
●	Linticlarus Cuvée '97	♆♆	5
○	A. A. Sauvignon Kirchleiten '99	♆♆	4
●	Linticlarus Cuvée '98	♆	5

CORTINA/KURTINIG (BZ)

Peter Zemmer - Kupelwieser
Strada del Vino, 24
39040 Cortina/Kurtinig (BZ)
Tel. 0471817143
E-mail: info@zemmer.com

Last year, the Italian edition only of the Guide erroneously merged the entries for Kupelwieser and Lun. The truth is, Kupelwieser is a winery in the same location as, and with much in common with, Helmut Zemmer's Peter Zemmer cellar. Together, they form a team capable of producing almost 600,000 bottles. In tandem, they presented us with many wines, some excellent, from the production of both cellars. The best of all of them is the Riesling '00 from Zemmer, which made it to our final taste-off. An aristocratic white, with citrus aromas, a typically acidulous flavour and good persistence. Again from Zemmer, we would point out the excellent Pinot Grigio '00, the Chardonnay Barrique '99, and, in descending order, two IGTs; the Cortinie Bianco '00, from chardonnay, pinot grigio, sauvignon and gewürztraminer, and Cortinie Rosso '99, from lagrein, merlot, cabernet sauvignon and cabernet franc; the Chardonnay '00; the Lagrein '99; the Merlot '99; and the fresh and simple Pinot Bianco '00. The Riesling and Chardonnay '00 were outstanding from the Kupelwieser wines and the Santa Maddalena '00, the Lagrein Intenditore '99 and the Sauvignon Intenditore '00 were not bad at all, either. As you can see, this is a very broad range with many quality peaks and a unique, delightful ability to interpret the two Rieslings. In itself, this is fairly unusual in a zone like Cortina/Kurtinig in Oltradige, way down in the south of Alto Adige.

○	A. A. Riesling '00	🍷🍷	4*
○	A. A. Chardonnay Kupelwieser '00	🍷🍷	4
○	A. A. Pinot Bianco Kupelwieser '00	🍷🍷	3*
○	A. A. Pinot Grigio '00	🍷🍷	4
○	A. A. Riesling Kupelwieser '00	🍷🍷	4*
●	A. A. Santa Maddalena Kupelwieser '00	🍷🍷	3*
○	A. A. Chardonnay Barrique '99	🍷🍷	5
●	Cortinie Rosso '99	🍷	5
○	A. A. Chardonnay '00	🍷	4
○	A. A. Pinot Bianco '00	🍷	3
○	A. A. Sauvignon Intenditore '00	🍷	4
○	Cortinie Bianco '00	🍷	5
●	A. A. Lagrein Scuro '99	🍷	4
●	A. A. Lagrein Scuro Intenditore '99	🍷	5
●	A. A. Merlot '99	🍷	5

EGNA/NEUMARKT (BZ)

Cantina H. Lun
Fraz. Villa
Via Villa, 22/24
39044 Egna/Neumarkt (BZ)
Tel. 0471813256
E-mail: contact@lun.it

Let us set things aright and dedicate an individual profile to Lun of Egna. This is the winery that we mistakenly lumped in with Kupelwieser last year, even though it has nothing to do with it. We apologize both to the wineries and our readers. A historic name in Alto Adige winemaking since 1840, H Lun has been recognized for a couple of years by the Cantina Produttori Cornaiano/Girlan and profits from the technical support of Georg Spitaler. The winery director is Manfred Waldthaler. The range presented this year was very sound. The Sandbichler Bianco '00, from pinot bianco, chardonnay and a smaller percentage of riesling, is once again the flagship wine for quality. Aged for six months in large barrels, it shows off very fruity aromas with notes that may be even a bit too citrussy, and a full flavour with a refreshing acidic vein. The Sauvignon Albertus Lun is also very good and the 2000 version confirmed the favourable impressions we already formed in 1999. Solid and varietal, the Lagrein Scuro Albertus Lun Riserva '98 may not have the explosive concentration of the very best wines but it is elegant and deliciously easy to drink. The rest of the range comprises well-made wines with the Cabernet Sauvignon Albertus Lun Riserva '98 in first place, followed closely by the Pinot Nero Sandbichler Riserva '98, which is not bad at all. The pleasant Santa Maddalena '00 is decent, as is the Gewürztraminer Albertus Lun '00, though the latter does not really seem like the house specialty.

○	A. A. Bianco Sandbichler '00	🍷🍷	4*
○	A. A. Sauvignon Albertus '00	🍷🍷	4
●	A. A. Lagrein Scuro Albertus Ris. '98	🍷🍷	5
○	A. A. Gewürztraminer Albertus '00	🍷	4
●	A. A. Santa Maddalena Föhrner '00	🍷	4
●	A. A. Cabernet Albertus Ris. '98	🍷	5
●	A. A. Pinot Nero Sandbichler Ris. '98	🍷	4
●	A. A. Cabernet Albertus Ris. '95	🍷🍷	5

MARLENGO/MARLING (BZ)

Cantina Produttori Burggräfler
Via Palade, 64
39020 Marlengo/Marling (BZ)
tel. 0473447137
e-mail: info@burggraefler.it

Year after year, the Cantina Produttori del Burgraviato, in German "Burggräfler", continues to put out well-made wines at very honest prices. This is a very important producer rooted firmly in the territory. The co-operative has existed for exactly a century and today includes 190 members from across the entire Merano area and part of the lower Adige valley. This year, it presented us with a good-quality range. The wine we enjoyed most was the Merlot-Cabernet Juvin Cuvée '98, a powerful, concentrated red that was as good as any from vineyards in Alto Adige. Right behind it was the Pinot Bianco Vendemmia Tardiva MerVin '98, a white from partially dried, botrytized grapes with unusual aromas of saffron and honey and a sweet, very well-balanced flavour. The Chardonnay Tiefenthaler '00 was even more elegant than the '99 version. All the other bottles are good and well-typed. There is a Pinot Nero Tiefenthaler MerVin '99 that perhaps suffers from the unexciting vintage, a decent Pinot Bianco Guggenberg '00 and a good Gewürztraminer '00, less concentrated than we expected but exquisitely vinified and matured. The Merlot-Lagrein '98, already reviewed in the last edition of the Guide, is fair. Though simple, the Meranese Schickenburg '00, the most typical wine from the territory, is fragrant and delightful to drink. The Moscato Giallo Schickenburg '00 is pleasantly aromatic.

MARLENGO/MARLING (BZ)

Popphof - Andreas Menz
Mitterterzerstrasse, 5
39020 Marlengo/Marling (BZ)
tel. 0473447180

The major new features of Andreas Menz's tiny Popphof winery are new wines and a new line-up in the range. In fact, neither the Cabernet nor the Pinot Nero were submitted for tasting. The only wine from the past still on the list is the Pinot Bianco '00, and this edition is on a par with the best. The straw yellow has light greenish highlights that introduce clean, varietal aromas. The other two wines presented by the talented Andreas were both new and, above all, did not carry a vintage year on the label. They are most likely a blend of several vintages. The Katharina Bianco from moscato giallo grapes is really interesting. A passito wine from partially dried grapes, it flaunts an amber colour and aromas of botrytis, saffron, honey and, in the background, cep mushrooms and autumn leaves. The taste is full, sweet and complex, with good definition and remarkable elegance. It lacks great length but this is a wine with personality. The Popphof Cuvée, a "vino da tavola", is a classic, powerful Alto Adige red with a fairly evident cabernet base and additions of lagrein and merlot. It has notes of red berries and liquorice on the nose while the palate comes through with excellent softness, compact but unassertive tannins, and good concentration. A wine that is as sound as they come, confirming the knack Andreas Menz has with all his wines, old and new. It's a talent he has demonstrated again and again over the past few years.

○ A. A. Chardonnay Tiefenthaler '00 ♟♟		4
● A. A. Merlot-Cabernet Juvin Cuvée '98	♟♟	5
○ A. A. Pinot Bianco MerVin V. T. '98	♟♟	6
○ A. A. Gewürztraminer '00	♟	4
● A. A. Meranese Schickenburg '00	♟	3
○ A. A. Moscato Giallo Schickenburg '00	♟	4
○ A. A. Pinot Bianco Guggenberg '00	♟	4
● A. A. Pinot Nero Tiefenthaler '99	♟	5
● A. A. Merlot-Lagrein '98	♟	5

○ A. A. Pinot Bianco '00	♟♟	4*
○ Katharina	♟♟	5
● Popphof Cuvée	♟♟	5
● A. A. Cabernet '97	♟♟♟	5
● A. A. Cabernet '95	♟♟	5
○ A. A. Pinot Bianco '97	♟♟	3
● A. A. Pinot Nero '97	♟♟	5
● A. A. Cabernet '98	♟♟	5
● A. A. Pinot Nero '98	♟	5

MELTINA/MÖLTEN (BZ)

VIVALDI - ARUNDA
CIVICO, 53
39010 MELTINA/MÖLTEN (BZ)
TEL. 0471668033
E-MAIL: arunda@dnet.it

The Vivaldi-Arunda winery – Vivaldi in Italy, Arunda for Alto Adige and non-domestic markets – is one of the most famous spumante-makers in Alto Adige, even though it is relatively small and produces no more than 70,000 bottles annually. Nonetheless, its fame is well deserved and due for the most part to the skill and charm of the owner, Josef Reiterer, who over the years has known how to conquer the respect and admiration of the many consumers who appreciate his products. Considering his overall production, the range he presented was fairly broad. The most prestigious spumante is probably the Riserva Millesimata di Arunda, this year in the '96 version. It comes from a "coupage" of 60 per cent Chardonnay and 40 per cent Pinot Nero and is particularly enjoyable because of its complex aromas, with very refined notes of fruit and minerals, and a full, concentrated palate. The impeccable Reiterer spumante technique does the rest and makes this as good a bottle of bubbly as you'll get anywhere. The other products in the range are correct and reliable, with special mention going to the Extra Brut Blanc de Blancs for its fragrant aromas and particularly delicate profile on the palate. The Vivaldi Brut and Vivaldi Extra Brut, both from '98, are very pleasant but definitely simpler.

MERANO/MERAN (BZ)

CANTINA PRODUTTORI DI MERANO
VIA SAN MARCO, 11
39012 MERANO/MERAN (BZ)
TEL. 0473235544
E-MAIL: info@meranerkellerei.com

The most representative wine from Meraner Kellerei, the Merlot Freiberg '99, was maturing slowly in barriques when we were tasting so instead we enjoyed a promising barrel sample that we would prefer not to evaluate this year to give it enough time to express its best. Great wines must be respected. However, we consoled ourselves with an excellent Pinot Nero Zenoberg '99 that proved to be among the best from its vintage and made it to our tasting finals. Though it didn't quite win its third Glass, it came close. The aromas are clean and varietal, the palate full and soft, just as an elegantly varietal Pinot Nero should be. It was the most interesting wine of the year from this large, famous co-operative winery but certainly not the only good one. The Lagrein Segenpichl '99 was almost as enjoyably expressive. Aromas of blackcurrants and pencil lead usher in excellent body, sweet tannins and good length. Outstanding among the whites were the Sauvignon Graf von Meran '00 and the Pinot Bianco Graf von Meran '00. They are fruity and varietal but, above all, technically very well-made. The Gewürztraminer Graf von Meran '00 was less enjoyable but this is not the winery's specialty. Correct and even, it lacks concentration on the nose.

○	A. A. Spumante Brut Arunda Ris. '96	🍷🍷	5
○	A. A. Spumante Blanc de Blancs Arunda	🍷🍷	5
○	A. A. Spumante Brut Vivaldi '98	🍷	5
○	A. A. Spumante Extra Brut Vivaldi '98	🍷	5
○	A. A. Spumante Brut Arunda Ris. '94	🍷🍷	5
○	A. A. Spumante Extra Brut Vivaldi '95	🍷🍷	5
○	A. A. Spumante Extra Brut Vivaldi Cuvée Marianna	🍷🍷	5

●	A. A. Pinot Nero Zenoberg '99	🍷🍷	5
○	A. A. Pinot Bianco Graf Von Meran '00	🍷🍷	4
○	A. A. Sauvignon Graf Von Meran '00	🍷🍷	4
●	A. A. Lagrein Scuro Segenpichl '99	🍷🍷	5
○	A. A. Gewürztraminer Graf Von Meran '00	🍷	4
●	A. A. Merlot Freiberg '97	🍷🍷🍷	5
●	A. A. Cabernet Sauvignon Graf Von Meran Ris. '97	🍷🍷	6
●	A. A. Cabernet-Merlot Graf Von Meran '97	🍷🍷	5
○	Sissi '98	🍷🍷	5

MONTAGNA/MONTAN (BZ)

Franz Haas
Via Villa, 6
39040 Montagna/Montan (BZ)
tel. 0471812280
e-mail: franz-haas@dnet.it

Franz Haas has done it again and for the second year in a row is in the Three Glass club. He is there because of another extraordinary version of his Moscato Rosa, this time from 2000. It must be said he is becoming a specialist with this very rare grape that is so difficult to interpret. Again, it is an aromatic red, with very clean, intense fragrances and notes of wild roses so clean they could be used at tasting courses to show how these wines should be. The flavour is elegant and harmonious, sweet but not cloying. A splendid example of how the moscato rosa grape should be vinified. But all of Haas' wines are particularly convincing this year. The Merlot '98 is from a barely average vintage but is especially varietal in its aromas and has a finesse we have rarely encountered in preceding versions. The Gewürztraminer '00 is very typical and elegant. Even the simplest wine, the Pinot Bianco '00, is pretty good. The Manna '99, a barrique-aged white from riesling, chardonnay, traminer and sauvignon grapes, is better than it was in '98, just like the Istante, a red IGT from a Bordeaux blend. In other words, it's a range with excellent overall quality that shows how, by carefully working the vineyards as Haas always has, excellent results can be obtained even in years that are not particularly favourable. However, this takes knowledge, skill and a refusal to accept compromises.

NALLES/NALS (BZ)

Cantina Produttori
Nalles Niclara Magrè
Via Heiligenberg, 2
39010 Nalles/Nals (BZ)
tel. 0471678626
e-mail: info@kellerei.it

Never before has the Cantina Produttori di Nalles Niclara Magré presented this good a range of wines: two wines in the finals and six with Two very full Glasses. Congratulations are definitely called for in cases like this. Absolutely the most convincing bottles, in our opinion, were the Chardonnay '99 and Gewürztraminer '00 from the Baron Salvadori line. The first, fermented and aged in small casks, is one of the finest of its vintage. The Gewürztraminer is a splendid, aromatic white with intense, varietal aromas and a soft, caressing flavour. But the basic Chardonnay and Riesling from 2000, the Merlot Levad '99, the Merlot-Cabernet Sauvignon Anticus '99, the Pinot Grigio Punggl '00 and the Terlano Pinot Bianco Sirmian '00 are all very good, in fact the last is a real house specialty. The Schiava Gallea '00 is simple and fragrant while the Terlano Sauvignon Mantele, again from 2000, is a bit below par. But the most impressive thing is the consistently high level of quality, coupled with prices that do not seem to have risen like most others, even in Alto Adige. We advise you to keep an eye out for this winery. Its progress is very encouraging. In the meantime, enjoy the excellent wines they presented to us this year.

●	A. A. Moscato Rosa Schweizer '00	🍷🍷🍷	5
○	A. A. Gewürztraminer '00	🍷🍷	4
●	A. A. Merlot Schweizer '99	🍷🍷	5
●	Istante '99	🍷🍷	5
○	Manna '99	🍷🍷	5
○	A. A. Pinot Bianco '00	🍷	4
●	A. A. Moscato Rosa Schweizer '99	🍷🍷🍷	5
●	A. A. Merlot Schweizer '93	🍷🍷	4
●	A. A. Pinot Nero Schweizer '95	🍷🍷	5
●	A. A. Pinot Nero Schweizer '97	🍷🍷	5
●	Istante '97	🍷🍷	5
○	A. A. Gewürztraminer '99	🍷🍷	3
●	Istante '98	🍷	5
○	Mitterberg Manna '98	🍷	5

○	A. A. Gewürztraminer Baron Salvadori '00	🍷🍷	5
○	A. A. Chardonnay Baron Salvadori '99	🍷🍷	5
○	A. A. Chardonnay '00	🍷🍷	4*
○	A. A. Pinot Grigio Punggl '00	🍷🍷	4*
○	A. A. Riesling '00	🍷🍷	4*
○	A. A. Terlano Pinot Bianco Sirmian '00	🍷🍷	4
●	A. A. Merlot Levad '99	🍷🍷	5
●	A. A. Merlot-Cabernet Sauvignon Anticus '99	🍷🍷	6
●	A. A. Schiava Gallea '00	🍷	3
○	A. A. Terlano Sauvignon Cl. Mantele '00	🍷	4
○	A. A. Pinot Grigio Punggl '98	🍷🍷	3
○	A. A. Pinot Bianco Sirmian '99	🍷🍷	3

NALLES/NALS (BZ)

Castello Schwanburg
Via Schwanburg, 16
39010 Nalles/Nals (BZ)
tel. 0471678622

Our comments on Castello Schwanburg and its wines for the 2002 Guide are not all positive. This can be partially explained by the missing Cabernet Sauvignon Castel Schwanburg and Cabernet Sauvignon Riserva, both from '99. In agreement with owner Dieter Rudolph Carli, we felt they were not yet ready and could not be adequately appraised at the time of the tastings. So we'll be reviewing them in the next edition. The rest of the range more or less confirms recent judgements. With all due respect, however, we would have expected something a bit more convincing from a winery with the track record of Castello Schwanburg and from such a committed owner. We felt the best of the samples submitted was the Alto Adige Bianco Pallas '00, a blend of pinot bianco and chardonnay with the addition of riesling and sauvignon. This is a wine with fine fruity aromas and a delicate flavour, though still not short on character or extractive weight. The rest of the wines in the range are correct, at times pleasant, but all just a little bit unchallenging. These include: the coherent and fruity Riesling and Sauvignon Castel Schwanburg '00; the two fairly one-dimensional Terlano Pinot Biancos, the classic Sonnenberg and the Pitzon, both from 2000; and the Merlot-Cabernet Sauvignon Geierberg '99 that may also be suffering from excessive youth, as well as its mediocre vintage. Finally, the fragrant Moscato Giallo '00 was among the best in its type. In other words, no disgrace but no particular praise either this year. These things happen.

NATURNO/NATURNS (BZ)

Tenuta Falkenstein - Franz Pratzner
Fraz. Val Venosta
Via Castello, 15
39025 Naturno/Naturns (BZ)
tel. 0473666054

The "Falcon's Rock" is once again among the top wineries in Alto Adige. Franz Pratzner, a master winemaker here in Valle Venosta, continues to amaze us with products born of his great sensitivity in interpreting the territory's wines. This year, he came back to win Three Glasses with a fascinating Riesling '00. It has very typical aromas, especially pineapple, but also clear mineral tones, perhaps resulting from letting the grapes ripen completely and particularly severe selection during the harvest. In other words, Pratzner's Riesling drinks like a dry Auslese. Though it may not have the cutting acidity of the '98, it has more body and concentration and outclasses the other wines in its category. Those who know wine will understand the difficulties Franz faced to keep such an aristocratically unco-operative variety as riesling renano. The Pinot Bianco '00 also cuts a nice figure. Obviously, it's much simpler but it's also very typical, although it could do with a little more concentration. The Sauvignon '00 was less enjoyable. An IGT wine with the curious label, "Vigneto delle Dolomiti" (Vineyard of the Dolomites), it seemed to us over-developed and lacking in the best characteristics of the variety. The same goes for the Gewürztraminer Vendemmia Tardiva '00, an indisputably powerful wine that needs fine-tuning.

○ A. A. Bianco Pallas '00	🍷	4*
○ A. A. Moscato Giallo '00	🍷	4
○ A. A. Riesling Castel Schwanburg '00	🍷	4
○ A. A. Sauvignon Castel Schwanburg '00	🍷	4
○ A. A. Terlano Pinot Bianco Pitzon '00	🍷	4
○ A. A. Terlano Pinot Bianco Sonnenberg '00	🍷	5
● A. A. Merlot - Cabernet Sauvignon Geierberg '99	🍷	6
● A. A. Cabernet Castel Schwanburg '96	🍷🍷🍷	6

○ A. A. Valle Venosta Riesling '00	🍷🍷🍷	5
○ A. A. Valle Venosta Gewürztraminer V. T. '00	🍷	5
○ A. A. Valle Venosta Pinot Bianco '00	🍷	4
○ Sauvignon '00	🍷	4
○ A. A. Valle Venosta Riesling '98	🍷🍷🍷	5
● A. A. Valle Venosta Pinot Nero '95	🍷🍷	5
○ A. A. Valle Venosta Gewürztraminer '98	🍷🍷	4
○ A. A. Valle Venosta Gewürztraminer '99	🍷🍷	4
○ A. A. Valle Venosta Pinot Bianco '99	🍷🍷	4
○ A. A. Valle Venosta Riesling '99	🍷🍷	5
● A. A. Valle Venosta Pinot Nero '97	🍷	4
● A. A. Valle Venosta Pinot Nero '98	🍷	4

SALORNO/SALURN (BZ)

HADERBURG
Loc. Pochi, 30
39040 Salorno/Salurn (BZ)
Tel. 0471889097

Luis and Christine Ochsenreiter continue to be the best exponents of spumante in Alto Adige. Once again, their Pas Dosé '95 and the non-vintage cuvée easily win a second Glass for their rock-solid technique. What is lacking in both wines is a touch of complexity, especially on the nose, but as far as the rest is concerned we feel we can again place Haderburg squarely in with the finest bubbly-makers in Italy. One of the southernmost wineries in Alto Adige, the cellar has a range that goes beyond spumantes, though these are excellent. This year, we had the good fortune to stumble on a very interesting version of Gewürztraminer Blaspichl, from the 2000 vintage, and it is a very convincing wine. It may not be enormous in terms of structure but the aromas are extremely varietal and the palate shows personality and nice finesse. The Chardonnay Hausmannhof, also a '00, has aromas of tropical fruit and well-integrated oak. The Pinot Nero Hausmannhof '99 was less successful in our opinion, paying the price of a lacklustre year, as were the two Sauvignons, the Hausmannhof '00 and Hausmannhof Selection '99. Both are correct enough but perhaps a bit too dominated by incisive acidity. Overall, however, this is a very well-run winery with many admirable qualities.

SALORNO/SALURN (BZ)

STEINHAUSERHOF
Pochi, 37
39040 Salorno/Salurn (BZ)
Tel. 0471889031

We knew very little about this winery in Salorno. We knew the name of its owner, Anton Ochsenreiter. Then we tasted his wines and were very impressed. All are very well made, in a first class style. In a nutshell, a real surprise. What can we tell you about these wines? The one we liked best was the Pinot Nero '99. It is not easy to make one this good, either in Alto Adige or even Burgundy, for that matter. It is varietal in its aromas, with fairly evident varietal notes of strawberry and though not possessing an enormous body, it still expresses itself with delicate elegance, just as a good Pinot Nero should. The '99 was better than the '98, which we also tasted. In our opinion, the earlier vintage had less clean, somewhat developed tones. The Sauvignon '00 is excellent, varietal but excessively gamey in its bouquet. It has good structure and real length in the mouth. The Gewürztraminer '00 is also good. An aromatic wine, it is coherent and elegant, and not excessively sweet. We close with the Chardonnay '00, which offers notes of pineapple on the nose and decent fullness on the mouth. Well done, Anton. We look forward to our next visit.

○	A. A. Chardonnay Hausmannhof '00	ΨΨ	4*
○	A. A. Gewürztraminer Blaspichl '00	ΨΨ	4
○	A. A. Spumante Haderburg Pas Dosé '95	ΨΨ	5
○	Spumante Haderburg Brut	ΨΨ	4*
○	A. A. Sauvignon Hausmannhof '00	Ψ	4
●	A. A. Pinot Nero Hausmannhof '99	Ψ	5
○	A. A. Sauvignon Hausmannhof Sel. '99	Ψ	5
○	A. A. Spumante Hausmannhof '90	ΨΨ	6
●	A. A. Pinot Nero Hausmannhof '95	ΨΨ	5
○	A. A. Gewürztraminer Blaspichl '98	ΨΨ	4
○	A. A. Chardonnay Hausmannhof '99	ΨΨ	3

○	A. A. Gewürztraminer '00	ΨΨ	4
○	A. A. Sauvignon '00	ΨΨ	4*
●	A. A. Pinot Nero '99	ΨΨ	5
○	A. A. Chardonnay '00	Ψ	4
●	A. A. Pinot Nero '98	Ψ	5

STAVA/STABEN (BZ)

Tenuta Unterortl-Castel Juval
Fraz. Juval, 1/B
39020 Stava/Staben (BZ)
tel. 0473667580
e-mail: familie.aurich@dnet.it

The Unterortl estate is in lower Val Venosta, on the hill where Reinhold Messner's Castel Juval sits, twenty kilometres west of Merano. Reinhold Messner is also the owner of the estate. Martin and Gisela Aurich are his tenants and the producers of these very good wines. The three hectares of vineyards tended by this oenology professor – Martin Aurich teaches at the San Michele agricultural college – are located at a remarkable altitude, from 600 to 850 meters above sea level with slopes of up to 45 per cent. Three varieties of grapes are cultivated on these steep hillsides: pinot bianco, riesling and pinot nero. Martin Aurich hit the Three Glasses mark with his Valle Venosta Riesling Castel Juval '00. It's a textbook white with a clean, straw yellow colour, nuanced with green highlights. Rich in intense peach, ripe apple and pineapple fruit, it has a structure that is sweet, full, minerally and tangy on the palate. It authentically expresses its site, climate and variety, as well as reflecting the tireless commitment of the producer himself. In addition to the nobler varieties of white grapes, the climate in the lower Val Venosta is also well adapted to pinot nero, which here shows off good, typical qualities. The Valle Venosta Pinot Nero Castel Juval '99 is a clear garnet ruby. Its very coherent bouquet has varietal and toasty notes, then shows typicity and pleasant drinkability on the palate, where it unveils mellow tannins. The Pinot Bianco Castel Juval '00 closes the range with its frank apple and pear fruit aromas.

TERLANO/TERLAN (BZ)

Cantina Terlano
Via Silberleiten, 7
39018 Terlano/Terlan (BZ)
tel. 0471257135
e-mail: office@cantina-terlano.com

Even if the Cantina di Terlano did not make it all the way to Three Glasses in this edition of the Guide, all it takes is one quick look at the scores at the bottom of the page to see that the quality level of the wines is very high. There can be no doubts. Terlano didn't get our top award but this does not alter our admiration for the commitment and dedication of its efforts. There are many very sound wines here and three reached our tasting finals. We felt the most interesting was the Sauvignon Quarz '99. A classic in its genre with varietal aromas, very elegant mineral notes and a balanced structure, it is perhaps not very concentrated though certainly not weak. The Lagrein Gries Riserva '98 is excellent, only a whisker less successful than the '97 version. The Terlano Pinot Bianco Vorberg '98 is always reliable and perhaps the most typical white from the Terlano area. But there is more. There is the Lagrein Porphyr '98, from Ora/Auer, a subzone that again shows itself to be very amenable to the grape type. Then we liked the complex, slightly developed aromas of the Terlano Nova Domus '98 and the more immediate and fragrant ones of the Terlano Classico '00. Equally good are the clean, varietal aromas of the Terlano Sauvignon Winkl '00. This is an extensive, varied range with an excellent overall quality level, completed by the Merlot Siebeneich '98, the Santa Maddalena Häusler '00 and the Terlano Sauvignon Classico, again from 2000. All are correct or better.

○ A. A. Valle Venosta Riesling '00	ŸŸŸ	4
● A. A. Valle Venosta Pinot Nero '99	ŸŸ	5
○ A. A. Valle Venosta Pinot Bianco '00	Ÿ	3
● A. A. Valle Venosta Pinot Nero '95	ŸŸ	5
○ A. A. Valle Venosta Riesling '96	ŸŸ	4
● A. A. Valle Venosta Pinot Nero '97	ŸŸ	5
○ A. A. Valle Venosta Riesling '97	ŸŸ	4
○ A. A. Valle Venosta Pinot Bianco '98	ŸŸ	3
○ A. A. Valle Venosta Riesling '98	ŸŸ	4
○ A. A. Valle Venosta Riesling '99	ŸŸ	4
● A. A. Valle Venosta Pinot Nero '96	Ÿ	5
○ A. A. Valle Venosta Pinot Bianco '97	Ÿ	4
● A. A. Valle Venosta Pinot Nero '98	Ÿ	5
○ A. A. Valle Venosta Pinot Bianco '99	Ÿ	3

● A. A. Lagrein Gries Ris. '98	ŸŸŸ	5
○ A. A. Terlano Sauvignon Quarz '99	ŸŸŸ	5
○ A. A. Terlano Cl. '00	ŸŸ	4
○ A. A. Terlano Pinot Bianco Vorberg '98	ŸŸ	5
○ A. A. Terlano Sauvignon Winkl '00	ŸŸ	5
● A. A. Lagrein Porphyr Ris. '98	ŸŸ	6
● A. A. Santa Maddalena Haüsler '00	Ÿ	3
○ A. A. Terlano Sauvignon Cl. '00	Ÿ	5
● A. A. Merlot Siebeneich '98	Ÿ	5
○ A. A. Terlano Pinot Bianco '79	ŸŸŸ	5
● A. A. Lagrein Gries Ris. '97	ŸŸŸ	5
○ A. A. Terlano Chardonnay '90	ŸŸ	6
○ A. A. Terlano Nova Domus '98	ŸŸ	5

TERMENO/TRAMIN (BZ)

Cantina Produttori Termeno
Strada del Vino, 122
39040 Termeno/Tramin (BZ)
tel. 0471860126
e-mail: info@tramin-wine.it

The Cantina Produttori di Termeno/Tramin has by now become one of the permanent fixtures on the quality winemaking scene in Alto Adige. More specifically, it is the best interpreter of Gewürztraminer and one of the best vinifiers of red varieties, including pinot grigio. Case in point, this year we stumbled on a majestic version of Gewürztraminer Nussbaumerhof '00 with a bouquet that is mineral as well as aromatic and truly exceptional concentration on the palate. Furthermore, the Gewürztraminer Passito Terminum '99 was sensational, with very evident notes of botrytis on the nose and a sweet, very full flavour with tremendous length. Two well deserved Three Glass accolades. We can also confidently recommend: the Lagrein Urbanhof '99; the Pinot Nero Mazzon '99, one of the best in its category; the Pinot Grigio Unterebnerhof '00; and even, something fairly unusual for this cellar, the Chardonnay Glassien '00 and the Sauvignon '00, which were surprises in this series. All the other wines were decent, with the Gewürztraminer Maratsch '00 at the top of the heap. The Pinot Bianco '00 and fragrant Schiava Freisingerhof, again obviously from 2000, were very well-typed and very honestly priced. So congratulations to all the co-operative members and especially to "kellermeister" Willi Stürz, talented technical manager and the man behind the estate's success.

TERMENO/TRAMIN (BZ)

Castel Ringberg
& Kastelaz Elena Walch
Via A. Hofer, 1
39040 Termeno/Tramin (BZ)
tel. 0471860172
e-mail: walch@cenida.it

Elena Walch made the grade again with her third Three Glass award in the last four years. The performance clearly shows the progress and entrepreneurial abilities of the woman who is currently the most famous lady of wine in Alto Adige. She took the prize with what, in our opinion, is her most classic wine, the Gewürztraminer '00 del Podere Kastelaz di Termeno, one of the best crus in the entire area. It is an aromatic white with a golden hue and the intense aromas of wild roses. Big, rich and full-bodied on the palate, it signs off with a faint, bitterish twist in the after-aroma. The other two whites are also very good, this time from the Podere Castel Ringberg di Caldaro. They are the Riesling '00 and, especially, the Pinot Grigio '00. Both manage to debunk the theory that would have only reds, apart from gewürztraminer, growing in the areas around Termeno and Caldaro, which are especially warm zones for Alto Adige. Other whites to note are the fragrant, fruit-rich Chardonnay Cardellino '00, the decent Sauvignon '00 from Castel Ringberg, and the Pinot Bianco '00 from Kastelaz. However, we were a bit puzzled by the reds. The Cabernet Istrice '99 was only fair. The Merlot Kastelaz '98 was a little disappointing, a consequence of an unexciting harvest. It is a shade over-developed on the nose and has no great concentration in the mouth. We would have liked something more from a wine of this type.

○ A. A. Gewürztraminer Nussbaumerhof '00 🍷🍷🍷	5
○ A. A. Gewürztraminer Passito Terminum '99 🍷🍷🍷	6
○ A. A. Chardonnay Glassien '00 🍷🍷	5
○ A. A. Pinot Grigio Unterbnerhof '00 🍷🍷	4
○ A. A. Sauvignon '00 🍷🍷	4*
● A. A. Lagrein Urbanhof '99 🍷🍷	4
● A. A. Pinot Nero Mazzon '99 🍷🍷	5
○ A. A. Gewürztraminer Maratsch '00 🍷	4
○ A. A. Pinot Bianco '00 🍷	3
● A. A. Schiava Hexenbichler '00 🍷	3
○ A. A. Gewürztraminer Passito Terminum '98 🍷🍷🍷	6
○ A. A. Gewürztraminer Nussbaumerhof '99 🍷🍷🍷	4

○ A. A. Gewürztraminer Kastelaz '00 🍷🍷🍷	5
○ A. A. Pinot Grigio Castel Ringberg '00 🍷🍷	5
○ A. A. Resling Castel Ringberg '00 🍷🍷	5
○ A. A. Chardonnay Cardellino '00 🍷	5
○ A. A. Pinot Bianco Kastelaz '00 🍷	4
○ A. A. Sauvignon Castel Ringberg '00 🍷	5
● A. A. Merlot Kastelaz Ris. '98 🍷	6
● A. A. Cabernet Sauvignon Castel Ringberg Ris. '97 🍷🍷🍷	5
○ A. A. Gewürztraminer Kastelaz '97 🍷🍷🍷	4
● A. A. Cabernet Istrice '98 🍷🍷	4
○ A. A. Gewürztraminer Kastelaz '98 🍷🍷	4
○ A. A. Gewürztraminer Kastelaz '99 🍷🍷	4

TERMENO/TRAMIN (BZ)

HOFSTÄTTER
P.ZZA MUNICIPIO, 5
39040 TERMENO/TRAMIN (BZ)
TEL. 0471860161
E-MAIL: info@hofstatter.com

We would advise Martin Foradori not to get upset if none of his wines took top honours in this year's Guide. The reason is largely to do with the fact that the Pinot Nero S. Urbano '98 had not yet been bottled at the time of our tastings and so we could not evaluate it. However, there were three wines in the series submitted by Hofstätter that came very close to a Third Glass and made it to our tasting finals. Above all, the Pinot Nero Riserva '98, the best of its vintage in Alto Adige, is varietal in its aromas and stylish, concentrated and soft on the palate. It has to be one of the best versions ever in spite of a harvest that was good but not exceptional. Then there is Martin's Gewürztraminer Kolbenhof '00, with its aromatic bouquet and good structure, though given the favourable harvest, we might have expected an attack on the palate with greater concentration. Finally, the Alto Adige Bianco Vigna San Michele '00, a blend of pinot bianco, chardonnay and riesling partially aged in small casks, was an eye-opener: a balanced wine with barely hinted-at oak integrated perfectly into the structure. In a word, it's great. The Lagrein Steinraffler '98 and undemanding standard-label '00 Chardonnay are also worth investigating. The Cabernet Sauvignon Riserva '98 was underperforming while the Pinot Bianco '00 and agreeable Schiava Kolbenhofer, again from 2000, are both merely correct.

○ A. A. Bianco S. Michele '00	♊	5
○ A. A. Gewürztraminer Kolbenhof '00	♊	5
● A. A. Pinot Nero Ris. '98	♊	5
● A. A. Lagrein Scuro Steinraffler '98	♊	6
● A. A. Cabernet Sauvignon Ris. '98	♉	5
○ A. A. Pinot Bianco '00	♉	4
● A. A. Schiava Kolbenhofer '00	♉	4
● A. A. Pinot Nero S. Urbano '93	♕	6
● A. A. Pinot Nero S. Urbano '95	♕	6
○ A. A. Gewürztraminer Kolbenhof '98	♕	4
○ A. A. Gewürztraminer Kolbenhof '99	♕	4

VADENA/PFATTEN (BZ)

CANTINA LAIMBURG
LOC. LAIMBURG, 6
39051 VADENA/PFATTEN (BZ)
TEL. 0471969700 - 0471969806
E-MAIL: laimburg@provinz.bz.it

If Laimburg did not exist, it would have to be invented. A laboratory for the adjacent agriculture and forestry experimental centre, this winery brings enormous benefits to Alto Adige. Every year, it turns out skilled, well-trained technicians, some in the wine sector, and supports the progress of viticulture in the region. Many of Alto Adige's "kellermeisters" and producers studied here, learning the basics for their subsequent careers. But Laimburg has also always made high quality wines. At present, the winery manager, Klaus Platter, and wine technician Urban Piccolruaz, can point to a range of wines that are not only correct but, in some cases, very good. This year, they submitted six to us for tasting. Two reached our finals. Not bad, don't you think? The most convincing was the Lagrein Scuro Riserva '98, now a classic for the estate. Varietal, concentrated and a little bit rough, it has the advantages that come with skilfully gauged oak. In other words, a Lagrein for those who love strong sensations. The Riesling '00 is also very good and is another wine that Laimburg has turned into a cellar specialty. Varietal, complex in its aromas and decisive, it has a hint of sharpness from the acidity in the structure. The Sauvignon '00 is almost as good. It, too, is varietal, with slightly gamy aromas and excellent structure. The Chardonnay Doa '99 is decent. It matures in small casks for around a year, which could be a bit too long. The Pinot Nero '99 is a better wine of its kind. Elegant, not excessively concentrated on the palate, it is very typical. The Gewürztraminer '00 was a minor disappointment because we have loved this wine in past versions. We might have expected more concentration from such a favourable harvest as the 2000.

○ A. A. Riesling Renano '00	♊	4*
● A. A. Lagrein Scuro Ris. '98	♊	6
○ A. A. Pinot Nero '99	♊	5
○ A. A. Sauvignon '00	♊	4
○ A. A. Gewürztraminer '00	♉	4
○ A. A. Chardonnay Doa '99	♉	5
○ A. A. Gewürztraminer '94	♕	4
● A. A. Cabernet Ris. '97	♕	5
○ A. A. Chardonnay Doa '97	♕	5
● A. A. Lagrein Scuro Ris. '97	♕	6
○ A. A. Riesling Renano '98	♕	4
○ A. A. Sauvignon '98	♕	4
○ A. A. Gewürztraminer '99	♕	4
○ A. A. Riesling Renano '99	♕	4
○ A. A. Sauvignon '99	♕	4

VARNA/VAHRN (BZ)

ABBAZIA DI NOVACELLA
FRAZ. NOVACELLA
VIA DELL'ABBAZIA, 1
39040 VARNA/VAHRN (BZ)
TEL. 0472836189
E-MAIL: info@kloster-neustift.it

The wines from Abbazia di Novacella are always good and well-made. One of the most northerly estates in Italy, it even managed to offer two wines that made it to our final taste-off, missing Third Glasses by a whisker. The first was the Valle Isarco Gewürztraminer '00 from the Praepositus line, the most prestigious in the entire range. It has a golden, straw-yellow colour and clear varietal bouquet with typical aromatic notes, a good, coherent body with a hint of residual sugar, and a finish that is just barely acidic. The second stunner was the Moscato Rosa '00 from the estate vineyards near Cornaiano/Girlan, south of Bolzano and therefore much further south. It is intense ruby with aromas of rose petal jam. The palate is sweet, firm and well-typed, with good persistence. But there are quite a lot of wines from this particular abbey. Among those to keep an eye on this year are the Valle Isarco Müller Thurgau '00, perhaps the best in its category, the standard-label Valle Isarco Gewürztraminer '00 and finally the Preapositus Weiss '99, a white from sylvaner, chardonnay and pinot grigio that ages for a year and a half in oak. Merely correct but worthwhile anyway are the Pinot Nero '00 and Valle Isarco Kerner '00, in both the flagship Praepositus and the basic version, and the two very famous Valle Isarco Sylvaners, the estate's calling cards, also in both standard-label version and the Praepositus edition. The team of estate manager Urban von Klebersberg and oenologist Celestino Lucin is obviously a winning one.

VARNA/VAHRN (BZ)

KÖFERERHOF
FRAZ. NOVACELLA
VIA PUSTERIA, 3
39040 VARNA/VAHRN (BZ)
TEL. 0472836649

The vineyards of this small estate in Valle Isarco could be the most northerly in Italy. Here, we are above the 47th parallel in one of the zones at the very limit for viticulture south of the Alps. Josef and Gunther Kerschbaumer perform small miracles every year to produce good quality wines. They have five hectares of vineyards with an average of 7,000 vines per hectare, producing around 5,000 kilograms per hectare to make barely 27,000 bottles. In a situation that is anything but easy, low yields are the key to creating wines full of personality and character. This year, we particularly liked the Sylvaner '00 for its typically grassy and slightly citrussy aromas, and unexpectedly robust structure. This is a very well-typed white, a wine that is born of its territory and the traditions of the zone. The other whites submitted were also good: the Kerner, the Gewürztraminer and the Pinot Grigio, all from the 2000 vintage. Well-made and typical, they were perhaps a bit closed when we tasted them but certainly interesting and rather special. What we should ask ourselves is why a DOC zone like Valle Isarco does not permit the production of Riesling. We hope this oversight can be corrected because a Riesling Renano produced by Köfererhof could be a really great wine.

●	A. A. Moscato Rosa '00	♟♟	5
○	A. A. Valle Isarco Gewürztraminer Praepositus '00	♟♟	5
○	A. A. Valle Isarco Gewürztraminer '00	♟♟	4
○	A. A. Valle Isarco Müller Thurgau '00	♟♟	4*
○	Praepositus Weiss '99	♟♟	5
●	A. A. Pinot Nero '00	♟	5
○	A. A. Valle Isarco Kerner '00	♟	4
○	A. A. Valle Isarco Kerner Praepositus '00	♟	5
○	A. A. Valle Isarco Pinot Grigio '00	♟	4
○	A. A. Valle Isarco Sylvaner '00	♟	4
○	A. A. Valle Isarco Sylvaner Praepositus '00	♟	5

○	A. A. Valle Isarco Sylvaner '00	♟♟	4*
○	A. A. Valle Isarco Gewürztraminer '00	♟	4
○	A. A. Valle Isarco Kerner '00	♟	4
○	A. A. Valle Isarco Pinot Grigio '00	♟	4
○	A. A. Valle Isarco Kerner '98	♟♟	4
○	A. A. Valle Isarco Pinot Grigio '98	♟♟	4
○	A. A. Valle Isarco Sylvaner '98	♟♟	4
○	A. A. Valle Isarco Kerner '99	♟♟	4
○	A. A. Valle Isarco Pinot Grigio '99	♟♟	4
○	A. A. Valle Isarco Sylvaner '99	♟♟	4
○	A. A. Valle Isarco Gewürztraminer '98	♟	4
○	A. A. Valle Isarco Gewürztraminer '99	♟	4

OTHER WINERIES

Lorenz Martini
Loc. Cornaiano/Girlan
Via Pranzol, 2/d
39050 Appiano/Eppan (BZ)
tel. 0471664136

A fine spumante from equal parts of chardonnay and pinot bianco grapes. Aroma-rich, delicate and elegant, although not very complex. A brief description of Comitissa Brut Riserva by Lorenz Martini, owner of a micro-winery at Cornaiano/Girlan.

○ A. A. Comitissa Brut Ris.	▼▼	5

K. Martini & Sohn
Via Lamm, 28
39050 Appiano/Eppan (BZ)
tel. 0471663156
e-mail: kmartini@dnet.it

A winery without peaks. There are lots of decent wines but none are particularly convincing. It's probably a case of vintage-related problems. A word to the wise, though: the Lagrein Maturum '99, Lagrein Rueslhof '99 and Chardonnay Palladium '00 are well-made.

○ A. A. Chardonnay Palladium '00	▼	3
● A. A. Lagrein Scuro Maturum '99	▼	5
● A. A. Lagrein Scuro Rueslhof '99	▼	4

Eberlehof - Zisser
Santa Magdalena, 26
39100 Bolzano/Bozen
tel. 0471978607

The Mabon '95 from Horst Zisser's Eberlehof winery is a fairly forward, complex Lagrein, both on the palate and especially the nose. One that shows the variety can age very well indeed.

● A. A. Lagrein Scuro Mabon '95	▼	4

Egger-Ramer
Fraz. Gries - Via Guncina, 5
39100 Bolzano/Bozen
tel. 0471280541 - 0471264004
e-mail: egger@suedtiroler-wein.de

Toni and Peter Egger are specialists in wines from Bolzano. Their Lagrein Gries Kristan Riserva, this year released in the '98 version, is always good, as is the basic Gries Kristan '00. The Santa Maddalena Classico '00 is a decent bottle.

● A. A. Lagrein Scuro Gries Kristan '00	▼	4
● A. A. Santa Maddalena Cl. '00	▼	3
● A. A. Lagrein Scuro Gries Kristan Ris. '98	▼	5

Thomas Mayr e Figli
Fraz. Gries - Via Mendola, 56
39100 Bolzano/Bozen
Tel. 0471281030
E-mail: thomas@mayr.cjb.net

The Mayr winery presented very few wines this year. As always, the Santa Maddalena Rumplerhof '00 is good. There are also many very promising barrel samples we will leave for another visit, particularly the Lagrein Riserva '99 and Schiava '00. The standard-label Lagrein '00 is decent.

● A. A. Lagrein Scuro '00	♀ 3*
● A. A. Santa Maddalena Cl. Rumplerhof '00	♀ 3*

Pfeifer Johannes Pfannenstielhof
Via Pfannestiel, 9
39100 Bolzano/Bozen
Tel. 0471970884 - 3388116623

A number of interesting products and a fairly good range. The Santa Maddalena Classico '00 is especially good, attractively varietal and fragrant. The Lagrein Riserva '98 and standarad-label Lagrein '99 are both well worth looking into. Considering the unfavourable vintage, future versions can be expected to do better.

● A. A. Santa Maddalena Cl. '00	♀♀ 4
● A. A. Lagrein Scuro Ris. '98	♀ 5
● A. A. Lagrein Scuro '99	♀ 4

Anton Schmid - Oberrautner
Fraz. Gries - Via M. Pacher, 3
39100 Bolzano/Bozen
Tel. 0471281440
E-mail: florianschmid@dnet.it

There were two rather interesting Lagreins, the Grieser Riserva '99 and Grieser '00, and a very promising barrel sample, the Lagrein Barrique '99. We will postpone our appraisal until next year but it is one to watch.

● A. A. Lagrein Scuro Grieser '00	♀ 3*
● A. A. Lagrein Scuro Grieser Ris. '99	♀ 4*

Taschlerhof
Via Mahr, 107
39042 Bressanone/Brixen (BZ)
Tel. 0472851091

Taschlerhof presented two typical wines from the Isarco valley, the Sylvaner '00 and the Gewürztraminer '00. Both are well-typed and well-executed. This was especially true of the Sylvaner, which was well-defined on the nose and had good structure on the palate.

○ A. A. Valle Isarco Gewürztraminer '00	♀ 4
○ A. A. Valle Isarco Sylvaner '00	♀ 4

Tenuta Ritterhof
Strada del Vino, 1
39052 Caldaro/Kaltern (BZ)
Tel. 0471963298

This year's Ritterhof selection is very good, above all the Lagrein Riserva Crescendo '98, Santa Maddalena Perlhof '00 and Merlot Riserva Crescendo '98. But the entire range continues to improve. In other words, keep your eye on this estate in the future.

● A. A. Lagrein Scuro Crescendo Ris. '98	♀♀ 4
● A. A. Santa Maddalena Perlhof '00	♀ 3
● A. A. Merlot Ris. '98	♀ 4

Markus Prackwieser Gumphof
Novale di Presule, 8
39050 Fié allo Sciliar/
Völs Am Schlern (BZ)
Tel. 0471601190

Two interesting whites and a worthy new entry for Markus Prackwieser and the Gumphof winery. We felt the Sauvignon Praesulius '00, in particular, was typical and elegant on the palate. The Pinot Bianco Praesulius '00 was correct and even, though a bit one-dimensional.

○ A. A. Pinot Bianco Praesulius '00	♀ 4
○ A. A. Sauvignon Praesulius '00	♀ 4

CASTELLO RAMETZ
VIA LABERS, 4
39012 MERANO/MERAN (BZ)
TEL. 0473211011 - 0473212152
E-MAIL: info@rametz.com

The Chardonnay '00, aged in steel vats, was very good. The Riesling '00 and Cabernet '98 were reasonable, after ageing in barriques for around two years. These are the best wines from Castello Rametz, a winery that has made steady progress over the last few years.

○ A. A. Chardonnay '00	♛♛	4*
○ A. A. Riesling '00	♛	4
● A. A. Cabernet '98	♛	6

TENUTA PFITSCHERHOF
VIA GLENO, 9
39040 MONTAGNA/MONTAN (BZ)
TEL. 0471819773

Only a few wines, but good ones. In particular, the Pinot Nero Matan '99 is one of the best in its category. The Pinot Nero Fuchsleiten '99, and the Pinot Nero Riserva '98 performed very well. Klaus Pfitscher is becoming one of Pinot Nero's most sensitive interpreters.

● A. A. Pinot Nero Matan '99	♛♛	5
● A. A. Pinot Nero Ris. '98	♛	4
● A. A. Pinot Nero Fuchsleiten '99	♛	5

BARON VON KRIPP STACHLBURG
39020 PARCINES/PARTSCHINS (BZ)
TEL. 0473968014

This winery is known particularly for its delicate Pinot Nero. We especially liked the two versions of Chardonnay, one a '99 and the other from 2000, with a slight preference for the former. Both are clean and varietal in their bouquets and have good structure.

○ A. A. Valle Venosta Chardonnay '99	♛♛	4
○ A. A. Valle Venosta Chardonnay '00	♛	4

OSWALD SCHUSTER BEFELNHOF
VIA VEZZANO, 14
39028 SILANDRO/SCHLANDERS (BZ)
TEL. 0473742197

The reason for including Oswald Schuster's Befelnhof winery in the Guide is a splendid Riesling '00 from Valle Venosta, a zone where the variety performs particularly well. It is a surprising wine, with a touch of mineral in its bouquet, and great character on the palate. Not to be missed.

○ A. A. Valle Venosta Riesling '00	♛♛	4

HOFKELLEREI
VIA JOSEF VON ZALLINGER, 4
39040 TERMENO/TRAMIN (BZ)
TEL. 0471860215

A good, late-harvest Gewürztraminer, Circe '99, is the best wine from the Hofkellerei winery owned by Willi and Gerlinde Walch. It has an aromatic bouquet and never cloys, despite the sugar content. The other wines presented were only fair.

○ Circe '99	♛	4

ROCKHOF
VIA S. VALENTINO, 9
39040 VILLANDRO/VILLANDERS (BZ)
TEL. 0472847130

From this small winery in the Isarco valley, owned by Konrad Augschöll, we picked out the very nice Müller Thurgau, with its typically aromatic bouquet. A well-executed wine.

○ A. A. Valle Isarco Müller Thurgau '00	♛	4

VENETO

There is renewed ferment in the Veneto, and it's not restricted to the cellars. This year's outstanding performance, with 18 Three Glasses wines, may even overshadow a more important phenomenon, which is that both small and large producers have realized that in focusing on quality they are also promoting the area in which they work. Having conquered a strong position on the market, some established wineries like Marion - and to an even greater extent, Serafini & Vidotto - have decided not to place their flagship products on the market at once because they are aware that these wines require a certain ageing period in bottles. Following in the footsteps of many such important wineries are numerous small producers that appear in the Guide for the first time, like Ca' La Bionda, I Scriani, Manara and Andreola Orsola. This demonstrates that Veneto winemaking is strongly developing and is no longer limited to one single area as it was in the past. The growth of co-operative wineries is also apparent as the Cantina della Valpantena enters the Guide, indicating that vineyard management is improving even faster than cellar techniques. There are no new entries from the provinces of Padua or Vicenza but the existing wineries demonstrate that they are continually making progress, vintage after vintage. Piovene, Emo Capodilista and Vigneto Due Santi are now benchmark wineries, just as in the Colli Trevigiani Sorelle Brona, Masottina and Bepin de Eto also embody the new approach. The quality of Proseccos this year is remarkable and evenly distributed. Producers like Bisol, Ruggeri and Adami are making a decisive contribution towards enhancing the reputation of the regional bubbly. Interesting results are emerging in Veneto from whites macerated on the skins, and Angiolino Maule of La Biancara is probably the most important exponent of this technique. The Soave zone is enjoying a boom period. Having won the White of the Year award in last year's edition of the Guide, this time the zone picked up six Three Glass awards. Roberto Anselmi wins Three Glasses again, following his decision to leave the DOC umbrella, with a very good version of Capitel Croce; and Pieropan, Ca' Rugate, Inama and Gini welcome Graziano Pra with his Montegrande to the Soave Three Glass club. In Valpolicella, Amarone and Recioto continue their upwards trend with increasingly significant high quality results. Alongside the impressive performance of Allegrini and Dal Forno, Bussola, Corte Sant'Alda and Viviani also confirm their position and Zenato moves up a gear with a really stylish Amarone. Lastly, Lorenzo Begali, Stefano Cesari, with his Brigaldara, and Sergio Castellani are rewarded for their commitment to quality with a top result, proving themselves to be among the very best. Polished performances as ever from Maculan with the Fratta, a more international-style product, and Vignalta, with a sumptuous version of the Gemola, which is more territory-driven.

BAONE (PD)

Il Filò delle Vigne
Via Terralba, 239
35030 Baone (PD)
tel. 042956243

Il Filò delle Vigne makes its second appearance in the Guide, confirming the quality of last year's tastings and contributing to improving the image of Colli Euganei wines. Owners Nicolò Voltan and Gino Giordani decided to set out along the tough road to quality, and this decision has paid off, especially if we bear in mind the potential of the area in question. Their other crucial move was securing the services of a skilled oenologist, Andrea Boaretti, with his in-depth knowledge of the DOC zone and its wines. This year, we tasted the products released in 2001 but preliminary tastings in the cellar promise an even rosier future. The Borgo delle Casette is the winery's leading light, in two vintages: '97 and '98. The former is very good, with a firm structure and character. It is stylish on the palate, and still young and healthy. The '98 has strikingly intense colour and the nose opens with vegetal aromas, developing into coffee, tobacco and autumn leaves. It is rounded and persistent, with good ageing prospects. The Vigna Cecilia is also very convincing. It's a Cabernet Riserva with a predominant percentage of cabernet franc aged in stainless steel. Purply ruby red, it shows minerally, gamey aromas, and intriguingly lively tannins. The Pinot Bianco could be a great wine if it was not a little in thrall to its high alcohol content.

● Colli Euganei Cabernet Borgo delle Casette Ris. '97 ♟♟	5
● Colli Euganei Cabernet Borgo delle Casette Ris. '98 ♟♟	5
● Colli Euganei Cabernet Vigna Cecilia di Baone Ris. '98 ♟♟	5
○ Colli Euganei Pinot Bianco '00 ♟	4
● Colli Euganei Cabernet Borgo delle Casette Ris. '96 ♟♟	5

BARDOLINO (VR)

Guerrieri Rizzardi
Via Verdi, 4
37011 Bardolino (VR)
tel. 0457210028
e-mail: mail@guerrieri-rizzardi.com

This large Bardolino winery is possibly the only privately owned producer in the Verona area with plots in all the province's DOC zones. Spreading the winery's activity across so many different types of wine may inevitably dilute the efforts made but, on the other hand, it allows Guerrieri Rizzardi to present good quality wines of various types. On the whole, this is a successful policy, as shown by the good results of our tastings. This year, the Amarone '96 stands out. Despite the poor year, it has engaging bottled fruit aromas giving way to subtler aromatic herb notes. On the palate, it may lack the richness and fruit pulp that a better year might have provided but it is stylish and elegant, with pleasantly rounded ripe fruit. The Dogoli, a white from aromatic grapes, maintains its high standard with a full, pervasive nose ranging from spring flowers to roses, candied fruit and spice, with a flinty undertone enhancing the range of nuances. On the palate, the mineral note gets the better of the fruit, making it a highly personal and interesting wine. The Soave Costeggiola is from a long-established cru, and demonstrates its class by coming close to Two Glasses, while the white Castello Guerrieri and the Chiaretto are particularly drinkable.

● Amarone della Valpolicella Cl. '96 ♟♟	6
○ Dogoli Bianco '99 ♟♟	4
⊙ Bardolino Chiaretto '00 ♟	4
○ Soave Cl. Costeggiola '00 ♟	4
○ Castello Guerrieri Bianco '99 ♟	4
● Valpolicella Cl. Sup. Poiega '99 ♟	4
○ Recioto di Soave '98	5

BARDOLINO (VR)

F.lli Zeni
Via Costabella, 9
37011 Bardolino (VR)
tel. 0457210022
e-mail: zeni@zeni.it

The Zeni dynasty is part of Garda's winemaking history. The estate was established at Bardolino in the second half of the 19th century and made its name primarily in exporting wines. About 20 years ago, Gaetano, or Nino, Zeni made the crucial decision to bottle on the estate and boost both production, now at around 800,000 bottles, and quality. The focus shifted to the local area and its winemaking heritage. In fact, the wine museum at the cellar, on the road that winds through the Bardolino hills, is a magnet for visitors. There are just three product lines: standard-label, Vigne Alte and Marogne, and a large number of wines were presented, as every year. Head and shoulders above the rest is the Amarone Vigne Alte '97, a creamy, rich wine with a floral, coffee-nuanced nose and a pulpy, stylishly well-sustained, clean palate. The Amarone aged in barriques is only slightly inferior. The nose is vegetal, and the palate shows bottled berry fruits and chocolate. Of the two Valpolicellas, the standard-label is better than the Vigne Alte while the opposite applies to the Recioto della Valpolicella. The series of Riviera wines is, as ever, well-typed and enjoyable. The grassy, floral Chiaretto Vigne Alte is followed by an interesting Bardolino Superiore, in both standard-label and Vigne Alte versions, and the simple, fragrantly floral Bianco di Custoza Vigne Alte. The Soave Vigne Alte is worth a mention.

BASSANO DEL GRAPPA (VI)

Vigneto Due Santi
V.le Asiago, 174
36061 Bassano del Grappa (VI)
tel. 0424502074
e-mail: info@duesanti.it

Stefano Zonta tends his vineyards with great care and commitment. Situated just outside Bassano, they extend over 13 hectares to the edge of the Valsugana. The valley is naturally cool in summer and mild in winter, and olive trees flourish here. It is protected by the mountains behind, and the Po valley opens out in front, making it an ideal place to grow vines. It's just a shame that every year, like clockwork, hail arrives to threaten a whole season's hard work. At last, after a decade of hail, 1999 passed without incident, enabling Stefano to bring in a great harvest that he transformed into an excellent Cabernet. The dark colour presages a nose that gradually opens out into mineral, gamey sensations, which in turn give way to black berry fruit and aromatic herbs. On the palate, the wine confirms the firmness and austerity of the nose. Good nose-palate consistency is backed up by dense, sweet tannins a the vein of acidity makes it fresher and more persistent. The excellent Sauvignon is enviably structured and mouthfilling, showing sage and red pepper aromas, with creamily sweet ripe fruit, especially peaches, on the palate. The other two whites, the Malvasia Campo di Fiori and the Breganze Bianco Rivana, are both interesting and more satisfying on the palate than on the nose. The standard-label Cabernet and Rosso are also very decent.

	Wine	Glasses	Price
●	Amarone della Valpolicella Cl. Vigne Alte '97	▼▼	6
◉	Bardolino Chiaretto Vigne Alte '00	▼	3
●	Amarone della Valpolicella Cl. Barrique '97	▼	6
●	Recioto della Valpolicella Cl. '98	▼	5
●	Recioto della Valpolicella Cl. Vigne Alte '98	▼	5
●	Bardolino Cl. Sup. '99	▼	2
●	Bardolino Cl. Sup. Vigne Alte '99	▼	3
●	Valpolicella Cl. Sup. '99	▼	3
●	Valpolicella Cl. Sup. Vigne Alte '99	▼	3
○	Bianco di Custoza Vigne Alte '00		3
○	Soave Cl. Vigne Alte '00		3
●	Amarone della Valpolicella Cl. '98	▼▼▼	6

	Wine	Glasses	Price
●	Breganze Cabernet Vigneto Due Santi '99	▼▼	5
○	Breganze Bianco Rivana '00	▼▼	3*
○	Breganze Sauvignon Vigneto Due Santi '00	▼▼	4
○	Malvasia Campo di Fiori '00	▼	3
●	Breganze Cabernet '99	▼	3
●	Breganze Rosso '99	▼	3
○	Prosecco		3
●	Breganze Cabernet Vigneto Due Santi '96	▽▽	4
●	Breganze Cabernet Vigneto Due Santi '97	▽▽	4
●	Breganze Cabernet Vigneto Due Santi '98	▽▽	4

BREGANZE (VI)

MACULAN
VIA CASTELLETTO, 3
36042 BREGANZE (VI)
TEL. 0445873733 - 0445873124
E-MAIL: maculan@netics.net

Some people believe that success breeds contentment. But Fausto Maculan is not resting on his laurels. In fact, he has begun a process of renewal in the last few years which is something of a revolution. Thanks also to the help of oenologist Massimo del Lago, his Breganze winery is slowly changing style and refining its techniques both in the vineyard and in the cellar, as well as rationalizing the wide range of products. The most obvious result of this labour is the Fratta, which again in the 1999 version gives a really outstanding performance. Concentration and strength are at the highest possible levels, and the precision and tidiness of expression are astounding. This is almost a cerebral wine, irresistibly dynamic with exemplary balance. A description of the individual components seems, for once, superfluous considering the profound nature of the wine, which is made from mainly cabernet sauvignon with a lower percentage of merlot, and takes its place among the world's great interpretations of the Bordeaux blend. Three Glasses were a formality. The other reds tasted are a simple Cabernet and the very fruity Brentino. The whites include the suave, subtle Breganze di Breganze, the warm, mature Chardonnay Riale and the Chardonnay Ferrata, which is still looking for a good balance of fruit and wood. The sweet wines are excellent, from the fragrant Dindarello to the spicy, exotic Torcolato and the exceptional, lively, velvet-smooth Acininobili.

●	Fratta '99	🍷🍷🍷	6
○	Acininobili '98	🍷🍷	6
○	Breganze Chardonnay Riale '99	🍷🍷	4
○	Breganze Torcolato '99	🍷🍷	6
○	Breganze di Breganze '00	🍷	3
○	Dindarello '00	🍷	4
○	Breganze Chardonnay Ferrata '99	🍷	5
●	Brentino '99	🍷	4
●	Cabernet Sauvignon Ferrata '90	🍷🍷🍷	6
●	Breganze Cabernet Sauvignon Ferrata '94	🍷🍷🍷	6
●	Fratta '97	🍷🍷🍷	6
●	Fratta '98	🍷🍷🍷	6

CAVAION VERONESE (VR)

LE FRAGHE
LOC. COLOMBARA, 3
37010 CAVAION VERONESE (VR)
TEL. 0457236832
E-MAIL: lefraghe@tiscalinet.it

Matilde Poggi is a determined woman. She knows that the hills between Garda and Valdadige can yield substantial wines, and is therefore totally committed to bottling the best of them. Of course, this is not easy land to work. The fluvio-glacial deposits seem to indicate a mild climate but in fact are often battered by winds or nipped by ice, despite the proximity of the lake. If you visit the winery, you will notice the curious contrast between the softness of the name - "fraghe" means strawberries – and the rather military appearance of the dovecote overlooking the old farmyard. The wines gush with grace and character. The Quaiare is an almost impenetrable red, from cabernet grapes, which improves over time, and has a promising future. The '97 has chocolate and ripe red fruit in the nose while the sweet, creamy palate is enriched with spice and coffee notes. The tannins are still harsh but further ageing will make this an extremely satisfying wine. The '98, still ageing in the cellar, is also very promising. The Bardolino has bags of personality. Its pleasant floral aromas enchant the nose, to emerge again on the palate with fruity notes from the partial drying of some of the grapes. The Chiaretto is fresh and drinkable, with remarkable body. Of the two whites, the Chardonnay and the Garganega, we preferred the former for its sweet ripe aromas, well reflected in the palate, where they mingle with hints of Mediterranean scrubland.

●	Bardolino Cl. '00	🍷	3*
●	Valdadige Quaiare '97	🍷🍷	5
⊙	Bardolino Chiaretto '00	🍷	2
○	Valdadige Chardonnay Montalto '99	🍷	3
○	Garganega del Veneto '00		3
●	Valdadige Quaiare '96	🍷🍷	4

CINTO EUGANEO (PD)

Ca' Lustra
Loc. Faedo
Via San Pietro, 50
35030 Cinto Euganeo (PD)
Tel. 042994128
E-mail: info@calustra.it

This is one of the most attractive wineries in the Colli Euganei. It is run with a steady hand by the Zanovello family, Franco, Ivano and Rita in particular, with the valuable assistance of oenologist Francesco Polastri and cellarmanager Andrea. Their strong point is undoubtedly an awareness of the specific nature of these hills of volcanic origin, from which they obtain wines like the Girapoggio, a Cabernet with a dense, impenetrable, purplish ruby red colour. The nose is complex and concentrated, with clear balsam and tobacco sensations. On the palate, a very pleasant sweet note revealing velvety, full-bodied morello cherry fruit, with a long chocolate and coffee finish. The Vigna Linda confirms it is the best Manzoni Bianco del Veneto. Delicate and minerally, it is also outstandingly fresh-tasting, full-bodied and persistent. The Colli Euganei Cabernet is an exemplary expression of the variety that comes close to earning Two Glasses. The Mosto Fior d'Arancio is enjoyable. A bright golden yellow, with an intense bouquet of pineapple and cakes, it offers a creamy, fragrant and delicately aromatic palate. The Barbera is a robust interpretation of the volcanic terroir. A warm wine, it has typical acidity and good structure. The Pinot Bianco and Sauvignon are good, though not up to the standard of the '99 versions. The Colli Euganei Bianco continues to surprise us with its textbook typing and appeal. Lastly, the Colli Euganei Rosso and the Merlot are two young, very well-made wines that offer instant appeal.

	Wine	Glasses	Score
○	Incrocio Manzoni Vigna Linda '00	YY	4
●	Colli Euganei Cabernet Girapoggio '99	YY	4
○	Colli Euganei Bianco '00	Y	3
●	Colli Euganei Merlot '00	Y	3
○	Colli Euganei Pinot Bianco '00	Y	3
●	Colli Euganei Rosso '00	Y	3
○	Colli Euganei Spumante Fior d'Arancio '00	Y	4
○	Sauvignon del Veneto '00	Y	4
●	Colli Euganei Cabernet '99	Y	3
●	Barbera del Veneto '99	Y	4

COLOGNOLA AI COLLI (VR)

Tenuta Sant'Antonio
Loc. San Zeno
Via Ceriani, 23
37030 Colognola Ai Colli (VR)
Tel. 0457650383 - 0456150913
E-mail: info@tenutasantantonio.it

Construction work on the new cellar in the Valle di Mezzane hills is proceeding briskly but as the complex is large, it is not likely to be ready soon. However, it does promise to be an attractive and functional building, useful for the work in hand as well as attractive to look at. After our visit to the vineyards, we tasted some of the winery's gems from the barrel, especially the Amarone Campo dei Gigli '97 and the Cabernet Sauvignon Vigna Capitello '99, two standard-bearers which will only be released next year. Moving on to the bottled wines, the Recioto della Valpolicella Argille Bianche in its first edition is an excellent example of the style. It is a deep purple in colour with notes of vanilla, bramble jelly and marmalade. There is plenty of acidity and body in a framework of elegance, from which coffee and chocolate emerge. Another very good dried-grape wine is the Colori d'Autunno, made from chardonnay grapes. We tasted the Valpolicella La Bandina for the first time. It's a strong, elegant wine from fruit dried for three weeks and aged for 30 months in Slovenian oak, showing sensations of tobacco, flowers, hay and plenty of berry fruit. The Cabernet Torre di Mellotti is very enjoyable, with mint and aromatic herb notes, while the Chardonnay Capitello '99 came close to a second Glass – its potential is clear as soon as you see its bright golden hue. Lastly, the simple Garganega Monte Ceriani is fruity and quite full, with a typical almond note enhancing the long finish.

	Wine	Glasses	Score
●	Recioto della Valpolicella Argille Bianche '97	Y	6
○	Passito Colori d'Autunno '97	YY	6
●	Valpolicella Sup. La Bandina '97	YY	6
●	Cabernet Sauvignon Torre di Mellotti '99	Y	5
○	Chardonnay Capitello '99	Y	5
○	Garganega Monte Ceriani '99	Y	4
●	Cabernet Sauvignon Vigna Capitello '97	YYY	6
●	Amarone della Valpolicella Campo dei Gigli '95	YY	6
●	Cabernet Sauvignon Vigna Capitello '95	YY	6
●	Amarone della Valpolicella Campo dei Gigli '96	YY	6
●	Cabernet Sauvignon Vigna Capitello '98	YY	6

CONEGLIANO (TV)

ZARDETTO SPUMANTI
FRAZ. OGLIANO
VIA MARCORÀ, 15
31015 CONEGLIANO (TV)
TEL. 0438208909
E-MAIL: bubbly@bubbly.it

After a few years' absence, Pino Zardetto's Conegliano winery returns to the Guide with a series of interesting wines and, above all, franker aromas throughout the range. This more assertive approach to aromatic profile has brought about an improvement in quality. The wines were already typical, extract-rich and harmonious, but now they are worthy of even more attention from winelovers. The sweeter bottles have benefited most from this renewal, starting with the Prosecco Dry Zeroventi. Its astonishing, highly individual, aniseed and jasmine nose is reflected on the palate with a pleasing extra aromatic note. This long, persistent wine is one of the most interesting dry spumantes in the area. The Cartizze is evidently mineral on the nose while the ripe fruit on the palate is well defined. Good creamy bubbles make it enjoyable and the sweetness is counterbalanced by the fresh acidic vein. The Extra Dry version is very lively, with peppery apple and pear aromas, then the palate is tangy and rounded. The Prosecco Frizzante is intriguing, offering sweet, ripe fruit notes on the palate, while the Prosecco Tranquillo is simpler and more drinkable.

O	Cartizze	4
O	P. di Conegliano Dry Zeroventi	4
O	Prosecco Extra Dry	3
O	P. di Conegliano Frizzante Brioso	3
O	P. di Conegliano Brut Bubbly	4
O	P. di Conegliano Tranquillo Lungo	3

DOLCE (VR)

ARMANI
VIA CERADELLO, 401
37020 DOLCE (VR)
TEL. 0457290033 - 0457290285
E-MAIL: info@albinoarmani.com

This part of Vallagarina, on the border between the Veneto region and the province of Trento, has always paid the price for its location in terms of visibility. Nonetheless, the little strip of land covered with vines and criss-crossed by roads, is a hive of activity. One of the promoters of this area's winemaking potential is Albino Armani, a young producer responsible for rediscovering a native vine variety threatened with extinction The foja tonda became acclimatized here long ago and has survived the ravages of phylloxera and the more modern perils of replanting with international varieties thanks to the Armanis. While we wait to taste the wines from the new vineyards, where strict clonal selection has been implemented, the '99 vintage provides us with another good interpretation of the Foja Tonda. The wine has a complex nose, as rich in character as the palate, which is well-balanced, offsetting the modern tones of the wood against the unusual aromatic characteristics of the varietal. The trial Corvara from a blend of cabernet, corvina and merlot is very good. The aromas have a Mediterranean-style note of thyme, mint and flowers while the palate is pulpy with a stylish finish. Moving on to the whites, the Pinot Grigio is very successful, offering a salty palate balanced with dried flower and apple notes. The typically aromatic Sauvignon Campo Napoleone is very enjoyable, like the Chardonnay Vigneto Capitel, which has hints of rennet apples and fascinating minerally nuances.

●	Corvara Rosso '98	5
●	Foja Tonda Rosso '99	4
O	Sauvignon Campo Napoleone '00	3
O	Trentino Chardonnay Vigneto Capitel '00	3
O	Valdadige Pinot Grigio Vigneto Corvara '00	3
●	Corvara Rosso '97	5
●	Foja Tonda Rosso '98	4

FARRA DI SOLIGO (TV)

Andreola Orsola
Via Cal Longa, 52
31010 Farra di Soligo (TV)
tel. 0438989379

For some years, this small winery at Col San Martino has been releasing increasingly substantial wines onto the market, attempting to find a niche among quality producers of Prosecco. Behind this move are Nazareno Pola and his son Stefano, who have decided to rely on their 12 hectars of vineyards, making and bottling wines exclusively from their own grapes, which is quite rare in this DOC zone. Direct supervision of all production phases allows Nazareno and Stefano to present an excellent Prosecco Extra Dry from the Dirupo vineyard, which is nicely delicate with floral and almond aromas. The palate reflects the nose well, the wine is creamy and harmonious, and both nose and palate are nicely perked up by well-sustained bubbly effervescence. A Brut version is also made. Although penalised by a lower sugar concentration, it is still expressive with clear flower and dried fruit aromas and a pleasant minerally note. On the palate, the robustness of the Brut style seems to be well controlled by the prickle and by a vein of acidity which is not intrusive. The Prosecco Tranquillo from the Romit vineyard is good, with immediate freshness and pleasant drinkability. There has to be a red, too, from this area halfway between Valdobbiadene and Felettano. The Cabernet Franc has managed to lose its trademark grassiness and express fresh floral sensations.

FUMANE (VR)

★ Allegrini
Corte Giara, 7
37022 Fumane (VR)
tel. 0456832011
e-mail: info@allegrini.it

Franco Allegrini has made a decisive leap forward with La Poja, Palazzo della Torre and La Grola. These wines are not made to DOC specifications but they are closely linked to the Valpolicella vine varieties. The most interesting features of the wines obtained from non-raisined grapes include their recognizable varietal nature, the effort put into preserving the integrity of the fruit, and the elegance and balance of the product. Of course, this project demands a great deal of work in the field so new plots of land are only purchased when their location, soil and aspect are just right. The La Poja, in another great version, has a dark, still youthful, ruby red colour. The explosion of aromas on the nose is very attractive while the fruit is ripe and almost chewy, enfolded in notes of roses and aromatic herbs. A strong mineral note runs through the oak sensations. On the palate, there is very good balance, with sweet tannins and acidity which easily support the richness of the very persistent fruit. The Amarone is for the first time fermented completely in new wood, perhaps pointing the way forward for the type. The fruit shows no signs of drying and is full and luscious while the rich, softly harmonious sensations promise a very pleasant future. Both the Amarone and the La Poja won Three Glasses. The excellent Recioto has fine overtones of dried fruit, gooseberries, mint and Alpine herbs on the nose while on the palate, the structure manages to contrast sweetness with style to produce a top quality sweet wine.

○ P. di Valdobbiadene Extra Dry Dirupo	♛♛	3*
● Cabernet Franc	♛	2
○ P. di Valdobbiadene Brut Dirupo	♛	3
○ P. di Valdobbiadene Tranquillo Romit	♛	2
○ P. di Valdobbiadene Frizzante Spago		3

● Amarone della Valpolicella Cl. '97	♛♛♛	6
● La Poja '97	♛♛♛	6
● Recioto della Valpolicella Cl. Giovanni Allegrini '98	♛♛	6
● Valpolicella Cl. '00	♛♛	4
● La Grola '98	♛♛	5
● Palazzo della Torre '98	♛♛	5
● Amarone della Valpolicella Cl. '93	♛♛♛	6
● La Poja '93	♛♛♛	6
● Amarone della Valpolicella Cl. '95	♛♛♛	6
● Recioto della Valpolicella Cl. Giovanni Allegrini '93	♛♛♛	6
● La Poja '95	♛♛♛	6
● Amarone della Valpolicella Cl. '96	♛♛♛	6
● La Poja '96	♛♛♛	6

FUMANE (VR)

Le Salette
Via Pio Brugnoli, 11/c
37022 Fumane (VR)
tel. 0457701027
e-mail: vinosal@tin.it

Following the well-deserved Three Glasses awarded for the Amarone Pergole Vece '95, Le Salette has not managed to repeat the result with the last two vintages released. Do not, however be deceived into thinking that this represents a lack of commitment by Franco Scamperle and his wife Monica to high quality. On the contrary, this year's tastings not only dispel any remaining doubt but also confirm the winery's progress. Many wines are very convincing indeed, above all the two Amarones, the Pergole Vece and its younger brother, the La Marega. The former has a range of aromas which is initially just slightly disturbed, showing clear vegetal and walnutskin notes. The palate is stylish and well-sustained, combining considerable texture with abundant tannins. The La Marega is also stylish and fresh-tasting on the palate, preceded by appealing balsam notes on the nose. Of the two Reciotos presented, the Le Traversagne is the more successful. More delicate, it has more immediately pleasant cherry jam aromas. To complete the excellent performance of the whole range, the Valpolicella Superiore Ca' Carnocchio, in particular, is well up to standard of the previous version and the Bianco Passito Cesare offers a no-nonsense, slightly rustic character. The standard-label Valpolicella is a further demonstration of Franco Scamperle's winemaking skills.

GAMBELLARA (VI)

La Biancara
Fraz. Sorio
C.da Biancara, 8
36053 Gambellara (VI)
tel. 0444444244

Comparing approaches with other winemakers, banning cellar techniques that do not respect the raw materials and the final consumer, and hard work in the vineyard are all pieces of the puzzle. When the jigsaw is complete, the authentic nature of wine can emerge and its roots in its territory respected. That, at least, is how Angiolino Maule sees things. Angiolino is the owner of the attractive La Biancara winery, one of the best in the Gambellara zone and beyond. The tastings of wines from the latest vintages confirm brilliant progress and improved focus in each wine's character. The range is pleasantly surprising with the mineral sensations that apparently derive from the volcanic subsoil of Gambellara. The standard Masieri has pleasant notes of freshly-picked grapes and the Sassaia has genuine, natural minerally hints in a pulpy body. The test wine at the Maule winery is the Pico de Laorenti '99. This selection embodies research work into the garganega variety, on which Angiolino has been conducting experiments for a couple of years now to obtain the best possible results. This wine has an enjoyably rustic character from its tannins - surprising in a white wine - and from its dynamic progression in the mouth. We will be following its progress over the next few years with great interest. The clean, easy-drinking Canà, from 80 per cent cabernet sauvignon and 20 per cent merlot, is the only red presented by La Biancara. Lastly, the Recioto '98 is an amber dessert wine with dried fruit and dates on the nose. On the palate, it is less sweet than you might expect, with rare complexity and a very satisfying, original profile.

● Amarone della Valpolicella Cl. La Marega '97	▼▼	6
● Amarone della Valpolicella Cl. Pergole Vece '97	▼▼	6
○ Cesare Passito Bianco '98	▼▼	5
● Recioto della Valpolicella Le Traversagne '98	▼▼	5
● Valpolicella Cl. Sup. Ca' Carnocchio '98	▼▼	4
● Valpolicella Cl. '00	▼	2*
● Recioto della Valpolicella Pergole Vece '98	▼	6
● Amarone della Valpolicella Cl. Pergole Vece '95	▼▼▼	6

○ Gambellara Cl. Sup. Sassaia '00	▼▼	3*
○ Recioto di Gambellara '98	▼▼	6
○ Pico de Laorenti '99	▼▼	4
○ Gambellara Cl. I Masieri '00	▼	2*
● Canà Rosso '99	▼	4
○ Recioto di Gambellara '97	▽▽	6
○ Pico de Laorenti '98	▽▽	4
○ Gambellara Cl. Sup. Sassaia '99	▽▽	3

GAMBELLARA (VI)

ZONIN
VIA BORGOLECCO, 9
36053 GAMBELLARA (VI)
TEL. 0444444031 - 0444640119
E-MAIL: zonin@zonin.it

We are used to surprises from Zonin every year, and this space will soon be insufficient even for the briefest description of this market leader, in Italy and abroad, in terms of both quantity and quality. There are now ten Zonin wineries and this year, a new winery in Sicily entered production with excellent results from the beginning. See our notes in the relevant section. The huge machine owned by the famous Gambellara-based family shows no signs of slowing down. With 3,000 hectares under vine, 35,000,000 bottles exported to 60 countries and a very significant turnover, Zonin is the second largest winemaking group in Italy today. It's not just a question of figures. The staff at Gambellara can call on skilled experts, Piedmont-born Franco Giacosa to name one, who in recent years have been able to make major improvements in quality for the Veneto winery. The results speak for themselves. We enjoyed the Amarone Maso Laito '97. Etheric, fresh-tasting and supple, it shows stylish raspberry and chocolate aromas. The Recioto di Gambellara, charming as ever, has become something of a flagship for Zonin. Its vibrant golden colour is reflected in the intense, dried fig and caramel aromas, followed by a sweet creamy palate, making it an ideal dessert wine. The Valpolicella '99, with fruit and aromatic herb notes, maintains the cellar's high standards. The Berengario '97 is well-made and the Gambellara il Giangio is pleasant and fresh-tasting.

○	Recioto di Gambellara Podere il Giangio Aristòs '98	ŸŸ 5
○	Gambellara Cl. Podere il Giangio '00	Ÿ 3
●	Amarone della Valpolicella Maso Laito '97	Ÿ 5
●	Berengario '97	Ÿ 5
●	Valpolicella Cl. Maso Laito '99	Ÿ 3
○	Recioto di Gambellara Podere il Giangio Aristòs '97	ŸŸ 5

ILLASI (VR)

★ ROMANO DAL FORNO
FRAZ. CELLORE
VIA LODOLETTA, 4
37030 ILLASI (VR)
TEL. 0457834923
E-MAIL: az.dalforno@tiscalinet.it

Spending a few hours with Romano Dal Forno is always enthralling. You are bound to learn something useful. Our long visits always begin with the vineyards – a new lot of land on the Illasi hills has been planted at 13,000 vines per hectare – and move on to the now rather small cellar (an extension is planned), where we taste the new wines from the wood or bottles. This skilled winegrower's wines have a distinguishing feature that makes them unique and unmistakeable. The key words to describe Romano Dal Forno's products are richness and elegance. Romano's wife, Loretta, and their children make a valuable, and very enthusiastic, contribution to production. We will restrict ourselves to a mouthwatering preview of two wines tasted "en primeur" which will see the light in a few years. The white dried-grape Nettare '95, still ageing in barriques, is absolutely sumptuous while the sublime Recioto '97, already bottled, is of international calibre. Average annual production is around 26,000 bottles and only two wines have been released this year, both from 1996 which was not as good as some other vintages. Nevertheless, the Amarone fully expresses the winegrower's skill. It is a dense, impenetrable ruby red in colour and develops into a bouquet of delicate violets, wild berries and spice. The tannins are well-defined on the palate, as is usual for such a young wine, but the juicy, extract-rich flesh enfolds them, heralding admirable velvetiness. This is a wine of considerable personality and the vintage, though not as rich as previous ones, is especially elegant. We awarded it Three well-earned Glasses. The Valpolicella from the same year is equally interesting and well-structured, and only a little simpler.

●	Amarone della Valpolicella Vigneto di Monte Lodoletta '96	ŸŸŸ 6
●	Valpolicella Sup. Vigneto di Monte Lodoletta '96	ŸŸ 6
●	Amarone della Valpolicella Vigneto di Monte Lodoletta '90	ŸŸŸ 6
●	Amarone della Valpolicella Vigneto di Monte Lodoletta '91	ŸŸŸ 6
●	Amarone della Valpolicella Vigneto di Monte Lodoletta '93	ŸŸŸ 6
●	Amarone della Valpolicella Vigneto di Monte Lodoletta '95	ŸŸŸ 6
●	Amarone della Valpolicella Vigneto di Monte Lodoletta '94	ŸŸ 6

ILLASI (VR)

SANTI
VIA UNGHERIA, 33
37031 ILLASI (VR)
TEL. 0456520077
E-MAIL: giv@giv.it

ILLASI (VR)

TRABUCCHI
LOC. MONTE TENDA
37031 ILLASI (VR)
TEL. 0457833233 - 0456528434
E-MAIL: raffaella.trabucchi@tin.it

Santi is one of the traditional wineries of the Gruppo Italiano Vini, and the largest in Italy in terms of bottles produced and turnover. The group owns cellars and vineyards in various areas of Italy and knows how to combine large numbers with an interesting quality profile. The leading GIV wineries are Conti Formentini in Friuli, Nino Negri in Lombardy and Machiavelli in Tuscany. In Veneto, interest focuses particularly on Santi, founded in the first half of the 19th century and still housed in an elegant old building in the centre of Illasi. The town lies at the foot of the Lessini mountains, in the northeast of the province of Verona. This year the jewel in the winery's crown was not presented. The Amarone Proemio '98, from new and more targeted selections of grapes, needs to mature further in the cellar. As we were able to ascertain from the barrels, it's going to be an intriguing version. The standard-label wines include two very enjoyable Soaves. The garganega grape comes through strongly on the nose of the Sanfederici, which has a good, tangy dynamic palate, while the Monteforte has ripe fruit and floral notes with sweet spice, and perfect nose-palate consistency. The Lugana Melibeo is also enjoyable, tangy and full of character. One Glass went to the Valpolicella Solane. The Valpolicella Le Caleselle and the Bardolino Ca' Bordenis are also worth mentioning.

Although mostly made with the grapes from the '98 harvest, which was inferior in quality to '97, the wines tasted this year mainly confirm the high standard of quality achieved by this small Valpolicella winery. The Trabucchi family's accumulated experience and financial investment are a guarantee of increasingly consistent wines, whatever the weather. The most positive developments are the more ambitious wines, starting with the Amarone, which although still young, has evolved, and complex features with a coherent rather than powerful flavour impact. The best wine is the Valpolicella Superiore Terre del Cereolo. A red with personality and an enjoyably profound nose, with pleasant jam and bottled fruit aromas, it then offers a harmonious palate that gradually expresses all its texture. If we turn to the dried-grape wines, the Recioto earned One Glass. Although impressive, it is simpler than the previous edition. The Sparvieri, made from partially dried garganega grapes, has impressive strength and character, and this is one of the best versions ever. The simpler wines are basically well-managed and nothing more. The Valpolicella Superiore Terre di San Colombano is actually a little disappointing.

○ Soave Cl. Sanfederici '00	ΨΨ	4
○ Lugana Melibeo '00	Ψ	4
○ Soave Cl. Monteforte '00	Ψ	3*
● Valpolicella Cl. Le Solane '99	Ψ	3
● Bardolino Cl. Vigneto Ca' Bordenis '00		3
● Valpolicella Cl. Le Caleselle '00		3
● Amarone della Valpolicella Proemio '95	ΨΨ	6
● Amarone della Valpolicella Proemio '97	ΨΨ	6

● Amarone della Valpolicella '98	ΨΨ	6
○ Passito Sparvieri '98	ΨΨ	5
● Valpolicella Sup. Terre del Cereolo '98	ΨΨ	5
● Recioto della Valpolicella '98	Ψ	5
● Amarone della Valpolicella '95	ΨΨ	6
● Amarone della Valpolicella '96	ΨΨ	6
● Amarone della Valpolicella '97	ΨΨ	6
● Valpolicella Sup. Terre del Cereolo '97	ΨΨ	5
● Valpolicella Sup. Terre di S. Colombano '97	ΨΨ	4

LAZISE (VR)

LE TENDE
FRAZ. COLÀ
LOC. LE TENDE
37010 LAZISE (VR)
TEL. 0457590748
E-MAIL: info@letende.it

This winery continues its quest for products with more individuality than the area can generally supply. Mauro Fortuna and Beatrice Lucillini, who own Le Tende, are moving towards the production of ambitious wines with a personal style from unexpected selections of Bardolino and Bianco di Custoza. Their best achievement this year is the most difficult wine, the Passito Bianco Amoroso, made from garganega with additional percentages of other local varieties. It manages to combine strong character, expressed in particular by the nose with typically intense grapeskin aromas, with a certain elegance, which enables its considerable body to spread delicately and gradually through the palate with a pleasant return of the aromas in the finish. The other leading wine is the Cicisbeo, from cabernet sauvignon grapes, which has surpassed the fuzzier previous version and now approaches Two Glasses. More definition in the nose with less intrusive wood would lend more character to the interesting development of the flavour. The Merlot lacks freshness but has plenty of texture. In the Bardolino and the two Bianco di Custoza the quest for a personal style is clear from the character but full harmony has yet to be achieved.

MARANO DI VALPOLICELLA (VR)

CA' LA BIONDA
FRAZ. VALGATARA
VIA BIONDA, 4
37020 MARANO DI VALPOLICELLA (VC)
TEL. 0456801198 - 0456837097
E-MAIL: casbionda@tin.it

After a few years of settling down following the split with his brother, Pietro Castellani makes a masterful return to the limelight with the wines that have made Valpolicella's tradition and fortune. He is helped in the wonderful cellar, built into the house where he was born, by his two sons. Alessandro gained work experience at the noble wineries of Tuscany before returning home to work as oenologist and Nicola has graduated with a diploma in agricultural science. The greatest achievement this year was building the new cellar, which is strikingly functional in its organization but also respects the simple country architecture of the building. The vineyards are all situated on hillslopes over an area of about 20 hectares along the Marano valley, at an altitude of between 200 and 300 metres above sea level. The Amarone is particularly successful, and made from top quality raw material. Concentrated in hue, it shows intense ripe fruit aromas that contrast with the light, intriguing mineral and aromatic herb notes that streamline and refresh the palate. The Passito Bianco is also very interesting and has striking combinations of aromas of vanilla, peach and super-ripe apricot on the one hand, and mint and rosemary on the other. The attractive flavour develops steadily. The Recioto is good, though it needs to rest a little to bring out its best features, and the Valpolicellas are nice, especially the Casal Vegri selection.

○ Amoroso '99	♈♈	4
○ Bianco di Custoza Lucillini '00	♈	3
● Garda Merlot '00	♈	3
● Bardolino Cl. Sup. '99	♈	3
● Garda Cabernet Sauvignon Cicisbeo '99	♈	4
○ Bianco di Custoza Oro '00		3
● Cicisbeo '97	♈♈	4
● Garda Cabernet Sauvignon Sorbo degli Uccellatori '98	♈	4

● Amarone della Valpolicella Cl. Vigneti di Ravazol '97	♈♈	6
○ Passito Bianco	♈♈	5
● Valpolicella Cl. Sup. Campo Casal Vegri '98	♈	4
● Valpolicella Cl. Sup. Vigneti di Ravazzol '98	♈	4
● Recioto della Valpolicella Cl. Vigneto le Tordare '99	♈	6
● Valpolicella Cl. '00		3

MARANO DI VALPOLICELLA (VR)

GIUSEPPE CAMPAGNOLA
LOC. VALGATARA
VIA AGNELLA, 9
37020 MARANO DI VALPOLICELLA (VR)
TEL. 0457703900
E-MAIL: campagnola@campagnola.com

Although the statistics for the Campagnola winery suggest an industrial enterprise, the most important wines, very much Veronese in character, give a glimpse of a family whose history is inextricably entwined with that of its vineyards and the production of good wines. Only three hectares of vineyards are actually owned by the estate but thanks to close collaboration with about 60 local growers, Giuseppe Campagnola obtains healthy ripe grapes for his best selections. One example of this is the Amarone '97. Its fresh floral aromas are flecked with mineral notes and demonstrate the attention paid to drying the fruit. The wine explodes vibrantly onto the palate, restrained by carefully gauged oak and dense, stylish tannins. The Amarone Caterina Zardini from the following year is less exuberant and more rigorous. Clean and sophisticated on nose and palate, it is a perfect accompaniment for richly flavoured meat dishes. The Valpolicella '99 is also very good, with a strong ripe fruit and flower impact on the nose before the flavour develops steadily. Irresistible and eminently drinkable. The Corte Agnella, from 100 per cent corvina, is just what you want if you're looking for an easy-going wine that is also satisfying and enjoyable. The Recioto still lacks density, and the interesting range of aromas is let down by inadequate development on the palate.

MARANO DI VALPOLICELLA (VR)

MICHELE CASTELLANI
FRAZ. VALGATARA
VIA GRANDA, 1
37020 MARANO DI VALPOLICELLA (VR)
TEL. 0457701253
E-MAIL: castellani.michele@tin.it

Vintage after vintage, Sergio Castellani demonstrates his knack for making great wines from partially dried grapes and always manages to combine strength and complexity with immediate impact and suppleness. Even his most prestigious wines are commendably accessible. This is true of the Recioto della Valpolicella Ca' del Pipa, with its ripe cherry and chocolate aromas and barely discernible oak sensations. On the palate, it is strong, rich and mouthfilling, as well as perfectly consistent with the nose. Despite its rich extract, this Amarone is delicate and stylish, easy going and drinkable and these characteristics merit the maximum accolade of Three Glasses. The more accessible Recioto Campo Casalin shows fresh floral aromas and a nice minerally note contrasting with the naturally explosive fruit. On the palate, it is fresh-tasting and very enjoyable. The Amarone from the Ca' del Pipa line has an interesting oxidized note followed by good, enfolding aromas of flowers and crushed fruit, then the silky, dry palate opens out well and closes with a slight burning sensation in the finish. The other Amarone, the Campo Casalin, has a strong oaky note while the ripe fruit is nicely freshened up by mineral and aromatic herb notes. The Passione is a very interesting sweet wine made from different varieties of dried grapes. This wine was invented almost by chance and only a few bottles are made. The aromas are profound and alluring, with fruit sensations followed by aromatic herbs, giving way to a nice mineral note. The nose is neatly echoed on the intriguing palate.

- Amarone della Valpolicella Cl. Caterina Zardini '98 ▼▼ 6
- Amarone della Valpolicella Cl. '97 ▼▼ 6
- Valpolicella Cl. Sup. Vigneti di Purano Le Bine '99 ▼▼ 3
- ○ Soave Cl. Sup. Vigneti Monte Foscarino Le Bine '00 ▼ 2*
- Corte Agnella Corvina Veronese '99 ▼ 4
- Valpolicella Recioto Cl. Casotto del Merlo '99 ▼ 4
- Amarone della Valpolicella Cl. Caterina Zardini '97 ▼▼ 6

- Recioto della Valpolicella Cl. Le Vigne Ca' del Pipa '99 ▼▼▼ 6
- Passione Rosso '97 ▼▼ 6
- Amarone della Valpolicella Cl. Campo Casalin I Castei '98 ▼▼ 6
- Amarone della Valpolicella Cl. Le Vigne Ca' del Pipa '98 ▼▼ 6
- Recioto della Valpolicella Cl. Campo Casalin I Castei '98 ▼▼ 6
- Cabernet Sauvignon I Castei '98 ▼ 4
- Amarone della Valpolicella Cl. Le Vigne Ca' del Pipa '97 ▼▼ 6
- Valpolicella Cl. Sup. Ripasso Ca' del Pipa '97 ▼ 4

MARANO DI VALPOLICELLA (VR)

CORTE RUGOLIN
FRAZ. VALGATARA
LOC. RUGOLIN, 1
37020 MARANO DI VALPOLICELLA (VR)
TEL. 0457702153
E-MAIL: rugolin@libero.it

As you go through the Marano valley, where the road begins to wind uphill and the vine-clad slopes draw closer, you come to the village of Valgatara. Here, the winery run by brother and sister Elena and Federico Coati continues to build on the progress begun a few years ago. The characteristics of the local terroir are reflected well in the wines from this little winery, where hard work in the vineyard, respect for tradition and a pinch of modernity are the order of the day. The long-awaited Amarone Monte Danieli still seems rather ruffled. It has substantial texture but doesn't seem to be as complete as it should. The aromas are warm and passionate, with ripe fruit, chocolate and a barely discernible mineral note. On the palate, it is very rich and hints at good ageing potential. It can only benefit from further maturing in bottles. The Recioto '99 has traditional sweet ripe fruit notes on the nose. The fresh acidic tang on the palate makes the wine supple and dynamic as it opens out stylishly, with the sweetness well under control. The standard-label Valpolicella is good. In addition to the usual fresh, immediate aromas, the palate is also dense, rich and very enjoyable. The Passito Aresco '99 and the Valpolicella Superiore '99 are not ready at the moment. They will be available later in 2002.

● Amarone della Valpolicella Cl. Vigneto Monte Danieli '97	♟♟	6
● Recioto della Valpolicella Cl. '99	♟♟	6
● Valpolicella Cl. '00	♟	3
● Amarone della Valpolicella Cl. Vigneto Monte Danieli '95	♟♟	6
○ Aresco Passito Veronese '98	♟♟	6
● Recioto della Valpolicella Cl. '98	♟♟	6

MARANO DI VALPOLICELLA (VR)

F.LLI DEGANI
FRAZ. VALGATARA
VIA TOBELE, 3/A
37020 MARANO DI VALPOLICELLA (VR)
TEL. 0457701850
E-MAIL: degani@valpolicella.it

The Degani brothers, Aldo, Luca and Zeno, work at Sant'Ambrogio and Valgatara, a village in the municipality of Marano famed for winegrowing where the soil type is classic Valpolicella. Again, the Deganis' wines lived up to our expectations and put on an enjoyable, exciting performance. The winery presented four Two Glasses wines and one of the best standard-label Valpolicellas ever. The Amarone La Rosta is dense, garnet-ruby and the nose opens with bottled fruit aromas, followed by chocolate, hay and tobacco. The tannic sensation on the palate is permeated by cherry fruit, coffee and cinnamon, which come together in a pleasantly persistent finish. The standard-label Amarone needn't fear comparison with its nobler brother. It, too, has an intense colour, with a fruity, gamey bouquet. The solid structure is well supported by the tannins, acidity and alcohol. The Recioto is rich and dense in colour and flaunts a delicate bouquet of Parma violets and morello cherry jam, good balance and considerable persistence. The Valpolicella Cicilio has a very good nose and a palate with clear chocolate, coffee and berry fruit aromas. The standard-label '98 selection is warm and velvety, with hints of tobacco, brambles and cherries, while the 2000 Valpolicella is ruby red in colour with faintly herbaceous notes, lifted by hints of sour cherries and raspberries.

● Amarone della Valpolicella Cl. '97	♟♟	6
● Amarone della Valpolicella Cl. La Rosta '97	♟♟	6
● Valpolicella Cl. Sup. Cicilio '98	♟♟	5
● Recioto della Valpolicella Cl. '99	♟♟	5
● Valpolicella Cl. '00	♟	3*
● Valpolicella Cl. Sup. '98	♟	4
● Amarone della Valpolicella Cl. '93	♟♟	5
● Amarone della Valpolicella Cl. '95	♟♟	5
● Amarone della Valpolicella Cl. La Rosta '95	♟♟	6

MARANO DI VALPOLICELLA (VR)

GIUSEPPE LONARDI
VIA DELLE POSTE, 2
37020 MARANO DI VALPOLICELLA (VR)
TEL. 0457755154 - 0457755001
E-MAIL: privilegia@lonardivini.it

In the wake of last year's success, Giuseppe Lonardi's wines have done equally well this time, demonstrating admirable continuity of production. The Amarone lives up to the last two versions, and again won Two Glasses. The '97 vintage, one of the best in recent years, was certainly beneficial for this wine, endowing it with unusual structure and concentration. The skill of the cellarmanager did the rest, adding elegance and finesse to excellent raw material. The nose opens gradually into a broad range of aromas. Sweet spices, vanilla and chocolate are followed by bottled morello cherries and fine herbs. The Privilegia maintains its high standard. This Cabernet Franc undergoes a second fermentation in winter with the addition of dried corvina grapes. The development of the nose is initially slightly disturbed by the rather intrusive wood, which detracts from the elegance, but as the aromas open out, it acquires a good fruity tone sprinkled with spice. The freshness on the palate makes this an enjoyable, robustly tannic wine. The ambitious Recioto Le Arele impressed us with its concentrated colour, delicate, profound nose with typical jammy notes, and balanced palate with good flesh and discernible tannins. Lastly, the two Valpolicellas. The Classico '00 and the Classico Superiore '98 both picked up One Glass, putting on little more than a correct performance.

- Amarone della Valpolicella Cl. '97 ♗♗ 6
- Privilegia Rosso '98 ♗♗ 5
- Recioto della Valpolicella Cl. Le Arele '98 ♗♗ 5
- Valpolicella Cl. '00 ♗ 2*
- Valpolicella Cl. Sup. '98 ♗ 4
- Amarone della Valpolicella Cl. '95 ♗♗ 5
- Amarone della Valpolicella Cl. '96 ♗♗ 5
- Privilegia Rosso '97 ♗♗ 5
- Recioto della Valpolicella Cl. Le Arele '97 ♗♗ 5

MARANO DI VALPOLICELLA (VR)

NOVAIA
VIA NOVAIA, 3
37020 MARANO DI VALPOLICELLA (VR)
TEL. 0457755129
E-MAIL: novaia@iper.net

The Vaona brothers continue their improvements in the vineyards, replacing the older, barely profitable, pergolas with rows of vines. In the next few years, these will yield richer grapes with more extract. The new cellar is now fully functional, boasting modern machinery and good quality barriques instead of the old barrels. However, we must admit that at the moment the wines are suffering the consequences of the new vineyards' youth. Although they are well made and enjoyable, they lack the depth that can only derive from more mature vines. The Recioto has a ruby red colour with purply highlights. On the nose, the ripe fruit aromas allow glimpses of nice ripe strawberries among the minerally folds. This wine makes a good entry on the palate, releasing wild berry fruit and mineral sensations and the fresh acidity helps make it light and drinkable. Despite the good '97 vintage, the Amarone is not wholly convincing. The nose opens out into pencil, chocolate and bottled fruit aromas which lead you to expect a good, pulpy, complex palate. The aromatic breadth is reflected in the palate but it is dynamic rather than beefy, and lacks adequate strength and structure. The Valpolicella Superiore is interesting, with bottled cherries and spice reflected well on the palate, and closes with a nice hint of bitter chocolate. The enjoyable Valpolicella '99 is a more upfront version of the Superiore.

- Recioto della Valpolicella Cl. '99 ♗♗ 5
- Amarone della Valpolicella Cl. '97 ♗ 6
- Valpolicella Cl. Sup. '98 ♗ 4
- Valpolicella Cl. '99 ♗ 2*
- Amarone della Valpolicella Cl. '95 ♗♗ 5

MEZZANE DI SOTTO (VR)

Corte Sant'Alda
Loc. Fioi
Via Capovilla, 28
37030 Mezzane di Sotto (VR)
Tel. 0458880006
E-mail: santalda@tin.it

Marinella Camerani's story is a strange one. She became a winemaker almost by chance, perhaps to escape from an unsatisfying, industry-centred world and has managed to make this little winery into one of the most popular in the whole of Valpolicella. The fact that she has no wine background has probably enabled Camerani to make to make improvements without the burden of received, and perhaps over-rigid, wisdom. That's how Ca' Fiui came about. It's a 2000 Valpolicella made with a blend of grapes from all the vineyards under ten years old. The red fruit aromas are enriched with hints of mineral and leather, while the palate is strong and rich. Having stunned us last year with an explosive Amarone '95, the Corte Sant'Alda presented its most important selection, the Mithas, this year, from a painstaking selection of partially dried grapes aged in small new barrels. The prevalent aromas of ripe fruit, cherry and plums are intertwined with intense veins of mint and thyme. The wood is imperceptible on the palate and the fruit is even riper and crunchier. Panache and an endless finish beautifully round off this outstanding wine, which is flanked by the standard selection from the same vintage, a wine we commended last year. The excellent Three Glass Mithas confirms the cellar's maturity. The Amarone '96 is also a success, with enjoyable flowery overtones and characterful mineral aromas. On the palate, the elegance of this fine red wine compensates for the inadequacies of the vintage.

MEZZANE DI SOTTO (VR)

Sartori - Roccolo Grassi
Via San Giovanni di Dio, 19
37030 Mezzane di Sotto (VR)
Tel. 0458880089

Along with Illasi, the Mezzane valley is the new face of Valpolicella winemaking. It has a great deal to offer in terms of growing, rather than just modernity and innovation. Unlike the Classico zone, which has been nudged along and promoted by the best producers for years, no one has so managed to assess Mezzane's full potential. Bruno Sartori's estate has about 12 hectares of vineyards, of which only six are currently in production. Helped increasingly by his son Marco, Bruno makes very exciting wines from partially dried grapes. One example is his Recioto della Valpolicella, which has a dark hue and a nose that alternates warm southern notes of chocolate and sultanas with mineral and Alpine herb nuances that add depth to the range. The wine is initially warm and sweet on the palate, and succeeds in the difficult task of combining style with strength. The Amarone is also very good. Well-sustained and mouthfilling, it again plays on nuances of very ripe fruit and crushed flowers. The Mezzane area also embraces part of the other noble Veronese designation and sure enough, here's a Recioto di Soave, with mineral and grapeskin aromas. The palate reflects the nose well, enriching it with honey and dried fruit notes. The two DOC warhorses are also a success: the Valpolicella has traditional aromas and the Soave shows more structure than elegance.

Wine	Glasses	Score
● Amarone della Valpolicella Mithas '95	▼▼▼	6
● Valpolicella Ca' Fiui '00	▼▼	3*
● Amarone della Valpolicella '96	▼▼	6
● Recioto della Valpolicella '98	▼▼	6
● Valpolicella Sup. '98	▼▼	5
● Valpolicella Sup. Mithas '98	▼	5
● Amarone della Valpolicella '90	▼▼▼	6
● Amarone della Valpolicella '95	▼▼▼	6
● Amarone della Valpolicella '93	▼▼	6
● Amarone della Valpolicella '94	▼▼	6
● Valpolicella Sup. Mithas '97	▼▼	5

Wine	Glasses	Score
● Recioto della Valpolicella Roccolo Grassi '97	▼▼	6
● Amarone della Valpolicella Roccolo Grassi '97	▼▼	6
○ Recioto di Soave La Broia '98	▼▼	5
● Valpolicella Sup. Roccolo Grassi '98	▼	5
○ Soave Sup. La Broia '99	▼	4
● Amarone della Valpolicella Roccolo Grassi '96	▼▼	6
○ Recioto di Soave La Broia '97	▼▼	5

MIANE (TV)

GREGOLETTO
FRAZ. PREMAOR
VIA SAN MARTINÒ, 1
31050 MIANE (TV)
TEL. 0438970463

Luigi Gregoletto is a skilled grower, whose wines come from his shrewd, practical approach to vineyard management. This attractive winery at Miane, the spiritual home of Prosecco – the flagship of the province of Treviso – also makes a series of remarkable still wines. The most convincing of these is the Albio, a characterful white of the Colli di Conegliano DOC. Luigi's selection again won Two Glasses for its habitual taut edge and elegance. The intense, subtle aromas include delicate green notes of summer flowers and lime blossom while the palate, supported by a pleasant vein of acidity, has good body and persistence. The Prosecco Tranquillo is still among the best in the category, thanks to its well-sustained fragrance and acidic freshness. The Prosecco Spumante, in contrast, is creamy and enjoyable but is also marked by pungent green apple notes. The Manzoni Bianco, from pinot bianco and riesling renano, is excellent. The straw yellow colour has greenish highlights and the new-cut grass aromas are reflected in the palate, with fresh fruit notes and rich body. The fruity, drinkable Pinot Bianco is very good. The Colli di Conegliano Rosso, from cabernet, merlot and marzemino, has hay and scrubland aromas then tannins and acidity prevail on the palate leaving an aftertaste which is not especially harmonious. The Cabernet and Merlot are both varietal, rustic and uncomplicated, through they could be fresher and more focused.

MONSELICE (PD)

BORIN
FRAZ. MONTICELLI
VIA DEI COLLI, 5
35043 MONSELICE (PD)
TEL. 042974384
E-MAIL: borin@protec.it

Professor Borin and his wife Teresa have run this smallish winery with scrupulous care for some time. The 25 hectares of vineyards are mainly situated on the high ground at Monticelli and the slopes of Monte Ventolone, near Arquà Petrarca. These grapes are used every year to make about 150,000 bottles, which are sold at very fair prices. Borin products are typically smooth and elegant, starting with the Mons Silicis, a cabernet sauvignon aged in barriques for 18 months. This selection is the cellar's most ambitious wine and here it maintains the standards set by its good debut last year. The grassy hints on the nose are followed by a pulpy, gradually intensifying flavour supported by smooth tannins thanks to the advanced stage of ripeness of the grapes. The enjoyable, balanced Cabernet Sauvignon Vigna Costa is the result of a less rigorous selection and lower contribution of wood than the Mons Silicis, and is simpler and more immediate. The Pinot Bianco Vigneto Archino is typically rounded, with a vegetal nose and refreshing nuances. The Passito Fior d'Arancio releases delicate aromas of dried fruit and fine herbs while the flavoursome entry on the palate is well controlled and delicate. The Merlot Vigna del Foscolo and the Moscato Fior d'Arancio Spumante are simple, well-made and enjoyable.

	Wine	Glasses	Score
○	Colli di Conegliano Bianco Albio '00	ŶŶ	3*
○	Manzoni Bianco '00	Ŷ	3
○	Pinot Bianco '00	Ŷ	3
●	Colli di Conegliano Rosso Gregoletto '96	Ŷ	5
●	Cabernet dei Colli Trevigiani '99	Ŷ	3
●	Merlot dei Colli Trevigiani '99	Ŷ	3
○	P. di Conegliano Extra Dry	Ŷ	3
○	P. di Conegliano Tranquillo '00	Ŷ	3
○	Colli di Conegliano Bianco Albio '99	ŶŶ	3

	Wine	Glasses	Score
●	Colli Euganei Cabernet Sauvignon Mons Silicis Ris. '98	ŶŶ	5
●	Colli Euganei Merlot Vigna del Foscolo '00	Ŷ	3
○	Colli Euganei Pinot Bianco Vigneto Archino '00	Ŷ	3
○	Colli Euganei Fior d'Arancio Passito '98	Ŷ	5
●	Colli Euganei Cabernet Sauvignon Vigna Costa '99	Ŷ	4
○	Colli Euganei Fior d'Arancio Spumante	Ŷ	4
○	Colli Euganei Bianco Vigna dei Mandorli '00		3
●	Colli Euganei Cabernet Mons Silicis Ris. '97	ŶŶ	5

MONTEBELLO VICENTINO (VI)

Domenico Cavazza & F.lli
Via Selva, 22
36054 Montebello Vicentino (VI)
Tel. 0444649166
E-mail: vini.cavazza@libero.it

Cavazza is a well-established name in the still dormant Gambellara and Colli Berici DOC zones and we hope that the progress recorded in the Colli line will soon be followed by a leap ahead in whites made from the native garaganega variety. The Gambellara La Bocara '00 is simple and pleasant, floral and slightly fruity on the nose, and the Sauvignon Santa Libera has smooth, sweet, lightly varietal tones, with a very enjoyable piquant finish. The Tocai Rosso is one of the best on the market and the fruity, refreshing tones make it especially suitable for summer drinking. The more structured reds are split up between the Capitel Santa Libera line and the Cicogna selection. The former includes a nicely made, drinkable Merlot with good impact and spice and flower sensations on the nose. The Cabernet Capitel Santa Libera is pleasant too, with fresh fruit, herbs and cloves in the mature nose. The long, persistent palate strongly reflects the herbs and spices. But the most ambitious wines are the Cicogna selections. The Merlot has super-ripe stewed fruit, aromatic herbs and toasty aromas in the nose, and the palate has plenty of texture. The spicy, smoky finish is reasonably long, though the fruit lacks subtlety and freshness. The Cabernet seems better this year, more austere and nearer to the Bordeaux model. The nose is still reserved but is already opening up with nuances of new wood and hints of cassis. The palate is also well defined, supported by acidity and fine-grained tannins.

● Colli Berici Cabernet Cicogna '98 ŸŸ		4
● Colli Berici Cabernet Capitel S. Libera '99	ŸŸ	3*
● Colli Berici Tocai Rosso '00	Ÿ	2*
○ Gambellara Cl. La Bocara '00	Ÿ	2*
● Colli Berici Merlot Cicogna '98	Ÿ	4
● Colli Berici Merlot Capitel S. Libera '99	Ÿ	3
○ Colli Berici Sauvignon Capitel S. Libera '00		3
● Colli Berici Merlot Cicogna '97	ŸŸ	4

MONTEBELLO VICENTINO (VI)

Luigino Dal Maso
Via Selva, 62
36054 Montebello Vicentino (VI)
Tel. 0444649104
E-mail: dalmaso@infinito.it

Since their son Nicola joined the firm, the Dal Maso family have shown that they are on the right road. They have built a modern, efficient cellar, planted new vineyards to obtain maximum quality, and are turning out reds from the Colli Berici DOC which bring out the as yet untapped potential of the area. In the meantime, our account of the wines tasted will have to be provisional, apart from the Recioto Riva dei Perari, which is now a triumphantly excellent product. The wine is only sold in the most successful years and the '99 has convincingly complex aromas, ranging from honey to tropical fruit, through coconut, caramelized pears and liquorice. The palate is appetizing and the sweetness is sustained by a pleasant vein of freshness. In the finish, there are attractive notes of almonds and light tannins from the garganega grapes. The Gambellara Ca' Cischele is presented in a delicately floral and immediately accessible version while the whites in the Casara Roveri line, a Chardonnay, a Sauvignon, and the monovarietal chardonnay Terra dei Rovi, need more definition in the aromas and greater integration with the wood. The reds from the Casara Roveri line, Merlot and Cabernet, are well-typed but did not earn more than One Glass. We look forward to the new red blend, as the advance tastings were more than promising.

○ Recioto di Gambellara Cl. Riva dei Perari '99	ŸŸ	5
○ Colli Berici Chardonnay Casara Roveri '00	Ÿ	3
○ Gambellara Cl. Ca' Cischele '00	Ÿ	2*
● Colli Berici Cabernet Casara Roveri '99	Ÿ	4
● Colli Berici Merlot Casara Roveri '99	Ÿ	4
○ Terra dei Rovi Bianco '99	Ÿ	4
○ Colli Berici Sauvignon Casara Roveri '00		3

MONTEFORTE D'ALPONE (VR)

Roberto Anselmi
Via S. Carlo, 46
37032 Monteforte d'Alpone (VR)
tel. 0457611488

MONTEFORTE D'ALPONE (VR)

Carlo Bogoni
Quartiere Aldo Moro, 1
37032 Monteforte d'Alpone (VR)
tel. 0456100385
e-mail: bogoniwine@tiscalinet.it

On meeting Roberto Anselmi, you can't help being impressed by his get up and go. Never content with the results achieved, he hurls himself without a safety net after his instincts and hopes, ready to gamble everything for an idea or an ideal. This is how his painful divorce from the DOC regulations came about. Roberto is convinced that qualitative improvement in the zone needs to start in the vineyard. And we can hardly disagree when the wines tasted for this edition of the Guide gave an excellent overall impression, appearing more balanced and more personal in character. The Capitel Croce has never been as enjoyable as it is this year. This white selection is aged in wood and has ripe, balsamic notes on the nose, while the well-sustained palate develops generously. This is a wonderful specimen, which brings together the best of the fruit aromas and toasty oak from the wood. The opulent structure is masterfully handled. It's a subtle, elegant wine that deserves our highest accolade. In confirmation of continuing quality, the I Capitelli is an excellent dried-grape wine which has abandoned opulence in favour of elegance and simplicity, and is delicious thanks to its fine poise and balance. However, the best indication of the quality of Roberto Anselmi's wines comes from the standard-label San Vincenzo, It's fresh and tangy on the palate, with lively, spicy ripe fruit notes. The moderate price tag is also an excellent feature. The Capitel Foscarino is different. Rich in colour, it shows still youthful apple aromas and nice tropical notes of banana and pineapple.

Carlo Bogoni runs this little winery in Monteforte d'Alpone with great enthusiasm. Founded around 1850 by Napoleone Bogoni, the cellar only began bottling in 1994. In fact, it still sells grapes from the flatland vineyards wholesale, using only those from the better hillslope plots for bottling. The aim is to achieve a wine that combines good ageing prospects with terroir. This quest has led to the most ambitious and successful white selection, La Ponsara, which is left long on the fine lees at a controlled temperature that takes into account the characteristics of the vintage. This intervention is never extreme but simply ensures that nature takes its course without unfortunate consequences for the wine. The aromas are very appealing and spicy with hints of botrytis and ripe, pulpy peaches and apricots. The palate reflects the nose well, and plays on elegance rather than strength. It is full and subtle, echoing the aromas on the nose with precision and intensity. The Recioto has an intense golden colour and a nose with typical butter and sour cream aromas, with light vegetal hints. On the palate, the smoothness cossets you through to a clean, satisfying finish. The 2000 Soave Classico is fresh and drinkable. The '98 Degorà is also successful. A Cabernet comes from vineyards situated in the Colli Berici. It has enjoyably profound, rich aromas.

○	Capitel Croce '99	🍷🍷🍷	5
○	I Capitelli '99	🍷🍷	6
○	Capitel Foscarino '00	🍷🍷	4
○	San Vincenzo '00	🍷🍷	3*
○	Recioto dei Capitelli '87	🍷🍷🍷	6
○	Recioto dei Capitelli '88	🍷🍷🍷	6
○	Recioto di Soave I Capitelli '93	🍷🍷🍷	6
○	Recioto di Soave I Capitelli '96	🍷🍷🍷	6
○	Capitel Croce '98	🍷🍷	5
○	I Capitelli '98	🍷🍷	6
○	Capitel Foscarino '99	🍷🍷	4

○	Soave Cl. Sup. La Ponsara '99	🍷🍷	3*
●	Degorà Cabernet Sauvignon '98	🍷🍷	5
○	Soave Cl. Sup. '00	🍷	3
○	Recioto di Soave '97	🍷	5
●	Degorà Cabernet Sauvignon '97	🍷🍷	5

MONTEFORTE D'ALPONE (VR)

CA' RUGATE
FRAZ. BROGNOLIGO
VIA MEZZAVILLA, 12
37032 MONTEFORTE D'ALPONE (VR)
TEL. 0456175082
E-MAIL: carugate@carugate.it

In its second edition, the Soave Classico Superiore Bucciato secures the most coveted award of Three Glasses, which it came close to winning in the first version of '98. This is an acknowledgement of the courage the Tessari family has put into making this supreme wine: the must ferments for five days on the skins, like a red wine, to obtain the maximum extract possible from the garganega grapes, making this a rich, complex bottle. The excellence of the selection is clear from the colour, an intense golden yellow that leads in to delicious exuberance and personality in both the nose and the palate. The aromas open into a rich swathe of sensations including flowers, honey, ripe fruit, tea and a nice closing note of liquorice. Thanks to a certain amount of tannin, the palate is unusually balanced for a white and the very smooth flavour is interspersed with considerable tanginess. This is a great wine, rich and opulent, which will be at its most expressive after a few years' ageing. The Monte Fiorentine is also a success. It's a Soave in a more orthodox style. The aroma range is more immediate than the Monte Fiorentine but is equally varied and stylish and the palate displays considerable texture. This characteristic is also seen in the two Passitos, the Recioto La Perlara and the Corte Durlo, made from garganega and chardonnay grapes. The Soave Monte Alto is another serious Ca' Rugate selection, which is aged for longer. We'll talk about it next year. Lastly, the Valpolicella Rovere '99 is very enjoyable.

MONTEFORTE D'ALPONE (VR)

FATTORI & GRANEY
VIA ZOPPEGA, 14
37030 MONTEFORTE D'ALPONE (VR)
TEL. 0457460041
E-MAIL: sgraney@tiscalinet.it

The most interesting newcomer this year is the Recioto di Soave, brought out for the first time by brothers Giovanni and Antonio Fattori. It's as welcome as last year's Soave, the oak-aged Motto Piane. So, it's one surprise after another at Fattori & Graney. If they carry on like this, the Fattoris will soon be presenting ranges of increasing complexity and, hopefully, quality. Let's look now at the wines reviewed for this edition of the Guide. The dense Recioto Motto Piane '99 is already a jewel in the Fattori crown. It is golden yellow in colour, with lighter highlights, indicating freshness. The nose has notes of apricot and mint, honey, hazelnuts and dried flowers, with intoxicating breadth. On the palate, the impact is subtle and the development gradual. The nose is reflected well and the sweetness is well sustained by the nice vein of acidity, and a light tannic weave. Our retasting of the Soave Motto Piane revealed an excellent wine. It is ripe and pulpy on the nose and the oak is integrating increasingly well. The palate opens out easily, showing that it has benefited from ageing in the bottle. The standard-label Soave has ripe fruit notes and is pleasantly drinkable and fresh on the palate, with ripe fruit. The Pinot Grigio is reliable and well-typed.

○ Soave Cl. Sup. Bucciato '99	♀♀♀	4
○ Soave Cl. Sup. Monte Fiorentine '00	♀♀	4
○ Passito Bianco Corte Durlo '97	♀♀	4
○ Recioto di Soave La Perlara '99	♀♀	5
● Valpolicella Sup. Rovere '99	♀	4
○ Soave Cl. Sup. Monte Alto '96	♀♀♀	4
● Valpolicella Sup. Rovere '98	♀♀	4
○ Soave Cl. Sup. Monte Alto '95	♀♀	4
○ Soave Cl. Sup. Monte Fiorentine '99	♀♀	3

○ Soave Cl. Sup. '00	♀♀	3*
○ Recioto di Soave Motto Piane '99	♀♀	5
○ Pinot Grigio delle Venezie '00	♀	3
○ Soave Cl. Sup. Motto Piane '99	♀♀	4

MONTEFORTE D'ALPONE (VR)

GINI
VIA MATTEOTTI, 42
37032 MONTEFORTE D'ALPONE (VR)
TEL. 0457611908
E-MAIL: az.agricolagini@tiscalinet.it

Anyone who thinks that it's impossible to make great whites in Italy from native grapes should taste the magnificent 2000 version of the Soave Salvarenza, which is arguably the most successful vintage ever. Old vines work miracles. The fruit is whistle-clean, the super-ripe notes recall Mediterranean scrubland and the fragrance is guaranteed by a subtle mineral balance which perks up the lovely finish. Here, wood really is a tool at the service of the wine, which still seems to be a long way from revealing all the nuances it will surely develop over the next few years. A well-deserved Three Glasses reward the reassuringly reliable quality of this Soave DOC winery. The standard-label Soave also confirms the winery's reliability while the Froscà is more severe and mineral than usual, with balanced immediacy, and flower and fruit sensations. This thoroughbred of a garganega can become yet more profound. From the vineyards situated higher up the slopes, the Ginis make two whites from international varieties. Both are subtle. They are the Chardonnay Sorai and the Macete Fumé, from sauvignon grapes, and a Pinot Nero, the Campo delle More, which in the best vintages is silky and uncommonly concentrated for an Italian wine of this category. The '98 is well-made, solid and earthy with a nice cherry and liquorice finish. The Renobilis '97, a great dessert wine, and the Recioto di Soave Col Foscarin '98 will come out next year.

MONTEFORTE D'ALPONE (VR)

LA CAPPUCCINA
FRAZ. COSTALUNGA
VIA SAN BRIZIO, 125
37030 MONTEFORTE D'ALPONE (VR)
TEL. 0456175840 - 0456175036
E-MAIL: lacappuccina@lacappuccina.it

The young Tessari family, enthusiastic and dynamic owners of this Soave DOC winery, divide their time between the vineyards and their restaurant. They are notably successful in both enterprises. The wines are typically elegant with a balanced flavour. The San Brizio, in particular, is a fine expression of the garganega grape. This is an intense, subtle and full-bodied wine, with fruit balanced by wisely used wood that gives it complexity without overwhelming the other components. The Arzìmo also put on a remarkable performance. A dried-grape wine, it shows a lustrous golden colour and cakey aromas and is opulent yet, at the same time, fresh and persistent on the palate. The Campo Bruni, a Cabernet Franc with distinctive personality, is back on form and refuses to yield an inch to the fashion for richly extracted wines. The Fontégo is very good. Floral and candid on the nose, with hints of peaches, it develops nicely on the palate to a finish with stylish almond sensations. The Soave '00 is enjoyable and youthful while the red Madégo '99 is grassy and peppery. The standard-label Sauvignon came close to earning Two Glasses. It shows a greenish straw yellow colour then hints of red peppers and tomato leaves on the nose. The palate is fresh-tasting and light, with plenty of fruit.

○ Soave Cl. Sup. Contrada Salvarenza Vecchie Vigne '00	▼▼▼	5
○ Soave Cl. Sup. La Froscà '00	▼▼	4
● Pinot Nero Sorai Campo alle More '98	▼▼	5
○ Chardonnay Sorai '99	▼▼	5
○ Soave Cl. Sup. '00	▼	3*
○ Sauvignon Maciete Fumé '99	▼	5
○ Soave Cl. Sup. Contrada Salvarenza Vecchie Vigne '96	▼▼▼	5
○ Soave Cl. Sup. Contrada Salvarenza Vecchie Vigne '98	▼▼▼	5
○ Soave Cl. Sup. La Froscà '99	▼▼▼	4
○ Recioto di Soave Renobilis '96	▼▼	6
○ Recioto di Soave Col Foscarin '97	▼▼	5

○ Soave Sup. S. Brizio '99	▼▼	5
○ Soave Sup. Fontégo '00	▼▼	4
○ Arzìmo Passito '98	▼▼	5
● Cabernet Franc Campo Buri '98	▼▼	5
● Cabernet Sauvignon Madégo '99	▼	4
○ Sauvignon '00	▼	4
○ Soave '00	▼	3
● Cabernet Franc Campo Buri '95	▼▼▼	5
○ Soave Sup. S. Brizio '97	▼▼	4
○ Recioto di Soave Arzìmo '98	▼▼	5
○ Soave Sup. S. Brizio '98	▼▼	5

MONTEFORTE D'ALPONE (VR)

Umberto Portinari
Fraz. Brognoligo
Via Santo Stefano, 2
37032 Monteforte d'Alpone (VR)
tel. 0456175087

Every year, Umberto Portinari's small winery succeeds in making wines of undisputed quality and – a rare thing in today's climate of globalized taste – with great personality, rejecting accessibility and immediacy in favour of the typical severity and vigour of garganega grapes. This is the result of the substantial amount of work in the vineyards, carried by Umberto with a calmly methodical thoroughness. As well as two hectares under vine at Albare and two in Ronchetto, on the Brognoligo hill, Umberto will be able to count on fruit from another vineyard he shares with a friend, from next year's harvest. He has high hopes. In this year's range, the Vigna Alabre stands out despite the fact that the grapes come from vineyards on the plains. Thanks to "doppia maturazione ragionata", a technique in which the bunch-bearing canes are cut in early September and left for a month on the vine, it has elegant aromas of dried flowers with almonds and hay. The fruit is ripe and deliciously sweet. On the palate, it is delicate and creamy, with good structure and imperceptible tannins that enliven the flavour. The Vigna Ronchetto is also good. Bolder and livelier, with ripe fruit aromas and a good vegetal note, it is rugged and dynamic on the palate. The Santo Stefano was good again. An oak-aged Soave, it is well-made and very enjoyable. We will have to wait a little longer for the dried grape wine because Umberto does not feel it is ready yet.

○	Soave Cl. Sup. Vigna Ronchetto '00	♟♟ 3*
○	Soave Sup. Vigna Albare Doppia Maturazione Ragionata '00	♟♟ 3
○	Soave Sup. S. Stefano '98	♟♟ 4
○	Soave Sup. Vigna Albare Doppia Maturazione Ragionata '97	♟♟♟ 4
○	Recioto di Soave Oro '97	♟♟ 5
○	Soave Cl. Sup. Vigna Ronchetto '98	♟♟ 3
○	Soave Sup. Vigna Albare Doppia Maturazione Ragionata '98	♟♟ 3
○	Soave Sup. Vigna Albare Doppia Maturazione Ragionata '99	♟♟ 3

MONTEFORTE D'ALPONE (VR)

Pra
Via della Fontana, 31
37032 Monteforte d'Alpone (VR)
tel. 0457612125

After several near misses, the Prà brothers have finally succeeded in earning Three Glasses for the Soave Superiore Monte Grande '00, crowning a long struggle. It is also to their credit that the other Soave Superiore, the Colle S. Antonio, gave a performance that is almost as good, demonstrating the high quality of the whole range. The bright straw yellow of the Monte Grande promises well, then the nose is striking, thanks to its lively aromatic range and complex sensations. There are flower and ripe fruit aromas, and a good almondy note with the addition of an intriguing mineral hint in the background. The palate it is vibrant and bold, showing perfect consistency with the nose, and is unusually persistent. Our compliments to the Prà brothers for this enjoyable, elegant and complex wine. The Colle S. Antonio has different characteristics but is still equally exciting. This Soave is fermented and aged in wood, and made exclusively from garganega grapes selected in the vineyard and part-dried on rush mats. It has a complex, rather than immediate, profile. Here, again, the aromas range wide, with ripe tones heralding a smooth, silky flavour, which is very tangy. The standard-label Soave is also good, and came close to Two Glasses, as did the Recioto Le Fontane.

○	Soave Cl. Sup. Vigneto Monte Grande '00	♟♟♟ 4
○	Soave Cl. Sup. Colle S. Antonio '98	♟♟ 4
○	Soave Cl. Sup. '00	♟ 3*
○	Recioto di Soave Le Fontane '98	♟ 5
○	Soave Cl. Sup. Colle S. Antonio '97	♟♟ 4
○	Soave Cl. Sup. Vigneto Monte Grande '98	♟♟ 3
○	Soave Cl. Sup. Vigneto Monte Grande '99	♟♟ 3

NEGRAR (VR)

BERTANI
FRAZ. ARBIZZANO
VIA NOVARE, 4
37020 NEGRAR (VR)
TEL. 0456011211
E-MAIL: upr@bertani.net

From this year, the Bertani family have taken their winery firmly in hand, relaunching the business through improvements in the quality of the wines. A new Soave has recently been presented for the '99 vintage, demonstrating the winery's success in the eastern part of the province as well. The Sereole, presented for the first time, is one of the most successful Soaves of the year, with plenty of character and personality. It is a bright straw yellow with greenish hues, indicating freshness and consistency on the palate. The aromas are well-defined and intensely balsamic with a barely perceptible hint of wood. On the palate, the fruit is more vigorous and nicely rounds off the flavour. The minerally notes and good acidity allow the palate to expand into a clean finish with elegantly returning almonds. The Cabernet Sauvignon Albion, from the lovely farm of Villa Novare at Negrar, has a rich, pulpy, ripe fruit nose, with hints of oak and herbs. The palate reflects the nose well, and a rich note of mineral and mint enhances the flavour. The Amarone '94, from a rather infelicitous year, still manages to show all the class a great wine should possess. The mineral aromas have a seductive complexity, thanks to gamey hints. It develops easily in the mouth, with plenty of breadth, nice texture and pleasantly rugged tannins caressing the whole palate. A good performance from the entire range.

○ Soave Cl. Sup. Sereole '99	🍷🍷	5
● Amarone della Valpolicella Cl. '94	🍷🍷	6
● Albion Cabernet Sauvignon Villa Novare '99	🍷🍷	6
○ Due Uve '00	🍷	3*
○ Soave Cl. Sup. '00	🍷	3
● Valpolicella Cl. Sup. Vigneto Ognisanti Villa Novare '98	🍷	4
○ Le Lave '99	🍷	4
● Valpantena Secco Bertani '99	🍷	4
● Valpolicella Cl. Sup. '99	🍷	4
● Albion Cabernet Sauvignon Villa Novare '97	🍷🍷🍷	6
● Amarone della Valpolicella Cl. '85	🍷🍷🍷	6

NEGRAR (VR)

TOMMASO BUSSOLA
LOC. SAN PERETTO
VIA MOLINO TURRI, 30
37024 NEGRAR (VR)
TEL. 0457501740
E-MAIL: t.bussola@tiscalinet.it

While respecting the traditions and specific features of the zone, Tommaso Bussola's wines have a personal hallmark that makes them instantly recognizable. These characteristics have established his winery as one of the best in Valpolicella, and beyond, in just a few years. Bussola's Amarone and Recioto are big hitters and do nothing to conceal the exuberance they have inherited from their creator, so evident when he is talking about his creations and plans, or striding tirelessly around his cellar and vineyards. The Recioto selection TB '98 is the winery's most emblematic wine and the new vintage again earned Three Glasses, making Tommaso Bussola the greatest Recioto della Valpolicella producer of them all. The two Amarones from '97, which was an especially good year for this type, also came close to earning the highest accolade. The BG seems to be readier to drink and is highly enjoyable with its sunny, almost tropical, profile. The nose is remarkably complex. In addition to morello cherry, there are the typical sensations of all Bussola's wines: pepper, flowers and herbs. The extreme smoothness does not mask a robust dose of tannins and in the mouthfilling, velvety finish there is a nice return of thyme and dried fruit. The flagship TB selection is even classier, thanks to its more seductive, opulent, warm, floral profile. The texture is lifted by echoes of spices and cocoa powder on the palate, lending it a wealth of subtle, elegant sensations. A wine with plenty of personality, which can only improve over time.

● Recioto della Valpolicella Cl. TB '98	🍷🍷🍷	6
● Amarone della Valpolicella Cl. TB '97	🍷🍷	6
● Amarone della Valpolicella Cl. BG '97	🍷🍷	6
● Recioto della Valpolicella Cl. TB '95	🍷🍷🍷	6
● Recioto della Valpolicella Cl. TB '97	🍷🍷🍷	6
● Amarone della Valpolicella Cl. BG '96	🍷🍷	6
● Valpolicella Cl. Sup. TB '97	🍷🍷	5

NEGRAR (VR)

CANTINA SOCIALE VALPOLICELLA
VIA CA' SALGARI, 2
37024 NEGRAR (VR)
TEL. 0457500070 - 0457500295
E-MAIL: info@cantinanegrar.it

Unlike Alto Adige, where quality is now the norm, in the Veneto region, co-operative wineries are only taking their first steps as producers of excellent wines. The fact is that the Cantina della Valpolicella, which has been in business since the early 1900s, showed the way in this field and is the steadiest, most reliable co-operative in the region. A decisive role is played by the current manager, Daniele Accordini. As well as supervising production, he invests a great deal of patience and enthusiasm in explaining to member growers that the only road to go down is the one that leads to quality. This means making sacrifices and monitoring production closely. We admit that the lesson finally appears to have been learned, at least to judge by the results, which are more convincing every year. We'll start with the Amarone Domini Veneti. Dark in the glass and closed on the nose, it strides confidently onto the palate, whose development benefits from the shrewd, intelligent use of wood. The two '99 Reciotos are also very good, and the Vigneti di Moron is particularly striking. The nose is still closed, with mineral and fragrant herb highlights, while clean tannins rein in the lively, mouthfilling fruit on the palate. The Domini Veneti is more immediate, and plays on its full, fleshy, explosive fruit. The Valpolicella La Casetta is also successful, and the winemaking skill that combines fruit with coffee, and elegance with power, is clear.

NEGRAR (VR)

LE RAGOSE
FRAZ. ARBIZZANO
VIA LE RAGOSE, 1
37024 NEGRAR (VR)
TEL. 0457513241
E-MAIL: leragose@libero.it

Marco and Paolo Galli, who own Le Ragose, are notable for their determination to allow their wines all the time they need to reach full expression, rejecting premature releases onto the market. These may satisfy some enthusiasts but are actually detrimental to the wine, which is often unco-ordinated and lacking in harmony. No fear of that with Le Ragose wines, which always enjoy at least six months in the bottle before they are sold. Again this year, the cellar's brilliant results confirm that this is the right approach. Let's take a look at the wines we tasted. In the rush for extract and opulence, the other typical qualities of Amarone, rigour and a noble expression of the terroir, often fall by the wayside. Despite the difficult year, the '96 Le Ragose version manages to combine these qualities, with mint and herbs on the nose. Crushed flowers peep out from a salty, iodate background, showing sensual complexity. On the palate, the wine makes no attempt to astonish with its extract but aims for elegance. Expansive and mature, its alcohol-rich, mouthfilling development denotes class and severity. The Valpolicella Le Sassine almost won Two Glasses, with typical aromas of ripe fruit and an attractive mineral note that also comes across on the palate. The Recioto has intense ripe fruit aromas on the nose with bitter chocolate, and the hints of spice and a pleasant acid vein make it supple and very elegant on the palate.

• Amarone della Valpolicella Cl. Domini Veneti '98	ŸŸ 6
• Recioto della Valpolicella Cl. Domini Veneti '99	ŸŸ 5
• Recioto della Valpolicella Cl. Vigneti di Moron '99	ŸŸ 5
• Valpolicella Cl. Sup. La Casetta di Ettore Righetti Domini Veneti '98	Ÿ 4
• Valpolicella Cl. Sup. Vigneti di Torbe '98	4
• Amarone della Valpolicella Cl. Manara '95	ŸŸ 6
• Amarone della Valpolicella Cl. Vigneti di Jago Sel. '97	ŸŸ 6

• Amarone della Valpolicella Cl. '96	ŸŸ 6
• Recioto della Valpolicella Cl. '98	ŸŸ 6
• Valpolicella Cl. Sup. Le Sassine '98	Ÿ 4
• Valpolicella Cl. '00	3*
• Amarone della Valpolicella Cl. '86	ŸŸŸ 6
• Amarone della Valpolicella Cl. '88	ŸŸŸ 6
• Amarone della Valpolicella Cl. '90	ŸŸ 6
• Amarone della Valpolicella Cl. '94	ŸŸ 6
• Amarone della Valpolicella Cl. '95	ŸŸ 6
• Amarone della Valpolicella Cl. Marta Galli '96	ŸŸ 6
• Garda Cabernet Le Ragose '97	ŸŸ 4

NEGRAR (VR)

Roberto Mazzi
Loc. San Peretto
Via Crosetta, 8
37024 Negrar (VR)
Tel. 0457502072
E-mail: robertomazzi@iol.it

The future of this winery, which already makes a nice series of classic Valpolicellas, is being forged by the passion of Stefano and Antonio Mazzi, sons of Roberto, who has made wine at Negrar since the early 1960s. New vineyards, planted in the best Negrar crus, will extend the family's vineyard property and enrich today's range of wines, which focus on elegance and sobriety rather than massive extract. The list includes all the zone's classics, from Valpolicellas, which will not be released onto the market this year, to Amarones, concluding with the sweet Recioto. Our retasting of the Valpolicella Poiega '98 confirms the skill of the Mazzis at handling the typical Veronese vine varieties. The Amarone Punta di Villa tempers the liveliness and natural warmth of partial drying with rare finesse. The floral and spicy aromas of roses and pepper are enhanced by notes of morello cherry and cocoa powder, then the palate continues stylishly, without excessive alcohol. The excellent Recioto is aromatic with dried fruit and herbs in the nose and has a ripe palate with a good dose of freshness. The red Libero aims to provide a valid alternative to the traditional local grapes: sangiovese, nebbiolo and cabernet combine to make a wine that is a little too one-dimensional, with gamey, earthy and mineral notes. The palate is long rather than strong, with good acidity and nice tannin.

NEGRAR (VR)

Giuseppe Quintarelli
Via Cerè, 1
37024 Negrar (VR)
Tel. 0457500016

It's always exciting to pay a call on Giuseppe Quintarelli. The cellar where Amarone has been made since the early 1900s is permeated by a magical silence which, during the long years of ageing, conjures up the richness that is the unmistakable trademark of both the winery and the wine. The whole world acknowledges that no one embodies the essence of Valpolicella and its wines better than Giuseppe Quintarelli. The Amarone '95 exemplifies, as ever, a special style and approach that is a skilful blend of spices, fruit and body, with excellent extract and etheric persistence. In the Valpolicella, there is a very pleasant note of freshness, unusual for a seven year old wine, and which comes across instantly in bottled fruit and chocolate sensations. The Alzero, a dried-grape Cabernet, is as usual a Lone Ranger of a wine. It's unique, in style, extract and the sheer volume of its aromas. Opulence and fullness prevail on the palate in an elegant framework. The Recioto also confirms Giuseppe Quintarelli's winemaking skill. Elegance and polish are the keywords to sum up this sound product, which is still developing eight years after the harvest. Lastly, the Bandito is possibly the best loved of the wines made by "Bepi", as Quintarelli is affectionately known. This white dried-grape wine, from garganega, trebbiano toscano and saorin grapes, is only released in the best years.

Wine	Rating
● Amarone della Valpolicella Cl. Punta di Villa '97	㊉㊉ 6
● Recioto della Valpolicella Cl. Le Calcarole '97	㊉㊉ 5
● Valpolicella Cl. Sup. '00	㊉ 3*
● Libero Rosso '97	㊉ 5
● Amarone della Valpolicella Cl. Punta di Villa '96	♀♀ 6
● Libero Rosso '96	♀♀ 5
● Valpolicella Cl. Sup. Vigneto Poiega '98	♀♀ 4

Wine	Rating
● Amarone della Valpolicella Cl. Sup. Monte Cà Paletta '95	㊉㊉ 6
○ Bianco Amabile del Cerè Bandito '90	㊉㊉ 6
● Recioto della Valpolicella Cl. '93	㊉㊉ 6
● Alzero Cabernet Franc '95	㊉㊉ 6
● Valpolicella Cl. Sup. '94	㊉ 5
● Amarone della Valpolicella Ris. '83	♀♀♀ 6
● Amarone della Valpolicella '84	♀♀♀ 6
● Amarone della Valpolicella Ris. '85	♀♀♀ 6
● Amarone della Valpolicella '86	♀♀♀ 6
● Alzero Cabernet Franc '90	♀♀♀ 6
● Amarone della Valpolicella Cl. Sup. Monte Cà Paletta '93	♀♀♀ 6

NEGRAR (VR)

VILLA SPINOSA
LOC. JAGO
37024 NEGRAR (VR)
TEL. 0457500093
E-MAIL: villaspinosa@tin.it

Jago is a beautiful part of the municipality of Negrar and here, Enrico Cascella has been busying himself with Villa Spinosa for around ten years. The 25,000 bottles made each year are divided among the traditional classics, aged rather slowly in the bottle. The Amarone '96 was released this year. It is not especially concentrated in colour because of the vintage, which was not particularly favourable. The aromas open on mineral and spicy notes with pepper in the foreground, followed by more delicate ripe fruit overtones. On the palate, it is surprisingly fresh-tasting and the firm tannins contrast with subtle aromatic herbs and raisins. The Valpolicella Superiore Jago is very interesting, with traditional-style aromas of tobacco and bottled fruit, rounded out by distinctive hints of flowers and new-mown grass. The entry on the palate is vigorous, then the tannic weave contrasts with the considerable warmth. The standard-label Valpolicella stands out for its sulphurous mineral note while the customary freshness gives the palate clear, fresh fruit overtones. The Recioto is a little below par, and lacks that dash of harmony that would bring it up to Two Glasses.

• Amarone della Valpolicella Cl. '96 ŶŶ	6
• Valpolicella Cl. '00 Ŷ	3
• Recioto della Valpolicella Cl. Francesca Finato Spinosa '98 Ŷ	5
• Valpolicella Cl. Sup. Jago '98 Ŷ	4
• Amarone della Valpolicella Cl. '95 ŶŶ	6
• Recioto della Valpolicella Cl. '97 ŶŶ	5
• Valpolicella Cl. Sup. Jago '97 ŶŶ	4

NEGRAR (VR)

VIVIANI
VIA MAZZANO, 8
37020 NEGRAR (VR)
TEL. 0457500286

Up in Mazzano, Claudio Viviani unflaggingly continues his quest for a wine that combines strength, elegance, immediate impact, terroir and complexity. The Amarone Tulipano Nero is the result of that search. It strives to find a personality that can take on the world without being classed as excessively typical, while still embodying the terroir. The colour is concentrated but not too dark, and the nose slowly unfolds with hints of dried flowers, aromatic herbs, dried fruit and a mineral note that is echoed on the palate. Tulipano Nero's considerable power comes out, but does not intrude, on the palate alongside hints of berry fruit and raisins, before the clean, dry, classy finish. This is a truly memorable achievement, which strolled away with Three Glasses. The Recioto is also very good indeed. The nose has immediate, but complex, impact and the aromas are strikingly stylish: fresh flowers, wild berries and herbs. On the palate, it is charming and lively, the framework of tannins, acidity and extract promising a radiant future. The Valpolicella Superiore is also a success, and discloses floral notes with nice personality. Which tells you all you need to know about the exposures of the vineyards.

• Amarone della Valpolicella Cl. Tulipano Nero '97 ŶŶŶ	6
• Recioto della Valpolicella Cl. '98 ŶŶ	5
• Valpolicella Cl. Sup. '98 ŶŶ	5
• Valpolicella Cl. '00 Ŷ	2*
• Amarone della Valpolicella Cl. Casa dei Bepi '95 ŶŶŶ	6
• Amarone della Valpolicella Cl. Casa dei Bepi '93 ŶŶ	5
• Amarone della Valpolicella Cl. Casa dei Bepi '94 ŶŶ	6
• Recioto della Valpolicella Cl. '97 ŶŶ	5

NERVESA DELLA BATTAGLIA (TV)

Serafini & Vidotto
Via Arditi, 1
31040 Nervesa della Battaglia (TV)
Tel. 0422773281

For the first time in six years, Serafini & Vidotto have not been awarded Three Glasses but this doesn't mean it wasn't a successful year. If you look through the list of wines tasted, the two flagship reds, Rosso dell'Abazia and Pinot Nero, are missing. Francesco and Antonello have decided to delay bringing out the '99 to allow the vintage to benefit fully from bottle ageing. This responsible decision further demonstrates the care they invest in their winemaking. So, in the absence of the big guns, our attention focused on the Phigaia, a Bordeaux blend that aims to combine immediacy with decent complexity and depth. This it did with great success in the '99 edition. There is a floral note on the nose that is enriched by fruity, minerally hints that lend interesting complexity. The entry on the palate is delicate and develops gradually, allowing the wine to express itself through its best quality, elegance. The Bianco is very good. Fresher and more supple than in previous versions, it is full-bodied and well-rounded with a pleasantly varietal minerally note and a lingering acid vein that gives it freshness and persistence. Although the duo make mainly reds, Francesco and Antonello also turn out a Prosecco that is anything but a lightweight. A rich wine with great structure, it is, in short, a must for lovers of strong sensations.

○ Il Bianco dell'Abazia '00	♀♀	4
● Phigaia After the Red '99	♀♀	4
○ Prosecco del Montello	♀♀	3*
● Il Rosso dell'Abazia '93	♀♀♀	6
● Il Rosso dell'Abazia '94	♀♀♀	6
● Il Rosso dell'Abazia '95	♀♀♀	6
● Il Rosso dell'Abazia '96	♀♀♀	6
● Il Rosso dell'Abazia '97	♀♀♀	6
● Il Rosso dell'Abazia '98	♀♀♀	6
● Pinot Nero '98	♀	5

PESCHIERA DEL GARDA (VR)

Ottella
Fraz. S. Benedetto di Lugana
Loc. Ottella, 1
37019 Peschiera del Garda (VR)
Tel. 0457551950

Trebbiano has always been grown in the difficult clay areas south of Lake Garda, and this variety is used to make Lugana wines. Firmly established as one of the best makers of Lugana is the Ottella winery, apparently named after octuplets born in this old farmhouse years ago, and commemorated by a crest with eight little heads sculpted in marble. The cellar is run with a sure hand by Francesco Montresor, using grapes from the vineyards near Lake Frassino to make three versions of Lugana. The best of these is the Molceo Superiore. The '99 edition is intense, spicy, pulpy and ready for drinking, although with further ageing it could become smoother. Exemplary as ever is the Lugana Le Creete, which shows good dense texture, length and cleanliness, while the standard-label Lugana is very drinkable. The Gimé is nicely aromatic and expressive. This, the winery's fourth white, is the result of a vineyard selection of incrocio Manzoni and chardonnay. A little below par compared to the good debut of the '97, the dried-grape Moscato Giallo Prima Luce is still appealingly drinkable with a nice blend of honey and grassy notes. The winery also makes two reds, the better of which is the Campo Sireso. This modern-style red is made from merlot, cabernet, sauvignon and corvina grapes and is mouthfilling with good fruit fragrance and texture, balanced by balsam from the wood. The Rosso Ottella is the simplest wine on the list.

● Campo Sireso '99	♀♀	5
○ Lugana Sup. Molceo '99	♀♀	4
○ Gimè Bianco '00	♀	4
○ Lugana Le Creete '00	♀	4
○ Prima Luce Passito '98	♀	5
● Rosso Ottella '00		3
● Campo Sireso '96	♀♀	4
● Campo Sireso '97	♀♀	4
○ Prima Luce Passito '97	♀♀	5
● Campo Sireso '98	♀♀	4

PESCHIERA DEL GARDA (VR)

ZENATO
FRAZ. S. BENEDETTO DI LUGANA
VIA S. BENEDETTO, 8
37019 PESCHIERA DEL GARDA (VR)
TEL. 0457550300

Zenato again turned out an exemplary batch of wines, from the company's own estate, Santa Cristina, and from other fruit bought in especially from Valpolicella, demonstrating how good the winery is at purchasing high quality grapes and then vinifying them. The Amarone '97 is a wonderful modern-style interpretation of a wine with close links to tradition. The grapes are from various plots scattered around Valpolicella and Zenato's careful drying has turned them into an exciting wine. The layered aromas emerge gradually, with red fruit jam giving way to flower and mineral hints, and roses developing into pepper. The same panache is evident on the palate, where the wine is noble and austere without excessively mature or warm tones. A very classy Three Glass wine. The Alberto is also very good. A blend of part-dried merlot, cabernet and corvina grapes, it has interesting iodine and mineral aromas with ripe, healthy fruit sensations. On the palate, the wine is tangy and harmonious, promising to develop well. The Cabernet Sauvignon Santa Cristina is of a high standard. The herb and fresh flower aromas are interlaced with hints of oak and are perfectly reflected on the palate. Of the Luganas, we preferred the Sergio Zenato, which is aged in small oak barrels, while the Ripassa was a step ahead of the other Valpolicellas.

●	Amarone della Valpolicella Cl. '97	🍷🍷🍷	6
●	Alberto Rosso '98	🍷🍷	5
●	Cabernet Sauvignon S. Cristina '98	🍷🍷	4
●	Valpolicella Cl. Sup. Ripassa '98	🍷🍷	4
○	Lugana Sergio Zenato '99	🍷🍷	4
○	Lugana '00	🍷	3
○	Lugana Vigneto Massoni S. Cristina '00	🍷	4
●	Valpolicella Cl. Sup. '98	🍷	4
●	Amarone della Valpolicella Cl. Ris. Sergio Zenato '88	🍷🍷🍷	6
●	Amarone della Valpolicella Cl. Ris. Sergio Zenato '95	🍷🍷	6

REFRONTOLO (TV)

VINCENZO TOFFOLI
VIA LIBERAZIONE, 26
31020 REFRONTOLO (TV)
TEL. 0438894240 - 0438978204
E-MAIL: toffoli@nline.it

Sante, Luciano and Gabriele are the sons of Vincenzo Toffoli, who founded this winery, and they put a great deal of enthusiasm into running the business. Their aim is to make the classic wines of the area that lies between Valdobbiadene and Vittorio Veneto. The range therefore includes red wines and Prosecco. This year, the panel were most impressed by the Prosecco Extra Dry, with its dried fruit and ripe pear aromas and fragrant apple notes on the palate, with delicate creamy prickle. The Prosecco Passito is excellent and rather unusual, compared to other sweet wines. The natural lightness and fragrance of the variety come through in a whirl of dried fruit sensations. Apricots, peaches and gooseberry are all mirrored well on the palate. The delicacy of the flavour prevents the sweetness from becoming intrusive, turning it instead into a convincingly smooth complement to the fruit. This is a wine more suited to cheeses and foie gras than to desserts. The red Amaranto dei Vanai is also good. It's a Colli del Conegliano blend but is not released as a DOC label. The ruby red is not too dark, then the aromas develop with flower notes and interesting mineral nuances. This pleasantly fragrant wine is delicate on the palate. The Prosecco Tranquillo is a success. Like the Prosecco Frizzante, it is uncompromising and frank.

○	Prosecco Passito '99	🍷🍷	5
○	P. di Conegliano Extra Dry	🍷	3
●	Amaranto dei Vanai Rosso dei Colli Trevigiani '00	🍷	3
○	P. di Conegliano Tranquillo '00	🍷	3
○	P. di Conegliano Frizzante		2

SALGAREDA (TV)

ORNELLA MOLON TRAVERSO
LOC. CAMPO DI PIETRA
VIA RISORGIMENTO, 40
31040 SALGAREDA (TV)
TEL. 0422804807
E-MAIL: info@molon.it

Ornella and Giancarlo Traverso are the enthusiastic owners of this attractive winery in the Piave DOC, which confirms its position as the best in the zone each year with a good selection of wines. As yet unsatisfied with the positive results achieved by their wide range, the Traversos continue to add enjoyable new wines to their list. For example, this year sees the debut of the Rosso di Villa '98, a pedigree Merlot that is bound to receive a great deal of attention. The aim is to create a wine that can aspire to the highest accolades and bring further recognition to this well-established Piave winery. The Rosso di Villa is richly extracted, which is evident from the deep ruby colour. This is confirmed in the rich, complex aromas which are slightly marked by the wood. The palate has a strong, tannic development. A very enjoyable Merlot, it promises well for the future. The winery also present classic selections at the usual high level of quality, starting with the whites. The Sauvignon is the best of recent versions, the Traminer is intensely fragrant and very tangy and the Chardonnay is particularly rich on the nose and the palate. Among the reds, the Vite Rossa stands out for its balsamic notes and good length while we encountered some flaws in the rather ill-defined nose of the Merlot. Lastly, the Cabernet is attractive, with a good balance of toasty and fruity notes.

SAN BONIFACIO (VR)

INAMA
VIA IV NOVEMBRE, 1
37047 SAN BONIFACIO (VR)
TEL. 0456104343
E-MAIL: inama@inamaaziendaagricola.it

The appearance of Stefano Inama's first wines was a turning point for the image of Soave. Without radically altering the type, he emphasized the zone's considerable, and perhaps under-rated, potential for mature wines of some texture that could take substantial oak. Over the years and harvests, he has fine-tuned his goal and achieved new balance across the range. The Du Lot is again a great wine, the product of a very personal approach. This Soave tempts the nose with intense notes of dried flowers and ripe peaches and apricots while a minerally vein recalls the wonderful volcanic landscape where the grapes are grown. The aromas are explosive on the palate and the flavour is soft. Spices appear and the fruit becomes riper and more diffuse. Very good now, it can only improve in the years to come and won another Three Glasses for Inama. The very interesting Vin Soave Cuvée Speciale has Alsace-style benzine and chamomile aromas and is severe and no-nonsense on the palate, where there is plenty of character and personality. One of the best whites in the area, it embodies the high quality of the wines made at Inama, combining freshness and pleasant drinkability with good structure. Last year, we mentioned the Campo dei Tovi '99 and the Vulcaia Fumé '99 from the multitude of labels. We retasted this year and they proved to be as reliable and rich as ever.

	Wine	Glasses	Score
○	Piave Chardonnay Ornella '00	♛♛	3
○	Sauvignon Ornella '00	♛♛	3
○	Traminer Ornella '00	♛♛	3
●	Vite Rossa '97	♛♛	4
●	Piave Merlot Rosso di Villa '98	♛♛	5
●	Piave Cabernet Ornella '98	♛	4
●	Piave Merlot Ornella '98		3
●	Piave Cabernet Ornella '97	♛♛	4
●	Piave Merlot Ornella '97	♛♛	4

	Wine	Glasses	Score
○	Soave Cl. Sup. Vigneto Du Lot '99	♛♛♛	6
○	Soave Cl. Sup. Vin Soave '00	♛♛	4
○	Soave Cl. Sup. Vin Soave Cuvée Speciale '98	♛♛	5
○	Chardonnay Campo dei Tovi '99	♛♛	5
○	Sauvignon Vulcaia Fumé '99	♛♛	6
○	Chardonnay '00	♛	4
○	Sauvignon Vulcaia Fumé '96	♛♛♛	5
○	Soave Cl. Sup. Vigneto Du Lot '96	♛♛♛	5
●	Bradisismo Cabernet Sauvignon del Veneto '98	♛♛	6

SAN FIOR (TV)

MASOTTINA
LOC. CASTELLO DI ROGANZOLO
VIA BRADOLINI, 54
31010 SAN FIOR (TV)
TEL. 0438400775

We are delighted to record an improvement in quality from this winery, run with clear-headed vision by the Dal Bianco brothers. This small winery makes three of the four DOC wines in the province of Treviso. Presentation of the Colli di Conegliano Rosso 1998 was delayed for one year and this decision proved to be the right one, as the wine has clearly benefited from its longer ageing. It has an austere profile with evolved and pleasantly complex notes in the long finish. Apart from the Rosso, which is the leading wine, the average quality of the range has never been as focused as this year. The Colli di Conegliano Bianco demonstrates its no-nonsense character and establishes itself as one of the most interesting whites in the area. Turning to the Spumantes, made from prosecco grapes, the Extra Dry is very good while the Cartizze, though well-typed, is slightly inferior in quality. The nicest surprises were the wines from the Piave DOC zone, which are usually the winery's least interesting bottles. The traditional-style Cabernet Sauvignon Riserva ai Palazzi is convincing and we preferred it to the Merlot Riserva, which is still well-typed. The standard-label Chardonnay and Pinot Bianco are enjoyable, with a pinch of character, and are good examples of wines that should be drunk while young.

	Wine	Rating	Score
O	Colli di Conegliano Bianco '99	¶¶	4
●	Colli di Conegliano Rosso '98	¶¶	5
●	Piave Cabernet Sauvignon ai Palazzi Ris. '98	¶¶	4
O	Piave Chardonnay '00	¶	2*
O	Piave Pinot Bianco '00	¶	2*
●	Piave Merlot ai Palazzi Ris. '98	¶	4
O	Cartizze	¶	5
O	P. di Conegliano Extra Dry	¶	3
●	Colli di Conegliano Rosso '97	¶¶	5
O	Colli di Conegliano Bianco '98	¶¶	4

SAN GERMANO DEI BERICI (VI)

VILLA DAL FERRO LAZZARINI
VIA CHIESA, 23
36040 SAN GERMANO DEI BERICI (VI)
TEL. 0444868025

The philosophy of the Lazzarini sisters is to shun fashions, keep production within reason and ignore barriques. Their wines are bottled and sold only when they are ready and not when the market demands them. They have kept faith with that philosophy this year, presenting only three wines, all of which are interesting. The Pinot Bianco won Two Glasses for its very clean aroma profile with discernible spring flowers, almonds and peaches. The delicate palate is refreshed with good fruit pulp and decent acidity. The Cabernet Rive Rosse, 30 per cent franc and 70 per cent sauvignon, is a disarmingly uncomplicated red obtained without pushing concentration and extraction to extremes. The colour is ruby red and the grassy notes on the nose mingle with hints of fruit, bramble and cassis. On the palate, it is lively with bright tannins. But the house classic is the Merlot Campo del Lago, with its legendary capacity for development over the years. The '98 edition still needs to age in the bottle but its absolute compliance with the house style and the typical features of a great wine are already noticeable. As expected, the colour is unimpressive, but the nose indicates that this is a thoroughbred. The aromas give plenty of scope to wild berry fruits, tobacco and spices, closing with a nice minerally tone. The palate is extremely delicate and well-sustained. Although not a paragon of roundness, the persistent elegance on the palate is appealing.

	Wine	Rating	Score
O	Colli Berici Pinot Bianco del Rocolo '00	¶¶	4
●	Colli Berici Merlot Campo del Lago '98	¶¶	6
●	Colli Berici Cabernet Le Rive Rosse '98	¶	5
●	Colli Berici Cabernet Ris. '93	¶¶	6
●	Colli Berici Merlot Campo del Lago '97	¶¶	6

SAN MARTINO BUON ALBERGO (VR)

Musella
Loc. Monte del Drago
37036 San Martino Buon Albergo (VR)
tel. 045973385
e-mail: musella@musella.it

When Emilio Pasqua first began working at the Musella estate, strolling among the vineyards and hills he saw his opportunity to create a major winery that would combine all the available modern technology with everything tradition has handed down over the centuries. This is how the "Musella project" was born, as Emilio Pasqua calls it. It's an ambitious, wide-ranging programme of renovation of the vineyards with new planting patterns, constant attention to remove anything that might disturb the birth and development of the wine, and absolute respect for the seasonal weather conditions and natural ageing times. It is no coincidence that the wines reviewed are only just becoming available on the market now. The bottle that made the greatest impression at our tastings was the Amarone. The complex nose releases its aromas little by little, first ripe fruit, then glimpses of mint and herb notes, before delicately intriguing mineral nuances emerge. The impact on the palate is warm and mouthfilling, without yielding to facile smoothness, while the tannins make their presence felt, easily supporting the huge body. The Chardonnay is very interesting. Straw yellow with greenish highlights, it shows mineral and dried flower aromas that are reflected well on the palate, where the wood is almost imperceptible. The Valpolicella Superiore and the Monte del Drago, a blend of cabernet and corvina, are both successful.

○	Garda Chardonnay '00	ŸŸ	4
●	Amarone della Valpolicella '97	ŸŸ	6
●	Monte del Drago Rosso '97	Ÿ	5
●	Valpolicella Sup. '98	Ÿ	4

SAN PIETRO DI FELETTO (TV)

Bepin de Eto
Via Colle, 32/A
31020 San Pietro di Feletto (TV)
tel. 0438486877

Ettore Ceschin is investing a lot of energy in his most recent creation, the ambitious Colli di Conegliano Rosso Croda Ronca. This is why the '98, which was to be tasted this year, has been postponed till 2002 to allow it to age further. This meticulousness has deprived this year's notes of the winery's most important wine, so the whites take the lion's share, starting with the Colli di Conegliano Bianco Greccio. The DOC is only a few years old and is still seeking a specific identity. Bepin de Eto's version could easily become the benchmark. His Bianco has all the characteristics of whites that are fermented and aged in steel, and the grape varieties in the blend, in this case, mainly incrocio Manzoni bianco, give it its personality. The wine has assumed the varietal's intense aromas, which are gradually released along with tropical fruit, spring flowers and mineral notes. The palate is vibrantly fresh-tasting and well-structured, and reflects the nose well. The monovarietal Incrocio Manzoni Bianco is in one of its best versions, and the range of aromas is in no way inferior to the Greccio. The rich nose is again followed by good thrust on the palate. The Prosecco Extra Dry has enjoyably elegant aromas and creamy prickle, followed by a good, balanced flavour.

○	Colli di Conegliano Bianco Il Greccio '00	ŸŸ	4
○	Incrocio Manzoni 6.0.13. '00	ŸŸ	3*
○	P. di Conegliano Extra Dry	Ÿ	3
○	Greccio Spumante		4
●	Colli di Conegliano Rosso Croda Ronca '96	ŸŸ	6
●	Colli di Conegliano Rosso Croda Ronca '97	ŸŸ	6

SAN PIETRO IN CARIANO (VR)

Stefano Accordini
Fraz. Pedemonte
Via Alberto Bolla, 9
37029 San Pietro in Cariano (VR)
tel. 0457701733
e-mail: stefano.accordini@tin.it

Three of the five Accordini wines were awarded Two Glasses this time and one, the Amarone Acinatico, came very close to Three, demonstrating the reliable quality of the whole range. The property has wisely been enlarged with the purchase of new land for future development. Stefano Accordini and his wife Giuseppina can be proud of their sons Tiziano and Daniele, who are leading figures in today's Valpolicella new wave. The strong Amarone Acinatico, from the wonderful '97 vintage, was very good. Colour and nose are concentrated, with subtle balsamic aromas of herbs and shrubs, and the palate is rich with notes of bitter chocolate and a finish that trails off like a shooting star. The Recioto is a purply ruby red with an enfolding, intensely fruity nose. The full flavour recalls bottled cherries and stewed plums. The Valpolicella Superiore, made using the "ripasso" technique of adding unpressed skins after fermentation to enhance alcohol and flavour, is an intense ruby red with cocoa powder, coffee and ripe cherry aromas. The balance is good and the finish is dense. The Passo is a dry red made primarily from corvina with small quantities of rondinella, cabernet sauvignon and merlot. The grapes are partially dried until November and after a short time in stainless steel, the wine is aged in barriques. It is garnet, with a nose of tobacco and brambles. The palate is very drinkable, with medium structure. Finally, the Valpolicella '00 is nice. The fresh herb, raspberry and bilberry in the nose are followed by wild cherry and light-skinned plums on the palate.

- Amarone della Valpolicella Cl. Acinatico '97 — 🍷🍷 6
- Passo Rosso '98 — 🍷🍷 5
- Recioto della Valpolicella Cl. Acinatico '99 — 🍷🍷 6
- Valpolicella Cl. Sup. Acinatico '99 — 🍷🍷 5
- Valpolicella Cl. '00 — 🍷 3*
- Amarone della Valpolicella Cl. Vigneto Il Fornetto '93 — 🍷🍷🍷 6
- Amarone della Valpolicella Cl. Acinatico '95 — 🍷🍷🍷 6
- Amarone della Valpolicella Cl. Vigneto Il Fornetto '95 — 🍷🍷🍷 6

SAN PIETRO IN CARIANO (VR)

Lorenzo Begali
Via Cengia, 10
37020 San Pietro in Cariano (VR)
tel. 0457725148
e-mail: tiliana@tiscalinet.it

At last, the moment has come for Lorenzo Begali and his little winery in San Pietro in Cariano. For years, we have doggedly praised his work and sensitive production of great wines from dried grapes. Now Lorenzo has stunned the competition with a magnificently meaty, warm Amarone. The dark but not impenetrable colour is followed by an engrossing nose that shows aromas of Alpine herbs and spring flowers. The super-ripe fruit is elegantly presented and the development on the palate is exemplary, rich in nuances and youthfully dynamic. The clear ripe fruit and minerally hints keep this very ageable wine firmly on course. It's an Amarone with bags of character, and the Three Glasses are well-deserved by a family that has always been passionately devoted to winemaking. The standard-label Amarone is further confirmation and benefits from ageing in larger wooden barrels. A charming wine, it has a less intriguing, more severe base, though it is a top quality sweet wine. The fresh flowers and new-mown grass on the nose succeed in the difficult task of complementing the lively chocolate note, and the mineral nuances complete the complex aroma profile. The Valpolicella Superiore is also good, with an enjoyable, mouthfilling and warm palate.

- Amarone della Valpolicella Cl. Vigneto Monte Ca' Bianca '97 — 🍷🍷🍷 6
- Recioto della Valpolicella Cl. '99 — 🍷🍷 6
- Amarone della Valpolicella Cl. '97 — 🍷🍷 6
- Valpolicella Cl. Sup. Vigneto La Cengia '99 — 🍷🍷 4
- Amarone della Valpolicella Cl. Vigneto Monte Ca' Bianca '95 — 🍷🍷 6
- Amarone della Valpolicella Cl. '96 — 🍷🍷 6
- Amarone della Valpolicella Cl. Vigneto Monte Ca' Bianca '96 — 🍷🍷 6
- Recioto della Valpolicella Cl. '97 — 🍷🍷 5
- Recioto della Valpolicella Cl. '98 — 🍷🍷 5

SAN PIETRO IN CARIANO (VR)

BRIGALDARA
FRAZ. SAN FLORIANO
VIA BRIGALDARA, 20
37029 SAN PIETRO IN CARIANO (VR)
TEL. 0457701055

Stefano Cesari's small winery is situated on the low San Pietro in Cariano hillsides at San Floriano. Here, the Po Valley and the nearby Adige river still have a benevolent influence, giving the grapes a Mediterranean warmth that they pass on to the wine. The 15 hectares of vineyards extend over these hillsides around the owner's lovely villa, which houses the cellars. Stefano has surprised us this year with a super Amarone. Dark in hue, tending to garnet, it delivers a nose of red fruit jam, enriched with aromatic herbs and a mineral vein streamlining the opulence of the aromas. The palate gradually reveals itself to be rich, pulpy, elegant and well-bred. This excellent Amarone manages to enfold the palate with great harmony, thrilling with a long fruity finish, where the ripe morello cherry sensation lingers almost forever. Thanks to this wonderful performance, Stefano picks up his first Three Glasses. The Recioto is missing because our hero does not consider it to be ready yet, so our attention is focused on the Valpolicella '99, of which only one version was released this year. The traditional vegetal, chocolate and tobacco aromas are well-reflected on the palate, where good alcohol makes it smoothly, warmly drinkable. We would also like to mention the pleasant Garda made from garganega grapes, with fresh floral notes on the nose and a pleasantly racy flavour.

● Amarone della Valpolicella Cl. '97	♟♟♟	6
● Valpolicella Cl. '99	♟♟	3
○ Garda Garganega '00	♟	3
● Amarone della Valpolicella Cl. '95	♟♟	5
● Amarone della Valpolicella Cl. '96	♟♟	5
● Recioto della Valpolicella '98	♟♟	5
● Valpolicella Il Vegro '98	♟♟	3

SAN PIETRO IN CARIANO (VR)

LUIGI BRUNELLI
VIA CARIANO, 10
37029 SAN PIETRO IN CARIANO (VR)
TEL. 0457701118
E-MAIL: cortecariano@tin.it

Making Amarone has become a matter of personal pride for Luigi Brunelli. This explains his excellent performance, even in less favourable years like '96. This time, we tasted the '98 selections, which are generally inferior to the exceptionally good '97 vintage. Quality was very high although no Three glasses were awarded. Two Amarones were placed on the market in autumn, the standard-label and the renowned Campo dei Titari, while the Campo Inferi, which made its successful debut last year, will come out later. The standard-label version gave a very fine performance with its concentrated hue and toasted hazelnuts on the nose. The concentration of the colour is echoed on the palate, which is a little bitter in the finish. The Campo dei Titari has denser flavour than the previous wine. It's muscular yet gradual, with clear tannins and considerable complexity in the nose, where unusual gamey and hay notes emerge with raisins. These wines would undoubtedly benefit from longer ageing in the cellars: extraordinary today, they will improve over time. The Recioto is convincing, with its good stuffing, and the three Valpolicellas we tasted also showed well. The standard-label made the best possible use of the good '00 vintage. The Pariondo selection has distinctive concentration and the Campo Praesel is more modern in style.

● Amarone della Valpolicella Cl. Campo del Titari '98	♟♟	6
● Amarone della Valpolicella Cl. '98	♟♟	6
● Recioto della Valpolicella Cl. '98	♟♟	5
● Valpolicella Cl. '00	♟	3
● Valpolicella Cl. Sup. Campo Praesel '99	♟	3
● Valpolicella Cl. Sup. Pariondo '99	♟	4
○ Pariondo Bianco '00		3
● Corte Cariano Rosso '99		3
● Amarone della Valpolicella Cl. Campo del Titari '96	♟♟♟	6
● Amarone della Valpolicella Cl. Campo del Titari '97	♟♟♟	6

SAN PIETRO IN CARIANO (VR)

Angelo Nicolis e Figli
Via Villa Girardi, 29
37029 San Pietro in Cariano (VR)
Tel. 0457701261
E-mail: vininicolis@libero.it

The good impression made by our visit last year to the Nicolis brothers' cellars has been confirmed by a great vintage. The excellent progress of the '97 harvest allowed Giuseppe, Giancarlo and Massimo to make optimum use of great fruit in two sumptuous Amarones, full of the warmth of enviable ripeness. The progress is clear throughout the range and belies a well thought-out estate management programme that can bend with the vagaries of the weather yet focuses on a quest for perfect fruit grown in nature's own time. This long-sighted company view means that the Amarone Ambrosan only goes into the bottle when it's good and ready, as in the case of the '97 vintage. The standard-label version has ripe fruit and aromatic herb aromas. On the palate, it has a strikingly immediate impact of chocolate and red fruit. The Ambrosan version is more complex with natural ripe fruit aromas mingling with mineral nuances of pencil lead and bottled cherries. On the palate, it fills the whole mouth with a no-nonsense, engrossing impact of dense fruit pulp, and seduces with smooth tannins and its mouthfilling creamy texture. The interesting Testal is a blend of the main traditional grape varieties of the area: it is vegetal on the nose with intense notes of flowers and new-mown grass, with an elegant, silky palate, and pleasant thyme and Alpine herb nuances.

SAN PIETRO IN CARIANO (VR)

Santa Sofia
Fraz. Pedemonte
Via Ca' Dedé, 61
37020 San Pietro in Cariano (VR)
Tel. 0457701074
E-mail: info@santasofia.com

This large winery in Pedemonte is relaunching production with wines seeking greater character within the ever-evolving Valpolicella overview. Extreme care over cleaning and the use of wood indicate the desire to develop and improve the quality of the products on offer, seeking new balance between the traditional and the modern. In this context, the wine that best represents this new direction is the Amarone '97 standard-label version. The ruby red colour tending to garnet is carefully made; the nose has mineral aromas giving way to an interesting gamy note which adds depth to the range of aromas. On the palate the wine is intriguing and appealing, with a good impact, while the warm alcoholic development strongly preserves the link with tradition. The Riserva Gioé is more classic, with evolved vegetal and tobacco notes; hints of toastiness also appear on the palate which prevents the wine from expressing itself fully. The Predaia and the Arleo are both pleasant and fragrant; these two red blends are based on local native varieties. The standard-label Valpolicella has an affable note of red fruits but its main virtue is freshness. If we move on to the whites, the Bianco di Custoza gives its usual good performance, its best feature being fruity freshness, and the Soave Monte Foscarin proves to be reliably drinkable.

● Amarone della Valpolicella Cl. '97 ♟♟	6
● Amarone della Valpolicella Cl. Ambrosan '97 ♟♟	6
☉ Chiaretto '00 ♟	3
● Valpolicella Cl. '00 ♟	3
● Recioto della Valpolicella Cl. '98 ♟	6
● Testal '98 ♟	5
● Valpolicella Cl. Sup. Seccal '98 ♟	4
● Valpolicella Cl. Sup. '98	4
● Amarone della Valpolicella Cl. Ambrosan '93 ♟♟♟	6
● Amarone della Valpolicella Cl. Ambrosan '95 ♟♟	6

● Amarone della Valpolicella Cl. '97 ♟♟	6
○ Bianco di Custoza Montemagrin '00 ♟	2
○ Soave Cl. Montefoscarin '00 ♟	2*
● Valpolicella Cl. '00 ♟	3
● Amarone della Valpolicella Cl. Gioé '95 ♟	6
● Arleo Rosso '97 ♟	5
● Predaia Rosso '97 ♟	4
● Recioto della Valpolicella Cl. '98 ♟	5

SAN PIETRO IN CARIANO (VR)

F.lli Speri
Fraz. Pedemonte
Via Fontana, 14
37020 San Pietro in Cariano (VR)
tel. 0457701154
e-mail: info@speri.com

Care in the vineyard and scrupulous attention to all stages of winemaking make the Speri family's traditional wines outstanding. The decision to adopt a modern version of the Veronese pergola vine training system, with low yields and high planting densities for quality, shows a refreshing vision of Valpolicella winemaking. And to buck the trend by making a completely dry Amarone demonstrates a self-confidence that only a winery with established production principles can afford. One might describe the Speri cousins' activity as a subtle interpretation of tradition in a modern key. Two complementary products have now emerged, the Amarone Monte Sant'Urbano and the Recioto La Roggia. The former, which is the result of an unfavourable vintage, makes no attempt to use sugar concentration as a passport to approachability. Quite the contrary, it maintains its dry, spare style despite the natural superabundance of fruit. The wine gradually opens onto the nose with mineral and aromatic herb aromas, and is invitingly drinkable. On the palate, it is candid and almost severe. The smoothness is never intrusive and the balance intriguing, with highly personal mineral notes. The Recioto has a totally different type of exuberance. Soft and creamy from the nose on, it has super-ripe fruit and mint at the beginning of a complex aromatic development that is still unfolding. Partly because of the indifferent vintage, the Valpolicella Sant'Urbano narrowly missed out on Two Glasses but confirmed its quality.

Wine		Score
● Amarone della Valpolicella Cl. Vigneto Monte Sant'Urbano '96	ΨΨ	6
● Recioto della Valpolicella Cl. La Roggia '97	ΨΨ	5
● Recioto della Valpolicella Cl. I Comunai '98	ΨΨ	5
● Valpolicella Cl. '00	Ψ	3*
● Valpolicella Cl. Sup. Sant'Urbano '98	Ψ	4
● Valpolicella Cl. Sup. La Roverina '99	Ψ	3
● Amarone della Valpolicella Cl. Vigneto Monte Sant'Urbano '93	ΨΨΨ	6
● Amarone della Valpolicella Cl. Vigneto Monte Sant'Urbano '95	ΨΨΨ	6

SAN PIETRO IN CARIANO (VR)

F.lli Tedeschi
Fraz. Pedemonte
Via Verdi, 4
37020 San Pietro in Cariano (VR)
tel. 0457701487
e-mail: tedeschi@tedeschiwines.com

With Sabrina firmly in the business and Antonietta and Riccardo increasingly expert, this Pedemonte winery has begun to look with renewed interest and conviction at the vineyards. The rediscovery of long-forgotten vines and the study of new planting systems are an important area of research, in addition to the usual experimentation in the cellars. It is no coincidence that this year the wines presented are among the best in the zone, starting with the Rosso della Fabriseria. Although this is the winery's most international product, it is made mainly from corvina grapes, which are an important local variety in Valpolicella. The colour is intense but not impenetrable, and does not instantly reveal the richness of the wine, then the aromas are attractively complex. Soft, sweet sensations of crushed fruit, strawberries and dried roses mingle with notes of thyme and mint, invigorating the aromatic range. On the palate, it lives up to its potential. Full and silky, with excellent nose-palate consistency, it closes with the return of the aromatic herbs and spices. The two Amarone selections are very good. The Monte Olmi is more traditional, pervasive and very warm, with bottled fruit and mineral notes. The Amarone La Fabriseria is richer with clearer fruit. We are convinced that ageing in the bottles will improve these two wines. Lastly, we note the good ageing prospects of Tedeschi products. Even decades later, they show a charm and integrity that few other wines possess.

Wine		Score
● Rosso della Fabriseria '99	ΨΨ	5
● Amarone della Valpolicella Cl. '98	ΨΨ	6
● Amarone della Valpolicella Cl. Capitel Monte Olmi '98	ΨΨ	6
● Amarone della Valpolicella Cl. La Fabriseria '98	ΨΨ	6
● Recioto della Valpolicella Cl. Capitel Monte Fontana '98	ΨΨ	5
● Capitel S. Rocco Rosso di Ripasso '98	Ψ	4
● Valpolicella Cl. Sup. Capitel dei Nicalò '98	Ψ	4
● Rosso della Fabriseria '97	ΨΨΨ	6
● Amarone della Valpolicella Cl. La Fabriseria '97	ΨΨ	6

SAN PIETRO IN CARIANO (VR)

VITICOLTORI TOMMASI
LOC. PEDEMONTE
VIA RONCHETTO, 2
37020 SAN PIETRO IN CARIANO (VR)
TEL. 0457701266
E-MAIL: info@tommasiwine.it

The Tommasi winery has been making traditional Veronese wines since the beginning of the last century, and despite the industrial-scale production, the standard of the leading labels is good. The winery owns an estate from which a label takes its name, Il Sestante, which monitors winemaking from the vineyard to the bottle. The Amarone Ca' Floria is only made in the most favourable years and is ruby red in colour, tending to garnet, with profound mineral aromas on the nose. The fruit is clearer on the palate, where it is flanked by typical vegetal, tobacco and leather notes, which make the wine well-typed and traditional. The Amarone Monte Masua is part aged in barriques and has a fresher nose with super-ripe fruit and aromatic herbs. On the palate, the smooth, warm impact develops harmoniously and openly with good nose-palate consistency. The Recioto Fiorato is a good interpretation of traditional style, with fruit jam and flower notes, though it hints at a density which is not fulfilled on the palate. The Valpolicella made using the "ripasso" technique of adding unpressed skins after fermentation is interesting. Alongside the usual crushed herb and mineral aromas, it offers a warm, mouthfilling palate. The Lugana San Martino is good with sweet, creamy sensations on the nose and a pleasant hint of butter. On the palate, it is fresh and supple, offsetting its smoothness and drinkability.

SAN PIETRO IN CARIANO (VR)

MASSIMINO VENTURINI
FRAZ. SAN FLORIANO
VIA SEMONTE, 20
37020 SAN PIETRO IN CARIANO (VR)
TEL. 0457701331 - 0457703320
E-MAIL: azagrventurinimassimo@tin.it

The Three Glasses won for the first time last year, with the wonderful Recioto Le Brugnine 1997, was an important landmark for the Venturini brothers, who have since redoubled their efforts to give all their products style and constant quality. The meticulous, rigorous work in the vineyards has been fine-tuned over the years and they are now turning their attention to the cellar, which was needing to adapt to the quality of the fruit at every stage of vinification. In the absence of Venturini's top wine, our attention is focused on its illustrious rival, the Amarone '97. Dark in colour, it has profound aromas of berry fruit, chocolate and scrubland, and a classy touch of wood. The impact on the palate is remarkable. Astounding texture is rigorously held in place by the close-knit tannins. The Valpolicella Semonte Alto is a good bottle, confirming the growth of all the winery's products. The sweet aromas of chocolate and ripe red fruit are followed by a warm, inviting palate that resists the temptation to mimic an Amarone. The Recioto in the standard-label version has interesting mineral peaks with its traditionally impatient vegetal notes. The well-controlled sweetness and fresh acidity make it supple and drinkable.

● Amarone della Valpolicella Cl. Ca' Florian '97	♟♟	6
● Amarone della Valpolicella Cl. Monte Masua Il Sestante '97	♟♟	6
○ Lugana Vigneto San Martino Il Sestante '00	♟	3
● Recioto della Valpolicella Cl. Fiorato '98	♟	5
● Valpolicella Cl. Sup. '98	♟	4
● Garda Merlot Le Prunee '99	♟	4

● Amarone della Valpolicella Cl. '97	♟♟	6
● Valpolicella Cl. Sup. Semonte Alto '98	♟♟	4
● Recioto della Valpolicella Cl. '99	♟♟	5
● Valpolicella Cl. '00	♟	2
● Valpolicella Cl. Sup. '98	♟	4
● Recioto della Valpolicella Cl. Le Brugnine '97	♟♟♟	5
● Amarone della Valpolicella Cl. '93	♟♟	5
● Amarone della Valpolicella Cl. '94	♟♟	5
● Amarone della Valpolicella Cl. '95	♟♟	5
● Amarone della Valpolicella Cl. '96	♟♟	5

SAN PIETRO IN CARIANO (VR)

Villa Bellini
Loc. Castelrotto di Negarine
Via dei Fraccaroli, 6
37020 San Pietro in Cariano (VR)
tel. 0457725630
e-mail: archivino@villafiorita.com

This small Castelrotto winery manages to produce a well-made Amarone every year from the property's few hectares of vineyards, showing sensitivity and care during the harvest and at the drying and vinification stages. In addition, selection of the grapes for the flagship has no repercussions on the character of the Valpolicellas. This respect for the countryside reflects Marco and Cecilia's production philosophy, poised between the modern and the traditional. The '97 Amarone is superbly balanced after ageing in 900-litre casks. On the nose, the fruit shows integrity and nice flesh with mineral and pepper notes that take it attractively into a more personal dimension. The palate shows medium structure and is made more enjoyable by its fruit sensations and the clean winemaking technique. The dry finish with a minerally tone brings things to a perfect close. The standard-label Valpolicella is always pleasant. Rounded, with fresh fruit and pepper tones, it has an acid vein that is never intrusive. The Superiore version is a little slow to open up on the nose but patient drinkers will be rewarded with minerally hints from bottle-ageing. On the palate, the pleasant rusticity is caressing rather than a disturbance. Please note Marco and Cecilia's laudable decision not to release their Amarone '96, which they felt was not up to the winery's standards.

- Amarone della Valpolicella Cl. '97 ⚜⚜ 6
- Valpolicella Cl. Il Brolo '00 ⚜ 3
- Valpolicella Cl. Sup. Il Taso '98 ⚜ 4
- Amarone della Valpolicella Cl. '93 ⚜ 5
- Amarone della Valpolicella Cl. '94 ⚜ 5
- Amarone della Valpolicella Cl. '95 ⚜ 6
- Recioto della Valpolicella Cl. '95 ⚜⚜ 5

SANT'AMBROGIO DI VALPOLICELLA (VR)

Masi
Fraz. Gargagnago
Via Monteleone, 2
37020 Sant'Ambrogio di Valpolicella (VR)
tel. 0456832511
e-mail: masi@masi.it

Masi is one of the most prestigious names in Veneto winemaking. The cellar belongs to the Boscaini family and has reached an annual production capacity of 3,000,000 bottles, with a further 2,000,000 from the recently purchased Lison-Pramaggiore winery. These figures might look threatening for quality but this has never been true at Masi. In fact recently, there has been a further improvement in the standard of the range. There are still just two lines, Masi and Serègo Alighieri, which comes from the farm belonging to Count Pieralvise. We tasted a wide range of wines this year and a special mention goes to the Osar '97, a red table wine made from local varieties, oseleta and corvina. It's a spontaneous, salty wine with mineral notes. Exceptionally enjoyable, it combines elegance and power on a palate enfolded by liquorice and aromatic herbs. The Amarones again are the leading reds. Both the Costasera '97 and the Mazzano '95 are very appealing, thanks to their sophisticated fruit and considerable structure, and both show class. The Valpolicella Serègo Alighieri is good while the Taor, from corvina, oseletta and rondinella, has the fresh flower notes we have enjoyed in the past. The Recioto Serègo Alighieri is well-typed, as are the Soave Colbaraca and the Bardolino La Vegrona.

- Amarone della Valpolicella Cl. Mazzano '95 ⚜⚜ 6
- Amarone della Valpolicella Cl. Costasera '97 ⚜⚜ 6
- Osar '97 ⚜⚜ 6
- Bardolino Cl. La Vegrona '00 ⚜ 3
- Recioto della Valpolicella Cl. Casal dei Ronchi Serègo Alighieri '97 ⚜ 6
- Toar '97 ⚜ 5
- Valpolicella Cl. Sup. Possessioni Rosso Serègo Alighieri '99 ⚜ 4
- ○ Soave Cl. Sup. Colbaraca '00 3
- Amarone della Valpolicella Cl. Mazzano '93 ⚜⚜⚜ 6

SANT'AMBROGIO DI VALPOLICELLA (VR)

RAIMONDI VILLA MONTELEONE
FRAZ. GARGAGNAGO
37020 SANT'AMBROGIO DI VALPOLICELLA (VR)
TEL. 0457704974

This Gargagnago winery seems able to present excellent wines despite the fact that professor Raimondi has passed away. A year after the sad event, it offered the panel a fine series of selections. Credit is due to Lucia, who has succeeded in the difficult task of maintaining continuity in both the good standard of quality achieved and also in the style of the wines. Lucia Raimondi's wines are characterized by elegance, charm and a strong link with the past. Frequently, they hover somewhere between tradition and modernity. A clear example of this is the Amarone '97, with its ripe red fruit and vegetal aromas, and penetrating mineral notes. The palate is rich and dense, with hints of dried fruit, dried flowers, leather and bottled cherries, all pervaded by an elegance and finesse that are rarely found in such a traditional-style Amarone. The other dried-grape wines are also very successful. The Recioto Pal Sun, although impressively concentrated, has enjoyable, immediate impact, and the Passito Bianco is more complex. The aromas include spring flowers, peaches and dried grass. Its unexpected freshness on the palate makes this a supple, intriguing wine. Very clean, it flaunts a long apricot and candied citrus finish.

- Amarone della Valpolicella Cl. '97 ΨΨ 6
- ○ Passito Bianco di Gargagnago '97 ΨΨ 5
- Recioto della Valpolicella Cl.
  Pal Sun '97 ΨΨ 6
- Valpolicella Cl. Sup.
  Campo S. Vito '98 Ψ 5
- Amarone della Valpolicella Cl. '94 ΨΨ 6
- Amarone della Valpolicella Cl.
  Campo S. Paolo '95 ΨΨ 6
- Amarone della Valpolicella Cl.
  Campo S. Paolo '97 ΨΨ 6
- Valpolicella Cl. Sup.
  Campo S. Vito '97 ΨΨ 5

SELVAZZANO DENTRO (PD)

LA MONTECCHIA
FRAZ. FERIOLE
VIA MONTECCHIA, 16
35030 SELVAZZANO DENTRO (PD)
TEL. 049637294
E-MAIL: lamontecchia@libero.it

Recently, the Colli Euganei DOC has demonstrated all its considerable potential, thanks to a close-knit circle of producers who have overcome difficulties with courage and followed the road to quality. The noble Giordano Emo Capodilista, owner of La Montecchia, is part of that circle and his selections are making the zone famous outside the region. Giordano's wines are not only typically elegant and delicate, but also strongly rooted in the territory, reflecting its salient features. The Rosso Montecchia is more convincing than in the past and bears witness to the cellar's continuing improvements. Despite the rather intrusive wood, the depth of the nose is striking and is followed by a full, meaty palate, again demonstrating very careful work in the vineyard. The Moscato Fior d'Arancio Passito declines to join the chase for extract, its intense, varied range of aromas opening delicately to introduce attractive balance on the palate. Among the other wines tasted, the standard-label Colli Euganei Rosso is well-typed while the Merlot Bandiera, presented this year in a more ambitious version, will need a more focused identity and a rethinking of the cask conditioning to express its full potential. The Cabernet Franc Godimondo is a stimulating and pleasant wine.

- Colli Euganei Rosso
  Montecchia '98 ΨΨ 5
- ○ Colli Euganei Moscato
  Fior d'Arancio Passito '99 ΨΨ 5
- ○ Colli Euganei Chardonnay
  Montecchia '00 Ψ 4
- Godimondo Cabernet Franc '00 Ψ 4
- Colli Euganei Rosso '98 Ψ 3*
- Colli Euganei Merlot Bandiera '99 Ψ 4
- Colli Euganei Rosso
  Montecchia '97 ΨΨ 5
- Colli Euganei Merlot Bandiera '98 ΨΨ 4

SOAVE (VR)

CANTINA DEL CASTELLO
CORTE PITTORA, 5
37038 SOAVE (VR)
TEL. 0457680093
E-MAIL: cantinacastello@cantinacastello.it

In the heart of the delightful town of Soave, surrounded by medieval walls, is the Cantina del Castello, which has been run enthusiastically by Arturi and Silvana Stocchetti for the last 20 years. The vineyards extend all around Soave as far as the eye can see, carpeting the gentle hills. The Stocchettis make their Soaves on these hillsides, in a well-aspected position. The vineyards are cared for like gardens, particularly on the Pressoni and Carniga hills. The wines express the rugged but light character of the land. In the tastings for this edition of the Guide, we particularly enjoyed the Carniga, a slightly super-ripe blend of garganega and trebbiano. Its bright straw yellow is followed by clear, intense aromas of flowers and ripe fruit, then there is an interesting minerally note on the palate that gives length to the flavour. The grapes for the Soave Acini Soavi are picked when even riper. The brighter colour ushers in aromas of spices and candied fruit, and the nose gains depth and character from its faint hints of botrytis. On the palate, the wine is full-flavoured and mouthfilling, with a very interesting note of petrol and there is pleasantly bitterish dried fruit in the finish. The successful Acini Dolci, made from dried garganega grapes, belongs to the Classico zone but does not use the Recioto designation. Pleasant balsamic, buttery notes are reflected on the palate, where the creamy sweetness contrasts nicely with the light tannic structure.

SOAVE (VR)

CANTINA DI SOAVE
V.LE VITTORIA, 100
37038 SOAVE (VR)
TEL. 0456139811
E-MAIL: cantina@cantinasoave.it

Soave boasts one of the largest co-operative wineries in Italy which represents 1,200 members over a total of more than 3,500 hectares, spread over the most important DOC zones in the province of Verona. As you might imagine, the Cantina is a point of reference for the Soave area, and especially for the growth in quality of the area in general. The fact that it is possible to select the growers' grapes allows the winery to dedicate the best of the harvest to the Rocco Sveva line. Amongst other things, we should point out that the total surface area of vineyards is representative of all the production zones in the Verona area. Again this year, the most interesting wine is the Amarone, from the great '95 vintage, with fascinating mineral notes on the nose lifting the super-ripe red fruit and light hints of oak. On the palate, the wine opens up gradually into sumptuous sensations of roasted hazelnuts and chocolate. The Cabernet from the Garda DOC is also a success. The grassy, dried flower aromas are fairly intense and are reflected on the palate, where the wine reveals an evolved, fruit-rich, mouthfilling flavour. Of the Soaves in the top range, we preferred the standard-label version, with its clean, ripe fruit and flower aromas, for it is instantly attractive on the palate. The Castelcerino selection has more complex aromas while the palate remains light and freshly drinkable.

	Wine	Rating
○	Soave Cl. Sup. Monte Carniga '00	♀♀ 4
○	Soave Cl. Sup. Monte Pressoni '00	♀♀ 4
○	Acini Dolci '98	♀♀ 6
○	Soave Cl. Sup. Acini Soavi '99	♀♀ 5
○	Soave Cl. Sup. '00	♀ 4
○	Recioto di Soave Corte Pittora '99	♀ 6
○	Soave Cl. Sup. Acini Soavi '98	♀♀ 5
○	Soave Cl. Sup. Monte Pressoni '99	♀♀ 4

	Wine	Rating
●	Amarone della Valpolicella Rocca Sveva '95	♀♀ 6
○	Soave Cl. Castelcerino Rocca Sveva '00	♀ 3
○	Soave Cl. Rocca Sveva '00	♀ 3
●	Garda Cabernet Sauvignon Rocca Sveva '99	♀ 4
○	Recioto di Soave Cl. Rocca Sveva '99	♀ 5
●	Valpolicella Sup. Rocca Sveva '99	3
●	Amarone della Valpolicella Rocca Sveva '94	♀♀ 5

SOAVE (VR)

COFFELE
VIA ROMA, 5
37038 SOAVE (VR)
TEL. 0457680007
E-MAIL: coffele@mbservice.it

In the old town centre, in the shadow of the castle of Soave, the small winery owned by Giuseppe and Alberto Coffele steadily continues to improve, as it has done for the past few years. The Coffeles are not after a wine with exaggeratedly explosive impact. They want one that will win the drinker's heart with its elegance. The objective brought about the Ca' Visco selection which, as ever, presents flower and fruit aromas of apples, pears, and especially peaches, gradually mingling with nuances of herbs and almonds. The opening on the palate is stylish and almost austere, echoing the nose and gradually revealing its creamy elegance. The long finish has a pleasantly bitterish note. At last, the Alzari, an oak-aged Soave, is an unqualified success, demonstrating improvements in cellar technique at Coffele as well. Its combination of structure and evolved primary aromas is astonishingly lucid. The Recioto Le Sponde has enjoyed DOCG status since the '99 vintage and is always reliable. It is the only product the Coffele family grants a little exuberant immediacy. The nose has apple and grapeskin aromas that are anything but predictable, then the stylish palate, with its well-controlled sweetness, make it supple and pleasantly drinkable. The standard-label Soave and the Chardonnay are both interesting, the latter showing an interesting aromatic note in its uncomplicated, well-managed structure.

SOAVE (VR)

MONTE TONDO
LOC. MONTE TONDO
VIA S. LORENZO, 89
37038 SOAVE (VR)
TEL. 0457680347
E-MAIL: info@montetondo.it

If you arrive in Soave from the east, you will see the impressive cellar buildings of Gino Magnabosco's winery on the first hill in the zone. Blending well with the landscape, the buildings are emblematic of the area – land, vineyards and hard work. Gino is certainly not one to shy away from a challenge. He is aided in the running of his 30-hectare estate by his son Luca, and over the years has managed to find his own way, respecting first the grapes and then the wine. Gino stays with some traditional varieties almost out of affection but at the same time he uses all the most modern cellar techniques. As well as Luca, his wife Paola and elder daughter Stefania work in the commercial side of the winery, and Marta has yet to complete her oenology studies. The whole range of products is a success and the Soave Casette Foscarin is outstanding. It spends a short time in small wooden barrels and the aromas are mature and creamy. But it performs best on the palate, and the ripe peach and apricot fruit, flowers and light spicy notes are rapturously, elegantly intriguing. The standard-label Soave greets the nose with nice almond and peachskin notes. The palate is very pleasant, and the wine is also sold at a very moderate price. Monte Tondo's first red is also a success. The Cabernet Sauvignon Giunone is stylish, and the variety is immediately recognizable on the nose.

○ Soave Cl. Sup. Ca' Visco '00	🍷🍷	4
○ Recioto di Soave Cl. Le Sponde '99	🍷🍷	5
○ Soave Cl. Sup. Alzari '99	🍷🍷	4
○ Chardonnay Castrum Icerini '00	🍷	4
○ Soave Cl. Sup. '00	🍷	3*
○ Recioto di Soave Cl. Le Sponde '98	🍷🍷	5
○ Soave Cl. Sup. Ca' Visco '99	🍷🍷	4

○ Soave Cl. Sup. Vigneti in Casette Foscarin '00	🍷🍷	3*
○ Soave Cl. Sup. Monte Tondo '00	🍷🍷	3*
○ Soave Spumante Brut '00	🍷	3
● Cabernet Sauvignon Giunone '99	🍷	3
○ Chardonnay Le Cingelle '00		3
○ Soave Cl. Sup. Vigneti in Casette Foscarin '99	🍷🍷	4
○ Recioto di Soave '98	🍷	4

SOAVE (VR)

Leonildo Pieropan
Via Camuzzoni, 3
37038 Soave (VR)
tel. 0456190171
e-mail: info@pieropan.it

One respected colleague has defined him as the watchmaker of wine, and no definition could be more accurate for an artist like Nino Pieropan. The value of a watch is on the inside, in the countless tiny mechanisms that seem unimportant but actually form a work of art, keeping perfect time. Pieropan's wines are like that: perfect and quiet. Astonishingly, when tasted again years later, they have not lost a second, and bear witness to the qualities of a far-off harvest. Named Best White Wine of the Year in the last edition, the Soave La Rocca is again of a very high standard, and earns Three more Glasses. Straw yellow with green highlights, it has a strong mineral note on the nose, flecked with fresh flowers and spices. The palate has a solid impact, stylish and no-nonsense at the same time, and the fruit is rich and ripe, leading to an elegant finish. The steel-aged Calvarino, which benefits from the generous contribution of trebbiano di Soave grapes, has intense dried flowers and citrus aromas, while the peach fruit is enfolded in almond and gunflint. Strong and very long on the palate, it almost seems reluctant to leave the mouth. The inimitable standard-label version, sold at a very moderate price, is as ever one of the best of the type. Lovers of dried-grape wines will have to wait another year to taste Nino and Teresita's products.

	Wine	Glasses	Price
O	Soave Cl. Sup. La Rocca '99	♛♛♛	5
O	Soave Cl. Sup. Calvarino '00	♛♛	4
O	Soave Cl. Sup. '00	♛♛	3*
O	Passito della Rocca '93	♛♛♛	6
O	Passito della Rocca '95	♛♛♛	6
O	Soave Cl. Sup. Vigneto La Rocca '95	♛♛♛	4
O	Soave Cl. Sup. Vigneto La Rocca '96	♛♛♛	4
O	Soave Cl. Sup. Vigneto Calvarino '98	♛♛♛	4
O	Soave Cl. Sup. Vigneto La Rocca '98	♛♛♛	5
O	Passito della Rocca '97	♛♛	6

SOAVE (VR)

Suavia
Fraz. Fittà
Via Centro, 14
37038 Soave (VR)
tel. 0457675089
e-mail: suavia@libero.it

"Suavia" was the ancient name of the town of Soave. The choice of name underlines the Tessari family's links to this area. The common denominator in this winery is garganega, an extremely tricky and unfashionable variety, but undeniably authentic. The Tessari vineyards are situated at about 300 metres above sea level with good exposure that ensures the fruit will be delicate and wonderfully ripe. The quest for ripeness is crucial in the wines made by the Tessari sisters, who are willing to run risks to obtain the right level of concentration in the grapes. Moving on to the wines themselves, the standard-label Soave is good. Already enjoyable, it is pleasantly drinkable and enriched with a touch of mineral complexity that makes it anything but dull. The Monte Carbonare has great texture. This wine can be profound and is typically very concentrated. The interesting nose, with flowers, almonds and pears, is reflected on the smooth, ripe palate, which is supremely stylish. This year, the Le Rive selection, aged in wood, could not match the performance of the famous Three Glass '98 vintage. Slightly hazy notes on the nose prevent the complex fruity sensations from developing as we would expect from a wine of this density. The flavour is quite sweet, though, with candied fruit and peaches while the almonds in the finish are typical of garganega-based wines. To conclude, the vibrantly sophisticated and velvety Recioto is worth a Glass.

	Wine	Glasses	Price
O	Soave Cl. Sup. Monte Carbonare '00	♛♛	4
O	Soave Cl. Sup. Le Rive '99	♛♛	5
O	Soave Cl. Sup. '00	♛	3
O	Recioto di Soave Acinatium '99	♛	5
O	Soave Cl. Sup. Le Rive '98	♛♛♛	5
O	Soave Cl. Sup. Monte Carbonare '99	♛♛	4

SOMMACAMPAGNA (VR)

CAVALCHINA
FRAZ. CUSTOZA
LOC. CAVALCHINA
37066 SOMMACAMPAGNA (VR)
TEL. 045516002
E-MAIL: cavalchina@cavalchina.com

Luciano Piona divides his time between the two family wineries, one at Custoza, in the province of Verona, and the other on the Mantua side of the Garda DOC. Together, they total 80 hectares of vineyards. Since last year, the wines have all been made at Cavalchina, which is why the notes are in the Veneto section and not Lombardy. They are classic Garda bottles, from the fresh-tasting Bianco di Custoza to the rich, complex Garda Rosso. Faial, a Merlot from the Colli Mantovani, proves to be one of the most successful Veneto reds. The dark, concentrated colour presages sensationally expressive aromas. Super-ripe fruit is enfolded by aromatic herbs and mint while the severe mineral tone is smoothed by sweet spice. On the smooth, mouthfilling palate, there is a hint of the slightly dried grapes, and the consistency and gradual progression are memorable. The other major red comes from the same area. Falcone is a Cabernet Sauvignon that shows floral tones that develop with dried herbs and almonds. The smooth palate has a no-nonsense impact and the sweet tannins back up the nice ripe cherry sensations. The dried-grape wine, Le Pergole del Sole, is very interesting. It is from müller thurgau grapes whose naturally aromatic nature develops into candied fruit, mint and roasted hazelnuts. On the palate, the sweetness contrasts well with the fresh acidity and the aromatic notes are well-supported by the wine's buttery overtones.

SOMMACAMPAGNA (VR)

LE VIGNE DI SAN PIETRO
VIA S. PIETRO, 23
37066 SOMMACAMPAGNA (VR)
TEL. 045510016
E-MAIL: carlo@nerozzi.org

Carlo Nerozzi owns this beautiful winery on the gentle slopes separating Lake Garda from Verona, immersed in the lush countryside and surrounded by vineyards. His enthusiasm for viticulture is deeply bound up with his desire to protect and promote the area, increasing awareness of the whole territory, not just this winery. This is the magnificent backdrop against which Carlo has devoted years to the production of classic local wines, Bianco di Custoza and Bardolino, with very positive results. One example is the Sanpietro, the best Bianco di Custoza on the market. The ripe apple and pear aromas are interwoven with elegant floral notes and on the palate the wine is rounded, mature, sweet and intriguing like the hills it comes from. The Bardolino is generous, with warm, profound mineral notes. As well as traditional wines, Carlo makes a good Cabernet Sauvignon in a Veronese style. The grapes are lightly dried, making the aromas warm, profound and enfolding, and the fruit is ripe and pulpy, with a nicely expressive hint of leather. The palate is warm and rounded, and reflects the nose well with a long persistent finish. The Due Cuori is very good. A dried-grape wine from moscato grapes, it is light and dynamic. The fresh, floral overtones are complemented by the sweetness on the palate, finding convincing harmony.

● Garda Merlot Faial La Prendina '99 ♟♟	5*
● Garda Cabernet Sauvignon Vigneto Il Falcone La Prendina '99 ♟♟	5
○ Le Pergole del Sole Cavalchina '99 ♟♟	5
● Bardolino Sup. S. Lucia Cavalchina '00 ♟	3
○ Bianco di Custoza Amedeo Cavalchina '00 ♟	3
○ Bianco di Custoza Cavalchina '00 ♟	2*
● Garda Merlot Rondinella La Prendina '00 ♟	3
○ Garda Sauvignon Valbruna La Prendina '00 ♟	4
● Garda Merlot La Prendina '98 ♟	3

○ Due Cuori Passito '98 ♟♟	5
● Refolà Cabernet Sauvignon '98 ♟♟	6
○ Bianco di Custoza Sanpietro '99 ♟♟	4
● Bardolino '00 ♟	3
⊙ Bardolino Chiaretto '00 ♟	3
○ Bianco di Custoza '00 ♟	3
● I Balconi Rosso '98 ♟	4
○ Sud '95 ♟♟♟	6
● Refolà Cabernet Sauvignon '93 ♟♟	6
● Refolà Cabernet Sauvignon '94 ♟♟	6
● Refolà Cabernet Sauvignon '96 ♟♟	6
○ Due Cuori Passito '97 ♟♟	5
● Refolà Cabernet Sauvignon '97 ♟♟	6

SUSEGANA (TV)

Conte Collalto
Via XXIV Maggio, 1
31058 Susegana (TV)
Tel. 0438738241
E-mail: collalto@collalto.it

The vineyards and cellars belonging to this important Susenaga winery have been renovated, and the investment has created a premium quality range of products, as was clearly demonstrated at this year's tastings. The Cabernet Torrai '96 has a nice concentrated colour. The nose ranges from interesting mineral notes to black berry fruit and stylish floral hints. Elegant and balanced on the palate, it shows good consistency and a clean finish. The Wildbacher and the Incrocio Manzoni 2.15 are especially intriguing. The former displays good ripe fruit and is warm, mouthfilling and clean on the palate, which has good support from the smooth tannins. The Incrocio Manzoni 2.15 has a good heady impact with fascinating fruit and flower overtones, and a smooth, full flavour with clean mineral hints. The Piave Cabernet Riserva and the Torrai are only slightly inferior in quality. The Piave has clear flowers and liquorice alongside balsamic notes and a smallish, if well-made, palate. The Torrai has prevalent vegetal notes, with herbs like thyme and mint, as well as minerally hints and an uncomplicated, silkily generous palate. The Prosecco Extra Dry is again one of the winery's best products this year. The Colli di Conegliano Bianco is green-appley and acidic, with a smooth palate and a few aromatic notes. The Merlot Piave is pleasant and drinkable. The Incrocio Manzoni 6.0.13 and Chardonnay Piave both deserve a mention, like the Colli di Conegliano Rosso.

● Incrocio Manzoni 2.15 '00	♉♉	3*
● Wildbacher '00	♉♉	3*
○ P. di Conegliano Extra Dry	♉♉	3
○ Colli di Conegliano Bianco '00	♉	3
● Piave Merlot '00	♉	3
● Cabernet Podere Torrai '96	♉	4
● Piave Cabernet Ris. '96	♉	4
○ P. di Conegliano Brut San Salvatore	♉	3
○ Incrocio Manzoni 6.0.13 '00		3
● Colli di Conegliano Rosso '97		4
○ Colli di Conegliano Bianco '99	♉♉	3

TORREGLIA (PD)

Vignalta
Fraz. Luvigliano
Via dei Vescovi, 5
35038 Torreglia (PD)
Tel. 0499933105 - 0429777225
E-mail: mrlunghe@tin.it

The success of this winery, owned by Lucio Gomiero, Franco Zanovello and Graziano Cardin, is due to a large extent to the vineyard manager Filippo Gianone and cellarmanager Marco Montecchio, who put the advice of the consultant oenologist Francesco Polastri into practice. Head and shoulders above the rest again is the Gemola, a blend of mainly merlot with cabernet franc. An intense red, its huge potential is already clear from the colour. The generous bouquet of aromatic herbs and flowers is subtle and stylish, with mineral and scrubland notes. The palate, too, is rich, with plenty of extract and finesse. It's a particularly good bottle this year, and more stylish than in the past, so a resounding Three Glasses. The Alpianae, a dried-grape wine from moscato, is no less successful and the Moscato Secco Sirio, increasingly reminiscent of Alsace wines, keeps up the standard. The Agno Casto '00 is on the same wavelength, and can develop well as demonstrated by our retasting of the previous vintage. Vignalta's third Moscato, the Il Nero, also brought home Glasses. The Pinot Bianco, Chardonnay and Colli Euganei Rosso show consistently respectable results. The highly unusual red Agno Tinto shines among the new wines. It's a blend of petite syrah and California zinfandel with a good percentage of marzemino, all aged in American oak. The colour is intense and the aromas show black pepper, cocoa powder and berry fruit. On the palate, it is full-bodied and pleasantly drinkable.

● Colli Euganei Rosso Gemola '99	♉♉♉	6
● Agno Tinto '00	♉♉	5
○ Colli Euganei Pinot Bianco Agno Casto '00	♉♉	5
○ Sirio '00	♉♉	4
○ Colli Euganei Moscato Fior d'Arancio Alpianae '99	♉♉	5
● Il Nero '99	♉♉	6
○ Colli Euganei Pinot Bianco '00	♉	4
○ Colli Euganei Chardonnay '99	♉	5
● Colli Euganei Rosso '99	♉	4
● Colli Euganei Rosso Gemola '95	♉♉♉	6
● Colli Euganei Rosso Gemola '97	♉♉♉	6
● Colli Euganei Rosso Gemola '98	♉♉♉	6

VALDOBBIADENE (TV)

Desiderio Bisol & Figli
Fraz. Santo Stefano
Via Fol, 33
31049 Valdobbiadene (TV)
tel. 0423900138

In the hilly prosecco-growing zone between Conegliano and Valdobbiadene, it is easy to be deceived into thinking that good bottle fermentation and a little sugar can cover the flaws in the grapes left by often inadequate vineyard techniques. Gianluca Bisol does not make this error. In fact, his vines yield a rather lower quantity of grapes than is allowed by the DOC regulations. For a delicate, light variety like prosecco, low yields do not make particularly highly-structured wines but they do give enviably rich, concentrated aromas. That's why for years now, the Prosecco Molera has managed to beat off the competition. It proves that even a light wine from prosecco grapes can have bags of character and personality. In the excellent Fol Extra Dry, the ripe apple and flower aromas are well-reflected on the palate, where the good structure ensures no-nonsense drinkability. The Cartizze is even more mature, with warm, enfolding tones that contrast wonderfully with the fresh citrus and thyme notes. The interesting Talento Eliseo Bisol '97, with honey and ripe fruit aromas, has a spicy feel and a deliciously aromatic note on the palate. As ever, the Garnei is one of the most interesting Proseccos around. The ripeness of the grapes, and the progress made during bottle ageing, give it a complexity and richness that are rarely found in other wines from the area.

○ P. di Valdobbiadene Extra Dry Vigneti del Fol '00	🍷🍷	4
○ P. di Valdobbiadene Extra Dry Garnei '00	🍷🍷	4
○ Talento Brut Bisol '97	🍷🍷	5
○ Talento Cuvée del Fondatore Eliseo Bisol '97	🍷🍷	5
○ Cartizze	🍷🍷	5
○ P. di Valdobbiadene Brut Crede	🍷🍷	3
○ P. di Valdobbiadene Tranquillo Molera	🍷🍷	3
○ Talento Pas Dosé '97	🍷	5
○ P. di Valdobbiadene Dry Salis	🍷	3

VALDOBBIADENE (TV)

F.lli Bortolin Spumanti
Fraz. Santo Stefano
Via Menegazzi, 5
31040 Valdobbiadene (TV)
tel. 0423900135
e-mail: posta@bortolin.com

Talking to Valeriano Bortolin, you realize that he is a serious winemaker. He knows that attention to detail is crucial and that the exuberant nature of the prosecco variety must be indulged without using force. Valeriano tries to pass on these principles to his children, who are now involved in running the winery. Claudia has a degree in agricultural science but is mainly busy with the commercial side of the business. Andrea and Diego are both oenologists. This year's wines are all of a high standard. The Cartizze is tried and true. The intense nose has fresh green apple aromas, the sweetness on the palate is well balanced by the other components and the flavour is long. The two Extra Dry versions are especially interesting. The Prosecco Extra Dry has fascinating almond and apple aromas, then a generous progression on the palate, where there is a nice fresh note that makes it lightly and pleasantly drinkable. The Rù version is a nice straw yellow. Stylish flower and golden delicious apple notes on the nose are continued on the palate, which is pleasantly smooth and well supported by the prickle. One step lower, but still enjoyable, is the Prosecco Brut, with its full, sinuous spring flower and citrus aromas. The palate is smooth, full-bodied and mouthfilling. The Dry version is successful, with ripe tropical notes before the palate opens gradually and enjoyably. The Colli di Conegliano Bianco has ripe fruit on the nose, with a smooth mouthfilling palate lifted by sweet notes.

○ Cartizze	🍷🍷	4
○ P. di Valdobbiadene Extra Dry	🍷🍷	3*
○ Colli di Conegliano Bianco '00	🍷	3
○ P. di Valdobbiadene Brut	🍷	3
○ P. di Valdobbiadene Dry	🍷	3
○ P. di Valdobbiadene Extra Dry Rù	🍷	3

VALDOBBIADENE (TV)

Bortolomiol
Via Garibaldi, 142
31049 Valdobbiadene (TV)
tel. 0423975794

As it does every year, this large, traditional Valdobbiadene winery showed consistent quality through the whole product range. The charismatic Giuliano Bortolomiol presides over the winery, which is active in Italy and international markets with its attractive wines at competitive prices. This is one of the reasons why Bortolomiol has become an important benchmark for the whole Treviso spumante-making area. Today, Giuliano's daughters and son-in-law, Daniele Buso, work alongside him. Best of the wines tasted this year is the Prosecco in its smoothest version, the captivating Dry, with its aromas of fresh golden delicious apples and sugared almonds. On the palate, the firm prickle is satisfyingly well sustained. The Cartizze is also a success, with floury ripe apple and hazelnuts on the nose, and light hints of dried flowers. It expands nimbly and with good balance on the palate, reflecting the aromas of the nose. The Extra Dry version is fresher tasting, with zesty citrus and herb notes, then shows an invigorating palate. It's a clean, lively, dynamic wine and definitely drinkable. This year, the Selezione Banda Rossa is rather too simple, and although pleasant enough, does not achieve the complexity we have admired in previous vintages.

○ P. di Valdobbiadene Dry	🍷🍷	3*
○ Cartizze	🍷	5
○ P. di Valdobbiadene Extra Dry	🍷	3
○ P. di Valdobbiadene Extra Dry Sel. Banda Rossa	🍷	4
○ P. di Valdobbiadene Frizzante Il Ponteggio	🍷	3
○ P. di Valdobbiadene Brut		3
○ P. di Valdobbiadene Tranquillo		3
○ Ris. del Governatore Extra Brut		4

VALDOBBIADENE (TV)

Canevel Spumanti
Via Roccat e Ferrari, 17
31049 Valdobbiadene (TV)
tel. 0423975940
e-mail: canevel@tiscalinet.it

After a few rather unexciting years, probably due to the inevitable problems resulting from a recent change of location for the cellars, Canevel has made a successful comeback to the big league, finding the quality that has characterized its products in the past. Two of the wines were especially impressive, Il Millesimato Extra Dry and the standard-label Extra Dry. The former confirms its usual excellent quality and is also one of the best Proseccos tasted this year. Its most salient feature is elegance, which makes it hard to resist as it gracefully expresses a rich array of aromas, from floral notes to ripe tropical fruit, via intriguing mineral notes. The development on the palate is more supple thanks to a pleasantly tangy freshness, and the prickle is delicate, creamy and well integrated. The standard-label Extra Dry is just as good as the Millesimato, just a little less complex. There was a nice surprise from the Brut. Recent versions have not always lived up to the winery's reputation but in this edition, the palate develops enjoyably with no-nonsense acidity and nice fruit pulp. The Cartizze is drinkable and subtle but less impressive and, in particular, less assertive than the other spumantes.

○ P. di Valdobbiadene Extra Dry Il Millesimato '00	🍷🍷	4
○ P. di Valdobbiadene Extra Dry	🍷🍷	3*
○ Cartizze	🍷	4
○ P. di Valdobbiadene Brut	🍷	3
○ Colli di Conegliano Bianco '00		3
○ P. di Valdobbiadene Frizzante Vigneto S. Biagio		3

VALDOBBIADENE (TV)

Col Vetoraz
Fraz. Santo Stefano
Via Tresiese, 1
31049 Valdobbiadene (TV)
Tel. 0423975291

Col Vetoraz is situated in one of the best areas for growing prosecco and is among the leading local wineries for quality, which was demonstrated and confirmed by the bottles we uncorked this year. It is unusual for a Col Vetoraz wine not to come up to scratch. That is further confirmation of the skill of the cellar staff. The top wine, the Dry Millesimato, is one of the best Proseccos ever and has elegantly expressive aromas with mineral hints, and enjoyable, captivating thrust on the palate. Running over the list of wines tasted, we note that the Extra Dry stands out. It offered a similar performance to the Dry Millesimato with its appealing drinkability and fragrant green apple aromas. The Cartizze and the Brut come close to Two Glasses and affirm the overall quality of the range. The Cartizze has very subtle floral aromas and a rich, pulpy palate with well-controlled residual sugar. The Brut is one of the best Proseccos of this type and the elegant range of aromas, a trademark of all Col Vetoraz products, is reflected in the balanced flavour. The Tranquillo Tresiese is as good as previous editions, easily earning One Glass, which is no mean feat for the type.

○ P. di Valdobbiadene Dry Millesimato '00	¶¶	4
○ P. di Valdobbiadene Extra Dry	¶¶	3*
○ P. di Valdobbiadene Tranquillo Tresiese '00	¶	3
○ Cartizze	¶	5
○ P. di Valdobbiadene Brut	¶	3

VALDOBBIADENE (TV)

Le Colture
Fraz. Santo Stefano
Via Follo, 5
31040 Valdobbiadene (TV)
Tel. 0423900192
E-mail: info@lecolture.it

We have come to expect great things from Le Colture, owing both to the quality of the vineyards and the vinification techniques. Care in the field and a love of the land are deep-rooted in the Ruggeri family. In recent years, they have begun producing a Colli di Conegliano Rosso, indicating that they are not standing still. They are willing to throw themselves into new challenges on unusual and uncertain terrain for a Prosecco producer. This is another reason why brothers Cesare and Renato Ruggeri unfashionably, at least around here, prefer to personally supervise their 34 or so hectares, which are scattered around Valdobbiadene, Vidor, Solighetto and San Pietro di Feletto. The Prosecco Extra Dry has good structure, delicate fruity aromas and ripe apple notes leading in to a smooth, generous palate where interesting aromatic features to emerge. The Prosecco Dry Funer has bright colour and remarkably delicate bubbles. On the nose, the typical floral aromas are enriched by hints of ripe fruit. Smooth, rounded and long on the palate, it has nice fleshy pulp well to the fore. The Brut is pale straw yellow with elegant floral aromas and a fresh, smooth palate that reveals intriguing tropical hints. The Cartizze is as good as ever. The floral nose has typical almond notes that offset a tangy, ripe palate. The Prosecco Tranquillo is uncomplicated and a little elusive.

○ Cartizze	¶¶	4
○ P. di Valdobbiadene Dry Funer	¶¶	3*
○ P. di Valdobbiadene Extra Dry	¶¶	3*
○ P. di Valdobbiadene Brut	¶	3
○ P. di Valdobbiadene Tranquillo Masaré '00		3

VALDOBBIADENE (TV)

NINO FRANCO
VIA GARIBALDI, 147
31049 VALDOBBIADENE (TV)
TEL. 0423972051

Primo Franco is the latest scion of this thriving dynasty of Valdobbiadene producers and his wines demonstrate that Prosecco is not the simple drink it may seem. Primo's selections aim for a complex, individual style that creates in a product with plenty of character. Prosecco is an important variety in Italy's viticultural heritage and when sensitively interpreted, it can offer the structure that lifts its rich aromas without becoming predictable. Nino Franco shows that there are many ways of interpreting prosecco and that the variety can enable each approach to find full expression. The selections we tasted have a style of their own, which is not always convincing and sometimes led to discussions among members of the tasting panel. The best wines we sampled for this year's Guide were: the Cartizze, with fine creamy fizz, fruity aromas and a pleasant, full-flavoured palate; the remarkable Dry Primo Franco, also full-flavoured with plenty of character and steady, well-sustained aromas; the attractive new Brut Rive di San Floriano; and the uncomplicated but enjoyable standard-label Brut. The classic Nino Franco label, Rustico, always performs well.

○ Cartizze	🍷🍷	5
○ P. di Valdobbiadene Dry Primo Franco	🍷🍷	4
○ P. di Valdobbiadene Brut	🍷	4
○ P. di Valdobbiadene Brut Rive di S. Floriano	🍷	4
○ P. di Valdobbiadene Rustico		3

VALDOBBIADENE (TV)

ANGELO RUGGERI
FRAZ. SANTO STEFANO
VIA FOLLO, 18
31049 VALDOBBIADENE (TV)
TEL. 0423900235

Remigio and Vittore Ruggeri's winery is situated in the heart of Santo Stefano, one of the best parts of Valdobbiadene to grow grapes, and high quality is constant across the whole range of products. From this year, the Bellerive trademark is more clearly visible on the labels to prevent confusion with the products of the much bigger Ruggeri & C. winery. The wines that made the biggest impact this year were the also smoothest, bottles where the sugar enables the aromas to emerge with greater intensity and generosity, enhancing texture and creaminess on the palate. The Prosecco Funer makes an immediate impression with its uncompromising traditional apple and ripe pear aromas. Nice liquorice and fresh hazelnut notes appear on the palate. The fizz stays through to the very end, giving it length and creaminess. The Cartizze also maintains a fresh vitality. The apple is even crunchier and floral notes emerge with a hint of citrus. We were won over by the palate, with its attractive parade of sweet, delicately fresh, sensations leading to a clean, very enjoyable finish. Apple appears again in the Extra Dry version as the common denominator of all Angelo Ruggeri wines, along with a pleasant dry note of bitter almonds. Thanks partly to a very warm year that encouraged ripening, the simpler Brut version is well-typed but lacks sufficient acid backbone.

○ Cartizze	🍷🍷	4
○ P. di Valdobbiadene Dry Funer	🍷🍷	4
○ P. di Valdobbiadene Extra Dry	🍷	3
○ P. di Valdobbiadene Brut		3

VALDOBBIADENE (TV)

RUGGERI & C.
VIA PRÀ FONTANA
31049 VALDOBBIADENE (TV)
TEL. 0423975716
E-MAIL: ruggeri@ruggeri.it

Paolo Bisol felt that something was missing from the prestigious range of products presented every year, a label that would complete the winery and take it beyond sparkling wine. In other words, he desperately wanted to make a red. A few years ago, Ruggeri did make reds but this was probably dictated by market demand rather than planning. The idea returned with the creation of the Colli di Conegliano DOC and Paolo began to think seriously about this new wine, with characteristic meticulous care. In its debut version, the Sant'Alberto comes close to winning Two Glasses and is clearly a Colli di Conegliano with a future. The sweet super-ripe fruit and chocolate notes on the nose are nicely reflected on the palate, where they develop to enrich the wine with balsamic herb aromas. In the series of very good Proseccos it is the Santo Stefano and Giustino B. that stand out this year, as every year. The former is exuberant as ever, with inebriating tropical overtones of pineapple and jasmine. It enfolds the palate caressingly and the structure is anything but light. The Giustino B. is a traditionally stylish wine, with subtle aromas of spring flowers and apples melding with faint citrus notes that make it appealingly drinkable. It is more complex on the palate, where the prickle is very pleasant. The Brut version is dense and very complete, thanks to scrupulous selection of the grapes and good spumante technique.

O	P. di Valdobbiadene Extra Dry Giustino B. '00	▼▼	4
O	Cartizze	▼▼	4
O	P. di Valdobbiadene Brut	▼▼	3*
O	P. di Valdobbiadene Dry S. Stefano	▼▼	4
O	P. di Valdobbiadene Extra Dry Giall'Oro	▼▼	3*
O	P. di Valdobbiadene Tranquillo La Bastia '00	▼	3
●	Colli di Conegliano Rosso S. Alberto '97	▼	4
O	P. di Valdobbiadene Extra Dry Giustino B. '99	▽▽	4

VALDOBBIADENE (TV)

SANTA EUROSIA
FRAZ. SAN PIETRO DI BARBOZZA
VIA DELLA CIMA, 8
31049 VALDOBBIADENE (TV)
TEL. 0423973236

Giuseppe Geronazzo's passion for cellar work is not limited to technical skills. He knows how to assess and transform his raw materials, enhancing their best features and giving the wine his personal stamp. Giuseppe has particular regard for the delicate, complex process of vinification and devotes special attention to the second fermentation involved in all the winery's products. Total production for '00 is about 400,000 bottles, mainly obtained from grapes bought in from trusted growers. The most interesting wine is certainly the Prosecco Extra Dry, which plays on stylish tones and delicately floral aromas. It may not have huge structure but the palate is subtle, pleasant and aromatic with nicely integrated effervescence. The Cartizze is balanced with light aromas on the nose, opening gradually on the palate and well supported by the fizz. It closes on an elegant note of almonds. The Prosecco Brut is slightly penalized by the structure of the generous vintage but there are discernible dried flower notes. The palate is a smooth, mouthfilling caress of subtlety and style. The Prosecco Tranquillo is quite enjoyable. Tangy on the palate, it has interesting fruit in the finish.

O	Cartizze	▼▼	4
O	P. di Valdobbiadene Extra Dry	▼▼	3*
O	P. di Valdobbiadene Brut	▼	3
O	P. di Valdobbiadene Tranquillo	▼	3

VALDOBBIADENE (TV)

Tanorè
Loc. San Pietro di Barbozza
Via Mont di Cartizze, 1
31049 Valdobbiadene (TV)
tel. 0423975770
e-mail: tanore@tin.it

The winery belonging to brothers Renato and Sergio Follador clings to a hillside from where the view encompasses almost the whole Cartizze zone. The vineyards are in the most favourable growing areas, San Pietro di Barbozza, Santo Stefano and Guia, which are in effect Prosecco crus. However, small quantities of grapes are also purchased from trusted local growers. The meticulous work in both field and cellar throughout the year has enabled Tanorè wines to consolidate their position of absolute quality year after year. This time, the smoothest product on the list is also the best. It's the Prosecco Dry Selezione, which has intriguing, gentle floral aromas with a note of ripe peaches and apricots, then a minerally nuance. The entry on the palate is delicate and the mid palate opens gradually, revealing good consistency with the nose in its generous aromas. The effervescence keeps up the pace through to the long finish, which has an enticing note of bitter almonds. The excellent Extra Dry has an immediate, more traditional nose of apples and ripe pears, with a fresh citrus note. On the palate, the lower percentage of sugar shows off the wine's intriguing vitality. The Prosecco Tranquillo and the Cartizze confirm that reliability at Tanorè is a given.

○ P. di Valdobbiadene Extra Dry	▼▼	3*
○ P. di Valdobbiadene Dry Sel.	▼▼	4
○ Cartizze	▼	5
○ P. di Valdobbiadene Tranquillo	▼	3

VALEGGIO SUL MINCIO (VR)

Corte Gardoni
Loc. Gardoni, 5
37067 Valeggio sul Mincio (VR)
tel. 0457950382

Year after year, Gianni Piccoli demonstrates how this part of the Garda hinterland, along the river Mincio towards the hills of Mantua, can show the way to the area's winemakers, with a style poised between the traditional and the modern. Corte Gardoni's often astonishing Bardolino and Bianco di Custoza are generously fragrant and engagingly drinkable. This year, the Bardolino has the edge on the Custoza, which is pleasant but inferior to previous versions. The Bardolino Le Fontane is exemplary. Nicely floral aromas mingle with ripe, crunchy berry fruit on a dense, well-sustained palate. The Bardolino Superiore is clean and stylish, and could offer pointers for the new DOCG. The Chiaretto is good, with cherry colour, and should be drunk while young and fresh. The Garda DOC is represented by a Merlot Vallidium that shows pulp, although the wood still needs to meld with the fruit. The jewel in the winery's crown is again I Fenili, a white dessert wine of remarkable character from a late harvest of garganega and other varieties. The aromas are enhanced by well-controlled sweetness that tends towards minerality. The Rosso di Corte achieved a satisfactory level of quality. This Bordeaux blend pays the price for the less than memorable '98 vintage but is still enjoyable, thanks to balanced density. Outside the DOC umbrella, the Nichesole has joined the list of products. It's an old-style white whose grapes come from old trebbianello vines that have been recovered.

● Bardolino Le Fontane '00	▼▼	3*
○ I Fenili '97	▼▼	5
◉ Bardolino Chiaretto '00	▼	3
○ Nichesole Bianco '00	▼	3
● Garda Merlot Vallidium '98	▼	4
● Rosso di Corte '98	▼	5
● Bardolino Sup. '99	▼	3
○ Bianco di Custoza '00	▼	3
○ I Fenili '93	▼▼	5
○ I Fenili '96	▼▼	5
● Rosso di Corte '97	▼▼	5

VERONA

CANTINA SOCIALE DELLA VALPANTENA
FRAZ. QUINTO
VIA COLONIA ORFANI DI GUERRA, 5/B
37100 VERONA
TEL. 045550032
E-MAIL: cantinavalpantena@tin.it

The Cantina della Valpantena is situated in Valpolicella, on the strip of Verona hills that begins where the DOC zone ends and extends along Val Tramigna, almost to the mediaeval gates of Soave. Valpantena is the valley of Grezzana, where growers must compete for space with quarries. The stony terrain is highly suitable for viticulture and still has considerable potential to be exploited. The most striking wine is the Amarone '98, with its individual, no-nonsense personality. The herb aromas and super-ripe fruit peek through the folds of mineral and leather aromas. On the palate, it is more traditional. Broad and alcohol-rich, it shows clear, pulpy fruit with tobacco notes and a nice hint of raspberries. The two Valpolicella Valpantenas are very good. The Ritocco has strikingly explosive floral aromas on the nose, enriched with nuances of aromatic herbs and gooseberries. The palate echoes the nose nicely and rounds off elegantly. The Ripasso Falasaco is in a more traditional style and the aromas are warm and evolved. The palate is warm with alcohol and silky, displaying upfront tannins. The Amarone Falasco is fairly convincing but lacks a little definition while the uncomplicated, pleasantly drinkable '00 Valpantena has fresh fruit aromas.

● Amarone della Valpolicella '98	🍷🍷	6
● Valpantena Ripasso Falasco '99	🍷🍷	3*
● Valpantena Ritocco '99	🍷🍷	3*
● Valpantena '00	🍷	3
● Amarone della Valpolicella Falasco '97	🍷	6
● Cabernet Sauvignon '99	🍷	3

VERONA

CECILIA BERETTA
LOC. SAN FELICE EXTRA
VIA BELVEDERE, 135
37131 VERONA
TEL. 0458402111
E-MAIL: pasqua@pasqua.it

Ever since the winery was founded in the early 1980s, it has been a kind of laboratory for Pasqua, where technicians evaluate and design the future production of traditional Verona wines for the whole group. This flagship estate embraces several vineyards in Valpolicella and Soave, with an important property near Verona that forms the focus of winemaking research, in collaboration with the Agricultural Faculty of the University of Milan. The Amarone Terre di Cariano is one product of that research and reveals interesting herbal notes that offset the sweetness of super-ripe fruit. The complexity develops over vegetal and mineral tones, already striking a good balance between freshness and evolved notes. The palate is warm, with evident alcohol well-supported by extract and tannins, before the hint of bitter chocolate in the finish. The Valpolicella is also interesting. Its fragrant chocolate and coffee notes tend to prevail over the fruit but on the palate it is ripe fruit and pleasant mineral notes that have the upper hand. The intriguing Soave shows a more convincing blend of wood and ripe fruit. The Recioto di Soave has fresh ripe aromas that are reflected on the palate while the best feature of the red Mizzole, a blend of corvina and merlot, is its drinkability.

● Amarone della Valpolicella Cl. Terre di Cariano '97	🍷🍷	6
○ Soave Cl. Brognoligo '00	🍷	3
○ Recioto di Soave Case Vecie '97	🍷	5
● Valpolicella Cl. Sup. Terre di Cariano '97	🍷	4
● Mizzole Rosso '98	🍷	4

VERONA

GIACOMO MONTRESOR
VIA CA' DEI COZZI, 16
37124 VERONA
TEL. 045913399
E-MAIL: montresor@tin.it

The historic house of Montresor has extended its considerable stock of vines in recent years to reach 100 hectares, distributed over four properties, Cavalcaselle in Castelnuovo del Garda, La Mandorla and Corte Quaiara at San Giorgio in Salici near Sona, and Siresol at San Peretto near Negrar. The Negrar winery receives most of Montresor's attention. It is here that grapes are grown for the most prestigious wines, the crus and special selections. Strictly speaking, we should also mention the other two estates, one, Domenico de Bertiol, in the Prosecco DOC zone and Wallenburg at Trento. As we move on to the wines tasted for this edition of the Guide, we find the usual impressive line-up, all of good quality. This year, our favourite was the Amarone Capitel Crosara. The trademark Amarone elegance and power are clear from the nose, which has subtle herb and bottled fruit notes. The palate is lean and rounded, the body robust but not rugged, and the finish long. The Passito Terranatia from sauvignon and garganega grapes is good as ever, with citron aromas and a sweet, pleasantly balanced palate. The Cabernet Sauvignon Vigneto Campo Madonna and the Recioto Re Teodorico are both good. The range of whites confirms last year's good impression. The Sauvignon Sansaia, the Bianco di Custoza Monte Fiera, the Lugana and the Soave Classico are all worth One full Glass.

● Amarone della Valpolicella Cl. Capitel della Crosara '98	▼▼ 6
○ Terranatia Passito '99	▼▼ 5
○ Bianco di Custoza Vigneto Monte Fiera '00	▼ 4
○ Lugana '00	▼ 3
○ Sauvignon Sansaia '00	▼ 4
○ Soave Cl. Capitel Alto '00	▼ 2
● Cabernet Sauvignon Vigneto Campo Madonna '99	▼ 5
● Recioto della Valpolicella Re Teodorico '99	▼ 5
● Santomío Rosso '98	▼▼ 5
○ Terranatia Passito '98	▼▼ 5

VERONA

PASQUA VIGNETI E CANTINE
VIA BELVIGLIERI, 30
37131 VERONA
TEL. 0458402111
E-MAIL: pasqua@pasqua.it

As we said last year, the new direction taken by this large traditional Veronese winery is beginning to show its first fruits, with a steady improvement in quality throughout the range. Consultancies from leading Italian experts enable the cellar to keep pace with the times and new planting systems. Renewed attention to the vineyards, thanks to drastic action taken by the new technical staff, led by Giancarlo Zanel, is allowing the wines made in Carlo, Umberto and Giorgio Pasqua's cellars to show more personality. The Amarone Villa Borghetti is remarkable, and takes full advantage of the potential of a good vintage. The super-ripe aromas mingle with mint and thyme notes that are reflected on the warm, mouthfilling palate. The quality boost is even more apparent in the Morago, a Veronese-style Cabernet Sauvignon. On the nose, there are distinct notes of ripe wild berry fruit, especially strawberries and raspberries, with dense hints of chocolate. The entry on the palate is firm and generous, indicative of a young wine with good ageing prospects. Good news from the vineyards in Val d'Illasi, on the Sagramaso property, which presents a flavoursome Soave Superior and a "ripasso" Valpolicella, to which unpressed skins were added after fermentation, with typical super-ripe and mineral tones. The Valpolicella Superiore has flowery aromas and an agile palate. The best feature of the Casterna and Villa Borghetti Valpolicellas is that they are well-typed.

● Amarone della Valpolicella Cl. Villa Borghetti '97	▼▼ 6
● Morago Cabernet Sauvignon '98	▼▼ 6
○ Soave Cl. Vigneti di Montegrande '00	▼ 3
○ Soave Sup. Sagramoso '00	▼ 4
● Valpolicella Sup. Sagramoso Ripasso '97	▼ 4
● Valpolicella Sup. Sagramoso '98	▼ 4
● Valpolicella Cl. Sup. Vigneti di Casterna '98	4
● Valpolicella Cl. Villa Borghetti '98	4
● Morago Cabernet Sauvignon '97	▼▼ 5

VIDOR (TV)

Adami
Fraz. Colbertaldo
Via Rovede, 21
31020 Vidor (TV)
tel. 0423982110

Armando and Franco Adami's story is that of a family with close ties to the land. It's not easy land to cultivate, either, here in the hills around Valdobbiadene. On these steep sunny slopes, viticulture becomes almost an art form. Franco and Armando Adami's wines always astonish us when we arrive for the Guide tastings. Consistently good, they unfailingly express the characteristics of the vintage. In 2000, the harvest yielded whole, healthy grapes brought to exceptional levels of ripeness. However, it would be wrong to expect wines like those from the preceding vintage, where acidity played a decisive role. The Cartizze has pleasant dried flower and golden delicious apple aromas, and almond notes that enhance its sweet creaminess. Immediacy takes a back seat on the full, subtle palate, which expands unhurriedly, sweetly filling the mouth. As always, the Adami cru, Giardino, is one of the best dry Proseccos in the whole DOC zone. The fresh, acidic apple aromas are perfectly reflected on the palate, which is admirably balanced with pleasant fizz. The entire Adami range is made to a very high standard but the Extra Dry and ever reliable Brut are far above the rest.

VIDOR (TV)

De Faveri
Fraz. Bosco
Via Sartori, 21
31020 Vidor (TV)
tel. 0423987673
e-mail: defaverispumanti@libero.it

De Faveri wines are excellent year after year, so much so that they have become a benchmark for the zone. Confidently, and with great technical expertise, Lucio De Faveri produces wines that bring out the best qualities in the superb grapes he carefully selects from a number of small growers scattered all over the area. The Dry Selezione, in its now-traditional black bottle, is exemplary and remains the winery's leading product. The balance and finesse with which it handles the considerable residual sugar is admirable. Freshness is its strong suit and comes through on the nose in attractive vegetal and tart fruit notes. Best of the other products is the Brut Selezione, another classic from this winery. The typical green apple nuances trace the development of the aromas, then the palate displays striking personality, good structure and vibrant acidity that contrasts attractively with the sweetness. The Extra Dry has delicate aromatic notes, ranging from almond nuances to acacia blossom, and the palate is remarkably fresh. The Frizzante is upfront and uncomplicated. Finally, the standard-label Brut is well-typed and worth a mention.

O P. di Valdobbiadene Dry Giardino '00	ŸŸ	4
O Cartizze	ŸŸ	5
O P. di Valdobbiadene Brut Bosco di Gica	ŸŸ	4
O P. di Valdobbiadene Extra Dry dei Casel	ŸŸ	4
O Incrocio Manzoni 6.0.13 Le Portelle '00	Ÿ	4
O P. di Valdobbiadene Tranquillo Giardino '00	Ÿ	4
O Spumante Brut Riserva Waldaz	Ÿ	4

O P. di Valdobbiadene Dry Sel.	ŸŸ	4
O P. di Valdobbiadene Brut Sel.	Ÿ	4
O P. di Valdobbiadene Extra Dry	Ÿ	3
O P. Frizzante Colli Trevigiani Sel. Spago	Ÿ	3
O P. di Valdobbiadene Brut		3

VIDOR (TV)

Sorelle Bronca
Fraz. Colbertaldo
Via Martiri, 20
31020 Vidor (TV)
tel. 0423987201

After years of sacrifice, during which the excellent grapes had to take their chances in a cellar that made up for its lack of technology and space with sheer hard work, Ersiliana, Antonella and Piero at last have a new cellar where the fruit get the treatment it deserves. To tell the truth, production is not enormous but it is divided into various wine types, each requiring a different approach. This means specific areas and techniques have to be available for each wine. Laudable vineyard management, respect for the hills and Piero's determination have produced an unusual Colli di Conegliano Rosso. Herb and flower aromas herald a wonderful palate where mineral and floral notes expand, with stylish tannins keeping the warmth of the ripe fruit under control and firming the wine. The same firmness is to be found in the Bianco. Despite the agile, dynamic style, with tropical fruit and unobtrusive fragrance, the palate is very interesting, with lots of finesse. The Delico is also good. It's an intriguing Prosecco Tranquillo with fresh, immediate fruit, like the mainly cabernet-based red Ardesco, which is clean and appealing on the nose, with good fruit and pleasant mineral notes on the palate.

○ Colli di Conegliano Bianco Ser Bele '00	▣▣	4
● Colli di Conegliano Rosso Ser Bele '98	▣▣	5
● Piave Cabernet Ardesco '99	▣	4
○ Livio Bronca Brut	▣	4
○ P. di Valdobbiadene Delico	▣	3*
○ P. di Valdobbiadene Extra Dry	▣	3*
● Colli di Conegliano Rosso Ser Bele '97	▣▣	5

VILLAGA (VI)

Piovene Porto Godi
Fraz. Toara
Via Villa, 14
36020 Villaga (VI)
tel. 0444885142
e-mail: tpiovene@protec.it

Tommaso Piovene and oenologist Flavio Prà have rationalized their vineyards in order to guarantee first class grapes. As we await the new products still in the cellars, which we will be reviewing next year, we note the progress of the whites, especially the Campigie selection. This late-harvested Sauvignon undergoes oak fermentation and has body and strength. Now, at last it has gained finesse, too. The wood mingles well with the peach and almond nuances, and is enhanced by good mineral notes, while the smooth entry in the mouth is sustained in mid palate by tangy sensations. The other Sauvignon, the Vigneto Fostine, has aromas of flowers and is very smooth on the palate while the Pinot Bianco offers the nose dried summer flowers, peaches and almonds, which return in the warm, appealing finish. The standard Tocai Rosso is arguably the best ever version from this winery and the finest from the Colli Berici DOC this year. It is pleasant and complex with significant texture that comes from 100 year old vines. The uncomplicated Merlot Fra i Boli is minerally and fruit-rich, as well as outstandingly clean and drinkable. The Cabernet Polviera is still very young, showing vegetal and green pepper notes on the nose. It is a little hard on the palate and fairly tannic. Lastly, the most successful of the reds is the Cabernet Pozzare, with its varietal cassis, pencil lead and tobacco aromas on a floral and mineral background. The palate is peppery, sophisticated and well-sustained, with a long aromatic finish.

○ Sauvignon Campigie '00	▣▣	4
● Colli Berici Cabernet Vigneto Pozzare '99	▣▣	4
● Colli Berici Cabernet Polveriera '00	▣	3*
○ Colli Berici Pinot Bianco Polveriera '00	▣	3*
○ Colli Berici Sauvignon Vigneto Fostine '00	▣	3*
● Colli Berici Tocai Rosso Vigneto Riveselle '00	▣	3*
● Colli Berici Merlot Fra i Broli '99	▣	4
● Colli Berici Cabernet Vigneto Pozzare '97	▣▣	4
● Colli Berici Merlot Fra i Broli '98	▣▣	4

OTHER WINERIES

Paladin & Paladin
Via Postumia, 12
30020 Annone Veneto (VE)
Tel. 0422768167
E-mail: paladin@paladin.it

Wine-grower Roberto Paladin divides production with scrupulous care between the line bearing his name and another made with organically-grown grapes, Bosco del Merlo. The Vigna degli Aceri is spicy, the 360 Ruber Capitae is complex and the Vineargenti is enjoyable.

●	Rosso Vineargenti Bosco del Merlo '97	5
●	Malbech Vigna degli Aceri Paladin '98	4
●	360 Ruber Capitae Rosso Bosco del Merlo '98	5

Dominio di Bagnoli
P.zza Marconi, 63
35023 Bagnoli di Sopra (PD)
Tel. 0495380008
E-mail: info@ildominiodibagnoli.it

The two Bagnoli Bianco singled out from one of the most recent DOCs in Italy stand out for their rich flavours. The S. Andrea has a higher percentage of sauvignon grapes and is fresh and no-nonsense, while the chewier, sweet Santissima Trinità has peach aromas.

○	Bagnoli Bianco S. Andrea '00	3
○	Bagnoli Bianco Santissima Trinità '00	3

Lenotti
Via S. Cristina, 1
37011 Bardolino (VR)
Tel. 0457210484
E-mail: info@lenotti.com

This Bardolino winery has always expressed the winemaking traditions of the Garda area well. The Soave Capocolle is good, with intense, ripe tropical fruit aromas, and surprisingly powerful on the palate. The Valpolicella Le Crosare has sweet, ripe aromas while the Bardolino is fresh-tasting and very drinkable.

●	Bardolino Cl. '00	2*
○	Soave Cl. Sup. Capocolle '00	2*
●	Valpolicella Cl. Sup. Le Crosare '98	3

Tinazzi Eugenio & Figli
Via Polichia
37010 Cavaion Veronese (VR)
Tel. 0457235394

The Tinazzi winery is situated in Cavaion Veronese and is the leader of the Tenuta Vallesele and Cà Isidora group of brand names, among the main Veronese designations. From the classic Bardolino to the firmly-structured, potent Amaroni della Valpolicella, not to mention the international varieties like Chardonnay.

●	Amarone della Valpolicella Cl. La Bastia '97	6
○	Chardonnay Arnasi Vallesele '99	4
○	Sauvignon Seregni Vallesele '98	4

Fasoli
Fraz. San Zeno - Via Battisti, 47
37030 Colognola ai Colli (VR)
tel. 0457650741
e-mail: fasoli.gino@mercurio.it

Amadio and Natalino Fasoli continue to run the business started by their father Gino, and since 1984 all the vineyards have been organically farmed. The wines are all well-made; outstanding are the excellent Soave Pieve Vecchia, the well-structured Merlot Orgno, and a pleasant basic Soave.

○	Soave Cl. Sup. Pieve Cecchia '99	♀♀	5
○	Soave Sup. '00	♀	2*
●	Merlot Orgno '99	♀	6

Carpenè Malvolti
Via Antonio Carpenè, 1
31015 Conegliano (TV)
tel. 0438364611
e-mail: carpene@pn.itnet.it

This traditional winery in Conegliano makes wines that are widely available throughout Italy. The Prosecco Dry Cuvée Oro is rich on the palate with very enjoyable aromatic hints and nice ripeness. The Extra Dry is no-nonsense and fragrant, and the Brut is fresh-tasting.

○	P. di Conegliano Dry Cuvée Oro	♀	4
○	P. di Conegliano Extra Dry	♀	3
○	P. di Conegliano Cuvée Brut		3

Scuola Enologica di Conegliano
G. B. Cerletti
Via XXVIII Aprile, 20
31015 Conegliano (TV)
tel. 043861421

After years of inactivity the Scuola Enologica di Conegliano has started bottling its own wines again. The Prosecco Extra Dry is good, the Colli Bianco is fresh and tangy, and the Incrocio Manzoni is pleasantly and intensely fragrant.

○	P. di Conegliano Extra Dry Millesimato '00	♀♀	2*
○	Colli di Conegliano Bianco '00	♀	2
○	Incrocio Manzoni 6.0.13 '00	♀	2

Merotto
Fraz. Col S. Martino
31010 Farra di Soligo (TV)
tel. 0438898195
e-mail: merottosnc@tin.it

Graziano Merotto is passionately attached to this land and makes 500,000 bottles of good wine per year from his grapes. The smoother Prosecco selections are good, the Colle Molina is floral and delicate and the riper, mouthfilling La Primavera di Barbara is good.

○	P. di Valdobbiadene Dry Colle Molina	♀♀	3*
○	P. di Valdobbiadene Dry La Primavera di Barbara	♀	4
○	P. di Valdobbiadene Extra Dry	♀	2

Santo Stefano
Via Cadorna, 92
30020 Fossalta di Piave (VE)
tel. 042167502
e-mail: santostefano@ronchiato.it

The De Stefani family make typical wines from this area, and show a particular aptitude for white wines, like the Chardonnay Terre Nobili. The Pinot Grigio is enjoyable and the Cabernet Terre Nobili promises to grow well.

○	Piave Chardonnay Terre Nobili '00	♀	3
○	Piave Pinot Grigio '00	♀	3
●	Piave Cabernet Terre Nobili '98		4

Santa Margherita
Via Ita Marzotto, 8
30025 Fossalta di Portogruaro (VE)
tel. 0421246111

The large Fossalta winery has worked for years to produce wines that combine competitive prices with accessibility. The Laudato di Malbech is widely available and shows good integration of fruit and oak wood. The Luna dei Feldi is vibrant and the Chardonnay Ca' d'Archi has good length

○	Luna dei Feldi '00	♀	4
●	Laudato di Malbech '97		4
○	A. A. Chardonnay Ca' d'Archi '99	♀	5

Corteforte
Via Osan, 45
37022 Fumane (VR)
Tel. 0456839104 - 0458388245
E-mail: studiocerruti@tin.it

This splendid winery is situated in the centre of a courtyard and has made wines since 1993 with distinctive care and attention. The Amandorlato is prestigious, rich and ripe. The Amarone is very good, and has nuances of aromatic herbs and flowers. The Passito Bianco is complex.

●	Recioto della Valpolicella Amandorlato '94 ▼▼	5
●	Amarone della Valpolicella Cl. '95 ▼	6
○	Passito Bianco Il Sole di Corteforte '97 ▼	5

I Scriani
Via Ponte Scrivan, 7
37022 Fumane (VR)
Tel. 0456839251 - 0456839093

Brothers Stefano and Paolo Cottini are young, promising wine growers. The Amarone is excellent: the super-ripe fruit and minerally hints blend well on the palate. The Recioto, the balanced Valpolicella Superiore and the vintage Valpolicella with its immediate appeal, are all interesting wines.

●	Amarone della Valpolicella Cl. '97 ▼▼	6
●	Valpolicella Cl. '00 ▼	2*
●	Recioto della Valpolicella Cl. '98 ▼	4
●	Valpolicella Cl. Sup. '98 ▼	3

Le Bertarole
Via Bertarole, 8/A
37022 Fumane (VR)
Tel. 0456839220

A deep Amarone with notes of chocolate and spice, and sweet, super-ripe fruit; on the palate this wine's exuberant liveliness is held in check by the structured tannin. This Amarone is followed by an intense Valpolicella Superiore and a traditionally-made Valpolicella Classico.

●	Amarone della Valpolicella Cl. '97 ▼▼	6
●	Valpolicella Cl. Sup. Le Portarine '98 ▼	4
●	Valpolicella Cl. '99	3

Lamberti
Via Gardesana
37017 Lazise (VR)
Tel. 0457580034
E-mail: giv@giv.it

This large winery guarantees typical quality products from the Garda area. The Bardolino Santepietre has fruity, floral aromas; the classy balanced palate makes it an excellent companion for typical local cuisine. The Soave Santepietre is fragrant and intense, and the Custoza Orchidea Platino is highly drinkable.

●	Bardolino Cl. Santepietre '00 ▼	2*
○	Bianco di Custoza Orchidea Platino '00 ▼	3
○	Soave Cl. Santepietre '00 ▼	2*

Basso Graziano
Via Casoni, 1
36023 Longare (VI)
Tel. 0444555114
E-mail: gbvini@libero.it

Graziano Basso's little winery makes wines that express the features of the local area, the Colli Berici, very well. One example of this is the Tocai Rosso, which is both fresh-tasting and dense in texture. The Garganego is fresh and harmonious and the young Cabernet is nicely drinkable.

●	Colli Berici Cabernet '00 ▼	3
●	Colli Berici Tocai Rosso '00 ▼	3
○	Garganego '00 ▼	2

Natalino Mattiello
Fraz. Costozza
Via Volto, 57
36023 Longare (VI)
Tel. 0444555258

Natalino Mattiello's wines are subdivided into a basic line and the Colle d'Elica line. The latter includes a Cabernet with good balance and clean aromas, and a fresh Chardonnay with strong aromatic overtones. The basic Garganega is well-managed.

○	Colli Berici Chardonnay Colle d'Elica '00 ▼	3
●	Colli Berici Cabernet Colle d'Elica '99 ▼	3
○	Colli Berici Garganega '00	2

San Rustico
Fraz. Valgatara - Via Pozzo, 2
37020 Marano di Valpolicella (VR)
Tel. 0457703348
E-mail: info@sanrustico.it

Luigi and Danilo Campagnola have been making wines from their vineyards in Valpolicella for many years. The Amarone Il Gaso has interesting, mature overtones. The Amarone '97 is fresher and the fruit expresses considerable sweetness. The Valpolicella is very pleasant.

● Valpolicella Cl. '00	🍷	3
● Amarone della Valpolicella Cl. Vigneti del Gaso '96	🍷	6
● Amarone della Valpolicella Cl. '97	🍷	6

Le Albare
Via Pergola, 69
37030 Montecchia di Crosara (VR)
Tel. 0456175131

Posenato's wines express the "suave" nature of their land of origin, with ripeness and above all, harmony. The Soave Vigna dello Stefano is sweetly mouthfilling with a pleasant bitter almond finish. The Recioto has interesting minerally nuances.

○ Recioto di Soave Vigna dello Stefano '97	🍷	5
○ Soave Cl. Sup. Vigna dello Stefano '99	🍷	3

Casa Vinicola Sartori
Via Casette, 2
37024 Negrar (VR)
Tel. 0456028011
E-mail: sartori@areacom.it

This large Negrar winery produces about 190 million bottles per year, and over a million of these are of superior quality. The Soave Vigneti di Sella has honey aromas and a hint of botrytis to open up the olfactory range; it is harmonious on the palate. The Bardolino and Recioto are both pleasant.

● Bardolino Cl. '00	🍷	3
○ Soave Cl. Sup. Vigneti di Sella '00	🍷	3
● Recioto della Valpolicella Cl. '99	🍷	6

Fraccaroli
Via Berra Vecchia, 4
37019 Peschiera del Garda (VR)
Tel. 0457550949
E-mail: info@fraccarolivini.it

The Fraccaroli brothers' winery makes traditional wines from the Garda area, with a particular preference for Lugana. The Vegne Vecie is full and pulpy, expressing its maturity with warm, mouthfilling sensations. The Vigneto Pansere is fruitier and fresh, and nicely vigorous on the palate. The Vigna Campo Serà is well-made.

○ Lugana Vigneto Pansere '00	🍷	3*
○ Lugana Vegne Vecie '99	🍷	5
○ Lugana Vigna Campo Serà '99		3

Tezza
Via Maioli, 4
37030 Poiano (VR)
Tel. 045550267
E-mail: vinitezza@tiscalinet.it

In the early Nineties the Tezza cousins took over from their parents and gave the winery a new impetus. The two Valpantenas are good: the Superiore is lovely and pulpy, with ripe fruit hints, while the '99 has aromatic herbs in the nose, and in nicely tangy on the palate.

● Valpolicella Valpantena Sup. Monte delle Fontane '97	🍷	4
● Valpolicella Valpantena '99	🍷	3

Case Bianche
Via Chisini, 79
31053 Pieve di Soligo (TV)
Tel. 0438841608

This splendid estate in Felettano has been owned for several years by Martino Zanetti, a well-known entrepreneur in the food sector. The Prosecco Extra Dry has nice, ripe, full aromatic nuances, the Merlot is enjoyable and the Colli di Conegliano Bianco is well-made.

● Merlot '99	🍷	3
○ P. di Conegliano Extra Dry	🍷	3
○ Colli di Conegliano Bianco Costa dei Falchi '00		3

Marion
Loc. Marcellise
Via Borgo, 1
37036 San Martino Buon Albergo (VR)
Tel. 0458740021

The Campedelli family have made an important decision this year which will have a positive effect on the whole production. The wines were not presented for tasting because they were not considered ready. This demonstrates the care taken over the important maturing stage of the wines.

● Cabernet Sauvignon del Veneto '97	ŶŶ	5
● Valpolicella Sup. '97	ŶŶ	5

Buglioni
Fraz. Corrubbio
Via Campagnola, 55
37029 San Pietro in Cariano (VR)
Tel. 0456760676

Alfredo Buglioni makes traditional wines from the Garda area. The Bardolino is well-structured with ripe fruit, while the Chiaretto has nicely fresh aromas. A Valpolicella and an Amarone are still maturing in the cellar, and will be on the market in the next few years.

● Bardolino '00	Ŷ	3
⊙ Bardolino Chiaretto '00	Ŷ	3

Giuseppe Fornaser
Fraz. Bure
Via Bure Alto, 1
37029 San Pietro in Cariano (VR)
Tel. 0457701651

The Fornaser family work their vineyards with great passion, and obtain grapes of a high quality. The Amarone Monte Faustino is a traditionally-styled wine. The Passito has well-controlled sweetness and is a good dessert wine.

● Amarone della Valpolicella Cl. Monte Faustino '97	ŶŶ	6
○ Passito Bianco Bure Alto '98	Ŷ	6

Guido Manara
Fraz. San Floriano
Via Don Cesare Biasi, 53
37020 San Pietro in Cariano (VR)
Tel. 0457701086

The change in generations has given this small winery's production a bit more impetus. The Valpolicella Superiore is good, and its international blend makes it fresh. The Amarone is richly extracted and dense in texture, with a nice minerally pencil sensation.

● Amarone della Valpolicella Cl. Costera '97	ŶŶ	6
● Valpolicella Cl. Sup. Le Morete '99	Ŷ	4

Casa Roma
Via Ormelle, 15
31020 San Polo di Piave (TV)
Tel. 0422855339

Gigi Peruzzetto believes in the raboso variety and is trying very hard to make a wine with good character. The Raboso '97 is minerally and generous in the nose, and has a pleasant flavour which manages to balance acidity and full body. The Incrocio Manzoni, ripe and pulpy and the sturdy Merlot, are both good.

○ Incrocio Manzoni 6.0.13 '00	Ŷ	3
● Piave Merlot '00	Ŷ	3
● Piave Raboso '97	Ŷ	4

Aleardo Ferrari
Fraz. Gargagnago
Via Giare, 15
37020 Sant'Ambrogio di Valpolicella (VR)
Tel. 0457701379

The ongoing renewal work in the vineyards, which started a few years ago, has inhibited production of the winery's full range. However the Valpolicella Corte Aleardi is good, with nice delicate dried flower and aromatic herb aromas. The Recioto is good, immediately accessible.

● Valpolicella Cl. Sup. Corte Aleardi '98	Ŷ	4
● Recioto della Valpolicella Cl. '99	Ŷ	5

Cooperativa Ottomarzo
Loc. Ca' Verde
37020 Sant'Ambrogio di Valpolicella (VR)
Tel. 0456861760

Ottomarzo has been making typical Valpolicella wines with organic methods for many years. The Amarone has traditional dried flower, tobacco and crushed fruit aromas, and is warm and mouthfilling on the palate. The Valpolicella Grola is fresh and makes a good impact.

● Amarone della Valpolicella Cl. Gnirega '98	🍷🍷	6
● Valpolicella Cl. Sup. Grola '99	🍷	3*

Mosole
Fraz. Corbollone
30029 Santo Stino di Livenza (VE)
Tel. 0421310404
E-mail: mosole@mosole.com

Lucio Mosole's winery is within the Lison-Pramaggiore DOC. The Merlot Ad Nonam is mature and pulpy. The Chardonnay is enjoyably fresh and tangy, but also rich in floral nuances and has a pleasant, persistent and drinkable character.

○ Lison-Pramaggiore Chardonnay '00	🍷	3
● Lison-Pramaggiore Merlot ad Nonam '99	🍷	5

Balestri Valda
Via Monti, 44
37038 Soave (VR)
Tel. 0457675393
E-mail: balestri.valda@tin.it

Guido Rizzotto runs one of the newer wineries that are emerging in the Soave area. His Soave has warm, mature tones, and the Lunalonga selection is more highly concentrated on the nose and on the palate. From next year a new Recioto will also be on sale.

○ Soave Cl. '00	🍷	3
○ Soave Cl. Lunalonga '00	🍷	3

Bisson
Via Bisson, 17
37038 Soave (VR)
Tel. 0457680775
E-mail: vinibisson@tin.it

Lino Battocchia's winery makes forthright, accessible and distinctly pleasant Soaves from the eight hectares of vineyards. The Soave Bisson is aromatic and spicy with a good appearance. The simpler Bissoncello and Classico Superiore are frank and drinkable.

○ Soave Bisson '00	🍷	2*
○ Soave Bissoncello '00	🍷	2*
○ Soave Cl. Sup. '00	🍷	2*

Tamellini
Via Tamellini, 4
37038 Soave (VR)
Tel. 0457675328

Gaetano and Pio Francesco Tamellini have run this winery in Soave for many years, but the real work towards quality only began in 1998. The Soave Le Bine is big and generous on the nose, and well-structured on the palate. The vintage Soave is pleasantly fresh. The Anguane is well-made.

○ Soave Sup. '00	🍷	3
○ Soave Cl. Sup. Le Bine '99	🍷	3
○ Soave Cl. Sup. Anguane '99		3

Albino Piona
Fraz. Custoza
Via Bellavista, 48
37060 Sommacampagna (VR)
Tel. 045516055

Albina Piona's winery is situated on the hills approaching Lake Garda. The winery makes the traditional local wines, mainly Bianco di Custoza and Bardolino. We also recommend the monovarietal Corvina, which is richly extracted, the enjoyable Bianco di Custoza and the fresh, floral Bardolino.

● Bardolino '00	🍷	3
○ Bianco di Custoza '00	🍷	2*
● Azobé Corvina Vigneto delle Pergole '98	🍷	3

Zamuner
Via Valecchia, 40
37060 Sona (VR)
Tel. 0458342168 - 0456081090
E-mail: info@zamuner.it

Daniele Zamuner divides his production between still and sparkling wine. The Demi Sec has complex aromas with a strong mineral overtone. The excellent nose-palate consistency is completed by stylish, elegant prickle. The Brut is full-bodied with a good impact and the Rosso Valecchia is highly expressive.

○ Spumante Demi Sec '93	♀	5
○ Spumante Brut	♀	5
● Rosso Valecchia Cabernet Sauvignon Merlot '98		5

La Primavera
Loc. Villa
Via Gazza, 29
35037 Teolo (PD)
Tel. 0499901332

La Primavera is the brand-name of Giuseppe Beccaro's winery, and has been joined by the more prestigious line bearing his name. We singled out the good Pinot Bianco, pleasant and well-structured, and especially the white blend Terre Bianche. Don't miss this wine, which deserves two glasses.

○ Colli Euganei Bianco Terre Bianche Beccaro Giuseppe '99	♀♀	4
○ Colli Euganei Pinot Bianco La Primavera '00	♀	3*

Cantina Produttori di Valdobbiadene
Via per San Giovanni, 65
31030 Valdobbiadene (TV)
Tel. 0423982070
E-mail: valdoca@valdoca.com

Cantina Produttori di Valdobbiadene plays an important role in the Valdobbiadene area. Production is divided between a basic line and the Val d'Oca. From the latter, we recommend the fragrant, full Prosecco Extra Dry Millesanto and the Prosecco Tranquillo, with intense floral and apple and pear nuances.

○ P. di Valdobbiadene Extra Dry Millesimato Val d'Oca '00	♀	4
○ P. di Valdobbiadene Tranquillo Minù Val d'Oca	♀	3

Ciodet
Via Piva, 104
31049 Valdobbiadene (TV)
Tel. 0423973131

Ciodet is a small winery situated opposite Villa dei Cedri in Valdobbiadene, and mainly works with purchased grapes. Great care taken during vinification allows the wines a good level of expression, as demonstrated by the mouthfilling Cartizze, the dynamic Brut and the pleasantly drinkable Extra Dry.

○ Cartizze	♀♀	4
○ P. di Valdobbiadene Brut	♀	3
○ P. di Valdobbiadene Extra Dry	♀	3

Dea - Rivalta
Via Garibaldi, 309/a
31049 Valdobbiadene (TV)
Tel. 0423971017
E-mail: deariva@tin.it

Rivalta is an emerging winery on the Valdobbiadene winemaking scene, and stands out for the care put into the whole range of wines. The Prosecco Extra Dry has a delicate bouquet with floral and pear aromas; it is creamy and stylish on the palate. The Tranquillo expresses tropical fruit and is very enjoyable.

○ P. di Valdobbiadene Extra Dry	♀♀	3*
○ P. di Valdobbiadene Tranquillo	♀	3

Paolo Zucchetto
Via Cima, 16
31040 Valdobbiadene (TV)
Tel. 0423972311

This small winery produces carefully-made wines from its own vineyards. The Cartizze has floral aromas perfectly backed up by the sweetness on the palate. The best feature of the Brut is its elegance while the Extra Dry has nice citrus overtones.

○ Cartizze	♀♀	5
○ P. di Valdobbiadene Brut	♀	3
○ P. di Valdobbiadene Extra Dry	♀	3

Corte Marzago
Loc. Le Bugne
37067 Valeggio sul Mincio (VR)
Tel. 0457945104
E-mail: info@cortemarzago.com

This winery stands on the moraine hills at the south-east edge of Lake Garda. The Passito Bianco Le Melghette has intense ripe fruit aromas with nice hints of botrytis. The Bardolino Chiaretto is forthright and tasty.

◎	Bardolino Chiaretto Vigna Le Ceresare '00	3
○	Passito Bianco Le Melghette '99	4

Giorgio Cecchetto
Fraz. Tezzeri Piave
Via Piave, 67
31020 Vazzola (TV)
Tel. 043828598

Giorgio Cecchetto devotes passion and care to the production of Piave wines, Raboso in particular. The Cabernet Sauvignon has simple aromas and a harmony on the palate that brings out the best of its expressive capacity. The Raboso still has room for improvement, and the Sauvignon is fresh with immediate impact.

●	Piave Cabernet Sauvignon '00	3
○	Sauvignon Marca Trevigiana '00	3
●	Piave Raboso '97	3

Baltieri
Loc. Mizzole
Via Villa Piatti, 5
37030 Verona
Tel. 045557616

Baltieri are still looking for the right compromise between strong extract and delicate aromas. Their wines are appreciably full-bodied and complex: the Valpolicella is minerally and fruity, and the Recioto is densely textured but lacks elegance.

●	Recioto della Valpolicella Dolce di Regina '96	5
●	Valpolicella Sup. Monte Paradiso '97	4

Dal Din
Via Montegrappa, 31
31020 Vidor (TV)
Tel. 0423987295

This Vidor winery is situated in the strip of land that separates the Valdobbiadene hills from the river Piave. The Prosecco Extra Dry is a success, with ripe fruit and floral aromas, and an enjoyable palate. The Tranquillo blends freshness and extract, while the Colli di Conegliano Bianco is well-made.

○	P. di Valdobbiadene Extra Dry	3
○	P. di Valdobbiadene Tranquillo	3
○	Colli di Conegliano Bianco '00	3

Bellenda
Fraz. Carpesica - Via Giardino, 90
31029 Vittorio Veneto (TV)
Tel. 0438920025
E-mail: info@bellenda.it

The Cosmo family makes classic local wines on the hills surrounding Vittorio Veneto. Among the many labels, we liked the rich and ripe Contrada di Concenigo, the strongly aromatic Prosecco Extra Dry and the pleasant Prosecco Brut.

●	Colli di Conegliano Rosso Contrada di Concenigo '97	4
○	P. di Conegliano Extra Dry	3*
○	P. di Conegliano Brut	3

Conte Loredan Gasparini Venegazzù
Fraz. Venegazzù
Via Martignago Alto, 23
31040 Volpago del Montello (TV)
Tel. 0423870024

The process of modernization begun at this classic Montello winery is starting to yield results. The Capo di Stato has ripe fruit aromas with nice mineral hints; it is full and harmonious on the palate. The Cabernet Sauvignon and the Bianco Falconera are nicely made and enjoyable.

○	Bianco Falconera '00	3
●	Montello Cabernet Sauvignon '00	3
●	Capo di Stato '98	6

FRIULI VENEZIA GIULIA

The '00 vintage is beginning to reveal just how good it actually was in Friuli-Venezia Giulia, although it was not quite on a par with the previous year. The weather during 2000 was similar to '99, with a significant difference from August onwards. Temperatures were high but the lack of rainfall restricted the range between daytime peaks and night-time lows. In consequence, the noses of more aromatic varieties, such as sauvignon and riesling, tended to suffer. Early tests in the cellar revealed biochemical parameters that were slightly inferior to those of the previous year, even though all grape types, including late-ripening reds, were able to express their full potential. Our random tastings from the vat confirmed that '00 was a seriously good year for many whites, beginning with native varieties like tocai friulano, malvasia and ribolla gialla. But pinot grigio and pinot bianco also seemed destined for an exceptionally good year while more modest success appeared on the cards for the chardonnays, especially those fermented and aged in stainless steel. In all the wines, we noted a very high alcohol content, comparable to the previous year, a consequence of the fruit's high sugar content. Overall, there was an improvement in the quality of the region's wines, confirming that the premium winemaking philosophy continues to gain new acolytes. Tastings confirmed the evidence of the early investigations and although the pages dedicated to Friuli-Venezia Giulia have increased, several cellars that earned four or more Glasses in total have had to be excluded. On the negative side, our tastings also showed that many Friulian producers have still to master the mysteries of making red wine. Acidity and tannin content were frequently aggressive, even in two superb vintages like '99 and '00. In contrast, those winemakers who have been making premium reds for a number of years presented us with some of the finest reds in the Italian peninsula, proving that Friuli, the land of great white wines, can also produce world-beating reds. There are more Friulian cellars in this year's Guide, and they have earned more Three Glass awards. Some famous names are missing from the list but there are also new entries, like Joe Bastianich, Mauro Drius, Adriano Gigante, Il Carpino, Aldo Polencic and Dario Raccaro. It should be pointed out that a large number of wines made it into the new Two and a Half Glasses category, providing solid support for their top-scoring compatriots. Moreover, we would also like to mention the superb performance of the Le Vigne di Zamò cellar, which carried off the White of the Year award with a stupendous Tocai Vigne Cinquant'Anni. Finally, a note on prices. A glance at the price lists from the last few vintages will give the lie to the reputation Friulian wines have of being good but expensive. Comparing like quality with like, which the simple act of tasting can verify, you will see that Friuli's winemakers are absolutely in line with price trends in other regions of Italy.

BAGNARIA ARSA (UD)

TENUTA BELTRAME
FRAZ. PRIVANO
LOC. ANTONINI, 6/8
33050 BAGNARIA ARSA (UD)
TEL. 0432923670
E-MAIL: tenuta.beltrame@libero.it

Is there any stopping young Cristian Beltrame? For some time, the quality of his wines has been surging ahead, this year matching that of the great hillslope estates. And he does it all in the Aquileia DOC zone, where premium-quality winemakers are thin on the ground. Tenuta Beltrame embraces 40 hectares, 25 of them planted to vine in neat, double Guyot-trained rows. In the middle stands the old residence, where the vinification and lovely barrel-ageing cellars are located. This is the source of the excellent range of wines that Cristian and the estate oenologist, Giuseppe Gollino have put together. We'll begin with the intense, mouthfilling Merlot Riserva, a complex bottle with notes of bramble tart, dried roses, Peruvian bark, balsam and cinnamon on the nose. It follows through on the palate with the same aromas, revealing nice progression and a robust tannic weave. Equally good are the Chardonnay, the pinot Bianco and the traditional-style Sauvignon. The Chardonnay has an upfront nose with nuances of yeasts accompanying the ripe white apples and pears. Well-structured on the palate, it has an attractively refreshing thrust. The flowery and very varietal Pinot Bianco might have been made in Alto Adige. For years, the Sauvignon has been collecting Two solid Glasses and this year's version has all the typical aromas of red pepper and tomato, nuanced with peach. Yet this is a wine that gives its best on the palate, the flavours of tomato leaf and green pepper lending it vibrancy and a freshness on the back palate. Finally, the first release of the oak-fermented Chardonnay Pribus promises well for future vintages.

○	Friuli Aquileia Chardonnay '00	▼▼	3*
○	Friuli Aquileia Pinot Bianco '00	▼▼	3*
○	Friuli Aquileia Sauvignon '00	▼▼	3*
●	Friuli Aquileia Merlot Ris. '98	▼▼	4
●	Friuli Aquileia Cabernet Sauvignon '00	▼	3
●	Friuli Aquileia Merlot '00	▼	3
○	Friuli Aquileia Pinot Grigio '00	▼	3
○	Friuli Aquileia Tocai Friulano '00	▼	3
●	Friuli Aquileia Cabernet Sauvignon Ris. '98	▼	4
●	Tazzelenghe Ris. '98	▼	4
○	Friuli Aquileia Chardonnay Pribus '99	▼	4
●	Friuli Aquileia Cabernet Sauvignon Ris. '97	▼▼	4

BAGNARIA ARSA (UD)

MULINO DELLE TOLLE
LOC. SEVEGLIANO
VIA MULINO DELLE TOLLE, 15
33050 BAGNARIA ARSA (UD)
TEL. 0432928113
E-MAIL: mulinodelletolle@tin.it

Until last year, preparations to open this attractive farm holiday centre, where the Italian customs house stood until the border moved in 1918, took up most of the attention of the Bertossi cousins. As a result, the cellar was down among the Other Wineries. The wines presented for this edition of the Guide, however, put Mulino delle Tolle back in the front rank of Friuli's wine producers. Giorgio and Eliseo are, respectively, a wine technician and an agricultural technician. Together, they manage 15 hectares of vineyards and have been bottling some of their wine for the past 13 vintages, last year turning out 60,000 units. The cellar has no frills so quality comes primarily from the vineyards, which are managed with scrupulous care. The estate sprawls across what were once the ancient Roman Via Postumia and Via Julia Augusta roads. It is no accident that numerous wine amphorae have been discovered among the vines, as well as a votive head which is reproduced on the Mulino delle Tolle labels. The Palmade Bianco comes from oak-conditioned malvasia, sauvignon and chardonnay, and again shows that it is an elegantly concentrated blend with forward notes of apple and a fresh-tasting, well-structured palate. But the Bertossis really surprised the panel with a fantastic Malvasia that offers generous, complex, fruit-rich aromas, a stylish, refreshing texture and lots of length. Another outstanding wine from the latest vintage is the Tocai Friulano, a wine that bursts onto the palate and signs off with rich notes of fruit. The Merlot has a remarkable palate, with good body and a leisurely finish while the Refosco tempts the nose with its varietal hints of spice. And to round off, the Chardonnay is pleasingly stylish.

○	Malvasia '00	▼▼	3*
○	Friuli Aquileia Bianco Palmade '00	▼▼	3*
○	Friuli Aquileia Tocai Friulano '00	▼▼	2*
○	Friuli Aquileia Chardonnay '00	▼	2
●	Friuli Aquileia Merlot '00	▼	2
●	Friuli Aquileia Refosco P. R. '99	▼	3
●	Friuli Aquileia Cabernet Franc '00		3

BERTIOLO (UD)

CABERT
VIA MADONNA, 27
33032 BERTIOLO (UD)
TEL. 0432917434
E-MAIL: bertiolo@tin.it

In 1960, a number of the oldest and most aristocratic farming estates in central Friuli decided to build at Bertiolo a large winery to vinify their grapes. Cabert, which since then has made wine only with its members' grapes, has been taking in fruit from all over Friuli, producing 800,000 bottles a year from vineyards totalling 314 hectares. Everything goes on, as the company slogan has it "from pruning to tasting", under the eagle eye of Daniele Calzavara, who for the past few years has been joined by consultants from the New World. The wonderfully elegant Chardonnay opens on flowery notes of wistaria, then goes on to reveal lime blossom, yellow peach and mango. This is followed up by a lovely entry on the palate, which is moderately buttery and echoes the nose delightfully as it unveils attractive freshness and plenty of style. Another big scorer was the Casali Roncali, its distinctive nose flaunting pineapple, orange peel and banana that lend it a very Mediterranean warmth. It follows through well on the front palate, rounding off with an invigoratingly fresh note of acidity in the finish. Both Merlots are excellent. The Riserva is very much in the international mould. Its full fragrances range from bramble and blackcurrant jam to coffee, cherry tart and cinnamon. The palate has still to settle down but the finish has warm alcohol and the tannins are already fairly mellow. The less challenging Merlot dei Colli Orientali is better on the palate than the nose. The round, soft mouthfeel takes you through to a long finish of berry fruit.

○	Friuli Grave Chardonnay '00	🍷🍷	3*
○	COF Chardonnay Casali Roncali '00	🍷	4
○	Friuli Grave Sauvignon '00	🍷	4
○	Friuli Grave Tocai Friulano '00	🍷	2*
●	Friuli Grave Merlot Ris. '95	🍷	4
●	COF Merlot Casali Roncali '99	🍷	4
○	COF Sauvignon Casali Roncali '00		4
○	Friuli Grave Pinot Grigio '00		3
●	Friuli Grave Refosco P. R. '00		3

BICINICCO (UD)

PRADIO
LOC. FELETTIS
VIA UDINE, 17
33050 BICINICCO (UD)
TEL. 0432990123

The Pradio winery, owned by the Cielo family, is a new entry in the Guide. The property, on the flatlands near Udine, was set up in the 1970s and today has a vine stock planted at 3-4,000 plants per hectare, where yields are kept strictly under control. Traditional techniques are used in the cellar, supplemented by cold maceration and hyperoxygenation of the musts. There are 30 hectares all told and annual production totals 200,000 bottles. The winemaking team comprises Giovanni Cielo, son Luca, who manages the winery, fruitmaker Beppe Gollino and wine technician Beppe Bassi. Both the Cabernet Sauvignon Crearo and the Pinot Grigio Priara are very good. The barrique-aged Crearo has an almost impenetrable purplish red colour that precedes an austere, well-balanced nose that unveils one after the other hints of bramble jam, chocolate, leather, pepper, cinnamon and cigar tobacco. The entry on is understated but the mid palate builds up into a rich softness, with firm, fine-grained tannins coming through in the finish. The Pinot Grigio Priara has taken full advantage of an excellent year for the variety, offering a fruit salad nose laced with balsam and wistaria. The palate mirrors these aromas well, showing a good balance of freshness and softness. The finish is lingering and irresistible. We can't overlook the Merlot Roncomoro, either. It's a tad stiff on the nose but has very decent structure. Also worth looking into are the Sauvignon Sobaia, with its curious fruit gum aromas, and the Tocai Gaiare, an elegant wine with a subtly smooth nose.

○	Friuli Grave Pinot Grigio Priara '00	🍷🍷	3*
●	Friuli Grave Cabernet Sauvignion Crearo '99	🍷🍷	3*
○	Friuli Grave Chardonnay Teraje '00	🍷	3
●	Friuli Grave Merlot Roncomoro '00	🍷	3
○	Friuli Grave Sauvignon Sobaja '00	🍷	3
○	Friuli Grave Tocai Friulano Gaiare '00	🍷	3
●	Friuli Grave Refosco P. R. Tuaro '00		3

BUTTRIO (UD)

Olivo Buiatti
Via Lippe, 23
33042 Buttrio (UD)
tel. 0432674316

BUTTRIO (UD)

Livio e Claudio Buiatti
Via Lippe, 25
33042 Buttrio (UD)
tel. 0432674317
e-mail: buiattivini@iol.it

We have to admit that were surprised to find Olivo Buiatti's wines had scored as highly as they did after each round of blind tastings. In the past, we have always encountered well-made, and sometimes good, products, which is why we regarded the winery as a borderline candidate for a full profile. The estate dates from 1911 but it was only in 1986 that brothers Olivo and Livio separated their cellars. For a few years now, Olivo has been letting his son Franco run the show. With help from his wife Simonetta, Franco now obtains 8,000 bottles of white wines and 4,000 of red every year from the property's seven hectares. But the real turning point came when Franco decided to take, at least in part, the advice of his brother's friend Enzo Pontoni, the artist of wine who owns the Miani cellar at Buttrio. Since then, bunch-thinning has been ruthless, artificial fertilizers are no longer used and sulphur-based treatments are the only ones allowed. The resulting fruit has a concentration of sugar which means that the wine is always good, if not excellent. The barrels used for ageing come from Enzo Pontoni and Paolo Meroi. Franco's Poanis Blanc is a gold-flecked blend of tocai, sauvignon and pinot grigio that releases elegant aromas of beeswax, honey and very ripe fruit, then showing hefty alcohol on the palate. It's a wine with considerable structure, like the full-bodied, well-sustained Tocai, a concentrated and very long wine reminiscent of almond leaf. But it is in the Cabernet that Pontoni's style shows through in the wealth of chewy fruit, the power, the structure, the notes of liquorice and spice, and the nicely mellowed tannins.

Claudio Buiatti graduated from the agricultural college at Cividale before joining, and then replacing, his father Livio on the family's eight hectares of hillslope vineyards at Buttrio. The relatively new cellar is near the family home and is fully equipped to vinify and age the property's production, all of which is made from estate-grown fruit. The roughly 50,000 bottles produced every year, about 65 per cent of which are whites, are sold almost entirely in Italy. The increasing attention Claudio devotes to vineyard management, with denser planting patterns and green covering of the rows, is paying off in the improved quality of the wines and reflected in the fine collection of Glassware the cellar has earned. The Pinot Grigio pleased the panel with its combination of rich fruit and freshness on the palate while for the Sauvignon it was the notes of rue and elderflower on the nose, along with the hint of citrus in the long finish. The Merlot '99 has a nose of plums, cherry and autumn leaves that are picked up on the well-structured palate, which also offers soft tannins. Partial drying of the grapes, barrique fermentation and ageing, then bottle ageing, all come together to make the Picolit fatty and deliciously drinkable. Best of the reds is the Refosco, which reveals spice and wild berry aromas on both nose and palate. In the mouth, rich red berry fruit and nice tannins delight the taste buds.

○ COF Bianco Poanis Blanc '00	ΨΨ	4
○ COF Tocai Friulano '00	ΨΨ	4
● COF Cabernet '99	ΨΨ	4
○ COF Pinot Grigio '00	Ψ	4
○ COF Sauvignon '00	Ψ	4

○ COF Pinot Grigio '00	ΨΨ	3*
○ COF Sauvignon '00	ΨΨ	3*
● COF Merlot '99	ΨΨ	3*
○ COF Pinot Bianco '00	Ψ	3
○ COF Verduzzo Friulano '00	Ψ	3
● COF Cabernet '99	Ψ	4
○ COF Picolit '99	Ψ	5
● COF Refosco P. R. '99	Ψ	4
○ COF Tocai Friulano '00		3
● COF Refosco P. R. '98	ΨΨ	4

BUTTRIO (UD)

Conte d'Attimis - Maniago
Via Sottomonte, 21
33042 Buttrio (UD)
tel. 0432674027

How much further can Alberto D'Attimis go? In recent vintages, the wines from his Sottomonte estate have been steadily improving, this year performing better than ever. We know he has replanted his vineyards with new clones, increasing the vine density. We know he has bought new barrel stock and has inaugurated a new bottle-ageing cellar. But what is clear is that is wines are now better made and more concentrated. And with those 110 hectares under vine, some on excellently aspected hillslopes, thing may improve even further. The Vignaricco Bianco is a stunner that timidly reveals notes of balsam and white chocolate as you raise it to your nose before adding apricot jam and citrus fruit. On the palate, the peach and apricot are superbly balanced by oak-derived nuances. It's a buttery yet fluent wine with a very long finish. Elegantly intense notes of sweet melon and papaya fruit are accompanied by wistaria on the nose of the Chardonnay. The entry on the palate is understated but softness emerges vigorously in mid palate to offset the refreshing acidity then the long finish signs off with notes of fruit salad. The velvety, harmonious Sauvignon is a riot of ripe fruit while the Refosco, from a native Friulian red variety that is gaining popularity, is soft, with notes of plums, brambles and pipe tobacco over silky tannins. Glasses also went to the subtly stylish Picolit and the spicy, varietal Cabernet.

○ COF Chardonnay '00	🍷🍷	4
● COF Refosco P. R. '00	🍷🍷	4
○ COF Sauvignon '00	🍷🍷	4
○ Vignaricco Bianco '96	🍷🍷	5
○ COF Picolit '00	🍷	6
○ COF Pinot Grigio '00	🍷	4
● Vignaricco Rosso '96	🍷	5
● COF Cabernet '99	🍷	4
● COF Merlot '99	🍷	4
● COF Cabernet '98	🍷🍷	4
○ COF Picolit '99	🍷🍷	6

BUTTRIO (UD)

★ Girolamo Dorigo
Via del Pozzo, 5
33042 Buttrio (UD)
tel. 0432674268
e-mail: girdorig@tin.it

The new winery set-up has still to find its feet, as may be inferred from a certain lack of continuity in the premium-quality and second-label ranges, as well as a little confusion over labelling. For example, the Sauvignon Ronc di Juri, should not be confused with the version reviewed last year. Having cleared that up, you can settle back to savour its hints of honey, citrus fruit and peaches as they meld seamlessly with the balsam of the oak and the rich, mellow mouthfeel with its refreshingly tangy vein of acidity. Not for the first time, the Chardonnay is a star, its hallmark subtle toastiness accompanying a nose of sage, thyme, bread and spring flowers, followed up by an elegantly long, tidy palate where the aromas of the nose are lifted by vanilla and tarragon. The customary Mediterranean notes of the Picolit display sweetness a tad too much to the fore. The panel was impressed by the Tocai, which lacks the extra thrust in the finish that would take it into the Three Glass zone, and by the '91 spumante. As usual, it is the finest sparkler in the region, tailor-made for those who like their bubbles mature. None of the three reds presented this year reached the heights of the past, partly because of the vintage and partly because of the consequent decision not to release the big guns – Montsclapade and Pignolo – whose fruit went into the more modest Rosso Dorigo. Best of the reds, however, were the deep-coloured Refosco, a spicy, complex wine with the over-edginess typical of the variety, and the "Tongue-cutter", Tazzelenghe, which as its name suggests is fairly hard and astringent in the mouth.

○ COF Chardonnay Vign. Ronc di Juri '99	🍷🍷	6
○ COF Picolit Vign. Montsclapade '99	🍷🍷	6
○ COF Sauvignon Ronc di Juri Vign. Montsclapade '99	🍷🍷	6
○ COF Tocai Friulano Vign. Montsclapade '00	🍷🍷	4
○ Dorigo Brut '91	🍷🍷	5
○ COF Sauvignon Vign. Ronc di Juri '00	🍷	4
● COF Refosco P. R. Vign. Montsclapade '98	🍷	6
● COF Rosso Dorigo '98	🍷	5
● COF Tazzelenghe di Buttrio Vign. Ronc di Juri '98	🍷	6
○ COF Chardonnay Vign. Ronc di Juri '98	🍷🍷🍷	6

BUTTRIO (UD)

DAVINO MEROI
VIA STRETTA DEL PARCO, 7
33042 BUTTRIO (UD)
TEL. 0432674025
E-MAIL: parco.meroi@libero.it

Restaurateur and winemaker Paolo Meroi is doing everything right. He has opted for premium quality and his wines are now concentrated, full-bodied and muscular yet very tidy and full of charm. Followers of the hoary old debate for and against barriques should taste Paolo's products to find out what is really meant by barrique wine, and how to handle what is after all, and will always be, simply a useful cellar tool. The richly extracted Tocai is firm and almost buttery on the palate, mingling its varietal notes of rennet, acacia blossom and bitter almonds with confectioner's cream. The Meroi Picolit has a sumptuous oiliness and Mediterranean notes of dried figs, almond paste and groundnuts to offset an elegance that does not cloy, despite the elevated sugar content, hints of polyflora honey and fragrant apple cider. The rustic soul of Paolo's traditional-style, baked apple and wild rose-nuanced Verduzzo is mellowed but not cowed by oak-derived vanilla, making this a wine that can compete with the best. And confirmation of the high quality levels reached, and the reliability of the cellar's products, comes from the Blanc di Buri, in which the yeast, milk and tropical fruit from the chardonnay ensure the aromas of the malvasia and the rich hue from the tocai will endure in the cellar. The Sauvignon is full-bodied and long, its hint of sinew coming through ripe fruit, tarragon and peach on the nose. Finally, the Ros di Buri, a blend of merlot and cabernet franc, releases notes of violets, cherry, printer's ink and butter.

BUTTRIO (UD)

★ MIANI
VIA PERUZZI, 10
33042 BUTTRIO (UD)
TEL. 0432674327

In recent years, the Friulian weather has alternated rain with much drier periods. This has had positive repercussions on the region's grapes, which have more robust skins, more phenolics and aroma-producing substances, and a more acid and sugar-rich pulp. That's precisely what Enzo Pontoni has been looking for since he first started making his own wine. Can he talk to the weather? What we have here is a local version of "vin de garage", although it would be more precise to call it "vino di ronc" – hillslope vineyard wine – since it comes from obsessively careful vineyard management. The vines are nurtured individually, day by day, and cellar intervention is kept to a minimum. In fact, Enzo's cellar is a wine technologist's nightmare. This year, however, the Pontoni magic worked again. We tasted the Merlot, which has more of everything you could wish for. We went on to a memorable Tocai, which was even better than in previous vintages, especially in terms of elegance, with a freshness that is nicely offset by the softness of the mouthfeel. Next the panel was enchanted by the Merlot '98. The deep vibrancy of the colour, with its brilliant purplish rim; the nose of warm cherry tart, tobacco and mint; the explosive and still spicy palate with magnificent breadth and concentration; all lead up to a quite sensational finish. Production of the stupendous Refosco Vigna Caliari is limited to 600 bottles so we decided not to review it even though it was easily worth Three Glasses. And that leaves the Sauvignon and the Ribolla. After all those other "tours de force", you might think they would be duly unpretentious but don't be fooled. Their clean aromas, weight on the palate and length make them very much premium wines.

○	COF Picolit '99	ΨΨ	6
○	COF Tocai Friulano '99	ΨΨ	5
○	Verduzzo '99	ΨΨ	5
○	COF Bianco Blanc di Buri '99	ΨΨ	5
●	COF Rosso Ros di Buri '99	ΨΨ	5
○	COF Sauvignon '99	ΨΨ	5
●	Dominin '97	Ψ	5
○	COF Picolit '98	Ψ	6
●	COF Rosso Ros di Buri '98	Ψ	5
○	COF Tocai Friulano '00	ΨΨΨ	6
●	COF Merlot '98	ΨΨΨ	6
○	COF Ribolla Gialla '00	ΨΨ	6
○	COF Sauvignon '00	ΨΨ	6
●	COF Merlot '94	ΨΨΨ	6
○	COF Bianco '96	ΨΨΨ	6
●	COF Rosso '96	ΨΨΨ	6
○	COF Sauvignon '96	ΨΨΨ	6
○	COF Tocai Friulano '96	ΨΨΨ	6
○	COF Bianco '97	ΨΨΨ	6
●	COF Rosso '97	ΨΨΨ	6
○	COF Tocai Friulano '98	ΨΨΨ	6
○	COF Tocai Friulano '99	ΨΨΨ	6
●	COF Merlot '97	ΨΨ	6
○	COF Ribolla Gialla '99	ΨΨ	6

BUTTRIO (UD)

PETRUCCO
VIA MORPURGO, 12
33042 BUTTRIO (UD)
TEL. 0432674387
E-MAIL: petruccovini@libero.it

You can always rely on Lina and Paolo Petrucco. The serious and enthusiastic winery owners never interfere with the careful work of oenologist Flavio Cabas. Instead, they back him up, giving him all the equipment needed by a modern cellar. The results are there for the tasting. The estate's 30 hectares include 20 under vine, enabling the Petruccos to release 100,000 bottles every year. It would be superfluous to add that vineyard management is, of course, scrupulous but we would like to point out that the cellar, only a few minutes away from the vineyards, is in a stunning location on the southern slopes of the Buttrio hills, looking out onto the flatlands of Friuli. The invariably hospitable Petrucco home and a tasting room large enough to accommodate groups complete the picture. But what about the wines? We could restrict ourselves to saying that none of them earned less than One Glass but we wanted to mention the best in more detail. The briefest of sojourns in oak – for some of the wine – has given the Chardonnay a full texture that is the perfect complement to the natural elegance of Flavio Cabas's winemaking style. Although the Pinot Grigio is fermented and aged only in stainless steel, it can still add notes of confectioner's cream to its fruit aromas. The Sauvignon softens the power of its aromas with warm alcohol, showing great structure and a lingering finish. And last but not least, the entire range is excellent value for money.

○ COF Chardonnay '00	♛♛	3*
○ COF Pinot Grigio '00	♛♛	3*
○ COF Sauvignon '00	♛♛	3*
○ COF Ribolla Gialla '00	♛	3
○ COF Tocai Friulano '00	♛	3
● COF Cabernet Franc '99	♛	3
● COF Merlot '99	♛	3
● COF Refosco P. R. '99	♛	3

CAPRIVA DEL FRIULI (GO)

CASTELLO DI SPESSA
VIA SPESSA, 1
34070 CAPRIVA DEL FRIULI (GO)
TEL. 0481639914
E-MAIL: info@castellospessa.com

The lovely, aristocratic Castello di Spessa, whose origins date back to the late 12th century, was purchased a few years ago by Loretto Pali, a dynamic businessman and lover of antiques. The residential part of the building has been lavishly furnished and is now used as a hospitality centre while the cellar, which lies at the foot of the castle and dates from the 14th century, is connected by an internal stairway to a bunker constructed in the 1930s. The advantage of this arrangement is that it is 15 metres underground and maintains a constant temperature of 13 degrees Centigrade all year round. That makes it the ideal place for barrique-ageing the Conte di Spessa red, a prevalently merlot-based Bordeaux blend which is one of the estate's leading products. Domenico Lovat and Alberto Pelos are in charge of the vineyards and the cellars, respectively. It is to them that we should pay tribute for the estate's consistently excellent results. The red Torriani '98, a blend of merlot and cabernet sauvignon, has the weaknesses of a poor harvest but the Conte di Spessa unveils all the rich body and power of the preceding year, which was one of the best in recent times. A newcomer for this estate is the Pinot Nero, dedicated to Casanova, who stayed in the castle in 1773. It's a good wine but struggles to bring out the varietal typicity of the grape. In contrast, the Pinot Bianco di Santarosa is a very good wine indeed, even if the sweet wood is still a little forward. The well-made Sauvignon Segrè, a tribute to one of the last families to own the estate, comes from fruit picked in three separate selections.

○ Collio Pinot Bianco '00	♛♛	4
○ Collio Pinot Grigio '00	♛♛	4
○ Collio Sauvignon Segrè '00	♛♛	5
○ Collio Tocai Friulano '00	♛♛	4
● Collio Rosso Conte di Spessa '97	♛♛	6
○ Collio Pinot Bianco di Santarosa '99	♛♛	5
○ Collio Ribolla Gialla '00	♛	4
○ Collio Sauvignon '00	♛	4
● Collio Pinot Nero Casanova '98	♛	5
● Collio Rosso Torriani '98		5
○ Collio Pinot Bianco '97	♛♛♛	4
● Collio Rosso Conte di Spessa '95	♛♛	6

CAPRIVA DEL FRIULI (GO)

PUIATTI
VIA AQUILEIA, 30
34070 CAPRIVA DEL FRIULI (GO)
TEL. 0481809922
E-MAIL: puiatti@puiatti.com

Unexpectedly and with no warning at all, Vittorio Puiatti passed away at the end of April. With him, we lost a man who brooked no half measures and whose frankness could often be mistaken for arrogance but which was profoundly inspired by his unwavering opinions and long experience of winemaking. The estate has been taken over by his children, Giovanni and Elisabetta. They have 11 hectares under vine in the Collio and 33 in the Isonzo DOC zone but they also buy in fruit from the same zones from about 30 other growers, who have always been paid for quality, not quantity. Vittorio Puiatti would point this out with pride as being the foundation for the consistently good quality of his wines. We continue to believe, however, that it was Vittorio's vast professional skill that brought those results, winning a fair number of prizes for the estate's wines. In recent years, the Archetipi range of wines for the cellar has been disappointing while the fresher, less demanding bottles have always been excellently made. The P range from Ruttars in the Collio is a very promising label but is handicapped by the relative youth of the vines. From the last vintage, we particularly like the DOC Friuli Isonzo Chardonnay and Pinot Grigio, both of which have attractive fruit, good balance and a nice tangy freshness, with the Pinot Grigio a nose ahead of its stablemate. We should also point out that the Puiatti slogan is "Save a tree, drink Puiatti" so don't expect any toasty oak or vanilla notes in their wines. Just enjoy the fruit.

CAPRIVA DEL FRIULI (GO)

RONCUS
VIA MAZZINI, 26
34070 CAPRIVA DEL FRIULI (GO)
TEL. 0481809349

Marco Perco continues to make progress in his own inimitable way and this year came close to winning Three Glasses with his Pinot Bianco and Sauvignon, even though they had only recently gone into the bottle. The estate's ten hectares produce a mere 30,000 bottles a year that express the owner's very personal approach to cellar and vineyard management in wines that are not so much made as crafted. Restless and dissatisfied with the excellent results he has turned out so far, Marco is now contemplating new, indeed innovative wine types, such as a very special white blend, fermented unhurriedly in oak, to be released in the future. As we said before, the Sauvignon and Pinot Bianco are immense. The Sauvignon opens slowly before offering a rich nose of melon and ripe peach with fumé nuances. This follows through on the soft, broad and very warm palate that takes you through to a mouthfilling finish of yellow peaches. The Pinot Bianco has vinous notes on the nose at first before it unfolds on the well-sustained palate with a roundness and a delicious fruit-derived softness that lingers nicely in the finish. Marco's other wines are worth Two full Glasses. We could mention the impenetrably dark Merlot, with its delightfully complex notes of Peruvian bark, black cherry syrup and earth; or the unabashedly Mediterranean Tocai that marries notes of citrus fruit and almonds with a full palate; or also the Roncùs Bianco, a malvasia-based blend from vines over 30 years old that offers balsamic notes over melon and vanilla, with hints of confectioner's cream, and whose thrust on the palate is intriguingly complex.

	Wine	Glasses	Score
O	Friuli Isonzo Pinot Grigio Giovanni Puiatti '00	ŸŸ	3*
●	Collio Cabernet Sauvignon Vittorio Puiatti '00	Ÿ	4
O	Collio Chardonnay P '00	Ÿ	4
O	Collio Pinot Bianco Vittorio Puiatti '00	Ÿ	4
O	Collio Sauvignon P '00	Ÿ	4
O	Friuli Isonzo Chardonnay Giovanni Puiatti '00	Ÿ	3
●	Collio Merlot P Blanchis '99	Ÿ	5
O	Collio Pinot Grigio Vittorio Puiatti '00		4
O	Collio Ribolla Vittorio Puiatti '00		4
O	Collio Sauvignon Archetipi '98		6
●	Collio Cabernet Sauvignon Blanchis Vittorio Puiatti '99		6

	Wine	Glasses	Score
O	Pinot Bianco '00	ŸŸ	4
O	Sauvignon '00	ŸŸ	4
O	Collio Tocai Friulano '00	ŸŸ	4
●	Merlot '00	ŸŸ	4
O	Roncùs Bianco '00	ŸŸ	5
●	Val di Miez '97	ŸŸ	5
●	Merlot '99	ŸŸ	4
O	Roncùs Bianco '99	ŸŸ	5

CAPRIVA DEL FRIULI (GO)

Russiz Superiore
Via Russiz, 7
34070 Capriva del Friuli (GO)
tel. 048199164 - 0481960270
Email: info@marcofelluga.it

This year, the Russiz Disôre came within an ace of winning Three Glasses. A blend of tocai, ribolla, pinot bianco and sauvignon fermented in 15 and 30 hectolitre barrels, it has an effortlessly elegant palate that is stylish, long and redolent of plums, pears and milk of almonds. Close on its heels was a pack of excellent wines, beginning with the Riserva degli Orzoni, a cabernet sauvignon-based blend with cabernet franc and merlot. Deep and rich in colour, it marries blackcurrant, spices and pencil lead over a close-knit, well-sustained palate that is a little edgy because of its substantial tannic weave. The Tocai has lustrous lemon-yellow highlights and ripe, juicy palate with a faint hint of almonds. Then came the Sauvignon, which is lifted nicely by the sweet notes on the nose before the palate lets it down a little. The Pinot Bianco is also attractive. Its ripe fruit and vanilla contribute to a lovely balance of acidity, alcohol and extract. The lovely golden yellow Verduzzo performed creditably, offering notes of honey, confectioner's cream and crusty bread, as well as velvet-soft alcohol and sweetness on the palate. The Pinot Grigio also earned a mention. Its palate is even but rather lightweight although it is a very drinkable bottle. The Merlot reveals wild cherries and autumn leaves in the retro after a palate with moderate structure and length while the Franc failed to live up to expectations, mainly because of its edginess in the mouth.

	Wine	Glasses	Price
○	Collio Bianco Russiz Disôre '99	ΥΥ	5
○	Collio Pinot Bianco '00	ΥΥ	4
●	Collio Rosso Ris. degli Orzoni '97	ΥΥ	6
○	Collio Sauvignon '00	ΥΥ	4
○	Collio Tocai Friulano '00	ΥΥ	4
○	Verduzzo '00	ΥΥ	6
●	Collio Cabernet Franc '99	Υ	5
●	Collio Merlot '99	Υ	5
○	Collio Pinot Grigio '00	Υ	4
●	Collio Rosso Ris. degli Orzoni '94	ΥΥΥ	6
○	Collio Sauvignon '98	ΥΥΥ	4
○	Collio Tocai Friulano '99	ΥΥΥ	4

CAPRIVA DEL FRIULI (GO)

★ Schiopetto
Via Palazzo Arcivescovile, 1
34070 Capriva del Friuli (GO)
tel. 048180332
e-mail: azienda@schioppetto.it

Mario Schiopetto can no longer surprise us with his wines. We're too used to trotting out the superlatives for them. Yet we can only continue to admire the man himself, who still manages to imbue his wines with ideas and personality despite being almost permanently confined to a wheelchair. Of course, it helps to have three children like Maria Angela, who looks after sales, and twins Giorgio and Carlo, who are busy managing the vineyards and the cellars. For several years, the 22 hectares of this Collio estate have been flanked by a further eight at Podere dei Blumeri in Rosazzo, in the Colli Orientali del Friuli DOC zone. This enables the family to exploit to the full the potential of their splendid and capacious cellar, built in the mid 1990s. Pinot Bianco is still the most elegant of the Schiopetto wines in absolute terms and the credit has to go to Mario himself. He knows how to bring out the grape's essence in notes of apple, an acidity and alcohol content that are always measured, and a delightfully long finish. Just as good, albeit with very different characteristics, is the Tocai Friulano, whose notes of pear and peach on the nose are complex and unusually elegant while the palate offers fruit in abundance and the variety's trademark tanginess. A hint of excessive acidity thins the palate of the extraordinary Pinot Grigio del Collio, which echoes the richness of the grape's aromas this year. The Podere dei Blumeri is only a notch or two below it. Finally, the part oak-aged versions of the Sauvignon Tarsia, the Pinot Bianco Amrità and the Tocai Friulano Pardes are interesting but will require further experimentation.

	Wine	Glasses	Price
○	Collio Pinot Bianco '00	ΥΥΥ	5
○	Collio Tocai Friulano '00	ΥΥΥ	5
○	Collio Pinot Grigio '00	ΥΥ	5
○	Blanc des Rosis '00	ΥΥ	5
○	COF Chardonnay Podere dei Blumeri '00	ΥΥ	5
○	COF Pinot Grigio Podere dei Blumeri '00	ΥΥ	5
○	COF Sauvignon Podere dei Blumeri '00	ΥΥ	5
○	Collio Sauvignon Tarsia '99	ΥΥ	6
○	Collio Pinot Bianco Amrità '99	Υ	6
○	Collio Tocai Friulano Pardes '99	Υ	6
○	Collio Pinot Bianco Amrità '97	ΥΥΥ	6
○	COF Sauvignon Podere dei Blumeri '99	ΥΥΥ	5
○	Collio Sauvignon '99	ΥΥ	4

CAPRIVA DEL FRIULI (GO)

Gestioni Agricole Vidussi
Via Spessa, 18
34070 Capriva del Friuli (GO)
Tel. 048180072 - 045913399

The winery was founded by Ferruccio Vidussi and is owned by his widow, Antonietta Causero. Since 1 August 2000, it has been managed by the Montresor family, who have their own winery in the Verona area. The new managers decided to give the cellar their full attention, since the vineyards were already capable of producing first-quality fruit, and called in to direct operations Luigino De Giuseppe, a young oenologist who has already built up an impressive track record. The 25 hectares in the Collio and seven in the Colli Orientali give excellent grapes in good years like 2000 so Luigino was able to get down to business straight away. The wines he uncorked for the panel put Vidussi firmly back into the Guide on merit. The overall level of quality looks as if it will get even better, if the Montresors' determination and De Giuseppe's commitment are anything to go by. The Chardonnay has vibrant golden highlights and a complex, elegantly soft, creamy palate where notes of citrus fruit and apple mingle with the top of the milk. The Malvasia is reminiscent of herbal tea and golden delicious apples. Its warm, caressing palate is so mellow and alcohol-rich that it seems almost sweet. The Pinot Grigio has intense fragrances that range from tropical fruit to pear with a faint hint of nail varnish. Broad on the palate, it offers well-integrated acidity in the finish. In the Collio Bianco Ronchi di Ravéz, malvasia predominates but other varieties add aromatic and citrus-fruit notes. It may still need a little fine-tuning but it is already close to a second Glass.

O	Collio Chardonnay '00	🍷🍷	4
O	Collio Malvasia '00	🍷🍷	4
O	Collio Pinot Grigio '00	🍷🍷	4
O	Collio Bianco Ronchi Ravéz '00	🍷	4
O	Collio Ribolla Gialla '00	🍷	4
O	Collio Sauvignon '00	🍷	4
O	COF Picolit '99	🍷	6
●	COF Schioppettino '00		5
O	Collio Tocai Friulano Croce Alta '00		4

CAPRIVA DEL FRIULI (GO)

★ Villa Russiz
Via Russiz, 6
34070 Capriva del Friuli (GO)
Tel. 048180047
E-mail: villarussiz@villarussiz.it

Year after year, Gianni Menotti makes astoundingly good wines that never fail to leave a mark in our final tastings. We tasted four bottles this time and just look at the results – one Three Glass giant and two more that made it to the taste-off. The 2000 vintage may not have been outstanding for sauvignon grapes but Gianni still manages to turn out a champion in the Graf del La Tour, an elegant, concentrated wine with rich fruit notes of citrus and peach, and an excellent standard-label Sauvignon whose slightly fresher aromas foreground nectarines. A poor vintage is obviously no obstacle to Gianni. Take the Merlot Graf de La Tour '98, for instance. Many winemakers in Friuli lost their red grapes that year but Menotti harvested his a few hours before the rain began to fall in earnest. His wine has incredible breadth and concentration on the nose, where very ripe plum and cherry, autumn leaves and chocolate all come through, and a full-bodied, tannin-rich structure that leads into a long finish. Pinot Bianco is the most elegant of the Menotti wines, an intense, generous wine with good breath and admirable length. But the pièce de résistance is the Chardonnay Gräfin de La Tour, which had all the panel members nodding in approval. Yeasts, confectioner's cream and golden delicious apples on the nose; tobacco, ripe fruit, mouthfilling structure, freshness and great length on the palate are just a few of the comments they jotted down. To round off, a historical note: the winery belongs to a charitable body and the count, or Graf, and countess – Gräfin – de La Tour were the last owners before the estate passed to Italian public ownership in 1918.

O	Collio Chardonnay Gräfin de La Tour '99	🍷🍷🍷	5
O	Collio Pinot Bianco '00	🍷🍷	4
●	Collio Merlot Graf de La Tour '98	🍷🍷	6
O	Collio Malvasia Istriana '00	🍷🍷	4
O	Collio Pinot Grigio '00	🍷🍷	4
O	Collio Sauvignon '00	🍷🍷	4
O	Collio Sauvignon de La Tour '00	🍷🍷	5
O	Collio Tocai Friulano '00	🍷🍷	4
O	Collio Ribolla Gialla '00	🍷	4
O	Collio Riesling '00	🍷	4
●	Collio Merlot '99		4
O	Collio Sauvignon de La Tour '97	🍷🍷🍷	5
O	Collio Sauvignon de La Tour '98	🍷🍷🍷	5
O	Collio Sauvignon de La Tour '99	🍷🍷🍷	5

CARLINO (UD)

Emiro Cav. Bortolusso
Via Oltregorgo, 10
33050 Carlino (UD)
tel. 043167596
e-mail: vinibortusso@bortusso.it

Sergio and Clara Bortolusso have a 38-hectare property and for several years, they have been releasing a range of well-made products in the modern style. And we shouldn't forget that this is not an easy area in which to produce premium-quality wines. We think the Bortolussos are doing an excellent job and sincerely hope that their example will be followed by others. The vines are planted at 3,500-3,800 to the hectare, yielding around 75-80 quintals, which is well below the limit stipulated by the DOC regulations. All the work in the cellar is done by the young estate wine technician, Luigino De Giuseppe. Two well-earned Glasses went to the Sauvignon, which has a fruit-rich nose of apricots, melon and tropical fruit. The well-rounded palate follows through with more sweet fruit and a long finish. The Bortolusso Pinot Bianco is traditionally a good one and this version has well-balanced, discreetly intense notes of green apples and spring flowers. Entry on the palate is delicious while the uncomplicated progression is refreshing and stylish. There are varietal notes of citrus in the Malvasia, which mingles with acacia blossom and white-skinned damsons. The characteristically tangy palate reveals a long, satisfying finish of apples and pears. We picked up notes of baked apples, ripe damsons and roasted almonds on the nose of the Tocai, which has a very varietal palate of bitter almonds and green apples leading into a warm after-aroma. 'Fresh on nose and palate' sums up the Pinot Grigio while the Merlot is a little stiff on the nose, although it offers good length and a reasonably soft mouthfeel. Finally, we enjoyed the typical baked apple aromas and slightly sweet palate of the Verduzzo.

○	Friuli Annia Sauvignon '00	🍷🍷	2*
●	Friuli Annia Merlot '00	🍷	2*
○	Friuli Annia Pinot Grigio '00	🍷	2*
○	Friuli Annia Malvasia '00	🍷	2*
○	Friuli Annia Pinot Bianco '00	🍷	2*
○	Friuli Annia Tocai Friulano '00	🍷	2*
○	Friuli Annia Verduzzo Friulano '00	🍷	3
●	Friuli Annia Refosco P. R. '00		2

CERVIGNANO DEL FRIULI (UD)

Ca' Bolani
Via Ca' Bolani, 1
33052 Cervignano del Friuli (UD)
tel. 043132670
e-mail: info@cabolani.it

The historic Ca' Bolani winery has belonged to the Zonin family since 1970. It takes its name from Domenico Bolani, the count who served as procurator of the Venetian Republic in Friuli in the first half of the 16th century. The Ca' Bolani estate of 95 hectares has been joined over the years by Ca' Vescovo, a 350-hectare estate with 230 hectares under vine, and Molin di Ponte, with 405 hectares, of which more than 230 are planted to vine. The cellar is everything you could wish for in this DOC zone and eminently capable of transforming into seriously good wine grapes that carefully managed planting densities, training systems and yields improve with each vintage. This is one of the cellars managed by Franco Giacosa, the expert Zonin oenologist who monitors operations to ensure that this improvement is constant. It is no coincidence that the Sauvignon earned Two Glasses, for the variety often excels at Ca' Bolani. Entry on the broad, long palate is impressive and the range of aromas includes red pepper, pennyroyal, nettles and white peaches. The Conte Bolani Rosso, a 60-40 blend of merlot and cabernet sauvignon, ages in small oak casks. Rich and remarkably well-structured on the palate, it has a fresh notes redolent of wild strawberries, among other things. The Pinot Grigio nearly won Two Glasses as it is distinctly more complex than the Opimio, a blend of chardonnay and tocai friulano that sees no wood. All in all, it was a very decent line-up of Glasses to mark the first full Guide profile for this promising winery.

○	Friuli Aquileia Sauvignon Gianni Zonin Vineyards '00	🍷🍷	4
●	Friuli Aquileia Merlot '00	🍷	3
●	Friuli Aquileia Refosco P. R. '00	🍷	3
○	Opimio Gianni Zonin Vineyards '00	🍷	4
●	Conte Bolani Rosso Gianni Zonin Vineyards '98	🍷	5
●	Friuli Aquileia Cabernet Franc '98	🍷	4
●	Friuli Aquileia Refosco P. R. Gianni Zonin Vineyards '98	🍷	4
○	Friuli Aquileia Pinot Grigio Gianni Zonin Vineyards '00	🍷	4
●	Friuli Aquileia Cabernet Franc Gianni Zonin Vineyards '99		3

CIVIDALE DEL FRIULI (UD)

GIOVANNI CROSATO
VIA CASTELMONTE, 1
33040 CIVIDALE DEL FRIULI (UD)
TEL. 0432701462
E-MAIL: ronchidifornaz_galasso@hotmail.com

Giovanni Crosato and his wife Lucia Galasso vinify together the grapes from their respective properties. Lucia owns five hectares of vineyards at Spessa near Cividale and Giovanni looks after six, some in the same area and others at Fornaz, also near Cividale. For commercial reasons, Giovanni has dropped the Ronchi di Fornaz label that has appeared in past editions of the Guide. Now his own name appears instead for he is known as one of the finest oenologists in Friuli. The bottles tasted were well received by the panel, starting with the Rosso Don.Giovanni '98 from Lucia's vines. The vintage may have been a poor one for reds but this cabernet sauvignon, cabernet franc, merlot and schioppettino blend flaunts austere aromas and a excellent front palate of lavish fruit and tannins. Capo d'Opera is a blend of 80 per cent refosco dal peduncolo rosso from 70 year old vines with merlot and offers a well-structured, fruity palate. The mouthfilling, full-bodied Pinot Grigio reveals minerally notes, pear and tropical fruit, all of which return in the leisurely finish. And last on the list is the Fumé Bianco is a blend of pinot bianco and pinot grigio harvested when super-ripe. It has a broad fruit salad nose dominated by apricots and pears and a palate that is nearly, but not quite, as good as you hoped.

○ Pinot Grigio '00	ΥΥ	3*
● Il Rosso Don.Giovanni Lucia Galasso '98	ΥΥ	4
○ Chardonnay '00	Υ	3
○ Fumé Bianco '00	Υ	4
○ Sauvignon '00	Υ	3
● Capo d'Opera Lucia Galasso '98	Υ	5

CIVIDALE DEL FRIULI (UD)

DAVIDE MOSCHIONI
LOC. GAGLIANO
VIA DORIA, 30
33043 CIVIDALE DEL FRIULI (UD)
TEL. 0432730210

When Davide Moschioni gave son Michele a free hand to run the winemaking side of the farm, Michele lost no time in changing things significantly. It should be said that the Moschionis, unlike most Friulian producers, had a vine stock that was three-quarters red and red varieties will soon account for 85 per cent of the total. In addition, Michele draws inspiration from several excellent winemaking models in Friuli and the Verona area. Yields are minimal in the 11 hectares of vineyards and the fruit is partially dried to achieve the sugar concentration desired. This means that the must-to-fruit ratio is below 50 per cent by weight. Michele also noticed that this procedure had to be carefully monitored otherwise all the wines tend to have the same note of raisining, which at times can be overpowering or render the wines very similar. But Michele has shown he has an old head on his young shoulders. Now his wines retain their varietal character while acquiring rare fullness and ageing potential. Michele is very much a traditionalist and concentrates primarily on native Friulian varieties. The results can be tasted in his splendid Picolit, a stupendous Pignolo, a variety that could take Friuli to the very pinnacle of world winemaking, an extraordinarily concentrated Schioppettino and a Refosco that needs a little more fine tuning. The cabernet sauvignon and tazzelenghe-based Rosso Moschioni is only available in magnums.

● COF Pignolo '99	ΥΥ	6
○ COF Picolit '99	ΥΥ	6
● COF Rosso Moschioni '99	ΥΥ	6
● COF Schioppettino '99	ΥΥ	6
● COF Refosco P. R. '00	Υ	5
● COF Pignolo '96	ΥΥ	6
● COF Schioppettino '97	ΥΥ	6
● COF Rosso Celtico '99	ΥΥ	5
● COF Pignolo '97	Υ	6
● COF Refosco P. R. '99	Υ	5

CIVIDALE DEL FRIULI (UD)

Paolo Rodaro
Fraz. Spessa
Via Cormons, 8
33040 Cividale del Friuli (UD)
tel. 0432716066

Paolo Rodaro has 35 hectares and an annual production of 200,000 bottles, and he continues to release excellent wines you can always rely on. But then the vineyards are well-aspected and their owner knows exactly what he is doing. Planting density is high at 4-5,000 vines per hectare and Paolo has also set up a small nursery to propagate endangered local clones so the quality of the wines isn't hard to explain. Tocai has always been the Rodaro strong suit and this year's was as good as any. The delicious nose foregrounds well-balanced ripe fruit, with peaches, oranges and williams pears prominent, following this up with broom and bitter almonds. Then the palate delivers a rounded, full-bodied mouthfeel and a long, fruity finish. Paolo's excellent Picolit is redolent of nuts, oranges and apricot peel on the nose. The dense palate unveils lingering notes of dates and figs before finishing on candied citron. The Verduzzo Pra Zenâr is from super-ripe, partially dried grapes that ferment in oak. The sophisticatedly complex nose is followed by a buttery palate reminiscent of honey and candied citrus peel. It's been years since Paolo presented us with a red as good as the Schioppettino, from the native variety of the same name. The complex nose hints at black pepper, cinnamon, plums and bramble, all echoed on the well-structured palate, which cossets the taste buds with fine-grained tannins. Last but not least, the Sauvignon is back on form, proffering attractive aromas of elderflower and ripe tomato.

O	COF Pinot Grigio '00	ŸŸ	4
O	COF Sauvignon '00	ŸŸ	4
O	COF Tocai Friulano '00	ŸŸ	4
O	COF Picolit '99	ŸŸ	6
●	COF Schioppettino '99	ŸŸ	5
O	COF Verduzzo Friulano Pra Zenâr '99	ŸŸ	5
O	COF Verduzzo Friulano '00	Ÿ	4
O	COF Pinot Bianco '00	Ÿ	4
O	COF Sauvignon Bosc Romain '96	ŸŸŸ	5
O	COF Picolit '98	ŸŸ	6
O	COF Verduzzo Friulano Pra Zenâr '98	ŸŸ	5

CORMONS (GO)

Tenuta di Angoris
Loc. Angoris, 7
34071 Cormons (GO)
tel. 048160923

Tenuta di Angoris is a large and long-established estate. One of the first in Friuli to bottle its own wines, it is constantly torn between conflicting needs and aspirations. The cellar is owned by Luciano Locatelli, who happens to have the same surname as Locatello Locatelli, the Friulian who in 1648 received as a gift part of the estate of the Austrian emperor, Ferdinand III. The property embraces 540 hectares, of which 130 are planted to vine in the Collio and Colli Orientali DOC zones, although most are located in the Isonzo DOC zone, near the large cellar. Annual production ranges from 700,000 to 1,000,000 bottles in a number of different ranges and labels. Vineyard selections, the Podere range as well as the Bianco Spìule and the Spumante Modolet, account for over 100,000 units. Claudia Locatelli, Luciano's daughter, has decided to devote her energies to the estate and she is ably backed up by Natale Favretto, who has been the wine technician for decades. Claudia wants to raise quality standards and to do so she will have to turn on its head a production strategy that has always put quantity first, as is evident from the planting densities and vineyard management techniques now being used. That's why she and Natale deserve particular praise for wines as good as Spìule, a softly delicious wine with good body and weight that comes from 70 per cent chardonnay, the rest of the blend being sauvignon with a touch of the native ucelùt variety. Oak-fermented, it ages in barriques for eight months. Another very attractive wine is the Pinot Brut Modolet, a sparkler from pinot bianco, chardonnay and pinot nero, of which 70,000 bottles have been released.

O	COF Bianco Spìule '99	ŸŸ	4
O	COF Picolit '00	Ÿ	6
O	COF Pinot Grigio Podere Ronco Antico '00	Ÿ	4
O	COF Ribolla Gialla Podere Stabili della Rocca '00	Ÿ	4
●	COF Refosco P. R. Podere Rocca Bernarda '99	Ÿ	4
O	Spumante Pinot Brut Modolet	Ÿ	3
O	Friuli Isonzo Chardonnay Podere Angoris '00		4

CORMONS (GO)

Borgo del Tiglio
Loc. Brazzano
Via San Giorgio, 71
34070 Cormons (GO)
tel. 048162166

We feel that when a wine is on the market, we should take into account how it is drinking now, and not just its cellar potential. This may have penalized some Borgo del Tiglio labels in the past. Nicola Manferrari almost always releases wines with above-average ageing potential but this time, he has managed to combine "drinking today" with "drinking tomorrow" and the results are stunning. The Chardonnay Selezione opens on flowery notes of wistaria and hawthorn with yellow plum and apple fruit, leading into a long, beautifully structured palate that is satisfying but never obvious. It's a stylish Three Glass wine with lots of character. The second-label Chardonnay is a little less of an aristocratic but still rather special. The Malvasia, too, is good, its honey and baked apple nose ushering in a complex yet tidy and elegant palate. The panel preferred the Tocai '99 to the more illustrious Ronco della Chiesa for it was more persuasive on the palate. Fresher and with more attractive fruit, it was undisturbed by the other's milky notes and forward alcohol. However, these are nuances rather than faults. The Bianco is a wine to watch that still needs to settle down and the Studio is a lovely example of how to offset toasty notes of tobacco and hazelnut with peach and mango fruit. As usual, the palate is powerful and the long finish ends with a faintly bitterish twist. Both reds were on a par with the other wines, the Rosso della Centa scoring a very full Two Glasses. It opens on nose and palate in textbook fashion, mingling bramble and spices with the dried flowers and tobacco of the finish, backed up by its austere, well-sustained structure.

O	Collio Chardonnay Sel. '99	♛♛♛	6
●	Collio Rosso della Centa '96	♛♛	6
O	Collio Malvasia Sel. '99	♛♛	6
●	Collio Rosso Ris. '96	♛♛	6
O	Collio Bianco '99	♛♛	5
O	Collio Bianco Ronco della Chiesa '99	♛♛	6
O	Collio Chardonnay '99	♛♛	5
O	Collio Studio di Bianco '99	♛♛	6
O	Collio Tocai Friulano '99	♛♛	5
O	Collio Tocai Ronco della Chiesa '90	♛♛♛	6
O	Collio Malvasia Sel. '97	♛♛	6
O	Collio Chardonnay Sel. '98	♛♛	6
O	Collio Studio di Bianco '98	♛♛	6

CORMONS (GO)

Borgo San Daniele
Via San Daniele, 16
34071 Cormons (GO)
tel. 048160552
e-mail: borgosandaniele@tin.it

Never as at this winery have winemaking decisions been so truly the fruit of reflection and personal convictions. Brother and sister Mauro and Alessandra Mauri have made oenology a philosophy of life. As you read the cellar's letter of presentation, the reasons for some of the choices are obvious. It's clear why they chose to reduce yields per hectare, and to cut the range to four wine types, as well as why the couple put the emphasis on substance rather than image. The resulting wines have a very individual style, with ever new hints of minerals from the soil and the carefully managed vineyards. They came within a whisker of winning Three Glasses but the entire range is admirably reliable and indeed has plenty of room to get even better with cellaring. The Pinot Grigio Olivers is worth Two and a Half Glasses. A complex, warm, richly fruity wine, it has a thrust on the palate that mingles fruity softness with attractively original, fresh-tasting sensations. The Tocai marries varietal notes of almond, rue and spring flowers with minerals and citrus fruit that come back on the stylish, lingering palate. Arbis Blanc is obtained from tocai, chardonnay, pinot bianco and sauvignon. It releases generous, complex aromas of dried flowers, williams pears and a hint of coffee, following through nicely on the tidy, stylish palate. The Arbis Rosso, a blend of cabernet and pignolo, is a wine to watch. Its delicious marriage of spice and ripe berry fruit on the nose, with a delicately elegant palate, is likely to age very well indeed.

O	Friuli Isonzo Pinot Grigio '00	♛♛	4
O	Friuli Isonzo Arbis Blanc '00	♛♛	4
O	Friuli Isonzo Tocai Friulano '00	♛♛	4
●	Arbis Rosso '99	♛♛	5
O	Friuli Isonzo Tocai Friulano '97	♛♛♛	4
O	Friuli Isonzo Pinot Grigio '99	♛♛♛	4
●	Gortmarin '97	♛♛	5
O	Friuli Isonzo Arbis Blanc '99	♛♛	4
O	Friuli Isonzo Tocai Friulano '99	♛♛	4

CORMONS (GO)

Branko - Igor Erzetic
Loc. Zegla, 20
34071 Cormons (GO)
tel. 0481639826

It's only been a few years since Igor Erzetic took over the family winery. Branko, the cellar label, is the name of Igor's father, who happily leaves the running of the estate to his outgoing and very able son. This small cellar is located between Novali and Zegla, two of the finest subzones in the Cormons area. Igor has four hectares of vineyards and the vine stock varies in age. Strict monitoring of yields enables Igor to turn out wines that have more than enough structure to age in oak tonneaux. Although a small percentage of the wine is aged in wood, drinkers will be able to tell only with great difficulty, perhaps because they detect the faintest hint of toastiness. Repeated tasting by the panel confirmed that the best wine of the vintage is the Tocai Friulano. Its complex, concentrated nose unveils hints of apple, pear, hawthorn and bitter almonds. After a fruit-rich entry, the palate follows through with a warm, rich progression to an invitingly long finish. The Pinot Grigio also has an elegantly deep, complex nose as well as serious structure on the well-sustained palate that echoes the nose before taking its leave on an intense, fruity finish. The Chardonnay tempts the nose with nicely gauged oak-derived hints of vanilla, confectioner's cream and banana but it is the concentration of the fruit that emerges in the aftertaste. Peach and sage characterize the attractive Sauvignon, which nearly earned a second Glass. Finally, the panel was pleasantly surprised by the complexity and body of the Rosso, a merlot and cabernet sauvignon blend that offers aromas of dried flowers and wild berries.

○	Collio Chardonnay '00	🍷🍷	4
○	Collio Pinot Grigio '00	🍷🍷	4
○	Collio Tocai Friulano '00	🍷🍷	4
●	Rosso '00	🍷🍷	4
○	Collio Sauvignon '00	🍷	4
○	Collio Chardonnay '99	🍷🍷	4
○	Collio Sauvignon '99	🍷🍷	4
○	Collio Tocai Friulano '99	🍷🍷	3
○	Collio Pinot Grigio '99	🍷	4

CORMONS (GO)

Maurizio Buzzinelli
Loc. Pradis, 20
34071 Cormons (GO)
tel. 048160902
e-mail: buzzinelli@libero.it

Despite his recently celebrated 30th birthday, Maurizio Buzzinelli still looks like a youngster. But don't let appearances deceive you. This kid continues to grow as a winemaker and the results he turns out provide incontrovertible proof of his progress. The cellar, increasingly in need of extra space, is on the hillside at Pradis, near the property's nine hectares under vine in the Collio DOC zone and not far away from the six hectares in the Isonzo DOC zone. Wines that are partly or entirely aged in wood are released under the Rond dal Luis labels. They are always good and repeated cellar tastings confirm that Maurizio still has plenty of potential in reserve. We'll be following this young man and his products with great interest. The Collio Bianco Frututis – which means "little girls" in Friulian – is based on tocai friulano, with malvasia and one third sauvignon vinified in stainless steel alone. Again it attained a Two Glass score for its close-knit weave on the palate, rich fruit and notes of almonds and dried leaves on the nose. Equally good is the Malvasia, a warm, tangy, lingering and richly fragrant wine with notes of apple, apricot and hawthorn that keep the intense oak-derived nuances in their place. But the big surprise was the Rosso Frututis, from 75 per cent merlot and 25 per cent cabernet sauvignon and cabernet franc. The complex, and in some respects austere, nose is followed by superb fruit on the front palate, which follows up with a full-bodied progression where prominent but unaggressive tannins precede a lingering finish.

○	Collio Bianco Frututis Ronc dal Luis '00	🍷🍷	4
○	Collio Malvasia Istriana Frututis Ronc dal Luis '00	🍷🍷	4
●	Collio Rosso Frututis Ronc dal Luis '00	🍷🍷	4
○	Collio Müller Thurgau '00	🍷	3
○	Collio Pinot Grigio '00	🍷	3
●	Friuli Isonzo Cabernet Sauvignon Ronc dal Luis '00	🍷	4
○	Collio Chardonnay '00		3
○	Collio Chardonnay Ronc dal Luis '00		4

CORMONS (GO)

PAOLO CACCESE
LOC. PRADIS, 6
34071 CORMONS (GO)
TEL. 048161062
E-MAIL: info@paolocaccese.com

Paolo Caccese may be, in many respects, a supremely likeable one-off but he is still emblematic of much of Friuli's hillslope winemaking. A law graduate, he left a promising professional career to look after the six hectares of vine that his father purchased at Pradis near Cormons. Not just that. He actually managed to convince Veronica, after they were married, to move from Gorizia to live in the vine-clad hills of Cormons. Even with so few hectares at his disposal, Paolo releases as many as 11 labels, including some varieties that many opine he would be better to drop, such as Riesling and Traminer Aromatico. Overall annual output is about 35-40,000 bottles, three quarters of which are white. This year, Paolo has added a minor masterpiece to his list in the shape of a stunning Malvasia. The nose offers notes of very ripe golden delicious apples and citrus fruits, followed by a rich, full-bodied palate that lingers, soft and fresh-tasting at the same time, and keeps the substantial alcohol content well under control. Two very full Glasses also went to the Pinot Grigio. Its ripe fruit nose mingles notes of apricot and herbs then an attractive hint of apples comes through on the tangy, full palate. Finally, the Tocai Friulano, its notes of milk of almonds overlaid with pears and apples, is another remarkably good wine.

○	Collio Malvasia '00	⚜⚜	4
○	Collio Pinot Grigio '00	⚜⚜	4
○	Collio Müller Thurgau '00	⚜	4
○	Collio Pinot Bianco '00	⚜	4
○	Collio Sauvignon '00	⚜	4
○	Collio Tocai Friulano '00	⚜	4
○	Collio Riesling '00		4
○	Collio Traminer Aromatico '00		4

CORMONS (GO)

CANTINA PRODUTTORI DI CORMONS
VIA VINO DELLA PACE, 31
34071 CORMONS (GO)
TEL. 048162471 - 048160579
E-MAIL: info@cormons.com

The best wine this from the Cantina Produttori di Cormons this year is the Collio Pinot Grigio. The old gold-flecked colour introduces a nose of yellow plums and williams pears, a mouthfilling texture that is soft at first and then dry, and very decent length. The Isonzo DOC Chardonnay also performed well. Yeasts and fruit salad come through on the nose to be mirrored satisfyingly on the palate, which has attractive thrust. The Collio version, however, is not quite so good. Its attractive notes of confectioner's cream, apple and pineapple are let down by a green palate with acidity too much to the fore. The panel made approving comments about the Ribolla, an uncomplicated yet elegant glass that unveils attractively citrus-laced apples and flowers. The fresh, stylish Tocai has hints of peach, apple, acacia blossom and almonds and the ebullient Collio Bianco also offers plenty of fruit. Then came the other wines. In the Collio range, the Sauvignon is a little dilute but has the classic varietal freshness on the palate while the Pinot Bianco lacks power but not balance. The Sauvignon in the Isonzo range is similar to its stablemate from the Collio. The slightly sweet Verduzzo opens on notes of walnut and summer flowers and is faintly tannic in the finish. The Madreterra is still rather harsh, revealing notes of chestnut, pepper and printer's ink. There is a certain lack of harmony between the richness of the nose and the concentration in the glass and mouth. As usual, the Vino della Pace, just the wine to give anyone who appreciates a maverick, deserves a mention of its own.

○	Collio Pinot Grigio '00	⚜⚜	3*
○	Friuli Isonzo Chardonnay '00	⚜⚜	3*
○	COF Ribolla Gialla '00	⚜	4
○	Collio Bianco '00	⚜	4
○	Collio Chardonnay '00	⚜	4
○	Collio Pinot Bianco '00	⚜	3
○	Collio Sauvignon '00	⚜	4
○	Collio Tocai Friulano '00	⚜	3
●	Friuli Isonzo Madreterra '00	⚜	3
○	Friuli Isonzo Sauvignon '00	⚜	3
○	Friuli Isonzo Verduzzo Dorè '00	⚜	3
○	Vino della Pace '98	⚜	6
○	Vino della Pace '97	⚜⚜	6

CORMONS (GO)

CARLO DI PRADIS
LOC. PRADIS, 22/BIS
34071 CORMONS (GO)
TEL. 048162272
E-MAIL: carlodipradis@tin.it

The Carlo di Pradis winery, named by Boris and David Buzzinelli after their father, Carlo, who passed it on to them, is a large building on the hillside of Pradis at Cormons. The very well-equipped cellar features an extremely inviting tasting room. The serious, professional attitude of the two brothers is giving their customers a lot to be happy about, particularly when you take into account their very consumer-friendly pricing policy. Their six hectares in the Collio DOC zone are very close to the cellar and produce the Carlo di Pradis range. They have a similar property in the Isonzo DOC zone on the flatlands near Cormons, which yields the fruit for their BorDavi wines. The '98 vintage was not a good one for red wines but the brothers still managed to turn out a Merlot with remarkable structure, complexity, rich fruit and tannic weave. The second Two Glass wine comes from the Isonzo DOC zone. It's the '99 Merlot, from a vintage to remember. The wine is well-structured and has a close-knit, fruit-rich mouthfeel, with fine-grained tannins and hints of cocoa powder on the nose that marry nicely with red berry tart. Just a neck behind came the BorDavi Rosso '98, from a blend of nine parts cabernet sauvignon with one part merlot. You hardly notice the year it spent in oak, so well are the aromas covered by intense notes of plum and warm cherry, melding with soft tannins. The Pradis Bianco is a blend of tocai, malvasia, pinot bianco and sauvignon. Aged in tonneaux, it came close to gaining a second Glass, as did the two Pinot Grigios.

- Collio Merlot '98 — ᵧᵧ 4
- Fruili Isonzo Merlot BorDavi '99 — ᵧᵧ 3*
- ○ Collio Pinot Grigio '00 — ᵧ 4
- ○ Collio Tocai Friulano '00 — ᵧ 4
- ○ Fruili Isonzo Chardonnay BorDavi '00 — ᵧ 3
- ○ Fruili Isonzo Pinot Grigio BorDavi '00 — ᵧ 3
- ● Fruili Isonzo Rosso BorDavi '98 — ᵧ 4
- ○ Collio Bianco Pradis '99 — ᵧ 4
- ● Fruili Isonzo Cabernet BorDavi '99 — 3
- ● Collio Merlot '97 — ᵧᵧ 4

CORMONS (GO)

COLLE DUGA
LOC. ZEGLA, 10
34071 CORMONS (GO)
TEL. 048161177

If you want to see just how little some international frontiers matter, then pay a visit to the home and cellar of Damian Princic. A few metres behind it, you will see the stone that marks the spot where Italy becomes Slovenia. Luckily, it has been some years since the frontier actually separated people who speak the same language and are often related to each other. For a few years, too, Damian has been bottling his own wines and has yet to put a foot wrong. He and his father, Luciano, manage six and a half hectares, obtaining no more than 300 hectolitres of wine. Only part of this ends up in their 14,000-bottle annual production because they make a second careful selection of the fruit at the cellar after selecting in the vineyard. Colle Duga, the estate's trademark, comes from the name of the spot where the cellar, and most of the vines, stand. The Collio Bianco, is a blend of equal parts of chardonnay, tocai and sauvignon, 40 per cent aged in pre-used small oak casks. The resulting wine is buttery and warm, revealing fresh flower aromas, intense fruit and remarkable structure. The entry and follow-through on the palate of the Tocai Friulano struggle to mask the robust alcohol – over 14 per cent in this vintage – despite intense notes of ripe apple. The Chardonnay flaunts a distinctively varietal personality, accompanied by complexity and elegance. Finally, Damian is waiting for new vines to come onstream to improve his Merlot, which even now is well worth One Glass.

- ○ Collio Bianco '00 — ᵧᵧ 4
- ○ Collio Chardonnay '00 — ᵧᵧ 3*
- ○ Collio Tocai Friulano '00 — ᵧᵧ 3*
- ● Collio Merlot '99 — ᵧ 4

CORMONS (GO)

Mauro Drius
Via Filanda, 100
34071 Cormons (GO)
tel. 048160998

Last year, we wrote that Mauro Drius had surpassed himself, so what could we say this time when his Pinot Bianco won Three Glasses and his Pinot Grigio came close to doing so as well? Visit his tiny, sparely equipped cellar, bearing in mind that he does everything, with no consultant winemaker, no posing, and laudable simplicity. The property comprises 11 hectares, nine of which are currently in production, and the cellar turns out 50,000 bottles a year. Vineyards are distributed over the Isonzo flatlands and the hillslopes of Monte Quarin. The Pinot Bianco is always a superior bottle but this year regales the nose with superbly rich and intense aromas, ranging from apple to pear-based fruit salad, wistaria and peach to finish on almonds. The subtle elegance never falters for a second. On the palate, it is concentrated, fragrant and tangy, with a very successful and attractive balance of fruit, which mirrors the nose, and the freshness of the back palate. Our admiring congratulations to Mauro. His Pinot Grigio is varietal and complex on nose and palate, showing balanced notes of williams pears and golden delicious apples backed up by impressive power. This is offset by well-gauged acidity that lends length to the finish. Mauro's excellent Tocais include a Mediterranean-style Collio version that offers hints of citrus fruit and hedgerow while the Isonzo Tocai is fattier and tangier. Well worth a mention is the Two Glass Riesling, one of the few decent versions of the type made in Friuli, and the Sauvignon, which reveals an intriguing contrast between ripe fruit and green notes.

O	Friuli Isonzo Pinot Bianco '00	ŶŶŶ	4
O	Friuli Isonzo Pinot Grigio '00	ŶŶ	4
O	Collio Sauvignon '00	ŶŶ	4
O	Collio Tocai Friulano '00	ŶŶ	4
O	Friuli Isonzo Bianco Vignis di Sìris '00	ŶŶ	4
O	Friuli Isonzo Riesling '00	ŶŶ	4
O	Friuli Isonzo Tocai Friulano '00	ŶŶ	4
O	Friuli Isonzo Malvasia '00	Ŷ	4
●	Friuli Isonzo Cabernet '99		4
●	Friuli Isonzo Merlot '99		4

CORMONS (GO)

★ Livio Felluga
Fraz. Brazzano
Via Risorgimento, 1
34070 Cormons (GO)
tel. 048160203
e-mail: info@liviofelluga.it

This winery was built up over several decades of steady work by Livio Felluga to become a paragon of consistently fine quality, as well as a source of new insights. Livio remains the cellar's guiding spirit but his children, Maurizio, Elda and their younger brothers Andrea and Filippo, play an increasingly large part in the running of the estate. For the past few years, the Fellugas have been making a series of major investments at their Brazzano cellar near Cormons. This enables them to vinify in exemplary fashion the fruit from their 135 hectare-property, most of which lies in the great natural amphitheatre around Rosazzo. Here, too, the Fellugas have their delightful hospitality facilities and it is here that the winery also plans to build a multipurpose centre and a barrel cellar. This year, the best wine in the Felluga range is the Terre Alte '99, a blend of tocai, pinot bianco and sauvignon. Last year, a slight toastiness let the palate down but the '99 version has only the faintest of echoes from the oak. Instead, it is the creaminess, fullness and elegance of the complex apple and peach-dominated fruit that grab the attention, following through to the long, unhurried finish. Despite the indifferent vintage, the Refosco '98 is on splendid form and the Picolit Riserva '97, with a very marked note of sweetness, shows that it is again a top-notch proposition. New wines include the Illivio, a barrique-fermented pinot bianco, but note, too, the scores attained by the merlot and cabernet sauvignon Vertigo not to mention the Shàrjs, from chardonnay and ribolla gialla; you would hardly know it had seen oak.

O	COF Rosazzo Bianco Terre Alte '99	ŶŶŶ	6
O	COF Rosazzo Picolit Ris. '97	ŶŶ	6
●	COF Refosco P. R. '98	ŶŶ	6
O	Shàrjs '00	ŶŶ	4
●	COF Rosazzo Sossò Ris. '98	ŶŶ	6
O	COF Bianco Illivio '99	ŶŶ	5
●	Vertigo '99	ŶŶ	4
O	COF Pinot Grigio '00	Ŷ	4
O	COF Sauvignon '00	Ŷ	4
O	COF Tocai Friulano '00	Ŷ	4
●	COF Refosco P. R. '97	ŶŶŶ	6
O	COF Rosazzo Bianco Terre Alte '97	ŶŶŶ	6

CORMONS (GO)

Edi Keber
Loc. Zegla, 17
34071 Cormons (GO)
tel. 048161184

There can be no doubting the consistently high quality of Edi Keber's range, even if there were no Three Glass winners this year. But before we review the wines, we would like to point out Edi's very unorthodox decision a few years ago to drastically cut back the number of labels he releases onto the market. The upshot is that he presents us with a Bianco and a Rosso, as well as his Tocai Friulano and Merlot – the Merlot only if the vintage is a good one. This is a courageous line to take in Friuli, where everyone wants to make everything. In recent years, Edi has of course been scrupulously tending his eight splendid hectares of vineyards, all near his home, but he has also expanded the cellar, adding an underground passage that links it to the family home. The tasting room is a very inviting one that frequently hosts exciting meetings where Friulian, and sometimes also Slovene, winemakers compare notes. The blend for the Collio Bianco contains malvasia, ribolla, pinot grigio, pinot bianco and sauvignon, as well as tocai. The resulting wine marries elegance and generous fruit, warm alcohol with notes of peach and rue, and buttery richness with excellent length. The Tocai Friulano has intense flecks of gold in the glass then the palate offers concentration, stylish elegance and the variety's trademark almondy finish. The tannic weave of the Merlot is close-knit and generous, the aromas redolent of autumn leaves and cherries, and the Collio Rosso, obtained from merlot and cabernet franc, reveals a tempting nose but lost points for a faint note of residual sugar.

○	Collio Bianco '00	🍷🍷	4
○	Collio Tocai Friulano '00	🍷🍷	4
●	Collio Merlot '99	🍷🍷	5
●	Collio Rosso '00	🍷	5
○	Collio Tocai Friulano '95	🍷🍷🍷	4
○	Collio Tocai Friulano '97	🍷🍷🍷	4
○	Collio Tocai Friulano '99	🍷🍷🍷	4
○	Collio Bianco '99	🍷🍷	4
●	Collio Rosso '99	🍷🍷	4

CORMONS (GO)

La Boatina
Via Corona, 62
34076 Cormons (GO)
tel. 048160445
e-mail: info@boatina.com

The 60-hectare Boatina estate, purchased in 1979 by Loretto Pali, has 20 hectares planted to vine, which have been extensively replanted to boost wine quality. For many years, oenologist Domenico Lovati has been managing both vineyards and cellar. And the cellar, a model of organization, technology and tradition, is well worth a visit. Part of the main complex underwent restructuring some time ago and five double guest rooms, with period furnishings, have been created, as well as a living room and kitchens. It's now a luxury farm holiday centre, hidden away in the middle of the countryside. Nearby, a small shop has been set up where visitors can taste not just the estate wines but also cheeses, salamis and cold meats from all over the world. The bright straw-yellow Chardonnay is a classic Friulian Chardonnay that has not seen wood. Superbly balanced, it unveils apples, pears and very ripe fruit leading in to a fresh, lingering palate. The Picol Maggiore '97 is a rather more serious wine, blended from 75 per cent merlot and cabernet sauvignon with a small proportion of cabernet franc. It's a very cellarable wine aged, after malolactic fermentation, in French barriques and large barrels of Slavonian oak. Its lustrous colour introduces a nose reminiscent of red berry fruit jam, prunes, cherries and black cherries. The palate is intense and harmonious. The Perle, from picolit and verduzzo, is very sweet, concentrated and full-bodied. Best of the other wines is the Tocai Friulano, which came within an ace of a second Glass.

○	Collio Chardonnay '00	🍷🍷	4
●	Collio Rosso Picol Maggiore '97	🍷🍷	5
○	Collio Pinot Bianco '00	🍷	4
○	Collio Pinot Grigio '00	🍷	4
○	Collio Ribolla Gialla '00	🍷	4
○	Collio Sauvignon '00	🍷	4
○	Collio Tocai Friulano '00	🍷	4
●	Collio Merlot '98	🍷	4
○	Perle '99	🍷	6

CORMONS (GO)

Roberto Picech - Le Vigne del Ribél
Loc. Pradis, 11
34071 Cormons (GO)
Tel. 048160347
E-mail: picech@libero.it

As is fitting, Roberto Picech has kept his father's nickname – "il Ribél", or "the Rebel" – on his labels. Egidio Picech passed away during 2001 and with him, we lost a man who could look back on decades of struggle, both by tenant farmers for the land they had worked for generations, and of partisans for the freedom of the country. Those values are now Roberto's, as he carries on his father's work on the small estate at Pradis. The five-hectare property on the hillslopes at Cormons produces about 20,000 units a year and the cellar, although cramped, is big enough to vinify the grapes, age some of the wines in wood and store the bottles until they are ready for release. Roberto is a skilful winemaker who believes that the estate blend should be a flagship wine, and not merely a convenient way to get rid of second-quality fruit. Not for the first time, he offered the panel a seriously good Bianco Jelka, which is the Slovene for Gabriella, his mother's name. An over-generous helping of oak marked the wine down a point or two in the final tastings but the full, fruit-rich structure, robust alcohol and fragrant aromas will fine-tune the toastiness in a few months. In any case, this blend of tocai friulano, malvasia and ribolla can be laid down for a number of years. The Passito di Pradis comes from malvasia istriana fruit that dries for several months. Slightly sweet, well-balanced and long on the palate, its keynote aromas are stewed apple and honey. The fresh-tasting, remarkably concentrated Tocai is almost lemony in colour, with heaps of fruit.

○	Collio Bianco Jelka '00	♢♢	4
○	Collio Tocai Friulano '00	♢♢	4
○	Passito di Pradis '99	♢♢	6
○	Collio Malvasia '00	♢	4
○	Collio Pinot Bianco '00	♢	4
●	Collio Rosso '00	♢	5
○	Collio Bianco Jelka '99	♢♢♢	4
●	Collio Rosso Ris. '97	♢♢	5

CORMONS (GO)

Ferdinando e Aldo Polencic
Loc. Plessiva, 13
34071 Cormons (GO)
Tel. 048161027

Father and son Ferdinando and Aldo Polencic busy themselves with seven hectares under vine in the Collio DOC zone. About 30 years ago, the Polencic family decided to grow grapes exclusively and make the necessary changes to the property's facilities. Although those facilities are showing their age, and are frankly inadequate by the canons of modern winemaking, you wouldn't know it from the final product and the 20,000 bottles sold every year are ample proof of the Polencic quality. The estate's success is confirmed this year by a range of very good wines indeed and a first full profile in the Guide. We have long been familiar with Polencic wines but for a number of reasons, the panel has been unable to review them. Happily, the problems of the past have been overcome and our tasters were able to get to work tasting the five wines proposed by the estate. And what a convincing range it was! The Tocai earned Three Glasses and another Polencic wine came very close indeed. The Tocai Friulano '00 is a splendid wine that tempts the nose with hints of tobacco and almonds, following up with a sumptuously concentrated, full-bodied palate whose tight-knit, fruit-rich texture is enhanced by a delicious fumé nuance. A wonderful wine, well worth Three Glasses. Traditionally the estate flagship wine, the Pinot Bianco is obtained from just over one hectare of 33 year old vines. As soon as the must has settled, it goes into large and small oak barrels, where it stays for several months. The results are impressive. The Merlot is also nice, with its red berry fruit, fine-grained tannins and a barely perceptible grassy note.

○	Collio Tocai Friulano '00	♢♢♢	4
○	Collio Pinot Bianco degli Ulivi '99	♢♢	5
●	Collio Merlot degli Ulivi '99	♢♢	5
○	Collio Sauvignon '00	♢	4
○	Collio Pinot Grigio '00		4

CORMONS (GO)

Isidoro Polencic
Loc. Plessiva, 12
34071 Cormons (GO)
Tel. 048160655

CORMONS (GO)

Alessandro Princic
Loc. Pradis, 5
34071 Cormons (GO)
Tel. 048160723

After this year's visit, Michele Polencic had a much longer list of Two Glass wines. He and his equally young sister, the delightful Elisabetta, manage to combine running the family winery with their studies at university, where both are close to graduation. Their father, Isidoro, has good reason to be proud of how his children are coping, as they carry on the fine tradition the family has created in past decades. Today, the Polencics have 22 hectares in the Collio, and a small parcel in the Isonzo DOC zone, from which they make 1,500 hectolitres of wine every year. Located right on the border with Slovenia, the spacious, modern cellar has more stainless steel than wood but the barrel cellar is far from empty. The Collio Bianco is a blend of 50 per cent tocai friulano, 30 per cent pinot bianco and chardonnay, with ribolla and malvasia. You can tell that this wine has been in wood but its main characteristics are rich fruit and refreshing acidity. The estate's other blend is the very successful Oblin Bianco, a young, soft, warm wine with good length, made from over half chardonnay blended with sauvignon and ribolla. All Isidoro Polencic wines give their best from the second year but the Tocai Friulano is drinking better now than the others. Fresh-tasting and well-structured, it takes its leave on a note of ripe fruit. The Pinot Grigio and the Sauvignon are both excellent, albeit a little grassy, while the Pinot Bianco, on the borderline for a second Glass, is destined to improve with time.

For some years, Sandro Princic has been turning out wines almost all of which earn a second Glass, even though we would like to see the peaks that in the past have taken him to the top flight of Italian winemaking. This is one of the estates that have written the story of premium wine in Friuli, thanks to Doro Princic, who ran the winery for decades to standards never before seen in the area. Doro may have celebrated his 90th birthday this year but he can still tell a great wine from a merely good one. The Princic residence and cellar is situated on the hill at Pradis. "Spectacular" is the only word for the view, which enhances the congenial welcome that Sandro and his wife Grazia offer their many visitors. This year, Sandro decided to keep separate several vats of Tocai that were very different from each other before bottling them under different labels. The Tocai Friulano Crôs Altis has clear notes of apple on a nose that introduces a warm, fruity palate and a long, caressing finish. In contrast, the standard version is drier and has more marked acidity on the palate. The Sauvignon's aromas may not be particularly emphatic but the wine is rich and tangy, with concentrated structure. As usual, the Pinot Bianco is one of Sandro Princic's strong suits, unveiling appley fruit on the nose against a backdrop of flowers and herbs. There is also a quite stunning unfiltered version of the same wine, bottled in magnums. Unfortunately, Sandro refuses to release it because he doesn't believe the market is ready for a product that could leave a deposit. What a pity!

○	Collio Bianco '00	🍷🍷	4
○	Collio Pinot Grigio '00	🍷🍷	4
○	Collio Sauvignon '00	🍷🍷	4
○	Collio Tocai Friulano '00	🍷🍷	4
○	Oblin Blanc '99	🍷🍷	5
○	Collio Chardonnay '00	🍷	4
○	Collio Pinot Bianco '00	🍷	4
●	Friuli Isonzo Cabernet Sauvignon '99		4
○	Collio Pinot Grigio '98	🍷🍷🍷	4
○	Oblin Blanc '98	🍷🍷	5

○	Collio Pinot Bianco '00	🍷🍷	4
○	Collio Sauvignon '00	🍷🍷	4
○	Collio Tocai Crôs Altis '00	🍷🍷	5
○	Collio Tocai Friulano '00	🍷🍷	4
○	Collio Pinot Grigio '00	🍷	4
○	Collio Tocai Friulano '93	🍷🍷🍷	5
○	Collio Pinot Bianco '95	🍷🍷🍷	5
●	Collio Merlot '98	🍷🍷	4
○	Collio Pinot Bianco '99	🍷🍷	4
○	Collio Tocai Friulano '99	🍷🍷	4

CORMONS (GO)

DARIO RACCARO
FRAZ. ROLAT
VIA SAN GIOVANNI, 87/B
34071 CORMONS (GO)
TEL. 048161425

Dario Raccaro is a small producer with four hectares of vines. He makes about 20,000 bottles a year, most of them sold privately. There was no question that sooner or later Dario would have a Three Glass award to tuck away in his trophy cupboard. It came from a Tocai of superb elegance and weight on the palate. A distinctly superior wine, it deserves to be savoured slowly on the palate after the nose has been enjoyed unhurriedly. Apple and pear are to the fore in the intensely concentrated fruit. Elegant and warm on entry, the palate follows through surefootedly, opening out delightfully and finishing with an extraordinarily rich, endlessly long after-aroma. Much hard work has gone into this wine over the years but credit must also go to the vineyard, first planted in the early years of the 20th century. Legend has it that the first plants came from Hungary and since then, cuttings grafted onto the same rootstock have been used to extend the vineyard. What we do know is that another estate won several Three Glass awards with tocai from this plot, which Dario has been renting for only a few years. When vines like these meet a winemaker like Dario, results are sure to follow. Not content, however, Dario also amazed the panel with a marvellous Merlot that had only gone into the bottle a few weeks before. In grateful appreciation, the panel noted plum, spices and cherries on the nose, echoed on a fruit-rich palate with a round, full-bodied thrust backed up by hefty tannins and over 14 per cent alcohol. Finally, the attractive Collio Bianco is a blend of 50 per cent tocai with equal parts of sauvignon and pinot grigio.

○	Collio Tocai Friulano '00	♛♛♛	4
●	Collio Merlot '00	♛♛	4
○	Collio Bianco '00	♛♛	4
○	Collio Malvasia '00	♛♛	4
●	Collio Merlot '97	♛♛	4
○	Collio Bianco '99	♛♛	4
●	Collio Merlot '99	♛♛	4
○	Collio Tocai Friulano '99	♛♛	4

CORMONS (GO)

RONCADA
LOC. RONCADA, 5
34071 CORMONS (GO)
TEL. 048161394
E-MAIL: roncada@hotmail.com

The Roncada estate has been in the Mattioni family for almost five decades. It comprises 22 hectares of vineyards at the edge of the Collio, where it descends to the flatlands. Its limestone and clay soil makes it an ideal place to grow premium-quality grapes and the owners who built the main residence in the 19th century made sure there was plenty of cellar space. The first thing that springs to mind about Roncada is the consistently high quality of its range. There may not be any world-shakers but you'd have difficulty in finding a bottle that isn't at least well-made. Results like these are guaranteed by the presence of Oscar Biasi, who has been the estate wine technician for about 20 years. Among his many skills, Oscar knows how to manage even-handedly all 14 varieties grown at Roncada. It gives us pleasure to note how reliable the Franconia is. It's a variety that few grow in Friuli: some producers even make an "amabile" medium-sweet version. The grape is known as Blaufrankisch in Burgenland and Alto Adige, where it goes into seriously good wines. The Roncada interpretation has a nose reminiscent of pepper, brambles and cassis, ushering in a dry palate rendered lean by forward tannins. The Pinot Grigio wins your praise for its lush fruit and long finish while what we liked about the Merlot was the tannic structure on the palate and the hints of cherry and black cherry in the bouquet. The Ribolla Gialla '00 is spot-on, the notes of very ripe yellow plums and trademark varietal acidity making it a perfect bottle to uncork when fish is on the menu.

○	Collio Pinot Grigio '00	♛♛	4
●	Collio Merlot '99	♛♛	4
○	Collio Ribolla Gialla '00	♛	4
○	Collio Sauvignon '00	♛	4
●	Franconia '99	♛	4
○	Collio Chardonnay '00		4
○	Collio Müller Thurgau '00		4
○	Collio Pinot Bianco '00		4
●	Collio Cabernet Sauvignon '98	♛♛	4

CORMONS (GO)

Ronco dei Tassi
Loc. Monte, 38
34071 Cormons (GO)
tel. 048160155
e-mail: roncodeitassi@libero.it

Little by little and step by prudent step, Fabio Coser has extended his estate's vineyards to their present ten hectares, to which we must add the three he rents, and his production to over 55,000 bottles a year. Work on the new cellar finished recently but for long the project absorbed much of Fabio's time and energy. Today, Fabio and his wife Daniela, with eldest son Matteo, can have plenty of elbow room and the right tools to make their wines to the highest standards. Fabio is one of the region's most respected and experienced oenologists. His wines are a touchstone of quality and honest pricing. Ronco dei Tassi grows eight grape types but only turns out five labels as some of the white varieties go into the Fosarin, while some reds into the Cjarandon, whose '99 version will be released in 2002. The Fosarin, a tocai and pinot bianco blend topped up with malvasia, has an elegant nose of stewed apple, peach and yellow plum nicely offset by faint hints of toastiness. Mouthfilling on the palate, it offers nice freshness and a long fruity after-aroma. The panel were impressed by the complexity of the Pinot Grigio on the nose, which ranges from pear to apple and yeasts. We also like the breadth on the palate, with its notes of citrus and tropical fruit, backed up by tangy acidity and warm alcohol. Finally, the Tocai unveils intense, stylish aromas of acacia blossom and elderflower before the full-bodied palate adds a backdrop of peach and almond, as well as a distinctly inviting twist of almonds in the finish.

O	Collio Bianco Fosarin '00	🍷🍷	4
O	Collio Pinot Grigio '00	🍷🍷	4
O	Collio Tocai Friulano '00	🍷🍷	4
O	Collio Sauvignon '00	🍷	4
O	Collio Bianco Fosarin '96	🍷🍷🍷	4
O	Collio Sauvignon '98	🍷🍷🍷	4
●	Collio Rosso Cjarandon '97	🍷🍷	5
O	Collio Bianco Fosarin '98	🍷🍷	4
O	Collio Bianco Fosarin '99	🍷🍷	4

CORMONS (GO)

Ronco del Gelso
Via Isonzo, 117
34071 Cormons (GO)
tel. 048161310
e-mail: roncodelgelso@libero.it

Year after year, Giorgio Badin manages his winemaking with the same scrupulous care, adjusting any procedures he thinks can be improved. That strategy has enabled him to make better and better wines, often winning Three Glasses for one bottle or another. There are about 15 hectares of vineyard on the estate, all lying around the cellar in the Isonzo DOC zone. We should add that Giorgio is very proud of the new cellar he opened a few years ago but he spent last summer overseeing work on now unavoidable extensions to his winemaking, barrel and bottle facilities. In the meantime, he was also nursing his vines through the hot, dry season. But let's move on to the wines. Badin employs his own special micro-oxygenation procedure to obtain wines that are drinking nicely only three months after the harvest but which then reduce during the following summer. This is true of Badin's whites but not his reds, which are evidently subject to another vinification process and evolve differently in the bottle. In any case, this situation makes special caution essential when tasting. You have to remember that the nose will be much tidier in a few weeks and the wines will gain in stature unbelievably in subsequent years. Giorgio's Sauvignon is a spectacular success, with its nose of elderflower, tomato leaf and citrus leading in to a lingering and beautifully structured palate. Also excellent are the Chardonnay, a textbook example of balance on nose and palate, with clear hints of golden delicious apples, and a Merlot that returns to the front rank in a warm, full-bodied version with remarkable fruit-rich texture.

O	Friuli Isonzo Sauvignon '00	🍷🍷🍷	4*
O	Friuli Isonzo Chardonnay '00	🍷🍷	4
●	Friuli Isonzo Merlot '99	🍷🍷	5
O	Friuli Isonzo Bianco Latimis '00	🍷🍷	4
O	Friuli Isonzo Pinot Bianco '00	🍷🍷	4
O	Friuli Isonzo Pinot Grigio Sot lis Rivis '00	🍷🍷	4
O	Friuli Isonzo Tocai Friulano '00	🍷🍷	4
●	Friuli Isonzo Cabernet Franc '00	🍷	4
O	Friuli Isonzo Riesling '00	🍷	4
O	Friuli Isonzo Tocai Friulano '97	🍷🍷🍷	5
O	Friuli Isonzo Sauvignon '98	🍷🍷🍷	4
O	Friuli Isonzo Pinot Grigio Sot lis Rivis '99	🍷🍷🍷	4

CORMONS (GO)

Oscar Sturm
Loc. Zegla, 1
34071 Cormons (GO)
tel. 048160720
e-mail: sturm@sturm.it

You can always bank on Oscar and Dunja Sturm's wines, even though the authors are engagingly modest about them. At some wineries, the bottles are trundled out to an accompanying chorus of praise but the Sturms have a very different style. In fact, Oscar and Dunja are sometimes the first to express reservations. But even the most casual of glances at the table below will reveal that Sturm wines are seriously good. The family name is Austrian in origin for their ancestors moved to Friuli a couple of centuries ago from Styria, a region with a proud wine heritage. Today, the Sturms have 11 hectares under vine around their home and cellar, most on hillslopes. The cellar itself is below ground and the temperature is almost always cool, which makes it an ideal place for barrel ageing and for storing the wines in the bottle before release. One of the finest of this year's products is an irresistible Collio Bianco, a blend of tocai and pinot grigio almost entirely aged in oak. Its oak-derived notes of vanilla and pipe tobacco meld deliciously with the broad swathe of fruit on both nose and palate, reaching a lovely peak in the unhurried finish. Sturm has the right sauvignon clones to turn out an excellent wine even when the weather has been unfavourable to the variety. His Tocai Friulano is broad and full-bodied, showing good complexity and length, while the equally long Merlot has nice weight in the mouth and aromas of black cherry tart and cherries.

O	Collio Bianco '00	🍷🍷	5
O	Collio Sauvignon '00	🍷🍷	4
O	Collio Tocai Friulano '00	🍷🍷	4
●	Collio Merlot '99	🍷🍷	4
O	Chardonnay Andritz '00	🍷	4
O	Collio Pinot Grigio '00	🍷	4
●	Cabernet Franc '00		4
O	Chardonnay Andritz '99	🍷🍷	3
O	Collio Tocai Friulano '99	🍷🍷	3

CORMONS (GO)

Subida di Monte
Loc. Monte, 9
34071 Cormons (GO)
tel. 048161011
e-mail: subida@libero.it

Subida di Monte was purchased in 1972 by Gigi Antonutti, who had decided to become a grower after years plying his trade as a wine merchant. His beautifully looked-after vines are decently aspected and stand near the winery itself. Space is not a problem and work proceeds unhampered. At present, the new generation of Antonuttis is settling in as Gigi hands over to his sons Cristian and Andrea, who are gradually taking charge of production and sales, respectively. A brace of Selezione wines, with Cristian Antonutti's name on the label, are the best of this year's offerings. The barrique and tonneau-aged Merlot Selezione '99 tempts the nostrils with notes of red berry fruit tart, cherries in syrup and plums. The complex, generous palate offers very ripe notes of fruit that mirror the nose. The Chardonnay Selezione, too, spent a long time in small oak casks, drawing from them hints of confectioner's cream, banana and apricot to mingle with the varietal hint of crusty bread that lead in to a soft, caressing mouthfeel. The panel particularly appreciated the nose of the Tocai Selezione while it was the palate of the standard-label Tocai that stood out. Finally, the Bianco Sotrari, a blend of sauvignon, traminer and riesling, was struggling to find its balance when we tasted.

O	Collio Chardonnay Sel. '00	🍷	5
●	Collio Merlot Sel. '99	🍷🍷	6
O	Collio Tocai Friulano '00	🍷	3
O	Collio Tocai Friulano Sel. '00	🍷	5
O	Collio Bianco Sotrari '00		4
O	Collio Pinot Grigio '00		3
O	Collio Sauvignon '00		3
●	Collio Rosso Poncaia '97	🍷🍷	5

CORMONS (GO)

Tiare - Roberto Snidarcig
Loc. Monte, 58
34071 Cormons (GO)
Tel. 048160064
E-mail: aztiare@tiscalinet.it

Roberto and Sandra Snidarcig are a very likeable young couple. Sandra spends most of her time looking after their restaurant on Monte Quarin, where diners can enjoy a spectacular view of the Friulian plain and Adriatic Sea in the distance. Husband Roberto is the winemaker, in charge of a winery he founded at a tender age in 1985. Today, he has about ten hectares of vineyards and turns out about 70,000 bottles a year under 11 labels. The modestly proportioned cellar is on a hillside at Mossa but Roberto has everything he needs to make wine. The top of the Snidarcig range is the Isonzo DOC Cabernet Sauvignon. There's a hint of tar over wild berry tart on the full complex nose, taking you in to a robust body and an intensely fruit-rich finish. The Merlot is another successful wine, at least as far as the fruit is concerned. It is slightly let down by over-sweet wood that leaves an intrusive note of vanilla and talcum powder. Roberto's Pinot Grigio is second only to the Sauvignon in terms of bottles produced. The '00 version is well-made, particularly if we bear in mind the vintage, and it has laudably rich fruit. Currently, the Ribolla Gialla is still shrugging off its residual sulphur dioxide. When we tasted it from the vat, it was very promising.

● Friuli Isonzo Cabernet Sauvignon '99	♟♟	3*
● Collio Cabernet Franc '00	♟	3
○ Collio Chardonnay '00	♟	3
○ Collio Pinot Grigio '00	♟	3
○ Collio Ribolla Gialla '00	♟	3
○ Collio Sauvignon '00	♟	3
● Friuli Isonzo Merlot '99	♟	3
● Friuli Isonzo Cabernet Sauvignon '98	♟♟	3

CORMONS (GO)

Franco Toros
Loc. Novali, 12
34071 Cormons (GO)
Tel. 048161327

You can't help liking Franco Toros, the genial winemaker from Novali near Cormons, particularly when he serves up a Three Glass wine for the second time in a row. The award went to a fantastic Pinot Bianco '00. Not content with an exploit that would satisfy much larger wineries, Franco cheerfully set in front of the panel a superb Tocai Friulano and two other whites, the Pinot Grigio and the Sauvignon, which promise great things for the future. It was a range of whites that the panel knew, having tasted them several times in the cellar, and one that confirms Franco as a great white winemaker. But what happened to the Merlot? There's no mystery. The disappointing '98 vintage simply didn't go into the bottle and we'll be tasting the '99 version for the next edition of the Guide. Franco has a densely planted vineyard of about eight hectares around his home, as well as one hectare he rents on the southern slopes of Monte Quarin, the hill that overlooks Cormons. Annual production is about 55,000 bottles, which tells you that the yields per vine and per hectare are kept very low. We were absolutely enchanted by this Pinot Bianco at the tastings. Warm and mouthfilling, it manages to conserve pinot bianco's varietal elegance despite its incredible weight on the palate. The Tocai Friulano is also very much a varietal wine, with its hints of almonds on the palate. These are married to a tangy freshness and remarkable structure. Finally, note that the Chardonnay is aged only in stainless steel.

○ Collio Pinot Bianco '00	♟♟♟	4*
○ Collio Tocai Friulano '00	♟♟	4
○ Collio Pinot Grigio '00	♟♟	4
○ Collio Sauvignon '00	♟♟	4
○ Collio Chardonnay '00	♟	4
● Collio Merlot Sel. '97	♟♟♟	6
● Collio Merlot '97	♟♟	4
○ Collio Pinot Bianco '99	♟♟	4
○ Collio Tocai Friulano '99	♟♟	4

CORMONS (GO)

VIGNA DEL LAURO
LOC. MONTE, 38
34071 CORMONS (GO)
TEL. 048160155
E-MAIL: roncodeitassi@libero.it

Vigna del Lauro is the winery founded by Fabio Coser, whom we have mentioned frequently in the Guide as he collaborates with several estates, and his friend Eberhard Spangenberg, a Bavaria-based importer of Italian wines. In its first two years, the cellar sent the entire production abroad but, heeding the advice of restaurateurs, wine merchants and Guide panellists, the partners have now also decided to sell their wines in Italy. Currently, Vigna del Lauro has six hectares in the municipalities of Cormons and San Floriano, straddling the adjoining DOC zones of Collio and Isonzo. The vintage was not a good one for Sauvignon, a wine that won Fabio and Eberhard Three Glasses in our last edition. Instead, it was the Pinot Grigio that shone, revealing intense apple aromas and a rich, complex structure on the palate with very ripe fruit and excellent length. The Bianco is a blend of tocai friulano, pinot bianco, malvasia and ribolla gialla whose curious hints of macaroons mingle with flowers on the nose, leading in to a palate dominated by tocai-inspired nuances of almonds. There's no mistaking the ripeness of the fruit in the very successful Merlot Isonzo '99, a wine whose tannins are deliciously swathed in a full, chewy palate. The other wines we tasted are also worth uncorking, including an exciting Collio Merlot that will be released in spring 2002. We'll be discussing it in more detail next time.

O Collio Bianco '00	YY	4
O Collio Pinot Grigio '00	YY	4
● Friuli Isonzo Merlot '99	YY	4
O Collio Tocai Friulano '00	Y	4
O Friuli Isonzo Chardonnay '00	Y	3
O Collio Sauvignon '99	YYY	4
O Collio Bianco '99	YY	4

CORNO DI ROSAZZO (UD)

VALENTINO BUTUSSI
VIA PRA' DI CORTE, 1
33040 CORNO DI ROSAZZO (UD)
TEL. 0432759194
E-MAIL: butussi@butussi.it

You can't miss Angelo Butussi's winery as you come into the small town of Corno di Rosazzo. It's not just a question of size; the facilities are also very attractive to look at. In the past year, a small outlet for cellar door sales has been added. It has the curious lines of a pre-Romanesque chapel, as if it has been erected in honour of the famously pious family's nickname, "Vaticano". The estate bears the name of the now 91 year old Valentino Butussi and the dynamic Angelo shares the work with his wife Pierina and their children Erika, Filippo and Tobia. Mattia, the youngest, is still studying. Currently, the Butussis have ten hectares of vineyard, some in the Colli Orientali DOC zone but most in Grave del Friuli. Production, largely of whites, hovers around 800 hectolitres a year, with a little help from bought-in fruit and a less than severe yield policy. Almost all of the wines we tasted were good but the Colli Orientali Pinot Grigio stood out. It has a concentrated nose with elegant notes of apple. The fresh, firmly structured palate mirrors the nose and has plenty of length. The Verduzzo, a local variety, has a vibrant gold hue that introduces a note of stewed apples, very ripe yellow peaches and roasted nuts. In the mouth, it is slightly sweet, with nuances of candied orange peel in the back palate. There was a long line of One Glass wines. The panel particularly liked the Ribolla Gialla, a refreshing wine redolent of golden delicious apples, herbs and spring flowers.

O COF Pinot Grigio '00	YY	3*
O COF Verduzzo Friulano '00	YY	3*
O Friuli Grave Pinot Bianco '00	Y	3
O COF Ribolla Gialla '00	Y	3
O COF Sauvignon '00	Y	3
O COF Tocai Friulano '00	Y	3
● COF Cabernet Sauvignon '99	Y	4
O COF Picolit '99	Y	6
● Friuli Grave Merlot '00		3

CORNO DI ROSAZZO (UD)

Eugenio Collavini
Loc. Gramogliano
Via Forum Julii, 2
33040 Corno di Rosazzo (UD)
tel. 0432753222
e-mail: collavini@collavini.it

The Eugenio Collavini winery continues to make satisfyingly steady progress under the guiding hand of the ever-enthusiastic Manlio, who directs operations from the old manor house that once belonged to the noble Zuccus di Cuccanea family. Until a few years ago, the accent at the property was on quantity but Manlio has now firmly embraced the doctrine of quality first. Anyone who, at tastings, has followed the birth and development of the wines presented will not be surprised at the results achieved. To supplement the fruit from the few hectares owned by the estate, Manlio buys in grapes from high-density vineyards, or from vines at least 20 years old. The technology in the cellar is very much cutting edge and, used in combination with more traditional techniques, means that intervention during vinification and ageing is kept to a minimum. This year, there was a long list of Two Glass products, led by the Chardonnay and the Merlot Collio '99, to testify to the excellent quality of the range. We can also tell you that there are some other very interesting wines presently ageing in the cellars. It is the complexity of the Chardonnay's aromas that impresses: the notes of very ripe citrus, fruit salad and yeasts. These are followed by a superbly balanced palate with nicely gauged acidity, lavish fruit and a full finish. The Merlot scored even higher, tempting the nose with plums, wild berries and bramble. A soft entry on the palate follows through with lusty, well-sustained fruit that never misses a beat. All in all, it looks as though Manlio will be turning out a couple of world-class bottles very soon.

○	Collio Chardonnay dei Sassi Cavi Collezione Privata '99	🍷🍷	5
●	Collio Merlot Collezione Privata '99	🍷🍷	5
○	COF Ribolla Gialla Turian '00	🍷🍷	4
○	Collio Pinot Grigio Collezione Privata '00	🍷🍷	4
○	Collio Sauvignon Poncenera Collezione Privata '00	🍷🍷	5
○	Collio Tocai Friulano Collezione Privata '00	🍷🍷	4
○	Friuli Isonzo Chardonnay dei Sassi Cavi '00	🍷🍷	4
●	Collio Cabernet Collezione Privata '99	🍷	4

CORNO DI ROSAZZO (UD)

Adriano Gigante
Via Rocca Bernarda, 3
33040 Corno di Rosazzo (UD)
tel. 0432755835
e-mail: gigantevini@libero.it

Here we have a family-run estate of 20 hectares, with 12 planted to vine. Adriano Gigante looks after sales while his cousin Ariedo manages the vineyards and cellars. Giuliana Veliscech takes care of public relations. The vines are either right next to the cellar or else very near. Winemaking facilities are a little cramped but perfectly well equipped to turn out 60,000 bottles of excellent wine every year. Last year, Adriano took us by surprise with a superb Sauvignon and only a few months later, the quite extraordinary virtues of his Tocai Storico have also emerged. Actually, in final taste-offs with other successful examples, this Tocai was always there or thereabouts. Obtained from vines more than 40 years old, the Tocai Storico '00 triumphed in this year's final round of tastings. Sweet almonds and apple nuanced with basil on the nose usher in a concentrated, full-flavoured palate with warm alcohol and plenty of length, where liquorice and mint peek through. Neither was it a flash in the Gigante pan. The standard-label Tocai, the Pinot Grigio, the Chardonnay, part-aged in tonneaux, and the classic "vino da meditazione" sipping wine, Picolit, aged in small oak casks, were all admirable. Another promising wine is the Giudizio red, from 50 per cent refosco with schioppettino and merlot. Its leather and red berry tart on the nose are backed up by a soft, lusciously rich palate.

○	COF Tocai Friulano Storico '00	🍷🍷🍷	4
○	COF Chardonnay '00	🍷🍷	4
○	COF Pinot Grigio '00	🍷🍷	4
○	COF Tocai Friulano '00	🍷🍷	4
○	COF Picolit '99	🍷🍷	6
○	COF Sauvignon '00	🍷	4
●	COF Merlot Ris. '97	🍷	5
●	COF Merlot '99	🍷	4
●	COF Refosco P. R. '99	🍷	4
●	COF Rosso Giudizio '99	🍷	4
●	COF Schioppettino '99	🍷	4
○	COF Verduzzo Friulano '99	🍷	4
○	COF Tocai Friulano Storico '99	🍷🍷	4

CORNO DI ROSAZZO (UD)

Le Due Torri
Via S. Martino, 19
33040 Corno di Rosazzo (UD)
Tel. 0432759150 - 0432753115
E-mail: info@le2torri.com

The panel has made many, very encouraging, visits to Le Due Torri in recent years and after this vintage, we could no longer defer the entry of this Corno di Rosazzo-based cellar. As is often the case with winemakers around here, the vineyards are scattered over the flatlands of the Friuli Grave DOC zone and the hillslopes of the Colli Orientali del Friuli. Antonino Volpe, the young owner, manages five and a half hectares of vines, as well as woodland and seed crops. Unfortunately, Antonino suffers from the "disease" that afflicts so many Friulian producers – his 22,000 bottles are released under as many as 15 labels. The winemaking consultant is Maurizio Michelini and Volpe uses Giuseppe Lipari's mobile bottling unit, a service that has helped so many local properties to get started with estate-bottled wines. For the past two years, the Ribolla Gialla has been drawing praise and high scores, thanks in part to the vintages but also to the skills of the winemaker who produced these excellent wines. Ribolla gialla is a native Friulian variety. It makes high-acidity wines that cry out for fish, whether grilled, boiled or fried, and in warm years, like the last two, manages to combine tanginess and alcohol wonderfully. In the Chardonnay '00, we liked the bouquet of citrus fruit, yeasts and apricots, the generous front palate and the fresh, inviting finish. The '98 version has a little less nose-palate consistency.

O	Friuli Grave Chardonnay '00	♉♉	2*
O	Ribolla Gialla '00	♉♉	2*
O	Friuli Grave Pinot Grigio '00	♉	2*
O	Friuli Grave Sauvignon '00	♉	2*
O	Friuli Grave Tocai Friulano '00	♉	2*
O	Friuli Grave Chardonnay '98	♉	3
O	Verduzzo Friulano '00		3

CORNO DI ROSAZZO (UD)

Leonardo Specogna
Via Rocca Bernarda, 4
33040 Corno di Rosazzo (UD)
Tel. 0432755840
E-mail: spek@inwind.it

Clamouring customers force the Specogna brothers, Graziano and Gianni, to release wine that will gain in stature after a further year in the bottle. For those of you who don't know Friuli, we're mainly talking whites here. But the Specognas don't make the lightweight quaffing wines that so often spring to mind when you hear the word "white". Graziano works mainly in the cellar and Gianni prefers life in the open air of the vineyards. Their property is on the hillslopes of Rocca Bernarda, in well-aspected, beautifully looked-after sites. Size isn't really a problem in the cellar but the brothers now need more dedicated space for their bottles and barrel stock, large and small. The Sauvignon '00 is half barrel fermented, although you'd never guess from nose or palate. What grabs your attention are the aromas of elderflower, apricot and tomato leaf, then the stylish peach in the lingering finish. No more than 20 per cent of the Pinot Grigio saw oak but the copper-tinged hue in the glass is remarkable. The Specognas are among the first winemakers to go back to this traditional technique, particularly appreciated by the UK market. Citrus and tropical fruit on the nose is followed up by refreshing gooseberry on the palate, which has all the suppleness of a very well-structured wine. As was the case last year, the Tocai Friulano evinces distinct sauvignon-like notes, which cost it points at our tasting, but it is still a very fine wine, if you're not too bothered about varietal typicity.

O	COF Sauvignon '00	♉♉	4
O	Pinot Grigio '00	♉♉	4
O	COF Tocai Friulano '00	♉	4
O	COF Chardonnay '99	♉	4
●	COF Refosco P. R. '99	♉	4
O	COF Verduzzo Friulano '00		4
●	COF Cabernet '99		4
●	COF Merlot '99		4
●	Oltre '96	♉♉	6

CORNO DI ROSAZZO (UD)

ANDREA VISINTINI
VIA GRAMOGLIANO, 27
33040 CORNO DI ROSAZZO (UD)
TEL. 0432755813
E-MAIL: info@vinivisintini.com

Andrea Visintini's estate embraces about 27 hectares of vineyard, which he and his son Oliviero manage personally. Oliviero also looks after the cellar and sister Cinzia, instantly likeable and herself a shrewd taster, runs sales. The house-cum-cellar incorporates a tower dating from 1560, built to replace a Roman construction that kept watch over the road from Aquileia to Cividale, the ancient city of Forum Julii. Andrea generally gives us a range that collects plenty of Glasses but as tastings proceeded this time, we began to note a worrying absence of wines that scored more than 80 points. It looked as if the Visintini cellar was shooting a tad below its traditionally high average. We were totally wrong, of course. The Pinot Bianco and the Malvasia are enough on their own to make up for shortcomings elsewhere. Both varieties were favoured by the weather but to that must be added Oliviero's skilful contribution. In the Pinot Bianco, he has managed to capture the grape's intrinsic elegance and fuse it into a concentrated mélange of fruit aromas where apple prevails. On the palate, there are even faint notes of honey tucked away in the rich, close-knit texture. The Malvasia offers notes of apple, fruit salad and herbal tea. There is nice nose-palate consistency in the aromas, with a pleasing hint of refreshing acidity that prolongs the finish. Finally, the Tocai won favourable comments, especially for its tangy, fruit-rich palate.

○	COF Pinot Bianco '00	🍷🍷	3*
○	Collio Malvasia '00	🍷🍷	3*
●	COF Merlot '00	🍷	3
○	COF Pinot Grigio '00	🍷	3
○	COF Ribolla Gialla '00	🍷	3
○	COF Sauvignon '00	🍷	3
○	Collio Tocai Friulano '00	🍷	3
○	COF Verduzzo Friulano '00		3
●	COF Merlot II Barrique '98	🍷🍷	4
●	COF Merlot '99	🍷🍷	3

CORNO DI ROSAZZO (UD)

ZOF
FRAZ. SANT'ANDREA DEL SUDRIO
VIA GIOVANNI XXIII, 32/A
33040 CORNO DI ROSAZZO (UD)
TEL. 0432759673
E-MAIL: info@zof.it

Daniele Zof runs a rather reassuring cellar, consistently turning out good wines. They may not be massive but you can bank on their quality. Daniele studied oenology and has put his knowledge into practice, adopting a very innovative approach to winemaking and engaging as his consultant, Donato Lanati, one of his former teachers. There are nine hectares on the estate and Zof rents six more to produce a total of 80,000 bottles a year and a further quantity of wine that is sold unbottled. His small cellar stands next to the farm holiday centre his mother runs and is sufficient for his needs. It takes only a few minutes for Daniele to reach his vines so the harvest is transported to the cellar swiftly and smoothly. Best of this year's offerings is the Pinot Bianco '00, which won Two Glasses with points to spare. Fermented without the skins, it offers cream and fruit aromas where honey prevails. The texture on the palate is close-knit and generously fruit-rich, showing good harmony and length. The golden Picolit has a complex nose redolent of apples, pears and peaches, with the odd sweet note. Elegant and slightly sweet, the palate mirrors the richness of the nose and lingers attractively. Va' Pensiero is a blend of cabernet sauvignon, merlot and schioppettino that reflects the limitations of the vintage.

○	COF Pinot Grigio '00	🍷🍷	3*
○	COF Picolit '99	🍷🍷	6
●	COF Cabernet Franc '00	🍷	3
○	COF Ribolla Gialla '00	🍷	3
○	COF Sauvignon '00	🍷	3
○	COF Tocai Friulano '00	🍷	3
●	Va' Pensiero '98	🍷	4
●	COF Merlot '00		3
●	COF Schioppettino '00		4

DOLEGNA DEL COLLIO (GO)

Ca' Ronesca
Via Lonzano, 15
34070 Dolegna del Collio (GO)
tel. 048160034
e-mail: caronesca@caronesca.it

Ca' Ronesca is a big winery, in every sense. Its 100 hectares in the Collio and Colli Orientali, 56 of them planted to vine, are matched by big quality, under the watchful eye of Paolo Bianchi. For years, Paolo has been flanked by oenologist Franco Della Rossa and together they produce 250,000 bottles every year in the superbly equipped cellar. Paolo devotes a lot of attention to vineyard management, as can be seen from the fairly dense planting patterns, low yields per vine and the setting aside of various plots for woodland to maintain the ecosystem. This also guarantees that nature's own brand of pest control is always available. Everything points to great results and those were duly achieved again this year. The Pinot Grigio and the Sauvignon Podere di Ipplis are irresistible. Butter-rich and almost opulent, the Pinot Grigio tempts the nose with honey, stewed apple and dried spring flowers before the palate reveals its contrast of appetite-reviving acidity and softness. The Sauvignon has notes of red pepper and rue, also unfurling definite notes of yellow peach that add complexity and varietal character. The palate follows through with sure-footed elegance, ending in a long, tangy finish. As soon as you lift the glass, the Sauvignon del Collio tells you that its vegetal notes of tomato leaf rub shoulders with peach and ripe melon sweetness. Both components are mirrored on the palate. If you didn't know, you might think the Saramago was from Alsace. Its sweetness never cloys and the fruit has notes of candied apricots, citrus and dried roses. Both the Tocai and the Marnà came close to a second Glass and the Sermar '99 has much improved since our last tasting.

○	COF Pinot Grigio Podere di Ipplis '00	▼▼ 4
○	COF Sauvignon Podere di Ipplis '00	▼▼ 4
○	Collio Sauvignon '00	▼▼ 4
○	Saramago '99	▼▼ 5
○	Collio Malvasia '00	▼ 4
○	Collio Tocai Friulano '00	▼ 4
○	Collio Bianco Marnà '99	▼ 4
●	Collio Cabernet Franc '99	▼ 4
○	Collio Chardonnay '00	4
●	COF Refosco P. R. '99	4
○	Saramago '98	▽▽ 4
○	COF Sauvignon Podere di Ipplis '99	▽▽ 4

DOLEGNA DEL COLLIO (GO)

Crastin
Loc. Ruttars, 33
34070 Dolegna del Collio (GO)
tel. 0481630310

Sergio Collarig, owner of the Crastin label, is a canny type who looks about him, tastes other cellars' wines and then rethinks his own products. As a result, his star is rising rapidly in the quality firmament. That was what the panel discovered when they went to taste Sergio's wines, a range that for the past couple of years has been showing a marked improvement over previous standards. We should point out that Sergio also runs a small and very inviting "agriturismo", or farm holiday centre, so in the past he has not always been able to concentrate on winemaking. However, he does have the support of oenologist Mauro Bressan. There are five hectares on the estate, with another one coming onstream next year, and the annual production of 35,000 bottles is sold exclusively in Italy. The Crastin Rosso comes from merlot and cabernet franc. Its garnet colour betrays its age but the nose and palate are wonderfully sprightly. Concentrated on the nose, with hints of cherry, black cherry, damson and autumn leaves, it follows through perfectly on the fruit and tannin-rich palate. In the Pinot Grigio, Sergio has managed to combine elegance with generous fresh fruit, a tight-knit mouthfeel, refreshing acidity and good length. His Collio Bianco is a blend of pinot bianco, tocai friulano and sauvignon and shows the breadth of the variety's complexity in youthful notes of apple, pear, peach and crusty bread, then the palate surges through to a sweet apple finish.

○	Collio Pinot Grigio '00	▼▼ 3*
●	Collio Rosso Crastin Rosso '97	▼▼ 5
○	Collio Bianco '00	▼ 4
○	Collio Tocai Friulano '00	▼ 4
●	Collio Cabernet Franc '99	▼ 4
○	Collio Sauvignon '00	4
●	Collio Merlot '99	4

DOLEGNA DEL COLLIO (GO)

VENICA & VENICA
LOC. CERO
VIA MERNICO, 42
34070 DOLEGNA DEL COLLIO (GO)
TEL. 048161264 - 048160177
E-MAIL: venica@venica.it

The Venica brothers, Gianni and Giorgio, have one of the finest wineries in Friuli, for the quality of the wines, the care lavished on the vineyards, the hospitality of the family and indeed everyone else on the estate, and finally by virtue of the lovely holiday centre. Let's drop a couple of names: Ornella, Gianni's wife, is now president of the Wine Tourism Movement and Gianni's son Gianpaolo has returned from his oenological studies and work experience across the Atlantic to concentrate on the family business. The Venicas have 28 hectares, all in the Collio DOC zone. This year, they delighted the panel with a superstar Tocai Friulano Cime. Intense and concentrated, its stylish notes of apple, pear and tea have a respectful hint of oak hovering in the background and the very warm, lingering palate has all the flavour you could want. The Sauvignon Ronco delle Mele also put on a fine show. Its nuances of rue and elderflower are less marked than usual before the tangy, mouthfilling palate unfurls notes of peach and tomato leaf laced with minerally hints. A word or two about some of the other wines. The Chardonnay Ronco Bernizza has enough complex, elegant tropical fruit to tame the oak-derived notes. There's a backdrop of onionskin in the nose of the Pinot Grigio that frames notes of yellow plum, apricot, apple and pear meet refreshing acidity in the long finish. Complexity is the keynote of the Tre Vignis, a blend of tocai and chardonnay with a little sauvignon. The nose ranges from peach leaf to hazelnut, tropical fruit and apple. Finally the Prime Note is equally rewarding. It's a blend, like the Tre Vignis, but with a robust proportion of ribolla.

○	Collio Tocai Friulano Ronco delle Cime '00	🍷🍷🍷	4
○	Collio Sauvignon Ronco delle Mele '00	🍷🍷	5
○	Collio Chardonnay Ronco Bernizza '00	🍷🍷	4
○	Collio Pinot Bianco '00	🍷🍷	4
○	Collio Ribolla Gialla '00	🍷🍷	4
○	Collio Sauvignon Ronco del Cerò '00	🍷🍷	4
●	Collio Merlot Perilla '98	🍷🍷	5
○	Collio Bianco Tre Vignis '99	🍷🍷	5
○	Collio Prime Note '99	🍷🍷	4
○	Collio Pinot Grigio '00	🍷	4
●	Refosco P. R. Bottaz '97	🍷	5

DUINO AURISINA (TS)

KANTE
LOC. PREPOTTO, 3
34011 DUINO AURISINA (TS)
TEL. 040200761

It's Malvasia that scored again this year at the Kante winery. And the panel is particularly pleased. For one thing, it confirms the standard Edi has achieved in the past and for another, this is a wine type that has huge market potential. You've got to take your hat off to Edi, though. He has believed in the variety right from the start, encouraged by having some very old rows he could nurture and lift with scrupulous fermentation and by blending lots from different vineyards. This year's version has a stunning range of aromas, including honey, broom, lemon verbena and vanilla, and a harmoniously soft, yet stylishly refreshing, palate. As usual, the Chardonnay and Sauvignon are big wines. The intense fruit of the Chardonnay offers notes of hazelnut and confectioner's cream, progressing solidly on the richly-textured palate, while the Sauvignon sets the sweetness of the nose against a pleasingly vibrant note. Both are excellent examples of Edi's trademark – elegant yet firm thrust on the palate. The Vitoska was a little off-form. It has decent body and length, with notes of dried flowers, chamomile and mint tea on the nose, but lacks its customary balance.

○	Carso Malvasia '99	🍷🍷	5
○	Carso Chardonnay '99	🍷🍷	5
○	Sauvignon '99	🍷🍷	6
○	Carso Vitovska '99	🍷	5
○	Carso Malvasia '98	🍷🍷🍷	5
○	Chardonnay '90	🍷🍷🍷	6
○	Chardonnay '94	🍷🍷🍷	6
○	Carso Sauvignon '91	🍷🍷🍷	6
○	Carso Sauvignon '92	🍷🍷🍷	6
○	Carso Chardonnay '98	🍷🍷	5
○	Carso Sauvignon '98	🍷🍷	5
○	Carso Vitovska '98	🍷🍷	5

DUINO AURISINA (TS)

Zidarich
Loc. Prepotto, 11/c
34011 Duino Aurisina (TS)
tel. 040201223
e-mail: zidarich@zidarich.com

The Guide profile for Beniamino Zidarich's winery is significant for it means an addition to the small but quality-enhanced band of producers in the Carso Triestino DOC zone. A harsh and challenging territory, the Carso forces growers to make incredible sacrifices in the struggle for quality. Beniamino has restructured the estate's old 19th century house and in 1988 and 1989, replanted the entire vine stock, which at the time came to a little over two and a half hectares. The new Guyot-trained vineyards have a density of 8-10,000 plants per hectare and the maximum yield is 35 hectolitres per hectare. Today, Beniamino has rented another half hectare and is planting more stock for a total of three new hectares. Zidarich currently bottles about 10,000 units and all the wine is aged in French or Slavonian oak. No sulphur dioxide is used during the winemaking process except at bottling. Prulke is a blend of vitovska, malvasia and sauvignon that ages for a year in barriques. Its intense straw hue introduces notes of hazelnut, banana, confectioner's cream and cream then a broad harmonious mouth with good freshness and body. In the Malvasia, the oak-derived hints of milky coffee and apricot mingle with apple on the nose, to be mirrored well on the soft, warm palate. Beniamino's Terrano is the best version of this very rustic wine we tasted. There are occasional creamy notes that lift the cherry and spice aromas.

FAEDIS (UD)

Paolino Comelli
Fraz. Colloredo
Via della Chiesa, 8
33040 Faedis (UD)
tel. 0432711226 - 0432504973
e-mail: comellip@tin.it

Colloredo is a tiny village on a very steep hill that rewards visitors with a glorious view of the Friulian plain. Pierluigi Comelli, a notary public in Udine by profession, also runs the family winery. Having made major investments out in the fields, he is now turning his attention to the cellar, especially the barrel cellars where he ages his reds and the chardonnay that goes into Locum Nostrum. Over the new facility, Comelli is building three holiday accommodation units and a small hospitality centre, with comfortable tasting facilities. For the past few months, there have been a number of changes on the technical side as Flavio Zuliani, an oenologist with a solid track record, has started to collaborate with the winery. Two promising youngsters, Michele Tomasin and Eros Zanini, look after the cellar. None of the wines the panel tasted scored lower than One Glass, which tells you all you need to know about general quality standards. Locum Nostrum is particularly good, its creamy vanilla backed up by uncommonly rich fruit. The reds, Cabernet Sauvignon, Cabernet Franc and the merlot-based Soffumbergo all came close to gaining a second Glass. These are young wines and will improve with time as the tannins mellow. For the time being, they have a hint of astringency. The stainless steel-vinified and aged whites, especially the cellar's flagship Tocai, are all well worth investigating.

○ Prulke '98	🍷🍷	5
○ Carso Malvasia '99	🍷🍷	5
● Carso Terrano '99	🍷🍷	5
○ COF Bianco Locum Nostrum '99	🍷🍷	4
○ COF Chardonnay '00	🍷	4
○ COF Pinot Grigio '00	🍷	4
○ COF Tocai Friulano '00	🍷	4
● COF Cabernet Sauvignon '99	🍷	4
● COF Merlot '99	🍷	4
● COF Rosso Soffumbergo '99	🍷	4
○ COF Bianco Locum Nostrum '98	🍷🍷	4

FARRA D'ISONZO (GO)

Borgo Conventi
Strada Colombara, 13
34070 Farra d'Isonzo (GO)
Tel. 0481888004
E-mail: vescovo@tmedia.it

Gian Luigi Vescovo is an important figure in Friulian winemaking. He runs one of the estates that count because he vinifies fruit not just from his own vineyards but also grapes he buys in. In short, he is one of the people that "make" the market. The Vescovo winery has some of the most modern equipment in the region and the barrel cellar can only be called spectacular. Most of the estate-owned vines are near the winery but there are also hillslope plots in the Collio Goriziano DOC zone. In recent years, Gianni has involved his daughters Barbara and Erica in the management of the estate so now they work alongside his wife, Genni (pronounced "Jenny"). Last year, Vescovo celebrated his quarter century in winemaking with the release of Braida Nuova '99, repeating the success of the previous auction a decade before. It all goes to show the esteem he enjoys with his numerous clientele around the world. In total, the Vescovo estate produces about 400,000 bottles a year. The best of this years wines is the Pinot Grigio '00. Fermented without the skins, it has a complex, elegant nose where apple is predominant. Its well-sustained structure on the palate has very attractive fruit, which comes through particularly in the finish. finally, we would like to point out how extensive the range of premium Vescovo wines is this year, including the Braida Nuova '98, with its cabernet franc vegetal notes.

	Wine	Glasses	Score
○	Collio Pinot Grigio '00	♟♟	4
○	Collio Chardonnay '00	♟	4
○	Collio Sauvignon '00	♟	4
○	Collio Tocai Friulano '00	♟	4
○	Friuli Isonzo Chardonnay I Fiori '00	♟	3*
●	Friuli Isonzo Refosco P. R. Colombara '99	♟	4
●	Braida Nuova '98	♟	6
○	Collio Chardonnay Colle Russian '99	♟	5
●	Friuli Isonzo Cabernet Sauvignon Colombara '99		4
●	Braida Nuova '91	♟♟♟	6
●	Braida Nuova '97	♟♟	6

FARRA D'ISONZO (GO)

Colmello di Grotta
Via Gorizia, 133
34170 Farra d'Isonzo (GO)
Tel. 0481888445 - 0481888162
E-mail: colmello@xnet.it

The Colmello di Grotta estate is at Villanova di Farra, where a few clay and marl hills rise out of the chalk and gravel flatlands to make an unusual patchwork of Collio DOC areas in the broad expanses of the Isonzo DOC zone. Established in 1985 by Luciana Bennati, Colmello di Grotta extends over 19 hectares, of which 15 are under vine. Sadly, Luciana is no longer with us so the estate is run by her daughter, Francesca Bortolotto. Thanks to their very different soil types, the two zones produce quite distinct wines, even when they are obtained from the same variety. Depending on the vintage, sometimes the Collio version is better and in other years, the Isonzo prevails. Reds and the Chardonnay Collio age in the wood while all the other wines are fermented and aged exclusively in stainless steel With the exception of the Collio and Isonzo Sauvignons, all the wines presented scored more than 75 out of 100, showing that quality is high. The Pinot Grigio Collio reveals an outstanding wealth of tropical citrus fruit whereas its partner from the Isonzo zone green note. The Tocai has good structure and a close-knit texture while the Chardonnay Isonzo is redolent of pineapple, dried fruit and tangerines on the nose, with apple and plum on the palate. The Rondon, a red from four parts merlot to one of cabernet sauvignon, is well-rounded and lingers on the palate, with hints of raspberry and plum.

	Wine	Glasses	Score
○	Collio Pinot Grigio '00	♟♟	4
○	Collio Tocai Friulano '00	♟♟	4
○	Friuli Isonzo Chardonnay '00	♟♟	3*
●	Friuli Isonzo Merlot '99	♟♟	4
○	Collio Chardonnay '00	♟	4
○	Collio Sauvignon '00	♟	4
○	Friuli Isonzo Pinot Grigio '00	♟	3
●	Friuli Isonzo Cabernet Sauvignon '99	♟	4
●	Rondon '99	♟	4
●	Rondon '97	♟♟	4

FARRA D'ISONZO (GO)

★ Vinnaioli Jermann
Loc. Villanova
Via Monte Fortino, 21
34070 Farra d'Isonzo (GO)
Tel. 0481888080
E-MAIL: info@jermannvinnaioli.it

The wines made by Silvio Jermann are impeccable, their quality a benchmark. One of the new developments this year is a proper bottling line, rendered necessary by the cellar's steadily growing production, which now tops 600,000 bottles a year. As well as an array of stainless steel, Jermann also has a huge barrel cellar tucked away under the estate's lovely main residence. Silvio is now experimenting with pignolo, a local red variety with loads of character, and franconia, another red that produces excellent results for Burgenland growers in Austria. For the time being, we can mention a new, excellent version of Vintage Tunina, the '00. Not for the first time, it is the finest of the Jermann wines. Not for the first time, it won Three Glasses. Chardonnay, sauvignon, picolit and other varieties all go into this blend, which is excellent when it is not sublime. Elegance and finesse in the mouth and intriguing aromas are the distinguishing, but not the only, characteristics of a champion that has brought honour to Friulian, and indeed Italian, winemaking. Capo Martino '99 is a blend of tocai and pinot bianco, with small proportions of malvasia and picolit, aged in eight hectolitre barrels. It too is a monster of elegance. Fresh notes of confectioner's cream and banana introduce an impressive palate with just the right note of acidity to take it through to a generous finish of fruit. Silvio's Dreams '00 is a Chardonnay. Banana, caffelatte and apricot lead in to a palate with a soft mouthfeel and excitingly attractive acidity in the finish. The cellar also makes many varietal wines, all of excellent quality.

○	Vintage Tunina '00	♛♛♛	6
○	Capo Martino '99	♛♛	6
○	Chardonnay '00	♛♛	5
○	Müller Thurgau '00	♛♛	5
○	Pinot Bianco '00	♛♛	5
○	Pinot Grigio '00	♛♛	5
○	Traminer Aromatico '00	♛♛	5
○	Were Dreams, Now It Is Just Wine! '00	♛♛	6
○	Were Dreams, Now It Is Just Wine! '99	♛♛	6
●	Red Angel '00	♛	4
○	Sauvignon '00	♛	5
○	Vinnae '00	♛	4
○	Capo Martino '97	♛♛♛	6
○	Vintage Tunina '97	♛♛♛	6
○	Vintage Tunina '99	♛♛♛	6

FARRA D'ISONZO (GO)

Tenuta Villanova
Loc. Villanova
Via Contessa Beretta, 29
34070 Farra d'Isonzo (GO)
Tel. 0481888593
E-MAIL: tenutavi@tin.it

Tenuta Villanova was founded in 1499, when it was common practice for estates to have vineyards, as well as orchards, woodland and cereal crops. In the 19th century, the estate was so famous that Louis Pasteur, at the time a guest of the Friulian chemist Luigi Chiozza, carried out here some of the studies on fermentation that were to gain him fame as a microbiologist. Today, the property extends over 200 hectares, equally distributed between the Isonzo and Collio DOC zones. Part of the main complex has been restructured as a marvellously attractive conference centre. Managed by Paolo Cora, with Graziano Ceccutto looking after the cellar, the Tenuta this year came up with a series of very good wines, beginning with the Sauvignon Ronco Cucco '00. Yellow peach mingles with sage on the nose, then the stylishly textured palate offers warm alcohol and good balance. The Pinot Grigio Collio has a faint onionskin hue and an intense, fruit-rich nose. It follows through well on the palate, with a nice balance of fruit and alcohol rounded off by more than decent length. The Chardonnay Monte Cucco has elegant, creamy aromas of banana and golden delicious apple with a hint of apricot in the after-aroma. Clean and fresh-tasting, the Malvasia Isonzo is another achiever that also has a lingering finish. A final note. Because of the creation of a Monte Cucco DOC zone, this estate, which for decades has sold its finest selections under the Monte Cucco label, will no longer be able to do so.

○	Collio Pinot Grigio '00	♛♛	4
○	Collio Sauvignon Ronco Cucco '00	♛♛	4
○	Friuli Isonzo Malvasia '00	♛♛	3*
○	Collio Chardonnay Monte Cucco '99	♛♛	4
○	Collio Pinot Bianco '00	♛	3
○	Collio Ribolla Gialla Ronco Cucco '00	♛	4
○	Menj Bianco '00	♛	4
●	Collio Cabernet Sauvignon Monte Cucco '97	♛	5
●	Collio Cabernet Franc '99		4
○	Collio Chardonnay Monte Cucco '97	♛♛♛	4
●	Fraja '95	♛♛	6

GONARS (UD)

DI LENARDO
LOC. ONTAGNANO
VIA BATTISTI, 1
33050 GONARS (UD)
TEL. 0432928633
E-MAIL: info@dilenardo.it

Massimo Di Lenardo is a busy man. He has extended the estate to 38 hectares; he is completing restoration work on the historic and very lovely winery headquarters at Gonars, improving hospitality facilities and putting in a new tasting room; and finally he is continuing his efforts to give his wines a distinctively personal image, without losing sight of international tastes. After the successes of recent years, Massimo has made further innovations to his Tocai. The search for a new tasting profile has taken him outside DOC regulations so has released the wine as Toh! ("What a surprise!"). It's a very nice white indeed, with aromas of crusty bread and ripe fruit but the palate is perhaps a tad too soft, even though it is well-sustained and has an attractive fruit finish. The Chardonnay Woody and Ronco Nolè are also excellent. The Chardonnay, aged in American oak, has an intriguing nose with a great balance of ripe melon and apricot fruit with milky and balsamic notes. Banana and tobacco are immediately apparent on the palate, then the development on the mid palate has breadth, generosity and lots of style. Ronco Nolè is a Bordeaux blend where oak-derived notes emerge over bramble jam, dried roses and milky coffee. There is good fruit on the soft palate then the finish offers lingering notes of milky coffee and cherries, backed up by firm tannins.

○	Friuli Grave Chardonnay Woody '00	▼▼	3*
●	Ronco Nolè Rosso '99	▼▼	3*
○	Friuli Grave Chardonnay Musque '00	▼	3*
○	Friuli Grave Pinot Grigio '00	▼	3
○	Toh! Tocai Friulano '00	▼	3
●	Friuli Grave Cabernet '00		3
●	Friuli Grave Merlot '00		3
●	Friuli Grave Refosco P. R. '00		3
○	Friuli Grave Pinot Blanc '00		3
○	Friuli Grave Sauvignon Blanc '00		3
●	Ronco Rosso Nolè '97	♀♀	3
○	Friuli Grave Chardonnay Woody '99	♀♀	3

GORIZIA

ATTEMS CONTE DOUGLAS
FRAZ. LUCINICO
VIA GIULIO CESARE, 36/A
34170 GORIZIA
TEL. 0481393619 - 0481888162
E-MAIL: claudia.kroimik@coattems.it

Conti Attems is one of Friuli's oldest wineries. Documents show that it was active as long ago as 1506. The Attems family was actually resident in Friuli several centuries earlier and over the years, its members have achieved distinction in the Austro-Hungarian Empire, the Church and various states. Sigismondo Douglas Attems, the current honorary chairman of the estate, founded the Consorzio Collio in 1964, chairing that organization, too, until 1999. Last year, Marchesi de' Frescobaldi joined forces with the winery, giving Attems access to a wealth of experience and a major distribution network. Today, the Attems estate embraces 75 hectares in total, with 28 hectares under vine in the Collio and four in the Isonzo DOC zone, but there are plans to plant a further 20. Virginia Attems, the chairman's daughter, looks after public relations and oenologist Fabio Coser continues to work alongside the new team, led by Vittorio Frescobaldi. Best of the bunch this year is the Pinot Grigio, which boasts a rich fruit palate and a confectioner's cream and apple nose. The Ribolla Gialla, from the native Friulian variety of the same name, is also outstanding. Butter-rich yet braced by acidity, it has oak-derived nuances that round out the freshness of the apple aromas and the grape's natural astringency. The Sauvignon has a lovely golden colour and its aromas of citrus fruits, rue and sage are equally attractive. Finally, the tocai, malvasia, ribolla and sauvignon Collio Bianco and the Collio Rosso Pelicans, an 80-20 blend of merlot and cabernet franc, are both well-made.

○	Collio Pinot Grigio '00	▼▼	4
○	Collio Ribolla Gialla '00	▼▼	4
○	Collio Sauvignon '00	▼	4
○	Collio Bianco '00		4
●	Collio Rosso Pelicans '00		5

GORIZIA

FIEGL
Fraz. Oslavia
Loc. Lenzuolo Bianco, 1
34170 Gorizia
tel. 048131072 - 0481547103
e-mail: info@fieglvini.com

Another step forward for Fiegl. All the wines tasted this year earned at least a Glass and two won a second. Yet Alessio, Giuseppe and Rinaldo know they could do even better and that recent favourable vintages should really have been exploited more consistently. The evidence is there: in some cases, the same wine has had wildly fluctuating reviews from year to year. But let's look at the best Fiegl wine, the delicious Tocai, which has balance, flower aromas and a fresh palate. The Sauvignon is a bright, sinewy wine that is easily recognizable, despite milky and oak-derived notes that are still prominent. The list continues, in descending order with the classically unassuming Pinot Grigio, a no-nonsense wine that delivers what it promises. Then comes the spicy, gamey Merlot '99 that softens out on the reasonably convincing palate after a very decisive attack. Next is the Leopold Cuvée Blanc, from sauvignon, tocai, pinot bianco and ribolla. It has nice colour and good extract but is slightly forward both on the nose and the after-aroma. The merlot and cabernet franc Leopold Cuvée Rouge is well-made but tends to put the accent on the two varieties' weaker points, combining the hardish palate of cabernet franc with merlot's gamey nuances. The hazelnut and banana Chardonnay has a muscular, mouthfilling attack but fades away on a greenish note, the Ribolla offers softish hints of cider and finally the slightly dusty and still unsettled Merlot '98 can show autumn leaves, dried cherries and pencil lead.

GORIZIA

LA CASTELLADA
Loc. Oslavia, 1
34170 Gorizia
tel. 048133670

It's hard to know just where Giorgio and Nicolò Bensa are going. Apart from their Ribolla and Bianco, are they perhaps returning to monovarietals, or do they make their decision year by year depending on how things go in the cellar? We'll have to leave the question open but in the meantime we can enjoy the delicious sensations the inimitably consistent La Castellada wines offer every time you uncork a bottle. The Bianco, a blend of tocai, sauvignon, pinot grigio and ribolla, to give typicity, sums up the cellar's approach to making white wine. Long fruit melds with attractive oak that has still to find its ideal point of equilibrium but the firm mouthfeel and presence on the palate let you know that this is a wine that will only get better. Three Glasses confirm that the Bensa brothers are big league winemakers. Their Chardonnay has similar weight, as well as forward notes of tropical fruit salad on the nose and a fresh palate of creamy vanilla, leading in to a long finish of orange blossom honey and yellow-skinned plums. Again, the remarkably reliable Ribolla is delicate and fruity, setting fresh, green notes against confectioner's cream, alcohol and extract. Despite the vintage, the merlot and cabernet sauvignon Rosso is a tad obvious. Its garnet ruby is less vibrant than usual and while the nose has nicely focused raisin, dried leaves and redcurrant, the palate doesn't quite find a balance of softness and tanginess.

○	Collio Sauvignon '00	♛♛	4
○	Collio Tocai Friulano '00	♛♛	4
○	Collio Chardonnay '00	♛	4
○	Collio Pinot Grigio '00	♛	4
○	Collio Ribolla Gialla '00	♛	4
●	Leopold Cuvée Rouge '97	♛	5
●	Collio Merlot '98	♛	4
●	Collio Merlot '99	♛	4
○	Leopold Cuvée Blanc '99	♛	4
○	Leopold Cuvée Blanc '98	♛♛	4

○	Collio Bianco della Castellada '99	♛♛♛	6
○	Collio Chardonnay '99	♛♛	6
○	Collio Ribolla Gialla '99	♛♛	6
●	Collio Rosso della Castellada '97	♛	6
○	Bianco della Castellada '92	♛♛♛	6
○	Collio Sauvignon '93	♛♛♛	6
○	Bianco della Castellada '94	♛♛♛	6
○	Collio Chardonnay '94	♛♛♛	6
○	Bianco della Castellada '95	♛♛♛	6
○	Collio Bianco della Castellada '98	♛♛♛	6
○	Collio Chardonnay '98	♛♛	6
○	Collio Sauvignon '98	♛♛	6

GORIZIA

DAMIJAN PODVERSIC
VIA BRIGATA PAVIA, 61
34170 GORIZIA
TEL. 048178217

Damijan Podversic produces 12,000 bottles a year, which will become 20,000 with the next vintage, selling them under two or three different labels. Damijan, 34, is married to Elena and the father of three children. His paternal grandfather was a grower but his father was mainly interested in running the family "osteria", or bar. However, he bought a hectare and a half of vineyard between Lucinico and Giasbana, near Gorizia, to make his own wine for the clientele. When he had finished his military service, Damijan decided that viticulture would be his future. In no hurry, he garnered advice, hints and lessons from the most successful growers in the Collio Goriziano as he patiently waited for grapes that would make wine genuinely worth bottling. The Podversic estate also continued to grow. Now there are four estate-owned hectares and one more is rented. Damijan's main plot is on the south-facing slope of Monte Calvario and is planted at 8,000 vines per hectare. With Franco Terpin, he uses a rented cellar at Dolegna del Collio and oak is very much part of the winemaking process. The Collio Bianco, blended from chardonnay, malvasia and tocai, is a complex, elegant and intense wine with dried apricot on the nose, to which the palate adds sweet citrus fruit and top of the milk. The Rosso is from super-ripe cabernet sauvignon and merlot fruit that imbues the wine with hints of baked berry fruit.

○ Collio Bianco '99	🍷🍷	5
● Collio Rosso '99	🍷	5

GORIZIA

PRIMOSIC
LOC. MADONNINA DI OSLAVIA, 3
34170 GORIZIA
TEL. 0481535153
E-MAIL: primosic@primosic.com

As we mentioned in last year's Guide, the Primosic family has opted for two quite distinct ranges, releasing under the Gmajne label the more prestigious wines that spend longer in the cellar and differentiating them from standard-label products. A wise decision, as is obvious both from our tastings and from the Klin '97, which we retasted and found much more convincing than it was last year. The most successful bottle this year is the Metamorfosis, a red from merlot, cabernet franc and cabernet sauvignon. Richly extracted, it has a nose of pepper and blackcurrant with cherry on the palate, which offers well-gauged tannins and nice structure. The Ribolla continues to be one of the cellar's most reliable wines. Green-flecked in the glass, it proffers discrete yet crisp fruit on the nose and a fresh, tangy alcohol-rich palate with a faint hint of oak from the 500-litre tonneaux used for ageing. "Elegance" and "balance" tend to be overused terms, especially when there isn't much else to say, but in the case of the Sauvignon, they neatly sum up our tasters' impressions. The Chardonnay, too, is worth looking into. Soft on the nose, it is, however, a little raw on the palate. The Pinot Grigio melds alcohol attractively with notes of flower but there is a bitter note in the finish. Finally, the Picolit, a rather drier version than one is used to, has a warm, caressing mouthfeel and notes of honey, hazelnuts and dried apple.

● Collio Rosso Metamorfosis '97	🍷🍷	6
○ Collio Ribolla Gialla Gmajne '99	🍷🍷	4
○ Collio Sauvignon Gmajne '99	🍷🍷	4
○ Collio Picolit Ris. '96	🍷	6
○ Collio Chardonnay Gmajne '99	🍷	4
○ Collio Pinot Grigio Gmajne '99	🍷	4
● Collio Rosso Ris. '97	🍷🍷	5

GRADISCA D'ISONZO (GO)

Marco Felluga
Via Gorizia, 121
34072 Gradisca d'Isonzo (GO)
Tel. 048199164 - 048192237
E-mail: info@marcofelluga.it

From Isola d'Istria to Grado, then to Gradisca, Capriva to Buttrio isn't such a long way. That is, it's nothing like as far as the Felluga family has come to become leading players in the region's winemaking scene. Marco Felluga is the cellar for big numbers. Its best performers at our tastings this year were the two estate crus, Carantan and Molamatta. The first is a blend of merlot, cabernet franc and cabernet sauvignon. Aged in large barrels of Slavonian oak, it has concentration and complexity, foregrounding bramble syrup and cherry notes over a firm structure that never wavers. Molamatta is from tocai, ribolla and pinot bianco. Fermented and aged in stainless steel, its strong suits are fruit-rich elegance and an irresistibly charming palate. The other Marco Felluga products are also worth investigating, starting with the Tocai, a tangy, dry wine with notes of pear drops, apricot and celery that shows good length. The green-flecked Ribolla reveals hints of lime blossom and green apples with bright, nicely controlled acidity and the Pinot Grigio, redolent of broom and pomegranate, is a little bit soft and a little bit minerally. The Chardonnay and Sauvignon are textbook varietals, the former rather sweeter and approachable, the latter greener, wilder and with more edginess. Moving on to the reds, the pleasantly spicy Refosco and the somewhat over-austere Merlot are very well-made. We will also review the Castello di Buttrio wines here, since there are only two, from oak-aged native varieties. The white, a blend of tocai and ribolla, is a tad heavy on the vanilla but the red is very successful. The Moscato Rosa is also nice.

○	Collio Bianco Molamatta '00	♟♟	4
○	Collio Pinot Grigio '00	♟♟	4
○	Collio Ribolla Gialla '00	♟♟	4
○	Collio Tocai Friulano '00	♟♟	4
●	Carantan '98	♟♟	6
●	Castello di Buttrio Marburg '98	♟♟	6
○	Collio Chardonnay '00	♟	4
○	Collio Sauvignon '00	♟	4
○	Castello di Buttrio Ovestein '99	♟	5
●	Collio Merlot '99	♟	4
●	Moscato Rosa '99	♟	5
●	Refosco '99	♟	4
●	Carantan '97	♟♟	6
●	Collio Merlot '98	♟♟	4

GRADISCA D'ISONZO (GO)

Sant'Elena
Via Gasparini, 1
34072 Gradisca d'Isonzo (GO)
Tel. 048192388
E-mail: sant.elena@libero.it

Dominic Nocerino, became the sole owner of Sant'Elena in 1997, since when he has managed in a very short time to radically transform the estate, taking it to an enviable level of quality. Helped by technician Marizio Drascek, he immediately set about reorganizing the vine stock, reducing yields per plant as he waited for new plots to come onstream. At the same time, he overhauled the cellar, not just equipping it with the technology required for the wines he had in mind but also restructuring the buildings to create barrel and bottle cellars. Bianco JN is dedicated to Dominic's wife Judith. A blend of chardonnay and sauvignon, it has a nose of apples, spring flowers and red pepper, laced with a hint of coffee. The impressive entry on the palate ushers in notes of fruit, backed up by good alcohol and acidity, then giving way to mineral and milk of almonds before the lingering finish. The Ròs di Rôl '99 is a cabernet sauvignon and merlot blend with black cherries, fresh-cut grass and hay on the nose that follow through nicely on the concentrated palate. The fresh acidity melds nicely with the well-integrated tannins. Much of the cellar's production consists of the Pinot Grigio that sells so well in the US, where Dominic runs a wine importing business. Italian wines only, of course. Sant'Elena has 14 hectares planted to the variety and the resulting wine has fumé notes and good, rich fruit on a long, tangy palate with a minerally nuance in the finish.

○	Bianco JN '99	♟♟	5
●	Friuli Isonzo Ròs di Rôl '99	♟♟	5
○	Pinot Grigio '00	♟	4
●	Merlot '99	♟	4
●	Friuli Isonzo Tato '97	♟♟	5
●	Friuli Isonzo Ròs di Rôl '98	♟♟	5

MANZANO (UD)

BANDUT - GIORGIO COLUTTA
VIA ORSARIA, 32
33044 MANZANO (UD)
TEL. 0432740315
E-MAIL: colutta@colutta.it

Giorgio Colutta is a determined viticulturist but also one who knows that all agriculture requires patience, as nature takes her own time. He is acquiring the equipment no modern cellar can be without and at the same time, he is making strenuous efforts in the vineyard. He is ably assisted by consultant Marco Simonit, a "preparatore d'uve" or fruitmaker, as he likes to call himself, and the first results are coming through. The estate's 15 hectares include three planted at 5,600 vines per hectare and the two now being replanted will have a similar density. Clizia Zambiasi, the young winemaker, has the task of vinifying the fruit that vineyard manager Antonio Maggio makes available. Together, they form a young and realistically ambitious team. Aged in 15-hectolitre barrels, the Cabernet Sauvignon offers intense notes of stewed cherries, dried grapes and bottled figs on the nose. It crashes onto the palate with great fruit and structure, driving through to a the fine-grained tannins in the finish without losing consistency. The Selenard '99, from pinot nero, cabernet sauvignon and refosco, came close to Two Glasses with its full fruit-rich aromas, hint of toastiness and tar nuances on the nose. Other nice reds included the Refosco, which has varietal spice and notes of autumn leaves, and the raspberry and wild berry Merlot. Finally, we'd like to put in a good word for the onionskin-hued Pinot Grigio and the sweet, concentrated Verduzzo.

●	COF Cabernet Sauvignon '00	🍷🍷	4
●	COF Merlot '00	🍷	3*
○	COF Pinot Grigio '00	🍷	4
○	COF Verduzzo Friulano '00	🍷	4
●	COF Refosco P. R. '00	🍷	4
●	COF Rosso Selenard '99	🍷	5
○	COF Bianco Nojâr '00		4
○	COF Sauvignon '00		4
○	COF Tocai Friulano '00		3

MANZANO (UD)

ROSA BOSCO
FRAZ. ROSAZZO
VIA ABATE COLONNA, 20
33044 MANZANO (UD)
TEL. 0432751522

Rosa Bosco, called Rosetta by her friends, is actually quite like ElleKappa's description in the cartoons that accompany her cases of wine, "a sort of good fairy with blue eyes and blond hair" who flits around the vineyard, cutting here, thinning there and selecting over there. Later, in her workshop cellar with consultant Donato Lanati, she concentrates flavours and aromas and above all, puts a little piece of her heart into each wine. The result is, of course, again a brace of very high quality wines. Fruit for the Sauvignon Blanc is selected by hand and then macerates on the skins. Alcoholic and malolactic fermentation take place in new barriques, where the wine remains to age. For the time being, the wine has rather marked toasty notes of coffee that penalize its elegance and balance on the palate but the structure has concentration, there is plenty of juicy fruit and the warm finish is satisfyingly long. Merlot grapes for the Boscorosso are also selected with near-fanatical care. The destemmed fruit is crushed and some of the must drawn off at the start of fermentation in new barriques to enhance concentration. This wine comes straight out of the top drawer, very nearly taking a third Glass for the intensity of its colour, its concentrated aromas of berry fruit, chocolate and herbs and its harmonious palate, where the tannins are mellowed by the creamy structure. Tar and plum take over in the remarkable finish.

●	COF Boscorosso '99	🍷🍷	6
○	COF Sauvignon Blanc '00	🍷🍷	5
●	COF Boscorosso '98	🍷🍷	6
○	COF Sauvignon Blanc '99	🍷🍷	5

MANZANO (UD)

WALTER FILIPUTTI
LOC. ROSAZZO
P.ZZA DELL'ABBAZIA, 15
33044 MANZANO (UD)
TEL. 0432759429
E-MAIL: w-filiputti@triangolo.it

People who know Walter and Patrizia Filiputti will be well aware that the couple are unlikely to subscribe to our review, which of course is based on strictly blind tastings. Nevertheless, we can only be dissatisfied when half of Walter's range is unquestionably premium quality while the other half is only well-made. He is, after all, a thoroughly competent wineman and a key figure on the winemaking scene in Friuli. For the past couple of vintages, Walter has been vinifying in the estate cellar, in the splendid surroundings of the abbey at Rosazzo, one of Friuli's historic sites for making both wine and olive oil. It has to be said that taking over from the former cellar management may have caused uncertainty over how to handle the vines, and this could have come through in the final product. So we'll be waiting to see what happens in the next few years because Walter is eminently capable of greater things. The Picolit '99 didn't let us down. As usual, it is stylish, fresh-tasting and sweet all at the same time, with aromas of dried apricots, very ripe banana and vanilla. The Ronco degli Agostiniani, a blend of chardonnay with a small proportion of tocai friulano, is equally elegant. Here, the wood has been handled beautifully and never threatens to prevail. Ronco dei Domenicani, from cabernet sauvignon and various local varieties, is very well-made, as is the monovarietal merlot-based Ronco dei Benedettini, even though it has to contend with a vintage, the '98, that was less than exciting for so many reds in Friuli.

MANZANO (UD)

LE VIGNE DI ZAMÒ
LOC. ROSAZZO
VIA ABATE CORRADO, 4
33044 MANZANO (UD)
TEL. 0432759693
E-MAIL: info@levignedizamo.com

Stunned was how the panel felt after tasting the incredible range of wines presented by brothers Pierluigi and Silvano. The new cellar is as spectacularly equipped with computer-controlled stainless steel as it is with barrels. Emilio Del Medico, under the watchful eye of Franco Bernabei, looks after the vineyards and sets the musts on their way in the cellar, then Barbara Maniacco takes over, adding her enthusiasm. We know that the estate plans to concentrate in future on the plots at Rosazzo and Ipplis while cutting back the number of labels released, which is still rather high. At all our tastings, whether blind or not, the Malvasia '00 left everyone speechless at its unbelievable richness, lifted by a seductive note of macaroon and liquorice in a finish that will make even the most blasé wine buff sit up. Two other native varieties also put on unforgettable performances, tocai friulano and ribolla gialla. We knew that the Tocai Vigne Cinquant'Anni was a fantastic wine and had further confirmation this year. Vibrant peach and summer flowers follow through from nose to palate and the finish signs off with tocai's hallmark twist of almond. The standard-label Tocai was only a shade less impressive and consistently stood out at our blind tastings. As we said, the Ribolla Gialla is a monster. Buttery rich and full-bodied, it tempts the nose with flowers and golden delicious apples. Other top scorers were the Ronco delle Acacie, from barrique-fermented tocai, chardonnay and pinot bianco, and the Ronco dei Roseti, a classic Bordeaux blend.

○ COF Bianco Ronco degli Agostiniani '99	♢♢	6
○ COF Picolit '99	♢♢	6
○ Pinot Grigio '00	♢	3
● COF Rosso Ronco dei Benedettini '98	♢	6
● COF Rosso Ronco dei Domenicani '98	♢	6
○ COF Bianco Ronco del Monastero '00		4
○ COF Chardonnay '00		3
○ COF Ribolla Gialla '00		4
○ COF Sauvignon Suvignis '00		4
● Broili di Filip '00		4
● COF Rosso Pignolo Ris. '97		6

○ COF Malvasia '00	♢♢♢	4*
○ COF Tocai Friulano Vigne Cinquant'Anni '00	♢♢♢	5
○ COF Rosazzo Ribolla Gialla '00	♢♢	4
○ COF Tocai Friulano '00	♢♢	4
○ COF Bianco Ronco delle Acacie '99	♢♢	5
● COF Rosso Ronco dei Roseti '97	♢♢	6
● COF Refosco P. R. '00	♢	4
○ COF Sauvignon '00	♢	4
● COF Cabernet '99		4
● COF Pinot Nero '99		5
● Ronco dei Roseti '94	♢♢♢	6
○ COF Tocai Friulano Vigne Cinquant'Anni '99	♢♢♢	5

MANZANO (UD)

RONCHI DI MANZANO
VIA ORSARIA, 42
33044 MANZANO (UD)
TEL. 0432740718 - 0432754098

Roberta Borghese is back in the big time. She only just missed a top award a couple of years ago with her Merlot Ronc di Subule, then again last year with the Tocai Superiore, and she has an eye-catching collection of Two Glass credits in any case. This time, the estate lined up a king, the '99 Merlot Ronc di Subule, flanking it with two high-ranking knights, the Chardonnay '00 and the Picolit Rosazzo '99. We didn't want an estate-influenced view of the reasons behind the success so we asked around. The secret seems to lie in the superbly aspected 45 hectares under vine on the hillslopes of Rosazzo and Manzano, and in the severe thinning of all the rows, which enables the cellar to work with very highly concentrated raw material. It's child's play after that for someone with Roberta's experience to keep that quality intact in the cellar, where she and Tonino Livon know exactly how to handle barriques, tonneaux and large barrels. The Merlot Ronc di Subule comes from a vineyard planted at 6,000 vines per hectare and a yield of only 900 grams per plant. After maceration, it goes into small French oak barrels, two thirds of which are new. Since no description can take the place of a glass of the real thing, we'll just say that the nose is impressive and the unflagging thrust on the palate even more so. Yields per plant are higher, sometimes as much as one kilogram, for the Chardonnay, only 60 per cent of which goes into wood. Finally, the sweet Picolit yields on 300 grams per plant and is then dried before pressing. It ferments and ages in 113-litre barrels of French oak.

MANZANO (UD)

RONCO DELLE BETULLE
LOC. ROSAZZO
VIA ABATE COLONNA, 24
33044 MANZANO (UD)
TEL. 0432740547

Some readers have criticized the Guide for paying too much attention to small producers. Others say that we neglect smaller premium hillslope wineries in favour of big number operators. The protests more or less even out, which shows that we're probably achieving our objective of being as impartial as possible. Yet we will admit to having a soft spot for smaller wineries that are trying to carve out a market niche and we can only express a certain disappointment when the results are only good and not excellent. That was the case this year with Ronco delle Betulle and its feisty owner, Ivana Adami. The Franconia continues to be a fine example of a niche wine that can stand comparison with the better-known examples made in Austria. The seriously good nose ranges over roses, pepper and coffee, which are mirrored nicely on the palate, but the wine's strongest suits are freshness and sheer drinkability. The Ribolla also continues to impress. We tasted it several times during the year as we have always considered it to be one of the best of its type, very varietal and deliciously well-balanced. Overall, the Cabernet is very decently made but fails to light any fires because of some rather gamey, roughish notes that poke through. Tocai, Pinot Bianco and Sauvignon made by the book but you can tell there is still potential to be exploited.

●	COF Merlot Ronc di Subule '99	♟♟♟	5
○	COF Chardonnay '00	♟♟	4
○	COF Rosazzo Picolit Ronc di Rosazzo '99	♟♟	6
○	COF Pinot Grigio '00	♟♟	4
●	Le Zuccule Rosso '98	♟♟	5
●	COF Merlot '99	♟♟	4
●	COF Rosazzo Rosso Ronc di Rosazzo '99	♟♟	4
○	COF Verduzzo Friulano Ronc di Rosazzo '99	♟♟	4
○	COF Rosazzo Bianco Ronc di Rosazzo '00	♟	4
○	COF Sauvignon '00	♟	4
○	COF Tocai Friulano Sup. '00	♟	4

○	COF Rosazzo Ribolla Gialla '00	♟♟	4
●	Franconia '99	♟♟	5
○	COF Pinot Bianco '00	♟	4
○	COF Sauvignon '00	♟	4
○	COF Tocai Friulano '00	♟	4
●	COF Cabernet Sauvignon '99	♟	5
●	Narciso Rosso '94	♟♟♟	6
●	COF Rosazzo Narciso Rosso '97	♟♟	6
○	COF Rosazzo Narciso Bianco '98	♟♟	5

MANZANO (UD)

Torre Rosazza
Fraz. Oleis
Loc. Poggiobello, 12
33044 Manzano (UD)
Tel. 0432750180

This year, the amiable sales manager at Torre Rosazza, Piero Totis, with the assistance of Donato Lanati, who has been estate consultant since 1999, was able to present the panel with an impressively consistent range. There were also two big hitters in the Picolit and the Altromerlot. Torre Rosazza has 80 hectares of marl-rich terrain on the beautiful slopes that form a natural amphitheatre around Rosazzo. From the estate's delightful main villa, you can pick out the vineyards of the various Torre Rosazza crus. The tidy, well-managed plots produce a total of 180,000 bottles a year. Since it dedicates fully four hectares to picolit, Torre Rosazza is probably one of the biggest producers of this native Friulian grapes, which is harvested in October and then in part dried on racks. Deep straw-yellow with golden highlights, it offers an elegant nose of apricot and candied peach, laced with stewed apple. It follows through well on the palate, where the fruit emerges distinctly, to finish on a long sweet note with an intriguing hint of strawberry. Altromerlot, the estate's flagship selection, is back on form and won Two Glasses for its impressive notes of bitter chocolate, bottled fruit, Peruvian bark and pipe tobacco. Equally awesome is the structure on the palate, where tannins and hints of bilberry and bramble jam prevail. And to round things off, the finish is mouthfilling and very warm. High marks also went to the clean-tasting and very Mediterranean Ribolla Gialla, the warm, complex Cabernet Franc and the Chardonnay, with its delicious palate of peach and pear.

	Wine	Score	
●	COF Merlot l'Altromerlot '98	♛♛	5
○	COF Picolit '99	♛♛	6
●	COF Cabernet Franc '00	♛	4
○	COF Chardonnay '00	♛	4
○	COF Pinot Bianco '00	♛	4
○	COF Pinot Bianco Ronco delle Magnolie '00	♛	4
●	COF Refosco P. R. '00	♛	4
○	COF Ribolla Gialla '00	♛	4
○	COF Sauvignon '00	♛	4
○	COF Sauvignon Silterra '00	♛	4
●	COF Merlot '99	♛	4
○	COF Verduzzo Friulano '99	♛	4

MARIANO DEL FRIULI (GO)

Eddi Luisa
Fraz. Corona
Via Cormons, 19
34070 Mariano del Friuli (GO)
Tel. 048169680
E-mail: azienda@viniluisa.com

Panel members were murmuring very favourable comments after the tasting: not one bottle failed to make the grade and the list of One Glass wines was a long one. We knew that Luisa was a winery with potential. The new cellar is well fitted out, the barrique cellar is splendid and the 55 hectares are carefully tended, which all shows how serious the estate is about quality. Eddi is in overall charge of affairs, ably backed up by his sons Michele and Davide. The two younger Luisas carry out the duties of fruitmaker and winemaker, respectively. The 300,000 bottles produced every year are released in two ranges, the standard label and I Ferretti. The Luisa vineyards lie in the triangle formed by Mariano, Gradisca and Cormons and their red soil is rich in iron hydrates, making it particularly suitable for the production of red wine. Just to confirm this fact, all three reds in the I Ferretti range scored well. The creamy, velvet-smooth Cabernet has a deliciously soft mouthfeel; the Cabernet Franc is very warm, stylish and clean-tasting; and the Merlot has intriguingly complex aromas of chocolate, bilberry jam and dried roses over delicious balsamic notes. The generally high level of quality also comes out in the Tocai, the Pinot Bianco and the standard-label Cabernet Franc. The Tocai has the variety's typical sauvignonesque nuances, offset by tropical fruit and yellow peach. The Pinot Bianco convinces with its newly-baked bread and golden delicious entry on the nose and fresh-tasting back palate. Finally, the Cabernet Franc is very varietal, showing warm notes of bramble, hay and ripe plum. We also liked its balance of spice and fruit on the palate.

	Wine	Score	
●	Friuli Isonzo Cabernet Franc '00	♛♛	3*
○	Friuli Isonzo Pinot Bianco '00	♛♛	3*
○	Friuli Isonzo Tocai Friulano '00	♛♛	3*
●	Friuli Isonzo Cabernet Sauvignon I Ferretti '98	♛♛	4
●	Friuli Isonzo Merlot I Ferretti '98	♛♛	4
●	Friuli Isonzo Cabernet Franc I Ferretti '99	♛♛	4
●	Friuli Isonzo Cabernet Sauvignon '00	♛	3
○	Friuli Isonzo Pinot Grigio '00	♛	3
○	Friuli Isonzo Sauvignon '00	♛	3
○	Friuli Isonzo Chardonnay '00	♛	3

MARIANO DEL FRIULI (GO)

Masut da Rive
Via Manzoni, 82
34070 Mariano del Friuli (GO)
tel. 048169200

It was 1979 when Silvano Gallo released his first 5,500 bottles onto the market. Since then, the cellar has had to change its name because of protests from a certain quarter in the US – "Masut da Rive" is the family nickname – and young Fabrizio Gallo has joined the team but the passage of time has not altered the quality of the wines. In fact this year, the Pinot Bianco came close to gaining Three Glasses. Masut da Rive is a flatlands winery with 18 hectares that supply 75,000 bottles each year, 60 per cent of which contain white wine, and Fabrizio is the driving spirit. His personality is reflected in all the estate products as he oversees cellar and vineyard with a scrupulous yet innovative eye. The Pinot Bianco is concentrated and buttery on the nose, nicely balancing crusty bread, williams pear and almonds with dried flowers. These notes are echoed on the palate, which reveals a satisfying broad, harmonious progression and a refreshing finish of apple. High marks went to the Cabernet Sauvignon for its hints of talcum powder, leather, cigars and pencil lead over bramble jam while the Chardonnay Maurùs, aged in new barriques, is definitely a wine to wait for. The nose may be a little heavy on the wood but the palate is well-made and juicy, the notes of melon pineapple and citrus fruit melding well with the oak. Good scores also went to the Merlot, for its depth on the nose and firm tannins, and the Pinot Grigio, which is true to type, with its minerals, broom, red delicious apples and pears, and has a satisfyingly well-balanced palate.

O	Friuli Isonzo Pinot Bianco '00	YY	4
O	Friuli Isonzo Pinot Grigio '00	YY	4
●	Friuli Isonzo Cabernet Sauvignon '99	YY	4
O	Friuli Isonzo Chardonnay Maurùs '99	YY	5
●	Friuli Isonzo Merlot '99	YY	4
O	Friuli Isonzo Chardonnay '00	Y	4
O	Friuli Isonzo Sauvignon '00	Y	4
O	Friuli Isonzo Tocai Friulano '00	Y	4
●	Friuli Isonzo Cabernet Franc '99	Y	4
O	Friuli Isonzo Chardonnay Maurùs '98	YY	4
●	Friuli Isonzo Merlot '98	YY	4

MARIANO DEL FRIULI (GO)

★ Vie di Romans
Loc. Vie di Romans, 1
34070 Mariano del Friuli (GO)
tel. 048169600
e-mail: viediromans@tiscalinet.it

Not infrequently, when you are reading about wines, there springs to mind the critic mentioned by Elias Canetti who only read books after he had written the review, so he would know what he thought. For example, when it comes to Gianfranco Gallo's wines, you often think you can take some things for granted but just as often, your certainties disappear as soon as you uncork the bottle. This year, five out of seven wines presented went into the final tastings. One of them was the Pinot Grigio, a wine about which we thought there was nothing left to say, at least in Friuli, but this bottle powered its way to Three Glasses. Broad and complex, with lactic and aromatic notes that are vaguely reminiscent of Alsace, it fills the palate with tight-knit texture of cream and fruit richness. Also outstanding are the Flor di Uis, where flowers and citrus from malvasia and riesling enhance the structure and fruit of the blend's chardonnay, and the two absolutely complementary monovarietal Chardonnays. Both have the charm that comes of breeding, the Ciampagnis standing out for its fresh notes of green apple and kiwi, and the rich texture of the yeasts that offset the tanginess of the palate. Yellow apples, bananas and cream are the keynotes of the Vie di Romans, which has a touch of oak that should mellow out in the cellar. There are also two Sauvignons. The Piere was as aristocratically powerful and stylish as ever while the Vieris, which the panel tasted several times, sometimes performed impeccably but on other occasions revealed a slight fuzziness on the nose that marked it down. Bringing up the rear is the estate's Bordeaux blend. It may not be a monster but it's still a very well-made wine.

O	Friuli Isonzo Pinot Grigio Dessimis '99	YYY	5
O	Friuli Isonzo Bianco Flors di Uis '99	YY	5
O	Friuli Isonzo Chardonnay Ciampagnis Vieris '99	YY	5
O	Friuli Isonzo Chardonnay Vie di Romans '99	YY	5
O	Friuli Isonzo Sauvignon Piere '99	YY	5
O	Friuli Isonzo Sauvignon Vieris '99	YY	5
●	Friuli Isonzo Rosso Voos dai Ciamps '98	Y	5
O	Friuli Isonzo Bianco Flors di Uis '96	YYY	6
O	Friuli Isonzo Sauvignon Piere '97	YYY	6

NIMIS (UD)

Dario Coos
Loc. Ramandolo
Via Pescia, 1
33045 Nimis (UD)
tel. 0432790320 - 0432797807
e-mail: dariocoos@libero.it

Guide deadlines just don't fit in with Dario Coos's idea of how long his wines should stay in the cellar. Although he also grows refosco, Dario's main variety is verduzzo di Ramandolo, the local variant of verduzzo friulano that here and immediately round about produces wines with a personality of their own. Naturally, much research and experimentation still needs to be done but in recent years, some seriously good wines have started to hit the market. The vineyards often stand on very steep slopes and the weather here at the northern edge of the Colli Orientali del Friuli brings bitter winds from the north east. The risk of hail is high and the grapes have to be dried to obtain Verduzzo's classic sweet flavour. Skin contact is a crucial factor since the high tannin content can easily be transferred to the wine. For the final product, this provides both a distinguishing characteristic and a potential limit to the elegance of the palate. The Ramandolo '99 is somewhere between old gold and copper. The concentrated nose reveals caramel, banana and bottled apricots that introduce a slightly sweet palate, nice fruit and the variety's signature tannic note. We find the same profile, albeit in a minor key due to the less favourable vintage, in the Ramandolo '98. The Romandus, another '98, has a distinctly high sugar content since the grapes were dried for rather longer than usual.

○ COF Ramandolo '99	ŸŸ	5
○ COF Ramandolo '98	Ÿ	5
○ COF Ramandolo Passito Romandus '98	Ÿ	6
○ COF Picolit Romandus '96	ŸŸ	6
○ COF Ramandolo Passito Romandus '97	ŸŸ	6
○ COF Ramandolo Il Longhino '99	ŸŸ	4

PASIAN DI PRATO (UD)

Antonutti
Fraz. Colloredo
Via D'Antoni, 21
33030 Pasian di Prato (UD)
tel. 0432662001
e-mail: info@antonuttivini.it

Last year, this Colloredo di Prato-based winery impressed us with an excellent Sauvignon Blanc and this time round, the Antonutti family, who founded the cellar in 1921, have a full Guide profile. In charge these days you will find Adriana and Paolo, third-generation winemaking Antonuttis, who are assisted by Lino Durandi. It's a classic Grave DOC estate, with poor, gravelly soil that enhances the varietal nature of the grapes. There are two ranges, the standard label and Le Selezioni. The Antonuttis kicked off again this year with a seriously good, stainless steel-fermented Sauvignon Blanc Le Selezioni, with a very vegetal, intense nose of red pepper, rue and tomato leaf. You wouldn't expect the palate to be soft but it is. Full-bodied, rich and well-sustained, it has delightful hints of peach and melon, offering an intriguing contrast between nose and palate. The standard-label Chardonnay is another very good wine. It is slow to open on the nose but the complexity comes through in tropical fruit, melon, yellow peach, butter and dried flowers that leave you with an overall impression of sweetness. On the palate, it is just as complex and mirrors the nose well. Clean-tasting, it could perhaps have been a little richer in the mouth. High marks went to the Pinot Grigio, which reveals curious hints of sultanas, pineapple and mango. The palate is full-bodied, with fruit salad flavours, and the sweet, long finish allows hints of peach to emerge. Moving over to the reds, we very much liked the Cabernet Sauvignon Le Selezioni, with its clean, elegant aromas of vanilla and cassis, nice balance and caressing mouthfeel.

○ Friuli Grave Chardonnay '00	ŸŸ	3*
○ Friuli Grave Sauvignon Blanc Le Selezioni '00	ŸŸ	4
○ Friuli Grave Pinot Bianco '00	Ÿ	3
○ Friuli Grave Pinot Grigio '00	Ÿ	3
○ Friuli Grave Sauvignon '00	Ÿ	3
○ Friuli Grave Tocai Friulano '00	Ÿ	3
● Friuli Grave Cabernet Sauvignon Le Selezioni '98	Ÿ	4
● Friuli Grave Merlot Poggio Alto '98		4
● Friuli Grave Refosco P. R. Le Selezioni '98		4
○ Friuli Grave Chardonnay Poggio Alto '99		4

PAVIA DI UDINE (UD)

F.lli Pighin
Fraz. Risano
V.le Grado, 1
33050 Pavia di Udine (UD)
Tel. 0432675444
E-mail: azpighin@tin.it

Pighin has 150 hectares under vine in the Friuli Grave DOC zone, as well as 30 in the Capriva depression in the Collio, making it one of the largest privately owned wineries in the region. The Pighin brothers' first sally into agriculture was in 1963, when they bought the Risano estate that runs along the main Udine-Aquileia-Grado road, and where four years later they built the imposing estate headquarters. The following year, the Pighins moved into the Collio, where they carried out major operations on the soil and the vine stock they found there. These were years when vine training systems were geared to volume, with obvious repercussions on quality, so recently the estate has had to make massive, urgent investments. These have brought the fruit into line with the quality-oriented philosophy the Pighins have adopted in order to make their mark in international markets. Technician Paolo Valdesolo looks after the vineyards and is even more active in the cellars. We feel we should point out that for years we have been making positive reviews of the entire Pighin range, which embraces 18 or 20 wines. Capriva is the second home of pinot bianco so it is no surprise to find the wine at the top of the Pighin range. It has all the elegance of the grape, marrying freshness with fruit, and complexity with length. The Pinot Bianco delle Grave has occasional notes of boiled sweets, which take nothing from the overall attractiveness of the wine.

PAVIA DI UDINE (UD)

Scarbolo
Fraz. Lauzacco
V.le Grado, 4
33050 Pavia di Udine (UD)
Tel. 0432675612

How Valter Scarbolo manages to do so many things at once, and well, is a matter for conjecture. He combines his profession as a restaurateur – he runs an attractive and always crowded restaurant – with that of pork butcher (he has some of his hams smoked by the legendary D'Osvaldo) and winemaker. To fill his idle moments, he also runs the winery of his friend Joe Bastianich, sharing with him the expertise of wine technician Emilio Del Medico and consultant Maurizio Castelli. The Scarbolo cellar vinifies fruit from nine hectares of estate-owned vineyard and a few more that are rented, as well as carefully selected bought-in grapes. Production hovers around 90,000 bottles a year and quality is steadily improving. Working on hillslopes as well as flatlands has taught Valter the importance of thinning and he has begun to believe in the potential of the Grave, the DOC zone on the plains where his own vines are located. for now, he has released a surprisingly impressive Tocai Friulano '00. Intense in hue, it grabs attention with the deliciously complex concentration of its ripe fruit, ranging from apple to plum and honeydew melon, echoed satisfyingly on the palate. The Chardonnay, too, offers good ripe fruit mingled with vanilla, yeasts and spices, which are picked up on the palate. Fresh-tasting and fairly buttery in the mouth, it signs off with a long finish. The Sauvignon is a supple wine whose aromas have suffered as a result of the warm, dry summer while the still youthful Merlot should be left to mature in the cellar for a time.

○	Collio Pinot Bianco '00	♟♟	4
○	Friuli Grave Pinot Bianco '00	♟♟	3*
○	Collio Sauvignon '00	♟	4
○	Friuli Grave Sauvignon '00	♟	3
○	Friuli Grave Tocai Friulano '00	♟	3
○	Friuli Grave Tocai Friulano Casette '00	♟	4
●	Baredo '97	♟	5
●	Friuli Grave Merlot Ris. '98	♟	4
●	Friuli Grave Refosco P. R. '99	♟	3
○	Soreli '99	♟	4
○	Collio Pinot Grigio '00		4
○	Friuli Grave Pinot Grigio '00		3

○	Friuli Grave Chardonnay '00	♟♟	3*
○	Friuli Grave Tocai Friulano '00	♟♟	3*
○	Friuli Grave Sauvignon '00	♟	3
●	Friuli Grave Merlot '99	♟	3

PINZANO AL TAGLIAMENTO (PN)

ALESSANDRO VICENTINI ORGNANI
FRAZ. VALERIANO
VIA SOTTOPLOVIA, 2
33094 PINZANO AL TAGLIAMENTO (PN)
TEL. 0432950107
E-MAIL: vicentiniorgnani@libero.it

The hills at Valeriano, where Alessandro Vicentini Orgnani has his splendid estate, are best-known for native local grapes varieties with evocative names such as sciaglin, piculit neri, forgiarin, ucelut and so on. Neither wine experts, nor Alessandro himself, have ever had much faith in the potential of these varieties and over the years, the plots have been replanted with international favourites. Quite rightly, though, Alessandro kept a parcel of ucelut, from which he rather timidly obtains a very decent dry white. We say rightly because this year, his technically impeccable Ucelut is very good indeed, coming within an ace of a third Glass. The vibrant golden yellow is flecked with amber and the wine is so concentrated that the legs on the glass hardly move. Mediterranean on the nose, it strikes a great balance between candied citrus peel and fresher notes of orange. On the oily rich palate, orange comes through again with figs and walnuts, lifted by a faint but very well-gauged and refreshing note of final acidity. All the other wines are good, including the reds, which in recent years have not quite managed to cut the mustard. For the fourth year in a row, the Pinot Bianco Braide Cjase picked up Two Glasses. On the nose, it opens on mint and white peach, giving way to hints of dry flowers and milky notes. It follows through well on the rich palate, where there is a nice contrast of fruit and oak-derived nuances.

○ Ucelut Bianco '99	🍷🍷	5
○ Friuli Grave Pinot Bianco Braide Cjase '00	🍷🍷	3*
● Friuli Grave Cabernet Sauvignon '00	🍷	3
● Friuli Grave Merlot '00	🍷	3
○ Friuli Grave Sauvignon '00	🍷	3
○ Friuli Grave Chardonnay Braide Cjase '00		3
○ Friuli Grave Pinot Grigio '00		3
○ Friuli Grave Pinot Grigio Braide Cjase '00		3

POVOLETTO (UD)

AQUILA DEL TORRE
FRAZ. SAVORGNANO DEL TORRE
VIA ATTIMIS, 25
33040 POVOLETTO (UD)
TEL. 0432666428
E-MAIL: aquiladeltorre@tin.it

Founded in the early 20th century, this estate was acquired by the Ciani family in 1996. In the 1970s, it was known as Podere del Sole, changing its name to Aquila del Torre in 1990. It was at that time that the barrel, bottle and vinification cellars, under the offices, were renovated, as were the hospitality and tasting rooms. The estate lies on a single 82-hectare property, with 25 planted to vine. The Ciani have under way a replanting programme that involves well over half of the area under vine. The vineyards themselves stand on excellent south-facing hillslopes at between 175 and 300 metres above sea level. As is the case with every cellar that is renewing stock, the range includes both premium-quality wines and less interesting bottles. Top of the range is the Picolit '99, a wine that has done much to make the estate's name. Golden in colour, it offers a nose of sultanas and dry figs, which return, more concentrated, on the palate. The other outstanding Aquila del Torre wine is the Merlot '99. Its notes of autumn leaves, fruit tart and cherry preserve blend nicely with the toastiness of the oak barrels used for ageing. Full-bodied and rich on the palate, it reveals notes of coffee that will soon disappear. In the Sauvignon, we find varietal aromas of peach and herbs as well as elegant notes of tea and chamomile. The palate is attractively fresh. Finally, Canticum Bianco, a blend of tocai friulano, sauvignon blanc and riesling renano, could do with a tad more concentration.

● COF Merlot Vocalis '99	🍷🍷	5
○ COF Picolit '99	🍷🍷	6
○ COF Bianco Canticum '00	🍷	5
○ COF Sauvignon Vocalis '00	🍷	5
● COF Merlot Canticum '97	🍷🍷	4

POVOLETTO (UD)

Teresa Raiz
Fraz. Marsure di Sotto
Via della Roggia, 22
33040 Povoletto (UD)
tel. 0432679071
e-mail: info@teresaraiz.com

This rapidly improving winery was founded in 1971 by brothers Paolo and Giovanni Tosolini. That improvement lies not just in the increasing number of Glasses earned but also in the high overall standards of quality maintained. There can be no doubt that the vineyards now coming onstream, totally different in conception from those of the past, are a major factor. Management policy now is to aim for ever higher standards of quality. The 20 hectares of vineyards provide little over half of the grapes vinified by the Tosolinis, whose annual production is about 200,000 bottles. Best of their offerings this year is the Tocai Friulano, which easily won Two Glasses. Intense and complex on the nose, where pear and apple dominate, it follows through with a firm entry on the palate that reveals all the richness of the fruit, as well as good structure, flavour and a very long after-aroma. It is surprising how complex the Sauvignon Rovel is, considering the indifferent vintage. Yet is shows nice peach, citrus fruit and rue in the mouth. The Sauvignon dei Colli Orientali has a more substantial mouthfeel, with elegant notes of tomato leaf and elderflower on the nose. The Tosolinis have also obtained an excellent Chardonnay with grapes from different DOC zones. It marries creamy aromas on the nose with a long, fresh-tasting palate reminiscent of apple and very ripe, yellow-skinned plum.

○	COF Sauvignon '00	🍷🍷	5
○	COF Tocai Friulano '00	🍷🍷	4
○	Friuli Grave Chardonnay Le Marsure '00	🍷🍷	4
○	Friuli Grave Sauvignon Rovel '00	🍷🍷	4
○	COF Pinot Grigio '00	🍷	4
○	COF Ribolla Gialla '00	🍷	5
○	Friuli Grave Pinot Grigio Le Marsure '00	🍷	4
●	COF Cabernet '00		4
●	COF Rosso Decano Rosso '97	🍷🍷	5

PRADAMANO (UD)

Fantinel
Via Cussignacco, 80
33040 Pradamano (UD)
tel. 0432670444
e-mail: fantinel@fantinel.com

Fantinel is a large concern whose 250 hectares are distributed over the Grave, Collio and Colli Orientali del Friuli DOC zones. It is run by the Fantinel family, who are determined to take the winery along the difficult path to premium quality. A long-standing relationship with professor Zironi from the University of Udine has enabled the cellar to invent shrewdly designed new quality products such as Trilogy, a white, and Platinum. Recently, work was completed on the large, modern cellar at Tauriano, where all the estate grapes are vinified. The results are good, indeed excellent, although there is of course room for further improvement. To go back to the new products, Platinum is an oak-aged blend of refosco, cabernet sauvignon and merlot that stays in the wood for 18 months; it has yet to find its balance. Instead, the Collio Trilogy really caught our attention. A carefully selected blend of the finest pinot bianco, tocai and sauvignon fruit from the plot at Vencò in the Collio, this barrique-fermented beauty has a full, fragrant nose redolent of peach, melon and apricot. Peach is to the fore in the front palate, staying with you through to the finish which has attractive hints of spring flowers. Progression on the palate is fresh and very supple. The Sauvignon also came close to a second Glass. Its rich, soft mouthfeel foregrounds ripe yellow peach and melon, with tomato in the finish. The Merlot Borgo Tesis has a very complex nose where cinnamon and clove spice emerges over bramble jam and milk chocolate. The palate mirrors the nose but lacks a little breadth, even though it is well-made.

○	Collio Bianco Trilogy '00	🍷🍷	5
○	Collio Bianco Santa Caterina '00	🍷	3
○	Collio Chardonnay Sant'Helena '00	🍷	4
○	Collio Pinot Grigio Sant'Helena '00	🍷	4
○	Collio Sauvignon Sant'Helena '00	🍷	4
○	COF Picolit I Principi '99	🍷	6
●	Friuli Grave Cabernet Sauvignon Sant'Helena '99	🍷	4
●	Friuli Grave Merlot Borgo Tesis '99	🍷	3
●	Collio Cabernet Franc Santa Caterina '99		4
●	Friuli Grave Refosco P. R. Sant'Helena '98	🍷🍷	4

PRATA DI PORDENONE (PN)

VIGNETI LE MONDE
FRAZ. LE MONDE
VIA GARIBALDI, 2
33080 PRATA DI PORDENONE (PN)
TEL. 0434626096 - 0434622087
E-MAIL: lemonde@iol.it

Piergiovanni Pistoni Salice, who chairs the Consorzio Grave, and his wife Antonella set before us possibly the best range of wines they have made in recent years. But we are still not satisfied and look forward, particularly for the reds, to perfomances similar to those achieved by the Cabernet Sauvignon Riserva '90 or the Pinot Nero '93. These are certainly within the cellar's grasp. The 25 hectares on clay and limestone soil, unusual for the Grave, give the 200,000 Le Monde bottles produced each year a distinctive character. A short head in front of the rest is the Sauvignon Puja, followed by the Pinot Grigio, Cabernet Sauvignon Riserva and Cabernet Franc. Barrique-fermented, the Sauvignon Puja is a selection from a vineyard that yields an average of 30 hectolitres per hectare. The complex entry on the nose reveals butter and vanilla that give way to hints of banana, peach and orange, nuanced with dried roses. Oak comes through on the palate, which has a keynote of banana and melon in the finish. The Pinot Grigio has taken full advantage of the favourable vintage, its inviting aromas of apples and pears mingling with dried spring flowers before the soft, rounded palate shows refreshing, well-balanced acidity in the finish. The Cabernet Sauvignon Riserva is intense and complex on the nose, hinting at hay, orange, black cherry syrup and Peruvian bark. The same notes return on the soft palate, which is discreetly full. Finally, there is lavish bramble, plum and blackcurrant fruit on nose and palate of the soft Cabernet Franc, backed by firm tannins.

○ Friuli Grave Sauvignon Puja '99	♟♟	4
○ Friuli Grave Bianco Pra' de Gai '00	♟	3
○ Friuli Grave Chardonnay '00	♟	3
○ Friuli Grave Pinot Grigio '00	♟	3
● Friuli Grave Refosco P. R. '00	♟	3
○ Friuli Grave Sauvignon '00	♟	3
● Friuli Grave Cabernet Sauvignon Ris. '97	♟	4
● Friuli Grave Cabernet Franc '99	♟	3
● Friuli Grave Rosso Ca' Salice '99	♟	3
● Friuli Grave Cabernet Sauvignon '99		3

PRATA DI PORDENONE (PN)

VILLA FRATTINA
LOC. GHIRANO
VIA PALAZZETTO, 68
33080 PRATA DI PORDENONE (PN)
TEL. 0434626105

Villa Frattina, a welcome new addition to the regional wine scene, is in the Lison Pramaggiore DOC zone. The 60 hectares of vineyards surround a beautiful late 16th century residence. Since 1989, the cellar has been owned by the Averna family. We are well aware of how hard it is to make a wine worthy of the region in this DOC zone, which is why in 1998 Villa Frattina engaged the services of celebrated winemaker Donato Lanati, assisted by oenologist Ivan Molaro. There were encouraging signs last year but this time the winery has released three seriously good products, the Chardonnay, the Merlot and the Rosso Corte dell'Abbà. The first has great fruit on the nose, where the ripe notes allow milky hints to peep through, then the tangy, broad palate follows through with admirable precision, expanding into a long banana-themed finish perked up by nicely gauged acidity. The Merlot, too, has good fruit and a full nose, with bramble jam and blackcurrant emerging over ripe cherry and prunes, attractively offset by hints of coffee. What you get on the nose is what you find on the soft, rich palate, which is well-sustained by mellow tannins. Rosso Corte dell'Abbà is a blend of cabernet sauvignon, refosco, merlot and cabernet franc that spends 15 months in barriques. Its strong suit is the well-structured, warm palate that finds a delightful point of equilibrium between the softness of the fruit and the assertiveness of the tannins. Worth a mention are the Sauvignon, the Cabernet Franc, pinot grigio and chardonnay-based Di Gale and the l'Ale di Gleise, a cask-conditioned blend of sauvignon, chardonnay, pinot grigio and tocai.

○ Lison-Pramaggiore Chardonnay '00	♟♟	3*
● Lison-Pramaggiore Merlot '00	♟♟	3*
● Rosso Corte dell'Abbà '98	♟♟	5
● Lison-Pramaggiore Cabernet Sauvignon '00	♟	3
● Refosco P. R. '99	♟	3
○ Di Gale '00		4
● Lison-Pramaggiore Cabernet Franc '00		3
○ Lison-Pramaggiore Sauvignon '00		3
○ Ale di Glesie '99		5

PRAVISDOMINI (PN)

PODERE DAL GER
FRAZ. FRATTINA
VIA STRADA DELLA MEDUNA, 13
33076 PRAVISDOMINI (PN)
TEL. 0434644452
E-MAIL: robspina@hotmail.com

Here we have a family business, run by father Gianluigi, mother Edda and son Robert Spinazzè, which for years has been manufacturing the concrete posts that support so much of Italy's vine stock. Add to that 50 hectares of land, 38 of which are planted to vine, at Frattina near Pravisdomini in the Lison Pramaggiore DOC zone and the collaboration – exclusive in Friuli, started in 1999 – of expert winemaker Romeo Taraborelli. Factor in unlimited passion and a modern, well-equipped cellar. And the result is Podere del Ger. Only four wines were presented but they are all excellent. Meanwhile, lurking in the cellars and waiting for release next year is evidence of just how good wines from this producer can be – a very exciting wood-fermented Verduzzo Secco and a promising red blend. The buttery Pinot Grigio is a very fine wine. Complex and concentrated on the nose, it hints at ripe citrus and williams pears, laced with intriguing dried roses, on the nose. These are echoed on the front palate, which follow through rich and broad, adding notes of melon. The Glass that the Chardonnay so effortlessly picked up was awarded for the balance of oak-derived vanilla and white chocolate with ripe pineapple and peach fruit. These are echoed on the nicely balanced palate, which has a lingering finish of banana. The Cabernet Franc is true to type, offering bramble jam, cinnamon and roasted coffee beans that lead in to a soft, clean palate. The tannins are mellowing nicely and the finish is packed with berry fruit. The Merlot is well-made and fruity.

○	Lison-Pramaggiore Pinot Grigio '00	3
○	Lison-Pramaggiore Chardonnay '00	3
●	Lison-Pramaggiore Cabernet Franc '99	3
●	Lison-Pramaggiore Merlot '99	3

PREMARIACCO (UD)

BASTIANICH
LOC. CASALI OTTELIO, 7
33040 PREMARIACCO (UD)
TEL. 0432675612

Joseph Bastianich, whose origins lie in the Istrian peninsula, is one of those entrepreneurs who show just how much interest there is in the world for the wines of Friuli. With mother Lidia and a select few others, Joe heads a market-leading group in the premium catering sector in New York, which means America. Years ago, Joe tasted Girolamo Dorigo's legendary '89 Pignolo and the sublime Tocai that the Zamòs make on the hillslopes at Buttrio. He decided this was where to invest. Today, his estate has five hectares and rents nine. He is also buying a further four and a half hectares. The cellar that is being completed will be able to implement the winery's strategy of releasing only supremely good wines, which involves appropriate barrel and bottle ageing. That's also the reason why on the Vespa Bianco '89 was released this year. The other wines, including a Pinot Grigio Plus '99 that we sampled at the cellar, will be put on the market next spring at the earliest. A word about the Bastianich team. The general manager is Walter Scarbolo, Emilio Del Medico is the oenologist and the consultant winemaker is Maurizio Castelli. The vineyards are scattered over the hills of Buttrio and Premariacco, in the southern part of the Colli Orientali del Friuli DOC zone. Vespa Bianco is obtained from sauvignon and chardonnay, half aged in lightly toasted barriques, with eight per cent of tonneau-aged picolit. The wine itself has golden highlights and intense, stylish aromas of fruit and flowers. Rich, broad and supple in the mouth, it shows great length with a hint of pepper in the finish. It may be a young wine but it has immense personality. It will age happily in the cellar for years; the Tocai Plus '99 we reviewed last year is already showing the way.

○	Vespa Bianco '99	5
○	COF Tocai Friulano Plus '98	5
●	Vespa Rosso '98	5
○	COF Tocai Friulano Plus '99	5

PREMARIACCO (UD)

Dario e Luciano Ermacora
Loc. Ipplis
Via Solzaredo, 9
33040 Premariacco (UD)
tel. 0432716250
e-mail: azermaco@tin.it

Dario and Luciano Ermacora missed out by a hair's breadth on Three Glasses for their Pinot Bianco. We are truly sorry because their wines are not only good; they are also expertly made and as typical of their variety as it is possible to be. The Ermacoras own 25 hectares, 19 under vine, and a lovely new cellar with plenty of space for entertaining. Their very shrewd management decisions include ageing their wines with prolonged lees contact and they are unfailingly hospitable. Not a bad profile for a winery. The Pinot Bianco has confectioner's cream on the nose, followed up by warm Mediterranean fruit. Citrus fruit and rue come through distinctly in the mouth, giving the palate softness and roundness, then a zesty freshness the finish. The Pinot Grigio shows power and intensity on the nose as soon as you lift the glass. Its banana and tropical fruit aromas introduce a very soft, almost creamy mouthfeel. The long, full-bodied palate features attractive fruit salad flavours. The Tocai is typical to a fault: intense on the nose, it offers varietal almonds, broom and williams pear aromas that follow through on the palate. There is nice acidity to back up the finish. The warm weather did nothing for the Sauvignon, which is delicate and well-made but a tad one-dimensional in the finish.

○	COF Pinot Bianco '00	🍷🍷	4
○	COF Pinot Grigio '00	🍷🍷	4
○	COF Tocai Friulano '00	🍷🍷	3*
○	COF Sauvignon '00	🍷	4
○	COF Verduzzo Friulano '00		4
●	COF Merlot '99		4
●	Rîul Rosso '97	🍷🍷	5

PREMARIACCO (UD)

Rocca Bernarda
Loc. Ipplis
Via Rocca Bernarda, 27
33040 Premariacco (UD)
tel. 0432716273 - 0432716914
e-mail: roccabernarda@roccabernarda.com

The much-decorated and still extraordinary Rocca Bernarda Picolit missed out on Three Glasses this year, perhaps because it is a shade over-sweet. But the winery stays in the top flight thanks to a stunning Merlot Centis '99. Its impenetrable ruby ushers in complex and deliciously balanced aromas of Peruvian bark, dried roses, bilberry and bramble jam, plain chocolate and the occasional note of leather. The entry on the palate is awesome, as are the elegance, progression and long finish backed up by fine-grained tannins. For some years, Centis has been agonizingly close to Three Glasses. This time it has made it. Estate manager Mario Zuliani is busy with the work at the Rocca which will soon restore one of the wings to its former glory. In the meantime, he has turned out an excellent Vineis. It's a white blend of the best oak-conditioned chardonnay grapes, with sauvignon and tocai. The aromas are delicate and vanilla nuances are nicely offset by apricot and orange. The palate is elegant and well-balanced, with a long finish of peaches. Marco Monchiero's expertise has also given us a fresh, varietal Ribolla Gialla with very inviting aromas of sage and golden delicious apples. The palate is clean-tasting and well-rounded. There is also a Pinot Grigio that offers the nose the variety's hallmark notes of mineral, fresh hints of green apples and rue, then a deliciously soft palate with intriguing aromas that return in the finish. Finally, the well-made Chardonnay has notes of vanilla, ripe pears and white damson. Broad and buttery in the mouth, it rounds off with a nice, sweet finish.

●	COF Merlot Centis '99	🍷🍷🍷	5
○	COF Picolit '99	🍷🍷	6
○	COF Bianco Vineis '00	🍷🍷	4
○	COF Chardonnay '00	🍷🍷	4
○	COF Pinot Grigio '00	🍷🍷	4
○	COF Ribolla Gialla '00	🍷🍷	4
○	COF Sauvignon '00	🍷	4
○	COF Tocai Friulano '00	🍷	4
○	COF Picolit '97	🍷🍷🍷	6
○	COF Picolit '98	🍷🍷🍷	6
●	COF Merlot Centis '95	🍷🍷	5
●	COF Merlot Centis '96	🍷🍷	5
●	COF Merlot Centis '97	🍷🍷	5

PREMARIACCO (UD)

SCUBLA
LOC. IPPLIS
VIA ROCCA BERNARDA, 22
33040 PREMARIACCO (UD)
TEL. 0432716258 - 048192550
E-MAIL: scublavini@tmedia.it

Roberto Scubla's personal kingdom is on the lower slopes of the Rocca Bernarda. Built a little at a time, with a touch of nostalgia and advice from friends, it embodies the rigour Roberto brings to his winemaking and the curiosity he devotes to his researches. There are three excellent results from all this, the Pomédes, the Graticcio and the Merlot. Roberto's Pomédes is a Dolomite-inspired blend of late-harvested tocai and pinot bianco with part-dried riesling. Again this year, it has supremely elegant fruit, reminiscent of candied orange peel, and a silky, caressing mouthfeel. Graticcio is from verduzzo grapes dried under the rafters by the "bora" gales. Delicious and velvet-smooth, it offers apple, apricot and fresh peanuts, accompanied by a lingering honeyed note that is nicely contrasted by the tannic weave. The rich-hued, full-bodied, complex Merlot confirms Scubla as an expert red winemaker and a man who knows how to handle fruit. The attack is soft, with hints of baked fruit, becoming warm and tannic before closing on notes of only faintly earthy autumn leaves. Other good performers in the range are pear, rue and bitter almond Tocai, which is a tad rugged on the palate but has good nose-palate consistency and is convincing; the attractively sauvignonesque Speziale, which has a slightly intrusive hint of sweetness this year; and the vivacious Sauvignon, a classic, fresh-tasting interpretation with a fine range of splendid aromas. Finally, the Cabernet, which has lovely colour and a nice nose, is a little too raw and edgy on the palate. The Pinot Bianco is fairly insubstantial and rather too lean.

○	COF Bianco Pomédes '99	▼▼▼	5
●	COF Merlot '99	▼▼	4
○	COF Tocai Friulano '00	▼▼	4
○	COF Verduzzo Friulano Graticcio '98	▼▼	5
○	COF Pinot Bianco '00	▼	4
○	COF Sauvignon '00	▼	4
○	COF Bianco Speziale '99	▼	4
●	COF Cabernet Sauvignon '99	▼	4
○	COF Bianco Pomédes '98	▼▼▼	5
○	COF Bianco Pomédes '97	▼▼	5
●	COF Rosso Scuro '97	▼▼	5

PREMARIACCO (UD)

LIVIO ZORZETTIG
LOC. IPPLIS
VIA DEL COLLIO, 14
33040 PREMARIACCO (UD)
TEL. 0432716030

This winery was established in 1986, when the Zorzettig brothers, taking over from father Min, decided to split up the family farm. Sadly, Livio passed away almost immediately afterwards and it was his wife Gabriella who carried on business while children Massimo and Marco were growing up. Massimo quickly took charge of the vineyards and cellar, then Marco joined him a couple of years later, also showing a lively interest in the countryside. In the meanwhile, the property continued to expand its vine stock, passing from the initial 23 hectares to the present 67. Much of the fruit used is bought in, however, giving the estate a strongly commercial, middle-of-the-range quality profile. That is why the family is changing the cellar name to mark the radical change in production philosophy. A young and very competent oenologist, Giuseppe Zamparo – known to one and all as "Luigino" – provides technical support for the winemaking. Only estate-grown grapes are used now and replantings ensure excellent quality raw material. Today's Zorzettig Ribolla Gialla is an elegant wine with intense flower and fruit aromas. The attack is impressive and the finish delicious. The Tocai, too, is a serious bottle, its notes of pear framed in a tidy, warm structure. The Picolit is sweet on nose and palate, offering dried fruit aromas, and good concentration, warmth and length. Good marks also went to the Pinot Grigio, the Cabernet Franc, the Refosco and the Bianco Nonalinda, a blend of tocai, ribolla and pinot bianco.

○	COF Picolit '00	▼▼	5
○	COF Ribolla Gialla '00	▼▼	3*
○	COF Tocai Friulano '00	▼▼	3*
●	COF Cabernet Franc '00	▼	3
●	COF Merlot '00	▼	3
○	COF Pinot Grigio '00	▼	3
●	COF Refosco P. R. '00	▼	3
○	COF Sauvignon '00	▼	3
○	COF Bianco Nonalinda '99	▼	5

PREPOTTO (UD)

IOLE GRILLO
LOC. ALBANA, 60
33040 PREPOTTO (UD)
TEL. 0432713201 - 0432713322
E-MAIL: grilloiole@lycosmail.com

It was in the early 1970s that Iole Grillo acquired this estate, which then passed to her daughter Anna Muzzolini, a dynamic young mother and winewoman. The vines stand next to the river Judrio, which forms the border between the province of Udine on one side and the province of Gorizia, and Slovenia, on the other. The winery is located in a lovely residence near to the bridge over the Judrio just outside Albana. Here the young and respected technician Lino Casella looks after winemaking and also supervises the vineyards. The fruit is soft-pressed and fermentation temperatures for white musts are controlled automatically. All the reds, except the Cabernet Franc, the Santa Justina white and the Verduzzo and Picolit dessert wines are aged in small and large barrels but you can hardly tell from the finished products. The oak is just sufficient to give the wines the structure that will extend their life in the cellar. For example, we retasted the '99 Verduzzo. Last year, it was only worth a mention but today would certainly win One Glass. The Santa Justina confirms that it is a very successful blend of chardonnay, tocai and malvasia, with distinct sauvignon-like aromas. The Pinot Grigio has a complex, fruit-rich weave and good length while the robust alcohol and glycerine of the Sauvignon are mellowed by lavish aromas that range from tomato leaf to rue, and from grapefruit to red pepper.

	Wine	Glasses	Price
○	COF Bianco Santa Justina '00	♈♈	4
○	COF Pinot Grigio '00	♈♈	4
○	COF Sauvignon '00	♈♈	4
●	COF Merlot '99	♈	4
○	COF Tocai Friulano '00	♈	4
●	COF Cabernet Franc '99		4
○	COF Picolit '99		6
○	COF Bianco Santa Justina '99	♛♛	4

PREPOTTO (TS)

LA VIARTE
FRAZ. NOVACUZZO
VIA NOVACUZZO, 50
33040 PREPOTTO (TS)
TEL. 0432/759458-0432/753354

The final vintage of the millennium was a memorable one. The growth cycle enjoyed excellent flowering and ripening of the fruit, which was a shade ahead at the beginning of August. Then a dry summer delayed the final stages, allowing the grapes sufficient time to recover aromas and the structure to carry the rather robust alcohol. It was a vintage for Tocai, Pinot Bianco and Pinot Grigio and it is these wines that are most complete. Particularly good was the Pinot Bianco, which came within an ace of Three Glasses for its mouthfilling texture, fresh elegance and balsamic notes that sign off with a hint of bitter almonds. The flowers and fruit on the nose of the Tocai augur well for the future. They are followed by a muscular, seriously impressive and well-orchestrated palate that hinges on warm alcohol, fresh-tasting acidity and the residual fragrance of the yeasts. The Pinot Grigio is a classic. Alcohol underpins the structure that looks a tad shaky but instead emerges well, especially when paired with difficult companions at table. Sìum is obtained from selected verduzzo and picolit grapes dried until December and then fermented for six months in new oak barriques. It's a wine you can always rely on, although this year a hint of sharp acidity subtracted a little pleasure from the dried apple, honey and sweet wood aromas. The tocai, pinot bianco, sauvignon, riesling and ribolla Liende also earned Two Glasses for its good weight on the front palate and lingering ripe fruit finish. Finally, the buttery, warm Chardonnay, the long Ribolla, with its slightly green notes of damson, and the Sauvignon, more dilute than usual and almost sweet, all performed very creditably.

	Wine	Glasses	Price
○	COF Pinot Bianco	♈♈	4
○	COF Bianco Liende '99	♈♈	5
○	COF Pinot Grigio '00	♈♈	4
○	COF Tocai Friulano '00	♈♈	4
○	Sìum '99	♈♈	6
○	COF Chardonnay '00	♈	5
○	COF Ribolla Gialla '00	♈	4
○	COF Sauvignon '00	♈	4
○	Sìum '97	♛♛	6
●	Tazzelenghe '96	♛♛	5

PREPOTTO (UD)

Le Due Terre
Via Roma, 68/b
33040 Prepotto (UD)
tel. 0432713189

No Three Glass awards this year for Le Due Terre, the splendid cellar owned by the delightful Flavio Basilicata and his wife Silvana. We do know, though, that we can expect truly great wines from them again in the future. The couple have five hectares under vine and yields hover around 40 quintals per hectare, with the exception of the picolit that goes into the Implicito, which has a yield of 30 quintals. You don't need a large cellar to make these quantities but you do need space if you release your wines two years after the vintage. The Basilicatas have a home-cum-winery in a lovely position overlooking the valley of the Judrio, the river that separates the provinces of Udine and Gorizia as well as the DOC zones of Colli Orientali del Friuli and Collio. It is unfortunate that our publishing schedule forced us to taste the Due Terre wines only a few days after they had gone into the bottle for this certainly penalized them. The Sacrisassi Bianco is from tocai, ribolla and sauvignon grapes that age for 18 months in oak barriques and tonneaux. Golden in the glass, it unveils fresh sweet notes of peach and yellow-skinned plums, laced with rue. As ever, the Implicito is a stunner. This is proof of just how massive and complex slowly fermented picolit fruit can be after scrupulous ageing in barrels that have left no trace in the final aromas. The refosco and schioppettino Sacrisassi Rosso, the Merlot and the Pinot Nero all show remarkably concentrated fruit, impressive structure, a close-knit weave and fine-grained tannins in the finish.

PREPOTTO (UD)

Valerio Marinig
Via Brolo, 41
33040 Prepotto (UD)
tel. 0432713012
e-mail: marinigvalerio@libero.it

When we say we are happy to see Valerio Marinig win his full Guide profile, it is not just a manner of speech. No one could resist the open friendliness and intelligent simplicity that the entire Marinig family brings to winemaking. For four generations, they have been growing grapes at Prepotto, where they cultivate six hectares under vine and a further six of woodland and seed crops. Sergio looks after the land, his wife Marisa entertains guests and their young son Valerio, a wine technician, keeps a watchful eye on the cellar. The cellar buildings are unsophisticated but any expansion has to come to terms with the limited spaces available. The part of the production that is bottled enables the family to release 25,000 units a year but there is plenty of margin for growth. The Verduzzo and the reds are aged in barrels of various sizes, mainly five-hectolitre tonneaux. Before we go on to the wines, we would like to point out the amazingly good value for money offered by the Marinig range, the Tocai in particular. As in previous years, the Tocai Friulano is seriously good, offering complex aromas of pear and apple on nose and palate, with attractive flavour and length. The Biel Cûr ("lovely heart"), a blend of cabernet sauvignon, schioppettino and refosco left to part-dry in cases before pressing, is aged in oak for about 20 months. The resulting bottle has superbly rich fruit, with notes of prunes and baked pears, as well as structure and character.

○	COF Bianco Sacrisassi '99	♀♀	5
●	COF Merlot '99	♀♀	5
●	COF Pinot Nero '99	♀♀	5
●	COF Rosso Sacrisassi '99	♀♀	5
○	Implicito '99	♀♀	6
●	COF Rosso Sacrisassi '97	♀♀♀	5
●	COF Rosso Sacrisassi '98	♀♀♀	5
○	COF Bianco Sacrisassi '98	♀♀	5
●	COF Merlot '98	♀♀	5
○	Implicito '98	♀♀	6

○	COF Tocai Friulano '00	♀♀	3*
●	Biel Cûr Rosso '99	♀♀	4
●	COF Cabernet Franc '00	♀	3
○	COF Chardonnay '00	♀	3
○	COF Pinot Bianco '00	♀	3
○	COF Sauvignon '00	♀	3
○	COF Verduzzo Friulano '99	♀	3

PREPOTTO (UD)

PETRUSSA
Loc. ALBANA, 49
33040 PREPOTTO (UD)
TEL. 0432713192
E-MAIL: paolo_petrussa@libero.it

Gianni and Paolo Petrussa are two brothers we have been following since they first started making premium wine. Now, they turn out 50,000 bottles a year from almost ten hectares of estate-owned vineyards and bought-in grapes. Their small cellar has been substantially altered and today has sufficient space for bottles, which are often released in the second or third year after the vintage. This year, the pair surprised us with a wine that is superior to anything they have produced in the past, a Bianco Petrussa that demands respect. It's a blend of field-selected grapes, half tocai and the rest chardonnay and pinot bianco topped up with a little sauvignon; 60 per cent of the wine is cask-conditioned. The colour of gold, it opens out delightfully on the palate, combining elegance with rich fruit, creaminess, fresh acidity, complexity and staying power. Despite the less than favourable weather, which has left some tannins that have still to mellow, the Rosso Petrussa '98 also scored an easy Two Glasses. It's a 90-10 blend of merlot and cabernet sauvignon with a rich full-bodied palate of black cherries, autumn leaves and attractive oak-derived nuances. The Petrussas also have an excellent sweet wine, the monovarietal Pensiero, which they make from verduzzo left to dry until Christmas. The must stays in oak for more than 14 months, then the wine ages in the bottle for at least a year. When you uncork it, you will find a lingeringly sweet wine with good depth that offers aromas of figs, lavender and baked apple.

○ COF Bianco Petrussa '99	♟♟	4
● COF Rosso Petrussa '98	♟♟	5
○ Pensiero '98	♟♟	5
● COF Cabernet '00	♟	4
○ COF Pinot Bianco '00	♟	4
○ COF Sauvignon '00	♟	4
○ COF Tocai Friulano '00	♟	4
● COF Schioppettino '98	♟	5
● COF Rosso Petrussa '97	♟♟	5
● COF Schioppettino '97	♟♟	5

PREPOTTO (UD)

RONCO DEI PINI
VIA RONCHI, 93
33040 PREPOTTO (UD)
TEL. 0432713239
E-MAIL: ronco.pini@katamail.com

For the past four years, we have been tasting all the wines made by brothers Giuseppe and Claudio Novello and we have never had to reject one. There were no real stars, though, but this year is different. The estate's roots lie in the Veneto, where the family arrived from in 1968 to buy the Rieppi vineyards at Prepotto. In recent years, the estate has been split into two distinct parts, one of which is Ronco dei Pini. There are four and a half hectares under vine in the Colli Orientali del Friuli and a further ten at Zegla near Cormons, in the Collio DOC zone. Part of the wine produced goes into the 140,000 bottles released each year. Vineyard management is in the hands of Renato de Noni while Damiano Stramare looks after the cellar. The Colli Orientali Pinot Bianco is one of the estate's flagship wines. This version has pear and apple on the nose and a well-structured, fruit-rich palate with a long finish. The Collio Sauvignon is a varietal wine, with evident notes of red pepper, rue and pennyroyal, followed by good weight and consistency on the palate and outstanding length. Leucos is a steel-fermented blend of 90 per cent pinot bianco with ten per cent tocai that ages unhurriedly in oak tonneaux. Vanilla and, particularly, apple are prominent. Limes is a red blend, with 90 per cent merlot and the rest cabernet sauvignon and cabernet franc. Aged for 12 months in tonneaux, it shows attractive cherry and a fresh-tasting structure but there is also room for improvement.

○ COF Pinot Bianco '00	♟♟	3*
○ Collio Sauvignon '00	♟♟	3*
● COF Cabernet '00	♟	3
● COF Merlot '00	♟	3
○ Leucos Bianco '00	♟	4
● Limes Rosso '99	♟	4
○ COF Tocai Friulano '00		3
○ Collio Chardonnay '00		3
○ Collio Pinot Grigio '00		3

TASTE AND CULTURE

Slow Food®
2002

Slow Food is an international movement which was founded in 1989 and is active in 46 countries worldwide, with 70,000 members and over 600 Convivia.

Slow Food has a cultural agenda:
It promotes a **philosophy of pleasure**, protects small food producers who make quality products, counters the degrading effects of industrial and fast food culture which standardize tastes, has a **taste education** program for adults and children, works towards **safeguarding** traditional food and wine heritage, provides **consumer information**, and promotes tourism that respects and cares for the environment.

Slow Food Events:
Each year Slow Food stages important food and wine events for enthusiasts and professionals: the two-yearly **Salone del Gusto** (Hall of Taste) in Turin, Italy; the two-yearly **Cheese** in Bra, Italy; the **Slow Food Festival** in Germany, one of the largest quality food markets in northern Europe; wine festivals such as **Superwhites**.

Each **Convivium** organizes social meetings, tastings, cooking courses, trips, visits to restaurants, and lectures for its members. The twinning of Convivia from different countries promotes the exchange of tastes and knowledge of different cultures.

An Ark to safeguard products and the planet of tastes:
An important project aimed at safeguarding and benefitting small-scale agricultural and food production, which risks dying out. Thousands of different kinds of *charcuterie*, cheeses, animal breeds and plants are in danger of disappearing forever: the homologation of tastes, the excessive power of industrial companies, distribution difficulties and disinformation are the causes of a process which could lead to the loss of an irreplaceable heritage of traditional recipes, knowledge and tastes. The Ark is a scientific research and documentation program which works towards relaunching businesses and outfits with important cultural and economic value.

Taste Education:
The Slow Food Movement has taken action to realize one of the objectives of the **Ark Manifesto** to promote taste education in grade schools. Besides staging numerous conferences on this subject, Slow Food has also published an instruction manual for teachers and parents on how to teach children to enjoy and understand their taste culture. Slow Food plans many more educational activities around the world during its "**Weeks of Taste**".

The Slow Food Award
The Slow Food Award for biodiversity is presented on a yearly basis to people who contribute to the protection of animal breeds, vegetable species, dishes and ecosystems in danger of extinction. The objective of the Award is to encourage people, in rich and poor areas alike, who are seeking to be models for a new agriculture that respects tradition, is sensitive to the environment and is attentive to quality. The nominations for the Slow Food Award are submitted by 600 experts (journalists, agronomists, chefs, researchers etc.) from over 80 countries. Winners receive a cash prize and their activity is publicized by Slow Food and the jury members. The third edition will be held in Turin on October 23, 2002.

Slow

Slow features in-depth and often off-the-wall stories about food culture across the globe, with related lifestyle topics of a truly international scope, unlike anything you've seen before on the newsstands. 140 well-designed pages in full color with exciting photography and articles by top authors, gourmets, wine experts, and food & travel writers worldwide. Just take your pick: English, German, French or Italian.

Italian Wines 2002

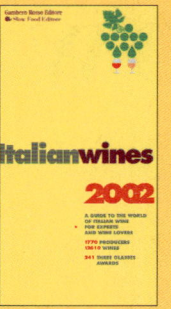

The most complete, reliable and influential guide to the best Italian wines. Published by Slow Food and Gambero Rosso, it is now in its 14th edition. It describes the history and production of 1,770 vineyards, describes and evaluates 12,610 wines and awards 241 wines with the "Tre Bicchieri" (Three Glasses) symbol - the élite of the great Italian wine-making tradition. Price € 28.50 or US$ 24.95

....

Registration Form

Slow Food is aimed at food and wine enthusiasts, those who do not want to lose the myriad of tastes in traditional foodstuffs from around the world, and those who share the snail's wise slowness. Annual membership includes:
- a personal membership card
- five issues of the quarterly magazine *Slow*
  (including one special issue dedicated to the Award)
- the new issues of *Slowine* (available in Spring 2002) and *SlowArk* (available in late Fall 2002)
- the right to attend all events organized by the Slow Food movement throughout the world
- a 20% discount on all Slow Food publications

If you have any questions, please feel free to contact us. We are only a fax, phone call or e-mail away. Phone: ++39 0172 419611 - Fax: ++39 0172 421293 E-mail: international@slowfood.com

I would like to:
❏ become a member   ❏ renew

....
Full Name

....
(of company or restaurant or other)

....
Street Address   City

....
State/Prov./County   Country   Postal Code

....
Home Tel.   Day Tel.   Fax

....
E-mail

....
Profession

I would prefer to receive Slow in: ❏ English   ❏ German   ❏ French   ❏ Italian

Membership fees to join Slow Food
    European Union   € 50.00   U.K.   £ 35.00
    Japan   ¥ 10,000   U.S.A. *and all other countries*   US$ 60.00

Method of Payment

❏ Cash   ❏ Eurocheque (no personal checks, please)
❏ Credit Card: ❏ Visa   ❏ AmEx   ❏ Mastercard   ❏ Diners

\# |__|__|__|__||__|__|__|__||__|__|__|__||__|__|__|__|

|__|__|/|__|__| X ....
Exp. Date   Signature

....
Cardholder   Amount

PREPOTTO (UD)

Vigna Petrussa
Loc. Albana, 47
33040 Prepotto (UD)
Tel. 0432713021

Albana is a small village that lies between rather forbidding hills and the Judrio, the river that forms the border with Slovenia and also divides the provinces of Udine and Gorizia. Hilde Petrussa Mecchia is a gracious woman who lived in Portogruaro for 25 years before persuading husband Renato to return to the family home and tend the five hectares of vines. That was in 1995. It is a moving sight to see this no longer young couple as, shears in hand, they move along the rows, clipping away damaged fruit or thinning the bunches. The first result is that the vineyards are kept perfectly. The cellar, too, reflects the owners' mentality and the same can be said of the wines, all of which the panel found up to scratch. The Picolit is obtained from fruit dried for about a month and spends a further ten in oak. It has warm aromas, where milk of almonds and very ripe figs come through, and a broad, sweet palate with plenty of style. The Tocai has intense aromas, a refreshingly tangy palate, and notes of pear and apple. Although not excessively varietal, the Sauvignon is a challenging, full-bodied wine with good structure. Bianco Richenza, named after a Lombard princess, comes from a various white grapes, selected and then dried before pressing. The wines are fermented and matured in barriques and then blended to produce a sweet, dense, elegant wine.

○	COF Sauvignon '00	♟♟	3*
○	COF Tocai Friulano '00	♟♟	3*
○	COF Picolit '99	♟♟	5
○	COF Bianco Richenza '99	♟	4
●	COF Cabernet Franc '99		3
●	COF Schioppettino '99		4

PREPOTTO (UD)

Vigna Traverso
Via Ronchi, 73
33040 Prepotto (UD)
Tel. 0432713072

Stefano Traverso is the owner of this winery, which is also named after him. The son of entrepreneurs from the Veneto – Giancarlo and the well-known Ornella Molon – he has made profound changes at the estate, which under the previous owners had a rather chequered career. There are just over seven hectares under vine, five of them in a single lot around the cellar. The winemaking team, assisted by consultant Luca D'Attoma, comprises oenologist Simone Casazza and Lauro Iacolettig, an expert fruitmaker and model cellarman. The '99 vintage was a very good one for reds in Friuli and the Traversos took full advantage, offering the panel a range of strikingly high quality with two wines nearly winning a third Glass. The Rosso Sottocastello is marvellous. A monovarietal merlot part aged for a year in new barriques, it has notes of cherry and ripe bramble, coffee and chocolate, with lots of concentration and weight on the palate. The Merlot '99 is equally good. It stays in the wood for eight months and perhaps for that reason has more prominent tannins in the finish. The entry on the palate is rich and full, and the powerful structure emerges in the follow through. In the Refosco, it is the notes of spice and chocolate, the close-knit weave and the rich fruity finish that impress. Finally, the Two Glass whites include a rather insistently varietal Tocai that can point to better than average texture.

●	COF Merlot '99	♟	4
●	COF Rosso Sottocastello Ris. '99	♟♟	5
○	COF Pinot Grigio '00	♟♟	4
●	COF Refosco P. R. '99	♟♟	4
○	COF Ribolla Gialla '00	♟♟	4
○	COF Sauvignon '00	♟♟	4
○	COF Tocai Friulano '00	♟♟	4
●	COF Cabernet Franc '99	♟	4
●	COF Schioppettino '99	♟	4
○	COF Chardonnay '00		4
●	COF Merlot '98	♟♟	4

RONCHI DEI LEGIONARI (GO)

Tenuta di Blasig
Via Roma, 63
34077 Ronchi dei Legionari (GO)
tel. 0481475480
e-mail: tenutadiblasig@tiscalinet.it

The Ronchi area has some very unusual features that derive from the nearby Carso. The plateau protects it from the cold, "bora" gales while breezes from the sea – a stone's throw away – help to moderate temperatures and encourage the growth of the vines. Another important factor is the Isonzo river, which over the centuries has created a series of distinct soil types that can each confer personality on the wines. Here at Tenuta di Blasig, winewoman Elisabetta Bortolotto Sarcinelli has been able to establish a consistency of quality that this year has touched levels of excellence, with the reds in particular. The Blasig family has been in the area for at least three centuries, which, together with the determination of Elisabetta, her mother Helga, young Ludovica and Letizia, and oenologist Erica Orlandino, has put this all-female winery where it is today. Among the reds, the excellent oak-aged Merlot Gli Affreschi has a warm, almost Tuscan, entry on the nose, where leather emerges over plums, bramble jelly, tobacco and Peruvian bark. The front palate is a little understated but it soon opens out with good body and fruit, nice structure and mellowing tannins. The standard-label Merlot may be a little straightforward on the nose but the palate is just as impressive as the premium bottle for its clean taste, well-integrated tannins and soft fruit. The very sweet Tocai with its fruit-rich nose came close to a second Glass. The nose is echoed on the palate, where curious balsamic hints emerge.

SACILE (PN)

Vistorta
Brandino Brandolini d'Adda
Via Vistorta, 82
33077 Sacile (PN)
tel. 043471135
e-mail: vistorta@iol.it

A stone's throw from the Veneto border lies the hamlet of Vistorta, for centuries the exclusive property of the noble Brandolini d'Adda family. The more modest dwellings housed the families of the estate workers and the lovely villa was the family residence. The nearby "barchessa" buildings were used as barns. Brandino Brandolini, the present owner, wanted to repopulate the long-abandoned village so he sold off some small lots and now the village has come to life again. The Conti Brandolini d'Adda estate covers more than 220 hectares, almost exactly half in Friuli and the rest in Veneto. Twenty-five of the 32 hectares under vine are in Friuli, where merlot is grown along with a few rows of cabernet franc and syrah. When Brandino Brandolini's entrepreneurship teamed up with the winemaking experience of Georges Pauli, the French technician who has Château Gruaud-Larose on his list of clients, the success of the Merlot Vistorta was assured. The '99 contains five per cent cabernet franc and two per cent syrah. It is aged in three equal parts in new, one year old and two year old barriques before it is bottled without filtration. We may have tasted it in extreme youth but we still found cherry tart and spices on nose and palate, remarkable complexity and plenty of evidence that it will evolve as well as editions from previous vintages.

● Friuli Isonzo Merlot '00	ŶŶ	4
● Friuli Isonzo Merlot Gli Affreschi '99	ŶŶ	4
○ Friuli Isonzo Chardonnay '00	Ŷ	3
○ Friuli Isonzo Tocai Friulano '00	Ŷ	3
○ Bianco Gli Affreschi '99	Ŷ	4
● Rosso Gli Affreschi '99	Ŷ	5
○ Friuli Isonzo Pinot Grigio '00		3
● Friuli Isonzo Cabernet Gli Affreschi '98	ŶŶ	4
● Friuli Isonzo Merlot Gli Affreschi '98	ŶŶ	4

● Friuli Grave Merlot Vistorta '99	ŶŶ	5
● Friuli Grave Merlot Vistorta '95	ŶŶ	5
● Friuli Grave Merlot Vistorta '97	ŶŶ	5
● Friuli Grave Merlot Vistorta '98	ŶŶ	5
● Friuli Grave Merlot Vistorta '96	Ŷ	5

SAGRADO (GO)

CASTELVECCHIO
VIA CASTELNUOVO, 2
34078 SAGRADO (GO)
TEL. 048199742
E-MAIL: info@castelvecchio.com

The five new hectares about to be planted will take the vine stock of this lovely Carso estate to a total of 40, all located around a splendid Renaissance villa and its parkland of oaks and cypresses. Vineyard and cellar management has always been in the expert hands of Giovanni Bignucolo. Old vines are being replaced and this year, for the first time, the estate is also releasing a small quantity of olive oil. There are two pieces of news this time. The first is the return to form, after an indifferent year, of the whites, with a Malvasia and a Pinot Grigio of real stature and two excellent blends, Sagrado Bianco and Sagrado Rosso. The Malvasia has plenty of alcohol but is fresh on the nose, where citrus fruit, especially citron, and wistaria come through. The palate is flavoursome, full-bodied and well-sustained. "Textbook" is the only way to describe the Pinot Grigio, which offers williams pear, white damson, mineral notes and yeasts on both nose and palate. Malvasia, sauvignon and traminer go into the blend for Sagrado Bianco, an elegant wine with generous notes of orange blossom, peaches in syrup and citrus on the nose, echoed nicely on the palate. Fresh apple perks up the finish. Sagrado Rosso is from cabernet sauvignon, cabernet franc and turmino. Aged for three years in small oak barrels, it tempts the nose with a complex entry whose spicy notes give way to wild roses, bilberry tart and milky coffee. Balanced and almost chewy in the mouth, it unveils spice and fruit aromas that return in the finish.

● Sagrado Rosso '97	🍷🍷	6
○ Carso Malvasia Istriana '00	🍷🍷	4
○ Carso Pinot Grigio '00	🍷🍷	4
● Carso Cabernet Franc '98	🍷🍷	5
○ Sagrado Bianco '99	🍷🍷	5
○ Carso Traminer Aromatico '00	🍷	4
● Terrano '00	🍷	4
● Carso Cabernet Sauvignon '98	🍷	5
● Carso Refosco P. R. '98	🍷	4
● Carso Rosso Turmino '98	🍷	4
● Carso Cabernet Franc '97	🍷🍷	4
● Carso Cabernet Sauvignon '97	🍷🍷	4
● Carso Refosco P. R. '97	🍷🍷	4
● Carso Rosso Turmino '97	🍷	3

SAN FLORIANO DEL COLLIO (GO)

ASCEVI - LUWA
VIA UCLANZI, 24
34070 SAN FLORIANO DEL COLLIO (GO)
TEL. 0481884140

Ascevi-Luwa is at San Floriano in the hills at Gorizia on the border with Slovenia. Soil and climate are ideal for making wine, especially whites with rich, complex aromas. So it's no surprise to find Sauvignon at the top of the list, either as a monovarietal or in blends. Unfortunately, we again noticed some differences in bottles with the same label, which means that our assessments are subject to reservations. Let's begin with the Sauvignon. As well as the two traditional labels, the more complex Ascevi and the quaffable Luwa, the cellar has also released a selection, Ronco dei Sassi. This was the most interesting of the three, a classically transparent wine with sweet notes of peaches in syrup and powerful fruit in the mouth. The Ascevi Sauvignon has a long, warm palate that suggests rue and apricot, in addition to peach, while the Luwa has comparable weight but rather greener, fresher aromas. The good, lively Col Martin, from sauvignon, tocai and pinot grigio, offers nice nose-palate consistency, with varietal green notes, and the sauvignon, chardonnay and ribolla-based Vigna Verdana is only a notch or two lower down. Again, sauvignon is prevalent but the palate lacks staying power. The two Ribollas are very varietal. Damson and pear mingle with apple and summer flowers on the nose of the long, fresh-tasting Ascevi while the finish of the soft, creamy Luwa nicely mirrors the nose. The Ascevi Tocai, Pinot Grigio and Pinot Bianco are all well up to the standards of a good vintage. And to finish, the Chardonnay and red Le Vigne, from 50 per cent cabernet franc, cabernet sauvignon and merlot, earned a mention in dispatches.

○ Col Martin Luwa '00	🍷🍷	4
○ Collio Ribolla Gialla Ascevi '00	🍷🍷	4
○ Collio Ribolla Gialla Luwa '00	🍷🍷	4
○ Collio Sauvignon Ascevi '00	🍷🍷	4
○ Collio Sauvignon Luwa '00	🍷🍷	4
○ Collio Sauvignon Ronco dei Sassi '00	🍷🍷	4
○ Collio Pinot Bianco Ascevi '00	🍷	4
○ Collio Pinot Grigio Ascevi '00	🍷	4
○ Collio Tocai Friulano Ascevi '00	🍷	4
○ Vigna Verdana Ascevi '00	🍷	4
○ Collio Chardonnay Luwa '00		4
● Le Vigne '99		4
○ Collio Sauvignon Ascevi '98	🍷🍷🍷	4
○ Col Martin Luwa '99	🍷🍷	4

SAN FLORIANO DEL COLLIO (GO)

Borgo Lotessa
Loc. Giasbana, 23
34070 San Floriano del Collio (GO)
Tel. 0481390302

Borgo Lotessa is a family-run winery at Lotessa and Crussoli, two elevations near the Italian-Slovene border. Roberto Fratepietro looks after winemaking and his sister Raffaella deals with marketing. The 16 hectares under vine are beautifully tended and tidily planted at 4,000 vines per hectare. The modern cellar, too, is spick and span, turning out around 80,000 bottles a year. The year 2000 was a great one for whites and Pinot Grigio and Pinot Bianco were the property's top scorers, expertly made to take full advantage of the vintage. The Pinot Grigio explodes onto the nose with fresh fruit aromas of pineapple, peach, orange and williams pear over dried spring flowers. On the palate, the very elegant mouthfeel is soft yet fresh, taking you through to a long finish of yellow peach. The Pinot Bianco has a varietal nose and palate of apple, wistaria and hedgerow. Well-defined on the palate, it shows good progression and a fresh finish. Only a mark or two lower comes the Cabernet Sauvignon '98, 5,000 bottles of which were released. Intense purple red, it proffers persuasive notes of berry fruit and chocolate with delicate spicy nuances. It's a shame that the lack of structure on the palate lets it down a little. Finally, the very decent Sauvignon has aromas of peach, tomato and dried roses, echoed on the fresh-tasting palate.

○ Collio Pinot Bianco '00	♟♟	4
○ Collio Pinot Grigio '00	♟♟	4
○ Collio Sauvignon '00	♟	4
● Friuli Isonzo Cabernet Sauvignon Ris. '98	♟	4
○ Collio Chardonnay '00		4

SAN FLORIANO DEL COLLIO (GO)

Conti Formentini
Via Oslavia, 5
34070 San Floriano del Collio (GO)
Tel. 0481884131
E-mail: giv@giv.it

The Formentinis are one of the families that have left their mark on the history of this land, for centuries the border between the Slav and Italian-speaking communities. When they established themselves in the castle in 1509, the Formentinis began farming and grapes were one of their crops. A recently discovered document shows that a Formentini who married a Hungarian took with her as a dowry 200 "toccai" vines. The find has set all Friuli talking about the strategy to follow to obtain EU approval of the region's right to keep the name Tocai Friulano for its vine and wine. Since the document predates the Hungarian name Tokaji, it would invalidate the agreement to relinquish the name Tocai Friulano by 2007. The Conti Formentini cellar buys in grapes from the Collio Goriziano and is today managed by the Gruppo Italiano Vini. Production is about 350,000 bottles a year and the cellar oenologist is Marco del Piccolo, who works in tandem with Marco Monchiero, the celebrated Piedmontese consultant who is currently enjoying enviable success in Friuli. With the exception of the Sauvignon, all the wines we tasted underwent malolactic fermentation, which has mellowed them out. The Chardonnay unites elegance with rich fruit aromas, showing apple and yellow-skinned plum over banana and yeasts. The young Merlot Tajut, which means "glass of wine" in Friulian, has already fulfilled its promise and the Pinot Nero reveals varietal notes that are hard to find in Friuli.

○ Collio Chardonnay Torre di Tramontana '99	♟♟	5
● Collio Merlot Tajut '99	♟♟	6
○ Collio Pinot Grigio '00	♟	4
○ Collio Sauvignon '00	♟	4
● Collio Pinot Nero Torre di Borea '99	♟	6
● Collio Merlot Tajut '97	♟♟	6
● Collio Merlot Tajut '98	♟	6

SAN FLORIANO DEL COLLIO (GO)

Gradis'ciutta
Loc. Giasbana, 10
34070 San Floriano del Collio (GO)
Tel. 0481390237
E-mail: robigradis@libero.it

Until 1997, this winery was called Isidoro Princic but to avoid confusion with the cellar of the same name in Cormons, it was decided to name the estate after the place where the main vineyard stands, Gradis'ciutta (the apostrophe separates the "s" and the "ci", pronounced "ch" in Italian). Over the last three years, we have watched the steady growth in quality of the wines that Robert, who works with his father Doro, has been releasing. The estate owns 13 hectares of vines and a further eight of woodland and seed crops. Annual output in bottles is limited to 55,000 units, most of them whites. It was in fact the whites that most impressed, partly because the cellar's red blend was not released in '98, an indifferent vintage here in Friuli. We'll have to be patient and wait for the '99, out next year. Bianco del Tùzz is a blend of barrique-aged chardonnay, pinot grigio, tocai and malvasia with marked golden highlights. Vanilla mingles with very ripe fruit on the nose then the palate offers breadth and structure that is fresh and soft at the same time. The Bianco del Bratinis comes from steel-aged chardonnay, pinot grigio, tocai and sauvignon. An elegant wine, it has concentration, a briny note and good length. What the panel liked about the Pinot Grigio was the rich ripeness of the fruit while the Tocai has a great attack, good progression and an inviting finish.

○	Collio Pinot Grigio '00	ŸŸ	4
○	Collio Tocai Friulano '00	ŸŸ	3*
○	Collio Bianco del Tùzz '99	ŸŸ	4
○	Collio Bianco del Bratinis '00	Ÿ	4
○	Collio Ribolla Gialla '00	Ÿ	4
○	Collio Sauvignon '00	Ÿ	4
●	Collio Cabernet Franc '00		4
○	Collio Chardonnay '00		4

SAN FLORIANO DEL COLLIO (GO)

Marcello e Marino Humar
Loc. Valerisce, 2
34070 San Floriano del Collio (GO)
Tel. 0481884094
E-mail: humarl@tiscalinet.it

It has been a pleasure to watch this winery come on in recent years. It has always produced good quality wines, although sometimes individual bottles have posed questions, a consequence of the large number of labels released. Now we note the confidence with which the fruit, from excellently located vineyards, is handled in the cellar. And talking about vineyards, the latest replanting of a hectare and a half below Valerisce at San Floriano is simply spectacular. It joins a further 23 hectares in the Collio and five in the Isonzo DOC zone. The estate is owned by brothers Marcello and Marino Humar, who currently turn out 130,000 bottles a year under 19 labels, including various blends and two spumantes. External relations are dealt with by Marcello's daughter Loretta, the winery trump card. As in the previous vintage, the two Collio Pinots are the pick of the list. We particularly liked the Pinot Bianco this year, an elegant wine with a concentrated nose that is reflected nicely on the well-structured, fruit-rich palate. An abundance of tropical fruit, as well as apple and pear, is the calling card of the Pinot Grigio, which might need to breathe for a moment or two to reveal its full breadth. Finally, one or two notes about the other wines: the elegant Chardonnay has a close-knit texture, the sweet Moscato Giallo offers wild roses and the Verduzzo varietal notes of baked apple. All came close to a second Glass.

○	Collio Pinot Bianco '00	ŸŸ	3*
○	Collio Pinot Grigio '00	ŸŸ	3*
○	Collio Chardonnay '00	Ÿ	3
○	Collio Traminer Aromatico '00	Ÿ	3
○	Moscato Giallo	Ÿ	4
○	Verduzzo Friulano	Ÿ	4
●	Collio Merlot '00		3
●	Collio Pinot Nero '00		3
○	Collio Tocai Friulano '00		3
●	Friuli Isonzo Cabernet Franc '00		3

SAN FLORIANO DEL COLLIO (GO)

IL CARPINO
LOC. SOVENZA, 14/A
34070 SAN FLORIANO DEL COLLIO (GO)
TEL. 0481884097
E-MAIL: ilcarpino@ilcarpino.com

Never before have we seen such a triumphal return to full Guide profile status as this but the long line of Glasses Il Carpino collected, including the Three that went to the Rubrum, speaks volumes. The panel had the opportunity to taste some of the wines as they aged in vats of barrels in the cellar and the picture we formed was a very positive one indeed. Silvano Cibini, daughter Anna and son-in-law Franco Sossol have taken giant strides forwards, enlisting help in the management of their 12 hectares from Marco Simonit and Pierpaolo Sirch, two names that are behind the progress made by many of the region's leading estates. For the cellar, they have called in Roberto Cipresso, whose name is familiar all over Italy, and the results have been quick to appear. The estate makes 70,000 bottles of barrique and tonneau-aged Il Carpino-label wines and Vigna Runc, a line of steel-aged whites and Merlot and Cabernet Sauvignon aged in wood. Rubrum is a monovarietal merlot from gravelly soil. Vine density is 5,000 plants per hectare and the wine is fermented, macerated and aged in seven-hectolitre tonneaux. Incredibly rich, it has a powerful but not austere structure, serious body and beautifully mellow tannins. A little lower down the pecking order is the very alcoholic Malvasia, fermented and aged for 15 months in barriques. Bianco Carpino, a 50-50 blend of chardonnay and sauvignon is a comfortable Two Glass wine and the Rosso Carpino, from four parts merlot to one of cabernet sauvignon, needs a little more cellar time.

SAN FLORIANO DEL COLLIO (GO)

MUZIC
LOC. BIVIO, 4
34070 SAN FLORIANO DEL COLLIO (GO)
TEL. 0481884201
E-MAIL: muzic.az.agr@libero.it

The cellar of Giovani Muzic – the last letter is pronounced "sh" – was completely renovated two years ago and today, it can call on the assistance of Sandro Facca, a wine technician who has many years' experience in various Friulian wineries. The first product of the new regime is Bric (pronounced "Breets"), a name used for residents of the Collio, which is known locally as Brda. The wine is a blend mainly of local varieties like tocai friulano, ribolla gialla and malvasia, with sauvignon adding its aromatic contribution. An interesting wine, it has a great nose and good dynamism in the mouth but it will need longer in the bottle if it is going to be equal to Giovanni's ambitious hopes. The estate has ten hectares in the Collio and a couple more in the Isonzo DOC zone, which provide the fruit for two rich, fruity reds, a Cabernet Franc and a Merlot. Ribolla Gialla is a Muzic classic, unfurling distinctly complex aromas of melon, summer flowers, zest of lemon, lavender and minerals, although the palate is fairly one-dimensional. In the Chardonnay, too, it was the nose that impressed more than the palate while the Tocai has original notes of honey and dried flowers with milky nuances. Creamy notes are also present in the aromas of the Pinot Grigio, perhaps from the malolactic fermentation that has left intact the fresh acidity of the fruity palate.

● Rubrum '99	♛♛♛	6
○ Collio Malvasia '99	♛♛	5
○ Collio Chardonnay Vigna Runc '00	♛♛	3*
○ Collio Bianco Carpino '99	♛♛	4
○ Collio Chardonnay '99	♛♛	5
○ Collio Sauvignon '99	♛♛	5
○ Collio Pinot Grigio Vigna Runc '00	♛	3
○ Collio Sauvignon Vigna Runc '00	♛	4
○ Collio Ribolla Gialla '99	♛	5
● Friuli Isonzo Merlot Vigna Runc '99	♛	4
● Rosso Carpino '99	♛	5

○ Collio Bianco Bric '00	♛♛	3*
○ Collio Chardonnay '00	♛	3
○ Collio Pinot Grigio '00	♛	3
○ Collio Ribolla Gialla '00	♛	3
○ Collio Tocai Friulano '00	♛	3
● Friuli Isonzo Cabernet Franc '99	♛	3
○ Collio Sauvignon '00		3
● Collio Cabernet Sauvignon '99		4
● Friuli Isonzo Merlot '99		4
● Friuli Isonzo Merlot Primo Legno '97	♛♛	4
● Collio Cabernet Sauvignon '98	♛♛	3

SAN FLORIANO DEL COLLIO (GO)

Matijaz Tercic
Loc. Bukuje, 9
34070 San Floriano del Collio (GO)
Tel. 0481884193

Matijaz Tercic is young and so shy that he hasn't even put a sign up to tell you where his small winery is located. A serious, scrupulous winemaker, he tends four hectares on the steep hillslopes around San Floriano del Collio. There are ten varieties in the vineyards but only seven labels on his wines. Nevertheless, since production totals about 22,000 bottles, it means that only a few labels will be released in 4,000 units or more. Commercial decisions like this restrict the growth potential of smaller producers since it becomes well nigh impossible to make any impact in the market. The cellar may be small but it is well equipped and we enjoyed some exciting tastings of wines that have yet to be released. Wines on show included the excellent Bianca Planta, a 90-10 blend of oak-aged chardonnay and pinot bianco. It is bottled without filtration, which means it may have some sediment, and offers aromas of white chocolate and confectioner's cream, leading in to a creamy, intense mouthfeel. The Pinot Grigio, of which fully 5,500 bottles are produced, is also delightfully complex and elegant, showing creamy fruit in the well-sustained, lingering palate. Vino degli Orti, a blend of tocai, malvasia istriana and riesling renano in order of quantity, is aged in stainless steel. Warm and lavishly fruity, it came very close to a second Glass.

○	Collio Pinot Grigio '00	▼▼	4
○	Collio Bianco Planta '99	▼▼	4
○	Collio Ribolla Gialla '00	▼	4
○	Vino degli Orti '00	▼	4
●	Collio Merlot '98	▼	4
○	Collio Chardonnay '00		4
○	Collio Sauvignon '00		4
●	Collio Merlot '97	♀♀	4
○	Collio Bianco Planta '98	♀♀	4

SAN FLORIANO DEL COLLIO (GO)

Franco Terpin
Loc. Valerisce, 6/a
34070 San Floriano del Collio (GO)
Tel. 0481884215

The Terpins have lived in the Collio for several generations and it was Teodoro Terpin who bought the first vines and started making wine. His son Franco now looks after the eight and a half hectares scattered over a number of small plots and from the last vintage, he made about 16,000 bottles. With his friend Damijan Podversic, Franco has rented a cellar at Dolegna del Collio, 20 or so kilometres away, because he could find nothing suitable any nearer home. Yet there are advantages to this, such as the opportunity to use shared hi-tech instruments, taking turns on duty in the cellar, if necessary, and the continuous exchange of information. The two friends also have as consultants Attilio Pagli and his team. Franco wanted to get his range down to just two labels, a Collio Bianco and a Collio Rosso, both oak-fermented and aged. In the meantime, he astonished the panel with his marvellous Collio Bianco '99, from cask-conditioned pinot grigio, sauvignon, chardonnay and tocai friulano. Its clear golden highlights introduce the intensely fruit-rich nose and palate, which has well-judged acidity and nicely amalgamated oak. The Sauvignon is remarkably complex, with a broad range of varietal aromas, good balance and robust alcohol. The cabernet sauvignon and cabernet franc Collio Rosso, which has five per cent merlot in the blend, was still trying to find its balance when we tasted it.

○	Collio Bianco '99	▼▼	5
○	Collio Sauvignon '00	▼▼	4
○	Collio Pinot Grigio '00		4
●	Collio Rosso '99		5
○	Collio Bianco '98	♀♀	5

SAN GIORGIO DELLA RICHINVELDA (PN)

FORCHIR
FRAZ. PROVESANO
VIA CIASUTIS, 1/B
33095 SAN GIORGIO DELLA RICHINVELDA (PN)
TEL. 042796037
E-MAIL: forchir@libero.it

The Forchir estate is celebrating its centenary. From Felettis near Bicinicco in the early 20th century to the present 221 hectares in various parts of the Friulian plain, and from Antonio Forchir to present owners Gianfranco Bianchini and Enzo Deana, the cellar has come a long way but quality has never wavered and the wines are very much terroir-driven. What really impresses, though, is the good all-round standard, for none of the wines went below One Glass. The panel also appreciated the special selections, like Sauvignon L'Altro and Pinot Bianco Campo dei Gelsi. To make these, very old vines have been recovered and some very bold winemaking decisions taken, considering this is a Grave DOC estate. The better of the two is the Pinot Bianco. Subtle and varietal on the nose, where elegant, complex notes of wistaria, melon and white damson come through, it follows through triumphantly on the palate, which is perked up by refreshing acidity in the finish. The Sauvignon L'Altro has a fine nose of ripe melon and tomato, acacia blossom and elderflower but falls off on the palate, where its suppleness and tangy freshness is not matched by the complexity. Outstanding in the long line of One Glass winners is the Bianco del Martin Pescatore, from oak-fermented chardonnay, riesling and traminer. It has a good balance of ripe wistaria and acacia fruit and white damson and pear flowers on the one hand, and vanilla notes on the other. The Rosso del Fondatore, a Bordeaux blend, is full and confident on the nose but a little one-dimensional in the mouth. Finally, the Merlot, redolent of hay, lucerne and black cherries in syrup, has very decent tannins.

○ Friuli Grave Pinot Bianco Campo dei Gelsi '00	ΨΨ	3*
● Friuli Grave Cabernet Sauvignon '00	Ψ	3
● Friuli Grave Merlot '00	Ψ	3
○ Friuli Grave Pinot Grigio '00	Ψ	3
● Friuli Grave Refosco P. R. '00	Ψ	3
○ Friuli Grave Sauvignon l'Altro '00	Ψ	3
○ Friuli Grave Traminer Aromatico '00	Ψ	3
○ Friuli Grave Bianco Martin Pescatore '99	Ψ	3

SAN GIOVANNI AL NATISONE (UD)

ALFIERI CANTARUTTI
VIA RONCHI, 9
33048 SAN GIOVANNI AL NATISONE (UD)
TEL. 0432756317
E-MAIL: alficant@tin.it

The future looks bright for Antonella, Fabrizio and their winery. It doesn't show entirely in the Glasses awarded, but the cellar's points total is growing year by year, in step with the new winemaking, organization and marketing initiatives introduced at this attractive estate. The best wines this year were: the Merlot, fermented slowly on the skins and aged in large and small barrels, which has depth and vigour on the nose, where sweet notes of morello cherry and cassis emerge, and a caressingly soft mouthfeel nicely offset by astringent notes; the elegantly fruity Tocai, with its soft notes on the front palate, followed by attractive sensations typical of the variety; and the Canto, a tocai-based wine with additions of sauvignon and pinot bianco. It's as exuberantly bright as Antonella herself, after whom it is named, and the ripe fruit and almond notes usher in a delightful and very quaffable palate. In the other white, Antizio, chardonnay takes the place of pinot. It performed well, offering sweet nuances of mint and lemon, which are echoed on the subtly elegant palate. The lime blossom and honey Pinot Grigio came close to winning Two Glasses for its elegance and balance. The red Antizio, a Bordeaux blend, was a little pale and underpowered. A pity, because its skilful execution and attractive aromas deserved better. The Sauvignon is well-sustained and varietal.

○ COF Bianco Canto '00	ΨΨ	4
○ COF Tocai Friulano '00	ΨΨ	4
○ Friuli Grave Bianco Antizio '00	ΨΨ	3*
● COF Merlot '99	ΨΨ	5
○ COF Pinot Grigio '00	Ψ	4
○ COF Sauvignon '00	Ψ	4
● Friuli Grave Rosso Antizio '00	Ψ	3
● COF Pinot Nero '99		5
● COF Rosso Carato '96	ΨΨ	5
○ COF Bianco Canto '99	ΨΨ	4

SAN GIOVANNI AL NATISONE (UD)

LIVON
LOC. DOLEGNANO
VIA MONTAREZZA, 33
33048 SAN GIOVANNI AL NATISONE (UD)
TEL. 0432757173 - 0432756231
E-MAIL: info@livon.it

Livon is hard to describe in a few words, because the range is so diversified. This profile will deal with the Collio products, sold under the Erté brand, itself split into the classic label for the middle of the market and the Cru range for more discriminating drinkers, as well as the Roncaltos, two wines from an estate that is still getting its house in order. Scoring high again is the Braide Alte, a blend of chardonnay, sauvignon, picolit and moscato giallo. Its concentrated tomato leaf, peach and citrus fruit is followed by lingering aroma-rich freshness on the palate. A great performance also came from the Merlot, whose concentrated fruit and smoky notes on the nose introduce a well-sustained tannic weave that backs up the warm, fruit-rich fullness of the palate. In the Cru series, there were good marks for the rich Tocai, an elegant, sweet infusion of flowers and pears. The Chardonnay did well, offering milky notes and hawthorn, then a palate that is first sweet, then fresh and a finish that needs more time, as did the Pinot, a complex medley of honey, apple and tangerines let down only by a slight uncertainty in the mid palate. There were good marks for the Roncaltos, especially the well-established Ribolla. It's a wine with personality, intense and weighty on the palate, with fresh and almost aromatic fruit. The newcomer, the Cabernet Sauvignon, is a wine to watch. Moving on to the classic range, the Pinot is a little off form but the Chardonnay is very good indeed, and can stand comparison with much more exalted versions. The Verduzzo is good but will find few takers outside the region without fine-tuning.

SAN GIOVANNI AL NATISONE (UD)

RONCO DEL GNEMIZ
VIA RONCHI, 5
33048 SAN GIOVANNI AL NATISONE (UD)
TEL. 0432756238 - 0432936297

Serena Palazzolo runs this estate in the hills just outside Rosazzo with Gabriele. Their discretion and determination has put the cellar firmly back on the road to the very top of winemaking in Friuli and, indeed, Italy. It's not a huge cellar but it is big enough to ferment and age the grapes from the estate. Barriques are stored on several floors but Gabriele has the situation well under control and keeps an eye on all of them. In spring, we were able to taste the Sauvignon Riserva '98 and we were left with the impression that it would never get on top of the oak. Well, we were wrong, as was apparent at summer tastings, so we decided to enter it for the final Three Glass tastings, where it missed out by a whisker. Notes of confectioner's cream, peach, apricot and zest of lemon on the nose meld into a chewy, fruit-rich mouthfeel on the robustly alcoholic palate. Sweet wood-derived tannins join in to make this a stupendous wine that can only improve in the next few years. The Bianco '99 Serena combines freshness with warmth, and elegance with intensity, and makes a great entry on the palate. The Chardonnay '98 is back on form, the wood perfectly dosed and with plenty of youthful notes. Knowing the winemakers, we would put serious money on its cellarability. Another surprise came from our retasting of the Rosso del Gnemiz '97. It wasn't so much the high quality of the wine as the softness of its tannins, which means that it is drinking well now. Generally, it would require seven or eight years in the cellar to reach this stage.

○	Braide Alte '99	🍷🍷	6
●	Merlot Tiare Mate '99	🍷🍷	5
○	Collio Chardonnay '00	🍷🍷	4
○	Collio Pinot Grigio Braide Grande '00	🍷🍷	5
○	Collio Ribolla Gialla Roncalto '00	🍷🍷	4
○	Collio Tocai Friulano Ronc di Zorz '00	🍷🍷	5
●	Collio Cabernet Sauvignon Roncalto '99	🍷🍷	5
○	Collio Chardonnay Braide Mate '99	🍷🍷	5
○	Collio Pinot Bianco '00	🍷	4
○	COF Verduzzo Friulano Casali Godia '99	🍷	5
○	Braide Alte '96	🍷🍷🍷	6
○	Braide Alte '97	🍷🍷🍷	6
○	Braide Alte '98	🍷🍷🍷	6

○	COF Sauvignon Ris. '98	🍷🍷	6
○	COF Chardonnay '98	🍷🍷	6
○	COF Serena Bianco '99	🍷🍷	6
○	COF Pinot Grigio '98	🍷	4
●	COF Schioppettino '98	🍷	6
○	COF Sauvignon '99		4
○	Chardonnay '90	🍷🍷🍷	6
○	COF Chardonnay '91	🍷🍷🍷	6
○	COF Chardonnay '97	🍷🍷	6
●	Rosso del Gnemiz '95	🍷🍷	6
●	Rosso del Gnemiz '97	🍷🍷	6
●	COF Schioppettino '97	🍷	6

SAN GIOVANNI AL NATISONE (UD)

VILLA CHIOPRIS
LOC. DOLEGNANO
VIA MONTAREZZA, 33
33048 SAN GIOVANNI AL NATISONE (UD)
TEL. 0432757173 - 0432756231
E-MAIL: info@livon.it

A Livon-group estate, Villa Chiopris specializes in making fresh-tasting, ready-to-drink wines. That doesn't mean that the wines are any less carefully made, though. Vineyard management and cellar equipment are cutting-edge stuff. The production philosophy simply acknowledges that there is a market for good wine to drink every day, without having to take out a second mortgage. Its consumers are looking for versatility at the table, freshness, delicacy and fruit-rich aromas, as well as decent length. That is the market Villa Chiopris caters for, with wines that deliver exactly what they promise. Our new assessments are a carbon copy of last year's. The Tocai came out on top. A cold-macerated wine fermented in stainless steel with lees contact, it offers the nose ripe fruit and spring flowers, and the palate good length and freshness. The similarly vinified Pinot Grigio is crystal-clear and lustrous in the glass, crisp on the nose and opens out soft and fresh on the palate with classic varietal aromas. The Chardonnay, which follows the same winemaking procedure, has its strong points in sweet fruit and summer flower aromas. The Sauvignon, made without lees contact, is softer than usual. The thrust on the palate is even and free of rough edges. Destemming, soft-pressing, low temperature fermentation and ageing in stainless steel is the procedure used for the Merlot and the Cabernet. Both and fresh and unobtrusive on the palate, where berry fruit is prominent. The Merlot has a hint of pennyroyal while the Cabernet offers spicy aromas.

○ Friuli Grave Tocai Friulano '00	♟♟	3*
● Friuli Grave Cabernet Sauvignon '00	♟	3
○ Friuli Grave Chardonnay '00	♟	3
● Friuli Grave Merlot '00	♟	3
○ Friuli Grave Pinot Grigio '00	♟	3
○ Friuli Grave Sauvignon '00	♟	3

SAN LORENZO ISONTINO (GO)

LIS NERIS - PECORARI
VIA GAVINANA, 5
34070 SAN LORENZO ISONTINO (GO)
TEL. 048180105
E-MAIL: lisneris@lisneris.it

It was going to be an emblem. A wine that embodied years of research and experimenting. A bottle that contained the best of the three vineyards, and the three grapes, that have made the Lis Neris reputation: chardonnay from Jurosa; sauvignon from Picol; and pinot grigio from Gris. It was going to be a stunning, irresistible wine. Inviting and unforgettable. A wine that caresses to conquer. Lis was going to be all of this. And it is. A perfect balance where the peach and freshness of sauvignon mingles with the tropical fruit and structure of chardonnay and the aroma-rich softness of pinot. But that's not all. As usual, Alvaro Pecorari wasn't satisfied with just one wine. He presented the panel with two other major bottles. The Tal Lûc is a dried-grape wine from verduzzo with a thimble-sized yield. Concentrated, sweet and fruity, it is only let down by a faint note of volatility. Alvaro's Pinot Grigio '00 is a textbook bottle. Fermented and aged in stainless steel, it outperformed the Pinot Gris above all for its rich aromas and firm, precise progression on the palate. We then moved on to the estate red, a Bordeaux blend that has had its ups and downs over the years. This was a good vintage, especially on the nose. After that came the two Chardonnays. Jurosa, a blend of steel and wood-aged wines, has generous ripe fruit and flowers with hazelnut, tobacco and toasty oak while the oak-aged Sant'Jurosa is almost a swansong for the label, which will be dropped in favour of Lis. The two Sauvignons scored slightly lower, although both came close to a second Glass. Remember that these are products which can spring some very pleasant surprises after a few months in the cellar.

○ Lis '99	♟♟♟	6
○ Tal Lûc '99	♟♟♟	6
○ Friuli Isonzo Pinot Grigio '00	♟♟	4
○ Friuli Isonzo Sauvignon Picòl '00	♟♟	5
○ Friuli Isonzo Chardonnay Jurosa '99	♟♟	5
○ Friuli Isonzo Chardonnay Sant'Jurosa '99	♟♟	5
○ Friuli Isonzo Pinot Grigio Gris '99	♟♟	5
● Lis Neris '99	♟♟	6
○ Friuli Isonzo Sauvignon '00	♟	4
○ Friuli Isonzo Sauvignon Dom Picòl '96	♟♟♟	5
○ Friuli Isonzo Pinot Grigio Gris '98	♟♟♟	5

SAN LORENZO ISONTINO (GO)

Pierpaolo Pecorari
Via Tommaseo, 36/c
34070 San Lorenzo Isontino (GO)
tel. 0481808775
e-mail: info@pierpaolopecorari.it

Pierpaolo Pecorari is giving an increasingly free rein in the winery to his son Alessandro. Educated in the humanities, Alessandro is proving that he knows how to give the estate wines a very stylish and attractive image. This cocktail of wisdom and youthful enterprise could take this already excellent winery on to even greater heights, particularly since eminent winemaker Donato Lanati has also come on board. The 25 Pecorari hectares produce three lines: steel-fermented varietal wines, the Altis selections, which start fermentation on the skins with ambient yeasts and are unfiltered, and the "vins de terroir" from the older vineyards, which are aged in 450-litre tonneaux for about a year. The results on all three fronts are splendid. The Pinot Grigio Olivers is a stunner. Aromas of tropical fruit and confectioner's cream return on the palate. Already good, it has the potential to improve with ageing. Exquisite is the word for the Sauvignon Kolàus, which has sweet, fragrant notes of peach, melon and vanilla on nose and palate, while the varietal Sauvignon and Chardonnay also delighted the panel. The Sauvignon is supple and elegant whereas the Chardonnay is fresh, aromas of banana, apricot and orange blossom leading in to refreshingly tangy finish. The Merlot Baolar is also delicious, its aromas of blackcurrant, morello cherry and dried flowers ushering in a subtle palate that mirrors the nose and offers nice breadth. We are looking forward to tracking the progress of the two Altis wines, especially the coppery, fruit-rich Pinot Grigio.

SAN QUIRINO (PN)

Russolo
Via San Rocco, 58/a
33080 San Quirino (PN)
tel. 0434919577 - 0434917361
e-mail: russolorino@libero.it

This estate, run by oenologist Iginio Russolo and his son Rino, lies on the "magredi", the poor, stony soil of alluvial origin in the flatlands around Pordenone. It is difficult terrain but excellent drainage is guaranteed and the clear air of the Carnian Prealps keeps the vines healthy. The winery has opted for very low yields, and vines that produce relatively little fruit, in order to make premium-quality bottles. Reports in the press that the chairman of a leading soccer club enjoys the red Borgo di Peuma blend have helped to generate interest in the Russolo estate. Reliable as ever, the Pinot Nero scored high marks. Entry on the nose is full and packed with fruit, where cherries, ripe blackcurrant, plum tart, lavender and sweet spices can all be perceived. Milky-soft in the mouth, it unveils nice warmth and breadth. Doi Raps is a convincing blend of super-ripe pinot and sauvignon fruit with two per cent moscato giallo. Fermented in four-hectolitre oak barrels, it has a delightfully rich nose of dried roses, ginger and candied orange peel. These aromas return on the soft yet well-structured palate, which has a dry finish. We should also mention the very good estate Müller Thurgau. Its subtle, penetrating nose has notes of tobacco, roses, peaches and tangerines, impeccably echoed on the palate, which is flavoursome and very full-bodied.

○ Pinot Grigio Olivers '99	ΨΨ	5
○ Friuli Isonzo Chardonnay '00	ΨΨ	4
○ Friuli Isonzo Sauvignon '00	ΨΨ	4
○ Chardonnay Sorìs '99	ΨΨ	5
● Merlot Baolar '99	ΨΨ	6
○ Sauvignon Kolàus '99	ΨΨ	5
○ Friuli Isonzo Pinot Grigio '00	Ψ	4
○ Friuli Isonzo Pinot Grigio Altis '99	Ψ	4
○ Friuli Isonzo Sauvignon Altis '99	Ψ	4
○ Pratoscuro '99		5
○ Sauvignon Kolàus '96	ΨΨΨ	5
● Merlot Baolar '97	ΨΨ	6
○ Pinot Grigio Olivers '98	ΨΨ	5

○ Doi Raps '99	ΨΨ	4
○ Müller Thurgau Mussignaz '00	ΨΨ	4
● Pinot Nero Grifo Nero '98	ΨΨ	5
● Borgo di Peuma '98	Ψ	5
● Cabernet I Legni '98	Ψ	4
○ Friuli Grave Pinot Grigio Ronco Calaj '00	Ψ	4
○ Friuli Grave Tocai Friulano Ronco Calaj '00	Ψ	4
● Merlot I Legni '98	Ψ	4
● Refosco P. R. I Legni '99	Ψ	4
○ Ronco Sesan '99	Ψ	4
○ Malvasia Istriana '00		4
● Pinot Nero Grifo Nero '97	ΨΨ	5

SPILIMBERGO (PN)

Borgo Magredo
Loc. Tauriano
Via Basaldella, 5
33090 Spilimbergo (PN)
Tel. 042751444

Borgo Magredo, owned by the Genagricola company, stands on characteristically lean, stony soil near Splimbergo, in the Grave DOC zone. There are 250 hectares all told, planted at an average density of 4,000 vines per hectare, and annual production is around 700,000 bottles. For years, the cellar has alternated good results with poor years, which can be attributed to changes in the management. Since the '99 harvest, Borgo Magredo has been assisted by winemaker Donato Lanati, who has shown what he can do, even on what is a relatively new soil type for him. As a result, the winery has regained its full Guide profile. The highest marks went to two whites, the Chardonnay Braida Longa and the Pinot Grigio. The Chardonnay is an attractive gold-flecked straw yellow, with complex oak aromas emerging against a backdrop of fresh fruit. Melon and banana come through to mingle with greener hints of sweet tobacco. We like the nicely handled contrast on the palate of the green fruit, which mirrors the nose, and nuances of vanilla. The Pinot Grigio takes full advantage of a favourable vintage to offer the nose fumé notes that make way for white damson and banana. It follows through well on the palate, where the wine shows buttery richness and well-sustained thrust through to the refreshingly acid-laced finish. One Glass wines include the Moscato Rosa, which discloses subtle notes of wild strawberries and freshly cut wild roses, and attractively understated sweetness.

○ Friuli Grave Chardonnay Braida Longa '00	🍷🍷	3*
○ Friuli Grave Pinot Grigio '00	🍷🍷	3*
● Friuli Grave Cabernet Franc '00	🍷	2*
○ Friuli Grave Chardonnay '00	🍷	3
● Friuli Grave Pinot Nero '00	🍷	2*
● Moscato Rosa Borgo della Rosa '00	🍷	3
○ Friuli Grave Sauvignon '00		3
○ Friuli Grave Tocai Friulano '00		2
● Friuli Grave Merlot Braida Moral '99		3

SPILIMBERGO (PN)

Plozner
Fraz. Barbeano
Via delle Prese, 19
33097 Spilimbergo (PN)
Tel. 04272902
E-mail: plozner@plozner.it

What surprises about the Plozner estate is not so much the consistently high quality as the fact that it is obtained on very lean, alluvial soil, where limestone makes up as much as 60-70 per cent of the terrain. This terroir, and the nearby mountains, creates a dry climate with a considerable range of temperatures during the course of the day and night, all of which keeps the vines healthy and the fruit excellent. There are 100 hectares on the property, which has a total output of 23,000 hectolitres, including wine sold unbottled. We have come to regard Sauvignon as the flagship Plozner wine, for it has enjoyed great commercial success for quite a number of years. On the nose, the fruit tumbles out in notes of rue, broom, tomato and peach in a balanced swathe that speaks volumes for the skills of winemaker Francesco Visentin. On the palate, it is stylish and elegant, setting off green notes of rue and red pepper nicely against softer hints of fruit. But the Grave can also produce serious reds, as the Plozner Merlot Riserva shows. About 15,000 bottles are released of this wine with its penetratingly warm nose of wild berry tart and bottled cherries with milk chocolate and vanilla. It follows through attractively on the palate, where softness and still roughish tannins find a nice point of equilibrium. The clean, well-made Pinot Bianco is good and tangy, in fact you would think it was made in Alto Adige. The green Tocai has hints of flowers and bitter almonds and the spicy, cinnamon and clove Cabernet Sauvignon Riserva proffers attractive aromas of violets and coffee.

○ Friuli Grave Sauvignon '00	🍷🍷	3*
● Friuli Grave Merlot Ris. '99	🍷🍷	4
○ Friuli Grave Pinot Bianco '00	🍷	3
○ Friuli Grave Tocai Friulano '00	🍷	3
● Friuli Grave Cabernet Sauvignon Ris. '97	🍷	4
○ Friuli Grave Chardonnay '00		3
○ Friuli Grave Pinot Grigio '00		3
○ Friuli Grave Chardonnay Ris. '97		4

TORREANO (UD)

JACUSS
FRAZ. MONTINA
V.LE KENNEDY, 35/A
33040 TORREANO (UD)
TEL. 0432715147
E-MAIL: jacuss@jacuss.com

Once upon a time, Torreano di Cividale was known for the quarries where a characteristic local stone was extracted. Now, its particular soil type has turned it into the home of several premium-quality wine producers. One of those is Jacuss, owned by the Iacuzzi brothers, and the winery can point to well-kept vineyards and cellar, a small vine stock – only ten hectares – and the determination to do well without outside assistance. The yearly output of 50,000 bottles is split equally between reds and whites. The estate has only been bottling for ten years, previously selling all its wine unbottled, so the results obtained so far are admirable. This year, we particularly like two wines from local varieties, Picolit and Schioppettino. The first has a complex nose of spring flowers, lime blossom honey, oranges and apricots. The stylish front palate reveals fruit flavours and dried roses come though in the lingering finish. Varietal is the word for the Schioppettino, with its signature spicy notes of nutmeg and white pepper mingling with bramble jam and black cherries. There's plenty of structure on the full palate, which has a nice tannic weave. The fresh-tasting, varietal Pinot Bianco and the very delicate Tocai, with its nice apple and acacia blossom aromas are good, as is the white Lindi Uà blend, from pinot bianco, sauvignon and tocai. Its nose is well up to scratch but the palate needs time to settle. Some of the reds, like the Merlot and the Rosso Lindi Uà, lack that little bit of balance which would make them complete.

TORREANO (UD)

VALCHIARÒ
FRAZ. LAURINI
VIA CASALI LAURINI, 3
33040 TORREANO (UD)
TEL. 0432712393
E-MAIL: info@valchiaro.com

Lauro De Vincenti affably chairs the group of five partners who decided, exactly ten years ago, to do a little more than just make a few demijohns of wine for themselves and their friends, and instead bottle their products. Emilio, Giampaolo, Armando and Galliano are the other members of the team, each one bringing some skill, as well as grapes, to their joint venture. Before the tastings, they are all as nervous as schoolkids with an exam the next day and it's hard to describe their enthusiasm when the "results" come out in the Guide. The vines are in one of the coolest valleys in the area but the partners' attentive vineyard management means that the fruit is perfectly ripe when it reaches the cellar. Sweet wines, such as Verduzzo and Picolit, the most recent versions of which will be released next year, are made with fruit that has been dried to concentrate the sugar in the grapes. The Valchiarò Tocai Friulano has elegantly concentrated aromas of apple, great nose-palate consistency and a rich, fruity thrust on the palate. The long, full finish is redolent of very ripe golden delicious apples. The Pinot Grigio is fresh and broad, with hints of apple to the fore, while the Sauvignon reveals delicious notes of citron and grapefruit. All the other wines were in the top half of the One Glass range, including El Clap, a blend of merlot cabernet franc and refosco from the '97 vintage, and La Clupa, a DOC white obtained from tocai, sauvignon and pinot bianco.

○ COF Picolit '98	🍷🍷	6
● COF Schioppettino '99	🍷🍷	4
○ COF Pinot Bianco '00	🍷	4
○ Tocai Friulano '00	🍷	3
○ COF Bianco Lindi Uà '99	🍷	4
○ COF Sauvignon '00		4
● COF Rosso Lindi Uà '97		4
● COF Merlot '99		3
○ COF Verduzzo Friulano '99		4
● COF Rosso Lindi Uà '96	🍷🍷	4

○ COF Pinot Grigio '00	🍷🍷	3*
○ COF Sauvignon '00	🍷🍷	3*
○ COF Tocai Friulano '00	🍷🍷	3*
● El Clap '97	🍷	4
○ COF Bianco La Clupa '99	🍷	4
● COF Merlot '99	🍷	4
● COF Refosco P. R. '99	🍷	4
● El Clap '96	🍷🍷	4
● COF Merlot '98	🍷🍷	3
● COF Refosco P. R. '98	🍷🍷	3

TORREANO (UD)

VOLPE PASINI
FRAZ. TOGLIANO
VIA CIVIDALE, 16
33040 TORREANO (UD)
TEL. 0432715151

Not for the first time, the dynamic Emilio Rotolo and his formidable winemaking team have achieved astounding results that put them firmly in the big league. So let's meet the team, starting with consultant oenologist Riccardo Cotarella. Internationally famous Riccardo has been able to breathe new life into all the Volpe Pasini wines, not just the reds, where his skills are legendary. Out in the vineyards are two equally well known and respected fruitmakers, Marco Simonit and Pierpaolo Sirch. Their job is to ensure that the fruit corresponds precisely to the winery's needs, and it seems they are eminently successful. In the cellar, Emilio can count on Alessandro Torresin's abilities while PR is the province of the delightful Rosa Tomaselli. There can be no denying that Emilio has been able to achieve, in very short order, absolutely outstanding results. A glance at the table below is enough to confirm that. Merlot Focus takes its place on Olympus thanks to a richly concentrated nose of caramel-covered berry fruit and a superbly generous palate that flanks warm, soft sensations with a bracing tannic weave. The stupendous Chardonnay was only a step or two behind. Its golden hue introduces notes of tobacco and toastiness that come through despite the abundance of fruit. And to round off, the Refosco is another great wine, its sweet spice and juniper combining with a rich, chewy mouthfeel, berry fruit tart and chocolate.

TRIVIGNANO UDINESE (UD)

FOFFANI
LOC. CLAUIANO
P.ZA GIULIA, 13/14
33050 TRIVIGNANO UDINESE (UD)
TEL. 0432999584

Giovanni and Elisabetta Foffani deservedly take their place in the Guide. The estate has ancient roots, having produced wines since 1789. That's the reason the nine-hectare property at Clauiano has a lovely, 16th-century residence which is sufficient reason on its own to visit the winery. The cellar turns out about 60,000 bottles a year from densely planted, Guyot-trained vines. All five wines presented passed muster, the Sauvignon winning Two Glasses. It has very bright greenish highlights that usher in very subtle aromas of tomato and elderflower, with distinct pear also emerging. Entry on the palate is rounded, with clear hints of ripe fruit and red pepper. The balance in the mid palate is perfect, and never wavers through to the long finish. Full Glasses went to the Tocai and the Pinot Grigio. The Tocai is a little straightforward at first on the nose but then opens into apple, crusty bread and dried fruit, giving an overall impression of elegance. Rich on the palate, it has complexity, pear peeking through in long finish. There are varietal notes of onionskin in the Pinot Grigio, as well as characteristic ripe pear with rue and wistaria to add complexity. The uncompromising entry on the palate follows through the fruit on the nose, expanding surefootedly in the mid palate. The Merlot won a Glass for its typicity, rich fruit flavours and a warm finish of bramble and black cherry.

● COF Merlot Focus '99	▼▼▼	6
○ COF Chardonnay Zuc di Volpe '99	▼▼	5
● COF Refosco P. R. Zuc di Volpe '99	▼▼	5
○ COF Pinot Bianco Zuc di Volpe '00	▼▼	5
○ COF Pinot Grigio Zuc di Volpe '00	▼▼	5
● COF Refosco P. R. '00	▼▼	4
○ COF Ribolla Gialla Zuc di Volpe '00	▼▼	5
○ COF Bianco Le Roverelle Zuc di Volpe '99	▼▼	6
○ COF Sauvignon Zuc di Volpe '00	▼	5
○ COF Tocai Friulano Zuc di Volpe '00	▼	5
● COF Cabernet Zuc di Volpe '99	▼	5

○ Friuli Aquileia Sauvignon Sup. '00	▼▼	3*
○ Friuli Aquileia Pinot Grigio Sup. '00	▼	3
○ Friuli Aquileia Tocai Friulano Sup. '00	▼	2*
● Friuli Aquileia Merlot '99	▼	4
○ Friuli Aquileia Chardonnay Sup. '00		3

OTHER WINERIES

FLAVIO PONTONI
VIA PERUZZI, 8
33042 BUTTRIO (UD)
TEL. 0432674352

Flavio Pontoni always turns out well-made wines and sometimes they can be seriously good. It's a classic Friulian winery, with five hectares under vine that produce 30,000 bottles a year. There are fully 11 labels, all offering excellent value for money. The Cabernet Franc is outstanding.

●	COF Cabernet Franc '00	ŸŸ	3*
●	COF Merlot '00	Ÿ	3
○	COF Picolit '00	Ÿ	5

VALLE
VIA NAZIONALE, 3
33042 BUTTRIO (UD)
TEL. 0432674289
E-MAIL: info@valle.it

This property is run by expert wineman Gigi Valle and his sons, Paolo and Marco. They have a large plot at Rutars, in the heart of the Collio, and a second at Rosazzo, in the Colli Orientali, and produce 200,000 bottles a year. The Sauvignon, Ribolla Gialla, Cabernet and L'Ambrosie are all good.

○	COF Sauvignon L'Araldo '00	Ÿ	5
●	COF Cabernet Sauvignon Ris. '97	Ÿ	5
○	COF Ribolla Gialla Sel. S. Blas '99	Ÿ	5
	L'Ambrosie S. Blas	Ÿ	5

BRUNNER
PIAZZA DE SENIBUS, 5
33040 CHIOPRIS VISCONE (UD)
TEL. 0432991184
E-MAIL: priviet@tin.it

The historic Brunner estate sprawls over 130 hectares, 20 of which are planted to vine. The beautifully looked after cellar is well worth a visit for its stock of 50-hectolitre barrels. The wines are all reliable and some are very good, like the Sauvignon and the Chardonnay.

○	Friuli Grave Chardonnay '00	Ÿ	3
○	Friuli Grave Pinot Grigio '00	Ÿ	3
○	Friuli Grave Sauvignon '00	Ÿ	3
○	Friuli Grave Tocai Friulano '00	Ÿ	3

DAL FARI
VIA DARNAZZACCO, 20
33043 CIVIDALE DEL FRIULI (UD)
TEL. 0432731219 - 0432706726
E-MAIL: dalfari@faber-italy.com

The obvious winemaking passion of the Toffoluttis is not always enough to produce good results. Their 12 hectares yield about 80,000 bottles and the average standard is very respectable. Well-earned Glasses went to the crisp, varietal Pinot Grigio and the complex Rosso D'Orsone, a characterful red blend.

○	COF Pinot Grigio '00	Ÿ	4
○	COF Sauvignon '00	Ÿ	4
●	COF Rosso d'Orsone '97	Ÿ	5
●	COF Schioppettino '99	Ÿ	4

Il Roncal
Loc. Montebello - Via Fornalis, 100
33043 Cividale del Friuli (UD)
Tel. 0432716156 - 0432730138
E-mail: ilroncal@tin.it

This well-organized and equipped property has a lovely barrel cellar and makes 90,000 bottles a year with the fruit from 15 hectares of vineyards. We have noted steady year-on-year progress, starting with the white Ploe di Stelis blend. The Civon, from refosco, schioppettino and a dash of cabernet franc, is also nice.

○	COF Bianco Ploe di Stelis '00	▼	4
○	COF Chardonnay '00	▼	4
●	COF Rosso Civon '99	▼	5
○	COF Tocai Friulano '00	▼	4

Magnàs
Via Corona, 47
34071 Cormons (GO)
Tel. 048160991

Magnàs has five hectares, four in the Isonzo DOC zone and one in the Collio. Luciano and his son Andrea make very decent wines, which they release at very attractive prices. Best of the bunch is the Chardonnay, which as smoky notes and pear on the nose, then a concentrated, well-sustained palate.

○	Friuli Isonzo Chardonnay '00	▼▼	4
○	Collio Tocai Friulano '00	▼	4
○	Friuli Isonzo Pinot Bianco '00	▼	3
○	Friuli Isonzo Pinot Grigio '00	▼	4

Stanislao Mavric
Loc. Novali, 11
34071 Cormons (GO)
Tel. 048160660

There may not have been any stars from Mavric this year but the general standard is as reliable as ever. The Rosso Vinko has more cabernet franc than merlot in the blend but there are no varietal herbaceous notes. The Bianco Rosa Mistica, from ribolla gialla, pinot bianco and a little traminer, seems one-dimensional.

●	Collio Pinot Nero '00	▼	4
○	Collio Sauvignon '00	▼	4
○	Collio Tocai Friulano '00	▼	4
●	Collio Rosso Vinko '99	▼	4

Ca di Bon
Via Casali Gallo, 1
33040 Corno di Rosazzo (UD)
Tel. 0432759316

This winery has stakes in three DOC zones, Collio, Colli Orientali del Friuli and Grave. This year, Gianni Bon has, despite the long list of labels, only managed to keep up standards of quality with his Sauvignons, both showing green pepper aromas, and the native Friulian reds, Refosco and Schioppettino.

○	Friuli Grave Sauvignon '00	▼▼	4
○	COF Sauvignon '00	▼	4
●	COF Refosco P. R. '00		4
●	COF Schioppettino '00		4

Perusini
Loc. Gramogliano, 13
33040 Corno di Rosazzo (UD)
Tel. 0432675018 - 0432759151
E-mail: info@perusini.com

Teresa Perusini and Gianpaolo de Pace are revamping this historic winery. It is clear that they are on the right road, even though the changes have inevitably caused problems. The whites are elegant and full-bodied but the reds are going to need a little more thought.

○	COF Pinot Bianco '00	▼	3
○	COF Pinot Grigio '00	▼	3
●	COF Merlot '99	▼	4
○	COF Picolit '99	▼	6

La Rajade
Loc. Restocina, 12
34070 Dolegna del Collio (GO)
Tel. 0481639897

It's been an indifferent year for La Rajade. The Chardonnay has personality, a close-knit weave and rich fruit while the Sauvignon, usually Romeo Rossi's flagship wine, has had problems in the hot weather. Finally, a mention for the unusual and full – particularly on the nose – Caprizi di Marceline.

○	Collio Chardonnay '00	▼▼	4
○	Collio Sauvignon '00	▼	4
○	Collio Bianco Caprizzi di Marceline '99	▼	4
●	Collio Cabernet Sauvignon Stratin '99		5

Casa Zuliani
Via Gradisca, 23
34070 Farra d'Isonzo (GO)
tel. 0481888506
e-mail: casazuliani@inwind.it

This winery was established in 1923 by Zuliano Zuliani and today is run by his heirs, who have installed Claudio Tomadin as manager. There are 16 hectares in all. Quality is good overall but there are no real peaks. The banana-themed Chardonnay is attractive, as is the fruity Pinot Bianco.

○ Collio Chardonnay '00	♀	3
○ Collio Pinot Bianco '00	♀	3
○ Collio Pinot Grigio '00	♀	3
○ Friuli Isonzo Pinot Grigio '00	♀	3

Radikon
Fraz. Oslavia
Loc. Tre Buchi, 4
34170 Gorizia
tel. 048132804

You've got to hand it to Stanislao Radikon. He sticks to his guns, even though his idea of wine is rather different from that of most tasters. The Merlot is good and thoroughly satisfying while the Ribolla Gialla is decent.

● Collio Merlot '90	♀♀	6
○ Collio Ribolla Gialla '98	♀	6

Il Roncat - Giovanni Dri
Loc. Ramandolo - Via Pescia, 7
33045 Nimis (UD)
tel. 0432478211
e-mail: info@drironcat.com

The nine beautifully looked after hectares of this estate yield 30,000 bottles every year. The Roncat Rosso is half refosco and the remainder cabernet sauvignon, franc, schioppettino and franconia, while the Monte dei Carpini is an 80-20 blend of schioppettino and refosco.

● COF Refosco '97	♀	5
● Il Roncat '97	♀	6
○ COF Picolit '99	♀	6
○ COF Ramandolo Il Roncat '99	♀	5

Ronco Vieri
Loc. Ramandolo
33045 Nimis (UD)
tel. 0432904726
e-mail: roncovieri@libero.it

Ronco Vieri is owned by a group of important Friulian oenologists, led by Alvaro Moreale, who have a very few hectares in a long-established hillslope vineyard. Ramandolo, the main wine, comes from a local variant of verduzzo friulano. The estate is also well-suited to the production of Picolit and Refosco.

○ COF Ramandolo '97	♀	4
○ COF Ramandolo '98	♀	4
○ COF Picolit '99	♀	6
● COF Refosco '99		4

Vigne Fantin Noda'r
Via Casali Ottelio
33040 Premariacco (UD)
tel. 043428735

Attilio Pignat's estate is on the hillslopes of Premariacco, where he has 18 hectares planted at 5,000 vines per hectare. None of this year's wines failed to make the grade, which tells you how well the winery is run. Best of the range were the Verduzzo Friulano and the Chardonnay.

○ COF Chardonnay '00	♀	3
○ COF Tocai Friulano '00	♀	3
● COF Merlot '99	♀	4
○ COF Verduzzo Friulano '99	♀	4

Ronco Severo
Via Ronchi, 93
33040 Prepotto (UD)
tel. 0432713144

Stefano Novello is an enthusiastic viticulturist who graduated as a wine technician before working in California and New Mexico, as well as in Italy. Today, he runs the family's seven hectares, turning out 25,000 bottles a year.

○ COF Pinot Grigio '00	♀♀	4
○ COF Sauvignon '00	♀	4
○ COF Tocai Friulano '00	♀	4
● COF Merlot '96		5

Evangelos Paraschos
Loc. Bukuje, 13/A
34070 San Floriano del Collio (GO)
Tel. 0481884154

Evangelos Paraschos came to Italy from Greece to study, took his degree and began to work as a restaurateur in Gorizia. Then he was bitten by the wine bug and today has nearly four hectares, where he makes 12,000 bottles a year. His tocai and chardonnay-based Collio Bianco blend is excellent.

○ Collio Bianco '00	♟♟	4
○ Collio Bianco Ris. '00	♟	4
○ Collio Pinot Grigio '00	♟	4
○ Collio Chardonnay '00		4

Tenuta Pinni
Via Sant'Osvaldo, 1
33096 San Martino al Tagliamento (PN)
Tel. 0434899464

This is the first Guide appearance for Tenuta Pinni, which has a 70-hectare estate, a splendid 17th-century villa and a restructured historic village, where the cellar is located. The Chardonnay Superiore '99 is excellent while the Cabernet Sauvignon Riserva '98 and the standard-label Pinot Grigio are both very pleasant bottles.

○ Friuli Grave Chardonnay Sup. '99	♟♟	4
○ Friuli Grave Pinot Grigio '00	♟	3
● Friuli Grave Cabernet Sauvignon Ris. '98	♟	4

Edi Gandin
Via San Zanut, 51
34070 San Pier d'Isonzo (GO)
Tel. 048170082
E-mail: egandin@spin.it

Edi Gandin confirmed his status as one of the region's rising stars with a range of very well-made wines. But there were none of the outstanding wines he has presented in previous vintages. The estate lies in the gravel and clay flatlands of the Isonzo DOC zone and embraces just over 12 hectares.

○ Friuli Isonzo Chardonnay Vigna Cristin '00	♟	3
● Il Falco di Castellamonte '97	♟	4
○ Filare Bianco Vigna Ronchetto '99	♟	4

Mangilli
Fraz. Flumignano - Via Tre Avieri, 12
33030 Talmassons (UD)
Tel. 0432766248
E-mail: mangilli@mangilli.com

The Mangilli label is best-known for spirits but the company also has several hectares under vine in the Grave and Collio, as well as small plots in the Colli Orientali del Friuli. The harvest is supplemented with bought-in fruit. The late-harvest Sauvignon is a cracker while the Progetto '95, a Bordeaux blend, is convincing.

○ Sauvignon '98	♟♟	5
○ Collio Pinot Bianco '00	♟	3
○ Collio Sauvignon '00	♟	4
● Progetto '95	♟	5

Brojli - Franco Clementin
Via G. Galilei, 5
33050 Terzo di Aquileia (UD)
Tel. 043132642
E-mail: fattoriaclementin@libero.it

Franco Clementin heads a family-run winery and an equally inviting farm holiday centre. His wines stand out for their consistency of quality and very good value for money. We were surprised by the Verduzzo, which is untypical for the zone, and his Pinot Bianco confirmed that it is a good wine.

○ Verduzzo del Piccolo Campo '00	♟♟	4
○ Friuli Aquileia Pinot Bianco '00	♟	2*
○ Friuli Aquileia Riesling '00		2

Guerra Albano
Loc. Montina
V.le Kennedy, 39/A
33040 Torreano (UD)
Tel. 0432715077

Guerra turns out as 11 wines, including whites, reds and two native sweet wines, a Verduzzo Friulano and a Picolit. Trauli is a blend of verduzzo, pinot grigio, sauvignon and tocai. Gritul is obtained from merlot and cabernet sauvignon. The Cabernet Franc is very good, as is the Picolit, but very few bottles are released.

● COF Cabernet Franc '00	♟♟	3
● COF Gritul '98	♟	5
○ COF Verduzzo Friulano '99	♟	3
○ Trauli Bianco '99	♟	4

EMILIA ROMAGNA

Wine professionals in Emilia Romagna have long been debating a thorny issue. How to define the region's viticultural identity more precisely. The crux of the problem is promoting the characteristics and potential of the territory, and of certain indigenous varieties, while at the same time launching the area's wines in the competitive global market against top quality products from other regions. In last year's edition of the Guide, we noted that the region lagged behind in the race for Three Glasses but this year we are happy to say that the results are more than gratifying. Indeed, no less than four wineries picked up Three Glass awards and at least another five or six wines are jostling for position with the best products available on the market today. The wines based on international varieties still impress for elegance and harmony but we would point out that they bear a firm imprint from the territory and Emilia Romagna's mesoclimates. The Three Glass winners include a new and, as always, splendid version of the Marzieno '99 from the Fattoria Zerbina estate which won top marks for the fourth time with this offering. Young Maurizio Vallona repeats the success of his '97 vintage with his Cabernet Sauvignon Selezione '99. The magnificent Terre del Cedro di San Patrignano estate has been promising us a surprise for years and bowled us over with its international red, the Montepirolo '97. We have a brand new offering – an encouraging sign for the Colli Piacentini territory – in the shape of the elegant, majestic Cabernet Sauvignon Corbeau from the Luretta winery. But these Three Glass awards, long an Emilia Romagna tradition as a careful look at the results of our tastings will attest, are only the tip of the iceberg. In our tasting profiles and even in the brief Other Wineries notes at the end of the section, there are clear indications that the products of all, or nearly all, of the zones have improved in quality across the board. The only thing lacking is a great wine from the region's hallmark variety, sangiovese. As you can see from the Guide, there are several excellent versions on offer, all quite capable of holding their own against similar products from other territories. We remain mystified, however, as to why we continue to find excessive quantities of rough tannins in many wines, disagreeable acidity in dozens of samples, and a murkiness that derives the old barrels used to condition the wine. In contrast, standard-label versions are very interesting for quality and for personality. As we have said on more than one occasion, the sophisticated techniques of highly skilled oenologists are no substitute for the unremitting and painstaking labours required to produce a great vintage. Powerful wines, over-concentrated and over the top, are popular with some connoisseurs but, as we well know, wine must ultimately be drunk by the consumer. It will feature on restaurant wine lists, and should be appreciated for the soul and the personality it expresses, even after several years in the cellar.

BERTINORO (FC)

Celli
Via Carducci, 5
47032 Bertinoro (FC)
tel. 0543445183
e-mail: celli@celli-vini.com

The Celli winery, which started out vinifying grapes bought in from other producers in the zone, is today a big name in growing, too. The estate tends its vineyards with care, researching into indigenous clones, and experiments with cutting-edge production techniques to obtain high quality wines. The selections we tasted this year attest to this quality, starting with the newest recruit to the ranks, the Bron e Rusèval '99. A blend of 40 per cent cabernet sauvignon and sangiovese, its sumptuous ruby attests to the richness of the extract. The exciting nose offers aromas ranging from wild berries to spice. There is also berry fruit on the palate, where it mingles with notes of vanilla from the oak, chocolate and liquorice. Well-rounded wine in flavour, it is velvet-soft, elegant and persistent. The Chardonnay Bron & Rusèval '00 is intriguing for its bouquet of butter, yeast and good oak, and a long, fleshy palate that finishes on a faintly bitterish note. It is probably the best Chardonnay to come out of this year's Romagna harvest. Of the local wines, which are also very well made, we liked the unusually dense Trebbiano Poggio Ferlina '00; the rather evolved and caramelly Albana Secco I Croppi '00; the Sangiovese Superiore Le Grillaie '00, with its not particularly refined nose; and the Sangiovese Riserva Le Grillaie '98, which shows rather over-ripe fruit. Rounding off the selection, there was a sweet, enticing Albana Passito Solara '99.

○	Bron & Rusèval Chardonnay '00	♟♟	3*
○	Albana di Romagna Passito Solara '99	♟♟	4
●	Bron & Rusèval Sangiovese-Cabernet '99	♟♟	4
○	Albana di Romagna Secco I Croppi '00	♟	2*
●	Sangiovese di Romagna Sup. Le Grillaie '00	♟	3
○	Trebbiano di Romagna Poggio Ferlina '00	♟	2
●	Sangiovese di Romagna Sup. Le Grillaie Ris. '98	♟	3
●	Sangiovese di Romagna Sup. Le Grillaie Ris. '97	♟♟	3

BERTINORO (FC)

Giovanna Madonia
Via de' Cappuccini, 130
47032 Bertinoro (FC)
tel. 0543444361 - 0543445085
e-mail: giovanna.madonia@libero.it

This small Bertinoro estate, which emerged during the recent years of upheaval in both Romagna and the wine world in general, continues to offer us wines of a consistently high quality that rank among the best in the region. The limited cellar space, which is very well equipped, has done little to curb the ambitions of Giovanna, a producer with flair, or the skills of famed Tuscan oenologist Attilio Pagli. The Sangiovese, the estate's flagship product, is enjoyable whether you uncork it straight away or leave it for a few years in the cellar. The younger version, the Sangiovese Superiore Fermavento '99, reviewed in error last year, is made with meticulous care and shrewdly judged barrique conditioning. The aromas are refined and graceful, and the palate displays extraordinary texture with a well-rounded, satisfying body. The Ombroso Riserva '98, a monovarietal sangiovese enhanced by an extended period of barrel ageing, is even more gratifying. The bouquet is sophisticated and charming then the aromas of delicate, clean oak play hide and seek with notes of blackcurrant, redcurrant and spice. The long, powerful yet harmonious palate hints at coffee and chocolate, with sweet tannins that are almost velvety. Excellent, too, is the Albana Passito Chimera '98. Its nose includes unusual nuances of botrytis, with traces of spice and aromatic herbs, while the palate displays warmth and ripe sweetness, with clear notes of honey, peach and apricot.

●	Sangiovese di Romagna Sup. Ombroso Ris. '98	♟♟	4
●	Sangiovese di Romagna Sup. Fermavento '99	♟♟	3*
○	Albana di Romagna Passito Chimera '98	♟	5
●	Sangiovese di Romagna Sup. Ombroso Ris. '97	♟♟	4
●	Sterpigno Merlot '98	♟♟	5

BERTINORO (FC)

Fattoria Paradiso
Loc. Capocolle
Via Palmeggiana, 285
47032 Bertinoro (FC)
Tel. 0543445044
E-mail: fattoriaparadiso@fattoriaparadiso.com

The blend of cabernet, merlot and syrah produced by this historic Bertinoro winery is being hailed as the event of the year. From time immemorial, they have cultivated the legendary, traditional variety of the region here and have named their new wine accordingly: Mito, or "legend". A prominent Italian celebrity, Nobel Prize winner Dario Fo, designed the label that graces the bottle. The new oenological direction taken by the winery can also be witnessed in the appearance of small, French oak casks alongside the big old barrels in the cellar. Of the two vintages we tasted, the '97 emerged readier for drinking and more balanced. Equilibrium is, in fact, the distinguishing feature of the Mito, which offers up hints of red and wild berry fruit laced with grassy undertones. The palate echoes the bouquet, revealing warmth and good structure. Yet, we preferred the '98 vintage, for its big structure and delicate persistence. It hasn't acquired a label yet and has still to be released. Varietal aromas melt into a more generous, complex bouquet dominated by elegant oakiness. It is the sheer sophistication of this wine that stays in the mind after tasting. Well balanced, but with less powerful characteristics, are the Barbarossa '97 and the Vigna delle Lepri '97. The first is more appealing on the nose than on the palate and Vigna delle Lepri is a Sangiovese Riserva that embodies all that is most sophisticated in the estate's tradition. This year's Sangiovese and the Albana Passito Gradisca are both well worth investigating.

BRISIGHELLA (RA)

La Berta
Via Pideura, 48
48013 Brisighella (RA)
Tel. 054684998
E-mail: be.gio@libero.it

Costantino Giovannini, a shy, retiring chap, can hardly believe his wines are so good and that they win such high points in our tastings. Today, his winery is well-established after a very low-key start and has a fine reputation in the sector, on a par with the great estates of Romagna. This has been a year of great transition for Costantino. His barrels, jealously watched over by the estate's technician, Stefano Chioccioli, contain a veritable treasure that is keeping us all on tenterhooks. In the meantime, however, we were very happy to sample products such as the Ca' di Berta '99, a Cabernet Sauvignon aged for several months in barriques, where it develops the rich, concentrated fruit that transforms it into a magnificent wine. This selection, which made it into the final Three Glass taste-offs, has rather an aggressive nose but once you are past this, it opens out on the palate to reveal mouthfilling roundness, with notes of ripe berry fruit. The finish is redolent of liquorice and spice, and has good, velvety length. The vintage Sangiovese Superiore Solano has a deceptively simple appearance and surprises with its texture, remarkably refined oaky aromas and powerful body. It also boasts length almost unheard of in such a young wine. The Sangiovese Riserva Olmatello '99 has a hay, cherry and violet nose, then a palate that stands out for sophistication and balance. It is let down slightly by a finish that does not do justice to a wine of this class.

● Mito '97	♟♟	5
● Mito '98	♟♟	5
● Barbarossa '97	♟	5
● Sangiovese di Romagna Castello di Ugarte Vigna delle Lepri Ris. '97	♟	5
● Sangiovese di Romagna Sup. Maestri di Vigna '00		3
○ Albana di Romagna Passito Gradisca '98		5
● Barbarossa '96	♟♟	5
● Sangiovese di Romagna Castello di Ugarte Vigna delle Lepri Ris. '96	♟♟	5

● Colli di Faenza Rosso Ca' di Berta '99	♟♟	5
● Sangiovese di Romagna Sup. Solano '00	♟♟	4
● Sangiovese di Romagna Olmatello Ris. '99	♟♟	4
● Sangiovese di Romagna Olmatello Ris. '97	♟♟	3
● Colli di Faenza Rosso Ca' di Berta '98	♟♟	4
● Sangiovese di Romagna Sup. Solano '99	♟♟	3

CASALECCHIO DI RENO (BO)

Tizzano
Via Marescalchi, 13
40033 Casalecchio di Reno (BO)
Tel. 051571208 - 051577665

Consistently good results in the cellars and in the vineyards, where new vines are always being planted. These are the two most important things to say about this estate on the first slopes of the Valle del Reno, owned by noble Luca Visconti di Modrone. Luca runs the estate himself with the help of Gabriele Forni, a demanding manager who knows what he is talking about. The wines, under the care of oenologist Giambattista Zanchetta in the cellar, are all of a very high quality. From the whites presented, we liked the three Pignolettos, starting with the Brut, a cuve close sparkler and long one of the estate's flagship products. The Pignoletto Superiore '00 releases lovely hints of flowers and aromatic herbs, leading in to a palate that is flavoursome, long and tangy. The Pignoletto Frizzante from the same vintage possesses a simple but attractively refreshing palate with good balance and a slightly bitterish varietal finish. We welcome a promising red newcomer in the shape of the estate's first Cabernet Sauvignon Riserva, from the '97 vintage. A first sniff of the bouquet suggests vanilla and spices, especially black pepper and cloves, then it opens out to embrace notes of ripe fruit and jam. Entry on the palate is full with just the right measure of tannins and great promise for the future. It is marred, however, by an acidulous vein that renders the finish rather hard. The Cabernet Sauvignon '99 is simpler. It has intense aromas of morello cherry and sweet tobacco, and a tangy, well-structured palate. The finish is faintly bitter, because of still edgy tannins. The Barbera '00 is refreshing and varietal with pleasant morello cherry tones and good persistence.

Wine	Rating	Score
● Colli Bolognesi Cabernet Sauvignon Ris. '97	♛♛	4
○ Colli Bolognesi Pignoletto '00	♛	2*
○ Colli Bolognesi Pignoletto Frizzante '00	♛	2
● Colli Bolognesi Cabernet Sauvignon '99	♛	3
○ Colli Bolognesi Pignoletto Brut	♛	4
● Colli Bolognesi Barbera '00		3
○ Colli Bolognesi Pinot Bianco '00		2
○ Colli Bolognesi Riesling '00		3
○ Colli Bolognesi Sauvignon '00		3
● Colli Bolognesi Cabernet Sauvignon '98	♛♛	3

CASTEL BOLOGNESE (RA)

Stefano Ferrucci
Via Casolana, 3045/2
48014 Castel Bolognese (RA)
Tel. 0546651068 - 054629789
E-mail: info@stefanoferrucci.it

For some years now, Stefano Ferrucci has pursued his own line of research, focused on the sun-drying of sangiovese grapes, mainly for use in the estate's two first-rank wines, Domus Caia and Bottale. The results have been more than gratifying so hats off to Stefano for having the courage of his convictions, and for the wines produced. The Domus Caia from the harvest of '98 has never been better. It is exquisitely sweet and smooth on the nose, which proffers rich, lingering red and black berry fruit aromas that mingle with notes of sultana, date, and sweet tobacco. The unusual palate, full-bodied and velvety, boasts tremendous structure, with excellent sinew and very tight-knit texture, while the sweet, spicy finish flaunts marvellous length. Stefano aged his Bottale '97 in a 500-litre barrel, which means that only 600 bottles were produced. The bouquet is rather closed but the very clean, fresh aromas of the super-ripe grapes make their presence felt. The palate reveals a mouthfilling, nicely structured body buttressed by generous alcohol, and a delicate vein of acidity that discreetly lifts the long, satisfying finish. This year's Sangiovese, the Centurion, has very sweet fresh fruit aromas, with strawberry and raspberry to the fore. The palate is fragrant and very clean, with rather strong acidity, but overall it is very well made. Of the sweet wines Stefano offered us, we liked the Vino da Uve Stramature Stefano Ferrucci, from malvasia grapes, for its unusual nose of rhubarb and roots, its substantial but not excessively sweet palate, and its singularly bitterish finish.

Wine	Rating	Score
● Sangiovese di Romagna Bottale Ris. '97	♛♛	6
● Sangiovese di Romagna Domus Caia Ris. '98	♛♛	5
○ Stefano Ferrucci Vino da Uve Stramature	♛♛	5
○ Albana di Romagna Dolce Lilaria '00	♛	3
● Sangiovese di Romagna Sup. Centurione '00	♛	3
○ Albana di Romagna Passito Domus Aurea '98	♛	5
● Sangiovese di Romagna Domus Caia Ris. '97	♛♛	5

CASTEL SAN PIETRO TERME (BO)

UMBERTO CESARI
FRAZ. GALLO BOLOGNESE
VIA STANZANO, 1120
40050 CASTEL SAN PIETRO TERME (BO)
TEL. 051941896 - 051940234
E-MAIL: umberto@cesari.dsnet.it

Sometimes in the world of wine, it is possible to find a combination of good quality and high volume. Although it produces 2,000,000 bottles a year, Umberto Cesari can point to a number of Two Glass products. This year, they bowled us over with their first Tauleto vintage, obtained from a selection of the best grapes from their own vineyards. The Tauleto '98 is superb and went all the way to the Three Glass final tastings, missing this coveted prize by a whisker. A dense, fleshy wine, with an austere nose of firm fruit and a good measure of oak, it reveals a palate full of flavour and personality, where muscular tannins are kept in check by well-gauged ageing and good extract. The finish is enhanced by lingering liquorice tones that lend harmony to the whole. The Liano '98, a blend of sangiovese and cabernet sauvignon, is also very good. It releases concentrated, velvety aromas of ripe fruit and the oak on the palate is nicely offset by the acidic vein and tight-knit, mellow tannins. But, as usual, the pick of the estate's crop is the Sangiovese Riserva, not least because of its value for money. The intriguing Cabernet Sauvignon Ca' Grande '99, also reasonably priced, possesses a clean, fruity nose with no grassy notes, a full-bodied palate and a soft finish. The standard-label Sangiovese, whose famous oval label has recently undergone minor modification, is also very drinkable and well made. The Albana Passito Colle del Re is up to its usual standards and shows delightful notes of candied apricot and sultanas. The entry on the palate is moderately sweet and the finish is quite dry.

● Tauleto Sangiovese '98	🍷🍷	5
○ Albana di Romagna Passito Colle del Re '96	🍷🍷	6
● Liano '98	🍷🍷	4
● Sangiovese di Romagna Ris. '98	🍷🍷	3*
● Colli di Imola Cabernet Sauvignon Ca' Grande '99	🍷🍷	3*
● Sangiovese di Romagna '00	🍷	2*
● Sangiovese di Romagna Sup. Ca' Grande '00	🍷	3
○ Trebbiano di Romagna Vigneto Parolino '00	🍷	2
○ Laurento Chardonnay '99	🍷	4
○ Albana di Romagna Secco Colle del Re '00		2
● Liano '97	🍷🍷	4

CASTELLO DI SERRAVALLE (BO)

VALLONA
FRAZ. FAGNANO
VIA SANT'ANDREA, 203
40050 CASTELLO DI SERRAVALLE (BO)
TEL. 0516703058

The new vines planted at Lamezzi have yielded their first fruit, although we will not be able to taste the wines themselves for a few years yet. In the meantime, we sampled the offerings from the Fagnano vineyards and they were very good indeed. This is, in fact, the best selection we have ever seen from the estate of young entrepreneur, Maurizio Vallona. His Cabernet Sauvignon Selezione '99 is a rich, vibrant ruby and has a bouquet of berry fruit layered over a vegetal vein, with hints of Peruvian bark and ample support from robust alcohol. The powerful, velvety palate is rounded off by a varietal finish lifted by lovely touches of charred oak. All this led the panel to award this past top scorer a further Three resounding Glasses. The Pignoletto Selezione, of which 3,000 bottles were released, is an interesting newcomer. It is obtained from grapes harvested late in the season, and matures partly in stainless steel vats and partly in barriques. On the nose, it proffers a cornucopia of aromas that range from apple to banana, then a sweet, complex, mouthfilling palate. This is the best Vallona Pignoletto ever. The extract-rich, balanced Chardonnay Selezione performs with its customary brio. Two Glasses go to one of the Cabernet '99s for a delightful nose and palate. Maurizio's skilled hand is also detectable in the estate's three classic DOC whites, which are perfectly clean on the nose, and display good balance on the palate. For many years now, these wines have provided us with good quality at a reasonable price. The Altreuve, a Passito obtained from albana grapes, is attractively quaffable.

● Colli Bolognesi Cabernet Sauvignon Sel. '99	🍷🍷🍷	4
○ Colli Bolognesi Pignoletto Sel. '00	🍷🍷	3*
● Colli Bolognesi Cabernet Sauvignon '99	🍷🍷	3*
○ Colli Bolognesi Chardonnay Sel. '99	🍷🍷	3*
○ Colli Bolognesi Chardonnay '00	🍷	3
○ Colli Bolognesi Pignoletto '00	🍷	3
○ Colli Bolognesi Pignoletto Vivace '00	🍷	2*
○ Colli Bolognesi Sauvignon '00	🍷	3
○ Altreuve Passito '98	🍷	5
● Colli Bolognesi Cabernet Sauvignon Sel. '97	🍷🍷🍷	4
● Colli Bolognesi Cabernet Sauvignon Sel. '98	🍷🍷	4

CASTELVETRO DI MODENA (MO)

Vittorio Graziano
Via Ossi, 30
41014 Castelvetro di Modena (MO)
tel. 059799162

From the estate's own high-yielding plots, which give an average of 60 quintals per hectare, the Vittorio Graziano cellar produces about 25,000 bottles a year. Lambrusco Grasparossa, the flagship wine of the estate, accounts for 18,000. Deep ruby with bright violet highlights in the glass, it offers light mousse and a refined nose full of fruity, almost vegetal, aromas topped off by a smoky tone. Its robust alcohol, rich texture, and effervescence all combine to soften the palate. The Sassoscuro is a blend of 60 per cent malbo gentile, with merlot and sangiovese harvested from a vineyard planted in 1946. The estate produces 4,000 bottles of the wine, which it cellars for three years before its release. Inky black, almost purple, in appearance, it releases notes of wild cherry buoyed up by alcohol and undertones of vanilla. The palate gives a first impression of fullness and softness, then follows through to reveal freshness and an intriguing acidity. The finish is strongly tannic, with great length. The Spargolino is a sparkling white obtained from two vintages, the '98 and the '99. A blend of sauvignon, chardonnay and pinot bianco, it matures for a minimum of two years on the yeasts before disgorging. The resulting wine is quite atypical, offering initial aromas of peach, apricot and American grapes that develop into minerally tones. The palate, instantly rendered soft and round by a delicate, enveloping effervescence, echoes the notes of American grapes and opens out slowly to finish on a more bitterish, dry, austere final note.

● Lambrusco Grasparossa di Castelvetro '00	♀	3
● Sassoscuro '98	♀	4
○ Spargolino Frizzante	♀	3

CIVITELLA DI ROMAGNA (FC)

Poderi dal Nespoli
Loc. Nespoli
Via Statale, 49
47012 Civitella di Romagna (FC)
tel. 0543989637

In the last few years, the Ravaioli estate has smoothed the rather rustic super-ripe corners that used to characterize its wines, and they now have a much cleaner profile on the nose. The flagship product is still the Borgo dei Guidi, a blend of 70 per cent sangiovese, 25 per cent cabernet sauvignon, and the rest raboso del Piave. This is a round, tannic wine that releases elegant notes of oak – it is aged in barriques – and berry fruits. Almost arrogantly full-bodied, it has enormous impact and very decent complexity. It also has all the length of a great, ambitious reds. The ace up the estate's sleeve is, however, the Nespoli '99, a sangiovese-based red enhanced by a sojourn in barriques. Its aromas of toastiness and berry fruit complement each other in an exciting duet then the palate oozes fruit, flesh and structure that give it length, sophistication and a velvety smoothness. Still young, this wine has enormous potential. The Damaggio '00 is another winner. Obtained from chardonnay grapes fermented in barrels and then in stainless steel vats, it is a dense, buttery white that unveils delicate notes of fruit and an alluring palate. The Sangiovese Vigneto Il Prugneto '00 is an bouncy red with a faint bouquet but can boasts solid structure, lifted by an abundance of tannins. Well done, then, to an estate whose perseverance has produced some excellent wines respect tradition yet offer an extra little something of their own.

○ Damaggio '00	♀♀	3*
● Borgo dei Guidi '99	♀♀	5
● Il Nespoli '99	♀♀	4
● Sangiovese di Romagna Vigneto Il Prugneto '00	♀	3
● Borgo dei Guidi '98	♀♀	5
● Borgo dei Guidi '97	♀♀	5
● Borgo dei Guidi '95	♀♀	5
● Il Nespoli '98	♀	4

CORIANO (RN)

SAN PATRIGNANO - TERRE DEL CEDRO
LOC. OSPEDALETTO
VIA SAN PATRIGNANO, 53
47852 CORIANO (RN)
TEL. 0541756436 - 0541756764
E-MAIL: comm3@sanpatrignano.org

The San Patrignano estate is destined to become one of the top wineries, not just in Romagna but beyond. It has everything it needs to take it to the top, including good organization, technical know-how, in-house resources at its disposal, the determination that drives the community – San Patrignano is a residential centre for recovering drug users – and the skilled management of Riccardo Cotarella. The colour of its reds is a good indication of the new direction the estate has taken. Until a few years ago, it hovered between pale and clear, but now the wines sport rich, ruby tones shot with brilliant purple highlights that are proof of the a quest for concentration. Witness the Montepirolo '99, obtained from a blend of cabernet sauvignon, merlot, cabernet franc and petit verdot, whose dense, almost opaque appearance announces its big personality. This is a very vigorous wine, with fabulously rich extract and fruit. The nose is refined and delicate, offering notes of ripe black cherry enhanced by the sweet toastiness of the wood that adds an agreeable balsamic note. The palate is a work of art, fleshy yet at the same time lifted by powerful tannins that will mellow to perfection over time. A superlative vintage that takes home Three full-to-the-brim Glasses, in recognition of the hard work done by Andrea Muccioli, Riccardo Cotarella and the entire San Patrignano community. The complex, harmonious Sangiovese Avi '98 is not far behind and will be a great wine after a few more years in the bottle. Time is on its side. Flanking these three champions, we have the lovely Sangiovese Superiore Zarricante '99, a muscular Sangiovese Superiore Aulente '00, and the easy-drinking Trebbiano Vintan.

	Wine	Glasses	Score
●	Montepirolo '99	♛♛♛	5
●	Sangiovese di Romagna Sup. Avi Ris. '98	♛♛	5
●	Sangiovese di Romagna Sup. Aulente '00	♛♛	4
○	Trebbiano di Romagna Vintan '00	♛	4
●	Sangiovese di Romagna Sup. Zarricante Ris. '99	♛	4
●	Sangiovese di Romagna Sup. Avi Ris. '97	♛♛	5
●	Sangiovese di Romagna Sup. Aulente '98	♛♛	3

FAENZA (RA)

FATTORIA ZERBINA
FRAZ. MARZENO
VIA VICCHIO, 11
48010 FAENZA (RA)
TEL. 054640022
E-MAIL: zerbina@zerbina.com

Fattoria Zerbina is the most interesting winery in Romagna. Each year, it moves up a rung in the national ladder, a tribute to the hard work of Maria Cristina Geminiani. In 2001, two versions of the Passito Scacco Matto were released onto the market, the '97 and '98. The first of these has a chewy, rich palate and a nose of citron and candied orange rind with lovely nuances of noble rot. The grapes from the '98 harvest, which were attacked by botrytis, giving us a sumptuous wine full of heady, exquisitely long fragrances. The palate is sophisticated, controlled and elegant. The Arrocco '98, the estate's other passito, is also very good. It releases aromas of candied apricot, exalted by botrytized hints, and the sweet palate has exceptional finesse. The Tergeno '99, a white obtained from chardonnay and sauvignon grapes, is also excellent. It shows perfectly gauged oak and unusual, lingering notes of redcurrant and gooseberry. The long list of reds starts with the Torre di Ceparano '99, which offers intense tones of ripe fruit and a dense, richly extracted palate. But the out-and-out winner is, yet again, the sangiovese and cabernet sauvignon Marzieno. The new vintage is austere, powerful and borne up by aromas of great elegance. Its a wine with great personality and each new vintage adds a further distinguished page to its already enviable CV. Another well deserved Three Glasses for this '99. Finally, the Sangiovese Pietramora '98 is one of the finest in the DOC zone, thanks to a very complex bouquet and a palate that revels in sweet fruit and dense, elegant, characterful tannins.

	Wine	Glasses	Score
●	Marzieno '99	♛♛♛	5
○	Albana di Romagna Passito Scacco Matto '98	♛♛	6
●	Sangiovese di Romagna Sup. Pietramora Ris. '98	♛♛	5
○	Albana di Romagna Passito Scacco Matto '97	♛♛	6
○	Albana di Romagna Passito Arrocco '98	♛♛	5
●	Sangiovese di Romagna Sup. Torre di Ceparano '99	♛♛	4
○	Tergeno '99	♛♛	4
●	Sangiovese di Romagna Sup. Ceregio '00	♛	2*
○	Albana di Romagna Passito Scacco Matto '96	♛♛♛	6
●	Marzieno '98	♛♛♛	5

FAENZA (RA)

**ISTITUTO PROFESSIONALE
PER L'AGRICOLTURA E L'AMBIENTE**
LOC. PERSOLINO - VIA FIRENZE, 194
48018 FAENZA (RA)
TEL. 054622932
E-MAIL: ipsaa.persolino@mbox.dinamica.it

Who knows if the young students that attend this school have been told of the brilliant results earned by the wines produced in their cellars. We would like to think that they have profited in some way from their success, if only in their end-of-year reports. The guru at this winery is Sergio Ragazzini, a man who now has many consultancy contracts. He has found his niche at this school, where he is able to research and experiment to his heart's content. The wines he offered us for this edition of the Guide are all very good and top of our list is again the Passito Rosso Amabile Persolino. The harvest of '99 has given us a wine that delights the taste receptors. Obtained from malbo gentile grapes fermented and conditioned slowly in oak, its velvety, classy sweetness shows satisfying length. The measured tones of fruit jam blend harmoniously with notes of chocolate and tobacco. The Rosso di Nero, based on pinot nero aged in small barrels for a minimum of eight months, also put on a good show. Its most surprising qualities are its pencil lead colour, its rich concentration and a warm, full, robust palate. We would also like to mention two "vini di meditazione" sipping wines, a school specialty. These are the Albana Passito Ultimo Giorno di Scuola '99, which possesses elegant aromas of botrytis, and the Poesia d'Inverno from malvasia grapes. The latter, unfortunately, is marred by insufficient acidity to balance its gratifying sweetness.

- ● Amabile Persolino Rosso
  Passito '99   4
- ● Rosso Di Nero '99   3*
- ○ Albana di Romagna Passito
  Ultimo Giorno di Scuola '99   4
- ○ Poesia d'Inverno '99   5
- ● Varrone '99   2

FAENZA (RA)

LEONE CONTI
LOC. SANTA LUCIA
VIA POZZO, 1
48018 FAENZA (RA)
TEL. 0546642149
E-MAIL: conti.vini@mbox.dinamica.it

Leone Conti, a young producer who is always juggling a thousand different activities and projects, this year presented us with another extensive, well put-together range of wines that he continues to develop. First to be tried was the Albana Passito Non Ti Scordar di Me '98, which we believe to be one of the best wines of its category in Romagna. Big and mouthfilling, with moderate sweetness, it is a well-rounded, unhurried wine that invites you to relax. We very much liked the Sangiovese Superiore Contiriserva '98 for its alluring, faintly vanillaed nose that suggests berry fruit jam, nuanced with violets and, in the finish, cocoa powder. The wonderful balance of body, strong tannins and good acidity give this wine a personality all of its own and a distinctive profile. We also liked the estate's other Sangiovese, the Poderepozzo Le Betule. This easy-drinking red is uncomplicated and well made. The Colli di Faenza Rosso Podereviacupa Le Ghiande '99's sojourn in barriques has left it with a rather dominant sensation of oak. Still, it has a spicy nose and a soft, weighty palate that displays good acidity and a slightly dry finish. Similar in concept is the Colli di Faenza Bianco Poderepalazzina '00, a chardonnay and sauvignon blend. Its fermentation in wood has left it rather too oaky but it has a lovely, rounded, fruit-rich base. The almost 100 per cent syrah Rossonero and the simple but tangy Trebbiano di Romagna are both decent.

- ○ Albana di Romagna Passito
  Non Ti Scordar di Me '98   5
- ● Sangiovese di Romagna Sup.
  Contiriserva '98   5
- ○ Colli di Faenza Bianco Poderepalazzina '00   3
- ○ Trebbiano di Romagna '00   2
- ● Colli di Faenza Rosso
  Podereviacupa Le Ghiande '99   4
- ● Rossonero '99   4
- ● Sangiovese di Romagna Sup.
  Poderepozzo Le Betulle '99   4
- ○ Albana di Romagna Passito
  Non Ti Scordar di Me '97   5
- ● Sangiovese di Romagna
  Poderepozzo Le Betulle '98   4

FAENZA (RA)

TRERÉ
LOC. MONTI CORALLI
VIA CASALE, 19
48018 FAENZA (RA)
TEL. 054647034
E-MAIL: trere@trere.com

The main features of the wines produced by this beautiful Faenza estate are charm and balance. Each and every one is vinified splendidly, which produces clean wines with plenty of personality, as we noted when we tasted the Sangiovese Renero. The 2000 version of this Sangiovese rises head and shoulders above the rest, even in a year that was disappointing for the category. Matured for several months in small barrels, it is deep red, with purple highlights, releasing heady varietal notes of violet. What is surprising, however, in a wine made last year, is how much structure and concentration it has. The Sangiovese Riserva Amarcord d'un Ross '98 is a bit more rustic but still has good extract. Not up to the standards of last year but still worth One Glass are the Sangiovese Superiore Vigna dello Sperone '00, which has small proportions of cabernet sauvignon and merlot, and the Vigna del Monte, a Sangiovese di Romagna vinified in stainless steel vats and noteworthy for its mature, evolved bouquet. The Montecorallo '98, a blend of sangiovese, merlot and cabernet aged in barriques for more than two years, has a robust palate slightly marked by bitter, tannic tones. The Albana Secco Vigna della Compadrona, which has a small proportion of super-ripe grapes in the blend, behaved well.

FORLÌ

DREI DONÀ TENUTA LA PALAZZA
LOC. MASSA DI VECCHIAZZANO
VIA DEL TESORO, 23
47100 FORLÌ
TEL. 0543769371
E-MAIL: dreidona@tin.it

Tenuta La Palazza, which belongs to the Drei Donà family – Claudio runs the business with his son, Enrico – has yet to realize its full potential, even if it has taken home Three Glasses on more than one occasion. It has everything necessary to make great wines, and make them very well. With a little fine-tuning, La Palazza, which already has a very able oenologist in the person of Franco Bernabei, will be set to achieve the position it deserves. This year, we were particularly impressed by the Cabernet Sauvignon Magnificat '97, a superb red that boasts a very deep, almost black colour and lovely notes of ripe berry fruit, sweetened by vanilla tones from its sojourn in barriques. This is a wine of character, austere and hard, but the palate is rather edgy and the finish a tad dry. These small imperfections put it just below the Three Glass level. The dark red Sangiovese di Romagna Riserva Pruno '97 is also good. It has a fairly distant nose that little by little opens out to reveal dense, concentrated, almost jammy fruit but unfortunately this is somewhat overwhelmed by oak notes from barrique-ageing. We expected more opulence on the palate but it is trapped between the oak and rather prominent acidity. Nevertheless, it is very well-structured and demands your full attention. The Tornese '99 is not up to the standards of the best vintages. Obtained from barrique-conditioned chardonnay grapes, the oak leaves it rather stiff and it has yet to express its full character. The sangiovese-based Notturno is worth a mention.

	Wine	Rating	Score
●	Colli di Faenza Sangiovese Renero '00	ŸŸ	3
○	Albana di Romagna Dolce Vigna della Ca' Lunga '00	Ÿ	3
○	Albana di Romagna Secco Vigna della Compadrona '00	Ÿ	2
●	Sangiovese di Romagna Vigna del Monte '00	Ÿ	3
●	Colli di Faenza Rosso Montecorallo '98	Ÿ	3
●	Sangiovese di Romagna Amarcord d'un Ross Ris. '98	Ÿ	3
○	Colli di Faenza Rebianco '00		2
●	Sangiovese di Romagna Sup. Vigna dello Sperone '00	Ÿ	3

	Wine	Rating	Score
●	Magnificat Cabernet Sauvignon '97	ŸŸ	6
●	Sangiovese di Romagna Sup. Pruno Ris. '97	ŸŸ	6
○	Il Tornese Chardonnay '99	Ÿ	5
●	Notturno Sangiovese '99		3
●	Magnificat Cabernet Sauvignon '94	ŸŸŸ	5
○	Il Tornese Chardonnay '95	ŸŸŸ	4
●	Graf Noir '95	ŸŸ	6
●	Magnificat Cabernet Sauvignon '95	ŸŸ	5
●	Sangiovese di Romagna Sup. Pruno Ris. '96	ŸŸ	5

IMOLA (BO)

TRE MONTI
LOC. BERGULLO
VIA LOLA, 3
40026 IMOLA (BO)
TEL. 0542657116
E-MAIL: tremonti@tremonti.it

The Navacchia family winery has decided to change direction commercially. They have eliminated a whole raft of wines from their catalogue, including the Turico, whose merlot grapes will be used to enrich the future Boldo '00. In their stead, the cellar offers just one series, sporting a new label that catches the eye and is readily identifiable. The logo of the Thea remains unchanged, as does the wine, a monovarietal sangiovese fermented in stainless steel and aged in barriques for approximately six months. The '99 vintage has a bouquet of toasty oak and ripe fruit while the palate is notable for its harmony and elegance. Robust, and with just the right amount of tannins, it only lacks a little more length. The Sangiovese Riserva '98 only spends three months in barriques. It offers a full, round palate of attractively complex fragrances. The Ciardo '00, a chardonnay fermented half in stainless steel and half in barriques, is also entirely successful. Dense and buttery, it flaunts a sweet, smooth nose and a well-developed, fruity palate with a bitterish note in the finish that lends elegance. The whites are excellent, and the Albana Secco Vigna della Rocca '00 is a very good example. Partly fermented in barrels, it has rare sophistication, which is supported by a full body and the warmth of the alcohol. The Salcerella '00 is obtained from a blend of 35 per cent steel-fermented chardonnay and 65 per cent albana fermented in small barrels. The nose has ripe fruit and the palate is soft and stylish. Finally, there is a welcome return by the Albana Passito to the quality levels of the past.

○	Albana di Romagna Secco Vigna della Rocca '00	♟♟	3*
○	Colli di Imola Chardonnay Ciardo '00	♟♟	3*
○	Colli di Imola Salcerella '00	♟♟	4
●	Sangiovese di Romagna Ris. '98	♟♟	3*
○	Albana di Romagna Passito '99	♟♟	4
●	Sangiovese di Romagna Sup. Thea '99	♟♟	4
●	Sangiovese di Romagna Sup. '00	♟	2*
○	Trebbiano di Romagna Vigna del Rio '00	♟	3
●	Colli di Imola Boldo '97	♟♟♟	5
●	Sangiovese di Romagna Sup. Thea '98	♟♟	4

MODIGLIANA (FC)

CASTELLUCCIO
LOC. POGGIOLO
VIA TRAMONTO, 15
47015 MODIGLIANA (FC)
TEL. 0546942486
E-MAIL: info@ronchidicastelluccio.it

If we were to generalize about the new wines presented by this Romagna winery, we might find ourselves saying that we were not particularly impressed. In fact, we might even express doubts about them. However, it is too early to pass judgement on the return of Vittorio Fiore, the well-known Tuscan oenologist who has come back to take the helm of this Modigliani estate. A new commercial strategy has excluded the Ronco della Simia from the wine list. It was an enjoyable enough wine but one that tended to go up and down in terms of results. The Ronco delle Ginestre '98, pure sangiovese matured in barrels of French oak, remains the estate's main product. It mingles alluring Bordeaux-style aromas with notes of toasty oak and black cherry, and has rather an edgy palate. Entry on the palate is well-structured and tannic, and there is a lovely alcohol-rich, soft finish that contains a certain austere elegance. The Ronco del Re, a white with a barrique-conditioned sauvignon base, returns to its old form. The nose declares the '98 vintage to be an impressive one, with varietal notes that meld very nicely into the more complex aromas of oak, citrus fruit and almond. The palate is also well-made and harmonious, showing great body and fine length, even if it fails to mirror the full complexity of the nose. The Sangiovese Le More merits One full Glass, as does another sauvignon-based wine, the Lunaria, the estate's least challenging white.

○	Ronco del Re '98	♟♟	5
●	Ronco delle Ginestre '98	♟♟	5
○	Lunaria '99	♟	4
●	Sangiovese di Romagna Sup. Le More '99	♟	3
●	Ronco delle Ginestre '90	♟♟♟	5
●	Ronco dei Ciliegi '96	♟♟	5
●	Ronco delle Ginestre '96	♟♟	5
●	Ronco dei Ciliegi '97	♟♟	5
●	Ronco delle Ginestre '97	♟♟	5
●	Sangiovese di Romagna Sup. Le More '98	♟	3

MONTE SAN PIETRO (BO)

Isola
Fraz. Mongiorgio
Via Bernardi, 3
40050 Monte San Pietro (BO)
tel. 0516768428
e-mail: isola1898@interfree.it

We have always been partial to Mario Franceschini's wines, finding them clean, easy to drink and very good value for money. This year, they performed even better than usual and show superb quality. In fact, the wines from the last few harvests at this lovely estate, which lies in the Colli Bolognesi area, have grown in richness and concentration without sacrificing any of the crispness or finesse on the nose that has always been their trademark. The best of the bunch, as it was last year, is the Chardonnay selection, which is fermented and matured briefly in new barriques. The bouquet hints faintly at coffee, with strong undertones of peach and apricot, which follow through well on the palate, where there is fresh acidity that leads into a coherent finish. Mario produces 5,000 bottles of this wine, although his ultimate goal is to increase this number over time. The Cabernet, which only just missed Two Glasses, is a lovely deep, vibrant ruby and flaunts a varietal nose that opens out to embrace stylish grassy tones. Entry on the palate is soft and well-balanced, with subdued tannins in mid palate, rich concentration, and medium length. The Pignoletto Superiore is proof that it is possible to obtain elegant, modern wines from a variety that is notoriously difficult. It has a well-defined, intense bouquet of fresh apples and pears, and a stylishly flavoursome palate with barely discernible vegetal hints. Finally, a mention for the clean Pignoletto Frizzante, which has a rather evolved nose and a delicately bitterish finish.

○ Colli Bolognesi Chardonnay Sel. '00	▼▼	3*
● Colli Bolognesi Cabernet Sauvignon '00	▼	2*
○ Colli Bolognesi Pignoletto Sup. '00	▼	3
○ Colli Bolognesi Chardonnay '00		2
○ Colli Bolognesi Pignoletto Frizzante '00		2
● Colli Bolognesi Barbera '99		3

MONTE SAN PIETRO (BO)

Santarosa
Fraz. San Martino in Casola
Via San Martino, 82
40050 Monte San Pietro (BO)
tel. 051969203
e-mail: santarosavini@katamail.com

Two big changes have occurred on this historic Colli Bolognesi estate. The first is the addition of the Adani brothers' plots to those of Giovanna Della Valentina, long-time proprietor of Santarosa. The new venture now boasts 10 hectares in full production and five more that have just been replanted. The second change is the support of the Matura group, who have brought in a highly skilled vineyard manager, Federico Curtaz, and very experienced Tuscan oenologist Alberto Antonini to run the cellars. Their arrival has changed not only the range but also the style of the wines. The Pignoletto Vivace has disappeared but the Pinot Bianco remains, although it is a little below par this year. The Chardonnay, however, is good. Vinified in stainless steel vats, it offers rich aromas of fresh fruit and has a buttery palate. An eminently drinkable wine, despite its generous level of alcohol, the Chardonnay Giòcoliere is even more fascinating. Its coffee and cocoa butter sensations tell you it aged in barriques and slightly dominate the initial fruitiness. Santarosa aims to produce each year a Cabernet Sauvignon and a Merlot aged for at least one year in barriques, and another wine from a blend of the same grapes aged only briefly in barrels. The first release of the Merlot-Sauvignon is a great success, a soft, smooth, full-bodied wine that is still very approachable. But the Giòrosso '99 is in another class altogether. Full and impenetrable, it flaunts austere aromas of berry fruit jam and elegant spices, and creamy weight on the palate invigorated by balanced acidic grip. The velvety finish leaves a fruity sweetness in the mouth.

○ Colli Bolognesi Chardonnay Giòcoliere '00	▼▼	4
● Colli Bolognesi Cabernet Sauvignon Giòrosso '99	▼▼	4
○ Colli Bolognesi Chardonnay '00	▼	3
○ Colli Bolognesi Pinot Bianco '00	▼	3
● Merlot–Cabernet '00	▼	3
○ Colli Bolognesi Pignoletto Cl. '00		3

MONTE SAN PIETRO (BO)

TENUTA BONZARA
VIA SAN CHIERLO, 37/A
40050 MONTE SAN PIETRO (BO)
TEL. 0516768324 - 051225772
E-MAIL: info@bonzara.it

Starting this year, Francesco Lambertini, owner of the Tenuta Bonzara, and Stefano Chioccioli, his knowledgeable, highly skilled oenologist, have decided to extend the period of ageing for their Bonzarone, a well-structured Cabernet Sauvignon that needs to mature before it loses its rough edges. Their intention is to do the same for the Rocca di Bonacciara, the estate's other great wine, probably starting from next year. Meanwhile, however, we found the Rocca di Bonacciara '99 to be excellent. While the bouquet is ever so slightly lacking in finesse, the palate is very good, if less complex than in the last few vintages. The estate's other Merlot, the Rosso del Poggio '00, has finally emerged from the shadow of its elder brother to assert itself a wine with a character of its own. The nose rather recalls the bouquet of the Rocca di Bonacciara, with its notes of liqueur cherries and spice. The full body is buttressed by just the right amount of alcohol and velvety tannins. But this is far from being a predictable wine and ideal if you are looking for a quaffable red. We were less enthusiastic about the whites. The Pinot Bianco Borgo di Qua is quite full-bodied and fairly evolved; the Pignoletto Vigna Antica is unusual but not very well balanced; and the Sauvignon Le Carrate is lightweight and not particularly varietal. The Û Pâsa, obtained from sauvignon blanc grapes sun-dried on the vine, is quite sweet and reveals aromas of candied pineapple. The palate has reasonable texture, good acidity and a lingering alcoholic vein that combine to make it refreshing and keep the sweetness in check. The finish is slightly marred by a bitterish tone.

- Colli Bolognesi Merlot
  Rosso del Poggio '00 ▼▼ 4
- Colli Bolognesi Merlot
  Rocca di Bonacciara '99 ▼▼ 5
- ○ Colli Bolognesi Pinot Bianco
  Borgo di Qua '00 ▼ 3
- ○ Û Pâsa '98 ▼ 4
- ○ Colli Bolognesi Pignoletto Cl.
  Vigna Antica '00 3
- ○ Colli Bolognesi Sauvignon Sup.
  Le Carrate '00 3
- Colli Bolognesi Cabernet
  Sauvignon Bonzarone '97 ▼▼▼ 5
- Colli Bolognesi Cabernet
  Sauvignon Bonzarone '98 ▼▼ 5

MONTEVEGLIO (BO)

GRADIZZOLO OGNIBENE
VIA INVERNATA, 2
40050 MONTEVEGLIO (BO)
TEL. 051830265

The Ognibene family has five hectares planted to vine in a prime spot on the steep slopes around the abbey at Monteveglio. These 40 year old vineyards have extremely low yields and are particularly well suited to the cultivation of barbera. The wines produced on the Gradizzolo estate have overcome the barrique-related problems they were having and have taken a huge step forward in terms of quality. We start our notes with the two wines that stood out in our tastings, the Barbera and the Merlot Calastrino. The former, of which 6,000 bottles are released, has a very stylish nose of berry fruit, with a barely discernible undertone of toastiness. The palate is very well-balanced, mouthfilling and well-sustained, striking a perfect balance between the tang of the variety and oak from its sojourn in new barriques. The Calastrino, which takes its name from the type of soil the vines grow on, a mixture of clay and stones, is a lovely rich ruby and unveils sweet aromas of ripe fruit with vegetal tones. Richly extracted, it is elegant and crisp on the palate, revealing remarkable softness. The Barbera Riserva '98 has a less sophisticated bouquet than the standard-label version but can point to excellent concentration. The estate only produced 2,000 bottles of this wine but it is big and powerful, with balanced tannins and alcohol supported by satisfying length. The traditional Barbera is good, too. It has a zesty, alcohol-rich nose redolent of violets, and a reasonably dense, tangy palate.

- Colli Bolognesi Barbera '99 ▼▼ 3*
- Colli Bolognesi
  Merlot Calastrino '99 ▼▼ 4
- Colli Bolognesi Barbera Ris. '98 ▼ 4
- Colli Bolognesi
  Barbera Frizzante ▼ 2
- ○ Colli Bolognesi
  Pignoletto Frizzante '00 2

PARMA

CARRA
Loc. Casatico - Fraz. Langhirano
Via la Nave, 10/B
43010 Parma
tel. 0521863510 - 0521355260
e-mail: beni.carra@libero.it

This young estate in the Colli di Parma has earned its place in the Guide with a glorious selection of wines. Lying among the Casatico hills, a stone's throw from the magnificent castle of Torrechiara, it embraces approximately 10 hectares planted to vine, cultivated according to the dictates of integrated vineyard management. The wines presented are the result of careful work in the vineyards and a good cellar technique. The refreshing, fruity Malvasia Frizzante embodies to perfection the varietal characteristics of its grape. The Sauvignon comes in two versions, a Frizzante and a Riserva. The first has an even, delicate nose but comes into its own on the palate, where a dash of sweetness in the final note reins in the acidity. The Riserva '00, conditioned briefly in barriques and matured for about eight months in stainless steel vats, has a discreetly citric nose and a well-structured, correct palate with a warm finish. Bonfiglio Carra selected pinot nero for his first major red. The '98 Riserva, obtained with low yields per hectare and left to age in barriques for approximately to two years, exhibits all the attractive softness and the rich expressiveness of the variety. We end with two sweet wines. The Malvasia & Moscato is fragrant and immediate, with a creamy, not too sweet palate. The Passito Eden '98, made from malvasia grapes, stays in barrels for almost two years and displays oaky notes on nose and the palate. That doesn't stop the excellent fruit coming through to balance things out, though.

○ Colli di Parma Malvasia Montefiore '00	♀	2
○ Colli di Parma Sauvignon Ris. '00	♀	3
○ Malvasia & Moscato Dolce '00	♀	3
○ Eden Passito '98	♀	4
● Pinot Nero Ris. '98	♀	5

PARMA

CANTINE DALL'ASTA
Via Toscana, 47
43100 Parma
tel. 0521484086
e-mail: cantinedallasta@libero.it

This famous estate in the Colli di Parma area makes its Guide debut this year. Established in 1910, it comprises about 15 hectares under vine at Torrechiara, which yield sufficient grapes for about half of the total production, now more than 250,000 bottles a year. The cellar, managed by Giovanni Dall'Asta, offered us a range of wines in the classic Frizzante category that rank among the most enjoyable and the best-made in the zone. The Malvasia Frizzante '00 is good, showing fruity aromas and a soft, even palate of rare elegance. We also liked the perky, refreshing Sauvignon for its clean nose, which is strongly reminiscent of the variety's aromas. The lowland reds, the Lambrusco and the Fortana, are particularly good. Neither is made to DOC regulations but both always feature among the most popular wines in the area. The Fortana, obtained from grapes of the same name grown on the sandy flatland soil, is the classic local wine of choice for sausages and salamis, particularly "spalla cotta". The ruby red 2000 vintage has a fragrant nose and a straightforward palate with a pleasant aromatic vein, tempered by delicious residual sweetness. The Lambrusco Le Viole is a great success. An estate classic, made with great care and attention, it is obtained from maestri grapes blended with 10 per cent fortana and displays an extraordinarily clean nose, as well as a seductively sweet, easy-drinking palate. Even more impressive is the 100 per cent lambrusco maestri-based Mefistofele '00, dark and impenetrable, with a bouquet of black berry fruit ripened to perfection. On the palate, its balanced, succulent sensations combine deliciously with the prickle.

○ Colli di Parma Malvasia '00	♀	3
○ Colli di Parma Sauvignon '00	♀	3
● Fortana dell'Emilia '00	♀	2*
● Lambrusco dell'Emilia Le Viole '00	♀	2*
● Lambrusco dell'Emilia Mefistofele '00	♀	2*

PREDAPPIO (FC)

PANDOLFA
FRAZ. FIUMANA
VIA PANDOLFA, 35
47016 PREDAPPIO (FC)
TEL. 0543940073
E-MAIL: info@pandolfa.it

The Tenuta Pandolfa boasts 90 hectares of vineyards, which fan out from the splendid 18th-century villa that houses the estate's brand new cellars. The Ricci family are the proud owners of this beautiful Romagna winery, established in 1997 and today one of the region's leading lights. They have made very shrewd choices in the vineyards, the cellars and, above all, the staff. Manager Claudio Gimelli and oenologist Paolo Inama bring a distinctly professional manner to operations. We tasted two Sangioveses. The first, the Canova '00, is a typical standard-label wine, with refreshingly fragrant aromas of ripe cherry, violet and mallow flowers, and a clean, uncomplicated palate that well-managed but not exceptionally intense. A pleasant, easy-to-drink wine. The second, the Sangiovese Superiore Pandolfo from the same vintage, is streets ahead in concentration. The nose has much greater complexity and good persistence, unveiling typically varietal hints of flowers and berry fruit. The palate is straight out of the textbook, with sustained acidity contrasting the velvety richness and decent texture. Very ripe fruit lends fullness and complexity to the Pezzolo, a barrique-conditioned Cabernet Sauvignon. The intense nose has oaky notes that make their presence felt but do not overwhelm, and the no-nonsense, rather rustic, palate has good grip. It's not a particularly soft red but it does possess good sinew and structure. The Chardonnay Cavina '00 is a shade lean but decent and nicely balanced.

- Pezzolo Cabernet Sauvignon '99 ♟♟ 4
- Sangiovese di Romagna
  Canova '00 ♟ 2
- Sangiovese di Romagna Sup.
  Pandolfo '00 ♟ 3
- O Cavina Chardonnay '00 2
- Pezzolo Cabernet Sauvignon '98 ♟♟ 4

REGGIO EMILIA

ERMETE MEDICI & FIGLI
LOC. GAIDA
VIA NEWTON, 13/A
42040 REGGIO EMILIA
TEL. 0522942135
E-MAIL: medici@medici.it

This year, the Medici family renovated an old farmhouse on their Tenuta Rampata estate to create a new visitors' area, featuring a tasting room, a wine museum and an educational tour of the zone's viticulture. Growing around here hinges on lambrusco salamino and malvasia grapes, the two varieties preferred by this estate. The cellar performs very well, even in disappointing years such as 2000, when the suffocating summer heat was detrimental, to the whites in particular. Of the wines presented for tasting, the best was the Concerto, a Lambrusco that has long enjoyed a good image and delivered high quality. Obtained from Tenuta Rampata's own grapes, this rich ruby wine has a fine mousse, a deliciously clean, intense, floral nose, and a well-rounded, harmonious palate. The Assolo, another lambrusco-based wine, came a close second in terms of quality. Its nose hints at sweet, ripe berry fruit while the palate is not excessively endowed with extract but nevertheless satisfying and flavoursome. The standard-label Lambrusco also merits a Glass for improvements in production technique. The delicate aromas of violets lead into a fairly well structured palate, whose very faint, elusive sparkle makes it most enjoyable. The two Malvasias, the Secca Daphne and the Dolce Nebbie d'Autunno, both well made, are worth investigating, although they lack some of the aromas we would expect from these wines. We much preferred the more attractive sweet version, whose substantial residual sugar takes the edge off the bitterish twist typical of the variety.

- Lambrusco Reggiano Secco
  Concerto '00 ♟ 2*
- Lambrusco Reggiano ♟ 1*
- Lambrusco Reggiano Secco
  Assolo ♟ 1*
- O Malvasia dell'Emilia
  Nebbie d'Autunno 2

RIVERGARO (PC)

La Stoppa
Loc. Ancarano
29029 Rivergaro (PC)
tel. 0523958159
e-mail: lastoppa@tin.it

It was a year of transition in 2001 for Elena Pantaloni's winery, and four of the estate's most important labels are missing from the list: the Alfeo and the Buca delle Canne were not produced; and the Macchiona and the Barbera, wines of remarkable structure and marked acidity, require more time in the cellar to reach their peak. In an area where turning out a many different types of wine is accepted practice, La Stoppa long ago chose to focus on reds and passitos. Above all, the team knows how to get the very best out of the territory, and has disproved the widely held opinion that it is only possible to produce semi-sparkling wines from these terrains. We start our tasting notes with one such frizzante, the Gutturnio '00. Its rich, violet colour heralds a bouquet of ripe red fruit that is echoed perfectly on the full-bodied, spice-rich palate whose prickle lifts its tangy freshness. The Stoppa '99 has a completely different slant to it. A barrique-aged blend of cabernet sauvignon and merlot, it has an immediacy that gives way to more complex aromas. The slightly evolved nose has a strong base of berry fruit and spice while the flavoursome, austere palate reveals strong but not domineering tannins. Two full Glasses go to the Malvasia Passito Vigna del Volta '99 for its varietal aromas of peach, apricots in syrup and candied fruit, mirrored on the big, round, pleasingly sweet palate.

O	Colli Piacentini Malvasia Passito Vigna del Volta '99	🍷🍷	5
●	Colli Piacentini Cabernet Sauvignon Stoppa '99	🍷🍷	5
●	Colli Piacentini Gutturnio Frizzante '00	🍷	2*
●	Stoppa '96	🍷🍷🍷	5
O	Colli Piacentini Malvasia Passito Vigna del Volta '97	🍷🍷🍷	5
●	Colli Piacentini Cabernet Sauvignon Stoppa '98	🍷🍷	5
O	Colli Piacentini Malvasia Passito Vigna del Volta '98	🍷🍷	5
●	Macchiona '98	🍷🍷	4

RUSSI (RA)

Tenuta Uccellina
Via Garibaldi, 51
48026 Russi (RA)
tel. 0544580144

Last year was a significant one for this small Ravenna winery. While the support of talented Romagna oenologist Sergio Ragazzini remains fundamental, the range presented this time was a little disappointing. The Ruchetto, the estate's flagship wine, is a rare example of a pinot nero-based wine in this zone. Its somewhat aggressive, rustic nose bears witness to a traditional vinification process. The wine recovers on the palate, where it reveals full body and good fruit. Just a little more balance would have made this the most interesting of the wines we tasted. The Albana Passito is rather half-hearted, both in terms of its fruit and juicy peach aromas and with regard to the palate. This is dominated by alcohol and fruit, and fails to achieve its traditional fullness, even though it is clean and enjoyable. The finish, mellowed by attractive sweetness, lacks the requisite complexity. The Burson, obtained from a legendary indigenous variety of the same name, is a more ambitious wine, full-bodied and tannic. An unusual red, it is very down to earth and draws its fascination from its sheer aggressiveness. The burson grape, which deserves to be included in the Slow Food Presidia of protected food products, is still vinified at this winery, even if, from the current year, the label will bear the logo of a new consortium set up at Bagnacavallo to defend this native grape type, the pride of the zone.

●	Burson	🍷🍷	3
●	Ruchetto dell'Uccellina '98	🍷	4
O	Albana di Romagna Passito '99	🍷	4
●	Ruchetto dell'Uccellina '97	🍷🍷	4
●	Sangiovese di Romagna Ris. '98	🍷🍷	4

SAN PROSPERO (MO)

Cantine Cavicchioli & Figli
Via A. Gramsci, 9
41030 San Prospero (MO)
tel. 059812411 - 059908828
e-mail: cantine@cavicchioli.it

The history of this winery is inextricably linked to the story of the Cavicchioli family, which has worked indefatigably for three generations now to win recognition for Lambrusco. Today's version has very little in common with the Lambrusco produced in the small cellars built behind the house in 1928. One thing has remained constant and that is the commitment to quality, starting with the selection of the plots themselves. Today, the Cavicchiolis are a benchmark for Lambrusco producers and recent tastings confirmed the quality of the estate's wines. There are two particularly interesting crus, the Tre Medaglie, and, from this year, the Croce della Pietra. Here are some statistics that show the potential of the estate: annual production is 15,000,000 bottles, and the wines featured in this year's edition of the Guide account for an astonishing 500,000 units. Again, it is the Col Sassoso that dominates. Rich in berry fruit, it boasts an almost toasty nose that is evolved but stylish. On the palate, it is round and faintly tannic, just as tradition dictates. Also very good is the austere Vigna del Cristo, which is however outclassed by the more seductive Sorbara Tre Medaglie, with its elegant bouquet echoed faithfully on the palate. Making its first appearance in the Guide is a Cavicchioli Lambrusco Reggiano, which earned One Glass. It is obtained from vines that the estate has rented for some years now and is vinified at San Prospero. The two Lambrusco di Modenas put on a good show. The standard version more closely resembles the Sorbara and the Salamino, while the new Croce della Pietra recalls the Grasparossa.

- Lambrusco Grasparossa
  di Castelvetro Col Sassoso '00   ΨΨ 3*
- Lambrusco di Sorbara
  Vigna del Cristo '00   Ψ   3
- Lambrusco di Modena   Ψ   2*
- Lambrusco di Modena
  Croce della Pietra   Ψ   2
- Lambrusco di Sorbara
  Tre Medaglie   Ψ   2*
- Lambrusco Reggiano
  Tre Medaglie   Ψ   2*

SANT'ILARIO D'ENZA (RE)

Moro - Rinaldo Rinaldini
Fraz. Calerno
Via Andrea Rivasi, 27
42040 Sant'Ilario d'Enza (RE)
tel. 0522679190 - 0522679964
e-mail: info@rinaldinivini.it

The Rinaldis have 15 hectares planted to vine in the province of Reggio Emilia, where it borders on Parma. From this terrain, the Rinaldis have produced 6,000 bottles of a very interesting wine. It is Vigna del Picchio, one of the very few lambrusco-based wines to win Two Glasses in the history of our Guide. It's a red obtained from lambrusco maestri and ancellotta varieties, harvested late, matured in oak for about one year, then aged in the bottle until ready to be released on the market some three years after the harvest. Inky dark, it offers etheric aromas that meld with notes of ripe fruit and new, but never intrusive, oak. The palate is full, velvety and packed with extract, and has nice length. While failing to repeat its 1997 performance, the Cabernet Sauvignon Riserva is still very good. It rather lacks the balsamic and vegetal fragrances of the earlier vintage and is more in line with the classic Emilia Cabernets that show good structure and mature bouquets, often hinting at red pepper. The estate's 30,000 bottles of Pjcol Ross are interesting. A Spumante Metodo Classico of immense character, with an intense nose that mingles fruit aromas with unusual, almost gamey notes that probably owe their presence to a long sojourn on the yeasts. The Malvasia, another Metodo Classico, is a lovely wine. Its squeaky clean, varietal nose ushers in a soft, flavoursome palate set off by a fine perlage. The finish is dry and reasonably persistent but not bitter. One Glass apiece also to the Lambrusco Reggiano, with its pleasant aromas of thyme, and the Grasparossa Vecchio Moro, a rich, round wine.

- Vigna del Picchio '98   ΨΨ 4
- Colli di Scandiano e di Canossa
  Cabernet Sauvignon Ris. '98   Ψ 4
- Colli di Scandiano e di Canossa
  Lambrusco Grasparossa
  Vecchio Moro   Ψ 2
○ Colli di Scandiano e di Canossa
  Malvasia Spumante M. Cl.   Ψ 2
- Lambrusco Reggiano   Ψ 2
- Lambrusco Spumante M. Cl. Pjcol Ross   Ψ 2*
- Colli di Scandiano e di Canossa
  Cabernet Sauvignon '99   2
○ Lambrusco Bianco Spumante M. Cl.   2
- Colli di Scandiano e di Canossa
  Cabernet Sauvignon Ris. '97   ΨΨ 4

SASSO MARCONI (BO)

Floriano Cinti
Fraz. San Lorenzo
Via Gamberi, 48
40037 Sasso Marconi (BO)
Tel. 0516751646
E-mail: cinti@collibolognesi.com

Young Floriano Cinti, a wineman of great character and no little experience, makes his third consecutive appearance in the Guide with his high quality line-up of wines, expanded to include three new labels, all reds. Without a doubt, the Merlot '00 is the best of these and we awarded it Two Glasses on its first time out. A substantial wine, dark, it has impressive aromas of very ripe fruit and a long, richly flavoured palate of a complexity almost unheard of in such a young wine. Then there is the Barbera '00, which is tangy, varietal, very clean and well-defined. It has good acidity which, combined with its sweet, black cherry finish, makes it an extremely pleasant tipple. The last, and the most unusual, of the newcomers is the Rubrum, a passito made from pinot nero and barbera grapes. This atypical offering is somewhat reminiscent a Recioto from Valpolicella but it is more tannic and not so sweet. The Cabernet Sauvignon '98 rounds off the reds. The barrique-conditioning lends overtones of spice to the nose of violet and cyclamen flowers, berry fruit and bitter orange peel. The robust structure and excellent balance make this a wine of great character and personality. The Pinot Bianco stands out for its aromas of spring flowers and fresh fruit – notably pineapple – and for the fullness of its soft, harmonious palate. The Pignoletto stops just short of Two Glasses. It has clean, crisp aromas of herbs and spring flowers, followed by a full palate with a slightly bitter, typical finish. The Sauvignon has a very varietal nose, and rather a light-bodied palate, while the Chardonnay has a nose of rich tropical fruit and a fairly buttery palate with just a trace too much acidity.

	Wine	Glasses	Score
●	Colli Bolognesi Merlot '00	♛♛	3*
○	Colli Bolognesi Pinot Bianco '00	♛♛	3*
○	Colli Bolognesi Cabernet Sauvignon '98	♛♛	3*
●	Colli Bolognesi Barbera '00	♛	3
○	Colli Bolognesi Chardonnay '00	♛	3
○	Colli Bolognesi Pignoletto Cl. '00	♛	3
○	Colli Bolognesi Pignoletto Frizzante '00	♛	2
○	Colli Bolognesi Sauvignon '00	♛	3
●	Rubrum Cor Laetificans '00	♛	4

SAVIGNANO SUL RUBICONE (FC)

Colonna - Vini Spalletti
Via Sogliano, 100
47039 Savignano sul Rubicone (FC)
Tel. 0541945111 - 0541943446
E-mail: info@spallettticolonnadipaliano.com

The huge property that belongs to the noble Colonna di Paliano family occupies a prime position on the slopes of Savignano sul Rubicone around the historic Ribano castle. There are 220 hectares, one quarter of which are planted to vine. Every year, the estate produces a long and impressive range of wines from both indigenous and international varieties. The 2001 selection, put together by talented oenologist and estate manager, Sergio Ragazzini, features a good list of reds, of which the star is the Monaco di Ribano '99. This Cabernet boasts ripe fruit that mingles beautifully with the toastiness of the oak, unveiling notes of spice, liquorice and chocolate. It is juicy, long, idiosyncratic and austere on the palate, where it reveals good structure and character. The Sabinio '99, the estate's second Cabernet, is a tad weak, revealing rather grassy notes and imperfect ripeness. The dense, dark Merlot Il Gianello '00 is very good, its clean, intense aromas highlighted by hints of jam and tamarind. The palate, although full-bodied and supported by a firm tannic weave, is still soft and harmonious. The Superiore '00, which is a bit gamey on the nose, and faintly acidic but with good structure on the palate, and the Riserva Villa Rasponi '98 are both sangiovese-based. The Riserva has a lovely nose of ripe fruit, spice and alcohol that fuse together and a nice rustic personality on the palate, which displays gorgeous velvetiness and a tannic but well-balanced finish. Lastly, the sweet, but not too sweet, Albana Passito Maolù never disappoints with its dry, agreeably honeyed palate.

	Wine	Glasses	Score
●	Il Gianello Merlot '00	♛♛	4
○	Albana di Romagna Passito Maolù '99	♛♛	5
●	Il Monaco di Ribano Cabernet '99	♛♛	5
○	Albana di Romagna Secco '00	♛	2
●	Sangiovese di Romagna Sup. Villa Rasponi Ris. '98	♛	5
●	Sangiovese di Romagna Sup. '00		2
●	Sabinio Cabernet '99		3
●	Il Monaco di Ribano Cabernet '98	♛♛	5
●	Sabinio Cabernet '98	♛♛	3

TRAVO (PC)

IL POGGIARELLO
LOC. SCRIVELLANO DI STATTO
29020 TRAVO (PC)
TEL. 0523957241 - 0523571610
E-MAIL: poggiarello@iol.it

In the campaign waged by producers in the Piacenza area to boost the image of Gutturnio around the world, the estate of Paolo and Stefano Perini is playing a leading role. After the brilliant performance of the '97 vintage, their Gutturnio Riserva La Barbona, a blend of barbera and bonarda, in name as well as in composition, is back with a superb '98 to confirm its status as one of the best wines in the DOC zone. Deep in colour, it offers a still austere nose that reveals toasty and sweeter jam aromas that spill over onto the palate, thanks to the fullness of the dense, vigorous texture. Its younger sibling, the Gutturnio Valandrea '99, is more upfront. On the palate, the marked acidic vein is absorbed to a certain extent into the substantial body. The Pinot Nero Le Giastre '99 displays lovely fragrances on the palate, and good length, but it lacks sufficient softness to do them justice. Excellent, as usual, the Cabernet Novarei '99 has a faint evolved note on the nose that does nothing to blunt its overall elegance. This is followed by a tight-knit varietal palate, tempered by muscular but sweet tannins. We'll finish our tasting notes with the whites, which leave some room for improvement in the use of oak. The Chardonnay La Piana '00 has seriously good texture. The initial sensation of ripe fruit gives way to a strong, final note of alcohol. The Sauvignon '00 is a bit simpler and has a smooth, supple palate enriched by mineral tones into which, unfortunately, creeps a final pungent note of wood resin.

- Colli Piacentini Gutturnio La Barbona Ris. '98 — 🍷🍷 5
- Colli Piacentini Cabernet Sauvignon Perticato del Novarei '99 — 🍷🍷 5
- Colli Piacentini Chardonnay Perticato La Piana '00 — 🍷 5
- Colli Piacentini Sauvignon Perticato Il Quadri '00 — 🍷 4
- Colli Piacentini Gutturnio Perticato Valandrea '99 — 🍷 4
- Colli Piacentini Pinot Nero Perticato Le Giastre '99 — 🍷 5
- Colli Piacentini Cabernet Sauvignon Perticato del Novarei '98 — 🍷🍷 4

VERNASCA (PC)

LURETTA
LOC. PAOLINI DI BACEDASCO
29010 VERNASCA (PC)
TEL. 0523895465 - 0523976500

Over the last two years, the Piacenza-based Luretta estate has made leaps and bounds in quality, so much so that this year it is the proud winner of a Three Glass award for its magnificent Corbeau '00. This is a new red obtained from cabernet sauvignon grapes and conditioned entirely in one year old barriques. Its black, almost opaque, appearance heralds an intense nose of cassis, bramble and blackcurrant that gives way to sweeter notes of beeswax and eucalyptus menthol. Entry on the palate is full-bodied and concentrated, revealing varietal fragrances framed by pleasant balsamic sensations. A truly great wine and a feather in the cap of this lovely winery that, from the outset, has always set its sights high. Not far behind, we have the Boccadirosa '00 and the Chardonnay Selin dl'Armari '00. The first of these is a malvasia, matured 80 per cent in barriques with distinctively crisp aromas that foreground citrus fruit and rose water. The Chardonnay proffers oaky aromas that accentuate its vanilla and mineral tones. The Come La Pantera e I Lupi nella Sera '00 selection is also generously extracted. The Lupi is a blend of barbera and bonarda, with an international touch from a small proportion of pinot nero. Its zesty, elegant nose of berry fruit, spice and vanilla ushers in a soft, close-knit mouthfeel. By contrast, the Sauvignon I Nani e Le Ballerine '00 flaunts a stylish structure that hardens in the finish on an acidulous, bitterish tone. Le Rane '00, a Vendemmia Tardiva di Malvasia fermented entirely in oak, is another welcome newcomer. Aromas of honey and of candied citrus fruit announce a well-structured palate that balances acidity, alcohol, and residual sugars beautifully.

- Colli Piacentini Cabernet Sauvignon Corbeau '00 — 🍷🍷🍷 6
- Colli Piacentini Chardonnay Selin dl'Armari '00 — 🍷🍷 5
- Colli Piacentini Malvasia Boccadirosa '00 — 🍷🍷 4
- Colli Piacentini Malvasia V. T. Le Rane '00 — 🍷🍷 6
- Come La Pantera e I Lupi nella Sera '00 — 🍷🍷 5
- Colli Piacentini Sauvignon I Nani e Le Ballerine '00 — 🍷 5
- Colli Piacentini Malvasia Boccadirosa '99 — 🍷🍷 4

VIGOLZONE (PC)

La Tosa
Loc. La Tosa
29020 Vigolzone (PC)
Tel. 0523870727 - 0523870168
E-mail: latosa@libero.it

Stefano Pizzamiglio's winery is a laboratory of ideas and a point of reference for all those seeking to produce good quality wines in the zone. His products always spark a reaction, even if at times it is one of perplexity or discussion. He has quite a following of admirers, who appreciate the sweetness and the concentration of fruit that distinguish the wines from La Tosa. The bottles are the result of lengthy research and very severe selections in the vineyard, as witnessed by the Sorriso di Cielo, the estate's impressive first selection obtained from malvasia di Candia, a grape often assumed to be ill-suited to the production of great wines. The '00 vintage is big and powerful. Paradoxically, its delicacy and pleasant residual sweetness are such that they actually restrict the fullness of the aromas on the palate. The Gutturnio Vignamorello '00, another big gun in the estate's arsenal, vaunts a richness of extract so extraordinary as to be almost chewy. Its intense nose of strawberry and raspberry ushers in a full-bodied, mouthfilling palate that hints at bramble and black cherry jam. The standard-label Gutturnio '00, a simpler and more immediate proposition, also performed very well. Underpinning its flavoursome palate is remarkable structure, buttressed by fully 14 per cent alcohol. The Cabernet Sauvignon Luna Selvatica '99 offers clean, fruity aromas and a palate with all the thick, fruity velvetiness and the varietal tones of the grape, laced with a barely discernible note of oak. The series is rounded off by the Sauvignon '00, a potent wine with delicate residual sweetness, and the Valnure '00, a very agreeable, semi-sparkling offering from a blend of malvasia, trebbiano and ortrugo.

- Colli Piacentini Gutturnio Vignamorello '00 — 4
- Colli Piacentini Gutturnio '00 — 3*
- ○ Colli Piacentini Malvasia Sorriso di Cielo '00 — 4
- Colli Piacentini Cabernet Sauvignon Luna Selvatica '99 — 5
- ○ Colli Piacentini Sauvignon '00 — 4
- ○ Colli Piacentini Valnure Frizzante '00 — 2*
- Colli Piacentini Cabernet Sauvignon Luna Selvatica '97 — 5
- Colli Piacentini Cabernet Sauvignon Luna Selvatica '98 — 5
- Colli Piacentini Gutturnio Vignamorello '99 — 4

VIGOLZONE (PC)

Conte Otto Barattieri
di San Pietro
Loc. Albarola
29020 Vigolzone (PC)
Tel. 0523875111

The loss of Francesco Rossi was unexpected. For many years, cellarman and general factotum for the house of Barattieri, his death gave rise to a period of re-organization and change on the estate. This year, the number of wines presented for tasting was smaller and in fact almost all the big reds were missing as they had not yet been bottled. The Gutturnio Selezione '99 took Two Glasses. Intense in hue, it has flower and spice aromas leading in to a well-balanced palate that fully reflects the nose. The Frizzante version is also very pleasant, obtained from the natural fermentation of the Gutturnio '00. Its lovely purplish mousse heralds a vinous, tangy, fruit-rich palate. We also liked the Ortrugo '00 frizzante for its apple and sage nose backed up by a creamy effervescence. The sweet wines were, as usual, very good. The Faggio '99, a red passito obtained from old brachetto vines that have an extremely low yield per hectare, is aged for two years in barrels. The resulting wine offers intense aromas of roses and raspberries. On the palate, the heavy sugar concentration gives the fruit a jammy taste. To finish with, we have the famous Vin Santo, made from malvasia di Candia fruit, which derives from the first racking sediment of a wine that goes all the way back to 1823. It is bottled after nine years and is entirely untreated. The limited number of bottles of '91, the vintage currently on the market, are, as ever, excellent. An intense bouquet, complex aromas, fullness of taste and a very long, lingering finish are but a few of the qualities to be found in this rare, superlative wine.

- ○ Colli Piacentini Vin Santo Albarola '91 — 6
- Colli Piacentini Gutturnio Sel. '99 — 3*
- Il Faggio Passito '99 — 5
- Colli Piacentini Gutturnio Frizzante '00 — 2
- ○ Colli Piacentini Ortrugo '00 — 2

ZIANO PIACENTINO (PC)

Gaetano Lusenti
Fraz. Vicobarone
Casa Piccioni, 57
29010 Ziano Piacentino (PC)
tel. 0523868479
e-mail: ludovica.lusenti@tin.it

The reliability of its leading wines, and a more focused attention to the work carried out in the vineyards, represent two more steps up the quality ladder for this estate. Of this year's offerings, the Gutturnio Superiore Riva al Sole is particularly good. The '99 vintage has lovely fruit wedded to spicy aromas that gain momentum on the full-bodied, nicely rounded palate. The Cabernet Sauvignon Il Villante '99 lacks the edge of previous vintages. Its wonderful colour gives way to a nose of less than elegant, slightly confused aromas but the wine comes back on the palate, which is mature and displays a solid richness of extract. The Malvasia di Case Piccioni '00 is clean, simple and enjoyably fruity. If we move over to the semi-sparkling wines, we find the coppery Pinot Grigio '00 performing well. Delicate and floral, it is softened by a subdued prickle. The Filtrato Dolce di Malvasia is also velvety, creamy and very pleasant. Rounding off the range, we have a wonderful newcomer, a '97 Spumante obtained using the metodo classico. It is an impressive rosé, a rarity indeed in the province of Piacenza, from pinot nero grapes with a dash of chardonnay. Its onionskin hue introduces a delicate, lingering perlage then a classy nose and a round, lively, well-made palate.

●	Colli Piacentini Gutturnio Sup. Riva al Sole '99	ŸŸ	3*
○	Colli Piacentini Malvasia di Case Piccioni '00	Ÿ	3
○	Colli Piacentini Pinot Grigio Frizzante '00	Ÿ	3
○	Filtrato Dolce di Malvasia '00	Ÿ	3
⊙	Colli Piacentini Pinot Nero Spumante Rosé '97	Ÿ	5
●	Colli Piacentini Cabernet Sauvignon Il Villante '99	Ÿ	4
●	Colli Piacentini Gutturnio '98	ŸŸ	3
●	Il Villante Cabernet Sauvignon '98	ŸŸ	4

ZIANO PIACENTINO (PC)

Torre Fornello
Loc. Fornello
29010 Ziano Piacentino (PC)
tel. 0523861001
e-mail: vini@torrefornello.it

Enrico Sgorbati's estate of more than 50 hectares at Valtidone has a brief but impressive history. It made its debut in the Guide last year and this year has an excellent series of wines that includes several Two Glass winners. The only minor disappointment is the Diacono Gerardo '99 which, although wonderfully concentrated, has bitter notes of Peruvian bark and rhubarb on the nose that mask the full body. It makes a comeback, however, on the palate where the rich velvetiness manages to take the edge off the robust tannic vein. The Gutturnio Superiore Sinsäl '00, meanwhile, repeats the success it enjoyed last year. Its red and black berry fruit aromas harmonize beautifully on the flavoursome, well-sustained palate, which is rounded off by a generous finish. The '00 vintage of the cabernet sauvignon-based Ca' Bernesca is quite superb. Its solid, chewy palate is a match for the balsamic tones of the oak and although it needs a bit more time, it is ready for uncorking even now. The whites have also progressed. The Vigna Pratobianco, from sauvignon, malvasia and chardonnay partially matured in barriques, has a delicate nose where barely discernible fumé tones blend in perfectly. Just shy of Two Glasses, the Sauvignon Ca' del Rio '00 boasts a crisp, varietal nose and a fruity palate that is nicely modulated by acidity. The Malvasia Donna Luigia '00 is also very decent, with alluring undertones of tropical fruit and rose-water while the Chardonnay La Jara '00 is less distinctive but still well-managed. Best of the frizzante wines on offer were the Malvasia Dolce, the Sauvignon and the warm, fragrant Bonarda.

●	Colli Piacentini Cabernet Sauvignon Ca' Bernesca '00	ŸŸ	4
●	Colli Piacentini Gutturnio Sup. Sinsäl '00	ŸŸ	3*
○	Vigna Pratobianco '00	ŸŸ	3*
●	Colli Piacentini Bonarda Frizzante '00	Ÿ	2
○	Colli Piacentini Chardonnay La Jara '00	Ÿ	3
○	Colli Piacentini Malvasia Donna Luigia '00	Ÿ	3
○	Colli Piacentini Sauvignon Ca' del Rio '00	Ÿ	3
●	Colli Piacentini Gutturnio Diacono Gerardo Ris. '99	Ÿ	4
●	Colli Piacentini Gutturnio Diacono Gerardo 1028 Ris. '98	ŸŸ	4

ZOLA PREDOSA (BO)

Maria Letizia Gaggioli
Vigneto Bagazzana
Fraz. Zola Chiesa
Via Raibolini detto il Francia, 55
40069 Zola Predosa (BO)
Tel. 051753489 - 0516189198

The Bagazzana estate, which extends across approximately 20 hectares in a beautiful natural valley, has an annual production of about 150,000 bottles, two thirds of which are dedicated to the two versions of Pignoletto produced, the Superiore and the Frizzante. We liked the Chardonnay Lavinio – 5,000 bottles a year – and awarded it Two well-deserved Glasses. The intense, stylish aroma has attractive notes of flowers and aromatic herbs while the extremely well-balanced palate is solid, rich and elegant. The Pinot Bianco is almost as good. It is a very clean-tasting, well-rounded product with sweet aromas and a fresh-tasting, persistent palate. The Il Francia Bianco is also rather nice. It is obtained from sauvignon, pignoletto and chardonnay grapes fermented and aged in barriques for one year. The oak still comes on a bit strong on the nose and the palate has yet to settle down. A bit longer in the bottle would make this a very interesting wine as it has great structure and lots of extract. We also liked the two Pignolettos, particularly the Superiore which has a classy nose and a powerful, tangy palate. The Frizzante is notable for its delicate, evanescent mousse and pleasantly fruity bouquet. The Sauvignon is good but, like other wines in this zone, it has suffered the effects of the excessive summer heat during 2000. This partially delayed the natural development of the fruit's aroma compounds.

○ Colli Bolognesi Chardonnay Lavinio '00	🍷	3*
● Colli Bolognesi Merlot '00	🍷	3
○ Colli Bolognesi Pignoletto Frizzante '00	🍷	3
○ Colli Bolognesi Pignoletto Sup. '00	🍷	3
○ Colli Bolognesi Pinot Bianco Crilò '00	🍷	3
○ Colli Bolognesi Sauvignon Sup. '00	🍷	3
○ Il Francia Bianco	🍷	3

ZOLA PREDOSA (BO)

Vigneto delle Terre Rosse
Via Predosa, 83
40068 Zola Predosa (BO)
Tel. 051755845 - 051759649

After a long absence, we are pleased to welcome back to the Guide Vigneto delle Terre Rosse, the Vallania family estate, run most efficiently by Adriana with the help of her children, Elisabetta and Giovanni, and, recently, Giovanni's son, Enrico. For more than 30 years, the Vallanias' wines have been distinctive for the fact that they are vinified entirely in stainless steel. Neither the reds nor the whites are go anywhere near oak at any time during the production process. This historic choice is now considered by many to be a modern, indeed almost trendy, decision. Of the estate whites, the excellent and very substantial Sauvignon '00 stands out for its softness and very varietal aromas. The Chardonnay '00 is also very good, offering an intense yet elegant nose of banana and tropical fruit, then a round, lingering palate topped off by a delicious banana finish. We shall have to wait until next year for the Chardonnay Cuvée '98 and the Merlot Petroso '98, which were not yet ready for release. We did, however, taste the Grannero '98, a Burgundy-style Pinot Nero with an original, well-structured palate, and the two '98 vintage Cabernets. The standard-label version is dense and almost black in hue, with rich, clean aromas of black cherry and pencil lead. The palate displays great power, structure, concentration and persistence. The Cuvée '98 is inky black and impenetrable to the eye, with very concentrated fruit that suggests bramble and bilberry jam. It's a very concentrated and cleanly made wine. The palate has a potent but complex tannic weave with perfect balance and a long, lingering finish that leaves a velvety sensation of ripe fruit in the mouth.

● Colli Bolognesi Cabernet Sauvignon Cuvée '98	🍷🍷	5
○ Colli Bolognesi Sauvignon '00	🍷🍷	3*
● Colli Bolognesi Cabernet Sauvignon '98	🍷🍷	4
○ Colli Bolognesi Chardonnay '00	🍷	3
○ Malvasia '00	🍷	3
● Grannero Pinot Nero '98	🍷	4

OTHER WINERIES

FRANCESCO BELLEI
VIA PER MODENA, 80
41030 BOMPORTO (MO)
TEL. 059818002

Christian Bellei represents the fourth generation of a family that has devoted itself to fizz. His Extra Brut Cuvée has delicate effervescence, floral aromas and a flavoursome, velvety, palate of good length. His Lambrusco sports a very fine mousse and a soft palate rounded off by a dry finish.

○ Bellei Extra Brut Cuvée		4
● Lambrusco di Sorbara		3

CANTINA SOCIALE VALTIDONE
VIA MORETTA, 58
29010 BORGONOVO VAL TIDONE (PC)
TEL. 0523864086

This estate is the largest in the Colli Piacentini area in terms of hectares under vine. We liked their flavoursome, tangy Ortrugo Frizzante Armonia '00 and the well-rounded, austere Cabernet Sauvignon '97, which is released under the label of the cellar's premium line, Castello di Rivalta.

○ Colli Piacentini Ortrugo Frizzante Armonia '00		2
● Colli Piacentini Cabernet Sauvignon Castello di Rivalta '97		4

TENUTA PERNICE
LOC. PERNICE
29010 BORGONOVO VAL TIDONE (PC)
TEL. 0523860050
E-MAIL: info@tenutapernice.com

This beautiful 25-hectare estate that lies on the slopes of the Valtidone area has added a still red to its well-made semi-sparkling selection, of which the Ortrugo is a particularly enjoyable example. The newcomer is the Collare Rosso, a blend of cabernet sauvignon and bonarda grapes.

○ Colli Piacentini Ortrugo Frizzante '00		2
● Collare Rosso '99		4

CARDINALI
LOC. MONTEPASCOLO
29014 CASTELL'ARQUATO (PC)
TEL. 0523803502
E-MAIL: info@cardinalidoc.it

Montepascolo is one of the areas of the Valle d'Arda best suited to viticulture. It is here that the Cardinali winery produces a good selection of Gutturnios. The Nicchio has intense black berry fruit on the nose while the Torquato Riserva '98, a muscular red, still shows rather mouth-drying oak.

● Colli Piacentini Gutturnio Cl. Nicchio '00		3*
● Colli Piacentini Gutturnio Cl. Torquato Ris. '98		4

Beghelli
Via Montalogno, 1243
40050 Castello di Serravalle (BO)
Tel. 0516704786

This is the first year of production for the Beghellis' cabernet sauvignon vines and the results are promising. The barrique-conditioned wine is packed with extract and offers sweet peachy aromas taking you through to a complex palate with elegant tannins. The Barbera '99 has good density and balance.

- Colli Bolognesi Cabernet Sauvignon '00 — 3*
- Colli Bolognesi Barbera '99 — 3

Sandoni
Via Valle del Samoggia, 780
40050 Castello di Serravalle (BO)
Tel. 0516703188

We liked the Barbera '98 for its classy, intense nose and full, elegant palate. The very original Sauvignon '98 has clean aromas, alcohol on the nose and marked residual sweetness. The Chardonnay proffers buttery aromas mingling with unusual green tones, then a medium-bodied palate.

- ○ Colli Bolognesi Chardonnay '00 — 3
- ● Colli Bolognesi Barbera '98 — 4
- ○ Colli Bolognesi Sauvignon '98 — 4

Corte Manzini
Via Modena 131/3
41014 Castelvetro di Modena (MO)
Tel. 059702658

We tasted three wines from this estate and awarded each of them One Glass, which is not bad going. The Acino has an intense fruity nose and a soft, tangy palate; the opaque purplish Amabile unveils sweet berry fruit aromas; and the slightly sparkling Trebbiano has a peach-themed nose and just the right amount of zesty acidity.

- Lambrusco Grasparossa di Castelvetro Amabile — 2*
- Lambrusco Grasparossa di Castelvetro L'Acino — 3
- ○ Trebbiano di Modena Rapsodia d'Autunno — 2*

Monte delle Vigne
Loc. Ozzano Taro - Via Costa, 27
43046 Collecchio (PR)
Tel. 0521809105
E-mail: montedellevigne@libero.it

Two of the wines from Andrea Ferrari's winery are worth closer investigation. The attractive Malvasia Dolce '00 is stylish and nicely balanced while the new barrique-conditioned Callas is a partially successful attempt to produce a Malvasia with more to it than the standard cheap 'n' cheerful offerings from this DOC zone.

- ○ Malvasia Dolce '00 — 3
- ○ Colli di Parma Malvasia Dolce Callas '99 — 4

Alessandro Morini
Via Firenze, 493
48018 Faenza (RA)
Tel. 054643042

This winery provides yet proof of the lush fertility of the Faenza hills, which are home to some really beautiful estates. The ever so elegant Albana Passito unfurls aromas of vanilla and almond that introduce a complex, mouthfilling palate. We also liked the Riserva di Sangiovese for its elegant nose and robust palate.

- ○ Albana di Romagna Passito Innamorato '99 — 5
- ● Sangiovese di Romagna Sup. Nonno Rico Ris. '98 — 4

Calonga
Via Castel Leone, 8
47100 Forlì
Tel. 0543753044

Of all the new estates emerging in Romagna, Calonga promises to become one of the most important. Six hectares planted to vine, and solid advice from Luca D'Attoma and Fabrizio Moltard, have created a Cabernet that stands out for its nose and a soft, rounded palate with lots of elegance.

- ● Cabernet Sauvignon Castellione '99 — 4

Guido Guarini Matteucci di Castelfalcino
Fraz. San Tome - Via Minarda, 2
47100 Forlì
Tel. 0543476147

This historic estate near Forlì is run by a member of the aristocracy so tradition is part of the way they do things here. A fine example is the Sangiovese Riserva, whose grassy aromas lead into a very agreeable palate full of ripe berry fruit, plums and cherries. The estate's Sangiovese is warm and easy drinking.

- Sangiovese di Romagna Sup. '00　2*
- Sangiovese di Romagna Sup.
  Mero Ris. '98　3

Tenuta Valli
Via delle Caminate, 38
47100 Forlì
Tel. 054524393
E-mail: info@tenutavalli.it

This estate has experimented with new training systems and new technology in the cellars. Results have been good and include the Arcadio '99, which stays for four months in French oak barrels, and has a buttery, harmonious palate with a faint bitterish twist in the finish. The Passito Mythos '99 is clean-tasting and pleasant.

- ○ Chardonnay Arcadio '00　3
- ○ Albana di Romagna Passito
  Mythos '99　4

Barbolini
Loc. Casinalbo di Formigine
Via Fiori, 40
41041 Formigine (MO)
Tel. 059550154

The semi-sparkling trebbiano-based Civolino is flowery and refreshing on the nose, with a dry palate. The Lambrusco di Modena Il Maglio unleashes fragrances of berry fruit, then a tangy, velvet-smooth palate. The Grasparossa offers a fruity nose and a moderately full, tannic palate.

- Lambrusco di Modena Il Maglio '00　2
- Lambrusco Grasparossa
  di Castelvetro '00　2
- ○ Trebbiano di Modena
  Il Civolino '00　2

La Macolina
Loc. Montecatone
Via Pieve Sant'Andrea, 2
40026 Imola (BO)
Tel. 051940234

The Cesari family has taken over this historic winery. Their Museum, a blend of sangiovese, cabernet and merlot, has a fruit-rich, velvety nose and a creamy, chewy palate. The Albana Passito is quite dry and long on the palate, after a nose of candied fruit and butter.

- Museum '98　4
- ○ Albana di Romagna Passito
  La Dolce Vita '96　4
- Sangiovese di Romagna Ris. '98　3

Isidoro Lamoretti
Fraz. Casatico - Strada della Nave, 6
43013 Langhirano (PR)
Tel. 0521863590
E-mail: lamoretti@tin.it

In the absence of any new versions of the Vignalunga and Vigna del Guasto reds, we tasted the well-managed frizzante wines, which to be honest, were a little below par. We can recommend the delicious Moscato '00, obtained from partially fermented must, and the Malvasia '00, which has a generous, tangy palate.

- ○ Colli di Parma Malvasia '00　3
- ○ Moscato '00　3

Il Pratello
Via Morana, 14
47015 Modigliana (FC)
Tel. 0546942038

Emilio Placci is a bit of a Renaissance man, dividing his time between his restaurant business and his winemaking activities. Now, both the grapes and the cellars are his. His first offerings include this intense ruby red Badia Raustignolo, which has an elegant nose and a generous, full-bodied palate, slightly marred by intrusive tannins.

- Badia Raustignolo '98　5

Bonfiglio
Via Cassola, 21
40050 Monteveglio (BO)
Tel. 051830758
E-mail: vinibonfiglio@libero.it

We awarded One Glass to three of the five Bonfiglio Pignolettos tasted. The Passito is good, with a complex palate and a balanced dose of oak. We also liked the elegant Superiore, which follows through well. The Prova d'Autore's bouquet is a bit closed as yet but it is soft and seductive on the palate.

○	Colli Bolognesi Pignoletto Sup. '00 🍷	2*
○	Colli Bolognesi Pignoletto Sup. Prova d'Autore '00 🍷	3
○	Colli Bolognesi Pignoletto Passito '99 🍷	4

La Mancina
Via Motta, 8
40050 Monteveglio (BO)
Tel. 051832691
E-mail: info@lamancina.it

Montebudello is one of the best zones for Colli Bolognesi reds. The Cabernet has faint green aromas layered over berry fruit and a velvety palate with well-integrated tannins. The complex Foriere has good length while the Merlot presents notes of fruit and Peruvian bark on the nose, then a very pleasant palate.

●	Colli Bolognesi Barbera Il Foriere '99 🍷	3
●	Colli Bolognesi Cabernet Sauvignon '99 🍷	3
●	Colli Bolognesi Merlot '99 🍷	3

San Vito
Fraz. Oliveto - Via Monte Rodano, 6
40050 Monteveglio (BO)
Tel. 051964521
E-mail: info@agricolasanvito.it

The hills of Oliveto are an acknowledged white frizzante-producing area and the Pignoletto San Vito is one of the best in this category. Slightly sparkling with delicate floral aromas, it has a well-rounded, dry, flavoursome palate. The soft, caressing Cabernet came within an ace of Two Glasses.

●	Colli Bolognesi Cabernet Sauvignon '00 🍷	3
○	Colli Bolognesi Pignoletto Frizzante '00 🍷	2

Ca' de' Medici
Loc. Cade
Via della Stazione, 34
42040 Reggio Emilia
Tel. 0522942141

Terra Calda is one of the best red frizzantes in the region. Fruity and faintly toasty on the nose, its flavoursome palate has a creamy mousse and good length. The Piazza San Prospero also put on a good show, with clean berry fruit aromas and a soft, full-bodied palate.

●	Lambrusco Reggiano Piazza San Prospero 🍷	2
●	Terra Calda Rosso 🍷	2
●	Lambrusco Reggiano Piazza San Giacomo Maggiore	2

San Valentino
Fraz. San Martino in Venti
47900 Rimini
Tel. 0541752231
E-mail: valerobi@libero.it

San Valentino is not far off a full Guide profile and after tasting the Luna Nuova, we are sure that it will not be long in coming. This wine balances aromas of hay with a long, velvety palate. The Terra is ripe, sunny and almost Mediterranean in style while the Fiore is a pleasant, harmonious white "vino da tavola".

●	Cabernet Sauvignon Luna Nuova '99 🍷🍷	3
○	Fiore '00 🍷	2
●	Sangiovese di Romagna Sup. Terra Ris. '97 🍷	4

Vigneti Calzetti
Loc. San Vitale Baganza
43030 Sala Baganza (PR)
Tel. 0521830117
E-mail: info@vigneticalzetti.it

Sergio Calzetti's wines come from 18 hectares of vineyards, some of which extend into the Boschi di Carrega regional nature park. We would like to draw your attention to two lovely semi-sparkling '00 wines, the varietal, well-structured Sauvignon and a fruity, refreshing Rosso Conventino Campo delle Lepri.

●	Colli di Parma Rosso Conventino Campo delle Lepri Frizzante '00 🍷	2*
○	Colli di Parma Sauvignon Frizzante '00 🍷	2*

Casali Viticultori
Fraz. Pratissolo - Via delle Scuole, 7
42019 Scandiano (RE)
tel. 0522855441
e-mail: casaliviticultori@tin.it

The range produced by this estate is excellent and keeps the Scandiano e Canossa appellation firmly in the spotlight. We particularly enjoyed the tangily fresh-tasting, sauvignon-based Altobrolo and the Casino dei Greppi. The latter is faintly vegetal, with balsamic nuances and good balance.

○	Colli di Scandiano e di Canossa Altobrolo Sauvignon '00	♀ 2*
●	Colli di Scandiano e di Canossa Casino dei Greppi Cabernet Sauvignon '97	♀ 3

Villa Pampini - F.lli Bernardi
Loc. Villa Verucchio
Via Tenuta, 91
47040 Verucchio (RN)
tel. 0541678622

At Villa Pampini, we were struck by three wines: a well-balanced, stylish Cabernet Sauvignon with a slight excess of tannins; the Sangiovese Superiore '99, which has a rustic nose, a ripe, mouthfilling palate and, again, a few too many tannins; and the harmonious Albana Dolce '00, which has fresh aromas and a sweet, satisfying palate.

○	Albana di Romagna Dolce '00	♀ 2
●	Colli di Rimini Cabernet Sauvignon '00	♀ 2
●	Sangiovese di Romagna Sup. '99	♀ 2

Campominosi
Via Carmiano Poggio, 54
29020 Vigolzone (PC)
tel. 0523877853

Hats off to the Campominosi winery. Their Gutturnio Superiore Vigna dei Cotorni '99 carried off Two Glasses and turned out to be one of the best from the vintage. The Valnure '00, a blend of malvasia, trebbiano and ortrugo, has sweet fruit over a soft, refreshing base.

●	Colli Piacentini Gutturnio Sup. Vigna dei Cotorni '99	♀♀ 4
○	Colli Piacentini Valnure Frizzante '00	♀ 2

Cantine Romagnoli
Loc. Villo - Via Genova, 20
29020 Vigolzone (PC)
tel. 0523870129 - 0523870904
e-mail: info@cantineromagnoli.it

Cantine Romagnoli only has an entry in the Other Wineries section this year because none of the riservas were available for tasting. The Gutturnio '00 is very good, offering balance, texture and lots of character. We also liked the fragrant Bonarda '00, which has an elegant palate and nicely gauged prickle.

●	Colli Piacentini Bonarda Frizzante '00	♀ 2
●	Colli Piacentini Gutturnio '00	♀ 2

Podere Casale
Loc. Vico Barone - Via Creta
29010 Ziano Piacentino (PC)
tel. 0523868302
e-mail: info@poderecasale.it

Podere Casale produces wines according to the tenets of integrated vineyard management. The fruity and very quaffable semi-sparkling reds are a great success. The Gutturnio Vigna del Castello Riserva '97 offers notes of fruit and spice on the nose and an attractive palate.

●	Colli Piacentini Bonarda Frizzante '00	♀ 2*
●	Colli Piacentini Gutturnio Frizzante '00	♀ 2*
●	Colli Piacentini Gutturnio Vigna del Castello Ris. '97	♀ 4

Alberto Lusignani
Loc. Vigoleno
Case Orsi, 9
29010 Vernasca (PC)
tel. 0523895178

From time immemorial, Vin Santo has been made at Vigoleno, a mediaeval village between the valleys of the Ongina and Stirone rivers. This '91 vintage is amber with a rustic nose then its dense, complex palate reveals notes of oxidation that are kept well under control.

○	Colli Piacentini Vin Santo di Vigoleno '91	♀♀ 5

TUSCANY

There has been a slight decline in the number of Three Glass awards for Tuscany: last year 55, and this time 52. In part, it is a question of vintages. The '98 is not on a par with the '97, and blessings were far from unmixed for Chianti Classico Riserva, Nobile di Montepulciano and lots of Supertuscans. In addition, the best wines from the newly emerging areas – the Maremma, where all the most important producers have been making investments, Montecucco, Monteregio and Cortona – will be making their appearance in a few years' time. Nevertheless, the average standard is very high. But perhaps what is taking place in the top ranks of Italian wines is a sort of decentralization, and Tuscany, although it is still one of the two lodestars of Italian oenology, the other being Piedmont, is not the only region in the centre or south of the country that can turn out first-class bottles. Of course, things are changing here as well, but there is no longer the irresistible impetus that brought about a real renaissance in years past. At the same time, the prices of the top wines have gone sky-high, and with things as they currently seem on the international market, this could become a serious problem in the near future. Calls for moderation tend to fall on deaf ears when money is at stake, and too many producers think a bird in hand is worth two in the bush. As a result, almost all the famous wines now cost nigh on € 50.00 if not more, in Italy. And it's even worse abroad. Will those of us who are passionate, but not necessarily well-heeled, winelovers find that the best Tuscan wines have been priced beyond our reach? This is what has started to happen, which is hardly good news. Especially when you think that the best wine in the world does not, or at any rate should not, cost more than € 10.00 a bottle to produce. But let's get down to business. This year, Brunello di Montalcino is back on form. Certainly, '95 was a good vintage and now some of the best selections, the Brunello Riservas, have been released. The Supertuscans are still outclassing the Chianti Classicos. Only a very few producers – Giampaolo Motta from La Massa in particular – are forging IGTs and staking their all on DOCs. This should be food for thought. Montepulciano is dragging its heels a bit, while the northern zones of the Maremma, most prominently Bolgheri, are putting in or repeating fine performances. There are a few small but interesting newcomers, not all of which won Three Glasses, in the Piombino district, which is worth keeping your eye on. Good performances are again to be found in Rufina and the Carmignano zone, where most notably Villa di Capezzana has come back to life with a number of excellent wines. Lastly, this year's Producer of the Year is Tuscan, indeed Tuscanissimo – Castello di Brolio, one of the glories of Italian oenology. All the details of this delightful story can be found in the profile.

AREZZO

FATTORIA SAN FABIANO
BORGHINI BALDOVINETTI
LOC. SAN FABIANO, 33
52100 AREZZO
TEL. 057524566 - 0575370368
E-MAIL: fattoriadisanfabiano@inwind.it

The San Fabiano winery is a model large Tuscan estate. It comprises a full 650 hectares, of which almost 140 are dedicated to viticulture, so it is vast in size and potential. Red grapes predominate in the vineyards, with sangiovese and some lesser native varieties, as well as a good bit of cabernet sauvignon and, more recently, merlot. Their most representative wine is unquestionably Armaiolo, a 50-50 blend of sangiovese and cabernet. The '99 has a distinctive style, with its emphasis on elegance and harmony rather than pure muscle. We can agree with the estate on that point, although a little more concentration would not have come amiss in the '99. It shows a brilliant but only moderately intense ruby with garnet highlights. The aromas are admirably drawn, the notes of berry fruit and faint vegetable nuances all carrying through onto the palate, which is balanced and stylish. The medium body does not manage to cover the acidity. The finish is clean but not very long. The interesting newcomer, Piocaia '99, a blend of sangiovese, cabernet and merlot, needs some fine-tuning. The colour shows signs of forwardness, and the nose is balsamic with distinct vegetal traces. The entry in the mouth is soft, the extract fair and the finish, with its incompletely ripened tannins, a bit rough. The Chianti '00, however, is delightfully fragrant.

● Armaiolo '99	♥♥	5
● Chianti '00	♥	2*
● Piocaia '99	♥	5
● Armaiolo '97	♥♥	5
● Armaiolo '98	♥♥	5
● Chianti '99	♥	3
○ Chiaro '99	♥	3

AREZZO

VILLA CILNIA
FRAZ. BAGNORO
LOC. MONTONCELLO, 27
52040 AREZZO
TEL. 0575365017
E-MAIL: villacilnia@interffre.it

Villa Cilnia is on its way back up the charts. It currently has a dozen hectares under vine to the south of Arezzo, at between 200 and 300 metres above sea level. A new wine has now joined their traditional assortment. Cign'Oro is a blend of sangiovese, cabernet and merlot, released in quite limited quantity – only 2,000 bottles – for the moment but the quality is definitely there. It is the only wine aged entirely in barriques, where it spends some 16 months before a further nine months of bottle-ageing. Our tasting notes include the following impressions: dense, clear ruby colour, well-defined nose dominated by black berry fruit, with vegetal hints and toasty oak. On the palate: good concentration, well-managed tannins and excellent balance. It does not show enormous personality but this is a very positive debut. The rest of the line is quite satisfactory, particularly the Vocato '98, from sangiovese and cabernet. It is a well-made, moderately structured and fairly expressive wine. The Mecenate '00, a mix of chardonnay and sauvignon, is interesting but perhaps too young for full enjoyment. The aromas are inviting but oak is still, as we write, in control of the situation. The Chiantis are more than acceptable: the Riserva is medium-bodied with some forward nuances and the uncomplicated Chianti '99 has vegetal tones.

● Cign'Oro '98	♥♥	5
○ Mecenate '00	♥	4
● Chianti Colli Aretini Ris. '98	♥	4
● Vocato '98	♥	4
● Chianti Colli Aretini '99	♥	3
● Vocato '93	♥♥	4
● Chianti Colli Aretini Ris. '97	♥♥	4
● Chianti Colli Aretini '98	♥♥	3
○ Mecenate '97	♥	4
● Vocato '97	♥	4

BAGNO A RIPOLI (FI)

Fattoria Le Sorgenti
Loc. Vallina
Via di Docciola, 8
50012 Bagno a Ripoli (FI)
tel. 055696004
e-mail: docciola@iol.it

The Ferrari family estate, just a few kilometres from Florence in a zone which is relatively new to top-flight winemaking, has made yet another good showing. First, a clarification regarding last year's profile: the two Chianti Colli Fiorentini vintages we reviewed there were, in fact, the '97 and the '98. But now let's start with a description of the Chianti '99: lovely purple highlights on a ruby ground; a nose with quite a broad range of fruit; grip and force on the palate, with lively, close-packed tannins and a balance that is matched on the rather long finish. The Sghiras, a monovarietal barrique-aged chardonnay, is good, too. The colour is a vivid straw yellow with lustrous golden highlights, and sweet vanilla blends with quite stylish apple and peach aromas, interlaced with delightful buttery notes. On the palate, a nervy attack, thanks to serious acidity, gives way to well-rounded flavour and a very long finish. But what really caught our fancy was the Scirus '99, a classic Bordeaux blend of cabernet and merlot. A lovely dense ruby colour leads in to a bouquet that ranges from blackcurrant to vanilla, with enchanting hints of mint. And then comes a powerful and extremely seductive attack on the palate, a full body perfectly supported by the tannins and a finish that goes on for ages.

●	Scirus '99	🍷🍷	5
○	Sghiras '00	🍷	4
●	Chianti Colli Fiorentini '99	🍷	3
●	Scirus '98	🍷🍷	5
○	Vin Santo '94	🍷	5
●	Chianti Colli Fiorentini '97	🍷	3
●	Chianti Colli Fiorentini '98	🍷	3
○	Sghiras '99	🍷	4

BARBERINO VAL D'ELSA (FI)

★ Isole e Olena
Loc. Isole, 1
50021 Barberino Val d'Elsa (FI)
tel. 0558072283 - 0558072763
e-mail: isolena@tin.it

The distinguished estate of Isole e Olena has taken the opportunity to thrill us yet again, this time with six wines that differ greatly in personality but show an admirable consistency of style. The '99 Cepparello is one of the best versions ever: a thoroughbred sangiovese, powerful and expressive, with enormous body and exceptional depth. The grapes were rigorously selected and the ageing process, and the handling of oak, are increasingly assured. Not far behind it, the Cabernet '98 from the Collezione De Marchi is elegant and supple with silky tannins and a lingering finish. The splendidly rich bouquet includes masses of fruit as well as notes of cedar and Oriental spice. These two wines are a hard act to follow and in fact, the Syrah '98, although powerful in impact, is not as stylish on the nose. In the mouth, the acidity is not fully integrated and perhaps the quest for concentration has involved some sacrifices. However, these are just minor details in a generally fine picture. The Chardonnay '99 is full-bodied and well-rounded and shows a nicely calibrated sweetness, but the nose, with its notes of vanilla and pear, is somewhat predictable. The Vin Santo '95, definitely up to standard, is characterized by notes of chestnut and plum jam on the nose, a sweet and stylish palate with some evidence of tannins, and a balanced but not over-long finish. The Chianti Classico '99, which almost got Two Glasses, seemed better than it has been in other years. The palate is firm, lively and medium-bodied, but just slightly dilute in the finish.

●	Cepparello '99	🍷🍷🍷	6
●	Cabernet Sauvignon '98	🍷🍷	6
●	Syrah '98	🍷🍷	6
○	Chardonnay '99	🍷🍷	5
○	Vin Santo '95	🍷🍷	6
●	Chianti Cl. '99	🍷	4
●	Cepparello '86	🍷🍷🍷	6
●	Cepparello '88	🍷🍷🍷	6
●	Cabernet Sauvignon '90	🍷🍷🍷	6
●	Cabernet Sauvignon '95	🍷🍷🍷	6
●	Cabernet Sauvignon '96	🍷🍷🍷	6
●	Cabernet Sauvignon '97	🍷🍷🍷	6
●	Cepparello '97	🍷🍷🍷	5
●	Cepparello '98	🍷🍷🍷	6

BARBERINO VAL D'ELSA (FI)

CASTELLO DI MONSANTO
VIA MONSANTO, 8
50021 BARBERINO VAL D'ELSA (FI)
TEL. 0558059000 - 0558059057
E-MAIL: monsanto@castellodimonsanto.it

It's years since Monsanto has been on such good form at our tastings. There was nothing really outstanding but Fabrizio Bianchi's estate gave a consistent performance with a new vitality that promises well for the future. The Riserva Il Poggio, for example, although never at its best around the time of release, is very interesting. We would not be a bit surprised if this selection – a real one – of sangiovese were to get a great deal better in the next few years. Its potential complexity is immediately evident on the nose, despite an initial hesitancy. The bouquet then opens up into characteristic sangiovese notes of violets, black cherry and liquorice with mineral nuances. Alcohol is in charge of the attack on the palate, and after a slightly dilute development, the wine acquires new energy for a lovely, elegant, full, deep finish. The Tinscvil '98, a sangiovese and cabernet sauvignon blend, did well, too. The bouquet is not yet entirely harmonious – there are earthy and vegetal notes – but the entry on the palate is powerful and the progression is as it should be. The tannins are still a bit rough, though, and the balance is not yet perfect. But the wine has lots of character, and time is on its side. The Nemo '98, on the other hand, a cabernet sauvignon, shows excellent balance and opens out evenly on the palate. Distinctly vegetal notes are much less to the fore here. The very agreeable if uncomplicated Chianti Classico '99 offers fruitiness and elegant flowery tones. Lastly, the Fabrizio Bianchi Chardonnay '99, although a little sweeter than it need be, is full-bodied and lingering.

	Wine	Glasses	Score
●	Chianti Cl. Il Poggio Ris. '98	♟♟	5
●	Nemo '98	♟♟	6
●	Tinscvil '98	♟♟	5
○	Fabrizio Bianchi Chardonnay '99	♟♟	5
●	Chianti Cl. '99	♟	4
●	Chianti Cl. Il Poggio Ris. '88	♟♟♟	5
●	Nemo '88	♟♟	5
●	Chianti Cl. Il Poggio Ris. '90	♟♟	5
●	Nemo '90	♟♟	5
●	Chianti Cl. Il Poggio Ris. '93	♟♟	5
●	Nemo '93	♟♟	5
●	Nemo '94	♟♟	5
●	Nemo '95	♟♟	6
●	Chianti Cl. Il Poggio Ris. '97	♟♟	5
●	Nemo '97	♟♟	6

BOLGHERI (LI)

TENUTA GUADO AL TASSO
LOC. BELVEDERE, 140
57020 BOLGHERI (LI)
TEL. 0565749735

The name of the Bolgheri estate that belongs to Florence-based Marchesi Antinori has been changed from Tenuta Belvedere to Tenuta Guado al Tasso. But if the form has changed, the substance remains the same. Indeed, there is lots more of it, as there has been a sizeable expansion of the area under vine, which will lead to a considerable increase in production once the vineyards have reached the appropriate age. The Antinoris, it is clear, are concentrating on their Bolgheri wines. Guado al Tasso will essentially become their upper range label, and also their biggest producer. As regards quality, the '98 Guado al Tasso is quite reassuring, although it is perceptibly different in style from recent vintages. To be more precise, it was already taking a new direction with the '97. The softness, which until '96 bordered on flabbiness, is underpinned by more substantial tannins and a more balanced acidity. The bouquet, too, is more compact, with no alternation between super-ripe and vegetal notes. In other words, the Guado al Tasso '98 has acquired the touch of austerity it needed and has increased in intensity. It's a more invigorating glass now. The cellar still has to put a couple of things right, like the slight unravelling of the acidity on the finish, but they are on the right path. Another good showing for the Vermentino too: the '00 offers attractive aromas, crispness and balance.

	Wine	Glasses	Score
●	Bolgheri Rosso Sup. Guado al Tasso '98	♟♟	6
○	Bolgheri Vermentino '00	♟♟	4*
●	Bolgheri Rosso Sup. Guado al Tasso '90	♟♟♟	6
●	Bolgheri Rosso Sup. Guado al Tasso '95	♟♟	6
●	Bolgheri Rosso Sup. Guado al Tasso '96	♟♟	6
●	Bolgheri Rosso Sup. Guado al Tasso '97	♟♟	6
○	Bolgheri Vermentino '99	♟♟	3

Enjoy Italy even more.

$18.95 4 issues

Gambero Rosso
the insider guide to
<u>top wines</u>
<u>best restaurants</u>
<u>delightful hotels</u>
<u>recipes and routes</u>
all chosen for you by our experts

Treat yourself to a subscription to Gambero Rosso
Italy's top wine, travel and food magazine

To subscribe, please call:
Speedimpex USA - 35-02 48th Avenue
L.I.C. NY 11101-2421 - Tel. 800-969-1258
mmorreale@speedimpex.com

For any other information, call:
Gambero Rosso Inc. - 636 Broadway suite 1111
New York - NY 10012 - Tel. 212-253-5653
gamberousa@aol.com

visit our website   **click on english**

www.gamberorosso.it

the tastiest news on the net

Italian wine travel food

Delightful hotels and restaurants • enticing food shops • easy-to-follow recipes • great chefs and young talents • key winemakers and smart wine buys • food artisans and itineraries

to know more click on www.gamberorosso.it

BOLGHERI (LI)

LE MACCHIOLE
LOC. CONTESSINE
VIA BOLGHERESE, 189
57020 BOLGHERI (LI)
TEL. 0565766092
E-MAIL: azagmacchiol@etruscan.li.it

For the fourth year in a row, Eugenio Campolmi has delivered a Three Glass wine. It's a sure sign that the strategic decisions taken brought his estate to a level of excellence from which it can be dislodged only by the sorts of disastrous climatic conditions that hardly ever occur in Bolgheri. Once again, it is the Messorio, his monovarietal merlot, that gets the honours, with its spectacular fruit-rich complexity, heady mineral aromas and simply extraordinary depth and structure. You might think that these were the qualities of a wine that offers mostly muscle but the great thing about the Messorio '98 is its balance, which makes the progression on the palate so very satisfying. The elegant and harmonious Paleo '98, while excellent, is a step down. The concentration is fine but not exceptional, and the vegetal notes tend to elbow aside the sensation of ripe fruit. In contrast, the syrah-based Scrio '98 makes a memorable impact. The palate is soft, powerful and very dense. The nose is somewhat less well-defined and the fruit tends to be overwhelmed by oak. Le Macchiole '99 is right on target. This is a blend of sangiovese with the cabernet, merlot and syrah grapes considered not quite good enough for the top wines of the estate. The nose, still partly dumb, reveals some black berry fruit and grassy notes. The palate is well-defined, with a vigorous structure, solid tannins and a succulent, fairly long finish. The Paleo Bianco '99 is pleasing and harmonious but somewhat predictable, with oak-derived vanilla in the ascendant.

BOLGHERI (LI)

TENUTA DELL' ORNELLAIA
VIA BOLGHERESE, 191
57020 BOLGHERI (LI)
TEL. 056571811
E-MAIL: info@ornellaia.it

The Tenuta dell'Ornellaia has gone into top gear. Their wines, which keep getting richer and better, show that their intense work is bearing fruit. The vineyards are the focus of attention and are tended with almost obsessive care. The quest for perfect ripeness is, of course, extremely risky but it is also the only road to true excellence, as our tastings confirmed. What can we say, for example, about the Masseto '98? It is a genuine masterpiece, one of the most complete and thrilling wines we have ever tasted. Its concentration, volume and depth are extraordinary, but that's not all. It also offers simply superb harmony and elegance. But we had better leave a few superlatives for the Ornellaia '98, which is also a great wine. The nose has the complexity of a Premier Cru, interlacing bramble, blackcurrant, pencil lead, cedar, mint and Oriental spice. The palate also goes straight to the point, with its dense, smooth structure and sumptuous tannins. Neither should the other wines be neglected. The Poggio alle Gazze '00, their sauvignon blanc, has again claimed a leading place among Tuscan whites. The inviting aromas are properly varietal, showing fresh sage, rue and lavender. After a balanced attack on the palate, it grows relentlessly in intensity to a long and elegant finish. The very good Serre Nuove '98 reveals a chewy structure and smooth tannins, its only defect being a rather vegetal nose. And the red Le Volte '99 is more delectable than ever.

●	Messorio '98	🍷🍷🍷	6
●	Bolgheri Rosso Sup. Paleo '98	🍷🍷	6
●	Scrio '98	🍷🍷	6
●	Le Macchiole '99	🍷🍷	5
○	Bolgheri Sauvignon Paleo '99	🍷	5
●	Bolgheri Rosso Sup. Paleo '95	🍷🍷🍷	6
●	Bolgheri Rosso Sup. Paleo '96	🍷🍷🍷	6
●	Bolgheri Rosso Sup. Paleo '97	🍷🍷🍷	6
●	Messorio '97	🍷🍷🍷	6
●	Le Macchiole '97	🍷🍷	5
●	Scrio '97	🍷🍷	6
○	Bolgheri Sauvignon Paleo '98	🍷🍷	4

●	Bolgheri Sup. Ornellaia '98	🍷🍷🍷	6
●	Masseto '98	🍷🍷🍷	6
○	Poggio alle Gazze '00	🍷🍷	4
●	Bolgheri Sup. Serre Nuove '98	🍷🍷	5
●	Le Volte '99	🍷	4
●	Masseto '93	🍷🍷🍷	6
●	Ornellaia '93	🍷🍷🍷	6
●	Masseto '94	🍷🍷🍷	6
●	Masseto '95	🍷🍷🍷	6
●	Bolgheri Sup. Ornellaia '97	🍷🍷🍷	6
●	Masseto '97	🍷🍷🍷	6
●	Ornellaia '94	🍷🍷	6
●	Ornellaia '95	🍷🍷	6
●	Masseto '96	🍷🍷	6
●	Ornellaia '96	🍷🍷	6

BOLGHERI (LI)

★ Tenuta San Guido
Loc. Capanne, 27
57020 Bolgheri (LI)
tel. 0565762003
e-mail: citaispa@infol.it

Of all the profiles in the Guide, that of the Tenuta San Guido is at once the easiest and the most difficult to write. It's the easiest because there is only one wine to discuss. And what a wine! The most famous Italian red, and one of the most famous red wines in the world. It's the most difficult profile to write because each time we have to ransack our vocabulary cupboard to pay due homage to the latest vintage, without either over-egging the critical pudding or neglecting to mention any defects there should happen to be. Here we go again, but with a categorical opening remark – the '98 Sassicaia is one of the best ever produced. The style is quite different from the benchmark '85. Where the earlier wine displayed power and tannic density, its younger brother evinces greater elegance of extract, greater drinkability, even purer fruit. Nor can the '98 be said to resemble the '88, one of the greatest of the former Sassicaia vintages and perhaps the most successful of them. It has a similar elegance, but the tannins are even finer-grained in the '98. At the estate, they would seem currently to be focused on reducing weight, "gravity" and phenolic earthiness in favour of a more subtle expressiveness. The '98 Sassicaia, in short, is transparently a red of impeccable breeding which will probably go down in history as one of the four or five best vintages. This leaves only the problem – and it is a challenging one – of getting hold of a few bottles. For speculators, and the wily few who will sink to any low stratagem, it is not so hard. For genuine enthusiasts, things can be a little more complicated.

BUCINE (AR)

Fattoria Santa Maria di Ambra
Loc. Ambra
52020 Bucine (AR)
tel. 055996806

Vittorio Zampi is not the sort of man to leave his plans for estate improvement half done. In fact, he has returned to the charge with more spirit than ever, presenting three notable wines from three different vineyards of some two hectares each. The Gavignano '97 is a blend of two parts cabernet sauvignon and one sangiovese aged in barriques, 70 per cent of which are new, for about 15 months. Our tasting notes indicate: a dark, vibrant ruby hue; the bouquet shows depth and is dominated by fruit, with light balsamic nuances; soft, concentrated palate, showing even progression and a slight oak-derived dryness. A more than sound performance that easily garnered Two Glasses. So did the Chianti La Bigattiera Riserva '98, which offers intense aromas of bramble and black pepper with vegetal hints. The palate displays a winning roundness and even distribution of tannins and flavour, leading in to a long finish that echoes the nose. The Casamurli '97, a sangiovese, is interesting if a tad forward. Black cherry jam, leather and liquorice are the dominant notes in the bouquet. The progression on the stylish palate is, however, hampered by rough, drying tannins. In short, this encouraging reappearance in the Guide of Santa Maria di Ambra bodes very well for the future.

Wine	Rating	Price
● Bolgheri Sassicaia '98	♟♟♟	6
● Sassicaia '83	♟♟♟	6
● Sassicaia '84	♟♟♟	6
● Sassicaia '85	♟♟♟	6
● Sassicaia '88	♟♟♟	6
● Sassicaia '90	♟♟♟	6
● Sassicaia '92	♟♟♟	6
● Sassicaia '93	♟♟♟	6
● Bolgheri Sassicaia '95	♟♟♟	6
● Bolgheri Sassicaia '96	♟♟♟	6
● Bolgheri Sassicaia '97	♟♟♟	6
● Sassicaia '87	♟♟	6
● Sassicaia '89	♟♟	6
● Sassicaia '91	♟♟	6
● Bolgheri Sassicaia '94	♟♟	6

Wine	Rating	Price
● Gavignano '97	♟♟	5
● Chianti V. La Bigattiera Ris. '98	♟♟	4
● Casamurli '97	♟	4
● Gavignano '92	♟♟	3
● Gavignano '93	♟♟	3
● Casamurli '95	♟♟	5
● Gavignano '95	♟♟	4
● Casamurli '96	♟♟	4
● Gavignano '90	♟	4
● Gavignano '94	♟	3
● Gavignano '96	♟	5

BUCINE (AR)

FATTORIA VILLA LA SELVA
LOC. MONTEBENICHI
52021 BUCINE (AR)
TEL. 055998203 - 055998200
E-MAIL: laselva@val.it

This Bucine estate has bounced straight back into the Guide. To tell the truth, the reason for its exclusion last year was lack of evidence: the wines were simply not ready in time for our tastings. From this year on, however, the dates should coincide and, quality permitting, the winery will not be overlooked over again. The owner, and also the life and soul, of Villa La Selva is Sergio Carpini, who after a distinguished career as a designer began, in 1988, to devote all his time to the family estate. There are almost 30 hectares under vine, with 10,000 vines per hectare in the most recently planted vineyards. But let's move on to the tastings. We have a good report of the Selvamaggio '97, a monovarietal cabernet sauvignon. The blackcurrant and capsicum aromas are intense, expressive and distinctly varietal. It is soft, elegant and well-proportioned in the mouth, in short a good wine that just wants more distinct character. The same can be said of the sangiovese, the Felciaia '98, which boasts admirable consistency but fails to show those rhythmic variations that make for real gustatory excitement. The bouquet is well-defined and delightfully fruity, palate rounded, meaty and controlled. The finish is austere, with tannins drying it just a bit. The Vin Santo Vigna del Papa '95 is not a great success. The nose hasn't got much to say and the flavour is sweet, syrupy and lacking in backbone, with a bitterish finish.

CAMPIGLIA MARITTIMA (LI)

JACOPO BANTI
VIA CITERNA, 24
57021 CAMPIGLIA MARITTIMA (LI)
TEL. 05658388021
E-MAIL: info@jacopobanti.it

Jacopo Banti was a pioneer among the winemakers of the Val di Cornia. He was one of the very first to bottle his wine and believe in the potential for excellence of the area. A few years ago, he suddenly passed away, and it seemed that that would be the end of his wines and all his plans. But happily this was not the case. His son Lorenzo has thrown himself wholeheartedly into the estate, discovering, with the passage of time, that he has a real passion for the vigneron's life. The winery has changed gear, the cellar is even now being remodelled and new vineyards have been planted. Il Peccato, a blend of sangiovese and cabernet sauvignon, stands out. It displays an intense ruby colour and a clear bouquet with black berry fruit and toasty notes of oak. The palate has good concentration, a close-knit, smooth tannic weave and a fairly long finish, just slightly over-awed by the oak. Banti's other wines are good as well, starting with the fruity, straightforward and well-rounded Di Campalto, made with merlot from young vines. In the Centomini, there is an interesting use of clairette, a grape that used to be found in the old Val di Cornia vineyards. It has produced an uncommon white which is not too fragrant but can boast a full, solid body. Another singular wine is the Ceragiolo, a red with admirable character made from monovarietal ciliegiolo. The tried and true, if less original, Poggio Angelica is a classic white fermented in oak. We have left for last the Aleatico '00, which really excited us with the intense and quite extraordinary purity of its fruit. We have not awarded any glasses, though, because so little was made – just 300 bottles.

● Selvamaggio '97	🍷🍷	5
● Felciaia '98	🍷🍷	5
○ Vin Santo Vigna del Papa '95		5
● Selvamaggio '90	🍷🍷	5
● Selvamaggio '91	🍷🍷	5
● Selvamaggio '92	🍷🍷	5
● Chianti Ris. '93	🍷🍷	5
● Selvamaggio '93	🍷🍷	5
● Felciaia '94	🍷🍷	5
● Felciaia '95	🍷🍷	5
● Selvamaggio '95	🍷🍷	5
● Selvamaggio '96	🍷🍷	5
● Felciaia '97	🍷🍷	5
● Chianti Evento '96	🍷	3

● Il Peccato Barrique '99	🍷🍷	5
● Ceragiolo '00	🍷	3
○ Val di Cornia Bianco Poggio Angelica '00	🍷	4
○ Val di Cornia Centomini '00	🍷	3
● Val di Cornia Di Campalto '00	🍷	4

CAPANNORI (LU)

Tenuta di Valgiano
Via di Valgiano, 7
55010 Capannori (LU)
tel. 0583402271
e-mail: valgiano@lunet.it

Another year's wait for their sangiovese vineyard selection, the Scasso dei Cesari '99 which will be released in 2002, has left centre stage clear for Moreno Petrini and Laura di Collobiano's new wine, the Tenuta di Valgiano '99. At this point, their policy, which other local producers might do well to consider, seems established and perfectly clear – to make a sangiovese cru in small quantities, a Bordeaux blend – the Tenuta – as the top of the line and the Rosso dei Palistorti as their basic red. And they are wisely not giving up their white wine, the Giallo dei Muri. The debut performance of the Tenuta di Valgiano '99 is very good. It is international in style but avoids excess. The palate offers deep full body, smooth tannins, well-integrated oak and great elegance. The nose seems less expressive, probably because of the wine's youth. The Rosso dei Palistorti '99 is edgier and more individual. There are some not altogether clean notes on the nose, which are more than made up for by a solid, austere palate that offers lively tannins. The Giallo dei Muri reveals inviting aromas of citrus and exotic fruit, and the flavour is both fragrant and balanced.

CAPRAIA E LIMITE (FI)

Fattoria di Bibbiani
Via Bibbiani, 7
50050 Capraia e Limite (FI)
tel. 057157338
e-mail: bibbiani@penteres.it

Although the Fattoria di Bibbiani is making its debut appearance in the Guide, it is not, like so many, a newcomer to wine. Bibbiani boasts a long tradition in the Montalbano zone and its splendid 16th-century villa, the winery headquarters, is justly famous. What is new is the dedication here to the production of first-class wine. The estate has discarded the trappings of a traditional Tuscan wine farm and is concentrating all its efforts in one direction. With the vineyard and cellar management advice of Stefano Chioccioli, Fattoria di Bibbiani is thus able to present a fine range of successful wines. First place goes to the Montereggi '99, a blend of sangiovese and merlot that gives tangible proof of the estate's potential. It offers all-round intensity on the senses, with a soft, full-bodied and distinctly fruity palate solidly underpinned by tannins, and a bouquet ranging from black berry fruit to vegetal and balsamic nuances. The engaging Pulignano '99, from sangiovese and cabernet, is their traditional red, which has cast off its old-fashioned character without sacrificing its attractive personality. It is a powerful, meaty and deep wine, even if the vegetal and animal notes on the nose are not exactly elegant. The interesting Treggiaia '99 is worth investigating, too. Although less ambitious, it has a good mouthfeel. We conclude with the Chianti Montalbano '99, which is simpler but nevertheless well-executed and decently structured.

●	Tenuta di Valgiano '99	♛♛	6
○	Colline Lucchesi Bianco Giallo dei Muri '00	♛	4
●	Colline Lucchesi Rosso dei Palistorti '99	♛	4
●	Scasso dei Cesari '95	♛♛	4
●	Scasso dei Cesari '96	♛♛	4
○	Colline Lucchesi Bianco Giallo dei Muri '97	♛♛	3
●	Scasso dei Cesari '97	♛♛	5
●	Colline Lucchesi Rosso Scasso dei Cesari '98	♛♛	6
○	Scasso del Bugiardo '99	♛♛	5
●	Colline Lucchesi Rosso dei Palistorti '98	♛	4

●	Montereggi '99	♛♛	5
●	Pulignano '99	♛♛	5
●	Chianti Montalbano '99	♛	2*
●	Treggiaia '99	♛	3

CARMIGNANO (PO)

Fattoria Ambra
Via Lombarda, 85
59015 Carmignano (PO)
Tel. 055486488 - 0558719049
E-mail: fattoria.ambra@libero.it

Beppe Rigoli is one of the champions of the excellence and typicity of Carmignano wines. Hence his technique keeps pace with the latest advances but his aim remains to produce wines that respect the classic Carmignano taste. He is the only producer hereabouts whose production policy is dictated by the divergent characteristics of his various vineyards, as is demonstrated by the three different Carmignanos he offers: the Elzana, which is almost all sangiovese, the Vigne Alte di Montalbiolo, from the vines in the hilly part of the estate, and the Santa Cristina a Pilli, from the flatter land, considered the basic red. But this year's tastings inverted the natural order. The wine we were most impressed by was, in fact, the Santa Cristina a Pilli. It could have more fruit and the finish is not endless but the nose opens onto intriguing mineral tones and the palate, punctuated by attractive tannins, is solid and vigorous. The Vigne Alte di Montalbiolo '98 is not altogether eloquent on the nose, although it is clean and harmonious. But the admirable tannic texture and, especially, the crescendo in the finish suggest that this is the most promising wine in the whole range. The Elzana, in contrast, is a respectable red with its own personality but proved disappointingly flat and forward. Lastly, the Barco Reale and the Vin Ruspo, both '00s, are correct but dilute.

Wine	Rating	Score
● Carmignano Le Vigne Alte di Montalbiolo '98	♟♟	4
● Carmignano Vigna S. Cristina a Pilli '98	♟♟	4
● Carmignano Elzana Ris. '98	♟	5
● Barco Reale '00		3
☉ Vin Ruspo '00		2
● Carmignano Elzana Ris. '95	♟♟	4
● Carmignano Elzana Ris. '96	♟♟	4
● Carmignano Le Vigne Alte Ris. '96	♟♟	4
● Carmignano Elzana Ris. '97	♟♟	4
● Carmignano Le Vigne Alte Montalbiolo '97	♟♟	4

CARMIGNANO (PO)

Capezzana
Loc. Seano
Via Capezzana, 100
59015 Carmignano (PO)
Tel. 0558706005 - 0558706091
E-mail: capezzana@capezzana.it

It was clear, even without immediate confirmation, that the wind had changed at Capezzana and the wines were really going places. In fact, for the second consecutive year, the Contini Bonacossi estate has won Three Glasses. We do not want to make too much of the figure of consultant oenologist or agronomist because it is always the winery itself that counts most, but we cannot help thinking that the arrival of Stefano Chioccioli at Carmignano made it all happen sooner, at the very least. It is also quite clear that the terroir was so naturally promising that it needed only the proper care to produce prodigies. The Villa di Capezzana '99 has taken highest honours for a remarkable performance. Although still a very young wine, with an as yet not fully developed bouquet, it boasts a remarkable concentration of fruit, robust tannins and a long finish. With time, it will grow in balance and elegance. Many of the same things can be said for the Ghiaie della Furba '99, a blend of cabernet and merlot with a pinch of syrah. It seemed a little backward, although it hinted at a powerful structure. The very good Villa di Trefiano '98 is solidly built and shows a captivating personality as well as excellent balance. It is held back only by some vegetal nuances and light traces of reduction on the nose. The Vin Santo Riserva '95, sweet, rich and elegant, although not exceptionally long, is a real classic. The wonderfully soft, fruity Barco Reale '00 is a gem of its kind. To conclude, both the Chardonnay '00 and the Vin Ruspo '00 are thoroughly successful and very good value for money.

Wine	Rating	Score
● Carmignano Villa di Capezzana '99	♟♟♟	5
● Ghiaie della Furba '99	♟♟	6
● Barco Reale '00	♟♟	3*
○ Vin Santo di Carmignano Ris. '95	♟♟	6
● Carmignano Villa di Trefiano '98	♟♟	5
○ Chardonnay '00	♟	2*
☉ Vin Ruspo '00	♟	2*
● Ghiaie della Furba '98	♟♟♟	5
○ Vin Santo di Carmignano Ris. '93	♟♟	5
● Ghiaie della Furba '95	♟♟	5
● Carmignano Villa di Trefiano Ris. '97	♟♟	5
● Ghiaie della Furba '97	♟♟	5

CASTAGNETO CARDUCCI (LI)

GRATTAMACCO
LOC. GRATTAMACCO
57022 CASTAGNETO CARDUCCI (LI)
TEL. 0565763840
E-MAIL: info@grattamacco.com

Let us restate the obvious – vintages make a significant difference to the quality and style of a wine. In Bolgheri, the '97 and the '98 were amongst the best vintages of the 1990s but we do not feel that this is sufficient to explain the very perceptible forward surge in Piermario Meletti Cavallari's Bolgheri Superiore in the two years in question. In addition to the ripeness of the grapes, there was probably more refinement in his use of oak and a better control of temperature. But whatever the reasons, the Grattamacco '98 is really lovely. Crystalline definition on the nose of wild berries, spice and Mediterranean scrubland precedes a splendid fragrant fruitiness that accompanies the development on the palate. The tannins are lively and substantial but never aggressive and the acidity, well covered by the body, makes its presence felt indirectly by the felicitous contrast it creates with the well-gauged sweetness. What then is the weak point of this wine? It could perhaps be said that it has limited complexity because of its youth. By way of comparison, we retasted the Grattamacco '97, which is excellent and markedly more complete than it was a year ago. Grattamacco is one of those wines you just have to wait for if you want to enjoy everything they have to offer. The Grattamacco Bianco, with its rich, luscious flavour, deserves a showcase. The well-judged oak neither masks nor trivializes the ripeness and fragrance of the fruit. At last we have a sunny, generous white, just right for drinking!

CASTAGNETO CARDUCCI (LI)

MICHELE SATTA
LOC. VIGNA AL CAVALIERE, 61
57022 CASTAGNETO CARDUCCI (LI)
TEL. 0565773041
E-MAIL: satta@infol.it

A reputable winery should know how to build on past triumphs, and we must say that Michele Satta has done just that, becoming one of the most reliable producers in the country. This year the Piastraia, a blend of sangiovese, merlot, syrah and cabernet, seemed more convincing and complete than usual. To its customary immediately appealing fruitiness, it has added a pinch more aromatic complexity, with notes of black berries, Oriental spice and sweet tobacco. It is satisfying on the palate where, though not outstandingly rich, it has good balance and length. The Costa di Giulia usually takes a good bit of time to come out but the '00 is already eloquent. The aromas are clear and stylish, and the palate invigoratingly tasty. This time we found a successful fusion of vermentino and sauvignon instead of the uneasy cohabitation of two obviously distinct varieties we noticed in the past. The Cavaliere '98 is good, but that is hardly news. After the parenthesis represented by the excellent '97, it is now again made exclusively from sangiovese, a grape that may not produce great density but does guarantee more personality. It has always been part of Michele Satta's winemaking philosophy to give space to his "lesser" wines. They are simple, uncomplicated wines that can be enjoyed by all. The Diambra is lively and agreeable, the Bolgheri Bianco refreshing and clean.

● Bolgheri Rosso Sup. Grattamacco '98	▼▼	6
○ Bolgheri Bianco '00	▼▼	4
● Grattamacco '85	▼▼▼	5
● Grattamacco '90	▼▼	5
● Grattamacco '91	▼▼	5
● Grattamacco '92	▼▼	4
● Grattamacco '93	▼▼	5
● Bolgheri Rosso Sup. Grattamacco '95	▼▼	6
● Bolgheri Rosso Sup. Grattamacco '97	▼▼	6
○ Bolgheri Bianco '99	▼▼	4

○ Costa di Giulia '00	▼▼	4*
● Vigna al Cavaliere '98	▼▼	6
● Bolgheri Rosso Piastraia '99	▼▼	5
● Bolgheri Rosso Diambra '00	▼	3
○ Bolgheri Bianco '00		3
● Vigna al Cavaliere '90	▼▼	5
● Bolgheri Rosso Piastraia '95	▼▼	3
● Vigna al Cavaliere '95	▼▼	4
● Bolgheri Rosso Piastraia '96	▼▼	4
● Vigna al Cavaliere '96	▼▼	5
● Bolgheri Rosso Piastraia '97	▼▼	4
● Vigna al Cavaliere '97	▼▼	5
● Bolgheri Rosso Piastraia '98	▼▼	5

CASTELLINA IN CHIANTI (SI)

CASTELLARE DI CASTELLINA
LOC. CASTELLARE
53011 CASTELLINA IN CHIANTI (SI)
TEL. 0577742903 - 0577740490
E-MAIL: isodi@tin.it

I Sodi di San Niccolò '97 is one of the best sangiovese-based reds we tasted this year. Or, as Paolo Panerai, the owner of this lovely estate, prefers to call the grape, sangioveto. It has both concentration and elegance, with complex, well-delineated aromas and firmness on the palate without the roughness of some previous editions. A great red that joins the other Three-Glass Olympians. But the excellent version of this flagship wine is, we feel, only the most obvious sign of a general improvement in the winery's output. All the bottles are much better than they ever have been, which suggests the presence of careful technical management, co-ordinated by Maurizio Castelli and Alessandro Cellai, that should produce other champions in the future. For the moment, we shall be satisfied with the fine '98 editions of the two Chianti Classico Riservas, the Vigna il Poggiale and the basic version. Despite the fact that this was not a very favourable vintage hereabouts, they reveal elegance and all the proper varietal characteristics of the sangiovese grape. The Chianti Classico '99, from a very different sort of vintage, is fair, and we shall have to wait to evaluate the Poggio ai Merli '99, their merlot-based Supertuscan. It had not yet been bottled at the time of our tastings although when we tried it from the barrel, it promised to be monumental.

CASTELLINA IN CHIANTI (SI)

FAMIGLIA CECCHI
LOC. CASINA DEI PONTI, 56
53011 CASTELLINA IN CHIANTI (SI)
TEL. 0577743024
E-MAIL: cecchi@cecchi.net

We are dedicating just one profile to the various estates that belong to the Cecchi family in different parts of Tuscany. In addition to the original Cecchi winery in Castellina, these now include Villa Cerna, also in Castellina, Castello di Montauto in San Gimignano and Val delle Rose in the Morellino di Scansano zone of the Maremma. Cecchi has turned into a viticultural empire, producing distinguished wines as well as bottles that are excellent value for money, always a priority for the Cecchis. We'll start with the best wine they presented, the Spargolo '98, a barrique-aged red made from their best selection of sangiovese. This version may not be quite up to the '97 but is elegant on the palate and satisfyingly varietal on the nose, which is not at all masked by the oak. Its strong suit is finesse, and if it does not have overwhelming body, the balance is extraordinary. The good, as ever, Morellino Val delle Rose Riserva '98 is soft and caressing. We actually preferred the attractive, upfront Chianti Classico '99 to the Riserva '98, which is somewhat forward on the nose, and to the Messer Piero di Teuzzo '99, which is still just a bit closed. The Vernaccia di San Gimignano '00 from Castello di Montauto is correctly executed, as is the fragrant Morellino di Scansano Val delle Rose '00, a very moreish if uncomplicated red. The Sagrato '00, a barrique-aged chardonnay, is distinctly good.

● I Sodi di San Niccolò '97	🍷🍷🍷	6
● Chianti Cl. Ris. '98	🍷🍷	5
● Chianti Cl. Vigna il Poggiale Ris. '98	🍷🍷	6
● Chianti Cl. '99	🍷	4
● Chianti Cl. Vigna il Poggiale Ris. '97	🍷🍷🍷	6
● I Sodi di San Niccolò '86	🍷🍷	6
● I Sodi di San Niccolò '90	🍷🍷	6
● I Sodi di San Niccolò '94	🍷🍷	6
● Chianti Cl. Vigna il Poggiale '95	🍷🍷	5
● Coniale '95	🍷🍷	6
● I Sodi di San Niccolò '95	🍷🍷	6
● I Sodi di San Niccolò '96	🍷🍷	6

○ Sagrato Chardonnay Castello di Montauto '00	🍷🍷	4
● Morellino di Scansano Val delle Rose Ris. '98	🍷🍷	4
● Spargolo '98	🍷🍷	6
● Chianti Cl. '99	🍷🍷	3*
● Morellino di Scansano Val delle Rose '00	🍷	3
○ Vernaccia di S. Gimignano Castello di Montauto '00	🍷	4
● Chianti Cl. Villa Cerna Ris. '98	🍷	4
● Chianti Cl. Messer Piero di Teuzzo '99	🍷	4
● Chianti Cl. Villa Cerna Ris. '97	🍷🍷	4
● Spargolo '97	🍷🍷	6

CASTELLINA IN CHIANTI (SI)

PODERE COLLELUNGO
LOC. COLLELUNGO
53011 CASTELLINA IN CHIANTI (SI)
TEL. 0577740489
E-MAIL: info@collelungo.com

This Castellina estate, which has climbed to remarkable heights in a very short time, has given an excellent performance this time. Credit must go again to the dedication of the owners, who have finished a radical restructuring, and to the help of their consultant oenologist Alberto Antonini. We'll start with the Roveto selection of the Chianti Classico '99, which made it to the final tastings. It presents a bright, vivid ruby hue and oak-derived vanilla nuances that are well integrated into the rich, varied underlying fruit. After a powerful entrance on the palate, it develops evenly, with the tannins balanced by substantial but harmonious alcohol. The basic version did extremely well too. Intense in colour, it offers a bouquet that ranges from coffee to balsamic hints that add to the complexity. Intriguing and delicious in the mouth, it has a distinct vein of acidity and a delightful, particularly captivating finish. The Riserva '98 displays a distinct fragrance of wild berries enriched by aromatic resin and refreshing notes of mint. After a silky-soft attack, there is a little slackness in mid-palate, but it gathers steam for the very persistent, well-balanced finish.

Chianti Cl. Roveto '99	♀♀	6
Chianti Cl. Ris. '98	♀♀	5
Chianti Cl. '99	♀♀	4
Chianti Cl. Ris. '97	♀♀	4
Chianti Cl. Roveto '97	♀♀	4
Chianti Cl. '98	♀	4

CASTELLINA IN CHIANTI (SI)

★ CASTELLO DI FONTERUTOLI
LOC. FONTERUTOLI
VIA OTTONE III DI SASSONIA, 5
53011 CASTELLINA IN CHIANTI (SI)
TEL. 057773571
E-MAIL: fonterutoli@fonterutoli.it

In the course of the last ten years, Fonterutoli has become one of the best wineries in the Chianti Classico zone, a fact now acknowledged even by its fiercest critics. This time they have walked off with their 15th Three Glass award in as many years, which is also as many as there have been editions of the Guide. This speaks for itself, as does the Siepi '99, a monumental wine made from sangiovese and merlot. It's true that it will lighten your wallet, but sometimes – not always, of course – you can see why a wine costs so much. Still, we hope that prices will not go completely off the scale. But back to the wine. The bouquet is a successful synthesis of the varietal characteristics of the two constituent grapes. The tobacco aroma of the merlot blends with the black cherry-dominated fruit notes of sangiovese. The wood remains in the background and the light vanilla is a harbinger of smoky tones that should develop later on, as was the case with preceding vintages. The concentration is extraordinary and the tannins are astonishingly smooth. In addition to this oenological gem, there is a range of admirable wines. The Chianti Classico Castello di Fonterutoli '98 made it to our finals but we found it slightly forward in fragrance. The Chianti Classico '99, which did just as well, is one of the best of its category. The Morellino di Scansano Belguardo '00 is better than ever, a velvety, mouth-filling and very typical wine. Even the simplest red on the list, the monovarietal sangiovese Poggio alla Badiola '00, is extremely good and anything but banal. There are not many wineries in Tuscany that can offer such a fine range of wines, and that is quite a compliment.

Siepi '99	♀♀♀	6
Chianti Cl. Castello di Fonterutoli '98	♀♀	6
Chianti Cl. '99	♀♀	5
Morellino di Scansano Belguardo '00	♀♀	4
Poggio alla Badiola '00	♀♀	4
Siepi '93	♀♀♀	5
Siepi '94	♀♀♀	6
Siepi '95	♀♀♀	6
Siepi '96	♀♀♀	6
Chianti Cl. Castello di Fonterutoli '97	♀♀♀	6
Siepi '97	♀♀♀	6
Siepi '98	♀♀♀	6

CASTELLINA IN CHIANTI (SI)

FATTORIA NITTARDI
LOC. NITTARDI, 76
53011 CASTELLINA IN CHIANTI (SI)
TEL. 0577740269
E-MAIL: fattorianittardi@chianticlassico.com

Peter Femfert has added another work of art to his collection. In this case, however, we are not talking about a painting or a sculpture but a wine. And not any wine, but his Chianti Classico Riserva '98. If the image seems forced, we insist that it has seldom seemed so appropriate to speak of a marriage of wine and art. Nestled as it is in the folds of the Chianti hills in an unspoiled landscape, Nittardi is a well worth a visit. And it is particularly worthwhile if you go to taste the Nittardi wines, of which there are only two, the Chianti Classico Casanuova and the Riserva. Peter Femfert has always firmly believed in the importance of the terroir and of respecting tradition. This does not perforce mean that Nittardi Chianti is still made with trebbiano or malvasia bianca. Obviously, he follows the dictates of the new DOC regulations, and his vinification and ageing techniques have kept pace with the times. Peter makes use of barriques and tonneaux as the grapes require and his oenologist Carlo Ferrini recommends. And so we come to the Riserva '98, which fully merited its Three Glasses for a quite exceptional character. The bouquet is rich and concentrated, and the intensity and volume expand as the wine develops on the palate. The tannins are solid yet rounded, and the finish is a constant crescendo of sensations. This is a great Chianti Classico. The Chianti Casanuova '99, which is good, suffers by comparison, but then you don't mass-produce works of art.

● Chianti Cl. Ris. '98	🍷🍷🍷	5
● Chianti Cl. Casanuova di Nittardi '99	🍷	4
● Chianti Cl. Ris. '88	🍷🍷	4
● Chianti Cl. Ris. '90	🍷🍷	5
● Chianti Cl. '93	🍷🍷	4
● Chianti Cl. Ris. '93	🍷🍷	4
● Chianti Cl. Ris. '94	🍷🍷	5
● Chianti Cl. '95	🍷🍷	4
● Chianti Cl. Ris. '95	🍷🍷	5
● Chianti Cl. '96	🍷🍷	4
● Chianti Cl. Ris. '96	🍷🍷	5
● Chianti Cl. '97	🍷🍷	4
● Chianti Cl. Ris. '97	🍷🍷	5
● Chianti Cl. '98	🍷🍷	4

CASTELLINA IN CHIANTI (SI)

ROCCA DELLE MACÌE
LOC. MACÌE
53011 CASTELLINA IN CHIANTI (SI)
TEL. 05777321
E-MAIL: rocca@roccadellemacie.com

Sergio Zingarelli has made a brilliant start on the new course at Rocca delle Macìe. This big, important Chianti Classico winery produces more than 4,000,000 bottles a year from 250 hectares of vineyards, some estate-owned, some rented. We say a new course because the fermentation technique, which in the past was anything but uniformly successful, now seems to have been sorted out. The wines are all at least well-made and in some cases really exciting. The most striking result is that the Roccato '98, from equal parts of sangiovese and cabernet sauvignon, made it into our finals. It's a modern-style, barrique-aged red, intense on eye, nose and mouth, with rich, lingering aromas and great balance on the palate, where the tannins are deliciously smooth. It lacks only a bit of complexity in the bouquet, probably because of the good, but not exceptional, vintage. The Ser Gioveto '98, a monovarietal sangiovese, is very sound as well. It is more one-dimensional than the Roccato, but shows crisp, well-expressed fruitiness. Another Two Glass wine is the Chianti Classico Fizzano Riserva '98, which is similar in many ways to the Ser Gioveto, but with less concentration on nose and palate. The brand new Morellino di Scansano Campomaccione '00 is most agreeable but a bit predictable. The quaffable Chianti Classico Sant'Alfonso '98 is, as usual, fair. The Chianti Classico Riserva '98, a winery mainstay, is only correct.

● Roccato '98	🍷🍷	6
● Chianti Cl. Fizzano Ris. '98	🍷🍷	5
● Ser Gioveto '98	🍷🍷	6
● Morellino di Scansano Campomaccione '00	🍷	3
● Chianti Cl. Ris. '98	🍷	5
● Chianti Cl. Tenuta S. Alfonso '98	🍷	4
● Chianti Cl. Fizzano Ris. '96	🍷🍷	5
● Roccato '96	🍷🍷	6
● Ser Gioveto '96	🍷🍷	6
● Chianti Cl. Fizzano Ris. '97	🍷🍷	5
● Roccato '97	🍷🍷	6
● Ser Gioveto '97	🍷🍷	6

CASTELLINA IN CHIANTI (SI)

San Fabiano Calcinaia
Loc. Cellole
53011 Castellina in Chianti (SI)
tel. 0577979232
e-mail: info@sanfabianocalcinaia.com

We are at the very edge of Chianti Classico here. The vineyards and winery of San Fabiano Calcinaia are on the western frontier of the zone, where the hills gradually open out and the view stretches westward as far as the eye can see. It is an area of powerful, soft wines without the bite characteristic of other Chiantis. And that's what the San Fabiano reds are like. It is clear that Guido Serio, the owner of the estate, and oenologist Carlo Ferrini respect those characteristics and make no attempt to tweak what nature has put into the grape. The most representative of their wines is, as usual, the Cerviolo Rosso, made from sangiovese with merlot and cabernet sauvignon. The '99 is even better than the last two versions we tasted and may be the best yet. Elegance, concentration, close-knit yet smooth tannins and great length. A masterpiece. Then there's the Cerviolo Bianco '00, a chardonnay aged in small barrels. We sometimes despair of finding a great white in Chianti but the captivating, mildly toasty aromas and the soft, lingering concentration of the flavour could convince us otherwise. Both the Chianti Classicos are good. We definitely prefer the Riserva '98 to the basic '99, which is much simpler. But that's the way it should be.

● Cerviolo Rosso '99	▼▼▼	6
○ Cerviolo Bianco '00	▼▼	5
● Chianti Cl. Cellole Ris. '98	▼▼	5
● Chianti Cl. '99	▼	4
● Cerviolo Rosso '96	▼▼▼	6
● Cerviolo Rosso '97	▼▼▼	6
● Cerviolo Rosso '98	▼▼▼	6
● Chianti Cl. Cellole Ris. '90	▼▼	5
● Cerviolo Rosso '95	▼▼	6
● Chianti Cl. Cellole Ris. '95	▼▼	5
● Chianti Cl. Cellole Ris. '97	▼▼	5
○ Cerviolo Bianco '98	▼▼	5
○ Cerviolo Bianco '99	▼▼	5
● Cerviolo Rosso '93	▼	6
● Cerviolo Rosso '94	▼	6

CASTELLINA MARITTIMA (PI)

Castello del Terriccio
Via Bagnoli, 20
56040 Castellina Marittima (PI)
tel. 050699709
e-mail: castello.terriccio@tin.it

For the fifth time in a row, Gian Annibale Rossi di Medelana has walked off with Three Glasses for his extraordinarily reliable Lupicaia. Apart from the excellent technical choices he has made, such as appointing Carlo Ferrini as his red wine consultant and Hans Terzer – from the '00 vintage – for the whites, he has the advantage of an exceptional terroir and the natural setting of his vineyards. These imbue all his wines with inimitable qualities and make the Lupicaia an instantly recognizable red with unique personality. The '99 version of this cabernet and merlot-based Supertuscan is one of the most successful yet produced. The masterful harmony of nose and palate are what make it so irresistible. The bouquet melds a wide range of aromas, from wild black berries to balsamic notes with undercurrents of Oriental spice. The fruit that comes out on the palate is lifted by the densely woven, soft tannins and then echoed unhurriedly on the finish. The Tassinaia '99, a blend of sangiovese, cabernet and merlot, is very good. Nothing new there. It shows excellent balance, admirable definition and good concentration. The Con Vento '00, from sauvignon, has definitely improved, even if it is not yet absolutely thrilling. Still, it is fragrant, clean and distinctly varietal. The Rondinaia '00, mostly chardonnay, is intensely fruity on the nose and full-bodied and deep on the palate. The Saluccio '99 does not have enough freshness and elegance to offset its remarkable structural complexity because the oak tends to dominate.

● Lupicaia '99	▼▼▼	6
○ Con Vento '00	▼▼	4
○ Rondinaia '00	▼▼	4
● Tassinaia '99	▼▼	5
○ Saluccio '99	▼	5
● Lupicaia '93	▼▼▼	5
● Lupicaia '95	▼▼▼	6
● Lupicaia '96	▼▼▼	6
● Lupicaia '97	▼▼▼	6
● Lupicaia '98	▼▼▼	6
● Tassinaia '97	▼▼	5
○ Saluccio '98	▼▼	5
● Tassinaia '98	▼▼	5

CASTELNUOVO BERARDENGA (SI)

Fattoria dell' Aiola
Loc. Vagliagli
53019 Castelnuovo Berardenga (SI)
tel. 0577322615
e-mail: aiola@chianticlassico.com

Last year, we were pleased to welcome this historic Chianti estate back to the Guide and this time we are happy to note that it wasn't just a flash in the pan. We'll start with the wine that struck us most, the Chianti Classico Riserva '98, which has a lovely ruby hue lightly tinged with purple. The nose, a little distant at first, opens out to reveal notes of animal skin with hints of ripe fruit. The entry in the mouth is austere and solid, and the prominent, tight-knit tannins give density to the palate. The good Logaiolo, a blend of sangiovese and cabernet sauvignon, shows an attractive ruby hue and pleasing aromas of blackcurrant and bilberry enriched by sweet notes of vanilla. The attack on the palate is soft and silky, and the follow-through consistent. We were slightly less taken with the Rosso del Senatore, another blend, but this time of sangiovese, colorino and merlot. The notes of black cherry and blackcurrant are joined by refreshingly lively, lingering balsamic nuances. The palate, however, is a bit shallow and not very concentrated, with an over-abundance of rather drying tannins. Lastly, the Chianti Classico '99 rates only a mention. It has undeveloped, neutral aromas and a lean body.

● Chianti Cl. Ris. '98	ΨΨ	4
● Logaiolo '98	ΨΨ	4
● Rosso del Senatore '99	Ψ	5
● Chianti Cl. '99		3
● Chianti Cl. Ris. '90	ΨΨ	5
● Chianti Cl. Ris. '94	ΨΨ	4
● Chianti Cl. Ris. '95	ΨΨ	4
● Chianti Cl. Cancello Rosso Ris. '97	ΨΨ	4
● Rosso del Senatore '95	Ψ	5
● Chianti Cl. '96	Ψ	3
● Chianti Cl. Ris. '97	Ψ	4
● Logaiolo '97	Ψ	4
● Chianti Cl. '98	Ψ	3
● Rosso del Senatore '98	Ψ	5

CASTELNUOVO BERARDENGA (SI)

Borgo Scopeto
Loc. Vagliagli
53019 Castelnuovo Berardenga (SI)
tel. 0577848390
e-mail: caparzo@libero.it

Borgo Scopeto is not a new name but we hadn't heard from the cellar for a while. Its reappearance in the Guide after a longish absence coincides with a change of ownership. It now belongs to the Tenuta di Caparzo company. The manager, Nuccio Turone, is hardly a novice when it comes to wine, and he can call upon the technical expertise of oenologist Vittorio Fiore, agronomist Remigio Bordini and Giovanni Sordi. Borgo Scopeto has been thoroughly restructured, with particular attention, naturally, lavished on the cellar and the vineyards. The primary focus is Chianti Classico, which appears in three versions, the standard-label and two Riservas. The tastings were most encouraging. The very good Riserva '98 even made it to our finals. It may perhaps not have the characteristics of a great wine but in its category, it is unquestionably one of the finest, and extremely well-made. It is a medium-bodied, well-balanced, soft and elegant wine, or in short, a lovely Chianti. The Riserva Misciano '98 is nice, too. Indeed it has more character and concentration but suffers from slight reduction on the nose. The Chianti '99, on the other hand, with its not very eloquent palate and somewhat ill-defined nose, failed to make the grade. But on the whole, there is plenty to be happy about here.

● Chianti Cl. Ris. '98	ΨΨ	4*
● Chianti Cl. Misciano Ris. '98	ΨΨ	5
● Chianti Cl. '99		3
● Chianti Cl. Ris. '90	ΨΨ	5
● Chianti Cl. Ris. '93	ΨΨ	4
● Chianti Cl. '91	Ψ	4
● Chianti Cl. '92	Ψ	4
● Chianti Cl. '93	Ψ	4

CASTELNUOVO BERARDENGA (SI)

CASTELLO DI BOSSI
LOC. BOSSI IN CHIANTI, 28
53019 CASTELNUOVO BERARDENGA (SI)
TEL. 0577359330 - 0577359177
E-MAIL: info@castellodibossi.it

This year, we witnessed an excellent performance from the estate headed by dedicated, enthusiastic Marco Bacci. The major efforts made over the last few years with the help of the oenologist Alberto Antonini were directed particularly towards clonal selection in the vineyards. Sangiovese produced the most interesting results and in fact they are planning the release of a wine made exclusively from the variety, to be called Di Marco. But signs of big changes are already to be seen in the Chianti Classico '99, which made it to our Three Glass finals. Intense ruby, it reveals a strikingly varied nose dominated by fruit and backed up by sweet notes of vanilla and toasted bread. Powerful on the palate, it can also point to sinew and structure, and the tannins are perfectly integrated with the alcohol. The finish is good and very persistent. The Girolamo '98, a monovarietal merlot of great character, did very well too. The clear-cut nose, with wild berries to the fore, includes very stylish nuances of coffee and chocolate. In the mouth, it is soft and silky, and the flavour lingers on. The lovely ruby-hued Riserva Berardo '97 reveals aromas of jam and ripe fruit. The entry on the palate is smooth and the length is just right. Lastly, the Corbaia '98, a blend of sangiovese and cabernet, offers a ripe fragrance of plum and cherry, combined with hints of tobacco. The attack on the palate is firm and full-bodied and the tannins are densely packed yet fine-grained. A perfect balance of alcohol and acidity makes it wonderfully quaffable.

● Chianti Cl. '99	♟♟	4
● Corbaia '98	♟♟	5
● Girolamo '98	♟♟	5
● Chianti Cl. Berardo Ris. '97	♟	5
● Chianti Cl. Ris. '94	♟♟	4
● Corbaia '94	♟♟	5
● Chianti Cl. Berardo Ris. '95	♟♟	5
● Chianti Cl. Ris. '95	♟♟	4
● Corbaia '95	♟♟	5
● Chianti Cl. Berardo Ris. '96	♟♟	5
● Chianti Cl. '94	♟	3
● Chianti Cl. '95	♟	3
● Corbaia '96	♟	5
● Girolamo '97	♟	5
● Chianti Cl. '98	♟	3

CASTELNUOVO BERARDENGA (SI)

CARPINETA FONTALPINO
FRAZ. MONTEAPERTI
LOC. CARPINETA
53019 CASTELNUOVO BERARDENGA (SI)
TEL. 0577369219 - 0577283228
E-MAIL: gioiacresti@interfree.it

Gioia Cresti never tires of astonishing us. Each year, her wines take a giant step forward. Do Ut Des is one of the best wines of the region and the Chianti Colli Senesi won Two Glasses of its own, which for a second wine that costs just over € 7.50 in the shops is no small achievement. Our astonishment, to tell the truth, is only relative, because it was clear that Carpineta Fontalpino had really got going, albeit a bit later than some of its fellows. The vine density is high and yields limited. Only barriques are used in the cellar and they are new for the most part. But to this careful planning is added the passionate dedication that propels Gioia Cresti past all obstacles, and that's what makes the difference. And her Do Ut Des '99 is an excellent red. It has a vivid concentrated ruby hue. The nose boasts depth and elegance, with layers of dark fruit nicely tempered with oak and the palate is dense and even in its progression. In the long finish, there is just the faintest trace of lively acidity – a sign of youth and a signature of the sangiovese grapes that, together with cabernet sauvignon and merlot, make up the blend of this Supertuscan. As we mentioned earlier, the Chianti Colli Senesi is not content with a supporting role. It is, of course, a more straightforward wine, but has surprising energy. The well-defined aromas evoke ripe fruit; the palate is warm, soft and lingering.

● Do Ut Des '99	♟♟	5
● Chianti Colli Senesi Gioia '99	♟♟	4
● Do Ut Des '97	♟♟	4
● Do Ut Des '98	♟♟	4
● Chianti Colli Senesi Gioia '97	♟	3
● Chianti Colli Senesi Gioia '98	♟	3

CASTELNUOVO BERARDENGA (SI)

Castell'in Villa
Loc. Castell'in Villa
53010 Castelnuovo Berardenga (SI)
Tel. 0577359074
E-mail: castellinvilla@interfree.it

The wines from Castell'in Villa are among the few that don't seem to fit into any pre-established categories. They are so individual that it is hard to compare them to other wines, even to others from the same DOC zone. This marked individuality seems quite unfettered by questions of possible consumer demand, or established marketing practices, as is also demonstrated by the release date, which is generally much later than most. Castell'in Villa reds are in fact wines made for the select few who are willing to wait for them and able to understand them. The Chianti Poggio delle Rose '97 is still young and has yet to develop complexity, but the signs are already perceptible. The nose foregrounds liquorice, mineral nuances and sweet tobacco. The fruit is lively and prominent, with lovely notes of black cherry, and there are also smoky oak-derived tones. The entry on the palate is generous, the mid-palate shows dense full body and the finish is tannic. The Chianti Riserva '95 is more open on the nose, offering dried flowers, balsamic notes, cinnamon and vanilla. It makes no attempt to curry favour with sweetness in the mouth but has an austere style which emphasizes balance and elegance, and the tannins are well-behaved. We thought the Santa Croce '95, from sangiovese, was more evolved. It has light bitterish notes but there is no shortage of personality.

● Chianti Cl. Ris. '95	🍷🍷	5
● Chianti Cl. Poggio delle Rose Ris. '97	🍷🍷	5
● Santa Croce '95	🍷	6
● Chianti Cl. Ris. '83	🍷🍷	4
● Chianti Cl. '86	🍷🍷	3
● Chianti Cl. Ris. '86	🍷🍷	4
● Chianti Cl. '87	🍷🍷	3
● Chianti Cl. '88	🍷🍷	3

CASTELNUOVO BERARDENGA (SI)

Fattorie Chigi Saracini
Via dell'Arbia, 2
53010 Castelnuovo Berardenga (SI)
Tel. 0577355113

The Chigi Saracini vineyards are still in the midst of upheavals. New plantings are appearing left and right, with a preference for sangiovese, but cabernet sauvignon and merlot are not being neglected either. The choices are carefully based on the varieties that have been seen to do well locally – the vineyards of this Colli Sienesi estate are right nextdoor to the Chianti Classico zone. It is too early to expect extraordinary results but it certainly looks as though they may be forthcoming in the near future. Nevertheless, this year's tastings were in some ways quite positive, thanks to well-judged investments in the cellar and the barrel stock. It was the intelligent use of oak that allowed Il Poggiassai '99, a blend of sangiovese and cabernet, to offer a denser, fuller body. And the fruit, sweet and succulent, is very much there, too. There is great variety on nose and palate, and the overall impression is delicious. Of the other two wines they presented, both of which we liked, we preferred the Chianti Colli Senesi '00 for its rich, full fruit and decent body. The '99 Chianti Superiore, if not actually superior, is certainly acceptable. The palate is well-rounded, but the finish is a little light.

● Il Poggiassai '99	🍷🍷	4*
● Chianti Colli Senesi '00	🍷	2*
● Chianti Sup. '99	🍷	3
● Il Poggiassai '97	🍷🍷	4
● Il Poggiassai '98	🍷🍷	4
● Chianti Sup. '97	🍷	3
● Chianti Colli Senesi '98	🍷	3
● Chianti Sup. '98	🍷	3
● Chianti Colli Senesi '99	🍷	3

CASTELNUOVO BERARDENGA (SI)

★ Fattoria di Felsina
S. S. 484 Chiantigiana
53010 Castelnuovo Berardenga (SI)
tel. 0577355117
e-mail: felsina@data.it

Fontalloro in the '98 version has now made its contribution to the Fattoria di Felsina's Three Glass hoard. It's a Fontalloro with original personality, and perhaps even unusual for this wine. On the nose, for example, there are very clear aromas of black pepper and violets side by side with notes of black cherry and liquorice. The palate offers a tannic weave of extraordinary quality and smoothness and a deep, well-sustained development held together by the vibrant energy of the sangiovese grape. It's a splendid red, perhaps less powerful than other versions, but outstanding for its elegance and aromatic personality. The Chianti Classico '99 is also very good. The nose, not fully defined, offers notes of red fruit with some vegetal and toasty oak undertones. It is considerably more assured and even on the palate, where it shows concentration, good progression, close-knit, well-rounded tannins and a refreshingly succulent finish. This is a real Chianti. The Riserva Rancia '98 was presented despite the poor vintage for sangiovese. And in fact there is some evidence of under-ripeness in the tannins and the aromatic tone. Both are just a bit green. These are minor points, though, that hardly affect the quality of a wine which is admirable for density, character and structure. The good chardonnay-based I Sistri '99 reveals an interesting mineral fragrance, a medium body and a slightly weak finish.

● Fontalloro '98	🍷🍷🍷	6
● Chianti Cl. Rancia Ris. '98	🍷🍷	5
● Chianti Cl. '99	🍷🍷	4
○ I Sistri '99	🍷	4
● Fontalloro '86	🍷🍷🍷	5
● Fontalloro '88	🍷🍷🍷	5
● Chianti Cl. Rancia Ris. '90	🍷🍷🍷	5
● Chianti Cl. Ris. '90	🍷🍷🍷	4
● Fontalloro '90	🍷🍷🍷	5
● Maestro Raro '91	🍷🍷🍷	5
● Chianti Cl. Rancia Ris. '93	🍷🍷🍷	5
● Fontalloro '93	🍷🍷🍷	6
● Maestro Raro '93	🍷🍷🍷	6
● Fontalloro '95	🍷🍷🍷	6
● Fontalloro '97	🍷🍷🍷	6

CASTELNUOVO BERARDENGA (SI)

Castello di Monastero
Loc. Monastero d'Ombrone, 19
53010 Castelnuovo Berardenga (SI)
tel. 05775701

We can report a brilliant debut for the Castello di Monastero, which has presented a fine, generally interesting range of wines. The star of the show – there were seven wines – was the Chianti Classico Riserva '98, a tidy, harmonious, well-executed red. The intense aromas include notes of red fruit, liquorice, spice and toasty hints of oak. The palate is not very weighty, but the progression is well-proportioned, elegant and deep. The sangiovese and cabernet sauvignon-based L'Infinito '99 is similar in style. Here, too, we noticed good ripeness with little space conceded to vegetal notes, but the volume was limited. It's a neatly made wine with an original bouquet of aromatic herbs, cinnamon and pepper. The palate is balanced, and oak lords it over the finish. The interesting Solo Chardonnay '99 may not have outstanding personality but it does offer clear-cut flowery, fruity and light boisé aromas. The pleasing palate progresses quietly, without thrills or disappointments. The well-made Chianti Monterotondo '99 is admirably varietal on the nose, with berry fruit and faint hints of vanilla, then uncomplicated, medium-bodied and agreeable in the mouth. We found rather prominent vegetal and oaky tones in the Chianti Classico '99. The Terre di Sasso '98 and the Sangiovese '99 are lighter but correct. The first has a more interesting range of aromas.

● Chianti Cl. Ris. '98	🍷🍷	4
● L'Infinito '99	🍷🍷	5
○ Terre di Sasso '98	🍷	4
● Chianti Cl. '99	🍷	4
● Chianti Sup. Monterotondo '99	🍷	3
○ Solo Chardonnay '99	🍷	4
● Sangiovese '99		4

CASTELNUOVO BERARDENGA (SI)

FATTORIA DI PETROIO
LOC. QUERCEGROSSA
VIA DI MOCENNI, 7
53010 CASTELNUOVO BERARDENGA (SI)
TEL. 0577328045 - 066798883
E-MAIL: g.l.lenzi@iol.it

After last year's Three Glasses for the excellent Riserva '97, Fattoria di Petroio has given further proof of its consistent high quality. The Riserva '98, from a decidedly less brilliant vintage, is nevertheless up to expectation stylistically. Sangiovese is still favoured over the other grapes permitted by Chianti Classico regulations. At Petroio, as we know, they rightly prefer to maintain the characteristics of the terroir rather than to jump onto the "big body" bandwagon, as the market seems to demand. This admirable constancy means that with Petroio wines, you know what you are buying. But let's get down to the wines themselves, which were most satisfactory. The Riserva '98 has a lovely ruby hue with bright highlights and offers a subtle, complex bouquet with notes of berry fruit, liquorice and faint tobacco nuances. The palate, after a convincing attack and a well-balanced development, shows the limits of the vintage in the finish, which is enjoyable but only moderately long. The Chianti '99 is really good. The style is simpler but immediately appealing, and based on sound, well-expressed fruit. The palate is concentrated, succulent and beautifully balanced.

●	Chianti Cl. Ris. '98	ΨΨ	5
●	Chianti Cl. '99	ΨΨ	4*
●	Chianti Cl. Ris. '97	ΨΨΨ	5
●	Chianti Cl. '90	ΨΨ	3
●	Chianti Cl. Ris. '90	ΨΨ	4
●	Chianti Cl. '91	ΨΨ	3
●	Chianti Cl. '93	ΨΨ	2
●	Chianti Cl. '95	ΨΨ	3
●	Chianti Cl. Ris. '95	ΨΨ	4
●	Chianti Cl. '96	ΨΨ	3
●	Chianti Cl. Ris. '96	ΨΨ	4
●	Chianti Cl. '97	ΨΨ	3
●	Chianti Cl. '98	ΨΨ	4
●	Chianti Cl. Ris. '93	Ψ	4
●	Chianti Cl. '94	Ψ	3

CASTELNUOVO BERARDENGA (SI)

POGGIO BONELLI
LOC. POGGIO BONELLI
53010 CASTELNUOVO BERARDENGA (SI)
TEL. 0577355382

Poggio Bonelli was recently acquired by Monte dei Paschi di Siena, which already owns the Fattorie Chigi nearby and the Tenimenti Fontanafredda in Piedmont. This Siena-based bank has revamped its oenological strategy and put all its weight behind the sort of management that should lead to serious improvement in its wines. That's why the estate has undergone extensive restructuring in both cellar and vineyard, of which there are currently about 15 hectares. The vines are sangiovese for the most part, but cabernet sauvignon and merlot can be found as well. Carlo Ferrini is in charge of production, which is in itself a sign of how high they are aiming. Of the four wines presented this year, the most notable is the Tramonto d'Oca '99, almost entirely from sangiovese and clear evidence of the ambitions of Poggio Bonelli. An expert hand has been at work selecting the fruit and in the use of oak which, if slightly prominent, is nonetheless essential for increasing tannic depth. The wine is solid, concentrated and even on the palate. The '98 Tramonto, which came close to getting Two Glasses, is not very eloquent on the nose but robust and characterful in the mouth. There are some sulphur aromas in the Chianti Classico '99 but the palate is clean, dense and vigorous, if rather austere on the finish. The Riserva '98 shows more evolved notes of leather and jam, then a rounded, more than acceptable palate.

●	Tramonto d'Oca '99	ΨΨ	5
●	Chianti Cl. Ris. '98	Ψ	4
●	Tramonto d'Oca '98	Ψ	5
●	Chianti Cl. '99	Ψ	4

CASTELNUOVO BERARDENGA (SI)

SAN FELICE
LOC. SAN FELICE
53010 CASTELNUOVO BERARDENGA (SI)
TEL. 0577359087 - 0577359088
E-MAIL: sfelice@val.it

San Felice is one of the historic estates of Chianti Classico. Its size – 200 hectares under vine – has never got in the way of the meticulous care devoted to all phases of wine production. Vigorello and the Riserva Poggio Rosso have always been the stars of their extensive range. But who is to say that the old rankings must always prevail? This year, for example, we were surprised to prefer the Riserva Il Grigio to Poggio Rosso. Is it a virtue of the former or a fault of the latter? A little of each, as is often the case. The Riserva Il Grigio '98 was in fine fettle, which has rarely been the case in the past. A robust, firm textured red with good extract, it is possibly a bit oak-dominated but still well worth Two Glasses. Poggio Rosso also got Two Glasses but although it shows impressive structure, it is more forward and the tannins are green and a bit over-extracted. High marks for the Vigorello '98, a blend of sangiovese and cabernet, despite some initial uncertainty on the nose. There is nothing uncertain about the attack on the palate, though, which proceeds apace, with densely packed tannins that fill the mouth, perhaps to excess. The laudable Belcaro '00 has an expressive bouquet of acacia blossom and sage, then a consistent, harmonious, lingering palate. Both the Chianti '99 and the white Ancherona '00 are enjoyable and well-executed.

CASTELNUOVO BERARDENGA (SI)

CASTELLO DI SELVOLE
FRAZ. VAGLIAGLI
LOC. SELVOLE
53010 CASTELNUOVO BERARDENGA (SI)
TEL. 0577322662
E-MAIL: vendite@selvole.com

Guido Busetto, who used to be a financial journalist with the Il Sole 24 Ore newspaper, is one of those people who at a certain point in their lives decide to change everything. He left Milan and his job, sold the little Cispiano property he had owned for years and purchased Selvole to live and work there, on one of the most beautiful estates in Chianti Classico. It is near Vagliagli in the western part of Castelnuovo Berardenga, in wildish countryside crisscrossed by dirt roads and baked in summer by a merciless sun. It's a place that produces powerful, alcohol-rich reds, much bigger and more muscular than those from other Chianti subzones. But the vines have to be properly looked after. Drought is a constant danger, and the yields have to be kept low. So Guido Busetto called in Stefano Porcinai, an agronomist and former oenologist of the Consorzio Chianti Classico. Stefano, too, left his job to set up on his own and has dedicated much of his time to Selvole. All of this is by way of introduction to the one wine we tasted this year, the Chianti Classico '99, their standard-label red. Well, it was sensational! Powerful and rich with a concentrated bouquet, it bore no relation whatsoever to a plain, run-of-the-mill product. And if that's the way things are going, what can we look forward to when we taste the Riserva '99 and the other wines from that vintage? But more about that next year.

● Vigorello '98	ŸŸ	6
○ Belcaro '00	ŸŸ	3*
● Chianti Cl. Il Grigio Ris. '98	ŸŸ	4
● Chianti Cl. Poggio Rosso Ris. '98	ŸŸ	5
○ Ancherona Chardonnay '00	Ÿ	4
● Chianti Cl. '99	Ÿ	4
● Vigorello '88	ŸŸŸ	5
● Chianti Cl. Poggio Rosso Ris. '90	ŸŸŸ	4
● Vigorello '97	ŸŸŸ	5
● Vigorello '95	ŸŸ	5
● Chianti Cl. Poggio Rosso Ris. '96	ŸŸ	5
● Chianti Cl. Poggio Rosso Ris. '97	ŸŸ	5

● Chianti Cl. '99	ŸŸ	4
● Chianti Cl. Ris. '96	ŸŸ	5
● Barullo '97	ŸŸ	6
● Chianti Cl. '98	ŸŸ	4
● Chianti Cl. '97	Ÿ	4

CASTELNUOVO BERARDENGA (SI)

Villa Arceno
Loc. Arceno
53010 Castelnuovo Berardenga (SI)
tel. 0577359346

Villa Arceno, which has belonged for some years to the well-known California-based Kendall-Jackson group, is a large estate of about 900 hectares, in a part of Castelnuovo Berardenga that is extraordinarily well-suited to viticulture. Both the land and its exposure are absolutely magnificent, and the American company made a wise decision investing here. It is probably no coincidence that the best wine – and what a wine it is! – to come out of Villa Arceno this year is a cabernet sauvignon, a variety that is second nature to Californians. It's a really lovely red, combining the warmth of the terroir with faultless technical execution. The oak, for example, is kept at a respectful distance by the richness of the fruit. And the racy energy and firm presence of the structure never mask the elegance of this Cabernet Sauvignon. The other estate wines are, it has to be said, way below this level. The Syrah '99 is generally successful, despite its medium body and overall simplicity. The quite good Arguzzio '98 shows firmness on a palate that fails to reflect the aromas of the slightly reduced nose. The '98 editions of the Chianti Classico Riserva and the Merlot need some fine-tuning. They both show signs of forwardness and harsh, dry tannins.

● Cabernet Sauvignon '99	▼▼	5
● Syrah '99	▼▼	5
● Arguzzio '98	▼	4
● Chianti Cl. Ris. '98		4
● Merlot '98		5

CIVITELLA PAGANICO (GR)

Le Capannacce
Loc. Pari
58040 Civitella Paganico (GR)
tel. 0564908848

In the northern reaches of the province of Grosseto, near the border with that of Siena, in what is now the Montecucco DOC zone, Fattoria Le Capannacce has taken centre stage with a cool assurance. For the first time, it has presented an extremely interesting red, the Poggio Crocino '98, an unusual blend of one half sangiovese, 20 per cent syrah and 30 per cent Grenache. It spent some 16 months in 450-litre tonneaux, and about 7,000 bottles were produced. At our tastings, it caused quite a stir. The bouquet is rich, intense and most original, a series of contrasting aromas including bramble jam, black pepper, earth, tobacco and Oriental spice. The palate is soft, full-bodied, voluptuous, seamless in its progression and long on the finish. A quite wonderful wine with an intriguing personality on both nose and palate, and a touch of the exotic. The estate, which covers 136 hectares, nine of which are under vine, is mostly engaged in the production of Capannacce (60,000 bottles), from sangiovese with one fifth syrah. This red offers lots of fruit, of which there is abundant evidence on the nose, together with riper tones of bramble jam. The attack on the palate is powerful, the concentration good and only a little tannic exuberance disturbs the finish.

● Poggio Crocino '98	▼▼	5
● Capannacce '99	▼	3

COLLE DI VAL D'ELSA (SI)

FATTORIA IL PALAGIO
FRAZ. CASTEL S. GIMIGNANO
LOC. IL PALAGIO
53030 COLLE DI VAL D'ELSA (SI)
TEL. 0577953004
E-MAIL: info@ilpalagio.it

Oenologist Walter Sovran, who is at the helm of the Zonin-owned Fattoria il Palagio, always manages to produce interesting, well-made wines, in keeping with the definite improvement that has marked group production in recent years. Of the various wines we tasted – and there are more on offer every year – both the Sauvignon '00 and the special selection Vernaccia La Gentilesca '00 fully deserve their Two Glasses. The well-executed Sauvignon is perfectly varietal on the intriguing nose, where classic aromas of tomato leaf, musk and aromatic herbs are joined by notes of apple, pear and tropical fruit, all carried through onto the palate, where the finish is dominated by delightful fruit. The excellent Vernaccia La Gentilesca, pale straw-yellow in hue, shows a stylish, intense nose with notes of peach and pineapple and a well-judged vanilla nuance. Good depth and balance are apparent on the palate; the finish is long and leisurely. Another wine that took our fancy was the Chardonnay '00, which came very close to winning Two Glasses. Vivid straw-yellow in colour, it displays an intense, lingering fragrance with rich notes of tropical fruit and butter, lifted by faint hints of well-amalgamated oak. The palate is soft, warm and structured but the finish is a bit weak. The Vernaccia Abbazia di Monte Oliveto is interesting, as usual, with its fruity, succulent nose and warm, enjoyable palate. Lastly, the successful Chianti Colli Senesi '00 is fruit-rich and clean in the mouth, with tannins just slightly out of control.

○ Il Palagio Sauvignon '00	🍷🍷	3*
○ Vernaccia di S. Gimignano La Gentilesca '00	🍷🍷	4
● Chianti Colli Senesi Il Palagio '00	🍷	3
○ Il Palagio Chardonnay '00	🍷	3
○ Vernaccia di S. Gimignano Abbazia di Monteoliveto '00	🍷	3
○ Il Palagio Sauvignon '97	🍷🍷	2
○ Il Palagio Sauvignon '98	🍷🍷	2
○ Vernaccia di S. Gimignano La Gentilesca '98	🍷🍷	4
○ Il Palagio Sauvignon '99	🍷🍷	3
○ Vernaccia di S. Gimignano La Gentilesca '99	🍷🍷	4
● Chianti Colli Senesi Il Palagio '99	🍷	3

CORTONA (AR)

TENIMENTI LUIGI D'ALESSANDRO
FRAZ. CAMUCIA
VIA DI MANZANO, 15
52044 CORTONA (AR)
TEL. 0575618667
E-MAIL: tenimenti.dalessandro@flashnet.it

The syrah-based Podere Il Bosco is unquestionably the flagship wine from the Tenimenti Luigi d'Alessandro. Indeed, the excellence of this shining star has encouraged other Tuscan producers to make serious efforts with syrah, which has consequently become more widespread in regional vineyards. Although the '99 Il Bosco just missed getting another Three Glass score, it does provide further evidence to show that it is a very serious red indeed. Well-meshed notes of wonderfully pure fruit greet the nose, together with a discreet oaky tone, and the hints of fresh spice and aromatic herbs make your mouth water. The palate is thoroughly satisfying, elegant and very surefooted. The fruit has clearly been given its head and is unencumbered by oak or the lively tannins. So what's missing? Concentration? No, there's plenty of that, and in any case you can't determine the value of a wine by its weight. Perhaps just a touch more of character, of caprice, of complexity wouldn't hurt. But it did win Two red Glasses, which is very nearly Three. D'Alessandro is not limited to syrah alone, however. Of their other wines, we were able to taste only the Podere Fontarca '00, and we must say that it, too, is a very good bottle indeed. The tropical fruit, honey, chamomile and vanilla aromas are rich, intense and very enjoyable. The palate is crisp and well-rounded, the finish leisurely. Lastly, the Vin Santo '93, which we retasted, again revealed itself to be an excellent and most interesting wine.

● Podere Il Bosco '99	🍷🍷	6
○ Podere Fontarca '00	🍷🍷	4*
● Podere Il Bosco '95	🍷🍷🍷	5
● Podere Il Bosco '97	🍷🍷🍷	5
● Vigna del Bosco '92	🍷🍷	5
● Vigna del Bosco '93	🍷🍷	4
○ Vin Santo '93	🍷🍷	5
○ Podere Fontarca '94	🍷🍷	4
● Podere Il Bosco '94	🍷🍷	5
● Podere Il Bosco '96	🍷🍷	5
● Migliara '97	🍷🍷	5
○ Podere Fontarca '98	🍷🍷	4
● Podere Il Bosco '98	🍷🍷	5
○ Podere Fontarca '99	🍷🍷	4

FAUGLIA (PI)

I Giusti e Zanza
Via dei Puntoni, 9
56043 Fauglia (PI)
tel. 058544354
e-mail: igiustiezanza@tin.it

Paolo Giusti and Fabio Zanza, well aware that they can't rush their vineyards if they are to make the major wines they have in mind, continue to work steadily. This year, they presented their customary brace of reds, which live up to expectations and are gradually acquiring more distinct identities. Both the Dulcamara, a blend of cabernet and merlot, and the Belcore, from sangiovese and merlot, again did very well. The two partners intend, with time, to make the former their top wine and the latter the "second vin" of the estate. At the moment, however, the class distinction is not so clear, because of the charmingly seductive sweetness of the fruit in the Belcore '99. Well-defined overtones of black cherry and ripe bramble, together with refreshing notes of black pepper, shape the bouquet. The palate, after an engaging entry, is soft and distinctly succulent. The finish, the wine's only evident weakness, is rather light and generally unexciting. The Dulcamara '98 is another story. Definitely better balanced than in the past, it has an elegant, silky progression and a long finish. The fruit makes less of an impact, but there is more complexity and depth. Meanwhile we expect the vines, in the fullness of time, to do the rest of the job, that is to confer a more complete ripeness and tone down the vegetal notes.

Wine	Rating	Score
● Dulcamara '98	🍷🍷	6
● Belcore '99	🍷🍷	4*
● Dulcamara '97	🍷🍷	5
● Belcore '98	🍷🍷	4

FAUGLIA (PI)

Fattoria Uccelliera
Via Pontita, 26
56043 Fauglia (PI)
tel. 050662747
e-mail: info@uccelliera.it

Fattoria dell'Uccelliera's top bottle, the Castellaccio, a blend of sangiovese with a little cabernet sauvignon, has again proved itself to be one of the most exciting wines in the province of Pisa. And it has also given further signs of the improvement that has quietly been going on at the estate for a number of years. Careful grape selection at harvest time means that perfectly ripe fruit is brought to the cellar. The Castellaccio is then aged in barriques, half of which are new, for about 15 months. The result is, as we found, an excellent wine, which came within an inch of Three Glasses. The most immediately striking characteristics are its balance and depth, but you soon also notice the richness of the fruit, the full body and the excellent amalgamation of tannins and wood. What then is wanting to make it that little bit better? Probably a tad more personality and rather less forward vegetal nuances. But we're splitting hairs. The Chianti '99, more modest in its aspirations, does have character. The intense bouquet includes bramble tones, toasty oak and a faint hint of animal notes. In the mouth, it reveals firm body, evident tannins and good length. The white Ficaia '00 seemed good enough but less crisply defined than it has been on other occasions.

Wine	Rating	Score
● Castellaccio Rosso '98	🍷🍷	5
○ Ficaia '00	🍷	3
● Chianti '99	🍷	3*
● Castellaccio Rosso '93	🍷🍷	4
● Castellaccio Rosso '95	🍷🍷	4
○ Castellaccio Bianco '96	🍷🍷	4
● Castellaccio Rosso '96	🍷🍷	4
○ Vin Santo Xantos '96	🍷🍷	5
● Castellaccio Rosso '97	🍷🍷	4
○ Castellaccio Bianco '98	🍷🍷	4
○ Castellaccio Bianco '99	🍷🍷	4
● Chianti '95	🍷	3
● Chianti '96	🍷	3
● Chianti '97	🍷	3
● Chianti '98	🍷	3

FIRENZE

★ MARCHESI ANTINORI
P.zza degli Antinori, 3
50123 Firenze
tel. 05523595
E-MAIL: antinori@antinori.it

It would seem that Antinori has no intention of giving up its role as leader in the Italian wine world. It has long held the position, thanks to the extraordinary merits of the team, made up of managers, technicians and ordinary agricultural workers, all of whom contribute to maintaining a really remarkable level of excellence. And it is all co-ordinated and inspired by Piero Antinori, the most lucid and intelligent entrepreneur that Italian wine can claim. For some years, he has been seconded at the helm by the able Renzo Cotarella as general manager and by his own three daughters, Albiera, Allegra and Alessia. Comment on the wines seems almost superfluous, as they are all classics. But e have a job to do, so we shall draw your attention to a good version of Solaia, the '98. It may not have the power and softness of the '97, but it had little trouble in picking up its Three Glasses. It is, of course, a blend of cabernet sauvignon with a little sangiovese. The Tignanello '98 is one of the best versions made in recent years and is obtained, as everyone knows, from sangiovese with a little cabernet sauvignon. Among the serried ranks of the other Antinori wines, all of which are at least well executed, we would point out the two Chianti Classicos – Tenute del Marchese Riserva '98 and Badia a Passignano Riserva '98 – but also the unassuming Santa Cristina '00, a direct, pleasing red of which this is a particularly successful version. So there's the usual cupboardful of Glasses and the usual reliability. Finally, it should also be noted that prices for most of the wines are by no means over the top. Real professionals.

FIRENZE

Tenute Folonari
Por Santa Maria, 8
50122 Firenze
tel. 055210771

We begin our profile with the news that Ambrogio Folonari and his son Giovanni are now the sole owners of these estates. And like the genuine winemen they are, they continue to present an excellent range that includes some outstanding bottles. This year, we were unable to taste the '99 versions of the two Cabreos, the red Il Borgo and the white La Pietra, so we shall have to review them on our next visit. The Pareto '98, however, the famous red made from cabernet sauvignon and produced on the Nozzole estate at Greve in Chianti, did extremely well. It has all the force of the best vintages together with an extraordinary elegance on the palate and particularly stylish balsamic and wild berry aromas. Three Glasses easily earned. Further good things from Nozzole are the excellent Chianti Classico La Forra Riserva '98 and the enjoyable Le Bruniche '00, predominantly chardonnay-based. As for the other estates, Gracciano Svetoni in Montepulciano and Spalletti in Rufina, we should mention a good version of Nobile '98, the Calvano, and of Rosso di Montepulciano '99, the Pancole. And then there's the super-traditional Chianti Rufina Poggio Reale Riserva '98, a genuine local classic. This is obviously a rich and varied range, which will be even more exciting next year with the two Cabreos and a surprise or two that could come from other parts of Tuscany. Perhaps even from Bolgheri or thereabouts.

● Solaia '98	▼▼▼	6
● Tignanello '98	▼▼	6
● Chianti Cl. Badia a Passignano Ris. '98	▼▼	5
● Chianti Cl. Tenute del Marchese Ris. '98	▼▼	5
● Santa Cristina '00	▼	3
● Tignanello '85	▼▼▼	6
● Solaia '90	▼▼▼	6
● Tignanello '93	▼▼▼	6
● Solaia '95	▼▼▼	6
● Chianti Cl. Badia a Passignano Ris. '97	▼▼▼	5
● Solaia '97	▼▼▼	6
● Tignanello '97	▼▼	6

● Il Pareto '98	▼▼▼	6
● Chianti Cl. La Forra Ris. '98	▼▼	5
● Nobile di Montepulciano Calvano '98	▼▼	5
○ Le Bruniche '00	▼	4
● Chianti Rufina Poggio Reale Ris. '98	▼	5
● Rosso di Montepulciano Pancole '99	▼	4
● Il Pareto '88	▼▼▼	6
● Chianti Cl. La Forra Ris. '90	▼▼▼	5
● Il Pareto '90	▼▼▼	6
● Il Pareto '93	▼▼▼	6
● Il Pareto '97	▼▼▼	6
● Cabreo Il Borgo '98	▼▼	6
○ Cabreo La Pietra '98	▼▼	6
● Chianti Cl. Nozzole '98	▼	4

FIRENZE

MARCHESI DE' FRESCOBALDI
VIA S. SPIRITO, 11
50125 FIRENZE
TEL. 05527141
E-MAIL: info@frescobaldi.it

Here's a summary of what the latest tastings of the wines from this historic Florentine estate revealed: the fine quality of past years has been maintained, with some pleasant surprises and, essentially, no disappointments. We did not get to try the Mormoreto, which will be released next year. The champion this time is the Montesodi, which won Three Glasses for the fifth time. It is still a very young wine, so it has to be judged for what it promises to offer. Wines from Rufina tend to last a very long time but are also slow to come out. But the Montesodi '99 is already quite eloquent. It shows great intensity of colour in the glass. The aromas are still developing and the oak makes its presence felt but notes of plum and spice are also evident. On the palate, it is firm, full-bodied and shows good depth. The Montesodi '98 is good but the structure is less striking. Here, too, oak rules the roost but the fruit doesn't seem to have the energy to assert itself. The Chianti Rufina Nipozzano '98 is well-defined, and the flavour is evenly distributed, but there is an insistent vegetal tone in the bouquet. The Pomino Il Benefizio '99, however, seemed very good. It boasts complexity on the nose and a firm, balanced palate with a long finish. The Pomino Bianco '00 is, naturally enough, a simpler white but a well-executed one. The Pomino Rosso '98 is straightforward, pleasing and fruitily fragrant, if a bit light on the finish. The clean, dense Chianti Castiglioni is surprisingly good, particularly for its price.

FIRENZE

ENRICO PIERAZZUOLI
LOC. CAPRAIA FIORENTINA
VIA VALICARDA, 35
50056 FIRENZE
TEL. 0571910078
E-MAIL: info@enricopierazzuoli.com

Young Enrico Pierazzuoli divides his wine-producing time among three different estates: Tenuta Le Farnete in Carmignano, Tenuta Cantagallo in Montalbano and Fattoria Matroneo in Chianti Classico. This inevitably leads to a certain amount of dissipated energy. And at this year's tastings, we did notice some inconsistencies in both quality and style. There were excellent bottles and some disappointments. This is, of course, quite normal when a winery is in the midst of expanding and the wines come from different places but Enrico will have to set about keeping his range of wines more even if he wants to establish himself as one of the most interesting and talented producers in the region. There's no doubt that the Gioveto '98 is very good. It may lack a little elegance and finesse but it offers lots of ripe fruit, nuances of bramble jam and a concentrated, lingering palate. The Chianti Classico Matroneo '98 starts off well with nice depth of colour and bouquet. Then the full-bodied palate reveals rich extract, silky tannins and a long finish. Altogether very good, but it needs a tad more personality and terroir-driven distinctiveness. The Carmignano '98 is soft and round, but excessive vegetal notes make it less interesting. The riesling-based Carleto '00 seemed pleasing but simple while we found the Carmignano '99 and the Chianti Montalbano '99 rather disappointing.

	Wine	Rating	Score
●	Chianti Rufina Montesodi '99	♕♕♕	6
○	Pomino Il Benefizio '99	♕♕	5
●	Chianti Rufina Montesodi '98	♕♕	6
●	Chianti Castiglioni '00	♕	2*
○	Pomino Bianco '00	♕	4
●	Chianti Rufina Nipozzano Ris. '98	♕	5
●	Pomino Rosso '98	♕	5
●	Pomino Rosso '85	♕♕♕	5
●	Chianti Rufina Montesodi '88	♕♕♕	6
●	Chianti Rufina Montesodi '90	♕♕♕	6
●	Chianti Rufina Montesodi '96	♕♕♕	6
●	Chianti Rufina Montesodi '97	♕♕♕	6
●	Mormoreto '97	♕♕♕	6
●	Chianti Rufina Nipozzano Ris. '97	♕♕	5
●	Pomino Rosso '97	♕♕	5

	Wine	Rating	Score
●	Chianti Cl. Matroneo '98	♕♕	4
●	Gioveto '98	♕♕	4
○	Carleto '00	♕	4
●	Carmignano Le Farnete Ris. '98	♕	5
●	Carmignano Le Farnete '99		4
●	Chianti Montalbano '99		3
●	Carmignano Le Farnete Ris. '97	♕♕♕	5
●	Carmignano Le Farnete Ris. '92	♕♕	4
●	Carmignano Le Farnete Ris. '93	♕♕	4
●	Chianti Montalbano Ris. '93	♕♕	3
●	Carmignano Le Farnete Ris. '94	♕♕	4
●	Chianti Montalbano Ris. '94	♕♕	4
●	Carmignano Le Farnete Ris. '96	♕♕	4
○	Carleto '97	♕♕	4
●	Chianti Montalbano Ris. '97	♕♕	4

FOIANO DELLA CHIANA (AR)

FATTORIA SANTA VITTORIA
LOC. POZZO
VIA PIANA, 43
52045 FOIANO DELLA CHIANA (AR)
TEL. 057566807 - 0575966026
E-MAIL: marnicc@@iol.it

This edition of the Guide bears ample evidence of an oenological resurgence in the province of Arezzo. Santa Vittoria made its Guide debut last year so what we were looking for this time was confirmation of our good impression. This the cellar provided, indeed with a certain nonchalance, presenting a consistently good range and evident improvement in the less ambitious wines. Yet Marta Niccolai, the owner of the estate, should not now rest on her laurels. Santa Vittoria takes advantage of its excellent exposure, and the vines are tended with intelligence and care, but there is still much room for improvement. The cellar, for example, which is currently being remodelled, needs a more radical renewal of its barrel stock. Nevertheless, we are encouraged by this year's performance, and things should get better with time. The Scannagallo, from sangiovese, cabernet and a little merlot, is again the top wine in the range. The '99 is more complete than ever. Vivid ruby, with bright highlights, it offers a nose of upfront fruit that keeps the oak well in check. The palate is soft and full-bodied, the well-integrated tannins are smooth and the finish is long. The convincing Vin Santo '96 boasts a broad array of aromas: chamomile, spice, almonds and vanilla. The dense palate favours elegance over fleshiness. Lastly, the Grechetto '00 is well-made, agreeable and fragrant.

FUCECCHIO (FI)

FATTORIA DI MONTELLORI
VIA PISTOIESE, 1
50054 FUCECCHIO (FI)
TEL. 0571260641
E-MAIL: montellori@tin.it

The wines presented by Fattoria di Montellori were so consistently good that we hardly missed their star of recent years, the Salamartano. The '99 vintage of that Bordeaux blend will not, in fact, be released until next year. Meanwhile, Alessandro Nieri's array of bottles absorbed all the panel's attention, with two standing out. The Castelrapiti '97, from sangiovese with a little cabernet, is probably the best version ever of this traditional Fucecchio red. It has the authentic character and sinew of sangiovese, as well as aromatic complexity, substantial structure and an intense, lively impact on the palate. The biggest surprise, however, was the sauvignon-based Sant'Amato '00, with its well-delineated varietal expression, crisp aromas and firm, energetic thrust on the palate. This is a wine that belies the widely held belief that you can't make a serious white in Tuscany, and the price is inviting as well. The mostly sangiovese-based Vigne del Moro '99 almost captured Two Glasses. The intense bouquet opens to notes of bramble and ripe blackcurrant, laced with hints of vanilla. The broad, rounded and fairly concentrated palate reveals lively tannins. The fragrant, enjoyable Vigne del Mandorlo '00 is made from a blend of Montellori's white grapes. Finally, a toast to the excellent Brut Montellori, a traditional-method, chardonnay-based bubbly we found really successful.

○	Vin Santo '96	ΨΨ	5
●	Scannagallo '99	ΨΨ	5
○	Val di Chiana Grechetto '00	Ψ	2*
○	Vin Santo '95	ΨΨ	5
●	Scannagallo '98	ΨΨ	4
○	Chardonnay '99	Ψ	3

●	Castelrapiti Rosso '97	ΨΨ	5
○	Montellori Brut	ΨΨ	4
●	Sant'Amato '00	ΨΨ	3*
○	Vigne del Mandorlo '00	Ψ	2*
●	Vigne del Moro '99	Ψ	3
●	Castelrapiti Rosso '92	ΨΨ	5
●	Salamartano '92	ΨΨ	5
●	Castelrapiti Rosso '93	ΨΨ	5
●	Salamartano '94	ΨΨ	5
●	Castelrapiti Rosso '95	ΨΨ	4
●	Salamartano '95	ΨΨ	5
●	Salamartano '96	ΨΨ	5
●	Salamartano '97	ΨΨ	5
●	Salamartano '98	ΨΨ	6

GAIOLE IN CHIANTI (SI)

AGRICOLTORI
DEL CHIANTI GEOGRAFICO
VIA MULINACCIO, 10
53013 GAIOLE IN CHIANTI (SI)
TEL. 0577749489
E-MAIL: info@chiantigeografico.it

If there is one winery in Tuscany – and a co-operative, to boot – that always manages to put together a good range of wines at reasonable prices, it is Agricoltori del Chianti Geografico. In addition, for the past two years it has had the capable young Lorenzo Landi as consultant oenologist, and good results can already be found in the wines. The best of the lot this year is the Pulleraia '99, a Merlot di Toscana IGT with well-expressed characteristic aromas of tobacco and violets, and a soft, not overly complex but concentrated palate. Their standard-bearer, the Chianti Classico Montegiachi Riserva '98, the fruit of an actual vineyard selection, is also good. The Chianti Classico Contessa di Radda '99, from a distinctly positive local vintage, is fair and correctly executed, and the standard-label Chianti Classico '99, although simple, is a well-made red, typical of its kind, not too concentrated and very affordable. Altogether, this year's was a fine performance from a winery that has long been a benchmark for producers throughout Chianti.

GAIOLE IN CHIANTI (SI)

★ CASTELLO DI AMA
FRAZ. LECCHI IN CHIANTI
LOC. AMA
53010 GAIOLE IN CHIANTI (SI)
TEL. 0577746031
E-MAIL: info@castellodiama.com

Finding great wines again at Castello di Ama after a few puzzling years is like bumping into an old friend you haven't seen for ages. You are surprised and pleased, and very excited. We are especially pleased because we know what dedication and ambition have always inspired Lorenza Sebasti, co-owner of Ama and driving spirit in the cellar, and Marco Pallanti, oenologist and her partner at work and in life. When we tasted the Chianti Classico La Casuccia '97, we knew at once that the anonymous sample couldn't be anything but the great Castello di Ama wine. It is not often that you find a sangiovese-based red that so successfully manages to unite the elegance typical of Ama wines with such prodigious concentration, or such noble tannins with that kind of velvety softness and yet such definite character. A magical, truly great, wine, and actually worth the small fortune it costs. For once, the celebrated merlot-based Vigna L'Apparita, although excellent in the '97 version – and way better than the '96 –, seemed to accept a supporting role to exalt the glorious complexity of the Chianti Classico. The range of standard wines includes a good version of the Chianti Classico '98 (there will be no Bellavista or La Casuccia from that vintage). In addition, there is a delicious Chardonnay Il Poggio '99, which is lightly barriqued. We're glad to have Lorenza and Marco back in the Three Glass club. They have earned their place.

Wine	Glasses	Score
Chianti Cl. Montegiachi Ris. '98	ΨΨ	4
Pulleraia '99	ΨΨ	5
Chianti Cl. '99	Ψ	3*
Chianti Cl. Contessa di Radda '99	Ψ	4
Chianti Cl. Montegiachi Ris. '94	ΨΨ	4
Chianti Cl. Montegiachi Ris. '95	ΨΨ	4
I Vigneti del Geografico '95	ΨΨ	5
I Vigneti del Geografico '96	ΨΨ	5
Chianti Cl. Montegiachi Ris. '97	ΨΨ	4
I Vigneti del Geografico '97	ΨΨ	5
Chianti Cl. '98	ΨΨ	3

Wine	Glasses	Score
Chianti Cl. La Casuccia '97	ΨΨΨ	6
Vigna l'Apparita Merlot '97	ΨΨ	6
Chianti Cl. Castello di Ama '98	ΨΨ	5
Chardonnay Il Poggio '99	ΨΨ	4*
Chianti Cl. Bellavista '85	ΨΨΨ	6
Chianti Cl. Bellavista '86	ΨΨΨ	6
Chianti Cl. Bertinga '88	ΨΨΨ	6
Vigna l'Apparita Merlot '88	ΨΨΨ	6
Chianti Cl. Bellavista '90	ΨΨΨ	6
Vigna l'Apparita Merlot '90	ΨΨΨ	6
Vigna l'Apparita Merlot '91	ΨΨΨ	6
Vigna l'Apparita Merlot '92	ΨΨΨ	6
Chianti Cl. La Casuccia '90	ΨΨ	5
Chianti Cl. Bellavista '97	ΨΨ	6
Chianti Cl. Castello di Ama '97	ΨΨ	5

GAIOLE IN CHIANTI (SI)

Barone Ricasoli
Loc. Brolio
53013 Gaiole in Chianti (SI)
tel. 05777301
e-mail: barone@ricasoli.it

A long and winding road brought this historic winery from the edge of disaster in the early 1990s to its present position as the Guide's Winery of the Year. There is something miraculous about the process. And behind it is the determined, intelligent Francesco Ricasoli, aided by a first-rate team consisting of Filippo Mazzei, managing director, Maurizio Ghiori, business manager, Carlo Ferrini, oenologist, Lucia Franciosi, in charge of public relations, and a host of cellar technicians, agronomists and agricultural workers, all of whom made it possible to reorganize and revive the estate in just over seven years. We can think of no similar exploit anywhere else in Italy. This year, everything they made was extraordinarily good, as has been the case for a while now. The Chianti Classico Castello di Brolio Riserva '98 is even better than the '97 and is the best in its category. A powerful red, it boasts a richly nuanced nose that ranges from typical sangiovese aromas to smoky, almost minerally tones. The Casalferro '99, from sangiovese with a little merlot, may be young but it shows enormous potential. The Chianti Classico Brolio '99 stands out for elegance and for its fantastic value for money. The predominantly chardonnay-based Torricella '00 is barrique-aged but not at all heavy: the oak is well integrated and the wine unfurls a pervasive, enchanting softness. The Formulae '99 and the Chianti Classico Rocca Guicciarda Riserva '98 may not be quite as good as they sometimes are but they are both technically well executed. Altogether, there were no disappointments, and the superb level achieved seems to be well entrenched.

● Chianti Cl. Castello di Brolio '98	ŸŸŸ	6
● Casalferro '99	ŸŸŸ	6
○ Torricella '00	ŸŸ	5
● Chianti Cl. Brolio '99	ŸŸ	4
● Formulae '99	Ÿ	3
● Chianti Cl. Rocca Guicciarda Ris. '98	Ÿ	5
● Casalferro '95	ŸŸŸ	6
● Casalferro '96	ŸŸŸ	6
● Casalferro '97	ŸŸŸ	6
● Chianti Cl. Castello di Brolio '97	ŸŸŸ	6
● Casalferro '98	ŸŸŸ	6
● Chianti Cl. Rocca Guicciarda Ris. '97	ŸŸ	5
○ Torricella '99	ŸŸ	5

Coltibuono
Loc. Badia a Coltibuono, 2
53013 Gaiole in Chianti (SI)
tel. 057774481
e-mail: info@coltibuono.com

The enthusiastic vitality of the owner, Emanuela Stucchi Prinetti, who is also the president of the Consorzio del Marchio Storico-Chianti Classico, has turned out to be contagious. Everyone who works with her at Coltibuono seems to have caught the bug, which is why wines that until recently were considered rather lacklustre have now acquired a new dimension. We refer in particular to the white Trappoline '00, with its lovely straw-yellow colour. This introduces a delicate but enjoyable fragrance of peach and green apple, and, in the mouth, good body, an attractive balance of alcohol and acidity, and nice length. In short, it's a white we wouldn't mind drinking every day. Now for the reds. The Sangioveto '99 made an excellent impression. An intense ruby red precedes a nose dominated by berries, with bramble and blackcurrant to the fore, ennobled by well-judged toasty nuances. The powerful attack on the palate already suggests that tannins and alcohol are meshing well. We then noted depth, mouthfilling body and intensity, and a finish of good length. We also liked the Riserva '98. The aromas, initially muffled and rather fuzzy, open to reveal notes of cherry and plum. The palate is well-rounded, thanks to powerful alcohol, and underpinned by close-knit tannins. The two vintage Chiantis, however, still get One Glass each. The R.S. selection is intriguing on the nose, with its scents of flint and ripe fruit, then harmonious on the palate, where forward acidity is balanced by body. The basic version is old-fashioned. Uncomplicated and enjoyable, it offers a fresh fruity fragrance and medium body. The Trappoline '00, which is very well made, nearly won Two Glasses.

● Chianti Cl. Ris. '98	ŸŸ	5
● Sangioveto '99	ŸŸ	6
○ Trappoline '00	Ÿ	3
● Chianti Cl. '99	Ÿ	4
● Chianti Cl. R. S. '99	Ÿ	3
● Sangioveto '95	ŸŸŸ	6
● Sangioveto '86	ŸŸ	6
● Chianti Cl. Ris. '88	ŸŸ	4
● Sangioveto '88	ŸŸ	6
● Chianti Cl. Ris. '90	ŸŸ	4
● Sangioveto '90	ŸŸ	6
● Sangioveto '94	ŸŸ	6
● Chianti Cl. Ris. '95	ŸŸ	5
● Chianti Cl. Ris. '96	ŸŸ	5
● Sangioveto '97	ŸŸ	6

GAIOLE IN CHIANTI (SI)

IL COLOMBAIO DI CENCIO
LOC. CORNIA
53013 GAIOLE IN CHIANTI (SI)
TEL. 0577747178

Il Colombaio di Cencio didn't carry off Three Glasses this time but is still one of the most interesting wineries in Chianti Classico. This year, it was the turn of the '98 Il Futuro, the Supertuscan from sangiovese and cabernet sauvignon which won top honours for the '95 and '97. But you can't win all the time, especially when the vintage is good but not exceptional. Il Futuro '98 did, however, make it to our finals, where it cut a fine figure. It is released, as usual, in a very heavy and rather awkward bottle, but it offers an intense bouquet with a note of fruit shot through with light balsamic nuances. The palate is full-bodied and very concentrated; it is the vintage's fault if the finish is insufficiently long. The very good Chianti Classico I Massi Riserva '98 did almost as well. It combines great elegance with considerable body and very smooth, not at all aggressive tannins. The nose is typical of a good Chianti Classico from Gaiole, with flowery notes of violets melding with more classic black cherry. It was well worth its Two Glasses. Werner Wilhelm, the owner of the estate, and Jacopo Morganti, the manager, have a lot to be proud of.

● Il Futuro '98	🍷🍷	6
● Chianti Classico I Massi Ris. '98	🍷🍷	6
● Il Futuro '95	🍷🍷🍷	6
● Il Futuro '97	🍷🍷🍷	6
● Chianti Cl. '95	🍷🍷	4
● Chianti Cl. Ris. '97	🍷🍷	4
● Chianti Cl. '96	🍷	4

GAIOLE IN CHIANTI (SI)

PODERE IL PALAZZINO
LOC. IL PALAZZINO
53013 GAIOLE IN CHIANTI (SI)
TEL. 0577747008
E-MAIL: palazzino@chianticlassico.com

Il Palazzino made a remarkably good showing this year. Alessandro Sderci's estate regained its full profile in the last edition of the Guide, having impressed with the well-defined expressiveness of its wines but we were not expecting such a fine performance this time. The setting here is, by the way, in one of the finest subzones of Chianti Classico and the owners have given their all to it, seeking particularly to bring out elegance and "goût de terroir" in their wines. In the past, it was not always possible to reconcile these qualities with thrust in the structure. But in the past few years, Il Palazzino has become more judicious in its use of oak, and we detected evidence of new, top-quality barrel stock. The Riserva Grosso Sanese '95, the top of the range, is a great Chianti Classico, powerful, rounded, luscious and deep. It's just as harmonious and elegant as it is big and rich. The Riserva '96 does not lag far behind it, with its intense aromas of black berries, violets and spice. The well-rounded, concentrated palate reveals tight-knit tannins. An excellent wine, and very fresh for a '96. The Riserva '98 fits neatly into this distinguished company with its solid, well-balanced structure, although rather noticeable oak makes it just a little less interesting. The Chianti Argenina '99 boasts lively concentrated fruit, positive progression on the palate and perfect balance. The Chianti La Pieve '99 is slightly unfocused on the nose but offers style, substance and complexity.

● Chianti Cl. Grosso Sanese Ris. '95	🍷🍷	5
● Chianti Cl. Grosso Sanese Ris. '96	🍷🍷	5
● Chianti Cl. Grosso Sanese '98	🍷🍷	5
● Chianti Cl. Argenina '99	🍷🍷	4
● Chianti Cl. La Pieve '99	🍷🍷	4
● Chianti Cl. Grosso Sanese Ris. '93	🍷🍷	5
● Chianti Cl. Grosso Sanese Ris. '94	🍷🍷	5
● Chianti Cl. '93	🍷	4

GAIOLE IN CHIANTI (SI)

Castello di Lucignano
Loc. Lucignano
53013 Gaiole in Chianti (SI)
tel. 0577747810
e-mail: gklucignano@libero.it

Castello di Lucignano embraces 53 hectares, 15 of which are under vine and almost all registered as Chianti Classico DOCG. This is the cellar's first appearance in the Guide and they earned with four distinctly attractive wines. The raw material is clearly very good and they know how to use oak so that it doesn't get in the way. Credit is due, obviously, to their oenologist, Fabrizio Ciufoli. We were very much struck by the Riserva '97, which combined sturdy structure with admirable character and recognizable territory-derived characteristics. The bouquet opens onto earthy and mineral tones against a backdrop of tobacco and liquorice. The palate reveals solid substance, well-integrated extract and the bright typicity of the sangiovese grape. The very interesting Solissimo '97 shows dense aromas of ripe fruit, hints of liquorice and toasty oak-derived undertones. After a warm, rounded attack, the palate develops satisfyingly and with a certain panache, then the sound finish is only slightly dried by tannins. The '98 version of the Solissimo is less distinguished, but then the vintage was not a great one. The taste profile is par for the course but it does have good balance. And the Chianti '99 is correct, if unexciting.

GAIOLE IN CHIANTI (SI)

Castello di Meleto
Loc. Cantina di Ponte di Meleto, 1
53013 Gaiole in Chianti (SI)
tel. 0577749217 - 0577749129
e-mail: info@castellomeleto.it

Castello di Meleto is one of the most important producers in the Chianti Classico zone, with more than 170 hectares of densely planted vines. The painstaking work of replanting the vineyards, which has been under way for some years, is beginning to bring results. The best of the four wines we tasted was the Rainero '99, a monovarietal sangiovese with an almost opaque intense ruby hue. The elegant, harmonious nose boasts wild berry notes enhanced by sweet nuances, with vanilla to the fore, all reflected on the palate, where neither the fine-grained tannins nor the alcohol prevails. The rising finish is succulent and meaty. The Fiore '98 did not seem quite so good. A purple-tinged ruby hue ushers in over-ripe aromas of plum, offset to some extent by spicy notes. It is lean in the mouth, and the acidity is rather forward, but it's still a very quaffable wine with a satisfying finish. The interesting Chianti Classico '99 offers an astonishing amount of fruit on the nose, where cherry leads the pack, but with no little style. The complex palate is soft almost to a fault but the finish perks up with acidity that adds just the right note of crispness. Lastly, the Riserva '98, which combines a youthful fragrance of strawberry and raspberry with a lean acidity-dominated body, is a straightforward, enjoyable wine.

● Chianti Cl. Ris. '97	♟♟	4
● Solissimo '97	♟♟	5
● Solissimo '98	♟	5
● Chianti Cl. '99	♟	4

● Chianti Cl. '99	♟♟	4
● Rainero '99	♟♟	5
● Chianti Cl. Ris. '98	♟	4
● Fiore '98	♟	5
● Fiore '97	♟♟	5
● Pieve di Spaltenna Alle Fonti '98	♟♟	5
● Chianti Cl. Ris. '97	♟	4
● Chianti Cl. Pieve di Spaltenna '98	♟	3
● Rainero '98	♟	5

GAIOLE IN CHIANTI (SI)

Montiverdi
Loc. Montiverdi
53013 Gaiole in Chianti (SI)
Tel. 0577749305 - 028378808

We have both compliments and criticism to offer Montiverdi this year. The compliments are for the wines they presented, which were generally good and often excellent. But we feel that there are simply too many different labels, which may well mean time and energy is being dissipated. It's not a much of a criticism, though, because in the end it is the excellent quality of the wines that counts. The really fine cabernet-based Le Borranine '97, which is clearly very well executed, displays remarkable elegance, smooth tannins and a long finish. High marks, too, for the Vigneto Cipressone '97, with its scents of sweet tobacco and bramble jam and powerful, full-bodied, lingering palate. The Riserva Ventesimo '97, in addition to its stylish presentation, offers other gustatory pleasures: depth on the nose, with notes of dark berries and spicy oak, and a well-balanced, weighty palate with a well-sustained development and just a hint of tannin-induced drying on the finish. The Riserva '97 did just as well. The bouquet is clean and not without finesse, showing nuances of red berries, liquorice and vanilla. In the mouth, it is medium-bodied, refreshing and well-balanced. The Villa di Maisano Quello '97 is convincing – we don't like the name, which means "That One" – although slightly overburdened with oak. It has a dense, concentrated structure with tannins that are just a bit too lively. The Villa Maisano '98 is round, agreeable and fairly characteristic. The Chianti '98 is admirably harmonious but light on the finish. The Riserva Villa Maisano '97, is well made but a little forward and the '97 Villa Maisano Questo ("This One"), also nicely crafted, has a woody tone that masks the fruit.

GAIOLE IN CHIANTI (SI)

S. M. Tenimenti Pile e Lamole
Loc. Vistarenni
53013 Gaiole in Chianti (SI)
Tel. 0577738186 - 0577738549
E-mail: a.ali@vistarenni.com

Once again the Riserva Campolungo is head of the class at Pile e Lamole. The colour of this Chianti Classico proclaims its youth – intense ruby with a garnet rim – and the fragrance tells the same tale, with its still evident fruit, few tertiary aromas, and discreetly emphasized oak. The attack in the mouth is dense and balanced, the mid palate is well-paced by the wood and the wine keeps expanding to a clear-cut finish. The Codirosso '99, from sangiovese, did well without thrilling us particularly. Colour and fragrance are a bit forward, in fact the wine is not particularly vigorous, but it is well conceived, and soft and harmonious in its development. The Riserva '97 Lamole di Lamole is reasonable although no heavyweight. Notes of toasty oak and black pepper on the nose lead into a pleasing and well co-ordinated, if not very dense, palate. The Lamole Barrique '98, which displays rather simple fruity scents and a medium-bodied palate with a bitterish finish, is an acceptable tipple. One small Glass goes to the Lamole di Lamole '99, which is correct and balanced but not especially irresistible, while the clean but not very energetic Villa Vistarenni '99 gets only a mention. Overall, the report is more than satisfactory but perhaps, with all these different labels, the cellar is in danger of spreading itself a bit thin.

● Chianti Cl. Ris. '97	♀♀	4
● Chianti Cl. Ventesimo Ris. '97	♀♀	5
● Chianti Cl. Vigneto Cipressone '97	♀♀	5
● Chianti Cl. Villa Maisano Quello '97	♀♀	5
● Le Borranine '97	♀♀	5
● Chianti Cl. Villa Maisano Questo '97	♀	5
● Chianti Cl. Villa Maisano Ris. '97	♀	4
● Chianti Cl. '98	♀	3
● Chianti Cl. Villa Maisano '98	♀	4
● Chianti Cl. Villa Maisano Quello '96	♀♀	5

● Chianti Cl. Campolungo Ris. '97	♀♀	5
● Codirosso '99	♀♀	5
● Chianti Cl. Lamole di Lamole Ris. '97	♀	4
● Chianti Cl. Lamole Barrique '98	♀	4
● Chianti Cl. Lamole di Lamole '99	♀	3
● Chianti Cl. Villa Vistarenni '99		3
● Chianti Cl. Campolungo Ris. '94	♀♀	4
● Chianti Cl. Campolungo Ris. '95	♀♀	4
● Chianti Cl. Lamole di Lamole Ris. '95	♀♀	4
● Chianti Cl. Villa Vistarenni '95	♀♀	4
● Codirosso '95	♀♀	5
● Chianti Cl. Lamole di Lamole '97	♀♀	3

GAIOLE IN CHIANTI (SI)

RIECINE
LOC. RIECINE
53013 GAIOLE IN CHIANTI (SI)
TEL. 0577749098 - 0577744046
E-MAIL: riecine@riecine.com

After a brief pause, Riecine has again put together a collection of crystal in keeping with its pedigree. Sean O'Callaghan hasn't exactly surprised us with this performance, because Riecine's wines have always done well, but the curious thing is that the winner of our highest award, as well as the Chianti Classico Riserva, which also came within an ace of Three Glasses, were both '98s, a vintage that many consider less than brilliant in the Chianti zone. But this, too, is comprehensible if you consider the exceptional qualities of the Riecine terroir and the meticulous care that is lavished on these vineyards. The sangiovese-based La Gioia '98 has become one of the jewels in Tuscany's oenological crown. Terroir and grape variety are beautifully interpreted, as is the Riecine style, which favours elegance. The admirable depth of colour and bouquet is reflected in the outstanding length of the finish and in the fascinatingly dense, full-bodied palate. As we mentioned, the Riserva '98 refused to retire quietly into the wings. This wine fought its way to the final tastings, vying with the Supertuscan for the spotlight. It offers considerable personality and a warm, well-rounded palate with close-knit, fine-grained tannins. We should add that both these champions reveal the masterly use of oak, which makes a significant contribution to their overall profile. We close with another success, the Chianti '99, which revealed enjoyable fruit, good control on the palate and excellent balance.

● La Gioia '98	▼▼▼	6
● Chianti Cl. Ris. '98	▼▼	5
● Chianti Cl. '99	▼▼	4
● Chianti Cl. Ris. '86	▼▼▼	5
● Chianti Cl. Ris. '88	▼▼▼	6
● La Gioia '95	▼▼▼	6
● Chianti Cl. Ris. '93	▼▼	5
● La Gioia '93	▼▼	5
● Chianti Cl. Ris. '94	▼▼	5
● La Gioia '94	▼▼	5
● Chianti Cl. Ris. '95	▼▼	6
● Chianti Cl. Ris. '96	▼▼	6
● La Gioia '96	▼▼	6
● Chianti Cl. Ris. '97	▼▼	5
● La Gioia '97	▼▼	6

GAIOLE IN CHIANTI (SI)

ROCCA DI CASTAGNOLI
LOC. CASTAGNOLI
53010 GAIOLE IN CHIANTI (SI)
TEL. 0577731004
E-MAIL: agricolarocca@libero.it

Rocca di Castagnoli is an important producer in Chianti Classico, both for its size – 1,320 hectares, of which 200 are under vine – and because of the constant improvement that have been made, particularly in the last few years. Not all the wines we tasted this time were wonderful, we must confess, but there is little one can do about the weather. The Riserva Capraia, as has been the case for a while now, is very good. It can't be said to have an outstanding aromatic personality. Indeed, we seem to find the duo "black berry fruit and toasty oak" wherever we turn in Tuscany, and it's there in the Riserva Capraia as well. Still, this is not always a bad thing, particularly when, as here, the palate answers the call of the nose with an appropriately dense, concentrated and complex structure. The Stielle '98, a classic Chianti blend of sangiovese and cabernet, was even more compelling. It's a lovely big wine, dense, powerful, long on the finish and well-balanced. The Chianti '99 is a relaxing wine. No racking your brains about how it was made or what with: it's enjoyable, direct, clean and quaffable. End of story. The Riserva Poggio ai Frati '98 is fair but rather forward, and the equally decent Cabernet Buriano '98 shows good body but has a super-ripe nose that is short on finesse.

● Chianti Cl. Capraia Ris. '98	▼▼	5
● Stielle '98	▼▼	5
● Buriano '98	▼	6
● Chianti Cl. '99	▼	3
● Chianti Cl. Poggio a' Frati Ris. '98	▼	5
● Buriano '96	▼▼	5
● Chianti Cl. Capraia Ris. '96	▼▼	4
● Stielle '96	▼▼	5
● Buriano '97	▼▼	5
● Chianti Cl. Capraia Ris. '97	▼▼	5
● Chianti Cl. Poggio a' Frati Ris. '97	▼▼	4
● Stielle '97	▼▼	5

GAIOLE IN CHIANTI (SI)

Rocca di Montegrossi
Fraz. Monti in Chianti
Loc. San Marcellino, 21
53013 Gaiole in Chianti (SI)
Tel. 0577747267
E-mail: rocca.di.montegrossi@chianticlassico.com

The restructuring and modernization of the cellar, completed in September 2000, have given the missing touch to Marco Ricasoli's Rocca di Montegrossi, propelling this historic estate into the front ranks of producers in Chianti. The 18 hectares of vineyard have also acquired a better profile, with 70 per cent planted to sangiovese, small amounts given over to other native varieties, and a little more than three hectares recently set aside for merlot and cabernet sauvignon. Starting with the 2002 harvest, the last two varieties will form part of the blend of the Geremia, the estate Supertuscan and previously a monovarietal sangiovese. But apart from all these promising plans, the cellar makes a wine which has always been a model of tradition and excellence: the Vin Santo. The little bottles of the '94 Rocca di Montegrossi are real gems. Unfortunately, they are also as rare as precious stones, too. This wine is at the very top of the range for density, complexity and aromatic length. But our tastings provided evidence of other interesting wines as well. The Chianti Classico '99, for example, while not ecstasy-inducing, does give real pleasure. Sound, well-balanced and substantial, it slips down very easily. The aforesaid sangiovese Geremia '98 is less rational and more impulsive. A bit fuzzy on the nose, it is nonetheless dynamic and full of character on the palate. Lastly, the Riserva San Marcellino, an admirably fresh wine, is by no means bad.

GAIOLE IN CHIANTI (SI)

San Giusto a Rentennano
Fraz. Monti in Chianti
Loc. San Giusto a Rentennano
53013 Gaiole in Chianti (SI)
Tel. 0577747121
E-mail: sangiustorentennano@chiantinet.it

Connoisseurs will need no introduction to the Martini di Cigala family's estate. But if you're new to Italian wine, you should know that San Giusto a Rentennano is a cornerstone of Tuscan oenology and makes, as opposed to just talking about, genuine "vins de terroir". San Giusto wines have always been closely bound up with their territory, and have tended to show a particular preference for sangiovese, the undisputed prince of Chianti Classico. They express typicity, but not hidebound, dusty traditionalism. A good example is La Ricolma, a merlot produced in small quantities which manages to suggest terroir more than variety, which is to say that when you taste it, you are reminded of the zone it comes from rather than of its grape. This is no small achievement. The nose of the '98 is warm, earthy and minerally. The palate has power, concentration and energy, while the vigorous tannins also emerge in the broad finish. The Percarlo '98 is, not surprisingly, better than good but not up to the level of its best vintages. The oak has things too much its own way, whereas it should be kept in line by the fruit. The Chianti Classico Riserva '98, a Two Glass winner, displays an austere style, full body and good balance. The fair Chianti '99 is a simpler but nonetheless coherent.

○ Vin Santo del Chianti Classico '94	♟♟	6
● Chianti Cl. '99	♟♟	4
● Chianti Cl. Vigneto S. Marcellino Ris. '98	♟	4
● Geremia '98	♟	5
● Vin Santo '88	♟♟	5
○ Vin Santo '91	♟♟	5
● Chianti Cl. Vigneto S. Marcellino '93	♟♟	4
● Chianti Cl. Ris. '95	♟♟	4
● Geremia '95	♟♟	5

● La Ricolma '98	♟♟	6
● Chianti Cl. Ris. '98	♟♟	5
● Percarlo '98	♟♟	6
● Chianti Cl. '99	♟	4
● Percarlo '88	♟♟♟	6
● Percarlo '97	♟♟♟	6
● Percarlo '90	♟♟	6
● Percarlo '92	♟♟	6
● Percarlo '93	♟♟	6
○ Vin Santo '93	♟♟	6
● Percarlo '94	♟♟	6
● Percarlo '95	♟♟	6
● Percarlo '96	♟♟	6
● Chianti Cl. Ris. '97	♟♟	5
● La Ricolma '97	♟♟	6

GAIOLE IN CHIANTI (SI)

San Vincenti
Loc. San Vincenti
Podere di Stignano, 27
53013 Gaiole in Chianti (SI)
Tel. 0577734047
E-mail: svincent@chiantinet.it

Yet again, Roberto Pucci and Roberta Vannini's estate has shown that it has what it takes. Their few hectares under vine are perfectly tended and the whole winemaking process is overseen by oenologist Carlo Ferrini. The only disappointment this time – and it's a small one – is the Chianti Classico Riserva '98, which is somewhat subdued compared to the standard version we tasted last year. The colour – garnet highlights are noticeable on a ruby ground – already shows signs of decline. The aromas, too, are already forward, jammy notes mingling with nuances of ripe fruit. The attack on the palate seems a bit muddled and the aggressive tannins are astringent, but in a substantial and powerful body. The faintly bitterish finish is moderately long. The very fine Chianti Classico '99, on the other hand, boasts a surprisingly well-defined nose, with clean, rich aromas where distinct fruity hints of plum and cherry come through to meld with spicy nuances of elegant toasty oak and coffee. The palate, after an excellent entry, shows dense, firm structure, softened by firm but not overbearing alcohol. The flavour is succulent and inviting, with a good rising finish. Lastly, the Stignano '98, their monovarietal sangiovese, lives up to expectations. A lovely limpid, intense ruby hue ushers in a big, varied bouquet where wild berries vie with fresh balsamic nuances. The mouthfillingly soft, silky palate gives way to a lingering finish.

● Stignano '98	▼▼	5
● Chianti Cl. '99	▼▼	4
● Chianti Cl. Ris. '98	▼	4
● Chianti Cl. Ris. '85	▼▼	4
● Chianti Cl. '88	▼▼	3
● Chianti Cl. Ris. '88	▼▼	4
● Chianti Cl. Ris. '95	▼▼	4
● Chianti Cl. Podere di Stignano '96	▼▼	3
● Chianti Cl. Ris. '96	▼▼	4
● Stignano '96	▼▼	5
● Chianti Cl. Ris. '97	▼▼	4
● Stignano '97	▼▼	5
● Chianti Cl. '98	▼▼	4
● Chianti Cl. '97	▼	3

GAMBASSI TERME (FI)

Villa Pillo
Fraz. Pillo
Via Volterrana, 24
50050 Gambassi Terme (FI)
Tel. 0571680212
E-mail: villapillo@leone.it

Syrah is again king at Villa Pillo. Although the '99 did not, like the '97, walk off with Three Glasses, it came very close. There must be something about the Gambassi site climate that favours this grape, but so do the intelligent choices made in vineyard and cellar. Varietal characteristics are immediately perceptible on the nose, with very lively fruit and delightful notes of black pepper. The palate is concentrated, the progression long and eloquent, and all it needs to lift it to the level of the '97 is more complexity. By way of consolation, the merlot selection, the Sant'Adele, made a fine debut. This very attractive, well-balanced red is constructed around the purity of its fruit. It never oversteps the limits but is just a touch straightforward. The standard-label Merlot is less brilliant but still satisfactory. The body is not so full, the tannins a bit raw, and the less ripe fruit marked by vegetal nuances. Similarly the cabernet franc-based Vivaldaia '99, although balanced and fluent, is distinctly vegetal and lacks character. We were happier, on the whole, with the sangiovese-based Borgoforte '98 which, in its evident simplicity, still manages to be admirably well-defined on the nose, and supple and harmonious on the palate. Our last notes, which are not exactly positive, regard the Vin Santo '96. It is unfocused on the nose and rather fuzzy in general.

● Syrah '99	▼▼	5
● Merlot Sant'Adele '99	▼▼	5
● Borgoforte '98	▼	3
● Merlot '99	▼	5
● Vivaldaia '99	▼	5
○ Vin Santo '96		5
● Syrah '97	▼▼▼	5
● Merlot '95	▼▼	5
● Cabernet Sauvignon '96	▼▼	5
● Merlot '96	▼▼	5
● Syrah '96	▼▼	5
● Cabernet Sauvignon '97	▼▼	5
● Merlot '97	▼▼	5
● Merlot '98	▼▼	5
● Syrah '98	▼▼	5

GREVE IN CHIANTI (FI)

CARPINETO
LOC. DUDDA
50020 GREVE IN CHIANTI (FI)
TEL. 0558549062 - 0558549086
E-MAIL: carpinet@hesp.it

This was a very positive year for Carpineto. Some of their wines were extremely interesting so this Greve estate is now beginning to play a role more in keeping with its potential. We have not reviewed the Riserva '98 of the Nobile di Montepulciano, since all the Nobiles have been assigned to next year's tastings but an advance tasting of the above-mentioned Riserva seemed most promising. Meanwhile, there was a very fine performance from the Chianti Classico Riserva '98, which displayed a lovely intense bright ruby hue, followed by clear-cut aromas with rich fruit to the fore and undertones of toasty oak. Our high expectations were confirmed by the firm entry on the palate, the seamless progression and the full, well-balanced body. The Chianti Classico '99 was less successful because of sulphurous notes on the nose. The structure, however, was admirable. The fairly good Farnito Cabernet Sauvignon '98 offers a clean but distinctly vegetal fragrance. The development in the mouth is well-balanced but overall it is rather forward, and drying tannins control the finish. We were pleasantly surprised by the Chardonnay Farnito '99, a very decent white. Rich aromas of clean tropical fruit, jasmine and vanilla with hazelnut nuances, follow through on a crisp, delightfully balanced palate with demure, well-integrated oak.

GREVE IN CHIANTI (FI)

MONTECALVI
VIA CITILLE, 85
50022 GREVE IN CHIANTI (FI)
TEL. 0558544665
E-MAIL: bollij@tin.it

There's no holding this wine. That's what we thought when we tasted the Montecalvi '98. It positively ran off with its Three Glasses, which is all the more impressive when you consider how far this Grevi estate has come in the last few years. They decided from the start to concentrate on producing one wine to which they would dedicate all their attention. The six hectares of vineyard are planted almost entirely to sangiovese, with no more than five per cent of the stock accounted for by cabernet sauvignon. Plantings are dense, some 9,000 vines per hectare, and the yield is less than one kilogram per vine. So the cellar starts with great raw material, and the aim of the owner, and oenologist Stefano Chioccioli, is then to marry the richness of the grape with the "goût de terroir". This latter quality has been the dominant characteristic of Montecalvi ever since its first release, which perhaps slowed the progress of Jacqueline Bolli's estate, but in the end has made for a glorious synthesis of strength and personality. The '98 Montecalvi is an unpredictable wine. Its energy seems at times almost uncontrollable. On entry, the nose, for example, has a moment of suspense: the richness of the fruit is joined for a couple of nanoseconds by animal and vegetal nuances, so fleeting as not to matter. The palate is like gliding across velvet: soft, silky, seamless in its progression and rhythmic variation. The finish goes on and on, just as you would expect from a great wine.

● Chianti Cl. Ris. '98	🍷🍷	4
○ Farnito Chardonnay '99	🍷🍷	4
○ Farnito Cabernet Sauvignon '98	🍷	5
● Chianti Cl. '99		3
● Farnito Cabernet Sauvignon '90	🍷🍷	5
● Farnito Cabernet Sauvignon '91	🍷🍷	5
● Chianti Cl. Ris. '93	🍷🍷	4
● Dogajolo '93	🍷🍷	4
● Farnito Cabernet Sauvignon '93	🍷🍷	5
● Chianti Cl. Ris. '94	🍷🍷	4
● Nobile di Montepulciano Ris. '94	🍷🍷	4
● Dogajolo '95	🍷🍷	3
● Farnito Cabernet Sauvignon '95	🍷🍷	5
● Chianti Cl. Ris. '97	🍷🍷	4
● Chianti Cl. '98	🍷🍷	3

● Montecalvi '98	🍷🍷🍷	6
● Montecalvi '94	🍷🍷	4
● Montecalvi '95	🍷🍷	5
● Montecalvi '96	🍷🍷	5
● Montecalvi '97	🍷🍷	6
● Montecalvi '93	🍷	4

GREVE IN CHIANTI (FI)

PODERE POGGIO SCALETTE
LOC. RUFFOLI
VIA BARBIANO, 7
50022 GREVE IN CHIANTI (FI)
TEL. 0558546108 - 0558549017
E-MAIL: j.fiore@tiscalinet.it

In the course of his career as an oenologist, Vittorio Fiore has been responsible for the creation of many great wines and has generously and unstintingly shared his knowledge and experience. Many wineries, and more than one oenologist, owe their success to him and his teachings. But Fiore is not the sort of man to live on past glories. He still has all the enthusiasm of a young man just starting out with a keen desire to test his mettle. The wine from his own estate is infused with Vittorio's knowledge and the philosophy that has always inspired him. He has managed to bring together three fundamental components in Il Carbonaione: a terroir with unique characteristics, Ruffoli in Chianti; the grape variety most characteristic of Tuscan tradition, sangiovese; and judicious use of technical skills in the service of the first two components. The result is a great "vin de terroir" with the look of the future. Another thing that becomes clear as you look back on Carbonaione's career is that, curiously enough, the best versions, or so they seem to us, come from vintages that were considered little better than mediocre in the rest of Chianti Classico: the '96 and the '98. We can only imagine that the conditions in Ruffoli make it possible to grow grapes of unusually balanced ripeness. The Carbonaione '98 from Poggio Scalette is an exceptional wine. The satisfyingly rich aromas offer notes of black berry fruit, violets, sweet spice and cocoa powder. The palate is concentrated, elegant and deep. Oak is integrated with a master's hand and the extremely fine-grained tannins are splendid.

GREVE IN CHIANTI (FI)

CASTELLO DI QUERCETO
LOC. QUERCETO - FRAZ. LUCOLENA
VIA DUDDA, 61
50020 GREVE IN CHIANTI (FI)
TEL. 05585921
E-MAIL: querceto@chiantipop.net

The wines from Castello di Querceto are Chianti country classics. The house style is fairly traditional, although you can also find reds that aren't Chianti Classico. The mesoclimatic conditions here – the vines grow at almost 500 metres above sea level – mean that ripening takes place slowly and late. In warmer years, they can produce wines that are both full-bodied and elegant. At this year's tastings, Castello di Querceto presented a number of wines from a vintage known for yielding beautifully ripe fruit – '97 – and these found the panel's favour. The cabernet-based Cignale especially stood out for its elegance, well-sustained palate and nicely gauged tannins. The nose has a light vegetal nuance, but it doesn't really get in the way. The somewhat more eccentric and uneven Querciolaia '97, from sangiovese and cabernet, doesn't follow any of the established rules. There is some uncertainty on the nose, and a slight roughness on the palate, but it has an interesting personality. The sangiovese-based La Corte '97 follows the same pattern, although with more moderation. Notes of cherry jam, tobacco and vanilla on the nose precede a soft, even palate which finishes with a slight tannic harshness. The Riserva Il Picchio is not entirely successful. It offers admirable grip, but also an unfocused nose and boisterous tannins. The Chianti Classico Riserva '97 is more docile but also less expressive. Lastly, the Chianti '99 seemed agreeable, although lean and forward.

● Il Carbonaione '98	🍷🍷🍷	6
● Il Carbonaione '96	🍷🍷🍷	5
● Il Carbonaione '92	🍷🍷	5
● Il Carbonaione '93	🍷🍷	5
● Il Carbonaione '94	🍷🍷	5
● Il Carbonaione '95	🍷🍷	5
● Il Carbonaione '97	🍷🍷	6

● Cignale '97	🍷🍷	6
● La Corte '97	🍷🍷	5
● Querciolaia '97	🍷🍷	5
● Chianti Cl. Il Picchio Ris. '97	🍷	5
● Chianti Cl. Ris. '97	🍷	4
● Chianti Cl. '99	🍷	4
● Chianti Cl. Ris. '90	🍷🍷	4
● Querciolaia '90	🍷🍷	5
● Chianti Cl. Il Picchio Ris. '93	🍷🍷	4
● Chianti Cl. Il Picchio Ris. '94	🍷🍷	4
● La Corte '94	🍷🍷	5
● Chianti Cl. '95	🍷🍷	3
● Chianti Cl. Ris. '95	🍷🍷	4
● Querciolaia '95	🍷🍷	5

GREVE IN CHIANTI (FI)

AGRICOLA QUERCIABELLA
LOC. RUFFOLI
VIA S. LUCIA A BARBIANO, 17
50022 GREVE IN CHIANTI (FI)
TEL. 055853834 - 0286452793

Sebastiano Castiglioni, the son of Giuseppe, or "Pepito", is now at the helm of Querciabella. He has decided to devote himself to the estate full-time, leaving his native Milan to move to his estate. We would have done the same in his shoes. Querciabella is heavenly. It has one of the most beautiful landscapes in Chianti and the wines are good. The property is situated in Ruffoli, between Greve and Panzano, not far from the estates of Lamole and Vignamaggio, and it's high up, 400 metres above sea level, where sangiovese ripens only if very well tended. Sebastiano refuses to deviate from the rule that there must be very few grapes per vine, and he always gets results. This time, it's his Camartina '97, an assemblage of sangiovese and cabernet sauvignon which has been released a year later than most Supertuscans. Sebastiano was right to wait. Only now has it achieved a perfect balance between the enchanting scents of bramble, black cherry and the hint of smokiness, as well as on the mouthfilling, enormously characterful palate. The balance will be maintained for many years. The Chianti Classico Riserva '98 is good too, despite the fact that 1998 was not a great vintage. By the way, the Camartina '98 will not be released. The mostly chardonnay-based Batàr '99 is less concentrated than usual but it reached our finals. The fair Chianti Classico '99 is a little grassy on the nose. This was a predictably triumphant performance. This Guide bears the ninth Querciabella Three Glass award. It's hard to imagine their not getting their Star for ten next time.

● Camartina '97	🍷🍷🍷	6
○ Batàr '99	🍷🍷	6
● Chianti Cl. Ris. '98	🍷🍷	5
● Chianti Cl. '99	🍷🍷	4
● Camartina '88	🍷🍷🍷	6
● Camartina '90	🍷🍷🍷	6
● Camartina '94	🍷🍷🍷	6
● Camartina '95	🍷🍷🍷	6
● Chianti Cl. Ris. '95	🍷🍷🍷	5
○ Batàr '97	🍷🍷🍷	6
○ Batàr '98	🍷🍷🍷	6
○ Vin Santo Orlando '90	🍷🍷	6
● Chianti Cl. Ris. '96	🍷🍷	5
● Chianti Cl. Ris. '97	🍷🍷	5
● Chianti Cl. '98	🍷🍷	4

GREVE IN CHIANTI (FI)

RISECCOLI
VIA CONVERTOIE, 9
50022 GREVE IN CHIANTI (FI)
TEL. 055853598
E-MAIL: info@riseccoli.com

The Tenuta di Riseccoli is located in the hills to the east of Greve in Chianti, with vineyards standing at more than 400 metres above sea level. This means the site climate does not exactly favour the perfect ripening of grapes. It's encouraging, then, to note the efforts, such as keeping yields low, made here to achieve this essential goal. After a couple of years' absence from the Guide, the Romanelli family's estate is back in form, thanks particularly to the surprisingly good performance of their Saeculum '99, a Supertuscan from half sangiovese and half cabernet sauvignon and merlot. The colour is very dark and intense. The aromas are clean and not yet fully expressed, but essentially focus on fruit, with vegetal traces and hints of toasty oak. After an exuberant attack, the palate expands on a dense body with remarkably close-knit tannins, and the finish is duly long. A really excellent wine, if perhaps a bit cold and cerebral, it came within an inch of winning Three Glasses. The next in line is quite a way behind it. The decent Vin Santo '96 is austere in style, and not spectacular on the nose, but intense, well-balanced and reasonably stylish on the palate. The quite good Chianti Classico Riserva '98 displays a dense, harmonious, ripe nose and a fresh flavour with lively, enjoyable fruit. The Chianti '99 left us with conflicting impressions because of a lack of clarity on the nose, which is a pity, because the wine has a fairly substantial structure.

● Saeculum '99	🍷🍷	5
● Vin Santo '96	🍷🍷	5
● Chianti Cl. Ris. '98	🍷	4
● Chianti Cl. '99		4
● Saeculum '94	🍷🍷	5
● Saeculum '95	🍷🍷	5
● Chianti Cl. Ris. '94	🍷	4
● Chianti Cl. '95	🍷	3
● Chianti Cl. Ris. '95	🍷	4
● Chianti Cl. '96	🍷	3

GREVE IN CHIANTI (FI)

TERRENO
VIA CITILLE, 4
50022 GREVE IN CHIANTI (FI)
TEL. 055854001
E-MAIL: info@fattoriaterreno.it

Terreno has been doing pretty well for a number of years. The wines are seldom disappointing but neither are they put forward for highest honours very often. However, they do, within the limits imposed by the vintage, seem to maintain a consistent quality. The estate covers about 130 hectares, 20 of which are planted to vine mainly for the production of Chianti Classico. The two wines we tasted this year earned Two Glasses each. The Chianti Classico '99 is unquestionably a well-made wine. No quibbles about its impeccably clean style, nor yet its balance, since everything is as it should be. Alcohol and acidity are well gauged and the oak and tannins lift the development, rather than dominate it. All in all, a pleasing wine. On the downside, it is held back by vegetal sensations that are a shade excessive for a Chianti Classico. The Chianti Riserva '98, meanwhile, is not fully defined on the nose. There is a slight fuzziness, due perhaps to the wood. The palate is admirably rounded on entry, the progression is enjoyable and the finish consistent, although it tends to be a little unchallenging. Here, too, tannins and oak have been nicely handled, and the flavour is attractively balanced. Its limitations are the occasional forward hint, in contrast with the freshness of the fruit in the mouth. Both these wines are, however, well-conceived and technically well-executed Chiantis that are abundantly satisfying to drink.

GREVE IN CHIANTI (FI)

CASTELLO DI VERRAZZANO
LOC. VERRAZZANO
50022 GREVE IN CHIANTI (FI)
TEL. 055854243 - 055290684
E-MAIL: info@verrazzano.com

Castello di Verrazzano presented only two wines this year but they are worth closer investigation. One of them, the curiously named '98 Bottiglia Particolare ("Special Bottle"), made it to our finals. This is a barrique-aged, predominantly sangiovese-based, red with a small addition of cabernet sauvignon, and it shows all the best characteristics of wine from the northern part of Greve in Chianti. It's not powerful and soft, the somewhat predictable combination one often finds in Supertuscans from the southern parts of Chianti Classico. This bottle is special mainly for its balance and elegance, with an intensely fruity bouquet where black cherries and wild berries set the pace and the wood blends in perfectly. On the palate, the tannins are fine-grained, smooth and not at all aggressive, while the structure is shot through with restrained acidulous notes. It clearly belongs to its territory, which is a very special compliment. The basic Chianti Classico '99 is very good but this is, by now, no surprise. The delicately and distinctly fruity aromas usher in an elegant palate, which is also typical of the zone. It may not be exceptionally long on the finish but technically it is faultless. We eagerly await the more promising '99s, in particular the Sassello, from which we expect great things.

| ● Chianti Classico Ris. '98 | 🍷🍷 | 4 |
| ● Chianti Classico '99 | 🍷🍷 | 4 |

● Bottiglia Particolare '98	🍷🍷	6
● Chianti Cl. '99	🍷🍷	4
● Chianti Cl. Ris. '90	🍷🍷🍷	5
● Sassello '97	🍷🍷🍷	6
● Bottiglia Particolare '90	🍷🍷	6
● Sassello '90	🍷🍷	6
● Sassello '93	🍷🍷	6
● Bottiglia Particolare '95	🍷🍷	6
● Sassello '95	🍷🍷	6
● Chianti Cl. Ris. '96	🍷🍷	5
● Bottiglia Particolare '97	🍷🍷	6
● Chianti Cl. '97	🍷🍷	4
● Chianti Cl. Ris. '97	🍷🍷	5
● Chianti Cl. '98	🍷	4

GREVE IN CHIANTI (FI)

CASTELLO DI VICCHIOMAGGIO
LOC. LE BOLLE
VIA VICCHIOMAGGIO, 4
50022 GREVE IN CHIANTI (FI)
TEL. 055854079
E-MAIL: vicchiomaggio@vicchiomaggio.it

We did not expect the '98 vintage to repeat the exceptional results of the '97, and so it was. Nevertheless, we must admit that Castello di Vicchiomaggio has achieved a notable consistency of quality and a style based on balance and technical mastery that manages to emerge, whatever the vintage is like. There may not be a Three Glass winner this time, but John Matta's estate has nothing to be ashamed of in the Ripa delle More '98, its flagship wine. A sangiovese-based wine that regularly reveals elegance and a refined use of oak, which discreetly underpins the excellent structure. The flavour has reasonable complexity that does not dwarf the fruit, and the finish is long and juicy. The two Riservas are very attractive as well. The Riserva La Prima '98 flaunts a nose of well-defined, lively fruit with notes of bramble and raspberry. We admired the fullness of body and excellent balance on the palate, but we might have wished for a bit more complexity and character. And this is what turned our fancy, just this once, to the Riserva Petri, also a '98. It offers a riper nose with nuances of jam and liquorice. The attack on the palate is vigorous, and the tannins are robust and tasty. The definitely more docile Chianti Classico San Jacopo '99 is an agreeable and even wine, if slightly dumb on the nose. The Ripa delle Mandorle '99 is straightforward but satisfactory.

GREVE IN CHIANTI (FI)

VILLA VIGNAMAGGIO
VIA DI PETRIOLO, 5
50022 GREVE IN CHIANTI (FI)
TEL. 055854661
E-MAIL: info@vignamaggio.com

Vignamaggio, with its nearly 50 hectares under vine, is one of the biggest estates in Chianti Classico. At this year's tastings, we found all their wines to be well executed, without, however, expressing any particular personality. The only one that seemed distinctly to embody the land from which it sprang was the Chianti Classico Riserva Monna Lisa '98. A vigorous wine with a strong character, it is still a bit undeveloped on the nose, where notes of liquorice and tobacco emerge. The palate shows the nervous energy of sangiovese, which never relents for a second but always provides intensity and lively contrasts. The good Obsession '98, a blend of cabernet and merlot, offers aromas of minerals and toasty oak, and a full-bodied, well-sustained palate with a slight harshness on the finish. The racy, stylish Vignamaggio '98, a monovarietal cabernet franc, reveals a soft, balanced, supple palate. The nose is less developed and has a distinct, but not unpleasant, vegetal cast. The successful Chianti Classico '99 offers clear, agreeable aromas and a succulent, structured flavour. The Vin Santo '96, austere in style and not very sweet, is dense and balanced, and the fairly long finish has a bitterish twist. The Chianti Terre di Prenzano '99 is less than successful: the nose is undefined and the palate a little hollow.

● Chianti Cl. La Prima Ris. '98	♟♟	5
● Chianti Cl. Petri Ris. '98	♟♟	4
● Ripa delle More '98	♟♟	6
● Chianti Cl. San Jacopo '99	♟	4
● Ripa delle Mandorle '99	♟	4
● Ripa delle More '94	♟♟♟	5
● Ripa delle More '97	♟♟♟	6
● Chianti Cl. La Prima Ris. '95	♟♟	5
● Ripa delle More '95	♟♟	5
● Ripa delle More '96	♟♟	5
● Chianti Cl. La Prima Ris. '97	♟♟	5
● Chianti Cl. Petri Ris. '97	♟♟	5

○ Vin Santo del Chianti Classico '96	♟♟	6
● Chianti Cl. Monna Lisa Ris. '98	♟♟	5
● Obsession '98	♟♟	6
● Vignamaggio '98	♟♟	5
● Chianti Cl. '99	♟	4
● Chianti Cl. Terre di Prenzano '99		3
● Chianti Cl. Monna Lisa Ris. '95	♟♟♟	4
● Chianti Cl. Monna Lisa Ris. '93	♟♟	4
● Chianti Cl. Monna Lisa Ris. '94	♟♟	4
● Gherardino '95	♟♟	5
○ Vin Santo '95	♟♟	5
● Vignamaggio '96	♟♟	6
● Chianti Cl. Monna Lisa Ris. '97	♟♟	5
● Chianti Cl. Vitigliano '97	♟♟	4
● Obsession '97	♟♟	5

GREVE IN CHIANTI (FI)

VITICCIO
VIA SAN CRESCI, 12/A
50022 GREVE IN CHIANTI (FI)
TEL. 055854210
E-MAIL: info@fattoriaviticcio.com

Viticcio is a regular guest on these pages, which means that each year's tastings – nobody gets a profile by divine right – show that the wines are up to scratch. This is greatly to the estate's credit, and should be borne in mind despite the absence of a Viticcio world-shaker so far. The Chianti Classico '99, lone representative of its vintage, gave a good performance, with its lovely bright ruby hue and clear-cut scents of bramble and cherry laced with faint vegetal hints. On the palate, it showed admirable weight, generous fruit and well-integrated oak. The good Chianti Classico Beatrice Riserva '98 is soft, velvety and elegant. Its major defect is a vegetal nuance that oversteps the limit for a Chianti Classico. The wine that has been most consistent over the years is, we think, the Monile, of which the '98 is a good example. It is a blend of two thirds cabernet sauvignon with sangiovese and, curiously, some nebbiolo, and revealed a sustained, rich, concentrated palate with tightly-knit tannins. The less clearly defined nose includes notes of mushrooms, which we found in several bottles. The sangiovese-based Prunaio '98 did well, although it showed the limitations of an imperfect vintage. The acidity is not well-masked by the body and the oak has rather a drying effect. The Chianti Classico Riserva '98 is more forward and equally in thrall to its wood.

● Chianti Cl. Beatrice Ris. '98	♀♀	5
● Monile '98	♀♀	5
● Chianti Cl. '99	♀♀	4
● Chianti Cl. Ris. '98	♀	4
● Prunaio '98	♀	5
● Monile '93	♀♀	5
● Prunaio '93	♀♀	5
● Monile '94	♀♀	5
● Prunaio '94	♀♀	5
● Monile '95	♀♀	5
● Prunaio '95	♀♀	5
● Monile '96	♀♀	5
● Prunaio '96	♀♀	5
● Monile '97	♀♀	5
● Prunaio '97	♀♀	5

GROSSETO

LE PUPILLE
LOC. ISTIA D'OMBRONE
PIAGGE DEL MAIANO, 92/A
58040 GROSSETO
TEL. 0564409517

Numbers never tell the whole story. If you were to judge by the series of Glasses, including sets of Three, won by Le Pupille in recent years, you might get the impression of a tranquil estate where the producers' only care is to turn out excellent wines. Of course, there is no denying that the excellent wines have been turned out but it would be a surprise to discover that, in the meantime, this Maremma estate has been in constant ferment. New vineyards and, most notably, the construction of a brand-new, efficient cellar have claimed vast quantities of physical and mental energy. All the more credit, then, to Stefano Rizzi and Elisabetta Geppetti for not having let themselves be sidetracked by the endless problems of restructuring and for having kept their attention focused on producing exceptional wines. One is tempted to say that if they have managed to get such good results in these conditions, there will be no holding them in the future. The Poggio Valente '99 repeated last year's triumph. It may not have the same overwhelming fruit, and the body is excellent without being extraordinary, but the execution is masterly. Tannins, oak and fruit have found a fair field and no favour: the wine is deliciously rounded and elegant. The difference from the '98 vintage, which was exceptional in the Maremma, is more evident in the Saffredi '99, a very soft and velvety wine but with a less compelling character. The excellent Solalto '99 is sweet and headily fragrant, with a faint smoky undertone. Both the Morellino '00 and the Poggio Argentato '00 are surefooted and good.

● Morellino di Scansano Poggio Valente '99	♀♀♀	5
● Saffredi '99	♀♀	6
● Morellino di Scansano '00	♀♀	3*
○ Poggio Argentato '00	♀♀	3*
○ Solalto '99	♀♀	4
● Saffredi '90	♀♀♀	6
● Saffredi '97	♀♀♀	6
● Morellino di Scansano Poggio Valente '98	♀♀♀	5
● Saffredi '94	♀♀	5
● Saffredi '95	♀♀	5
● Morellino di Scansano Poggio Valente '97	♀♀	5
● Saffredi '98	♀♀	6

GROSSETO

POGGIO ARGENTIERA
LOC. BANDITELLA - FRAZ. ALBERESE
S. S. 1, 54
58010 GROSSETO
TEL. 0564405099
E-MAIL: info@poggioargentiera.com

There's been a lot of talk in recent years about the Maremma as the new frontier of Tuscan, and indeed Italian, wine. In fact, results from the copious investments, made largely by producers from elsewhere, are still embryonic. So at the moment, most bottled wine from the Maremma comes from the historic local estates. Poggio Argentiera, although fairly recently established, has native roots and is, in our opinion, amongst the most interesting producers to emerge in the Maremma in these exciting years. Giampaolo Paglia, the owner of Poggio Argentiera, is a young producer who knows what he wants and is determined to get it. First of all, he means to produce perfectly ripe, rich, concentrated grapes. Then he uses nothing but barriques to age his Morellino. The results speak for themselves, and the Morellino CapaTosta '99 is indeed one of the most expressive reds from this warm part of Tuscany. It's a wine with a strong character that dynamically interprets its terroir. The bouquet reveals the richness of ripe fruit, with aromas of bramble and black cherry jam, but also notes of spice and minerals. The attack on the palate is powerful and vigorous, the progression dense and mouthfilling. The impetuousness of the wine comes through on the finish, where boisterous tannins lend a hint of edginess. Giampaolo Paglia's second wine, the Morellino BellaMarsilia '00, is also good and has a similar character to its big brother's. Overall, though, it is less challenging and intense, with the oak having the last word.

IMPRUNETA (FI)

LANCIOLA
LOC. POZZOLATICO
VIA IMPRUNETANA PER POZZOLATICO, 210
50023 IMPRUNETA (FI)
TEL. 055208324 - 055208362
E-MAIL: info@lanciola.net

They are hard at work finishing the new cellar at the Guarneri family's small but well-run estate. It had become practically impossible to continue using the old facilities, given the new direction mapped out with the help of oenologist Stefano Chioccioli, who again has produced good results. We were unable to taste the Terricci and the Riccionero, two major selections that we'll be reviewing next year. For now, we'll start with the Chianti Colli Fiorentini '99, which is a well-made wine, if a little quiet and inexpressive on the nose. The good Chianti Classico Le Masse di Greve '99 has an attractive ruby hue, followed by powerful fruity aromas that blend harmoniously with a note of toasty oak. After an excellent, fairly mouthfilling attack on the palate, the tannins amalgamate nicely with the alcohol, and the rising finish is just as it should be. The Riserva '98 of Le Masse di Greve made a very fine showing. An opaque ruby colour with violet highlights leads in to a lovely minty notes that fuse with wild berry aromas. The wine makes a great impact on the palate; the structure is substantial, the tannins are lively but enjoyable, the alcohol is well-judged and the finish lingers. The Terricci Chardonnay '99 displays mineral aromas and notes of aromatic herbs against a fruity backdrop. The palate is medium-bodied and well-made, although the acidity tends to make its presence felt, and the finish is satisfyingly long.

- Morellino di Scansano CapaTosta '99 — 5
- Morellino di Scansano BellaMarsilia '00 — 4
- Morellino di Scansano CapaTosta '98 — 5
- Morellino di Scansano BellaMarsilia '98 — 4
- Morellino di Scansano BellaMarsilia '99 — 4

- Chianti Cl. Le Masse di Greve Ris. '98 — 4
- Chianti Cl. Le Masse di Greve '99 — 3*
- ○ Terricci Chardonnay '99 — 4
- Chianti Colli Fiorentini '99 — 3
- Terricci '86 — 4
- Terricci '88 — 4
- Terricci '95 — 4
- Terricci '96 — 4
- Chianti Cl. Le Masse di Greve Ris. '97 — 4
- Chianti Colli Fiorentini Ris. '97 — 3
- Riccionero '97 — 3
- Terricci '97 — 4
- Chianti Cl. Le Masse di Greve Ris. '95 — 4
- Chianti Cl. Le Masse di Greve '98 — 3
- Chianti Colli Fiorentini '98 — 2

LUCCA

TERRE DEL SILLABO
LOC. CAPPELLA
FRAZ. PONTE DEL GIGLIO
VIA PER CAMAIORE TRAV. V
55060 LUCCA - TEL. 0583394487
E-MAIL: clara.giampi@lunet.it

Giampi Moretti is in the midst of a revolution. Having rethought his winemaking methods, he has now changed the name of his estate as well. His wines will no longer be labelled Le Murelle but will now be marshalled under the new banner of Terre del Sillabo. A further innovation is the extension of the range. Two new wines have been added to the traditional line-up: Spante, a chardonnay, and Gana, a sauvignon. Both are oak-fermented, which seems to have been a good idea. The estate produces only one red wine, a blend of cabernet sauvignon, cabernet franc, sangiovese, colorino and canaiolo called Niffo, and the '99 is excellent, in fact it very nearly won Three Glasses. It delighted us with full rich fruit we had never before encountered in Giampi Moretti's wines. But its most captivating quality is its remarkable elegance. The tannic weave is silky, the oak is beautifully blended and the finish is deep and persistent. Then the debut performance of the Gana '00 was a great success for it shows some complexity, a lingering finish and excellent balance. The very good Spante '00 is young and promising, with many of the same qualities but can also point to very decent density on the palate. The Colline Lucchesi Chardonnay and Sauvignon, both '00s, get One Glass each. On balance, we preferred the former for its more clearly defined varietal characteristics.

MAGLIANO IN TOSCANA (GR)

FATTORIA MANTELLASSI
LOC. BANDITACCIA
SAN GIUSEPPE, 26
58051 MAGLIANO IN TOSCANA (GR)
TEL. 0564592037
E-MAIL: info@fatt.mantellasi.it

As usual, the Morellino Le Sentinelle is the best wine at Fattoria Mantellassi. The '98 seems particularly successful but that is no surprise, because for the Maremma, unlike the interior of Tuscany, this was a splendid vintage. The wine is a blend of 85 per cent morellino (sangiovese) and 15 per cent alicante, and is warm, rich and characteristic of its terroir. Spice sets the tone in the bouquet, which also includes notes of refreshing liquorice and black cherry jam. The admirably stylish palate shows, but is not dominated by, its alcohol, the tannins are well integrated and the long finish echoes the nose elegantly: an excellent Morellino. The other wines fill their supporting roles well. The Morellino San Giuseppe '00 is simpler, of course, but quite up to expectations. Clean, fruity and enjoyable, it also reveals substance and good texture. The '99 version is leaner-bodied and shorter on the finish but pleasing and easy to drink all the same. The well-made Querciolaia '98, a monovarietal alicante, displays ripe notes of bramble jam with a faint vegetal undertone on the nose. The progressive expansion on the palate takes you through to a rather simple finish. The Riserva '98 is correctly executed but not very compelling, and alcohol tends to have the upper hand.

● Niffo '99	🍷🍷	5
○ Gana '00	🍷🍷	5
○ Spante '00	🍷🍷	5
○ Colline Lucchesi Chardonnay '00	🍷	4
○ Colline Lucchesi Sauvignon '00	🍷	4
○ Colline Lucchesi Sauvignon '98	🍷🍷	3
● Niffo '98	🍷🍷	5
○ Colline Lucchesi Chardonnay '99	🍷🍷	4
○ Colline Lucchesi Chardonnay '98	🍷	3
○ Colline Lucchesi Sauvignon '99	🍷	4

● Morellino di Scansano Le Sentinelle Ris. '98	🍷🍷	4
● Morellino di Scansano San Giuseppe '00	🍷	3
● Morellino di Scansano Ris. '98	🍷	4
● Querciolaia '98	🍷	4
● Morellino di Scansano San Giuseppe '99	🍷	3
● Morellino di Scansano Ris. '96	🍷🍷	3
● Querciolaia '96	🍷🍷	4
● Morellino di Scansano Le Sentinelle '97	🍷🍷	4

MANCIANO (GR)

La Stellata
Via Fornacina, 18
58014 Manciano (GR)
tel. 0564620190
e-mail: lastellata@tiscalinet.it

It will soon be the 20th anniversary of the founding of this little winery. It is almost two decades since Manlio Giorni and Clara Divizia left their work in Rome and came here to live and labour. By now, they no longer look like a couple of white-collar farmers but real vignerons and their winery is considered one of the leaders of the zone. When they first started out at La Stellata, they were pretty much on their own, and for years their Lunaia was, apart from the white produced by the Cantina Sociale, the only Bianco di Pitigliano and indeed the only good wine made in the entire area from Manciano to Pitigliano. The '00 version is true to its origins and rather a nice wine. Manlio and Clara have always been faithful to malvasia and trebbiano, eschewing fancy varieties. In consequence, the Lunaia Bianco is never going to be an enormous wine. The '00 again offers a delicate fragrance and a light, fairly well-balanced flavour that is not overwhelmingly deep. But the mostly sangiovese-based Lunaia Rosso '98 is another story. The concentration is good, the fruit on the nose very intense and the structure admirable. One last note. If you happen to be in these parts, do drop in. Manlio and Clara are delightful people. They still have all the enthusiasm they had at the outset and can also accommodate paying guests.

●	Lunaia Rosso '98	🍷🍷	4
○	Bianco di Pitigliano Lunaia '00	🍷	3
●	Lunaia Rosso '97	🍷🍷	3*

MASSA

Cima
Loc. San Lorenzo
Fraz. Romagnano
Via del Fagiano, 1
54100 Massa
tel. 0585830835 e-mail: candia.cima@libero.it

There are no half measures in the wines from Cima. The main focus is on fruit, an extreme richness achieved by taking ripening to the limits, great concentration and first-class new, small barrels. This is the essence of Aurelio Cima's recipe for wine, in addition to grape varieties and blend. The results are excellent, although we do have a bone or two to pick. Particularly when young, Aurelio's wines are not markedly different from one another. This does not mean they are identical but just that they don't seem to have very distinctive characters. The quality is high so perhaps the problem is simply that we usually taste them too soon. The Massaretta '99, made from the grape of the same name, is very interesting. It offers breadth, solidity and depth, with oak still making itself felt and some vegetal nuances. The Montervo '99, a merlot, is characterized by super-ripe tones and extraordinarily rich fruit. We would have liked to taste it later to see how the complexity develops. At the moment, it is impressive but needs more refinement. The Romalbo '99, a blend of sangiovese and massaretta, also offers a super-ripe nose. Dark in colour, it has rich extract and a heady impact. The tannins are tightly knit but not particularly stylish. The Sangiovese '99 is super-concentrated, and has been generously dosed with new oak, but wants breeding and distinction. The very good white Candia '00 displays scents of apricot, almond and vanilla. The palate offers good weight and a rather long finish.

○	Candia dei Colli Apuani '00	🍷🍷	4
●	Massaretta '99	🍷🍷	6
●	Montervo '99	🍷🍷	6
●	Romalbo '99	🍷🍷	6
●	Sangiovese '99	🍷	5
●	Montervo '98	🍷🍷	6
●	Romalbo '98	🍷🍷	6
●	Sangiovese '98	🍷🍷	5
○	Candia dei Colli Apuani '99	🍷	4
○	Candia dei Colli Apuani Vigneto Candia Alto '99	🍷	5
○	Vermentino '99	🍷	4

MASSA MARITTIMA (GR)

Massa Vecchia
Loc. Le Rocche
Podere Fornace, 11
58024 Massa Marittima (GR)
tel. 0566904144 - 0566904031

Massa Vecchia wines, as we have had occasion to observe in the past, are difficult to classify: no standard taste, no recognizable category. Tasting them is a curious and entertaining experience. But please don't assume that we like Niccolaini's wines because they are unusual. We like them because they're very good. And this year, it seems to us that the producer is showing signs of greater maturity: there was less eccentricity, which used at times to emerge in a rustic style, and increasing refinement in the interpretation of each wine. The cabernet-based Fonte di Pietrarsa – we tasted the '98 – is again excellent. It is the one wine Niccolaini produces that comes close to making concessions to the international style. Without, however, sacrificing any of its own identity. It's mouthfilling and solid, with lots of meaty fruit and beautifully integrated oak. The very good Matto delle Giuncaie '99 has the brusque character of the aleatico grape as well as its rough tannic tone. However, the wine also displays a succulent sweetness and intense attractive scents of wild herbs, oregano and black cherry. The debut performance of the sangiovese-based Poggio ai Venti '98 was interesting. Despite a rather pallid colour and fairly forward aromas, the engaging profile gradually reveals the true nature of the grape: a measured sweetness that is both soft and vibrant. The Terziere '98, from alicante, is more dilute, although eloquent. The Ariento '98 and the Veglie di Neri '97 are original but border on the picturesque.

MASSA MARITTIMA (GR)

Moris Farms
Loc. Curanuova
Fattoria Poggetti
58024 Massa Marittima (GR)
tel. 0566919135
e-mail: avvoltore@cometanet.it

Although the Avvoltore '99 has netted Moris Farms its first Three Glasses, this is not quite an epoch-making development. We have long thought very well indeed of this estate, managed by Adolfo Parentini, which several times in the past came within an inch of winning highest honours. Only two wines were presented this time, since the Morellino Riserva '99 will not be released until next year and the new red Monteregio '00 was not yet ready for tasting. But the Avvoltore '99 does its duty and then some as the cellar's standard-bearer. It is, we feel, better than ever, with its complete structure and a harmony of fragrance and body it has never before shown. A very intense dark ruby introduces a deep, dense bouquet with wonderfully ripe fruit underpinned by refreshing spice, pepper and cocoa. The attack on the palate is round, mouthfilling and engrossing; the tannins are remarkably close-knit but not in the least rough or astringent. On the long finish, intense fruit comes out in force. It's a great wine that is certain to age wonderfully. A brief note on the Morellino '00, which is a correctly executed, unpretentious One Glass wine.

● La Fonte di Pietrarsa '98	🍷🍷	5
● Poggio ai Venti '98	🍷🍷	5
● Il Matto delle Giuncaie '99	🍷🍷	4
● Terziere '98	🍷	4
● Le Veglie di Neri '97	🍷	4
○ Monteregio di Massa Marittima Bianco Ariento '98		4
● Terziere '93	🍷🍷	4
● La Fonte di Pietrarsa '94	🍷🍷	4
● La Fonte di Pietrarsa '95	🍷🍷	4
● La Fonte di Pietrarsa '96	🍷🍷	4
● Il Matto delle Giuncaie '97	🍷🍷	4
● La Fonte di Pietrarsa '97	🍷🍷	5
● Il Matto delle Giuncaie '98	🍷🍷	4

● Avvoltore '99	🍷🍷🍷	6
● Morellino di Scansano '00	🍷	3
● Avvoltore '94	🍷🍷	5
● Morellino di Scansano Ris. '94	🍷🍷	4
● Avvoltore '95	🍷🍷	5
● Avvoltore '97	🍷🍷	5
● Morellino di Scansano Ris. '97	🍷🍷	4
● Avvoltore '98	🍷🍷	5
● Morellino di Scansano Ris. '98	🍷🍷	4
● Avvoltore '93	🍷	5
● Morellino di Scansano Ris. '93	🍷	4
● Morellino di Scansano '94	🍷	2
● Morellino di Scansano '95	🍷	2
● Morellino di Scansano '98	🍷	2
● Morellino di Scansano '99	🍷	2

MONTALCINO (SI)

ALTESINO
LOC. ALTESINO
53028 MONTALCINO (SI)
TEL. 0577806208
E-MAIL: altesino@iol.it

Altesino was one of the first producers in Montalcino to add reds made from non-traditional blends to its roster of Brunellos and Rossos. This decision was subsequently imitated by so many other estates that it must have been justified by substantial consumer demand. It is somewhat less clear why the estate produces so many different labels here (Alte, Palazzo, Borgo and Quarto d'Altesi), making it arduous, at least for us, to characterize the individual wines. The most structured of the group is the Alte di Altesi, which is mouthfilling, enticing and fairly long, but held back by a forward, not entirely clean bouquet where distinct notes of sulphur come through. The Palazzo Altesi offers some of the same sensations: animal notes on the nose are followed by a broad, solid flavour with a slight tannic rusticity in the finish. But this, too, is basically a wine with character. Neither is the nose of the Borgo d'Altesi very convincing but this time the palate, with its signs of over-extraction and bitter notes, fails to come to the rescue. But let's consider the Brunellos. Our tasting notes for the '96 are positive. Given the vintage, it seemed well-made, intense and invigorating on the palate, where alcohol and acidity were in pleasing contrast and the flavour was clean, if simple. The Riserva '95, meanwhile, has a fairly dense structure, prominent wood and slightly rough and astringent tannins.

MONTALCINO (SI)

TENUTA DI ARGIANO
LOC. S. ANGELO IN COLLE, 54
53020 MONTALCINO (SI)
TEL. 0577844037

Tenuta di Argiano is emblematic of a good chunk of the history of Montalcino and its wines. Enviably situated in the southwest of the Brunello zone, it boasts vineyards with exceptional soil and aspects. Up to now, this has always resulted in excellent wines. But all these advantages are less obvious in this year's range, which is moderately good but is not up to the estate's reputation. The Solengo '99 doesn't not have the qualities of the '95 and '97, which both won Three Glasses. The scents are heady and earthy, with somewhat intrusive oak. On entry, the palate is powerful and promising but then it falls off, losing intensity without growing in elegance. It is a good wine, of course, but not a great one. And unfortunately, we were no more encouraged by the Brunello '96. The palate has good stylistic coherence but the tannins are drying and astringent. It must be said in the wine's defence that the '96 vintage was not a memorable one in these parts. This excuse is not available, however, for the Rosso di Montalcino, as the '99 vintage was excellent. The wine, however, is unfocused on the nose and bitterish in the mouth. We can but hope that things will go better next year.

● Brunello di Montalcino '96	ŸŸ	6
● Brunello di Montalcino Ris. '95	Ÿ	6
● Alte d'Altesi '98	Ÿ	5
● Palazzo Altesi '98	Ÿ	5
● Borgo d'Altesi '98		4
● Brunello di Montalcino '93	ŸŸ	5
● Brunello di Montalcino Montosoli '93	ŸŸ	6
● Brunello di Montalcino '95	ŸŸ	6
● Brunello di Montalcino Montosoli '95	ŸŸ	6
● Alte d'Altesi '97	ŸŸ	5

● Solengo '99	ŸŸ	6
● Brunello di Montalcino '96	Ÿ	6
● Rosso di Montalcino '99		4
● Brunello di Montalcino Ris. '85	ŸŸŸ	5
● Brunello di Montalcino Ris. '88	ŸŸŸ	6
● Solengo '95	ŸŸŸ	6
● Solengo '97	ŸŸŸ	6
● Brunello di Montalcino Ris. '90	ŸŸ	6
● Brunello di Montalcino Ris. '91	ŸŸ	6
● Brunello di Montalcino '92	ŸŸ	6
● Brunello di Montalcino '93	ŸŸ	6
● Brunello di Montalcino '94	ŸŸ	6
● Brunello di Montalcino '95	ŸŸ	6
● Solengo '96	ŸŸ	6
● Solengo '98	ŸŸ	6

MONTALCINO (SI)

★ BANFI
LOC. SANT' ANGELO
CASTELLO DI POGGIO ALLE MURA
53024 MONTALCINO (SI)
TEL. 0577840111
E-MAIL: banfi@banfi.it

Banfi has been one of the great phenomena of Italian winemaking in recent years. Founded in 1978, it now boasts 850 hectares under vine, more than 8,000,000 bottles produced every year and an annual turnover of over € 40,000,000.00. Furthermore, the cellar produces an unusually reliable range of wines and has become a benchmark for the Montalcino zone. For a little over a year, Banfi has been doing without the person who was, to a great extent, responsible for the development of the winery. Ezio Rivella has retired but he has already set up four cellars of his own. Meanwhile, the Mariani family has been joined at the helm of the Banfi cellar by Enrico Viglierchio and his mother Giuseppina is still in charge of marketing. Technical operations are directed by the young and very capable oenologist Rudi Buratti. This year's wines are formidable. The Brunello di Montalcino Poggio all'Oro Riserva '95, a simply monumental red, secured Three Glasses. But the Excelsus '98, from cabernet sauvignon and merlot, is equally splendid and made it to our final taste-offs. The delicious Rosso di Montalcino '99 may be the best in its category. The Col di Sasso '99, a blend of sangiovese and cabernet, of which a million and a half bottles are released, is very convincing. The Summus '98, from sangiovese, cabernet and syrah, and the Tavernelle '98, a monovarietal cabernet sauvignon, are both sound. The Brunello '96, the syrah-based Colvecchio '98 and the Mandrielle '98, a merlot, are fair. We could go on: the cellar makes about 30 wines, which is perhaps too many, but instead we'll conclude by saying we wouldn't mind at all if other Banfis were to spring up across the country.

MONTALCINO (SI)

FATTORIA DEI BARBI
LOC. PODERNOVI, 170
53024 MONTALCINO (SI)
TEL. 0577841111

Stefano Cinelli Colombini presented quite an array of wines this time and the results were generally encouraging. There were no misfires. Everything was in excellent form, although we failed to glimpse any hints of ambition. The Vigna del Fiore was perhaps a little below par but it comes from a less than splendid vintage. In almost all the wines we tasted, fractious tannins were the norm – in some cases they positively took over – and the oak was not always perfectly judged. The wine that stood out was the Riserva '95, a Brunello with aromatic density, an austere classical style and a finish somewhat roughened by nonetheless flavoursome, robust tannins. The Brunello '96, similarly conceived, is admirable in style, but insufficient fruit leaves the door wide open to tannins that make short work of the finish. As we mentioned, the Brunello Vigna del Fiore '96 is dominated by oak and less than eloquent. The Rosso di Montalcino '99 reveals a lively and energetic palate but suffers from an unfocused bouquet. The Brigante dei Barbi '97, a blend of sangiovese and merlot, is well-balanced and enjoyable, but vegetal tones are too much in evidence. A grassy pungent note also appears in the Brusco dei Barbi '99, a blend of sangiovese and canaiolo which is correctly executed but could do with more concentration.

Wine	Rating	Score
● Brunello di Montalcino Poggio all'Oro Ris. '95	▼▼▼	6
● Excelsus '98	▼▼	6
● Rosso di Montalcino '99	▼▼	5
● Brunello di Montalcino '96	▼▼	6
● Summus '98	▼▼	6
● Tavernelle Cabernet '98	▼▼	5
● Col di Sasso '99	▼▼	4*
● Colvecchio Syrah '98	▼	5
● Mandrielle Merlot '98	▼	5
● Brunello di Montalcino Poggio all'Oro Ris. '93	▼▼▼	6
● Excelsus '93	▼▼▼	6
● Summus '97	▼▼▼	6

Wine	Rating	Score
● Brunello di Montalcino Ris. '95	▼▼	6
● Brunello di Montalcino '96	▼	5
● Brunello di Montalcino V. del Fiore Ris. '96	▼	6
● Brigante dei Barbi '97	▼	5
● Brusco dei Barbi '99	▼	3
● Rosso di Montalcino '99	▼	5
● Brunello di Montalcino V. del Fiore Ris. '88	▼▼	6
● Brunello di Montalcino V. del Fiore Ris. '91	▼▼	6
● Brunello di Montalcino '93	▼▼	5
● Brunello di Montalcino V. del Fiore Ris. '93	▼▼	6
● Brunello di Montalcino V. del Fiore Ris. '95	▼▼	6
● Brunello di Montalcino '95	▼	5
● Brigante dei Barbi '96	▼	5

MONTALCINO (SI)

CASTELLO DI CAMIGLIANO
LOC. CAMIGLIANO
VIA D'INGRESSO, 2
53024 MONTALCINO (SI)
TEL. 0577816061 - 0577844058
E-MAIL: camigliano@sienane.it

After years of turning out well-made, somewhat anonymous, wines, Camigliano has finally emerged from its shell. This is important news, not just for the estate itself but also for Montalcino as a whole, as this is a large estate with great potential. We're not yet shouting it from the rooftops because the wines, while good, show room for improvement, which is what we hope will arrive in the coming years. Still, something has definitely happened, as you can tell by tasting the wines. The Riserva '95 made it to Two Glasses with grip and substance that had not previously been the norm at Camigliano. It is also true that the oak still wants some fine-tuning, as it's a bit intrusive on nose and palate, but the wine is generally admirable. The Poderuccio '99, despite a distinct vegetal note on the nose, is good too. The medium-bodied palate, complex and persistent, is not without elegance. The successful Brunello '96 came quite close to a second Glass. The nose is well-typed but not very eloquent. The palate has much more to say for itself: the attack is rounded, the well-sustained progression never falters and the finish shows only the faintest hint of edginess. The nose of the good Sant'Antimo is not perfectly defined but the palate is solid and substantial, if also a bit raw and tannic. We are putting off our review of the Rosso di Montalcino '99 until next time because it has yet to settle down.

MONTALCINO (SI)

TENUTA CAPARZO
LOC. CAPARZO
S. P. DEL BRUNELLO KM 1,700
53024 MONTALCINO (SI)
TEL. 0577848390 - 0577847166
E-MAIL: ntrune@caparzo.com

Over the last ten years, the wines from Tenuta Caparzo have generally been very good, with the odd Three Glass winner, vintage permitting. Usually, the Brunello La Casa stands out but no '96 was presented. The well-ordered Brunello Riserva '95 revealed a clean nose with characteristic ripe black cherry notes. The palate is even and smooth, with an elegant progression. The tannins, which are a bit astringent but basically sound, have their say in the finish. The Rosso di Montalcino La Caduta '99 gave a good performance. The dense aromas are nicely balanced between notes of berry fruit and agreeable nuances of oak. Style, elegance and body characterize the palate. The satisfactory Caparzo Rosso '98 offers substance and an orderly development. The finish is moderate in length and the nose needs more definition. The Ca' del Pazzo '97, from sangiovese and cabernet, did very well. It shows a distinctive ripe bouquet with earthy and vegetal tones. The palate may not be overly impressive on entry but it gradually gains momentum, finishing fairly long, despite slightly raw tannins. The Rosso '99 is uncomplicated, intense and enjoyably fragrant but the Brunello '96 is disappointing because of a tannic punch that would be appropriate to rather more body. The very fine Moscadello '98 boasts intriguing aromas of lavender, honey and dried figs.

Wine	Glasses	Score
● Brunello di Montalcino Ris. '95	ŶŶ	6
● Poderuccio '99	ŶŶ	4
● Brunello di Montalcino '96	Ŷ	5
● Sant'Antimo Rosso '99	Ŷ	3
● Brunello di Montalcino Ris. '90	ŶŶ	6
● Brunello di Montalcino '91	ŶŶ	5

Wine	Glasses	Score
● Brunello di Montalcino Ris. '95	ŶŶ	6
○ Moscadello V. T. '98	ŶŶ	6
● Rosso di Montalcino La Caduta '99	ŶŶ	5
● Ca' del Pazzo '97	ŶŶ	5
● Caparzo Rosso '99	Ŷ	4
● Brunello di Montalcino '96		6
● Brunello di Montalcino La Casa '88	ŶŶŶ	6
● Brunello di Montalcino La Casa '93	ŶŶŶ	6
● Brunello di Montalcino Ris. '88	ŶŶ	6
● Brunello di Montalcino La Casa '91	ŶŶ	5
● Brunello di Montalcino '93	ŶŶ	6
● Brunello di Montalcino Ris. '93	ŶŶ	6
● Brunello di Montalcino La Casa '94	ŶŶ	6
● Brunello di Montalcino Ris. '94	ŶŶ	6
● Brunello di Montalcino La Casa '95	ŶŶ	6

MONTALCINO (SI)

CASANOVA DI NERI
PODERE CASANOVA
53028 MONTALCINO (SI)
TEL. 0577834455 - 0577834029
E-MAIL: giacner@tin.it

Giacomo Neri may not have netted Three Glasses this time but he did make one of the best Brunellos to be found from the difficult '96 vintage. This was another excellent performance from Cerretalto. It is bound to leave its mark in future years partly because we'll have fruit from better vintages, starting with the '97, and partly because it is clear that this Torrenieri estate is getting better every year. The new vineyards have now been planted and the cellars boast many new barrels whose size varies according to the type and characteristics of the wines they are destined to receive. Since Brunello DOC regulations reduced the minimum ageing in oak to two years, small and medium sizes are finding more favour. But let's get back to the Cerretalto '96, which again has a strong character. It's an expressive, powerful, solidly tannic and fruit-rich wine. You couldn't accuse it of being soft or velvety but for a Brunello that is considered a compliment and a sign of personality. Of the other wines presented, the Rosso di Montalcino '99 stands out for its good substance and pleasing personality. The Brunello Tenuta Nuova '96 made less of an impression than usual. Showing the defects of its vintage, it has an acidity that fails to mesh totally with the substantial body and there is a slight lack of focus on the nose.

MONTALCINO (SI)

FATTORIA DEL CASATO
DONATELLA CINELLI COLOMBINI
LOC. CASATO PRIME DONNE
53024 MONTALCINO (SI)
TEL. 0577849421 - 0577662108
E-MAIL: vino@cinellicolombini.it

Donatella Cinelli Colombini continues to work on her Prime Donne project. This involves a selection of Brunello di Montalcino which is chosen and tasted by a panel consisting exclusively of female tasters. The '96 version, although it evidently comes from a vintage that was by no means magnificent in the Brunello zone, magically manages to rise above it in most ways. In fact, the aromas are very well defined and include a particularly characteristic black cherry note, then the palate, which is not overly tannic, is full-bodied and suitably long. A slight acid tang accompanies the flavour and is perhaps the only reminder left by this less than glorious vintage. We were not quite so enthusiastic about the basic Brunello '96, which has a slightly forward bouquet and a less structured, more dilute palate than the Prime Donne. Perhaps the female tasters were too efficient, creaming off all the best batches for their own wine and leaving little for the standard Brunello. The Leone Rosso '99, a new red from sangiovese and merlot, is by no means bad. Modern in style, with only moderate density, it can still point to fairly concentrated fruit on the nose and a soft, decently persistent palate. The Rosso di Montalcino '99 is reasonable: a bit simple but well executed.

Wine	Rating	Score
Brunello di Montalcino Cerretalto '96	▼▼	6
Brunello di Montalcino Tenuta Nuova '96	▼	6
Rosso di Montalcino '99	▼	4
Brunello di Montalcino Cerretalto '95	▼▼▼	6
Brunello di Montalcino '90	▼▼	5
Brunello di Montalcino '93	▼▼	5
Brunello di Montalcino Tenuta Nuova '93	▼▼	6
Brunello di Montalcino Tenuta Nuova '94	▼▼	6
Brunello di Montalcino Tenuta Nuova '95	▼▼	6

Wine	Rating	Score
Brunello di Montalcino Prime Donne '96	▼▼	6
Brunello di Montalcino '96	▼	6
Leone Rosso '99	▼	4
Rosso di Montalcino '99	▼	4
Brunello di Montalcino '93	▼▼	5
Brunello di Montalcino Prime Donne '93	▼▼	6
Brunello di Montalcino Prime Donne '94	▼▼	6
Brunello di Montalcino '95	▼▼	6
Brunello di Montalcino Prime Donne '95	▼▼	6
Rosso di Montalcino '98	▼▼	4

MONTALCINO (SI)

CASISANO COLOMBAIO
LOC. PODERE COLOMBAIO
53024 MONTALCINO (SI)
TEL. 0577849087

Tatiana Schwarze's estate just outside Montalcino is making its debut appearance in the Guide this time, thanks to the progress of the last few years. The vineyards are now tended with much greater care and the barrel stock has grown, confirming the rule that new oak can work miracles in Montalcino, vintage permitting. Fermentation still takes place in temperature-controlled stainless steel vats and the oak barrels vary from medium to large in size. The Brunello Riserva '95 stands out for its dense, very vigorous and well-sustained structure. It's a wine with loads of character, our only deriving from the untypical hints of peach on the nose and the exuberance of acidity-boosted tannins in the finish. The Brunello Vigne del Colombaio '96 also made a good impression. It is broad, round and mouthfilling, with lots of flavoursome tannins and admirable cleanness. Although less successful stylistically, as it is not really characteristic of a sangiovese-based product, it is still a nice bottle of wine. The Brunello '96, a few marks lower down, is sound. The clear-cut nose includes lively notes of black cherry and bramble. Medium-bodied and well-balanced on the palate, despite somewhat prominent tannins, it's an altogether tasty and enjoyable tipple.

● Brunello di Montalcino Ris. '95	♟♟	6
● Brunello di Montalcino Vigna del Colombaio '96	♟♟	6
● Brunello di Montalcino '96	♟	5

MONTALCINO (SI)

CASTELGIOCONDO
LOC. CASTELGIOCONDO
53024 MONTALCINO (SI)
TEL. 05527141

The extensive Marchesi de' Frescobaldi estate at Montalcino lies in one of the most propitious parts of the zone, where vineyard aspects are enviable. Sangiovese, obviously, is king here, but merlot, a grape that adapts nicely to clayey soil, has its say too. Merlot is, in fact, the basis of the Lamaione, which seems to get more complete with each passing year. The '98 is very good. Its bouquet has not fully opened up yet but the fruit is remarkably concentrated and when the wine has been allowed to breathe, it unfurls a toasty note of oak as well as spicy and mineral tones. The entry on the palate is soft and subdued but the structure gradually emerges and the long finish shows very decent complexity. These characteristics are typical of a young wine that is still developing, perhaps not yet eloquent, but definitely promising. Another hard to pin down wine is the Brunello Riserva '95. The complex nose includes distinct notes of liquorice, black cherry jam, tar and minerals. The palate is powerful, severe and a little high strung but the dynamic thrust takes you through nicely to a finish where the tannins emerge. Again, only bottle age will reveal what the wine is really like. The Brunello '96 offers heady aromas laced with earthy tones, notes of bramble jam and balsamic nuances. The palate reveals a well-sustained structure and a slightly tannic finish.

● Brunello di Montalcino Ris. '95	♟♟	6
● Lamaione '98	♟♟	6
● Brunello di Montalcino '96	♟♟	6
● Brunello di Montalcino Ris. '88	♟♟♟	6
● Brunello di Montalcino Ris. '90	♟♟♟	6
● Brunello di Montalcino '91	♟♟	5
● Lamaione '91	♟♟	5
● Lamaione '92	♟♟	5
● Brunello di Montalcino '93	♟♟	5
● Lamaione '94	♟♟	5
● Brunello di Montalcino '95	♟♟	5
● Lamaione '95	♟♟	5
● Lamaione '96	♟♟	5
● Lamaione '97	♟♟	5

MONTALCINO (SI)

CASTIGLION DEL BOSCO
LOC. CASTIGLION DEL BOSCO
53024 MONTALCINO (SI)
TEL. 0577807078
E-MAIL: castbosco@iol.it

Castiglion del Bosco is hardly a newcomer to wine or Montalcino. The cellar was among the founding members of the Consorzio at the end of the 1960s and has been producing the classic reds of this zone for decades. As one of the largest estates hereabouts, with its 50 hectares under vine, it has considerable potential, which has not been fully exploited in recent years. Vineyard and cellar management have had ups and downs but are now in the safe hands of Riccardo Cotarella, Italy's most celebrated oenologist. It would be unreasonable to expect miracles straight away, though. Good as he is, Riccardo will need time to get to know the region and its peculiarities. Meanwhile, we tasted some very fine reds. For starters, the Brunello Riserva '95, is very successful. A headily elegant nose precedes the full-bodied, stylishly expressive palate with its surefooted progression and support from robust tannins. The Brunello '96 is perforce less rich but nonetheless characterful. The Rosso di Montalcino has rather unforgiving acidity and lacks length. We were unable to taste the Bernaia, a blend of sangiovese and cabernet.

MONTALCINO (SI)

CIACCI PICCOLOMINI D'ARAGONA
FRAZ. CASTELNUOVO DELL'ABATE
B.GO DI MEZZO, 62
53024 MONTALCINO (SI)
TEL. 0577835616
E-MAIL: info@ctacci-piccolomini.com

Ciacci Piccolomini, together with a select group of other estates, contributed significantly to enhancing Montalcino's prestige in the late 1980s. We still fondly remember the wonderful versions of Brunello Vigna di Pianrosso from '88 and '90, and also the excellent Rosso di Montalcino '90. Then there was a decline and the estate seemed destined to occupy a supporting role until last year, when there were signs of resurgence with the Brunello '95 and, particularly, the Fabius, a very fine syrah which almost won Three Glasses. We were expecting something good from Giuseppe Bianchini this time but he has gone beyond our expectations with a great Brunello Vigna di Pianrosso Riserva '95. It is a subtly nuanced, richly textured wine with distinct fruit on the nose, where the oak is kept well under control. The palate is broad yet concentrated, the progression luscious. But this wine is no a one-off for the whole range is admirable. The Fabius '99 confirms that it is a wine to be watched. It may not have the clear-cut bouquet or the overall harmony of the '98 but its energy is really impressive. Power, rather than elegance, is its strong suit, and it also reveals original hints of aromatic herbs. The weaker but still good Brunello '96 is soft and concentrated, revealing lovely succulent fruit, but also some vegetal notes on the nose. The fine Rosso di Montalcino '99 boasts a dynamic finish, but the Ateo '98, with its marked vegetal tone, is only fair.

● Brunello di Montalcino Ris. '95	ŸŸ 6
● Brunello di Montalcino '96	ŸŸ 6
● Rosso di Montalcino '99	Ÿ 4

● Brunello di Montalcino Vigna di Pianrosso Ris. '95	ŸŸŸ 6
● Brunello di Montalcino Vigna di Pianrosso '96	ŸŸ 6
● Rosso di Montalcino Vigna della Fonte '99	ŸŸ 4
● Sant'Antimo Fabius '99	ŸŸ 5
● Ateo '98	Ÿ 5
● Brunello di Montalcino Vigna di Pianrosso '88	ŸŸŸ 6
● Brunello di Montalcino Vigna di Pianrosso '90	ŸŸŸ 5
● Brunello di Montalcino Vigna di Pianrosso '95	ŸŸ 6
● Sant'Antimo Fabius '98	ŸŸ 6

MONTALCINO (SI)

TENUTA COL D'ORCIA
LOC. SANT'ANGELO IN COLLE
53020 MONTALCINO (SI)
TEL. 0577808001
E-MAIL: coldorcia.direzione@tin.it

Quantity and quality do not always go hand in hand. At Col d'Orcia, however, all the wines in the vast range, which are also produced in serious numbers, reveal the meticulous and constant care that goes into them year after year. The Brunello Poggio al Vento Riserva is the gem of the collection but you probably knew that. The '95 has imposing structure yet also reveals elegance, and should get better with time. The nose is bouquet is that of a wine with character, an earthy tone mingling with notes of liquorice, tobacco and spice accompanied by balsamic nuances. The palate is soft, smooth and even, and the finish is still under the influence of wood tannins. The Brunello Riserva '95 made a very good showing. Elegant, complex aromas of flowers, tobacco, liquorice and pepper precede a nicely ordered, sustained and stylish palate with a long finish. The Rosso di Montalcino '99 acquitted itself well. Although simpler, it reveals some aromatic richness with notes of black cherry, violet and toasty oak. The attack on the palate is warm and round, tannins are present but well under control and all the aromas are delightfully echoed on the finish. The Moscadello Pascena '98 is less clear-cut but interesting, all the same. The nose foregrounds gooseberry and anise while the palate is well-balanced, even and stylish rather than powerful. The acceptable Brunello '96 is fairly forward, and dry tannins appear in the finish. The somewhat disappointing cabernet sauvignon-based Olmaia '97, although nicely structured, is distinctly forward. The rest of the range is uncomplicated but well executed.

- Brunello di Montalcino Poggio al Vento Ris. '95 — 6
- Brunello di Montalcino Ris. '95 — 6
- O Moscadello di Montalcino V. T. Pascena '98 — 6
- Rosso di Montalcino '99 — 4
- Chianti Gineprone '99 — 2*
- Rosso degli Spezieri '00 — 2*
- Brunello di Montalcino '96 — 5
- Olmaia '97 — 6
- O Ghiaie Bianche '99 — 4
- Brunello di Montalcino Poggio al Vento Ris. '88 — 6
- Brunello di Montalcino Poggio al Vento Ris. '90 — 6
- Olmaia '94 — 5

MONTALCINO (SI)

ANDREA COSTANTI
COLLE AL MATRICHESE
53024 MONTALCINO (SI)
TEL. 0577848195
E-MAIL: costanti@inwind.it

The Ardingo was a surprise. In Andrea Costanti's line-up of wines, which performed very well as a whole, it was this blend of two parts merlot to one of cabernet sauvignon that shone with special brilliance. An intense, lively dark ruby precedes the deep nose of dark berry fruit and captivating notes of pepper. The flavour, while not explosive, is well-balanced, elegant and underpinned but not overwhelmed by the oak. That's not to say the other wines didn't perform well for they did, starting with the Rosso di Montalcino Calbello '99, which is close to the Ardingo in style, balance and elegance, offering medium body and moderate length. The good Brunello '96 suffers from slight reduction on the nose but reveals concentration, densely knit tannins and a lingering finish. Neither is the Vermiglio, a sangiovese, to be overlooked. The fragrance, with its earthy tone, is more forward, the attack on the palate is quite powerful and the development is well proportioned but the finish is tannic and lacks refinement. The Brunello Riserva '95 is more austere but also a little in thrall to animal and vegetal aromas. The palate is generous and dynamic on entry but a little rough in the finish. Lastly, the Rosso di Montalcino '99 is well conceived and soundly put together but boisterous oak upstages the fruit.

- Ardingo '98 — 5
- Brunello di Montalcino Ris. '95 — 6
- Vermiglio '98 — 4
- Rosso di Montalcino Calbello '99 — 4
- Brunello di Montalcino '96 — 6
- Rosso di Montalcino '99 — 4
- Brunello di Montalcino '88 — 6
- Brunello di Montalcino Ris. '83 — 6
- Brunello di Montalcino Ris. '88 — 6
- Brunello di Montalcino '90 — 6
- Brunello di Montalcino Ris. '90 — 6
- Brunello di Montalcino '93 — 6
- Brunello di Montalcino '95 — 6

MONTALCINO (SI)

TENUTA DI SESTA
LOC. CASTELNUOVO DELL'ABATE
53020 MONTALCINO (SI)
TEL. 0577835612 - 0577596014
E-MAIL: giovanni.ciacci@tin.it

For some time now we've been waiting for Tenuta di Sesta to show us what it can do. It is, after all, located in the most sought-after part of Castelnuovo dell'Abate, with spectacular exposure that lets the grapes ripen perfectly even in less favourable vintages. And then the cellar can pick and choose from the fruit of almost 15 hectares of vineyards so that this is potentially one of the most interesting producers in Montalcino. Yet in the past, we have not encountered the hoped-for consistent excellence: one good wine and one decent one was the long and short of it. But this year's tastings were decidedly more encouraging. The Brunello Riserva '95 is a very good wine indeed. It may not have the complexity and character that make a Brunello really great but it does have several other strings to its bow. The aromas are well-defined and the fruit is clearly in evidence with notes of black cherry and bramble. We liked the soft texture of the palate, the beautifully amalgamated tannins and the well-behaved oak, not to mention the intensity of the fruit in the finish. The Rosso di Montalcino '99 is pretty good, too. The colour on the rim is already fairly evolved, and the nose is dominated by wood, but things look up on the palate. A well-rounded attack is followed up by a progression that expands nicely to finish with tight-knit, dry but pleasing tannins. A good performance from Tenuta di Sesta, and we hope they'll consolidate their gains in the future.

● Brunello di Montalcino Ris. '95	♀♀	6
● Rosso di Montalcino '99	♀	4

MONTALCINO (SI)

FANTI - LA PALAZZETTA
FRAZ. CASTELNUOVO DELL'ABATE
B.GO DI SOTTO, 25
53020 MONTALCINO (SI)
TEL. 0577835631

Do we have to recite the truism about how good wine is made in the vineyard? Well in Montalcino, the best results are obtained by producers who tend their vines with care, plant them densely and keep yields low. In other words, it is not sufficient to focus obsessively on the fermentation process, buy lots of new barrels and change the lighting in the cellar. Not that we are wine technicians but it does seem to us that a lot of the raw material in Montalcino is a little too dilute. The groundwork must, unsurprisingly, be done in the field. A few years ago, Flavio Fanti, owner of La Palazzetta, decided to apply the old adage. And this year's tastings bear out the wisdom of that decision. The Brunello di Montalcino '96 may not be a paragon of rich extract and complexity but it is graceful and well-balanced, despite slightly intrusive oak. To Flavio's credit, it's an honest interpretation of a less than captivating vintage. The Rosso di Montalcino '99 is riper and meatier, a broad, fruity wine with attractive tannins. It too is over-generous with the oak but the raw material is excellent and the finish beautifully clean.

● Brunello di Montalcino '96	♀♀	6
● Rosso di Montalcino '99	♀♀	4
● Brunello di Montalcino '93	♀♀	5
● Brunello di Montalcino '94	♀♀	5
● Brunello di Montalcino '95	♀♀	5
● Rosso di Montalcino '96	♀♀	4
● Rosso di Montalcino '97	♀♀	4
● Rosso di Montalcino '98	♀	4

MONTALCINO (SI)

Fanti - San Filippo
Loc. San Filippo
Fraz. Castelnuovo dell'Abate
B.go di Mezzo, 15
53020 Montalcino (SI)
Tel. 0577835628 - E-mail: balfanti@tin.it

We share neither of the extreme opinions about Montalcino and its wines that one hears bandied about. For some, Brunello is an exemplary, if not perfect, wine while others mutter that the market is fed up with these old-fashioned, over-rated bottles. Montalcino did go through a period of decline, as we pointed out at the time, but cannot ignore its enormous potential. That's why we note with great pleasure the evidence of increased commitment from many of the producers in the area. Filippo Baldassare Fanti is one of them. This year, he may have strolled off with an effortless Three Glasses, and a number of other very high scores, but he remains well aware that this is only a beginning. Filippo is, in fact, his own severest critic. At times, he can be too severe. Still, his Riserva '95 is quite frankly a superb wine. It shows all the warmth and richness you expect from a Brunello but also unveils remarkable tannic depth, excellent balance and perfectly calibrated oak. The Brunello '96, also well designed, offers notes of blackcurrant and bramble on the nose, followed by a round, mouthfilling and balanced, if not very complex, palate. The admirable Vin Santo reveals aromas of leather, cigar box, wax and dried figs. The attack on the palate is very sweet and succulent, the finish lingering and mildly tannic. Finally, the Sant'Antimo '00 is fruity and pleasing.

● Brunello di Montalcino Ris. '95	🍷🍷🍷	6
● Brunello di Montalcino '96	🍷🍷	6
○ Vin Santo	🍷🍷	5
● Sant'Antimo '00	🍷	3
● Brunello di Montalcino '93	🍷🍷	5
● Brunello di Montalcino '95	🍷🍷	6
● Rosso di Montalcino '96	🍷🍷	4
● Rosso di Montalcino '97	🍷🍷	4
● Brunello di Montalcino Ris. '93	🍷	6
● Brunello di Montalcino '94	🍷	5
● Rosso di Montalcino '98	🍷	4
● Sant'Antimo '98	🍷	3

MONTALCINO (SI)

Eredi Fuligni
Via S. Saloni, 32
53024 Montalcino (SI)
Tel. 0577848039 - 0577848127

We're still waiting for the brilliant performance that Roberto Guerrini's estate is going to give us sooner or later. We feel there can be no doubt on the point because so much progress has been made already and everything is in place for a great leap forward. It is also true that Fuligni's wines do not have the kick of those from the slopes of Montalcino further south, and that they take longer to come out, but they can boast a reliable consistency of style and an elegance that is hard to match in the Montalcino DOC zone. It is altogether possible that the next few vintages to be released, those warm ripeness-friendly years 1997 on, will give Roberto's wines that extra touch of chewy richness. The first piece of evidence to this effect is provided by the Rosso di Montalcino Ginestreto '99, which offers a broad, very well-defined bouquet with delightful aromas of black cherry and modest oaky notes. The palate is full-bodied, energetic, balanced and persistent. This is a successful wine that offers elegance and pleasing sweet, ripe fruit, perhaps without great complexity, which is in any case not a quality we expect from a Rosso. The Brunello Riserva '95, more austere and less straightforward, is hindered by oak-derived tannins that get in the way of a relaxed progression. The flavoursome and vibrant Brunello '96 reveals somewhat noticeable oak, with a clean and enjoyable if only moderately long finish.

● Brunello di Montalcino Vigneti dei Cottimelli Ris. '95	🍷🍷	6
● Brunello di Montalcino Vigneti dei Cottimelli '96	🍷🍷	6
● Rosso di Montalcino Ginestreto '99	🍷🍷	4
● Brunello di Montalcino '90	🍷🍷	5
● Brunello di Montalcino Ris. '90	🍷🍷	6
● Brunello di Montalcino '93	🍷🍷	5
● Brunello di Montalcino Ris. '93	🍷🍷	6
● Brunello di Montalcino '94	🍷🍷	6
● Brunello di Montalcino '95	🍷🍷	6
● Rosso di Montalcino Ginestreto '95	🍷🍷	4

MONTALCINO (SI)

GREPPONE MAZZI
TENIMENTI RUFFINO
LOC. GREPPONE
53024 MONTALCINO (SI)
TEL. 05583605 - 05778313677
E-MAIL: ruffino@ruffino.it

After the amicable divorce that saw the estates split between the two branches of the Folonari family, the Ruffino side still has Greppone Mazzi, the important Montalcino property. From almost ten hectares under vine, they harvest the grapes for the only wine they make, which is a Brunello, of course. The last few vintages have demonstrated that the raw material is more reliable than it used to be. The Brunello di Montalcino '96 was inevitably somewhat diminished by its not very propitious year. But its style comes through in the well-defined bouquet and obvious character. The brilliant, moderately saturated ruby hue shows a classic garnet rim. The dominant tones on the nose are alcohol-rich and fruity, foregrounding black cherry, liqueur cherry and redcurrant, and oak is kept under control. After a somewhat uncertain attack on the palate, the development is confident, even and full-bodied, with a moderately persistent finish. It's a wine to be drunk within the next four to five years but then longevity is not characteristic of most '96 Brunellos.

MONTALCINO (SI)

TENUTA IL GREPPO
LOC. GREPPO, 183
53024 MONTALCINO (SI)
TEL. 0577848087
E-MAIL: biondisanti@biondisanti.it

This profile covers all the wines marketed by Biondi Santi so, leaving aside the wines produced at Il Greppo, which were not available in time for our tastings, we are reviewing those from the Poggio Salvi estate and from Jacopo Biondi Santi's new property, Castello di Montepò, which is located in the Morellino di Scansano zone. First up is the Morellino di Scansano Riserva '98, with its fine vivid ruby and nicely blended fruity and spicy aromas, followed by a satisfying, concentrated flavour. Two Glasses well earned. The same award was easily won by the red Sassoalloro '98, another thoroughly reliable wine. On the intense nose, fruity and spicy tones cover the grassy nuance, which is in any case unobtrusive. Although the tannins are a bit hard, they are not bitter nor do they dry the palate. The Brunello di Montalcino Poggio Salvi '96 did very nicely. The ruby colour verges on garnet then the broad bouquet offers scents of tobacco and vanilla, in addition to the classic fruit note of morello cherry. The palate shows signs of the less than brilliant vintage but the fine-grained tannins and well-judged acidity offset nicely the rather lightweight body. The elegance of the whole, with a succulent finish, earned Two Glasses. Lastly, there is only a mention for the Lavischio, with its unfocused nose and rather one-dimensional palate.

● Brunello di Montalcino '96	ŶŶ	6
● Brunello di Montalcino Ris. '82	ŶŶ	6
● Brunello di Montalcino Ris. '83	ŶŶ	6
● Brunello di Montalcino Ris. '90	ŶŶ	6
● Brunello di Montalcino Ris. '95	ŶŶ	6
● Brunello di Montalcino Ris. '85	Ŷ	6
● Brunello di Montalcino Ris. '88	Ŷ	6
● Brunello di Montalcino '91	Ŷ	5
● Brunello di Montalcino Ris. '91	Ŷ	6
● Brunello di Montalcino '93	Ŷ	5
● Brunello di Montalcino '94	Ŷ	6

● Brunello di Montalcino Poggio Salvi '96	ŶŶ	6
● Morellino di Scansano Ris. Montepò '98	ŶŶ	4
● Sassoalloro '98	ŶŶ	5
● Lavischio Poggio Salvi '98		3
● Sassoalloro '94	ŶŶ	5
● Sassoalloro '95	ŶŶ	5
● Sassoalloro '96	ŶŶ	5
● Brunello di Montalcino Poggio Salvi '95	Ŷ	6
● Lavischio di Poggio Salvi '96	Ŷ	4
● Rosso di Montalcino Poggio Salvi '98	Ŷ	4

MONTALCINO (SI)

IL POGGIOLO
LOC. POGGIOLO, 259
53024 MONTALCINO (SI)
TEL. 0577848412 - 3483411848
E-MAIL: info@ilpoggiolomontalcino.com

Rodolfo Cosimi is an original producer and to judge from the number of wines he presented – ten – he certainly doesn't lack imagination. The merits of the '99 vintage are obvious in his two versions of Rosso di Montalcino. The Sassello is very good, thanks to spot-on balance. A rounded, full-bodied and thoroughly enjoyable wine, it reveals well-gauged tannins and nice wood. The other Rosso, Terra Rossa, is not bad, either. Here, the style is more forward but there's still lots of balance, the progression is orderly and well-sustained, and the tannins are softly flavoursome. The less successful Brunello Beato '96 is a bit sulphurous on the nose, and bitterish on the palate. The other Brunello '96, the sound Terra Rossa, offers notes of bramble and more mature aromas, followed by a dense palate with plenty of oak and a somewhat closed finish. The Brunello Five Stars Riserva '95 did well, revealing a compact, deep bouquet with notes of black cherry, liquorice and cinnamon mingling with toasty notes of oak. The entry on the palate is excellent – broad and round – but mid palate and finish, although nicely complex, are less concentrated. The Brunello Riserva Sassello '95 is aromatically interesting and not without complexity. The well-sustained palate labours under too much oak, which hinders the expansion. The Brunello Beato Riserva '95 seemed acceptable but a bit unfocused, less than perfectly defined on the nose, and shot through with bitterish notes in the mouth. The sangiovese-based In Riva al Fosso is good, although marked by wood-derived dryness on the finish. The 10 Anni, a simple, vegetal and correct cabernet sauvignon, is fair.

● Brunello di Montalcino Five Stars Ris. '95	ŶŶ	6
● Rosso di Montalcino Sassello '99	ŶŶ	4
● Rosso di Montalcino Terra Rossa '99	ŶŶ	5
● Brunello di Montalcino Terra Rossa '96	Ŷ	6
● Brunello di Montalcino Beato Ris. '95	Ŷ	6
● Brunello di Montalcino Sassello Ris. '95	Ŷ	6
● Brunello di Montalcino Beato '96	Ŷ	6
● Brunello di Montalcino Sassello '96	Ŷ	6
● In Riva al Fosso '97	Ŷ	6
● 10 Anni '97	Ŷ	5

MONTALCINO (SI)

TENUTA IL POGGIONE
FRAZ. SANT'ANGELO IN COLLE
VIA CASTELLO, 14
53020 MONTALCINO (SI)
TEL. 0577844029
E-MAIL: ilpoggione@tin.it

The 50 hectares of vineyards, all basking in the warmth of the southern slopes of Montalcino, make Il Poggione one of the richest historic estates in the Brunello zone, in terms of potential for both quality and quantity. Its appearance in the Guide year after year is due to the stylistic consistency of its wines. These are of the traditional persuasion, by which we mean that they age in large barrels and barriques tend to be shunned. But it is not the size of containers that determines the worth of a producer, it is what you find when you uncork the bottle, and we are pleased to say that this year's range is more than acceptable, starting with the San Leopoldo '98. A blend of sangiovese and cabernet, it reveals powerful notes of black pepper and an equally distinctive palate that is soft, persistent and full-bodied. The Brunello Riserva '95, another Two Glass winner, is rounded, rich in alcohol and very enjoyable, although not awfully complex and somewhat markedly vanillaed on the nose, thanks to the oak. The simple, fruity Rosso di Montalcino '99 has the obvious merit of a fragrant palate enlivened by attractive tannins. The Brunello '96 is quite respectable but a tad forward. The bubbly version of the Moscadello is very simple but quite pleasant.

● Brunello di Montalcino Ris. '95	ŶŶ	6
○ Moscadello di Montalcino '00	Ŷ	5
● Brunello di Montalcino '96	Ŷ	5
● Rosso di Montalcino '99	Ŷ	4
● Brunello di Montalcino '88	ŶŶ	5
● Brunello di Montalcino Ris. '88	ŶŶ	6
● Brunello di Montalcino '90	ŶŶ	5
● Brunello di Montalcino '92	ŶŶ	5
● Rosso di Montalcino '92	ŶŶ	3
● Brunello di Montalcino Ris. '93	ŶŶ	5
● Rosso di Montalcino '93	ŶŶ	3
● Rosso di Montalcino '95	ŶŶ	3
● San Leopoldo '98	ŶŶ	5
● Brunello di Montalcino Ris. '90	Ŷ	6

MONTALCINO (SI)

PODERE LA FORTUNA
LOC. PODERE LA FORTUNA
53024 MONTALCINO (SI)
TEL. 0577848308

Podere La Fortuna is one of the many small Montalcino estates that make their wine with a craft-oriented approach. The group becomes smaller if you only include those who work with care and passion but Podere La Fortuna is still in it. From just over three hectares under vine, the winery harvests good grapes, which are fermented expertly and with no little flair, to judge from the unexpected success of wines they produced from less than inspiring vintages, such as '84. Curiously, very good vintages don't always seem to lead to correspondingly good results at Podere La Fortuna. The Brunello di Montalcino Riserva '95 has a moderately vivid ruby hue, intensely varietal aromas of bay leaf, violet and black cherry, and good weight on the palate where, however, the progression lacks breadth. The Rosso di Montalcino '99 offers fair structure, a not entirely focused nose and a rather austere palate with strong acidity. At this point, we were very nearly wishing the owners a mediocre vintage next time.

● Brunello di Montalcino Ris. '95	ŸŸ	6
● Rosso di Montalcino '99	Ÿ	4
● Brunello di Montalcino '91	ŸŸ	6
● Brunello di Montalcino '93	ŸŸ	6
● Brunello di Montalcino Ris. '93	ŸŸ	6
● Brunello di Montalcino '94	ŸŸ	6
● Brunello di Montalcino '95	ŸŸ	6
● Rosso di Montalcino '98	ŸŸ	4

MONTALCINO (SI)

LA GERLA
LOC. CANALICCHIO
PODERE COLOMBAIO, 5
53024 MONTALCINO (SI)
TEL. 0577848599
E-MAIL: lagerla@tin.it

Consistency used not to be La Gerla's strong suit. Their wines had tended to vary greatly, according to vintage and also to type. There were some very good bottles but they seemed to be the exception rather than the rule. Results last year, however, were most encouraging and at this year's tastings, our favourable impression was confirmed. Sergio Rossi's estate has come up with a range of good wines, and some are better than just good. The mostly sangiovese-based Birba '98, for a start, has many attractive qualities, if not a distinctive personality. A fine lively ruby introduces the clean bouquet of fruit with light toasty notes and a vegetal undertone. The palate confirms the quality of the fruit and the careful vinification. Soft, dense and nicely proportioned, it is lifted by beautifully integrated tannins. The Brunello '96 also impressed. Here, too, the panel appreciated the well-calibrated use of oak, and also the pleasingly sweet, sustained palate with its succulent fruit and lingering finish. The Brunello Riserva '95 also did well, despite some volatility on the nose. The development in the mouth is well co-ordinated, although perhaps somewhat under the thumb of sweet alcohol, while the finish is marked by lively tannins. The Rosso '99 offers appealingly meaty fruit on the palate but the nose is a tad unfocused and the oak has yet to settle down. A satisfactory wine, nevertheless.

● Brunello di Montalcino Ris. '95	ŸŸ	6
● Brunello di Montalcino '96	ŸŸ	6
● Birba '98	ŸŸ	5
● Rosso di Montalcino '99	Ÿ	4
● Brunello di Montalcino Ris. '88	ŸŸ	6
● Birba '90	ŸŸ	5
● Brunello di Montalcino Ris. '91	ŸŸ	6
● Birba '95	ŸŸ	5
● Brunello di Montalcino '88	Ÿ	5
● Brunello di Montalcino '93	Ÿ	5
● Rosso di Montalcino '95	Ÿ	4
● Rosso di Montalcino '96	Ÿ	4

MONTALCINO (SI)

La Poderina
Fraz. Castelnuovo dell'Abate
Loc. Poderina
53020 Montalcino (SI)
Tel. 0577835737
E-mail: fattoriadelcerro@tin.it

The style of La Poderina's Brunello sets it apart from the rest. The simplest description would be "atypical" but typicity is a thorny subject for a wine like Brunello. The DOC regulations permit back blending with younger wine, a process known as "ringiovanimento", or "refreshing". This can make considerable changes to the wine's sensory profile. So, it would perhaps be more appropriate to say that the Brunello from SAI Agricola's Montalcino estate is unconventional. This does not mean that it isn't good for the Riserva '95 is excellent. It is dark ruby, with a garnet rim, then the fruit-centred nose includes undertones of bramble jam and perhaps a touch too much oak. The palate is very concentrated, the tannins substantial and fine-grained, and the development is even. The quality is undeniable and in fact, our only criticism is subjective: the wine is a bit coldly technological and not very exciting. The impeccable Moscadello Vendemmia Tardiva is just as good, which is to say excellent, and also rather more engrossing. The absolutely pure nose offers notes of peach blossom, lavender, acacia and orange peel, all expressed with exemplary elegance. The sweet palate is glycerine-rich, but not cloying, and toasty tones emerge on the long finish. Both the Brunello '96, solid and with a rather inelegant super-ripe timbre, and the clean and well-balanced Rosso di Montalcino '99 are more fairly run of the mill.

MONTALCINO (SI)

La Togata
Loc. Argiano
53024 Montalcino (SI)
Tel. 0577849363 - 066880300

This small but feisty Montalcino winery is carrying forward its programme of improvement. The results of a more rational distribution of technical resources – fermentation rooms are now separate from the ageing cellar – get better every year. The Brunello di Montalcino Riserva '95, in fact, ended up at the Three Glass taste-offs. Full-bodied, with great depth of both bouquet and flavour, it is a very harmonious, rich and elegant red. It didn't miss by much – it has perhaps just a pinch too much acid tang – but at this rate, next year's offering may well win the big prize. The Rosso di Montalcino '99, which is delightfully and distinctly fruity, with very attractive if slightly insistent oak, was also in contention until the very end, further evidence of a high all-round standard. The standard-label Brunello '96 is a successful wine, too. Not so impressively structured as the Riserva – not surprisingly – it develops evenly on the palate, revealing prominent tannins in the finish. The IGT Azzurreta '99, a monovarietal sangiovese, is moderately good. The aromas are muffled and not very vibrant, the palate is attractively firm but the finish is fleeting.

● Brunello di Montalcino Ris. '95	🍷🍷	6
○ Moscadello V. T. '99	🍷🍷	5
● Brunello di Montalcino '96	🍷	6
● Rosso di Montalcino '99	🍷	4
● Brunello di Montalcino Ris. '88	🍷🍷🍷	6
● Brunello di Montalcino '88	🍷🍷	5
● Brunello di Montalcino Ris. '90	🍷🍷	6
● Brunello di Montalcino Ris. '93	🍷🍷	6
● Brunello di Montalcino '95	🍷🍷	5
○ Moscadello V. T. '98	🍷🍷	5
● Brunello di Montalcino '89	🍷	5
● Brunello di Montalcino '90	🍷	5
● Brunello di Montalcino '94	🍷	5
○ Moscadello V. T. '97	🍷	5

● Brunello di Montalcino Ris. '95	🍷🍷	6
● Rosso di Montalcino '99	🍷🍷	4
● Brunello di Montalcino '96	🍷🍷	6
● Azzurreta '99	🍷	5
● Brunello di Montalcino '90	🍷🍷	6
● Brunello di Montalcino '91	🍷🍷	6
● Brunello di Montalcino '94	🍷🍷	6
● Brunello di Montalcino '95	🍷🍷	6
● Azzurreta '96	🍷🍷	5
● Rosso di Montalcino '98	🍷	4

MONTALCINO (SI)

Maurizio Lambardi
Podere Canalicchio di Sotto, 8
53024 Montalcino (SI)
tel. 0577848476

Maurizio Lambardi deserves our respect and trust, not just because of the wines that emerge from his cellar year after year but also because he is a real vigneron whose primary concern is his grapes. Maurizio isn't one to waste time on self-advertisement. His scanty regard for publicity has kept him out of the limelight but in the long run, this makes him a more authentic and unaffected figure. And then his bottles of Brunello and Rosso do the talking for him. These bottles are never showy or flamboyant but remain resolutely true to the style of the estate. Maurizio's wines give you the real measure of sangiovese and of each single vintage, with no fudging. To start with, the Brunello '96 is one of the best of its vintage. The nose is redolent of its terroir, unveiling liquorice, tobacco and a firm minerally note. The palate is densely knit and substantial, with prominent tannins that have yet to settle down. This is not one of your accommodating or docile Brunellos; it's a wine with strong character. The Rosso di Montalcino '99 is less spunky but still good. The nose, well-defined and distinctive, offers lots of black cherry fruit and delightfully fragrant notes of black pepper. The wine is very satisfying in the mouth, proffering a well-rounded body, flavourful tannins and a long finish that mirrors the palate. It's a harmonious and pleasing Rosso, made to drunk and enjoyed without inhibition.

MONTALCINO (SI)

Luce
Loc. Castelgiocondo
53024 Montalcino (SI)
tel. 0577848492

When Marchesi de' Frescobaldi and Mondavi, the Californian winemakers, joined forces to set up this winery in Montalcino, there were those who thought it just an exercise in marketing, and that wines in the international style would be the only result. But we have been tasting Luce year after year, and its stylistic characteristics have become increasingly evident. We have seen that it has not only achieved a very high standard but has even succeeded in becoming a genuine "vin de terroir", which is equally significant. The colour of the Luce '98 – ruby with a garnet rim – suggests a more forward wine than one might expect. This impression is confirmed by the aromas, which show some tertiary hints of leather, liquorice and red berry jam. It's an interesting nose which, if not very fresh, is complex and resonantly reminiscent of the Montalcino terroir. The palate elicits a range of impressions. The attack is a little uncertain and lacks force but from mid palate on, the wine opens out remarkably and finishes long. If wines, and their future development, are to be judged by their finish, then the Luce '98, a blend of sangiovese and merlot, is great. If impact on nose and palate count, then it's only good. We tend to favour the first of these interpretations but only time will tell. Both vintages of Lucente were good and stylistically consistent. We slightly prefer the '99, which is much better balanced and succulent, with just the right concentration and soft, smooth tannins. The '98 is similar but a bit more forward.

● Brunello di Montalcino '96	ŶŶ 6
● Rosso di Montalcino '99	ŶŶ 4
● Brunello di Montalcino '88	♀ 5
● Brunello di Montalcino '90	♀♀ 5
● Rosso di Montalcino '90	♀♀ 4
● Brunello di Montalcino '91	♀♀ 5
● Rosso di Montalcino '91	♀♀ 4
● Rosso di Montalcino '92	♀♀ 4
● Brunello di Montalcino '93	♀♀ 5
● Rosso di Montalcino '93	♀♀ 4
● Brunello di Montalcino '95	♀♀ 6
● Rosso di Montalcino '95	♀♀ 4
● Rosso di Montalcino '98	♀♀ 4

● Luce '98	ŶŶ 6
● Lucente '99	ŶŶ 5
● Lucente '98	Ŷ 5
● Luce '94	♀♀♀ 6
● Luce '95	♀♀ 6
● Lucente '95	♀♀ 5
● Luce '96	♀♀ 6
● Lucente '96	♀♀ 5
● Luce '97	♀♀ 6
● Lucente '97	♀♀ 5

MONTALCINO (SI)

MASTROJANNI
FRAZ. CASTELNUOVO DELL'ABATE
PODERI LORETO E SAN PIO
53024 MONTALCINO (SI)
TEL. 0577835681
E-MAIL: mastrojanni.vini@tiscalinet.it

Many estates in Montalcino regularly present a range of up-and-down wines whose quality varies significantly according to type and vintage. One of the notable merits of the Mastrojanni cellar is that it manages to maintain a consistent level in the wines it produces. The characteristics of each vintage do make a difference, of course, but in disappointing years Mastrojanni succeeds in mitigating the negative effects by skilful vineyard management and enormous care during fermentation. In recent years, there have been some mild surprises. In last year's Guide, for instance, the best wine was the Botrys, a sweet white made from moscato. This time, less surprisingly but still significantly, we preferred the Brunello Riserva '95 to the celebrated Schiena d'Asino selection from the same vintage. The Riserva is rounder, more balanced and rich in complex aromas ranging from ripe fruit to spicy and faintly animal nuances. The Schiena d'Asino, which had been long and eagerly awaited, is more inscrutable. We tried it three or four times and our impressions were always the same: great raw material but a not very eloquent nose and a certain hardness on the palate – mostly tannin-derived – that may be a sign of slight over-extraction. Perhaps they went too far, or else the wine may just be going through a difficult phase and will become more harmonious as it develops. We shall see. Meanwhile, we very much liked the Brunello '96, with its etheric nose and close-knit palate, the San Pio, a blend of sangiovese and cabernet which is tasty if not extremely elegant, and the soft, fragrant Botrys '97. We conclude with the Rosso di Montalcino '99, which performed less excitingly.

● Brunello di Montalcino Ris. '95	¶¶	6
● Brunello di Montalcino Schiena d'Asino '95	¶¶	6
● Brunello di Montalcino '96	¶¶	5
○ Botrys '97	¶¶	5
● San Pio '98	¶¶	4
● Rosso di Montalcino '99	¶	5
● Brunello di Montalcino Ris. '88	¶¶¶	6
● Brunello di Montalcino '90	¶¶¶	6
● Brunello di Montalcino Schiena d'Asino '90	¶¶¶	6
● Brunello di Montalcino Schiena d'Asino '93	¶¶¶	6
● Brunello di Montalcino Ris. '93	¶¶	5
● San Pio '95	¶¶	5
○ Botrys '96	¶¶	5

MONTALCINO (SI)

MOCALI
LOC. MOCALI
53024 MONTALCINO (SI)
TEL. 0577849485

Tiziano Ciacci is a man of few words and many deeds. Without fuss, he has steadily restructured his entire estate, from vineyards to cellar, while continuing to turn out good wine. Shrewd management policies, in pricing as in other matters, have helped maintain Mocali's solid reputation for reliability over the years. At this year's tastings, the only wine that really stood out was the Brunello Riserva '95. The bouquet may not be particularly intense but it is tidy and clear-cut. The palate is much more expressive, the flavour being evenly distributed, concentrated and underpinned by lively, smooth tannins of excellent quality. The oak is perfectly integrated and the finish long. All that it wants to be great is a touch more verve. The Brunello '96 did less brilliantly. The nose is not very well defined and the palate is leaner, though still even. There is more substance in the Rosso di Montalcino '99, a pleasingly fruity wine with admirable sweetness, although oak tends to dominate nose and finish. Neither of the other two wines is particularly exciting. The acceptable I Piaggioni has fruit and flowers on the nose and an agreeable, if rather simple, flavour. The Moscadello '99 is well made but not very impressive. The aromas struggle to emerge and the palate is marked by an almost cloying sweetness.

● Brunello di Montalcino Ris. '95	¶¶	6
● Brunello di Montalcino '96	¶	5
● I Piaggioni '99	¶	3
● Rosso di Montalcino '99	¶	4
○ Moscadello di Montalcino '99		5
● Brunello di Montalcino '93	¶¶	5
● Brunello di Montalcino Ris. '93	¶¶	5
● Brunello di Montalcino '95	¶¶	5
● Rosso di Montalcino '98	¶¶	3
● Brunello di Montalcino '94	¶	5

MONTALCINO (SI)

Siro Pacenti
Loc. Pelagrilli, 1
53024 Montalcino (SI)
tel. 0577848662
e-mail: pacentisiro@libero.it

It is no secret that Giancarlo Pacenti is a beacon among Montalcino producers for his dedication, consistent excellence and ability to grow and change while remaining true to the bases of local tradition. Recently, we have often had occasion to underline his determination to improve and find new ways of dealing with the peculiar characteristics of each vintage. His latest wines are, as usual, very successful. He has walked off with the same awards as last time, Three Glasses for the Brunello and Two for the Rosso. Giancarlo's Rosso di Montalcino '99 is one of the best of its year. Ruby-hued, with youthful highlights, it reveals aromas of very ripe plum, sour cherry jam and bay leaf. The palate, also characterized by the great ripeness of its raw material, shows roundness and, at this early stage of its development, a fairly marked note of sweet oak. The Brunello di Montalcino '96 claimed Three Glasses at our finals with its customary poise. This rich and chewy red opens with impressive breadth on both nose and palate, then succeeds in combining softness with impeccable style, not an easy trick to pull off. From a mediocre vintage like the '96, this is a particularly splendid performance.

● Brunello di Montalcino '96	♛♛♛ 6
● Rosso di Montalcino '99	♛♛ 5
● Brunello di Montalcino '88	♛♛♛ 6
● Brunello di Montalcino '95	♛♛♛ 6
● Brunello di Montalcino '90	♛♛ 6
● Brunello di Montalcino Ris. '90	♛♛ 6
● Brunello di Montalcino '91	♛♛ 6
● Rosso di Montalcino '92	♛♛ 4
● Brunello di Montalcino '93	♛♛ 6
● Rosso di Montalcino '93	♛♛ 4
● Rosso di Montalcino '95	♛♛ 4
● Rosso di Montalcino '96	♛♛ 4
● Rosso di Montalcino '97	♛♛ 5
● Rosso di Montalcino '98	♛♛ 5
● Brunello di Montalcino '94	♛ 6

MONTALCINO (SI)

Piancornello
Fraz. Castelnuovo dell'Abate
Loc. Piancornello
53024 Montalcino (SI)
tel. 0577844105

The number of craft winewomen in Montalcino is growing. Silvana Pieri is certainly amongst them, partly because of the small area of her estate, which covers about three hectares near Castelnuovo dell'Abate. Her style is traditional, involving the use of medium-sized barrels for ageing. The excellent potential of her vineyards and the renewal of her barrel collection have helped her in recent years to make great progress. When soil and aspect are as they should be, Brunello di Montalcino has no need of hocus-pocus to come out well. One point to reflect on, however, is that excellence in Montalcino wines often seems to coincide with the introduction of new oak barrels, whatever their size. The two Piancornello wines presented this year are a case in point. The very good Rosso '99 is one of the best of its vintage. The nose exhibits the typical qualities of a sangiovese from a warm area, flaunting earthy and mineral tones, and the odd animal nuance that disappears when the wine has had some time to breathe. The palate is even more exciting. The entry is powerful, the development broad and well-proportioned, and the expressive finish is appropriately long. The Brunello '96 is surprisingly good, given the limitations of its vintage, and it also took part in our finals. Although it did not win Three Glasses, it held its own as an excellent Brunello. The enticing bouquet of ripe black cherry leads to a palate that clearly reveals the character of the sangiovese grape. Succulent and full-bodied, it has the varietal acidity that gives it extra vitality, rounded off by perfectly extracted flavoursome tannins.

● Brunello di Montalcino '96	♛♛ 6
● Rosso di Montalcino '99	♛♛ 4
● Brunello di Montalcino '93	♛♛ 5
● Brunello di Montalcino '95	♛♛ 6
● Rosso di Montalcino '96	♛ 3
● Rosso di Montalcino '98	♛ 4

MONTALCINO (SI)

AGOSTINA PIERI
LOC. PIANCORNELLO
VIA FABBRI, 2
53024 MONTALCINO (SI)
TEL. 0577375785 - 0577844163

Agostina Pieri's estate continues to stand out on the Brunello horizon, despite being a relative newcomer. Agostina's wines attracted critical attention very early because of the dynamic modern style that puts the emphasis on richness of fruit. Barrels of various sizes are to be found in her cellar but barriques are favoured. At this year's tastings, we noticed wines with very imposing structures that were not always accompanied by well-calibrated oak. We were not, for example, entirely persuaded by what should have been the star, the Brunello Riserva '95, whose substantial structure fails to open out properly or to amalgamate successfully with the wood. The body of the Brunello '96 is less impressive but, given the vintage, quite acceptable. The wine reveals aromas of black cherry and vanilla, then a round, soft palate which, however, lacks a little breadth and finishes dry under the influence of wood-derived tannins. All in all, the Rosso di Montalcino '99 performed best. It may show less complexity and body but the balance is right and the flavour is soft, rounded and well sustained. The acidity is kept within bounds and the tannins are perceptible, but not predominant, on the finish.

MONTALCINO (SI)

POGGIO DI SOTTO
FRAZ. CASTELNUOVO DELL'ABATE
LOC. POGGIO DI SOPRA, 222
53020 MONTALCINO (SI)
TEL. 0577835502
E-MAIL: palmuccipds@libero.it

The Three very well-earned Glasses we awarded to the classic Brunello from Poggio di Sotto is more evidence that we do not make our decisions on ideological lines. We are not modernists or traditionalists, although it is debatable whether producers can really be divided up in such a schematic fashion. In the wines from Poggio di Sotto, you will find none of the characteristics flaunted by the celebrated new-generation reds, such as hints of new oak and toastiness, primary aromas of fruit, intimidatingly high extract, near-black hues and oily mouthfeel. And yet we still admire the style of Piero Palmucci and his famous master taster, Giulio Gambelli, a style made up of subtle shades, composed elegance, and structure that emphasizes depth of alcohol rather than tannic force. Such is the style of the refined and richly nuanced Brunello di Montalcino Riserva '95. In addition, it has a greater volume of extract and a longer finish than other recent vintages. It should be remembered that Poggio di Sotto produces a Riserva only in the best years, which means that there have not been many in the last decade. This first Three Glass award is also recognition of the ability and discretion with which they do their job here, at a great remove from the sort of media hype that seems to have become part and parcel of the work of oenologists and vignerons everywhere. A few final words for the Brunello '96, the child of a lesser vintage. It is harmonious, full-bodied and surprisingly long.

Wine	Glasses	Price
Rosso di Montalcino '99	♛♛	4
Brunello di Montalcino Ris. '95	♛	6
Brunello di Montalcino '96	♛	6
Rosso di Montalcino '95	♛♛♛	4
Brunello di Montalcino '94	♛♛	6
Rosso di Montalcino '94	♛♛	4
Brunello di Montalcino '95	♛♛	6
Rosso di Montalcino '96	♛♛	4
Rosso di Montalcino '97	♛	4
Rosso di Montalcino '98	♛	4

Wine	Glasses	Price
Brunello di Montalcino Ris. '95	♛♛♛	6
Brunello di Montalcino '96	♛♛	6
Brunello di Montalcino '94	♛♛	6
Rosso di Montalcino '94	♛♛	4
Brunello di Montalcino '95	♛♛	6
Brunello di Montalcino '91	♛	6

MONTALCINO (SI)

CASTELLO ROMITORIO
LOC. ROMITORIO, 279
53024 MONTALCINO (SI)
TEL. 0577897220 - 0577847212
E-MAIL: inf@castelloromitorio.it

Sandro Chia's estate is now well-established as a source of reliably high quality Montalcino wines. Fervent admirers of Chia, the celebrated "transavanguardia" artist, eagerly collect bottles from Castello Romitorio because their favourite painter has designed the label. Meanwhile Sandro is working to further improve the contents by enlarging the cellar next to the beautiful former monastery where the main offices are located. The estate includes about eight hectares of Brunello. A further 12 are planted to other varieties, such as cabernet sauvignon and chardonnay. Three wines were presented at our tastings this year, the Chardonnay being left out because it wasn't ready in time. The best was the Brunello '96, which easily picked up Two Glasses. A concentrated, lustrous ruby, verging on pigeon's blood, precedes a broad intense bouquet with lots of morello and sour cherry fruit that blend nicely with sweet oak-derived spice. The palate is satisfyingly rich in fruit and reveals powerful yet ripe, close-knit tannins and a long, dense finish. Another Two Glasses went to the Romito del Romitorio '99, a blend of cabernet sauvignon and sangiovese. The nose offers notes of raspberry, geranium and candied fruit, while the concentrated, mellow palate reveals solid and still slightly aggressive tannins. It should develop well in the bottle. The agreeable, medium-bodied Rosso di Montalcino '99 gets One Glass.

MONTALCINO (SI)

SALICUTTI
PODERE SALICUTTI, 174
53024 MONTALCINO (SI)
TEL. 0577847003 - 03357013552

Salicutti, only recently established, has already aroused interest because of its rich, concentrated, radiantly powerful wines. Frequent use is made here of new barriques, which generally lead to fuller, firmly fruity wines with more rounded tannins. It has to be said that we have occasionally noticed an excess of oak that compromised the balance and elegance of the palate. But Francesco Leanza's winery is definitely on the right path, and we offer this criticism because we feel that a more controlled use of wood will lead to a fuller exploitation of Salicutti's great potential. The Rosso di Montalcino '99 is a wonderfully solid wine with a structural richness that would be enviable in a Brunello, but overweening oak masks other aromatic sensations and produces a slightly bitter aftertaste. The Brunello '96 is less spectacular but much better balanced; the palate is full, round, very complex and rounded off by a tannic finish. The very good cabernet sauvignon-based Dopoteatro '99 shows admirable depth on the nose with notes of black berry fruit and vegetal hints. The palate is soft, velvety, elegant and lingering.

● Brunello di Montalcino '96	ŸŸ	6
● Sant'Antimo Rosso		
Romito del Romitorio '99	ŸŸ	6
● Rosso di Montalcino '99	Ÿ	4
● Romito del Romitorio '90	ŸŸ	5
● Brunello di Montalcino '93	ŸŸ	6
● Brunello di Montalcino '95	ŸŸ	6
● Romito del Romitorio '96	ŸŸ	5
● Romito del Romitorio '98	ŸŸ	6

● Brunello di Montalcino '96	ŸŸ	6
● Dopoteatro '99	ŸŸ	5
● Rosso di Montalcino '99	Ÿ	4
● Brunello di Montalcino '95	ŸŸ	5
● Rosso di Montalcino '97	ŸŸ	4
● Rosso di Montalcino '98	ŸŸ	4

MONTALCINO (SI)

SALVIONI - LA CERBAIOLA
P.ZZA CAVOUR, 19
53024 MONTALCINO (SI)
TEL. 0577848499

It is with great regret that we continue to chart a decline in the wines produced by Giulio Salvioni, one of the most celebrated and respected winemakers in Montalcino. Of course, it could be that our tasting panels have failed to appreciate the qualities of La Cerbaiola's reds in recent years. A lighter style has been favoured, and the intensely fruity tone that made Salvioni's Brunello famous in the past is now more fleeting. A headier, less structured wine is the rule, as is, to tell the truth, rather less clarity on the nose. The '96 version, which was certainly not helped by the vintage, reveals a certain olfactory opacity, together with a fairly tenacious sulphurous note that is scarcely improved with breathing time. On the palate, the wine shows attractive body, very solid tannins and nicely gauged acidity but the various components fail to mesh, even taking the youth of the wine into account – this is a Brunello, after all. It is altogether possible, even probable, that it will improve as it ages. Meanwhile, we have high hopes for the next vintage, which has already given signs of being significantly better.

Wine	Rating	Score
● Brunello di Montalcino '96	♀	6
● Brunello di Montalcino '85	♀♀♀	6
● Brunello di Montalcino '87	♀♀♀	6
● Brunello di Montalcino '88	♀♀♀	6
● Brunello di Montalcino '89	♀♀♀	6
● Brunello di Montalcino '90	♀♀♀	6
● Brunello di Montalcino '91	♀♀	6
● Brunello di Montalcino '92	♀♀	6
● Brunello di Montalcino '93	♀♀	6
● Brunello di Montalcino '95	♀♀	6

MONTALCINO (SI)

SOLARIA - CENCIONI
PODERE CAPANNA, 102
53024 MONTALCINO (SI)
TEL. 0577849426
E-MAIL: solaria.cencioni@infinito.it

Patrizia Cencioni hasn't let us down. Her wines have been showing increasing confidence and are acquiring a distinctive style. Sound and concentrated but never showy, they show full respect for their vintages, without excessive recourse to back blending. All this was clear when we tasted the Brunello '96. The colour has the garnet highlights of a mature wine, and the bouquet also reveals, in its distinctly forward – but not faded – timbre, that this was not a great vintage. The very good palate is caressing and stylish. The new cabernet sauvignon, the Solarianne '98, had a very fine debut and is in line with the estate style, which values harmony and elegance over muscle. The oak is excellent and not at all intrusive on the palate, which reveals smooth, juicy tannins. The wine is still young and wants more complexity but it should evolve well. As for the Rosso di Montalcino '99, we were not taken with its nose, which exhibited distinct but not new wood, as well as a light vegetal tone. But these characteristics vanish on the palate, where the tannins are nicely judged and the well-ordered progression is enlivened by refreshing acidity: indeed, it becomes very enjoyable.

Wine	Rating	Score
● Brunello di Montalcino '96	♀♀	6
● Solarianne '98	♀♀	5
● Rosso di Montalcino '99	♀	4
● Brunello di Montalcino '95	♀♀	6
● Rosso di Montalcino '98	♀	4

MONTALCINO (SI)

Tenimenti Angelini - Val di Suga
Loc. Val di Cava
53024 Montalcino (SI)
tel. 057780411

Just as we have given highest honours to a representative of the classic Montalcino tradition in Poggio di Sotto, we are also happy to award Three Glasses to Val di Suga, considered by many a modernist winery. The quality of what we find in the glass is what counts, of course: we are attracted neither by anachronistic wines bowed down by faults and strong smells nor by bottles that are too clever by half, monsters of softness and overwhelming fruit. So Three Glasses go to the Brunello di Montalcino Vigna Spuntali '95, a red with rich yet beautifully controlled extract. It is also a wine that gives a convincing interpretation of the best elements of the Montalcino tradition, such as the austere eloquence of alcohol and the warmth of fruit. Vivid ruby in colour, it has an already complex bouquet, rich in notes of black cherry, violet and liquorice, while the toasty notes of oak – this is quite normal in Val di Suga reds during their first few years – are a little too much in evidence. On the palate, it shows excellent body, warm alcohol and a long finish that sublimely mirrors the nose. Unfortunately, no such results were achieved by the rest of the range. The Brunello '96 is decidedly less successful. The colour is intense, but there are some problems on the nose, and the palate is not very well-orchestrated. There are prominent, edgy tannins and, in particular, a rather short finish. The Rosso di Montalcino '99 is equally modest and in fact gets no more than a mention. A final note to express our hearty approval of the Angelini policy of staggering releases of the two best '95 crus: the Vigna del Lago won Three Glasses last year.

MONTALCINO (SI)

Tenuta Valdicava
Loc. Val di Cava
53024 Montalcino (SI)
tel. 0577848261

Vincenzo Abruzzese, the owner of Valdicava, is a young winemaker with quite a number of vintages behind him. He's no dabbler who hits pay dirt one year and never manages to repeat the feat. Vincenzo has his own view of what a wine should be like, especially one with deep territorial and traditional roots like Brunello. Occasionally, his bottles are a little uneven, and show signs of reduction on the nose, but they all have genuine character and respect for their grape variety, their terroir and their vintage. In short, personality is there in spades. These characteristics are often not fully understood at tastings – sometimes the wines are underrated while on other occasions quite the opposite takes place. But this is the nature of Valdicava wines: strong and authentic, even if they don't always follow all the rules. The Brunello Riserva Madonna del Piano '95 needs breathing time after pouring but emerges rich and generous on the palate, which boasts elegantly velvety tannins. The very successful Rosso di Montalcino '99 has a clean, concentrated, complex bouquet. The palate shows medium weight and a substantial progression underpinned by smooth tannins. The '96 vintage was mediocre in these parts and Abruzzese doesn't try to pass it off as a great one. His Brunello is more than satisfactory but not particularly energetic.

● Brunello di Montalcino Vigna Spuntali '95	🍷🍷🍷	6
● Brunello di Montalcino '96	🍷	6
● Rosso di Montalcino '99		4
● Brunello di Montalcino Vigna del Lago '90	🍷🍷🍷	6
● Brunello di Montalcino Vigna del Lago '93	🍷🍷🍷	6
● Brunello di Montalcino Vigna Spuntali '93	🍷🍷🍷	6
● Brunello di Montalcino Vigna del Lago '95	🍷🍷🍷	6
● Brunello di Montalcino '95	🍷🍷	6
● Rosso di Montalcino '98	🍷	4

● Brunello di Montalcino Madonna del Piano Ris. '95	🍷🍷	6
● Rosso di Montalcino '99	🍷🍷	4
● Brunello di Montalcino '96	🍷	6
● Brunello di Montalcino Madonna del Piano Ris. '90	🍷🍷	6
● Brunello di Montalcino '93	🍷🍷	5
● Rosso di Montalcino '96	🍷🍷	4
● Brunello di Montalcino '90	🍷	5

MONTALCINO (SI)

VILLA LE PRATA
LOC. LE PRATA, 261
53024 MONTALCINO (SI)
TEL. 0577848325

Villa Le Prata was established just for fun, or very nearly. Dr. Losapio, the owner, rightly felt that a property in Montalcino should not be just a bucolic retreat for his own use and delectation. He would have to try to produce some wine there. So he chose an oenologist, Roberto Cipresso, who in addition to knowing the territory as few others do, is sensitive enough to respond to an unusual challenge: one hectare under vine at 500 metres above sea level! What began as a pastime slowly turned into a serious enterprise. Subsequently, the estate has grown, although not very much, and now includes another plot, near Castelnuovo dell'Abate, in a warmer location just right for producing riper grapes. This means the wines can have all the distinctive aromatic qualities offered by the cool climate in the higher vineyard while tempering the austerity of flavour with the rounded sweetness of the grapes from Castelnuovo. The wines we tasted this year showed remarkably good quality, despite the absence of the Brunello '96. The Rosso di Montalcino Tirso '99 has an engagingly delightful nose with clearly defined hints of cherry, wild cherry and black cherry, leading to a caressing, succulent and beautifully balanced palate with tasty, well-calibrated tannins. The red Le Prata '99, a blend of sangiovese and merlot, is less complex on the nose but has plenty of structure. It's a concentrated, fruit-rich, broad and powerful wine.

MONTE SAN SAVINO (AR)

SAN LUCIANO
LOC. SAN LUCIANO, 90
52048 MONTE SAN SAVINO (AR)
TEL. 0575848518

San Luciano takes its place in the Guide as a dynamic representative of the Val di Chiana. The estate covers about 100 hectares, 60 of which are under vine. The main red grapes are sangiovese, merlot, cabernet sauvignon and montepulciano d'Abruzzo; white grapes include trebbiano, chardonnay, grechetto and vermentino. Ovidio Ziantoni and his sons Marco and Stefano follow every phase of production with the technical assistance of Fabrizio Ciufoli. Things are well organized here: fermentation vats and ageing cellar are temperature-controlled. The D'Ovidio '98, a blend of sangiovese, montepulciano d'Abruzzo, cabernet and merlot with a distinctive character, stood out at our tastings. It shows a dense, soft and mouth-filling structure and easily walked off with Two Glasses. The Colle Carpito '99, from sangiovese and montepulciano, has an original fragrance with notes of black cherry and anise. The palate is rounded, even and just slightly tannic on the finish. The third red, the Boschi Salviati '99, made from sangiovese, montepulciano and cabernet, has a nicely ripe bouquet with aromas of tobacco, black cherry jam and liquorice. The palate is medium-bodied but very well balanced and not without elegance. The two whites, Resico and Luna di Monte, are very successful as well: clean, consistent and attractively aromatic.

● Le Prata '99	ŸŸ	5
● Rosso di Montalcino Tirso '99	ŸŸ	4
● Brunello di Montalcino '93	ŸŸ	6

● D'Ovidio '98	ŸŸ	5
● Boschi Salviati '99	ŸŸ	4*
○ Luna di Monte '00	Ÿ	2*
○ Resico '00	Ÿ	3
● Colle Carpito '99	Ÿ	3*

MONTECARLO (LU)

FATTORIA DEL BUONAMICO
LOC. CERCATOIA
VIA PROVINCIALE DI MONTECARLO, 43
55015 MONTECARLO (LU)
TEL. 058322038
E-MAIL: buonamico@sole.it

There are few perceptible results as yet from the serious efforts this winery has been making in recent years. Of course, when it is a question of replanting old vineyards and creating new ones, you just have to be patient. But we should not have to wait much longer before the Fattoria del Buonamico provides us with some delightful surprises. At the moment, their range of wines is admirably consistent in style and quality. We should mention the improvement, which is not reflected in the number of Glasses awarded, in the standard-label Montecarlos. The Montecarlo Rosso '00 is a perfect example of its category. A straightforward wine, naturally, but one that offers absolutely uncontaminated pure fruit that is sheer pleasure. Inviting aromas of raspberry and cherry on the nose are followed by an equally enjoyable palate with balance, roundness and surprisingly substantial body. Had it not been for the finish, which is a bit short, we might well have given it Two Glasses. Which is what we awarded to the Cercatoja Rosso '97, a blend of sangiovese, cabernet sauvignon, cabernet franc and syrah. The nose, a bit dumb at first, opens after a time into a decently broad range of aromas, including blackberry jam, pepper, cinnamon and vegetal nuances. In the mouth, it is elegant, supple and lingering. The Vasario '98, from pinot bianco, sauvignon and semillon, is a soft, alluring white but needs the contrast that a little more acidic bite would provide. The nose features notes of exotic fruit, honey and vanilla. Lastly, the Montecarlo Bianco is fragrant and agreeable.

MONTECARLO (LU)

GINO FUSO CARMIGNANI
FRAZ. CERCATOIA ALTA
VIA DELLA TINAIA, 7
55015 MONTECARLO (LU)
TEL. 058322381

Gino Fuso has extended his range of wines to include some magnums. We are accustomed to the weird and wonderful names he gives his creations, ranging from mythical mediaeval warriors to the cellar guard dog, so we can hardly claim to be surprised by his latest, the zoologically challenged "Il Merlo della Topa Nera" (the name is an innocuous pun on "merlo", the Italian for "thrush", combined with a less innocent Tuscan colloquialism that looks as if it means "female mouse" but in fact refers to an intimate region of the feminine anatomy: "The Thrush with the Black ..."). It's a good Merlot, too, albeit of a very different kind from the giants on the Tuscan coast. Gino's avian creation has a style of its own: succulent, vibrant and also rich, without seeming heavy. Another very good wine is the For Duke '99, from sangiovese with a little syrah: dense and concentrated, but without going too far, because Fuso's wines are always balanced and quaffable. These are not show wines bred for competitions: they're made to be drunk at table, with whatever, and whomever, you fancy. They can also be drunk a few years from now because they have the kind of structure that guarantees staying power. The Sassonero '00, his Montecarlo Rosso, on the other hand, is for immediate drinking. It's so rounded, fruity and direct yet flavoursome that you keep reaching for another glass. Finally, we were by no means disappointed by the Montecarlo Bianco Stati d'Animo, which is crisp and pleasing, the oak doing its part with discretion.

	Wine	Glasses	Score
●	Cercatoja Rosso '97	▼▼	5
○	Montecarlo Bianco '00	▼	3
●	Montecarlo Rosso '00	▼	3
○	Vasario '98	▼	4
●	Cercatoja Rosso '90	▼▼	5
●	Il Fortino Cabernet/Merlot '91	▼▼	5
●	Il Fortino Syrah '92	▼▼	5
●	Il Fortino Cabernet/Merlot '93	▼▼	5
●	Fort'Yrah '94	▼▼	5
●	Il Fortino Cabernet/Merlot '94	▼▼	5
●	Cercatoja Rosso '95	▼▼	5
●	Il Fortino Syrah '95	▼▼	5
●	Cercatoja Rosso '96	▼▼	5
●	Il Fortino Syrah '96	▼▼	6
○	Vasario '96	▼▼	4

	Wine	Glasses	Score
●	Il Merlot della Topa Nera '98	▼▼	5
●	For Duke '99	▼▼	5
○	Montecarlo Bianco Stati d'Animo '00	▼	3
●	Montecarlo Rosso Sassonero '00	▼	3*
●	For Duke '90	▼▼	4
●	For Duke '94	▼▼	4
●	For Duke '95	▼▼	4
●	For Duke '97	▼▼	5
●	Montecarlo Rosso Sassonero '97	▼▼	2
●	For Duke '98	▼▼	5
○	Montecarlo Bianco Stati d'Animo '99	▼▼	4

MONTECARLO (LU)

Fattoria di Montechiari
Via Montechiari, 27
55015 Montecarlo (LU)
tel. 058322189 - 058322189

Montechiari may not rival Bolgheri for tall cypresses, which here too line the drive and appear on all the labels, but it can be said to compete with its wines, which are frank, dependable and excellent in quality. The keenest competition is provided by the Cabernet, the '98 version of which came within a hair's breadth of winning Three Glasses and confirmed the excellent impression made in past vintages. It is elegant in style, substantial in structure, concentrated and packed with smooth, fine-grained tannins. The long finish is redolent of spice and dark berry fruit, with faint vegetal undertones. The interesting, original Nero '98 is a monovarietal pinot nero. Although the bouquet may not have the trademark finesse of the Burgundian grape, it is not lacking in personality, which comes through in distinct spicy notes of cinnamon and clove, as well as black cherry aromas and nuances of oak. The vigour on the palate is unusual for this variety, the tannins make their presence felt and the finish is lingering, if not very elegant. The Montechiari Rosso '98, from sangiovese, seems a bit unfocused and unsettled on the nose but the more successful palate is soft-textured and vibrant. The Chardonnay '99 is also not entirely balanced on the nose. With a bit of breathing time, though, it reveals notes of honey and chamomile blending with mineral hints. The palate is slightly forward but also succulent and enjoyably meaty.

MONTECARLO (LU)

Wandanna
Fraz. San Salvatore
Via Don Minzoni, 38
55015 Montecarlo (LU)
tel. 0583228989 - 0583228226

Ever since Ivaldo Fantozzi decided to devote all his time to winemaking, he hasn't put a foot wrong. His wines have gradually made a name for themselves and are deservedly viewed as the last word in reliability. The range is extensive – Ivano has something for every taste and every pocket-book. This ought to be enough to make a producer content, and Fantozzi is just that. But it is easy to slide from contentment into complacency, and the owner of Wandanna is ever on his guard. The estate is a hive of activity: new barriques keep appearing in the cellar and activity in the vineyards is never-ending. The Virente '98 is still the flagship red but something has changed: there is no more ciliegiolo in the blend, which now consists of cabernet sauvignon, cabernet franc, merlot and syrah. It has, however, maintained its familiar style, which hinges on dense, well-balanced structure and aromatic richness. The fruit notes of bramble and bilberry are enhanced by spicy and toasty hints, and light vegetal nuances. The Terre dei Cascinieri Rosso '99 has a more characterful, less elegant and orderly nature than the Virente. The palate is concentrated and just a touch angular on the finish. The rest of the range is well-executed: the pleasingly structured Terre dei Cascinieri Bianco '99 reveals a light vanilla undertone; the Terre della Gioiosa '00 is correct and agreeable; and the Roussanne '00 has an attractive tang. Our preview taste of the Labirinto, which we shall be reviewing next year, aroused considerable interest.

● Montechiari Cabernet '98	🍷🍷	6
● Montechiari Nero '98	🍷🍷	6
○ Montechiari Chardonnay '99	🍷🍷	5
● Montechiari Rosso '98	🍷	5
● Montechiari Cabernet '97	🍷🍷🍷	6
● Montechiari Nero '95	🍷🍷	5
● Montechiari Rosso '95	🍷🍷	4
● Montechiari Cabernet '96	🍷🍷	6
○ Montechiari Chardonnay '96	🍷🍷	4
● Montechiari Pinot Nero '96	🍷🍷	5
● Montechiari Pinot Nero '97	🍷🍷	6
○ Montechiari Chardonnay '98	🍷🍷	5
● Montechiari Rosso '96	🍷	4

● Virente '98	🍷🍷	5
● Montecarlo Rosso Terre dei Cascinieri '99	🍷🍷	4
○ Montecarlo Bianco Terre della Gioiosa '00	🍷	2*
○ Roussanne '00	🍷	3
○ Montecarlo Bianco Terre dei Cascinieri '99	🍷	4
● Virente '95	🍷🍷	5
● Virente '96	🍷🍷	5
● Montecarlo Rosso Terre dei Cascinieri '97	🍷🍷	4
● Virente '97	🍷🍷	5
○ Montecarlo Bianco Terre dei Cascinieri '98	🍷🍷	4
● Terre dei Cascinieri '98	🍷🍷	4

MONTECATINI VAL DI CECINA (PI)

FATTORIA SORBAIANO
LOC. SORBAIANO
56040 MONTECATINI VAL DI CECINA (PI)
TEL. 058830243
E-MAIL: fattoriasorbaiano@libero.it

Fattoria Sorbaiano is one of the most firmly rooted and widely known estates in Val di Cecina. Its wines have always met with general approval, as they combine good quality with very reasonable prices. It has, however, also been the case for some time that this general framework of absolute reliability has shown no signs of a striving for more ambitious goals. That is why we are particularly pleased to report that the Picciolini family seem once again to be throwing themselves enthusiastically into the running of Sorbaiano: the vineyards, which currently cover some 25 hectares, are being extended, and they are adapting the cellar to this increase in quantity and, presumably, quality. This year's tastings showed no really significant innovations but there were some signs of change. The Pian del Conte, for example, a beautifully expressive monovarietal sangiovese, has definitely moved up a notch. The scents are harmonious and richly redolent of berry fruit and toasty oak. Not an explosive wine on the palate, it has strong suits in elegance and balance. The Rosso delle Miniere '98 is certainly up to snuff: the flavour is soft-textured, well structured and nicely rounded by delightful notes of liquorice and pepper, together with a less commendable vegetal undertone. The interesting, well-executed Lucestraia '99 offers balsamic, flower and citrus notes on the nose and a palate with both depth and length. The two standard-label Montescudaios are well-made and admirably full-bodied.

MONTEFOLLONICO (SI)

VITTORIO INNOCENTI
VIA LANDUCCI, 10/12
53040 MONTEFOLLONICO (SI)
TEL. 0577669537

Vittorio Innocenti is continuing to produce wines that show enormous personality, concede very little to current fashion and faithfully express their terroir. They are often a little spiky their first few years out, a quality not always fully understood or appreciated by those who are used to the monotonous softness of many of today's wines. His splendid cellar beneath the historic Palazzo Muccinelli has made it possible to rationalize both the fermentation space and the ageing rooms, where there are ever more barriques. In recent years, this estate has astonished us all with its excellent Vin Santo, and the '96 version, which carries on the tradition, is in fact one of the best ever produced here. A warm amber hue introduces a bouquet in which the scent of walnutskin blends with notes of candied fruit, sultana and dried apricot. The harmonious palate perfectly balances the substantial sugar with acidity. Mid palate is lovely, but the fleshy finish is slightly heavy. Two Glasses go to the red Acerone '97, which shows its stuff in a good attack on the palate but has, as usual, a somewhat prominent tannic note as it develops. It ends well, expanding easily and without bitter notes, so that one can assume bottle age will take care of the tannic unevenness. The Nobile di Montepulciano Riserva '97 exhibits a lively classic floral bouquet with violets, peach and apricot, and the flavour is dense. The Rosso di Montepulciano '99, a generally successful wine, has netted Two Glasses.

● Montescudaio Rosso delle Miniere '98	🍷🍷 5
○ Montescudaio Bianco Lucestraia '99	🍷🍷 4*
● Pian del Conte '99	🍷🍷 4*
○ Montescudaio Bianco '00	🍷 2*
● Montescudaio Rosso '00	🍷 2*
● Montescudaio Rosso delle Miniere '94	🍷🍷 4
● Montescudaio Rosso delle Miniere '95	🍷🍷 4
● Montescudaio Rosso delle Miniere '96	🍷🍷 4
● Montescudaio Rosso delle Miniere '97	🍷🍷 4
○ Montescudaio Bianco Lucestraia '98	🍷🍷 4
● Pian del Conte '98	🍷 3

○ Vin Santo '96	🍷🍷 6
● Acerone '97	🍷🍷 5
● Rosso di Montepulciano '99	🍷🍷 3
● Nobile di Montepulciano Ris. '97	🍷 5
● Nobile di Montepulciano Ris. '88	🍷🍷🍷 5
● Acerone '90	🍷🍷 5
○ Vin Santo '90	🍷🍷 6
● Acerone '93	🍷🍷 5
○ Vin Santo '95	🍷🍷 6
● Nobile di Montepulciano Ris. '96	🍷 5
● Nobile di Montepulciano '97	🍷 4

MONTEMURLO (PO)

Tenuta di Bagnolo
dei Marchesi Pancrazi
Fraz. Bagnolo
Via Montalese, 156
50045 Montemurlo (PO)
Tel. 0574652439 - 03356916329

This year, we should really assign a profile to Marchesi Pancrazi's second property. The review should concentrate not on the Tenuta di Bagnolo but the Fattoria di San Donato, which presented some rather surprising wines that have, for once, pushed the famous Pinot Nero into the background. This is not a permanent change in ranking, in part because other wines in general, quite apart from the others produced by Marchesi Pancrazi, can hardly be compared to the unusual Pinot Nero. We were particularly pleased to see evidence of the renewed attention that has been lavished on San Donato, which thoroughly deserves to be cosseted. The Casaglia, a monovarietal colorino, is becoming denser and less edgy. The '99 displays an imposing structure with a broad and very impressive attack. This is a great step forward for the wine and indeed for the grape variety. Here too, though, there is still a need for some fine-tuning of the nose, which shows a little reduction, and of the tannins, which have it all their own way on the palate. The two San Donatos, the '99 and the '00, almost won Two Glasses. Each has a very enjoyable, vibrant palate and fruit-rich, flower and spice aromas with, in the '00, a bitterish note. It is harder to come to grips with the Pinot Nero '99. The palate has substantial body but the nose is somewhat problematic. It's a good wine in any case, but since it was bottled shortly before our tastings, and given the rather special personality of the pinot nero grape, we have decided to put off a complete review until next year's edition.

MONTEPULCIANO (SI)

Avignonesi
Via di Gracciano nel Corso, 91
53045 Montepulciano (SI)
Tel. 0578757872 - 0578724304
E-mail: elena.falvo@avignonesi.it

Yet another Three Glasses for this historic estate in the lovely Valiano area. This time, the prize went to the cellar's flagship wine, the Vin Santo Occhio di Pernice. The '89 finds a marvellous balance on the palate. The residual sugar attractively offsets a lively acidity that lends elegance and a welcome drinkability to this extremely rich and concentrated wine. The impressively clean bouquet offers intense scents of black cherry jam, plum and candied red berries. The extremely dense palate is, happily, well sustained by acidity. The Nobile '98 did very well, too. Although full-bodied, it is easy and satisfying to drink, thanks to its remarkable balance. Another Two Glass wine, the Vin Santo '91, displays a very vivid amber hue and distinct aromas of baked apple, candied apricot and tobacco. The attack on the palate is sweet; concentration and progression are both big. The very good Desiderio '98 is an assemblage of merlot and cabernet. Its intense ruby lightens at the rim, and on the nose notes of red berry jam alternate with a vegetal tone. The Bianco Avignonesi is harmonious and delightful while the Rosso Avignonesi is less brilliant. The Nobile Grandi Annate Riserva '97 is the only disappointment in a series of convincing wines from Avignonesi.

● Casaglia '99	ŸŸ	4
● San Donato '00	Ÿ	2*
● San Donato '99	Ÿ	2*
● Pinot Nero Villa di Bagnolo '89	ŸŸ	5
● Pinot Nero Villa di Bagnolo '91	ŸŸ	5
● Pinot Nero Villa di Bagnolo '92	ŸŸ	5
● Pinot Nero Villa di Bagnolo '93	ŸŸ	5
● Pinot Nero Villa di Bagnolo '94	ŸŸ	5
● Pinot Nero Villa di Bagnolo '95	ŸŸ	5
● Pinot Nero Villa di Bagnolo '97	ŸŸ	5
● Pinot Nero Villa di Bagnolo '98	ŸŸ	5
● Pinot Nero Villa di Bagnolo '90	Ÿ	5
● Pinot Nero Villa di Bagnolo '96	Ÿ	5
● San Donato '97	Ÿ	3
● San Donato '98	Ÿ	2

○ Vin Santo Occhio di Pernice '89	ŸŸŸ	6
○ Vin Santo '91	ŸŸ	6
○ Bianco Avignonesi '00	ŸŸ	3*
● Merlot Desiderio '98	ŸŸ	6
● Nobile di Montepulciano '98	ŸŸ	4
● Rosso di Montepulciano '00	Ÿ	3
● Nobile di Montepulciano Grandi Annate Ris. '97	Ÿ	6
● Rosso Avignonesi '99	Ÿ	3
○ Vin Santo '88	ŸŸŸ	6
○ Vin Santo '89	ŸŸŸ	6
● 50 & 50 Avignonesi e Capannelle '97	ŸŸŸ	6
● Desiderio '97	ŸŸ	6
● Merlot Desiderio '97	ŸŸ	6
○ Il Marzocco '98	ŸŸ	4

MONTEPULCIANO (SI)

BINDELLA
FRAZ. ACQUAVIVA
VIA DELLE TRE BERTE, 10/A
53040 MONTEPULCIANO (SI)
TEL. 0578767777
E-MAIL: info@bindella.it

At Bindella, they are anxiously awaiting the day when the new vineyards come onstream: production here is already well below market demand. But viticulture has its own rhythms, and estate standards forbid the use of grapes from vines that are too young. The very capable wine technician, Signor Mazzamurro, believes that the new vineyards, which are densely planted with special clone selections, will significantly increase quality. In the lovely spacious cellar, fermentation takes place in wooden vats as well as in the more traditional temperature-controlled stainless steel vats. For ageing, there are small barrels and an increasing number of barriques and tonneaux. The intense ruby red Rosso di Montepulciano Fosso Lupaio '00 flaunts berry fruit and a light grassy note on the nose. The very fresh palate is consistent and the finish echoes the bouquet. No '98 Vallocaia was produced, as the cellar felt it fell below Bindella standards. The Nobile '98 was the subject of heated discussion at our tastings. The very successful palate is rich and well-balanced, and the finish is good, but the nose, at least in the bottles we tried, is closed and too unfocused. The wine that everybody liked, however, was the Dolce Sinfonia, a '96 Vin Santo that is, fortunately, far less cloying than its name ("Sweet Symphony"). It has a brilliant amber hue and a complex bouquet with notes of quince, citron and dried fruit. The palate is very rich, yet fresh, with a broad and mouthfilling finish.

○	Vin Santo Dolce Sinfonia '96	🍷🍷	6
●	Rosso di Montepulciano Fosso Lupaio '00	🍷	3
●	Nobile di Montepulciano '98	🍷	5
●	Nobile di Montepulciano '90	🍷🍷	4
●	Nobile di Montepulciano Ris. '90	🍷🍷	5
●	Nobile di Montepulciano '91	🍷🍷	4
●	Nobile di Montepulciano '92	🍷🍷	4
●	Nobile di Montepulciano '94	🍷🍷	4
●	Vallocaia '94	🍷🍷	5
●	Vallocaia '95	🍷🍷	5
●	Nobile di Montepulciano '97	🍷🍷	5
●	Vallocaia '96	🍷	5
●	Vallocaia '97	🍷	6

MONTEPULCIANO (SI)

BOSCARELLI
FRAZ. CERVOGNANO
VIA DI MONTENERO, 28
53040 MONTEPULCIANO (SI)
TEL. 0578767277 - 0578767608

The historic De Ferrari family estate is still a benchmark for Montepulciano. Ruthless selection at harvest time and painful commercial sacrifices are the virtues that have made it so reliable over the years. The estate style is based on a profound respect for both the terroir and the various vintages, as a consequence of which the owners have, in fact, forgone two extremely successful wines: there is no '98 version of either the celebrated Nobile di Montepulciano cru, Vigna del Nocio, or the house Supertuscan, Boscarelli. This was a courageous decision, and one we greatly admire. As a result, there were only two wines for us to taste, and, predictably, they did well. The '99 De Ferrari is an enjoyable red. Its intense ruby introduces a fresh, rich bouquet with fruity notes of cherry and a well-integrated, enticing vegetal undertone. The palate is medium-bodied and well-balanced throughout. The Nobile di Montepulciano '98 is another story, and a greater wine. Here, too, we find an intense ruby hue but this time it is followed by a complex, generous and altogether captivating bouquet with some slightly unusual notes, such as medicinal herbs. The palate makes an equally good impression. The admirable development, with tightly knit tannins, leads to a clean and well-defined finish. It's a wine that reflects the best qualities of its terroir: the Cervognano cru is, in fact, known for its ability to unite power and elegance in its wines, and to give them long life.

●	Nobile di Montepulciano '98	🍷🍷	4
●	De Ferrari '99	🍷	3
●	Nobile di Montepulciano Ris. '88	🍷🍷🍷	5
●	Nobile di Montepulciano Vigna del Nocio Ris. '91	🍷🍷🍷	5
●	Boscarelli '95	🍷🍷	6
●	Boscarelli '97	🍷🍷	5
●	Nobile di Montepulciano Vigna del Nocio '97	🍷🍷	5
●	Nobile di Montepulciano '97	🍷	4

MONTEPULCIANO (SI)

Fattoria del Cerro
Fraz. Acquaviva
Via Grazianella, 5
53040 Montepulciano (SI)
tel. 0578767722
e-mail: fattoriadelcerro@tin.it

After repeatedly coming close, Fattoria del Cerro has finally won Three Glasses. Honours went to the '98 version of the estate standard-bearer, the Nobile di Montepulciano Antica Chiusina. The general excellence of this winery is confirmed by the abundance of Glasses netted by the rest of the range. For starters, the reds made a good showing and some were very good indeed. Among the One Glass winners we find the Chianti Colline Senesi '00, which offers very pleasing scents of bilberry and raspberry, and the Rosso di Montepulciano '00, with a nose enriched by notes of incense and morello cherry that usher in a soft-textured, fresh palate. Two red Glass winners include the merlot-based Poggio Golo '99, a wine that stands out for richness of extract and excellent balance in the mouth. The same score goes to the Nobile '98 for its remarkably harmonious bouquet and enormous depth of flavour. The very good Manero is a monovarietal sangiovese with rich notes of morello cherry and ripe cherry that mingle well with an oaky timbre. Next came the Chardonnay, with its scents of ripe banana and invigorating palate that never cloys palate, which almost picked up a second Glass. We've saved the Nobile Antica Chiusina for last: a rich, intense nose embraces notes of black cherry and dark berry fruit fused with perfectly judged, supremely elegant overtones of oak. On the palate, there is splendid elegance and balance, with very fine-grained tannins melding wonderfully into the wine's dense texture.

MONTEPULCIANO (SI)

Contucci
Via del Teatro, 1
53045 Montepulciano (SI)
tel. 0578757006
e-mail: info@contucci.it

Alemanno Contucci has been re-elected president of the Consorzio del Vino Nobile, but that's only part of the good news. Our tastings showed that his wines are definitely getting better, which confirms the wisdom of the decisions made in the last few years. For there have been some radical changes at this historic winery. The most visible one is the shift to barrels of Slavonian oak with a capacity of 25-30 hectolitres. There are also some tonneaux of French oak while barriques, although they have been tried, are used only intermittently. The wines presented are the local classics: Rosso di Montepulciano, Nobile di Montepulciano and Nobile Riserva. The Nobile '98 easily won its Two Glasses, incidentally pointing the way the new estate wines are going. Vibrantly intense ruby, it has a rich fruit nose of cherry and raspberry, pleasingly accompanied by oak-derived vanilla nuances. The interesting palate, after a robust yet harmonious attack, reveals attractive ripe tannins. One Glass goes to the Rosso di Montepulciano '98, which boasts a very clean fragrance with fresh fruity scents of berry fruit, then light tannins. The finish may not be explosive, but it is free of bitter notes. The Nobile Riserva '97 is interesting but no more. The nose is traditional in style and the palate is somewhat austere.

Wine	Glasses	Score
Nobile di Montepulciano Vigneto Antica Chiusina '98	🍷🍷🍷	6
Manero '99	🍷🍷	5
Poggio Golo '99	🍷🍷	5
Vin Santo Sangallo '96	🍷🍷	5
Nobile di Montepulciano Ris. '97	🍷🍷	5
Nobile di Montepulciano '98	🍷🍷	4
Braviolo '00	🍷	2*
Cerro Bianco '00	🍷	2
Chianti Colli Senesi '00	🍷	2*
Rosso di Montepulciano '00	🍷	3
Nobile di Montepulciano '90	🍷🍷🍷	4*
Nobile di Montepulciano Vigneto Antica Chiusina '97	🍷🍷	5
Poggio Golo '98	🍷🍷	5

Wine	Glasses	Score
Nobile di Montepulciano '98	🍷🍷	4
Nobile di Montepulciano Ris. '97	🍷	5
Rosso di Montepulciano '99	🍷	3
Vin Santo '86	🍷🍷	6
Nobile di Montepulciano '90	🍷🍷	4
Vin Santo '90	🍷🍷	4
Nobile di Montepulciano Pietrarossa '96	🍷	4
Nobile di Montepulciano '97	🍷	4

MONTEPULCIANO (SI)

DEI
LOC. VILLA MARTIENA, 35
53045 MONTEPULCIANO (SI)
TEL. 0578716878

The estate run by Caterina Dei is replanting its vineyards, which means that only about 40 hectares are currently producing. The cellar has now been enlarged and restructured and the very handsome completed building fits nicely into the landscape. It's a delight inside as well, where clever use of terracotta brickwork and travertine stone complements a décor otherwise composed of barrels, tonneaux and an increasing number of barriques. Caterina has not agreed with our evaluations of her Nobile di Montepulciano in the last few editions of the Guide: she found the wines underrated compared to the house Supertuscan, the Sancta Catharina. This year, there is less of a gap between their respective ratings, as the Vino Nobile Riserva '97 performed beautifully. A very dense, intense ruby hue leads to a clean, eloquent bouquet with clear hints of berry fruit, including particularly captivating notes of ripe bramble. The well-balanced palate has smooth tannins and a broad, lingering finish that perfectly echoes the nose. A step down, the standard-label Nobile '98 exhibits sour cherry aromas and a very pleasing flowery note of oleander. The palate shows great balance, the tannins fusing perfectly with glycerine and alcohol. The violet-hued Sancta Catharina '98 offers a rich bouquet and a well-balanced, very stylish palate.

MONTEPULCIANO (SI)

FASSATI
FRAZ. GRACCIANO
VIA DI GRACCIANELLO, 3/A
53040 MONTEPULCIANO (SI)
TEL. 0578708708 - 06844311
E-MAIL: info@fazibattaglia.it

Fassati is more or less the red winemaking heart of the well-known Fazi Battaglia company. The estate is growing: new high-density vineyards are about to start producing. Estate executives are counting particularly on these new vines, which will be total seven hectares, because of the special sangiovese clones planted and the position of the land. Four wines were presented at our tastings and three of them won Two Glasses. We'll begin with the Chianti Le Gaggiole Riserva '98, which is very successful. The deep ruby introduces a range of fruit aromas with very attractive hints of coffee and cocoa. The palate shows density and smooth tannins. The Nobile Salarco Riserva '97 is just as convincing, starting with its intense, lustrous colour. The palate is restrained and well-balanced, taking you through to a clean, reasonably long finish. The Nobile Pasiteo '98 has a lively ruby hue with violet highlights. The oak makes itself felt on the nose, although the cocoa and vanilla tones never smother the fruit. Elegance is the strong suit on the palate of this quaffable wine. The simpler Rosso di Montepulciano '00 is very neat and easy to drink.

● Nobile di Montepulciano Ris. '97	ŸŸ	5
● Sancta Catharina '98	ŸŸ	5
● Nobile di Montepulciano '98	Ÿ	4
● Nobile di Montepulciano '90	ŸŸ	4
● Nobile di Montepulciano '93	ŸŸ	4
● Sancta Catharina '94	ŸŸ	5
● Sancta Catharina '95	ŸŸ	5
● Sancta Catharina '96	ŸŸ	5
● Sancta Catharina '97	ŸŸ	5
● Nobile di Montepulciano Ris. '95	Ÿ	4
● Rosso di Montepulciano '96	Ÿ	3
● Nobile di Montepulciano '97	Ÿ	4

● Nobile di Montepulciano Salarco Ris. '97	ŸŸ	5
● Chianti Le Gaggiole Ris. '98	ŸŸ	3*
● Nobile di Montepulciano Pasiteo '98	ŸŸ	4
● Rosso di Montepulciano Selciaia '00	Ÿ	3
● Nobile di Montepulciano '95	ŸŸ	4
● Nobile di Montepulciano Salarco '95	ŸŸ	5
● Nobile di Montepulciano '96	ŸŸ	4
● Nobile di Montepulciano Pasiteo '97	ŸŸ	4
● Rosso di Montepulciano Selciaia '99	Ÿ	3

MONTEPULCIANO (SI)

FATTORIA LA BRACCESCA
LOC. GRACCIANO - S. S. 326, 15
53040 MONTEPULCIANO (SI)
TEL. 0578724252
E-MAIL: antinori@antinori.it

This was a transitional year for the Montepulciano outpost of the Antinori empire. The lovely winery at Maestrelle, near Valiano, is now almost complete, although the underground ageing cellar has still to be constructed. For the moment, the estate continues to use the equally charming subterranean cellar at the Badia, or abbey, of Montepulciano. The total surface planted to vine is a hefty 300 hectares, give or take a hectare, but not all of it is producing yet. La Braccesca makes two DOC wines and one monovarietal merlot. Of this year's range, we particularly liked the Nobile di Montepulciano '98. The ruby hue is intense, lightening a bit at the rim, and a note of rhubarb on the nose blends nicely with the berry fruit. The palate has muscle and lots of body but the tannins are fine-grained. The Rosso di Montalcino '00 is, in keeping with the natural order of things, simpler. The nose is distinctly fruity and the palate, if not muscular, is well-balanced and appealing, making for an eminently quaffable wine. The Merlot '99 also got One Glass. It is flavoursome and mouthfilling but the bouquet is not altogether clear-cut and the tannins get slightly out of hand. A few years of bottle age should take care of these problems.

Wine	Rating	Score
● Nobile di Montepulciano '98	♟♟	5
● Rosso di Montepulciano Sabazio '00	♟	3
● Merlot '99	♟	6
● Nobile di Montepulciano '95	♟♟	4
● Merlot '96	♟♟	5
● Nobile di Montepulciano '96	♟♟	4
● Merlot '97	♟♟	5
● Nobile di Montepulciano '97	♟♟	5
● Rosso di Montepulciano Sabazio '97	♟♟	3
● Merlot '98	♟♟	6
● Rosso di Montepulciano Sabazio '99	♟	3

MONTEPULCIANO (SI)

LA CALONICA
FRAZ. VALIANO
VIA DELLA STELLA, 27
53040 MONTEPULCIANO (SI)
TEL. 0578724119
E-MAIL: lacalonica@libero.it

With admirable regularity, Ferdinando Cattani produces well-made, characterful wines. He says that what does the trick is his location, particularly in very hot years, when Lake Trasimeno plays an essential role in keeping vine stress to a minimum. Recently, he has planted some additional hectares to varieties other than sangiovese – merlot and cabernet sauvignon, for example. All five of the wines he presented this year did well. The Signorelli has, in its second year out, taken over the position of flagship wine. The '99 version of this barrique-aged monovarietal merlot has a very intense colour. After a slightly grassy attack, the bouquet opens onto notes of dark berry fruit that meld nicely with the underlying oak. The palate is still hard, and the tannins make their presence felt, but there is nice concentration; both entry and progression are good. High marks go to the Nobile di Montepulciano '98 as well, although the aromas are neither particularly intense nor very clear-cut. It does better in the mouth, where good extract emerges. The Sangiovese '00 is attractive and delicately fruity. Then the Vin Santo '96 offered the panel hints of hazelnut, walnutskin, tobacco and tea on the nose but was less exciting on the palate. The Rosso di Montepulciano '00 is a straightforward red with well-tamed tannins.

Wine	Rating	Score
● Nobile di Montepulciano '98	♟♟	4
● Signorelli '99	♟♟	5
● Rosso di Montepulciano '00	♟	3
● Sangiovese '00	♟	2*
○ Vinsanto '96	♟	6
● Girifalco '95	♟♟	5
● Signorelli '98	♟♟	5
● Girifalco '96	♟	5
● Nobile di Montepulciano '96	♟	4
● Girifalco '97	♟	6
● Nobile di Montepulciano '97	♟	4
● Girifalco '98	♟	6
● Rosso di Montepulciano '99	♟	3

MONTEPULCIANO (SI)

La Ciarliana
Fraz. Gracciano
Via Ciarliana, 31
53040 Montepulciano (SI)
Tel. 0578758423 - 03355652718

We have noticed that a number of owners of small estates in Montepulciano have decided to become independent producers. The changeover from supplier of grapes to winemaker often coincides with a generation shift and in many cases the younger people can count on their parents' professional skills in vineyard management. Luigi Frangiosa's estate, which is making its debut in the Guide, belongs to this category. The location of his vineyards is particularly propitious: they are in Gracciano, which is known for the force and cellarability it gives to its wines. La Ciarlana has nine hectares dedicated to Vino Nobile. The little cellar is almost entirely taken up by barriques, and will be replaced within the coming year, in time for the 2002 vintage, by a construction more in keeping with the future requirements of the winery. Three wines were presented: two are Nobile di Montepulciano and one is a Rosso. The Nobile '98 shows an intense, very concentrated ruby hue and distinct scents of berry fruit, with secondary notes of incense. The texture on the palate is dense and the broad finish is marked by fine-grained tannins. A well-judged use of oak provides an agreeable undertone without distorting the wine's personality. The Nobile Riserva '97 is quite different in style, and even in appearance, as the ruby is lighter at the rim. More intense oak accompanies notes of peach and apricot on the nose, and the lovely tannins will need more time to blend into the texture of the wine. The very correctly executed Rosso di Montepulciano '00 also has substantial tannins.

● Nobile di Montepulciano Ris. '97	♟♟	5
● Nobile di Montepulciano '98	♟♟	4
● Rosso di Montepulciano '00	♟	3

MONTEPULCIANO (SI)

Nottola
Loc. Nottola
S. S. 326, 15
53045 Montepulciano (SI)
Tel. 0578707060 - 0577684711
E-mail: nottola@bccmp.com

Progress continues apace at this highly respected Montepulciano estate. Investments have been made in every aspect of production. The vineyards are not yet completely renewed but year by year, further sectors are replanted and new lots are acquired. The cellar, meanwhile, has been completely refitted in record time. It is now temperature-controlled throughout, and more barriques and tonneaux are finding a home there. Three wines were presented this year, two of which easily won Two Glasses. Actually, the Nobile di Montepulciano Vigna del Fattore '98 seemed better than ever. It is rather modern in style, with a fresh bouquet featuring notes of cedar, blackcurrant and bilberry nicely underpinned by an unobtrusive vegetal nuance. The full-bodied palate starts encouragingly and the progression is lifted by very fine-grained tannins. The long finish echoes the vegetal nuances. The other Two Glass winner, the Nobile di Montepulciano '98, is more traditional, although its colour is impressive. Again, the nose is very youthful, with intense notes of morello cherry and raspberry simply but crisply presented. The Rosso di Montepulciano '99 is less successful, largely because of its slightly unfocused nose. In addition, the palate is rather one-dimensional and elusive.

● Nobile di Montepulciano '98	♟♟	4
● Nobile di Montepulciano Vigna del Fattore '98	♟♟	5
● Rosso di Montepulciano '00		3
● Nobile di Montepulciano Vigna del Fattore '95	♟♟	5
● Nobile di Montepulciano Vigna del Fattore '97	♟♟	5
● Nobile di Montepulciano '96	♟	4
● Nobile di Montepulciano Vigna del Fattore '96	♟	5

MONTEPULCIANO (SI)

Fattoria di Paterno
Fraz. Sant'Albino
Via Fontelellera, 11
53045 Montepulciano (SI)
tel. 0578799194 - 0685301102
e-mail: fattoriapaterno@tiscalinet.it

After a few years' absence, Fattoria di Paterno is back in the Guide with its own profile. We feel certain that the new policy, which was already perceptible in the wines we tasted last year, will continue to give good results. Five hectares are currently dedicated to the production of Vino Nobile but when the newly planted vines come onstream, that number will grow to nine. In addition to the classic prugnolo gentile grape, the cellar is experimenting with other varieties, including native ones. A significant influence in the changes that have taken place here has been exercised by the new consultant, Lorenzo Landi, who was quick to spot the great potential of the Paterno vineyards and has been able to bring it out in characterful wines. The Nobile di Montepulciano Riserva '97 is a very intense ruby. The bouquet includes notes of oleander, almond and berry fruit. The good points of the palate are balance and the finish which, if not extremely long, is fairly long. Perhaps the tannins are a bit exposed in the back palate but they couldn't be described as bitter. The Nobile '98 seemed even better. A very dense ruby colour introduces the complex fruit fragrance of morello cherry, cherry and mulberry jam. The development on the palate is intriguing, finding a consummate balance of tannins and alcohol.

MONTEPULCIANO (SI)

★ Poliziano
Loc. Montepulciano Stazione
Via Fontago, 1
53040 Montepulciano (SI)
tel. 0578738171
e-mail: az.agr.poliziano@iol.it

This is another first-class performance from the estate owned by Federico Carletti, a well-known and much esteemed figure in these parts. Every year, his winery walks off with at least one Three Glass award and places at least one other wine in the finals. And even the simplest wines are always very good, too. The basis of this success is constant dedication to oenological and viticultural research and experimentation. In the modern and very practical cellar, the Poliziano team tries out new fermentation vessels and their loyalty to small barrels is now total. The estate standard-bearers are super, as usual: star billing goes to the Nobile Asinone '98, which won Three Glasses. It flaunts a dense, intense colour and a sumptuous bouquet with fruity notes of bramble, wild cherry and bilberry enhanced by delicate, very discreet suggestions of elegant oak. The palate is complex and substantial, its smooth tannins well integrated into the structure. What a wine. Le Stanze '99, a blend of cabernet sauvignon and merlot aged in French oak, is almost as brilliant. A very dense violet introduces well-defined fruit aromas and an enticing note of candied citron peel. The palate is not yet at its peak and there are some rough edges that require a little more bottle age. The other wines get One Glass each: the Nobile '98 is very enjoyable and elegant but lacks power. The Rosso di Montepulciano '00 stumbles a bit on the nose but is pleasing on the palate. Lastly, the Morellino di Scansano Lohsa '00, from the Scansano property, is technically well-made but the structure and general balance are not exceptional.

● Nobile di Montepulciano Ris. '97	♈♈	5
● Nobile di Montepulciano '98	♈♈	4
● Nobile di Montepulciano Ris. '88	♉♉	4
● Nobile di Montepulciano Ris. '90	♉♉	4
● Nobile di Montepulciano Ris. '91	♉♉	4
● Nobile di Montepulciano '91	♉	4
● Nobile di Montepulciano '92	♉	4

● Nobile di Montepulciano Asinone '98	♈♈♈	6
● Le Stanze '99	♈♈	6
● Morellino di Scansano Lohsa '00	♈	3
● Rosso di Montepulciano '00	♈	3
● Nobile di Montepulciano '98	♈	4
● Nobile di Montepulciano Vigna dell'Asinone '93	♉♉♉	5
● Elegia '95	♉♉♉	5
● Le Stanze '95	♉♉♉	5
● Nobile di Montepulciano Vigna dell'Asinone '95	♉♉♉	5
● Le Stanze '97	♉♉♉	6
● Nobile di Montepulciano Asinone '97	♉♉♉	6
● Le Stanze '98	♉♉♉	6

MONTEPULCIANO (SI)

REDI
VIA DI COLLAZZI, 5
53045 MONTEPULCIANO (SI)
TEL. 0578757102
E-MAIL: info@cantinadelredi.com

What began as the centre for technological research of Vecchia Cantina, the only wine co-operative in Montepulciano, continues to make progress in terms of both quantity and quality. At Redi, they are still improving their wines. They plan to spend roughly 10,000,000 lire renovating the cellar, installing new equipment to make control temperatures during fermentation, and increasing the stock of small oak barrels. At our tastings, four Redi wines won Two Glasses, and the Nobile di Montepulciano Briareo '98 is at the top of the list. Concentrated ruby with violet highlights, it offers crisp, clean notes of cherries and morello cherries. The palate makes an equally good impression, with solid, well-integrated tannins and a vigour that bodes well for the future. The similarly impressive '98 Vino Nobile displays aromas of blackcurrants and cherries, as well as a light grassy note which is never excessive. Orbaio, the most recent addition to the list, is a blend of cabernet and merlot aged in small barrels. The '99 has light vegetal overtones on a bilberry base; the palate is attractive and elegant, thanks to nice tannins and good length. The '93 Vin Santo is very good. The nose may be a touch unexciting but the palate is substantial. The Argo '00 is a simple but very pleasurable wine while the Rosso di Montepulciano merits only a mention, as the nose is a little unfocused.

MONTEPULCIANO (SI)

SALCHETO
LOC. SANT'ALBINO
VIA DI VILLA BIANCA, 15
53045 MONTEPULCIANO (SI)
TEL. 0578799031
E-MAIL: posta@salcheto.it

First, an important note. We make no comment on the Rosso di Montepulciano '99 because it hadn't been released when we were tasting. As for the rest of the range, we can only offer our compliments to the Piccins and Michele Manelli, who run the estate with conviction and enthusiasm. The are doing a very good job, especially in the vineyards, where they are experimenting with some sangiovese clones which will show results in coming years. There is also good news regarding this year's wines. The Nobile di Montepulciano Riserva '97 was looking very good. Great colour, clean and intense on the nose, it mingles nice fruit with well-gauged oak. In the mouth, it is never heavy, the smooth, ripe tannins giving it elegance and a pleasing personality. The Rosso di Montepulciano '00 also did well and is one of this year's best. The very intense fragrance embraces sour cherries and raspberries while the rich, well-balanced palate is underpinned by unobtrusive acidity. The Nobile '98 also gets Two Glasses. It needs to breathe a while before it opens on the nose but quickly reveals its personality and elegance on the palate. The Chianti Colline Senesi '00 earned a Glass.

	Wine	Glasses	Score
○	Vin Santo '93	ŸŸ	6
●	Nobile di Montepulciano '98	ŸŸ	4
●	Nobile di Montepulciano Briareo '98	ŸŸ	6
●	Orbaio '99	ŸŸ	5
●	Argo '00	Ÿ	2*
●	Rosso di Montepulciano '00		3
○	Vin Santo '90	ŸŸ	6
○	Vin Santo '92	ŸŸ	6
●	Nobile di Montepulciano Briareo '96	ŸŸ	5
●	Nobile di Montepulciano Briareo '97	ŸŸ	6
○	Riccio '97	ŸŸ	4
●	Argo '99	Ÿ	3

	Wine	Glasses	Score
●	Nobile di Montepulciano Ris. '97	ŸŸ	5
●	Rosso di Montepulciano '00	ŸŸ	3
●	Nobile di Montepulciano '98	ŸŸ	5
●	Chianti Colline Senesi '00	Ÿ	3
●	Nobile di Montepulciano '97	ŸŸŸ	5
●	Salcheto '90	ŸŸ	4
●	Nobile di Montepulciano '91	ŸŸ	4
●	Nobile di Montepulciano Ris. '93	ŸŸ	5
●	Nobile di Montepulciano Ris. '95	ŸŸ	5

MONTEPULCIANO (SI)

TENIMENTI ANGELINI
TENUTA TREROSE
FRAZ. VALIANO
VIA DELLA STELLA, 3
53040 MONTEPULCIANO (SI)
TEL. 057880411 - 0578724018

The wines from Trerose did brilliantly at our tastings. No great surprise, when you consider the investments that the Angelini group has made here. The new vines are planted densely and the experiments with various grape varieties are going well. Large as it is, the cellar is showing signs of strain because so many big barrels have been replaced by space-consuming barriques. The Nobile di Montepulciano La Villa '98 came very close to winning Three Glasses. It is a prugnolo and cabernet sauvignon blend with a very modern style, which some people like and others abhor, and is aged only in barriques. The very intense ruby colour is firm to the rim of the glass, introducing a full, clean nose. The oak on the nose blends nicely with the fruit – we noted blackcurrants, sour cherries and citron. The richly extracted palate also convinces, unfurling serious tannins. The good but less expressive Nobile Simposio '98, a monovarietal sangiovese, has trouble keeping up the pressure on the palate, probably because it is a very young youth. Rich and powerful, it lacks the elegance which won the last version Three Glasses. The standard Nobile '98, aged in Slavonian oak, is classic in style. The white Busillis, a monovarietal viognier, is even more nicely balanced and full-bodied in this year's version.

MONTEPULCIANO (SI)

TENUTA VALDIPIATTA
VIA CIARLIANA, 25/A
53040 MONTEPULCIANO (SI)
TEL. 0578757930
E-MAIL: valdipiatta@bccmp.com

Valdipiatta has been expanding both its cellar space and its vine stock. The cellar, which is beautiful, boasts a large number of barriques and tonneaux, and much of the vinification is done in wooden vats. The overall results justify the decisions made by this reliable producer. Four wines received Two Glasses, two reaching our new Two Plus category, indicating Three Glass finalists. The very fine Tre Fonti, a blend of cabernet sauvignon, prugnolo gentile and canaiolo, has a very intense colour and rich aromas of cherries with caramel and vanilla. The palate, after a clean, sharp attack, follows through well to reveal fine-grained tannins. The finish is free of bitter notes and delightfully long. The Nobile Riserva '97 is a very interesting wine with an intense ruby hue. There is breadth and depth on the nose, with notes of more, bilberry and blackcurrant sweetened by wood-derived spiciness. It lacks perhaps the touch of elegance that could net it Three Glasses but it is still an excellent wine. Both the Nobile '98 and the Trincerone '99 are also persuasive, the latter – a blend of merlot and canaiolo – showing an attractive nose and good length on the palate. The Rosso di Montepulciano '99, with its slightly unfocused nose and light structure, and the white Nibbiano '00, both get only a mention.

● Nobile di Montepulciano La Villa '98	♟♟	6
● Nobile di Montepulciano Simposio '98	♟♟	6
○ Busillis '99	♟♟	4
● Nobile di Montepulciano '98	♟	4
● Nobile di Montepulciano Simposio '97	♟♟♟	6
● Nobile di Montepulciano La Villa '95	♟♟	5
● Nobile di Montepulciano Simposio '95	♟♟	5
● Nobile di Montepulciano La Villa '97	♟♟	6
○ Busillis '98	♟♟	4

● Nobile di Montepulciano Ris. '97	♟♟	5
● Tre Fonti '98	♟♟	5
● Nobile di Montepulciano '98	♟♟	4
● Trincerone '99	♟♟	5
○ Nibbiano '00		2
● Rosso di Montepulciano '00		3
● Nobile di Montepulciano Ris. '90	♟♟♟	5
● Nobile di Montepulciano Ris. '93	♟♟	5
● Nobile di Montepulciano '95	♟♟	4
● Nobile di Montepulciano Ris. '95	♟♟	5
● Nobile di Montepulciano '96	♟♟	4
● Tre Fonti '96	♟♟	5
● Nobile di Montepulciano '97	♟♟	4
● Tre Fonti '97	♟♟	5
● Trincerone '97	♟♟	5

MONTEPULCIANO (SI)

VILLA SANT'ANNA
LOC. ABBADIA
53040 MONTEPULCIANO (SI)
TEL. 0578708017 - 03355283775
E-MAIL: simona@villasantanna.it

In the general improvement in Montepulciano, we are pleased to note that Simona and Anna Fabroni's estate is holding its own. Their new oenologist, Carlo Ferrini, has suggested some important changes that will soon lead, among other things, to a larger barrique stock. This year's wines also show progress. The vibrant, dense violet-tinged Rosso di Montepulciano '00 has a refreshing nose of red and black berry notes that mingle delightfully with nicely calibrated wood. The rich palate reveals very good balance, despite its youth. The fine-grained tannins are particularly attractive and in fact, this is one of the best Rossos we tasted. Though different in style, the Nobile '98 is no less impressive. It, too, has fruity aromas but there is more ripeness, with hints of cherry jam and bottled cherries. The oak peeks through flirtatiously while the thrust on the palate favours finesse over power. The Valloni '97 is not new wine but the former Il Vallone Supertuscan under a new name. It has a medium ruby colour that tends towards garnet at the rim while wood-derived coffee and vanilla notes tend to suppress the fruit on the nose. Medium-bodied with good tannins, this wine is pleasant enough to drink, but a bit on the simple side.

MONTEROTONDO MARITTIMO (GR)

SERRAIOLA
FRAZ. FRASSINE
LOC. SERRAIOLA
58020 MONTEROTONDO MARITTIMO (GR)
TEL. 0566910026 - 056640157

Blessed with a strong character, Fiorella Lenzi has always been an oenological nonconformist. While other producers struggled to turn out a major red, she set about making whites and planted greco, sauvignon, fiano and vermentino alongside her trebbiano and malvasia. She does make just a small amount of steel-fermented and aged red, which is accessible to everyone's palate and pocket. Although not bubbling with enthusiasm, Fiorella did try in '98 to make a blend of cabernet and merlot, the Campo Montecristo. The results, while not extraordinary, were encouraging. Now the second edition, the '99, has come out, and it's a distinctly good, clean-tasting, full-bodied wine. Although it is still a tad heavy on the oak, the fruit is definitely there, lively and concentrated. Her trump card, the white Violina, also did well at our tastings. It unveils aromas of citrus fruits, sage and butter. Refreshingly tangy in the mouth, it has good length and finishes pleasantly with ripe fruit. The Vermentino '00 is just as good, with its lovely aromas of fresh herbs and lively, persistent, pleasantly complex flavours. The Monteregio Rosso Lentisco '99 is an unabashedly straightforward, lively and technically correct wine.

● Rosso di Montepulciano '00	ΥΥ	3
● Nobile di Montepulciano '98	ΥΥ	4
● I Valloni '97	Υ	5
● Nobile di Montepulciano '93	ΥΥ	4
● Chianti '94	ΥΥ	2
● Nobile di Montepulciano '94	ΥΥ	4
● Chianti Colli Senesi '95	ΥΥ	2
● Vigna Il Vallone '95	ΥΥ	5
● Nobile di Montepulciano '96	ΥΥ	4
○ Vin Santo '93	Υ	5
● Nobile di Montepulciano '97	Υ	4
● Chianti Colli Senesi '99	Υ	3
● Rosso di Montepulciano '99	Υ	3

○ Monteregio Bianco di Massa Marittima Violina '00	ΥΥ	4*
● Campo Montecristo '99	ΥΥ	5
○ Vermentino '00	Υ	3
● Monteregio Rosso di Massa Marittima Lentisco '99		3

MONTESCUDAIO (PI)

Poggio Gagliardo
Loc. Poggio Gagliardo
56040 Montescudaio (PI)
tel. 0586630775
e-mail: info@poggiogagliardo.com

The years go by but Poggio Gagliardo continues to produce wines that are only slightly better than average. We are not happy about starting on a negative note but perhaps a gentle nudge will be helpful. Poggio Gagliardo has a history that few others in this coastal area can boast. Actually, it watched of a number of local estates come into being and then go on to surpass it in quality. Poggio Gagliardo's wines are reliable and well-made but we feel that there is lots of unexploited potential. Now on to the wines. Il Gobbo ai Pianacci '98 starts of with decent raw material, which is properly handled to produce good body underpinned by nicely balanced oak: in short a nice soft, clean-tasting red with good length. What it lacks, though is more character. Vigna Lontana '00 is similar: well-balanced and round with wood dominant. A few years ago, this was enough to make a wine stand out but more effort is needed today. The Linaglia '00 is consistent, correct and pleasurable. It has no great pretensions but won't let you down, either. It was the Rovo '98 that failed to live up to expectations. It is well-made and earns its Glass but lacks vigour. In short, it is a little forward and over the hill.

MONTESPERTOLI (FI)

Le Calvane
Fraz. Montagnana
Via Castiglioni, 1/5
50020 Montespertoli (FI)
tel. 0571671073

Thanks to the hard work of a few estates, the historic area of Montespertoli is regaining its lustre. No longer does it hitch its wagon to local colour. Instead, the subzone is adapting to the new requirements of the wine market. Le Calvane is the most up-to-date and vital winery in the area. They made the straightforward decision to use cabernet sauvignon in their flagship wine. For the '98 version of this excellent red, the cellar followed the excellent plan of harvesting the grapes, weather permitting, at the moment of perfect ripeness, both to avoid unpleasant vegetal excesses, and to obtain adequate phenolic stability. Small barrels, new for the most part, are used with discretion in the cellar to give the wine an elegant structure. The '98 version of the Borro del Boscone, with just a bit more verve, would have netted Three Glasses, as it did last year. Dense and concentrated wine, it reveals excellent balance and a long finish. It has no great complexity but is still a wine of a very high standard indeed. The Chianti Riserva Trecione '98 is good, too, offering aromas of liquorice, wild cherries and minerals. In the mouth, it is both substantial and well-conceived. The Chianti Quercione '99 is, as expected, a simple wine but a delicious, well-made and nicely balanced one.

	Wine	Rating	Score
●	Montescudaio Rosso Gobbo ai Pianacci '98	🍷🍷	5
○	Montescudaio Bianco Linaglia '00	🍷	4
○	Montescudaio Bianco Vigna Lontana '00	🍷	4
●	Montescudaio Rosso Rovo '98	🍷	5
●	Montescudaio Rosso Malemacchie '92	🍷🍷	3
●	Montescudaio Rosso Gobbo ai Pianacci '97	🍷🍷	5
●	Montescudaio Rosso Rovo '97	🍷🍷	5
○	Montescudaio Bianco Vigna Lontana '98	🍷🍷	4
○	Montescudaio Bianco Vigna Lontana '99	🍷🍷	4
○	Montescudaio Bianco '99	🍷	3
●	Montescudaio Rosso '99	🍷	3
●	Borro del Boscone '98	🍷🍷	6
●	Chianti Colli Fiorentini Il Trecione Ris. '98	🍷🍷	4
●	Chianti Colli Fiorentini Quercione '99	🍷	3
●	Borro del Boscone '97	🍷🍷🍷	5
●	Borro del Boscone '91	🍷🍷	4
●	Chianti Colli Fiorentini Il Trecione Ris. '91	🍷🍷	4
●	Borro del Boscone '94	🍷🍷	4
●	Borro del Boscone '95	🍷🍷	5
●	Borro del Boscone '96	🍷🍷	5
●	Chianti Colli Fiorentini Il Trecione Ris. '96	🍷🍷	4
●	Chianti Colli Fiorentini Il Trecione Ris. '97	🍷🍷	4

MONTESPERTOLI (FI)

CASTELLO DI POPPIANO
VIA DI FEZZANA, 45
50025 MONTESPERTOLI (FI)
TEL. 05582315
E-MAIL: poppiano@mclink.it

This historic winery, a Marchesi Guicciardini property, makes a comeback to the Guide this year. That is in itself an encouraging sign but we are only half way there. All the wines have improved but the upper end of the range still has to make further progress. The line is a long one and all the wines are well-made, the Tricorno '97 being the star of the show. A compact wine, it has a clean bouquet and is not without a certain complexity. The palate is even and develops well, offering pleasure and showing character. The Toscoforte '98 does not have much to say to the nose but displays good balance and consistency in the mouth. The rest of the line has, as we have already suggested, a certain dignified correctness and quaffability. The Sassaia del Virginio '00, a monovarietal Chardonnay, has notes of aromatic herbs mingling with inviting mineral sensations. The entry on the palate is good, lively and enjoyable, with marked acidity balanced by the alcohol. The Colli Fiorentini Il Cortile '99 does quite well, too. It unveils admirable fruit with just a hint of super-ripeness on the nose. Similarly, the Syrah '99 does not take full advantage of fruit's potential but still makes a decent showing. The Riserva '97 is a little shy on the nose, where tobacco and leather emerge, but reveals admirable grip in the mouth. The Morellino di Scansano Massi di Mandorlaia '99 fails to convince entirely. Its colour and nose are a bit weak and evolved, and the palate is quite vegetal and bitter in the finish.

MONTESPERTOLI (FI)

POGGIO A POPPIANO
VIA DI POPPIANO, 19
50025 MONTESPERTOLI (FI)
TEL. 055213084 - 0552335313
E-MAIL: pezilevi@tin.it

Poggio a Poppiano has done well its second year in the Guide, with good scores and high ambitions. Only two wines were presented, very different in kind but similar in quality. The Flocco '99, from mostly cabernet sauvignon with some merlot and sangiovese, made an excellent impression. The nose is not yet very expressive, for the wine is still very young, but the aromas are clean and concentrated, revealing hints of plums and blackberries, as well as toasty notes from the oak. Pleasingly robust tannins blend well into the richly extracted body; the oak is already well integrated, if still rather noticeable, and the finish is long and flavoursome. This may not be very complex wine but it definitely has promise. The Vin Santo '99 was a pleasant surprise: it has lots of character and a very rich nose of almonds, cinnamon, dried figs, candied fruit and autumn leaves. It is markedly volatile but with Vin Santo one can't be too picky. In the mouth, it is very sweet, mellow and dense. The finish is a bit short and tannic but the wine has nice style and personality.

● Tricorno '97	⍦⍦	5
○ Sassaia del Virginio '00	⍦	3
● Chianti Colli Fiorentini Ris. '97	⍦	3
● Toscoforte '98	⍦	4
● Chianti Colli Fiorentini Il Cortile '99	⍦	3
● Syrah '99	⍦	4
● Morellino di Scansano Massi di Mandorlaia '99		3
● Chianti Colli Fiorentini Ris. '93	⍦⍦	3
● Tricorno '93	⍦⍦	4
● Chianti Colli Fiorentini Il Cortile '95	⍦	2
● Syrah '96	⍦	3
● Toscoforte '96	⍦	3

○ Vin Santo '89	⍦⍦	5
● Flocco '99	⍦⍦	5
● Flocco '97	⍦⍦	5
● Flocco '98	⍦⍦	5
● Calamita '99	⍦⍦	4

MONTEVARCHI (AR)

Fattoria Petrolo
Loc. Galatrona
Fraz. Mercatale Valdarno
Via Petrolo, 30
52020 Montevarchi (AR)
tel. 0559911322 e-mail: petrolo@petrolo.it

Another triumph for the merlot, Galatrona, which continues the winning run it began with the '97. It is a wine that has changed Petrolo, and probably also the winery's production strategy, with its continuing success. This does not mean that the cellar is going to forget the sangiovese, which may well keep its dominant position in the Sanjust family's vineyards. The Galtrona has yet to make a false move, and has shone every year. It is a powerful and very concentrated wine with copious and energetic tannins. There is no point sniffing around for subtle undertones or delicate refinement in this wine: the impetuous structure and mineral tones of the bouquet brook no argument. This is a Merlot that is neither easy nor ingratiating; instead, it's got attitude. We did not, however, taste the Torrione '99, a sangiovese which is the godfather, as it were, of Petrolo reds. The vintage, to judge by the other wines, was excellent, which bodes well for its release next year. The estate's third wine, Terre di Galatrona, a blend of sangiovese and merlot, nearly won Two Glasses. The '99 seemed quite successful with its pleasing aromas of aniseed and vanilla, joined by balsamic notes. The attack on the palate is intense and convincingly full; the progress in the mouth is well-ordered, letting up slightly only on the finish.

● Galatrona '99	▼▼▼	6
● Terre di Galatrona '99	▼	4
● Galatrona '97	▼▼▼	6
● Galatrona '98	▼▼▼	6
● Torrione '90	▼▼	5
○ Vin Santo '93	▼▼	5
● Torrione '94	▼▼	5
● Galatrona '95	▼▼	6
● Torrione '95	▼▼	5
● Torrione '97	▼▼	5
● Torrione '98	▼▼	5
● Terre di Galatrona '98	▼	4

ORBETELLO (GR)

La Parrina
Loc. Albinia
58010 Orbetello (GR)
tel. 0564862636 - 0564862626
e-mail: parrina@dada.it

A winery with an entire DOC zone to itself, La Parrina has up to now had to deal more with the difficulties of isolation than with the advantages of uniqueness. Fortunately, the estate has reacted energetically and the good results are already there to be seen. None of the wines are outstanding but they are all carefully made, revealing good raw material. And if we look ahead, things are even more encouraging. Our preview tasting of the Parrina Riserva '99, for example, was very exciting. Rich and full, it offers beautifully ripe fruit perfectly fused with the oak, which very properly keeps its distance. The interesting Riserva '98 displays good but insufficiently ripe fruit, as rather evident vegetal tones and still dominant wood indicate. In the mouth, however, it shows good balance and body, though it closes a bit stiffly. The successful Ansonica '00 is very enjoyable with its captivating aromas of tropical fruit and its solid, expressive body. The uncomplicated but pleasant Parrina Rosso '00, fermented and aged in stainless steel, is a quaffable wine that wins you over straight away. The well-made Parrina Bianco '00 has substantial body and succulent fruit. The Parrina Muraccio '99 is not bad either, and though still somewhat undefined on the nose, has a good robust structure. We close with the least challenging wine presented, the Capalbio Violetto '00, which is straightforward and agreeable, and can be found in the shops for little more than € 2.50.

● La Parrina Rosso Ris. '98	▼▼	4
○ Ansonica '00	▼	3
● La Parrina Rosso '00	▼	3
○ Parrina Bianco '00	▼	2*
● La Parrina Rosso Muraccio '99	▼	4
○ Capalbio Bianco '00		1*

PALAIA (PI)

SAN GERVASIO
LOC. SAN GERVASIO
56030 PALAIA (PI)
TEL. 0587483360
E-MAIL: sangervasio@sangervasio.com

They are working for the future at San Gervasio. The vineyards planted in recent years are becoming increasingly impressive as they relentlessly invade the hills surrounding Luca Tommasini's winery. Clearly, plans are ambitious: the cellar and the barrique cellar are ready and prospects are encouraging. But we must be patient because, though it is true that great wine is born from excellent grapes, it is also true that it takes time to produce them. Few wines were presented at this year's tastings, with A Sirio, a wine based mostly on sangiovese, conspicuous by its absence. The '99 version will be released next year. That leaves us with I Renai, a merlot, and the Chianti, Le Stoppie. San Gervasio's merlot has a potentially excellent structure, as was clear when we tasted it. It is also true that I Renai '99 will only get better with more time in the bottle, since oak lords it over nose and palate at the moment. Yet, the wine left an indelible impression of enormous energy. The Chianti Le Stoppie, as might be expected, has more modest ambitions. It is fruity and enjoyable, if a bit emphatically super-ripe on the nose.

PANZANO (FI)

CAROBBIO
VIA SAN MARTINO A CECIONE, 26
50020 PANZANO (FI)
TEL. 0558560133
E-MAIL: saati@saati.it

Carobbio has been maintaining high standards for some time and this year is no exception: the whole range is very good. Indeed, their cabernet, Pietraforte del Carobbio '97, came within an inch of Three Glasses. It's a wine with depth, elegance, balance and tasty tannins. Only its somewhat insistent vegetal tone denied it higher honours, although it is still excellent. Curiously, grassy notes can be found as well in their sangiovese, the Leone '97, which is, however, interestingly complex and grows in intensity if left to breathe. The Panzano estate has nearly ten hectares under vine of which about half are dedicated to Chianti Classico. Their efforts with this wine were readily evident at our tastings. The nicely structured Chianti Classico '99 is round and full-flavoured, with pleasing notes of vanilla and red berries in evidence on the lingering finish. The '98 Riserva commands respect as well. It has a lively ruby colour and a concentrated if not yet fully eloquent nose. The attack on the palate is dense and underpinned by oak; the progression is full-bodied and invigorating, and the finish is still young and just a bit undisciplined, but promising nonetheless.

Wine	Rating	Score
● I Renai '99	ŸŸ	6
● Chianti Le Stoppie '00	Ÿ	3
● A Sirio '96	ŸŸ	4
● A Sirio '97	ŸŸ	5
○ Marna '97	ŸŸ	4
● A Sirio '98	ŸŸ	5
● I Renai '98	ŸŸ	6
○ Vin Santo '95	Ÿ	4
○ Marna '96	Ÿ	4
● Chianti Le Stoppie '97	Ÿ	3
● Chianti Le Stoppie '98	Ÿ	3
● Chianti Le Stoppie '99	Ÿ	3

Wine	Rating	Score
● Pietraforte del Carobbio '97	ŸŸ	6
● Leone del Carobbio '97	ŸŸ	6
● Chianti Cl. Ris. '98	ŸŸ	5
● Chianti Cl. '99	ŸŸ	4
● Chianti Cl. Ris. '93	ŸŸ	5
● Leone del Carobbio '93	ŸŸ	5
● Pietraforte del Carobbio '93	ŸŸ	5
● Leone del Carobbio '94	ŸŸ	5
● Chianti Cl. '95	ŸŸ	4
● Chianti Cl. Ris. '95	ŸŸ	5
● Pietraforte del Carobbio '95	ŸŸ	5
● Chianti Cl. Ris. '96	ŸŸ	5
● Chianti Cl. '97	ŸŸ	4
● Chianti Cl. Ris. '97	ŸŸ	5
● Chianti Cl. '98	ŸŸ	4

PANZANO (FI)

FATTORIA CASALOSTE
VIA MONTAGLIARI, 32
50020 PANZANO (FI)
TEL. 055852725
E-MAIL: casaloste@casaloste.it

Whenever we write about this estate, the passion and resolution that inspire Giovanni Battista and Emilia d'Orsi come clearly to mind, as does their close collaboration with their consultant oenologist, Gabriella Tani. That's why it's so hard when we have to be critical, which is the case this year after an infelicitous vintage. Let's begin at once with the wine we liked least, the Riserva '98. Its impenetrable colour ushers in not altogether clean aromas of caramel and butter. It tends to fade in the mouth, despite its fleshy pulp and tight-knit tannins. The Don Vincenzo '97, on the other hand, is very good, its intensely clean ruby colour and intriguing aromas of cinnamon and pepper uniting perfectly with the concentrated, almost pungent notes of cherries and wild strawberries. The excellent entry in the mouth is soft and velvety; the tannins seem perfectly integrated with alcohol and sustained by good body. The Chianti Classico '99 is eminently enjoyable: intense notes of cherries mingle with particularly enticing hints of cloves on the nose. Acidity dominates alcohol on the palate, making it a very easy wine to drink.

Wine	Glasses	Score
● Chianti Cl. Don Vincenzo Ris. '97	ΨΨ	5
● Chianti Cl. Ris. '98	Ψ	4
● Chianti Cl. '99	Ψ	3
● Chianti Cl. Ris. '94	ΨΨ	4
● Chianti Cl. Don Vincenzo Ris. '95	ΨΨ	5
● Chianti Cl. Ris. '95	ΨΨ	4
● Chianti Cl. Don Vincenzo Ris. '96	ΨΨ	5
● Chianti Cl. '98	ΨΨ	3
● Chianti Cl. Ris. '96	Ψ	4
● Chianti Cl. '97	Ψ	3
● Chianti Cl. Ris. '97	Ψ	4

PANZANO (FI)

CENNATOIO
VIA DI SAN LEOLINO, 37
50020 PANZANO (FI)
TEL. 055852134 - 0558963230
E-MAIL: info@cennatoio.it

Cennatoio has presented a long list of wines this year, partly because some of their wines were not yet ready at the time of last year's tastings. The Chianti Riserva '97 is more than acceptable, displaying a maturity on the nose, while still lively and fruity in the mouth. The '99 Chianti, also very good, its intense aromas with sound fruit predominating, accompanied by spiciness and vegetal notes. It is well-behaved on the palate, revealing elegant body and good length. The Riserva O'Leandro '98 shows a lovely brilliant ruby colour and a fairly substantial palate, hindered by notes that are rather too herbal to be desirable in a Chianti. A grassy note is also present in the '98 Chianti Riserva, which shows admirable balance and medium body. Of the other labels, the Arcibaldo '97 has an earthy and vegetal nose but is more convincing in the mouth, where it shows good body. The tannins are perhaps a little dry on the finish. The Arcibaldo '98 scored about the same with its clean, if not very expressive, aromas and a palate well-sustained by oak. Very much like each other, the Mammolo '97 and '98 are simple and well-balanced but, more's the pity, dominated by vegetal sensations. We also found these present in the cabernet-based Rosso Fiorentino '97 and '98. The '97 has more density and elegance than the leaner '98. In conclusion, the Etrusco '98 is a good sangiovese, well-balanced and even on the palate, with boisé on the nose.

Wine	Glasses	Score
● Chianti Cl. Ris. '97	ΨΨ	4
● Rosso Fiorentino '97	ΨΨ	5
● Etrusco '98	ΨΨ	5
● Chianti Cl. '99	ΨΨ	4
● Arcibaldo '97	Ψ	5
● Mammolo '97	Ψ	4
● Arcibaldo '98	Ψ	5
● Chianti Cl. O'Leandro Ris. '98	Ψ	5
● Chianti Cl. Ris. '98	Ψ	4
● Mammolo '98	Ψ	4
● Rosso Fiorentino '98	Ψ	5
● Etrusco '94	ΨΨΨ	5
● Etrusco '95	ΨΨ	5
● Rosso Fiorentino '95	ΨΨ	5
● Etrusco '97	ΨΨ	5

PANZANO (FI)

★ Tenuta Fontodi
Via San Leolino, 87
50020 Panzano (FI)
Tel. 055852005
E-mail: fontodi@dada.it

To say that this is one of the most beautiful estates in Chianti Classico would be putting it mildly. The vineyards are kept like gardens and the cellar is modern but respectful of its surroundings. Moreover, Giovanni and Letizia Manetti are passionate winemakers, their oenologist, Franco Bernabei, is a great one, and Panzano has a fantastic terroir, capable of producing wines of inimitable elegance. At Fontodi, the Manettis made several fine wines this year but our favourite, the Three Glass winner, is their Syrah Case Via '98, which is one of the innovative, indeed almost experimental, wines that Giovanni Manetti has produced in recent years. With the '98 version, Fontodi's Syrah has come of age technically. It is a great wine, very varietal, with spicy and fruity scents and a powerfully concentrated structure. As we proceeded through the range, we found this was a good but not exceptional year for the Flaccianello della Pieve and the Chianti Classico Vigna del Sorbo Riserva. Both are '98s and somewhat closed on the nose, although intense on the palate. But then '98 was not one of the best sangiovese vintages in Panzano. Their successful standard-label Chianti '99 is very good: intensely fruity with the notes of violets typical of this wine. We were not altogether happy, however, with the Pinot Nero Case Via '99. Pinot nero is tricky to deal with, and this version did not seem to reflect the grape's varietal characteristics.

Wine	Rating	Score
● Syrah Case Via '98	♟♟♟	6
● Chianti Cl. Vigna del Sorbo Ris. '98	♟♟	6
● Flaccianello della Pieve '98	♟♟	6
● Chianti Cl. '99	♟♟	5
● Pinot Nero Case Via '99	♟	6
● Chianti Cl. Vigna del Sorbo Ris. '86	♟♟♟	6
● Chianti Cl. Vigna del Sorbo Ris. '90	♟♟♟	6
● Flaccianello della Pieve '90	♟♟♟	6
● Syrah Case Via '95	♟♟♟	6
● Flaccianello della Pieve '97	♟♟♟	6
● Chianti Cl. '98	♟♟	5

PANZANO (FI)

La Massa
Via Case Sparse, 9
50020 Panzano (FI)
Tel. 055852722
E-mail: fattoria.lamassa@tin.it

Seven Three Glasses in a row for the Chianti Classico Giorgio Primo. Few successes have been as long-running in the more than decade-long history of the Guide. But Giancarlo Motta, La Massa's owner, and his oenologist Carlo Ferrini don't leave anything to chance. Every aspect of the wine's production is followed with almost obsessive attention. The '99 Giorgio Primo is worthy of its predecessors. The colour, to begin with, is not dark and impenetrable like many (indeed, too many) fashionable reds. It has the brilliant and intense ruby colour of the best sangiovese-based wines. On the nose, the progression is clear and precise, fruit and wood are perfectly integrated and there are delightful balsamic undertones. After a refreshing attack, the palate is harmonious and the finish reveals notably fine-grained tannins. A wine of remarkable ripeness, it is already drinkable, with no hard edges demanding more time in the bottle. The Chianti Classico '99 is a wine of the same style: soft, well-balanced, with excellent basic material.

Wine	Rating	Score
● Chianti Cl. Giorgio Primo '99	♟♟♟	6
● Chianti Cl. '99	♟♟	4
● Chianti Cl. Giorgio Primo '93	♟♟♟	4
● Chianti Cl. Giorgio Primo '94	♟♟♟	5
● Chianti Cl. Giorgio Primo '95	♟♟♟	5
● Chianti Cl. Giorgio Primo '96	♟♟♟	5
● Chianti Cl. Giorgio Primo '97	♟♟♟	6
● Chianti Cl. Giorgio Primo '98	♟♟♟	6
● Chianti Cl. '94	♟♟	4
● Chianti Cl. '95	♟♟	4
● Chianti Cl. '96	♟♟	4
● Chianti Cl. '97	♟♟	4
● Chianti Cl. '98	♟♟	4

PANZANO (FI)

PODERE LE CINCIOLE
VIA CASE SPARSE, 83
50020 PANZANO (FI)
TEL. 055852636
E-MAIL: cinciole@chianticlassico.com

As we have been saying for years, Valeria Viganò and Luca Orsini faithfully interpret both sangiovese and their terroir. They do this without flummery or playing to the crowds. Sangiovese in Tuscany has become a highly marketable name, and lots of people have jumped on the bandwagon for just this reason. Such is not the case at Le Cinciole, where they fervently believe in their land and its vines. Perhaps they are somewhat romantic but they are clearly not out for quick profits. As for the wines, the Chianti Classico Petresco Riserva '98 did very well indeed. It hasn't got exotic richness on the nose or an overwhelming structure. Its approach is discreet, almost reserved, eschewing showiness on nose and palate. The bouquet, initially reticent, gradually reveals black and bottled cherries, violets and pepper. Similarly, the heady warmth of the wine is not immediately apparent on the palate, which grows in intensity, going from gentle to vibrant, with densely layered, invigorating tannins. This is a genuine, yet original, Chianti, made not for casual quaffers but for those who like to think about what they're drinking with some attention. The Chianti Classico '99 shows the same characteristics to a lesser degree. The bouquet is slightly too woody but the palate reveals balance and energy.

Wine	Rating	Score
Chianti Cl. Petresco Ris. '98	🍷🍷	5
Chianti Cl. '99	🍷	4
Chianti Cl. '93	🍷🍷	3
Chianti Cl. '94	🍷🍷	3
Chianti Cl. '95	🍷🍷	3
Chianti Cl. Valle del Pozzo Ris. '95	🍷🍷	4
Chianti Cl. Petresco Ris. '97	🍷🍷	4
Chianti Cl. Valle del Pozzo Ris. '94	🍷	4
Chianti Cl. '97	🍷	3
Chianti Cl. '98	🍷	3

PANZANO (FI)

FATTORIA LE FONTI
LE FONTI
50020 PANZANO (FI)
TEL. 055852194
E-MAIL: info@fatorialefonti.it

Work continues apace at this small winery in Panzano where the team made up of the owner Konrad Schmitt, agronomist Marco Pierucci and consulting oenologist Stefano Chioccioli continue to do a good job. Of course, we had hoped for more from the Chianti Classico Riserva, the only kind of Chianti made here, inasmuch as its recent versions have accustomed us to bottles of distinction. Yet the overall results are certainly satisfactory. We'll begin with a description of the Fontissimo '98, a blend of mostly sangiovese with the addition, which varies in amount each year, of some cabernet sauvignon. It has a lovely ruby colour with clear hints of purple and offers a vast array of aromas. These begin with notes of leather, open to coffee and chocolate, and then make way for ripe fruit. The entry on the palate is elegantly seductive and velvety, the structure full but soft and pleasantly creamy, becoming refreshing on the finish thanks to a nicely dosed vein of acidity underpinning the impressive length. The '98 Chianti Classico Riserva has a not particularly intense ruby colour. The nose is pleasant, showing notes of strawberries and blackcurrants, with elegant hints of spices and coffee. It is a bit disappointing in the mouth, where the texture is not very densely woven. The body is also a bit thin, the tannins intrude a little and the aftertaste is slightly bitter.

Wine	Rating	Score
Fontissimo '98	🍷🍷	5
Chianti Cl. Ris. '98	🍷	4
Fontissimo '91	🍷🍷	5
Chianti Cl. Ris. '95	🍷🍷	4
Fontissimo '95	🍷🍷	5
Chianti Cl. Ris. '96	🍷🍷	4
Fontissimo '96	🍷🍷	5
Chianti Cl. Ris. '97	🍷🍷	4
Fontissimo '97	🍷🍷	5
Chianti Cl. Ris. '90	🍷	3
Chianti Cl. Ris. '91	🍷	4
Chianti Cl. Ris. '93	🍷	4
Fontissimo '93	🍷	5
Chianti Cl. '96	🍷	4

PANZANO (FI)

MONTE BERNARDI
VIA SAN LEONINO, 68
50020 PANZANO (FI)
TEL. 055852400 - 055852305

PANZANO (FI)

CASTELLO DEI RAMPOLLA
VIA CASE SPARSE, 22
50020 PANZANO (FI)
TEL. 055852001
E-MAIL: castellodeirampolla.cast@tin.it

Monte Bernardi has produced a very good line-up of wines this year, although there were no out-and-out champions. The best – a distinction which is also reflected in its price – is their cabernet-merlot blend, Tzingana '99. In addition to a splendid colour, it displays an elegant and profound nose. Attack and mid palate are both convincing, and only the finish misfires a little because of dominant tannins. But some more time in the bottle will probably clear up this problem. Although simpler, the Chianti Classico '99 also did very well. It is pleasurably fruity, spicy, concentrated and consistent but too heavily marked by the presence of wood. The sangiovese-based Sa'etta '99, which is still very young and not fully developed, is already interesting. An intense ruby colour with lively highlights precedes aromas now dominated by red and black berry fruit, with a distinct but aristocratic note of oak. In the mouth, the wine shows plenty of extract underpinned by robust tannins. It broadens out more on the fairly long finish.

What strikes us most in a wine like Vigna d'Alceo is the highly individual style, maintained year after year. Of course, we have to remember that this is only the fourth year that it has been bottled so the track record is not a long one. Yet the cellar's desire to make a technically perfect wine is evident, as their focus shifts from the richness of their raw material, from drastically reduced yields, to a greater emphasis on style and elegance. In other words, the '99 Vigna d'Alceo has plenty of muscle but doesn't flex it, preferring a silky, velvety insouciance. The purity and richness of its fruit are, however, extraordinary, as is its miraculous balance. The éclat of this cabernet cru relegates Sammarco, the other splendid Di Napoli wine, from three parts cabernet and one sangiovese, to a secondary role. It is undoubtedly a great red but it has a more austere and less accessible character, especially on the nose, which has yet to open up completely. The palate, however, is broad and full, driving through vigorously to a long, complex finish which suggests that it will have a long life in the cellar. It will also certainly lose some of its austerity. Most of the estate's 40 hectares under vine are dedicated to the production of Chianti Classico. Although the '98 Riserva was not ready at the time of our tastings, the standard-label Chianti '99 does full justice to the excellent vintage.

● Chianti Cl. Paris '99	ŸŸ	5
● Sa'etta '99	ŸŸ	6
● Tzingana '99	ŸŸ	6
● Tzingana '97	ŸŸŸ	6
● Chianti Cl. '97	ŸŸ	4
● Chianti Cl. Ris. '97	ŸŸ	5
● Sa'etta '97	ŸŸ	6
● Chianti Cl. Paris '98	ŸŸ	5
● Sa'etta '98	ŸŸ	6
● Tzingana '98	ŸŸ	6

● La Vigna di Alceo '99	ŸŸŸ	6
● Sammarco '98	ŸŸ	6
● Chianti Cl. '99	ŸŸ	5
● Sammarco '85	ŸŸŸ	6
● Sammarco '86	ŸŸŸ	6
● Sammarco '94	ŸŸŸ	6
● La Vigna di Alceo '96	ŸŸŸ	6
● La Vigna di Alceo '97	ŸŸŸ	6
● La Vigna di Alceo '98	ŸŸŸ	6
● Sammarco '88	ŸŸ	6
● Sammarco '93	ŸŸ	6
● Sammarco '95	ŸŸ	6
● Sammarco '96	ŸŸ	6
● Chianti Cl. Ris. '97	ŸŸ	5
● Sammarco '97	ŸŸ	6

PANZANO (FI)

FATTORIA SANT'ANDREA
LOC. CASE SPARSE
50020 PANZANO (FI)
TEL. 0558549090

The wines of the Fattoria Sant'Andrea, often known as Panzanello, are becoming increasingly self-confident. They did brilliantly at our tastings this year but they still have a way to go. They show progress in the ripeness of the fruit, as demonstrated by reduced vegetal sensations, which were strongly present in past versions. The cellar makes shrewder use of wood, which is now very much better gauged. Complexity and an individual personality are still lacking but one shouldn't ask too much all at once of this youthful winery. The Manuzzio '99 performed well. A wine made only from sangiovese, it has a lively ruby colour and a nose that has still to develop, hardly a surprise in a young wine. It does reveal red berry fruit accompanied by an oaky tone. The palate develops pleasantly and offers good body but is still somewhat stiff in the finish. The '98 Riserva is very good. It may not be strikingly original but it has a full, succulent palate, with lip-smacking tannins. A well-executed wine, it is a bit vegetal on the nose well on top of its wood. The '99 Chianti is similar in style, if less exalted. The quite mature nose has a vanilla timbre; the palate is soft, nicely balanced and attractively structured.

● Chianti Cl. Panzanello Ris. '98	♟♟	4
● Manuzzio '99	♟♟	5
● Chianti Cl. Panzanello '99	♟	4
● Chianti Cl. '97	♟♟	3
● Chianti Cl. Panzanello '98	♟♟	3
● Chianti Cl. Ris. '95	♟	4
● Chianti Cl. Ris. '96	♟	4
● Chianti Cl. Panzanello Ris. '97	♟	4
● Il Mastio '97	♟	4

PANZANO (FI)

VECCHIE TERRE DI MONTEFILI
VIA SAN CRESCI, 45
50022 PANZANO (FI)
TEL. 055853739
E-MAIL:
ten.vecchie-terre-montefili@inwind.it

This historic estate in Panzano continues to be a guarantee of high quality, thanks in part to the winning two-man team of owner, Roccaldo Acuti, and oenologist Vittorio Fiore. Let's begin with their white, Vigna Regis '99, made mostly from chardonnay with some traminer and sauvignon blanc. Deep straw with attractive golden highlights, it offers a variety of aromas, with peaches and apples in the foreground enhanced by suggestions of vanilla. On the palate, the acidity stands out in the lean body and the finish is correct if not thrilling. The selections are better, starting with the Anfiteatro '98, a pure sangiovese with a not very intense ruby colour. The nose is quite lively and fruity, with ripe plums and cherries clearly noticeable. The palate, after an easy attack, acquires depth and well-sustained evenness, with prominent tannins and good staying power. The Bruno di Rocca '98, a blend of cabernet sauvignon and sangiovese, did well too. Intense ruby with purple highlights, it presents quite pronounced vegetal scents, mingling with confident notes of blackcurrants and bilberries. The entry on the palate is pleasantly soft but firm nonetheless; the structure is powerful and supple, and the long finish is very satisfying.

● Anfiteatro '98	♟♟	6
● Bruno di Rocca '98	♟♟	6
○ Vigna Regis '99	♟	4
● Chianti Cl. Ris. '85	♟♟♟	6
● Chianti Cl. Anfiteatro Ris. '88	♟♟♟	6
● Anfiteatro '94	♟♟♟	6
● Bruno di Rocca '93	♟♟	6
● Bruno di Rocca '94	♟♟	6
● Anfiteatro '95	♟♟	6
● Bruno di Rocca '95	♟♟	6
● Anfiteatro '96	♟♟	6
● Bruno di Rocca '96	♟♟	6
● Anfiteatro '97	♟♟	6
● Bruno di Rocca '97	♟♟	6
● Chianti Cl. '98	♟♟	4

PANZANO (FI)

VILLA CAFAGGIO
VIA SAN MARTINO IN CECIONE, 5
50020 PANZANO (FI)
TEL. 0558549094 - 055852949
E-MAIL: basilica.cafaggio@tiscalinet.it

Stefano Farkas seems unstoppable. The quality of his wines is no longer a surprise, nor is the ease with which he systematically picks up his Three Glasses. We "only" awarded him one this year, perhaps because we were too strict, but our overall judgement is certainly unchanged. All the wines we tasted were superbly rich with crisp, clean fruit, indeed superlatively so in the cases of the San Martino and the Cortaccio. They were also extraordinarily harmonious. The San Martino '98, mostly sangiovese, shows a breathtakingly massive structure. Only its aromas, which include spices and chocolate, are slightly lacking in finesse: indeed there are notes of super-ripeness. There are no awkward pauses as the San Martino enthrals the palate, reaching never before plumbed depths and expanding constantly. Alcohol, tannins and acidity merge together in a seamless velvety smoothness. The Cortaccio '98, 100 per cent cabernet, has a similar profile but it goes so far that it becomes less exciting. All the structural components cry out for the adjective "extraordinary", perhaps a little too often. The two Chiantis are very good, and rather more "human". The Chianti Classico '99 displays a range of perhaps not altogether characteristic aromas of wild dark berry fruit and toasty oak with grassy undertones. After an intense entry on the palate, it drives on apace, concluding with a convincing display of tasty tannins. The '98 Riserva shows beautifully clean fruit and a substantial if not very complex palate with well-balanced tannins and elegant progression.

Wine	Rating	Score
● San Martino '98	♛♛♛	6
● Cortaccio '98	♛♛	6
● Chianti Cl. Ris. '98	♛♛	5
● Chianti Cl. '99	♛♛	4
● Cortaccio '93	♛♛♛	6
● Cortaccio '97	♛♛♛	6
● San Martino '97	♛♛♛	5
● Cortaccio '90	♛♛	6
● San Martino '94	♛♛	5
● Chianti Cl. Solatio Basilica Ris. '95	♛♛	5
● Cortaccio '95	♛♛	6
● San Martino '95	♛♛	5
● San Martino '96	♛♛	5
● Chianti Cl. Ris. '97	♛♛	5
● Chianti Cl. '98	♛♛	4

PECCIOLI (PI)

TENUTA DI GHIZZANO
FRAZ. GHIZZANO
VIA DELLA CHIESA, 1
56030 PECCIOLI (PI)
TEL. 0587630096
E-MAIL: info@tenutadighizzano.com

The Tenuta di Ghizzano has given a significant performance this year. The estate has made great progress recently, starting from what was already a fairly strong position. They may not have won Three Glasses but producers are not to be judged only by awards and prizes. The fact is that Ghizzano's wines seemed in the best form ever: already a delight to drink and perfectly balanced. The Nambrot '99, mostly merlot with a touch of cabernet, has a very solid and concentrated body with the advantage (or is it a disadvantage?) of not flaunting it. Indeed, elegance is its most outstanding quality, perceptible in the refined equilibrium of its components and silky tannins. The finish, it goes without saying, is appropriately long. What could be missing? Perhaps their wines could be more driven and competitive; or do they want a little more complexity, which some bottle age will give them? The Veneroso '99, from sangiovese, cabernet and merlot, is the best version to have come out of the Ghizzano cellars. Is that putting it too strongly? Try it. You'll see that we're right. The bouquet is not immediately warm but reveals itself gradually in rich oriental spices, cocoa and blackcurrants, with a delicate vegetal nuance. The palate is deep and beautifully even. The mid palate is dense, and the stylish tannins are fully integrated. Lastly, the Chianti just keeps getting better every year. Its structure is way ahead of the pack for this wine type. But that's nothing new.

Wine	Rating	Score
● Nambrot '99	♛♛	6
● Veneroso '99	♛♛	5
● Chianti Colline Pisane '00	♛	3
● Veneroso '88	♛♛	5
● Veneroso '90	♛♛	5
● Veneroso '91	♛♛	4
● Veneroso '93	♛♛	4
● Veneroso '94	♛♛	4
● Veneroso '95	♛♛	5
● Nambrot '96	♛♛	6
● Veneroso '96	♛♛	5
● Nambrot '97	♛♛	6
● Veneroso '97	♛♛	5
● Nambrot '98	♛♛	6
● Veneroso '98	♛♛	5

PIOMBINO (LI)

SAN GIUSTO
LOC. SALIVOLI
57025 PIOMBINO (LI)
TEL. 056541198

We were very curious to see how Piero Bonti's wines would do after their debut in the Guide last year. Our curiosity was satisfied as the clinking of the Glasses awarded grew louder, with their Rosso degli Appiani showing all the qualities of a future star. These results crown years of hard work in obscurity, and have come at just the right moment. The Rosso degli Appiani '98, from two parts sangiovese and one of montepulciano d'Abruzzo, does not go in for half measures. Its impact is overwhelming, and the ripeness of its fruit and tannins is simply spectacular – no wonder that it came within a hair's breadth of winning Three Glasses. Without any claims to finesse, it offers a bouquet that opens to super-ripe tones of blackberry jam, but spicy and mineral notes soon follow. The palate is powerful and commanding. There simply isn't time to stop and consider subtleties. But then this is not a subtle wine; it is "matière" in the primal state. You either take it or leave it. Although it may sound like another super-endowed muscular wine, it is in its way very much a "vin de terroir". You only need to see the sunny exposure of Salivoli's vines, a stone's throw from the sea, to understand that this is the way these wines have to be. Piero Bonti's Rosso embodies its territory. The other wines are up to snuff: the red San Giusto '99 is densely structured and nicely oaked; the white San Giusto is fragrant, round and very reliable.

● Rosso degli Appiani '98	ΨΨ	5
● San Giusto '99	ΨΨ	4
○ Val di Cornia Bianco San Giusto '00	Ψ	3
● Rosso degli Appiani '97	ΨΨ	5
● San Giusto '98	ΨΨ	4
○ Bontesco Bianco '99	Ψ	2
● Bontesco Rosso '99	Ψ	2
○ Val di Cornia Bianco San Giusto '99	Ψ	3

PIOMBINO (LI)

PODERE SAN LUIGI
VIA DELL'ARSENALE, 16
57025 PIOMBINO (LI)
TEL. 0565220578 - 056530380

Anna and Elio Toni have made wine all their lives. They used to sell it unbottled, with the occasional flagon of red and a few bottles of Vermentino. This was how it was for years, and now that they are old enough to retire, they have been bitten by the bottling bug and are making ambitious plans for the future. Their idea was to make a good red wine, but in tiny quantities. Even if it wasn't a good bet financially, what a pleasure it would be! They used some grapes from their own vines, rented a few small vineyards nearby, and called in Alberto Antonini because without a good oenologist, you don't get very far, at least at the beginning. The first vintage, '95, produced excellent results. The '96 was good but not so strong and in '97, another excellent year, they decided to give the wine a name of its own, instead of just San Luigi Rosso. They chose Fidenzio, in memory of Anna's father who had run a legendary trattoria in Piombino. We have never included them in the Guide, apart from a mention in Other Wineries, simply because the quantity was so limited - there were practically no bottles available. There are only a few thousand bottles of the Fidenzio '98 but we can no longer keep quiet about it. It is a superlative wine that demands attention. A brilliant and very intense colour precedes the richness and ripeness of first-class fruit on the nose. In the mouth, the sweetness of the fruit, the extremely fine-grained tannins, and the mouth-filling, overwhelming density finish the job. We almost forgot to mention the vermentino, La Goccia, that Anna and Elio Toni continue to make very well: a pleasing and easy-to-drink wine.

● Fidenzio '98	ΨΨ	5
○ La Goccia '00	Ψ	2*

PITIGLIANO (GR)

TENUTA ROCCACCIA
LOC. ROCCACCIA
58017 PITIGLIANO (GR)
TEL. 0564617976

The Goraccis' estate has again shown it has what it takes to produce fine wine. With the careful support of oenologist Alberto Antonini, the family has turned out another very successful range of wines. This was particularly true of their reds, which seem more responsive to the character of the soil. We'll begin with the Roccaccia '00. It has a lovely intense ruby colour. Jammy aromas, ennobled by spicy notes of pepper and cloves, whet the appetite. The palate offers a powerful, solid structure with silky tannins offsetting the alcohol in an admirable balance; the finish is long and convincing. The excellent Fontenova '99, a blend of ciliegiolo and sangiovese, is a vibrantly intense ruby. It surprises and delights the nose with clear notes of blackberries and bilberries mingling with hints of various spices. The entry on the palate is straightforward and enjoyable, with good depth while nice hints of pepper emerge in the finish. The very decent Chardonnay '00 is straw yellow with golden highlights. The bouquet includes hints of resin, sweeter nuances of honey and vanilla, and fruity notes of apple and apricot. It convinces at once in the mouth, the refreshing well-balanced acidity balanced in a good, well-structured body. The Bianco Pitigliano '00 was the least successful of the Roccaccia wines: one-dimensional, slight of body, and a bit short.

POGGIBONSI (SI)

FATTORIA LE FONTI
LOC. SAN GIORGIO
53036 POGGIBONSI (SI)
TEL. 0577935690 - 035711067
E-MAIL: fattorialefonti@tin.it

This Poggibonsi estate, after a year in the wilderness, is back in the Guide with a good performance. There are 142 hectares, of which about 23 – soon to become 25 – are under vine, mostly planted to sangiovese. We'll start by looking at the Chianti Classico '99, with its surprisingly rich and varied aromas, ranging from vanilla to coffee, with lashings of fruit. The mouthfeel, after a good attack, is soft and shows fine-grained, tightly-woven tannins, but is also somewhat thin. The finish is correct if not imposing. Similar in style but perfectly executed, the Chianti Classico '98 Riserva has a ruby colour with purple highlights, and a nose that shows ripe fruit lifted by hints of chocolate and vanilla. In the mouth, it has good, sustained body, generous, well-defined tannins, nice depth of flavour, satisfying density and a long, pleasing finish. The Vito Arturo '98, a monovarietal sangiovese aged in barriques, also did very well. It's impenetrable in hue but does have sparkling ruby glints. These introduce a nose whose rich, toasty aromas mingle with coffee and chocolate, before the fruit finally emerges in hints of plums and cherries. The front palate is juicy and convincing, broad, silky tannins underpinning the creaminess of the body, and the finish signs off with a pleasing array of sensations.

● La Roccaccia '00	ΨΨ	3*
● Fontenova '99	ΨΨ	4
○ Chardonnay '00	Ψ	3
○ Bianco di Pitigliano '00		2
● La Roccaccia Fontenova '98	ΨΨ	4
● La Roccaccia '99	ΨΨ	3

● Chianti Cl. Ris. '98	ΨΨ	4
● Vito Arturo '98	ΨΨ	5
● Chianti Cl. '99	Ψ	3
● Chianti Cl. Ris. '96	ΨΨ	4
● Vito Arturo '95	ΨΨ	5
● Vito Arturo '96	ΨΨ	5
● Chianti Cl. '97	ΨΨ	3*
● Chianti Cl. Ris. '95	Ψ	4
● Chianti Cl. '96	Ψ	3

POGGIBONSI (SI)

MELINI
LOC. GAGGIANO
53036 POGGIBONSI (SI)
TEL. 0577989001
E-MAIL: giv@giv.it

The most interesting news from Melini this year is the release of the Bonorli '99, made from merlot and aged in barriques. Powerful and enticing, it seems almost Australian in style, with its softness and concentration. It is not incredibly complex but the opulent palate is very enjoyable. There is no doubt that it will be a success, easily earning Two Glasses and making us very curious about future versions. The Chianti Classico La Selvanella Riserva '98, on the other hand, has given a fine repeat performance. The vineyard has been replanted, and one already notes the greater concentration in its colour, and a greater softness of flavour. It is a more traditional wine than the others: it isn't aged in barriques but in large barrels of Allier oak, and has been sharper-tasting in other versions. It should, as usual, last a good long time. The Chianti Classico Massovecchio Riserva '98 is more modern and soft, but also more predictable. And the '98 doesn't have the concentration of the '97. The Vernaccia di San Gimignano Le Grillaie '00 seemed less convincing than the '99: it is lighter, and perhaps just a bit dilute. Correct and reasonably priced, as is its wont, the Chianti Classico I Sassi '99 is a soft, uncomplicated pleaser, though its aromas are a tad past their best.

● Chianti Cl. La Selvanella Ris. '98	▼▼	5
● Bonorli '99	▼▼	5
○ Vernaccia di S. Gimignano Le Grillaie '00	▼	4
● Chianti Cl. Massovecchio Ris. '98	▼	5
● Chianti Cl. I Sassi '99	▼	3*
● Chianti Cl. La Selvanella Ris. '86	▼▼▼	5
● Chianti Cl. La Selvanella Ris. '90	▼▼▼	5
● Chianti Cl. La Selvanella Ris. '93	▼▼	5
● Chianti Cl. La Selvanella Ris. '95	▼▼	5
● Chianti Cl. La Selvanella Ris. '96	▼▼	5
● Chianti Cl. La Selvanella Ris. '97	▼▼	5

POGGIO A CAIANO (PO)

PIAGGIA
VIA CEGOLI, 47
59016 POGGIO A CAIANO (PO)
TEL. 0558705401

We had little doubt that Mauro Vanucci's range of wines would again be at the top in Carmignano. The uncompromising quality choices that this winemaker from Prato continues to make in both vineyard and cellar mean that even poor climatic conditions can have only a limited effect. And poor years are rare here thanks to the zone's fortunate mesoclimate. His recipe is a simple one: very limited yields, the fullest ripening possible, and the use of all new wood, obviously of the highest quality. Then of course his chosen blend plays its part: he takes full advantage of the 30 per cent of cabernet sauvignon and merlot permitted by local DOC regulations. The exciting news here is not so much that he has again walked off with Three Glasses, this time for the '98 Riserva, but the first appearance of a second wine, Il Sasso, with which he has been experimenting for several years. And it is an excellent red with rich, juicy fruit, made from grapes, and in barriques, that do not meet the high standards he has set for his Carmignano. It is a very extraordinary "ordinary" wine made 60-30-10 from sangiovese, cabernet and merlot. The Piaggia Riserva '98 is another great wine from Mauro Vanucci's cellars. The fruit is first-rate and the wine has great concentration without flaunting it. The nose is deep, and still developing. Rich fruit dominates, but spicy and very faint vegetal tones can be perceived. The final flourish is a very long finish, which promises a very long life.

● Carmignano Ris. '98	▼▼▼	6
● Il Sasso '99	▼▼	5
● Carmignano Ris. '97	▼▼▼	5
● Carmignano Ris. '94	▼▼	4
● Carmignano Ris. '95	▼▼	4
● Carmignano Ris. '96	▼▼	4

PONTASSIEVE (FI)

★ Tenimenti Ruffino
Via Aretina, 42/44
50065 Pontassieve (FI)
tel. 05583605
e-mail: ruffino@ruffino.it

Luigi Folonari has rolled up his sleeves and Ruffino is rapidly changing. From 2002 on, there will be no more Rosatello, a fate that awaits many of their more commercial wines. Meanwhile all the vineyards, not just those in Chianti Classico, are being renewed. The vines are more densely planted, careful clone selection is the order of the day, and the wines that are starting to come out are already distinctly better. But, keeping in mind that we are here talking only about Ruffino properties in Chianti, let's get down to the business of tasting. Il Romitorio di Santedame '99, made from sangiovese and colorino, is a triumph, as usual. Very concentrated in colour, it unveils a complex bouquet of berries, graphite, and smoky nuances. Exceptional concentration on the palate is accompanied by closely woven tannins and considerable length. This is absolutely one of Tuscany's most remarkable wines. Less original but still very good, the Modus '99 is a blend of sangiovese and cabernet. It is clearly better than the somewhat experimental '98 which there is no point in describing, since it can no longer be found. The Chianti Classico Riserva Ducale Oro '97 is the best version in recent years. The surprise of the group, though, is Solatia '99, a barrique-aged chardonnay and one of the most interesting whites in all of Chianti. The Libaio '00, also a chardonnay, is fruity and simple but very charming. To learn more about the wine from their Montalcino estate, Greppone Mazzi, and their Montepulciano holding, Lodola Nuova, we encourage the reader to turn to their separate entries. Lodola Nuova is to be found among the Other Wineries, but only because of the vintages considered.

PONTASSIEVE (FI)

Fattoria Selvapiana
Loc. Selvapiana, 43
50065 Pontassieve (FI)
tel. 0558369848
e-mail: selvapiana@tin.it

Federico Giuntini's commitment to, and enthusiasm for, this historic estate in Chianti Rufina are undiminished. The great leap forward we hoped for last year has not yet taken place, and we still feel that the wines here could improve considerably. They will, with a little more determination. Let's turn to the wine we liked most, the Fornace Riserva '98. It has a ruby colour with purple highlights, and ripe scents of plums and cherries with some cloves and cinnamon mixed in. It follows through firmly on the front palate, then rich, silky tannins meld into a full, ripe body. The finish is long and irresistible. We did not taste the Riserva Bucerchiale '98, a wine which always likes to take its time, so we must put off our review until next year. The Chianti Rufina '99 is simply disappointing: pallid ruby, with a young and very vinous nose, it soldiers on into a rather graceless palate, with edgy tannins and a bitter finish. The Vin Santo '95 did better, though not so well as previous versions. A lustrous amber introduces a bouquet of hazelnuts and honey, enhanced by distinct, elegant notes of vanilla. After a velvety, seductive entry on the palate, it reveals a lean body lacking in density, but it is well-balanced and lingers enjoyably.

	Wine		Score
●	Romitorio di Santedame '99	♛♛♛	6
●	Modus '99	♛♛	6
○	Solatia '99	♛♛	5
●	Chianti Cl. Ris. Ducale Oro '97	♛♛	5
○	Libaio '00	♛	3
●	Chianti Cl. Ris. Ducale Oro '88	♛♛♛	5
●	Chianti Cl. Ris. Ducale Oro '90	♛♛♛	5
●	Romitorio di Santedame '96	♛♛♛	6
●	Romitorio di Santedame '97	♛♛♛	6
●	Romitorio di Santedame '98	♛♛♛	6
●	Romitorio di Santedame '93	♛♛	6
●	Romitorio di Santedame '94	♛♛	6
●	Chianti Cl. Ris. Ducale Oro '95	♛♛	5
●	Romitorio di Santedame '95	♛♛	6
●	Nero del Tondo '98	♛♛	6

	Wine		Score
○	Vin Santo della Rufina '95	♛♛	5
●	Chianti Rufina Fornace Ris. '98	♛♛	5
●	Chianti Rufina '99		3
●	Chianti Rufina Ris. '88	♛♛	4
●	Chianti Rufina Bucerchiale Ris. '90	♛♛	5
●	Chianti Rufina '91	♛♛	3
○	Vin Santo della Rufina '93	♛♛	5
●	Chianti Rufina Bucerchiale Ris. '94	♛♛	5
●	Chianti Rufina Fornace Ris. '94	♛♛	5
●	Chianti Rufina Bucerchiale Ris. '95	♛♛	5
●	Chianti Rufina Ris. '95	♛♛	4
●	Chianti Rufina Ris. '96	♛♛	4
●	Chianti Rufina Ris. '97	♛♛	4
●	Chianti Rufina Bucerchiale Ris. '96	♛	5
●	Chianti Rufina Fornace Ris. '96	♛	5

RADDA IN CHIANTI (SI)

CASTELLO D' ALBOLA
LOC. PIAN D'ALBOLA, 31
53017 RADDA IN CHIANTI (SI)
TEL. 0577738019
E-MAIL: info@albola.it

RADDA IN CHIANTI (SI)

LA BRANCAIA
LOC. POPPI, 42/B
53017 RADDA IN CHIANTI (SI)
TEL. 0577742007
E-MAIL: brancaia@brancaia.it

Castello d'Albola is one of the leading estates in the Zonin group. It sits on a hill overlooking Radda in Chianti, and for several years now has been offering excellent wines, the best of which is doubtless the Acciaiolo '98. A cabernet/sangiovese blend, it continues to be the wine we have come to know and love in previous versions. Perhaps the '98 has less structure than the '95 or the '97, but its intense and complex nose and concentrated, elegant flavour, with well-integrated tannins, make it a red to be reckoned with. The barrique-aged Chardonnay Le Fagge '99 is also very good, and as harmonious as it was in its best years. The wood is not excessive, and the nose ranges from notes of tropical fruits to hints of vanilla and green almonds. In the mouth, it is fat, rich and substantial. All the other wines presented were good. The pinot nero-based Le Marangole '99 and the Chianti Classico '99 both repeated the favourable impressions they made at previous tastings. The Chianti Classico Le Ellere '98 suffered from the less than perfect harvest on the highest slopes of this zone.

The '99 Brancaia, a blend of sangiovese and one third merlot with just a drop of cabernet sauvignon, is the best version in recent years. Enticing scents of black cherries, vanilla, blackberries and tobacco, together with smoky nuances, precede a full-bodied, soft palate with densely knit, smooth tannins and impressive length. This is a superb wine from Chianti, although the blend prevents it from being called Chianti Classico. Bruno and Brigitte Widmer, two Swiss citizens with a passion for Chianti and its wines, have been successful in a difficult undertaking. At present, they have 18 hectares under vine and produce 80,000 bottles. This is no longer merely the pastime of a couple of dabblers. The Widmers keep their eyes on everything, sometimes from a distance, such as when they leave commercial management in the competent hands of Francesco Mazzei, co-owner of Castello di Fonterutoli and a close family friend. Their daughter Barbara, with the help of the legendary Carlo Ferrini, is in charge of the technical side. In addition to the Brancaia, they make a Chianti Classico, and this year they presented the '99. The wine is less powerful and concentrated than its big brother but in some versions comes up at least to its shoulder. The '99 is one of those versions.

● Acciaiolo '98	♟♟	6
○ Le Fagge Chardonnay '99	♟♟	4
● Chianti Cl. Le Ellere '98	♟	5
● Chianti Cl. '99	♟	4
● Le Marangole '99	♟	5
● Acciaiolo '95	♟♟♟	6
● Acciaiolo '93	♟♟	6
○ Le Fagge Chardonnay '95	♟♟	4
● Acciaiolo '96	♟♟	6
○ Le Fagge Chardonnay '96	♟♟	4
● Le Marangole '96	♟♟	5
● Acciaiolo '97	♟♟	6
● Chianti Cl. Ris. '97	♟♟	5
● Le Marangole '97	♟♟	5
● Acciaiolo '90	♟	6

● Brancaia '99	♟♟♟	6
● Chianti Cl. '99	♟♟	5
● Brancaia '94	♟♟♟	6
● Brancaia '97	♟♟♟	6
● Brancaia '98	♟♟♟	6
● Brancaia '88	♟♟	6
● Brancaia '90	♟♟	6
● Brancaia '91	♟♟	6
● Brancaia '93	♟♟	5
● Brancaia '95	♟♟	6
● Chianti Cl. '95	♟♟	5
● Brancaia '96	♟♟	5
● Chianti Cl. '96	♟♟	5
● Chianti Cl. '97	♟♟	5
● Chianti Cl. '98	♟♟	5

RADDA IN CHIANTI (SI)

LIVERNANO
LOC. LIVERNANO, 67/A
53017 RADDA IN CHIANTI (SI)
TEL. 0577738353
E-MAIL: info@livernano.it

We must confess that we are very fond of the wines from Livernano. It's easy to explain why: they have a sinuous elegance, great harmony of form, and a subtle clarity in their aromas. It should also be mentioned, however, that both Puro Sangue and Livernano have notable structure, although they are in no way vulgar or overblown. To put it simply, these are bottles destined to last for many years but even if opened today, they will offer considerable pleasure. That's no small thing in these days of very concentrated, but not very drinkable, wines. Three Glasses were awarded this year too, but it was neck and neck up to the finish between Livernano and Puro Sangue, with the honours going again to Livernano, a blend of merlot, cabernet sauvignon, cabernet franc, carmènere and sangiovese. As is usually the case with Marco Montanari's wines, it impresses with its great harmony of bouquet and flavour. There are rich aromas of blackberries, plums, graphite and cedar, and in the mouth it is equally satisfying, with good structure, fine-grained tannins and a finish of excellent length. High marks, as we said, for the Sangiovese Puro Sangue '99, which offers the nose delicious aromas of sour cherries, pepper, violets and spices. In the mouth, it is full and dense with nice weight and elegance. The white, Anima '99, from chardonnay and sauvignon, seems somewhat uncertain of itself. It has a good full body but is already showing less welcome signs of evolution.

RADDA IN CHIANTI (SI)

CASTELLO DI MONTERINALDI
LOC. LUCARELLI
53017 RADDA IN CHIANTI (SI)
TEL. 0577733533
E-MAIL: info@monterinaldi.it

The wines from Castello di Monterinaldi did well at our tastings, and not for the first time. It would be better, however, if this winery were more consistent for it certainly has great potential. With its 105 hectares under vine at an altitude of some 300 metres, it has a size that very few winemakers in Tuscany can match. The Chianti Classico '99 is quite simple but very pleasant. The nose is very clean and shows berry fruit, raspberries, cherries, bilberries and brambles. The palate echoes the nose, and offers well-balanced touches of oak, supple tannins, and lively, intense fruit. The '97 Riserva is also good, and, unusually for a Chianti, reveals mint and raspberries on the nose. Pleasingly concentrated in the mouth, it has a nice balance of tannins and oak. The Sangiovese Pesanella '95 has a mineral nose, lively tannins and an admirably tight-knit texture. Unburdened by any great pretensions, the Gottizio '00 is very simple and fruity. We'll close with the two Vin Santos. The '75 opens with the classic aromas of sweet biscuits and almonds. In the mouth, it is not excessively sweet and has an austere style. It could, however, do with some more flesh. The Vin Santo '77 has a rich, intense nose of custard cream, zabaione and candied apricots. The palate is sweet, quite full and pleasurable, but without the length we expected.

●	Livernano '99	▼▼▼	6
●	Puro Sangue '99	▼▼	6
○	Anima '99	▼	6
●	Livernano '97	▼▼▼	6
●	Livernano '98	▼▼▼	6
●	Nardina '95	▼▼	5
●	Puro Sangue '95	▼▼	6
○	Anima '96	▼▼	5
●	Livernano '96	▼▼	6
●	Puro Sangue '97	▼▼	6
○	Anima '98	▼▼	5
●	Puro Sangue '98	▼▼	6
○	Anima '97	▼	5

○	Vin Santo del Chianti Cl. Ris. '75	▼▼	6
○	Vin Santo del Chianti Cl. Ris. '77	▼▼	6
●	Chianti Cl. '99	▼▼	4
●	Gottizio '00	▼	3
●	Pesanella '95	▼	4
●	Chianti Cl. Ris. '97	▼	4
●	Chianti Cl. Ris. '95	▼▼	4
●	Chianti Cl. '96	▼	3

RADDA IN CHIANTI (SI)

FATTORIA DI MONTEVERTINE
LOC. MONTE VERTINE
53017 RADDA IN CHIANTI (SI)
TEL. 0577738009

We would have preferred not to have to write these notes. Sergio Manetti is no longer with us, and in him we have lost an extraordinary figure who helped Italian wine to grow and become great. He was a real champion of sangiovese and of the Chianti Classico territory with which he was deeply in love. He leaves an enormous gap, which no one else can fill, but he has also left us the unforgettable memories of his wines, and the sensations and emotions they aroused. Describing this year's tastings inevitably seems of secondary importance. It is a task we must face, however, and it is with enormous regret that we cannot laud his Pergole Torte. The '98 is, unfortunately, well below its usual standard. It is already quite evolved and lacks vitality, and only its good balance in the mouth spares it from disaster. The good but not exciting Sodaccio '98 also shows signs of premature age and lack of clarity on the nose. But things go decidedly better on the palate, where sangiovese comes into its own, transmitting a sense of depth and elegance despite its only moderate body. We also liked the Montevertine Riserva '98, which starts to display a distinct personality in its bouquet of flowery notes, together with a hint of reduction in the suggestion of anchovies you so often find in a sangiovese from Chianti. The palate is neither exceptionally long nor concentrated but it is lively and rigorous, and shows just the right amount of sinew.

RADDA IN CHIANTI (SI)

POGGERINO
LOC. POGGERINO, 6
53017 RADDA IN CHIANTI (SI)
TEL. 0577738958
E-MAIL: info@poggerino.com

Poggerino presented only two wines at our tastings this year, a Chianti Classico and the Primamateria, both from the '99 vintage, and they confirm the overall style of production from this Radda in Chianti winery. A noticeable difference between the two wines, however, is readily apparent, much to the advantage of the Primamateria. This half sangiovese and half merlot blend is distinctly convincing. Our notes report an intense, vibrant ruby colour, a concentrated nose with fresh spices on a base of ripe black berry fruit and a well-judged touch of wood. The attack on the palate is full, solid and well-balanced. Mid palate reveals good extract with round, smooth tannins and the finish is decently long, although the acidity of the sangiovese has yet to integrate. All in all, it's a very good wine. We tasted it very young and it is destined to improve in balance though not, probably, in complexity. The Chianti Classico '99 is decent but less captivating. The nose, in particular, has not entirely attractive notes of super-ripeness. Things improve on the palate, which exhibits good balance, medium body and an agreeable, if slightly predictable, finish.

● Il Sodaccio '98	🍷🍷	6
● Montevertine Ris. '98	🍷🍷	6
● Le Pergole Torte '98	🍷	6
● Le Pergole Torte '83	🍷🍷🍷	6
● Le Pergole Torte '86	🍷🍷🍷	6
● Le Pergole Torte '88	🍷🍷🍷	6
● Le Pergole Torte '90	🍷🍷🍷	6
● Le Pergole Torte '92	🍷🍷🍷	6
● Le Pergole Torte '96	🍷🍷	6
● Il Sodaccio '97	🍷🍷	5
● Le Pergole Torte '97	🍷🍷	6
● Montevertine Ris. '97	🍷🍷	5

● Primamateria '99	🍷🍷	5
● Chianti Cl. '99	🍷	5
● Chianti Cl. Ris. '90	🍷🍷🍷	5
● Vigna di Bugialla '91	🍷🍷	5
● Vigna di Bugialla '93	🍷🍷	5
● Chianti Cl. '94	🍷🍷	3
● Chianti Cl. Bugialla Ris. '94	🍷🍷	5
● Chianti Cl. '95	🍷🍷	3
● Chianti Cl. Bugialla Ris. '95	🍷🍷	5
● Chianti Cl. '96	🍷🍷	3
● Chianti Cl. Bugialla Ris. '96	🍷🍷	5
● Chianti Cl. '97	🍷🍷	3
● Chianti Cl. Bugialla Ris. '97	🍷🍷	5
● Chianti Cl. '98	🍷🍷	3
● Primamateria '98	🍷🍷	5

RADDA IN CHIANTI (SI)

Fattoria di Terrabianca
Loc. San Fedele a Paterno
53017 Radda in Chianti (SI)
Tel. 0577738544
E-mail: info@terrabianca.com

Terrabianca may not have made the earth move at our tastings but the wines did reveal a distinguished style. The estate, in the heart of Chianti Classico near Siena, covers 124 hectares, and the vines enjoy southern and south-eastern exposures at an altitude of between 250 and 500 metres above sea level. In addition to the wines from the Chianti estate, Terrabianca vinifies grapes from Il Tesoro, the estate property near Massa Marittima, from which come the sangiovese La Fonte, and some of the cabernet sauvignon and merlot fruit that goes into the Ceppate. In fact the '98 Ceppate was our favourite from the cellar this year. It is an elegant red, intense in colour and in its aromas of bramble, blackcurrants and coffee, which are accompanied by some light vegetal hints. In the mouth, it is smooth, soft and well-balanced. The special selection Campaccio '97 did very well, too. The nose unveils notes of vanilla, liquorice, and violets with admirable finesse while the concentrated, well-calibrated flavour is supported by a moderate amount of oak. The interesting Piano del Cipresso '97 displays unusual scents of sour cherries and mint. On the palate, the attack is well sustained by the alcohol and the wine opens out appealingly, revealing medium concentration. The Campaccio '97 is lighter and well-made but does present some vegetal nuances. The Chianti Classico Croce Riserva '98 is fair but struck us as a bit weak and old. The La Fonte '99 and the Chianti Scassino '99 are both acceptable. The former has good extract but is a little imprecise on the nose while the latter is correct but rather lean.

● Campaccio Sel. Speciale '97	ŶŶ	6
● Piano del Cipresso '97	ŶŶ	5
● Ceppate '98	ŶŶ	6
● Campaccio '97	Ŷ	5
● Chianti Cl. Vigna della Croce Ris. '98	Ŷ	5
● Tenuta Il Tesoro La Fonte '99	Ŷ	4
● Chianti Cl. '99		4
● Campaccio '93	ŶŶ	5
● Campaccio Sel. Speciale '93	ŶŶ	6
● Campaccio '94	ŶŶ	6
● Campaccio '95	ŶŶ	5
● Campaccio Sel. Speciale '95	ŶŶ	6
● Campaccio Sel. Speciale '96	ŶŶ	5
● Ceppate '97	ŶŶ	6

RADDA IN CHIANTI (SI)

Vignavecchia
Sdrucciolo di Piazza, 7
53017 Radda in Chianti (SI)
Tel. 0577738090 - 0577738326
E-mail: vignavecchia@vignavecchia.com

The Beccari siblings, Franco and Orsola, should be very pleased with the way things are going at Vignavecchia. The whole winemaking process has been completely overhauled and is now much more in keeping with this historic estate's potential. The wines generally did very well indeed, showing excellent structure and signs of skilful execution. What is still missing is strong personality, and also a hint of terroir. In all the red wines we tasted, we noted a constant presence of vegetal tones, at times quite strong. Even in the Canvalle '98, from sangiovese and cabernet, the tones come through, although they are more than offset by the wine's very positive characteristics. The fruit is crisp and clean, the wood well-dosed. Remarkable concentration is sustained on the palate and the long finish is laced with very fine-grained tannins. The chardonnay-based Titanum '00 is surprising. Scents of tropical fruits and hazelnuts lead in to a full, substantial and even palate. This is a very good white, which is something of a rarity in Tuscany. All it needs is a bit more force in the finish. The Raddese '98 and the Chianti Classico Riserva '98 had our tasters repeat the comments made above. Although both are well put together, with nice balance and concentration, they are let down by grassy and green pepper aromas. We hope that this can be laid at the door of a vintage, the '98, which made it difficult for grapes to ripen in Chianti Classico.

● Canvalle '98	ŶŶ	5
○ Titanum '00	ŶŶ	4
● Chianti Cl. Ris. '98	Ŷ	4
● Raddese '98	Ŷ	5
● Raddese '90	ŶŶ	5
● Canvalle '93	ŶŶ	5
● Canvalle '96	ŶŶ	5
● Chianti Cl. Ris. '96	ŶŶ	4
● Chianti Cl. Ris. '97	ŶŶ	4
○ Titanum '99	ŶŶ	4
● Canvalle '97	Ŷ	5
● Raddese '97	Ŷ	5

RADDA IN CHIANTI (SI)

CASTELLO DI VOLPAIA
LOC. VOLPAIA
P.ZZA DELLA CISTERNA, 1
53017 RADDA IN CHIANTI (SI)
TEL. 0577738066
E-MAIL: info@volpaia.com

There are 45 hectares of vines in an enchanting location that dominates the entire Radda in Chianti zone. Above the vineyards sits the restored mediaeval village with the estate olive press. The name of this little corner of paradise is Castello di Volpaia, and here Giovannella Stianti and her husband Carlo Mascheroni have put together one of the most beautiful cellars in Chianti Classico. They are assisted by Stefano Borsa, their estate manager and agronomist, and Maurizio Castelli, their long-time oenologist. The wines, as we have noted in the past, reflect the location and, particularly, the altitude of the vineyards. Fine and elegant, rather than powerful – delicacy is the watchword – the fruit does best when the vines have not had to suffer drought. This year, the standard-label Chianti Classico '99 seemed especially good to us and, although the simplest of all the estate wines, made it to the finals, where it proved one of the best of its category. It's a cut above the Chianti Classico Riserva '98, which is not as good as usual. In fact, if we allow for the difference in categories, it is better than the Balifico '98, the Supertuscan from sangiovese with a bit of cabernet sauvignon, which is interesting, but not up to standard set by the excellent '97. Lastly, the '93 Vin Santo is a real speciality of the house but, sadly, very little is made.

	Wine		Score
●	Chianti Cl. '99	▼▼	4*
○	Vin Santo del Chianti Cl. '93	▼▼	6
●	Balifico '98	▼▼	6
●	Chianti Cl. Ris. '98	▼	5
●	Balifico '88	♀♀	6
●	Balifico '91	♀♀	6
●	Chianti Cl. Ris. '95	♀♀	5
●	Coltassala '95	♀♀	6
●	Balifico '97	♀♀	6
●	Chianti Cl. '97	♀♀	4
●	Chianti Cl. Ris. '97	♀♀	5
●	Coltassala '97	♀♀	6
●	Balifico '90	♀	6
●	Balifico '94	♀	6
●	Balifico '95	♀	6

RAPOLANO TERME (SI)

CASTELLO DI MODANELLA
LOC. SERRE
53040 RAPOLANO TERME (SI)
TEL. 0577704604

The wines of Castello di Modanella did not do brilliantly at our tastings this time. Only the Cabernet Le Voliere '98 made a really good showing whereas the others hardly rose above average. Not all vintages are excellent and in the life of a winery, there can be ups and downs, so we hope for a quick upturn beginning next year. There is plenty of potential. Meanwhile, Le Voliere made a good impression. The bouquet includes vegetal notes as well as hints of wild berries and some light toastiness from the wood. In the mouth, it reveals concentration, good tannic density, and a moderately long finish that earned it Two Glasses. We were not altogether charmed by the merlot-based Poggio Mondino '98. It is correct and well-balanced but has neither an imposing structure nor a long finish. It's well-made but the raw material could have been better. The Campo d'Aia '98, a sangiovese, did a little better. Although fairly forward, it reveals a meaty mid palate. The finish is still rather austere and dominated by rigid tannins. We shall have to try the Poggio Ajole '99 again, as the sample we tasted was untypical of the product, or at least we hope so.

	Wine		Score
●	Le Voliere Cabernet Sauvignon '98	▼▼	5
●	Campo d'Aia '98	▼	4
●	Poggio Mondino '98	▼	4
●	Campo d'Aia '95	♀♀	3
●	Le Voliere Cabernet Sauvignon '95	♀♀	4
●	Le Voliere Cabernet Sauvignon '96	♀♀	4
●	Campo d'Aia '97	♀♀	4
●	Le Voliere Cabernet Sauvignon '97	♀♀	4
●	Poggio Mondino '97	♀♀	4

RIPARBELLA (PI)

LA REGOLA
VIA A. GRAMSCI, 1
56046 RIPARBELLA (PI)
TEL. 0586699216 - 3485858530
E-MAIL: dr.nuti@multinet.it

Something new has been needed in the Montescudaio zone for some time. The energy perceptible in nearby Bolgheri was absent. The usual good wineries did their usual good job. But Luca Nuti, owner of La Regola, has done something different. This is the second year his wines have been released and he has already made a name for himself on the Tuscan coast, showing that he knows what he wants and is aiming high. First of all, he engaged the excellent Piedmontese oenologist, Giovanni Bailo. Luca Nuti himself tends the eight hectares of vineyards. In the cellar, he uses new barriques, selected with care and absolute respect for quality, in addition to his temperature-controlled fermentation vats. The results speak for themselves. The Montescudaio La Regola '99 is a great success. Right from the colour, an intense limpid ruby, it promises well and the nose more than delivers. Distinct scents of red and black berry fruit, hints of chocolate, and a very well-behaved undertone of excellent oak all come through. The palate is broad, velvety, dense-textured and crowned by a long finish that delightfully echoes the nose. The Vallino '99, which nearly got Two Glasses, has a sound bouquet with notes of bramble and vanilla, shaded with faint vegetal nuances. In the mouth, it is well-balanced and substantial, showing well-distributed tannins but the finish is just a tad acidic. The Steccaia '00, a Montescudaio Bianco, is more than decent, with its fragrant aromas of citrus fruits and lean but energetic flavour. The Rosso Ligustro '00 is correct and pleasant.

ROCCALBEGNA (GR)

VILLA PATRIZIA
LOC. CANA
58050 ROCCALBEGNA (GR)
TEL. 0564982028

Making good wines is both a question of pride and a financial necessity for any serious producer. The winemaker who goes even further and tries to encourage wines to reflect their territory is admirable in these times of globalization. And this is the trump card of Villa Patrizia. This devotion to terroir is precisely what you perceive when tasting the wines from Roccalbegna. There are no bombshells but personality is not in short supply. Let's begin with the Orto di Boccio '98, made from sangiovese with one quarter cabernet and merlot. The nose shows pleasing and original notes of violets, pepper and berry fruit. The palate is not imposing but there is appropriate weight, a soft tastiness and a finish with good tannic grip. Similar aromatic characteristics are again on display in the Morellino Riserva '98. The terroir here, it would seem, confers its own stamp no matter what grapes are used. It is not a hot Morellino like those from nearer the seashore but does have a freshness and elegance of its own, medium body and a finish that mirrors the nose. In contrast, the Sciamareti '00, a monovarietal malvasia, has both warmth and alcoholic power. It's a characterful, if not particularly aromatic, wine.

● Montescudaio Rosso La Regola '99	🍷🍷	5
○ Montescudaio Bianco Steccaia '00	🍷	3
● Montescudaio Rosso Ligustro '00	🍷	3
● Montescudaio Rosso Vallino '99	🍷	4

● Morellino di Scansano Ris. '98	🍷🍷	4
● Orto di Boccio '98	🍷🍷	5
○ Sciamareti '00	🍷	3
○ Alteta '96	🍷🍷	4
○ Alteta '97	🍷🍷	4
● Morellino di Scansano Ris. '97	🍷🍷	4
● Orto di Boccio '97	🍷🍷	5
● Orto di Boccio '94	🍷	4
● Orto di Boccio '95	🍷	4
● Morellino di Scansano '96	🍷	2
● Orto di Boccio '96	🍷	4
● Morellino di Scansano '97	🍷	3
● Albatraia '98	🍷	1
● Morellino di Scansano '98	🍷	2
● Morellino di Scansano '99	🍷	2
○ Sciamareti '99	🍷	2

ROCCASTRADA (GR)

MELETA
FRAZ. ROCCATEDERIGHI
LOC. MELETA
58028 ROCCASTRADA (GR)
TEL. 0564567155

We were generally content with Meleta's wines this year, although there was nothing earth-shaking. Great wines are not easily made, of course, but we are sure that this winery in Roccatederighi has what it takes. In the light of our tastings, we feel that they need to concentrate on rethinking vineyard management. From a technical point of view, all the wines are well-made but there seems to have been a dearth of really ripe grapes. Of the many wines, the merlot-based Massaio '98 particularly intrigued the panel. The intense, clean bouquet boasts out of the ordinary mineral, fruity and faintly vegetal tones. In the mouth, the attack is well-balanced but the wine loses density at mid palate, picking up again in the finish, where it displays enticing notes of black pepper. The Vin Santo '96 is good, though there are rather tiresome oak-derived vanilla notes. Still, it is even, sweet and undeniably attractive. The Rosso della Rocca '98, a blend of sangiovese, cabernet and merlot, stays in the One Glass band. Pleasant enough and well-balanced, it lacks bite and complexity. Although somewhat evolved and flat, the sangiovese-based Pietrello d'Oro '98 is at least acceptable. The Pietrello '00 is thin, acidulous and little more than well-made. The rosé Rocchigiano '00, on the other hand, is supple and fragrant, with fresh scents of raspberries.

RUFINA (FI)

FATTORIA DI BASCIANO
V.LE DUCA DELLA VITTORIA, 161
50068 RUFINA (FI)
TEL. 0558397034
E-MAIL: masirenzo@virgilio.it

The Masi family winery performed well this year. Although they do not make wines that are typical of their area, what they do produce is of excellent quality. Let's begin with the purple-hued Chianti Rufina '99. Sweet scents of vanilla almost cover the not very assertive fruit on the nose. In the mouth, it shows good weight, dense structure, well-tamed tannins and sufficient length. The bouquet of the very good '98 Riserva is a pleasant mixture of berry fruit and spices. The palate, after a decisive attack, reveals a seamless, mouthfilling and velvety progression through to a broad, relaxed finish. From equal amounts of cabernet and sangiovese, I Pini '99 presents ripe aromas of plum and jam with notable finesse. The flavour is soft, smooth and caressing, and the tannins are well integrated but character is wanting. The Corto '99, made from sangiovese with a drop of cabernet, is less good than usual. The somewhat forward nose includes notes of leather, although the fruit is abundant and varied. There is excellent balance on the medium-bodied palate, and the finish is pleasing but a bit simple. The Erta e China '99 is a surprise, and also great value for money. Purple in the glass, its aromas of wild berries are rounded off by nuances of coffee and a distinct vegetal after-aroma. The development on the palate is well co-ordinated, even and balanced, and the finish is fairly long. The fair Vin Santo '96 offers sweet but not very pronounced aromas and a balanced body without much personality.

○	Vin Santo '96	▮▮	5	●	Chianti Rufina Ris. '98	▮▮	3*
●	Massaio '98	▮▮	6	●	Erta e China '99	▮▮	3*
◉	Rocchigiano '00	▮	2*	●	I Pini '99	▮▮	4
●	Rosso della Rocca '98	▮	5	●	Il Corto '99	▮▮	4
●	Pietrello '00		3	○	Vin Santo Rufina '96	▮	4
●	Rosso della Rocca '93	▯▯	5	●	Chianti Rufina '99	▮	2*
●	Merlot '94	▯▯	6	●	Chianti Rufina Ris. '95	▯▯	2
●	Rosso della Rocca '94	▯▯	5	●	Chianti Rufina Ris. '96	▯▯	2
○	Vin Santo '94	▯▯	5	●	I Pini '96	▯▯	3
●	Rosso della Rocca '95	▯▯	5	●	Il Corto '96	▯▯	3
○	Vin Santo '95	▯▯	5	●	I Pini '97	▯▯	3
○	Bianco della Rocca '98	▯▯	5	●	Il Corto '97	▯▯	3
●	Rosso della Rocca '96	▯	5	●	Chianti Rufina '98	▯▯	3
●	Rosso della Rocca '97	▯	5	●	I Pini '98	▯▯	3
●	Pietrello d'Oro '98	▯	4	●	Il Corto '98	▯▯	3

SAN CASCIANO DEI BAGNI (SI)

Giacomo Mori
Fraz. Palazzone
P.zza Sandro Pertini, 8
53040 San Casciano dei Bagni (SI)
tel. 0578227005
e-mail: giacomo.mori@libero.it

Giacomo Mori's two wines were in excellent form at our tastings this year, as they demonstrated by the ease with which they scooped up their respective awards. And if those awards were not in the top category, the performance was an improvement on last year and there is definitely more style on show this time. There has been more extensive use of new oak, and grapes other than sangiovese are finding a place in the blends. The Chianti Castelrotto '99 is a very intense dark ruby, which is itself sufficient to justify these impressions. The nose then confirms them, showing deep layers of black berry fruit mingling with clear nuances of new oak. The attack on the palate is powerful, broad and very soft, the smooth tannins are perfectly integrated and the very superior oak plays a significant, though complementary, role. The finish is good but not very long. Following in the footsteps of its big brother, the Chianti '00 displays a notably concentrated colour, scents of fruit and oak, and softness, roundness and substance on the palate. However, the helpings of oak have been overgenerous, which leads to some bitterness. The wines are good overall but they tend to lack personality. In short, they are a little predictable and not very representative of the terroir.

● Chianti Castelrotto '99	▼▼	4
● Chianti '00	▼	3
● Chianti Castelrotto '98	▽▽	4
● Chianti '99	▽	3

SAN CASCIANO IN VAL DI PESA (FI)

Castelli del Grevepesa
Loc. Mercatale Val di Pesa
Via Grevigiana, 34
50024 San Casciano in Val di Pesa (FI)
tel. 055821911
e-mail: castelgreve@chianticlassico.co

Never have the wines of Castelli del Grevepesa been as convincing as they were this year. This large co-operative in Mercatale Val di Pesa really surprised us with a whole series of splendid bottles. The Coltifredi '97, a monovarietal sangiovese with a modern style and faultless execution, is a very different matter from the '96 version, which was a little under par. In fact, it made it to the finals. An intense bouquet with notes of black cherries and light smoky nuances leads to a confident, concentrated palate with a touch of acidity that adds to its character and sinew. The finish, if not very long, is very good. The Guado al Luco '97, a blend of cabernet and sangiovese, is a bit less complex and the balsamic note that it acquires from the French grape is quite noticeable. Yet the structure is excellent and the tannins are smooth. The Chianti Classico Sant'Angelo '97, another Two Glass winner, is forceful and full-bodied, thanks to the exceptionally good local vintage. Even the Chianti Classico Castelgreve Riserva '98 is very convincing, so much so that it hardly seems like a '98 at all. The Chianti Classico Clemente VII '99 and the standard-label Chianti Classico Grevepesa '99 are agreeable but simpler and more dilute. This is a range of wines worthy of one of the best cellars in the area. With wines this good, congratulations are in order.

● Coltifredi '97	▼▼	5
● Chianti Cl. S. Angelo Vico l'Abate '97	▼▼	5
● Guado al Luco '97	▼▼	5
● Chianti Cl. Castelgreve Ris. '98	▼▼	4*
● Chianti Cl. Castelgreve '99	▼	3
● Chianti Cl. Clemente VII '99	▼	4
● Guado al Luco '93	▽▽	5
● Chianti Cl. Castelgreve Ris. '95	▽▽	4
● Coltifredi '95	▽▽	5
● Guado al Luco '95	▽▽	5
● Guado al Luco '96	▽▽	5
● Chianti Cl. Castelgreve Ris. '97	▽▽	4
● Chianti Cl. Castelgreve Ris. '96	▽	4
● Coltifredi '96	▽	5
● Chianti Cl. Castelgreve '98	▽	3

SAN CASCIANO IN VAL DI PESA (FI)

FATTORIA CORZANO E PATERNO
LOC. SAN PANCRAZIO IN VAL DI PESA
VIA PATERNO, 8
50024 SAN CASCIANO IN VAL DI PESA (FI)
TEL. 0558249114 - 0558248179
E-MAIL: corzpaterno@falcc.it

Even if the estate didn't collect another Three Glasses, Fattoria di Corzano e Paterno gave an excellent performance at our tastings. For some years now, their wines have shown character, thanks to careful attention to the ripeness of the grapes, good judgement in the extraction of phenolics, and a more skilful, discreet use of wood. From this very high level to that of supreme excellence there are many obstacles, such as weather and the myriad imponderables that together make all the difference. The Corzano '98, a blend of sangiovese and cabernet, is still the leading wine and has its own distinct character. The nose, although still closed, shows intriguingly characteristic scents of minerals. The development on the palate is quite confident, although it lacks the plumpness of fruit to be found in the best years, and the finish brings out both the tannins and the oak. The Chianti I Tre Borri '98 makes an interesting debut. Here, too, character and density abound, and there is plenty of elegance, but the oak, at least for the time being, is very evident. The Vin Santo '94 is truly excellent. The intense, complex bouquet includes hints of spices, marrons glacés and fig jam, as well as the trace of volatility that seems inevitable in this category of wine. In the mouth, it has elegance, concentration and depth. The very pleasant if a little monotonous chardonnay-based Aglaia '00 has clean aromas of pears and vanilla. Lastly, the Chianti Terre di Corzano '99 is more than just acceptable.

SAN CASCIANO IN VAL DI PESA (FI)

IL MANDORLO
VIA CERTALDESE, 2/B
50024 SAN CASCIANO IN VAL DI PESA (FI)
TEL. 0558228211

The Conticelli brothers' estate, situated not far from the centre of San Casciano in Val di Pesa, made its presence felt at our tastings this year. All three of the wines did well, with the cabernet and sangiovese-based Terrato '98 standing out. It's an elegant wine, very well-balanced on the palate, with close-knit, flavourful tannins, but just a little vegetal on the nose and on the finish. Still, it is very interesting and in fact made it as far as the Three Glass finals. A single wine, however, does not by itself provide a clear, complete picture of how a winery is doing so we welcome the corroboration offered by the Chianti Classico '99, a simpler wine, but very well made. The clean fragrance has a distinctive mineral nuance. The lively, tasty fruit and overall harmony of the palate are admirable. The Riserva Il Rotone '98 missed a second Glass because of a not entirely successful nose. The characterful palate reveals fine-grained tannins that get just a bit out of hand on the finish. Il Mandorlo now needs to show perseverance and we are sure that it will, given the aspirations of the owners. Their new cellar, which is nearly ready, will be a great help.

○ Vin Santo '94	🍷🍷	6
● Chianti I Tre Borri '98	🍷🍷	5
● Il Corzano '98	🍷🍷	6
○ Aglaia '00	🍷	4
● Chianti Terre di Corzano '99	🍷	4
● Il Corzano '97	🍷🍷🍷	5
● Il Corzano '88	🍷🍷	5
● Chianti Terre di Corzano Ris. '90	🍷🍷	4
○ Vin Santo '90	🍷🍷	5
○ Vin Santo '93	🍷🍷	5
● Chianti Terre di Corzano Ris. '95	🍷🍷	4
● Il Corzano '95	🍷🍷	5
● Il Corzano '96	🍷🍷	5
● Chianti Terre di Corzano '97	🍷🍷	3
● Chianti Terre di Corzano Ris. '97	🍷🍷	4

● Terrato '98	🍷🍷	5
● Chianti Cl. '99	🍷🍷	4
● Chianti Cl. Ris. '98	🍷	4

SAN CASCIANO IN VAL DI PESA (FI)

ISPOLI
LOC. MERCATALE VAL DI PESA
VIA SANTA LUCIA, 2
50024 SAN CASCIANO IN VAL DI PESA (FI)
TEL. 055821613
E-MAIL: ispoli@tin.it

For some years now, Ispoli hasn't put a foot wrong and the wines released have been admirable. The estate has very few hectares under vine and these are being replanted in line with the dictates of organic farming. Only two wines were presented at our tastings. We'll begin with the Chianti Classico '99. A vivid and wonderfully clear ruby introduces a vast array of aromas ranging from fresh blackcurrant and cherry fruit to sweet spices like vanilla and, faintly, cinnamon. The palate, after a good entry, shows a richly meaty structure and tannins perfectly blended with alcohol. Possessed of good length and depth, it has a very satisfying finish. We are glad to say that their Ispolaia '98, a blend of cabernet and sangiovese, has had another good year. Its lively ruby colour is tinged with purple, and the broad, varied aromas include forest fruits like wild strawberries, raspberries and bilberries, and aromatic spices such as cloves and pepper, all sweetened by an intense note of vanilla. Though not over-powering, the attack in the mouth is full-bodied and confident, and mid palate is round and soft, with smooth, densely knit tannins. There is just the right amount of acidity to perk things up. This is an eminently drinkable wine, with a tasty, well-balanced finish.

SAN CASCIANO IN VAL DI PESA (FI)

LA SALA
LOC. PONTEROTTO
VIA SORRIPA, 34
50024 SAN CASCIANO IN VAL DI PESA (FI)
TEL. 055828111
E-MAIL: info@lasala.it

La Sala is a female-oriented estate not just because of the name that it bears but also because its owner, Laura Baronti, avails herself of the technical services of the able, reserved Gabriella Tani. Three wines are produced from the 15 hectares under vine and all were presented at our tastings. We have not reviewed the '99 Chianti because its obvious defects are probably due to a provisional bottling. The Riserva '98, on the other hand, is very successful. It has a good, full structure with tannins very much present, and indeed a touch excessive on the finish. The aromas are well-defined and concentrated, with notes of berry fruit melding into noticeable oak-derived spicy and toasty tones. This year, however, Signora Baronti prepared a surprise for us. Her Supertuscan, Campo all'Albero '98, a blend of sangiovese and cabernet sauvignon, scored very high indeed at our tastings. The bouquet has intensity and depth, with aromas of chocolate and coffee that come largely from the excellent wood over a base of black berry fruit with vegetal nuances. In the mouth, it is concentrated without being showy or aggressive. The orderly progression is accompanied by respectful oak and by docile tannins. The wine would not be harmed by a bit more complexity and a touch less wood but is nonetheless excellent and fully deserved its place in our finals.

Wine	Rating	Score
● Ispolaia Rosso '98	♟♟	4
● Chianti Cl. '99	♟♟	4
● Ispolaia Rosso '96	♟♟	4
● Chianti Cl. '97	♟♟	3
● Chianti Cl. Ris. '97	♟♟	4
● Chianti Cl. '98	♟♟	3
○ Chardonnay '99	♟	3

Wine	Rating	Score
● Campo all'Albero '98	♟♟	5
● Chianti Cl. Ris. '98	♟♟	4
● Campo all'Albero '94	♟♟	4
● Campo all'Albero '95	♟♟	4
● Campo all'Albero '96	♟♟	5
● Chianti Cl. '96	♟♟	3
● Chianti Cl. Ris. '96	♟♟	4
● Campo all'Albero '97	♟♟	5
● Chianti Cl. Ris. '97	♟♟	4
● Chianti Cl. '93	♟	3
● Chianti Cl. Ris. '93	♟	4
● Chianti Cl. '95	♟	3
● Chianti Cl. Ris. '95	♟	4
● Chianti Cl. '97	♟	3
● Chianti Cl. '98	♟	3

SAN CASCIANO IN VAL DI PESA (FI)

Fattoria Le Corti - Corsini
Loc. Le Corti
Via San Piero di Sotto, 1
50024 San Casciano in Val di Pesa (FI)
Tel. 055820123
E-mail: info@principecorsini.com

Could the Don Tommaso keep coming close to Three Glasses without ever getting them? The answer is easy to guess but the distinction awarded to Duccio Corsini's wine is not so much a recognition of consistent quality as of the leap forward we were predicting last year. With the help of the kinder '99 vintage, it has at last taken place. The Don Tommaso is an excellent Chianti Classico, unabashedly modern in its elegant use of oak, and the rich constant presence of its fruit, but with an elegance found in excellent wines whatever their grape or origins. The colour is extremely intense and fairly youthful while the nose offers plenty of ripe fruit, along with spicy and toasty notes of oak. The tannins, solid and perfectly integrated, seem to suggest the remarkable ageing potential. The Chianti Classico '99 did very well, too, despite some haziness on the nose from wood that was probably not new. The full, well-balanced palate is nicely underpinned by tannins, and the finish lingers. The Riserva Cortevecchia '98 was less brilliant, though. The colour shows signs of evolution, the nose is troubled by reduction, and the palate reveals good extractive weight but not much harmony. It should be noted that '98 was a poor year in Chianti Classico. You can't win them all.

● Chianti Cl. Don Tommaso '99	🍷🍷🍷	5
● Chianti Cl. '99	🍷🍷	4
● Chianti Cl. Cortevecchia Ris. '98	🍷	4
● Chianti Classico '98	🍷🍷	3*
● Chianti Cl. Cortevecchia Ris. '95	🍷🍷	5
● Chianti Cl. Cortevecchia Ris. '97	🍷🍷	5
● Chianti Classico Don Tommaso '94	🍷🍷	5
● Chianti Classico Don Tommaso '95	🍷🍷	5
● Chianti Classico Don Tommaso '96	🍷🍷	5
● Chianti Classico Don Tommaso '97	🍷🍷	5
● Chianti Classico Don Tommaso '98	🍷🍷	5

SAN CASCIANO IN VAL DI PESA (FI)

Machiavelli
Loc. Sant'Andrea in Percussina
50024 San Casciano in Val di Pesa (FI)
Tel. 055828471
E-mail: giv@giv.it

As we have already mentioned a number of times, '98 was not a stellar vintage in Chianti Classico. As the oenologists hereabouts say, it was a "leopard-spot" harvest, meaning that in some subzones it went quite well and in others less so. The "spot" at Machiavelli was neither all dark nor all light. The Chianti Classico Vigna di Fontalle Riserva '98 certainly came out well. Aromas and flavour are absolutely "comme il faut", as in the best versions of this wine. It is less interesting than the '97, however, and so much less complex than the '95. Nor is it likely to have the long cellar life of its predecessors but it will be drinking very well for the next five years. Il Principe '98, made from pinot nero, boasts an intense, inviting fragrance, again without the concentration of the '95. But it is still a red with remarkable structure, which is unusual for wines from this grape, but typical of this particular wine. The terroir has had more to say than the variety so the characteristics of a Chianti red are easier to identify than the delicate strawberries and blackcurrants of a pinot nero. The same is true of the Ser Niccolò '98, a cabernet sauvignon that behaves almost like a sangiovese. These are not defects, obviously, but they are worth mentioning. Altogether, the wines did quite well this year, and the leopard spots didn't do much damage.

● Chianti Cl. V. di Fontalle Ris. '98	🍷🍷	5
● Il Principe '98	🍷🍷	5
● Ser Niccolò Solatio del Tani '98	🍷	5
● Chianti Cl. V. di Fontalle Ris. '95	🍷🍷🍷	5
● Il Principe '95	🍷🍷🍷	4
🍷🍷🍷		5
● Chianti Cl. V. di Fontalle Ris. '93	🍷🍷	5
● Ser Niccolò Solatio del Tani '93	🍷🍷	5
● Chianti Cl. V. di Fontalle Ris. '94	🍷🍷	5
● Il Principe '94	🍷🍷	4
● Il Principe '96	🍷🍷	5
● Il Principe '97	🍷🍷	5
● Ser Niccolò Solatio del Tani '94	🍷	5
● Ser Niccolò Solatio del Tani '97	🍷	5

SAN CASCIANO IN VAL DI PESA (FI)

Fattoria Poggiopiano
Via di Pisignano, 28/30
50024 San Casciano in Val di Pesa (FI)
tel. 0558229629
e-mail: poggiopiano@ftbcc.it

The Fattoria Poggiopiano's wines were again in excellent form at our tastings. We'll get back to the Rosso di Sera, which gave the Bartolli brothers their usual Three Glasses, and bring on first the Chianti Classico '99, which is better than it has ever been. It may seem strange but this was an especially pleasing development. It means that Poggiopiano has really got it together, incidentally backing up in our positive overall evaluation. A really reliable winery looks after all of its wines, two in this case. This Chianti shows considerable density, thanks to abundant ripe fruit, and nicely integrated, good quality oak. The flavour is, in fact, concentrated and composed, the tannins are tightly woven, and balance and elegance play their part as well. The star turn, as usual, is the Rosso di Sera, made from sangiovese and colorino. Its exceptional richness floods through on the nose in a wide range of scents including spices, dark berry fruit, vanilla, coffee and mineral notes. The palate is powerful and chewy, and simply gets better and better as it progresses. It's a very young wine, and the oak and tannins are still prominent.

● Rosso di Sera '99	▼▼▼	6
● Chianti Cl. '99	▼▼	4*
● Rosso di Sera '95	▼▼▼	5
● Rosso di Sera '97	▼▼▼	5
● Rosso di Sera '98	▼▼▼	6
● Rosso di Sera '96	▼▼	5
● Chianti Cl. '98	▼▼	4
● Chianti Cl. '95	▼	3
● Chianti Cl. '96	▼	3
● Chianti Cl. '97	▼	4

SAN GIMIGNANO (SI)

Ca' del Vispo
Loc. Le Vigne
Via Fugnano, 31
53037 San Gimignano (SI)
tel. 0577943053

Ca' del Vispo has made an impressive debut in the Guide. The winery was founded in 1994 by three young men, Roberto, originally from Piedmont, and Marco and Massimo, two growers from Trentino. Their first efforts were encouraging. This year, they presented a selection of wines that is well thought out and reliable. Let's begin with their Crueter '99, a 100 per cent merlot. It offers lots of good fruit, excellent balance and velvety tannins that hint at the skilful use of oak, and earns Two Glasses. The expertise with wood is confirmed in the Basolo '99, a blend of cabernet sauvignon and sangiovese with a nose of berry fruit and undertones of spices and caramel. The full, seductive palate progresses well to a moderately long finish. The Rovai '99, from merlot, cabernet sauvignon and sangiovese, has an intense nose with notes of liquorice and raspberries. The well-balanced palate is mouthfilling and the tannins are well integrated with the slightly prominent alcohol. The Colle Leone '99, a blend of sangiovese and merlot, presents light vegetal notes and a succulent, if not extremely vigorous, flavour. The Poggio Solivo '99 rounds off the range of IGT wines and seems a little weaker than the others. The trio also has a neat touch with whites. The Vernaccia di San Gimignano Vigna in Fiore '00 is a well-made wine with aromas of ripe fruit and notes of oak. The palate displays good structure and softness. The standard-label version earns One Glass for its freshness and sheer drinkability, and reveals the characteristic Vernaccia almondy finish.

● Basolo '99	▼▼	4
● Crueter '99	▼▼	4
○ Vernaccia di S. Gimignano '00	▼	3
○ Vernaccia di S. Gimignano Vigna in Fiore '00	▼	3
● Colle Leone '99	▼	4
● Poggio Solivo '99	▼	4
● Rovai '99	▼	4
● Chianti Colli Senesi '00		3
○ Segumo '99		4

SAN GIMIGNANO (SI)

CASA ALLE VACCHE
FRAZ. PANCOLE
LOC. LUCIGNANO, 73/A
53037 SAN GIMIGNANO (SI)
TEL. 0577955103 - 0577955089
E-MAIL: casaallevacche@cyber.dada.it

This year's tastings of the Casa alle Vacche range confirmed the winery's determination to produce consistent wines with a recognizable style, even in less memorable years. The Aglieno '00, which won Two Glasses, has a dark ruby colour that hints at the complexity of the nose, where black berry fruit blends well with sweet vanilla. The palate is full and concentrated from the start, the tannins are smooth, elegant and well-balanced, and the lingering finish is sweetly fruity. The Chianti Colli Senesi Cinabro '99 is equally well-made. It displays a dense ruby that ushers in rich, sound fruit and spice aromas. The palate is concentrated, soft and full-bodied, and the finish is less astringent than last year's version. The standard-label Chianti Colli Senesi '00 gives a lot of simple pleasure. The whites show clear signs of improvement. The Vernaccia di San Gimignano Crocus '00 easily picked up Two Glasses. The attractive bouquet includes lots of tropical fruit mingling with notes of citrus fruits and flowers. The entry on the palate is sweet and substantial, the development meaty and balanced, and the long finish is enjoyably fruity. The successful Vernaccia I Macchioni '00 has a delicate fragrance of almonds and vegetal nuances, a soft, enticing mouthfeel, and a typically varietal finish. The standard-label Vernaccia is correctly executed, with a refreshing, agreeable flavour.

SAN GIMIGNANO (SI)

VINCENZO CESANI
FRAZ. PANCOLE
VIA PIAZZETTA, 82/D
53037 SAN GIMIGNANO (SI)
TEL. 0577955084
E-MAIL: cesanivini@novamedia.it

The aim of the Cesanis, a husband and wife team, has always been to make excellent wines with a definite imprint from their terroir. For this reason, they have relied on local grapes such as sangiovese and colorino – the basis of their Luenzo – so as to avoid the risk of standardization that the use of cabernet and merlot often entails. Perhaps it is this very firm bond with the territory that has won the Luenzo '99 its Three Glasses. It's a splendid wine with a complex bouquet of red berry fruit layered with coffee, spices and hints of oak. The especially concentrated and fruity palate reveals dense, smooth tannins smothered in a velvety softness. The Chianti Colli Senesi '00 is one the best of its category. It is a violet-tinged ruby, with pleasing aromas of plums and morello cherries laced with faint hints of oak. The enjoyable, soft flavour shows fine-grained tannins that are slightly prominent in the finish. Since the Sanice was still ageing in the wood at the time of our tastings, the only white considered is the Vernaccia di San Gimignano '00. Pale straw yellow, it shows good fruit on the nose with some vegetal notes. The palate is fresh, soft and well-balanced with a typical twist of almonds in the aftertaste.

● Aglieno '00	ŸŸ	4
○ Vernaccia di S. Gimignano Crocus '00	ŸŸ	4
● Chianti Colli Senesi '00	Ÿ	3
○ Vernaccia di S. Gimignano I Macchioni '00	Ÿ	3
● Chianti Colli Senesi Cinabro '99	Ÿ	3
○ Vernaccia di S. Gimignano '00		2
● Chianti Colli Senesi Cinabro '97	ŸŸ	4
○ Vernaccia di S. Gimignano Crocus '98	ŸŸ	3
● Chianti Colli Senesi Cinabro '95	Ÿ	3
● Chianti Colli Senesi Cinabro '98	Ÿ	4
● Aglieno '99	Ÿ	4
● Chianti Colli Senesi '99	Ÿ	2

● Luenzo '99	ŸŸŸ	5
● Chianti Colli Senesi '00	Ÿ	3
○ Vernaccia di S. Gimignano '00	Ÿ	3
● Luenzo '97	ŸŸŸ	5
● Luenzo '95	ŸŸ	4
● Luenzo '96	ŸŸ	4
● Luenzo '98	ŸŸ	5
○ Vernaccia di S. Gimignano Sanice '98	ŸŸ	4
○ Vernaccia di S. Gimignano Sanice '99	ŸŸ	4
● Chianti Colli Senesi '93	Ÿ	2
● Chianti Colli Senesi '94	Ÿ	2
● Chianti Colli Senesi '98	Ÿ	2
● Chianti Colli Senesi '99	Ÿ	3

SAN GIMIGNANO (SI)

Guicciardini Strozzi
Fattoria Cusona
Loc. Cusona, 5
53037 San Gimignano (SI)
tel. 0577950028
e-mail: guicciardinistrozzi@iol.it

At last year's tastings, the wines from Cusona seemed to have more energy and personality, signs that changes were under way at the estate. And indeed progress was driven by serious work in the vineyards and greater use of new oak in the cellar. This admirable commitment has yielded Three Glasses for Cusona's top wine, the Millani '99, a red that brilliantly fuses the qualities of its component grapes. You note the enormous character of the sangiovese melding into the elegance of the cabernet sauvignon and the enveloping seductiveness of the merlot. In short, it's a tremendous wine. A dark ruby introduces an intense nose with lots of berry fruit, hints of coffee, and scents of Mediterranean underbrush. The palate is broad, deep and mouthfilling, with impressive tannic structure and a long, dense finish. The Selvascura '99 easily added another Two Glasses to the haul. The bouquet reveals intense aromas of berry fruit and tobacco with a light vegetal nuance and well-amalgamated tones of oak. The well-sustained, elegant flavour shows rounded tannins and considerable length. The quite convincing Sodole '99 is a sangiovese thoroughbred with an elegant, eminently varietal nose. The Chianti Titolato '00 is as exemplary a representative of its category as ever, though a little on the simple side. The Vernaccia Riserva '99 is, however, merely decent. Its nose, somewhat undefined at first, opens up to fruity and woody notes. In the mouth, it is well-balanced and soft, with a typically bitter finish. The Vernaccia Perlato '00 is correctly made and redolent of almonds. On the other hand, the Vermentino Luna Verde is disappointing and rather untypical.

SAN GIMIGNANO (SI)

Il Lebbio
Loc. San Benedetto, 11/c
53037 San Gimignano (SI)
tel. 0577944725 - 057794461

At our tastings, Il Lebbio's reds seemed to be holding their own while their versions of the typical wine from this zone, Vernaccia, are somewhat improved. We'll start with the Polito '98, an IGT made from colorino and sangiovese which confirms the expert Il Lebbio technique in the cellar. It has a violet-tinged ruby colour, and an intense, enticing nose of ripe bramble and raspberries blending well with notes of oak. The full, caressingly soft palate shows a fine tannic structure that nicely balances the alcohol. Just below the Two Glass level, the violet-tinged ruby Grottoni '00 exhibits an intensely fruity nose with faint notes of pepper and mint as well as some vegetal hints. It is not a big wine but has good balance and drinkability. The Cicogio '00 is a respectable red made from ciliegiolo, colorino and sangiovese. Intense varietal fragrances and notes of ripe sour cherries lead in to a well-balanced, nicely tannic palate that lacks something in complexity but is attractively upfront and fruity. Among the whites, the Vernaccia di San Gimignano Tropie '00 seems to have improved. It shows a pale, not very vivid straw-yellow colour and aromas of ripe fruit with hints of yeast and vanilla. In the mouth, it is sweet, tangy and soft, but the wood is still in evidence. The successful standard-label Vernaccia is fresh, well-balanced and very attractive. Finally, the Malvasia '00 is less convincing.

● Millanni '99	🍷🍷🍷	6
● Selvascura '99	🍷🍷	5
● Sodole '99	🍷🍷	5
● Chianti Colli Senesi Titolato '00	🍷	3
○ Vernaccia di S. Gimignano Perlato '00	🍷	4
○ Vernaccia di S. Gimignano Ris. '99	🍷	4
○ Luna Verde '00		3
○ Vernaccia di S. Gimignano S. Biagio '00		4
● Millanni '95	🍷🍷	6
● Millanni '96	🍷🍷	6
● Millanni '97	🍷🍷	6
● Millanni '98	🍷🍷	6
● Selvascura '98	🍷🍷	5

● Polito '98	🍷🍷	4
● Cicogio '00	🍷	3
● I Grottoni '00	🍷	3
○ Vernaccia di S. Gimignano '00	🍷	2*
○ Vernaccia di S. Gimignano Tropie '00	🍷	3
○ Malvasia '00		2
● I Grottoni '97	🍷🍷	2
● Polito '97	🍷🍷	4
● Cicogio '98	🍷🍷	3
● I Grottoni '99	🍷🍷	3
● Chianti '97	🍷	2
● I Grottoni '98	🍷	3
● Cicogio '99	🍷	3

SAN GIMIGNANO (SI)

Poderi del Paradiso
Loc. Strada, 21/a
53037 San Gimignano (SI)
Tel. 0577941500
E-mail: 0577941500@iol.it

In recent years, the Poderi del Paradiso winery frequently came close to winning Three Glasses. This time, the Saxa Calida '99, a magnificent blend of cabernet sauvignon and merlot, actually did so, a testimony to the strength of will of two determined vignerons, Vasco Cetti and his wife Graziella. This excellent red is as dark as ink. The intense, lingering bouquet shows a rich array of dark berry fruit with notes of coffee and spices. The palate reveals a meaty fullness and a generous structure underpinned by perfectly ripe fruit. The sangiovese-based Paterno II also showed breeding and elegance for it almost walked away with a second Three Glasses. It's a concentrated wine with an intensely ruby red hue that ushers in an immediately engrossing fragrance of ripe fruit with notes of violets and spices. The powerful flavour is backed up by well-gauged extract and smooth, soft tannins that mingle well with the fruit and the oak-derived spice. Poderi del Paradiso has also produced the best Chianti Colli Senesi of the '00 vintage. It is intensely redolent of raspberries, with a voluptuously velvet mouthfeel. Two Glasses without any trouble. Among the whites, the Vernaccia Biscondola '00 is again interesting, while the standard-label version is aromatic and well-structured. Il Bottaccio '99 reveals softness and good weight in the mouth, as well as plenty of tannin.

SAN GIMIGNANO (SI)

La Lastra
Fraz. Santa Lucia
Via R. De Grada, 9
53037 San Gimignano (SI)
Tel. 0577941781 - 0577236423
E-mail: staff@lalastra.it

There is no lack of commitment on the part of Nadia Betti and Renato Spanu, who are both expert growers and run one of the recently most interesting estates in the area. Their range of wines, despite vintage problems, was very well received by the panel although there was nothing absolutely outstanding. The Rovaio '98, a blend of sangiovese, cabernet sauvignon and merlot in equal parts, won Two Glasses. The ruby colour maintains its concentration all the way to the rim then the basically fruity nose reveals some vegetal hints. In the mouth, there is good concentration, rounded tannins, good balance and a moderately long finish. In short, it did well, though we it lacks the character we hope to find in future versions. Not quite as good as it has been recently, the Vernaccia Riserva '99 shows a vivid straw colour introducing delicate aromas of golden delicious apples and citrus fruits, with faint toasty notes. The palate shows fair depth and is lively if a little rustic, a varietal note of almonds appearing in the finish. The Vernaccia di San Gimignano '00 is correct on the nose if not terribly convincing in the mouth but the Chianti Colli Senesi '00 performed better. It has pleasing aromas of berry fruit and a fresh, moderately concentrated palate with a decent progression.

Wine	Glasses	Score
● Saxa Calida '99	▼▼▼	5
● Paterno II '98	▼▼	5
● Chianti Colli Senesi '00	▼▼	2*
○ Vernaccia di S. Gimignano '00	▼	2
○ Vernaccia di S. Gimignano Biscondola '00	▼	4
● Bottaccio '99	▼	4
● Saxa Calida '96	▼▼	4
● Bottaccio '97	▼▼	4
● Paterno II '97	▼▼	5
● Saxa Calida '98	▼▼	5
○ Vernaccia di S. Gimignano Biscondola '98	▼▼	4
● Saxa Calida '95	▼	4
● Paterno II '96	▼	4

Wine	Glasses	Score
● Rovaio '98	▼▼	5
● Chianti Colli Senesi '00	▼	3
○ Vernaccia di S. Gimignano '00	▼	3
○ Vernaccia di S. Gimignano Ris. '99	▼	4
○ Vernaccia di S. Gimignano Ris. '95	▼▼	3
○ Vernaccia di S. Gimignano Ris. '96	▼▼	3
● Rovaio '97	▼▼	5
○ Vernaccia di S. Gimignano Ris. '97	▼▼	3
○ Vernaccia di S. Gimignano '98	▼▼	2
○ Vernaccia di S. Gimignano Ris. '98	▼▼	4
● Rovaio '95	▼	4
● Rovaio '96	▼	5
● Chianti Colli Senesi '97	▼	4
● Chianti Colli Senesi '98	▼	2
● Chianti Colli Senesi '99	▼	3

SAN GIMIGNANO (SI)

La Rampa di Fugnano
Via di Fugnano, 55
53037 San Gimignano (SI)
Tel. 0577941655
E-mail: larampad@cyber.dada.it

La Rampa di Fugnano has recently added some underground rooms to its cellar in order to offer the wines time to age properly. This year, we tasted some very fine bottles and one thrilling product, the Gisèle '99, which nearly won Three Glasses. The dense, dark ruby goes all the way to the rim, and the deep nose of very ripe fruit includes traces of vanilla and spicy notes, as well as evident vegetal nuances. It develops with breadth and power, only slightly disturbed by exuberant tannins, which reappear prominently on the still slightly raw finish. Nor is the sangiovese-based Bombereto '99 disappointing and it, too, easily gains Two Glasses. The bouquet is varietal, and the juicy, flavoursome palate shows good balance and tannic structure, then a sweet finish. However, it lacks the complexity of a truly serious wine. The whites reveal some personality and good technical execution although vintage problems come into play. The Vernaccia Riserva Privato '99 wins One Glass. It shows a straw colour and a nose of some finesse, with fruity and vegetal notes and an undertone of vanilla. In the mouth, it is fresh, soft and moderately dense, vanilla triumphing in the finish. The Vernaccia di San Gimignano Alata '00 is redolent of apples and hedgerow then the palate is direct and refreshing, revealing fair balance and a not very long but quite pleasing finish. The agreeable and well-balanced Chianti Colli Senesi '00 has a pinch more sinew than usual.

SAN GIMIGNANO (SI)

Tenuta Le Calcinaie
Loc. Monteoliveto, 36
53037 San Gimignano (SI)
Tel. 0577943007

Simone Santini is so deeply wrapped up in the task of imbuing his wines with character and serious body that he sometimes overlooks the most elementary details, particularly olfactory ones. The overall result is still very good, though, and his wines have the great virtue of possessing authentic personality, an increasingly rare quality these days, especially among whites. His Vernaccia Vigna ai Sassi '00 won Two Glasses. An intense straw introduces a bouquet of ripe fruit, citrus fruits, and a hint of spring flowers. The rich, sweet, harmonious flavour reveals an attractive bitterish undertone. The standard-label Vernaccia di San Gimignano also gave a convincing performance, and is one of the best of its kind this year. A lovely straw with green highlights, it boasts aromas of golden delicious apples, peaches and chocolate mints. The tangy, fruity palate has a harmonious, well-balanced progression and a pleasingly long fruity finish. The Teodoro '98, made from sangiovese with a bit of merlot, also gets Two Glasses. It shows a dark hue and aromas of ripe fruit, slightly marked by vegetal nuances. The palate displays remarkable, if not perfectly balanced, extract. The Chianti Colli Senesi '00 did well again. Its purplish ruby introduces a nose that slowly opens out with notes of berry fruit and slight vegetal hints. After a sweet fruity attack, the palate reveals somewhat insistent tannins.

● Gisèle '99	🍷🍷	6
● Bombereto '99	🍷🍷	5
● Chianti Colli Senesi Via dei Franchi '00	🍷	3
○ Vernaccia di S. Gimignano Alata '00	🍷	3
○ Vernaccia di S. Gimignano Privato Ris. '99	🍷	4
● Gisèle '97	🍷🍷🍷	5
● Bombereto '97	🍷	5
● Bombereto '98	🍷🍷	5
● Gisèle '98	🍷🍷	6
○ Vernaccia di S. Gimignano Privato Ris. '98	🍷🍷	4
● Bombereto '93	🍷	4

○ Vernaccia di S. Gimignano Vigna ai Sassi '00	🍷🍷	4
● Teodoro '98	🍷🍷	4
● Chianti Colli Senesi '00	🍷	3
○ Vernaccia di S. Gimignano '00	🍷	3
○ Vernaccia di S. Gimignano Vigna ai Sassi '98	🍷🍷	4
○ Vernaccia di S. Gimignano '99	🍷🍷	3
○ Vernaccia di S. Gimignano Vigna ai Sassi '99	🍷🍷	4
● Teodoro '94	🍷	4
● Teodoro '95	🍷	4
● Teodoro '96	🍷	4
● Chianti Colli Senesi '97	🍷	4
● Chianti Colli Senesi '98	🍷	3

SAN GIMIGNANO (SI)

MORMORAIA
LOC. SANT'ANDREA
53037 SAN GIMIGNANO (SI)
TEL. 0577940096
E-MAIL: info@mormoraia.it

In a few short years, Mormoraia has made a name for itself as an innovative producer. In fact, it is surprisingly well-known by critics and the public at large. Behind this feat lie a good number of hectares under vine in an enviable position for climate, soil and exposure. They are managed with an eye to excellence, as is the very well-equipped cellar and it is all thanks to the tireless dedication of Giuseppe Passoni, once a publicity-shunning businessman, who has transformed himself into a gifted grower. The wines have been satisfying from the first, although we are still waiting for a champion that would place the estate in the winners' circle where it belongs. The Vernaccia Riserva '99, one of the best of its vintage, shows an elegant, varied bouquet that ranges from ripe peaches and grapefruit to an oak-derived vanilla tone. The flavour is tangy, mouthfilling, rich and well sustained. The red Neitea '98 has an attractive ruby red hue with a purple rim and a lovely intense fruity fragrance with a faint vegetal undertone. The full-bodied, warm, even palate is underpinned by noble tannins, and finishes long. The nose of the standard-label Vernaccia has distinct personality, with fruit and flower notes taking turns and then carrying through on the palate, where the structure provides good support. The other white, the Ostrea Grigia '99, also did well. We noted aromas of several kinds of fruit, wild flowers and vanilla, and a soft-textured palate with nice acidity and a decent amount of body.

SAN GIMIGNANO (SI)

PALAGETTO
VIA MONTEOLIVETO, 46
53037 SAN GIMIGNANO (SI)
TEL. 0577943090 - 0577942098
E-MAIL: palagetto@iol.it

The only criticism we can offer Simone Niccolai, if we were wanting to be rather severe, is that he had got us used to expecting the very best. This year is different. It's a vintage problem – not all years are kind – and we feel sure that next time, Simone's wines will be at their customary high level. Meanwhile, we must admit that his red Sottobosco '99, a blend of sangiovese and 20 per cent cabernet sauvignon, is no disappointment, and has again won Two Glasses. An intense ruby introduces a bouquet laced with aromas of berry fruit with spicy and vegetal notes over oak. The palate is dense and very rich in delicious extract but there are some rough edges that give a dry sensation to the finish. The satisfactory, mostly sangiovese-based, Solleone '99 shows a characteristic varietal nose, a soft, full but rather monotonous palate and a slightly short finish. The Vernaccia Riserva '99, which is less successful than it has been, offers aromas of flowers with vanilla nuances. The moderately intense palate with notes of almond and fruit leads in to a pleasing but not very persistent finish. The standard Vernaccia is a reliable wine that regularly offers good value for money while the Vernaccia Vigna Santa Chiara '00 has not yet really found a length. Finally, we liked the well-rounded flavour of the Chianti Colli Senesi '99 but the nose was rather dumb.

○	Vernaccia di S. Gimignano Ris. '99	ΨΨ	4
●	Neitea '98	ΨΨ	5
○	Vernaccia di S. Gimignano '00	Ψ	3
○	Ostrea Grigia '99	Ψ	4
●	Neitea '95	ΨΨ	4
○	Ostrea '95	ΨΨ	4
●	Neitea '96	ΨΨ	4
○	Ostrea '96	ΨΨ	4
●	Neitea '97	ΨΨ	4
○	Ostrea '97	ΨΨ	4
○	Vernaccia di S. Gimignano Ris. '97	ΨΨ	4
○	Ostrea Grigia '98	ΨΨ	4
○	Vernaccia di S. Gimignano Ris. '98	ΨΨ	4

●	Sottobosco '99	ΨΨ	5
○	Vernaccia di S. Gimignano '00	Ψ	3
●	Solleone '99	Ψ	4
○	Vernaccia di S. Gimignano Ris. '99	Ψ	4
○	Vernaccia di S. Gimignano Vigna Santa Chiara '00		3
●	Chianti Colli Senesi '99		3
●	Sottobosco '97	ΨΨ	5
○	Vernaccia di S. Gimignano Ris. '97	ΨΨ	4
●	Sottobosco '98	ΨΨ	5
●	Sottobosco '94	Ψ	3
●	Sottobosco '95	Ψ	4
●	Sottobosco '96	Ψ	4
●	Chianti Colli Senesi '98	Ψ	3
●	Solleone '98	Ψ	4

SAN GIMIGNANO (SI)

Giovanni Panizzi
Loc. Racciano
Podere Santa Margherita, 34
53037 San Gimignano (SI)
tel. 0577941576 - 0290938796
e-mail: panizzi@ciber.data.it

Giovanni Panizzi was well aware that it would not be easy to produce a Vernaccia that could reconcile current taste with the basic characteristics of Tuscany's most classic white wine. He believed it could be done, though. That's how his style was born, modern, vibrant, authentic and unmistakable, as well as extremely enjoyable. It just missed out on Three Glasses for the second year in a row but it still is the best wine of its kind. The sweet bouquet shows finesse and elegance in its notes of tropical fruits, melding with vanilla and toasty tones. It is a little less complex than last year's but the wonderful refreshing flavour is enlivened by fruity sensations. There is notable energy and balance, and a finish that is in no hurry to ease up. The other whites did well, too. The standard-label Vernaccia '00 is particularly satisfying on the palate this time round while the Bianco di Gianni '99 shows a more focused nose of tropical fruits, butter and vanilla and a succulent, soft, well-balanced palate. The debut of a new wine was another pleasant surprise. It's the San Gimignano Rosso '99, which already shows style and personality. Purplish ruby, it has a fragrance in which dark bramble and blackcurrant fruit offer a perfect counterweight to the oak. The entry in the mouth is sweet, fruity, solid and concentrated, and the finish is a long. The Chianti Colli Senesi Vertunno '99 is solid, if a bit austere because of its youth, while the Ceraso '00 is pleasing.

O	Vernaccia di S. Gimignano Ris. '99	ΨΨ	6
O	San Gimignano Rosso Folgore '99	ΨΨ	5
●	Ceraso '00	Ψ	3
O	Vernaccia di S. Gimignano '00	Ψ	4
O	Bianco di Gianni '99	Ψ	5
●	Chianti Colli Senesi Vertunno '99	Ψ	4
O	Vernaccia di S. Gimignano Ris. '98	ΨΨΨ	6
O	Vernaccia di S. Gimignano Ris. '94	ΨΨ	5
O	Vernaccia di S. Gimignano Ris. '95	ΨΨ	5
O	Vernaccia di S. Gimignano Ris. '96	ΨΨ	5
●	Chianti Colli Senesi '97	ΨΨ	4
O	Vernaccia di S. Gimignano Ris. '97	ΨΨ	5
●	Ceraso '98	Ψ	3
●	Chianti Colli Senesi Vertunno '98	Ψ	4
●	Ceraso '99	Ψ	3

SAN GIMIGNANO (SI)

Pietrafitta
Loc. Cortennano
53037 San Gimignano (SI)
tel. 0577943200
e-mail: sapsrl@temainf.it

Pietrafitta continues to send out strong signals that a new style has been introduced. This year, we were favourably impressed by the Vernaccia Borghetto '00, which effortlessly earned Two Glasses. It has a lively straw colour while the nose reveals personality and aromatic complexity, underpinned by intense fruit. It fills the mouth on entry and the well-judged acidity is nicely balanced by alcohol that gives the wine a soft overall harmony. The finish is pleasingly almondy. The barrique-fermented Vernaccia Riserva La Costa '99 is less expressive but it's probably just paying the price of a poor vintage. The colour is an intense, lively straw-yellow and distinct, sound aromas of ripe banana and melon fruit are shot through with light nuances of oak. In the mouth, it is soft and refreshing, the prominent wood adding a tannic note, and in the fair finish varietal almonds make their traditional appearance. The normal Vernaccia is a respectable effort with fruity aromas and a soft, fresh-tasting, well-balanced flavour but the finish is simple and short. The San Gimignano Rosso La Sughera '99 also gets One Glass. It is admirably direct, without being predictable or simple, but it needs more definition on nose and palate. The Vin Santo '96 almost won Two Glasses. It has an amber hue and an intense, etheric nose in which notes of jam, figs, and nougat stand out. The palate, however, is thinner than expected. It progresses evenly but fades rather soon.

O	Vernaccia di S. Gimignano V. Borghetto '00	ΨΨ	4
O	Vernaccia di S. Gimignano '00	Ψ	3
O	Vin Santo '96	Ψ	5
●	S. Gimignano Rosso La Sughera '99	Ψ	4
O	Vernaccia di S. Gimignano Vigna La Costa Ris. '99	Ψ	4
O	Vin Santo '93	ΨΨ	4
O	Vernaccia di S. Gimignano Vigna La Costa Ris. '98	ΨΨ	4
●	S. Gimignano Rosso La Sughera '98	Ψ	4
O	Vernaccia di S. Gimignano V. Borghetto '99	Ψ	3

SAN GIMIGNANO (SI)

Signano
P.zza San Agostino, 17
53037 San Gimignano (SI)
tel. 0577940164 - 0577942587

This year's wines from Signano are nicely finished, confident and, most important, capable once again of expressing their customary style. The one that showed most personality was the San Gimignano Rosso '98, which has a more clearly defined bouquet than last year's version, showing aromas of liqueur cherries, blackcurrants and vanilla. The palate is soft and supple, with a smooth, elegant tannic weave, and a finish of some depth. The Vernaccia Selezione '99 is better than fair. At first the nose is dumb but then it opens to a rich variety of fruit aromas mixed with notes of vanilla and hints of oak. The structure on the palate is moderate, sustained by a little fleshiness, but the finish is somewhat short. The Vernaccia Poggiarelli '00 is not in good form. It has a weak colour and a faint nose of apples, pears and citrus fruits. In the mouth, it doesn't show much structure but it is well-balanced. On a similar level is the standard-label Vernaccia, which offers good balance between acidity and softness, as well as an admirably varietal finish. The Chianti Colli Senesi Poggiarelli '99 is well sustained. The palate is soft, warm and structured, and the finish somewhat astringent. The Chianti Colli Senesi '00 is fragrant and pleasant to drink.

SAN GIMIGNANO (SI)

Teruzzi & Puthod
Via Casale, 19
53037 San Gimignano (SI)
tel. 0577940143
e-mail: info@teruzzieputhod.com

Enrico Teruzzi is generally considered one of the leading producers in San Gimignano. The experience he has accumulated over the years, his state-of-the-art cellar, the enviably aspected vineyards he has acquired and the innovative assistance he receives from his fine oenologist, Pierluca Freddi, have all made it possible for him to produce really excellent wines. The Terre di Tufi '99, a splendidly seamless white, is one of the best versions in recent years. At our tastings, the nose was a little reluctant at first but then opened out into quite an intense array of aromas of tropical fruits and mineral notes, slightly challenged by hints of new oak. The palate is confident, full-bodied, well-balanced and fruity, and the finish is captivating but not very long. The Vigna a Rondolino '00 reveals aromas of peaches with sweet hints of vanilla that are mirrored on the palate. The debut of the Vernaccia Riserva is fairly successful. The nose shows some complexity and the flavour has softness but the balance is less than perfect. The standard-label Vernaccia, is as good as usual, unveiling aromas of ripe tropical fruits, a fresh, dry flavour and a faintly almondy finish. The Peperino '99, which we reviewed in error last year, is admirably varietal whereas the Carmen '99 is disappointing. The nose is fuzzy and the palate inexpressive.

	Wine	Rating	Score
●	San Gimignano Rosso '98	♛♛	5
○	Vernaccia di S. Gimignano Poggiarelli '00	♛	3
●	Chianti Colli Senesi Poggiarelli '99	♛	4
○	Vernaccia di S. Gimignano Sel. '99	♛	4
●	Chianti Colli Senesi '00		2
○	Vernaccia di S. Gimignano '00		2
○	Vernaccia di S. Gimignano Sel. '97	♛♛	4
○	Vin Santo '90	♛	4
●	Chianti Colli Senesi Poggiarelli '94	♛	3
●	Chianti Colli Senesi Poggiarelli '95	♛	4
●	Chianti Colli Senesi Poggiarelli '96	♛	4
●	Chianti Colli Senesi Poggiarelli '97	♛	4
○	Vernaccia di S. Gimignano Ris. '97	♛	3
○	Vernaccia di S. Gimignano '98	♛	2

	Wine	Rating	Score
○	Terre di Tufi '99	♛♛	5
○	Vernaccia di S. Gimignano Vigna a Rondolino '00	♛♛	4
○	Vernaccia di S. Gimignano '00	♛	3
●	Peperino '99	♛	3*
○	Vernaccia di S. Gimignano Ris. '99	♛	3
○	Carmen '99		4
○	Carmen '95	♛♛	4
○	Terre di Tufi '95	♛♛	5
○	Carmen '96	♛♛	4
○	Terre di Tufi '96	♛♛	5
○	Carmen '97	♛♛	4
○	Terre di Tufi '97	♛♛	5
○	Carmen '98	♛♛	4
○	Terre di Tufi '98	♛♛	4

SAN GIMIGNANO (SI)

F.lli Vagnoni
Loc. Pancole, 82
53037 San Gimignano (SI)
tel. 0577955077

SCANSANO (GR)

Podere Aia della Macina
Loc. Fosso Lombardo, 87
58054 Scansano (GR)
tel. 0577940600

The wines presented by Fratelli Vagnoni are, as always, reliable, clean, and good. The unstinting energy they have profused on vineyards and cellar is the prerequisite for producing solidly structured wines. And to prove it, there is the Mocali, a barrique-fermented selection of Vernaccia which has consistently been one of the best of its kind in recent years. The '99 earned its Two Glasses with no difficulty. A vibrant straw yellow with greenish highlights, it reveals an intense, intriguing nose that ranges from tropical fruits and spring flowers to well-judged notes of oak. The palate, underpinned by dense extract, is enticing and full-bodied, and the oak-derived vanilla merges with a very elegant fresh, fruity tone. The standard-label Vernaccia is exemplary. Delicacy and finesse come through better on the nose than on the nonetheless satisfying palate, which is well-balanced and varietally bitter in the finish. I Sodi Lunghi '98, a bit under par, still earns One Glass and is more admirable for harmony and structure in the mouth than for its fairly distant, austere nose. The Chianti Colli Senesi '99 has a supple, pleasing flavour while the traditional Vin Brusco '00 is fragrant, fresh, correct and unpretentious.

In 1997, Bruna Baroncini and Franco Azara bought a lovely estate in Scansano, Aia della Macina, covering over 40 hectares, about 30 of which are under vine although not all are as yet productive. Franco and Bruna have high ambitions for their winery, which specializes in Morellino di Scansano that they produce using modern techniques, while carefully observing the spirit of tradition. The cellar is just finished and boasts up-to-the-minute equipment as well as ageing rooms for the red wines where 30-hectolitre oak barrels and barriques are on view. Bruna made a successful job of winemaking for the first few vintages, which we review in this column, but starting with the 2001 vintage Riccardo Cotarella will be their consultant oenologist, which promises well. The Morellino di Scansano '00 has walked off with Two Glasses for its violet-tinged dark ruby hue, its intense aromas of berry fruit and spices, and its delicate nuances of oak. These lead in to a powerful, fruit-rich palate with perfectly ripe fruit framed in a firm tannic structure, and a lingering finish. The interesting Terra Nera Riserva '98 is fairly concentrated, reasonably stylish and rich in fruit but it is more austere and less of an extrovert than the standard version. The white Labruna '00, made from vermentino and ansonica, displays a lovely brilliant straw colour and an intense fruit and flower nose. The confident palate reveals good tangy acidity and lots of tropical fruit. The Maiano '00 is good too. It's a sangiovese-based blend made for fresh, fruity quaffability.

○ Vernaccia di S. Gimignano Mocali '99	▼▼	4
○ Vernaccia di S. Gimignano '00	▼	2
● I Sodi Lunghi '98	▼	4
○ Vinbrusco '00		2
● Chianti Colli Senesi '99		3
○ Vernaccia di S. Gimignano Mocali '96	▼▼	4
● I Sodi Lunghi '97	▼▼	4
○ Vernaccia di S. Gimignano Mocali '97	▼▼	4
○ Vernaccia di S. Gimignano Mocali '98	▼▼	4
● I Sodi Lunghi '95	▼	4
● I Sodi Lunghi '96	▼	4

○ Labruna '00	▼▼	3*
● Morellino di Scansano '00	▼▼	3*
● Morellino di Scansano Terra Nera Ris. '98	▼	4
● Maiano '00	▼	3

SINALUNGA (SI)

Tenuta Farneta
Loc. Farneta, 161
53048 Sinalunga (SI)
Tel. 0577631025

Sinalunga definitely has a way with reds. A huge gap divides their Bongoverno and Bentivoglio from the two Bonagrazia wines, one white and one rosé, both of which were quite weak in their '00 versions. On the other hand, the Bongoverno '97 is excellent, indeed one of the best ever. It is a strikingly fresh sangiovese that promises excellent cellarability. The colour is an intense ruby with a faint garnet tinge at the rim. From the bouquet, you can tell it came from warm, sunny year. There are jammy notes of black cherries and bramble, with earthy and mineral notes. The flavour is mouthfilling and dense, with well-behaved tannins and a long, fresh and elegant finish. In a nutshell, a lovely wine. The Bentivoglio '98 is only slightly less rich and complex. It has a mature appearance, the garnet shading into brownish red at the edges. The impression is confirmed by the nose of cherry jam and autumn leaves. The entry on the palate is much more energetic, as well as being soft and fruity, while the progression is impeccably well sustained, finishing on a concentrated note of fruitiness. As we have already suggested, the white and rosé are less exciting. Unpretentious standard bottles, they are lightweight and very simple, and are priced accordingly.

SINALUNGA (SI)

Farnetella
Fraz. Farnetella
Strada Siena-Bettolle, km 37
53048 Sinalunga (SI)
Tel. 0577355117
E-mail: felsina@dada.it

Castello di Farnetella's Poggio Granoni is generally released later than any other Tuscan wine. This year, for example, they presented the '95 version, which looks far from over the hill. It has complexity and ripe fruit that is still incisively present. Poggio Granoni is made mostly from sangiovese, with the addition of some cabernet sauvignon, and is sold only in magnums. Notes of liquorice, leather and sweet tobacco on a base of black cherries and blackcurrants make up the nose. The palate is meaty, solid and distinctly reminiscent of its terroir. It's one of those wines that lets you know where it comes from rather than what grapes went into it. The Three Glass score was a formality. This year, Giuseppe Mazzocolin's estate brought out a new wine, the Lucilla '99, which made a respectable debut. It is made from more or less the same grape blend as the Poggio Granoni but is a much simpler wine. An earthy, mineral tone on the nose is accompanied by some vegetal hints. The palate is admirable for its complexity, the chewy smoothness of the tannins, and the balance that makes it so pleasant to drink. The Chianti Colli Senesi, slightly below par, has substantial structure with rather prominent tannins, as well as a nose dominated by notes of super-ripeness.

Wine	Glasses	Score
● Bongoverno '97	🍷🍷	6
● Bentivoglio '98	🍷🍷	4
○ Bonagrazia Bianco '00		2
◉ Bonagrazia Rosato '00		2
● Bongoverno '88	🍷🍷	6
● Bentivoglio '89	🍷🍷	2
● Bongoverno '90	🍷🍷	6
● Bentivoglio '91	🍷🍷	2
● Bongoverno '91	🍷🍷	6
● Bongoverno '92	🍷🍷	6
● Bongoverno '93	🍷🍷	6
● Bongoverno '94	🍷🍷	6
● Bongoverno '95	🍷🍷	6
● Bongoverno '96	🍷🍷	6
● Bentivoglio '97	🍷🍷	4

Wine	Glasses	Score
● Poggio Granoni '95	🍷🍷🍷	6
● Chianti Colli Senesi '99	🍷	3
● Lucilla '99	🍷	4
● Poggio Granoni '93	🍷🍷🍷	6
○ Sauvignon '91	🍷🍷	4
○ Sauvignon '95	🍷🍷	4
● Chianti Colli Senesi '96	🍷🍷	3
○ Sauvignon '97	🍷🍷	4
● Chianti Colli Senesi '98	🍷🍷	3
● Chianti Colli Senesi '91	🍷	3
● Nero di Nubi '93	🍷	5
● Nero di Nubi '94	🍷	5
● Nero di Nubi '95	🍷	5
● Chianti Colli Senesi '97	🍷	3
● Nero di Nubi '97	🍷	5

SORANO (GR)

PODERE SOPRA LA RIPA
FRAZ. SOVANA
LOC. PODERE SOPRA RIPA
58010 SORANO (GR)
TEL. 0564616885
E-MAIL: info@sopralaripa.com

This is the debut appearance – and rather an impressive one – in the Guide for this Pitigliano estate which only recently, under the able management of Alberto Antonini, started producing wines of high quality. The wines presented at our tastings surprised us both for their complexity and for the way that they reflect their terroir. Let's begin with the Ea '00, which has an opaque, lustrous ruby colour. Fresh, inviting hints of mint blend with distinct notes of fresh blackcurrant and bilberry fruit on the nose. The excellent attack on the palate is seductive and fleshy, with well-integrated tannins, and the full-bodied, juicy progression leads to a good long finish. The Ripa '00 did well, too. An attractively vivid, concentrated ruby introduces a nose of some finesse, with elegant aromas of blackcurrants and bilberries lifted by very enjoyable spicy hints of cinnamon and pepper. The palate reveals a soft, dense body with tightly woven, silky tannins. Although it loses pace a little at mid palate, the finish is captivating and full of flavour. We found the white Perla del Mare '00 less convincing. The colour is a rather pale straw while the aromas, which include notes of ripe apples, are simple and not very intense. The attack on the palate is one-dimensional, acidity gets the upper hand, and the finish is rather bitter.

● Ea '00	🍷🍷	4
● Ripa '00	🍷🍷	3*
● Perla del Mare '00		3

SORANO (GR)

SASSOTONDO
FRAZ. SOVANA
LOC. PIANI DI CONATI, 52
58010 SORANO (GR)
TEL. 0564614218
E-MAIL: sassotondo@ftbce.it

If every grape could select its own patron saint, ciliegiolo would certainly choose San Lorenzo, or St. Lawrence, which is also the name of Carla and Edoardo Ventimiglia's flagship wine. This is not just a pleasantry because it is partly thanks to this wine that ciliegiolo has regained in some areas a certain dignity and consideration. The '99 version received Two Red Glasses, which means that it came quite close to getting Three. This is, of course, excellent in itself but it is quite exceptional for a wine of this kind. It is faithful to the style of previous versions, with aromas of wild berries, toasted oak, and spices, especially black pepper. The palate is mouthfilling, well sustained with good progression, underpinned by new oak, and just a bit austere on the finish where the tannins are more conspicuous. It's still young, and should acquire more balance and elegance of flavour with more time in the bottle. Potential future elegance is already discernible in the sangiovese-based Franze '99 which shows a coherent progression and a fruit-themed nose with the inevitable black pepper, a constant in Sovana wines whatever their grape. The Sassotondo Bianco '00 is also successful. Aromas of sage, pears and apples introduce a fair-textured palate and a clean, moderately long finish. Lastly, the Sassotondo Rosso '00 reveals a clean, pleasing flavour.

● San Lorenzo '99	🍷🍷	5
● Franze '99	🍷🍷	4
○ Sovana Bianco Sassotondo '00	🍷	3
● Sovana Rosso Sassotondo '00	🍷	3
● San Lorenzo '97	🍷🍷	4
● Franze '98	🍷🍷	4
● San Lorenzo '98	🍷🍷	5
● Sassotondo Rosso '98	🍷🍷	3
● Sassotondo Rosso '99	🍷🍷	3

SUVERETO (LI)

Lorella Ambrosini
Loc. Tabaro, 96
57028 Suvereto (LI)
tel. 0565829301
e-mail: lorellaambrosini@jumpy.it

This small Suvereto winery is getting down to serious business. The wines that they presented at our tastings brook no argument. They are really good, although some fine-tuning would not come amiss. Lorella Ambrosini and her husband Roberto Fanetti must be aware that the full potential of their vineyards has yet to be discovered. The Riflesso Antico, made from 100 per cent montepulciano, has no end of character and grip, as well as considerable structure. This wine, we feel sure, could be even better with greater care at harvest time, that is to say with more rigorous selection. But it is particularly in the cellar that they could make a difference, changing the relationship between the wine and the oak and adjusting the contact time and barrel size to suit the richness of the raw material. Our tastings of the Riflesso Antico '98 showed both strong and weak points. The least convincing part is the impact on the nose, which is dominated by strong animal and phenolic aromas. On the palate, however, it offers remarkable energy, breadth, power and tight-knit tannins. The Subertum '99 is very good. The colour is dark and concentrated, and the nose is themed around ripe, if not perfectly clean, fruit and plenty of oak. Densely woven tannins and generous extract appear on the palate, which is still a bit cramped in its development. The fair Val di Cornia Tabarò '00 is a simple, fruity, tangy wine with notes of cherries, medium body, lively tannins and a finish of some length.

SUVERETO (LI)

Gualdo del Re
Loc. Notri, 77
57028 Suvereto (LI)
tel. 0565829888 - 0565829361
e-mail: gualdo@infol.it

Lumen, a pinot bianco, is the wine that struck us most from Nico and Teresa Rossi's extensive range. This is an unusual in a part of the country where reds rule the roost, so one naturally tends to wonder whether it has come about entirely on the strengths of this white or whether failings on the part of the reds were responsible. In fact, it's a little of each. The Lumen is a surprisingly good wine. The nose makes an astonishing impact with notes of tropical fruits and Mediterranean flowers, and the palate is round, full and persistent. Perhaps it could use a pinch more acidic grip to guarantee it a long life but it is drinking beautifully at present. The red wines, as we mentioned, are less convincing. They are good by and large, but we think they could be better. The Gualdo Riserva, 100 per cent sangiovese, is interesting and varietal but already shows signs of age and has very little fruit. The wine which has not been able to find itself, however, is the Federico Primo. Obtained from cabernet and merlot, it is well-balanced and pleasant but has none of the character you might expect from a grape blend that has made the oenological fortune of the Tuscan coast. The rest of the range is respectable but not exciting.

●	Riflesso Antico '98	♟♟	5
●	Subertum '99	♟♟	5
○	Val di Cornia Bianco Tabarò '00	♟	3
●	Riflesso Antico '94	♟♟	4
●	Riflesso Antico '97	♟♟	5
●	Subertum '97	♟♟	5
●	Subertum '98	♟♟	5
●	Riflesso Antico '93	♟	4
●	Val di Cornia Rosso Ambrosini '93	♟	2
●	Subertum '94	♟	4
●	Subertum '96	♟	5
●	Val di Cornia Rosso Tabarò '98	♟	3
○	Val di Cornia Bianco Tabarò '99	♟	3
●	Val di Cornia Rosso Tabarò '99	♟	3

○	Lumen '00	♟♟	4
●	Federico Primo '98	♟	5
●	Val di Cornia Gualdo del Re Ris. '98	♟	5
○	Val di Cornia Bianco Esordio '00		3
●	Val di Cornia Rosso Esordio '99		4
●	Federico Primo '93	♟♟	5
●	Val di Cornia Gualdo del Re Ris. '95	♟♟	5
○	Vigna Valentina '95	♟♟	3
●	Federico Primo '96	♟♟	5
○	Lumen '98	♟♟	4
○	Lumen '99	♟♟	4
●	Val di Cornia Gualdo del Re Ris. '97	♟	5
○	Vigna Valentina '99	♟	4

SUVERETO (LI)

Montepeloso
Loc. Montepeloso, 82
57028 Suvereto (LI)
Tel. 0565828180

SUVERETO (LI)

Russo
Via Forni, 71
57028 Suvereto (LI)
Tel. 0565845105

Fabio Chiarellotto's commitment to his wines is admirable. He has recently planted a new vineyard to cabernet to increase production, which is currently unable to meet demand, and to help balance the books as well. The wines from the '99 vintage are very good but have not yet acquired, we feel, a perfect balance between fruit and wood. On the other hand, these are solidly built wines that need some time to blend harmoniously. But our preview tasting of some '00s, which were excellent, showed more successful integration, at least at the moment. The Gabbro '99, from cabernet sauvignon, presents aromas of blackcurrants and bramble with faint vegetal nuances. The palate is full-bodied, soft and even, with a good finish that doesn't show quite the depth we were expecting. It wants just a bit more complexity. The Nardo '99, made from sangiovese with a little cabernet, displays more personality. The intense nose includes balsamic, vanilla and mineral notes, and the invigorating palate reveals concentration and grip, as well as a rather tannic finish. The surprisingly successful Val di Cornia Rosso '99 also gets Two Glasses, and is the readiest to drink bottle on the list. It is simpler than the others, which also means that it offers less resistance to the overbearing oak. But it still manages to be soft, fairly full-bodied and enjoyable.

The Russo brothers, originally from Campania, are all-round farmers. They grow cereal crops, raise animals and keep dairy cattle. Yet they couldn't resist the temptation to produce wine. So far, they have six hectares under vine, planted mostly to sangiovese, but there is also some merlot and white grapes too - vermentino and trebbiano. These are still early days for the winery: the cellar, although modern, is a bit cramped. The ageing cellar contains only 225-litre barriques for their flagship Barbicone and Sassobucato. Despite their limited experience, the brothers seem to know what they are about, thanks, in part, to the oenological advice of Alberto Antonini. The Barbicone '99, a monovarietal sangiovese, is a solid, concentrated wine with oak still noticeable at first impact on the nose. It is at its best on the palate, where it shows character and tannic vigour. The merlot-based Sassobucato '99, is no less impressive. It is still young and a little closed on the nose, but notes of bramble and spices peek through. The structure is dense and the tannins are remarkably promising, if not yet perfectly balanced. The fairly interesting Ceppitaio '00, their standard red, is full-bodied, succulent and very good value for money. The Vermentino Pietrasca '00 is merely correct.

● Gabbro '99	🍷🍷	6
● Nardo '99	🍷🍷	6
● Val di Cornia Rosso Montepeloso '99	🍷🍷	4
● Nardo '95	🍷🍷	5
● Val di Cornia Rosso Montepeloso '95	🍷🍷	4
● Gabbro '97	🍷🍷	5
● Nardo '97	🍷🍷	6
● Gabbro '98	🍷🍷	6
● Nardo '98	🍷🍷	6
● Nardo '94	🍷	5
● Nardo '96	🍷	6
● Val di Cornia Rosso '98	🍷	4

● Barbicone '99	🍷🍷	4*
● Sassobucato '99	🍷🍷	5
● Val di Cornia Rosso Ceppitaio '00	🍷	2*
○ Pietrasca '00		3

SUVERETO (LI)

Tua Rita
Loc. Notri, 81
57025 Suvereto (LI)
Tel. 0565829237

TAVARNELLE VAL DI PESA (FI)

Il Poggiolino
Loc. Sambuca
Via Chiantigiana, 32
50020 Tavarnelle Val di Pesa (FI)
Tel. 0558071635

This Suvereto estate is still advancing on all fronts. There is no let-up for Rita and Virgilio Bisti, or for their son-in-law Stefano Frascolla, who is now working with them full-time. All this, however, in no way interferes with the minute attention they dedicate to every phase of production and indeed their wines are increasingly special, despite ever fiercer competition. The merlot-based Redigaffi '99 is an extraordinary wine. Each year it gains in elegance of execution – richness of structure has long been one of its qualities. It reveals great power and concentration but also a beautifully defined bouquet, balance and admirable depth. The extremely good Giusto di Notri '99, from cabernet and merlot, is wonderfully dense and energetic. The aromas are intensely rich but still youthful and in need of a little more time to settle. The estate's lesser wines are also better than they were. The Perlato del Bosco Rosso '99 is a lovely sangiovese with a concentrated palate that reveals an excellent balance of fruit and oak, as well as good texture and length. The Lodano '00, a blend of chardonnay, riesling and traminer, has replaced their Sileno, and is very convincing, thanks to complex aromas of tropical fruits, minerals and vanilla. In the mouth, it is pleasingly fleshy without sacrificing either freshness or elegance. The Perlato Bianco '00 is improving, too. A blend of trebbiano and vermentino, it has may not have a very pronounced nose but the palate is impressively structured, succulent and lingering.

The Pacini family's estate did very well this year. They have only a few hectares under vine at Tavernelle but they have managed to produce a range of interesting and very distinctive wines which we found remarkably impressive. Le Balze '97, a barrique-aged pure sangiovese, made it into our finals. An inviting ruby with purple highlights introduces firm, very agreeable fruity aromas. The palate is even and deep, with silky tannins in an understated but austere structure that leads to a very successful rising finish. The very good Chianti Classico has youthful aromas of fresh fruit mixed with subtle and elegant riper tones. The palate is solid and dense, with well-integrated, tightly woven, flavoursome tannins and a long, very satisfying finish. The Riserva did equally well. A lovely deep ruby introduces clean notes of grass and green pepper that give way to scents of ripe fruit. The palate is delightfully integrated, also offering lively chewy tannins and a finish of increasing intensity. A good wine, though it allows too much space to vegetal notes. Lastly, we enjoyed the rosé immensely, simple as it is. It offers bewitchingly powerful aromas of fresh flowers together with notes of strawberries, adequate body, perfectly judged acidity and good length.

● Redigaffi '99	🍷🍷🍷	6
● Giusto di Notri '99	🍷🍷	6
○ Lodato '00	🍷🍷	4
● Perlato del Bosco Rosso '99	🍷🍷	5
○ Perlato del Bosco Bianco '00	🍷	3
● Giusto di Notri '94	🍷🍷🍷	5
● Redigaffi '96	🍷🍷🍷	6
● Redigaffi '98	🍷🍷🍷	6
● Giusto di Notri '92	🍷🍷	5
● Giusto di Notri '93	🍷🍷	5
● Redigaffi '95	🍷🍷	6
● Giusto di Notri '96	🍷🍷	5
● Giusto di Notri '97	🍷🍷	5
● Redigaffi '97	🍷🍷	6
● Giusto di Notri '98	🍷🍷	6

● Chianti Cl. Ris. '98	🍷🍷	4
● Le Balze '97	🍷🍷	4
● Chianti Cl. '99	🍷🍷	3*
⊙ Rosato '00	🍷	3
● Chianti Cl. '97	🍷🍷	3
● Chianti Cl. Ris. '97	🍷🍷	4
● Chianti Cl. '98	🍷🍷	3
● Le Balze '95	🍷	4
● Chianti Cl. Ris. '96	🍷	4
● Le Balze '96	🍷	4

TAVARNELLE VAL DI PESA (FI)

PODERE LA CAPPELLA
FRAZ. SAN DONATO IN POGGIO
STRADA CERBAIA, 10/A
50028 TAVARNELLE VAL DI PESA (FI)
TEL. 0558072727
E-MAIL: poderelacappella@libero.it

La Cappella presented two wines, each of which won Two Glasses. It all goes to show that Bruno Rossini's estate continues to work with great care, consolidating a position from which it can aim even higher. Within the context of our positive review of this San Donato estate, there are a few points we should like to make. We had eagerly awaited the debut of the merlot-based Cantico '98, not least because our preview tasting, before it went into the bottle, whetted our appetites. And the wine did certainly seem good. It was attractive and well-made on our second tasting but frankly we had expected something more. The aromas are clean, clear-cut and basically fruity with vegetal undertones. The warm, soft palate is well balanced but rather lacking in character, and the finish soon fades in intensity. Given its category the Chianti Classico Querciolo '99 cuts a better figure. The colour is very intense and the not yet fully expressive nose is somewhat oak-dominated. The attack on the palate is powerful, dense and concentrated, tannins and wood are well integrated, and the finish is appropriately long. It may be an untypical Chianti but it is a very good wine.

TAVARNELLE VAL DI PESA (FI)

FATTORIA LA RIPA
LOC. SAN DONATO IN POGGIO
50028 TAVARNELLE VAL DI PESA (FI)
TEL. 0558072948 - 0558072121
E-MAIL: laripa@ftbcc.it

This year, Fattoria La Ripa confirmed past good impressions. There are 14 hectares under vine, mostly in the Chianti Classico zone, and the cellar can call on the expert advice of the oenologist Marco Chellini. The Chianti Classico '99 has a clear, not very intense ruby colour, and simple but inviting aromas of fresh cherry and raspberry fruit. The palate is solid, with soft tannins and a tangy acidity that makes it enticingly, enjoyably quaffable. The vividly purple-tinged '98 Riserva offers an array of aromas that includes berry fruit, vanilla and spicy, well-modulated hints of cloves. It does not make much of an immediate impression in the mouth, but is still pleasing and well-balanced, if not very long. The Santa Brigida '98, a blend of sangiovese and cabernet sauvignon, is very good. The intense ruby hue shades into purple. The nose is equally concentrated, with vegetal notes and green peppers prominent without being disturbing. The palate, after a powerful attack, is mouthfilling with firm, densely packed, well-integrated tannins. The excellent, very long finish includes notes of coffee and chocolate. A mention only for the estate white, the Tiratari '00, which is correct, balanced and invitingly fragrant, but a bit lean and short.

● Cantico '98	🍷🍷	5
● Chianti Cl. Querciolo '99	🍷🍷	4
● Corbezzolo '96	🍷🍷	5
● Corbezzolo '97	🍷🍷	5
● Chianti Cl. Querciolo '98	🍷🍷	4
● Corbezzolo '98	🍷🍷	5
● Chianti Cl. Querciolo '96	🍷	4
● Chianti Cl. Querciolo '97	🍷	4

● Santa Brigida '98	🍷🍷	5
● Chianti Cl. '99	🍷🍷	3*
● Chianti Cl. Ris. '98	🍷	4
○ Tiratari '00		3
● Chianti Cl. Ris. '90	🍷🍷	4
● Chianti Cl. Ris. '97	🍷🍷	4
● Chianti Cl. '98	🍷🍷	3
● Chianti Cl. '93	🍷	3

TAVARNELLE VAL DI PESA (FI)

Poggio al Sole
Loc. Sambuca Val di Pesa
50020 Tavarnelle Val di Pesa (FI)
Tel. 0558071504
E-mail: poggiosole@ftbc.it

The ascent of Giovanni Davaz's wines seems unstoppable. The hard work of recent years is bearing abundant fruit for this estate. Poggio al Sole doesn't go in much for publicity, but, quite rightly, lets the wines do the talking. Or rather shouting, for this year the cellar walked off with two Three Glass ratings. No magic is involved in the production of these wines. The basic requirements are the usual ones: the right kind of land, careful vineyard management, limited yields and a clean cellar with good oak barrels. Easy, isn't it? The reality is that patience is necessary, and great wines aren't just improvised. Giovanni Davaz has spent several years, as was proper, waiting for the vines to reach maturity, and for the experience he had acquired in cellar technique to suggest the right moves. Now he is gathering in the harvest with his Casasilia, which has become a star among modern Chianti Classicos. It is an elegant, concentrated wine without excesses or exaggeration. The category's aromatic personality has been respected and shows the effects of the weather during '98: the earthy and mineral tones that accompany the generous fruit are probably a consequence of that very dry summer. The Syrah '99 is also a magnificent wine. The ripeness of the grapes is exemplary, indeed absolutely faultless. The well-conceived structure reveals taut energy and the complex aromas offer varietal tones of dark berry fruit and pepper that never get out of hand. The Chianti Classico '99, with its fuzzy nose but full body, nearly won Two Glasses while the Seraselva '98, a blend of cabernet and merlot, is again too hard.

Wine	Rating	Score
● Chianti Cl. Casasilia '98	🍷🍷🍷	6
● Syrah '99	🍷🍷🍷	6
● Seraselva '98	🍷	6
● Chianti Cl. '99	🍷	4
● Chianti Cl. Casasilia '97	🍷🍷🍷	6
● Seraselva '94	🍷🍷	5
● Chianti Cl. Casasilia Ris. '95	🍷🍷	5
● Seraselva '95	🍷🍷	5
● Seraselva '96	🍷🍷	5
● Seraselva '97	🍷🍷	6
● Syrah '97	🍷🍷	5
● Syrah '98	🍷🍷	6

TERRANUOVA BRACCIOLINI (AR)

Tenuta Sette Ponti
Loc. Oreno
52020 Terranuova Bracciolini (AR)
Tel. 055977443

Tenuta Sette Ponti has claimed a place in the front rank of Italian wines. Antonio Moretti makes no secret of his ambitions, and his wines, in just their second year of production, have already made their mark. His farm also grows cereal crops and the highly prized Chianina breed of cattle are raised, as well as herds of Cinta Senese, a rare native variety of pigs reared in the wild. There are about 10 hectares under vine, almost entirely planted to sangiovese, cabernet and merlot, but with a little malvasia and trebbiano from which the cellar makes a sweet dried grape wine, the Grisoglia. The technical staff consists of Carlo Ferrini and Gioia Cresti, with help from agricultural technicians Gilbert Bouvet and Benedetto d'Anna. Their objectives, as we said, are ambitious and backed up by specific choices in the vineyard, where yields are severely limited, and in the cellar, where small barrels – either 225-litre barriques or 500-litre tonneaux - are the rule. Not counting the occasional, very limited production of Grisoglia, there are two wines made, the sangiovese-based Crognolo and the Oreno, from cabernet and merlot. Our opinion of the former is very positive. It's a lovely Sangiovese, dense and concentrated, with dynamic thrust on the palate, although the oak is a little too outspoken just at the moment. But we liked the Oreno '99 even more. It offers masses of very rich fruit, densely packed and expertly extracted tannins, and excellent balance despite its extreme youth. The future, at Sette Ponti, has already begun.

Wine	Rating	Score
● Oreno '99	🍷🍷	6
● Crognolo '99	🍷🍷	4
● Crognolo '98	🍷🍷	4

TERRICCIOLA (PI)

Badia di Morrona
Loc. Badia di Morrona
La Badia, 8
56030 Terricciola (PI)
tel. 0587658505
e-mail: info@badiamorrona.it

Badia di Morrona is one of the most important producers in the Pisa area. For some years now, it has attracted attention for a range of wines that are more than just good, and sometimes are almost outstanding. The estate, which belongs to the noble Gaslini family, is in a state of continual expansion so data about the area under vine always risk obsolescence. The results of this year's tastings are in part satisfactory, because the performance is up to previous standards, and partly a disappointment because we had hoped for something more from their top wines. We refer particularly to the Vigna Alta and the N'Antia, the former made from sangiovese and the latter a Tuscan-Bordeaux blend of cabernet, merlot and sangiovese. The N'Antia '98 has dark berry fruit aromas and a marked presence of oak-derived vanilla and toasty notes. On the palate, it shows good body and balance and is pleasant, but a bit simple on the finish and not very characterful. The Vigna Alta '98, as usual, reveals more personality but the scents of earth, vanilla and quinine are less than elegant. The attack on the palate is vigorous, the structure is even and well-calibrated, but oak gets the upper hand in the finish. Best of the rest is the very simple Chianti Sodi del Paretaio '00, which boasts a pleasingly fragrant nose of raspberries and black pepper. The San Torpè Felciaio '00 is well made and correct.

VINCI (FI)

Cantine Leonardo da Vinci
Via Provinciale Mercatale, 291
50059 Vinci (FI)
tel. 0571902444
e-mail: info@cantineleonardo.it

They don't waste any time at the Cantine Leonardo da Vinci. A new wine has done well, as have the other bottles presented at our tastings. So, this model co-operative winery continues to follow the path of excellence it set out on not many years ago. Everything is going well, although we could make some small criticisms of the style of their wines, which are generally very fruity and dark-hued, frequently very concentrated, and by and large similar one to the other. Our positive notes begin with the Sant'Ippolito '99, a blend of merlot and syrah. Very full-bodied and robust, it is a classic example of an international wine, showing lots of rich fruit, a well-judged use of small barrels, and tightly woven tannins, all expressed with great balance. It is very good, but not terribly complex or expressive of its terroir. The Vigna degli Artisti '99, made solely from merlot, is another big wine: muscular, hyper-concentrated, and all fruit. It is good and well made but it, too, fails to thrill. The mostly sangiovese-based San Zio '99 is a further example of a felicitous marriage between fruit and oak, with dark berry fruit and chocolate abounding. The Chianti Leonardo offers remarkable value for money. It has a very dark colour and aromas of blackcurrants and bramble jam. The flavour is soft and round, and the finish just faintly bitter. The well-made Ser Piero, from chardonnay, is nice and fat. The Vin Santo Tegrino d'Anchiano, on the other hand, has a distinctly oxidized style and is less successful.

● N'Antia '98	♛♛	5
● Vigna Alta '98	♛♛	6
● Chianti Sodi del Paretaio '00	♛	2*
○ S. Torpè Felciaio '00	♛	2*
● N'Antia '91	♛♛	5
● N'Antia '93	♛♛	5
● N'Antia '94	♛♛	5
● Vigna Alta '94	♛♛	5
● N'Antia '95	♛♛	5
● N'Antia '96	♛♛	5
● Vigna Alta '96	♛♛	6
● N'Antia '97	♛♛	5
● Vigna Alta '97	♛♛	6
● Chianti Sodi del Paretaio '97	♛	2
● Chianti Sodi del Paretaio '99	♛	2

● Sant'Ippolito '99	♛♛	5
● San Zio '99	♛♛	4
● Vigna degli Artisti '99	♛♛	5
● Chianti '00	♛	2*
○ Ser Piero '00	♛	3
○ Vin Santo Tegrino d'Anchiano		4
● Sant'Ippolito '96	♛♛	4
● San Zio '96	♛♛	4
● Sant'Ippolito '97	♛♛	5
● San Zio '97	♛♛	4
● Sant'Ippolito '98	♛♛	5
● San Zio '98	♛♛	4
○ Vin Santo Tegrino d'Anchiano '93	♛	4
○ Vin Santo Tegrino d'Anchiano '94	♛	4
● Chianti '98	♛	2

OTHER WINERIES

Podere Il Carnasciale
Fraz. Galatrona
Loc. San Leonino, 82
52020 Arezzo
tel. 0559911142

Only one wine and not much of it: just 1,500 magnums. The Caberlot is made from the grape of the same name, which, in its turn, is derived from a curious genetic cross. The wine shows great breeding and inimitable personality.

● Caberlot '98	6

Fattoria Lilliano
Loc. Grassina
Via Lilliano e Meoli, 82
50015 Bagno a Ripoli (FI)
tel. 055642602

This Florentine estate produces well-executed wines without faults but also without any really outstanding qualities. The two wines presented are even and well-made: the Chianti is sober and typical while the Bruzzico makes much of its fruit.

● Bruzzico '98	4
● Chianti Colli Fiorentini '99	2*

Casa Emma
Loc. San Donato in Poggio
S. P. di Castellina in Chianti, 3/5/7
50021 Barberino Val d'Elsa (FI)
tel. 0558072859 - 0558072239

This was a slightly disappointing year for Casa Emma, but these things happen. The Riserva '98 has good substance and a little too much oak. The Soloìo, a monovarietal merlot, is penalized by rather unappealing animal and vegetal nuances.

● Chianti Cl. Ris. '98	5
● Soloìo '98	5
● Chianti Cl. '99	4

Fattoria Casa Sola
Fraz. Cortine - Via Cortine, 5
50021 Barberino Val d'Elsa (FI)
tel. 0558075028
e-mail: casasola@chianticlassico.com

A mixed bag this year from the Chianti-based Fattoria Casa Sola estate. The Chianti '99 is very good, with delightful black cherry scents, rich mouthfeel and well-balanced, characteristic flavour. The less successful Riserva '98, however, is simple and offers a somewhat super-ripe bouquet.

● Chianti Cl. '99	4*
● Chianti Cl. Ris. '98	4

I Balzini
Loc. Pastine, 19
50021 Barberino Val d'Elsa (FI)
Tel. 0558085503 - 0557323845
E-mail: w-filiputti@triangolo.it

Vincenzo D'Isanto and Walter Filipputti produce only one wine on their estate, the sangiovese and cabernet blend I Balzini. The vintage '97 is really good: a robust, meaty red with oak-rich aromas.

● I Balzini Rosso '97	🍷🍷 6

Le Filigare
Loc. San Donato il Poggio
Fraz. Le Filigare - Via Sicelle, 35
50020 Barberino Val d'Elsa (FI)
Tel. 0558072796 - 0558072302

This was not the best year ever for Le Filigare. The Chianti '99 was good enough to get Two Glasses. The other wines, although not so convincing, are decently made.

● Chianti Cl. '99	🍷🍷 4
● Podere Le Rocce '98	🍷 5
● Chianti Cl. Ris. '98	🍷 4

Castello della Paneretta
Strada della Paneretta, 35
50021 Barberino Val d'Elsa (FI)
Tel. 0558059003
E-mail: stefano.paneretta@tin.it

This leading Chianti estate did not give one of its best performances but when you are faced with a tricky vintage like '98, this is often the case. We expect Castello della Paneretta to bounce back next year.

● Chianti Cl. Torre a Destra Ris. '98	🍷 5
● Quattrocentenario '98	🍷 5
● Chianti Cl. '99	🍷 4

Sant'Appiano
Sant'Appiano, 11
50021 Barberino Val d'Elsa (FI)
Tel. 0558075541
E-mail: pierfrancesco17@supereva.it

Sant'Appiano is a winery with limited experience but very good prospects. Their Monteloro, from sangiovese and colorino, is very encouraging. It has lots of good fruit on the nose and a concentrated, well-balanced palate. The Chianti is great value for money.

● Monteloro '99	🍷🍷 4
● Chianti '99	🍷 2*

Le Ginestre
Fraz. San Pancrazio
Loc. Greti, 56 - 52020 Bucine (AR)
Tel. 0559918032
E-mail: ginestre@val.it

This estate near Arezzo produces many different wines, some of which are outstanding. The Vin Santo '94 is rich in fragrance, balanced and pleasing in flavour. The decidedly good sangiovese-based I Greti '98 is full-bodied and intense, if a bit vegetal.

○ Vin Santo '94	🍷🍷 5
● I Greti '98	🍷 4
○ Le Ginestre Brut	🍷 4

Agricola Valle
Loc. Arcille
Podere ex E.M., 348
58050 Campagnatico (GR)
Tel. 0564998142 E-mail: uvalle@tiscalinet.it

Umberto and Bernardo Valle's winery started up in 1999. This means they are producing from vine stock that was already in place. Their wines are good, and going to get better.

● Morellino di Scansano Valle '00	🍷 3*
● Morellino di Scansano Larcille '99	🍷 4

Artimino
Fraz. Artimino
V.le Papa Giovanni XXIII, 1
59015 Carmignano (PO)
tel. 0558751424 e-mail: fattoria@artimino.com

The largest estate in Carmignano presented some interesting wines at this year's tastings. We were particularly impressed by the Vigna Iris, a blend of cabernet and sangiovese with excellent structure. The very successful Villa Artimino almost won a second Two Glass rating.

● Vigna Iris '99	🍷🍷 6
● Carmignano Villa Artimino '98	🍷 4

Il Poggiolo
Via Pistoiese, 76
50042 Carmignano (PO)
tel. 0558711242

This estate generally gives a solid performance. Unfailingly, the Vin Santo stands out for its elegant style. This year, we also liked the Barco Reale '99, which is fruity, well-rounded and very enjoyable. The Carmignano '98 is acceptable.

○ Vin Santo di Carmignano '93	🍷🍷 6
● Barco Reale '99	🍷 3
● Carmignano '98	4

Pratesi
Loc. Seano - Via Rizzelli, 10
59011 Carmignano (PO)
tel. 0558706400 - 0558953531
e-mail: lolocco@libero.it

Fabrizio Pratesi is an ambitious young man who has changed the orientation of his family estate, planting new vineyards and building a practical, efficient cellar. His Carmignano '99, which is a very good, though not remarkably complex wine, represents just one step along the path to future excellence.

● Carmignano '99	🍷🍷 5

Vinca
Via Candia Bassa 27/bis
tel. 0585834217
54033 Carrara (MS)

Vinca wines did very well indeed. The excellent Vermentino '00 is a full-bodied white with clearly defined aromas. The Gialosguardo is a simple but enjoyable merlot with a good structure. The Candia is correct.

○ Vermentino Vinca '00	🍷🍷 4
○ Candia dei Colli Apuani '00	🍷 4
● Gialosguardo '00	🍷 4

Enrico Santini
Loc. Campo alla Casa, 74
57022 Castagneto Carducci (LI)
tel. 0565774375

This young Bolgheri producer is making his debut with the 2000 vintage. His two basic wines already show that the estate will be aiming high. The Poggio al Moro came within an inch of a second Glass.

○ Bolgheri Bianco Campo della Casa '00	🍷 3
● Bolgheri Rosso Poggio al Moro '00	🍷 3

Parmoleto
Loc. Montenero d'Orcia
Strada Prov.le Cipressino Km. 14
58033 Castel del Piano (GR)
tel. 0564954131

Parmoleto presented only one wine but it was enough to make a good showing. It is a sangiovese that offers depth of structure but whose nose needs some fine-tuning.

● Montecucco Sangiovese '99	4

Perazzeta
Loc. Montenero d'Orcia
Via Grandi
58033 Castel del Piano (GR)
Tel. 0564954065

Perazzeta is one of the most dynamic estates in the Montecucco zone and is beginning to show signs of interestingly good quality, although there is still room for improvement. We were particularly struck by the Alfeno '00, a meaty and fruity wine that almost wrested Two Glasses from the panel.

• Montecucco Alfeno '00	🍷	4
• Montecucco Sangiovese '00	🍷	3
• Lupinello '00		3

Castagnoli
Loc. Castagnoli
53011 Castellina in Chianti (SI)
Tel. 0577740446

We liked the Castagnoli Syrah best. It has a well-defined nose of pepper, plum and spice, combined with excellent length. The Chianti '98 is a bit forward but fair to good. The Merlot is straightforward but very drinkable.

• Syrah '98	🍷🍷	5
• Chianti Cl. '97	🍷	4
• Merlot '98	🍷	5

Gagliole
Loc. Gagliole, 42
53011 Castellina in Chianti (SI)
Tel. 0577740369
E-mail: gagliole@tin.it

Thomas Bar puts his all into one wine, the Gagliole, a sangiovese with a small amount of cabernet. It is still a young wine but shows a good tannic weave and nicely gauged alcoholic strength.

• Gagliole Rosso '99	🍷🍷	5

La Castellina
Via Ferruccio, 26
53011 Castellina in Chianti (SI)
Tel. 0577740454
E-mail: lacastellinasas@tin.it

The Aureo '99, a blend of sangiovese, cabernet and merlot, is very good. It has nice balance but a faint vegetal note as well. The fair Chianti '99 is fruity and agreeable, if a bit short. The Reale '97 is acceptable, although forward.

• Aureo '99	🍷🍷	5
• Reale '97	🍷	4
• Chianti Classico '99	🍷	4

Castello La Leccia
Loc. La Leccia
53011 Castellina in Chianti (SI)
Tel. 0577743148
E-mail: laleccia@chianticlassico.com

This was not the best year for Francesco Daddi's estate. The Chianti '99 did very well, displaying energy, depth and the classic tension on the palate of the sangiovese grape. The Riserva was less impressive, because of distinct signs of reduction on the nose.

• Chianti Cl. '99	🍷🍷	4
• Chianti Cl. Ris. '98		4

Castello di Lilliano
Loc. Lilliano
53011 Castellina in Chianti (SI)
Tel. 0577743070

This is one of the estates that have contributed most to the reputation of Chianti Classico. In general, the wines show rich structure and loads of character. The most distinguished of their various bottles is the Anagallis '99, a blend of sangiovese and colorino.

• Anagallis '99	🍷🍷	6
• Chianti Cl. '99	🍷	4
• Vigna Catena '99	🍷	5

Poggio al Sorbo
Loc. Poggio al Sorbo
53001 Castellina in Chianti (SI)
Tel. 0577749731
E-mail: poggioalsorbo.c@tin.it

There is no really outstanding wine this year but the general impression is favourable. The Chianti '99 came close to getting Two Glasses, as did the Riserva '97. They are stylistically correct wines which are well-made and attractively expressive of the sangiovese grape.

● Chianti Classico Ris. '97	🍷	4
● Chianti Classico Ris. '98	🍷	4
● Chianti Classico '99	🍷	4

Poggio Amorelli
Loc. Poggio Amorelli
53011 Castellina in Chianti (SI)
Tel. 0571668733 - 03483954884
E-mail: poggioamorelli@libero.it

Good signs emerged from our tastings. The Chianti Classico is extremely successful. Its concentration and balance are admirable and the oak is well judged. It just needs a bit more personality. The Oracolo has a less well-defined nose.

● Chianti Cl. '99	🍷🍷	4
● Oracolo '99	🍷	5

Rodano
Loc. Rodano, 84
53011 Castellina in Chianti (SI)
Tel. 0577743107

The wines from Rodano this year showed definite notes of reduction. Is it just a temporary glitch? Perhaps, but only the Monna Claudia overcame it at our tasting with a powerful, concentrated and satisfyingly long palate.

● Monna Claudia '97	🍷🍷	5
● Chianti Cl. Viacosta Ris. '97		4

Villa Rosa
Loc. Villa Rosa
53011 Castellina in Chianti (SI)
Tel. 0577743003

The two Chiantis from Villa Rosa were distinguished by the super-ripe tones of their aromas. The Chianti '99 was much more successful: it may not be extremely elegant, but it's powerful and vigorous.

● Chianti Cl. '99	🍷🍷	4
● Chianti Cl. Ris. '97		4

Villa Trasqua
Loc. Trasqua
53001 Castellina in Chianti (SI)
Tel. 0577743047

We were not entirely won over by this year's offerings from this Chianti estate. The Chianti Classicos rather poorly focused on the nose. But we were surprised by the Trasgaia '95, which showed remarkable concentration and persistence.

● Trasgaia '95	🍷🍷	4

Caiano
Loc. Caiano
53019 Castelnuovo Berardenga (SI)
Tel. 0577355244

The Chianti Riserva is admirably consistent, the tannins are lively, the palate flavoursome and the balance is good. The Chianti '99 is a tad simpler but shows fairly solid structure, underpinned by firm tannins, and then a well-balanced finish.

● Chianti Classico Ris. '98	🍷🍷	4
● Chianti Classico '99	🍷	4

Fattoria di Dievole
Fraz. Vagliagli - Loc. Dievole
53019 Castelnuovo Berardenga (SI)
Tel. 0577322613 - 0577322712
E-mail: dievole@iol.it

We were not very excited by Dievole's wines this year. They are correct and well-executed but lack personality. The Broccato is rather forward and the Riserva '97, despite its good body, is over-oaked.

● Chianti Cl. Ris. '97	5
● Broccato '98	5

Le Trame
Loc. Podere Le Bonce
53019 Castelnuovo Berardenga (SI)
Tel. 0577359116
E-mail: gmorganti@nettuno.it

Giovanna Morganti gets only a brief review because she produces only one wine. But it is true nonetheless that her Chianti continues to be excellent, faithful to its terroir, and absolutely typical of its category.

● Chianti Classico Le Trame '98	4

Pacina
Loc. Pacina
53019 Castelnuovo Berardenga (SI)
Tel. 0577355044 - 0577355037

Giovanna Tiezzi's estate at the edge of the Chianti Classico zone produces just two wines. The Malena, a blend of sangiovese and syrah, displays a fruity fragrance and excellent tannins. The Chianti is an appealingly typical and vibrant sangiovese.

● Chianti Colli Senesi '98	4
● Malena '98	4

La Pievuccia
Loc. Santa Lucia, 118
52043 Castiglion Fiorentino (AR)
Tel. 0575651007
E-mail: info@lapievuccia.it

The Vin Santo '96 is the best of the range presented by La Pievuccia. It's a concentrated, characterful wine with scents of walnut, almond and dried fig. The Chianti '99, on the other hand, seems a bit flat and forward.

○ Vin Santo '96	4

Fattoria di Petriolo
Via di Petriolo, 7
50050 Cerreto Guidi (FI)
Tel. 0571509491

This is a successful debut. Villa Petriolo's wines are decidedly modern in style, offering lots of fruit, softness and concentration. The Golpaja, from sangiovese and merlot, is very good indeed and not without elegance.

● Golpaja '99	4
● Chianti Villa Petriolo '00	2*

Fattoria di Fiano
Loc. Fiano
Via di Firenze, 11
50050 Certaldo (FI)
Tel. 0571669048

Ugo Bing's range of wines is definitely interesting. The Fianesco displays lots of lovely fruit on the nose with light vegetal hints, and a soft, full-bodied palate. The finish that is slightly held back by tannins. The two Chiantis are equally good.

● Fianesco '99	4
● Chianti Colli Fiorentini '99	2*
● Chianti Colli Fiorentini Ris. '99	4

Ficomontanino
Loc. Ficomontanino
53043 Chiusi (SI)
tel. 057821180
e-mail: luca.giannelli2@tin.it

Ficomontanino has again presented good wines. The outstanding one, as usual, is the monovarietal cabernet sauvignon, the Lucumone, an elegant and well-balanced, if rather grassy, wine. The nicely executed Chianti Tutulus boasts attractive texture.

● Lucumone '99	🍷🍷 5
● Chianti Colli Senesi Tutulus '99	🍷 4

Il Palagione
Via per Castel San Gimignano, 36
53030 Colle di Val d'Elsa (SI)
tel. 0577953134

The two wines presented by this recently established winery are sufficient to show that they know what they're about. Planning carefully for the future, the owners already have about ten hectares under vine: six are planted to red varieties, the rest to vernaccia.

● Chianti Colli Senesi '00	🍷 3
○ Vernaccia di S. Gimignano '00	🍷 3

Frascole
Via di Frascole, 27
50062 Dicomano (FI)
tel. 0558386340

The most striking of the wines from this Rufina estate is the Vin Santo '93. Very sweet and mouthfilling, it lacks a little balance on the nose, which offers notes of chestnut and crème brulée. The Chianti Rufina '99 doesn't perform at all badly, either.

○ Vin Santo del Chianti Rufina '93	🍷🍷 5
● Chianti Rufina '99	🍷 2*

Fattoria di Piazzano
Via di Piazzano, 5
50053 Empoli (FI)
tel. 0571999044 - 0571994032
e-mail: fattoriadipiazzano@libero.it

Piazzano needs still to make a decisive leap forward but results are, on the whole, satisfactory. The Vin Santo almost got Two Glasses but there was no "almost" about the Chianti Riserva '98, which has concentration and good tannic density.

● Chianti Ris. '98	🍷🍷 4
○ Vin Santo '91	🍷 5
● Chianti Rio Camerata '00	2

Fossi
Loc. Signa - Via Privata Fossi
50058 Firenze
tel. 0558732174
e-mail: agrifossi@libero.it

Enrico Fossi's wines flaunt solid structure, power and concentration. Their weaker points are finesse and correctness of execution. The eloquent, original Malbec '99 is undeniably very good, though.

● Malbec '99	🍷🍷 5

Marchesi Torrigiani
Loc. Vico d'Elsa
P.zza Torrigiani, 15
50050 Firenze
tel. 0558073001 e-mail: az.torri@tin.it

The general renovation under way at this estate is showing its first tangible results. The Guidaccio '99 is a solid, concentrated wine, nicely underpinned by oak. The very interesting Torre di Ciardo picked up Two Glasses.

● Guidaccio '99	🍷🍷 5
● Torre di Ciardo '99	🍷 4

Pasolini Dall'Onda
P.zza Mazzini, 10
50021 Firenze
Tel. 0558075019
E-mail: info@pasolinidallonda.com

The extensive Pasolini dall'Onda estate generally produces a wide range of decently made wines. Of the bottles we tasted, we admired the Chardonnay Le Macchie and the respectable, fairly substantial San Zenobi.

○ Cardonnay Le Macchie '98	🍷🍷	4
● San Zenobi '97	🍷	4
● Chianti Cl. Badia a Sicelle '99	🍷	3

Podere Lavandaro
Via Rocca, 1
54035 Fosdinovo (MS)
Tel. 018768202

Something's on the move in Lunigiana. Vermentino is the unchallenged champion amongst white grapes while the Vignanera, a blend of sangiovese and merlot, is a worthwhile red. The Masero, with its attractive aromatic character, is also making a name for itself.

○ Masero '99	🍷🍷	4
● Vignanera '98	🍷	4
● Vignanera '99	🍷	4
○ Vermentino dei Colli di Luni '00		4

Podere Terenzuola
Via Vercalda, 14
54035 Fosdinovo (MS)
Tel. 018768943 - 03332607077
E-mail: podereterenzuola@interfree.it

When Ivan Giuliani releases the red wine he has tucked away in his cellar, we shall dedicate a full profile to him. Meanwhile, his Fosso di Corsano continues to do well, even if the '00 seems less expressive than usual.

○ Colli di Luni Vermentino Fosso di Corsano '00	🍷🍷	5

Castello di Cacchiano
Fraz. Monti in Chianti
Loc. Cacchiano
53010 Gaiole in Chianti (SI)
Tel. 0577747018

Castello di Cacchiano presented only one wine this year, the Chianti Classico '99, which is good without being earth-shaking. It shows an admirable typicity but the palate is only medium-bodied, as is the finish.

● Chianti Cl. '99	🍷	4

Le Miccine
Loc. Miccine
53013 Gaiole in Chianti (SI)
Tel. 0577749526

Le Miccine's wines show fair depth but both reds suffer from a rather ill-defined nose. This is a pity, because it's clear that the grapes were very good.

● Chianti Cl. Don Alberto Ris. '97	🍷	4
● Chianti Cl. '99	🍷	3

Rietine
Loc. Rietine, 27
53013 Gaiole in Chianti (SI)
Tel. 0577738482 - 0577731110

The wines from Rietine gave a very encouraging performance this year. The very good Riserva '97 boasts elegance and a velvety tannic weave. The original, robust merlot-based Tiziano almost won Two Glasses. The Rietine Bianco is refreshing and agreeable.

● Chianti Cl. Ris. '97	🍷🍷	4
○ Rietine Bianco '00	🍷	3
● Tiziano '97	🍷	5

San Martino
Via B. Bandinelli, 13/17
53013 Gaiole in Chianti (SI)
Tel. 0577749517
E-mail: enotecamontagnani@si.technet.it

The Chianti Riserva '98 is a very good wine indeed. Rich in structure, dense and warm on the palate, starting with the attack. The aromas are crystal clear. The other San Martino wines are not on the same level, though. The Chianti '98 is thin and the Pian della Cava is cowed by its tannins.

Wine	Rating
Chianti Cl. Ris. '98	ŶŶ 4
Pian della Cava '98	Ŷ 4
Chianti Cl. '98	3

Fattoria Valtellina
Fraz. Rietine - Loc. Valtellina, 47
53013 Gaiole in Chianti (SI)
Tel. 0577731005
E-mail: info@fattoria-valtellina.com

This is a serious estate that can turn out excellent wines at times but is somewhat inconsistent. The Chianti Riserva '98, for example, is very good but we were less struck by the Convivio, with its super-ripe timbre, or by the hardly acceptable Chianti '99.

Wine	Rating
Chianti Cl. Ris. '98	ŶŶ 4
Convivio '98	Ŷ 6

Le Piagge
Loc. Le Piagge
S. Maria a Chianni, 70
50050 Gambassi Terme (FI)
Tel. 0571638851

This youthful Florentine estate presented just one wine, a really enjoyable, well-made, clean and fruit-rich Chianti. Of course, it is a very straightforward wine but it came close to winning Two Glasses.

Wine	Rating
Chianti '00	Ŷ 2*

La Doccia
Via Casole, 56
50022 Greve in Chianti (FI)
Tel. 0558549049 - 0558547071

For some years now, this minuscule estate in Lamole has been producing a Chianti Classico that rarely disappoints. The Riserva '97 makes a good showing, too. It has a substantial palate and good tannic grip, but also faint signs of forwardness.

Wine	Rating
Chianti Cl. Ris. '97	ŶŶ 5

La Madonnina - Triacca
Loc. Strada in Chianti
V.lo Abate, 1
50027 Greve in Chianti (FI)
Tel. 055858003 E-mail: info@triacca.com

This large estate – 100 hectares under vine – has not managed in recent years to pull itself up to a higher level. The wines are well made, but they need more fruit and energy.

Wine	Rating
Chianti Cl. V. La Palaia '98	Ŷ 4
Il Mandorlo '98	Ŷ 4
Chianti Cl. Ris. '98	4
Chianti Classico Bello Stento '99	4

Savignola Paolina
Via Petriolo, 58
50022 Greve in Chianti (FI)
Tel. 055853139
E-mail: savignola@ftbcc.IT

This was a satisfactory performance, with the odd hiccough. The most successful wine was the Riserva '98, which came very close to winning Two Glasses: robust, concentrated, appealingly tannic. The Granaio '98 is a bit forward but fair; the Granaio '99, well-ordered but light.

Wine	Rating
Chianti Cl. Ris. '98	Ŷ 4
Granaio '98	Ŷ 5
Granaio '99	Ŷ 5
Chianti Cl. '99	4

Torraccia di Presura
Loc. Strada in Chianti
Via della Montagnola, 130
50027 Greve in Chianti (FI)
Tel. 0558588656 - 055490563

The consistently good wines from La Torraccia di Presura usually show solid structure, not always accompanied by commensurate elegance. The Riserva '98 just made it into the Two Glass category.

● Chianti Cl. Il Tarocco '98	▼▼ 4
● Lucciolaio '97	▼ 5
● Chianti Cl. Il Tarocco '99	▼ 4

Villa Buonasera
Loc. La Panca - Via Cintoia Alta, 32
50027 Greve in Chianti (FI)
Tel. 0558547932
E-mail: info@villabuonasera.it

Barbara Schwenniger is the owner of this Chianti estate, which has eight hectares under vine. The Chianti Casa Eri did brilliantly at our tastings. It's an enjoyable, invigorating and nicely balanced wine.

● Chianti Cl. Casa Eri '97	▼▼ 4
● Chianti Cl. Ris. '97	4

Villa Calcinaia
Via Citille, 84
50022 Greve in Chianti (FI)
Tel. 055854008
E-mail: villacalcinaia@villacalcinaia.it

The wines from Villa Calcinaia are well enough made but could do with more distinctive character. The merlot-based Casarsa is faintly vegetal on the nose and shows only medium body. The other wines were less challenging.

● Casarsa '98	▼ 5
● Chianti Cl. Ris. '98	▼ 3
● Chianti Cl. '99	▼ 4

Villa Casale
Loc. Greti
50022 Greve in Chianti (FI)
Tel. 0558544859

This small estate has little more than three hectares under vine. The wines are not, at the moment, altogether consistent in quality and share a distinct note of oak. The most successful is the Chianti La Cappella '99, which boasts excellent concentration.

● Chianti Classico La Cappella '99 ▼▼	4
● Chianti Classico '99	4

I Campetti
Loc. Casa Campetti - Fraz. Ribolla
Via della Collacchia, 2
58027 Grosseto
Tel. 0564579663

Yet again, the white Almabruna, made from viognier, is the best wine from this Maremma estate. It has lots going for it on nose and palate. The only other interesting offering is the red Baccio.

○ Almabruna '00	▼▼ 4
● Montereggio di Massa Marittima Rosso Baccio '98	▼ 4

Santa Lucia
Fraz. Fonteblanda
Via Aurelia Nord, 66
58010 Grosseto
Tel. 0564885474 - E-mail: az.santalucia@tin.it

There may not be any absolutely fantastic wines among those presented by Santa Lucia but the general quality is encouragingly high. We were favourably impressed by the Capalbio Rosso Losco '00, which is whistle-clean and decently structured. All the other wines are pleasing.

○ Ansonica Costa dell'Argentario '00	▼ 3
● Capalbio Rosso Losco '00	▼ 3
● Betto '99	▼ 4

Fattoria Collazzi
Loc. Tavarnuzze
Via Colleramole, 101
50029 Impruneta (FI)
tel. 0552022528

This is the first release of the Collazzi, a blend of cabernet and merlot. It is a wine worth watching because even on its debut it showed extremely well, revealing remarkable concentration and excellent balance.

● Collazzi '99	ΨΨ	5

Fattoria di Bagnolo
Via Imprunetana per Tavarnuzze, 48
50023 Impruneta (FI)
tel. 0552313403

Things are changing in the Colli Fiorentini. Fattoria di Bàgnolo is showing signs of having well-justified ambitions. The Caprorosso stands out for its dense structure. The other wines are fair: the Chianti '99 is fresh and fruity; the Riserva is somewhat old-fashioned but perfectly respectable.

● Caprorosso '99	ΨΨ	4
● Chianti Colli Fiorentini Ris. '98	Ψ	3
● Chianti Colli Fiorentini '99	Ψ	2*

Fattoria Le Querce
Via Imprunetana per Tavarnuzze, 41
50023 Impruneta (FI)
tel. 0552011380

Considerable progress has been made at Le Querce, which presented two straightforward but good wines. The Chianti La Torretta is remarkably dense, and very redolent of oak. The Sorrettole is more direct.

● Chianti Colli Fiorentini La Torretta '00	ΨΨ	3*
● Chianti Colli Fiorentini Sorrettole '00	Ψ	3

Cecilia
Loc. La Pila
57034 Livorno
tel. 0565977322 - 024989864
e-mail: gcamerini@tin.it

This estate on the isle of Elba, which for some years has been preparing itself for a quality quantum leap, presented a fair range of wines. The Riserva '98 is quite good, still a bit uncertain but characterful.

○ Elba Bianco '00	Ψ	3
● Elba Rosso Ris. '98	Ψ	4
● Aleatico dell'Elba '99	Ψ	5

Tenuta Il Borro
Fraz. San Giustino Valdarno
Loc. Il Borro, 1
52020 Loro Ciuffenna (AR)
tel. 055977864

The vintage released is the first one produced by the Ferragamo family estate and it was a most encouraging debut. The Borro '99, a Bordeaux blend, is a fine red that already has a distinctive personality of its own.

● Il Borro '99	ΨΨ	6

Cohens Gervais
Loc. Massa Macinaia
55100 Lucca
tel. 058390431

This splendid villa in Massa Macinaia includes a gem of a mini-vineyard planted to international varieties: cabernet and merlot for their red, Tempietto, and chardonnay and sauvignon for the Sorbus, a white with a fleshy, exotic flavour and attractive personality.

○ Sorbus '99	ΨΨ	5
● Tempietto '98	Ψ	5

Valle del Sole
Loc. La Cappella
55100 Lucca
Tel. 0583395093

Surprises will never end! The Ebrius, at its debut performance, did beautifully. The fragrance includes scents of dark berry fruit, leather and earth, as well as mineral tones. The palate is soft-textured and dense.

● Ebrius '99	4

Malfatti
Loc. Colle di Lupo
58051 Magliano in Toscana (GR)
Tel. 0564592535

This is the first release of wines from this estate and it has started off with a winner: a Morellino with solid structure, lots of very ripe fruit and toasty hints of oak on the nose followed by a soft, mouthfilling flavour.

● Morellino di Scansano '99	3*

Podere Scurtarola
Via dell'Uva, 3
54100 Massa
Tel. 0585833523 - 0585831560
E-mail: lorieri@tin.it

The wines from Scurtarola have a definite, distinctly traditional character. Their style is very much their own, which all to the good. We particularly enjoyed the admirable Brut and the original Candia.

○ Candia dei Colli Apuani '00	4
○ Brut Scurtarola	4

Fattoria Coliberto
Fraz. Valpiana - Loc. Coliberto
58024 Massa Marittima (GR)
Tel. 0566919039 - 0566919337
E-mail: az.agr.az.coliberto@libero.it

Coliberto is one of the estates in the Monteregio DOC zone that are making a name for themselves. The red Thesan, in particular, is very good, with its concentration and intense aromas of black cherry, toasty oak and black pepper. The other wines are correct and show good weight.

● Monteregio di Massa Marittima Rosso Thesan '98	5
● Monteregio di Massa Marittima Rosso '00	3
● Monteregio di Massa Marittima Ris. '98	4

Castelli Martinozzi
Loc. Villa S. Restituta
53024 Montalcino (SI)
Tel. 057784856

Here's a very promising newcomer! Castelli Martinozzi is located in one of the most sought-after areas of Montalcino. Their intense and clean Rosso is among the best of its vintage. And the Brunello shows outstanding balance.

● Rosso di Montalcino '99	4
● Brunello di Montalcino '96	5

Centolani
Loc. Friggiali - Strada Maremmana
53024 Montalcino (SI)
Tel. 0577849314 - 0577849454
E-mail: agricolacentolani@libero.it

Friggiali has long been a name to conjure with in Montalcino. The wines are always good but so far there have been no great ones. The best this time are the Brunello '96 and the Riserva '95, both of which came close to winning Two Glasses.

● Brunello di Montalcino Friggiali Pietranera Vigna della Sughera Ris. '95	6
● Brunello di Montalcino Friggiali Pietranera '96	6

Coldisole
Loc. I Verbi
53024 Montalcino (SI)
tel. 0577355789

The Coldisole estate presented us with a memorable Brunello '96. It may not be very eloquent on the nose but it drives along confidently on the palate. The attack is powerful and nicely underpinned by tannins, and the mid palate is full-bodied.

● Brunello di Montalcino '96	🍷🍷 5
● Rosso di Montalcino '99	4

Tenuta di Collosorbo
Loc. Villa a Sesta, 25
53020 Montalcino (SI)
tel. 0577835534

A disappointing Brunello and a really good Rosso: that, in a nutshell, is what we found at the Tenuta di Collosorbo. There are super-ripe notes on the nose of the Rosso '99 but the palate is powerful, revealing solid tannins and a long finish.

● Rosso di Montalcino '99	🍷🍷 4
● Brunello di Montalcino '96	6

Corte Pavone
Loc. Casanova
53024 Montalcino (SI)
tel. 0577848110
e-mail: lo@cker.it

Corte Pavone turned out two good wines that show lots of grip on the palate. The use of wood, however, seems a little less than skilful, and the oak in the Rosso is almost aggressive. But these are defects that can be overcome.

● Brunello di Montalcino '96	🍷 5
● Rosso di Montalcino '99	🍷 4

Due Portine - Gorelli
Via Cialdini, 51/53
53024 Montalcino (SI)
tel. 0577848098

As usual, Giuseppe Gorelli's wines are well made. Their distinctive style is based on balance and elegance, rather than power, and the use of oak is well judged. The Brunello '96 is docile and harmonious; the Rosso '99 is more expressive and lively.

● Rosso di Montalcino Le Potazzine '99	🍷🍷 5
● Brunello di Montalcino '96	🍷 6

Fornacina
Podere Fornacina, 153
53024 Montalcino (SI)
tel. 0577848464

This little Montalcino estate produced a good performance that also promises well for the future. The outstanding wine is their very fine Brunello Riserva '95, with rich aromas of liquorice, jam and spice and good structure as well. The other wines are also well-made.

● Brunello di Montalcino Ris. '95	🍷🍷 6
● Brunello di Montalcino '96	🍷 6
● Rosso di Montalcino '99	🍷 4

Il Marroneto
Loc. Madonna delle Grazie
53024 Montalcino (SI)
tel. 0577849382 - 0577846075
e-mail: ilmarroneto@ftbcc.it

The hectare and a half of vineyard at Alessandro Mori's estate is dedicated to only one wine, a Brunello of course. The '96 offers earthy tones of underbrush, earth and leather. The flavour is supple and balanced, but a little hard on the finish.

● Brunello di Montalcino '96	🍷 6

Il Palazzone
Loc. Due Porte, 245
53024 Montalcino (SI)
Tel. 0577847080 - 0577849375

The wines from Il Palazzone are somewhat puzzling: the aromas leave room for improvement while the structure is imposing. This applies to the Riserva '95 as well, which has a very successful palate, solid and well-balanced.

- Brunello di Montalcino Ris. '95 — 6
- Brunello di Montalcino '96 — 6
- Rosso di Montalcino '99 — 4

La Fiorita
Loc. Castelnuovo dell'Abate
Piaggia della Porta, 3
53024 Montalcino (SI)
Tel. 0577835521 E-mail: lafiorita@tiscalinet.it

This small estate has presented excellent wines in the recent past. The '96 vintage offered little opportunity to shine but the Brunello is well-made, clean and balanced.

- Brunello di Montalcino '96 — 6
- Laurus '98 — 4

La Fornace
Podere Fornace, 154/a
53024 Montalcino (SI)
Tel. 0577848465 - 03485181644
E-mail: lafornace@tin.it

La Fornace is a modestly sized estate which has been producing very fine wines with increasing frequency. The Riserva '95 is well-balanced and soft; the Brunello '96 is disappointing; and the Rosso '99 very nearly won Two Glasses.

- Brunello di Montalcino Ris. '95 — 6
- Rosso di Montalcino '99 — 4
- Brunello di Montalcino '96 — 6

Tenuta La Fuga
Loc. Camigliano
53024 Montalcino (SI)
Tel. 0577816039
E-mail: tenutalafuga@tin.it

The small Tenuta La Fuga estate produces good reds in the southern part of Montalcino. The wines are of a consistent quality, with the exception of the standard-label Brunello '96, which is less well-defined on the nose than the Riserva '95 and the good Rosso '99.

- Brunello di Montalcino Ris. '95 — 6
- Rosso di Montalcino '99 — 4
- Brunello di Montalcino '96 — 6

La Lecciaia
Loc. Vallafrico
53024 Montalcino (SI)
Tel. 0577849287
E-mail: lecciaia@pacinimauro.com

In recent years, La Lecciaia has produced wines that were neither very good nor particularly bad. This time, however, the Riserva '95 struck us as very successful, thanks to its remarkable structure.

- Rosso di Montalcino Ris. '95 — 6
- Il Baccanale '97 — 5

La Serena
Loc. Podere Rasa I°, 133
53024 Montalcino (SI)
Tel. 0577848659

The wines from La Serena have been attracting notice for a few years. What they need now is a greater consistency throughout the range. The Rosso '99 was adjudged very good by the panel.

- Rosso di Montalcino '99 — 4
- Brunello di Montalcino '96 — 5

Le Chiuse
Loc. Pullera, 228
53024 Montalcino (SI)
Tel. 0577848595 - 055597052
E-mail: n.magnelli@infinito.it

The Riserva '95 has a rounded, full flavour. The nose of the Brunello '96 is not very clear-cut but things look up on the palate, with its enjoyable tannic texture. The nose of the Rosso '99 is pleasing but the palate is rather lightweight.

● Brunello di Montalcino Ris. '95	▼▼	6
● Brunello di Montalcino '96	▼	6
● Rosso di Montalcino '99	▼	4

Le Gode di Ripaccioli
Loc. Le Gode
53024 Montalcino (SI)
Tel. 0577847089

Only two wines were presented and both did well. The Brunello '96 takes pride of place with its solid, meaty, deep palate. The nose is also good, and not without complexity. The Rosso is simpler but still enjoyable.

● Brunello di Montalcino '96	▼▼	6
● Rosso di Montalcino '99	▼	4

Cantina di Montalcino
Loc. Val di Cava
53024 Montalcino (SI)
Tel. 0577848704
E-mail: info@cantinadimontalcino.it

Cantina di Montalcino produces reliable wines that could do with more personality. The best this time around was the Villa di Corsano '99, which is very good but also very 'technological', which is to say without any apparent connection to its terroir.

● Villa di Corsano '99	▼▼	5
● Brunello di Montalcino '96	▼	6

Tenute Silvio Nardi
Loc. Casale del Bosco
53024 Montalcino (SI)
Tel. 0577808269
E-mail: tenutenardi@tin.it

At Tenute Nardi, it's full steam ahead with the program of expansion and renovation. This year's tastings were not, however, quite up to expectations. The Brunello '96 is a correct, well-made and balanced wine, but not very eloquent.

● Brunello di Montalcino '96	▼	6
● Brunello di Montalcino '90	▼▼	5
● Brunello di Montalcino '93	▼▼	5
● Brunello di Montalcino Ris. '93	▼▼	5

Oliveto
Fraz. Castelnuovo dell'Abate
Loc. Oliveto
53020 Montalcino (SI)
Tel. 0577807170 - 0577835542

Oliveto could be said to be a small estate with a big future. They have not yet presented a Brunello, but judging from the Rosso, we can expect something really remarkable. The Leccio '99 did well, too, and in fact almost got Two Glasses.

● Rosso di Montalcino Il Roccolo '99	▼▼	5
● Il Leccio '99	▼	5

Pian delle Vigne
Loc. Pian delle Vigne
53024 Montalcino (SI)
Tel. 0577816066

The Antinori-group Brunello again shows admirable quality and style. Tertiary aromas have the upper hand in the bouquet, and the flavour is pleasing, well-ordered and attractively energetic.

● Brunello di Montalcino '96	▼▼	6

San Filippo - Rosi
Loc. San Filippo, 134
53024 Montalcino (SI)
Tel. 0577848705

San Filippo, which had made quite a name for itself with its wines from the 1980s, is back again with a successful range. Three of the wines are worthy of the estate's reputation, and one, the Brunello '96, is particularly good.

● Brunello di Montalcino '96	🍷🍷	6
● Brunello di Montalcino Ris. '95	🍷	6
● Rosiano '98	🍷	4

Talenti - Podere Pian di Conte
Fraz. Sant'Angelo in Colle
Loc. Pian di Conte, 98
53020 Montalcino (SI)
Tel. 0577844064 - E-mail: az.talenti@tin.it

Work has started on the winery's renovation. Signs are not yet forthcoming in the wines themselves but we should be seeing definite improvement by next year. Meanwhile, the Riserva '95 is an attractively rigorous exercise in style.

● Brunello di Montalcino Ris. '95	🍷	6
● Pian di Conte '99	🍷	4
● Brunello di Montalcino '96	🍷	6

Tornesi
Loc. Le Benducce, 207
53024 Montalcino (SI)
Tel. 0577848689

The average quality of wines from Montalcino is gradually improving. Further proof of this is provided by Tornesi, with two very successful wines. The Rosso is a well-conceived product with generous body. The Brunello '96 has good balance.

● Rosso di Montalcino '99	🍷🍷	4
● Brunello di Montalcino '96	🍷	6

Uccelliera
Fraz. Castelnuovo dell'Abate
Pod. Uccelliera, 45
53020 Montalcino (SI)
Tel. 0577835729

Andrea Cortonesi knows what he wants. In his wines, he strives to respect both terroir and vintage. And we have to admit that he pulls it off admirably, despite the fact that '96 was not a brilliant year.

● Rapace '98	🍷🍷	5
● Brunello di Montalcino '96	🍷	6
● Rosso di Montalcino '99	🍷	4

Verbena
Loc. Verbena, 100
53024 Montalcino (SI)
Tel. 0577848432

This little Montalcino estate is changing gear, as we noted when we tasted their latest wine, the firm-structured Rosso '99. The Brunello '96 is not bad, either.

● Rosso di Montalcino '99	🍷🍷	4
● Brunello di Montalcino '96	🍷	5

Vitanza
Podere Renaione, 291
53024 Montalcino (SI)
Tel. 0577846031 - 03479731898
E-mail: tenutavitanza@hotmail.com

The first wines presented by this compact, recently established estate are interesting and promise great things for the future. We were particularly impressed by the well-made, and equally well-balanced, Rosso '99.

● Rosoo di Montalcino '99	🍷🍷	4
● Brunello di Montalcino Ris. '95	🍷	6
● Brunello di Montalcino '96	🍷	6

GIACOMO MARENGO
FRAZ. CAPRAIA - LOC. PALAZZUOLO
52048 MONTE SAN SAVINO (AR)
TEL. 0575847083
E-MAIL: marengoe@tin.it

Giacomo Marengo presented the panel with an excellent wine but the rest of the range lags behind. The mostly cabernet-based Stroncoli '97 is warm and dense, with good complexity on the nose.

● Stroncoli '97	🍷🍷 5
● Chianti Castello di Rapale '97	3

MAZZINI FRANCESCHI
VIA ROMA, 12
55015 MONTECARLO (LU)
TEL. 058322010

Mazzini is no newcomer and has recently produced some very interesting wines, although a consistent range has yet to be assembled. The Rosso Casalta is a good red with depth, concentration and a shade too much oak.

● Montecarlo Rosso Casalta '99	🍷🍷 4
○ Montecarlo Bianco La Salita '00	🍷 4

FATTORIA DEL TESO
VIA POLTRONIERA
55015 MONTECARLO (LU)
TEL. 0583286288
E-MAIL: info@fattoriadelteso.com

We are beginning to see good results from the changes being made at this Montecarlo estate, although the star of the range is the Vin Santo '90. The other wines have all clearly moved up a step and are now denser and more expressive.

○ Vin Santo '90	🍷🍷 5
○ Montecarlo Bianco '00	🍷 2*
● Montecarlo Rosso '00	🍷 2*
● Montecarlo Rosso Anfidiamante '98	🍷 4

FATTORIA VIGNA DEL GREPPO
VIA DEL MOLINETTO, 24/25
55015 MONTECARLO (LU)
TEL. 058322593 - 0583276667
E-MAIL: info@fattoriavignadelgreppo.com

Commendator Virgilio Vettori deserves praise for the passionate care he has always dedicated to his vineyards. The Bianco di Napoleone made a very good showing, and the other wines we have listed are just as well-made and enjoyable.

○ Bianco di Napoleone '00	🍷 3
○ Montecarlo Bianco '00	🍷 2*
● Montecarlo Rosso Carlo IV Ris. '97	🍷 4

PODERE AIONE
LOC. AIONE
56040 MONTECATINI VAL DI CECINA (PI)
TEL. 058830339

The Aione '98 is a wine to keep in mind. It may not make an overwhelming impact on the nose, or on the palate, but it grows in intensity and finishes deliciously long.

● Aione '98	🍷🍷 4

CANNETO
VIA DEI CANNETI, 14
53045 MONTEPULCIANO (SI)
TEL. 0578758277
E-MAIL: canneto@dccmp.com

The signs from Canneto are generally positive. The wines, if not paragons of finesse, do show impressive structure. The Rosso '00 is successful, and the fair Nobile '98 is powerful and dense, albeit a bit sulphurous on the nose.

● Rosso di Montepulciano '00	🍷 2*
● Nobile di Montepulciano '98	🍷 4

Crociani
Via del Poliziano, 15
53045 Montepulciano (SI)
tel. 0578757919
e-mail: crocianig@bccmp.com

The Crociani wines are promising. The Nobile Riserva '97 impressed us with its rich bouquet and dense flavour. The Nobile '98 offers super-ripe notes on the nose and good body.

● Nobile di Montepulciano Ris. '97	♛	4
● Nobile di Montepulciano '98	♛	4

Ercolani
S. S. per Chianciano, 146
53045 Montepulciano (SI)
tel. 0578716764 - 0578788711

We were very pleasantly surprised by the wines presented by this young Montepulciano producer. The Nobile '98 shows good body and careful execution, the Rosso '00 is balanced and enjoyable and the Chianti is upfront and clean. A very encouraging range.

● Nobile di Montepulciano '98	♛♛	4
● Chianti Colli Senesi '00	♛	2*
● Rosso di Montepulciano '00		3

Fanetti - Tenuta S. Agnese
Via Antica Chiusina, 15
53045 Montepulciano (SI)
tel. 0578716716 - 0578757266

The Fanetti wines are a bit old-fashioned. The fruit is understated and the tannins tend towards astringency. This is all true of the Riserva '97, which is, however, also admirable for its personality. The decent Vin Santo '87 avoids excessive sweetness.

○ Vin Santo '87	♛	5
● Nobile di Montepulciano Ris. '97	♛	4

Agricola Gavioli
Loc. Argiano
Via delle Tre Berte
53042 Montepulciano (SI)
tel. 057863995

The Gavioli Brut is well-conceived and rather good – fresh, clean and balanced. The Nobile '98 also appealed to the panel with its balanced, medium-bodied palate and clear-cut fragrance. The Riserva '97 is rather forward.

● Nobile di Montepulciano '98	♛	4
○ Gavioli Brut	♛	4
● Nobile di Montepulciano Ris. '97		4

Podere Le Berne
Loc. Cervognano
Via Poggio Golo, 7
53040 Montepulciano (SI)
tel. 0578767328

The Le Berne wines show considerable potential but still vary considerably. The Nobile '98 reveals notable structure, character and austere tannins. The Riserva is pleasing but somewhat forward. The Rosso '00, which is thin and not very clean, needs some serious rethinking.

● Nobile di Montepulciano '98	♛♛	4
● Nobile di Montepulciano Ris. '97	♛	4
● Rosso di Montepulciano '00		2

Fattoria Le Casalte
Loc. S. Albino
Via del Termine, 2
53045 Montepulciano (SI)
tel. 0578799138 - 069323090

No wine from Le Casalte managed to win Two Glasses but the Nobile '98 came very close, thanks to its excellent balance and attractive tannic texture. The Riserva '97 is a bit forward but stylish.

○ Celius '00	♛	2
● Nobile di Montepulciano Ris. '97	♛	4
● Nobile di Montepulciano '98	♛	4
● Rosso di Montepulciano '00		3

Lodola Nuova - Tenimenti Ruffino
Loc. Valiano
Via Lodola, 1
53045 Montepulciano (SI)
tel. 0578724032

This estate is part of Tenimenti Ruffino, and its wines are very carefully made, but could do with more personality. The Nobile '98 is a little vegetal but well-balanced, the Rosso Alauda no more than acceptable.

● Rosso di Montepulciano Alàuda '00	2
● Nobile di Montepulciano '98	4

Eredi Antonino Lombardo
Fraz. Gracciano - Via Umbria, 59
53040 Montepulciano (SI)
tel. 0578708321
e-mail: cantina.lombardo@iol.it

Lombardo produces a reliably consistent range. Usually, there are no poor wines but neither is there anything particularly characterful. This time, the Riserva '97 stands out for density and harmony.

● Nobile di Montepulciano Ris. '97	4
● Nobile di Montepulciano '98	4
● Rosso di Montepulciano '00	2

Palazzo Vecchio
Loc. Valiano
Via Terrarossa, 5
53040 Montepulciano (SI)
tel. 0578724170 - e-mail: marcosbernadori@tin.it

This historic Montepulciano estate did very well this year. The intense, well-balanced and lingering Nobile Riserva '97 is very good. The Nobile '98 is interesting as well: the nose is a bit vegetal but the finish on the palate is unreserved and convincing.

● Nobile di Montepulciano Ris. '97	4
● Nobile di Montepulciano '98	4
● Nobile di Montepulciano '91	4
● Nobile di Montepulciano Ris. '90	4

Massimo Romeo
Loc. Nottola di Gracciano
Via di Totona, 29
53045 Montepulciano (SI)
tel. 0578757127

Massimo Romeo is trying to establish a style of his own, an admirable ambition. His Nobile Riserva, which has the classic characteristics of the sangiovese grape, is a bit pale in colour but shows good balance in the mouth. The other wines we tasted seemed a little forward.

● Nobile di Montepulciano Ris. dei Mandorli '97	5
● Lipitiresco '98	6
● Nobile di Montepulciano '98	4

Suveraia
Loc. Bacucco
58025 Monterotondo Marittimo (GR)
tel. 0566910106

The Bacucco is a very fine red, with flavoursome tannins and solid body. The oak is perhaps slightly out of control but this is a problem that can – and should – be dealt with in the future.

● Monteregio di Massa Marittima Bacucco Ris. '99	4
● Monteregio di Massa Marittima '00	3

Tenuta La Cipressaia
Loc. Montagnana Val di Pesa
Via Romita, 38
50025 Montespertoli (FI)
tel. 0571670868

La Cipressaia produces simple but well-crafted wines. The one that has most to offer is, we think, the Borgoricco. Without being outstanding, it can point to good structure and a well-focused nose. The Colli Fiorentini is succulent and enjoyable.

● Chianti Colli Fiorentini '00	3
● Borgoricco '99	4
● Chianti '00	3

Fattorie Parri
Via Ribaldaccio, 80
50025 Montespertoli (FI)
tel. 0571609154
e-mail: info@fattorieparri.it

Parri offered the panel a generous selection of wines, all honest and correct. The cabernet-based Le Bronche is the pick of the bunch. We also liked the Vin Santo, which is not too sweet.

● Le Bronche '96	ŸŸ	4
○ Vin Santo del Chianti Ris. '91	Ÿ	5
● Le Bronche '97	Ÿ	4
● Chianti Montespertoli '99	Ÿ	2*

Poggio Capponi
Fraz. Pulica - Via Montelupo, 184
50025 Montespertoli (FI)
tel. 0571671914
e-mail: poggiocapponi@dada.it

The range of wines is fairly wide, and so is the range of quality. The good Tinorso '99 is solid and concentrated but not remarkably elegant. The Chardonnay came within an inch of winning a second Two Glasses for the estate.

● Tinorso '99	ŸŸ	5
○ Chardonnay '00	Ÿ	4
● Chianti Montespertoli Petriccio '00	Ÿ	2

Fattoria Castello Sonnino
Via Volterrana Nord, 10
50025 Montespertoli (FI)
tel. 0571609198 - 0571657481
e-mail: sonnino@mbr.it

Barone De Renzis' winery is being overhauled with an eye to radical improvement. The wines presented this year are the product of a transitional phase, and not as good as they might otherwise have been.

○ Vin Santo del Chianti '97	Ÿ	5
● Sanleone '99	Ÿ	5

Fattoria di Rendola
Loc. Rendola, 85
52025 Montevarchi (AR)
tel. 0559707594

We do not feel that there has been any notable progress in recent years at this estate near Arezzo. The wines are fair but structure is not their strong suit and oak tends to take the upper hand. The Merlot has more grip than the rest of the range.

● L'Incanto '99	Ÿ	4
● Merlot '99	Ÿ	5
● La Pineta '99		4

Giovanna Giannaccini
Via Zeri, 13
54038 Montignoso (MS)
tel. 0585348305

This estate started up, almost by chance, in January 2000, so this is its very first vintage. To our amazement, the Vermentino is extremely good, as you can see from its Two Glasses.

○ Pagus '00	ŸŸ	3*

Varramista
Loc. Varramista
Fraz. Casteldelbosco - Via Ricavo, 31
56020 Montopoli in Val d'Arno (PI)
tel. 0571468121 - 0571468122

We have not taken away Varramista's full profile because of any lapse in quality. It is simply that the estate produced only one wine this year, and not much of that. However, the Varramista '99, made mostly from syrah, is a seriously good bottle.

● Varramista '99	ŸŸ	6

La Borsa
Loc. Casciano
53010 Murlo (SI)
Tel. 0577818002
E-mail: assfata@tiscali.net

Guido Pieralisi is the owner of this estate in the province of Siena. From his 22 hectares under vine, he produces two wines, a Chianti Superiore and Crevole, a monovarietal sangiovese. We tasted the latter and was more than promising; indeed it won Two Glasses.

● Crevole '99	🍷🍷	4

La Marcellina
Via Case Sparse, 74
50020 Panzano (FI)
Tel. 055852126
E-mail: marcellina@ftbcc.it

The range is inconsistent, with some good wines and others not worth uncorking. One good wine is the Camporosso '97, from sangiovese and cabernet, an energetic red with firm, if not particularly fine-grained, tannins. The Sassocupo is a little bitter.

● Camporosso '97	🍷🍷	5
● Chianti Classico Sassocupo '99	🍷	4

Vignole
Loc. La Massa - Via Case Sparse, 14
50022 Panzano (FI)
Tel. 0574592025 - 055852197
E-mail: vinisistri@tin.it

The wines we tasted were all decent, except for the Congius '98, which we liked a lot. Its nose is clean and multi-faceted, and the palate is admirably dense, if somewhat markedly oaky.

● Congius '98	🍷🍷	5
● Chianti Cl. Ris. '97	🍷	4
● Chianti Cl. '99	🍷	4

Il Vignale
Loc. Vignale Riotorto
57025 Piombino (LI)
Tel. 056520812

Il Vignale did surprisingly well this year. The Vermentino Campo degli Albicocchi is fragrant, well-rounded and persistent. The intense, concentrated and promising Vinivo almost got Two Glasses as well.

○ Val di Cornia Vermentino Campo degli Albicocchi '00	🍷🍷	3*
● Val di Cornia Rosso Vinivo '99	🍷	4

Cantina Cooperativa di Pitigliano
Loc. Vignagrande
58017 Pitigliano (GR)
Tel. 0564616133
E-mail: info@cantinadipitigliano.it

Things are changing at the Cantina di Pitigliano. The first sign is the Vignamurata '00, which displays intense, clean fruit and a broad flavour well supported by tannins. Who knows what wonders are to follow!

● Sovana Sup. Vignamurata '00	🍷🍷	4

Fattoria Ormanni
Loc. Ormanni, 1
53036 Poggibonsi (SI)
Tel. 0577937212

With just a bit more energy, the Ormanni wines – the two Chiantis in particular – would have picked up more Glassware. But basically this Poggibonsi estate again demonstrated its commitment, and the wines did well.

● Julius '99	🍷🍷	5
● Chianti Cl. Ris. '98	🍷	5
● Chianti Cl. '99	🍷	4

Fattoria Lavacchio
Via di Montefiesole, 55
50065 Pontassieve (FI)
Tel. 0558317472 - 0558396168
E-mail: agrlavac@ftbcc.it

Unusually for these parts, Lavacchio appears to favour its whites, which often do better than the correct but not very charactertful reds. The late-harvested Oro del Cedro, a Traminer, is fragrant and pleasing.

○ Oro del Cedro '00		4
● Cortigiano '98		4
● Chianti Rufina '99		3

Tenuta di Bossi
Loc. Bossi
Via dello Stracchino, 32
50065 Pontassieve (FI)
Tel. 0558317830

As usual, the star turn at Tenuta di Bossi is the Vin Santo. Other good wines are the two Chianti Rufina Riservas. We were a bit disappointed by the Mazzaferrata, a blend of sangiovese and cabernet with a rather noticeable grassy tone.

○ Vin Santo Rufina '96		5
● Chianti Rufina Villa di Bossi Ris. '97		4
● Chianti Rufina Ris. '98		4
● Mazzaferrata '97		4

Mola
Loc. Gelsarello, 2
57031 Porto Azzurro (LI)
Tel. 0565222089
E-mail: pavoletti@infol.it

The general level of Mola's wines is only just acceptable but the Aleatico is outstanding. A bouquet of black cherry and fresh spice is followed by a sweet, full-bodied, juicy flavour which is a shade tannic on the finish.

● Aleatico dell'Elba '99		5

Sapereta
Loc. Mola
Via Provinciale Ovest, 73
57036 Porto Azzurro (LI)
Tel. 056595033 E-mail: info@sapereonline.it

This greatly improved historic Elba estate gave us a delightful surprise. Their Moscato is really excellent, a sweet, fragrant and very flavoursome wine. The Aleatico and the Thea are both quite good as well.

○ Moscato dell'Elba '00		5
● Aleatico dell'Elba '00		5
● Elba Rosso Thea '00		4

Acquabona
Loc. Acquabona, 1
57037 Portoferraio (LI)
Tel. 0565933013
E-mail: acquabona.elba@tiscalinet.it

There are no faults to be found in these satisfactory wines but none of this year's range did stunningly well. The Voltraio made an interesting, if somewhat unpolished, debut.

○ Acquabona di Acquabona '00		4
● Aleatico dell'Elba '98		6
● Elba Rosso Ris. '98		4
● Voltraio '99		5

Tenuta La Chiusa
Loc. Magazzini, 93
57037 Portoferraio (LI)
Tel. 0565933046

Like many other estates on Elba, La Chiusa shows to greatest advantage in its Aleatico. The other wines presented were not particularly successful. The Aleatico '99 is extremely good: fragrant, sweet, persistent and well-balanced.

● Aleatico dell'Elba '99		5

Borgo Salcetino
Loc. Lucareli
53017 Radda in Chianti (SI)
Tel. 0577757173 - 0577733541

Borgo Salcetino is the Tuscan branch of the noted Friuli-based producer Livon. The wines are good but not yet in keeping with the company's ambitions. The next few vintages may well show a clearer improvement.

• Rossole '99	🍷🍷 5
• Chianti Cl. Lucarello Ris. '98	🍷 5

Colle Bereto
Loc. Colle Bereto
53017 Radda in Chianti (SI)
Tel. 0577738083 - 0554299330
E-mail: colle.bereto@collebereto.it

It is a pity that Colle Bereto's range is still patchy because we have more than once found really excellent wines here. One example is the extremely good Tocco '99, which is soft, elegant and deep.

• Il Tocco '99	🍷🍷 5
• Il Cenno '99	🍷 5

Podere Capaccia
Loc. Capaccia
53017 Radda in Chianti (SI)
Tel. 0577738385 - 0574582426
E-mail: capaccia@chianticlassico.com

Podere Capaccia presented only one wine this time. The Querciagrande, their flagship bottle, will be released next year so the Chianti '98 was left to defend the estate colours. It is good and well-rounded, and reveals lively tannins.

• Chianti Cl. '98	🍷 4

Podere Terreno alla Via della Volpaia - Via della Volpaia
53017 Radda in Chianti (SI)
Tel. 0577738312
E-mail: podereterreno@chiantinet.it

The Chianti Classico '98 is not all it might be on the nose, which is a shame because the structure is good. The Riserva '97 is soft and characterful, and shows a certain aromatic depth. It only just failed to win Two Glasses.

• Chianti Cl. Ris. '97	🍷 4
• Chianti Cl. '98	🍷 4

Monte Morioni
Loc. Sassofortino
Loc. Monte Morioni
58036 Roccastrada (GR)
Tel. 0564567501 E-mail: gdweine@datacomm.ch

The estate wines, Gioioso, Grassotto and Focoso ("Joyful", "Chubby" and "Fiery"), sound like Snow White's second-string dwarfs. Gioioso and the Grassotto are poorly focused but Focoso is very interesting and easily gathered up Two Glasses.

• Focoso '98	🍷🍷 4

Colognole
Loc. Colognole - Via del Palagio 15
50068 Rufina (FI)
Tel. 0558319870
E-mail: info@colognole.it

Colognole, long a producer in the Rufina zone, has turned out an excellent Chianti Rufina this time. A bouquet of clean, intense fruit leads in to a soft, dense, lingering palate.

• Chianti Rufina '99	🍷🍷 3*

Fattoria Castelvecchio
Loc. San Casciano Val di Pesa
Via Certaldese, 30
50020 San Casciano in Val di Pesa (FI)
Tel. 0558248032

An encouraging performance for this estate in the Colli Fiorentini. The star was the Brecciolino '99, which nearly won Two Glasses with its deliciously lean, well-balanced palate. The other wines are fair.

○ Vin Santo del Chianti '90	♀	5
● Chianti Colli Fiorentini '99	♀	2*
● Il Brecciolino '99	♀	4

La Loggia
Loc. Montefiridolfi
Via Collina, 40
50020 San Casciano in Val di Pesa (FI)
Tel. 0558244288

The Nearco '97 is the most distinguished of the wines we tasted from La Loggia. It has admirable balance, the flavour is even and the body fairly substantial, although vegetal tones are in evidence. The other two wines are also well made.

● Nearco '97	♀♀	4
● Chianti Classico '98	♀	3
● Chianti Classico Ris. '96	♀	4

Baroncini
Loc. Casale, 43
53037 San Gimignano (SI)
Tel. 0577940600

Baroncini is one of the most important wineries in San Gimignano. Stefano and Bruna Baroncini have extended their range to include not only Vernaccia but also other typical Tuscan wines, such as Brunello di Montalcino and Chianti.

○ Faina '99	♀♀	4
● Chianti Colli Senesi Sup. Vigna S. Domenico Sovestro '00	♀	3
○ Vernaccia di S. Gimignano Dometaia Ris. '99	♀	4

Canneta
Loc. Santa Lucia, 27
53037 San Gimignano (SI)
Tel. 0577941540
E-mail: podcanneto@hotmail.com

Stefano and Valeria Grandi's estate is back in the limelight with two good wines. The partly barrique-fermented Vernaccia La Luna e le Torri is soft, intense and lingering. The basic Vernaccia makes a good showing as well.

○ Vernaccia di S. Gimignano '00	♀	3
○ Vernaccia di S. Gimignano La Luna e le Torri '00	♀	4

Cappella Sant'Andrea
Loc. Casale, 26
53037 San Gimignano (SI)
Tel. 0577940456

Only 2,000 bottles of the Vernaccia Rialto '00 were produced. Fermented and aged in oak, it displays notable structure and, if allowed more bottle age, will acquire greater breadth.

○ Vernaccia di S. Gimignano Rialto '00	♀♀	4

Casale - Falchini
Via di Casale, 40
53037 San Gimignano (SI)
Tel. 0577941305 - 0577940819
E-mail: casale_falchini@tin.it

Not all the wines did well at our tastings. The most successful was the cabernet-based Campora '97, which is concentrated but a bit vegetal on the nose. The Vernaccia Ab Vinea Doni, with its super-ripe timbre, is very decent.

● Campora '97	♀♀	6
○ Vernaccia di S. Gimignano Ab Vinea Doni '99	♀	4

Pietraserena
Loc. Casale, 5
53037 San Gimignano (SI)
Tel. 0577940083

The Ser Gervasio '97 was this year's best offering from Pietraserena. It's a monovarietal merlot with aromas of berry fruit and a faint grassy undertone. The palate is soft, with smooth tannins, and there are some forward notes on the finish.

● Ser Gervasio '97	🍷🍷	5

San Quirico
Via Pancole, 39
53037 San Gimignano (SI)
Tel. 0577955007

San Quirico is one of the historic estates of San Gimignano and its wines are in the traditional mould. The San Gimignano Rosso is agreeably fruity while the Vernaccia Riserva has a varietal bitterish twist.

● San Gimignano Rosso '99	🍷	3
○ Vernaccia di S. Gimignano Ris. '99	🍷	4

Fattoria di Sassolo
Loc. La Serra
Via Bucciano, 59
56020 San Miniato (PI)
Tel. 0571460001 - 035625564

Vin Santo is the standard-bearer of Sassolo as the other wines failed to put in an appearance this time. The '95 version of the Fiorile is excellent, as usual, with notes of plum and chestnut on the nose and a powerful, fat, long palate. The Vin Santo '95 is less concentrated but good all the same.

○ Vin Santo San Torpé Fiorile '95	🍷🍷	5
○ Vin Santo San Torpé '95	🍷	5

Podere San Michele
Via della Caduta, 3/A
57027 San Vincenzo (LI)
Tel. 0565798038

The Allodio is based for the most part on sangiovese. The '99 has a dense, vibrant structure, with distinct, energetically expressed fruit. The estate also produces a white wine and a syrah, but they were not ready in time for our tastings.

● Allodio Rosso '99	🍷🍷	5

San Michele a Torri
Loc. San Michele a Torri
Via Michele a Torri, 36
50018 Scandicci (FI)
Tel. 055769111

San Michele a Torri keeps improving. The Murtas '99 shows good extractive weight; the Chianti Riserva La Gabbiola has distinct notes of bay leaf and spice, ushering in a soft, well-balanced flavour.

○ Vin Santo '97	🍷	4
● Chianti Classico La Gabbiola Ris. '98	🍷	4
● Murtas '99	🍷	4

Vigliano
Via di Carcheri, 309
50055 Lastra a Signa (FI)
Tel. 0558727006
E-mail: info@vigliano.com

They know what they are doing at Vigliano and the future looks very promising. The Vigna dell'Erta '99, a blend of sangiovese and cabernet, is a dynamic, powerful wine with lots of youthful exuberance. This very good red also has considerable character.

● Vigna dell'Erta '99	🍷🍷	5
○ Bricoli '99		4

CANTINA COOP. DEL MORELLINO
DI SCANSANO - LOC. SARAGIOLO
58054 SCANSANO (GR)
TEL. 0564507288 - 0564507979
E-MAIL: coopmorel@libero.it

We can recommend the wines from the Cantina Cooperativa. Technically faultless, they occasionally show a touch of brilliance, as in the case of the Roggiano '00, with its fresh, inviting fragrance and extremely enjoyable palate.

- Morellino di Scansano
  Roggiano '98   ♀♀ 3*
- Morellino di Scansano Roggiano '00 ♀ 3
- Morellino di Scansano
  Vigna Benefizio '00   ♀   3

PROVVEDITORE-BARGAGLI
LOC. SALAIOLO, 174
58054 SCANSANO (GR)
TEL. 0564599237
E-MAIL: provveditore@tin.it

The Provveditore '00 is Bargagli's top wine this year. It offers immediate, attractive fruit as well as fair structure. The Primo Riserva also made a good impression on our tasters.

- Morellino di Scansano
  Provveditore '00   ♀♀ 3*
- Morellino di Scansano
  Primo Ris. '98   ♀   4

CASTELPUGNA
STRADA VALDIPUGNA, 12/14
53100 SIENA
TEL. 0577222461
E-MAIL: info@castelpugna.com

They are just starting out here but plans for the future are ambitious. To judge from the wines presented, which were straightforward by definition, the estate should be able to achieve its goals. The Chianti '00, in particular, is a pleasing wine with substantial body.

- Chianti Colli Senesi '00   ♀   3
- Chianti Colli Senesi '99   ♀   3

POGGIO SAN POLO
FRAZ. MONTALCINO
LOC. PODERE DI SAN POLO, 161
53024 SIENA
TEL. 0577835522

The Mezzopane '99 was the best of the wines presented by San Polo. Rich, clean fruit on the nose, with a heady, long palate. The Brunello '96 has a convincing flavour and a less successful bouquet. The Rosso '99, however, is over-evolved.

- Mezzopane '99   ♀♀ 4
- Brunello di Montalcino '96   ♀   6
- Rosso di Montalcino '99   4

SAN GIORGIO A LAPI
VIA COLLE PINZUTO, 30
53100 SIENA
TEL. 0577356836
E-MAIL: sangiorgioalapi@libero.it

This fairly new winery near Siena has already aroused interest. Its wines are well-made and have decent structure. The Chianti Colli Senesi was the pick of the pack and in fact almost won Two Glasses.

- Chianti Classico '99   ♀   4
- Chianti Colli Senesi '99   ♀   3*

POGGIO SALVI
LOC. POGGIO SALVI, 251
53018 SOVICILLE (SI)
TEL. 0577349045 - 057745237
E-MAIL: info@poggiosalvi.it

This estate near Siena produces reliably consistent wines, without great highs or lows. Apart from the Vin Santo, we would draw your attention to the density of the sangiovese-based Campo del Bosco and the aromatic freshness of the Refola.

- ○ Vin Santo '96   ♀♀ 5
- ○ Refola '00   ♀   3
- Campo del Bosco '99   ♀   5
- Chianti Colli Senesi '99   ♀   3

Tenuta di Trecciano
Loc. Trecciano
53018 Sovicille (SI)
Tel. 0577314357
E-mail: trecciano@libero.it

It is worth keeping your eye on the wines from Trecciano, particularly the Daniello, a blend of sangiovese and cabernet that has harmony, elegance and a seamless progression. The other wines are correct and well-made but not earth-shaking.

● Daniello '99	🍷🍷 5
● Chianti Colli Senesi Terra di Siena '00	🍷 3
● Cabernet Sauvignon '99	🍷 4

Bulichella
Loc. Bulichella, 131
57028 Suvereto (LI)
Tel. 0565829892
E-mail: bulichella@etruscan.li.it

Bulichella is making remarkable progress. These are just the first signs but the commitment here augurs very well for the future. For now, the Tuscanio is doing well, although the oak is perhaps a little too generous.

● Val di Cornia Rosso Tuscanio '99	🍷🍷 5
○ Val di Cornia Bianco Tuscanio '00	🍷 4

Incontri
Loc. Fossoni, 38
57028 Suvereto (LI)
Tel. 0565829401
E-mail: blocloko@hotmail.com

This estate has changed gear and name for it was formerly Martelli Busdraghi. The red Lagobruno is very good, revealing concentration and an expert use of oak. The Vermentino Ildebrandino nearly won Two Glasses. The Rubizzo is a decent, well-made wine.

● Lagobruno '99	🍷🍷 5
● Val di Cornia Rosso Rubizzo '00	🍷 3
○ Val di Cornia Vermentino Ildebrandino '00	🍷 4

Monte Rico
Loc. Poggio Cerro
57028 Suvereto (LI)
Tel. 0565829550

Monte Rico has always focused its efforts on the production of a monovarietal sangiovese, the Villa Monte Rico, which is stylistically correct, austere and expressive. The successful '98 came close to getting Two Glasses.

● Villa Monte Rico '98	🍷 4

Petra
Loc. S. Lorenzo
57028 Suvereto (LI)
Tel. 0565845180

Petra, in Val di Cornia, is the Tuscan holding of the Moretti family, of Bellavista fame (in Franciacorta, of course). They have invested heavily here in extensive vineyards and a brand-new cellar. The plans are ambitious and these wines are the first results.

● Petra '97	🍷🍷 5
● Val di Cornia Rosso '98	🍷 4

Petricci del Pianta
Loc. S. Lorenzo, 20
57028 Suvereto (LI)
Tel. 0565845140
E-mail: petricci@etruscan.li.it

This small estate has high ambitions. The sweet, varietal Aleatico is well-made and dense. The Buca di Cleonte has interesting structure but the aromas are not unfocused. The other wines are quite satisfactory.

● Aleatico '00	🍷🍷 5
○ Fabula '00	🍷 4
● Buca di Cleonte '98	🍷 5
● Cerosecco '99	🍷 4

Le Chiantigiane
Via Ponte Nuovo, 15/23
50028 Tavarnelle Val di Pesa (FI)
tel. 0558070031

The Cooperativa Le Chiantigiane offered the panel some interesting wines. The Riserva Santa Trinità is a bit forward but can point to a well-balanced flavour, nicely underpinned by alcohol. The Cardinale '98 did quite well, too.

- Cardinale '98 — 3
- Chianti Classico S. Trinita Ris. '98 — 3*
- Chianti Classico S. Trinita '99 — 2

Fattoria Poggio Romita
Loc. La Romita - Via Del Cerro, 10
50028 Tavarnelle Val di Pesa (FI)
tel. 0558077253
e-mail: poggioromita@tin.it

Young Andrea Sestini's Poggio Romita does better every year. His Chianti Frimaio '99 is a wine to watch. A shade fuzzy on the nose, it has a very attractive, muscular palate with dense, flavoursome tannins.

- Chianti Classico Frimaio '99 — 4
- Chianti Classico Frimaio Ris. '98 — 4
- La Sassaia '99 — 5

Cooperativa Agricola Valdarnese
Loc. Paterna, 96
52028 Terranuova Bracciolini (AR)
tel. 055977052

The Cooperativa Valdarnese Paterna provided one of the most pleasant surprises at this year's tastings. The sangiovese-based Vignanova '98 is a revelation. It has balance, concentration, sweet, polished tannins and a lingering finish. In short, it's excellent.

- Vignanova '98 — 4*
- Chianti '99 — 2*

Elyane & Bruno Moos
Fraz. Soiana
Via Pier Capponi, 98
56030 Terricciola (PI)
tel. 0587654180

Bruno and Elyane Moos have gone back to Canada. Their name remains but the estate is now run by a Swiss couple, Ursula and Peter Mock. The very successful sangiovese-based Fontestina '99 proffers dense structure, well backed up by oak.

- Fontestina '99 — 5
- Soianello '99 — 4

Camposilio
Fraz. Pratolino - Via Basciano, 8
50036 Vaglia (FI)
tel. 055696456 - 055696486
e-mail: alerusti@tin.it

This Vaglia-based estate concentrates its energies on one wine, the Camposilio, a blend of sangiovese and cabernet. The '98 vintage has again done very well. It is a well-balanced product with good structure, but rather vegetal.

- Camposilio '98 — 5

Ortaglia
Loc. Pratolino - Via San Jacopo, 331
50036 Vaglia (FI)
tel. 055409136
e-mail: ortaglia@iol.it

This estate near Florence produces unusual wines for its zone. They are, in fact, all white, and mostly based on chardonnay and sauvignon. The structure is so good, though, that they both came close to winning a second Glass.

- ○ Bianca Capello '00 — 4
- ○ Ortaglia N° 1 '99 — 5

MARCHE

Steady progress in quality has been made in much of the Marche wine-producing sector. We noted this last year in the Guide, allotting much more space to the region. A significant number of wines were awarded Three Glasses. In confirmation of this progress, the tasting results for this year are, again, in many cases brilliant. A few statistics: overall annual production quantity is close to 200,000,000 litres, with an increase in DOC production, which currently accounts for around 30 per cent of the total. This brings us to the region's seriously good products – there are nine Three Glass winners in this edition of the Guide – starting with a white that is no newcomer, the wonderful Verdicchio dei Castelli di Jesi Podium '99. The best Verdicchio di Jesi from 2000 is the San Michele di Bonci. We have always enjoyed Ampelio Bucci's long, elegant Verdicchios and always given them high scores so the Villa Bucci '98 is something of an old friend, and further proof of the potential that Verdicchio undoubtedly has. Moving on to the interesting red wine scene, the latest exploit of white winemaker Aldo Cifola from La Monacesca, known for his Verdicchio di Matelica, is the red Camerte '99. A Three Glass winner is the Sangiovese Moggio '98 selection presented by San Savino, which is highly indicative of developments around Ascoli Piceno. Similar in many ways is the achievement of the other newcomer from the area, the Anghelos '99 from De Angelis. It is a wine that sets the pattern for the new Offida DOC zone, which takes effect from the 2001 harvest. Another new element, but only in terms the score it achieved, is the Rosso Conero Fibbio '99 selection from Lanari. Staying with Rosso Conero, Fattoria Le Terrazze di Numana again chalked up Three Glasses for Sassi Neri '99. Cabernet sauvignon grapes are behind a record-breaking achievement by Boccadigabbia's Akronte, which claimed Three Glasses for the sixth year running. Continuing with this year's exciting red tastings, there are quite a few label that deserve a mention: Dezi's Solo '99, the Kurni '99 from Oasi degli Angeli, Rosso Conero Traiano '99 from Strologo, Rosso Piceno Nero di Vote '98 by Le Caniette, Rosso Piceno Superiore '98 Roggio del Filare from Velenosi, Mancini's Impero Selezione F M '98, and Moroder's Rosso Conero Dorico '98. Moving on to the whites, La Monacesca's Mirum '98, Belisario's Verdicchio di Matelica '98 Cambrugiano, the Stefano Antonucci Bianco '99 selection presented by Santa Barbara, Moncaro's Verdicchio dei Castelli di Jesi Vigna Novali '98, Verdicchio Tufico '99 by Colonnara, yet another Verdicchio, Serra Fiorese '98 from Garofoli, and lastly the sweet Maximo by Umani Ronchi and Fazi Battaglia's Arkezia all attracted very favourable comments.

ANCONA

LANARI
FRAZ. VARANO
VIA POZZO, 142
60029 ANCONA
TEL. 0712861343

Lanari continues its dogged pursuit of quality, refusing to release wines that are not up to scratch, as happened after the disastrous '95 vintage. Thanks to the strict standards maintained in the field, with low yields guaranteed by weeding out imperfect bunches several times, Lanari can make great wines even from quite ordinary harvests. The wines are also outstanding in more favourable years, like 2000. The standard-label Rosso Conero 2000 has already been widely praised. An impenetrably dark purple in colour, it is smooth and supple. The nose has firm notes of morello cherry, bramble and ripe plums and the enrty on the palate has incredible power, but no rough edges. A Rosso Conero with a perfect balance of concentration, acidity and tannin from the fruit, which is fully ripe and very sweet. There was an excellent performance from the winery's flagship selection, the Rosso Conero Fibbio '99, which may not come from a particularly great vintage but does put on a good show, thanks to the particular care taken during winemaking. A first Three Glass award for a winery that has done much to merit it. Ageing in barriques gives the wine depth and concentration, rounding out its elegance. Dark purple, with ripe cherry and bilberry aromas mingling with spicy notes on the nose, it has an astoundingly elegant, complex structure with a wealth of soft, sweet tannins. The palate opens out well into cocoa powder and roasted coffee beans, closing with a finish that is both elegant and persistent.

● Rosso Conero Fibbio '99	♟♟♟♟	5
● Rosso Conero '00	♟♟	3*
● Rosso Conero Fibbio '97	♟♟	5
● Rosso Conero Fibbio '98	♟♟	5
● Rosso Conero '99	♟♟	3

ANCONA

MARCHETTI
FRAZ. PINOCCHIO
VIA DI PONTELUNGO, 166
60131 ANCONA
TEL. 071897386 - 071897385
E-MAIL: info@marchettiwines.it

Founded in the 19th century, this winery, now run by the Marchetti family, is located just outside Ancona. The 11 hectares of vineyards around the winery are mainly planted to montepulciano, with another eight in the classic Verdicchio zone. The once technical, well-made wines are slowly becoming more concentrated and fragrant, following the current trend in Rosso Conero and Marche wines in general. The winery's products have therefore lost a lot of their original rustic nature and become softer, more elegant and complex. The Villa Bonomi '98 Riserva di Rosso Conero is generally good. The nose has rich, ripe fruit notes of stewed plums and sweet spices. On the palate, good concentration and sweet tannins emerge to sustain the flavour through to the tidily persistent finish. The complex texture guarantees ageing potential. The standard-label '99 Rosso Conero bears witness to the special care taken in the vineyard. The slightly super-ripe fruit lifts the aromas, which are reminiscent of jam rather than fresh fruit. This is a good wine for everyday drinking, with no emphatic tannic astringency and a well-managed finish. The Verdicchio Tenuta del Cavaliere is less balanced than the reds, with shy aromas and limited character in the palate. But then, 2000 wasn't a great year for whites.

● Rosso Conero Villa Bonomi Ris. '98	♟♟	4
○ Verdicchio dei Castelli di Jesi Cl. Sup. Tenuta del Cavaliere '00	♟	4
● Rosso Conero '99	♟	3
● Rosso Conero Villa Bonomi Ris. '97	♟♟	4

ANCONA

ALESSANDRO MORODER
VIA MONTACUTO, 112
60062 ANCONA
TEL. 071898232
E-MAIL: moroder@libero.it

Over the last decade, the Rosso Conero DOC has experienced a period of steady growth in quality and interest from the market, thanks to the conscientious efforts of the few wineries in the area, which lies in the national park of the same name. Alessandro and Serenella Moroder's is one of those wineries and their best product, the Rosso Conero Dorico selection has won Three Glasses on several occasions. Of the winery's 45 hillslope hectares, 26 are planted to specialist vines at a height of about 200 metres above sea level. The cellar buildings are inside the farm complex, which also has a very pleasant restaurant, the Aiòn, which often hosts enjoyable dinners and other events. Let's look at the wines themselves, starting, naturally, with the Dorico '98 – one of the better vintages – which is now in the shops. It has a good ruby red colour tending towards garnet, with complex aromas ranging from plum and bramble to spice and tobacco. The nice complexity of the nose is reflected in the smooth, firm palate. Dorico is produced in considerable quantities, which is of course to the winery's credit, and is one of the best wines in the DOC zone. The standard-label Rosso Conero, which is good value for money as usual, pays the price of that rather lean '99 harvest. Still, it is well-made, which brings out the best in its fruit. The Rosa di Montacuti is pleasant as ever, with prominent fruit. Lastly, the Oro di Moroder is an enjoyable dessert wine made from dried trebbiano, malvasia and moscato grapes.

APPIGNANO (MC)

FATTORIA DI FORANO
C.DA FORANO, 40
62010 APPIGNANO (MC)
TEL. 073357102

Conte Lucangeli's winery puts a lot of effort into raising the quality of local DOCs. Consultant oenologist Giancarlo Soverchia has laid down the guidelines and timescale for winning results: look after the vineyard and make full use of all the vinification techniques available to a modern, functional winery. All the requirements for premium quality are there and the wines presented demonstrate the potential of the estate – no predictable flavours in these deliciously appealing wines. The best example of this is the Rosso Piceno '99: its rather intense aromas include liquorice, bilberries and a pleasant gamey note, while the palate is concentrate and dynamic, with a ripe berry fruit finish. This is a top quality wine sold at a very moderate price. The series continues with Colli Maceratesi Monteferro '99, obtained from selected grapes. Straw yellow with an initial chlorophyll note on the nose, it expands into yellow plums and broom. The palate is broad and mouthfilling with vigorous acidity and a fruity character. Just a step below is the Colli Maceratesi Bianco Vulla Forano '00. The aromas feature peach and apricot fruit and the wine is soft and substantial on the palate.

● Rosso Conero Dorico '98	🍷🍷 5
○ L'Oro di Moroder '99	🍷🍷 5
● Rosso Conero '99	🍷 3*
⊙ Rosa di Montacuti '00	3
● Rosso Conero Dorico '90	🍷🍷🍷 5
● Rosso Conero Dorico '93	🍷🍷🍷 5
● Rosso Conero Dorico '97	🍷🍷 5

○ Colli Maceratesi Bianco Monteferro '99	🍷🍷 3*
● Rosso Piceno '99	🍷🍷 3*
○ Colli Maceratesi Bianco Villa Forano '00	🍷 2*
● Rosso Piceno Bulciano '98	🍷🍷 4

ASCOLI PICENO

Ercole Velenosi
Via dei Biancospini, 11
63100 Ascoli Piceno
Tel. 0736341218
E-mail: info@velenosivini.com

There have been no changes in set-up at the winery. Ercole Velenosi and oenologist Romeo Taraborrelli still supervise vineyard and cellar while Angelo Velenosi and Luisa Acciarri are in charge of the commercial side. However, there is something new in the product range. The Ludi '98, a blend of montepulciano with a touch of cabernet and merlot performed well. It is deep ruby red with a spicy nose that has bramble to the fore. The taut, sustained front palate is followed by fat tannins and a long, warm finish. The Roggio del Filare '98 is even better. More balanced and denser on the palate, it has a range of well-focused aromas. The Rosso Piceno Superiore Il Brecciarolo is punching above its weight with rich structure and intense, fruit-rich flavours. The Velenosi Brut is at last mature and complex on the palate, with an attractive hint of iodine on the nose. The standard-label Villa Angela is also convincing. Made from chardonnay grapes vinified in stainless steel, it is enjoyably tangy with banana and melon aromas. The Rêve di Villa Angela '99, also made with chardonnay grapes, is less successful. The structure is a touch light and it is still overpowered by the wood. The Falerio Vigna Solaria '00 is drinking nicely now and will be even better after a few months more in the bottle. The aromas have a good fruit impact while the flavour is still developing, sustained by a good alcohol content. Lastly, the Falerio Brecciarolo and the standard-label Linagre are correctly made: the former is a little lightweight and the Linagre has rather fuzzy aromas.

● Rosso Piceno Sup. Roggio del Filare '98	🍷🍷	5
○ Falerio dei Colli Ascolani Vigna Solaria '00	🍷🍷	3*
○ Villa Angela Chardonnay '00	🍷🍷	3*
● Ludi '98	🍷🍷	5
● Rosso Piceno Sup. Il Brecciarolo '98	🍷🍷	3*
○ Velenosi Brut M. Cl.	🍷🍷	5
○ Rêve di Villa Angela '99	🍷	4
○ Falerio dei Colli Ascolani Il Brecciarolo '00		2
○ Linagre Sauvignon di Villa Angela '00		3
● Rosso Piceno Sup. Roggio del Filare '97	🍷🍷	5

BARBARA (AN)

Santa Barbara
B.go Mazzini, 35
60010 Barbara (AN)
Tel. 0719674249
E-mail: info@vinisantabarbara.it

When Stefano Antonucci took over his father and uncle's winery in 1986, he decided to devote his energies full-time to the business for which he was developing a real passion. A modern style was what he brought to the range, starting of course with the Verdicchio dei Castelli di Jesi. The standard-label Verdicchio and the Pignocco selection, both correct and varietal in the '00 version, are followed by the Le Vaglie selection, a Verdicchio with character and personality in the latest version. The pronounced vegetal and mineral aromas are followed by a persistent, almondy flavour. The long list of products has been extended with the Nidastore and the Riserva Stefano Antonucci. The latter is aged in wood and has a bright, intense straw yellow colour, with spicy notes on the nose of beeswax and tropical fruit, leading in to a broad, rather boisé palate. Stefano Antonucci's alter ego is Silvio Brocani, a well-known figure in the world of wines in Marche and elsewhere. Since 1993, he has been acting as marketing director for the winery. The reds include an excellent Stefano Antonucci selection from merlot and cabernet. Spicy on the nose and easy-drinking on the palate, it has a rich, intriguing and delicately fruity finish. The San Bartolo '99 is good, though penalized by the difficult year. A blend of cabernet and merlot, it is pleasant and drinkable, like all Santa Barbara wines, and also sold at a reasonable price, considering the quality of the product. The Pignocco Rosso '00 makes a good impact, and has plenty of no-nonsense body, as well as being enjoyably quaffable.

○ Verdicchio dei Castelli di Jesi Cl. Stefano Antonucci Ris. '99	🍷🍷	4
● Pignocco Rosso '00	🍷🍷	3*
○ Verdicchio dei Castelli di Jesi Cl. Le Vaglie '00	🍷🍷	3*
● Stefano Antonucci Rosso '99	🍷🍷	5
○ Muscatell '00	🍷	3
○ Verdicchio dei Castelli di Jesi Cl. '00	🍷	2*
○ Verdicchio dei Castelli di Jesi Cl. Nidastore '00	🍷	3
○ Verdicchio dei Castelli di Jesi Cl. Pignocco '00	🍷	2*
● San Bartolo Rosso '99	🍷	3*
○ Verdicchio dei Castelli di Jesi Cl. Stefano Antonucci Ris. '98	🍷🍷	4

BARCHI (PU)

Valentino Fiorini
Via Giardino Campioli, 5
61030 Barchi (PU)
tel. 072197151
e-mail: carla@fioriniwines.it

Carla Fiorini, daughter of Valentino, is working alongside consultant oenologist Roberto Potentini to achieve commendable consistency of quality for this traditional winery from the Pesaro area. The new version of the Sangiovese dei Colli Pesaresi Luigi Fiorini was not among the wines tasted this year, although we did confirm the stature of the '97 at a recent retasting. Still, the whole range showed very reliable quality. The analysis begins with the most traditional wine from the Fiorini stable, the Bianchello del Metauro. The Vigna Sant'Ilario '00 version is, as usual, fresh, vegetal and easy-going, with a nice complex palate. The Tenuta Campioli '00 is weightier and more mouthfilling, with clearly-defined spring flower aromas preceding a hefty palate rounded off by a twist of almonds. The red Bartis '98 has aroused a great deal of interest. A sangiovese, montepulciano and cabernet blend, it has distinctive sweet aromas of violets and cherries, alternating with toastiness. On the palate, it is elegant, drinkable and smooth, with good balance. Our closing comment is reserved for the Monsavium '95, a monovarietal bianchello. This dried grape wine has intense aromas of stewed apple, vanilla and madeira. On the palate, it has well-controlled sweetness and a rather evident hint of oxidation.

● Bartis Rosso '98	🍷🍷	4
○ Bianchello del Metauro Tenuta Campioli '00	🍷	3
○ Bianchello del Metauro Vigna Sant'Ilario '00	🍷	2*
○ Monsavium Passito '95	🍷	5
● Colli Pesaresi Rosso Luigi Fiorini '97	🍷🍷	4

BELVEDERE OSTRENSE (AN)

Luciano Landi
Via Gavigliano, 16
60030 Belvedere Ostrense (AN)
tel. 073162353

Luciano Landi's winery is one of many that were founded and developed to promote wines from the Jesi area, rescuing them from an undeserved oblivion. The youth of the owners, reliable guidance from oenologist Sergio Paolucci, and substantial investment have allowed the property to close the quality and image gaps accumulated by the area, despite its evident suitability for viticulture. The standard-label Verdicchio has strong ripe fruit aromas and warm softness on the palate which are not, however, supported by sufficient vigorous acidity. Moving on to the reds, the standard-label Lacrima has a nice crimson colour although the nose - which offers green, rather than flower and fruity, notes - is not without defects. This rather tannic wine also has vegetal sensations on the palate. The Lacrima Vecchi Sapori is a deep purple in colour with clear dried roses on the nose over the other fruit and flower aromas. The palate reflects the nose, adding soft tannins. The Gavigliano selection, also a Lacrima, has a more firmly stated profile. Deep purple in the glass, it yields dried rose, raspberry and violet aromas. The tannins on the palate are more prominent, and the fruit sensations on the nose return to blossom with the support of the good structure. The Goliardo Rosso has an almost impenetrable purple colour. The nose brims with dried morello cherry and bramble aromas while the palate is concentrated, with discernible but delicate tannins, and a triumphant finish that recalls the fruit and spice. The Lacrima Passito opens with aromas ranging from Parma violets to sweet spices. The palates develops around very respectable structure, with pleasant softness conferred by the residual sugar.

● Goliardo Rosso '00	🍷🍷	5
● Lacrima di Morro d'Alba Gavigliano '00	🍷🍷	4
● Lacrima di Morro d'Alba '00	🍷	3
● Lacrima di Morro d'Alba Passito '00	🍷	5
● Lacrima di Morro d'Alba Vecchi Sapori '00	🍷	3
○ Verdicchio dei Castelli di Jesi Cl. '00	🍷	2*

CAMERANO (AN)

Silvano Strologo
Via Osimana, 89
60021 Camerano (AN)
tel. 071732359 - 071731104

The soft hills at the foot of Monte Conero are the home of one of the most important grape varieties in Italy, montepulciano. Temperamental if treated badly, this variety becomes versatile and generous if handled with care. It is no coincidence that montepulciano has for years been used as a pick-me-up for feeble, tired wines, even from other regions of Italy. Silvano Strologo's estate, where oenologist Giancarlo Soverchia makes an expert contribution, is completely given over to montepulciano, either in old vineyards or in new plantings, with the high density that modern growing techniques demand. All this montepulciano is used to make just two wines, a standard-label and a selection, both Rosso di Conero. The Julius has a hearteningly generous price-quality ratio and is deep, concentrated red in colour. The broad aromas of ripe cherry jam, blackcurrants and crushed brambles mingle with spicy notes. On the palate, power and serious huge extract combine with a dense weave of sweet tannins to sustain the fullness of the flavour. Despite an unfortunate year, the Traiano selection maintains a high standard of quality. This characterful red is the result of repeated and rigorous selections in the vineyard. The wine is dark vermilion with ruby highlights then ripe fruit aromas, with hints of spice, pepper, tar and liquorice, blend with the toasty oak from the wood. There is nice complexity on the palate, thanks to mellow tannins and a powerful, compact structure. The clear, assertive spice is echoed in the long finish.

• Rosso Conero Traiano '99	5
• Rosso Conero Julius '00	3*
• Rosso Conero Julius '98	3
• Rosso Conero Traiano '98	4

CASTEL DI LAMA (AP)

Tenuta De Angelis
Via San Francesco, 10
63030 Castel di Lama (AP)
tel. 073687429

This winery, run by Quinto Fausti, has over 50 hectares of vineyards. Cellar operations are supervised by well-known oenologist Roberto Potentini. This year our tasting notes show the red wines firmly in the lead. For the last three years, the best wine has been the Anghelos, made from montepulciano, sangiovese and cabernet sauvignon, and the '99 was gained Three well-deserved Glasses in recognition of its enviably consistent standard of quality. The dense ruby red colour is followed by a nose with a distinctly floral entry, shading into berry fruit and faint nuances of spice. It shows good thrust on the palate, where there are plenty of close-knit tannins. Richly extracted, it signs off with a delectably lingering finish. The Rosso Piceno Superiore '98 is deep ruby red, with strong liquorice and clove sensations on the nose that alternate with distinct boisé notes. These aromas are mirrored on the warm, compact palate, where assertive tannins back up good overall structure. The nose of the Rosso Piceno '00 is not especially intense but there are well-defined notes of fruit while the palate offers rather rugged tannins. The Falerio '00 shows vegetal notes and acidity while the Chardonnay Prato Grande from the same year stands out for its broad aromas and smooth drinkability.

• Anghelos '99	4
• Rosso Piceno Sup. '98	3*
○ Prato Grande Chardonnay '00	2
• Rosso Piceno '00	2
○ Falerio dei Colli Ascolani '00	1
• Anghelos '97	4
• Rosso Piceno Sup. '97	3
• Anghelos '98	4

CASTELPLANIO (AN)

Fazi Battaglia
Via Roma, 117
60032 Castelplanio (AN)
Tel. 0731813444 - 06844311
E-mail: info@fazibattaglia.it

This historic Castelplanio winery was responsible for inventing the famous amphora-shaped "sex bottle", with its seductively sinuous curves, that ensured the success of Verdicchio. It has also become a benchmark for this white wine type. Fazi Battaglia owns 34 hectares in various municipalities around the classic Castelli di Jesi DOC zone and releases an interesting range of products. The technical staff, consisting of oenologist Dino Porfiri and agronomists Mario Ghergo and Antonio Verdolini with consultant Franco Bernabei, continue their experiments, hoping to produce, for example, a Verdicchio Vendemmia Tardiva to sell alongside the tried and tested versions. The classic standard-label Verdicchio, Titulus, is as ever well-made in the 2000 version. Le Moie, the result of careful clonal research, shows good consistency in the flavour, as well as pronounced and still rather vegetal aromas. We tasted the '98 Riserva S. Sisto, fermented and aged in small oak casks, which has rather strong toasty sensations but bags of texture. The Arkezia Muffo di S. Sisto '98 is only made in special vintage years, that is when the Verdicchio can develop botrytis. There are ripe fruit and elegant honey notes on the nose, with moderate complexity on the palate and dates, apricots and quince in the flavour. The reds are also coming along nicely. The Rosso Conero Passo del Lupo '97 has a deep amaranth-purple colour, broad aromas and good extract on the palate. The standard-label is rich and stylish, just a point or two behind the Sangiovese '00.

○	Arkezia Muffo di S. Sisto '98	👓👓	6
●	Rosso Conero '00	👓👓	3*
○	Verdicchio dei Castelli di Jesi Cl. Sup. Le Moie '00	👓👓	3*
●	Rosso Conero Passo del Lupo Ris. '97	👓👓	5
○	Verdicchio dei Castelli di Jesi Cl. S. Sisto Ris. '98	👓👓	4
●	Sangiovese '00	👓	2*
○	Verdicchio dei Castelli di Jesi Cl. Titulus '00	👓	3
●	Rosso Conero Passo del Lupo Ris. '95	👓👓	5
○	Arkezia Muffo di S. Sisto '97	👓👓	6
○	Verdicchio dei Castelli di Jesi Cl. S. Sisto Ris. '97	👓👓	4

CINGOLI (MC)

Lucangeli Aymerich di Laconi
Loc. Tavignano
62011 Cingoli (MC)
Tel. 0733617303

Don't be misled by the fact that this winery is situated in the province of Macerata. Tavignano is actually much nearer to Staffolo and Cupramontana than the provincial capital, and shares the same mid-hill soil and site climate as these two municipalities. The conditions are eminently suitable for growing splendid bunches of verdicchio, sangiovese and montepulciano grapes. The property currently owns over 20 hectares of vineyards, mainly verdicchio, and a modern, well-organized cellar. Oenologist Giancarlo Soverchia is head of the technical team. Of the three wines tasted, the Verdicchio Tavignano '00 is the most successful interpretation of this varietal. Aromas of lime blossom and ripe apples are followed by a fresh, tangy palate that echoes the nose satisfyingly. The Verdicchio Misco '00 is straw yellow in colour with greenish highlights, and has a very subtle nose that unveils aniseed and sweet almond aromas. On the palate, the wine has a marked vein of acidity, backed up by reasonably good structure. The purplish Rosso Piceno '00 has intense rustic aromas of ripe cherries and coffee while the dense, fruity palate is adequately braced by tannins. For the immediate future, we can look forward to a scrupulously made Rosso Piceno selection that will give the cellar a serious red. It will be a pleasure to taste this newcomer.

○	Verdicchio dei Castelli di Jesi Cl. Sup. Sel. Misco '00	👓👓	4
●	Rosso Piceno Tavignano '00	👓	3
○	Verdicchio dei Castelli di Jesi Cl. Sup. Tavignano '00	👓	3

CIVITANOVA MARCHE (MC)

Boccadigabbia
Loc. Fontespina
C.da Castelletta, 56
62012 Civitanova Marche (MC)
tel. 073370728
e-mail: info@boccadigabbia.com

Elvio Alessandri, an explosive character with a finger in countless pies, has never openly admitted the fact that his greatest satisfaction comes from wine. His Akronte has been awarded Three Glasses several times, hardly ever missing out, proving that competence – his assistants are Fabrizio Ciufoli and Giovanni Basso – and passion contribute to quality in the Marche as they do elsewhere. Alongside this outstanding wine, which won top honours again this year, we find a range of other labels, some obtained from local varieties. The Garbì is a freshly drinkable standard-label with a decent range of aromas, the nose revealing lime fruit and blossom. The Montalperti, from chardonnay grapes aged in small barrels, has a bright straw yellow colour and oaky aroma that lets the ripe fruit come through. On the palate, it is subtle and quite concentrated while the flavour echoes the vanilla notes on the nose. The Bianco Monsanulus '98 has excellent structure and an interesting progression. The Sangiovese Saltapicchio is deep garnet red with warm ripe fruit aromas and powerful, rich extracted on the palate. The Rosso Piceno '99 has a ruby hue, berry fruit on the nose and a smooth, fairly dense mouthfeel. The monovarietal cabernet sauvignon Akronte is deep red with majestic purple highlights. There are no herbal notes on the nose, which offers instead vanilla, bramble, sweet tobacco and tar. The assertiveness of the still-mellowing tannins cannot impair the stylish concentration and tanginess of the fruit. This wine is still developing and shows remarkable cellar potential.

CUPRA MARITTIMA (AP)

Oasi degli Angeli
C.da S. Egidio, 50
63012 Cupra Marittima (AP)
tel. 0735778569

Marco Casolanetti and Eleonora Rossi have decided to make just one wine, Kurni, and want it to be a unique. They have never baulked at imposing very low yields on their four and a half hectares of vineyards but in a year like '99, which was really hard on late ripening grapes like montepulciano, the yield was microscopic – less than 20 quintals per hectare, or two bunches per plant. One could almost call it quintessential. After nine months in new barriques, the wine is racked into other new barriques, and there it remains for a further nine months. As Marco says, "It's a question of controlled oxidation". Another six months in the bottle, and there you have the Kurni '99. Ruby red, flecked with blue, it is so dark it is almost impenetrable. The nose opens on less than perfectly defined notes but these clear up with lengthy aeration. The nose progresses well with dense aromas of black berry fruit, ripe black cherries, coffee and plums mingling with balsamic, spicy notes. The rich palate has a firm mouthfeel and develops steadily, thanks to the impressive tannic weave, leading you through to an intense and very persistent finish. This wine was just ready for uncorking at the time of tasting and promises to develop well over the next few years, when it will probably lose those minor blemishes on the nose.

● Akronte '98	▼▼▼	6
○ Monsanulus Bianco Villamagna '98	▼▼	4
● Saltapicchio Sangiovese '98	▼▼	6
○ Montalperti Chardonnay '99	▼▼	5
○ Garbì Bianco '00	▼	3
● Rosso Piceno '99	▼	4
● Akronte '93	▼▼▼	6
● Akronte '94	▼▼▼	6
● Akronte '95	▼▼▼	6
● Akronte '97	▼▼▼	6
● Akronte '96	▼▼	6
● Girone '96	▼▼	6

● Kurni '99	▼▼	6
● Kurni '97	▼▼▼	6
● Kurni '98	▼▼▼	6

CUPRAMONTANA (AN)

Colonnara Viticultori
in Cupramontana
Via Mandriole, 6
60034 Cupramontana (AN)
tel. 0731780273
e-mail: info@colonnara.it

Winds of change can be discerned in the various Verdicchio dei Castelli di Jesi presented by this co-operative. Founded in 1959 in one of the traditional DOC municipalities, it numbers almost 200 members – most small growers – working the 270 hectares situated at about 450 metres above sea level. Consultant oenologists Cesare Ferrari and Corrado Cugnasco are assisted by Pierluigi Gagliardini, the indefatigable cellar manager. The most immediate and positive evidence of innovation is provided by the two new selections of Verdicchio dei Castelli di Jesi, Tufico and Vigna San Marco. The former is definitely the keynote product in the range, and the '99 vintage currently available has the typical lime blossom and chamomile aromas of the variety and mineral notes of striking clarity in the mouth. This is a pleasant wine with good weight. The other selection, Vigna San Marco, proffers aromas of sun-kissed ripeness, a consequence of the heat in 2000. On the palate, it is smooth and pleasantly drinkable, finding plenty of support in the serious alcohol content. There were good marks for the classic Cuprese selection, also from 2000, which is fresh-tasting yet substantial, and the elegant, almost creamy Colonnara Metodo Classico, the feather in the cap of Colonnara's not insignificant sparkling wine production. The tradition of making spumante has been established in the Jesi area since the 19th century, as is also shown by the competitively priced cuve close sparkler from verdicchio grapes. Lastly, a good performance from the solid, fairly soft Tornamagno '97, made from sangiovese and montepulciano grapes.

CUPRAMONTANA (AN)

Vallerosa Bonci
Via Torre, 13
60034 Cupramontana (AN)
tel. 0731789129
e-mail: vallerosabonci@tiscalinet.it

Cupramontana is located in an especially good position in the Castelli di Jesi DOC zone, which enables it to produce some of its most representative wines. Vallerosa Bonci has taken full advantage of that potential. The winery has 35 hectares of vineyards in excellent positions, like San Michele, Colonnara, Torre, Carpaneto, Alvareto and Pietrone. Some of these plots provide the grapes for the selections, like the now-celebrated San Michele. This is arguably the most characteristic of the cellar's wines and is the undisputed champion from the 2000 vintage, at least if we consider the labels now available. A white with typical greenish highlights flashing against its deep yellow, it shows intense green varietal aromas with hints of lime blossom and hay. The flavour is full and supported by substantial alcohol – a characteristic of the vintage – but there is also tangy acidity and sinew. The thoroughly deserved Three Glass award is a tribute to the winery's consistent quality, also evident in the other products. The Verdicchio dei Castelli di Jesi Via Torre '00 selection – what a great price-quality ratio! – is fresh-tasting yet dense and enjoyable, while the Le Case, another Verdicchio selection that benefits from a brief sojourn in wood, emerges after breathing for a while as it still has faint oak-derived notes. The new Passito Rojano has a rather toasty spicy nose with fragrant nuances of cakes, which all come tidily together on the palate. Finally, the correctly-made and enjoyable Spumante Brut Bonci is highly representative of this variety's other vocation, sparkling wines.

	Wine	Glasses	Score
○	Verdicchio dei Castelli di Jesi Cl. Sup. Tufico '99	▼▼	4*
○	Verdicchio dei Castelli di Jesi Cl. Sup. Cuprese '00	▼▼	3*
○	Verdicchio dei Castelli di Jesi Cl. Sup. Vigna San Marco '00	▼▼	3*
○	Colonnara Spumante Brut M. Cl. Millesimato '95	▼▼	4
●	Tornamagno '97	▼▼	4
●	Rosso Piceno '98	▼	3
○	Verdicchio dei Castelli di Jesi Cl. Spumante Brut	▼	3
●	Tornamagno '96	▼▼	4
○	Verdicchio dei Castelli di Jesi Cl. Cuprese Ris. '97	▼▼	4

	Wine	Glasses	Score
○	Verdicchio dei Castelli di Jesi Cl. Sup. S. Michele '00	▼▼▼	4
○	Verdicchio dei Castelli di Jesi Cl. Sup. Le Case '00	▼▼	4
○	Verdicchio dei Castelli di Jesi Cl. Passito Rojano '99	▼▼	5
○	Verdicchio dei Castelli di Jesi Cl. Via Torre '00	▼	3*
○	Verdicchio dei Castelli di Jesi Cl. Spumante Brut Bonci	▼	3
○	Verdicchio dei Castelli di Jesi Cl. Sup. S. Michele '96	▼▼▼	4
○	Verdicchio dei Castelli di Jesi Cl. Sup. S. Michele '97	▼▼▼	4

FABRIANO (AN)

Enzo Mecella
Via Dante, 112
60044 Fabriano (AN)
tel. 073221680
e-mail: enzo.mecella@fabriano.nettuno.it

Not all of Enzo Mecella's wines were convincing this year. Nothing serious enough to compromise his reputation as an expert winemaker and skilled selector of grapes, of course. Just a couple of hiccoughs along the way which, in the case of the Verdicchio, can in part be attributed to the difficulties of the vintage. More specifically, we noticed that the Rosso Conero Rubelliano is far and away the best of the products tasted, as usual. The '98 has a ruby red colour, still purple at the edge, with strong morello cherry in the nose that mingles well with stylish toasty notes. A no-nonsense entry on the palate, with concentrated fruit and tannins that integrate well with the body, also let you know this is a wine of breeding. The Braccano '98, from ciliegiolo with a touch of merlot, did not quite come up to our expectations. It's a little more edgy and dilute than usual and lacks the tidy structure of the past. The less prestigious Rosso Conero I Lavi selection from the same year is good, though. It has Parma violet and cherry aromas, with medium body and a soft flavour, making a feature of balance rather than power. Moving on to the whites, the Verdicchio di Matelica Pagliano is always correctly-made and the acacia blossom on the nose heralds a distinctly fresh vegetal note on the palate. The Verdicchio Casa Fosca '00 is a bit disappointing, as it lacks density on the palate and has a less than convincing aroma profile.

● Rosso Conero Rubelliano '98	▼▼	5
○ Verdicchio di Matelica Pagliano '00	▼	3
● Rosso Conero I Lavi '98	▼	3
○ Verdicchio di Matelica Casa Fosca '00		3
● Braccano Rosso '98		5
● Braccano Rosso '97	▼▼	4
● Rosso Conero Rubelliano '97	▼▼	4
● Longobardo Rosso '98	▼▼	5

FANO (PU)

Claudio Morelli
V.le Romagna, 47/b
61032 Fano (PU)
tel. 0721823352

Claudio Morelli is one of the producers who are synonymous with DOC Bianchello del Metauro, a designation founded in 1969. This winery has consolidated experience of over 70 years in winemaking and its vineyards are among the most beautiful in the Pesaro area. Each year, the winery presents some very exciting selections of this wine, which is still largely unknown. We recommend you visit the Roncosambaccio vineyard, on a sort of natural terrace overlooking the Adriatic. Claudio is a specialist in white wine production and with this vintage, he has again presented a series of very enjoyable Bianchello del Metauros. The Borgo Torre, as you might expect, "towers" above the rest. It has a complex persistent nose, reminiscent of summer flowers, and the palate is warm, intense, rich and structured as never before. The San Cesareo is next on the list, but on a rather lower level. The faint fruit on the nose comes through better on the palate, which has good body and a gently bitterish finish. Last of the whites is the La Vigna delle Terrazze, which has slightly rustic apple aromas and a candid, well-measured palate finishing with a distinctly salty note. The most noteworthy of the reds is the DOC Colli Pesaresi La Vigna delle Terrazze, also a '00. Ruby red with a slightly vinous raspberry nose, it is light on the palate with moderate structure and somewhat intrusive tannins.

○ Bianchello del Metauro Borgo Torre '00	▼▼	3*
○ Bianchello del Metauro La Vigna delle Terrazze '00	▼	3
○ Bianchello del Metauro S. Cesareo '00	▼	2*
● Colli Pesaresi Rosso La Vigna delle Terrazze '00		3
● Suffragium '97	▼▼	4

GROTTAMMARE (AP)

Vinicola del Tesino
Via San Leonardo
63013 Grottammare (AP)
tel. 0735735869
e-mail: carminucci@carminucci.com

This restructured and very motivated winery deserves a full profile in the Guide this year, though last year we already mentioned one of its wines, which caught our attention. The estate has a long winemaking tradition and is run by Piero Carminucci, assisted by his son with the technical support of oenologist Pierluigi Lorenzetti. The production trend has become much more clear-cut in the last few years, following the decision to gradually and definitively reduce the amount of wine sold unbottled, and improve quality. For the time being, it is the Naumachos range, which includes a good extravirgin olive oil made in the farm's own press, that leads the quality crusade. The Chardonnay from this range is good out and last year we reviewed the '99 vintage, which has developed well. This year, we tasted the '00 version. An attractive wine with intense acacia and ripe fruit aromas, it is fresh and persistent on the palate. It has benefited from ageing in oak, which is seamlessly absorbed and in perfect balance with the fruit. The Rosso Piceno Superiore '98 also received Two Glasses. Flavoursome and eminently drinkable, it has lots of personality.

JESI (AN)

Mario e Giorgio Brunori
V.le della Vittoria, 103
60035 Jesi (AN)
tel. 0731207213
e-mail: brunorivini@libero.it

The Brunori family are well-known among winemakers in the Jesi area for their contribution towards making Verdicchio famous in the mid-1980s. As well as making a softer, more muscular wine, the Brunoris also developed their own special style – partial fermentation with only a small quantity of skins allowed to stay in the must, and for only a short time: sufficient obtain extract and colour. This technique may be old-fashioned but it is carefully executed and scrupulously monitored, enabling Brunori to produce seriously cellarable wines. The Verdicchio Classico is the keystone of the range. Pale straw yellow flecked with green, it offers a pleasantly fruity nose. The palate has well-modulated freshness, accompanied by appealingly delicate structure. The San Nicolò selection is a Verdicchio Classico Superiore with more pronounced characteristics. Lustrous, deep straw yellow, it has a broad nose with ripe fruit, walnutskin, sweet almond and ripe apricot notes. The palate has sinew and personality, pleasing fragrance and decent length while the finish is typically bitterish. A safe bet for the cellar.

○ Chardonnay Naumachos '00	🍷🍷	4
● Rosso Piceno Sup. '98	🍷🍷	4
○ Falerio dei Colli Ascolani '00	🍷	3

○ Verdicchio dei Castelli di Jesi Cl. Sup. San Nicolò '00	🍷🍷	4
○ Verdicchio dei Castelli di Jesi Cl. '00	🍷	3

LORETO (AN)

Gioacchino Garofoli
Loc. Villa Musone
Via Arno, 9
60025 Loreto (AN)
tel. 0717820163
e-mail: mail@garofolivini.it

The year 2001 marks the 100th anniversary of the Garofoli winery. In 1901, Giacchino Garofoli turned the family passion into a business. We would like to take this opportunity to wish the winery and all those who work there all the best for the future. This is one of the finest examples of a Marche winery as it offers a full range of wines, created with style and flair by owner-oenologist Carlo Garofoli. Again this year, his Podium '99 delighted the panel and secured Three Glasses for the fourth year running. The attractive flower, ripe apple, honey and sweet almond notes on the nose are perfectly mirrored on the concentrated palate with its effortlessly elegant finish. The Serra Fiorese '98 is on a par, its long fruity notes sweetened by a hint of vanilla, and the soft, mouthfilling palate leading in to a lingering finish. The Macrina '00 is a model for the DOC zone, a powerful, rounded, perfectly varietal bottle, while the Garofoli Brut, also from Verdicchio grapes, has great nose-palate consistency, making it one of the best spumantes in the region. The Rosso Conero Grosso Agontano '97 is very good. Austere and well-balanced, it will presumably cellar very well. To round off, the Dorato is good as ever, an enjoyable aromatic wine to sip at the end of the meal.

O	Verdicchio dei Castelli di Jesi Cl. Sup. Podium '99	ƳƳƳ	4*
O	Verdicchio dei Castelli di Jesi Cl. Serra Fiorese Ris. '98	ƳƳ	4
O	Verdicchio dei Castelli di Jesi Cl. Sup. Macrina '00	ƳƳ	3*
●	Rosso Conero Grosso Agontano '97	ƳƳ	5
O	Garofoli Brut	ƳƳ	3*
O	Dorato	Ƴ	4
O	Verdicchio dei Castelli di Jesi Cl. Sup. Podium '96	ƳƳƳ	4
O	Verdicchio dei Castelli di Jesi Cl. Sup. Podium '97	ƳƳƳ	4
O	Verdicchio dei Castelli di Jesi Cl. Sup. Podium '98	ƳƳƳ	4

MAIOLATI SPONTINI (AN)

Monteschiavo
Fraz. Monteschiavo
Via Vivaio
60030 Maiolati Spontini (AN)
tel. 0731700385 - 0731700297

Monteschiavo was founded in 1978 as the Cooperativa Vinicola di Produttori del Verdicchio. In 1994, the winery became part of the Pieralisi group, one of the largest producers in the region, and a world leader in the industrial farm machinery sector. From the very beginning, Monteschiavo decided to differentiate its Verdicchio selections, respecting the specific nature of the various vineyards and presenting wines with very different characteristics. Our analysis of the five Verdicchios we were offered begins with Il Pallio di San Floriano '00, with its nice varietal aromas, nicely mirrored on the palate. The Bando di San Settimio is a similar proposition, smooth and faintly redolent of oak in this new version. The Coste del Molino, a classic wine for everyday drinking, holds its own in comparison with the nobler selections. The Colle del Sole is well-typed and fresh-tasting but destined for export, again at a very affordable price. These products have recently been joined by the Classico Riserva Le Giuncare, made from carefully selected Verdicchio grapes, which is typically cellarable in the '99 version. The wine has a signature minerally note in the aromas and a softness of flavour. Going on to the reds, we liked the Rosso Conero Conti Cortesu '99, with its nice wild cherry aromas and fruity, harmonious palate. The Rosso Piceno Sassaiolo, Lacrima di Morro d'Alba and the new Montepulciano d'Abruzzo Croce del Moro are from the 2000 vintage and all well-made and quaffable. Our review concludes with the best-ever version of the red Esio. The '99 is a delight, with its morello cherry and pepper aromas.

O	Verdicchio dei Castelli di Jesi Cl. Sup. Pallio di S. Floriano '00	ƳƳ	3*
●	Esio Rosso '99	ƳƳ	5
●	Rosso Conero Conti Cortesi '99	ƳƳ	3
O	Verdicchio dei Castelli di Jesi Cl. Bando di S. Settimio '99	ƳƳ	4
O	Verdicchio dei Castelli di Jesi Cl. Le Giuncare Ris. '99	ƳƳ	4
●	Lacrima di Morro d'Alba '00	Ƴ	3
●	Montepulciano d'Abruzzo Croce del Moro '00	Ƴ	3
●	Rosso Piceno Sassaiolo '00	Ƴ	3
O	Verdicchio dei Castelli di Jesi Cl. Colle del Sole '00	Ƴ	2*
O	Vigna Tassanare Brut '00	Ƴ	3

MATELICA (MC)

**Belisario Cantina Sociale
di Matelica e Cerreto d'Esi**
Via Merloni, 12
62024 Matelica (MC)
tel. 0737787247
e-mail: vinibelisario@libero.it

The small Verdicchio di Matelica DOC zone covers a valley nestling between the mountains, the only valley in Marche not to slope down to the sea. This is where the Cantina Sociale di Matelica and Cerreto d'Esi, now called Belisario, organizes and manages the production of a host of small growers. Manager Roberto Potentini is one of the best oenologists in the Marche region and has managed to give his white wines a commendably consistent level quality and create a distinctive style for each cru. The ageing potential of this wine, which often has aniseed and chlorophyll notes, is best exemplified by the fresh-tasting Terre di Valbona '00. This surprising standard-label Verdicchio di Matelica is produced in very large quantities and put on an extremely good performance at our tastings. But the Vigneti del Cerro from the same year is equally fresh, with a more powerful structure. The excellent Belisario '00 selection has a softer flavour. Its fragrant varietal aromas of lemon and chamomile are joined by hints of fruit. Next, we come to the mineral notes on the nose and full flavour of the complex Cambrugiano. The '98 is one of the best versions ever. If memory serves us well, the '88 had comparable richness. The range of Verdicchios is supported by the very approachable Esino Bianco Ferrante and by a several reds, which are helping to recover the old red winemaking tradition of the Matelica area. We liked the scarlet Esino Colferraio '99, an easy-going crowd-pleaser with sweet spicy aromas, and the San Leopardo '99, a purplish ruby red with oak-derived notes and acidity that doesn't quite mesh with the tannins.

MATELICA (MC)

La Monacesca
C.da Monacesca, 1
62024 Matelica (MC)
tel. 0733812602
e-mail: monacesca@tin.it

The estate run by Casimiro Cifola, enthusiastically and competently assisted by son Aldo, takes its name from the Benedictine monks who made the area their source of agricultural produce. At this very comfortable, restructured farmhouse as elsewhere, it was monks who kept the skills of viticulture alive. The soil and unique site climates in the foothills around Matelica make the Verdicchio produced here very different from that of the Castelli di Jesi DOC zone. La Monacesca's cellar, a remarkably consistent producer of high quality wines, interprets the local terroir to perfection. The enviable line-up of whites has in recent vintages been extended with a very exciting red, Camerte, which won Three Glasses in its latest incarnation. From sangiovese grosso and merlot, the '99 that has now been released is elegant on the spicy, berry-rich nose and remarkably tidy on the palate, which is destined to improve further with bottle age. For the panel, it was a genuine surprise, confirming the potential of the local territory to make reds as well as whites. And when we moved on to the more traditional wines, the La Monacesca '00 selection, the cellar's trademark bottle, revealed aromas of aniseed, pears and apples, leading in to a warmly satisfying palate. The concentrated, lingering standard-label Verdicchio is almost as good as the selection. In contrast, Ecclesia is an opulent Chardonnay. Last in line was the Mirum, one of Italy's finest whites and excellent again this year. Obtained from 80 per cent verdicchio, with small proportions of chardonnay and sauvignon, it captivates the nose with notes of aromatic herbs and fruit that return delightfully on the palate.

○	Verdicchio di Matelica Cambrugiano Ris. '98	🍷🍷	4
○	Verdicchio di Matelica Vigneti Belisario '00	🍷🍷	3*
○	Verdicchio di Matelica Vigneti del Cerro '00	🍷🍷	3*
○	Esino Bianco Ferrante '00	🍷	1*
○	Verdicchio di Matelica Terre di Valbona '00	🍷	2*
●	Esino Rosso Colferraio '99	🍷	1*
●	San Leopardo '99		3
○	Verdicchio di Matelica Cambrugiano Ris. '97	🍷🍷	4

●	Camerte '99	🍷🍷🍷	5
○	Mirum '99	🍷🍷	4
○	Ecclesia Chardonnay '00	🍷🍷	4
○	Verdicchio di Matelica '00	🍷🍷	3*
○	Verdicchio di Matelica La Monacesca '00	🍷🍷	4
○	Mirus '91	🍷🍷🍷	5
○	Mirum '94	🍷🍷🍷	5
○	Verdicchio di Matelica La Monacesca '94	🍷🍷🍷	5
●	Camerte '98	🍷🍷	5
○	Mirum '98	🍷🍷	5

MONTECAROTTO (AN)

LAURENTINA
VIA SAN PIETRO
60036 MONTECAROTTO (AN)
TEL. 073189435

This recently established winery is housed in an efficiently designed building equipped with the latest technology, and its inclusion in the Guide in its second year of production is well deserved. Laurentina has made strategic decisions which overturn the usual vineyard management criteria for the area, with new plantations of 4,800 plants per hectare ensuring optimal yields. Black grapes account for about 60 per cent of the total production, rather than the verdicchio and lacrima white grapes grown extensively in the Jesi area. The wines produced do not follow international trends. Instead, they are solidly rooted in local tradition. The winery is supported in its explicit ambition of reaching premium quality standards quickly by oenologist Giancarlo Soverchia. A total of 35,000 bottles are obtained from the 11 hectares of vineyards. Two types are made, Verdicchio and Rosso Piceno. The Verdicchio Vigneto di Tobia is a good example of a traditional wine with a hint of innovation. The subtle, not especially insistent, aromas of lime blossom, geraniums and summer flowers are followed by a tangy, firm-structured palate, supported more by the backbone of the extract than by the vein of acidity. The Rosso Piceno has a deep purple colour. The nose is initially vegetal, opening out into red fruit aromas, then the densely textured palate, with its soft tannins, reveals ripe, juicy morello cherry before closing with a clean finish. The promising Rosso Piceno is still maturing in its barriques so we'll be telling you about it next year.

○ Verdicchio dei Castelli di Jesi Cl. Il Vigneto di Tobia '00	3*
● Rosso Piceno '00	3

MONTECAROTTO (AN)

TERRE CORTESI MONCARO
VIA PIANDOLE, 7/A
60036 MONTECAROTTO (AN)
TEL. 073189245
E-MAIL: terrecortesi@moncaro.com

This is one of the largest co-operatives in central Italy and its recent history has been encouraging. Following an ideological battle among the member growers that focused production on increasingly selective standards, Moncaro has been able to put together a highly respectable range, in both its premium line and the standard-label wines. One important feature is the attention given to environmental impact and the integrity of the wines, evident in the adoption of integrated vineyard management and the production of an organic Verdicchio. Let's begin our analysis of the wines with the Geo, the organic 2000 Verdicchio, supervised - like all Moncaro products - by oenologist Giulio D'Ignazi with the assistance of consultant Marco Monchiero. The wine is fresh-tasting and weighty, like the Le Vele selection from the same year. The rather more challenging Verde di Ca' Ruptae has intense aromas and rich, balanced palate. The best white, though, is the Verdicchio dei Castelli di Jesi Classico Superiore Vigna Novali 1998, which has great ageing potential and a typically varietal style. The Verdicchio dei Castelli di Jesi Classico Passito Tordiruta '98 couldn't repeat the previous year's performance but is still an exciting wine. Sweet, with a fairly complex nose of ripe fruit and dried figs, it is a shade too generous with the honey on the palate. The very good Riserva di Rosso Conero '97 Vigneti del Parco won Two Glasses while the Riserva di Rosso Conero '97 is reasonably expressive. The new DOC Rosso Piceno bottles, which have just joined the Terre Cortesi Moncaro range, are wines to watch.

○ Verdicchio dei Castelli di Jesi Cl. Sup. Vigna Novali '98	4
○ Verdicchio dei Castelli di Jesi Cl. Sup. Verde di Ca' Ruptae '00	3*
● Rosso Conero Vigneti del Parco Ris. '97	4
○ Verdicchio dei Castelli di Jesi Cl. Passito Tordiruta '98	5
○ Falerio dei Colli Ascolani Castello d'Acquaviva '00	2
○ Verdicchio dei Castelli di Jesi Biologico Geo '00	3
○ Verdicchio dei Castelli di Jesi Cl. '00	2*
○ Verdicchio dei Castelli di Jesi Cl. Le Vele '00	3
● Rosso Conero Ris. '97	3

MONTEGRANARO (AP)

Rio Maggio
C.da Vallone, 41
63014 Montegranaro (AP)
Tel. 0734889587

Graziano Santucci decided to invest in wine during the industrial boom of the early 1970s, although his experience lay in very different areas, and he made extensive plantings in the Montegranaro hills. Over 20 years later, his son Simone, helped by his wife Tiziana, found himself at the helm of a flourishing winery with an annual output of 100,000 bottles, all reliable and very fairly priced. The jewel in the estate crown is the Rosso Piceno GrAnarijS, which is supervised at every stage by oenologist Giancarlo Soverchia. The '99 is the product of a rather poor year but still shows a dense ruby red, with morello cherry and chocolate on the nose. The palate is concentrated and rounded, thanks to robust alcohol and soft, sweet tannins, then the finish is long and sound. The other flagship wine is the Artias Sauvignon, which returns to its usual high standard with the 2000 vintage. The distinct sensations of sage and elderflower are reflected in the delicately salty, intense palate. The Chardonnay can't keep up with them, though. It is soft but lacks personality. Moving on to the DOC whites, we note a fine performance by the '00 Falerio Telusiano, with typical spring flower and sweet almond aromas, and an attractively mouthfilling palate. The impressive standard-label wines include the Rosso Piceno '00, with its upfront, fruity character, and the Falerio '00, which offers summer flowers on the nose and a soft flavour.

O	Artias Sauvignon '00	ΨΨ	3*
O	Falerio dei Colli Ascolani Telusiano '00	ΨΨ	3*
●	Rosso Piceno GrAnarijS '99	ΨΨ	5
O	Falerio dei Colli Ascolani '00	Ψ	3
●	Rosso Piceno '00	Ψ	2*
O	Artias Chardonnay '00		3
●	Rosso Piceno GrAnarijS '97	ΨΨ	5
●	Rosso Piceno GrAnarijS '98	ΨΨ	5

MORRO D'ALBA (AN)

Stefano Mancinelli
Via Roma, 62
60030 Morro d'Alba (AN)
Tel. 073163021
E-mail: manvin@tin.it

The Mancinelli winery has been the guiding light in the Lacrima area for years, and a source of techniques to copy by other producers who want to endow the hard-to-handle variety with a noble style it certainly did not possess in the past. Despite an increase in competition with the emergence of many new wineries, Stefano Mancinelli is still the undisputed leader of Marche winemaking, although the 2000 vintage brought with it occasional quality blips. The Verdicchio Classico has delicate chamomile and acacia overtones on the nose and reasonable texture on a palate with well-balanced components. A little lower down the scale is the Verdicchio Classico Superiore, where ripe fruit and stewed apple aromas dominate the nose. The Terre dei Goti, a monovarietal Verdicchio, is a '97 white aged in barriques. Its aromas are rather reticent, although it is pleasantly fresh-tasting on the palate, which doesn't let the vintage down. The red Terre dei Goti is a very successful blend of lacrima grapes, part raisined and part subject to carbonic maceration. The colour, aromas and palate are consistent with the richness of the bouquet and the wine's lively personality recalls stewed plums, with notes of dried roses. Next, we retasted an excellent wine we reviewed last year. The Rosso Piceno San Michele has overtones of roses and alcohol-rich aromas that are echoed in the mouth, where they are backed up by no-nonsense acidity. The Lacrima, with its typical fruity aromas, is warm on the palate with lightweight tannins. Overall, it is correctly made wine but it is less exciting than previous versions.

●	Lacrima di Morro d'Alba S. Maria del Fiore '00	Ψ	3
●	Rosso Piceno S. Michele '00	Ψ	3
O	Verdicchio dei Castelli di Jesi Cl. S. Maria del Fiore '00	Ψ	3
O	Verdicchio dei Castelli di Jesi Cl. Sup. '00	Ψ	2*
O	Terre dei Goti Bianco	Ψ	4
●	Terre dei Goti Rosso	ΨΨ	5
●	Rosso Piceno S. Michele '99	Ψ	3

MORRO D'ALBA (AN)

Marotti Campi
Loc. Sant'Amico, 14
60030 Morro d'Alba (AN)
tel. 0731618027
e-mail: wine.marotticampi@tin.it

Sant'Amico is a traditional production area for Lacrima Morro d'Alba. This imposing hill overlooks the sea and has a favourable position, which enables the variety to express to the full its typically complex, fragrant aromas. The Marotti Campi winery is in its second year of production and owes its rapid ascent to shrewd investments that have permitted the construction of a modern cellar in record time. The guidance of the prudent and very competent oenologist Roberto Potentini has also been a factor. The barrique-aged Salmariano stands the archetypal fresh, fragrant profile for Verdicchio on its head. Bright straw yellow, with sweet notes of cakes, honey and stewed fruit on the nose that follow through on a well-rounded, voluptuously textured palate. A wine of structure, vanillaed and very stimulating. The traditional-style Luzano has a more fragrant character and a floral nose. The lime blossom and acacia are muted at first but then emerge more vigorously. The Rùbico may not have an impeccable nose but the classic rose and violet notes are still there. The palate shows rough-edged tannins that mask the fruity notes. The Xyris is a seductive attempt to produce a sparkling lacrima with low alcohol while preserving the variety's rich primary aromas. It could well be a good alternative as a dessert wine to some better known competitors.

○ Verdicchio dei Castelli di Jesi Cl. Salmariano '00	♆♆	4
● Lacrima di Morro d'Alba Rùbico '00	♆	3
○ Verdicchio dei Castelli di Jesi Cl. Luzano '00	♆	2*
● Xyris Filtrato di Lacrima		4

NUMANA (AN)

Conte Leopardi Dittajuti
Via Marina II, 26
60026 Numana (AN)
tel. 0717390116
e-mail: leopar@tin.it

The Leopardi Dittajuti vineyards currently cover about 20 hectares, although a further 15 are planned. Located in the Conero DOC zone, they are excellently aspected for quality wine production. In fact, everything is in place for distinctive interpretations of a unique terroir and this is exactly what Piervittorio Leopardi is aiming for, with the support of one of the most skilled oenologists in Marche, Giancarlo Soverchia. The sauvignon-based Bianco di Coppo is bright straw yellow with strong varietal characteristics in the nose that hints at tomatoes and sage leaf. The palate is sinewy and the smoothness of the flavour will emerge with greater precision over time. The straw yellow Calcare has typically vegetal sauvignon aromas, reasonably elegantly expressed. The overall impression is further enhanced on the palate. Richly extracted, tangy and fragrant, it shows some room for improvement, as did previous versions. The Fructus, as the name suggests, should be the cellar's freshest and fruitiest Rosso Conero. The 2000 version has achieved its aim on the palate but the nose is less successful. The Rosso Conero Vigneti del Coppo is an attractively clear ruby red with purple highlights. The grassy, heady aromas are followed by a palate with well-gauged acidity, concentration and soft tannins. The line-up of Rosso Coneros closes with the Pigmento, a dark ruby red wine with vibrant tinges of amaranth. The nose is a little unsophisticated but the palate is smooth, with soft tannins and fairly good balance.

○ Bianco del Coppo Sauvignon '00	♆♆	3*
○ Calcare Sauvignon '00	♆♆	4
● Rosso Conero Fructus '00	♆	3
● Rosso Conero Pigmento '97	♆	5
● Rosso Conero Vigneti del Coppo '99	♆	4
● Rosso Conero Pigmento '96	♆♆	5

NUMANA (AN)

Fattoria Le Terrazze
Via Musone, 4
60026 Numana (AN)
tel. 0717390352

OFFAGNA (AN)

Malacari
Via Enrico Malacari, 6
60020 Offagna (AN)
tel. 0717207606

Despite the weather in 1999, which seemed determined to making it difficult for the grapes to ripen, Le Terrazze obtained excellent products, proving that shoot thinning and field selection are strong weapons in challenging years. Antonio and Giorgina Terni, with the help of vineyard manager Leonardo Valenti and oenologist Attilio Pagli, made wines that are very different from the class of '98. There is shade less concentration but the elegance and complexity are still there. The Sassi Neri selection again won Three Glasses this year, compensating the lack of fleshy fruit in the vintage with barrique-derived toasty oak that is immediately evident on the nose. The wine then opens up with fruity aromas, recovering some freshness. The smooth tannic framework focuses on balance rather than strength and the finish is clean and deliciously lingering. The Chaos, a blend of montepulciano, syrah and merlot, has a dark, impenetrable hue. The restrained vanilla from the oak avoids masking the bilberry, bramble and elderberry fruit or spicy notes of cloves, cocoa powder and tar on the nose while the concentration on the palate allows the fruit and spice sensations to show through in the flavour. The standard-label Rosso Conero has decent fruit notes on a light, grassy palate. Not massive, but generally well managed. The chardonnay-based Le Cave is worth a Glass for its rich flavour but the aromas lack finesse. The wine is densely textured, with honeyed nuances, but the finish is one-dimensional and lacks freshness.

The attractive Offagna area is the natural extension to the west of Monte Conero, both in geographical and winemaking terms, because montepulciano is grown here. Vineyards have always been a characteristic feature of the Marche countryside hereabouts, along with olive groves and arable farmland. Part of this landscape are the south-facing properties of the Malacari winery, founded in 1668, at Baviera and Grigiano. Owner Alessandro Starabba and oenologist Sergio Paolucci have brought this winery out of its former obscurity. Alessandro has always believed in the potential of the montepulciano grape and in 1997, he began to make Rosso Conero, soon achieving excellent standards of quality. The winning ingredients are repeated selections in the vineyard at harvesting, thorough fermentation on the skins in stainless steel vats, and unhurried ageing in large and small wooden barrels. The Rosso Conero '99, with its scarlet colour, has dried roses and cherry notes in the nose. It is moderately well-structured on the palate – despite the difficult year, good work was done in the vineyard – with discernible but fundamentally soft tannins. The flavour reflects the nose with fruity characteristics that open and linger on the palate till the persistent finish. The Grigiano '98 selection is still available and has reached a perfect balance in these last few months of ageing. In fact, it is one of the most stylish Rosso Coneros ever made in the DOC zone.

● Rosso Conero Sassi Neri '99	🍷🍷🍷	5
● Chaos Rosso '99	🍷🍷	6
○ Le Cave Chardonnay '00	🍷	3
● Rosso Conero '99	🍷	3
● Chaos Rosso '97	🍷🍷🍷	6
● Rosso Conero Visions of J '97	🍷🍷🍷	6
● Rosso Conero Sassi Neri '98	🍷🍷🍷	5
● Rosso Conero Sassi Neri '95	🍷🍷	5
● Rosso Conero Sassi Neri '96	🍷🍷	5
● Rosso Conero Sassi Neri '97	🍷🍷	5

● Rosso Conero '99	🍷	3
● Rosso Conero Grigiano '98	🍷🍷	5

OFFIDA (AP)

Ciù Ciù
C.da Ciafone, 106
63035 Offida (AP)
tel. 0736810001
e-mail: info@ciuciu.com

It is always a pleasure to note a winery's success and include it in the Guide. Our satisfaction is even greater when the owners are young and motivated like brothers Massimiliano and Walter Bartolomei. The Ciù Ciù winery possesses about 70 hectares in the municipalities of Offida and Acquaviva and benefits from the input of skilled oenologist Pierluigi Lorenzetti. The top wine is the Oppidum '98, made from 100 per cent montepulciano harvested when fairly super-ripe. The wine is impenetrable. Its ruby red hue leads in to bottled cherries and raisins on the nose, then the tannins on the palate emerge, swathed in alcohol and rich extract. The impressive body is backed up by nice sinew and the finish reflects the nose with intense warmth. The Rosso Piceno Superiore Gotico '98 has cherry jam, liquorice and coffee on the nose. In the mouth, it is meaty but lacks elegance. The Rosso San Carro '00 is a blend of red varieties, including merlot and barbera. A light wine, it shows a fair amount of residual sugar. Turning to the whites, we enjoyed the Falerio dei Colli Ascolani '00, with its brightish straw yellow hue introducing broom and sweet almond aromas. The palate is full and well-rounded, with good grip and a fairly intense, bitterish finish. Lastly, we should mention that all the grapes are organically grown.

○ Falerio dei Colli Ascolani '00	🍷🍷	2*
● Oppidum Rosso '98	🍷🍷	4
● Rosso Piceno Sup. Gotico '98	🍷	3
● San Carro Rosso '00		3

OFFIDA (AP)

San Giovanni
C.da Ciafone, 41
63035 Offida (AP)
tel. 0736889032
e-mail: sangiovanni@vinisangiovanni.it

With the help of young oenologist Primo Narcisi from Piceno, Gianni De Lorenzo began aiming for quality wines a few years ago, very low yields enabling him to obtain top quality grapes. The drastic thinning of grapes in the vineyards, especially over the last two harvests, has resulted in very well-extracted wines. From next year, eight new vineyards will enter production. They are planted to both native and international varieties. Another innovation is the Rosso Piceno '00 Ophites, which – in contrast to previous years – is no longer a Superiore. Now it is a fresh-tasting wine, with immediate impact. At the tastings, however, its immediacy proved not to be synonymous with simplicity for the wine is very attractive and substantial. The Leo Guelfus '99 is a Rosso Piceno Superiore selection from a rather unfavourable year yet it still manages to express the typical features of the variety with a certain panache. The Rosso del Nonno '99 is a very good selection of Rosso Piceno Superiore, obtained from a blend that contains the maximum permitted proportion of montepulciano grapes. The wine is aged in 50-hectolitre oak barrels for eight months, and in barriques for a further six months. There is also a nice range of whites. The Falerio Leo Guelfus '00 stands out for its elegance and consistency while the white Ophites is appealingly fresh-tasting. The Marta '99 is an interesting attempt to make a more serious Falerio, although greater balance is needed between fruit and wood.

● Rosso Piceno Sup. Rosso del Nonno '99	🍷🍷	5
○ Falerio dei Colli Ascolani Leo Guelfus '00	🍷🍷	3*
○ Falerio dei Colli Ascolani Ophites '00	🍷	2*
● Rosso Piceno Ophites '00	🍷	3
○ Falerio dei Colli Ascolani Marta V. T. Ris. '99	🍷	4
● Rosso Piceno Sup. Leo Guelfus '99	🍷	3
● Rosso Piceno Sup. Rosso del Nonno '98	🍷🍷	5
● Rosso Piceno Sup. Leo Guelfus '98	🍷	3

OFFIDA (AP)

Villa Pigna
C.da Ciafone, 63
63035 Offida (AP)
Tel. 073687525 - 073687526
E-mail: villapigna@villapigna.com

This winery, with over 300 hectares of vineyards in Offida, is the largest in the DOC zone both in terms of production capacity and numbers of bottles produced of the various types. The wines maintain a constantly high level of quality across both native and international varieties. Winemaking is supervised by oenologist Massimo Uriani and it is the reds that are preferred, which reflects the potential of the vineyards. The top wine is once again the Cabernasco, obtained as you might guess from cabernet grapes. The spicy aromas are picked up on the soft palate. The Rozzano '98 was reviewed last year and we tasted again this year to gauge its ageing potential. It can still look to the future with confidence. The Rosso Piceno Superiore Vergaio '98 is not up to the level of the previous version but its best features are the consistency of its medium impact nose and the neat tannin-rich palate. The Briccaio Vellutato '98, obtained from 100 per cent montepulciano grapes, did equally well. It has rather vegetal aromas and a well-managed flavour that is enjoyable but not terribly generous. The Rosso Piceno Superiore '98 from the lower-priced range is upfront and great value for money. The Villa Pigna Brut, a cuve close sparkler, won a Glass, as did the Falerio dei Colli Ascolani Pliniano '00, a warm, alcohol-rich wine that lacks a touch of acidic structure. The Colle Malerbì '00, made from chardonnay grapes, has better balance. The standard-label Falerio '00 is well-made and also has an attractive price-quality ratio, while the Rugiasco, a direct chardonnay and riesling-based white, is only worth a mention.

● Cabernasco '98	¶¶	4
○ Colle Malerbì '00	¶	3
○ Falerio dei Colli Ascolani '00	¶	2*
○ Falerio dei Colli Ascolani Pliniano '00	¶	3
● Briccaio Vellutato '98	¶	3
● Rosso Piceno Sup. '98	¶	2*
● Rosso Piceno Sup. Vergaio '98	¶	3
○ Villa Pigna Brut	¶	3
○ Rugiasco '00		3
● Rozzano '98	¶¶	4

OSIMO (AN)

Umani Ronchi
S. S. 16, Km. 310+400, 74
60027 Osimo (AN)
Tel. 0717108019
E-mail: wine@umanironchi.it

This Osimo-based winery has 90 hectares of vineyards in the Rosso Conero zone, 40 of which are rented, and 100 in the Castelli di Jesi zone, where the Verdicchio cellar is located. The winery's main cellar buildings have been refurbished. Umani Ronchi belongs to the Bernetti family, who have turned it into a major player, both in Italy and beyond, for the range enjoys success in foreign markets. Verdicchio and montepulciano are the main varieties grown, though they have been joined over the years by chardonnay, sauvignon, cabernet sauvignon and merlot. The Pelago '98 is made from cabernet, merlot and montepulciano. Its peppery, slightly vegetal nose is followed by a more satisfying palate. The Rosso Conero Cùmaro and San Lorenzo '98 selections are excellent. Both express the typical features of montepulciano well in their aromas and plum-themed flavours. The Montepulciano d'Abruzzo Jorio '99 is very good and varietal while the Sangiovese Medoro from the same year was a pleasant surprise. The range of Verdicchios includes a series of top quality crus, thanks to the care and skill of oenologist Umberto Trombelli, who works effectively in tandem with Giacomo Tachis. The Plenio '98 has a generous, no-nonsense flavour while the Casal di Serra '00 offers herbal aromas and mineral sensations. The Villa Bianchi '00 is commendable for nose-palate consistency. But the most interesting product is the sweet Maximo wine. The '98 is different from previous versions, with more generous dried fruit and jam aromas echoed in the full and opulent flavour. The Le Busche '99, from chardonnay and verdicchio, is pleasant and harmonious.

○ Maximo '98	¶¶	5
○ Verdicchio dei Castelli di Jesi Cl. Sup. Casal di Serra '00	¶¶	4
○ Verdicchio dei Castelli di Jesi Cl. Villa Bianchi '00	¶¶	4
● Pelago '98	¶¶	6
● Rosso Conero Cùmaro '98	¶¶	5
● Rosso Conero S. Lorenzo '98	¶¶	4
○ Verdicchio dei Castelli di Jesi Cl. Plenio Ris. '98	¶¶	4
● Montepulciano d'Abruzzo Jorio '99	¶¶	4
○ Le Busche '99	¶	4
● Medoro Sangiovese '99	¶	3
○ Verdicchio dei Castelli di Jesi Cl. Sup. Casal di Serra '99	¶¶¶	4

OSTRA VETERE (AN)

F.lli Bucci
Via Cona, 30
60010 Ostra Vetere (AN)
tel. 071964179 - 026570558
e-mail: bucciwines@villabucci.com

The Bucci winery has always stood apart from others in the Castelli di Jesi zone. The winery's guarantee of high quality, instantly recognizable wines is a watchword with demanding consumers. This is also because Ampelio Bucci likes to take his time when marketing his deep, drinkable wines, which have the potential to develop over quite long periods of time. The winery has 18 hectares of vineyards, 14 planted with verdicchio and four with black grape varieties, especially sangiovese and montepulciano. Verdicchio comes from five, variously aspected vineyards at altitudes from 200 to 350 metres above sea level. The grapes are vinified separately and then used in different blends. We tasted the latest vintage of the Riserva Villa Bucci, which is the '98. A wine with of soberly expressive aromas, it offers hints of hazelnut and almond, and an elegantly soft palate. Three Glasses for its rich extract, confirming the absolute quality of the cellar's selections. Previous vintages are usually kept on the list, and we warmly recommend tasting these as this is a wine that has already amply demonstrated its ability to age for years, or even decades. The standard-label Verdicchio also performed creditably. The 2000 vintage is more robust than usual but maintains the traditional aplomb. Last, but definitely not least, the Rosso Piceno Pongelli '99 is stylish, with well-measured tannins.

O	Verdicchio dei Castelli di Jesi Cl. Villa Bucci Ris. '98	🍷🍷🍷	5
O	Verdicchio dei Castelli di Jesi Cl. '00	🍷	3*
●	Rosso Piceno Tenuta Pongelli '99	🍷	3
O	Verdicchio dei Castelli di Jesi Cl. Villa Bucci Ris. '95	🍷🍷	5
O	Verdicchio dei Castelli di Jesi Cl. Villa Bucci Ris. '97	🍷🍷	5

PESARO

Fattoria Mancini
Strada dei Colli, 35
61100 Pesaro
tel. 072151828
e-mail: fattoriamancini@libero.it

The Luigi Mancini winemaking credo is summed up in his driving passion for pinot nero. This variety, as we all know, can be tricky and tiresome to deal with but the Impero Rosso Selezione Fattoria Mancini '98 shows that Luigi's efforts in vineyard and cellar were not wasted. The wine has a good garnet ruby colour and an intense peppery nose, with autumn leaves and violets. The palate is brilliantly stylish in echoing the notes on the nose, and the tannins and acidity are well-balanced with the body. The long finish fully expresses the spicy hints of the variety. The pinot nero-based Blu '98 is also very good. More floral, with red fruit aromas, it reveals an intense thrust on the palate and a substantial finish. The Colli Pesaresi Focara 1999 from pinot nero and sangiovese is also good, with intense aromas evoking black pepper. The fresh-tasting, pleasant palate makes it a delicious, outstandingly drinkable wine. Turning to the whites, we found the Valserpe 1999, from sauvignon and pinot nero fermented without the skins, was not particularly convincing. The nose is vaguely mineral and the palate is marked by immature acidity and a leanish structure. The Colli Pesaresi Roncaglia '00, obtained from albanella and pinot nero fermented without the skins, is different again, its sweet almond and peach aromas nicely reflected in the smooth, fruit-rich palate.

●	Impero Pinot Nero Selezione F M '98	🍷🍷	6
O	Colli Pesaresi Bianco Roncaglia '00	🍷	3*
●	Blu '98	🍷🍷	5
●	Colli Pesaresi Rosso Focara '99	🍷	4
O	Valserpe '99		4
●	Impero Rosso '98	🍷🍷	4

POGGIO SAN MARCELLO (AN)

SARTARELLI
VIA COSTE DEL MOLINO, 24
60030 POGGIO SAN MARCELLO (AN)
TEL. 073189732
E-MAIL: info@sartarelli.it

We have come to expect Sartarelli to present Verdicchios of a particularly high standard every year, providing a benchmark that can stand comparison with other great Italian and non-domestic whites. The cellar have, in the past, shown just how good this wine can get with the Balciana selection and the Tralivio. If fermented and aged carefully, Verdicchio is a wine that can hold its head high in the most exalted company. Let's begin our analysis with the standard-label Verdicchio, which is admirably well-made. The typically intense, fragrant aromas are followed by a well-balanced structure with measured acidity. The long, concentrated finish guarantees a comfortable sojourn in the cellar for a further couple of years and the price-quality ratio is very good. The Tralivio, however, does not quite cut the mustard. Its limited aromatic range is coupled with a body where the dominant notes are alcohol and softness. Acidic backbone is lacking and this renders the palate rather flat and the flavours neutral and monotonous. The Contrada Balciana is the winery's leading selection. A bright straw yellow, flecked with green and gold, it proffers a fairly aromatic nose with notes of ripe apples, honey and thyme. On the palate, it has remarkable concentration, with a butteriness and rounded flavour that is perhaps excessively smooth from the discernible residual sugar. It's a white with considerable impact that does not, however, come up to the standards of previous vintages.

RIPATRANSONE (AP)

TENUTA COCCI GRIFONI
LOC. SAN SAVINO
C.DA MESSIERI, 12
63030 RIPATRANSONE (AP)
TEL. 073590143
E-MAIL: info@tenutacoccigrifoni.it

Guido Cocci Grifoni is something of a pioneer in recovering native vine varieties from Piceno, including passerina and pecorino, which will be able to count on a new DOC from next year's harvest. He is also an indefatigable champion of Rosso Piceno Superiore. Guido has focused on typicity since 1969 and put a great deal of effort into in tests and experiments. These have yielded good results. Last year, he presented the new Rosso Piceno Superiore Il Grifone, which is an unexpected development for the winery as it was aged in barriques instead of the large wooden barrels tradition demands. We tasted the '98 vintage, which is intended to be the flagship of the winery's entire list. The colour is fairly evolved and the aromas lack a little definition, though the cherry fruit comes through well. The palate, too, is leanish. The other selection we tasted, the Vigna Messieri from '99, which was not a good year locally, is a fruity, stylish and drinkable wine. The more economical Rosso Piceno Superiore selection, Le Torre '99, is quite a good middle-of-the-road product, which sticks to type. Also worth uncorking is the immediate and fairly rustic Rosso Piceno '00. Moving on to the whites, we recommend the Passerina Brut, an always well-made Charmat method sparkler from passerina grapes, the Falerio Vigneti San Basso '00 selection and the standard-label Falerio. The best white is the Podere Colle Vecchio 2000, from pecorino grapes. Vibrant straw yellow, it offers ripe fruit aromas and a fairly full flavour.

○ Verdicchio dei Castelli di Jesi Cl. '00	♟♟	3*
○ Verdicchio dei Castelli di Jesi Cl. Sup. Contrada Balciana '99	♟♟	6
○ Verdicchio dei Castelli di Jesi Cl. Sup. Tralivio '00	♟	4
○ Verdicchio dei Castelli di Jesi Cl. Sup. Contrada Balciana '94	♟♟♟	6
○ Verdicchio dei Castelli di Jesi Cl. Sup. Contrada Balciana '95	♟♟♟	6
○ Verdicchio dei Castelli di Jesi Cl. Sup. Contrada Balciana '97	♟♟♟	6
○ Verdicchio dei Castelli di Jesi Cl. Sup. Contrada Balciana '98	♟♟♟	6
○ Verdicchio dei Castelli di Jesi Cl. Sup. Tralivio '99	♟♟	4

○ Podere Colle Vecchio '00	♟♟	3*
○ Falerio dei Colli Ascolani '00	♟	2*
○ Falerio dei Colli Ascolani Vigneti San Basso '00	♟	3
○ Passerina Brut	♟	3
● Rosso Piceno Sup. Il Grifone '98	♟	5
● Rosso Piceno Sup. Vigna Messieri '99	♟	4
● Rosso Piceno Sup. Le Torri '99		3
● Rosso Piceno '00		2
● Rosso Piceno Sup. Il Grifone '97	♟♟	5

RIPATRANSONE (AP)

LA CANTINA DEI COLLI RIPANI
VIA TOSCIANO, 28
63038 RIPATRANSONE (AP)
TEL. 07359505 - 073599940
E-MAIL: info@colliripani.com

Colli Ripiani makes a well deserved entry into the Guide this year. This co-operative winery has invested a great deal in a bottling system, cellar door sales outlet and other winemaking and ancillary areas. It has also set up a quality programme with selected members to identify criteria for getting the very best out of the grapes through low yields and field selection. The standard-label products are very competitively priced but still suffer from the quantity-oriented choices typical of many co-operatives. The most emblematic product of the winery's new approach is the convincing Pharus line, supervised by Fabrizio Ciufoli, the co-operative's ever-competent oenologist. Brezzolino is a pleasant Falerio whose slightly unfocused nose makes way for a concentrated palate with a nice tangy finish. The Leukon, a chardonnay aged in barriques, has a delicately fumé nose with liquorice notes and the palate evokes the sweetness of the wood, with fruity freshness. The Castellano is aged in large barrels but has preserved its aroma-rich acidity, with clear, fruity notes of prunes, brambles and elderberry on both the nose and the palate. The Leo Ripanus has tangy ripe cherry aromas and a substantial palate, its texture harmonized by well-gauged tannins. This austere yet pleasant red is certain to cellar well. The Passito has an amber yellow colour and a dense, dried fruit nose. Sadly, the rounded but dullish palate doesn't live up to expectations.

● Rosso Piceno Sup. Castellano '97	▼▼	4
● Rosso Piceno Sup. Leo Ripanus '98	▼▼	4
○ Chardonnay Leukon '00	▼	3
○ Falerio dei Colli Ascolani Brezzolino '00	▼	2*
○ Passito Anima Mundi	▼	4
● Rosso Piceno Sup. Castellano '96	▽▽	4
● Rosso Piceno Sup. Leo Ripanus '97	▽▽	4

RIPATRANSONE (AP)

LE CANIETTE
C.DA CANALI, 23
63038 RIPATRANSONE (AP)
TEL. 07359200
E-MAIL: info@lecaniette.it

In last year's Guide, we were happy to note the improvements at the winery run by Raffaele, Luigi and Giovanni Vagnoni. The hoped for results were promptly forthcoming at this year's tasting. The prize for the best wine in the range goes to the Nero di Vite 1998, a Rosso Piceno making its debut on the market and which the winery's releases as a Riserva. It is deep ruby red, with cherry jam, coffee and chocolate on the nose. On the palate, the lively tannins and alcohol combine to weave a dense texture that signs off with a warm persistent finish. The Morellone '99 selection is good but not as good as the '98 version. In general, 1999 was not a good year for montepulciano and this is evident in the tannins, which are still a bit edgy. The nose is convincing, with cherry and coffee overtones, as is the generous, well-sustained palate, and the wine is likely to improve with further bottle ageing. The last Rosso Piceno is the Bello 1999, the winery's standard-label wine. A clean-tasting, fruity wine with astringent tannins, it reveals a bitterish twist in the finish. The Falerio Lucrezia '00 has summer flowers, chamomile and ripe fruit on the nose while the mouthfilling, smooth palate focuses on sweet almonds. Irresistible as ever, the new version of the Vino Santo di Ripatransone Sibilla Agrippa, from 100 per cent passerina, has distinct notes of oxidation on the nose that are moderated on the palate by sensations of stewed apple and dried apricot. A honeyed, but not cloying, sweetness provide the keynote on the palate.

● Rosso Piceno Nero di Vite '98	▼▼	5
● Rosso Piceno Morellone '99	▼▼	4
○ Vino Santo di Ripatransone Sibilla Agrippa	▼▼	6
○ Falerio dei Colli Ascolani Lucrezia '00	▼▼	3*
● Rosso Piceno Rosso Bello '99	▼	3
● Rosso Piceno Morellone '98	▽▽	4
● Rosso Piceno Rosso Bello '98	▽▽	3
○ Vino Santo di Ripatransone Sibilla Delphica	▽▽	6

RIPATRANSONE (AP)

San Savino
Loc. San Savino
C.da Santa Maria in Carro, 13
63038 Ripatransone (AP)
tel. 073590107

Owned and run by Domenico Capecci with the help of his son Simone and oenologist Federico Giotto, San Savino makes an interesting debut. The estate comprises 25 hectares of vineyards in a fine growing area but its long history of winemaking was interrupted when the family decided to sell the grapes to co-operatives. More recently, the restoration of the cellar buildings coincided with the realization that the fruit was of excellent quality. And the series of reds presented this year is comparable to any in the region. The Moggio '98, from 100 per cent sangiovese, is so good that it trotted off with Three Glasses on its first outing. A strikingly intense red with a richly complex nose, it tempts with fruity nuances and hints of violets mingling with measured hints of coffee and vanilla. On the palate, it is warm and harmonious, with sweet tannins that soften a richly extracted finish with delicious notes of ripeness. The Mito '98, from 100 per cent stainless steel-aged montepulciano, has a deep ruby red colour. Its aromas of morello cherry and liquorice are laced with varietal gamey overtones and spicy notes from the mineral-rich terroir. The palate is generous. An excellent performance also came from the Rosso Piceno Superiore Rubbio '97. Ruby red tending to garnet, it unveils berry fruit and balsam notes on the nose and a warm, structured palate. The same can be said of the Rosso Piceno Superiore '99, with its dense colour and evocative nose leading in to enviable texture on the palate. Finally, the white Colle di Guardia '99, from pecorino grapes, has complex citrus aromas and a full, fruity flavour.

● Sangiovese Moggio '98	🍷🍷🍷	5
● Mito '98	🍷🍷	5
● Rosso Piceno Sup. Rubbio Sel. '97	🍷🍷	5
○ Colle di Guardia '99	🍷🍷	3*
● Rosso Piceno Sup. '99	🍷🍷	3*

SAN PAOLO DI JESI (AN)

Amato Ceci
Via Battinebbia, 4
60038 San Paolo di Jesi (AN)
tel. 0731779197 - 0731779052
e-mail: info@vignamato.com

This winery confirmed its right to the profile earned last year in the Guide. Run by Maurizio Ceci with the help of oenologist Sergio Paolucci, its distinctive winemaking style foregrounds Verdicchio. And how could it be otherwise? The 10 hectares or so of part estate-owned vineyards are situated in one of the areas where the variety feels most at home: the hills that rise softly above the southern slopes of the Esino river valley. The winery's Verdicchio is absolutely typical and richly extracted, with the trademark bitterish twist in the finish. The Vignamato, almost archetypal for the DOC zone, is ripe on nose and palate. The gentle hints of lime blossom and elderflower are echoed on the palate, where they meld seamlessly into the robust, concentrated structure. The low acidity never jeopardizes the overall balance, which is nicely managed. The Valle delle Lame has a fresher nose, and the sensations on the palate are more polished, where there is good, but rather lighter, structure. The Rosso Vignamato has a clear garnet colour, boisé notes on the nose and overtones of vanilla, from ageing in small wooden barrels, on the fairly weighty palate. Finally, the Rosolaccio is a very enjoyable Rosso Piceno with peony highlights in the glass and echoes of ripe plums and brambles on the nose. The attractively structured palate shows very nice balance.

○ Verdicchio dei Castelli di Jesi Cl. Sup. Vignamato '00	🍷🍷	3*
● Rosso Piceno Rosolaccio '00	🍷	2*
○ Verdicchio dei Castelli di Jesi Cl. Valle delle Lame '00	🍷	2*
● Vignamato Rosso '99	🍷	3

SERRA DE' CONTI (AN)

CASALFARNETO
VIA FARNETO, 16
60030 SERRA DE' CONTI (AN)
TEL. 0731889001
E-MAIL: info@casalfarneto.it

This fairly young winery, founded in 1995, has staked an immediate claim to fame as an interpreter of Verdicchio. Sheltered by the foothills of the Apennines, at altitudes ranging from 300 to 350 metres above sea level, its 23 hectares are planted mainly to white varieties. The cellar is situated in a group of restructured farmhouses with all the modern technology necessary to make wines of a consistently high quality. The warm weather in 2000 lowered the acidity of the fruit so the whites lack the fragrance that enables them to develop and become really drinkable. But although this problem affects many wines of that year, Casalfarneto skilfully parried the blow by focusing on extract and concentration of the fruit. The Grancasale was fermented at low temperatures after brief skin contact. The super-ripe grapes give the wine warm aromatic tones and plenty of extract, with alcohol prevailing over acidity. The Fontevecchia is fresher. Its attractive aromas harmoniously offset the pulpy structure then intense after-aromas echo the notes of lime blossom, acacia and geraniums on the nose. The Verdicchio Cimaio '98 has ripe, fairly complex aromas but the wood is a little too evident.

SERRAPETRONA (MC)

ALBERTO QUACQUARINI
VIA COLLI, 1
62020 SERRAPETRONA (MC)
TEL. 0733908180

The Vernaccia di Serrapetrona DOC is small both in terms of surface area and in the number of wineries. Almost extreme in terms of altitude and climate, two factors which prompted the triple fermentation technique, it lies in wonderful countryside. We hear through the grapevine, if you'll pardon the pun, that the over the next few years the four local wineries intend to seek DOCG status. This is a good thing, if only for the rediscovered sense of belonging to the territory. The decision will save a unique variety and wine from becoming a fairground curiosity. Meanwhile, let's take a look at the results achieved by Mauro, Luca and Alberto Quacquarini, who make bold, innovative wines like the Petronio '98. This red was reviewed last year and is now on sale. From 100 per cent raisined vernaccia grapes, it has a slightly lower concentration of sugar than is required for sparkling wines. It undergoes a fairly protracted maceration, fermenting until all the sugar is transformed into alcohol. The ripe berry fruit on the nose is reflected on the satisfying, well-gauged palate. The brand new Colli della Serra '98 is a blend of 25 per cent vernaccia and 25 per cent sangiovese with 50 per cent merlot and cabernet. The vernaccia does not really come across and seems to be overpowered by the severe, fairly tight-knit texture. As well as the two wines the panel tasted, the cellar offers classic Vernaccias, in both dry and 'amabile' versions. For the 2000 vintage, we prefer the dry bottle, with its purple-flecked hue and floral aromas. On the palate, it is attractively warm and flavoursome.

○ Verdicchio dei Castelli di Jesi Cl. Sup. Fontevecchia '00	ΨΨ	3*
○ Verdicchio dei Castelli di Jesi Cl. Sup. Grancasale '00	ΨΨ	4
○ Verdicchio dei Castelli di Jesi Cl. Cimaio Ris. '98	Ψ	4
● Vernaccia di Serrapetrona Secco '00	Ψ	4
● Colli della Serra Rosso '98	Ψ	4
● Vernaccia di Serrapetrona Amabile '00		4
● Petronio '98	ΨΨ	6

SERVIGLIANO (AP)

FATTORIA DEZI
C.DA FONTE MAGGIO, 14
63029 SERVIGLIANO (AP)
TEL. 0734750408 - 0734740077
E-MAIL: Mauridez@tin.it

Stefano Dezi went to great lengths to convince his father, Romolo, uncle Remo and brother Maurizio that they needed to work harder in the vineyard, refurbish the cellars and purchase expensive French oak barriques to put their winery on the map. We are now starting to witness the results – with no little satisfaction. But the road to the region's winemaking heights is paved with hazards. For example, it is not always possible to obtain tip-top fruit. That is what happened in 1999, when the montepulciano was just not good enough for Regina del Bosco, the winery's leading selection. Stefano kept these grapes for the Dezio Vigneto Beccaccia, and obtained a fragrant, highly drinkable red with well-defined, typical fruit. The sangiovese used for the Solo selection, on the other hand, turned out extremely well. The nose is an inebriating bouquet of stylish Parma violet, black cherry and Peruvian bark aromas, layered with spicy tones. The Solo has firm, fine-grained tannins in an intriguing palate that signs off with a very long finish. Stefano's passion and spirit of adventure have also taken him into uncharted territory with white wines. While the Le Solagne '00 from verdicchio, trebbiano and pecorino is deliberately fresh-tasting and zesty, with apple and hazelnut flavours, the Le Solagne Vendemmia Tardiva, vinified in stainless steel only, packs all the vigorous aromatic punch of its malvasia toscana and verdicchio blend. The intense aromas are reminiscent of pineapple and broom, which return on the generous, persistent palate, where acidity and softer alcohol, sugar and glycerine extract components find a perfect balance.

	Wine	Rating	Score
●	Solo Sangiovese '99	♟♟	4
○	Le Solagne V. T. '00	♟♟	4
○	Le Solagne '00	♟	3
●	Dezio Vigneto Beccaccia '99	♟	3
●	Rosso Piceno Regina del Bosco '97	♟♟	4
●	Rosso Piceno Regina del Bosco '98	♟♟	4
○	Le Solagne V. T. '99	♟♟	4

SPINETOLI (AP)

SALADINI PILASTRI
VIA SALADINI, 5
63030 SPINETOLI (AP)
TEL. 0736899534
E-MAIL: saladpil@tin.it

The attractive Saladini Pilastri winery at Spinetoli, in the heart of the Piceno wine area is underneath an interesting 15th-century farmhouse that has been renovated in recent years. The wines are noteworthy for the consistently high quality that has been achieved and maintained in recent years. Efforts have also been made to keep prices affordable. Of the wines we tasted this year, presented by expert oenologist Domenico D'Angelo, the best was definitely the Vigna Montetinello 1998, one of the best Rosso Piceno Superiore selections around. This deep, tight-knit wine has intense aromas, with plums to the fore, and a richly extracted palate. The winery also uncorked the new '99 Rosso Piceno Superiore, a nicely typical wine from a less than memorable year. Moving on to the whites, we would first of all draw you attention to the Vigna Palazzi '00, a Falerio selection which Saladini Pilastri has been releasing to an appreciative market for a few years. The latest edition has a nice bright yellow colour, ripe fruit aromas and an enjoyably weighty flavour with robust alcohol. The well-managed Falerio '00 is more quaffable, though. As well as traditional labels from this area, the winery also offers an interesting red and white under the Pregio del Conte label. The white has good alcohol and is obtained from fiano and falanghina grapes. It shows citrus aromas and a nice, concentrated flavour.

	Wine	Rating	Score
○	Falerio dei Colli Ascolani Vigna Palazzi '00	♟♟	2*
○	Pregio del Conte Bianco '00	♟♟	2*
●	Rosso Piceno Sup. Vigna Montetinello '98	♟♟	4
●	Rosso Piceno Sup. '99	♟	2*
○	Falerio dei Colli Ascolani '00		1
●	Rosso Piceno Sup. Vigna Monteprandone Conte Saladino '97	♟♟	4
●	Pregio del Conte Rosso '98	♟♟	3
●	Rosso Piceno Sup. Vigna Monteprandone Conte Saladino '98	♟♟	4

STAFFOLO (AN)

Fattoria Coroncino
C.da Coroncino, 7
60039 Staffolo (AN)
tel. 0731779494
e-mail: coroncino@libero.it

Luca Canestrari only makes white wine. Over the years, he has shown that he can do so very well indeed, earning the Guide's highest accolade. Thanks to the unique climatic conditions in the Staffolo hills and Luca's limited yields, his Verdicchios are always sumptuous and richly alcoholic. In the last two years, Luca has become enamoured of barriques and tonneaux, a development that has prompted him to make Gaiospino Fumé. The '98 vintage is a first attempt, with a limited release. Golden yellow, it unveils an intense nose where toasty oak notes mingle with cake and butter sensations. The palate has plenty of stuffing and moderately intense oak-derived aromas, as well as excellent length. This muscular wine will be at its best in a few years when the boisé edge has mellowed a shade. The Gaiospino '99 well-balanced and drinking nicely. It, too, has fumé hints on the nose but these are much less intrusive. The palate combines generous flavour and remarkable style. Moving on to the wines vinified and aged exclusively in stainless steel, we particularly enjoyed the Coroncino '99, with its typical sweet almond nose and soft, warm, structured palate. It was the best of the range. The Bacco '00 is fresh-tasting, intriguing and anything but run-of-the-mill while the Staffolo from the same year has an immediately appealing impact while remaining true to the winery's sophisticated style.

○ Verdicchio dei Castelli di Jesi Cl. Coroncino '99	♈♈	3*
○ Verdicchio dei Castelli di Jesi Cl. Sup. Gaiospino '99	♈♈	4
○ Verdicchio dei Castelli di Jesi Cl. Bacco '00	♈	3
○ Verdicchio dei Castelli di Jesi Cl. Staffolo '00	♈	2*
○ Verdicchio dei Castelli di Jesi Cl. Sup. Gaiospino Fumé '98	♈	6
○ Verdicchio dei Castelli di Jesi Cl. Sup. Gaiospino '97	♈♈♈	4
○ Verdicchio dei Castelli di Jesi Cl. Sup. Gaiospino '98	♈♈	4

STAFFOLO (AN)

Fonte della Luna
Medoro Cimarelli
Via San Francesco, 1
60039 Staffolo (AN)
tel. 0731779307

Young Luca Cimarelli and oenologist Giancarlo Soverchia know what is needed to achieve premium quality – tenacity, a competitive spirit and hard work in the vineyard. Now that the wonderful grapes they grow on their Staffolo terroir have a modern, restructured cellar at their disposal, the winery's upwardly mobile momentum has moved up a gear. We welcome these laudable decisions with just one, tiny regret. Sometimes, the Rosso Piceno Grizio does not go into the bottle in time for Guide. Unfortunately, there's little point in writing about it after the event for it sells out to the last bottle before the next Guide is published. So you'll just have to take our word for it that the Grizio 1999, despite the tricky harvest period which made it rather a poor year, was a treasure. Utterly drinkable, stylish and with exemplary definition of the fruit. Turning to the two new products we tasted, we found the Verdicchio dei Castelli di Jesi Classico Fra Moriale '00 to be a textbook exercise in strength and typicity. Sweet almonds, ripe apples and acacia blossom on the nose usher in a good attack on the palate, where alcohol, juicy fruit and great structure all come through. The standard-label 2000 Verdicchio is not far short of the selection in quality. Almonds are still there on the nose, with sweet glycerine overtones, and the palate may be a little less intense and persistent, but it's still very mouthfilling.

○ Verdicchio dei Castelli di Jesi Cl. '00	♈♈	3*
○ Verdicchio dei Castelli di Jesi Cl. Sup. Fra Moriale '00	♈♈	4

OTHER WINERIES

ALBERTO SERENELLI
VIA DEL CONERO, 20/C
60129 ANCONA
TEL. 07131343

The best products this year are the Rosso Conero Varano 1998, with morello cherries and tar in the nose and a rather over-generously extracted palate, and the Verdicchio dei Castelli di Jesi Sora Elvira '00 which weighty, glycerine-rich and very soft.

○ Verdicchio dei Castelli di Jesi Cl. Sora Elvira '00	♀	4
● Rosso Conero Varano '98	♀	5

CATIA SPINSANTI
VIA GALLETTO, 29
60021 CAMERANO (AN)
TEL. 071731797

Catia Spinsanti's winery is situated at Camerano, in the Parco del Conero. This second edition of the Camars is a modern-style monovarietal red from montepulciano grapes. Ruby red with good extract, it offers pleasant, pronounced aromas of cocoa powder and red peppers.

● Camars '00	♀	4

COLLE STEFANO
LOC. COLLE STEFANO
62022 CASTELRAIMONDO (MC)
TEL. 0737640439
E-MAIL: info@collestefano.com

A small, organically farmed estate that has been producing a successful Verdicchio di Matelica selection for several years. The 2000 Colle Stefano has delicate herbal and floral aromas and a tangy, complex flavour. Even better, it also sells for a very competitive price.

○ Verdicchio di Matelica Colle Stefano '00	♀	2*

CANTINA COOPERATIVA CASTIGNANESE
C.DA SAN VENANZO, 31
63032 CASTIGNANO (AP)
TEL. 0736822216
E-MAIL: scac@topnet.it

Our favourites from this winery's extensive range were, in order of presentation: the Gramelot '99, a white blend with good floral aromas and a well-sustained palate; the light but deliciously smooth Falerio dei Colli Ascolani '00; and lastly the full-bodied, pleasantly rustic Rosso Piceno Superiore '98.

○ Falerio dei Colli Ascolani '00	♀	1*
● Rosso Piceno Sup. '98	♀	2
○ Gramelot '99	♀	3

Saputi
C.da Fiastra, 2
62020 Colmurano (MC)
tel. 0733508137

The Saputi winery focuses on local DOCs. White maceratino grapes and red montepulciano and sangiovese respectively go into Castru Vecchiu '00, with its floral nose and fresh-tasting palate, and the Rosso Piceno Castru Vecchiu 1999, a red with cherry aromas and rich extract but rather a rustic flavour.

● Rosso Piceno Castru Vecchiu '99 ❦	3
○ Colli Maceratesi Bianco Castru Vecchiu '00	2

Mancini
Via Santa Lucia, 19
60030 Maiolati Spontini (AN)
tel. 0731702975

We recommend this winery from Maiolati for its two selections of Verdicchio dei Castelli di Jesi: Ghibellino is fresher and more immediate; Santa Lucia is straw yellow with pale green highlights and pronounced notes of aromatic herbs and hay in the nose. The palate is backed up by good alcohol.

○ Verdicchio dei Castelli di Jesi Cl. Sup. Santa Lucia '00 ❦	4
○ Verdicchio dei Castelli di Jesi Cl. Ghibellino '00 ❦	3

Bisci
Via Fogliano, 120
62024 Matelica (MC)
tel. 0737787490
e-mail: bisciwines@libero.it

The Bisci winery extends over 105 hectares in the Verdicchio di Matelica DOC zone. The Vigneto Fogliano '98 selection has intense lime blossom aromas and a robust, very ripe palate. The interesting '99 Villa Castglioni red shows good extract.

● Villa Castiglioni '99 ❦	4
○ Verdicchio di Matelica Vigneto Fogliano '98 ❦	4

Gino Gagliardi
Via Aristide Merloni, 5
62024 Matelica (MC)
tel. 073785611
e-mail: vinigagliardig@libero.it

One of the best Gagliardi products, apart from the Verdicchios, is the merlot-based Pianero. The 2000 version has a concentrated colour, vibrant spice-nuanced aromas and a satisfying flavour. The Maccagnano '000 has intense, fragrant aromas that are mirrored well on the palate.

● Pianero '00 ❦	3
○ Verdicchio di Matelica Maccagnano '00 ❦	4

San Biagio
Via San Biagio, 32
62024 Matelica (MC)
tel. 073783997

The Verdicchio di Matelica we tasted was the Vigneto Braccano '99, which has medium weight in the mouth and a pale straw yellow hue. The nose has vegetal notes and there is a distinct note of acidity in the mouth. The sangiovese and ciliegiolo Bragnolo '99 is pleasant and the Grottagrifone '99 is stylish and balanced.

● Bragnolo Rosso '99 ❦	4
● Grottagrifone Rosso '99 ❦	5
○ Verdicchio di Matelica Vigneto Braccano '99 ❦	4

Fattoria Laila
Via S. Filippo sul Cesano, 27
61040 Mondavio (PU)
tel. 0721979357

Fattoria Laila's winery is situated in 30 acres just outside the province of Ancona, where this stylish, evocative Verdicchio dei Castelli di Jesi is made. Lime blossom and herbs herald a palate with nicely gauged alcohol. The Rosso Piceno '00 is also good.

● Rosso Piceno '00 ❦	3*
○ Verdicchio dei Castelli di Jesi '00 ❦	2*

Donatella Paoloni
Via Sabbionare, 10
60036 Montecarotto (AN)
Tel. 0731889004
E-mail: sabbionare@libero.it

Sergio Paolucci is the oenologist at Donatella Paoloni's winery, which is beginning to get into its stride. The Verdicchio Sabbionare '00 has intense golden delicious apples in the nose and an overall elegance with good alcohol. The other Verdicchio, I Pratelli '00, is also more than just decent.

○ Verdicchio dei Castelli di Jesi Cl. Sabbionare '00	♀	3
○ Verdicchio dei Castelli di Jesi Cl. I Pratelli '00	♀	2*

Azzoni Avogadro Carradori
Via Carradori, 13
62010 Montefano (MC)
Tel. 0733850002 - 0733850219
E-mail: fdeglia@tin.it

This 850-hectare estate has 130 planted to vine. The grechetto-based Cantalupo '00 is an attractive white with forthright herb and hay aromas; the palate has good alcohol. The Colli Maceratesi Bianco, also from the '00 vintage, is well-made with a moderately full-bodied palate.

○ Cantalupo Bianco '00	♀	3
○ Colli Maceratesi Bianco '00	♀	2

F.lli Badiali
Via Marconi, 26
60030 Morro d'Alba (AN)
Tel. 073163510

The historic Morro d'Alba winery has updated its Lacrima, turning it into a fresh, quaffable wine with soft tannins. The Paucca '00 – about 6,500 bottles are made – has depth on the nose, offering hints of dried roses and ripe brambles, followed up by a palate that has you reaching for a second glass.

● Lacrima di Morro d'Alba Paucca '00	♀	4

Lucchetti
Via Santa Maria del Fiore, 17
60030 Morro d'Alba (AN)
Tel. 073163314

This small winery is strongly committed to the local DOCs and presents two versions of Lacrima. Only the black label distinguishes the selection from the standard product. The former has more style on the nose and a very inviting palate while its stablemate is enjoyable and uncomplicated.

● Lacrima di Morro d'Alba '00	♀	3
● Lacrima di Morro d'Alba Sel. Etichetta Nera '00	♀	4

Capinera
C.da Crocette, 16
62010 Morrovalle (MC)
Tel. 0733222444

The Capinera bothers have decided that quality is the way to go. They make local wines, with the occasional foray into the international arena, under the watchful eye of oenologist Giovanni Basso. This year, they presented a good Rosso Piceno Duca Guarnerio 1999 and an enjoyable Chardonnay La Capinera.

● Rosso Piceno Duca Guarnerio '99	♀	4
○ Chardonnay La Capinera '00		4

Aurora
C.da Ciafone, 98
63035 Offida (AP)
Tel. 0736810007
E-mail: enrico@viniaurora.it

Aurora was one of the first estates to adopt the organic credo. This year, they presented a Rosso Piceno '00 with a brilliant ruby red colour and pleasant, clean-tasting palate with no tannin-inspired edginess. The pecorino-based Fiorile '00 is also good, showing apple and spring flower aromas, and a tangy, persistent palate.

○ Fiorile '00	♀	3
● Rosso Piceno '00	♀	2

Castello Fageto
Via Valdaso, 52
63016 Pedaso (AP)
Tel. 0734931784
E-mail: castellofageto@castellofageto.it

Claudio Di Ruscio's winery turned out a very decent range this year, the best of these being the Rusus '98, with clean cherry aromas and warmth on the palate, and the Alido, a sweet white with a raisin and honey nose that is echoed in the full-bodied palate.

○ Alido '00	🍷	4
● Rosso Piceno Rusus '98	🍷	3

Santa Cassella
C.da Santa Cassella, 7
62018 Potenza Picena (MC)
Tel. 0733671507

Santa Cassella presented the panel with a good, spice-and-fruit Rosso Piceno '99 and a series of whites. The Guardia Vecchia '00, for example, has a varietal nose and an attractively straightforward palate that fades early. The white Donna Angela '00 is also good, with fragrant aromas and a fresh flavour.

○ Chardonnay Guardia Vecchia '00	🍷	2*
○ Donna Angela '00	🍷	3
● Rosso Piceno '99	🍷	2*

Maurizio Marconi
Via Melano, 23
60030 San Marcello (AN)
Tel. 0731267223

The winery has more than 20 hectares of vineyards. Production is supervised by oenologist Sergio Paolucci and the high point this year is the Verdicchio Corona Reale. Evocative lime blossom and elderflower lead in to a concentrated, well-sustained palate. The lacrima-based Falconiere is fragrant and alcohol-rich.

● Lacrima di Morro d'Alba Sel. Falconiere '00	🍷	4
○ Verdicchio dei Castelli di Jesi Cl. Sup. Sel. Corona Reale '00	🍷	4

Massimo Serboni
Via Case Sparse Borgiano, 6
62020 Serrapetrona (MC)
Tel. 0733904088

This small winery, run by Massimo Serboni, specializes in the production of the local Vernaccia di Serrapetrona DOC and offers several versions. The most interesting are the Selezione Passita, with more generous alcohol, less prickle and vernaccia's signature flowery notes, and the I Serboni Secco.

● Vernaccia di Serrapetrona I Serboni Secco '00	🍷	4
● Vernaccia di Serrapetrona Sel. Passita Dolce '00	🍷	5

Angelo Accadia
Fraz. Castellaro
Via Ammorto, 19
60040 Serra San Quirico (AN)
Tel. 0731857009

Angelo Accadia offered the panel two selections of Verdicchio dei Castelli di Jesi. The Classico Conscio '00 has rather vegetal aromas and a good fresh flavour. The Classico Cantori '00 is obtained from slightly super-ripe, more carefully selected fruit. Intense on the nose, it has good weight in the mouth.

○ Verdicchio dei Castelli di Jesi Cl. Cantorì '00	🍷	3
○ Verdicchio dei Castelli di Jesi Cl. Conscio '00	🍷	2*

F.lli Zaccagnini & C.
Via Salmagina, 9/10
60039 Staffolo (AN)
Tel. 0731779892
E-mail: info@zaccagnini.it

The Zaccagnini vineyards are situated at about 450 metres above sea level. We recommend the oak-aged Pier delle Vigne '97. The standard-label Verdicchio dei Castelli di Jesi Classico is always well-made and this version has clean aromas and a forthright, flavoursome palate.

○ Verdicchio dei Castelli di Jesi Cl. '00	🍷	3
○ Verdicchio dei Castelli di Jesi Cl. Pier delle Vigne Ris. '97	🍷	5

UMBRIA

Another year, another six Three Glass wines. It wouldn't be unreasonable to call it the "Umbrian miracle", given that only a decade ago, the focus of the region was large quantities of good-value reds and whites, a sector to which Orvieto and the surrounding area seemed irremediably relegated. Umbria's geographical proximity to the front-line estates of Tuscany certainly didn't do much to speed winemaking development, quality-wise. The region remained as little more than a convenient source of decent quality red and, more important, white wines to fill out the portfolios of the larger Chianti producers. Still, there wasn't a complete dearth of high quality Umbrian estates. Take, for example, Lungarotti from Torgiano, its name long synonymous world-wide with the best of Umbrian winemaking. Or Castello della Sala, which the intrepid, far-seeing Antinori family transformed into a hotspot of winemaking research for the new millennium. It was here that one of the outstanding bottles on Italy's new wine scene, the white Cervaro, was born. But this was just small fry, quantitatively speaking, and eventually the mass of the region's producers refused to be also-rans any longer. During the 1980s and, especially, the 1990s, many opted to completely rethink their wines, reaching quality levels undreamt of ten years earlier. Montefalco and Sagrantino are emblematic of what happened. The Caprai family have always believed strongly in this singular indigenous variety and invested large sums in research and technology. The results are there for all to see: their Sagrantino di Montefalco 25 Anni has become one of Italy's new classics and Sagrantino in general has gained international renown. Moreover, vineyard terrain in Montefalco is now some of the most sought-after in the Peninsula. This and other examples have been crucial in stimulating development in the wine sector as a whole and now innumerable estates of all sizes, from tiny "boutique wineries" to large co-operatives, are all bent on the pursuit of ever better quality. This year, there are a further four stars on the podium beside Cervaro and Caprai's Sagrantino. There's the Sagrantino from Còlpetrone, another Three Glass habitué, and two red wines from the Orvieto zone. Fobiano from Carraia is back for the second year running and "IL" from Decugnano dei Barbi has newly risen to the highest ranks. Finally, the extraordinary Campoleone '99, from La Fiorita-Lamborghini, lifts the Colli del Trasimeno zone into the elite. The saga of great wines from Umbria is a long way from being over. Watch this space.

BASCHI (TR)

PODERE VAGLIE
VIA AMELIA, 48
05023 BASCHI (TR)
TEL. 0744957425
E-MAIL: a.lumini@tiscalinet.it

Umbria has recently seen a significant transformation in the hierarchy of its top wine estates. Naturally, our Guide has to reflect such changes and that's why we have given the high-performing Vaglie estate its own entry. It is based in Baschi, an area that falls into three DOC zones, Orvieto Classico, Rosso Orvietano and Lago di Corbara. There are ten hectares of vineyard and the reliable Maurilio Chioccia is consultant winemaker. It is the reds that have made the biggest advances in quality. The Umbria Rosso Momenti '00, a sangiovese-merlot blend, is dark red in colour and has subtle but fruity aromas, mainly of mulberry and blackcurrant, overlain with delicate wafts of incense. The palate is broad, well-structured and complex, revealing flavours of mulberry and ripe cherry, with a long, elegant finish. The equally fine Umbria Rosso Masseo '99 is spicier, recalling cinnamon and vanilla. The two Orvietos both have reasonable structure and overall balance. The Classico Superiore Matricale '00 is a deep straw yellow, leading in to a clean, flowery nose with golden delicious apple and nectarine fruitiness. The palate is fresh with just a hint of bitterness on the finish. The other Orvieto, the Classico Podere Vaglie '00, is more forward, with white peach and ripe damson scents that precede a fruity, fresh, well-structured palate.

BEVAGNA (PG)

AGRICOLA ADANTI
VOC. ARQUATA
06031 BEVAGNA (PG)
TEL. 0742360295
E-MAIL: info@cantineadanti.com

Adanti, a long-established estate from the Bevagna area, retains its full entry in the Guide. The wines are, as usual, well-typed, although in general they don't scale the quality heights of previous years. An intriguing '00 Bianco di Montefalco kicks off the range. Dark straw in the glass, it unveils a nose of lavender and jasmine, with a hint of bitter apple fruit. The palate is clean, showing delicate tropical fruit flavours, let down by an unimpressive structure. The '00 Grechetto dei Colli Martani turned out fairly similar. The colour is straw yellow. The nose has aromas of apple with touches of summer flowers, especially broom, then the first impression on the palate is warmth, followed by good body and structure. The reds, too, show good overall balance. Rosso Montefalco '99 has a nice deep ruby colour. Fruity on the nose, it shows a light vegetal note with hints of wild berries and ripe plum. The palate is full and evolved, with ripe fruit flavours of blackcurrant and bramble, and a firm vegetal note on the finish. The '97 Sagrantino di Montefalco Passito, however, is less impressive than previous vintages. While still attractive, with its dark violet-red colour and its intense, deep nose full of sweet spiciness, it is thrown out of kilter by too much sweetness and cloys a little. The '97 Sagrantino di Montefalco is also below par. The nose is not perfectly clean and the palate poorly-knit.

●	Momenti '00	🍷🍷	3*
●	Masseo '99	🍷🍷	4
○	Orvieto Cl. '00	🍷	2*
○	Orvieto Cl. Sup. Matricale '00	🍷	4

○	Bianco di Montefalco '00	🍷	3
○	Colli Martani Grechetto '00	🍷	3
●	Montefalco Sagrantino Passito '97	🍷	5
●	Montefalco Rosso '99	🍷	4
●	Umbria Rosso Arquata '91	🍷🍷	4
●	Umbria Rosso Arquata '97	🍷🍷	5
●	Montefalco Sagrantino Passito '89	🍷	4
●	Montefalco Sagrantino '96	🍷	5
●	Montefalco Sagrantino Passito '96	🍷	5
●	Nispero Rosso '98	🍷	3

BEVAGNA (PG)

FATTORIA MILZIADE ANTANO
LOC. COLLE ALLODOLE
06031 BEVAGNA (PG)
TEL. 0742360371

Once more, the continually improving wines of this estate, especially its traditional Montefalco reds, bear witness to its high standing in the region. Fattoria Milziade Antano is now a Guide regular. Sagrantino Colle delle Allodole '98 starts us off. It is a good violet ruby red. The nose is complex and powerful, with a ripe plummy fruitiness, and the palate has a rich, spicy taste. The standard and dried-grape "passito" versions, both from '98, are no less attractive, both claiming Two Glasses. The former has a violet red hue introducing an elegant nose with aromas of small berry fruits, most notably mulberry and bilberry. On the full, rich palate, it offers a sweet spiciness and ripe, finely-honed tannins. However, it is the Sagrantino Passito that is the estate's best wine. Dark violet red, it has a rich, ripe fruitiness on the nose, evoking plum, bramble and bilberry, overlain with oaky and sweetly spicy tones. The ample palate then contributes soft tannins and well-judged residual sweetness. The two '99 Rosso di Montefalcos are good, too. The standard version has a good ruby red colour and an elegant, spicy, fruity nose, with cherry and plum clearly in evidence. The palate is super-ripe, gently tannic, and very clean and spicy. The Riserva also has a good ruby colour. There is concentration on the fruit-rich nose, and a delicate, sweet spiciness on the palate, leading to warm, gentle tannins and good fruit.

● Montefalco Sagrantino '98	🍷🍷	5
● Montefalco Sagrantino Colle delle Allodole '98	🍷🍷	6
● Montefalco Sagrantino Passito '98	🍷🍷	5
● Montefalco Rosso '99	🍷	4
● Montefalco Rosso Ris. '99	🍷	5
● Montefalco Sagrantino Passito '94	🍷🍷	5
● Montefalco Sagrantino '95	🍷🍷	5
● Montefalco Sagrantino Passito '96	🍷🍷	5
● Montefalco Sagrantino '97	🍷🍷	5
● Montefalco Sagrantino Colle delle Allodole '97	🍷🍷	5

CANNARA (PG)

DI FILIPPO
VIA CONVERSINO, 160
06033 CANNARA (PG)
TEL. 0742731242
E-MAIL: difilippo@bcsnet.it

Italo and Roberto Di Filippo are experienced, professional and certainly not lacking in commitment. They have been running their estate, which operates organically, for some years now and their continued success speaks for itself. As usual, the cellar's most distinctive wines are its reds and the one that showed best this year is the Rosso dell'Umbria Poggio Madrigale, the '97, from merlot, montepulciano and sangiovese. It gained Two effortless Glasses. The colour is an attractive violet ruby. The nose is rich and full with a lingering berry fruitiness of morello cherry, bilberry and ripe plum, overlain with nuances of sweet spice and mint. It opens out well on the palate, which has good intensity, a fruit jam sweetness and a stylish spiciness. Both structure and nose-palate harmony are excellent. The Sangiovese dei Colli Martani Riserva Properzio '98 also showed well, if on a less exalted plane. It is a good deep ruby and has aromas of ripe berry fruit well knit into its subtle spiciness. There is fair tannic attack on the palate, which has good body and an elegant fruity finish. The strongly fruity Umbria Rosso Villa Conversino '00 is also characterful, with aromas of cherry and strawberry, a fresh, fragrant palate and good drinkability. The estate's newest wine, the Umbria Bianco Farandola '99, is a blend of 70 per cent grechetto with 30 per cent pinot bianco, barrique-aged. The colour is straw yellow with coppery tinges, the nose is full with notes of sweet oak and ripe tropical fruits while the palate has good structure and complexity.

● Poggio Madrigale '97	🍷🍷	4
● Villa Conversino Rosso '00	🍷	2*
● Colli Martani Sangiovese Properzio Ris. '98	🍷	3
○ Farandola Bianco '99	🍷	3
● Poggio Madrigale '96	🍷🍷	4
● Terre di S. Nicola Rosso '97	🍷🍷	3
● Colli Martani Sangiovese Properzio '96	🍷	3
● Terre di S. Nicola Rosso '96	🍷	3
● Colli Martani Sangiovese Properzio '97	🍷	3
● Villa Conversino Rosso '98	🍷	1
● Villa Conversino Rosso '99	🍷	1

CASTEL VISCARDO (TR)

Cantina Monrubio
Fraz. Monterubiaglio
Loc. Le Prese, 22
05010 Castel Viscardo (TR)
tel. 0763626064
e-mail: cantina.monrubio@tiscalinet.it

Cantina Monrubio was set up in 1957 at the instigation of several local growers. Now, with around 300 members contributing grapes, it has become one of the most quality conscious co-operatives. None other than the redoubtable Riccardo Cotarella is consultant and the cellar turns out a fine range of wines that also score highly for value for money. This year's tastings confirmed their standing. Again it was the Umbria Rosso Palaia, from an unusual blend of merlot, cabernet sauvignon and pinot nero, that came out top of the range. It is violet-ruby red and has an intense, stylish nose, with clove and black pepper spiciness and the classic wild berry fruitiness. The palate has a soft but precise attack with good extractive weight on the mid palate and ripe tannins. Naturally fruity, it shows hints of mulberry and bilberry, and is nicely clean, without any fuzziness round the edges. The Orvieto Classico Superiore Soana '00 has a floral, well-fruited nose with aromas of citron and lemon liqueur, and a clean, well-delineated palate, supported by good acidic zest. The two Orvieto Classicos also surge past the One Glass barrier. The Roio '00 is fresh and attractive, with aromas of apple and citrus fruits and good nose-palate balance, while Salceto '00 is bigger and fuller-bodied.

CASTIGLIONE DEL LAGO (PG)

Fanini
Loc. Petrignano del Lago
Voc. I Cucchi
06060 Castiglione del Lago (PG)
tel. 0755171241 - 0755173122
e-mail: mldp@unipg.it

This small but sound estate seems set to become a fixture in the Guide. The vineyards it owns are all situated on the gentle hills around Lake Trasimeno, on the bank adjacent to Tuscany. They are cultivated mainly with the zone's traditional varieties: sangiovese, gamay, ciliegiolo and grechetto. The sole exception is chardonnay, which this year as before, produced Fanini's best wine, Chardonnay Robbiano. The '00 is deep straw yellow. The nose is pervasive and floral, enlivened by a tang of citrus, and the warm, rich, full palate has good power, gaining character from complex notes of ripe tropical fruit and toasted oak. The estate's newest wine, Sangiovese dell'Umbria Vigna la Pieve '98, impressed us right from our first glimpse of its intense, dark, violet-ruby hue. The initial aromas open smoothly into an intense ripe plum and berry fruitiness while the powerful, elegant, whistle-clean palate has a firm structure that leads it to a long, balsam-like finish. The Colli del Trasimeno Rosso Morello del Lago is as good as ever, the clean, highly drinkable '98 being of similar quality to the previous vintage. Colli del Trasimeno Rosato Balestrino '00, with its fresh, fruity nose, giving primary aromas of strawberry and cherry, is also at the One Glass level.

● Palaia '99	🍷 5	○ Chardonnay Robbiano '00	🍷🍷 4
● Monrubio '00	🍷 2	● Sangiovese Vigna La Pieve '98	🍷🍷 5
○ Orvieto Cl. Roio '00	🍷 2*	○ C. del Trasimeno Balestrino Rosato '00	🍷 3
○ Orvieto Cl. Salceto '00	🍷 2*	● C. del Trasimeno Rosso Morello del Lago '98	🍷 3
○ Orvieto Cl. Sup. Soana '00	🍷 3	● C. del Trasimeno Rosso Morello del Lago '95	🍷🍷 3
● L'Olmaia '96	🍷🍷 4	○ Chardonnay Robbiano '96	🍷🍷 3
● Monrubio '98	🍷🍷 2	○ Chardonnay Robbiano '97	🍷🍷 3
● Palaia '98	🍷🍷 5	○ Chardonnay Robbiano '98	🍷🍷 3
● Palaia '97	🍷 3	○ Chardonnay Robbiano '99	🍷🍷 3
● Monrubio '99	🍷 2	● C. del Trasimeno Rosso Morello del Lago '97	🍷 3
○ Orvieto Cl. Roio '99	🍷 2		
○ Orvieto Cl. Salceto '99	🍷 2		
○ Orvieto Macchia del Pozzo '99	🍷 1		

CASTIGLIONE DEL LAGO (PG)

POGGIO BERTAIO
FRAZ. CASAMAGGIORE
FRATTAVECCHIA, 29
06061 CASTIGLIONE DEL LAGO (PG)
TEL. 075956921

The Poggio Bertaio estate was set up in 1972 when Fabio Ciufoli moved to Castiglione del Lago from the Castelli Romani and bought a small property, planting nine hectares of vineyard to gratify his passion for winemaking. For many years, production was solely for private consumption but as time went by, Fabio's two sons, Ugo and Fabrizio, also fell in love with wine. The rest, as they say, is history. By '98 Fabrizio had become a highly esteemed oenologist and that year the brothers first made the wine now called Cimbolo, from 100 per cent Sangiovese. Released in autumn '00, it sailed into the Two Glass category in last year's Guide. This year, the '99 performed even better, reaching the final round of tastings for the coveted Three Glasses. It has a bright, lively, ruby red colour, tinged with violet. Its aromas are intense and very distinct with a marked, still rather dominant, oakiness. The palate is powerful with good alcoholic weight and assertive tannins which, while not particularly fine-grained, avoid any bitterness on the finish. In short, it is a vigorous number which will appeal to those who like their wines meaty and full-bodied.

● Cimbolo '99	♟♟	5
● Cimbolo '98	♟♟	5

CITTÀ DELLA PIEVE (PG)

DUCA DELLA CORGNA
VIA PO' DI MEZZO
06064 CITTÀ DELLA PIEVE (PG)
TEL. 0759653210
E-MAIL: ducacorgna@libero.it

The Duca della Corgna estate has achieved a real feat. After several years when the jury stayed out, this co-operative cellar has shown just what it is capable of, and we are not exaggerating when we say that its performance was one of the best in the region. Frankly, we cannot remember ever tasting such a great range of wines from this cellar. President Biavati, a notary, was very keen to gain the services of oenologist Lorenzo Landi, and his contribution is tangible. The flagship wine is Colli del Trasimeno Rosso Corniolo and the '00 easily gains Two Glasses with its elegant nose, its rich fruit, its silky spiciness, and muscular, full, abundantly fruity bilberry and mulberry palate. The tannins are ripe and the finish intense and long. Colli del Trasimeno '00 Baccio del Rosso is also very good. More immediate, it has a nose of red berry fruit with a vegetal hint, and a fresh, fruity flavour reminiscent of liqueur cherries. Colli del Trasimeno Gamay Divina Villa '00 Etichetta Nera – the name means "Black Label" – is of similar quality. A glance at the deep violet hue gives you an idea of its structure. The nose has good fruit with alluring notes of bramble and bilberry, plus a sweet spiciness. Even the White Label version, Etichetta Bianca, vinified without oak, showed well. Colli del Trasimeno Baccio del Bianco '00, fresh on the nose, acidulous and full-bodied, with ripe peach and apricot flavours, is also good while the Colli del Trasimeno Grechetto Nutricante '00, redolent of golden delicious apples, is simple but tasty.

● C. del Trasimeno Rosso Corniolo '00	♟♟	4
● C. del Trasimeno Baccio del Rosso '00	♟♟	3*
● C. del Trasimeno Gamay Divina Villa et. Nera '00	♟♟	4
● C. del Trasimeno Baccio del Bianco '00	♟	2*
● C. del Trasimeno Gamay Divina Villa et. Bianca '00	♟	4
○ C. del Trasimeno Grechetto Nuricante '00	♟	3
● C. del Trasimeno Rosso Corniolo '97	♟♟	3
● C. del Trasimeno Rosso Corniolo '98	♟♟	4

CORCIANO (PG)

PIEVE DEL VESCOVO
VIA G. LEOPARDI, 82
06073 CORCIANO (PG)
TEL. 0756978874
E-MAIL: lucciaio@pievedelvescovo.com

It is still full speed ahead at this classic Colli del Trasimeno estate, despite the recent changes of ownership, and quality remains enviably consistent. Colli del Trasimeno Rosso Lucciaio is again the leading wine. Despite steady modifications to the grape blend, which now has a good 40 per cent of cabernet sauvignon alongside the 45 per cent merlot and 15 per cent sangiovese, this barrique-aged wine continues to perform excellently. The '99 is a beautifully deep red with extremely bright violet tinges. The nose is broad, complex and refined, with aromas of nutmeg, black pepper and pencil lead gently overlain by fresh berry fruit. The palate is full and well-structured, with a good weight of tannin making for a dense mid palate and a long finish. Good, too, is the Colli del Trasimeno Rosso '00, from a sangiovese-dominated blend with 20 per cent canaiolo and ciliegiolo. This has notable concentration, flavours of berry fruit jam and good nose-palate harmony. Finally, the estate's sole white wine, Colli del Trasimeno Etesiaco, gains One Glass again this year with the '00. Clean, with good golden delicious apple and white peach fruit, it shows alcohol that is maybe just a little too overt.

FICULLE (TR)

★ CASTELLO DELLA SALA
LOC. SALA
05016 FICULLE (TR)
TEL. 076386051

Cervaro della Sala has gained its 11th Three Glass award. This consistency of quality at the highest level backs up the claim that it is one of the best two or three whites in Italy. What can we say about the '99 Cervaro, a wine that blew us away with the purity of its aromas and the complexity of its palate? The appearance is stunningly bright, with a deep straw yellow colour that, as usual, tends slightly towards over-concentration. The nose has a broad spectrum of very clearly defined aromas, centred on elegant notes of ripe tropical fruit and well-judged oaking. The palate is powerful, harmonious and long, with flavours that are decisive but at the same time discreet, and has a marvellous thrust of crystal-pure but unassertive acidity that refreshes. Both the '00 Sauvignon and the '00 Chardonnay are in simper vein, as one might expect. That doesn't mean they can't be well-rounded and harmonious, though. The '98 Pinot Nero is as impressive as ever. Its ruby colour tends to garnet, it has good varietal character and is stylish and pervasive on the nose, where blackcurrant, leather and spices emerge. The palate is warm, with well-defined berry flavours and a generous stamp of oak. The three Orvieto Classicos are all from '00. The Campo Grande, the Superiore and the sweetish "abboccato" version, Casa Sole, are all good, clean and free of edginess. Umbria Bianco Conte della Vipera '99, from sauvignon with a little chardonnay, has breadth on the nose, with aromas of quince enhanced by delicate touches of balsam, and a mid-structured palate.

	Wine	Glasses	Score
●	C. del Trasimeno Rosso Lucciaio '99	♟♟	5
○	C. del Trasimeno Bianco Etesiaco '00	♟	3
●	C. del Trasimeno Rosso '00	♟	2*
●	C. del Trasimeno Rosso Lucciaio '94	♟♟	3
●	C. del Trasimeno Rosso Lucciaio '95	♟♟	3
●	C. del Trasimeno Rosso Lucciaio '96	♟♟	4
●	C. del Trasimeno Rosso Lucciaio '97	♟♟	4
●	C. del Trasimeno Rosso Lucciaio '98	♟♟	4
○	Cervaro della Sala '99	♟♟♟	6
○	Chardonnay della Sala '00	♟♟	4*
○	Sauvignon della Sala '00	♟♟	3*
●	Pinot Nero Vigneto Consola '98	♟♟	5
○	Orvieto Cl. Abboccato Casa Sole '00	♟	2*
○	Orvieto Cl. Campogrande '00	♟	2*
○	Orvieto Cl. Sup. '00	♟	3
○	Conte della Vipera '99	♟	4
○	Cervaro della Sala '93	♟♟♟	5
○	Cervaro della Sala '94	♟♟♟	5
○	Cervaro della Sala '95	♟♟♟	5
○	Cervaro della Sala '96	♟♟♟	5
○	Cervaro della Sala '97	♟♟♟	5
○	Cervaro della Sala '98	♟♟♟	6

GUALDO CATTANEO (PG)

CÒLPETRONE
Loc. Madonnuccia - Fraz. Marcellano
Via della Collina, 4
06035 Gualdo Cattaneo (PG)
Tel. 0578767722
E-mail: fattoriadelcerro@tin.it

That Còlpetrone has scaled the heights of Umbrian winemaking is clear for all to see, not just the Guide's tasters. But in case there were any residual doubts, the estate, part of the Saiagricola group, has picked up a Three Glass award for the third consecutive year. Lorenzo Landi, the oenologist responsible for these results, is showing an ever surer hand. Whichever way you approach it, Sagrantino di Montefalco '98 consistently shows good aromas and impressive flavours. As is Landi's style, the colour, a deep, dark ruby, has remarkable depth and saturation, reflecting the light with great intensity. The aromas are fruit-driven, perfectly focused and very concentrated, although at this early stage of the wine's life they are still very youthful. The palate has weight and a good thrust of alcohol, but also grace and balance, while the tannins are robust yet soft and ripe. You might have expected the Rosso di Montefalco '99 to be a simple, easy-drinker. Instead, it is powerful and long, with plentiful extract giving it surprising verve, although the oak toast is still very much to the fore. Finally comes Sagrantino di Montefalco Passito, a style that can easily become heavy and cloying. Còlpetrone's '98, while classically rich and sweet, has also managed to retain an attractive drinkability.

MONTECASTRILLI (TR)

FATTORIA LE POGGETTE
Loc. Le Poggette
05026 Montecastrilli (TR)
Tel. 0744940338

Our tasting panels were struck by the quality of Fattoria Le Poggette's wines. The estate is situated near to Montecastrilli and has 12 hectares of enviably sited vineyards, mainly planted with red varieties such as canaiolo, sangiovese and montepulciano. It is with a wine made solely from montepulciano that the estate really shows its paces. The '98 Montepulciano, like its predecessors, easily slots into the Two Glass category. The colour is a beautifully dense ruby red. There is great vibrancy of ripe red berry, plum and liqueur cherry fruit on the well-integrated, clean nose. The palate is full and rich, and has ripe tannins. In contrast, the Canaiolo '99 is more immediate, with a strawberry and cherry-like nose, and a full-bodied palate with marked youthful, primary flavours. Next on the list is the Umbria Grechetto '00, which shows well. The colour is a deep golden yellow, introducing a good array of ripe apple, citrus fruit, damson and summer flower aromas. The palate is intense, full and rich, with a fruitiness strongly reminiscent of quince. The Colli Amerini Superiore '99 is naturally more simple but its aromas are flawless and it has good drinkability.

● Montefalco Sagrantino '98	🍷🍷🍷	5
● Montefalco Sagrantino Passito '98	🍷🍷	6
● Montefalco Rosso '99	🍷🍷	4
● Montefalco Sagrantino '96	🍷🍷🍷	4
● Montefalco Sagrantino '97	🍷🍷🍷	5
● Montefalco Rosso '95	🍷🍷	3
● Montefalco Sagrantino '95	🍷🍷	4
● Montefalco Rosso '97	🍷🍷	3
● Montefalco Sagrantino Passito '97	🍷🍷	6
● Montefalco Rosso '98	🍷🍷	3
● Montefalco Sagrantino '93	🍷	4

○ Grechetto '00	🍷🍷	3*
● Montepulciano '98	🍷🍷	5
● Canaiolo '99	🍷🍷	4
● C. Amerini Rosso Sup. '99	🍷	3
● Montepulciano '95	🍷🍷	5
● Montepulciano '96	🍷🍷	5
● Montepulciano '97	🍷🍷	5
● C. Amerini Rosso Sup. '96	🍷	3
● C. Amerini Rosso Sup. '97	🍷	3
● Canaiolo '98	🍷	3

MONTEFALCO (PG)

ANTONELLI - SAN MARCO
LOC. SAN MARCO, 59
06036 MONTEFALCO (PG)
TEL. 0742379158
E-MAIL: info@antonellisanmarco.it

This year's tastings of the Antonelli-San Marco wines was anything but a let down. They are increasingly reliable and impressive, proving that owner Filippo Antonelli and his oenologist Manlio Erba are supremely skilled at extracting the full essence of their grapes. These excellent wines fully realize the Montefalco zone's potential. All the wines tasted performed valiantly but a particular note of merit must go to the '98 Sagrantino di Montefalco, which is one of the best of the vintage. This has a good, dark, violet-ruby colour and a rich, powerful nose, characterized by an elegant fruitiness with clear notes of mulberry and plum. The palate is powerful yet soft. The Rosso Montefalco '99 also showed well and easily gained Two Glasses. It is a violet-tinged ruby red and has inviting aromas of red berry fruit and an intense, pervasive toastiness. The palate is full, warm and attractively complex, with the tannins in particular showing notable finesse. One Glass goes to the Colli Martani Grechetto '00. The colour is a deep straw yellow. The nose has good fruit, elegance and harmony and a good attack of alcohol gives the palate warmth.

● Montefalco Sagrantino '98	🍷	6
● Montefalco Rosso '99	🍷🍷	4
○ Colli Martani Grechetto '00	🍷	2*
● Montefalco Sagrantino '94	🍷🍷	4
● Montefalco Sagrantino '95	🍷🍷	4
● Montefalco Sagrantino Passito '95	🍷🍷	4
● Montefalco Sagrantino '96	🍷🍷	4
○ Colli Martani Grechetto Vigna Tonda '97	🍷🍷	3
● Montefalco Sagrantino '97	🍷🍷	6
● Montefalco Sagrantino Passito '97	🍷🍷	6
● Montefalco Sagrantino '93	🍷	4
● Montefalco Rosso '98	🍷	4

MONTEFALCO (PG)

ARNALDO CAPRAI
VAL DI MAGGIO
LOC. TORRE
06036 MONTEFALCO (PG)
TEL. 0742378802 - 0742378523
E-MAIL: info@arnaldocaprai.it

There are not many wineries that, having achieved a Three Glass award, are capable of repeating the success. But Marco Caprai has managed just that. For six vintages on the trot. That is consistency at the highest level. The wine, Sagrantino di Montefalco 25 Anni, has come to represent a turning point in the Umbria wine scene, notably in Montefalco itself. The '98 has the stylistic power you would expect, set into a weighty structure that brings out the monumental concentration of its extract more than the charm of its character. Full of aroma, with its oak well integrated into the fruit, the palate has a significant but restrained attack and is full and chewy in mid palate, with an extremely long finish. In short, it is sumptuous. A new wine, the ripe, full-bodied Sagrantino di Montefalco Colle Piano '98, makes a good second lead. Its super-clean, forest-floor aromas are less intense than the 25 Anni but there is only a little less structure and it has good density of extract, particularly tannin, and packs a plentiful alcoholic punch. The Rosso di Montefalco Riserva '98 is well-judged on both the nose and the palate, where the fruit just hints at over-ripeness. And don't expect the younger, non-Riserva Rosso di Montefalco to be all that much simpler. It may be a tad more vegetal on the nose, and have a touch more bitterness on the finish, but it is very attractive. Next in line is a fruity Grechetto '00, with notes of white peach, damson and ripe apple, which has a warm, soft palate and good acidity. And we finish with a less full, but just as praiseworthy, Bianco di Montefalco.

● Montefalco Sagrantino 25 Anni '98	🍷🍷🍷	6
● Montefalco Rosso Ris. '98	🍷🍷	6
● Montefalco Sagrantino Colle Piano '98	🍷🍷	6
○ Colli Martani Grechetto Grecante '00	🍷🍷	4
○ Montefalco Bianco '00	🍷🍷	3*
● Montefalco Rosso '99	🍷🍷	4
● Montefalco Sagrantino 25 Anni '93	🍷🍷🍷	5
● Montefalco Sagrantino 25 Anni '94	🍷🍷🍷	6
● Montefalco Sagrantino 25 Anni '95	🍷🍷🍷	6
● Montefalco Sagrantino 25 Anni '96	🍷🍷🍷	6
● Montefalco Sagrantino 25 Anni '97	🍷🍷🍷	6

MONTEFALCO (PG)

ROCCA DI FABBRI
LOC. FABBRI
06036 MONTEFALCO (PG)
TEL. 0742399379
E-MAIL: roccafabbri@tin.it

Rocca di Fabbri wines have made a significant leap forward in quality and a good four were judged worthy of Two Glasses. Even better, this estate, belonging to the Vitali family and situated in the excellent Montefalco DOC zone, manages to combine quality with quantity, producing 250,000 bottles from the 60 hectares of vineyard. Once more, it is Faroaldo that makes the strongest impression. A deep red wine with a super-clean, complex nose, it proffers a wide spectrum of finely-nuanced, fruit-based aromas, including gooseberry, redcurrant and wild cherry. The palate is full and well-balanced, the tannins in particular being beautifully behaved. The Sagrantino di Montefalco '98 also showed excellently. It is marked by gamey aromas of leather and fur with hints of over-ripeness that lead in to a complex, full palate of good tannic presence. The Sangiovese dei Colli Martani Satiro has improved significantly with the '99. Its nose is fresh and well-fruited, with slightly vegetal, cherry-like aromas and a mellow, rounded taste, making for good nose-palate balance. The '97 Sagrantino di Montefalco Passito is probably the best version the cellar has ever produced and has glorious balance of sweetness with acidic freshness. The '99 Rosso di Montefalco is less complex in aroma but has good depth on its warm, spicy palate.

MONTEFALCO (PG)

SCACCIADIAVOLI
LOC. CANTINONE, 31
06036 MONTEFALCO (PG)
TEL. 0742378272 - 0742371210
E-MAIL: scacciadiavoli@tin.it

Scacciadiavoli enters the Guide in grand style. Owned by the Pambuffetti brothers, it extends over 130 hectares, of which 25 are vineyard, planted mainly with sagrantino, sangiovese and grechetto. The cellars are situated in an enormous building, built in the second half of the 19th century and used even then for vinification. The current winery, however, was founded in the 1950s and now produces around 60,000 bottles under the supervision of chief winemaker Guido Guardigli. The Sagrantino di Montefalco '98 shows great extractive power and good overall harmony. It is intense and full on the nose, with aromas of ripe cherry, jam and spice. The palate is warm, with firm tannins, a full mid palate and a long finish. Rosso di Montefalco '99, from sangiovese with a little sagrantino, also shows well. The colour is a violet ruby, then the nose is refined and delicate with clean aromas of red berry fruit, mainly bramble and bilberry. The equally well-fruited palate has good body, good structure, a good dose of tannin and a long finish. The tannins are still slightly raw on the finish but the wine is young and needs time.

- Montefalco Sagrantino Passito '97 ᵧᵧ 5
- Faroaldo '98 ᵧᵧ 5
- Montefalco Sagrantino '98 ᵧᵧ 5
- Colli Martani Sangiovese Satiro '99 ᵧᵧ 3*
- Montefalco Rosso '99 ᵧ 3
- Umbria Pinot Nero '90 ᵧᵧ 5
- Faroaldo '97 ᵧᵧ 5
- Montefalco Sagrantino '96 ᵧ 4
- Montefalco Sagrantino Passito '96 ᵧ 5
- Montefalco Rosso '97 ᵧ 3
- Montefalco Sagrantino '97 ᵧ 5
- Colli Martani Sangiovese Satiro '98 ᵧ 2

- Montefalco Sagrantino '98 ᵧᵧ 5
- Montefalco Rosso '98 ᵧ 4

ORVIETO (TR)

Barberani - Vallesanta
Loc. Cerreto
Via Michelangeli, 8
05018 Orvieto (TR)
tel. 0763341820
e-mail: barberani@barberani.it

Barberani is situated a few kilometres from Orvieto and has 45 hectares of vineyard, a large ampelographic park and high-tech cellars. The estate has always presented high quality wines, apart from the past two years, which were rather iffy. Hence, we were expecting something a bit better than last year's showing, and so it was for the tasting scores did indeed show a small improvement. The best of the range is Lago di Corbara Foresco '99. It is violet-red, with intense, pervasive aromas. Vegetal in character, it offers elegant sensations of blackcurrant and wild berries, and a distinct oaky sweetness. The palate is full and powerful, revealing plentiful tannin and spiciness. Another Two Glass wine is the Moscato Passito Villa Monticelli '99. Golden yellow with faint hints of amber, it has a nose of very clean, intense, ultra-ripe aromas of tropical fruit, pineapple, mango and apricot. There are clear, ripe, appley flavours on the palate, which has a well-judged, attractive sweetness. The '98 vintage of the more traditional, sweet Orvieto Classico, Calcaia, is also good. It has an intense golden yellow colour tinged with amber. The aromas are elegant and refined, flaunting an intense, complex fruitiness. The palate has good body but lacks the structure and complexity necessary to bring it a second Glass. Frankly, though, both the Grechetto '00 and the Orvieto Classico Superiore Castagnolo '00 disappoint, lacking structure and cleanliness of aroma.

ORVIETO (TR)

Bigi
Loc. Ponte Giulio, 3
05018 Orvieto (TR)
tel. 0763316291
e-mail: giv@giv.it

Founded in 1880, Bigi is probably the winery of greatest historical importance in the Orvieto zone. Now owned by Gruppo Italiano Vini, there are 193 hectares of vineyard and annual production hovers around 3,000,000 bottles, oenologist Francesco Bardi overseeing the technical side. Once more, the wines live up to expectations. Take, for example, the '00 Orvieto Classico Vigneto Torricella, which easily gains Two Glasses, as did the previous vintage. Its deep straw yellow ushers in a nose that is elegant and clean, with good green apple and citrus fruit, and distinct aromas of spring flowers. The palate is complex and well-structured, with a pervasive fruitiness and a whistle-clean finish. The Orvieto Classico Secco '00 is also good. The nose is characterized by a good weight of fruit and a fresh, delicate florality reminiscent of broom and lemon liqueur. The palate foregrounds primary fruit flavours with an appealing streak of refreshing acidity, good body and a hint of balsam on the finish. Even the one red wine, the excellent Sangiovese dell'Umbria '00, keeps up the Bigi consistency of quality. It is violet-ruby and offers a nose of fresh red berry fruitiness, most notably mulberry, blackcurrant and cherry. The fresh, clean palate has good body, appealing fruit and soft, well-gauged tannins that make for easy drinking.

	Wine		Score
●	Lago di Corbara Foresco '99	♟♟	5
○	Moscato Passito Villa Monticelli '99	♟♟	6
○	Orvieto Cl. Sup. Calcaia '98	♟	5
○	Orvieto Cl. Sup. Calcaia '92	♟♟	5
●	Foresco '93	♟♟	4
○	Orvieto Cl. Sup. Calcaia '93	♟♟	5
○	Orvieto Cl. Sup. Calcaia '94	♟♟	5
○	Orvieto Cl. Sup. Calcaia '95	♟♟	5
○	Moscato Passito Villa Monticelli '97	♟♟	6
○	Orvieto Cl. Sup. Calcaia '97	♟♟	5
●	Lago di Corbara Foresco '98	♟♟	5
○	Orvieto Cl. Castagnolo '99	♟♟	4
●	Foresco '95	♟	4
●	Foresco '96	♟	4
●	Foresco '97	♟	4

	Wine		Score
○	Orvieto Cl. Vigneto Torricella '00	♟♟	3*
○	Orvieto Cl. '00	♟	2*
●	Umbria Sangiovese '00	♟	2*
○	Marrano '93	♟♟	4
○	Marrano '94	♟♟	4
●	Umbria Sangiovese '97	♟♟	2
○	Orvieto Cl. Vigneto Torricella '98	♟♟	3
○	Orvieto Cl. Vigneto Torricella '99	♟♟	3
●	Sangiovese Tenuta Corbara '98	♟	3
●	Umbria Sangiovese '98	♟	2
●	Umbria Sangiovese '99	♟	2

ORVIETO (TR)

Co.Vi.O.
Fraz. Sferracavallo
Loc. Cardeto, 18
05019 Orvieto (TR)
Tel. 0763341286 - 0763343189
E-mail: infcarde@tin.it

This co-operative is still one of the best wineries in Umbria. It has around 350 members, who tend 1,000 hectares of vineyard, growing mainly Orvieto's classic white varieties. A broad range of wines emerges and the reds in particular were on good form. Let's begin with the excellent Umbria Rossos Rupestro '00 and Arciato '99. Both have good structure, a solid fruit base and a full palate, well balanced with tannin. The Umbria Rosso Nero della Greca '99 is pitched higher. Elegant and spicy on the nose, with wild berry fruitiness and a sweet oaky overlay, it delivers a palate with good body and fairly ripe tannins. The super-ripe '99 Pinot Nero is distinctive. Colli Amerini Rosso Terre Arnolfe '00 is fruity, with a swathe of fresh acidity and a good level of tannin, while finesse is the strong suit of the Umbria Rosso Alborato '00. Orvieto Classico Superiore '00 comes in several versions, all straightforward but reliable. There is white peach, damson and mango on the delicate Colbadia, while Febeo has primary, green apple aromas. Best of the sweet wines is an excellent Orvieto L'Armida '00. It has considerable complexity on its nose of tropical fruit, dates and figs, and a good dose of glycerine. The Passito Mandoleo '96, with scents of dried figs and spices, is also good if simpler.

ORVIETO (TR)

Decugnano dei Barbi
Loc. Fossatello di Corbara, 50
05019 Orvieto (TR)
Tel. 0763308255
E-mail: info@decugnanodeibarbi.com

At last! After so many near misses, Decugnano dei Barbi, historically one of the most impeccably archetypal of Orvieto estates, finally sweeps up Three Glasses with its Umbria Rosso "IL". Owners Claudio and Marina and their oenologist Corrado Cugnasco must be delighted that all their efforts, year after year, to bring the wine to such awesome heights have finally paid off. "IL" is made from sangiovese, montepulciano and canaiolo, with small amounts of cabernet and syrah. The winning '98 is a dark violet red. The nose is a little reticent at first, then opens out to give great intensity of primary fruit aromas. The palate is powerful, with excellent structure, a slight herbaceousness on the mid palate and a long finish. The '00 white "IL", an Orvieto Classico Superiore, is also excellent. Full of rich tropical fruit aromas, the palate has a well-judged dose of oak which harmonizes nicely with the fruit. Other successful Decugnano wines include: Lago di Corbara '99, with a youthful cherry and strawberry fruitiness; Orvieto Classico Superiore '00, characterized by peachy pink grapefruit aromas, and good freshness of taste; and the complex, well-structured Brut Metodo Classico '97. Orvieto Classico Superiore Pourriture Noble '99, attractive on the nose but slightly cloying on the palate, is also good but less exceptional. The fresh Pojo del Ruspo '99 and the two standard-label Barbi wines are right on target. For price, too.

O	Orvieto Cl. Sup. L'Armida '00	🍷🍷	4
●	Rupestro '00	🍷🍷	2*
●	Arciato '99	🍷🍷	3*
●	Nero della Greca '99	🍷🍷	4
●	Alborato '00	🍷	3
O	Orvieto Cl. Sup. Colbadia '00	🍷	3
O	Orvieto Cl. Sup. Febeo '00	🍷	3
O	Mandoleo Passito '96	🍷	4
●	Pinot Nero '99	🍷	6
●	Fantasie del Cardeto Rosso '96	🍷🍷	3
●	Arciato '98	🍷🍷	3
●	Nero della Greca '98	🍷🍷	4
●	Pinot Nero '98	🍷🍷	6
O	Orvieto Cl. Dolce V. T. Cardeto '99	🍷🍷	4

●	"IL" Rosso '98	🍷🍷🍷	5
O	Orvieto Cl. Sup. Decugnano dei Barbi '00	🍷🍷	3*
O	Orvieto Cl. Sup. "IL" '00	🍷🍷	4
O	Decugnano dei Barbi Brut M. Cl. '97	🍷🍷	5
O	Orvieto Cl. Barbi '00	🍷	2*
●	Lago di Corbara '99	🍷	4
●	Lago di Corbara Barbi '99	🍷	2*
O	Orvieto Cl. Sup. Pourriture Noble '99	🍷	5
●	Pojo del Ruspo Barbi '99	🍷	3
●	"IL" Rosso '94	🍷🍷	5
●	"IL" Rosso '95	🍷🍷	5
●	"IL" Rosso '96	🍷🍷	5
●	"IL" Rosso '97	🍷🍷	5

ORVIETO (TR)

GIULIO FREDDANO
LOC. FOSSATELLO
05018 ORVIETO (TR)
TEL. 0763308248

We welcome Freddano to the Guide. The estate was founded in 1927 when Sante Freddano returned to Italy after seeking his fortune in the United States and bought the property for a few thousand lire. It lies 15 kilometres from Orvieto, nestling in the hills facing Lake Corbara and embraces 22 hectares, of which nine are planted to vine. Maurilio Chioccia is the consultant oenologist. The Lago di Corbara Fontauro '99 is made from 60 per cent cabernet sauvignon, 30 per cent cabernet franc and sangiovese. With its rounded, fine-grained palate, its fruit, its elegant spicy tones and its excellent tannins, it has turned out very successfully and picked up Two Glasses. Umbria Rosso Campo de' Massi '00, from an 80-20 sangiovese and cabernet sauvignon blend, is also good. It is violet red and while there may be a touch too much herbaceousness on the nose, this is offset by a rich, fresh cherry fruitiness. The palate shines for good body, balanced tannins and subtle red berry fruit on the finish.

● Lago di Corbara Fontauro '99	ՄՄ	4
● Campo de' Massi '00	Մ	1*

ORVIETO (TR)

LA CARRAIA
LOC. TORDIMONTE, 56
05018 ORVIETO (TR)
TEL. 0763304013
E-MAIL: lacarraia@libero.it

For the second year running, Odoardo Gialletti and Riccardo Cotarella, joint owners of this estate situated in the heart of the Orvieto zone, have hit the bull's eye. Three Glasses again go to the flagship wine, Fobiano. Indeed, the entire La Carraia range has been spot-on for some time now but Fobiano is indisputably at the top of the tree. This year's '99 vintage is a dark ruby red tinged with violet. The aromas are well-defined, intense and powerful, and overt notes of black berry fruit, mulberry and bilberry alternate satisfyingly with the spiciness of black pepper, clove and cinnamon notes ceded by the oak. The palate is full, soft and elegant, with the fruit hinting at great ripeness. Good, too, is the Umbria Sangiovese '00. Violet red, it has a fresh and very clean nose, followed by a warm, well-fruited palate with nicely firm tannins. Neither are the whites a let down. In fact, Orvieto Classico Poggio Calvelli is another of the estate's highlights. The '00 has delicate florality, reminiscent of orange blossom and elderflower, on the nose while the palate is complex and harmonious, with a fresh acidic zestiness. The Orvieto Classico '00 is also good. Its nose has a rich peach and damson fruitiness, with a lemon liqueur florality, then the palate shows good body. Inevitably less complex than the Poggio Calvelli, it is just as enjoyable to drink.

● Fobiano '99	ՄՄՄ	6
○ Orvieto Cl. Poggio Calvelli '00	ՄՄ	3*
○ Orvieto Cl. '00	Մ	2*
● Umbria Sangiovese '00	Մ	2*
● Fobiano '98	ՄՄՄ	5
● Fobiano '95	ՄՄ	4
● Fobiano '96	ՄՄ	4
● Fobiano '97	ՄՄ	4
● Umbria Sangiovese '97	ՄՄ	3
○ Orvieto Cl. Poggio Calvelli '98	ՄՄ	3
○ Orvieto Cl. Poggio Calvelli '99	ՄՄ	2

ORVIETO (TR)

Tenuta Le Velette
Loc. Le Velette, 23
05019 Orvieto (TR)
tel. 076329090

Situated in the heart of the Orvieto Classico production zone, this estate, owned by Corrado and Cecilia Bottai, has everything it needs to become – and remain – one of Umbria's best. Certainly, the Bottais seem to be working flat out for ever enhanced quality and the entire range has taken a big step forwards. So there is no reason why they shouldn't secure Three Glasses again and this year they came very close, with two wines reaching the final taste-off. The first was Gaudio '98, the second release of this monovarietal Merlot. It has intense, complex aromas, primarily of black pepper, black berry fruits and ripe cherry. The palate is full, soft and very long, with ripe berry fruit and a sweet oakiness. The second contender was Calanco '98, which nearly reached the heights of the '95. It has good fruit on the nose along with vegetal notes of green pepper. The palate is dense and full, with rich spiciness lifted by flavours of plum and cherry. The third estate red, Rosso di Spicca '00, a sangiovese and canaiolo blend, is also very good and has great overall harmony that includes lively fruit, body and length. A comfortable Two Glasses. The Orvieto Classico Superiore Lunato '00, stylish, floral and with a note of tropical fruit, gains a single but brimming Glass, as does Traluce Sauvignon '00, with its generous freshness and its apples-and-pears fruitiness. Good, too, are the estate's other two Orvieto Classicos: the Velico '00 is super-ripe and well structured while the sweetish "amabile" Rasenna '00, is ripe and fat but could do with a touch more acidity.

ORVIETO (TR)

Palazzone
Loc. Rocca Ripesena, 68
05010 Orvieto (TR)
tel. 0763344921
e-mail: palazzone@palazzone.com

Palazzone, owned by Giovanni Dubini, has 22 hectares of vineyard and is one of Umbria's best wineries. It has not, though, achieved Three Glass status yet, despite engaging the legendary Riccardo Cotarella as consultant oenologist. This year, it was the whites that showed best, notably the two Orvietos, each of which scored Two Glasses. Orvieto Classico Campo del Guardiano '99 is beautifully clear and bright, with a straw yellow hue. Its apple, pear and spring flower aromas have good definition then the palate is full, complex and mouthfilling. Orvieto Classico Terre Vineate '00 has instead a more subtle, fruitier touch on the nose, with aromas of pink grapefruit and citron, nuanced with delicate minerality. The palate is rich and full, and there is exemplary nose-palate harmony. The other two whites each gain One Glass. Grechetto '00 has sweetly fruited perfumes and a mid-weight palate and L'Ultima Spiaggia '00 is a fine barrique-aged Viognier, although the oak is perhaps a little too intrusive. Rubbio '00 was the most impressive of the reds. The colour is violet red, preceding herbaceous notes that intertwine with wild berry fruit on the nose and a palate that is full with fairly fine-grained tannins. The estate's flagship Armaleo is, however, a little under par with somewhat simplistic aromas and a palate that despite reasonable structure has a touch of rawness to its tannins. Finally, the Vendemmia Tardiva '00 is worthy of mention for its citron and tropical fruit aromas and its fresh, well-fruited palate.

● Calanco '98	🍷🍷	5
● Gaudio '98	🍷🍷	4
● Rosso Orvietano Rosso di Spicca '00	🍷🍷	2*
○ Orvieto Cl. Amabile Rasenna '00	🍷	2*
○ Orvieto Cl. Sup. Lunato '00	🍷	3
○ Orvieto Cl. Velico '00	🍷	4
○ Traluce '00	🍷	4
● Calanco '95	🍷🍷🍷	5
● Calanco '96	🍷🍷	5
● Calanco '97	🍷🍷	5
● Gaudio '97	🍷🍷	4
● Rosso Orvietano Rosso di Spicca '99	🍷🍷	2

○ Orvieto Cl. Terre Vineate '00	🍷🍷	3*
● Rubbio '00	🍷🍷	3*
● Armaleo '99	🍷🍷	5
○ Orvieto Cl. Campo del Guardiano '99	🍷🍷	4
○ Grechetto '00	🍷	3
○ L'Ultima Spiaggia '00	🍷	4
○ Vendemmia Tardiva '00	🍷	5
● Armaleo '95	🍷🍷🍷	4
● Armaleo '97	🍷🍷🍷	5
● Armaleo '98	🍷🍷🍷	5
● Armaleo '92	🍷🍷	5
● Armaleo '94	🍷🍷	4
○ Muffa Nobile '97	🍷🍷	4
○ Muffa Nobile '98	🍷🍷	4

PANICALE (PG)

La Fiorita - Lamborghini
Loc. Soderi, 1
06064 Panicale (PG)
Tel. 0758350029
E-mail: info@lamborghini.cc

This time round, Umbria Rosso Campoleone has finally done it. After coming so close in recent years, it has at last joined the Three Glass top flight and its deserved success confirms Patrizia Lamborghini's Trasimeno estate as one of the most distinctive in all Italy. Patrizia is the daughter of Ferruccio Lamborghini, founder of the famous automobile company, and her able management of the estate, just a few kilometres from Lake Trasimeno, is backed up by the presence of Riccardo Cotarella as consultant oenologist. Campoleone '99 stakes its claim to excellence with your first glance at its dark violet-ruby colour. Powerful on the nose, it unfurls a broad array of richly fruited aromas, from ripe mulberry, bilberry and cherry to wild berries. There is also a delicate gamey hint which adds complexity. The palate is powerful, warm and intense, characterized by primary, red berry fruitiness and underscored by toasted oak. Lamborghini's second wine, Umbria Rosso Trescone '99, is also excellent and well deserves its Two Glasses. The colour is violet-ruby, introducing a beautifully clean, youthful nose with aromas of fresh cherry and ripe strawberry. The palate has good body, a note of acidic freshness and a solid tannic core.

● Campoleone '99	🍷🍷🍷	6
● Trescone '99	🍷🍷	3*
● Campoleone '97	🍷🍷	5
● Campoleone '98	🍷🍷	5
● C. del Trasimeno Trescone '97	🍷	3
● C. del Trasimeno Trescone '98	🍷	3

PENNA IN TEVERINA (TR)

Rio Grande
Loc. Montecchie
05028 Penna in Teverina (TR)
Tel. 0744993102 - 0666416440
E-mail: pastore.dme@interbussiness.it

Situated in at Penna in Teverina, just a hop, skip and a jump from the Lazio border, this estate produces consistently high quality wines from its two vineyards, planted in '90 and '91 respectively, and totalling 12 hectares. Cabernet sauvignon seems particularly successful here and the Cabernet Casa Pastore '99 performed with aplomb in the final Three Glass taste-off, although it just missed this final accolade. A wine of great power, with a richness of extract that almost goes over the top, it will need a few years before its characteristics express themselves to the full. On the nose, the wild berry and ripe cherry fruit aromas remain happily unobscured by the grape's typical vein of vegetality. The palate has good structure, good balance and abundant but fine-grained tannins. The estate's other reds, Cabernet I Ricordi '98 and Poggio Muralto '00 also won Two Glasses. The former is evolved on the nose, which is rich in ripe berry fruit aromas, and has a concentrated, tannic palate, with notes of sweet spice and red fruit jam. The mouthfilling Poggio Muralto is from merlot, cabernet and sangiovese and has a rather vegetal nose, overlain with aromas of black pepper and berry fruit. The '00 Chardonnay Colle delle Montecchie is as well made as ever, although less assertive than usual. Golden delicious apples and floral scents of broom mark out the nose, and the palate is fresh with good acidic backbone.

● Casa Pastore Rosso '99	🍷🍷	5
● Poggio Muralto '00	🍷🍷	3*
● I Ricordi '98	🍷🍷	4
○ Chardonnay Colle delle Montecchie '00	🍷	4
○ Chardonnay Colle delle Montecchie '94	🍷🍷	3
● Casa Pastore Rosso '95	🍷🍷	4
○ Chardonnay Colle delle Montecchie '95	🍷🍷	3
● Casa Pastore Rosso '97	🍷🍷	4
● Casa Pastore Rosso '98	🍷🍷	4
● Poggio Muralto '98	🍷🍷	3
○ Chardonnay Colle delle Montecchie '99	🍷🍷	3

PERUGIA

CASTELLO DI ANTIGNANO
BROGAL VINI
LOC. BASTIA UMBRA
VIA DEGLI OLMI, 9 - 06083 PERUGIA
TEL. 0758001501
E-MAIL: vignabaldo@vignabaldo.it

The excellent showing of the Castello di Antignano wines this year brings Brogal Vini its first full entry in the Guide. It is no coincidence. For some time now, winemaking has been overseen by Riccardo Cotarella who, however widely he spreads his skills, still has more than enough technical know-how and professionalism to go round. The estate's grapes come from vineyards in the most important zones in Umbria, Torgiano and Montefalco. The most distinctive wine from the Torgiano vineyards is Rosso Riserva Santa Caterina '97, which sails into the Two Glass category. The colour is dark violet red and there are berry fruit notes on the nose, notably cherry, bilberry and mulberry. The palate is full, warm and excellently structured. The Torgiano Rosso '98 is not quite as concentrated but still good, with greater freshness of fruit and less marked acidity and tannins on the palate. Torgiano Cabernet Sauvignon '97 is not overly complex but avoids any excess of vegetal, green pepper aromas and benefits from attractive scents of spices and liquorice. The Montefalco area furnishes two more good wines, Sagrantino '98 and Rosso '99. The former has a good violet-ruby hue and a finely-tuned, evolved nose full of a ripe fruitiness that comes through on the palate too, where hints of cinnamon and citrus peel emerge. The Montefalco Rosso is less complex, revealing light scents of ripe berry fruit and slightly raw tannins.

PERUGIA

FRANCA CHIORRI
LOC. SANT' ENEA
VIA TODI, 98
06070 PERUGIA
TEL. 075607141
E-MAIL: info@chiorri.it

This small estate is situated in the Perugia hills, overlooking the Tiber valley, across the river from Torgiano. It was founded in 1978 but took on its current form in the early 1990s when the owner, Tito Mariotti, was finally able to retire and dedicate his efforts full-time to his first love, viticulture. There are now 13 hectares of vineyard, planted with sangiovese, merlot, montepulciano, cabernet sauvignon and grechetto, which go into around 40,000 bottles of Colli Perugini DOC. These are produced by Tito, who studied as an agricultural technician in his youth, with his daughters Marta and Monica. The best wine this year was the Colli Perugini Rosso '00, which took Two Glasses with ease. It is an almost opaque violet red and proffers an intense nose with a marked vegetality offset by a ripe fruitiness of mulberries, bilberries and cherries. The palate is rich and powerful, with reasonably fine-grained tannins, and has lots of sweet spiciness. The '99 vintage of the same wine is also characterful and highly drinkable, although less interesting than its younger brother. The nose is vegetal, with strong well-integrated balsamic tones then the palate emerges light on tannin but with good body. Finally, the Colli Perugini Rosato is also good. The colour is pale, and tinged lightly with orange. The aromas are floral and vegetal, leading in to a palate that is fairly intense, warm, fruity, and long.

● Torgiano Rosso Ris. Santa Caterina '97	▼▼	4
● Torgiano Cabernet Sauvignon '97	▼	4
● Montefalco Sagrantino '98	▼	5
● Torgiano Rosso '98	▼	2*
● Montefalco Rosso '99	▼	3

● Colli Perugini Rosso '00	▼▼	2*
☉ Colli Perugini Rosato '00	▼	2
● Colli Perugini Rosso '99	▼	2*

PERUGIA

GISBERTO GORETTI
LOC. PILA
STRADA DEL PINO, 4
06070 PERUGIA
TEL. 075607316
E-MAIL: goretti@vinigoretti.com

Brothers Stefano and Gianluca Goretti have a good 60 hectares of vineyard scattered across the hills above Perugia. This geographical spread allows them to cope well with vintage variations and harvest grapes that are generally of good quality. The estate's flagship wine, Colli Perugini Rosso L'Arringatore, comes from sangiovese, montepulciano, merlot and ciliegiolo. The '98 has a notable aromatic elegance, with fruit that is interwoven with hints of pencil lead and spices. The palate is both rich and elegant, with good extract and good fruit definition. Overall, it is attractive and should evolve well over the next few years. The '00 vintage of the estate's standard-label wine, Umbria Rosso Fontanella, is also good. In fact, we have never seen it so elegant and fruity. The newest addition to the range, Il Moggio '99, is a monovarietal Chardonnay fermented and aged in barrique. Bright, deep straw yellow, it has a nose of alluring tropical fruit, plus hints of fresh butter, toasted hazelnuts and cinnamon from the oak. The palate has good body and fair length. The Colli Perugini Chardonnay '00 has a well-fruited, floral nose. Its palate is even and not too strong in alcohol. Fruity aromas of peach and damson characterize the Colle Perugini Bianco Torre del Pino '00, along with good acidic freshness. The Umbria Bianco Fontanella '00 has primary aromas and an attractively acidulous palate with good fruit. The Vin Santo, deep amber yellow, shows richness and complexity on the nose, with notes of dried fruit and iodine salts.

●	Fontanella Rosso '00	♀♀	2*
●	Colli Perugini Rosso L'Arringatore '98	♀♀	4
○	Colli Perugini Bianco Torre del Pino '00	♀	2*
○	Colli Perugini Chardonnay '00	♀	3
○	Fontanella Bianco '00	♀	2*
○	Umbria Chardonnay Il Moggio '99	♀	4
○	Umbria Vin Santo	♀	4
●	Colli Perugini Rosso L'Arringatore '95	♀♀	3
●	Colli Perugini Rosso L'Arringatore '96	♀	3
●	Colli Perugini Rosso L'Arringatore '97	♀	4

SPELLO (PG)

F.LLI SPORTOLETTI
LOC. CAPITANLORETO
VIA LOMBARDIA, 1
06038 SPELLO (PG)
TEL. 0742651461
E-MAIL: office@sportoletti.com

Although brothers Remo and Ernesto Sportelli's estate didn't manage a Three Glass award this year, the whole range oozes quality. With 20 hectares under vine nestling in the Spello and Assisi hills, it is one of the prettiest farms in the region and with the famed Riccardo Cotarella acting as consultant oenologist, it is no surprise that both wines in the top Villa Fidelia range made it through to our tasting finals. The Villa Fidelia Rosso '99, a merlot-led Bordeaux blend, has a spicy nose whose fruit component evokes ripe cherry and prune. Its palate is warm and powerful with marked vegetal notes and austere, firm tannins that are still a touch boisterous. The barrique-aged '99 Bianco, from equal proportions of grechetto and chardonnay, is also marvellous - one of the best white wines of the region. Ripe tropical fruit, vanilla and a sweet oakiness on the nose are followed by a full, complex, warm palate, well supported by fruit. All in all, a very successful wine and excellent value for money. Assisi Rosso '00, a sangiovese and merlot blend in which the characteristics of both are clearly apparent, is rich, well-fruited, attractively complex and nicely balanced. The Assisi Grechetto '00 is a simpler wine and oak dominates both nose and palate.

○	Villa Fidelia Bianco '99	♀♀	5
●	Villa Fidelia Rosso '99	♀♀	6
●	Assisi Rosso '00	♀♀	4*
○	Assisi Grechetto '00	♀	3
●	Villa Fidelia Rosso '98	♀♀♀	6
●	Villa Fidelia Rosso '91	♀♀	4
○	Villa Fidelia Bianco '95	♀♀	4
●	Villa Fidelia Rosso '97	♀♀	4
○	Villa Fidelia Bianco '98	♀♀	4
●	Assisi Rosso '99	♀♀	4
●	Villa Fidelia Rosso '94	♀	4
●	Assisi Rosso '96	♀	1
●	Villa Fidelia Rosso '96	♀	5
●	Assisi Rosso '98	♀	2
●	Pinot Nero '98	♀	6

STRONCONE (TR)

La Palazzola
Loc. Vascigliano
05039 Stroncone (TR)
Tel. 0744607735 - 0744272357

Happily, quality standards are as high as usual at Stefano Grilli's La Palazzola estate, a long-standing star on the Umbrian wine scene. The property lies in the Stroncone hills, a few kilometres from Terni, and has 14 hectares of vineyard, from which Grilli produces a wide range of wines. This year a good five of them were awarded Two Glasses. The '99 Merlot is as stylish as in previous vintages. Its intense wild berry aromas are interlaced with gamey notes of leather and fur, and the palate is excellently structured. The Rubino, a cabernet sauvignon-led Bordeaux blend, of dark red hue tinged with violet, is also good. Perhaps not destined to be a wine of enormous complexity, it is however full of stuffing and the tannins are already silky soft. The '99 Vendemmia Tardiva is also as good as usual. The colour is almost amber and an intense, powerful nose full of sweet tropical fruits and citrus peel takes you in to the expected super-ripeness on the palate. No matter, though, for it is offset by good fresh acidity. The Riesling Brut '97, a classic method sparkling wine, is particularly rich and full, with aromas of sage and bread crusts, and huge intensity on the palate. Finally, the Vin Santo '97, with predominant flavours of dried fig, jam and pineapple, is not particularly typical but good nonetheless.

●	Merlot '99	ŸŸ	5
○	Riesling Brut M. Cl. '97	ŸŸ	4
○	Vin Santo '97	ŸŸ	5
○	La Palazzola V. T. '99	ŸŸ	5
●	Rubino '99	ŸŸ	5
●	Merlot '97	ŸŸŸ	5
●	Rubino '93	ŸŸ	3
●	Rubino '94	ŸŸ	4
●	Merlot '95	ŸŸ	4
●	Rubino '95	ŸŸ	4
●	Rubino '96	ŸŸ	5
●	Rubino '97	ŸŸ	5
○	La Palazzola V. T. '98	ŸŸ	5
●	Merlot '98	ŸŸ	5
●	Rubino '98	ŸŸ	5

TORGIANO (PG)

Cantine Lungarotti
Via Mario Angeloni, 16
06089 Torgiano (PG)
Tel. 075988661

The endeavours of the late Giorgio Lungarotti, the uncontested father-figure of Umbrian winemaking, are now being furthered with skill and love by his two daughters, Chiara and Teresa. In particular, their great efforts to improve and renew every aspect of the estate should not go unnoticed. The vast range of wines, which all share high quality and reliability, are already beginning to show the effects of the new oenological consultancies they have taken on. For example, the newest arrival to the range, Aurente '99, is a deep straw yellow. The nose is pervasive and stylish, full of florality and tropical fruits, with elegant, complex, sweetly spicy notes that meld perfectly with the fruit. The palate is beautifully textured, well balanced in its oak tenor, and shows distinct flavours of apples and citrus peel. San Giorgio '93, a red with a particularly elegant nose and a careful balance on the palate between fruit and oak, is another Two Glass certainty. The Torgiano Cabernet Sauvignon '98 has well-judged varietal aromas, enhanced by black pepper and cinnamon nuances. It develops well on the palate, with good initial impact, fullness in the centre of the mouth and an even finish. Giubilante '98 is well made, almost overshadowing the '93 vintage of that Lungarotti classic, Torgiano Rosso Rubesco Riserva Vigna Monticchio, which appeared a little below par. Finally, a round of applause for the excellent drinkability and the rich seam of fruit in the classic Torgiano Bianco Torre di Giano '00.

●	San Giorgio '93	ŸŸ	6
●	Cabernet Sauvignon '98	ŸŸ	4
○	Chardonnay Aurente '99	ŸŸ	5
○	Torgiano Bianco Torre di Giano '00	Ÿ	3
●	Torgiano Rosso Vigna Monticchio Ris. '93	Ÿ	6
●	Giubilante '98	Ÿ	5
●	San Giorgio '88	ŸŸ	5
●	Torgiano Rosso Vigna Monticchio Ris. '88	ŸŸ	5
●	Torgiano Rosso Vigna Monticchio Ris. '90	ŸŸ	5
●	San Giorgio '92	ŸŸ	5
●	Cabernet Sauvignon '95	ŸŸ	4
●	Il Vessillo '97	ŸŸ	5

OTHER WINERIES

Cantina dei Colli Amerini
Loc. Fornole
05020 Amelia (TR)
tel. 0744989721
e-mail: carbio@net4free.it

An open verdict for the Cantina dei Colli Amerini which, after years of excellent results, has to be relegated to the "other wineries" list due to the absence of their top reds. The flowery Chardonnay Rocca Nerina and the acidulous, fruity Terre Arnolfe are both good.

○ C. Amerini Bianco Terre Arnolfe '00		2*
● C. Amerini Rosso Terre Arnolfe '00		2*
○ C. Amerini Chardonnay Rocca Nerina '98		4
● C. Amerini Rosso Sup. Carbio '98		4

Zanchi
Via Ortana, 122
05022 Amelia (TR)
tel. 0744970011 - 0744402323

Founded in 1970, this Amelia estate retains its listing thanks to its Rosso dei Colli Amerini Sciurio '97 with a fruit-driven nose and powerful, spicy palate

● C. Amerini Rosso Sup. Sciurio '97		4

Tenuta di Salviano
Loc. Civitella del Lago
Voc. Salviano, 44
05020 Baschi (TR)
tel. 0744950459 e-mail: fattoria@orvieto.it

Situated on the shores of Lake Corbara, straddling the River Tiber between Todi and Orvieto, Tenuta di Salviano turns out typically well made wines. The Lago di Corbara Turlò '99 has a ripe cherry character, the Orvieto Classico Superiore is floral and balanced.

○ Orvieto Cl. Sup. '00		4
● Lago di Corbara Turlò '99		4
○ Orvieto Cl. Sup. '96		3
○ Orvieto Cl. Sup. '97		3

Il Poggio
Loc. Macchie
Via Petrarca, 8
06060 Castiglione del Lago (PG)
tel. 0759589923

The wines of this small estate situated on the hills surrounding Lake Trasimeno and run by Anna Gattobigio are showing well. The typical wines of the zone, the Colli del Trasimeno Rosso and Bianco, are well typed.

○ C. del Trasimeno Bianco '00		2*
○ C. del Trasimeno Bianco Scelto '00		2*
● C. del Trasimeno Rosso '99		2*

Podere Marella
Loc. Ferretto
06061 Castiglione del Lago (PG)
tel. 075954139

Run by Fiammetta Inga, this estate has been going since 1974. There are seven hectares of vineyard, all cultivated organically. It is the two reds that are the most interesting: the intense, fruity Umbria Rosso Caluna '99 and the pleasingly complex Colli del Trasimeno Rosso '98.

● C. del Trasimeno Rosso '98	2*
● Caluna '99	3

Villa Po' del Vento
Via Po' del Vento, 6
06062 Città della Pieve (PG)
tel. 0578299950
e-mail: podelvento@tiscalinet.it

The estate is owned by Francesco Anichini and has 12 hectares of vineyard. The wines showed well, most notably the Umbria Bianco Riesling with its fresh nose and the fruity Colli del Trasimeno Rosso which had pepper and clove spiciness.

○ Umbria Riesling '00	2*
● C. del Trasimeno Rosso '99	2*
● C. del Trasimeno Rosso '94	2
○ C. del Trasimeno Bianco '96	2*

San Lorenzo
Loc. San Lorenzo Vecchio
06034 Foligno (PG)
tel. 074222553

Situated on the hills overlooking Foligno, this estate, owned by Flaminia De Luca, makes its debut in the Guide with an interesting Umbria Rosso '99 which is herbaceous on the nose and has a concentrated, fruity palate.

● De Luca Rosso '99	3

Terre de' Trinci
Via Fiamenga, 57
06034 Foligno (PG)
tel. 0742320165 - 0742320243
e-mail: cantina@terredetrinci.com

With 300 hectares of vineyard, Terre de' Trinci is certainly no small estate. Its Umbria Rosso Cajo '99, with its subtle tones of undergrowth, and the full-bodied Sagrantino di Montefalco '97, nicely complex on the nose, are both good.

● Montefalco Sagrantino '97	5
● Cajo '99	4

Terre del Carpine
Via Formanuova, 87
06063 Magione (PG)
tel. 075840298
e-mail: cit@trasinet.com

Terre del Carpine is the new name for the wines of the Cantina Intercomunale del Trasimeno The co-operative has 400 members owning a good 420 hectares of vineyard. This year the two red Colli del Trasimeno wines, the concentrated Barca '99 and the fresh, fruity Erceo '00, topped the range.

● C. del Trasimeno Rosso Erceo '00	2
● C. del Trasimeno Rosso Barca '99	3

Umbria Viticoltori Associati
Loc. Cerro
Zona Industriale
06055 Marsciano (PG)
tel. 0758748989

The Umbria Viticoltori Associati, known as UVA, slips into the "other wineries" section despite the good showing of several of its wines, most notably the Umbria Trebbiano '00 with its complex floral tones, and the vegetal, somewhat evolved Umbria Sangiovese.

● Umbria Sangiovese '00	2*
○ Umbria Trebbiano '00	2*
○ Chardonnay Vigne Umbre '98	2
● Montefalco Sagrantino Vigne Umbre '95	5

Piero Virili
Loc. Belvedere
Via Montepennino, 40
06036 Montefalco (PG)
Tel. 0742379602 e-mail: virilipiero@libero.it

The Virili family has been cultivating the sagrantino variety with care and skill on their estate in the Montefalco hills for many years now and it is the variety that gives them their best results, as exemplified by the Sagrantino Passito '97.

● Montefalco Sagrantino Passito '97	♀	5

Luciano Sassara
Loc. Pian del Vantaggio, 43
05019 Orvieto (TR)
Tel. 076325119

The wines of this Orvieto estate remain interesting, most notably the Umbria Rosso Vantaggio '99 which has ripe red berry fruit on the nose and a mid-length, nicely tannic palate.

● Vantaggio '99	♀	3

La Querciolana
Via Vieniche, 4
06064 Panicale (PG)
Tel. 075837477

Situated near to Lake Trasimeno, this estate retains its listing due to its good overall performance but particularly that of its two red '98 Colli del Trasimenos: Boldrino and Riserva Grifo del Boldrino.

● C. del Trasimeno Rosso di Boldrino '98	♀	3
● C. del Trasimeno Rosso Grifo di Boldrino Ris. '98	♀	3

Spoletoducale
Loc. Petrognano, 54
06049 Spoleto (PG)
Tel. 074356224
e-mail: collispoletini@mail.caribusiness.it

Results from this winery are encouraging. The two traditional Montefalco wines are both at One Glass level. The Rosso di Montefalco has an attractive subtle spiciness, the Sagrantino evokes red fruit jam.

● Montefalco Sagrantino '97	♀	5
● Montefalco Rosso '98	♀	3

Todini
Loc. Collevalenza
06059 Todi (PG)
Tel. 075887122 - 075887222
e-mail: agrtodi@libero.it

This is Todini's first appearance in the Guide. The fresh, fruity Grechetto di Todi is successful, the Sangiovese Rubro has good body and length.

○ Grechetto di Todi '00	♀	3
● Colli Martani Sangiovese Rubro '99	♀	3

I Girasoli di Sant'Andrea
Loc. Molino Vitelli
06019 Umbertide (PG)
Tel. 0759410837

Owned by the Gritti, the noble Venetian family, this estate joins the Guide for the first time with its major red wine, Il Doge '00, which is full, powerful and nicely spicy.

● Il Doge '00	♀	6

LAZIO

So slow, so slow. Watching this region haul itself forward is excruciating, although, in truth, there have been some signs of less tortoise-like movement, at least on the red front. Not with the '00 whites, sadly, because the weather during the year was capricious, to put it mildly, and many of the wines are lacking in primary aromas. Some producers opted to pick early and involuntarily impoverished the complexity of their wines' perfumes without managing to achieve their main objective of retaining acidity. Others left the grapes on the vines until they were fully ripe in the hope of gaining complexity but the fierce heat that plagued the summer months and part of autumn meant that the grapes became over-ripe. The result was wines with over-evolved aromas and not enough fixed acidity. They appeared lumberingly heavy in structure – exactly what isn't required with wines that are supposed to be light, fresh and fragrant. Anyway, enough of this depressing news. Let's turn our attention to the numerous good reds that were produced. Once more Riccardo Cotarella hit a bull's eye with Montiano. His powerful '99 gained Three Glasses and was the only wine in the region to do so. Cotarella also sailed high into the Two Glass category with the revamped Merlot Umbria '00. Another well deserved Two Glasses went to the Ferretti brothers from Cori for a brilliant Colle Amato '99. These outsiders are joined by Giulio Santarelli with Quattro Mori '99, Casale del Giglio with Mater Matuta '98, Colle Picchioni with the ever-reliable Vigna del Vassallo '99 and Roberto Trappolini, who has excelled himself with an incredible '99 Paterno, which is also priced low enough to keep anyone's bank manager happy. There's little to complain about with Giovanni Palombo's '99 Cabernet Riserva, although it doesn't match up to the glories of the '97. After a few wobbles, the Cantina di Cerveteri's Vigna Grande Rosso has bounced back to give an impressive showing. The parade finishes with a newcomer to the Guide, Colle di Maggio, from Velletri, which has hit the spotlight with an impeccable red, Le Anfore '98. For the '00 whites, things were, as we have said, anything but easy. As ever, though, some people managed to buck the trend. So up pop Fontana Candida with a faultless release of its evergreen Frascati Santa Teresa, again unrivalled, and Santarelli with Frascati Vigna Adriana '00, which scored a distinguished Two Glasses. Sergio Mottura's captivating "vin français", Latour a Civitella '99, was also on form, as was Paolo D'Amico's Falesia '99 and Poggio dei Gelsi '00 from Falesco. We applaud the return of Christine Vaselli to the Other Wineries page with her muscular Torre Sant'Andrea '99, as well as the arrival of Marco Carpineti's small estate at Cori and its promising range of organic wines.

APRILIA (LT)

Casale del Giglio
Loc. Le Ferriere
Strada Cisterna-Nettuno, km 13
04011 Aprilia
tel. 0692902530
e-mail: casaledelgiglio@tin.it

Years of ceaseless effort and unwavering commitment at Casale del Giglio are bringing their reward. This year's achievements include two wines, Shiraz '99 and Antinoo '98, which gain acclaim for value for money and one, Mater Matuta '98, which reached the final taste-off for those magic Three Glasses. The whole range, though, is distinguished, right down to the two "basics". The Chardonnay '00 has a delicious aroma of not-quite-ripe peaches and the Sauvignon '00 shows a very intense, strongly varietal aroma of great finesse. Antinoo '98, from chardonnay and viognier, is as characterful as ever. A solid wine, its good pale gold ushers in notes of vanilla that sink into a savoury yet fresh fruity aroma. The reds are also good news, with the sumptuous Mater Matuta '98 at the top of the tree. It is a caressingly elegant, dense, tightly-knit wine of great depth, with excellent fruit, warmth and length. It was well worth its place at the final tastings, not to mention its brimming Two Glass score. The Cabernet Sauvignon Riserva '98 is also excellent. Deep and concentrated, it shows a range of aromas that is as complex as it is impressive. The punchy, solid Shiraz '99 is stunningly good. Tight and densely woven, balanced in tannin, tangy and spicy, it reveals hints of animal skin and a light touch of bitterness on the finish. Both the Merlot '99 and the Madreselva '97 are sound wines, the latter with good breadth of aroma and moderate structure yet also with fair complexity. Finally, a tip of the hat to the striking, fresh Albiola '00 with its delicious aromatic fragrance.

ATINA (FR)

Giovanni Palombo
C.so Munanzio Planco
03042 Atina (FR)
tel. 0776610200
e-mail: margiuri@jumpy.it

Perhaps we haven't quite got to grips with what drives Giovanni Palombo. We'd hate to see this capable guy overlooking some detail in his enthusiasm to realize his ambition of hitting it big time as a quality wine producer. He set off with a bang. The highly lauded '97 Duca Cantelmi was marvellous but later vintages haven't done as well. And that is a real shame. Maybe he produces too many wines. Maybe the vines are still too young. Whatever it is, this year's Atina Cabernet Riserva Duca Cantelmi, the '99, managed to win a second Glass but not by much. The rest of the reds, apart from Atina Cabernet '99 which we assessed for last year's Guide, include a rather good Colle della Torre '99, a fruit-driven, merlot-led Bordeaux blend with decent complexity and concentration, and Rosso delle Chiaie '00, again merlot-based but vinified and aged without any oak. The outcome is a delightful wine with a youthful attack and overt varietal character. From the whites, the pleasing Somiglò, from sémillon and sauvignon, always makes its mark. The '00 has good mouthfeel although the nose is rather toned down compared with the previous vintage. The effect of the vintage was also apparent on the '00 Bianco delle Chiaie. A malvasia and vermentino blend it is still attractive but lacks some of its habitual fresh, fragrant aroma.

● Mater Matuta '98	🍷🍷	4
○ Sauvignon '00	🍷🍷	2*
○ Antinoo '98	🍷🍷	3*
● Cabernet Sauvignon '98	🍷🍷	4
● Shiraz '99	🍷🍷	3*
⊙ Albiola '00	🍷	2
○ Chardonnay '00	🍷	2
○ Lazio Bianco Satrico '00	🍷	2
● Madreselva '97	🍷	4
● Merlot '99	🍷	3
● Mater Matuta '95	🍷🍷	4
● Madreselva '96	🍷🍷	4
● Mater Matuta '96	🍷🍷	4
○ Antinoo '97	🍷🍷	3
● Cabernet Sauvignon '97	🍷🍷	4

● Cabernet Duca Cantelmi '99	🍷🍷	6
● Rosso delle Chiaie '00	🍷	3
○ Somiglò '00	🍷	4
● Colle della Torre '99	🍷	5
○ Bianco delle Chiaie '00		2
● Cabernet Duca Cantelmi '97	🍷🍷	5
● Colle della Torre '97	🍷🍷	4
● Cabernet Duca Cantelmi '98	🍷🍷	5
● Colle della Torre '98	🍷🍷	4
● Rosso delle Chiaie '97	🍷	3
● Rosso delle Chiaie '98	🍷	3
○ Somiglò '98	🍷	3
● Atina Cabernet '99	🍷	4

BOLSENA (VT)

Italo Mazziotti
Loc. Mecona-Bonvino
Via Cassia Km 110
01023 Bolsena (VT)
Tel. 0761799049 - 0644291377
E-mail: mazziott@tin.it

After a brief absence last year, the wines of Mazziotti, a long-standing Montefiascone estate, are back in our sights and the Mazziotti family looks to be squaring up firmly to the future's challenges. For starters, the range has been embellished by the arrival of a charming late-harvest wine, Terre di Melona. Made from a grechetto and malvasia blend, it is particularly intense in fruit aromas and has flavours of apricot jam interwoven with subtle hints of tropical fruit. It may not be powerful in structure but it has more than decent texture. The traditionally styled Est Est Est di Montefiascone continues to perform reliably. The '00 has a fair spread of aromas and an intriguing streak of citrus. The '00 barrique-aged version Canuleio is just a shade better. This has a broad, dense, richly nuanced nose, from which vanilla emerges strongly. The palate is lent complexity by all its components, from its warm ripe peach fruitiness, to its seams of vanilla and considerable length. From the reds produced by winemaker Flaminia, we happily nominate a fine Volgente '99 as the best bottle. Made from merlot, sangiovese and montepulciano, and given around a year's ageing in barriques, it has quite a complex bouquet dominated by spices, tobacco and coffee, good nose-palate consistency and plentiful length.

CASTIGLIONE IN TEVERINA (VT)

Paolo d'Amico
Fraz. Vaiano
Loc. Palombaro
01024 Castiglione in Teverina (VT)
Tel. 0761948868 - 0668134079

The d'Amico husband and wife team continue to reap success. They certainly do not lack initiative and their wines are full of personality, even though we felt that this year, of the two Chardonnays, the Falesia was more impressive than the Calanchi di Vaiano. Indeed, the Falesia '99, with 12 months' oak ageing, explodes with sensations. The colour is bright gold. The dense nose is punctuated by vanilla, oak toast and ripe tropical fruit, then the palate is deep and mouthfilling, with vanilla that melds into its buttery, fruity flavours. The finish is all-enveloping, warm and very long. The Calanchi di Vaiano '99, on the other hand, puzzled us because it came over as rather heavy on the nose and surprisingly untogether. It didn't look like an error in winemaking, though, an unlikely event in any case given that their vineyard manager, Fabrizio Moltard, and their oenologist, Carlo Corino, are two of Italy's top specialists. In any event our esteem for the d'Amicos remains undimmed and we are impatient to see their new wine, due out shortly and already announced as a very serious red.

● Volgente Rosso '99	🍷🍷	4
○ Est Est Est di Montefiascone Canuleio '00	🍷	4
○ Terre di Melona '99	🍷	4
○ Est Est Est di Montefiascone '00		2
○ Est Est Est di Montefiascone Canuleio '94	🍷🍷	4
● Volgente Rosso '97	🍷🍷	4
○ Est Est Est di Montefiascone '96	🍷	2
○ Est Est Est di Montefiascone '97	🍷	2
○ Est Est Est di Montefiascone Canuleio '97	🍷	4
○ Est Est Est di Montefiascone '99	🍷	2
○ Est Est Est di Montefiascone Filò '99	🍷	2

○ Falesia '99	🍷🍷	5
○ Calanchi di Vaiano '99	🍷	4
○ Falesia '98	🍷🍷	5
○ Calanchi di Vaiano '98	🍷	4

CASTIGLIONE IN TEVERINA (VT)

TRAPPOLINI
VIA DEL RIVELLINO, 65
01024 CASTIGLIONE IN TEVERINA (VT)
TEL. 0761948381
E-MAIL: trappolini@tin.it

Paterno. Don't forget the name. We were astounded when we discovered how highly the '99 had scored when the results of our tastings were revealed. It was one of the top wines. A monovarietal Sangiovese this dense and concentrated has never before been seen in Lazio. It was so good we sent it through to the final Three Glass taste-off. What is even more amazing is that Roberto Trappolini sells a wine of such complexity for so little. The Chardonnay dell'Umbria '00, though, was not overshadowed by it. This is tightly knit and has perfect fruit-oak balance, an enchanting note of toast and a broad range of elegant fruit. The estate's other wines were a notch or two below. The Grechetto dell'Umbria Brecceto '00 is mid-structured. The nose has rather evolved fruit and fair complexity but shows good persistence, as does the palate, which finishes on a thread of bitterness. Even if the Est Est Est di Montefiascone '00 isn't particularly muscular, it still wins friends for its varietal fragrance and its freshness and vitality. The Orvieto '00, too, is a touch subdued yet with its delicate fruit and zestiness, it comes over as "small but perfectly formed". Idea '00 is from aleatico. It seemed thinner than the previous vintage, perhaps because of the poor weather, and the mixture of fruit and hints of dried rose flowers we so liked last year seemed diluted and supported by a less firm structure.

Paterno '99	🍷🍷	3*
Chardonnay '00	🍷🍷	3
Idea '00	🍷	4
Umbria Grechetto Brecceto '00	🍷	3
Est Est Est di Montefiascone '00		2
Orvieto '00		3
Paterno '96	🍷🍷	3
Chardonnay '98	🍷🍷	3
Idea '98	🍷🍷	4
Paterno '98	🍷🍷	3
Chardonnay '99	🍷🍷	3
Idea '99	🍷🍷	4
Umbria Grechetto Brecceto '99	🍷	3

CERVETERI (RM)

CANTINA COOPERATIVA DI CERVETERI
VIA AURELIA KM 42.700
00052 CERVETERI (RM)
TEL. 069905697 - 069905677
E-MAIL: cantina@caerenet.it

Once again, we have doubts about Cerveteri. Nothing dramatic, you understand, just a sign of the difficulties a large co-operative can find itself having to confront. The most serious is the variability of quality in its members' grapes, something only an expert oenologist like Riccardo Cotarella can remedy, and even then only sometimes. For example, Cerveteri Bianco Vigna Grande '00 is disappointing. It has slightish aromas and a drying palate that tends to fall apart on the finish. Yet the more basic Cerveteri Bianco Fontana Morella '00 is surprisingly good, earning itself a well-deserved One Glass, not to mention our esteem for its incredible value for money. Then again, the '00 Malvasia Villanova was clearly affected by the warm year and is over-weighty compared with the previous vintage. Both Cerveteri's top reds showed very well. Cerveteri Rosso Vigna Grande, back in the frame with the '98 after a gap of one year, has a wealth of potential. Its nose is full and spicy. The warm, zesty palate is spicy, too, and given depth by its notes of toast, while holding together very well as a whole. Tertium '99, from malvasia nera, sangiovese and cabernet, is muscular and has enviable complexity and great concentration of aroma. All this makes for a firm wine that shouldn't have any problems in ageing. The Cerveteri Rosso Fontana Morella '00 is more modest and rather one-dimensional but the price is excellent.

Cerveteri Rosso Vigna Grande '98	🍷🍷	3*
Tertium '99	🍷🍷	4
Cerveteri Bianco Fontana Morella '00	🍷	1*
Cerveteri Bianco Vigna Grande '00	🍷	2
Cerveteri Rosso Fontana Morella '00	🍷	1
Malvasia del Lazio Villanova '00		2
Cerveteri Rosso Vigna Grande '95	🍷🍷	3
Cerveteri Rosso Vigna Grande '97	🍷🍷	3
Cerveteri Rosso Vigna Grande '94	🍷	3
Cerveteri Rosso Fontana Morella '96	🍷	1
Cerveteri Rosso Vigna Grande '96	🍷	3
Cerveteri Bianco Vigna Grande '98	🍷	2
Tertium '98	🍷	3
Cerveteri Bianco Vigna Grande '99	🍷	2
Malvasia del Lazio '99	🍷	2

CIVITELLA D'AGLIANO (VT)   CORI (LT)

Tenuta Mottura
Loc. Rio Chiaro
Via Poggio della Costa, 1
01020 Civitella d'Agliano (VT)
Tel. 0761914533
E-mail: mottura@isa.it

Colle San Lorenzo
Via Gramsci, 52
04010 Cori (LT)
Tel. 069677151

There is always something bubbling away on this estate. This year, it is the Civitella Rosso, made from merlot and montepulciano d'Abruzzo, which has been given a makeover by the ever-busy Sergio Mottura. In fact, the '00 isn't all that different from previous vintages. It has a good ruby colour. The nose is full of spice and classy oak then the palate, is held together by tannins that support without overwhelming. There are intense, long-lasting nuances of small red berry fruit, coffee and chocolate. Next comes the stately Latour a Civitella '99, from grechetto vinified in stainless steel and then aged in barriques supplied by Burgundy's Louis Latour. It has warm notes of vanilla that meld harmoniously into its fruit and the palate is full, warm and pervasive. Two comfortable Glasses. The Orvieto Vigna Tragugnano '00, while reflecting the problems of the hot year, has managed to retain its habitual array of aromas almost intact. These are set in a good, solid framework which lasts right through the mouth, breaking up only slightly on the finish. The Grechetto Poggio della Costa '00 came out similarly, with its rather evolved fruity aromas offset by a most attractive freshness on the palate, with hints of rhubarb. Usually we go into raptures over Muffo but this year we can't because the new release, the '00, is not yet ready. We'll just have to wait patiently.

Little and good. This small, feisty estate at Cori is sending out incontrovertible signals of where it's at. The Fratelli brothers who run it produce just three wines but all three won unanimous approval. Top of the trio is a fascinating cabernet and syrah blend, Colle Amato. The '99 showed magnificently this year, with not a single glitch in its styling. The full, dense nose is pervasive and spicy with elegant wafts of morello cherry. The palate, also spicy, is warm, deep and very long, with ripe but not obtrusive tannins. In short, it has all the distinguishing characteristics of a final taste-off candidate. Its almost equally good partner, Cori Costa Vecchia '99, is a merlot and petit verdot blend. It, too, shines and is excellently put together with a lightly spicy nose of good intensity and a warm, long, fruit-forward palate, punctuated by notes of vanilla and caramel. The Pietra Pinta white, Chardonnay del Lazio '00, has a good spectrum of harmonious varietal aromas, with plentiful fruit, some tropical, softened by notes of honey. The palate is silky and supple. It had no trouble gaining a Two generous Glasses.

● Civitella Rosso '00	ŦŦ	3
○ Grechetto Latour a Civitella '99	ŦŦ	4
○ Grechetto Poggio della Costa '00	Ŧ	3
○ Orvieto Cl. Vigna Tragugnano '00	Ŧ	2
○ Grechetto Poggio della Costa '95	ŦŦ	3
○ Muffo '95	ŦŦ	4
○ Grechetto Latour a Civitella '96	ŦŦ	4
○ Grechetto Latour a Civitella '97	ŦŦ	4
○ Muffo '97	ŦŦ	3
○ Grechetto Latour a Civitella '98	ŦŦ	4
○ Grechetto Poggio della Costa '98	ŦŦ	3
○ Muffo '98	ŦŦ	3
○ Grechetto Poggio della Costa '99	ŦŦ	3
○ Muffo '94	Ŧ	4
○ Orvieto Cl. Vigna Tragugnano '99	Ŧ	2

● Colle Amato '99	ŦŦ	5
○ Chardonnay del Lazio '00	ŦŦ	3
● Cori Rosso Costa Vecchia '99	ŦŦ	3*

FRASCATI (RM)

CASALE MARCHESE
VIA DI VERMICINO, 68
00044 FRASCATI (RM)
TEL. 069408932
E-MAIL: marchese@microelettra.it

This has been a less than great year for the Carletti family's Vigna del Cavaliere, a prestigious red produced from cabernet sauvignon, cabernet franc, merlot and a touch of montepulciano, grown on the Frascati hills. The '98 did not enjoy the weather conditions of previous vintages and so, although still a wine that is a great pleasure to drink, it lacks a bit of impact on the nose and its palate is looser. We are really looking forward to the '00, though, given that the more basic version from the same grape blend, Rosso di Casale Marchese, is already showing excellently – and with the montepulciano strongly in evidence. The nose has a good array of aromas, primarily cherry, lightly supported by spice. The palate is cleanly defined, fresh and supple and the finish soft, clean and tight. The heat of the '00 vintage meant that the Frascati Superiore has lost some of its characteristic exuberance of aroma and resembles a more typical Frascati. Still, it well deserves its One Glass. The fairly aromatic nose has refinement and persistence, with lively notes of summer flowers, then the palate is pleasingly soft, remaining fruity right through to the finish. The Cortesia also showed improvements, the '00 offering more weight than the rather thin versions of previous years. It remains softly sweet but with more conviction, has good length and retains sweetness on the warm finish.

GROTTAFERRATA (RM)

CASTEL DE PAOLIS
VIA VAL DE PAOLIS, 41
00046 GROTTAFERRATA (RM)
TEL. 069413648
E-MAIL: info@casteldepaolis.it

Giulio Santarelli should be very proud of himself this year. For a start, two wines, Quattro Mori and Vigna Adriana, made it to the Three Glasses tasting finals. In addition, almost all the other wines gained Two Glasses, and deservedly so. This is obviously not just chance. We shouldn't forget that the attentive Franco Bernabei has been looking after the Castel De Paolis wines for some time now. The Quattro Mori has always scored very highly in tasting but the '99 is sumptuous, elegant and quite simply great. "Great" also describes the '00 Frascati Vigna Adriana. Never has it been so complex, with honey, pineapple and vanilla on the imposing nose and fresh yet refined palate that fills the mouth with a silky seductiveness. The standard-label Frascati Superiore has also made a similar quality leap, the '00 having overt aromas of tropical fruit, warmth, fragrance and a firm but not overweening structure that allows elegance and softness to come through. Frascati Superiore Campo Vecchio '00, full of elegant, lively aroma, is another very good wine, as is the spicy Campo Vecchio Rosso '99, rich in red berry fruit. Among the sweet wines, a delicious Muffa Nobile '00, intensely sweet and elegant, stands out although the Frascati Cannellino '00 and Rosathea '00, with its hints of dried rose petals, are both good sound wines.

○ Cortesia di Casale Marchese '00	♀	3
○ Frascati Sup. '00	♀	2
● Rosso di Casale Marchese '00	♀	3
● Vigna del Cavaliere '98	♀	5
○ Cortesia di Casale Marchese '93	♀♀	3
○ Cortesia di Casale Marchese '94	♀♀	3
○ Cortesia di Casale Marchese '95	♀♀	3
● Vigna del Cavaliere '96	♀♀	4
● Rosso di Casale Marchese '97	♀♀	3
● Vigna del Cavaliere '97	♀♀	4
● Rosso di Casale Marchese '98	♀	3
● Rosso di Casale Marchese '99	♀	3

● Quattro Mori '99	♀♀	5
○ Frascati Sup. Campo Vecchio '00	♀♀	3*
○ Frascati Sup. Castel De Paolis '00	♀♀	4
○ Frascati Sup. V. Adriana '00	♀♀	5
○ Muffa Nobile '00	♀♀	5
● Rosathea '00	♀♀	5
○ Frascati Sup. Cannellino '00	♀	5
● Campo Vecchio Rosso '99	♀	3
● Quattro Mori '97	♀♀	5
● Quattro Mori '98	♀♀	5
● Selve Vecchie '98	♀♀	5
○ Frascati Sup. '99	♀♀	4
○ Frascati Sup. V. Adriana '99	♀♀	5
○ Muffa Nobile '99	♀♀	5
● Rosathea '99	♀♀	5

MARINO (RM)

Paola Di Mauro - Colle Picchioni
Loc. Frattocchie
Via Colle Picchione, 46
00040 Marino (RM)
tel. 0693546329
e-mail: p.dm.dimauro@flashnet.it

Colle Picchioni, with only nine hectares of lovingly tended vineyards and an annual production of just over 100,000 bottles, is almost a "boutique winery". Indeed, if the Marino zone has any renown at all internationally, it is all down to Paola di Mauro and her son Armando. To start with, they have to their credit a series of excellent vintages of their Bordeaux blend, Vigna del Vassallo. The latest, the 99, is emblematic and again one of the region's best reds. It is a dark, dense ruby and the nose is full and rich, with an initial ripe black berry fruit that tends towards roast coffee beans, cocoa powder, vanilla and sweet spices. The palate is dense and meaty, with smooth tannins, good progression and a long finish. The only question mark is the slight bitterness on the finish, possibly due to oak that isn't quite up to the quality of the wine. Both the '99 and the '00 Colle Picchioni Rosso, made predominantly from montepulciano and merlot, are very successful. Wines of substance, they also offer an attractive softness that comes from their fruit notes of ripe plum and ripe mulberry. Marino Colle Picchioni Oro '00 has a deep straw hue then classy aromas of ripe fruit, with mineral and vanilla touches, that introduce a concentrated, balanced, well-fruited palate. The Marino '00 Etichetta Verde – the name means "Green Label" – is less complex but still fresh and lively. We have no doubts that once the new cellars currently under construction are completed, the Di Mauros and their oenologist Riccardo Cotarella will gain the momentum to wow us with even more exciting wines.

MONTE PORZIO CATONE (RM)

Fontana Candida
Via Fontana Candida, 11
00040 Monte Porzio Catone (RM)
tel. 069420066
e-mail: giv@giv.it

In difficult years, class shines through and Franco Bardi has once more shown his oenological pedigree. His is a titanic undertaking, given the vast quantities of wines handled at Fontana Candida. No one can perform miracles but just try the '00 Frascati Superiore Santa Teresa, still one of Lazio's best whites, and see how close Bardi can come. Fragrant peachy notes add to a delicious fresh zestiness. The structure is not conspicuous but is supported by a good weight of alcohol and a well-integrated flavour the finish remains soft and long. The '00 standard Frascati Superiore is, as ever, a greatly appealing wine. It may not be as striking as the previous vintage but is nevertheless fresh and very attractive. From the Terre dei Grifi line, the Malvasia del Lazio is as well styled as usual, the '00 having the right balance of aroma, freshness, notes of almond and a good finish. The Terre dei Grifi Frascati Superiore '00 is delicately fresh and fruity. However, the real interest this year is focused on a new wine, Kron, the first red the winery has ever produced. It is a monovarietal Merlot aged in small oak barrels and a pre-release sample of the '99 showed notable depth and indisputable complexity, although it is still too early to give a definitive assessment. We shall return to it next year.

● Vigna del Vassallo '99	ŶŶ	5*
● Colle Picchioni Rosso '00	ŶŶ	4*
○ Marino Colle Picchioni Oro '00	ŶŶ	4*
● Colle Picchioni Rosso '99	ŶŶ	4
○ Marino Etichetta Verde '00	Ŷ	3
● Vigna del Vassallo '85	ŶŶŶ	5
● Vigna del Vassallo '88	ŶŶŶ	5
● Vigna del Vassallo '95	ŶŶ	5
● Vigna del Vassallo '96	ŶŶ	5
○ Marino Colle Picchioni Oro '97	ŶŶ	4
● Vigna del Vassallo '97	ŶŶ	5
○ Marino Colle Picchioni Oro '98	ŶŶ	4
● Vigna del Vassallo '98	ŶŶ	5
○ Marino Colle Picchioni Oro '99	ŶŶ	4
○ Marino Etichetta Verde '99	Ŷ	3

○ Frascati Sup. Santa Teresa '00	ŶŶ	3
○ Frascati Sup. Terre dei Grifi '00	Ŷ	2
○ Malvasia del Lazio Terre dei Grifi '00	Ŷ	3
○ Frascati Sup. '00		2
○ Frascati Sup. Terre dei Grifi '95	ŶŶ	2
○ Malvasia del Lazio '95	ŶŶ	2
○ Frascati Sup. Santa Teresa '96	ŶŶ	2
○ Malvasia del Lazio '96	ŶŶ	2
○ Frascati Sup. Santa Teresa '97	ŶŶ	2
○ Malvasia del Lazio '97	ŶŶ	2
○ Frascati Sup. Santa Teresa '98	ŶŶ	2
○ Malvasia del Lazio '98	ŶŶ	2
○ Frascati Sup. Santa Teresa '99	ŶŶ	3
○ Malvasia del Lazio Terre dei Grifi '99	ŶŶ	3
○ Frascati Sup. Terre dei Grifi '99	Ŷ	2

MONTE PORZIO CATONE (RM)

Villa Simone - Piero Costantini
Via Frascati Colonna, 29
00040 Monte Porzio Catone (RM)
tel. 069449717
e-mail: info@pierocostantini.it

In a surge of renewed self-respect, Piero Costantini's Frascati Superiore returns to a quality level more in keeping with its status. For some time, this standard-label wine of the estate had seemed stuck on the sidelines but the '00 has delightfully fragrant aromas, perfect nose-palate consistency and is fresh and delightfully drinkable. The habitual richness of Frascati Superiore Villa dei Preti is toned down in the '00. It is still a very well-styled wine but its fruit is less impressive and its complexity more subdued than in the vintages that have seen this wine standing out from the crowd. Such things happen. The '00 Frascati Filonardi, however, sees no fall from grace. The fruit on the nose is evolved but without any signs of tiredness and its flavour is beautifully fresh. Complex, full and long, it is a wine of distinct personality, made for sophisticated palates. The sweet '99 Cannellino version is, as usual, a well-defined wine of character. Its dense, warm, silky, texture, with a broad array of interweaving perfumes from honey through to apricot, risks being almost too sweet, but it is a wine of great structure and a superb partner for sweet biscuits.

○ Frascati Sup. Vign. Filonardi '00	ŶŶ	3
○ Frascati Sup. Cannellino '99	ŶŶ	4
○ Frascati Sup. V. dei Preti '00	Ŷ	2
○ Frascati Sup. Villa Simone '00	Ŷ	2
○ Frascati Sup. Cannellino '91	ŶŶ	5
○ Frascati Sup. Cannellino '92	ŶŶ	5
○ Frascati Sup. V. dei Preti '94	ŶŶ	2
○ Frascati Sup. V. dei Preti '95	ŶŶ	2
○ Frascati Sup. Vign. Filonardi '95	ŶŶ	3
○ Frascati Sup. Cannellino '97	ŶŶ	5
○ Frascati Sup. V. dei Preti '97	ŶŶ	2
○ Frascati Sup. Vign. Filonardi '97	ŶŶ	3
○ Frascati Sup. Cannellino '98	ŶŶ	4
○ Frascati Sup. V. dei Preti '99	ŶŶ	2
○ Frascati Sup. Vign. Filonardi '99	ŶŶ	3

MONTEFIASCONE (VT)

Falesco
Loc. Artigiana Le Guardie
01027 Montefiascone (VT)
tel. 0761825669 - 0761834011
e-mail: falesco@leonet.it

Going through the wines produced by the much fêted and discussed winemaker of the moment, Riccardo Cotarella, prompted us to reflect that he has no need to make up stories to defend his reputation. When someone knows what they're doing, it stands out a mile and Cotarella is a master of his trade. Quite simply, his wines are among the best in the region. Once again Montiano, this time the '99, is a multi-faceted stream of aromas and flavours and Lazio's only Three Glass wine while Riccardo's Merlot dell'Umbria '00 is the year's most exciting newcomer, offering a wonderful mix of printer's ink, oak toast, spices, coffee and goodness knows what else. Vitiano showed well again, the '00 easily gaining Two Glasses for its refined spiciness, not to mention its excellent value for money. Then when in a duff vintage like '00, Cotarella manages to produce an absolutely delicious Est Est Est di Montefiascone, bringing improvements even to the basic version, it can only mean that he has absolutely everything well in hand. And where does that leave the Poggio dei Gelsi selection? With a fabulously broad spectrum of aromas and a firm, elegantly fruity palate and a warm, soft finish, that's where. The Grechetto '00 is soundly made and a more than valid alternative to the ever more popular Chardonnay. The '99 Vendemmia Tardiva is notable, too. Made from typical local varieties harvested when past normal ripeness, there is an impressive breadth of fruit character overlain with acacia honey. No doubt, though, there are further surprises in the pipeline.

● Montiano '99	ŶŶŶ	6
○ Est Est Est di Montefiascone Poggio dei Gelsi '00	ŶŶ	3*
● Merlot dell'Umbria '00	ŶŶ	5
● Vitiano '00	ŶŶ	3*
○ Est Est Est di Montefiascone V. T. '99	ŶŶ	5
○ Est Est Est di Montefiascone Falesco '00	Ŷ	2
○ Grechetto '00	Ŷ	3
● Montiano '94	ŶŶŶ	5
● Montiano '95	ŶŶŶ	5
● Montiano '96	ŶŶŶ	5
● Montiano '97	ŶŶŶ	5
● Montiano '98	ŶŶŶ	5
○ Ferentano '99	ŶŶ	5

ROMA

CONTE ZANDOTTI
VIA VIGNE COLLE MATTIA, 8
00132 ROMA
TEL. 0620609000 - 066160335

VELLETRI (RM)

COLLE DI MAGGIO
VIA FIENILI SNC
00049 VELLETRI (RM)
TEL. 0696453072

The negative effects of a difficult vintage are usually even more evident when a producer is first and foremost a "récoltant", or grower. There is rarely any way to compensate for deficiencies, short of acquiring grapes from other areas and Count Zandotti certainly has no interest in "correcting" his wines with those from elsewhere. Yet despite all this Zandotti and his skilled oenologist, Marco Ciarla, have managed to turn out some more than promising wines. For example, we really admired the delicate aromatics of the Malvasia del Lazio Rumon '00. It has great elegance in its notes of apple and acacia blossom, the palate is tangily complex and there is beautiful nose-palate harmony. The '00 Frascati Superiore, even though a bit more muscular than usual, has a lovely, warm nose rich in fruit and a fresh, zesty palate that finishes long. The '00 Frascati Cannellino, on the other hand, seems to have stood up less well to the difficult weather conditions and is weaker than usual, with lower acidity. This leaves it a little flabby, with over-evolved aromas. We can not assess the red La Petrosa '00 as it had not been released in time for our tastings. We'll be back for it next year.

We decided it was time to give Colle di Maggio a full profile in the Guide because the wines are now too good to ignore. Started in the 1970s by Domenico Tulino to realize his winemaking ambitions, it took several years of experimentation before it came together as a workable undertaking, with experts of the calibre of Paolo Peira contributing to the modern, efficient set-up. Not all the 17 hectares under vine are in production yet but the current output of around 20,000 bottles is more than enough to give a good idea of the estate's potential. A fairly large number of grape varieties are grown, leading to wide diversity in the wines produced. From these, Velitrae Bianco '99, focused on floral-fruity notes and with a fresh, exuberant liveliness, is of particular interest, as is Porticato '99, from a multi-grape blend, which has an intriguing, fruity nose of apple and citrus, and a well-sustained, long palate. There is, naturally, a barriqued Chardonnay, Villa Tulino Bianco '99. It has a more than decent array of aromas, led by vanilla and leather. The fruit and oak are already well in balance, although the wine is still coming round. Standing out from the rest of the reds is a fabulous merlot and cabernet sauvignon blend, Le Anfore '98. It is solidly structured, deep and tightly woven, densely spicy and threaded through with mint. Then we tasted Velitrae Rosso '99, with its aromas of walnutskins and eucalyptus. There is also a red version of the Villa Tulino but we'll come back to it later.

O	Malvasia del Lazio Rumon '00	YY	3*
O	Frascati Sup. '00	Y	2
O	Frascati Cannellino '00		3
O	Frascati Sup. '94	YY	2
O	Frascati Cannellino '95	YY	3
O	Frascati Sup. '95	YY	2
O	Frascati Cannellino '96	YY	3
O	Frascati Sup. '98	YY	2
●	La Petrosa '98	YY	4
O	Malvasia del Lazio Rumon '98	YY	3
O	Frascati Cannellino '99	YY	3
O	Frascati Sup. '99	YY	2
●	La Petrosa '99	YY	4
O	Frascati Cannellino '98	Y	3

●	Le Anfore '98	YY	4
O	Porticato Bianco '99	YY	4
O	Velitrae Bianco '99	Y	4
●	Velitrae Rosso '99	Y	4
O	Villa Tulino Bianco '99	Y	5

OTHER WINERIES

COLACICCHI
LOC. ROMAGNANO
03012 ANAGNI (FR)
TEL. 064469661

A "slap" from Anagni. Nothing to do with history of the Papacy, just the new early-drinking red from Colacicchi, Schiaffo '00 ("schiaffo" means "slap"). Romagnano Rosso '98, aged in oak for 12 months, and Romagnano Bianco '00, from native grapes, are both good.

○ Romagnano Bianco '00	🍷	4
● Schiaffo '00	🍷	4
● Romagnano Rosso '98	🍷	5

ANTONELLO COLETTI CONTI
VIA VITTORIO EMANUELE, 116
03012 ANAGNI (FR)
TEL. 0775728610
E-MAIL: coletticonti@libero.it

Antonello Coletti Conti has around 14 hectares of vineyard in the Anagni-Piglio area. Year after year, his Cesanese del Piglio gains depth and interest. This year, it is joined by Poggio del Cotoverio '99, an oak-aged cabernet-cesanese blend.

● Cesanese del Piglio Haernicus '00	🍷	4
● Poggio del Cotoverio '99		4

PAOLO PERINELLI
LOC. LA GLORIA, 79
03012 ANAGNI (FR)
TEL. 077556031 - 066865913

Paolo Perinelli is a rising star on the Lazio wine scene. This year, he won us over with a delightful Cesanese Casale della Ioria '00 and an elegant, oak-aged Cesanese del Piglio Torre del Piano '00. In addition, the Passerina del Frusinate '00 is very well typed.

● Cesanese del Piglio Torre del Piano '00	🍷🍷	5
● Cesanese del Piglio '00	🍷	3*
○ Passerina del Frusinate '00		3

VASELLI
P.ZZA DEL POGGETTO, 12
01024 CASTIGLIONE IN TEVERINA (VT)
TEL. 0761948305

This long-standing Lazio wine name returns to prominence. Christine Vaselli, now with the ineffable Riccardo Cotarella as her righthand man, has released Torre Sant'Andrea '99, a splendid wine that makes a real impact with its tight texture and complexity.

○ Orvieto Cl. Torre Sant'Andrea '99	🍷🍷	5

Vini Pallavicini
Via Casilina Km. 25,500
00030 Colonna (RM)
Tel. 069438816
E-MAIL: saitacolonna@vinipallavicini.com

This winery produces a wide range, best of which are the well-made, nicely complex Rosso Riserva Pallavicini '97 and the delightful Malvasia del Lazio '00. The latter might be in the running for Two Glasses if it could gain a little more concentration.

○ Malvasia del Lazio '00	🍷	2
● Rosso Ris. Pallavicini '97	🍷	3

Cantina Cooperativa di Cincinnato
Via Cori - Cisterna, km 2
04010 Cori (LT)
Tel. 069679380
E-MAIL: cincinnato@tiscalinet.it

A co-operative that works well is always a good sign. Take, for example, Cincinnato's Cori Rosso '00. Elegant, fruity and long on the palate, it costs less than € 2.50. Rosso dei Dioscuri '00 is not bad either. There is room for improvement but it is still very enjoyable.

● Cori Rosso '00	🍷	1
● Rosso dei Dioscuri '00		2

Marco Carpineti
Via delle Colonne, 25
04010 Cori (LT)
Tel. 069679642

From this organic estate's range, we most liked: Moro '00, from greco; Collesanti '00, from bellone, with its unusual nose of aniseed and golden delicious apples; and Ditirambo '98 from good quality nero buono di Cori and montepulciano.

● Moro '00	🍷	2*
● Ditirambo '98	🍷	4
○ Collesanti '00		2

Casale Mattia
Via Buttarelli, 16
00044 Frascati (RM)
Tel. 069426249 - 069486930
E-MAIL: info@casalemattia.it

Even with the '00 vintage, we prefer the Frascati Superiore to the reds, which still have quite some way to go. In contrast, the Frascati has all the qualities one would expect on both nose and palate. Attractively styled, it is a joy to drink.

○ Frascati Sup. '00	🍷	2
● Merlot Lazio Costamagna '00		3

L'Olivella
Via di Colle Pisano, 1
00044 Frascati (RM)
Tel. 069424527
E-MAIL: info@racemo.it

This year, L'Olivella has come out with two new reds of great character. Racemo Rosso '97 has intense, persistent aromas and good complexity. Even better is the Shiraz-Cesanese '00. The blend may be unusual but the result is very promising.

● Shiraz-Cesanese	🍷🍷	4
● Racemo Rosso '97	🍷	4
○ Frascati Sup. Racemo '00		3

Cantine San Marco
Loc. Vermicino
Via di Mola Cavona, 26
00044 Frascati (RM)
Tel. 069409403 - 069422689

The Frascati Superiore is always San Marco's top wine and the '00 is no exception, retaining fragrance of aroma and fresh vitality. The red Meraco '97 is of interest. It has good structure even though it is not overly powerful.

○ Frascati Sup. Sel. '00	🍷	3
● Meraco Rosso '97		4

Camponeschi
Via Piastrarelle, 10
00040 Lanuvio (RM)
Tel. 069374390
E-mail: campones@mbox.miganet.it

Camponeschi's wines showed well this year. The Carato Rosso '99, with a carefully thought-out grape blend and a tight yet supple texture, stands out. The easy-drinking Colli Lanuvini Superiore '00, fresh and graceful on the palate, is as attractive as ever.

● Carato Rosso '99	🍷	4
○ Colli Lanuvini Sup. '00		2

Gotto d'Oro
Loc. Frattocchie
Via del Divino Amore, 115
00040 Marino (RM)
Tel. 069302221 E-mail: info@gottodoro.it

Gotto d'Oro with its super-equipped cellars strides ever forward. The wines are excellently typed and the prices very reasonable. Best of the bunch are Marino '00, with appley, varietal aromas, Frascati Superiore '00 and the red Castelli Romani '00.

● Castelli Romani '00	🍷	2
○ Frascati Sup. '00	🍷	2
○ Marino Sup. '00	🍷	2

Tenuta Le Quinte
Via delle Marmorelle, 71
00040 Montecompatri (RM)
Tel. 069438756

The Papi family is keeping up quality levels. Virtù Romane '00, with its soft, fresh aromas, is straightforward. Rasa di Marmorata '99 is well styled and Dulcis Vitis '00 has a subtle but clearly evident elegant sweetness.

○ Dulcis Vitis '00	🍷	4
○ Montecompatri Colonna Sup. Virtù Romane '00		2
● Rasa di Marmorata '99		2

Cantina Sociale Cesanese del Piglio
Via Prenestina, km 42
03010 Piglio (FR)
Tel. 0775502355 - 0775502356
E-mail: c.cantinasocialecesanese@tin.it

This is another co-operative that is emerging from the shadows, albeit with some difficulty. The best wine in the range is Oro di Cesanese del Piglio '00. Dense, tight and perhaps a tad unbalanced from lack of ageing, it is a cut above previous vintages.

● Cesanese del Piglio Etichetta Oro '00	🍷	4

Massimi Berucci
Via Prenestina, km 42
03010 Piglio (FR)
Tel. 0775501303 - 0668307004

The charismatic Manfredi Berucci, long-time leading producer in Ciociaria, continues to craft his wines unperturbed by changes around him. With the '00, his Cesanese del Piglio Casal Cervino is back on form. It has firm structure and splendid style.

● Cesanese del Piglio Casal Cervino '00	🍷	4

Cantina di Sant'Andrea
Loc. Borgovodice
Via Renibbio, 1720
04019 Terracina (LT)
Tel. 0773755028

This winery must be complimented for its role in the rebirth of Moscato di Terracina. The Moscato Secco '00 is really good news, winning Two Glasses. The Circeo Rosso Il Sogno '99 has good character, too.

○ Moscato Secco di Terracina '00	🍷🍷	2*
● Circeo Rosso Il Sogno '99	🍷	4

ABRUZZO AND MOLISE

Improvements in viticultural and winemaking Improvements in viticultural and winemaking techniques have touched every region of Italy, if to different extents in north and south. Abruzzo, though, has approached this new wave of quality wine in a uniquely eclectic way. There is no longer any definitive Abruzzo style. There are endless ways of getting from a bunch of grapes to a bottle of Montepulciano d'Abruzzo, and just as many variations on Trebbiano d'Abruzzo. There are "tendone", or arbour trained, and wire trained systems, ageing may be in "botti", large old barrels, or barriques and there are very young wines as well as others released after six or seven years' ageing. But could it be that this diversity of styles is the reason for the growing success of the region? Only one thing is certain: with the exception of '96, and '99 in some areas, the quality of grapes handled in Puglia recently has been extraordinarily good. It has been an enabling factor in the huge progress in quality that has been seen throughout the region. But tasters have a duty to tastings and results show that between the two extremes in winemaking philosophy and style, one represented by Edoardo Valentini, the other by Gianni Masciarelli, you can find almost every approach imaginable. "The Master of Loreto Aprutino", Valentini, presented an awesome Montepulciano d'Abruzzo, the '95. It's a wine of unique personality, enormous intensity and richness of stuffing, kaleidoscopic in its sensations on nose and palate. From across the divide came Gianni Masciarelli's response and he summoned two pearls from his futuristic cellars at San Martino sulla Marrucina, both made from montepulciano: the brilliant '97 Villa Gemma, powerful, complex and as opulent as ever; and a wonderful Marina Cvetic. Most other producers have made steady progress. Some are relatively new names, such as Sabatino Di Properzio of Fattoria La Valentina, Luigi Valori, Riccardo De Cerchio of Torre Zambra, Marina Orlandi Contucci, whose Teramo winery is named after her, Alessandro and Elena Nicodemi, Enrico Marramiero, Nicola D'Auria of Sarchese; others are evergreens like Dino Illuminati, Marcello Zaccagnini, Luigi Cataldi Madonna, Rocco Pasetti and Camillo Montori. Looking to the future, it is comforting to note that both groups are spurred on by the same credo: absolute quality without compromise. These pages are also home to Molise, a region that, despite its small size, is showing great potential. Some production is already in the hands of go-ahead folk from elsewhere. But the producers who have brought the region from obscurity are not standing back to watch. Borgo di Colloredo makes a welcome entry to the Guide and Di Majo Norante picks up Three Glasses. This is not just due to the wine, however good. It is also a tribute to young, ambitious Alessio Di Majo himself, who has long preached the gospel of quality in a region long impervious to change.

BOLOGNANO (PE)

Ciccio Zaccagnini
C.da Pozzo
65020 Bolognano (PE)
tel. 0858880195 - 0858880155
e-mail: zaccaginiwines@tin.it

Marcello Zaccagnini's winery overlooks the spectacular Orta valley, which has remained spectacular, despite the construction of a new industrial complex. The wines that emerge from Marcello's cellar are as impressive as ever. They come from 50 hectares of vineyard, are produced by skilled oenologist Concezio Marulli and the range is broad, perhaps almost too extensive. Topping it are the two S. Clemente wines. The S. Clemente Montepulciano d'Abruzzo is fleshy, richly fruity with some spice and mouthfilling balanced palate, even though it was seriously penalized by the disappointing vintage. The white, from barrique-vinified chardonnay, is attractive and elegant both in its structure and its persistent ripe peach and apricot flavours. Two further Montepulciano d'Abruzzos, the standard version and the Cuveé dell'Abate, have intense aromas of violet and red berry fruits in common, as they do a most pleasing firmness allied with good drinkability. A third, the Castello di Salle '98, has rather more evolved fruit and additional complexity from notes of spices and liquorice. The Cerasuolo Myosotis is one of the top wines of its type this year. It has perfect typicity with a deep cherry colour, aromas that range from dried rose petals to vibrant fruit, and a fresh, well-structured palate that finishes on a long almondy note. Bianco di Ciccio, from trebbiano and chardonnay, the riesling-based Ibisco Bianco and the basic Cerasuolo are all well-honed on the nose with good definition on the palate. To close, the '00 Passito, from moscato, is probably its best release ever. There is good candied fruit character on both nose and palate, and no hint of cloying.

	Wine		Score
●	Capsico Rosso '97	🍷🍷	4
◉	Montepulciano d'Abruzzo Cerasuolo Myosotis '00	🍷🍷	3*
●	Montepulciano d'Abruzzo Castello di Salle '98	🍷🍷	4
●	Montepulciano d'Abruzzo '99	🍷🍷	3*
●	Montepulciano d'Abruzzo Abbazia S. Clemente '99	🍷🍷	5
●	Montepulciano d'Abruzzo Cuvée dell'Abate '99	🍷🍷	4
○	S. Clemente Bianco '99	🍷🍷	4
○	Bianco di Ciccio '00	🍷	3
○	Ibisco Bianco '00	🍷	3
◉	Montepulciano d'Abruzzo Cerasuolo '00	🍷	3
○	Passito Bianco '00	🍷	4

CAMPOMARINO (CB)

Borgo di Colloredo
Fraz. Nuova Cliternia
C.da Zezza, 8
86042 Campomarino (CB)
tel. 087557453
e-mail: info@borgocolloredo.it

It is a great pleasure to give this Molise estate a full profile in the Guide. Situated on the hills of Campomarino, it was converted around six years ago by the Di Giulio family and the cellars, built by brothers Enrico, the winemaker, and vineyard manager Pasquale were designed with an eye to architecture as much as to the practicalities of winemaking. Its 60 hectares under vine, planted with montepulciano, aglianico, falanghina, malvasia and trebbiano, as well as cabernet sauvignon and merlot, have been zoned in order to sequence vineyard improvements. The bottled range homes in on good value in both the Gironia labels three wines and the less expensive line. It is the two reds that showed best of the latest releases. The Gironia Rosso is from montepulciano and aglianico, aged partly in large old barrels, partly in barrique. It has a deep ruby colour and the nose is a little closed at first but then reveals full, ripe aromas of black cherry and small black berry fruit. These come through strongly on the palate too, where they linger, supported by good overall structure. The simpler red is made solely from montepulciano and is a delightfully attractive wine of intense fruitiness with light vegetal notes. The Sangiovese is also good, although it seemed too young and green to express its potential to the full. The whites are less interesting but are still well typed and attractive.

	Wine		Score
●	Molise Montepulciano '00	🍷🍷	2*
●	Biferno Rosso Gironia '98	🍷🍷	4
○	Biferno Bianco Gironia '00	🍷	3
◉	Biferno Rosato Gironia '00	🍷	3
○	Molise Trebbiano '00	🍷	2*
●	Sangiovese '00	🍷	3
○	Molise Falanghina '00		2

CAMPOMARINO (CB)

Di Majo Norante
Fraz. Nuova Cuternia
C.da Ramitello, 4
86042 Campomarino (CB)
tel. 087557208
e-mail: dimajo@tin.it

This year Molise's best known estate joins the Three Glass ranks for the first time ever. This achievement is down to the hard work of Alessio Di Majo, guided by Riccardo Cotarella, whom he took on as consultant two years ago. We hope that his success will give a jolt to the rather dozy Molise wine scene. The range of wines from Di Majo's 60 hectares of vineyard is excellent. The prize-winning Don Luigi is made from montepulciano and tintilia, a variety that some think is a version of bovale. The two grapes interact with perfect synergy to give an almost opaque wine of dark ruby tinged with violet. Its nose has complex aromas of small black berry fruit, highlighted with spiciness. First impressions on the palate are of slight stalkiness but it quickly opens out to fill the mouth with a perfect play-off between the fruit and the oak, both of which remain on the long, well-defined finish. There are no let-downs among any of the other reds, which in general are very well priced. The classic Ramitello, this year better than ever, and the modern-styled, fruit-driven Molì, which is exceedingly attractive yet has enough firm structure to be the envy of a great red, are cases in point. As are the Prugnolo, the Contado and even the Sangiovese, whose varietal characteristics are augmented by good fruit extract and excellently-balanced tannins, which are some of the most impressive found anywhere outside Tuscany. The whites are good too, most notably the Fiano which is fresh without being simplistic and which brings together florality and fruitiness in a style that is almost perfumed.

	Wine	Rating	Score
●	Molise Don Luigi '99	🍷🍷🍷	5
●	Biferno Molì Rosso '00	🍷🍷	2*
●	Sangiovese Terra degli Osci '00	🍷🍷	2*
●	Molise Aglianico Contado '98	🍷🍷	3*
●	Biferno Rosso Ramitello '99	🍷🍷	3*
●	Prugnolo '99	🍷🍷	3*
○	Molise Fiano '00	🍷🍷	3*
○	Biferno Molì Bianco '00	🍷	1*
○	Molise Falanghina '00	🍷	3
○	Molise Greco '00	🍷	3
○	Apianae '99	🍷	4
○	Biblos '99	🍷	4
○	Apianae '93	🍷🍷	4
●	Biferno Rosso Ramitello '97	🍷🍷	3
●	Molise Don Luigi '98	🍷🍷	5

COLONNELLA (TE)

Lepore
C.da Civita
64010 Colonnella (TE)
tel. 086170860 - 0854222835

Previously, we have not been all that free with compliments for this estate. The reason is that right from its formation a decade ago, we felt that the wines rarely matched up to the potential we saw in its 30 hectares of hillside vineyard and the technical abilities of its team (Gaspare Lepore is in charge, assisted by Giampiero Cichetti and oenologist Umberto Svizzeri). We believe that criticism, if it is honest and constructive, can spur a producer on to aim higher and achieve higher quality standards. So this year, we are concentrating on two wines, both Montepulciano d'Abruzzos, which scored pretty well. The first is the estate's classically-styled version from selected grapes. It is intense ruby, and initially reticent on the nose but then opens to give concentrated aromas of bilberry and blackcurrant. The palate is soft, the fruit enhanced by sensations of printer's ink and pencil lead, and reveals smooth tannins. The second wine Re – the name refers to D, the second note on the musical scale – comes under the Colline Teramane subzone, a denomination that the area's producers are backing very heavily and which, from this year, is being utilized massively. Re is as intense on the nose as the selection but with slightly less distinct aromas. The palate has good extractive weight and slightly green tannins. There is a touch of bitterness on the finish, where the fruit, coffee and liquorice sensed earlier return. The rest of the range is, as usual, well-typed even though the basic Montepulciano d'Abruzzo '99 is still coming round, as is the white Passera delle Vigne '00, from passerina, with its characteristic floral and tropical fruit aromas.

	Wine	Rating	Score
●	Montepulciano d'Abruzzo Luigi Lepore '97	🍷🍷	5
⊙	Montepulciano d'Abruzzo Cerasuolo '00	🍷	3
○	Passera delle Vigne '00	🍷	3
○	Trebbiano d'Abruzzo '00	🍷	3
●	Montepulciano d'Abruzzo Colline Teramane Re '98	🍷	4
●	Montepulciano d'Abruzzo '99	🍷	3
●	Passito dei Lepore '95	🍷	5
●	Montepulciano d'Abruzzo '96	🍷	3
●	Montepulciano d'Abruzzo '97	🍷	3
●	Montepulciano d'Abruzzo Colline Teramane Re '97	🍷	4
●	Montepulciano d'Abruzzo '98	🍷	3

CONTROGUERRA (TE)

Dino Illuminati
Via San Biagio, 18
64010 Controguerra (TE)
tel. 0861808008
e-mail: info@illuminativini.it

Last year, this celebrated estate received the ultimate accolade of Three Glasses for its Lumen. Although oenologist Claudio Cappellacci and consultant Giorgio Marone have made further quality progress across the board, there is no repeat performance this year: the '98 Lumen came just short of Three Glasses. It is concentrated ruby colour, intense but slightly off-key aromas of mulberry and blackcurrant. The palate is full and pervasive with fine-grained, ripe tannins and good fruit, highlighted by subtle notes of roast coffee beans, but the alcohol is a touch intrusive. The Montepulciano d'Abruzzo Zanna scored nearly as highly, returning in strong form after a year's absence, the '96 having been considered not up to scratch. This year's '97 is along traditional lines. A garnet-tinged red, it has a nose of ripe black and red cherry aromas which are well integrated with the oak. Both fruit and oak reappear on the palate, which is full, structured and develops well in the mouth. The consistent, inexpensive Riparosso is, as usual, one of the best of its type. It is bright red, with good fruit and evenness throughout, and excellent drinking. The other wines in this quality band, comprising several whites and a Cerasuolo, have the merit of having absorbed the roundness and warmth of the '00 vintage without losing freshness of aroma. Ciafré, a blend of trebbiano, passerina and riesling, is the best in the group. And if the noble rot wine Loré is still Abruzzo's best dessert wine, and the Spumante Brut remains Abruzzo's best sparkler, Nicò clinched Two Glasses for being much better than a run-of-the-mill "passito". It's a late harvest wine of real excellence.

	Wine	Glasses	Score
●	Montepulciano d'Abruzzo Zanna Vecchio '97	ŸŸ	4
●	Controguerra Lumen '98	ŸŸ	6
●	Montepulciano d'Abruzzo Riparosso '00	ŸŸ	3*
●	Controguerra Nicò '98	ŸŸ	5
○	Loré Muffa Nobile	ŸŸ	4
○	Controguerra Chardonnay Cenalba '00	Ÿ	3*
○	Controguerra Ciafré '00	Ÿ	3
○	Controguerra Costalupo '00	Ÿ	2*
○	Montepulciano d'Abruzzo Cerasuolo Campirosa '00	Ÿ	2*
○	Trebbiano d'Abruzzo Daniele '99	Ÿ	4
○	Spumante Brut	Ÿ	3
●	Controguerra Lumen '97	ŸŸŸ	6

CONTROGUERRA (TE)

Camillo Montori
Piane Tronto, 23
64010 Controguerra (TE)
tel. 0861809900

The criticisms we have laid at Lepore's door over the past few years are probably even more valid for Camillo Montori. Here we have another 30-hectare estate but this time with a producer of great personality who has been a player in the high quality sector of the market for decades. This year, Montori fielded a brace of Two Glass wines which lead a more than respectable range. Montepulciano d'Abruzzo Fonte Cupa '97, produced under the Colline Teramane DOC subzone, is a wine with concentrated colour. Its fleshy, rich, fruit aromas of wild cherry and mulberry are suffused with a hint of balsam then the rounded palate develops with elegance and length, revealing a certain complexity on the finish. Leneo Moro '97, a red from montepulciano and cabernet sauvignon, has benefited from long bottle maturation that has given it exemplary definition. On the nose, there is perfect harmony between the maturity of the fruit and the herbaceous tones given by the two varieties in the blend. This is followed by a soft, velvety palate with good structure and delicate oakiness on the finish. The whites are led by Trebbiano d'Abruzzo Fonte Cupa. Its appearance may not be perfectly bright but it has delightful delicate aromas of golden delicious apple on the nose and excellent weight of extract, which lends softness to its fruit-rich palate. The standard Trebbiano d'Abruzzo is fresh and attractive, as are the oak-fermented Leneo d'Oro '99, made from chardonnay and trebbiano, and the Fauno, whose fine aromatic impact is echoed on the nicely acidic palate.

	Wine	Glasses	Score
○	Controguerra Leneo Moro '97	ŸŸ	4
●	Montepulciano d'Abruzzo Fonte Cupa Colline Teramane '97	ŸŸ	4
○	Controguerra Fauno '00	Ÿ	2*
○	Trebbiano d'Abruzzo Fonte Cupa '00	Ÿ	3
○	Controguerra Leneo Moro '99	Ÿ	4
○	Controguerra Leneo d'Oro '99	Ÿ	4
◉	Montepulciano d'Abruzzo Cerasuolo Fonte Cupa '00		3
○	Trebbiano d'Abruzzo '00		2
●	Leneo Moro '94	ŸŸ	5
●	Leneo Moro '95	ŸŸ	5
○	Leneo Moro '96	Ÿ	4
○	Controguerra Leneo d'Oro '98	Ÿ	4
●	Montepulciano d'Abruzzo '98	Ÿ	2

FRANCAVILLA AL MARE (CH)

Franco Pasetti
C.da Pretaro - Via San Paolo, 21
66023 Francavilla al Mare (CH)
Tel. 08561875 - 0856920041
E-mail: vignetipasetti@hotmail.com

Year after year, we have recorded the steady growth in both size and quality of this estate, run by Mimmo and Rocco Pasetti. They certainly seem to be going about things in the right way, with improvements to every aspect of production, and the resulting set-up surely cannot fail to give excellent results sooner or later. For instance, Testarossa Bianco, from oak-vinified chardonnay, trebbiano and pecorino, performed very well last year but is even better this. It has a good intense straw colour, introducing a wide spectrum of aromas that range from apple, to banana, to ripe peach and on to grapefruit. Everything is nicely held together by the sage-like herbiness that pervades throughout. There is richness and good softness on the palate, which mirrors the sensations on the nose and is underscored by delicate acidity, finishing long, with an almondy aftertaste. The '99 Montepulciano d'Abruzzo is noteworthy, as usual, for its deep ruby colour, its fruitiness, its restrained structure and its excellent value for money. The '98 release of the Tenuta di Testarossa selection is the first to break through the Two Glasses barrier. There is great concentration in the colour and the nose has a good array of berry fruit and spices. The palate is fresh but rich with good tannic balance and flavours of mulberry, tobacco and Peruvian bark that open progressively to give a well orchestrated finish. Finally come the '00 Cerasuolo, an intense, structured rosé with distinct notes of cherry and raspberry – it won the Gran Medaglia d'Oro at the 2001 Vinitaly wine fair – and the Trebbiano d'Abruzzo from the same line, an attractive citrus-like white with reassuring nose-palate consistency.

	Wine	Glasses	Score
○	Tenuta di Testarossa Bianco '00	ŸŸ	4
●	Montepulciano d'Abruzzo Tenuta di Testarossa '98	ŸŸ	4
●	Montepulciano d'Abruzzo '99	ŸŸ	3*
⊙	Montepulciano d'Abruzzo Cerasuolo '00	Ÿ	2*
○	Trebbiano d'Abruzzo '00	Ÿ	2*
●	Montepulciano d'Abruzzo '98	ŸŸ	3
○	Tenuta di Testarossa Bianco '99	ŸŸ	4
●	Montepulciano d'Abruzzo '96	Ÿ	2
●	Montepulciano d'Abruzzo '97	Ÿ	2
●	Montepulciano d'Abruzzo Tenuta di Testarossa '97	Ÿ	4

GIULIANOVA (TE)

Faraone
Loc. Colleranesco
Via Nazionale per Teramo, 290
64020 Giulianova (TE)
Tel. 0858071804
E-mail: faraone.vino@tin.it

Giovanni Faraone's small estate swiftly returns to the Guide after a year in the wilderness due more to the absence of some of his wines than to quality problems. In the meantime, Faraone has been busy renovating his vineyards and re-equipping his cellars. The return happily coincides Giovanni's first Two Glass rating, awarded to the estate's top wine, Montepulciano d'Abruzzo S. Maria dell'Arco. This is a deep, lively ruby, with a nose that is initially closed but quickly opens to give ripe berry fruits and spices. The initial impact on the palate is quite austere with hardly any tannin, but a fine underlying structure soon emerges, allowing softer tones to take over and bring the wine to a well-fruited, liquorice-nuanced finish. The Le Vigne selection is less imposing. It is similar to its "big brother" but its characteristics are scaled down to give more emphasis to drinkability. The Cerasuolo successfully harnesses the fruit and freshness bestowed by the vintage. Then the two Trebbiano d'Abruzzos, which Faraone notoriously makes to last, both showed well. The S. Maria dell'Arco selection no longer has the oxidized character that penalized former releases. Instead, it shows more elegance on the nose, and fruit-rich aromas recalling banana and mango, but the palate is a little over acidic. The same holds true to a certain extent for the Le Vigne version. This has a more attractive, fragrant nose, with tenuous aromas of spring flowers, sage and citrus, and is more immediate and delicate on the palate.

	Wine	Glasses	Score
●	Montepulciano d'Abruzzo S. Maria dell'Arco '98	ŸŸ	4
⊙	Montepulciano d'Abruzzo Cerasuolo Le Vigne '00	Ÿ	3
○	Trebbiano d'Abruzzo Le Vigne '00	Ÿ	3
○	Trebbiano d'Abruzzo S. Maria dell'Arco '98	Ÿ	4
●	Montepulciano d'Abruzzo Le Vigne '99	Ÿ	3
○	Brut M. Cl. '95	Ÿ	4
●	Montepulciano d'Abruzzo '97	Ÿ	3
○	Trebbiano d'Abruzzo S. Maria dell'Arco '97	Ÿ	4
○	Trebbiano d'Abruzzo Le Vigne '98	Ÿ	2

LORETO APRUTINO (PE)

★ Edoardo Valentini
Via del Baio, 2
65014 Loreto Aprutino (PE)
tel. 0858291138

Edoardo Valentino and his son Francesco Paolo have given us another fabulous Montepulciano d'Abruzzo, one of the best of recent times. Once more we find ourselves up against a wine that can be described as "country-style" and yet is at the same time "international", or do the two go hand in hand? In any case, it's a wine of great individuality with a strong territorial identity. The '95, like all its predecessors, will mature over very many years but in the meantime… It has a deep, dark colour. The nose is astounding in its intensity and range of nuances, with ripe cherry, black berry fruit, coffee, chocolate and mineral notes following one after the other. These evocative aromas gain further complexity on the palate as the mineral elements become more tobacco-like and the fruit veers towards liquorice. The tannins are tightly-woven, the wine's power is already easing into roundness, and the fine overall balance gives perspective to the long finish. And this is just for starters. In contrast, the Trebbiano d'Abruzzo seemed almost ready for drinking. The appearance is bright and lively, there are ripe citrus fruits and characteristic mineral tones on the nose, and the palate has its usual elegance and fullness. There's plenty of complexity in the fruit, although it does not have the carry through of the best vintages. Finally comes the Cerasuolo di Montepulciano which is, of course, quite distinct from all others, not only because it is released two years after the harvest. Its colour is onionskin and the aromas are of roses, bottled white cherries and bread crusts. Citrus fruit and light toastiness come through on the palate, underscored by a structure that would not be out of place in a red.

● Montepulciano d'Abruzzo '95	ㅠㅠㅠ	6
○ Trebbiano d'Abruzzo '98	ㅠㅠ	5
◉ Montepulciano d'Abruzzo Cerasuolo '98	ㅠㅠ	5
● Montepulciano d'Abruzzo '77	ㅠㅠㅠ	6
● Montepulciano d'Abruzzo '85	ㅠㅠㅠ	6
● Montepulciano d'Abruzzo '88	ㅠㅠㅠ	6
○ Trebbiano d'Abruzzo '88	ㅠㅠㅠ	5
● Montepulciano d'Abruzzo '90	ㅠㅠㅠ	6
● Montepulciano d'Abruzzo '92	ㅠㅠㅠ	6
○ Trebbiano d'Abruzzo '92	ㅠㅠㅠ	5
● Montepulciano d'Abruzzo '94	ㅠㅠ	6
◉ Montepulciano d'Abruzzo Cerasuolo '95	ㅠㅠ	5
◉ Montepulciano d'Abruzzo Cerasuolo '96	ㅠㅠ	5
◉ Montepulciano d'Abruzzo Cerasuolo '97	ㅠㅠ	5

NOTARESCO (TE)

Bruno Nicodemi
C.da Veniglio - S. P. 19
64024 Notaresco (TE)
tel. 085895493 - 085895135

When Alessandro and Elena Nicodemi, helped by Ida Carlini, took over the reins of this estate, there was the promise of new energy and new stimuli. Expectations have already been fulfilled and further improvements are on the cards with the arrival of their new technical consultant, Paolo Caciorgna. For now, we enjoyed this year's two releases in the Bacco line – never before have they been so fleshy and so concentrated. The Montepulciano d'Abruzzo '98, which is now bottled under the Colline Teramane subzone, was tasted in June 2001, still in its initial phase of development. It was an explosion of ripe fruit, which will benefit greatly from bottle maturation. The panel noted the typical violet, black cherry and mulberry aromas of montepulciano, allied with a delicate spiciness. There is solidity on the palate, as well as tannins that are still settling down and fruit that is beginning to gain complexity. Contrastingly, the Trebbiano d'Abruzzo '00 seems to have broken with its usual styling and may be more intriguing as a result. Intense straw yellow, it reveals a nose that is atypical, with aromas of candied fruit and orange blossom, then the palate, after a firm, fresh initial impact, tends towards a delicate herbaceousness before finishing on attractive almondy notes. The standard-label Trebbiano is in simpler style, with gentle florality and fruit, and although it loses out in mid palate, it comes back strongly with a good finish and aftertaste. Its partnering Montepulciano, from '99, is deeply coloured and has the well-defined fruit typical of this style.

○ Trebbiano d'Abruzzo Bacco '00	ㅠㅠ	3*
● Montepulciano d'Abruzzo Colline Teramane Bacco '98	ㅠㅠ	5
◉ Montepulciano d'Abruzzo Cerasuolo '00	ㅠ	2
○ Trebbiano d'Abruzzo '00	ㅠ	2
● Montepulciano d'Abruzzo '99	ㅠ	3
● Montepulciano d'Abruzzo Bacco '97	ㅠㅠ	5
● Montepulciano d'Abruzzo '98	ㅠ	3
◉ Montepulciano d'Abruzzo Cerasuolo '98	ㅠ	2
○ Trebbiano d'Abruzzo Bacco '98	ㅠ	4

OFENA (AQ)

Tenuta Cataldi Madonna
Loc. Piana
67025 Ofena (AQ)
tel. 0854911680

The new slant that Luigi Cataldi Madonna and his winemaker Giovanni Bailo have put on production at this classic inland estate is beginning to show. Cellar and vineyard refinements were not aimed at giving immediate results but the rapid improvements in grape quality have already had an effect. Let's start with the Montepulciano d'Abruzzo selection Tonì, the '98 again scoring a reassuring Two Glasses. The colour is a deep, intense ruby lightly tinged with garnet. There are pervasive scents of cherry and ripe plum, overlain with toastiness. The first impact on the palate is of power and richness, followed by densely-woven tannins. The wine is marred only by a slightly short finish with marginally overly-invasive sensations of caramel. The well-structured, highly drinkable standard-label version is also excellent, the '99 having more substance and definition on the palate than usual. From the same vintage comes the best Occhiorosso Cabernet Sauvignon that Cataldi Madonna has ever produced. The colour is intense, there is good concentration, attractive notes of green pepper and tomato leaf, and vigour and richness of fruit on the palate, which we also noted vegetal tones and very slightly raw-edged tannins. Cerasuolo Pié delle Vigne is, as ever, a fine rosé, with an intense cherry colour and attractively fruity notes on both nose and palate. Apart from the Trebbiano d'Abruzzo, the range of whites includes a noteworthy Pecorino. Partly vinified in barriques, it has a deep colour, aromas of citrus fruit and vanilla, and a harmonious palate, with good acid-alcohol balance but an overly bitter finish.

● Montepulciano d'Abruzzo Tonì '98	🍷🍷	5
● Montepulciano d'Abruzzo '99	🍷🍷	3*
● Occhiorosso '99	🍷🍷	4
◎ Montepulciano d'Abruzzo Cerasuolo '00	🍷	2
◎ Montepulciano d'Abruzzo Cerasuolo Pié delle Vigne '00	🍷	3
○ Pecorino '00	🍷	3
● Malandrino '99	🍷	4
○ Trebbiano d'Abruzzo '00	🍷	2*
● Montepulciano d'Abruzzo Tonì '97	🍷🍷	5
◎ Montepulciano d'Abruzzo Cerasuolo Pié delle Vigne '99	🍷🍷	3

ORTONA (CH)

Agriverde
Loc. C.da Caldari
Via Monte Maiella, 118
66020 Ortona (CH)
tel. 0859032101

This is Agriverde's second year with a full profile in the Guide. It is run by Giannicola Di Carlo, with Paride Marino on the commercial side and the skilled youngster Riccardo Brighigna looking after the winemaking. Our wait for the new Montepulciano d'Abruzzo Plateo was not in vain. From the '95 vintage and aged in small oak casks, it seems much younger than it actually is. The colour is still deep and purple-tinged, the nose yields elegant spiciness alongside berry fruit and the palate is full, with a soft attack. The fruit is only just masked by the oak, the tannins are dense and there are sensations of bitter chocolate. The other two Montepulcianos are quite different in style. Natum '00, from organically grown grapes, has an intense, purplish colour, a nose full of fruit, and a dense, tannic palate with flavours of tobacco and plum. In contrast, the Riseis '99 is much more traditionally styled, with less overt oak. The Cerasuolo Riseis, a fresh, fruity rosé, is distinctly good while of the two Chardonnays presented, the rather ambitious, barrique-vinified Vallée du Vin was probably the more successful. It has an intense, bright straw colour and elegant varietal aromas highlighted by mineral notes. The palate is structured but the oak is still masking the fruit and the alcohol is just a little too invasive. Both Trebbiano d'Abruzzos are good. The Natum has golden delicious apple and spring flower aromas, and a full palate with an almond aftertaste. The Riseis has a more aromatic nose and greater acidity.

● Montepulciano d'Abruzzo Natum '00	🍷🍷	2*
● Montepulciano d'Abruzzo Plateo '95	🍷🍷	5
○ Chardonnay Tresor '00	🍷	2
○ Chardonnay Vallée du Vin '00	🍷	3
◎ Montepulciano d'Abruzzo Cerasuolo Riseis '00	🍷	2
○ Trebbiano d'Abruzzo Riseis '00	🍷	2
● Montepulciano d'Abruzzo Riseis '99	🍷	2
○ Trebbiano d'Abruzzo Natum '00	🍷	3
● Montepulciano d'Abruzzo Riseis '97	🍷	3
○ Chardonnay Tresor '99	🍷	2
◎ Montepulciano d'Abruzzo Cerasuolo Riseis '99	🍷	2
● Montepulciano d'Abruzzo Natum '99	🍷	2

ORTONA (CH)

SARCHESE DORA
C.DA CALDARI
66026 ORTONA (CH)
TEL. 0859031249
E-MAIL: sarchesedora@tin.it

This is Sarchese Dora's first full entry in the Guide following several years of steady improvements in its wines. It is not a huge estate, comprising around 15 hectares, and is run by highly motivated siblings Esmeralda and Nicola D'Auria. We feel that the remarks we have made on other occasions, that a winery can emerge from obscurity by grafting modern ideas onto traditional practices, are valid in this case, too. Having seen consistently good typing in the Sarchese Dora wines over the last few years, we believe that the estate could possibly be making headway more quickly. This year, the pattern continues with a mass of wines gaining good scores. The '98 Montepulciano d'Abruzzo selection Rosso di Macchia emerges at the peak, with over 80/100 and Two Glasses. It has an intense, garnet-tinged colour and a nose that marries aromas of black berry fruits with those of spices, particularly pepper. The palate is soft and mouthfilling, with a good fruit presence that lingers attractively through to a complex finish with a liquorice aftertaste. The simpler Montepulciano d'Abruzzo, the Pietrosa, also from '98, is not far behind. It is classically styled, with rich fruit on the nose as well as on the more confident palate. Here, the wine gains substance, and the fruit is interwoven with balsam and chocolate notes. Another good wine is the Montepulciano Cerasuolo Pietrosa, which has deep colour, aromas of cherry, softness and a final note of almond. The other two whites in the Pietrosa line are of similar quality but Bianco della Rocca, from late-harvest chardonnay, fell short of expectations.

●	Montepulciano d'Abruzzo Rosso di Macchia '98	♛♛	5
●	Montepulciano d'Abruzzo Pietrosa '99	♛♛	3*
○	Chardonnay Pietrosa '00	♛	2
☉	Montepulciano d'Abruzzo Cerasuolo Pietrosa '00	♛	2
○	Trebbiano d'Abruzzo Pietrosa '00	♛	2
○	Bianco della Rocca '00		3
●	Montepulciano d'Abruzzo Rosso di Macchia '96	♛	5
●	Montepulciano d'Abruzzo Pietrosa '98	♛	3
☉	Montepulciano d'Abruzzo Cerasuolo Pietrosa '99	♛	2

ROSCIANO (PE)

MARRAMIERO
C.DA SANT'ANDREA, 1
65010 ROSCIANO (PE)
TEL. 0858505766
E-MAIL: azmarram@tin.it

There was almost a "full house" at this estate, which is run by Enrico Marramiero, assisted by director Antonio Chiavaroli and consultant Romeo Taraborrelli. No longer do they present just one headline-grabbing wine, the Montepulciano d'Abruzzo Inferi. Now three whites of distinct personality sit alongside. The Inferi is deep in colour. It has clean, vanilla and ripe berry fruit aromas of good intensity. These are followed by a palate with good definition, good weight, good tannic presence and good consistency of fruit, given complexity by notes of tobacco and liquorice. Small oak has also been used to good effect in the Trebbiano Altare and Chardonnay Punta di Colle. The Altare is intense in colour. The nose is rich in fruit with light toasty notes then the palate reveals itself to be soft, fresh, fragrant and fruity. The Chardonnay a much heftier wine. Almost cloying on the nose, where the oak has impacted heavily on the clarity of the fruit, it shows better on the palate, where there are more clearly defined notes of pineapple and candied apricot. The Trebbiano Anima is the third high-scoring white, mainly because it marries outstanding freshness of fruit with an imposing structure. The Dama line is characterized by sound wines that offer good value and the level between Dama and Inferi is now called Incanto. The Incanto Montepulciano showed very well. It has characterful aromas and a well-structured palate, although we did pick up some bottle variation.

●	Montepulciano d'Abruzzo Inferi '97	♛♛	5
○	Chardonnay Punta di Colle '98	♛♛	4
●	Montepulciano d'Abruzzo Incanto '98	♛♛	4
○	Trebbiano d'Abruzzo Altare '99	♛♛	5
○	Trebbiano d'Abruzzo Anima '00	♛	4
○	Trebbiano d'Abruzzo Dama '00	♛	3
☉	Montepulciano d'Abruzzo Cerasuolo Dama '98	♛	3
●	Montepulciano d'Abruzzo Dama '98	♛	3
●	Montepulciano d'Abruzzo Inferi '93	♛♛	4
●	Montepulciano d'Abruzzo Inferi '94	♛♛	4
●	Montepulciano d'Abruzzo Inferi '95	♛♛	4
●	Montepulciano d'Abruzzo Inferi '96	♛♛	5

ROSETO DEGLI ABRUZZI (TE)

ORLANDI CONTUCCI PONNO
LOC. C.DA VOLTARROSTO
VIA PIANA DEGLI ULIVI, 1
64026 ROSETO DEGLI ABRUZZI (TE)
TEL. 0858944049
E-MAIL: orlandi.contucci@libero.it

We are used to high quality from Maria Orlandi Contucci's estate and this year was no exception. Indeed, it wasn't just the two leading reds that scored highly. There were also two surprisingly good whites, which were remarkably good value, too. But let's not get ahead of ourselves. Cabernet Sauvignon Colle Funaro leads us off. This, as usual, is rich in colour and full of small berry fruit that melds well with its oaky notes. These sensations are reflected on the palate, where the initial impression is one of elegance. The mid palate then remains firm and round through to the finish, where there is no falling away of fruit. Liburnio, from a blend of cabernet sauvignon with sangiovese and montepulciano, has just a touch less glycerine. There are vegetal aromas and fruity notes of bramble, blackcurrant and printer's ink but then the palate appears to have less ripeness and depth. The Trebbiano Colle della Corte and Chardonnay Roccesco are two delicious whites. The Trebbiano has a good bright colour, a well-fruited nose with aromas lying somewhere between apple and ripe citrus, and an elegant, soft palate, led by a firm streak of acidity and finishing on an attractive note of bitter almond. The Chardonnay has good varietal character with distinct aromas of banana and spring flowers on the nose, underscored by nuances of balsam and spice. The initial sensation of the palate is slightly flabby but the wine soon recovers and finishes long. Montepulciano d'Abruzzo '99 is a tad closed on the nose but is more expressive on the palate where the variety's fruit knits well into its vegetal notes. Donato Lanati is the consulting oenologist.

○ Chardonnay Roccesco '00	♟♟	3*
○ Trebbiano d'Abruzzo Colle della Corte '00	♟♟	3*
● Cabernet Sauvignon Colle Funaro '98	♟♟	4
● Liburnio '98	♟♟	5
◉ Montepulciano d'Abruzzo Cerasuolo Vermiglio '00	♟	2
● Montepulciano d'Abruzzo La Regia Specula '99	♟	3
○ Sauvignon Ghiaiolo '00		3
● Cabernet Sauvignon Colle Funaro '95	♟♟	3
● Liburnio '95	♟♟	5
● Cabernet Sauvignon Colle Funaro '97	♟♟	4
● Liburnio '97	♟♟	5

SAN MARTINO SULLA MARRUCINA (CH)

GIANNI MASCIARELLI
VIA GAMBERALE, 1
66010 SAN MARTINO
SULLA MARRUCINA (CH)
TEL. 087185241

Gianni Masciarelli never ceases to amaze. Alongside his mind-blowing Villa Gemma is a series of bottles good enough to become collectors' items. The '97 Villa Gemma is as good as it gets. Depth of colour, aromatic length in its notes of mulberry and chocolate, depth and elegance of flavour in its sensations of coffee, tar and liquorice. Montepulciano Marina Cvetic '98, which we erroneously listed last year and of which there were 70,000 bottles at its second production run, is hardly less good. Vinified in oak vats and aged in French oak barriques, it is a deep ruby colour tinged with dark violet. There are intense aromas of ripe berry fruits, pencil lead and tobacco on the nose. The palate is intriguing, and fully expressive of the wine's "terroir", and the powerful initial impact is followed by complexity with good, fleshy fruit and intense, long spicy notes. A further tiny step downwards brings us to the two barrique-fermented whites. Trebbiano d'Abruzzo Marina Cvetic has extraordinary depth of colour, suggesting a powerful wine rich in extract. There is ripe apricot, well integrated with the oak, on the nose. These sensations are echoed on the palate, where they are lengthened by almondy notes. The second white, the Chardonnay, is similar in style but has greater varietal character, most notably from the prominent tropical fruit on the nose, as well as freshness, elegance, richness and ripeness. Equally noteworthy are the quaffable yet well-structured Montepulciano d'Abruzzo '99, and the fruity, fresh Cerasuolo Villa Gemma, one of the best Cerasuolos produced this year.

● Montepulciano d'Abruzzo Villa Gemma '97	♟♟♟	6
● Montepulciano d'Abruzzo Marina Cvetic S. Martino Rosso '98	♟♟	4*
○ Chardonnay Marina Cvetic '99	♟♟	5
○ Trebbiano d'Abruzzo Marina Cvetic '99	♟♟	5
◉ Montepulciano d'Abruzzo Cerasuolo Villa Gemma '00	♟♟	3
● Montepulciano d'Abruzzo '99	♟♟	2*
○ Villa Gemma Bianco '99	♟♟	3*
◉ Rosato '00	♟	2
○ Trebbiano d'Abruzzo '00	♟	2
● Montepulciano d'Abruzzo Villa Gemma '95	♟♟♟	6
○ Trebbiano d'Abruzzo Marina Cvetic '98	♟♟♟	4

SPOLTORE (PE)

FATTORIA LA VALENTINA
VIA COLLE CESI, 10
65010 SPOLTORE (PE)
TEL. 0854478158
E-MAIL: info@fattorialavalentina.it

As if to prove that the decision to take on Luca D'Attoma as oenologist was a winner, one of Sabatino Di Properzio's wines moved right up the scales – to within an inch of a Three Glass award. The wine is the Montepulciano d'Abruzzo Spelt '97. It is somewhat atypical for the denomination but has great complexity. Deep ruby in colour, it offers a multi-faceted bouquet that goes from small red berry fruit to spices, such as pepper, and aromatic herbs, such as rosemary, then on to mineral notes of pencil lead. However, it shows its character to the full on the palate, where it is initially soft and charming, then foregrounding nuanced elegance rather than power, which, however, it does not lack. It closes on a long, spicy finish. Despite a none too brilliant vintage, the standard-label Montepulciano d'Abruzzo shows worthily too, with distinct aromas of fruit and printer's ink, and reasonable body allied to immediacy and drinkability. Its Trebbiano d'Abruzzo stablemate easily earned One Glass, with its light fruitiness and gentle softness, as did the single vineyard version, Vigneto Spilla. This, though, is more complex and structured, with better fruit extract, and richer in the mouth, with more alcohol and greater length. Finally, the Cerasuolo, which offers a deep cherry colour, a youthful, fruity, fresh nose with an almondy on finish, and the young, easy-drinking Punta Rossa are both praiseworthy.

	Wine	Glasses	Score
●	Montepulciano d'Abruzzo Spelt '97	YY	4
⊙	Montepulciano d'Abruzzo Cerasuolo '00	Y	2
●	Punta Rossa '00	Y	2
○	Trebbiano d'Abruzzo '00	Y	2
○	Trebbiano d'Abruzzo Vigneto Spilla '00	Y	3
●	Montepulciano d'Abruzzo '99	Y	2
●	Montepulciano d'Abruzzo Spelt '96	YY	4
●	Montepulciano d'Abruzzo Binomio '98	YY	5
○	Trebbiano d'Abruzzo '99	Y	2

TOCCO DA CASAURIA (PE)

FILOMUSI GUELFI
VIA F. FILOMUSI GUELFI, 11
65028 TOCCO DA CASAURIA (PE)
TEL. 08598353 - 085986908

Last year, we mentioned that Lorenzo Filomusi Guelfi and his oenologist Romano D'Amario were working on two new wines, a white and a red. For the red at least the wait has been worthwhile. It is a Montepulciano d'Abruzzo in the traditional style, in the positive sense of the word. The concentrated ruby colour is tinged with garnet and ushers in aromas of cherry, mulberry and ripe black cherry. On the palate, it has good initial impact, with hardly any tannin, then the fruit comes through, sweetly and elegantly, before the long, liquorice-tinged finish. The classic Montepulciano d'Abruzzo is just a touch less intense and, although from a less than brilliant vintage, has a most attractive character. There is not a great deal on the nose but the wine has more to say for itself on the palate, where the fruit is well in evidence, as well as good structure and fairly fine-grained tannins. The Cerasuolo is spot-on. It has perfect depth of colour, there are clean-cut aromas of cherry and roses in full bloom and the palate marries fresh acidity with a structure worthy of a red. There is good fruit in the mouth and an almondy edge on the finish. As for the two whites, the malvasia, chardonnay and sauvignon-based Scuderie del Cielo is as clean and clear-cut as ever in its aromas of apple and citrus fruit while its palate is fragrantly fruity with a decent waft of acidity. The second white, the Alegio, has the same grape blend but is oak-aged. This, the estate's other new wine, still needs some work, we reckon, not so much on its overall shape as on the over-evolved character that comes through on both nose and palate.

	Wine	Glasses	Score
●	Montepulciano d'Abruzzo Cerasuolo '00	YY	3*
●	Montepulciano d'Abruzzo Vigna Fonte Dei '97	YY	4
○	Alegio '00	Y	4
○	Le Scuderie del Cielo '00	Y	3
●	Montepulciano d'Abruzzo '99	Y	3
●	Montepulciano d'Abruzzo '90	Y	3
●	Montepulciano d'Abruzzo '91	Y	3
●	Montepulciano d'Abruzzo '92	Y	3
●	Montepulciano d'Abruzzo '97	Y	3
○	Le Scuderie del Cielo '98	Y	3
○	Le Scuderie del Cielo '99	Y	3
⊙	Montepulciano d'Abruzzo Cerasuolo '99	Y	3

TOLLO (CH)

CANTINA TOLLO
VIA GARIBALDI, 68
66010 TOLLO (CH)
TEL. 087196251 - 0871961726
E-MAIL: ordinivino@cantinatollo.it

Two wines were left out, the '98 Cagiòlo Rosso, which was not yet ready for release, and a new wine due to appear at the beginning of 2002, but Cantina Tollo still presented a good selection of wines for tasting. All were up to the standards we have come to expect from this leading co-operative. After a couple of attempts, marred by unhelpful vintages, Cagiòlo Bianco, from chardonnay vinified in French oak barriques, finally strides into the Two Glasses category. The colour has good intensity and the nose is complex, offering a series of aromas that range from florality to ripe fruit and on to balsam. The palate is rich with sensations of acacia honey, apricot and, on the finish, caramel. Colle Secco Rubino is one of the most popular and best value for money wines in the region, selling at under € 4.00 in wine shops. The '98 is as good as this wine gets. Bright in appearance, it has aromas of cherry and small red berry fruit, together with delicate spiciness. The palate is well structured, light in tannin and attractive in its ripe fruitiness and overall balance. Just one step below is the more traditionally styled Colle Secco with its distinctive black label. It has a dark colour that tends to garnet, more immediacy of aroma and more overt alcohol on the palate plus greater tannic grip. The Trebbiano Colle Secco is as attractive as the Rubino. It is a delicate wine, focusing on florality and an acid balance that gives it a pleasing finish. The two Valle d'Oro wines are as reliably good as ever, particularly the fruity, fragrant Cerasuolo.

○ Cagiòlo Bianco '00	₹₹	4
● Montepulciano d'Abruzzo Colle Secco Rubino '98	₹₹	2*
⊙ Montepulciano d'Abruzzo Cerasuolo Valle d'Oro '00	₹	2
○ Trebbiano d'Abruzzo Colle Secco '00	₹	2
● Montepulciano d'Abruzzo Colle Secco '98	₹	2
● Montepulciano d'Abruzzo Valle d'Oro '98	₹	2
● Montepulciano d'Abruzzo Cagiòlo '94	₹₹	3
● Montepulciano d'Abruzzo '97	₹₹	4

VILLAMAGNA (CH)

TORRE ZAMBRA
V.LE REGINA MARGHERITA, 20
66010 VILLAMAGNA (CH)
TEL. 0871300121 - 03356223114

Riccardo De Cerchio was once a footballer. Perhaps this gave him a taste for a challenge, because he started in wine a number of years ago, bottling the output of several producers in and around Villamagna, one of the most densely planted parts of Abruzzo. With the help of consultant Romeo Taraborrelli, the quality of the wines has improved rapidly so that now, after several years in the Other Wineries listings, the estate has earned its spurs and moves up to a full profile. In particular, the '97 vintage of its flagship wine, Brume Rosse, is a great success and scored very highly. A garnet-tinged ruby leads in to developed aromas of wild mulberry, and morello and black cherries, interwoven with oak. The palate has an initially powerful attack and then develops evenly, with smooth tannins and a sweetly fruited, full finish. The Montepulciano d'Abruzzo Colle Maggio is similarly conceived. Deep in colour and tinged with violet, it shows berry fruit aromas augmented by notes of vanilla and tobacco then the decently structured palate is nicely oaky, although the tannins have a slightly bitter edge. The Chardonnay is more immediate in its ripe apple and banana aromas. The palate is both soft and fresh. In contrast, the Trebbiano d'Abruzzo Colle Maggio is limited by excessive acidity, making it overly tangy and citrus-dominated.

● Montepulciano d'Abruzzo Brume Rosse '97	₹₹	4
● Montepulciano d'Abruzzo Colle Maggio '98	₹₹	3*
○ Chardonnay Colle Maggio '00	₹	3
○ Trebbiano d'Abruzzo Colle Maggio '00	₹	3

OTHER WINERIES

SPINELLI
FRAZ. PIAZZANO DI ATESSA
VIA PIANA LA FARA, 90
66041 ATESSA (CH)
TEL. 0872897916

The Spinelli brothers produce an almost too extensive range of wines but this year they have done particularly well. All their reds are well-made and attractive.

- Montepulciano d'Abruzzo Quartana '00 🍷🍷 2*
- Montepulciano d'Abruzzo
  Tenute di Pallano '00 🍷 2
- Montepulciano d'Abruzzo
  Terra d'Aligi '99 🍷 3

MADONNA DEI MIRACOLI
C.DA TERMINE, 38
66021 CASALBORDINO (CH)
TEL. 0873918107 - 0873918420
E-MAIL: msic@vinicasalbordino.com

This co-operative's wines, shaped by oenologist Beniamino Di Domenica, are decidedly promising. That goes particularly for the well-fruited, complex oaked white. The wood is less well-gauged on the red, and masks the varietal character.

- ○ Chardonnay Castel Verdino '99 🍷🍷 4
- Montepulciano d'Abruzzo
  Badia dei Miracoli '98 🍷 4

SAN LORENZO
C.DA PLAVIGNANO, 2
64075 CASTILENTI (TE)
TEL. 0861999325

The San Lorenzo estate has just started to bottle and has ambitious plans. It has taken on as consultant Riccardo Brighigna, who has created a range of most attractive wines, in particular the Montepulciano selection and the rich, well-fruited Chardonnay.

- ○ Chardonnay Chioma di Berenice '00 🍷🍷 3
- Montepulciano d'Abruzzo Antares '97 🍷🍷 3*
- ○ Trebbiano d'Abruzzo Antares '00 🍷 3

ANTONIO E ELIO MONTI
C.DA PIGNOTTO, 62
64010 CONTROGUERRA (TE)
TEL. 086189042
E-MAIL: mon@tin.it

From the moment of Riccardo Cotarella's arrival as consultant, Monti wines have taken a turn for the better. There can be no doubt that the estate is now starting to realize its potential.

- Montepulciano d'Abruzzo Pignotto '00 🍷🍷 5
- Montepulciano d'Abruzzo '00 🍷 3

CANTINA MIGLIANICO
VIA SAN GIACOMO, 40
66010 MIGLIANICO (CH)
TEL. 0871951262 - 0871950240

As usual, the Cantina Miglianico range is more than respectable. This year, though, the winery did not present its top wines, leaving Montepulciano Fondatore '97, which marries fair structure with good drinkability, to keep its banner aloft.

● Montepulciano d'Abruzzo Fondatore '97	🍷🍷	4
● Montepulciano d'Abruzzo Montupoli '99	🍷	2
○ Trebbiano d'Abruzzo Fondatore '97	🍷	4

NESTORE BOSCO
C.DA CASALI, 7
65010 NOCCIANO (PE)
TEL. 085847345 - 085847139
E-MAIL: info@nestoreboschi.com

While waiting for the release of its two Montepulciano d'Abruzzo selections, this long-established winery offered the panel a pair of young, easy-drinking reds, both of good personality.

● Montepulciano d'Abruzzo '00	🍷	3
● Il Grappolo Rosso '00	🍷	3

CHIUSA GRANDE
C.DA CASALI
65010 NOCCIANO (PE)
TEL. 085847460 - 0858470818
E-MAIL: fdeusan@libero.it

Franco D'Eusanio's estate is run on organic lines and looks likely to have plenty to say for itself in the future. For now, the Roccosecco is full and fruity and the white Matté fully reflects the trebbiano grape's fragrant character.

○ Trebbiano d'Abruzzo Matté '00	🍷	2
● Montepulciano d'Abruzzo Rocco Secco '99	🍷	3

CITRA
C.DA CUCULLO
66026 ORTONA (CH)
TEL. 0859031342
E-MAIL: citra@citra.it

This is another winery that is represented by its standard-label red this year. The Caroso selection Caroso, and the additions to the range introduced by the new technical staff, were not available at the time of our tasting. Villa Torre is fruity, attractive, lightly tannic and well-structured.

● Montepulciano d'Abruzzo Villa Torre '00	🍷	3

CHIARIERI
VIA SANT'ANGELO, 10
65019 PIANELLA (PE)
TEL. 085971365 - 085973313

The wines at Chiarieri produced one of this year's surprises, especially the traditionally styled but impressively flavoursome reds. Hannibal is the more complex, Granaro the more immediate and attractive, and also great value for money.

● Montepulciano d'Abruzzo Hannibal '97	🍷🍷	4
● Montepulciano d'Abruzzo Granaro '00	🍷	2*

CANTINA SOCIALE FRENTANA
VIA PERAZZA, 32
66020 ROCCA SAN GIOVANNI (CH)
TEL. 087260152
E-MAIL: info@cantinafrentana.it

The input of the skilled oenologist Gianni Pasquale is beginning to produce results. The barrique-aged Rubesto, of the two reds, has the substance to age well while the Frentano is excellent value for money.

● Montepulciano d'Abruzzo Rubesto '98	🍷🍷	3*
● Montepulciano d'Abruzzo Frentano '00	🍷	2*

CASA VINICOLA ROXAN
FRAZ. TRATTURO - C.DA TRATTURO, 1
65020 ROSCIANO (PE)
TEL. 0858505683
E-MAIL: roxanvini@tin.it

This is one of the most promising co-operatives in the region, especially for its great value reds. The Trebbiano d'Abruzzo showed well this year, too.

● Montepulciano d'Abruzzo Roxan '00	🍷	2*
○ Trebbiano d'Abruzzo Roxan '00	🍷	2
● Montepulciano d'Abruzzo Galelle '99	🍷	3

VALORI
VIA TORQUATO AL SALINELLO
64027 SANT'OMERO (TE)
TEL. 086188461 - 0861796340

The quality of the wines of this estate, owned by Luigi Valori, is improving visibly. The standard-label Montepulciano stands out from the crowd of Abruzzo reds thanks to its modern style, which gives it good extractive weight. Attilio Pagli is in charge of winemaking.

● Montepulciano d'Abruzzo '00	🍷🍷	3*
○ Trebbiano d'Abruzzo Preludio '00	🍷	3

TENUTA CARACCIOLO
DUCHI DI CASTELLUCCIO
C.DA ZAPPINO, 99
VIA TIBURTINA KM 200
65027 SCAFA (PE) - TEL. 0858541508

The new owners of this estate, the Franceschelli family, are heading determinedly down the road to high quality. Their better wines already have a new image and, more important, a new style, which has been fashioned for them by oenologist Vittorio Festa.

● Montepulciano d'Abruzzo Rosso di Crosta '98	🍷🍷	5
○ Trebbiano d'Abruzzo Bianco di Crosta '00	🍷	4

BARONE CORNACCHIA
C.DA TORRI
64010 TORANO NUOVO (TE)
TEL. 0861887412

Barone Cornacchia finds himself listed here, rather than with a full profile, simply because of the absence of the leading wines, Vigna Le Coste and Poggio Varano. There is, though, a new wine, Cabernet Sauvignon Villa Torri, which comes very close to the Two Glass standard.

● Controguerra Cabernet Sauvignon Villa Torri '98	🍷	4
● Montepulciano d'Abruzzo '00	🍷	2
○ Trebbiano d'Abruzzo '00	🍷	1

POGGIO LE GAZZE
CANTINE DEL PALAZZETTO
VIA R. MARGHERITA, 29
64010 TORANO NUOVO (TE)
TEL. 0861856933

This is the first appearance in the Guide of this newish estate, owned by the Guglielmana family, who have already given it a distinctive approach. Among the wines worthy of mention are the barrique-aged Colle Creta and Terre dei Gechi, and the more traditional Sasso Arso.

● Montepulciano d'Abruzzo Colle Creta '97	🍷🍷	4
● Montepulciano d'Abruzzo Terre dei Gechi '98	🍷🍷	3*
● Montepulciano d'Abruzzo Sasso Arso '98	🍷	4

BUCCICATINO
FRAZ. C.DA STERPANA
C.DA STERPANA
66010 VACRI (CH)
TEL. 0871720273

Here we have another winery temporarily bereft of its top wines. The efforts of Umberto Buccicatino to ensure consistent high quality will, though, make the wait worth while.

○ Trebbiano d'Abruzzo '00	🍷	2
● Montepulciano d'Abruzzo '99	🍷	3

CAMPANIA

This has been a year to remember in Campania. Things have probably not been so propitious in the region of Cecubo, Falerno, Apianum and Cauda Vulpium since Roman times. A good six wines achieved Three Glasses – that is 50 per cent more than last year and the region's best result ever. In addition, when you leaf through the pages in this section you will find a goodly number of wines printed in colour, indicating those that reached the taste-offs for top honours. Further proof of the substantial improvements that have been made in the region. Neither are all the top wines concentrated in Irpinia, the area that has generally been considered the epicentre of premium quality wine production in Campania. Two of them come from the province of Caserta, making this the prime candidate for the role of "up and coming area". The '99 release of Galardi's Terre di Lavoro is the best ever and offers a dense, powerful wine of huge concentration and tremendous personality while the '98 Vigna Camarato, from neighbouring Villa Matilde, is terrific proof of the maturity of style that the Avallone siblings have achieved in their wines. But there are a whole lot more dynamic producers in the province, especially in the new Galluccio DOC, not to mention those further south around Massico and Volturno, where there has been a veritable explosion of estates old and new whose quality levels have skyrocketed. Things are slightly different in the province of Naples where the main fascination still seems to be traditional reds and whites made from classic local varieties. Yet, if the output of DOCs like Vesuvio is mainly unexceptional wines that offer good value for your euro, along the Sorrento peninsula and the Amalfi coast, not forgetting Ischia, the emphasis is much more on wines of great presence and character, often based on once-ignored indigenous varieties. Indeed, Campania seems to have almost endless potential on this front. The province of Benevento now has its first world-class wine. It's an Aglianico called Bue Apis from the Cantina del Taburno, a co-operative winery that is just as on the ball as its more renowned Alto Adige cousins. And it is not the only one in the area to have invested money and manpower to bring major success. In fact, it is a racing certainty that the next few years will see the Benevento DOCs making their mark in a big way. In Irpinia, despite a large number of good quality estates, the scene is dominated by the giant Feudi di San Gregorio, which this year collected two Three Glasses awards, one with Serpico, a fabulous aglianico-based red, the other with Pàtrimo, one of the best Merlots anywhere this year. Incontrovertible proof, if any were still needed, that you can track market trends and global fashions yet still keep one foot based firmly in tradition. Finally, the province of Salerno also gains a Three Glass award this time. The laureate is the superb Montevetrano from Silvia Imparato. We are sure that we will also shortly be seeing top-ranking wines from that other area of huge potential, Cilento.

ATRIPALDA (AV)

MASTROBERARDINO
VIA MANFREDI, 75/81
83042 ATRIPALDA (AV)
TEL. 0825614111
E-MAIL: mastro@mastro.it

Atripalda's Mastroberardino winery has a history spanning more than a century and is one of the best loved and most widely recognized Italian names. At the helm of the estate is Antonio Mastroberardino, who has been responsible for its winemaking strategies since 1945. He reigns over 330 hectares of vineyard, some owned outright, the rest controlled by the company in one way or another, and annual production averages 2,600,000 bottles, all of excellent quality. A retaste of the Naturalis Historia '97, first examined last year, revealed encouraging development for it has now gained really promising balance and softness. However, the wine that showed best this year was the mature, complex Fiano di Avellino More Maiorum '97. This is the result of an experiment to give Fiano di Avellino three years' ageing before release, partly in barrique, partly in bottle. It is pale straw tinged with gold, ushering in ripe fruit that tends to minerality on the nose, which also has elegant tertiary notes. The palate is beautifully balanced, with good oaking, and has finesse and harmony. The Taurasi Radici is a bright, deep ruby and has fairly ripe berry fruit on both nose and palate, which is well-defined, full and spicy, if not particularly deep. Best of the rest in the vast range are Greco di Tufo Nova Serra '00 and Aglianico Avellanio '99.

CASTELLABATE

LUIGI MAFFINI
LOC. SAN MARCO
84071 CASTELLABATE
TEL. 0974966345 - 03383495193
E-MAIL: maffini@costacilento.it

If some of Campania's major estates appear to be going through a period of stagnation and seem to lack enthusiasm and drive, this is anything but the case with the young, highly motivated group of producers to which Luigi Maffini belongs. After graduating in agricultural studies, he decided to set up his own estate, taking as a starting point the small vineyard his family owned, adjacent to their country house at San Marco di Castellabate. He got right down to the job, experimenting with vinifying in new wood while also working to restore some old vineyards which had excellent exposures but were in a state of semi-abandonment. Now, five years on, the estate produces 35,000 bottles a year and has three different wines, led by Cenito. This is a fabulous red from equal parts of aglianico and piedirosso, aged for a year and a half in small French casks. The '99 is full of ripe fruit, spices, tobacco and vanilla, and has good structure, good depth, plentiful extractive weight, rounded tannins and a long finish. Kléos '00 is also a terrific, full-bodied red from piedirosso, sangiovese and aglianico. It has excellent texture, good balance and complexity, and overall attractiveness. The third member of the team is Kràtos, a delicious, zesty Fiano whose richness of fruit, aromatic breadth and tropical nuances are quite captivating.

○ Fiano di Avellino More Maiorum '97	🍷🍷	6
○ Greco di Tufo Novaserra '00	🍷	4
● Aglianico Avellanio '99	🍷	4
● Taurasi Radici '97	🍷	6
● Taurasi Radici '90	🍷🍷🍷	6
○ Fiano di Avellino More Maiorum '96	🍷🍷	5
● Taurasi Radici '96	🍷🍷	6
● Naturalis Historia '97	🍷🍷	6

● Cenito '99	🍷🍷	6
● Kléos '00	🍷🍷	4*
○ Kràtos '00	🍷🍷	4*
● Cenito '97	🍷🍷	5
● Cenito '98	🍷🍷	6
● Kléos '98	🍷🍷	3
● Kléos '99	🍷🍷	3

CELLOLE (CE)

VILLA MATILDE
S. S. DOMITIANA, 18 - KM. 4,700
81030 CELLOLE (CE)
TEL. 0823932088
E-MAIL: info@fattoriavillamatilde.com

There are very, very few estates in Campania, maybe in the entire country, that can boast an output of the quality and impact of brother and sister Tani and Ida Avallone's Villa Matilde. The estate was founded in 1963 and today comprises 100 hectares, of which 70 are planted to vine, and an annual production of over half a million bottles. In addition, their oenological consultant is one who has no need of introduction, the top-ranking Riccardo Cotarella. Villa Matilde's list of prize-winning wines is astonishing and this year gained another Three Glasses trophy, awarded, hardly surprisingly, to the new vintage of Vigna Camarato, the '98. This is a monovarietal Aglianico which reflects both the distinction of its terroir, the volcanic massif of Roccamonfina, and the attention given to every detail of its production, in both vineyard and cellar. It is deep, dense, tightly-knit, and as concentrated in colour as it is on the nose, where it displays a vast repertoire of red and black berry fruit threaded through with extremely elegant notes of spice, vanilla and tobacco. The palate is tight and powerful, full of muscle yet perfectly balanced, revealing fleshy fruit, the most elegant array of tannins and a perfectly judged oak component. In short, it is just incredible. Nevertheless, it would be unjust to let it overshadow the rest of the estate's range, the spicy Cecubo, for example, or the soft Falerno del Massico '99, the floral Falerno Bianco Vigna Caracci or the fruity Aglianico di Roccamonfina, all of which are superb wines.

● Falerno del Massico Vigna Camarato '98	¶¶¶	6
○ Aglianico di Roccamonfina '00	¶¶	3*
○ Falerno del Massico Bianco Vigna Caracci '00	¶¶	4*
● Cecubo '99	¶¶	4*
● Falerno del Massico Rosso '99	¶¶	4*
○ Falerno del Massico Bianco '00	¶	3*
◉ Terre Cerase '00	¶	3*
● Vigna Camarato '95	¶¶¶	5
● Falerno del Massico Vigna Camarato '97	¶¶¶	6
○ Falerno del Massico Bianco Vigna Caracci '99	¶¶	4
● Aglianico di Roccamonfina '98	¶	3
○ Eleusi Passito '98	¶	4

FOGLIANISE (BN)

CANTINA DEL TABURNO
VIA SALA
82030 FOGLIANISE (BN)
TEL. 0824871338 - 082421765
E-MAIL: info@cantinadeltaburno.it

Bue Apis '99, a red made exclusively from aglianico, scored spectacularly highly in our tastings and was judged a runaway Three Glasses winner. However, its vertiginous rise shouldn't be allowed to outweigh the incredible amount of work carried out at Cantina del Taburno to bring it to superstardom. The co-operative is owned by the Consorzio Agrario di Benevento and produces wine from 500 hectares of vines owned by its 330 members. Oenologist Filippo Colandrea is technical director and Alfonso Pedicini the vineyard manager, while valuable consultancy comes from Professor Luigi Moio and research assistance is provided by the faculty of agriculture at the University of Naples. The grapes for Bue Apis are from a vineyard that is an almost unbelievable 180 years old and the wine has a power, an elegance and a concentration rarely seen. It is a dark ruby colour, tinged with purple. The nose is rich and complex, with intense bramble and blackcurrant fruit that knits perfectly with its notes of tobacco, black pepper and oak toast. The palate is dense, powerful, exuberantly fruity and has notable tannic impact of almost perfect refinement. The wine develops evenly, filling the mouth and finishing long, with soft tones of ripe black berry fruit, tobacco and roast coffee beans on the aftertaste. Aglianico Delius is another surprisingly good wine. The colour is dark ruby with a violet-tinged rim. The nose is soft and fruity with overt aromas of, mainly, blackcurrant, bramble and other wild berries then the palate is mouthfilling, fleshy and warm, with notable backbone, great elegance, balance and length, and a long, fruity, balsamic finish. The remaining wines are excellent, too.

● Bue Apis '99	¶¶¶	6
● Delius '99	¶¶	6
○ Greco del Taburno '00	¶¶	3*
● Aglianico del Taburno Fidelis '98	¶¶	3*
○ Taburno Falanghina Cesco dell'Eremo '00	¶¶	4*
◉ Aglianico del Taburno Rosato Alba Rosa '00	¶	3
○ Taburno Coda di Volpe Amineo '00	¶	3
○ Taburno Coda di Volpe Serra Docile '00	¶	4
○ Taburno Falanghina '00	¶	3
○ Falanghina Passita Ruscolo '99	¶	6

FORIO (NA)

D'AMBRA VINI D'ISCHIA
FRAZ. PANZA
VIA MARIO D'AMBRA, 16
80075 FORIO (NA)
TEL. 081907246 - 081907210
E-MAIL: info@dambravini.com

D'Ambra has represented Ischia on the world stage since 1888. Its biancolella-based whites and its reds from per''e palummo embrace the perfumes and aromas of this Mediterranean island and its thousands of years of winemaking traditions. Andrea d'Ambra's worthy aim is to express the potential of its fabulous vineyards to the full, plots such as the starry Frassitelli, for example, which are rooted in the terraces of Mount Epodo and which continually risk abandonment or grubbing up because of difficulties in cultivation and the competing interests of tourism. The '00 Biancolella from Tenuta Frassitelli is a great drop of wine. It is a deep straw colour and has an intense, fresh nose of ripe fruit, notably pear, and distinct scents of flowers and Mediterranean scrub. The soft, well-defined, long palate has good acidity and is full of fleshy fruitiness. On a second look, the Dedicato a Mario d'Ambra '98, from guarnaccia and per''e palummo first tasted as a cask sample a year ago, was in splendid form. The tightness of its structure, its balance and its excellent fruity and spicy finish, gave it far more class than we found first time round. We have therefore decided to make an exception to our rule and revise its score upwards. All the remaining d'Ambra wines are worth investigating.

FORIO (NA)

PIETRATORCIA
FRAZ. CUOTTO
VIA PROVINCIALE PANZA, 267
80075 FORIO (NA)
TEL. 081908206 - 081907232

Pietratorcia was founded less than ten years ago when three families, the Iaconos, the Regines and the Verdes, got together to explore the potential of their vineyards on Ischia. This was a noble venture, especially given that viticulture risks extinction on this wonderful Mediterranean island because agricultural land is progressively being lost on all fronts to the ever-encroaching demands of tourism. However, helped by technical support from the agricultural school at San Michele all'Adige, the team now produces around 100,000 bottles a year, all wines with distinct personalities that remain firmly rooted in the thousands of years of winemaking tradition on the island. You can understand what this means when you taste the '98 Scheria, a barrique-aged white from fiano and biancolella. It has a deep straw colour and the first impact on the nose is of pineapple and apricot, followed by more developed, complex aromas which tend to an elegantly evolved minerality. The palate is powerful, with good fruit and acidity, and an array of tertiary flavours that give the wine good ageing potential. The "passito", or dried grape wine, Meditandum '99 has exuberant aromas of apricot jam, fig and orange blossom honey. It is sweet and dense on the palate, giving a wealth of warm Mediterranean sensations. Ischia Bianco Vigne del Cuotto '00 is quite well-knit and has aromas of balsam but seems a little over-ripe while Scheria Rosso '98 is a slim-bodied, but well balanced, red with a delicate vein of tannin and sweet scents of cherry and very ripe berry fruit.

○ Ischia Biancolella Tenuta Frassitelli '00	ΨΨ	4*
● Rosso Dedicato a Mario d'Ambra '98	Ψ	5
○ Ischia Biancolella '00	Ψ	3
○ Ischia Forastera '00	Ψ	3
● Ischia Per''e Palummo '00	Ψ	3
○ Ischia Biancolella Tenuta Frassitelli '99	ΨΨ	4

○ Scheria Bianco '98	ΨΨ	5
○ Meditandum '99	ΨΨ	6
○ Ischia Bianco Sup. Vigne del Cuotto '00	Ψ	4
● Scheria Rosso '98	Ψ	6
○ Ischia Bianco Ris. '97	ΨΨ	5
○ Ischia Bianco Ris. '98	ΨΨ	5
● Pietratorcia Rosso Ris. '98	ΨΨ	5

FURORE (SA)

CANTINE GRAN FUROR
DIVINA COSTIERA
VIA G. B. LAMA, 14
84010 FURORE (SA)
TEL. 089830348
E-MAIL: info@granfuror.it

It might be the influence of the name ("furore" means frenzy) but Marisa Cuomo and her husband Andrea Ferraioli seem to be in the grip of some religious excitation as they doggedly fight each year to pluck ripe bunches of grapes from the precipitous rocky slopes of their vineyards. They have ten hectares to cope with, only part of which they own directly. All are pergola-trained or trellised to the rock face, the only options in such conditions. It could be termed "heroic" viticulture, as arduous and labour-intensive as that carried out in the mountains of the north. And it is no coincidence that the ridges to which Furore itself clings so tightly are of Dolomitic rock. This year's tastings brought us the extraordinary Fior d'Uva, made from the rare indigenous varieties fenile and ginestra, and one of southern Italy's most exciting whites. It is a bright, deep straw colour. The nose is full and intense with alluring aromas of apples, tropical pineapple and papaya fruit, and apricot. The palate is powerful yet elegant, broad and complex and has very carefully gauged oak. It is without doubt Campania's best white this year. The estate's other wines are as good as ever: Furore Bianco '00 has power on the nose and fresh acidity; Ravello Bianco, also '00, is fleshy and long; Furore Rosso Riserva '98 has a super-ripe plumy sweetness, spiciness and is full, harmonious and mouthfilling on the palate. Professor Luigi Moio consults.

GALLUCCIO (CE)

TELARO
COOPERATIVA LAVORO E SALUTE
LOC. CINQUE PIETRE
81045 GALLUCCIO (CE)
TEL. 0823925841
E-MAIL: info@vinitelaro.it

The Telaro brothers' Lavoro e Salute co-operative is without doubt one of the wineries that has made the greatest improvements in quality in the past year. Massimo, Pasquale and Luigi Telaro set up the undertaking in 1987, opting to follow the dictates of organic farming and throwing themselves wholeheartedly into salvaging old vine varieties and restoring traditional wine styles. They now produce a wide range of wines, all made from their good 35 hectares of vines, which cling onto the slopes of the volcanic massif at Roccamonfina. Monte Caruso is a DOC Galluccio and made mainly from aglianico, with ten per cent piedirosso. The '99 is a fine deep ruby tinged with violet. There is a good, sweet fruit-rich impact on the nose, which has lots of ripe fruit and hints of spice. The dense palate follows on well, and has smooth tannins, good balance and a long finish, leaving hints of vanilla on the aftertaste. The wine clearly has the potential to mature well over several years. The Galluccio Falanghina Ripa Bianca '00 is intense and richly fruited, with attractive touches of citron and pink grapefruit and nuances of broom and hedgerows. The Falanghina di Roccamonfina is nicely fruity with pleasing undertones of medicinal herbs on the nose and a soft, supple palate. Next up was the Galluccio Riserva Calivierno '97, a full red, rich in soft, fleshy fruitiness and subtly tannic. The rest of the range is also of good quality.

○	Costa d'Amalfi Furore Bianco Fiord'uva '00	♥♥	5*
○	Costa d'Amalfi Furore Bianco '00	♥♥	4*
○	Costa d'Amalfi Ravello Bianco '00	♥♥	3*
●	Costa d'Amalfi Furore Rosso Ris. '98	♥♥	5
●	Costa d'Amalfi Furore Rosso '00	♥	4
●	Costa d'Amalfi Furore Rosso Ris. '97	♀♀	5
○	Costa d'Amalfi Furore Bianco Fiord'uva '99	♀♀	5

●	Galluccio Aglianico Monte Caruso '99	♥♥	3*
○	Falanghina di Roccamonfina '00	♥	2*
○	Galluccio Falanghina Ripabianca '00	♥	3
●	Galluccio Ara Mundi Ris. '97	♥	5
●	Galluccio Calivierno Ris. '97	♥	5
●	Aleatico Passito delle Cinque Pietre '00		5
●	Aglianico di Roccamonfina '97	♀♀	3
●	Aglianico di Roccamonfina '98	♀	3

GUARDIA SANFRAMONDI (BN)

CORTE NORMANNA
C.DA SAPENZIE, 20
82034 GUARDIA SANFRAMONDI (BN)
TEL. 0824817004 – 0824817008
E-MAIL: info@cortenormanna.it

Gaetano and Alfredo Falluto own 18 hectares of vineyard at Guardia Sanframondi, in the heart of the Sannio area. They currently produce around 50,000 bottles a year and, with assistance from consultant oenologist Roberto Mazzer who has worked with the estate for several years now, they turn out wines of admirably consistent quality. It was the Aglianico del Sannio '00 that we liked best this year. It is a good ruby colour, tinged with violet. There are ripe red berry fruits, most notably plum, on the nose, and delicate vegetal and balsamic notes. This soft fruitiness is reflected on the palate, which has decent structure and good astringency. Falanghina del Sannio '00 is a bright straw. It has inviting aromas of flowers and ripe golden delicious apples, with a gently balsamic underlay. The palate is clean, fresh, supple and fruity. Falanghina La Palombaia, also from the '00 vintage, comes from selected grapes and ages for three months in new oak barriques. This gives it fullness on both nose and palate, and it has an attractive mix of vanilla, ripe apples and more flowery notes, supported by a seam of fresh acidity. Both the red and white versions of Solopaca DOC Guiscardo have attractive fruit and drinkability, and provide further proof of the quality of the '00 vintage.

Wine		Score
● Sannio Aglianico '00	♟	4
○ Sannio Falanghina '00	♟	3
○ Sannio Falanghina La Palombaia '00	♟	5
○ Solopaca Bianco Guiscardo '00	♟	2*
● Solopaca Rosso Guiscardo '00	♟	3*
○ Sannio Falanghina Passito Porta dell'Olmo '99		5
● Sannio Aglianico '99	♟	4

GUARDIA SANFRAMONDI (BN)

DE LUCIA
C.DA STARZE
82034 GUARDIA SANFRAMONDI (BN)
TEL. 0824864259
E-MAIL: c.delucia@tin.it

Carlo De Lucia's 18 hectares of vineyard are situated at Guardia Sanframondi in the heart of the Sannio, an area that is starting to gain itself a name for quality, thanks to the outstanding efforts of De Lucia himself and others. Carlo's great care in vine cultivation, and his collaboration with consultant oenologist Roberto Mazzer, have produced a fine range of wines. Aglianico del Sannio Vigna la Corte '99 has an intense ruby colour, suggesting good concentration and ripeness of fruit. This is confirmed on the clean, elegant nose, with its cherry and ripe small black berry fruitiness, and well-integrated oak. The palate is full, structured, soft, fleshy and long. Despite the youthful exuberance of the Aglianico del Sannio '00, it has good maturity in its fruit, which is soft and succulent, but held in by an elegant astringency. There is also a pleasing harmony right across the board. The two DOC Falanghinas, the standard version and La Vigna delle Ginestre, both '00, were pleasant surprises. The latter has a broad spectrum of aroma, with the oak supporting rather than masking its ripe apply fruit, and a fresh, supple palate. The standard-label wine is simpler but has an elegant nose with ripe fruit, florality and notes of broom, and a palate of good body and balance.

Wine		Score
● Sannio Aglianico '99	♟♟	4
● Sannio Aglianico Vigna La Corte '99	♟♟	5
○ Sannio Falanghina '00	♟	3
○ Sannio Falanghina Vigna delle Ginestre '00	♟	4
● Sannio Aglianico Adelchi '97	♟♟	4
● Sannio Aglianico Adelchi '98	♟♟	5
○ Sannio Falanghina '99	♟	3
● Solopaca Rosso Vassallo '99	♟	2

MONDRAGONE (CE)

Michele Moio
V.le Regina Margherita, 6
81034 Mondragone (CE)
Tel. 0823978017
E-mail: info@moio.it

Campania's wine history would be incomplete without the Moio family, which has been in the business since 1880. Quality is now rising rapidly at their Mondragone estate, which directly controls 11 hectares of vineyard as well as buying in grapes from other growers in the zone. Total annual production is 100,000 bottles. Working alongside brothers Bruno and Luigi, a lecturer in oenology at the University of Naples, is their father Michele, who is a Primitivo specialist. So naturally Primitivo has always been very much part of their production. It is now made in three different versions. Falerno del Massico Primitivo '98 has a dark ruby colour with a violet rim. The nose is deep and full of sweet, ripe, red-berried fruitiness and spice, then the palate is rich, full, powerful and tightly knit, and finishes long with flavours of ripe morello cherry. Gaurano comes from primitivo grapes allowed to become over-ripe. Recent vintages have made great strides and the '98 has a dark, deep hue. The nose is exuberant, with toasty and spicy notes melding elegantly into its cherry and wild berry fruitiness. The soft, finely-tuned palate is full of tannins of great finesse and has good length. The '99 vintage of Rosso 57, named for the memorable '57 vintage, is a wine of great substance with a gorgeous over-ripe red berried fruitiness set into a full, well balanced structure. The two whites, Falanghina Villa dei Marchi '00, with its intense, multi-faceted florality, and the fresh, white peach and ripe damson-scented Falerno del Massico Bianco '00, also from falanghina, are both good, too.

● Falerno del Massico Primitivo '98	♛♛	4*
● Gaurano '98	♛♛	4*
● Rosso 57 '99	♛♛	4*
○ Falanghina Villa dei Marchi '00	♛	3
○ Falerno del Massico Falanghina '00	♛	3
● Falerno del Massico Primitivo '97	♟	4
● Rosso 57	♟	4

MONTEFUSCO (AV)

Colli Irpini - Montesolae
Via Serra di Montefusco
83030 Montefusco (AV)
Tel. 0825963972
E-mail: Info@colliirpini.com

With an annual production of 700,000 bottles and 15 different wines, Colli Irpini is one of the most prolific wineries in Irpinia. It doesn't own any vineyards but buys in grapes according to requirements from a group of reliable growers in the provinces of Avellino and Benevento. Winemaking is in the hands of Rosa Pesa, an agronomist and the winery's owner, assisted by oenologist Massimo De Renzo. As in previous years, it was the whites that were the most characterful wines. And, just as in previous years, the pick of the bunch was the Fiano di Avellino and the Greco di Tufo from the most recent vintage, the '00 this year. The Fiano has a good, bright straw colour, with greenish tinges. Its nose is open, fresh and full of well-defined fruit aromas, then the palate is fully structured, with great freshness and good length, enlivened by an apply finish. The Greco di Tufo has marked intensity and cleanliness, and is floral and ripely fruity. There is good quality on both versions of the '00 Falanghina. The Simposium Sannio DOC has good balance and freshness, and an attractive balsamic character that is picked up on the end of the palate. The Falanghina del Beneventano is fresh, with pure tones of golden delicious apple, good texture and attractive suppleness. A retaste of the '96 Taurasi confirmed the good quality we found previously. In general, though, we would expect greater things from the estate's cru wines, which were very variable.

○ Falanghina del Beneventano '00	♛	3*
○ Fiano di Avellino '00	♛	4
○ Greco di Tufo '00	♛	4
○ Sannio Falanghina Simposium '00	♛	5
● Taurasi '96	♟	4
○ Fiano di Avellino '99	♟	3
○ Greco di Tufo '99	♟	3

MONTEFUSCO (AV)

TERREDORA DI PAOLO
VIA SERRA
83030 MONTEFUSCO (AV)
TEL. 0825968215
E-MAIL: info@terradora.com

This estate belongs to Walter Mastroberardino and his children Paolo, Lucio and Daniela, a family of longstanding importance on the regional wine scene. It now makes 800,000 bottles a year and controls a good 150 hectares of vineyard, much of it directly owned. There are also some new plantings which, when they come into production, will increase output further. The wines do justice to the efforts made in producing them and two of them leapt with ease into the Two Glass category. One is the '97 Taurasi Fatica Contadina, possibly the best vintage ever of the wine. It has a good dark ruby colour, still tinged with violet, introducing a nose that is initially a little reticent before opening out to reveal cherry and plum jam fruit, underscored by a delicate touch of balsam. There is appreciable body on the warm, velvety palate, which has elegant tannins, good balance and considerable length. The other biggy is the first-rate Fiano di Avellino Terre di Dora '00 with its deep straw colour. The nose of tropical fruit, summer flowers and honey ushers in an intense, powerful palate, full of lively acidity and beautifully clean fruit. Greco di Tufo Loggia della Serra '00 had less impact but made up for it in attractiveness, with well-defined floral and apple and pear-fruit aromas and a pink grapefruit-like citrus note. We found good character on the Irpinia Bianco Gioie di Vitae '00 but were less enthused by the rest of the vast range. However, with the amount of work that the Mastroberardinos are putting into both vineyard and cellar, it would be very surprising if wines of great class didn't emerge sooner or later.

	Wine	Glasses	Score
○	Fiano di Avellino Terre di Dora '00	♛♛	4*
●	Taurasi Fatica Contadina '97	♛♛	6
○	Gioie di Vitae '00	♛	3
○	Greco di Tufo Loggia della Serra '00	♛	4
○	Fiano di Avellino Campo Re '99	♛	5
○	Falanghina d'Irpinia '00		3
●	Irpinia Aglianico '00		3
●	Taurasi Fatica Contadina '94	♛♛	5
○	Fiano di Avellino Terre di Dora '98	♛♛	4
○	Greco di Tufo Terra degli Angeli '98	♛♛	3

MONTEMARANO (AV)

SALVATORE MOLETTIERI
VIA MUSANNI, 19/B
83040 MONTEMARANO (AV)
TEL. 082763722 - 082763424

Salvatore and Giovanni Molettieri put both enthusiasm and love into cultivating their seven hectares of aglianico, planted at Montemarano in the Taurasi zone. The well-aspected site lies at 500-600 metres above sea level and the vines are old. This means that yields are necessarily low and grape quality is excellent. The crop is vinified skilfully into two glorious reds by the Molettieris themselves, who use the Matura Group for consultancy. If we were intrigued by the Taurasi previously, this year we were bowled over. It has gained depth, finesse and an additional touch of elegance, and now can rightfully be cited as one of the best examples of this celebrated DOCG. Just try it. You'll love the rich opulence of its fruit, its delicate astringency and its fine array of aromas. You'll be equally impressed by the finely-judged level of new oak. Cinque Querce is also from aglianico and is the Taurasi's fresher, younger and more immediate counterpart. But beware, it's no insignificant droplet. Cherry, mulberry and raspberry may well follow each other playfully on the nose but the palate has good texture, ripe, velvety tannins and great richness of fruit. This estate is certainly one to watch.

	Wine	Glasses	Score
●	Taurasi Vigna Cinque Querce '97	♛♛	6
●	Cinque Querce Rosso '99	♛♛	4*
●	Taurasi Vigna Cinque Querce '94	♛♛	4
●	Cinque Querce Rosso '96	♛♛	3
●	Taurasi Vigna Cinque Querce '96	♛♛	5
●	Cinque Querce Rosso '97	♛	4
●	Cinque Querce Rosso '98	♛♛	4

PONTE (BN)

OCONE
FRAZ. LA MADONNELLA
VIA DEL MONTE, 56
82030 PONTE (BN)
TEL. 0824874040
E-MAIL: admocone@tin.it

Domenico Ocone carries on his family's almost century-long tradition of wine production with great enthusiasm. The estate now has a good 35 hectares of vineyard, all in fabulous positions on the slopes of the Taburno massif, and Domenico and his partners concentrate on the traditional varieties: falanghina, aglianico, greco, coda di volpe and piedirosso, grapes which have settled in here over thousands of years. The estate turns out a large range of wines from this fruit and the best this year was easily the '00 Falanghina cru Vigna del Monaco. The wine has a good pale straw colour with greenish tinges. The nose is clean, fresh and pervasive with soft aromas of golden delicious apple and summer flowers. Its soft palate has good structure, marked zestiness, an excitingly lively, fleshy fruitiness and plentiful length. We expected a bit more from the Aglianico Diomede '97 whose ruby colour is still tinged with violet. The nose is a little masked even though sweet notes of bramble and blackcurrant do emerge, while the palate has good complexity, elegance of tannin and good fruit but sadly lacks the underlying density of texture that it needs. A retaste of the Aglianico del Taburno '97 found it still on good form while the Coda di Volpe '00 has attractive aromas of white peach and damson, and a pleasing softness. The Falanghina del Taburno '00 is also attractive but seems a little too evolved for its age. Finally, the Piedirosso DOC from the same vintage is light bodied and is fresh and highly drinkable.

○ Taburno Falanghina Vigna del Monaco '00	₶₶	4*
○ Taburno Coda di Volpe '00	₶	3*
○ Taburno Falanghina '00	₶	3*
● Taburno Piedirosso '00	₶	3*
● Aglianico del Taburno Diomede '97	₶	5
● Aglianico del Taburno Vigna Pezza la Corte '93	₶₶	4
● Aglianico del Taburno Vigna Pezza la Corte '95	₶₶	4
● Aglianico del Taburno Diomede '96	₶₶	4
● Aglianico del Taburno Vigna Pezza la Corte '96	₶₶	4

PRIGNANO CILENTO (SA)

VITICOLTORI DE CONCILIIS
LOC. QUERCE, 1
84060 PRIGNANO CILENTO (SA)
TEL. 0974831090
E-MAIL: deconcillis@hotmail.com

If Cilento is now being touted as the new up-and-coming area of Campania, it is due to just a few people who bet on the potential of its terrain a few years back and then put heart and soul into trying to prove themselves right. The place of honour in the group goes to Bruno De Conciliis, who not only involved his whole family in the enterprise but brought in Severio Petrilli as consultant oenologist. His estate now has 19 hectares of vineyard and produces a range of wines of great class, topped by a gem of a red called Naima (remember John Coltrane?), made from 100 per cent aglianico. This year the '99, just like previous vintages, is up there with the region's most eminent wines. It is a dark, dense ruby, still tinged with violet. There is immediate impact on the nose, which is intense and clearly defined, with ripe red berry fruit, primarily cherry, mulberry and plum, and the complexity of beautifully calibrated new oak, tobacco and Mediterranean scrub. The palate is powerful, warm, pervasive and harmonious, with supreme balance, ripeness of fruit and smoothness of tannins, developing evenly through the mouth before coming to a long, aromatic finish. Zero '99, a wine produced in the De Conciliis cellars for D'Orta-De Conciliis, a company formed from a partnership between Winny D'Orta and Bruno de Conciliis, is just as fascinating. It, too, has power, refinement and depth. There are elegant aromas of wild berry fruits and spices, and the palate is firm and vigorous. All the estate's other wines are very good, especially the Aglianico Donnaluna.

● Naima '99	₶₶	5
● Donnaluna Aglianico '00	₶₶	4*
● Zero - D'Orta-De Conciliis '99	₶₶	5
○ Donnaluna Fiano '00	₶	3
○ Vigna Perella '00	₶	5
● Naima '98	₶₶	5
● Zero - D'Orta-De Conciliis '98	₶₶	5
○ Vigna Perella '99	₶₶	5
○ Donnaluna '99	₶	3

QUARTO (NA)

Cantine Grotta del Sole
Via Spinelli, 2
80010 Quarto (NA)
tel. 0818762566 - 0818761320
e-mail: grottadelsole@iol.it

For years now, the Martusciello family has been engaged in rediscovering the qualities of ancient, often disregarded or abandoned vine varieties and wines and bringing them back to public attention. They own just five hectares of vineyard but work with numerous small growers scattered across five of the region's zones, whom they follow closely to ensure good quality grapes. Their work is at its most intense in Aversa and Campi Flegrei but efforts are also dedicated to the Sorrento peninsula, the Vesuvius area and the wine country of the province of Avellino. Quarto di Sole '98 turned out to be the most interesting of their wines this year. It comes from a blend of piedirosso and aglianico, grown in the IGT area of Pompei and aged in new wood. It has a dark ruby colour, elegant aromas of red berry fruit and spices, and a structured, powerful palate of fair length. It is partnered by the white Quarto di Luna, also IGT Pompei, made from falanghina and caprettone (an indigenous Campanian variety). It is a deep straw colour, heralding sweet aromas of ripe fruit and vanilla, and its nicely balanced palate has good structure. But Grotta del Sole's classic wines are the lively, fruity Gragnano, which goes perfectly with the local cuisine, and Asprinio di Aversa, whose vines grow on the ancient "alberata" system where they are looped high over trees. This has an intensely citrus-like nose, a slim structure and a vigorous, cutting acidity. Montegauro, Piedirosso dei Campi Flegrei, also deserves a mention. It scores for its good structure, its rounded tannins and its attractively fruity and spicy notes on both nose and palate.

● Quarto di Sole '98	♉♉	5
○ Asprinio d'Aversa '00	♉	3
○ Quarto di Luna '99	♉	5
● Campi Flegrei Piedirosso Montegauro Ris. '97	♉	5
● Penisola Sorrentina Gragnano '00	♉	3
○ Campi Flegrei Falanghina Coste di Cuma '00		4
● Campi Flegrei Piedirosso Montegauro Ris. '96	♉	4
● Aglianico '98	♉	3

SAN CIPRIANO PICENTINO (SA)

Montevetrano
Via Montevetrano
84099 San Cipriano Picentino (SA)
tel. 089882285
e-mail: montevetrano@tin.it

Silvia Imparato is a professional photographer with a passionate love of wine who has become rather like the wine equivalent of a Formula One racing car. She's used to going fast and winning major awards. It is no great surprise that she has gained another Three Glasses – it would have been more of a story if she hadn't – given that for several years now her star has soared high above Montevetrano and her wines are among those most eagerly sought-after by collectors in both Italy and the United States. Her estate's production has fortunately been growing, however slowly, and has now just about reached 20,000 bottles. It should also soon expand further, although not much. But let's look at the wine itself, produced under the guidance of Riccardo Cotarella, one of Italy's most brilliant oenologists. It's a blend of 60 per cent cabernet sauvignon, 30 per cent merlot and aglianico. The '99 has the typical opaque, dark ruby colour, tinged with violet on the rim. The nose has extraordinary intensity and stylishness in an irresistible blend of red berry fruit, led by mulberry, spices (primarily pepper and clove), and the elegance of new oak. Showing great consistency, the same characteristics also appear on the palate but are amplified by its firm, powerful structure and balanced by velvety texture and tannins of astounding finesse. It develops excellently throughout the mouth, steadily gaining depth, and has a sweetly fruity finish underlined by a hint of tobacco and more spice. A wine not to miss.

● Montevetrano '99	♉♉♉	6
● Montevetrano '93	♉♉♉	5
● Montevetrano '95	♉♉♉	5
● Montevetrano '96	♉♉♉	5
● Montevetrano '97	♉♉♉	5
● Montevetrano '98	♉♉♉	6
● Montevetrano '94	♉♉	5

SESSA AURUNCA (CE)

GALARDI
Loc. Vallemarina - Fraz. S. Carlo
Prov.le Sessa-Mignano
81030 Sessa Aurunca (CE)
tel. 0823925003
e-mail: galardi@napoli.com

The story of Galardi's Terra di Lavoro takes us from the experiments of a group of hobbyists to a wine of international status, which has now been rewarded by Three Glasses. Francesco Catello, Dora Catello and her husband Arturo Celentano, Maria Luisa Murena and husband Roberto Selvaggi were all firmly convinced by the potential of their terrain, a corner of Campania of rare beauty, lying between the slopes of the extinct volcano of Roccamonfina and the sea. They therefore transformed their family inheritance into first a "garage winery" and then, with help from friend and oenologist Riccardo Cotarella, a "boutique winery". If the first ('94) and subsequent vintages of this brilliant red from 80 per cent aglianico and piedirosso were hardly more than rumours for most of those who attempted to get their hands on one of the few bottles produced, now, with the '99, there are almost 10,000 bottles and quantities are due to increase further, significantly so, in the future. For Galardi has turned into a fully-fledged estate with a modern cellar, 11 hectares of vineyard and a soon-to-be-opened Relais with restaurant attached. In the meantime, we have the best vintage so far in the shops. It is a thick, dark ruby, almost black in colour. Its aromas are intense and elegant with ripe black berry fruits, ranging from morello cherry to bramble and blackcurrant, strong hints of spice and tobacco, and delicate suggestions of oak. It is concentrated and powerful on the palate, perfectly firm - not even a hint of a wobble – and has the most elegant of tannins. What balance and extraordinary length! It's a stunner of a wine with huge personality. Congratulations!

● Terra di Lavoro '99	🍷🍷🍷	6
● Terra di Lavoro '94	🍷🍷	5
● Terra di Lavoro '95	🍷🍷	5
● Terra di Lavoro '97	🍷🍷	5
● Terra di Lavoro '98	🍷🍷	6
● Terra di Lavoro '96	🍷	5

SORBO SERPICO (AV)

FEUDI DI SAN GREGORIO
Cerza Grossa
83050 Sorbo Serpico (AV)
tel. 0825986611 - 0825986627
e-mail: feudi@feudi.it

It is always difficult to write this estate's entry. One problem is lack of space, which makes it almost impossible to discuss each wine as fully as it deserves. Another snag is that there are not enough superlatives in our language to avoid repeating ourselves. The Capaldo and Ercolino families who own Feudi are naturally not trying to make our lives easier. But let's see what we can do. Pàtrimo '99, a Merlot produced from a seven-hectare vineyard at Pietradefusi, in the Taurasi zone, is one of the best wines in the entire country. It is a miracle of concentration, power and elegance whose nose will dazzle you with its aromas of bramble and blackcurrant, its spicy, balsamic notes and its delicate toastiness, while its palate will wow you with incredible depth, a wealth of the finest-grained tannins, complexity, structure and extraordinary aromatic length. Then there is Serpico '99, a fabulous Aglianico from sensational vineyards with, in one part, non-grafted vines of over 100 years old. It has a hefty structure but this is carried with rare finesse. Throughout, there is an over-riding sweet fruitiness of ripe cherry with some morello and plum that melds wonderfully on both nose and palate into an irresistible mix of spices, tobacco and coffee. The length is, apparently, infinite. Everything else, from the supremely elegant Taurasi Piano di Montevergine '97, to the white Campanaro '00 and Privilegio '99, both from fiano, is nothing short of excellent. We can only congratulate Enzo Ercolino, who is in charge of the estate, Riccardo Cotarella, the oenologist, and Attilio Scienza, the agricultural consultant.

● Pàtrimo '99	🍷🍷🍷	6
● Serpico '99	🍷🍷🍷	6
○ Campanaro '00	🍷🍷	5
● Taurasi Piano di Montevergine Ris. '97	🍷🍷	6
○ Fiano di Avellino Pietracalda V. T. '00	🍷🍷	4*
○ Greco di Tufo '00	🍷🍷	4*
○ Greco di Tufo Cutizzi '00	🍷🍷	4*
● Idem '00	🍷🍷	5
○ Privilegio '00	🍷🍷	5
● Rubrato '00	🍷🍷	4
● Taurasi Selve di Luoti '97	🍷🍷	6
○ Fiano di Avellino '00	🍷	4
○ Sannio Falanghina '00	🍷	3
● Taurasi Piano di Montevergine '96	🍷🍷🍷	6
○ Fiano di Avellino Pietracalda V. T. '99	🍷🍷🍷	4

TAURASI (AV)

Antonio Caggiano
C.da Sala
83030 Taurasi (AV)
tel. 082774043 - 03389820074
e-mail: info@cantinecaggiano.it

In ten years, Antonio Caggiano has brought his estate from nowhere to become one of Campania's leading lights. This is due not only to the quality of the vast range but, just as important, to its enviable consistency. This becomes immediately evident on tasting the Taurasi Vigna Macchia dei Goti '98. It has a deep ruby colour. There is complexity on the nose, which is full of the sweetness of ripe small berry fruits supported by elegant nuances of balsam, and has beautifully integrated new oak showing signs of development. The palate reveals ripe, velvety tannins, a firm structure and good aromatic length. The Aglianico from the Salae Domini vineyard will also win you over with its intensity, its youthful attack, the raciness that goes right through it, the cleanliness of its wild berry fruit on both nose and palate, and a ripe cherry aftertaste that stays long in the mouth. Taurì '99, from aglianico again, is focused on an attractive strawberry-cherry character, given additional charm by notes of spice and balsam. It also has good fleshy fruit and eucalyptus on the aftertaste. The first release of Fiano d'Avellino Béchar has concentration and elegance, and the new oak is in good balance. Fiagrè '00, from fiano and greco, has invitingly rounded tropical fruits and vanilla, supported by a freshness that makes it delightfully drinkable. Mel '99 is a sweet wine, a sumptuous concentrate of honey and tropical fruits that is sweet without cloying, and has balance and length.

● Taurasi Vigna Macchia dei Goti '98	ΨΨ	5
● Taurì '99	ΨΨ	4
○ Fiagrè '00	ΨΨ	4*
○ Fiano di Avellino Béchar '00	ΨΨ	5
○ Mel '99	ΨΨ	6
● Salae Domini '99	ΨΨ	5
● Taurasi Vigna Macchia dei Goti '95	ΨΨ	6
● Taurasi Vigna Macchia dei Goti '97	ΨΨ	6
○ Mel '98	ΨΨ	6
● Salae Domini '98	ΨΨ	5
● Taurì '98	ΨΨ	4

TEVEROLA (CE)

Cantine Caputo
Via Garibaldi, 64
81030 Teverola (CE)
tel. 0815033955
e-mail: cantine@caputo.it

A welcome return to the Guide for this large winery. It has an output of 1,500,000 bottles each year, which comes partly from the 30 hectares it owns but mainly from grapes bought in. Now that Lorenzo Landi has become consultant oenologist, it has shifted up a gear and its wines have already acquired new depth, cleanliness and freshness, all of which bodes very well for the future. The most engaging wine is currently Aglianico del Sannio '00. This has a dark ruby colour tinged with violet. There are exuberantly fruity aromas of ripe and over-ripe red berries, most notably cherry and redcurrant, then it offers a rounded, full-bodied palate with fruit characteristics that echo the nose. The white Lacryma Christi del Vesuvio '00 is a bright straw yellow. Fresh fruitiness on the nose is lifted by an attractive touch of summer flowers. The palate is fresh and full, and has sweet lemon flavours on the finish. Falanghina del Sannio Frattasi '00 has a chamomile florality and decent balance, while Fiano di Avellino, also from the '00 vintage, has fresh aromas of apples and pears, a delicate florality and an attractive supple freshness.

● Sannio Aglianico '00	ΨΨ	3*
○ Fiano di Avellino '00	Ψ	4
○ Sannio Falanghina Frattasi '00	Ψ	4
○ Vesuvio Lacryma Christi Bianco '00	Ψ	3
○ Asprinio d'Aversa '00		3

TORRECUSO (BN)

FONTANAVECCHIA - ORAZIO RILLO
C.DA FONTANAVECCHIA
82030 TORRECUSO (BN)
TEL. 0824876275
E-MAIL: orarillo@tin.it

There is increasing evidence that the role of the Taburno zone in Campania's varied wine scene is anything but marginal. Among those putting in greatest efforts to secure its renown for high quality is Orazio Rillo, owner of the Fontanvecchia estate. His family has been involved in grape growing for over a century but he has been bottling only since 1990. Most of the grapes come from his own vineyards but some are bought in from selected local growers. The current vintage, the '97, of the estate's flagship wine, Aglianico Vigna Cataratte, had not been released at the time of our tastings, so we will leave its assessment until next year. In the meantime, we can thoroughly recommend Orazio '00, a fabulous new red from 60 per cent aglianico, 35 per cent cabernet sauvignon and merlot, aged in new oak, a wine that signals a further step forward for the estate. It has a good dark ruby colour tinged with violet. The nose is refined and inviting, with aromas of small red berry fruits, ripe plum and balsam-tinged undergrowth. The palate is big, powerful, full of extract and yet well balanced. Facetus '00, from falanghina and coda di volpe, aged briefly in barrique, is also highly promising. It has freshness and personality, with a good array of floral notes and ripe apply fruit. All the other wines showed well, too.

●	Orazio '00	❦❦	6
●	Aglianico del Taburno '00	❦	4
◉	Aglianico del Taburno Rosato '00	❦	3
○	Facetus '00	❦	5
○	Taburno Falanghina '00	❦	3
●	Aglianico del Taburno Vigna Cataratte Ris. '94	❦❦	5
●	Aglianico del Taburno Vigna Cataratte Ris. '95	❦❦	5
●	Aglianico del Taburno '96	❦❦	3
●	Aglianico del Taburno Vigna Cataratte '96	❦❦	4

TUFO (AV)

BENITO FERRARA
FRAZ. S. PAOLO, 14/A
83010 TUFO (AV)
TEL. 0825998194
E-MAIL: info@benitoferrara.it

Gabriella Ferrara's estate is small, with just three hectares at San Paolo, near Tufo, and produces a mere 25,000 bottles each year. Moreover, it only makes one wine, albeit in two versions. It merits its entry in the Guide in any case because the efforts put into maximizing quality on the estate are remarkable and its Greco di Tufo Vigna Cicogna '00 is an outstandingly fine wine. It is a good, bright, straw yellow. The nose is softly intense with a clean, well-defined, ripe apple, peach and apricot fruitiness, which swiftly develops into a more complex florality with subtle undertones of aromatic herbs. The fleshy palate has good balance and structure, a soft fruitiness and finishes long. So, what is the wine's secret? It is partly the "terroir", a clayey limestone soil that lends unusual finesse, and partly the high planting density, with 6,000-7,000 Guyot-trained vines per hectare, which along with the low yields, gives fabulous grape quality. Last but not least, there is the individual touch of the skilled oenologists Attilio Pagli and Paolo Caciorgna from the Matura Group. The standard-label Greco di Tufo '00 has similar characteristics but in a minor key.

○	Greco di Tufo Vigna Cicogna '00	❦	5
○	Greco di Tufo '00	❦	5
○	Greco di Tufo '99	❦❦	4
○	Greco di Tufo Vigna Cicogna '99	❦❦	4

OTHER WINERIES

Marianna
Via Filande, 6
83100 Avellino
Tel. 0825627252 - 0825627224
E-mail: info@vinimarianna.it

Ciriaco Coscia has built up an estate for production of around 300,000 bottles a year of DOC and IGT wines from Irpinia and Sannio. There are 23 hectares of vineyard and other grapes are bought in from reliable growers.

○ Irpinia Coda di Volpe '00	▼	4
● Taurasi '97	▼	6

Vestini - Campagnano
Fraz. S.S. Giovanni e Paolo
Via Barracone, 5
81013 Caiazzo (CE)
Tel. 0823862770 - 03355878791

We are going to hear much more of this name. Masina and Giuseppe Mancini are working with extreme commitment on their five hectares of vineyard to repropagate rare local varieties such as pallagrello and casavecchia. Results so far are surprisingly good.

● Terre del Volturno Pallagrello Rosso '00	▼▼	5*
○ Terre del Volturno Pallagrello Bianco Le Ortole '00	▼	5

Agricola La Caprense
Via Provinciale Marina Grande, 203/a
80037 Capri (NA)
Tel. 0818376835 - 0818376990

This co-operative has been working for years to safeguard Capri's viticultural heritage. The varieties grown are analogous to those on nearby Ischia, with the addition of falanghina, greco and aglianico. Quality levels are encouraging.

○ Capri Bianco Bordo '00	▼	3*

Cooperativa Val Calore
Via Donato Riccio, 30
84049 Castel San Lorenzo (SA)
Tel. 0828944035 - 0828944036
E-mail: esabattino@valcalorescrl.it

A co-operative winery in the province of Salerno that makes still and sparkling wines under the Castel San Lorenzo DOC. The wines are uncomplicated but clean. Best of the bunch are Castel San Lorenzo Rosso and the Moscato Spumante.

● Castel San Lorenzo Rosso '00	▼	3
○ Castel San Lorenzo Moscato Spumante	▼	3

Antica Masseria Venditti
Via Sannitica, 122
82030 Castelvenere (BN)
Tel. 0824940306
E-mail: masseria@venditti.it

Nicola Venditti, an oenologist, produces a carefully honed range of wines from the Solopaca and Sannio DOCs. This year the clean, well-structured Sannio wines were more impressive, especially the reds.

	Wine		Score
●	Sannio Barbera Barbetta Vàndari '00	🍷	4
○	Sannio Falanghina Vàndari '00	🍷	4
●	Sannio Rosso '00	🍷	3

Vinicola del Sannio
Via Sannitica, 171
82030 Castelvenere (BN)
Tel. 0824940207
E-mail: r.pengue@tin.it

Founded in 1997, Vinicola del Sannio handles grapes from its own vineyards and from selected growers in the DOC territories of Guardiolo, Sannio and Solopaca. Its cellars are in Castelvenere, where it produces around 300,000 bottles a year of good quality wine.

	Wine		Score
●	Sannio Aglianico '00	🍷	3

La Guardiense
Loc. Santa Lucia, 104/105
82034 Guardia Sanframondi (BN)
Tel. 0824864034
E-mail: guardiense@laguardiense.com

La Guardiense has set up an ambitious programme to monitor and improve the vineyards of its members and modernize the winery's own cellars. The '97 vintage brought the first results of this work.

	Wine		Score
○	Guardiolo Falanghina '00	🍷	3*
●	Guardiolo Rosso Ris. '97	🍷	4

Colli di Lapio - Clelia Romano
Fraz. Arianiello
83030 Lapio (AV)
Tel. 0825982191 - 0825982184

This is a small, family-run estate specializing in the production of Fiano di Avellino, made entirely from grapes grown on the estate. The '00, full, zesty and with good complexity on both nose and palate, is one of the best of the vintage.

	Wine		Score
○	Fiano di Avellino '00	🍷🍷	4*

D'Antiche Terre - Vega
C.da Lo Piano - S. S. 7 bis
83030 Manocalzati (AV)
Tel. 0825675359 - 0825675358

With a good 40 hectares of vineyard, Vega is one of the largest estates in Irpinia. It was founded in 1993 and produces around 300,000 bottles a year of good quality wine. The Taurasi deserves particular attention.

	Wine		Score
●	Taurasi '97	🍷	5

Cantine Monte Pugliano
C.da San Vito
84090 Montecorvino Pugliano (SA)
Tel. 3283412515 - 3476970167
E-mail: cesare.cavallo@tiscalinet.it

This small estate, based in the province of Salerno, has been set up recently as a three-way partnership. There are five hectares of vine, all cultivated organically. The most interesting of the wines is the red from aglianico, barbera and merlot.

	Wine		Score
●	Castellacio '00	🍷	5

Ettore Sammarco
Via Civita, 9
84010 Ravello (SA)
tel. 089872774
e-mail: esamarco@amalficoast.it

Ettore Sammarco produces a series of good wines in the Ravello subzone of the Costiera Amalfitana. The meaty, full, rich white Selva delle Monache with its citrus hints is particularly noteworthy.

○ Costa d'Amalfi Ravello Bianco Selva delle Monache '00	4
● Costa d'Amalfi Ravello Rosso Selva delle Monache Ris. '98	4

Francesco Rotolo
Via San Cesario, 18
84070 Rutino (SA)
tel. 0974830050

Rotolo is a producer from the Cilento who makes three wines under the Paestum IGT. The most interesting is the Fiano Valentina, which has rich, clean aromas, good structure and intense fruit.

○ Fiano Valentina '00	3

Di Meo
C.da Coccovoni, 1
83050 Salza Irpina (AV)
tel. 0825981419
e-mail: info@dimeo.it

Roberto Di Meo, an oenologist, and his sister Erminia have dedicated themselves heart and soul to running their 250-hectare estate, of which 30 hectares are vineyard. There is a good range of wines, mainly those typical of the province of Avellino.

○ Fiano di Avellino Colle dei Cerri '00	4
○ Sannio Falanghina '00	3
● Taurasi '97	5

De Falco Vini
Via Figliola
80040 San Sebastiano al Vesuvio (NA)
tel. 0817713755
e-mail: defalcovini@tin.it

Gabriele De Falco selects grapes and wines from various parts of the region to produce a vast range of decent quality and very good value. As well as wines from Vesuvius, the province of Benevento and the Sorrento peninsula, there is a good DOC Greco and a good DOC Fiano.

○ Fiano di Avellino '00	4*
○ Greco di Tufo '00	4

Di Marzo
Via Gaetano Di Marzo, 17
83010 Tufo (AV)
tel. 0825998022

The Di Marzo family own 30 hectares of vineyard in the Tufo zone, planted to greco and aglianico. They produce 200,000 bottles a year and make two wines, both of good quality.

○ Greco di Tufo '00	3
● Irpinia Rosso '99	1*

Villa San Michele
Via Appia km. 198
81050 Vitulazio (CE)
tel. 081666773 - 0823963775
e-mail: villasanmichelesrl@libero.it

This attractive holding with 33 hectares of vineyard is owned by the Galeno family. They grow falanghina, aglianico, greco and piedirosso, and produce elegant sparkling wines as well as a well-honed range of still wines.

○ Terre del Volturno Greco '00	3
○ Don Carlos Brut M. Cl.	4

BASILICATA

At last, a wine from Basilicata gains Three Glasses. It is the extraordinary Aglianico del Vulture Rotondo from Paternoster, a marvellous red that marries to perfection traditional values with modern winemaking know-how. This is of course a fabulous result for the estate but also a terrific result for the region as a whole, which has made tremendous progress over the past five years in the quality of its wines. This is confirmed also by the goodly number of Three Glass finalists that Basilicata fielded this year. We have no doubt that Paternoster's is only the first of a long series of top awards that the region can expect. The number of premium-quality producers in Basilicata is constantly growing too, a fact that we would have liked to underline by increasing the number of entries for the region. Unfortunately, it just wasn't possible this year but ought to be next time. Vulture is far and away the leading zone, indeed to all intents and purposes the only zone. The long-standing estates here are working assiduously to maximize the territory's potential and it is now attracting new investors from other parts of Italy. Vulture's aglianico-based reds have power, elegance, openness and depth: we offer a good selection in the following pages, although this year Martino and Di Palma had to drop out. Their high quality wines will assuredly feature next year, as will those of the large new estate, Terre degli Svevi, situated in Venosa. Part of Gruppo Italiano Vini, it released its first offerings this year. Things are much quieter in the province of Matera but even there, there is no staying the march of quality. This year, we list just one estate from the province even though Dragone, from Matera itself, and Pisani from Viggiano, who had not released their latest wines at the time of our tastings, deserve serious attention.

BARILE (PZ)

Tenuta Le Querce
Fraz. Le Querce
Via Appia, 123
85100 Barile (PZ)
tel. 0971470709
e-mail: tenutalequerce@tin.it

The Pietrafesa family bought this attractive 85-hectare holding in 1997 and threw themselves headlong into Aglianico del Vulture production. There are 60 hectares of vineyard, a part of which has been recently replanted. All is excellently sited in Barile itself, on the slopes of the Vulture massif. Current production is around 300,000 bottles a year but is due to increase. Both viticulture and winemaking are in the hands of Leonardo Valenti, who makes three versions of Aglianico del Vulture for the estate. We liked Rosso di Costanza '99 best of the trio. It has a good, dark, concentrated ruby colour. The nose is full of red and black cherry, tobacco and vanilla, then the palate is deep, fleshy and rich in soft tannins. Balanced and long overall, it falls from grace only for seeming slightly more developed than one would expect for its age. The Federico II has a similar profile on the nose and it, too, has considerable depth and softness, along with a firm backbone. Elegant and attractively astringent, it is a shade less concentrated than the Costanza. Viola '99 is different from its two stablemates in that it does not age in new oak. It is true to its name, having a clear violet rim to its dark ruby hue. The nose was still a bit reticent when we were tasting but the palate is fresh, modern and attractively full, the typical strengths of Aglianico produced in these parts.

BARILE (PZ)

Consorzio Viticoltori
Associati del Vulture
S. S. 93
85022 Barile (PZ)
tel. 0972770386
e-mail: covir@tiscalinet.it

Once again, the Viticoltori Associati di Barile collected enviably high scores in the Guide, confirming its position as one of the best and most reliable wineries in Vulture. Set up in 1977, this consortium brings together and bottles the wines of six co-operatives in the area, producing several versions of Aglianico and two sparkling wines, for an annual production of 200,000 bottles. This year its oenologist, Sergio Paternoster, has produced an Aglianico del Vulture Carpe Diem, the '99, of rare elegance and concentration. It has a good deep, dense ruby, almost black colour. The soft, elegant nose has aromas of ripe plum and mulberry, with hints of balsam and delicate wafts of vanilla and oak toast. The palate is warm, concentrated, austere and full of stuffing, backed by fine-grained tannins. It is a wine of great balance with good freshness and considerable ageing potential. The '98 Vetusto showed very well, as usual, and is another Aglianico of class. The appearance is dense and dark, introducing a deep, intense nose dominated by black berry fruit and tobacco. The palate has good extract and is full, deep and tannic, with just a hint of bitterness on the finish. This is a wine to recommend without fear or favour. The straight Aglianico del Vulture '99 is less impressive but is still very good and is excellent value for money. A special word should go to the consortium's two sparkling wines, an attractively sweet Moscato, full of aroma, and the sweet, red Ellenico, made from aglianico and beautifully fresh and supple.

- Aglianico del Vulture Federico II '99 — 5
- Aglianico del Vulture Rosso di Costanza '99 — 6
- Aglianico del Vulture Il Viola '99 — 4
- Aglianico del Vulture Rosso di Costanza '98 — 6
- Aglianico del Vulture Federico II '98 — 5
- Aglianico del Vulture Il Viola '98 — 4

- Aglianico del Vulture Carpe Diem '99 — 4*
- Aglianico del Vulture Vetusto '98 — 5
- Aglianico del Vulture '99 — 2*
- Aglianico Spumante Ellenico — 3
- ○ Moscato Spumante — 2*
- Aglianico del Vulture Vetusto '97 — 4
- Aglianico del Vulture Carpe Diem '97 — 4

BARILE (PZ)

Paternoster
Via Nazionale, 23
85022 Barile (PZ)
tel. 0972770224
e-mail: paternoster.vini@tiscalinet.it

For winelovers, Paternoster, founded in 1925, is synonymous with Aglianico del Vulture. The estate has always produced wines to high standards but for some years now Vito Paternoster has dedicated his efforts to improving quality. The results of this are now being seen. Alongside the estate's classics, such as Aglianico del Vulture Don Anselmo and the fine Aglianico del Vulture Synthesi, Vito and consultant Leonardo Palumbo have come out this year with an Aglianico del Vulture of spectacular richness and depth. It is a cru, from the wonderfully aspected Rotondo vineyard, situated on the edge of Barile. The wine is possibly the region's best ever. It is dark ruby, almost black, and still tinged with violet on the rim. It has intense aromas of black berry fruit interwoven with balsam and spice. But it is on the palate that it shows its beefy character. The imposing structure has not yet been calmed by ageing and the elegance and stylistic purity are almost without equal. The overwhelming richness of its tannins is not intrusive, thanks to good balance and a full body. These smooth, elegant tannins will ensure an ageing curve of well over ten years. The wine's Three Glasses were very well merited. Don Anselmo '97 is almost as captivating and as deep, powerful, elegant, refined and balanced on the nose as it is on the palate, which has terrific length. Even the basic Aglianico, Synthesi, is a concentrated wine of good body with rich of fruit. Barigliòtt, a lightly sparkling red from aglianico is inviting, as are Fiano Bianco di Corte '99 and the aromatic Moscato Clivus '00.

RIONERO IN VULTURE (PZ)

Basilisco
Via Umberto I, 129
85028 Rionero in Vulture (PZ)
tel. 0972720032 - 03392700296
e-mail: basilisco@interfrre.it

Michele Cutolo is a doctor by profession but he has always been passionate about wine – great, time-defying red wine, that is – exactly the sort, in fact, that his homeland can produce. So in 1992, he decided to turn his great love into a second occupation and planted seven and a half hectares of vines on his family's land in Rionero, all aglianico. He entrusted the winemaking to the Piedmontese oenologist Rossano Abbona, a choice in keeping with Aglianico del Vulture's reputation as the "Barolo of the South". For viticultural matters, he took on Giuseppe Avigliano as consultant vineyard manager, a specialist with a deep knowledge of the aglianico grape. Thus emerged the first vintages of Aglianico del Vulture Basilisco and it immediately took its place up with Vulture's best. It is a concentrated, structured, soft wine, aged in new oak and demonstrably on the modern side of Aglianico. The immediate success of the '97 was repeated with the '98 but the '99 is even better, good enough to gain the estate a full profile in this Guide. It is a deep, dark ruby with a violet rim. There are intense, but beautifully elegant and balanced, aromas of ripe, red berry fruits, tobacco and oak toast. The mouthfilling palate is also exuberantly fruity, as well as deep, soft and full of ripe tannins. It is a wine that can stand on equal terms with the region's best and which needs to shed just a little excess roundness, due perhaps to a touch of residual sugar, to soar into the Three Glass category.

● Aglianico del Vulture Rotondo '98	🍷🍷🍷	5*
● Aglianico del Vulture Ris. Don Anselmo '97	🍷🍷	5
● Barigliòtt '00	🍷	3
○ Moscato della Basilicata Clivus '00	🍷	3
● Aglianico del Vulture Synthesi '99	🍷	4
○ Bianco di Corte '99	🍷	4
● Aglianico del Vulture Don Anselmo Ris. '95	🍷🍷	5
● Aglianico del Vulture Rotondo '97	🍷🍷	4
● Aglianico del Vulture '98	🍷🍷	4

● Aglianico del Vulture Basilisco '99	🍷🍷	5

RIONERO IN VULTURE (PZ)

D'ANGELO
VIA PROVINCIALE, 8
85028 RIONERO IN VULTURE (PZ)
TEL. 0972721517

Donato and Lucio D'Angelo represent Basilicata winemaking traditions at their best. Their Aglianicos form the denomination's benchmark, especially for traditionalists who see the firm, almost harsh, structure and the sober styling of these wines – attributes that go hand in hand with extraordinary longevity – as the true expression of Aglianico del Vulture. The '98 Canneto is again the estate's top wine. Made exclusively from aglianico, it has a deep, dark ruby colour. The spice and vanilla on the nose do not mask the ripeness and good definition of the small berry fruit aromas. The palate is structured, rich in fine-grained tannins and develops evenly and consistently throughout the mouth. Aglianico del Vulture Vigna Caselle Riserva '97 is another superb wine that eloquently expresses the Vulture "terroir". It is an intense, deep ruby and there are complex, clean aromas of ripe cherry, red berry and wild berry fruit. The palate reveals a firm, smooth tannic structure that integrates well with the wine's rich fruitiness and gives considerable length. The standard-label Aglianico del Vulture '98 – last year we tasted the '97, not the '98 – is ruby, tending to garnet on the rim. Full on the nose, it has aromas of liquorice and tar that usher in a powerful palate, just very slightly marred by signs of ageing. Serra delle Querce '98 is a spot-on blend of aglianico with 20 per cent merlot, barrique-aged, that has considerable richness on both nose and palate. The estate's offerings are brought to a close by the fragrant, fruity white Vigna dei Pini '00, from a blend of chardonnay, incrocio Manzoni 6.0.13 and pinot bianco.

● Canneto '98		5
● Aglianico del Vulture Ris. Vigna Caselle '97		5
● Serra delle Querce '98		6
○ Vigna dei Pini '00		3
● Aglianico del Vulture '98		4
● Aglianico del Vulture Vigna Caselle Ris. '95		5
● Canneto '97		5
● Aglianico del Vulture '97		3

RIONERO IN VULTURE (PZ)

AGRICOLA EUBEA - FAM. SASSO
VIA ROMA, 209
85028 RIONERO IN VULTURE (PZ)
TEL. 0972723574

If this area with its ancient winemaking traditions has a long history, so does the Sasso family, who have been producing Aglianico del Vulture for almost 80 years. But now, at Eubea, their new property at Rionero run by Eugenia Sasso, they join the Guide with a really excellent wine, one that puts them firmly among the region's top up-and-coming estates. There are six hectares of vineyard and, for now, just the one wine. We tasted two vintages. The one that really struck us was the '99. It has everything a red needs to be considered great: a deep, dark ruby colour; an open, inviting nose, still youthful, with aromas of wild berry fruit, blackberry, mulberry and ripe cherry, highlighted by nuances of oak and cinchona; a dense palate that opens gradually to reveal plentiful fruit; a huge attack of tannin, so typical of Aglianico, yet also tremendous finesse that balances the wine's fullness and fleshiness; and many years' ageing potential. Aglianico del Vulture Il Covo dei Briganti '98 is immediate, sound and well made, with good concentration, but its new oak is a little too marked. Their new dried-grape white "passito" Seduzione is still at the experimental stage. We'll be reviewing it next year.

● Aglianico del Vulture Il Covo dei Briganti '99		6
● Aglianico del Vulture Il Covo dei Briganti '98		4

RIONERO IN VULTURE (PZ)

Cantine del Notaio
Via Roma, 159
85028 Rionero in Vulture (PZ)
Tel. 0972717111 - 03356842483
E-mail: gerardo.giura@tin.it

Gerardo Giuratrabocchetti's story is emblematic of the new direction in Basilicata winemaking. As the estate's name suggests, Gerardo, who has a degree in agriculture, inherited the vineyards from his father, a notary. Gerardo's enthusiasm for wine grew to the extent that he decided to become a producer and set himself the mission of restoring Aglianico del Vulture back to its ancient glories. To achieve that goal, he first set about increasing vineyard density and reducing yields. A meeting with Professor Luigi Moio, lecturer in oenology at the University of Naples, was the pivotal moment for Gerardo. He took Moio on as consultant and started his new life as producer in earnest. The estate's evocative cellars were once owned by Franciscan monks and comprise a group of ten underground grottoes. There are seven and a half hectares of vineyard, of which two and a half are in the municipality of Maschito and represent the estate's "grand cru". Two wines are made, both DOC Aglianico, La Firma and Il Repertorio. The '99 vintage of the latter is full and rich, with deep colour and ripe tannins. There are sophisticated notes of tobacco and chocolate on the nose and good length of fruit on the palate. La Firma '99, produced from the vines at Maschito, takes us up a couple of steps. It is a dark, dense, opaque ruby. The nose is full and complex, with ripe red berry fruit sweetness enhanced by elegant tones of vanilla, tobacco and spices. The palate is elegant and complex, with a wealth of structure and concentration, not to mention a significant but not dominant presence of new oak.

- Aglianico del Vulture La Firma '99   🍷🍷   6
- Aglianico del Vulture Il Repertorio '99   🍷🍷   5

VENOSA (PZ)

Cantina Riforma Fondiaria di Venosa
C.da Vignali
85029 Venosa (PZ)
Tel. 097236702

Basilicata can look Alto Adige squarely in the eye given that, from the results of our tastings, practically all the co-operatives are producing wines that equal, if not outperform, many private estates. This is certainly the case with the Cantina della Riforma Fondiaria of Venosa, a modern, efficient undertaking of around 480 members, which handles their more than 700 hectares of vineyard in the Vulture DOC zone and produces something like 240,000 bottles a year. A good deal of the credit for the wines goes to technicians Rocco Manieri and Oronzo Alò, who respectively co-ordinate the vineyard work and cellar activities. On retasting the leading wine, Aglianico del Vulture Carato Venusio '97, we found it still one of the most interesting in the area. It gives us great expectations of future vintages. Aglianico del Vulture Terre di Orazio '99 is full of sweet notes of ripe red berry fruit on the nose and has a deep, full, elegant palate, rich is soft tannins, that finishes long with notes of spice, printer's ink and morello cherry. The red Vignali '00, from aglianico, is a marvel of fresh, attractive drinkability. You'll be swept away by the intense raspberry and redcurrant on both nose and palate, where there is also depth, finesse and soft, easy tannins. The intense, well-typed, balanced Aglianico del Vulture Vignali '99 is good, as is the white Vignali '00, from greco, chardonnay and malvasia bianca. In general, this winery is moving forward rapidly and combines quality with good prices.

- Basilicata Rosso Vignali '00   🍷🍷   2*
- Aglianico del Vulture Terre di Orazio '99   🍷🍷   3*
- ○ Basilicata Bianco Vignali '00   🍷   1*
- Aglianico del Vulture Vignali '99   🍷   2*
- Aglianico del Vulture Carato Venusio '97   🍷🍷   4
- Aglianico del Vulture Terre di Orazio '98   🍷🍷   3

OTHER WINERIES

BASILIUM
C.DA PIPOLI
85011 ACERENZA (PZ)
TEL. 0971741449
E-MAIL: basilium@freenet.com

This is one of the most reliable co-operatives in the region. It vinifies grapes from its members' 350 hectares in the Vulture zone. The '98 vintage of the Aglianico Valle del Trono selection is characterful. All the other wines are well-typed, attractive and easy drinking.

○ Basilicata Pipoli Chiaro '00	🍷	3
● Aglianico del Vulture Valle del Trono '98	🍷	6
● Aglianico del Vulture Pipoli '99	🍷	3

TENUTA DEL PORTALE
LOC. LE QUERCE
85022 BARILE (PZ)
TEL. 0972724691

Filena Ruppi, assisted by oenologist Enzo Michelet, produces around 100,000 bottles of Aglianico del Vulture, in three styles. Our preference is for the standard version, with its elegant aromas, good structure and complexity.

● Aglianico del Vulture '98	🍷🍷	4

F.LLI NAPOLITANO
VIA MATTEOTTI, 40
85028 RIONERO IN VULTURE (PZ)
TEL. 0972721040
E-MAIL: giulio.napolitano1@tin.it

F.lli Napolitano, founded in 1930, is one of the traditional Basilicata estates now showing major signs of renewed vigour. There are around 100,000 bottles a year, all from bought-in grapes.

● Aglianico del Vulture '98	🍷🍷	4
● Aglianico del Vulture Elea '98	🍷🍷	5

PROGETTO DIVINO
VIA NAZIONALE, 76
75100 MATERA
TEL. 0835262851 - 0835259549
E-MAIL: progettodivino@hsh.it

Sante Lomurno and his team produce an excellent red, San Biagio, from aglianico and merlot, in the estate's evocative ancient cellars. The '99 is a carefully honed, modern-style wine with elegance and intensity on nose and palate.

● San Biagio '99	🍷🍷	5
● San Biagio '97	🍷🍷	4
● San Biagio '98	🍷🍷	4

PUGLIA

This year, we can again report on significant increase in the overall quality of Puglia's output. The region, with its wealth of fine "terroirs" and indigenous varieties, is undeniably fascinating, an allure that hasn't escaped astute producers from numerous other regions, who have arrived in search of vineyard land to buy. There is Antinori, for example, Zonin, Feudi di San Gregorio and many others, who have either just bought or are about to do so. Naturally, it is not only good prices or the chance of acquiring 100 to 200 hectares in a single plot – a possibility that exists only here and in Sicily - that so appeals. Despite the region's fine wines that already have a solid reputation, the new wines that are making waves and well-established areas like the Salento, Puglia is still in many ways wide open to development. And this goes both for its terroirs and its vine varieties. For example, the northern part of the region, comprising the province of Foggia and its DOCs, is still no more than good on paper. We are still waiting for the vineyard improvements and cellar modernization that will bring premium-quality production. In the meantime, the DOCs of the province of Bari are beginning to make their mark. Castel del Monte is in the lead but Locorotondo and Gravina are also enjoying deserved success in the marketplace, thanks mainly to their unbeatable value for money, and Gioia del Colle is rapidly becoming an alternative to Manduria and Sava as the production hub of Primitivo. This is the wine that has recently had phenomenal success, on both sides of the Atlantic, following a spate of publicity in America hailing it as the parent of Zinfandel. Finally, we are seeing the consolidation of the Salento's high reputation, which is based primarily on the negroamaro variety, and the red and rosé wines made from it. The only thing holding back future development is the excessive number of almost identical red wine DOCs in the area, which reduces the impact of the region's wines on the market. If we could change things, we'd like to see all these denominations merged into just two or three, conceived specifically for high quality production - or maybe into just one, at DOCG level. This could make a tremendous difference in commercial terms. But these are only minor peccadilloes. As we have already said, quality is rising continuously in every one of the region's wine zones. Moreover, every zone is also seeing increased involvement from savvy youngsters with an intelligent approach and very clear, quality-driven ideas. All these currents come together in this year's two prize-winning wines, the excellent Nero from Conti Zecca of Leverano, up in the stratosphere for the second year running, and Albano Carrisi's terrific Platone, another innovative Salento red of stunning style. But it should not be forgotten that there are many others just a heartbeat away from similar stardom. The future looks rosy for wine production in Puglia.

ALEZIO (LE)

Rosa del Golfo
Via Garibaldi, 56
73011 Alezio (LE)
tel. 0331993198
e-mail: calo@rosadelgolfo.com

As winelovers know well, Rosa del Golfo is probably one of the four or five best rosés in Italy. This is nothing new. The wine has been at or near the top of the tree for at least 15 years now. The credit goes to its creator, Mino Calò, but also to his son Damiano who is now enthusiastically following in his footsteps assisted, as ever, by Angelo Solci, the estate's oenologist. Rosa del Golfo, with annual production running at 100,000 bottles, is made from negroamaro from the estate's 40 hectares or so of vineyard, part owned, part leased. The '00 has a bright, deep pink colour that never wavers into orange. The nose is clean, intense and fruity, with wild strawberry, bilberry, raspberry and bramble apparent. The attractive palate is fresh, zesty, structured and fruity, with a delicate touch of tannin in the background and good length. Damiano Calò also submitted Quarantale for tasting, a classy red from negroamaro with a little primitivo and aglianico he produces only in better vintages. The '97 is dark in hue, with a garnet rim. The nose is intense and rich, with aromas of plum and morello cherry jam that are underpinned by hints of smouldering logs, strawberry tree and Mediterranean scrub. The dense, structured, attractively warm palate has good backbone and a subtle but well-balanced astringency. A retasting of Portulano '97, another Negroamaro, confirmed its class, and the good texture and fruity richness we found last year. The red Scaliere '00, from negroamaro with 20 per cent aglianico, and the white verdeca-based Bolina '00, are both pleasant and well made.

ANDRIA (BA)

Rivera
C.da Rivera
S. S. 98, km 19.800
70031 Andria (BA)
tel. 0883569501 - 0883569510
e-mail: info@rivera.it

If we had to choose one estate to represent each region's winemaking, Rivera could be the embodiment of Puglia. The Corato family has entrusted the winemaking to the able Leonardo Palumbo, whose forte is shaping modern-style wines that still reflect their origin. As a result, the uva di troia and montepulciano Il Falcone '98 came within a hair of Three Glasses. It is a deep, opaque ruby. The red berry fruit jam nose is delicately spicy, then the palate is complex and elegant, with an almost super-ripe character and flavours of Mediterranean scrub. Tightly knit, rounded tannins take you through to a firm, long finish. Its only fall from grace is that it fades a touch on the mid palate. Cappellaccio, from aglianico, is also excellent. It is deep ruby tinged with violet, the nose is sweet, pervasive and balsamic, and the aromas of red berry fruits are moderately ripe. Good alcoholic structure comes through on the palate, which is initially soft and rich, and finishes long. The Primitivo Triusco '98 has good concentration of colour and a delightfully spicy nose, with herbaceous notes. The fleshy, tannic palate offers flavours of red berries supported by good alcoholic weight. The final red of the series is simpler, mid-weight Rupicolo. In the same price range are the Rosé, as fresh and vibrantly fruity as ever, and the white Dama di Svevia, from indigenous grapes, which has surprising intensity of flowers and fruit on the nose. The same notes give softness and density to the palate. Chardonnay Preludio n.1 is more complex and structured, with clean aromas of white peach and apple.

⊙ Salento Rosato Rosa del Golfo '00	♟♟	3*
● Salento Rosso Quarantale '97	♟♟	5
○ Salento Bianco Bolina '00	♟	3
● Salento Rosso Scaliere '00	♟	2*
⊙ Salento Rosato Rosa del Golfo '97	♟♟	3
● Salento Rosso Portulano '97	♟♟	3
⊙ Salento Rosato Rosa del Golfo '98	♟♟	3
⊙ Salento Rosato Rosa del Golfo '99	♟♟	4

● Castel del Monte Rosso Il Falcone Ris. '98	♟♟	4
○ Castel del Monte Chardonnay Preludio N° 1 '00	♟♟	3*
● Castel del Monte Aglianico Cappellaccio Ris. '98	♟♟	4*
● Primitivo Triusco '98	♟♟	3*
○ Castel del Monte Bianco Dama di Svevia '00	♟	2*
⊙ Castel del Monte Rosé di Rivera '00	♟	2*
○ Castel del Monte Sauvignon Terre al Monte '00	♟	3*
● Castel del Monte Rosso Rupicolo di Rivera '99	♟	3*
○ Moscato di Trani Piani di Tufara '99	♟	3*
● Castel del Monte Aglianico Cappellaccio Ris. '97	♟♟	4
● Castel del Monte Rosso Il Falcone Ris. '97	♟♟	4
○ Moscato di Trani Piani di Tufara '98	♟♟	3

AVETRANA (TA)

Sinfarosa
S. S. 174, km 3
74020 Avetrana (TA)
tel. 0999735235
e-mail:
accademia@accademiadeiracemi.it

Sinfarosa's Mimma and Salvatore Mero with Arcangelo My, other partners and the assistance of oenologist Fabrizio Perrucci, have become leading players on the Puglian wine scene. Ten hectares of alberello-trained vineyard produce the primitivo grapes used for the estate's two wines, the standard Primitivo, immediate, clean, modern and remarkably inexpensive, and the selection called Zinfandel. After the frosts that hit production in '99, the team announced the '00 vintage as being one of the best of recent years. Their – and our – expectations have not been disappointed. The Zinfandel almost reached our Three Glass category. It is a deep ruby tinged with dark violet. Spicy and balsamic notes on the nose overlay a wild bramble fruitiness. The firm, highly structured yet soft palate has well-judged levels of tannin and well-extracted fruit nicely integrated into the oak, which only briefly threatens to dominate. The finish is complex and fairly long. The Primitivo also has a dark ruby hue and an equally fine nose with sharply defined red berry fruits mingling with tobacco and vanilla. First impact on the palate is full and pervasive, the mid palate is firm, with a fleshy richness and good balance, and the finish is long, with oak well integrated into the fruit, and liquorice on the aftertaste.

BRINDISI

Tenute Rubino
Via Medaglie d'Oro, 15/a
72100 Brindisi
tel. 0831571955 - 0831502912
e-mail: info@tenuterubino.it

Luigi Rubino made his debut in quality wine only last year. And 12 months later, he has made significant progress. The vines, 160 hectares of them, are still young but the cellar is as modern as you could wish. The arrival of Riccardo Cotarella as consultant has reduced the range of wines from seven to four, giving each more weight and depth of character. This becomes evident in the '00 Brindisi Rosso Gallico, from negroamaro, montepulciano and malvasia nera. The nose has opulent fruit and elegant toasty, cocoa powder and coffee notes that interweave with fresh scents of balsam and vanilla. They return on the palate, whose richness is held in check by a firm tannic frame and acidity that accentuates the persistence without compromising its elegance. Primitivo del Salento Visellio '00 has the variety's typical mulberry and ripe plum characteristics. It is full-bodied, without being heavy, and shows fine-grained tannins. There is also an intriguing spiciness, predominantly of white pepper, which emerges on both nose and palate. Next comes the red Marmorelle, from negroamaro with 15 per cent malvasia nera. This is spectacular, with freshness and upfront soft fruitiness as well as an underlying elegant complexity. New oak brings balance to the nose and the palate finishes long with wild berry fruits jam and new oak. Note the price too. At just over € 5.00 in Italian wine shops, the value is just amazing. The final wine is Marmorelle Bianco '00, from chardonnay and malvasia. It has an attractive, ripe appley fruitiness with tropical fruit overtones, and an incisive finish.

● Primitivo di Manduria Zinfandel '00	♟♟	4*
● Primitivo di Manduria '00	♟♟	3*
● Primitivo di Manduria Zinfandel '98	♟♟♟	4
● Primitivo di Manduria '98	♟♟	4
● Primitivo di Manduria Zinfandel '99	♟♟	4
● Primitivo di Manduria '99	♟	4

● Brindisi Rosso Gallico '00	♟♟	5*
● Salento Primitivo Visellio '00	♟♟	4*
● Salento Rosso Marmorelle '00	♟♟	3*
○ Salento Bianco Marmorelle '00	♟	3*
● Salento Rosso Gallico '99	♟	3

CAMPI SALENTINA (LE)

CALATRASI PUGLIA
VIA CELLINO SAN MARCO, KM 1,5
73012 CAMPI SALENTINA (LE)
TEL. 0918576767

L'Accademia del Sole is a brand name belonging to Sicily's Calatrasi, owned by the Miccichè family. They used it for the wines from the best vineyards that the estate owns or leases in Sicily, Puglia and Tunisia. In Puglia, Calatrasi controls 300 hectares in Salento, which coalesce into two lines. D'Istinto comprises simpler wines, aimed mainly at export markets, and Allora is reserved for quality selections. The Puglian cellars are based at Campi Salentina and are overseen, as is customary with Calatrasi, by an Australian winemaker. This is Lisa Gilbee, who gained considerable experience working on large estates in her homeland. Two wines stood out at our tastings, an Aglianico and a Primitivo. The Aglianico Allora '00 is a good, deep, dark ruby. The nose is sweet and inviting, with red and black berry fruit aromas that initially emerge distinctly then meld elegantly with the new oak spiciness. The wine is clean and modern on the soft, fleshy palate, which echoes the fruit of the nose with its ripe cherry and bramble flavours, and has a firm but velvety tannic presence on the finish with an aftertaste of cocoa powder and roast coffee beans. The Primitivo Allora '00 also boasts a rich spectrum of colour and aroma, with ripe plum and freshly ground black pepper most obvious. The well-rounded palate has great ripeness of fruit yet avoids any flabbiness, indeed it is pleasingly fresh overall and has a neat touch of astringency. It finishes, like its companion, with undertones of ripe fruit and smokiness – a profile that will doubtless make it a bestseller on the international market.

● Allora Aglianico '00	♙♙	4*
● Allora Primitivo '00	♙♙	4*

CELLINO SAN MARCO (BR)

TENUTE ALBANO CARRISI
C.DA BOSCO, 13
72020 CELLINO SAN MARCO (BR)
TEL. 0831619211 - 0831618777
E-MAIL: albano@tin.it

It's probably not widely known that Albano Carrisi, a well known personality in Italian music, has been working all out – other engagements permitting – on his farm and wine production since the early 1970s. Recently, he upgraded the set-up at his estate, situated at Cellino San Marco in the heart of the Salento peninsula, and is now going full speed ahead for ultimate quality. There are 20 hectares of vineyard planted with the traditional negroamaro and malvasia nera varieties, and also chardonnay, sauvignon blanc and cabernet sauvignon, which here give full, richly fruited wines, typical of hot climates. Indeed, Albano's wines are a successful mix of tradition and innovation. They are exemplified by Platone '98, a 50-50 blend of negroamaro and cabernet matured in new oak. The vintage has given the wine that additional weight and depth it needed to really hit the mark, so much so that it has joined the Three Glass club. An elegant wine, it has enticing aromas of black berry fruits and ripe plum, given complexity by nuances of herbaceousness and sweet spices. The palate is warm, mouthfilling, powerful and well-fruited, and finishes long with a fabulous aftertaste of cocoa powder, mint and eucalyptus. The rest of the range, from the rosé Mediterraneo, to the Negroamaro Don Carmelo, not forgetting the whites from the Felicità line, are all of excellent quality and sold at very fair prices. We'd like to ask Albano: if Felicità is, as he says, simply "a glass of wine", how does it feel to have Three Glasses?

● Platone '98	♙♙♙	6
⊙ Salento Rosato Mediterraneo '00	♙♙	3*
● Salento Rosso Don Carmelo '97	♙♙	2*
○ Salento Bianco Felicità '00	♙	3
○ Salento Bianco Villa Carrisi '00	♙	3
○ Salento Chardonnay Don Carmelo '00	♙	2*
● Salento Rosso Villa Carrisi '99	♙	3
● Salento Rosso Nostalgia '96	♙♙	3
● Salice Salentino Albano Carrisi '96	♙♙	2
● Salento Rosso Nostalgia '97	♙♙	3
● Platone '97	♙♙	6

CELLINO SAN MARCO (BR)

Marco Maci
Via San Marco, 61
72020 Cellino San Marco (BR)
Tel. 0831617689 - 0831617120
E-mail: marcomaci@libero.it

To review the full range of wines that Marco Maci produces would take a lot more than one column of this Guide. He isn't short on quantity either, producing around 1,000,000 bottles on his La Mea estate at Cellino San Marco near Brindisi, where he owns a good 120 hectares of vineyard. The core is planted to negroamaro, malvasia nera and primitivo, though there is also some chardonnay and sauvignon blanc. Taking things in perspective, maybe the range should be a more compact but it is what it is. However, apart from this minor gripe, one can only admire the excellent quality of most bottles. The best showing this year came from the red negroamaro and cabernet Salento Vita '98. The colour is a deep, dark ruby and the nose has an exuberant, super-ripe red and black berry fruitiness, predominantly bramble, with balsamic and toasty notes of considerable finesse. The palate has concentration, power and robust alcohol but also wonderful fruit and balance. The '98 Bella Mojgan, from negroamaro and malvasia nera, has its usual almost opaque ruby hue and an opulent, sweet, super-clean, complex nose with black berry fruitiness underscored with delicate and discreet toasty, vanilla notes. The evenly structured, fleshy and softly concentrated palate fully expresses the rich character of the wine's terroir and the careful touch in its vinification. Equally successful are the deep, dense Negroamaro Sire '98 and the merlot-negroamaro blend, Dragonero '98. The Rosato Sarì '00, Sauvignon Villa di Grazia '00 and Squinzano Zephir '98 are also good. The rest of the range is less exciting.

●	Bella Mojgan '98	🍷🍷	6
●	Dragonero '98	🍷🍷	6
●	Sire '98	🍷🍷	6
●	Vita '98	🍷🍷	6
○	Arabesco Chardonnay '00	🍷	4
⊙	Sarì '00	🍷	4
○	Villa di Grazia '00	🍷	4
●	Squinzano Rosso Zephir '98	🍷	5
●	Bella Mojgan '97	🍷🍷	6
●	Dragonero '97	🍷🍷	5
●	Vita '97	🍷🍷	6
●	Primitivo del Salento Fra Diavolo '99	🍷🍷	5

CORATO (BA)

Santa Lucia
Strada Comunale San Vittore, 1
70033 Corato (BA)
Tel. 0808721168 - 0817642888
E-mail: info@vinisantalucia.com

Father and son, Giuseppe and Roberto Perrone Capano are the owners of an ancient estate that the family has owned since the early 17th century. It lies in the Murge area on the slopes of Castel del Monte, which has always yielded fine quality grapes. The estate currently has 15 hectares of vineyard, all around Corato, growing mainly local varieties such as uva di troia, aleatico, bombino nero and montepulciano for the reds, and fiano for the whites. There is also a little malbec, which has been in the area for centuries, and chardonnay. Recently, the cellar has been completely revamped and much investment has gone into the vineyards. The Castel del Monte Rosso Riserva '98 demonstrates the Perrone Capano production philosophy, put into effect by oenologist Luigi Cantatore, and bears elegant witness to the estate's surging quality. It is a dark ruby, violet-tinged at the rim. The nose is sweet and complex, with wild berry fruits topped by delicate notes of spice and printer's ink. The palate is full and warm, not very big but balanced and elegant, finishing on a stylish note of ripe cherry. The Aleatico di Puglia '00 is one of the best sweet wines in the region. Full, fleshy, rich and sweet, it is held together by a good vein of acidity. Castel del Monte Rosso '99 Vigna del Melograno has an alluring ripe fruitiness, good structure, prominent but well-behaved tannins and a comforting fullness. The range is completed by a good Rosato, Vigna Lama di Carro '00, slim, fruity and supple, and the white Vigna Tufaroli, from chardonnay with small quantities of pampanuto and bombino bianco.

●	Puglia Aleatico '00	🍷🍷	4*
●	Castel del Monte Rosso Ris. '98	🍷🍷	5
○	Castel del Monte Bianco Vigna Tufaroli '00	🍷	3*
⊙	Castel del Monte Rosato Vigna Lama di Carro '00	🍷	3
●	Castel del Monte Rosso Vigna del Melograno '99	🍷	3*
●	Castel del Monte Rosso Ris. '95	🍷🍷	3
●	Castel del Monte Rosso '97	🍷🍷	2
●	Castel del Monte Rosso Ris. '97	🍷🍷	5
●	Puglia Aleatico '99	🍷🍷	4
⊙	Castel del Monte Rosato Vigna Lama di Carro '99	🍷	2

CORATO (BA)

TORREVENTO
Loc. Castel del Monte
S. S. 170, km 28
70033 Corato (BA)
tel. 0808980923 - 0808980929
e-mail: torrevento@libero.it

Torrevento is a substantial estate producing over 700,000 bottles annually. It has over 100 hectares of land, 80 of which are vineyard. Not all is in production yet. There are 25 hectares planted only recently, so the estate is still some way from its maximum output. Nevertheless, we don't believe Francesco Liantonio is solely interested in quantity. Each year, our tastings show that he and his oenologist Lino Carparelli are also, nay primarily, working towards better quality. The '99 vintage of Torrevento's flagship, Castel del Monte Vigna Pedale, was not ready in time for our tastings so judgement is held over until next year, even though cask samples showed well. However, the '00 release of the delicious Moscato di Trani was ready and was a joy to taste. It is intensely perfumed with sage, lavender and candied fruit, and is sweet, intense and long on the palate with fresh acidity and pervasive aromatic flavours. Also showing excellently this year is the '99 Salice Salentino. Its ruby colour is still violet tinged then the nose gives ultra-ripe plum and morello cherry. The structure is firm, the tannins are soft and ripe, and it should develop well for another few years. The fresher, Castel del Monte Rosato '00, with its meaty yet fruit-rich character, is on form while the red Torre del Falco '98, from 50 per cent cabernet sauvignon, 30 per cent cabernet franc and uva di troia, is better than when tasted last year.

FASANO (BR)

BORGO CANALE
V.le Canale di Pirro, 23
72015 Fasano (BR)
tel. 0804331351
e-mail: info@borgocanale.it

We have to say right out that we were disappointed with the Borgo Canale wines this year. Given the potential that they have been showing recently, we were looking forward to seeing rather better quality, but it wasn't to be. However, we should also say that there has been a change in oenologists. The expert Manlio Erba has taken over, putting a completely new stylistic slant on the entire range. It's going to take time for this to bed down. The winery buys grapes from selected growers and manages about 50 hectares of leased vineyard, whose quality it aims to improve further. The best of the wines tasted was Maestro. With the '00 vintage, this is no longer solely from primitivo but is now a blend with pinot nero, uva di troia and montepulciano. It is a dark ruby with violet tinges and the nose is characterized by a touch of balsam and oak toast that almost masks the fruit. The palate has good structure and fleshiness but the tannins are slightly green and oak dominates the finish, which is mid-length. Rosa del Selva is attractive, as usual, with a nice cherry colour. The nose seems a little stalky but the palate is soft with an enlivening but gentle acidity that gives freshness. The best of the whites is Divo, from verdeca, vermentino and chardonnay. This is a straw yellow, with delicate fruity perfumes, medium weight and fair length. The Locorotondo Talné, from verdeca, bianco d'Alessano and fiano, is fresh and with a light florality but somewhat evanescent. It will need a second look, as will the verdeca and bianco d'Alessano Agorà, which suffers from a closed nose.

○ Moscato di Trani Dulcis in Fundo '00	ҰҰ	4*
● Salice Salentino Rosso '99	ҰҰ	2*
⊙ Castel del Monte Rosato '00	Ұ	2*
● Castel del Monte Rosso '99	Ұ	2*
○ Castel del Monte Bianco '00		2
● Castel del Monte Rosso Vigna Pedale Ris. '94	ҰҰ	2
● Castel del Monte Rosso Vigna Pedale Ris. '96	ҰҰ	2
● Castel del Monte Rosso '97	ҰҰ	1
● Castel del Monte Rosso Vigna Pedale Ris. '98	ҰҰ	3
○ Torre del Falco '98	Ұ	3

○ Divo '00	Ұ	4
● Maestro '00	Ұ	4
⊙ Puglia Rosa di Selva '00	Ұ	2
○ Agorà Bianco '00		2
○ Locorotondo Talné '00		2
● Primitivo Maestro '96	Ұ	3
● Primitivo Maestro '98	Ұ	3

GRAVINA IN PUGLIA (BA)

CANTINA COOPERATIVA BOTROMAGNO
VIA F.LLI CERVI, 12
70024 GRAVINA IN PUGLIA (BA)
TEL. 0803265865
E-MAIL: bortomagno@tiscalinet.it

Botromagno has had a Guide profile for a long time. With an annual production of 350,000 bottles, all of good quality, and 80 hectares of vineyard, some owned and others leased, Beniamino d'Agostino's winery is one of the main contenders in the province of Bari. In addition, the 2001 vintage will see the new, state-of-the-art cellar in operation for the first time, which can only give Botromagno a further shift upward in quality. But even this year's tastings gave inspiring results, for which credit obviously goes to oenologist Severino Garofano, almost an institution in south Italian winemaking. D'Agostino and Garofano's sweet wine, Gravisano, is one of southern Italy's best. From malvasia bianca grapes dried on rush mats for around a month, it is vinified and aged in French oak barriques. The '97 is a deep straw yellow tinged with amber-gold. The nose is intense, sweet but fresh, with apricot jam and candied citrus peel aromas that meld into hints of vanilla. The full-flavoured palate is sweet, balanced by fresh acidity, and echoes the fruit and spiciness of the nose. The red Pier delle Vigne '96 from montepulciano and aglianico has a nice bright ruby colour, firm structure and elegant tannins, plus tones of ripe fruit, liquorice and balsam that make it very inviting. But the estate's high spot is Gravina, a white from greco and malvasia, with an annual run of 200,000 bottles. The '00 is one of its best vintages. Bright straw, it releases intense perfumes of apples, flowers and herbs, then the well-balanced palate has good body and character.

GUAGNANO (LE)

ANTICA MASSERIA DEL SIGILLO
VIA PROVINCIALE, 143
73010 GUAGNANO (LE)
TEL. 0832706331
E-MAIL: commercial@vinisigillo.com

The Antica Masseria del Sigillo is a small estate in Salento terms – it has about ten hectares of vineyard and produces around 120,000 bottles annually. Set up as recently as 1998, it first gained a place in the Guide last year and this year amply confirms its position, with one wine, Terre del Guiscardo, in the running for Three Glasses. This is an amazing success for such a young estate and inspires optimism for the rosiest of futures. For Terre del Guiscardo, oenologist Oronzo Alò came up with a 60 per cent primitivo-based blend with the rest divided equally between cabernet sauvignon and merlot. The wine ages for almost a year, partly in stainless steel and partly in new barriques. The result is a dark ruby hue tinged with violet, ushering in has soft, intense aromas of red and black berry fruit, a decisive spicy note of white pepper, elegant but not overbearing toasted oak, vanilla and India ink. The palate is full, fat and rounded, rich in soft, ripe tannins and with good aromatic length. But Masseria's flagship is Sigillo Primo, a juicy Primitivo with a run of 80,000 bottles that appeals – scoring Two Glasses – for its commanding presence, its firm structure combined with a comforting softness, and its attractive toasty and tobacco-like notes that pervade both nose and palate. Sigillo Primo Chardonnay '00 is very slightly super-ripe but works well overall.

○ Gravina '00	🍷🍷	3*
○ Gravisano '97	🍷🍷	6
● Murgia Rosso Pier delle Vigne '96	🍷	3
● Pier delle Vigne '93	🍷🍷	2
● Pier delle Vigne '94	🍷🍷	2

● Terre del Guiscardo '99	🍷🍷	4*
● Primitivo Sigillo Primo '00	🍷🍷	2*
○ Sigillo Primo Chardonnay '00	🍷	3
● Terre del Guiscardo '98	🍷🍷	4
● Sigillo Primo Primitivo '99	🍷🍷	2

GUAGNANO (LE)

COSIMO TAURINO
S. S. 605 SALICE-SANDONACI
73010 GUAGNANO (LE)
TEL. 0832706490
E-MAIL: taurino@tin.it

Francesco Taurino is devoting all his time to running the estate founded by his father Cosimo. It has a good 150 hectares of vineyard, mostly bush-trained, and a state-of-the-art cellar, while oenologist Severino Garofano, who helped Cosimo create the wines that made the estate's name, continues to oversee the winemaking. The top wine is Brindisi Rosso Patriglione, made with super-ripe grapes from the Patriglione vineyard. It is a concentrated, austere red of great power, driven by a super-ripe red and black berry fruitiness and superb tannic structure. It has the balance and power to mature for many years. This year's release, the '95, is again one of the most complex and fascinating of south Italy's reds but didn't quite reach Three Glasses because of a slight lack of definition on the nose and a finish in a lower key than the best vintages. There was also a tad too much bitterness. However, the '95 is perhaps the best release ever of Notarpanaro. From negroamaro with 15 per cent malvasia nera, it has its usual dark ruby hue with an orange rim while the nose is sweet, rich and complex with an initial ripe, red berry fruit that softens elegantly into aromas of balsam and Mediterranean scrub. It is warm, succulent and mouthfilling on the palate, which is long and develops well throughout. Rosato Scaloti '00 is one of the best rosés of the vintage. Bright, deep pink, it releases wonderfully clean red fruit aromas and the palate is fresh, structured and very long. Salice Riserva '98 has good style but the '00 I Sierri, from chardonnay and malvasia, is a little under par.

● Patriglione '95	🍷🍷	6
◉ Salento Rosato Scaloti '00	🍷🍷	3*
● Notarpanaro '95	🍷🍷	4*
● Salice Salentino Rosso Ris. '98	🍷	3
○ I Sierri '00		4
● Patriglione '85	🍷🍷🍷	5
● Patriglione '88	🍷🍷🍷	5
● Patriglione '94	🍷🍷🍷	6
● Salice Salentino Rosso Ris. '93	🍷🍷	3
● Notarpanaro '94	🍷🍷	4
● Salice Salentino Rosso Ris. '94	🍷🍷	3

LECCE

CANTELE
VIA VINCENZO BALSAMO, 13
73100 LECCE
TEL. 0832240962
E-MAIL: cantele@cantele.it

Augusto and Domenico Cantele set up their estate in 1979 and today boast an output that combines high quality with high quantity. They turn out 2,500,000 million bottles annually, making this one of the largest wineries in Puglia. The Canteles own no land but buy in from 243 growers, giving them 200 hectares-worth of grapes. A good proportion of the wines are exported, which goes some way to explaining their international tenor, even in traditional DOCs such as Salice Salentino, as well as the importance of the various Chardonnays in the vast range. However, this year it was a red that stole the scene, a 60-40 primitivo and negroamaro blend, part-aged in new oak barriques. Amativo '99 is a dark, opaque ruby and its nose is intense with exuberant, super-ripe black berry fruits, tobacco and oriental spices. The palate is full, succulent and soft, with firm tannic structure, balance, freshness, oak that is well integrated into the fruit, and a long, black cherry jam finish, although we found this just a touch too sweet. But flavours of chocolate, tobacco and red berry fruit linger and Amativo earns its place among Puglia's best reds. Chardonnay Teresa Manara '00 is fresh, full of fruit and has an elegant oakiness. Equally successful is the red Varius '99, from negroamaro, cabernet and montepulciano, which interweaves rich fruit with mellow tannins. All the rest of the range showed well.

● Amativo '99	🍷🍷	6
○ Salento Chardonnay Teresa Manara '00	🍷🍷	5
● Varius '99	🍷🍷	5
○ Salento Chardonnay '00	🍷	4
◉ Salice Salentino Rosato Cenobio '00	🍷	3*
● Salice Salentino Rosso Cenobio '97	🍷	3*
● Salento Primitivo '98	🍷	4
● Salice Salentino Rosso Ris. '98	🍷	4
● Salice Salentino Rosso Ris. '96	🍷🍷	4
● Salice Salentino Rosso Ris. '97	🍷🍷	4
○ Salento Chardonnay Teresa Manara '99	🍷🍷	4

LECCE

AGRICOLE VALLONE
VIA XXV LUGLIO, 5
73100 LECCE
TEL. 0832308041

Sisters Vittoria and Maria Teresa Vallone run their 660-hectare family estate with great diligence. It has been producing classic Salento wines since the early 1930s and the vineyards now extend over 150 hectares. Annual production is past the 600,000-bottle mark. Severino Garofano provides invaluable oenological consultancy and the wines are sold with great success both in Italy and abroad. The range is led by Graticciaia, a fine red from late-picked, slightly raisined negroamaro grapes, a sort of "southern-style Amarone". The latest vintage, the '96, is on similar lines to its predecessors. It is a dark, almost opaque ruby with a violet rim. The nose is complex and rich with deep aromas of redcurrant jam, mulberry and plum, interwoven with sweet spices, cocoa powder, vanilla and liqueur cherries. The palate is big, with a powerful thrust of alcohol. Rich in residual sugar, elegant in its tannins and very long, it leaves intense fruit and sensations of vanilla and spices on the aftertaste. These, combined with its sweetness, make it more a wine for drinking after the meal than with it. The '98 Brindisi Rosso Vigna Flaminio is as good as ever and has a rich array of ripe red berry fruit on both nose and palate, together with smooth tannins and good balance. The fruit, robust structure and delicate, balanced astringency of the '00 Rosato gives it great allure while the '98 Salice Vereto luxuriates in aromas of leather and old wood, and a full, tannic, evenly textured palate. The white Corte Valesio '00, from Sauvignon, is promising but lacks definition.

● Graticciaia '96	🍷🍷	6
● Brindisi Rosso Vigna Flaminio '98	🍷🍷	2*
◉ Brindisi Rosato Vigna Flaminio '00	🍷	2*
● Salice Salentino Rosso Vereto '98	🍷	2*
○ Salento Sauvignon Corte Valesio '00		2
● Graticciaia '93	🍷🍷	5
● Graticciaia '94	🍷🍷	5
● Brindisi Rosso V. Flaminio '95	🍷🍷	2
● Graticciaia '95	🍷🍷	6
● Brindisi Rosso V. Flaminio '96	🍷🍷	2
● Brindisi Rosso V. Flaminio '97	🍷🍷	2

LEVERANO (LE)

CONTI ZECCA
VIA CESAREA
73045 LEVERANO (LE)
TEL. 0832925613
E-MAIL: info@contizecca.it

Nero is a great red. Any remaining doubts should be dispelled by Three Glasses for the second year running, this time for the '99. It could be even more complex and fascinating than the '98 for it has greater maturity of style. It's a highly successful blend of 70 per cent negroamaro, 20 per cent cabernet sauvignon and malvasia nera, aged in French oak barriques. The colour is as you would expect ("nero" is Italian for "black"), showing purple and violet tinges only on the rim. The nose gives immediate impact, with intensity and complexity, and has a rich array of red berry fruit that dissolves elegantly in nuances of oak and delicate balsam-like tones. The palate is dense, extraordinarily elegant, perfectly balanced and succulent, with velvety tannins and great length. In short, it is fabulous. But don't underrate the rest of the large range. There are around 320 hectares of vineyard and annual production of runs at over 1,500,000 bottles. Salice Salentino Cantalupi '99 is a lively ruby colour. It has the typical aromas of negroamaro and malvasia nera, and is richly evocative of the Mediterranean, but with a clean, modern slant. On the palate, fruit and velvety tannins knit elegantly into notes of cocoa powder and oak toast. Leverano '99 Vigna del Saraceno acts as its alter ego, with a bright, lively ruby hue, sweet, spicy nose and fresh, harmonious palate. The rest of the large range is excellent and priced more than reasonably. The Conti Zecca locomotive, under estate manager and oenologist Antonio Romano, with consultant Giorgio Marone at his side, thunders on.

● Nero '99	🍷🍷🍷	5*
● Leverano Rosso Vigna del Saraceno '99	🍷🍷	3*
● Salice Salentino Rosso Cantalupi '99	🍷🍷	3*
○ Leverano Bianco Vigna del Saraceno '00	🍷	3*
◉ Leverano Rosato Vigna del Saraceno '00	🍷	3*
● Salento Primitivo Zinfandel '00	🍷	3*
◉ Salento Rosato Donna Marzia '00	🍷	2*
● Salento Rosso Donna Marzia '98	🍷	2*
● Nero '98	🍷🍷🍷	5
● Leverano Rosso Vigna del Saraceno Ris. '96	🍷🍷	2
● Nero '97	🍷🍷	4
● Salice Salentino Rosso Cantalupi '97	🍷🍷	2
○ Leverano Malvasia Vigna del Saraceno '98	🍷	4

LIZZANO (TA)

CANTINA SOCIALE DI LIZZANO
C.SO EUROPA, 37/39
74020 LIZZANO (TA)
TEL. 0999552013 - 0999552014
E-MAIL: lizzano@cantinelizzano.it

The L. Ruggieri co-operative winery gained its entry this year simply from the high scores its wines achieved in our tastings. However, we must emphasize that this ranking is not a one-off. The wines have shone for quality and pricing for several years now. The co-operative produces over 500,000 bottles annually, with grapes coming from the 665 hectares of vineyard belonging to its 571 members. The technical side is controlled by oenologist Angelo Pinto. He has produced, among others, an excellent Primitivo del Tarantino '98. It is a dark ruby tinged with garnet. The nose is clean, decisive, deep and rich, driven by its terroir and redolent of ripe black berry fruit and spices. The palate has body but avoids heaviness, showing long-lasting flavours of fruit, tobacco and white pepper, all enlivened by a herbaceous freshness. Lizzano Rosato Porvica '00 Collezione Le Masserie is one of the best Puglian rosés we tasted this year. The colour is a bright, deep pink, introducing a well-fruited, full, elegant nose whose scents are echoed on the well-structured palate, which has impressive ripe morello cherry fruitiness. Lizzano Bianco '00 Torretta, from trebbiano and pinot bianco, is also good. It has a bright straw colour and there are fresh, clean aromas of ripe apple on the nose. The palate is soft, fresh, clean and well-defined, almost winning a second Glass. Lizzano Rosso Belvedere '98, from 60-40 negroamaro and montepulciano, has good character but maybe suffers a little from being made in a more traditional style, which means it is rather closed.

LOCOROTONDO (BA)

CANTINA COOPERATIVA
DEL LOCOROTONDO
VIA MADONNA DELLA CATENA, 99
70010 LOCOROTONDO (BA)
TEL. 0804311644 - 0804311298
E-MAIL: info@locorotondodoc.com

The Cantina Sociale di Locorotondo is an institution in Puglia, first because it was founded in 1932 and is the region's oldest co-operative, next because of its huge output of over 3,500,000 bottles a year, and finally for the sound quality of its wines. Those bottles are also brilliant value for money. Benedetto Lorusso, the oenologist, has excellent grapes to work with from the members' 1,000 hectares of vineyard (that's right, three zeros). The Locorotondo cru Vigneti in Tallinajo has rarely shown as well as with the '00. It is a bright, pretty straw colour and has fresh, fruity perfumes with floral and vanilla nuances. These are echoed on the soft, well-structured and long palate. Casale San Giorgio Rosato, also '00, has a very bright cherry colour, fresh, red berry fruit on the nose, and a supple, well-fruited palate. Another rosé, Cummerse, is fairly similar but is distinguished by ringing tones of ripe cherry. The standard Locorotondo '00 is very attractive. Full of simple, fresh fruitiness on the nose, it is delightfully full and supple on the palate, which has a dominant surge of youthful acidity to support its clean, tightly-knit fruit. Finally, the '98 Casale San Giorgio Rosso, from negroamaro and primitivo, offers complexity of character and a nicely defined structure with ripe, soft tannins and a well-fruited, rounded finish.

○ Lizzano Rosato Porvica '00	2*
● Primitivo del Tarantino '98	2*
○ Lizzano Bianco Torretta '00	2*
● Lizzano Rosso Belvedere '99	3*

○ Casale San Giorgio Rosato '00	2*
○ Cummerse Rosato '00	3
○ Locorotondo '00	2*
○ Locorotondo Vigneti in Tallinajo '00	3
○ Roccia Bianco '00	1*
○ Roccia Rosato '00	1*
● Casale San Giorgio Rosso '98	3
● Cummerse Rosso '97	4
● Roccia Rosso '99	1

MANDURIA (TA)

Felline
Via N. Donadio, 20
74024 Manduria (TA)
tel. 0999739060
e-mail: accademia@accademiadeiracemi.it

With the weather problems that plagued the previous vintage now well behind them, Felline's wines are back to the sort of quality levels that do justice to the estate. In addition, the collaboration between the Perrucci brothers and oenologist Roberto Cipresso is working very nicely. The result is three more wines of great distinction. Vigna del Feudo '00, a blend of primitivo and montepulciano with small amounts of cabernet and merlot, comes top of the range, thanks mainly to the solidity of its structure. The dark ruby is tinged with garnet and the nose has ripe plumy fruit and sensations of balsam. The oak on the palate is well judged, the tannins are ripe and there is complexity with distinct, soft tones of black berry fruit overlain by tobacco and cocoa powder. In short, it is one of Puglia's top reds. The '00 Primitivo is also remarkably good. Surprisingly concentrated in aroma, it shows clear tones of mulberry, blackcurrant and oriental spices. There is marked oak on the succulent, rich palate but this does not mask the fruit, adding complexity to the wine. The tannins are elegant and finely grained, and there are sensations of coffee, chocolate and liquorice on the finish. Alberello, from primitivo and negroamaro, was one of the wines that last year helped give Puglian winemaking a jolt with its clean style and its remarkable value for money. It's good again this time. The fruit on the nose is supported by good weight of alcohol, and the palate is full, round and gently tannic but finishes rather short.

● Vigna del Feudo '00	♟♟	4*
● Primitivo di Manduria '00	♟♟	4*
● Salento Rosso Alberello '00	♟	3*
● Vigna del Feudo '97	♟♟♟	4
● Primitivo di Manduria '98	♟♟	3
● Primitivo di Manduria '99	♟♟	4

MANDURIA (TA)

Pervini
C.da Acuti
Via Santo Stasi Primo - Z. I.
74024 Manduria (TA)
tel. 0999738929
e-mail: accademia@accademiadeiracemi.it

Owned by the Perrucci brothers, this is the leading estate in the Accademia dei Racemi grouping of several small Salento cellars. Pervini has a wide range of wines, in which the Primitivo Archidamo '00 is the star. It is purple, with typical aromas of plum and tobacco on the nose, and has a well-structured, lightly tannic, intense, long palate with pervasive tones of vanilla and ripe fruit. Giravolta, another Primitivo, is quite different in style. Deep and dark, it has a nose with incisive but not excessive oaking and a palate whose toastiness is well integrated into the black berry fruit. Powerful, big, vigorous and deep, it flaunts ripe tannins and hazelnut on the finish. Other interpretations of the variety come from the straight Primitivo '00, which sports a brightly-coloured label. Deeply coloured, it is complex on the nose and well-structured on the palate. I Monili '99 is another Primitivo which, despite the less than exciting vintage, has a good deep ruby colour, bitter-sweet cherry aromas on the nose, and a firmly weighty palate with a subtle streak of acidity supporting a good finish. However, even with all these Primitivos, one of Pervini's top wines is a Salice Salentino, the Riserva Te Deum Laudamus '98, sumptuous in name and character. It is a concentrated ruby tinged with garnet, the aromas marrying a black berry fruitiness with a minerally tang. The elegant palate reflects the nose and has a dense tannic weave while there are pervasive notes of tar on the finish. The late-harvest Moscato, Grelise, and the three wines from the Bizantino line are the best of the rest.

● Primitivo di Manduria Archidamo '00	♟♟	3*
● Primitivo di Manduria Giravolta Tenuta Pozzopalo '00	♟♟	4*
● Salice Salentino Rosso Te Deum Laudamus Ris. Casale Bevagna '98	♟♟	4*
● Primitivo di Manduria '00	♟	3*
○ Salento Bianco Bizantino '00	♟	2*
⊙ Salento Rosato Bizantino '00	♟	2*
● Salento Rosso Bizantino '00	♟	2*
○ Moscato Grelise V. T. '98	♟	4
● Primitivo di Manduria Primo Amore '98	♟	3*
● Primitivo del Tarantino I Monili '99	♟	2*
● Solaria Ionica Ferrari '59	♟♟	6
● Finibusterre Antica Masseria Torre Mozza '97	♟♟	6
● Primitivo di Manduria Archidamo '98	♟♟	3

MARUGGIO (TA)

MASSERIA PEPE
LOC. CASTIGNO
74020 MARUGGIO (TA)
TEL. 0999711660
E-MAIL:
accademia@accademiadeiracemi.it

If we had one wish, we would like to reach the age of 90 and still have the vitality and enthusiasm of Alberto Pagano, the owner of this delightful estate in the Primitivo di Manduria zone. Alberto, originally a pharmacist, made the switch to his real love, wine, some years ago and started to vinify his grapes and sell the results. His almost nine hectares of bush-trained vines lie just a few metres from the Ionian coastline and their roots dig into the coastal sand dunes. His Primitivos are elegant, modern and concentrated, and practically epitomize the DOC. There are currently 70,000 bottles produced annually, although this will increase when new vineyards come into production, and just two wines. Dunico is the better of the pair. The '00 is the trademark dark ruby, violet-tinged on the rim. There is bramble and plum jam on the nose, denoting the great ripeness, or maybe even super-ripeness, of the grapes, and an array of spicy, barbecue notes, with white pepper prominent. The palate is full-bodied and kept in balance by a well-judged streak of freshness and perfectly ripe tannins. These also enliven its dense, rich texture. The second wine, Primitivo Il Portile, also '00, is just as attractive but less complex. It's a soft, full red with sweet, juicy fruit, then spices and mint on the finish.

NOCI (BA)

BARSENTO
C.DA SAN GIACOMO
70015 NOCI (BA)
TEL. 0804979657

This estate, owned by the Colucci family, is only in its first year of marketing wine in the bottle yet fully deserves its Guide profile. Founded in the 1970s and recently modernized with a new vinification plant, Barsento, in the person of the skilled oenologist Leonardo Palumbo, oversees and vinifies the output of several growers in an area that straddles the provinces of Brindisi and Taranto. There are three wines, all worthy of note. The rosé, Magilda '00, is obtained from briefly macerated malvasia nera grapes and is one of the best of its type. It has a good, deep cherry – almost ruby – colour and an intense, raspberry and ripe cherry nose. The palate is structured and full but remains fresh, supple and fruity, with an attractive note of bitter almond on the finish. The red Paturno '00, from a blend of three of central-southern Italy's finest varieties, montepulciano, primitivo and negroamaro, is also a delight. It has a concentrated ruby colour, pervasive aromas of ripe red berry fruit and light, tobacco-nuanced spiciness. The well balanced, elegant, even palate has soft tannins, and a good, if not particularly long finish. Malicchia Mapicchia is as strangely labelled as it is named but what you uncork is a sweet Primitivo of deep violet colour with primary aromas of grape must, ripe bramble and black fig fruit and delicate vegetal touches. The palate is soft, with evident sweetness of fruit, but doesn't cloy and has just a hint of soft tannin and fair length.

● Primitivo di Manduria Dunico '00	ΨΨ	5
● Primitivo Il Portile '00	ΨΨ	4*
● Primitivo di Manduria Dunico '98	ΨΨ	5
● Primitivo di Manduria Dunico '99	ΨΨ	5
● Primitivo Il Portile '99	ΨΨ	4

● Paturno '00	ΨΨ	4*
⊙ Magilda Rosato '00	ΨΨ	3*
● Malicchia Mapicchia '00	Ψ	4

SALICE SALENTINO (LE)

LEONE DE CASTRIS
VIA SENATORE DE CASTRIS, 50
73015 SALICE SALENTINO (LE)
TEL. 0832731112 - 0832733608
E-MAIL: info@leonedecastris.net

The Leone de Castris family has owned land in Puglia since the middle of the 17th century. Currently, Salvatore Leone de Castris is at the helm of the estate, although his workload is shared with son Piernicola. They have as much as 380 hectares of vineyard but still need to buy in grapes, which they do from a group of trusted growers, to reach their production requirements of over 3,500,000 bottles. Scanning the list of wines is rather like running through the last half century or so of Puglia's wine history. Some are classics, like the celebrated Five Roses, the first Puglian wine to be marketed in bottle after the Second World War; others, like Salice Salentino Riserva Donna Lisa, are classics in the making. In fact, the latter wine has really been making waves over the past few years. The '97, though, does not match the standards set by its predecessors. Make no mistake, it is still a terrific red, full-bodied, deep, modern-styled. It's just that it lacks a little of the concentration and stylistic purity that have shot previous vintages to stardom. On the other hand, the Five Roses selection Anniversario '00 does nothing to dent the wine's fame as one of Italy's best rosés. Expectations are fulfilled by its very bright colour, its intense red berry fruit aromas and the fresh, elegant, supple, long palate of good body. Salice Salentino Riserva '98, agreeably fruity and oaky, is also excellent, as is the sweet, spicy Primitivo di Manduria Santera '99 with its intense notes of tobacco and coffee. All the estate's other offerings are also very good.

	Wine	Rating	Score
●	Salice Salentino Rosso Donna Lisa Ris. '97	♛♛	6*
⊙	Five Roses Anniversario '00	♛♛	3*
●	Salice Salentino Rosso Ris. '98	♛♛	3*
●	Primitivo di Manduria Santera '99	♛♛	3*
⊙	Five Roses '00	♛	3*
○	Puglia Moscato Pierale '00	♛	4
○	Salice Salentino Bianco Donna Lisa '00	♛	4
○	Salice Salentino Bianco Imago '00	♛	3*
●	Salento Rosso Illemos '97	♛	5
●	Aleatico Negrino '99	♛	4
●	Salice Salentino Rosso Maiana '99	♛	2*
●	Salice Salentino Rosso Donna Lisa Ris. '93	♛♛♛	4
●	Salice Salentino Rosso Donna Lisa Ris. '95	♛♛♛	5
●	Salice Salentino Rosso Donna Lisa Ris. '96	♛♛	5

SAN DONACI (BR)

FRANCESCO CANDIDO
VIA A. DIAZ, 46
72025 SAN DONACI (BR)
TEL. 0831635674 - 0831635674
E-MAIL: candido.wines@tin.it

Candido is one of Puglian winemaking's classic names. The '95 Duca d'Aragona, from negroamaro with 20 per cent montepulciano, is one of the region's top scoring reds this year but still lacks that touch of depth and length that would take it to the top. Never has it come closer, though. The colour is an intense ruby and the nose is highly impressive, focusing on ripe, concentrated red berry fruit. The palate is structured, with good tannic balance, and finishes sweet and balsamic. A notch below is Immensum '99, from negroamaro and cabernet sauvignon. It is a deep ruby and the nose is full of spice and wild berry fruit jam. The palate is round and full, with a touch of toastiness showing good use of oak, and there is a long, delicately astringent finish. The '97 vintage of Cappello di Prete, a Candido classic, seemed a little under par. The nose is closed and the wine reveals itself only on the palate, where light fruit is supported by good alcohol. The '97 Salice Salentino Riserva is more characterful with its deep colour and a clean nose showing red berry fruitiness. The palate picks up the theme, knitting the fruit into an elegant, velvety tannic weave. Among the whites, the sweet Paule Calle, a chardonnay and malvasia bianca blend, did well. Golden straw, it has a nose of acacia honey and the palate is well-structured and elegant, with candied fruits and toasty notes. Both Vigna Vinera, which is a vibrant straw yellow, with a structured but rather rough palate, and the Salice Salentino Bianco are decent but simpler wines. The rosé Le Pozzelle '00 has appealing fruitiness.

	Wine	Rating	Score
●	Duca d'Aragona '95	♛♛	5*
○	Paule Calle '98	♛♛	4*
●	Immensum '99	♛♛	4*
○	Salento Bianco Vigna Vinera '00	♛	3*
⊙	Salice Salentino Rosato Le Pozzelle '00	♛	2*
●	Cappello di Prete '97	♛	3
●	Salice Salentino Ris. '97	♛	2*
○	Salice Salentino Bianco '00		2
●	Duca d'Aragona '90	♛♛	5
●	Duca d'Aragona '93	♛♛	5
●	Duca d'Aragona '94	♛♛	5
●	Cappello di Prete '95	♛♛	3
●	Cappello di Prete '96	♛♛	3

SAN PIETRO VERNOTICO (BR)

SANTA BARBARA
VIA MATERNITÀ E INFANZIA, 23
72027 SAN PIETRO VERNOTICO (BR)
TEL. 0831652749
E-MAIL: santabarba@mails.clio.it

Santa Barbara wins back its Guide profile after several years' absence, thanks to a sound line-up of wines. The winery is a co-operative of around 80 members, led with competence and total commitment by oenologist, Pietro Giorgiani. Their members' vine stock, in San Pietro Vernotico and thereabouts, amounts to approximately 150 hectares and annual production reaches around 1,500,000 bottles. Primitivo del Salento '98 topped the range. We admired its dark ruby colour and its viscosity, the tight aromas of impeccably varietal black berry fruits, and the subtle underlying vegetal, spicy and tobacco-like notes. We also liked the full but not heavy palate with its abundant soft tannins and flavours of plum jam and chocolate. The Sauvignon, Cantamessa '00, also nearly scored Two Glasses. It is a bright, greenish straw colour. There are plentiful green and vegetal aromas, and an exotic, musky touch typical of the variety. It has flavours of sage and ripe fruit on the round, full palate, which is supported by good freshness. However, the estate's workhorse is a delightful red, Squinzano. The '98 has a bright ruby colour, intense, rich aromas of morello cherry and ripe plum, with an attractive note of undergrowth. Then follows a palate of well-balanced structure and elegant tannicity. The Brindisi Rosso and Salice Salentino, both also '98, are both attractive and well made, as is the white Ursa Maior '99, from chardonnay and sauvignon. The other wines presented were all characterful and well priced.

● Primitivo '98	♟♟	2*
● Brindisi Rosso '98	♟	2*
● Salento Rosso Ursa Maior '98	♟	2*
● Salice Salentino '98	♟	2*
● Squinzano '98	♟	2*
○ Salento Bianco Cantamessa '00	♟	1*
○ Salento Bianco Ursa Maior '99	♟	2*

SAN PIETRO VERNOTICO (BR)

TORMARESCA
VIA MATERNITÀ ED INFANZIA, 21
72027 SAN PIETRO VERNOTICO (BR)
TEL. 0804771392
E-MAIL: tormaresca@tormaresca.it

Since 1998, the Antinoris have bought over 600 hectares in Puglia, in two distinct blocks, the first in the Murge area in the Castel del Monte DOC, and the other in Salento, at San Pietro Vernotico. Currently, the holding totals 350 hectares, some already under vine and some newly planted. The figure is due to grow. In 2000, production reached 800,000 bottles, split among four wines. The standard line comprises Tormaresca Bianco and Tormaresca Rosso; we tasted the '00 vintage of both. The white, from chardonnay fermented and aged in small oak, is golden straw, with an intense nose of apples, pears and vanilla. It is soft on the palate, with good structure, although it lacks a touch of freshness. The red is from 70 per cent aglianico with cabernet sauvignon and is dark ruby. Full of red berry fruitiness on both nose and palate, it has ripe tannins and good depth, balance and length. Petrabianca '00, chardonnay once more, is on a different plane. Bright straw, it flaunts an intense, fresh nose, fragrant with ripe fruit and florality and elegantly nuanced with oak. The palate is fruity, racy and yet soft, elegant, complex and long. Bocca di Lupo '99, from the same blend as the Tormaresca Rosso, is the best of the group, as you can sense from its deep, dense ruby hue. It is still very young but has a stunningly rich and complex nose, focused primarily on ripe, but not cooked, red and black berry fruit, with some spice. The palate is deep, mouthfilling, beautifully defined and develops evenly to a long finish. It is one of Puglia's best reds and future vintages may well be starry.

● Castel del Monte Rosso Boccadilupo '99	♟♟	5*
○ Castel del Monte Chardonnay Pietrabianca '99	♟♟	5
○ Tormaresca Bianco '00	♟	3*
● Tormaresca Rosso '00	♟	3*
○ Tormaresca Bianco '98	♟♟	2
○ Tormaresca Bianco '99	♟♟	2
● Tormaresca Rosso '98	♟	2

SCORRANO (LE)

Duca Carlo Guarini
L.go Frisari, 1
73020 Scorrano (LE)
tel. 0836460288
e-mail: ducaguarini@tin.it

The Guarini family has owned land at Scorrano, in the province of Lecce, for almost 1,000 years. They currently control a good 700 hectares, producing various crops, including olives, and 65 hectares of vine. Negroamaro is the principal variety but there is also primitivo, montepulciano and malvasia rossa, not forgetting the international cabernet sauvignon and sauvignon blanc. For some years now, Giovanbattista and Fabrizio Guarini, assisted by their oenologist Giuseppe Pizzolante Leuzzi, have been throwing themselves enthusiastically into vineyard and cellar work and they now have a well-honed range, producing 100,000 bottles a year. The most interesting of the wines is, surprisingly, the white Murà '00, a monovarietal sauvignon blanc that is dedicated to Joachim Murat, Napoleon's Marshall and much-loved King of Naples. Despite being grown so far south, this sauvignon has most of the variety's typical characteristics: a bright, deep greenish straw colour; tomato leaf, elderflower and musky, vegetal notes on the nose; and a fleshy, structured, freshly acidic, elegant palate of good depth with hints of tropical fruit and herbs on its finish. The Piutri holding furnishes the grapes for the attractive Rosato '00, with its intense aromas of ripe red berry fruit and good body, and for the negroamaro-based Salento Rosso '99, which despite a slightly closed nose is rounded and characterful on the palate.

TRICASE (LE)

Castel di Salve
Fraz. Depressa
P.zza Castello, 8
73030 Tricase (LE)
tel. 0833771012 - 0833771206
e-mail: casteldisalve@tiscalinet.it

Francesco Marra and Francesco Winspeare have been turning out wines with personality for some time now and the enthusiasm of their approach has made its mark on the stylistic development of the region's wines. On their 40 hectares, they grow mainly negroamaro but also some malvasia nera, montepulciano, sangiovese and primitivo, and these varieties naturally form the base of their production. One of their most successful wines this year is Volo di Alessandro '00, a Sangiovese. Ruby red tinged with violet, it reveals an intense, deep nose with distinct damson and plum fruit. First impressions on the palate are of softness and depth, followed by well-judged tannins and well-defined fruit, then there is an attractive, long, liquorice-nuanced finish. Equally good is Santi Medici Rosso '00, a negroamaro-led blend. The colour is a bright, dark violet-ruby. There is ripe fruit and spiciness on both nose and palate, where they are more distinct and complex. The palate also has a nice balance of richness, oak and tannin. Armecolo '00, from negroamaro and malvasia nera, has good structure and is neither too serious nor too simple. Focusing on wild red berry fruit and tobacco, it melds fruit and oak attractively on the soft palate. Of the other two wines in the Santi Medici line, the Rosato '00 appealed for its deep, bright colour, its delicate floral perfumes and its fresh, attractive palate.

○ Salento Sauvignon Murà '00	ΨΨ	3*
⊙ Salento Rosato Tenuta Piutri '00	Ψ	3*
● Salento Rosso Negroamaro Tenuta Piutri '99	Ψ	3

● Armecolo '00	ΨΨ	3*
● Il Volo di Alessandro '00	ΨΨ	4*
● Salento Rosso Santi Medici '00	ΨΨ	2*
⊙ Salento Rosato Santi Medici '00	Ψ	2*
○ Salento Bianco Santi Medici '00		2
● Lama del Tenente '98	ΨΨ	4
● Armecolo '99	ΨΨ	3

OTHER WINERIES

I PASTINI - CARPARELLI
LOC. CASTEL DEL MONTE
S. S. 170, KM 28 - 70033 ANDRIA (BA)
TEL. 0808980923 - 0804434557
E-MAIL: nicola.carparelli@libero.it

The Carparelli brothers' estate has three wines, all good, but the two modern-styled reds are especially interesting and very well priced. The better of the pair is Murgia Rosso '98, from cabernets sauvignon and franc, and montepulciano.

○ Locorotondo '00	🍷	3
● Murgia Rosso '98	🍷	2*
● Primitivo del Tarantino '99	🍷	3

CANTINA DUE PALME
VIA SAN MARCO, 130
72020 CELLINO SAN MARCO (BR)
TEL. 0831617865 - 0831619728
E-MAIL: duepalme@tin.it

Due Palme is one of the largest agricultural properties in the province of Brindisi. Angelo Maci produces a wide range of DOC and IGT wines here, totalling 20,000 bottles a year. Quality is good and prices very reasonable throughout.

● Brindisi Rosso '98	🍷	2*
● Squinzano '99	🍷	2*

CANTINA SOCIALE COOPERATIVA COPERTINO
VIA MARTIRI DEL RISORGIMENTO, 6
73043 COPERTINO (LE)
TEL. 0832947031

With 600 members, 350 hectares of vine and Severino Garofano as consultant oenologist, this cellar has been, and remains, one of the region's lynchpins. In general, the reds are traditionally styled and quality is excellent.

○ Salento Bianco Cigliano '00	🍷	3
● Copertino Rosso Ris. '98	🍷	3

VALLE DELL'ASSO
VIA GUIDANO, 18
73013 GALATINA (LE)
TEL. 0836561470

One of the surprises of this year's tastings was the success of Macàro, a sweet red from aleatico and malvasia nera, but made from an 18-vintage blend! Also good are Galatina Rosso and the attractive Piromàfo, with its enjoyable fruit and spiciness.

● Macàro Metodo Solera	🍷🍷	4
● Galatina Rosso '99	🍷	2*
● Salento Rosso Piromàfo '99	🍷	4

Lomazzi & Sarli
C.da Partemio
S. S. 7 Brindisi-Taranto
72022 Latiano (BR)
Tel. 0831725898 - 0337282775

This long-standing winery now produces large quantities of good wine from 100 hectares or so of vine stock, most of it owned by the estate.

● Primitivo del Salento Latias '99	♛	3
○ Salento Bianco Terra di Tacco '00	♛	2*

Cantina Sociale Cooperativa Leverano
Via Marche, 1
73045 Leverano (LE)
Tel. 0832925053 - 0832921985

Leverano is one of the co-operatives in Puglia most worth watching. All the wines are of good quality, particularly the reds, but the soft, structured and excellently typed Primitivo '98 is head and shoulders above the rest.

● Salento Primitivo Vecchia Torre '98	♛♛	2*
☉ Leverano Rosato '00	♛	1*
● Salice Salentino Vecchia Torre '98	♛	2*

Vini classici Cardone
Via Martiri della Libertà, 28
70010 Locorotondo (BA)
Tel. 0804311624 - 0804312561
E-mail: info@cardonevini.com

The Cardone wines are based on primitivo and are reliably well styled and made. The '98s and '97s have more complexity on nose and palate while the Primaio is slim-bodied but harmonious and most attractive.

● Primitivo Primaio '00	♛	2*
● Salento Primitivo '97	♛	3
● Gioia del Colle Primitivo Ris. '98	♛	3*

Consorzio Produttori Vini
Via Fabio Massimo, 19
74024 Manduria (TA)
Tel. 0999735332
E-mail: consvini@libero.it

With grapes supplied by 490 member growers, this co-operative approaches the production and marketing of Primitivo di Manduria with intelligence. It turns out the wine in numerous styles, all of good quality.

● Primitivo di Manduria Antiche Contrade '99	♛	3*
● Primitivo di Manduria Lirica '99	♛	3

Soloperto
S. S. 7 ter
74024 Manduria (TA)
Tel. 0999794286
E-mail: soloperto@soloperto.it

Giovanni Soloperto has been selling Primitivo in various styles since the end of the 1960s. Produced from grapes from his 50 hectares of vineyard, scattered mainly around Manduria, they are good quality bottles with a traditional stamp.

● Primitivo di Manduria Vecchio Ceppo '91	♛	4
● Primitivo di Manduria '99	♛	2*

Vinicola Miali
Via Madonnina, 1
74015 Martina Franca (TA)
Tel. 0804303222
E-mail: cantine-miali@libero.it

The Miali family has been producing wine since 1886. They have modern cellars in Martina Franca where they turn out a large range of wines, produced from grapes bought in the best zones of Puglia and Basilicata. Value for money is excellent.

● Aglianico del Vulture '98	♛	1*
● Castel del Monte Rosso '99	♛	2*
● Primitivo di Manduria '99	♛	1*

Cantina Cooperativa della Riforma Fondiaria
Via Madonna delle Grazie, 8/A
70037 Ruvo di Puglia (BA)
tel. 0803601611

The Riforma Fondiaria di Ruvo co-operative is beginning to get itself noticed thanks to the care taken in making the wines from its members' 800 hectares of vine. The range is huge and pricing is fair.

- Murgia Rosso Le Carraie '98 ♈ 3
- Murgia Sangiovese '99 ♈ 1*

Vinicola Resta
Loc. Squinzano - Via Campi, 7
72027 San Pietro Vernotico (BR)
tel. 0831671182
e-mail: vinicolaresta@libero.it

The Resta family has characterful wines at competitive prices. The firmly structured Salice Salentino is partnered by two others of similar quality, all made under the aegis of oenologist Stefano Porcinai.

- Primitivo di Manduria '99 ♈ 2*
- Salento Rosso
  Vigna del Gelso Moro '99 ♈ 2*
- Salice Salentino '99 ♈ 2*

Vinicola Mediterranea
Via Maternità Infanzia, 22
72027 San Pietro Vernotico (BR)
tel. 0831676323 - 0831659329
e-mail: medvini@libero.it

Vinicola Mediterranea has risen from the ashes of the San Pietro Vernotico co-operative. Its modern cellars handle around 4,000,000 kilograms of grapes each year and a carefully made range of good value wines results.

- Primitivo di Manduria '99 ♈♈ 3*
- Salice Salentino Rosso '00 ♈ 3*

Giovanni D'Alfonso del Sordo
C.da Sant'Antonino - S. S. 89, km 5
71016 San Severo (FG)
tel. 0882221444
e-mail: g.dalfonso@fg.nettuno.it

There are improvements year after year in the quality of this winery's output, as clearly demonstrated by the San Severo Bianco and the Rosato Posta Arignano.

- ○ San Severo Bianco
  Posta Arignano '00 ♈ 2*
- ○ San Severo Rosato
  Posta Arignano '00 ♈ 2*

Pichierri - Vinicola Savese
Via Ippolita Prato, 3
74028 Sava (TA)
tel. 0999726232
e-mail: vinicolasavese@vinipichierri.com

From the wines presented this year, the best performers were the Primitivo '99, a well-structured red with a full, round palate, and the sweet '96, with its plum jam character.

- Primitivo di Manduria
  Dolce Naturale '96 ♈ 4
- Primitivo di Manduria
  16° Tradizione del Nonno '99 ♈ 3

Michele Calò & Figli
Via Masseria Vecchia, 1
73058 Tuglie (LE)
tel. 0833596242
e-mail: michelecalo@staff.it

Michele Calò's estate is one of the names of highest renown in the Salento. Specializing in Alezio Rosato, Calò also has good whites and reds of excellent structure, all marketed under the Mjère brand.

- ○ Alezio Rosato Mjère '00 ♈ 4
- Salento Rosso Grecantico '00 ♈ 4

CALABRIA

Something is finally on the move, even in Calabria. There are several new estates arriving on the marketplace and highly regarded oenologists are beginning to work in areas such as Cirò and Lamezia. So, after years of depressing news, at last we have something more positive to report, even though, with soils and climates that are so well suited to viticulture, it is absurd that Calabria is still awash with producers who can't, or don't want to, move up into the premium quality bracket. Still, the exceptions to the rule are beginning to shine more brightly. Take for example the Librandi brothers, whose Gravello '98 is back up to the level of previous top vintages and claimed Three well-earned Glasses. As if by magic, the entire Librandi range has made considerable progress, suggesting that with just a bit more work, the wines could be phenomenal. It is not magic, though. It is all down to carefully planned changes at the estate and the input of leading oenologist Donato Lanati and his "wine angels", led by Dora Marchi and Franca Ratti, who work with him at his Enosis company in Cuccaro Monferrato. But obviously there is more to Calabria than Gravello. Francesco Siciliani, who is assisted by Fabrizio Ciufoli, another prominent oenologist, submitted a Cirò Rosso Ronco dei Quattro Venti '99 that missed Three Glasses by a whisker. It is a modern wine, impeccably well made, without oxidation or even any premature ageing. In short, it's a wine that shouts class. There is none of the unacceptable lack of cleanliness that too many examples of Cirò still manifest. It could well be emblematic of the way styles are going, a marker for its competitors and a blueprint for the Cirò of the future. If so, we should soon be seeing the exciting atmosphere in Calabria that is already pervading its neighbouring regions. In Sicily, Basilicata and Campania, it is as if a sort of phoenix has risen from the flames of archaic wine styles, bringing quality-directed set-ups and winemaking professionalism. But there's more back in Calabria. Odoardi, even without his Vigna Mortilla and Vigna Garrone selections ready for release, nor the new vintage of Valeo, submitted an absolutely glorious Savuto '99. Serracavallo, a highly promising newcomer to the Guide, presented a well-made, impressive range led by its Rosso Riserva '98. There were good showings from Caparra & Siciliani, and from Vintripodi and Statti, not to mention the Lamezia Rosso Riserva '95 from the Cantine Lento di Lamezia. In addition, Dattilo and Vivacqua, listed in the Other Wineries section, are well worth watching. The former has Fabrizio Ciufoli as consultant, the latter works with the D'Attoma-Moltard duo. Improvements are practically assured.

CIRÒ (KR)

FATTORIA SAN FRANCESCO
LOC. QUATTROMANI
S. P. EX S. S. 106
88813 CIRÒ (KR)
TEL. 096232228
E-MAIL: info@fattoriasanfrancesco.it

Francesco Siciliani came pretty close to winning a Three Glass award this year. His '99 Cirò Rosso Classico Ronco dei Quattro Venti is a truly sumptuous wine. It shows not just how skilled Siciliani and his oenologist Fabrizio Ciufoli are in shaping impeccable wines but also the additional benefits of having modern, functional cellars, new oak to work with and, above all, better organized vineyards. The result is this deeply coloured wine with aromas of wild cherry jam and tobacco, threaded through with the floral hints that are so typical of Cirò, and a soft, elegant palate of decisive flavour. It is years since we last tasted a Cirò of such quality. It needs just a touch more complexity and length to conquer those Three Glasses and in fact we have no doubt that sooner or later it will do so. Just as important, though, the other wines in the range have improved, too. The more traditionally styled Cirò Rosso Donna Madda '99 is a very confidently-made wine and there were other more than decent bottles. The Martà '99, from gaglioppo and merlot, the white Pernicolò '00, from greco and chardonnay, the Cirò Bianco '00 and the popular Cirò Rosato '00, the winery's speciality, are all sound.

CIRÒ MARINA (KR)

CAPARRA & SICILIANI
BIVIO S. S. 106
88811 CIRÒ MARINA (KR)
TEL. 0962371435
E-MAIL: caparra&siciliani@cirol.it

It looks as if things are beginning to go a lot better at Caparra & Siciliani. Six wines were submitted for tasting and all scored well. This is one of Cirò's long-standing wineries and so the improvements are particularly encouraging. We are even more pleased as the zone has recently been struggling to keep pace with the rapid developments on the quality front in the rest of southern Italy. But let's have a look at the wines themselves. Cirò Rosso Classico Superiore Riserva comes top of the range and the '98 has turned out very well, with fullness, structure, good concentration and great typicity. The Cirò Classico Superiore Volvito '96 has good character, despite coming from a so-so vintage, but the '00 Cirò Bianco Curiale was rather a let-down after the impressive '99, which almost gained Two Glasses in last year's Guide. The other wines, Cirò Rosato '00, Cirò Bianco '00 and Cirò Rosso Classico '99 are all sound and well made, marking the winery out for reliability. Pricing is also very much in the consumer's favour.

● Cirò Rosso Cl. Ronco dei Quattro Venti '99	♀♀	5
● Cirò Rosso Cl. Sup. Donna Madda '99	♀♀	5
○ Cirò Bianco '00	♀	2
⊙ Cirò Rosato '00	♀	2
● Martà '99	♀	5
○ Pernicolò '00	♀	4
● Cirò Rosso Cl. Donna Madda '97	♀♀	5
● Cirò Rosso Cl. Ronco dei Quattro Venti '97	♀♀	4
● Cirò Rosso Cl. Ronco dei Quattro Venti '98	♀♀	5

○ Cirò Bianco '00	♀	3
○ Cirò Bianco Curiale '00	♀	3
⊙ Cirò Rosato '00	♀	3
● Cirò Rosso Cl. Sup. Volvito '96	♀	4
● Cirò Rosso Cl. Sup. Ris. '98	♀	3
● Cirò Rosso Cl. '99	♀	3
○ Cirò Bianco Curiale '99	♀♀	3
● Cirò Rosso Cl. Sup. Volvito '95	♀	3

CIRÒ MARINA (KR)

LIBRANDI
LOC. SAN GENNARO
S. S. 106
88811 CIRÒ MARINA (KR)
TEL. 096231518 - 096231519
E-MAIL: librandi@librandi.it

Having tasted our way through this year's output from Antonio, Cataldo and Nicodemo Librandi, we can sum it up quite simply as, well, a spectacular range of excellent wines. This is patently the result of a very clearly thought-out production philosophy, co-ordinated by oenologist Donato Lanati with he team from his Enosis company, based in Cuccaro Monferrato. The finest of them all, and the one that brings the Librandis back into the Three Glass club after several years' absence, is the '98 Gravello. Probably Librandi's most acclaimed wine, Gravello is made from almost equal proportions of gaglioppo and cabernet sauvignon given just over a year's ageing in small casks. The '98 is elegant, with plenty of fruit on the nose as well as light balsamic touches, and a harmonious palate of good length with ripe tannins. Close by comes Magno Megonio '99, made exclusively from magliocco. Possibly, it is not quite as good as the previous vintage but nevertheless it shows considerable body and depth. Next follows a series of wines that are well styled, if not more, most notably Le Passule '98, a sweet white from mantonico, and Critone '00, from chardonnay with a little sauvignon. Ciro Classico Riserva Duca Sanfelice '98 and the rosé Terre Lontane '00 are, as usual, attractive, The straightforward, simply-styled Cirò Rosato and Cirò Bianco, both from '00, bring this classy range to a close.

COSENZA

GIOVAN BATTISTA ODOARDI
V.LE DELLA REPUBBLICA, 143
87100 COSENZA
TEL. 098429961

Odoardi's Savuto '99 exemplifies exactly the sort of product a winelover with only moderately deep pockets is generally looking out for. It may not have huge complexity but it is so deliciously inviting that the bottle empties far too quickly. It is beautifully constructed, with an intensely fruity nose, plenty of body giving roundness and character, soft tannins, good length and terrific balance. What more can you ask from a price of € 7.50 or so on the shelves of a good wine shop? And remember that Odoardi also makes a Savuto selection, Vigna Mortilla. The latest vintage was not released in time for our tastings but we will be reviewing it for next year's Guide. If it lives up to expectations, you can be sure that we will have a fabulous wine on our hands, one to bring confidence in the way the estate, not to mention Calabrian winemaking in general, is headed. Next year, you'll be able to read about Valeo too, a sweet wine from moscato which did not reach us before we went to press. The '99 Savuto is not Odoardi's sole wine this year, though. It is flanked by two other good wines, Scavigna Bianco Pian della Corte and Scavigna Rosato, both '00. They are straightforward but well made, reflecting the style and traditions of this most dependable estate, a winery Calabria can be proud of.

● Gravello '98	🍷🍷🍷	5
● Magno Megonio '99	🍷🍷	6
○ Critone '00	🍷🍷	3*
○ Le Passule '98	🍷🍷	4
○ Cirò Bianco '00	🍷	3
⊙ Cirò Rosato '00	🍷	3
⊙ Terre Lontane '00	🍷	3
● Cirò Rosso Cl. Sup. Duca Sanfelice Ris. '98	🍷	4
● Gravello '89	🍷🍷🍷	5
● Gravello '90	🍷🍷🍷	5
● Magno Megonio '98	🍷🍷	6

● Savuto '99	🍷🍷	3*
○ Scavigna Bianco Pian della Corte '00	🍷	3*
⊙ Scavigna Rosato '00	🍷	3
● Savuto Sup. Vigna Mortilla '98	🍷🍷	4
○ Valeo '99	🍷🍷	5
● Scavigna Vigna Garrone '98	🍷	5
○ Scavigna Pian della Corte '99	🍷	4

COSENZA

SERRACAVALLO
FRAZ. BISIGNANO
VIA PIAVE - COSENZA, 51
87100 COSENZA
TEL. 098421144 - 33552722586

LAMEZIA TERME (CZ)

CANTINE LENTO
VIA DEL PROGRESSO, 1
88046 LAMEZIA TERME (CZ)
TEL. 096828028
E-MAIL: lento@cantinelento.com

In Calabria's rather wishy-washy high-quality wine scene, it is wonderfully reassuring to see a newcomer like Serracavallo sweep into the Guide in such grand style. The wines come entirely from the estate's own 18 hectares or so of vineyard and are all produced as IGTs ("indicazione geografica tipica", more or less equivalent to France's "vin de pays"). The one that impressed us most was Serracavallo Rosso Riserva '98, made from equal proportions of magliocco and cabernet sauvignon and aged for around 16 months in small French oak casks. It is a powerful, concentrated red with an intensely fruity nose laced through with very delicate hints of balsam. The palate is firm and full with nicely ripe tannins and very good length. It is partnered by the estate's two basic wines, both from '00. Serracavallo Bianco, from greco with a little sauvignon and, surprisingly, riesling, is joined by the most attractive, though not overly complex, Serracavallo Rosso, made from cabernet sauvignon with some magliocco. A further point to note is that about a quarter of the grapes grown here are magliocco, a highly characteristic indigenous variety which is more than likely to form the base for a whole raft of new wines across the region.

This is one of southern Italy's most modern wineries with a production capacity of around 500,000 bottles, including several remarkably fine wines. Moreover this year, the standard overall was particularly good, giving a clear indication of the way quality winemaking in Calabria is headed. As regards specifics, we were particularly impressed by the '95 Lamezia Rosso Riserva, from greco nero, gaglioppo and nerello. It has a developed, pervasive nose of wild cherry jam, with lightly smoky notes that enhance its complexity. There is considerable structure on the palate but also a softness and perfectly balanced tannins that come from its long maturation, first in small oak then in bottle. Both Lamezia Rosso Tenuta Romeo '99 and Federico II '98, from cabernet sauvignon, are also very good wines, as are the excellent unoaked Sauvignon, Contessa Emburga '00, and the classic Lamezia Greco, also '00, with its exotic, ripe aromas and softness on the palate. Together, these wines provide further insight into the great winemaking potential that lies under the surface in and around Lamezia. Salvatore Lento should be proud.

● Serracavallo Rosso Ris. '98	4
○ Serracavallo Bianco '00	3*
● Serracavallo Rosso '00	3

● Lamezia Rosso Ris. '95	5
○ Contessa Emburga '00	4
● Federico II '98	5
● Lamezia Rosso Tenuta Romeo '99	4
○ Lamezia Greco '00	4
● Lamezia Rosso Ris. '94	5
● Federico II '97	5
○ Contessa Emburga '99	4

LAMEZIA TERME (CZ)

Statti
Tenuta Lenti
88046 Lamezia Terme (CZ)
tel. 0968456138 - 0968453655
e-mail: statti@statti.com

This year has once more seen a series of ups and downs in the Statti wines, although with the work being put in by the estate's owners, Antonio and Alberto, and their winemaking staff, there is bound to be a lasting improvement before too long. For now, the wines remain well made but in several cases seem to lack something or other. The classic Lamezia Greco '00, though, was clearly one of the better examples. It has a fairly developed nose with aromas of ripe tropical fruit, and a rounded, mouthfilling palate given warmth, softness and proportion by its substantial weight of alcohol. The white Ligeia '00, from chardonnay and sauvignon aged briefly in small French oak barrels, is another good wine. Even and well made, it lacks that touch of complexity necessary to emerge from the crowd. Arvino '99, from gaglioppo and cabernet sauvignon, has one or two edges on the palate that reveal the paucity of its underlying structure but otherwise it is a decent wine. Cauro '98, from an intelligent mix of gaglioppo, magliocco and cabernet sauvignon, is the top red in the range. It did indeed show more positively, with its only partially suppressed richness of extract giving an idea of how little it would take to bring significant improvements.

REGGIO CALABRIA

Vintripodi
Fraz. Archi
Via Vecchia Comunale, 28
89051 Reggio Calabria
tel. 096548438 - 0965895009
e-mail: info@vintripodi.it

Vintripodi is without doubt the most eminent of the few winemaking estates in the province of Reggio Calabria. Without wishing to belittle Vintripodi's achievements, it comes hard to have to admit that a province renowned since ancient times for its wines now has so little to offer that is worthy of its past. At least Ignazio Tripodi is trying his best and, despite highs and lows, always manages to come up with something of interest. This year, one wine struck us in particular. The sweet white Mantonico, from mantonico grapes grown in the zone of another "desaparecido" wine, Greco di Bianco. The '96 evokes the splendour of this great wine of ancient origin. It has an amber hue, introducing an intense, lightly perfumed nose giving aromas of jam, honey and bottled fruit. The palate is sweet, highly concentrated, soft and rich in alcohol. In addition, the wine makes an excellent partner for Calabria's rich pastries. The Magna Grecia Bianco '00, IGT Calabria, from grecanico, inzolia and trebbiano, showed well enough, its style having much in common with the wines of its near neighbour, Sicily. The red Pellaro '98, also IGT and from nerello, alicante and castiglione, is highly typical of the zone and, although possibly rather simple, has good character and is technically unimpeachable.

○ Lamezia Greco '00	🍷	3
○ Ligeia '00	🍷	3
● Cauro '98	🍷	5
● Arvino '99		3
○ Ligeia '98	🍷🍷	3
● Cauro '97	🍷	5
○ Ligeia '99	🍷	3

○ Mantonico di Bianco '96	🍷🍷	5
○ Magna Grecia Bianco '00	🍷	3
● Pellaro '98	🍷	4

OTHER WINERIES

Cantina Enotria
Loc. San Gennaro - S. S. 106
88811 Cirò Marina (KR)
tel. 0962371181
e-mail: cantinaenotria@infinito.it

Around 1,500,000 bottles are produced each year and quality levels are decent. We point you particularly to the winery's most noted wine, Cirò Rosso Classico Superiore Riserva Piana delle Fate '97, which is well made and traditionally styled.

- Cirò Rosso Cl. Sup.
  Piana delle Fate Ris. '97 — 4

Vincenzo Ippolito
Via Tirone, 118
88811 Cirò Marina (KR)
tel. 096231106
e-mail: ippolito1845@ippolito1845.it

Founded back in 1845, this is one of Cirò's best known estates. There is a vast range of wines, topped by the Cirò Classico Superiore Colli del Mancuso Riserva '91, a fully evolved, very traditionally styled red with complex aromas and a decisive flavour.

- Cirò Rosso Cl. Sup.
  Colli del Mancuso Ris. '91 — 4

Dattilo
Loc. Marina di Strongoli
C.da Dattilo - 88815 Crotone
tel. 0962865613
e-mail: dattilo@genesi.it

The Dattilo wines have made improvements. We particularly liked the Amineo Bianco Donnacaterina '00, from chardonnay briefly aged in barrique. Amineo Rosso '99, from gaglioppo, cabernet and montepulciano, is also very nice.

- ○ Amineo Bianco
  Donnacaterina '00 — 4
- ● Amineo Rosso '99 — 3

Luigi Vivacqua
C.da San Vito
87040 Luzzi (CS)
tel. 0984543404 - 098428825
e-mail: luigi@vivacqua.it

The red Marinò, from gaglioppo and merlot, is the top Vivacqua wine. It ages in barrique for a year and has an intensely fruity nose, then a palate of notable finesse. Donna Aurelia '00, from greco, malvasia and chardonnay given a touch of new oak, is also good.

- ○ Donna Aurelia Chardonnay '00 — 3
- ● Marinò Rosso '98 — 4

SICILY

Sicily is turning into one of the world's great winemaking powers. The perhaps rather casual prediction we made some years back, that Sicily would become the California of the Mediterranean, was not just us trying to be cleverer than the rest. The truth is that in Sicily it is easier to make a good wine than a bad one. And that speaks volumes for the short-sightedness of the many producers in the 1970s and 1980s who ignored quality in a mad rush to turn out huge quantities of anonymous wines, motivated solely by cash and quick returns, however small. If only they had taken a longer term view, and used a bit more business nous, they could have reaped some extraordinary benefits. In those days, there were only a few wineries, principally Corvo and Tasca d'Almerita, who took up the quality cudgels and even fewer wines – Duca Enrico, Regaleali's Cabernet and their Chardonnay, Marco De Bartoli's Vecchio Samperi – that managed to express the enormous potential of the land and its exceptional vine-growing terrain. It is to these wines and wineries that we owe the start of the revolution – the term is no exaggeration – whose results we are now celebrating. It has been enormously satisfying to watch all this, to see just how much that is good and positive has come from the achievements of the new generation of Sicilian producers, and to have such confidence that the future will bring further improvements. For four years now, a little provocatively, we've made the once tiny estate, Planeta, from Sambuca di Sicilia, Winery of the Year. This year, a good three of its wines scored Three Glasses, which means that the three youngsters running the estate, Alessio, Francesca and Santi Planeta, have notched up an achievement that few other cellars - Gaja, La Spinetta, San Michele Appiano and Miani – can match. If we then consider their overall output, the Planetas have a better batting average than even Antinori and Ruffino. With the difference that the Planetas are in Sicily, not Piedmont, Tuscany or Alto Adige. And they are not the only stars in the Sicilian firmament. What about the large estate, Feudo Principi di Butera, that Gianni Zonin has recently created in the south east of the island? Or Morgante, Abbazia di Santa Anastasia, Pantelleria's Salvatore Murana? Or then again, the Cantina Sociale di Trapani and Cusumano from Partinico? And the rising stars, Cottanera, Spadafora, the tiny Ceuso and Abraxas? In addition, Tasca d'Almerita, Donnafugata, Benanti, Firriato and De Bartoli shine as brightly as ever, albeit without a bandleading Three Glass wine this year. Then there's Duca di Salaparuta, a winery of fundamental importance to the Sicilian scene, and one that merits separate comment. It has at last been sold by the Sicilian regional authority to Illva Saronno, which also owns Florio. There is now no reason why this famous, prestigious estate should not return in grand style, and the first signs are already appearing. We can only wish the new owners all the success in the world. Corvo is one of Italy's most important wine brands and it deserves the support of all those who, like us, believe that it's not such a great idea to sell off the family silver.

ACATE (RG)

Cantine Torrevecchia
C.da Torrevecchia
97011 Acate (RG)
Tel. 0916882064 - 0932990951
E-mail: cantinetorrevecchia@libero.it

It has been another good year for the congenial Beppe and Daniele Favuzza. The already large, well-diversified range from this sizeable winery has been augmented by some interesting new wines and, throughout, the lynchpins of the new Sicily – quality and reliability – are well in evidence. Four wines shone. First, let's take Bianco Biscari '99, from inzolia and chardonnay. It has admirable fruit-oak balance and is attractive, concentrated and long. The '00 vintage of Fontanabianca, a successful blend of syrah, cabernet sauvignon and merlot, is excellent. Soft and elegant, it has captivating spice and red berry fruit. Casale dei Biscari, made exclusively from nero d'Avola, remains one of the island's best indigenous reds. The '98 is deep ruby. It has a broad, complex array of attractive aromas with liqueur black cherries, blackcurrant and coffee to the fore. The palate is concentrated and meaty, with firm, fine-grained tannins. A new wine, Mont Serrat A.D. 1668, Cerasuolo di Vittoria '98, is basically a careful selection of grapes from particularly good sites. It shows nice character with clear scents of ripe fruit, cinnamon and liquorice, then an attractive, concentrated palate with a seductively warm, enveloping Mediterranean style. The rest of the range is well made, well styled and excellent value for money, too.

● Fontanabianca '00	▼▼	5
● Casale dei Biscari '98	▼▼	4
● Cerasuolo di Vittoria Mont Serrat A.D. 1668 '98	▼▼	4
○ Bianco Biscari '99	▼▼	4
○ Alcamo '00	▼	2*
○ Chardonnay '00	▼	2*
● Frappato '00	▼	3
○ Inzolia '00	▼	2*
● Pietra di Zoe '00	▼	1*
● Syrah '00	▼	4
● Cerasuolo di Vittoria '99	▼	2*
● Casale dei Biscari '97	▽▽	4
● Fontanabianca '99	▽▽	5
● Frappato '99	▽▽	3

ACATE (RG)

Cantina Valle dell'Acate
C. da Bidini
97011 Acate (RG)
Tel. 0932874166
E-mail: valledellecate@tin.it

Gaetana Jacono's relentless pursuit of wines that fully express the characteristics of their territory is really good news, even more so now that attractive wines with personality are emerging. Let's start with the wine we liked best this year, Bidis '99, curiously the only one not based on indigenous varieties. It comes, in fact, predominantly from chardonnay with some inzolia, and spends a year in oak. It has a good deep straw yellow colour, a nose of great elegance with intense aromas of spring flowers and banana, and a most attractively fresh, zesty palate. The successful, eminently drinkable '00 Inzolia is clean and has delicate floral perfumes. On to the reds. The first release of Il Moro, made solely from nero d'Avola, has a good ruby colour ushering in an intense, refined nose with balsamic notes, then a well-balanced palate. It will doubtless improve further with bottle maturation. Two other reds were assessed, both local classics in their way. The Frappato is rich in attractive morello cherry and red berry fruit flavours and a delight to drink. Neither does the frappato and nero d'Avola-based Cerasuolo di Vittoria disappoint. It offers delicate yet full aromas of green pepper, black pepper and spice, and a well-structured palate with good breadth and quite finely grained tannins.

○ Bidis '99	▼▼	2*
● Il Moro '99	▼	3
● Frappato '00	▼	2*
○ Inzolia '00	▼	2*
● Cerasuolo di Vittoria '99	▼	2*
● Frappato '97	▽▽	2
● Cerasuolo di Vittoria '94	▽	2
● Cerasuolo di Vittoria '95	▽	2
● Frappato '95	▽	2
● Cerasuolo di Vittoria '96	▽	3
● Frappato '96	▽	2
● Cerasuolo di Vittoria '98	▽	2
● Frappato '98	▽	2
● Frappato '99	▽	2

BUTERA (CL)

Feudo Principi di Butera
C.da Deliella
93011 Butera (CL)
tel. 0934347726

Raise your glasses to an extraordinary new Sicilian winery, the estate so eagerly desired by Gianni Zonin, a man who needs no introduction, and Franco Giacosa, the highly professional Piedmontese oenologist who worked to excellent effect for many years at Duca di Salaparuta, which means that he knows Sicily like the back of his hand. The Zonin Group made all sorts of pre-launch announcements but it was still difficult for those impatiently awaiting the wines to predict what they were going to be like. The reason is simple. Butera's climate and soils mean it has the potential to produce wines rivalling the world's best, or at least those from hot and usually dry areas, such as Napa, Barossa and Maipo. We finally had the chance to taste the wines in April '01 at Vinitaly, the major wine fair held each year in Verona. The Merlot '00 was extremely highly rated by practically all the tasters. Soft, fat, powerful and concentrated, it was a marvel. But then we got our lips and our tongues round the Cabernet '00 and the Merlot, great as it was, faded in comparison. Lightly balsamic notes duetted, like Ella and Satchmo, with sensations of wild berry fruits and jam. In the end, it was almost impossible not to swallow it and to spit it as professionalism demanded. Alongside these two giants, up popped another member of the band, an attractive, well fruited Chardonnay '00 that conceded nothing to the vanilla from the barriques. And they've only just started.

CASTELBUONO (PA)

Abbazia Santa Anastasia
C.da Santa Anastasia
90013 Castelbuono (PA)
tel. 0921671959 - 091201593
e-mail: info@abbaziasantanastasia.it

That great Sicilian red, Litra, is back in the Three Glass club with an imposing, concentrated '99 vintage. Still young, it hasn't yet shed its more austere tannic elements; even so, it will never have the mouthfilling softness of the '96 or the '97. It's partly vintage variation but more is due to the different direction that Abbazia di Santa Anastasia wines are now taking. This style shift has much to do with the technical credo of Riccardo Cotarella, the estate's consultant. Beside Litra, there is a distinctive version of Montenero, also '99, from nero d'Avola with some syrah and merlot. It is more elegant than the Litra at this stage but has a less powerful, less intense palate. The Passomaggio, from nero d'Avola with 20 per cent merlot, is another good wine and the '99 is one of its most successful vintages ever. Santa Anastasia, another '99 and the estate's standard-label wine, is made solely from nero d'Avola and showed well enough. Of course, it is a simpler wine but it offers reasonable body, despite an acidulous edge that is slightly at odds with its alcohol-glycerine softness. The whites, Zurrica '00, from inzolia with small amounts of pinot bianco and chardonnay, and Gemelli '00, from chardonnay with some sauvignon, are well made but lack great interest. They're a tad simple and neutral.

● Cabernet '00	🍷🍷🍷	6
● Merlot '00	🍷🍷	6
○ Chardonnay '00	🍷🍷	5

● Litra '99	🍷🍷🍷	5
● Montenero '99	🍷🍷	5
○ Gemelli '00	🍷	4
○ Zurrica '00	🍷	4
● Passomaggio '99	🍷	4
● Santa Anastasia Rosso '99	🍷	3
● Litra '96	🍷🍷🍷	5
● Litra '97	🍷🍷🍷	6
● Montenero '98	🍷🍷	5

CASTELDACCIA (PA)

Duca di Salaparuta - Vini Corvo
Via Nazionale, S. S. 113
90014 Casteldaccia (PA)
tel. 091945201
e-mail: vinicorvo@vinicorvo.it

The new regime at Duca di Salaparuta and the Corvo brand is now in place. After years of haggling and an auction that lasted over a year, the Sicilian regional authority has at last sold the concern. It went to Illva Saronno, which owns Florio as well as the famous liqueur Disaronno, once known as Amaretto. At the head of the operation is the Gianfranco Caci, who boasts a long career in management, first with Gruppo Italiano Vini, then with Cinzano and latterly at Saronno. On the technical side, Giacomo Tachis remains in control, which is excellent news. Even more comforting, though, is that the '96 Duca Enrico from nero d'Avola, which appeared erroneously in last year's Guide (we tasted a barrel sample), reached the tasting finals this year and came within an inch of collecting Three Glasses. It is certainly the best release in the past four years. Bianca di Valguarnera '98, from inzolia, also showed well, with its nose less masked by oak and displaying better defined fruit. Triskelé '98, from nero d'Avola, and the mainly frappato Terre d'Agala '98, are both decent while the aroma of Colomba Platino '00 was just a little too neutral. Corvo Rosso '99 seemed the most successful of the more classic wines, followed by Corvo Glicine '00 and then Corvo Bianco '00. All are well made, reliable but without any soaring quality peaks. We were less impressed, though, by the third nero d'Avola, Bennoto '98, which we found a bit too rustic and aggressive. Still, it's not an insurmountable problem. The important thing is that this is a completely new start for a key Sicilian estate.

●	Duca Enrico '96	▼	6
○	Bianca di Valguarnera '98	▼▼	5
○	Corvo Bianco '00	▼	3
○	Corvo Colomba Platino '00	▼	3
○	Corvo Glicine '00	▼	3
●	Terre d'Agala '98	▼	4
●	Corvo Rosso '99	▼	3
○	Bianca di Valguarnera '97	▼▼	5
●	Nero d'Avola Triskelè '98	▼	4

CASTIGLIONE DI SICILIA (CT)

Cottanera
C.da Iannuzzo
95030 Castiglione di Sicilia (CT)
tel. 0942963601

Cottanera is the hottest new property on the Sicilian wine scene. There are 50 hectares of vineyard, planted mainly with international varieties, and ownership is in the hands of brothers Guglielmo and Vincenzo Cambrìa, with Professor Leonardo Talenti from the University of Milan acting as technical supervisor. Two of his pupils, Giulio Vecchio and Luciana Biondo, partners in life as well as work, look after winemaking and grape growing respectively, and produce a small range of fascinating wines. In short, the estate is a gem. Let's begin with Ardenza '99, which does not refer to the Livorno football stadium of the same name but is a red wine from mondeuse, a variety from Savoie that arrived in the area by chance. The result is terrific: spicy aromas, great body, the ripest of tannins. Perhaps someone should make a more thorough study of the variety's potential in Mediterranean climates, and not just in eastern Sicily. The soft, concentrated Grammonte '99, from merlot, is also excellent while with Sole di Sesta, also '99, the syrah on which it is based gives a spicy, very varietal nose and considerable body. It's a wine of great personality, even if it is a little simpler than the first two. Fatagione '99, from nerello mascalese and nero d'Avola, is sound but less powerful. The two base wines, Barbazzale Bianco '00, from inzolia, and the Rosso '00, from the same blend as Fatagione but with a shorter time in oak, are also both sound and keenly priced. All this is just the beginning. You can be sure we'll be hearing more about this estate before too long.

●	Grammonte '99	▼	5
●	L'Ardenza '99	▼▼	5
●	Sole di Sesta '99	▼▼	5
○	Barbazzale Bianco '00	▼	3
●	Barbazzale Rosso '00	▼	3*
●	Fatagione '99	▼	4

CATANIA

BENANTI
LOC. VIAGRANDE
VIA G. GARIBALDI, 475
95029 CATANIA
TEL. 0957893438 - 0957893533
E-MAIL: benanti@sifi.it

The wines of Etna are not the easiest to deal with. We are in Sicily but sometimes you forget that the vineyards may be at altitudes more than 600 or 700 metres above sea level. This means that latitude can lead you astray. Etna's wines have more Nordic characteristics than you might imagine. At times, they need longer ageing. On other occasions, the acidity, particularly in the whites, is appreciable. It has to be said, though, that there are very few Sicilian wines that develop with time, gaining in overall complexity, like those from Etna. That said, let's look the wines from Benanti, indisputably the best winery in the area. This year, the estate's "monovarietals" operation has been implemented rigorously. The idea is to produce a series of yardstick wines, one for each of the main varieties cultivated on the property. Of the six wines presented, we liked the Nero d'Avola and, particularly, the Cabernet Sauvignon, both from '98, while the other four, the Nerello Cappuccio, the Nerello Mascalese, the Carricante and the Chardonnay, also '98s, were less impressive. However, all except the Cabernet had also been reviewed last year. Moving on to the DOC Etna wines, the '97 Pietramarina is excellent, as usual. There is complexity of aroma and, with its acidulous, citrus notes, great personality of taste. The Bianco di Caselle '00 is simpler but satisfactory.

GROTTE (AG)

MORGANTE
C.DA RACALMARE
92020 GROTTE (AG)
TEL. 0922945579
E-MAIL: camorg@tin.it

Right on cue, Three Glasses arrived at Morgante for the second year running, an attainment that catapults the Grotte estate into the front rank of Italian wine. In truth, this renewed success doesn't come to us as much of a surprise. It is simply the logical outcome of a strategy inaugurated some years back, part of which saw technical management entrusted to the leading oenologist, Riccardo Cotarella. Not all the credit is Cotarella's, though. The accomplishment is also due to Carmelo and Giovanni Morgante who, with their father Antonio, to whom the estate's top wine is dedicated, spend the entire day in their extensive vineyards, which spread over the fine countryside of Racalmare and Poggio Scintilia. The profile of the '99 Don Antonio is similar to last year's star performer. A magnificent monovarietal Nero d'Avola, with a deep ruby colour, it shows a broad spectrum of aromas, centred on ripe red berry fruits, spices and dark chocolate. The palate is powerful, almost meaty in consistency, and very well balanced, with solid, ripe tannins. It ought not, though, be allowed to overshadow the '99 Nero d'Avola, which is a deep ruby with delightful aromas of red berries and damson, and has a strong yet soft palate with notable extractive weight.

	Wine	Glasses	Score
○	Etna Bianco Sup. Pietramarina '97	⚜⚜	5
●	Cabernet Sauvignon '98	⚜⚜	5
○	Etna Bianco Bianco di Caselli '00	⚜	4
●	Lamoremio '97	⚜⚜	5
●	Etna Rosso Rovittello '97	⚜	5
○	Carricante '98	⚜	5
○	Chardonnay '98	⚜	5
●	Nerello Cappuccio '98	⚜	5
●	Nerello Mascalese '98	⚜	5
●	Nero d'Avola '98	⚜	5

	Wine	Glasses	Score
●	Don Antonio '99	⚜⚜⚜	5
●	Nero d'Avola '99	⚜⚜	3*
●	Don Antonio '98	⚜⚜⚜	5
●	Nero d'Avola '98	⚜	3

LICATA (AG)

BARONE LA LUMIA
C.DA CASAL POZZILLO
92027 LICATA (AG)
TEL. 0922770057 - 0922806194
E-MAIL: info@vogliedisicilia.it

Barone Nicolò La Lumia produces fine grapes. His terrain lies close to the crystal-clear waters that separate Sicily from Africa and has magnificent exposure to its sea breezes. Landscapes are parched here, baked by a hot sun that beats down powerfully for seven months each year. And the Baron's wines reflect this Mediterranean warmth. We must also acknowledge his commitment to producing wines from local varieties. Nero d'Avola and inzolia form the base of practically all the estate's output. Let's start with Nikao, a dried-grape "passito" from nero d'Avola. Intense red, it has pervasive aromas and a youthful palate with body and ripe tannins. Don Totò, also from nero d'Avola, is an almost opaque ruby red. It offers a broad spectrum of aromas and a long, full palate. Limpiados and Signorio Rosso '98, another two nero d'Avola monovarietals, are aged and matured differently but share the same principal characteristic – heady warmth. Delizia del Conte '98, a nerello mascalese and frappato blend, has delicate aromas of morello cherry and a fresh drinkability. But the wine we liked most this year was Halykàs, made solely from inzolia, with a proportion of the grapes allowed to become super-ripe. The nose has pervasive, well-defined aromas of tropical fruit overlain with more subtle secondary candied fruit scents. The palate develops evenly, with good intensity and superb balance. The run finishes with Gloria and Sogno di Dama. The former, from inzolia blended with other local varieties, is fresh and immediate while the monovarietal inzolia Sogno di Dama has intriguing green pepper notes.

MARSALA (TP)

MARCO DE BARTOLI
C.DA FORNARA, 292
91025 MARSALA (TP)
TEL. 0923962093 - 0923918344

Marco De Bartoli is one of the pioneers of quality Sicilian wine, holding the banner aloft even when no one else seemed to believe that the island really was suited to fine wine production. He started and continued on his difficult course with commitment and dogged intransigence, despite a thousand and one obstacles and pitfalls, now thankfully all behind him. And the "old lion" can at last enjoy his moment of glory, in the knowledge that time has finally proved him right. Indomitable and combative as ever, he now has two talented "pups" at his side, his sons Renato and Sebastiano, both in their 20s and both successful oenologists. They may be less fiercely vehement than their father but are just as passionate. The wines sent for tasting demonstrated that great care had been taken with their vinification. The results were very gratifying indeed. Pietra Nera '00, a soft, perfumed dry Zibibbo, is delicate and alluring. The equally good Grappoli del Grillo '00 has excellent fruit and an imposing structure. The Passito di Pantelleria Bukkuram '98, has a lovely amber colour and penetrating notes of honey and dates. It's as delicious as ever. The Marsala Superiore, a fabulous wine for cheese, is superb, as is Vecchio Samperi Ventennale with its dried fruit, leather and tobacco, and Marsala Superiore Riserva 20 Anni, deep, full of character and with unforgettable toasty aromas. The rest of the range is impeccable, too.

○ Halykas '00	♉♉	3*
○ Gloria '00	♉	3
○ Sogno di Dama '00	♉	4
● Stemma '00	♉	3
● Cadetto Rosso '98	♉	3
● Don Totò '98	♉	4
● Limpiados '98	♉	3
● Nikao '98	♉	3
● Signorio Rosso '98	♉	3
● Delizia del Conte '99	♉	3
● Don Totò '97	♉♉	4
○ Sogno di Dama '99	♉♉	4
● Signorio Rosso '96	♉	3
● Delizia del Conte '98	♉	3

○ Grappoli del Grillo '00	♉♉	4
○ Pietranera '00	♉♉	4
○ Passito di Pantelleria Bukkuram '98	♉♉	6
○ Marsala Sup.	♉♉	5
○ Marsala Sup. Ris. 20 Anni	♉♉	5
○ Vecchio Samperi Ventennale	♉♉	6
○ Sole e Vento '00	♉	4
● Rosso di Marco '99	♉	4
○ Vigna La Miccia	♉	6
○ Passito di Pantelleria Bukkuram '94	♉♉	5
○ Marsala Sup. 20 Anni	♉♉	5
○ Vecchio Samperi	♉♉	5

MARSALA (TP)

Tenuta di Donnafugata
Via Sebastiano Lipari, 18
91025 Marsala (TP)
tel. 0923724200
e-mail: info@donnafugatatin.it

Donnafugata's wines put in a good team effort this year. Sadly, there was no crowning glory of Three Glasses but with two wines reaching the final taste-off, the cellar wasn't far off. In any event, the overall class of the estate is unimpeachable and the improvements seen in the last few years are turning it into one of the region's leaders. Credit for this is due to the clear-sighted acumen of Giacomo Rallo and his offspring, José and Antonio. This year, the best wine in the range was the '00 Pantelleria Ben Ryé, possibly its best release ever. It has remarkably well-defined perfumes, with overt aromatics, and a palate that is full and sweet without cloying. Tancredi '99, from nero d'Avola and cabernet sauvignon, is also top notch, being fuller and more even than in the past. Indeed, we found it even better than the predominantly nero d'Avola Milleunanotte '97. This may be more powerful and concentrated but it is also a tad over-evolved on the nose. Chiarandà del Merlo '00, a barrique-aged Chardonnay, is as elegant and even as ever though the nose is less complex than the previous vintage and it has a little less body. However, the real surprise this year, is Angheli '99, from nero d'Avola and merlot, which beautifully combines softness with good structure. Both the chardonnay-based La Fuga '00 and Vigna di Gabri '00, from inzolia, or ansonica as it is called in these parts, seemed more or less at their usual standard. Good news all round, then, as the winery's profile continues to rise and gain individuality with each year that passes.

O	Passito di Pantelleria Ben Ryé '00	♟♟	5
●	Tancredi '99	♟♟	5
O	Contessa Entellina Chiarandà del Merlo '00	♟♟	5
●	Milleunanotte '97	♟♟	6
●	Angheli '99	♟♟	5
O	Contessa Entellina Chardonnay La Fuga	♟	4
O	Contessa Entellina Vigna di Gabri '00	♟	4
O	Contessa Entellina Chiarandà del Merlo '98	♟♟♟	5
O	Contessa Entellina Chiarandà del Merlo '99	♟♟♟	5

MARSALA (TP)

Cantine Florio
Via Vincenzo Florio, 1
91025 Marsala (TP)
tel. 0923781111
e-mail: marsala@cantineflorio.com

You could make a film about the history of the Florios. They were the undisputed leaders of Sicilian trade at the beginning of the century and presided over an economic empire of banks, construction and shipping companies. They also sponsored a motor race, the famous Targa Florio, and owned agricultural and wine estates, including the one that still bears their name. Today the shareholding may be in the hands of Illva di Saronno but the wines still mature in Florio's fascinating ancient cellars carved out of the tufa rock, just as they always have done. But let us come to this year's wines. Targa Riserva '91, a Marsala Superiore based on inzolia and grillo, has a bright amber hue and is soft and mellow on the nose. The full-flavoured, grillo and catarratto-based Vecchio Florio Riserva Marsala '93 is similarly soft and silky, and an ideal partner for dainty Sicilian biscuits. Another good showing came from Terre Arse '90, which is redolent of tobacco and dried fruits, and the inviting Baglio Florio '98, with aromas of honey, hazelnut and liquorice. The '98 Morsi di Luce, from moscato, is as good as usual, with an attractive golden colour and sensual aromas of elderflower, toasted hazelnut and dates. But the final word goes to Grecale '00, a sweet white of surprising freshness, which fully expresses the character of the grapes from which it comes. Moreover, just try it with a hunk of moderately mature cheese.

O	Marsala Sup. Ris. Targa 1840 '91	♟♟	4
O	Marsala Sup. Vecchioflorio Ris. '93	♟♟	4
O	Morsi di Luce '98	♟♟	5
O	Marsala Vergine Terre Arse '90	♟	4
O	Marsala Vergine Baglio Florio '98	♟	4
O	Grecale Vino Liquoroso	♟	2*
O	Marsala Soleras Oro Baglio Florio '79	♟♟	6
O	Marsala Vergine Baglio Florio '85	♟♟	5
O	Marsala Vergine Baglio Florio '86	♟♟	5
O	Marsala Sup. Vecchioflorio Ris. '91	♟♟	4
O	Morsi di Luce '95	♟♟	4
O	Morsi di Luce '97	♟♟	5

MARSALA (TP)

CARLO PELLEGRINO
VIA DEL FANTE, 37
91025 MARSALA (TP)
TEL. 0923719911
E-MAIL: info@carlopellegrino.it

Pellegrino has been celebrating its 120 glorious years of activity in grand style. And why not? It has a large turnover that is growing exponentially and a range of reliable, well made wines that are drunk by millions of consumers – enough to make anyone happy. All the wines, from the simplest to the most serious, which are sold under the Duca di Castelmonte label, clearly express the company strategy. Resolutely championed by Michele Sala and Massimo Bellina, managing director and export director respectively, the aim is to offer well differentiated wines of quality, drinkability and practically unrivalled value for money. This year, we greatly admired the Cabernet Sauvignon '98, produced under the new Delia Nivolelli DOC. It is an exemplary, dark ruby wine with delicate aromas of blackcurrant and spices. Forward on the palate, it shows depth, great textured and a caressing mouthfeel. Gorgo Tondo Bianco '00, with delicate florality and fruit, is also very good while the '99 release of Passito Nes is the best ever. Long, and absolutely delicious, it's a real treat to drink. Dom Pellegrino, an excellent Marsala Superiore Riserva scored just as highly. All the other wines showed well, too, but those that were particularly attractive turned out to be the Ulysse '99, an impeccable Etna Rosso, and the Gorgo Tondo Rosso '98.

O	Gorgo Tondo Bianco '00	ΨΨ	3*
●	Delia Nivolelli Cabernet Sauvignon '98	ΨΨ	4
O	Passito di Pantelleria Nes '99	ΨΨ	5
O	Marsala Sup. Ris. Dom Pellegrino	ΨΨ	4
O	Cent'Are Bianco '00	Ψ	2
O	Moscato di Pantelleria '00	Ψ	4
O	Passito di Pantelleria '00	Ψ	4
O	Traimani '00	Ψ	2
●	Cent'Are Rosso '98	Ψ	3
●	Gorgo Tondo Rosso '98	Ψ	3
●	Ulysse '99	Ψ	3
●	Marsala Fine Ruby	Ψ	3
O	Marsala Sup. Oro	Ψ	3

MARSALA (TP)

CANTINE RALLO
VIA VINCENZO FLORIO, 2
91025 MARSALA (TP)
TEL. 0923721633 - 092372163

Marsala Vergine Soleras Riserva 12 Anni is the most impressive wine from Rallo this year. This is especially gratifying because Rallo started out as an important Marsala producer and the fact that this ancient tradition still forms a significant part of its winemaking philosophy is something we are pleased to document. Reasonably enough, though, despite this historical and symbolic importance, the winery does not live by Marsala alone and a series of modern, innovative wines line up with it in the catalogue. The first and the best is without doubt the '99 Merlot, one of the best from Sicily we tasted this year. Next come Vesco Bianco '00, from inzolia and chardonnay; Areté, also white, also '00 and, unusually, for Sicily, from müller thurgau; and Passito di Pantelleria Mare d'Ambra, which is already one of the estate's classics. All are well made technically and perfectly correct but lack any real hint of excitement. Both the Chardonnay '00 and the Vesco Rosso '99, from nero d'Avola and cabernet, are also commendable although possibly less impressive than the other wines presented. In any event, it is good to see once more that behind this prestige label there is substance and not just the memory of past glories, as is still the case sometimes elsewhere in Sicily and indeed on the mainland.

●	Merlot '99	ΨΨ	4
O	Marsala Vergine Soleras Ris. 12 anni	ΨΨ	4
O	Areté '00	Ψ	2
O	Chardonnay '00	Ψ	4
O	Vesco Bianco '00	Ψ	4
●	Vesco Rosso '99	Ψ	4
O	Passito di Pantelleria Mare d'Ambra	ΨΨ	4
O	Grillo '99	ΨΨ	3
●	Vesco Rosso '96	Ψ	4
●	Vesco Rosso '97	Ψ	3
●	Vesco Rosso '98	Ψ	3
O	Marsala Sup. Ambra Semisecco	Ψ	3

MENFI (AG)

Settesoli
S. S. 115
92013 Menfi (AG)
tel. 092577111

Settesoli is an astounding co-operative for all sorts of reasons. It has a large number of members; it handles vast quantities of grapes; its turnover is constantly growing, in fact the winery is the powerhouse that drives the local economy; the high average quality of the wines is high; their styling is technically impeccable; and the price asked are very competitive. Obviously, all this hasn't happened by chance. Indeed, everything grew from a clearly thought-out, rational plan. But the real triumph stemmed from the abilities of Settesoli's clear-sighted, intelligent president, Diego Planeta, a man of great determination, and the long-term thinking and sense of unity of purpose he managed to inspire in everyone involved. This means all the co-operative's grape-supplying members now have great faith in both Planeta and the project itself, as well as Carlo Corino, the internationally renowned consultant who undertook the practical work. The wines reviewed are all from the well-known Mandrarossa line. The Merlot '00 is a fine bottle, with clean blackberry and cherry aromas, and a soft, silky palate. Equally good is the concentrated, attractive and very drinkable Rosso di Sicilia '00. Bendicò '99, a barrique-aged blend of nero d'Avola, merlot and syrah, is a welcome newcomer to the range. Cherry and ripe red berry fruit dominate its nose and it has a well-structured, velvety palate with ripe, elegant tannins. Sheer delight in the mouth! The remainder of the range is consistently well made and all the wines deserve praise for their superb value for money.

MESSINA

Palari
Loc. Santo Stefano Briga
C.da Barna
98137 Messina
tel. 090630194 - 090694281
e-mail: vinipalari@tin.it

The '99 Faro Palari missed Three Glasses by a hair's breadth, leaving the '96 and '98 alone on their podium. Nonetheless, it is an elegant wine, with great finesse, something that is still pretty rare in Sicily. But the question is will Turi Geraci, urbane Messina-based architect that he is, be able with his personality to accept this judgement? We hope so, because we esteem and admire him, and we have to admit that we will miss him at the Three Glass wine presentations we'll be holding in the United States and Germany. He's like a sort of good luck charm. When he's around things always go well. And he is a cultured man with an attractive personality and is always ready with a witty remark. Indeed, the '99 Faro Palari, with its elegance, its well-contained structure and its excellent balance, resembles him more than a little. And maybe Turi Gerace should have nudged it into being even more like himself, giving it a little more depth and a little more complexity. But there's always another chance, and another vintage to improve things. The technical side is still being looked after excellently by Donato Lanati's Enosis team and this is very reassuring. The estate's second wine, Rosso di Soprano, is, like the Palari, made from nerello mascalese and nerello cappuccio. The '99 vintage is performing very well. It has a clear resemblance to its stablemate but is simply a little less classy. Nevertheless, it is still easily a Two Glass wine. And so the tale of this tiny but remarkable estate goes on.

●	Mandrarossa Rosso '00	♛♛	3
●	Merlot Mandrarossa '00	♛♛	3
●	Mandrarossa Bendicò '99	♛♛	4
●	Cabernet Sauvignon Mandrarossa '00	♛	3
○	Chardonnay Mandrarossa '00	♛	3
○	Grecanico Mandrarossa '00	♛	3
○	Mandrarossa Bianco '00	♛	3
●	Nero d'Avola Mandrarossa '00	♛	3
●	Bonera '94	♛♛	3
○	Feudo dei Fiori '97	♛♛	2
●	Nero d'Avola '98	♛♛	3
●	Nero d'Avola/Cabernet '98	♛♛	3
○	Chardonnay Mandrarossa '99	♛♛	3
●	Merlot Mandrarossa '99	♛♛	3

●	Faro Palari '99	♛♛	6
●	Rosso del Soprano '99	♛♛	5
●	Faro Palari '96	♛♛♛	5
●	Faro Palari '98	♛♛♛	6
●	Faro Palari '94	♛♛	5
●	Faro Palari '95	♛♛	5
●	Faro Palari '97	♛♛	6
●	Rosso del Soprano '98	♛♛	5

MILO (CT)

Barone di Villagrande
Via del Bosco
95025 Milo (CT)
Tel. 0957082175 - 0957494339

It is a great pleasure to be able to dedicate a full profile to Carlo Asmundo Nicolosi's fine estate at Milo, right under Etna, Europe's most active volcano, as many had the opportunity to observe last summer. The wines that were sent for tasting impressed us greatly. Let's start with the '98 Sciara, which is a blend of merlot and nerello mascalese with some other local varieties. It eclipsed even last year's highly successful version with its ruby-red colour, its complex nose of musk, liquorice and spice, and its beautifully balanced palate that shows power alongside roundness and harmony. The dry Etna Rosso, mainly from nerello mascalese, is simple and immediate. Fiore di Villagrande '99, a white made solely from carricante, takes Two Glasses with style for its fresh flowers, green apple and vanilla nose, and its harmonious palate with good aromatic length. The Etna Bianco '00 and the Fiore '00, both based on carricante grown on different parts of Etna's slopes, are well-styled and attractive. Both have flower and fruit aromas, a balanced but not overweening structure and a mid-length finish.

● Sciara di Villagrande Rosso '98	🍷🍷	4
● Fiore di Villagrande '99	🍷🍷	3*
○ Etna Bianco '00	🍷	3
○ Fiore '00	🍷	3
● Etna Rosso '98	🍷	3
○ Malvasia delle Lipari Passito		5
● Etna Rosso '94	🍷	3

MONREALE (PA)

Pollara
C.da Malvello - S. P. 4 bis km 2
90046 Monreale (PA)
Tel. 0918462922 - 0918463512
E-mail: pollara@principedicorleone.it

Year by year, the wines of brothers Giuseppe and Vincenzo Pollara have been slowly edging forward in quality. Now they have reached highly encouraging levels. Principe di Corleone Cabernet Sauvignon is the best of the bunch. A brightly tinged deep red, it has a pervasive nose with a bouquet of red berry fruit, plum, leather, spice and cocoa powder, then a rounded palate of good presence. Next comes Il Rosso '98, a fine Nero d'Avola from grapes grown at Malvello, which is well balanced, with a clearly defined array of aromas. Equally good is the fragrant and richly aromatic standard-label Nero d'Avola '99. The whites match the reds for style. Chardonnay Vigna di Corte has good nose-palate harmony with attractive aromas of oak toast and green banana, and a fresh, decisive palate. The Pinot Bianco and the Giada '00, mainly from damaschino, are of similar quality and, with their delicate florality and refreshing flavours, are both wines made to give simple, immediate pleasure. They are also ideal with lightly fried anchovies, sardines or mackerel. The '00 Alcamo, though, stands apart. From catarratto and damaschino, it is richly fruited, correctly structured, and harmonious and zesty on the palate. In short, a very good wine.

● Cabernet Sauvignon Principe di Corleone '99	🍷🍷	3*
○ Alcamo Principe di Corleone '00	🍷	2
○ Chardonnay Vigna di Corte '00	🍷	3
○ Giada Bianco '00	🍷	2*
○ Pinot Bianco Principe di Corleone '00	🍷	2*
● Il Rosso '99	🍷	3
● Nero d'Avola '99	🍷	2*
○ Inzolia '00		2
● Cabernet Sauvignon Principe di Corleone '96	🍷	3
● Cabernet Sauvignon Principe di Corleone '97	🍷	3

PACECO (TP)

Casa Vinicola Firriato
Via Trapani, 4
91027 Paceco (TP)
tel. 0923882755
e-mail: info@firriato.it

Girolamo and Salvatore Di Gaetano may have missed Three Glasses by a hair but three magnificent wines from an excellent range reached our final taste-offs and their winery remains one of the brightest stars in the Sicilian wine firmament. Let's have a look at their offerings. Camelot '99 is a wine of extraordinary power and complexity, further enhanced by seductively soft, palate-caressing tannins. The '99 Santagostino Baglio Soria is excellent, as usual, and furthermore very well priced. It is an opaque ruby colour. There is a wonderful ripe berry fruitiness on the nose, most notably of blackcurrant, then on the palate there is perfect balance between the vibrancy of the nero d'Avola and the finesse of the syrah. The third star is a new wine, Harmonium '99, made solely from the classy nero d'Avola variety. A magnificent dark ruby colour precedes a wide ranging swathe of aromas, with liquorice, cocoa powder and plum most dominant. Attractive, warm and vigorous, with tightly-knit, velvety tannins, it is a fascinating wine and a masterpiece of harmony and elegance. The remaining wines in the range are all well made and show great technical prowess, not to mention admirable overall quality. However, particular mention should go to the elegant Santagostino '00 Baglio Soria, from a catarratto and chardonnay blend, and the Altavilla della Corte wines, the '00 white and the '99 red, both exemplary and sold at surprisingly good prices.

PALERMO

Calatrasi - Terre di Ginestra
Loc. San Cipirello
C.da Piano Piraino
90040 Palermo
tel. 0918576767 - 0918578080
e-mail: calat@gestelnet.it

Antonio Miccichè, owner of Calatrasi, has an excellent business head on his shoulders. In less than a decade, he's built up what amounts to a wine empire, with an annual production capacity of several million bottles, and comprising two lines, Terre di Ginestra and D'Istinto. In addition, he has even set up a small wine business in Tunisia, producing a good Carignan called Selian, which we can't comment on further as this is an Italian wine guide! That said, let's review the wines presented for tasting this time round. The estate's two classic wines, Terre di Ginestra Bianco '00 from catarratto and Terre di Ginestra Rosso '99 from nero d'Avola are as well styled as ever. Of the many wines from the D'Istinto range, the one that impressed us most was the '00 Sangiovese-Merlot. With over 1,000,000 bottles produced annually, it is quite simply a fabulously drinkable fruit-driven wine sold at an excellent price. The simple, attractive Catarratto-Chardonnay '00 is good stuff, as are Nero '99, from nero d'Avola and Magnifico '98. This latter, which was well received when it was first tasted last year, is from nero d'Avola, cabernet, syrah and merlot, with 18 months in barrique. The '99 Syrah paled a little in comparison but this is barely significant in a range that shows good winemaking and correctness of style throughout.

● Camelot '99	🍷🍷	6
● Harmonium '99	🍷🍷	6
● Santagostino Rosso Baglio Soria '99	🍷🍷	4
○ Alcamo '00	🍷🍷	2*
○ Altavilla della Corte Bianco '00	🍷🍷	3*
○ Santagostino Bianco Baglio Soria '00	🍷🍷	4
● Altavilla della Corte Rosso '99	🍷🍷	3*
○ Primula Bianco '00	🍷	1*
● Etna Rosso '98	🍷	2*
● Primula Rosso '99	🍷	1*
● Camelot '98	🍷🍷🍷	5
● Etna Rosso '97	🍷🍷	2
● Altavilla della Corte Rosso '98	🍷🍷	3

● D'Istinto Sangiovese-Merlot '00	🍷🍷	3*
○ Terre di Ginestra Bianco '00	🍷🍷	3*
○ D'Istinto Catarratto-Chardonnay '00	🍷	3
● D'Istinto Nero '99	🍷	4
● Terre di Ginestra Rosso '99	🍷	4
● D'Istinto Syrah '99		4
● D'Istinto Magnifico '98	🍷🍷	4

PALERMO

CUSUMANO
S. S. 113 - C.DA SAN CARLO
90047 PALERMO
TEL. 0918903456
E-MAIL: cusumano@cusumano.it

The Cusumano winery, listed last year under the name Cadivin and owned by two young brothers, the congenial, brilliant Alberto and Diego Cusumano, has seen a spectacular upsurge in the quality of its wines. So much so that one of them picked up Three Glasses, and with a very high score. The wine is the fabulous Noa' '00, from a blend of nero d'Avola, merlot and cabernet sauvignon. But there's more: Sagana '00, a monovarietal nero d'Avola of exceptional quality also made it to the final taste-off. Beside these two superstars, the magic touch of Mario Ronco, famed Piedmontese winemaker, has created a range of surprisingly high quality to project this new estate straight into the top echelon of Sicilian wineries. Now for the wines themselves. Noa' '00 has a lovely dark red colour. The nose has clear-cut, deeply intense notes of ripe fruit and spices, underscored with unusual nuances of oregano and Mediterranean scrub. The palate captivates with its power, its seductive, silky ripe tannins and its incredible length. Challenging it for quality is the perfumed, pervasive Sagana '00 with its great concentration and persistence on both nose and palate. Finally, Benuara '00, a successful blend of nero d'Avola and syrah, Jalè '00, from barrique-fermented chardonnay, and the excellent Angimbé '00, from chardonnay and inzolia, are all well worth investigating. All the other wines presented showed well too.

PALERMO

AZIENDE VINICOLE MICELI
VIA DENTI DI PIRAINO, 9
90142 PALERMO
TEL. 0916396111
E-MAIL: midi@midmiceli.it

This has been a very good year for the go-ahead Aziende Vinicole Miceli. All the efforts of the past few years, and all the work lavished on the two properties at Castelvetrano and on the island of Pantelleria, are now paying off. Well-made, characterful wines are emerging from the two state-of-the-art cellars, wines that will no doubt bring excellent returns to manager Giuseppe Lo Re. Starting at the top, the '00 Ymm is probably the best release ever of this fascinating dry Zibibbo di Pantelleria. Soft, gentle and Mediterranean in character, it's ideal to drink with seafood starters. Similarly impressive are the '99 Cabernet Sauvignon and Chiana d'Inserra '98. The former, made exclusively from cabernet sauvignon, is a concentrated ruby and has a complex mix of bottled red berry fruits, plum and liquorice. The Chiana d'Inserra, from a successful blend of nero d'Avola and cabernet sauvignon, is the perfect marriage of power and elegance, plus its beautifully fine-grained tannins give fabulous mouthfeel. The intriguing new Entelechia, a Moscato di Pantelleria, from the volcanic soils of the most fascinating of Mediterranean islands, is an absolute gem, spellbinding with its delicate, soft notes of honey and dates. The remainder of the wines this year also showed well.

● Noà '00	▼▼▼	5
● Sagana '00	▼▼	5
○ Angimbé '00	▼▼	3*
● Benuara '00	▼▼	4*
○ Jalé '00	▼▼	4
○ Cubia '00	▼	4
○ Nadarìa Alcamo '00	▼	2*
○ Nadarìa Inzolia '00	▼	2*
● Nadaria Nero d'Avola '00	▼	2*
● Nadaria Syrah '00	▼	2*

○ Yrnm '00	▼	4
● Cabernet Sauvignon '99	▼▼	5
○ Chiana d'Inserra '99	▼▼	4
○ Passito di Pantelleria Entelechia	▼▼	6
○ Chardonnay '00	▼	5
○ Guggino '00	▼	5
● Nero d'Avola '00	▼	3
○ Organza '00	▼	3
○ Dedicato '99	▼	6
○ Initio '99	▼	5
● Majo San Lorenzo '99	▼	5
● Syrah '99	▼	5
○ Garighe Zibibbo	▼	4
○ Passito di Pantelleria Nun	▼	5
○ Passito di Pantelleria Tanit	▼	4

PALERMO

Tenute Rapitalà
Via Segesta, 9
90141 Palermo
tel. 091332088
e-mail: cantinarapitala@giv.it

The comments in last year's Guide hold good this year, too. Rapitalà wines are pleasing, well styled and well made. The new controlling interest by GIV, and the work of able Piedmontese oenologist Marco Monchiero, are beginning to bear fruit and we are convinced that in a few years, Conte Hugues de la Gatinais, his wife Gigi and son Laurent will be more than happy with the changes. Let us start with Rapitalà Conte Hugues '99, a good catarratto and chardonnay blend. It has a delightful nose, clean, floral and well fruited, while the palate has good character and a surprisingly full, long aftertaste for a white wine. Next comes Casalj '00. Made from the same varieties, it has a stylish nose and an immediate, fresh, intriguing personality. The Rapitalà DOC Alcamo showed well with the typical aromas of its varieties, a fresh, zesty palate and an attractive almondy aftertaste. The final white is Bouquet '00, a blend of sauvignon and catarratto blend. Water white, it has attractive floral perfumes with hints of green pepper. The reds are led by Nuhar '00, from the unusual mix of nero d'Avola and pinot nero. It has intense, well-knit fruity perfumes, with notes of tobacco and chocolate, followed by a soft, balanced palate. Finally, Rapitalà Rosso is well styled and easy drinking. It comes from nero d'Avola, nerello mascalese and perricone, the last of these an ancient Sicilian variety that is practically extinct.

PALERMO

Spadafora
Via Ausonia, 90
90100 Palermo
tel. 091514952 - 0916703322
e-mail: info@spadafora.com

Francesco Spadafora's estate missed Three Glasses by a whisker with Schietto. Nevertheless, the highly successful '99 vintage submitted this year was the best we have ever tasted. It is a good, deep red, ushering in rich, pervasive aromas of bitter cherry, plum, pencil lead and tobacco. The palate is full and firm with balanced, fine-grained tannins, In a nutshell, it is a wine that the Sicilian tasting panel had to rate very highly. Don Pietro '99, a wine full of red berry aromas and with a decisive attack of ripe tannins, showed almost as well. Another well-constructed wine is the Rosso Virzì '00, a nero d'Avola and syrah blend that is concentrated in colour, intense in aroma, redolent of small berries and liqueur black cherries, and well supported on the palate by balanced acidity. Coming to the whites, the Schietto Chardonnay is only at its first release but already has good character. It would benefit though with less invasive oak. Divino, from an intriguing blend of inzolia, grillo and chardonnay, is not dissimilar to the previous vintage. Pale straw in colour, it has refined flower and fruit aromas on the nose, following up with freshness and balance on the palate.

○	Rapitalà Conte Hugues '99	▼▼	4
○	Alcamo Rapitalà '00	▼	3
○	Bouquet '00	▼	3
○	Casalj '00	▼	3
●	Nuhar '00	▼	4
●	Rapitalà Rosso '99	▼	3
○	Alcamo Rapitalà Grand Cru '95	▽▽	4
●	Rapitalà Rosso '95	▽	3
●	Rapitalà Rosso '96	▽	3
○	Alcamo Rapitalà Grand Cru '98	▽	4
●	Nuhar '98	▽	4
●	Rapitalà Rosso '98	▽	3
○	Alcamo Rapitalà '99	▽	3
○	Bouquet '99	▽	3
○	Casalj '99	▽	3

●	Schietto Rosso '99	▼▼	5
●	Don Pietro Rosso '99	▼▼	3
●	Vigna Virzì Rosso '00	▼▼	3*
○	Divino '00	▼	2
○	Schietto Chardonnay '00	▼	3
○	Alcamo Alahambra '00		2
○	Vigna Virzì Bianco '00		3
●	Don Pietro Rosso '95	▽▽	3
●	Don Pietro Rosso '96	▽▽	3
●	Schietto Rosso '97	▽▽	3
●	Don Pietro Rosso '98	▽▽	3
●	Schietto Rosso '98	▽▽	3
●	Vigna Virzì Rosso '98	▽▽	2

PANTELLERIA (TP)

AGRICOLA BONSULTON
C.DA CIMILLIA
91017 PANTELLERIA (TP)
TEL. 0923918353
E-MAIL: info@bonsulton.it

We well recall our first visit to this estate many years ago and the cordial welcome we received from Salvatore Casano, a gentleman in the true sense of the word and the pioneer of quality wine on Pantelleria. We remember what a pleasure it was to talk unhurriedly about the problems surrounding wine production on the island at the time, then going on to taste some superb vintages of Bonsulton, a tasting that fixed that wonderful day in our minds for ever. Salvatore Casano is now enjoying his well-deserved retirement and his son Roberto has taken over, the fourth generation to run the estate. He has kept family prestige high by turning out some impeccable wines that are a delight to drink. Of those presented, the one that stands head and shoulders above the rest is the '98 Passito di Pantelleria Bonsulton, which sailed into the Three Glass taste-offs. The colour is bright amber, introducing perfumes of figs, honey, dates and Mediterranean scrub. It opens out on the palate with unusual distinction and personality, and is soft, velvety and long. The '99 Passito Bonsulton is along very similar lines. It has the same characteristics and qualities but just needs a few more months bottle age to show at its best. The Moscato Bonsulton '00 is also a delicate, good quality wine.

○ Passito di Pantelleria '98	🍷🍷	6
○ Passito di Pantelleria '99	🍷🍷	6
○ Moscato di Pantelleria '99	🍷	5

PANTELLERIA (TP)

D'ANCONA
C.DA KADDIUGGIA
91017 PANTELLERIA (TP)
TEL. 0923913016

This small family-run estate continues its successful run. It is led by Giacomo D'Ancona, producer and oenologist of high standing, and his wife Solidea, from whom the estate's well-known line of wines takes its name. The couple, with just over 60 years between them, have shown themselves to be superbly gifted at shaping the delicious "moscatellone", or moscato d'Alessandria, better known as zibibbo, into an exemplary wine. They follow the island's traditional winemaking practices, traditions that they have seen passed down from father to son over the generations, and the wines have gained them many fans among winelovers and wine writers alike. The '00 Passito Solidea, like the previous release, is a fascinating, very expressive wine that captivates at once with the brightness of its amber hue. Its nose is whistle-clean, rich and concentrated, with an array of aromas in which acacia honey, dried figs and candied fruit take centre stage, while the soft, elegant, mouthfilling palate gives full rein to the wine's best qualities. We can see it accompanying full-flavoured, creamy blue cheeses magnificently and being an excellent foil to almond-based petits fours. The '00 Moscato Solidea also showed well although it was a little more closed than the previous vintage. No doubt a few more months in bottle will bring it round and impart greater softness and harmony.

○ Passito di Pantelleria Solidea '00	🍷🍷	5
○ Moscato di Pantelleria Solidea '00	🍷	5
○ Passito di Pantelleria Solidea '98	🍷🍷🍷	5
○ Passito di Pantelleria Solidea '93	🍷🍷	5
○ Passito di Pantelleria Solidea '95	🍷🍷	5
○ Scirocco '96	🍷🍷	2
○ Bianco Scuvaki '97	🍷🍷	3
○ Moscato di Pantelleria Solidea '99	🍷🍷	5
○ Passito di Pantelleria Solidea '99	🍷🍷	5
○ Moscato di Pantelleria	🍷🍷	3
○ Passito di Pantelleria	🍷🍷	3

PANTELLERIA (TP)

SALVATORE MURANA
C.DA KHAMMA, 276
91017 PANTELLERIA (TP)
TEL. 0923915231

RAGUSA

VITIVINICOLA AVIDE
CORSO ITALIA, 131
97100 RAGUSA
TEL. 0932967456 - 0932621358
E-MAIL: avide@avide.it

The aroma of dates that characterizes Salvatore Murana's Martingana, the uncontested number one Passito di Pantelleria, is simply unforgettable. Just like its intense amber colour and that sweet, comforting taste that becomes more enchanting with each sip. Murana has given dignity and a solid reputation to the wines of the island of Pantelleria like no one else and deserves recognition for it. Nowadays, Martingana is a wine known to everyone around the world who loves wines that express their terroir. It doesn't matter if they are white, red or sparkling or if, as in this case, they form part of the exclusive group of dessert wines, perhaps the most difficult of all to make well. The '98 is no exception and in addition to great concentration it is very firmly territory-driven. Alongside Martingana are the '99 Passito di Pantelleria Khamma and Mueggen, also '99, both more delicate and less concentrated, the Mueggen in particular, but both also rich in extraordinary concentration and typicity. The whole is garnished with a sort of peasant farmer dignity that manages to give elegance to something that would otherwise seem rustic, a concept that the writer Luigi Veronelli has captured with one of his ingenious neologisms. Veronelli has come up with the term "zergo" for a wine that manages to marry these apparently contradictory characteristics, and nothing can be more "elegantly rustic" than Salvatore Murana's amazing wines.

Avide has long been one of the leading wineries in south east Sicily. It makes attractive, well-styled wines that people like. They are bottles that reflect the characteristics of the local grapes, predominantly frappato, nero d'Avola and inzolia. The Cerasuolo di Vittoria Barocco is as excellent as ever and even seemed a little softer than usual. The colour is the classic ruby red and the nose has clear-cut notes of red berry fruits, particularly mulberry. The palate is harmoniously youthful, dry and offers good body. Sigillo '99 is firm and immediate on the palate, which is well structured with a clean finish. Herea Rosso has a ruby hue shading into garnet, and fair body with balanced, unobtrusive tannins. The other Cerasuolo, the Etichetta Nera, which has a higher proportion of frappato, is also exceedingly attractive. Appealingly aromatic, with excellent definition, it displays just the right balance of softness and freshness on the palate. Vigne d'Oro, from inzolia, is a good deep straw yellow and has light aromas of vanilla and banana, then a rather simple, but clean and lively, palate. Herea Bianca is good too. Greenish-tinged in colour, it has delicate floral perfumes and a perfect acid-alcohol balance on the palate, which has a soft, gentle fruitiness. But the final surprise is the second release of Avide's sweet wine, Lacrimae Bacchi, made exclusively from inzolia. It has great character. The concentrated, bright gold ushers in an array of soft tropical fruit perfumes and a rich, ripe fleshy palate.

○	Moscato Passito di Pantelleria Martingana '98	♛♛♛	6
○	Moscato Passito di Pantelleria Khamma '99	♛♛	5
○	Moscato Passito di Pantelleria Mueggen '99	♛♛	5
○	Moscato Passito di Pantelleria Martingana '97	♛♛♛	6
○	Moscato Passito di Pantelleria Khamma '98	♛♛	5
○	Moscato Passito di Pantelleria Mueggen '98	♛♛	5

●	Cerasuolo di Vittoria Barocco '98	♛♛	4
○	Lacrimæ Bacchi	♛♛	5
○	Dalle Terre di Herea Bianco '00	♛	2*
●	Dalle Terre di Herea Rosso '00	♛	2*
●	Sigillo Rosso '99	♛	4
○	Vigne d'Oro '99	♛	3
●	Cerasuolo di Vittoria Etichetta Nera '99		2
●	Cerasuolo di Vittoria Barocco '95	♛♛	4
●	Cerasuolo di Vittoria Barocco '96	♛♛	4
○	Vigne d'Oro '96	♛♛	3
●	Sigillo Rosso '98	♛♛	4
○	Vigne d'Oro '98	♛♛	3
●	Cerasuolo di Vittoria Etichetta Nera '98	♛	2

SAMBUCA DI SICILIA (AG)

Planeta
C.da Dispensa
92013 Sambuca di Sicilia (AG)
Tel. 092580009 - 091327965
E-mail: planeta@planeta.it

The Planetas have excelled themselves. It is difficult to find words to do justice to the commitment, the determination and the intelligent, businesslike approach of young Alessio, Francesca and Santi Planeta. More professional than ever, they have become a team capable of scaling the dizziest heights of fine wine production. All the Planeta wines are splendid this year and a good three of them get Three Glasses, an achievement that no one else from the centre or south of the country has ever managed. And that includes Tuscany. There's Cometa '00, from fiano, a grape that is going to be pivotal to Sicily in the next few years. As powerful as Chardonnay, it is more citrus-like on the nose and gives more acidic support to the wine's body. Then there's the '00 Chardonnay, which is more even and elegant than usual, closer in style to the '96 than the sturdy '99. The third star is the stunning '99 Merlot, which has tobacco, bramble and balsam on the nose, and softness and power on the palate. It has finesse worthy of Italy's best for it is neither over-elaborate, nor simply attractive for its own sake. In short, it is flawless. Among the other wines, the '99 Cabernet Burdese is a welcome release. Santa Cecilia '99, from nero d'Avola, and Syrah '99 have great typicity and Alastro '00, from grecanico and chardonnay, is almost too good for its price. Then there's La Segreta Bianco '00, also grecaninco and chardonnay but without any oak, and La Segreta Rosso '99, from nero d'Avola and merlot. Even the least good Planeta wine easily attained Two Glasses. So we must have been right to nominate Planeta Winery of the Year four years ago.

○	Chardonnay '00	♛♛♛	5
○	Cometa '00	♛♛♛	5
●	Merlot '99	♛♛♛	5
●	Syrah '99	♛♛	5
○	Alastro '00	♛♛	4
○	La Segreta Bianco '00	♛♛	3
●	Cabernet Sauvignon Burdese '99	♛♛	5
●	La Segreta Rosso	♛♛	3
●	Santa Cecilia '99	♛♛	5
○	Chardonnay '96	♛♛♛	5
●	Santa Cecilia '97	♛♛♛	5
○	Chardonnay '98	♛♛♛	5
○	Chardonnay '99	♛♛♛	5

TRAPANI

Cantina Sociale di Trapani
Loc. Fontanelle
C.da Ospedaletto
91100 Trapani
Tel. 0923539349
E-mail: cantinatp@libero.it

We've been saying it for several years now – the provinces of Trapani and Agrigento are the most promising in Sicily. We were also among the first to speak highly of the Cantina Sociale di Trapani because we were impressed not only by the quality of its wines but also by the business skills of its president, Roberto Adragna, and the team spirit pervading the entire staff. This year's tastings have further convinced us of the co-operative's dependability and, for the third year running, one extraordinary wine, Forti Terre di Sicilia Cabernet Sauvignon '99, stood well above the rest. It comes from Valderice, where the countryside opens out onto the sea at Bonagia, cool lands shaded by the Erice massif. The wine's colour is a concentrated red. Its nose is intense, with notes of red berry fruits, newly-mown grass and spices, then the palate is silky, full and beautifully balanced. Its Three Glasses were well deserved. The '00 Forti Terre di Sicilia Rosso, from nero d'Avola and cabernet sauvignon, is as impressive as ever. There are aromas of redcurrant, bramble and raspberry with undertones of tobacco and the palate is full-bodied, soft and balanced. The Nero d'Avola is not dissimilar but warmer and more mouthfilling. The first release of a Chardonnay showed very well. Deep straw, it has fair complexity of both aroma and flavour, characterized by vanilla, fresh butter, banana, melon and citrus fruit.

●	Forti Terre di Sicilia Cabernet Sauvignon '99	♛♛♛	5
○	Forti Terre di Sicilia Chardonnay '00	♛♛	3*
●	Forti Terre di Sicilia Il Rosso '00	♛	3
●	Forti Terre di Sicilia Nero d'Avola '99	♛	3
●	Forti Terre di Sicilia Cabernet Sauvignon '97	♛♛	3
●	Forti Terre di Sicilia Cabernet Sauvignon '98	♛♛	3
●	Forti Terre di Sicilia Il Rosso '99	♛♛	2

VALLELUNGA PRATAMENO (CL)

★ Tasca d'Almerita
C.da Regaleali
90029 Vallelunga Pratameno (CL)
Tel. 0921544011 - 0921542522

Again, Tasca d'Almerita presented a huge range of wines, as many as 14, perhaps a few too many for a fair-sized but not enormous winery. Still, it's not for us to comment on their marketing strategies. Naturally, we can not review all 14 here but will concentrate on the pleasant surprises, most notably the '99 Rosso del Conte, the best release of the wine ever. Made predominantly from nero d'Avola, it has at last developed real elegance and class, and has a complexity of bouquet never before attained. There is a new-found mineral and smoky overlay, as well as excellent concentration on the palate. The '99 Chardonnay is also back on form. It is less powerful than before but more even and better constructed. No longer does the oak squash the varietal aromas. The two nero d'Avola and cabernet-based Cygnus reds, from nero the '98 and '99 vintages, are both showing well. Camastra '99, from nero d'Avola with merlot, is even better. But the biggest surprise came from the Regaleali wines, the '99 Rosso and the '00 Rosato. Both are very sound, attractive and, above all, great value for money. The simple but pleasant '00 Regaleali Bianco is more than decent. To round up this very brief run-down come Tasca d'Almerita Brut '98, the only Sicilian sparkling wine of note, and Nozze d'Oro '99, from the sauvignon tasca variety, which seemed a touch under par. We will pass over the '99 Cabernet Sauvignon for now, as it is still too young to be judged fairly, but our impression was positive. For the future, we wait with interest to see how Gaetano Zangara, formerly of Corvo, will mould these wines.

VITTORIA (RG)

COS
P.zza del Popolo, 34
97019 Vittoria (RG)
Tel. 0932864042
E-mail: info@cosvittoria.it

They are committed, inventive, tenacious, in love with their work. They refuse to cut corners. They work all hours. They, Giusto Occhipinti and "Titta" Cilia, were around before Sicily had gained its current success on the international market. They were around and, being both stubborn and articulate, would talk for hours about how their wines, and Sicilian wines in general, were different – nay better – than the rest. They are still around and happier than ever, we imagine, at Sicily's new prestige, a success that even a short time ago was unimaginable. The Cerasuolo di Vittorio, from frappato and nero d'Avola, their first love, is greatly admired and in great demand all over the world, even in Japan. This year, the '99 is firmly incisive, with a good deep ruby leading in to attractive, distinct, fruity and spicy aromas, then an attractive, well-structured, long palate with tightly-knit, elegant tannins. Scyri '98 is of similar standing, although it no longer sports Cerasuolo di Vittoria DOC status as it is now made exclusively from nero d'Avola. There are notes of bottled fruit, liquorice and humus, the tannins are well-balanced and attractive and, together with the wine's great length, give it warmth and pure Mediterranean style. Cerasuolo di Vittoria Vigna di Bastonaca '00 is also good while Ramì '00, made solely from inzolia, was not ready in time for our tastings.

○ Chardonnay '99	🍷🍷	6
● Rosso del Conte '99	🍷🍷	5
◉ Regaleali Rosato '00	🍷🍷	3*
○ Almerita Brut '98	🍷🍷	5
● Cygnus '98	🍷🍷	5
● Camastra '99	🍷🍷	5
● Cygnus '99	🍷🍷	5
● Regaleali Rosso '99	🍷🍷	3*
○ Regaleali Bianco '00	🍷	3*
○ Nozze d'Oro '99	🍷	4
● Cabernet Sauvignon '98	🍷🍷🍷	6

● Scyri '98	🍷🍷	5
● Cerasuolo di Vittoria '99	🍷🍷	4
● Cerasuolo di Vittoria V. di Bastonaca '00	🍷	3
● Cerasuolo di Vittoria '94	🍷🍷	3
● Cerasuolo di Vittoria '95	🍷🍷	3
● Cerasuolo di Vittoria Sciri '95	🍷🍷	4
● Cerasuolo di Vittoria V. di Bastonaca '95	🍷🍷	4
● Le Vigne di Cos Rosso '95	🍷🍷	4
● Cerasuolo di Vittoria '96	🍷🍷	3
● Cerasuolo di Vittoria Sciri '96	🍷🍷	4
● Cerasuolo di Vittoria Sciri '97	🍷🍷	5

OTHER WINERIES

CEUSO
VIA ENEA, 18
91011 ALCAMO (TP)
TEL. 0924507860 - 0924228336
E-MAIL: info@ceuso.it

This year, the Melia brothers' Ceuso Custera will again delight aficionados. From nero d'Avola, cabernet sauvignon and merlot, with a complex array of aromatics and a velvety palate, it is a marvellous wine that deservedly reached the final Three Glass taste-off.

● Ceuso Custera '99	🍷🍷	6
● Ceuso '96	🍷🍷	5
● Ceuso Custera '97	🍷🍷	5
● Ceuso Custera '98	🍷🍷	5

FATTORIE AZZOLINO
C.DA AZZOLINO
90043 CAMPOREALE (PA)
TEL. 3358448437
E-MAIL: fattorieazzolino@tiscalinet.it

The Nomi co-operative from Trentino has "married" this Camporeale estate and the immediate result is this lovely, perfumed yet firmly structured Chardonnay. Franco Sacco, the Sicilian partner who was behind the deal, and is highly committed to it, should be pleased!

○ Chardonnay '00	🍷	5

TENUTA SCILIO DI VALLE GALFINA
V.LE DELLE PROVINCIE, 52
95014 GIARRE (CT)
TEL. 095933694
E-MAIL: scilio@infinito.it

The vineyards are 650 metres above sea level on the slopes of Etna. Views are panoramic, the climate attractive and the vineyards organically cultivated. Orpheus is an Etna Rosso with good nose-palate balance. The round Tenuta Scilio Etna Rosso and the fruity Scilio Bianco are both pleasant.

○ Tenuta Scilio Bianco '00	🍷	2*
● Tenuta Scilio Rosso '00	🍷	2*
● Orpheus Etna Rosso '98	🍷	3

CANTINE MONTHIA
VIA SAPPUSI, 12
91025 MARSALA (TP)
TEL. 0923737295

The Bonomo family continues to turn out characterful wines. Vela Latina '00, from grillo and chardonnay, is delicate with nice purity of aroma. Hammon, from cabernet sauvignon and nero d'Avola, has fine-grained tannins and shows well. The white Saline is also good.

○ Saline '00	🍷	3
○ Vela Latina '00	🍷	3
● Hammon '99	🍷	3

AJELLO
C.DA GIUDEO
91025 MAZARA DEL VALLO (TP)
TEL. 091309107
E-MAIL: azajello@tin.it

With his first releases, Salvatore Ajello has come up with two serious, technically exemplary wines. Furat, from nero d'Avola, cabernet sauvignon, merlot and syrah, is complex and harmonious. Bizir, from chardonnay, grillo and inzolia, is elegant.

● Furat '99	🍷🍷	4
○ Bizir '00	🍷	4

PROMED
VIA TOSCANINI, 6
91026 MAZARA DEL VALLO (TP)
TEL. 0923670214
E-MAIL: promed@promed.it

Manager Francesco Rossi wants "to give consumers the emotions of the Mediterranean" and in the sensual, soft Passito di Pantelleria Rihali '98 there are sensations of the island's hot sun and volcanic terrain. Moscato Rihali '96 is similar in quality but more delicate in aroma.

○ Passito di Pantelleria Rihali '98	🍷🍷	5
○ Moscato di Pantelleria Rihali '96	🍷	4

AGARENO
C.DA SANT'ANTONIO
92013 MENFI (AG)
TEL. 0925570409
E-MAIL: agareno@libero.it

Seven friends from Menfi, all with clear ideas for the future, run this winery founded in '99. There are two wines. Moscafratta, from nero d'Avola and cabernet sauvignon, has a plummy nose and good body, and the monovarietal nero d'Avola Gurra is great.

● Moscafratta '99	🍷	5
● Gurra '99	🍷	3

BAGLIO SAN VINCENZO
C.DA SAN VINCENZO
92013 MENFI (AG)
TEL. 33924226103

This is a classic "baglio", or walled property, surrounded by superb vineyards. Don Neli Bianco, from grecanico and chardonnay, is zesty, nero d'Avola and cabernet-based Don Neli Rosso is spicy, but the Terre dell'Istrice, a cabernet sauvignon-merlot mix, is simply terrific.

● Terre dell'Istrice '98	🍷🍷	4
○ Don Neli Bianco '00	🍷	3
● Don Neli Rosso '00	🍷	3

CASA VINICOLA GRASSO
VIA ALBERO, 5
98057 MILAZZO (ME)
TEL. 0909281082
E-MAIL: casavinieolagrasso@tiscalinet.it

This was a disappointing year for Paola and Alessio Grasso. Only Sulleria showed really well with its intense bouquet, soft, balanced palate and super-clean, pleasant finish. The fresh, perfumed white Mamertino was reasonably good.

○ Mamertino Bianco '00	🍷	2*
● Sulleria Rosso '00	🍷	5
○ Passito di Pantelleria Ergo '92	🍷🍷	5
● Caporosso '98	🍷🍷	2

TAMBURELLO
C.DA PIETRANIELLA
90046 MONREALE (PA)
TEL. 0918465272
E-MAIL: dagala@libero.it

The wines of Tamburello, which now has the skilled Fabrizio Zardini as oenologist, are making progress. Dagala Rosso, from nero d'Avola and cabernet sauvignon is fruity and balanced. Dagala Bianco, from catarratto and inzolia, is well-styled, up-front and easy drinking,

○ Dagala Bianco '00	🍷	1*
● Dagala Rosso '99	🍷	1*

Abraxas
Fraz. Bukkuram - E. Albanese, 29
91017 Pantelleria (TP)
Tel. 0916110051 - 3381458517
E-mail: customer@winesabraxas.com

From the inland zone of Bukkuram comes this bright amber coloured Passito with rich perfumes of ripe apricot, dates and figs. That, and the round, seductive, very long palate, was more than enough to take it to the Three Glass taste-off.

○ Passito di Pantelleria	🍷🍷	6

Case di Pietra
C.da Nikà
91017 Pantelleria (TP)
Tel. 0659280220
E-mail: casedipietra@tiscalinet.it

Case di Pietra, a new estate, produced an excellent Passito di Pantelleria, Nikà, which went through to the Three Glass finals. It has well-defined notes of candied orange and honey, then a creamily all-enveloping palate. The dry Zibibbo, Nikà, is also well made.

○ Passito di Pantelleria Nikà '99	🍷🍷	5
○ Nikà '00	🍷	4

Cantina Sociale Cellaro
S. S. 188 - C.da Anguilla
92017 Sambuca di Sicilia (AG)
Tel. 0925941230 - 0924942310
E-mail: cellaro@futuralink.it

The wines from this co-operative were a pleasant surprise. Cellaro Rosso, from nero d'Avola and sangiovese, is soft, fresh and good drinking. Batìa Rosso is from the same varieties but more mature. Batìa Bianco, an Inzolia, has summer fruits aromas.

○ Batia Bianco '99	🍷	2
● Batia Rosso '99	🍷	2
● Cellaro Rosso '99	🍷	2

Di Prima
Via G. Guasto, 27
92017 Sambuca di Sicilia (AG)
Tel. 0925941201
E-mail: info@diprimavini.it

This estate, near Sambuca di Sicilia, is one to watch. The grapes are entrusted to the noted oenologist Luca D'Attoma. We tasted two wines. An extraordinarily complex, concentrated monovarietal Syrah and a white, Pepita, with a flower and fruit nose.

● Villamaura Syrah '99	🍷🍷	4
○ Pepita '00	🍷	2*

Barone Scammacca del Murgo
Via Zafferana, 13
95010 Santa Venerina (CT)
Tel. 095950520
E-mail: murgo@murgo.it

Tenuta San Michele is always this estate's leading wine. From selected cabernet sauvignon grapes, it is a concentrated red with expressive varietal aromas and a warm, soft, attractive palate. Arbiato '99, a promising Chardonnay, is already showing well.

● Tenuta San Michele '98	🍷	4
○ Arbiato '99	🍷	4
● Tenuta San Michele '95	🍷🍷	4
● Tenuta San Michele '97	🍷🍷	4

Antonino Pupillo
C.da Targia
96100 Siracusa
Tel. 0931494029

Nino Pupillo deserves credit for having resurrected moscato di Siracusa when it was almost extinct. Polio '99, from super-ripe fruit, is intriguing and has notes of apricot, honey and chamomile. Solacium, with inviting scents of candied fruit, is almost as good.

○ Moscato di Siracusa '99	🍷🍷	4
○ Moscato di Siracusa Solacium '99	🍷	4

SARDINIA

Historically, Sardinia has not been the most dynamic of wine regions. Cultural resistance, intransigence on the technical front, unshakeable convictions passed down from generation to generation and all sorts of suspicious attitudes have long held back any real aspirations or initiative. Yet, things have begun to change. In the past few years, many producers and oenologists of a certain age have decided to hand over to the next generation. It is as if a page has turned and a new era has begun. A few "oldies" have hung on and continue to produce old-style, or at least anachronistic, wines that have no real place in today's market. But the leading players are now the young growers whose enthusiasm is giving a much-needed jolt to the whole quality wine sector. Results are beginning to be seen throughout and with them the first real high-fliers. Whizzing through those most representative of this new Sardinia, and their most emblematic wines, we have Addis from the Cantina Sociale Gallura with Vermentino di Gallura Canayli and Piras, Murru from Argiolas with Turriga and Angialis, Cella from the Cantina Sociale di Santadi with Terre Brune and Latinia, and Parpinello from the Cantina Sociale di Santa Maria La Palma with the new Chardonnay and Sauvignon. These are all wines that scored over 80/100 this year and were, in general, happily free of faults or simplistic styling. Moving higher up the scale, Three Glasses awards go to four wines. Two are repeat performances: the red Marchese di Villamarina of Sella & Mosca and Turriga from Argiolas, which is a regular award-winner. The other two are newcomers to the top ranks: Capichera, with a late-harvest Vermentino, and Santadi with Latinia. The 2000 vintage was not problematic in any way but it was definitely kinder to the whites and dessert wines than to the reds. However, some brilliant young reds have still been produced – Karana, for instance, based on nebbiolo – as well as delightful rosés like Serralori, Sibiola and Campos. Other excitement comes from estates which, more or less coyly, are bringing out traditional wines which have had a makeover to give them new character. These include estates such as Depperu from Luras, in the Gallura and Dettori in the Sorso Sennori zone. And there are two young producers to watch from the Valle del Quirra winery at Ogliastra, in the Cannonau area. All in all, there is a lot more going on in the region than ever before.

ALGHERO (SS)

Cantina Sociale
Santa Maria La Palma
Loc. Santa Maria La Palma
07041 Alghero (SS)
tel. 079999008 - 079999044
e-mail: vini@santamarialapalma.it

There is much afoot at this co-operative situated on the outskirts of Alghero. With the arrival of the new general manager Paolo Parpinello, the range of wines has been enlarged and restyled. The fresh look applies most dramatically to the new Chardonnay and Sauvignon, bottled under the Alghero DOC. Both are beautifully clean, well-made and characterful, particularly in their aromas and fruit intensity, which is well balanced by alcohol. The Sauvignon, from '99, is the fuller on the palate and is very attractive, although it could perhaps do with a touch more refreshing acidity. The Chardonnay, also a '99, has a more evolved flavour and is characterized by greater softness. In any event, attempts like these to innovate with wines new to the area are highly encouraging and, given the winery's technical expertise, future vintages are sure to impress even further. Turning to more traditional styles, of the two Vermentino di Sardegna selections, both '00, we preferred the Aragosta to the I Papiri. Technically faultless, it is more harmonious, better balanced, and was fresh and simple on the palate. When we moved on to the reds, we found a first-rate Alghero Cagnulari, freshly bottled at the time of tasting but already with a wonderful concentration of aromas and great roundness on the palate. The '00 Cannonau di Sardegna Le Bombarde is as characterful as ever, with its fresh, pervasive aromas and soft, longish palate. The '99 Cannonau di Sardegna '99, entitled Grand Cru, is a little ill-defined and unfocused on the nose although the palate is full, with considerable structure and reasonably fine-grained tannins.

	Wine		Score
○	Alghero Chardonnay '99	♟	5
○	Alghero Sauvignon '99	♟	5
●	Alghero Cagnulari '00	♟	4
●	Cannonau di Sardegna Le Bombarde '00	♟	3
○	Vermentino di Sardegna Aragosta '00	♟	3
●	Cannonau di Sardegna Grand Cru '99	♟	3
●	Cannonau di Sardegna Le Bombarde '93	♟♟	2
●	Alghero Rosso Vigne del Mare '96	♟	2
●	Cannonau di Sardegna Le Bombarde '97	♟	2

ALGHERO (SS)

Tenute Sella & Mosca
Loc. I Piani
07041 Alghero (SS)
tel. 079997700
e-mail: sella-mosca@alghero.it

Sella & Mosca continues to put a lot of effort into conquering ever more important markets. As an estate, its strategy has for many years been to operate independently of the competition but without losing sight of what is going on elsewhere. The estate has made investments in the Gallura zone, where it produces Vermentino di Gallura Monteoro, and the '00 edition is full and round, with almondy aromas. Its most recent purchase has been in the Sulcis zone. The wine, Carignano del Sulcis Terrerare '98, is still developing but already has considerable intensity on the nose and an excellent palate that hasn't yet lost its suggestions of vanilla and pepper. The more classic Vermentino di Sardegna La Cala '00, stylish and delicate on the nose, and attractive on the palate, is up to speed, as are the two Algheros, Terre Bianche, from torbato, and Le Arenarie '00, from sauvignon. But the most important news is that the Alghero Marchese di Villamarina has again won Three Glasses, this time with the '97. It is a concentrate of intense, persistent aromas that pervade the nose to form a rich, complex bouquet with subtle scents of balsam. It is full and caressing on the palate, too, and finishes very long. The other leading red, Alghero Tanca Farrà, confirmed that '97 was a top-notch vintage for the winery. It is balanced and harmonious with ethereal vegetal notes, and aromas and flavours that are still fresh. Anghelu Ruju is one of Sella & Mosca's most renowned wines, produced only in particularly sunny years that allow the grapes to dry outdoors on mats after picking. The Riserva '94 is striking, with marked notes of spices, rhubarb and walnutskins on the nose, and a full, deep, balanced, harmonious palate.

	Wine		Score
●	Alghero Marchese di Villamarina '97	♟♟♟	6
○	Alghero Le Arenarie '00	♟♟	4
○	Alghero Torbato Terre Bianche '00	♟♟	3
○	Vermentino di Gallura Monteoro '00	♟♟	3
○	Vermentino di Sardegna La Cala '00	♟♟	3
●	Anghelu Ruju Ris. '94	♟♟	4
●	Alghero Tanca Farrà '97	♟♟	4
●	Carignano del Sulcis Terrerare '98	♟♟	4
●	Marchese di Villamarina '93	♟♟♟	6
●	Alghero Marchese di Villamarina '95	♟♟	6

ARZACHENA (SS)

CAPICHERA
LOC. CAPICHERA
07021 ARZACHENA (SS)
TEL. 078980612 - 078980654
E-MAIL: capighera@tiscalinet.it

Things are changing at the Ragnedda brothers' Capichera winery. Not only is there a new cellar, at Spridda. And not only are there eight hectares of new vineyard, bringing the total vine stock to around 60 hectares of estate-owned and rented plots. The Ragneddas are now bottling their Vermentino simply as a "vino da tavola" rather than DOCG Vermentino di Gallura. This unexpected and rather daring move naturally gives their estate's name more prominence on the label and emphasizes their confidence in the quality of the wine. Nomenclature aside, there is little to criticize in the range, with the Capichera Vendemmia Tardiva '00 even reaching the starry heights of Three Glasses. It takes the best elements of traditional Vermentino di Gallura styling – fullness, alcoholic power and character – and works them into a wine of great fragrance and harmony, on both nose and palate. In addition, the force of the alcohol on the palate is cushioned by softness, length and beautiful balance. Capichera Vigna 'Ngena '00 is also a terrific wine, with a deep straw colour, nicely persistent aromas, and a full, lightly honeyed palate that remains fresh. Capichera '00 is aged for a short while in barriques, a proportion of which are new. The lightly floral aromas are fleeting but there is more character on the palate, where the flavours stay longer. The red Assajè '00, a Carignano, has heady aromas, with geranium tones, and is still youthful on the palate. The new red, Mantenghia '99, also from carignano, is most promising, with a more than respectable structure and considerable tannic drive giving it good ageing potential.

○	Capichera V.T. '00	🍷🍷🍷	6
○	Capichera '00	🍷🍷	5
○	Capichera Vigna 'Ngena '00	🍷🍷	4
●	Mantenghia '99	🍷🍷	5
●	Assajè Rosso '00	🍷	4
○	Vermentino di Gallura V. T. '97	🍷🍷	5
○	Vermentino di Gallura Capichera '98	🍷🍷	5
○	Vermentino di Gallura V. T. '98	🍷🍷	5
○	Vermentino di Gallura Capichera '99	🍷🍷	5
○	Vermentino di Gallura V. T. '99	🍷🍷	6
○	Vermentino di Gallura Vigna 'Ngena '99	🍷🍷	4
●	Assajè Rosso '99	🍷	4

CABRAS (OR)

ATTILIO CONTINI
VIA GENOVA, 48/50
09072 CABRAS (OR)
TEL. 0783290806 - 0783399466
E-MAIL: vinicontini@tiscalinet.it

We'd like to avoid our usual tone of resignation on the condition of the Vernaccia di Oristano DOC. We have tried on numerous occasions to awaken producers and officials to the precarious state of this celebrated wine. We prefer to concentrate on the growers, such as Contini, who have tried to change things and who are paying more attention to the market rather than merely wax lyrical about Vernaccia di Oristano's ancient glories. A long-standing estate like Contini cannot, though, simply abandon the wine. As usual, it is all about balancing the traditional side with a more innovative layer. These days, there is great demand for territory-focused wines, in the sense of those made with indigenous varieties, and Contini answers the call with a well-made Niedderra Rosso '98. There is breadth of aroma, with tar and balsam, and the palate is attractive without losing its touch of astringency. The Niedderra Rosato is also worthy of mention. Contini's Cannonau di Sardegna comes from the traditional, hilly production zones of the province of Nuoro and the Riserva '98 is fairly full on the nose, then soft and round on the palate. Karmis '00, from low-yielding Vernaccia, is a very successful wine. It has fresh, fruity aromas, and the full, soft Vernaccia character comes through on the palate, which also has the trademark almondy finish. However, we are delighted that Contini's top scorer, with Two Glasses, was the classic wine itself, Vernaccia di Oristano Riserva '83. The hefty alcohol brings vigour to the nose, the palate has a wealth of flavours, all typical of the wine, and there is great structure and wonderful overall harmony.

○	Vernaccia di Oristano Ris. '83	🍷🍷	4
●	Cannonau di Sardegna '98	🍷	3
○	Karmis '98	🍷	3
●	Niedderra Rosso '98	🍷	3
◉	Niedderra Rosato '00		2
○	Vernaccia di Oristano Ris. '80	🍷🍷	3
○	Vernaccia di Oristano '88	🍷🍷	3
○	Vernaccia di Oristano Ris. '90	🍷🍷	3
●	Niedderra Rosso '91	🍷🍷	3
○	Vernaccia di Oristano '92	🍷🍷	3
○	Elibaria '93	🍷🍷	2
○	Karmis '96	🍷🍷	2
○	Antico Gregori	🍷🍷	6
●	Cannonau di Sardegna Ris. '97	🍷	3

CARDEDU (NU)

ALBERTO LOI
S. S. 125 CARDEDU
08040 CARDEDU (NU)
TEL. 070240866 - 078275807
E-MAIL: albertoloi@libero.it

This estate returns to the Guide after a year of absence and improvements to both vineyards and cellars. The vines are situated in one of the best areas for Cannonau production and a good part of them have been replanted and renewed, some even with international varieties. These are present, though, in small percentages and are used only for blending. The estate was initially founded by Alberto Loi, the father of the current owners, with the aim of pushing Cannonau, Sardinia's most typical and representative wine, to ever greater renown. His offspring are working in the same spirit but with an eye to the marketplace, too. The wines we tasted were in general well-typed but do not yet fully express the potential of cannonau in this area. Cannonau di Sardegna Riserva Alberto Loi '97 gains Two Glasses, mainly for its comforting fullness. The nose is somewhat straightforward but has plentiful super-ripe fruit. The palate is rounded and warm, with the tannins still very evident. The Cannonau di Sardegna Cardedo Riserva '98 is almost as good. Rich in vegetal aromas on the nose, its palate has well-judged tannins and good weight of extract. It is already showing well but could improve further over the next three or four years. The Loi siblings are very bullish about Tuvara, a barrique-aged red. The '96 is very encouraging, with morello cherry and tar on the nose, and while not huge on the palate, it has warmth and fleshiness. Finally, the straightforward, well-typed Cannonau di Sardegna Sa Mola '99 is worth a mention.

DOLIANOVA (CA)

CANTINE DI DOLIANOVA
LOC. SANT'ESU
S. S. 387 KM. 17,150
09041 DOLIANOVA (CA)
TEL. 070744101 - 07074410226
E-MAIL: cantinedolianova@tiscalinet.it

Maintaining high quality levels is not easy for a co-operative producing 4,000,000 bottles a year, especially with a large variety of wines that range from the traditional Monica, Nasco and Nuragus to the modern Chardonnay and Sauvignon. Yet Dolianova has strengthened the position of its wines in important markets abroad as well as in Italy, even though, as yet, there are no earth-shakers on the list to focus interest. On the other hand, it does have a well-respected group of dessert wines. This year's tastings showed similar quality levels between the whites, from '00, and the reds, from '99, and apart from Nuragus di Cagliari '00, which appeared to have little to offer on the nose, all scored over 70/100. Vermentino di Sardegna Naèli '00 has good balance, and is good easy drinking, while the new Andias '00, from vermentino and nuragus, has more interest on the nose. The '99 Falconaro, made from cannonau, carignano and montepulciano, seemed more fragile in structure and less rich in aroma than we remembered from previous vintages, although it was still good enough to pick up One Glass. Monica di Sardegna Dolia '99 is lively, with fresh, youthful aromas and light tannins. Sibiola, a rosé made from indigenous varieties, is one of Dolianova's most reliable wines. The '00 has a well-fruited nose and a fresh, zesty, attractive palate. Moscato di Cagliari '98 came very close to gaining Two Glasses, providing further evidence of the suitability of this area for sweet wine production. Typically, they are rich, deep on the palate and are full of aroma.

● Cannonau di Sardegna Alberto Loi Ris. '97	♀♀	4
● Tuvara '96	♀	6
● Cannonau di Sardegna Cardedo '98	♀	4
● Cannonau di Sardegna Sa Mola Rubia '99		3
● Cannonau di Sardegna Alberto Loi Ris. '93	♀♀	4
● Cannonau di Sardegna Alberto Loi Ris. '95	♀	4
● Cannonau di Sardegna Cardedo '95	♀	3
● Cannonau di Sardegna Ris. '96	♀	4

○ Andias '00	♀	2*
◉ Sibiola Rosato '00	♀	2*
○ Vermentino di Sardegna Naeli '00	♀	2
○ Moscato di Cagliari '98	♀	4
● Falconaro '99	♀	4
● Monica di Sardegna '99	♀	2*
○ Nuragus di Cagliari '00		2
○ Dolicante '96	♀♀	3
● Falconaro '97	♀♀	3
○ Moscato di Cagliari '97	♀♀	4
● Cannonau di Sardegna '98	♀	2
● Falconaro '98	♀	3
○ Nuragus di Cagliari '99	♀	2
○ Caralis Brut	♀	3
○ Scaleri Démi Sec	♀	3

DORGALI (NU)

Cantina Sociale Dorgali
Via Piemonte, 11
08022 Dorgali (NU)
tel. 078496143
e-mail: info@c.s.dorgali.com

We have often stressed that, in our opinion, the Cannonau di Sardegna DOC, and others like it, are too generic. Things would work better, we feel, if they were split into sub-denominations, or even into microzones and single crus. Maybe our views have not fallen completely on deaf ears as more and more producers are coming out with wines made from particular vineyard selections. The revitalized Dorgali co-operative is a case in point. It concentrates its efforts on cannonau and the best of its more serious wines made from the grape this year is the second release of Fuili, the '99, which nudged Three Glasses. Full of heady, primary aromas of strawberry and jam, it is balanced on the palate despite still rather abrasive tannins. Cannonau di Sardegna Vigna Isalle '00 scored well over 70/100. Its vegetal and fruity aromas give it character on the nose and softness and decent length on the palate. One Glass also goes to Filieri '00, a red full of fruity and vegetal aromas, most notably cherry and geranium. The Cannonau di Sardegna Viniola '99 adds a further One Glass to Dorgali's collection. It is rather overtly herbaceous on the nose but the wine develops nicely on the palate. Another red of interest is Noriolo '98, based on cannonau with small amounts of other local red varieties. The nose is not all that intense but it is clean and there is good softness on the palate.

JERZU (NU)

Antichi Poderi Jerzu
Via Umberto I, 1
08044 Jerzu (NU)
tel. 078270028
e-mail: antichipoderi@tiscalinet.it

The new set-up at the Jerzu winery is a million miles away from the stereotypical co-operative it used to be. Its members were used to producing grapes that were all lumped together without any attempt at selection by quality or origin. The situation in those days meant that the aim had to be to produce as much as possible to retain a foothold in the larger markets. Now strategies are different, there is more care in the choice of vineyards and grapes, and production techniques have been adopted to give more sharply honed varietal character. The winery has also set in place a series of marketing initiatives, another aspect that was once ignored. During this period of change, the most recent vintages are not necessarily always available: there were several wines we could not taste as they had not yet been released. The newest wine in the range is a Cannonau di Sardegna Riserva '97 Josto Miglior, named after the winery's founder. The grapes come from low-yielding vines and the wine is aged in barrique for approximately a year. It is not yet ready and should improve with time but for now it has an intense, fairly persistent nose, dominated by vanilla from the oak. Its youth is emphasized by firm tannins on the palate, which is nonetheless warm and ripe. Radames, from cannonau, carignano and cabernet, and barrique-aged, is another successful wine, giving aromas of ripe bramble and jam, then an immediate, soft palate of great structure.

● Fuili '99	ŸŸ	5
● Cannonau di Sardegna Vigna di Isalle '00	Ÿ	3
● Filieri Rosso '00	Ÿ	2*
● Noriolo '98	Ÿ	4
● Cannonau di Sardegna Viniola '99	Ÿ	3
● Fuili '98	ŸŸ	5
● Filieri Rosso '96	Ÿ	2
● Filieri Rosso '97	Ÿ	2
● Noriolo '97	Ÿ	4
● Filieri Rosso '98	Ÿ	2
● Cannonau di Sardegna Vigna di Isalle '99	Ÿ	3

● Cannonau di Sardegna Riserva Josto Miglior '97	Ÿ	4
● Radames '98	Ÿ	4
● Cannonau di Sardegna Ris. '91	ŸŸ	3
● Cannonau di Sardegna Ris. Chuerra '97	ŸŸ	4
● Cannonau di Sardegna Ris. '95	Ÿ	3
● Cannonau di Sardegna '96	Ÿ	2
● Cannonau di Sardegna '97	Ÿ	2
● Radames '97	Ÿ	4
● Cannonau di Sardegna Marghia '98	Ÿ	4
● Cannonau di Sardegna Ris. '98	Ÿ	3

MONTI (SS)

CANTINA SOCIALE DEL VERMENTINO
VIA SAN PAOLO, 1
07020 MONTI (SS)
TEL. 078944012 - 078944631
E-MAIL: cantina@vermentinomonti.it

If we were asked to sum up the 2000 wines from this co-operative in a single phrase, we would have to write, "good but not exceptional, another year without any real peaks". The estate's flagship, Vermentino di Gallura Funtanaliras, made a good impression as usual. The '00 has very intense, pervasive perfumes and fresh, vegetal notes come through on the palate too, making it very approachable. Another of the winery's classics is Vermentino di Gallura Superiore Aghiloia. Its style is closer to traditions in Gallura some time ago, when the grapes were harvested so late they had almost dried out but had great concentration of sugars. The '00 gives the fullness and depth of the wines of those days, especially on the palate. Both aroma and flavour linger and there is a slightly almondy note in the finish. The Vermentino di Gallura S'Eleme '00 is in a lower price bracket but also manages to grab One Glass, more for its palate than its nose. There is nothing particularly new among the reds. Abbaìa '00, from a blend of cannonau, pascale, malaga and monica, is as good, clean and well-styled as ever. The forward, delicately fruity, rosé version, Thaora '00, is also attractive. There are also a couple of sparkling wines in the range, a Sec and a Démi Sec from vermentino, a sweet wine from moscato, and a Vermentino Passito called Aldiola.

●	Abbaìa '00	♀	2*
○	Vermentino di Gallura Funtanaliras '00	♀	3
○	Vermentino di Gallura S'Eleme '00	♀	2*
○	Vermentino di Gallura Sup. Aghiloia '00	♀	2*
◉	Thaora Rosato '00		2
○	Vermentino di Gallura Sup. Aghiloia '94	♀♀	2
○	Vermentino di Gallura Funtanaliras '98	♀♀	3
●	Abbaìa '99	♀	2
○	Vermentino di Gallura Funtanaliras '99	♀	3
○	Vermentino di Gallura Sup. Aghiloia '99	♀	2

MONTI (SS)

PEDRA MAJORE
VIA ROMA, 106
07020 MONTI (SS)
TEL. 078943185

It is now several years since Pedra Majore changed to quality-led winemaking. There is much in the estate's favour, in particular its vineyards which are in a enviable position at 500 metres above sea level, ideally sited for producing top-rate Vermentino but also excellent for fine red wine production. The plots, situated between Monti and Calangianus, are surrounded by imposing masses of granite and centuries'-old cork-oak woods. Producing wine runs in the family of the estate's owners, the Isoni siblings. For many years, their forebears were leading players in the local winemaking sector. Vermentino I Graniti '00 has good character. The nose is full and persistent with clear notes of ripe fruit. The palate is full, round and has just enough alcoholic impact. The Vermentino Hysonj '00 is almost as good. Attractive on the nose, it lacks its stablemate's length on the palate, which has a lightly acidulous streak. Vermentino di Sardegna Le Conche '00 has ripe tropical fruit on the nose while the palate is soft throughout. It was not a good year for the red Murighessa, which is bottled only in the best vintages. The range also includes a Brut sparkling wine based on Vermentino and a very good non-vintage sweet wine from "passito", or part-dried, grapes. It should also be remembered that this estate uses organic cultivation methods.

○	Vermentino di Gallura I Graniti '00	♀♀	3*
○	Vermentino di Gallura Hysonj '00	♀	3
○	Vermentino di Sardegna Le Conche '00	♀	3
○	Mirju Passito '98	♀	5
●	Murighessa '98	♀	3
○	Vermentino di Gallura I Graniti '98	♀	3
●	Murighessa '99	♀	3
○	Vermentino di Gallura Hysonj '99	♀	3
○	Vermentino di Gallura I Graniti '99		3

NUORO

Giuseppe Gabbas
Via Trieste, 65
08100 Nuoro
Tel. 078431351 - 078433745

QUARTU SANT'ELENA (CA)

Villa di Quartu
Via Garibaldi, 39/90
09045 Quartu Sant'Elena (CA)
Tel. 070820947 - 070826997

Giuseppe Gabbas is not the type to talk animatedly about his wines, as do so many other producers. His products reflect the character of their origin and it would be fair to say that territory, wine and man all live in symbiosis. Of the 13 hectares under vine, practically all renovated, eight are planted to cannonau and one of these has vines of about 60 years of age, from a local cannonau clone. The remainder is used, in variable proportions, for montepulciano, merlot, colorino, sangiovese, cabernet and syrah. The wines showed very well in tasting. Clearly, the work of oenologist Gori is having its effect. Dule '00 stood out in particular. It has great intensity on the nose with plentiful fruit and, the wine having been aged in new barriques, some vanilla. Youthful but not raw tannins are quite marked on the well-structured palate and the wine has great ageing potential. Arbeskia '99, from an unusual mix of cannonau, sangiovese, merlot and cabernet, stayed in barrique for around a year. It has intense aromas of ripe wild berry fruits interwoven with tobacco and coffee. The palate is tannic, warm and well-sustained, and in fact this wine, too, has a structure that will happily allow it to age for some years. Cannonau di Sardegna Lillovè '00 is simpler and more immediate but nevertheless not lacking in substance. The latest arrival to the range, Avra, is a red dessert wine from grapes that are left to dry and concentrate on the vine. Aged in barriques for 18 months, it is warm and pervasive on the nose, with aromas of wild berries and walnutskins, and nicely full on the palate.

Villa di Quartu is a young estate which sees its future in traditionally styled wines. The area was once renowned for sweet wine production and, after our numerous tastings over the past few years, we believe that this is the route that is likely to bring greatest success. However, coming to the wines presented this year, the two whites, Nuragus di Cagliari '00 and Vermentino di Sardegna '00, were not particularly exciting. The former seemed a bit tired and not perfectly clean on the nose. The Vermentino had evanescent aromas and was not all that long. Cepola Bianco, from vermentino and nasco, was another proposition altogether. The nose is fairly intense and fruity, then the palate has appreciable weight and balance. However, it is the series of dessert wines that really makes waves. The Malvasia di Cagliari '98 sailed through the Two Glasses barrier. It has sensual aromas of Mediterranean scrub and resin on the nose. The palate is sweet but not cloying and develops confidently, finishing on a note of ripe peach. Moscato di Cagliari '98 is also attractive but less "complete". Its aromas of sage are fleeting but are echoed on the mid-length palate. The trio is completed by Nasco di Cagliari '98. Nasco is a variety that has almost disappeared, thanks to those producers who preferred to make easy wines. They thought they were switching to modern wines but the results were often simply insignificant. Villa di Quartu's Nasco is full of aroma, even though the variety is not particularly aromatic. But they are secondary aromas, from fermentation, and give developed notes of nuts and dried fruits. The wine's energy and character comes through forcibly on the palate where, it is full, rich and succulent.

● Dule '00	🍷🍷	4
● Arbeskia '99	🍷🍷	5
● Avra '99	🍷🍷	4
● Cannonau di Sardegna Lillovè '00	🍷	4
● Dule '94	🍷🍷	4
● Dule '95	🍷🍷	4
● Cannonau di Sardegna Lillovè '96	🍷🍷	3
● Dule '96	🍷🍷	4
● Cannonau di Sardegna Lillovè '97	🍷🍷	3
● Dule '97	🍷🍷	4
● Cannonau di Sardegna Lillovè '98	🍷🍷	3
● Dule '98	🍷🍷	4
● Arbeskia '97	🍷	5
● Cannonau di Sardegna Lillovè '99	🍷	3

○ Malvasia di Cagliari '98	🍷🍷	4
○ Moscato di Cagliari '98	🍷🍷	4
○ Cepola Bianco '00	🍷	3
○ Nasco di Cagliari '98	🍷	4
○ Malvasia di Cagliari '97	🍷	4
● Cepola Rosso '98	🍷	3
○ Cepola Bianco '99	🍷	2

SANTADI (CA)

Cantina Sociale di Santadi
Via Su Pranu, 12
09010 Santadi (CA)
Tel. 0781950127 - 0781953007
E-mail: pgserafini@cantinadisantadi.it

The executives of this co-operative should be very satisfied with the large number of Glasses collected in just one year, even if they "flooded" the tasting, as usual, with a vast number of wines. Santadi is a winery that gained its reputation from reds and is now doing good things with its whites, too. Even so, we didn't think we would find ourselves awarding Three Glasses to one of their dessert wines. After all, Sulcis is known as a red wine zone. But the extraordinary sweet Latinia '99, made from bush-trained nasco, a variety that is uncommon in the area, walked off with Three Glasses. It is full of aromas of ripe fruit and honey, expressed with rare cleanliness and intensity. Sweet, alluring, creamy and harmonious on the palate, it can still point to a firm structure with plentiful extract and great length. The two whites, Villa di Chiesa '00 and Vermentino di Sardegna Cala Silente '00, are also notable. The former is oaky on the nose and very full on the palate while the Vermentino is fresher and more elegant. Nuragus di Cagliari Pedraia '00 comes slightly lower down the scale but is still attractive and well balanced. Carignano del Sulcis Superiore Terre Brune '97 stands out among the reds. It has a rich, intense, morello cherry and cooked plum nose, followed by a palate that is rich in extract and has considerable tannic presence. Baje Rosse, a heftily-structured wine, from bush-trained carignano vines, also acquits itself well. To round off the range, One Glass each goes to Carignano del Sulcis Rocca Rubia '98, Carignano del Sulcis Grotta Rossa '99, Monica di Sardegna Antigua '00 and Araja '99.

SELARGIUS (CA)

Meloni Vini
Via Gallus, 79
09047 Selargius (CA)
Tel. 070852822

This estate, one of the most important in the province of Cagliari, was founded at the end of the 19th century and has now seen three generations at the helm. The property incorporates three separate properties, situated in Campidano di Cagliari, each with distinct characteristics of site climate and terrain. Great importance is also given to organic cultivation, with highly satisfactory results, although only part of the estate is organically managed. The organic Vermentino di Sardegna '00 is fresh, attractive and averagely long. The Cannonau di Sardegna '98, also organic, is fuller, mid-bodied and has lively fresh fruit. Cannonau di Sardegna Le Ghiaie '97, the cannonau augmented by ten per cent of other varieties, including some cabernet, has attractive red berry fruits aromas. It is soft and warm on the palate, which is moderately tannic, a typical feature of many of the island's wines, whose tannins are usually unobtrusive. There is also a range of traditional sweet wines, all of good quality. Nasco di Cagliari '95 from the Donna Jolanda line has resin-like aromas and is soft and caressing on the palate, which has a gently bitterish finish. The best of the series, though, is Moscato di Cagliari '95. The high alcohol makes it a touch biting on the nose but it is fat on the palate without cloying, and gives richly fruited sensations of very ripe grapes.

○ Latinia '99	▼▼▼	4*
○ Vermentino di Sardegna Cala Silente '00	▼▼	4
○ Villa di Chiesa '00	▼▼	4
● Carignano del Sulcis Sup. Terre Brune '97	▼▼	6
● Carignano del Sulcis Baje Rosse '98	▼▼	5
● Monica di Sardegna Antigua '00	▼	2*
○ Nuragus di Cagliari Pedraia '00	▼	2*
● Carignano del Sulcis Rocca Rubia '98	▼	4
● Araja '99	▼	3
● Carignano del Sulcis Grotta Rossa '99	▼	3
● Terre Brune '93	▼▼▼	6
● Terre Brune '94	▼▼▼	6

○ Moscato di Cagliari Donna Jolanda '95	▼▼	4
○ Nasco di Cagliari Donna Jolanda '95	▼	4
● Cannonau di Sardegna Le Ghiaie '97	▼	4
● Cannonau di Sardegna '98	▼	3
○ Vermentino di Sardegna '00		3
○ Moscato di Cagliari Donna Jolanda '91	▼▼	4
● Cabernet di Sardegna '92	▼▼	4
○ Nasco di Cagliari Donna Jolanda '94	▼▼	4
● Monica di Sardegna '98	▼▼	2
● Cannonau di Sardegna Le Ghiaie '96	▼	3

SENNORI (SS)

Tenute Dettori
Loc. Badde Nigolosu
S. P. 29, Km 10
07036 Sennori (SS)
Tel. 079514711 - 0795041013
E-mail: info@tenutedettori.it

This is Dettori's first profile in the Guide. A newish estate, it operates in Romangia, an area of Sardinia close to the coast north of Sassari, and well noted for wine production, primarily from cannonau and moscato. These varieties yield excellent quality grapes here, grapes that give fat, concentrated wines. Nowadays, many of the vines have been grubbed up and, of those that remain, most are still bush trained, including those that furnish Dettori's grapes. Yields are very low, not exceeding 3,500 kilos of grapes per hectare, and the cellar has the modern technology to allow, amongst other things, temperature-controlled fermentation. The range currently comprises three reds, one white and a Moscato and the estate has decided to release them all outside the DOC umbrella. Dettori Rosso '00, made solely from cannonau, is very intense on the nose, with aromas of super-ripe fruit. The palate is dense and warm, with sweet notes that emphasize its residual sugar. Tenores '00, another Cannonau, is less rich in aroma but has a similar profile on the palate, with more stress on roundness and sweetness than zip. On Tuderi '00, from cannonau once more, the aromas are more vegetal, with notes of geranium, and the palate is fairly soft but concentrated. Dettori Bianco '00, from 100 per cent vermentino, is still a little closed on the nose but very lively on the palate. Muscadeddu '00 is rather uninteresting on the nose. Its aromas of honey and very ripe fruit sadly just don't sing. The typicity of Moscato from this area shows much more clearly on the palate which is full, round and has good balance in its sweetness.

● Dettori Rosso '00	♙	6
○ Muscadeddu '00	♙	6
● Tenores '00	♙	6
● Tuderi '00	♙	6
○ Dettori Bianco '00		5

SENORBI (CA)

Cantina Sociale della Trexenta
V.le Piemonte, 28
09040 Senorbi (CA)
Tel. 0709808863 - 0709809005
E-mail: trexentavini@tiscalinet.it

The administrators of this co-operative have a strong sense of the importance of continual change and development. This doesn't necessarily imply overturning tradition completely. It tends to mean, for example, ever new and better wines from traditional grape varieties and, since the directors are aware of developments on world markets, great attention is paid to the international varieties, too. On the cellar front, they are adopting more modern techniques for vinification and ageing, such as the use of barriques of various types of wood. The winery has also been enlarged, with the construction of a tasting room, a meeting room and a sales outlet. As for the wines themselves, there has been no earth-shattering development over the past 12 months. Some wines suffered from vintage problems but overall whites and reds put on a more or less equal showing. Let's start with one of this winery's standards, Monica di Sardegna Duca di Mandas. The '00 has a fresh, youthful nose with aromas of raspberry and black cherry. The palate has delightful suppleness and drinkability, set within good structure. Cannonau di Sardegna Baione '97 has simple but clean aromas. Tanca Su Conti '97, a barrique-aged red, is more characterful and gives great pleasure on the palate with its softness and balanced tannins. The whites include a One Glass winner in the delicately aromatic and attractively acidulous Vermentino di Sardegna Donna Leonora '00. Nuragus di Cagliari '00 is also a One Glass bottle but Vermentino di Sardegna Tanca Sa Contissa '00 is less attractive than the '99.

● Monica di Sardegna Duca di Mandas '00	♙♙	2*
○ Nuragus di Cagliari Tenute San Mauro '00	♙	2*
○ Vermentino di Sardegna Donna Leonora '00	♙	2*
● Cannonau di Sardegna Baione '97		3
● Tanca Su Conti '97	♙	5
○ Vermentino di Sardegna Tanca Sa Contissa '00		2
● Tanca Su Conti '96	♙♙	4
● Monica di Sardegna '97	♙♙	1
● Cannonau di Sardegna Baione '95	♙	3
● Tanca Su Conti '95	♙	4
● Cannonau di Sardegna Baione '96	♙	3

SERDIANA (CA)

Antonio Argiolas
Via Roma, 56/58
09040 Serdiana (CA)
Tel. 070740606 - 070743264
E-mail: argiolasspa@tin.it

Each year Argiolas adds a new piece to its oenological "mosaic" and while Turriga remains one of the best reds in Sardinia, if not all Italy, Angialis moves closer year by year to stealing its thunder as best wine of the estate. The '98 is refined and pervasive on the nose, complex and elegant on the palate. If it continues in like vein it will soon take over Argiolas' top spot. Whatever happens, it is unchallenged as Sardinia's most consistently good high-quality dessert wine. Coming back to Turriga, the '97 has an aromatic spectrum of superb breadth, taking in mulberry, morello cherry, pencil lead, chocolate, and a meaty palate of fabulous appeal. Powerful yet restrained, it has excellent definition and is very long. No problem about the Three Glasses, and this is the seventh vintage of the wine to win them. Moving on, Two Glasses go to the red Korem for fullness on a nose with notes of mulberry jam and conserve and the warmth on its palate. Cannonau di Sardegna Costera '99 is also very good and certainly better than the previous vintage. The '00 vintage of the white named after the estate, Argiolas, entices with its sensations of balsam and ripe fruit on both nose and palate. Vermentino di Sardegna Costamolino '00 is worth investigating, too, for its tropical fruit aromas, which are not overly intense but beautifully harmonious, and for the overall pleasure it gives in drinking. We were favourably impressed by the '99 Monica di Sardegna Perdera's good stamp of fruit. The Rosato Serralori '00 has good impact on the nose, and is light and balanced, making it one of the best of its style.

● Turriga '97	🍷🍷🍷	6
○ Argiolas '00	🍷🍷	4
○ Vermentino di Sardegna Costamolino '00	🍷🍷	3*
○ Angialis '98	🍷🍷	6
● Cannonau di Sardegna Costera '99	🍷🍷	4
● Korem '99	🍷🍷	6
○ Nuragus di Cagliari S'Elegas '00	🍷	3
⊙ Serralori Rosato '00	🍷	3
● Monica di Sardegna Perdera '99	🍷	3
● Turriga '92	🍷🍷🍷	6
● Turriga '93	🍷🍷🍷	6
● Turriga '94	🍷🍷🍷	6
● Turriga '95	🍷🍷🍷	6

SERDIANA (CA)

Pala
Via Verdi, 7
09040 Serdiana (CA)
Tel. 070740284 - 070740284
E-mail: cantinapala@tiscalinet.it

Despite being one of Sardinia's smallest estates, Pala is a significant and growing presence on the island. It is owned by brothers Mario and Enrico Pala and both their families are involved with the estate. Indeed, they have been working with vines and wines for generations but only recently have they come out with their own, more than respectable, range of wines. The main aim is to avoid being wooed by fashion. The Palas have no intention of letting imported varieties take over and they concentrate as much as possible on local grapes. All the wines we tasted this year were well-made and characterful. The white Entemari '00, based on malvasia and vermentino, has intense, fresh, attractive aromas, with vegetal notes that are echoed on the palate. S'Arai '99, from an intriguing blend of cannonau, carignano, bovale and barbera sardo, is destined to become the estate's top wine. It is clean on the nose with notes of balsam and well defined fruit. The attractive, even, but not overly close-knit, palate has plentiful flavour and fair body. Vermentino di Sardegna Crabilis '00 stands out among the DOC wine. It is clean and perfumed, with tomato leaf in particular on the nose, and good weight of extract and length on the palate. The '00 Nuragus di Cagliari Salnico is not as impressive as the previous vintage but is straightforward on the nose and reasonably balanced on the palate. The two reds, Monica di Sardegna Elima '99 and Cannonau di Sardegna Triente '00, are both good, fresh, easy-drinking wines.

○ Entemari '00	🍷🍷	4
○ Vermentino di Sardegna Crabilis '00	🍷🍷	3*
● S'Arai '99	🍷🍷	5
● Cannonau di Sardegna Triente '00	🍷	3
○ Nuragus di Cagliari Salnico '00	🍷	2*
● Monica di Sardegna Elima '99	🍷	3
● S'Arai '98	🍷🍷	5
○ Nuragus di Cagliari Salnico '99	🍷🍷	2
● Monica di Sardegna Elima '98	🍷	3
○ Vermentino di Sardegna Crabilis '99	🍷	2

TEMPIO PAUSANIA (SS)

CANTINA SOCIALE GALLURA
VIA VAL DI COSSU, 9
07029 TEMPIO PAUSANIA (SS)
TEL. 079631241
E-MAIL: info@cantinagallura.it

This winery's production strategy aims at good value for money in its wines but what really impresses us are the serious attitude to vineyard management, right through the year, and the care it takes in all aspects of winemaking. This year, there is a new wine, Vermentino di Gallura Gemellae. It is a successful white with clean, intense aromas of citrus fruit and ripe apple, and excellent balance on the palate. However, the Vermentino di Gallura Canayli continues to win acclaim with the '00 even bordering on Three Glasses. It has an intense, persistent nose of tropical fruit with floral nuances. The palate is full, rich and round, verging on fatness. The third Vermentino di Gallura, Piras '00, is almost as good and its nose is more directed towards Mediterranean herbs. Even Vermentino di Gallura Mavriana '00 has stolen a march, despite being considered the most "commercial" wine of the group. It picks up Two Glasses for its beautiful harmony of flavour. Balajana, aged first in barrique then in bottle, is unbeatable value given its quality and should sell like hot cakes. On the red front Karana, made from nebbiolo, continues to amaze us. It is youthful, heady and fresh, simple and easy drinking, but this year fuller than usual. Two Glasses also go to its big brother, Dolmen, from a special selection of nebbiolo grapes and aged in oak. It has ripe fruit and aromatic wood scents on the nose then the palate reveals ripe, dense tannins, giving the impression of a wine that will mature slowly and well. The rosé Campos is attractive and the Moscato Spumante has great elegance on both nose and palate.

○	Vermentino di Gallura Sup. Canayli '00	🍷	2
○	Balajana '00	🍷🍷	4
●	Nebbiolo dei Colli del Limbara Karana '00	🍷🍷	1
○	Vermentino di Gallura Gemellae '00	🍷🍷	2*
○	Vermentino di Gallura Mavriana '00	🍷🍷	1*
○	Vermentino di Gallura Piras '00	🍷🍷	3*
○	Moscato di Tempio Pausania	🍷🍷	4
⊙	Campos Rosato del Limbara '00	🍷	1*
●	Dolmen '97	🍷	4
●	Nebbiolo dei Colli del Limbara Karana '99	🍷🍷	1

USINI (SS)

GIOVANNI CHERCHI
VIA OSSI, 22
07049 USINI (SS)
TEL. 079380273 - 079380273
E-MAIL: vinicolacherchi@tiscalinet.it

There are great changes afoot at the Cherchi estate. The ever-present Giovanni has started to give his son more space. This doesn't mean that a change of generation is imminent, as Giovanni is still a long way from retirement, but it is certainly a first step towards it. As for the wines themselves, there is nothing of great moment to report. Vermentino di Sardegna Tuvaoes has always been the most noted for quality but it has been rather variable in recent years. The '00 is attractive on both nose and palate and retains its distinct personality. It is partnered by Boghes, another Vermentino di Sardegna, aged for several months in barriques. This was interesting on the nose, with evident oak, but the fruit still well apparent. The traditionally styled Vermentino di Sardegna Pigalva is simple, well-typed and good. The reds have character but without any real excitement. That could be because the weather in recent vintages has not been ideal. Luzzana '99, from cannonau and cagnulari, and barrique-aged, is not particularly intense or persistent on the nose but is nonetheless attractive on its warm, slightly rustic palate. Cagnulari is no longer bottled under the Alghero DOC but as IGT Calaresu. It is clean and well-styled but could probably be improved, although its makers know that it is anything but a docile wine to produce. Giovanni Cherchi deserves all the credit for having brought the variety back from extinction and we are certain that his efforts, and those of his son, will brings us wines that are ever better.

○	Vermentino di Sardegna Boghes '00	🍷🍷	5
●	Calaresu '00	🍷	2*
○	Vermentino di Sardegna Pigalva '00	🍷	3
○	Vermentino di Sardegna Tuvaoes '00	🍷	4
●	Luzzana '99	🍷	5
○	Vermentino di Sardegna Tuvaoes '99	🍷🍷	4
●	Luzzana '91	🍷	4
●	Luzzana '93	🍷	4
●	Luzzana '94	🍷	4
●	Luzzana '96	🍷	4
●	Luzzana '97	🍷	4
●	Luzzana '98	🍷	4

OTHER WINERIES

Cantina Sociale Giogantinu
Via Milano, 30
07022 Berchidda (SS)
tel. 079704163 - 079704939

The wines presented this year included some vintages we had tasted previously. New offerings showed primarily increasing attention to Vermentino production. Terra Mala '99 confirms the area's proclivity for good reds.

● Nastarrè '00	▼	1*
○ Vermentino di Gallura '00	▼	1*
○ Vermentino di Gallura Sup. '00	▼	2*
● Terra Mala Vigne Storiche '99	▼	4

Gigi Picciau
Fraz. Pirri
Via Italia, 196
09134 Cagliari
tel. 070560224

Gigi Picciau was born and bred among Cagliari's vineyards and he is still particularly drawn by local varieties. He is convinced of semidano's potential and has been producing it for several years with good results. Nasco and Malvasia also form part of the range.

○ Sardegna Semidano '00	▼	3
● Cannonau di Sardegna '97	▼	3
● Cannonau di Sardegna '94	▽	2
○ Sardegna Semidano '95	▽	2

Tenute Soletta
Loc. Codrongianos - Reg. Signar'Anna
07030 Florinas (SS)
tel. 079438160 - 079435067
e-mail: pina.soletta@tiscalinet.it

The Soletta siblings are unflaggingly active and motivated. They produce a comprehensive spread of styles in what is a pretty vast range. We liked the Cannonau di Sardegna Firmadu '98, which is still fresh on the nose as well as being attractive on the palate, and Dolce Valle, a Moscato Passito.

● Cannonau di Sardegna Firmadu '98	▼	2*
○ Dolce Valle Moscato Passito '98	▼	3
○ Vermentino di Sardegna Prestizu '99	▼▼	3

Depperu
Via Udine, 2
07025 Luras (SS)
tel. 079648121 - 079647314

This small estate, with just five hectares in the upper Gallura, makes its first appearance in the Guide. Low yields and carefully selected grapes are behind the success of a Vermentino that was an immediate sell-out.

○ Vermentino di Gallura Saruinas '00	▼▼	3*

GIANVITTORIO NAITANA
VIA ROMA, 2
08010 MAGOMADAS (NU)
TEL. 078535333 - 03490801807

This small producer continues to play his part in bringing out the class in the area's Malvasia. The well-typed fruity wines have elegance and finesse of aroma, as well as great length.

○ Planargia Murapiscados '00	🍷🍷	5
○ Planargia Murapiscados '97	🍷🍷	4
○ Planargia Murapiscados '98	🍷🍷	4
○ Planargia Murapiscados '99	🍷🍷	4

CANTINA SOCIALE MARRUBIU
S. S. 126, KM 117.600
09094 MARRUBIU (OR)
TEL. 0783859213
E-MAIL: cantinadimarrubiu@tiscalinet.it

There is little new at this co-operative, one of the largest in the province of Oristano. The whites, Vermentino for example, are straightforward, although the reds are a little more interesting. Work on re-establishing here the local variety bovale, produced under the denomination Campidano di Terralba Madrigal, is meritorious.

● Arborea Sangiovese '00	🍷	2*
● Campidano di Terralba Bovale Madrigal '99	🍷	2*
● Arborea Sangiovese '95	🍷	2

F.LLI PORCU
LOC. SUPIRINU
08019 MODOLO (NU)
TEL. 078535420

This is a small estate of around three hectares, situated in the Modolo valley. It produces Malvasia di Bosa, which is given a minimum of two years' ageing. The '96 has an amber colour, aromas of almond blossom and walnuts, and a warm, long palate.

○ Malvasia di Bosa '96	🍷	3

CANTINA SOCIALE IL NURAGHE
S. S. 131, KM 62
09095 MOGORO (OR)
TEL. 0783990285
E-MAIL: nuraghe@essenet.it

The standard wines, comprising red and white DOCs, have been joined by two barrique-aged selections, a Cannonau and a Monica. The Cannonau is particularly interesting and has aromas of liqueur cherries.

● Monica di Sardegna Nabui '98	🍷	3
● Cannonau di Sardegna Chio '99	🍷	3
● Cannonau di Sardegna Vigna Ruja '93	🍷	2

PERDARUBIA
VIA ASPRONI, 29
08100 NUORO
TEL. 0782615367
E-MAIL: perdarubia@tin.it

This producer sticks with the same vinification techniques that he always used. His wines are distinguished by good structure and a certain rusticity. Cannonau di Sardegna '99 is evolved, warm and fairly long.

● Cannonau di Sardegna '99	🍷	3

PIERO MANCINI
LOC. CALA SACCAIA
07026 OLBIA (SS)
TEL. 078950717
E-MAIL: poero.mancini@tiscalinet.it

This is a dynamic, efficiently run winery. The wines are well-styled but there is room for improvement, particularly with the two whites, Vermentino di Gallura Cucaione and Saraina. This latter has delicate aromas of aromatic herbs and is close to a second Glass. The Cannonau di Sardegna has somewhat more to offer than the red Saccaia.

○ Vermentino di Gallura Cucaione '00	🍷	3
○ Vermentino di Gallura Saraina '00	🍷	4
● Cannonau di Sardegna '99	🍷	3

Cantina Cooperativa di Oliena
Via Nuoro, 112
08025 Oliena (NU)
Tel. 0784287509

This winery, like all producers hereabouts, is very proud of its Nepente, a subzone of the Cannonau di Sardegna DOC. The Riserva '98 is already on sale. Its nose is full of vanilla while the palate has firm acidity.

● Cannonau di Sardegna Corrasi Nepente di Oliena Ris. '98	ŸŸ 5

Josto Puddu
Via San Lussorio, 1
09070 San Vero Milis (OR)
Tel. 078353329
E-mail: puddu.vini@tiscalinet.it

Josto Puddu is known for his aged Vernaccias. But for a number of years, he has been producing a wider range of wines to satisfy market demands. The best of these is a nicely made, simple but well-balanced, Monica di Sardegna.

● Monica di Sardegna Torremora '98	Ÿ	3
○ Vernaccia di Oristano Ris. '86	Ÿ	3

Fattoria Mauritania
09010 Santadi (CA)
Tel. 070401465

This is an estate with great potential that has yet to be exploited to the full. Its best wines are the reds, made mostly from carignano. Both Antas '99 and Barrua '98 have ripe fruit aromas and are warm and well-structured.

● Barrua '98	Ÿ	6
● Antas '99	Ÿ	4

Cantine Sardus Pater
Via Rinascita, 46
09017 Sant'Antioco (CA)
Tel. 0781800274
E-mail: cantine@cantinesarduspater.com

Another co-operative which is showing signs of greater dynamism. Production concentrates on carignano and monica. The wines showing best are the reasonably balanced Carignano del Sulcis Solus '99 and the attractively youthful, immediate Monica di Sardegna Insula '00.

● Monica di Sardegna Insula '00	Ÿ	2*
● Carignano del Sulcis Solus '99	Ÿ	1*
● Carignano del Sulcis Rosso '95	Ÿ	1
● Monica di Sardegna '95	Ÿ	2

Arcone
V.le Italia, 3
07100 Sassari
Tel. 079233721 - 03356183448
E-mail: gabrielepalmas@tiscalinet.it

This estate, run by its young owner, is about to make major changes to both vineyards and cellars. Currently, it produces just the one wine, Arcone, made from sangiovese together with some indigenous varieties. It is an attractive red that is set to become the estate's flagship.

● Arcone '99	Ÿ	2*
● Arcone '96	ŸŸ	3

Valle del Quirra
Via S. Melis, 59
08047 Tertenia (NU)
Tel. 078293770

The estate is run by three youngsters who are making their first sally onto the market. Things look very promising all round. Corriga '99 is made from cannonau, bovale and girò, with small amounts of sangiovese and cabernet. It is deep, full-bodied and still a little tannic.

● Corriga '99	Ÿ	3

INDEX OF WINES

10 Anni, Il Poggiolo	483
11 Novembre, C. Soc. di Avio	216
360 Ruber Capitae Rosso Bosco del Merlo, Paladin & Paladin	323
50 & 50 Avignonesi e Capannelle, Avignonesi	497
A. A. Bianco, Kössler - Praeclarus	243
A. A. Bianco Abtei, C. Convento Muri-Gries	246
A. A. Bianco Cuvée Anna, Tiefenbrunner	257
A. A. Bianco Mondevinum, Josef Sölva - Niklaserhof	255
A. A. Bianco Pallas, Castello Schwanburg	262
A. A. Bianco Passito Dorado, Graf Pfeil Weingut Kränzel	256
A. A. Bianco Passito Peperum, Heinrich Plattner - Waldgries	250
A. A. Bianco S. Michele, Hofstätter	266
A. A. Bianco Sandbichler, C. H. Lun	258
A. A. Cabernet, A. Berger -Thurnhof	245
A. A. Cabernet, Castel Sallegg - Graf Kuenburg	253
A. A. Cabernet, Popphof - Andreas Menz	259
A. A. Cabernet, Castello Rametz	270
A. A. Cabernet Albertus Ris., C. H. Lun	258
A. A. Cabernet Castel Schwanburg, Castello Schwanburg	262
A. A. Cabernet Freienfeld, C. Prod. Cortaccia	257
A. A. Cabernet Istrice, Castel Ringberg & Kastelaz Elena Walch	265
A. A. Cabernet Kastlet, Loacker Schwarzhof	248
A. A. Cabernet Kastlet Ris., Loacker Schwarzhof	248
A. A. Cabernet Kirchhügel, C. Prod. Cortaccia	257
A. A. Cabernet Kössler & Ebner, Kössler - Praeclarus	243
A. A. Cabernet Mumelterhof, C. Prod. S. Maddalena	247
A. A. Cabernet Puntay, Prima & Nuova/Erste & Neue	254
A. A. Cabernet Ris., C. Convento Muri-Gries	246
A. A. Cabernet Ris., C. Prod. S. Michele Appiano	242
A. A. Cabernet Ris., Castel Sallegg - Graf Kuenburg	253
A. A. Cabernet Ris., C. Laimburg	266
A. A. Cabernet Ris., R. Malojer Gummerhof	248
A. A. Cabernet Sauvignon, J. Mayr - Erbhof Unterganzner	249
A. A. Cabernet Sauvignon, Heinrich Plattner - Waldgries	250
A. A. Cabernet Sauvignon Campaner Ris., C. Viticoltori di Caldaro	253
A. A. Cabernet Sauvignon Castel Ringberg Ris., Castel Ringberg & Kastelaz Elena Walch	265
A. A. Cabernet Sauvignon Graf Von Meran Ris., C. Prod. di Merano	260
A. A. Cabernet Sauvignon Lafoa, C. Prod. Colterenzio	241
A. A. Cabernet Sauvignon Maso Castello, Kettmeir	254
A. A. Cabernet Sauvignon Pfarrhof Ris., C. Viticoltori di Caldaro	253
A. A. Cabernet Sauvignon Ris., A. Berger -Thurnhof	245
A. A. Cabernet Sauvignon Ris., C. Prod. Cornaiano	241
A. A. Cabernet Sauvignon Ris., Hofstätter	266
A. A. Cabernet Sauvignon-Merlot Sagittarius, Graf Pfeil Weingut Kränzel	256
A. A. Cabernet Select Ris, Hans Rottensteiner	251
A. A. Cabernet Tor di Lupo, C. Prod. Andriano	240
A. A. Cabernet Wienegg Ris., A. Berger -Thurnhof	245
A. A. Cabernet-Lagrein Bautzanum, R. Malojer Gummerhof	248
A. A. Cabernet-Lagrein Bautzanum Ris., R. Malojer Gummerhof	248
A. A. Cabernet-Merlot Cornelius Rosso, C. Prod. Colterenzio	241
A. A. Cabernet-Merlot Feld, Prima & Nuova/Erste & Neue	254
A. A. Cabernet-Merlot Graf Von Meran, C. Prod. di Merano	260
A. A. Cabernet-Merlot Putz Ris., H. & T. Rottensteiner	251
A. A. Cabernet-Merlot S. Pauls, Kössler - Praeclarus	243
A. A. Cabernet-Merlot Soma, C. Prod. Cortaccia	257
A. A. Chardonnay, Josef Brigl	240
A. A. Chardonnay, C. Prod. Nalles Niclara Magrè	261
A. A. Chardonnay, C. Prod. Valle Isarco	256
A. A. Chardonnay, Castello Rametz	270
A. A. Chardonnay, Steinhauserhof	263
A. A. Chardonnay, Peter Zemmer - Kupelwieser	258
A. A. Chardonnay Ateyon, Loacker Schwarzhof	248
A. A. Chardonnay Baron Salvadori, C. Prod. Nalles Niclara Magrè	261
A. A. Chardonnay Barrique, Peter Zemmer - Kupelwieser	258
A. A. Chardonnay Ca' d'Archi, S. Margherita	324
A. A. Chardonnay Cardellino, Castel Ringberg & Kastelaz Elena Walch	265
A. A. Chardonnay Castel Turmhof, Tiefenbrunner	257
A. A. Chardonnay Ceolan, La Vis	224
A. A. Chardonnay Cornell, C. Prod. Colterenzio	241
A. A. Chardonnay Doa, C. Laimburg	266
A. A. Chardonnay Eberlehof, C. Prod. Cortaccia	257
A. A. Chardonnay Felsenhof, C. Prod. Cortaccia	257
A. A. Chardonnay Glassien, C. Prod. Termeno	265
A. A. Chardonnay Hausmannhof, Haderburg	263
A. A. Chardonnay Kleinstein, C. Prod. S. Maddalena	247
A. A. Chardonnay Kupelwieser, Peter Zemmer - Kupelwieser	258
A. A. Chardonnay Maso Rainer, Kettmeir	254
A. A. Chardonnay Palladium, K. Martini & Sohn	268
A. A. Chardonnay Pinay, C. Prod. Colterenzio	241
A. A. Chardonnay Puntay, Prima & Nuova/Erste & Neue	254
A. A. Chardonnay Salt, Prima & Nuova/Erste & Neue	254
A. A. Chardonnay Schwarzhaus, Stroblhof	244
A. A. Chardonnay Select Art Flora, C. Prod. Cornaiano	241
A. A. Chardonnay St. Valentin, C. Prod. S. Michele Appiano	242
A. A. Chardonnay Tiefenthaler, C. Prod. Burggräfler	259
A. A. Chardonnay Tor di Lupo, C. Prod. Andriano	240
A. A. Chardonnay Torculum, Viticoltori Alto Adige	245
A. A. Chardonnay Wadleith, C. Viticoltori di Caldaro	253
A. A. Comitissa Brut Ris., Lorenz Martini	268
A. A. Gewürztraminer Lage Doss, Josef Niedermayr	244
A. A. Gewürztraminer Puntay, Prima & Nuova/Erste & Neue	254
A. A. Gewürztraminer Sel. Sonnengut, C. Prod. Andriano	240
A. A. Gewürtztramier Kleinstein, C. Prod. S. Maddalena	247
A. A. Gewürztraminer, C. Prod. Burggräfler	259
A. A. Gewürztraminer, Castel Sallegg - Graf Kuenburg	253
A. A. Gewürztraminer, Franz Haas	261
A. A. Gewürztraminer, C. Laimburg	266
A. A. Gewürztraminer, Steinhauserhof	263
A. A. Gewürztraminer, Stroblhof	244
A. A. Gewürztraminer, Tiefenbrunner	257
A. A. Gewürztraminer Albertus, C. H. Lun	258
A. A. Gewürztraminer Baron Salvadori, C. Prod. Nalles Niclara Magrè	261
A. A. Gewürztraminer Blaspichl, Haderburg	263
A. A. Gewürztraminer Brenntal, C. Prod. Cortaccia	257
A. A. Gewürztraminer Campaner, C. Viticoltori di Caldaro	253
A. A. Gewürztraminer Cancenai, Hans Rottensteiner	251
A. A. Gewürztraminer Cornell, C. Prod. Colterenzio	241
A. A. Gewürztraminer Graf Von Meran, C. Prod. di Merano	260
A. A. Gewürztraminer Kastelaz, Castel Ringberg & Kastelaz Elena Walch	265
A. A. Gewürztraminer Kolbenhof, Hofstätter	266
A. A. Gewürztraminer Maratsch, C. Prod. Termeno	265
A. A. Gewürztraminer Nussbaumerhof, C. Prod. Termeno	265
A. A. Gewürztraminer Passito, Graf Pfeil Weingut Kränzel	256
A. A. Gewürztraminer Passito Nectaris, C. Prod. Valle Isarco	256
A. A. Gewürztraminer Passito Terminum, C. Prod. Termeno	265
A. A. Gewürztraminer Pigeno, Stroblhof	244
A. A. Gewürztraminer St. Valentin, C. Prod. S. Michele Appiano	242
A. A. Gewürztraminer Windegg, Josef Brigl	240
A. A. Lago di Caldaro Scelto Cl., Josef Sölva - Niklaserhof	255
A. A. Lago di Caldaro Scelto Cl. Sup. Pfarrhof, C. Viticoltori di Caldaro	253
A. A. Lago di Caldaro Scelto Haslhof, Josef Brigl	240
A. A. Lago di Caldaro Scelto Puntay, Prima & Nuova/Erste & Neue	254
A. A. Lagrein Aus Gries Ris., Josef Niedermayr	244
A. A. Lagrein Ceolan, La Vis	224
A. A. Lagrein Cornell, C. Prod. Colterenzio	241
A. A. Lagrein Gries Ris., C. Terlano	264
A. A. Lagrein Porphyr Ris., C. Terlano	264
A. A. Lagrein Ris., C. Prod. Cornaiano	241
A. A. Lagrein Ris., Castel Sallegg - Graf Kuenburg	253
A.A. Lagrein Riserva Sel. Sonnengut, C. Prod. Andriano	240
A. A. Lagrein Rosato, C. Convento Muri-Gries	246
A. A. Lagrein Rosato, C. Gries	246
A. A. Lagrein Scuro, A. Berger -Thurnhof	245
A. A. Lagrein Scuro, Josef Brigl	240
A. A. Lagrein Scuro, Franz Gojer Glögglhof	247
A. A. Lagrein Scuro, Kössler - Praeclarus	243
A. A. Lagrein Scuro, Thomas Mayr e Figli	269
A. A. Lagrein Scuro, J. Mayr - Erbhof Unterganzner	249
A. A. Lagrein Scuro, Pfeifer Johannes Pfannenstielhof	269
A. A. Lagrein Scuro, Peter Zemmer - Kupelwieser	258
A. A. Lagrein Scuro Abtei, C. Convento Muri-Gries	246
A. A. Lagrein Scuro Abtei Ris., C. Convento Muri-Gries	246
A. A. Lagrein Scuro Albertus Ris., C. H. Lun	258
A. A. Lagrein Scuro Berger Gei, Ignaz Niedrist	243
A. A. Lagrein Scuro Berger Gei Ris., Ignaz Niedrist	243
A. A. Lagrein Scuro Briglhof, Josef Brigl	240
A. A. Lagrein Scuro Castel Turmhof, Tiefenbrunner	257
A. A. Lagrein Scuro Crescendo Ris., Tenuta Ritterhof	269
A. A. Lagrein Scuro DiVinus Ris., C. Prod. S. Paolo	242
A. A. Lagrein Scuro Forhof, C. Prod. Cortaccia	257
A. A. Lagrein Scuro Grafenleiten Ris., H. & T. Rottensteiner	251
A. A. Lagrein Scuro Gries, C. Convento Muri-Gries	246
A. A. Lagrein Scuro Gries Kristan, Egger-Ramer	268

Entry	Page
A. A. Lagrein Scuro Gries Kristan Ris., Egger-Ramer	268
A. A. Lagrein Scuro Grieser, C. Gries	246
A. A. Lagrein Scuro Grieser, Anton Schmid - Oberrautner	269
A. A. Lagrein Scuro Grieser Baron Carl Eyrl Ris., C. Gries	246
A. A. Lagrein Scuro Grieser Prestige Line Ris., C. Gries	246
A. A. Lagrein Scuro Grieser Ris., Anton Schmid - Oberrautner	269
A. A. Lagrein Scuro Grieser Select Ris., Hans Rottensteiner	251
A. A. Lagrein Scuro Intenditore, Peter Zemmer - Kupelwieser	258
A. A. Lagrein Scuro Mabon, Eberlehof - Zisser	268
A. A. Lagrein Scuro Maturum, K. Martini & Sohn	268
A. A. Lagrein Scuro Perlhof, C. Prod. S. Maddalena	247
A. A. Lagrein Scuro Pitz Thurù Ris., Loacker Schwarzhof	248
A. A. Lagrein Scuro Ris., A. Berger -Thurnhof	245
A. A. Lagrein Scuro Ris., Franz Gojer Glögglhof	247
A. A. Lagrein Scuro Ris., C. Laimburg	266
A. A. Lagrein Scuro Ris., R. Malojer Gummerhof	248
A. A. Lagrein Scuro Ris., J. Mayr - Erbhof Unterganzner	249
A. A. Lagrein Scuro Ris., Georg Mumelter	249
A. A. Lagrein Scuro Ris., Pfeifer Johannes Pfannenstielhof	269
A. A. Lagrein Scuro Ris., Heinrich Plattner - Waldgries	250
A. A. Lagrein Scuro Ris., Georg Ramoser - Untermoserhof	250
A. A. Lagrein Scuro Ris., Hans Rottensteiner	251
A. A. Lagrein Scuro Rueslhof, K. Martini & Sohn	268
A. A. Lagrein Scuro Segenpichl, C. Prod. di Merano	260
A. A. Lagrein Scuro Steinraffler, Hofstätter	266
A. A. Lagrein Scuro Taberhof Ris., C. Prod. S. Maddalena	247
A. A. Lagrein Scuro Tor di Lupo, C. Prod. Andriano	240
A. A. Lagrein Scuro Torculum Ris., Viticoltori Alto Adige	245
A. A. Lagrein Scuro Weingutt Rahmhütt, R. Malojer Gummerhof	248
A. A. Lagrein Urbanhof, C. Prod. Termeno	265
A. A. Lagrein-Cabernet Klaser, Josef Sölva - Niklaserhof	255
A. A. Lagrein-Merlot, Peter Sölva & Söhne - Paterbichl	255
A. A. Lagrein-Merlot Cuvée Girlan, C. Prod. Cornaiano	241
A. A. Meranese, Graf Pfeil Weingut Kränzel	256
A. A. Meranese Schickenburg, C. Prod. Burggräfler	259
A. A. Merlot, Castel Sallegg - Graf Kuenburg	253
A. A. Merlot, Ignaz Niedrist	243
A. A. Merlot, Georg Ramoser - Untermoserhof	250
A. A. Merlot, Peter Zemmer - Kupelwieser	258
A. A. Merlot Brenntal, C. Prod. Cortaccia	257
A. A. Merlot - Cabernet Sauvignon Geierberg, Castello Schwanburg	262
A. A. Merlot DiVinus, C. Prod. S. Paolo	242
A. A. Merlot Freiberg, C. Prod. di Merano	260
A. A. Merlot Kastelaz Ris., Castel Ringberg & Kastelaz Elena Walch	265
A. A. Merlot Levad, C. Prod. Nalles Niclara Magrè	261
A. A. Merlot Ris., Castel Sallegg - Graf Kuenburg	253
A. A. Merlot Ris., R. Malojer Gummerhof	248
A. A. Merlot Ris., Tenuta Ritterhof	269
A. A. Merlot Schweitzer, Franz Haas	261
A. A. Merlot Siebeneich, C. Prod. Andriano	240
A. A. Merlot Siebeneich, C. Terlano	264
A. A. Merlot Siebeneich Tor di Lupo, C. Prod. Andriano	240
A. A. Merlot Spitz, Franz Gojer Glögglhof	247
A. A. Merlot Windegg, Josef Brigl	240
A. A. Merlot-Cabernet Juvin Cuvée, C. Prod. Burggräfler	259
A. A. Merlot-Cabernet Sauvignon Anticus, C. Prod. Nalles Niclara Magrè	261
A. A. Merlot-Lagrein, C. Prod. Burggräfler	259
A. A. Merlot-Lagrein Ebner, Kössler - Praeclarus	243
A. A. Moscato Giallo, A. Berger -Thurnhof	245
A. A. Moscato Giallo, Castello Schwanburg	262
A. A. Moscato Giallo Passito, H. & T. Rottensteiner	251
A. A. Moscato Giallo Schickenburg, C. Prod. Burggräfler	259
A. A. Moscato Giallo Vinalia, C. Gries	246
A. A. Moscato Rosa, Abbazia di Novacella	267
A. A. Moscato Rosa, Castel Sallegg - Graf Kuenburg	253
A. A. Moscato Rosa, Heinrich Plattner - Waldgries	250
A. A. Moscato Rosa Schweizer, Franz Haas	261
A. A. Müller Thurgau Hofstatt, C. Prod. Cortaccia	257
A. A. Pinot Bianco, C. Prod. S. Maddalena	247
A. A. Pinot Bianco, C. Prod. Termeno	265
A. A. Pinot Bianco, Graf Pfeil Weingut Kränzel	256
A. A. Pinot Bianco, Franz Haas	261
A. A. Pinot Bianco, Hofstätter	266
A. A. Pinot Bianco, Popphof - Andreas Menz	259
A. A. Pinot Bianco, Josef Sölva - Niklaserhof	255
A. A. Pinot Bianco, Peter Zemmer - Kupelwieser	258
A. A. Pinot Bianco Brunar, Prima & Nuova/Erste & Neue	254
A. A. Pinot Bianco Carnol, Hans Rottensteiner	251
A. A. Pinot Bianco Fritz Dellago, C. Gries	246
A. A. Pinot Bianco Graf Von Meran, C. Prod. di Merano	260
A. A. Pinot Bianco Guggenberg, C. Prod. Burggräfler	259
A. A. Pinot Bianco Helios, Graf Pfeil Weingut Kränzel	256
A. A. Pinot Bianco Kastelaz, Castel Ringberg & Kastelaz Elena Walch	265
A. A. Pinot Bianco Kupelwieser, Peter Zemmer - Kupelwieser	258
A. A. Pinot Bianco MerVin V. T., C. Prod. Burggräfler	259
A. A. Pinot Bianco Plattenriegl, C. Prod. Cornaiano	241
A. A. Pinot Bianco Praesulius, Markus Prackwieser Gumphof	269
A. A. Pinot Bianco Puntay, Prima & Nuova/Erste & Neue	254
A. A. Pinot Bianco Schulthauser, C. Prod. S. Michele Appiano	242
A. A. Pinot Bianco Sirmian, C. Prod. Nalles Niclara Magrè	261
A. A. Pinot Bianco Strahler, Stroblhof	244
A. A. Pinot Bianco Vial, C. Viticoltori di Caldaro	253
A. A. Pinot Bianco Weisshaus, C. Prod. Colterenzio	241
A. A. Pinot Grigio, C. Convento Muri-Gries	246
A. A. Pinot Grigio, Peter Zemmer - Kupelwieser	258
A. A. Pinot Grigio Anger, C. Prod. S. Michele Appiano	242
A. A. Pinot Grigio Castel Ringberg, Castel Ringberg & Kastelaz Elena Walch	265
A. A. Pinot Grigio Griesbauerhof, Georg Mumelter	249
A. A. Pinot Grigio Maso Reiner, Kettmeir	254
A. A. Pinot Grigio Puiten, C. Prod. Colterenzio	241
A. A. Pinot Grigio Punggl, C. Prod. Nalles Niclara Magrè	261
A. A. Pinot Grigio Söll, C. Viticoltori di Caldaro	253
A. A. Pinot Grigio St. Valentin, C. Prod. S. Michele Appiano	242
A. A. Pinot Grigio Unterbnerhof, C. Prod. Termeno	265
A. A. Pinot Nero, Abbazia di Novacella	267
A. A. Pinot Nero, Graf Pfeil Weingut Kränzel	256
A. A. Pinot Nero, C. Laimburg	266
A. A. Pinot Nero, Ignaz Niedrist	243
A. A. Pinot Nero, Popphof - Andreas Menz	259
A. A. Pinot Nero, Steinhauserhof	263
A. A. Pinot Nero Briglhof, Josef Brigl	240
A. A. Pinot Nero DiVinus, C. Prod. S. Paolo	242
A. A. Pinot Nero Fuchsleiten, Tenuta Pfitscherhof	270
A. A. Pinot Nero Greel, C. Prod. S. Maddalena	247
A. A. Pinot Nero Haslhof, Josef Brigl	240
A. A. Pinot Nero Hausmannhof, Haderburg	263
A. A. Pinot Nero Matan, Tenuta Pfitscherhof	270
A. A. Pinot Nero Mazon Trattmannhof, C. Prod. Cornaiano	241
A. A. Pinot Nero Mazzon, C. Prod. Termeno	265
A. A. Pinot Nero Mazzon Select Ris., Hans Rottensteiner	251
A. A. Pinot Nero Patricia, C. Prod. Cornaiano	241
A. A. Pinot Nero Pigeno, Stroblhof	244
A. A. Pinot Nero Ris., C. Prod. S. Michele Appiano	242
A. A. Pinot Nero Ris., C. Viticoltori di Caldaro	253
A. A. Pinot Nero Ris., Castel Sallegg - Graf Kuenburg	253
A. A. Pinot Nero Ris., Hofstätter	266
A. A. Pinot Nero Ris., Josef Niedermayr	244
A. A. Pinot Nero Ris., Tenuta Pfitscherhof	270
A. A. Pinot Nero Ris., Stroblhof	244
A. A. Pinot Nero S. Urbano, Hofstätter	266
A. A. Pinot Nero Saltnerhof, C. Viticoltori di Caldaro	253
A. A. Pinot Nero Sandbichler Ris., C. H. Lun	258
A. A. Pinot Nero Sandlahner Ris., C. Prod. S. Maddalena	247
A. A. Pinot Nero Schweizer, Franz Haas	261
A. A. Pinot Nero Strahler Ris., Stroblhof	244
A. A. Pinot Nero Tiefenthaler, C. Prod. Burggräfler	259
A. A. Pinot Nero Vorhof, C. Prod. Cortaccia	257
A. A. Pinot Nero Zenoberg, C. Prod. di Merano	260
A. A. Praeclarus Brut, Kössler - Praeclarus	243
A. A. Praeclarus Rosé, Kössler - Praeclarus	243
A. A. Resling Castel Ringberg, Castel Ringberg & Kastelaz Elena Walch	265
A. A. Riesling, C. Prod. Nalles Niclara Magrè	261
A. A. Riesling, Castello Rametz	270
A. A. Riesling, Peter Zemmer - Kupelwieser	258
A. A. Riesling Castel Schwanburg, Castello Schwanburg	262
A. A. Riesling Kupelwieser, Peter Zemmer - Kupelwieser	258
A. A. Riesling Leitach, C. Prod. S. Maddalena	247
A. A. Riesling Montiggl, C. Prod. S. Michele Appiano	242
A. A. Riesling Renano, C. Laimburg	266
A. A. Riesling Renano, Ignaz Niedrist	243
A. A. S. Maddalena, C. Prod. Andriano	240
A. A. S. Maddalena, Georg Mumelter	249
A. A. S. Maddalena Cl., C. Prod. S. Maddalena	247
A. A. S. Maddalena Cl., Egger-Ramer	268
A. A. S. Maddalena Cl., Franz Gojer Glögglhof	247
A. A. S. Maddalena Cl., R. Malojer Gummerhof	248
A. A. S. Maddalena Cl., J. Mayr - Erbhof Unterganzner	249
A. A. S. Maddalena Cl., Pfeifer Johannes Pfannenstielhof	269
A. A. S. Maddalena Cl., Heinrich Plattner - Waldgries	250
A. A. S. Maddalena Cl., Georg Ramoser - Untermoserhof	250
A. A. S. Maddalena Cl., H. & T. Rottensteiner	251
A. A. S. Maddalena Cl. Egger-Larcherhof, Josef Niedermayr	244
A. A. S. Maddalena Cl. Huck am Bach, C. Prod. S. Maddalena	247
A. A. S. Maddalena Cl. Premstallerhof, Hans Rottensteiner	251
A. A. S. Maddalena Cl. Rumplerhof, Thomas Mayr e Figli	269
A. A. S. Maddalena Cl. Tröglerhof, C. Gries	246
A. A. S. Maddalena Föhrner, C. H. Lun	258
A. A. S. Maddalena Haüsler, C. Terlano	264
A. A. S. Maddalena Kupelwieser, Peter Zemmer - Kupelwieser	258
A. A. S. Maddalena Perlhof, Tenuta Ritterhof	269
A. A. S. Maddalena Reierhof, Josef Brigl	240
A. A. S. Maddalena Rondell, Franz Gojer Glögglhof	247
A. A. S. Maddalena Tenuta De Ferrari, Viticoltori Alto Adige	245
A. A. Sauvignon, A. Berger -Thurnhof	245
A. A. Sauvignon, Josef Brigl	240
A. A. Sauvignon, C. Gries	246
A. A. Sauvignon, C. Prod. Termeno	265
A. A. Sauvignon, Castel Sallegg - Graf Kuenburg	253
A. A. Sauvignon, C. Laimburg	266
A. A. Sauvignon, H. & T. Rottensteiner	251
A. A. Sauvignon, Josef Sölva - Niklaserhof	255
A. A. Sauvignon, Steinhauserhof	263
A. A. Sauvignon Albertus, C. H. Lun	258
A. A. Sauvignon Allure, Josef Niedermayr	244

Entry	Page
A. A. Sauvignon Castel Ringberg, Castel Ringberg & Kastelaz Elena Walch	265
A. A. Sauvignon Castel Schwanburg, Castello Schwanburg	262
A. A. Sauvignon Exclusiv Gfilhof, C. Prod. S. Paolo	242
A. A. Sauvignon Graf Von Meran, C. Prod. di Merano	260
A. A. Sauvignon Gur zur Sand Classic, R. Malojer Gummerhof	248
A. A. Sauvignon Hausmannhof, Haderburg	263
A. A. Sauvignon Hausmannhof Sel., Haderburg	263
A. A. Sauvignon Intenditore, Peter Zemmer - Kupelwieser	258
A. A. Sauvignon Kirchleiten, Tiefenbrunner	257
A. A. Sauvignon Lafoa, C. Prod. Colterenzio	241
A. A. Sauvignon Lahn, C. Prod. S. Michele Appiano	242
A. A. Sauvignon Milla, C. Prod. Cortaccia	257
A. A. Sauvignon Mockhof, C. Prod. S. Maddalena	247
A. A. Sauvignon Praesulius, Markus Prackwieser Gumphof	269
A. A. Sauvignon Prail, C. Prod. Colterenzio	241
A. A. Sauvignon Premstalerhof, C. Viticoltori di Caldaro	253
A. A. Sauvignon Select Art Flora, C. Prod. Cornaiano	241
A. A. Sauvignon St. Valentin, C. Prod. S. Michele Appiano	242
A. A. Sauvignon Stern, Prima & Nuova/Erste & Neue	254
A. A. Schiava Exclusiv Sarner, C. Prod. S. Paolo	242
A. A. Schiava Gallea, C. Prod. Nalles Niclara Magrè	261
A. A. Schiava Grigia Castel Turmhof, Tiefenbrunner	257
A. A. Schiava Grigia Sonnntaler, C. Prod. Cortaccia	257
A. A. Schiava Gschleier, C. Prod. Cornaiano	241
A. A. Schiava Hexenbichler, C. Prod. Termeno	265
A. A. Schiava Kolbenhofer, Hofstätter	266
A. A. Schiava S. Giustina, C. Prod. Andriano	240
A. A. Schiava Schloss Baslan, Graf Pfeil Weingut Kränzel	256
A. A. Spumante Blanc de Blancs Arunda, Vivaldi - Arunda	260
A. A. Spumante Brut, Kettmeir	254
A. A. Spumante Brut Arunda Ris., Vivaldi - Arunda	260
A. A. Spumante Brut Vivaldi, Vivaldi - Arunda	260
A. A. Spumante Extra Brut Vivaldi, Vivaldi - Arunda	260
A. A. Spumante Extra Brut Vivaldi Cuvée Marianna, Vivaldi - Arunda	260
A. A. Spumante Haderburg Pas Dosé, Haderburg	263
A. A. Spumante Hausmannhof, Haderburg	263
A. A. Spumante Praeclarus Noblesse Ris., Kössler - Praeclarus	243
A. A. Terlano Chardonnay, C. Terlano	264
A. A. Terlano Cl., C. Terlano	264
A. A. Terlano Hof zu Pramol, Josef Niedermayr	244
A. A. Terlano Müller Thurgau Cl., C. Prod. Andriano	240
A. A. Terlano Nova Domus, C. Terlano	264
A. A. Terlano Pinot Bianco, Josef Brigl	240
A. A. Terlano Pinot Bianco, C. Terlano	264
A. A. Terlano Pinot Bianco Cl. Sonnengut, C. Prod. Andriano	240
A. A. Terlano Pinot Bianco Exclusiv Plötzner, C. Prod. S. Paolo	242
A. A. Terlano Pinot Bianco Pitzon, Castello Schwanburg	262
A. A. Terlano Pinot Bianco Riol, Heinrich Plattner - Waldgries	250
A. A. Terlano Pinot Bianco Sirmian, C. Prod. Nalles Niclara Magrè	261
A. A. Terlano Pinot Bianco Sonnenberg, Castello Schwanburg	262
A. A. Terlano Pinot Bianco Vorberg, C. Terlano	264
A. A. Terlano Sauvignon, Ignaz Niedrist	243
A. A. Terlano Sauvignon Cl., C. Terlano	264
A. A. Terlano Sauvignon Cl., Viticoltori Alto Adige	245
A. A. Terlano Sauvignon Cl. Mantele, C. Prod. Nalles Niclara Magrè	261
A. A. Terlano Sauvignon Preciosa Tor di Lupo, C. Prod. Andriano	240
A. A. Terlano Sauvignon Quarz, C. Terlano	264
A. A. Terlano Sauvignon Winkl, C. Terlano	264
A. A. Traminer aromatico Cresta, Hans Rottensteiner	251
A. A. Valle Isarco Gewürztraminer, Abbazia di Novacella	267
A. A. Valle Isarco Gewürztraminer, C. Prod. Valle Isarco	256
A. A. Valle Isarco Gewürztraminer, Köfererhof	267
A. A. Valle Isarco Gewürztraminer, Kuenhof - Peter Pliger	252
A. A. Valle Isarco Gewürztraminer, M. Nössing - Hoandlhof	252
A. A. Valle Isarco Gewürztraminer, Taschlerhof	269
A. A. Valle Isarco Gewürztraminer Praepositus, Abbazia di Novacella	267
A. A. Valle Isarco Kerner, Abbazia di Novacella	267
A. A. Valle Isarco Kerner, C. Prod. Valle Isarco	256
A. A. Valle Isarco Kerner, Köfererhof	267
A. A. Valle Isarco Kerner, M. Nössing - Hoandlhof	252
A. A. Valle Isarco Kerner Praepositus, Abbazia di Novacella	267
A. A. Valle Isarco Klausener Laitacher, C. Prod. Valle Isarco	256
A. A. Valle Isarco Müller Thurgau, Abbazia di Novacella	267
A. A. Valle Isarco Müller Thurgau, C. Prod. S. Maddalena	247
A. A. Valle Isarco Müller Thurgau, C. Prod. Valle Isarco	256
A. A. Valle Isarco Müller Thurgau, M. Nössing - Hoandlhof	252
A. A. Valle Isarco Müller Thurgau, Rockhof	270
A. A. Valle Isarco Pinot Grigio, Abbazia di Novacella	267
A. A. Valle Isarco Pinot Grigio, C. Prod. Valle Isarco	256
A. A. Valle Isarco Pinot Grigio, Köfererhof	267
A. A. Valle Isarco Sylvaner, Abbazia di Novacella	267
A. A. Valle Isarco Sylvaner, C. Prod. Valle Isarco	256
A. A. Valle Isarco Sylvaner, Köfererhof	267
A. A. Valle Isarco Sylvaner, Kuenhof - Peter Pliger	252
A. A. Valle Isarco Sylvaner, M. Nössing - Hoandlhof	252
A. A. Valle Isarco Sylvaner, Taschlerhof	269
A. A. Valle Isarco Sylvaner Aristos, C. Prod. Valle Isarco	256
A. A. Valle Isarco Sylvaner Praepositus, Abbazia di Novacella	267
A. A. Valle Isarco Veltliner, C. Prod. Valle Isarco	256
A. A. Valle Isarco Veltliner, Kuenhof - Peter Pliger	252
A. A. Valle Venosta Chardonnay, Baron von Kripp Stachlburg	270
A. A. Valle Venosta Gewürztraminer, Tenuta Falkenstein - Franz Pratzner	262
A. A. Valle Venosta Gewürztraminer V. T. , Tenuta Falkenstein - Franz Pratzner	262
A. A. Valle Venosta Pinot Bianco, Tenuta Falkenstein - Franz Pratzner	262
A. A. Valle Venosta Pinot Bianco, Tenuta Unterortl-Castel Juval	264
A. A. Valle Venosta Pinot Nero, Tenuta Falkenstein - Franz Pratzner	262
A. A. Valle Venosta Pinot Nero, Tenuta Unterortl-Castel Juval	264
A. A. Valle Venosta Riesling, Oswald Schuster Befelnhof	270
A. A. Valle Venosta Riesling, Tenuta Falkenstein - Franz Pratzner	262
A. A. Valle Venosta Riesling, Tenuta Unterortl-Castel Juval	264
A Sirio, S. Gervasio	510
Abbaia, C. Soc. del Vermentino	724
Acciaiolo, Castello d' Albola	521
Accordo Bianco, Degiorgis	95
Acerone, Vittorio Innocenti	496
Acini Dolci, C. del Castello	308
Acini Rari Passito, Enoteca Bisson	159
Acinobili, Maculan	274
Acquabona di Acquabona, Acquabona	570
Aglaia, Fattoria Corzano e Paterno	529
Aglianico, Cantine Grotta del Sole	662
Aglianico Avellaino, Mastroberardino	654
Aglianico del Taburno, Fontanavecchia - Orazio Rillo	665
Aglianico del Taburno Diomede, Ocone	661
Aglianico del Taburno Fidelis, C. del Taburno	655
Aglianico del Taburno Rosato, Fontanavecchia - Orazio Rillo	665
Aglianico del Taburno Rosato Alba Rosa, C. del Taburno	655
Aglianico del Taburno Vigna Cataratte, Fontanavecchia - Orazio Rillo	665
Aglianico del Taburno Vigna Cataratte Ris., Fontanavecchia - Orazio Rillo	665
Aglianico del Taburno Vigna Pezza la Corte, Ocone	661
Aglianico del Vulture, Consorzio Viticoltori Associati del Vulture	670
Aglianico del Vulture, D'Angelo	672
Aglianico del Vulture, Vinicola Miali	691
Aglianico del Vulture, F.lli Napolitano	674
Aglianico del Vulture, Paternoster	671
Aglianico del Vulture, Tenuta del Portale	674
Aglianico del Vulture Basilisco, Basilisco	671
Aglianico del Vulture Carato Venusio, C. Riforma Fondiaria di Venosa	673
Aglianico del Vulture Carpe Diem, Consorzio Viticoltori Associati del Vulture	670
Aglianico del Vulture Don Anselmo Ris., Paternoster	671
Aglianico del Vulture Elea, F.lli Napolitano	674
Aglianico del Vulture Federico II, Tenuta Le Querce	670
Aglianico del Vulture Il Covo dei Briganti, Agricola Eubea - Fam. Sasso	672
Aglianico del Vulture Il Repertorio, Cantine del Notaio	673
Aglianico del Vulture Il Viola, Tenuta Le Querce	670
Aglianico del Vulture La Firma, Cantine del Notaio	673
Aglianico del Vulture Pipoli, Basilium	674
Aglianico del Vulture Ris. Don Anselmo, Paternoster	671
Aglianico del Vulture Ris. Vigna Caselle, D'Angelo	672
Aglianico del Vulture Rosso di Costanza, Tenuta Le Querce	670
Aglianico del Vulture Rotondo, Paternoster	671
Aglianico del Vulture Synthesi, Paternoster	671
Aglianico del Vulture Terre di Orazio, C. Riforma Fondiaria di Venosa	673
Aglianico del Vulture Valle del Trono, Basilium	674
Aglianico del Vulture Vetusto, Consorzio Viticoltori Associati del Vulture	670
Aglianico del Vulture Vigna Caselle Ris., D'Angelo	672
Aglianico del Vulture Vignali, C. Riforma Fondiaria di Venosa	673
Aglianico di Roccamonfina, Telaro - Coop. Lavoro e Salute	657
Aglianico di Roccamonfina, Villa Matilde	655
Aglianico Spumante Ellenico, Consorzio Viticoltori Associati del Vulture	670
Aglieno, Casa alle Vacche	533
Agno Tinto, Vignalta	312
Agorà Bianco, Borgo Canale	680
Ailanpa, Foradori	228
Aione, Podere Aione	565
Akronte, Boccadigabbia	584
Alastro, Planeta	714
Albaciara Bianco, Barni	44
Albana di Romagna Dolce, Villa Pampini - F.lli Bernardi	428
Albana di Romagna Dolce Lilaria, S. Ferrucci	406
Albana di Romagna Dolce Vigna della Ca' Lunga, Treré	411
Albana di Romagna Passito, Tenuta Uccellina	417
Albana di Romagna Passito, Tre Monti	412
Albana di Romagna Passito Arrocco, Fattoria Zerbina	409
Albana di Romagna Passito Chimera, Giovanna Madonia	404
Albana di Romagna Passito Colle del Re, Umberto Cesari	407
Albana di Romagna Passito Domus Aurea, S. Ferrucci	406

Albana di Romagna Passito Gradisca, Fattoria Paradiso	405
Albana di Romagna Passito Innamorato, Alessandro Morini	425
Albana di Romagna Passito La Dolce Vita, La Macolina	426
Albana di Romagna Passito Maolù, Colonna - Vini Spalletti	419
Albana di Romagna Passito Mythos, Tenuta Valli	426
Albana di Romagna Passito Non Ti Scordar di Me, Leone Conti	410
Albana di Romagna Passito Scacco Matto, Fattoria Zerbina	409
Albana di Romagna Passito Solara, Celli	404
Albana di Romagna Passito Ultimo Giorno di Scuola, Istituto Professionale per l'Agricoltura e l'Ambiente	410
Albana di Romagna Secco, Colonna - Vini Spalletti	419
Albana di Romagna Secco Colle del Re, Umberto Cesari	407
Albana di Romagna Secco I Croppi, Celli	404
Albana di Romagna Secco Vigna della Compadrona, Treré	411
Albana di Romagna Secco Vigna della Rocca, Tre Monti	412
Albatraia, Villa Patrizia	526
Alberto Rosso, Zenato	297
Albiola, Casale del Giglio	628
Albion Cabernet Sauvignon Villa Novare, Bertani	292
Alborato, Co.Vi.O.	617
Alcamo, Casa Vinicola Firriato	709
Alcamo, Cantine Torrevecchia	700
Alcamo Alahambra, Spadafora	711
Alcamo Principe di Corleone, Pollara	708
Alcamo Rapitalà, Tenute Rapitalà	711
Alcamo Rapitalà Grand Cru, Tenute Rapitalà	711
Ale di Glesie, Villa Frattina	378
Aleatico, Petricci del Pianta	575
Aleatico dell'Elba, Acquabona	570
Aleatico dell'Elba, Cecilia	559
Aleatico dell'Elba, Tenuta La Chiusa	570
Aleatico dell'Elba, Mola	570
Aleatico dell'Elba, Sapereta	570
Aleatico Negrino, Leone de Castris	687
Aleatico Passito delle Cinque Pietre, Telaro - Coop. Lavoro e Salute	657
Alegio, Filomusi Guelfi	648
Alezio Rosato Mjère, Michele Calò & Figli	692
Alghero Cagnulari, C. Soc. S. Maria La Palma	720
Alghero Chardonnay, C. Soc. S. Maria La Palma	720
Alghero Le Arenarie, Tenute Sella & Mosca	720
Alghero Marchese di Villamarina, Tenute Sella & Mosca	720
Alghero Rosso Vigne del Mare, C. Soc. S. Maria La Palma	720
Alghero Sauvignon, C. Soc. S. Maria La Palma	720
Alghero Tanca Farrà, Tenute Sella & Mosca	720
Alghero Torbato Terre Bianche, Tenute Sella & Mosca	720
Alido, Castello Fageto	606
Allodio Rosso, Podere S. Michele	573
Allora Aglianico, Calatrasi Puglia	678
Allora Primitivo, Calatrasi Puglia	678
Almabruna, I Campetti	558
Almerita Brut, Tasca d'Almerita	715
Alta Langa Brut M. Cl., Vigne Regali	133
Altavilla della Corte Bianco, Casa Vinicola Firriato	709
Altavilla della Corte Rosso, Casa Vinicola Firriato	709
Alte d'Altesi, Altesino	473
Alterego, Luigi Coppo e Figli	52
Alteta, Villa Patrizia	526
Altreuve Passito, Vallona	407
Alzero Cabernet Franc, Giuseppe Quintarelli	294
Amabile Persolino Rosso Passito, Istituto Professionale per l'Agricoltura e l'Ambiente	410
Amaranto dei Vanai Rosso dei Colli Trevigiani, Vincenzo Toffoli	297
Amarone della Valpolicella, C. Soc. della Valpantena	319
Amarone della Valpolicella, Corte Sant'Alda	285
Amarone della Valpolicella, Musella	300
Amarone della Valpolicella, Giuseppe Quintarelli	294
Amarone della Valpolicella, Trabucchi	280
Amarone della Valpolicella Campo dei Gigli, Tenuta Sant'Antonio	275
Amarone della Valpolicella Cl., Allegrini	277
Amarone della Valpolicella Cl., Lorenzo Begali	301
Amarone della Valpolicella Cl., Bertani	292
Amarone della Valpolicella Cl., Brigaldara	302
Amarone della Valpolicella Cl., Luigi Brunelli	302
Amarone della Valpolicella Cl. , Giuseppe Campagnola	282
Amarone della Valpolicella Cl., Corteforte	325
Amarone della Valpolicella Cl., F.lli Degani	283
Amarone della Valpolicella Cl., Guerrieri Rizzardi	207
Amarone della Valpolicella Cl., I Scriani	325
Amarone della Valpolicella Cl., Le Bertarole	325
Amarone della Valpolicella Cl., Le Ragose	293
Amarone della Valpolicella Cl., Giuseppe Lonardi	284
Amarone della Valpolicella Cl., Angelo Nicolis e Figli	303
Amarone della Valpolicella Cl., Novaia	284
Amarone della Valpolicella Cl., Raimondi Villa Monteleone	307
Amarone della Valpolicella Cl., S. Rustico	326
Amarone della Valpolicella Cl., S. Sofia	303
Amarone della Valpolicella Cl., F.lli Tedeschi	207
Amarone della Valpolicella Cl., Massimo Venturini	305
Amarone della Valpolicella Cl., Villa Bellini	306
Amarone della Valpolicella Cl., Villa Spinosa	295
Amarone della Valpolicella Cl., Zenato	297
Amarone della Valpolicella Cl., F.lli Zeni	273
Amarone della Valpolicella Cl. Acinatico, Stefano Accordini	301
Amarone della Valpolicella Cl. Ambrosan, Angelo Nicolis e Figli	303
Amarone della Valpolicella Cl. Barrique, F.lli Zeni	273
Amarone della Valpolicella Cl. BG, Tommaso Bussola	292
Amarone della Valpolicella Cl. Ca' Florian, Viticoltori Tommasi	305
Amarone della Valpolicella Cl. Campo Casalin I Castei, Michele Castellani	282
Amarone della Valpolicella Cl. Campo del Titari, Luigi Brunelli	302
Amarone della Valpolicella Cl. Campo S. Paolo, Raimondi Villa Monteleone	307
Amarone della Valpolicella Cl. Capitel della Crosara, Giacomo Montresor	320
Amarone della Valpolicella Cl. Capitel Monte Olmi, F.lli Tedeschi	207
Amarone della Valpolicella Cl. Casa dei Bepi, Viviani	295
Amarone della Valpolicella Cl. Caterina Zardini, Giuseppe Campagnola	282
Amarone della Valpolicella Cl. Costasera, Masi	306
Amarone della Valpolicella Cl. Costera, Guido Manara	327
Amarone della Valpolicella Cl. Domini Veneti, C. Soc. Valpolicella	293
Amarone della Valpolicella Cl. Gioé, S. Sofia	303
Amarone della Valpolicella Cl. Gnirega, Coop. Ottomarzo	328
Amarone della Valpolicella Cl. La Bastia, Eugenio & Figli Tinazzi	323
Amarone della Valpolicella Cl. La Fabriseria, F.lli Tedeschi	207
Amarone della Valpolicella Cl. La Marega, Le Salette	278
Amarone della Valpolicella Cl. La Rosta, F.lli Degani	283
Amarone della Valpolicella Cl. Le Vigne Ca' del Pipa, Michele Castellani	282
Amarone della Valpolicella Cl. Manara, C. Soc. Valpolicella	293
Amarone della Valpolicella Cl. Marta Galli, Le Ragose	293
Amarone della Valpolicella Cl. Mazzano, Masi	306
Amarone della Valpolicella Cl. Monte Faustino, Giuseppe Fornaser	327
Amarone della Valpolicella Cl.Monte Masua Il Sestante, Viticoltori Tommasi	305
Amarone della Valpolicella Cl. Pergole Vece, Le Salette	278
Amarone della Valpolicella Cl. Punta di Villa, Roberto Mazzi	294
Amarone della Valpolicella Cl. Ris. Sergio Zenato, Zenato	297
Amarone della Valpolicella Cl. Sup. Monte Cà Paletta, Giuseppe Quintarelli	294
Amarone della Valpolicella Cl. TB, Tommaso Bussola	292
Amarone della Valpolicella Cl. Terre di Cariano, Cecilia Beretta	319
Amarone della Valpolicella Cl. Tulipano Nero, Viviani	295
Amarone della Valpolicella Cl. Vigne Alte, F.lli Zeni	273
Amarone della Valpolicella Cl. Vigneti del Gaso, S. Rustico	326
Amarone della Valpolicella Cl. Vigneti di Jago Sel., C. Soc. Valpolicella	293
Amarone della Valpolicella Cl. Vigneti di Ravazol, Ca' La Bionda	281
Amarone della Valpolicella Cl. Vigneto Il Fornetto, Stefano Accordini	301
Amarone della Valpolicella Cl. Vigneto Monte Ca' Bianca, Lorenzo Begali	301
Amarone della Valpolicella Cl. Vigneto Monte Danieli, Corte Rugolin	283
Amarone della Valpolicella Cl. Vigneto Monte Sant'Urbano, F.lli Speri	304
Amarone della Valpolicella Cl. Villa Borghetti, Pasqua Vigneti e Cantine	320
Amarone della Valpolicella Falasco, C. Soc. della Valpantena	319
Amarone della Valpolicella Maso Laito, Zonin	279
Amarone della Valpolicella Mithas, Corte Sant'Alda	285
Amarone della Valpolicella Proemio, Santi	280
Amarone della Valpolicella Ris., Giuseppe Quintarelli	294
Amarone della Valpolicella Rocca Sveva, C. di Soave	308
Amarone della Valpolicella Roccolo Grassi, Sartori - Roccolo Grassi	285
Amarone della Valpolicella Vigneto di Monte Lodoletta, Romano Dal Forno	279
Amativo, Cantele	682
Amineo Bianco Donnacaterina, Dattilo	698
Amineo Rosso, Dattilo	698
Amistar Bianco, Peter Sölva & Söhne - Paterbichl	255
Amistar Rosso, Peter Sölva & Söhne - Paterbichl	255
Amoroso, Le Tende	281
Anagallis, Castello di Lilliano	552
Ancherona Chardonnay, S. Felice	448
Andias, Cantine di Dolianova	722
Anfiteatro, Vecchie Terre di Montefili	515
Angheli, Tenuta di Donnafugata	705
Anghelos, Tenuta De Angelis	582
Anghelu Ruju Ris., Tenute Sella & Mosca	720
Angialis, Antonio Argiolas	728
Angimbé, Cusumano	710
Anima, Livernano	522
Ansonica, La Parrina	509

Ansonica Costa dell'Argentario, S. Lucia	558
Antas, Fattoria Mauritania	732
Anthos, Prima & Nuova/Erste & Neue	254
Antico Gregori, Attilio Contini	721
Antinoo, Casale del Giglio	628
Apianae, Di Majo Norante	641
Arabesco Chardonnay, Marco Maci	679
Araja, C. Soc. di Santadi	726
Arbeskia, Giuseppe Gabbas	725
Arbiato, Barone Scammacca del Murgo	713
Arbis Rosso, Borgo S. Daniele	344
Arborea Sangiovese, C. Soc. Marrubiu	731
Arcana Bianco, Terre Bianche	161
Arcana Rosso, Terre Bianche	161
Arcass V. T., Cascina Chicco	47
Arciato, Co.Vi.O.	617
Arcibaldo, Cennatoio	511
Arcone, Arcone	732
Ardingo, Andrea Costanti	479
Aresco Passito Veronese, Corte Rugolin	283
Areté, Cantine Rallo	706
Argiolas, Antonio Argiolas	728
Argo, Redi	504
Arguzzio, Villa Arceno	449
Arkezia Muffo di S. Sisto, Fazi Battaglia	583
Arleo Rosso, S. Sofia	303
Armaiolo, Fattoria S. Fabiano - Borghini Baldovinetti	430
Armaleo, Palazzone	619
Armecolo, Castel di Salve	689
Arneis Passito Poch ma Bon, Cascina Pellerino	109
Arte, Domenico Clerico	98
Artias Chardonnay, Rio Maggio	591
Artias Sauvignon, Rio Maggio	591
Arvino, Statti	697
Arzimo Passito, La Cappuccina	290
Asprinio d'Aversa, Cantine Caputo	664
Asprinio d'Aversa, Cantine Grotta del Sole	662
Assajè Rosso, Capichera	721
Assisi Grechetto, F.lli Sportoletti	622
Assisi Rosso, F.lli Sportoletti	622
Asti, Cascina Fonda	95
Asti, Fontanafredda	129
Asti, I Vignaioli di S. Stefano	127
Asti, Vigne Regali	133
Asti Cascina Palazzo, F.lli Bera	116
Asti De Miranda M. Cl., Giuseppe Contratto	51
Asti Driveri M. Cl., Cascina Fonda	95
Asti La Selvatica, Caudrina	61
Ateo, Ciacci Piccolomini D'Aragona	478
Atina Cabernet, Giovanni Palombo	628
Aura, Vallis Agri	218
Aureo, La Castellina	552
Aureus, Josef Niedermayr	244
Avra, Giuseppe Gabbas	725
Avvoltore, Moris Farms	472
Azobé Corvina Vigneto delle Pergole, Albino Piona	328
Azzurreta, La Togata	485
Badia Raustignolo, Il Pratello	426
Bagnoli Bianco S. Andrea, Dominio di Bagnoli	323
Bagnoli Bianco Santissima Trinità, Dominio di Bagnoli	323
Balajana, C. Soc. Gallura	729
Balifico, Castello di Volpaia	525
Ballistarius, Letrari	230
Barbanico, Nicola Balter	230
Barbasiolo, Batasiolo	83
Barbaresco, Giacomo Borgogno & Figli	36
Barbaresco, Ca' Rome' - Romano Marengo	29
Barbaresco, Fontanabianca	112
Barbaresco, Gaja	31
Barbaresco, Gastaldi	112
Barbaresco, I Paglieri	32
Barbaresco, Gianluigi Lano	25
Barbaresco, Fiorenzo Nada	136
Barbaresco, Pelissero	137
Barbaresco, Vignaioli Elvio Pertinace	137
Barbaresco, Pio Cesare	25
Barbaresco, Prunotto	26
Barbaresco, Punset	151
Barbaresco, Cascina Vano	115
Barbaresco Ad Altiora, Michele Taliano	106
Barbaresco Asili, Ca' del Baio	135
Barbaresco Asili, Michele Chiarlo	45
Barbaresco Asili, Bruno Giacosa	113
Barbaresco Asili Barrique, Ca' del Baio	135
Barbaresco Asili Ris., Bruno Giacosa	113
Barbaresco Asji, Ceretto	24
Barbaresco Basarin, Moccagatta	33
Barbaresco Bernardot Bricco Asili, Bricco Rocche - Bricco Asili	58
Barbaresco Bric Balin, Moccagatta	33
Barbaresco Bric Turot, Prunotto	26
Barbaresco Bricco, Pio Cesare	25
Barbaresco Bricco Asili Bricco Asili, Bricco Rocche - Bricco Asili	58
Barbaresco Bricco Libero, Rino Varaldo	35
Barbaresco Bricco Mondino, Piero Busso	111
Barbaresco Camp Gros, Tenute Cisa Asinari dei Marchesi di Gresy	30
Barbaresco Campo Quadro, Punset	151
Barbaresco Cascina Bordino, Tenuta Carretta	120
Barbaresco Cichin, Ada Nada	136
Barbaresco Cole, Moccagatta	33
Barbaresco Coparossa, Bruno Rocca	35
Barbaresco Costa Russi, Gaja	31
Barbaresco Coste Rubin, Fontanafredda	129
Barbaresco Cottà, Sottimano	115
Barbaresco Cottà Vigna Brichet, Sottimano	115
Barbaresco Crichèt Pajé, I Paglieri	32
Barbaresco Curà, C. del Glicine	151
Barbaresco Currà Vigna Masué, Sottimano	115
Barbaresco Faset, Marziano e Enrico Abbona	69
Barbaresco Faset Bricco Asili, Bricco Rocche - Bricco Asili	58
Barbaresco Fausoni, Sottimano	115
Barbaresco Fausoni Vigna del Salto, Sottimano	115
Barbaresco Gaiun, Tenute Cisa Asinari dei Marchesi di Gresy	30
Barbaresco Gallina, Ugo Lequio	114
Barbaresco Lancaia, Teo Costa	145
Barbaresco Marcorino, C. del Glicine	151
Barbaresco Maria di Brun, Ca' Rome' - Romano Marengo	29
Barbaresco Martinenga, Tenute Cisa Asinari dei Marchesi di Gresy	30
Barbaresco Masseria, Vietti	60
Barbaresco Montefico, Carlo Giacosa	31
Barbaresco Morassino, Cascina Morassino	144
Barbaresco Narin, Carlo Giacosa	31
Barbaresco Ovello, C. del Pino	29
Barbaresco Ovello, Cascina Morassino	144
Barbaresco Pajoré, Sottimano	115
Barbaresco Rabajà, Castello di Verduno	139
Barbaresco Rabajà, Giuseppe Cortese	30
Barbaresco Rabajà, Cascina Luisin	32
Barbaresco Rabajà, Bruno Rocca	35
Barbaresco Rio Sordo, F.lli Giacosa	113
Barbaresco Ris., I Paglieri	32
Barbaresco Rombone, Fiorenzo Nada	136
Barbaresco Roncaglie, Bel Colle	138
Barbaresco Rongallo, Orlando Abrigo	154
Barbaresco Santo Stefano, Bruno Giacosa	113
Barbaresco Serraboella, F.lli Cigliuti	111
Barbaresco Sorì Burdin, Fontanabianca	112
Barbaresco Sorì Loreto, Rino Varaldo	35
Barbaresco Sörì Montaribaldi, Montaribaldi	33
Barbaresco Sorì Paitin, Paitin	114
Barbaresco Sorì Paolin, Cascina Luisin	32
Barbaresco Sori Rio Sordo, Ca' Rome' - Romano Marengo	29
Barbaresco Sorì S. Lorenzo, Gaja	31
Barbaresco Sorì Tildin, Gaja	31
Barbaresco Tenuta Roncaglia, Poderi Colla	26
Barbaresco Valeirano, Ada Nada	136
Barbaresco Valgrande, Ca' del Baio	135
Barbaresco Vanotu, Pelissero	137
Barbaresco Vigna Borgese, Piero Busso	111
Barbaresco Vigna Montersino, Orlando Abrigo	154
Barbaresco Vigneti in Asili Ris., Prod. del Barbaresco	34
Barbaresco Vigneti in Moccagatta Ris., Prod. del Barbaresco	34
Barbaresco Vigneti in Montefico Ris., Prod. del Barbaresco	34
Barbaresco Vigneti in Montestefano Ris., Prod. del Barbaresco	34
Barbaresco Vigneti in Ovello Ris., Prod. del Barbaresco	34
Barbaresco Vigneti in Pajé Ris., Prod. del Barbaresco	34
Barbaresco Vigneti in Pora Ris., Prod. del Barbaresco	34
Barbaresco Vigneti in Rabajà Ris., Prod. del Barbaresco	34
Barbaresco Vigneti in Rio Sordo Ris., Prod. del Barbaresco	34
Barbaresco Vigneto Brich Ronchi, Albino Rocca	34
Barbaresco Vigneto Castellizzano, Vignaioli Elvio Pertinace	137
Barbaresco Vigneto Gallina, La Spinetta	54
Barbaresco Vigneto Loreto, Albino Rocca	34
Barbaresco Vigneto Marcarini, Vignaioli Elvio Pertinace	137
Barbaresco Vigneto Nervo, Vignaioli Elvio Pertinace	137
Barbaresco Vigneto Starderi, La Spinetta	54
Barbaresco Vigneto Valeirano, La Spinetta	54
Barbarossa, Fattoria Paradiso	405
Barbazzale Bianco, Cottanera	702
Barbazzale Rosso, Cottanera	702
Barbera d'Alba, F.lli Alessandria	138
Barbera d'Alba, Gianfranco Alessandria	97
Barbera d'Alba, Elio Altare - Cascina Nuova	82
Barbera d'Alba, F.lli Bera	116
Barbera d'Alba, Enzo Boglietti	83
Barbera d'Alba, Giacomo Borgogno & Figli	36
Barbera d'Alba, Cascina Ca' Rossa	47
Barbera d'Alba, C. del Pino	29
Barbera d'Alba, Aldo Conterno	98
Barbera d'Alba, Giovanni Corino	85
Barbera d'Alba, Matteo Correggia	48
Barbera d'Alba, Damilano	37
Barbera d'Alba, Degiorgis	95
Barbera d'Alba, Destefanis	108
Barbera d'Alba, Fontanabianca	112
Barbera d'Alba, Gabutti - Franco Boasso	130
Barbera d'Alba, Filippo Gallino	49
Barbera d'Alba, Attilio Ghisolfi	101

Entry	Page
Barbera d'Alba, Hilberg - Pasquero	120
Barbera d'Alba, Gianluigi Lano	25
Barbera d'Alba, Giuseppe Mascarello e Figlio	96
Barbera d'Alba, Moccagatta	33
Barbera d'Alba, Monfalletto - Cordero di Montezemolo	87
Barbera d'Alba, Monti	102
Barbera d'Alba, Stefanino Morra	55
Barbera d'Alba, Cascina Pellerino	109
Barbera d'Alba, Fabrizio Pinsoglio	56
Barbera d'Alba, Pio Cesare	25
Barbera d'Alba, Prunotto	26
Barbera d'Alba, F.lli Revello	89
Barbera d'Alba, Bruno Rocca	35
Barbera d'Alba, Luciano Sandrone	39
Barbera d'Alba, Giorgio Scarzello e Figli	40
Barbera d'Alba, Poderi Sinaglio	27
Barbera d'Alba, Michele Taliano	106
Barbera d'Alba, G. D. Vajra	41
Barbera d'Alba, Cascina Val del Prete	121
Barbera d'Alba, Cascina Vano	115
Barbera d'Alba, Rino Varaldo	35
Barbera d'Alba, Mauro Veglio	149
Barbera d'Alba, Vielmin	146
Barbera d'Alba Affinata in Carati, Paolo Scavino	59
Barbera d'Alba Armujan, Podere Ruggeri Corsini	150
Barbera d'Alba Ars Vivendi, Pajana - Renzo Seghesio	150
Barbera d'Alba Asili, Cascina Luisin	32
Barbera d'Alba Asili Barrique, Cascina Luisin	32
Barbera d'Alba Aves, G. B. Burlotto	139
Barbera d'Alba Basarin, Moccagatta	33
Barbera d'Alba Bramè, Deltetto	48
Barbera d'Alba Brea, F.lli Brovia	58
Barbera d'Alba Bric Bertu, Angelo Negro & Figli	108
Barbera d'Alba Bric La Rondolina, Fabrizio Pinsoglio	56
Barbera d'Alba Bric Loira, Cascina Chicco	47
Barbera d'Alba Bric Torretta, Porello	145
Barbera d'Alba Bricco dei Fagiani, Silvano e Elena Boroli	24
Barbera d'Alba Bricco dei Merli, Elvio Cogno	118
Barbera d'Alba Bricco delle Viole, G. D. Vajra	41
Barbera d'Alba Bricco Marun, Matteo Correggia	48
Barbera d'Alba Bricco Quattro Fratelli, Silvano e Elena Boroli	24
Barbera d'Alba Bricco Volpiana, Valerio Aloi	150
Barbera d'Alba Brunet, Fontanabianca	112
Barbera d'Alba Bussia, F.lli Giacosa	113
Barbera d'Alba Campolive, Paitin	114
Barbera d'Alba Cannubi, Giacomo Brezza & Figli	36
Barbera d'Alba Cascina Francia, Giacomo Conterno	99
Barbera d'Alba Cascina Nuova, Mauro Veglio	149
Barbera d'Alba Ciabot Camerano, Poderi Marcarini	86
Barbera d'Alba Ciabot della Luna, Gianni Voerzio	91
Barbera d'Alba Ciabot du Re, F.lli Revello	89
Barbera d'Alba Ciabot Pierin, Funtanin	49
Barbera d'Alba Codana, Giuseppe Mascarello e Figlio	96
Barbera d'Alba Croere, Terre da Vino	41
Barbera d'Alba Donatella, Luigi Baudana	129
Barbera d'Alba dü Gir, Montaribaldi	33
Barbera d'Alba Fides, Pio Cesare	25
Barbera d'Alba Flin, Cascina Flino	147
Barbera d'Alba Fondo Prà, Gianluigi Lano	25
Barbera d'Alba Fontanile, Silvio Grasso	85
Barbera d'Alba Gallina, Ugo Lequio	114
Barbera d'Alba Gepin, Albino Rocca	34
Barbera d'Alba Giada, Andrea Oberto	88
Barbera d'Alba Ginestra, Paolo Conterno	99
Barbera d'Alba Gisep, Vigna Rionda - Massolino	131
Barbera d'Alba Giuli, Cascina Ballarin	84
Barbera d'Alba Goretta, F.lli Ferrero	149
Barbera d'Alba Granera Alta, Cascina Chicco	47
Barbera d'Alba I Piani, Pelissero	137
Barbera d'Alba Il Ciotto, Gianfranco Bovio	84
Barbera d'Alba La Gamberaja, Ca' Rome' - Romano Marengo	29
Barbera d'Alba La Romualda, Ferdinando Principiano	103
Barbera d'Alba La Serra, Giovanni Manzone	102
Barbera d'Alba Laboriosa, Michele Taliano	106
Barbera d'Alba Le Masche, Bel Colle	138
Barbera d'Alba Le Masserie, Boschis	147
Barbera d'Alba Lina, Carlo Giacosa	31
Barbera d'Alba Maggior, Cascina Luisin	32
Barbera d'Alba Mancine, Osvaldo Viberti	149
Barbera d'Alba Maria Gioana, F.lli Giacosa	113
Barbera d'Alba Marun, Matteo Correggia	48
Barbera d'Alba MonBirone, Monchiero Carbone	50
Barbera d'Alba Mucin, Carlo Giacosa	31
Barbera d'Alba Mulassa, Cascina Ca' Rossa	47
Barbera d'Alba Nicolon, Angelo Negro & Figli	108
Barbera d'Alba Ornati, Armando Parusso	103
Barbera d'Alba Pairolero, Sottimano	115
Barbera d'Alba Pajarell, Marchesi di Barolo	37
Barbera d'Alba Papagena, Fontanafredda	129
Barbera d'Alba Pian Romualdo, Prunotto	26
Barbera d'Alba Piana, Ceretto	24
Barbera d'Alba Pistìn, Giacomo Grimaldi	144
Barbera d'Alba Pozzo, Giovanni Corino	85
Barbera d'Alba Preda, F.lli Barale	144
Barbera d'Alba Raimonda, Fontanafredda	129
Barbera d'Alba Regia Veja, Gianfranco Bovio	84
Barbera d'Alba Rinaldi, Marziano e Enrico Abbona	69
Barbera d'Alba Rocche delle Rocche, Rocche Costamagna	90
Barbera d'Alba Roscaleto, Enzo Boglietti	83
Barbera d'Alba Ruvei, Marchesi di Barolo	37
Barbera d'Alba S. Cristoforo, Marsaglia	146
Barbera d'Alba Salgà, Ada Nada	136
Barbera d'Alba Scarrone, Vietti	60
Barbera d'Alba Scarrone Vigna Vecchia, Vietti	60
Barbera d'Alba Serra Boella, Paitin	114
Barbera d'Alba Serraboella, F.lli Cigliuti	111
Barbera d'Alba Sòri della Roncaglia, Terre del Barolo	60
Barbera d'Alba Sorito Mosconi, Podere Rocche dei Manzoni	104
Barbera d'Alba Sovrana, Batasiolo	83
Barbera d'Alba Sup., F.lli Bera	116
Barbera d'Alba Sup., Destefanis	108
Barbera d'Alba Sup., Funtanin	49
Barbera d'Alba Sup., Filippo Gallino	49
Barbera d'Alba Sup., Hilberg - Pasquero	120
Barbera d'Alba Sup., Armando Parusso	103
Barbera d'Alba Sup., Giorgio Scarzello e Figli	40
Barbera d'Alba Sup., Terre del Barolo	60
Barbera d'Alba Sup. Bricco delle Viole, Tenuta La Volta - Cabutto	40
Barbera d'Alba Sup. Carolina, Cascina Val del Prete	121
Barbera d'Alba Sup. Gran Madre, Cascina Pellerino	109
Barbera d'Alba Surì di Mù, Icardi	61
Barbera d'Alba Tenuta Roncaglia, Poderi Colla	26
Barbera d'Alba Torriglione, Renato Ratti	89
Barbera d'Alba Trevigne, Domenico Clerico	98
Barbera d'Alba V. T., Pira	71
Barbera d'Alba Valbianchera, Giovanni Almondo	106
Barbera d'Alba Valdinera, Giovanni Almondo	106
Barbera d'Alba Valdisera, Terre del Barolo	60
Barbera d'Alba Valletta, Claudio Alario	68
Barbera d'Alba Vigna Bruseisa, Cascina Fonda	95
Barbera d'Alba Vigna Clara, Eraldo Viberti	91
Barbera d'Alba Vigna dei Dardi, Alessandro e Gian Natale Fantino	100
Barbera d'Alba Vigna dei Romani, Enzo Boglietti	83
Barbera d'Alba Vigna del Cuculo, F.lli Cavallotto	59
Barbera d'Alba Vigna della Madre, Ettore Germano	130
Barbera d'Alba Vigna Erta, Poderi Sinaglio	27
Barbera d'Alba Vigna Fontanelle, Ascheri	44
Barbera d'Alba Vigna Gattere, Mauro Molino	87
Barbera d'Alba Vigna Lisi, Attilio Ghisolfi	101
Barbera d'Alba Vigna Majano, Piero Busso	111
Barbera d'Alba Vigna Martina, Elio Grasso	101
Barbera d'Alba Vigna Pierin, Ada Nada	136
Barbera d'Alba Vigna Pozzo, Giovanni Corino	85
Barbera d'Alba Vigna S. Lorenzo, Bartolo Mascarello	38
Barbera d'Alba Vigna Vigia, Bricco Maiolica	69
Barbera d'Alba Vigneto Boscato, G. B. Burlotto	139
Barbera d'Alba Vigneto della Chiesa, F.lli Seghesio	105
Barbera d'Alba Vigneto Gallina, La Spinetta	54
Barbera d'Alba Vigneto Pozzo dell'Annunziata Ris., R. Voerzio	92
Barbera d'Alba Vigneto Punta, Azelia	57
Barbera d'Alba Vignota, Conterno Fantino	100
Barbera d'Alba Vittoria, Gianfranco Alessandria	97
Barbera d'Asti, A. Baldizzone – Cascina Lana	151
Barbera d'Asti, Cascina Barisél	51
Barbera d'Asti, Ca' Bianca	28
Barbera d'Asti, C. Soc. di Vinchio e Vaglio Serra	142
Barbera d'Asti, Cascina Giovenale	151
Barbera d'Asti, Castello del Poggio	152
Barbera d'Asti, F. Fidanza	145
Barbera d'Asti, Sergio Grimaldi - Ca' du Sindic	127
Barbera d'Asti, Tenuta Olim Bauda	149
Barbera d'Asti, Claudio Rosso	66
Barbera d'Asti, Valfieri	67
Barbera d'Asti Banin, Vigne Regali	133
Barbera d'Asti Bassina, Marenco	133
Barbera d'Asti Bric dei Banditi, Franco M. Martinetti	135
Barbera d'Asti Bric Stupui, Isabella	110
Barbera d'Asti Bricco Battista, G. Accornero e Figli	140
Barbera d'Asti Bricco Blina, Agostino Pavia e Figli	23
Barbera d'Asti Bricco Crea, Tenuta La Tenaglia	132
Barbera d'Asti Bricco dell'Uccellone, Braida	122
Barbera d'Asti Bricco della Bigotta, Braida	122
Barbera d'Asti Bricco Garitta, Cascina Garitina	55
Barbera d'Asti Ca' di Pian, La Spinetta	54
Barbera d'Asti Caminata, Cascina Orsolina	150
Barbera d'Asti Camp du Rouss, Luigi Coppo e Figli	52
Barbera d'Asti Castello di Calosso Rodotiglia, F. Fidanza	145
Barbera d'Asti Castello di Calosso Vignali, L'Armangia	145
Barbera d'Asti Chersì, Ca' Bianca	28
Barbera d'Asti Ciresa, Marenco	133
Barbera d'Asti Costamiòle, Prunotto	26
Barbera d'Asti Cremosina, Bersano & Riccadonna	116
Barbera d'Asti Emozioni, Tenuta La Tenaglia	132
Barbera d'Asti Fiulòt, Prunotto	26
Barbera d'Asti Giarone, Poderi Bertelli	65
Barbera d'Asti Giorgio Tenaglia, Tenuta La Tenaglia	132
Barbera d'Asti Gratia Plena, Vignaioli Elvio Pertinace	137
Barbera d'Asti Grivò, Elio Perrone	62
Barbera d'Asti 'I Suli, La Zucca	110
Barbera d'Asti Il Bergantino, Bricco Mondalino	140

Entry	Page
Barbera d'Asti Is, Tenuta dei Fiori	46
Barbera d'Asti La Barbatella, Cascina La Barbatella	117
Barbera d'Asti La Carlotta, Tenuta dell'Arbiola	125
Barbera d'Asti La Crena, Vietti	60
Barbera d'Asti La Cricca, Roberto Ferraris	143
Barbera d'Asti La Luna e i Falò, Terre da Vino	41
Barbera d'Asti La Marescialla, Agostino Pavia e Figli	23
Barbera d'Asti La Solista, Caudrina	61
Barbera d'Asti La Tota, Marchesi Alfieri	124
Barbera d'Asti Martinette, Alfonso Boeri	146
Barbera d'Asti Martizza, La Zucca	110
Barbera d'Asti Martleina, Maurizio Nervi	145
Barbera d'Asti Moliss, Agostino Pavia e Figli	23
Barbera d'Asti Montetusa, Poderi Bertelli	65
Barbera d'Asti Nuj Suj, Icardi	61
Barbera d'Asti Panta Rei, Giuseppe Contratto	51
Barbera d'Asti Pian del Bosco, K. e R. Hohler	53
Barbera d'Asti Pian del Bosco Barrique, K. e R. Hohler	53
Barbera d'Asti Pomorosso, Luigi Coppo e Figli	52
Barbera d'Asti Quorum, Hastae	122
Barbera d'Asti Rodotiglia Castello di Calosso, Tenuta dei Fiori	46
Barbera d'Asti Rouvé, F.lli Rovero	28
Barbera d'Asti Rubermillo, Paolo Casalone	94
Barbera d'Asti Rubermillo Sel., Paolo Casalone	94
Barbera d'Asti S. Antonio Vieilles Vignes, Poderi Bertelli	65
Barbera d'Asti S. Martino, Luigi Nebiolo	147
Barbera d'Asti S. Nicolao, Terre da Vino	41
Barbera d'Asti Sanbastiàn, Dacapo	22
Barbera d'Asti SanSì, Scagliola	45
Barbera d'Asti SanSì Sel., Scagliola	45
Barbera d'Asti Sel. Gaudium Magnum, Bricco Mondalino	140
Barbera d'Asti Solus Ad, Giuseppe Contratto	51
Barbera d'Asti Sup., Guido Berta	153
Barbera d'Asti Sup., C. Soc. di Vinchio e Vaglio Serra	142
Barbera d'Asti Sup., La Spinetta	54
Barbera d'Asti Sup., Luigi Nebiolo	147
Barbera d'Asti Sup., Olim Bauda	149
Barbera d'Asti Sup., Valfieri	67
Barbera d'Asti Sup. Acsé, Franco e Mario Scrimaglio	118
Barbera d'Asti Sup. Ajan, Villa Giada	52
Barbera d'Asti Sup. Alfiera, Marchesi Alfieri	124
Barbera d'Asti Sup. Ansemma, Cascina Giovenale	151
Barbera d'Asti Sup. Arbest, Bava	63
Barbera d'Asti Sup. Balau, Carlo Benotto	65
Barbera d'Asti Sup. Beneficio, Sciorio	67
Barbera d'Asti Sup. Bric d'Alì, Renzo Beccaris	146
Barbera d'Asti Sup. Bricco Dani, Villa Giada	52
Barbera d'Asti Sup. Bricco della Volpettona, E. e A. Brema	81
Barbera d'Asti Sup. Bricco S. Ippolito, F. e M. Scrimaglio	118
Barbera d'Asti Sup. Bricco Sereno, Tenuta La Meridiana	107
Barbera d'Asti Sup. Bricconizza, E. e A. Brema	81
Barbera d'Asti Sup. Cala delle Mandrie, La Giribaldina	144
Barbera d'Asti Sup. Camparò, Cascina La Ghersa	96
Barbera d'Asti Sup. Campasso, Tenuta Castello di Razzano	143
Barbera d'Asti Sup. Canto di Luna, Guido Berta	153
Barbera d'Asti Sup. Cardin, Claudio Rosso	66
Barbera d'Asti Sup. Cascina Croce, E. e A. Brema	81
Barbera d'Asti Sup. Cavalé, Cantine Sant'Agata	128
Barbera d'Asti Sup. Cipressi della Court, Michele Chiarlo	45
Barbera d'Asti Sup. Collina della Vedova, Alfiero Boffa	125
Barbera d'Asti Sup. Croutin, F. e M. Scrimaglio	118
Barbera d'Asti Sup. Favà, Tenuta Garetto	22
Barbera d'Asti Sup. Galana, Malgrà	150
Barbera d'Asti Sup. Generala, Bersano & Riccadonna	116
Barbera d'Asti Sup. I Bricchi di Castelrocchero, Scarpa - Antica Casa Vinicola	117
Barbera d'Asti Sup. I Filari Lunghi, Valfieri	67
Barbera d'Asti Sup. Il Giorgione, Villa Fiorita	146
Barbera d'Asti Sup. Il Sogno, F. e M. Scrimaglio	118
Barbera d'Asti Sup. In Pectore, Tenuta Garetto	22
Barbera d'Asti Sup. La Bogliona, Scarpa - Antica Casa Vinicola	117
Barbera d'Asti Sup. La Cappelletta, Cascina Barisél	51
Barbera d'Asti Sup. La Court, Michele Chiarlo	45
Barbera d'Asti Sup. La Romilda IV, Tenuta dell'Arbiola	125
Barbera d'Asti Sup. La Romilda V, Tenuta dell'Arbiola	125
Barbera d'Asti Sup. La Vignassa, Cascina La Ghersa	96
Barbera d'Asti Sup. Le Cascine, E. e A. Brema	81
Barbera d'Asti Sup. Litina, Cascina Castlèt	66
Barbera d'Asti Sup. Mora di Sassi, Malgrà	150
Barbera d'Asti Sup. Monte Venere, Caudrina	61
Barbera d'Asti Sup. Montruc, Franco M. Martinetti	135
Barbera d'Asti Sup. Neuvsent, Cascina Garitina	55
Barbera d'Asti Sup. Nobbio, Roberto Ferraris	143
Barbera d'Asti Sup. Passum, Cascina Castlèt	66
Barbera d'Asti Sup. Piano Alto, Bava	63
Barbera d'Asti Sup. Piatin, Cantine Sant'Agata	128
Barbera d'Asti Sup. Pörlapà, Alfonso Boeri	146
Barbera d'Asti Sup. Rive, Araldica - Il Cantinone	54
Barbera d'Asti Sup. Rossoboldo, La Giribaldina	144
Barbera d'Asti Sup. Rouvé, F.lli Rovero	28
Barbera d'Asti Sup. Rupestris, Carlo Benotto	65
Barbera d'Asti Sup. S. Lorenzo, Renzo Beccaris	146
Barbera d'Asti Sup. Sciorio, Sciorio	67
Barbera d'Asti Sup. Sel., Sciorio	67
Barbera d'Asti Sup. Stradivario, Bava	63
Barbera d'Asti Sup. Tardiva, Michele Chiarlo	45
Barbera d'Asti Sup. Testimonium, Alfiero Boffa	125
Barbera d'Asti Sup. Titon, L'Armangia	145
Barbera d'Asti Sup. Tra Terra e Cielo, Tenuta La Meridiana	107
Barbera d'Asti Sup. Vigna Cua Longa, Alfiero Boffa	125
Barbera d'Asti Sup. Vigna del Beneficio, Tenuta Castello di Razzano	143
Barbera d'Asti Sup. Vigna del Noce, Trinchero	143
Barbera d'Asti Sup. Vigna dell'Angelo, Cascina La Barbatella	117
Barbera d'Asti Sup. Vigna delle More, Alfiero Boffa	125
Barbera d'Asti Sup. Vigna delle Rose, Franco Mondo	153
Barbera d'Asti Sup. Vigna Muntrivé, Alfiero Boffa	125
Barbera d'Asti Sup. Vigna Ronco, Alfiero Boffa	125
Barbera d'Asti Sup. Vigne Vecchie, C. Soc. di Vinchio e Vaglio Serra	142
Barbera d'Asti Sup. Vigneto Casot, Carlo Benotto	65
Barbera d'Asti Sup. Vigneto Guera, Il Mongetto	154
Barbera d'Asti Sup. Vigneto Gustin, F.lli Rovero	28
Barbera d'Asti Sup. Vigneto La Quercia, Villa Giada	52
Barbera d'Asti Tonneau, Liedholm	68
Barbera d'Asti Tra Nueit e Dì, Tenuta Garetto	22
Barbera d'Asti Tre Vigne, Vietti	60
Barbera d'Asti Truccone, Isabella	110
Barbera d'Asti Varmat, La Morandina	62
Barbera d'Asti Vigna Dacapo, Dacapo	22
Barbera d'Asti Vigna del Salice, Franco Mondo	153
Barbera d'Asti Vigna delle More, Cascina Gilli	56
Barbera d'Asti Vigna Minerva, Saccoletto	152
Barbera d'Asti Vigna Stramba, Castello di Lignano	74
Barbera d'Asti Vigneto del Tulipano Nero, Tenuta dei Fiori	46
Barbera d'Asti Vin ed Michen, A. Baldizzone – Cascina Lana	151
Barbera d'Asti Zucchetto, La Morandina	62
Barbera del M.to, Tenuta S. Sebastiano	94
Barbera del M.to Alessandra, Colonna	141
Barbera del M.to Bricco Morlantino, Paolo Casalone	94
Barbera del M.to Gallianum, Tenuta Gaiano	46
Barbera del M.to Giulin, G. Accornero e Figli	140
Barbera del M.to I Cheini, Cascina Bertolotto	132
Barbera del M.to La Monella, Braida	122
Barbera del M.to La Rossa, Colonna	141
Barbera del M.to Mepari, Tenuta S. Sebastiano	94
Barbera del M.to Ornovo, La Guardia	109
Barbera del M.to Rapet, Marco Canato	141
Barbera del M.to Rossa d'Ocra, Cascina La Maddalena	121
Barbera del M.to Sup., Vicara	123
Barbera del M.to Sup. Bricco Battista, G. Accornero e Figli	140
Barbera del M.to Sup. Cantico della Crosia, Vicara	123
Barbera del M.to Sup. Cima, G. Accornero e Figli	140
Barbera del M.to Sup. La Baldea, Marco Canato	141
Barbera del M.to Sup. Tenaglia è, Tenuta La Tenaglia	132
Barbera del M.to Sup. Valisenda, Castello di Lignano	74
Barbera del M.to Sup. Vigneto della Amorosa, La Scamuzza	154
Barbera del M.to Sup. Vigneto Mongetto, Il Mongetto	154
Barbera del M.to Vigna della Torretta, Tenuta Gaiano	46
Barbera del M.to Vigna di Dante, La Guardia	109
Barbera del M.to Vigna I Filari Lunghi, Saccoletto	152
Barbera del M.to Vivace Bricco Montemà, Isabella	110
Barbera del M.to Volpuva, Vicara	123
Barbera del M.to Zerolegno, Bricco Mondalino	140
Barbera del Veneto, Ca' Lustra	275
Barbicone, Russo	544
Barco Reale, Fattoria Ambra	437
Barco Reale, Capezzana	437
Barco Reale, Il Poggiolo	551
Bardolino, Buglioni	327
Bardolino, Le Vigne di S. Pietro	311
Bardolino, Albino Piona	328
Bardolino Chiaretto, Buglioni	327
Bardolino Chiaretto, Corte Gardoni	318
Bardolino Chiaretto, Guerrieri Rizzardi	207
Bardolino Chiaretto, Le Fraghe	274
Bardolino Chiaretto, Le Vigne di S. Pietro	311
Bardolino Chiaretto Vigna Le Ceresare, Corte Marzago	330
Bardolino Chiaretto Vigne Alte, F.lli Zeni	273
Bardolino Cl., Le Fraghe	274
Bardolino Cl., Lenotti	323
Bardolino Cl., Casa Vinicola Sartori	326
Bardolino Cl. La Vegrona, Masi	306
Bardolino Cl. Santepietre, Lamberti	325
Bardolino Cl. Sup., Le Tende	281
Bardolino Cl. Sup., F.lli Zeni	273
Bardolino Cl. Sup. Vigne Alte, F.lli Zeni	273
Bardolino Cl. Vigneto Ca' Bordenis, Santi	280
Bardolino Le Fontane, Corte Gardoni	318
Bardolino Sup., Corte Gardoni	318
Bardolino Sup. S. Lucia Cavalchina, Cavalchina	311
Baredo, F.lli Pighin	375
Barigliòtt, Paternoster	671
Barolo, F.lli Alessandria	138
Barolo, Gianfranco Alessandria	97
Barolo, Elio Altare - Cascina Nuova	82
Barolo, Azelia	57
Barolo, Batasiolo	83

Barolo, Luigi Baudana	129
Barolo, Cascina Bongiovanni	57
Barolo, G. B. Burlotto	139
Barolo, Ca' Bianca	28
Barolo, Cascina Ballarin	84
Barolo, Aldo Conterno	98
Barolo, Giovanni Corino	85
Barolo, Damilano	37
Barolo, Poderi Luigi Einaudi	70
Barolo, Gabutti - Franco Boasso	130
Barolo, Gianni Gagliardo	149
Barolo, Silvio Grasso	85
Barolo, Bartolo Mascarello	38
Barolo, Mauro Molino	87
Barolo, Andrea Oberto	88
Barolo, F.lli Oddero	88
Barolo, Pio Cesare	25
Barolo, Luigi Pira	131
Barolo, E. Pira & Figli - Chiara Boschis	38
Barolo, Prunotto	26
Barolo, F.lli Revello	89
Barolo, Flavio Roddolo	104
Barolo, Podere Ruggeri Corsini	150
Barolo, Luciano Sandrone	39
Barolo, Giorgio Scarzello e Figli	40
Barolo, Paolo Scavino	59
Barolo, Aurelio Settimo	150
Barolo, Eraldo Viberti	91
Barolo, Vigna Rionda - Massolino	131
Barolo Arborina, Mauro Veglio	149
Barolo Bofani, Batasiolo	83
Barolo Boscareto, Batasiolo	83
Barolo Boscareto, Ferdinando Principiano	103
Barolo Boscato, Bel Colle	138
Barolo Bric dël Fiasc, Paolo Scavino	59
Barolo Bricco, Giuseppe Mascarello e Figlio	96
Barolo Bricco Boschis, F.lli Cavallotto	59
Barolo Bricco delle Viole, G. D. Vajra	41
Barolo Bricco Fiasco, Azelia	57
Barolo Bricco Francesco Rocche dell'Annunziata, Rocche Costamagna	90
Barolo Bricco Luciani, Silvio Grasso	85
Barolo Bricco Rocca, Cascina Ballarin	84
Barolo Bricco Rocche Bricco Rocche, Bricco Rocche - Bricco Asili	58
Barolo Bricco Viole, Mario Marengo	86
Barolo Bricco Visette, Attilio Ghisolfi	101
Barolo Brunate, Enzo Boglietti	83
Barolo Brunate, Poderi Marcarini	86
Barolo Brunate, Mario Marengo	86
Barolo Brunate, Vietti	60
Barolo Brunate, R. Voerzio	92
Barolo Brunate Bricco Rocche, Bricco Rocche - Bricco Asili	58
Barolo Brunate Ris., Poderi Marcarini	86
Barolo Brunate-Le Coste, Giuseppe Rinaldi	39
Barolo Bussia, Silvano e Elena Boroli	24
Barolo Bussia, Bussia Soprana	150
Barolo Bussia, Cascina Ballarin	84
Barolo Bussia, F.lli Giacosa	113
Barolo Bussia, Prunotto	26
Barolo Bussia Dardi Le Rose, Poderi Colla	26
Barolo Bussia Soprana, Aldo Conterno	98
Barolo Bussia Vigna Munie, Armando Parusso	103
Barolo Bussia Vigna Rocche, Armando Parusso	103
Barolo Ca' Mia, F.lli Brovia	58
Barolo Cannubi, Giacomo Brezza & Figli	36
Barolo Cannubi, Michele Chiarlo	45
Barolo Cannubi, Damilano	37
Barolo Cannubi, Marchesi di Barolo	37
Barolo Cannubi, E. Pira & Figli - Chiara Boschis	38
Barolo Cannubi, Paolo Scavino	59
Barolo Cannubi Boschis, Luciano Sandrone	39
Barolo Cannubi S. Lorenzo-Ravera, Giuseppe Rinaldi	39
Barolo Carobric, Paolo Scavino	59
Barolo Cascina Francia, Giacomo Conterno	99
Barolo Case Nere, Enzo Boglietti	83
Barolo Castellero, F.lli Barale	144
Barolo Castellero Ris., Giacomo Brezza & Figli	36
Barolo Castelletto, Mauro Veglio	149
Barolo Castello Ris., Terre del Barolo	60
Barolo Cerequio, Batasiolo	83
Barolo Cerequio, Michele Chiarlo	45
Barolo Cerequio, R. Voerzio	92
Barolo Cerequio Tenuta Secolo, Giuseppe Contratto	51
Barolo Cerretta, Ettore Germano	130
Barolo Cerretta, Giovanni Rosso	153
Barolo Cerretta Piani, Luigi Baudana	129
Barolo Ciabot Manzoni, Silvio Grasso	85
Barolo Ciabot Mentin Ginestra, Domenico Clerico	98
Barolo Cicala, Aldo Conterno	98
Barolo Cl., Giacomo Borgogno & Figli	36
Barolo Codana, Terre del Barolo	60
Barolo Colonnello, Aldo Conterno	98
Barolo Corda della Briccolina, Batasiolo	83
Barolo Costa Grimaldi, Poderi Luigi Einaudi	70
Barolo Coste di Rose, Marchesi di Barolo	37
Barolo di Castiglione Falletto, Terre del Barolo	60
Barolo Enrico VI, Monfalletto - Cordero di Montezemolo	87
Barolo Estate Vineyard, Marchesi di Barolo	37
Barolo Falletto, Bruno Giacosa	113
Barolo Fossati, Enzo Boglietti	83
Barolo Gabutti, Gabutti - Franco Boasso	130
Barolo Gattera, Mauro Veglio	149
Barolo Gavarini Vigna Chiniera, Elio Grasso	101
Barolo Ginestra, Paolo Conterno	99
Barolo Ginestra Ris., Paolo Conterno	99
Barolo Ginestra Vigna Casa Maté, Elio Grasso	101
Barolo Gramolere, Giovanni Manzone	102
Barolo Gramolere Bricat, Giovanni Manzone	102
Barolo Gramolere Ris., Giovanni Manzone	102
Barolo Gran Bussia Ris., Aldo Conterno	98
Barolo La Brunella, Silvano e Elena Boroli	24
Barolo La Rocca e La Pira, I Paglieri	32
Barolo La Serra, Poderi Marcarini	86
Barolo La Serra, Gianni Voerzio	91
Barolo La Serra, R. Voerzio	92
Barolo Lazzarito, Vietti	60
Barolo Le Coste, Giacomo Grimaldi	144
Barolo Le Coste, Ferdinando Principiano	103
Barolo Le Rocche del Falletto, Bruno Giacosa	113
Barolo Le Vigne, Luciano Sandrone	39
Barolo Liste, Giacomo Borgogno & Figli	36
Barolo Manzoni, F.lli Ferrero	149
Barolo Marasco, Franco M. Martinetti	135
Barolo Marcenasco, Renato Ratti	89
Barolo Margheria, Vigna Rionda - Massolino	131
Barolo Mariondino, Armando Parusso	103
Barolo Massara, Castello di Verduno	139
Barolo Mondoca di Bussia Soprana, F.lli Oddero	88
Barolo Monfalletto, Monfalletto - Cordero di Montezemolo	87
Barolo Monfortino Ris., Giacomo Conterno	99
Barolo Monprivato, F.lli Brovia	58
Barolo Monprivato, Giuseppe Mascarello e Figlio	96
Barolo Monprivato Ca' d' Morissio, Giuseppe Mascarello e Figlio	96
Barolo Monvigliero, F.lli Alessandria	138
Barolo Monvigliero, Bel Colle	138
Barolo Monvigliero, Castello di Verduno	139
Barolo Monvigliero, Mauro Sebaste	27
Barolo Mosconi, Bussia Soprana	150
Barolo nei Cannubi, Poderi Luigi Einaudi	70
Barolo Ornato, Pio Cesare	25
Barolo Paesi Tuoi, Terre da Vino	41
Barolo Pajana, Domenico Clerico	98
Barolo Pajana, Pajana - Renzo Seghesio	150
Barolo Parafada, Vigna Rionda - Massolino	131
Barolo Parafada Ris., Vigna Rionda - Massolino	131
Barolo Parej, Icardi	61
Barolo Parussi, Conterno Fantino	100
Barolo Percristina, Domenico Clerico	98
Barolo Pernanno, Cascina Bongiovanni	57
Barolo Piccole Vigne, Armando Parusso	103
Barolo Poderi Parussi, Terre da Vino	41
Barolo Prapò, Ettore Germano	130
Barolo Prapò Bricco Rocche, Bricco Rocche - Bricco Asili	58
Barolo Preve, Gianni Gagliardo	149
Barolo Rapet, Ca' Rome' - Romano Marengo	29
Barolo Ravera, Elvio Cogno	118
Barolo Ravera, Flavio Roddolo	104
Barolo Ris., Marchesi di Barolo	37
Barolo Ris., E. Pira & Figli - Chiara Boschis	38
Barolo Ris. Collina Rionda, Bruno Giacosa	113
Barolo Ris. del Fondatore, Tenuta La Volta - Cabutto	40
Barolo Riva, Claudio Alario	68
Barolo Rocche, Giovanni Corino	85
Barolo Rocche, Aurelio Settimo	150
Barolo Rocche, Vietti	60
Barolo Rocche dei Brovia, F.lli Brovia	58
Barolo Rocche dei Rivera di Castiglione, F.lli Oddero	88
Barolo Rocche dell'Annunziata, F.lli Revello	89
Barolo Rocche dell'Annunziata, Rocche Costamagna	90
Barolo Rocche dell'Annunziata, Paolo Scavino	59
Barolo Rocche di Castiglione, F.lli Oddero	88
Barolo Rocche di Castiglione, Vietti	60
Barolo Rocche di Castiglione Falletto, Bruno Giacosa	113
Barolo Rocche Marcenasco, Renato Ratti	89
Barolo Rocchettevino, Gianfranco Bovio	84
Barolo Runcot, Elio Grasso	101
Barolo S. Giovanni, Gianfranco Alessandria	97
Barolo S. Lorenzo, F.lli Alessandria	138
Barolo S. Rocco, Azelia	57
Barolo S. Stefano di Perno, Giuseppe Mascarello e Figlio	96
Barolo Sarmassa, Giacomo Brezza & Figli	36
Barolo Sarmassa, Marchesi di Barolo	37
Barolo Serra dei Turchi, Osvaldo Viberti	149
Barolo Serralunga d'Alba, Fontanafredda	129
Barolo Sorano, Ascheri	44
Barolo Sorì Ginestra, Conterno Fantino	100
Barolo Vecchie Vigne, Giovanni Corino	85
Barolo Vecchi Viti dei Capalot e delle Brunate Ris., R. Voerzio	92
Barolo Vigna Arborina, Gianfranco Bovio	84

Name	Page
Barolo Vigna Big 'd Big, Podere Rocche dei Manzoni	104
Barolo Vigna Big Ris., Podere Rocche dei Manzoni	104
Barolo Vigna Bricco Gattera, Monfalletto - Cordero di Montezemolo	87
Barolo Vigna Cappella di S. Stefano, Podere Rocche dei Manzoni	104
Barolo Vigna Cerrati, Cascina Cucco	153
Barolo Vigna Cerretta, Ca' Rome' - Romano Marengo	29
Barolo Vigna Colonnello, Bussia Soprana	150
Barolo Vigna Conca, Mauro Molino	87
Barolo Vigna Conca, F.lli Revello	89
Barolo Vigna Cucco, Cascina Cucco	153
Barolo Vigna d'la Roul, Podere Rocche dei Manzoni	104
Barolo Vigna d'la Roul Ris., Podere Rocche dei Manzoni	104
Barolo Vigna dei Dardi, Alessandro e Gian Natale Fantino	100
Barolo Vigna dei Pola, Ascheri	44
Barolo Vigna del Colonnello, Aldo Conterno	98
Barolo Vigna del Gris, Conterno Fantino	100
Barolo Vigna di Aldo, Rino Varaldo	35
Barolo Vigna Elena, Elvio Cogno	118
Barolo Vigna Gancia, Mauro Molino	87
Barolo Vigna Gattera, Gianfranco Bovio	84
Barolo Vigna Giachini, Giovanni Corino	85
Barolo Vigna Giachini, F.lli Revello	89
Barolo Vigna La Volta, Tenuta La Volta - Cabutto	40
Barolo Vigna Mandorlo, F.lli Giacosa	113
Barolo Vigna Merenda, Giorgio Scarzello e Figli	40
Barolo Vigna Prapò, Mauro Sebaste	27
Barolo Vigna Rionda, F.lli Oddero	88
Barolo Vigna Rionda Ris., Vigna Rionda - Massolino	131
Barolo Vigna S. Giuseppe, F.lli Cavallotto	59
Barolo Vigna S. Giuseppe Ris., F.lli Cavallotto	59
Barolo Vigne La Delizia, Fontanafredda	129
Barolo Vigne La Rosa, Fontanafredda	129
Barolo Vigne La Villa, Fontanafredda	129
Barolo Vigne La Villa-Paiagallo, Fontanafredda	129
Barolo Vigne Lazzarito, Fontanafredda	129
Barolo Vigneti in Cannubi, Tenuta Carretta	120
Barolo Vigneto Albarella, Andrea Oberto	88
Barolo Vigneto Arborina, Elio Altare - Cascina Nuova	82
Barolo Vigneto Arborina, Giovanni Corino	85
Barolo Vigneto Cannubi, G. B. Burlotto	139
Barolo Vigneto La Villa, F.lli Seghesio	105
Barolo Vigneto Marenca, Luigi Pira	131
Barolo Vigneto Margheria, Luigi Pira	131
Barolo Vigneto Rocche, Giovanni Corino	85
Barolo Vigneto Rocche, Andrea Oberto	88
Barolo Vigneto Rocche, Mauro Veglio	149
Barolo Vigneto Terlo Ravera, Marziano e Enrico Abbona	69
Barolo Vignolo Ris., F.lli Cavallotto	59
Barolo Villero, Silvano e Elena Boroli	24
Barolo Villero, F.lli Brovia	58
Barolo Villero, Giuseppe Mascarello e Figlio	96
Barolo Villero, Vietti	60
Barolo Zonchera, Ceretto	24
Barrua, Fattoria Mauritania	732
Bartis Rosso, Valentino Fiorini	581
Barullo, Castello di Selvole	448
Basilicata Bianco Vignali, C. Riforma Fondiaria di Venosa	673
Basilicata Pipoli Chiaro, Basilium	674
Basilicata Rosso Vignali, C. Riforma Fondiaria di Venosa	673
Basolo, Ca' del Vispo	532
Batàr, Agricola Querciabella	465
Batia Bianco, C. Soc. Cellaro	713
Batia Rosso, C. Soc. Cellaro	713
Belcaro, S. Felice	448
Belcore, I Giusti e Zanza	451
Bella Mojgan, Marco Maci	679
Bellei Extra Brut Cuvée, Francesco Bellei	424
Benaco Bresciano Bianco Balì, Trevisani	208
Benaco Bresciano Marzemino Le Mazane, Costaripa	190
Benaco Bresciano Ronchedone, Ca' dei Frati	201
Benaco Bresciano Rosso Mal Borghetto, Le Chiusure	213
Benaco Bresciano Rosso S. Gioan I Carati, Pasini Prod.	212
Benaco Bresciano Rosso Sùer, Trevisani	208
Benaco Bresciano Rosso Vigne Sparse, Visconti	207
Bentivoglio, Tenuta Farneta	541
Benuara, Cusumano	710
Bera Brut, F.lli Bera	116
Berengario, Zonin	279
Berillo d'Oro, Alessandro Secchi	216
Betto, S. Lucia	558
Bianca Capello, Ortaglia	576
Bianca di Valguarnera, Duca di Salaparuta - Vini Corvo	702
Bianchello del Metauro Borgo Torre, Claudio Morelli	586
Bianchello del Metauro La Vigna delle Terrazze, Claudio Morelli	586
Bianchello del Metauro S. Cesareo, Claudio Morelli	586
Bianchello del Metauro Tenuta Campioli, Valentino Fiorini	581
Bianchello del Metauro Vigna Sant'Ilario, Valentino Fiorini	581
Bianco Amabile del Cerè Bandito, Giuseppe Quintarelli	294
Bianco Avignonesi, Avignonesi	497
Bianco Biscari, Cantine Torrevecchia	700
Bianco del Coppo Sauvignon, Conte Leopardi Dittajuti	592
Bianco della Bergamasca Riera, C. Soc. Val S. Martino	211
Bianco della Boemia, Liedholm	68
Bianco della Castellada, La Castellada	366
Bianco della Rocca, Meleta	527
Bianco della Rocca, Sarchese Dora	646
Bianco delle Chiaie, Giovanni Palombo	628
Bianco di Alberico, La Brugherata	200
Bianco di Castelnuovo, Castel Noarna	228
Bianco di Ciccio, Ciccio Zaccagnini	640
Bianco di Corte, Paternoster	671
Bianco di Custoza, Corte Gardoni	318
Bianco di Custoza, Le Vigne di S. Pietro	311
Bianco di Custoza, Albino Piona	328
Bianco di Custoza Amedeo Cavalchina, Cavalchina	311
Bianco di Custoza Cavalchina, Cavalchina	311
Bianco di Custoza Lucillini, Le Tende	281
Bianco di Custoza Montemagrin, S. Sofia	303
Bianco di Custoza Orchidea Platino, Lamberti	325
Bianco di Custoza Oro, Le Tende	281
Bianco di Custoza Sanpietro, Le Vigne di S. Pietro	311
Bianco di Custoza Vigne Alte, F.lli Zeni	273
Bianco di Custoza Vigneto Monte Fiera, Giacomo Montresor	320
Bianco di Gianni, Giovanni Panizzi	538
Bianco di Montefalco, Agricola Adanti	608
Bianco di Napoleone, Fattoria Vigna del Greppo	565
Bianco di Pitigliano, Tenuta Roccaccia	518
Bianco di Pitigliano Lunaia, La Stellata	471
Bianco Falconera, Conte Loredan Gasparini Venegazzù	330
Bianco Faye, Pojer & Sandri	219
Bianco Ghibellino, Aldo Rainoldi	179
Bianco Gli Affreschi, Tenuta di Blasig	386
Bianco Imperiale, Guido Berlucchi & C.	183
Bianco JN, Sant'Elena	368
Bianco Maso Bergamini, Maso Bergamini	238
Bianco Scuvaki, D'Ancona	712
Biblos, Di Majo Norante	641
Bidis, C. Valle dell'Acate	700
Biel Cûr Rosso, Valerio Marinig	383
Biferno Bianco Gironia, Borgo di Colloredo	640
Biferno Molì Bianco, Di Majo Norante	641
Biferno Molì Rosso, Di Majo Norante	641
Biferno Rosato Gironia, Borgo di Colloredo	640
Biferno Rosso Gironia, Borgo di Colloredo	640
Biferno Rosso Ramitello, Di Majo Norante	641
Bigarò Rosso, Elio Perrone	62
Birba, La Gerla	484
Birbarossa, Tenuta Gaiano	46
Bizir, Ajello	717
Blanc des Rosis, Schiopetto	339
Blu, Fattoria Mancini	596
Blu Perla, Bailoni	238
Bolgheri Bianco, Grattamacco	438
Bolgheri Bianco, Michele Satta	438
Bolgheri Bianco Campo della Casa, Enrico Santini	551
Bolgheri Rosso Diambra, Michele Satta	438
Bolgheri Rosso Piastraia, Michele Satta	438
Bolgheri Rosso Poggio al Moro, Enrico Santini	551
Bolgheri Rosso Sup. Grattamacco, Grattamacco	438
Bolgheri Rosso Sup. Guado al Tasso, Tenuta Guado al Tasso	432
Bolgheri Rosso Sup. Paleo, Le Macchiole	433
Bolgheri Sassicaia, Tenuta S. Guido	434
Bolgheri Sauvignon Paleo, Le Macchiole	433
Bolgheri Sup. Ornellaia, Tenuta dell' Ornellaia	433
Bolgheri Sup. Serre Nuove, Tenuta dell' Ornellaia	433
Bolgheri Vermentino, Tenuta Guado al Tasso	432
Bombereto, La Rampa di Fugnano	536
Bonagrazia Bianco, Tenuta Farneta	541
Bonagrazia Rosato, Tenuta Farneta	541
Bonera, Settesoli	707
Bongoverno, Tenuta Farneta	541
Bonmé, Poderi Colla	26
Bonorli, Melini	519
Bontesco Bianco, S. Giusto	517
Bontesco Rosso, S. Giusto	517
Borgo d'Altesi, Altesino	473
Borgo dei Guidi, Poderi dal Nespoli	408
Borgo di Peuma, Russolo	395
Borgoforte, Villa Pillo	462
Borgoricco, Tenuta La Cipressaia	567
Borro del Boscone, Le Calvane	507
Boscarelli, Boscarelli	498
Boschi Salviati, S. Luciano	493
Botrys, Mastrojanni	487
Bottaccio, Il Paradiso	535
Botticino Faja d'Or Ris., Emilio Franzoni	205
Bottiglia Particolare, Castello di Verrazzano	466
Bouquet, Tenute Rapitalà	711
Braccano Rosso, Enzo Mecella	586
Brachetto d'Acqui, Braida	122
Brachetto d'Acqui Castelgaro, Bersano & Riccadonna	116
Brachetto d'Acqui Pineto, Marenco	133
Brachetto d'Acqui Spumante Contero, La Giustiniana	78
Bradisismo Cabernet Sauvignon del Veneto, Inama	298
Bragnolo Rosso, S. Biagio	206

Braida Nuova, Borgo Conventi	363
Braide Alte, Livon	393
Bramaterra, Sella	92
Brancaia, La Brancaia	521
Braviolo, Fattoria del Cerro	499
Breganze Bianco Rivana, Vigneto Due Santi	273
Breganze Cabernet, Vigneto Due Santi	273
Breganze Cabernet Sauvignon Ferrata, Maculan	274
Breganze Cabernet Vigneto Due Santi, Vigneto Due Santi	273
Breganze Chardonnay Ferrata, Maculan	274
Breganze Chardonnay Riale, Maculan	274
Breganze di Breganze, Maculan	274
Breganze Rosso, Vigneto Due Santi	273
Breganze Sauvignon Vigneto Due Santi, Vigneto Due Santi	273
Breganze Torcolato, Maculan	274
Brentino, Maculan	274
Bric du Liun Passito, Deltetto	48
Briccaio Vellutato, Villa Pigna	595
Bricco Appiani, Flavio Roddolo	104
Bricco dell'Uccellone, Braida	122
Bricco Sturnel, Bellaria	206
Bricoli, Vigliano	573
Brigante dei Barbi, Fattoria dei Barbi	474
Brindisi Rosato Vigna Flaminio, Agricole Vallone	683
Brindisi Rosso, C. Due Palme	690
Brindisi Rosso, S. Barbara	688
Brindisi Rosso Gallico, Tenute Rubino	677
Brindisi Rosso V. Flaminio, Agricole Vallone	683
Brindisi Rosso Vigna Flaminio, Agricole Vallone	683
Broccato, Fattoria di Dievole	554
Broili di Filip, Walter Filiputti	370
Brolo dei Passoni, Ricci Curbastro	173
Bron & Rusèval Chardonnay, Celli	404
Bron & Rusèval Sangiovese-Cabernet, Celli	404
Brunello di Montalcino, Altesino	473
Brunello di Montalcino, Tenuta di Argiano	473
Brunello di Montalcino, Banfi	474
Brunello di Montalcino, Fattoria dei Barbi	474
Brunello di Montalcino, Castello di Camigliano	475
Brunello di Montalcino, Tenuta Caparzo	475
Brunello di Montalcino, Casanova di Neri	476
Brunello di Montalcino, Fattoria del Casato - Donatella Cinelli Colombini	476
Brunello di Montalcino, Casisano Colombaio	477
Brunello di Montalcino, Castelgiocondo	477
Brunello di Montalcino, Castelli Martinozzi	560
Brunello di Montalcino, Castiglion del Bosco	478
Brunello di Montalcino, Tenuta Col d'Orcia	479
Brunello di Montalcino, Coldisole	561
Brunello di Montalcino, Tenuta di Collosorbo	561
Brunello di Montalcino, Corte Pavone	561
Brunello di Montalcino, Andrea Costanti	479
Brunello di Montalcino, Due Portine - Gorelli	561
Brunello di Montalcino, Fanti - La Palazzetta	480
Brunello di Montalcino, Fanti - S. Filippo	481
Brunello di Montalcino, Fornacina	561
Brunello di Montalcino, Eredi Fuligni	481
Brunello di Montalcino, Greppone Mazzi - Tenimenti Ruffino	482
Brunello di Montalcino, Il Marroneto	561
Brunello di Montalcino, Il Palazzone	562
Brunello di Montalcino, Tenuta Il Poggione	483
Brunello di Montalcino, La Fiorita	562
Brunello di Montalcino, La Fornace	562
Brunello di Montalcino, Podere La Fortuna	484
Brunello di Montalcino, Tenuta La Fuga	562
Brunello di Montalcino, La Gerla	484
Brunello di Montalcino, La Poderina	485
Brunello di Montalcino, La Serena	562
Brunello di Montalcino, La Togata	485
Brunello di Montalcino, Maurizio Lambardi	486
Brunello di Montalcino, Le Chiuse	563
Brunello di Montalcino, Le Gode di Ripaccioli	563
Brunello di Montalcino, Mastrojanni	487
Brunello di Montalcino, Mocali	487
Brunello di Montalcino, C. di Montalcino	563
Brunello di Montalcino, Tenute Silvio Nardi	563
Brunello di Montalcino, Siro Pacenti	488
Brunello di Montalcino, Pian delle Vigne	563
Brunello di Montalcino, Piancornello	488
Brunello di Montalcino, Agostina Pieri	489
Brunello di Montalcino, Poggio di Sotto	489
Brunello di Montalcino, Poggio S. Polo	574
Brunello di Montalcino, Castello Romitorio	490
Brunello di Montalcino, Salicutti	490
Brunello di Montalcino, Salvioni - La Cerbaiola	491
Brunello di Montalcino, S. Filippo - Rosi	564
Brunello di Montalcino, Solaria - Cencioni	491
Brunello di Montalcino, Talenti - Podere Pian di Conte	564
Brunello di Montalcino, Tenimenti Angelini - Val di Suga	492
Brunello di Montalcino, Tornesi	564
Brunello di Montalcino, Uccelliera	564
Brunello di Montalcino, Tenuta Valdicava	492
Brunello di Montalcino, Verbena	564
Brunello di Montalcino, Villa Le Prata	493
Brunello di Montalcino, Vitanza	564
Brunello di Montalcino Beato, Il Poggiolo	483
Brunello di Montalcino Beato Ris., Il Poggiolo	483
Brunello di Montalcino Cerretalto, Casanova di Neri	476
Brunello di Montalcino Five Stars Ris., Il Poggiolo	483
Brunello di Montalcino Friggiali Pietranera, Centolani	560
Brunello di Montalcino Friggiali Pietranera Vigna della Sughera Ris., Centolani	560
Brunello di Montalcino La Casa, Tenuta Caparzo	475
Brunello di Montalcino Madonna del Piano Ris., Tenuta Valdicava	492
Brunello di Montalcino Montosoli, Altesino	473
Brunello di Montalcino Poggio al Vento Ris., Tenuta Col d'Orcia	479
Brunello di Montalcino Poggio all'Oro Ris., Banfi	474
Brunello di Montalcino Poggio Salvi, Tenuta Il Greppo	482
Brunello di Montalcino Prime Donne, Fattoria del Casato - Donatella Cinelli Colombini	476
Brunello di Montalcino Ris., Altesino	473
Brunello di Montalcino Ris., Tenuta di Argiano	473
Brunello di Montalcino Ris., Fattoria dei Barbi	474
Brunello di Montalcino Ris., Castello di Camigliano	475
Brunello di Montalcino Ris., Tenuta Caparzo	475
Brunello di Montalcino Ris., Casisano Colombaio	477
Brunello di Montalcino Ris., Castelgiocondo	477
Brunello di Montalcino Ris., Castiglion del Bosco	478
Brunello di Montalcino Ris., Tenuta Col d'Orcia	479
Brunello di Montalcino Ris., Andrea Costanti	479
Brunello di Montalcino Ris., Tenuta Di Sesta	480
Brunello di Montalcino Ris., Fanti - S. Filippo	481
Brunello di Montalcino Ris., Fornacina	561
Brunello di Montalcino Ris., Eredi Fuligni	481
Brunello di Montalcino Ris., Greppone Mazzi - Tenimenti Ruffino	482
Brunello di Montalcino Ris., Il Palazzone	562
Brunello di Montalcino Ris., Tenuta Il Poggione	483
Brunello di Montalcino Ris., La Fornace	562
Brunello di Montalcino Ris., Podere La Fortuna	484
Brunello di Montalcino Ris., Tenuta La Fuga	562
Brunello di Montalcino Ris., La Gerla	484
Brunello di Montalcino Ris., La Poderina	485
Brunello di Montalcino Ris., La Togata	485
Brunello di Montalcino Ris., Le Chiuse	563
Brunello di Montalcino Ris., Mastrojanni	487
Brunello di Montalcino Ris., Mocali	487
Brunello di Montalcino Ris., Siro Pacenti	488
Brunello di Montalcino Ris., Agostina Pieri	489
Brunello di Montalcino Ris., Poggio di Sotto	489
Brunello di Montalcino Ris., S. Filippo - Rosi	564
Brunello di Montalcino Ris., Talenti - Podere Pian di Conte	564
Brunello di Montalcino Ris., Vitanza	564
Brunello di Montalcino Sassello, Il Poggiolo	483
Brunello di Montalcino Sassello Ris., Il Poggiolo	483
Brunello di Montalcino Schiena d'Asino, Mastrojanni	487
Brunello di Montalcino Tenuta Nuova, Casanova di Neri	476
Brunello di Montalcino Terra Rossa, Il Poggiolo	483
Brunello di Montalcino Vigna del Colombaio, Casisano Colombaio	477
Brunello di Montalcino Vigna del Fiore Ris., Fattoria dei Barbi	474
Brunello di Montalcino Vigna del Lago, Tenimenti Angelini - Val di Suga	492
Brunello di Montalcino Vigna di Pianrosso, Ciacci Piccolomini D'Aragona	478
Brunello di Montalcino Vigna di Pianrosso Ris., Ciacci Piccolomini D'Aragona	478
Brunello di Montalcino Vigna Spuntali, Tenimenti Angelini - Val di Suga	492
Brunello di Montalcino Vigneti dei Cottimelli, Eredi Fuligni	481
Brunello di Montalcino Vigneti dei Cottimelli Ris., Eredi Fuligni	481
Bruno di Rocca, Vecchie Terre di Montefili	515
Bruno Giacosa Extra Brut, Bruno Giacosa	113
Brusco dei Barbi, Fattoria dei Barbi	474
Brut Carato Oro, Villa Mazzucchelli	209
Brut Cl. Costaripa, Costaripa	190
Brut Cl. Il Calepino, Il Calepino	177
Brut Cl. Ris. Fra Ambrogio, Il Calepino	177
Brut Conte Giammaria Ris., Villa Mazzucchelli	209
Brut M. Cl., Faraone	643
Brut M. Cl. Linea 2000, Il Calepino	177
Brut Sauvage, Villa Mazzucchelli	209
Brut Scurtarola, Podere Scurtarola	560
Bruzzico, Fattoria Lilliano	549
Buca di Cleonte, Petricci del Pianta	575
Bue Apis, C. del Taburno	655
Burgò Rosso, La Colombera	154
Buriano, Rocca di Castagnoli	460
Burson, Tenuta Uccellina	417
Busillis, Tenimenti Angelini - Tenuta Trerose	505
C. Amerini Bianco Terre Arnolfe, C. dei Colli Amerini	624
C. Amerini Chardonnay Rocca Nerina, C. dei Colli Amerini	624
C. Amerini Rosso Sup., Fattoria Le Poggette	613
C. Amerini Rosso Sup. Carbio, C. dei Colli Amerini	624
C. Amerini Rosso Sup. Sciurio, Zanchi	624
C. Amerini Rosso Terre Arnolfe, C. dei Colli Amerini	624
C. del Trasimeno Baccio del Bianco, Duca della Corgna	611
C. del Trasimeno Baccio del Rosso, Duca della Corgna	611

C. del Trasimeno Balestrino Rosato, Fanini	610	Campidano di Terralba Bovale Madrigal,	
C. del Trasimeno Bianco, Il Poggio	624	C. Soc. Marrubiu	731
C. del Trasimeno Bianco, Villa Po' del Vento	625	Campo all'Albero, La Sala	530
C. del Trasimeno Bianco Etesiaco, Pieve del Vescovo	612	Campo d'Aia, Castello di Modanella	525
C. del Trasimeno Bianco Scelto, Il Poggio	624	Campo de' Massi, Giulio Freddano	618
C. del Trasimeno Gamay Divina Villa et. Bianca, Duca della Corgna	611	Campo del Bosco, Poggio Salvi	574
		Campo Montecristo, Serraiola	506
C. del Trasimeno Gamay Divina Villa et. Nera, Duca della Corgna	611	Campo Sireso, Ottella	296
		Campo Vecchio Rosso, Castel De Paolis	632
C. del Trasimeno Grechetto Nuricante, Duca della Corgna	611	Campoleone, La Fiorita - Lamborghini	620
C. del Trasimeno Rosso, Il Poggio	624	Campora, Casale - Falchini	572
C. del Trasimeno Rosso, Podere Marella	625	Camporosso, La Marcellina	569
C. del Trasimeno Rosso, Pieve del Vescovo	612	Campos Rosato del Limbara, C. Soc. Gallura	729
C. del Trasimeno Rosso, Villa Po' del Vento	625	Camposilio, Camposilio	576
C. del Trasimeno Rosso Barca, Terre del Carpine	625	Canà Rosso, La Biancara	278
C. del Trasimeno Rosso Corniolo, Duca della Corgna	611	Canaiolo, Fattoria Le Poggette	613
C. del Trasimeno Rosso di Boldrino, La Querciolana	626	Canavese Bianco Castello di Loranzé, Ferrando	82
C. del Trasimeno Rosso Erceo, Terre del Carpine	625	Canavese Rosso Cieck, Cieck	23
C. del Trasimeno Rosso Grifo di Boldrino Ris., La Querciolana	626	Canavese Rosso Montodo, Ferrando	82
		Canavese Rosso Neretto, Cieck	23
C. del Trasimeno Rosso Lucciaio, Pieve del Vescovo	612	Candia dei Colli Apuani, Cima	471
C. del Trasimeno Rosso Morello del Lago, Fanini	610	Candia dei Colli Apuani, Podere Scurtarola	560
C. del Trasimeno Trescone, La Fiorita - Lamborghini	620	Candia dei Colli Apuani, VIN.CA	551
Ca' del Forte Rosso, Barni	44	Candia dei Colli Apuani Vigneto Candia Alto, Cima	471
Ca' del Pazzo, Tenuta Caparzo	475	Canneto, D'Angelo	672
Cabanon Noir, Cabanon	188	Cannonau di Sardegna, Antichi Poderi Jerzu	723
Caberlot, Podere Il Carnasciale	549	Cannonau di Sardegna, Cantine di Dolianova	722
Cabernasco, Villa Pigna	595	Cannonau di Sardegna, Attilio Contini	721
Cabernet, Feudo Principi di Butera	701	Cannonau di Sardegna, Piero Mancini	731
Cabernet dei Colli Trevigiani, Gregoletto	286	Cannonau di Sardegna, Meloni Vini	726
Cabernet della Bergamasca Messernero, Le Corne	208	Cannonau di Sardegna, Perdarubia	731
Cabernet di Sardegna, Meloni Vini	726	Cannonau di Sardegna, Gigi Picciau	730
Cabernet Duca Cantelmi, Giovanni Palombo	628	Cannonau di Sardegna Alberto Loi Ris., Alberto Loi	722
Cabernet Franc, Andreola Orsola	277	Cannonau di Sardegna Baione, C. Soc. della Trexenta	727
Cabernet Franc, Oscar Sturm	354	Cannonau di Sardegna Cardedo, Alberto Loi	722
Cabernet Franc Campo Buri, La Cappuccina	290	Cannonau di Sardegna Chio, C. Soc. Il Nuraghe	731
Cabernet I Legni, Russolo	395	Cannonau di Sardegna Corrasi Nepente di Oliena Ris., C. Coop. di Oliena	732
Cabernet Podere Torrai, Conte Collalto	312		
Cabernet Sauvignon, Benanti	703	Cannonau di Sardegna Costera, Antonio Argiolas	728
Cabernet Sauvignon, C. Soc. della Valpantena	319	Cannonau di Sardegna Firmadu, Tenute Soletta	730
Cabernet Sauvignon, Casale del Giglio	628	Cannonau di Sardegna Grand Cru, C. Soc. S. Maria La Palma	720
Cabernet Sauvignon, Isole e Olena	431		
Cabernet Sauvignon, Cantine Lungarotti	623	Cannonau di Sardegna Le Bombarde, C. Soc. S. Maria La Palma	720
Cabernet Sauvignon, Aziende Vinicole Miceli	710		
Cabernet Sauvignon, Alessandro Secchi	216	Cannonau di Sardegna Le Ghiaie, Meloni Vini	726
Cabernet Sauvignon, Tasca d'Almerita	715	Cannonau di Sardegna Lillovè, Giuseppe Gabbas	725
Cabernet Sauvignon, Tenuta di Trecciano	575	Cannonau di Sardegna Marghìa, Antichi Poderi Jerzu	723
Cabernet Sauvignon, Villa Arceno	449	Cannonau di Sardegna Ris., Antichi Poderi Jerzu	723
Cabernet Sauvignon, Villa Pillo	462	Cannonau di Sardegna Ris., Attilio Contini	721
Cabernet Sauvignon Burdese, Planeta	714	Cannonau di Sardegna Ris., Alberto Loi	722
Cabernet Sauvignon Castellione, Calonga	425	Cannonau di Sardegna Ris. Chuerra, Antichi Poderi Jerzu	723
Cabernet Sauvignon Colle Funaro, Orlandi Contucci Ponno	647	Cannonau di Sardegna Riserva Josto Miglior, Antichi Poderi Jerzu	723
Cabernet Sauvignon del Veneto, Marion	327	Cannonau di Sardegna Sa Mola Rubia, Alberto Loi	722
Cabernet Sauvignon Ferrata, Maculan	274	Cannonau di Sardegna Sa Mola Rubia Ris., Alberto Loi	722
Cabernet Sauvignon Giunone, Monte Tondo	309	Cannonau di Sardegna Trieste, Pala	728
Cabernet Sauvignon I Castei, Michele Castellani	282	Cannonau di Sardegna Vigna di Isalle, C. Soc. Dorgali	723
Cabernet Sauvignon Luna Nuova, S. Valentino	427	Cannonau di Sardegna Vigna Ruja, C. Soc. Il Nuraghe	731
Cabernet Sauvignon Madégo, La Cappuccina	290	Cannonau di Sardegna Vinìola, C. Soc. Dorgali	723
Cabernet Sauvignon Mandrarossa, Settesoli	707	Cantalupo Bianco, Azzoni Avogadro Carradori	605
Cabernet Sauvignon Principe di Corleone, Pollara	708	Cantico, Podere La Cappella	546
Cabernet Sauvignon S. Cristina, Zenato	297	Canvalle, Vignavecchia	524
Cabernet Sauvignon Torre di Mellotti, Tenuta Sant'Antonio	275	Capalbio Bianco, La Parrina	509
Cabernet Sauvignon Vigna Capitello, Tenuta Sant'Antonio	275	Capalbio Rosso Losco, S. Lucia	558
Cabernet Sauvignon Vigneto Campo Madonna, Giacomo Montresor	320	Capannacce, Le Capannacce	449
		Caparzo Rosso, Tenuta Caparzo	475
Cabreo Il Borgo, Tenute Folonari	452	Capichera, Capichera	721
Cabreo La Pietra, Tenute Folonari	452	Capichera V.T., Capichera	721
Cadetto Rosso, Barone La Lumia	704	Capichera Vigna 'Ngena, Capichera	721
Cagiòlo Bianco, C. Tollo	649	Capineto, Tenuta Castellino	180
Cajo, Terre de' Trinci	625	Capitel Croce, Roberto Anselmi	288
Calamita, Poggio a Poppiano	508	Capitel Foscarino, Roberto Anselmi	288
Calanchi di Vaiano, Paolo d'Amico	629	Capitel S. Rocco Rosso di Ripasso, F.lli Tedeschi	304
Calanco, Tenuta Le Velette	619	Capo d'Opera Lucia Galasso, Giovanni Crosato	342
Calaresu, Giovanni Cherchi	729	Capo di Stato, Conte Loredan Gasparini Venegazzù	330
Calcare Sauvignon, Conte Leopardi Dittajuti	592	Capo Martino, Vinnaioli Jermann	364
Caluna, Podere Marella	625	Caporosso, Casa Vinicola Grasso	717
Caluso Bianco Vignot S. Antonio, Orsolani	124	Cappello di Prete, Francesco Candido	687
Caluso Passito Alladium Vigneto Runc, Cieck	23	Capri Bianco Bordo, Agricola La Caprense	666
Caluso Passito La Rustìa, Orsolani	124	Capriano del Colle Bianco, Cascina Nuova	171
Caluso Passito Sulé, Orsolani	124	Capriano del Colle Rosso, Cascina Nuova	171
Caluso Passito Vigneto Cariola, Ferrando	82	Capriano del Colle Rosso Monte Bruciato Ris., La Vigna	205
Camars, Catia Spinsanti	603	Capriano del Colle Rosso Vigna Tenuta Anna, Cascina Nuova	171
Camartina, Agricola Querciabella	465		
Camastra, Tasca d'Almerita	715	Caprorosso, Fattoria di Bagnolo	559
Camelot, Casa Vinicola Firriato	709	Capsico Rosso, Ciccio Zaccagnini	640
Camerte, La Monacesca	589	Caralis Brut, Cantine di Dolianova	722
Campaccio, Fattoria di Terrabianca	524	Carantan, Marco Felluga	368
Campaccio Sel. Speciale, Fattoria di Terrabianca	524	Caratello Passito, Enoteca Bisson	159
Campanaro, Feudi di S. Gregorio	663	Carato Rosso, Camponeschi	638
Campi Flegrei Falanghina Coste di Cuma, Cantine Grotta del Sole	662	Cardinale, Le Chiantigiane	576
		Cardonnay Le Macchie, Pasolini Dall'Onda	556
Campi Flegrei Piedirosso Montegauro Ris., Cantine Grotta del Sole	662	Carema Carema, C. dei Prod. Nebbiolo di Carema	53
		Carema Cl., C. dei Prod. Nebbiolo di Carema	53
Campi Sarni, Vallarom	217	Carema Etichetta Nera, Ferrando	82
Campi Sarni Bianco, Vallarom	217	Carema Le Tappie, Orsolani	124

Carema Sel., C. dei Prod. Nebbiolo di Carema	53
Carialoso, Marenco	133
Carignano del Sulcis Baje Rosse, C. Soc. di Santadi	726
Carignano del Sulcis Grotta Rossa, C. Soc. di Santadi	726
Carignano del Sulcis Rocca Rubia, C. Soc. di Santadi	726
Carignano del Sulcis Rosso, Cantine Sardus Pater	732
Carignano del Sulcis Solus, Cantine Sardus Pater	732
Carignano del Sulcis Sup. Terre Brune, C. Soc. di Santadi	726
Carignano del Sulcis Terrerare, Tenute Sella & Mosca	720
Carleto, Enrico Pierazzuoli	453
Carlozadra Cl. Brut, Carlozadra	189
Carlozadra Cl. Brut Nondosato, Carlozadra	189
Carlozadra Extra Dry Liberty, Carlozadra	189
Carmen, Teruzzi & Puthod	539
Carmenèro, Ca' del Bosco	185
Carmignano, Il Poggiolo	551
Carmignano, Pratesi	551
Carmignano Elzana Ris., Fattoria Ambra	437
Carmignano Le Farnete, Enrico Pierazzuoli	453
Carmignano Le Farnete Ris., Enrico Pierazzuoli	453
Carmignano Le Vigne Alte di Montalbiolo, Fattoria Ambra	437
Carmignano Le Vigne Alte Ris., Fattoria Ambra	437
Carmignano Ris., Piaggia	519
Carmignano Vigna S. Cristina a Pilli, Fattoria Ambra	437
Carmignano Villa Artimino, Artimino	551
Carmignano Villa di Capezzana, Capezzana	437
Carmignano Villa di Trefiano, Capezzana	437
Carmignano Villa di Trefiano Ris., Capezzana	437
Carolus, Antichi Vigneti di Cantalupo	80
Carricante, Benanti	703
Carso Cabernet Franc, Castelvecchio	387
Carso Cabernet Sauvignon, Castelvecchio	387
Carso Chardonnay, Kante	361
Carso Malvasia, Kante	361
Carso Malvasia, Zidarich	362
Carso Malvasia Istriana, Castelvecchio	387
Carso Pinot Grigio, Castelvecchio	387
Carso Refosco P. R., Castelvecchio	387
Carso Rosso Turmino, Castelvecchio	387
Carso Sauvignon, Kante	361
Carso Terrano, Zidarich	362
Carso Traminer Aromatico, Castelvecchio	387
Carso Vitovska, Kante	361
Cartizze, Adami	321
Cartizze, Desiderio Bisol & Figli	313
Cartizze, F.lli Bortolin Spumanti	313
Cartizze, Bortolomiol	314
Cartizze, Canevel Spumanti	314
Cartizze, Ciodet	329
Cartizze, Col Vetoraz	315
Cartizze, Le Colture	315
Cartizze, Masottina	299
Cartizze, Nino Franco	316
Cartizze, Angelo Ruggeri	316
Cartizze, Ruggeri & C.	317
Cartizze, S. Eurosia	317
Cartizze, Tanorè	318
Cartizze, Zardetto Spumanti	276
Cartizze, Paolo Zucchetto	329
Casa Pastore Rosso, Rio Grande	620
Casaglia, Tenuta di Bagnolo dei Marchesi Pancrazi	497
Casale dei Biscari, Cantine Torrevecchia	700
Casale S. Giorgio Rosato, C. Coop. del Locorotondo	684
Casale S. Giorgio Rosso, C. Coop. del Locorotondo	684
Casalferro, Barone Ricasoli	456
Casalj, Tenute Rapitalà	711
Casamurli, Fattoria S. Maria di Ambra	434
Casarsa, Villa Calcinaia	558
Casorzo Malvasia Brigantino, G. Accornero e Figli	140
Casorzo Malvasia Passito Pico, G. Accornero e Figli	140
Casotte, Bellavista	185
Cassabò Rosso, Valfieri	67
Castel del Monte Aglianico Cappellaccio Ris., Rivera	676
Castel del Monte Bianco, Torrevento	680
Castel del Monte Bianco Dama di Svevia, Rivera	676
Castel del Monte Bianco Vigna Tufaroli, S. Lucia	679
Castel del Monte Chardonnay Pietrabianca, Tormaresca	688
Castel del Monte Chardonnay Preludio N° 1, Rivera	676
Castel del Monte Rosato, Torrevento	680
Castel del Monte Rosato Vigna Lama di Carro, S. Lucia	679
Castel del Monte Rosé di Rivera, Rivera	676
Castel del Monte Rosso, Vinicola Miali	691
Castel del Monte Rosso, S. Lucia	679
Castel del Monte Rosso, Torrevento	680
Castel del Monte Rosso Boccadilupo, Tormaresca	688
Castel del Monte Rosso Il Falcone Ris., Rivera	676
Castel del Monte Rosso Ris., S. Lucia	679
Castel del Monte Rosso Rupicolo di Rivera, Rivera	676
Castel del Monte Rosso Vigna del Melograno, S. Lucia	679
Castel del Monte Rosso Vigna Pedale Ris., Torrevento	680
Castel del Monte Sauvignon Terre al Monte, Rivera	676
Castel S. Lorenzo Moscato Spumante, Coop. Val Calore	666
Castel S. Lorenzo Rosso, Coop. Val Calore	666
Castellaccio Bianco, Fattoria Uccelliera	451
Castellaccio Rosso, Fattoria Uccelliera	451
Castellacio, Cantine Monte Pugliano	667
Castelli Romani, Gotto d'Oro	638
Castellinaldo Barbera d'Alba, Raffaele Gili	146
Castellinaldo Barbera d'Alba, Marsaglia	146
Castellinaldo Barbera d'Alba, Stefanino Morra	55
Castellinaldo Barbera d'Alba, Vielmin	146
Castellinaldo Barbera d'Alba Castelli di Castellinaldo, Teo Costa	145
Castello di Buttrio Marburg, Marco Felluga	368
Castello di Buttrio Ovestein, Marco Felluga	368
Castello Guerrieri Bianco, Guerrieri Rizzardi	272
Castelrapiti Rosso, Fattoria di Montellori	454
Cauro, Statti	697
Cavina Chardonnay, Pandolfa	416
Cecubo, Villa Matilde	655
Celius, Fattoria Le Casalte	566
Cellarius Brut Ris., Guido Berlucchi & C.	183
Cellaro Rosso, C. Soc. Cellaro	713
Cenito, Luigi Maffini	654
Cent'Are Bianco, Carlo Pellegrino	706
Cent'Are Rosso, Carlo Pellegrino	706
Cepola Bianco, Villa di Quartu	725
Cepola Rosso, Villa di Quartu	725
Cepparello, Isole e Olena	431
Ceppate, Fattoria di Terrabianca	524
Ceragiolo, Jacopo Banti	435
Ceraso, Giovanni Panizzi	538
Cerasuolo di Vittoria, COS	715
Cerasuolo di Vittoria, Cantine Torrevecchia	700
Cerasuolo di Vittoria, C. Valle dell'Acate	700
Cerasuolo di Vittoria Barocco, Vitivinicola Avide	713
Cerasuolo di Vittoria Etichetta Nera, Vitivinicola Avide	713
Cerasuolo di Vittoria Mont Serrat A.D. 1668, Cantine Torrevecchia	700
Cerasuolo di Vittoria Sciri, COS	715
Cerasuolo di Vittoria V. di Bastonaca, COS	715
Cercatoja Rosso, Fattoria del Buonamico	494
Cerosecco, Petricci del Pianta	575
Cerro Bianco, Fattoria del Cerro	499
Cervaro della Sala, Castello della Sala	612
Cerveteri Bianco Fontana Morella, C. Coop. di Cerveteri	630
Cerveteri Bianco Vigna Grande, C. Coop. di Cerveteri	630
Cerveteri Rosso Fontana Morella, C. Coop. di Cerveteri	630
Cerveteri Rosso Vigna Grande, C. Coop. di Cerveteri	630
Cerviolo Bianco, S. Fabiano Calcinaia	442
Cerviolo Rosso, S. Fabiano Calcinaia	442
Cesanese del Piglio, Paolo Perinelli	636
Cesanese del Piglio Casal Cervino, Massimi Berucci	638
Cesanese del Piglio Etichetta Oro, C. Soc. Cesanese del Piglio	638
Cesanese del Piglio Haernicus, Antonello Coletti Conti	636
Cesanese del Piglio Torre del Piano, Paolo Perinelli	636
Cesare Passito Bianco, Le Salette	278
Ceuso, Ceuso	716
Ceuso Custera, Ceuso	716
Chaos Rosso, Fattoria Le Terrazze	593
Char-de S., Elio Perrone	62
Chardonnay, Fattorie Azzolino	716
Chardonnay, Benanti	703
Chardonnay, Capezzana	437
Chardonnay, Casale del Giglio	628
Chardonnay, Giovanni Crosato	342
Chardonnay, Feudo Principi di Butera	701
Chardonnay, Inama	298
Chardonnay, Isole e Olena	431
Chardonnay, Ispoli	530
Chardonnay, Kante	361
Chardonnay, La Cadalora	236
Chardonnay, Aziende Vinicole Miceli	710
Chardonnay, Planeta	714
Chardonnay, Poggio Capponi	568
Chardonnay, Cantine Rallo	706
Chardonnay, Tenuta Roccaccia	518
Chardonnay, Ronco del Gnemiz	393
Chardonnay, Fattoria S. Vittoria	454
Chardonnay, Tasca d'Almerita	715
Chardonnay, Cantine Torrevecchia	700
Chardonnay, Trappolini	630
Chardonnay, Vinnaioli Jermann	364
Chardonnay Andritz, Oscar Sturm	354
Chardonnay Arcadio, Tenuta Valli	426
Chardonnay Arnasi Valleselle, Eugenio & Figli Tinazzi	323
Chardonnay Aurente, Cantine Lungarotti	623
Chardonnay Campo dei Tovi, Inama	298
Chardonnay Capitello, Tenuta Sant'Antonio	275
Chardonnay Castel Verdino, Madonna dei Miracoli	650
Chardonnay Castrum Icerini, Coffele	309
Chardonnay Chioma di Berenice, S. Lorenzo	650
Chardonnay Colle delle Montecchie, Rio Grande	620
Chardonnay Colle Maggio, Torre Zambra	649
Chardonnay del Lazio, Colle S. Lorenzo	631
Chardonnay della Sala, Castello della Sala	612
Chardonnay Guardia Vecchia, S. Cassella	606
Chardonnay Il Poggio, Castello di Ama	455
Chardonnay La Capinera, Capinera	605
Chardonnay Le Cingelle, Monte Tondo	309
Chardonnay Leukon, La C. dei Colli Ripani	598

Chardonnay Mandrarossa, Settesoli	707
Chardonnay Marina Cvetic, Gianni Masciarelli	647
Chardonnay Naumachos, Vinicola del Tesino	587
Chardonnay Pietrosa, Sarchese Dora	646
Chardonnay Polzina, Barone Pizzini	182
Chardonnay Punta di Colle, Marramiero	646
Chardonnay Robbiano, Fanini	610
Chardonnay Roccesco, Orlandi Contucci Ponno	647
Chardonnay Sorai, Gini	290
Chardonnay Soris, Pierpaolo Pecorari	395
Chardonnay Sottobosco, Ronco Calino	178
Chardonnay Tresor, Agriverde	645
Chardonnay Vallée du Vin, Agriverde	645
Chardonnay Vigna di Corte, Pollara	708
Chardonnay Vigne Umbre, Umbria Viticoltori Associati	625
Chaudelune Bianco, Cave du Vin Blanc de Morgex et de La Salle	18
Chiana d'Inserra, Aziende Vinicole Miceli	710
Chianti, Il Lebbio	534
Chianti, Tenuta La Cipressaia	567
Chianti, Le Piagge	557
Chianti, Cantine Leonardo da Vinci	548
Chianti, Giacomo Mori	528
Chianti, Fattoria S. Fabiano - Borghini Baldovinetti	430
Chianti, Sant'Appiano	550
Chianti, Fattoria Uccelliera	451
Chianti, Coop. Agricola Valdarnese	576
Chianti, Villa Sant'Anna	506
Chianti Castello di Rapale, Giacomo Marengo	565
Chianti Castelrotto, Giacomo Mori	528
Chianti Castiglioni, Marchesi de' Frescobaldi	453
Chianti Cl., Agricola Querciabella	465
Chianti Cl., Agricoltori del Chianti Geografico	455
Chianti Cl., Borgo Scopeto	443
Chianti Cl., Caiano	553
Chianti Cl., Carobbio	510
Chianti Cl., Carpineto	463
Chianti Cl., Casa Emma	549
Chianti Cl., Castagnoli	552
Chianti Cl., Castell'in Villa	445
Chianti Cl., Castellare di Castellina	439
Chianti Cl., Castello d' Albola	521
Chianti Cl., Castello dei Rampolla	514
Chianti Cl., Castello della Paneretta	550
Chianti Cl., Castello di Bossi	444
Chianti Cl., Castello di Cacchiano	556
Chianti Cl., Castello di Fonterutoli	440
Chianti Cl., Castello di Lilliano	552
Chianti Cl., Castello di Lucignano	458
Chianti Cl., Castello di Meleto	458
Chianti Cl., Castello di Monastero	446
Chianti Cl., Castello di Monsanto	432
Chianti Cl., Castello di Monterinaldi	522
Chianti Cl., Castello di Querceto	464
Chianti Cl., Castello di Selvole	448
Chianti Cl., Castello di Verrazzano	466
Chianti Cl., Castello di Volpaia	525
Chianti Cl., Castello La Leccia	552
Chianti Cl., Cennatoio	511
Chianti Cl., Coltibuono	456
Chianti Cl., Famiglia Cecchi	439
Chianti Cl., Fattoria Casa Sola	549
Chianti Cl., Fattoria Casaloste	511
Chianti Cl., Fattoria dell' Aiola	443
Chianti Cl., Fattoria di Felsina	446
Chianti Cl., Fattoria di Petroio	447
Chianti Cl., Fattoria di Terrabianca	524
Chianti Cl., Fattoria La Ripa	546
Chianti Cl., Fattoria Le Corti - Corsini	531
Chianti Cl., Fattoria Le Fonti	513
Chianti Cl., Fattoria Le Fonti	518
Chianti Cl., Fattoria Nittardi	441
Chianti Cl., Fattoria Ormanni	569
Chianti Cl., Fattoria Poggiopiano	532
Chianti Cl., Fattoria Sant'Andrea	515
Chianti Cl., Il Colombaio di Cencio	457
Chianti Cl., Il Mandorlo	529
Chianti Cl., Il Poggiolino	545
Chianti Cl., Isole e Olena	431
Chianti Cl., Ispoli	530
Chianti Cl., La Brancaia	521
Chianti Cl., La Castellina	552
Chianti Cl., La Loggia	572
Chianti Cl., La Massa	512
Chianti Cl., La Sala	530
Chianti Cl., Le Filigare	550
Chianti Cl., Le Miccine	556
Chianti Cl., Monte Bernardi	514
Chianti Cl., Montiverdi	459
Chianti Cl., Podere Capaccia	571
Chianti Cl., Podere Collelungo	440
Chianti Cl., Podere Il Palazzino	457
Chianti Cl., Podere Le Cinciole	513
Chianti Cl., Podere Terreno alla Via della Volpaia	571
Chianti Cl., Poggerino	523
Chianti Cl., Poggio al Sole	547
Chianti Cl., Poggio al Sorbo	553
Chianti Cl., Poggio Amorelli	553
Chianti Cl., Poggio Bonelli	447
Chianti Cl., Riecine	460
Chianti Cl., Riseccoli	465
Chianti Cl., Rocca di Castagnoli	460
Chianti Cl., Rocca di Montegrossi	461
Chianti Cl., S. Fabiano Calcinaia	442
Chianti Cl., S. Felice	448
Chianti Cl., S. Giorgio a Lapi	574
Chianti Cl., S. Giusto a Rentennano	461
Chianti Cl., S. Martino	557
Chianti Cl., S. Vincenti	462
Chianti Cl., Savignola Paolina	557
Chianti Cl., Tenuta Fontodi	512
Chianti Cl., Terreno	466
Chianti Cl., Vecchie Terre di Montefili	515
Chianti Cl., Vignole	569
Chianti Cl., Villa Cafaggio	516
Chianti Cl., Villa Calcinaia	558
Chianti Cl., Villa Casale	558
Chianti Cl., Villa Rosa	553
Chianti Cl., Villa Vignamaggio	467
Chianti Cl., Viticcio	468
Chianti Cl. Anfiteatro Ris., Vecchie Terre di Montefili	515
Chianti Cl. Argenina, Podere Il Palazzino	457
Chianti Cl. Badia a Passignano Ris., Marchesi Antinori	452
Chianti Cl. Badia a Sicelle, Pasolini Dall'Onda	556
Chianti Cl. Beatrice Ris., Viticcio	468
Chianti Cl. Bellavista, Castello di Ama	455
Chianti Cl. Bello Stento, La Madonnina - Triacca	557
Chianti Cl. Berardo Ris., Castello di Bossi	444
Chianti Cl. Bertinga, Castello di Ama	455
Chianti Cl. Brolio, Barone Ricasoli	456
Chianti Cl. Bugialla Ris., Poggerino	523
Chianti Cl. Campolungo Ris., S. M. Tenimenti Pile e Lamole	459
Chianti Cl. Cancello Rosso Ris., Fattoria dell' Aiola	443
Chianti Cl. Capraia Ris., Rocca di Castagnoli	460
Chianti Cl. Casa Eri, Villa Buonasera	558
Chianti Cl. Casanuova di Nittardi, Fattoria Nittardi	441
Chianti Cl. Casasilia Ris., Poggio al Sole	547
Chianti Cl. Casasilia, Poggio al Sole	547
Chianti Cl. Castelgreve Ris., Castelli del Grevepesa	528
Chianti Cl. Castelgreve, Castelli del Grevepesa	528
Chianti Cl. Castello di Ama, Castello di Ama	455
Chianti Cl. Castello di Brolio, Barone Ricasoli	456
Chianti Cl. Castello di Fonterutoli, Castello di Fonterutoli	440
Chianti Cl. Cellole Ris., S. Fabiano Calcinaia	442
Chianti Cl. Clemente VII, Castelli del Grevepesa	528
Chianti Cl. Contessa di Radda, Agricoltori del Chianti Geografico	455
Chianti Cl. Cortevecchia Ris., Fattoria Le Corti - Corsini	531
Chianti Cl. Don Alberto Ris., Le Miccine	556
Chianti Cl. Don Tommaso, Fattoria Le Corti - Corsini	531
Chianti Cl. Don Vincenzo Ris., Fattoria Casaloste	511
Chianti Cl. Fizzano Ris., Rocca delle Macìe	441
Chianti Cl. Frimaio Ris., Fattoria Poggio Romita	576
Chianti Cl. Frimaio Ris., Fattoria Poggio Romita	576
Chianti Cl. Giorgio Primo, La Massa	512
Chianti Cl. Grosso Sanese Ris., Podere Il Palazzino	457
Chianti Cl. Grosso Sanese, Podere Il Palazzino	457
Chianti Cl. I Massi Ris., Il Colombaio di Cencio	457
Chianti Cl. I Sassi, Melini	519
Chianti Cl. Il Grigio Ris., S. Felice	448
Chianti Cl. Il Picchio Ris., Castello di Querceto	464
Chianti Cl. Il Poggio Ris., Castello di Monsanto	432
Chianti Cl. Il Tarocco Ris., Torraccia di Presura	558
Chianti Cl. Il Tarocco, Torraccia di Presura	558
Chianti Cl. La Cappella, Villa Casale	558
Chianti Cl. La Casuccia, Castello di Ama	455
Chianti Cl. La Forra Ris., Tenute Folonari	452
Chianti Cl. La Gabbiola Ris., S. Michele a Torri	573
Chianti Cl. La Pieve, Podere Il Palazzino	457
Chianti Cl. La Prima Ris., Castello di Vicchiomaggio	467
Chianti Cl. La Selvanella Ris., Melini	519
Chianti Cl. Lamole Barrique, S. M. Tenimenti Pile e Lamole	459
Chianti Cl. Lamole di Lamole Ris., S. M. Tenimenti Pile e Lamole	459
Chianti Cl. Lamole di Lamole, S. M. Tenimenti Pile e Lamole	459
Chianti Cl. Le Ellere, Castello d' Albola	521
Chianti Cl. Le Masse di Greve Ris., Lanciola	469
Chianti Cl. Le Masse di Greve, Lanciola	469
Chianti Cl. Le Trame, Le Trame	554
Chianti Cl. Lucarello Ris., Borgo Salcetino	571
Chianti Cl. Massovecchio Ris., Melini	519
Chianti Cl. Matroneo, Enrico Pierazzuoli	453
Chianti Cl. Messer Piero di Teuzzo, Famiglia Cecchi	439
Chianti Cl. Misciano Ris., Borgo Scopeto	443
Chianti Cl. Monna Lisa Ris., Villa Vignamaggio	467
Chianti Cl. Montegiachi Ris., Agricoltori del Chianti Geografico	455
Chianti Cl. Nozzole, Tenute Folonari	452
Chianti Cl. O'Leandro Ris., Cennatoio	511
Chianti Cl. Panzanello Ris., Fattoria Sant'Andrea	515
Chianti Cl. Panzanello, Fattoria Sant'Andrea	515

Chianti Cl. Paris, Monte Bernardi	514
Chianti Cl. Petresco Ris., Podere Le Cinciole	513
Chianti Cl. Petri Ris., Castello di Vicchiomaggio	467
Chianti Cl. Pieve di Spaltenna, Castello di Meleto	458
Chianti Cl. Podere di Stignano, S. Vincenti	462
Chianti Cl. Poggio a' Frati Ris., Rocca di Castagnoli	460
Chianti Cl. Poggio delle Rose Ris., Castell'in Villa	445
Chianti Cl. Poggio Rosso Ris., S. Felice	448
Chianti Cl. Querciolo, Podere La Cappella	546
Chianti Cl. R. S., Coltibuono	456
Chianti Cl. Rancia Ris., Fattoria di Felsina	446
Chianti Cl. Ris. Ducale Oro, Tenimenti Ruffino	520
Chianti Cl. Ris., Agricola Querciabella	465
Chianti Cl. Ris., Borgo Scopeto	443
Chianti Cl. Ris., Caiano	553
Chianti Cl. Ris., Carobbio	510
Chianti Cl. Ris., Carpineto	463
Chianti Cl. Ris., Casa Emma	549
Chianti Cl. Ris., Castell'in Villa	445
Chianti Cl. Ris., Castellare di Castellina	439
Chianti Cl. Ris., Castello d' Albola	521
Chianti Cl. Ris., Castello dei Rampalli	514
Chianti Cl. Ris., Castello di Bossi	444
Chianti Cl. Ris., Castello di Lucignano	458
Chianti Cl. Ris., Castello di Meleto	458
Chianti Cl. Ris., Castello di Monastero	446
Chianti Cl. Ris., Castello di Monterinaldi	522
Chianti Cl. Ris., Castello di Querceto	464
Chianti Cl. Ris., Castello di Selvole	448
Chianti Cl. Ris., Castello di Verrazzano	466
Chianti Cl. Ris., Castello di Volpaia	525
Chianti Cl. Ris., Castello La Leccia	552
Chianti Cl. Ris., Cennatoio	511
Chianti Cl. Ris., Coltibuono	456
Chianti Cl. Ris., Fattoria Casa Sola	549
Chianti Cl. Ris., Fattoria Casaloste	511
Chianti Cl. Ris., Fattoria dell' Aiola	443
Chianti Cl. Ris., Fattoria di Dievole	554
Chianti Cl. Ris., Fattoria di Felsina	446
Chianti Cl. Ris., Fattoria di Petroio	447
Chianti Cl. Ris., Fattoria La Ripa	546
Chianti Cl. Ris., Fattoria Le Fonti	513
Chianti Cl. Ris., Fattoria Le Fonti	518
Chianti Cl. Ris., Fattoria Nittardi	441
Chianti Cl. Ris., Fattoria Ormanni	569
Chianti Cl. Ris., Fattoria Sant'Andrea	515
Chianti Cl. Ris., Fattoria Valtellina	557
Chianti Cl. Ris., Il Colombaio di Cencio	457
Chianti Cl. Ris., Il Mandorlo	529
Chianti Cl. Ris., Il Poggiolino	545
Chianti Cl. Ris., Ispoli	530
Chianti Cl. Ris., La Doccia	557
Chianti Cl. Ris., La Loggia	572
Chianti Cl. Ris., La Madonnina - Triacca	557
Chianti Cl. Ris., La Sala	530
Chianti Cl. Ris., Le Filigare	550
Chianti Cl. Ris., Monte Bernardi	514
Chianti Cl. Ris., Montiverdi	459
Chianti Cl. Ris., Podere Collelungo	440
Chianti Cl. Ris., Podere Terreno alla Via della Volpaia	571
Chianti Cl. Ris., Poggerino	523
Chianti Cl. Ris., Poggio al Sorbo	553
Chianti Cl. Ris., Poggio Bonelli	447
Chianti Cl. Ris., Riecine	460
Chianti Cl. Ris., Rietine	556
Chianti Cl. Ris., Riseccoli	465
Chianti Cl. Ris., Rocca delle Macìe	441
Chianti Cl. Ris., Rocca di Montegrossi	461
Chianti Cl. Ris., S. Giusto a Rentennano	461
Chianti Cl. Ris., S. Martino	557
Chianti Cl. Ris., S. Vincenti	462
Chianti Cl. Ris., Savignola Paolina	557
Chianti Cl. Ris., Terreno	466
Chianti Cl. Ris., Vecchie Terre di Montefili	515
Chianti Cl. Ris., Vignavecchia	524
Chianti Cl. Ris., Vignole	569
Chianti Cl. Ris., Villa Arceno	449
Chianti Cl. Ris., Villa Buonasera	558
Chianti Cl. Ris., Villa Cafaggio	516
Chianti Cl. Ris., Villa Calcinaia	558
Chianti Cl. Ris., Villa Rosa	553
Chianti Cl. Ris., Viticcio	468
Chianti Cl. Rocca Guicciarda Ris., Barone Ricasoli	456
Chianti Cl. Roveto, Podere Collelungo	440
Chianti Cl. S. Angelo Vico l'Abate, Castelli del Grevepesa	528
Chianti Cl. S. Jacopo, Castello di Vicchiomaggio	467
Chianti Cl. S. Trinita Ris., Le Chiantigiane	576
Chianti Cl. S. Trinita Ris., Le Chiantigiane	576
Chianti Cl. Sassocupo, La Marcellina	569
Chianti Cl. Solatio Basilica Ris., Villa Cafaggio	516
Chianti Cl. Tenuta S. Alfonso, Rocca delle Macìe	441
Chianti Cl. Tenute del Marchese Ris., Marchesi Antinori	452
Chianti Cl. Terre di Prenzano, Villa Vignamaggio	467
Chianti Cl. Torre a Destra Ris., Castello della Panerretta	550
Chianti Cl. V. di Fontalle Ris., Machiavelli	531
Chianti Cl. V. La Palaia, La Madonnina - Triacca	557
Chianti Cl. Valle del Pozzo Ris., Podere Le Cinciole	513
Chianti Cl. Ventesimo Ris., Montiverdi	459
Chianti Cl. Viacosta Ris., Rodano	553
Chianti Cl. Vigna del Sorbo Ris., Tenuta Fontodi	512
Chianti Cl. Vigna della Croce Ris., Fattoria di Terrabianca	524
Chianti Cl. Vigna il Poggiale Ris., Castellare di Castellina	439
Chianti Cl. Vigna il Poggiale, Castellare di Castellina	439
Chianti Cl. Vigneto Cipressone, Montiverdi	459
Chianti Cl. Vigneto S. Marcellino Ris., Rocca di Montegrossi	461
Chianti Cl. Vigneto S. Marcellino, Rocca di Montegrossi	461
Chianti Cl. Villa Cerna Ris., Famiglia Cecchi	439
Chianti Cl. Villa Maisano Quello, Montiverdi	459
Chianti Cl. Villa Maisano Questo, Montiverdi	459
Chianti Cl. Villa Maisano Ris., Montiverdi	459
Chianti Cl. Villa Maisano, Montiverdi	459
Chianti Cl. Villa Vistarenni, S. M. Tenimenti Pile e Lamole	459
Chianti Cl. Vitigliano, Villa Vignamaggio	467
Chianti Colli Aretini, Villa Cilnia	430
Chianti Colli Aretini Ris., Villa Cilnia	430
Chianti Colli Fiorentini, Fattoria Castelvecchio	572
Chianti Colli Fiorentini, Fattoria di Bagnolo	559
Chianti Colli Fiorentini, Fattoria di Fiano	554
Chianti Colli Fiorentini, Fattoria Lilliano	549
Chianti Colli Fiorentini, Tenuta La Cipressaia	567
Chianti Colli Fiorentini, Lanciola	469
Chianti Colli Fiorentini, Fattoria Le Sorgenti	431
Chianti Colli Fiorentini Il Cortile, Castello di Poppiano	508
Chianti Colli Fiorentini Il Trecione Ris., Le Calvane	507
Chianti Colli Fiorentini La Torretta, Fattoria Le Querce	559
Chianti Colli Fiorentini Quercione, Le Calvane	507
Chianti Colli Fiorentini Ris., Fattoria di Bagnolo	559
Chianti Colli Fiorentini Ris., Fattoria di Fiano	554
Chianti Colli Fiorentini Ris., Lanciola	469
Chianti Colli Fiorentini Ris., Castello di Poppiano	508
Chianti Colli Fiorentini Sorrettole, Fattoria Le Querce	559
Chianti Colli Senesi, Ca' del Vispo	532
Chianti Colli Senesi, Casa alle Vacche	533
Chianti Colli Senesi, Castelpugna	574
Chianti Colli Senesi, Fattoria del Cerro	499
Chianti Colli Senesi, Vincenzo Cesani	533
Chianti Colli Senesi, Fattorie Chigi Saracini	445
Chianti Colli Senesi, Ercolani	566
Chianti Colli Senesi, Farnetella	541
Chianti Colli Senesi, Il Palagione	555
Chianti Colli Senesi, Il Paradiso	535
Chianti Colli Senesi, La Lastra	535
Chianti Colli Senesi, Tenuta Le Calcinaie	536
Chianti Colli Senesi, Pacina	554
Chianti Colli Senesi, Palagetto	537
Chianti Colli Senesi, Giovanni Panizzi	538
Chianti Colli Senesi, Poggio Salvi	574
Chianti Colli Senesi, S. Giorgio a Lapi	574
Chianti Colli Senesi, Signano	539
Chianti Colli Senesi, F.lli Vagnoni	540
Chianti Colli Senesi, Villa Sant'Anna	506
Chianti Colli Senesi Cinabro, Casa alle Vacche	533
Chianti Colli Senesi Gioia, Carpineta Fontalpino	444
Chianti Colli Senesi Il Palagio, Fattoria Il Palagio	450
Chianti Colli Senesi Poggiarelli, Signano	539
Chianti Colli Senesi Sup. Vigna S. Domenico Sovestro, Baroncini	572
Chianti Colli Senesi Terra di Siena, Tenuta di Trecciano	575
Chianti Colli Senesi Titolato, Guicciardini Strozzi - Fattoria Cusona	534
Chianti Colli Senesi Tutulus, Ficomontanino	555
Chianti Colli Senesi Vertunno, Giovanni Panizzi	538
Chianti Colli Senesi Via dei Franchi, La Rampa di Fugnano	536
Chianti Colline Pisane, Tenuta di Ghizzano	516
Chianti Colline Senesi, Salcheto	504
Chianti Evento, Fattoria Villa La Selva	435
Chianti Gineprone, Tenuta Col d'Orcia	479
Chianti I Tre Borri, Fattoria Corzano e Paterno	529
Chianti Le Gaggiole Ris., Fassati	500
Chianti Le Stoppie, S. Gervasio	510
Chianti Montalbano, Fattoria di Bibbiani	436
Chianti Montalbano, Enrico Pierazzuoli	453
Chianti Montalbano Ris., Enrico Pierazzuoli	453
Chianti Montespertoli, Fattorie Parri	568
Chianti Montespertoli Petriccio, Poggio Capponi	568
Chianti Rio Camerata, Fattoria di Piazzano	555
Chianti Ris., Fattoria di Piazzano	555
Chianti Ris., Fattoria Villa La Selva	435
Chianti Rufina, Fattoria di Basciano	527
Chianti Rufina, Colognole	571
Chianti Rufina, Frascole	555
Chianti Rufina, Fattoria Lavacchio	570
Chianti Rufina, Fattoria Selvapiana	520
Chianti Rufina Bucerchiale Ris., Fattoria Selvapiana	520
Chianti Rufina Fornace Ris., Fattoria Selvapiana	520
Chianti Rufina Montesodi, Marchesi de' Frescobaldi	453
Chianti Rufina Nipozzano Ris., Marchesi de' Frescobaldi	453
Chianti Rufina Poggio Reale Ris., Tenute Folonari	452
Chianti Rufina Ris., Fattoria di Basciano	527
Chianti Rufina Ris., Fattoria Selvapiana	520
Chianti Rufina Ris., Tenuta di Bossi	570
Chianti Rufina Villa di Bossi Ris., Tenuta di Bossi	570

Entry	Page
Chianti Sodi del Paretaio, Badia di Morrona	548
Chianti Sup., Fattorie Chigi Saracini	445
Chianti Sup. Monterotondo, Castello di Monastero	446
Chianti Terre di Corzano, Fattoria Corzano e Paterno	529
Chianti Terre di Corzano Ris., Fattoria Corzano e Paterno	529
Chianti V. La Bigattiera Ris., Fattoria S. Maria di Ambra	434
Chianti Villa Petriolo, Fattoria di Petriolo	554
Chiaretto, Angelo Nicolis e Figli	303
Chiaro, Fattoria S. Fabiano - Borghini Baldovinetti	430
Ciapin Bianco, Claudio Rosso	66
Cicisbeo, Le Tende	281
Cicogio, Il Lebbio	534
Cign'Oro, Villa Cilnia	430
Cignale, Castello di Querceto	464
Cimbolo, Poggio Bertaio	611
Cinerino Bianco, Marziano e Enrico Abbona	69
Cinque Querce Rosso, Salvatore Molettieri	660
Cinque Terre, Walter De Battè	165
Cinque Terre, Forlini e Cappellini	168
Cinque Terre, La Pollenza	168
Cinque Terre Marea, Enoteca Bisson	159
Cinque Terre Sciacchetrà, Walter De Battè	165
Cinque Terre Sciacchetrà Ris., Walter De Battè	165
Circe, Hofkellerei	270
Circeo Rosso Il Sogno, C. di Sant'Andrea	638
Cirò Bianco, Caparra & Siciliani	694
Cirò Bianco, Librandi	695
Cirò Bianco, Fattoria S. Francesco	694
Cirò Bianco Curiale, Caparra & Siciliani	694
Cirò Rosato, Caparra & Siciliani	694
Cirò Rosato, Librandi	695
Cirò Rosato, Fattoria S. Francesco	694
Cirò Rosso Cl., Caparra & Siciliani	694
Cirò Rosso Cl. Donna Madda, Fattoria S. Francesco	694
Cirò Rosso Cl. Ronco dei Quattro Venti, Fattoria S. Francesco	694
Cirò Rosso Cl. Sup. Colli del Mancuso Ris., Vincenzo Ippolito	698
Cirò Rosso Cl. Sup. Donna Madda, Fattoria S. Francesco	694
Cirò Rosso Cl. Sup. Duca Sanfelice Ris., Librandi	695
Cirò Rosso Cl. Sup. Piana delle Fate Ris., C. Enotria	698
Cirò Rosso Cl. Sup. Ris., Caparra & Siciliani	694
Cirò Rosso Cl. Sup. Volvito, Caparra & Siciliani	694
Civitella Rosso, Tenuta Mottura	631
Clarae, Nicola Balter	230
Codirosso, S. M. Tenimenti Pile e Lamole	459
COF Bianco, Miani	336
COF Bianco Blanc di Buri, Davino Meroi	336
COF Bianco Canticum, Aquila del Torre	376
COF Bianco Canto, Alfieri Cantarutti	392
COF Bianco Illivio, Livio Felluga	348
COF Bianco La Clupa, Valchiarò	397
COF Bianco Le Roverelle Zuc di Volpe, Volpe Pasini	398
COF Bianco Liende, La Viarte	382
COF Bianco Lindi Uà, Jacuss	397
COF Bianco Locum Nostrum, Paolino Comelli	362
COF Bianco Nojâr, Bandut - Giorgio Colutta	369
COF Bianco Nonalinda, Livio Zorzettig	381
COF Bianco Petrussa, Petrussa	384
COF Bianco Ploe di Stelis, Il Roncal	400
COF Bianco Poanis Blanc, Olivo Buiatti	334
COF Bianco Pomédes, Scubla	381
COF Bianco Richenza, Vigna Petrussa	385
COF Bianco Ronco degli Agostiniani, Walter Filiputti	370
COF Bianco Ronco del Monastero, Walter Filiputti	370
COF Bianco Ronco delle Acacie, Le Vigne di Zamò	370
COF Bianco Sacrisassi, Le Due Terre	383
COF Bianco S. Justina, Iole Grillo	382
COF Bianco Speziale, Scubla	381
COF Bianco Spìule, Tenuta di Angoris	343
COF Bianco Vineis, Rocca Bernarda	380
COF Boscorosso, Rosa Bosco	369
COF Cabernet, Livio e Claudio Buiatti	334
COF Cabernet, Olivo Buiatti	334
COF Cabernet, Conte d'Attimis-Maniago	335
COF Cabernet, Le Vigne di Zamò	370
COF Cabernet, Petrussa	384
COF Cabernet, Ronco dei Pini	384
COF Cabernet, Leonardo Specogna	358
COF Cabernet, Teresa Raiz	377
COF Cabernet Franc, Iole Grillo	382
COF Cabernet Franc, Guerra Albano	402
COF Cabernet Franc, Valerio Marinig	383
COF Cabernet Franc, Petrucco	337
COF Cabernet Franc, Flavio Pontoni	399
COF Cabernet Franc, Torre Rosazza	372
COF Cabernet Franc, Vigna Petrussa	385
COF Cabernet Franc, Vigna Traverso	385
COF Cabernet Franc, Zof	359
COF Cabernet Franc, Livio Zorzettig	381
COF Cabernet Sauvignon, Bandut - Giorgio Colutta	369
COF Cabernet Sauvignon, Valentino Butussi	356
COF Cabernet Sauvignon, Paolino Comelli	362
COF Cabernet Sauvignon, Ronco delle Betulle	371
COF Cabernet Sauvignon, Scubla	381
COF Cabernet Sauvignon Ris., Valle	399
COF Cabernet Zuc di Volpe, Volpe Pasini	398
COF Chardonnay, Paolino Comelli	362
COF Chardonnay, Conte d'Attimis-Maniago	335
COF Chardonnay, Walter Filiputti	370
COF Chardonnay, Adriano Gigante	357
COF Chardonnay, La Viarte	382
COF Chardonnay, Valerio Marinig	383
COF Chardonnay, Petrucco	337
COF Chardonnay, Rocca Bernarda	380
COF Chardonnay, Il Roncal	400
COF Chardonnay, Ronchi di Manzano	371
COF Chardonnay, Ronco del Gnemiz	393
COF Chardonnay, Leonardo Specogna	358
COF Chardonnay, Torre Rosazza	372
COF Chardonnay, Vigna Traverso	385
COF Chardonnay, Vigne Fantin Noda'r	401
COF Chardonnay Casali Roncali, Cabert	333
COF Chardonnay Podere dei Blumeri, Schiopetto	339
COF Chardonnay Vign. Ronc di Juri, Girolamo Dorigo	335
COF Chardonnay Zuc di Volpe, Volpe Pasini	398
COF Gritul, Guerra Albano	402
COF Malvasia, Le Vigne di Zamò	370
COF Merlot, Bandut - Giorgio Colutta	369
COF Merlot, Livio e Claudio Buiatti	334
COF Merlot, Alfieri Cantarutti	392
COF Merlot, Paolino Comelli	362
COF Merlot, Conte d'Attimis-Maniago	335
COF Merlot, Dario e Luciano Ermacora	380
COF Merlot, Adriano Gigante	357
COF Merlot, Iole Grillo	382
COF Merlot, Jacuss	397
COF Merlot, Le Due Terre	383
COF Merlot, Miani	336
COF Merlot, Perusini	400
COF Merlot, Petrucco	337
COF Merlot, Flavio Pontoni	399
COF Merlot, Ronchi di Manzano	371
COF Merlot, Ronco dei Pini	384
COF Merlot, Ronco Severo	401
COF Merlot, Scubla	381
COF Merlot, Leonardo Specogna	358
COF Merlot, Torre Rosazza	372
COF Merlot, Valchiarò	397
COF Merlot, Vigna Traverso	385
COF Merlot, Vigne Fantin Noda'r	401
COF Merlot, Andrea Visintini	359
COF Merlot, Zof	359
COF Merlot, Livio Zorzettig	381
COF Merlot Canticum, Aquila del Torre	376
COF Merlot Casali Roncali, Cabert	333
COF Merlot Centis, Rocca Bernarda	380
COF Merlot Focus, Volpe Pasini	398
COF Merlot Il Barrique, Andrea Visintini	359
COF Merlot l'Altromerlot, Torre Rosazza	372
COF Merlot Ris., Adriano Gigante	357
COF Merlot Ronc di Subule, Ronchi di Manzano	371
COF Merlot Vocalis, Aquila del Torre	376
COF Picolit, Tenuta di Angoris	343
COF Picolit, Aquila del Torre	376
COF Picolit, Livio e Claudio Buiatti	334
COF Picolit, Valentino Butussi	356
COF Picolit, Conte d'Attimis-Maniago	335
COF Picolit, Walter Filiputti	370
COF Picolit, Adriano Gigante	357
COF Picolit, Iole Grillo	382
COF Picolit, Il Roncat - Giovanni Dri	401
COF Picolit, Jacuss	397
COF Picolit, Davino Meroi	336
COF Picolit, Davide Moschioni	342
COF Picolit, Perusini	400
COF Picolit, Flavio Pontoni	399
COF Picolit, Rocca Bernarda	380
COF Picolit, Paolo Rodaro	343
COF Picolit, Ronco Vieri	401
COF Picolit, Torre Rosazza	372
COF Picolit, Gestioni Agricole Vidussi	340
COF Picolit, Vigna Petrussa	385
COF Picolit, Zof	359
COF Picolit, Livio Zorzettig	381
COF Picolit I Principi, Fantinel	377
COF Picolit Romandus, Dario Coos	374
COF Picolit Vign. Montsclapade, Girolamo Dorigo	335
COF Pignolo, Davide Moschioni	342
COF Pinot Bianco, Livio e Claudio Buiatti	334
COF Pinot Bianco, Dario e Luciano Ermacora	380
COF Pinot Bianco, Jacuss	397
COF Pinot Bianco, La Viarte	382
COF Pinot Bianco, Valerio Marinig	383
COF Pinot Bianco, Perusini	400
COF Pinot Bianco, Petrussa	384
COF Pinot Bianco, Paolo Rodaro	343
COF Pinot Bianco, Ronco dei Pini	384
COF Pinot Bianco, Ronco delle Betulle	371
COF Pinot Bianco, Scubla	381
COF Pinot Bianco, Torre Rosazza	372
COF Pinot Bianco, Andrea Visintini	359

COF Pinot Bianco Ronco delle Magnolie, Torre Rosazza	372
COF Pinot Bianco Zuc di Volpe, Volpe Pasini	398
COF Pinot Grigio, Bandut - Giorgio Colutta	369
COF Pinot Grigio, Livio e Claudio Buiatti	334
COF Pinot Grigio, Olivo Buiatti	334
COF Pinot Grigio, Valentino Butussi	356
COF Pinot Grigio, Alfieri Cantarutti	392
COF Pinot Grigio, Paolino Comelli	362
COF Pinot Grigio, Conte d'Attimis-Maniago	335
COF Pinot Grigio, Dal Fari	399
COF Pinot Grigio, Dario e Luciano Ermacora	380
COF Pinot Grigio, Livio Felluga	348
COF Pinot Grigio, Adriano Gigante	357
COF Pinot Grigio, Iole Grillo	382
COF Pinot Grigio, La Viarte	382
COF Pinot Grigio, Perusini	400
COF Pinot Grigio, Petrucco	337
COF Pinot Grigio, Rocca Bernarda	380
COF Pinot Grigio, Paolo Rodaro	343
COF Pinot Grigio, Ronchi di Manzano	371
COF Pinot Grigio, Ronco del Gnemiz	393
COF Pinot Grigio, Ronco Severo	401
COF Pinot Grigio, Teresa Raiz	377
COF Pinot Grigio, Valchiarò	397
COF Pinot Grigio, Vigna Traverso	385
COF Pinot Grigio, Andrea Visintini	359
COF Pinot Grigio, Zof	359
COF Pinot Grigio, Livio Zorzettig	381
COF Pinot Grigio Podere dei Blumeri, Schiopetto	339
COF Pinot Grigio Podere di Ipplis, Ca' Ronesca	360
COF Pinot Grigio Podere Ronco Antico, Tenuta di Angoris	343
COF Pinot Grigio Zuc di Volpe, Volpe Pasini	398
COF Pinot Nero, Alfieri Cantarutti	392
COF Pinot Nero, Le Due Terre	383
COF Pinot Nero, Le Vigne di Zamò	370
COF Ramandolo, Dario Coos	374
COF Ramandolo, Ronco Vieri	401
COF Ramandolo Il Longhino, Dario Coos	374
COF Ramandolo Il Roncat, Il Roncat - Giovanni Dri	401
COF Ramandolo Passito Romandus, Dario Coos	374
COF Refosco, Il Roncat - Giovanni Dri	401
COF Refosco, Ronco Vieri	401
COF Refosco P. R., Bandut - Giorgio Colutta	369
COF Refosco P. R., Livio e Claudio Buiatti	334
COF Refosco P. R., Ca di Bon	400
COF Refosco P. R., Ca' Ronesca	360
COF Refosco P. R., Conte d'Attimis-Maniago	335
COF Refosco P. R., Livio Felluga	348
COF Refosco P. R., Adriano Gigante	357
COF Refosco P. R., Le Vigne di Zamò	370
COF Refosco P. R., Davide Moschioni	342
COF Refosco P. R., Petrucco	337
COF Refosco P. R., Leonardo Specogna	358
COF Refosco P. R., Torre Rosazza	372
COF Refosco P. R., Valchiarò	397
COF Refosco P. R., Vigna Traverso	385
COF Refosco P. R., Volpe Pasini	398
COF Refosco P.R., Livio Zorzettig	381
COF Refosco P. R. Podere Rocca Bernarda, Tenuta di Angoris	343
COF Refosco P. R. Vign. Montsclapade, Girolamo Dorigo	335
COF Refosco P. R. Zuc di Volpe, Volpe Pasini	398
COF Ribolla Gialla, Valentino Butussi	356
COF Ribolla Gialla, C. Prod. di Cormons	346
COF Ribolla Gialla, Walter Filiputti	370
COF Ribolla Gialla, La Viarte	382
COF Ribolla Gialla, Miani	336
COF Ribolla Gialla, Petrucco	337
COF Ribolla Gialla, Rocca Bernarda	380
COF Ribolla Gialla, Teresa Raiz	377
COF Ribolla Gialla, Torre Rosazza	372
COF Ribolla Gialla, Vigna Traverso	385
COF Ribolla Gialla, Andrea Visintini	359
COF Ribolla Gialla, Zof	359
COF Ribolla Gialla, Livio Zorzettig	381
COF Ribolla Gialla Podere Stabili della Rocca, Tenuta di Angoris	343
COF Ribolla Gialla Sel. S. Blas, Valle	399
COF Ribolla Gialla Turian, Eugenio Collavini	357
COF Ribolla Gialla Zuc di Volpe, Volpe Pasini	398
COF Rosazzo Bianco Ronc di Rosazzo, Ronchi di Manzano	371
COF Rosazzo Bianco Terre Alte, Livio Felluga	348
COF Rosazzo Narciso Bianco, Ronco delle Betulle	371
COF Rosazzo Narciso Rosso, Ronco delle Betulle	371
COF Rosazzo Picolit Ris., Livio Felluga	348
COF Rosazzo Picolit Ronc di Rosazzo, Ronchi di Manzano	371
COF Rosazzo Ribolla Gialla, Le Vigne di Zamò	370
COF Rosazzo Ribolla Gialla, Ronco delle Betulle	371
COF Rosazzo Rosso Ronc di Rosazzo, Ronchi di Manzano	371
COF Rosazzo Sossò Ris., Livio Felluga	348
COF Rosso, Miani	336
COF Rosso Carato, Alfieri Cantarutti	392
COF Rosso Celtico, Davide Moschioni	342
COF Rosso Civon, Il Roncal	400
COF Rosso d'Orsone, Dal Fari	399
COF Rosso Decano Rosso, Teresa Raiz	377
COF Rosso Dorigo, Girolamo Dorigo	335
COF Rosso Giudizio, Adriano Gigante	357
COF Rosso Lindi Uà, Jacuss	397
COF Rosso Moschioni, Davide Moschioni	342
COF Rosso Petrussa, Petrussa	384
COF Rosso Pignolo Ris., Walter Filiputti	370
COF Rosso Ronco dei Benedettini, Walter Filiputti	370
COF Rosso Ronco dei Domenicani, Walter Filiputti	370
COF Rosso Ronco dei Roseti, Le Vigne di Zamò	370
COF Rosso Ros di Buri, Davino Meroi	336
COF Rosso Sacrisassi, Le Due Terre	383
COF Rosso Scuro, Scubla	381
COF Rosso Selenard, Bandut - Giorgio Colutta	369
COF Rosso Soffumbergo, Paolino Comelli	362
COF Rosso Sottocastello Ris., Vigna Traverso	385
COF Sauvignon, Bandut - Giorgio Colutta	369
COF Sauvignon, Olivo Buiatti	334
COF Sauvignon, Livio e Claudio Buiatti	334
COF Sauvignon, Valentino Butussi	356
COF Sauvignon, Ca di Bon	400
COF Sauvignon, Alfieri Cantarutti	392
COF Sauvignon, Conte d'Attimis-Maniago	335
COF Sauvignon, Dal Fari	399
COF Sauvignon, Dario e Luciano Ermacora	380
COF Sauvignon, Livio Felluga	348
COF Sauvignon, Adriano Gigante	357
COF Sauvignon, Iole Grillo	382
COF Sauvignon, Jacuss	397
COF Sauvignon, La Viarte	382
COF Sauvignon, Le Vigne di Zamò	370
COF Sauvignon, Valerio Marinig	383
COF Sauvignon, Davino Meroi	336
COF Sauvignon, Miani	336
COF Sauvignon, Petrucco	337
COF Sauvignon, Petrussa	384
COF Sauvignon, Rocca Bernarda	380
COF Sauvignon, Paolo Rodaro	343
COF Sauvignon, Ronchi di Manzano	371
COF Sauvignon, Ronco del Gnemiz	393
COF Sauvignon, Ronco delle Betulle	371
COF Sauvignon, Ronco Severo	401
COF Sauvignon, Scubla	381
COF Sauvignon, Leonardo Specogna	358
COF Sauvignon, Teresa Raiz	377
COF Sauvignon, Torre Rosazza	372
COF Sauvignon, Valchiarò	397
COF Sauvignon, Vigna Petrussa	385
COF Sauvignon, Vigna Traverso	385
COF Sauvignon, Andrea Visintini	359
COF Sauvignon, Zof	359
COF Sauvignon, Livio Zorzettig	381
COF Sauvignon Blanc, Rosa Bosco	369
COF Sauvignon Bosc Romain, Paolo Rodaro	343
COF Sauvignon Casali Roncali, Cabert	333
COF Sauvignon L'Araldo, Valle	399
COF Sauvignon Podere dei Blumeri, Schiopetto	339
COF Sauvignon Podere di Ipplis, Ca' Ronesca	360
COF Sauvignon Ris., Ronco del Gnemiz	393
COF Sauvignon Ronc di Juri Vign. Montsclapade, Girolamo Dorigo	335
COF Sauvignon Silterra, Torre Rosazza	372
COF Sauvignon Suvignis, Walter Filiputti	370
COF Sauvignon Vign. Ronc di Juri, Girolamo Dorigo	335
COF Sauvignon Vocalis, Aquila del Torre	376
COF Sauvignon Zuc di Volpe, Volpe Pasini	398
COF Schioppettino, Ca di Bon	400
COF Schioppettino, Dal Fari	399
COF Schioppettino, Adriano Gigante	357
COF Schioppettino, Jacuss	397
COF Schioppettino, Davide Moschioni	342
COF Schioppettino, Petrussa	384
COF Schioppettino, Paolo Rodaro	343
COF Schioppettino, Ronco del Gnemiz	393
COF Schioppettino, Gestioni Agricole Vidussi	340
COF Schioppettino, Vigna Petrussa	385
COF Schioppettino, Vigna Traverso	385
COF Schioppettino, Zof	359
COF Tazzelenghe di Buttrio Vign. Ronc di Juri, Girolamo Dorigo	335
COF Tocai Friulano, Bandut - Giorgio Colutta	369
COF Tocai Friulano, Livio e Claudio Buiatti	334
COF Tocai Friulano, Olivo Buiatti	334
COF Tocai Friulano, Valentino Butussi	356
COF Tocai Friulano, Alfieri Cantarutti	392
COF Tocai Friulano, Paolino Comelli	362
COF Tocai Friulano, Dario e Luciano Ermacora	380
COF Tocai Friulano, Livio Felluga	348
COF Tocai Friulano, Adriano Gigante	357
COF Tocai Friulano, Iole Grillo	382
COF Tocai Friulano, La Viarte	382
COF Tocai Friulano, Le Vigne di Zamò	370
COF Tocai Friulano, Valerio Marinig	383
COF Tocai Friulano, Davino Meroi	336
COF Tocai Friulano, Miani	336
COF Tocai Friulano, Petrucco	337
COF Tocai Friulano, Petrussa	384

Entry	Page
COF Tocai Friulano, Rocca Bernarda	380
COF Tocai Friulano, Paolo Rodaro	343
COF Tocai Friulano, Il Roncal	400
COF Tocai Friulano, Ronco dei Pini	384
COF Tocai Friulano, Ronco delle Betulle	371
COF Tocai Friulano, Ronco Severo	401
COF Tocai Friulano, Scubla	381
COF Tocai Friulano, Leonardo Specogna	358
COF Tocai Friulano, Teresa Raiz	377
COF Tocai Friulano, Valchiarò	397
COF Tocai Friulano, Vigna Petrussa	385
COF Tocai Friulano, Vigna Traverso	385
COF Tocai Friulano, Vigne Fantin Noda'r	401
COF Tocai Friulano, Zof	359
COF Tocai Friulano, Livio Zorzettig	381
COF Tocai Friulano Plus, Bastianich	379
COF Tocai Friulano Storico, Adriano Gigante	357
COF Tocai Friulano Sup., Ronchi di Manzano	371
COF Tocai Friulano Vign. Montsclapade, Girolamo Dorigo	335
COF Tocai Friulano Vigne Cinquant'Anni, Le Vigne di Zamò	370
COF Tocai Friulano Zuc di Volpe, Volpe Pasini	398
COF Verduzzo Friulano, Bandut - Giorgio Colutta	369
COF Verduzzo Friulano, Livio e Claudio Buiatti	334
COF Verduzzo Friulano, Valentino Butussi	356
COF Verduzzo Friulano, Dario e Luciano Ermacora	380
COF Verduzzo Friulano, Adriano Gigante	357
COF Verduzzo Friulano, Guerra Albano	402
COF Verduzzo Friulano, Jacuss	397
COF Verduzzo Friulano, Valerio Marinig	383
COF Verduzzo Friulano, Paolo Rodaro	343
COF Verduzzo Friulano, Leonardo Specogna	358
COF Verduzzo Friulano, Torre Rosazza	372
COF Verduzzo Friulano, Vigne Fantin Noda'r	401
COF Verduzzo Friulano, Andrea Visintini	359
COF Verduzzo Friulano Casali Godia, Livon	393
COF Verduzzo Friulano Graticcio, Scubla	381
COF Verduzzo Friulano Pra Zenâr, Paolo Rodaro	343
COF Verduzzo Friulano Ronc di Rosazzo, Ronchi di Manzano	371
Col di Sasso, Banfi	474
Col Martin Luwa, Ascevi - Luwa	387
Collare Rosso, Tenuta Pernice	424
Collazzi, Fattoria Collazzi	559
Colle Amato, Colle S. Lorenzo	631
Colle Carpito, S. Luciano	493
Colle della Torre, Giovanni Palombo	628
Colle di Guardia, S. Savino	599
Colle Leone, Ca' del Vispo	532
Colle Malerbì, Villa Pigna	595
Colle Picchioni Rosso, Paola Di Mauro - Colle Picchioni	633
Collesanti, Marco Carpineti	637
Colli Berici Cabernet, Basso Graziano	325
Colli Berici Cabernet Capitel S. Libera, Domenico Cavazza & F.lli	287
Colli Berici Cabernet Casara Roveri, Vinicola Luigino Dal Maso	287
Colli Berici Cabernet Cicogna, Domenico Cavazza & F.lli	287
Colli Berici Cabernet Colle d'Elica, Natalino Mattiello	325
Colli Berici Cabernet Le Rive Rosse, Villa dal Ferro Lazzarini	299
Colli Berici Cabernet Polveriera, Piovene Porto Godi	322
Colli Berici Cabernet Ris., Villa dal Ferro Lazzarini	299
Colli Berici Cabernet Vigneto Pozzare, Piovene Porto Godi	322
Colli Berici Chardonnay Casara Roveri, Vinicola Luigino Dal Maso	287
Colli Berici Chardonnay Colle d'Elica, Natalino Mattiello	325
Colli Berici Garganega, Natalino Mattiello	325
Colli Berici Merlot Campo del Lago, Villa dal Ferro Lazzarini	299
Colli Berici Merlot Capitel S. Libera, Domenico Cavazza & F.lli	287
Colli Berici Merlot Casara Roveri, Vinicola Luigino Dal Maso	287
Colli Berici Merlot Cicogna, Domenico Cavazza & F.lli	287
Colli Berici Merlot Fra i Broli, Piovene Porto Godi	322
Colli Berici Pinot Bianco del Rocolo, Villa dal Ferro Lazzarini	299
Colli Berici Pinot Bianco Polveriera, Piovene Porto Godi	322
Colli Berici Sauvignon Capitel S. Libera, Domenico Cavazza & F.lli	287
Colli Berici Sauvignon Casara Roveri, Vinicola Luigino Dal Maso	287
Colli Berici Sauvignon Vigneto Fostine, Piovene Porto Godi	322
Colli Berici Tocai Rosso, Basso Graziano	325
Colli Berici Tocai Rosso, Domenico Cavazza & F.lli	287
Colli Berici Tocai Rosso Vigneto Riveselle, Piovene Porto Godi	322
Colli Bolognesi Barbera, Beghelli	425
Colli Bolognesi Barbera, Floriano Cinti	419
Colli Bolognesi Barbera, Gradizzolo Ognibene	414
Colli Bolognesi Barbera, Isola	413
Colli Bolognesi Barbera, Sandoni	425
Colli Bolognesi Barbera, Tizzano	406
Colli Bolognesi Barbera Frizzante, Gradizzolo Ognibene	414
Colli Bolognesi Barbera Il Foriere, La Mancina	427
Colli Bolognesi Barbera Ris., Gradizzolo Ognibene	414
Colli Bolognesi Cabernet Sauvignon, Beghelli	425
Colli Bolognesi Cabernet Sauvignon, Floriano Cinti	419
Colli Bolognesi Cabernet Sauvignon, Isola	413
Colli Bolognesi Cabernet Sauvignon, La Mancina	427
Colli Bolognesi Cabernet Sauvignon, S. Vito	427
Colli Bolognesi Cabernet Sauvignon, Tizzano	406
Colli Bolognesi Cabernet Sauvignon, Vallona	407
Colli Bolognesi Cabernet Sauvignon, Vigneto delle Terre Rosse	423
Colli Bolognesi Cabernet Sauvignon Bonzarone, Tenuta Bonzara	414
Colli Bolognesi Cabernet Sauvignon Cuvée, Vigneto delle Terre Rosse	423
Colli Bolognesi Cabernet Sauvignon Giòrosso, Santarosa	413
Colli Bolognesi Cabernet Sauvignon Ris., Tizzano	406
Colli Bolognesi Cabernet Sauvignon Sel., Vallona	407
Colli Bolognesi Chardonnay, Floriano Cinti	419
Colli Bolognesi Chardonnay, Isola	413
Colli Bolognesi Chardonnay, Sandoni	425
Colli Bolognesi Chardonnay, Santarosa	413
Colli Bolognesi Chardonnay, Vallona	407
Colli Bolognesi Chardonnay, Vigneto delle Terre Rosse	423
Colli Bolognesi Chardonnay Giòcoliere, Santarosa	413
Colli Bolognesi Chardonnay Lavinio, Maria Letizia Gaggioli Vigneto Bagazzana	423
Colli Bolognesi Chardonnay Sel., Isola	413
Colli Bolognesi Chardonnay Sel., Vallona	407
Colli Bolognesi Merlot, Floriano Cinti	419
Colli Bolognesi Merlot, Maria Letizia Gaggioli Vigneto Bagazzana	423
Colli Bolognesi Merlot, La Mancina	427
Colli Bolognesi Merlot Calastrino, Gradizzolo Ognibene	414
Colli Bolognesi Merlot Rocca di Bonacciara, Tenuta Bonzara	414
Colli Bolognesi Merlot Rosso del Poggio, Tenuta Bonzara	414
Colli Bolognesi Pignoletto, Tizzano	406
Colli Bolognesi Pignoletto, Vallona	407
Colli Bolognesi Pignoletto Brut, Tizzano	406
Colli Bolognesi Pignoletto Cl., Floriano Cinti	419
Colli Bolognesi Pignoletto Cl., Santarosa	413
Colli Bolognesi Pignoletto Cl. Vigna Antica, Tenuta Bonzara	414
Colli Bolognesi Pignoletto Frizzante, Floriano Cinti	419
Colli Bolognesi Pignoletto Frizzante, Maria Letizia Gaggioli Vigneto Bagazzana	423
Colli Bolognesi Pignoletto Frizzante, Gradizzolo Ognibene	414
Colli Bolognesi Pignoletto Frizzante, Isola	413
Colli Bolognesi Pignoletto Frizzante, S. Vito	427
Colli Bolognesi Pignoletto Frizzante, Tizzano	406
Colli Bolognesi Pignoletto Passito, Bonfiglio	427
Colli Bolognesi Pignoletto Sel., Vallona	407
Colli Bolognesi Pignoletto Sup., Bonfiglio	427
Colli Bolognesi Pignoletto Sup., Maria Letizia Gaggioli Vigneto Bagazzana	423
Colli Bolognesi Pignoletto Sup., Isola	413
Colli Bolognesi Pignoletto Sup. Prova d'Autore, Bonfiglio	427
Colli Bolognesi Pignoletto Vivace, Vallona	407
Colli Bolognesi Pinot Bianco, Floriano Cinti	419
Colli Bolognesi Pinot Bianco, Santarosa	413
Colli Bolognesi Pinot Bianco, Tizzano	406
Colli Bolognesi Pinot Bianco Borgo di Qua, Tenuta Bonzara	414
Colli Bolognesi Pinot Bianco Crilò, Maria Letizia Gaggioli Vigneto Bagazzana	423
Colli Bolognesi Riesling, Tizzano	406
Colli Bolognesi Sauvignon, Floriano Cinti	419
Colli Bolognesi Sauvignon, Sandoni	425
Colli Bolognesi Sauvignon, Tizzano	406
Colli Bolognesi Sauvignon, Vallona	407
Colli Bolognesi Sauvignon, Vigneto delle Terre Rosse	423
Colli Bolognesi Sauvignon Sup., Maria Letizia Gaggioli Vigneto Bagazzana	423
Colli Bolognesi Sauvignon Sup. Le Carrate, Tenuta Bonzara	414
Colli della Serra Rosso, Alberto Quacquarini	600
Colli di Conegliano Bianco, F.lli Bortolin Spumanti	313
Colli di Conegliano Bianco, Canevel Spumanti	314
Colli di Conegliano Bianco, Conte Collalto	312
Colli di Conegliano Bianco, Dal Din	330
Colli di Conegliano Bianco, Masottina	299
Colli di Conegliano Bianco, Scuola Enologica di Conegliano G. B. Cerletti	324
Colli di Conegliano Bianco Albio, Gregoletto	286
Colli di Conegliano Bianco Costa dei Falchi, Case Bianche	326
Colli di Conegliano Bianco Il Greccio, Bepin de Eto	300
Colli di Conegliano Bianco Ser Bele, Sorelle Bronca	322
Colli di Conegliano Rosso, Conte Collalto	312
Colli di Conegliano Rosso, Masottina	299
Colli di Conegliano Rosso Contrada di Concenigo, Bellenda	330
Colli di Conegliano Rosso Croda Ronca, Bepin de Eto	300
Colli di Conegliano Rosso Gregoletto, Gregoletto	286
Colli di Conegliano Rosso S.Alberto, Ruggeri & C.	317
Colli di Conegliano Rosso Ser Bele, Sorelle Bronca	322
Colli di Faenza Bianco Poderepalazzina, Leone Conti	410
Colli di Faenza Rebiano, Treré	411
Colli di Faenza Rosso Ca' di Berta, La Berta	405
Colli di Faenza Rosso Montecorallo, Treré	411
Colli di Faenza Rosso Podereviacupa Le Ghiande, Leone Conti	410
Colli di Faenza Sangiovese Renero, Treré	411
Colli di Imola Boldo, Tre Monti	412

Colli di Imola Cabernet Sauvignon Ca' Grande, Umberto Cesari	407
Colli di Imola Chardonnay Ciardo, Tre Monti	412
Colli di Imola Salcerella, Tre Monti	412
Colli di Luni Bianco, S. Caterina	166
Colli di Luni Bianco Giuncaro, S. Caterina	166
Colli di Luni Rosso, Il Torchio	158
Colli di Luni Rosso, S. Caterina	166
Colli di Luni Rosso Ghiaretolo, S. Caterina	166
Colli di Luni Rosso Maniero, Ottaviano Lambruschi	159
Colli di Luni Rosso Poggio dei Magni, Il Monticello	165
Colli di Luni Rosso Rupestro, Il Monticello	165
Colli di Luni Vermentino, Giacomelli	158
Colli di Luni Vermentino, Il Monticello	165
Colli di Luni Vermentino, Il Torchio	158
Colli di Luni Vermentino, La Pietra del Focolare	163
Colli di Luni Vermentino, Ottaviano Lambruschi	159
Colli di Luni Vermentino, 'R Mesueto	167
Colli di Luni Vermentino, S. Caterina	166
Colli di Luni Vermentino Costa Marina, Ottaviano Lambruschi	159
Colli di Luni Vermentino Fosso di Corsano, Podere Terenzuola	556
Colli di Luni Vermentino Podere Paterno, Il Monticello	165
Colli di Luni Vermentino Poggi Alti, S. Caterina	166
Colli di Luni Vermentino Santo Paterno, La Pietra del Focolare	163
Colli di Luni Vermentino Sarticola, Ottaviano Lambruschi	159
Colli di Luni Vermentino Solarancio, La Pietra del Focolare	163
Colli di Luni Vermentino Villa Linda, La Pietra del Focolare	163
Colli di Parma Malvasia, Cantine Dall'Asta	415
Colli di Parma Malvasia, Isidoro Lamoretti	426
Colli di Parma Malvasia Dolce Callas, Monte delle Vigne	425
Colli di Parma Malvasia Montefiore, Carra	415
Colli di Parma Rosso Conventino Campo delle Lepri Frizzante, Vigneti Calzetti	427
Colli di Parma Sauvignon, Cantine Dall'Asta	415
Colli di Parma Sauvignon Frizzante, Vigneti Calzetti	427
Colli di Parma Sauvignon Ris., Carra	415
Colli di Rimini Cabernet Sauvignon, Villa Pampini - F.lli Bernardi	428
Colli di Scandiano e di Canossa Altobrolo Sauvignon, Casali Viticultori	428
Colli di Scandiano e di Canossa Cabernet Sauvignon, Moro - Rinaldo Rinaldini	418
Colli di Scandiano e di Canossa Cabernet Sauvignon Ris., Moro - Rinaldo Rinaldini	418
Colli di Scandiano e di Canossa Casino dei Greppi Cabernet Sauvignon, Casali Viticultori	428
Colli di Scandiano e di Canossa Lambrusco Grasparossa Vecchio Moro, Moro - Rinaldo Rinaldini	418
Colli di Scandiano e di Canossa Malvasia Spumante M. Cl., Moro - Rinaldo Rinaldini	418
Colli Euganei Bianco, Ca' Lustra	275
Colli Euganei Bianco Vigna dei Mandorli, Borin	286
Colli Euganei BiancoTerre Bianche Beccaro Giuseppe, La Primavera	329
Colli Euganei Cabernet, Ca' Lustra	275
Colli Euganei Cabernet Borgo delle Casette Ris., Il Filò delle Vigne	272
Colli Euganei Cabernet Girapoggio, Ca' Lustra	275
Colli Euganei Cabernet Mons Silicis Ris., Borin	286
Colli Euganei Cabernet Sauvignon Mons Silicis Ris., Borin	286
Colli Euganei Cabernet Sauvignon Vigna Costa, Borin	286
Colli Euganei Cabernet Vigna Cecilia di Baone Ris., Il Filò delle Vigne	272
Colli Euganei Chardonnay, Vignalta	312
Colli Euganei Chardonnay Montecchia, La Montecchia	307
Colli Euganei Fior d'Arancio Passito, Borin	286
Colli Euganei Fior d'Arancio Spumante, Borin	286
Colli Euganei Merlot, Ca' Lustra	275
Colli Euganei Merlot Bandiera, La Montecchia	307
Colli Euganei Merlot Vigna del Foscolo, Borin	286
Colli Euganei Moscato Fior d'Arancio Alpianae, Vignalta	312
Colli Euganei Moscato Fior d'Arancio Passito, La Montecchia	307
Colli Euganei Pinot Bianco, Ca' Lustra	275
Colli Euganei Pinot Bianco, Il Filò delle Vigne	272
Colli Euganei Pinot Bianco, Vignalta	312
Colli Euganei Pinot Bianco Agno Casto, Vignalta	312
Colli Euganei Pinot Bianco La Primavera, La Primavera	329
Colli Euganei Pinot Bianco Vigneto Archino, Borin	286
Colli Euganei Rosso, Ca' Lustra	275
Colli Euganei Rosso, La Montecchia	307
Colli Euganei Rosso, Vignalta	312
Colli Euganei Rosso Gemola, Vignalta	312
Colli Euganei Rosso Montecchia, La Montecchia	307
Colli Euganei Spumante Fior d'Arancio, Ca' Lustra	275
Colli Lanuvini Sup., Camponeschi	638
Colli Maceratesi Bianco, Azzoni Avogadro Carradori	605
Colli Maceratesi Bianco Castru Vecchiu, Saputi	604
Colli Maceratesi Bianco Monteferro, Fattoria di Forano	579
Colli Maceratesi Bianco Villa Forano, Fattoria di Forano	579
Colli Martani Grechetto, Agricola Adanti	608
Colli Martani Grechetto, Antonelli - S. Marco	614
Colli Martani Grechetto Grecante, Arnaldo Caprai - Val di Maggio	614
Colli Martani Grechetto Vigna Tonda, Antonelli - S. Marco	614
Colli Martani Sangiovese Properzio, Di Filippo	609
Colli Martani Sangiovese Properzio Ris., Di Filippo	609
Colli Martani Sangiovese Rubro, Todini	626
Colli Martani Sangiovese Satiro, Rocca di Fabbri	615
Colli Perugini Bianco Torre del Pino, Gisberto Goretti	622
Colli Perugini Chardonnay, Gisberto Goretti	622
Colli Perugini Rosato, Franca Chiorri	621
Colli Perugini Rosso, Franca Chiorri	621
Colli Perugini Rosso L'Arringatore, Gisberto Goretti	622
Colli Pesaresi Bianco Roncaglia, Fattoria Mancini	596
Colli Pesaresi Rosso Focara, Fattoria Mancini	596
Colli Pesaresi Rosso La Vigna delle Terrazze, Claudio Morelli	586
Colli Pesaresi Rosso Luigi Fiorini, Valentino Fiorini	581
Colli Piacentini Bonarda Frizzante, Podere Casale	428
Colli Piacentini Bonarda Frizzante, Cantine Romagnoli	428
Colli Piacentini Bonarda Frizzante, Torre Fornello	422
Colli Piacentini Cabernet Sauvignon Ca' Bernesca, Torre Fornello	422
Colli Piacentini Cabernet Sauvignon Castello di Rivalta, C. Soc. Valtidone	424
Colli Piacentini Cabernet Sauvignon Corbeau, Luretta	420
Colli Piacentini Cabernet Sauvignon Il Villante, Gaetano Lusenti	422
Colli Piacentini Cabernet Sauvignon Luna Selvatica, La Tosa	421
Colli Piacentini Cabernet Sauvignon Perticato del Novarei, Il Poggiarello	420
Colli Piacentini Cabernet Sauvignon Stoppa, La Stoppa	417
Colli Piacentini Chardonnay La Jara, Torre Fornello	422
Colli Piacentini Chardonnay Perticato La Piana, Il Poggiarello	420
Colli Piacentini Chardonnay Selin dl'Armari, Luretta	420
Colli Piacentini Gutturnio, La Tosa	421
Colli Piacentini Gutturnio, Gaetano Lusenti	422
Colli Piacentini Gutturnio, Cantine Romagnoli	428
Colli Piacentini Gutturnio Cl. Nicchio, Cardinali	424
Colli Piacentini Gutturnio Cl. Torquato Ris., Cardinali	424
Colli Piacentini Gutturnio Diacono Gerardo 1028 Ris., Torre Fornello	422
Colli Piacentini Gutturnio Diacono Gerardo Ris., Torre Fornello	422
Colli Piacentini Gutturnio Frizzante, Conte Otto Barattieri di S. Pietro	421
Colli Piacentini Gutturnio Frizzante, La Stoppa	417
Colli Piacentini Gutturnio Frizzante, Podere Casale	428
Colli Piacentini Gutturnio La Barbona Ris., Il Poggiarello	420
Colli Piacentini Gutturnio Perticato Valandrea, Il Poggiarello	420
Colli Piacentini Gutturnio Sel., Conte Otto Barattieri di S. Pietro	421
Colli Piacentini Gutturnio Sup. Riva al Sole, Gaetano Lusenti	422
Colli Piacentini Gutturnio Sup. Sinsäl, Torre Fornello	422
Colli Piacentini Gutturnio Sup. Vigna dei Cotorni, Campominosi	428
Colli Piacentini Gutturnio Vigna del Castello Ris., Podere Casale	428
Colli Piacentini Gutturnio Vignamorello, La Tosa	421
Colli Piacentini Malvasia Boccadirosa, Luretta	420
Colli Piacentini Malvasia di Case Piccioni, Gaetano Lusenti	422
Colli Piacentini Malvasia Donna Luigia, Torre Fornello	422
Colli Piacentini Malvasia Passito Vigna del Volta, La Stoppa	417
Colli Piacentini Malvasia Sorriso di Cielo, La Tosa	421
Colli Piacentini Malvasia V. T. Le Rane, Luretta	420
Colli Piacentini Ortrugo, Conte Otto Barattieri di S. Pietro	421
Colli Piacentini Ortrugo Frizzante, Tenuta Pernice	424
Colli Piacentini Ortrugo Frizzante Armonia, C. Soc. Valtidone	424
Colli Piacentini Pinot Grigio Frizzante, Gaetano Lusenti	422
Colli Piacentini Pinot Nero Perticato Le Giastre, Il Poggiarello	420
Colli Piacentini Pinot Nero Spumante Rosé, Gaetano Lusenti	422
Colli Piacentini Sauvignon, La Tosa	421
Colli Piacentini Sauvignon Ca' del Rio, Torre Fornello	422
Colli Piacentini Sauvignon I Nani e Le Ballerine, Luretta	420
Colli Piacentini Sauvignon Perticato Il Quadri, Il Poggiarello	420
Colli Piacentini Valnure Frizzante, Campominosi	428
Colli Piacentini Valnure Frizzante, La Tosa	421
Colli Piacentini Vin Santo Albarola, Conte Otto Barattieri di S. Pietro	421
Colli Piacentini Vin Santo di Vigoleno, Alberto Lusignani	428
Colli Tortonesi Barbera, Paolo Poggio	144
Colli Tortonesi Barbera Boccanera, Luigi Boveri	64
Colli Tortonesi Barbera Derio, Paolo Poggio	144
Colli Tortonesi Barbera Poggio delle Amarene, Luigi Boveri	64
Colli Tortonesi Barbera Sup. Amaranto, Cascina Montagnola	142
Colli Tortonesi Barbera Sup. Rodeo, Cascina Montagnola	142
Colli Tortonesi Barbera Vignalunga, Luigi Boveri	64
Colli Tortonesi Bianco Filari di Timorasso, Luigi Boveri	64
Colli Tortonesi Bianco La Vetta, Terralba	42
Colli Tortonesi Bianco Martin, Franco M. Martinetti	135
Colli Tortonesi Bianco Profilo, Claudio Mariotto	154
Colli Tortonesi Bianco Sull'Aia, Mutti	128

Colli Tortonesi Bianco Timorasso, Paolo Poggio	144	Collio Chardonnay, Fiegl	366
Colli Tortonesi Bianco Timorasso Castagnoli, Mutti	128	Collio Chardonnay, Gradis'ciutta	389
Colli Tortonesi Bigolla, Vigneti Massa	105	Collio Chardonnay, Marcello e Marino Humar	389
Colli Tortonesi Brillo, La Colombera	154	Collio Chardonnay, Il Carpino	390
Colli Tortonesi Cerreta, Vigneti Massa	105	Collio Chardonnay, La Boatina	349
Colli Tortonesi Cortese Casareggio, Vigneti Massa	105	Collio Chardonnay, La Castellada	366
Colli Tortonesi Cortese Vigna del Prete, Luigi Boveri	64	Collio Chardonnay, La Rajade	400
Colli Tortonesi Costa del Vento Timorasso, Vigneti Massa	105	Collio Chardonnay, Livon	393
Colli Tortonesi Monleale, Vigneti Massa	105	Collio Chardonnay, Muzic	390
Colli Tortonesi Pertichetta Croatina, Vigneti Massa	105	Collio Chardonnay, Isidoro Polencic	351
Colli Tortonesi Pietra del Gallo Freisa, Vigneti Massa	105	Collio Chardonnay, Roncada	352
Colli Tortonesi Rosso Monleale, Terralba	42	Collio Chardonnay, Ronco dei Pini	384
Colli Tortonesi Rosso Montegrande, Terralba	42	Collio Chardonnay, Matijaz Tercic	391
Colli Tortonesi Rosso Rivadestra, Mutti	128	Collio Chardonnay, Tiare - Roberto Snidarcig	355
Colli Tortonesi Rosso S. Ruffino, Mutti	128	Collio Chardonnay, Franco Toros	355
Colli Tortonesi Rosso Strà Loja, Terralba	42	Collio Chardonnay, Gestioni Agricole Vidussi	340
Colli Tortonesi Rosso Terralba, Terralba	42	Collio Chardonnay Braide Mate, Livon	393
Colli Tortonesi Vegia Rampana, La Colombera	154	Collio Chardonnay Colle Russian, Borgo Conventi	363
Collina del Milanese Verdea La Tonsa, Enrico Riccardi	213	Collio Chardonnay dei Sassi Cavi Collezione Privata,	
Colline del Milanese Banino, Antonio Panigada - Banino	212	Eugenio Collavini	357
Colline Lucchesi Bianco Giallo dei Muri, Tenuta di Valgiano	436	Collio Chardonnay Gmajne, Primosic	367
Colline Lucchesi Chardonnay, Terre del Sillabo	470	Collio Chardonnay Gräfin de La Tour, Villa Russiz	340
Colline Lucchesi Rosso Brania delle Ghiandaie,		Collio Chardonnay Luwa, Ascevi - Luwa	387
Fattoria Colle Verde	199	Collio Chardonnay Monte Cucco, Tenuta Villanova	364
Colline Lucchesi Rosso dei Palistorti, Tenuta di Valgiano	436	Collio Chardonnay P, Puiatti	338
Colline Lucchesi Rosso Scasso dei Cesari,		Collio Chardonnay Ronc dal Luis, Maurizio Buzzinelli	345
Tenuta di Valgiano	436	Collio Chardonnay Ronco Bernizza, Venica & Venica	361
Colline Lucchesi Sauvignon, Terre del Sillabo	470	Collio Chardonnay Sant'Helena, Fantinel	377
Colline Novaresi Agamium, Antichi Vigneti di Cantalupo	80	Collio Chardonnay Sel., Borgo del Tiglio	344
Colline Novaresi Bianco, Rovellotti	81	Collio Chardonnay Sel., Subida di Monte	354
Colline Novaresi Nebbiolo, Dessilani	73	Collio Chardonnay Torre di Tramontana, Conti Formentini	388
Colline Novaresi Nebbiolo Tre Confini,		Collio Chardonnay Vigna Runc, Il Carpino	390
Torraccia del Piantavigna	149	Collio Malvasia, Ca' Ronesca	360
Colline Novaresi Rosso, Rovellotti	81	Collio Malvasia, Paolo Caccese	346
Colline Savonesi Passito, La Vecchia C.	157	Collio Malvasia, Il Carpino	390
Collio Bianco, Attems Conte Douglas	365	Collio Malvasia, Roberto Picech - Le Vigne del Ribél	350
Collio Bianco, Borgo del Tiglio	344	Collio Malvasia, Dario Raccaro	352
Collio Bianco, C. Prod. di Cormons	346	Collio Malvasia, Gestioni Agricole Vidussi	340
Collio Bianco, Colle Duga	347	Collio Malvasia, Andrea Visintini	359
Collio Bianco, Crastin	360	Collio Malvasia Istriana, Villa Russiz	340
Collio Bianco, Evangelos Paraschos	402	Collio Malvasia Istriana Frututis Ronc dal Luis,	
Collio Bianco, Edi Keber	349	Maurizio Buzzinelli	345
Collio Bianco, Damijan Podversic	367	Collio Malvasia Sel., Borgo del Tiglio	344
Collio Bianco, Isidoro Polencic	351	Collio Merlot, Carlo di Pradis	347
Collio Bianco, Dario Raccaro	352	Collio Merlot, Colle Duga	347
Collio Bianco, Oscar Sturm	354	Collio Merlot, Crastin	360
Collio Bianco, Franco Terpin	391	Collio Merlot, Marco Felluga	368
Collio Bianco, Vigna del Lauro	356	Collio Merlot, Fiegl	366
Collio Bianco Bric, Muzic	390	Collio Merlot, Marcello e Marino Humar	389
Collio Bianco Caprizzi di Marceline, La Rajade	400	Collio Merlot, Edi Keber	349
Collio Bianco Carpino, Il Carpino	390	Collio Merlot, La Boatina	349
Collio Bianco del Bratinis, Gradis'ciutta	389	Collio Merlot, Alessandro Princic	351
Collio Bianco del Tùzz, Gradis'ciutta	389	Collio Merlot, Dario Raccaro	352
Collio Bianco della Castellada, La Castellada	366	Collio Merlot, Radikon	401
Collio Bianco Fosarin, Ronco dei Tassi	353	Collio Merlot, Roncada	352
Collio Bianco Frututis Ronc dal Luis, Maurizio Buzzinelli	345	Collio Merlot, Russiz Superiore	339
Collio Bianco Jelka, Roberto Picech - Le Vigne del Ribél	350	Collio Merlot, Oscar Sturm	354
Collio Bianco Marnà, Ca' Ronesca	360	Collio Merlot, Matijaz Tercic	391
Collio Bianco Molamatta, Marco Felluga	368	Collio Merlot, Franco Toros	355
Collio Bianco Planta, Matijaz Tercic	391	Collio Merlot, Villa Russiz	340
Collio Bianco Pradis, Carlo di Pradis	347	Collio Merlot Collezione Privata, Eugenio Collavini	357
Collio Bianco Ris., Evangelos Paraschos	402	Collio Merlot degli Ulivi, Ferdinando e Aldo Polencic	350
Collio Bianco Ronchi Ravéz, Gestioni Agricole Vidussi	340	Collio Merlot Graf de La Tour, Villa Russiz	340
Collio Bianco Ronco della Chiesa, Borgo del Tiglio	344	Collio Merlot P Blanchis, Puiatti	338
Collio Bianco Russiz Disòre, Russiz Superiore	339	Collio Merlot Perilla, Venica & Venica	361
Collio Bianco S. Caterina, Fantinel	377	Collio Merlot Sel., Subida di Monte	354
Collio Bianco Sotrari, Subida di Monte	354	Collio Merlot Sel., Franco Toros	355
Collio Bianco Tre Vignis, Venica & Venica	361	Collio Merlot Tajut, Conti Formentini	388
Collio Bianco Trilogy, Fantinel	377	Collio Müller Thurgau, Maurizio Buzzinelli	345
Collio Cabernet Collezione Privata, Eugenio Collavini	357	Collio Müller Thurgau, Paolo Caccese	346
Collio Cabernet Franc, Ca' Ronesca	360	Collio Müller Thurgau, Roncada	352
Collio Cabernet Franc, Crastin	360	Collio Picolit Ris., Primosic	367
Collio Cabernet Franc, Gradis'ciutta	389	Collio Pinot Bianco, Borgo Lotessa	338
Collio Cabernet Franc, Russiz Superiore	339	Collio Pinot Bianco, Paolo Caccese	346
Collio Cabernet Franc, Tenuta Villanova	364	Collio Pinot Bianco, C. Prod. di Cormons	346
Collio Cabernet Franc, Tiare - Roberto Snidarcig	355	Collio Pinot Bianco, Casa Zuliani	401
Collio Cabernet Franc S. Caterina, Fantinel	377	Collio Pinot Bianco, Castello di Spessa	337
Collio Cabernet Sauvignon, Muzic	390	Collio Pinot Bianco, Marcello e Marino Humar	389
Collio Cabernet Sauvignon, Roncada	352	Collio Pinot Bianco, La Boatina	349
Collio Cabernet Sauvignon Blanchis Vittorio Puiatti, Puiatti	338	Collio Pinot Bianco, Livon	393
Collio Cabernet Sauvignon Monte Cucco, Tenuta Villanova	364	Collio Pinot Bianco, Mangilli	402
Collio Cabernet Sauvignon Roncalto, Livon	393	Collio Pinot Bianco, Roberto Picech - Le Vigne del Ribél	350
Collio Cabernet Sauvignon Stratin, La Rajade	400	Collio Pinot Bianco, F.lli Pighin	375
Collio Cabernet Sauvignon Vittorio Puiatti, Puiatti	338	Collio Pinot Bianco, Isidoro Polencic	351
Collio Chardonnay, Borgo Conventi	363	Collio Pinot Bianco, Alessandro Princic	351
Collio Chardonnay, Borgo del Tiglio	344	Collio Pinot Bianco, Roncada	352
Collio Chardonnay, Borgo Lotessa	338	Collio Pinot Bianco, Russiz Superiore	339
Collio Chardonnay, Branko - Igor Erzetich	345	Collio Pinot Bianco, Schiopetto	339
Collio Chardonnay, Maurizio Buzzinelli	345	Collio Pinot Bianco, Tenuta Villanova	364
Collio Chardonnay, Ca' Ronesca	360	Collio Pinot Bianco, Franco Toros	355
Collio Chardonnay, C. Prod. di Cormons	346	Collio Pinot Bianco, Venica & Venica	361
Collio Chardonnay, Casa Zuliani	401	Collio Pinot Bianco, Villa Russiz	340
Collio Chardonnay, Colle Duga	347	Collio Pinot Bianco Amrità, Schiopetto	339
Collio Chardonnay, Colmello di Grotta	363	Collio Pinot Bianco Ascevi, Ascevi - Luwa	387
Collio Chardonnay, Evangelos Paraschos	402	Collio Pinot Bianco degli Ulivi,	
Collio Chardonnay, Marco Felluga	368	Ferdinando e Aldo Polencic	350

Entry	Page
Collio Pinot Bianco di Santarosa, Castello di Spessa	337
Collio Pinot Bianco Vittorio Puiatti, Puiatti	338
Collio Pinot Grigio, Attems Conte Douglas	365
Collio Pinot Grigio, Borgo Conventi	363
Collio Pinot Grigio, Borgo Lotessa	338
Collio Pinot Grigio, Branko - Igor Erzetich	345
Collio Pinot Grigio, Maurizio Buzzinelli	345
Collio Pinot Grigio, Paolo Caccese	346
Collio Pinot Grigio, C. Prod. di Cormons	346
Collio Pinot Grigio, Carlo di Pradis	347
Collio Pinot Grigio, Casa Zuliani	401
Collio Pinot Grigio, Castello di Spessa	337
Collio Pinot Grigio, Colmello di Grotta	363
Collio Pinot Grigio, Conti Formentini	388
Collio Pinot Grigio, Crastin	360
Collio Pinot Grigio, Evangelos Paraschos	402
Collio Pinot Grigio, Marco Felluga	368
Collio Pinot Grigio, Fiegl	366
Collio Pinot Grigio, Gradis'ciutta	389
Collio Pinot Grigio, Marcello e Marino Humar	389
Collio Pinot Grigio, La Boatina	349
Collio Pinot Grigio, Muzic	390
Collio Pinot Grigio, F.lli Pighin	375
Collio Pinot Grigio, Isidoro Polencic	351
Collio Pinot Grigio, Ferdinando e Aldo Polencic	350
Collio Pinot Grigio, Alessandro Princic	351
Collio Pinot Grigio, Roncada	352
Collio Pinot Grigio, Ronco dei Pini	384
Collio Pinot Grigio, Ronco dei Tassi	353
Collio Pinot Grigio, Russiz Superiore	339
Collio Pinot Grigio, Schiopetto	339
Collio Pinot Grigio, Oscar Sturm	354
Collio Pinot Grigio, Subida di Monte	354
Collio Pinot Grigio, Tenuta Villanova	364
Collio Pinot Grigio, Matijaz Tercic	391
Collio Pinot Grigio, Franco Terpin	391
Collio Pinot Grigio, Tiare - Roberto Snidarcig	355
Collio Pinot Grigio, Franco Toros	355
Collio Pinot Grigio, Venica & Venica	361
Collio Pinot Grigio, Gestioni Agricole Vidussi	340
Collio Pinot Grigio, Vigna del Lauro	356
Collio Pinot Grigio, Villa Russiz	340
Collio Pinot Grigio Ascevi, Ascevi - Luwa	387
Collio Pinot Grigio Braide Grande, Livon	393
Collio Pinot Grigio Collezione Privata, Eugenio Collavini	357
Collio Pinot Grigio Gmajne, Primosic	367
Collio Pinot Grigio Sant'Helena, Fantinel	377
Collio Pinot Grigio Vigna Runc, Il Carpino	390
Collio Pinot Grigio Vittorio Puiatti, Puiatti	338
Collio Pinot Nero, Marcello e Marino Humar	389
Collio Pinot Nero, Stanislao Mavric	400
Collio Pinot Nero Casanova, Castello di Spessa	337
Collio Pinot Nero Torre di Borea, Conti Formentini	388
Collio Prime Note, Venica & Venica	361
Collio Ribolla Gialla, Attems Conte Douglas	365
Collio Ribolla Gialla, Castello di Spessa	337
Collio Ribolla Gialla, Marco Felluga	368
Collio Ribolla Gialla, Fiegl	366
Collio Ribolla Gialla, Gradis'ciutta	389
Collio Ribolla Gialla, Il Carpino	390
Collio Ribolla Gialla, La Boatina	349
Collio Ribolla Gialla, La Castellada	366
Collio Ribolla Gialla, Muzic	390
Collio Ribolla Gialla, Radikon	401
Collio Ribolla Gialla, Roncada	352
Collio Ribolla Gialla, Matijaz Tercic	391
Collio Ribolla Gialla, Tiare - Roberto Snidarcig	355
Collio Ribolla Gialla, Venica & Venica	361
Collio Ribolla Gialla, Gestioni Agricole Vidussi	340
Collio Ribolla Gialla, Villa Russiz	340
Collio Ribolla Gialla Ascevi, Ascevi - Luwa	387
Collio Ribolla Gialla Gmajne, Primosic	367
Collio Ribolla Gialla Luwa, Ascevi - Luwa	387
Collio Ribolla Gialla Roncalto, Livon	393
Collio Ribolla Gialla Ronco Cucco, Tenuta Villanova	364
Collio Ribolla Vittorio Puiatti, Puiatti	338
Collio Riesling, Paolo Caccese	346
Collio Riesling, Villa Russiz	340
Collio Rosso, Edi Keber	349
Collio Rosso, Roberto Picech - Le Vigne del Ribél	350
Collio Rosso, Damijan Podversic	367
Collio Rosso, Franco Terpin	391
Collio Rosso Cjarandon, Ronco dei Tassi	353
Collio Rosso Conte di Spessa, Castello di Spessa	337
Collio Rosso Crastin Rosso, Crastin	360
Collio Rosso della Castellada, La Castellada	366
Collio Rosso della Centa, Borgo del Tiglio	344
Collio Rosso Frututis Ronc dal Luis, Maurizio Buzzinelli	345
Collio Rosso Metamorfosis, Primosic	367
Collio Rosso Pelicans, Attems Conte Douglas	365
Collio Rosso Picol Maggiore, La Boatina	349
Collio Rosso Poncaia, Subida di Monte	354
Collio Rosso Ris., Borgo del Tiglio	344
Collio Rosso Ris., Roberto Picech - Le Vigne del Ribél	350
Collio Rosso Ris., Primosic	367
Collio Rosso Ris. degli Orzoni, Russiz Superiore	339
Collio Rosso Torriani, Castello di Spessa	337
Collio Rosso Vinko, Stanislao Mavric	400
Collio Sauvignon, Attems Conte Douglas	365
Collio Sauvignon, Borgo Conventi	363
Collio Sauvignon, Borgo Lotessa	338
Collio Sauvignon, Branko - Igor Erzetich	345
Collio Sauvignon, Ca' Ronesca	360
Collio Sauvignon, Paolo Caccese	346
Collio Sauvignon, C. Prod. di Cormons	346
Collio Sauvignon, Castello di Spessa	337
Collio Sauvignon, Colmello di Grotta	363
Collio Sauvignon, Conti Formentini	388
Collio Sauvignon, Crastin	360
Collio Sauvignon, Mauro Drius	348
Collio Sauvignon, Marco Felluga	368
Collio Sauvignon, Fiegl	366
Collio Sauvignon, Gradis'ciutta	389
Collio Sauvignon, Il Carpino	390
Collio Sauvignon, La Boatina	349
Collio Sauvignon, La Castellada	366
Collio Sauvignon, La Rajade	400
Collio Sauvignon, Mangilli	402
Collio Sauvignon, Stanislao Mavric	400
Collio Sauvignon, Muzic	390
Collio Sauvignon, F.lli Pighin	375
Collio Sauvignon, Isidoro Polencic	351
Collio Sauvignon, Ferdinando e Aldo Polencic	350
Collio Sauvignon, Alessandro Princic	351
Collio Sauvignon, Roncada	352
Collio Sauvignon, Ronco dei Pini	384
Collio Sauvignon, Ronco dei Tassi	353
Collio Sauvignon, Russiz Superiore	339
Collio Sauvignon, Schiopetto	339
Collio Sauvignon, Oscar Sturm	354
Collio Sauvignon, Subida di Monte	354
Collio Sauvignon, Matijaz Tercic	391
Collio Sauvignon, Franco Terpin	391
Collio Sauvignon, Tiare - Roberto Snidarcig	355
Collio Sauvignon, Franco Toros	355
Collio Sauvignon, Gestioni Agricole Vidussi	340
Collio Sauvignon, Vigna del Lauro	356
Collio Sauvignon, Villa Russiz	340
Collio Sauvignon Archetipi, Puiatti	338
Collio Sauvignon Ascevi, Ascevi - Luwa	387
Collio Sauvignon de La Tour, Villa Russiz	340
Collio Sauvignon Gmajne, Primosic	367
Collio Sauvignon Luwa, Ascevi - Luwa	387
Collio Sauvignon P, Puiatti	338
Collio Sauvignon Poncanera Collezione Privata, Eugenio Collavini	357
Collio Sauvignon Ronco Cucco, Tenuta Villanova	364
Collio Sauvignon Ronco dei Sassi, Ascevi - Luwa	387
Collio Sauvignon Ronco del Cerò, Venica & Venica	361
Collio Sauvignon Ronco delle Mele, Venica & Venica	361
Collio Sauvignon Sant'Helena, Fantinel	377
Collio Sauvignon Segrè, Castello di Spessa	337
Collio Sauvignon Tarsia, Schiopetto	339
Collio Sauvignon Vigna Runc, Il Carpino	390
Collio Studio di Bianco, Borgo del Tiglio	344
Collio Tocai Crôs Altis, Alessandro Princic	351
Collio Tocai Friulano, Borgo Conventi	363
Collio Tocai Friulano, Borgo del Tiglio	344
Collio Tocai Friulano, Branko - Igor Erzetich	345
Collio Tocai Friulano, Ca' Ronesca	360
Collio Tocai Friulano, Paolo Caccese	346
Collio Tocai Friulano, C. Prod. di Cormons	346
Collio Tocai Friulano, Carlo di Pradis	347
Collio Tocai Friulano, Castello di Spessa	337
Collio Tocai Friulano, Colle Duga	347
Collio Tocai Friulano, Colmello di Grotta	363
Collio Tocai Friulano, Crastin	360
Collio Tocai Friulano, Mauro Drius	348
Collio Tocai Friulano, Marco Felluga	368
Collio Tocai Friulano, Fiegl	366
Collio Tocai Friulano, Gradis'ciutta	389
Collio Tocai Friulano, Marcello e Marino Humar	389
Collio Tocai Friulano, Edi Keber	349
Collio Tocai Friulano, La Boatina	349
Collio Tocai Friulano, Magnàs	400
Collio Tocai Friulano, Stanislao Mavric	400
Collio Tocai Friulano, Muzic	390
Collio Tocai Friulano, Roberto Picech - Le Vigne del Ribél	350
Collio Tocai Friulano, Ferdinando e Aldo Polencic	350
Collio Tocai Friulano, Isidoro Polencic	351
Collio Tocai Friulano, Alessandro Princic	351
Collio Tocai Friulano, Dario Raccaro	352
Collio Tocai Friulano, Ronco dei Tassi	353
Collio Tocai Friulano, Roncùs	338
Collio Tocai Friulano, Russiz Superiore	339
Collio Tocai Friulano, Schiopetto	339
Collio Tocai Friulano, Oscar Sturm	354
Collio Tocai Friulano, Subida di Monte	354
Collio Tocai Friulano, Franco Toros	355
Collio Tocai Friulano, Vigna del Lauro	356
Collio Tocai Friulano, Villa Russiz	340
Collio Tocai Friulano, Andrea Visintini	359

Entry	Page
Collio Tocai Friulano Ascevi, Ascevi - Luwa	387
Collio Tocai Friulano Collezione Privata, Eugenio Collavini	357
Collio Tocai Friulano Croce Alta, Gestioni Agricole Vidussi	340
Collio Tocai Friulano Pardes, Schiopetto	339
Collio Tocai Friulano Ronc di Zorz, Livon	393
Collio Tocai Friulano Ronco delle Cime, Venica & Venica	361
Collio Tocai Friulano Sel., Subida di Monte	354
Collio Tocai Ronco della Chiesa, Borgo del Tiglio	344
Collio Traminer Aromatico, Paolo Caccese	346
Collio Traminer Aromatico, Marcello e Marino Humar	389
Colonnara Spumante Brut M. Cl. Millesimato, Colonnara Viticultori in Cupramontana	585
Coltassala, Castello di Volpaia	525
Coltifredi, Castelli del Grevepesa	528
Colvecchio Syrah, Banfi	474
Come La Pantera e I Lupi nella Sera, Luretta	420
Cometa, Planeta	714
Comprino Mirosa Ris., Montelio	181
Comprino Rosso, Montelio	181
Comprino Rosso Legno, Montelio	181
Comtess, C. Prod. S. Michele Appiano	242
Con Vento, Castello del Terriccio	442
Congius, Vignole	569
Coniale, Castellare di Castellina	439
Conte Bolani Rosso Gianni Zonin Vineyards, Ca' Bolani	341
Conte della Vipera, Castello della Sala	612
Contessa Emburga, Cantine Lento	696
Contessa Entellina Chardonnay La Fuga, Tenuta di Donnafugata	705
Contessa Entellina Chiarandà del Merlo, Tenuta di Donnafugata	705
Contessa Entellina Vigna di Gabri, Tenuta di Donnafugata	705
Controguerra Cabernet Sauvignon Villa Torri, Barone Cornacchia	652
Controguerra Chardonnay Cenalba, Dino Illuminati	642
Controguerra Ciafré, Dino Illuminati	642
Controguerra Costalupo, Dino Illuminati	642
Controguerra Fauno, Camillo Montori	642
Controguerra Leneo d'Oro, Camillo Montori	642
Controguerra Leneo Moro, Camillo Montori	642
Controguerra Lumen, Dino Illuminati	642
Controguerra Nicò, Dino Illuminati	642
Convivio, Fattoria Valtellina	557
Copertino Rosso Ris., C. Soc. Coop. Copertino	690
Coppo Brut Ris., Luigi Coppo e Figli	52
Corbaia, Castello di Bossi	444
Corbezzolo, Podere La Cappella	546
Cori Rosso, C. Coop. di Cincinnato	637
Cori Rosso Costa Vecchia, Colle S. Lorenzo	631
Corindone Rosso, Alessandro Secchi	216
Corriga, Valle del Quirra	732
Cortaccio, Villa Cafaggio	516
Corte Agnella Corvina Veronese, Giuseppe Campagnola	282
Corte Cariano Rosso, Luigi Brunelli	302
Cortese dell'Alto M.to Ciarea, Cantine Sant'Agata	128
Cortesia di Casale Marchese, Casale Marchese	632
Cortigiano, Fattoria Lavacchio	570
Cortinie Bianco, Peter Zemmer - Kupelwieser	258
Cortinie Rosso, Peter Zemmer - Kupelwieser	258
Corvara Rosso, Armani	276
Corvo Bianco, Duca di Salaparuta - Vini Corvo	702
Corvo Colomba Platino, Duca di Salaparuta - Vini Corvo	702
Corvo Glicine, Duca di Salaparuta - Vini Corvo	702
Corvo Rosso, Duca di Salaparuta - Vini Corvo	702
Costa d'Amalfi Furore Bianco, Cantine Gran Furor Divina Costiera	657
Costa d'Amalfi Furore Bianco Fiord'uva, Cantine Gran Furor Divina Costiera	657
Costa d'Amalfi Furore Rosso, Cantine Gran Furor Divina Costiera	657
Costa d'Amalfi Furore Rosso Ris., Cantine Gran Furor Divina Costiera	657
Costa d'Amalfi Ravello Bianco, Cantine Gran Furor Divina Costiera	657
Costa d'Amalfi Ravello Bianco Selva delle Monache, Ettore Sammarco	668
Costa d'Amalfi Ravello Rosso Selva delle Monache Ris., Ettore Sammarco	668
Costa di Giulia, Michele Satta	438
Coste del Roccolo, Anteo	197
Coste della Sesia Bianco La Doranda, Sella	92
Coste della Sesia Nebbiolo Juvenia, Antoniolo	75
Coste della Sesia Rosso, Nervi	75
Coste della Sesia Rosso Orbello, Sella	92
Coste della Sesia Rosso Piccone, Sella	92
Coste della Sesia Torrearsa, Barni	44
Coteau Barrage, Lo Triolet - Marco Martin	18
Crevole, La Borsa	569
Critone, Librandi	695
Crognolo, Tenuta Sette Ponti	547
Crueter, Ca' del Vispo	532
Cubia, Cusumano	710
Cummerse Rosato, C. Coop. del Locorotondo	684
Cummerse Rosso, C. Coop. del Locorotondo	684
Cuveé Extra Brut, Pojer & Sandri	219
Cuvée Imperiale Brut, Guido Berlucchi & C.	183
Cuvée Imperiale Brut Extrême, Guido Berlucchi & C.	183
Cuvée Imperiale Max Rosé, Guido Berlucchi & C.	183
Cuvée Imperiale Pas Dosé, Guido Berlucchi & C.	183
Cuvée Jus Osculi, Loacker Schwarzhof	248
Cuvée Storica Spumante M. Cl., Orsolani	124
Cuvée Storica Spumante M. Cl. Gran Ris., Orsolani	124
Cygnus, Tasca d'Almerita	715
D'Istinto Catarratto-Chardonnay, Calatrasi - Terre di Ginestra	709
D'Istinto Magnifico, Calatrasi - Terre di Ginestra	709
D'Istinto Nero, Calatrasi - Terre di Ginestra	709
D'Istinto Sangiovese-Merlot, Calatrasi - Terre di Ginestra	709
D'Istinto Syrah, Calatrasi - Terre di Ginestra	709
D'Ovidio, S. Luciano	493
Dagala Bianco, Tamburello	717
Dagala Rosso, Tamburello	717
Dalle Terre di Herea Bianco, Vitivinicola Avide	713
Dalle Terre di Herea Rosso, Vitivinicola Avide	713
Damaggio, Poderi dal Nespoli	408
Daniello, Tenuta di Trecciano	575
De Ferrari, Boscarelli	498
De Luca Rosso, S. Lorenzo	625
Decugnano dei Barbi Brut M. Cl., Decugnano dei Barbi	617
Dedicato, Aziende Vinicole Miceli	710
Degorà Cabernet Sauvignon, Carlo Bogoni	288
Delia Nivolelli Cabernet Sauvignon, Carlo Pellegrino	706
Delius, C. del Taburno	655
Delizia del Conte, Barone La Lumia	704
Desiderio, Avignonesi	497
Dettori Bianco, Tenute Dettori	727
Dettori Rosso, Tenute Dettori	727
Dezio Vigneto Beccaccia, Fattoria Dezi	601
Di Gale, Villa Frattina	378
Di Giorgio Bianco, Il Torchio	158
Diano d'Alba, Bricco Maiolica	69
Diano d'Alba Cascina Flino Vigna Vecchia, Cascina Flino	147
Diano d'Alba Cascinotto, Terre del Barolo	60
Diano d'Alba Costa Fiore, Claudio Alario	68
Diano d'Alba Montagrillo, Claudio Alario	68
Diano d'Alba Montagrillo, Terre del Barolo	60
Diano d'Alba Rizieri, Ricchino - Tiziana Menegaldo	147
Diano d'Alba Sorba, Massimo Oddero	147
Diano d'Alba Sörì Bricco Maiolica, Bricco Maiolica	69
Diano d'Alba Sörì Bricco Maiolica, Poderi Sinaglio	27
Diano d'Alba Vigna La Lepre, Fontanafredda	129
Dindarello, Maculan	274
Dioniso Rosso, S. Seraffa	148
Ditirambo, Marco Carpineti	637
Divino, Spadafora	711
Divo, Borgo Canale	680
Do Ut Des, Carpineta Fontalpino	444
Docetto d'Alba, Damilano	37
Dogajolo, Carpineto	463
Dogoli Bianco, Guerrieri Rizzardi	272
Doi Raps, Russolo	395
Dolce Valle Moscato Passito, Tenute Soletta	730
Dolcetto d'Acqui, Ca' Bianca	28
Dolcetto d'Acqui Argusto, Vigne Regali	133
Dolcetto d'Acqui Bric Maioli, Villa Sparina	80
Dolcetto d'Acqui d'Giusep, Villa Sparina	80
Dolcetto d'Acqui L'Ardì, Vigne Regali	133
Dolcetto d'Acqui La Cresta, Cascina Bertolotto	132
Dolcetto d'Acqui La Muiètte, Cascina Bertolotto	132
Dolcetto d'Acqui La Selva di Moirano, Scarpa - Antica Casa Vinicola	117
Dolcetto d'Acqui Marchesa, Marenco	133
Dolcetto d'Alba, Gianfranco Alessandria	97
Dolcetto d'Alba, F.lli Alessandria	138
Dolcetto d'Alba, Elio Altare - Cascina Nuova	82
Dolcetto d'Alba, Cascina Bongiovanni	57
Dolcetto d'Alba, Giacomo Borgogno & Figli	36
Dolcetto d'Alba, C. del Pino	29
Dolcetto d'Alba, Aldo Conterno	98
Dolcetto d'Alba, Giovanni Corino	85
Dolcetto d'Alba, Destefanis	108
Dolcetto d'Alba, Giacomo Grimaldi	144
Dolcetto d'Alba, Gianluigi Lano	25
Dolcetto d'Alba, Ugo Lequio	114
Dolcetto d'Alba, Giovanni Manzone	102
Dolcetto d'Alba, Monfalletto - Cordero di Montezemolo	87
Dolcetto d'Alba, Cascina Morassino	144
Dolcetto d'Alba, F.lli Mossio	123
Dolcetto d'Alba, Fiorenzo Nada	136
Dolcetto d'Alba, Andrea Oberto	88
Dolcetto d'Alba, F.lli Oddero	88
Dolcetto d'Alba, Vignaioli Elvio Pertinace	137
Dolcetto d'Alba, Luigi Pira	131
Dolcetto d'Alba, Prunotto	26
Dolcetto d'Alba, F.lli Revello	89
Dolcetto d'Alba, Podere Ruggeri Corsini	150
Dolcetto d'Alba, Luciano Sandrone	39
Dolcetto d'Alba, Giorgio Scarzello e Figli	40
Dolcetto d'Alba, Paolo Scavino	59
Dolcetto d'Alba, G. D. Vajra	41
Dolcetto d'Alba, Cascina Vano	115
Dolcetto d'Alba, Rino Varaldo	35
Dolcetto d'Alba, Mauro Veglio	149

Voce	Pag.
Dolcetto d'Alba Augenta, Pelissero	137
Dolcetto d'Alba Barturot, Ca' Viola	107
Dolcetto d'Alba Bordini, Fontanabianca	112
Dolcetto d'Alba Boschetti, Marchesi di Barolo	37
Dolcetto d'Alba Boschi di Berri, Poderi Marcarini	86
Dolcetto d'Alba Bric del Salto, Sottimano	115
Dolcetto d'Alba Bric Trifùla, Cascina Luisin	32
Dolcetto d'Alba Bricco, Giuseppe Mascarello e Figlio	96
Dolcetto d'Alba Bricco Bastia, Conterno Fantino	100
Dolcetto d'Alba Bricco Caramelli, F.lli Mossio	123
Dolcetto d'Alba Bricco dell'Oriolo, Azelia	57
Dolcetto d'Alba Bricco di Vergne, Batasiolo	83
Dolcetto d'Alba Bricco Peso, Degiorgis	95
Dolcetto d'Alba Brusalino, Cascina Fonda	95
Dolcetto d'Alba Bussia, F.lli Barale	144
Dolcetto d'Alba Bussia, Cascina Ballarin	84
Dolcetto d'Alba Campot, Castello di Verduno	139
Dolcetto d'Alba Cascina Francia, Giacomo Conterno	99
Dolcetto d'Alba Colombè, Renato Ratti	89
Dolcetto d'Alba Coste & Fossati, G. D. Vajra	41
Dolcetto d'Alba Cottà, Sottimano	115
Dolcetto d'Alba Cuchet, Carlo Giacosa	31
Dolcetto d'Alba Dabbene, Gianfranco Bovio	84
Dolcetto d'Alba Galletto, Osvaldo Viberti	149
Dolcetto d'Alba Gavarini Vigna dei Grassi, Elio Grasso	101
Dolcetto d'Alba Ginestra, Paolo Conterno	99
Dolcetto d'Alba La Pria, R. Voerzio	92
Dolcetto d'Alba La Serra, Giovanni Rosso	153
Dolcetto d'Alba Le Passere, Terre del Barolo	60
Dolcetto d'Alba Lodoli, Ca' del Baio	135
Dolcetto d'Alba Madonna di Como, Silvano e Elena Boroli	24
Dolcetto d'Alba Madonna di Como, F.lli Giacosa	113
Dolcetto d'Alba Meriane, Gabutti - Franco Boasso	130
Dolcetto d'Alba Monrobiolo e Ruè, Bartolo Mascarello	38
Dolcetto d'Alba Monte Aribaldo, Tenute Cisa Asinari dei Marchesi di Gresy	30
Dolcetto d'Alba Moriolo, Gastaldi	112
Dolcetto d'Alba Munfrina, Pelissero	137
Dolcetto d'Alba Nicolini, Montaribaldi	33
Dolcetto d'Alba Piani Noci, Armando Parusso	103
Dolcetto d'Alba Piano delli Perdoni, F.lli Mossio	123
Dolcetto d'Alba Raviole, Terre del Barolo	60
Dolcetto d'Alba Rocchettevino, Gianni Voerzio	91
Dolcetto d'Alba Ronchella, Gianluigi Lano	25
Dolcetto d'Alba Rubis, Rocche Costamagna	90
Dolcetto d'Alba S. Anna, Ferdinando Principiano	103
Dolcetto d'Alba S. Lorenzo, Giacomo Brezza & Figli	36
Dolcetto d'Alba S. Rocco, Ascheri	44
Dolcetto d'Alba S. Stefano di Perno, Giuseppe Mascarello e Figlio	96
Dolcetto d'Alba Sant'Anna, Vietti	60
Dolcetto d'Alba Serra dei Fiori, Braida	122
Dolcetto d'Alba Serraboella, F.lli Cigliuti	111
Dolcetto d'Alba Solatio, F.lli Brovia	58
Dolcetto d'Alba Sörì Baudana, Luigi Baudana	129
Dolcetto d'Alba Sorì Paitin, Paitin	114
Dolcetto d'Alba Sup., F.lli Mossio	123
Dolcetto d'Alba Sup., Flavio Roddolo	104
Dolcetto d'Alba Sup. Moriolo, Gastaldi	112
Dolcetto d'Alba Tigli Neri, Enzo Boglietti	83
Dolcetto d'Alba Trifolera, Giuseppe Cortese	30
Dolcetto d'Alba Vigna Buschin, Viticoltori Associati di Rodello	152
Dolcetto d'Alba Vigna Campasso, Viticoltori Associati di Rodello	152
Dolcetto d'Alba Vigna del Mandorlo, Elvio Cogno	118
Dolcetto d'Alba Vigna Deserto, Viticoltori Associati di Rodello	152
Dolcetto d'Alba Vigna Fornaci, Pira	71
Dolcetto d'Alba Vigna La Volta, Tenuta La Volta - Cabutto	40
Dolcetto d'Alba Vigna Majano, Piero Busso	111
Dolcetto d'Alba Vigna Melera, F.lli Cavallotto	59
Dolcetto d'Alba Vigna Monia Bassa, Destefanis	108
Dolcetto d'Alba Vigna Nirane, Ascheri	44
Dolcetto d'Alba Vigna Scot, F.lli Cavallotto	59
Dolcetto d'Alba Vigna Trifolé, Bruno Rocca	35
Dolcetto d'Alba Vignalunga, Albino Rocca	34
Dolcetto d'Alba Vigneti Ca' d'Gal, Ca' d'Gal	126
Dolcetto d'Alba Vigneto Castellizzano, Vignaioli Elvio Pertinace	137
Dolcetto d'Alba Vigneto della Chiesa, F.lli Seghesio	105
Dolcetto d'Alba Vigneto Lorenzino, Ettore Germano	130
Dolcetto d'Alba Vigneto Neirane, G. B. Burlotto	139
Dolcetto d'Alba Vigneto Nervo, Vignaioli Elvio Pertinace	137
Dolcetto d'Alba Vigneto Pra di Pò, Ettore Germano	130
Dolcetto d'Alba Vigneto S. Francesco, Andrea Oberto	88
Dolcetto d'Alba Vigneto Vantrino Albarella, Andrea Oberto	88
Dolcetto d'Alba Vilot, Ca' Viola	107
Dolcetto d'Asti Vigna Impagnato, E. e A. Brema	81
Dolcetto d'Ovada, La Smilla	43
Dolcetto d'Ovada Nsè Pesa, La Smilla	43
Dolcetto delle Langhe Monregalesi Il Colombo, Il Colombo - Barone Riccati	97
Dolcetto delle Langhe Monregalesi Sup. Monteregale, Il Colombo - Barone Riccati	97
Dolcetto delle Langhe Monregalesi Vigna della Chiesetta, Il Colombo - Barone Riccati	97
Dolcetto di Dogliani, Bricco del Cucù	42
Dolcetto di Dogliani, S. Romano	72
Dolcetto di Dogliani Autin Lungh, Eraldo Portale	148
Dolcetto di Dogliani Briccolero, Quinto Chionetti & Figlio	70
Dolcetto di Dogliani Cursalet, Giovanni Battista Gillardi	74
Dolcetto di Dogliani I Filari, Poderi Luigi Einaudi	70
Dolcetto di Dogliani Maioli, Anna Maria Abbona	73
Dolcetto di Dogliani Monetti, Ribote	148
Dolcetto di Dogliani Papà Celso, Marziano e Enrico Abbona	69
Dolcetto di Dogliani Puncin, Osvaldo Barberis	147
Dolcetto di Dogliani Ribote, Ribote	148
Dolcetto di Dogliani S. Fereolo, S. Fereolo	72
Dolcetto di Dogliani S. Luigi, Quinto Chionetti & Figlio	70
Dolcetto di Dogliani S. Luigi, F.lli Pecchenino	71
Dolcetto di Dogliani S. Matteo, Eraldo Portale	148
Dolcetto di Dogliani Sirì d'Jermu, F.lli Pecchenino	71
Dolcetto di Dogliani Sorì dij But, Anna Maria Abbona	73
Dolcetto di Dogliani Sup. 1593, S. Fereolo	72
Dolcetto di Dogliani Sup. Bricco Botti, F.lli Pecchenino	71
Dolcetto di Dogliani Sup. Bricco S. Bernardo, Bricco del Cucù	42
Dolcetto di Dogliani Sup. Dolianum, S. Romano	72
Dolcetto di Dogliani Sup. Maioli, Anna Maria Abbona	73
Dolcetto di Dogliani Vigna Bricco dei Botti, Pira	71
Dolcetto di Dogliani Vigna dei Prey, Boschis	147
Dolcetto di Dogliani Vigna del Pilone, S. Romano	72
Dolcetto di Dogliani Vigna Landes, Pira	71
Dolcetto di Dogliani Vigna Sorì S. Martino, Boschis	147
Dolcetto di Dogliani Vigna Tecc, Poderi Luigi Einaudi	70
Dolcetto di Dogliani Vigneto Maestra, Giovanni Battista Gillardi	74
Dolcetto di Dogliani Vigneto Muntâ, Marziano e Enrico Abbona	69
Dolcetto di Ovada, Il Rocchin	148
Dolcetto di Ovada, Cascina La Maddalena	121
Dolcetto di Ovada Bricco del Bagatto, Cascina La Maddalena	121
Dolcetto di Ovada Sup. Drac Rosso, Domenico Ghio	144
Dolcetto di Ovada Sup. Il Gamondino, La Guardia	109
Dolcetto di Ovada Sup. Vigneto Bricco Riccardo, La Guardia	109
Dolcetto di Ovada Sup. Villa Delfini, La Guardia	109
Dolcetto di Ovada Vigna Oriali, Verrina	152
Dolcetto Tormento, Ca' del Gé	190
Dolicante, Cantine di Dolianova	722
Dolmen, C. Soc. Gallura	729
Dominin, Davino Meroi	336
Don Antonio, Morgante	703
Don Carlos Brut M. Cl., Villa S. Michele	668
Don Ludovico Pinot Nero, Carlozadra	189
Don Neli Bianco, Baglio S. Vincenzo	717
Don Neli Rosso, Baglio S. Vincenzo	717
Don Pietro Rosso, Spadafora	711
Don Totò, Barone La Lumia	704
Donna Angela, S. Cassella	606
Donna Aurelia Chardonnay, Luigi Vivacqua	698
Donna Nunzia Moscato Giallo, Carlozadra	189
Donnaluna Aglianico, Viticoltori De Conciliis	661
Donnaluna Fiano, Viticoltori De Conciliis	661
Dopoteatro, Salicutti	490
Dorado, Graf Pfeil Weingut Kränzel	256
Dorato, Gioacchino Garofoli	588
Dorigo Brut, Girolamo Dorigo	335
Dragonero, Marco Maci	679
Duca d'Aragona, Francesco Candido	687
Duca Enrico, Duca di Salaparuta - Vini Corvo	702
Due Cuori Passito, Le Vigne di S. Pietro	311
Due Uve, Bertani	292
Dulcamara, I Giusti e Zanza	451
Dulcis Vitis, Tenuta Le Quinte	638
Dule, Giuseppe Gabbas	725
Ea, Podere Sopra la Ripa	542
Ebrius, Valle del Sole	560
Ecclesia Marche Chardonnay, La Monacesca	589
Eden Passito, Carra	415
Edys, Maso Bastie	238
El Calié Moscato, Borgo Maragliano	93
El Clap, Valchiarò	397
El Filò, Pravis	222
Elba Bianco, Cecilia	559
Elba Rosso Ris., Acquabona	570
Elba Rosso Ris., Cecilia	559
Elba Rosso Thea, Sapereta	570
Elegia, Poliziano	503
Eleusi Passito, Villa Matilde	655
Elfo 10, Ca' del Bosco	185
Elibaria, Attilio Contini	721
Elisa Rosso, La Colombera	154
Élite, Institut Agricole Régional	16
Eloise Bianco, Bianchi	153
Enantio, C. Soc. di Avio	216
Enantio, Concilio	235
Entemari, Pala	728

Erbaluce di Caluso, Antoniolo	75		Fianesco, Fattoria di Fiano	554
Erbaluce di Caluso, Cieck	23		Fiano di Avellino, Cantine Caputo	664
Erbaluce di Caluso Calliope, Cieck	23		Fiano di Avellino, Colli di Lapio - Clelia Romano	667
Erbaluce di Caluso Cariola Etichetta Nera, Ferrando	82		Fiano di Avellino, Colli Irpini - Montesolae	659
Erbaluce di Caluso Cariola Etichetta Verde, Ferrando	82		Fiano di Avellino, De Falco Vini	668
Erbaluce di Caluso Cella Grande, La Cella di S. Michele	154		Fiano di Avellino, Feudi di S. Gregorio	663
Erbaluce di Caluso La Rustìa, Orsolani	124		Fiano di Avellino Béchar, Antonio Caggiano	664
Erbaluce di Caluso Spumante Brut Calliope, Cieck	23		Fiano di Avellino Campo Re, Terredora di Paolo	660
Erbaluce di Caluso Spumante S. Giorgio Brut, Cieck	23		Fiano di Avellino Colle dei Cerri, Di Meo	668
Erbaluce di Caluso Vigna delle Chiusure, Favaro	152		Fiano di Avellino More Maiorum, Mastroberardino	654
Erbaluce di Caluso Vigna Misobolo, Cieck	23		Fiano di Avellino Pietracalda V. T., Feudi di S. Gregorio	663
Eretico Pigato, Maria Donata Bianchi	160		Fiano di Avellino Terre di Dora, Terredora di Paolo	660
Eretico Vermentino, Maria Donata Bianchi	160		Fiano Valentina, Francesco Rotolo	668
Erta e China, Fattoria di Basciano	527		Ficaia, Fattoria Uccelliera	451
Esegesi, Eugenio Rosi	238		Fidenzio, Podere S. Luigi	517
Esino Bianco Ferrante,			Filare Bianco Vigna Ronchetto, Edi Gandin	402
Belisario C. Soc. di Matelica e Cerreto d'Esi	589		Filieri Rosso, C. Soc. Dorgali	723
Esino Rosso Colferraio,			Filtrato Dolce di Malvasia, Gaetano Lusenti	422
Belisario C. Soc. di Matelica e Cerreto d'Esi	589		Finibusterre Antica Masseria Torre Mozza, Pervini	685
Esino Rosso, Monteschiavo	588		FiorDesAri Rosso, Valditerra	152
Essenza Moscato, Degiorgis	95		Fiore, Castello di Meleto	458
Essenzia Vendemmia Tardiva, Pojer & Sandri	219		Fiore, S. Valentino	427
Est Est Est di Montefiascone, Italo Mazziotti	629		Fiore di Villagrande, Barone di Villagrande	708
Est Est Est di Montefiascone, Trappolini	630		Fiorile, Aurora	605
Est Est Est di Montefiascone Canuleio, Italo Mazziotti	629		Five Roses, Leone de Castris	687
Est Est Est di Montefiascone Falesco, Falesco	634		Five Roses Anniversario, Leone de Castris	687
Est Est Est di Montefiascone Filò, Italo Mazziotti	629		Flaccianello della Pieve, Tenuta Fontodi	512
Est Est Est di Montefiascone Poggio dei Gelsi, Falesco	634		Flocco, Poggio a Poppiano	508
Est Est Est di Montefiascone Vendemmia Tardiva, Falesco	634		Fobiano, La Carraia	618
Etna Bianco, Barone di Villagrande	708		Focoso, Monte Morioni	571
Etna Bianco Bianco di Caselle, Benanti	703		Foja Tonda Rosso, Armani	276
Etna Bianco Sup. Pietramarina, Benanti	703		Fojaneghe Rosso, Conti Bossi Fedrigotti	237
Etna Rosso, Casa Vinicola Firriato	709		Fontalloro, Fattoria di Felsina	446
Etna Rosso, Barone di Villagrande	708		Fontanabianca, Cantine Torrevecchia	700
Etna Rosso Rovittello, Benanti	703		Fontanella Bianco, Gisberto Goretti	622
Etrusco, Cennatoio	511		Fontanella Rosso, Gisberto Goretti	622
Euforius, Josef Niedermayr	244		Fontenova, Tenuta Roccaccia	518
Excelsus, Banfi	474		Fontestina, Elyane & Bruno Moos	576
Extra Brut M. Cl., Il Calepino	177		Fontissimo, Fattoria Le Fonti	513
Fabrizio Bianchi Chardonnay, Castello di Monsanto	432		For Duke, Gino Fuso Carmignani	494
Fabula, Petricci del Pianta	575		Foresco, Barberani - Vallesanta	616
Facetus, Fontanavecchia - Orazio Rillo	665		Formulae, Barone Ricasoli	456
Falanghina d'Irpinia, Terredora di Paolo	660		Fort'Yrah, Fattoria del Buonamico	494
Falanghina del Beneventano, Colli Irpini - Montesolae	659		Fortana dell'Emilia, Cantine Dall'Asta	415
Falanghina di Roccamonfina,			Forti Terre di Sicilia Cabernet Sauvignon, C. Soc. di Trapani	714
Telaro - Coop. Lavoro e Salute	657		Forti Terre di Sicilia Chardonnay, C. Soc. di Trapani	714
Falanghina Passita Ruscolo, C. del Taburno	655		Forti Terre di Sicilia Il Rosso, C. Soc. di Trapani	714
Falanghina Villa dei Marchi, Michele Moio	659		Forti Terre di Sicilia Nero d'Avola, C. Soc. di Trapani	714
Falconaro, Cantine di Dolianova	722		Fossa Bandita, Letrari	230
Falerio dei Colli Ascolani, C. Coop. Castignanese	603		Fraja, Tenuta Villanova	364
Falerio dei Colli Ascolani, Ciù Ciù	594		Franciacorta 30 anni di Doc, F.lli Berlucchi	182
Falerio dei Colli Ascolani, Tenuta Cocci Grifoni	597		Franciacorta Ante Omnia Satèn, Majolini	195
Falerio dei Colli Ascolani, Rio Maggio	591		Franciacorta Brut, Al Rocol	210
Falerio dei Colli Ascolani, Saladini Pilastri	601		Franciacorta Brut, Barone Pizzini	182
Falerio dei Colli Ascolani, Tenuta De Angelis	582		Franciacorta Brut, F.lli Berlucchi	182
Falerio dei Colli Ascolani, Villa Pigna	595		Franciacorta Brut, Bersi Serlini	197
Falerio dei Colli Ascolani, Vinicola del Tesino	587		Franciacorta Brut, Bettinzana - Cascina Ronco Basso	207
Falerio dei Colli Ascolani Brezzolino,			Franciacorta Brut, Ca' del Bosco	185
La C. dei Colli Ripani	598		Franciacorta Brut, Ca' del Vent	206
Falerio dei Colli Ascolani Castello d'Acquaviva,			Franciacorta Brut, Tenuta Castellino	180
Terre Cortesi Moncaro	590		Franciacorta Brut, Castelveder	192
Falerio dei Colli Ascolani Il Brecciarolo, Ercole Velenosi	580		Franciacorta Brut, Catturich-Ducco	205
Falerio dei Colli Ascolani Leo Guelfus, S. Giovanni	594		Franciacorta Brut, Battista Cola	204
Falerio dei Colli Ascolani Lucrezia, Le Caniette	598		Franciacorta Brut, Contadi Castaldi	170
Falerio dei Colli Ascolani Marta V. T. Ris., S. Giovanni	594		Franciacorta Brut, Cornaleto	170
Falerio dei Colli Ascolani Ophites, S. Giovanni	594		Franciacorta Brut, Lorenzo Faccoli & Figli	180
Falerio dei Colli Ascolani Pliniano, Villa Pigna	595		Franciacorta Brut, Marchesi Fassati di Balzola	211
Falerio dei Colli Ascolani Telusiano, Rio Maggio	591		Franciacorta Brut, Ferghettina	186
Falerio dei Colli Ascolani Vigna Palazzi, Saladini Pilastri	601		Franciacorta Brut, Enrico Gatti	187
Falerio dei Colli Ascolani Vigna Solaria, Ercole Velenosi	580		Franciacorta Brut, Il Mosnel	196
Falerio dei Colli Ascolani Vigneti S. Basso,			Franciacorta Brut, La Boscaiola	181
Tenuta Cocci Grifoni	597		Franciacorta Brut, La Montina	192
Falerno del Massico Bianco, Villa Matilde	655		Franciacorta Brut, Lantieri de Paratico	173
Falerno del Massico Bianco Vigna Caracci, Villa Matilde	655		Franciacorta Brut, Le Marchesine	211
Falerno del Massico Falanghina, Michele Moio	659		Franciacorta Brut, Lo Sparviere	193
Falerno del Massico Primitivo, Michele Moio	659		Franciacorta Brut, Longhi de Carli	207
Falerno del Massico Rosso, Villa Matilde	655		Franciacorta Brut, Majolini	195
Falerno del Massico Vigna Camarato, Villa Matilde	655		Franciacorta Brut, Monzio Compagnoni	183
Falesia, Paolo d'Amico	629		Franciacorta Brut, Principe Banfi	207
Fantasie del Cardeto Rosso, Co.Vi.O.	617		Franciacorta Brut, Ricci Curbastro	173
Fara Caramino, Dessilani	73		Franciacorta Brut, Ronco Calino	178
Fara Lochera, Dessilani	73		Franciacorta Brut, S. Cristoforo	187
Farandola Bianco, Di Filippo	609		Franciacorta Brut, Ugo Vezzoli	210
Farnito Cabernet Sauvignon, Carpineto	463		Franciacorta Brut, Villa	193
Farnito Chardonnay, Carpineto	463		Franciacorta Brut Antica C. Fratta, Guido Berlucchi & C.	183
Faro Palari, Palari	707		Franciacorta Brut Arcadia, Lantieri de Paratico	173
Faroaldo, Rocca di Fabbri	615		Franciacorta Brut Bagnadore I, Barone Pizzini	182
Fatagione, Cottanera	702		Franciacorta Brut Bagnadore V, Barone Pizzini	182
Febo, Agricola Gatta	206		Franciacorta Brut Blanc de Blancs, Cavalleri	186
Federico II, Cantine Lento	696		Franciacorta Brut Cabochon, Monte Rossa	178
Federico Primo, Gualdo del Re	543		Franciacorta Brut Cabochon Rosé, Monte Rossa	178
Felciaia, Fattoria Villa La Selva	435		Franciacorta Brut Cuvée Millennio, Bersi Serlini	197
Feldmarschall von Fenner zu Fennberg, Tiefenbrunner	257		Franciacorta Brut Cuvée n. 4, Bersi Serlini	197
Ferentano, Falesco	634		Franciacorta Brut Francesco I, Uberti	188
Feudo dei Fiori, Settesoli	707		Franciacorta Brut I Cuvée, Monte Rossa	178
Fiagre, Antonio Caggiano	664		Franciacorta Brut Magnificentia, Uberti	188

Entry	Page
Franciacorta Brut Monogram Cuvée Giunone, CastelFaglia	206
Franciacorta Brut Monogram mill., CastelFaglia	206
Franciacorta Brut Rosé, Lorenzo Faccoli & Figli	180
Franciacorta Brut Satèn, F.lli Berlucchi	182
Franciacorta Brut Secolo Novo, Le Marchesine	211
Franciacorta Brut Sel., Villa	193
Franciacorta Brut Tetellus, Conti Bettoni Cazzago	177
Franciacorta Casa delle Colonne Brut, F.lli Berlucchi	182
Franciacorta Collezione Brut, Cavalleri	186
Franciacorta Collezione Esclusiva Brut, Cavalleri	186
Franciacorta Cuvée Annamaria Clementi, Ca' del Bosco	185
Franciacorta Cuvée Brut, Bellavista	185
Franciacorta Cuvette Sec, Villa	193
Franciacorta Démi Sec, Ricci Curbastro	173
Franciacorta Dosage Zéro, Ca' del Bosco	185
Franciacorta Electo Brut, Majolini	195
Franciacorta Extra Brut, Bersi Serlini	197
Franciacorta Extra Brut, CastelFaglia	206
Franciacorta Extra Brut, Castelveder	192
Franciacorta Extra Brut, Battista Cola	204
Franciacorta Extra Brut, Lorenzo Faccoli & Figli	180
Franciacorta Extra Brut, Marchesi Fassati di Balzola	211
Franciacorta Extra Brut, Il Mosnel	196
Franciacorta Extra Brut, La Montina	192
Franciacorta Extra Brut, Lantieri de Paratico	173
Franciacorta Extra Brut, Lo Sparviere	193
Franciacorta Extra Brut, Monte Rossa	178
Franciacorta Extra Brut, Monzio Compagnoni	183
Franciacorta Extra Brut, Ricci Curbastro	173
Franciacorta Extra Brut, Villa	193
Franciacorta Extra Brut Bagnadore V, Barone Pizzini	182
Franciacorta Extra Brut Cabochon, Monte Rossa	178
Franciacorta Extra Brut Comarì del Salem, Uberti	188
Franciacorta Extra Brut Francesco I, Uberti	188
Franciacorta Extra Brut Vittorio Moretti Ris., Bellavista	185
Franciacorta Extra Dry, Barone Pizzini	182
Franciacorta Gran Cuvée Brut, Bellavista	185
Franciacorta Gran Cuvée Pas Operé, Bellavista	185
Franciacorta Gran Cuvée Rosé, Bellavista	185
Franciacorta Gran Cuvée Satèn, Bellavista	185
Franciacorta Magno Brut, Contadi Castaldi	170
Franciacorta Non Dosato, Mirabella	212
Franciacorta Pas Dosé, Cavalleri	186
Franciacorta Pas Dosé Torre Ducco, Catturich-Ducco	205
Franciacorta Rosé, Barone Pizzini	182
Franciacorta Rosé, F.lli Berlucchi	182
Franciacorta Rosé, Contadi Castaldi	170
Franciacorta Rosé, Mirabella	212
Franciacorta Rosé Brut Francesco I, Uberti	188
Franciacorta Rosé Demi Sec, La Montina	192
Franciacorta Rosé Démi Sec, Villa	193
Franciacorta Satèn, Barone Pizzini	182
Franciacorta Satèn, F.lli Berlucchi	182
Franciacorta Satèn, Bersi Serlini	197
Franciacorta Satèn, Conti Bettoni Cazzago	177
Franciacorta Satèn, Ca' del Bosco	185
Franciacorta Satèn, Tenuta Castellino	180
Franciacorta Satèn, Cavalleri	186
Franciacorta Satèn, Contadi Castaldi	170
Franciacorta Satèn, Ferghettina	186
Franciacorta Satèn, Enrico Gatti	187
Franciacorta Satèn, Il Mosnel	196
Franciacorta Satèn, La Montina	192
Franciacorta Satèn, Lantieri de Paratico	173
Franciacorta Satèn, Longhi de Carli	207
Franciacorta Satèn, Majolini	195
Franciacorta Satèn, Monte Rossa	178
Franciacorta Satèn, Monzio Compagnoni	183
Franciacorta Satèn, Principe Banfi	207
Franciacorta Satèn, Ricci Curbastro	173
Franciacorta Satèn, Ronco Calino	178
Franciacorta Satèn, Attilio Vezzoli	208
Franciacorta Satèn, Villa	193
Franciacorta Sec, Monte Rossa	178
Franciacorta Zéro, Contadi Castaldi	170
Franconia, Roncada	352
Franconia, Ronco delle Betulle	371
Franze, Sassotondo	542
Frappato, Cantine Torrevecchia	700
Frappato, C. Valle dell'Acate	700
Frascati Cannellino, Conte Zandotti	635
Frascati Sup., Casale Marchese	632
Frascati Sup., Casale Mattia	637
Frascati Sup., Castel De Paolis	632
Frascati Sup., Conte Zandotti	635
Frascati Sup., Fontana Candida	633
Frascati Sup., Gotto d'Oro	638
Frascati Sup. Campo Vecchio, Castel De Paolis	632
Frascati Sup. Cannellino, Castel De Paolis	632
Frascati Sup. Cannellino, Villa Simone - Piero Costantini	634
Frascati Sup. Castel De Paolis, Castel De Paolis	632
Frascati Sup. Racemo, L'Olivella	637
Frascati Sup. S. Teresa, Fontana Candida	633
Frascati Sup. Sel., Cantine S. Marco	637
Frascati Sup. Terre dei Grifi, Fontana Candida	633
Frascati Sup. V. Adriana, Castel De Paolis	632
Frascati Sup. V. dei Preti, Villa Simone - Piero Costantini	634
Frascati Sup. Vign. Filonardi, Villa Simone - Piero Costantini	634
Frascati Sup. Villa Simone, Villa Simone - Piero Costantini	634
Fratta, Maculan	274
Freisa d'Asti, La Zucca	110
Freisa d'Asti Luna di Maggio, Cascina Gilli	56
Freisa d'Asti Vigna del Forno, Cascina Gilli	56
Freisa d'Asti Vivace, Cascina Gilli	56
Friuli Annia Malvasia, Cav. Emiro Bortolusso	341
Friuli Annia Merlot, Cav. Emiro Bortolusso	341
Friuli Annia Pinot Bianco, Cav. Emiro Bortolusso	341
Friuli Annia Pinot Grigio, Cav. Emiro Bortolusso	341
Friuli Annia Refosco P. R., Cav. Emiro Bortolusso	341
Friuli Annia Sauvignon, Cav. Emiro Bortolusso	341
Friuli Annia Tocai Friulano, Cav. Emiro Bortolusso	341
Friuli Annia Verduzzo Friulano, Cav. Emiro Bortolusso	341
Friuli Aquileia Bianco Palmade, Mulino delle Tolle	332
Friuli Aquileia Cabernet Franc, Ca' Bolani	341
Friuli Aquileia Cabernet Franc, Mulino delle Tolle	332
Friuli Aquileia Cabernet Franc Gianni Zonin Vineyards, Ca' Bolani	341
Friuli Aquileia Cabernet Sauvignon, Tenuta Beltrame	332
Friuli Aquileia Cabernet Sauvignon Ris., Tenuta Beltrame	332
Friuli Aquileia Chardonnay, Tenuta Beltrame	332
Friuli Aquileia Chardonnay, Mulino delle Tolle	332
Friuli Aquileia Chardonnay Pribus, Tenuta Beltrame	332
Friuli Aquileia Chardonnay Sup., Foffani	398
Friuli Aquileia Merlot, Tenuta Beltrame	332
Friuli Aquileia Merlot, Ca' Bolani	341
Friuli Aquileia Merlot, Foffani	398
Friuli Aquileia Merlot, Mulino delle Tolle	332
Friuli Aquileia Merlot Ris., Tenuta Beltrame	332
Friuli Aquileia Pinot Bianco, Tenuta Beltrame	332
Friuli Aquileia Pinot Bianco, Brojli - Franco Clementin	402
Friuli Aquileia Pinot Grigio, Tenuta Beltrame	332
Friuli Aquileia Pinot Grigio Gianni Zonin Vineyards, Ca' Bolani	341
Friuli Aquileia Pinot Grigio Sup., Foffani	398
Friuli Aquileia Refosco P. R., Ca' Bolani	341
Friuli Aquileia Refosco P. R., Mulino delle Tolle	332
Friuli Aquileia Refosco P. R. Gianni Zonin Vineyards, Ca' Bolani	341
Friuli Aquileia Riesling, Brojli - Franco Clementin	402
Friuli Aquileia Sauvignon, Tenuta Beltrame	332
Friuli Aquileia Sauvignon Gianni Zonin Vineyards, Ca' Bolani	341
Friuli Aquileia Sauvignon Sup., Foffani	398
Friuli Aquileia Tocai Friulano, Tenuta Beltrame	332
Friuli Aquileia Tocai Friulano, Mulino delle Tolle	332
Friuli Aquileia Tocai Friulano Sup., Foffani	398
Friuli Grave Bianco Antizio, Alfieri Cantarutti	392
Friuli Grave Bianco Martin Pescatore, Forchir	392
Friuli Grave Bianco Pra' de Gai, Vigneti Le Monde	378
Friuli Grave Cabernet, Di Lenardo	365
Friuli Grave Cabernet Franc, Borgo Magredo	396
Friuli Grave Cabernet Franc, Vigneti Le Monde	378
Friuli Grave Cabernet Sauvignion Crearo, Pradio	333
Friuli Grave Cabernet Sauvignon, Forchir	392
Friuli Grave Cabernet Sauvignon, Alessandro Vicentini Orgnani	376
Friuli Grave Cabernet Sauvignon, Vigneti Le Monde	378
Friuli Grave Cabernet Sauvignon, Villa Chiopris	394
Friuli Grave Cabernet Sauvignon Le Selezioni, Antonutti	374
Friuli Grave Cabernet Sauvignon Ris., Plozner	396
Friuli Grave Cabernet Sauvignon Ris., Tenuta Pinni	402
Friuli Grave Cabernet Sauvignon Ris., Vigneti Le Monde	378
Friuli Grave Cabernet Sauvignon Sant'Helena, Fantinel	377
Friuli Grave Chardonnay, Antonutti	374
Friuli Grave Chardonnay, Borgo Magredo	396
Friuli Grave Chardonnay, Brunner	399
Friuli Grave Chardonnay, Cabert	333
Friuli Grave Chardonnay, Le Due Torri	358
Friuli Grave Chardonnay, Plozner	396
Friuli Grave Chardonnay, Scarbolo	375
Friuli Grave Chardonnay, Vigneti Le Monde	378
Friuli Grave Chardonnay, Villa Chiopris	394
Friuli Grave Chardonnay Braida Longa, Borgo Magredo	396
Friuli Grave Chardonnay Braide Cjase, Alessandro Vicentini Orgnani	376
Friuli Grave Chardonnay Le Marsure, Teresa Raiz	377
Friuli Grave Chardonnay Musque, Di Lenardo	365
Friuli Grave Chardonnay Poggio Alto, Antonutti	374
Friuli Grave Chardonnay Ris., Plozner	396
Friuli Grave Chardonnay Sup., Tenuta Pinni	402
Friuli Grave Chardonnay Teraje, Pradio	333
Friuli Grave Chardonnay Woody, Di Lenardo	365
Friuli Grave Merlot, Valentino Butussi	356
Friuli Grave Merlot, Di Lenardo	365
Friuli Grave Merlot, Forchir	392
Friuli Grave Merlot, Scarbolo	375
Friuli Grave Merlot, Alessandro Vicentini Orgnani	376
Friuli Grave Merlot, Villa Chiopris	394
Friuli Grave Merlot Borgo Tesis, Fantinel	377
Friuli Grave Merlot Braida Moral, Borgo Magredo	396
Friuli Grave Merlot Poggio Alto, Antonutti	374
Friuli Grave Merlot Ris., Cabert	333

Entry	Page
Friuli Grave Merlot Ris., F.lli Pighin	375
Friuli Grave Merlot Ris., Plozner	396
Friuli Grave Merlot Roncomoro, Pradio	333
Friuli Grave Merlot Vistorta, Vistorta - Brandino Brandolini d'Adda	386
Friuli Grave Pinot Bianco, Antonutti	374
Friuli Grave Pinot Bianco, Valentino Butussi	356
Friuli Grave Pinot Bianco, Di Lenardo	365
Friuli Grave Pinot Bianco, F.lli Pighin	375
Friuli Grave Pinot Bianco, Plozner	396
Friuli Grave Pinot Bianco Braide Cjase, Alessandro Vicentini Orgnani	376
Friuli Grave Pinot Bianco Campo dei Gelsi, Forchir	392
Friuli Grave Pinot Grigio, Antonutti	374
Friuli Grave Pinot Grigio, Borgo Magredo	396
Friuli Grave Pinot Grigio, Brunner	399
Friuli Grave Pinot Grigio, Cabert	333
Friuli Grave Pinot Grigio, Di Lenardo	365
Friuli Grave Pinot Grigio, Forchir	392
Friuli Grave Pinot Grigio, Le Due Torri	358
Friuli Grave Pinot Grigio, F.lli Pighin	375
Friuli Grave Pinot Grigio, Plozner	396
Friuli Grave Pinot Grigio, Tenuta Pinni	402
Friuli Grave Pinot Grigio, Alessandro Vicentini Orgnani	376
Friuli Grave Pinot Grigio, Vigneti Le Monde	378
Friuli Grave Pinot Grigio, Villa Chiopris	394
Friuli Grave Pinot Grigio Braide Cjase, Alessandro Vicentini Orgnani	376
Friuli Grave Pinot Grigio Le Marsure, Teresa Raiz	377
Friuli Grave Pinot Grigio Priara, Pradio	333
Friuli Grave Pinot Grigio Ronco Calaj, Russolo	395
Friuli Grave Pinot Nero, Borgo Magredo	396
Friuli Grave Refosco P. R., Cabert	333
Friuli Grave Refosco P. R., Di Lenardo	365
Friuli Grave Refosco P. R., Forchir	392
Friuli Grave Refosco P. R., F.lli Pighin	375
Friuli Grave Refosco P. R., Vigneti Le Monde	378
Friuli Grave Refosco P. R. Le Selezioni, Antonutti	374
Friuli Grave Refosco P. R. Sant'Helena, Fantinel	377
Friuli Grave Refosco P. R. Tuaro, Pradio	333
Friuli Grave Rosso Antizio, Alfieri Cantarutti	392
Friuli Grave Rosso Ca' Salice, Vigneti Le Monde	378
Friuli Grave Sauvignon, Antonutti	374
Friuli Grave Sauvignon, Borgo Magredo	396
Friuli Grave Sauvignon, Brunner	399
Friuli Grave Sauvignon, Ca di Bon	400
Friuli Grave Sauvignon, Cabert	333
Friuli Grave Sauvignon, Le Due Torri	358
Friuli Grave Sauvignon, F.lli Pighin	375
Friuli Grave Sauvignon, Plozner	396
Friuli Grave Sauvignon, Scarbolo	375
Friuli Grave Sauvignon, Alessandro Vicentini Orgnani	376
Friuli Grave Sauvignon, Vigneti Le Monde	378
Friuli Grave Sauvignon, Villa Chiopris	394
Friuli Grave Sauvignon Blanc, Di Lenardo	365
Friuli Grave Sauvignon Blanc Le Selezioni, Antonutti	374
Friuli Grave Sauvignon l'Altro, Forchir	392
Friuli Grave Sauvignon Puja, Vigneti Le Monde	378
Friuli Grave Sauvignon Rovel, Teresa Raiz	377
Friuli Grave Sauvignon Sobaja, Pradio	333
Friuli Grave Tocai Friulano, Antonutti	374
Friuli Grave Tocai Friulano, Borgo Magredo	396
Friuli Grave Tocai Friulano, Brunner	399
Friuli Grave Tocai Friulano, Cabert	333
Friuli Grave Tocai Friulano, Le Due Torri	358
Friuli Grave Tocai Friulano, F.lli Pighin	375
Friuli Grave Tocai Friulano, Plozner	396
Friuli Grave Tocai Friulano, Scarbolo	375
Friuli Grave Tocai Friulano, Villa Chiopris	394
Friuli Grave Tocai Friulano Casette, F.lli Pighin	375
Friuli Grave Tocai Friulano Gaiare, Pradio	333
Friuli Grave Tocai Friulano Ronco Calaj, Russolo	395
Friuli Grave Traminer Aromatico, Forchir	392
Friuli Isonzo Arbis Blanc, Borgo S. Daniele	344
Friuli Isonzo Bianco Flors di Uis, Vie di Romans	373
Friuli Isonzo Bianco Latimis, Ronco del Gelso	353
Friuli Isonzo Bianco Vignis di Siris, Mauro Drius	348
Friuli Isonzo Cabernet, Mauro Drius	348
Friuli Isonzo Cabernet BorDavi, Carlo di Pradis	347
Friuli Isonzo Cabernet Franc, Marcello e Marino Humar	389
Friuli Isonzo Cabernet Franc, Eddi Luisa	372
Friuli Isonzo Cabernet Franc, Masut da Rive	373
Friuli Isonzo Cabernet Franc, Muzic	390
Friuli Isonzo Cabernet Franc, Ronco del Gelso	353
Friuli Isonzo Cabernet Franc I Ferretti, Eddi Luisa	372
Friuli Isonzo Cabernet Gli Affreschi, Tenuta di Blasig	386
Friuli Isonzo Cabernet Sauvignon, Colmello di Grotta	363
Friuli Isonzo Cabernet Sauvignon, Eddi Luisa	372
Friuli Isonzo Cabernet Sauvignon, Masut da Rive	373
Friuli Isonzo Cabernet Sauvignon, Isidoro Polencic	351
Friuli Isonzo Cabernet Sauvignon, Tiare - Roberto Snidarcig	355
Friuli Isonzo Cabernet Sauvignon Colombara, Borgo Conventi	363
Friuli Isonzo Cabernet Sauvignon I Ferretti, Eddi Luisa	372
Friuli Isonzo Cabernet Sauvignon Ris., Borgo Lotessa	338
Friuli Isonzo Cabernet Sauvignon Ronc dal Luis, Maurizio Buzzinelli	345
Friuli Isonzo Chardonnay, Tenuta di Blasig	386
Friuli Isonzo Chardonnay, C. Prod. di Cormons	346
Friuli Isonzo Chardonnay, Colmello di Grotta	363
Friuli Isonzo Chardonnay, Eddi Luisa	372
Friuli Isonzo Chardonnay, Magnàs	400
Friuli Isonzo Chardonnay, Masut da Rive	373
Friuli Isonzo Chardonnay, Pierpaolo Pecorari	395
Friuli Isonzo Chardonnay, Ronco del Gelso	353
Friuli Isonzo Chardonnay, Vigna del Lauro	356
Friuli Isonzo Chardonnay BorDavi, Carlo di Pradis	347
Friuli Isonzo Chardonnay Ciampagnis Vieris, Vie di Romans	373
Friuli Isonzo Chardonnay dei Sassi Cavi, Eugenio Collavini	357
Friuli Isonzo Chardonnay Giovanni Puiatti, Puiatti	338
Friuli Isonzo Chardonnay I Fiori, Borgo Conventi	363
Friuli Isonzo Chardonnay Jurosa, Lis Neris - Pecorari	394
Friuli Isonzo Chardonnay Maurùs, Masut da Rive	373
Friuli Isonzo Chardonnay Podere Angoris, Tenuta di Angoris	343
Friuli Isonzo Chardonnay Sant'Jurosa, Lis Neris - Pecorari	394
Friuli Isonzo Chardonnay Vie di Romans, Vie di Romans	373
Friuli Isonzo Chardonnay Vigna Cristin, Edi Gandin	402
Friuli Isonzo Madreterra, C. Prod. di Cormons	346
Friuli Isonzo Malvasia, Mauro Drius	348
Friuli Isonzo Malvasia, Tenuta Villanova	364
Friuli Isonzo Merlot, Tenuta di Blasig	386
Friuli Isonzo Merlot, Colmello di Grotta	363
Friuli Isonzo Merlot, Mauro Drius	348
Friuli Isonzo Merlot, Masut da Rive	373
Friuli Isonzo Merlot, Muzic	390
Friuli Isonzo Merlot, Ronco del Gelso	353
Friuli Isonzo Merlot, Tiare - Roberto Snidarcig	355
Friuli Isonzo Merlot, Vigna del Lauro	356
Friuli Isonzo Merlot BorDavi, Carlo di Pradis	347
Friuli Isonzo Merlot Gli Affreschi, Tenuta di Blasig	386
Friuli Isonzo Merlot I Ferretti, Eddi Luisa	372
Friuli Isonzo Merlot Primo Legno, Muzic	390
Friuli Isonzo Merlot Vigna Runc, Il Carpino	390
Friuli Isonzo Pinot Bianco, Mauro Drius	348
Friuli Isonzo Pinot Bianco, Eddi Luisa	372
Friuli Isonzo Pinot Bianco, Magnàs	400
Friuli Isonzo Pinot Bianco, Masut da Rive	373
Friuli Isonzo Pinot Bianco, Ronco del Gelso	353
Friuli Isonzo Pinot Grigio, Tenuta di Blasig	386
Friuli Isonzo Pinot Grigio, Borgo S. Daniele	344
Friuli Isonzo Pinot Grigio, Casa Zuliani	401
Friuli Isonzo Pinot Grigio, Colmello di Grotta	363
Friuli Isonzo Pinot Grigio, Mauro Drius	348
Friuli Isonzo Pinot Grigio, Lis Neris - Pecorari	394
Friuli Isonzo Pinot Grigio, Eddi Luisa	372
Friuli Isonzo Pinot Grigio, Magnàs	400
Friuli Isonzo Pinot Grigio, Masut da Rive	373
Friuli Isonzo Pinot Grigio, Pierpaolo Pecorari	395
Friuli Isonzo Pinot Grigio Altis, Pierpaolo Pecorari	395
Friuli Isonzo Pinot Grigio BorDavi, Carlo di Pradis	347
Friuli Isonzo Pinot Grigio Dessimis, Vie di Romans	373
Friuli Isonzo Pinot Grigio Giovanni Puiatti, Puiatti	338
Friuli Isonzo Pinot Grigio Gris, Lis Neris - Pecorari	394
Friuli Isonzo Pinot Grigio Sot lis Rivis, Ronco del Gelso	353
Friuli Isonzo Refosco P. R. Colombara, Borgo Conventi	363
Friuli Isonzo Riesling, Mauro Drius	348
Friuli Isonzo Riesling, Ronco del Gelso	353
Friuli Isonzo Ròs di Ròl, Sant'Elena	368
Friuli Isonzo Rosso BorDavi, Carlo di Pradis	347
Friuli Isonzo Rosso Voos dai Ciamps, Vie di Romans	373
Friuli Isonzo Sauvignon, C. Prod. di Cormons	346
Friuli Isonzo Sauvignon, Lis Neris - Pecorari	394
Friuli Isonzo Sauvignon, Eddi Luisa	372
Friuli Isonzo Sauvignon, Masut da Rive	373
Friuli Isonzo Sauvignon, Pierpaolo Pecorari	395
Friuli Isonzo Sauvignon, Ronco del Gelso	353
Friuli Isonzo Sauvignon Altis, Pierpaolo Pecorari	395
Friuli Isonzo Sauvignon Dom Picòl, Lis Neris - Pecorari	394
Friuli Isonzo Sauvignon Picòl, Lis Neris - Pecorari	394
Friuli Isonzo Sauvignon Piere, Vie di Romans	373
Friuli Isonzo Sauvignon Vieris, Vie di Romans	373
Friuli Isonzo Tato, Sant'Elena	368
Friuli Isonzo Tocai Friulano, Tenuta di Blasig	386
Friuli Isonzo Tocai Friulano, Borgo S. Daniele	344
Friuli Isonzo Tocai Friulano, Mauro Drius	348
Friuli Isonzo Tocai Friulano, Eddi Luisa	372
Friuli Isonzo Tocai Friulano, Masut da Rive	373
Friuli Isonzo Tocai Friulano, Ronco del Gelso	353
Friuli Isonzo Verduzzo Dorè, C. Prod. di Cormons	346
Fuili, C. Soc. Dorgali	723
Fumé Bianco, Giovanni Crosato	342
Furat, Ajello	717
Futuro Bianco, F. e M. Scrimaglio	118
Gabbro, Montepeloso	544
Gagliole Rosso, Gagliole	552
Galatina Rosso, Valle dell'Asso	690
Galatrona, Fattoria Petrolo	509
Galluccio Aglianico Monte Caruso, Telaro - Coop. Lavoro e Salute	657
Galluccio Ara Mundi Ris., Telaro - Coop. Lavoro e Salute	657
Galluccio Calivierno Ris., Telaro - Coop. Lavoro e Salute	657

Entry	Page
Galluccio Falanghina Ripabianca, Telaro - Coop. Lavoro e Salute	657
Gamba di Pernice, Carlo Benotto	65
Gamba di Pernice, Tenuta dei Fiori	46
Gambellara Cl. Ca' Cischele, Vinicola Luigino Dal Maso	287
Gambellara Cl. I Masieri, La Biancara	278
Gambellara Cl. La Bocara, Domenico Cavazza & F.lli	287
Gambellara Cl. Podere Il Giangio, Zonin	279
Gambellara Cl. Sup. Sassaia, La Biancara	278
Gana, Terre del Sillabo	470
Garbi Bianco, Boccadigabbia	584
Garda Cabernet Le Ragose, Le Ragose	293
Garda Cabernet Ribò, Ricchi	210
Garda Cabernet Sauv. Pradamonte, Costaripa	190
Garda Cabernet Sauvignon Cicisbeo, Le Tende	281
Garda Cabernet Sauvignon Rocca Sveva, C. di Soave	308
Garda Cabernet Sauvignon Sorbo degli Uccellatori, Le Tende	281
Garda Cabernet Sauvignon Vigneto Il Falcone La Prendina, Cavalchina	311
Garda Chardonnay, Musella	300
Garda Cl. Chiaretto, Provenza	184
Garda Cl. Chiaretto Le Sincette, Cascina La Pertica	196
Garda Cl. Chiaretto Molmenti, Costaripa	190
Garda Cl. Groppello Maim, Costaripa	190
Garda Cl. Groppello Vigneto Le Castelline, Costaripa	190
Garda Cl. Rosso Campo delle Starme, Costaripa	190
Garda Cl. Rosso Chr. Barnard, Costaripa	190
Garda Cl. Rosso Le Sincette, Cascina La Pertica	196
Garda Cl. Rosso Negresco, Provenza	184
Garda Cl. Rosso Sel. Fabio Contato, Provenza	184
Garda Cl. Rosso Sup. Cap del Priu, Pasini Prod.	212
Garda Cl. Rosso Sup. Corte Ialidy, Marangona	211
Garda Cl. Sup. Rosso Brol, Cantine Valtenesi - Lugana	209
Garda Colli Mantontovani Cabernet Ris., Reale Boselli	214
Garda Colli Mantovani Rubino Vigna del Moro, Reale Boselli	214
Garda Garganega, Brigaldara	302
Garda Marzemino Vigna Balosse, Cantine Valtenesi - Lugana	209
Garda Merlot, Le Tende	281
Garda Merlot, Ricchi	210
Garda Merlot Faial La Prendina, Cavalchina	311
Garda Merlot La Prendina, Cavalchina	311
Garda Merlot Le Prunee, Viticoltori Tommasi	305
Garda Merlot Rondinella La Prendina, Cavalchina	311
Garda Merlot Vallidium, Corte Gardoni	318
Garda Pinot Nero Corteccio, Cantrina	204
Garda Sauvignon Valbruna La Prendina, Cavalchina	311
Garganega del Veneto, Le Fraghe	274
Garganega Monte Ceriani, Tenuta Sant'Antonio	275
Garganego, Basso Graziano	325
Garighe Zibibbo, Aziende Vinicole Miceli	710
Garofoli Brut, Gioacchino Garofoli	588
Gastaldi Rosso, Gastaldi	112
Gatinera Brut Talento, Fontanafredda	129
Gatti Bianco, Enrico Gatti	187
Gatti Rosso, Enrico Gatti	187
Gattinara, Antoniolo	75
Gattinara, Dessilani	73
Gattinara, Nervi	75
Gattinara, Torraccia del Piantavigna	149
Gattinara, Giancarlo Travaglini	76
Gattinara Ris., Giancarlo Travaglini	76
Gattinara Ris. Numerata, Giancarlo Travaglini	76
Gattinara Tre Vigne, Giancarlo Travaglini	76
Gattinara Vigneto Castelle, Antoniolo	75
Gattinara Vigneto Molsino, Nervi	75
Gattinara Vigneto Osso S. Grato, Antoniolo	75
Gattinara Vigneto S. Francesco, Antoniolo	75
Gattinara Vigneto Valferana, Bianchi	153
Gaudio, Tenuta Le Velette	619
Gaurano, Michele Moio	659
Gavi, Pio Cesare	25
Gavi Brut, La Scolca	79
Gavi Ca' Bianca, Ca' Bianca	28
Gavi Ca' da Bosio, Terre da Vino	41
Gavi Ca' di Maggio, S. Seraffa	148
Gavi Camghé, La Guardia	109
Gavi Cascine dell'Aureliana, Prod. del Gavi	79
Gavi Castello di Tassarolo, Castello di Tassarolo	134
Gavi dei Gavi Etichetta Nera, La Scolca	79
Gavi del Comune di Gavi, Nicola Bergaglio	76
Gavi del Comune di Gavi, Il Rocchin	148
Gavi del Comune di Gavi, La Smilla	43
Gavi del Comune di Gavi, Morgassi Superiore	148
Gavi del Comune di Gavi, Villa Sparina	80
Gavi del Comune di Gavi Bruno Broglia, Gian Piero Broglia - Tenuta La Meirana	77
Gavi del Comune di Gavi La Chiara, La Chiara	78
Gavi del Comune di Gavi La Meirana, Gian Piero Broglia - Tenuta La Meirana	77
Gavi del Comune di Gavi Lugarara, La Giustiniana	78
Gavi del Comune di Gavi Marchese Raggio, Bersano & Riccadonna	116
Gavi del Comune di Gavi Minaia, Nicola Bergaglio	76
Gavi del Comune di Gavi Monte Rotondo, Villa Sparina	80
Gavi del Comune di Gavi Montessora, La Giustiniana	78
Gavi del Comune di Gavi Pelöia, S. Bartolomeo	148
Gavi del Comune di Gavi Rolona, Castellari Bergaglio	77
Gavi del Comune di Gavi Vigna del Bosco, Il Rocchin	148
Gavi del Comune di Gavi Vigneto Groppella, La Chiara	78
Gavi di Rovereto Vigna Il Poggio, Cascina La Ghersa	96
Gavi Etichetta Bianca, Tenuta La Marchesa	151
Gavi Etichetta Nera, Tenuta La Marchesa	151
Gavi Fornaci, Castellari Bergaglio	77
Gavi Fornaci di Tassarolo, Michele Chiarlo	45
Gavi I Bergi, La Smilla	43
Gavi I Filagnotti, Cascina Ulivi	151
Gavi La Scolca, La Scolca	79
Gavi La Zerba, La Zerba	134
Gavi Le Colombare, S. Seraffa	148
Gavi Maddalena, Prod. del Gavi	79
Gavi Masseria dei Carmelitani, Terre da Vino	41
Gavi Primuva, Prod. del Gavi	79
Gavi Principessa Gavia, Vigne Regali	133
Gavi Ricella Alta, Vigne del Pareto	119
Gavi Rovereto Vignavecchia, Castellari Bergaglio	77
Gavi Sel. Valditerra, Valditerra	152
Gavi Tassarolo S, Castello di Tassarolo	134
Gavi Terrarossa, La Zerba	134
Gavi Vigne Alte, Il Vignale	119
Gavi Vigne del Pareto, Vigne del Pareto	119
Gavi Vigneto Alborina, Castello di Tassarolo	134
Gavi Villa Scolca, La Scolca	79
Gavi Vilma Cappelletti, Il Vignale	119
Gavignano, Fattoria S. Maria di Ambra	434
Gavioli Brut, Agricola Gavioli	566
Gemelli, Abbazia S. Anastasia	701
Geremia, Rocca di Montegrossi	461
Ghemme, Antichi Vigneti di Cantalupo	80
Ghemme, Rovellotti	81
Ghemme, Torraccia del Piantavigna	149
Ghemme Colle Baraggiole, Bianchi	153
Ghemme Collis Breclemae, Antichi Vigneti di Cantalupo	80
Ghemme Collis Carellae, Antichi Vigneti di Cantalupo	80
Ghemme Ris., Rovellotti	81
Ghemme Signore di Bayard, Antichi Vigneti di Cantalupo	80
Gherardino, Villa Vignamaggio	467
Ghiaie Bianche, Tenuta Col d'Orcia	479
Ghiaie della Furba, Capezzana	437
Giacomelli Bianco, Giacomelli	158
Giada Bianco, Pollara	708
Gialosguardo, VIN.CA	551
Gilat Rosso, Eraldo Viberti	91
Gimè Bianco, Ottella	296
Gioia del Colle Primitivo Ris., Vini Classici Cardone	691
Gioie di Vitae, Terredora di Paolo	660
Gioveto, Enrico Pierazzuoli	453
Girifalco, La Calonica	501
Girolamo, Castello di Bossi	444
Girone, Boccadigabbia	584
Giséle, La Rampa di Fugnano	536
Giubilante, Cantine Lungarotti	623
Giulio Cocchi Brut, Bava	63
Giulio Ferrari, Ferrari	234
Giuseppe Galliano Brut M. Cl., Borgo Maragliano	93
Giuseppe Galliano Chardonnay Brut, Borgo Maragliano	93
Giusto di Notri, Tua Rita	545
Gloria, Barone La Lumia	704
Godimondo Cabernet Franc, La Montecchia	307
Golfo del Tigullio Bianchetta Genovese U Pastine, Enoteca Bisson	159
Golfo del Tigullio Rosso Il Musaico, Enoteca Bisson	159
Golfo del Tigullio Rosso Il Musaico Barrique, Enoteca Bisson	159
Golfo del Tigullio Vermentino Vigna Erta, Enoteca Bisson	159
Goliardo Rosso, Luciano Landi	581
Golpaja, Fattoria di Petriolo	554
Gonzialer, Grigoletti	237
Gorgo Tondo Bianco, Carlo Pellegrino	706
Gorgo Tondo Rosso, Carlo Pellegrino	706
Gortmarin, Borgo S. Daniele	344
Gottizio, Castello di Monterinaldi	522
Graf Noir, Drei Donà Tenuta La Palazza	411
Gramelot, C. Coop. Castignanese	603
Grammonte, Cottanera	702
Granaio, Savignola Paolina	557
Granato, Foradori	228
Grannero Pinot Nero, Vigneto delle Terre Rosse	423
Grappoli del Grillo, Marco De Bartoli	704
Graticciaia, Agricole Vallone	683
Grattamacco, Grattamacco	438
Gravello, Librandi	695
Gravina, C. Coop. Botromagno	681
Gravisano, C. Coop. Botromagno	681
Grecale Vino Liquoroso, Cantine Florio	705
Grecanico Mandrarossa, Settesoli	707
Greccio Spumante, Bepin de Eto	300
Grechetto, Falesco	634
Grechetto, Fattoria Le Poggette	613
Grechetto, Palazzone	619
Grechetto di Todi, Todini	626

Name	Page
Grechetto Latour a Civitella, Tenuta Mottura	631
Grechetto Poggio della Costa, Tenuta Mottura	631
Greco del Taburno, C. del Taburno	655
Greco di Tufo, Colli Irpini - Montesolae	659
Greco di Tufo, De Falco Vini	668
Greco di Tufo, Di Marzo	668
Greco di Tufo, Benito Ferrara	665
Greco di Tufo, Feudi di S. Gregorio	663
Greco di Tufo Cutizzi, Feudi di S. Gregorio	663
Greco di Tufo Loggia della Serra, Terredora di Paolo	660
Greco di Tufo Novaserra, Mastroberardino	654
Greco di Tufo Terra degli Angeli, Terredora di Paolo	660
Greco di Tufo Vigna Cicogna, Benito Ferrara	665
Grignolino d'Asti, Braida	122
Grignolino d'Asti, C. Soc. di Vinchio e Vaglio Serra	142
Grignolino d'Asti, Castello del Poggio	152
Grignolino d'Asti, Agostino Pavia e Figli	23
Grignolino d'Asti Miravalle, Cantine Sant'Agata	128
Grignolino d'Asti Pian delle Querce, Villa Fiorita	146
Grignolino d'Asti S. Giacu, Cascina Orsolina	150
Grignolino d'Asti Sandefendente, Scarpa - Antica Casa Vinicola	117
Grignolino d'Asti Vigneto La Casalina, F.lli Rovero	28
Grignolino del M.to Casalese, Bricco Mondalino	140
Grignolino del M.to Casalese, Tenuta La Tenaglia	132
Grignolino del M.to Casalese, Liedholm	68
Grignolino del M.to Casalese, Vicara	123
Grignolino del M.to Casalese Bricco del Bosco, G. Accornero e Figli	140
Grignolino del M.to Casalese Bricco Mondalino, Bricco Mondalino	140
Grignolino del M.to Casalese Celio, Marco Canato	141
Grignolino del M.to Casalese Cré Marcaleone, Carlo Quarello	64
Grignolino del M.to Casalese Montecastello, Isabella	110
Grignolino del M.to Casalese Sansin, Colonna	141
Grignolino del M.to Casalese Vigna del Convento, Tenuta Gaiano	46
Grignolino del M.to Casalese Vigna Tufara, Castello di Lignano	74
Grillo, Cantine Rallo	706
Grottagrifone Rosso, S. Biagio	604
Guado al Luco, Castelli del Grevepesa	528
Guardiolo Falanghina, La Guardiense	667
Guardiolo Rosso Ris., La Guardiense	667
Guggino, Aziende Vinicole Miceli	710
Guidaccio, Marchesi Torrigiani	555
Gurra, Agareno	717
Halykas, Barone La Lumia	704
Hammon, Cantine Monthia	716
Harmonium, Casa Vinicola Firriato	709
Harys, Giovanni Battista Gillardi	74
I Balconi Rosso, Le Vigne di S. Pietro	311
I Balzini Rosso, I Balzini	550
I Campi Rosso, Giacomelli	158
I Capitelli, Roberto Anselmi	288
I Fenili, Corte Gardoni	318
I Greti, Le Ginestre	550
I Grottoni, Il Lebbio	534
I Piaggioni, Mocali	487
I Pini, Fattoria di Basciano	527
I Renai, S. Gervasio	510
I Ricordi, Rio Grande	620
I Sierri, Cosimo Taurino	682
I Sistri, Fattoria di Felsina	446
I Sodi di S. Niccolò, Castellare di Castellina	439
I Sodi Lunghi, F.lli Vagnoni	540
I Valloni, Villa Sant'Anna	506
I Vigneti del Geografico, Agricoltori del Chianti Geografico	455
Ibisco Bianco, Ciccio Zaccagnini	640
Idea, Trappolini	630
Idem, Feudi di S. Gregorio	663
Il Baccanale, La Lecciaia	562
Il Bianco dell'Abazia, Serafini & Vidotto	296
Il Borro, Tenuta Il Borro	559
Il Brecciolino, Fattoria Castelvecchio	572
Il Carbonaione, Podere Poggio Scalette	464
Il Cenno, Colle Bereto	571
Il Conte, Carlotta	43
Il Corto, Fattoria di Basciano	527
Il Corzano, Fattoria Corzano e Paterno	529
Il Doge, I Girasoli di Sant'Andrea	626
Il Faggio Passito, Conte Otto Barattieri di S. Pietro	421
Il Falco di Castelmonte, Edi Gandin	402
Il Fortino Cabernet/Merlot, Fattoria del Buonamico	494
Il Fortino Syrah, Fattoria del Buonamico	494
Il Francia Bianco, Maria Letizia Gaggioli Vigneto Bagazzana	423
Il Futuro, Il Colombaio di Cencio	457
Il Gianello Merlot, Colonna - Vini Spalletti	419
Il Grappolo Rosso, Nestore Bosco	651
Il Leccio, Oliveto	563
Il Mandorlo, La Madonnina - Triacca	557
Il Marzocco, Avignonesi	497
Il Mastio, Fattoria Sant'Andrea	515
Il Matto delle Giuncaie, Massa Vecchia	472
Il Merlot della Topa Nera, Gino Fuso Carmignani	494
Il Monaco di Ribano Cabernet, Colonna - Vini Spalletti	419
Il Moro, C. Valle dell'Acate	700
Il Nero, Vignalta	312
Il Nespoli, Poderi dal Nespoli	408
Il Palagio Chardonnay, Fattoria Il Palagio	450
Il Palagio Sauvignon, Fattoria Il Palagio	450
Il Pareto, Tenute Folonari	452
Il Paturno, Barsento	686
Il Peccato Barrique, Jacopo Banti	435
Il Poggiassai, Fattorie Chigi Saracini	445
Il Principe, Machiavelli	531
Il Roncat, Il Roncat - Giovanni Dri	401
Il Rosso, Pollara	708
Il Rosso dell'Abazia, Serafini & Vidotto	296
Il Rosso Don Giovanni Lucia Galasso, Giovanni Crosato	342
Il Saloncello, Conti Sertoli Salis	202
Il Sasso, Piaggia	519
Il Sodaccio, Fattoria di Montevertine	523
Il Tocco, Colle Bereto	571
Il Tornese Chardonnay, Drei Donà Tenuta La Palazza	411
Il Vento Chardonnay, Tenuta dei Fiori	46
Il Vessillo, Cantine Lungarotti	623
Il Villante Cabernet Sauvignon, Gaetano Lusenti	422
Il Volo di Alessandro, Castel di Salve	689
"IL" Rosso, Decugnano dei Barbi	617
Immensum, Francesco Candido	687
Impero Pinot Nero Selezione F M, Fattoria Mancini	596
Impero Rosso, Fattoria Mancini	596
Implicito, Le Due Terre	383
In Riva al Fosso, Il Poggiolo	483
Incrocio Manzoni, Vignaiolo Giuseppe Fanti	224
Incrocio Manzoni 2.15, Conte Collalto	312
Incrocio Manzoni 6.0.13., Bepin de Eto	300
Incrocio Manzoni 6.0.13, Casa Roma	327
Incrocio Manzoni 6.0.13, Conte Collalto	312
Incrocio Manzoni 6.0.13, Scuola Enologica di Conegliano G. B. Cerletti	324
Incrocio Manzoni 6.0.13 Le Portelle, Adami	321
Incrocio Manzoni Vigna Linda, Ca' Lustra	275
Initio, Aziende Vinicole Miceli	710
Inzolia, Pollara	708
Inzolia, Cantine Torrevecchia	700
Inzolia, C. Valle dell'Acate	700
Irpinia Aglianico, Terredora di Paolo	660
Irpinia Coda di Volpe, Marianna	666
Irpinia Rosso, Di Marzo	668
Isarcus, Georg Mumelter	249
Ischia Bianco Ris., Pietratorcia	656
Ischia Bianco Sup. Vigne del Cuotto, Pietratorcia	656
Ischia Biancolella, D'Ambra Vini d'Ischia	656
Ischia Biancolella Tenuta Frassitelli, D'Ambra Vini d'Ischia	656
Ischia Forastera, D'Ambra Vini d'Ischia	656
Ischia Per"e Palummo, D'Ambra Vini d'Ischia	656
Ispolaia Rosso, Ispoli	530
Istante, Franz Haas	261
Jalé, Cusumano	710
Julius, Fattoria Ormanni	569
Just Bianco, La Giustiniana	78
Justinus Kerner, Josef Sölva - Niklaserhof	255
Kaiton, Kuenhof - Peter Pliger	252
Karanar, Foradori	228
Karmis, Attilio Contini	721
Katharina, Popphof - Andreas Menz	259
Kléos, Luigi Maffini	654
Korem, Antonio Argiolas	728
Kràtos, Luigi Maffini	654
Kurni, Oasi degli Angeli	584
L'Ambrosie S. Blas, Valle	399
L'Ardenza, Cottanera	702
L'Incanto, Fattoria di Rendola	568
L'Infinito, Castello di Monastero	446
L'Insieme, Gianfranco Alessandria	97
L'Insieme, Elio Altare - Cascina Nuova	82
L'Insieme, Silvio Grasso	85
L'Insieme, Mauro Molino	87
L'Insieme, F.lli Revello	89
L'Insieme, Mauro Veglio	149
L'Olmaia, C. Monrubio	610
L'Oro di Moroder, Alessandro Moroder	579
L'Ultima Spiaggia, Palazzone	619
La Bernardina Brut, Ceretto	24
La Corte, Castello di Querceto	464
La Faina, Baroncini	572
La Fonte di Pietrarsa, Massa Vecchia	472
La Gioia, Riecine	460
La Goccia, Podere S. Luigi	517
La Grola, Allegrini	277
La Macchia, Bellaria	206
La Palazzola V. T., La Palazzola	623
La Parrina Rosso, La Parrina	509
La Parrina Rosso Muraccio, La Parrina	509
La Parrina Rosso Ris., La Parrina	509
La Petrosa, Conte Zandotti	635
La Pineta, Fattoria di Rendola	568
La Poja, Allegrini	277

La Ricolma, S. Giusto a Rentennano	461	Langhe Bianco Centobricchi, Mauro Sebaste	27
La Roccaccia, Tenuta Roccaccia	518	Langhe Bianco di Busso, Piero Busso	111
La Roccaccia Fontenova, Tenuta Roccaccia	518	Langhe Bianco Dives, G. B. Burlotto	139
La Sassaia, Fattoria Poggio Romita	576	Langhe Bianco Gastaldi, Gastaldi	112
La Segreta Bianco, Planeta	714	Langhe Bianco Graffagno, Paolo Saracco	63
La Segreta Rosso, Planeta	714	Langhe Bianco Il Fiore, Braida	122
La Vigna di Alceo, Castello dei Rampolla	514	Langhe Bianco L'Aura, Monti	102
La Vigna di Sonvico, Cascina La Barbatella	117	Langhe Bianco La Rocca, Albino Rocca	34
Labruna, Podere Aia della Macina	540	Langhe Bianco Lorenso, Luigi Baudana	129
Lacrima di Morro d'Alba, Luciano Landi	581	Langhe Bianco Matteo Correggia, Matteo Correggia	48
Lacrima di Morro d'Alba, Lucchetti	605	Langhe Bianco Printanié, Aldo Conterno	98
Lacrima di Morro d'Alba, Monteschiavo	588	Langhe Bianco Rolando, Bricco Maiolica	69
Lacrima di Morro d'Alba Gavigliano, Luciano Landi	581	Langhe Bianco Suasì, Deltetto	48
Lacrima di Morro d'Alba Passito, Luciano Landi	581	Langhe Bianco Tamardì, Monchiero Carbone	50
Lacrima di Morro d'Alba Paucca, F.lli Badiali	605	Langhe Bianco Tre Uve, Malvirà	50
Lacrima di Morro d'Alba Rùbico, Marotti Campi	592	Langhe Bianco Vigna Maestro, F.lli Pecchenino	71
Lacrima di Morro d'Alba S. Maria del Fiore, Stefano Mancinelli	591	Langhe Bric Quercia, Tenuta Carretta	120
		Langhe Bricco del Drago, Poderi Colla	26
Lacrima di Morro d'Alba Sel. Etichetta Nera, Lucchetti	605	Langhe Chardonnay, Ca' d'Gal	126
Lacrima di Morro d'Alba Sel. Falconiere, Maurizio Marconi	606	Langhe Chardonnay, Tenute Cisa Asinari dei Marchesi di Gresy	30
Lacrima di Morro d'Alba Vecchi Sapori, Luciano Landi	581	Langhe Chardonnay, Gastaldi	112
Lacrimæ Bacchi, Vitivinicola Avide	713	Langhe Chardonnay, Ettore Germano	130
Lago di Corbara, Decugnano dei Barbi	617	Langhe Chardonnay, La Morandina	62
Lago di Corbara Barbi, Decugnano dei Barbi	617	Langhe Chardonnay, Moccagatta	33
Lago di Corbara Fontauro, Giulio Freddano	618	Langhe Chardonnay, Poderi Sinaglio	27
Lago di Corbara Foresco, Barberani - Vallesanta	616	Langhe Chardonnay, Vigna Rionda - Massolino	131
Lago di Corbara Turlò, Tenuta di Salviano	624	Langhe Chardonnay Alessandra, Gianfranco Bovio	84
Lagobruno, Incontri	575	Langhe Chardonnay Ampelio, Fontanafredda	129
Lama del Tenente, Castel di Salve	689	Langhe Chardonnay Barricello, Valfieri	67
Lamaione, Castelgiocondo	477	Langhe Chardonnay Barrique, Destefanis	108
Lamarein, J. Mayr - Erbhof Unterganzner	249	Langhe Chardonnay Bastia, Conterno Fantino	100
Lambrusco Bianco Spumante M. Cl., Moro - Rinaldo Rinaldini	418	Langhe Chardonnay Bianch del Luv, Paolo Saracco	63
		Langhe Chardonnay Boccabarile, Poderi Sinaglio	27
Lambrusco dell'Emilia Le Viole, Cantine Dall'Asta	415	Langhe Chardonnay Buscat, F.lli Alessandria	138
Lambrusco dell'Emilia Mefistofele, Cantine Dall'Asta	415	Langhe Chardonnay Buschet, Moccagatta	33
Lambrusco di Modena, Cantine Cavicchioli & Figli	418	Langhe Chardonnay da Bertù, Albino Rocca	34
Lambrusco di Modena Croce della Pietra, Cantine Cavicchioli & Figli	418	Langhe Chardonnay Educato, Elio Grasso	101
		Langhe Chardonnay Elioro, Monfalletto - Cordero di Montezemolo	87
Lambrusco di Modena Il Maglio, Barbolini	426	Langhe Chardonnay Flavo, Rocche Costamagna	90
Lambrusco di Sorbara, Francesco Bellei	424	Langhe Chardonnay Gaia & Rey, Gaja	31
Lambrusco di Sorbara Tre Medaglie, Cantine Cavicchioli & Figli	418	Langhe Chardonnay Gresy, Tenute Cisa Asinari dei Marchesi di Gresy	30
Lambrusco di Sorbara Vigna del Cristo, Cantine Cavicchioli & Figli	418	Langhe Chardonnay La Bernardina, Ceretto	24
Lambrusco Grasparossa di Castelvetro, Barbolini	426	Langhe Chardonnay Le Masche, Bel Colle	138
Lambrusco Grasparossa di Castelvetro, Vittorio Graziano	408	Langhe Chardonnay Livrot, Mauro Molino	87
Lambrusco Grasparossa di Castelvetro Amabile, Corte Manzini	425	Langhe Chardonnay Morino, Batasiolo	83
		Langhe Chardonnay PiodiLei, Pio Cesare	25
Lambrusco Grasparossa di Castelvetro Col Sassoso, Cantine Cavicchioli & Figli	418	Langhe Chardonnay Prasuè, Paolo Saracco	63
		Langhe Chardonnay Roera, F.lli Giacosa	113
Lambrusco Grasparossa di Castelvetro L'Acino, Corte Manzini	425	Langhe Chardonnay Scapulin, Giuseppe Cortese	30
		Langhe Chardonnay Serbato, Batasiolo	83
Lambrusco Mantovano, Lebovitz	204	Langhe Chardonnay Sermine, Ca' del Baio	135
Lambrusco Mantovano Banda Blu, C. Soc. Coop. di Quistello	212	Langhe Chardonnay Stissa d'le Favole, Montaribaldi	33
		Langhe Dolcetto, Anna Maria Abbona	73
Lambrusco Mantovano Banda Rossa, C. Soc. Coop. di Quistello	212	Langhe Dolcetto, Bricco del Cucù	42
		Langhe Dolcetto Visadi, Domenico Clerico	98
Lambrusco Mantovano Rosso dei Concari, Lebovitz	204	Langhe Eremo, Fontanafredda	129
Lambrusco Provincia di Mantova Etichetta Blu, Stefano Spezia	209	Langhe Fabio, Andrea Oberto	88
		Langhe Favorita, F.lli Alessandria	138
Lambrusco Reggiano, Ermete Medici & Figli	416	Langhe Favorita, Bel Colle	138
Lambrusco Reggiano, Moro - Rinaldo Rinaldini	418	Langhe Favorita, Cascina Chicco	47
Lambrusco Reggiano Piazza S. Giacomo Maggiore, Ca' de' Medici	427	Langhe Favorita, Gianluigi Lano	25
		Langhe Favorita, Pelissero	137
Lambrusco Reggiano Piazza S. Prospero, Ca' de' Medici	427	Langhe Freisa, C. del Pino	29
Lambrusco Reggiano Secco Assolo, Ermete Medici & Figli	416	Langhe Freisa, F.lli Cavallotto	59
Lambrusco Reggiano Secco Concerto, Ermete Medici & Figli	416	Langhe Freisa, Moccagatta	33
		Langhe Freisa Kyè, G. D. Vajra	41
Lambrusco Reggiano Tre Medaglie, Cantine Cavicchioli & Figli	418	Langhe Freisa La Violetta, Piero Gatti	126
		Langhe Freisa S. Rosalia, Giacomo Brezza & Figli	36
Lambrusco Spumante M. Cl. Pjcol Ross, Moro - Rinaldo Rinaldini	418	Langhe Freisa S. Lucia, Gianfranco Bovio	84
		Langhe Furesté, F.lli Oddero	88
Lamezia Greco, Cantine Lento	696	Langhe La Castella, F.lli Pecchenino	71
Lamezia Greco, Statti	697	Langhe La Villa, Elio Altare - Cascina Nuova	82
Lamezia Rosso Ris., Cantine Lento	696	Langhe Larigi, Elio Altare - Cascina Nuova	82
Lamezia Rosso Tenuta Romeo, Cantine Lento	696	Langhe Nebbiolo, F.lli Bera	116
Lamoremio, Benanti	703	Langhe Nebbiolo, Giacomo Borgogno & Figli	36
Langhe Arbarei, Ceretto	24	Langhe Nebbiolo, Castello di Verduno	139
Langhe Arborina, Elio Altare - Cascina Nuova	82	Langhe Nebbiolo, Giuseppe Cortese	30
Langhe Arneis, Fontanabianca	112	Langhe Nebbiolo, Fontanabianca	112
Langhe Arneis, Ugo Lequio	114	Langhe Nebbiolo, Cascina Luisin	32
Langhe Arneis, Monfalletto - Cordero di Montezemolo	87	Langhe Nebbiolo, Mario Marengo	86
Langhe Arneis, Pio Cesare	25	Langhe Nebbiolo, Giuseppe Mascarello e Figlio	96
Langhe Arneis Blangé, Ceretto	24	Langhe Nebbiolo, Monfalletto - Cordero di Montezemolo	87
Langhe Arte, Domenico Clerico	98	Langhe Nebbiolo, Montaribaldi	33
Langhe Barilot, Michele Chiarlo	45	Langhe Nebbiolo, Cascina Morassino	144
Langhe Bianco, Bricco del Cucù	42	Langhe Nebbiolo, Pelissero	137
Langhe Bianco, Tenute Cisa Asinari dei Marchesi di Gresy	30	Langhe Nebbiolo, Giorgio Scarzello e Figli	40
Langhe Bianco, La Spinetta	54	Langhe Nebbiolo, G. D. Vajra	41
Langhe Bianco, G. D. Vajra	41	Langhe Nebbiolo, Rino Varaldo	35
Langhe Bianco Asso di Fiori, Braida	122	Langhe Nebbiolo, Vigna Rionda - Massolino	131
Langhe Bianco Ballarin, Cascina Ballarin	84	Langhe Nebbiolo Annunziata, Gianfranco Bovio	84
Langhe Bianco Bel Amì, Silvano e Elena Boroli	24	Langhe Nebbiolo Batié, Gianni Gagliardo	149
Langhe Bianco Binel, Ettore Germano	130	Langhe Nebbiolo Bric del Baio, Ca' del Baio	135
Langhe Bianco Boccabarile, Poderi Sinaglio	27	Langhe Nebbiolo Castellero, Araldica - Il Cantinone	54
Langhe Bianco Bricco Rovella, Armando Parusso	103		

Entry	Page
Langhe Nebbiolo Ciabot della Luna, Gianni Voerzio	91
Langhe Nebbiolo Conteisa, Gaja	31
Langhe Nebbiolo Lasarin, Poderi Marcarini	86
Langhe Nebbiolo Martinenga, Tenute Cisa Asinari dei Marchesi di Gresy	30
Langhe Nebbiolo Sperss, Gaja	31
Langhe Nebbiolo Surisjvan, Icardi	61
Langhe Nebbiolo Terranìn, Silvano e Elena Boroli	24
Langhe Paitin, Paitin	114
Langhe Pe Mol, Luciano Sandrone	39
Langhe Rosso, Hilberg - Pasquero	120
Langhe Rosso, F.lli Mossio	123
Langhe Rosso, Terre del Barolo	60
Langhe Rosso Acanzio, Mauro Molino	87
Langhe Rosso Alta Bussia, Attilio Ghisolfi	101
Langhe Rosso Balàu, Ettore Germano	130
Langhe Rosso Ballarin, Cascina Ballarin	84
Langhe Rosso Bouquet, F.lli Seghesio	105
Langhe Rosso Bric du Luv, Ca' Viola	107
Langhe Rosso Bric Quercia, Tenuta Carretta	120
Langhe Rosso Bricco Manzoni, Podere Rocche dei Manzoni	104
Langhe Rosso Bricco Rovella, Armando Parusso	103
Langhe Rosso Bricco Serra, F.lli Cigliuti	111
Langhe Rosso Briccobotti, Pira	71
Langhe Rosso Brich Ginestra, Paolo Conterno	99
Langhe Rosso Brumaio, S. Fereolo	72
Langhe Rosso Buio, Enzo Boglietti	83
Langhe Rosso Cadò, Anna Maria Abbona	73
Langhe Rosso Carlin, Attilio Ghisolfi	101
Langhe Rosso Castlé, Gastaldi	112
Langhe Rosso Centobricchi, Mauro Sebaste	27
Langhe Rosso Corale, Paolo Scavino	59
Langhe Rosso Costa Russi, Gaja	31
Langhe Rosso Curdè, Monfalletto - Cordero di Montezemolo	87
Langhe Rosso Da Pruvé, Ca' Rome' - Romano Marengo	29
Langhe Rosso Darmagi, Gaja	31
Langhe Rosso Dossi Rossi, Monti	102
Langhe Rosso Duetto, Cascina Vano	115
Langhe Rosso Faletto, Cascina Bongiovanni	57
Langhe Rosso Fantasia 4.20, Rino Varaldo	35
Langhe Rosso I Due Ricu, Marziano e Enrico Abbona	69
Langhe Rosso Il Nebbio, Pio Cesare	25
Langhe Rosso La Bisbetica, Ada Nada	136
Langhe Rosso La Malora, Terre da Vino	41
Langhe Rosso Livraie, Orlando Abrigo	154
Langhe Rosso Lorenso, Luigi Baudana	129
Langhe Rosso Lorié, Bricco Maiolica	69
Langhe Rosso Luigi Einaudi, Poderi Luigi Einaudi	70
Langhe Rosso Luna, F.lli Alessandria	138
Langhe Rosso Martin Sec, S. Romano	72
Langhe Rosso Mondaccione, Luigi Coppo e Figli	52
Langhe Rosso Monprà, Conterno Fantino	100
Langhe Rosso Monsordo La Bernardina, Ceretto	24
Langhe Rosso Montegrilli, Elvio Cogno	118
Langhe Rosso Nej, Icardi	61
Langhe Rosso Pafoj, Icardi	61
Langhe Rosso Pi Cit, Marchesi di Barolo	37
Langhe Rosso Pian del Gäje, Ca' d'Gal	126
Langhe Rosso Piria, Vigna Rionda - Massolino	131
Langhe Rosso Quatr Nas, Podere Rocche dei Manzoni	104
Langhe Rosso Rangone, Ca' Viola	107
Langhe Rosso Riella, Degiorgis	95
Langhe Rosso S. Guglielmo, Malvirà	50
Langhe Rosso Seifile, Fiorenzo Nada	136
Langhe Rosso Serrapiù, Gianni Voerzio	91
Langhe Rosso Sinaij, Poderi Sinaglio	27
Langhe Rosso Sorì S. Lorenzo, Gaja	31
Langhe Rosso Sorì Tildin, Gaja	31
Langhe Rosso Status, Giuseppe Mascarello e Figlio	96
Langhe Rosso Suo di Giacomo, Eugenio Bocchino	143
Langhe Rosso Tris, Giovanni Manzone	102
Langhe Rosso Vignaserra, R. Voerzio	92
Langhe Rosso Virtus, Tenute Cisa Asinari dei Marchesi di Gresy	30
Langhe Rosso Yeta, Giovanni Battista Gillardi	74
Langhe Sassisto, F.lli Bera	116
Langhe Vendemmiaio, Tenuta La Volta - Cabutto	40
Latinia, C. Soc. di Santadi	726
Laudato di Malbech, S. Margherita	324
Laurento Chardonnay, Umberto Cesari	407
Laurus, La Fiorita	562
Lavischio di Poggio Salvi, Tenuta Il Greppo	482
Lavischio Poggio Salvi, Tenuta Il Greppo	482
Lazio Bianco Satrico, Casale del Giglio	628
Le Anfore, Colle di Maggio	635
Le Balze, Il Poggiolino	545
Le Banche, Cascina delle Terre Rosse	162
Le Borranine, Montiverdi	459
Le Bronche, Fattorie Parri	568
Le Bruniche, Tenute Folonari	452
Le Busche, Umani Ronchi	595
Le Cave Chardonnay, Fattoria Le Terrazze	593
Le Fagge Chardonnay, Castello d' Albola	521
Le Ginestre Brut, Le Ginestre	550
Le Lave, Bertani	292
Le Macchiole, Le Macchiole	433
Le Marangole, Castello d' Albola	521
Le Monache Passito, Poderi Sinaglio	27
Le Passule, Librandi	695
Le Pergole del Sole Cavalchina, Cavalchina	311
Le Pergole Torte, Fattoria di Montevertine	523
Le Prata, Villa Le Prata	493
Le Scuderie del Cielo, Filomusi Guelfi	648
Le Sincette Brut, Cascina La Pertica	196
Le Solagne, Fattoria Dezi	601
Le Solagne V. T., Fattoria Dezi	601
Le Stanze, Poliziano	503
Le Veglie di Neri, Massa Vecchia	472
Le Vigne, Ascevi - Luwa	387
Le Vigne di Cos Russo, COS	715
Le Voliere Cabernet Sauvignon, Castello di Modanella	525
Le Volte, Tenuta dell' Ornellaia	433
Le Zalte Rosso, Cascina La Pertica	196
Le Zuccule Rosso, Ronchi di Manzano	371
Leneo Moro, Camillo Montori	642
Leone del Carobbio, Carobbio	510
Leone Rosso, Fattoria del Casato - Donatella Cinelli Colombini	476
Leopold Cuvée Blanc, Fiegl	366
Leopold Cuvée Rouge, Fiegl	366
Lessona, Sella	92
Lessona Il Chioso, Sella	92
Lessona S. Sebastiano allo Zoppo, Sella	92
Leucos Bianco, Ronco dei Pini	384
Leverano Bianco Vigna del Saraceno, Conti Zecca	683
Leverano Malvasia Vigna del Saraceno, Conti Zecca	683
Leverano Rosato, C. Soc. Coop. Leverano	691
Leverano Rosato Vigna del Saraceno, Conti Zecca	683
Leverano Rosso Vigna del Saraceno, Conti Zecca	683
Leverano Rosso Vigna del Saraceno Ris., Conti Zecca	683
Liano, Umberto Cesari	407
Libaio, Tenimenti Ruffino	520
Libero Rosso, Roberto Mazzi	294
Liburnio, Orlandi Contucci Ponno	647
Ligeia, Statti	697
Limes Rosso, Ronco dei Pini	384
Limpiados, Barone La Lumia	704
Linagre Sauvignon di Villa Angela, Ercole Velenosi	580
Linticlarus Cuvée, Tiefenbrunner	257
Lipitiresco, Massimo Romeo	567
Lis, Lis Neris - Pecorari	394
Lis Neris, Lis Neris - Pecorari	394
Lison-Pramaggiore Cabernet Franc, Podere dal Ger	379
Lison-Pramaggiore Cabernet Franc, Villa Frattina	378
Lison-Pramaggiore Cabernet Sauvignon, Villa Frattina	378
Lison-Pramaggiore Chardonnay, Mosole	328
Lison-Pramaggiore Chardonnay, Podere dal Ger	379
Lison-Pramaggiore Chardonnay, Villa Frattina	378
Lison-Pramaggiore Merlot, Podere dal Ger	379
Lison-Pramaggiore Merlot, Villa Frattina	378
Lison-Pramaggiore Merlot ad Nonam, Mosole	328
Lison-Pramaggiore Pinot Grigio, Podere dal Ger	379
Lison-Pramaggiore Sauvignon, Villa Frattina	378
Litra, Abbazia S. Anastasia	701
Livernano, Livernano	522
Livio Bronca Brut, Sorelle Bronca	322
Lizzano Bianco Torretta, C. Soc. di Lizzano	684
Lizzano Rosato Porvica, C. Soc. di Lizzano	684
Lizzano Rosso Belvedere, C. Soc. di Lizzano	684
Loazzolo Borgo Maragliano V. T., Borgo Maragliano	93
Loazzolo Piasa Rischei, Forteto della Luja	93
Locorotondo, C. Coop. del Locorotondo	684
Locorotondo, I Pastini - Carparelli	690
Locorotondo Talné, Borgo Canale	680
Locorotondo Vigneti in Tallinajo, C. Coop. del Locorotondo	684
Lodato, Tua Rita	545
Logaiolo, Fattoria dell' Aiola	443
Loghetto, Agnes	198
Longobardo Rosso, Enzo Mecella	586
Loré Muffa Nobile, Dino Illuminati	642
Lucciolaio, Torraccia di Presura	558
Luce, Luce	486
Lucente, Luce	486
Lucilla, Farnetella	541
Lucumone, Ficomontanino	555
Ludi, Ercole Velenosi	580
Luenzo, Vincenzo Cesani	533
Lugana, Costaripa	190
Lugana, Giacomo Montresor	320
Lugana, Tenuta Roveglia	211
Lugana, Zenato	297
Lugana Brolettino Grande Annata, Ca' dei Frati	201
Lugana Brut, Pasini Prod.	212
Lugana Brut Cl. Cà Maiol, Provenza	184
Lugana Brut Cl. Cuvèe dei Frati, Ca' dei Frati	201
Lugana Brut Sebastian, Provenza	184
Lugana Cà Maiol, Provenza	184
Lugana Collo Lungo, Visconti	207
Lugana Il Brolettino, Ca' dei Frati	201
Lugana Il Rintocco, Marangona	211

Name	Page
Lugana Le Creete, Ottella	296
Lugana Melibeo, Santi	280
Lugana S. Onorata, Visconti	207
Lugana Sergio Zenato, Zenato	297
Lugana Sup., Ca' Lojera	213
Lugana Sup., Visconti	207
Lugana Sup. Cà Molin, Provenza	184
Lugana Sup. Cios, Cantine Valtenesi - Lugana	209
Lugana Sup. Filo di Arianna, Tenuta Roveglia	211
Lugana Sup. Molceo, Ottella	296
Lugana Sup. Sel. Fabio Contato, Provenza	184
Lugana Sup. Vigne di Catullo, Tenuta Roveglia	211
Lugana Vegne Vecie, Fraccaroli	326
Lugana Vigna Campo Serà, Fraccaroli	326
Lugana Vigna Silva, Ca' Lojera	213
Lugana Vigneto Massoni S. Cristina, Zenato	297
Lugana Vigneto Pansere, Fraccaroli	326
Lugana Vigneto S. Martino II Sestante, Viticoltori Tommasi	305
Lumen, Gualdo del Re	543
Luna dei Feldi, S. Margherita	324
Luna di Monte, S. Luciano	493
Luna Verde, Guicciardini Strozzi - Fattoria Cusona	534
Lunaia Rosso, La Stellata	471
Lunaria, Castelluccio	412
Lupicaia, Castello del Terriccio	442
Lupinello, Perazzeta	552
Luzzana, Giovanni Cherchi	729
LV Passito, Tenuta S. Sebastiano	94
Macàro Metodo Solera, Valle dell'Asso	690
Macchiona, La Stoppa	417
Madreselva, Casale del Giglio	628
Maestro, Borgo Canale	680
Maestro Raro, Fattoria di Felsina	446
Magilda Rosato, Barsento	686
Magna Grecia Bianco, Vintripodi	697
Magnificat Cabernet Sauvignon, Drei Donà Tenuta La Palazza	411
Magno Megonio, Librandi	695
Maiano, Podere Aia della Macina	540
Majere, La Cadalora	236
Majo S. Lorenzo, Aziende Vinicole Miceli	710
Malandrino, Tenuta Cataldi Madonna	645
Malbec, Fossi	555
Malbech Vigna degli Aceri Paladin, Paladin & Paladin	323
Malena, Pacina	554
Malicchia Mapicchia, Barsento	686
Malvasia, Il Lebbio	534
Malvasia, Mulino delle Tolle	332
Malvasia, Vigneto delle Terre Rosse	423
Malvasia Campo di Fiori, Vigneto Due Santi	273
Malvasia del Lazio, C. Coop. di Cerveteri	630
Malvasia del Lazio, Fontana Candida	633
Malvasia del Lazio, Vini Pallavicini	637
Malvasia del Lazio Rumon, Conte Zandotti	635
Malvasia del Lazio Terre dei Grifi, Fontana Candida	633
Malvasia del Lazio Villanova, C. Coop. di Cerveteri	630
Malvasia dell'Emilia Nebbie d'Autunno, Ermete Medici & Figli	416
Malvasia delle Lipari Passito, Barone di Villagrande	708
Malvasia di Bosa, F.lli Porcu	731
Malvasia di Cagliari, Villa di Quartu	725
Malvasia di Castelnuovo Don Bosco, Cascina Gilli	56
Malvasia di Castelnuovo Don Bosco Rosa Canina, Bava	63
Malvasia Dolce, Monte delle Vigne	425
Malvasia Istriana, Russolo	395
Malvasia & Moscato Dolce, Carra	415
Mamertino Bianco, Casa Vinicola Grasso	717
Mammolo, Cennatoio	511
Mandolaia, La Vis	224
Mandoleo Passito, Co.Vi.O.	617
Mandrarossa Bendicò, Settesoli	707
Mandrarossa Bianco, Settesoli	707
Mandrarossa Rosso, Settesoli	707
Mandrielle Merlot, Banfi	474
Manero, Fattoria del Cerro	499
Manna, Franz Haas	261
Mantenghia, Capichera	721
Mantonico di Bianco, Vintripodi	697
Manuzzio, Fattoria Sant'Andrea	515
Manzoni Bianco, Gregoletto	286
Marconero, Contadi Castaldi	170
Marino Colle Picchioni Oro, Paola Di Mauro - Colle Picchioni	633
Marino Etichetta Verde, Paola Di Mauro - Colle Picchioni	633
Marinò Rosso, Luigi Vivacqua	698
Marino Sup., Gotto d'Oro	638
Marna, S. Gervasio	510
Marrano, Bigi	616
Marsala Fine Ruby, Carlo Pellegrino	706
Marsala Soleras Oro Baglio Florio, Cantine Florio	705
Marsala Sup., Marco De Bartoli	704
Marsala Sup. 20 Anni, Marco De Bartoli	704
Marsala Sup. Ambra Semisecco, Cantine Rallo	706
Marsala Sup. Oro, Carlo Pellegrino	706
Marsala Sup. Ris. 20 Anni, Marco De Bartoli	704
Marsala Sup. Ris. Dom Pellegrino, Carlo Pellegrino	706
Marsala Sup. Ris. Targa 1840, Cantine Florio	705
Marsala Sup. Vecchioflorio Ris., Cantine Florio	705
Marsala Vergine Baglio Florio, Cantine Florio	705
Marsala Vergine Soleras Ris. 12 anni, Cantine Rallo	706
Marsala Vergine Terre Arse, Cantine Florio	705
Martà, Fattoria S. Francesco	694
Mary Grace, Carlo Giacosa	31
Marzieno, Fattoria Zerbina	409
Masero, Podere Lavandaro	556
Masetto Bianco, Endrizzi	232
Masetto Nero, Endrizzi	232
Maso Furli Rosso, Maso Furli	225
Maso Torresella, Cavit - Consorzio di Cantine Sociali	233
Maso Torresella Cuvée, Cavit - Consorzio di Cantine Sociali	233
Massaio, Meleta	527
Massaretta, Cima	471
Masseo, Podere Vaglie	608
Masseto, Tenuta dell' Ornellaia	433
Mataossu Vigneto Reinè, Filippo Ruffino	167
Maté Rosso, Sottimano	115
Mater Matuta, Casale del Giglio	628
Mauritius, C. Gries	246
Maximo, Umani Ronchi	595
Mazzaferrata, Tenuta di Bossi	570
Mecenate, Villa Cilnia	430
Meditandum, Pietratorcia	656
Meditandum ad 2000, C. Soc. di Nomi	229
Medoro Sangiovese, Umani Ronchi	595
Mel, Antonio Caggiano	664
Menj Bianco, Tenuta Villanova	364
Meraco Rosso, Cantine S. Marco	637
Merlot, Casale del Giglio	628
Merlot, Case Bianche	326
Merlot, Castagnoli	552
Merlot, Feudo Principi di Butera	701
Merlot, Fattoria La Braccesca	501
Merlot, La Palazzola	623
Merlot, Meleta	527
Merlot, Melini	519
Merlot, Planeta	714
Merlot, Cantine Rallo	706
Merlot, Fattoria di Rendola	568
Merlot, Roncùs	338
Merlot, Sant'Elena	368
Merlot, Villa Arceno	449
Merlot, Villa Pillo	462
Merlot Baladello, Ferghettina	186
Merlot Baolar, Pierpaolo Pecorari	395
Merlot–Cabernet, Santarosa	413
Merlot dei Colli Trevigiani, Gregoletto	286
Merlot dell'Umbria, Falesco	634
Merlot Desiderio, Avignonesi	497
Merlot I Legni, Russolo	395
Merlot Lazio Costamagna, Casale Mattia	637
Merlot Mandrarossa, Settesoli	707
Merlot Orgno, Fasoli	324
Merlot Sant'Adele, Villa Pillo	462
Merlot Sebino, Ferghettina	186
Merlot Sebino, Ferghettina	186
Merlot Tiare Mate, Livon	393
Mesolone Rosso, Barni	44
Messorio, Le Macchiole	433
Mezzopane, Poggio S. Polo	574
Migliara, Tenimenti Luigi D'Alessandro	450
Millanni, Guicciardini Strozzi - Fattoria Cusona	534
Milleunanotte, Tenuta di Donnafugata	705
Minaia, Franco M. Martinetti	135
Mirju Passito, Pedra Majore	724
Mirum, La Monacesca	589
Mirus, La Monacesca	589
Mito, Fattoria Paradiso	405
Mito, S. Savino	599
Mitterberg Manna, Franz Haas	261
Mizzole Rosso, Cecilia Beretta	319
Modus, Tenimenti Ruffino	520
Molise Aglianico Contado, Di Majo Norante	641
Molise Don Luigi, Di Majo Norante	641
Molise Falanghina, Borgo di Colloredo	640
Molise Falanghina, Di Majo Norante	641
Molise Fiano, Di Majo Norante	641
Molise Greco, Di Majo Norante	641
Molise Montepulciano, Borgo di Colloredo	640
Molise Trebbiano, Borgo di Colloredo	640
Momenti, Podere Vaglie	608
Monferrato Alterego, Luigi Coppo e Figli	52
Monferrato Barbera Rivalta, Villa Sparina	80
Monferrato Bianco Airales, Vicara	123
Monferrato Bianco Altesserre, Bava	63
Monferrato Bianco Camillona, Araldica - Il Cantinone	54
Monferrato Bianco dei Marchesi, Marchesi Alfieri	124
Monferrato Bianco Eliseo, Cantine Sant'Agata	128
Monferrato Bianco Grisello, Castello di Lignano	74
Monferrato Bianco I Fossaretti, Poderi Bertelli	65
Monferrato Bianco Il Barigi, Cascina Bertolotto	132
Monferrato Bianco Munsret, Paolo Casalone	94
Monferrato Bianco Non è, Cascina La Barbatella	117

Monferrato Bianco Pafoj, Icardi	61
Monferrato Bianco Sarni, Vicara	123
Monferrato Bianco Sauvignon, F.lli Rovero	28
Monferrato Bianco Sauvignon Barrique, F.lli Rovero	28
Monferrato Bianco Sivoj, Cascina La Ghersa	96
Monferrato Bianco Tra Donne Sole, Terre da Vino	41
Monferrato Cabernet Fossaretti, Poderi Bertelli	65
Monferrato Casalese Cortese, Tenuta S. Sebastiano	94
Monferrato Cortese, La Guardia	109
Monferrato Countacc!, Michele Chiarlo	45
Monferrato Dolcetto Fiordaliso, Tenuta dei Fiori	46
Monferrato Dolcetto Nibiô, Cascina Ulivi	151
Monferrato Freisa Bioc, Isabella	110
Monferrato Freisa La Frassinella, Castello di Lignano	74
Monferrato Freisa La Selva di Moirano, Scarpa - Antica Casa Vinicola	117
Monferrato Freisa Vivace Sobric, Isabella	110
Monferrato Müller Thurgau, Villa Sparina	80
Monferrato Pomona, Bersano & Riccadonna	116
Monferrato Rosso, Gian Piero Broglia - Tenuta La Meirana	77
Monferrato Rosso, Cascina Gilli	56
Monferrato Rosso, Tenuta dei Fiori	46
Monferrato Rosso Amis, Cascina Garitina	55
Monferrato Rosso Antico Vitigno, Sciorio	67
Monferrato Rosso Bigio, Colonna	141
Monferrato Rosso Bricco Maddalena, Cascina La Maddalena	121
Monferrato Rosso Bricco S. Tomaso, La Scamuzza	154
Monferrato Rosso Bruno Broglia, Gian Piero Broglia - Tenuta La Meirana	77
Monferrato Rosso Cabernet, Colonna	141
Monferrato Rosso Cabernet, F.lli Rovero	28
Monferrato Rosso Cabernet, Tenuta dei Fiori	46
Monferrato Rosso Cascina Bricco del Sole, Icardi	61
Monferrato Rosso Castello di Tassarolo, Castello di Tassarolo	134
Monferrato Rosso Centenario, G. Accornero e Figli	140
Monferrato Rosso Crebarné, Carlo Quarello	64
Monferrato Rosso dei Marchesi, Marchesi Alfieri	124
Monferrato Rosso di Malì, Il Vignale	119
Monferrato Rosso Dom, Tenuta dell'Arbiola	125
Monferrato Rosso Estremis, Cascina Garitina	55
Monferrato Rosso Genesi, Cantine Sant'Agata	128
Monferrato Rosso Innominabile, La Guardia	109
Monferrato Rosso Just, La Giustiniana	78
Monferrato Rosso l'Uccelletta, Vicara	123
Monferrato Rosso La Ghersa, Cascina La Ghersa	96
Monferrato Rosso Le Grive, Forteto della Luja	93
Monferrato Rosso Le Pernici, Gian Piero Broglia - Tenuta La Meirana	77
Monferrato Rosso Lhennius, Castello di Lignano	74
Monferrato Rosso Luce Monaca, Araldica - Il Cantinone	54
Monferrato Rosso Matot, Valfieri	67
Monferrato Rosso Mon Mayor, Poderi Bertelli	65
Monferrato Rosso Mondone, Colonna	141
Monferrato Rosso Monterovere, Cantine Sant'Agata	128
Monferrato Rosso Mystère, Cascina La Barbatella	117
Monferrato Rosso Piagé, Cascina La Ghersa	96
Monferrato Rosso Pin, La Spinetta	54
Monferrato Rosso Pinot Nero, F.lli Rovero	28
Monferrato Rosso Policalpo, Cascina Castlèt	66
Monferrato Rosso Reginal, Sciorio	67
Monferrato Rosso Renero, Araldica - Il Cantinone	54
Monferrato Rosso Rivaia, Tenuta La Meridiana	107
Monferrato Rosso Rivalta, Villa Sparina	80
Monferrato Rosso Rubello, Vicara	123
Monferrato Rosso Rus, Paolo Casalone	94
Monferrato Rosso S. Germano, Marchesi Alfieri	124
Monferrato Rosso Sacroprofano, La Guardia	109
Monferrato Rosso Sonvico, Cascina La Barbatella	117
Monferrato Rosso Sul Bric, Franco M. Martinetti	135
Monferrato Rosso Tantra, F. e M. Scrimaglio	118
Monferrato Villa Pattono, Renato Ratti	89
Monica di Sardegna, C. Soc. della Trexenta	727
Monica di Sardegna, Cantine di Dolianova	722
Monica di Sardegna, Meloni Vini	726
Monica di Sardegna, Cantine Sardus Pater	732
Monica di Sardegna Antigua, C. Soc. di Santadi	726
Monica di Sardegna Duca di Mandas, C. Soc. della Trexenta	727
Monica di Sardegna Elima, Pala	728
Monica di Sardegna Insula, Cantine Sardus Pater	732
Monica di Sardegna Nabui, C. Soc. Il Nuraghe	731
Monica di Sardegna Perdera, Antonio Argiolas	728
Monica di Sardegna Torremora, Josto Puddu	732
Monile, Viticcio	468
Monna Claudia, Rodano	553
Monprà, Conterno Fantino	100
Monrubio, C. Monrubio	610
Monsanulus Bianco Villamagna, Boccadigabbia	584
Monsavium Passito, Valentino Fiorini	581
Montalperti Chardonnay, Boccadigabbia	584
Montalupa Bianco, Ascheri	44
Montalupa Rosso, Ascheri	44
Monte del Drago Rosso, Musella	300
Montecalvi, Montecalvi	463
Montecarlo Bianco, Fattoria del Buonamico	494
Montecarlo Bianco, Fattoria del Teso	565
Montecarlo Bianco, Fattoria Vigna del Greppo	565
Montecarlo Bianco La Salita, Mazzini Franceschi	565
Montecarlo Bianco Stati d'Animo, Gino Fuso Carmignani	494
Montecarlo Bianco Terre dei Cascinieri, Wandanna	495
Montecarlo Bianco Terre della Gioiosa, Wandanna	495
Montecarlo Rosso, Fattoria del Buonamico	494
Montecarlo Rosso, Fattoria del Teso	565
Montecarlo Rosso Anfidiamante, Fattoria del Teso	565
Montecarlo Rosso Carlo IV Ris., Fattoria Vigna del Greppo	565
Montecarlo Rosso Casalta, Mazzini Franceschi	565
Montecarlo Rosso Sassonero, Gino Fuso Carmignani	494
Montecarlo Rosso Terre dei Cascinieri, Wandanna	495
Montechiari Cabernet, Fattoria di Montechiari	495
Montechiari Chardonnay, Fattoria di Montechiari	495
Montechiari Nero, Fattoria di Montechiari	495
Montechiari Pinot Nero, Fattoria di Montechiari	495
Montechiari Rosso, Fattoria di Montechiari	495
Montecompatri Colonna Sup. Virtù Romane, Tenuta Le Quinte	638
Montecucco Alfeno, Perazzeta	552
Montecucco Sangiovese, Parmoleto	551
Montecucco Sangiovese, Perazzeta	552
Montefalco Bianco, Arnaldo Caprai - Val di Maggio	614
Montefalco Rosso, Agricola Adanti	608
Montefalco Rosso, Fattoria Milziade Antano	609
Montefalco Rosso, Antonelli - S. Marco	614
Montefalco Rosso, Arnaldo Caprai - Val di Maggio	614
Montefalco Rosso, Castello di Antignano - Brogal Vini	621
Montefalco Rosso, Còlpetrone	613
Montefalco Rosso, Rocca di Fabbri	615
Montefalco Rosso, Scacciadiavoli	615
Montefalco Rosso, Spoletoducale	626
Montefalco Rosso Ris., Fattoria Milziade Antano	609
Montefalco Rosso Ris., Arnaldo Caprai - Val di Maggio	614
Montefalco Sagrantino, Agricola Adanti	608
Montefalco Sagrantino, Fattoria Milziade Antano	609
Montefalco Sagrantino, Antonelli - S. Marco	614
Montefalco Sagrantino, Castello di Antignano - Brogal Vini	621
Montefalco Sagrantino, Còlpetrone	613
Montefalco Sagrantino, Rocca di Fabbri	615
Montefalco Sagrantino, Scacciadiavoli	615
Montefalco Sagrantino, Spoletoducale	626
Montefalco Sagrantino, Terre de' Trinci	625
Montefalco Sagrantino 25 Anni, Arnaldo Caprai - Val di Maggio	614
Montefalco Sagrantino Colle delle Allodole, Fattoria Milziade Antano	609
Montefalco Sagrantino Colle Piano, Arnaldo Caprai - Val di Maggio	614
Montefalco Sagrantino Passito, Agricola Adanti	608
Montefalco Sagrantino Passito, Fattoria Milziade Antano	609
Montefalco Sagrantino Passito, Antonelli - S. Marco	614
Montefalco Sagrantino Passito, Còlpetrone	613
Montefalco Sagrantino Passito, Rocca di Fabbri	615
Montefalco Sagrantino Passito, Piero Virili	626
Montefalco Sagrantino Vigne Umbre, Umbria Viticoltori Associati	625
Montello Cabernet Sauvignon, Conte Loredan Gasparini Venegazzù	330
Montellori Brut, Fattoria di Montellori	454
Monteloro, Sant'Appiano	550
Montenero, Abbazia S. Anastasia	701
Montenetto di Brescia Merlot, Cascina Nuova	171
Montepirolo, S. Patrignano - Terre del Cedro	409
Montepulciano, Fattoria Le Poggette	613
Montepulciano d'Abruzzo, Barone Cornacchia	652
Montepulciano d'Abruzzo, Nestore Bosco	651
Montepulciano d'Abruzzo, Buccicatino	652
Montepulciano d'Abruzzo, Tenuta Cataldi Madonna	645
Montepulciano d'Abruzzo, Faraone	643
Montepulciano d'Abruzzo, Filomusi Guelfi	648
Montepulciano d'Abruzzo, Fattoria La Valentina	648
Montepulciano d'Abruzzo, Lepore	641
Montepulciano d'Abruzzo, Gianni Masciarelli	647
Montepulciano d'Abruzzo, Antonio e Elio Monti	650
Montepulciano d'Abruzzo, Camillo Montori	642
Montepulciano d'Abruzzo, Bruno Nicodemi	644
Montepulciano d'Abruzzo, Franco Pasetti	643
Montepulciano d'Abruzzo, C. Tollo	649
Montepulciano d'Abruzzo, Edoardo Valentini	644
Montepulciano d'Abruzzo, Valori	652
Montepulciano d'Abruzzo, Ciccio Zaccagnini	640
Montepulciano d'Abruzzo Abbazia S. Clemente, Ciccio Zaccagnini	640
Montepulciano d'Abruzzo Antares, S. Lorenzo	650
Montepulciano d'Abruzzo Bacco, Bruno Nicodemi	644
Montepulciano d'Abruzzo Badia dei Miracoli, Madonna dei Miracoli	650
Montepulciano d'Abruzzo Binomio, Fattoria La Valentina	648
Montepulciano d'Abruzzo Brume Rosse, Torre Zambra	649
Montepulciano d'Abruzzo Cagiòlo, C. Tollo	649
Montepulciano d'Abruzzo Castello di Salle, Ciccio Zaccagnini	640
Montepulciano d'Abruzzo Cerasuolo, Tenuta Cataldi Madonna	645

Entry	Page
Montepulciano d'Abruzzo Cerasuolo, Filomusi Guelfi	648
Montepulciano d'Abruzzo Cerasuolo, Fattoria La Valentina	648
Montepulciano d'Abruzzo Cerasuolo, Lepore	641
Montepulciano d'Abruzzo Cerasuolo, Bruno Nicodemi	644
Montepulciano d'Abruzzo Cerasuolo, Franco Pasetti	643
Montepulciano d'Abruzzo Cerasuolo, Edoardo Valentini	644
Montepulciano d'Abruzzo Cerasuolo, Ciccio Zaccagnini	640
Montepulciano d'Abruzzo Cerasuolo Campirosa, Dino Illuminati	642
Montepulciano d'Abruzzo Cerasuolo Dama, Marramiero	646
Montepulciano d'Abruzzo Cerasuolo Fonte Cupa, Camillo Montori	642
Montepulciano d'Abruzzo Cerasuolo Le Vigne, Faraone	643
Montepulciano d'Abruzzo Cerasuolo Myosotis, Ciccio Zaccagnini	640
Montepulciano d'Abruzzo Cerasuolo Pié delle Vigne, Tenuta Cataldi Madonna	645
Montepulciano d'Abruzzo Cerasuolo Pietrosa, Sarchese Dora	646
Montepulciano d'Abruzzo Cerasuolo Riseis, Agriverde	645
Montepulciano d'Abruzzo Cerasuolo Valle d'Oro, C. Tollo	649
Montepulciano d'Abruzzo Cerasuolo Vermiglio, Orlandi Contucci Ponno	647
Montepulciano d'Abruzzo Cerasuolo Villa Gemma, Gianni Masciarelli	647
Montepulciano d'Abruzzo Colle Creta, Poggio Le Gazze - Cantine del Palazzetto	652
Montepulciano d'Abruzzo Colle Maggio, Torre Zambra	649
Montepulciano d'Abruzzo Colle Secco, C. Tollo	649
Montepulciano d'Abruzzo Colle Secco Rubino, C. Tollo	649
Montepulciano d'Abruzzo Colline Teramane Bacco, Bruno Nicodemi	644
Montepulciano d'Abruzzo Colline Teramane Re, Lepore	641
Montepulciano d'Abruzzo Croce del Moro, Monteschiavo	588
Montepulciano d'Abruzzo Cuvée dell'Abate, Ciccio Zaccagnini	640
Montepulciano d'Abruzzo Dama, Marramiero	646
Montepulciano d'Abruzzo Fondatore, C. Miglianico	651
Montepulciano d'Abruzzo Fonte Cupa Colline Teramane, Camillo Montori	642
Montepulciano d'Abruzzo Frentano, C. Soc. Frentana	651
Montepulciano d'Abruzzo Galelle, Casa Vinicola Roxan	652
Montepulciano d'Abruzzo Granaro, Chiarieri	651
Montepulciano d'Abruzzo Hannibal, Chiarieri	651
Montepulciano d'Abruzzo Incanto, Marramiero	646
Montepulciano d'Abruzzo Inferi, Marramiero	646
Montepulciano d'Abruzzo Jorio, Umani Ronchi	595
Montepulciano d'Abruzzo La Regia Specula, Orlandi Contucci Ponno	647
Montepulciano d'Abruzzo Le Vigne, Faraone	643
Montepulciano d'Abruzzo Luigi Lepore, Lepore	641
Montepulciano d'Abruzzo Marina Cvetic S. Martino Rosso, Gianni Masciarelli	647
Montepulciano d'Abruzzo Montupoli, C. Miglianico	651
Montepulciano d'Abruzzo Natum, Agriverde	645
Montepulciano d'Abruzzo Pietrosa, Sarchese Dora	646
Montepulciano d'Abruzzo Pignotto, Antonio e Elio Monti	650
Montepulciano d'Abruzzo Plateo, Agriverde	645
Montepulciano d'Abruzzo Quartana, Spinelli	650
Montepulciano d'Abruzzo Riparosso, Dino Illuminati	642
Montepulciano d'Abruzzo Riseis, Agriverde	645
Montepulciano d'Abruzzo Rocco Secco, Chiusa Grande	651
Montepulciano d'Abruzzo Rosso di Crosta, Tenuta Caracciolo - Duchi di Castelluccio	652
Montepulciano d'Abruzzo Rosso di Macchia, Sarchese Dora	646
Montepulciano d'Abruzzo Roxan, Casa Vinicola Roxan	652
Montepulciano d'Abruzzo Rubesto, C. Soc. Frentana	651
Montepulciano d'Abruzzo S. Maria dell'Arco, Faraone	643
Montepulciano d'Abruzzo Sasso Arso, Poggio Le Gazze - Cantine del Palazzetto	652
Montepulciano d'Abruzzo Spelt, Fattoria La Valentina	648
Montepulciano d'Abruzzo Tenuta di Testarossa, Franco Pasetti	643
Montepulciano d'Abruzzo Tenute di Pallano, Spinelli	650
Montepulciano d'Abruzzo Terra d'Aligi, Spinelli	650
Montepulciano d'Abruzzo Terre dei Gechi, Poggio Le Gazze - Cantine del Palazzetto	652
Montepulciano d'Abruzzo Toni, Tenuta Cataldi Madonna	645
Montepulciano d'Abruzzo Valle d'Oro, C. Tollo	649
Montepulciano d'Abruzzo Vigna Fonte Dei, Filomusi Guelfi	648
Montepulciano d'Abruzzo Villa Gemma, Gianni Masciarelli	647
Montepulciano d'Abruzzo Villa Torre, Citra	651
Montepulciano d'Abruzzo Zanna Vecchio, Dino Illuminati	642
Montereggi, Fattoria di Bibbiani	436
Monteregio Bianco di Massa Marittima Violina, Serraiola	506
Monteregio di Massa Marittima, Suveraia	567
Monteregio di Massa Marittima Bacucco Ris., Suveraia	567
Monteregio di Massa Marittima Bianco Ariento, Massa Vecchia	472
Monteregio di Massa Marittima Rosso, Fattoria Coliberto	560
Monteregio di Massa Marittima Rosso Baccio, I Campetti	558
Monteregio di Massa Marittima Rosso Ris., Fattoria Coliberto	560
Monteregio di Massa Marittima Rosso Thesan, Fattoria Coliberto	560
Monteregio Rosso di Massa Marittima Lentisco, Serraiola	506
Montervo, Cima	471
Montescudaio Bianco, Poggio Gagliardo	507
Montescudaio Bianco, Fattoria Sorbaiano	496
Montescudaio Bianco Linaglia, Poggio Gagliardo	507
Montescudaio Bianco Lucestraia, Fattoria Sorbaiano	496
Montescudaio Bianco Steccaia, La Regola	526
Montescudaio Bianco Vigna Lontana, Poggio Gagliardo	507
Montescudaio Rosso, Poggio Gagliardo	507
Montescudaio Rosso, Fattoria Sorbaiano	496
Montescudaio Rosso delle Miniere, Fattoria Sorbaiano	496
Montescudaio Rosso Gobbo ai Pianacci, Poggio Gagliardo	507
Montescudaio Rosso La Regola, La Regola	526
Montescudaio Rosso Ligustro, La Regola	526
Montescudaio Rosso Malemacchie, Poggio Gagliardo	507
Montescudaio Rosso Rovo, Poggio Gagliardo	507
Montescudaio Rosso Vallino, La Regola	526
Montevertine Ris., Fattoria di Montevertine	523
Montevetrano, Montevetrano	662
Montiano, Falesco	634
Morago Cabernet Sauvignon, Pasqua Vigneti e Cantine	320
Morellino di Scansano, Podere Aia della Macina	540
Morellino di Scansano, Le Pupille	468
Morellino di Scansano, Malfatti	560
Morellino di Scansano, Moris Farms	472
Morellino di Scansano, Villa Patrizia	526
Morellino di Scansano Belguardo, Castello di Fonterutoli	440
Morellino di Scansano BellaMarsilia, Poggio Argentiera	469
Morellino di Scansano Campomaccione, Rocca delle Macìe	441
Morellino di Scansano CapaTosta, Poggio Argentiera	469
Morellino di Scansano Larcille, Agricola Valle	550
Morellino di Scansano Le Sentinelle, Fattoria Mantellassi	470
Morellino di Scansano Le Sentinelle Ris., Fattoria Mantellassi	470
Morellino di Scansano Lohsa, Poliziano	503
Morellino di Scansano Massi di Mandorlaia, Castello di Poppiano	508
Morellino di Scansano Poggio Valente, Le Pupille	468
Morellino di Scansano Primo Ris., Provveditore-Bargagli	574
Morellino di Scansano Provveditore, Provveditore-Bargagli	574
Morellino di Scansano Ris., Fattoria Mantellassi	470
Morellino di Scansano Ris., Moris Farms	472
Morellino di Scansano Ris., Villa Patrizia	526
Morellino di Scansano Ris. Montepò, Tenuta Il Greppo	482
Morellino di Scansano Roggiano, C. Coop. del Morellino di Scansano	574
Morellino di Scansano S. Giuseppe, Fattoria Mantellassi	470
Morellino di Scansano Terra Nera Ris., Podere Aia della Macina	540
Morellino di Scansano Val delle Rose, Famiglia Cecchi	439
Morellino di Scansano Val delle Rose Ris., Famiglia Cecchi	439
Morellino di Scansano Valle, Agricola Valle	550
Morellino di Scansano Vigna Benefizio, C. Coop. del Morellino di Scansano	574
Mormoreto, Marchesi de' Frescobaldi	453
Moro, Marco Carpineti	637
Morsi di Luce, Cantine Florio	705
Moscadello di Montalcino, Tenuta Il Poggione	483
Moscadello di Montalcino, Mocali	487
Moscadello di Montalcino Vendemmia Tardiva Pascena, Tenuta Col d'Orcia	479
Moscadello V. T., Tenuta Caparzo	475
Moscadello V. T., La Poderina	485
Moscafratta, Agareno	717
Moscato, Isidoro Lamoretti	426
Moscato d'Asti, Cascina Barisél	51
Moscato d'Asti, F.lli Bera	116
Moscato d'Asti, Ca' del Baio	135
Moscato d'Asti, Cascina Fonda	95
Moscato d'Asti, I Vignaioli di S. Stefano	127
Moscato d'Asti, Paolo Saracco	63
Moscato d'Asti Aureum, Silvano e Elena Boroli	24
Moscato d'Asti Biancospino, La Spinetta	54
Moscato d'Asti Bricco Quaglia, La Spinetta	54
Moscato d'Asti Ca' du Sindic Capsula Argento, Sergio Grimaldi - Ca' du Sindic	127
Moscato d'Asti Ca' du Sindic Capsula Oro, Sergio Grimaldi - Ca' du Sindic	127
Moscato d'Asti Caudrina, Caudrina	61
Moscato d'Asti Clarté, Elio Perrone	62
Moscato d'Asti Contero, La Giustiniana	78
Moscato d'Asti di Serralunga, Vigna Rionda - Massolino	131
Moscato d'Asti Ferlingot, Tenuta dell'Arbiola	125
Moscato d'Asti La Caliera, Borgo Maragliano	93
Moscato d'Asti La Galeisa, Caudrina	61
Moscato d'Asti La Mimosa, Poderi Sinaglio	27
Moscato d'Asti La Morandina, La Morandina	62
Moscato d'Asti La Rosa Selvatica, Icardi	61
Moscato d'Asti La Serra, Tenute Cisa Asinari dei Marchesi di Gresy	30
Moscato d'Asti Moncalvina, Luigi Coppo e Figli	52
Moscato d'Asti Scrapona, Marenco	133
Moscato d'Asti Smentiò, Michele Chiarlo	45

Moscato d'Asti Sorì del Re, Degiorgis	95
Moscato d'Asti Sourgal, Elio Perrone	62
Moscato d'Asti Su Reimond, F.lli Bera	116
Moscato d'Asti Tenuta dei Ciombi, Tenuta Il Falchetto	153
Moscato d'Asti Tenuta del Fant, Tenuta Il Falchetto	153
Moscato d'Asti Vigna Lupa, Alfiero Boffa	125
Moscato d'Asti Vigna Senza Nome, Braida	122
Moscato d'Asti Vigna Vecchia, Ca' d'Gal	126
Moscato d'Asti Vigneti Ca' d'Gal, Ca' d'Gal	126
Moscato d'Asti Volo di Farfalle, Scagliola	45
Moscato d'Asti Zagara, Marchesi di Barolo	37
Moscato dell'Elba, Sapereta	570
Moscato della Basilicata Clivus, Paternoster	671
Moscato di Cagliari, Cantine di Dolianova	722
Moscato di Cagliari, Villa di Quartu	725
Moscato di Cagliari Donna Jolanda, Meloni Vini	726
Moscato di Pantelleria, Agricola Bonsulton	712
Moscato di Pantelleria, D'Ancona	712
Moscato di Pantelleria, Carlo Pellegrino	706
Moscato di Pantelleria Rihali, Promed	717
Moscato di Pantelleria Solidea, D'Ancona	712
Moscato di Scanzo Don Quijote, Monzio Compagnoni	183
Moscato di Scanzo Passito Doge, La Brugherata	200
Moscato di Siracusa, Antonino Pupillo	713
Moscato di Siracusa Solacium, Antonino Pupillo	713
Moscato di Tempio Pausania, C. Soc. Gallura	729
Moscato di Trani Dulcis in Fundo, Torrevento	680
Moscato di Trani Piani di Tufara, Rivera	676
Moscato Giallo, Marcello e Marino Humar	389
Moscato Giallo Passito Aureo, C. Soc. Bergamasca	199
Moscato Giallo Passito Perseo, C. Soc. Bergamasca	199
Moscato Grelise V. T., Pervini	685
Moscato Passito di Pantelleria Khamma, Salvatore Murana	713
Moscato Passito di Pantelleria Martingana, Salvatore Murana	713
Moscato Passito di Pantelleria Mueggen, Salvatore Murana	713
Moscato Passito Villa Monticelli, Barberani - Vallesanta	616
Moscato Rosa, Marco Felluga	368
Moscato Rosa, Maso Bastie	238
Moscato Rosa Borgo della Rosa, Borgo Magredo	396
Moscato Secco di Terracina, C. di Sant'Andrea	638
Moscato Spumante, Consorzio Viticoltori Associati del Vulture	670
Muffa Nobile, Castel De Paolis	632
Muffa Nobile, Palazzone	619
Muffo, Tenuta Mottura	631
Müller Thurgau, Vinnaioli Jermann	364
Müller Thurgau della Val di Cembra, Nilo Bolognani	222
Müller Thurgau Mussignaz, Russolo	395
Murgia Rosso, I Pastini - Carparelli	690
Murgia Rosso Le Carraie, C. Coop. della Riforma Fondiaria	692
Murgia Rosso Pier delle Vigne, C. Coop. Botromagno	681
Murgia Sangiovese, C. Coop. della Riforma Fondiaria	692
Murighessa, Pedra Majore	724
Murtas, S. Michele a Torri	573
Muscadeddu, Tenute Dettori	727
Muscaté, Vigneti Massa	105
Muscatell, S. Barbara	580
Museum, La Macolina	426
Musica Moscato, Tenuta dei Fiori	46
Myrto, Foradori	228
N'Antia, Badia di Morrona	548
Nadaria Alcamo, Cusumano	710
Nadaria Inzolia, Cusumano	710
Nadaria Nero d'Avola, Cusumano	710
Nadaria Syrah, Cusumano	710
Naima, Viticoltori De Conciliis	661
Nambrot, Tenuta di Ghizzano	516
Narciso Rosso, Ronco delle Betulle	371
Nardina, Livernano	522
Nardo, Montepeloso	544
Nas-Cetta, Elvio Cogno	118
Nasco di Cagliari, Villa di Quartu	725
Nasco di Cagliari Donna Jolanda, Meloni Vini	726
Nastarrè, C. Soc. Giogantinu	730
Naturalis Historia, Mastroberardino	654
Nearco, La Loggia	572
Nebbiolo d'Alba, Destefanis	108
Nebbiolo d'Alba, Hilberg - Pasquero	120
Nebbiolo d'Alba, Fabrizio Pinsoglio	56
Nebbiolo d'Alba, Poderi Colla	26
Nebbiolo d'Alba, Flavio Roddolo	104
Nebbiolo d'Alba, Vielmin	146
Nebbiolo d'Alba Bricco S. Cristoforo, Bel Colle	138
Nebbiolo d'Alba Bricco S. Giacomo, Ascheri	44
Nebbiolo d'Alba Cascinotto, Claudio Alario	68
Nebbiolo d'Alba Cumot, Bricco Maiolica	69
Nebbiolo d'Alba Giachét, Poderi Sinaglio	27
Nebbiolo d'Alba La Val dei Preti, Matteo Correggia	48
Nebbiolo d'Alba Lantasco, Ceretto	24
Nebbiolo d'Alba Mompissano, Cascina Chicco	47
Nebbiolo d'Alba Occhetti, Prunotto	26
Nebbiolo d'Alba Ochetti, Renato Ratti	89
Nebbiolo d'Alba Rapalin, Massimo Oddero	147
Nebbiolo d'Alba Sansivé, Raffaele Gili	146
Nebbiolo d'Alba Valmaggiore, Bruno Giacosa	113
Nebbiolo d'Alba Valmaggiore, Luciano Sandrone	39
Nebbiolo d'Alba Vigna di Lino, Cascina Val del Prete	121
Nebbiolo dei Colli del Limbara Karana, C. Soc. Gallura	729
Nebbiolo Passito Vigna dei Dardi, Alessandro e Gian Natale Fantino	100
Neitea, Mormoraia	537
Nemo, Castello di Monsanto	432
Nepas Rosso, Alessandro e Gian Natale Fantino	100
Nerello Cappuccio, Benanti	703
Nerello Mascalese, Benanti	703
Nero, Conti Zecca	683
Nero d'Avola, Benanti	703
Nero d'Avola, Aziende Vinicole Miceli	710
Nero d'Avola, Morgante	703
Nero d'Avola, Pollara	708
Nero d'Avola, Settesoli	707
Nero d'Avola Mandrarossa, Settesoli	707
Nero d'Avola Triskelè, Duca di Salaparuta - Vini Corvo	702
Nero d'Avola/Cabernet, Settesoli	707
Nero del Tondo, Tenimenti Ruffino	520
Nero della Greca, Co.Vi.O.	617
Nero di Nubi, Farnetella	541
Nibbiano, Tenuta Valdipiatta	505
Nichesole Bianco, Corte Gardoni	318
Nieddera Rosato, Attilio Contini	721
Nieddera Rosso, Attilio Contini	721
Niergal, Pravis	222
Niffo, Terre del Sillabo	470
Nikà, Case di Pietra	713
Nikao, Barone La Lumia	704
Nispero Rosso, Agricola Adanti	608
Noà, Cusumano	710
Nobile di Montepulciano, Avignonesi	497
Nobile di Montepulciano, Bindella	498
Nobile di Montepulciano, Boscarelli	498
Nobile di Montepulciano, Canneto	565
Nobile di Montepulciano, Fattoria del Cerro	499
Nobile di Montepulciano, Contucci	499
Nobile di Montepulciano, Crociani	566
Nobile di Montepulciano, Dei	500
Nobile di Montepulciano, Ercolani	566
Nobile di Montepulciano, Fassati	500
Nobile di Montepulciano, Agricola Gavioli	566
Nobile di Montepulciano, Vittorio Innocenti	496
Nobile di Montepulciano, Fattoria La Braccesca	501
Nobile di Montepulciano, La Calonica	501
Nobile di Montepulciano, La Ciarliana	502
Nobile di Montepulciano, Podere Le Berne	566
Nobile di Montepulciano, Fattoria Le Casalte	566
Nobile di Montepulciano, Lodola Nuova - Tenimenti Ruffino	567
Nobile di Montepulciano, Eredi Antonino Lombardo	567
Nobile di Montepulciano, Nottola	502
Nobile di Montepulciano, Palazzo Vecchio	567
Nobile di Montepulciano, Fattoria di Paterno	503
Nobile di Montepulciano, Poliziano	503
Nobile di Montepulciano, Redi	504
Nobile di Montepulciano, Massimo Romeo	567
Nobile di Montepulciano, Salcheto	504
Nobile di Montepulciano, Tenimenti Angelini - Tenuta Trerose	505
Nobile di Montepulciano, Tenuta Valdipiatta	505
Nobile di Montepulciano, Villa Sant'Anna	506
Nobile di Montepulciano Asinone, Poliziano	503
Nobile di Montepulciano Brareo, Redi	504
Nobile di Montepulciano Calvano, Tenute Folonari	452
Nobile di Montepulciano Grandi Annate Ris., Avignonesi	497
Nobile di Montepulciano La Villa, Tenimenti Angelini - Tenuta Trerose	505
Nobile di Montepulciano Pasiteo, Fassati	500
Nobile di Montepulciano Pietrarossa, Contucci	499
Nobile di Montepulciano Ris., Bindella	498
Nobile di Montepulciano Ris., Boscarelli	498
Nobile di Montepulciano Ris., Carpineto	463
Nobile di Montepulciano Ris., Fattoria del Cerro	499
Nobile di Montepulciano Ris., Contucci	499
Nobile di Montepulciano Ris., Crociani	566
Nobile di Montepulciano Ris., Dei	500
Nobile di Montepulciano Ris., Fanetti - Tenuta S. Agnese	566
Nobile di Montepulciano Ris., Agricola Gavioli	566
Nobile di Montepulciano Ris., Vittorio Innocenti	496
Nobile di Montepulciano Ris., La Ciarliana	502
Nobile di Montepulciano Ris., Podere Le Berne	566
Nobile di Montepulciano Ris., Fattoria Le Casalte	566
Nobile di Montepulciano Ris., Eredi Antonino Lombardo	567
Nobile di Montepulciano Ris., Palazzo Vecchio	567
Nobile di Montepulciano Ris., Fattoria di Paterno	503
Nobile di Montepulciano Ris., Salcheto	504
Nobile di Montepulciano Ris., Tenuta Valdipiatta	505
Nobile di Montepulciano Ris. dei Mandorli, Massimo Romeo	567
Nobile di Montepulciano Salarco, Fassati	500
Nobile di Montepulciano Salarco Ris., Fassati	500
Nobile di Montepulciano Simposio, Tenimenti Angelini - Tenuta Trerose	505
Nobile di Montepulciano Vigna del Fattore, Nottola	502
Nobile di Montepulciano Vigna del Nocio, Boscarelli	498
Nobile di Montepulciano Vigna del Nocio Ris., Boscarelli	498

Entry	Page
Nobile di Montepulciano Vigna dell'Asinone, Poliziano	503
Nobile di Montepulciano Vigneto Antica Chiusina, Fattoria del Cerro	499
Noriolo, C. Soc. Dorgali	723
Nosiola Le Frate, Pravis	222
Notarpanaro, Cosimo Taurino	682
Notturno Sangiovese, Drei Donà Tenuta La Palazza	411
Nozze d'Oro, Tasca d'Almerita	715
Nuhar, Tenute Rapitalà	711
Nuragus di Cagliari, Cantine di Dolianova	722
Nuragus di Cagliari Pedraia, C. Soc. di Santadi	726
Nuragus di Cagliari S'Elegas, Antonio Argiolas	728
Nuragus di Cagliari Salnico, Pala	728
Nuragus di Cagliari Tenute S. Mauro, C. Soc. della Trexenta	727
Nuvola Démi Sec, Bersi Serlini	197
Oblin Blanc, Isidoro Polencic	351
Obsession, Villa Vignamaggio	467
Occhiorosso, Tenuta Cataldi Madonna	645
Olivar, Cesconi	223
Olmaia, Tenuta Col d'Orcia	479
Oltre, Leonardo Specogna	358
Onero Rosso, Tenuta Castello di Razzano	143
OP . Pinot Nero, La Scolca	79
OP Barbera Campo del Marrone, Bruno Verdi	172
OP Barbera Clà, Vercesi del Castellazzo	194
OP Barbera Costa del Sole, Percivalle	205
OP Barbera del Marrone, Bruno Verdi	172
OP Barbera Frizzante, Isimbarda	199
OP Barbera I due Draghi, Tenuta La Costaiola	191
OP Barbera La Strega, la Gazza, il Pioppo, Martilde	198
OP Barbera Magenga, Monsupello	202
OP Barbera Piccolo Principe, Cabanon	188
OP Barbera Pivena, Monsupello	202
OP Barbera Prunello, Cabanon	188
OP Barbera Safrana, Tenuta Pegazzera	176
OP Barbera Viga Varmasì, Ca' del Gé	190
OP Barbera Vigna Varmasì, Ca' del Gé	190
OP Barbera Vigna Varmasì, Ca' del Gé	190
OP Barbera Vivace, Marco Giulio Bellani	206
OP Barbera Vivace, Pietro Torti	209
OP Barbera, Ca' del Gé	190
OP Barbera, Cascina Gnocco	210
OP Barbera, Isimbarda	199
OP Barbera, Martilde	198
OP Barbera, Montelio	181
OP Barbera, Tenimenti Castelrotto - Torti	209
OP Bonabà, Franco Bazzini	212
OP Bonarda Campo del Monte, Agnes	198
OP Bonarda Cresta del Ghiffi, Agnes	198
OP Bonarda Fatila, Vercesi del Castellazzo	194
OP Bonarda Frizzante Ca' Bella, C. Soc. La Versa	200
OP Bonarda Frizzante Vigna dei Frati, Cascina Gnocco	210
OP Bonarda Frizzante Vigna dei Frati, Montini	213
OP Bonarda Frizzante, Bagnasco	213
OP Bonarda Frizzante, Montelio	181
OP Bonarda Frizzante, Riccardo Albani	174
OP Bonarda Frizzante, Vanzini	213
OP Bonarda Ghiro Rosso d'Inverno, Martilde	198
OP Bonarda La Casetta, Ca' di Frara	195
OP Bonarda La Rubiosa, Le Fracce	175
OP Bonarda Luogo della Milla, Vercesi del Castellazzo	194
OP Bonarda Millenium, Agnes	198
OP Bonarda Pentagonon, C. Soc. La Versa	200
OP Bonarda Possessione del Console, Agnes	198
OP Bonarda Ris., Cabanon	188
OP Bonarda Staffolo, Anteo	197
OP Bonarda Vigna Butas, Franco Bazzini	212
OP Bonarda Vigna del Vespero, Il Montù	194
OP Bonarda Vignazzo, Agnes	198
OP Bonarda Vivace Frambos, C. di Casteggio	174
OP Bonarda Vivace Giada, Tenuta La Costaiola	191
OP Bonarda Vivace La Brughera, F.lli Giorgi	172
OP Bonarda Vivace Le Cento Pertiche, Clastidio	206
OP Bonarda Vivace Poggio Pelato, Tenuta Il Bosco	203
OP Bonarda Vivace Possessione di Vargomberra, Bruno Verdi	172
OP Bonarda Vivace Riva degli Zingari, Ca' del Santo	209
OP Bonarda Vivace Vigna Il Modello, Monterucco	211
OP Bonarda Vivace, C. Soc. La Versa	200
OP Bonarda Vivace, Ca' del Gé	190
OP Bonarda Vivace, Cabanon	188
OP Bonarda Vivace, Francesco Quacquarini	205
OP Bonarda Vivace, Isimbarda	199
OP Bonarda Vivace, Marco Giulio Bellani	206
OP Bonarda Vivace, Pietro Torti	209
OP Bonarda Zaffo, Martilde	198
OP Bonarda, Bruno Verdi	172
OP Bonarda, C. di Casteggio	174
OP Bonarda, C. Soc. La Versa	200
OP Bonarda, Cabanon	188
OP Bonarda, Martilde	198
OP Bonarda, Riccardo Albani	174
OP Bonarda, Tenuta Mazzolino	184
OP Brut Cl. Blanc de Blanc, Ruiz de Cardenas	176
OP Brut Cl. Réserve, Ruiz de Cardenas	176
OP Brut Cl. Vergomberra, Bruno Verdi	172
OP Brut Class. Classese, Travaglino	171
OP Brut Il Bosco, Tenuta Il Bosco	203
OP Brut Metodo Martinotti, Anteo	197
OP Brut Regal Cuvée, Tenuta Il Bosco	203
OP Buttafuoco Casa del Corno, F.lli Giorgi	172
OP Buttafuoco Frizzante, Francesco Quacquarini	205
OP Buttafuoco Vigna Letizia, Il Montù	194
OP Buttafuoco Vigna Montarzolo, Tenuta La Costa - Calvi	205
OP Buttafuoco Vivace La Manna, F.lli Giorgi	172
OP Cabernet Sauvignon Aplomb, Monsupello	202
OP Cabernet Sauvignon Corvino, Tenuta Mazzolino	184
OP Cabernet Sauvignon Ligna, Tenuta Pegazzera	176
OP Cabernet Sauvignon, C. di Casteggio	174
OP Cabernet Sauvignon, F.lli Giorgi	172
OP Chardonnay Bianco del Cardinale, Tenuta Pegazzera	176
OP Chardonnay Blanc, Tenuta Mazzolino	184
OP Chardonnay Senso, Monsupello	202
OP Chardonnay Vigna del Mattino, Il Montù	194
OP Chardonnay, C. Soc. La Versa	200
OP Chardonnay, Ca' di Frara	195
OP Chardonnay, Il Montù	194
OP Chardonnay, Marco Vercesi	210
OP Chardonnay, Monsupello	202
OP Cortese, Montelio	181
OP Extra Brut Cl., Ruiz de Cardenas	176
OP Malvasia Dolce, F.lli Giorgi	172
OP Malvasia Frizzante, Tenuta Il Bosco	203
OP Malvasia Il Raro, Ca' di Frara	195
OP Malvasia Passito, Il Montù	194
OP Malvasia Piume, Martilde	198
OP Malvasia, C. di Casteggio	174
OP Malvasia, Tenuta Il Bosco	203
OP Moscato Fiori di Campo, Tenuta La Costaiola	191
OP Moscato La Volpe e L'Uva, Anteo	197
OP Moscato Passito Lacrimae Vitis La Soleggia, C. Soc. La Versa	200
OP Moscato Spumante, C. Soc. La Versa	200
OP Moscato Spumante, Vanzini	213
OP Moscato Volpara, Bruno Verdi	172
OP Moscato, C. di Casteggio	174
OP Moscato, Ca' del Gé	190
OP Muller Thurgau, Ca' del Gé	190
OP Passito Oro, Cabanon	188
OP Pinot Grigio V. T., Ca' di Frara	195
OP Pinot Grigio, Bruno Verdi	172
OP Pinot Grigio, C. di Casteggio	174
OP Pinot Grigio, Cabanon	188
OP Pinot Grigio, Le Fracce	175
OP Pinot Grigio, Monsupello	202
OP Pinot Nero 3309, Monsupello	202
OP Pinot Nero Baloss, Ruiz de Cardenas	176
OP Pinot Nero Bellarmino, Tenuta La Costaiola	191
OP Pinot Nero Brumano, Ruiz de Cardenas	176
OP Pinot Nero Brut Cl. Elith, F.lli Giorgi	172
OP Pinot Nero Brut Cl. Philèo, Tenuta Il Bosco	203
OP Pinot Nero Brut Cl. Regal Cuvée, Tenuta Il Bosco	203
OP Pinot Nero Brut Cl., Anteo	197
OP Pinot Nero Brut Cl., C. di Casteggio	174
OP Pinot Nero Brut Cl., Ca' del Gé	190
OP Pinot Nero Brut Cl., Francesco Quacquarini	205
OP Pinot Nero Brut Cl., Il Montù	194
OP Pinot Nero Brut Cl., Monsupello	202
OP Pinot Nero Brut Cl., Tenuta Il Bosco	203
OP Pinot Nero Brut Cl., Tenuta Pegazzera	176
OP Pinot Nero Brut Class. Grand Cuvée, Travaglino	171
OP Pinot Nero Brut Mise en Cave, C. Soc. La Versa	200
OP Pinot Nero Brut, C. Soc. La Versa	200
OP Pinot Nero Brut, Il Montù	194
OP Pinot Nero Brut, Monsupello	202
OP Pinot Nero Brut, Tenuta Pegazzera	176
OP Pinot Nero Cl. Anteo Nature, Anteo	197
OP Pinot Nero Cl. Nature, Monsupello	202
OP Pinot Nero Extra Dry, Vanzini	213
OP Pinot Nero Il Raro, Ca' di Frara	195
OP Pinot Nero in bianco Ca' dell'Oca, Anteo	197
OP Pinot Nero in bianco Gugiarolo, Vercesi del Castellazzo	194
OP Pinot Nero in bianco Querciolo, Doria	191
OP Pinot Nero Luogo dei Monti, Vercesi del Castellazzo	194
OP Pinot Nero Martuffo, Martilde	198
OP Pinot Nero Monte Roso, F.lli Giorgi	172
OP Pinot Nero Noir, Tenuta Mazzolino	184
OP Pinot Nero Petrae, Tenuta Pegazzera	176
OP Pinot Nero Poggio della Buttinera, Travaglino	171
OP Pinot Nero Querciolo, Doria	191
OP Pinot Nero Vigna Miraggi, Ruiz de Cardenas	176
OP Pinot Nero, Ca' del Gé	190
OP Pinot Nero, Frecciarossa	175
OP Pinot Nero, Isimbarda	199
OP Pinot Nero, Ruiz de Cardenas	176
OP Pinot Nero, Tenimenti Castelrotto - Torti	209
OP Pinot Nero, Tenuta Mazzolino	184
OP Provincia di Pavia Moscato Adagetto, Cascina Gnocco	210
OP Riesling Italico Gelo, Martilde	198

Entry	Page
OP Riesling Italico, Ca' del Gé	190
OP Riesling Italico, Montelio	181
OP Riesling La Fojada, Travaglino	171
OP Riesling Renano Apogeo, Ca' di Frara	195
OP Riesling Renano Attimo, Tenuta La Costaiola	191
OP Riesling Renano Bellarmino, Tenuta La Costaiola	191
OP Riesling Renano Parsua, Percivalle	205
OP Riesling Renano Roncobianco V. Tesi, Doria	191
OP Riesling Renano Roncobianco, Doria	191
OP Riesling Renano Vigna Martina, Isimbarda	199
OP Riesling Renano Vigneto Costa, Bruno Verdi	172
OP Riesling Renano, Cabanon	188
OP Riesling Renano, Frecciarossa	175
OP Riesling Renano, Le Fracce	175
OP Riesling Renano, Riccardo Albani	174
OP Riesling V. Belvedere, Isimbarda	199
OP Riesling Vendemmia Tardiva Pajarolo, Travaglino	171
OP Riesling Vivace I Soli, C. di Casteggio	174
OP Riesling, Monsupello	202
OP Rosato, Montelio	181
OP Rosso Botte n. 18, Cabanon	188
OP Rosso Cardinale, Tenuta Pegazzera	176
OP Rosso Cavariola Ris., Bruno Verdi	172
OP Rosso Cirgà, Le Fracce	175
OP Rosso Donelasco, C. Soc. La Versa	200
OP Rosso Great Ruby, Monsupello	202
OP Rosso Il Frater, Ca' di Frara	195
OP Rosso Infernot Ris., Cabanon	188
OP Rosso Io, Ca' di Frara	195
OP Rosso Monplò, Isimbarda	199
OP Rosso Montezavo Ris., Isimbarda	199
OP Rosso Narbusto, Clastidio	206
OP Rosso Orto di S. Giacomo, Vercesi del Castellazzo	194
OP Rosso Pezzalunga, Vercesi del Castellazzo	194
OP Rosso Ris. Donelasco, C. Soc. La Versa	200
OP Rosso Ris. Marc'Antonio, Travaglino	171
OP Rosso Ris. Vigna Solarolo, Montelio	181
OP Rosso Riserva Eventi, Montini	213
OP Rosso Riserva Mosaico, Monsupello	202
OP Rosso Riserva Solarolo, Montelio	181
OP Rosso Roncorosso V. Siura, Doria	191
OP Rosso Roncorosso, Doria	191
OP Rosso Vigna Casa del Corno, F.lli Giorgi	172
OP Rosso Vigna del Tramonto, Isimbarda	199
OP Rosso Vigna della Casona Ris., Riccardo Albani	174
OP Rosso Villa Odero Ris., Frecciarossa	175
OP Rosso Vino Cuore, Cabanon	188
OP Rosso, Isimbarda	199
OP Rosso, Montelio	181
OP Sangue di Giuda Dolce Paradiso, Bruno Verdi	172
OP Sangue di Giuda, Bagnasco	213
OP Sangue di Giuda, Il Montù	194
OP Sauvignon, C. di Casteggio	174
OP Sauvignon, Monsupello	202
Opera Prima Cabanon Blanc, Cabanon	188
Opera Prima XIII, I Paglieri	32
Opera Prima XIV, I Paglieri	32
Opimio Gianni Zonin Vineyards, Ca' Bolani	341
Oppidum Rosso, Ciù Ciù	594
Oracolo, Poggio Amorelli	553
Orazio, Fontanavecchia - Orazio Rillo	665
Orbaio, Redi	504
Oreno, Tenuta Sette Ponti	547
Organza, Aziende Vinicole Miceli	710
Ornellaia, Tenuta dell' Ornellaia	433
Oro del Cedro, Fattoria Lavacchio	570
Orpheus Etna Rosso, Tenuta Scilio di Valle Galfina	716
Ortaglia N° 1, Ortaglia	576
Orto di Boccio, Villa Patrizia	526
Orvieto, Trappolini	630
Orvieto Cl., Bigi	616
Orvieto Cl., La Carraia	618
Orvieto Cl., Podere Vaglie	608
Orvieto Cl. Abboccato Casa Sole, Castello della Sala	612
Orvieto Cl. Amabile Rasenna, Tenuta Le Velette	619
Orvieto Cl. Barbi, Decugnano dei Barbi	617
Orvieto Cl. Campo del Guardiano, Palazzone	619
Orvieto Cl. Campogrande, Castello della Sala	612
Orvieto Cl. Castagnolo, Barberani - Vallesanta	616
Orvieto Cl. Dolce V. T. Cardeto, Co.Vi.O.	617
Orvieto Cl. Poggio Calvelli, La Carraia	618
Orvieto Cl. Roio, C. Monrubio	610
Orvieto Cl. Salceto, C. Monrubio	610
Orvieto Cl. Sup., Castello della Sala	612
Orvieto Cl. Sup., Tenuta di Salviano	624
Orvieto Cl. Sup. Calcaia, Barberani - Vallesanta	616
Orvieto Cl. Sup. Colbadia, Co.Vi.O.	617
Orvieto Cl. Sup. Decugnano dei Barbi, Decugnano dei Barbi	617
Orvieto Cl. Sup. Febeo, Co.Vi.O.	617
Orvieto Cl. Sup. IL, Decugnano dei Barbi	617
Orvieto Cl. Sup. L'Armida, Co.Vi.O.	617
Orvieto Cl. Sup. Lunato, Tenuta Le Velette	619
Orvieto Cl. Sup. Matricale, Podere Vaglie	608
Orvieto Cl. Sup. Pourriture Noble, Decugnano dei Barbi	617
Orvieto Cl. Sup. Soana, C. Monrubio	610
Orvieto Cl. Terre Vineate, Palazzone	619
Orvieto Cl. Torre Sant'Andrea, Vaselli	636
Orvieto Cl. Velico, Tenuta Le Velette	619
Orvieto Cl. Vigna Tragugnano, Tenuta Mottura	631
Orvieto Cl. Vigneto Torricella, Bigi	616
Orvieto Macchia del Pozzo, C. Monrubio	610
Osar, Masi	306
Ostrea, Mormoraia	537
Ostrea Grigia, Mormoraia	537
P. di Conegliano Brut, Bellenda	330
P. di Conegliano Brut Bubbly, Zardetto Spumanti	276
P. di Conegliano Brut S. Salvatore, Conte Collalto	312
P. di Conegliano Cuvée Brut, Carpenè Malvolti	324
P. di Conegliano Dry Cuvée Oro, Carpenè Malvolti	324
P. di Conegliano Dry Zeroventi, Zardetto Spumanti	276
P. di Conegliano Extra Dry, Bellenda	330
P. di Conegliano Extra Dry, Bepin de Eto	300
P. di Conegliano Extra Dry, Carpenè Malvolti	324
P. di Conegliano Extra Dry, Case Bianche	326
P. di Conegliano Extra Dry, Conte Collalto	312
P. di Conegliano Extra Dry, Gregoletto	286
P. di Conegliano Extra Dry, Masottina	299
P. di Conegliano Extra Dry, Vincenzo Toffoli	297
P. di Conegliano Extra Dry Millesimato, Scuola Enologica di Conegliano G. B. Cerletti	324
P. di Conegliano Frizzante, Vincenzo Toffoli	297
P. di Conegliano Frizzante Brioso, Zardetto Spumanti	276
P. di Conegliano Tranquillo, Gregoletto	286
P. di Conegliano Tranquillo, Vincenzo Toffoli	297
P. di Conegliano Tranquillo Lungo, Zardetto Spumanti	276
P. di Valdobbiadene Brut, F.lli Bortolin Spumanti	313
P. di Valdobbiadene Brut, Bortolomiol	314
P. di Valdobbiadene Brut, Canevel Spumanti	314
P. di Valdobbiadene Brut, Ciodet	329
P. di Valdobbiadene Brut, Col Vetoraz	315
P. di Valdobbiadene Brut, De Faveri	321
P. di Valdobbiadene Brut, Le Colture	315
P. di Valdobbiadene Brut, Nino Franco	316
P. di Valdobbiadene Brut, Angelo Ruggeri	316
P. di Valdobbiadene Brut, Ruggeri & C.	317
P. di Valdobbiadene Brut, S. Eurosia	317
P. di Valdobbiadene Brut, Paolo Zucchetto	329
P. di Valdobbiadene Brut Bosco di Gica, Adami	321
P. di Valdobbiadene Brut Crede, Desiderio Bisol & Figli	313
P. di Valdobbiadene Brut Dirupo, Andreola Orsola	277
P. di Valdobbiadene Brut Rive di S. Floriano, Nino Franco	316
P. di Valdobbiadene Brut Sel., De Faveri	321
P. di Valdobbiadene Delico, Sorelle Bronca	322
P. di Valdobbiadene Dry, F.lli Bortolin Spumanti	313
P. di Valdobbiadene Dry, Bortolomiol	314
P. di Valdobbiadene Dry Colle Molina, Merotto	324
P. di Valdobbiadene Dry Funer, Le Colture	315
P. di Valdobbiadene Dry Funer, Angelo Ruggeri	316
P. di Valdobbiadene Dry Giardino, Adami	321
P. di Valdobbiadene Dry La Primavera di Barbara, Merotto	324
P. di Valdobbiadene Dry Millesimato, Col Vetoraz	315
P. di Valdobbiadene Dry Primo Franco, Nino Franco	316
P. di Valdobbiadene Dry S. Stefano, Ruggeri & C.	317
P. di Valdobbiadene Dry Salis, Desiderio Bisol & Figli	313
P. di Valdobbiadene Dry Sel., De Faveri	321
P. di Valdobbiadene Dry Sel., Tanorè	318
P. di Valdobbiadene Extra Dry, F.lli Bortolin Spumanti	313
P. di Valdobbiadene Extra Dry, Bortolomiol	314
P. di Valdobbiadene Extra Dry, Canevel Spumanti	314
P. di Valdobbiadene Extra Dry, Ciodet	329
P. di Valdobbiadene Extra Dry, Col Vetoraz	315
P. di Valdobbiadene Extra Dry, Dal Din	330
P. di Valdobbiadene Extra Dry, De Faveri	321
P. di Valdobbiadene Extra Dry, Dea - Rivalta	329
P. di Valdobbiadene Extra Dry, Le Colture	315
P. di Valdobbiadene Extra Dry, Merotto	324
P. di Valdobbiadene Extra Dry, Angelo Ruggeri	316
P. di Valdobbiadene Extra Dry, S. Eurosia	317
P. di Valdobbiadene Extra Dry, Sorelle Bronca	322
P. di Valdobbiadene Extra Dry, Tanorè	318
P. di Valdobbiadene Extra Dry, Paolo Zucchetto	329
P. di Valdobbiadene Extra Dry dei Casel, Adami	321
P. di Valdobbiadene Extra Dry Dirupo, Andreola Orsola	277
P. di Valdobbiadene Extra Dry Garnei, Desiderio Bisol & Figli	313
P. di Valdobbiadene Extra Dry Giall'Oro, Ruggeri & C.	317
P. di Valdobbiadene Extra Dry Giustino B., Ruggeri & C.	317
P. di Valdobbiadene Extra Dry Il Millesimato, Canevel Spumanti	314
P. di Valdobbiadene Extra Dry Millesimato Val d'Oca, C. Prod. di Valdobbiadene	329
P. di Valdobbiadene Extra Dry Rù, F.lli Bortolin Spumanti	313
P. di Valdobbiadene Extra Dry Sel. Banda Rossa, Bortolomiol	314
P. di Valdobbiadene Extra Dry Vigneti del Fol, Desiderio Bisol & Figli	313
P. di Valdobbiadene Frizzante Il Ponteggio, Bortolomiol	314
P. di Valdobbiadene Frizzante Spago, Andreola Orsola	277
P. di Valdobbiadene Frizzante Vigneto S. Biagio, Canevel Spumanti	314
P. di Valdobbiadene Rustico, Nino Franco	316

P. di Valdobbiadene Tranquillo, Bortolomiol	314		Piave Cabernet Sauvignon, Giorgio Cecchetto	330
P. di Valdobbiadene Tranquillo, Dal Din	330		Piave Cabernet Sauvignon ai Palazzi Ris., Masottina	299
P. di Valdobbiadene Tranquillo, Dea - Rivalta	329		Piave Cabernet Terre Nobili, Santo Stefano	324
P. di Valdobbiadene Tranquillo, S. Eurosia	317		Piave Chardonnay, Masottina	299
P. di Valdobbiadene Tranquillo, Tanorè	318		Piave Chardonnay Ornella, Ornella Molon Traverso	298
P. di Valdobbiadene Tranquillo Giardino, Adami	321		Piave Chardonnay Terre Nobili, Santo Stefano	324
P. di Valdobbiadene Tranquillo La Bastia, Ruggeri & C.	317		Piave Merlot, Casa Roma	327
P. di Valdobbiadene Tranquillo Masaré, Le Colture	315		Piave Merlot, Conte Collalto	312
P. di Valdobbiadene Tranquillo Minù Val d'Oca, C. Prod. di Valdobbiadene	329		Piave Merlot ai Palazzi Ris., Masottina	299
			Piave Merlot Ornella, Ornella Molon Traverso	298
P. di Valdobbiadene Tranquillo Molera, Desiderio Bisol & Figli	313		Piave Merlot Rosso di Villa, Ornella Molon Traverso	298
			Piave Pinot Bianco, Masottina	299
P. di Valdobbiadene Tranquillo Romit, Andreola Orsola	277		Piave Pinot Grigio, Santo Stefano	324
P. di Valdobbiadene Tranquillo Tresiese, Col Vetoraz	315		Piave Raboso, Casa Roma	327
P. Extra Dry, Zardetto Spumanti	276		Piave Raboso, Giorgio Cecchetto	330
P. Frizzante Colli Trevigiani Sel. Spago, De Faveri	321		Pico de Laorenti, La Biancara	278
Pagus, Giovanna Giannaccini	568		Piemonte Barbera, Poderi Luigi Einaudi	70
Palai, Pojer & Sandri	219		Piemonte Barbera Bricco del Tempo, Domenico Ghio	144
Palaia, C. Monrubio	610		Piemonte Barbera Briccobotti, Pira	71
Palazzo Altesi, Altesino	473		Piemonte Barbera Brichat, Osvaldo Barberis	147
Palazzo della Torre, Allegrini	277		Piemonte Barbera Crown Cap, F. e M. Scrimaglio	118
Paradiso, Tenuta La Tenaglia	132		Piemonte Barbera Identità, Terralba	42
Paradiso Rosso, Tenuta La Tenaglia	132		Piemonte Barbera Mounbè, Cascina Ulivi	151
Pariondo Bianco, Luigi Brunelli	302		Piemonte Barbera Sentieri, Vigneti Massa	105
Parrina Bianco, La Parrina	509		Piemonte Barbera Territorio, Claudio Mariotto	154
Passaurum, A. Berger -Thurnhof	245		Piemonte Barbera Vho, Claudio Mariotto	154
Passera delle Vigne, Lepore	641		Piemonte Barbera Vivace, Sergio Grimaldi - Ca' du Sindic	127
Passerina Brut, Tenuta Cocci Grifoni	597		Piemonte Bonarda, Cascina Gilli	56
Passerina del Frusinate, Paolo Perinelli	636		Piemonte Brachetto, Cascina Fonda	95
Passione Rosso, Michele Castellani	282		Piemonte Brachetto, Piero Gatti	126
Passito Anima Mundi, La C. dei Colli Ripani	598		Piemonte Brachetto Ca' du Sindic, Sergio Grimaldi - Ca' du Sindic	127
Passito Bianco, Ca' La Bionda	281			
Passito Bianco, Ciccio Zaccagnini	640		Piemonte Brachetto Carlotta, E. e A. Brema	81
Passito Bianco Bure Alto, Giuseppe Fornaser	327		Piemonte Brachetto Forteto Pian dei Sogni, Forteto della Luja	93
Passito Bianco Corte Durlo, Ca' Rugate	289			
Passito Bianco di Gargagnago, Raimondi Villa Monteleone	307		Piemonte Brut M. Cl., Araldica - Il Cantinone	54
Passito Bianco Il Sole di Corteforte, Corteforte	325		Piemonte Chardonnay, Paolo Casalone	94
Passito Bianco Le Melghette, Corte Marzago	330		Piemonte Chardonnay, Tenuta La Tenaglia	132
Passito Colori d'Autunno, Tenuta Sant'Antonio	275		Piemonte Chardonnay, Luigi Nebiolo	147
Passito dei Lepore, Lepore	641		Piemonte Chardonnay, Scagliola	45
Passito della Rocca, Leonildo Pieropan	310		Piemonte Chardonnay Bric di Bric, Marco Canato	141
Passito di Pantelleria, Abraxas	713		Piemonte Chardonnay Costebianche, Luigi Coppo e Figli	52
Passito di Pantelleria, Agricola Bonsulton	712		Piemonte Chardonnay Crevoglio, Borgo Maragliano	93
Passito di Pantelleria, D'Ancona	712		Piemonte Chardonnay Diversamente, Tenuta Garetto	22
Passito di Pantelleria, Carlo Pellegrino	706		Piemonte Chardonnay Galet, Marenco	133
Passito di Pantelleria Ben Ryé, Tenuta di Donnafugata	705		Piemonte Chardonnay Giarone, Poderi Bertelli	65
Passito di Pantelleria Bukkuram, Marco De Bartoli	704		Piemonte Chardonnay L'Altro, Pio Cesare	25
Passito di Pantelleria Entelechia, Aziende Vinicole Miceli	710		Piemonte Chardonnay La Sabauda, Giuseppe Contratto	51
			Piemonte Chardonnay Lydia, La Spinetta	54
Passito di Pantelleria Ergo, Casa Vinicola Grasso	717		Piemonte Chardonnay Marajan, Borgo Maragliano	93
Passito di Pantelleria Mare d'Ambra, Cantine Rallo	706		Piemonte Chardonnay Mej, Caudrina	61
Passito di Pantelleria Nes, Carlo Pellegrino	706		Piemonte Chardonnay Monteriolo, Luigi Coppo e Figli	52
Passito di Pantelleria Nikà, Case di Pietra	713		Piemonte Chardonnay Piasì, Marco Canato	141
Passito di Pantelleria Nun, Aziende Vinicole Miceli	710		Piemonte Chardonnay Roleto, Araldica - Il Cantinone	54
Passito di Pantelleria Rihali, Promed	717		Piemonte Chardonnay Surissara, Icardi	61
Passito di Pantelleria Solidea, D'Ancona	712		Piemonte Chardonnay Thou Bianc, Bava	63
Passito di Pantelleria Tanit, Aziende Vinicole Miceli	710		Piemonte Cortese DiVino, Prod. del Gavi	79
Passito di Pantelleria Yanir, Aziende Vinicole Miceli	710		Piemonte Cortese Lacrime di Gioia, Carlo Benotto	65
Passito di Pradis, Roberto Picech - Le Vigne del Ribél	350		Piemonte Grignolino, Paolo Casalone	94
Passito di Roveglia, Tenuta Roveglia	211		Piemonte Grignolino, Pelissero	137
Passito Sparavieri, Trabucchi	280		Piemonte Grignolino, Tenuta S. Sebastiano	94
Passo Rosso, Stefano Accordini	301		Piemonte Grignolino Sansoero, Marchesi Alfieri	124
Passomaggio, Abbazia S. Anastasia	701		Piemonte Moscato, Piero Gatti	126
Paterno, Trappolini	630		Piemonte Moscato d'Asti Moscato d'Autunno, Paolo Saracco	63
Paterno II, Il Paradiso	535			
Patriglione, Cosimo Taurino	682		Piemonte Moscato Passito Avié, Cascina Castlèt	66
Pàtrimo, Feudi di S. Gregorio	663		Piemonte Moscato Passito La Bella Estate, Terre da Vino	41
Paule Calle, Francesco Candido	687		Piemonte Venta Quemada, Cascina Ulivi	151
Pecorino, Tenuta Cataldi Madonna	645		Pier delle Vigne, C. Coop. Botromagno	681
Pelago, Umani Ronchi	595		Pietraforte del Carobbio, Carobbio	510
Pellaro, Vintripodi	697		Pietranera, Marco De Bartoli	704
Pen. Sorr. Gragnano, Cantine Grotta del Sole	662		Pietrasca, Russo	544
Pensiero, Petrussa	384		Pietratorcia Rosso Ris., Pietratorcia	656
Peperino, Teruzzi & Puthod	539		Pietrello, Meleta	527
Pepita, Di Prima	713		Pietrello d'Oro, Meleta	527
Percarlo, S. Giusto a Rentennano	461		Pieve di Spaltenna Alle Fonti, Castello di Meleto	458
Perdaudin Passito, Angelo Negro & Figli	108		Pigmento Rosso, Cascina Montagnola	142
Perla del Mare, Podere Sopra la Ripa	542		Pignocco Rosso, S. Barbara	580
Perlato del Bosco Bianco, Tua Rita	545		Pilin Bianco, Castellari Bergaglio	77
Perlato del Bosco Rosso, Tua Rita	545		Pinèro, Ca' del Bosco	185
Perle, La Boatina	349		Pinodisé, Contadi Castaldi	170
Pernicolò, Fattoria S. Francesco	694		Pinot Bianco, Gregoletto	286
Pesanella, Castello di Monterinaldi	522		Pinot Bianco, Roncùs	338
Petra, Petra	575		Pinot Bianco, Vinnaioli Jermann	364
Petronio, Alberto Quacquarini	600		Pinot Bianco Principe di Corleone, Pollara	708
Pezzolo Cabernet Sauvignon, Pandolfa	416		Pinot Brut, C. Soc. Bergamasca	199
Phigaia After the Red, Serafini & Vidotto	296		Pinot Grigio, Giovanni Crosato	342
Pian del Conte, Fattoria Sorbaiano	496		Pinot Grigio, Walter Filiputti	370
Pian del Tufo Bianco, Barni	44		Pinot Grigio, Sant'Elena	368
Pian della Cava, S. Martino	557		Pinot Grigio, Leonardo Specogna	358
Pian di Conte, Talenti - Podere Pian di Conte	564		Pinot Grigio, Vinnaioli Jermann	364
Pianero, Gino Gagliardi	604		Pinot Grigio delle Venezie, Fattori & Graney	289
Piano del Cipresso, Fattoria di Terrabianca	524		Pinot Grigio Graminè, Longariva	231
Piave Cabernet Ardesco, Sorelle Bronca	322		Pinot Grigio Olivers, Pierpaolo Pecorari	395
Piave Cabernet Ornella, Ornella Molon Traverso	298		Pinot Nero, Barone Pizzini	182
Piave Cabernet Ris., Conte Collalto	312		Pinot Nero, Ca' del Santo	209

Pinot Nero, Co.Vi.O.	617	Prosecco del Montello, Serafini & Vidotto	296
Pinot Nero, Pojer & Sandri	219	Prosecco Passito, Vincenzo Toffoli	297
Pinot Nero, Alessandro Secchi	216	Provincia di Mantova Lambrusco Etichetta Rossa,	
Pinot Nero, Serafini & Vidotto	296	Stefano Spezia	209
Pinot Nero, F.lli Sportoletti	622	Provincia di Pavia Müller Thurgau, Montelio	181
Pinot Nero Case Via, Tenuta Fontodi	512	Provincia di Pavia Müller Thurgau La Giostra, Montelio	181
Pinot Nero Grifo Nero, Russolo	395	Provincia di Pavia Rosso Vespolino,	
Pinot Nero L'Arturo, Ronco Calino	178	Vercesi del Castellazzo	194
Pinot Nero Ris., Carra	415	Provincia di Pavia Uva Rara, Frecciarossa	175
Pinot Nero Ris., Pojer & Sandri	219	Prugnolo, Di Majo Norante	641
Pinot Nero Sebino, Il Mosnel	196	Prulke, Zidarich	362
Pinot Nero Sebino, Ricci Curbastro	173	Prunaio, Viticcio	468
Pinot Nero Sorai Campo alle More, Gini	290	Puglia Aleatico, S. Lucia	679
Pinot Nero Vigneto Consola, Castello della Sala	612	Puglia Moscato Pierale, Leone de Castris	687
Pinot Nero Villa di Bagnolo,		Puglia Rosa di Selva, Borgo Canale	680
Tenuta di Bagnolo dei Marchesi Pancrazi	497	Pulignano, Fattoria di Bibbiani	436
Piocaia, Fattoria S. Fabiano - Borghini Baldovinetti	430	Pulleraia, Agricoltori del Chianti Geografico	455
Planargia Murapiscados, Gianvittorio Naitana	731	Punta Rossa, Fattoria La Valentina	648
Plissé Traminer, Poderi Bertelli	65	Puro Sangue, Livernano	522
Podere Colle Vecchio, Tenuta Cocci Grifoni	597	Pusterla Bianco, Pusterla	212
Podere Fontarca, Tenimenti Luigi D'Alessandro	450	Pusterla Rosso, Pusterla	212
Podere Il Bosco, Tenimenti Luigi D'Alessandro	450	Quarto di Luna, Cantine Grotta del Sole	662
Podere Le Rocce, Le Filigare	550	Quarto di Sole, Cantine Grotta del Sole	662
Poderuccio, Castello di Camigliano	475	Quattro Marzo Bianco, Anteo	197
Poesia d'Inverno,		Quattro Mori, Castel De Paolis	632
Istituto Professionale per l'Agricoltura e l'Ambiente	410	Quattrocentenario, Castello della Panereta	550
Poggio ai Venti, Massa Vecchia	472	Querciolaia, Fattoria Mantellassi	470
Poggio alla Badiola, Castello di Fonterutoli	440	Querciolaia, Castello di Querceto	464
Poggio alle Gazze, Tenuta dell' Ornellaia	433	Racemo Rosso, L'Olivella	637
Poggio Argentato, Le Pupille	468	Radames, Antichi Poderi Jerzu	723
Poggio Crocino, Le Capannucce	449	Raddese, Vignavecchia	524
Poggio del Cotoverio, Antonello Coletti Conti	636	Rafé Bianco, Cascina Gilli	56
Poggio Golo, Fattoria del Cerro	499	Rainero, Castello di Meleto	458
Poggio Granoni, Farnetella	541	Rairi Moscato, Tenuta dei Fiori	46
Poggio Madrigale, Di Filippo	609	Rapace, Uccelliera	564
Poggio Mondino, Castello di Modanella	525	Rapitalà Conte Hugues, Tenute Rapitalà	711
Poggio Muralto, Rio Grande	620	Rapitalà Rosso, Tenute Rapitalà	711
Poggio Solivo, Ca' del Vispo	532	Rasa di Marmorata, Tenuta Le Quinte	638
Poiema Marzemino dei Ziresi, Eugenio Rosi	238	Re di Bric, Marco Vercesi	210
Pojo del Ruspo Barbi, Decugnano dei Barbi	617	Reale, La Castellina	552
Polito, Il Lebbio	534	Recioto Cl. della Valpolicella Giovanni Allegrini, Allegrini	277
Pomino Bianco, Marchesi de' Frescobaldi	453	Recioto dei Capitelli, Roberto Anselmi	288
Pomino Il Benefizio, Marchesi de' Frescobaldi	453	Recioto della Valpolicella, Brigaldara	302
Pomino Rosso, Marchesi de' Frescobaldi	453	Recioto della Valpolicella, Corte Sant'Alda	285
Popphof Cuvée, Popphof - Andreas Menz	259	Recioto della Valpolicella, Trabucchi	280
Porticato Bianco, Colle di Maggio	635	Recioto della Valpolicella Amandorlato, Corteforte	325
Portico Rosso, Vignaiolo Giuseppe Fanti	224	Recioto della Valpolicella Argille Bianche,	
Praepositus Weiss, Abbazia di Novacella	267	Tenuta Sant'Antonio	275
Prato Grande Chardonnay, Tenuta De Angelis	582	Recioto della Valpolicella Cl., Lorenzo Begali	301
Pratoscuro, Pierpaolo Pecorari	395	Recioto della Valpolicella Cl., Luigi Brunelli	302
Pratto, Ca' dei Frati	201	Recioto della Valpolicella Cl., Corte Rugolin	283
Predaia Rosso, S. Sofia	303	Recioto della Valpolicella Cl., F.lli Degani	283
Pregio del Conte Bianco, Saladini Pilastri	601	Recioto della Valpolicella Cl., Aleardo Ferrari	327
Pregio del Conte Rosso, Saladini Pilastri	601	Recioto della Valpolicella Cl., I Scriani	325
Prima Luce Passito, Ottella	296	Recioto della Valpolicella Cl., Le Ragose	293
Primamateria, Poggerino	523	Recioto della Valpolicella Cl., Angelo Nicolis e Figli	303
Primigenia, Antichi Vigneti di Cantalupo	80	Recioto della Valpolicella Cl., Novaia	284
Primitivo, S. Barbara	688	Recioto della Valpolicella Cl., Giuseppe Quintarelli	294
Primitivo del Salento Fra Diavolo, Marco Maci	679	Recioto della Valpolicella Cl., S. Sofia	303
Primitivo del Salento Latias, Lomazzi & Sarli	691	Recioto della Valpolicella Cl., Casa Vinicola Sartori	326
Primitivo del Tarantino, C. Soc. di Lizzano	684	Recioto della Valpolicella Cl., Massimino Venturini	305
Primitivo del Tarantino, I Pastini - Carparelli	690	Recioto della Valpolicella Cl., Villa Bellini	306
Primitivo del Tarantino I Monili, Pervini	685	Recioto della Valpolicella Cl., Villa Spinosa	295
Primitivo di Manduria, Felline	685	Recioto della Valpolicella Cl., Viviani	295
Primitivo di Manduria, Vinicola Miali	691	Recioto della Valpolicella Cl., F.lli Zeni	273
Primitivo di Manduria, Pervini	685	Recioto della Valpolicella Cl. Acinatico, Stefano Accordini	301
Primitivo di Manduria, Vinicola Resta	692	Recioto della Valpolicella Cl. Campo Casalin I Castei,	
Primitivo di Manduria, Sinfarosa	677	Michele Castellani	282
Primitivo di Manduria, Soloperto	691	Recioto della Valpolicella Cl. Capitel Monte Fontana,	
Primitivo di Manduria, Vinicola Mediterranea	692	F.lli Tedeschi	304
Primitivo di Manduria 16° Tradizione del Nonno,		Recioto della Valpolicella Cl. Casal dei Ronchi	
Pichierri - Vinicola Savese	692	Serègo Alighieri, Masi	306
Primitivo di Manduria Antiche Contrade,		Recioto della Valpolicella Cl. Domini Veneti,	
Consorzio Prod. Vini	691	C. Soc. Valpolicella	293
Primitivo di Manduria Archidamo, Pervini	685	Recioto della Valpolicella Cl. Fiorato,	
Primitivo di Manduria Dolce Naturale,		Viticoltori Tommasi	305
Pichierri - Vinicola Savese	692	Recioto della Valpolicella Cl. Francesca Finato Spinosa,	
Primitivo di Manduria Dunico, Masseria Pepe	686	Villa Spinosa	295
Primitivo di Manduria Giravolta Tenuta Pozzopalo, Pervini	685	Recioto della Valpolicella Cl. Giovanni Allegrini, Allegrini	277
Primitivo di Manduria Lirica, Consorzio Prod. Vini	691	Recioto della Valpolicella Cl. I Comunai, F.lli Speri	304
Primitivo di Manduria Primo Amore, Pervini	685	Recioto della Valpolicella Cl. La Roggia, F.lli Speri	304
Primitivo di Manduria Santera, Leone de Castris	687	Recioto della Valpolicella Cl. Le Arele, Giuseppe Lonardi	284
Primitivo di Manduria Vecchio Ceppo, Soloperto	691	Recioto della Valpolicella Cl. Le Brugnine,	
Primitivo di Manduria Zinfandel, Sinfarosa	677	Massimino Venturini	305
Primitivo Il Portile, Masseria Pepe	686	Recioto della Valpolicella Cl. Le Calcarole, Roberto Mazzi	294
Primitivo Maestro, Borgo Canale	680	Recioto della Valpolicella Cl. Le Vigne Ca' del Pipa,	
Primitivo Primaio, Vini Classici Cardone	691	Michele Castellani	282
Primitivo Sigillo Primo, Antica Masseria del Sigillo	681	Recioto della Valpolicella Cl. Pal Sun,	
Primitivo Triusco, Rivera	676	Raimondi Villa Monteleone	307
Primosole Rosso, Bianchi	153	Recioto della Valpolicella Cl. TB, Tommaso Bussola	292
Primula Bianco, Casa Vinicola Firriato	709	Recioto della Valpolicella Cl. Vigne Alte, F.lli Zeni	273
Primula Rosso, Casa Vinicola Firriato	709	Recioto della Valpolicella Cl. Vigneti di Moron,	
Privilegia Rosso, Giuseppe Lonardi	284	C. Soc. Valpolicella	293
Privilegio, Feudi di S. Gregorio	663	Recioto della Valpolicella Cl. Vigneto le Tordare,	
Progetto, Mangilli	402	Ca' La Bionda	281
Prosecco, Vigneto Due Santi	273	Recioto della Valpolicella Dolce di Regina, Baltieri	330

Entry	Page
Recioto della Valpolicella Le Traversagne, Le Salette	278
Recioto della Valpolicella Pergole Vece, Le Salette	278
Recioto della Valpolicella Re Teodorico, Giacomo Montresor	320
Recioto della Valpolicella Roccolo Grassi, Sartori - Roccolo Grassi	285
Recioto di Gambellara, La Biancara	278
Recioto di Gambellara Cl. Riva dei Perari, Vinicola Luigino Dal Maso	287
Recioto di Gambellara Podere il Giangio Aristòs, Zonin	279
Recioto di Soave, Carlo Bogoni	288
Recioto di Soave, Guerrieri Rizzardi	272
Recioto di Soave, Monte Tondo	309
Recioto di Soave Acinatium, Suavia	310
Recioto di Soave Arzìmo, La Cappuccina	290
Recioto di Soave Case Vecie, Cecilia Beretta	319
Recioto di Soave Cl. Le Sponde, Coffele	309
Recioto di Soave Cl. Rocca Sveva, C. di Soave	308
Recioto di Soave Col Foscarin, Gini	290
Recioto di Soave Corte Pittora, C. del Castello	308
Recioto di Soave I Capitelli, Roberto Anselmi	288
Recioto di Soave La Broia, Sartori - Roccolo Grassi	285
Recioto di Soave La Perlara, Ca' Rugate	289
Recioto di Soave Le Fontane, Prà	291
Recioto di Soave Motto Piane, Fattori & Graney	289
Recioto di Soave Oro, Umberto Portinari	291
Recioto di Soave Renobilis, Gini	290
Recioto di Soave Vigna dello Stefano, Le Albare	326
Red Angel, Vinnaioli Jermann	364
Redigaffi, Tua Rita	545
Refola, Poggio Salvi	574
Refolà Cabernet Sauvignon, Le Vigne di S. Pietro	311
Refosco, Marco Felluga	368
Refosco P. R., Villa Frattina	378
Refosco P. R. Bottaz, Venica & Venica	361
Refosco P. R. I Legni, Russolo	395
Regaleali Bianco, Tasca d'Almerita	715
Regaleali Rosato, Tasca d'Almerita	715
Regaleali Rosso, Tasca d'Almerita	715
Resico, S. Luciano	493
Rêve di Villa Angela, Ercole Velenosi	580
Ribolla Gialla, Le Due Torri	358
Riccio, Redi	504
Riccionero, Lanciola	469
Riesling Brut M. Cl., La Palazzola	623
Rietine Bianco, Rietine	556
Riflesso Antico, Lorella Ambrosini	543
Ripa, Podere Sopra la Ripa	542
Ripa delle Mandorle, Castello di Vicchiomaggio	467
Ripa delle More, Castello di Vicchiomaggio	467
Ris. del Governatore Extra Brut, Bortolomiol	314
Risveglio Chardonnay, Cascina Montagnola	142
Ritratto, La Vis	224
Ritratto Bianco, La Vis	224
Rìul Rosso, Dario e Luciano Ermacora	380
Riviera Ligure di Ponente Ormeasco, Cantine Calleri	167
Riviera Ligure di Ponente Ormeasco Sup. Le Braje, Tommaso e Angelo Lupi	163
Riviera Ligure di Ponente Pigato, A Maccia	164
Riviera Ligure di Ponente Pigato, Anfossi	167
Riviera Ligure di Ponente Pigato, Laura Aschero	168
Riviera Ligure di Ponente Pigato, Maria Donata Bianchi	160
Riviera Ligure di Ponente Pigato, Cascina Feipu dei Massaretti	156
Riviera Ligure di Ponente Pigato, La Rocca di S. Nicolao	160
Riviera Ligure di Ponente Pigato, La Vecchia C.	157
Riviera Ligure di Ponente Pigato, Tommaso e Angelo Lupi	163
Riviera Ligure di Ponente Pigato, Terre Bianche	161
Riviera Ligure di Ponente Pigato, Cascina delle Terre Rosse	162
Riviera Ligure di Ponente Pigato, Claudio Vio	166
Riviera Ligure di Ponente Pigato Apogeo, Cascina delle Terre Rosse	162
Riviera Ligure di Ponente Pigato Artemide, Maria Donata Bianchi	160
Riviera Ligure di Ponente Pigato Costa de Vigne, Massimo Alessandri	168
Riviera Ligure di Ponente Pigato Le Petraie, Tommaso e Angelo Lupi	163
Riviera Ligure di Ponente Pigato Le Russeghine, Bruna	164
Riviera Ligure di Ponente Pigato Piansoprano, Fiorenzo Guidi	168
Riviera Ligure di Ponente Pigato U Bacan, Bruna	164
Riviera Ligure di Ponente Pigato Vigna La Torretta, Colle dei Bardellini	162
Riviera Ligure di Ponente Pigato Vigna Proxi, La Rocca di S. Nicolao	160
Riviera Ligure di Ponente Pigato Villa Torrachetta, Bruna	164
Riviera Ligure di Ponente Rossese, A Maccia	164
Riviera Ligure di Ponente Rossese, Bruna	164
Riviera Ligure di Ponente Vermentino, Maria Donata Bianchi	160
Riviera Ligure di Ponente Vermentino, Colle dei Bardellini	162
Riviera Ligure di Ponente Vermentino, Tenuta Giuncheo	157
Riviera Ligure di Ponente Vermentino, La Rocca di S. Nicolao	160
Riviera Ligure di Ponente Vermentino, La Vecchia C.	157
Riviera Ligure di Ponente Vermentino, Tommaso e Angelo Lupi	163
Riviera Ligure di Ponente Vermentino, Terre Bianche	161
Riviera Ligure di Ponente Vermentino, Cascina delle Terre Rosse	162
Riviera Ligure di Ponente Vermentino, Claudio Vio	166
Riviera Ligure di Ponente Vermentino Barricato, La Rocca di S. Nicolao	160
Riviera Ligure di Ponente Vermentino I Muzzazzi, Cantine Calleri	167
Riviera Ligure di Ponente Vermentino Le Palme, Tenuta Giuncheo	157
Riviera Ligure di Ponente Vermentino Le Serre, Tommaso e Angelo Lupi	163
Riviera Ligure di Ponente Vermentino Vigna Proxi, La Rocca di S. Nicolao	160
Riviera Ligure di Ponente Vermentino Vigna U Munte, Colle dei Bardellini	162
Roccato, Rocca delle Macìe	441
Rocchigiano, Meleta	527
Roccia Bianco, C. Coop. del Locorotondo	684
Roccia Rosato, C. Coop. del Locorotondo	684
Roccia Rosso, C. Coop. del Locorotondo	684
Roceja, Carlotta	43
Roero, Cascina Ca' Rossa	47
Roero, Matteo Correggia	48
Roero, Filippo Gallino	49
Roero, Malvirà	50
Roero, Cascina Pellerino	109
Roero, Fabrizio Pinsoglio	56
Roero, Cascina Val del Prete	121
Roero Arneis, Bel Colle	138
Roero Arneis, Tenuta Carretta	120
Roero Arneis, Matteo Correggia	48
Roero Arneis, Funtanin	49
Roero Arneis, Filippo Gallino	49
Roero Arneis, Bruno Giacosa	113
Roero Arneis, Raffaele Gili	146
Roero Arneis, Malvirà	50
Roero Arneis, Montaribaldi	33
Roero Arneis, Stefanino Morra	55
Roero Arneis, Prunotto	26
Roero Arneis, Mauro Sebaste	27
Roero Arneis, Vietti	60
Roero Arneis Anterisio, Cascina Chicco	47
Roero Arneis Boneur, Cascina Pellerino	109
Roero Arneis Bricco Cappellina, Gianni Voerzio	91
Roero Arneis Bricco delle Ciliegie, Giovanni Almondo	106
Roero Arneis Camestrì, Porello	145
Roero Arneis Daivej, Deltetto	48
Roero Arneis Gianat, Angelo Negro & Figli	108
Roero Arneis Luet, Cascina Val del Prete	121
Roero Arneis Merica, Cascina Ca' Rossa	47
Roero Arneis Perdaudin, Angelo Negro & Figli	108
Roero Arneis Pierin di Soc, Funtanin	49
Roero Arneis Re Cit, Monchiero Carbone	50
Roero Arneis Renesio, Malvirà	50
Roero Arneis S. Michele, Deltetto	48
Roero Arneis Saglietto, Malvirà	50
Roero Arneis Sernì, Michele Taliano	106
Roero Arneis Sorilaria, Araldica - Il Cantinone	54
Roero Arneis Trinità, Malvirà	50
Roero Arneis Vigna Canorei, Tenuta Carretta	120
Roero Arneis Vigne Sparse, Giovanni Almondo	106
Roero Arneis Vigneto Malinot, Fabrizio Pinsoglio	56
Roero Braja, Deltetto	48
Roero Bric Torretta, Porello	145
Roero Bric Valdiana, Giovanni Almondo	106
Roero Bricco Morinaldo, Valerio Aloi	150
Roero Madonna dei Boschi, Deltetto	48
Roero Mompissano, Cascina Ca' Rossa	47
Roero Mulino della Costa, Cascina Chicco	47
Roero Ròche d'Ampsèj, Matteo Correggia	48
Roero Ròche dra Bòssora, Michele Taliano	106
Roero Srù, Monchiero Carbone	50
Roero Sup., Cornarea	145
Roero Sup., Filippo Gallino	49
Roero Sup., Malvirà	50
Roero Sup., Stefanino Morra	55
Roero Sup. Bric d'America, Marsaglia	146
Roero Sup. Bric Paradiso, Tenuta Carretta	120
Roero Sup. Bricco Barbisa, Funtanin	49
Roero Sup. Giovanni Almondo, Giovanni Almondo	106
Roero Sup. Printi, Monchiero Carbone	50
Roero Sup. Sodisfà, Angelo Negro & Figli	108
Roero Valmaggiore, Cascina Chicco	47
Roero Vicot, Cascina Pellerino	109
Roero Vigna Audinaggio, Cascina Ca' Rossa	47
Romagnano Bianco, Colacicchi	636
Romagnano Rosso, Colacicchi	636
Romalbo, Cima	471
Romito del Romitorio, Castello Romitorio	490
Romitorio di Santedame, Tenimenti Ruffino	520
Ronco dei Ciliegi, Castelluccio	412
Ronco dei Roseti, Le Vigne di Zamò	370
Ronco del Re, Castelluccio	412

Entry	Page
Ronco delle Ginestre, Castelluccio	412
Ronco Nolè Rosso, Di Lenardo	365
Ronco Sesan, Russolo	395
Roncùs Bianco, Roncùs	338
Rondinaia, Castello del Terriccio	442
Rondon, Colmello di Grotta	363
Rosa di Montacuto, Alessandro Moroder	579
Rosathea, Castel De Paolis	632
Rosato, Il Poggiolino	545
Rosato, Gianni Masciarelli	647
Rosiano, S. Filippo - Rosi	564
Rosserto Bianco, Giovanni Manzone	102
Rossese di Dolceacqua, Tenuta Giuncheo	157
Rossese di Dolceacqua, Terre Bianche	161
Rossese di Dolceacqua Bricco Arcagna, Terre Bianche	161
Rossese di Dolceacqua Sup. Vigneto Arcagna, Giobatta Mandino Cane	161
Rossese di Dolceacqua Sup. Vigneto Morghe, Giobatta Mandino Cane	161
Rossese di Dolceacqua Vigneto Pian del Vescovo, Tenuta Giuncheo	157
Rossinot, Nicola Balter	230
Rosso, Branko - Igor Erzetich	345
Rosso 57, Michele Moio	659
Rosso A.D., Doria	191
Rosso Avignonesi, Avignonesi	497
Rosso Carpino, Il Carpino	390
Rosso Conero, Fazi Battaglia	583
Rosso Conero, Lanari	578
Rosso Conero, Fattoria Le Terrazze	593
Rosso Conero, Malacari	593
Rosso Conero, Marchetti	578
Rosso Conero, Alessandro Moroder	579
Rosso Conero Conti Cortesi, Monteschiavo	588
Rosso Conero Cùmaro, Umani Ronchi	595
Rosso Conero Dorico, Alessandro Moroder	579
Rosso Conero Fibbio, Lanari	578
Rosso Conero Fructus, Conte Leopardi Dittajuti	592
Rosso Conero Grigiano, Malacari	593
Rosso Conero Grosso Agontano, Gioacchino Garofoli	588
Rosso Conero I Lavi, Enzo Mecella	586
Rosso Conero Julius, Silvano Strologo	582
Rosso Conero Passo del Lupo Ris., Fazi Battaglia	583
Rosso Conero Pigmento, Conte Leopardi Dittajuti	592
Rosso Conero Ris., Terre Cortesi Moncaro	590
Rosso Conero Rubelliano, Enzo Mecella	586
Rosso Conero S. Lorenzo, Umani Ronchi	595
Rosso Conero Sassi Neri, Fattoria Le Terrazze	593
Rosso Conero Traiano, Silvano Strologo	582
Rosso Conero Varano, Alberto Serenelli	603
Rosso Conero Vigneti del Coppo, Conte Leopardi Dittajuti	592
Rosso Conero Vigneti del Parco Ris., Terre Cortesi Moncaro	590
Rosso Conero Villa Bonomi, Marchetti	578
Rosso Conero Villa Bonomi Ris., Marchetti	578
Rosso Conero Visions of J, Fattoria Le Terrazze	593
Rosso Conte Kuenburg, Castel Sallegg - Graf Kuenburg	253
Rosso Corte dell'Abbà, Villa Frattina	378
Rosso Dedicato a Mario d'Ambra, D'Ambra Vini d'Ischia	656
Rosso degli Appiani, S. Giusto	517
Rosso degli Spezieri, Tenuta Col d'Orcia	479
Rosso dei Dioscuri, C. Coop. di Cincinnato	637
Rosso dei Massaretti, Cascina Feipu dei Massaretti	156
Rosso del Cardinale, Barone de Cles	227
Rosso del Conte, Tasca d'Almerita	715
Rosso del Gnemiz, Ronco del Gnemiz	393
Rosso del Notaio, Massimo Oddero	147
Rosso del Senatore, Fattoria dell' Aiola	443
Rosso del Soprano, Palari	707
Rosso della Boemia, Liedholm	68
Rosso della Fabriseria, F.lli Tedeschi	304
Rosso della Rocca, Meleta	527
Rosso delle Chiaie, Giovanni Palombo	628
Rosso di Alberico, La Brugherata	200
Rosso di Casale Marchese, Casale Marchese	632
Rosso di Corte, Corte Gardoni	318
Rosso di Marco, Marco De Bartoli	704
Rosso di Montalcino, Tenuta di Argiano	473
Rosso di Montalcino, Banfi	474
Rosso di Montalcino, Fattoria dei Barbi	474
Rosso di Montalcino, Casanova di Neri	476
Rosso di Montalcino, Fattoria del Casato - Donatella Cinelli Colombini	476
Rosso di Montalcino, Castelli Martinozzi	560
Rosso di Montalcino, Castiglion del Bosco	478
Rosso di Montalcino, Tenuta Col d'Orcia	479
Rosso di Montalcino, Coldisole	561
Rosso di Montalcino, Tenuta di Collosorbo	561
Rosso di Montalcino, Corte Pavone	561
Rosso di Montalcino, Andrea Costanti	479
Rosso di Montalcino, Tenuta Di Sesta	480
Rosso di Montalcino, Fanti - La Palazzetta	480
Rosso di Montalcino, Fanti - S. Filippo	481
Rosso di Montalcino, Fornacina	561
Rosso di Montalcino, Il Palazzone	562
Rosso di Montalcino, Tenuta Il Poggione	483
Rosso di Montalcino, La Fornace	562
Rosso di Montalcino, Podere La Fortuna	484
Rosso di Montalcino, Tenuta La Fuga	562
Rosso di Montalcino, La Gerla	484
Rosso di Montalcino, La Poderina	485
Rosso di Montalcino, La Serena	562
Rosso di Montalcino, La Togata	485
Rosso di Montalcino, Maurizio Lambardi	486
Rosso di Montalcino, Le Chiuse	563
Rosso di Montalcino, Le Gode di Ripaccioli	563
Rosso di Montalcino, Mastrojanni	487
Rosso di Montalcino, Mocali	487
Rosso di Montalcino, Tenute Silvio Nardi	563
Rosso di Montalcino, Siro Pacenti	488
Rosso di Montalcino, Piancornello	488
Rosso di Montalcino, Agostina Pieri	489
Rosso di Montalcino, Poggio di Sotto	489
Rosso di Montalcino, Poggio S. Polo	574
Rosso di Montalcino, Castello Romitorio	490
Rosso di Montalcino, Salicutti	490
Rosso di Montalcino, Solaria - Cencioni	491
Rosso di Montalcino, Tenimenti Angelini - Val di Suga	492
Rosso di Montalcino, Tornesi	564
Rosso di Montalcino, Uccelliera	564
Rosso di Montalcino, Tenuta Valdicava	492
Rosso di Montalcino, Verbena	564
Rosso di Montalcino, Vitanza	564
Rosso di Montalcino Calbello, Andrea Costanti	479
Rosso di Montalcino Ginestreto, Eredi Fuligni	481
Rosso di Montalcino Il Roccolo, Oliveto	563
Rosso di Montalcino La Caduta, Tenuta Caparzo	475
Rosso di Montalcino Le Potazzine, Due Portine - Gorelli	561
Rosso di Montalcino Poggio Salvi, Tenuta Il Greppo	482
Rosso di Montalcino Ris., La Lecciaia	562
Rosso di Montalcino Sassello, Il Poggiolo	483
Rosso di Montalcino Terra Rossa, Il Poggiolo	483
Rosso di Montalcino Tirso, Villa Le Prata	493
Rosso di Montalcino Vigna della Fonte, Ciacci Piccolomini D'Aragona	478
Rosso di Montepulciano, Avignonesi	497
Rosso di Montepulciano, Canneto	565
Rosso di Montepulciano, Fattoria del Cerro	499
Rosso di Montepulciano, Contucci	499
Rosso di Montepulciano, Dei	500
Rosso di Montepulciano, Ercolani	566
Rosso di Montepulciano, Vittorio Innocenti	496
Rosso di Montepulciano, La Calonica	501
Rosso di Montepulciano, La Ciarliana	502
Rosso di Montepulciano, Podere Le Berne	566
Rosso di Montepulciano, Fattoria Le Casalte	566
Rosso di Montepulciano, Eredi Antonino Lombardo	567
Rosso di Montepulciano, Nottola	502
Rosso di Montepulciano, Poliziano	503
Rosso di Montepulciano, Redi	504
Rosso di Montepulciano, Salcheto	504
Rosso di Montepulciano, Tenuta Valdipiatta	505
Rosso di Montepulciano, Villa Sant'Anna	506
Rosso di Montepulciano Alàuda, Lodola Nuova - Tenimenti Ruffino	567
Rosso di Montepulciano Fosso Lupaio, Bindella	498
Rosso di Montepulciano Pancole, Tenute Folonari	452
Rosso di Montepulciano Sabazio, Fattoria La Braccesca	501
Rosso di Montepulciano Selciaia, Fassati	500
Rosso di Nero, Istituto Professionale per l'Agricoltura e l'Ambiente	410
Rosso di Nero, Monzio Compagnoni	183
Rosso di Sera, Fattoria Poggiopiano	532
Rosso Faye, Pojer & Sandri	219
Rosso Fiorentino, Cennatoio	511
Rosso Giublot, Anteo	197
Rosso Gli Affreschi, Tenuta di Blasig	386
Rosso La Tia, Cascina Bertolotto	132
Rosso La Vigna Bricca Ris., Tenuta La Costaiola	191
Rosso Merlorso, Pusterla	212
Rosso Orvietano Rosso di Spicca, Tenuta Le Velette	619
Rosso Ottella, Ottella	296
Rosso Piceno, Aurora	605
Rosso Piceno, Boccadigabbia	584
Rosso Piceno, Tenuta Cocci Grifoni	597
Rosso Piceno, Colonnara Viticultori in Cupramontana	585
Rosso Piceno, Fattoria di Forano	579
Rosso Piceno, Fattoria Laila	604
Rosso Piceno, Laurentina	590
Rosso Piceno, Rio Maggio	591
Rosso Piceno, S. Cassella	606
Rosso Piceno, Tenuta De Angelis	582
Rosso Piceno Bulciano, Fattoria di Forano	579
Rosso Piceno Castru Vecchiu, Saputi	604
Rosso Piceno Duca Guarnerio, Capinera	605
Rosso Piceno GrAnarijS, Rio Maggio	591
Rosso Piceno Morellone, Le Caniette	598
Rosso Piceno Nero di Vite, Le Caniette	598
Rosso Piceno Ophites, S. Giovanni	594
Rosso Piceno Regina del Bosco, Fattoria Dezi	601
Rosso Piceno Rosolaccio, Amato Ceci	599
Rosso Piceno Rosso Bello, Le Caniette	598

Rosso Piceno Rusus, Castello Fageto	606
Rosso Piceno S. Michele, Stefano Mancinelli	591
Rosso Piceno Sassaiolo, Monteschiavo	588
Rosso Piceno Sup., C. Coop. Castignanese	603
Rosso Piceno Sup., Saladini Pilastri	601
Rosso Piceno Sup., S. Savino	599
Rosso Piceno Sup., Tenuta De Angelis	582
Rosso Piceno Sup., Villa Pigna	595
Rosso Piceno Sup., Vinicola del Tesino	587
Rosso Piceno Sup. Castellano, La C. dei Colli Ripani	598
Rosso Piceno Sup. Gotico, Ciù Ciù	594
Rosso Piceno Sup. Il Brecciarolo, Ercole Velenosi	580
Rosso Piceno Sup. Il Grifone, Tenuta Cocci Grifoni	597
Rosso Piceno Sup. Le Torri, Tenuta Cocci Grifoni	597
Rosso Piceno Sup. Leo Guelfus, S. Giovanni	594
Rosso Piceno Sup. Leo Ripanus, La C. dei Colli Ripani	598
Rosso Piceno Sup. Roggio del Filare, Ercole Velenosi	580
Rosso Piceno Sup. Rosso del Nonno, S. Giovanni	594
Rosso Piceno Sup. Rubbio Sel., S. Savino	599
Rosso Piceno Sup. Vergaio, Villa Pigna	595
Rosso Piceno Sup. Vigna Messieri, Tenuta Cocci Grifoni	597
Rosso Piceno Sup. Vigna Monteprandone Conte Saladino, Saladini Pilastri	601
Rosso Piceno Sup. Vigna Montetinello, Saladini Pilastri	601
Rosso Piceno Tavignano, Lucangeli Aymerich di Laconi	583
Rosso Piceno Tenuta Pongelli, F.lli Bucci	596
Rosso Poculum, Agnes	198
Rosso Ris. Pallavicini, Vini Pallavicini	637
Rosso Teodote, Tenuta Il Bosco	203
Rosso Valecchia Cabernet Sauvignon Merlot, Zamuner	329
Rosso Vineargenti Bosco del Merlo, Paladin & Paladin	323
Rossole, Borgo Salcetino	571
Rossonero, Leone Conti	410
Rouchet Bricco Rosa, Scarpa - Antica Casa Vinicola	117
Rouge du Prieur, Institut Agricole Régional	16
Roussanne, Wandanna	495
Rovai, Ca' del Vispo	532
Rovaio, La Lastra	535
Rozzano, Villa Pigna	595
Rubbio, Palazzone	619
Rubino, La Palazzola	623
Rubrato, Feudi di S. Gregorio	663
Rubrum, Il Carpino	390
Rubrum Cor Laetificans, Floriano Cinti	419
Ruché di Castagnole M.to 'Na Vota, Cantine Sant'Agata	128
Ruchetto dell'Uccellina, Tenuta Uccellina	417
Rugiasco, Villa Pigna	595
Rupestro, Co.Vi.O.	617
S'Arai, Pala	728
S. Clemente Bianco, Ciccio Zaccagnini	640
S. Gimignano Rosso La Sughera, Pietrafitta	538
S. Torpè Felciaio, Badia di Morrona	548
Sa'etta, Monte Bernardi	514
Sabinio Cabernet, Colonna - Vini Spalletti	419
Saeculum, Riseccoli	465
Saffredi, Le Pupille	468
Sagana, Cusumano	710
Sagittarius, Graf Pfeil Weingut Kränzel	256
Sagrado Bianco, Castelvecchio	387
Sagrado Rosso, Castelvecchio	387
Sagrato Chardonnay Castello di Montauto, Famiglia Cecchi	439
Salae Domini, Antonio Caggiano	664
Salamartano, Fattoria di Montellori	454
Salcheto, Salcheto	504
Salento Bianco Bizantino, Pervini	685
Salento Bianco Bolina, Rosa del Golfo	676
Salento Bianco Cantamessa, S. Barbara	688
Salento Bianco Cigliano, C. Soc. Coop. Copertino	690
Salento Bianco Felicità, Tenute Albano Carrisi	678
Salento Bianco Marmorelle, Tenute Rubino	677
Salento Bianco Santi Medici, Castel di Salve	689
Salento Bianco Terra di Tacco, Lomazzi & Sarli	691
Salento Bianco Ursa Maior, S. Barbara	688
Salento Bianco Vigna Vinera, Francesco Candido	687
Salento Bianco Villa Carrisi, Tenute Albano Carrisi	678
Salento Chardonnay, Cantele	682
Salento Chardonnay Don Carmelo, Tenute Albano Carrisi	678
Salento Chardonnay Teresa Manara, Cantele	682
Salento Primitivo, Cantele	682
Salento Primitivo, Vini Classici Cardone	691
Salento Primitivo Vecchia Torre, C. Soc. Coop. Leverano	691
Salento Primitivo Visellio, Tenute Rubino	677
Salento Primitivo Zinfandel, Conti Zecca	683
Salento Rosato Bizantino, Pervini	685
Salento Rosato Donna Marzia, Conti Zecca	683
Salento Rosato Mediterraneo, Tenute Albano Carrisi	678
Salento Rosato Rosa del Golfo, Rosa del Golfo	676
Salento Rosato Santi Medici, Castel di Salve	689
Salento Rosato Scaloti, Cosimo Taurino	682
Salento Rosso Tenuta Piutri, Duca Carlo Guarini	689
Salento Rosso Alberello, Felline	685
Salento Rosso Bizantino, Pervini	685
Salento Rosso Don Carmelo, Tenute Albano Carrisi	678
Salento Rosso Donna Marzia, Conti Zecca	683
Salento Rosso Gallico, Tenute Rubino	677
Salento Rosso Grecantico, Michele Calò & Figli	692
Salento Rosso Illemos, Leone de Castris	687
Salento Rosso Marmorelle, Tenute Rubino	677
Salento Rosso Negroamaro Tenuta Piutri, Duca Carlo Guarini	689
Salento Rosso Nostalgia, Tenute Albano Carrisi	678
Salento Rosso Piromàfo, Valle dell'Asso	690
Salento Rosso Platone, Tenute Albano Carrisi	678
Salento Rosso Portulano, Rosa del Golfo	676
Salento Rosso Quarantale, Rosa del Golfo	676
Salento Rosso Santi Medici, Castel di Salve	689
Salento Rosso Scaliere, Rosa del Golfo	676
Salento Rosso Ursa Maior, S. Barbara	688
Salento Rosso Vigna del Gelso Moro, Vinicola Resta	692
Salento Rosso Villa Carrisi, Tenute Albano Carrisi	678
Salento Sauvignon Corte Valesio, Agricole Vallone	683
Salento Sauvignon Murà, Duca Carlo Guarini	689
Salice Salentino, Vinicola Resta	692
Salice Salentino, S. Barbara	688
Salice Salentino Albano Carrisi, Tenute Albano Carrisi	678
Salice Salentino Bianco, Francesco Candido	687
Salice Salentino Bianco Donna Lisa, Leone de Castris	687
Salice Salentino Bianco Imago, Leone de Castris	687
Salice Salentino Ris., Francesco Candido	687
Salice Salentino Rosato Cenobio, Cantele	682
Salice Salentino Rosato Le Pozzelle, Francesco Candido	687
Salice Salentino Rosso, Torrevento	680
Salice Salentino Rosso, Vinicola Mediterranea	692
Salice Salentino Rosso Cantalupi, Conti Zecca	683
Salice Salentino Rosso Cenobio, Cantele	682
Salice Salentino Rosso Donna Lisa Ris., Leone de Castris	687
Salice Salentino Rosso Maiana, Leone de Castris	687
Salice Salentino Rosso Ris., Cantele	682
Salice Salentino Rosso Ris., Leone de Castris	687
Salice Salentino Rosso Ris., Cosimo Taurino	682
Salice Salentino Rosso Te Deum Laudamus Ris. Casale Bevagna, Pervini	685
Salice Salentino Rosso Vereto, Agricole Vallone	683
Salice Salentino Vecchia Torre, C. Soc. Coop. Leverano	691
Saline, Cantine Monthia	716
Saltapicchio Sangiovese, Boccadigabbia	584
Saluccio, Castello del Terriccio	442
Sammarco, Castello dei Rampolla	514
S. Bartolo Rosso, S. Barbara	580
S. Biagio, Progetto DiVino	674
S. Carlo, Barone Pizzini	182
S. Carro Rosso, Ciù Ciù	594
S. Colombano Banino Ris. La Merla, Antonio Panigada - Banino	212
S. Colombano Rosso Banino, Antonio Panigada - Banino	212
S. Colombano Rosso I Chiostri, Enrico Riccardi	213
S. Colombano Rosso Roverone, Enrico Riccardi	213
S. Cristoforo Uno, S. Cristoforo	187
S. Donato, Tenuta di Bagnolo dei Marchesi Pancrazi	497
S. Gimignano Rosso, S. Quirico	573
S. Gimignano Rosso, Signano	539
S. Gimignano Rosso Folgore, Giovanni Panizzi	538
S. Giorgio, Cantine Lungarotti	623
S. Giusto, S. Giusto	517
S. Leonardo, Tenuta S. Leonardo	217
S. Leopoldo, Belisario C. Soc. di Matelica e Cerreto d'Esi	589
S. Leopoldo, Tenuta Il Poggione	483
S. Lorenzo, Sassotondo	542
S. Marsan Bianco, Poderi Bertelli	65
S. Marsan Rosso, Poderi Bertelli	65
S. Martino, Villa Cafaggio	516
S. Martino della Battaglia Liquoroso, Spia d'Italia	208
S. Pio, Mastrojanni	487
S. Severo Bianco Posta Arignano, Giovanni D'Alfonso del Sordo	692
S. Severo Rosato Posta Arignano, Giovanni D'Alfonso del Sordo	692
S. Vincenzo, Roberto Anselmi	288
S. Zenobi, Pasolini Dall'Onda	556
S. Zio, Cantine Leonardo da Vinci	548
Sancta Catharina, Dei	500
Sangiovese, Borgo di Colloredo	640
Sangiovese, Cima	471
Sangiovese, Fazi Battaglia	583
Sangiovese, La Calonica	501
Sangiovese, Castello di Monastero	446
Sangiovese di Romagna, Umberto Cesari	407
Sangiovese di Romagna Amarcord d'un Ross Ris., Treré	411
Sangiovese di Romagna Bottale Ris., S. Ferrucci	406
Sangiovese di Romagna Canova, Pandolfa	416
Sangiovese di Romagna Castello di Ugarte Vigna delle Lepri Ris., Fattoria Paradiso	405
Sangiovese di Romagna Domus Caia Ris., S. Ferrucci	406
Sangiovese di Romagna Olmatello Ris., La Berta	405
Sangiovese di Romagna Poderepozzo Le Betulle, Leone Conti	410
Sangiovese di Romagna Ris., Umberto Cesari	407
Sangiovese di Romagna Ris., La Macolina	426
Sangiovese di Romagna Ris., Tenuta Uccellina	417
Sangiovese di Romagna Ris., Tre Monti	412

Entry	Page
Sangiovese di Romagna Sup., Colonna - Vini Spalletti	419
Sangiovese di Romagna Sup., Guido Guarini Matteucci di Castelfalcino	426
Sangiovese di Romagna Sup., Tre Monti	412
Sangiovese di Romagna Sup., Villa Pampini - F.lli Bernardi	428
Sangiovese di Romagna Sup. Aulente, S. Patrignano - Terre del Cedro	409
Sangiovese di Romagna Sup. Avi Ris., S. Patrignano - Terre del Cedro	409
Sangiovese di Romagna Sup. Ca' Grande, Umberto Cesari	407
Sangiovese di Romagna Sup. Centurione, S. Ferrucci	406
Sangiovese di Romagna Sup. Ceregio, Fattoria Zerbina	409
Sangiovese di Romagna Sup. Contiriserva, Leone Conti	410
Sangiovese di Romagna Sup. Fermavento, Giovanna Madonia	404
Sangiovese di Romagna Sup. Le Grillaie, Celli	404
Sangiovese di Romagna Sup. Le Grillaie Ris., Celli	404
Sangiovese di Romagna Sup. Le More, Castelluccio	412
Sangiovese di Romagna Sup. Maestri di Vigna, Fattoria Paradiso	405
Sangiovese di Romagna Sup. Mero Ris., Guido Guarini Matteucci di Castelfalcino	426
Sangiovese di Romagna Sup. Nonno Rico Ris., Alessandro Morini	425
Sangiovese di Romagna Sup. Ombroso Ris., Giovanna Madonia	404
Sangiovese di Romagna Sup. Pandolfo, Pandolfa	416
Sangiovese di Romagna Sup. Pietramora Ris., Fattoria Zerbina	409
Sangiovese di Romagna Sup. Poderepozzo Le Betulle, Leone Conti	410
Sangiovese di Romagna Sup. Pruno Ris., Drei Donà Tenuta La Palazza	411
Sangiovese di Romagna Sup. Solano, La Berta	405
Sangiovese di Romagna Sup. Terra Ris., S. Valentino	427
Sangiovese di Romagna Sup. Thea, Tre Monti	412
Sangiovese di Romagna Sup. Torre di Ceparano, Fattoria Zerbina	409
Sangiovese di Romagna Sup. Vigna dello Sperone, Treré	411
Sangiovese di Romagna Sup. Villa Rasponi Ris., Colonna - Vini Spalletti	419
Sangiovese di Romagna Sup. Zarricante Ris., S. Patrignano - Terre del Cedro	409
Sangiovese di Romagna Vigna del Monte, Treré	411
Sangiovese di Romagna Vigneto Il Prugneto, Poderi dal Nespoli	408
Sangiovese Moggio, S. Savino	599
Sangiovese Tenuta Corbara, Bigi	616
Sangiovese Terra degli Osci, Di Majo Norante	641
Sangiovese Vigna La Pieve, Fanini	610
Sangioveto, Coltibuono	456
Sanleone, Fattoria Castello Sonnino	568
Sannio Aglianico, Cantine Caputo	664
Sannio Aglianico, Corte Normanna	658
Sannio Aglianico, De Lucia	658
Sannio Aglianico, Vinicola del Sannio	667
Sannio Aglianico Adelchi, De Lucia	658
Sannio Aglianico Vigna La Corte, De Lucia	658
Sannio Barbera Barbetta Vàndari, Antica Masseria Venditti	667
Sannio Falanghina, Corte Normanna	658
Sannio Falanghina, De Lucia	658
Sannio Falanghina, Di Meo	668
Sannio Falanghina, Feudi di S. Gregorio	663
Sannio Falanghina Frattasi, Cantine Caputo	664
Sannio Falanghina La Palombaia, Corte Normanna	658
Sannio Falanghina Passito Porta dell'Olmo, Corte Normanna	658
Sannio Falanghina Simposium, Colli Irpini - Montesolae	659
Sannio Falanghina Vàndari, Antica Masseria Venditti	667
Sannio Falanghina Vigna delle Ginestre, De Lucia	658
Sannio Rosso, Antica Masseria Venditti	667
Sant'Amato, Fattoria di Montellori	454
Sant'Antimo, Fanti - S. Filippo	481
Sant'Antimo Fabius, Ciacci Piccolomini D'Aragona	478
Sant'Antimo Rosso, Castello di Camigliano	475
Sant'Antimo Rosso Romito del Romitorio, Castello Romitorio	490
Sant'Ippolito, Cantine Leonardo da Vinci	548
S. Anastasia Rosso, Abbazia S. Anastasia	701
S. Brigida, Fattoria La Ripa	546
S. Cecilia, Planeta	714
S. Cristina, Marchesi Antinori	452
S. Croce, Castell'in Villa	445
Santagostino Bianco Baglio Soria, Casa Vinicola Firriato	709
Santagostino Rosso Baglio Soria, Casa Vinicola Firriato	709
Santomio Rosso, Giacomo Montresor	320
Saramago, Ca' Ronesca	360
Sarastro, Morgassi Superiore	148
Sardegna Semidano, Gigi Picciau	730
Sarì, Marco Maci	679
Sarica, Pisoni	221
Saros V. T., Giulio Poli	238
Sassaia del Virginio, Castello di Poppiano	508
Sassello, Castello di Verrazzano	466
Sassicaia, Tenuta S. Guido	434
Sassoalloro, Tenuta Il Greppo	482
Sassobucato, Russo	544
Sassoscuro, Vittorio Graziano	408
Sassotondo Rosso, Sassotondo	542
Sauvignon, Casale del Giglio	628
Sauvignon, Giovanni Crosato	342
Sauvignon, Tenuta Falkenstein - Franz Pratzner	262
Sauvignon, Farnetella	541
Sauvignon, Kante	361
Sauvignon, La Cappuccina	290
Sauvignon, Mangilli	402
Sauvignon, Roncùs	338
Sauvignon, Vinnaioli Jermann	364
Sauvignon Atesino, Castel Noarna	228
Sauvignon Atesino, Pojer & Sandri	219
Sauvignon Campigie, Piovene Porto Godi	322
Sauvignon Campo Napoleone, Armani	276
Sauvignon Del Frate, Triacca	203
Sauvignon del Veneto, Ca' Lustra	275
Sauvignon della Sala, Castello della Sala	612
Sauvignon Ghiaiolo, Orlandi Contucci Ponno	647
Sauvignon Kolàus, Pierpaolo Pecorari	395
Sauvignon Maciete Fumé, Gini	290
Sauvignon Marca Trevigiana, Giorgio Cecchetto	330
Sauvignon Ornella, Ornella Molon Traverso	298
Sauvignon Sansaia, Giacomo Montresor	320
Sauvignon Seregni Valleselle, Eugenio & Figli Tinazzi	323
Sauvignon Vulcaia Fumé, Inama	298
Savuto, Giovan Battista Odoardi	695
Savuto Sup. Vigna Mortilla, Giovan Battista Odoardi	695
Saxa Calida, Il Paradiso	535
Scaleri Démi Sec, Cantine di Dolianova	722
Scannagallo, Fattoria S. Vittoria	454
Scasso dei Cesari, Tenuta di Valgiano	436
Scasso del Bugiardo, Tenuta di Valgiano	436
Scavigna Bianco Pian della Corte, Giovan Battista Odoardi	695
Scavigna Pian della Corte, Giovan Battista Odoardi	695
Scavigna Rosato, Giovan Battista Odoardi	695
Scavigna Vigna Garrone, Giovan Battista Odoardi	695
Scheria Bianco, Pietratorcia	656
Scheria Rosso, Pietratorcia	656
Schiaffo, Colacicchi	636
Schiava Valle dei Laghi, Giulio Poli	238
Schietto Chardonnay, Spadafora	711
Schietto Rosso, Spadafora	711
Sciamareti, Villa Patrizia	526
Sciara di Villagrande Rosso, Barone di Villagrande	708
Scirocco, D'Ancona	712
Scirus, Fattoria Le Sorgenti	431
Scrio, Le Macchiole	433
Scyri, COS	715
Sebino Giuliana C., La Boscaiola	181
Segumo, Ca' del Vispo	532
Seifile, Fiorenzo Nada	136
Selva Rosa La Selva di Moirano, Scarpa - Antica Casa Vinicola	117
Selvamaggio, Fattoria Villa La Selva	435
Selvascura, Guicciardini Strozzi - Fattoria Cusona	534
Selve Vecchie, Castel De Paolis	632
Ser Gervasio, Pietraserena	573
Ser Gioveto, Rocca delle Macìe	441
Ser Niccolò Solatio del Tani, Machiavelli	531
Ser Piero, Cantine Leonardo da Vinci	548
Seraselva, Poggio al Sole	547
Serena Bianco, Ronco del Gnemiz	393
Serpico, Feudi di S. Gregorio	663
Serra delle Querce, D'Angelo	672
Serracavallo Bianco, Serracavallo	696
Serracavallo Rosso, Serracavallo	696
Serracavallo Rosso Ris., Serracavallo	696
Serralori Rosato, Antonio Argiolas	728
Sghiras, Fattoria Le Sorgenti	431
Shàrjs, Livio Felluga	348
Shiraz, Casale del Giglio	628
Shiraz-Cesanese, L'Olivella	637
Sibiola Rosato, Cantine di Dolianova	722
Siepi, Castello di Fonterutoli	440
Sigillo Primo Chardonnay, Antica Masseria del Sigillo	681
Sigillo Primo Primitivo, Antica Masseria del Sigillo	681
Sigillo Rosso, Vitivinicola Avide	713
Signorelli, La Calonica	501
Signorio Rosso, Barone La Lumia	704
Sire, Marco Maci	679
Sirio, Vignalta	312
Sirius, Tenuta Giuncheo	157
Sissi, C. Prod. di Merano	260
Siùm, La Viarte	382
Soave, La Cappuccina	290
Soave Bisson, Bisson	328
Soave Bissoncello, Bisson	328
Soave Cl., Balestri Valda	328
Soave Cl. Brognoligo, Cecilia Beretta	319
Soave Cl. Capitel Alto, Giacomo Montresor	320
Soave Cl. Castelcerino Rocca Sveva, C. di Soave	308
Soave Cl. Costeggiola, Guerrieri Rizzardi	272

Entry	Page
Soave Cl. Lunalonga, Balestri Valda	328
Soave Cl. Monteforte, Santi	280
Soave Cl. Montefoscarin, S. Sofia	303
Soave Cl. Rocca Sveva, C. di Soave	308
Soave Cl. Sanfederici, Santi	280
Soave Cl. Santepietre, Lamberti	325
Soave Cl. Sup., Bertani	292
Soave Cl. Sup., Bisson	328
Soave Cl. Sup., Carlo Bogoni	288
Soave Cl. Sup., C. del Castello	308
Soave Cl. Sup., Coffele	309
Soave Cl. Sup., Fattori & Graney	289
Soave Cl. Sup., Gini	290
Soave Cl. Sup., Leonildo Pieropan	310
Soave Cl. Sup., Prà	291
Soave Cl. Sup., Suavia	310
Soave Cl. Sup. Acini Soavi, C. del Castello	308
Soave Cl. Sup. Alzari, Coffele	309
Soave Cl. Sup. Anguane, Tamellini	328
Soave Cl. Sup. Bucciato, Ca' Rugate	289
Soave Cl. Sup. Ca' Visco, Coffele	309
Soave Cl. Sup. Calvarino, Leonildo Pieropan	310
Soave Cl. Sup. Capocolle, Lenotti	323
Soave Cl. Sup. Colbaraca, Masi	306
Soave Cl. Sup. Colle S. Antonio, Prà	291
Soave Cl. Sup. Contrada Salvarenza Vecchie Vigne, Gini	290
Soave Cl. Sup. La Froscà, Gini	290
Soave Cl. Sup. La Ponsara, Carlo Bogoni	288
Soave Cl. Sup. La Rocca, Leonildo Pieropan	310
Soave Cl. Sup. Le Bine, Tamellini	328
Soave Cl. Sup. Le Rive, Suavia	310
Soave Cl. Sup. Monte Alto, Ca' Rugate	289
Soave Cl. Sup. Monte Carbonare, Suavia	310
Soave Cl. Sup. Monte Carniga, C. del Castello	308
Soave Cl. Sup. Monte Fiorentine, Ca' Rugate	289
Soave Cl. Sup. Monte Pressoni, C. del Castello	308
Soave Cl. Sup. Monte Tondo, Monte Tondo	309
Soave Cl. Sup. Motto Piane, Fattori & Graney	289
Soave Cl. Sup. Pieve Vecchia, Fasoli	324
Soave Cl. Sup. Sereole, Bertani	292
Soave Cl. Sup. Vigna dello Stefano, Le Albare	326
Soave Cl. Sup. Vigna Ronchetto, Umberto Portinari	291
Soave Cl. Sup. Vigneti di Sella, Casa Vinicola Sartori	326
Soave Cl. Sup. Vigneti in Casette Foscarin, Monte Tondo	309
Soave Cl. Sup. Vigneti Monte Foscarino Le Bine, Giuseppe Campagnola	282
Soave Cl. Sup. Vigneto Calvarino, Leonildo Pieropan	310
Soave Cl. Sup. Vigneto Du Lot, Inama	298
Soave Cl. Sup. Vigneto La Rocca, Leonildo Pieropan	310
Soave Cl. Sup. Vigneto Monte Grande, Prà	291
Soave Cl. Sup. Vin Soave, Inama	298
Soave Cl. Sup. Vin Soave Cuvée Speciale, Inama	298
Soave Cl. Vigne Alte, F.lli Zeni	273
Soave Cl. Vigneti di Montegrande, Pasqua Vigneti e Cantine	320
Soave Spumante Brut, Monte Tondo	309
Soave Sup., Fasoli	324
Soave Sup., Tamellini	328
Soave Sup. Fontégo, La Cappuccina	290
Soave Sup. La Broia, Sartori - Roccolo Grassi	285
Soave Sup. S. Brizio, La Cappuccina	290
Soave Sup. S. Stefano, Umberto Portinari	291
Soave Sup. Sagramoso, Pasqua Vigneti e Cantine	320
Soave Sup. Vigna Albare Doppia Maturazione Ragionata, Umberto Portinari	291
Sodole, Guicciardini Strozzi - Fattoria Cusona	534
Sogno di Dama, Barone La Lumia	704
Soianello, Elyane & Bruno Moos	576
Sol Doré, Provenza	184
Solaia, Marchesi Antinori	452
Solalto, Le Pupille	468
Solaria Ionica Ferrari, Pervini	685
Solarianne, Solaria - Cencioni	491
Solatia, Tenimenti Ruffino	520
Solativo, Ferrando	82
Soldati La Scolca Brut, La Scolca	79
Sole d'Autunno, Maso Martis	235
Sole di Dario, Cantrina	204
Sole di Sesta, Cottanera	702
Sole e Vento, Marco De Bartoli	704
Solengo, Tenuta di Argiano	473
Solissimo, Castello di Lucignano	458
Solitario, Cascina delle Terre Rosse	162
Solleone, Palagetto	537
Solo Chardonnay, Castello di Monastero	446
Solo Sangiovese, Fattoria Dezi	601
Soloìo, Casa Emma	549
Solopaca Bianco Guiscardo, Corte Normanna	658
Solopaca Rosso Guiscardo, Corte Normanna	658
Solopaca Rosso Vassallo, De Lucia	658
Somigliò, Giovanni Palombo	628
Sorbus, Cohens Gervais	559
Soreli, F.lli Pighin	375
Sottobosco, Palagetto	537
Sovana Bianco Sassotondo, Sassotondo	542
Sovana Rosso Sassotondo, Sassotondo	542
Sovana Sup. Vignamurata, C. Coop. di Pitigliano	569
Spante, Terre del Sillabo	470
Spargolino Frizzante, Vittorio Graziano	408
Spargolo, Famiglia Cecchi	439
Spigàu, Fausto De Andreis	156
Spigàu Crociata, Fausto De Andreis	156
Spumante Brut, Dino Illuminati	642
Spumante Brut, Zamuner	329
Spumante Brut Riserva Waldaz, Adami	321
Spumante Classico Cuvée Testarossa Extra Dry, C. Soc. La Versa	200
Spumante Demi Sec, Zamuner	329
Spumante Haderburg Brut, Haderburg	263
Spumante M. Cl. Brut Ris. Giuseppe Contratto, Contratto	51
Spumante Pinot Brut Modolet, Tenuta di Angoris	343
Squinzano, C. Due Palme	690
Squinzano, S. Barbara	688
Squinzano Rosso Zephir, Marco Maci	679
Stefano Antonucci Rosso, S. Barbara	580
Stefano Ferrucci Vino da Uve Stramature, S. Ferrucci	406
Stemma, Barone La Lumia	704
Sterpigno Merlot, Giovanna Madonia	404
Stielle, Rocca di Castagnoli	460
Stignano, S. Vincenti	462
Stoppa, La Stoppa	417
Stravino di Stravino, Pravis	222
Stroncoli, Giacomo Marengo	565
Subertum, Lorella Ambrosini	543
Sud, Le Vigne di S. Pietro	311
Suffragium, Claudio Morelli	586
Sul Bric, Franco M. Martinetti	135
Sulleria Rosso, Casa Vinicola Grasso	717
Summus, Banfi	474
Syra's, Cabanon	188
Syrae, Pravis	222
Syrah, Castagnoli	552
Syrah, Isole e Olena	431
Syrah, Aziende Vinicole Miceli	710
Syrah, Planeta	714
Syrah, Poggio al Sole	547
Syrah, Castello di Poppiano	508
Syrah, Cantine Torrevecchia	700
Syrah, Vallarom	217
Syrah, Villa Arceno	449
Syrah, Villa Pillo	462
Syrah Case Via, Tenuta Fontodi	512
Taburno Coda di Volpe, Ocone	661
Taburno Coda di Volpe Amineo, C. del Taburno	655
Taburno Coda di Volpe Serra Docile, C. del Taburno	655
Taburno Falanghina, C. del Taburno	655
Taburno Falanghina, Fontanavecchia - Orazio Rillo	665
Taburno Falanghina, Ocone	661
Taburno Falanghina Cesco dell'Eremo, C. del Taburno	655
Taburno Falanghina Vigna del Monaco, Ocone	661
Taburno Piedirosso, Ocone	661
Tal Lûc, Lis Neris - Pecorari	394
Talento Banfi Brut M. Cl., Vigne Regali	133
Talento Brut Bisol, Desiderio Bisol & Figli	313
Talento Cuvée del Fondatore Eliseo Bisol, Desiderio Bisol & Figli	313
Talento Pas Dosé, Desiderio Bisol & Figli	313
Tamino, Morgassi Superiore	148
Tanca Su Conti, C. Soc. della Trexenta	727
Tancredi, Tenuta di Donnafugata	705
Tarasco Bianco, Cornarea	145
Tassinaia, Castello del Terriccio	442
Tauleto Sangiovese, Umberto Cesari	407
Taurasi, Colli Irpini - Montesolae	659
Taurasi, D'Antiche Terre - Vega	667
Taurasi, Di Meo	668
Taurasi, Marianna	666
Taurasi Fatica Contadina, Terredora di Paolo	660
Taurasi Piano di Montevergine, Feudi di S. Gregorio	663
Taurasi Piano di Montevergine Ris., Feudi di S. Gregorio	663
Taurasi Radici, Mastroberardino	654
Taurasi Selve di Luoti, Feudi di S. Gregorio	663
Taurasi Vigna Cinque Querce, Salvatore Molettieri	660
Taurasi Vigna Macchia dei Goti, Antonio Caggiano	664
Taurì, Antonio Caggiano	664
Tavernelle Cabernet, Banfi	474
Tazzelenghe, La Viarte	382
Tazzelenghe Ris., Tenuta Beltrame	332
TdF Bianco, Barone Pizzini	182
TdF Bianco, Bellavista	185
TdF Bianco, F.lli Berlucchi	182
TdF Bianco, Guido Berlucchi & C.	183
TdF Bianco, Bersi Serlini	197
TdF Bianco, Ca' del Bosco	185
TdF Bianco, Tenuta Castellino	180
TdF Bianco, Castelveder	192
TdF Bianco, Cavalleri	186
TdF Bianco, Contadi Castaldi	170
TdF Bianco, Lorenzo Faccoli & Figli	180
TdF Bianco, Ferghettina	186
TdF Bianco, Enrico Gatti	187
TdF Bianco, Il Mosnel	196

Entry	Page
TdF Bianco, La Montina	192
TdF Bianco, Lantieri de Paratico	173
TdF Bianco, Lo Sparviere	193
TdF Bianco, Ricci Curbastro	173
TdF Bianco, S. Cristoforo	187
TdF Bianco, Ugo Vezzoli	210
TdF Bianco, Villa	193
TdF Bianco Anna, La Boscaiola	181
TdF Bianco Augustus, Uberti	188
TdF Bianco Campolarga, Il Mosnel	196
TdF Bianco Colzano, Lantieri de Paratico	173
TdF Bianco Convento dell'Annunciata, Bellavista	185
TdF Bianco dei Frati Priori, Uberti	188
TdF Bianco della Seta, Monzio Compagnoni	183
TdF Bianco Dossi delle Querce, F.lli Berlucchi	182
TdF Bianco Favento, Ferghettina	186
TdF Bianco Giuliana C., La Boscaiola	181
TdF Bianco Le Arzelle, Guido Berlucchi & C.	183
TdF Bianco Lo Sparviere Ris., Lo Sparviere	193
TdF Bianco Manca Pane, Contadi Castaldi	170
TdF Bianco Marengo, Villa	193
TdF Bianco Maria Medici, Uberti	188
TdF Bianco Pian della Villa, Villa	193
TdF Bianco Pio Elemosiniere, Bredasole	210
TdF Bianco Rampaneto, Cavalleri	186
TdF Bianco Ris., Lo Sparviere	193
TdF Bianco Ronchello, Majolini	195
TdF Bianco Ronco della Seta, Monzio Compagnoni	183
TdF Bianco Seradina, Cavalleri	186
TdF Bianco Solicano, Tenuta Castellino	180
TdF Bianco Sottobosco, Ronco Calino	178
TdF Bianco Sulif, Il Mosnel	196
TdF Bianco Tetellus, Conti Bettoni Cazzago	177
TdF Bianco Uccellanda, Bellavista	185
TdF Bianco V. Saline, Cornaleto	170
TdF Bianco Vign. Palanca, La Montina	192
TdF Chardonnay, Ca' del Bosco	185
TdF Gatti Bianco, Enrico Gatti	187
TdF Rosso, Barone Pizzini	182
TdF Rosso, Bellavista	185
TdF Rosso, Bersi Serlini	197
TdF Rosso, Tenuta Castellino	180
TdF Rosso, Castelveder	192
TdF Rosso, Cavalleri	186
TdF Rosso, Contadi Castaldi	170
TdF Rosso, Ferghettina	186
TdF Rosso, Enrico Gatti	187
TdF Rosso, Lo Sparviere	193
TdF Rosso, Principe Banfi	207
TdF Rosso, Ricci Curbastro	173
TdF Rosso, Ronco Calino	178
TdF Rosso, S. Cristoforo	187
TdF Rosso, Attilio Vezzoli	208
TdF Rosso, Ugo Vezzoli	210
TdF Rosso, Villa	193
TdF Rosso Augustus, Uberti	188
TdF Rosso Barricato, Cornaleto	170
TdF Rosso Borbone, Al Rocol	210
TdF Rosso Colzano, Lantieri de Paratico	173
TdF Rosso Cornaleto, Cornaleto	170
TdF Rosso dei Dossi, La Montina	192
TdF Rosso Dordaro, Majolini	195
TdF Rosso Dossi delle Querce, F.lli Berlucchi	182
TdF Rosso Fontècolo, Il Mosnel	196
TdF Rosso Gradoni, Villa	193
TdF Rosso Il Sergnana, Lo Sparviere	193
TdF Rosso Maniero, Mirabella	212
TdF Rosso Poligono, Cornaleto	170
TdF Rosso Ritorno, La Boscaiola	181
TdF Rosso Ronco della Seta, Monzio Compagnoni	183
TdF Rosso Ruc di Gnoc, Majolini	195
TdF Rosso Santella del Gröm, Ricci Curbastro	173
TdF Rosso Sarese, Cornaleto	170
TdF Rosso Spigolato, Bredasole	210
TdF Rosso Tajardini, Cavalleri	186
TdF Rosso Tamino, Battista Cola	204
TdF Rosso Vigna Monte della Rosa, Castelveder	192
TdF Rosso Vino del Cacciatore, Lo Sparviere	193
Tempietto, Cohens Gervais	559
Tener Brut N. M., Vigne Regali	133
Tenores, Tenute Dettori	727
Tenuta di Testarossa Bianco, Franco Pasetti	643
Tenuta di Valgiano, Tenuta di Valgiano	436
Tenuta Il Tesoro La Fonte, Fattoria di Terrabianca	524
Tenuta S. Michele, Barone Scammacca del Murgo	713
Tenuta Scilio Bianco, Tenuta Scilio di Valle Galfina	716
Tenuta Scilio Rosso, Tenuta Scilio di Valle Galfina	716
Teodoro, Tenuta Le Calcinaie	536
Tergeno, Fattoria Zerbina	409
Teroldego Atesino Cernidor, Vigneti delle Meridiane	238
Teroldego Ris., Endrizzi	232
Teroldego Rotaliano, C. Rotaliana	227
Teroldego Rotaliano, Marco Donati	225
Teroldego Rotaliano, F.lli Dorigati	226
Teroldego Rotaliano, Foradori	228
Teroldego Rotaliano, Gaierhof	229
Teroldego Rotaliano, Zeni	233
Teroldego Rotaliano Bottega Vinai, Cavit - Consorzio di Cantine Sociali	233
Teroldego Rotaliano Braide, Concilio	235
Teroldego Rotaliano Clesurae, C. Rotaliana	227
Teroldego Rotaliano Diedri Ris., F.lli Dorigati	226
Teroldego Rotaliano Due Vigneti, Cipriano Fedrizzi	237
Teroldego Rotaliano Le Cervare, Zanini	237
Teroldego Rotaliano Maso Camorz, Endrizzi	232
Teroldego Rotaliano Maso Cervara, Cavit - Consorzio di Cantine Sociali	233
Teroldego Rotaliano Maso Scari, Barone de Cles	227
Teroldego Rotaliano Pieve Francescana, C. Rotaliana	227
Teroldego Rotaliano Pini, Zeni	233
Teroldego Rotaliano Ris., C. Rotaliana	227
Teroldego Rotaliano Ris., MezzaCorona	226
Teroldego Rotaliano Sangue del Drago, Marco Donati	225
Teroldego Rotaliano Sgarzon, Foradori	228
Teroldego Rotaliano Sup. Sel., Endrizzi	232
Terra Calda Rosso, Ca' de' Medici	427
Terra dei Rovi Bianco, Vinicola Luigino Dal Maso	287
Terra di Lavoro, Galardi	663
Terra Mala Vigne Storiche, C. Soc. Giogantinu	730
Terranatia Passito, Giacomo Montresor	320
Terrano, Castelvecchio	387
Terrato, Il Mandorlo	529
Terre Brune, C. Soc. di Santadi	726
Terre Cerase, Villa Matilde	655
Terre d'Agala, Duca di Salaparuta - Vini Corvo	702
Terre dei Cascinieri, Wandanna	495
Terre dei Goti Bianco, Stefano Mancinelli	591
Terre dei Goti Rosso, Stefano Mancinelli	591
Terre del Guiscardo, Antica Masseria del Sigillo	681
Terre del Noce Bianco, Marco Donati	225
Terre del Volturno Greco, Villa S. Michele	668
Terre del Volturno Pallagrello Bianco Le Ortole, Vestini - Campagnano	666
Terre del Volturno Pallagrello Rosso, Vestini - Campagnano	666
Terre dell'Istrice, Baglio S. Vincenzo	717
Terre di Galatrona, Fattoria Petrolo	509
Terre di Ginestra Bianco, Calatrasi - Terre di Ginestra	709
Terre di Ginestra Rosso, Calatrasi - Terre di Ginestra	709
Terre di Melona, Italo Mazziotti	629
Terre di S. Nicola Rosso, Di Filippo	609
Terre di Sasso, Castello di Monastero	446
Terre di Tufi, Teruzzi & Puthod	539
Terre Lontane, Librandi	695
Terricci, Lanciola	469
Terricci Chardonnay, Lanciola	469
Tertium, C. Coop. di Cerveteri	630
Terziere, Massa Vecchia	472
Testal, Angelo Nicolis e Figli	303
Thaora Rosato, C. Soc. del Vermentino	724
Tignanello, Marchesi Antinori	452
Tinorso, Poggio Capponi	568
Tinscvil, Castello di Monsanto	432
Tiratari, Fattoria La Ripa	546
Titanum, Vignavecchia	524
Tiziano, Rietine	556
Toar, Masi	306
Tocai Friulano, Jacuss	397
Toh! Tocai Friulano, Di Lenardo	365
Torgiano Bianco Torre di Giano, Cantine Lungarotti	623
Torgiano Cabernet Sauvignon, Castello di Antignano - Brogal Vini	621
Torgiano Rosso, Castello di Antignano - Brogal Vini	621
Torgiano Rosso Ris. S. Caterina, Castello di Antignano - Brogal Vini	621
Torgiano Rosso Vigna Monticchio Ris., Cantine Lungarotti	623
Tormaresca Bianco, Tormaresca	688
Tormaresca Rosso, Tormaresca	688
Tornamagno, Colonnara Viticultori in Cupramontana	585
Torre della Sirena, Conti Sertoli Salis	202
Torre di Ciardo, Marchesi Torrigiani	555
Torricella, Barone Ricasoli	456
Torrione, Fattoria Petrolo	509
Toscoforte, Castello di Poppiano	508
Traimani, Carlo Pellegrino	706
Traluce, Tenuta Le Velette	619
Traminer Aromatico, Vinnaioli Jermann	364
Traminer Ornella, Ornella Molon Traverso	298
Tramonto d'Oca, Poggio Bonelli	447
Trappoline, Coltibuono	456
Trasgaia, Villa Trasqua	553
Trauli Bianco, Guerra Albano	402
Tre Filer, Ca' dei Frati	201
Tre Fonti, Tenuta Valdipiatta	505
Trebbiano d'Abruzzo, Barone Cornacchia	652
Trebbiano d'Abruzzo, Buccicatino	652
Trebbiano d'Abruzzo, Tenuta Cataldi Madonna	645
Trebbiano d'Abruzzo, Fattoria La Valentina	648
Trebbiano d'Abruzzo, Lepore	641
Trebbiano d'Abruzzo, Gianni Masciarelli	647
Trebbiano d'Abruzzo, Camillo Montori	642
Trebbiano d'Abruzzo, Bruno Nicodemi	644
Trebbiano d'Abruzzo, Franco Pasetti	643

Trebbiano d'Abruzzo, Edoardo Valentini	644
Trebbiano d'Abruzzo Altare, Marramiero	646
Trebbiano d'Abruzzo Anima, Marramiero	646
Trebbiano d'Abruzzo Antares, S. Lorenzo	650
Trebbiano d'Abruzzo Bacco, Bruno Nicodemi	644
Trebbiano d'Abruzzo Bianco di Crosta, Tenuta Caracciolo - Duchi di Castelluccio	652
Trebbiano d'Abruzzo Colle della Corte, Orlandi Contucci Ponno	647
Trebbiano d'Abruzzo Colle Maggio, Torre Zambra	649
Trebbiano d'Abruzzo Colle Secco, C. Tollo	649
Trebbiano d'Abruzzo Dama, Marramiero	646
Trebbiano d'Abruzzo Daniele, Dino Illuminati	642
Trebbiano d'Abruzzo Fondatore, C. Miglianico	651
Trebbiano d'Abruzzo Fonte Cupa, Camillo Montori	642
Trebbiano d'Abruzzo Le Vigne, Faraone	643
Trebbiano d'Abruzzo Marina Cvetic, Gianni Masciarelli	647
Trebbiano d'Abruzzo Matté, Chiusa Grande	651
Trebbiano d'Abruzzo Natum, Agriverde	645
Trebbiano d'Abruzzo Pietrosa, Sarchese Dora	646
Trebbiano d'Abruzzo Preludio, Valori	652
Trebbiano d'Abruzzo Riseis, Agriverde	645
Trebbiano d'Abruzzo Roxan, Casa Vinicola Roxan	652
Trebbiano d'Abruzzo S. Maria dell'Arco, Faraone	643
Trebbiano d'Abruzzo Vigneto Spilla, Fattoria La Valentina	648
Trebbiano di Modena Il Civolino, Barbolini	426
Trebbiano di Modena Rapsodia d'Autunno, Corte Manzini	425
Trebbiano di Romagna, Leone Conti	410
Trebbiano di Romagna Poggio Ferlina, Celli	404
Trebbiano di Romagna Vigna del Rio, Tre Monti	412
Trebbiano di Romagna Vigneto Parolino, Umberto Cesari	407
Trebbiano di Romagna Vintan, S. Patrignano - Terre del Cedro	409
Treggiaia, Fattoria di Bibbiani	436
Trentino Bianco, C. Soc. di Avio	216
Trentino Bianco Castel S. Michele, Istituto Agrario Provinciale S. Michele all'Adige	232
Trentino Bianco Résorso Le Comete, C. Soc. di Nomi	229
Trentino Bianco Sommolago, Madonna delle Vittorie	236
Trentino Bianco Vigna Prà dei Fanti, Vallis Agri	218
Trentino Brut M. Cl., Casata Monfort	223
Trentino Cabernet, Cesconi	223
Trentino Cabernet, Concilio	235
Trentino Cabernet, C. d'Isera	220
Trentino Cabernet, F.lli Dorigati	226
Trentino Cabernet, Tenuta S. Leonardo	217
Trentino Cabernet, Armando Simoncelli	231
Trentino Cabernet Fratagranda, Pravis	222
Trentino Cabernet Pianilonghi, de Tarczal	220
Trentino Cabernet Quartella, Longariva	231
Trentino Cabernet Romeo, Castel Noarna	228
Trentino Cabernet Sauvignon, Nicola Balter	230
Trentino Cabernet Sauvignon, Letrari	230
Trentino Cabernet Sauvignon, Vallarom	217
Trentino Cabernet Sauvignon Marognon Ris., Longariva	231
Trentino Cabernet Sauvignon Mercuria, Castel Noarna	228
Trentino Cabernet Sauvignon Oltresarca, MezzaCorona	226
Trentino Cabernet Sauvignon Ris., Letrari	230
Trentino Cabernet Sauvignon Ritratti, La Vis	224
Trentino Cabernet Sauvignon Rosso di Pila, Maso Cantanghel	218
Trentino Cabernet Sauvignon Sant'Ilario, Vallis Agri	218
Trentino Cabernet Sauvignon Vign. Belvedere, Vallarom	217
Trentino Chardonnay, Bailoni	238
Trentino Chardonnay, Nicola Balter	230
Trentino Chardonnay, Barone de Cles	227
Trentino Chardonnay, Nilo Bolognani	222
Trentino Chardonnay, Casata Monfort	223
Trentino Chardonnay, Castel Noarna	228
Trentino Chardonnay, Cesconi	223
Trentino Chardonnay, Concilio	235
Trentino Chardonnay, Dalzocchio	237
Trentino Chardonnay, de Tarczal	220
Trentino Chardonnay, Vignaiolo Giuseppe Fanti	224
Trentino Chardonnay, Maso Furli	225
Trentino Chardonnay, Maso Martis	235
Trentino Chardonnay, MezzaCorona	226
Trentino Chardonnay, Pojer & Sandri	219
Trentino Chardonnay, Istituto Agrario Provinciale S. Michele all'Adige	232
Trentino Chardonnay, Vallarom	217
Trentino Chardonnay, Vigneti delle Meridiane	238
Trentino Chardonnay Bottega Vinai, Cavit - Consorzio di Cantine Sociali	233
Trentino Chardonnay Campo Grande, Castel Noarna	228
Trentino Chardonnay Collezione, Endrizzi	232
Trentino Chardonnay Costa Erta, Gaierhof	229
Trentino Chardonnay di Faedo, Graziano Fontana	219
Trentino Chardonnay I Giardini, Zanini	237
Trentino Chardonnay L'Incanto, Maso Martis	235
Trentino Chardonnay L'Opera, Grigoletti	237
Trentino Chardonnay Praistel, Longariva	231
Trentino Chardonnay Ritratti, La Vis	224
Trentino Chardonnay Robur, Vignaiolo Giuseppe Fanti	224
Trentino Chardonnay Vigna Brioni, Vallarom	217
Trentino Chardonnay Vigna Piccola, Maso Cantanghel	218
Trentino Chardonnay Vigneto Capitel, Armani	276
Trentino Chardonnay Vigneto Lavine, Vallarom	217
Trentino Chardonnay Villa Gentilotti, Lunelli	234
Trentino Chardonnay Villa Margon, Lunelli	234
Trentino Enantio, C. Soc. di Avio	216
Trentino Gewürztraminer, Enrico Spagnolli	221
Trentino Lagrein, Barone de Cles	227
Trentino Lagrein, Casata Monfort	223
Trentino Lagrein, Arcangelo Sandri	236
Trentino Lagrein, Armando Simoncelli	231
Trentino Lagrein di Faedo, Graziano Fontana	219
Trentino Lagrein Maso Baldazzini, La Vis	224
Trentino Lagrein Rosato, Marco Donati	225
Trentino Lagrein Rosato, F.lli Dorigati	226
Trentino Lagrein Sel., Casata Monfort	223
Trentino Marzemino, Riccardo Battistotti	237
Trentino Marzemino, Conti Bossi Fedrigotti	237
Trentino Marzemino, C. Soc. di Avio	216
Trentino Marzemino, C. Soc. di Nomi	229
Trentino Marzemino, Grigoletti	237
Trentino Marzemino, Alessandro Secchi	216
Trentino Marzemino, Armando Simoncelli	231
Trentino Marzemino, Enrico Spagnolli	221
Trentino Marzemino, Vallarom	217
Trentino Marzemino, Vallis Agri	218
Trentino Marzemino d'Isera Husar, de Tarczal	220
Trentino Marzemino dei Ziresi, Vallis Agri	218
Trentino Marzemino dei Ziresi Vigna Fornàs, Vallis Agri	218
Trentino Marzemino Etichetta Verde, C. d'Isera	220
Trentino Marzemino Le Fornas, C. Soc. di Nomi	229
Trentino Marzemino Mozart, Concilio	235
Trentino Marzemino Sel., Letrari	230
Trentino Marzemino Vigneto Capitello, Vallarom	217
Trentino Merlot, C. Soc. di Nomi	229
Trentino Merlot, Cesconi	223
Trentino Merlot, C. d'Isera	220
Trentino Merlot, MezzaCorona	226
Trentino Merlot, Tenuta S. Leonardo	217
Trentino Merlot, Istituto Agrario Provinciale S. Michele all'Adige	232
Trentino Merlot Borgosacco, Vallis Agri	218
Trentino Merlot Campiano, de Tarczal	220
Trentino Merlot di Nomi, Grigoletti	237
Trentino Merlot Le Campagne, C. Soc. di Nomi	229
Trentino Merlot Novaline Ris., Concilio	235
Trentino Merlot Ris., Gaierhof	229
Trentino Merlot Tajaprenda, Maso Cantanghel	218
Trentino Merlot Tovi, Longariva	231
Trentino Moscato Giallo, Nilo Bolognani	222
Trentino Moscato Giallo, C. d'Isera	220
Trentino Moscato Giallo, Vallis Agri	218
Trentino Moscato Giallo Le Comete, C. Soc. di Nomi	229
Trentino Moscato Rosa, Riccardo Battistotti	237
Trentino Moscato Rosa, Endrizzi	232
Trentino Moscato Rosa, Gaierhof	229
Trentino Moscato Rosa, Letrari	230
Trentino Moscato Rosa, Maso Bergamini	238
Trentino Moscato Rosa, Maso Martis	235
Trentino Moscato Rosa, Zeni	233
Trentino Müller Thurgau, Nilo Bolognani	222
Trentino Müller Thurgau, Casata Monfort	223
Trentino Müller Thurgau, Concilio	235
Trentino Müller Thurgau, C. d'Isera	220
Trentino Müller Thurgau, Graziano Fontana	219
Trentino Müller Thurgau, Arcangelo Sandri	236
Trentino Müller Thurgau, Enrico Spagnolli	221
Trentino Müller Thurgau dei Settecento, Gaierhof	229
Trentino Müller Thurgau di Faedo, Graziano Fontana	219
Trentino Müller Thurgau St. Thomà, Pravis	222
Trentino Nosiola, Nilo Bolognani	222
Trentino Nosiola, C. Soc. di Toblino	236
Trentino Nosiola, Castel Noarna	228
Trentino Nosiola, Cesconi	223
Trentino Nosiola, Marco Donati	225
Trentino Nosiola, Vignaiolo Giuseppe Fanti	224
Trentino Nosiola, Gaierhof	229
Trentino Nosiola, Pisoni	221
Trentino Nosiola, Pojer & Sandri	219
Trentino Nosiola, Enrico Spagnolli	221
Trentino Nosiola, Vallis Agri	218
Trentino Nosiola Casot, Castel Noarna	228
Trentino Pinot Bianco, C. Soc. di Avio	216
Trentino Pinot Bianco, de Tarczal	220
Trentino Pinot Bianco, Istituto Agrario Provinciale S. Michele all'Adige	232
Trentino Pinot Bianco, Armando Simoncelli	231
Trentino Pinot Bianco, Vallarom	217
Trentino Pinot Bianco, Vallis Agri	218
Trentino Pinot Bianco Canevaire, C. Rotaliana	227
Trentino Pinot Bianco Pergole, Longariva	231
Trentino Pinot Bianco Sortì, Zeni	233
Trentino Pinot Grigio, Nilo Bolognani	222
Trentino Pinot Grigio, C. Soc. di Avio	216
Trentino Pinot Grigio, Casata Monfort	223

Trentino Pinot Grigio, Cesconi	223
Trentino Pinot Grigio, Concilio	235
Trentino Pinot Grigio, F.lli Dorigati	226
Trentino Pinot Grigio, Gaierhof	229
Trentino Pinot Grigio, MezzaCorona	226
Trentino Pinot Grigio, Istituto Agrario Provinciale S. Michele all'Adige	232
Trentino Pinot Grigio Canevarie, C. Rotaliana	227
Trentino Pinot Grigio Graminè, Longariva	231
Trentino Pinot Grigio Maso Guà, Concilio	235
Trentino Pinot Grigio Maso Poli, Gaierhof	229
Trentino Pinot Grigio Ritratti, La Vis	224
Trentino Pinot Grigio Vigna Reselé, Vallis Agri	218
Trentino Pinot Nero, C. Soc. di Avio	216
Trentino Pinot Nero, Dalzocchio	237
Trentino Pinot Nero, MezzaCorona	226
Trentino Pinot Nero, Enrico Spagnolli	221
Trentino Pinot Nero, Vallarom	217
Trentino Pinot Nero Bottega Vinai, Cavit - Consorzio di Cantine Sociali	233
Trentino Pinot Nero di Faedo, Graziano Fontana	219
Trentino Pinot Nero Maso Montalto, Lunelli	234
Trentino Pinot Nero Novaline Ris., Concilio	235
Trentino Pinot Nero Ris., Endrizzi	232
Trentino Pinot Nero Ritratti, La Vis	224
Trentino Pinot Nero Spiazol, Zeni	233
Trentino Pinot Nero Vignalet, La Cadalora	236
Trentino Pinot Nero Vigneto Ventrat, Vallarom	217
Trentino Pinot Nero Zabini, Maso Cantanghel	218
Trentino Pinot Nero Zinzèle, Longariva	231
Trentino Rebo, F.lli Dorigati	226
Trentino Rebo, Istituto Agrario Provinciale S. Michele all'Adige	232
Trentino Rebo Novecentosette, C. d'Isera	220
Trentino Rebo Rigotti, Pravis	222
Trentino Rosso Castel S. Michele, Istituto Agrario Provinciale S. Michele all'Adige	232
Trentino Rosso Maso Le Viane, Lunelli	234
Trentino Rosso Maso Lodron, Letrari	230
Trentino Rosso Mori Vecio, Concilio	235
Trentino Rosso Navesèl, Armando Simoncelli	231
Trentino Rosso Novecentosette, C. d'Isera	220
Trentino Rosso Résorso, C. Soc. di Nomi	229
Trentino Rosso Résorso Le Comete, C. Soc. di Nomi	229
Trentino Rosso Ris., C. Soc. di Avio	216
Trentino Rosso S. Siro, Pisoni	221
Trentino Rosso Sentieri, C. d'Isera	220
Trentino Rosso Tebro, Enrico Spagnolli	221
Trentino Rosso Tre Cesure Ris., Longariva	231
Trentino Rosso Tre Cesure Sel. 25°., Longariva	231
Trentino Sauvignon, Nicola Balter	230
Trentino Sauvignon, Nilo Bolognani	222
Trentino Sauvignon, Castel Noarna	228
Trentino Sauvignon, Cesconi	223
Trentino Sauvignon, C. d'Isera	220
Trentino Sauvignon, La Cadalora	236
Trentino Sauvignon, Maso Furli	225
Trentino Sauvignon, Istituto Agrario Provinciale S. Michele all'Adige	232
Trentino Sauvignon di Faedo, Graziano Fontana	219
Trentino Sauvignon Solitaire, Maso Cantanghel	218
Trentino Sauvignon Villa S. Nicolò, Lunelli	234
Trentino Sorni Bianco Maso Poli, Gaierhof	229
Trentino Traminer, Barone de Cles	227
Trentino Traminer, Pojer & Sandri	219
Trentino Traminer Aromatico, Casata Monfort	223
Trentino Traminer Aromatico, Cesconi	223
Trentino Traminer Aromatico, Maso Furli	225
Trentino Traminer Aromatico, Enrico Spagnolli	221
Trentino Traminer di Faedo, Graziano Fontana	219
Trentino Vendemmia Tardiva, C. Soc. di Avio	216
Trentino Vino Santo, C. Soc. di Toblino	236
Trentino Vino Santo, Pisoni	221
Trentino Vino Santo Aréle, Cavit - Consorzio di Cantine Sociali	233
Trento Brut, Nicola Balter	230
Trento Brut, Ferrari	234
Trento Brut, Maso Martis	235
Trento Brut, Pisoni	221
Trento Brut, Armando Simoncelli	231
Trento Brut Antàres, C. Soc. di Toblino	236
Trento Brut Firmato, Cavit - Consorzio di Cantine Sociali	233
Trento Brut Firmato mill., Cavit - Consorzio di Cantine Sociali	233
Trento Brut Incontri, Ferrari	234
Trento Brut M. Cl., Zeni	233
Trento Brut Maximum, Ferrari	234
Trento Brut Perlé, Ferrari	234
Trento Brut Perlé Rosé, Ferrari	234
Trento Brut Ris., Maso Martis	235
Trento Brut Ris., Pisoni	221
Trento Graal Brut Ris., Cavit - Consorzio di Cantine Sociali	233
Trento Methius Ris., F.lli Dorigati	226
Trento Rotari Brut Arte Italiana, MezzaCorona	226
Trento Rotari Brut Ris., MezzaCorona	226
Trento Rotari Ris., MezzaCorona	226
Trento Talento Brut, Madonna delle Vittorie	236
Trescone, La Fiorita - Lamborghini	620
Trésor du Caveau, Institut Agricole Régional	16
Tricorno, Castello di Poppiano	508
Trincerone, Tenuta Valdipiatta	505
Tuderi, Tenute Dettori	727
Turriga, Antonio Argiolas	728
Tuvara, Alberto Loi	722
Tzingana, Monte Bernardi	514
Û Pâsa, Tenuta Bonzara	414
Ucelut Bianco, Alessandro Vicentini Orgnani	376
Ulysse, Carlo Pellegrino	706
Umbria Chardonnay Il Moggio, Gisberto Goretti	622
Umbria Grechetto Breccheto, Trappolini	630
Umbria Pinot Nero, Rocca di Fabbri	615
Umbria Riesling, Villa Po' del Vento	625
Umbria Rosso Arquata, Agricola Adanti	608
Umbria RossoTrescone, La Fiorita - Lamborghini	620
Umbria Sangiovese, Bigi	616
Umbria Sangiovese, La Carraia	618
Umbria Sangiovese, Umbria Viticoltori Associati	625
Umbria Trebbiano, Umbria Viticoltori Associati	625
Umbria Vin Santo, Gisberto Goretti	622
Va' Pensiero, Zof	359
Val di Chiana Grechetto, Fattoria S. Vittoria	454
Val di Cornia Bianco Esordio, Gualdo del Re	543
Val di Cornia Bianco Poggio Angelica, Jacopo Banti	435
Val di Cornia Bianco S. Giusto, S. Giusto	517
Val di Cornia Bianco Tabarò, Lorella Ambrosini	543
Val di Cornia Bianco Tuscanio, Bulichella	575
Val di Cornia Centomini, Jacopo Banti	435
Val di Cornia Di Campalto, Jacopo Banti	435
Val di Cornia Gualdo del Re Ris., Gualdo del Re	543
Val di Cornia Rosso, Montepeloso	544
Val di Cornia Rosso, Petra	575
Val di Cornia Rosso Ambrosini, Lorella Ambrosini	543
Val di Cornia Rosso Ceppitaio, Russo	544
Val di Cornia Rosso Esordio, Gualdo del Re	543
Val di Cornia Rosso Montepeloso, Montepeloso	544
Val di Cornia Rosso Rubizzo, Incontri	575
Val di Cornia Rosso Tabarò, Lorella Ambrosini	543
Val di Cornia Rosso Tuscanio, Bulichella	575
Val di Cornia Rosso Vinivo, Il Vignale	569
Val di Cornia Vermentino Campo degli Albicocchi, Il Vignale	569
Val di Cornia Vermentino Ildebrandino, Incontri	575
Val di Miez, Roncùs	338
Val Polcevera Bianchetta Genovese, Enoteca Bruzzone	168
Valcalepio Bianco, C. Soc. Bergamasca	199
Valcalepio Bianco, C. Soc. Val S. Martino	211
Valcalepio Bianco, Castello di Grumello	208
Valcalepio Bianco, Il Calepino	177
Valcalepio Bianco, Medolago Albani	204
Valcalepio Bianco Colle della Luna, Monzio Compagnoni	183
Valcalepio Bianco Ripa di Luna, Caminella	207
Valcalepio Bianco Vescovado, La Brugherata	200
Valcalepio Rosso, C. Soc. Bergamasca	199
Valcalepio Rosso, La Tordela	214
Valcalepio Rosso, Tallarini	208
Valcalepio Rosso Colle del Calvario, Castello di Grumello	208
Valcalepio Rosso Colle della Luna, Monzio Compagnoni	183
Valcalepio Rosso Orologio, C. Soc. Bergamasca	199
Valcalepio Rosso Ripa di Luna, Caminella	207
Valcalepio Rosso Ris., Medolago Albani	204
Valcalepio Rosso Ris. Doglio, La Brugherata	200
Valcalepio Rosso Riserva Akros Vigna La Tordela, C. Soc. Bergamasca	199
Valcalepio Rosso Riserva Akros Vigneto Palma, C. Soc. Bergamasca	199
Valcalepio Rosso Riserva S. Giovannino, Tallarini	208
Valcalepio Rosso Surie, Il Calepino	177
Valcalepio Rosso Vescovado, La Brugherata	200
Valdadige Chardonnay Montalto, Le Fraghe	274
Valdadige Pinot Grigio Vigneto Corvara, Armani	276
Valdadige Quaiare, Le Fraghe	274
Valdadige Schiava, C. Soc. di Nomi	229
Valdenrico Bianco, Rovellotti	81
Valentino Brut Ris. Elena, Podere Rocche dei Manzoni	104
Valeo, Giovan Battista Odoardi	695
Valle d'Aosta Blanc de Morgex et de La Salle, Cave du Vin Blanc de Morgex et de La Salle	18
Valle d'Aosta Blanc de Morgex et de La Salle, Maison Albert Vevey	20
Valle d'Aosta Blanc de Morgex et de La Salle M. Cl., Cave du Vin Blanc de Morgex et de La Salle	18
Valle d'Aosta Blanc de Morgex et de La Salle Rayon, Cave du Vin Blanc de Morgex et de La Salle	18
Valle d'Aosta Chambave Moscato Passito, La Crotta di Vegneron	17
Valle d'Aosta Chambave Muscat, La Crotta di Vegneron	17
Valle d'Aosta Chambave Rouge, La Crotta di Vegneron	17
Valle d'Aosta Chardonnay, Cave des Onze Communes	20
Valle d'Aosta Chardonnay Barrique, Institut Agricole Régional	16
Valle d'Aosta Chardonnay Cuvée Frissonière Les Crêtes, Les Crêtes	17
Valle d'Aosta Chardonnay Cuvée Frissonière Les Crêtes Cuvée Bois, Les Crêtes	17
Valle d'Aosta Chardonnay Élevé en Fût de Chêne, Renato Anselmet	19

Valle d'Aosta Fumin, F.lli Grosjean	19
Valle d'Aosta Fumin, La Crotta di Vegneron	17
Valle d'Aosta Fumin Vigne La Tour, Les Crêtes	17
Valle d'Aosta Gamay, F.lli Grosjean	19
Valle d'Aosta Gamay, Lo Triolet - Marco Martin	18
Valle d'Aosta Müller Thurgau, Renato Anselmet	19
Valle d'Aosta Müller Thurgau, Cave des Onze Communes	20
Valle d'Aosta Müller Thurgau, Institut Agricole Régional	16
Valle d'Aosta Müller Thurgau, La Crotta di Vegneron	17
Valle d'Aosta Nus Malvoisie Flétri, La Crotta di Vegneron	17
Valle d'Aosta Petite Arvine, F.lli Grosjean	19
Valle d'Aosta Petite Arvine, Institut Agricole Régional	16
Valle d'Aosta Petite Arvine Vigne Champorette, Les Crêtes	17
Valle d'Aosta Pinot Gris, Renato Anselmet	19
Valle d'Aosta Pinot Gris, Institut Agricole Régional	16
Valle d'Aosta Pinot Gris Élevé en Fût de Chêne, Lo Triolet - Marco Martin	18
Valle d'Aosta Pinot Gris Lo Triolet, Lo Triolet - Marco Martin	18
Valle d'Aosta Pinot Noir, Institut Agricole Régional	16
Valle d'Aosta Pinot Noir Élevé en Barrique, F.lli Grosjean	19
Valle d'Aosta Pinot Noir Élevé en Fût de Chêne, Renato Anselmet	19
Valle d'Aosta Pinot Noir Vigne La Tour, Les Crêtes	17
Valle d'Aosta Prëmetta, Costantino Charrere	16
Valle d'Aosta Torrette, Renato Anselmet	19
Valle d'Aosta Torrette, Costantino Charrere	16
Valle d'Aosta Torrette, F.lli Grosjean	19
Valle d'Aosta Torrette Sup., Cave des Onze Communes	20
Valle d'Aosta Torrette Vigne Les Toules, Les Crêtes	17
Vallée d'Aoste Blanc de Morgex et de La Salle, Carlo Celegato	20
Vallée d'Aoste Müller Thurgau, Gabriella Minuzzo	20
Vallocaia, Bindella	498
Valon Chardonnay, Maurizio Nervi	145
Valpantena, C. Soc. della Valpantena	319
Valpantena Ripasso Falasco, C. Soc. della Valpantena	319
Valpantena Ritocco, C. Soc. della Valpantena	319
Valpantena Secco Bertani, Bertani	292
Valpolicella Ca' Fiui, Corte Sant'Alda	285
Valpolicella Cl., Stefano Accordini	301
Valpolicella Cl., Allegrini	277
Valpolicella Cl., Brigaldara	302
Valpolicella Cl., Luigi Brunelli	302
Valpolicella Cl., Ca' La Bionda	281
Valpolicella Cl., Corte Rugolin	283
Valpolicella Cl., F.lli Degani	283
Valpolicella Cl., I Scriani	325
Valpolicella Cl., Le Bertarole	325
Valpolicella Cl., Le Ragose	293
Valpolicella Cl., Le Salette	278
Valpolicella Cl., Giuseppe Lonardi	284
Valpolicella Cl., Angelo Nicolis e Figli	303
Valpolicella Cl., Novaia	284
Valpolicella Cl., S. Rustico	326
Valpolicella Cl., S. Sofia	303
Valpolicella Cl., F.lli Speri	304
Valpolicella Cl., Massimo Venturini	305
Valpolicella Cl., Villa Spinosa	295
Valpolicella Cl., Viviani	295
Valpolicella Cl. Il Brolo, Villa Bellini	306
Valpolicella Cl. Le Caleselle, Santi	280
Valpolicella Cl. Le Solane, Santi	280
Valpolicella Cl. Maso Laito, Zonin	279
Valpolicella Cl. Sup., Bertani	292
Valpolicella Cl. Sup., F.lli Degani	283
Valpolicella Cl. Sup., I Scriani	325
Valpolicella Cl. Sup., Giuseppe Lonardi	284
Valpolicella Cl. Sup., Roberto Mazzi	294
Valpolicella Cl. Sup., Angelo Nicolis e Figli	303
Valpolicella Cl. Sup., Novaia	284
Valpolicella Cl. Sup., Giuseppe Quintarelli	294
Valpolicella Cl. Sup., Viticoltori Tommasi	305
Valpolicella Cl. Sup., Massimino Venturini	305
Valpolicella Cl. Sup., Viviani	295
Valpolicella Cl. Sup., Zenato	297
Valpolicella Cl. Sup., F.lli Zeni	273
Valpolicella Cl. Sup. Acinatico, Stefano Accordini	301
Valpolicella Cl. Sup. Ca' Carnocchio, Le Salette	278
Valpolicella Cl. Sup. Campo Casal Vegri, Ca' La Bionda	281
Valpolicella Cl. Sup. Campo Praesel, Luigi Brunelli	302
Valpolicella Cl. Sup. Campo S. Vito, Raimondi Villa Monteleone	307
Valpolicella Cl. Sup. Capitel dei Nicalò, F.lli Tedeschi	304
Valpolicella Cl. Sup. Cicilio, F.lli Degani	283
Valpolicella Cl. Sup. Corte Aleardi, Aleardo Ferrari	327
Valpolicella Cl. Sup. Grola, Coop. Ottomarzo	328
Valpolicella Cl. Sup. Il Taso, Villa Bellini	306
Valpolicella Cl. Sup. Jago, Villa Spinosa	295
Valpolicella Cl. Sup. La Casetta di Ettore Righetti Domini Veneti, C. Soc. Valpolicella	293
Valpolicella Cl. Sup. La Roverina, F.lli Speri	304
Valpolicella Cl. Sup. Le Crosare, Lenotti	323
Valpolicella Cl. Sup. Le Morete, Guido Manara	327
Valpolicella Cl. Sup. Le Portarine, Le Bertarole	325
Valpolicella Cl. Sup. Le Sassine, Le Ragose	293
Valpolicella Cl. Sup. Pariondo, Luigi Brunelli	302
Valpolicella Cl. Sup. Poiega, Guerrieri Rizzardi	272
Valpolicella Cl. Sup. Possessioni Rosso Serègo Alighieri, Masi	306
Valpolicella Cl. Sup. Ripassa, Zenato	297
Valpolicella Cl. Sup. Ripassa Ca' del Pipa, Michele Castellani	282
Valpolicella Cl. Sup. Sant'Urbano, F.lli Speri	304
Valpolicella Cl. Sup. Seccal, Angelo Nicolis e Figli	303
Valpolicella Cl. Sup. Semonte Alto, Massimino Venturini	305
Valpolicella Cl. Sup. TB, Tommaso Bussola	292
Valpolicella Cl. Sup. Terre di Cariano, Cecilia Beretta	319
Valpolicella Cl. Sup. Vigne Alte, F.lli Zeni	273
Valpolicella Cl. Sup. Vigneti di Casterna, Pasqua Vigneti e Cantine	320
Valpolicella Cl. Sup. Vigneti di Purano Le Bine, Giuseppe Campagnola	282
Valpolicella Cl. Sup. Vigneti di Ravazzol, Ca' La Bionda	281
Valpolicella Cl. Sup. Vigneti di Torbe, C. Soc. Valpolicella	293
Valpolicella Cl. Sup. Vigneto La Cengia, Lorenzo Begali	301
Valpolicella Cl. Sup. Vigneto Ognisanti Villa Novare, Bertani	292
Valpolicella Cl. Sup. Vigneto Poiega, Roberto Mazzi	294
Valpolicella Cl. Villa Borghetti, Pasqua Vigneti e Cantine	320
Valpolicella Il Vegro, Brigaldara	302
Valpolicella Recioto Cl. Casotto del Merlo, Giuseppe Campagnola	282
Valpolicella Recioto Cl. TB, Tommaso Bussola	292
Valpolicella Sup., Corte Sant'Alda	285
Valpolicella Sup., Marion	327
Valpolicella Sup., Musella	300
Valpolicella Sup. La Bandina, Tenuta Sant'Antonio	275
Valpolicella Sup. Mithas, Corte Sant'Alda	285
Valpolicella Sup. Monte Paradiso, Baltieri	330
Valpolicella Sup. Rocca Sveva, C. di Soave	308
Valpolicella Sup. Roccolo Grassi, Sartori - Roccolo Grassi	285
Valpolicella Sup. Rovere, Ca' Rugate	289
Valpolicella Sup. Sagramoso, Pasqua Vigneti e Cantine	320
Valpolicella Sup. Sagramoso Ripasso, Pasqua Vigneti e Cantine	320
Valpolicella Sup. Terre del Cereolo, Trabucchi	280
Valpolicella Sup. Terre di S. Colombano, Trabucchi	280
Valpolicella Sup. Vigneto di Monte Lodoletta, Romano Dal Forno	279
Valpolicella Valpantena, Tezza	326
Valpolicella Valpantena Sup. Monte delle Fontane, Tezza	326
Valserpe, Fattoria Mancini	596
Valsusa Costadoro, Carlotta	43
Valsusa Rocca del Lupo, Carlotta	43
Valsusa Vignacombe, Carlotta	43
Valtellina Casa La Gatta, Triacca	203
Valtellina Prestigio, Triacca	203
Valtellina Prestigio Millennium, Triacca	203
Valtellina Sforzato, Fay	201
Valtellina Sforzato, Casa Vinicola Nera	207
Valtellina Sforzato, Triacca	203
Valtellina Sforzato Albareda, Mamete Prevostini	189
Valtellina Sforzato Canua, Conti Sertoli Salis	202
Valtellina Sforzato Ronco del Picchio, Fay	201
Valtellina Sfursat, Nino Negri	179
Valtellina Sfursat, Aldo Rainoldi	179
Valtellina Sfursat 5 Stelle, Nino Negri	179
Valtellina Sfursat Fruttaio Ca' Rizzieri, Aldo Rainoldi	179
Valtellina Sfurzat Vin da Ca', Plozza	214
Valtellina Sup. Capo di Terra, Conti Sertoli Salis	202
Valtellina Sup. Corte della Meridiana, Conti Sertoli Salis	202
Valtellina Sup. Corte di Cama, Mamete Prevostini	189
Valtellina Sup. Crespino, Aldo Rainoldi	179
Valtellina Sup. Grumello Vigna Sassorosso, Nino Negri	179
Valtellina Sup. Inferno, Aldo Rainoldi	179
Valtellina Sup. Inferno Mazer, Nino Negri	179
Valtellina Sup. Inferno Prodigio, F.lli Bettini	214
Valtellina Sup. Inferno Ris., Casa Vinicola Nera	207
Valtellina Sup. Inferno Ris. Barrique, Aldo Rainoldi	179
Valtellina Sup. Ris. La Scala, Plozza	214
Valtellina Sup. Ris. Triacca, Triacca	203
Valtellina Sup. Sassella, Aldo Rainoldi	179
Valtellina Sup. Sassella, Conti Sertoli Salis	202
Valtellina Sup. Sassella, Triacca	203
Valtellina Sup. Sassella Il Glicine, Fay	201
Valtellina Sup. Sassella Le Tense, Nino Negri	179
Valtellina Sup. Sassella Ris., Aldo Rainoldi	179
Valtellina Sup. Sassella Sommarovina, Mamete Prevostini	189
Valtellina Sup. Sfursat, F.lli Bettini	214
Valtellina Sup. Valgella Ca' Morei, Fay	201
Valtellina Sup. Valgella Carteria, Fay	201
Valtellina Sup. Valgella Carteria Trentennale, Fay	201
Valtellina Sup. Valgella Fracia Oro, Nino Negri	179
Vantaggio, Luciano Sassara	626
Vareij Rosso, Hilberg - Pasquero	120
Varius, Cantele	682
Varramista, Varramista	568
Varrone, Istituto Professionale per l'Agricultura e l'Ambiente	410
Vasario, Fattoria del Buonamico	494
Vecchio Samperi, Marco De Bartoli	704
Vecchio Samperi Ventennale, Marco De Bartoli	704
Vela Latina, Cantine Monthia	716
Velenosi Brut M. Cl., Ercole Velenosi	580
Velitrae Bianco, Colle di Maggio	635
Velitrae Rosso, Colle di Maggio	635

Entry	Page
Velo di Maya, Alfiero Boffa	125
Vendemmia Tardiva, Cascina Fonda	95
Vendemmia Tardiva, Palazzone	619
Veneroso, Tenuta di Ghizzano	516
Verasis Bianco, La Morandina	62
Verbeia, Piero Gatti	126
Verde Luna Bianco, Caminella	207
Verd. Castelli di Jesi Cl. Ghibellino, Mancini	604
Verd. dei Castelli di Jesi, Fattoria Laila	604
Verd. dei Castelli di Jesi Biologico Geo, Terre Cortesi Moncaro	590
Verd. dei Castelli di Jesi Cl., Mario e Giorgio Brunori	587
Verd. dei Castelli di Jesi Cl., F.lli Bucci	596
Verd. dei Castelli di Jesi Cl., Fonte della Luna - Medoro Cimarelli	602
Verd. dei Castelli di Jesi Cl., Luciano Landi	581
Verd., dei Castelli di Jesi Cl., S. Barbara	580
Verd. dei Castelli di Jesi Cl., Sartarelli	597
Verd. dei Castelli di Jesi Cl., Terre Cortesi Moncaro	590
Verd. dei Castelli di Jesi Cl., F.lli Zaccagnini & C.	606
Verd. dei Castelli di Jesi Cl. Bacco, Fattoria Coroncino	602
Verd. dei Castelli di Jesi Cl. Bando di S. Settimio, Monteschiavo	588
Verd. dei Castelli di Jesi Cl. Cantorì, Angelo Accadia	606
Verd. dei Castelli di Jesi Cl. Cimaio Ris., Casalfarneto	600
Verd. dei Castelli di Jesi Cl. Colle del Sole, Monteschiavo	588
Verd. dei Castelli di Jesi Cl. Conscio, Angelo Accadia	606
Verd. dei Castelli di Jesi Cl. Coroncino, Fattoria Coroncino	602
Verd. dei Castelli di Jesi Cl. Cuprese Ris., Colonnara Viticultori in Cupramontana	585
Verd. dei Castelli di Jesi Cl. I Pratelli, Donatella Paoloni	605
Verd. dei Castelli di Jesi Cl. Il Vigneto di Tobia, Laurentina	590
Verd. dei Castelli di Jesi Cl. Le Giuncare Ris., Monteschiavo	588
Verd. dei Castelli di Jesi Cl. Le Vaglie, S. Barbara	580
Verd. dei Castelli di Jesi Cl. Le Vele, Terre Cortesi Moncaro	590
Verd. dei Castelli di Jesi Cl. Luzano, Marotti Campi	592
Verd. dei Castelli di Jesi Cl. Nidastore, S. Barbara	580
Verd. dei Castelli di Jesi Cl. Passito Rojano, Vallerosa Bonci	585
Verd. dei Castelli di Jesi Cl. Passito Tordiruta, Terre Cortesi Moncaro	590
Verd. dei Castelli di Jesi Cl. Pier delle Vigne Ris., F.lli Zaccagnini & C.	606
Verd. dei Castelli di Jesi Cl. Pignocco, S. Barbara	580
Verd. dei Castelli di Jesi Cl. Plenio Ris., Umani Ronchi	595
Verd. dei Castelli di Jesi Cl. S. Maria del Fiore, Stefano Mancinelli	591
Verd. dei Castelli di Jesi Cl. S. Sisto Ris., Fazi Battaglia	583
Verd. dei Castelli di Jesi Cl. Sabbionare, Donatella Paoloni	605
Verd. dei Castelli di Jesi Cl. Salmariano, Marotti Campi	592
Verd. dei Castelli di Jesi Cl. S. Sisto Ris., Fazi Battaglia	583
Verd. dei Castelli di Jesi Cl. S. Lucia, Mancini	604
Verd. dei Castelli di Jesi Cl. Serra Fiorese Ris., Gioacchino Garofoli	588
Verd. dei Castelli di Jesi Cl. Sora Elvira, Alberto Serenelli	603
Verd. dei Castelli di Jesi Cl. Spumante Brut, Colonnara Viticultori in Cupramontana	585
Verd. dei Castelli di Jesi Cl. Staffilo, Fattoria Coroncino	602
Verd. dei Castelli di Jesi Cl. Stefano Antonucci Ris., S. Barbara	580
Verd. dei Castelli di Jesi Cl. Sup., Stefano Mancinelli	591
Verd. dei Castelli di Jesi Cl. Sup. Casal di Serra, Umani Ronchi	595
Verd. dei Castelli di Jesi Cl. Sup. Contrada Balciana, Sartarelli	597
Verd. dei Castelli di Jesi Cl. Sup. Cuprese, Colonnara Viticultori in Cupramontana	585
Verd. dei Castelli di Jesi Cl. Sup. Fontevecchia, Casalfarneto	600
Verd. dei Castelli di Jesi Cl. Sup. Fra Moriale, Fonte della Luna - Medoro Cimarelli	602
Verd. dei Castelli di Jesi Cl. Sup. Gaiospino, Fattoria Coroncino	602
Verd. dei Castelli di Jesi Cl. Sup. Gaiospino Fumé, Fattoria Coroncino	602
Verd. dei Castelli di Jesi Cl. Sup. Grancasale, Casalfarneto	600
Verd. dei Castelli di Jesi Cl. Sup. Le Case, Vallerosa Bonci	585
Verd. dei Castelli di Jesi Cl. Sup. Le Moie, Fazi Battaglia	583
Verd. dei Castelli di Jesi Cl. Sup. Macrina, Gioacchino Garofoli	588
Verd. dei Castelli di Jesi Cl. Sup. Pallio di S. Floriano, Monteschiavo	588
Verd. dei Castelli di Jesi Cl. Sup. Podium, Gioacchino Garofoli	588
Verd. dei Castelli di Jesi Cl. Sup. S. Michele, Vallerosa Bonci	585
Verd. dei Castelli di Jesi Cl. Sup. S. Nicolò, Mario e Giorgio Brunori	587
Verd. dei Castelli di Jesi Cl. Sup. Sel. Corona Reale, Maurizio Marconi	606
Verd. dei Castelli di Jesi Cl. Sup. Sel. Misco, Lucangeli Aymerich di Laconi	583
Verd. dei Castelli di Jesi Cl. Sup. Tavignano, Lucangeli Aymerich di Laconi	583
Verd. dei Castelli di Jesi Cl. Sup. Tenuta del Cavaliere, Marchetti	578
Verd. dei Castelli di Jesi Cl. Sup. Tralivio, Sartarelli	597
Verd. dei Castelli di Jesi Cl. Sup. Tufico, Colonnara Viticultori in Cupramontana	585
Verd. dei Castelli di Jesi Cl. Sup. Verde di Ca' Ruptae, Terre Cortesi Moncaro	590
Verd. dei Castelli di Jesi Cl. Sup. Vigna Novali, Terre Cortesi Moncaro	590
Verd. dei Castelli di Jesi Cl. Sup. Vigna S. Marco, Colonnara Viticultori in Cupramontana	585
Verd. dei Castelli di Jesi Cl. Sup. Vignamato, Amato Ceci	599
Verd. dei Castelli di Jesi Cl. Titulus, Fazi Battaglia	583
Verd. dei Castelli di Jesi Cl. Valle delle Lame, Amato Ceci	599
Verd. dei Castelli di Jesi Cl. Via Torre, Vallerosa Bonci	585
Verd. dei Castelli di Jesi Cl. Villa Bianchi, Umani Ronchi	595
Verd. dei Castelli di Jesi Cl. Villa Bucci Ris., F.lli Bucci	596
Verd. dei castelli di Jesi Spumante Brut Bonci, Vallerosa Bonci	585
Verd. di Matelica, La Monacesca	589
Verd. di Matelica Cambrugiano Ris., Belisario C. Soc. di Matelica e Cerreto d'Esi	589
Verd. di Matelica Casa Fosca, Enzo Mecella	586
Verd. di Matelica Colle Stefano, Colle Stefano	603
Verd. di Matelica La Monacesca, La Monacesca	589
Verd. di Matelica Maccagnano, Gino Gagliardi	604
Verd. di Matelica Pagliano, Enzo Mecella	586
Verd. di Matelica Terre di Valbona, Belisario C. Soc. di Matelica e Cerreto d'Esi	589
Verd. di Matelica Vigneti Belisario, Belisario C. Soc. di Matelica e Cerreto d'Esi	589
Verd. di Matelica Vigneti del Cerro, Belisario C. Soc. di Matelica e Cerreto d'Esi	589
Verd. di Matelica Vigneto Braccano, S. Biagio	604
Verd. di Matelica Vigneto Fogliano, Bisci	604
Verduno Pelaverga, F.lli Alessandria	138
Verduno Pelaverga, Bel Colle	138
Verduno Pelaverga, G. B. Burlotto	139
Verduno Pelaverga, Castello di Verduno	139
Verduzzo, Davino Meroi	336
Verduzzo, Russiz Superiore	339
Verduzzo del Piccolo Campo, Brojli - Franco Clementin	402
Verduzzo Friulano, Marcello e Marino Humar	389
Verduzzo Friulano, Le Due Torri	358
Vergato Cortese, Cascina Montagnola	142
Vermentino, Cima	471
Vermentino, Serraiola	506
Vermentino dei Colli di Luni, Podere Lavandaro	556
Vermentino di Gallura, C. Soc. Giogantinu	730
Vermentino di Gallura Capichera, Capichera	721
Vermentino di Gallura Cucaione, Piero Mancini	731
Vermentino di Gallura Funtanaliras, C. Soc. del Vermentino	724
Vermentino di Gallura Gemellae, C. Soc. Gallura	729
Vermentino di Gallura Hysonj, Pedra Majore	724
Vermentino di Gallura I Graniti, Pedra Majore	724
Vermentino di Gallura Mavriana, C. Soc. Gallura	729
Vermentino di Gallura Monteoro, Tenute Sella & Mosca	720
Vermentino di Gallura Piras, C. Soc. Gallura	729
Vermentino di Gallura S'Eleme, C. Soc. del Vermentino	724
Vermentino di Gallura Saraina, Piero Mancini	731
Vermentino di Gallura Saruinas, Depperu	730
Vermentino di Gallura Sup., C. Soc. Giogantinu	730
Vermentino di Gallura Sup. Aghiloia, C. Soc. del Vermentino	724
Vermentino di Gallura Sup. Canayli, C. Soc. Gallura	729
Vermentino di Gallura V. T., Capichera	721
Vermentino di Gallura Vigna 'Ngena, Capichera	721
Vermentino di Sardegna, Meloni Vini	726
Vermentino di Sardegna Aragosta, C. Soc. S. Maria La Palma	720
Vermentino di Sardegna Boghes, Giovanni Cherchi	729
Vermentino di Sardegna Costamolino, Antonio Argiolas	728
Vermentino di Sardegna Crabilis, Pala	728
Vermentino di Sardegna Donna Leonora, C. Soc. della Trexenta	727
Vermentino di Sardegna La Cala, Tenute Sella & Mosca	720
Vermentino di Sardegna Le Conche, Pedra Majore	724
Vermentino di Sardegna Naeli, Cantine di Dolianova	722
Vermentino di Sardegna Pigalva, Giovanni Cherchi	729
Vermentino di Sardegna Prestizu, Tenute Soletta	730
Vermentino di Sardegna Tanca Sa Contissa, C. Soc. della Trexenta	727
Vermentino di Sardegna Tuvaoes, Giovanni Cherchi	729
Vermentino di Sardegna Villa Solais, C. Soc. di Santadi	726
Vermentino Eclis, Tenuta Giuncheo	157
Vermentino Vinca, VIN.CA	551
Vermiglio, Andrea Costanti	479
Vernaccia di Oristano, Attilio Contini	721
Vernaccia di Oristano Ris., Attilio Contini	721
Vernaccia di Oristano Ris., Josto Puddu	732
Vernaccia di S. Gimignano, Ca' del Vispo	532
Vernaccia di S. Gimignano, Canneta	572
Vernaccia di S. Gimignano, Casa alle Vacche	533
Vernaccia di S. Gimignano, Vincenzo Cesani	533
Vernaccia di S. Gimignano, Il Lebbio	534
Vernaccia di S. Gimignano, Il Palagione	555
Vernaccia di S. Gimignano, Il Paradiso	535
Vernaccia di S. Gimignano, La Lastra	535
Vernaccia di S. Gimignano, Tenuta Le Calcinaie	536
Vernaccia di S. Gimignano, Mormoraia	537
Vernaccia di S. Gimignano, Palagetto	537
Vernaccia di S. Gimignano, Giovanni Panizzi	538
Vernaccia di S. Gimignano, Pietrafitta	538
Vernaccia di S. Gimignano, Signano	539
Vernaccia di S. Gimignano, Teruzzi & Puthod	539

Name	Page
Vernaccia di S. Gimignano, F.lli Vagnoni	540
Vernaccia di S. Gimignano Ab Vinea Doni, Casale - Falchini	572
Vernaccia di S. Gimignano Abbazia di Monteoliveto, Fattoria Il Palagio	450
Vernaccia di S. Gimignano Alata, La Rampa di Fugnano	536
Vernaccia di S. Gimignano Biscondola, Il Paradiso	535
Vernaccia di S. Gimignano Castello di Montauto, Famiglia Cecchi	439
Vernaccia di S. Gimignano Crocus, Casa alle Vacche	533
Vernaccia di S. Gimignano Dometaia Ris., Baroncini	572
Vernaccia di S. Gimignano I Macchioni, Casa alle Vacche	533
Vernaccia di S. Gimignano La Gentilesca, Fattoria Il Palagio	450
Vernaccia di S. Gimignano La Luna e le Torri, Canneta	572
Vernaccia di S. Gimignano Le Grillaie, Melini	519
Vernaccia di S. Gimignano Mocali, F.lli Vagnoni	540
Vernaccia di S. Gimignano Perlato, Guicciardini Strozzi - Fattoria Cusona	534
Vernaccia di S. Gimignano Poggiarelli, Signano	539
Vernaccia di S. Gimignano Privato Ris., La Rampa di Fugnano	536
Vernaccia di S. Gimignano Rialto, Cappella Sant'Andrea	572
Vernaccia di S. Gimignano Ris., Guicciardini Strozzi - Fattoria Cusona	534
Vernaccia di S. Gimignano Ris., La Lastra	535
Vernaccia di S. Gimignano Ris., Mormoraia	537
Vernaccia di S. Gimignano Ris., Palagetto	537
Vernaccia di S. Gimignano Ris., Giovanni Panizzi	538
Vernaccia di S. Gimignano Ris., S. Quirico	573
Vernaccia di S. Gimignano Ris., Signano	539
Vernaccia di S. Gimignano Ris., Teruzzi & Puthod	539
Vernaccia di S. Gimignano S. Biagio, Guicciardini Strozzi - Fattoria Cusona	534
Vernaccia di S. Gimignano Sanice, Vincenzo Cesani	533
Vernaccia di S. Gimignano Sel., Signano	539
Vernaccia di S. Gimignano Tropie, Il Lebbio	534
Vernaccia di S. Gimignano V. Borghetto, Pietrafitta	538
Vernaccia di S. Gimignano Vigna a Rondolino, Teruzzi & Puthod	539
Vernaccia di S. Gimignano Vigna ai Sassi, Tenuta Le Calcinaie	536
Vernaccia di S. Gimignano Vigna in Fiore, Ca' del Vispo	532
Vernaccia di S. Gimignano Vigna La Costa Ris., Pietrafitta	538
Vernaccia di S. Gimignano Vigna S. Chiara, Palagetto	537
Vernaccia di Serrapetrona Amabile, Alberto Quacquarini	600
Vernaccia di Serrapetrona I Serboni Secco, Massimo Serboni	606
Vernaccia di Serrapetrona Secco, Alberto Quacquarini	600
Vernaccia di Serrapetrona Sel. Passita Dolce, Massimo Serboni	606
Vertigo, Livio Felluga	348
Vesco Bianco, Cantine Rallo	706
Vesco Rosso, Cantine Rallo	706
Vespa Bianco, Bastianich	379
Vespa Rosso, Bastianich	379
Vespolino, Vercesi del Castellazzo	194
Vesuvio Lacryma Christi Bianco, Cantine Caputo	664
Vigna al Cavaliere, Michele Satta	438
Vigna Alta, Badia di Morrona	548
Vigna Camarato, Villa Matilde	655
Vigna Catena, Castello di Lilliano	552
Vigna degli Artisti, Cantine Leonardo da Vinci	548
Vigna dei Pini, D'Angelo	672
Vigna del Bosco, Tenimenti Luigi D'Alessandro	450
Vigna del Cavaliere, Casale Marchese	632
Vigna del Feudo, Felline	685
Vigna del Picchio, Moro - Rinaldo Rinaldini	418
Vigna del Vassallo, Paola Di Mauro - Colle Picchioni	633
Vigna dell'Erta, Vigliano	573
Vigna di Bugialla, Poggerino	523
Vigna Il Vallone, Villa Sant'Anna	506
Vigna Iris, Artimino	551
Vigna l'Apparita Merlot, Castello di Ama	455
Vigna La Miccia, Marco De Bartoli	704
Vigna Perella, Viticoltori De Conciliis	661
Vigna Pratobianco, Torre Fornello	422
Vigna Regis, Vecchie Terre di Montefili	515
Vigna Tassanare Brut, Monteschiavo	588
Vigna Valentina, Gualdo del Re	543
Vigna Verdana Ascevi, Ascevi - Luwa	387
Vigna Virzì Bianco, Spadafora	711
Vigna Virzì Rosso, Spadafora	711
Vignamaggio, Villa Vignamaggio	467
Vignamare, Tommaso e Angelo Lupi	163
Vignamato Rosso, Amato Ceci	599
Vignanera, Podere Lavandaro	556
Vignanova, Coop. Agricola Valdarnese	576
Vignaricco Bianco, Conte d'Attimis-Maniago	335
Vignaricco Rosso, Conte d'Attimis-Maniago	335
Vigne d'Oro, Vitivinicola Avide	713
Vigne del Mandorlo, Fattoria di Montellori	454
Vigne del Moro, Fattoria di Montellori	454
Vigneto Ca' Brione Bianco, Nino Negri	179
Vigneto del Malaga, Tenuta La Meridiana	107
Vigorello, S. Felice	448
Villa Angela Chardonnay, Ercole Velenosi	580
Villa Castiglioni, Bisci	604
Villa Conversino Rosso, Di Filippo	609
Villa di Chiesa, C. Soc. di Santadi	726
Villa di Corsano, C. di Montalcino	563
Villa di Grazia, Marco Maci	679
Villa Fidelia Bianco, F.lli Sportoletti	622
Villa Fidelia Rosso, F.lli Sportoletti	622
Villa Gemma Bianco, Gianni Masciarelli	647
Villa Horta, Antichi Vigneti di Cantalupo	80
Villa Monte Rico, Monte Rico	575
Villa Pigna Brut, Villa Pigna	595
Villa Sparina Brut M. Cl., Villa Sparina	80
Villa Tulino Bianco, Colle di Maggio	635
Villamaura Syrah, Di Prima	713
Vin de La Sabla, Costantino Charrere	16
Vin dei Molini Rosato, Pojer & Sandri	219
Vin du Prévôt, Institut Agricole Régional	16
Vin Les Fourches, Costantino Charrere	16
Vin Ruspo, Fattoria Ambra	437
Vin Ruspo, Capezzana	437
Vin Santo, Avignonesi	497
Vin Santo, Contucci	499
Vin Santo, Fattoria Corzano e Paterno	529
Vin Santo, Tenimenti Luigi D'Alessandro	450
Vin Santo, Fanetti - Tenuta S. Agnese	566
Vin Santo, Fanti - S. Filippo	481
Vin Santo, Vittorio Innocenti	496
Vin Santo, Isole e Olena	431
Vin Santo, La Palazzola	623
Vin Santo, La Pievuccia	554
Vin Santo, Le Ginestre	550
Vin Santo, Fattoria Le Sorgenti	431
Vin Santo, Meleta	527
Vin Santo, Fattoria Petrolo	509
Vin Santo, Fattoria di Piazzano	555
Vin Santo, Pietrafitta	538
Vin Santo, Poggio a Poppiano	508
Vin Santo, Poggio Salvi	574
Vin Santo, Redi	504
Vin Santo, Riseccoli	465
Vin Santo, Rocca di Montegrossi	461
Vin Santo, S. Gervasio	510
Vin Santo, S. Giusto a Rentennano	461
Vin Santo, S. Michele a Torri	573
Vin Santo, Fattoria S. Vittoria	454
Vin Santo, Signano	539
Vin Santo, Fattoria del Teso	565
Vin Santo, Villa Vignamaggio	467
Vin Santo, Villa Pillo	462
Vin Santo, Villa Sant'Anna	506
Vin Santo del Chianti, Fattoria Castelvecchio	572
Vin Santo del Chianti, Fattoria Castello Sonnino	568
Vin Santo del Chianti Cl., Castello di Volpaia	525
Vin Santo del Chianti Classico, Rocca di Montegrossi	461
Vin Santo del Chianti Classico, Villa Vignamaggio	467
Vin Santo del Chianti Classico Ris., Castello di Monterinaldi	522
Vin Santo del Chianti Ris., Fattorie Parri	568
Vin Santo del Chianti Rufina, Frascole	555
Vin Santo della Rufina, Fattoria Selvapiana	520
Vin Santo di Carmignano, Il Poggiolo	551
Vin Santo di Carmignano Ris., Capezzana	437
Vin Santo Dolce Sinfonia, Bindella	498
Vin Santo Occhio di Pernice, Avignonesi	497
Vin Santo Orlando, Agricola Querciabella	465
Vin Santo Rufina, Fattoria di Basciano	527
Vin Santo Rufina, Tenuta di Bossi	570
Vin Santo S. Torpé, Fattoria di Sassolo	573
Vin Santo S. Torpé Fiorile, Fattoria di Sassolo	573
Vin Santo Sangallo, Fattoria del Cerro	499
Vin Santo Tegrino d'Anchiano, Cantine Leonardo da Vinci	548
Vin Santo Vigna del Papa, Fattoria Villa La Selva	435
Vin Santo Xantos, Fattoria Uccelliera	451
Vinbrusco, F.lli Vagnoni	540
Vinnae, Vinnaioli Jermann	364
Vino degli Orti, Matijaz Tercic	391
Vino del Maso Rosso, Marco Donati	225
Vino della Pace, C. Prod. di Cormons	346
Vino Santo di Ripatransone Sibilla Agrippa, Le Caniette	598
Vino Santo di Ripatransone Sibilla Delphica, Le Caniette	598
Vinsanto, La Calonica	501
Vintage Tunina, Vinnaioli Jermann	364
Virente, Wandanna	495
Vita, Marco Maci	679
Vite Rossa, Ornella Molon Traverso	298
Vitiano, Falesco	634
Vito Arturo, Fattoria Le Fonti	518
Vivaldaia, Villa Pillo	462
Vocato, Villa Cilnia	430
Volgente Rosso, Italo Mazziotti	629
Voltraio, Acquabona	570
Were Dreams, Now It Is Just Wine!, Vinnaioli Jermann	364
Wildbacher, Conte Collalto	312
Xyris Filtrato di Lacrima, Marotti Campi	592
Yrnm, Aziende Vinicole Miceli	710
Zero - D'Orta-De Conciliis, Viticoltori De Conciliis	661
Zurrica, Abbazia S. Anastasia	701

INDEX OF PRODUCERS

A Maccia	164	Badia di Morrona	548
Abbazia di Novacella	267	Badiali, F.lli	605
Abbazia Santa Anastasia	701	Baglio San Vincenzo	717
Abbona, Anna Maria	73	Bagnasco	213
Abbona, Marziano e Enrico	69	Bagnolo dei Marchesi Pancrazi,	
Abraxas	713	Tenuta di	497
Abrigo, Orlando	154	Bailoni	238
Accadia, Angelo	606	Baldizzone – Cascina Lana, Antonio	151
Accordini, Stefano	301	Balestri Valda	328
Accornero e Figli, Giulio	140	Balter, Nicola	230
Acquabona	570	Baltieri	330
Adami	321	Bandut - Giorgio Colutta	369
Adanti, Agricola	608	Banfi	474
Agareno	717	Banti, Jacopo	435
Agnes	198	Barale, F.lli	144
Agricoltori del Chianti Geografico	455	Barattieri di San Pietro, Conte Otto	421
Agriverde	645	Barberani - Vallesanta	616
Aia della Macina, Podere	540	Barberis, Osvaldo	147
Aiola, Fattoria dell'	443	Barbi, Fattoria dei	474
Ajello	717	Barbolini	426
Al Rocol	210	Barisél, Cascina	51
Alario, Claudio	68	Barni	44
Albani, Riccardo	174	Baroncini	572
Albano Carrisi, Tenute	678	Barone Cornacchia	652
Albola, Castello d'	521	Barone de Cles	227
Alessandri, Massimo	168	Barone Pizzini	182
Alessandria, F.lli	138	Barone Ricasoli	456
Alessandria, Gianfranco	97	Barsento	686
Alfieri, Marchesi	124	Basciano, Fattoria di	527
Allegrini	277	Basilisco	671
Almondo, Giovanni	106	Basilium	674
Aloi, Valerio	150	Basso Graziano	325
Altare - Cascina Nuova, Elio	82	Bastianich	379
Altesino	473	Batasiolo	83
Ama, Castello di	455	Battistotti, Riccardo	237
Ambra, Fattoria	437	Baudana, Luigi	129
Ambrosini, Lorella	543	Bava	63
Andreas Berger -Thurnhof	245	Bazzini, Franco	212
Andreola Orsola	277	Beccaris, Renzo	146
Anfossi	167	Befelnhof, Oswald Schuster	270
Angoris, Tenuta di	343	Begali, Lorenzo	301
Anselmet, Renato	19	Beghelli	425
Anselmi, Roberto	288	Bel Colle	138
Antano, Fattoria Milziade	609	Belisario Cantina Sociale di Matelica	
Anteo	197	e Cerreto d'Esi	589
Antica Masseria del Sigillo	681	Bellani, Marco Giulio	206
Antichi Poderi Jerzu	723	Bellaria	206
Antichi Vigneti di Cantalupo	80	Bellavista	185
Antinori, Marchesi	452	Bellei, Francesco	424
Antonelli - San Marco	614	Bellenda	330
Antoniolo	75	Beltrame, Tenuta	332
Antonutti	374	Benanti	703
Aquila del Torre	376	Benotto, Carlo	65
Araldica - Il Cantinone	54	Bepin de Eto	300
Arcone	732	Bera, F.lli	116
Argiano, Tenuta di	473	Bergaglio, Nicola	76
Argiolas, Antonio	728	Berlucchi, F.lli	182
Armani	276	Berlucchi & C., Guido	183
Artimino	551	Bersano & Riccadonna	116
Ascevi - Luwa	387	Bersi Serlini	197
Ascheri	44	Berta, Guido	153
Aschero, Laura	168	Bertani	292
Attems Conte Douglas	365	Bertelli, Poderi	65
Aurora	605	Bertolotto, Cascina	132
Avide, Vitivinicola	713	Bettini, F.lli	214
Avignonesi	497	Bettinzana - Cascina Ronco Basso	207
Azelia	57	Bettoni Cazzago, Conti	177
Azzolino, Fattorie	716	Bianchi	153
Azzoni Avogadro Carradori	605	Bianchi, Maria Donata	160

Bibbiani, Fattoria di	436	Ca' Bolani	341
Bigi	616	Ca' d'Gal	126
Bindella	498	Ca' de' Medici	427
Bisci	604	Ca' dei Frati	201
Bisol & Figli, Desiderio	313	Ca' del Baio	135
Bisson	328	Ca' del Bosco	185
Bisson, Enoteca	159	Ca' del Gé	190
Blasig, Tenuta di	386	Ca' del Santo	209
Boccadigabbia	584	Ca' del Vent	206
Bocchino, Eugenio	143	Ca' del Vispo	532
Boeri, Alfonso	146	Ca di Bon	400
Boffa, Alfiero	125	Ca' di Frara	195
Boglietti, Enzo	83	Ca' La Bionda	281
Bogoni, Carlo	288	Ca' Lojera	213
Bolognani, Nilo	222	Ca' Lustra	275
Bonfiglio	427	Ca' Rome' - Romano Marengo	29
Bongiovanni, Cascina	57	Ca' Ronesca	360
Bonsulton, Agricola	712	Ca' Rossa, Cascina	47
Borgo Canale	680	Ca' Rugate	289
Borgo Conventi	363	Ca' Viola	107
Borgo del Tiglio	344	Cabanon	188
Borgo di Colloredo	640	Cabert	333
Borgo Lotessa	388	Caccese, Paolo	346
Borgo Magredo	396	Cacchiano, Castello di	556
Borgo Maragliano	93	Caggiano, Antonio	664
Borgo Salcetino	571	Caiano	553
Borgo San Daniele	344	Calatrasi Puglia	678
Borgo Scopeto	443	Calatrasi - Terre di Ginestra	709
Borgogno & Figli, Giacomo	36	Calleri, Cantine	167
Borin	286	Calò & Figli, Michele	692
Boroli, Silvano e Elena	24	Calonga	425
Bortolin Spumanti, F.lli	313	Camigliano, Castello di	475
Bortolomiol	314	Caminella	207
Bortolusso, Emiro Cav.	341	Campagnola, Giuseppe	282
Boscarelli	498	Campominosi	428
Boschis	147	Camponeschi	638
Bosco, Nestore	651	Camposilio	576
Bosco, Rosa	369	Canato, Marco	141
Bossi Fedrigotti, Conti	237	Candido, Francesco	687
Botromagno, Cantina Cooperativa	681	Cane, Giobatta Mandino	161
Boveri, Luigi	64	Canevel Spumanti	314
Bovio, Gianfranco	84	Canneta	572
Braida	122	Canneto	565
Branko - Igor Erzetich	345	Cantarutti, Alfieri	392
Bredasole	210	Cantele	682
Brema, Ermanno e Alessandra	81	Cantina Convento Muri-Gries	246
Brezza & Figli, Giacomo	36	Cantina Cooperativa Castignanese	603
Bricco del Cucù	42	Cantina Cooperativa	
Bricco Maiolica	69	del Locorotondo	684
Bricco Mondalino	140	Cantina Cooperativa	
Bricco Rocche - Bricco Asili	58	della Riforma Fondiaria	692
Brigaldara	302	Cantina Cooperativa di Cerveteri	630
Brigl, Josef	240	Cantina Cooperativa	
Broglia - Tenuta La Meirana, Gian Piero	77	di Cincinnato	637
Brojli - Franco Clementin	402	Cantina Cooperativa di Oliena	732
Brovia, F.lli	58	Cantina Cooperativa di Pitigliano	569
Bruna	164	Cantina dei Colli Amerini	624
Brunelli, Luigi	302	Cantina dei Produttori	
Brunner	399	Nebbiolo di Carema	53
Brunori, Mario e Giorgio	587	Cantina del Castello	308
Bruzzone, Enoteca	168	Cantina del Pino	29
Bucci, F.lli	596	Cantina del Taburno	655
Buccicatino	652	Cantina di Casteggio	174
Buglioni	327	Cantina di Sant'Andrea	638
Buiatti, Livio e Claudio	334	Cantina di Soave	308
Buiatti, Olivo	334	Cantina Gries	246
Bulichella	575	Cantina Produttori Andriano	240
Buonamico, Fattoria del	494	Cantina Produttori Burggräfler	259
Burlotto, G. B.	139	Cantina Produttori Colterenzio	241
Bussia Soprana	150	Cantina Produttori Cornaiano	241
Busso, Piero	111	Cantina Produttori Cortaccia	257
Bussola, Tommaso	292	Cantina Produttori di Cormons	346
Butussi, Valentino	356	Cantina Produttori di Merano	260
Buzzinelli, Maurizio	345	Cantina Produttori	
Ca' Bianca	28	di Valdobbiadene	329

Cantina Produttori Nalles Niclara Magrè	261	Casanova di Neri	476
Cantina Produttori San Michele Appiano	242	Casata Monfort	223
		Casato - Donatella Cinelli Colombini, Fattoria del	476
Cantina Produttori San Paolo	242	Cascina Ballarin	84
Cantina Produttori Santa Maddalena	247	Cascina Chicco	47
Cantina Produttori Termeno	265	Cascina Cucco	153
Cantina Produttori Valle Isarco	256	Cascina Fonda	95
Cantina Riforma Fondiaria di Venosa	673	Cascina Giovenale	151
Cantina Rotaliana	227	Cascina Gnocco	210
Cantina Sociale Bergamasca	199	Cascina Montagnola	142
Cantina Sociale Cesanese del Piglio	638	Cascina Nuova	171
Cantina Sociale Cooperativa Copertino	690	Cascina Orsolina	150
Cantina Sociale Cooperativa di Quistello	212	Cascina Ulivi	151
Cantina Sociale Cooperativa Leverano	691	Case Bianche	326
Cantina Sociale del Vermentino	724	Case di Pietra	713
Cantina Sociale della Trexenta	727	Casisano Colombaio	477
Cantina Sociale della Valpantena	319	Castagnoli	552
Cantina Sociale di Avio	216	Castel De Paolis	632
Cantina Sociale di Lizzano	684	Castel di Salve	689
Cantina Sociale di Nomi	229	Castel Noarna	228
Cantina Sociale di Santadi	726	Castel Sallegg - Graf Kuenburg	253
Cantina Sociale di Toblino	236	CastelFaglia	206
Cantina Sociale di Trapani	714	Castelgiocondo	477
Cantina Sociale di Vinchio e Vaglio Serra	142	Castell'in Villa	445
		Castellani, Michele	282
Cantina Sociale Dorgali	723	Castellare di Castellina	439
Cantina Sociale Frentana	651	Castellari Bergaglio	77
Cantina Sociale Gallura	729	Castelli del Grevepesa	528
Cantina Sociale Giogantinu	730	Castelli Martinozzi	560
Cantina Sociale Il Nuraghe	731	Castellino, Tenuta	180
Cantina Sociale Marrubiu	731	Castello del Poggio	152
Cantina Sociale Santa Maria La Palma	720	Castello della Sala	612
		Castello di Antignano - Brogal Vini	621
Cantina Sociale Val San Martino	211	Castello di Bossi	444
Cantina Sociale Valpolicella	293	Castello di Grumello	208
Cantina Sociale Valtidone	424	Castello di Razzano, Tenuta	143
Cantina Terlano	264	Castello di Spessa	337
Cantina Viticoltori di Caldaro	253	Castello di Verduno	139
Cantine di Dolianova	722	Castello Fageto	606
Cantrina	204	Castelluccio	412
Caparra & Siciliani	694	Castelpugna	574
Caparzo, Tenuta	475	Castelrotto - Torti, Tenimenti	209
Capezzana	437	Castelvecchio	387
Capichera	721	Castelvecchio, Fattoria	572
Capinera	605	Castelveder	192
Cappella Sant'Andrea	572	Castiglion del Bosco	478
Caprai - Val di Maggio, Arnaldo	614	Castlèt, Cascina	66
Caputo, Cantine	664	Cataldi Madonna, Tenuta	645
Cardinali	424	Catturich-Ducco	205
Cardone, Vini Classici	691	Caudrina	61
Carlo di Pradis	347	Cavalchina	311
Carlotta	43	Cavalleri	186
Carlozadra	189	Cavallotto, F.lli	59
Carmignani, Gino Fuso	494	Cavazza & F.lli, Domenico	287
Carobbio	510	Cave des Onze Communes	20
Carpenè Malvolti	324	Cave du Vin Blanc de Morgex et de La Salle	18
Carpineta Fontalpino	444	Cavicchioli & Figli, Cantine	418
Carpineti, Marco	637	Cavit - Consorzio di Cantine Sociali	233
Carpineto	463	Cecchetto, Giorgio	330
Carra	415	Cecchi, Famiglia	439
Carretta, Tenuta	120	Ceci, Amato	599
Casa alle Vacche	533	Cecilia	559
Casa Emma	549	Cecilia Beretta	319
Casa Roma	327	Celegato, Carlo	20
Casa Sola, Fattoria	549	Cellaro, Cantina Sociale	713
Casa Zuliani	401	Celli	404
Casale del Giglio	628	Cennatoio	511
Casale - Falchini	572	Centolani	560
Casale Marchese	632	Ceretto	24
Casale Mattia	637	Cerro, Fattoria del	499
Casalfarneto	600	Cesani, Vincenzo	533
Casali Viticultori	428	Cesari, Umberto	407
Casalone, Paolo	94	Cesconi	223
Casaloste, Fattoria	511		

Ceuso	716
Charrere, Costantino	16
Cherchi, Giovanni	729
Chiarieri	651
Chiarlo, Michele	45
Chigi Saracini, Fattorie	445
Chionetti & Figlio, Quinto	70
Chiorri, Franca	621
Chiusa Grande	651
Ciacci Piccolomini D'Aragona	478
Cieck	23
Cigliuti, F.lli	111
Cima	471
Cinti, Floriano	419
Ciodet	329
Cisa Asinari dei Marchesi di Gresy, Tenute	30
Citra	651
Ciù Ciù	594
Clastidio	206
Clerico, Domenico	98
Co.Vi.O.	617
Cocci Grifoni, Tenuta	597
Coffele	309
Cogno, Elvio	118
Cohens Gervais	559
Col d'Orcia, Tenuta	479
Col Vetoraz	315
Cola, Battista	204
Colacicchi	636
Coldisole	561
Coletti Conti, Antonello	636
Coliberto, Fattoria	560
Collalto, Conte	312
Collavini, Eugenio	357
Colle Bereto	571
Colle dei Bardellini	162
Colle di Maggio	635
Colle Duga	347
Colle San Lorenzo	631
Colle Stefano	603
Collelungo, Podere	440
Colli di Lapio - Clelia Romano	667
Colli Irpini - Montesolae	659
Collosorbo, Tenuta di	561
Colmello di Grotta	363
Colognole	571
Colonna	141
Colonna - Vini Spalletti	419
Colonnara Viticoltori in Cupramontana	585
Còlpetrone	613
Coltibuono	456
Comelli, Paolino	362
Concilio	235
Consorzio Produttori Vini	691
Consorzio Viticoltori Associati del Vulture	670
Contadi Castaldi	170
Conte d'Attimis-Maniago	335
Conte Zandotti	635
Conterno, Aldo	98
Conterno, Giacomo	99
Conterno, Paolo	99
Conterno Fantino	100
Conti, Leone	410
Conti Formentini	388
Conti Zecca	683
Contini, Attilio	721
Contratto	51
Contucci	499
Coos, Dario	374
Coppo e Figli, Luigi	52
Corino, Giovanni	85
Cornaleto	170
Cornarea	145
Coroncino, Fattoria	602
Correggia, Matteo	48
Corte Gardoni	318
Corte Manzini	425
Corte Marzago	330
Corte Normanna	658
Corte Pavone	561
Corte Rugolin	283
Corte Sant'Alda	285
Corteforte	325
Cortese, Giuseppe	30
Corzano e Paterno, Fattoria	529
COS	715
Costa, Teo	145
Costanti, Andrea	479
Costaripa	190
Cottanera	702
Crastin	360
Crociani	566
Crosato, Giovanni	342
Cusumano	710
D'Alessandro, Tenimenti Luigi	450
D'Alfonso del Sordo, Giovanni	692
D'Ambra Vini d'Ischia	656
d'Amico, Paolo	629
D'Ancona	712
D'Angelo	672
D'Antiche Terre - Vega	667
d'Isera, Cantina	220
Dacapo	22
Dal Din	330
Dal Fari	399
Dal Forno, Romano	279
Dal Maso, Vinicola Luigino	287
Dall'Asta, Cantine	415
Dalzocchio	237
Damilano	37
Dattilo	698
De Andreis, Fausto	156
De Bartoli, Marco	704
De Battè, Walter	165
De Conciliis, Viticoltori	661
De Falco Vini	668
De Faveri	321
De Lucia	658
de Tarczal	220
Dea - Rivalta	329
Decugnano dei Barbi	617
Degani, F.lli	283
Degiorgis	95
Dei	500
Deltetto	48
Depperu	730
Dessilani	73
Destefanis	108
Dettori, Tenute	727
Dezi, Fattoria	601
Di Filippo	609
Di Lenardo	365
Di Majo Norante	641
Di Marzo	668
Di Mauro - Colle Picchioni, Paola	633
Di Meo	668
Di Prima	713
Di Sesta, Tenuta	480
Dievole, Fattoria di	554
Dittajuti, Conte Leopardi	592
Dominio di Bagnoli	323
Donati, Marco	225
Donnafugata, Tenuta di	705
Doria	191
Dorigati, F.lli	226
Dorigo, Girolamo	335
Drei Donà Tenuta La Palazza	411
Drius, Mauro	348
Duca Carlo Guarini	689

Duca della Corgna	611	Forano, Fattoria di	579
Duca di Salaparuta - Vini Corvo	702	Forchir	392
Due Palme, Cantina	690	Forlini e Cappellini	168
Due Portine - Gorelli	561	Fornacina	561
Eberlehof - Zisser	268	Fornaser, Giuseppe	327
Egger-Ramer	268	Forteto della Luja	93
Einaudi, Poderi Luigi	70	Fossi	555
Elena Walch, Castel Ringberg & Kastelaz	265	Fraccaroli	326
Endrizzi	232	Franzoni, Emilio	205
Enotria, Cantina	698	Frascole	555
Ercolani	566	Frecciarossa	175
Ermacora, Dario e Luciano	380	Freddano, Giulio	618
Eubea - Fam. Sasso, Agricola	672	Frescobaldi, Marchesi de'	453
Evangelos Paraschos	402	Fuligni, Eredi	481
F.lli Ferrero	149	Funtanin	49
Faccoli & Figli, Lorenzo	180	Gabbas, Giuseppe	725
Falesco	634	Gabutti - Franco Boasso	130
Falkenstein - Franz Pratzner, Tenuta	262	Gaggioli Vigneto Bagazzana, Maria Letizia	423
Fanetti - Tenuta S. Agnese	566	Gagliardi, Gino	604
Fanini	610	Gagliardo, Gianni	149
Fanti, Vignaiolo Giuseppe	224	Gagliole	552
Fanti - La Palazzetta	480	Gaiano, Tenuta	46
Fanti - San Filippo	481	Gaierhof	229
Fantinel	377	Gaja	31
Fantino, Alessandro e Gian Natale	100	Galardi	663
Faraone	643	Gallino, Filippo	49
Farneta, Tenuta	541	Gandin, Edi	402
Farnetella	541	Garetto, Tenuta	22
Fasoli	324	Garitina, Cascina	55
Fassati	500	Garofoli, Gioacchino	588
Fassati di Balzola, Marchesi	211	Gastaldi	112
Fattori & Graney	289	Gatta, Agricola	206
Fattoria Collazzi	559	Gatti, Enrico	187
Fattoria di Bagnolo	559	Gatti, Piero	126
Fattoria di Fiano	554	Gavioli, Agricola	566
Fattoria Lilliano	549	Germano, Ettore	130
Fattoria Zerbina	409	Ghio, Domenico	144
Favaro	152	Ghisolfi, Attilio	101
Fay	201	Ghizzano, Tenuta di	516
Fazi Battaglia	583	Giacomelli	158
Fedrizzi, Cipriano	237	Giacosa, Bruno	113
Feipu dei Massaretti, Cascina	156	Giacosa, Carlo	31
Felline	685	Giacosa, F.lli	113
Felluga, Livio	348	Giannaccini, Giovanna	568
Felluga, Marco	368	Gigante, Adriano	357
Felsina, Fattoria di	446	Gili, Raffaele	146
Ferghettina	186	Gillardi, Giovanni Battista	74
Ferrando	82	Gilli, Cascina	56
Ferrara, Benito	665	Gini	290
Ferrari	234	Giorgi, F.lli	172
Ferrari, Aleardo	327	Giuncheo, Tenuta	157
Ferraris, Roberto	143	Glicine, Cantina del	151
Ferrucci, Stefano	406	Gojer Glögglhof, Franz	247
Feudi di San Gregorio	663	Goretti, Gisberto	622
Feudo Principi di Butera	701	Gotto d'Oro	638
Ficomontanino	555	Gradis'ciutta	389
Fidanza, Fabio	145	Gradizzolo Ognibene	414
Fiegl	366	Graf Pfeil Weingut Kränzel	256
Filiputti, Walter	370	Gran Furor Divina Costiera, Cantine	657
Filomusi Guelfi	648	Grasso, Casa Vinicola	717
Fiorini, Valentino	581	Grasso, Elio	101
Firriato, Casa Vinicola	709	Grasso, Silvio	85
Flino, Cascina	147	Grattamacco	438
Florio, Cantine	705	Graziano, Vittorio	408
Foffani	398	Gregoletto	286
Folonari, Tenute	452	Greppone Mazzi - Tenimenti Ruffino	482
Fontana, Graziano	219	Grigoletti	237
Fontana Candida	633	Grillo, Iole	382
Fontanabianca	112	Grimaldi, Giacomo	144
Fontanafredda	129	Grimaldi - Ca' du Sindic, Sergio	127
Fontanavecchia - Orazio Rillo	665	Grosjean, F.lli	19
Fonte della Luna - Medoro Cimarelli	602	Grotta del Sole, Cantine	662
Fonterutoli, Castello di	440	Guado al Tasso, Tenuta	432
Fontodi, Tenuta	512	Gualdo del Re	543
Foradori	228	Guerra Albano	402

Guerrieri Rizzardi	272	Kuenhof - Peter Pliger	252
Guicciardini Strozzi - Fattoria Cusona	534	L'Armangia	145
Guidi, Fiorenzo	168	L'Olivella	637
Guido Guarini Matteucci di Castelfalcino	426	La Barbatella, Cascina	117
Gumphof, Markus Prackwieser	269	La Berta	405
Haas, Franz	261	La Biancara	278
Haderburg	263	La Boatina	349
Hastae	122	La Borsa	569
Hilberg - Pasquero	120	La Boscaiola	181
Hofkellerei	270	La Braccesca, Fattoria	501
Hofstätter	266	La Brancaia	521
Hohler, Karin e Remo	53	La Brugherata	200
Humar, Marcello e Marino	389	La Cadalora	236
I Balzini	550	La Calonica	501
I Campetti	558	La Cantina dei Colli Ripani	598
I Girasoli di Sant'Andrea	626	La Cappella, Podere	546
I Giusti e Zanza	451	La Cappuccina	290
I Paglieri	32	La Caprense, Agricola	666
I Pastini - Carparelli	690	La Carraia	618
I Scriani	325	La Castellada	366
I Vignaioli di S. Stefano	127	La Castellina	552
Icardi	61	La Cella di San Michele	154
Il Borro, Tenuta	559	La Chiara	78
Il Bosco, Tenuta	203	La Chiusa, Tenuta	570
Il Calepino	177	La Ciarliana	502
Il Carnasciale, Podere	549	La Cipressaia, Tenuta	567
Il Carpino	390	La Colombera	154
Il Colombaio di Cencio	457	La Costa - Calvi, Tenuta	205
Il Colombo - Barone Riccati	97	La Costaiola, Tenuta	191
Il Falchetto, Tenuta	153	La Crotta di Vegneron	17
Il Filò delle Vigne	272	La Doccia	557
Il Greppo, Tenuta	482	La Fiorita	562
Il Lebbio	534	La Fiorita - Lamborghini	620
Il Mandorlo	529	La Fornace	562
Il Marroneto	561	La Fortuna, Podere	484
Il Mongetto	154	La Fuga, Tenuta	562
Il Monticello	165	La Gerla	484
Il Montù	194	La Ghersa, Cascina	96
Il Mosnel	196	La Giribaldina	144
Il Palagio, Fattoria	450	La Giustiniana	78
Il Palagione	555	La Guardia	109
Il Palazzino, Podere	457	La Guardiense	667
Il Palazzone	562	La Lastra	535
Il Paradiso	535	La Leccia, Castello	552
Il Poggiarello	420	La Lecciaia	562
Il Poggio	624	La Loggia	572
Il Poggiolino	545	La Lumia, Barone	704
Il Poggiolo	551	La Maddalena, Cascina	121
Il Poggiolo	483	La Madonnina - Triacca	557
Il Poggione, Tenuta	483	La Mancina	427
Il Pratello	426	La Marcellina	569
Il Rocchin	148	La Marchesa, Tenuta	151
Il Roncat - Giovanni Dri	401	La Massa	512
Il Torchio	158	La Meridiana, Tenuta	107
Il Vignale	119	La Monacesca	589
Il Vignale	569	La Montecchia	307
Illuminati, Dino	642	La Montina	192
Inama	298	La Morandina	62
Incontri	575	La Palazzola	623
Innocenti, Vittorio	496	La Parrina	509
Institut Agricole Régional	16	La Pertica, Cascina	196
Ippolito, Vincenzo	698	La Pietra del Focolare	163
Isabella	110	La Pievuccia	554
Isimbarda	199	La Poderina	485
Isola	413	La Primavera	329
Isole e Olena	431	La Querciolana	626
Ispoli	530	La Rajade	400
Istituto Professionale		La Rampa di Fugnano	536
per l'Agricoltura e l'Ambiente	410	La Regola	526
Jacuss	397	La Ripa, Fattoria	546
Kante	361	La Rocca di San Nicolao	160
Keber, Edi	349	La Sala	530
Kettmeir	254	La Scamuzza	154
Köfererhof	267	La Scolca	79
Kössler - Praeclarus	243	La Serena	562

La Smilla	43	Leonardo da Vinci, Cantine	548
La Spinetta	54	Leone de Castris	687
La Stellata	471	Lepore	641
La Stoppa	417	Lequio, Ugo	114
La Tenaglia, Tenuta	132	Les Crêtes	17
La Togata	485	Letrari	230
La Tordela	214	Librandi	695
La Tosa	421	Liedholm	68
La Valentina, Fattoria	648	Lignano, Castello di	74
La Vecchia Cantina	157	Lilliano, Castello di	552
La Versa, Cantina Sociale	200	Lis Neris - Pecorari	394
La Viarte	382	Livernano	522
La Vigna	205	Livon	393
La Vis	224	Lo Sparviere	193
La Zerba	134	Lo Triolet - Marco Martin	18
La Zucca	110	Loacker Schwarzhof	248
Laila, Fattoria	604	Lodola Nuova - Tenimenti Ruffino	567
Laimburg, Cantina	266	Loi, Alberto	722
Lambardi, Maurizio	486	Lomazzi & Sarli	691
Lamberti	325	Lombardo, Eredi Antonino	567
Lambruschi, Ottaviano	159	Lonardi, Giuseppe	284
Lamoretti, Isidoro	426	Longariva	231
Lanari	578	Longhi de Carli	207
Lanciola	469	Loredan Gasparini Venegazzù, Conte	330
Landi, Luciano	581	Lucangeli Aymerich di Laconi	583
Lano, Gianluigi	25	Lucchetti	605
Lantieri de Paratico	173	Luce	486
Laurentina	590	Lucignano, Castello di	458
Lavacchio, Fattoria	570	Luisa, Eddi	372
Lavandaro, Podere	556	Luisin, Cascina	32
Le Albare	326	Lun, Cantina H.	258
Le Berne, Podere	566	Lunelli	234
Le Bertarole	325	Lungarotti, Cantine	623
Le Calcinaie, Tenuta	536	Lupi, Tommaso e Angelo	163
Le Calvane	507	Luretta	420
Le Caniette	598	Lusenti, Gaetano	422
Le Capannacce	449	Lusignani, Alberto	428
Le Casalte, Fattoria	566	Machiavelli	531
Le Chiantigiane	576	Maci, Marco	679
Le Chiuse	563	Macolina, La	426
Le Chiusure	213	Maculan	274
Le Cinciole, Podere	513	Madonia, Giovanna	404
Le Colture	315	Madonna dei Miracoli	650
Le Corne	208	Madonna delle Vittorie	236
Le Corti - Corsini, Fattoria	531	Maffini, Luigi	654
Le Due Terre	383	Magnàs	400
Le Due Torri	358	Majolini	195
Le Filigare	550	Malacari	593
Le Fonti, Fattoria	513	Malfatti	560
Le Fonti, Fattoria	518	Malgrà	150
Le Fracce	175	Malojer Gummerhof, R.	248
Le Fraghe	274	Malvirà	50
Le Ginestre	550	Manara, Guido	327
Le Gode di Ripaccioli	563	Mancinelli, Stefano	591
Le Macchiole	433	Mancini	604
Le Marchesine	211	Mancini, Fattoria	596
Le Miccine	556	Mancini, Piero	731
Le Piagge	557	Mangilli	402
Le Poggette, Fattoria	613	Mantellassi, Fattoria	470
Le Pupille	468	Manzone, Giovanni	102
Le Querce, Fattoria	559	Marangona	211
Le Querce, Tenuta	670	Marcarini, Poderi	86
Le Quinte, Tenuta	638	Marchesi di Barolo	37
Le Ragose	293	Marchesi Torrigiani	555
Le Salette	278	Marchetti	578
Le Sorgenti, Fattoria	431	Marconi, Maurizio	606
Le Tende	281	Marella, Podere	625
Le Terrazze, Fattoria	593	Marenco	133
Le Trame	554	Marengo, Giacomo	565
Le Velette, Tenuta	619	Marengo, Mario	86
Le Vigne di San Pietro	311	Marianna	666
Le Vigne di Zamò	370	Marinig, Valerio	383
Lebovitz	204	Marion	327
Lenotti	323	Mariotto, Claudio	154
Lento, Cantine	696	Marotti Campi	592

Marramiero	646	Montepeloso	544
Marsaglia	146	Monterinaldi, Castello di	522
Martilde	198	Monterucco	211
Martinetti, Franco M.	135	Monteschiavo	588
Martini, Lorenz	268	Montevertine, Fattoria di	523
Martini & Sohn, K.	268	Montevetrano	662
Mascarello, Bartolo	38	Monthia, Cantine	716
Mascarello e Figlio, Giuseppe	96	Monti	102
Masciarelli, Gianni	647	Monti, Antonio e Elio	650
Masi	306	Montini	213
Maso Bastie	238	Montiverdi	459
Maso Bergamini	238	Montori, Camillo	642
Maso Cantanghel	218	Montresor, Giacomo	320
Maso Furli	225	Monzio Compagnoni	183
Maso Martis	235	Moos, Elyane & Bruno	576
Masottina	299	Morassino, Cascina	144
Massa Vecchia	472	Morelli, Claudio	586
Masseria Pepe	686	Morellino di Scansano, Cantina Coop. del	574
Massimi Berucci	638		
Mastroberardino	654	Morgante	703
Mastrojanni	487	Morgassi Superiore	148
Masut da Rive	373	Mori, Giacomo	528
Mattiello, Natalino	325	Morini, Alessandro	425
Mauritania, Fattoria	732	Moris Farms	472
Mavric, Stanislao	400	Mormoraia	537
Mayr e Figli, Thomas	269	Moroder, Alessandro	579
Mayr - Erbhof Unterganzner, Josephus	249	Morra, Stefanino	55
Mazzi, Roberto	294	Moschioni, Davide	342
Mazzini Franceschi	565	Mosole	328
Mazziotti, Italo	629	Mossio, F.lli	123
Mazzolino, Tenuta	184	Mottura, Tenuta	631
Mecella, Enzo	586	Mulino delle Tolle	332
Medici & Figli, Ermete	416	Mumelter, Georg	249
Medolago Albani	204	Murana, Salvatore	713
Meleta	527	Musella	300
Meleto, Castello di	458	Mutti	128
Melini	519	Muzic	390
Meloni Vini	726	Nada, Ada	136
Meroi, Davino	336	Nada, Fiorenzo	136
Merotto	324	Naitana, Gianvittorio	731
MezzaCorona	226	Napolitano, F.lli	674
Miali, Vinicola	691	Nardi, Tenute Silvio	563
Miani	336	Nebiolo, Luigi	147
Miceli, Aziende Vinicole	710	Negri, Nino	179
Miglianico, Cantina	651	Negro & Figli, Angelo	108
Minuzzo, Gabriella	20	Nera, Casa Vinicola	207
Mirabella	212	Nervi	75
Mocali	487	Nervi, Maurizio	145
Moccagatta	33	Nicodemi, Bruno	644
Modanella, Castello di	525	Nicolis e Figli, Angelo	303
Moio, Michele	659	Niedermayr, Josef	244
Mola	570	Niedrist, Ignaz	243
Molettieri, Salvatore	660	Nino Franco	316
Molino, Mauro	87	Nittardi, Fattoria	441
Molon Traverso, Ornella	298	Nössing - Hoandlhof, Manfred	252
Monastero, Castello di	446	Notaio, Cantine del	673
Monchiero Carbone	50	Nottola	502
Mondo, Franco	153	Novaia	284
Monfalletto - Cordero di Montezemolo	87	Oasi degli Angeli	584
Monrubio, Cantina	610	Oberto, Andrea	88
Monsanto, Castello di	432	Ocone	661
Monsupello	202	Oddero, F.lli	88
Montalcino, Cantina di	563	Oddero, Massimo	147
Montaribaldi	33	Odoardi, Giovan Battista	695
Monte Bernardi	514	Olim Bauda, Tenuta	149
Monte delle Vigne	425	Oliveto	563
Monte Morioni	571	Orlandi Contucci Ponno	647
Monte Pugliano, Cantine	667	Ormanni, Fattoria	569
Monte Rico	575	Ornellaia, Tenuta dell'	433
Monte Rossa	178	Orsolani	124
Monte Tondo	309	Ortaglia	576
Montecalvi	463	Ottella	296
Montechiari, Fattoria di	495	Ottomarzo, Cooperativa	328
Montelio	181	Pacenti, Siro	488
Montellori, Fattoria di	454	Pacina	554

Paitin	114	Planeta	714
Pajana - Renzo Seghesio	150	Plattner - Waldgries, Heinrich	250
Pala	728	Plozner	396
Paladin & Paladin	323	Plozza	214
Palagetto	537	Podere Aione	565
Palari	707	Podere Capaccia	571
Palazzo Vecchio	567	Podere Casale	428
Palazzone	619	Podere dal Ger	379
Pallavicini, Vini	637	Podere San Michele	573
Palombo, Giovanni	628	Podere Terreno alla Via della Volpaia	571
Pandolfa	416	Poderi Colla	26
Paneretta, Castello della	550	Poderi dal Nespoli	408
Panigada - Banino, Antonio	212	Podversic, Damijan	367
Panizzi, Giovanni	538	Poggerino	523
Paoloni, Donatella	605	Poggio, Paolo	144
Paradiso, Fattoria	405	Poggio a Poppiano	508
Parmoleto	551	Poggio al Sole	547
Parri, Fattorie	568	Poggio al Sorbo	553
Parusso, Armando	103	Poggio Amorelli	553
Pasetti, Franco	643	Poggio Argentiera	469
Pasini Produttori	212	Poggio Bertaio	611
Pasolini Dall'Onda	556	Poggio Bonelli	447
Pasqua Vigneti e Cantine	320	Poggio Capponi	568
Paterno, Fattoria di	503	Poggio di Sotto	489
Paternoster	671	Poggio Gagliardo	507
Pavia e Figli, Agostino	23	Poggio Le Gazze - Cantine del Palazzetto	652
Pecchenino, F.lli	71	Poggio Romita, Fattoria	576
Pecorari, Pierpaolo	395	Poggio Salvi	574
Pedra Majore	724	Poggio San Polo	574
Pegazzera, Tenuta	176	Poggio Scalette, Podere	464
Pelissero	137	Poggiopiano, Fattoria	532
Pellegrino, Carlo	706	Pojer & Sandri	219
Pellerino, Cascina	109	Polencic, Ferdinando e Aldo	350
Perazzeta	552	Polencic, Isidoro	351
Percivalle	205	Poli, Giulio	238
Perdarubia	731	Poliziano	503
Perinelli, Paolo	636	Pollara	708
Pernice, Tenuta	424	Pollenza, La	168
Perrone, Elio	62	Pontoni, Flavio	399
Pertinace, Vignaioli Elvio	137	Popphof - Andreas Menz	259
Perusini	400	Poppiano, Castello di	508
Pervini	685	Porcu, F.lli	731
Petra	575	Porello	145
Petricci del Pianta	575	Portale, Tenuta del	674
Petriolo, Fattoria di	554	Portinari, Umberto	291
Petroio, Fattoria di	447	Prà	291
Petrolo, Fattoria	509	Pradio	333
Petrucco	337	Pratesi	551
Petrussa	384	Pravis	222
Pfannenstielhof, Pfeifer Johannes	269	Prevostini, Mamete	189
Pfitscherhof, Tenuta	270	Prima & Nuova/Erste & Neue	254
Piaggia	519	Primosic	367
Pian delle Vigne	563	Princic, Alessandro	351
Piancornello	488	Principe Banfi	207
Piazzano, Fattoria di	555	Principiano, Ferdinando	103
Picciau, Gigi	730	Produttori del Barbaresco	34
Picech - Le Vigne del Ribél, Roberto	350	Produttori del Gavi	79
Pichierri - Vinicola Savese	692	Progetto DiVino	674
Pierazzuoli, Enrico	453	Promed	717
Pieri, Agostina	489	Provenza	184
Pieropan, Leonildo	310	Provveditore-Bargagli	574
Pietrafitta	538	Prunotto	26
Pietraserena	573	Puddu, Josto	732
Pietratorcia	656	Puiatti	338
Pieve del Vescovo	612	Punset	151
Pighin, F.lli	375	Pupillo, Antonino	713
Pile e Lamole, S. M. Tenimenti	459	Pusterla	212
Pinsoglio, Fabrizio	56	Quacquarini, Alberto	600
Pio Cesare	25	Quacquarini, Francesco	205
Piona, Albino	328	Quarello, Carlo	64
Piovene Porto Godi	322	Querceto, Castello di	464
Pira	71	Querciabella, Agricola	465
Pira, Luigi	131	Quintarelli, Giuseppe	294
Pira & Figli - Chiara Boschis, E.	38	'R Mesueto	167
Pisoni	221	Raccaro, Dario	352

Radikon	401	Ruiz de Cardenas	176
Raimondi Villa Monteleone	307	Russiz Superiore	339
Rainoldi, Aldo	179	Russo	544
Rallo, Cantine	706	Russolo	395
Rametz, Castello	270	Saccoletto	152
Ramoser - Untermoserhof, Georg	250	Saladini Pilastri	601
Rampolla, Castello dei	514	Salcheto	504
Rapitalà, Tenute	711	Salicutti	490
Ratti, Renato	89	Salviano, Tenuta di	624
Reale Boselli	214	Salvioni - La Cerbaiola	491
Redi	504	Sammarco, Ettore	668
Rendola, Fattoria di	568	San Bartolomeo	148
Resta, Vinicola	692	San Biagio	604
Revelli, Eraldo	148	San Cristoforo	187
Revello, F.lli	89	San Fabiano - Borghini Baldovinetti, Fattoria	430
Ribote	148	San Fabiano Calcinaia	442
Riccardi, Enrico	213	San Felice	448
Ricchi	210	San Fereolo	72
Ricchino - Tiziana Menegaldo	147	San Filippo - Rosi	564
Ricci Curbastro	173	San Francesco, Fattoria	694
Riecine	460	San Gervasio	510
Rietine	556	San Giorgio a Lapi	574
Rinaldi, Giuseppe	39	San Giovanni	594
Rinaldini, Moro - Rinaldo	418	San Giusto	517
Rio Grande	620	San Giusto a Rentennano	461
Rio Maggio	591	San Guido, Tenuta	434
Riseccoli	465	San Leonardo, Tenuta	217
Ritterhof, Tenuta	269	San Lorenzo	650
Rivera	676	San Lorenzo	625
Rocca, Albino	34	San Luciano	493
Rocca, Bruno	35	San Luigi, Podere	517
Rocca Bernarda	380	San Marco, Cantine	637
Rocca delle Macìe	441	San Martino	557
Rocca di Castagnoli	460	San Michele a Torri	573
Rocca di Fabbri	615	San Michele all'Adige,	
Rocca di Montegrossi	461	Istituto Agrario Provinciale	232
Roccaccia, Tenuta	518	San Patrignano - Terre del Cedro	409
Rocche Costamagna	90	San Quirico	573
Rocche dei Manzoni, Podere	104	San Romano	72
Rockhof	270	San Rustico	326
Rodano	553	San Savino	599
Rodaro, Paolo	343	San Sebastiano, Tenuta	94
Roddolo, Flavio	104	San Valentino	427
Romagnoli, Cantine	428	San Vincenti	462
Romeo, Massimo	567	San Vito	427
Romitorio, Castello	490	Sandoni	425
Roncada	352	Sandri, Arcangelo	236
Roncal, Il	400	Sandrone, Luciano	39
Ronchi di Manzano	371	Sant'Agata, Cantine	128
Ronco Calino	178	Sant'Andrea, Fattoria	515
Ronco dei Pini	384	Sant'Antonio, Tenuta	275
Ronco dei Tassi	353	Sant'Appiano	550
Ronco del Gelso	353	Sant'Elena	368
Ronco del Gnemiz	393	Santa Barbara	580
Ronco delle Betulle	371	Santa Barbara	688
Ronco Severo	401	Santa Cassella	606
Ronco Vieri	401	Santa Caterina	166
Roncùs	338	Santa Eurosia	317
Rosa del Golfo	676	Santa Lucia	679
Rosi, Eugenio	238	Santa Lucia	558
Rosso, Claudio	66	Santa Margherita	324
Rosso, Giovanni	153	Santa Maria di Ambra, Fattoria	434
Rotolo, Francesco	668	Santa Seraffa	148
Rottensteiner, Hans	251	Santa Sofia	303
Rottensteiner, Heinrich & Thomas	251	Santa Vittoria, Fattoria	454
Roveglia, Tenuta	211	Santarosa	413
Rovellotti	81	Santi	280
Rovero, F.lli	28	Santini, Enrico	551
Roxan, Casa Vinicola	652	Santo Stefano	324
Rubino, Tenute	677	Sapereta	570
Ruffino, Filippo	167	Saputi	604
Ruffino, Tenimenti	520	Saracco, Paolo	63
Ruggeri, Angelo	316	Sarchese Dora	646
Ruggeri & C.	317	Sardus Pater, Cantine	732
Ruggeri Corsini, Podere	150	Sartarelli	597

Sartori, Casa Vinicola	326	Tallarini	208
Sartori - Roccolo Grassi	285	Tamburello	717
Sassara, Luciano	626	Tamellini	328
Sassolo, Fattoria di	573	Tanorè	318
Sassotondo	542	Tasca d'Almerita	715
Satta, Michele	438	Taschlerhof	269
Savignola Paolina	557	Tassarolo, Castello di	134
Scacciadiavoli	615	Taurino, Cosimo	682
Scagliola	45	Tedeschi, F.lli	304
Scammacca del Murgo, Barone	713	Telaro - Cooperativa Lavoro e Salute	657
Scarbolo	375	Tenimenti Angelini - Tenuta Trerose	505
Scarpa - Antica Casa Vinicola	117	Tenimenti Angelini - Val di Suga	492
Scarzello e Figli, Giorgio	40	Tenuta Bonzara	414
Scavino, Paolo	59	Tenuta Caracciolo - Duchi di Castelluccio	652
Schiopetto	339	Tenuta De Angelis	582
Schmid - Oberrautner, Anton	269	Tenuta dei Fiori	46
Schwanburg, Castello	262	Tenuta dell'Arbiola	125
Scilio di Valle Galfina, Tenuta	716	Tenuta di Bossi	570
Sciorio	67	Tenuta di Trecciano	575
Scrimaglio, Franco e Mario	118	Tenuta La Volta - Cabutto	40
Scubla	381	Tenuta Pinni	402
Scuola Enologica di Conegliano		Tenuta Uccellina	417
G. B. Cerletti	324	Tenuta Valli	426
Scurtarola, Podere	560	Tenuta Villanova	364
Sebaste, Mauro	27	Tercic, Matijaz	391
Secchi, Alessandro	216	Terenzuola, Podere	556
Seghesio, F.lli	105	Teresa Raiz	377
Sella	92	Terpin, Franco	391
Sella & Mosca, Tenute	720	Terrabianca, Fattoria di	524
Selvapiana, Fattoria	520	Terralba	42
Selvole, Castello di	448	Terre Bianche	161
Serafini & Vidotto	296	Terre Cortesi Moncaro	590
Serboni, Massimo	606	Terre da Vino	41
Serenelli, Alberto	603	Terre de' Trinci	625
Serracavallo	696	Terre del Barolo	60
Serraiola	506	Terre del Carpine	625
Sertoli Salis, Conti	202	Terre del Sillabo	470
Sette Ponti, Tenuta	547	Terre Rosse, Cascina delle	162
Settesoli	707	Terredora di Paolo	660
Settimo, Aurelio	150	Terreno	466
Signano	539	Terriccio, Castello del	442
Simoncelli, Armando	231	Teruzzi & Puthod	539
Sinaglio, Poderi	27	Teso, Fattoria del	565
Sinfarosa	677	Tezza	326
Solaria - Cencioni	491	Tiare - Roberto Snidarcig	355
Soletta, Tenute	730	Tiefenbrunner	257
Soloperto	691	Tinazzi	323
Sölva - Niklaserhof, Josef	255	Tizzano	406
Sölva & Söhne - Paterbichl, Peter	255	Todini	626
Sonnino, Fattoria Castello	568	Toffoli, Vincenzo	297
Sopra la Ripa, Podere	542	Tollo, Cantina	649
Sorbaiano, Fattoria	496	Tommasi, Viticoltori	305
Sorelle Bronca	322	Tormaresca	688
Sottimano	115	Tornesi	564
Spadafora	711	Toros, Franco	355
Spagnolli, Enrico	221	Torraccia del Piantavigna	149
Specogna, Leonardo	358	Torraccia di Presura	558
Speri, F.lli	304	Torre Fornello	422
Spezia, Stefano	209	Torre Rosazza	372
Spia d'Italia	208	Torre Zambra	649
Spinelli	650	Torrevecchia, Cantine	700
Spinsanti, Catia	603	Torrevento	680
Spoletoducale	626	Torti, Pietro	209
Sportoletti, F.lli	622	Trabucchi	280
Stachlburg, Baron von Kripp	270	Trappolini	630
Statti	697	Travaglini, Giancarlo	76
Steinhauserhof	263	Travaglino	171
Stroblhof	244	Tre Monti	412
Strologo, Silvano	582	Treré	411
Sturm, Oscar	354	Trevisani	208
Suavia	310	Triacca	203
Subida di Monte	354	Trinchero	143
Suveraia	567	Tua Rita	545
Talenti - Podere Pian di Conte	564	Uberti	188
Taliano, Michele	106	Uccelliera	564

Name	Page
Uccelliera, Fattoria	451
Umani Ronchi	595
Umbria Viticoltori Associati	625
Unterortl-Castel Juval, Tenuta	264
Vaglie, Podere	608
Vagnoni, F.lli	540
Vajra, G. D.	41
Val Calore, Cooperativa	666
Val del Prete, Cascina	121
Valchiarò	397
Valdarnese, Cooperativa Agricola	576
Valdicava, Tenuta	492
Valdipiatta, Tenuta	505
Valditerra	152
Valentini, Edoardo	644
Valfieri	67
Valgiano, Tenuta di	436
Vallarom	217
Valle	399
Valle, Agricola	550
Valle del Quirra	732
Valle del Sole	560
Valle dell'Acate, Cantina	700
Valle dell'Asso	690
Vallerosa Bonci	585
Vallis Agri	218
Vallona	407
Vallone, Agricole	683
Valori	652
Valtellina, Fattoria	557
Valtenesi - Lugana, Cantine	209
Vano, Cascina	115
Vanzini	213
Varaldo, Rino	35
Varramista	568
Vaselli	636
Vecchie Terre di Montefili	515
Veglio, Mauro	149
Velenosi, Ercole	580
Venditti, Antica Masseria	667
Venica & Venica	361
Venturini, Massimino	305
Verbena	564
Vercesi, Marco	210
Vercesi del Castellazzo	194
Verdi, Bruno	172
Verrazzano, Castello di	466
Verrina	152
Vestini - Campagnano	666
Vevey, Maison Albert	20
Vezzoli, Attilio	208
Vezzoli, Ugo	210
Viberti, Eraldo	91
Viberti, Osvaldo	149
Vicara	123
Vicchiomaggio, Castello di	467
Vicentini Orgnani, Alessandro	376
Vidussi, Gestioni Agricole	340
Vie di Romans	373
Vielmin	146
Vietti	60
Vigliano	573
Vigna del Greppo, Fattoria	565
Vigna del Lauro	356
Vigna Petrussa	385
Vigna Rionda - Massolino	131
Vigna Traverso	385
Vignalta	312
Vignamaggio, Villa	467
Vignavecchia	524
Vigne del Pareto	119
Vigne Fantin Noda'r	401
Vigne Regali	133
Vigneti Calzetti	427
Vigneti delle Meridiane	238
Vigneti Le Monde	378
Vigneti Massa	105
Vigneto delle Terre Rosse	423
Vigneto Due Santi	273
Vignole	569
Villa	193
Villa Arceno	449
Villa Bellini	306
Villa Buonasera	558
Villa Cafaggio	516
Villa Calcinaia	558
Villa Casale	558
Villa Chiopris	394
Villa Cilnia	430
Villa dal Ferro Lazzarini	299
Villa di Quartu	725
Villa Fiorita	146
Villa Frattina	378
Villa Giada	52
Villa La Selva, Fattoria	435
Villa Le Prata	493
Villa Matilde	655
Villa Mazzucchelli	209
Villa Pampini - F.lli Bernardi	428
Villa Patrizia	526
Villa Pigna	595
Villa Pillo	462
Villa Po' del Vento	625
Villa Rosa	553
Villa Russiz	340
Villa San Michele	668
Villa Sant'Anna	506
Villa Simone - Piero Costantini	634
Villa Sparina	80
Villa Spinosa	295
Villa Trasqua	553
Villagrande, Barone di	708
VIN.CA	551
Vinicola del Sannio	667
Vinicola del Tesino	587
Vinicola Mediterranea	692
Vinnaioli Jermann	364
Vintripodi	697
Vio, Claudio	166
Virili, Piero	626
Visconti	207
Visintini, Andrea	359
Vistorta - Brandino Brandolini d'Adda	386
Vitanza	564
Viticcio	468
Viticoltori Alto Adige	245
Viticoltori Associati di Rodello	152
Vivacqua, Luigi	698
Vivaldi - Arunda	260
Viviani	295
Voerzio, Gianni	91
Voerzio, Roberto	92
Volpaia, Castello di	525
Volpe Pasini	398
Wandanna	495
Zaccagnini, Ciccio	640
Zaccagnini & C., F.lli	606
Zamuner	329
Zanchi	624
Zanini	237
Zardetto Spumanti	276
Zemmer - Kupelwieser, Peter	258
Zenato	297
Zeni	233
Zeni, F.lli	273
Zidarich	362
Zof	359
Zonin	279
Zorzettig, Livio	381
Zucchetto, Paolo	329